RHB

12-25-06

"SECRETARIAT, HIS LAST PORTRAIT" BY TONY LEONARD

CHAMPIONS

The Lives, Times, and Past Performances

of

America's Greatest Thoroughbreds

Revised Edition | Champions from 1893–2004

Published by
Daily Racing Form Press
100 Broadway, 7th Floor
New York, NY 10005

ISBN: 1–932910–02–6
Library of Congress Control Number: 2005929756

Cover photo, "Man o' War," oil on canvas, 1979, by Anthony M. Alonso
Back cover photo by Tony Leonard
Cover and jacket designed by Chris Donofry
Text design by Neuwirth and Associates
Printed in the United States of America

All entries, results, charts and related information provided by

EQUIBASE
COMPANY

821 Corporate Drive • Lexington, KY 40503-2794 Toll Free (800) 333-2211 or
(859) 224-2860; Fax (859) 224-2811 • Internet: www.equibase.com

The Thoroughbred Industry's Official Database for Racing Information

CONTENTS

Acknowledgments

A work such as *Champions* could not have been completed without considerable help from many varied resources. Information for British, European, South African, and some South American races was supplied by the International Racing Bureau. Detailed race lines on the Chilean starts by Iceberg II, Cougar II, and Gran Kan were supplied by Racing Manager Beltran A. Montt of the Sociedad Hipodromo Chile S.A. Alan Shuback provided invaluable assistance in obtaining and sorting foreign race records and past performances.

Data for starts that predate the publication of *Daily Racing Form* was obtained from Goodwin's Turf Guide, which ceased production in 1908. Some past performances created from *Daily Racing Form* charts also contain supplementary data from Goodwin's, primarily information regarding purses, which were often listed in incomplete fashion in very early *Daily Racing Form* charts.

Some of the photographs were provided from collections maintained by the Keeneland library, the National Museum of Racing, the New York Racing Association, and the California Thoroughbred Breeders' Association. Other photographs were by Horsephotos.

The cover portrait of Man o' War is by Anthony M. Alonso.

Past performances were proofread by Steve Hill, Dan Illman, Chuck Kuehhas, Paul Malecki, Pat Mannion, Pam Ohanesian, Barbara Ransom, and Carmine Sicuranza. Additional support was provided by Mike Beer, Lonnie Goldfeder, and Meg Wren.

Pauline Neuwirth and John Nora of Neuwirth and Associates were responsible for layout and design. Chris Donofry designed the cover.

The text was edited by Robin Foster.

Champions would not have been possible without the dedication and perseverance of Paula Welch, who not only conceived the idea of collecting the past performances of the 20th century's greatest horses into one volume, but practically assembled many of them with her bare hands. The existence of this book is due in great part to her tireless efforts.

FOREWORD

WHEN *Champions: The Lives, Times, and Past Performances of the 20th Century's Greatest Thoroughbreds* was first published in July 2000, it set out to capture the first 100 years of the modern Thoroughbred era in words and past performances, to underline the greatness of racing immortals, and to revive the memories of those who, for one splendid season, were called champion.

Since then, the best-selling book *Seabiscuit: An American Legend* and its successful movie adaptation revived a piece of racing's great past, and the feel-good stories of Funny Cide and Smarty Jones helped raise the sport's profile to its highest level since the glory days of the late 1970's.

At first glance, Seabiscuit, Funny Cide, and Smarty Jones all seemed unlikely candidates to reach the pinnacle of the sport, but in reality, each had a pedigree that allowed him to excel at the highest level. The success of these horses confirms the cliché that "a good horse can come from anywhere."

And that is the common thread that runs through the nearly 500 horses whose past performances appear in this second edition of *Champions.* Equal treatment is given to the regally bred, such as Secretariat and Easy Goer, and to the products of seemingly haphazard matings such as Kelso and John Henry.

Champions has no barriers for longevity, either. It allows for the inclusion of Vindication, whose career was cut short after just four starts, though his last was a victory over the best of his division in the Breeders' Cup Juvenile, as well as Imp and Pan Zareta, each of whom made in excess of 150 trips to the post. And though it is rare among these pages to find the merely ordinary, those non-immortals still occupy space without prejudice alongside Cigar, Citation, Dr. Fager, Equipoise, Native Dancer, and Spectacular Bid.

All are measured by the single most important gauge used in the sport: the past-performance line. Over two dozen elements are used to define and summarize each race in the past-performance profile, yet a single glance can sometimes distill a historic moment such as Secretariat's unforgettable victory in the 1973 Belmont Stakes:

Secretariat — **ch. c. 1970, by Bold Ruler (Nasrullah)–Somethingroyal, by Princequillo** — **Lifetime record: 21 16 3 1 $1,316,808**
Own.– Meadow Stable
Br.– Meadow Stud Inc (Va)
Tr.– L. Laurin
9Jun73- 8Bel fst 1$\frac{1}{2}$:46^{1} 1:09^{4} 1:59 2:24 Belmont-G1 1 1 1^{hd} 1^{20} 1^{28} 1^{31} Turcotte R 126 b *.10 113-05 Secretariat126^{31}TwiceaPrince126$\frac{1}{2}$MyGllnt126^{13} Ridden out 5

Yet statistics often do not offer a complete picture of a moment, and certainly not of an era. To that end, *Champions* provides decade-by-decade accounts of Thoroughbred history by some of the sport's most celebrated journalists. Glenye Cain, Steven Crist, David Grening, Joe Hirsch, Jay Hovdey, Dave Litfin, Jay Privman, and Paula Welch provide a more elaborate context for the numbers, bringing the horses, and the people who nurtured and cajoled their talent, to life.

One very recognizable difference between the past performances in the first and second editions of *Champions* is the inclusion of Beyer Speed Figures for Eclipse Award winners beginning in 1992. First appearing in the late 1980's as part of a statistical service, Beyer Speed Figures emerged in wider distribution in 1991, when they were included in past-performance lines in *The Racing Times*, and later in *Daily Racing Form*. Their addition has been the single most important change in the evolution of past performances. They have leveled the playing field for the everyday handicapper, arming him with a tool to identify the fastest horse in a given race.

Equally important, at least to devotees of the sport and its history, is the fact that Beyer Speed Figures provide a way to compare the best horses of the past two decades against each other. Was Ghostzapper, who earned the highest speed figure in this book—a 128 in the 2004 Philip Iselin Handicap—superior to Cigar, whose career best was a 121 in the 1995 Oaklawn Park Handicap? Historians and supporters from both camps can debate deep into the night, but by the numbers, Ghostzapper was the faster horse.

Other spirited discussion is likely to arise from the rich vein of information in *Champions*. Throughout racing history, those inspired by the competition of great Thoroughbreds have earnestly discussed their relative merit, raising questions and setting the standards by which greatness is measured. The best indicators of the ultimate truth lie within these pages.

—**Irwin Cohen**

FOUNDATIONS

1890's–1920's

by Paula Welch

EVOLUTION IS A GRADUAL process. It is easy to compare something now and then to see how it has changed, but it is not so easy to pinpoint the precise moment that the change occurred.

During the 1800's, horse racing in the United States went from being a sport characterized by relatively tiny purses and hard campaigns at advanced ages to one of astronomical purses offered to the very young, with the spotlight shifting from grueling heat racing for older horses to so-called dashes for younger ones. While there are many milestones marking this transformation, it is not unreasonable to single out August 29, 1893, as one day in particular that racing in this country took shape in its modern form. In the 1:12⅘ that it took the undefeated Domino to negotiate about six furlongs in the Futurity Stakes at Sheepshead Bay, the past was erased and the present took its place.

In the course of securing the rich race, worth almost $49,000 to the winner, Domino became America's leading earning horse, unseating the still–racing Kingston in one quick blow. Then a 9-year-old, Kingston would retire a year later with 89 victories, which still stands as an American record. That tally, and his final lifetime earnings of $138,917, required 138 starts during nine seasons. The 2-year-old Domino surpassed Kingston's total earnings in just seven starts over barely three months.

Kingston and Domino were tied together not just as former leading earner and successor, but by a man who was one of the dominant influences on American racing of his time. James R. Keene, who had twice earned a fortune in stocks and once lost it, bred Kingston. When he and his son, Foxhall, merged their racing stables, he became the co–owner of Domino, whom the younger Keene had bought as a yearling for $3,000. Keene had campaigned stars such as Spendthrift years before, and in the 1890's, with a lost fortune recovered, much glory lay ahead – and it all started with Domino.

The pedigree of Domino's sire, Himyar, reflected the culture clash that was occurring in the mid-19th century in American racing and breeding. Heat racing had begun falling out of favor in England decades earlier, and American breeders looked there for sources of speed. Eclipse, a stakes winner at 2 and 3, brought speed with him when imported to the United States, and among his offspring was Alarm, a record setter at a mile.

Himyar was by the sprinter-miler Alarm out of the Lexington mare Hira. The most dominant stallion the United States has ever seen, Lexington was the leading sire from 1861 through 1874, and twice again thereafter. During his racing career in the 1850's, he covered four miles in 7:19¾ against time and won 6 of 7 official races, all run in heats at distances ranging from one to four miles. Himyar, however, was more a speedster like his sire, and he transmitted that quality in abundance to his greatest son, Domino.

As brilliant as the "Black Whirlwind" was, he had an obvious weakness: stamina. Beaten just once in 19 starts at a mile or less, he won only one race at nine furlongs or more, and that was a dead heat in a match race.

Domino suffered the worst defeat of his career in the 1½-mile American Derby, fighting an effort by jockey Fred Taral to rate him and finishing last. The younger Keene claimed the colt had exited the race lame, and it was two months before he ran again. This debacle did not discourage the Keenes and trainer Billy Lakeland from trying Domino in routes again at 4, with little success. Kept to shorter distances, he remained a dominant force.

With his prodigious fleetness came a dose of unsoundness. After spectacular speed trials as a yearling, the colt suffered bowed tendons and always raced in bandages. A bad foot troubled him at 3 and 4 and, eventually, he refused to train on it and was retired to Keene's Castleton Stud near Lexington, Kentucky.

Domino was not only a star on the racetrack, but also became a significant influence in American pedigrees.

Domino – against tremendous odds – became a significant influence in American pedigrees. He died in 1897, the year his first crop was born, and despite siring only 20 foals – and only four surviving colts who were not gelded – Domino's name peppers the distant recesses of pedigrees of virtually every Thoroughbred alive today. From those two small crops, Domino produced eight stakes winners, and despite his own distance limitations, his offspring included Cap and Bells, who was the first American-bred to win the English Oaks, and Commando, winner of the Belmont.

Domino's first crop of five foals, which included three stakes winners, were 2-year-olds of 1899; Commando was a member of the second and last crop and he proved an immediate sensation, winning five straight races before losing his last outing of the season under a notably careless ride.

James Rowe Sr., a leading jockey of his day, had become an enormously successful trainer, developing stars such as Hindoo and Miss Woodford – even before joining forces with Keene. He had ridden two winners of the Belmont and eventually would train eight of them, more than anyone else in history. He sent Commando into the then-11-furlong classic for his 3-year-old debut, and the colt galloped to victory over the two rivals that dared to challenge him. An easy win in the Carlton followed, and then came the Lawrence Realization. According to accounts, Commando was lame before the race, and after a game but losing effort behind The Parader, whom he had beaten easily in the Belmont, the colt was virtually broken down. It was to be his last start.

Like Domino, Commando proved both an astonishingly successful stallion and a tragically unlucky one. He died of tetanus in 1905, siring just 27 foals in the end. This small total included 10 stakes winners, headlined by the fabulous Colin.

Barely a year and a month separate Colin's first and last racecourse appearances, but in that brief time, he established himself as one of the sport's superstars. Observers rated him the best American racehorse ever – better than stablemate Sysonby, and better, some would later maintain, than Man o' War.

Colin, the last major undefeated horse in America for 80 years, won the Belmont Stakes in a driving rainstorm over a sloppy track, despite suffering from severe soundness problems.

He went undefeated in 15 starts, his two close calls attributable to the sporadic leg troubles that eventually would end his career.

Only once was Colin challenged in 12 races at 2 – in the Eclipse, his third start. A week before, he had easily won his debut and in the intervening days had set a track record in the National Stallion Stakes. In the Eclipse, however, he never was able to get a clear lead and won by a head, emerging from the race with sore shins. That didn't prevent the Keene colt from returning after a short rest to sweep through nine more races before the season's end, setting an American record at seven furlongs in his 2-year-old finale.

Colin won the Withers in his return at 3, but after a swift 1¼-mile workout, it was announced that he had bowed tendons in his forelegs and would not run in the Belmont. In a last-minute surprise, however, he contested the race, held in a driving rainstorm over a sloppy track. The weather conditions prevented a time from being taken and also made it impossible to discern the horses until the final quarter-mile, in which Colin lost all but a head of a five-length lead, just edging Fair Play for the victory. The chart noted that rider error nearly cost Colin the win; jockey Joe Notter claimed that he was told to give the colt an easy race and that Colin had little left to offer against Fair Play's late run.

Antigambling legislation was passed on June 11, 1908, severely restricting betting in New York, but 20,000 were reported to be on hand at Sheepshead Bay for Colin's finale, a comfortable victory in the Tidal Handicap.

Like many American-owned racehorses of the day, Colin was sent to England, but he never raced there. After an impressive trial as a 4-year-old, he proved irretrievably broken down.

Unlike Commando and Domino, Colin lived to an advanced age, but he proved unable to produce a worthy successor on the track. Although other sons of Commando – Ultimus, Celt, and Peter Pan – were much more successful stallions, it is Colin who provides the sire-line link from Domino to the present, through Neddie, grandsire of Alsab and progenitor of the sire line that leads to Ack Ack.

Among the best of Keene's fillies was Maskette, whose somewhat disappointing 4-year-old campaign could not erase her accomplishments at 2 and 3. A daughter of the Domino stallion Disguise out of a Hamburg mare, Maskette suffered her only defeat at 2 behind the year's best 2-year-old colt, Sir Martin, who was subsequently sold for $70,000 and sent to England. Keene reportedly proclaimed her the fastest horse he yet had bred. Following her retirement, Maskette produced an Ultimus filly in the United States before being sold and sent to France.

One of the last stars campaigned by Keene was Sweep. By Ben Brush and out of the Domino mare Pink Domino, Sweep went 9 for 13 and was never unplaced in a career highlighted by victories in the Futurity, Belmont, and Lawrence Realization.

A two-time leading sire, Sweep produced good stallions in Eternal and The Porter, but his lasting prominence in pedigrees is mainly through his daughters. He is the broodmare sire of Triple Crown winners War Admiral and Whirlaway, of champion El Chico, and of Kentucky Derby winner Bubbling Over, among others.

Not all of the Keenes' superstars were homebred descendants of Domino, however. Sysonby was bred in England by American Marcus Daly, who had bought Optime and sent her to dual classicist Melton. Daly died before the foal was born, however, and when his England-based stock was auctioned, the elder Keene purchased the mare. Sysonby was foaled at Castleton Stud the following February.

It was fortuitous that Sysonby campaigned in America in Keene colors at all. James Keene wanted to sell the colt as a yearling, but Foxhall convinced him otherwise; later, Sysonby was slated to be shipped to England to race, but Rowe bundled up the little bay colt so it would be thought that he was in too poor a condition to make the trip. Actually, there was nothing wrong with him.

In fact, unlike Domino, Commando, and Colin, Sysonby was not troubled by unsoundness. He won the Lawrence Realization off three days' rest and won stakes races from 5½ furlongs to 2¼ miles. In most of his victories, he was not under urging at the end; the exception was a dead heat for

The versatile Sysonby won stakes races from 5 ½ furlongs to 2 ¼ miles, and lost only once in his career.

first in the Metropolitan Handicap, his 3-year-old debut, in which he gave 10 pounds to the older Race King. His lone defeat, to the good filly Artful in the 1904 Futurity, was later ascribed to foul play.

It was intended to race Sysonby at 4, but an irritating skin condition kept him sidelined through the spring. He suddenly developed a high fever and died shortly thereafter of blood poisoning. For Castleton, which had lost its two best stallions early, the ill fortune continued.

Racing in New York persisted until 1910, with betting on a man-to-man basis, until further legislation prohibited even that. Racing would not return to the state until 1913, and some storied tracks, such as Sheepshead Bay and Gravesend, shut down, never to reopen. Although he maintained a few horses in England, Keene sold his American interests, and he died before racing returned to Belmont in May 1913.

Henry of Navarre may have been the best of his time going long. As a 3-year-old, he won the Belmont and Travers, and also won the Suburban among other major stakes as a handicap star.

Henry of Navarre had not been good enough to beat Domino at a mile in the 1894 Withers, but after winning 11 of his next 12 starts, including the Belmont and the Travers, he was ready for a rematch. Gravesend featured a match race between the 3-year-old stars at nine furlongs, in which they hit the finish line together. Their connections opted against a runoff, and the race stood as a dead heat. It would be Domino's only victory beyond a mile, and the last time he got that close to Henry of Navarre at the finish of a race.

A week later, Henry of Navarre lost narrowly to the older Clifford, a horse Domino had beaten in a one-mile match race, thus setting up a contest among the three early the following month to determine the season's best. Longshot Henry of Navarre won, dueling Domino into defeat and holding off Clifford late; favored Domino finished last with an injured foot.

Midway through his 4-year-old season, Henry of Navarre was purchased by August Belmont II for $35,000. Although the colt won 6 of 8 starts for Belmont, including the 1896 Suburban Handicap despite suffering a career-ending injury, he didn't come close to earning back his purchase price. After a disappointing career at stud, he was given away to the U.S. government for its cavalry program.

Belmont had more bad luck with Beldame, whom he bred but leased as a 2-year-old to Newton Bennington. She won 12 of 14 starts at 3 for Bennington, dominating fillies in the 1904 Gazelle and the Alabama and squashing older males in the Saratoga Cup and the First and Second Specials. Belmont reacquired her in time for her 4-year-old season, during which she took the Suburban but won only 2 of 10 starts. (Belmont's poor luck would hold; the very best horse he ever bred, and among the best horses anyone ever bred, would be sold as a yearling in 1918 for $5,000. That horse was Man o' War.)

Earlier on the very card in which Domino's career had come to a close with a whimper behind Henry of Navarre in the 1895 First Special, the sport's newest sensation exploded onto the scene. Ben Brush had been a star in the Midwest, winning his first five starts easily, but had come up short in New York, losing three of his first four starts there. In the Holly Handicap, he began an eight-race winning streak that would include the Champagne and the 1896 Kentucky Derby.

Roseben, "The Big Train," was a prodigious weight-carrier, once winning while spotting the runner-up 60 pounds. His seven-furlong record of 1:22 set in 1906 stood for 41 years.

Following the impressive Holly Handicap victory, the colt was bought by Mike Dwyer, who, with his brother, Phil, had campaigned a long stream of American champions such as Kingston, Hindoo, Miss Woodford, and Hanover, as well as Ben Brush's sire, Bramble. Mike had parted company with his brother and Ben Brush would be the last major horse he would own.

In his final start, Ben Brush, then 4, failed to give 36 pounds to a John E. Madden 2-year-old named Plaudit in an all-ages race, losing by a head to a colt who would go on to win the Kentucky Derby. After the race, Ben Brush was sold to James Keene to stand at Castleton Stud. He proved to be both an outstanding sire and a sire of sires; the leading stallion of 1909, he was represented by classic winners Delhi and Sweep. Sweep and Broomstick would lead the annual sire list themselves for five years between them.

Madden would figure prominently in the story of another 2-year-old of 1897: In 1895, the year that Domino retired, a near-relative was born who would later be hailed as the best of his crop. By Hanover out of a half-sister to Domino, Hamburg was purchased as a youngster by Madden, who was in the process of switching from Standardbred to Thoroughbred racing.

Although he lost 4 of his 16 starts at 2, Hamburg was considered far and away the standout of his generation. He won 10 stakes races, under 127 pounds or more in eight of them and once under 135 pounds, giving 15 to Futurity winner L'Alouette. He closed his campaign with six starts in a little more than two weeks, winning the last four. Late in the year, Marcus Daly purchased Hamburg for just over $40,000, an American record for a Thoroughbred in training. With the proceeds, Madden purchased Hamburg Place near Lexington.

Early the next season, it looked as if the wily Madden had come out best in the deal. The colt he kept, Plaudit, won the Kentucky Derby, while Hamburg was beaten in the Belmont in his season debut by Bowling Brook, whom he had handled easily at 2. But Hamburg, under the care of Domino's former trainer, Billy Lakeland, never lost again, capping his career with a victory over Plaudit in the Lawrence Realization and annihilating older horses in the 2¼-mile Brighton Cup by a margin officially estimated at 100 lengths.

Hamburg was America's leading sire in 1905, but his lasting contribution to the breed came with his daughters, such as the stellar racer Artful, who gave Sysonby his lone defeat, and Jersey Lightning, dam of Regret.

■ ■ ■

If Domino represented the modern era of American racing, with its new emphasis on youthful brilliance and shorter campaigns, there was still room for troupers such as Imp, Roseben, and Pan Zareta.

Imp, a handicap mare referred to as My Coal Black Lady after a popular song of the time, contested 96 races at 2, 3, and 4 before achieving national prominence as a 5-year-old in 1899.

Little more than a sprinter at first, the Ohio-bred proved a useful middle-distance stakes horse at the Chicago-area tracks at 4, but it was at 5, when she became the first filly or mare to win the Suburban, that she secured her place in history. Succeeding where legendary females such as Firenze had failed, Imp not only won the 1¼-mile handicap classic by daylight but also set a stakes record of 2:05⅘. Before her career ended, she set track records at 10, 12, and 14 furlongs in New York, and in addition to her Suburban score she won 16 other stakes, including the Advance, the Brighton Handicap, and the First and Second Specials.

The itinerant Pam Zareta was a brilliant weight-carrying mare who won a record 76 times while racing over 24 different tracks.

Roseben, "The Big Train," was renowned for his speed and weight-carrying ability: The huge gelding once won a six-furlong race in near-track-record time while giving the runner-up 60 pounds, and he won four times under 147 pounds and 38 times under 126 or more. He set records at six, seven, and 7½ furlongs, and at Belmont Park in 1906, he established an American record of 1:22 for seven furlongs around a turn, taking almost three seconds off the previous mark of 1:24⅘. The American record would last for 41 years, while the track record survived until 1957, when Bold Ruler finally laid it to rest.

Considering that he was a brilliant sprinter, Roseben reached prominence surprisingly late in life. Over 17 hands at maturity, the big horse raced just once at 2 and finished up the track. It was not until his 19th start that he finally won a stakes race, the Toboggan Handicap at the brand-new Belmont facility. Among the beaten was Race King, who had finished in a dead heat with Sysonby in the opening-day Metropolitan Handicap.

Between 1905 and 1907, Roseben was in the top three nearly 90 percent of the time despite weight assignments of up to 150 pounds. He was retired after bowing a tendon in 1909, ending his career with 52 victories from 111 starts.

From the fringes of racing in 1912 came one of the sport's enduring legends, the female equivalent to Roseben. Pan Zareta was a record-setting, weight-carrying sprinter who ran at 24 different tracks in Mexico, Canada, and eight states during her six-year career. Although she set a track record at a mile, she was most effective at six furlongs and under. She never won a race of significance, and aside from a victory over Old Rosebud early in his first comeback, she never defeated a top-level horse. What she did was run fast and win often.

Pan Zareta's dam, Caddie Griffith, was the offspring of the Thoroughbred stallion Rancocas out of a mare of somewhat more questionable breeding, and neither Caddie Griffith nor her famous daughter appears in the American Stud Book. That didn't keep Pan Zareta out of the winner's circle, which she visited 76 times – more than any other mare in U.S. racing history.

Ultimately, "Panzy," named after Panzy Zareta, the daughter of the former mayor of Juarez, set six track records at distances ranging from five furlongs to a mile, including a world record at five furlongs that would stand until 1951. She won under 146 pounds – giving 46 pounds to the runner-up – and carried 126 pounds or more 48 times, including 21 of her victories. Despite this, and a pronounced dislike of off tracks, Pan Zareta finished in the top three 128 times – 85 percent of her starts.

Pan Zareta died of pneumonia while in training at Fair Grounds, where she was buried.

Having outlived Mike Dwyer and James Keene, for whom he had trained a long stream of champions, and having waited out the dark days of no racing in New York, James Rowe was back on May 30, 1913, opening day at Belmont, with a new star for Harry Payne Whitney. Like many top American owners, Whitney had kept a stable in England, and among his better horses campaigning there was Whisk Broom. Classic-placed behind Neil Gow at 3, the Broomstick colt was a decent stakes-class performer in his adopted home.

The 6-year-old, racing in his native country under the name Whisk Broom II, came with a glowing reputation that earned him high weight in the opening-day Metropolitan Handicap, and he didn't disappoint. After his Met Mile victory, he took the Brooklyn and Suburban Handicaps before being sidelined by injury, sweeping the series that would later be recognized as the Handicap Triple Crown.

Whisk Broom II's U.S. finale was a performance that would earn him "greatest ever" accolades from contemporary observers, but the achievement had its share of controversy. Under 139 pounds, the horse officially traveled the 1¼ miles of the Suburban in 2:00, almost three seconds faster than the American record of the time set by his sire. But no independent clocker matched W. H. Barretto's official time. Among those on hand was James Fitzsimmons, who timed the race in 2:02⅗ – still an American record.

The following year, Whitney and Rowe had the country's best 2-year-old in the filly Regret, who proved her superiority in a rapid succession of three stakes victories against colts. Between August 8 and August 22, she won the Saratoga Special, Sanford, and Hopeful and was put away for the season.

Rowe, who had sent out Commando to win the Belmont in his 3-year-old debut, brought the filly back in the 1915 Kentucky Derby, where she was favored despite a nine-month layoff and the fact that she had never run farther than six furlongs. She won easily, leading throughout.

Whisk Broom II wins the Suburban Handicap under 139 pounds, going a mile and a quarter in 2:00, almost three seconds faster than the American record.

On one hand, Regret was campaigned in remarkably conservative fashion – in four years of racing, she had only 11 starts. But much was asked of her in most of those starts. At 4, she suffered the worst of two career losses when she took on an outstanding field in the 1¼-mile Saratoga Handicap in her first start in nearly a year, a race in which she led early and stopped abruptly, finishing 16 lengths behind Stromboli. Her other defeat came in the 1917 Brooklyn Handicap.

The Brooklyn featured a matchup of three Kentucky Derby winners – Regret, year-older Old Rosebud, and 3-year-old Omar Khayyam – and three of the best handicap horses of the time in Stromboli, Roamer, and Regret's stablemate, Borrow. Whitney had declared that he wanted to win with the mare, but in the stretch, with Regret on the lead and Old Rosebud looming dangerously, Willie Knapp aboard Borrow drove on to victory in track-record time over his own stablemate. Regret had been able to hold off Old Rosebud but fell a nose short against Borrow.

Roamer was not at his best for the 1917 Brooklyn, finishing fifth, but the tough gelding had done enough to prove his worth before the race. Even at 6, he still had important races yet to win. In fact, just a week before, he had beaten Borrow by daylight in the Excelsior Handicap.

Like Regret, he had scored his first stakes win in the Saratoga Special at 2 and went on to greatness at 3, winning 12 of 16 starts. The versatile runner had beaten older horses at seven furlongs in the Carter Handicap, won the Travers by 10, and so sufficiently scared away the opposition that he took the 1½-mile Autumn Weight-for-Age in a walkover. During the season, he set track records at seven, nine, and 10 furlongs. He was again dominant at 4 but afterward had to settle for being among a top-class set of handicap horses rather than being the leader.

With his best behind him, Roamer nevertheless had one particularly notable performance left in him even after the 1917 Brooklyn. At 7, after lowering his own 1¼-mile record at Saratoga, he ran a mile around two turns at Saratoga against time in 1:34⅘, becoming the first horse in history to run a

Despite being off for nine months and never having raced beyond six furlongs, Regret became the first filly to win the Kentucky Derby, in 1915.

sub-1:35 mile around at least one turn. Years before, Salvator had set the standard of 1:35½ on a straight course; the track record at Saratoga at the time was 1:36⅕.

In the winter after his 8-year-old season, the only year he failed to win a stakes event, Roamer died as a result of a paddock accident.

As good as Roamer was, he had an old rival who was, more often than not, better. He would try Old Rosebud 11 times over his career, with the latter finishing in front of him on six occasions.

Old Rosebud and Roamer met on the track for the first time as 2-year-olds in Kentucky, and though Roamer would go on to be a stakes-winning juvenile, he was no match for Old Rosebud, clearly the best 2-year-old of the year. It was not Roamer who would prove Old Rosebud's nemesis at 2, however, but Little Nephew, who was responsible for both of the gelding's losses that season. After losing the Bashford Manor, Old Rosebud romped through nine straight races before minor injury ended his campaign in August.

After a prep-race victory, Old Rosebud went to Churchill Downs for the Kentucky Derby, which was only then beginning to surge into prominence under Matt Winn, and there he won by eight

A bowed tendon sidelined 1914 Kentucky Derby winner Old Rosebud for more than 2 ½ years, but he came back as a star going shorter distances.

lengths while setting a track record. It was to be his last hurrah for quite some time, however, as he came out of his next start, the Withers, dead lame. A bowed tendon put the gelding on the sidelines for more than 2½ years.

In early 1917, Old Rosebud made it back to the track, and it wasn't long before he had established himself at the top again. The Derby record holder was no longer capable of handling 1¼ miles – he was unplaced both times he tried – but at shorter distances, he won 15 of 19 and was not worse than third. Then, injury intervened again and he sat out the 1918 season.

Returned to the races again the following year, Old Rosebud continued to win, but never again at the stakes level. In 1921, at age 10, he had only a couple of starts, both claiming events. When he pulled up lame winning the second, he was sidelined one last time, and after two races in his final comeback try, he broke down in a workout and was destroyed two days later.

Old Rosebud was in fact the first of five Kentucky Derby winners foaled at the farm named for Hamburg. Madden sold Old Rosebud as a yearling, but the second member of the quintet, the well-bred Sir Barton, raced for Madden at 2 until Commander J. K. L. Ross purchased the Star Shoot colt.

Madden had high expectations for Sir Barton; he was a half-brother to Sir Martin, who had handed Maskette her only loss at 2. Sir Barton debuted in a stakes event, and he showed little. Madden nevertheless sent him to Saratoga, where he ran even worse. He had not earned a penny when Ross, who already had bought a better 2-year-old in Billy Kelly, purchased him. In his final start of the season, though, he was a late-running second in the Futurity, at last showing a glimmer of his true racing ability.

Sir Barton made his 3-year-old debut in the Kentucky Derby, in which he did two things he had never before done: show speed from the gate and win. The Derby was contested in the mud and Sir Barton was getting weight from race favorites Eternal and Billy Kelly, but he returned four days later to beat Eternal at equal weights on a fast track in the Preakness. Victories in the Withers and the Belmont followed, though Sir Barton would not be recognized as America's first Triple Crown winner for years.

At the time, Sir Barton was best known for a race he lost – the famous match race against Man o' War at Kenilworth Park in October 1920. Before that, however, Sir Barton had put together a brilliant

In between Sir Barton's not-yet-recognied sweep of the Triple Crown and his match race loss to Man o' War was a brilliant four-race winning streak which included a track-record victory over Exterminator in the Saratoga Cup.

four-race winning streak that included a track-record victory in the 1¼-mile Saratoga Handicap against Exterminator and an American-record performance in the 1$\frac{3}{16}$-mile Merchants' and Citizens', also at Saratoga. Man o' War had tied the former record in winning the Travers and had won the Miller Stakes in a second slower time than the latter, causing interest in a match race between the country's best 3- and 4-year-old. The showdown proved anticlimactic as Sir Barton never offered a challenge to his younger rival, who galloped to an easy victory. It was generally reported that Sir Barton, who suffered from the bad feet common to Star Shoot offspring, was not at his best on the hard track.

The Merchants' and Citizens' was to prove the last highlight for Sir Barton. He never won another race, losing his final three starts after the match race, and after a mediocre career at stud, he died in Wyoming in 1937 as a U.S. Army Remount stallion.

The Madden-bred Paul Jones won the Derby that Man o' War skipped, and the following year, Grey Lag almost gave Madden a chance at three in a row, but a stone bruise caused the colt to be scratched from the race.

Grey Lag was sold as a yearling to trainer Max Hirsch, who campaigned him until Sam Hildreth and Harry F. Sinclair purchased him for $50,000 after his victory in the Champagne. The colt raced in trainer Hildreth's name for the remainder of his 2-year-old season, then in the name of Sinclair's Rancocas Stable thereafter. A good 2-year-old but a notch below the best of his crop, the son of Star Shoot returned to dominate the division for the next three years.

Grey Lag's stellar career was interrupted several times by injury and once by a failed attempt at stud duty.

Starting with the Belmont, Grey Lag won eight straight stakes events, six of them in July alone, before losing his final three outings of the season. During the streak, he beat older horses, including Exterminator, in the Brooklyn Handicap, equaled an American record, and set a Canadian record. Like Sir Barton, he was troubled by bad feet and had two short campaigns at 4 and 5, losing only twice before being retired.

After proving a failure at stud, siring only a handful of foals before becoming sterile, he was back at the track at 9, when he won both starts, and at 10, when he only won 1 of 4. Retired once again to a supposed life of ease, the old horse changed ownership and eventually ended up racing three years later in claiming races in Canada, in which he was unable to win. When news of the matter reached Sinclair, the 13-year-old was bought back and sent, finally, to retirement at Rancocas.

Only two years after Grey Lag missed his Derby, another Madden-bred, Rancocas-owned horse earned the roses at Churchill Downs. This was Zev, who had lost the Preakness as the favorite the week before and was sent off at 19-1 in the Derby.

A good 2-year-old, Zev entered the Preakness having never gone beyond six furlongs, and his dismal showing in the nine-furlong event suggested that he could not handle the distance. A mid-week sprint victory proved his fitness but did little to convince anyone that he could manage 10 furlongs. His front-running Derby victory did, however, and Zev kept on winning despite added distance. The Belmont at 1⅜ miles was no problem, nor was the 1⅝-mile Lawrence Realization.

Having established himself as the best 3-year-old in the country, Zev took on Epsom Derby winner Papyrus in a 1½-mile match race at Belmont in October. The International Race, worth a fabulous

$100,000, was contested in deep slop, and Zev won it in a romp by five lengths.

Despite all that he had accomplished, the Latonia Championship nearly upended Zev's season. In the 1¾-mile race, In Memoriam replaced Zev as the division's leader in the eyes of many when he won by six lengths. A later match race between the two was inconclusive, won by a nose in rather unimpressive fashion by Zev over the Kentucky-based colt. Many went away feeling that In Memoriam was better, but Zev had won 12 of 14, including many of the season's most important contests, and his 3-year-old season earnings alone were enough to eclipse Man o' War as the country's leading money winner.

Zev returned to the races at 4 and won a pair of stakes, but he was no longer the kingpin. He took part in two of the three International Specials with French invader Epinard but failed to finish in the top three in either of them. On the day of the climactic International Special #3, he was in action, but in a sprint allowance, not the day's feature.

Instead, the star of the International Special #3 was the 3-year-old gelding Sarazen. By the remarkably inbred High Time, who was the product of a son of two Domino offspring bred to a Domino mare, Sarazen had been an undefeated sensation at 2 and was among the best of the crop at 3. In the International Special #3, he was trying 10 furlongs for the first time and proved spectacularly able, winning decisively in a brilliant 2:00⅘. Given the controversial nature of Whisk Broom II's 1913 Suburban record timing, it was probably the fastest 10 furlongs in the history of the sport.

Midway through his 5-year-old season, Sarazen began to sulk habitually in his races. After taking the Mount Vernon Handicap in July 1926, he never won another race. Eventually his connections, despairing of ever getting the horse to run again, retired him after he lost 16 straight over three seasons.

Also in action in the International Special #3 was another Madden-bred, the 3-year-old filly Princess Doreen. Already she had accounted for the Kentucky Oaks by disqualification, with Preakness winner Nellie Morse among the beaten, and an easy victory in the Coaching Club American Oaks. She came into the race with two straight stakes victories against older males and was well regarded in the Special, going off at 5-1. It was Sarazen's day to shine, however, and Princess Doreen finished a well-beaten fifth. But in years to come, when Sarazen's best days were behind him, the tough mare still had important races to win. Racing almost entirely in open company, Princess Doreen was a perennial star of the Midwest and competitive against the best in the East, winning races such as the Saratoga Handicap, Bowie Handicap, and the valuable Independence Handicap at Latonia twice.

In 1925, Princess Doreen passed Miss Woodford to become America's leading female earner, and the well-traveled mare ultimately retired in 1927 with $174,745 from 34 wins in 94 starts.

Just a week after Princess Doreen won the Coaching Club American

Princess Doreen, a winner 34 times in 94 starts, retired in 1927 as the richest female of all time, with $174,745 in earnings.

Oaks, a legendary career came quietly to a close in Canada. At 9, the great gelding Exterminator was long past his prime, but he was still good enough to win 3 of 7 outings, all three in different countries. A career that had seen him win 50 of 100 starts, recording victories in 33 stakes at distances ranging from six furlongs to 2¼ miles, ended with a third-place finish at Dorval Park.

Exterminator had won a pair of races at 2 without looking like a future star, but while in training at 3 he caught the eye of Henry McDaniel, who trained Kentucky Derby favorite Sun Briar for Willis Sharpe Kilmer. In the days before the 1918 Derby, Exterminator was purchased by Kilmer for $15,000 from J. C. Milam, who had obtained him as a yearling for $1,500. Although Exterminator was supposedly purchased as a workmate for Sun Briar, it was Exterminator who represented Kilmer in the Derby, and the gelding won as the longshot in an eight-horse field. He would not win again until the fall, eventually closing the season with a narrow victory in the 2¼-mile Latonia Cup.

Early in his 4-year-old campaign, Exterminator returned to the site of his Derby triumph to take the Kentucky Handicap over 10 furlongs but failed to win another stakes race at less than 1¾ miles through a long, hard campaign. His late season was highlighted by a victory in the Pimlico Cup over 2 ¼ miles, a race he would win the next two years.

Over the next three seasons, the marathon star, who previously had been outrun at middle distances against better company, suddenly proved dangerously proficient at all distances. At nine furlongs, he won the Brooklyn and Long Beach Handicaps, the latter twice in track-record time; at 9½, the Merchants' and Citizens' Handicap; and at 10, the Toronto Autumn Cup three straight years. Such was the respect for him that in 33 starts at ages 6 and 7, he never carried less than 126 pounds.

In a brief three-start campaign at 8, Exterminator earned his final stakes triumph in the Philadelphia Handicap, and he was no longer capable of winning against stakes company at 9. But with the last few thousand dollars he earned that season, he inched past Man o' War's former earnings record to retire with $252,996, good enough to place him second behind Zev among American runners.

Exterminator beat almost all of the good horses of his day, but although they competed at the same track on the same day on more than one occasion, Exterminator and the mighty Man o' War never met.

In fact, Man o' War raced only one horse not foaled in 1917 during his entire career, and that occurred in his final start, when he decisively

A moderate horse at 3, Exterminator won the Kentucky Derby as a longshot, but didn't really hit his stride until he turned 5.

Man o' War was so dominant that few horses would run against him. He won the Lawrence Realization by 100 lengths against just one other rival.

downed 1919 Triple Crown winner Sir Barton in the match race. But while his competition was limited, his performances were so brilliant that by the time he retired he was hailed almost universally as the best racehorse ever bred in the United States.

A son of Fair Play, who had almost beaten the great Colin in the 1908 Belmont, Man o' War was generally regarded as the best racehorse since that Keene runner by the end of his 2-year-old campaign. He had suffered one defeat in 10 starts when he was away poorly in the Sanford Memorial at Saratoga, losing by a half-length to Upset. He won under 130 pounds on five occasions while winning races at five to six furlongs, but the closest he came to a track record at 2 was in his lone loss.

The big red colt's performances at 3, virtually unvarying demonstrations of brilliance, effectively established him as a legend. After winning his season debut in the Preakness, he set five American records at distances ranging from a mile to 1⅝ miles while winning many of the most important races of the season. He won the Lawrence Realization by 100 lengths and took the Potomac Handicap under 138 pounds, believed to be the highest weight carried to victory by a 3-year-old in a flat race at a major track since at least the Civil War. So dominant was Man o' War that few would run their horses against him. Only once after the Preakness did he face as many as four rivals.

Man o' War's career ended with an anticlimactic gallop over Sir Barton in the $75,000 Kenilworth Park Gold Cup, at that time the richest horse race in history. It was enough to propel his earnings to nearly $250,000, well past Domino's standing record. Concerned about the weights that would be assigned to the colt in further campaigns, owner Samuel D. Riddle retired his champion shortly thereafter.

Man o' War made an immediate impression at stud. From his first crop, he sired American Flag, Maid at Arms, and Florence Nightingale, winners of the Belmont, Alabama, and Coaching Club American Oaks, respectively. From the second crop came Travers winner Mars, another CCA Oaks winner in Edith Cavell, and Crusader, the best of Man o' War's early foals.

Although he had previously won a stakes, it wasn't until the 1926 Suburban Handicap that Crusader began his ascent. Part of a favored entry with stablemate American Flag and under a feathery 104 pounds as a 3-year-old against his elders, he led American Flag home five lengths in front, then returned a week later to win the Belmont. The other highlight of a successful classic season was his victory in the Jockey Club Gold Cup, in which he produced a final quarter of just under 23 seconds to win the two-mile race going away.

He returned at 4 to win the Suburban by an even wider margin, but in his next outing he was kicked at the start and never returned to his best form. He already had done enough to earn a place in the record books, however. No other horse has won the Suburban Handicap, Belmont, and Jockey Club Gold Cup in the same season and it would be close to 60 years before Devil His Due won consecutive runnings of the Suburban, once America's premier contest for older horses.

Crusader went to stud amid great expectations but proved a dismal failure. Although Man o' War would eventually establish a surviving sire line, it would not be through Crusader or his other best racing son, War Admiral, but through War Relic, grandsire of sprint champion Intentionally.

As the 1920's drew to a close, racing lost one of its most noteworthy figures when James Rowe Sr. died in August 1929. Rowe had seen a heroic age of American racing from many angles: He had ridden classic winners during his stint as a racing official, he had set the field for Domino's Futurity on its way, and he had trained many of the legends of his time. Rowe had been a constant in a period of change, and his passing served well to mark the ending of an era.

Champions

Past Performances

1890's–1920's

Beldame

ch. f. 1901, by Octagon (Rayon d'Or)–Bella-Donna, by Hermit

Lifetime record: 31 17 6 4 $102,570

Own.– A. Belmont

Br.– August Belmont (Ky)

Tr.– A.J. Joyner

Date	Track	Fractions	Race	Running line	Jockey	Wt	Odds	Figures	Top finishers	Comment
19Aug05- 4Sar	fst 1¾	:51 2:08 2:341 3:004	3↑ Sar Cup 7.5k	1 1 12 1hd 21½ 21½	O'Neill F	121 w	3.60	84-11	Caughnawaga1271½Beldame1213Cairngorm113	Gamely 3
8Aug05- 4Sar	fst 1	:244 :483 1:13 1:392	3↑ Delaware H 2.6k	1 1 1hd 31 46 52½	O'Neill F	122 w	3.20	89-13	MollyBrnt1132DollySpnkr108noCrngorm109hd	Fast pace,tired 7
31Jly05- 4Sar	sl 1¼	:474 1:132 1:41 2:07	3↑ Saratoga H 10k	8 6 65¼ 51½ 44 33½	O'Neill F	120 w	4.50e	86-15	Caughnawaga1193WaterLight108½Beldm1208	Wide,game at end 9
8Jly05- 4Bri	sly 1¼	:482 1:131 1:391 2:044	3↑ Brighton H 25k	4 4 42½ 44 36 39	O'Neill F	125 w	3.20	81-12	Artful1031Ort Wells1258Beldame1253	Impeded first turn 7
5Jly05- 4Bri	fst 1	:243 :483 1:131 1:381	3↑ Brighton Mile 3.8k	1 1 11½ 11½ 1½ 2¾	O'Neill F	121 w	*.80	98-08	OrtWells126¾Beldame1217Delhi1268	Sulked when challenged 4
Previously trained by F. Burlew										
24Jun05- 4She	hy 1⅜	:494 1:151 1:411 2:204	3↑ Advance 15k	3 1 11½ 11½ 1hd 2no	O'Neill F	121 w	*.20	84-14	Agile111noBeldame12150Graziallo126	Just missed 3
15Jun05- 4She	fst 1¼	:484 1:133 1:393 2:052	3↑ Suburban H 20k	3 2 23 22 11½ 11	O'Neill F	123 w	3.50	96-07	Beldame1231Proper1094First Mason118¾	Easily 11
8Jun05- 4Gra	hy 1¼	:49 1:144 1:413 2:073	3↑ Standard 5.8k	2 2 2nk 2hd 1hd 11	O'Neill F	121 w	*.70	89-15	Beldame1211Cairngorm11110MajorDaingerfld128	Dueled,best 3
5Jun05- 3Gra	fst 1 1/16	:24 :48 1:133 1:47	3↑ Handicap 1405	7 1 1½ 11½ 1nk 21½	O'Neill F	126 w	4.00	93-08	Garnish1071½Beldame1264Kehailan1024	Second best 12
4May05- 4Bel	fst 1	:253 :49 1:413	3↑ Metropolitan H 12k	4 3 33 33½ 72 915	O'Neill F	122 w	4.00	- -	DHSysonby107DHRace King975Colonial Girl1114	Tired 12
Previously owned by N. Bennington										
24Sep04- 4Gra	fst 1½	:50 1:153 2:073 2:352	3↑ Second Spl 5.7k	4 1 12 13 16 15	O'Neill F	112 w	*.55	88-10	Beldame1125Broomstick1101McChesney121hd	Easing up 4
19Sep04- 4Gra	fst 1¼	:484 1:14 1:402 2:06	3↑ First Spl 5.9k	2 1 14 13 12 11½	O'Neill F	114 w	*1.00	97-06	Beldame1141½Caughnawaga1263Stalwart11710	Easily 5
7Sep04- 4She	fst 1⅜	:49 1:142 1:402 2:193	September 4.8k	4 2 11½ 12 13 12½	O'Neill F	123	*1.20	97-05	Beldame1232½Graziallo122¾Ort Wells1261	Easily 4
30Aug04- 4She	fst 1⅛	:49 1:141 1:402 1:53	Dolphin 3.6k	3 1 12 12 13 14	O'Neill F	126 w	*.14	96-09	Beldame1264Ormonde's Right1143Aurumaster1052	4
Repelled stretch challenge										
20Aug04- 4Sar	sly 1¾	:50 2:082 2:36 3:034	3↑ Sar Cup 10k	5 1 16 15 14 14	O'Neill F	108 w	*1.80	71-21	Beldame1084Africandr126½ThPckt1262	Never fully extended 5
4Aug04- 4Sar	fst 1⅛	:49 1:14 1:402 1:533	ⒻAlabama 5k	1 1 15 16 18 16	O'Neill F	124 w	*.05	89-08	Beldame1246Dimple1164Ishlana116	Easing up late 3
6Jly04- 4Bri	fst 1	:241 :48 1:123 1:38	3↑ Test H 5k	1 3 21½ 22 22 21	O'Neill F	115 w	1.40	99-07	Hermis1331Beldame1155Dainty1034	Off slowly,poor ride 5
30Jun04- 2She	gd 1	:242 :48 1:13 1:392	3↑ ⒻAlw 1140	2 1 16 16 14 12	O'Neill F	111 w	*.35	92-05	Beldame1112Lux Casta1105Hortensia1013	Bumped at start 6
22Jun04- 4She	fst 1⅛	:483 1:14 1:41 1:542	ⒻMermaid 6.3k	6 1 13 15 16 17	O'Neill F	126 w	*.60	89-11	Beldame1267Little Em1112½Possession1113½	Easing up 6
9Jun04- 4Gra	sly 1 1/16	:24 :50 1:173 1:523	ⒻGazelle 4.6k	4 1 12 13 15 110	O'Neill F	124 w	*.17	67-27	Beldame12410Graceful1211Little Em1135	Easily 5
1Jun04- 1Gra	sly *6f	:234 :481 1:11	3↑ ⒻAlw 1220	3 3 32 21 11 11	O'Neill F	106 w	*.50	88-17	Beldame1061Mamie Worth1155Graceful1016	Easily 8
21May04- 4MP	fst 1	:243 :50 1:153 1:411	ⒻLadies 5.6k	4 1 11½ 1½ 14 1¾	Hildebrand	121 w	*.60	87-10	Beldame121¾Audience1215Marjoram12110	4
Bolted before start and returned to stable area,won easing up										
5May04- 4MP	fst 1	:242 :48 1:142 1:40	3↑ Metropolitan H 13k	9 7 73¼ 77 45 34	Brennan A	98 w	20.00	89-09	Irish Lad1232Toboggan1032Beldame98½	Gamely 17
15Apr04- 4Aqu	fst 7f	:24 :494 1:141 1:27	3↑ Carter H 8.7k	5 1 11 11 11¼ 12	O'Neill F	103 w	7.00	96-09	Beldame1032Peter Paul985Wotan1001½	Speed in reserve 17
5Nov03- 5Aqu	sly 6f	:251 1:154	Handicap 880	- 2 11½ 11½ 11 14	O'Neill F	121 w	1.70	90-11	Beldame1214Harangue1221Palette1056	Easily 5
Previously owned by A. Belmont;previously trained by J. Hyland										
3Oct03- 3MP	fst *6f	1:102	Nursery H 7.6k	- 2 51¾ 62¼ 61½ 42½	Cochran H	116 w	15.00	89-11	Race King1141½Grenade115hdDivination108¾	Finished fast 12
28Sep03- 3MP	gd *6f	1:101	ⒻMatron 7k	- 4 57½ 44½ 43½ 32	Cochran H	123 w	6.00e	90-07	Armenia112hdFor Luck1092Beldame123½	Fast finish 8
2Sep03- 3She	gd *6f	1:124	ⒻGreat Filly 17k	- 2 32½ 2½ 2½ 1hd	Bullman	116wb	15.00	76-20	Beldame116hdOcean Tide116noMineola1166	Dueled,just up 15
22Aug03- 5Sar	fst 5½f	:232 :47 1:002 1:07	Alw 740	- 11 75¾ 55 77¾ 68	Bullman	114 w	9.00	87-00	Hamburg Belle1141½Long Shot1171½Race King1172	Bad start 11
1Jly03- 4She	fst 5f	1:012	ⒻVernal 4.9k	- 3 11 11 12 11	Bullman	107 w	*.90e	85-15	Beldame1071Monsoon107hdTepee107hd	Gamely 13
10Jun03- 3Gra	my 5f	:244 :50 1:03	ⒻClover 2.6k	- 12 76¼ 72½ 32 21½	Minder	112 w	*2.50	81-20	Contentous1121½Bldm112½Mordll1124	Bad start,fast finish 12

Ben Brush

b. c. 1893, by Bramble (Bonnie Scotland)–Roseville, by Reform

Lifetime record: 40 25 5 5 $65,217

Own.– Michael F. Dwyer

Br.– Clay & Woodford (Ky)

Tr.– Hardy Campbell

Date	Track	Fractions	Race	Running line	Jockey	Wt	Odds	Figures	Top finishers	Comment
29Sep97- 4Gra	fst 1 1/16	:25 :49½ 1:14½ 1:47½	2↑ Alw 1050	- 4 42½ 32 33 2hd	Simms	126	*.29	- -	Plaudit90hdBenBrush126hdDr.Ctltt1143	Driving throughout 5
25Sep97- 4Gra	gd 1¼	:53½ 1:18¾ 1:43½ 2:10	3↑ Second Spl 2.3k	- 1 1½ 1¾ 12 13	Simms	126	*.80	- -	Ben Brush1263Ornament117	Best,good ride 2
23Sep97- 3Gra	hy 1		2↑ Alw 340	- 1 1 1 1 1	Simms	120	-	- -	Ben Brush120	Walked over 1
No times taken										
18Sep97- 4Gra	sl 1 1/16	:25 :50¼ 1:16 1:48¼	3↑ First Spl 2.5k	- 2 23 22½ 1½ 12	Simms	120	*1.00	- -	Ben Brush1202Hastings1205Requital120	Easily 3
14Sep97- 4Gra	gd 1¼	:50 1:15½ 1:42¾ 2:08	3↑ Oriental H 3k	- 2 22 2½ 1½ 2no	Simms	127	4.00		Havoc113noBen Brush1272½Maurice99½	Used early 8
4Sep97- 4She	hy 1⅛	:511 1:17 1:421 1:55	3↑ Omnium H 2k	- 2 1hd 1hd 1½ 1¾	Simms	126	3.00	- -	Ben Brush126¾Hastings1231Clifford127½	Best,handily 7
30Aug97- 5She	gd 1⅛	:503 1:154 1:432 1:561	3↑ Handicap 1170	- 9 64¾ 72¾ 53 31	Hewitt	127	3.50	- -	Sir Walter117hdFree Advice1081Ben Brush1274	Bad ride 10
21Aug97- 5Bri	gd 2¼	:52½ 2:38½ 2:51½ 3:56½	3↑ Brighton Cup 5k	- 3 35 35 35 310	Simms	130	*.60	- -	TheFriar115hdSunnySlope11110BenBrush130	Challenged,quit 3
10Aug97- 4Sar	fst 1¼	:50¼ 1:15¾ 1:41¾ 2:07½	3↑ Citizens' 2.5k	- 2 21 21½ 2½ 11	Simms	126	2.00	- -	Ben Brush1261Clifford1264Howard Mann126	Gamely 4
31Jly97- 3Sar	hy 1	:26 :51 1:16½ 1:44	2↑ Midsummer H 2k	- 3 31¼ 31¾ 45 31	Simms	126	*1.40	- -	Sir Walter111hdHavoc1121Ben Brush1266	Pulled up lame 7
12Jly97- 4Bri	gd 1¼	:49¼ 1:14¼ 1:41¼ 2:09	3↑ Brighton H 2.5k	- 2 2½ 2hd 11 12	Simms	126	1.00	- -	Ben Brush1262The Friar1076Volley98	Easily 3
8Jly97- 4She	gd 1⅛	:504 1:16 1:411 1:542	3↑ Long Island H 2k	- 3 21½ 31 33½ 42½	Simms	126	2.50	- -	Clifford127½Sir Walter1092Lehman114hd	5
Eased up,passed late for 3rd										
5Jly97- 5She	gd 1	:242 :49 1:15 1:41	3↑ Sheepshead Bay H 1.5k	- 8 7 7 8 69¾	Simms	128	2.00	- -	Havoc108nkLehman111½The Swain101.58	Eased up late 10
Other margins unavailable										
22Jun97- 4She	gd 1¼	:511 1:161 1:464 2:071	3↑ Suburban H 7.5k	- 4 41½ 3½ 1½ 11	Simms	123	*2.00	- -	Ben Brush1231The Winner115½Havoc1028	Best,handily 9
17Jun97- 5Gra	gd 1	:25 :50¼ 1:15¾ 1:41¾	3↑ Alw 660	- 3 32½ 2hd 12 13	Simms	118	*.60	- -	Ben Brush1183Belmar1205The Swain108½	Much the best 5
12Jun97- 5Gra	hy 1 1/16	:25½ :51 1:17 1:48¼	3↑ Alw 680	- 4 51½ 31 3½ 2nk	Simms	118	3.00	- -	Premier118nkBen Brush1181Caldron91hd	All out 10
18Aug96- 3She	gd 1	:262 :523 1:174 1:42	3↑ Handicap 890	- 4 31 32 1nk 1no	Simms	111	*.90	- -	DBen Brush111noSouffle1003Hanwell112½	4
Disqualified										
15Aug96- 3She	gd 6f-FC	:251 :494 1:021 1:15	3↑ Fall H 1.5k	- 5 64½ 64½ 62¼ 4nk	Simms	113	5.00	- -	Gotham121hdHanwell110hdBuck Massie121hd	Closed gap 8
25Jun96- 4Lat	hy 1½	:53 1:20¼ 2:13¼ 2:40½	Lat Derby 13k	- 5 21 2hd 1½ 11½	Simms	122	*.25e	- -	Ben Brush1221½Ben Eder1225Loki1223	Entry much best 5
20Jun96- 4StL	fst 1½	:51½ 1:17 2:08 2:34	National Derby 20k	- 3 23 22 2hd 2hd	Simms	127	*1.00e	- -	PrinceLief127hdBenBrush1275BenEder1228	All out effort 7
13Jun96- 4Oky	fst 1⅛	:50½ 1:15 1:40¾ 1:54	Buckeye 7k	- 3 2½ 2hd 1hd 1hd	Simms	122	1.60	- -	Ben Brush122hdPrince Lief1252Loki1191	Dueled,good ride 4
21May96- 4Oky	gd 1¼	:52 1:17 1:42 2:08¼	Oakley Derby 12k	- 4 31¼ 31½ 22 31½	Simms	122	*.50e	- -	Prince Lief1171½Ben Eder122hdBen Brush1221½	Not enough 5
16May96- 4CD	my 1	:27 :53 1:19 1:44¼	Schulte 2k	- 1 1½ 12 1nk 110	Thorpe	122	*.40	- -	DHBen Brush122DHLady Inez11710Semper Ego11510	Driving 4
16May96- 0CD	my 1	:25½ :50¾ 1:16¼ 1:43	Run-Off	- 1 11 12 11 11	Thorpe	122	.90	- -	Ben Brush1221Lady Inez117	Easily 2
Run off of dead heat										
6May96- 3CD	fst 1¼	:49½ 1:15½ 1:42 2:07¾	Ky Derby 6k	- 4 21½ 21½ 11 1no	Simms	117	*.50	- -	Ben Brush117noBen Eder1175Semper Ego1175	Driving,lasted 8
31Oct95- 4MP	gd 7f	:25¼ :49½ 1:02¼ 1:27	Champagne 3k	- 2 2hd 24 1nk 1½	Simms	120	*.33	- -	Ben Brush120½Prince Lief1104Merry Prince1108	Handily 5
19Oct95- 3MP	fst 6f-EC	:24½ :49¼ 1:01½ 1:14	Albany 2k	- 2 11 1½ 1nk 1¾	Simms	128	*.10	- -	Ben Brush128¾Merry Prince1158Cassette1054	Very easily 4
15Oct95- 4MP	sly 6f-EC	:25½ :51¾ 1:04½ 1:11¾	Nursery H 3.2k	- 4 31½ 2½ 2hd 1½	Simms	127	*.80	- -	Ben Brush127½Hazlet111½Woodvine1044	Handily 6
12Oct95- 1Gra	hy 6f	:25¾ 1:03 1:17½	2↑ Handicap 650	- 1 1hd 11 11 11½	Simms	108	*.30	- -	Ben Brush1081½Salvable98nkCuckoo973	Cantering 5
5Oct95- 3Gra	fst 6f	:24¼ 1:01½ 1:15½	Prospect H 3k	- 2 2nk 1nk 11 12	Simms	124	*1.00	- -	Ben Brush1242Crescendo1211½Handspring125nk	Handily 7

30Sep95- 5Gra	fst 5½f	:25¼ :50½ 1:04¼ 1:11	Alw 500	- 1 2hd 1½ 1½	1½	Simms	118	*.35	- -	Ben Brush118½Margrave1132Karma103	In a canter	3
	Previously owned and trained by Ed Brown & Eugene Leigh											
17Sep95- 3Gra	gd 5f	:23¾ :48¼ 1:01½	Holly H 2k	- 3 21 1nk 1½	11	Williams R	121	3.50	- -	Ben Brush1211Margrave1152Crescendo1221	Easily	7
14Sep95- 4She	gd *6f-FC	1:101	Great Eastern H 5k	- -	8	Williams R	126	4.50	- -	One I Love122hdMargrave110½Hazlet112hd	Never a threat	13
10Sep95- 4She	fst 7f	1:26	Flatbush 3k	- -	22	Williams R	110	3.00	- -	Requital1152Ben Brush1103Crescendo115	Led til late	4
5Sep95- 1She	fst 5f	1:002	Handicap 700	- -	11	Williams R	114	*.45	- -	BenBrush1141Mussulman95hdIntermission101.5hd	Led,easily	5
27Aug95- 1She	fst 6f	1:131 2↑	Alw 590	- -	35	Perkins	103	*.40	- -	RightRoyal824FlorettaIV103.51BenBrush103	Never a threat	6
23Jly95- 4Oky	fst 5½f	1:08	Diamond 3.5k	- -	11	Williams R	125	*.50	- -	Ben Brush1251Ben Eder1232Prince Lief111	Easily	5
9Jly95- 4Oky	fst 5f	1:02¼	ⒸEmerald 2.5k	- -	12	Williams R	123	*.60	- -	Ben Brush1232Ramiro118hdBen Holladay118	Easily	5
6Jun95- 4Lat	gd 5f	:25 :49½ 1:02¾	ⒸHarold 2.7k	- 3 22 21 2½	13	Williams R	121	*.60	- -	Ben Brush1213Nimrod111½The Dragon1111	Galloping	6
15May95- 4CD	hy 4½f	:25¼ :51¼ :58	ⒸCadet 2k	- 1 1nk 1½ 11	13	Williams R	118	*1.60	- -	Ben Brush1182Del Coronado115hdBen Eder118½	Easily	6
7May95- 2CD	fst 5f	1:02¼	ⒸAlw 400	- -	15	Perkins	108	1.60	- -	Ben Brush1085Captive1134Concession113		5

Black Maria

blk. f. 1923, by Black Toney (Peter Pan)–Bird Loose, by Sardanapale

Lifetime record: 52 18 14 6 $110,350

Own.– W.R. Coe
Br.– E.R. Bradley (Ky)
Tr.– J. Lowe

21Nov28- 5Bow	gd 1 1/16	:25 :501 1:15 1:464 3↑	Handicap 1900	2 3 32 34¼ 35	37½	Bejshak J	117wb	4.30	81-14	Victorian120½Misstep1187Black Maria117	Outrun late	3
6Nov28- 5Pim	gd 1½	:493 1:153 2:072 2:342 3↑	Bowie H 13k	7 6 68½ 615 617	623¾	Fator L	116wb	9.65	57-21	Genie1171½Display1266Edith Cavell104nk	Never a factor	7
27Oct28- 5Lrl	fst 1¼	:463 1:12 1:373 2:033 3↑	Washington H 32k	9 10 1011 115 106¼	105¾	Fator L	122wb	*2.65e	86-11	Mike Hall124hdDisplay1262½Sir Harry113½	Tired	13
13Oct28- 5Lrl	fst 1	:234 :474 1:131 1:384 2↑	Laurel 14k	8 9 913 97 34½	2nk	Barnes E	113wb	8.20	94-12	Osmand123nkBlackMaria1131PrincessTina107½	Crowded start	9
8Oct28- 5Lrl	fst 6f	:23 :464 1:122 2↑	Handicap 1500	7 3 52¾ 75¼ 76¾	65	Barnes E	125wb	6.10	90-13	Knapsack104.5hdPrince of Wales1281½Wellet1051½	Outrun	8
25Aug28- 5Sar	my 1 3/16	:50 1:16 1:43 2:031 3↑	Merchants & Cits H 9k	3 2 12 1½ 1nk	2nk	Fator L	123wb	*1.10	62-34	ChanceShot123nkBlackMr1236Dngrous11015	Rushed up,gamely	4
11Aug28- 5Sar	fst 1¼	:471 1:124 1:39 2:06 3↑	Whitney 8.2k	1 2 21½ 21 1nk	1¾	Fator L	121wb	1.50	79-19	Black Maria121¾Chance Shot1264Whiskery12615	Driving	4
30Jly28- 5Sar	gd 1¼	:483 1:13 1:39 2:06 3↑	Saratoga H 9.7k	5 2 21 2hd 1hd	21½	Fator L	115wb	10.00	77-15	Chance Shot1221½Black Maria1152Edith Cavell1061½	Gamely	8
16Jun28- 4Aqu	fst 1⅛	:464 1:13 1:372 1:511 3↑	Brooklyn H 17k	9 6 64¼ 53¼ 55	64¼	Fator L	114wb	*2.20	83-21	Black Panther105½Victorian112½Diavolo1061½	Poor effort	9
12Jun28- 4Aqu	fst 1	:233 :47 1:123 1:383 3↑	Handicap 1200	2 2 13 15 13	12	Fator L	126wb	*.45	87-17	BlackMaria1262Dangerous11515Lasso'Gowrie109	Won eased	3
2Jun28- 4Bel	fst 1¼	:483 1:13 1:40 2:063 3↑	Suburban H 17k	2 3 43 86¾ 811	917½	Fator L	120wb	5.00	49-26	Dolan1054Chance Shot120½Scapa Flow120no	Quit	9
24May28- 4Bel	fst 6½f	:224 :47 1:12 1:184 3↑	ⒻHandicap 1275	3 5 43 21 23	22	Coltiletti F	126wb	*1.60	90-17	BlackCurl1202BlackMaria1262Snobbish988	Tired in stretch	5
	Previously trained by W.H. Karrick											
29Oct27- 5Lrl	fst 1¼	:47 1:114 1:372 2:022 3↑	Washington H 36k	5 2 2hd 2hd 2hd	2hd	Coltiletti F	117wb	4.20	98-10	Display112hdBlack Maria1171Mars1281	Just missed	9
15Oct27- 5Lrl	fst 1	:233 :47 1:133 1:381 2↑	Laurel 13k	5 8 62 62 21	2nk	Coltiletti F	117wb	3.85	97-14	Osmand115nkBlack Maria1171Macaw1161½	Getting to winner	8
8Oct27- 4Jam	sly 1 1/16	:233 :492 1:133 1:451 3↑	Continental H 6k	1 2 1hd 2hd 1hd	11½	Fator L	125wb	*.08	87-17	Black Maria1251½Rip Rap105	Won under restraint	2
1Oct27- 4Aqu	fst 1⅛	:47 1:12 1:36 1:494 3↑	Aqueduct H 7.4k	1 3 21 2½ 1½	12	Fator L	122wb	*.40	94-14	BlackMaria1222ⒹKentuckyII1062LightCarbin1082	Drew away	4
24Sep27- 4Aqu	fst 1⅛	:474 1:124 1:37 1:504 3↑	Edgemere H 7k	2 1 11½ 11½ 11½	12	Coltiletti F	116wb	*.55	89-12	BlackMaria1162LghtCrbn10810Pnuts122	Won under restraint	3
7Sep27- 4Bel	fst 1	:232 :462 1:111 1:372 2↑	Manhattan H 5.2k	8 2 2½ 2½ 2½	51	Coltiletti F	118wb	*2.00	89-14	Valorous114nkKiev109noOsmand117½	Forced pace,tired late	9
27Aug27- 5Sar	sly 1 3/16	:49 1:141 1:393 1:591 3↑	Merchants & Cits H 9.7k	4 1 11 1hd 2hd	21	McAuliffe D	116wb	*1.50e	81-19	Chance Play1241Black Maria1164Pompey1174	Tired	6
9Aug27- 4Sar	hy 1	:242 :474 1:134 1:403 3↑	Delaware H 5.3k	4 3 35 22 22	44¾	Coltiletti F	120wb	*.17e	73-26	LightCarbin106nkByrd1001½Pompy1193	Tired badly in drive	5
1Aug27- 5Sar	hy 1¼	:503 1:153 1:403 2:073 3↑	Saratoga H 9.5k	5 2 21 1nk 1hd	21½	Coltiletti F	119wb	3.20	69-21	Mars1221½Black Maria1193Light Carbine1073	Second best	5
4Jly27- 4Aqu	fst 7f	:23 :461 1:112 1:241 3↑	Carter H 10k	9 9 93½ 41½ 21½	2nk	Sande E	124wb	4.00e	94-10	HappyArgo119nkBlckMr1243Mcw124hd	Swerved final furlong	14
18Jun27- 4Aqu	fst 1⅛	:471 1:12 1:36 1:484 3↑	Brooklyn H 17k	3 5 44 35 47	76¼	Coltiletti F	123wb	7.00e	93-09	Peanuts112hdChance Play1214Display1121	Poor effort	10
4Jun27- 4Bel	fst 1¼	:464 1:11 1:371 2:022 3↑	Suburban H 15k	3 2 1hd 1hd 22	27	Coltiletti F	120wb	3.00	81-14	Crusadr1277BlckMaria1202Macw1202	Forced pace,no match	8
30May27- 4Bel	fst 1	:231 :47 1:112 1:372 3↑	Metropolitan H 9.7k	1 5 31¼ 21 21	11	Coltiletti F	116wb	4.00	90-16	BlackMaria1161Osmnd1122Vlorous108.55	Forced wide,gamely	8
21May27- 5Bel	gd 1	:231 :464 1:122 1:394 3↑	ⒻLadies H 4.4k	1 3 33½ 21½ 1nk	15	Coltiletti F	127wb	*.45	78-24	Black Maria1275Jumbo110½Corvette1111½	Cantering	5
14May27- 1Jam	fst 6f	:24 :471 1:121 3↑	ⒻHandicap 1255	2 4 2no 21 1hd	11½	Breuning B	126wb	*.60	94-07	BlackMaria1261½Accomplish1041Corvette115no	Won eased up	4
6Oct26- 4Jam	sly 1 1/16	:242 :473 1:122 1:452 3↑	October H 4.4k	3 1 14 13 14	12	McAuliffe D	115wb	*.65e	86-19	Black Maria1152Sanford1065Pompey1164	Won eased up	5
2Oct26- 5HdG	hy 1 1/16	:241 :484 1:134 1:47	Potomac H 16k	3 2 2½ 21 21	4¾	Johnson A	116 w	1.35e	88-21	ChancePlay123¾Gffsmn112hdPompy121no	Tired final furlong	6
25Sep26- 4Aqu	my 1⅛	:472 1:12 1:371 1:512 3↑	Aqueduct H 7.4k	1 1 12 15 14	15	Callahan J	112wb	*.13e	88-26	Black Maria1125Pompey1184Dazzler1008	Speed in reserve	5
18Sep26- 4Aqu	fst 1⅛	:454 1:102 1:36 1:483 3↑	Edgemere H 7.5k	4 2 11½ 11 11½	31¾	Fator L	113wb	*.35e	100-11	Peanuts114nkPompey1181½Black Maria113hd	Resolutely	7
14Sep26- 6Bel	fst 1¼	:484 1:121 1:37 2:024 3↑	Twin City H 5.9k	7 1 12 12 15	14	Fator L	110wb	4.50	86-17	BlackMaria1104Sanford108.5hdEdithCvll1051½	Won eased up	7
6Sep26- 6Bel	my 1¼	:473 1:123 1:391 2:074	ⒻChampion Filly 5.5k	1 1 12 14 16	15	Fator L	123wb	*.40	61-28	Black Maria1235Rapture123	Eased final 16th	2
24Aug26- 4Sar	my 1 3/16	:49 1:142 1:393 1:593	Huron H 5.1k	1 4 42½ 21½ 33	36½	Breuning B	112wb	6.00	73-20	Crusader1261½Espino1145Black Maria1124	Tired	7
19Aug26- 4Sar	fst 1	:242 :481 1:141 1:392	Sar Sales 3.8k	4 3 1hd 11½ 12	15	Breuning B	115wb	*.30	84-19	Black Maria1155Nomad1202Nurmi120hd	In a canter	4
10Aug26- 4Sar	fst 1¼	:473 1:131 1:392 2:06	ⒻAlabama 12k	3 1 13 11 1hd	22	Breuning B	126wb	2.50	77-15	Rapture1242Black Maria12610Ruthenia1174	Tired,gamely	6
31Jly26- 6Was	fst 1½	:48 1:131 2:043 2:301	American Derby 106k	4 4 35 42½ 33	34	Breuning B	116wb	2.80	- -	Boot to Boot1212Display1262Black Maria1166	Tired,gamely	5
24Jly26- 5Was	gd 1⅛	:49 1:134 1:394 1:54	ⒻIll Oaks 11k	3 1 13 16 16	16	Breuning B	121wb	*.10	- -	Black Maria1216In Bounds11610Spanish Star116	Cantering	3
3Jly26- 5Lat	fst 1¼	:464 1:121 1:38 2:03	ⒻLat Oaks 13k	4 3 21 2½ 21	21½	Mortensen A	126wb	3.70	87-11	EdithCavell1261½BlackMaria1262Helen'sBb121½	Outfinished	10
9Jun26- 4Bel	fst 1⅜	:50 1:154 1:412 2:203	ⒻC C A Oaks 13k	1 1 31 2½ 22	22	Fator L	121wb	*1.20	66-33	EdithCavell1172BlackMaria1214Rptur1177	Challenged,tired	6
31May26- 5CD	sly 1⅛	:491 1:143 1:414 1:552	ⒻKy Oaks 13k	6 2 2½	14	Mortensen A	121wb	4.00	72-20	BlckMria1214DarkPhantom116hdHelen'sBab1163	Going away	10
22May26- 4Bel	fst 1	:233 :473 1:132 1:384 3↑	ⒻLadies H 4k	5 1 11½ 13 11½	12	Fator L	120wb	7.00	83-20	Black Maria1202Extra Dry1197Rapture1222	Easily	7
5May26- 4Pim	fst 1 1/16	:234 :483 1:133 1:454	ⒻPim Oaks 6k	5 8 86 75¾ 611	312	Fator L	113wb	*1.15	81-17	Rapture11312Ingrid121hdBlack Maria1131½		8
	Outrun early,finished well											
1May26- 4Jam	fst 1 70	:234 :483 1:123 1:42	Wood 10k	7 4 42 44 44	46½	Mortensen A	105wb	*.29e	89-09	Pompey1201½Navigator1204Espino1101	Rated,outside	7
	Geldings not eligible;Previously campaigned in name of Shoshone Stable											
12Oct25- 3Jam	fst 5½f	:23 :47 1:054	ⒻHiawatha H 3.9k	5 5 56¾ 45¼ 33	42¼	Fator L	126wb	*1.00	93-12	Ethereal108hdPatricJ.121hdMdl1072	Hard ridden,slow gain	5
14Sep25- 4Bel	fst 5½f	:232 :473 1:053	ⒻTomboy H 4.6k	5 5 54½ 43 22	21½	Kummer C	125 w	5.00	92-16	Ruthenia1171½Black Maria1254Martha Washington1141		10
	Shuffled back,wide,finished fast											
5Sep25- 5Bel	fst 6f	:233 :471 1:12	Clm	2 2 21½ 24 23	11	Fator L	108wb	8.00	92-11	BlackMaria1081ColorSergeant1104RockStar1181	Going away	7
29Aug25- 3Sar	fst 6½f	:23 :461 1:113 1:174	Hopeful 51k	14 14 147¾ 1314 118½	915¼	Fator M	112wb	*3.20e	97-10	Pompey1275FlightofTime1254ChancePlay1223	Not a factor	15
25Aug25- 6Sar	fst 6½f	:23 :47 1:131 1:191	Alw 1000	6 3 21 11½ 13	14	Callahan J	99wb	3.60	105-11	Black Maria994Nurmi108noBlondin108½	Easily	7
15Aug25- 3Sar	hy 6f	:23 :48 1:152	ⒻSpinaway 8.9k	12 12 1220 1217 76¾	55¼	Fator L	109 w	4.50e	70-31	Cinema1121Asn1122Ruthn113nk	Left at start,closed ground	13
11Aug25- 6Sar	gd 5f	:233 :473 1:004	Alw 1000	8 10 98¼ 105¾ 62½	35	Fator L	108wb	6.00e	80-19	Rockslide118hdRemedy1135BlackMari1083	Began in a tangle	10
5Aug25- 6Sar	sl 5½f	:233 :474 1:072	Md Sp Wt	10 15 138 1313 1013	1016	Fairbrother C	115wb	40.00	70-17	Haste1182Vespasian1185Blondin1181	Not a factor	17

Colin

b. c. 1905, by Commando (Domino)–Pastorella, by Springfield — Lifetime record: 15 15 0 0 $180,912

Own.– J.R. Keene
Br.– James R. Keene (Ky)
Tr.– J. Rowe

20Jun08- 4She	fst 1¼	:47 1:113 1:38 2:04	Tidal 20k	3 1 12 11½ 13 12	Notter	126 w	*.20	103-06	Colin1262Dorante1264Stamin1218	Bore out,tiring slightly	4
30May08- 3Bel	sly 1⅜		Belmont 25k	2 - 11½ 1hd	Notter	126 w	*.50	- -	Colin126hdFair Play12615King James12610	Eased up	4
Driving rainstorm,no time taken											
23May08- 4Bel	hy 1	:24 :48 1:14 1:41	Withers 14k	2 1 13 13 14 12	Notter	126 w	*.40	82-19	Colin1262Fair Play126¾King James1268	Eased up	6
16Oct07- 3Bel	fst 7f-Str	1:23	Champagne 7.2k	2 1 13 14 15 16	Miller W	122 w	*.14	103-06	Colin1226Stamina119	Drawing away	2
7Oct07- 2Bel	fst 6f-Str	1:12	©Matron 10k	3 1 24 15 14 13	Miller W	129 w	*.14	90-11	Colin1293Fair Play1224Royal Tourist119½	Easing up	4
30Sep07- 4Bri	my 6f	:242 :474 1:123	©Produce (2nd half) 12k	1 1 11½ 14 14 15	Miller W	125 w	*.25	96-13	Colin1255Fair Play119hdRoyal Tourist11920	Eased up	4
7Sep07- 3She	fst 7f-FC	1:244	Flatbush 10k	6 1 11½ 11½ 13 13	Miller W	120 w	*.35e	100-00	Colin1203Celt1055Bar None105½	Hard held	7
31Aug07- 4She	fst 6f-FC	1:111	Futurity 28k	5 1 21 22 1½ 11½	Miller W	125 w	*.33	97-03	Coln1251½BrNon1171Chpultpc1171½	Blocked,as rider pleased	8
14Aug07- 3Sar	fst 6f	:241 :482 1:13	Grand Union Hotel 10k	3 4 2hd 2hd 1hd 12	Miller W	127 w	*.13e	95-05	Colin1272Jim Gaffney1123Ben Fleet1171	Hard held	6
10Aug07- 3Sar	fst 6f	:233 :47 :582 1:12	Sar Spl 9.5k	2 2 1hd 1hd 11 11	Miller W	122 w	*.40	100-04	Colin1221Uncle122	Decisively	2
27Jly07- 4Bri	fst 6f	:232 :471 1:121	Brighton Junior 15k	2 2 1½ 11½ 11½ 11½	Miller W	127 w	*.65	99-06	Coln1271½Chpultpc1256BrNon112½	Repelled stretch challenge	8
29Jun07- 3She	sl 6f-FC	1:122	Great Trial 25k	7 2 21 11 12 12	Miller W	129 w	*2.60e	91-09	Colin1292Meelick1221½Monopolist1221½	Mild restraint	14
5Jun07- 3Bel	my 5½f-Str	1:063	Eclipse 9.2k	6 2 1nk 1hd 1hd 1hd	Mountain	125 w	*.60	94-07	Colin125hdBeaucoup11710WvCrst1175	Under pressure,gamely	6
1Jun07- 3Bel	fst 5f-Str	:58	National Stallion 10k	3 1 11½ 11½ 12 13	Miller W	122 w	*.75	102-00	Colin1223Bar None1174Ben Fleet122hd	Never threatened	6
29May07- 2Bel	gd 5f-Str	1:01	Md Sp Wt	10 1 12 13 12 12	Miller W	110 w	*1.20	87-17	Colin1102Bar None1108Harcourt1101½	Easily	23

Commando

b. c. 1898, by Domino (Himyar)–Emma C., by Darebin — Lifetime record: 9 7 2 0 $58,196

Own.– J.R. Keene
Br.– James R. Keene (Ky)
Tr.– James Rowe

4Jly01- 4She	my 1⅝	:492 1:433 2:10 2:494	Lawrence Realizatn 16k	- 2 24 21 1½ 22	Spencer	121	*.20	91-13	TheParader1262Cmmndo12112Mortllo116hd	Tired badly,game	4
Previously owned by J.R. & F.P. Keene											
1Jun01- 4Gra	fst 1	:242 :482 1:13 1:392	Carlton 5k	- 1 11 1¾ 14 14	Spencer	126	*.20	106-08	Commando1264Blues111	Never extended	2
23May01- 4MP	fst 1⅜	:502 1:162 2:21	Belmont 13k	- 1 1hd 1¾ 13 1½	Spencer	126	*.70	101-12	Commando126½The Parader12650All Green126	Tired at end	3
20Oct00- 3MP	fst *6f-EC	1:101	Matron 21k	- 3 11½ 1½ 12 2½	Spencer	125	*.40	91-09	Beau Gallant125½Commando125nkThe Parader1173	Poor ride	10
11Sep00- 3Gra	fst 6f	:231 :472 1:003 1:134	Jr Champion 15k	- 3 11 1½ 11½ 11	Spencer	127	*.33e	98-07	Commando1271Bellario117hdOlympian1072	Eased up at end	7
7Aug00- 5Bri	fst 6f	:233 :48 1:002 1:131	Brighton Junior 10k	- 1 2hd 1hd 1hd 1hd	Spencer	125	*.20e	100-02	Commando125hdOlympian1121½All Green1122	Best	5
6Jly00- 3Bri	fst 6f	:234 :474 1:141	Montauk 3k	- 1 13 13 15 18	Spencer	122	*.07	95-02	Commando1228Cresson1076Bedeck107	Outclassed rest	3
30Jun00- 3She	fst *6f-FC	1:114	Great Trial 20k	- 9 1½ 14 14 13	Spencer	122	*1.80e	81-15	Commando1223The Parader1222Elkhorn1171½	Eased up	11
25Jun00- 3She	fst *6f-FC	1:092	Zephyr 1.1k	- 4 1hd 11 11½ 11½	Spencer	112	*.70	93-05	Commando1121½Holstein112½King Pepper1126	Much the best	5

Crusader

ch. c. 1923, by Man o' War (Fair Play)–Star Fancy, by Star Shoot — Lifetime record: 42 18 8 4 $203,261

Own.– Glen Riddle Stable
Br.– Samuel D. Riddle (Ky)
Tr.– G. Conway

27Oct28- 5Lrl	fst 1¼	:463 1:12 1:373 2:033 3↑	Washington H 32k	1 6 77½ 72¾ 75¾ 63½	Walls P	122wb	5.65	88-11	Mike Hall124hdDisplay1262½Sir Harry113½	Outrun	13
24Oct28- 5Lrl	fst 1 1/16	:232 :47 1:124 1:452 3↑	Alw 2000	5 3 35¼ 21 23 2½	Walls P	111wb	1.75	89-20	Victorian114½Crusader1116Display1208	Gamely	5
11Oct28- 5Haw	fst 1¼	:473 1:12 1:371 2:03 3↑	Haw Gold Cup 26k	6 7 46½ 51½ 53½ 32	Walls P	126wb	2.91	103-06	Display126noMike Hall1262Crusader126hd	Hard urged	9
29Sep28- 5HdG	sly 1⅛	:48 1:131 1:411 1:534 3↑	H de Grace Cup H 24k	3 8 88 78 78½ 33	Walls P	124wb	4.05	78-19	Osmand121½Sun Beau1142½Crusader1241½	Outrun early	8
26Sep28- 6HdG	fst 1 1/16	:231 :474 1:122 1:442 3↑	Alw 2000	4 5 35½ 33 22 23	Walls P	117wb	3.25	98-14	Victorian1133Crusdr1173StrollngPlyr106.51	Game,no match	6
19Sep28- 4HdG	my 1 70	:22 :46 1:122 1:444 3↑	Alw 2500	6 3 36 24 23 24	Walls P	117wb	3.00	82-19	Victorian1154Crusader117hdSun Beau1075	Game,tiring	6
30Jly28- 5Sar	gd 1¼	:483 1:13 1:39 2:06 3↑	Saratoga H 9.7k	2 6 55½ 52 52¾ 55	Workman R	127wb	4.00	74-15	Chance Shot1221½Black Maria1152Edith Cavell1061½	Tired	8
29Oct27- 5Lrl	fst 1¼	:47 1:114 1:372 2:022 3↑	Washington H 36k	2 8 84½ 62½ 41½ 42	Sande E	128wb	*3.30	96-10	Display112hdBlack Maria1171Mars1281	Impeded,tired	9
24Oct27- 5Lrl	fst 1⅛	:473 1:12 1:392 1:514 3↑	Handicap 2000	1 5 51¼ 43 42½ 21	Sande E	130wb	*1.00	88-16	DMars1281Crusader1302½Gaffsman1161		6
Placed first by disqualification											
18Oct27- 5Lrl	sly 1⅛	:492 1:151 1:403 1:532 3↑	Handicap 2000	2 1 1½ 1½ 1½ 11	Sande E	126wb	*.30	81-23	Crusader1261Sir Harry112hdDolan105	Handily	3
1Oct27- 5HdG	fst 1⅛	:47 1:123 1:383 1:52 3↑	H de Grace Cup H 24k	3 6 64¼ 42¼ 32½ 43¾	Sande E	129wb	*.75	86-14	ChancePly1241EdthCvll1031½Bostonn1131¼	Tired,eased late	7
28Sep27- 5HdG	fst 1 1/16	:242 :483 1:132 1:454 3↑	Delaware H 2k	1 3 32 21 1nk 13	Sande E	128wb	*.45	95-16	Crusader1283Bostonian1171Navigtor1052½	As rider pleased	4
18Jun27- 4Aqu	fst 1⅛	:471 1:12 1:36 1:484 3↑	Brooklyn H 17k	4 8 88½ 45½ 79¼ 66¼	Sande E	132wb	*1.10	93-09	Peanuts112hdChance Play1214Display1121	No threat	10
4Jun27- 4Bel	fst 1¼	:464 1:11 1:371 2:022 3↑	Suburban H 15k	5 5 43 3nk 12 17	Kummer C	127wb	3.00	88-14	Crusader1277Black Maria1202Macaw1202	Won easily	8
14May27- 4Jam	fst 1 1/16	:24 :474 1:122 1:44 3↑	Excelsior H 7.7k	4 4 55 45½ 44 43½	Fator L	127wb	*.33	89-07	Amber Jack1022½Cherry Pie110hdNavigator1081	Poor effort	5
23Apr27- 5HdG	gd 1 1/16	:232 :473 1:132 1:452 3↑	Philadelphia H 12k	3 5 31 32 53¼ 53	Fator L	128wb	*.80	94-14	Single Foot114½Canter112hdMontferrat1031½		10
Traffic on turn,dropped back											
13Nov26- 4Pim	fst 2¼	:50 2:34 3:01 3:521 3↑	Pim Cup H 12k	1 3 416 38¼ 2½ 22½	Sande E	126wb	*.25	101-15	Edith Cavell932½Crusader12640Princess Doreen110hd		4
Rated,tired late											
1Nov26- 4Pim	my 1½	:49 1:144 2:06 2:323	Riggs Mem H 30k	2 3 64 2½ 11½ 11¼	Sande E	130wb	*.65	90-12	Crusader1301¼Mars1195Gaffsman1101½	Rated,easily	7
23Oct26- 5Lrl	sl 1¼	:472 1:123 1:392 2:052	Maryland H 12k	1 1 52 31¼ 1nk 13	Ellis G	126wb	*.45	83-17	Crusader1263Chance Play1195Gaffsman10812	Won easing up	5
16Oct26- 5Lrl	fst 1	:23 :472 1:123 1:38 2↑	Laurel 14k	8 7 82½ 53 52¼ 43	Coltiletti F	124wb	*1.75	95-11	Croyden107.52Sarazen126hdMrs1171	Shuffled back 1st turn	11
25Sep26- 5HdG	fst 1⅛	:473 1:122 1:38 1:50 3↑	Havre de Grace H 17k	8 7 63½ 31 11 15	Sande E	122wb	*.85	100-06	Crusader1225Son of John108hdDisplay114nk	In a canter	12
11Sep26- 5Bel	fst 2	:502 2:36 3:024 3:26 3↑	J C Gold Cup 17k	2 2 23 22 21½ 11½	Maiben J	114wb	*1.40	79-17	Crusader1141½Espino1145Altawood125no	Going away	5
4Sep26- 5Bel	fst 1⅝	:481 1:392 2:044 2:423	Lawrence Realizatn 29k	5 2 12 12 11½ 2hd	Maiben J	126wb	*.80	91-16	Espino126hdCrusader1265Mars12615	Outfinished	5
24Aug26- 4Sar	my 1 3/16	:49 1:142 1:393 1:593	Huron H 5.1k	7 1 11 11½ 13 11½	Sande E	126wb	*.55	80-20	Crusader1261½Espino1145Black Maria1124	Speed to spare	7
14Aug26- 5Sar	fst 1¼	:463 1:123 1:383 2:043	Travers 18k	4 6 43½ 22 31¼ 44½	Sande E	129wb	*.80	81-16	Mrs1231½Pompy1231½Dsply1231½	Left at start,rushed up,tired	8
24Jly26- 6CI	fst 1¼	:464 1:112 1:362 2:02	Cincinnati Derby 28k	3 3 21½ 2hd 13 13	Sande E	126wb	*.80	101-09	Crsdr1263Dsply126½BoottoBoot1262	Wide 1st turn,drew away	8
3Jly26- 4Aqu	fst 1½	:491 1:14 2:052 2:293	Dwyer 19k	2 5 57½ 43 21 1no	Sande E	123wb	1.60e	127-07	Crusader123noChance Play1203Espino1084	Just up	5
12Jun26- 5Bel	sly 1½	:50 1:14 2:063 2:321	Belmont 56k	2 2 51¾ 34 2½ 11	Johnson A	126wb	*.70	83-22	Crusader1261Espino1264Haste1262	Handily	9
5Jun26- 4Bel	fst 1¼	:47 1:114 1:373 2:03 3↑	Suburban H 16k	2 3 21½ 1nk 15 15	Callahan J	104wb	*1.00e	85-17	Crusadr1045AmrcnFlg1241KngSolomon'sSl1071½	In a canter	9
26May26- 4Bel	fst 1	:232 :464 1:112 1:373	Withers 25k	4 13 106½ 98¼ 56½ 21	Johnson A	118wb	7.00	88-24	Haste1181Crusader118hdEspino1181½	Impeded,finished fast	15
20May26- 3Jam	fst 6f	:233 :473 1:12 3↑	Handicap 1260	5 2 21½ 21 22 21	Johnson A	126wb	2.00	94-12	Claptrap1201Crusader1263Pheasant112hd	Gamely	5
Previously trained by G.R. Tompkins											
6Nov25- 4Pim	fst 1	:232 :472 1:13 1:404	Pim Futurity 61k	2 13 1215 1212 78½ 53	Johnson A	117 w	3.45e	81-19	Canter117noBubblingOver1221½Disply1191	Crowded 1st turn	14
Geldings not eligible											
24Oct25- 4Lrl	hy 1	:241 :492 1:152 1:414	Manor H 14k	4 1 11½ 13 16 110	Johnson A	116wb	7.55e	79-28	Crusader11610Corvette107½Blondin1094	In a canter	10
10Oct25- 5Lrl	fst 6f	:234 :48 1:141	National 7.5k	4 2 66 47 34 31¼	Johnson A	115 b	*.45e	85-20	Gaffsman1181¼Corvtt112hdCrusdr1154	Finished with a rush	6
30Sep25- 4HdG	fst 5½f	:231 :47 1:06	Alw 1300	2 6 64¾ 35 21½ 13½	Callahan J	114 w	2.10	96-14	Crusader1143½UrsaMajor1176TheEngineer1081	Won eased up	6
26Sep25- 4HdG	fst 6f	:231 :472 1:122	Alw 1300	3 1 54½ 31 26 37	Johnson A	112wb	1.35	86-17	Macaw1127Welshot106noCrusader1126	Tiring	7

Date/Race	Cond/Dist	Fractions/Time	Race	Running line	Fin	Jockey	Wt	Odds	Speed	Top finishers	Comment	Field
8Sep25-5Bel	my 5½f	:243 :482 1:072	Alw 1000	6 6 43½ 31¼ 3¾	14	Johnson A	117wb	*1.60	85-22	Crusader1174Deviner1122Mars1124	Easily	9
3Jun25-6Bel	fst 5f-Str	:582	Alw 1200	4 4 2½ 2hd	11	Maiben J	107wb	2.20	86-17	Crusader1071Mars1071Sandstorm107no	Finished fast	9
28May25-3Bel	fst 4½f-Str	:52	Alw 1200	1 3 21 2½	2½	Johnson A	112 w	3.00	94-08	Punjab112½Crusader1124Euclid1152	Tired in drive	7
13May25-1Pim	fst 4½f	:232 :473 :542	Md Sp Wt	8 6 54½ 45 21½	1hd	Johnson A	115 w	12.75	96-04	Crusader115hdGaffsman1152Zeppelin1153	Wide,just up	9
1May25-2Pim	sl 4f	:233 :493	Md Alw 1500	6 6 64 56½	77¼	Scobie E	115 w	25.05	83-11	Welshot115hdShampoo1121½Foretell1155	Never a factor	12
16Apr25-3HdG	fst 4f	:23 :471	©Md Sp Wt	2 10 1319 1017	817	Babin G	118 w	39.55	82-01	Canter118½Fiddlstcks1183HrvyStdmn1181½	Crowded at start	14

Domino

br. c. 1891, by Himyar (Alarm)–Mannie Gray, by Enquirer
Own.– J.R. & F.P. Keene
Br.– Maj B.G. Thomas (Ky)
Tr.– William Lakeland

Lifetime record: 25 19 2 1 $193,550

Date/Race	Cond/Dist	Fractions/Time	Race	Running line	Fin	Jockey	Wt	Odds	Speed	Top finishers	Comment	Field
17Sep95-4Gra	gd 1¼	:53 1:17½ 1:43½ 2:09	3↑ First Spl 2.5k	- 4 53 4¾ 51¼	56¼	Taral	122	5.00	- -	Henry of Navarre1221½Clifford117nkSir Walter1103		5
11Sep95-5She	fst 1⅛	1:532	Swpst 3500	- -	2nk	Taral	122	1.60	- -	Henry of Navarre122nkDomino1223Rey el Santa Anita122		3
	Led,just missed											
24Aug95-2She	fst *6f-FC	1:094	3↑ Fall H 1.5k	- -	2hd	Taral	133	*.70	- -	Butterflies109hdDomino1336ReyDelCarrs112	Dueled,missed	8
29Jun95-4She	gd 1	:26 :493 1:134 1:411	3↑ Sheepshead Bay H 1.5k	- 1 12 12	12	Taral	127	*1.40	- -	Domino1272Dorian118hdSir Walter1232	Handily	6
22Jun95-4She	fst *6f-FC	:233 :473 :59 1:10	3↑ Coney Island H 1.5k	- 2 11 11	12	Taral	120	*1.20	- -	Domino1202Wernberg116hdRedskin109nk	Very easily	6
18Jun95-1She	fst 5½f	:24⅗ :50 1:01⅗ 1:08	3↑ Alw 720	- 2 21 2½ 2nk	13	Taral	122	*.50	- -	Domino1223Factotum112hdRey del Carreras1091	Easily	5
15Jun95-4She	fst 1¼	:51½ 1:17 1:42 2:074	3↑ Suburban H 6.2k	- 3 3¾ 3½ 21½	43¼	Taral	123	*.40	- -	Lazzarone1151½Sir Walter1261½Song and Dance103nk		6
	Eased up after mile											
15May95-1Gra	hy 6f	1:17	2↑ Swpst 690	- -	12	Taral	122	*.50	- -	Domino1222Wernberg112¾Patrician112	Led final ¼,easily	4
6Oct94-5MP	fst 1⅛	1:52¼	3↑ Special 5k	- -	310¾	Taral	113	*1.20	- -	Henry of Navarre113¾Clifford12210Domino113	Led,faltered	3
15Sep94-5Gra	gd 1⅛	1:55½	3rd Spl 5k	- -	1↓	Taral	122	*.55	- -	DH Domino122 DH Henry of Navarre122	Led,dueled late	2
11Sep94-4Gra	gd 6f	1:13⅗	2↑ Culver 2.1k	- -	11½	Taral	116	*.25	- -	Domino1161½Stonenell12210Lissak91	Led final ¼	3
6Sep94-5She	fst 1	1:392	3↑ Match Race 5k	- -	1¾	Taral	112	1.05	- -	Domino112¾Clifford122	Led,drawing away	2
30Aug94-4She	fst 1	1:401	3↑ Ocean H 2k	- -	1hd	Taral	116	*.65	- -	Domino116hdDucat1141½Saragossa106	Easily	4
27Aug94-4She	fst *6f-FC	1:10	Flying 1.9k	- -	13	Taral	130	*.55	- -	Domino1303Peacemaker1195Harrington112		6
23Jun94-3OWP	fst 1½	:52¼ 1:19⅗ 2:10 2:36	American Derby 25k	- -	9	Taral	125	*1.40	- -	ReyelSantaAnita1226SntorGrdy1222Dspot122	Never a threat	9
12Jun94-4MP	fst 1	1:40	Withers 7.9k	- -	1hd	Taral	122	1.80	- -	Domino122hdHenry of Navarre1223Dobbins122	Driving	5
29Sep93-3MP	fst 6f	1:09	Matron 27k	- -	11	Taral	128	*.25	- -	Domino1281Peacemaker109.53Jack of Spades121		11
	Dueled,drew away rapidly											
31Aug93-0She	fst *6f-FC	1:123	Match Race 22k	- -	1↓	Taral	118	-	- -	DH Domino118 DH Dobbins118	Dueled throughout	2
	Match and mutuels called off - off at odds of *.50											
29Aug93-4She	hy *6f-FC	1:124	Futurity 56k	- -	1hd	Taral	130	*1.20	- -	Domino130hdGallilee115hdDobbins130	Rapid finish	20
19Aug93-4OMP	gd 6f-Str	1:14½	Produce 22k	- -	1¾	Taral	128	*.50	- -	Domino128¾Discount108nkDeclare118	Led throughout	11
13Jly93-3OWP	fst 6f	1:14	Hyde Park 18k	- -	12	Taral	123	*.20e	- -	Domino1232Peter the Great118nkVassal123	Handily	9
27Jun93-3She	hy *6f-FC	1:14	Great Trial 26k	- -	1nk	Garrison	125	*.60	- -	Domino125nkHyderAbad1182Dobbns125	Led throughout,easily	9
10Jun93-4MP	fst 6f	1:12¾	Great Eclipse 20k	- -	12	Taral	118	*.33	- -	Domino1182Dobbins118¾Declare118	Led throughout	6
27May93-3Gra	fst 5f	1:01¾	Great American	- -	14	Taral	118	*1.00	- -	Domino1184Dobbins1181Joe Ripley119		8
22May93-2Gra	fst 5f	1:02	Swpst	- -	16	Taral	112	*.80	- -	Domino1126Fonso111¾Patrician111	Led throughout	13

Exterminator

ch. g. 1915, by McGee (White Knight)–Fair Empress, by Jim Gore
Own.– W.S. Kilmer
Br.– F.D. Knight (Ky)
Tr.– H. McDaniel

Lifetime record: 100 50 17 17 $252,996

Date/Race	Cond/Dist	Fractions/Time	Race	Running line	Fin	Jockey	Wt	Odds	Speed	Top finishers	Comment	Field
21Jun24-5Dor	gd 1$\frac{1}{16}$	:232 :474 1:132 1:47	3↑ Queen's Hotel H 3k	4 3 31¼ 3¾ 42½	35½	Wallace J	113 w	*1.30	84-13	SpotCash1282½ForestLor1033Extrmntor113nk	Pulled up lame	5
7Jun24-6BB	gd 1	:232 :473 1:132 1:394	3↑ Alw 1000	1 4 21½ 21 22	11	Wallace J	111 w	1.85	90-14	Exterminator1111Golden Rule1134Opperman1116	Handily	5
1May24-6Pim	fst 1	:242 :483 1:13 1:383	3↑ Handicap 2000	4 5 42½ 55¼ 46¼	310½	Johnson A	126 w	4.80	84-11	Martingale120½SpicndSpn10610Extrmntor1261	Always outrun	6
19Apr24-5HdG	hy 1$\frac{1}{16}$	:232 :482 1:153 1:492	3↑ Philadelphia H 5.1k	6 5 65½ 63 56¾	58¼	Johnson A	125 w	*1.20e	69-25	SpotCash111hdFlintStone118nkNewHampshire1124	No mishap	6
17Apr24-5HdG	fst 1 70	:244 :49 1:14 1:44	3↑ Alw 2000	2 2 21½ 1hd 1hd	1½	Walls P	107 w	*.50	92-11	Exterminator107½GoldenSpher103½SttngSun10615	Ridden out	5
30Mar24-6Tij	fst 1¼	:474 1:124 1:39 2:052	3↑ Coffroth H 51k	11 7 65¾ 54½ 53	41½	Johnson A	130 w	*1.60e	97-14	Runstar123noOsprey123noCherryTree1171½	Challenged,tired	18
17Feb24-4Tij	fst 1 70	:241 :483 1:133 1:443	4↑ Alw 700	4 2 2¾ 21 11	11	Johnson A	113 w	*.30	89-12	Extermintor1131Suprcrgo1161VnPtrck1011	Gentle hand ride	5
	Previously trained by W. Shields											
28Apr23-5HdG	my 1 70	:242 :493 1:143 1:452	3↑ Handicap 2500	3 4 31½ 21 2½	2no	Johnson A	132 w	*1.10	85-21	Chickvl101noExtrmntor1321PulJons10810	Getting to winner	5
21Apr23-5HdG	fst 1$\frac{1}{16}$	:24 :48 1:123 1:454	3↑ Philadelphia H 5.1k	2 4 53½ 42¼ 2¾	1nk	McAtee L	129 w	*.80	95-10	Exterminator129nkPaul Jones1092Fair Phantom107nk	Gamely	6
16Apr23-4HdG	my 6f	:24 :49 1:15	3↑ Harford H 5.1k	4 5 64 62¾ 42½	31¼	Sande E	132 w	3.70	80-32	Blazes106nkCareful116½Exterminator1326	Finished fast	8
	Previously trained by E. Wayland											
11Nov22-4Pim	fst 2¼	:50 2:34 3:04 3:532	3↑ Pim Cup H 10k	5 2 2hd 46 418	331½	Marineli B	126 w	*.65	66-13	CaptanAlcock1061½PulJons9930Extrmntor126100	Forced pace	5
28Oct22-5Lrl	fst 1¼	:47 1:122 1:382 2:044	3↑ Washington H 28k	8 5 54 44½ 45	43½	Johnson A	132 w	*.90	82-17	Oceanic104½Lucky Hour1202Paragon II1211	Finished fast	8
21Oct22-5Lrl	fst 1	:244 :49 1:14 1:40	2↑ Laurel 13k	1 5 53 42 31½	12½	Johnson A	132 w	2.25	88-15	Extermintor1322½ D PrgonII1251½Trystr123hd	Won easing up	8
14Oct22-4Lrl	fst 6f	:23 :47 1:124	3↑ Handicap 2000	8 2 86¾ 64½ 65	41½	Johnson A	133 w	*2.25	92-16	CalamityJane113hdOnWatch1241TipptyWtcht112½	Steady gain	8
30Sep22-5Haw	fst 1¼	:514 1:183 1:451 2:10	Special	- 1 1 1 1	1	Johnson A	126 w	-	73-19	Exterminator126	Good run	1
	Race against time											
20Sep22-5OW	fst 1¼	:463 1:113 1:382 2:051	3↑ Toronto Aut Cup H 16k	5 5 53¼ 42½ 3½	11½	Johnson A	132 w	*.80	95-09	Exterminator1321½Guy102hdBitofWhit1001	Rated,going away	8
31Aug22-4Sar	gd 1¾	:50 2:10 2:35 3:002	3↑ Sar Cup 8.3k	1 1 11 11 11	1nk	Johnson A	126 w	1.40	80-18	Exterminatr126nkMdHttr12612BonHomm126	Outstayed rivals	3
1Aug22-4Sar	fst 1¼	:481 1:123 1:38 2:031	3↑ Saratoga H 9.2k	1 4 52 53½ 57	510¼	Johnson A	137 w	5.00	83-09	Grey Lag130½Bon Homme1091¼Prudery1146	Hard ridden	5
4Jly22-5Lat	gd 1½	:482 1:122 2:041 2:302	3↑ Independence H 18k	2 4 44½ 59½ 68	612	Johnson A	140 w	*.90	84-14	Firebrand1163Devastation1026Minto II1161		8
	Appeared in distress after mile											
16Jun22-4Aqu	fst 1⅛	:473 1:123 1:37 1:50	3↑ Brooklyn H 9.8k	2 3 32 2½ 2hd	1hd	Johnson A	135 w	1.50	95-10	Exterminator135hdGreyLag1264PollyAnn103hd	Strong finish	5
13Jun22-4Bel	fst 1$\frac{1}{16}$	:234 :48 1:131 1:44	3↑ Handicap 1635	5 4 21½ 22 11	11½	Johnson A	135 w	1.40	96-12	Exterminator1351½Mad Hatter1286Devastation102nk	Rated	6
5Jun22-4Bel	gd 1⅛	:47 1:122 1:382 1:522	3↑ Handicap 1470	2 1 1no 1½ 1½	1½	Johnson A	133 w	*.07	83-11	Exterminator133½Be Frank107	Won hard held	2
27May22-5CD	sl 1¼	:48 1:122 1:382 2:042	3↑ Kentucky H 12k	1 2 2hd 11 11½	11½	Johnson A	138 w	*.45	94-15	Exterminator1381½Firebrand1195Blarney Stone958	Easily	4
20May22-5CD	fst 1⅛	:471 1:12 1:37 1:50	3↑ Clark H 13k	5 4 51½ 2nk 1½	11½	Johnson A	133 w	*.60	99-10	Exterminator1331½Lady Madcap1111Rouleau1074	Drew away	9
6May22-6Pim	sl 1$\frac{1}{16}$	:243 :493 1:14 1:454	3↑ Pim Spring H 5.6k	3 2 21 1nk 1hd	1hd	Johnson A	133 w	*.75	97-18	Exterminator133hdBoniface12510Registrar1022	Hard drive	7
22Apr22-5HdG	fst 1$\frac{1}{16}$	:244 :483 1:141 1:45	3↑ Philadelphia H 5.5k	2 2 31¼ 31½ 2hd	2no	Johnson A	133 w	*.65	99-09	Boniface122noExterminator1336BungaBuck110nk	Cut off ⅜	6
15Apr22-4HdG	hy 6f	:234 :481 1:141	3↑ Harford H 5.2k	7 4 64½ 43 42	11	Johnson A	132wb	4.95	85-24	Exterminator1321Billy Kelly1321Dexterous1021	Going away	12
	Previously trained by W. Knapp											
12Nov21-5Pim	hy 2¼	:55 2:462 3:12 4:081	3↑ Pim Cup H 9.8k	1 1 1½ 1½ 1hd	1hd	Johnson A	126 w	*.70	- -	Exterminator126hdBoniface12120Lady Emmeline96	Held on	3
29Oct21-5Lxt	fst 1½	:502 1:161 2:07 2:313	3↑ Lex Cup H 6.2k	5 3 33 23 32½	36½	Johnson A	135 w	*.80	84-10	Firbrnd1181½UntdVrd1055Extrmntor1352	Tired under impost	5
22Oct21-4Lrl	fst 1¼	:471 1:12 1:382 2:042	3↑ Handicap 2038	6 3 37 34 2nk	11	Johnson A	132 w	*1.65	88-14	Exterminator1321My Dear1151½Bygone Days961½	Driving	6
8Oct21-4Lrl	sly 1½	:483 1:141 2:06 2:35	3↑ Annapolis H 12k	6 4 1hd 21 33	38½	Kelsay W	135 w	*2.15	64-23	ThePorter1202½MyDer1146Extrmntr1351½	Eased when beaten	8
24Sep21-5OW	fst 1¼	:48 1:132 1:383 2:051	3↑ Toronto Aut Cup H 7.9k	6 4 43½ 2½ 1½	1nk	Kelsay W	137 w	*1.40	95-12	Exterminator137nkMy Dear1172Golden Sphere1061	Gamely	9

16Sep21- 4Bel	fst	2	:493 2:352 3:02 3:291	3↑ Autumn Gold Cup H 5.7k	2 2 1hd 11 13 16	Kelsay W	130	w	*.33	63-19	Exterminator1306Bellsolar104	In a canter	2
31Aug21- 4Sar	sl	1¾	:554 2:132 2:393 3:043	3↑ Sar Cup 4.5k	- 1 1 1 1 1	Kelsay W	126	w	-	59-22	Exterminator126	Galloped	1
	Walkover												
27Aug21- 4Sar	fst	1 3/16	:472 1:114 1:373 1:572	3↑ Merchants & Cits H 8.7k	6 5 51¾ 21 1½ 11	Kelsay W	130	w	6.00	91-10	Exterminator1301MadHattr132¾Bllsolr104hd	Outside,gamely	7
	Previously trained by F. Curtis												
12Jly21- 4Wnr	fst	1⅛	:471 1:12 1:382 1:512	3↑ Frontier H 12k	7 4 51¾ 32½ 31½ 32	Simpson R	132	w	4.20	97-07	BestPal1191½IrishKiss108½Extrmntor1328	Closed with rush	8
9Jly21- 5Lat	fst	1 3/16	:473 1:122 1:373 1:561	3↑ Daniel Boone H 14k	7 4 21 1½ 21½ 32	Haynes E	135	w	2.20	100-08	Best Pal1191La Rablee1061Exterminator1356		8
	Cut off by winner final ⅛												
4Jly21- 5Lat	fst	1½	:493 1:141 2:052 2:301	3↑ Independence H 19k	5 3 32 21 1½ 11	Haynes E	130	w	*.55	97-07	Exterminator1301Woodtrap1111½La Rablee1086	Handily	7
	Previously trained by W. McDaniel												
17Jun21- 4Aqu	gd	1⅛	:462 1:11 1:362 1:494	3↑ Brooklyn H 9.8k	10 7 74 42½ 42½ 33	Ensor L	129	w	4.00	94-08	GreyLag1121½JohnP.Grier1241½Extrmntor1291	Inside,gamely	11
4Jun21- 4Bel	fst	1¼	:473 1:12 1:361 2:021	3↑ Suburban H 11k	8 5 58½ 59½ 59½ 58¾	Johnson A	133	w	*1.20	80-09	Audacious120¾MadHattr1306SennngsPrk110no	Always outrun	8
21May21- 4Jam	fst	1⅛	:48 1:123 1:372 1:50	3↑ Long Beach H 5.8k	3 2 21½ 1hd 1½ 1¾	Johnson A	130	w	*1.00	106-03	Exterminator130¾Mad Hatter1305Cirrus1287	Drew clear	4
14May21- 4Jam	my	1 1/16	:233 :481 1:14 1:471	3↑ Excelsior H 10k	1 5 53 42½ 31½ 21	Johnson A	129	w	3.60	89-15	Blazes1181Exterminator1296Naturalist126¾	Slow late gain	7
7May21- 4Jam	fst	1 1/16	:233 :472 1:12 1:45	3↑ Kings County H 6.1k	3 3 44½ 35 25 23	Haynes E	129	w	2.20	98-08	MadHatter1243Extrmintr1293YllowHnd1101½	Closed gamely	5
12Nov20- 4Pim	fst	2¼	:472 2:321 2:583 3:53	3↑ Pim Cup H 10k	2 3 21 11 1½ 1no	Ensor L	126	w	*.75	20- -	Exterminator126noBonifc11410PulJons110.56	Rated,all out	7
8Nov20- 4Pim	fst	1½	:483 1:142 2:051 2:313	3↑ Bowie H 11k	3 7 73½ 53½ 63¾ 53½	Fairbrother C	135	w	2.80	94-08	Mad Hatter120noBoniface1221½The Porter128no	In a pocket	9
20Oct20- 5OW	hy	2¼	:513 2:393 3:094 4:044	3↑ Ont Jockey Club Cup 7.7k	1 1 22 22 1nk 11¼	Fairbrother C	134	w	*.15	49-26	Exterminator1341¼Bondage1106St. Germain901½	Easily	4
25Sep20- 5OW	fst	1¼	:482 1:133 1:394 2:042	3↑ Toronto Aut Cup 7.8k	4 2 11 11 1½ 1hd	Fairbrother C	132	w	*.25	99-10	Exterminator132hdMy Dear9212Bondage1081	Driving	5
	Previously trained by J.S. Healey												
15Sep20- 4Bel	fst	2	:482 2:293 3:214	3↑ Autumn Gold Cup 6.3k	2 3 32½ 32 2½ 1hd	Fairbrother C	128	w	*.70	- -	Exterminator128hdDamask982½Cleopatra105	Rated,driving	3
31Aug20- 4Sar	sl	1¾	:502 2:043 2:294 2:562	3↑ Sar Cup 5.6k	2 1 11 11½ 13 16	Fairbrother C	126	w	*.55	108-12	Exterminator1266Cleopatra111	Easily	2
28Aug20- 4Wnr	fst	1 1/16	:23 :472 1:12 1:444	3↑ George Hendrie H 8.6k	4 3 31½ 31¼ 2½ 11	Fairbrother C	131	w	*1.15	98-09	Exterminator1311Wildair1143My Dear95hd	Rated,going away	6
21Aug20- 4Wnr	sl	1⅛	:48 1:132 1:384 1:511	3↑ Wnr Jockey Club H 11k	1 3 21½ 21½ 2nk 11¼	Fairbrother C	125	w	2.50	100-17	Exterminator1251¼Wildair11010Boniface130nk	Drew away	7
14Aug20- 4Sar	gd	1⅛	:484 1:14 1:402 1:531	3↑ Champlain H 4.1k	1 4 21 31½ 1½ 21½	Schuttinger A	128	w	*2.20	82-19	Gnome1091½Extrminatr1281MadHatter1175	Inside,no match	7
2Aug20- 4Sar	fst	1¼	:474 1:11 1:36 2:014	3↑ Saratoga H 6.7k	3 5 54¼ 21½ 22½ 22	Schuttinger A	126	w	7.00	100-06	SirBarton1292Exterminator1263Wildar1153	Gamely,no match	5
14Jly20- 4Wnr	hy	1⅛	:492 1:182 1:47 2:011	3↑ Frontier H 12k	5 3 44 22 32½ 32½	Davies T	127	w	*1.25	47-48	Slippery Elm109½The Porter1292Exterminator1275	Tired	8
3Jly20- 4Aqu	my	1⅛	:481 1:124 1:373 1:501	3↑ Brookdale H 4.2k	2 3 3½ 21 2½ 11½	Schuttinger A	129	w	2.00	96-11	Exterminator1291½Cirrus1234Gladiator1126	Hard ridden	4
29Jun20- 4Aqu	fst	1 1/16	:233 :462 1:11 1:44	3↑ Handicap 1290	3 3 34 33 31 1¾	Schuttinger A	126	w	3.00	101-18	Exterminator126¾Naturalist120½Wildair11412	Drew away	5
24Jun20- 4Aqu	fst	1⅛	:47 1:11 1:363 1:50	3↑ Brooklyn H 7.3k	7 7 75 76 46 48¼	Schuttinger A	124	w	6.00	89-09	Cirrus108hdBoniface1228Mad Hatter115hd	Steadily	7
19Jun20- 4Jam	gd	1⅛	:474 1:13 1:382 1:511	3↑ Long Beach H 4k	2 3 1½ 11 11 11	Schuttinger A	119	w	2.20	102-06	Exterminator1191Cirrus1098Naturalist1203	Handily	5
5Jun20- 4Bel	my	1¼	:52 1:163 1:432 2:093	3↑ Suburban H 7.8k	5 5 58½ 46½ 47 36	Rice T	123	w	*2.20	46-30	Paul Jones106hdBoniface1156Exterminator123½	Game try	5
29May20- 5Bel	fst	1 1/16	:242 :48 1:13 1:443	3↑ Handicap 1605	4 3 21½ 31 1½ 2nk	Davies T	128	w	*2.00	97-10	Alibi107nkExterminator1282Sea Mint98no	Led,tired	5
	Previously trained by H. McDaniel												
13Nov19- 4Pim	hy	2¼	:523 2:50 3:182 4:13	3↑ Pim Cup H 4.9k	1 1 22 14 12 14	Kummer C	121	w	*1.00	- -	Extrminatr1214RoycRools1058½Woodtrp1023	Won easing up	3
8Nov19- 4Pim	fst	1½	:493 1:15 2:072 2:334	3↑ Bowie H 10k	5 3 52¾ 55½ 511 513½	Kummer C	128	w	2.90	73-11	Royce Rools1071½Cudgel1314Mad Hatter1132	Quit badly	5
18Oct19- 5Lat	hy	2¼	:54 2:50 3:184 4:17	3↑ Lat Cup 8.7k	4 3 11 2hd 21½ 22	Knapp W	134	w	*.45	- -	Be Frank1222Exterminator13420Legal10520	Tired	4
11Oct19- 4Lrl	fst	1½	:473 1:13 2:033 2:293	3↑ Annapolis H 8.3k	3 3 34½ 21 21½ 2hd	Knapp W	128	w	2.05	107-06	Thunderclp108hdExtrmntor1283Cudgl1321	Getting to winner	5
3Oct19- 3Lrl	fst	1 1/16	:242 :49 1:153 1:461	3↑ Alw 1200	2 1 11 1hd 1½ 1nk	Knapp W	120	w	*.05	86-15	Exterminator120nkOrestes12010Douglass S.113	Hard ridden	3
27Sep19- 5HdG	fst	1⅛	:471 1:122 1:373 1:50	3↑ Havre de Grace H 10k	5 6 64¾ 4¾ 41¾ 2½	Knapp W	126	w	10.50	105-05	Cudgel129½Extrmntr126noSrBrton1242	Impeded,game finish	8
22Sep19- 5HdG	fst	1 1/16	:24 :48 1:13 1:45	3↑ Purse 2527	1 2 22 21½ 21 1¾	Schuttinger A	124	w	5.05	100-11	Exterminator124¾Cudgel1291Slippery Elm993	Gamely	5
11Sep19- 4HdG	my	1 70	:25 :49 1:143 1:45	3↑ Harford County H 5.4k	4 2 3½ 23 24 24	Schuttinger A	125	w	*.35	83-25	The Porter1214Exterminator1258Slippery Elm1033	No match	5
30Aug19- 4Sar	sl	1¾	:48 2:07 2:32 2:58	3↑ Sar Cup 6.3k	3 1 11½ 12 1½ 11½	Schuttinger A	126	w	2.50	100-14	Extrmntr1261½Purchs11650ThTrump116	Challenged,drew away	3
23Aug19- 4Sar	fst	1 3/16	:484 1:133 1:372 1:572	3↑ Merchants & Cits H 3.4k	1 1 11 2½ 32½ 33	Loftus J	126	w	*1.10e	90-08	Cudgel1321Star Master1222Exterminator1261½	No menace	5
9Aug19- 4Sar	fst	1⅛	:48 1:123 1:371 1:50	3↑ Champlain H 3.4k	6 4 42¼ 31 21 21	Loftus J	120	w	*.90e	106-09	SunBriar1281Extermintor120½Hollstr1151½	Not hard ridden	6
5Aug19- 4Sar	fst	1	:232 :462 1:112 1:361	3↑ Delaware H 3.4k	6 5 44½ 34 33½ 31	Loftus J	121	w	*1.20e	99-08	FairyWand107hdSunBriar1281Exterminator121½	Fast finish	8
14Jun19- 4Jam	fst	1 1/16	:244 :482 1:13 1:452	3↑ Excelsior H 4.8k	8 5 44½ 45½ 68 53¾	Loftus J	124	w	8.00	96-07	Naturalist1221Star Master1191Boniface108nk	No threat	8
7Jun19- 4Bel	fst	1¼	:463 1:113 1:38 2:021	3↑ Suburban H 6.7k	1 4 57½ 75¼ 76¾ 55¼	Rice T	128	w	5.00	84-16	Corn Tassel108nkSweep On1081½Boniface1073	Outrun	8
24May19- 5CD	hy	1¼	:482 1:143 1:42 2:102	3↑ Kentucky H 14k	1 4 1½ 1hd 1hd 31	Morys J	134	w	*2.15	64-31	Midway1221Beaverkill108noExterminator1342	Gamely	7
22May19- 6CD	my	1	:25 :50 1:153 1:423	3↑ Handicap 1660	4 1 11½ 12 11½ 15	Morys J	134	w	*.60	74-39	Exterminator1345Flyaway97nkDrastic11210	Ridden out	4
15May19- 4CD	fst	1	:25 :493 1:143 1:391	3↑ Alw 1800	4 1 1½ 11 2hd 2no	Morys J	115	w	*.20	91-11	Under Fire103noExterminator1151½Bribed Voter1088		4
	Tight restraint,tired												
8May19 4Lxt	my	1¼	:403 1:152 1:42 2:073	3↑ Camden H 2.5k	1 1 11 11 11 11	Morys J	132	w	*.35	81-28	Exterminator1321Midway118	Drawing away	2
1May19- 4Lxt	hy	1 1/16	:243 :491 1:16 1:502	3↑ Ben Ali H 2.9k	4 3 21½ 21½ 11½ 13	Morys J	124	w	*.60	70-33	Exterminator1243AmericanAc996Mdwy120hd	As rider pleased	5
31Mar19- 4OP	fst	6f	:233 :48 1:124	3↑ Handicap 800	3 1 31½ 32 1hd 11½	Haynes E	123	w	*1.00	96-09	Extrmntor1231½UltmThul1141½A.N.Akn1072	As rider pleased	6
22Mar19- 4OP	fst	1 70	:242 :48 1:13 1:432	3↑ Handicap 800	2 2 2½ 11½ 11½ 13	Schuttinger A	126	w	*.80	109-09	Exterminator1263Lucky B.1111½Drastic1113	Won eased up	4
28Nov18- 5Lat	my	1 1/16	:243 :493 1:153 1:503	2↑ Handicap 2090	2 4 3½ 12 14 12½	Loftus J	126	w	*.85	64-37	Exterminator1262½Drastic1046WrMchn1095	As rider pleased	8
23Nov18- 5Lat	hy	2¼	:54 2:433 3:11 4:063	3↑ Lat Cup H 8.9k	6 6 11½ 11 1hd 1no	Loftus J	121	w	*1.25	- -	Exterminator121noBeaverkill1105Moscowa1153	Gamely	6
12Nov18- 4Pim	fst	1½	:49 1:142 2:043 2:311	3↑ Bowie H 12k	4 5 1½ 24 22 31¼	Loftus J	120	w	6.85	102-06	GeorgeSmith130¾OmarKhayyam115½Extrmntr1206	Resolutely	15
6Nov18- 4Pim	fst	1¼	:492 1:141 1:393 2:053	Pim Autumn H 5.4k	2 2 1hd 2hd 11 1½	Ensor L	118	w	3.20	99-09	Extrmntor118½Forground107nkThPortr1276	Outstayed rivals	5
31Oct18- 4Lrl	hy	1⅛	:50 1:16 1:414 1:542	3↑ National H 3k	1 1 1nk 1nk 1nk 2hd	Knapp W	117	w	1.75	76-25	Midway117hdExterminator11720Tombolo98	Wide	3
26Oct18- 6Lrl	fst	1⅛	:49 1:141 1:393 1:521	Ellicott City H 2.5k	5 1 1nk 13 11½ 12½	Knapp W	113	w	*.30	87-08	Extermintor1132½Aurum104.51½RdSox105.5nk	Never extended	5
12Oct18- 5Lrl	gd	1⅛	:49 1:143 1:402 1:512	3↑ Washington H 2.5k	3 1 1¾ 22 32 33½	Knapp W	114	w	3.15	87-13	Midway111.52Cudgel1301½Exterminator113.51½	Tired badly	4
8Oct18- 4Lrl	fst	1 1/16	:231 :464 1:124 1:441	Carrollton H 1.9k	4 1 1nk 1½ 1½ 1hd	Knapp W	118	w	12.70	96-11	Exterminator118hdThe Porter1265Sunny Slope1304	Gamely	4
4Oct18- 4Lrl	fst	1 1/16	:24 :481 1:15 1:461	3↑ Alw 1408	4 1 12 11½ 11 11	Kummer C	103	w	*.65	86-11	Exterminator1031Franklin1122John I. Day100no	Ridden out	4
30Aug18- 4Sar	hy	1¼	:501 1:171 1:451 2:122	3↑ Handicap 1313	4 2 22 42½ 47 39½	Knapp W	115	w	*2.20	48-34	Ticket1061½Bondage1068Extermntr1151½	Impeded by winner	5
17Aug18- 4Sar	fst	1¼	:49 1:133 1:382 2:031	Travers 10k	2 2 44½ 47 48 412	Schuttinger A	123	w	*1.10e	92-05	Sun Briar120hdJohren1266War Cloud1266	Outrun	4
3Aug18- 4Sar	fst	1 3/16	:483 1:132 1:383 1:563	Kenner 4k	3 2 32½ 33 31¾ 22	Knapp W	129	w	5.00	105-02	Enfilade1142Exterminator129nkTippityWitcht1235	Game try	5
22Jun18- 5Lat	fst	1½	:494 1:142 2:063 2:33	Lat Derby 12k	5 4 42½ 35½ 31½ 22	Knapp W	124	w	8.75	85-11	Johren1272Exterminator124½Frecuttr1228	Hard ridden late	6
25May18- 4BPT	fst	1		3↑ Turf and Field H .7k	- - 21	Knapp W	122		*.45	- -	Kilts II1261Exterminator1221Square Dealer1262	Driving	6
	No time taken												
11May18- 5CD	my	1¼	:491 1:161 1:433 2:104	Ky Derby 18k	5 5 42½ 1hd 2hd 11	Knapp W	114	w	29.60	63-25	Exterminator1141Escoba1178Viva America1134	Saved ground	8
	Previously owned and trained by J.C. Milam												
26Jly17- 2Knw	fst	5½f	:233 :473 1:004 1:071	Alw 800	3 7 64¾ 45 66¾ 4½	Morys J	112	w	*1.55	102-00	MissBryn112noOwnRoeO'Neil104½Salvstr112no	Finished fast	11
17Jly17- 3Wnr	hy	5½f	:244 :51 1:052 1:13	Alw 800	2 6 43½ 3nk 13 11	Kelsay W	105	w	7.85	63-41	Exterminator1051Fern Handley1031Lady Eileen1103	Handily	6
14Jly17- 2Wnr	gd	5f	:23 :473 1:011	Alw 800	11 3 48 79¾ 49 410	Morys J	105	w	14.35	84-18	Jack Hare Jr.1111High Cost1153Viva America1156	Bumped	11
30Jun17- 1Lat	fst	6f	:233 :483 1:144	Md Sp Wt	2 2 12 12 11½ 13	Morys J	109	w	5.20	81-12	Exterminator1093Mistress Polly1091Quito112½	Easily	12

Grey Lag

ch. c. 1918, by Star Shoot (Isinglass)–Miss Minnie, by Meddler

Lifetime record: 47 25 9 6 $136,715

Own.– Mrs J. Casson
Br.– Mr John E. Madden (Ky)
Tr.– W. Casson

Date/Race	Cond/Dist	Fractions	Race	Running line	Jockey	Wt	Odds	Figs	Top finishers	Comment	Field
1Jly31- 6Dor	fst 1⅛	:493 1:152 1:421 1:541	3↑ Clm	1 6 913 914 914 917¾	Fisher D	113wb	10.10	69-11	AlLivingston112hdJunMoon1044HghPlyr109nk	Never a factor	10
24Jun31- 3Dor	fst 6f	1:121	3↑ Clm	3 10 98¼ 98 96½ 710	Fisher D	115wb	22.10	82-15	Scotland110¾Zaidee1073Hogarty110¾	No factor	10
18Jun31- 6BB	fst 7f	:234 :49 1:142 1:273	3↑ Clm 2000	2 1 2hd 31½ 36 38	Simpson R	116wb	9.15	76-21	Scotland1125FairOrb1153GreyLg116hd	Hard ridden,game try	10
13Jun31- 2BB	fst 6f	:233 :482 1:141	3↑ Clm 2500	8 12 1212 1214 912 76¾	Drake V	115wb	18.90	79-18	Wacket1151½Vacillate1131½Zaidee107½	Closed fast	12
Previously owned by Rancocas Stable;previously trained by S.C. Hildreth											
12May28- 4Jam	fst 1 1/16	:24 :48 1:13 1:462	3↑ Excelsior H 7.7k	1 1 11 2hd 31¼ 33	Sande E	118wb	*.90e	78-15	Brown Flash114noHerodian1053Grey Lag118hd	Showed speed	6
4May28- 4Jam	fst 1 1/16	:23 :464 1:122 1:463	3↑ Handicap 1250	1 4 49 45¾ 11 13	Fator L	120wb	*1.10	80-13	GreyLg1203ChrryP1172Flmkr1105	Rated early,won easing up	5
30Apr28- 2Jam	hy 1 70	:243 :494 1:15 1:46	3↑ Alw 1000	3 4 43 42½ 42¼ 33½	Fator L	128wb	6.00	72-23	Gormond1181½Ironsides1152Grey Lag128½	Rated,gamely	7
25Apr28- 6Jam	sl 1 1/16	:24 :483 1:14 1:48	3↑ Handicap 1350	3 4 48 410 48½ 49	Pasc'ma A	126wb	*1.20	64-22	Retaliate1112Sanford1186Oh Say1101	Pulled up lame	4
22Jun27- 3Aqu	fst 1	:241 :473 1:121 1:374	3↑ Alw 1000	4 3 21½ 21 11 13	Fator L	122wb	*.17	91-11	Grey Lag1223Our General1191½John J. Williams1151	Easily,pulled up lame	6
17Jun27- 2Aqu	fst 1	:233 :47 1:12 1:38	3↑ Alw 1000	5 2 2½ 21½ 12 12	Fator L	115wb	*.50	90-14	GreyLag1152LordBroom111hdRoyalPlay1158	Under restraint	5
2Jun23- 4Bel	fst 1¼	:483 1:132 1:373 2:03	3↑ Suburban H 10k	3 3 32 2hd 11½ 11½	Sande E	135wb	*.33e	85-14	Grey Lag1351½Snob II1152Exodus1092	Easily	6
24May23- 4Bel	fst 1	:232 :464 1:113 1:38	3↑ Metropolitan H 9.2k	7 5 32 1½ 13½ 13	Sande E	133wb	*1.40e	88-10	Grey Lag1333Dinna Care107hdExodus110½	Won eased up	7
19May23- 4Jam	fst 1 1/16	:233 :473 1:113 1:43	3↑ Long Beach H 6k	1 2 23 23 23 22	Fator M	133wb	*.65	104-06	SnobII116.52GreyLag1338KingAlbrt100.52	Steady late gain	5
12May23- 4Jam	fst 1 1/16	:24 :48 1:123 1:45	3↑ Excelsior H 7.3k	3 1 12 12 13 13	Fator L	130wb	*.50	96-06	Grey Lag1303Exodus1114Prince James112nk	Won eased up	6
5May23- 4Jam	fst 1 1/16	:24 :481 1:123 1:444	3↑ Kings County H 5.9k	3 2 22 21 1½ 11¾	Sande E	128wb	*.60	97-07	Grey Lag1281¾Snob II11110Prince James1204	Going away	4
1Aug22- 4Sar	fst 1¼	:481 1:123 1:38 2:031	3↑ Saratoga H 9.2k	5 5 41½ 2½ 11 1½	Fator L	130wb	*.70	93-09	Grey Lag130½Bon Homme1091½Prudery1146	Hard ridden late	5
19Jly22- 4Emp	gd 1 70	:24 :483 1:14 1:452	3↑ Mount Kisco 4.1k	2 2 21 12 13 12¼	Fator L	125wb	*.08	87-14	Grey Lag1252¼Letterman102	Won under pull	2
8Jly22- 4Emp	sl 1⅛	:484 1:142 1:402 1:54	3↑ Empire City H 8k	3 4 42 42½ 1½ 11½	Fator L	132wb	*1.00	85-13	GreyLg1321½BonHomme111¾Devastton1021½	Rated,going away	5
24Jun22- 4Aqu	fst 1	:233 :464 1:102 1:38	3↑ Queens County H 7.9k	3 2 33 31 3½ 11½	Fator L	127wb	*.40	90-13	GreyLg1271½SenningsPark1203CaptanAlcock112¾	Going away	5
16Jun22- 4Aqu	fst 1⅛	:473 1:123 1:37 1:50	3↑ Brooklyn H 9.8k	1 2 21 1½ 1hd 2hd	Fator L	126wb	*.70	95-10	Exterminator135hdGrey Lag1264Polly Ann103hd	Gamely	5
9Jun22- 4Bel	fst 1	:231 :462 1:102 1:36	3↑ Handicap 1588	3 2 21 1hd 1no 12	Fator L	126wb	*.60	98-12	GreyLag1262Frigate1051Bersglr1095	Long drive,going away	5
17Sep21- 5Lat	my 1¾	:481 2:09 2:47 3:053	Lat Championship 29k	2 2 21 21 31½ 43¼	Fator L	126wb	*.60	53-29	SportngBlood1262BlckSrvnt1261Humphry126nk	Disliked going	5
10Sep21- 4Bel	fst 2	:48 2:292 2:552 3:222	3↑ J C Gold Cup 13k	4 3 33 23 24 22½	Fator L	114wb	*.60e	94-04	Mad Hatter1252½Grey Lag11415Touch Me Not1148	Rated	4
3Sep21- 4Bel	fst 1⅝	:474 1:39 2:043 2:431	Lawrence Realizatn 20k	2 4 2½ 21½ 22 21½	Fator L	126wb	*.70	83-09	TouchMNot1261½GryLg1265SprtngBlood12120	Rated,tired late	4
Geldings not eligible											
30Jly21- 5Dev	fst 1⅛	:472 1:112 1:38 1:50	Dev Int'l 21k	1 2 22 22 2½ 1no	Sande E	126wb	*.48	113-03	GreyLag126noBlackServnt1238BygonDys1172	In final stride	5
26Jly21- 4Emp	fst 1 70	:244 :474 1:122 1:434	3↑ Mount Kisco 4.3k	2 1 12¼ 14 16 17	Sande E	121wb	*.03	95-08	Grey Lag1217Copper Demon111	Won easing up	2
23Jly21- 4Emp	fst 1 1/16	:232 :47 1:122 1:45	Knickerbocker H 5.1k	3 3 31¾ 11½ 12½ 12½	Sande E	135wb	*.29e	98-09	Grey Lg1352½Careful1083Copper Demon11012	Won easing up	4
16Jly21- 4Emp	sl 1¼	:493 1:133 1:403 2:071	Emp Derby 8k	3 4 21½ 11 12 1¾	Fator L	129wb	*.25e	84-16	GryLg129¾SportngBlood1115CopprDmon11015	Hard ridden late	4
11Jly21- 6Emp	gd 1	:25 :482 1:134 1:40	Alw 1200	2 3 2½ 11 11½ 13	Sande E	130wb	*.10	93-08	Grey Lag1303Quecreek11310Parader110	Cantering	3
7Jly21- 4Aqu	fst 1⅛	:461 1:101 1:352 1:49	Dwyer 8.6k	5 4 22 11 13 14	Sande E	123wb	*.40	101-06	GreyLag1234SportingBlood1124CopperDemon1081	Easing up	6
17Jun21- 4Aqu	gd 1⅛	:462 1:11 1:362 1:494	3↑ Brooklyn H 9.8k	1 5 63 31 1½ 11½	Fator L	112 w	*2.00	97-08	GreyLag1121½JohnP.Grier1241½Exterminator1291	Going away	11
11Jun21- 4Bel	fst 1⅜	:47 1:113 1:37 2:164	Belmont 10k	3 4 21½ 1½ 13 13	Sande E	126wb	2.00	87-12	GreyLag1263Sporting Blood126hdLeonardo II12610	Slight restraint late	4
2Jun21- 4Bel	fst 1	:23 :46 1:102 1:372	Withers 6.4k	1 4 32½ 21 25 34½	Sande E	118 w	*1.00	87-09	Leonardo II1182Sporting Blood1182½Grey Lag1181½	Tired final furlong	7
31May21- 2Bel	fst 6f	:232 :463 1:121	Handicap 1345	8 6 62¾ 31 1½ 11	Sande E	126 w	*1.10	92-12	GreyLag1261DryMoon1061Messins1071	Slow start,going away	9
Previously owned by S.C. Hildreth											
6Nov20- 5CD	fst 1	:233 :47 1:122 1:382	Ky Jockey Club 26k	2 6 32 31½ 22 21	Sande E	122 w	5.30	94-11	Tryster1221GreyLag1221BehaveYourself1225	Gamely,tiring	6
21Oct20- 4Emp	fst 5½f	:223 :463 1:00 1:06	Autumn Days 3.3k	3 3 44 45½ 32½ 1½	Ensor L	125 w	*.45	99-10	Grey Lag125½Mulciber1226Curfew118hd	Gamely	5
11Oct20- 4Jam	fst 6f	:24 :48 1:13	Oceanus H 4.2k	3 1 1hd 1hd 21½ 22	Fator L	128 w	*1.80	92-11	Mulciber1112Grey Lag1283Knobbie1256	Tired late	6
6Oct20- 4Jam	fst 6f	:24 :48 1:13	Remsen H 4.6k	4 2 21½ 2hd 31 1nk	Ensor L	123 w	*.70	94-11	Grey Lag123nkKnobbie1221½Care Free1091½	Forced wide	5
28Sep20- 4Aqu	sly 6f	:234 :48 1:134	Babylon H 5.1k	4 4 44½ 43½ 34 35	Ensor L	126 w	*.70	81-19	Knobbie1163½Mulciber1091½Grey Lag1263	Slow to begin	4
20Sep20- 4Aqu	fst 6f	:24 :473 1:13	Oakdale H 4.7k	1 1 1½ 21 22 21½	Fator L	126 w	*1.00	88-15	Knobbie1061½Grey Lag1262Dry Moon1126	Gamely	5
Previously owned and trained by M. Hirsch											
14Sep20- 4Bel	fst 7f-Str	1:242	Champagne 5.7k	3 4 42½ 21 11½ 16	Ensor L	111.5 w	*1.00	90-17	Grey Lag111.56Banksia105.51Our Flag115¾	Rated,easily	6
11Sep20- 3Bel	fst 6f-Str	1:121	Futurity 42k	5 15 107 104¼ 31½	Pierce J	119 w	15.00	80-21	Step Lightly1161Star Voter127½Grey Lag119hd	Closed gap	18
8Sep20- 1Bel	fst 5½f-Str	1:072	Handicap 1488	8 8 51¼ 32 1hd	Ensor L	114 w	4.50	82-23	Grey Lag114hdQuecreek109noStar Voter125½	Vigorous ride	8
4Sep20- 3Bel	fst 6f-Str	1:103	Nursery H 6.4k	10 7 64 67 44¾	Johnson A	112 w	4.00	85-13	Hildur1143Smoke Screen1151Oriole118¾	Finished fast	12
31Aug20- 3Sar	sl 6f	:223 :464 1:122	Hopeful 38k	11 12 1411 1315 1112 1012¼	McAtee L	115 w	30.00	78-12	Leonardo II115hdPrudery127½Oriole1155	No factor	15
26Aug20- 6Sar	fst 5½f	:222 :461 :591 1:051	Alw 1000	10 3 21 2hd 21½ 21	Kelsay W	108.5 w	*2.00	96-06	Broom Spun107.51Grey Lag108.52Normal1158	Chased winner	10
18Aug20- 6Sar	fst 6f	:233 :481 1:133	Md Sp Wt	3 6 44 54½ 52½ 2nk	Ponce C	115 w	50.00	84-13	Dartmoor115nkGrey Lag1151Bermont1151	Gaining	14

Hamburg

b. c. 1895, by Hanover (Hindoo)–Lady Reel, by Fellowcraft

Lifetime record: 21 16 3 2 $61,455

Own.– Marcus Daly
Br.– C.J. Enright (Ky)
Tr.– William Lakeland

Date/Race	Cond/Dist	Fractions	Race	Running line	Jockey	Wt	Odds	Figs	Top finishers	Comment	Field
30Jly98- 5Bri	hy 2¼	:55¼ 2:42¼ 3:08½ 4:02¾	3↑ Brighton Cup 7.5k	- 1 150 150 150 1100	Sloan T	112	*.05e	69-15	Hamburg112100Ogden13010Howard Mann133	Easing up	3
4Jly98- 5She	gd 1⅝	:494 1:17 1:43 2:511	Lawrence Realizatn 16k	- 1 13 16 16 12	Sloan T	122	*.90	86-13	Hamburg1222Plaudit12210George Boyd1121	Easing up late	6
23Jun98- 4She	gd 7f	:232 :47 1:13 1:271	Swift 1.7k	- 1 13 110 110 18	Taral	126	*.20	91-11	Hamburg1268Lotrr1166Murllo116	Very easily,eased up late	3
8Jun98- 3Gra	gd 1 1/16	:25¼ :49¼ 1:14½ 1:49	3↑ Spring Spl .8k	- 1 16 18 18 18	Sloan T	105	*.80	90-13	Hamburg1058SlyFox1084Hndbll105	Galloping,easing up late	3
26May98- 4MP	my 1⅜	:53 1:19½ 1:47¾ 2:32	Belmont 9.7k	- 2 2hd 21½ 35 316	Taral	122	*1.00	40-51	BowlngBrook1228Prvous1228Hmbrg12240	Eased last furlong	4
Previously owned and trained by John E. Madden											
16Sep97- 3Gra	sl 6f	:24 :48¼ 1:15	Excelsior 2.5k	- 2 11½ 12 13 12	Taral	115	*.17	--	Hamburg1152Handbll115½EstrGft115½	Easily,pulled up lame	4
14Sep97- 3Gra	gd 6f	:24 :49 1:15	Prospect 3k	- 3 12 11½ 12 12	Taral	127	*.60	--	Hamburg1272Handball122hdArchduke1154	Very easily	7
11Sep97- 3She	gd *6f-FC	:24 :482 1:00 1:101	Great Eastern H 5k	- 1 12 12 12 11½	Taral	135	*1.60	--	Hamburg1351½Kitefoot111½Briar Sweet1092	Easily	14
6Sep97- 3She	gd *6f-FC	1:11	Autumn 3k	- 1 1hd 1½ 13 12½	Taral	129	*1.40	--	Hamburg1292½Archduke1223The Huguenot1223	Easing up	6
4Sep97- 3She	hy 7f	:244 :491 1:144 1:281	Flatbush 3k	- 2 2hd 1½ 1hd 2hd	Taral	120	*.60	--	Previous115hdHamburg120½Firearm115½	Rated,hung	9
1Sep97- 3She	gd 7f	:232 :473 1:133 1:263	2↑ Flight 2.5k	- 1 11½ 11½ 2hd 22	Simms	105	2.00	--	Requital1252Hamburg10510Flying Dutchman1256	Gamely	4
21Aug97- 4Bri	gd 6f	:23½ :48½ 1:00½ 1:14¼	Electric H 2k	- 1 11½ 11½ 13 11½	Simms	132	*.17	--	Hmbrg1321½Hndbll12010FrstFrut8810	Never extended,easing up	5
17Aug97- 4Bri	fst 6f	:24 :48½ 1:15	Rising Generation 2k	- 1 13 14 15 13	Simms	127	*.13	--	Hamburg1273CentralTrust12210JuliusCaesar1108	Easing up	6
7Aug97- 3Sar	sl 6f	:24¾ :50 1:15	Grand Union Hotel 2k	- 2 2½ 2½ 11 2hd	Wilhite	129	*.33	--	Archduke117hdHamburg12915Harvey117	Driving,poor ride	3
4Aug97- 3Sar	sl 5f	:24 :47 1:01½	Congress Hall 2k	- 4 22 2¾ 1hd 11	Wilhite	134	*1.00	--	Hamburg1341Archduke1198Harvey119½	Easily	7
28Jly97- 3Sar	hy 4f	:24¾ :50	Flash 2k	- 2 3½ 1hd 11½	Wilhite	129	*.50	--	Hamburg1291½Handball129hdLoiterer1225	Galloping	4
10Jly97- 3She	fst *6f-FC	:233 :481 1:002 1:111	Double Event (2) 5k	- 2 21 1hd 12 12	Wilhite	129	*1.20	--	Hamburg1292Uriel1223Mont d'Or122½	Easily	10

5Jly97- 4She gd *6f-FC :251 :511 1:121 Great Trial 20k - 2 2½ 21 13 14 Wilhite 122 6.00 -- Hamburg1224Previous1292George Keene1222 Much best 12
22Jun97- 3She gd 5½f-FC :252 :504 1:03 1:091 Double Event (1) 5k - 5 3nk 22 51½ 33½ Wilhite 122 *.80 -- Bowling Brook122½Laudeman1173Hamburg122nk Bumped 8
15Jun97- 5Gra fst 5f :25¼ :49¾ 1:02¼ Alw 700 - 1 12 12 13 12 Wilhite 122 *2.00 -- Hamburg1222Previous122nkColonial Dame1013 Fast start 7
9Jun97- 1Gra hy 5f :24 :49¾ 1:03¼ Alw 710 - 2 11 11 11 11 Wilhite 104 2.00 -- Hamburg1041Previous1151Swango104½ Handily 8

Henry of Navarre

ch. c. 1891, by Knight of Ellerslie (Eolus)–Moss Rose, by The Ill-Used — Lifetime record: 42 29 8 3 $68,985

Own.– August Belmont II
Br.– L.O. Appleby (NJ)
Tr.– John J. Hyland

23Jun96- 4She fst 1¼ :51¾ 1:163 1:414 2:07 3↑ Suburban H 7.5k - 6 2hd 2½ 2nk 11 Griffin 129 2.00 -- HenryofNavarre1291ThCommonr113½Clfford1261 Driving,best 7
21May96- 3MP sl 1 :27 :53¾ 1:19¼ 1:44 3↑ Alw 500 - 2 22 2nk 1½ 13 Griffin 126 - -- Henry of Navarre1263Mingo II10120Ventanna98 Very easily 3
Odds not offered on Henry of Navarre
24Oct95- 5MP fst 1¾ :55¾ 2:37½ 3:02 3↑ Municipal H 3.5k - 2 2nk 11 11 11 Griffin 130 *.60 -- HenryofNavarre1301ReyelSantaAnt1268Clfford12815 Handily 4
15Oct95- 5MP sly 1¼ :55¼ 1:20 1:42½ 2:07 3↑ Manhattan H 3.5k - 4 42¼ 32 3½ 11 Griffin 127 *1.20 -- HenryofNavarre1271CounterTenor1002SirWalter1076 Handily 4
21Sep95- 4Gra fst 1¼ :55¼ 1:19½ 1:43½ 2:07½ 3↑ Oriental H 3k - 7 5 51¼ 41¼ 32½ Griffin 128 *1.20 -- Clifford1211SirExcess1071½HenryofNavrr1284 Lacked speed 7
17Sep95- 4Gra gd 1¼ :53 1:17½ 1:43½ 2:09 3↑ First Spl 2.5k - 3 31½ 3nk 2hd 11½ Griffin 122 *1.80 -- HenryofNavarre1221½Clifford117nkSirWalter1103 Handily 5
11Sep95- 5She fst 1⅛ 1:532 Swpst 3500 - - 1nk Perkins 122 *1.00 -- HenryofNavarre122nkDomino1223ReyelSantaAnit122 Cleverly 3
2Sep95- 4She fst 1¼ 2:07 3↑ Twin City H 2.2k - - 22 Perkins 127 *.60 -- Rey el Santa Anita1202Henry of Navarre1278Sir Excess115 4
Second best;Previously owned and trained by B. McClelland
13Jly95- 2Oky fst 1 :50 1:02¾ 1:15¼ 1:40¾ 3↑ Alw 500 - 1 1½ 1½ 11 11 Perkins 110 *.04 -- Henry of Navarre1101Orinda1053Lehman11010 Easily 5
29Jun95- 4Oky fst 1⅛ :51½ 1:17¼ 1:43 1:55½ 3↑ Country Club 2.5k - 2 22 21½ 1½ 12 Perkins 125 *.20 -- Henry of Navarre1252Lehman112hd[D]Selika1071 4
11Jun95- 4Lat fst 1⅛ :50½ 1:16 1:42 1:55 3↑ Merchant 1.9k - 3 32 22 2hd 1hd Perkins 117 *.04 -- Henry of Navarre117hdBrendoo9710Ray S117 Under a pull 3
23May95- 1Lat fst 1 1:41¾ 3↑ Alw 500 - - 1¾ Perkins 117 *.17 -- Henry of Navarre117¾Selika107¾Tariff Reform109 6
6Oct94- 5MP fst 1⅛ 1:52¼ 3↑ Special 5k - - 1¾ Clayton A 113 4.00 -- HenryofNavarre113¾Clifford12210Domino113 Led final ½ 3
22Sep94- 4Gra fst 1⅛ 1:54¾ 3↑ 2nd Spl 1.8k - - 2no Doggett 112 *.40 -- Clifford122noHenry of Navarre112 Led to ¼ 2
15Sep94- 5Gra gd 1⅛ 1:55½ 3rd Spl 5k - - 1↓ Doggett 122 1.80 -- [DH]Domino122[DH]Henry of Navarre122 Dueled last 3f 2
5Sep94- 5She fst 1 3/16 2:023 2↑ Bay 3.2k - - 1nk Taral 112 *.60 -- Henry of Navarre112nkBanquet11912Yo Tambien119 4
25Aug94- 3She fst 1⅛ 1:534 Dolphin 1.9k - - 1hd Clayton A 122 *1.20 -- Henry of Navarre122hdDorian1106Sir Knight106.5 4
18Aug94- 3Sar fst 1 1:43 Iroquois 2.5k - - 11½ Clayton 122 *.20 -- Henry of Navarre1221½Peacemaker1191½Lakeshore110 4
14Aug94- 2Sar gd 6½f 1:20¼ Alw 600 - - 11 Clayton 122 *.22 -- Henry of Navarre1221Potentate1154Lakeshore112 3
7Aug94- 4Sar fst 1⅛ 1:53¾ Foxhall 2.5k - - 13 Clayton 122 *.90 -- HenryofNavarre1223JohnCooper1224ReyelSantaAnita122 3
23Jly94- 4Sar gd 1¼ 2:10¼ Travers 3k - - 1½ Taral 125 *.33 -- HenryofNavarre125½JoeRipley1104ReyelSantaAnita125 5
7Jly94- 3She gd 1⅛ 1:55 3↑ Handicap 1145 - - 11 Doggett 112 *.33 -- Henry of Navarre1121Herald1081½Redskin99 6
5Jly94- 4She fst 1⅛ 1:561 Spindrift 2.5k - - 11 Doggett 125 *.90 -- Henry of Navarre1251Dorian1128Our Jack112 4
3Jly94- 1She fst 7f 1:262 3↑ Alw 1165 - - 13 Jones H 103 *.90 -- HnryofNvrr1033Glnmoyn1093MrryMonrch106 Led throughout 3
21Jun94- 5She fst 1¼ 2:061 3↑ Suburban H 16k - - 5 Perkins J 108 6.00 -- Ramapo1201Banquet1192Sport114 Prominent early 12
19Jun94- 4MP fst 1⅛ 1:56½ Belmont 7.4k - - 11½ Simms 117 *.10 -- HenryofNavarre1171½Prig11910Assign115 Led final furlong 3
15Jun94- 1MP fst 6f 1:11 3↑ Swpst 1180 - - 11½ Perkins 107 *.40 -- HenryofNavarre1071½Melba108hdMerryMonarch113 Led late 5
12Jun94- 4MP fst 1 1:40 Withers 7.9k - - 2hd Garrison 122 *1.30 -- Domino122hdHenry of Navarre1223Dobbins122 Driving 5
2Jun94- 4MP gd 1⅛ 1:52½ 3↑ Metropolitan H 7.6k - - 33½ Doggett 106 5.00 -- Ramapo1171½Roche1052HnryofNavrr106 Late bid,not enough 12
29May94- 4Gra gd 1⅛ 1:55¼ Fort Hamilton H - - 21½ Doggett 121 4.00 -- JohnCooper1101½HenryofNavarre1212Hornpipe122 Late bid 11
21May94- 4Gra hy 1⅛ 1:58 3↑ Standard 2.5k - - 21½ Griffin 106 *.33 -- Don Alonzo1221½Henry of Navarre106 Led for mile 2
15May94- 4Gra fst 1¼ 2:07¼ 3↑ Brooklyn H 25k - - 21 Clayton A 100 7.00 -- Dr. Rice1121Henry of Navarre1002Sir Walter120 14
Prominent throughout
19Sep93- 3Gra fst 6f 1:15 Algeria H - - 12 Taral 116 *1.40 -- Henry of Navarre1162Dobbins1231½Ornus100 11
2Sep93- 2She gd 5f 1:012 Dash 2.4k - - 1hd Bryant 115 *2.00 -- HenryofNavarr115hdPotntt1042Wrnbrg104 Led final furlong 13
1Sep93- 6She gd 7f(T) 1:30 Golden Rod 1.3k - - 1½ Bryant 110 *.40 -- Henry of Navarre110½Figaro1104Queenlike110 Led,easily 6
19Aug93- 2OMP gd 6f-Str 1:15 Alw 1060 - - 11 Bryant 119 *.33 -- HnryofNvrr1191Illuson104.56Ornus119 Pressed pace,galloping 5
12Aug93- 2OMP fst 5f-Str :58¾ Alw 1120 - - 11½ Hamilton 119 *.40 -- HenryofNavarre1191½Senella1191½Dorian119 Led throughout 8
8Aug93- 3OMP fst 6f-Str 1:13¼ Jr Champion 23k - - 31¼ Overton 118 8.00 -- Senator Grady1181Hornpipe118nkHenry of Navarre118 8
5Aug93- 3OMP sl 6f-Str 1:13¼ Select 5.7k - - 2½ Hamilton 113 8.00 -- Senator Grady113½Henry of Navarre113¾Hornpipe118 9
Led early,pressed pace late
25Jly93- 3OMP fst 5½f-Str 1:05 Sapling 8k - - 21½↓ Hamilton 111 8.00 -- SenatorGrady1111½[DH]HyderAbad118[DH]HenryofNavarre111 6
8May93- 3Lxt hy 5f 1:04½ Breeders - - 1½ Bryant 118 5.50 -- Henry of Navarre118½La Joya1205Lazzarone118 6
1May93- 3Lxt hy 5f 1:07¼ Melbourne - - 6 118 4.00 -- La Joya115nkLazzarone118nkOh No115 7

Hermis

ch. c. 1899, by Hermence (Isonomy)–Katy of the West, by Spendthrift — Lifetime record: 55 29 8 6 $84,135

Own.– E.R. Thomas
Br.– H.A. Engman (Ky)
Tr.– J. Shields

27Jly05- 4Bri fst 1 :24 :474 1:131 1:391 3↑ Test H 4.1k 5 2 2hd 21½ 57½ 512 Redfern 132wb *1.20 82-11 Wild Mint109hdHambrg Belle1232Buttling1044 Wide,bumped 5
15Jly05- 3Bri fst 1⅛ :48 1:13 1:39 1:52 3↑ Islip H 3k 10 1 11 11 11½ 1½ Redfern 132wb *2.60 95-06 Hermis132½Buttling1022½Bad News114hd Gamely 10
11Jly05- 2Bri fst 6f :24 :474 1:131 4↑ Alw 1080 5 1 14 14 13 11 Knapp W 125wb *.33 94-08 Hermis1251Jocund1153½Incubator1153 Cantered 6
6Jly04- 4Bri fst 1 :241 :48 1:123 1:38 3↑ Test H 5k 2 1 11½ 12 12 11 Redfern 133wb *1.30 100-07 Hermis1331Beldame1155Dainty1034 Bore out,best 5
25Jun04- 4StL hy 1¼ :50¼ 1:16½ 1:43 2:09½ 3↑ World's Fair H 50k 2 1 16 15 21 23 Redfern 130wb *1.60 75-32 Colonial Girl973Hermis1306Moharib1038 No match 12
16Jun04- 4She fst 1¼ :482 1:13 1:382 2:05 3↑ Suburban H 20k 6 1 11 13 13 12½ Redfern 127wb 4.00 98-06 Hermis1272½The Picket124noIrish Lad12710 Very easily 6
14Jun04- 4Gra fst 1⅛ :49 1:132 1:391 1:524 3↑ Brookdale H 4.2k 3 1 12 11½ 12 11 Redfern 125wb *.60 96-08 Hermis1251½Dainty1005Africander1272½ Won easing up 5
7Jun04- 4Gra my 1¼ :50 1:16 1:43 2:10 3↑ Standard 6.3k 2 1 2hd 35 32½ 325¾ Phillips H 128wb 1.50 51-24 MajorDaingerfild128¾Afrcndr12625Hrms1283½ Brushed,eased 6
26May04- 4Gra fst 1¼ :482 1:13 1:392 2:063 3↑ Brooklyn H 20k 6 2 2hd 21 2hd 43 Redfern 127wb 4.00 91-06 ThePckt119hdIrshLd1252Propr1101 Carried wide final turn 16
21May04- 6MP fst 1 :24 :483 1:141 1:392 3↑ Handicap 1365 6 1 1hd 12 15 14 Redfern 128wb 7.00 96-10 Hermis1284Toboggan1134Hello97¾ In a canter 7
29Oct03- 4Aqu fst 1⅛ :49 1:141 1:401 1:53 2↑ Edgemere 1.7k - 1 13 12 12 14 Redfern 126wb *.14 105-00 Hermis1264Stolen Moments11515Warranted126 In a canter 3
20Oct03- 4Bri fst 2¼ :49 2:33 2:592 3:532 3↑ Brighton Cup 8.8k - 1 1½ 11½ 1hd 18 Redfern 124wb 1.60 79-10 Hermis1248MajorDaingerfield1243Ignitr12420 Won eased up 4
13Oct03- 4Bri gd 1½ :49 1:141 2:053 2:321 3↑ Cup Preliminary 2.4k - 1 11½ 11½ 12 11 Fuller 126wb *.65 106-05 Hermis1261Major Daingerfield12620Igniter126 Rated,best 3
3Oct03- 1MP fst 7f :25 :492 1:132 1:26 2↑ Alw 1120 - 2 22 21 2hd 2hd Redfern 122wb *.20 100-05 MamieWorth107hdHrmis1222HighChancellor1103 Just missed 4
1Oct03- 6MP fst 1⅛ :484 1:142 1:40 1:522 3↑ Handicap 1255 - 1 11½ 13 1½ 11½ Fuller 134wb *1.10 95-07 Hermis1341½RiverPirate1101½Colonsay861 Speed in reserve 5
25Sep03- 4Gra fst 1 1/16 :233 :474 1:141 1:461 2↑ Handicap 1285 - 1 13 12 13 13 Fuller 134wb *.50 99-06 Hermis1343Colonsay86½Mabel Richardson95¾ Speed to spare 7
7Sep03- 4She fst 1¼ :474 1:122 1:383 2:043 3↑ Twin City H 7.2k - 1 16 14 2hd 21½ Odom 129wb 4.00e 100-00 McChesney1291½Hermis1291His Eminence1004 Second best 12
5Sep03- 4She fst 1½ :491 1:143 2:05 2:313 3↑ Century 20k - 1 1hd 24 35½ 412½ Odom 126wb *1.80 89-02 Water Bay1262½The Picket1154Heno1266 Tired badly 5
2Sep03- 4She gd 1 :232 :471 1:122 1:394 3↑ Ocean H 2.6k - 1 11½ 12 12 1½ Odom 127wb *.60 90-10 Hermis127½Molly Brant1051½Douro1193 Driving,sulked 8
18Aug03- 4Sar fst 1⅛ :49 1:131 1:383 1:513 3↑ Merchants & Citizens 7k - 3 12 13 13 13 Odom 124wb 1.60 99-02 Hermis1243Irish Lad1206Rigodon1035 Easily 4
15Aug03- 4Sar fst 1¼ :482 1:132 1:384 2:05 3↑ Sar Champion 6.9k - 2 21 2½ 21½ 21½ Odom 126wb 4.00 101-09 Irish Lad1161½Hermis1261½Heno1263 No match 4

13Aug03- 1Sar gd 7f :233 :482 1:144 1:282 2↑ Handicap 960 - 3 22 2½ 2½ 11 Odom 128wb *.50 83-21 Hermis1281Molly Brant1036Rigodon1148 Away slowly 4
8Aug03- 1Sar sl 7f :24 :474 1:141 1:282 2↑ Handicap 810 - 1 14 15 110 112 Rice 126wb 3.20 83-24 Hermis12612Major Daingerfield124¾Stamping Ground1088 5
Won eased up
3Aug03- 4Sar fst 1¼ :491 1:142 1:401 2:053 3↑ Saratoga H 12k - 2 2hd 21 77¼ 714¼ Rice 123 ws 7.00 86-06 WaterBoy127¾HunterRaine1073Caughnawg1091½ Quit after 7f 11
24Jun03- 7She yl 1$\frac{1}{16}$Ⓣ :252 :514 1:184 1:53 3↑ Alw 1040 - 4 21½ 2hd 34 33½ Rice 126 w *.45 62-34 FlorhamQun961½FlyngJb1012Hrms126¾ Bad start,poor effort 5
18Jun03- 4She sly 1¼ :492 1:152 1:43 2:102 3↑ Suburban H 19k - 1 2hd 32 96¼ 1224¼ Redfern 128wsb 10.00e 49-25 Africander110hdHrbrt1184HuntrRn986 Pulled up after mile 15
12Jun03- 2Gra my 1$\frac{1}{16}$:233 :473 1:134 1:471 3↑ Alw 1080 - 2 22 22½ 23 2¾ Rice 106wb *.29 93-17 RiverPirate91¾Hrms10620StmpngGround86 Rated,closed gap 3
3Jun03- 4Gra fst 1$\frac{1}{16}$:232 :472 1:132 1:46 3↑ Handicap 1370 - 3 21 21½ 22 57 Burns T 126 w *.60 93-07 Dublin1141½Water Boy1112½Herbert1101 Tired 7
Previously owned by L.V. Bell;previously trained by J. McCorm'ck
13Oct02- 3MP cpy 1¼ :504 1:16 1:42 2:081 2↑ Mamaroneck H 2.5k - 2 32½ 31½ 1hd 11½ Rice 126 w *2.00 87-13 Hermis1261½Warranted87½Advance Guard1243 6
Unruly start,wide turn,speed to spare
7Oct02- 5MP fst 1¼ :51 1:172 2:061 Jerome H 2.9k - 3 32½ 33 2hd 13 Rice 126 w *.50 97-08 Hermis1263Hunter Raine100hdOom Paul1101½ Won easing up 4
2Oct02- 4Gra gd 1$\frac{1}{16}$:244 :50 1:154 1:48 Ocean View H 2.1k - 2 41½ 31 1hd 13 Rice 126 w 2.50 90-14 Hermis1263Huntressa98hdIgniter1161 Easily 4
15Sep02- 4Gra fst 1¼ :491 1:143 1:401 2:061 3↑ First Spl 3.6k - 2 21½ 21 1hd 11½ Odom 117 ws 3.00 96-07 Hermis1171½Articulate1261Gunfire114hd Easily 6
28Aug02- 3Sar fst 1⅛ :482 1:132 1:384 1:512 Saranac H 5k - 2 21 2hd 1hd 1hd Rice 122 w 10.00 104-02 Hermis122hdWhiskey King1043Cunard115no Driving 10
9Aug02- 4Sar cpy 1⅛ :493 1:15 1:413 1:544 Travers 10k - 5 54¾ 52¾ 4½ 1hd Rice 111 w *.90 87-13 Hermis111hdGold Cure116noCunard1111 Wide,going away 7
Previously owned by H.M. Ziegler,trainer C. Hughes
4Aug02- 1Sar gd 7f :243 :491 1:15 1:28 2↑ Alw 860 - 2 31 2hd 1hd 12 Odom 110 w *1.40 90-06 Hermis1102Monograph119½Maud Gonne1142 Easily 14
21Jly02- 1Bri my 1$\frac{1}{16}$:251 :51 1:174 1:51 3↑ Alw 885 - 1 11½ 11½ 13 14 Wonderly 114 w *.03 71-23 Hermis1144Fair Knight106 Hard held 2
17Jly02- 3Bri fst 1$\frac{1}{16}$:234 :48 1:131 1:46 Alw 960 - 1 1½ 1hd 11½ 14 Wonderly 116 w *.70 96-05 Hermis1164LadySterling111hdParExcellence1114 Much best 5
21Jun02- 3OWP sl 1½ :501 1:171 2:102 2:401 American Derby 25k - 12 1247 1253 - - McCue 122 w 10.00 - - Wyth1221½LucnApplby1223Alddn1223 Faltered,pulled up lame 12
5Jun02- 2Gra fst 1½ :494 1:162 2:071 2:333 3↑ Handicap 1605 - 6 63 52¾ 62¾ 31½ Shea 98 w 7.00 96-07 Monarka106¾WaterCur104½Hrms98no Poor ride,finished fast 8
2Jun02- 5Gra fst 1$\frac{1}{16}$:234 :482 1:14 1:463 3↑ Handicap 1125 - 5 42½ 62½ 32¾ 32½ Jackson L 114 w 6.00 95-08 Highlander110¾Colonel Bill891½Hermis1142½ Bad start 9
Previously owned by H.A. Engman
28May02- 4Gra hy 1$\frac{1}{16}$:234 :483 1:15 1:481 3↑ Handicap 1085 - 2 21½ 31 21 11 Jackson L 108 w *1.80 89-15 Hermis1081Himself1103Oom Paul116¾ Impeded,up with rush 5
26May02- 5Gra fst 1$\frac{1}{16}$:24 :482 1:133 1:462 Alw 1060 - 3 3½ 41½ 21½ 21 Jackson L 109 w 3.00 97-06 Hyphen1091Hermis10915Bessie McCarthy10410 Good finish 4
12Nov01- 5Lat my 6f :25¼ :51 1:18½ Alw 300 - 6 51¼ 41¼ 1½ 14 Lyne 110 *.60e 73-33 Hermis1104Kaloma1152Moderator103½ Easily 6
9Nov01- 2Lat fst 5½f :24 :49 1:01¾ 1:08 Alw 300 - 1 2hd 1½ 1½ 12 Lyne 107 5.00 96-12 Hermis1072Inventor1072Setauket1072 Easily 7
31Oct01- 2Lat fst 5½f :24 :49½ 1:01½ 1:08 ©Alw 300 - 4 21 21½ 21 3½ Lyne 109 2.60 95-08 BalmofGilead106.5noHarryNew109½Hrms109½ Bumped stretch 10
28Oct01- 5Lat fst 5½f :23¾ :49½ 1:01¾ 1:08 ©Alw 250 - 1 22 22 41½ 14 Lyne 106 7.00 96-11 Hermis1064Inventor106½Harry New1105 Easily 11
26Oct01- 3Lat fst 5f :24 :49 1:01½ Alw 300 - 9 52½ 53½ 32 23 Lyne 105 10.00 98-06 Jack Rattlin1133Hermis1051Inventor1051 Tiring,swerved 12
26Sep01- 6Haw fst 6f :24 :48½ 1:14 Alw 400 - 8 43 42½ 43 69¾ Coburn 112 4.00 83-08 TommyFostr1122½Emathion109nkRosePlume1122 Not a factor 10
18Sep01- 7Haw gd 6½f :25 :49¾ 1:15½ 1:22¼ Alw 400 - 5 87¼ 810 - - Jackson L 110 13.00 - - SouthTrimble105¾DarkSecret1101St.Tmmny1101 Cut off,fell 9
Previously owned by W.A. Engman
16Sep01- 2Haw gd 5f :24½ :49½ 1:02¾ Alw 500 - 5 55½ 33½ 34½ 21½ Jackson L 102 12.00 82-19 Evening Star1041½Hermis1021Amirante1076 Finished well 8
30Aug01- 1Haw fst 5½f :24¾ :49 1:02 1:09 ©Md Alw 400 - 4 21½ 21½ 12 13 Winkfield J 109 *2.00 90-13 Hermis1093Huzzah1132½Tommy Foster1061 As rider pleased 11
13Aug01- 1Hrm fst 6f :242 :492 1:153 ©Md Alw 400 - 2 14 13 12 32 Knight T 110 4.50 81-09 Landseer1081Ravensbury1101Hermis1101 Tired 15
6Aug01- 1Hrm fst 5f :492 1:014 ©Md Alw 400 - 12 78½ 72¾ 51½ 55¼ Mitchell C 106 *2.60 83-12 Emathion1051Landseer1021Pompey1063 Nearly left 15
2Aug01- 1Haw fst 5½f :25¼ :50¼ 1:03¼ 1:10 ©Md Alw 400 - 9 32½ 31½ 2nk 43 Nutt 107 12.00 82-13 Harry Wilson1122Fullen104hdHuzzah1071 Faltered late 12
22Jly01- 2Haw fst 5f :25 :49¾ 1:02½ Alw 400 - 12 1027 1020 1015 1017 Dominick 103 20.00 68-10 RedTip1104ISamuelson103hdBrdg115½ Slow start,closed gap 13

Imp

br. or blk. f. 1894, by Wagner (Prince Charlie)–Fondling, by Fonso **Lifetime record: 171 62 35 29 $70,119**
Own.– Daniel R. Harness
Br.– D.R. Harness (Oh)
Tr.– P. Wimmer

9Nov01- 4Aqu fst 1$\frac{1}{16}$:234 :482 1:142 1:474 2↑ Farmingdale H .8k - 5 54½ 53½ 44½ 66¼ Odom 126 *1.50 92-10 Oom Paul1122Ben Mac Dhui1142Handicapper982 Poor effort 6
7Nov01- 1Aqu fst 7f :242 :483 1:14 1:274 2↑ Oakdale H .8k - 6 72¾ 71½ 62 51¼ Odom 126 2.60 83-12 Paul Clifford113hdShoreham1001Unmasked120hd Closed gap 9
5Nov01- 4Aqu gd 1$\frac{1}{16}$:243 :50 1:491 2↑ Idlewild H .8k - 2 1hd 2hd 2hd 2¾ Odom 126 *2.00 90-11 Potente110¾Imp1262St. Finnan115hd Good try 5
26Oct01- 4MP fst 2¼ :50 2:351 3:56 3↑ Morris Park 4.7k - 3 32 46½ 612 517 Bullman 121 7.00 90-05 GoldHeels1112Hernando111noWtrColor1113 Lacked condition 8
25Oct01- 6MP fst 1¼ :514 1:17 1:42 2:072 3↑ Handicap 1045 - 1 12 12 13 14 Odom 122 5.00 91-10 Imp1224Advance Guard1264Rafaello1053 Never extended 4
22Oct01- 5MP fst 1 :252 :50 1:15 1:40 3↑ Handicap 660 - 1 1nk 1hd 1hd 1hd Shaw 109 3.50 95-09 Imp109hdSt. Finnan1046Decanter1142 Driving 5
19Oct01- 3MP fst *6f-EC 1:10 2↑ Handicap 885 - 7 8 78¾ 73½ 77 Bullman 116 15.00 86-09 Rockwater99½Roxane1091BelleofLxngton103½ Never a factor 10
6Sep01- 6She fst 1½Ⓣ :50 1:161 2:08 2:332 3↑ Handicap 1445 - 1 1nk 45 48½ 422½ Fairgood 110 3.50 81-00 Trigger97½Baron Pepper1022Maid of Harlem9220 Speed,quit 4
2Sep01- 4She gd 1¼ :491 1:143 1:404 2:07 3↑ Twin City H 6.3k - 2 33 43 64¼ 78½ Woods J 117 10.00 81-07 Herbert116hdTerminus108½Trigger951 Disliked going 10
24Aug01- 4Sar my 1⅝ :51 1:45 2:522 3↑ Sar Cup 5k - 2 23 315 325 338 Odom 122 2.60 - - Blues1138Baron Pepper11330Imp122 Disliked going 3
20Aug01- 3Sar fst 1$\frac{1}{16}$:243 :491 1:15 1:464 3↑ Alw 770 - 1 1hd 21 21½ 26 Fairgood 111 *1.20 87-06 Roe Hampton1066Imp11112The Rhymer985 Poor ride 4
13Aug01- 4Sar fst 1 70 :243 :494 1:161 1:452 3↑ Alw 790 - 2 21 21 21 1¾ Fairgood 113 *.90 - - Imp113¾Smoke11312Admonition110 Poor ride,much best 3
5Aug01- 4Sar fst 1⅛ :493 1:15 1:403 1:531 3↑ Saratoga H 10k - 5 4¾ 42½ 34 53½ Odom 123 20.00 91-09 Rockton1162Water Cure1071Water Color115nk Good try 11
Previously trained by C.E. Brossman,owned by Harness & Brossman
23Nov00- 6Ben fst 1 100 :252 :50 1:163 1:492 3↑ Handicap 445 - 1 1½ 1hd 2hd 2no Rutter 123 *.90 93-07 First Whip112noImp1234Asquith99no Tired 4
14Nov00- 1Aqu fst *7f :232 :483 1:14 1:252 2↑ Handicap 585 - 6 53¼ 55¼ 41 31 Rutter 126 *3.00 95-08 Bastile95hdTrumpet1171Imp1262 Hung 12
8Nov00- 4Aqu fst 1½ :501 1:17 2:092 2:373 2↑ Alw 525 - 1 1¾ 1½ 2hd 21½ Burns T 123 *.50 108-06 McMeekin1171½Imp12312Compensation126 Saved ground 3
3Nov00- 4Emp hy 1⅛ :501 1:151 1:411 1:55 2↑ Wakefield H 1.4k - 3 52¼ 52¾ 510 611¼ Burns T 126 4.00 - - James1121KingBarleycorn1062PinkCoat107no Disliked going 6
1Nov00- 6Emp sl 1$\frac{1}{16}$:243 :483 1:15 1:474 2↑ Handicap 700 - 2 1hd 1hd 2½ 21½ Burns T 128 2.00 - - McMeekin1131½Imp1282Herbert1061 Disliked going 5
25Oct00- 4Emp sl 1$\frac{1}{16}$:25 :481 1:141 1:47 3↑ ⒻMahopac H 1.1k - 1 1½ 11 11½ 11½ Burns T 126 *.70 - - Imp1261½Kamara104hdOneck Queen951 Won easing up 4
22Oct00- 4Emp fst 1¼ :484 1:13 1:39 2:04 2↑ Emp City H 3.2k - 1 1hd 1hd 1½ 2hd O'Conner 124 *1.60 - - Charentus106hdImp1241Pink Coat105no Just missed 7
13Oct00- 5MP fst 1¾ :49 2:084 2:333 2:583 3↑ Municipal H 3.9k - 1 1½ 12 11½ 2hd Burns T 126 4.00 103-05 Ethelbert126hdImp1266Maid of Harlem1005 Gamely 5
22Sep00- 4Gra fst 1⅛ :484 1:142 1:404 1:534 2↑ Occidental H 2.3k - 2 1hd 4¾ 73¼ 79¾ McJoynt 126 *3.00 86-07 PinkCoat1021½JckPont1163Chrntus103hd Tired under impost 9
15Sep00- 4Gra fst 1½ :502 1:17 2:083 2:341 3↑ Second Spl 3.2k - 1 11 11 11 11 Burns T 118 7.00 99-06 Imp1181Kinley Mack126noEthelbert1211 Handily 4
11Sep00- 4Gra fst 1¼ :512 1:171 1:431 2:081 3↑ First Spl 3.1k - 1 11 11 1hd 34 Odom 123 *.90 86-07 Kinley Mack126hdMcMeekin1174Imp123 Speed,tired 3
3Sep00- 6She fst 1$\frac{1}{16}$Ⓣ :242 :483 1:143 1:464 3↑ Handicap 1120 - 1 11½ 1½ 1hd 11½ Odom 128 3.50 101-00 Imp1281½Intrusive1171½Maximo Gomez1148 Gamely 6
4Aug00- 4Bri fst 2¼ :501 2:323 2:574 3:491 3↑ Brighton Cup 8.3k - 1 14 16 11½ 2¾ Jenkins 121 8.00 135-00 Ethelbert124¾Imp12110Sidney Lucas10910 Good try 4
1Aug00- 6Bri fst 1⅛ :483 1:141 1:40 1:53 3↑ Alw 880 - 1 2hd 2hd 22 23 Clawson 121 *.70 104-00 Belle of Troy1063Imp1212Gonfalon106no Second best 5
25Jly00- 4Bri fst 1 :24 :481 1:142 1:40 3↑ Islip 2.5k - 1 2hd 2hd 35½ 35½ Mitchell 121 2.20 92-05 Ethlbrt1264SkyScrpr1071½Imp121 Speed,tired,pulled up lame 3
23Jly00- 2Bri fst 1⅛ :472 1:122 1:393 1:53 3↑ Alw 670 - 2 22 23 1hd 11½ Mitchell 115 *.45 107-00 Imp1151½Water Cure902Plucky95 Easily 3
7Jly00- 4Bri fst 1¼ :473 1:13 1:382 2:043 3↑ Brighton H 11k - 5 44 3nk 31 32 Odom 129 8.00 102-03 Jack Point1091½The Kentuckian109½Imp1293 Good effort 9
3Jly00- 4She fst 1⅛ :50 1:144 1:404 1:54 3↑ Long Island H 2.5k - 4 2hd 1hd 2hd 2no Odom 130 *2.20 95-08 Charentus99noImp130noGreyfeld1006 Driving 6
30Jun00- 4She fst 1¾ :491 2:05 2:32 2:591 3↑ Advance 5.3k - 1 120 130 130 130 Odom 113 *.10 110-01 Imp11330MaidofHarlem1038PostHst95 Restrained throughout 3
23Jun00- 4She fst 1 :24 :49 1:144 1:404 3↑ Sheepshead Bay H 2k - 3 64¼ 54½ 23 34 Tabor 133 6.00 87-09 Greyfeld911Bendoran1213Imp133hd Tired under impost 10
20Jun00- 3She fst 1$\frac{3}{16}$:501 1:153 1:413 2:003 3↑ Handicap 1270 - 1 12 11½ 11½ 11½ Tabor 131 *.80 98-09 Imp1311½Col. Roosevelt1016David Garrick1135 Easily 4
16Jun00- 4She fst 1¼ :491 1:15 1:411 2:064 3↑ Suburban H 10k - 2 21 2hd 42 410½ O'Conner 128 4.00 80-09 Kinley Mack1251½Ethelbert1304Gulden1005 Speed,tired 10
13Jun00- 2Gra fst 1¼ :50 1:152 1:413 2:08 3↑ Handicap 1080 - 1 12 13 13 11½ Tabor 126 *1.40 91-08 Imp1261½Gulden99noLothario106no Easily 7

5Jun00- 4Gra	fst	1⅛	:49	1:141	1:404	1:541	3↑ Brookdale H 2k	-	2	2½	2hd	1hd	2no	O'Connor	127	*.70	94-08	Jean Beraud127noImp1271½Charentus101hd	Gamely	4
30May00- 4Gra	fst	1 1/16	:25	:492	1:144	1:464	3↑ Parkway H 2.1k	-	1	1hd	12	1hd	12	O'Connor	124	*1.80	97-04	Imp1242Kinley Mack1274Survivor104hd	Easily	6
26May00- 4Gra	hy	1¼	:491	1:161	1:431	2:10	3↑ Brooklyn H 10k	-	4	32	41¼	61½	64¾	Clawson	128	8.00	76-15	Kinley Mack1221Rafaello113¾Herbert98hd	Disliked going	9
15May00- 1MP	fst	6½f	:234	:494	1:143	1:21	3↑ Alw 590	-	3	31	31	3½	31¾	Clay P	124	*.90	93-07	Vulcain1131Unmasked103¾Imp1241½	Urged,not enough	6
9May00- 4MP	sl	7f	:244	:511	1:164	1:30¼	3↑ ⒻAlw 690	-	2	32	3½	41¾	25	Vest	129	*.60	74-28	SparrowWing1135Imp129noStarChime106no	Poor ride,outrun	5
5May00- 4MP	fst	1	:234	:483	1:15	1:41¼	3↑ Metropolitan H 7.7k	-	7	51¾	32	22	33	Clawson	127	8.00	86-13	Ethelbert1263Box121noImp1271½	Driving	11
14Apr00- 5Ben	sl	7f	:242	:494	1:162	1:31	3↑ 2nd Ben Spring H 1.1k	-	2	31½	43	43½	35	Clay	132	*1.10	85-13	Charentus1125Boney Boy116hdImp132nk	Impeded	4
2Apr00- 4Ben	gd	6f	:241	:50	1:03	1:161	3↑ 1st Bennings Spring H .9k	-	1	3nk	3nk	41¼	31½	Clay P	132	*1.20	91-09	Boney Boy106½Charentus1101Imp132hd	Impeded½	7
30Sep99- 4Gra	fst	1¼	:492	1:141	1:41	2:073	2↑ Oriental H 2.5k	-	1	12	12	14	14	Clay P	128	*.50	94-08	Imp1284Charentus106	Eased in stretch	2
23Sep99- 4Gra	fst	1½	:50	1:16	2:08	2:34	2↑ Second Spl 3.3k	-	1	12	13	15	11½	Clay P	124	3.50	107-04	Imp1241½BenHolldy12110ThBchlor118hd	Eased final furlong	4
16Sep99- 4Gra	fst	1⅛	:49	1:143	1:411	1:542	3↑ Occidental H 2.3k	-	2	1hd	2hd	31	53¼	Clay P	129	3.50	95-06	Previous122hdCharentus1091Prince McClurg115hd	Tired	7
12Sep99- 4Gra	gd	1¼	:494	1:15	1:42	2:094	3↑ First Spl 3.5k	-	2	2nk	1nk	11½	12	Clay P	119	*1.60	83-11	Imp1192May Hempstead1121½Maxine119¾	Restrained at end	6
4Sep99- 4She	gd	1¼	:491	1:16	1:44	2:10	3↑ Twin City H 6k	-	1	1hd	2hd	6	8	Clay P	130	4.00	- -	Previous1144Bangle1201½Bannockburn1261	Disliked footing	9
1Sep99- 6She	fst	1¼Ⓣ	:49	1:141	1:401	2:071	3↑ Turf H 1.7k	-	1	13	14	12	12	Clay P	128	3.00	100-00	Imp1282Decanter1173Bon Ino973	Never threatened	6
30Aug99- 4She	fst	1	:242	:482	1:141	1:401	3↑ Ocean H 1.5k	-	1	1hd	1hd	1hd	1hd	Clay P	123	8.00	94-09	Imp123hdCharentus1092Batten112hd	Driving	9
26Aug99- 3She	fst	6f	:232	:473		1:132	3↑ Fall H 1.5k	-	1	2hd	2hd	21	33½	Clay	124	5.00	91-10	Previous111½Batten1143Imp1242	Outpaced	7
31Jly99- 5Bri	fst	1	:241	:482	1:141	1:403	3↑ Islip 2.3k	-	2	31	21	2hd	1hd	Clay	111	1.80	95-05	Imp111hdFirearm1132Peep o' Day1114	Just up	4
24Jly99- 3Bri	hy	1 1/16	:25	:502	1:162	1:50	3↑ Handicap 775	-	1	2nk	41	34½	46	Clay P	124	3.50	79-15	Kirkwood1041½Maxine1144Tamor98½	Poor ride	4
18Jly99- 3Bri	fst	1	:25	:501	1:16	1:412	3↑ Handicap 735	-	1	11	1½	1½	1½	Clay P	126	*1.00	91-08	Imp126½Charentus1065Cambrian1052	Driving	4
11Jly99- 4Bri	fst	6f	:232	:481	1:012	1:144	2↑ Flight H 1.8k	-	5	53	65¾	66¼	44	Clay P	126	6.00	88-08	Firearm1082Bendoran1262Swiftmas115hd	Finished fast	6
6Jly99- 4Bri	fst	1¼	:491	1:143	1:40	2:052	3↑ Brighton H 9.9k	-	1	11	11	11	11	O'Leary	115	8.00	110-02	Imp1151Ethelbert1071Bangle112nk	Mild drive	7
3Jly99- 3She	fst	1⅛	:50	1:144	1:401	1:53	3↑ Handicap 1080	-	1	11	11	1hd	32	Turner N	126	*3.50	98-04	Tragedian1062Survivor107hdImp1264	Driving	7
29Jun99- 4She	hy	1⅛	:49	1:15	1:411	1:541	3↑ Long Island H 2k	-	1	11	1hd	1hd	34½	O'Leary	119	2.60	89-06	Bangle1093Maxine1131½Imp1195	Dueled,tired	5
24Jun99- 4She	fst	1	:232	:471	1:123	1:394	3↑ Sheepshead Bay H 1.5k	-	2	25	35	33¼	78¼	Taral	125	3.50	88-06	Fly by Night108¾Azucena982Bendoran123hd	Weakened	9
20Jun99- 4She	fst	6f	:234	:472	1:00	1:132	3↑ Coney Island H 1.5k	-	4	47	45½	23	21½	Taral	128	*3.50	93-10	Bendoran1181½Imp1282St. Cloud122nk	Second best	12
17Jun99- 4She	fst	1¼	:492	1:141	1:393	2:054	3↑ Suburban H 10k	-	3	31	11	13	12	Turner N	114	6.00	96-06	Imp1142Bannockburn1123Warrenton114nk	Never threatened	13
14Jun99- 2Gra	fst	1⅛	:494	1:151	1:41	1:534	3↑ Handicap 1100	-	1	12	13	14	13	Clawson	126	3.20	101-06	Imp1263Pirate M.971Warrenton1251	Never extended	6
8Jun99- 2Gra	fst	1 1/16	:24	:49	1:152	1:49	3↑ ⒻAlw 700	-	4	21	11	1½	11½	Taral	123	3.50	90-08	Imp1231½Gaze983Azucena106½	Easily	7
5Jun99- 5Gra	fst	1 1/16	:251	:503	1:152	1:483	3↑ Handicap 875	-	2	21	31½	33	34½	Mitchell	122	4.00	87-07	Intrusive1123Charentus1101½Imp1222	Weak handling	9
27May99- 4Gra	fst	1¼	:491	1:142	1:392	2:061	3↑ Brooklyn H 10k	-	5	53½	62¼	15	15	Clayton	110	15.00	- -	Banastar1103Lanky Bob1051Filigrane982	Outrun	16
23May99- 6MP	fst	1⅛	:502	1:15	1:41	1:533	3↑ Handicap 850	-	2	2hd	2hd	11	11	Taral	125	*2.00	89-05	Imp1251Glonoine108hdJefferson1083	Handily	8
18May99- 5MP	fst	6½f	:24	:49	1:14	1:202	3↑ Claremont Hwt H 1.5k	-	3	1nk	11	11	3½	Taral	119	*3.50	100-01	Kinnikinnick124½Dr. Eichberg106hdImp1191	Good effort	8
16May99- 4MP	fst	7f	:24	:492	1:141	1:263	3↑ New Rochelle H 1.6k	-	5	31¼	41	2nk	22	Taral	112	5.00	102-01	Previous1132Imp1122Kingdon112no	Good try	10
13May99- 5MP	fst	1 1/16	:26	:51	1:153	1:471	3↑ Handicap 900	-	9	4¾	2nk	2½	2¾	O'Connor	113	4.00	95-04	Don D'Oro128¾Imp1136Free Lance105½	Second best	10
11May99- 6MP	my	1	:251	:501	1:16	1:43	3↑ Handicap 880	-	1	22	22	25	42¾	Taral	117	*1.60	84-10	Don D'Oro1222Twinkler98½Charentus107nk	Tired	6
9May99- 4MP	fst	*6f-EC	:231	:47	:58	1:09	3↑ Toboggan H 2.1k	-	4	2½	63¼	63½	8	McGlone	120	8.00	- -	Banastar116¾Sanders1213Octagon1303	Pulled up	10
6May99- 4MP	fst	1	:242	:49	1:14	1:394	3↑ Metropolitan H 8.2k	-	5	52¼	41¾	42	43	McGlone	112	6.00	100-00	Filigrane1022Ethelbert106hdSanders1101	Outrun	14
12Apr99- 5Ben	fst	1 1/16	:254	:501	1:161	1:503	3↑ Handicap 350	-	1	12	14	13	13	McGlone	126	1.60	- -	Imp1263Alice Farley1161Double Dummy109hd	Cantering	5
8Apr99- 5Ben	sl	1 100	:25	:51	1:194	1:522	3↑ Handicap 335	-	2	1hd	21½	43	412	Scherrer	126	*.50	- -	Beau Ideal1002Imperator1046Alice Farley1144	Weakened	5
15Nov98- 3Lak	hy	1 1/16	:25¼	:52	1:19	1:53½	3↑ Handicap 400	-	1	15	112	16	18	McNickle	116	1.40	68-27	Imp1168Macy1142Al Fresco97	Galloping	3
14Nov98- 3Lak	hy	6f	:26¼	:52½	1:05	1:17½	3↑ Handicap 400	-	1	2nk	2nk	2½	23	McNickle	125	*.60	81-29	O'Connell1173Imp1255Timemakr1113	Carried wide by winner	6
8Nov98- 4Lak	gd	1⅛	:50	1:14½	1:42	1:55¾	Handicap 400	-	1	1¾	13	11	15	McNickle	112	1.40	88-14	Imp1125Macy1163Storm King992	Easily	5
5Nov98- 4Lak	hy	1 1/16	:25¼	:50¾	1:16½	1:52¾	3↑ Handicap 400	-	1	2¾	23	24	35	Ellis	115	*.90	67-25	Macy1113Storm King972Imp1155	Dull effort	4
29Oct98- 4Lak	hy	1 100	:25¼	:50¼	1:15¾	1:46¼	Alw 400	-	1	12	12	1nk	21½	Sheppard	119	3.00	- -	Macy1041½Imp1198Storm King96¾	Second best	5
12Oct98- 3Haw	sl	7f	:25½	:50	1:15¾	1:29	3↑ Dash 1.3k	-	2	1½	11½	12½	11	Rutter	118	*.60	- -	Imp1181May W.1024Lady Ellerslie976	Hand ride	5
1Oct98- 4Hrm	gd	6f	:23¼	:47¾	1:01	1:13	2↑ Speed 1.5k	-	3	24	25	23	12½	Rutter	115	*.60	96-10	Imp1152½Frank Bell923Traverser1132½	In hand	5
28Sep98- 4Hrm	gd	1 70	:24¾	:49¾	1:15¼	1:44½	Alw 400	-	1	15	18	13	11	Rutter	119	*.70	94-15	Imp1191Dare II947Carnero945	Easily	4
19Sep98- 4Hrm	gd	7f	:25	:49¾	1:15¼	1:27¾	3↑ Austin 1.7k	-	1	1nk	1hd	11½	12½	Rutter	119	3.50	92-16	Imp1192½Hugh Penny1082Found95no	Easily	9
17Sep98- 3Haw	hy	1⅛	:53	1:19	1:47¼	2:01½	3↑ Monadnock 1.1k	-	1	12	15	11½	12	McNickle	114	*.95	- -	Imp1142Hugh Penny114	Easily	2
12Sep98- 3Haw	fst	1⅛	:49¾	1:14¾	1:40½	1:53	3↑ Alw 500	-	1	12	16	15	12	McNickle	109	1.80	- -	Imp1092Crocket9910John Bright1072	Eased up	5
8Sep98- 3Haw	gd	1	:26	:51	1:16½	1:42	4↑ Alw 500	-	2	2½	1nk	21	25	Conley	111	4.50	- -	Hugh Penny1115Imp1116David1042	Good try	5
3Sep98- 5Hrm	fst	1 70	:25	:50¼	1:15¾	1:44	Alw 400	-	2	2hd	21	33½	410½	Sheppard	112	9.00	85-07	Storm King981David Tenny1121½What Next1008	Stopped	4
1Sep98- 3Hrm	fst	6f	:24	:48¾	1:01	1:13¾	3↑ Alw 400	-	3	32	34	34½	34¾	Sheppard	109	4.50	88-07	EugeniaWickes1044FloraLouis98¾Imp1092	Driving,lost whip	7
30Jly98- 5Hrm	hy	6f	:24¾	:50¼	1:03¾	1:17¼	3↑ Alw 400	-	2	25	23	24	25	Thorpe	112	*1.00	70-36	Mary Black1055Imp11250Storm King117100	Good try	4
23Jly98- 3OWP	fst	1¼	:48¼	1:13¼	1:39	2:04½	3↑ Wheeler H 5.4k	-	3	44	56	44¾	721¼	Reiff L	115	15.00	- -	Algol1075Goodrich107½Pink Coat109¾	No threat	10
16Jly98- 5OWP	fst	1	:24½	:48¾	1:13½	1:39	3↑ Alw 400	-	3	1nk	1nk	2hd	22	Caywood	109	*.70	- -	Azucena972Imp1098Miss Gussie97nk	Wide,careless ride	5
11Jly98- 5OWP	fst	6¼f	:24	:49	1:13¾	1:17	3↑ Alw 500	-	3	22	22	31¾	42½	Turner N	112	*1.00	- -	Satsuma109nkAlgol1171½Abuse119¾	Dull	5
9Jly98- 2OWP	fst	1⅛	:48¼	1:14	1:39¼	1:51¾	4↑ Alw 595	-	1	11½	12	11½	11½	Caywood	112	1.30	- -	Imp1121½Macy117	Best	2
5Jly98- 3OWP	fst	1 1/16	:25	:50¼	1:15¾	1:46	3↑ Alw 600	-	1	11	12½	12	13	Caywood	110	*.55	- -	Imp1103The Devil10010The Roman110	Easily	3
2Jly98- 3OWP	fst	1⅛	:49½	1:14¼	1:39¼	1:51¾	3↑ Oakwood H 2.4k	-	1	1¾	11½	1nk	31½	Caywood	118	7.00	- -	Fervor103noWhat Er Lou1081½Imp1186	Faltered late	6
22Jun98- 1She	gd	6½f	:232	:49	1:153	1:221	3↑ HiW H 845	-	4	33	43	54½	68	McCafferty	135	6.00	78-16	Swiftmas1201Hanlon106½Mainstay1123	Eased up late	10
18Jun98- 4She	gd	1¼	:51	1:16	1:412	2:081	3↑ Suburban H 10k	-	6	4nk	21	31	610½	Clawson	102	5.00	73-14	Tillo119½Semper Ego106hdOgden1093	Faltered	11
13Jun98- 2Gra	gd	1⅛	:51	1:16	1:41¾	1:55½	3↑ Handicap 875	-	1	11½	11½	11½	11	Spencer	108	2.00	93-10	Imp1081Havoc1261½Knight of the Garter934	Tiring	5
3Jun98- 5Hrm	fst	6f	:24½	:48½	1:01	1:14¼	3↑ Handicap 400	-	2	21	22½	21½	11½	Martin W	124	*.50	90-17	Imp1241½Dave Waldo108¾Cherry Leaf955	Driving	6
30May98- 5Hrm	sl	1 1/16	:25	:51¼	1:18¼	1:51½	3↑ Memorial Day H 1.9k	-	1	14	16	13	110	Caywood	118	*.80	70-31	Imp11810Dr. Sheppard10925Goodrich100	Won eased up	3
24May98- 5Hrm	gd	1	:26	:49¾	1:16½	1:44	3↑ Alw 500	-	1	11	11½	12½	1¾	Turner N	105	*.25	73-21	Imp105¾Frank Thompson946J.H.C.11012	Won eased up	4
21May98- 6Lak	hy	1⅛	:52	1:18¾	1:45¾	1:59¼	3↑ Handicap 400	-	1	13	15	18	16	Turner N	117	*.50	70-29	Imp1176Moncreith1055Banquo II10510	Won eased up	4
18May98- 5Lak	hy	1 1/16	:24¾	:50½	1:16¾	1:54½	4↑ Alw 400	-	1	115	125	120	16	Turner N	102	*.17	63-29	Imp1026Kirk108noArrezzo10210	Won pulled up	4
7May98- 5Lak	fst	5f	:23¼	:48½		1:01	3↑ Alw 400	-	1	22½	33¼	32¼	22	Turner N	109	*.70	93-10	Abuse1102Imp1094Peter McCue951½	Outrun,driving	8
5May98- 4Lak	sly	1	:24¼	:49¾	1:16¼	1:44	3↑ Alw 400	-	1	18	115	112	112	Sheppard	102	*.25	81-23	Imp10212Dr. Sheppard107nkMyth1045	Won eased up	4
22Apr98- 4Nwp	fst	5½f	:22¼	:46¾	1:00¾	1:07	3↑ Alw 250	-	5	79	67½	44½	11	Sheppard	111	*.40	101-10	Imp1111Richard J.104noAunt Bird943	Driving	10
21Apr98- 3Nwp	fst	1	:25	:49¾	1:14½	1:40	3↑ Handicap 450	-	1	12	15	13	12	Sheppard	116	*1.60	100-08	Imp1162What Next110½Marito895	Easily	8
12Apr98- 3Nwp	fst	1 50	:24	:48¾	1:13½	1:43	3↑ Alw 250	-	1	12	12	1½	13	Sheppard	106	*1.00	107-03	Imp1063What Next1082Sister Stella1038	In a gallop	8
9Apr98- 1Nwp	fst	6f	:24½	:49	1:02¼	1:15	4↑ Alw 250	-	2	1nk	11	12	16	Sheppard	109	*1.20	88-16	Imp1096Lufra112½Box1212	Galloping	5

Previously owned by Daniel R. Brossman

15Nov97- 5Lak	hy	1	:25	:50¼	1:17¼	1:45	3↑ Handicap 400	-	1	18	18	112	115	Waldo	80	*.60	- -	Imp8015Harry Thoburn808Ben Waddell821	Easily	5
12Nov97- 4Lak	gd	7f	:24¼	:48¼	1:14	1:26¾	3↑ Alw 400	-	1	1¾	12	12	14	Dupee	90	1.60	- -	Imp904The Elector1043Laureate90	Speed to spare	3
9Nov97- 3Lak	my	7f	:25½	:51	1:18½	1:32	3↑ Alw 400	-	2	1nk	2nk	2nk	21½	Dupee	104	1.30	- -	Laureate1091½Imp1048LadyCallhn1003	Handicapped by going	8
6Nov97- 5Lak	fst	5f	:23½	:48½		1:01	2↑ Alw 400	-	2	31¾	32½	3¾	21½	Dupee	105	4.00	- -	Abuse1131½Imp1053Lady Callahan103nk	Good try	8
4Nov97- 5Lak	fst	7f	:24½	:48¾	1:15	1:27¾	3↑ Alw 400	-	4	21	2nk	1½	1¾	Dupee	89	6.00	- -	Imp89¾Gath1071Timemaker1001½	Hand ride	5
1Nov97- 3Lak	hy	7f	:24¼	:49	1:16½	1:30¼	3↑ Alw 400	-	4	42½	42¼	44¼	46	Dupee	90	7.00	- -	Macy922May W924Lady Callahan100no	Tired,disliked going	8
23Oct97- 4Hrm	fst	5½f	:23½	:49	1:01¼	1:07½	2↑ Handicap 400	-	4	41¾	63	56¾	511¼	Burns T	103	4.00	- -	Gath1181St. Alfonses D854Judge Wardell97nk	Poor effort	6

21Oct97- 5Hrm	fst	6f	:23½ :48 1:00½ 1:13¾	3↑ Alw 400	-	2	31¾	32¼	44	49	Clay	104	7.00	- -	Timemaker1052May W1023Abuse1124	Showed little	4
19Oct97- 6Hrm	fst	7f	:23¾ :48½ 1:14¼ 1:27	2↑ Alw 400	-	1	1nk	1nk	2nk	67	Everett	104	7.00	- -	May W102½Lieber Karl943Gath119no	Dueled,tired	7
16Oct97- 5Hrm	fst	6f	:24¼ :48½ 1:01¼ 1:13¼	2↑ Speed .6k	-	1	2nk	32¾	41	41½	Everett	105	30.00	- -	May W102noGath117noDFlora Louise871½	Impeded stretch	5
Placed third through disqualification																	
12Oct97- 3Hrm	hy	5½f	:25¾ :52 1:05¾ 1:12¾	3↑ Alw 400	-	4	32¾	313	312	316	Clay	99	3.00	- -	Gath1146B & W10210Imp9912	Disliked going	4
9Oct97- 5Hrm	fst	5½f	:23 :48½ 1:01 1:07¼	2↑ Alw 400	-	1	31	32¾	41¼	45	Clay	102	4.50	- -	Flora Louise881Charm1074Judge Wardell88hd	Good effort	5
18Sep97- 4Hrm	gd	6f	:24½ :49½ 1:01¼ 1:13½	2↑ Alw 400	-	3	44	44¼	21½	21	Connolly	105	4.00	- -	Harry Duke1071Imp1052½The Swain1076	Driving	8
15Sep97- 4Hrm	fst	6f	:24 :48½ 1:01¾ 1:14½	3↑ Handicap 400	-	2	41¼	43¼	31½	46½	Clay	115	*1.60	- -	Laureate110½Preston983Simmons983	Poor ride	5
11Sep97- 5Hrm	fst	6f	:24 :48½ 1:00½ 1:13¼	2↑ Alw 400	-	1	12½	1½	1nk	11½	Clay	108	4.50	- -	Imp1081½HrryDuk109½Prsbytrn885	Rated,drew away cleverly	5
9Sep97- 5Hrm	fst	7f	:24½ :49¾ 1:14½ 1:26¾	3↑ Alw 400	-	1	11	1¾	1nk	1no	Clay	104	6.00	- -	Imp104noThe Swain104½Macy1011½	Tired,well ridden	5
2Sep97- 4Hrm	fst	6f	:23½ :47½ 1:00¾ 1:13	3↑ Alw 400	-	1	11	11	1½	1½	Clay	97	*1.40	- -	Imp97½Harry Duke105.5¾Abuse11310	All out drive	4
30Aug97- 5Hrm	fst	7f	:22¾ :47 1:12½ 1:26¼	2↑ Alw 400	-	1	18	16	12	11	Clay	97	*1.10	- -	Imp971Fretful1046Irene Woods1094	Tiring	5
28Aug97- 5Hrm	fst	6f	:23¾ :48½ 1:00¼ 1:12¾	2↑ Alw 400	-	1	13	11½	1nk	2½	Clay	99	8.00	- -	Flora Louise85½Imp991½Timemaker110hd	Driving	5
24Aug97- 3Hrm	fst	6½f	:23½ :48¾ 1:13¼ 1:19¾	2↑ Alw 400	-	3	2½	2¾	3nk	34½	Clay	103	8.00	- -	Timemaker1081½Irene Woods1103Imp103hd	Used,tired	5
19Aug97- 4Hrm	fst	1	:24 :48 1:13½ 1:40	Alw 400	-	2	2½	2hd	21½	35½	Woods J	89	7.00	- -	Lady Callahan892½Serrano963Imp89hd	Appeared lame	4
16Aug97- 3Hrm	fst	1	:24 :49 1:13¾ 1:39¾	Alw 400	-	2	2hd	2hd	21½	37½	Caywood	102	1.60	- -	Lady Callahan981½Dunois986Imp10210	Dueled,tired	6
13Aug97- 4Hrm	fst	7f	:24¼ :49 1:14½ 1:27¾	3↑ Alw 400	-	1	1¾	12	11½	15	Burns T	97	5.00	- -	Imp975Greyhurst1042½Nimrod1072	Handily	7
11Aug97- 6Hrm	fst	6f	:24¼ :48¼ 1:01¼ 1:13¾	3↑ Alw 400	-	6	57¾	46	53	53	Hicks J	95	8.00	- -	IreneWoods1091½LadyCallahn95noThDuc105no	Never a threat	11
29Jly97- 4Oky	fst	7f	:23¾ :48¼ 1:14¼ 1:27	Ohio Selling 1k	-	1	1hd	2½	2hd	33½	Everett	97	8.00	- -	Taluca1031½Remember Me902Imp971	Gave way	6
27Jly97- 4Oky	hy	6f	:24½ :49 1:16½	Press 1.5k	-	1	2½	21	22	21	Piggott	103	2.50	- -	Abe Furst1081Imp1035Eugenia Wickes103	Driving,no match	3
17Jly97- 6Oky	hy	6½f	:25 :50¼ 1:16½ 1:23½	3↑ Alw 300	-	6	66½	614	611	717½	Reiff C	103	3.00	- -	Box984Arlington1064Geyser1063	Bad start	7
8Jly97- 5Oky	fst	1	:25¼ :50 1:15½ 1:43	Ⓕ Alw 350	-	1	1½	11	12	1hd	Reiff C	104	2.50	- -	Imp104hdPerformance1041½BelleBramble1078	Tiring,held on	5
1Jly97- 1Oky	fst	6f	:24½ :49¼ 1:14½	3↑ Inaugural Dash .5k	-	2	42	42½	31½	42½	Burns T	98	4.00	- -	Panmure101hdGeyser1061Boanerges1131½	No threat	7
29Jun97- 5Lat	fst	1	:24½ :48¾ 1:14¼ 1:41¾	Clm	-	3	2½	1nk	32	45	Everett	97	3.50	- -	LordZeni1041½Viscount932AbFurst1021½	Stopped in stretch	6
24Jun97- 5Lat	fst	1	:24½ :49 1:15 1:41¾	Handicap 500	-	2	2no	11	12	21	Burns T	97	5.00	- -	Donna Rita951Imp972Boanerges1142	Second best	4
14Jun97- 4Lat	fst	1	:24½ :48½ 1:13¾ 1:41¼	3↑ Alw 300	-	2	2½	2½	21	53½	Burns T	102	3.00	- -	Cavalero1071½FredBarr102.51JoClrk100no	Stopped in drive	8
10Jun97- 4Lat	fst	6f	:24¼ :49 1:14¼	3↑ Milldale 1.5k	-	6	52¼	33	44½	62½	Nutt	111	20.00	- -	Taluca101.51Byron McClelland112½Pete114hd	No threat	8
8Jun97- 5Lat	gd	6f	:24¼ :49 1:14½	3↑ Alw 300	-	1	11	11	1½	2hd	Nutt	106	*1.40	- -	Geyser97hdImp1062Orimar973	Speed,just missed	8
1Jun97- 4Lat	fst	6f	:24½ :48¾ 1:14	3↑ Handicap 480	-	1	11	12	11½	11½	Everett	104	10.00	- -	Imp1041½Byron McClelland1061Sangamon100hd	Cleverly	8
29May97- 5Lat	fst	6f	:24¼ :48½ 1:13¾	3↑ Alw 350	-	2	22	2½	21	2½	Burns T	100	15.00	- -	Pete109½Imp1001Sharon1103	No match	10
26May97- 6Lat	gd	6f	:24½ :49 1:14	3↑ Clm	-	3	41	55½	31½	512	Hill J	103	8.00	- -	J.A. Gray1091½Balk Line108.5hdW C T10910	Bid,tired	10
18May97- 4Nwp	fst	6f	:24 :48¾ 1:01¾ 1:14½	Ⓕ Alw 250	-	2	22	41½	31	4nk	Sheedy	115	5.00	- -	Suisun105noHer Excellency115noTrimuda105no	Driving	8
15May97- 4Nwp	fst	7f	:23¾ :48¾ 1:15¼ 1:28½	3↑ Clm 1500	-	1	11	12	1½	21	Sheedy	105	*2.00	- -	Irksome1051Imp105½Miss Ross105½	Stopped when challenged	9
13May97- 1Nwp	gd	6f	:25 :50 1:03 1:16¼	Alw 250	-	3	21	11	11	1½	Sheedy	109	2.00	- -	Imp109½Box1092Myth1062	Handily	6
7May97- 1Nwp	fst	5f	:24 :49 1:02	Alw 250	-	3	64½	44½	43	31	Knapp	112	3.00	- -	Lady Juliet1071Her Excellency107hdImp1123	Good try	9
4May97- 4Nwp	hy	7f	:25 :51½ 1:19½ 1:34¼	3↑ Clm 1400	-	1	12	12	12	12	Hill J	104	3.50	- -	Imp1042J H C1026Banquo II986	Handily	8
1May97- 2Nwp	sly	1	:27¼ :54 1:20¼ 1:46½	3↑ Alw 250	-	1	13	11	2½	26	Chenault	86	1.60	- -	Skate1046Imp863Jamboree1083	Used,tired	8
29Apr97- 6Nwp	fst	6f	:23½ :48½ 1:01½ 1:14½	3↑ Clm 1200	-	1	11	12	13	13	Reiff C	105	*2.50	- -	Imp1053J. Walter100nkGooding1111	Easily	8
19Apr97- 4Nwp	gd	6f	:23¾ :48 1:01½ 1:14¾	3↑ Alw 300	-	1	35	36	55	49	Hill J	100	10.00	- -	Flotow1053Winker1055Abe Furst1101	Outrun	6
16Apr97- 3Nwp	hy	1 50	:25¼ :51¼ 1:17¼ 1:50	3↑ Clm 1500	-	1	11	1½	2½	33½	Reiff C	101	2.50	- -	John Sullivan103½Parson1043Imp1018	Weakened	6
14Apr97- 1Nwp	hy	6f	:25 :50½ 1:05 1:19¾	Ⓕ Alw 250	-	2	1hd	13	12	15	Hill J	115	*.70	- -	Imp1155Adalid1158Carlotta C.1156	Much best	8
10Apr97- 3Nwp	sl	1	:25½ :52 1:20¾ 1:50¾	Ⓕ Queen City Oaks 1.3k	-	1	12	2hd	1½	49	Reiff C	112	12.00	- -	Faunette107hdNannieL'sSister1121PanchitaII1128	Stopped	5
8Apr97- 1Nwp	hy	6f	:25 :50½ 1:04 1:19	Alw 300	-	3	2½	24	36	54½	Scherrer	102	*.90	- -	Vengeance104½Suydam1072Cynthia II1021	Stopped	6
1Apr97- 4Nwp	fst	1	1:41¾	Alw 300	-	-	1	1	1	33½	Scherrer	107	3.50	- -	Winker109½Vengeance1043Imp107		9
25Jly96- 5Lat	sl	5½f	:25 :51½ 1:11¾	Ⓕ Alw 400	-	3	1hd	1½	1nk	36	Sherrin	115	*2.20	- -	Truelight1121Lady Keith1005Imp115no	Quit badly	6
24Jly96- 2Lat	hy	5f	:26 :53¼ 1:06¾	Ⓕ Alw 300	-	1	1½	12½	15	12½	Sherrin	112	*1.30	- -	Imp1122½Black Heart105.51Carlotta C112no	Never extended	13
14Jly96- 5Lat	sly	5f	:25¾ :51¼ 1:04	Ⓕ Alw 400	-	1	12	12	12	13	Sherrin	107	*2.00	- -	Imp1073Carlotta C1072Pouting1074	Easily	8
9Jly96- 5Lat	hy	5f	:26 :52¼ 1:05½	Ⓕ Alw 400	-	2	1½	1hd	12	21	Sherrin	107	7.00	- -	Mertie Reed1071Imp1071Adowa1103	Tiring badly	9
7Jly96- 4Lat	sl	5f	:25 :49¾ 1:01¾	Ⓕ Clipsetta 2.5k	-	4	43	54½	34½	48½	Van Kuren	110	15.00	- -	Midlight105½EugeniaWcks1188BllBrmbl115hd	Never a threat	9
23Jun96- 3Oky	hy	5f	:25 :50 1:04	Alw 400	-	1	1½	2hd	21	22	Thorpe	112	*1.20	- -	Orion1152Imp1125Red115hd	Second best	6
15Jun96- 3Oky	gd	5f	:24¼ :49¼ 1:03	Alw 400	-	3	54¼	1no	2½	41	Snedeker	110	6.00	- -	Burlsqu1131ChrryLf108noOron113no	Taken up,altered course	8
12Jun96- 3Oky	gd	5f	:24 :48½ 1:02½	Alw 400	-	2	31	2½	21	22	Snedeker	108	3.00	- -	Eugenia Wickes1072Imp1083Cavalero110hd	Outrun	7
2Jun96- 1Oky	fst	5f	:24¼ :49 1:01¾	Ⓕ Alw 400	-	1	1hd	11½	11	2½	Thorpe	115	3.00	- -	White Frost105½Imp1156Charina1052	Used in pace	6
26May96- 4Oky	sl	4f	:24½ :50¾	Ⓕ Sapphire 2.5k	-	2		32	32	33	Perkins	115	4.00	- -	Cleophus1202Amiable1151Imp1151	No threat to winner	5
22May96- 1Oky	sl	4f	:25 :50¾	Ⓕ Md Sp Wt	-	4		12	15	11	Snedeker	110	2.50	- -	Imp1101Dulcenea1055Scarf Pin1055	Urged at end	8

Man o' War

ch. c. 1917, by Fair Play (Hastings)–Mahubah, by Rock Sand
Own.– S.D. Riddle
Br.– August Belmont (Ky)
Tr.– L. Feustel

Lifetime record: 21 20 1 0 $249,465

12Oct20- 4Knw	fst	1¼	:462 1:114 1:372 2:03	3↑ Ken Park Gold Cup 75k	2	1	12	15	16	17	Kummer C	120	w	*.05	132-03	Man o' War1207Sir Barton126	Never extended	2
18Sep20- 5HdG	fst	1 1/16	:23 :473 1:113 1:444	Potomac H 10k	4	1	11½	11	11½	11½	Kummer C	138	w	*.15	101-16	Man o' War1381½Wildair10815Blazes104.52	Easing late	4
11Sep20- 4Bel	fst	1½	:493 1:141 2:032 2:284	3↑ Jockey Club 6.8k	2	1	15	18	112	115	Kummer C	118	w	*.01	117-02	Man o' War11815Damask118	Under a pull	2
4Sep20- 4Bel	fst	1⅝	:474 1:382 2:033 2:404	Lawrence Realizatn 16k	2	1	120	130	150	1100	Kummer C	126	w	*.01	134-00	Man o' War126100Hoodwink116	Restrained at end	2
21Aug20- 4Sar	fst	1¼	:463 1:10 1:353 2:014	Travers 12k	1	1	12	14	14	12½	Schuttinger A	129	w	*.22	102-08	Mano'War1292½Upset1237JohnP.Grier115	Restrained in str	3
7Aug20- 4Sar	fst	1 3/16	:481 1:124 1:374 1:563	Miller 5.7k	2	1	11½	13	14	16	Sande E	131	w	*.03	97-09	Mano'War1316Donnacona1194KingAlbert114	Never extended	3
10Jly20- 4Aqu	fst	1⅛	:46 1:093 1:36 1:491	Dwyer 5.5k	1	1	1hd	1hd	1½	11½	Kummer C	126	w	*.20	101-08	Man o' War1261½John P. Grier108	Hard ridden,drew away	2
22Jun20- 4Jam	gd	1	:253 :49 1:141 1:413	Stuyvesant H 4.5k	1	1	14	17	18	18	Kummer C	135	w	*.01	86-13	Man o' War1358Yellow Hand103	Eased final ⅛	2
12Jun20- 4Bel	fst	1⅜	2:141	Belmont 9.2k	1	1	12	17	112	120	Kummer C	126	w	*.04	116-10	Man o' War12620Donnacona126	Taken up final 1/16	2
29May20- 4Bel	fst	1	:24 :471 1:11 1:354	Withers 5.8k	2	1	11½	12	12	12	Kummer C	118	w	*.14	104-10	Man o' War1182Wildair11812David Harum118	Won under pull	3
18May20- 4Pim	fst	1⅛	:473 1:122 1:381 1:513	Preakness 29k	7	1	11½	14	12	11½	Kummer C	126	w	*.80	97-10	Man o' War1261½Upset1225Wildair1145	Speed in reserve	9
13Sep19- 3Bel	fst	6f-Str	1:113	Futurity 31k	8	2	31½	1½	12	12½	Loftus J	127	w	*.50	85-21	Mano'War1272½JohnP.Grier1174Dominiqu122nk	Won easing up	10
30Aug19- 3Sar	sl	6f	:23 :47 1:13	Hopeful 29k	3	4	22	21	15	14	Loftus J	130	w	*.45	87-14	Man o' War1304Cleopatra1124Constancy1242	Easily	8
23Aug19- 3Sar	fst	6f	:223 :462 1:12	Grand Union Hotel 9.8k	2	3	1hd	13	13	11	Loftus J	130	w	*.55	92-08	Man o' War1301Upset1254Blazes122½	Eased final 16th	10
13Aug19- 4Sar	fst	6f	:231 :464 1:111	Sanford Memorial 4.9k	6	5	41½	32	31½	2½	Loftus J	130	w	*.55	95-09	Upst115½Mno'Wr1303GoldnBroom1302	Slow start,gaining	7
2Aug19- 3Sar	fst	6f	:23 :471 1:122	U S Hotel 9.8k	8	1	13	13	14	12	Loftus J	130	w	*.90	90-13	Man o' War1302Upset1151Homely1121	Eased final 16th	10
5Jly19- 3Aqu	fst	6f	:233 :472 1:13	Tremont 5.8k	2	2	11	11	11½	11	Loftus J	130	w	*.10	90-12	Man o' War1301Ralco11520Ace of Aces112	Never extended	3
23Jun19- 3Aqu	fst	5f	1:013	Hudson 3.4k	2	1	1½	11	11	11½	Loftus J	130	w	*.10e	83-12	Mano'War1301½VioletTip1094Shoal11512	Broke thru barrier	5
21Jun19- 3Jam	gd	5½f	:231 :473 1:001 1:063	Youthful 4.8k	4	3	11	12	14	12½	Loftus J	120	w	*.50	92-09	Mno'War1202½OnWtch1082LdyBrumml10510	Easing final 16th	4
9Jun19- 4Bel	sl	5½f-Str	1:053	Keene Mem 5.2k	3	2	2½	3¾	31	13	Loftus J	115	w	*.70	91-17	Man o' War1153On Watch115½Anniversary1154	Drew away	6
6Jun19- 6Bel	fst	5f-Str	:59	Md Sp Wt	7	1	2nk	2½	13	16	Loftus J	115	w	*.60	83-18	Man o' War1156Retrieve112½Neddam1154	Easily	7

Maskette

br. f. 1906, by Disguise (Domino)–Biturica, by Hamburg — Lifetime record: 17 12 3 0 $77,090

Own.– J.R. Keene
Br.– James R. Keene (Ky)
Tr.– J. Rowe

6Aug10- 4Sar	gd	1	:24^4 :48 1:12^4 1:40	3↑	Delaware H	6	2	2^1	3^{1½}	4^{5½}	5^{13½}	Notter	125	w	*.50	74-14	SirJohnJohnson124^{hd}StanlyFy104^{5}Dnoscr105½	Quit after 5f	6
23Jun10- 4She	fst	1	:23^2 :47^2 1:12 1:37^3	3↑	Sheepshead Bay H 2k	4	3	3^{1½}	2^{1½}	2^{1½}	2½	Powers V	123	w	1.80	99-05	King James129½Maskette123^{8}Czar110^{hd}	Gamely,impeded late	6
9Jun10- 5Gra	fst	1$\frac{1}{16}$	:24^1 :48^1 1:13^1 1:46^3	3↑	Ⓕ Handicap	1	1	1^1	1^{1½}	1^2	1^1	Powers V	128	w	*.14	94-07	Maskette128^{1}Hill Top103^{10}Imitator95^3	Won easing up	5
13May10- 4Bel	fst	1	:23^3 :47^2 1:12^2 1:37^4	3↑	Metropolitan H	5	3	2^{1½}	2^{hd}	1½	6^8	Butwell	123	w	2.50	90-03	Fashion Plate105^{1}Prince Imperial97^{1}Jack Atkin129½	Tired	9
5May10- 4Aqu	fst	6½f	:22^4 :47^2 1:11^1 1:18	3↑	Handicap	2	2	1^{hd}	1½	1^{hd}	1^{nk}	Butwell	122	w	*.33	109-00	Maskett122^{nk}Dlmtn105½RockyO'Brn107^{15}	Not fully extended	4
26Oct09- 4Aqu	fst	1$\frac{1}{16}$	:24 :49 1:13^2 1:48^2	2↑	Aqueduct H 2.5k	3	1	1^1	1½	1^{hd}	2no	Butwell	126	w	*.25	85-16	Firestone113^{no}Maskette126^{1}Olambala119^{hd}	Just missed	4
12Oct09- 4Jam	gd	1⅛	:50 1:15 1:41^3 1:54^2	2↑	Pierrepont H 2.5k	5	4	1^{hd}	1^{1½}	1^{1½}	1^2	Butwell	124	w	*.50	92-12	Maskette124^{2}Huck98^{1½}Firston118¾	Bad start,wide 1st turn	6
5Aug09- 4Sar	sly	1⅛	:50 1:17 1:45^3 1:59^2		Ⓕ Alabama 5k	3	1	1^2	1^3	1^2	1^{1½}	Scoville	124	w	*.30	60-27	Maskette124^{1½}MissKearney116^{3}Petticot116^3	Disliked going	6
7Jly09- 4She	fst	1⅛	:47^2 1:12^2 1:38^3 1:52		Ⓕ Mermaid	1	1	1^{1½}	1^{1½}	1^2	1^3	Scoville	126	w	*.13	97-03	Maskette126^{3}Lady Bedford111^{6}Petticoat111	Won easing up	3
17Jun09- 3Gra	fst	1$\frac{1}{16}$	:24^4 :48^2 1:14 1:48		Ⓕ Gazelle	1	1	1^2	1^{1½}	1^1	1^2	Scoville	121	w	*.25	87-14	Maskette121^{2}Petticoat111^{2}Lady Bedford111^6	Much best	4
20May09- 4Bel	fst	1	:24^1 :48^2 1:13^3 1:39		Ⓕ Ladies	4	1	1^1	1^6	1^3	1^5	Butwell	121	w	*.25e	92-08	Maskette121^{5}Lady Bedford121^{4}Field Mouse121^4	Much best	4
8Oct08- 3Bel	fst	6f-Str	1:20^4		Ⓕ Matron 6.5k	2	2	2^{hd}	1^{hd}	1^1	1^{1½}	Notter	124			- -	Masktt124^{1½}Afflcton106	Stablemates cantered throughout	2
5Sep08- 3She	fst	7f-FC	1:25^2		Flatbush 13k	5	2	2½	1½	2½	2^4	Notter	117	w	*.50e	93-10	Sir Martin115^{4}Maskette117^{1½}Fayette115^2	Bumped,tired	5
2Sep08- 3She	fst	6f-FC	1:12^3		Ⓕ Great Filly 12k	2	2	1½	1^2	1^2	1^1	Notter	127	w	*.25e	90-10	Maskette127^{1}Wedding Bells119^{4}Lady Bedford116^{hd}	Easily	5
29Aug08- 4She	fst	6f-FC	1:11^1		Futurity 29k	3	2	1^1	1^2	1^2	1^3	Notter	118	w	*.70e	97-06	Maskette118^{3}Sir Martin127^{hd}Helmet123^4	Never extended	9
5Aug08- 3Sar	fst	5½f	:22^2 :47 :58^4 1:05^4		Ⓕ Spinaway 10k	5	2	1½	1½	1^1	1^{1½}	Notter	112	w	*.29e	101-18	Masktte112^{1½}WeddngBlls112^{no}MssHubbrd112^2	Much the best	6
3Aug08- 6Sar	fst	5½f	:23 :47^2 :59^3 1:06^3		Alw 455	6	7	3^1	2^1	3^2	1½	Notter	101	w	*.25	97-10	Maskette101½Miss Kearney103^{6}Louise Bell99½		8
	Open to fillies and geldings																		

Old Rosebud

b. g. 1911, by Uncle (Star Shoot)–Ivory Bells, by Himyar — Lifetime record: 80 40 13 8 $74,729

Own.– F.D. Weir
Br.– J.E. Madden (Ky)
Tr.– F.D. Weir

17May22- 1Jam	fst	6f	:24^2 :49^3 1:15	3↑	Alw 1000	6	7	2^{hd}	2^2	3^3	7^{9¼}	Sande E	110	w	5.00	74-10	Victor S.107^{1}Ogarite96.5^{3}Ting-a-Ling110^1	Quit badly	11
6May22- 6Jam	gd	5½f	:24 :48^3 1:01^1 1:07^3	3↑	Clm	3	5	4^2	2½	1^2	2½	Sande E	114	w	*1.60	86-10	Liberty Girl109½Old Rosebud114^{1½}Dare106^3	Rated,tired	8
6Sep21- 1Bel	fst	6½f	:23^3 :47^1 1:13 1:19^3	3↑	Clm	3	2	3^2	2½	1^{1½}	1^3	Fator L	110	w	6.00	88-09	Old Rosebud110^{3}Old Sinner114^{hd}Gem97^2	Pulled up lame	9
20Apr21- 3HdG	fst	6f	:23^2 :47^3 1:13^3	3↑	Clm	3	3	2^{1½}	2^{nk}	2^1	6^{3¾}	McAtee L	111	w	*1.25	84-16	Panaman108^{nk}Pickwick117^{1}Uncle's Lassie109^{1½}	Speed,tired	9
14Jun20- 5Jam	fst	5½f	:23^1 :46^4 :59^3 1:05^3	3↑	Handicap 1620	9	10	7^7	7^8	6^9	6^{9½}	McCabe J	119	w	10.00	87-06	PeterPiper130^{3}IrishDream105^{1½}Liond'Or126^2	Never a factor	10
31May20- 4Bel	fst	6f-Str	1:09^3	3↑	Toboggan H 4k	2	4	6^5	6^4	6^{6½}	5^{5½}	McCabe J	113	wb	8.00	87-11	Lion d'Or107.5^{hd}Motor Cop128^{no}Naturalist126^4	Swerved	7
27May20- 4Bel	fst	6f-Str	1:11^2	3↑	Handicap 1195	2	1	3^{1½}	2^2	2^1	1^{1½}	McCabe J	123	wb	5.00	84-13	Old Rosebud123^{1½}Peter Piper134½Leading Star110^4	Easily	8
22May20- 6Jam	sl	6f	:24^4 :49 1:15	3↑	Handicap 1155	1	7	5^{2¾}	5^3	2½	2^{hd}	McCabe J	124	wb	6.00	84-15	Padriac116^{hd}OldRosbud124½Tcklsh124^{1½}	Hard ridden,gamely	8
15May20- 4Jam	sl	6f	:23^3 :46^4 1:12^2	3↑	Paumonok H 4.8k	2	2	3^2	2^1	2^4	4^{4½}	McCabe J	111	wb	12.00	92-13	Dunboyne115^{2}Billy Kelly126½Ticklish107.5^2	Speed,tired	9
27Apr20- 3HdG	my	6f	:24 :47^3 1:14^1	4↑	Alw 1200	3	4	1^3	1^1	1^{hd}	2^{1¼}	McCabe J	116	wb	3.40	84-26	WarPennant109.5^{1¼}OldRosebud116^{5}Quietude110^2		4
	Speed,gave way																		
20Apr20- 4HdG	fst	6f	:23^2 :46^4 1:13^1	3↑	Alw 1674	7	4	4^{3¾}	4^{3½}	4^{3½}	5^6	McCabe J	116	w	7.35	84-11	Dr. Clark104½Fruit Cake111^{2½}War Pennant108^3	Speed,tired	7
16Apr20- 5HdG	gd	6f	:23^4 :47^3 1:13	3↑	Harford H 5.6k	5	6	4^3	4^{2½}	6^{7¼}	6^{11¾}	McCabe J	122	w	15.95	79-15	BillyKelly127^{nk}StarMaster122^{8}MidnghtSun105^1	Speed,tired	7
29Nov19- 4Bow	fst	1	:24^3 :48^4 1:15^2 1:42^2	2↑	Handicap 1500	3	1	1^1	1^1	1½	2^{nk}	Stirling D	117	w	5.30e	93-13	Slippery Elm112^{nk}Old Rosebud117^{1}Ballet Dancer II103^4		7
	Tired in drive																		
27Nov19- 5Bow	fst	1$\frac{1}{16}$	:25 :50 1:15 1:49^3	2↑	Thanksgiving H 2.6k	5	3	6^{5½}	6^{4½}	3^{1¾}	3^{1½}	Stirling D	117	w	6.50	90-14	Ormonda118^{no}Slippery Elm111^{1½}Old Rosebud117½	Resolutely	7
25Nov19- 5Bow	fst	1 70	:24^3 :50 1:14^3 1:46	3↑	Handicap 1500	2	2	2^2	2^4	2^2	3^5	Stirling D	120	w	16.45	91-10	Ophelia114^{4}Salvestra108^{1}Old Rosebud120^{1½}	Tired late	5
22Nov19- 3Bow	fst	6½f	:23^2 :46^4 1:13^2 1:20	2↑	Handicap 1200	5	4	2^{hd}	2^{1½}	2^3	2^5	McCabe J	122	w	3.30	91-12	Flags128^{5}Old Rosebud122^{hd}Quietude104^1	Held place	5
15Nov19- 3Bow	fst	7f	:23^1 :47^2 1:13^4 1:27^2	2↑	Alw 1000	1	2	1½	1^{1½}	1^2	1^2	McCabe J	112	w	*.70	95-13	OldRosebud112^{2}CharlieLeydecker102^{8}ArrahGoOn102^2	Easily	6
12Nov19- 5Pim	hy	6f	:23^4 :48^1 1:14^4	2↑	Handicap 1863	1	4	1^1	1^{nk}	2½	3^{5½}	McCabe J	113	w	2.70	79-26	TippityWtcht104^{1½}Dr.Johnson93^{4}OldRosbud113^6	Tired badly	4
21Oct19- 3Emp	fst	*6f	:22^4 :46^4 1:10	2↑	Handicap 1199	8	1	2^1	2½	1^3	1^2	McCabe J	126	w	4.50	89-12	Old Rosebud126^{2}Flags132^{1}Bill McCloy111^{nk}	Won easing up	9
15Oct19- 4Emp	hy	*6f	:23^2 :48^4 1:11^2	3↑	Kingsbridge Hwt H 2.9k	2	7	6^3	5^{2¼}	6^4	6^{5¼}	Fairbrother C	125	w	3.50e	77-24	FruitCake120^{hd}Pickwick120^{hd}UltimaThul118^2	Always beaten	7
13Oct19- 3Emp	hy	*6f	:23 :47^2 1:10^3	2↑	Alw 1361	3	1	2^{hd}	4^8	4^{4½}	4^7	McCabe J	116	w	4.00	79-19	Ormonda103^{hd}Ultima Thule107^{5}Flags106^2	Tired	6
11Oct19- 6Jam	fst	6f	:23^1 :47^2 1:12^3	2↑	Handicap 920	3	8	4^{3½}	4^4	3^3	3^{3½}	McCabe J	126	w	3.60	92-09	Flags116^{2}Arnold111^{1½}Old Rosebud126^2	Away poorly	8
23Sep19- 3Aqu	my	7f	:24 :48^3 1:13 1:26^2	2↑	Handicap 1658	4	1	1^1	1^2	1^2	1^2	McCabe J	111	w	*1.20	83-18	Old Rosebud111^{2}Nutcracker106^{1}Homely95^6	As rider pleased	5
17Sep19- 4Aqu	fst	6f	:23^1 :47^1 1:11^4	3↑	Arverne H 3.2k	5	5	3^4	4^2	4^{1¾}	4^{1¾}	McCabe J	118	w	12.00	94-10	Lord Brighton114^{hd}Enfilade112^{1½}Hollister123^{nk}	No mishap	7
15Sep19- 1Aqu	fst	6½f	:23 :47 1:11^3 1:18^2	2↑	Handicap 1920	8	12	8^{7½}	8^{7½}	7^{6½}	7^{7½}	McCabe J	120	w	20.00	90-10	FaryWnd112^{1}CornTssl113^{no}Hollstr125^1	Close quarters late	13
4Sep19- 3Bel	gd	6f-Str	1:11^3	2↑	Autumn Hwt H 3.5k	4	-	-	-	-	-	McCabe J	126	w	20.00	- -	Naturalist140^{no}BillyKelly124^{3}Enfilade116^{1½}	Left at post	7
1Sep19- 1Bel	fst	6f	:23 :46^4 1:10^3	3↑	Alw 1025	3	4	3^1	4^{5½}	4^4	5^{9½}	McCabe J	123	w	7.00	94-03	Lucullite130^{5}Peter Piper113^{4}Fruit Cake108½	Tired late	7
29Aug19- 2Sar	fst	6f	:23 :46^4 1:11^3	3↑	Handicap 1145	7	2	1^{hd}	1^{1½}	1^1	3^3	McCabe J	125	w	10.00	92-10	Startling112^{1}Lord Brighton110^2 [D] Old Rosebud125½	Tired	7
	Impeded rival turn;Disqualified																		
26Jly19- 4Emp	fst	1$\frac{1}{16}$	:23^3 :47^4 1:13^2 1:45^3	3↑	Yonkers H 2.9k	1	1	1^{nk}	4^3	5^{6½}	5^{18½}	Loftus J	127	w	3.00	76-11	Bally109^{2}Roamer120^{3}Spur113^{1½}	Eased when beaten	5
17Jly19- 4Emp	gd	1	:24^1 :48^2 1:13^2 1:40^2	3↑	Mount Vernon H 2.9k	4	3	2^2	2^3	2^3	2^4	Lunsford H	126	w	4.00	87-18	Lucullite127^{4}Old Rosebud126^{1}Sun Briar128^8	Chased winner	4
5Jly19- 4Lat	fst	1	:24 :48 1:36^4	3↑	Handicap 2000	2	1	1^{nk}	1^1	1½	2^{nk}	Murray T	126	w	1.45	103-06	SenningsPark118^{nk}OldRosebd126^{10}Ginger100^3	Saved ground	4
1Jly19- 5Lat	fst	1$\frac{1}{16}$	:23^3 :46^4 1:11^4 1:43^4	3↑	Handicap 2500	1	1	1½	1½	2½	3^{2½}	Howard J	128	w	3.20	95-09	BarneyShannon102^{2}VivaAmerica108½OldRosebud128^{hd}	Tired	7
25Jun19- 4Lat	my	6f	:23^3 :47^4 1:14	3↑	Handicap 2500	2	5	6^7	6^{11}	6^{13}	5^{16}	Van Dusen C	133	w	*1.50	69-25	Beaverkill108^{1}Top Coat101^{1}Green Grass105^8	Poor effort	6
12Jun19- 4Lat	fst	6f	:23 :46^2 1:11^1	3↑	Alw 2000	2	2	2^1	2^{nk}	1^{hd}	1^{hd}	Murray T	117	w	*.50	99-10	OldRsbd117^{hd}Topo'th'Mornng112^{8}BroomPddlr110.5^{1½}	Gamely	6
5Jun19- 4Lat	fst	1	:24^2 :48^1 1:13 1:38^2	3↑	Sp Wt 1868	7	1	1^{1½}	1^{1½}	1^3	1^{1½}	Murray T	118	w	*.30	95-10	Old Rosebud118^{1½}Buford118^{2}Dodge115^5	Won easing up	7
27May19- 3Bel	fst	6f	:23^3 :47^1 1:12^2	3↑	Alw 920	2	3	2½	1^1	1^1	1^{1½}	Loftus J	128	w	*.25	95-07	OldRosebud128^{1½}CrystalFord107½Crimper113^{1½}	Unruly start	10
22May19- 1Bel	sly	5½f-Str	1:07^4	3↑	Alw 930	3	3	3^2	1^1	1^2	1^6	Dreyer J	124	w	*.33	80-19	OldRosebud124^{6}BullyBoy115^{2½}BillMcCloy118^{15}	In a canter	4
15May19- 4Jam	fst	6f	:23^1 :47^1 1:12^2	3↑	Paumonok H 5.8k	14	6	5^7	4^3	3^2	2^{1½}	Dreyer J	134	w	7.00	95-08	Flgs126^{1½}OldRosbud134^{1½}Lucullt119½	Interference at start	14
10May19- 5Pim	hy	6f	:23^3 :48^3 1:16^2	3↑	Handicap 1120	6	5	3^{2¼}	3^{2¼}	3^2	2^1	Dreyer J	132	w	*1.15	76-25	Papp111^{1}Old Rosebud132^{nk}L'Errant105^{nk}	Poor ride	7
6May19- 6Pim	fst	1	:24^3 :49^2 1:15^2 1:42	3↑	Alw 1000	2	1	1^4	1^4	1^{nk}	2no	Dreyer J	124	w	*.30	85-15	Sweep On108^{no}Old Rosebud124^{6}Polka Dot90^{15}	Tiring	6
1May19- 6Pim	sly	6f	1:15	3↑	Alw 1078	1	-			1^{1½}	1^2	Dreyer J	118	w	*.45	84-18	Old Rosebud118^{2}Flags118^{5}Peter Piper118^3	In a canter	7
	Early calls unavailable due to fog																		
25Apr19- 3HdG	gd	5½f	:23^3 :47^2 1:00^2 1:06^3	3↑	Alw 1176	1	4	1^{1½}	1^{1½}	1^2	1^2	Dreyer J	123	w	1.45	94-16	OldRosebud123^{2}Bonifc118½Mlkmd110^{hd}	Restrained final ⅛	7
17Sep17- 4Aqu	fst	1$\frac{1}{16}$	:24^4 :48 1:12^1 1:44^3	3↑	Bayview H 1.6k	4	1	1^1	1^2	1^2	1^2	Peak C	133	w	*1.30	100-06	OldRosebud133^{2}Capra105^{nk}StraghtForwrd103^1	Easing at end	7
7Aug17- 4Sar	fst	1	:23^3 :47^1 1:13^3 1:38^2	3↑	Delaware H 3.5k	2	3	3^2	2^1	2½	1^{hd}	Molesworth G	133	w	2.60	95-10	Old Rosebud133^{hd}Capra104½Roamer127^4	Gamely	6
1Aug17- 4Sar	my	1¼	:50^3 1:15^4 1:41^2 2:06^1	3↑	Saratoga H 5.8k	4	4	3^{2½}	3^2	5^6	5^{12½}	Molesworth G	132	w	*1.70	76-14	Roamer122½Spur123^{1}Ticket107^1	Rated,tired	7
24Jly17- 5Knw	fst	1 70	:23^4 :47^4 1:13^1 1:43^2	3↑	Handicap 1200	1	2	2½	2½	1^{nk}	1^2	Molesworth G	132	w	*.15	108-00	Old Rosebud132^{2}Kinney108^{hd}Franklin107½	Easily	6
14Jly17- 4Wnr	gd	1⅛	:49^3 1:15 1:40^3 1:54^1	3↑	Frontier H 13k	3	2	3^1	1^1	1^1	1^{1½}	Molesworth G	129	w	3.25	85-18	Old Rosebud129^{1½}Boots129^{3}Hodge117^5	Hard ridden	8
9Jly17- 4Aqu	sl	1$\frac{1}{16}$	:24^1 :48 1:12^4 1:46^2	3↑	Handicap 1625	3	3	1^{nk}	1^1	1½	1^{nk}	Knapp W	130	w	*.80	91-13	Old Rosebud130^{nk}Bromo120^{5}Chiclet110	Gamely	3
4Jly17- 4Aqu	fst	7f	:24 :48^1 1:12^4 1:25^4	3↑	Carter H 3.4k	1	1	1^1	1^{1½}	1^1	1½	Schuttinger A	130	w	*2.20	93-11	OldRosebud130½Bromo122^{no}TheFinn130½	Repelled challenges	9
30Jun17- 4Aqu	fst	1	:24^1 :46^4 1:11^4 1:37^3	3↑	Queens County H 4.3k	1	2	1^{hd}	1^1	1^{1½}	1^{1½}	Robinson F	125	w	*2.40	94-12	Old Rosebud125^{1½}Roamer129^{1½}Chiclet110^2	Easily	7

25Jun17-4Aqu	fst	1⅛	:47 1:12^{2} 1:36^{3} 1:49^{2}	3↑ Brooklyn H 5.8k	$5\ 5\ 5^{4\frac12}\ 4^{2\frac12}\ 3^{2}\ 3^{1}$	Connelly D	120 w	8.00	102-04	Borrow117^{no}Rgrt122^{10}OldRosbud120^{1}	Gamely,swerved last ¼	11
11Jun17-5Lat	fst	1$\frac{1}{16}$	:24^{1} :48^{4} 1:14 1:45	3↑ Inaugural H 3k	$4\ 3\ 3^{1\frac12}\ 2^{hd}\ 1^{1\frac12}\ 1^{2}$	Connelly D	124 w	*2.30	92-13	OldRosebd124^{2}KingGorn119$^{1\frac12}$Mdwy103^{1}	Rated,won easing up	6
2Jun17-5DoP	gd	1¼	:47^{4} 1:12^{1} 1:38^{4} 2:04^{1}	3↑ Kentucky H 14k	$2\ 1\ 2^{hd}\ 2^{1}\ 7^{5\frac34}\ 9^{13}$	Connelly D	120 w	*1.80	80-13	King Gorin108^{nk}Cudgel103$^{\frac12}$Roamer126^{2}	Speed,tired	11
30May17-5DoP	fst	1⅛	:49 1:13 1:38^{1} 1:51^{1}	3↑ Handicap 1000	$4\ 2\ 2^{hd}\ 1^{\frac12}\ 1^{1}\ 1^{1\frac12}$	Connelly D	126 w	*1.00	99-09	Old Rosebud126$^{1\frac12}$King Gorin113^{1}Hodge121^{5}	Easily	5
26May17-5DoP	fst	1$\frac{1}{16}$	:25 :49^{2} 1:13 1:45	3↑ Alw 1000	$5\ 2\ 2^{hd}\ 1^{1\frac12}\ 1^{5}\ 1^{1\frac12}$	Connelly D	115 w	*.65	94-09	Old Rosebud115$^{1\frac12}$Leo Skolny111^{4}Pif Jr.116no	Won eased up	5
19May17-5CD	fst	1$\frac{1}{16}$	:25 :49^{3} 1:13 1:45^{1}	3↑ Clark H 2.8k	$2\ 1\ 1^{\frac12}\ 1^{1}\ 1^{\frac12}\ 1^{1}$	Connelly D	117 w	3.85	96-14	OldRosbd117^{1}Romr128^{8}Embrodry106$^{1\frac12}$	Rated,ridden strongly	4
12May17-3CD	fst	1$\frac{1}{16}$	:23^{4} :47^{3} 1:12^{3} 1:44^{3}	4↑ Alw 1000	$1\ 1\ 1^{\frac12}\ 1^{\frac12}\ 2^{1}\ 3^{6\frac12}$	Connelly D	119 w	*.50	92-06	Roamer119$^{1\frac12}$Ed Crump122^{5}Old Rosebud119^{6}	Tired badly	4
6Apr17-3OP	fst	7f	:24 :47 1:12^{1} 1:25^{1}	3↑ Alw 500	$-\ 2\ 1^{1\frac12}\ 1^{1\frac12}\ 1^{3}\ 1^{2}$	Molesworth G	105 w	*.90	105-06	Old Rosebud105^{2}Robert Bradley106.5^{2}Pan Zareta103		3
	Won under restraint											
30Mar17-4Esx	fst	1	:24 :47^{3} 1:13 1:38^{4}	3↑ Handicap 750	$-\ 1\ 1^{1\frac12}\ 1^{3}\ 1^{1\frac12}\ 1^{hd}$	Peak C	130 w	*.55	106-01	Old Rosebud130^{hd}Little String101^{no}Gordon Russell101^{12}		6
	Careless ride											
24Mar17-3OP	fst	6f	:23^{3} :47^{1} 1:12^{3}	3↑ Handicap 600	$-\ 6\ 3^{3\frac12}\ 2^{1\frac12}\ 2^{1\frac12}\ 3^{6}$	Peak C	137 w	1.30	95-05	PanZareta113^{hd}ColonelVenn123^{6}OldRosbd137^{hd}	Away poorly	6
12Mar17-4OP	sl	6f	:24 :47^{4} 1:15	3↑ Handicap 500	$-\ 2\ 1^{3}\ 1^{5}\ 1^{1}\ 1^{3}$	Peak C	130 w	*.55	89-22	Old Rosebud130^{3}David Craig106^{nk}Bob Hensley112^{1}		5
	Won under restraint											
8Mar17-4OP	gd	6f	:23^{4} :47^{4} 1:13^{1}	3↑ Handicap 500	$-\ 2\ 1^{1\frac12}\ 1^{1\frac12}\ 1^{1\frac12}\ 1^{2}$	Peak C	120 w	*.80	98-13	Old Rosebud120^{1}Aldebaran106^{5}Robert Bradley108^{nk}	Easily	6
18Feb17-4Jua	fst	5½f	:23^{2} :47^{4} 1:00^{1} 1:06^{2}	3↑ Handicap	- - 2	Molesworth G	122		- -	Zim108Old Rosebud122Belle Bird90		5
30May14-4Bel	fst	1	:23^{2} :47^{4} 1:13^{3} 1:39^{4}	Withers 3.4k	$3\ 1\ 1^{1}\ 3^{\frac12}\ 5^{6\frac14}\ 5^{16}$	McCabe J	115 w	*.20	72-14	Charlestonian115^{no}Gainer118^{8}Roamr115^{5}	Bore out far turn	5
9May14-4CD	fst	1¼	:47^{4} 1:13 1:38^{4} 2:03^{2}	Ky Derby 12k	$6\ 1\ 1^{1\frac12}\ 1^{2}\ 1^{6}\ 1^{8}$	McCabe J	114 w	*.85	107-09	Old Rosebud114^{8}Hodge114$^{1\frac12}$Bronzewing117^{4}	Hard held	7
25Apr14-4Lxt	sl	1	:24^{2} :48 1:15^{2} 1:42	Alw 600	$5\ 1\ 1^{2}\ 1^{3}\ 1^{6}\ 1^{6}$	McCabe J	112 w	*.30	77-22	Old Rosebud112^{6}Christophine98^{5}Ivan Gardner112^{6}		7
	Under restraint throughout											
13Aug13-3Sar	fst	6f	:23^{2} :47^{2} 1:13^{2}	U S Hotel 2.8k	$1\ 2\ 1^{3}\ 1^{6}\ 1^{4}\ 1^{3}$	McCabe J	125 w	*.17	91-08	OldRsbd125^{3}BlckBroom107$^{1\frac12}$PomttBlu111$^{1\frac12}$	Easing up at end	6
2Aug13-3Sar	fst	5½f	:23 :47^{2} 1:00 1:07	Flash 1.1k	$4\ 1\ 1^{2}\ 1^{1\frac12}\ 1^{2}\ 1^{2}$	McCabe J	124 w	*.60	94-09	Old Rosebud124^{2}Stromboli112^{10}Black Broom109^{3}	Easily	6
5Jly13-4Lat	fst	6f	:23^{2} :46^{4} 1:12^{4}	Cincinnati Trophy 5.7k	$2\ 3\ 1^{2}\ 1^{6}\ 1^{8}\ 1^{6}$	McCabe J	124 w	*.25	95-07	Old Rosebud124^{6}Pebeco111^{4}O'Hagan114^{hd}	In a canter	4
18Jun13-4Lat	my	5f	:23^{4} :49^{3} 1:01^{3}	©Harold 3.5k	$2\ 1\ 1^{1}\ 1^{3}\ 1^{4}\ 1^{5}$	McCabe J	120 w	*.15	87-20	Old Rosebud120^{5}Big Spirit106^{4}O'Hagan113	Easily	3
7Jun13-4DoP	fst	5f	:23 :46^{2} :58^{2}	Spring Trial 4.5k	$5\ 1\ 1^{1\frac12}\ 1^{1}\ 1^{1\frac12}\ 1^{2}$	McCabe J	115 w	*.55	113-04	Old Rosebud115^{2}Little Nephew118^{10}Imperator121^{3}	Easily	5
4Jun13-3DoP	fst	5f	:23^{1} :46^{3} :58^{3}	Alw 850	$1\ 2\ 2^{1}\ 2^{1\frac12}\ 1^{1\frac12}\ 1^{1}$	McCabe J	115 w	*.45	112-00	Old Rosebud115^{1}Little Nephew118^{8}Roamer100^{5}	Easily	5
31May13-3DoP	fst	5f	:22^{4} :46^{2} :58^{4}	Sp Wt 1030	$2\ 2\ 2^{nk}\ 2^{nk}\ 1^{1\frac12}\ 1^{4}$	McCabe J	112 w	2.20	111-00	OldRosebd112^{4}LittleNephew112$^{1\frac12}$Imprtor112	Won easing up	3
26May13-2DoP	fst	5f	:23 :47 1:00^{2}	Alw 750	$3\ 2\ 1^{1\frac12}\ 1^{2}\ 1^{4}\ 1^{6}$	McCabe J	111 w	*.25	103-00	OldRosbud111^{6}Vndrgrft114^{3}BlckToney114^{2}	Eased up last $\frac{1}{16}$	5
23May13-6CD	hy	4½f	:23 :47^{4} :54^{2}	Alw 600	$2\ 1\ 1^{10}\ 1^{10}\ 1^{10}$	McCabe J	115 w	*.45	92-08	Old Rosebud115^{10}The Norman111^{3}Harwood105^{1}	Easily	7
19May13-4CD	gd	4½f	:23^{2} :46^{3} :53	©Bashford Manor 1k	$3\ 2\ 2^{hd}\ 2^{hd}\ 2^{1}$	McCabe J	118 w	*.55	98-07	Little Nephew118^{1}Old Rosebud118^{10}Black Toney118^{8}		5
	Impeded start,wide,tired											
17May13-2CD	hy	4½f	:23^{4} :48 :54	Alw 600	$2\ 1\ 1^{3}\ 1^{4}\ 1^{6}$	Peak C	115 w	*.40	94-06	OldRosebd115^{6}Roamer108^{5}BraveCunardr105^{12}	Won easing up	5
1May13-4Lxt	fst	4½f	:23^{3} :47^{2} :53^{4}	Idle Hour 1.6k	$3\ 2\ 2^{hd}\ 1^{1\frac12}\ 2^{hd}$	McCabe J	115 w	*.50	99-05	Little Nephew115^{hd}Old Rosebud115^{6}Francis110$^{1\frac12}$	Gamely	9
5Mar13-1Jua	fst	4f	:23^{2} :47	Alw 300	$8\ 3\ 2^{2}\ 1^{3}\ 1^{5}$	McCabe J	118 w	*.40	96-04	Old Rosebud118^{5}Shadrach115$^{2\frac12}$Gladys Y.107^{3}	Won easing up	8
9Feb13-4Jua	hy	3½f	:24^{3} :43	©Yucatan .9k	$5\ 3\ 1^{2\frac12}\ 1^{6}$	Peak C	110 w	3.00	82-18	Old Rosebud110^{6}Blarney118$^{1\frac12}$Manganese118$^{2\frac12}$	In a canter	6

Pan Zareta

ch. f. 1910, by Abe Frank (Hanover)–Caddie Griffith, by Rancocas **Lifetime record: 151 76 31 21 $39,082**

Own.– J. Marrone
Br.– J.F. Newman (Tx)
Tr.– J.C. Kirkpatrick

10Nov17-4Lat	fst	6f	:23 :46^{2} 1:11^{4}	2↑ Handicap 1580	$3\ 3\ 6^{3}\ 4^{2}\ 1^{\frac12}\ 2^{nk}$	Willis O	123wb	4.60	96-08	Atalanta109^{nk}Pan Zareta123^{3}Solly129^{1}	Impeded	7
7Nov17-5Lat	fst	6f	:22^{4} :46^{3} 1:11^{4}	2↑ Ladies H 2.1k	$3\ 7\ 5^{3}\ 4^{3\frac12}\ 5^{4\frac12}\ 6^{7\frac12}$	Gentry L	125wb	2.75	88-09	Solly122$^{1\frac12}$Atalanta105^{3}Ocean Sweep105^{hd}	Quit badly	8
29Oct17-5Lat	my	6f	:24 :48^{1} 1:15	2↑ Handicap 1000	$1\ 3\ 5^{2\frac14}\ 5^{5}\ 4^{1\frac34}\ 4^{4\frac14}$	Garner M	127wb	6.00	76-28	Harry Kelly113^{hd}J.J. Murdock113^{nk}Fruit Cake110^{4}	Outrun	7
26Oct17-5Lat	sl	6f	:23^{1} :46^{4} 1:12^{3}	3↑ Handicap 1000	$2\ 1\ 1^{hd}\ 1^{hd}\ 1^{2}\ 1^{\frac12}$	Garner M	122wb	3.00	92-19	Pan Zareta122$^{\frac12}$J.J. Murdock110^{4}Phocion107^{5}	Tiring	5
22Oct17-5Lat	fst	6f	:23 :46^{4} 1:11^{3}	2↑ Handicap 1000	$3\ 5\ 4^{2\frac12}\ 3^{\frac34}\ 6^{2\frac34}\ 5^{5}$	Garner M	126wb	*1.30	92-11	Atalanta100$^{1\frac12}$BelieveMeBoys106^{hd}Bradley'sChoice113^{2}	Outrun	8
15Oct17-4Lat	gd	6f	:23 :46^{4} 1:12^{3}	2↑ Handicap 1000	$3\ 3\ 2^{hd}\ 2^{2}\ 4^{nk}\ 5^{5\frac14}$	Garner M	128wb	3.25	87-13	Believe Me Boys100^{nk}Prince of Como119$^{1\frac12}$Vogue120^{2}		6
	Dropped out after ½											
4Oct17-4CD	sl	6f	:23^{2} :47^{1} 1:13	3↑ Falls City H 2.7k	$5\ 1\ 1^{1\frac12}\ 1^{1\frac12}\ 1^{1}\ 3^{1}$	Garner M	131wb	5.70	89-20	Vogue113^{1}Bradley's Choice108^{hd}Pan Zareta131^{2}	Tired	10
28Sep17-5DoP	fst	6f	:23 :46^{1} 1:12	2↑ Handicap 1000	$3\ 3\ 1^{\frac12}\ 3^{4\frac12}\ 2^{5}\ 5^{6\frac14}$	Howard J	133wb	*1.70	87-14	Prince of Como108.5^{5}Vogue110^{nk}Believe Me Boys99$^{\frac12}$	Tired	6
26Sep17-4DoP	fst	6f	:22^{3} :45^{3} 1:12^{1}	3↑ Alw 1000	$1\ 3\ 2^{1\frac12}\ 2^{1\frac12}\ 1^{1}\ 1^{1}$	Garner M	123wb	*1.35	92-09	Pan Zareta123^{1}Marion Goosby112$^{\frac12}$Blind Baggage126^{3}		5
	Rated,won restrained											
20Sep17-4Lxt	fst	6f	:23 :46^{2} 1:12	3↑ Alw 650	$2\ 1\ 1^{1\frac12}\ 1^{1\frac12}\ 1^{1}\ 1^{nk}$	Garner M	115wb	1.15	96-10	Pan Zareta115^{nk}Blind Baggage118^{12}Franklin105^{6}	Lasted	6
15Sep17-3Lxt	fst	6f	:23^{2} :47^{3} 1:12^{4}	3↑ Handicap 700	$4\ 1\ 1^{1}\ 1^{1\frac12}\ 1^{2}\ 1^{1\frac12}$	Howard J	125wb	*.80	92-14	Pan Zareta125$^{1\frac12}$Marion Goosby114^{5}John Jr.109^{1}	Easily	5
12Sep17-1Lxt	fst	6f	:23^{3} :47^{4} 1:14	3↑ Alw 700	$4\ 3\ 1^{hd}\ 2^{hd}\ 2^{\frac12}\ 4^{1\frac14}$	Howard J	125wb	2.35	85-12	Blind Baggage128^{nk}Marion Goosby115^{hd}John Jr.103^{1}	Tired	6
	Previously owned and trained by E.T. Colton											
6Aug17-2Sar	fst	6f	:23^{1} :47^{4} 1:13^{2}	3↑ Handicap 875	$3\ 3\ 3^{2}\ 2^{3}\ 3^{2\frac12}\ 6^{4\frac14}$	Mott A	142wb	4.50	84-14	Corn Tassel112^{hd}High Noon120^{hd}Tom McTaggart112$^{1\frac12}$	Tired	14
31Jly17-3Emp	fst	*6f	:22^{2} :46^{3} 1:08^{2}	3↑ Handicap 600	$4\ 2\ 1^{1\frac12}\ 1^{1\frac12}\ 1^{2}\ 1^{1}$	Mott A	140wb	3.20	98-04	Pan Zareta140^{1}High Noon122^{hd}Leochares126^{3}	Gamely	6
26Jly17-3Emp	fst	*6f	:23 :47 1:09^{2}	3↑ Katonah H 1.1k	$5\ 7\ 2^{hd}\ 2^{hd}\ 1^{1}\ 1^{\frac34}$	Mott A	137wb	4.50	93-08	Pan Zareta137$^{\frac34}$Leochares127^{hd}Whimsy114^{3}	Dueled,gamely	7
20Jly17-4Emp	fst	*6f	:23 :48^{3} 1:10^{2}	3↑ ⒻHandicap 660	$1\ 2\ 1^{1}\ 1^{hd}\ 1^{3}\ 1^{2}$	Mott A	135wb	*1.60	88-11	Pan Zareta135^{2}Capra127$^{2\frac12}$Diamond100^{1}	Dueled	6
5Jly17-5Aqu	fst	6½f	:23 :47^{1} 1:12^{1} 1:19	3↑ Handicap 710	$5\ 3\ 1^{1}\ 1^{1}\ 2^{\frac12}\ 2^{1\frac12}$	Mott A	135wb	3.00	93-11	Startling124$^{1\frac12}$PanZart135^{nk}[D]Whmsy118^{4}	Hard ridden,tired	6
29Jun17-2Aqu	sly	6½f	:24 :47^{4} 1:14^{4} 1:22	3↑ ⒻHandicap 670	$4\ 5\ 4^{4\frac12}\ 3^{3}\ 2^{\frac12}\ 1^{\frac12}$	Mott A	123 w	4.00	80-24	PanZarta123$^{\frac12}$RhineMaiden108^{2}FairyWand103^{2}	Saved ground	7
26Jun17-1Aqu	fst	6½f	:23 :47^{1} 1:12^{1} 1:19	3↑ Alw 700	$4\ 2\ 1^{hd}\ 2^{1\frac12}\ 3^{5}\ 5^{13}$	Troxler R	128wb	*2.00	82-14	Bromo119^{2}Hank O'Day123^{8}Madame Curie103^{no}	Quit badly	8
19Jun17-5Jam	fst	5½f	:23 :47^{3} :59^{3} 1:05^{3}	3↑ Handicap 815	$3\ 1\ 1^{1\frac12}\ 1^{1}\ 1^{2}\ 1^{2}$	Troxler R	128wb	10.00	102-07	PanZrta128^{2}Topo'th'Morning140^{1}HighNoon137$^{1\frac12}$	Drew away	10
21May17-7OW	fst	6f	:23^{1} :47^{2} 1:13^{3}	3↑ ⒻAlw 840	$7\ 1\ 1^{\frac12}\ 1^{hd}\ 1^{1}\ 1^{2}$	Mott A	125wb	7.15	90-11	Pan Zareta125^{2}Arriet116^{nk}Graphic103^{nk}	Easily	7
18May17-4Dev	fst	6f	:23^{4} :49 1:13	3↑ Handicap 1000	$6\ 6\ 5^{3\frac12}\ 4^{3\frac12}\ 4^{2\frac12}\ 3^{3\frac12}$	Mott A	132wb	*1.50	91-15	Skiles Knob105$^{\frac12}$Tiajan98^{3}Pan Zareta132^{2}	Slow start,tired	6
16May17-4Dev	fst	5½f	:23^{4} :48^{1} 1:01 1:07^{4}	3↑ Handicap 1000	$3\ 7\ 4^{3\frac12}\ 4^{4\frac12}\ 3^{3\frac12}\ 3^{3}$	Mott A	130wb	*.90	90-18	Etruscan116^{1}ArthurMiddleton100^{2}PanZareta130^{3}	Slow start	8
14May17-4Dev	fst	6f	:24^{2} :49 1:15^{2}	3↑ Handicap 1000	$4\ 7\ 4^{2\frac12}\ 3^{6}\ 2^{1}\ 1^{hd}$	Mott A	126wb	*1.15	83-25	Pan Zareta126^{hd}Etruscan108^{5}Pesky110^{1}	Flat-footed start	8
9Apr17-4OP	fst	6f	:24 :48^{3} 1:13^{2}	3↑ Handicap 550	$-\ 6\ 4^{1}\ 4^{1}\ 3^{\frac12}\ 2^{no}$	Dominick J	126wb	*.80	97-10	Opportunity104^{no}PanZrt126^{no}CaneRun110^{hd}	Away slowly,wide	6
6Apr17-3OP	fst	7f	:24 :47 1:12^{1} 1:25^{1}	3↑ Alw 500	$-\ 3\ 2^{1\frac12}\ 2^{1\frac12}\ 2^{3}\ 3^{4}$	Lykes L	103wb	2.60	101-06	Old Rosebud105^{2}Robert Bradley106.5^{2}Pan Zareta103		3
	Away slowly,tired											
3Apr17-3OP	fst	6f	:23^{3} :48 1:13^{1}	3↑ Handicap 700	$-\ 1\ 3^{2}\ 3^{1\frac34}\ 3^{\frac34}\ 3^{1\frac34}$	Peak C	126wb	1.60	96-08	CaneRun101$^{1\frac12}$MarieMiller106^{nk}PanZareta126^{5}	Tired,gamely	4
	Previously owned by H.S. Newman, trained by E. Foucon											
28Mar17-5OP	fst	6f	:23^{3} :47 1:12^{2}	3↑ Handicap 600	$-\ 3\ 2^{hd}\ 1^{hd}\ 1^{1}\ 1^{1\frac12}$	Kederis J	120wb	*.70	102-08	Pan Zareta120$^{1\frac12}$Hanovia116$^{\frac12}$Wise Man102^{2}	Briefly urged	6
24Mar17-3OP	fst	6f	:23^{3} :47^{1} 1:12^{3}	3↑ Handicap 600	$-\ 1\ 1^{3}\ 1^{1\frac12}\ 1^{1\frac12}\ 1^{hd}$	Kederis J	113wb	*1.00	101-05	PanZarta113^{hd}ColonelVennie123^{6}OldRosbd137^{hd}	Hard ridden	6
20Mar17-4OP	fst	6f	:23^{2} :47^{1} 1:12^{1}	3↑ Handicap 600	$-\ 3\ 3^{1}\ 3^{2}\ 2^{1}\ 2^{\frac12}$	Kederis J	112wb	5.00	102-08	Brumley106.5$^{\frac12}$PanZareta112$^{\frac12}$JackO'Dowd105^{hd}	Finished fast	8
17Feb17-3FG	fst	1	:23^{4} 1:13^{2} 1:40	3↑ Alw 600	$-\ 2\ 2^{hd}\ 2^{\frac12}\ 6^{4\frac12}\ 8^{16\frac12}$	Lykes L	103 ws	*2.60	72-14	Half Rock109^{hd}Wise Man104^{6}McAdoo106^{1}	Tired badly	9
15Feb17-5FG	sl	6f	:23^{4} :47^{3} 1:14	3↑ Handicap 700	$-\ 3\ 1^{hd}\ 2^{1}\ 2^{1}\ 3^{1\frac12}$	Kederis J	116 ws	2.50	88-17	J.J.Murdock111$^{1\frac12}$RobertBradley108^{hd}PanZareta116^{1}	Tired	7
12Jan17-4FG	fst	1	:24 :48 1:13^{2} 1:40^{4}	4↑ Alw 500	$-\ 1\ 1^{1\frac12}\ 1^{\frac12}\ 2^{1}\ 3^{2}$	Kederis J	106wb	*.80	83-15	DavidCraig104$^{1\frac12}$Woodstone97$^{\frac12}$PanZaret106^{3}	Tired after ¾	7
4Jan17-4FG	sl	6f	:23^{3} :48 1:15^{1}	3↑ Handicap 600	$-\ 1\ 2^{nk}\ 2^{1\frac12}\ 3^{\frac12}\ 4^{2}$	Kederis J	122wb	*.80	82-21	BarsandStars100$^{1\frac12}$PrinceofComo114^{hd}ArchPlotter95$^{\frac12}$	Tired	5
30Mar16-4OP	fst	5½f	:23^{3} :48^{1} 1:00^{2} 1:07	3↑ Handicap 500	$1\ 1\ 1^{hd}\ 2^{hd}\ 1^{\frac12}\ 1^{1\frac12}$	Murphy F	142wb	*.80	96-09	PanZareta142$^{1\frac12}$MarsCassidy110^{no}Korfhage110^{no}	Hard ridden	5
17Mar16-4OP	fst	6f	:23^{1} :47^{3} 1:12^{4}	3↑ Handicap 300	$3\ 1\ 1^{\frac12}\ 1^{\frac12}\ 1^{\frac12}\ 1^{1}$	Kederis J	135wb	*.80	100-06	PanZareta135^{1}Korfhage107$^{\frac12}$Dr.Larrick126^{nk}	Saved ground	5

11Mar16- 4OP	fst 1	:25 :49 1:143 1:39	3 ↑ Handicap 300	2 1 1½ 1½ 1¹	1³	Kederis J	118wb	*.60	103-05	PanZaret118³Grumpy106nkBobHnsly102nk	Finished easing up	6
4Mar16- 5FG	fst 6f	:224 :463 1:121	5 ↑ Sp Wt 600	1 1 2hd 2¹ 2¹	2¾	Garner M	110wb	1.10	98-05	Bringhurst110¾Pan Zareta110	Tired	2
26Feb16- 4FG	fst 1 1/16	:234 :474 1:133 1:453	3 ↑ New Orleans Hotel H 3.9k	11 1 1½ 1²	1½	3²	Kederis J	115wb	6.00	94-08	Marion Goosby110²Skeerface103hdPan Zareta115hd	Tired	14
23Feb16- 4FG	fst 1	:233 :471 1:123 1:391	5 ↑ Sp Wt 600	1 2 2½ 1½ 1²	1²	Kederis J	108wb	*.65	97-07	Pan Zareta108²J.J. Lillis108	Rated	2
19Feb16- 4FG	fst 1 1/16	:233 :474 1:122 1:45	3 ↑ Merchants H 3.3k	14 1 1½ 1½ 1²	3¹	Kederis J	112wb	6.00	98-04	MarionGoosby103¹SkeerFace98hdPnZareta112hd	Not enough	15
5Feb16- 3FG	fst 5½f	:224 :47 :592 1:061	3 ↑ Handicap 600	8 3 5³½ 4²½ 4¾	1½	Kederis J	140wb	*1.40	98-06	Pan Zareta140½J.J. Lillis125noCarbide108³	Gamely	11
29Jan16- 3FG	gd 6f	:23 :473 1:132	3 ↑ Handicap 600	1 2 3¹ 3¹ 1¹½	1¹½	Kederis J	124wb	*1.60	93-13	PnZareta124¹½MronGoosby105½Dr.Lrrck110hd	Won easing up	6
15Jan16- 3FG	fst 6f	:231 :463 1:12	3 ↑ Handicap 500	4 4 3nk 2hd 3¹½	3³	Kederis J	126wb	*1.40	97-06	J.J. Lillis108¹½Bringhurst113¹½Pan Zareta126⁴	Gamely	6
7Jan16- 4FG	fst 6f	:23 :472 1:123	3 ↑ Handicap 400	6 5 2nk 1hd 1½	1½	Kederis J	124wb	*.80	97-08	Pan Zareta124½Ahara106.5½Carbide103no	Hard ridden	6
5Oct15- 3CD	hy 6f	:241 :48 1:14	3 ↑ ⒻAlw 700	4 1 1² 1⁴ 1⁶	1⁶	Kederis J	110wb	*.50	85-18	Pan Zareta110⁶Vogue100⁶Lady J. Grey103⁶		4
		Imped rivals at start,won easily										
29Sep15- 4CD	gd 6f	:234 :474 1:131	3 ↑ Falls City H 2.8k	7 5 1¹½ 1¹ 2nk	3¹½	Rice T	125wb	3.50	87-14	PrinceHermis108noVogue107¹½PanZareta125½	Tired near end	11
22Sep15- 6OW	fst 6f	:22 :454 1:114	2 ↑ Handicap 745	3 2 2¹ 3² 3²	3¹½	Rice T	126wb	*1.00	97-09	Water Lady105hdKewessa110¹½Pan Zareta126¹	Rated,tired	6
20Sep15- 6OW	fst 7f	:24 :473 1:131 1:263	2 ↑ ⒻHandicap 640	4 1 1nk 1² 1³	1¹½	Rice T	124wb	*.70	99-11	Pan Zareta124¹½Water Lady108noVenetia107⁴	Won easing up	5
16Sep15- 4Dor	fst 6f	:224 :463 1:11	2 ↑ Handicap 600	1 1 2hd 1nk 1nk	2no	Smyth J	123wb	*1.00	112-00	Back Bay113noPan Zareta123½Kewessa109¹½	Just missed	5
8Sep15- 5BB	sly 6f	:231 :473 1:133	2 ↑ Handicap 640	5 2 3³ 3⁶ 2²	2nk	Rice T	125wb	3.50	94-16	Water Lady102nkPan Zareta125¹Venetia106½	Good try	7
2Sep15- 5BB	fst 7f	:23 :47 1:12 1:25	2 ↑ Handicap 700	7 2 2⁴ 2⁴ 2½	2²	Cooper F	122wb	*1.50	95-11	Back Bay107²Pan Zareta122½Ten Point124½	Led,tired	8
26Aug15- 4Con	gd 6f	:234 :481 1:142	2 ↑ Handicap 500	2 2 1hd 2hd 1½	2½	Cooper F	129wb	*1.60	95-15	SirEdgar107½PanZareta129¹½BackBy110³	Saved ground,tired	5
10Aug15- 4FE	gd 6f	:224 :47 1:141	3 ↑ Handicap 700	2 5 4²¼ 3² 4²¼	3²½	Cooper F	130 w	*.75	83-21	Kewessa102½Sir Edgar103¹Pan Zareta130¾	Outrun	7
28Jly15- 5Ham	sly 6f	:234 :484 1:142	3 ↑ Handicap 670	5 1 2nk 5⁹ 5¹⁵	5¹¹	Cooper F	139wb	*1.40	72-20	Dr. Larrick100²Ed Howard97noCarbide106¹	Quit	5
24Jly15- 3Ham	fst 6f	:233 :472 1:114	3 ↑ Handicap 680	4 3 2² 2½ 1nk	2nk	Cooper F	140wb	*.70	96-04	SirEdgar99nkPanZareta140¾Dr.Larrick101hd	Resolute drive	8
20Jly15- 3Wnr	fst 6f	:241 :473 1:122	3 ↑ Handicap 700	4 4 1½ 1¹½ 1⁴	1¹½	Cooper F	136wb	*.60	98-11	PanZrta136¹½Commonada105¹Ed Howard98hd	Won easing up	5
14Jly15- 3Wnr	fst 6f	:232 :463 1:112	3 ↑ Alw 700	3 3 1¹½ 1¹ 1¹½	1²	Cooper F	118wb	*.80	103-07	Pan Zareta118²Back Bay103²Iron Mask108⁴	Easily	6
28Jun15- 3Ham	fst 5½f	:231 :47 :594 1:061	3 ↑ Handicap 690	2 3 1hd 1¹ 1³	1⁵	Cooper F	131wb	*1.60	98-12	Pan Zareta131⁵Sir Edgar95.5²Ed Howard99½	Drew away	9
25Jun15- 3Ham	fst 6f	:223 :471 1:122	3 ↑ Handicap 680	3 5 2² 3¹ 3²¼	1½	Cooper F	127wb	2.20	93-10	PnZreta127½Carbide96²½Kewessa107⁶	Inside move,drew clear	7
		Previously owned by J.F. Newman & H.S. Newman										
22Jun15- 3Con	gd 6f	:24 :482 1:144	3 ↑ Handicap 500	4 1 2hd 1¹½ 1³	1hd	Cooper F	129wb	*1.60	94-09	PanZarta129hdSouthernMaid94⁵BckBy116⁴	Ridden out,lasted	5
17Jun15- 5Con	sl 6f	:24 :483 1:141	3 ↑ Handicap 500	2 3 2² 2¹ 2¹½	3¹½	Burns G	134wb	*1.20	95-15	Recoil90hdBack Bay116¹½Pan Zareta134³	Tired	4
9Jun15- 3BB	fst 6f	:24 :474 1:133	3 ↑ Handicap 630	2 1 1¹ 1hd 1½	1¹	Burns G	134wb	*.80	94-14	Pan Zareta134¹Carbide105²½Deposit104nk	Swerved ⅛	5
28May15- 4OW	fst 6f	:222 :463 1:122	3 ↑ Handicap 770	1 1 2hd 1½ 1³	1¹	Rice T	129wb	*1.05	96-10	Pan Zareta129¹Kewessa112³Back Bay117½	Ridden out	6
24May15- 7OW	fst 6f	:23 :471 1:13	3 ↑ ⒻAlw 630	4 1 1² 1² 1³	1²	Rice T	123wb	*.10	93-09	Pan Zareta123²Recoil113¹½Shyness103¹	Under restraint	6
		Previously trained by H.S. Newman										
26Mar15- 4Jua	fst 6f	:232 :47 1:114	3 ↑ Handicap 300	2 2 1½ 1nk 1¾	1nk	Loftus J	146wb	*.80	89-17	PanZrta146nkSeneca100³Kootny115²½	Ridden out vigorously	5
22Mar15- 4Jua	fst 5½f	:221 :46 :59 1:052	3 ↑ Handicap 300	5 4 2² 2¹½ 1¹	1²½	Loftus J	140wb	*.70	90-16	PanZarta140²½Kootenay112¹½Manganese95¹½	Won easing up	7
7Mar15- 4Jua	fst 7f	:232 :463 1:121 1:243	3 ↑ Dos Republicas H 1.4k	6 2 2² 2²½ 1nk	2hd	Loftus J	135wb	*1.40	94-13	Kootenay107hdPan Zareta135½Rash112¹½	Gamely	12
21Feb15- 5Jua	gd 1	:241 :49 1:154 1:413	3 ↑ Alw 400	6 2 1¹½ 1³ 1²½	1¹	Rice T	108wb	*.70	76-24	PnZreta108¹Roadmstr103⁵GnrlMrchmont104¹	Easing up late	7
10Feb15- 3Jua	fst 5f	:213 :444 :571	3 ↑ Sp Wt 400	2 2 2³ 2²½ 2hd	1²	Loftus J	120 w	*.50	105-07	Pan Zareta120²Joe Blair110	Rated,easing late	2
18Jan15- 4Jua	fst 5½f	:23 :471 :594 1:062	3 ↑ Handicap 400	1 1 1² 1³ 1²	1³	Loftus J	136wb	*.13	85-19	Pan Zareta136³Little Will92¹New Haven103⁴	Won easing up	4
13Dec14- 4Jua	fst 6f	:232 :473 1:111	2 ↑ Handicap 500	2 2 1¹½ 1² 1²½	1hd	Loftus J	132wb	*.70	92-14	PnZrt132hdHocnir116³SirDyke96¹½	Eased late,almost caught	4
		Previously trained by E. Foucon										
10Oct14- 3CD	my 6f	:233 :472 1:13	3 ↑ Alw 600	4 3 1¹½ 1¹½ 1²	1¹½	Loftus J	112wb	*.40	90-18	Pan Zareta112¹½Bob Hensley106⁶Korfhage103⁸	Cantering	7
2Oct14- 4DoP	fst 6f	:23 :461 1:112	3 ↑ Handicap 760	1 3 1½ 1¹ 1nk	1hd	Loftus J	116wb	3.35	97-10	PanZareta116hdLeoSkolny106nkLeochares113⁴	Saved ground	6
26Sep14- 2OW	fst 6f	:221 :453 1:113	2 ↑ Handicap 725	5 1 2¹ 2² 2nk	2nk	Burns G	122wb	*1.12	101-05	BackBay117nkPanZareta122⁶SouthernMaid100²	Second best	5
19Sep14- 1OW	fst 6f	:244 :463 1:12	2 ↑ Handicap 730	1 4 1nk 2½ 2¹½	2¹½	Burns G	124wb	*1.35	97-10	Back Bay115¹½Pan Zareta124¹½Rockville106²	Tired	6
14Sep14- 4Dor	fst 6f	:233 :482 1:144	3 ↑ Rapids H 1.7k	3 1 1² 1¹ 1nk	2hd	Burns G	126wb	*1.40	99-07	Water Lady91hdPan Zareta126⁴Brave Cunarder94¹	Gamely	5
28Aug14- 4Con	fst 6f	:24 :484 1:14	2 ↑ Handicap 600	1 4 1³ 1² 1⁴	1¾	Callahan J	120wb	*1.80	98-09	Pan Zareta120¾Back Bay115²Southern Maid105⁵	Tiring	8
5Aug14- 6FE	fst 6f	:224 :461 :584 1:112	3 ↑ Alw 600	5 1 2hd 2nk 3½	4²½	Burns G	115wb	*1.50	99-04	Leochares102²BackBy102½LttlNphw104hd	Tired under impost	7
31Jly14- 4Ham	fst 5½f	:241 :482 :594 1:054	3 ↑ Handicap 650	2 1 1¹½ 1½ 1¹	1³	Burns G	126wb	*2.00	100-03	PanZareta126³Useeit100½KnightsDiffer103¹	Won easing up	5
29Jly14- 1Ham	fst 6f	:233 :481 1:13	3 ↑ Handicap 740	1 1 1² 1² 1²	1²	Burns G	123wb	*.90	90-13	PanZrta123²Nightstck117½MovngPctur97¹½	Never extended	4
25Jly14- 5Ham	fst 6f	:233 :462 1:122	3 ↑ Handicap 690	3 2 2nk 2½ 2¹½	2²	Burns G	124wb	*2.60	91-09	Back Bay112²Pan Zareta124nkElwah100½	Game try	8
21Jly14- 4Wnr	fst 6f	:234 :472 1:12	3 ↑ Handicap 700	1 1 1¹ 1¹½ 1²	1nk	Burns G	120wb	2.50	100-04	Pan Zareta120nkBack Bay111²Miramichi103²	Hard ridden	5
8Jly14- 5FE	fst 6f	:224 :47 1:13	3 ↑ Handicap 600	4 1 1½ 1½ 1⁴	1²	Burns G	119wb	1.50	94-09	PanZarta119²MeetingHous124nkShrwood114⁶	Easing up late	4
4Jly14- 5FE	fst 6f	:232 :472 1:123	3 ↑ Alw 700	5 3 4¹½ 3¹½ 2½	2¹	Burns G	112wb	*.80	95-08	SouthrnMaid102¹PanZarta112nkMeetngHouse117⁸	Wide,tired	5
27Jun14- 1Ham	fst 6f	:24 :483 1:121	3 ↑ Alw 530	2 4 2² 2² 2¹	2³	Callahan J	109wb	*.40	91-08	Back Bay112³Pan Zareta109¹½Dorothy Dean115³	Lost whip	6
25Jun14- 3Ham	fst 6f	:231 :464 1:12	3 ↑ Alw 640	7 2 2½ 2¹ 1½	1no	Callahan J	106wb	*1.00	95-08	Pan Zareta106noNightstick105³Marjorie A.107⁶	Lasted	7
20Jun14- 5Con	sl 6f	:241 :493 1:162	3 ↑ Handicap 500	5 3 3² 2nk 1²	1¹	Peak C	117 w	5.00	88-23	Pan Zareta117¹Sir Blaise104¹Fathom104⁴	Ridden out	9
11Jun14- 4Dor	fst 6f	:234 :484 1:144	3 ↑ Caughnawaga H 2.2k	8 2 1nk 1½ 1³	4³¼	Peak C	120wb	*3.00	104-00	Bwana Tumbo112hdSherwood112³Marjorie A.112nk	Tired	9
2Jun14- 3BB	fst 6f	:233 :474 1:124	3 ↑ Handicap 755	5 3 3²½ 2nk 1¹½	2½	Peak C	126wb	3.60	97-15	SirBlaise109½PanZareta126⁴Recol102no	Tired under impost	7
29May14- 3OW	fst 6f	:23 :474 1:13	3 ↑ Handicap 820	4 2 2hd 1hd 2¹½	3⁶	Peak C	126wb	4.20	88-12	Cabaret115²Marjorie A.112⁴Pan Zareta126hd	Dueled,tired	11
		Previously trained by H.S. Newman										
22Mar14- 4Jua	fst 5½f	:23 :472 :591 1:052	3 ↑ Handicap 500	4 4 5³¾ 3³ 3⁴	4²½	Woods H	132wb	*.60	99-05	Lady Panchita98½Seneca108¹Furlong100¹	Tired	6
17Mar14- 4Jua	fst 7f	:223 :461 1:113 1:241	3 ↑ Handicap 500	4 1 1²½ 1²½ 1²	1²	Cavanaugh H	122wb	*.60	101-09	PanZarta122²NewHaven95nkSwish87²	Went to knees at start	5
11Mar14- 4Jua	fst 1	:232 :452 1:113 1:364	3 ↑ Handicap 600	4 3 2hd 2hd 3¹¼	5⁶	Cavanaugh H	126wb	4.00	97-06	Christophine102¹BertGetty105²Curlicue102no		7
		Forced pace,tired										
8Mar14- 4Jua	fst 7f	:232 :46 1:102 1:24	3 ↑ Dos Republicas H 1.4k	6 1 1hd 2nk 2nk	3¹¾	Van Dusen C	130wb	*2.00	100-01	Orb105¹Dorothy Dean122¾Pan Zareta130nk	Tired	7
16Feb14- 4Jua	fst 7f	:231 :464 1:114 1:24	3 ↑ Handicap 400	3 1 1¹½ 1² 1²½	2¾	Van Dusen C	135wb	2.20	101-05	Dorothy Dean112¾Pan Zareta135½Barsac112⁴	Resolute	6
13Feb14- 4Jua	fst 6f	:222 :471 1:12	3 ↑ Handicap 400	4 3 1² 1²½ 1³	1³	Van Dusen C	132wb	*.80	96-06	Pan Zareta132³Cosgrove102nkColquitt97²½	Never extended	4
27Jan14- 4Jua	fst 6f	:222 :47 1:113	3 ↑ Handicap 400	2 3 1¾ 1¹ 1²½	1¹	Loftus J	124wb	*.50	98-11	Pan Zareta124¹New Haven100noBarsac103¹½	Eased last 100y	5
4Jan14- 3Jua	fst 6f	:213 :45 :564 1:093	3 ↑ Alw 500	1 1 2½ 2²½ 2²½	2⁵	Kirschbaum C	110wb	1.50	103-02	Iron Mask115⁵Pan Zareta110	No match	2
13Dec13- 4Jua	fst 5½f	:222 :461 :583 1:043	2 ↑ Handicap 500	1 2 1¾ 1² 1²½	1¹½	Kirschbaum C	126 w	*.80	103-03	Pan Zareta126¹½Useeit105²Orb92⁹	Won easing up	4
6Dec13- 4Jua	fst 5½f	:222 :461 :582 1:043	2 ↑ Handicap 500	2 1 1¹ 1² 1²½	1²½	Kirschbaum C	124wb	*1.00	103-06	Pan Zareta124²½Florence Roberts112¹½Gold of Ophir102²		4
		Won easing up										
2Dec13- 4Jua	fst 6f	:223 :471 1:114	2 ↑ Handicap 500	5 1 2hd 1hd 1nk	2¾	Kirschbaum C	124wb	*1.00	96-06	VestedRights102¾PnZrt124nkHnryWlbnk101½	Led,just missed	8
27Nov13- 4Jua	fst 6f	:224 :47 1:12	2 ↑ Juarez H 1.4k	4 1 1¹½ 1¹½ 1²	1hd	Kirschbaum C	118wb	*1.60	96-08	Pan Zareta118hdMimorioso105⁴Useeit110nk	Gamely	10
		Previously owned by J.F. Newman										
23Oct13- 2Dal	sl 6f	:283 :583 1:29	Handicap 300	- -	5¹³¾	Small R	122	--		Furlong116nkHusky Lad104³Suffragist106¹⁰		5
21Oct13- 3Dal	sl 6f	:253 :52 1:19	3 ↑ Alw 200	- -	1³	Small R	119	--		Pan Zareta119³Furlong122³Suffragist115⁴		7
3Oct13- 4DoP	fst 6f	:23 :463 1:104	3 ↑ Handicap 760	2 3 1nk 6⁶¾ 6⁹¼	6¹⁴¼	Taylor WW	108wb	40.00	89-05	Leochares109⁵Helios108nkIron Mask132¹	Dropped back	6
20Sep13- 1OW	fst 6f	:233 :473 1:124	2 ↑ Handicap 745	5 2 2hd 1¹ 1½	2¹½	Peak C	119wb	1.95	93-09	Rockville105¹½Pan Zareta119½Plate Glass126¹	Tired	6
11Sep13- 3BB	fst 6f	:24 :473 1:124	2 ↑ Handicap 625	2 2 1¹½ 1¹½ 1⁴	1³	Peak C	116wb	*.70	98-10	Pan Zareta116³Sir Blaise105½Cowl104³	Easily	5
1Sep13- 2Con	fst 5½f	:23 :473 1:002 1:064	2 ↑ Handicap 655	1 4 2¹½ 2¹½ 2²	1¹½	Kederis J	115wb	*1.60	104-02	Pan Zareta115¹½Three Links102¹Sir Blaise110¹	Handily	5
29Aug13- 4Con	sl 6f	:24 :48 1:14	3 ↑ Handicap 600	5 2 2nk 1² 1²	1¹	Kederis J	110wb	*1.80	101-05	Pan Zareta110¹Towton Field103¹½Yorkville102⁴	Easily	6

27Aug13- 3Con	hy	6f	:242 :50 1:152	2↑ Handicap 600	4 2 11 1½ 11½ 11½	Kederis J	105wb	*.80	94-12	Pan Zareta1051½Sherwood1146Sir Blaise112½	Gamely	5
22Aug13- 4Wnr	hy	6f	:243 :494 1:174	2↑ St. Clair H 1.4k	1 3 21½ 31¼ 33½ 22	Kederis J	104wb	3.00	69-35	Flabbergast1082PanZareta1044HelenBarbee1141	Second best	4
19Aug13- 1Wnr	fst	6f	:24 :471 1:122	Alw 600	3 3 2hd 2½ 2nk 2nk	Kederis J	100wb	2.00	98-04	[D]Great Britain107nkPan Zareta1003Grosvenor1021½		4
	Carried wide by winner;Placed first by disqualification											
11Aug13- 3FE	hy	6f	:24 :49 1:171	3↑ Alw 600	4 2 11 1hd 11 11	Kederis J	98.5 w	*1.10	73-36	Pan Zareta98.51Joe Knight108.5hdDuquesne1081½	Gamely	6
6Aug13- 5FE	fst	6f	:223 :462 1:13	3↑ Alw 600	1 3 21 2½ 31½ 41¾	Callahan J	96.5 w	7.00	92-07	Calgary100hdUseeit105.5hdLeochares1111½	Tired	6
2Aug13- 3Ham	fst	6f	:231 :472 1:123	3↑ Alw 635	1 3 11½ 1hd 1½ 2hd	Callahan J	99 w	3.00	92-07	MarjorieA.102hdPanZareta994SirBlaise1123	Tiring,gamely	5
28Jly13- 6Ham	fst	6f	:233 :464 1:113	3↑ Handicap 755	1 5 1hd 2hd 11½ 31½	Gross C	103.5 w	*2.20	95-06	Sir Blaise107½Sun Queen1051Pan Zareta103.5hd	Slow start	5
26Jly13- 4Ham	fst	6f	:241 :473 1:113	3↑ Alw 640	4 3 21 32½ 34½ 24	Kederis J	98 w	6.00	93-05	Leochares1044Pan Zareta98hdTen Point1123	Good try	8
23Jly13- 1Wnr	fst	6f	:232 :471 1:122	3↑ Alw 600	5 2 11½ 11½ 1nk 2hd	Kederis J	98 w	3.50	98-05	Plate Glass113hdPan Zareta985Sir Blaise1091½	Held well	8
18Jly13- 3Wnr	hy	6f	:25 :494 1:17	Alw 600	4 4 31 34 31¾ 32	Gross C	106 w	10.00	73-32	MovingPicture102.5noLeochars1122PnZrt10610	Saved ground	4
1Jly13- 4Lat	fst	6f	:23 :464 1:122	3↑ Handicap 870	3 2 1hd 31 31 21	Kederis J	100 w	3.40	96-09	Casey Jones1141Pan Zareta100noBenanet1055	Came on again	6
28Jun13- 4Lat	fst	6f	:23 :462 1:112	3↑ Quickstep 3.4k	2 4 22 24 24 57	Kederis J	100 w	10.50f	95-07	Helios1083Presumption109hdGowell1103	Tired badly	11
24Jun13- 4Lat	hy	6f	:232 :482 1:141	Alw 700	1 1 11½ 1½ 2½ 42¼	Estep	105 w	3.80	86-19	Helios108hdUSteppa1102Benanet108hd	In deep going,tiring	7
18Jun13- 5Lat	my	6f	:24 :484 1:134	Alw 700	2 4 42½ 35½ 33 35¼	Kederis J	107 w	7.40	85-20	Maria C.1025Flying Tom109nkPan Zareta107hd	Game finish	8
20May13- 3CD	fst	6f	:232 :47 1:124	Alw 700	1 1 77 712 77¾ 715¼	Gross C	107 w	5.10	77-09	Silver Bill1042McCorkle1102Flying Tom106hd		8
	Knocked out of contention at start											
17May13- 3CD	hy	6f	:233 :472 1:14	3↑ Handicap 700	2 2 21½ 33½ 49 413	Gross C	104 w	9.00	73-18	HelenBarbee1121SamulR.Myr105.54JimBasey1138	Quit after ¼	4
2Mar13- 4Jua	fst	6f	:232 :48 1:131	Chapultepec H 1.1k	1 2 11 1½ 12 12	Loftus J	122 w	*2.00	90-12	Pan Zareta1222Colquitt95¾Truly1122	Won easing up	10
22Feb13- 4Jua	fst	5½f	:222 :461 :594 1:061	3↑ Handicap 400	2 1 22½ 23 22½ 21	Gross C	106 w	*1.20	94-15	Pride of Lismore1121Pan Zareta1062Kootenay1021	Gaining	5
5Feb13- 4Jua	fst	6f	:23 :471 1:122	Alw 300	1 2 3½ 41½ 3nk 11	Gross C	114 w	3.00	94-11	Pan Zareta1141Truly98hdEl Palomar1163	Rated,going away	7
2Feb13- 4Jua	fst	6f	:222 :471 1:131	Chihuahua 1.1k	6 4 21½ 2nk 1¾ 1½	Rightmire	112 w	*.80	90-10	PanZareta112½TheCindr112¾Gskt1002½	Stumbled badly start	6
25Jan13- 5Jua	fst	6f	:23 :481 1:131	Alw 300	1 2 1½ 11 11 11	Gross C	110 w	*.60	90-11	PanZareta1101Truly1072½GordonRussell1081	Never extended	5
19Jan13- 4Jua	sl	6f	:231 :483 1:141	3↑ Rio Grande 1.1k	5 5 1¾ 31¼ 22 1no	Gross C	102 w	9.00	85-21	Pan Zareta102noFlorence Roberts1002Chapultepec108½		10
	Taken back,game finish											
17Dec12- 1Jua	fst	5½f	:232 :481 1:004 1:071	Alw 300	1 1 2½ 21 1hd 1½	Gross C	112 w	*.80	90-12	PanZareta112½Mrs.Gamp1095TheCinder1082	Impeded ½ post	5
14Dec12- 4Jua	fst	5½f	:24 :482 1:003 1:07	2↑ Handicap 400	1 2 11½ 1nk 11½ 1hd	Hill	95 w	*1.80	91-12	Pan Zareta95hdLady Panchita100¾Pawhuska1096	Gamely	5
11Dec12- 1Jua	gd	5f	:24 :483 1:013	Clm	2 1 12 11 13 13	Gross C	112 w	*1.00	82-19	Pan Zareta1123Real Star104¾Bula Welsh100¾	Easily	6
24Sep12- 3Hel	fst	5f	1:02	Wonderland H .4k	- - 32½	Rooney	119		- -	Envy1152O'Konite107½Pan Zareta1193	Driving	6
4Sep12- 3Bue	sly	5f	:241 :492 1:02	Handicap 350	- - 11	Rooney	116	*1.60	87-17	Pan Zareta1161Gasket1015Mollie Richards1075	Handily	6
22Aug12- 1Bue	fst	5f	:234 :483 1:003	Clm	7 1 2hd 1nk 12½ 12½	Buxton	115 w	*.40	94-07	PnZrta1152½Coeurd'Alen1052½JohnHurie107½	Won easing up	7
17Aug12- 3Bue	sl	5f	:241 :483 1:01	Handicap 350	5 3 2nk 1hd 11½ 2½	Buxton	115 w	*2.00e	91-11	Orlin Kripp115½Pan Zareta1152Envy115hd	No match	6
6Aug12- 3Bue	fst	4f	:24 :473	Alw 300	3 2 12 1½ 11	Buxton	109 w	*.75e	94-11	Pan Zareta1091Envy1091Al Bloch110no	Swerved in str	5
23Jly12- 2Lag	fst	5f	:231 :472 1:002	Clm	5 4 12 13 14 14	Buxton	109 w	*.65	95-03	Pan Zareta1094Auto Run1051Bells1042	Never extended	8
9Jly12- 2Lag	fst	4½f	:23 :46 :524	Alw 300	4 4 22½ 22 22½ 24	Anderson E	109 w	1.80e	104-05	FloralPark1074PanZareta1093OrlinKripp1043	Chased winner	7
4Jly12- 2Lag	fst	4f	:233 :49	Alw 300	6 4 12 12½ 12	Gross C	117 w	1.30	93-07	Pan Zareta1172John Hurie1124O'Konite1077	Easily	6
19Jun12- 3CDA	fst	5f	:234 :483 1:012	Alw 300	2 4 11 11½ 1¾ 1¾	Carter	103 w	*.40e	93-04	PanZareta103¾Camia99noVestedRights1036	Hard ridden late	7
14May12- 1CDA	fst	4f	:241 :49	Clm	7 6 13 13 14	Buxton	107 w	*.60	93-00	PanZareta1074VelieForty106¾JessiPortr1084	Won easing up	7
2Mar12- 1Jua	fst	4f	:232 :472	Alw 300	1 4 21½ 23 33½	Murray A	110 w	3.50	90-06	Inquieta115½Negligee1083Pan Zareta1108	Tired	5
11Feb12- 1Jua	fst	4f	:23 :48	Alw 300	4 2 1hd 1hd 1¾	Prior	117 w	*1.60	91-09	[DH]StoutHeart105[DH]PanZrta117¾Oldsmobl1023	Stretch duel	5
31Jan12- 1Jua	fst	3½f	:223 :401	Alw 300	8 2 1nk 12	Murray A	112 w	4.00	96-04	PanZareta1122Palatable115nkOldsmobile1053	Bore out turn	9
14Jan12- 4Jua	fst	3½f	:23 :402	(F)Senoritas .7k	1 2 22 1nk 1¾	Borel	110 w	*1.40	95-05	Pan Zareta110¾Truly1103Velie Forty1156	Bore out,gamely	5
10Jan12- 1Jua	fst	3f	:233 :361	(F)Alw 300	3 7 45 2¾	Murray A	110 w	10.00	- -	Velie Forty110¾Pan Zareta1101Tildy Wolffarth1103		11
	May have won if kept straight											
7Jan12- 1Jua	fst	3f	:222 :342	Alw 300	7 8 76¾ 78¾	Murray A	110 w	5.00e	- -	Hawthorne1153Palatable1132½Pat Gannon1101½	Greenly	10

Princess Doreen

b. f. 1921, by Spanish Prince II (Ugly)–Lady Doreen, by Ogden **Lifetime record: 94 34 15 17 $174,745**

Own.– Audley Farm Stable
Br.– J.E. Madden (Ky)
Tr.– K. Spence

24Nov27- 5Bow	fst	1 3/16	:482 1:131 1:391 1:59	3↑ Thanksgiving H 12k	9 6 51¾ 52 83½ 86	Ambrose E	118 w	5.40	86-02	BlackPanther111noDisplay1264LightView103.5nk	Poor effort	10
26Oct27- 5Lrl	fst	1 1/16	:232 :47 1:124 1:444	3↑ Alw 2000	3 4 53¼ 4¾ 42½ 41	Ellis G	117wb	2.60	92-12	Display123noBostonian1141Jock114no	Good try	7
24Oct27- 5Lrl	fst	1⅛	:473 1:12 1:392 1:514	3↑ Handicap 2000	2 2 3nk 32 32½ 44½	Ellis G	116wb	4.65	84-16	[D]Mars1281Crusader1302½Gaffsman1161	Used,tired	6
	Placed third by disqualification											
3Sep27- 4Haw	fst	1 1/16	:231 :47 1:12 1:44	3↑ Oak Park H 6.3k	2 1 11½ 11½ 11½ 32½	Pool E	128wb	*1.35	97-10	Chicago116½Flat Iron1262Princess Doreen1282		5
	Set fast pace,tired late											
27Aug27- 5Haw	fst	1 1/16	:232 :47 1:123 1:45	3↑ Greater Chicago H 5k	2 1 12 13 11 11½	Pool E	124wb	*.97	95-11	Princess Doreen1241½Mix-Up101nkChicago1171½	Hand ride	6
10Aug27- 5LF	fst	1 1/16	:233 :47 1:113 1:433	3↑ Handicap 1800	3 1 13 16 16 13	Pool E	118wb	2.07	98-11	Princess Doreen1183Handy Mandy1084Yeddo105hd	Cantering	8
6Aug27- 5LF	fst	1	:232 :453 1:11 1:363	3↑ Steger H 8.4k	12 8 96 94 73¼ 77	Crump W	120 w	3.91	90-09	Chicago1102Nor'Easter1141½Cudgeller1081	Never a factor	13
23Jly27- 5LF	fst	1 1/16	:24 :472 1:13 1:442	3↑ Marquette H 8.1k	8 8 63 87 118½ 1223½	Crump W	123 w	*1.99	70-09	Rothermel109½Chicago108hdNor'Easter1075	Impeded	14
9Jly27- 5LF	fst	1¼	:483 1:122 1:38 2:041	3↑ Lincoln H 30k	11 6 2hd 32 33 35½	Crump W	122 w	9.12	107-03	ChancePlay1221½FlatIron1214PrincessDoreen122hd	All out	13
4Jly27- 5Lat	fst	1 3/16	:471 1:123 1:374 1:562	3↑ Independence H 15k	6 3 61¾ 62¼ 2½ 1no	Crump W	120 w	6.00	97-10	PrincessDoren120noRhnock1102Prcusson100hd	Tiring,gamely	13
25Jun27- 6FP	fst	1 1/16	:232 :474 1:13 1:453	3↑ Hotel Statler H 7.3k	6 1 2nk 23 21 2no	Legere E	122 w	*.90	97-10	Banton106noPrincssDreen122½Helen'sBabe1171½	Just missed	6
17Jun27- 5FP	fst	6f	:231 :463 1:121	3↑ Handicap 1235	4 3 21 21½ 21 1hd	Legere E	126 w	*.55	98-11	PrincssDrn126hdReputation112hdLoungr1108	Gamely,up late	4
25Nov26- 4Bow	fst	1 3/16	:473 1:122 1:373 1:572	3↑ Thanksgiving H 12k	1 5 74½ 1214 1211 1317	McTague J	118 w	11.00	106-00	Backbone114nkPeanuts1215Joy Smoke121hd	Tired badly	13
13Nov26- 4Pim	fst	2¼	:50 2:34 3:01 3:521	3↑ Pim Cup H 12k	2 2 212 28 331 342½	McTague J	110 w	6.90e	61-15	EdithCavell932½Crusader12640PrincessDoreen110hd	Outrun	4
12Nov26- 5Pim	fst	1⅛	:492 1:143 1:402 1:54	2↑ Serial WFA #3 5.2k	1 1 1nk 2hd 21½ 21½	McTague J	123 w	2.30	83-16	Mars1201½Princess Doreen123	No match	2
6Nov26- 4Pim	fst	1½	:50 1:15 2:043 2:311	3↑ Bowie H 13k	5 2 63 31 2½ 22	McTague J	112 w	10.60e	95-13	Peanuts1152PrincessDoren1121Dsply1172½	Challenged,tired	11
3Nov26- 5Pim	fst	1 3/16	:48 1:132 1:392 1:59	3↑ Handicap 1550	3 4 42 42 2hd 1nk	McTague J	115 w	3.85	97-14	PrincessDoreen115nkSeventhSon105hdJoySmoke1192	Lasted	8
30Oct26- 5Lrl	fst	1¼	:472 1:123 1:373 2:03	3↑ Washington H 29k	7 5 72 103¼ 105¾ 95½	Lang C	113 w	11.65	89-10	Mars118½Peanuts114½Display1141½	No factor	13
27Oct26- 5Lrl	fst	1 70	:232 :473 1:124 1:422	3↑ Purse 2000	2 2 21 2nk 2½ 31½	Lang C	116 w	5.20	97-14	Gaffsman1121PrinceofWales116½PrncssDorn116hd	Raced well	5
16Oct26- 5Lrl	fst	1	:23 :472 1:123 1:38	2↑ Laurel 14k	5 4 51¾ 43 74¼ 85¾	McTague J	117 w	35.75	92-11	Croyden107.52Sarazen126hdMars1171	No factor	11
5Oct26- 5Lrl	fst	6f	:222 :461 1:113	3↑ Capitol H 7.7k	11 6 1113 107 84½ 62¼	McTague J	117 w	7.15e	97-06	Prince of Wales1071Noah119hdCroyden114hd	Closed gap	13
25Sep26- 5HdG	fst	1⅛	:473 1:122 1:38 1:50	3↑ Havre de Grace H 17k	1 8 96¼ 96¼ 1012 812¼	Lang C	115 w	25.05	88-06	Crusader1225Son of John108hdDisplay114nk	Never a factor	12
15Sep26- 4OW	my	1¼	:492 1:142 1:413 2:07	3↑ Toronto Aut Cup H 10k	7 8 75 84¼ 66 63¼	McTague J	120 w	3.55	83-16	Edisto122hdGaffsman1081Harry Baker105nk	Always beaten	13
28Aug26- 5Sar	sl	1¾	:50 2:09 2:34 3:002	3↑ Sar Cup 9.1k	3 1 11½ 11 31 37	Sande E	121 w	7.00	73-20	Espino1162Display1165PrincessDoreen12110	Rated,no match	5
21Aug26- 5Sar	fst	1 3/16	:483 1:132 1:394 1:59	3↑ Merchants & Cits H 9.4k	2 1 12 2hd 23 44½	McTague J	123 w	*1.50	78-16	Flagstaff1082Peanuts1172Blondin109½	Tired	5
30Jly26- 4Sar	my	1¼	:49 1:141 1:402 2:082	3↑ Saratoga H 10k	7 1 15 15 15 14	McTge J	116 w	20.00	67-24	PrincessDoren1164Blondn1083KngSolomon'sSl1093	Cantering	8
5Jly26- 5Lat	gd	1 3/16	:463 1:113 1:374 1:571	3↑ Independence H 14k	2 8 67 53¼ 1hd 2½	McTague J	124 w	3.80e	92-11	Rothermel103½Princess Doreen1241Rhinock1084	Second best	8
19Jun26- 5Lat	fst	1 1/16	:231 :463 1:12 1:433	3↑ Enquirer H 7.9k	5 4 54 54 55½ 510	Scobie E	127 w	*1.30e	86-12	Barcolo107hdRhinock1063Heln'sBabe1002	Tired under impost	8
8Jun26- 5Lat	fst	6f	:223 :46 1:12	3↑ (F)Alw 1615	2 4 55 34½ 2½ 11½	Scobie E	113 w	*.50	89-16	PrincessDoreen1131½Teak1054LittleVstor1151½	Wide,easily	6
3Jun26- 5Lat	fst	1 1/16	:241 :472 1:124 1:45	3↑ Inaugural H 7.8k	1 4 32¼ 22 2½ 11½	Legere E	122 w	*.60	89-12	PrincssDrn1221½Trymore1088Tangara1091½	Wide into stretch	8

22May26-5CD	fst 1¼		:472 1:124 1:391 2:043	3↑ Grainger Mem H 14k	5	5	55	32¼	21½	21½	ZcchiniR	123	w	7.20	91-12	King Nadi1191½Princess Doreen1235Captain Hal1222		7
	Finished well,no match																	
19May26-5CD	fst 6f		:224 :462 1:12	3↑ Handicap 1868	3	4	55	57	42½	44	Zucchini R	118	w	5.30	91-14	King Nadi1171Arcady1102Lee O. Cotner1171	Good effort	6
3May26-5Pim	fst 1 3/16		:474 1:132 1:383 2:004	3↑ Dixie H 32k	1	4	55	64¼	86¼	98¾	Lang C	118	w	10.00	79-14	Sarazen128nkSunPal1051GeneralThtchr118nk	Never a factor	11
4Apr26-8Tij	fst 1 70		:224 :464 1:114 1:414	3↑ Handicap 1200	1	2	21½	2½	11	1no	McTague J	120	w	*1.60	101-10	Princess Doreen120noSanford923Cherry Tree115no	Lasted	7
28Mar26-7Tij	fst 1¼		:461 1:101 1:354 2:023	3↑ Coffroth H 80k	4	5	615	517	612	714¼	Sande E	123	w	2.20	97-10	Carlaris1008Roycrofter1001Cherry Tree1134	Outrun	9
24Mar26-6Tij	fst 1⅛		:482 1:124 1:381 1:504	3↑ Handicap 1000	3	4	41½	41¾	31½	1hd	McTague J	120	w	*.90	105-10	PrincessDorn120hdKntuckyCrdnl1121½Roycroftr1033	Just up	5
21Mar26-7Tij	fst 1⅛		:463 1:103 1:363 1:492	3↑ Handicap 1500	1	2	22½	24	23	43	McTague J	123	w	5.00	109-10	Carlaris1061½Kentucky Cardinal112hdCherry Tree1151½		8
	Dropped back late																	
25Feb26-7Tij	fst 6f		:224 :463 1:114	3↑ Handicap 1000	3	5	55¼	54½	43	35½	McTague J	123	w	*1.50e	89-17	Glister951½Serenader1184PrincessDoreen1232	Finished fast	6
26Nov25-5Bow	fst 1 3/16		:492 1:14 1:412 2:021	3↑ Thanksgiving H 12k	6	3	43½	32½	31½	22	Lang C	117	w	*3.05e	97-12	JoySmoke1142PrincessDorn117nkSenatorNorrs109hd	Gamely	13
21Nov25-4Bow	fst 1		:24 :482 1:133 1:402	2↑ G D Bryan Mem H 18k	1	5	42½	43½	3¾	32½	Stutts H	117	w	3.95	100-05	Sarazen1261Joy Smoke1151½Princess Doreen117nk		15
	In close start,gamely																	
14Nov25-4Pim	gd 2¼		:503 2:38 3:023 3:58	3↑ Pim Cup H 11k	4	1	11	11	2hd	32	Lang C	116	w	*.90e	73-23	Rockminister102½Harrovin1121½PrncssDorn1166	Good effort	6
10Nov25-5Pim	fst 1½		:493 1:15 2:063 2:342	3↑ Bowie H 12k	5	3	42¼	11	14	12	Lang C	118	w	2.75	81-17	PrincessDoreen1182AgaKhan1211MyOwn115nk	Won easing up	6
31Oct25-5Lrl	sly 1¼		:482 1:14 1:423 2:094	3↑ Washington H 29k	5	6	52¾	43	46½	410	Stutts H	119	w	7.30	51-36	Joy Smoke1123Big Blaze1226Aga Khan1221	Tired	8
19Sep25-5Lat	fst 6f		:224 :454 1:112	3↑ Autumn H 6.7k	9	1	105	83	21	1no	Stutts H	133	w	*3.60	92-12	PrincessDoreen133noArcady1111BrownSugr1131	Wide,just up	10
12Sep25-5Lat	fst 1 1/16		:242 :48 1:13 1:451	3↑ Covington H 6.5k	5	7	31	1½	13	11½	Stutts H	130	w	2.00	88-13	PrincessDoreen1301½Starbeck1033NancyLanghorn107½		7
	Won easing up																	
7Sep25-5CI	fst 1⅛		:472 1:112 1:371 1:492	3↑ Cincinnati Enquirer H 10k	6	7	74	2hd	11	1½	Stutts H	129	w	5.10	- -	PrincssDreen129½KentckyCardinal1101Boon Companion113hd		8
	Slow to start,wide																	
22Aug25-4Haw	fst 1 3/16		:473 1:12 1:363 1:562	3↑ Chicago Spl 22k	3	2	21½	21½	3½	33	Stutts H	121	w	2.60	101-06	Mad Play1261Kentucky Cardinal1182Princess Doreen1218		5
	Forced wide,tired																	
15Aug25-5CI	gd 1 3/16		:481 1:13 1:394 1:592	3↑ Western Hills H 7.9k	5	1	13	15	15	15	Stutts H	126	w	*.45	- -	Princess Doreen1265Tall Grass98nkOld Slip1022	Easily	5
8Aug25-6Tdn	sl 1		:24 :482 1:141 1:40	3↑ Flint Stone Mem H 10k	9	8	53	42½	43½	32	Stutts H	129	w	*.60	- -	John T.D.104hdCherry Pie1142Princess Doreen1291½		9
	Slow to start,tired																	
1Aug25-4CI	fst 1 1/16		:242 :48 1:12 1:433	3↑ Commercial Trib H 6.4k	4	2	2hd	13	12	11½	Stutts H	124	w	*.25	- -	PrincessDrn1241½GustofHonor1061NncyLnghrn103hd	Rated	4
18Jly25-6CI	fst 1⅛		:463 1:102 1:354 1:491	3↑ Handicap 1800	4	1	12	12	11½	1½	Stutts H	122	w	*1.20	- -	PrincessDoreen122½SirPeter1174KingGorinII1026	Driving	4
11Jly25-5CI	gd 1 1/16		:234 :471 1:114 1:44	3↑ Cin Times-Star H 6.5k	3	2	21	11½	12	11	Stutts H	118	w	*.50	- -	Princess Doreen1181King Gorin II1052Tangara99hd		5
	Won under restraint																	
4Jly25-4Lat	gd 1 3/16		:47 1:114 1:374 1:573	3↑ Independence H 14k	9	1	110	110	15	13	Stutts H	115	w	4.55	91-16	Princess Doreen1153Progress1024King Gorin II1072	Easily	9
1Jly25-5Lat	fst 1 70		:23 :464 1:104 1:421	3↑ Handicap 1700	1	2	22	21	21½	21½	Stutts H	114	w	*.65	96-12	SirPeter1071½PrcssDrn1146Graeme1056	Gamely,no match	5
27Jun25-4Lat	fst 6f		:231 :464 1:121	3↑ Handicap 1765	3	1	2hd	11	12	11½	Stutts H	113	w	*1.15	88-15	PrincessDoreen1131½LordGranite108½Lathrop1005		4
	Won easing up																	
18Jun25-4Lat	gd 6f		:232 :463 1:122	3↑ Alw 1720	6	1	1hd	12	12	12	Scobie E	109	w	*1.50	87-13	PrincessDoren1092Dudly109noDryMoon1094	As rider pleased	6
13Jun25-5Lat	fst 1 1/16		:243 :481 1:132 1:443	3↑ Enquirer H 7.4k	1	3	31	42	3¾	33	Garner M	112	w	*1.30	88-13	Sir Peter1031½Guest of Honor1081½Princess Doreen112hd		6
	Finished gamely																	
2Jun25-5Lat	fst 1 1/16		:24 :464 1:113 1:44	3↑ Inaugural H 7.5k	5	3	43½	32½	2½	32	Lang C	113	w	3.20	92-09	CaptainHal110noHopeless1072PrincssDorn1131	Tired at end	11
23May25-5CD	fst 1¼		:473 1:12 1:38 2:041	3↑ Grainger Mem H 13k	7	4	46	34	1hd	31½	Connelly D	112	w	3.35	93-09	King Nadi102hdCaptain Hal1091½Princess Doreen1121		7
	Impeded by runner-up																	
15May25-6CD	fst 1 1/16		:242 :482 1:131 1:441	3↑ Handicap 2500	6	1	1nk	32	2½	2½	Pool E	113	w	*2.10	98-12	BeauButlr108½PrncssDrn1136Stanwix1046	Getting to winner	6
1May25-5Pim	sl 1 3/16		:482 1:133 1:403 2:02	3↑ Dixie H 33k	11	9	73¾	126½	1216	1320½	Lang C	115	w	8.45f	61-24	Sarazen1301¼Spot Cash115½Joy Smoke1043	Never a factor	14
25Apr25-5HdG	fst 1 70		:231 :472 1:122 1:42	3↑ Handicap 2000	3	3	33	31½	43½	45¾	Lang C	112	w	*1.05	96-03	Transmute1123TenMinutes1061¼TheRollCll1011½	Hard ridden	8
15Apr25-5HdG	gd 6f		:223 :46 1:122	3↑ Harford H 5.7k	7	4	57½	58	33½	33½	Lang C	110	w	12.85f	90-14	Noah1051½Leopardess1102PrincessDoren1101	Tired in drive	8
22Nov24-5Bow	hy 1		:242 :49 1:142 1:421	2↑ G D Bryan Mem H 11k	11	9	108¼	44½	42½	22	Stutts H	109	w	7.10	92-14	Donaghee1102PrincessDrn1093MssWhsk96hd	Closed big gap	15
17Nov24-4Bow	fst 1⅛		:493 1:142 1:412 1:552	Prince George H 7.9k	3	2	22	21½	22	25	Lang C	112	w	*.35	98-07	Donaghee1095PrincessDrn1122PrinceHamlet963	Tired badly	5
6Nov24-7Pim	fst 1 1/16		:23 :463 1:12 1:452	ⓕAlw 1300	1	1	16	110	18	15	Lang C	123	w	*.85	95-12	PrincessDoreen1235PrscllRuly1235Sunyr108	Never extended	3
1Nov24-5Lrl	fst 1¼		:462 1:114 1:381 2:041	3↑ Washington H 31k	6	4	43½	53¼	67¼	75½	Stutts H	110	w	20.55	83-14	Big Blaze1061¼Aga Khan106noRustic107hd	Good effort	10
25Oct24-5CD	fst 1⅛		:473 1:133 1:384 1:513	3↑ Falls City H 6.6k	5	6	55½	12	12	13	Stutts H	111	w	4.80	91-14	PrincessDrn1113Hopeless1076JustDavid102½	Won easing up	7
18Oct24-4Lat	fst 1		:233 :472 1:112 1:362	3↑ Handicap 1800	3	2	21½	2½	2nk	31¾	Stutts H	115	w	2.30	99-08	Zev129nkPostillion981½Princess Doreen115	Tired	3
11Oct24-5Lat	fst 1¼		:451 1:102 1:354 2:004	3↑ Int'l Spl #3 65k	8	6	53¼	52	55½	59½	Stutts H	117	w	5.15	98-07	Sarazen1201½Epinard126noMad Play120no	Outrun	8
13Sep24-5Lat	gd 1 1/16		:223 :471 1:114 1:441	3↑ Covington H 6.6k	5	3	1½	15	14	15	Stutts H	114	w	*.60e	94-15	Princess Doreen1145Graeme1091J.G. Denny1043	Easily	8
1Sep24-4Haw	fst 1¼		:481 1:124 1:383 2:042	3↑ Labor Day H 6.3k	2	1	11	12	14	18	Stutts H	119	w	*.35	99-04	PrincessDrn1198Laveen1091PrinceTiiTii106nk	Much the best	7
23Aug24-4Haw	fst 1 3/16		:47 1:12 1:373 1:571	3↑ Chicago Spl 15k	3	3	21½	2nk	2nk	2nk	Stutts H	113	w	1.30	114-07	Giblon118nkPrincess Doreen1135Hopeless12615	Wide,gamely	5
12Aug24-4Sar	sly 1¼		:502 1:161 1:413 2:084	ⓕAlabama 12k	2	2	21½	21	21	21	Stutts H	126	w	*.40	64-23	Priscilla Ruley1171Princess Doreen1262½Sunayr117		3
	Rated,second best																	
6Aug24-3Sar	my 1		:24 :47 1:134 1:401	3↑ Handicap 1305	1	4	34½		1½	12	Stutts H	122	w	*1.10	80-20	Princess Doreen1222Initiate1148Sunayr1112	Going away	7
	Second call unavailable due to rain storm																	
5Jly24-5Lat	fst 1¼		:47 1:121 1:374 2:022	ⓕLat Oaks 11k	4	1	12	12	1hd	2nk	Stutts H	130	w	*.60	101-06	Befuddle121nkPrinccsDorn13012Lvn1218	Tired under impost	4
13Jun24-4Bel	fst 1⅜		:472 1:124 1:384 2:191	ⓕC C A Oaks 14k	8	3	31	2½	11	12	Stutts H	121	w	4.00	75-12	Princess Doreen1212Relentless114½Priscilla Ruley111hd		9
	Won easing up																	
31May24-5CD	fst 1⅛		:48 1:132 1:39 1:514	ⓕKy Oaks 12k	3	5	53	52	2½	22	Stutts H	116	w	5.40	88-11	DGlide1162Princess Doreen116½Nellie Morse121hd		8
	Close quarters final turn;Placed first by disqualification																	
27May24-5CD	my 7f		:233 :473 1:131 1:264	ⓕAlw 1558	1	2	11½	13	13	12	Stutts H	112	w	3.70	82-25	Princess Doreen1122Beautiful Agnes1011½Befuddle1076		6
	Speed in reserve																	
17May24-3CD	fst 1		:221 :452 1:102 1:363	3↑ Handicap 2000	6	4	53¼	45½	45	57	Kennedy B	100	w	16.35	91-09	Actuary1104Moonraker1101½Ten-Lec109½	Needed race	8
13May24-5CD	gd 1		:23 :46 1:112 1:374	Alw 2000	1	4	66	75½	69	616¼	Stutts H	114	w	34.15	76-11	BlackGold1198WildAster119nkKingGorinII1191	Brief speed	8
14Nov23-5CD	fst 6f		:223 :46 1:12	Handicap 1500	7	5	32	1hd	13	13	Pool E	111	w	5.15e	95-13	Princess Drn1113Chilhowee112nkBattlCrk115no	easily	7
12Nov23-6CD	fst 6f		:231 :472 1:13	Alw 1100	1	6	41¾	31	2hd	11½	Pool E	112	w	3.00e	90-13	Princess Doreen1121½Clarence1081Stage Coach105no		11
	Saved ground,drew away																	
9Nov23-6CD	gd 6f		:232 :472 1:124	ⓕAlw 1200	4	3	1hd	12	1hd	1hd	Scobie E	115	w	*1.20	91-16	PrincessDoreen115hdBeautifulAgns103hdMhJong1061½	Lasted	9
23Oct23-5Lat	fst 6f		:23 :464 1:124	Handicap 1700	7	4	63½	75	65½	65¼	Scobie E	109	w	3.50	81-16	ColonelGilmore111.5nkBeauButler1122Glide1051	Poor effort	7
16Oct23-4Lat	fst 1		:233 :481 1:132 1:384	Alw 1700	7	1	11	2½	53½	511¾	Woods L	99	w	3.25e	78-13	Dare Say952Beau Butler1071½King Gorin II102nk	Tired	8
13Oct23-4Lat	fst 6f		:23 :462 1:12	Fort Thomas H 7.9k	7	3	31	1½	2hd	2no	Scobie E	109	w	9.10	90-11	Chilhowee118noPrincessDoreen1091Sanola108nk	Just missed	13
3Oct23-6Lat	fst 5½f		:23 :473 1:001 1:07	ⓕAlw 1500	2	4	21	2nk	1½	12	Scobie E	115	w	*1.45e	92-12	PrincssDoreen1152MahJong110nkButfulAgns1102	Going away	8
2Oct23-2Lat	fst 5½f		:23 :471 :594 1:07	Md Clm	9	6	3½	11½	11½	12	Scobie E	115	w	*.70e	92-11	PrincessDoreen1152BreakfastBell115½PhyllsLous1153	Easily	12
10Sep23-4Bel	fst 6f		:232 :461 1:113	ⓕMatron 5.2k	1	5	42	42¼	44	32	Scobie E	105.5	w	*3.60	92-06	Tree Top109hdNellie Morse1222Princess Doreen105.51		13
	Eased in final strides																	
5Sep23-3Bel	fst 5½f		:461 :591 1:051	ⓕTomboy H 4.8k	1	1	43	54½	69	43	Pool W	106	w	*2.00	93-08	Lady Diana1071½Tree Top1091Anna MarroneII123½	Crowded	9
30Aug23-6Sar	gd 5½f		:232 :472 :594 1:06	Md Alw 1000	7	5	55	55¼	44½	2no	Pool W	112	w	8.00	93-10	Sun Pal115noPrincess Doreen1123Mr. Mutt115½	Just missed	8
25Aug23-3Sar	fst 6f		:224 :462 1:123	ⓕSpinaway 9.1k	3	10	96¾	97	109¼	98	Pool W	109	w	6.00	81-07	AnnaMarroneII117nkNellMors1241TrTop112nk	Never a factor	11
21Aug23-6Sar	fst 5f		:224 :454 :584	Alw 1000	5	8	96	96¾	68	44	Pool W	105	w	*1.60e	91-11	TreeTop106.51LadyDiana1102DearMaria1051	Finished fast	9

Regret

ch. f. 1912, by Broomstick (Ben Brush)–Jersey Lightning, by Hamburg **Lifetime record: 11 9 1 0 $35,093**

Own.– H.P. Whitney
Br.– H.P. Whitney (NJ)
Tr.– J. Rowe

25Sep17- 1Aqu fst 7f :234 :472 1:112 1:241 2↑ Handicap 764 2 1 12 12 13 13 Robinson F 127 w *.08 101-09 Regret1273Ima Frank109 Speed in reserve 2
10Jly17- 4Aqu gd 1 1/16 :241 :48 1:152 1:452 3↑ ⒻGazelle H 3.1k 6 1 12 13 13 13 Loftus J 129 w *.17 96-11 Regret1293Bayberry Candle123hdWistful1051 Won eased up 6
25Jun17- 4Aqu fst 1⅛ :47 1:122 1:363 1:492 3↑ Brooklyn H 5.8k 3 1 12 11 11½ 2no Robinson F 122 w 3.60e 103-04 Borrow117noRegret1221Old Rosebud1201 Overconfident ride 11
31May17- 3Bel fst 5½f-Str 1:042 3↑ ⒻAlw 880 2 1 11 13 15 18 Robinson F 128 w *.17 97-09 Regret1288YankeeWitch118½Admiration1061½ Won pulling up 5
18Aug16- 3Sar fst 1 :25 :49 1:14 1:392 3↑ Alw 710 4 1 11½ 13 12 11½ Keogh F 107.5 w *.07 90-10 Regret107.51½Flittergold1154Polroma1041½ 5
Under restraint throughout
31Jly16- 4Sar fst 1¼ :50 1:144 1:40 2:051 3↑ Saratoga H 4.8k 6 1 11 2nk 21½ 816 Notter J 123 w *.90 78-10 Stromboli1211½EdCrump1231½FriarRock107hd Set pace,tired 8
17Aug15- 4Sar gd 1 :25 :49 1:151 1:42 Saranac H 1.4k 2 1 12 11 12 11½ Notter J 123 w *.33 77-21 Rgrt1231½TrlbyJury1143LdyRotha1061 Under stout restraint 8
8May15- 5CD fst 1¼ :483 1:133 1:392 2:052 Ky Derby 14k 2 1 1½ 1½ 11½ 12 Notter J 112 w *2.65 90-09 Regret1122Pebbles1172Sharpshooter1141 Won easing up 16
22Aug14- 3Sar hy 6f :241 :491 1:162 Hopeful 10k 2 2 56½ 66¾ 31½ 1½ Notter J 127 w *1.60 76-27 Regret127½AndrewM.1143Pebbles1304 In heavy going,gamely 11
15Aug14- 3Sar sl 6f :23 :471 1:132 Sanford Mem 3.4k 1 3 11 12 11½ 11½ Notter J 127 w *.80e 91-17 Rgrt1271½Solly1132DinahDo1075 Under restraint throughout 8
8Aug14- 3Sar fst 6f :23 :47 1:113 Sar Spl 4.1k 8 1 13 1½ 12 11 Notter J 119 w *1.60e 100-03 Regret1191Pebbles1223Paris122no Speed in reserve 8

Roamer

b. g. 1911, by Knight Errant (Trenton)–Rose Tree II, by Bona Vista **Lifetime record: 98 39 26 9 $98,828**

Own.– A. Miller
Br.– Clay Brothers (Ky)
Tr.– A.J. Goldsborough

26Jly19- 4Emp fst 1 1/16 :233 :474 1:132 1:453 3↑ Yonkers H 2.9k 3 2 2nk 11 2hd 22 Schuttinger A 120wb 2.60 93-11 Bally1092Roamer1203Spur1131½ Tired 5
11Jly19- 2Aqu gd 6f :233 :472 1:12 3↑ Handicap 1468 3 3 31½ 3¾ 32¼ 1¾ Schuttinger A 114wb 4.00 95-12 Roamer114¾Sun Briar1302L'Errant98.58 Driving 4
21Jun19- 4Jam gd 1 1/16 :242 :48 1:133 1:46 3↑ Long Beach H 4.8k 5 4 43 66 611 711½ Schuttinger A 116 w 8.00 85-09 Naturalist128½Lanius1153Star Master1221 Speed,eased up 7
14Jun19- 4Jam fst 1 1/16 :244 :482 1:13 1:452 3↑ Excelsior H 4.8k 6 2 22 23 34½ 611¾ Schuttinger A 121wb 7.00 88-07 Naturalist1221Star Master1191Boniface108nk Tired badly 8
9Jun19- 5Bel sl 1 :242 :48 1:133 1:374 3↑ Alw 879 3 3 33½ 37 36 315 Schuttinger A 122wb 3.00 79-20 Lucullite1145Natural Bridge10110Roamer122 Not a factor 3
4Jun19- 4Bel fst 1 :241 :472 1:123 1:372 3↑ Alw 1340 2 1 13 14 11 21 Schuttinger A 127wb *.14 95-08 Natural Bridge971Roamer12715Henry G.100 3
Tired under confident ride
19Oct18- 4Emp fst 1 1/16 :243 :484 1:123 1:462 3↑ Pelham Bay H 2k 1 4 21½ 21 21½ 21 Schuttinger A 126wb *1.80 90-08 Naturalist1231Roamer126hdCorn Tassel109no Wide on turn 4
16Oct18- 4Emp fst 1 70 :24 :474 1:133 1:43 2↑ Scarsdale H 2.1k 3 3 21½ 22 22 32 Schuttinger A 128wb *.90 97-07 War Cloud1171½Corn Tassel109½Roamer1286 Bumped 1st turn 4
12Oct18- 4Jam fst 1⅛ :483 1:131 1:382 1:513 3↑ Continental H 2.8k 3 1 12 11½ 11 2½ Schuttinger A 127wb 3.50 101-06 Star Master115½Roamer1271George Smith1285 Gamely 4
5Oct18- 4Jam fst 1⅛ :49 1:14 1:393 1:523 3↑ Pierrepont H 3.3k 3 3 21½ 2½ 2½ 1nk Schuttinger A 127wb *.55 97-08 Roamer127nkManister Toi1031War Cloud121 Rated 3
28Sep18- 4Aqu fst 1⅛ :474 1:13 1:381 1:501 3↑ Edgemere H 3.4k 2 2 21 11 1nk 34¼ Robinson F 130wb 3.20 92-15 George Smith1234War Cloud124nkRoamer1305 Wide,tired 5
31Aug18- 4Sar hy 1¾ :502 2:081 2:342 3:021 3↑ Sar Cup 5.9k 2 2 21½ 21 24 25 Schuttinger A 127wb 1.60 74-15 Johren1135Roamer127 Tired 2
21Aug18- 0Sar fst 1 :233 :46 1:101 1:344 Special .5k 1 1 1 1 1 1 Schuttinger A 110wb - 113-00 Roamer110 Outran pacesetter from start 1
Race against time
1Aug18- 4Sar fst 1¼ :481 1:12 1:371 2:021 3↑ Saratoga H 6.8k 6 4 22 21½ 13 13 Robinson F 129wb 3.60 109-02 Roamer1293Cudgel1332Bondage105nk Won easing up 6
17Jly18- 4Emp gd 1 :25 :484 1:144 1:401 3↑ Mount Vernon H 2.9k 1 3 31½ 31 3¾ 12 Lyke L 133wb *.40 92-11 Roamer1332Old Koenig1262Papp112 Rated,drew away 3
13Jly18- 4Emp fst 1⅛ :48 1:123 1:383 1:51 3↑ Emp City H 4.8k 3 1 11½ 15 15 18 Lyke L 128wb *.55e 100-07 Roamer1288Hollister1143Spur1166 In a canter 4
4Jly18- 4Aqu fst 7f :224 :464 1:102 1:234 3↑ Carter H 3.4k 3 4 53 32 32 2nk Lyke L 130wb *1.30 102-03 OldKoenig122nkRoamr1301½Polymelian1282 Impeded at start 9
29Jun18- 4Aqu fst 1 :23 :463 1:111 1:363 3↑ Queens County H 4.3k 2 1 13 12 12 12½ Lyke L 123wb *.60 99-08 Rmr1232½TomMcTaggart1094HandGrenad1051 Won easing up 6
24Jun18- 4Aqu fst 1⅛ :473 1:13 1:373 1:501 3↑ Brooklyn H 5.8k 7 1 13 12 11½ 21 Schuttinger A 120wb 6.00e 95-05 Cudgel1291Roamer1202½George Smith1223 Held well 8
17Jun18- 4Jam fst 1 1/16 :233 :473 1:122 1:452 3↑ Excelsior H 4.8k 2 3 31½ 43 3¾ 22 Loftus J 120wb *3.20 98-08 George Smith1172Roamer120noWesty Hogan1221½ Gamely 11
30May18- 4Bel sly 6f-Str 1:10 3↑ Toboggan H 4.4k 3 6 75¼ 87½ 88½ 97½ Schuttinger A 130wb 8.00 85-11 Naturalist1071½MotorCop1131½OldKoeng1202 Never a factor 11
27May18- 4Bel fst 1 :232 :472 1:131 1:382 3↑ Metropolitan H 4.8k 2 1 11 1nk 2½ 56 Schuttinger A 126wb 3.00 85-13 TrompeLaMort1021½OldKoenig1181PriscillaMullns104½ Tired 8
5Nov17- 4Pim fst 1 3/16 :473 1:124 1:39 1:584 3↑ Monumental H 2.2k 1 1 11½ 21½ 45 48 Schuttinger A 129wb *.55 96-05 Spur118noWalnut Hall109noHendrie1168 Tired badly 5
1Nov17- 4Pim sl 1 1/16 :233 :481 1:133 1:47 3↑ Arlington H 2.3k 5 2 21½ 1hd 12 12 Schuttinger A 126wb *.95 95-16 Roamer1262Sunbonnet1151Ed Roche106¾ Speed in reserve 7
17Oct17- 5Lrl fst 1 1/16 :232 :473 1:124 1:443 2↑ Handicap 1309 3 1 13 15 14 14 Schuttinger A 126wb *.30 94-10 Romr1264Wstful1113PrscllMullns1065 Restrained throughout 6
6Oct17- 4Aqu sl 1 1/16 :25 :492 1:14 1:471 3↑ Edgemere H 2k 1 1 1hd 2½ 22 22½ McTaggart J 130wb *.50 84-14 Chiclet1142½Roamer1306Capra108 Tired 3
29Sep17- 4Aqu fst 1⅛ :462 1:112 1:364 1:501 3↑ Aqueduct H 2.8k 2 1 11 12 12 13 Schuttinger A 127wb *.33 96-12 Roamer1273Manister Toi108hdRunes101 Won easing up 3
21Sep17- 4Aqu fst 1 1/16 :244 :492 1:141 1:443 2↑ Handicap 1018 2 1 15 12 11 13½ Schuttinger A 126wb *.50 100-07 Roamer1263½Runes1031½Daddy's Choice104hd Drew away 4
7Aug17- 4Sar fst 1 :233 :471 1:133 1:382 3↑ Delaware H 3.5k 3 4 53½ 32 31½ 3½ Butwell J 127wb *1.50 94-10 Old Rosebud133hdCapra104½Roamer1274 Tired 6
1Aug17- 4Sar my 1¼ :503 1:154 1:412 2:061 3↑ Saratoga H 5.8k 3 1 1½ 11 11 1½ Butwell J 122wb 5.00 89-14 Roamer122½Spur1231Ticket1071 Hard ridden 7
18Jly17- 4Emp sl 1 :25 :492 1:143 1:401 3↑ Mount Vernon H 2.9k 2 1 11 11 1hd 41½ Schuttinger A 125wb *.70 90-16 St. Isidore1111½Daddy's Choice107noWistful101no 6
Tired when challenged
13Jly17- 4Emp hy 1⅛ :511 1:17 1:432 1:563 3↑ Emp City H 4.8k 4 1 1½ 1hd 1hd 44 Schuttinger A 126wb *1.70 68-29 Spur1122Borrow124½Daddy's Choice1021½ Tired 4
7Jly17- 4Aqu fst 1⅛ :471 1:114 1:362 1:492 3↑ Brookdale H 4.4k 8 1 12 1½ 1½ 2½ Buxton M 126wb 3.00e 99-11 Boots127½Roamer1262Borrow124¾ Held gamely 8
30Jun17- 4Aqu fst 1 :241 :464 1:114 1:373 3↑ Queens County H 4.3k 3 4 31 21 21½ 21½ Schuttinger A 129wb 3.50 92-12 Old Rosebud1251½Roamer1291½Chiclet1102 Gamely,no match 7
25Jun17- 4Aqu fst 1⅛ :47 1:122 1:363 1:492 3↑ Brooklyn H 5.8k 6 4 32½ 21 53½ 53½ Schuttinger A 128wb 4.00 99-04 Borrow117noRegret1221Old Rosebud1201 Tired badly 11
18Jun17- 4Jam fst 1 1/16 :241 :48 1:123 1:452 3↑ Excelsior H 3.4k 4 1 2hd 2hd 2hd 11½ Schuttinger A 123 w 3.00 101-07 Roamer1231½Borrow117hdOld Koenig1124 Drew away 9
2Jun17- 5DoP gd 1¼ :474 1:121 1:384 2:041 3↑ Kentucky H 14k 5 3 3½ 11 3nk 3¾ Schuttinger A 126wb 4.80 92-13 King Gorin108nkCudgel103½Roamer1262 No mishaps 11
19May17- 5CD fst 1 1/16 :25 :493 1:13 1:451 3↑ Clark H 2.8k 3 2 2½ 21 2½ 21 Goose R 128wb *.45 95-14 Old Rosebd1171Roamer1288Embroidery1061½ Stumbled start 4
12May17- 3CD fst 1 1/16 :234 :473 1:123 1:443 4↑ Alw 1000 4 2 2½ 2½ 11 11½ Schuttinger A 119wb 4.20 99-06 Roamer1191½Ed Crump1225Old Rosebud1196 Won easing up 4
7Oct16- 4Lrl fst 1 1/16 :233 :473 1:124 1:432 3↑ Baltimore H 2.8k 6 2 21 31 89¼ 812 Byrne G 124wb 3.15 89-04 Boots1161Spur1181½Stromboli1252 Tired 9
23Sep16- 4HdG sl 1⅛ :483 1:141 1:392 1:521 3↑ Havre de Grace H 3.8k 5 3 73¾ 55½ 53½ 54½ Davies T 126wb 4.25 90-15 The Finn1291Spur117.5½Borrow1181 Crowded 8
16Sep16- 4HdG gd 1 1/16 :241 :49 1:143 1:453 3↑ Chesterbrook H 3.9k 4 4 51¼ 42 23 22 Loftus J 126wb 1.90 97-15 The Finn1252Roamer1262Stromboli1261 Forced wide,gamely 8
4Sep16- 4Bel fst 1½ 2:391 3↑ Municipal H 2.5k 2 1 11 11 1½ 2½ Butwell J 124wb *.60 64-25 Stromboli123½Roamer124 Gamely,tiring 2
26Aug16- 4Sar gd 1¾ :55 2:363 3:03 3↑ Sar Cup 3.7k 1 1 32½ 21 2hd 22 Butwell J 127wb 4.50 73-20 Friar Rock1132Roamer1276The Finn126 Saved ground,tired 3
19Aug16- 4Sar fst 1 3/16 :48 1:132 1:38 1:58 3↑ Merchants & Cits H 2.4k 2 1 11 1hd 22 35 Butwell J 127wb *1.20 95-06 The Finn1233Ed Crump1182Roamer127½ Saved ground 5
29Jly16- 4Emp fst 1 :25 :491 1:133 1:39 3↑ Mount Vernon H 2.6k 5 2 31¼ 32½ 43½ 44½ Butwell J 130wb *1.10 94-11 Boots104.52½He Will117½Spur1141½ Rated,no gain 5
22Jly16- 4Emp sly 1⅛ :502 1:162 1:43 1:56 3↑ Yonkers H 2.3k 1 1 11 11 11 1¾ Butwell J 127wb 4.00 75-23 Roamer127¾Spur1115Ed Crump1231 Easing up late 4
12Jly16- 4Emp fst 1⅛ :482 1:13 1:391 1:511 3↑ Emp City H 4.2k 7 5 52½ 31 1hd 21 Butwell J 129wb *1.40 98-10 ShortGrass1271Roamer129hdSpur1051 Tired when challenged 9
1Jly16- 4Aqu fst 1 :23 :461 1:104 1:362 3↑ Queens County H 3.4k 5 1 11 11 11 23 Butwell J 129wb *1.40 99-09 Short Grass1143Roamer1291½Gainer1083 Gamely 9
24Jun16- 4Aqu fst 1⅛ :47 1:11 1:372 1:50 3↑ Brooklyn H 4.8k 4 5 43½ 42 31 56¾ Butwell J 131wb *2.20 96-09 Friar Rock1082Pennant1231½Slumber II111nk Tired 8
3Jun16- 5DoP fst 1¼ :481 1:131 1:39 2:043 3↑ Kentucky H 13k 10 5 2hd 11½ 1½ 2½ Butwell J 132wb *3.90 90-11 Ed Crump121½Roamer1321Water Witch1071 Tired 11
20May16- 4Jam fst 1 1/16 :24 :472 1:123 1:453 3↑ Kings County H 3.4k 10 1 2hd 42 46¼ 912 Butwell J 133wb *1.40 88-07 Capra98½The Finn1203Boots106½ Tired 10
30Oct15- 4Lrl fst 1⅛ :472 1:114 1:381 1:50 3↑ National H 3k 3 1 11 12 13 13 Butwell J 132wb *1.00 98-09 Roamer1323Stromboli1231½Short Grass1236 Won easing up 4
18Sep15- 4HdG fst 1⅛ :483 1:133 1:391 1:511 3↑ Havre de Grace H 1.8k 1 1 13 12 12 13 Butwell J 129wb *.65 104-09 Roamer1293Slumber II1131½Stromboli1201 Speed in reserve 4
28Aug15- 4Sar fst 1¾ :491 2:083 2:352 3:014 3↑ Sar Cup 2.4k 2 1 1½ 12 15 18 Butwell J 123wb *.13 81-14 Roamer1238Virile12410Star Gaze127 Under restraint 4
21Aug15- 4Sar fst 1 3/16 :49 1:14 1:391 1:59 3↑ Merchants & Cits H 1.9k 3 1 11 11½ 11½ 1½ Butwell J 129wb *1.40 95-11 Roamer129½Borrow1233Stromboli1215 Gamely 8
14Aug15- 4Sar sl 1⅛ :494 1:153 1:42 1:552 3↑ Champlain H 2.4k 2 3 34½ 33½ 45 49¾ Butwell J 132wb *.75 70-25 Star Jasmine110¾Gainer1145Stromboli1244 Never a threat 6

Date/Race	Cond/Dist	Fractions	Race	Running line	Jockey	Wt	Odds	Speed	Top finishers	Comment	Field
2Aug15-4Sar	fst 1¼	:48 1:132 1:392 2:042	3↑ Saratoga H 2.9k	2 1 12 13 15 110	Butwell J	128wb	*3.00	98-11	Roamer12810Saratoga1031StarJsmn103½	Won under restraint	7
24Jly15-4Bel	fst 1⅛	:473 1:13 1:382 1:513	3↑ Emp City H 3.5k	2 2 2½ 44 56½ 710¼	Butwell J	129wb	*.80	88-18	Gainer1092AddieM.995SamJackson105¾	Close quarters early	7
10Jly15-4Aqu	fst 1⅛	:473 1:12 1:373 1:503	3↑ Brookdale H 2.5k	1 1 11½ 12 13 15	Butwell J	128wb	*.55	107-10	Roamer1285Stromboli12410Rock View114	In a canter	3
5Jly15-4Aqu	sly 7f	:242 :482 1:144 1:30	3↑ Carter H 2.4k	2 8 89¾ 710 69½ 612	Butwell J	130wb	*2.50	62-30	Phosphor1161Pomette Bleu1041Leo Skolny1053		8
	Shuffled back at start,not persevered with										
29Jun15-4Aqu	fst 1	:232 :462 1:132 1:392	3↑ Queens County H 2.8k	6 3 32 31½ 21 1no	Butwell J	127wb	*1.10	93-12	Roamer127noStromboli125½Harmonicon1214	Gamely	6
26Jun15-4Aqu	fst 1⅛	:48 1:12 1:38 1:503	3↑ Brooklyn H 4.8k	3 1 13 12 2hd 21	Butwell J	125wb	*1.50	106-06	Tartar1031Roamer125hdBorrow1286	Tired in drive	6
29May15-4DoP	hy 1¼	:493 1:151 1:432 2:102	3↑ Kentucky H 13k	3 1 11 1nk 43 814¼	Butwell J	127wb	*1.65	48-33	Borrow1261½Hodge109½Prince Hermis103no	Tired badly	9
8May15-4CD	fst 1	:233 :472 1:123 1:39	3↑ Alw 700	4 2 11½ 11½ 11½ 1½	Butwell J	112wb	*.30	92-09	Romr112½ShortGrss108hdPrncHrms104hd	Won under restraint	8
10Oct14-4Lrl	fst 1⅛	:463 1:113 1:363 1:493	3↑ Washington H 2.5k	3 1 12 12 12 11½	Butwell J	124wb	*1.40	105-02	Roamer1241½Tartar1022Buskin1101½	As rider pleased	6
1Oct14-4Lrl	fst 1 1/16	:232 :47 1:121 1:433	3↑ Baltimore H 2.7k	7 1 12 11½ 1hd 21½	Butwell J	123wb	*.73	102-04	Stromboli1171½Roamer1235Tartar1041	Tired late	10
19Sep14-4Bel	fst 1½	3:04	3↑ Autumn WFA .8k	1 1 1 1 1 1	Butwell J	112wb	-	--	Roamer112	Walked over	1
12Sep14-4Bel	fst 1¼	:483 1:14 1:393 2:04	3↑ Municipal H 2.7k	2 1 11 12 11½ 11	Butwell J	122wb	*.20	80-12	Roamer1221Addie M.981½Pandean1042	Tiring,ridden out	4
5Sep14-3Syr	fst 1¼	:472 1:112 1:361 2:02	3↑ State Fair 10k	1 1 11½ 13 14 18	Butwell J	114wb	*.07	--	Roamer1148Gainer117	In a canter	2
25Aug14-4Sar	gd 1¼	:503 1:153 1:411 2:064	Huron H 3.2k	3 1 11½ 12 13 14	Butwell J	128wb	*.50	89-15	Roamer1284Punch Bowl1092Gainer1145	In a canter	4
8Aug14-4Sar	fst 1¼	1:141 1:392 2:04	Travers 3.5k	3 1 11 13 15 110	Butwell J	123wb	*1.10	103-03	Roamer12310Surprising126¾Gainer121no	Cantering	7
22Jly14-4Emp	fst 1½	:532 2:133 2:401	Midsummer 3.4k	1 1 12 13 14 13	Butwell J	123wb	*.02	69-13	Roamer1233Robert Oliver123	Hard held throughout	2
18Jly14-4Emp	gd 1⅛	:49 1:14 1:41 1:54	3↑ Emp City H 3.9k	1 1 11 11½ 1½ 31	Butwell J	116wb	*.90	84-15	Buckhorn1201G.M.Mllr104hdRomr1166	Tired when challenged	5
9Jly14-4Aqu	fst 1¼	:49 1:14 2:053	Brooklyn Derby 2.8k	2 1 11½ 12 14 18	Butwell J	117wb	*.70	119-04	Roamer1178Gainer1205Charlestonin123	Won under restraint	3
1Jly14-3Aqu	fst 7f	:224 :463 1:12 1:25	3↑ Handicap 580	2 1 11½ 12 12 12½	Butwell J	115wb	*.65	105-07	Roamer1152½Hocnir1028HestrPrynn1003	Won under restraint	7
27Jun14-4Aqu	fst 7f	:231 :47 1:121 1:244	3↑ Carter H 2.4k	8 1 15 13 12 12	Buxton M	109wb	6.00	106-06	Roamer1092Borrow1293Flying Fairy1173	Won easing up	12
20Jun14-2Bel	fst 6f-Str	1:13	3↑ Handicap 625	9 1 11 12 13 13	Butwell J	107wb	4.50	78-19	Roamer1073Yankee Notions1021½Hester Prynne100nk	Easily	9
11Jun14-4Bel	fst 6f-Str	1:121	3↑ Toboggan 3k	9 14 108¾ 1312 1314 1424½	Kederis J	106 w	20.00	57-23	Rock View126nkFiginny1001½Ten Point1283	Never a factor	15
30May14-4Bel	fst 1	:232 :474 1:133 1:394	Withers 3.4k	4 4 42¾ 2½ 3¾ 38	Davies T	115 w	10.00	80-14	Charlestonian115noGainer1188Roamer1155	Ran well	5
27May14-3Bel	sly 6f		3↑ Handicap 570	1 1 1½ 14	Turner C	104 w	*1.40	--	Roamer1044Yankee Notions1142Leo Skolny1076	Easily	6
	No time taken,rainstorm prevented view of horses										
30Oct13-3Lrl	gd 5½f	:24 :484 1:014 1:081	Handicap 620	5 1 2nk 3nk 32½ 43	Wolfe H	111 w	2.00	93-13	Gotelus124hdBraveCunarder1022WaterLdy96.51	Showed speed	7
17Oct13-3Lrl	fst 5½f	:233 :472 1:002 1:064	Handicap 625	5 1 55½ 42¾ 42¼ 67½	Musgrave P	114 w	5.00	95-08	Surprising1171Gainer1253Addie M.109hd	Stumbled start	6
23Sep13-4HdG	fst 5½f	:23 :48 1:003 1:07	Eastern Shore H 1.5k	8 1 54¾ 67½ 64¾ 810	Glass J	121 w	*2.50	82-12	Tranid1022Northerner1021½Uncle Mun1091	Impeded	9
16Sep13-4HdG	fst 5½f	:223 :472 1:00 1:062	Lafayette H 1.5k	1 3 22 22 21½ 21½	Byrne G	123 w	*3.00	93-11	Gainer1201½Roamer1231Mr.Sniggs1081½	No match for winner	9
27Aug13-4Sar	sl 6f	:233 :482 1:15	Adirondack H 2.4k	4 1 41½ 56 55½ 52½	Byrne G	118 w	4.00	80-17	Little Nephew125¾Black Broom116¾Spearhead106hd		9
	Shuffled back start										
20Aug13-1Sar	fst 6f	:234 :473 1:123	2↑ Handicap 630	2 3 21 21 31¼ 21½	Byrne G	105 w	3.50	93-09	Isirose1061½Roamer105noSebago120hd	Gamely	7
15Aug13-2Sar	fst 5½f	:224 :593 1:063	Handicap 635	9 3 41¼ 41½ 64½ 812	Byrne G	123 w	3.00	84-07	Gracilla1061Uncle Mun110½Flittergold120½	Tired	11
9Aug13-3Sar	fst 6f	:232 :47 1:13	Sar Spl 6k	10 2 1hd 2hd 1hd 11½	Byrne G	119 w	7.00	93-08	Roamer1191½Gainer1222Black Toney1221	Going away	12
5Aug13-1Sar	fst 5½f	:23 :471 1:002 1:064	Handicap 615	5 1 21½ 21½ 21½ 21	Byrne G	107 w	6.00	94-13	Little Nephew1201Roamer1071½Surprising1153	No match	8
	Previously owned by Clay Brothers;previously trained by F. Brooks										
15Jly13-3Bel	fst 5½f-Str	1:07	Clm 2000	5 6 11 12 13 14	McTaggart T	109 w	2.50	85-13	Roamer1094Delft1093Gallop112¾	Much best	8
19Jun13-3Lat	gd 5½f	:233 :474 1:003 1:07	Alw 670	4 3 55 55½ 56½ 512	Martin E	112 w	*1.70	80-09	Bringhurst1122BootsandSaddle115noMinda1065	Dropped back	6
11Jun13-2Lat	fst 5f	:233 :482 1:004	Alw 710	1 1 13 14 16 16	Martin E	109 w	*.55	91-07	Roamer1096Candy Box1091½O'Reilly109no	Much best	8
4Jun13-3DoP	fst 5f	:231 :463 :583	Alw 850	2 3 33 39½ 39½ 39	Callahan J	100 w	21.00	103-00	Old Rosebud1151Little Nephew1188Roamer1005	Best of rest	5
17May13-2CD	hy 4½f	:234 :48 :54	Alw 600	5 2 23 24 26	Taplin	108 w	5.00	88-06	OldRosebud1156Roamer1085BraveCunarder10512	Second best	5
13May13-2CD	fst 4½f	:24 :482 :54	©Alw 600	3 1 2nk 22 25	Ganz	109 w	*.35	89-05	The Norman1105Roamer1093Old Ben1085	Tired	5
6May13-5Lxt	fst 4½f	:233 :48 :543	©Alw 390	4 1 1½ 1hd 2nk	Ganz	111 w	1.90	95-05	Imperatore109nkRoamer1115Bird Man112nk	Tired	4
1May13-2Lxt	fst 4½f	:241 :49 :552	Md Sp Wt	7 5 11 12 15	Ganz	111.5wb	*.65	91-05	Roamer111.55Destino1121½Tiktok112nk	Easily	11

Roseben

b. g. 1901, by Ben Strome (Bend Or)–Rose Leaf, by Duke of Montrose — **Lifetime record: 111 52 25 12 $74,910**

Own.– D.C. Johnson
Br.– Mrs T.J. Carson (Ky)
Tr.– F.D. Weir

Date/Race	Cond/Dist	Fractions	Race	Running line	Jockey	Wt	Odds	Speed	Top finishers	Comment	Field
1Jly09-2She	fst 7f	:24 :471 1:131 1:26	3↑ Clm	6 1 12 12½ 1½ 22½	Dugan E	105wb	5.00	91-06	Nimbus1112½Roseben1054Casque94½	Quit badly	7
2Jun09-6Bel	sly 6f	:24 :474 1:13	3↑ Clm	7 6 52 45 33 23	McIntyre J	110wb	*1.00	90-07	Dreamer1083Roseben110hdSirJohnJohnson113½	Belated rally	10
29May09-3Bel	gd 6½f	:224 :48 1:14 1:201	3↑ Clm 1000	4 3 32 31 11 13	McIntyre J	115wb	1.60	86-10	Roseben1153Black Mate1104McCarter113hd	Won easing up	4
20May09-3Bel	fst 6f-Str	1:103	3↑ Norwood Selling	6 5 4¾ 42 63 54½	McIntyre J	111wb	*1.80	85-08	Chapultepec118½Dreamer1111½Horace E.111½	Poor effort	8
31Mar09-4Oak	sl *6f-FC	1:12	3↑ Clm 1500	6 2 22½ 1nk 1¾ 13	Walsh A	107wb	*.90	84-16	Roseben1073Westbury107noBellwether1111	Easily	9
22Feb09-4SAP	fst 6f	:23 :46 :59 1:114	3↑ Speed H 6k	6 4 2hd 32 32 22	Walsh A	139 w	4.00	97-03	King James1422Roseben139hdMagazine126½	Resolute finish	10
30Jan09-4SAP	fst 6f	:224 :463 :582 1:113	3↑ Alhambra H 2.5k	5 5 52½ 43 55 52¼	Goldstein	129wb	10.00	98-05	Jack Atkin138nkDominus Arvi1131Magazine1071	Gamely	11
23Jan09-6Oak	sly *6f-FC	1:123	3↑ Handicap 600	4 4 21 15 14 14	Mentry	130wb	*.50	81-19	Roseben1304Rose Queen917Sevenfull935	Flatfooted start	4
16Jan09-4Oak	sly 6½f	:232 :49 1:151 1:22	3↑ Andrew Selling	4 4 31 2hd 2½ 2hd	Goldstein	119wb	4.60	82-27	BoogerRed100hdRosbn1195Bllwthr1021	Slow start,weak ride	8
9Jan09-4Oak	hy 7f	:24 :484 1:162 1:29	3↑ Follansbee Hwt H	2 3 24 26 24 57	Lee J	145wb	4.00e	74-25	SmileyCorbett1303GracG.110noLghtWool1362	Failed to stay	9
19Dec08-6Oak	gd *6f-FC	1:091	2↑ Handicap 600	3 6 58 57¼ 58¼ 57½	Miller W	140wb	*1.20	90-06	Pajaroita108½Smiley Corbett1123Berry Maid1144	Outrun	8
14Dec08-4Oak	hy 7f	:23 :481 1:15 1:274	2↑ Alw 700	1 2 2nk 12 2½ 22	McCarthy D	107wb	*.20	85-22	Firestone1062Roseben1074Hanbridge1066	Broke slowly	5
12Dec08-6Oak	hy *6f-FC	1:104	2↑ Handicap 600	1 2 12 13 13 13	Miller W	135wb	*.60	90-10	Rosebn1353CollctorJssup1005RoylTourst1153	Won easing up	7
5Dec08-6Oak	my *6f-FC	1:103	2↑ Handicap 600	3 5 43¼ 14 16 14	Holmes	128wb	*.55	91-09	Roseben1284Berry Maid1152Collector Jessup1027		5
	Unready for start,won easing up										
26Nov08-3Oak	sl *6f-FC	1:103	2↑ Alw 500	4 3 12½ 13 13 14	Holmes	112wb	*.80	91-09	Rosebn1124CollctorJssup11012J.C.Core1075	Won under pull	6
25Sep08-5Gra	fst *6f	:221 :472 1:00 1:10	3↑ Clm 3000	5 2 13 13 14 13	Notter	123wb	*.50	92-10	Roseben1233Stargowan100½Saracinesca1018	Never extended	8
15Sep08-4Gra	fst *6f	:224 :471 :594 1:093	3↑ Bayshore Selling	3 4 22 22 23 34½	Holmes	123wb	2.00	89-09	Besom1044Westbury108½Roseben1235	Pulled up sore	4
10Sep08-4She	fst 7f	:24 :473 1:122 1:26	2↑ Flight 5k	5 5 31½ 31 43 59¼	Garner	122wb	*1.60	85-08	BabyWolf1074HalfSovereign1054Arcite110¾	Tired,pulled up	5
5Sep08-1She	fst 6½f	:22 :47 1:122 1:192	2↑ HiW H 795	6 4 33½ 32½ 13 15	Garner	140wb	*2.50	95-01	Roseben1405Tom McGrath1173De Mund1231	Drew away	16
29Aug08-3She	fst 6½f	:222 :464 1:11 1:181	3↑ Fall H 1.4k	4 3 813 814 811 916¼	Garner	129wb	*1.00	85-01	Half Sovereign984Dorante1095Westbury1091	Rough trip	10
20Aug08-3Emp	fst 6f	:222 :46 1:122	3↑ Handicap 675	5 1 1hd 2hd 21 2¾	Garner	128wb	6.00	--	Nimbus111¾Roseben1282Rialto1036	Not urged	5
6Jly08-2She	fst 7f	:231 :464 1:12 1:254	3↑ Handicap 720	2 1 11½ 12 21 31¾	Garner	130wb	*3.00	93-05	Peter Quince1121Dreamer118¾Roseben1301½	Tired	9
3Jly08-5She	fst 6½f(T)	:222 :474 1:121 1:183	3↑ Alw 590	5 4 1hd 2½ 2nk 2hd	Garner	127wb	*.60	106-00	Nimbus106hdRoseben1271Peter Quince1141	Wide,just missed	7
27Jun08-1She	fst 6½f	:221 :47 1:12 1:19	3↑ HiW H 755	7 5 32 32 32½ 22	Notter	142wb	*1.20	95-05	Westbury1062Roseben142¾De Mund1192	Away slowly	11
25Jun08-1She	fst 6½f	:231 :491 1:12 1:19	3↑ Alw 580	4 1 1½ 12 12 11½	Notter	137wb	*1.60	97-04	Roseben1371½Bouquet1025Jubilee1128	Never extended	4
22Jun08-4She	fst 6f-FC	1:12	3↑ Coney Island H 4.5k	8 12 106¼ 105¼ 95¼ 912¼	Garner	140wb	6.00	81-10	Dreamer1121Jack Atkin1353De Mund115hd	Away poorly	13
18Jun08-4Gra	fst *6f	:222 :473 :593 1:091	2↑ Handicap 1090	4 8 824 714 711 612	Garner	142wb	*.80	84-08	Rialto1002Pantoufle1071Bat Masterson1041		8
	Caught in barrier,closed gap										
11Jun08-6Gra	fst *6f	:221 :472 :594 1:093	2↑ Handicap 1080	4 3 42 42 41 31	Notter	142wb	*.70	93-05	Dreamer110hdBat Masterson971Roseben1423	Held well	6
5Jun08-1Gra	fst *6f	:23 :472 :591 1:091	2↑ Handicap 1100	2 1 12 13 13 14	Notter	135wb	*.65	96-05	Roseben1354Pantoufle1094Gold Lady1131	Never extended	7
1Jun08-1Gra	fst *6f	:222 :473 1:00 1:10	2↑ Handicap 1120	1 4 22 21½ 2hd 1nk	Notter	130wb	*2.60	92-08	Roseben130nkBerry Maid1092King Cobalt1114	Going away	10

26May08-5Bel	fst 6f	:242 :481	1:132	3↑ Handicap 1070	8 4 2½ 21½ 22 24	Shaw	132wb	*1.60	87-12	Royal Tourist1124Roseben132½Pantoufle1141½		8
Impeded by barrier,held 2nd												
22May08-3Bel	sly 6½f	:233 :483 1:141	1:211	3↑ Claremont H 2.7k	4 2 2hd 2hd 32 35½	Shaw	129wb	*2.00	75-24	Priscillian1111½King Cobalt1024Roseben1295	Tired badly	5
20May08-1Bel	sly 6f		1:15	3↑ HiW H 1050	2 1 11½ 12 13 16	Shaw	140wb	1.60	83-21	Roseben1406Aletheuo1275King Sol1163	Cantering	4
16May08-4Bel	gd 6f-Str		1:113	3↑ Toboggan H 4.9k	4 9 104¾ 106 106¼ 107¾	Shaw	130wb	5.00	84-06	BerryMaid100nkBabyWolf118nkRestgouch1052	Never a threat	13
30Apr08-4Jam	fst 6f	:242 :482	1:123	3↑ Paumonok H 2.1k	6 1 3½ 31½ 65½ 610	Shaw	130wb	*1.50	88-10	RedRiver1132Restigouche104½Rlto1022	Quit,not ridden out	6
27Apr08-2Aqu	fst 5f-Str		:592	3↑ Alw 890	1 5 65¼ 54 43½ 43	Shaw	130wb	*1.60	95-01	Berry Maid104noKing Cobalt991½Red River1181½	Impeded	7
12Sep07-4She	hy 7f	:234 :472 1:124	1:253	2↑ Flight 5.8k	5 1 11½ 13 12 12	Knapp W	110wb	*1.00	96-15	Roseben1102Far West11210Keator1098	Easily	5
10Sep07-1She	fst 6f	:24 :473	1:123	2↑ Alw 1300	1 2 23 1½ 11 1¾	Knapp W	137wb	*.20	97-07	Roseben137¾Veil1136First Premium123½	Lasted	8
3Sep07-1She	my 6f	:243 :49	1:143	2↑ Alw 1340	6 1 12 14 15 13	Knapp W	132wb	*.60	87-21	Roseben1323Firestone1102½King Cole1154	Never extended	8
25Jly07-3Bri	fst 6f	:23 :47	1:121	3↑ Handicap 1105	1 2 11 21½ 21½ 21½	Martin J	150wb	*1.00	97-03	Ben Ban921½Roseben1501Red River108hd	Tired,gamely	9
17Jly07-1Bri	fst 6f	:232 :47	1:121	2↑ Handicap 1330	2 3 11½ 13 13 13	Martin J	147wb	*2.20	99-07	Roseben1472Smoker87¾Dreamer116hd	Never extended	9
10Jly07-1Bri	fst 6f	:233 :471	1:12	3↑ Handicap 1365	10 3 11 11½ 1½ 11	Martin J	140wb	4.00	100-02	Roseben1401Suffrage1275Herodotus103hd	Handily	12
6Jly07-1She	fst 6f	:24 :474	1:124	3↑ HiW H 1290	3 1 1½ 1½ 2nk 23	Martin J	140wb	*.50	93-07	Dreamer1133Roseben1404Comedienne1026	Quit	7
3Jly07-1She	fst 6f	:241 :481	1:134	3↑ Alw 1060	1 1 21½ 22 11 14	Martin J	130wb	*.20	91-12	Roseben1304Haensel1073Berwick107¾	Easily	6
24Jun07-4She	fst 1			3↑ Equality 5.5k	6 1 1½ 11 2hd 32	Martin J	115wb	*2.00	--	Frank Gill1151½Charles Edward107½Roseben1152	Tired	10
No time taken due to fog												
22Jun07-1She	fst 6f	:242 :48	1:13	3↑ HiW H 1275	4 5 21 21½ 2nk 22	Martin J	140wb	*.45	93-12	Prince Hamburg1202Roseben14010La Londe94½	Away slowly	5
20Jun07-2She	fst 6f	:233 :474	1:124	3↑ Alw 1090	1 1 11½ 13 13 11	Martin J	137wb	*1.20	96-07	Roseben1371Prince Hamburg1235Gold Lady10510	Easing up	5
16May07-5Bel	fst 6f-Str		1:124	3↑ Crotona H 2.7k	3 6 63¼ 64 63¾ 64¼	Martin J	140wb	*1.20	82-11	Suffrage1132Jack Atkin1061½Pantoufle103hd	No gain	11
9May07-3Bel	hy 1	:241 :482 1:14	1:404	3↑ Metropolitan H 13k	1 4 42½ 41 1hd 33½	Martin J	124wsb	*1.60	79-26	Glorifier1191½Okenite992Roseben124hd	Tired	15
15Apr07-4Aqu	sl 7f	:25 :484 1:15	1:281	3↑ Carter H 10k	5 15 12 11 83¼ 21½	Beckman	135wsb	8.00	87-10	Glorifir1191½Rosbn135noDonDgo1081½	Bumped,finished fast	16
12Nov06-4Aqu	sly 7f	:25 :49 1:143	1:272	2↑ Bayview H 2.1k	3 1 11½ 11 1½ 12	Shaw	146wb	2.20	93-14	Roseben14620Oxford1196Ormonde's Right1042	Ridden out	5
5Nov06-1Aqu	fst 6f	:24 :48	1:124	2↑ Handicap 905	5 1 1hd 1½ 13 12½	Shaw	147wb	*.55	100-05	Roseben1472½Zienap956Gambrinus100hd	Easily	5
31Oct06-4Jam	my 6f	:24 :484	1:134	2↑ Richmond H 2k	2 2 1¾ 11½ 2½ 31½	Shaw	148wb	*.33	90-15	Oxford121no[D]Jacobite1141½Rosebn1488	Tiring,impeded str	4
Placed second by disqualification												
16Oct06-5Bel	fst 7f	:234 :464 1:102	1:22	2↑ Alw 1130	2 1 18 110 120 120	Shaw	126wb	*.01	116-00	Roseben12620Beauclare85	Ridden out	2
12Oct06-3Bel	fst 6f-Str		1:121	2↑ Manhattan H 3.2k	2 1 12 13 14 16	Shaw	147wb	*1.00	93-12	Roseben1476Suffrage111¾Handzarra11210	Won easing up	5
19Sep06-1Gra	fst *6f	:222 :474 1:02	1:10	2↑ Handicap 1145	4 3 12 1½ 1hd 22	Lyne	150wb	*.45	91-10	Comedienne1092Roseben1501½Wtrgrss1072	Tired,good effort	5
15Sep06-1She	fst 6f	:24 :472	1:123	2↑ HiW H 1390	6 1 1½ 11 1hd 1½	Lyne	144wb	*.33	99-08	Roseben144¾Suffrage1003Far West1151	Never extended	11
13Sep06-4She	gd 7f	:233 :462 1:13	1:261	2↑ Flight 5.9k	5 2 13 12½ 13 13	Lyne	122wb	*.33	96-09	Roseben1223Sanfara1058Deutschland1104	Never extended	5
6Sep06-1She	fst 6f	:232 :47	1:121	2↑ Alw 1130	5 1 11½ 14 15 16	Shaw	137wb	*.33	101-05	Roseben1376Rusk1151Pretension130hd	In a canter	8
1Sep06-3She	fst 6f	:24 :473	1:122	3↑ Fall H 3.5k	5 2 1½ 12 12 12	Lyne	132 w	3.50	100-04	Roseben1322Neva Lee1071Ormondale116hd	Never extended	11
5Jly06-5She	fst 6f	:24 :473	1:124	3↑ Alw 1060	3 2 2¾ 2¾ 1hd 2hd	Lyne	137 w	2.20	98-14	Kiamesha128hdRoseben137½Hndzrr1138	Bore out,just missed	4
28Jun06-1She	fst 6f	:24 :471	1:122	3↑ Alw 1050	3 5 32 33 34 34½	Lyne	137wb	*.90	95-00	Kiamesha1134Handzarra113½Roseben137hd	Bad start	5
25Jun06-2She	fst 6½f	:222 :47 1:13	1:19	3↑ Alw 1070	4 3 11 1½ 1½ 24	O'Neill F	137wb	1.80	93-05	Timber1124Roseben1372Handzarra1152	Disliked going	5
22Jun06-4She	fst 6f	:24 :474	1:122	3↑ Coney Island H 4k	5 5 43 34 34 33	Miller W	143wb	*1.40	97-04	King'sDaughter1131PrinceHmburg1242Rsbn1431½	Away badly	8
18Jun06-1Gra	my *6f	:234 :484 1:014	1:113	2↑ Handicap 1355	3 5 52½ 31¼ 32 32½	Lyne	149wb	3.50	82-20	Shot Gun1301½Bohemia1031Roseben1492	Rated,belated rally	7
21May06-4Gra	fst 1¼	:484 1:13 1:392	2:053	3↑ Brooklyn H 20k	2 2 11½ 12 23 77¾	Lyne	119wb	20.00	90-09	Tokalon108noDandelion1072ThePicket1204	Tired after mile	14
19May06-1Bel	fst 7½f	:231 :471 1:124	1:321	3↑ Handicap 1080	3 1 12 12 11½ 1½	Lyne	133 w	*.60	113-00	Roseben133½Tommy Waddell1063Cinna97½	Driving	5
17May06-1Bel	fst 6f	:243 :482	1:13	3↑ HiW H 1125	5 3 32 31 41½ 2nk	Lyne	140wb	*.90	93-11	Guiding Star112nkRoseben1402Samson1042	Troubled trip	8
10May06-3Bel	gd 1	:242 :47 1:134	1:39	3↑ Metropolitan H 13k	17 1 1½ 1½ 2hd 54¼	Lyne	129wb	*3.50	88-12	Grapple106¾Dandelion108hdOxford1093	Gamely,tiring	22
28Apr06-4Jam	fst 1 1/16	:241 :492 1:143	1:471	3↑ Excelsior H 10k	6 1 11½ 12 21½ 54¼	Lyne	120wb	*.70	87-07	MerryLark1061½Ormonde'sRight1111EugeniaBurch1101½	Quit	10
25Apr06-4Aqu	fst 1	:231 :48 1:134	1:401	3↑ Sterling 2.4k	2 1 14 14 16 12	Lyne	127wb	*.80	89-09	Roseben1272Ram's Horn1266Phil Finch1278	Never extended	4
16Apr06-4Aqu	fst 7f	:234 :474 1:132	1:262	3↑ Carter H 10k	12 1 11 13 12 1hd	Lyne	129wb	*2.20	98-03	Roseben129hdSouthern Cross1061Red Knight108no	Held on	13
13Oct05-6Bel	fst 6f	:232 :474	1:121	2↑ Alw 1050	3 1 18 112 115 120	O'Neill F	130wb	*.04	--	Roseben13020Consideration1154Torchello110	Won easily	3
10Oct05-5Bel	fst 7f	:244 :482	1:251	2↑ Alw 1150	3 1 18 110 110 110	O'Neill F	126wb	*.05	--	Roseben12610Chimney Sweep107hdMonet109	Won easing up	3
6Oct05-3Bel	fst 6f	:24 :47	1:113	2↑ Manhattan H 2.5k	2 1 11½ 11 12 15	O'Neill F	147wb	*.60	--	Roseben1475Aeronaut1056Race King1044	Never extended	5
4Oct05-5Bel	fst 6f	:233 :473	1:12	2↑ Bronx Highweight H 2.2k	7 1 11 11 12 15	O'Neill F	140wb	*1.10	--	Roseben1405Ancestor90¾RaceKing103½	Never fully extended	9
18Sep05-3Gra	my *6f	:242 :483 1:014	1:111	2↑ Handicap 1210	2 3 2nk 1hd 11½ 11½	Lyne	137wb	*1.80	87-17	Roseben1371½Schulamite104½NnnHodg115nk	Bad start,easily	10
15Sep05-1Gra	fst *6f	:222 :48 1:00	1:092	2↑ Handicap 1130	5 1 1½ 12 12 15	O'Neill F	132wb	2.00	96-10	Roseben1325Lady Amelia122¾Rapid Water1191½	In a canter	6
31Aug05-2She	sl 6f	:25 :49	1:141	2↑ Alw 1040	2 1 1hd 21 23 25	O'Neill F	137 w	*.29	86-10	Jocund1205Roseben1376Blucher116	Wide,poor effort	3
26Aug05-3She	sl 6f	:244 :49	1:141	3↑ Fall H 3.5k	5 1 42 32 31½ 21	O'Neill F	129 w	*.90	90-12	PrinceHamburg1121Rosbn129hdLadyAmel1236	Troubled trip	11
22Aug05-1Sar	fst 6f	:234 :48	1:13	2↑ Handicap 935	7 2 11 11 1½ 1hd	O'Neill F	140 w	3.60	96-09	Roseben140hdMarjoram1046Right and True108hd	Lasted	12
8Aug05-4Sar	fst 1	:244 :483 1:13	1:392	3↑ Delaware H 2.6k	3 2 2hd 53 68 68½	Buchanan W	120 w	3.50	83-13	MollyBrant1132DollySpanker108noCairngorm109hd	Pulled up	7
25Jly05-3Bri	fst 6f	:244 :49	1:144	3↑ Alw 1070	1 2 1hd 1hd 14 11½	Lyne	137 w	*.13	86-10	Roseben1371½Israelite1101Robador1055	Won eased up	7
15Jly05-6Bri	fst 6f	:241 :48	1:13	3↑ Handicap 1170	2 1 1½ 11½ 12 11½	O'Neill F	140 w	*1.20	95-06	Roseben1401½Incantation1051½Lady Uncas100½	Easily	13
5Jly05-1Bri	fst 6f	:231 :472	1:122	3↑ Alw 1330	2 2 22 21 2hd 13½	O'Neill F	135 ws	*1.00	98-08	Roseben1353½Lady Amelia123noBad News1158	Won easing up	8
1Jly05-2She	sl 6f	:242 :481	1:13	3↑ HiW H 1380	8 3 21½ 21 21 11	O'Neill F	140 ws	*1.60	97-08	Roseben1401Druid10510Prince Hamburg110hd	Handily	15
24Jun05-2She	hy 6f	:24 :484	1:144	3↑ HiW H 1405	4 1 32 32 11½ 16	O'Neill F	137 ws	*1.50	88-14	Roseben1376SparklingStar112hdDmondFlush1045	Wide,easily	8
Previously trained by C. Oxx												
16Jun05-4She	fst 6f	:234 :472	1:123	3↑ Coney Island H 3.8k	10 4 2hd 21 21½ 22	O'Neill F	120 ws	4.00	97-05	HamburgBelle1242Roseben1201½WildMnt1131½	Tired,bore out	13
14Jun05-1Gra	gd *6f	:224 1:003	1:10	2↑ Handicap 1350	9 2 32½ 32 31¼ 33	O'Neill F	123 w	5.00	90-10	Marjoram1043Incantation95hdRoseben1231½	Careless ride	9
22May05-1Bel	fst 7f-Str		1:282	3↑ HiW H 1130	3 3 51¼ 3nk 1½ 12	O'Neill F	140 ws	*1.60	--	Roseben1402Neptunus117½Delcanta1164	Won easing up	8
15May05-4Bel	gd 6½f	:24 :48 1:134	1:204	3↑ Claremont H 2.4k	3 2 31 31 31 11½	Burns T	115 ws	*2.40e	--	Roseben1151½Race King1062Oxford108hd	Going away	8
8May05-4Bel	gd 6f-Str		1:13	3↑ Crotona H 2.1k	6 2 2½ 3nk 3½ 622¼	O'Neill F	115 w	5.00	--	Wild Mint105hdSpring108hdSparkling Star898		10
Stumbled,bumped badly late str												
6May05-4Bel	gd 6f-Str		1:13	3↑ Toboggan H 3.2k	1 2 1½ 11 1hd 1no	O'Neill F	112 w	8.00	--	Roseben112noSparkling Star871½Pasadena105½	Lasted	12
22Apr05-4Aqu	fst 1	:243 :483 1:14	1:391	3↑ Queens County H 2.1k	9 4 45½ 43 41½ 47	O'Neill F	122	6.00	87-04	St. Valentine112hdRapid Water1255Sinister1042	Tired	10
15Apr05-4Aqu	fst 7f	:242 :472 1:13	1:264	3↑ Carter H 8.1k	3 3 32 63¼ 2½ 2¾	Fuller	113 w	10.00	95-08	Ormonde'sRight110¾Rosbn1135LttlEm105¾	Getting to winner	18
4Apr05-4Ben	fst 6f	:244 :493	1:15	3↑ Alw 540	1 1 1hd 2hd 1hd 1hd	Fuller	122 w	1.40	93-12	Roseben122hdSanta Catalina1028Monacodor101	Went wide	3
1Apr05-3Ben	fst 6f	:24 :482	1:14	3↑ Alw 565	2 2 11½ 1½ 2½ 22	Fuller	115 w	*.55	96-11	Santa Catalina922Roseben115	No mishap	2
27Mar05-1Ben	gd 5½f	:242 :494 1:041	1:104	3↑ Handicap 595	2 1 31 21½ 1½ 1no	Fuller	128 w	*2.00	83-28	Roseben128noRockland938Right and True1143	Gamely	6
17Feb05-3OP	hy 5½f	:252 :504	1:111	3↑ Alw 600	4 5 27 22½ 12 15	Smithson	98 w	*.33	--	Roseben985Incense911½Grenade9815	In a canter	5
1Feb05-4Esx	hy 6f	:25 :50½	1:18	3↑ Handicap 600	2 3 31½ 2½ 31 3½	Hildebrand	130 w	*.60	75-32	Mame Worth120hdToscan121½Roseben13025	Weak ride	5
18Jan05-4Esx	my 6f	:25 :50½	1:18	3↑ Handicap 500	2 2 12 15 110 112	Smithson	117 w	*1.00	76-24	Roseben11712Buttons12010Neversuch986	Won eased up	5
24Nov04-4FG	fst 6f	:244 :472	1:133	2↑ Inaugural H 2.2k	4 2 1hd 1½ 2hd 23	Gannon	116 w	12.00	91-08	Floral King1183Roseben116hdRam's Horn1011	Tired	13
12Nov04-1Aqu	hy 6f	:25 :504	1:162	2↑ Handicap 880	6 7 41½ 41½ 4¾ 41	Martin J	114 w	6.00	81-16	Atwood105½Ascension119hdMonet112½	Good try	11
9Nov04-1Aqu	hy 7f	:25 :493 1:15	1:28	2↑ Handicap 785	3 2 23 33½ 42 3½	Martin J	122 w	2.20	90-12	Bank105hdMonet118½Roseben1222	Bumped	5
4Nov04-3Aqu	fst 6f	:25 :481	1:133	Handicap 775	3 1 1½ 11 1½ 1½	Martin J	123 w	1.20	96-03	Roseben123½Crown Prince1205Rob Roy112	Gamely	3
31Oct04-1Jam	fst 6f	:234 :472	1:13	Handicap 855	3 3 2hd 2hd 1hd 1no	O'Neill F	106 w	*1.00	98-04	Roseben106noCrown Prince1086Rapid Water126	Driving	3
24Oct04-3Jam	fst 6f	:24 :474	1:132	Handicap 885	6 1 11 11 1hd 2nk	O'Neill F	108 w	4.00	95-06	Crown Prince105nkRoseben108½Israelite1075	Gamely	6
Previously owned by J.A. Drake;previously trained by E. Wishard												

11Oct04- 1MP	sl	6½f	:242 :49 1:16 1:23	3↑ Md Alw 1050	14 4 14 14 14 13	O'Neill F	107 w	*1.20e	82-18	Roseben1073Water Pansy108¾Tide1071½	Easily 14
21Sep04- 1Gra	gd	*6f	:241 :483 1:013 1:113	2↑ Handicap 1185	10 12 88¼ 86¾ 88½ 89¼	Sperling	98 w	100.00	76-16	Invincible98½Divination982½Shot Gun125nk	Away badly 14
7Jly04- 2Bri	my	6f	:24 :482 1:144	Alw 1090	4 5 42 48 410 416½	Sperling	98 w	*2.20e	69-19	Mineola1061½Jocund1085EtTuBrute10810	Showed brief speed 5
28Apr03- 4Nvl	fst	4½f	:23¼ :48¾ :56	©Alw 300	- 11 10 10 10	Meade T	107	8.00e	--	Council1038EmperorofIndia1051Paris107hd	Never a factor 11

Sarazen

ch. g. 1921, by High Time (Ultimus)–Rush Box, by Box

Own.– Fair Stable

Br.– M.E. Johnston (Ky)

Tr.– A.B. Gordon

Lifetime record: 55 27 2 6 $225,000

9Jun28- 4Bel	fst	1	:24 :474 1:13 1:394	3↑ Alw 1265	2 2 31¼ 42½ 33¼ 33	Pasc'ma A	126 w	*1.60	75-23	Ingrid1122Knapsack1121Sarazen126hd	Impeded,sulked 4
30May28- 3Bel	fst	7f	:23 :463 1:12 1:253	3↑ Handicap 2115	3 6 64¼ 53¾ 53¾ 31¾	Fields G	120 w	15.00	80-21	BlackCurl113nkBuddyBauer1111½Sarazen120nk	Finished well 10
26May28- 4Bel	sly	1	:23 :47 1:133 1:40	3↑ Metropolitan H 10k	4 7 722 713 613 616	Fields G	124 w	20.00	61-25	Nimba1141½ChanceShot1184ScapFlow1251½	Refused to extend 7
21May28- 4Bel	hy	6f	:231 :48 1:144	3↑ Handicap 1375	4 6 1115 106¼ 85¾ 45¾	Fator L	126 w	8.00	72-28	IndianLovCll107¾Byrd1144GnrlDskn1011	Dropped back start 13
	Previously trained by M. Hirsch										
17May28- 4Bel	fst	6f-WC	1:112	3↑ Toboggan H 10k	8 3 52¼ 62½ 64½ 79¼	Pasc'ma A	126 w	15.00	85-07	Osmand124nkScapa Flow1241½Happy Argo125hd	No factor 9
1Aug27- 4Sar	hy	7f	:233 :472 1:133 1:262	3↑ Handicap 1365	4 7 64¼ 53 54 413½	O'Donell S	127 w	4.00	72-21	Pompey1186Brown Bud1021½Byrd1006	Sulked late 7
4Jly27- 4Aqu	fst	7f	:23 :461 1:112 1:241	3↑ Carter H 10k	2 5 62¼ 74½ 118 97½	O'Donell S	129 w	7.00e	86-10	Happy Argo119nkBlack Maria1243Macaw124hd	No factor 14
2May27- 4Pim	fst	1 3/16	:473 1:132 1:39 1:592	3↑ Dixie H 34k	6 9 114 158 1516 1425¼	O'Donell S	127 w	12.35	70-17	Mars124½Display120½Edisto1132	Never a factor 15
27Apr27- 4Jam	gd	6f	:232 :472 1:13	3↑ Handicap 1320	8 6 41¼ 2hd 21½ 32¼	O'Donell S	130 w	2.20	88-16	Cntnkrous107nkCelidon1172Srzn130hd	Fractious before start 8
20Nov26- 5Bow	hy	1	:242 :492 1:152 1:43	2↑ G D Bryan Mem H 26k	5 8 85½ 89 86½ 86	O'Donell S	126 w	*2.60	81-16	Glister104nkBackbone114½Willie K.94hd	Impeded 15
2Nov26- 4Pim	fst	6f	:23 :464 1:122	2↑ Fall Serial WFA #1 3.9k	3 2 41 41¾ 45 47¾	O'Donell S	130 w	3.05	84-16	Croyden1271½Prince of Wales1271¼Nedana1275	Sulked 6
16Oct26- 5Lrl	fst	1	:23 :472 1:123 1:38	2↑ Laurel 14k	10 5 2½ 21 21½ 22	O'Donell S	126 w	9.10	96-11	Croyden107.52Sarazen126hdMars1171	Second best 11
2Oct26- 4Jam	fst	1 1/16	:24 :481 1:13 1:44	3↑ Continental H 6.4k	1 3 42 43 34¼ 37	O'Donell S	128 w	*1.70	86-11	Catalan1154High Star1063Sarazen1281½	Ran well 7
25Sep26- 5HdG	fst	1⅛	:473 1:122 1:38 1:50	3↑ Havre de Grace H 17k	3 2 21½ 21 21 45¼	O'Donell S	127 w	5.35	95-06	Crusader1225Son of John108hdDisplay114nk	Tired late 12
4Aug26- 4Sar	sl	1	:24 :473 1:13 1:40	3↑ Delaware H 5.6k	8 3 2½ 21½ 4¾ 97½	O'Donell S	130 w	4.00	73-21	Single Foot115noDress Parade1163Rock Man108hd	9
	Impeded,quit,not persevered with										
30Jly26- 4Sar	my	1¼	:49 1:141 1:402 2:082	3↑ Saratoga H 10k	3 3 25 38 511 514	Weiner F	129 w	3.20	53-24	PrincssDoreen1164Blondin1083KingSolomon'sSeal1093	Tired 8
10Jly26- 4Emp	fst	1 70	:241 :481 1:13 1:424	3↑ Mount Vernon H 6.4k	5 3 42½ 31½ 1nk 11½	Weiner F	128 w	*2.20	99-06	Sarazen1281½Senalado112½Single Foot1121½	Going away 6
5Jly26- 4Aqu	fst	7f	:231 :464 1:112 1:243	3↑ Carter H 10k	2 7 69 67¼ 67½ 66¾	Weiner F	132 w	4.00	85-15	DH Macaw123 DH Nedana1191½Extra Dry99.54	Dwelt 7
14Jun26- 4Aqu	fst	1⅛	:463 1:122 1:382 1:502	3↑ Brooklyn H 14k	1 1 11 11½ 1nk 66	Weiner F	130 w	5.00	87-10	Single Foot110noPeanuts1114Dangerous108hd	Tired 10
31May26- 4Bel	gd	1	:232 :463 1:124 1:38	3↑ Metropolitan H 10k	1 2 21½ 2nk 1nk 11	Weiner F	129 w	4.00	87-19	Sarazen1291Senalado115½Rock Star1052	Held on 10
3May26- 5Pim	fst	1 3/16	:474 1:132 1:383 2:004	3↑ Dixie H 32k	3 1 11 11 12 1nk	Weiner F	128 w	*1.80e	88-14	Sarazen128nkSun Pal1051General Thatcher118nk	Ridden out 11
28Apr26- 4HdG	fst	6f	:23 :463 1:122	3↑ Handicap 1500	2 6 57¾ 58¼ 55¼ 55	Weiner F	130 w	*.80	88-12	Sun Pal982Postillion94noTamarind92no	Worked extra ¼ 6
20Apr26- 5HdG	fst	1 70	:242 :492 1:133 1:444	3↑ Handicap 2000	2 2 21 2½ 1nk 1hd	Weiner F	128 w	*.90	86-17	Sarazen128hdJoy Smoke1182½Edisto111.56	Ridden out 4
21Nov25- 4Bow	fst	1	:24 :482 1:133 1:402	2↑ G D Bryan Mem H 18k	14 3 32½ 2nk 1½ 11	Weiner F	126 w	*3.35	103-05	Sarazen1261JoySmoke1151½PrincessDoreen117nk	Going away 15
10Nov25- 4Pim	fst	6f	:23 :472 1:13	3↑ Handicap 1500	4 5 89 84¾ 62¼ 41½	Weiner F	129 w	*.85	87-17	Bigheart103nkWorthmore132nkLuckyPlay1221	9
	Finished fastest of all										
6Oct25- 5Lrl	fst	6f	:231 :47 1:12	3↑ Capital H 6.6k	1 4 67 68½ 58¼ 35	Sande E	132 w	*1.05	92-12	WisCounsllor130hdSnglFoot1125Srzn1324	Fractious at post 7
28Sep25- 4Aqu	fst	6f	:24 :47 1:113	3↑ Arverne H 4.2k	2 2 11 12 13 11½	Sande E	130 w	*2.00	96-11	Sarzn1301½ExtraDry98½AnnaMarroneII114no	Never threatened 5
5Aug25- 4Sar	sl	1	:241 :48 1:124 1:384	3↑ Delaware H 4.3k	4 2 2nk 2nk 43¾ 723½	Sande E	130wb	*2.50	63-17	Blind Play106.52Mad Play1332Big Blaze1175	Tired,eased 8
30Jly25- 4Emp	fst	*6f	:214 :463 :591 1:082	3↑ Fleetwing H 5.1k	1 1 2hd 13 13 1½	Sande E	130wb	*1.40	97-18	Sarazen130½Lucky Play1154Worthmore126½	6
	Fractious,unseated rider before start,ridden out										
2Jly25- 4Aqu	fst	7f	:223 :462 1:11 1:242	3↑ Carter H 9.6k	1 5 54¾ 53¼ 56 56	Sande E	132 w	*.75	87-12	SilvrFox1141Worthmor1282CndyKd105.5no	Refused to extend 5
22May25- 4Bel	fst	1	:222 :453 1:102 1:37	3↑ Metropolitan H 10k	1 7 74¾ 64¼ 78¾ 713½	Sande E	128 w	*1.00	78-10	Sting1142Shuffle Along1124Serenader106hd	In close early 8
1May25- 5Pim	sl	1 3/16	:482 1:133 1:403 2:02	3↑ Dixie H 33k	6 1 1½ 11 12 11¼	Sande E	130 w	*1.25	82-24	Sarazen1301¼Spot Cash115½Joy Smoke1043	Easily 14
21Apr25- 5HdG	fst	6f	:223 :46 1:11	3↑ Handicap 2000	1 5 42 2hd 11 11½	Sande E	129 w	*.65	101-09	Sarazn1291½BigBlaze115¾ThVintner1098	Under light restraint 6
1Nov24- 5Lrl	fst	1¼	:462 1:114 1:381 2:041	3↑ Washington H 31k	9 3 32½ 31 3¾ 51½	Babin G	126 w	*1.10	87-14	BigBlaze1061¼AgaKhan106noRustic107hd	Pressed pace,tired 10
25Oct24- 5Lrl	fst	1¼	:45 1:102 1:364 2:022	Maryland H 12k	4 2 23 21 21 1hd	Babin G	126 w	*.60	98-11	Sarazen126hdRustic1071½Aga Khan1083½	Tiring,held on 6
11Oct24- 5Lat	fst	1¼	:451 1:102 1:354 2:004	3↑ Int'l Spl #3 65k	3 2 2nk 11 11 11½	Babin G	120 w	5.70	108-07	Sarazen1201½Epinard126noMad Play120no	Easily 8
24Sep24- 4Aqu	fst	6f	:232 :464 1:112	3↑ Arverne H 4.5k	5 4 31¾ 21 2½ 11	Babin G	128 w	*.60	97-11	Sarazen1281Zev130noMiss Star1144	Speed in reserve 5
12Sep24- 4Bel	fst	6f	:23 :46 1:113	2↑ Fall Highweight H 5.4k	12 9 96¾ 64¼ 43¼ 3½	Maiben J	135 w	*1.20	93-12	Worthmore126½ShuffleAlong125hdSarazen1353	Slow to start 12
1Sep24- 5Bel	fst	1	:23 :47 1:113 1:362	2↑ Manhattan H 4.4k	1 2 21 21½ 11½ 11	Maiben J	122 w	*.45	94-11	Sarazen1221Cherry Pie1085Mad Play116	Won easing up 3
26Aug24- 4Sar	my	1 3/16	:50 1:163 1:44 2:024	Huron H 4.9k	5 1 11 11 11 11½	Maiben J	126 w	*2.20	64-32	Sarazen1261½Aga Khan1122Big Blaze1154	Easily 5
9Aug24- 4Sar	gd	1	:234 :47 1:121 1:373	Saranac H 9.7k	6 4 31 21 3½ 1½	Maiben J	120 w	*1.40	93-17	Sarazen120½Klondyke1141½Wise Counsellor1222	Away slowly 7
30Jly24- 4Emp	fst	*6f	:221 :461 :591 1:082	3↑ Fleetwing H 5.4k	2 3 32 11½ 13 13	Maiben J	126 w	*.45	97-07	Sarazen1263H.T. Waters110hdMiss Star11810	Won easing up 4
12Jly24- 4Emp	fst	1	:24 :473 1:132 1:38	3↑ Mt. Vernon H 8.1k	4 4 11½ 1½ 2½ 68½	McAtee L	120 w	*1.20	92-10	Ordinance112.5¾Sunsini1022Mad Play1152	Eased in stretch 7
4Jly24- 4Aqu	fst	7f	:23 :463 1:11 1:233	3↑ Carter H 8.4k	6 6 11½ 11½ 12 12½	Sande E	118 w	*1.60	97-12	Sarazen1182½Brainstorm112½Ordinance1153	Won eased up 7
2May24- 4Jam	fst	6f	:233 :463 1:12	3↑ Handicap 1335	5 1 31½ 31½ 31½ 21¼	Kummer C	115 w	*.33	95-06	Bracadale1071¼Sarazen115½Brainstorm1084	Slow gain 8
5Nov23- 5Pim	gd	1	:24 :482 1:132 1:40	2↑ Fall Serial #2 3.5k	2 1 11½ 12 13 11½	Callahan J	100 w	*.15	90-13	Sarazen1001½GeneralThatcher1206Blazes126	Never extended 3
26Oct23- 5Lrl	gd	6f	:233 :48 1:14	Lrl Spl 15k	2 1 14 15 16 12	Sande E	118 w	*.30	88-22	Sarazen1182Happy Thoughts115	Won eased up 2
6Oct23- 5Lrl	fst	6f	:23 :474 1:122	National 7.3k	3 2 21½ 2½ 12 11½	Kummer C	122 w	*.10	96-10	Sarazen1221½Moon Star112nkAga Khan1084	Easily 5
2Oct23- 6Lrl	fst	1	:24 :481 1:133 1:383	2↑ Alw 2000	1 1 12 12 13 12	Callahan J	91 w	*.35	95-10	Sarazen912Flagstaff1094Bigheart115hd	As rider pleased 4
20Sep23- 4Aqu	fst	6f	:232 :463 1:12	Oakdale H 5.2k	3 1 11½ 12 12 12	Kummer C	127 w	*.35	95-12	Sarazen1272Sun Pal1083½Elvina113¾	Easily 5
12Sep23- 4Bel	fst	7f	:23 :461 1:103 1:243	Champagne 6.8k	3 1 11 12 15 12	Sande E	112 w	*.30	87-11	Sarazen1122Aga Khan107hdSunspero1191½	Under restraint 9
7Sep23- 3Bel	fst	5½f	:23 :454 :59 1:05	Alw 1000	3 1 12 13 15 14½	Sande E	118 w	*.33	97-06	Sarazen1184½McAuliffe1081½Bonaparte118hd	Under restraint 11
	Previously owned by P.T. Chinn; previously trained by C.E. Patterson										
28Aug23- 6Sar	my	5½f	:244 :472 1:054	Alw 1000	6 1 11½ 11½ 13 14	Garner M	115 w	*.90	94-13	Sarazen1154H.T. Waters1154Bob Tail115hd	Never extended 6
19Jly23- 1Haw	fst	5f	:23 :462 :591	Alw 700	2 1 11½ 14 15 18	Garner M	108 w	*1.20e	101-04	Sarazen1088Sanola1131Time Exposure1032	As rider pleased 6
7Jly23- 1Haw	hy	5f	:25 :502 1:052	Md Sp Wt	6 5 3¾ 11½ 12 12½	Martinez P	115 w	*1.40	70-31	Sarazen1152½Brandeis1151½No Lady1152	Under restraint 7

Sir Barton

ch. c. 1916, by Star Shoot (Isinglass)–Lady Sterling, by Hanover — **Lifetime record: 31 13 6 5 $116,857**

Own.– J.K.L. Ross
Br.– Madden & Gooch (Ky)
Tr.– H.G. Bedwell

10Nov20- 4Pim	fst 1⅛	:473 1:122 1:382 1:513	2↑ Fall Serial #3 4.2k	3	1	47½	35	31¼	21½	Keogh F	126 w	1.65e	95-10	Billy Kelly1261½Sir Barton126noMad Hatter1265		5
Led early,good finish																
5Nov20- 4Pim	fst 1	:234 :473 1:12 1:38	2↑ Fall Serial #2 3.6k	1	1	2nk	24	33½	31¼	Keogh F	126wb	*.45e	104-04	Mad Hatter1261Billy Kelly126nkSir Barton1265		4
Led early,fast finish																
23Oct20- 3Lrl	fst 1	:233 :474 1:14 1:40	2↑ Laurel 11k	5	2	2½	33	31½	32	O'Brien WJ	125wb	*.85	86-18	Blazes1201ThePorter1251SirBarton125no	Forced early pace	6
12Oct20- 4Knw	fst 1¼	:462 1:114 1:372 2:03	3↑ Ken Park Gold Cup 75k	1	2	22	25	26	27	Keogh F	126wb	5.55	125-03	Man o' War1207Sir Barton126	Unable to gain	2
28Aug20- 4Sar	fst 1 3/16	:472 1:123 1:362 1:553	3↑ Merchants & Cits H 6.7k	2	1	1¾	11	1hd	1no	Sande E	133wb	*.80	102-03	Sir Barton133noGnome1153Jack Stuart109	Saved ground	3
11Aug20- 5FE	sl 1¼	:473 1:122 1:383 2:06	3↑ Dominion H 11k	3	1	1hd	11	12	11½	Sande E	134wb	*.25	84-18	Sir Barton1341½Bondage1173The Porter1244	Mild hand ride	4
2Aug20- 4Sar	fst 1¼	:474 1:11 1:36 2:014	3↑ Saratoga H 6.7k	2	1	1hd	11½	12½	12	Sande E	129wb	2.60	102-06	SirBarton1292Extrmntor1263Wldr1153	Drew clear,easing up	5
4May20- 5Pim	fst 1	:243 :492 1:143 1:404	4↑ Rennert H 2.5k	2	2	2nk	2hd	1½	11	Sande E	132wb	*.60	91-15	Sir Barton1321Foreground1135Bondage103.56	All out	5
30Apr20- 4HdG	fst 1 1/16	:234 :48 1:122 1:452	3↑ Philadelphia H 5.4k	9	3	42	42½	43¼	41½	Kummer C	132wb	*.55e	96-13	CrystlFord100nkStrMstr127nkBllyKlly1261	Finished gamely	10
27Apr20- 5HdG	my 1 1/16	:25 :501 1:153 1:49	3↑ Marathon H 2k	3	2	23	24	33	34	Sande E	135wb	*.30	76-26	Wildair110noBolster1064Sir Barton135	Wide,tired	3
24Apr20- 3HdG	fst 6f	:231 :474 1:131	3↑ Handicap 1845	2	4	11	12½	11	11½	Kummer C	133wb	*.65e	90-11	SirBarton1331½Mlkmd1222Tcklsh1023	Slight restraint late	7
19Apr20- 5HdG	gd 6f	:234 :472 1:133	3↑ Belair H 2.7k	4	1	2½	2nk	3nk	42½	Kummer C	133wb	*.25e	85-21	Billy Kelly1321¼War Mask107nkTicklish1031	Speed,tired	6
11Nov19- 4Pim	sly 1⅛	:493 1:143 1:42 1:563	2↑ Fall Serial #3 4k	3	2	1½	12	13	13	Kummer C	120wb	*.30e	72-28	Sir Barton1203Billy Kelly1204Lucullite126	Easily	3
7Nov19- 4Pim	fst 1	:24 :482 1:142 1:40	2↑ Fall Serial #2 3.1k	2	1	1nk	2hd	1½	12	Kummer C	120wb	2.60e	95-15	SirBarton1202ThePorter1265BillyKelly120nk	Won easing up	4
5Nov19- 4Pim	sl 1¼	:503 1:154 1:424 2:091	Autumn H 5.4k	5	4	43½	31¼	36	312	Loftus J	132wb	*.45e	69-26	Mad Hatter1114Bridesman1078Sir Barton13212	Tired,eased	5
4Oct19- 4Lrl	fst 1¼	:463 1:12 1:373 2:022	Maryland H 11k	6	4	51¾	31	2½	12	Loftus J	133wb	*1.25	98-08	SrBrtn1332MdHttr1061½Audcous118½	Forced wide,going away	6
27Sep19- 5HdG	fst 1⅛	:471 1:122 1:373 1:50	3↑ Havre de Grace H 10k	8	1	13	1½	2½	3½	Metcalf J	124wb	*.75e	105-05	Cudgel129½Exterminator126noSirBrton1242	Held resolutely	8
24Sep19- 4HdG	hy 1	:242 :49 1:151 1:422	3↑ Alw 2708	3	2	2hd	24	23	25	Sande E	110wb	*.60	- -	ThePorter1145SirBarton1103WarMask1008	Gamely,no match	5
13Sep19- 5HdG	gd 1 1/16	:242 :492 1:15 1:462	Potomac H 10k	5	1	11	13	11	11½	Nolan T	132wb	*.15e	93-10	SirBarton1321½BillyKelly125hdMlkmd117nk	Outran the rest	5
11Sep19- 3HdG	my 6f	:233 :482 1:14	3↑ Alw 1115	1	5	12	11	2nk	21	Troxler R	120wb	*.10e	87-25	Billy Kelly1201Sir Barton120hdMidnight Sun1052	Tired	7
10Jly19- 4Aqu	sly 1⅛	:481 1:132 1:39 1:523	Dwyer 5.8k	3	1	11½	11	1½	23	Loftus J	127wb	*.80	81-21	Purchase1183Sir Barton12715Crystal Ford109	Tired	3
11Jun19- 4Bel	fst 1⅜	2:172	Belmont 14k	1	2	23	21	13	15	Loftus J	126wb	*.35	102-05	Sir Barton1265Sweep On1268Natural Bridge126		3
Fast start, eased up late																
24May19- 4Bel	gd 1	:24 :48 1:13 1:384	Withers 9k	2	1	21½	22	11	12½	Loftus J	118wb	*.35	89-12	SirBrtn1182½Etrnl1188PstorlSwn118½	Rated,eased up late	6
14May19- 4Pim	fst 1⅛	:471 1:13 1:391 1:53	Preakness 30k	8	1	11	12	16	14	Loftus J	126wb	*1.40e	90-11	Sir Barton1264Eternal1263Sweep On1262	eased up at finish	12
10May19- 5CD	hy 1¼	:482 1:14 1:414 2:094	Ky Derby 24k	1	1	1½	12	1½	15	Loftus J	112wb	2.60e	68-28	SirBarton112.55BillyKelly1191UnderFire1221	Rated,easily	12
14Sep18- 3Bel	fst 6f-Str	1:124	Futurity 29k	13	6	47½	31	21½	22½	Sande E	117wb	15.00	76-19	Dunboyne1272½Sir Barton117½Purchase1192	Held second	15
31Aug18- 3Sar	hy 6f	:232 :481 1:133	Hopeful 35k	6	13	15	17	17	16	Sande E	115 w	12.00	- -	Eternal1153Daydue1158War Marvel115hd	Never a factor	20
Beaten lengths unavailable;Previously owned by J.E. Madden;previously trained by W.S. Walker																
14Aug18- 4Sar	sly 6f	:232 :484 1:143	Sanford Mem 4.9k	7	7	711	710	710	719	Collins A	112wb	25.00	63-25	BillyKelly1308Liond'Or1155ColonelLvngston1222	No factor	8
3Aug18- 3Sar	fst 6f	:23 :471 1:122	U S Hotel 11k	11	13	1111	98½	108¾	916	Collins A	112 w	25.00	77-02	Billy Kelly1271½Dunboyne1301½Terentia1241½	No factor	14
1Aug18- 3Sar	fst 5½f	:222 :464 :583 1:053	Flash 5.1k	9	11	1019	1116	118½	915½	Collins A	107 w	8.00	84-02	BillyKelly1195LadyRosebud113½StarRealm1101½	Slow start	15
6Jly18- 3Aqu	fst 6f	:233 :473 1:124	Tremont 6.8k	7	8	74½	76	77	56	Collins A	112 w	8.00	85-10	Lord Brighton1251Sweep On1153War Pennant1121	Greenly	9

Sweep

br. c. 1907, by Ben Brush (Bramble)–Pink Domino, by Domino — **Lifetime record: 13 9 2 2 $63,948**

Own.– J.R. Keene
Br.– James R. Keene (Ky)
Tr.– J. Rowe

4Jly10- 4She	fst 1⅝	:501 1:47 2:27 2:53	Lawrence Realization	3	1	110	115	12	15	Notter	126 w	*.01e	60-18	Sweep1265Suffragist1165Hindoo Star116	eased up	3
14Jun10- 4Gra	gd 1¼	:461 1:14 1:402 2:07	Brooklyn Derby 3k	4	2	21½	41½	33½	34	Powers V	126 w	*.70	78-12	Dalmatian1221PrinceImperial1223Swep126hd	Failed to stay	4
8Jun10- 4Gra	fst 1	:242 :483 1:134 1:391	Carlton 2.5k	6	1	12	11½	12	1¾	Powers V	126 w	*.90	98-10	Sweep126¾ThTurk1265Dlmtn1224	Easily withstood challenge	6
30May10- 4Bel	fst 1⅜	:51 1:16 1:41 2:22	Belmont	1	1	14	15	15	16	Butwell	126 w	*.10	90-10	Sweep1266Duke of Ormonde126	Never extended	2
14May10- 2Bel	fst 7f	:241 :483 1:132 1:261	Alw	4	2	21	21½	1½	12	Butwell	121 w	*.17	79-23	Sweep1212KngOlympn1162Sndrian11510	Carried out in stretch	5
30Aug09- 4She	fst 6f-FC	1:114	Futurity	12	2	32½	31	11½	16	Butwell	126 w	*.90e	94-08	Sweep1266Candleberry117½Grasmere1221½		13
Impeded,drew off when clear																
14Aug09- 3Sar	fst 6f	:233 :472 1:131	Hopeful	9	5	53¼	42½	31	21½	Butwell	130 w	*1.30e	91-08	RockyO'Brn1221½Sweep130¾Barleythpe115½	Slow start	9
12Aug09- 1Sar	fst 6f	:233 :472 1:124	Handicap	7	5	2½	1½	11	1hd	Butwell	120 w	*1.50	95-07	Sweep120hdLouiseS.1072Fauntleroy109¾	Away badly,impeded	12
7Aug09- 3Sar	gd 6f	:25 :49 1:154	Sar Spl	1	3	33½	34	32	23	Scoville	122 w	*.90	77-21	Waldo1223Sweep122hdHerkmr122	Slow start,just up for 2nd	3
3Jly09- 3She	fst 6f-FC	1:132	Great Trial 2.5k	3	1	1hd	2½	32	36	Scoville	130 w	*.45	80-14	Dalmatian122hdLovetie1226Sweep1302	Set pace,tired	6
31May09- 3Bel	fst 5½f-Str	1:081	Natl Stallion	5	2	12	13	15	18	Burns G	122 w	*.90	79-21	Sweep1228Newmarket122½Big Stick122½	Won easing up	5
29May09- 1Bel	gd 5f-Str	1:012	Alw	1	1	11	12	14	15	Scoville	119 w	*.33	83-20	Sweep1195Medallion1221Perry Johnson1142	Never extended	9
20May09- 1Bel	fst 5f-Str	:584	©Md Sp Wt	5	5	1½	1hd	12	18	Butwell	110 w	*1.10	96-08	Sweep1108Beau Nash1104Firebox111hd	Easily	7

Sysonby

b. c. 1902, by Melton (Master Kildaire)–Optime, by Orme — **Lifetime record: 15 14 0 1 $184,438**

Own.– J.R. Keene
Br.– Marcus Daly (Ky)
Tr.– J. Rowe

9Sep05- 4She	fst 2¼	:491 2:341 2:594 3:54	3↑ Annual Champion 25k	3	1	12	12	14	14	Nicol	115 w	*.17	98-08	Sysonby1154Oiseau10825Broomstick119	With ease	3
2Sep05- 4She	gd 1½	:51 1:183 2:092 2:35	3↑ Century 20k	1	1	12	13	13	12	Nicol	115 w	*.05	81-12	Sysnby1152Broomstick1261½EurgeniaBurch123no	Very easily	4
12Aug05- 4Sar	gd 1¼	:482 1:132 1:394 2:07	3↑ Great Republic 50k	5	2	1½	13	15	13	Nicol	119 w	*.45	90-12	Sysonby1193Oiseau1161Broomstick12620	Away slowly	5
29Jly05- 4Bri	fst 1½	:493 1:154 2:063 2:331	Brighton Derby 15k	3	1	11½	13	13	15	Nicol	126 w	*.25	95-06	Sysonby1265Agile12630Pasadena118	Easing up	3
20Jly05- 4Bri	fst 1¼	:491 1:15 1:411 2:062	Iroquois 7.5k	1	1	11½	11½	13	11½	Martin J	126 w	*.03	82-08	Sysonby1261½Migraine11615Pasadena119	Easily	3
4Jly05- 4She	fst 1⅝	:474 1:394 2:06 2:47	Lawrence Realizatn 20k	4	1	12	12½	15	15	Nicol	126 w	*.40	91-06	Sysonby1265Tanya1213Migraine1166	Easing up	4
1Jly05- 4She	sl 1¼	:49 1:141 1:40 2:07	3↑ Commonwealth H 15k	1	1	12	12	13	14	Nicol	111 w	*1.00	88-08	Sysonby1114Proper1143Mabel Richardson958	Kicked at post	6
17Jun05- 4She	fst 1¼	:483 1:133 1:392 2:05	Tidal 20k	3	1	14	14	13	15	Nicol	126 w	*.90	98-08	Sysonby1265Agile1264Cairngorm12612	Easily	4
4May05- 4Bel	fst 1	:253 :49 1:413	3↑ Metropolitan H 12k	12	1	11½	11½	11½	15	Shaw	107 w	*2.00	- -	[DH]Sysonby107[DH]RaceKing975ColonialGirl1114	Hand ridden	12
19Sep04- 3Gra	fst *6f	:231 :48 1:093	Jr Champion 10k	3	2	14	11	15	13	Redfern	127 w	*.33e	95-06	Sysonby1273Wild Mint1171Cairngorm110hd	Easing up	5
27Aug04- 4She	fst 6f-FC	1:114	Futurity 48k	16	8	12	1hd	21½	35	Redfern	127 w	*.65e	76-17	Artful1145Tradition127hdSysonby1273		16
Broke sideways,slow into stride																
6Aug04- 3Sar	fst 5½f	:223 :471 1:00 1:07	Sar Spl 10k	1	2	13	15	15	16	Redfern	122 w	*.05	95-06	Sysonby1226Hot Shot1224Britisher122	Easily	3
1Aug04- 3Sar	fst 5½f	:233 :474 1:001 1:064	Flash 6k	4	1	13	15	15	16	Redfern	125 w	*.40e	96-05	Sysonby1256Augur1192Glorifier1255	Easing up	4
16Jly04- 4Bri	fst 6f	:24 :481 1:13	Brighton Junior 15k	4	7	2hd	11½	13	14	Martin J	112 w	*.80e	95-03	Sysnby1124Jonquil107½Britisher1123	Away last,under a pull	7
14Jly04- 6Bri	fst 5½f	:232 :48 1:004 1:074	Md Sp Wt	6	1	11½	12	13	16	Martin J	107 w	*.60	94-12	Sysonby1076Linda Lee104noGotowin1041½	Under restraint	11

Whisk Broom II

ch. c. 1907, by Broomstick (Ben Brush)–Audience, by Sir Dixon — **Lifetime record: 26 10 7 1 $38,545**

Own.– H.P. Whitney
Br.– Clarence H. Mackay (Ky)
Tr.– James Rowe

28Jun13- 4Bel	fst 1¼	:471 1:12 1:364 2:00	3↑ Suburban H 3.5k	4 2 23 1hd 1nk	1½	Notter	139 w	*.40	121-00	Whisk Broom II139½Lahore1125Meridian1193	Fully extended	6
21Jun13- 4Bel	fst 1¼	:482 1:131 1:39 2:032	3↑ Brooklyn H 3.6k	6 1 11½ 1½ 12	11½	Notter	130 w	*.50	104-06	Whisk Broom II1301½G.M. Miller1061½Sam Jackson108½		7
	Loafed in stretch											
30May13- 4Bel	fst 1	1:39	3↑ Metropolitan H 4k	1 11 10 45½ 12	11½	Notter	126	*1.60	92-08	Whisk Broom II1261½G.M. Miller1003Meridian120½		12
	Previously trained by Andrew Jackson Joyner											
30Oct12♦ Newmarket(GB)	gd 1⅛ⓉStr	1:554	3↑ Cambridgeshire H Hcp5800		7	Maher D	130	33.00		Adam Bede110½La Boheme II1071Drinmore100		20
16Oct12♦ Newmarket(GB)	gd 1ⓉStr	1:402	3↑ Select Stakes Stk1340		2no	Maher D	132	*.65		Long Set132noWhisk Broom II1326The Story132		4
3Oct12♦ Newmarket(GB)	gd 5fⓉStr		2↑ Snailwell Stakes Alw800		1	Maher D	138	-		Whisk Broom II138	Walkover.Time not taken	1
19Jun12♦ Ascot(GB)	gd *7½fⓉStr	1:413	3↑ Royal Hunt Cup H Hcp10700		6	Maher D	133	10.00		Eton Boy1083Long Set1301½Matelot97		28
28May12♦ Hurst Park(GB)	gd 7fⓉStr		3↑ Victoria Cup H Hcp5200		11½	Maher D	128	*2.50		Whisk Broom II1281½Prince San1043Eton Boy111	Time not taken	14
11May12♦ Kempton(GB)	hd 1¼ⓉRH	2:054	3↑ Great Jubilee H Hcp12000		24	Maher D	125	7.50		Bachelor's Hope1004Whisk Broom II1256Mustapha121		12
8Sep11♦ Derby(GB)	gd 1ⓉStr		3↑ Peril of the Peak H Hcp4000		1nk	Martin JH	126	4.50		Whisk Broom II126nkSunspot1221½Mustapha122	Time not taken	12
14Jly11♦ Sandown(GB)	gd 1¼ⓉRH	2:09	3↑ Eclipse Stakes Stk40000		4	Martin JH	134	9.00		Swynford1404Lemberg1404Pietri125	Started slowly	7
28Jun11♦ Newmarket(GB)	gd 1ⓉStr	1:41	3↑ Duke of Cambridge H Hcp4000		2hd	Martin JH	126	7.00		Bannockburn103hdWhisk Broom II126½Sandal96		13
10Jun11♦ Manchester(GB)	gd 6fⓉStr	1:111	3↑ Salford Borough H Hcp4000		11½	Martin JH	123	14.25		Whisk Broom II1231½Great Surprise994Spinner86		8
29Apr11♦ Hurst Park(GB)	gd 7fⓉStr	1:302	3↑ Victoria Cup H Hcp5000		5	Martin JH	117	4.50		Spanish Prince1124Orphah1012Golden Rod119		9
26Oct10♦ Newmarket(GB)	gd 1⅛ⓉStr	1:562	3↑ Cambridgeshire H Hcp6300		4	Martin JH	110	*3.00		Christmas Daisy1141½Mustapha118¾Halcyon109		21
12Oct10♦ Newmarket(GB)	gd 1ⓉStr	1:41	3↑ Select Stakes Stk1300		14	Martin JH	124	*.25		Whisk Broom II1244Dean Swift131St Crispin109		3
21Jly10♦ Aintree(GB)	gd 1¼ⓉLH	2:073	Knowsley Dinner Stakes Stk4000		2hd	Martin JH	126	1.60		Willonyx122hdWhisk Broom II1261½Merry Task126		4
17Jun10♦ Ascot(GB)	gd 1½ⓉRH		3↑ Hardwicke Stakes Stk15200		6	Martin JH	117	*2.25		Swynford105¾Marajax1102Sanctuary112	Time not taken	7
14Jun10♦ Ascot(GB)	gd *7½fⓉStr	1:42	3↑ Trial Stakes Alw2500		12	Martin JH	106	*.30		Whisk Broom II1062Dean Swift1263Yellow Slave111		8
27Apr10♦ Newmarket(GB)	gd 1ⓉStr	1:402	2000 Guineas Stakes Stk27200		32	Martin JH	126	14.25		Neil Gow126noLemberg1262Whisk Broom II126		13
14Apr10♦ Newmarket(GB)	gd 1ⓉStr	1:44	Craven Stakes Stk2180		23	Martin JH	129	6.00		Neil Gow1323Whisk Broom II129nkTressady132		6
28Oct09♦ Newmarket(GB)	hy 7fⓉStr	1:314	Dewhurst Plate Stk6500		25	Martin JH	125	2.75		Lemberg1315Whisk Broom II125		2
15Oct09♦ Newmarket(GB)	gd 6fⓉStr	1:144	Middle Park Plate Stk13300		2nk	Martin JH	126	3.50		Lemberg129nkWhisk Broom II126¾Admiral Hawke129		8
7Sep09♦ Doncaster(GB)	sf *5½fⓉStr	1:094	Champagne Stakes Stk6920		4	Martin JH	126	7.00		Neil Gow1261½Admiral Hawke1261Lemberg126		4
24Aug09♦ York(GB)	sf 5fⓉStr	1:024	Prince of Wales Plate Alw4000		12	Martin JH	119	3.00		Whisk Broom II1192Galatine1242Woolacombe119		10
2Aug09♦ Sandown(GB)	gd 5fⓉStr	1:054	Holiday Stakes Alw1600		4	Martin JH	115	8.00		MountFelix116¾BlueBlazes1124Unnamed filly byCyllene123		7

Zev

br. c. 1920, by The Finn (Ogden)–Miss Kearney, by Planudes — **Lifetime record: 43 23 8 5 $313,639**

Own.– Rancocas Stable
Br.– J.E. Madden (Ky)
Tr.– S.C. Hildreth

8Nov24- 4Pim	fst 1	:23 :472 1:123 1:392	2↑ Fall Serial #2 4.3k	4 3 36½ 33 33¼	34	Fator L	126wb	*1.10	87-14	Sun Flag1203Master Charlie1001Zev126nk	Rated,tired	4
7Nov24- 3Pim	fst 6f	:222 :453 1:111	2↑ Alw 2000	3 5 52½ 41¼ 1½	4nk	Fator L	125wb	*.65	98-10	Swinging90noMainmast115nkShuffle Along125no	Wide,tired	6
4Nov24- 4Pim	fst 6f	:223 :462 1:12	2↑ Fall Serial #1 3.8k	4 1 23 21½ 2½	1½	Fator L	130wb	*.35	94-12	Zev130½Goshawk1304½Lucky Play127½	Drew away	4
18Oct24- 4Lat	fst 1	:233 :472 1:112 1:362	3↑ Handicap 1800	1 3 33 34½ 31¾	1nk	Fator L	129wb	*.55	101-08	Zv129nkPostllon981½PrncssDorn115	Appeared beaten,just up	3
13Oct24- 5Lat	fst 6f	:231 :454 1:101	3↑ Alw 1800	1 3 21 1nk 11	12	Fator L	117wb	*35	98-10	Zev1172Baffling1176Best Pal117no	Easily	4
11Oct24- 3Lat	fst 6f	:231 :462 1:104	3↑ Alw 1615	6 2 11½ 11 12	12	Fator L	110wb	1.30	95-07	Zev1102Pegasus115½AliceB.Gown1091½	Won under restraint	6
10Oct24- 5Lat	fst 6f	:23 :461 1:111	3↑ Alw 1660	6 3 1hd 1½ 11	11	Fator L	108wb	*.70	93-13	Zev1081SnooksieBradly101hdRightonTime1108	Finished well	7
4Oct24- 4Jam	fst 1⅛	:473 1:123 1:373 1:493	3↑ Continental H 7.1k	5 1 1hd 1hd 33½	34¼	Kummer C	127wb	*.60e	98-07	MadPlay1154PriscillRuly106nkZv127nk	Tired,came on again	6
1Oct24- 4Jam	sl 1 1/16	:242 :472 1:123 1:444	3↑ Interborough H 5.3k	1 1 1½ 1nk 11	22	Fator L	130wb	*1.00e	89-15	Big Blaze1082Zev130¾Stanwix1023	Wide,tired under impost	5
27Sep24- 4Aqu	fst 1	:23 :454 1:103 1:362	3↑ Int'l Spl #2 35k	4 3 45¼ 44½ 45¼	43½	Fator L	126 w	5.00	94-09	Ladkin119noEpinard1261½Wise Counsellor1192	Outrun	6
24Sep24- 4Aqu	fst 6f	:232 :464 1:112	3↑ Arverne H 4.5k	1 1 43¼ 43½ 43	21	Fator L	130 w	8.00	96-11	Sarazen1281Zev130noMiss Star1144	Finished fast	5
8Sep24- 3Bel	fst 6f	:23 :461 1:122	2↑ Handicap 1420	8 9 911 97¼ 913	913¾	Fator L	130wb	*.80e	76-15	ⒹShuffle Along1141¼Rival1121½Dinna Care1172		9
	Unprepared for start,left,not persevered with											
1Sep24- 4Bel	fst 6f	:23 :46 1:114	3↑ Int'l Spl #1 36k	8 6 42¾ 2nk 2hd	56¼	Fator L	130wb	4.00	87-11	WiseCounsellor125¾Epnrd1303Ladkin1251	Tired final furlong	9
14Jun24- 4Aqu	fst 1⅛	:471 1:123 1:373 1:504	3↑ Brooklyn H 9.9k	5 2 2½ 2½ 2½	73¾	Sande E	130wb	*1.80e	87-07	Hephaistos106½Sunsini1021ⒹDunlin111hd	Impeded,tired	12
10May24- 4Jam	sl 1 1/16	:24 :474 1:13 1:46	3↑ Excelsior H 7.3k	1 3 21½ 32½ 3¾	31	Fator L	133wb	*.50e	84-17	Rialto115hdSunsini1021Zev1333	Wide,tired	6
3May24- 4Jam	fst 1 1/16	:234 :48 1:123 1:44	3↑ Kings County H 6.7k	3 1 11 11 12	12	Sande E	130wb	*.17e	95-08	Zev1302Mad Play107½Sunsini10210	Easily	5
29Apr24- 4Jam	fst 6f	:23 :47 1:113	3↑ Paumonok H 5.8k	1 1 21 22 22	23	Sande E	130wb	*.45e	95-07	St. James1123Zev1302½Dunlin1196	Close quarters early	8
17Nov23- 6CD	fst 1¼	:50 1:152 1:411 2:063	©Match Race 30k	2 2 21½ 21 11½	1no	Sande E	126wb	*.40	83-13	Zev126noIn Memoriam126	Lasted	2
8Nov23- 3Pim	gd 1⅛	:492 1:15 1:404 1:533	2↑ Fall Serial #3 3.9k	3 2 2nk 12 12	13	Sande E	120wb	*.15	87-15	Zev1203Homestretch12010Tryster126	Easily	3
3Nov23- 5Lat	fst 1¾	:491 2:081 2:344 3:004	Lat Championship 61k	2 1 11½ 12 21½	26	Sande E	126wb	*.40	68-18	In Memoriam1266Zev12610My Own126	Tired final ½	4

31Oct23-4Emp	sl	1	:24^3	:47^3	1:13^2	1:40^3	2↑	Aut Championship 11k	3	2	3^1	1^1	1^2	1^4	Sande E	120wb	*.07e	88-11	Zev120^{4}Bracadale101.5^{15}Tryster126	Speed in reserve	4
20Oct23-4Bel	sly	1½	:50^2	1:15	2:07^3	2:35^2		International Race 105k	1	1	1^1	1$^{1\frac{1}{2}}$	1^3	1^5	Sande E	126wb	*.80	67-19	Zev126^{5}Papyrus126	Ridden out	2
8Sep23-4Bel	fst	1⅝	:47	1:37^2	2:03^2	2:44^3		Lawrence Realizatn 27k	3	2	2^2	2^2	1^2	1$^{2\frac{1}{2}}$	Sande E	126wb	*.33	81-12	Zev126$^{2\frac{1}{2}}$Untidy123$^{2\frac{1}{2}}$Rialto119^1	Won easing up	5
1Sep23-1Bel	fst	6f	:22^3	:46^1		1:11^1	3↑	Alw 1238	1	1	1^{hd}	1$^{\frac{1}{2}}$	1^2	1$^{2\frac{1}{2}}$	Sande E	125wb	*.17	97-06	Zev125$^{2\frac{1}{2}}$Bigheart112^{1}Runviso110$^{\frac{1}{2}}$	In a canter	4
23Jun23-4Aqu	fst	1	:22^2	:46	1:11	1:37	3↑	Queens County H 8.6k	7	1	1^1	1^1	1^2	1$^{3\frac{1}{2}}$	Sande E	117 w	*.65e	95-13	Zev117$^{3\frac{1}{2}}$Dunlin107^{2}Nedna103$^{\frac{3}{4}}$	Going away	8
9Jun23-4Bel	gd	1⅜	:47^2	1:12^4	1:38^1	2:19		Belmont 46k	2	1	1^2	1^5	1^4	1$^{1\frac{1}{2}}$	Sande E	126wb	*.80	76-17	Zev126$^{1\frac{1}{2}}$Chickvale126$^{3\frac{1}{2}}$Rialto126$^{1\frac{1}{2}}$	Tiring late	8
26May23-4Bel	fst	1	:23	:46^4	1:11	1:37^2		Withers 20k	5	1	1^1	1^2	1^3	1$^{\frac{1}{2}}$	Sande E	118wb	*.90	91-09	Zev118$^{\frac{1}{2}}$Martingale118$^{4\frac{1}{2}}$Barbary Bush118$^{2\frac{1}{2}}$		7
	Eased up,almost caught																				
19May23-5CD	fst	1¼	:47^2	1:12^2	1:39	2:05^2		Ky Derby 63k	10	1	1^2	1$^{\frac{1}{2}}$	1^2	1$^{1\frac{1}{2}}$	Sande E	126wb	19.20	89-11	Zev126$^{1\frac{1}{2}}$Martingale126^{1}Vigil126^1	Gamely	21
15May23-4Jam	gd	6f	:23^3	:46^4		1:12	3↑	Rainbow H 4.1k	7	3	1^2	1^2	1^2	1$^{\frac{1}{2}}$	Sande E	114wb	2.40e	96-11	Zev114$^{\frac{1}{2}}$Dominique125^{no}Rigel107^{no}	Best	8
12May23-4Pim	fst	1⅛	:47^4	1:13	1:39^4	1:53^3		Preakness 62k	6	3	4$^{2\frac{1}{4}}$	11^{18}	12^{29}	12$^{26\frac{1}{4}}$	Sande E	126wb	*4.35	61-12	Vigil114$^{1\frac{1}{4}}$General Thatcher114^{1}Rialto114^{hd}	Quit	13
	Geldings not eligible																				
2May23-4Jam	fst	6f	:23^1	:46^3		1:12	3↑	Paumonok H 5.8k	1	2	1$^{\frac{1}{2}}$	1^2	1$^{2\frac{1}{2}}$	1^{nk}	Fator L	109wb	*2.50	96-07	Zev109^{nk}Dominique123^{6}Galantman106.5^{no}		10
	Tired,hard hand ride																				
16Sep22-3Bel	fst	6f-Str				1:11		Futurity 55k	15	3			2$^{1\frac{1}{2}}$	2^3	Sande E	124 w	*5.00	85-12	Sally's Alley116^{3}Zev124$^{\frac{1}{2}}$Wilderness119^1	Tired	23
31Aug22-3Sar	gd	6f	:23^2	:47^2		1:12^2		Hopeful 43k	12	2	2^{hd}	1^1	1^1	3$^{1\frac{1}{4}}$	Sande E	130wb	5.00	89-18	Dunlin115$^{\frac{3}{4}}$Goshawk130$^{\frac{1}{2}}$Zev130^1	Saved ground,tired	12
28Aug22-4Sar	hy	6f	:23^4	:48^2		1:15^3		Albany H 4.9k	2	5	1$^{1\frac{1}{2}}$	1^2	1^3	1$^{2\frac{1}{2}}$	Sande E	126wb	*.60	74-31	Zev126$^{2\frac{1}{2}}$Vigil106^{5}Boys Believe Me110^4	Never threatened	6
19Aug22-3Sar	hy	6f	:23^4	:47^4		1:15		Grand Union Hotel 12k	3	4	1^1	1^4	1^2	1^2	Fator L	115wb	*2.20e	77-31	Zev115^{2}Dunlin115^{2}Bud Lerner127^2	Ridden out	10
15Aug22-6Sar	fst	5f	:23^1	:46^1		:59		Alw 1476	11	4	1^1	1^1	1^4	1$^{\frac{1}{2}}$	Sande E	125wb	*2.50e	94-11	Zev125$^{\frac{1}{2}}$Enchantment115^{2}Dunlin119^2	Ridden out	11
8Aug22-6Sar	hy	5f	:24	:49		1:03		Alw 1000	5	2	1^2	1^3	1^5	1^4	Fator L	115wb	*.60	74-34	Zev115^{4}Wilderness110^{3}Nassau115^8	Easily	5
5Aug22-6Sar	hy	5½f	:24	:48	1:02	1:08^2		Md Sp Wt	4	3	1^3	1^5	1^8	1^5	Sande E	115wb	*1.40	81-29	Zev115^{5}Doughoregan115^{6}Beatitude112$^{\frac{1}{2}}$	Won eased up	14
1Aug22-6Sar	fst	5f	:23^4	:46^3		:59^3		Md Sp Wt	17	7	2$^{2\frac{1}{2}}$	2$^{1\frac{1}{2}}$	2^1	2$^{3\frac{1}{2}}$	Sande E	115wb	*2.00	87-09	Comixa112$^{3\frac{1}{2}}$Zev115$^{2\frac{1}{2}}$Betty Beall112^2	Chased winner	20
21Jly22-6Emp	fst	5½f	:22^3	:46^4	:59^4	1:06		Alw 1058	2	1	1$^{2\frac{1}{2}}$	1^1	1^1	2$^{\frac{3}{4}}$	Fator L	104wb	1.80	98-09	Dunlin103$^{\frac{3}{4}}$Zev104^{4}William Tell103^{12}	Tired late	5
19Jun22-6Aqu	gd	5f				1:00		Md Sp Wt	3	10			2$^{1\frac{1}{2}}$	3^2	Sande E	115wb	*1.60e	87-12	Cyclops115^{2}General Thatcher115^{hd}Zev115$^{1\frac{1}{2}}$	Tired	18
17Jun22-3Aqu	fst	5f				:59^2		Hudson H 6.5k	2	6		3$^{2\frac{1}{2}}$	2$^{\frac{1}{2}}$	4$^{2\frac{3}{4}}$	Fator L	112 w	2.60e	89-14	Sunference114^{nk}Cherry Pie130^{2}Bud Lerner127$^{\frac{1}{2}}$	Tired	13
14Jun22-6Bel	fst	5f-Str				:57^4		Alw 1113	4	2		3^1	3^2	2no	Fator L	108wb	*.22e	89-16	Prince Regent108^{no}Zev108^{1}Whirlwind115^8	Just missed	6

Legacies

The 1930's

by Glenye Cain

Few decades have had such a diverse and lasting impact on North American racing as the 1930's. The prevalence of racetracks around the country, the shapes of our prime circuits, and some of our most prestigious stakes races have their roots in the thirties, as do several of the conveniences that racegoers today take for granted. From starting gate to photo finish, the thirties left an impressive legacy for the Thoroughbred sport – in bloodstock, history, and mechanical invention.

"The Fox of Belair," Gallant Fox, kicked off the 1930's by winning the Triple Crown. The tall, talented colt lured legendary jockey Earl Sande out of retirement to ride him as a 3-year-old.

After the Crash, the nation was slipping deeper into the economic devastation that drove hordes of people out of work and into breadlines. State governments were also hungry, but for tax revenue, and they saw a convenient opportunity in the daily attendance figures at places such as Pimlico, Belmont, and Churchill Downs. If citizens across the nation wanted diversion, their state governments, hunting for income, would give it to them in the form of more racetracks.

Thus began, paradoxically, a Depression boom as racing, demonized and shunned the generation before, was revived state by state to help fund government. Maryland, Kentucky, New York, and New England had been the predominant racing venues, but in the thirties racing appeared (or reappeared) in other areas, too. In New Hampshire, Thoroughbreds returned to Rockingham Park, while Massachusetts built Suffolk Downs. Rhode Island got Narragansett Park, and racing came to Delaware. In Kentucky, Keeneland debuted. Out west, still a relatively new frontier for racing,

California opened Santa Anita, Del Mar, Hollywood, and Bay Meadows that decade, and Texas got Arlington Downs. In south Florida, Tropical Park joined Hialeah in the Miami market in 1931, followed by Gulfstream Park in 1939.

The growth spurred unprecedented tinkering, too, as regulation-minded states looked for better ways to run the races for the benefit of the public; the electric timer and the photo-finish camera were among the developments in the 1930's, the amplified race call began and became an audio icon in the decade, and experimentation with starting gates ultimately resulted in the gate we know today.

Suddenly, racing was everywhere – and so were the opportunities for owners and trainers to make a little purse money, though the purse money was exactly that: little. In 1932, thanks to the general economic condition, the average purse slipped from $1,100 to $920, making it harder for racing stables to offset their expenses and for great racehorses to set new earnings records. At the top of the world's earnings list was Sun Beau, who had won much of his money by 1929, when he already was the nation's top older horse. When he retired in October 1931, Sun Beau had amassed a lifetime bankroll of $376,744. The horses that followed him in the 1930's were racing in a trench, so to speak, and it wasn't until 1940 that Seabiscuit finally climbed past Sun Beau's purse mark.

The history of the Thoroughbred is as cyclical as any other, and the decade of the thirties is especially rich in sporting and bloodstock regenerations. As new tracks sprang up, young members of old families took the helms of stables, while great racehorses went to stud and sired or produced another generation of champions. Some of the legacies of that time have faded in the 60 years since, but others are still etched in our collective memory and in the record books.

The Fox of Belair was his nickname. It is appropriate that the names of Gallant Fox and Belair Stud should be linked so closely, because together they dominated the 1930's and produced one of the era's most famous racing dynasties.

Gallant Fox was, in a sense, the bellwether for the era, a propitious sign. How better to begin a decade, after all, than with a Triple Crown winner? In 1930, thanks to Belair's blaze-faced bay colt, turf writers dusted off the record books and created a royal designation for sweeping the Kentucky Derby, Preakness, and Belmont Stakes. Sir Barton had been the first to do so 11 years before, when the feat was highly notable but not titled; Gallant Fox's repetition of it prompted someone to christen the events racing's Triple Crown.

In 1929, Gallant Fox had been a lanky, ungainly 2-year-old who, it was hoped, would help justify a risk taken in 1925 by Belair owner William Woodward Sr. Gallant Fox, out of Belair's Celt mare Marguerite, was a member of the first American crop sired by the English stallion Sir Gallahad III, whom Woodward and three other men, including Arthur B. Hancock Sr., had purchased in partnership for the fantastic sum of $125,000 and imported to stand at Hancock's Claiborne Farm.

Gallant Fox proved to be a talented, but not champion, 2-year-old, winning just two stakes. But his large size and awkward manner suggested that time and distance would bring him along. The hint was strong enough to induce three-time leading jockey Earl Sande to come out of retirement to ride the colt at 3, and he even forwent his usual monthly retainer on the agreement that he would instead get 10 percent of Gallant Fox's earnings.

The speculation paid off like a slot machine. Returning from winter quarters in April 1930, Gallant Fox was mature, coordinated, and practically invincible. After winning his season debut in the Wood Memorial by four lengths, he skated through the Preakness on May 9, the Derby just 10 days later, and the Belmont on June 7. And he went on from there, knitting together a skein of stakes wins that galvanized his reputation as an unbeatable foe.

He was not invulnerable, however, and the story of the one that got away has always stained Gallant

Fox's record like a brushstroke gone awry across a fine oil. It happened, as so many legendary defeats have, at Saratoga, when Gallant Fox, now the undisputed king of the 3-year-olds, met what should have been a docile field of three rivals in the 1930 Travers. Sent off the 1–2 favorite for the race over a heavy, muddy strip, Gallant Fox hooked into an early duel with Whichone, who had finished second to him in the Belmont. On the turn, the pair drifted wide, and into the breach stepped one of the turf's most unlikely spoilers: a 100-1 shot named Jim Dandy. Spurting through on the inside, Jim Dandy took the fastest route home and sailed in eight lengths ahead of the "invincible" 3-year-old, with Whichone another six lengths back. It was, without a doubt, Jim Dandy's finest hour – he made half of his career earnings in the Travers – and Gallant Fox's most humiliating one.

Still, when he retired at the end of the season, Gallant Fox had a bed of laurels on which to rest: He was the first horse ever to earn more than $300,000 in a single season, his career earnings totaled $328,165, and he was the first Triple Crown winner in 11 years. He had repaid everyone associated with him, from the casual bettor to Earl Sande, whose 10-percent deal netted him more than 3½ times the amount his monthly retainer would have brought.

Gallant Fox marked a turning point for his owner as well. Belair's white silks with red dots had been carried to new heights on the colt's back and he had resoundingly justified the investment in Sir Gallahad III. In fact, Sir Gallahad became a four-time leading sire in his adopted country, and his runners later included two stakes-winning full brothers to Gallant Fox: Foxbrough, who was a champion 2-year-old in England, and Fighting Fox. What Woodward suspected but didn't know at the time was that Gallant Fox also would add immense value to Belair's thirties legacy with his own progeny.

Four years later, Omaha, one of just 18 foals from Gallant Fox's first crop, arrived in trainer Sunny Jim Fitzsimmons's barn. Omaha, though chestnut, had his sire's flashy blaze and big frame. Like Gallant Fox, he was awkward and long-striding, which augured better success at 3 than at 2. He matured into a long, elegant horse and set experts nodding in anticipation when he scored his first time out at 3, but enthusiasm dampened slightly when he failed to reproduce his sire's win in the Wood Memorial the following week; he finished third.

Between Gallant Fox's 1930 Derby and his son's in 1935, the race's purse had plummeted from $60,000 to $49,000. Nonetheless, after the winter-book favorite, Chance Sun, bowed out with an injury, the Derby appeared up for grabs, and 18 contested the race. Omaha was sent off at 4-1 and won, as the chart said, "easily," a word that also described his victories in the Preakness and the Belmont.

After Omaha's Triple Crown, newspaper columnist W. J. Macbeth noted that "Fitzsimmons is anxious to have Omaha duplicate all of Gallant Fox's stakes victories and to retrieve the sire's reputation in the Travers at Saratoga." That hope failed. Omaha, who could not win at Saratoga at 2, never ran there at all at 3, then was shipped to England, where he won two good races and narrowly lost

After an eventful early 3-year-old campaign, Granville won the Belmont and every succeeding race in which he ran in 1936 to become the first elected Horse of the Year.

the Ascot Gold Cup. But in winning the Triple Crown, Omaha offset Gallant Fox's black-mark Travers with an honor that was equally indelible: with Omaha, Gallant Fox became the only Triple Crown winner to date to sire a Triple Crown winner, and he did it in his first crop of runners.

While Omaha was winning the 1935 Triple Crown, a 2-year-old son of Gallant Fox was also in the hands of "Mr. Fitz" and training for his career debut at Saratoga. Named Granville, the colt showed some talent when he ran third in his first stakes, the Babylon Handicap, in September. Behind him in sixth place that day, incidentally, was another Fiztsimmons trainee, a hard-campaigned but obscure 2-year-old named Seabiscuit, who was making his 26th start.

Granville hit the board several times at 2, winning just once, in a $1,000 allowance race, and he was put away for the season having failed to raise any eyebrows. Typical of his sire and Omaha, however, Granville rocketed out of the barn at 3. He won his 1936 debut by five lengths under a hold and was nosed out in the Wood Memorial, suggesting that a third Triple Crown for the Gallant Fox males could be in the offing.

But in the Derby, now run before the Preakness, Granville bobbled at the start, and any Triple Crown hopes hit the track with jockey Jimmy Stout. Granville galloped off, stirrups flopping empty on their leathers, as front-runner Bold Venture won by a head from Brevity. Nor did Granville win the Preakness, though he came close: Having gained the lead in the stretch, he battled a fierce challenge by Bold Venture but could not hold the Derby winner off and lost by a nose. Two weeks later, he veered from the Triple Crown path to try older horses in the Suburban and was handed another nose defeat by the well-regarded Firethorn. But that 1¼-mile performance – and Bold Venture's retirement after he bowed a tendon in the Preakness – set Granville up well for the Belmont six days later, when he finally came out on the right side of a close decision. Pushed to his limit by longshot Mr. Bones, Granville dug in and kept his nose in front at the wire.

Granville never lost again, and that year he helped atone for his sire's Travers defeat. It was a messy victory that was threatened by the stewards: Granville won by a head, but only after hampering second-placed Sun Teddy. The officials, in a quirky decision, let the result stand after determining that Granville also had been bothered earlier by another horse and thus was already at a disadvantage when he bumped Sun Teddy.

In his next start, Granville defeated the great handicapper Discovery by eight lengths in the Saratoga Cup, a much-hyped match race. Discovery was the 4-5 choice in the 1¼-mile contest, which was run over a sloppy track at weight-for-age conditions. Carrying 116 pounds to Discovery's 126, Granville jumped out to an early lead and won by eight. There were extenuating circumstances, however, as Discovery was found to have thrown a shoe in Saratoga's deep going.

Granville won once more, easily taking the Lawrence Realization. Crowned Horse of the Year – the first so named – he retired, the most successful member of Gallant Fox's 19-horse second crop, which also included the good English stakes winner Flares.

From 1930 through 1936, Gallant Fox, in one way or another, was responsible for some of the finest racetrack performances of the decade. Having contributed, along with Fitzsimmons and his prodigious talents, to Belair's dominance of the era, Gallant Fox promptly lost cachet as a stallion, slipping off the top 20 sires list and finally getting 20 stakes winners from 320 foals.

Gallant Fox's own sire, ultimately, provided a more comprehensive breeding legacy. Sir Gallahad III appears early in the pedigrees of several other greats from the 1930's. His daughter La France, mated with the good handicapper Jamestown, produced Johnstown, who was purchased by Belair and won the Derby and Belmont. Laura Gal, another daughter of Sir Gallahad III owned by W. L. Brann's Branncastle Farm, produced Johnstown's chief rival, Challedon, a two-time Horse of the Year. And a son of Sir Gallahad III, Insco, sired two of the era's best fillies, Herbert Woolf's homebreds

Inscoelda and Unerring, whose long and distinguished records extended into the early 1940's.

Among the swells in Pimlico's clubhouse on November 5, 1930, was young Cornelius Vanderbilt Whitney, who was hoping not to be noticed. It was the day of the Pimlico Futurity, and the assembled throng that raw, damp afternoon was focused on the coming race, which pitted the country's top 2-year-olds against each other; the outcome would almost certainly settle the divisional crown. C. V. Whitney, who previously had not cared one way or the other about racing, found himself in the strange position of owning one of the leading contenders, a great crowd-pleaser later nicknamed the Chocolate Soldier – Equipoise.

It was, in fact, C. V. Whitney's first day at the races as an owner, and he was in that capacity to fulfill a family obligation. Whitney had arrived in the sport almost by accident 10 days earlier on the death of his father, the renowned owner-breeder Harry Payne Whitney, who had left a string of racehorses and his breeding stock. The younger Whitney, 31, encouraged by another great Thoroughbred sportsman, Joseph E. Widener, took his father's place at the helm.

Equipoise, the popular "Chocolate Soldier," was one of the first horses to run in the colors of C. V. Whitney.

The heir to Harry Payne Whitney's stable may have hoped for a relatively quiet entrance into his father's sport, but he got more fanfare, and probably more fun, than he bargained for. At the Pimlico Futurity, the stewards insisted that he and trainer Freddy Hopkins view the race from their stand, and when Whitney finally consented, the crowd, catching sight of him, broke into a spontaneous ovation.

As it happened, Equipoise's most contentious rival that day – all season, in fact – was also owned by a Whitney. Helen Hay Whitney, widow of C. V.'s uncle, Payne, campaigned the immensely popular Twenty Grand under the name of her Greentree Stable. Twenty Grand had beaten Equipoise twice, both times over a fast track at a mile. This time, the two were meeting at 1$\frac{1}{16}$ miles over a muddy strip, and the betting crowd gave Equipoise the edge.

The Futurity was more than the expected coronation; it was one of the decade's epic clashes, and those who saw Equipoise's victory in it never forgot it. Not just beaten but distanced after sideswiping another horse at the break, C.V. Whitney's liver chestnut unexpectedly shot forward and started passing his rivals with a mere half-mile left in the race. Strenuously, yard by yard, he began picking up the 2-year-old championship for his new owner. He caught Twenty Grand in the stretch, matched strides with him, and those two joined the leader, Mate. As they swept past the wire, Equipoise was a half-length in front of Twenty Grand, with Mate a neck farther back.

In the running, Equipoise had gotten a bad start, been shuffled back into the deepest going, lost both front shoes, cut a front foot, popped open a recurring quarter crack, and still won. He retired for the season after the Futurity with top earnings for his division, $156,835. Even so, there were some who argued that Whitney's aunt owned the better horse, especially considering that, during his earlier defeat of Equipoise in the Kentucky Jockey Club Stakes, Twenty Grand had posted the fastest mile time, 1:36, that had ever been run by a 2-year-old in the United States.

Twenty Grand and Equipoise met only once the following year, when Mate beat them both to win the Preakness. Twenty Grand was second that day, but went on to win the Derby from Sweep All a week later, with Mate third. Equipoise, fourth in the Preakness, withdrew from the Derby and sat out the rest of the year with his troublesome quarter crack, which sometimes bled so badly that "you could track him all the way back to the barn," according to George Mohr, who worked as a teenager in trainer Al Weston's stable at Pimlico, across the horse path from Equipoise's barn.

Despite Equipoise's layoff, C.V. Whitney's stable was far from dormant in 1931. Just a month after Equipoise left the track, Whitney entered a 2-year-old Dis Donc filly in her first race, the five-furlong Clover Stakes at Aqueduct. Carrying 107 pounds, Top Flight cruised home by a length over Polonaise, who had 122 pounds. Top Flight proved the performance was a result of talent rather than a break in the weights when she traveled to Arlington Park for the Lassie Stakes. Carrying 120 pounds, the same as Polonaise, Top Flight won again, this time by five while giving seven pounds to second-placed Modern Queen and three to third runner Princess Camellia. Polonaise finished fourth.

Top Flight provided plenty of entertainment for the Whitney stable the rest of the year, and plenty of dust for her competitors. She went on to be undefeated in 1931, skipping home by 1¼ lengths against colts in the Saratoga Special, by five again in the Spinaway, and by 1¼ in the Matron, seemingly oblivious to her 127-pound burden. In the fall, Top Flight stepped back into the boys division and handily whipped them again, coasting clear of well-regarded Mad Pursuit and Morfair, who both carried 122 to her 127, in Belmont's six-furlong Futurity. A month later, she beat males yet again – by the uncharacteristically slender margin of a neck – at 1 1/16 miles in the

Twenty Grand, winner of two legs of the Triple Crown in 1931, was a brilliant 3-year-old, defeating handicap star Sun Beau by 10 lengths in the Saratoga Cup.

Pimlico Futurity. Behind her that day was Burgoo King, who went on to win the Derby the following year.

While one Whitney runner sewed up the 2-year-old division, another Whitney horse pocketed the 3-year-old title with nearly equal ease. Greentree's trainer, Thomas W. Murphy, had resigned but offered a reported $125,000 to take Twenty Grand with him. Mrs. Whitney refused and was amply rewarded, as the St. Germans colt proceeded to win the Belmont (by 10), the Dwyer, and the Travers, with a third in the Arlington Classic for good measure. True proof of his hardiness came in the Saratoga Cup, when he faced the reigning handicap king, 6-year-old Sun Beau, who was enjoying a banner season that made him the world's leading earner in his last year at the races. Twenty Grand beat him by 10 in a gallop, then followed up by airing in the Lawrence Realization and the Jockey Club Gold Cup. In the latter, he hit his left front pastern, injuring the splint bone and tendon, and he hung up his bridle for the year.

Mrs. Whitney's Greentree Stable, which she started with her husband, Payne, in 1911, was a turf dynasty that had built its foundation with steeplechasers. Though her watermelon-pink silks with black-striped sleeves became increasingly prominent on the flat, Mrs. Whitney's stable in the 1930's also fielded one of the prominent jumpers of the era, Jungle King. The connection points to yet another breeding legacy of the time, that of the horse St. Germans. Payne Whitney had bought the English horse for $125,000 in 1925 – the same price and year of Sir Gallahad III's acquisition.

St. Germans sired both Jungle King and Twenty Grand, and the latter nearly single-handedly boosted the stallion to the top of America's sire list in 1931. Jungle King began as a flat runner but proved more successful over fences; despite a four-year career, though, he never quite equaled the dominance of another steeplechase champion of the time, Joe Widener's Bushranger, who won 11 of 21 career starts and carried 172 pounds to victory in the 1936 Grand National. Jungle King, carrying 140, lost his rider in that contest, precluding a true battle.

C. V. Whitney and his aunt Helen were to keep the Whitney name in the fore throughout the thirties, though their standard-bearers, Equipoise and Twenty Grand, did not meet again until their careers were near an end, in 1935.

Santa Anita Park near Los Angeles had opened on Christmas Day, 1934, to much fanfare, and the new hot spot, in an effort to attract horses from around the country and Mexico for high-class winter racing, was staging its inaugural $100,000-added Santa Anita Handicap in February. When the race had been announced, many greeted the plan with skepticism, but the horses pointing for it included a number of great runners from the East, among them old rivals Twenty Grand, Mate, and Equipoise, who was gunning for Sun Beau's all-time earnings title.

The story behind Twenty Grand's appearance was a sad one. Greentree trainer James Rowe Jr. had died soon after the 1931 Jockey Club Gold Cup, and his replacement, William Brennan, brought the now-4-year-old Twenty Grand back from his injury to start twice in 1932, but to little avail. He won his seasonal debut, but then pulled up lame in the slop at Laurel after running second. Deemed too valuable to risk any longer, he was retired to stud, where he was found to be infertile. Mrs. Whitney returned him to the racetrack in 1935. He was 7.

Equipoise also was struggling increasingly with his fragile feet and notorious quarter crack, which had required much of one hoof to be cut away and regrown. But heart and talent still got him to the wire. In a February 18 prep for the Santa Anita Handicap, Equipoise, carrying 125 and giving nine pounds to Twenty Grand, beat the Greentree runner by one length. But he also bothered him, resulting in Equipoise's third career disqualification. The crowd nonetheless saw that Twenty Grand was no longer the horse he had been, and five days later, they favored Equipoise – highweight at 130 pounds to Twenty Grand's 126 – among the 20 runners in the big event.

It was the last race for the three-time handicap champion. Breaking slowly from the gate, Equipoise was positioned to strike as the field headed home, but this time a tendon failed him, and he never improved from seventh. Twenty Grand finished a distant tenth. Fred Alger's Azucar, a former steeplechaser carrying 117, had lifted the prize. In doing so, Azucar made $108,400, the most a horse had ever earned in a single race; it would have been more than enough to catapult Equipoise past Sun Beau's famous earnings mark. Even the winner did not escape unscathed, though. It was reported some days later in the Detroit News that Azucar had been "slightly burned by electric wires when he became frightened and ran away after the finish of the Santa Anita Handicap."

And so the two great Whitney horses left the track, at least in America. Equipoise was retired with 29 wins from 51 starts, and total purses of $338,610, some $40,000 short of the world record. Twenty Grand was sent briefly to trainer Cecil Boyd-Rochfort in England, where he was easily put away by local runners in two races. In the fall of 1935, the old hero was taken home and turned out to pasture.

In 1935, the public and racing press hungered for a successor to Equipoise, and they found one in Discovery, who had never met Equipoise, though their careers had overlapped. This changing of the guard in the handicap division was reflected in the Thoroughbred industry's human leadership, as well.

On September 22, 1933, Alfred Gwynne Vanderbilt turned 21 and became, officially, a millionaire in his own right. Like his cousin C.V. Whitney, Vanderbilt also inherited a foothold in Thoroughbred racing, which he was to parlay into a role of immense influence. On his 21st birthday, he received a $2 million installment, the first of four, from the estate of his father, who had died on the Lusitania, as well as a birthday gift from his mother: her Sagamore Farm in Maryland and all of its Thoroughbreds.

Vanderbilt moved quickly to bolster Sagamore's homebreds with outside purchases. Discovery, a good 2-year-old of 1933, was among the early draftees. Bred and owned early by Mr. and Mrs. Walter Salmon, Discovery had been the subject of some haggling before Vanderbilt, preparing to board the Aquitania at the start of a safari journey, made a final offer of $25,000. On November 2, 1933, Vanderbilt received an answer via his mother in a Cunard Line telegraph: "Discovery yours ok love Mother." Two days later, Discovery carried Alfred Vanderbilt's silks for the first time, getting within a neck of Chicstraw in Pimlico's Walden Handicap, his final start as a 2-year-old. Six lengths farther back that afternoon was Cavalcade, who would prove to be Discovery's nemesis the following year.

Prepping for the Derby, Discovery had a public work between races at Havre de Grace on April 21, 1934. Joined by a stablemate midway through it, Discovery went three-quarters in 1:12 2/5, prompting the three clockers on duty, each sure he'd made an error, to quickly compare times. Discovery zipped past the wire under a tight hold in a final mile time of 1:37 4/5, a second better than the track record. Vanderbilt and trainer J. H. Stotler "expressed satisfaction with the trial," *Daily Racing Form* noted.

Discovery was overshadowed by Cavalcade during his 3-year-old season, but went on to become a superior weight-carrier and handicap champion.

Cavalcade spoiled Discovery's Derby hopes, however. Discovery finished second, then came back to be third behind High Quest and Cavalcade in the Preakness. He was forced to skip the Belmont; the Salmons had never nominated him, and the deadline was past when Vanderbilt acquired him.

Stotler and Vanderbilt turned their attention to the late-season races, where Discovery was untouchable against almost all comers. Running at a dozen tracks in the Northeast and Midwest, he won half his 16 starts in 1934, six of them stakes. In his easiest race, the Whitney, he carried just 105 pounds and won off by 10; after that, he never carried less than 119. By the end of the season, his weight assignment reached 130 for the Maryland Handicap, and he won that, too, by a half-length over Good Goods.

There was one runner, however, he had been unable to beat all year long: Cavalcade. Mrs. Isabel Dodge Sloane's Brookmeade Stable campaigned the Lancegaye colt through a brilliant season that was further gilded by his routine drubbing of the obviously high-caliber Discovery. Even when he gave Discovery weight, as he did in the Detroit and American Derbies, Cavalcade beat Vanderbilt's colt. "Cavalcade strikes human fancy hardest by the destruction and havoc he causes among his rivals with one short but very explosive burst of speed," the *Form*'s Norris Royden wrote after Cavalcade, conceding five pounds, beat Discovery for the sixth and final time that season in the Arlington Classic.

With Cavalcade out the rest of 1934 with a hoof ailment, Discovery took advantage and won 5 of 7 races, setting a world record of 1:55 for 1 3⁄16 miles in the Rhode Island Handicap. On the heels of Equipoise's retirement, he was hailed as the Chocolate Soldier's successor.

Discovery met Cavalcade only once more, in the 1935 Suburban, when Cavalcade lost his rider at the start. Head Play won under 114 pounds, with Discovery, carrying 123, second. Though he returned in 1936 for two races at Narragansett and his stable kept hope alive that he was training to meet the best of the day, Cavalcade never won again and was retired.

The years 1935 and '36 belonged to Discovery, whose burdens had crept up to groaning levels. In 1935, he won five times carrying more than 130 pounds. In one of those races, Saratoga's 1 3⁄16-mile Merchants' and Citizens' Handicap, often thought to be his best performance, he lugged 139 pounds to a two-length score.

Northeastern handicappers, trainer Stotler felt, were especially harsh on Discovery. In 1936, after he had lost the Santa Anita Handicap thanks to getting bumped, he was given 135 pounds for his first race back at Aqueduct, which he won by four. Ten days later, on June 27, he aced his third consecutive Brooklyn Handicap, carrying 136. His assignments reached their peak in the 1936 Merchants' and Citizens', where he lugged 143 pounds over a sloppy track and finished fifth. The situation prompted a group of owners to call for a 138-pound ceiling on handicaps, citing the weight put on Discovery as "bad practice."

Vanderbilt generally remained quiet about the loads Discovery was asked to haul. "I wanted to see how good he was," he said 60 years later. In reference to the outcome of the Merchants' and Citizens', he added, "The thing I liked about that was that after he got beaten, they said he sulked, which said to me that they thought if he'd tried he could have done it."

When he retired at the end of the season, Discovery had won $195,287 and 27 races from 67 starts. He was third or better 47 times, he set a world mark, and he carried 130 pounds or more into the winner's circle nine times. In that respect, at least, he was able to beat Cavalcade, who never ran under more than 127.

As for Discovery's legacy, Vanderbilt noted in 1999, "In a way, the most important thing about Discovery is that for probably 20 years, give or take a little, the two major stallions in North America were Native Dancer and Bold Ruler. Both of them were out of Discovery mares."

Vanderbilt, too, made lasting contributions to the sport. As the head of Pimlico, and later

War Admiral, the great Man o' War's best son, was undefeated in eight starts as a 3-year-old.

Belmont, he brought innovation in track management. He helped usher in parimutuel wagering to New York, among other things, and sought to improve customer service for race fans. One of his first moves in power at Pimlico was to remove the infield hill that gave the track the moniker Old Hilltop and obstructed many fans' view of the backstretch; another was the installation of a public-address system. He also developed a stable full of talented runners, including the champion Now What, whom Stotler called the best filly he ever trained. She flew the Vanderbilt flag high late in the decade by winning the Astoria, Demoiselle, Arlington Lassie, and Spinaway Stakes in 1939.

On November 1, 1938, Vanderbilt, who was just 27 but had already acquired controlling interest in Pimlico, fulfilled something of a coup for the track by staging a match race between War Admiral and Seabiscuit, by far the best handicap horses of the day. Belmont Park previously had tried to put the match on for a $100,000 purse, but that event fell apart when owner Charles S. Howard withdrew Seabiscuit. Amid suggestions that he was ducking War Admiral, Howard agreed to Vanderbilt's suggestion to run the two in the $15,000 Pimlico Special.

The match race marked a neat conjunction in the revival of a great name from the 1920's: Man o' War. War Admiral, who carried the black and gold silks of Man o' War's owner-breeder, Samuel D. Riddle, was a Triple Crown-winning son of the great horse; Seabiscuit, by hot-blooded Hard Tack, was a grandson of Man o' War campaigned by Howard, a California-based Buick dealer. The Pimlico Special was the first and only meeting of two of the decade's best horses.

War Admiral, for his part, was the best thing Man o' War had sired. At 2, he was overshadowed by the precocious champion Pompoon. But as a 3-year-old of 1937, he literally could not be caught. He was undefeated in eight starts – with Pompoon second to him twice. In the Belmont Stakes, War Admiral had clinched both the Triple Crown and a reputation for courage: Stumbling at the start, he had torn off a section of his right front hoof, which bled profusely. Driven on to the lead, he finished three lengths in front. Along the way, he had broken his sire's 17-year track record for 1½ miles, lowering the mark by one-fifth to 2:28⅗, which also was an American record for the distance.

At 4, War Admiral won eight races leading up to the Pimlico Special. He had little trouble with his competition, though the champion filly Esposa ran him to a neck in the sloppy Saratoga Handicap.

Setting records was old hat to Seabiscuit, who spent much of 1937 lowering track marks from Santa Anita to Suffolk Downs. Originally trained by Sunny Jim Fitzsimmons for the Wheatley Stable of Mrs. Henry Carnegie Phipps and her brother, Ogden Mills, he evidently failed to impress his connections at 2 and 3; he started 35 times at 2 and could have been claimed for $2,500 more than once. Shortly after a victory in the Mohawk Claiming Stakes at Saratoga in August 1936, in which he was entered for a $6,000 tag, the Wheatley principals happily sold the 3-year-old colt to Howard for $7,500.

Under the care of Silent Tom Smith, Seabiscuit gradually developed into something almost otherworldly. By the time the 5-year-old horse met War Admiral in the 1938 Pimlico Special, he owned track marks over a mile, 1³⁄₁₆, and 1⅛ at Bay Meadows (1:36, 1:55⅘, and 1:49); 1⅛ miles at Santa Anita (1:48 ⅘); 1 ¹⁄₁₆ miles at Empire State (1:44 ⅕); 1⅛ miles at Suffolk (1:49); 1³⁄₁₆ miles at Pimlico (1:57⅖); 1¼ miles at Hollywood (2:03 ⅘); and 1 ⅛ miles at Del Mar (1:49).

Since War Admiral had been known to kick up a fuss at the starting gate, Riddle insisted on a walk-up start for the Pimlico Special. He also demanded that the race be run without the participation of starter James Milton, whom he disliked. At Milton's own request, he was temporarily replaced by George Cassidy of New York

The start, everyone knew, was crucial. Tom Smith knew it, and he knew that Seabiscuit, who sometimes was a slow starter, was at a disadvantage in this regard. The week of the race, according to fellow trainer George Mohr, who also was stabled at Pimlico by this time, "They'd gallop Seabiscuit around, pull him up, then let him walk four or five strides and break him off sharp."

After two attempts at a true start, and in front of a record crowd of 40,000, War Admiral and Seabiscuit put on a memorable race. Seabiscuit was struck twice by jockey George Woolf, who was substituting for injured regular rider Red Pollard, and unexpectedly jumped to the lead, tracked by War Admiral 2½ lengths behind. At the three-quarter mark in the 1³⁄₁₆-mile contest, jockey Charley Kurtsinger plied whip and heel to War Admiral, who hooked Seabiscuit at the half. It appeared to be over for Seabiscuit as War Admiral headed him for

Seabiscuit returns to the winner's circle following his victory over War Admiral in the 1938 Pimlico Special. The popular star trumped the 1937 Triple Crown winner by four lengths in track-record time.

about 100 yards. But Seabiscuit switched into high gear, and at the top of the stretch, he began drawing away powerfully, though War Admiral was under vigorous whipping. At the wire, it was Seabiscuit by four lengths in a track-record time of 1:56⅗. The defeat cost War Admiral the championship that season, though he won the Rhode Island Handicap 11 days later. He only raced once the following season, taking a Hialeah allowance, before retiring with a wrenched ankle.

Seabiscuit took the winter off after the Pimlico Special but returned in 1939 for a special task. It was his owner's fond hope to win the Santa Anita Handicap. The race had been an annual heartbreaker for him with Seabiscuit, who lost by a nose twice, to Rosemont in 1936 and to Stagehand in 1938. Unfortunately, Seabiscuit returned lame from a prep race, and he took the rest of the year off, at least from racing: While at his owner's northern California farm, he was bred to a handful of mares. Howard, as it happened, got lucky in the race anyway: His imported Kayak II drew away to win, and, in Seabiscuit's absence, proceeded to lock up the year's handicap championship. Seabiscuit would return briefly in 1940, finally surpassing Sun Beau's record and winning the Santa Anita Handicap on his third try.

Seabiscuit and War Admiral were not the only horses descended from Man o' War and his own sire, Fair Play, in the 1930's. Sun Beau was out of a Fair Play mare, as was Stagehand, who beat Pompoon and Bull Lea in addition to Seabiscuit. Discovery and Now What were by sons of Fair Play.

In their bloodlines and their ownership, many of the great runners of the 1930's harked back to an older world in racing that would one day fade almost entirely from view. The monarchies of the turf would eventually be replaced by increasingly diverse ownership interests, an upswing in strictly commercial breeding, and a more egalitarian clubhouse. But these champions of the 1930's, while representing the legacies that brought them into being, also created legacies of their own. They passed Fair Play's name into the future, but they also contributed their own to future pedigrees of import. Even if they proved infertile or unsuccessful at stud, like Twenty Grand, their place in the record books made them standards, marks for future runners to aim for.

And, perhaps as importantly, they lifted the sport and the people who watched them run. The colts were men's men, never-say-die warriors; the fillies were courageous and glamorous, too, exemplified by the brilliance and class of Top Flight, so merciless against all comers, and the Blue Larkspur blazer Myrtlewood, who won 15 of her 22 starts, including nine stakes and two matches, and set three track records.

In general, the greatest Depression-era runners were, in some respects, like the survivors who filled grandstands to watch them: hard-bitten, tough, and burdened by misfortune or physical frailty, as in Equipoise's case, or, in Discovery's case, by crushing weight. And still they fought hard, playing out on racing's stage the allegories of the era: struggle and win, or at least go down fighting.

Champions

Past Performances

The 1930's

Year by Year Champions

•1936•
•2-Year-Old Male *Pompoon* •3-Year-Old Male *Granville* •Handicap Horse *Discovery*
•Sprinter *Myrtlewood* •Steeplechase *Bushranger*
•**HORSE OF THE YEAR** Granville

•1937•
•2-Year-Old Male *Menow* •3-Year-Old Male *War Admiral* •Handicap Horse *Seabiscuit*
•Steeplechase *Jungle King*
•**HORSE OF THE YEAR** War Admiral

•1938•
•2-Year-Old Male *El Chico* •2-Year-Old Filly *Inscoelda* •3-Year-Old Male *Stagehand*
•Handicap Horse *Seabiscuit* •Handicap Mare *Marica*
•**HORSE OF THE YEAR** Seabiscuit

•1939•
•2-Year-Old Male *Bimelech* •2-Year-Old Filly *Now What* •3-Year-Old Male *Challedon*
•3-Year-Old Filly *Unerring* •Handicap Horse *Kayak II* •Handicap Mare *Lady Maryland*
•**HORSE OF THE YEAR** Challedon

Bushranger

ch. g. 1930, by Stefan the Great (The Tetrarch)–War Path, by Man o' War — **Lifetime record: 21 11 3 1 $20,635**

Own.– J.E. Widener
Br.– Joseph E. Widener (Ky)
Tr.– J.H. Lewis

3Oct36- 2Bel	fst	*3	S'Chase 5:47	4↑ Grand National H 7.5k	5	4	$4^{5½}$	2^{1}	$1^{½}$	1^{2}	Little H	172 w	*1.00	--	Bushranger172^{2}Rioter156^{10}Amagansett157^{nk}	Speed to spare	5
26Sep36- 2Bel	fst	*2½	S'Chase $4:46^{1}$	4↑ Brook H 3.7k	6	1	1^{1}	1^{nk}	1^{3}	1^{5}	Little H	165 w	*1.80	--	Bushrangr165^{5}Rioter157^{3}GoldenMeadow154^{7}	Speed to spare	6
17Sep36- 2Bel	fst	*2	S'Chase $3:42^{3}$	3↑ Broad Hollow H 1.9k	4	2	$1^{1½}$	1^{2}	$1^{1½}$	$1^{1½}$	Little H	159 w	*.60	--	Bushranger$159^{1½}$Prattler139^{10}Spinach143	Much the best	4
30May36- 2Bel	fst	*2	S'Chase $3:43^{3}$	4↑ Corinthian H 1.9k	2	1	1^{4}	1^{hd}	1^{1}	1^{2}	Little H	157 w	*.75	--	Bushranger157^{2}Birmingham$139^{1½}$Jungle King143		3
	Bobbled several fences,won in hand																
16May36- 6Bel	fst	$1\frac{1}{16}$	$:23^{4}$ $:47^{3}$ $1:12^{3}$ $1:44^{1}$	3↑ Handicap 1230	6	5	$5^{3½}$	5^{7}	$5^{5¾}$	$5^{8¼}$	Wright WD	123wb	4.00	82-14	Rust107^{nk}Esposa107^{3}Chance Ray110^{2}	Quit	7
5Nov35- 3Bel	gd	1½	$:48^{1}$ $1:13^{3}$ $2:06^{2}$ $2:32^{3}$	3↑ Whitney Trophy H 1.5k	1	3	2^{2}	$2^{1½}$	1^{hd}	1^{3}	Wright WD	118 w	*1.50	--	Bushranger118^{3}Fortification105^{no}Chance Ray100^{40}		4
	Fractious post,speed to spare																
30Sep35- 2Bel	fst	*2	S'Chase 3:45	3↑ Broad Hollow H 1.8k	2	1	1^{6}	1^{3}	1^{hd}	1^{1}	Little H	153 w	*.50	--	Bushranger153^{1}Amagansett154	Speed in reserve	2
25May35- 2Bel	fst	*2	S'Chase $3:42^{1}$	4↑ C L Appleton Mem 3.7k	7	3	$5^{3¾}$	$4^{3½}$	1^{1}	$1^{1½}$	Little H	143 w	*1.80	--	Bushranger$143^{1½}$Rideaway140^{2}Spinach$142^{1½}$	Speed to spare	8
18May35- 2Bel	fst	*2	S'Chase 3:41	4↑ International H 2.1k	2	1	2^{5}	$2^{1½}$	2^{2}	$2^{1½}$	Little H	142 w	2.20	--	Amagansett$143^{1½}$Bushrangr142^{6}JunglKng148^{10}	Finished well	5
	Previously trained by D. Byers																
12Nov34- 1Pim	fst	2	S'Chase $3:45^{2}$	4↑ Alw 1000	6	1	1^{1}	1^{hd}	1^{hd}	$1^{1¼}$	Little H	140 w	*1.30	--	Bushranger$140^{1¼}$Amagansett142^{10}Help Me138^{4}	Drawing away	7
5Nov34- 1Pim	sl	2	S'Chase 3:54	4↑ Alw 1000	2	2	1^{nk}	1^{1}	$1^{1½}$	1^{2}	Little H	135 w	2.40	--	Bushranger135^{2}Snap Back143^{12}Nesconset133^{15}	Won in hand	6
17Sep34- 5Aqu	sly	1	$:23^{4}$ $:48^{1}$ $1:13^{3}$ $1:38^{1}$	2↑ Md Sp Wt	5	2	3^{2}	$3^{3½}$	$2^{1½}$	1no	Wright WD	120 w	3.00	89-10	Bushranger120^{no}Parma105^{3}Sir Thomas117^{4}		6
	Up final strides,impeded rival																
3Sep34- 2Bel	fst	*2	S'Chase $3:45^{2}$	3↑ Broad Hollow H 2.2k	7	6	5^{11}	-	-	-	Bauman A	137 w	2.00	--	RockLad142^{7}ThistlePlay135^{no}Poppyman135^{6}	Lost rider 9th	7
9Jun34- 2Bel	fst	*2	S'Chase 3:42	4↑ Alw 1000	3	1	1^{3}	$1^{1½}$	1^{nk}	$1^{1½}$	Bauman A	133 w	*1.40	--	Bushranger$133^{1½}$Nesconset137^{20}Dock Light136^{20}		5
	Bad landing 8th,recovered																
30May34- 2Bel	fst	*2	S'Chase $3:47^{2}$	4↑ Alw 1000	4	1	2^{1}	1^{1}	2^{hd}	$2^{1½}$	Bauman A	136 w	2.50	--	Nsconst$136^{1½}$Bshrngr136^{50}HolHgh135^{4}	Saved ground,gamely	7
16May34- 2Bel	gd	*2	S'Chase $3:44^{2}$	4↑ International H 2.4k	5	3	$4^{3¼}$	$4^{2¾}$	-	-	Slate F	130 w	*1.40e	--	Amagansett130^{5}RockyRun131.5^{5}Benedictn142^{hd}	Fell at 11th	8
	Previously trained by H. McDaniel																
8Nov32- 2Pim	hy	1 70	:24 $:49^{1}$ $1:15^{2}$ $1:47^{1}$	2↑ Md Sp Wt	5	3	$3^{3½}$	3^{6}	3^{9}	3^{14}	Studley W	108wb	3.90	61-27	BandWagon108^{12}FrenchKnight108^{2}Bshrngr108^{5}	No excuses	12
3Nov32- 1Pim	gd	1 70	:24 $:49^{2}$ $1:14^{3}$ $1:46^{4}$	©Md Sp Wt	12	2	1^{hd}	1^{hd}	1^{hd}	2no	Garner M	116wb	3.20	77-17	PolarBrush116^{no}Bushrngr$116^{1½}$JudgJudy$116^{1½}$	Dueled,gamely	12
24Oct32- 1Lrl	fst	6f	$:23^{3}$ $:48^{2}$ $1:14^{4}$	©Md Sp Wt	3	8	$7^{3¼}$	$8^{3¾}$	$6^{4¼}$	$5^{2¼}$	Garner M	115 w	4.10	80-12	Sky Haven115^{no}Chatterfol115^{2}Band Wagon115^{hd}	Fast finish	12
10Aug32- 3Sar	fst	5½f	$:23^{1}$ $:47^{1}$ $1:00^{1}$ 1:07	Alw 800	6	12	$7^{9½}$	$6^{4½}$	$6^{7¼}$	6^{5}	Garner M	110 w	3.60	83-16	WeddingRing115^{1}Sarada110^{1}JungleKing120^{2}	Dwelt at start	12
4Aug32- 6Sar	my	5½f	$:23^{3}$ $:48^{2}$ 1:02 1:09	Md Sp Wt	9	10	$8^{8¾}$	$8^{7½}$	6^{6}	$5^{6½}$	Garner M	117 w	7.00	71-26	RushHour$117^{1½}$Pompoleon117^{4}CarrytheNws117^{1}	Slow to start	11

Cavalcade

br. c. 1931, by Lancegaye (Swynford)–Hastily, by Hurry On — **Lifetime record: 22 8 5 3 $127,165**

Own.– Brookmeade Stable
Br.– F. Wallis Armstrong Sr (NJ)
Tr.– R.A. Smith

12Sep36- 5Nar	fst	$1\frac{1}{16}$	:24 $:48^{1}$ $1:13^{2}$ $1:44^{4}$	3↑ Handicap 1400	2	6	$7^{8¼}$	8^{16}	9^{15}	9^{23}	Woolf G	120wb	4.10	70-13	Sun Teddy$119^{½}$Mountainy Man108^{1}Pundit103.5^{hd}	Outrun	9
9Sep36- 5Nar	fst	$1\frac{1}{16}$	$:23^{3}$ $:47^{2}$ $1:12^{3}$ $1:44^{1}$	3↑ Alw 1100	4	6	$6^{9¼}$	$5^{9½}$	5^{8}	$6^{12¼}$	Woolf G	121 w	*.60	84-08	Chancing106^{nk}Piccolo110^{3}Boston Brook106^{1}	No excuses	7
30May35- 5Bel	fst	1¼	:46 $1:10^{3}$ $1:36^{1}$ 2:02	3↑ Suburban H 15k	4	-	-	-	-	-	Gilbert J	127 w	*1.40	--	Head Play$114^{1½}$Discovery123^{3}Only One110^{3}	Lost rider	7
22May35- 4Bel	fst	1	$:23^{4}$ $:47^{1}$ $1:11^{2}$ $1:37^{1}$	3↑ Handicap 1230	1	3	2^{4}	2^{4}	2^{4}	2^{3}	Gilbert J	127 w	*.50	86-09	Head Play114^{3}Cavalcade127^{10}Carry Over104^{5}	Evenly	4
14Jly34- 6AP	fst	1¼	$:47^{3}$ 1:12 $1:36^{3}$ $2:02^{4}$	Classic 40k	6	7	7^{8}	3^{1}	1^{3}	1^{4}	Garner M	126 w	*.37e	95-08	Cavalcade126^{4}Discovery$121^{½}$Hadagal121^{3}	In hand	9
16Jun34- 6Det	fst	$1\frac{3}{16}$	$:47^{3}$ $1:12^{4}$ $1:39^{3}$ $1:58^{1}$	Det Derby 29k	7	11	$10^{6¾}$	11^{10}	6^{3}	$1^{1½}$	Garner M	126 w	*.50e	107-04	Cavalcade$126^{1½}$Plight123^{2}New Deal119^{3}	Handily	12
2Jun34- 6Was	fst	1¼	$:46^{4}$ $1:11^{4}$ $1:38^{1}$ 2:04	American Derby 28k	1	9	$8^{9¾}$	6^{4}	1^{hd}	1^{2}	Garner M	126 w	*1.07e	90-09	Cavalcade126^{2}Discovery118^{6}Singing Wood121^{1}	Drew out	9
12May34- 5Pim	fst	$1\frac{3}{16}$	$:47^{3}$ $1:12^{2}$ $1:37^{3}$ $1:58^{1}$	Preakness 29k	5	7	$6^{4¾}$	$5^{3½}$	2^{hd}	2no	Garner M	126 w	*.45e	99-11	High Quest126^{no}Cavalcade126^{1}Discovery$126^{1½}$	Gaining	7
	Geldings not eligible																
5May34- 6CD	fst	1¼	$:47^{1}$ $1:12^{1}$ $1:37^{2}$ 2:04	Ky Derby 36k	8	11	$7^{7½}$	3^{2}	2^{nk}	$1^{2½}$	Garner M	126 w	*1.50e	89-11	Cavalcade$126^{2½}$Discovery126^{4}Agrarian126^{no}	Handily	13
28Apr34- 5HdG	fst	$1\frac{1}{16}$	$:23^{2}$:47 $1:11^{3}$ $1:43^{3}$	Chesapeake 9.3k	8	3	$1^{½}$	1^{1}	1^{2}	$1^{1¼}$	Garner M	119 w	*1.10e	102-07	Cavalcade$119^{1¼}$Agrarian114^{no}Discovery$114^{½}$	Driving	9
25Apr34- 5HdG	fst	1 70	$:23^{3}$ $:47^{3}$ $1:12^{3}$ $1:41^{4}$	Alw 1000	6	4	$3^{2½}$	2^{2}	$1^{1½}$	1^{2}	Garner M	113 w	*1.55e	100-07	Cavalcade113^{2}Agrarian106^{4}Jabot$108^{1½}$	Easily	7
4Nov33- 4Pim	fst	$1\frac{1}{16}$	$:23^{3}$ $:47^{3}$ 1:12 $1:44^{3}$	Walden H 6.5k	6	8	$5^{3¾}$	$5^{7¼}$	3^{8}	$3^{6¼}$	Jones R	121 w	*3.00	93-07	Chicstraw118^{nk}Discovery113^{6}Cavalcade121^{3}	Closed fast	10
28Oct33- 4Lrl	fst	1	$:23^{2}$ $:47^{3}$ $1:12^{3}$ $1:38^{4}$	S Lowe Jenkins H 3.8k	3	4	$7^{2¼}$	$5^{2¼}$	$3^{2½}$	2^{1}	Bellizzi D	118 w	4.80	91-11	Bazaar116^{1}Cavalcade118^{no}Vicar106^{3}	Belated rush	8
7Oct33- 5Lrl	fst	6f	:23 $:46^{2}$ $1:11^{1}$	Richard Johnson 3.8k	3	6	$6^{1¼}$	$6^{2¼}$	$4^{3½}$	4^{1}	Bellizzi D	112 w	2.70	93-11	Chicstraw$116^{1½}$WiseDughtr119^{1}Dscovry$113^{1½}$	Closed stoutly	6
3Oct33- 4Lrl	fst	5½f	$:23^{3}$ $:47^{2}$ $1:06^{1}$	Alw 800	4	6	$5^{5½}$	$5^{3¾}$	$3^{½}$	1^{1}	Meade D	122 w	*1.00	92-14	Cavalcade122^{1}Cant Remember107^{1}Polly Egret107^{2}	Drew out	6
27Sep33- 5HdG	fst	6f	$:22^{4}$:46 $1:11^{3}$	Eastern Shore H 13k	1	9	$9^{4¼}$	$8^{4¾}$	3^{1}	2^{1}	Bellizzi D	115 w	8.00e	96-12	HighQuest117^{1}Cavalcade115^{1}WiseDaughtr$122^{1½}$	Belated rush	9
23Aug33- 4Sar	hy	6f	$:23^{3}$ $:48^{2}$ 1:15	Sanford 3.5k	3	2	$3^{1¾}$	$3^{1¾}$	2^{nk}	2^{2}	Fronk W	123 w	*3.50e	75-27	FirstMinstrel113^{2}Cavalcade123^{no}SoonOver116^{5}	Game finish	10
8Aug33- 3Sar	fst	5½f	$:23^{1}$ $:46^{4}$ 1:06	Sar Sales 2.4k	4	8	$6^{8¾}$	$5^{4¼}$	3^{2}	3^{4}	Bellizzi D	122 w	6.00e	89-11	WiseDaughter119^{3}BlackBuddy122^{1}Cavalcade122^{2}	Closed fast	8
5Aug33- 3Sar	gd	6f	$:23^{3}$ $:47^{4}$ 1:14	U S Hotel 8.1k	4	6	$6^{1½}$	6^{2}	$4^{2¼}$	$4^{6¾}$	Horn F	125 w	4.00e	75-19	Red Wagon$117^{1¼}$Black Buddy127^{4}Sainted$115^{1½}$	Shuffled back	7
1Jly33- 6AP	my	5½f	:23 $:48^{3}$ $1:01^{3}$ $1:08^{4}$	Hyde Park 14k	14	13	$10^{7½}$	$8^{4¼}$	$3^{4½}$	1^{nk}	Bellizzi D	112 w	90.57f	77-34	Cavalcade112^{nk}Singing Wood114^{1}Dartle117^{6}	Hard drive	14
28Jun33- 1AP	fst	5½f	$:22^{3}$ $:45^{3}$ $:57^{3}$ $1:04^{3}$	©Md Sp Wt	6	9	$8^{8¼}$	6^{13}	5^{11}	$3^{7½}$	Bellizzi D	118 w	6.73	90-09	Singing Wood118^{6}Sir Ten$118^{1½}$Cavalcade118^{3}	Closed fast	10
27May33- 3Bel	fst	4½f-WC	$:52^{3}$	Alw 600	2	5		$4^{1½}$	$4^{1¼}$	4^{5}	Bellizzi D	112 w	12.00	87-10	Billy M.118^{no}Foghound112^{no}Salaam115^{5}	Tired	8

Challedon

b. c. 1936, by Challenger II (Swynford)–Laura Gal, by Sir Gallahad III — **Lifetime record: 44 20 7 6 $334,660**

Own.– W.L. Brann
Br.– Branncastle Farm (Md)
Tr.– E.A. Christmas

17Nov42- 6Bow	fst	1⅛	$:49^{4}$ $1:15^{3}$ $1:41^{4}$ $1:55^{4}$	3↑ Handicap 1035	1	4	3^{3}	3^{1}	3^{1}	5^{5}	Keiper P	122wb	*2.10	79-19	SirAlfred$107^{1½}$KsrofAudly$116^{2½}$AbbPrr$111^{½}$	Tired at finish	5
4Nov42- 7Pim	gd	$1\frac{1}{16}$	$:23^{2}$ $:47^{3}$ $1:13^{1}$ 1:47	3↑ Handicap 2000	4	2	$1^{1½}$	1^{hd}	2^{hd}	$3^{2¼}$	Woolf G	122wb	2.90	81-23	Ksar of Audley107^{nk}Bushwhacker115^{2}Challedon$122^{½}$	Tired	7
17Oct42- 7Lrl	sl	$1\frac{1}{16}$	$:24^{3}$ $:49^{3}$ $1:15^{1}$ $1:47^{4}$	3↑ Handicap 2500	2	3	$4^{4½}$	$4^{6½}$	$4^{4¾}$	5^{8}	Woolf G	120 w	2.65	70-28	Equifox$108.5^{1¼}$Rosetown111^{3}He Rolls114^{3}	Tired	5
26Sep42- 5HdG	fst	1⅛	$:47^{3}$ 1:12 $1:37^{3}$ 1:50	3↑ Havre de Grace H 18k	2	6	$7^{8¾}$	8^{10}	8^{11}	$8^{14½}$	Woolf G	122 w	*1.30e	84-12	TolaRose$109^{½}$Aonbarr$114^{1½}$Pctor116^{4}	Outrun,pulled up sore	9
26May42- 6Bel	fst	1⅛	:47 1:12 $1:36^{2}$ $1:48^{4}$	3↑ Handicap 3035	4	3	$3^{2½}$	2^{hd}	2^{2}	2^{5}	Woolf G	126 w	1.25	93-08	Shut Out112^{5}Challedon126^{4}Reading II118^{5}	Second best	4
6May42- 6Pim	fst	$1\frac{3}{16}$	$:47^{2}$ $1:11^{4}$ $1:37^{4}$ 1:57	3↑ Dixie H 25k	6	7	7^{13}	7^{10}	3^{nk}	$4^{1¼}$	Woolf G	124 w	5.90	97-12	Whirlaway$128^{¾}$Attention$124^{½}$Mioland126^{hd}	Weakened	8
25Apr42- 5HdG	fst	$1\frac{1}{16}$	$:24^{1}$ $:48^{2}$ 1:13 $1:45^{2}$	3↑ Philadelphia H 11k	6	7	$7^{8¼}$	$7^{3¾}$	$3^{1½}$	1no	Woolf G	122 w	3.20	91-21	Challedon122^{no}Mioland$124^{1½}$Cape Cod112^{3}	Hard drive	7
18Apr42- 7HdG	fst	$1\frac{1}{16}$	:24 $:48^{3}$ $1:13^{2}$ $1:45^{2}$	3↑ Handicap 3000	4	4	$4^{2½}$	3^{3}	3^{2}	2^{hd}	Woolf G	124wb	*.80	91-18	Alaking112^{hd}Challedon124^{3}Warlock$108^{1½}$	Just missed	6
7Mar42- 6Hia	fst	1¼	:47 $1:12^{2}$ $1:37^{4}$ $2:05^{1}$	3↑ Widener H 67k	12	14	16^{14}	$12^{9¾}$	$10^{3¾}$	$6^{1½}$	Woolf G	126wb	13.85e	81-17	The Rhymer111^{hd}Best Seller112^{hd}Olympus107^{nk}	Off slowly	17
28Feb42- 5Hia	fst	1⅛	$:46^{2}$ $1:11^{2}$ $1:36^{4}$ $1:49^{3}$	4↑ Sp Wt 2500	8	5	$7^{3¾}$	$7^{3½}$	6^{6}	$5^{6¼}$	Woolf G	122wb	3.55e	87-14	Market Wise$120^{1½}$Attention$120^{½}$War Relic120^{nk}	No mishaps	9
24Feb42- 6Hia	sl	7f	$:22^{4}$ $:46^{3}$ $1:11^{4}$ $1:24^{3}$	4↑ Alw 1400	5	4	$5^{8¼}$	$4^{3½}$	3^{2}	1^{3}	Woolf G	117 w	*1.25	89-21	Challedon117^{3}Signator110^{hd}Doublrab109^{4}	Going away	6
16Feb42- 6Hia	fst	1⅛	$:48^{3}$ $1:12^{3}$ $1:37^{3}$ $1:50^{4}$	4↑ Alw 1400	4	5	$5^{4½}$	4^{4}	$4^{1¾}$	2^{5}	Woolf G	126 w	*.65	82-23	Ponty106^{5}Challedon126^{no}Choppy Sea106^{3}	Dwelt at start	6
7Feb42- 7Hia	fst	7f	$:23^{1}$ $:46^{3}$ $1:11^{3}$ 1:24	4↑ Alw 1500	2	6	5^{7}	3^{7}	3^{4}	2^{2}	Woolf G	124 w	14.55	90-13	SheriffCulkin105^{2}Challedon$124^{1¼}$WarRelic122^{6}	Closed fast	7
	Previously trained by L.T. Whitehill																
4Jly41- 7Hol	fst	1⅛	$:46^{2}$ $1:10^{4}$ $1:36^{4}$ $1:49^{2}$	3↑ American H 22k	8	8	$9^{7¾}$	$10^{6¾}$	9^{9}	8^{8}	Woolf G	126 w	*2.60	90-09	Mioland126^{no}Woof Woof114^{1}Big Pebble$117^{½}$	Dull effort	10
1Mar41- 6SA	sly	1¼	:47 $1:12^{1}$ $1:38^{3}$ $2:05^{2}$	3↑ S Anita H 124k	7	7	10^{7}	13^{22}	13^{22}	$14^{17¾}$	Woolf G	130 w	3.20	61-29	Bay View108^{nk}Mioland124^{4}Bolingbroke106^{2}	Outrun	16

Date	Cond	Dist	Fractions	Race	PP	St	1st call	2nd call	Str	Fin	Jockey	Wt	Odds	Speed	Top finishers	Comment
22Feb41- 6SA	sl	1 1/16	:234 :473 1:121 1:452 3↑	San Antonio H 12k	11	9	910	1014	815	77	Woolf G	128 w	3.70	78-23	Mioland128noHysterical1111Bay View1051	Raced wide 11
		Previously trained by G.D. Cameron														
1Nov40- 7Pim	sl	1 3/16	:52 1:18 1:444 2:031 3↑	Pim Spl 10k	2	1	13	12½	12½	12	Woolf G	126 w	*.20	67-24	Challedon1262Can't Wait126	Easily 2
28Sep40- 5HdG	fst	1⅛	:483 1:124 1:38 1:502 3↑	Havre de Grace H 16k	1	3	43¼	31	1hd	13	Woolf G	130 w	*.25	97-13	Challdn1303HoneyCloud110½MaskedGeneral1125	Going away 4
21Sep40- 6Nar	fst	1 3/16	:472 1:13 1:381 1:57 3↑	Nar Spl 31k	1	3	48	31	12	2½	Woolf G	130 w	*.70	89-16	Hash122½Challedon130½Viscounty1165	Tired badly 9
		Previously trained by L.J. Schaefer														
27Aug40- 5Sar	fst	1¼	:484 1:131 1:381 2:031 3↑	Whitney 3.7k	3	1	22	21	1hd	1no	Woolf G	126 w	*.20	93-14	Challdon126noIsoltr1267¾DuskyFox117	Driving,forced wide 3
27Jly40- 7Hol	fst	1¼	:461 1:11 1:36 2:02 3↑	Hol Gold Cup 53k	9	6	89½	53	23	11¼	Woolf G	133 w	2.70	103-07	Challedon1331¼Specify1172½Can't Wait1151½	Going away 11
17Jly40- 7Suf	fst	1⅛	:471 1:104 1:353 1:49 3↑	Mass H 65k	8	8	87¾	64¾	64¾	32½	Woolf G	130 w	*.90	97-12	Eight Thirty1261Hash1151½Challedon130½	Closed fast 11
9Jly40- 0Suf	fst	1 1/16	:243 :474 1:121 1:441 4↑	Alw 1500	2	1	11	11½	13	12½	Woolf G	126 w	-	95-12	Challedon1262½Many Stings118	Easily 2
1Nov39- 5Pim	gd	1 3/16	:512 1:163 1:404 1:59 3↑	Pim Spl 10k	2	2	11	1½	2hd	1½	Arcaro E	120 w	*.45	88-19	Challedon120½Kayak II12612Cravat126	Going away 3
21Oct39- 5Lrl	fst	1¼	:47 1:112 1:363 2:023	Maryland H 8.8k	4	1	45½	1hd	12	14	Woolf G	128 w	*.15	97-14	Challedon1284General Mowlee1001Hostility1066	Going away 5
10Oct39- 5Kee	fst	1 3/16	:471 1:114 1:361 1:543 3↑	Tranter 5.4k	5	5	53¾	2hd	12	14	Woolf G	120 w	*.40	144-02	Challedon1204Hash1168Chief Onaway1082	Ridden out 5
30Sep39- 5HdG	my	1⅛	:482 1:141 1:40 1:523 3↑	Havre de Grace H 18k	1	3	33	31½	12	14	Woolf G	122 w	*.70	86-22	Challedon1224RobertL.107nkManieO'Hara105.51½	Going away 6
16Sep39- 6Haw	fst	1¼	:471 1:12 1:373 2:031 3↑	Haw Gold Cup H 16k	4	5	65	42	1½	1¾	Richards H	120 w	*.30	92-12	Challedon120¾Gridiron106noChief Onaway108¾	Drew away 8
2Sep39- 5Nar	fst	1 3/16	:482 1:124 1:374 1:563 3↑	Nar Spl H 31k	6	6	64¼	52	1½	13	Richards H	118 w	2.60	92-14	Challedon1183Kayak II1284Sorteado116½	Going away 6
26Aug39- 5Nar	hy	1⅛	:472 1:131 1:394 1:524	J C Thornton Mem H 6.1k	2	6	66¾	32	21	21½	Richards H	128 w	*.55	81-23	Porter's Mite1161½Challedon1282½Montsin10410	No excuse 6
22Jly39- 6AP	fst	1¼	:47 1:112 1:36 2:02	Classic 47k	4	4	59½	21½	1½	1nk	Richards H	126 w	13.60	96-11	Challedon126nkSun Lover1216Johnstown1262	Hard drive 5
12Jly39- 7Suf	sly	1⅛	:482 1:13 1:391 1:52 3↑	Mass H 68k	8	11	118¼	97	66¾	46	Richards H	113 w	*1.30	79-19	Fighting Fox113½Pompoon1203Burning Star1102½	Late foot 12
4Jly39- 6Suf	fst	1 3/16	:464 1:104 1:37 1:562	Yankee H 18k	2	4	68	45	11	11	Richards H	124 w	*.90	99-11	Challedon1241Hash1172Silent Witness106no	Easily 6
24Jun39- 5Del	fst	1 1/16	:24 :472 1:13 1:444	Kent H 12k	1	6	63¾	52	32	32	Seabo G	126 w	*1.90	93-11	SunLover117noEightThirty1202Challedon1261½	Closed well 9
17Jun39- 5Aqu	fst	1⅛	:46 1:103 1:353 1:482	Dwyer 12k	1	2	22	24	23	37	Seabo G	126 w	8.00	92-05	Johnstown1261Sun Lover1166Challedon1266	Weakened 5
13May39- 6Pim	my	1 3/16	:473 1:133 1:394 1:594	Preakness 70k	2	2	44½	34½	11½	11¼	Seabo G	126 w	6.20	84-19	Challedon1261¼Gilded Knight1263Volitant1263	Ridden out 6
6May39- 7CD	fst	1¼	:472 1:124 1:38 2:032	Ky Derby 56k	7	5	78	45	35	28	Seabo G	126 w	6.60	84-11	Johnstown1268Challedn1261Heather Broom126½	Good effort 8
22Apr39- 5HdG	fst	1 1/16	:232 :48 1:131 1:453	Chesapeake 17k	3	8	77¾	53	44½	32½	Seabo G	122 w	*2.60	87-14	Gilded Knight1141Impound1191½Challedon1221½	Closed fast 9
12Nov38- 6Pim	fst	1 1/16	:232 :473 1:124 1:454	Pim Futurity 33k	3	7	64¾	33¼	2hd	11½	Seabo G	119 w	3.95	91-13	Challedon1191½ThirdDegree1191GildedKnght1222	Going away 8
		Geldings not eligible														
29Oct38- 6Nar	hy	1 70	:231 :47 1:14 1:462	New England Fut 42k	6	6	64¼	1hd	13	12	Seabo G	114 w	14.70	73-30	Challedon1142Impound114nkGilded Knight1144	Handily 7
		Geldings not eligible														
15Oct38- 4Lrl	fst	6f	:234 :473 1:132	[S]Md Futurity 6.4k	7	5	71¾	62¾	31	1no	Seabo G	111 w	*2.30	87-12	Challedon111noWar Moon1091Mystery Miss1133	Just up 12
17Sep38- 5HdG	fst	6f	:232 :464 1:124	Eastern Shore H 15k	7	13	138¼	138¼	1215	126½	Laidley O	116 w	8.25	82-14	Time Alone1091Sweet Nancy110hdT.M. Dorsett112½	Outrun 15
7Sep38- 2Nar	fst	6f	:224 :462 1:121	Md Sp Wt	3	3	11½	13	14	14	Laidley O	116 w	2.50	90-11	Challedon1164Greedan1162½Top Queen1132	Much best 8
6Jly38- 5Del	fst	5½f	:234 :49 1:004 1:072	Alw 1000	2	4	53¾	54¼	47	36	Laidley O	112 w	31.10	89-11	Birch Rod1182Buds Bell1154Challedon112hd	Closed fast 7

Discovery

ch. c. 1931, by Display (Fair Play)–Ariadne, by Light Brigade
Own.– A.G. Vanderbilt
Br.– Mereworth Stud (Ky)
Tr.– J.H. Stotler

Lifetime record: 63 27 10 10 $195,287

Date	Cond	Dist	Fractions	Race	PP	St	1st call	2nd call	Str	Fin	Jockey	Wt	Odds	Speed	Top finishers	Comment
30Sep36- 5HdG	sly	1⅛	:48 1:131 1:373 1:51 3↑	Havre de Grace H 11k	1	4	44	45½	46½	54½	Bejshak J	128wsb	*.75	89-16	RomnSldier1182WhereAway1102DrkHop110½	Not enough late 8
16Sep36- 5Nar	fst	1 3/16	:48 1:123 1:373 1:562 3↑	Nar Spl 37k	5	8	88½	87¾	32	2hd	Bejshak J	130wb	*1.55	93-11	Rosemont121hdDiscovery1301½Time Supply1216	Just missed 8
29Aug36- 5Sar	sly	1¾	:502 2:083 2:341 3:004 3↑	Sar Cup 7.7k	1	2	21½	21	25	28	Bejshak J	126 w	*.40	63-22	Granville1168Discovery126	Outrun 2
22Aug36- 5Sar	my	1¼	:483 1:131 1:392 2:064 3↑	Whitney 4.4k	1	1	410	13	15	110	Bejshak J	126wsb	*.20	75-27	Discovery12610Esposa1218Rust1061	Eased up 4
		Geldings not eligible														
8Aug36- 5Sar	sl	1 3/16	:492 1:143 1:403 2:002 3↑	Merchants & Cits H 11k	4	4	44½	32½	55¼	56½	Bejshak J	143wsb	*.70	69-22	Esposa1001Count Arthur107hdMantagna1081½	Tired 5
5Aug36- 4Sar	fst	1	:241 :481 1:132 1:384 3↑	Wilson 4.5k	1	1	12	15	14	18	Bejshak J	126wsb	*.04e	87-17	Discovery1268St. Bernard115.55Purple Knight114	Easily 3
		Geldings not eligible														
1Aug36- 5Sar	fst	1¼	:48 1:121 1:382 2:05 3↑	Saratoga H 10k	1	3	12	13	14	16	Bejshak J	132wsb	*.60e	84-12	Discovery1326Mantagna1091½Isolater103nk	Easily 6
22Jly36- 5Suf	fst	1⅛	:472 1:12 1:373 1:494 3↑	Mass H 32k	2	7	102¾	94½	78¾	89½	Fallon L	136wsb	*1.10e	88-07	Time Supply1213Gov. Sholtz1003Stand Pat1191	Impeded 11
4Jly36- 6AP	fst	1⅛	:474 1:12 1:371 1:493 3↑	Stars & Stripes H 13k	5	8	77¼	88	810	98¾	Fallon L	138wsb	*1.00	90-09	Stand Pat1161½Corinto108noWhopper122no	Swerved 12
27Jun36- 5Aqu	fst	1⅛	:472 1:122 1:372 1:50 3↑	Brooklyn H 14k	3	4	23	22	21½	14	Fallon L	136wb	*.29e	91-12	Discovery1364Good Gamble1104Roman Soldier126hd	Easily 5
17Jun36- 4Aqu	fst	1⅛	:47 1:113 1:371 1:50 3↑	Handicap 1165	2	2	12	14	14	14	Fallon L	135wb	*.45	91-14	Discovery1354Palma1063Observant110	Easily 3
22Feb36- 6SA	gd	1¼	:46 1:104 1:372 2:041 3↑	S Anita H 122k	12	12	109	114½	108½	75¾	Bejshak J	130wsb	*1.50	84-17	Top Row116½Time Supply114½Rosemont116½	Bumped 15
8Feb36- 6SA	fst	1⅛	:472 1:12 1:37 1:492 3↑	San Antonio H 8.6k	8	6	52¾	51¼	46	58	Bejshak J	138wsb	*.70e	93-10	TimeSupply1166PompeysPillar1051ArlCross106½	Dull effort 9
1Feb36- 6SA	sly	1 1/16	:232 :472 1:122 1:452 3↑	San Carlos H 5.7k	3	6	59	46½	2½	15	Bejshak J	130wsb	*.60	87-20	Discovery1305Ariel Cross1065Beefsteak1041½	Easily best 6
26Oct35- 5Lrl	fst	1¼	:461 1:113 1:371 2:023 3↑	Washington H 12k	7	9	99¾	63½	53½	45	Bejshak J	138wsb	*.65	92-13	Firethorn1193CountArthur112noOnlyOne1142	Closed ground 9
22Oct35- 6CI	my	1¼	:483 1:133 1:392 2:062 3↑	Cincinnati H 12k	6	5	35	16	110	112	Bejshak J	132wb	*.20	78-26	Discovry13212GoldenRockII10412OpenHearth1031	Much best 6
16Oct35- 6Suf	fst	1⅛	:473 1:12 1:364 1:492 3↑	Mass H 27k	7	3	31	2hd	3nk	3nk	Bejshak J	138wsb	*.70	112-02	Top Row116nkWhopper108noDiscovery1382	Good effort 8
5Oct35- 6Haw	fst	1¼	:472 1:112 1:372 2:042 3↑	Haw Gold Cup 16k	3	1	21	14	15	18	Bejshak J	126wsb	*.10	86-11	Discovery1263Top Dog1208Spanish Babe1174	Eased up 4
24Aug35- 5Sar	fst	1¼	:48 1:13 1:38 2:043 3↑	Whitney 4.3k	2	1	22	1hd	11	12	Bejshak J	126wsb	*.10e	86-14	Discovery1262Esposa1001½Good Goods1147	Easily 4
		Geldings not eligible														
21Aug35- 5Nar	fst	1 3/16	:484 1:123 1:37 1:554 3↑	Nar Spl 30k	2	1	11½	2hd	21	21½	Bejshak J	139wsb	*.25	94-08	Top Row1101½Discovery1391Howard1072	No mishap 5
10Aug35- 5Sar	fst	1 3/16	:482 1:132 1:38 1:572 3↑	Merchants & Cits H 10k	5	1	12	12	12	12	Bejshak J	139wsb	*.60e	91-14	Discovery1392Stand Pat1172Top Row1175	In hand 6
31Jly35- 4Sar	fst	1	:244 :48 1:121 1:371 3↑	Wilson 4.5k	2	2	2hd	13	13	16	Bejshak J	126wb	*.10e	95-11	Discovery1266Identify122nkPsychic Bid112	Eased up 3
		Geldings not eligible														
27Jly35- 6AP	fst	1¼	:472 1:11 1:36 2:011 3↑	Arlington H 12k	6	5	32	1½	13	15	Bejshak J	135wsb	*.30	103-06	Discovery1355Stand Pat1154Riskulus1162	Easily 7
20Jly35- 6Suf	gd	1⅛	:484 1:133 1:392 1:514 3↑	Bunker Hill H 10k	5	3	2hd	13	16	115	Bejshak J	131wsb	*.20	- -	Discovery13115Gov.Sholtz1071AdvisingAnna103½	Galloping 5
13Jly35- 5Emp	sl	1⅛	:484 1:13 1:39 1:53 3↑	Butler H 15k	4	4	48	33¼	31¾	11½	Bejshak J	132wsb	*.90	90-11	Discovery1321½Only One1132Top Row1163	Easily 6
4Jly35- 6AP	gd	1⅛	:482 1:13 1:382 1:504 3↑	Stars & Stripes H 12k	4	4	2½	1hd	13	16	Bejshak J	126wsb	*.30	93-18	Discovery1266Chief Cherokee1061½Riskulus1182	Easily 8
29Jun35- 6Det	my	1 3/16	:464 1:12 1:381 1:581 3↑	Det Challenge Cup 13k	1	1	16	110	118	130	Bejshak J	126wb	*.20	100-25	Discovery12630Azucar127	Easily 2
22Jun35- 5Aqu	fst	1⅛	:461 1:112 1:353 1:481 3↑	Brooklyn H 13k	2	2	22	21½	1nk	18	Bejshak J	123wb	5.00	102-13	Discovery1238King Saxon1274Omaha1146	Driven out 6
15Jun35- 5Rkm	my	1⅛	:47 1:122 1:39 1:522 3↑	Rock Park H 10k	1	4	22	33	32½	33	Bejshak J	128wsb	*1.20e	84-18	Identify1138Dark Hope113hdDiscovery1282½	Closed well 11
10Jun35- 5Aqu	gd	1	:232 :463 1:113 1:371 3↑	Queens County H 4.7k	5	4	42½	43¾	43¾	57	Bejshak J	123wsb	2.60	87-09	King Saxon1181Only One1103Singing Wood113hd	Faltered 6
30May35- 5Bel	fst	1¼	:46 1:103 1:361 2:02 3↑	Suburban H 15k	6	6	68	66½	42¾	21½	Bejshak J	123wsb	2.60e	88-12	Head Play1141½Discovery1233Only One1103	Closed well 7
18May35- 4Bel	fst	1	:233 :471 1:121 1:381 3↑	Metropolitan H 8.8k	4	5	52¼	43¾	43¼	41	Bejshak J	127wsb	5.00	83-16	King Saxon118nkSinging Wood114nkOnly One113½	Swerved 9
15May35- 4Bel	fst	6f-WC	1:113 3↑	Toboggan H 5.2k	12	7		53	44½	52½	Bejshak J	130wb	*1.80e	86-11	Identify1081½Ajaccio1161Pompeys Pillar102no	Evenly 12
20Oct34- 5Lrl	fst	1¼	:461 1:102 1:364 2:03	Maryland H 6k	3	1	11½	12	13	1½	Bejshak J	130wsb	*.30	95-09	Discovery130½Good Goods1095Maine Chance105nk	Hard drive 5
29Sep34- 5HdG	fst	1⅛	:473 1:114 1:38 1:504 3↑	Havre de Grace H 12k	5	9	62½	32	33	31	Bejshak J	126wsb	*.55	94-10	Faireno122noAzucar1081Discovery1261½	Impeded 9
15Sep34- 5HdG	gd	1 1/16	:243 :49 1:134 1:451	Potomac H 11k	5	5	32½	3½	14	14	Bejshak J	128wsb	*.60	92-17	Discovery1284Chicstraw116noOnly One1061	Easily 6
3Sep34- 6Nar	fst	1 3/16	:472 1:132 1:373 1:55 3↑	Rhode Island H 16k	1	5	11½	11½	12	12	Bejshak J	119wb	*1.00	- -	Discovery1192Hadagal1192½Good Goods1041	Easily 6
1Sep34- 5Rkm	fst	1 1/16	:234 :474 1:131 1:431 3↑	Bennington H 10k	8	10	86	54	65¼	56½	Bejshak J	124wb	*.40	98-07	Advising Anna1022Fleam1073Larranaga1131½	Impeded 10
25Aug34- 5Sar	hy	1¼	:503 1:162 1:413 2:074 3↑	Whitney 3.3k	3	1	23	13	15	110	Meade D	105wb	*.33	70-24	Discovery10510Fleam1074Time Clock1121	Eased up 4
14Aug34- 4Sar	fst	1 3/16	:481 1:122 1:373 1:571	Kenner 2.4k	2	1	15	16	13	12	Bejshak J	113wsb	*.10	92-10	Discovery1132Somebody1068Cleves106	Easily 3
14Jly34- 6AP	fst	1¼	:473 1:12 1:363 2:024	Classic 40k	4	1	43½	2hd	23	24	Bejshak J	121wsb	4.91	91-08	Cavalcade1264Discovery121½Hadagal1213	Held well 9

4Jly34- 4Aqu fst 1⅛ :481 1:13 1:373 1:494 3↑ Brooklyn H 4.3k 4 2 21 23 22 16 Bejshak J 113wb *.60 94-14 Discovery1136Dark Secret1266Fleam1081 Easily 4
28Jun34- 4Aqu fst 7f :232 :464 1:112 1:233 Alw 1200 4 2 2hd 12 13 16 Bejshak J 112wsb *1.80 97-10 Discovery1126Fleam1103Somebody1153 In hand 7
16Jun34- 6Det fst 1 3/16 :473 1:124 1:393 1:581 Det Derby 29k 2 1 64 53¼ 108 1114½ Workman R 119wsb 3.50 92-04 Cavalcade1261½Plight1232New Deal1193 Outrun 12
2Jun34- 6Was fst 1¼ :464 1:114 1:381 2:04 American Derby 28k 6 6 57½ 42 2hd 22 Bejshak J 118wb 2.74 88-09 Cavalcade1262Discovery1186Singing Wood1211 Troubled 9
25May34- 3Bel sly 7f :232 :471 1:12 1:25 Alw 1000 6 1 14 15 16 110 Bejshak J 112wsb *.20 85-17 Discovery11210War Letter115½Rebel Yell1093 In hand 7
12May34- 5Pim fst 1 3/16 :473 1:122 1:373 1:581 Preakness 29k 2 2 31 32 3nk 31 Bejshak J 126wsb 7.40 98-11 High Quest126noCavalcade1261Discovery1261½ Gamely 7
Geldings not eligible
5May34- 6CD fst 1¼ :471 1:121 1:372 2:04 Ky Derby 36k 6 4 33 12 1nk 22½ Bejshak J 126wb 12.10 86-11 Cavalcade1262½Discovery1264Agrarian126no Held well 13
28Apr34- 5HdG fst 1 1/16 :232 :47 1:113 1:433 Chesapeake 9.3k 1 2 31 21 22 31¼ Bejshak J 114wb 3.60 101-07 Cavalcade1191¼Agrarian114noDiscovery114½ Faltered 9
4Nov33- 4Pim fst 1 1/16 :233 :473 1:12 1:443 Walden H 6.5k 7 3 2hd 1hd 2hd 2nk Humphries L 113wb 4.40 99-07 Chicstraw118nkDiscovery1136Cavalcade1213 Just missed 10
Previously owned by A. Pons,previously trained by J.R. Pryce
28Oct33- 6Lat fst 1 :232 :464 1:124 1:394 Ky Jockey Club 19k 10 5 36 35½ 24 22½ Allen CE 122wb 3.60 80-18 Mata Hari1192½Discovery1222Collateral1222½ Closed well 11
21Oct33- 6Lat fst 6f-FC :222 :461 :592 1:093 Breeders' Futurity 21k 6 5 86½ 79½ 47½ 32¾ Allen CE 122wb 3.20 98-18 Mata Hari1242½Giggling119nkDiscovery122no Belated rush 12
7Oct33- 5Lrl fst 6f :23 :462 1:114 Richard Johnson 3.8k 1 4 53¾ 31½ 31½ 32½ Steffen E 113wb 13.60 94-11 Chicstraw1161½WiseDughtr1191Dscovry1131½ Close quarters 6
27Sep33- 5HdG fst 6f :224 :46 1:113 Eastern Shore H 13k 8 5 62 63¾ 66½ 66 Steffen E 116wb 25.90 91-12 High Quest1171Cavalcade1151Wise Daughter1221½ Even race 9
21Sep33- 4HdG fst 6f :233 :472 1:122 Alw 800 3 1 2½ 21 1½ 12½ Gilbert J 113wb *.80 93-11 Discovery1132½Prince Pompey1134Collateral115hd Easily 6
2Sep33- 4Sar fst 6½f :232 :47 1:121 1:19 Hopeful 38k 3 14 106 98¼ 85 34 Gilbert J 117wb 15.00 86-14 Bazaar1194High Quest117noDiscovery117no Belated rush 14
28Aug33- 5Sar gd 6f :232 :474 1:13 Alw 600 2 3 34 32 31¼ 33½ Robertson A 111wb 12.00 83-19 High Quest1112Soon Over1181½Discovery1113 Closed well 8
29Jly33- 5AP fst 6f :223 :46 1:111 Arl Futurity 42k 4 6 84¾ 811 711 710½ Corbett C 117wb 69.33 84-11 Far Star1161½Hadagal1176Singing Wood1171½ Outrun 8
18Jly33- 4AP fst 5½f :23 :463 :592 1:053 Alw 800 3 5 31½ 21 21½ 23 Jones R 115wb 3.52 90-13 Hadagal1153Discovery115½Spy Hill1111 Closed well 7
6Jly33- 1AP fst 5½f :223 :463 :592 1:06 ©Md Sp Wt 11 6 52½ 31½ 11 15 Jones R 118wb 6.98 91-12 Discovery1185GoldSignet118nkCottonClub1181 Easily best 12
28Jun33- 1AP fst 5½f :223 :453 :573 1:043 ©Md Sp Wt 7 6 3½ 36½ 48½ 511¼ Woolf G 118wb *2.40 86-09 Singing Wood1186Sir Ten1181½Cavalcade1183 Tired 10
8Jun33- 5Bel fst 5f-WC 1:00 Md Sp Wt 2 1 31 31 32½ Mills H 115wb *1.50 77-14 Galabang1152½Willow King115noDiscovery115nk Faltered 7
3Jun33- 6Bel fst 5f-WC :593 Md Sp Wt 1 7 55¼ 46 48¾ Robertson A 117 w 3.60 73-19 Watch Her1147Koterito1171½Galabang117nk Closed well 8

El Chico

ch. c. 1936, by John P. Grier (Whisk Broom II)–La Chica, by Sweep
Lifetime record: 18 9 3 1 $88,050
Own.– W. Ziegler Jr
Br.– Leslie Combs Jr trustee (Ky)
Tr.– M. Brady

7Oct39- 4Lrl fst 6f :233 :463 1:114 3↑ Handicap 1500 5 3 41¼ 52 62¼ 52¼ Wall N 117 w 3.10 93-14 Joe Schenck114hdAllegro1111½Bill Farnsworth119nk 7
Hard urged,no excuse
3Oct39- 5Lrl my 6f :243 :483 1:132 3↑ Capital H 9.3k 5 2 3nk 73½ 88½ 810 Wall N 119 w 3.85 77-22 Sun Egret1201½Clodion1121½Rough Time122½ Tired 8
23Sep39- 5HdG fst 1 1/16 :24 :472 1:124 1:444 Potomac H 11k 1 1 11 11 2½ 33¼ Wall N 115 w 6.70 91-15 Third Degree1143Porter's Mite116nkEl Chico1151½ Tired 7
13Sep39- 5Aqu fst 6½f :222 :453 1:101 1:163 3↑ Bay Shore H 7.6k 9 7 54 41½ 2nk 68½ Workman R 126 w *2.60e 91-08 ThirdDegree1161½BillFarnsworth1213WsBrrstr106hd Impeded 12
14Aug39- 5Nar fst 6f :223 :46 1:11 3↑ Nar H 6.7k 3 5 61½ 1hd 1½ 2no Wall N 115 w *.35 96-12 Olney108noEl Chico1152½Prairie Dog103hd No excuse 10
10Aug39- 5Sar fst 6f :224 :461 1:103 Alw 1000 4 1 11½ 13 14 13 Wall N 119 w *.33 99-08 ElChico1193ThirdDegree1162NoCompetition1192 Easily best 4
1Aug39- 5Sar fst 1 :232 :471 1:112 1:373 3↑ Alw 1200 3 1 14 15 16 15 Wall N 105 w *.90 93-12 El Chico1055Pernie113noMy Porter1094 Much best 7
30May39- 3Bel fst 6f :224 :462 1:12 Alw 1200 3 3 21 1hd 2hd 22 Wall N 117 w *.50 88-20 Golden Voyage1132El Chico1171½Black Bun1136 Hung 4
6May39- 7CD fst 1¼ :472 1:124 1:38 2:032 Ky Derby 56k 1 1 22 613 617 623½ Wall N 126 w 8.20 68-11 Johnstown1268Challedon1261Heather Broom126½ Quit 8
29Apr39- 5Jam fst 1 70 :23 :464 1:112 1:42 Wood Memorial 24k 4 5 59½ 58½ 613 615¼ Wall N 120 w 3.60 79-11 Johnstown1208Volitant1201Impound120¾ Impeded 8
15Apr39- 4Jam fst 6f :223 :46 1:112 Alw 1200 3 1 1½ 11 1hd 2no Wall N 116 w *.14e 95-14 Gilded Knight116noEl Chico1163Sea Captain1135 Not urged 5
10Sep38- 5Aqu fst 6½f :224 :46 1:114 1:18 Jr Champion 13k 2 2 1hd 1hd 2hd 11 Wall N 122 w *.45 96-06 El Chico1221Volitant114noJohnstown1145 Driving 4
27Aug38- 4Sar fst 6½f :231 :463 1:121 1:182 Hopeful 48k 10 1 11 14 12 12 Wall N 126 w *.33 93-08 El Chico1262Ariel Toy1161Johnstown116hd In hand 11
6Aug38- 4Sar fst 6f :224 :46 1:102 Sar Spl 8k 8 1 11½ 11½ 11 13 Wall N 122 w *.40 100-05 El Chico1223Eight Thirty1224Third Degree1225 Going away 8
30Jly38- 4Sar sl 6f :224 :47 1:131 U S Hotel 12k 6 3 1½ 12 13 18 Wall N 122 w *2.00 86-16 El Chico1228Invader1162Eight Thirty122no Much best 11
25Jun38- 4Aqu fst 6f :23 :47 1:131 Great American 4.7k 1 1 34½ 34½ 3¾ 14 Wall N 119 w 2.50e 88-12 El Chico1194Lovely Night1154Maeline1191 Going away 6
11Jun38- 5Del fst 5f :224 :46 :591 Dover 7.1k 10 4 31 21½ 1½ 11 Wall N 122 w *2.40 100-03 El Chico1221Star Runner1164Cherry Jam1162 Drew out 10
16Apr38- 4Jam fst 5f :231 :474 1:00 Youthful 4.2k 3 3 11½ 1nk 11½ 14 Wall N 114 w *2.20 93-13 El Chico1144Jack Horner119hdWise Shine1141 Going away 8

Equipoise

ch. c. 1928, by Pennant (Peter Pan)–Swinging, by Broomstick
Lifetime record: 51 29 10 4 $338,610
Own.– C.V. Whitney
Br.– H.P. Whitney (Ky)
Tr.– T.J. Healey

23Feb35- 6SA fst 1¼ :45 1:10 1:36 2:021 3↑ S Anita H 125k 19 12 1213 1213 74¼ 77½ Workman R 130wb *1.70e - - Azucar1172Ladysman1171Time Supply1182 20
Off slowly,close quarters
18Feb35- 5SA fst 1 1/16 :24 :473 1:12 1:432 3↑ Handicap 1200 4 3 31½ 31 1hd 11 Workman R 125wb *.60 - - [D]Equipos1251TwntyGrnd1163Srd1051½ Bumped rival,bore in 5
Disqualified
13Feb35- 5SA fst 1 :23 :463 1:102 1:363 3↑ Handicap 1000 5 5 45 33 3½ 21 Workman R 128wb *.30 - - Sweping Light1091Equipoise128nkTed Clark1111½ Impeded 8
6Nov34- 3Bel sly 1¼ :493 1:143 1:404 2:063 3↑ Whitney Trophy H 5.5k 5 1 51 21½ 2hd 11½ Workman R 128wb *.55 67-23 Equipoise1281½Faireno1222Mr. Khayyam1204 Ridden out 6
31Oct34- 6Nar fst 6f :23 :453 1:104 3↑ Invitation 5.1k 5 2 45½ 44½ 43¾ 3½ Workman R 130wb *.45 100-07 Okapi130½All Forlorn127noEquipoise130hd Closed fast 5
30May34- 5Bel fst 1¼ :471 1:12 1:371 2:023 3↑ Suburban H 7.4k 1 4 53¼ 31¼ 2½ 2no Robertson A 134wb *.50 87-16 Ladysman114noEquipoise13410War Glory1151½ Just missed 8
19May34- 4Bel fst 1 :233 :47 1:112 1:37 3↑ Metropolitan H 4.3k 6 8 82¾ 4½ 1hd 12 Workman R 132wb *.70 90-15 [D]Equipoise1322Mr.Khyym1191SunArchr1065 Swerved stretch 9
Disqualified
5May34- 5Pim fst 1 3/16 :483 1:14 1:40 2:014 3↑ Dixie H 5.9k 4 1 2nk 2½ 14 11½ Workman R 130wb *.10 81-19 Equipoise1301½Chatmoss1103Flaming Mamie1027 Easily 4
21Apr34- 5HdG fst 1 1/16 :232 :472 1:122 1:442 3↑ Philadelphia H 8.4k 4 4 32½ 21 11½ 11 Workman R 130wb *.50 98-08 Equipoise1301Springsteel1174Larranaga1136 In hand 5
30Sep33- 5HdG fst 1⅛ :48 1:114 1:371 1:494 3↑ Havre de Grace H 11k 1 4 42 31½ 21 21 Workman R 132wb *1.60 100-09 Osculator1041Equipoise1321½Mate1101½ Closed well 9
16Sep33- 5Bel my 2 :50 2:341 3:251 3↑ J C Gold Cup 8.1k 1 2 21½ 21 31¼ 312 Workman R 125wb *.45 71-16 Dark Secret1254Gusto1258Equipoise1257 No excuses 4
2Sep33- 5Sar fst 1¾ :52 2:092 2:344 3:00 3↑ Sar Cup 6.9k 3 2 21½ 21 11 11½ Workman R 126 w *.12 75-14 Equipoise1261½Gusto1268Keep Out118 Going away 3
24Aug33- 6Haw fst 1¼ :483 1:132 1:383 2:024 3↑ Haw Gold Cup 27k 3 1 33 2½ 1hd 12 Workman R 126wb *.18 94-14 Equipoise1262GallantSir1261½Mr.Khayyam1171½ Going away 5
3Aug33- 5Sar fst 1 :242 :48 1:133 1:39 3↑ Wilson 3.3k 3 3 31¾ 3nk 1hd 13 Workman R 126wb *.20 86-15 Equipoise1263Tambour1062Mate1113 Eased up 5
22Jly33- 6AP fst 1¼ :471 1:114 1:37 2:023 3↑ Arlington H 12k 4 5 42 31½ 2nk 11½ Workman R 135wb *.75 96-13 Equipoise1351½Watch Him1065Gallant Sir125no Going away 7
7Jun33- 4Bel fst 1¼ :47 1:111 1:36 2:02 3↑ Suburban H 8.9k 7 2 43½ 21½ 2hd 12 Workman R 132wb *.40 90-18 Equipoise1322Osculator1076Apprentice112nk Eased up 7
3Jun33- 5Bel fst 1 :232 :464 1:114 1:372 3↑ Metropolitan H 5.8k 7 5 32 2½ 11 14 Workman R 128wb *.90 88-15 Equipoise1284Okapi1021Scotch Gold1061 Eased up 10
22Apr33- 5HdG fst 1 1/16 :232 :472 1:12 1:443 3↑ Philadelphia H 8.9k 1 5 43 41¼ 12 11½ Workman R 128wb *.90 99-05 Equipoise1281½Tred Avon1122Osculator1051 Won easily 8
Previously trained by F. Hopkins
29Oct32- 5Lrl gd 1¼ :48 1:134 1:393 2:053 3↑ Washington H 18k 6 4 86 21 2½ 2hd Workman R 129wb *1.10 82-25 Tred Avon112hdEquipoise129noMate1126 Finished fast 9
15Oct32- 5Lrl fst 1 :233 :473 1:13 1:371 2↑ Laurel 7.1k 1 7 54 41½ 3½ 31½ Workman R 126wb *.70 100-11 Jack High118noGallant Sir1081½Equipoise1263 No excuse 7
1Oct32- 5HdG fst 1⅛ :461 1:11 1:364 1:501 3↑ H de Grace Cup H 26k 4 6 34½ 2½ 11½ 11 Workman R 128wb *1.05 99-06 Equipoise1281Gallant Sir1073Tred Avon1103 Handily 13
24Sep32- 3HdG gd 6f :23 :464 1:12 3↑ Handicap 1500 3 5 54 53½ 58½ 59 Workman R 129wb *.65 86-08 Pairbypair107½Jack High1231½Con Amore1125 Dull effort 5
13Aug32- 5Sar fst 1¼ :50 1:142 1:40 2:053 3↑ Whitney 6.9k 2 1 11½ 14 14 13 Workman R 126wb *.14 81-16 Equipoise1263Gusto1178Rocky News116 Easily 3
6Aug32- 5Sar fst 1 :233 :462 1:113 1:381 3↑ Wilson 7.8k 2 3 32½ 31 11 12 Workman R 126wb *.13 90-11 Equipoise1262Blind Bowboy1216Pompeius113 Easily 3
23Jly32- 6AP fst 1¼ :48 1:13 1:372 2:021 3↑ Arlington H 27k 3 4 32½ 2½ 2hd 2nk Workman R 134wb *.82 98-08 Plucky Play111nkEquipoise1346Pittsburgher1053 Hard try 6

9Jly32- 6AP fst 1¼ :482 1:131 1:37 2:024 3↑ Arl Gold Cup 24k 3 1 21½ 12½ 15 14 Workman R 126wb *.24 95-04 Equipoise1264Gusto1143½Mate126 Easily 3
4Jly32- 5AP hy 1⅛ :492 1:15 1:412 1:544 3↑ Stars & Stripes H 27k 1 2 1hd 1hd 13 1¾ Workman R 129wb *.34 73-31 Equipoise129¾Tred Avon1075Dr. Freeland1103 Easily 6
30Jun32- 5AP fst 1 :231 :46 1:091 1:342 3↑ Handicap 1450 1 2 21½ 21½ 21 13 Workman R 128wb *.90 106-02 Equipoise1283Jamestown1183½Spanish Play106 Easily 3
21May32- 4Bel fst 1 :224 :462 1:102 1:37 3↑ Metropolitan H 9k 6 5 33¼ 21½ 2hd 12½ Workman R 127 w *.60 90-15 Equipoise1272½Sun Meadow1181½Mate1284 Easily 7
12May32- 4Bel fst 6f-WC 1:093 3↑ Toboggan H 8.2k 10 6 21 1hd 11 Workman R 129wb *1.00 99-02 Equipoise1291Ironclad1081½Helianthus1104 Handily 10
16Apr32- 5HdG fst 6f :232 :472 1:122 3↑ Harford H 13k 9 5 72¼ 41½ 11½ 13 Workman R 128wb *.55 93-16 Equipoise1283Happy Scot106.5hdEvening1051 Easily 12
13Apr32- 4Bow fst 5f :231 :46 :592 3↑ Handicap 1400 7 2 51¾ 31½ 2nk 1½ Workman R 126wb *1.40 109-14 Equipoise126½Hygro112½Brandon Mint1046 Drew out 7
9May31- 5Pim fst 1 3/16 :483 1:132 1:383 1:59 Preakness 58k 2 7 63¼ 62¼ 41¾ 42¾ Workman R 126wb 1.95 94-10 Mate1261½Twenty Grand126nkLadder1261 Impeded early 7
Geldings not eligible
25Apr31- 5HdG fst 1 1/16 :24 :483 1:143 1:464 Cheseapeake 13k 6 6 64¼ 62¼ 611 613½ Robertson A 122wb *.15 74-13 Anchors Aweigh114noSoll Gills1143Levante1121 Distressed 6
13Apr31- 4HdG fst 6f :231 :47 1:113 Alw 1400 4 1 21 2½ 11½ 12½ Robertson A 123wb *.25 97-14 Equipoise1232½Panetian1084DarkHero1083 Outclassed field 5
5Nov30- 5Pim my 1 1/16 :234 :482 1:142 1:483 Pim Futurity 58k 2 8 87½ 54¾ 22 1½ Workman R 119wb *.95 79-26 Equipoise119½TwentyGrand119nkMat1194 Driving,great rush 8
Geldings not eligible;Previously owned by H.P. Whitney
16Oct30- 5CD fst 1 :231 :464 1:111 1:36 Ky Jockey Club 31k 4 2 2½ 12 2hd 2no Workman R 122wb *.76 101-13 Twenty Grand122noEquipoise12210Knight's Call1225 7
Going best at end
4Oct30- 3Aqu fst 1 :233 :473 1:13 1:38 Jr Champion 9.8k 4 5 53¼ 31¾ 21 21 Workman R 122wb *.20 89-15 Twenty Grand1111Equipoise1223Ormesby1168 Driving 7
27Sep30- 5HdG fst 6f :224 :463 1:122 Eastern Shore H 31k 2 8 52 2½ 11 15 Workman R 126wb *.60e 93-12 Equipoise1265Don Leon1192½Magnifico110hd Closed fast 15
13Sep30- 4Bel fst *7f-WC 1:203 Futurity 114k 7 6 2nk 32 2hd Workman R 130wb 3.60 92-11 Jamestown130hdEquipoise1303Mate1221 Driving,interfered 15
Geldings not eligible
6Sep30- 4Bel fst *7f-WC 1:214 Champagne 7.6k 9 6 2½ 1hd 2hd Workman R 132 w *1.20 86-15 Mate119hdEquipoise1323Sunny Lassie1135 Driving,faltered 10
9Aug30- 4Sar fst 6f :23 :46 1:112 Sar Spl 14k 1 4 21½ 21½ 21½ 22½ Workman R 122wb *.70 92-09 Jamestown1222½Eqpoise1228SunMedow1222 Not good enough 4
21Jun30- 3Aqu fst 5f 1:001 Great American 16k 3 1 11 12 12 Workman R 130wb *.45e 86-15 Equpos1302Polydorus1154Hlnthus1152½ Cleverly,mild drive 7
7Jun30- 3Bel fst 5f-WC :593 National Stallion 26k 7 4 21 13 16 Workman R 122wb *.40e 82-20 Equipoise1226Polydorus1222Baba Kenny119hd Easily 8
27May30- 4Bel gd 5f-WC :59 Juvenile 17k 1 4 34 31½ 1nk Workman R 125wb *.40e 85-24 Equipoise125nkHappy Scot122½Panasette1146 Driving 7
17May30- 3Bel sl 4½f-WC :523 Keene Mem 8.6k 2 2 3½ 2hd 12 Workman R 122wb *.60 92-13 Equipoise1222Happy Scot1228Avaricious1172 Easily 5
10May30- 3Jam fst 5f :231 :47 :591 Youthful 11k 1 2 4¾ 1nk 11 14 Workman R 117wb 3.50 97-14 [D]Equipoise1174Vander Pool1254Chouette1254 Drew away 8
Disqualified for impeding runner-up
2May30- 5Pim fst 4½f :223 :47 :534 Pim Nursery 7.6k 2 2 - - - - Workman R 122 w *1.65 - - Happy Scot1224Up1225St. Agnes1191 8
Stumbled after start,lost rider
23Apr30- 5HdG fst 4½f :23 :463 :53 Aberdeen 15k 7 9 55¼ 32¼ 34 Robertson A 122 w 4.25e 96-05 Vander Pool1221Up1173Equipoise1221½ Driving,closed well 10
15Apr30- 2HdG fst 4½f :233 :481 :542 Alw 1200 1 2 1½ 11½ 11½ Robertson A 118 w *.90 93-07 Equipoise1181½Schooner1123Uncle Sam1121 Driving 15
7Apr30- 3Bow hy 4f :232 :481 Alw 1200 8 4 1hd 1nk 14 Robertson A 111 w *2.15 92-08 Equipoise1114Glidelia1103Dry Dock112hd Won easily 11

Gallant Fox

b. c. 1927, by Sir Gallahad III (Teddy)–Marguerite, by Celt **Lifetime record: 17 11 3 2 $328,165**
Own.– Belair Stud Stable
Br.– Belair Stud (Ky)
Tr.– J. Fitzsimmons

17Sep30- 4Bel fst 2 :50 2:34 3:242 3↑ J C Gold Cup 13k 3 2 21 11 11½ 13 Sande E 118.5wb *.04e 87-19 Gallant Fox118.53Yarn11412Frisius125 Speed in reserve 3
6Sep30- 3Bel fst 1⅝ :483 1:374 2:024 2:411 Lawrence Realizatn 33k 2 2 22 22 1nk 1hd Sande E 126wb *.70 98-12 Gallant Fox126hdQuestionnaire1235Yarn1163 Outlasted 4
30Aug30- 5Sar fst 1¾ :483 2:052 2:30 2:56 3↑ Sar Cup 10k 5 3 35½ 22 11 11½ Sande E 117.5wb *.20e 95-06 Gallant Fox117.51½Frisius1261Gone Away1165 In hand late 6
16Aug30- 5Sar hy 1¼ 1:133 1:42 2:08 Travers 33k 4 4 2½ 21½ 23 28 Sande E 126wb *.50 61-26 Jim Dandy1208Gallant Fox1266Whichone1263 Wide,no match 4
12Jly30- 5AP fst 1¼ :474 1:122 1:372 2:034 Classic 78k 3 4 21½ 1hd 1½ 1nk Sande E 126wb *.32 99-00 GallntFox126nkGllntKnght1236NdO.12110 Hard stretch duel 6
28Jun30- 4Aqu gd 1½ :49 1:142 2:063 2:322 Dwyer 15k 2 1 22 11½ 12 11½ Sande E 126wb *.13e 86-18 Gallant Fox1261½Xenofol1107Limbus110nk Loafed 5
7Jun30- 5Bel gd 1½ :501 1:16 2:07 2:313 Belmont 77k 1 2 12 12 11 13 Sande E 126wb 1.60 86-18 GallantFox1263Whichon1263Qustonnr12620 Speed in reserve 4
17May30- 5CD gd 1¼ :474 1:14 1:404 2:073 Ky Derby 60k 7 8 43 12 12 12 Sande E 126wb *1.19 78-15 GallantFox1262GallantKnght1262NdO.1261 Speed in reserve 15
9May30- 5Pim fst 1 3/16 :48 1:133 1:39 2:003 Preakness 61k 1 2 87 3nk 1hd 1¾ Sande E 126wb *1.00 89-20 Gallant Fox126¾Crack Brigade1266Snowflake1211½ 11
Geldings not eligible
26Apr30- 4Jam fst 1 70 :243 :483 1:142 1:433 Wood Memorial 13k 1 3 32 3¾ 1nk 14 Sande E 120wb *1.60 88-18 GallantFox1204CrackBrigad1201½DsrtLght1205 Drawing away 5
28Sep29- 3Aqu fst 1 :24 :473 1:12 1:38 Jr Champion 9.5k 3 3 45 35 1½ 12 Maiben J 116wb *.90 90-17 GallantFox1162DesrtLght1118SrJohrn1111 Speed in reserve 4
14Sep29- 4Bel fst *7f-WC 1:193 Futurity 119k 12 11 23 33½ 33 McAuliffe D 122wb 20.00 94-09 Whichone1253Hi-Jack122noGallant Fox122no Held well 17
10Sep29- 3Bel gd 6f-WC 1:113 Alw 1200 6 3 4nk 21 2nk McAuliffe D 120wb *2.00 93-14 Polygamous117nkGallant Fox1201½Stanton115½ 12
Impeded,swerved,finished fast
3Aug29- 3Sar fst 6f :232 :47 1:12 U S Hotel 16k 10 8 21½ 2hd 2hd 21½ Burke JH 122wb 2.00 90-16 Caruso1221½GallantFox1223Hi-Jck1146 No match for winner 10
29Jly29- 3Sar fst 5½f :23 :47 1:06 Flash 6.8k 3 8 64¼ 66½ 33 11½ Burke JH 112wb 10.00 93-08 GllntFox1121½Cruso1254H-Jck112hd Outrun early,drawing away 13
29Jun29- 3Aqu gd 6f :24 :472 1:144 Tremont 15k 6 12 1212 1111 119¾ 86¾ McAuliffe D 110wb 3.50 73-22 SarznII1251Moktm125hdPromthus1153 Dropped back at start 13
24Jun29- 5Aqu fst 5f 1:004 Alw 1000 6 8 88½ 32 31 Burke JH 113wb *2.40e 82-20 Desert Light113½Peto118½Gallant Fox1133 Greenly 10

Granville

b. c. 1933, by Gallant Fox (Sir Gallahad III)–Gravita, by Sarmatian **Lifetime record: 18 8 4 3 $111,820**
Own.– Belair Stud
Br.– Belair Stud (Ky)
Tr.– J. Fitzsimmons

26Sep36- 5Bel fst 1⅝ :48 1:38 2:034 2:433 Lawrence Realizatn 23k 1 1 23 11 13 12 Stout J 126wb *.13 86-16 Granville1262GiantKiller1161½MmoryBook126½ In hand late 5
Geldings not eligible
29Aug36- 5Sar sly 1¾ :502 2:083 2:341 3:004 3↑ Sar Cup 7.7k 2 1 11½ 11 15 18 Stout J 116wb 1.80 71-22 Granville1168Discovery126 Easily 2
15Aug36- 5Sar my 1¼ :49 1:133 1:394 2:054 Travers 19k 5 3 32¼ 31 2hd 1hd Stout J 127wb *1.00e 80-19 Granville127hdSun Teddy1224Count Morse1122 Hard drive 5
11Aug36- 5Sar gd 1 3/16 :482 1:133 1:394 1:583 Kenner 5k 1 1 25 22 2hd 1nk Stout J 126wb *.60 85-17 Granville126nkMemory Book1231½Pullman108 Hard drive 3
25Jly36- 6AP fst 1¼ :47 1:112 1:371 2:031 Classic 35k 1 3 41½ 3½ 1hd 12½ Stout J 126wb *1.60e 90-12 Granville1262½Mr. Bones1211¼Hollyrood1234 Going away 10
6Jun36- 5Bel fst 1½ :493 1:14 2:051 2:30 Belmont 41k 9 6 65¼ 41¼ 2hd 1no Stout J 126wb 3.20e 94-09 Granville126noMr. Bones1268Hollyrood126½ Just up 10
30May36- 5Bel fst 1¼ :474 1:13 1:382 2:043 3↑ Suburban H 15k 2 3 34 12 11½ 2no Stout J 108wb *2.50e 77-19 Firethorn116noGranville1082Whopper1191 Just missed 12
16May36- 5Pim fst 1 3/16 :473 1:123 1:39 1:59 Preakness 31k 11 6 2hd 1½ 2hd 2no Stout J 126wb 3.95e 95-17 BoldVenture126noGranville1268JeanBart126hd Just missed 11
2May36- 6CD fst 1¼ :474 1:123 1:374 2:033 Ky Derby 47k 4 - - - - - Stout J 126wb 10.60e - - Bold Venture126hdBrevity1266Indian Broom1263 Lost rider 14
25Apr36- 5Jam fst 1 70 :233 :471 1:12 1:431 Wood Memorial 14k 1 3 31½ 2hd 11 2no Stout J 117wb *1.00e 90-16 Teufel112noGranville1176Delphinium1171 Nosed out 7
21Apr36- 4Jam fst 1 70 :234 :473 1:122 1:432 Alw 1200 2 1 11 11 13 15 Stout J 110wb 1.50e 89-14 Granville1105Ned Reigh1141Pullman110nk Eased up 5
12Oct35- 4Bel fst 6½f-WC 1:172 Futurity 84k 1 1 115 52½ 62¼ Rainey C 122wb 3.60e 94-04 Tintagel1221Hollyrood122noJean Bart122hd Went well 18
3Oct35- 5Bel fst 6½f-WC 1:172 Champagne 5.9k 12 11 41½ 35 35 Merritt R 113wb *1.80e 91-09 Brevity113noSnark1135Granville113hd Closed gamely 14
13Sep35- 6Aqu fst 6f :234 :481 1:124 Alw 1000 2 3 76¾ 55 42¾ 13 Litzenberger E 107wb *1.30e 90-12 Granville1073Go Home112noDark Wizard112hd Easily 11
7Sep35- 5Aqu gd 6½f :23 :463 1:121 1:183 Jr Champion 8.7k 3 4 89¾ 75 67½ 53¾ Litzenberger E 105 w 2.60e 90-11 Ned Reigh115½The Fighter1172Pullman110nk Impeded 9
2Sep35- 3Aqu fst 6f :241 :49 1:12 Babylon H 4.2k 6 5 46½ 43 32¼ 3hd Wright WD 114 w 1.50e 94-09 NedReigh116noSpeedtoSpare115noGranville1145 Game finish 6
22Aug35- 4Sar fst 5½f :231 :473 1:07 Alw 1000 10 7 85 73¼ 23 21 Malley T 110 w 3.60 87-16 BoldVenture114.51Granvill1102Trnsportr110hd Game finish 12
16Aug35- 3Sar fst 5½f :232 :472 1:06 Alw 1000 10 2 2nk 42¾ 42¼ 33½ Malley T 108 w 15.00e 89-13 Brevity1082Aneroid1131½Granville108hd Closed gamely 13

Inscoelda

br. f. 1936, by Insco (Sir Gallahad III)–Griselda, by Wrack — Lifetime record: 42 12 4 8 $38,970

Own.– King Ranch
Br.– Herbert M. Woolf (Kan)
Tr.– W.J. Hirsch

3Feb42- 6Hia	fst 7f	:232 :472 1:121 1:25	4↑ ⒻAlw 1500	2 5 44½ 55½ 54½ 58	Garza I	109wb	12.75	79-16	Transient993Moon Maiden1051Silvestra1031½	Some str gain 8
Previously trained by M. Hirsch										
21Oct41- 5Emp	fst 1⅛	:49 1:14 1:394 1:524	3↑ Hannibal H 3.5k	1 2 21 21½ 2hd 11	Garza I	108wb	5.60	86-12	Inscoelda1081Hypocrite1212City Talk110hd	Drew out 5
Previously owned by Woolford Farm;previously trained by R.O. Higdon										
10Oct41- 5Jam	sly 6f	:23 :472 1:131	3↑ ⒻAlw 2000	6 7 79¾ 78½ 63 31½↓	Strickler W	103wb	5.05	84-21	YarrowMaid117¾FivtoOn117¾DHDrkImp111	Dwelt,fast finish 7
5Sep41- 6Aqu	fst 6f	:23 :462 1:113	3↑ ⒻAlw 2000	4 7 88 711 76½ 57½	Strickler W	105wb	5.50	88-11	Pelisse1053½Thorn Apple1052Fleetborough112hd	Outrun 9
25Jly41- 5AP	fst 6f	:23 :462 1:122	3↑ Alw 1200	2 2 43 3½ 2½ 1nk	Strickler W	106wb	4.30	85-18	Inscoelda106nkJack Twink105hdWoodsaw1112	Hard drive 7
12Nov40- 6Pim	sly 1$\frac{1}{16}$	:241 :481 1:143 1:503	3↑ ⒻLady Baltimore H 3.4k	4 6 69½ 68½ 69½ 512¾	Vedder RL	116wb	5.95	54-34	Rosetown1095Bright View104nkRaise Up1111½	Outrun 6
5Nov40- 6Pim	fst 1$\frac{3}{16}$	:481 1:121 1:384 1:593	3↑ Riggs H 13k	4 2 77 88¼ 97¼ 89½	Vedder RL	110wb	16.75	75-21	Rough Pass1053Burning Star113½War Beauty1011½	Outrun 10
22Oct40- 5Emp	fst 1$\frac{1}{16}$	:234 :474 1:123 1:444	3↑ Handicap 3030	4 5 610 610 52¾ 44¼	Vedder RL	109wb	3.45	91-08	Get Off1221½No Sir1122Foxbrough118¾	No excuse 6
5Oct40- 3Bel	fst 1$\frac{1}{16}$	:223 :461 1:104 1:432	3↑ Handicap 1520	4 3 46 36 32¼ 2nk↓	Vedder RL	114wb	8.85	94-09	ThirdCovey116nkDHVolitant119DHInscold1148	Finished well 4
21Sep40- 5Aqu	fst 1⅛	:472 1:12 1:372 1:504	3↑ ⒻBeldame H 19k	7 15 1414 139 1111 1011¾	Vedder RL	116wb	20.65	90-02	Fairy Chant1191¼Dotted Swiss1141Dolly Val1212½	Outrun 16
12Sep40- 4Aqu	fst 7f	:23 :47 1:122 1:244	3↑ Handicap 2030	4 3 31½ 1hd 1hd 11	Roberts P	107wb	13.25	92-09	Inscoelda1071Roman Flag119¾Dini1201	Drew out 4
17Aug40- 6Was	gd 1	:233 :471 1:122 1:383	3↑ ⒻBeverly H 5.9k	3 3 32½ 55½ 56½ 57¼	Ashcroft J	113 w	5.40	78-31	BusyMorn1152Montsin1152½ShineO'Night1122	Close quarters 8
31Jly40- 7Was	fst 1	:232 :471 1:114 1:371	3↑ Handicap 1200	4 3 43 31½ 42 34	Craig A	108 w	*.90e	88-12	Detroit Bull110hdTown Boy1044Inscoelda108nk	Weakened 8
29Jun40- 6AP	fst 1	:224 :451 1:10 1:361	3↑ ⒻArl Matron H 9.1k	8 11 98¼ 89 77¼ 45	Richard J	108 w	*.90e	86-18	Shine O'Night1033Montsin1101Manie O'Hara1091	Late foot 14
25Jun40- 5AP	fst 1	:23 :46 1:102 1:371	3↑ Alw 1200	3 2 22 23 11½ 12¾	Richard J	109 w	2.70	86-16	Inscoelda1092¾Bucking116½Loque1012	Going away 5
30May40- 6LF	sl 1$\frac{1}{16}$	:252 :51 1:17 1:503	3↑ F S Peabody Mem H 5.8k	3 2 22 21 42 44	Vedder RL	110 w	4.00	59-34	Mucho Gusto1121½Shot Put110½Gray Jack1092	Tired 7
6May40- 6CD	gd 7f	:232 :472 1:132 1:271	3↑ Alw 1000	9 4 33½ 21½ 1hd 11½	Roberts P	110 w	*2.30	80-23	Inscoelda1101½TrueStar1102SouthlandBeau115nk	Going away 9
2Mar40- 6Hia	fst 1¼	:471 1:111 1:363 2:03	3↑ Widener H 66k	6 13 1113 1011 1422 1516¾	Roberts P	110 w	25.15e	77-09	Many Stings1091Big Pebble1065DHDay Off110	Outrun 16
21Feb40- 6Hia	fst 7f	:23 :471 1:113 1:241	3↑ Handicap 1500	3 7 73½ 73¾ 64 52½	Smith FA	112 w	4.60e	89-13	Armor Bearer107¾Dunade1111½Dolly Val109hd	Off slowly 7
14Feb40- 5Hia	fst 6½f	:233 :472 1:111 1:172	3↑ Handicap 1500	2 4 32½ 42½ 45½ 35¼	Smith FA	111 w	*1.60e	87-12	Many Stings118nkArmor Bearer1095Inscoelda1111½	5
No response late,worked mile in 1:37										
26Jan40- 6Hia	fst 7f	:232 :471 1:123 1:251	4↑ Alw 1200	1 6 53½ 32 23 2¾	Ryan P	112 w	*2.20	86-13	DMythicalKing110¾Inscold1121½Bllotr102.55	Impeded turn 8
Placed first through disqualification										
11Jan40- 6Hia	fst 7f	:23 :462 1:111 1:242	4↑ Alw 1200	7 7 911 910 88¾ 65	Ryan P	109 w	28.45	86-10	Napper Tandy1161Galsun1042One Jest1091½	Outrun 10
8Nov39- 6Pim	fst 1$\frac{1}{16}$	:24 :483 1:14 1:472	3↑ ⒻLady Baltimore H 3.9k	2 6 73¾ 63 97¾ 99¾	Robertson A	113 w	*1.55e	73-21	Manie O'Hara1084Bala Ormont109½Hostility110½	No excuse 12
26Oct39- 5Lrl	fst 6f	:231 :47 1:123	3↑ Handicap 1200	3 5 55½ 54¼ 45½ 54¼	Ryan P	108 w	41.70	87-16	Allegro114hdBill Farnsworth1172½Cravat1241½	No mishaps 6
Previously trained by B.A. Jones										
4Feb39- 5Hia	fst 7f	:223 :454 1:104 1:234	Bahamas H 6.5k	4 10 106¾ 106¼ 75½ 73¾	Smith FA	121 w	*2.00e	90-09	RoyalPam113nkTechnician1192ErlyMorn112hd	Close quarters 12
28Jan39- 6Hia	fst 7f	:23 :462 1:111 1:234	Alw 1200	2 5 52¼ 52¼ 42 41	Yarberry W	112 w	*1.85	93-11	Cherry Jam113nkHeather Time114½Search110nk	Good try 6
8Nov38- 5Pim	sl 1$\frac{1}{16}$	:233 :482 1:143 1:49	Walden 10k	5 8 52¼ 31½ 22 1hd	Longden J	116 w	4.75	75-34	Inscoelda116hdVolitant1164Ciencia1101½	Just up 9
22Oct38- 4Lrl	sl 1	:241 :48 1:142 1:41	ⒻSelima 29k	14 16 104½ 51½ 2hd 2¾	Gilbert J	119 w	4.60	80-16	Big Hurry114¾Inscoelda1191½Dinner Date1221	Weakened 16
11Oct38- 4Jam	fst 6f	:23 :473 1:12	ⒻAlw 1000	5 6 66½ 46 45 34½	Rollins C	122 w	2.60e	87-13	SmartCrack1091½Matterhorn1143Inscoelda122hd	Closed fast 6
27Sep38- 4Bel	fst 6f-WC	1:103	Handicap 1265	2 1 64½ 44½ 38	Rollins C	117 w	4.50	86-06	Johnstown1225Birch Rod1123Inscoelda117hd	Closed well 7
16Jly38- 6AP	fst 6f	:223 :454 1:113	ⒻArl Lassie 26k	5 7 65½ 45½ 1hd 11	Rollins C	117 w	*.90e	89-07	Inscoelda1171Dinner Date1172½Unerring1195	Drew out 9
12Jly38- 4AP	fst 5½f	:23 :46 :583 1:044	ⒻAlw 1000	8 2 22 21½ 11 14	Rollins C	112 w	3.80	97-12	Inscoelda1124Bold Fay1093Smart Trick115no	Going away 8
17Jun38- 5LF	fst 5f	:233 :472 1:00	Alw 1000	6 6 54½ 43 21½ 11½	Rollins C	107 w	3.60e	99-15	Inscoelda1071½Maetown110nkBala Ormont105hd	Going away 9
30May38- 6CD	fst 5f	:232 :462 :59	Bashford Manor 7.1k	5 3 99 811 62½ 66¾	Dotter R	119 w	3.10e	93-13	Royal Pam1192Unerring119hdCherry Jam1223	Outrun 11
3May38- 1CD	fst 4½f	:23 :464 :532	ⒻAlw 800	5 5 21 2½ 1¾	Perkins C	107 w	*.90	95-08	Inscold107¾Espn113.56MssAlrt1102	Awkward start,drew out 6
30Apr38- 4CD	sl 4½f	:233 :473 :541	Alw 800	4 6 612 69½ 56½	Perkins C	106 w	4.50	85-14	American Byrd113¾Dolly Whisk1104Range Dust1151½	Outrun 7
26Feb38- 1Hia	fst 3f	:22 :34	Alw 800	6 7 63½ 21	Haas L	112 w	3.10e	--	CherryJam1151Inscoelda112noSweetPatrice112nk	Great rush 9
17Feb38- 1Hia	fst 3f	:221 :343	ⒻAlw 800	8 5 45 3hd	Haas L	118 w	4.45e	--	OddesaBeulah118noSwetPtrc118hdInscold1182	Strong finish 12
11Feb38- 1Hia	fst 3f	:221 :344	Md Sp Wt	11 5 2hd 12½	Haas L	113 w	*1.00f	--	Inscoelda1132½Pradis116noHenryels Pick1162	Going away 13
28Jan38- 1Hia	fst 3f	:221 :334	ⒻAlw 800	2 7 45 32	Haas L	114 w	5.30	--	CharlotteGirl1181KentyMiss1181Inscoelda1145	Closed gap 7
20Jan38- 1Hia	fst 3f	:223 :344	Md Sp Wt	8 6 41 2½	Haas L	113	*1.25	--	HigherBracket116½Inscoelda1131½Matown1113	Strong finish 9
12Jan38- 1Hia	fst 3f	:223 :343	ⒻMd Sp Wt	14 8 46½ 35½	Haas L	118	7.75f	--	CharlotteGirl1181½SweetPatrc1184Inscold1185	Closed well 14

Johnstown

b. c. 1936, by Jamestown (St. James)–La France, by Sir Gallahad III — Lifetime record: 21 14 0 3 $169,315

Own.– Belair Stud
Br.– A.B. Hancock Sr. (Ky)
Tr.– J. Fitzsimmons

22Jly39- 6AP	fst 1¼	:47 1:112 1:36 2:02	Classic 47k	1 2 13 11½ 31½ 36¼	Stout J	126wb	*.20	90-11	Challedon126nkSun Lover1216Johnstown1262	Tired badly 5
17Jun39- 5Aqu	fst 1⅛	:46 1:103 1:353 1:482	Dwyer 12k	2 1 12 14 13 11	Stout J	126wb	*.20	99-05	Johnstown1261Sun Lover1166Challedon1266	Ridden out 5
3Jun39- 5Bel	fst 1½	:481 1:122 2:023 2:293	Belmont 45k	1 1 11½ 16 14 15	Stout J	126wb	*.13e	95-12	Johnstown1265Belay1261½Gilded Knight1261½	In hand 6
27May39- 5Bel	fst 1	:23 :461 1:10 1:354	Withers 19k	2 1 14 14 16 16	Stout J	118wb	*.13e	96-10	Johnstown1186Hash118hdPorter's Mite1186	Much best 5
Geldings not eligible										
13May39- 6Pim	my 1$\frac{3}{16}$	:473 1:133 1:394 1:594	Preakness 70k	4 1 11½ 11½ 59 511¼	Stout J	126wb	*.45e	73-19	Challedon1261¼GildedKnight1263Volitnt1263	Stopped badly 6
6May39- 7CD	fst 1¼	:472 1:124 1:38 2:032	Ky Derby 56k	5 2 12 14 15 18	Stout J	126wb	*.60	92-11	Johnstown1268Challedon1261HthrBroom126½	Under restraint 8
29Apr39- 5Jam	fst 1 70	:23 :464 1:112 1:42	Wood Memorial 24k	6 2 21½ 11½ 15 18	Stout J	120wb	*.55	94-11	Johnstown1208Volitant1201Impound120¾	Much left 8
25Apr39- 4Jam	fst 1 70	:23 :463 1:113 1:404	Alw 1500	1 1 13 14 16 16	Stout J	120wb	*.33	102-06	Johnstwn1206LovlyNght1136EghtThrty11620	Under restraint 4
15Apr39- 5Jam	fst 6f	:221 :452 1:111	3↑ Paumonok H 9.5k	2 1 11½ 14 14 16	Stout J	112wb	*1.30	96-14	Johnstown1126Pagliacci1073EarlyDelivry1161½	Easily best 6
22Oct38- 5Kee	fst 6f	:223 :462 1:112	Breeders' Futurity 14k	5 3 3½ 31 2hd 1no	Stout J	119wb	*.60	97-09	Johnstown119noAllegro117hdLightspur1171¼	Hard drive 7
15Oct38- 5Jam	fst 6f	:223 :454 1:11	Remsen H 8.8k	1 1 1nk 13 16 17	Stout J	126wb	*.80e	97-11	Johnstown1267Lovely Night1224Beau James1203	Much best 6
8Oct38- 5Lrl	fst 6f	:23 :461 1:114	Richard Johnson 7.5k	2 4 2hd 1hd 13 1nk	Stout J	115wb	*1.25	95-11	Johnstown115nkImpound1123Time Alone1221½	Hard drive 7
1Oct38- 4Bel	fst 6½f-WC	1:164	Futurity 69k	3 1 32½ 43 43	Stout J	119wb	*2.00	85-12	Porter'sMite119½EightThirty1221½ThirdDgr1191	No mishaps 11
Geldings not eligible										
27Sep38- 4Bel	fst 6f-WC	1:103	Handicap 1265	6 4 1hd 13 15	Stout J	122wb	*.60	94-06	Johnstown1225Birch Rod1123Inscoelda117hd	Much best 7
10Sep38- 5Aqu	fst 6½f	:224 :46 1:114 1:18	Jr Champion 13k	3 3 2hd 2hd 1hd 31	Stout J	114wb	2.50	95-06	El Chico1221Volitant114noJohnstown1145	Good effort 4
5Sep38- 4Aqu	fst 6f	:224 :461 1:111	Babylon H 4k	5 4 1nk 11 13 14	Stout J	119wb	5.00	98-07	Johnstown1194Birch Rod1151T.M. Dorsett1121½	Much best 10
27Aug38- 4Sar	fst 6½f	:231 :463 1:121 1:182	Hopeful 48k	9 6 92¾ 34½ 42½ 33	Stout J	116 w	15.00	90-08	El Chico1262Ariel Toy1161Johnstown116hd	Closed well 11
22Aug38- 4Sar	fst 6f	:23 :472 1:132	Alw 1000	6 7 53½ 51½ 2hd 1hd	Stout J	116 w	*2.20e	85-15	Johnstown116hdPontius116noDRollandToss116½	Hard drive 14
25Jly38- 4Sar	fst 5½f	:223 :462 1:051	Flash 5.9k	3 5 42 42½ 42¾ 47	Stout J	110 w	*2.60e	90-06	Eight Thirty117hdMaeline1193Ariel Toy1104	No mishap 15
27Apr38- 3Jam	fst 5f	:23 :461 :592	©Md Sp Wt	4 2 1½ 11 12 11½	Stout J	117 w	*1.50	96-12	Johnstown1171½Hash1174King Cotton1173	Never headed 10
23Apr38- 4Jam	fst 5f	:23 :473 1:003	Alw 1000	4 4 2hd 31 43½ 42¾	Stout J	111 w	*.70	87-11	Our Mat1142Rosemain112nkKate Smith114½	Raced greenly 5

Jungle King

b. g. 1930, by St. Germans (Swynford)–Leopardess, by Dominant
Own.– Greentree Stable
Br.– Greentree Stable (Ky)
Tr.– V. Powers

Lifetime record: 77 15 13 11 $32,605

13Aug38- 2Sar	gd	*2	S'Chase	4:134	3↑ North American H 2.6k	3	3	35½	33	414	417	Collins W	148	w	3.60	--	Ossabaw1426Gay Charles1363Ship Executive1408	Faltered	4
18Jun38- 2Aqu	sly	*2½	S'Chase	5:003	4↑ Old Glory H 2k	1	1	11	11	15	18	Little H	143	w	3.00	--	Jungle King1438Yemasee160	Easily	3
11Jun38- 2Aqu	fst	*2	S'Chase	4:054	4↑ Lion Heart H 1.7k	2	4	23	33	49	418	Little H	147	w	1.20e	--	Yemasee1566Gay Charles1394Sumatra1418	Challenged,quit	4
4Jun38- 2Bel	fst	*2½	S'Chase	4:451	4↑ Meadow Brook H 2.1k	2	5	31½	55	411	412	Collins W	150	w	*1.20e	--	Rioter1511SailorBeware1598LittleMarty1473	Rated,no gain	6
30May38- 2Bel	fst	*2	S'Chase	3:462	4↑ Corinthian H 4.2k	2	3	55½	23	25	45	Collins W	149	w	*1.50e	--	Annibal1463NationalAnthem1401½RedRain152½	Faltered late	8
14May38- 2Bel	fst	*2	S'Chase	3:44	4↑ International H 2k	5	5	55½	44½	43½	35	Little H	149	w	4.50	--	RedRain1401NationalAnthem1394JungleKing1491	No threat	6
8Nov37- 4Pim	fst	2½	S'Chase	4:531	4↑ Manley Mem H 6.5k	1	5	58½	46	2hd	2no	Little H	143	w	*2.40	--	[D]LittleMarty148noJungleKing14312CduII146½	Forced wide	7
			Placed first through disqualification																
2Nov37- 4Bel	fst	*2½	S'Chase	4:474	4↑ Temple Gwathmey H 2.6k	3	2	32	2½	14	11½	Little H	147	w	*1.30e	--	Jungle King1471½Cadeau II1473Galsac1502	Speed to spare	5
20Oct37- 4Lrl	my	*2	S'Chase	4:211	3↑ Chevy Chase H 3.3k	2	5	57	44	417	416½	Little H	146	w	*2.15e	--	Cadeau II1414Swimalong138½Rideaway14412	No factor	8
4Sep37- 2Aqu	fst	*2½	S'Chase	4:472	4↑ Glendale H 5.8k	3	3	59½	49½	522	525	Baldwin E	146	w	*.60e	--	Yemasee1404Galsac1486National Anthem1408	Rated,no gain	6
28Aug37- 1Sar	hy	*2½	S'Chase	5:102	4↑ Saratoga H 3.8k	2	4	37	35	33¼	34	Baldwin E	147	w	1.80e	--	Galsac145noLondon Town1464Jungle King147	Gamely	4
21Aug37- 1Sar	fst	*2	S'Chase	4:153	3↑ Beverwyck H 2.4k	3	3	25	2hd	12	14	Baldwin E	142	w	*.08e	--	Jungle King1424Galsac142	Speed in reserve	3
14Aug37- 1Sar	fst	*2	S'Chase	4:111	3↑ North American H 2.7k	6	2	314	315	38¼	37	Baldwin E	143	w	2.50e	--	Sailor Beware1453London Town1494Jungle King143	Outrun	6
26Jun37- 2Aqu	fst	*2½	S'Chase	4:544	4↑ Old Glory H 2.8k	1	3	41¼	21	11	12½	Collins W	140	w	5.00	--	JungleKing1402½MaskedKnight144½St.Francis1548	Drew away	8
17Jun37- 2Aqu	fst	*2	S'Chase	4:064	4↑ Handicap 1380	2	7	84	63½	76½	612½	Collins W	140	w	*4.00	--	Masked Knight1371½Prattler139noSaluda1436		10
			Bad landing 13th,faltered																
5Jun37- 2Bel	fst	*2½	S'Chase	4:432	4↑ Meadow Brook H 2.2k	5	8	62¼	61½	69¼	617	Collins W	142	w	5.00	--	Birmingham1422ShipExecutiv1426St.Frncs1403	Bobbled 14th	10
29May37- 2Bel	fst	*2	S'Chase	3:441	4↑ Corinthian H 2.1k	1	5	35	31	11½	13	Collins W	140	w	4.00	--	Jungle King1403Rioter1644Saluda14410	Easily	5
15May37- 2Bel	my	*2	S'Chase	3:45	4↑ International H 2.1k	1	5	24	23	49	516	Collins W	143	w	7.00	--	Rioter1592Birminghm1408Rhdmnthus1484	Faltered final ¼	5
3Nov36- 4Bel	fst	2½	S'Chase	4:484	4↑ Temple Gwathmey H 2.1k	1	2	25	21	21	21½	McGinnis P	139	w	*1.00e	--	Sailor Beware1421½Jungle King1393Arc Light1546	No match	4
21Oct36- 4Lrl	fst	*2	S'Chase	3:551	3↑ Chevy Chase H 2.9k	1	4	43	42½	49½	411	Collins W	141	w	8.35	--	Rioter1602Lord Johnson1351Birmingham1408	No threat	4
12Oct36- 2Lrl	fst	*2	S'Chase	3:553	3↑ Handicap 1000	1	4	43	21	21½	21½	Collins W	140	w	5.45	--	Amagansett1601½JngleKing1401½Brmnghm1403	Finished well	6
3Oct36- 2Bel	fst	*3	S'Chase	5:47	4↑ Grand National H 7.5k	4	5	59½	-	-	-	Collins W	140	w	20.00	--	Bushranger1722Rioter15610Amaganstt157nk	Lost rider 13th	5
26Sep36- 2Bel	fst	*2½	S'Chase	4:461	4↑ Brook H 3.7k	5	5	55	55¼	412	415	Collins W	143	w	20.00	--	Bushranger1655Rioter1573Golden Meadow1547	No excuse	6
23Sep36- 2Bel	fst	*2	S'Chase	3:494	3↑ Alw 1000	4	2	22	43¼	414	415	Baldwin E	151	w	4.00	--	Golden Meadow1474St. Francis1525Navarino1486	No excuse	4
29Aug36- 2Sar	sly	*2½	S'Chase	5:242	4↑ Sar H 3.3k	4	4	47	-	-	-	Collins W	142	w	*1.40	--	Rioter1501½Birmingham14012Redshank142	Fell at 13th	4
22Aug36- 1Sar	my	*2	S'Chase	4:224	3↑ North American H 2.2k	3	3	33	22	12	13	Collins W	140	w	*1.20	--	JungleKing1403NtonlAnthm139½Prttlr1384	Drew away easily	4
13Aug36- 2Sar	fst	*2	S'Chase	4:104	4↑ Alw 900	2	2	22	21½	1nk	2no	Baldwin E	142	w	1.20	--	Prattler137noJungle King142	Saved ground,gamely	3
5Aug36- 2Sar	fst	*2	S'Chase	4:064	4↑ Alw 1000	1	3	35½	34½	36	312	Collins W	148	w	2.20	--	Golden Meadow1438Escapade1524Jungle King14812	Hung	5
1Aug36- 2Sar	fst	*2	S'Chase	4:12	3↑ Beverwyck H 2.1k	1	4	42¾	34¼	23	23	Collins W	142	w	4.00	--	Rioter1463Jungle King14212National Anthem1426	No match	4
6Jun36- 2Bel	fst	*2½	S'Chase	4:48	4↑ Meadow Brook H 1.9k	3	3	35	36½	23	22	Collins W	143	w	1.80	--	NationalAnthem1352JungleKing1433SnapBack146	Slow start	3
30May36- 2Bel	fst	*2	S'Chase	3:433	4↑ Corinthian H 1.9k	3	3	38	2hd	21	33½	Collins W	143	w	8.00	--	Bushranger1572Birmingham1391½JungleKing143	Bid,faltered	3
5Oct35- 2Bel	fst	*2½	S'Chase	4:464	4↑ Brook H 3.2k	3	-	-	-	-	-	Williams F	143	w	1.60e	--	ArcLight1544BorderWarrant138	Pulled up lame after 1st	4
31Aug35- 2Sar	fst	*2½	S'Chase	5:084	4↑ Sar H 3.8k	6	7	713	64¾	32	11½	Williams F	139	w	*2.20	--	Jungle King1391½Red Flash1443Amagansett1504	Driving	7
24Aug35- 2Sar	fst	*2	S'Chase	4:14	3↑ Alw 1200	8	6	41¾	21	1nk	2nk	Collins W	150	w	*2.20	--	Driver130nkJungle King1505Benedictine1542	Gamely	8
17Aug35- 2Sar	fst	*2	S'Chase	4:15	3↑ North American H 2.4k	4	4	32¼	42½	24	35½	Collins W	138	w	4.50	--	Rhadamanthus1452½Amaganstt1483JnglKng1388	Bid,faltered	5
14Aug35- 2Sar	gd	*2	S'Chase	4:183	3↑ Alw 1000	4	3	2nk	2nk	140	140	Collins W	141	w	*1.40	--	Jungle King14140Staunch Pal136Galyarrow133	Easily	5
1Aug35- 2Sar	fst	*2	S'Chase	4:183	3↑ Beverwyck H 2.4k	4	-	-	-	-	-	Collins W	136	w	*1.60e	--	Red Flash142½Amagansett1496Spinach1402	Lost rider 3rd	8
8Jun35- 2Bel	gd	*2½	S'Chase	4:442	4↑ Meadow Brook H 2.2k	1	4	35	33	21½	34¼	Collins W	139	w	4.00	--	IrishBullet1564ArcLight155nkJungleKng1392	Faltered late	6
25May35- 2Bel	fst	*2	S'Chase	3:421	4↑ C L Appleton Cup 3.7k	6	8	77¼	78	616	615	Collins W	150	w	12.00	--	Bushranger1431½Rideaway1402Spinach1421½		8
			Impeded by riderless horse																
18May35- 2Bel	fst	*2	S'Chase	3:41	4↑ International H 2.1k	3	4	49	45¾	38	37½	Collins W	148	w	10.00	--	Amagansett1431½Bushrngr1426JunglKng14810	Outrun on flat	5
6Nov34- 4Bel	sly	*2½	S'Chase	5:043	4↑ Temple Gwathmey H 2.4k	1	4	21	2hd	2nk	2hd	Collins W	142	w	4.00	--	Kummel136hdJungle King14210Bagatelle141½	Finished well	6
24Oct34- 3Lrl	fst	*2	S'Chase	3:55	3↑ Chevy Chase H 2.9k	2	3	43	31½	1hd	1nk	Collins W	136	w	5.40	--	JungleKing136nkTanaringo1391Rideaway1431½	Game in drive	6
22Sep34- 2Aqu	sly	2	S'Chase	4:07	3↑ Handicap 1670	2	2	13	15	16	112	Collins W	132	w	5.00	--	Jungle King13212National Anthem135	In hand	3
20Sep34- 2Aqu	fst	2	S'Chase	3:564	3↑ Md Sp Wt	2	2	3½	12	23	27	Collins W	145	w	*.90e	--	Black Bean1337Jungle King14510Lei1456	Swerved	7
30Aug34- 2Sar	hy	*2	S'Chase	4:133	3↑ Md Sp Wt	4	4	613	614	618	512	Collins W	142	w	3.50e	--	National Anthem1332Axon1354Surf Board1321	No mishap	10
			Previously trained by M.C. Lilly																
5Jun34- 5Det	fst	1		:243 :482 1:131 1:391	3↑ Alw 800	7	5	43½	45	55½	55	Jacobs J	106	w	7.20	94-08	Bamboula1032½Money Getter99hdDark Conquest1042		7
			Lost ground throughout																
21May34- 5Det	fst	1		:24 :473 1:122 1:371	3↑ Alw 1000	2	4	44	45	45½	48½	Jacobs J	104	w	5.30	100-02	Elf Lock89.5½Polydorus1065Projectile1063	No factor	5
7May34- 4Pim	fst	1 70		:233 :48 1:132 1:44	3↑ Alw 800	9	7	73¼	65¼	35½	34	Jacobs J	117	w	8.00e	87-13	Sea Fox1171Swiftsport106.53Jungle King1171	Good try	10
30Apr34- 6Pim	fst	6f		:232 :472 1:12	3↑ Alw 800	7	6	67	69½	611	69¾	Jacobs J	118	wb	26.25	84-14	CrowningGlory118¾BrightHaven1022HappyGo1042½	No threat	8
14Apr34- 5Bow	fst	1 70		:234 :482 1:133 1:46	3↑ Handicap 1500	6	6	52¼	53	511	58½	Coucci S	103	wb	4.80	76-21	Gay World120½Chatmoss1062½Chance Flight1084	No threat	7
10Mar34- 5Hia	fst	1⅛		:461 1:102 1:353 1:482	3↑ J McLennan Mem H 2.4k	5	3	46½	46	69	614	Stout J	102	wb	11.20	90-04	BlessedEvent1112Somebody1011½FlyingSailor1054	Quit late	6
3Mar34- 5Hia	fst	1¼		:474 1:122 1:37 2:024	3↑ Jockey Club H 3.5k	5	4	21½	22	44½	55½	Porter E	100	wb	15.40	98-01	BlessedEvent1081Springsteel1262BigBeu107.51½	Speed,quit	9
6Feb34- 5Hia	fst	1		:233 :464 1:114 1:38	4↑ Alw 1000	3	4	53¾	54¾	44	42½	Coucci S	113	w	3.90	87-10	Repaid115nkMountain Elk110¾Big Beau1121½	Saved ground	5
3Feb34- 6Hia	fst	1		:231 :463 1:114 1:371	3↑ Handicap 1000	6	5	65	63¼	65¼	67¼	Coucci S	105	w	*1.20e	87-08	SwpngLght116nkCurco110½MdFrmp1092½	Not persevered with	7
26Jan34- 5Hia	fst	1		:234 :464 1:111 1:364	4↑ Alw 1000	6	2	41½	43¼	34	36½	Coucci S	102	w	*1.20	89-05	Repaid103½Pastry1076Jungle King1022	Pinched back	6
28Jun33- 6AP	fst	1		:23 :463 1:111 1:37	Alw 1000	1	4	42½	44½	2½	21	Coucci S	108	w	*1.63	86-09	Esseff1041JungleKng1085Pompolon107½	Impeded after start	6
17Jun33- 5Aqu	fst	1		:24 :482 1:133 1:38	Alw 800	3	3	32½	31¾	32	23	Coucci S	112	w	2.20	87-14	Balios1123Jungle King1123Caesars Ghost1071		5
			Blocked,knocked off stride																
11Mar33- 5Hia	fst	1⅛		:47 1:113 1:37 1:493	Florida Derby 13k	2	5	32	41¾	22	23	Coucci S	118	w	*.80	102-01	Charley O.1183Jungle King1182½Inlander1164	No match	10
4Mar33- 6Hia	fst	1		:233 :47 1:11 1:364	Alw 1000	6	5	54	54	41½	1½	Coucci S	120	w	2.35	98-00	Jungle King120½Pot Au Brooms110nkCharacter1201	Driving	7
11Feb33- 4Hia	fst	7f		:23 :463 1:133 1:253	Bahamas 2.9k	5	5	64¼	63¼	42	2hd	Coucci S	122	w	3.15	89-10	Character121hdJungleKng1221½Algr113hd	Getting to winner	8
3Feb33- 4Hia	fst	1		:233 :47 1:12 1:381	Alw 1000	3	2	23	2½	11½	12½	Coucci S	111	w	2.90	91-14	Jungle King1112½Bubbler107nkPre War1061½	Easily	7
28Jan33- 4Hia	fst	6f		:23 :462 1:121	Hialeah 3k	6	7	87¼	67½	59	44½	Coucci S	114	w	14.30	86-09	Character1161½GoldBasis111hdThePelican1163	Hard ridden	9
23Jan33- 4Hia	fst	6f		:232 :47 1:124	Alw 1000	5	2	52½	42½	31	1hd	Coucci S	110	w	5.35	88-13	Jungle King110hdBubbler110noDaudet110hd	Up late	9
			Previously trained by W. Brennan																
18Nov32- 3Bow	my	6f		:232 :473 1:13	Alw 1000	2	6	128¾	1214	1116	811¼	Jones R	111	wb	32.95	77-22	Filter1081½Cruising1081Character1113	No factor	12
9Nov32- 3Pim	hy	1 70		:242 :50 1:172 1:501	Alw 1000	1	3	52¾	54¾	54	53¼	Kurtsinger C	111	wb	14.25	57-35	SilentShot114hdWhiteThorn1141½BurningFeet114nk	Good try	11
3Nov32- 4Pim	gd	6f		:232 :473 1:13	Pim Home-Bred 1.5k	2	5	62½	64¼	67	54½	Kurtsinger C	113	wb	69.75	84-17	Iseult1102Acautaw1152The Pelican113½	No mishap	10
14Oct32- 5Lrl	fst	1 70		:233 :482 1:132 1:442	Alw 1200	11	3	31	63¾	912	1012	Kurtsinger C	110	wb	13.20	77-15	Mr. Khayyam110hdPoppyman1152Keep Out1103	Quit	11
10Oct32- 3Lrl	gd	6f		:233 :483 1:142	Alw 1000	8	7	84¼	85¾	45½	43	Kurtsinger C	110	wb	15.65f	81-21	BoldLover110½Snaplock1142BrightShadow109.5½	Fast finish	12
21Sep32- 3HdG	fst	6f		:23 :461 1:114	Alw 1200	7	3	74¼	85¾	109¼	1010½	Kurtsinger C	108	wb	17.05	85-10	Poppyman110hdWhite Lies1055Okapi108hd	No factor	11
10Sep32- 3Bel	fst	*7f-WC		1:204	Champagne 5k	3	2	1½	52¾	712	65	Robertson A	116	wb	5.00e	86-12	Dynastic1191Kerry Patch116noDe Valera1102	Quit,mate won	9

24Aug32- 3Sar	fst 5½f	:23 :463 :593 1:062	Alw 800	2 2 51¾ 53¼ 51¾ 2no	Workman R	118wb	15.00	91-09	Bold Lover108noJungle King1181Llandaff111nk	Driving	9
18Aug32- 3Sar	sly 6f	:231 :471 1:124	Grab Bag H 3.4k	8 7 109¾ 1012 95½ 98¾	Coucci S	120wb	15.00	79-13	Sun Archer1153Garden Message1121½Grand Time125no		10
	Struggled in going										
10Aug32- 3Sar	fst 5½f	:231 :471 1:001 1:07	Alw 800	5 5 35 32½ 43 32	Kurtsinger C	120wb	5.00e	86-16	Wedding Ring1151Sarada1101Jungle King1202	Tired	12
6Aug32- 3Sar	fst 6f	:23 :47 1:123	U S Hotel 13k	10 1 63¾ 85 85½ 79½	Kurtsinger C	118wb	30.00	79-11	Ladysman1253De Valera1142Happy Gal122½	Early speed	10
2Aug32- 6Sar	fst 5½f	:231 :464 1:00 1:064	©Md Sp Wt	9 5 47 45¼ 43¼ 1no	Kurtsinger C	116wb	*2.00	89-12	JunglKng116noBlssdEvnt116½CrckFlyr1161	Away in a tangle	12
9Jun32- 3Bel	fst 5f-WC	1:001	Alw 1000	9 6 52¾ 51¼ 43	Kurtsinger C	108wb	10.00	76-17	CrzyJn1131RomnHoldy116½LoughPort1161½	Blocked final ⅛	11
4Jun32- 6Bel	fst 4½f-WC	:52	Alw 1000	2 5 88¼ 915 813½	Kurtsinger C	112 w	8.00	81-08	Kerry Patch1121Bronze Saint112noPuchero1122	Outrun	9

Kayak II (Arg)

br. c. 1935, by Congreve (Copyright)–Mosquita, by Your Majesty — **Lifetime record: 26 14 8 1 $213,205**

Own.– C.S. Howard
Br.– J.V. Roca (Arg)
Tr.– T. Smith

16Jan41- 6SA	gd 6f	:223 :462 1:111 4↑	Alw 2500	1 5 56 31½ 3½ 21½	Haas L	126wb	*.90	91-14	Augury1151½Kayak II1261Carmenita1052½		7
	Wide,worked mile in 1:37 4/5										
2Sep40- 6Was	fst 1¼	:494 1:144 1:391 2:04 3↑	Wash Park H 31k	5 5 53½ 56 68 610¾	Adams J	130wb	*.80	79-14	War Plumage110¾Viscounty1183Burning Star1094	Gave way	6
3Aug40- 7Hol	fst 1½	:481 1:131 2:041 2:301 3↑	Sunset H 20k	7 4 55 32½ 2½ 1hd	Adams J	131wb	*1.40e	94-06	Kayak II131hdSpecify1161½Big Flash1093	Hard drive	8
27Jly40- 7Hol	fst 1¼	:461 1:11 1:36 2:02 3↑	Hol Gold Cup 53k	11 8 67 73¾ 67¾ 79¾	Rodriguez E	133wb	*1.10e	93-07	Challedon1331¼Specify1172½Can't Wait1151½	No excuse	11
2Mar40- 6SA	fst 1¼	:471 1:111 1:36 2:011 3↑	S Anita H 121k	2 13 1311 62½ 31½ 21½	Haas L	129wb	*.70e	99-11	Seabiscuit1301½Kayak II1291Whichcee1141½	Good effort	13
24Feb40- 6SA	fst 1 1/16	:231 :464 1:111 1:422 3↑	S Antonio H 13k	5 10 95 54½ 42 22½	Shelhamer A	128wb	*1.70e	97-07	Seabiscuit1242½Kayak II128½Viscounty1104	Closed strong	13
17Feb40- 6SA	fst 7f	:223 :453 1:103 1:232 3↑	San Carlos H 12k	7 9 72¾ 63½ 710 87½	Adams J	130wb	*.80e	87-14	Specify1151¼Lassator105hdViscounty1093	Dull effort	11
1Jan40- 6SA	fst 1	:224 :463 1:112 1:372 3↑	New Year H 11k	7 5 33 33½ 23 24	Adams J	128wb	*.80	87-16	Whichcee1164Kayak II1284Heelfly1172	Second best	7
15Nov39- 6Pim	fst 1⅝	:494 1:402 2:05 2:442 3↑	Bowie H 12k	3 3 49½ 35 2hd 12	Woolf G	126wb	*.40	104-10	Kayak II1262Heelfly113noChallephen1131	Going away	8
1Nov39- 5Pim	gd 1 3/16	:512 1:163 1:404 1:59 3↑	Pim Spl 10k	3 1 21 2½ 1hd 2½	Woolf G	126wb	2.55	87-19	Challedon120½Kayak II12612Cravat126	Second best	3
21Oct39- 5Jam	fst 1 1/16	:231 :47 1:121 1:45 3↑	Continental H 12k	4 3 45½ 33 2½ 11	Adams J	128wb	*.90	88-13	Kayak II1281Hash118noJourney On1124	Eased up	6
2Sep39- 5Nar	fst 1 3/16	:482 1:124 1:374 1:563 3↑	Nar Spl H 31k	3 2 31¾ 3nk 2½ 23	Woolf G	128wb	*.50e	89-14	Challedon1183Kayak II1284Sorteado116½	Led,no excuse	6
22Jly39- 7Hol	fst 1¼	:472 1:121 1:371 2:023 3↑	Hol Gold Cup 52k	4 4 32 1hd 14 15	Woolf G	125wb	*.40	106-10	Kayak II1255Cravat126¾Specify118nk	Easily	7
4Jly39- 7Hol	fst 1⅛	:47 1:114 1:371 1:494 3↑	American H 15k	4 2 21 13 12½ 15	Woolf G	120wb	*.60	101-10	Kayak II1205Gosum1073½Olimpo107no	Going away	8
4Mar39- 6SA	fst 1¼	:461 1:102 1:353 2:012 3↑	S Anita H 126k	16 10 73¾ 43½ 31½ 11¼	Adams J	110wb	*3.00e	101-11	Kayak II1101¼Whichcee1121Main Man1171½	Going away	16
18Feb39- 6SA	fst 1 1/16	:231 :464 1:11 1:422 3↑	San Carlos H 13k	10 5 54½ 32 22½ 1no	Adams J	110wb	4.20	102-11	Kayak II110noSpecify1194½Whichcee1124½	Just up	13
14Feb39- 5SA	fst 1 1/16	:231 :463 1:104 1:423 4↑	Alw 2000	2 2 2hd 1½ 12 34¼	Craigmyle J	120wb	*.30	97-06	Bottle Top1071½Patty Cake1053Kayak II1205	Tired badly	6
25Jan39- 7SA	fst 1	:224 :462 1:11 1:36 4↑	Alw 1500	7 1 15 14 16 14½	Neves R	118wb	*.60	99-08	Kayak II1184½Quick Devil1181½Masker1152½	Easily best	8
14Jan39- 4SA	fst 6f	:221 :453 1:102 4↑	Handicap 1500	1 7 68½ 47 32 1hd	Neves R	116wb	*2.00	98-07	Kayak II116hdFirst Kiss1064½Lavengro1151	Just up	8
15Nov38- 4Pim	fst 6f	:23 :462 1:12	Alw 1200	6 3 2hd 21 1nk 1¾	Peters M	116wb	*1.00	94-15	Kayak II116¾Rissa104hdRoar113hd	Drew out	8
29Oct38- 2Lrl	hy 1 70	:234 :48 1:15 1:464	Alw 1100	5 2 1hd 13 11 21	Smith FA	118wb	*.70	74-30	SunAlexandria1151KayakII1184JohnOne1182	Tired in drive	5
17Oct38- 6Lrl	fst 1 70	:233 :463 1:121 1:423	Alw 1100	7 1 13 12 12 1nk	Smith FA	112wb	*1.25	96-13	Kayak II112nkPernie1121John One112½	Just lasted	7
13Oct38- 5Lrl	fst 6f	:231 :464 1:121	Alw 1200	1 5 11 11½ 12 11	Smith FA	110wb	2.95	93-13	Kayak II1101Court Dance107nkRissa1071	Driving	8
27Jun38- 6Suf	sly 1 70	:231 :47 1:114 1:433	Alw 1000	5 1 11½ 12 13 12½	Smith FA	113wb	*1.90	88-20	Kayak II1132½Mama's Boy1071Landlubber104no	In hand	6
23Jun38- 1Suf	fst 6f	:23 :453 1:11 3↑	Md Sp Wt	5 3 11½ 12 12½ 15	Smith FA	110wb	*1.70	93-13	Kayak II1105Sport Heel1101½Running Scale1053	Going away	9
10Jun38- 6Aqu	fst 6½f	:233 :47 1:122 1:192 3↑	Md Sp Wt	7 6 2hd 11 1hd 22	Pollard J	118 w	3.00	88-13	Billy Van Nuys1182Kayak II1182Trojan Racket1262	Hung	7

Lady Maryland

gr. f. 1934, by Sir Greysteel (Roi Herode)–Palestra, by Prince Palatine — **Lifetime record: 82 18 14 14 $31,067**

Own.– G. Ring
Br.– Mrs Helena S. Raskob (Md)
Tr.– A.G. Robertson

12Oct40- 3Jam	fst 6f	:224 :462 1:121 3↑	ⒻAlw 2000	7 8 817 819 814 813	Seabo G	114 w	10.45	78-13	Dini1221½Flota105½Colosseum1141¼	Never a factor	8
	Previously trained by L.G. Bedwell										
22Jun40- 6Del	fst 1 1/16	:233 :464 1:113 1:451 3↑	ⒻNewcastle H 13k	10 12 105¾ 117 1113 1010¾	Driscoll D	124 w	7.65	82-08	Tedbriar108.5½War Beauty1062Orcades107hd	Outrun	12
7Jun40- 6Bel	fst 1 1/16	:224 :453 1:103 1:433 3↑	ⒻTop Flight H 7.9k	4 8 67 64¼ 53 56½	Charlton C	126 w	4.45e	86-15	True Call1071Piquet106hdDolly Val120½	No mishap	9
27May40- 6Bel	fst 1 1/16	:231 :464 1:111 1:441 3↑	ⒻHandicap 2040	2 6 69½ 58½ 23 1hd	Charlton C	122 w	*1.50e	90-13	Lady Maryland122hdRosetown105½One Jest1174	Hard drive	8
16May40- 5Bel	fst 7f	:23 :461 1:121 1:25 3↑	ⒻHandicap 2035	1 3 32 33½ 23 2hd	Charlton C	122 w	*1.10	85-16	Torchlight116hdLadyMrylnd1226HstyWddng1062	Just missed	5
11May40- 5Pim	fst 6f	:223 :464 1:12 3↑	WFBR H 1.5k	4 4 54½ 41½ 1½ 12	Charlton C	114 w	2.30	94-15	LadyMrylnd1142SlowMotion1223LegalLight1122	Going away	7
6May40- 6Pim	fst 6f	:222 :454 1:112 3↑	Jennings H 6k	1 6 42¾ 64¾ 53¼ 43	Charlton C	111 w	8.45	94-15	BattleJack120½SpeedtoSpare1182SlowMotion117½	No mishap	9
29Apr40- 6Pim	fst 6f	:222 :46 1:111 3↑	Baltimore Spring H 3.2k	6 6 56 43 32 31¼	Charlton C	111 w	5.05	97-17	BattleJack1171SpeedtoSpar118nkLdyMrylnd1111	Closed fast	6
15Apr40- 5HdG	fst 6f	:234 :462 1:12 3↑	Harford H 6.7k	5 8 913 96½ 94½ 45	Charlton C	111 w	7.25e	88-14	Sun Egret1222Battle Jack1152Jay Jay1141	Late foot	10
30Jan40- 5Hia	fst 7f	:23 :462 1:103 1:232 4↑	ⒻAlw 1200	4 7 54½ 55½ 42¾ 51¼	Durando C	115 w	3.30	95-09	Flying Lill115nkDolly Val115hdUnerring118½	Swerved	8
27Jan40- 4Hia	fst 6f	:224 :463 1:102 4↑	Alw 1400	3 4 55½ 55½ 32½ 33	Smith FA	111 w	7.10	94-12	EasyMon1142TheChief108.51LadyMaryland1115	Closed well	5
17Jan40- 6Hia	fst 6f	:23 :461 1:10 3↑	Handicap 1500	4 6 74¼ 74½ 55½ 43½	Donoso R	113 w	7.15	95-07	Easy Mon1133Mar Le108½Speed to Spare118no	Late foot	7
10Jan40- 6Hia	gd 6f	:221 :453 1:114 3↑	Inaugural H 6.7k	4 13 1320 1325 1123 1119¾	Smith FA	115 w	6.10	70-18	Maetall114hdCardinalis1103Great Union120hd	Dull race	13
11Nov39- 6Pim	fst 6f	:221 :453 1:112 3↑	Ritchie H 7.5k	12 8 76 53½ 41½ 1hd	Smith FA	108 w	9.10	97-12	Lady Maryland108hdJay Jay113noAirflame1102	Hard drive	12
7Nov39- 6Pim	gd 6f	:224 :464 1:13 2↑	ⓈHeiser H 3.1k	1 1 43¾ 52¼ 31½ 2hd	Robertson A	111 w	10.80	89-25	SlowMotion116hdLadyMrylnd111noSpdtoSpr1181	Just missed	6
3Nov39- 5Pim	fst 1 1/16	:241 :484 1:14 1:464 3↑	Handicap 1500	5 4 43¼ 31½ 21½ 21	Shelhamer A	115 w	*1.25	85-17	FlyingLee1111LadyMrylnd1152NoCompetiton1093	No excuse	5
21Oct39- 6Lrl	fst 1 1/16	:232 :464 1:122 1:45 3↑	Handicap 1500	4 4 42¾ 32 45½ 45¼	Peters M	112 w	1.95	87-14	Challephen1111Nedayr116nkManie O'Hara1034	No excuse	6
14Oct39- 5Lrl	fst 1	:232 :463 1:12 1:374 2↑	Laurel 9.7k	7 7 74½ 63½ 34 34	Robertson A	111 w	5.90	92-13	Sun Egret1184Nedayr113hdLady Maryland1114	Closed well	8
	Previously trained by P.D. Watts										
7Oct39- 6Lrl	fst 1 1/16	:232 :472 1:123 1:443 3↑	Handicap 2000	5 3 4¾ 2½ 2hd 2nk	Robertson A	111 w	4.40	94-14	WarMinstrel109nkLadyMaryland1112RobertL.1113	Game try	6
3Oct39- 5Lrl	my 6f	:243 :483 1:132 3↑	Capital H 9.3k	6 8 88¼ 86½ 78 79	Hardy L	110 w	20.40	78-22	Sun Egret1201½Clodion1121½Rough Time122½	Outrun	8
25Sep39- 4HdG	fst 6f	:232 :462 1:121 3↑	Handicap 1200	4 4 43¼ 43 21 2nk	Hardy L	116 w	3.35	92-17	BunnyBaby104nkLadyMaryland1161RobertL.1164	Just missed	5
18Sep39- 5HdG	fst 6f	:23 :463 1:114 3↑	Susquehanna H 2.5k	3 10 107 107¼ 105½ 82¾	Stevenson C	116 w	11.95	91-12	Sun Egret120½Jay Jay115hdRedlin116½	Off slowly	11
9Sep39- 5Aqu	fst 1 1/16	:233 :462 1:103 1:43 3↑	ⒻBeldame H 13k	6 8 74¾ 42 41¾ 63¾	Arcaro E	124 w	8.00	94-03	Nellie Bly102noUnerring1203Bala Ormont115hd	No mishap	18
5Sep39- 5Aqu	fst 7f	:231 :464 1:123 1:243 3↑	ⒻAlw 1200	3 5 65¾ 52¼ 3¾ 12	Arcaro E	115 w	3.20	91-10	Lady Maryland1152Pixey Dell1154Chicluna105½	Going away	9
7Aug39- 5Sar	fst 1	:242 :481 1:124 1:381 3↑	ⒻHandicap 1230	1 5 57½ 57 52¼ 67½	Peters M	122 w	6.00	82-11	Solar Flight1021½Hostility1121One Jest1122	No excuse	7
29Jly39- 5Emp	sly 1 1/16	:24 :473 1:123 1:453 3↑	Yonkers H 9.9k	6 6 68½ 67½ 57¼ 58½	Peters M	112 w	12.00	84-16	Sickle T.108hdHe Did116½The Chief1165	Outrun	7
1Jly39- 5AP	fst 1	:23 :454 1:103 1:363 3↑	ⒻArl Matron H 6.1k	5 6 65½ 44 35 34¼	Smith G	120 w	7.00	85-17	FlyingLill107nkUnerring1084LadyMaryland1202	Closed well	9
10Jun39- 6Del	fst 1 1/16	:24 :48 1:124 1:46 3↑	ⒻNewcastle H 12k	2 9 82¾ 72¾ 2hd 3nk	Smith G	118 w	4.40	89-11	ShangayLily113noBunnyBaby108nkLadyMrylnd118no	Game try	12
3Jun39- 7Del	fst 1 70	:232 :472 1:123 1:431 4↑	ⒻAlw 1000	2 4 42½ 41¾ 1½ 1¾	Smith G	117 w	2.45	100-07	LadyMaryland117¾PixeyDell1134ShortDistanc1031½	Drew out	7
30May39- 5Del	fst 6f	:23 :46 1:114 3↑	Wilmington H 5.4k	2 6 74½ 75¾ 54¾ 32	Smith G	108 w	4.95	97-07	FightingFox1261Preeminent1131LdyMrylnd108hd	Closed fast	8
20May39- 5Bel	fst 1	:231 :463 1:12 1:371 3↑	Metropolitan H 10k	6 6 65½ 56 69¾ 67½	Smith G	109 w	10.00	81-13	Knickerbocker1001½Heelfly116noJacola115hd	Outrun	8
11May39- 6Pim	fst 6f	:23 :463 1:121 3↑	ⒻCarroll H 3.3k	2 5 43½ 3½ 11½ 14	Smith G	116 w	*2.05	93-16	Lady Maryland1164Rehearsal1151Bunny Baby1143	Easily	7
6May39- 4Pim	fst 6f	:23 :463 1:122 3↑	Handicap 1200	1 6 83¾ 64¾ 4¾ 1nk	Smith G	110 w	6.15	92-15	LadyMaryland110nkSlowMotion111noRehersl1111½	Hard drive	9
15Apr39- 5HdG	fst 6f	:23 :463 1:114 3↑	Harford H 7k	6 13 135½ 135¼ 129¼ 119½	Smith G	109 w	5.40f	84-15	Sun Egret1164Fighting Fox1221Old Rosebush1141½	Outrun	14

Race	Cond	Dist	Times	Race	PP St 1C 2C Str Fin	Jockey	Wt	Odds	Spd	Top finishers	Comment	Field
8Apr39- 4Bow	gd	6f	:232 :473 1:14	3↑ Handicap 1065	8 2 97¾ 53¾ 41½ 31¾	Smith G	110 w	8.40	81-23	Pagliacci1121½Drudgery115nkLady Maryland110hd	Late foot	10
30Mar39- 5Bow	sly	6f	:231 :472 1:131	3↑ Rowe Mem H 6.3k	9 9 97½ 99 911 76¾	Mora H	108 w	16.90	80-25	Rough Time1161½Benjam1083Old Rosebush116hd	Outrun	10
16Nov38- 5Bow	fst	6f	:231 :472 1:12	2↑ W P Burch Mem H 2.6k	11 2 73½ 65 84 62¾	Seabo G	112 w	16.20	90-22	HoneyCloud1151½Clingendaal112noRyeBeach121no	No mishap	13
11Nov38- 6Pim	fst	6f	:23 :462 1:121	3↑ Ritchie H 7.5k	7 13 94 51¾ 32 2¾	Yarberry W	109 w	19.70	92-16	HoneyCloud110¾LadyMaryland109¾HighLark107½	Closed fast	14
7Nov38- 6Pim	hy	1 70	:233 :483 1:142 1:46	3↑ ⓈHeiser H 2.7k	3 3 3nk 11 1½ 1¾	Wall N	115 w	2.25	81-26	Lady Maryland115¾Unheralded1076Toddle On111	Drew out	3
2Nov38- 6Pim	fst	6f	:23 :463 1:114	2↑ Baltimore Autumn H 3.8k	3 9 82¾ 92 42 32¼	Yarberry W	107 w	32.05	93-13	SunEgrt1142Mowr116noDHTheFightr126	Close quarters early	11
17Oct38- 5Lrl	fst	1 1/16	:232 :471 1:122 1:444	3↑ Alw 1200	4 2 23 22 22 21½	Renick J	109 w	3.60	91-13	Conquer1201½LadyMrylnd1093SirJimJames1201	Good effort	5
12Oct38- 5Lrl	fst	1 70	:232 :47 1:123 1:431	3↑ Handicap 1200	4 6 66½ 43¼ 32 3½	Renick J	111 w	4.95	92-16	JohnOne111.5noJourneyOn111½LadyMrylnd1114	Strong finish	6
5Oct38- 4Lrl	fst	6f	:231 :463 1:123	3↑ Handicap 1200	5 4 42½ 31½ 31 3hd	Scheih F	113 w	2.65	91-14	Benjam115noHappy Code108noLady Maryland1132	Game try	6
24Sep38- 4HdG	fst	6f	:234 :47 1:12	3↑ Clm 4500	8 4 43 32 2nk 2¾	Dupps L	112 w	3.15	92-10	Infidox114¾Lady Maryland1123Carvola1041½	Weakened	9
16Sep38- 4HdG	fst	6f	:241 :472 1:121	3↑ Susquehanna H 2.5k	4 9 95¾ 85¼ 75½ 54	Seabo G	108 w	13.40	88-16	Lavengro114noSunEgret1131MaskedGnrl1141½	Close quarters	10
20Aug38- 4Nar	fst	6f	:231 :462 1:104	3↑ Clm 6000	5 4 33½ 33 2½ 1hd	Krovitz H	95 w	*2.20	97-09	Lady Maryland95hdHappy Knot1041Pordina101½	Hard drive	6
3Aug38- 5Nar	fst	1 70	:233 :472 1:114 1:422	3↑ ⒻMary Dyer H 6.7k	10 2 3nk 21½ 44 67½	Scheih F	107wb	23.55	85-14	Marica1292Patty Cake112noFair Stein1142	Tired	10
1Aug38- 5Nar	fst	6f	:23 :452 1:104	3↑ Nar H 6.6k	1 10 106½ 107¼ 106 104¾	Smith E	112wb	33.80	92-14	Accolade1132Merry Lassie1101The Fighter114hd	Outpaced	11
18Jly38- 4Emp	fst	5½f	:231 :464 1:09	3↑ Handicap 1030	2 4 44 33½ 31¼ 1nk	Wall N	117wb	*1.50	94-12	Lady Maryland117nkSunport120noLakeview1091½	Just up	5
7Jly38- 6Del	fst	6f	:241 :461 1:12	3↑ Handicap 2000	3 7 51¾ 5½ 42 43¼	Vedder RL	113wb	7.10	95-11	James A.108¾Sun Egret1201½Bull Whip1111	No mishaps	10
18Jun38- 4Del	fst	6f	:224 :46 1:12	3↑ Alw 1200	1 4 31¼ 31 2½ 21	Wall N	111wb	7.80	97-10	Sun Egret1131Lady Maryland111hdNedayr113no	Good effort	5
15Jun38- 5Del	fst	6f	:24 :473 1:131	3↑ Handicap 1000	1 3 21 2nk 12 11	Vedder RL	108wb	8.60	92-11	Lady Maryland1081Sun Celerina1081Conquer1263	Driving	7
				Previously owned by B.B. Archer								
8Jun38- 5Del	sl	6f	:24 :473 1:142	4↑ Clm 4000	1 4 2hd 11½ 11½ 1no	Wall N	115wb	2.00	86-16	LadyMaryland115noWinningChance1154Crvol1141½	Hard drive	5
				Previously trained by B.B. Archer								
11May38- 3Pim	fst	6f	:231 :473 1:124	4↑ Clm 3250	5 4 21½ 2½ 14 11	Wall N	112wb	2.80	90-13	LadyMaryland1121ChiefCherokee1172Tddy'sStr107hd	Driving	7
6May38- 2Pim	fst	6f	:232 :472 1:122	4↑ Clm c-2500	6 8 73¾ 41¾ 21½ 2hd	Adleman W	114wb	*1.55	92-13	PostageDue121hdLadyMaryland1145Sachem1181½	Just missed	8
				Claimed from Mrs R.H. Heighe, trainer J.A. Boniface								
3May38- 3Pim	fst	6f	:232 :473 1:122	4↑ ⒻClm 2250	5 8 52¼ 32 1½ 15	Adleman W	108wb	*2.25	92-11	Lady Maryland1085Sheknows1111½Deflate1152	Going away	10
27Apr38- 2HdG	fst	6f	:232 :473 1:13	4↑ Clm 2500	8 11 72 3nk 1hd 3nk	Adleman W	108wb	5.20f	88-18	Golden Vein115nkEarly Times118noLady Maryland1081	Hung	12
22Mar38- 4TrP	fst	6f	:223 :461 1:114	4↑ Clm 2500	4 5 85½ 75¼ 62¼ 31½	Adleman W	106wb	6.30	89-11	DHMixwell113DHLadfield1161½LadyMaryland106nk	Great rush	8
17Mar38- 7TrP	fst	5½f	:23 :462 1:061	4↑ Clm 2500	1 6 75¾ 65½ 43½ 32½	Adleman W	106wb	4.80	86-14	Rebekah1111½Mixwell1161Lady Maryland106hd	Closed fast	8
14Mar38- 6TrP	fst	6f	:23 :462 1:12	4↑ Clm 3000	1 6 53½ 54½ 42½ 53¾	Adleman W	106wb	9.60	86-14	Noble Boy1141½My Kin109noGold Buckle1141½	Hung	7
12Feb38- 3Hia	fst	6½f	:23 :463 1:133 1:181	4↑ Clm 3500	5 3 53½ 42½ 56 88½	Kurtsinger C	110wb	7.15	79-14	Sunphantom110nkSachem111¾My Kin1102	No excuse	9
3Feb38- 4Hia	fst	6f	:23 :46 1:112	4↑ Clm 4000	6 7 710 78 78 611	Adleman W	106wb	4.30	81-18	Indomitable1133Time Signal1142Max B.1131	Outrun	8
24Jan38- 6Hia	fst	1	:234 :464 1:111 1:373	4↑ Alw 1200	4 4 32 31 68½ 1014½	Smith FA	96wb	16.05	73-19	Mucho Gusto1161½Maecloud921Pageboy1141½	Quit	11
19Jan38- 4Hia	fst	6f	:223 :461 1:112	3↑ Handicap 1000	2 8 72¾ 74¼ 46½ 46	Adleman W	118wb	14.35	86-16	Joyride1101Black River124hdGene Wagers1165	No mishaps	11
27Jly37- 5Sar	sl	6f	:24 :473 1:14	Seneca Claiming 4k	7 2 54¼ 52¼ 41¼ 43½	Wagner J	109wb	4.00	78-19	Golden Era108½Mahdi106noBitter Berry1053	No mishaps	7
3Jly37- 4Del	fst	6f	:233 :463 1:131	ⒻAlw 1000	5 2 32 32 2hd 1hd	Adelman W	106wb	*1.20	- -	LadyMaryland106hdEarlyAutumn1034CareFor1035	Hard drive	6
26Jun37- 4Del	fst	6f	:23 :462 1:123	Clm 4000	2 1 41¼ 3½ 1hd 14	McDermott P	104wb	*1.20	- -	LadyMaryland1044CareFor101hdAlexandrine1051	Going away	5
15Jun37- 6Aqu	fst	7f	:233 :48 1:121 1:244	Handicap 1055	4 3 34 35 33½ 24	Ray W	106wb	7.00	87-15	Drudgery1184LadyMaryland106½EarlySettlr1072	Closed well	5
4Jun37- 5Bel	fst	1	:233 :471 1:12 1:374	3↑ Handicap 1065	8 1 2hd 2hd 55¾ 610½	Peters M	111wb	4.00	75-14	Buginarug109½Danger Point1042Night Bud1105	Speed,quit	8
29May37- 4Bel	fst	6f	:223 :454 1:12	ⒻAlw 1000	1 3 45 55 32½ 34½	Hanford C	111wb	6.00	85-17	North Riding1151½Rosenna1113Lady Maryland111½	Wide	7
11May37- 5Bel	fst	6f	:23 :464 1:13	ⒻAlw 1000	7 4 33 32½ 2½ 22½	Peters M	113wb	10.00	86-19	NorthRiding1172½LadyMaryland1134Flyanett109hd	Wide,hung	7
30Apr37- 6Pim	fst	6f	:232 :473 1:134	Alw 1000	3 3 3½ 2hd 42 54¾	Peters M	111wb	11.75	80-21	Carnarvon112.5½PrairiDog111nkGrndPly1114	Faltered drive	7
19Apr37- 3HdG	fst	6f	:233 :48 1:144	ⒻAlw 1000	2 3 1hd 1hd 1hd 1½	Peters M	110wb	8.95	79-24	Lady Maryland110.5½Care For112½My Elsie1124		7
				Driving,slowly drew clear								
18Sep36- 2HdG	fst	6f	:24 :482 1:144	Alw 1000	1 5 43½ 43½ 43½ 6¾	Renick J	111wb	18.45f	78-18	Alexandrine108noAngloSaxon111hdLiveGrant117no	No factor	12
30Jly36- 3Sar	fst	5½f	:232 :482 1:082	ⒻMd Sp Wt	2 2 43¼ 3¾ 1nk 11	Fallon L	115wb	15.00	81-14	Lady Maryland1151Janeen115hdCare For1151½	Wide	14
20Jun36- 1Aqu	fst	5f	1:002	ⒻMd Sp Wt	5 2 63 62¾ 65¾	Richards H	115wb	4.00	79-09	Devil's Pace1102Sunfeathers115hdCeltic Legend1153		11
				Slow into stride								
4Jun36- 3Bel	fst	4½f-WC	:523	ⒻMd Sp Wt	14 7 11½ 1hd 42	Peters M	112wb	50.00	90-15	Richmond Rose1121Premiere1121Scottish Mary112hd		14
				Faltered under urging								
1Jun36- 1Bel	fst	5f-WC	1:001	Clm 3500	6 7 75½ 77¼ 713	Peters M	113wb	15.00	66-16	Pass 'Em By1141½Papenie1191½Thomas C.1115	Trailed	7
25Feb36- 2Hia	fst	3f	:344	Md Sp Wt	13 2 22 2hd	Renick J	113wb	5.95f	- -	BravoCaruso116hdLadyMaryland1132MayRo1141	Just missed	13
13Feb36- 2Hia	gd	3f	:35	ⒻAlw 800	6 3 55½ 47½	Renick S	115 w	19.40	- -	Owaller1182Moss Gal1181½Little Empress1184	No mishaps	7
5Feb36- 2Hia	fst	3f	:35	Clm 2500	1 1 1½ 21½	Meade D	113 w	4.55	- -	Oddesa Girl1151½Lady Maryland1131½Greedy113hd	Bore out	14
27Jan36- 2Hia	fst	3f	:34	ⒻMd Sp Wt	2 3 44 45½	Workman R	116 w	73.90	- -	Owaller116½Peggy Porter116noClouds1165	Evenly	12

Marica

blk. f. 1933, by Epinard (Badajoz)–Canberra, by Craigangower
Own.– French Lick Springs Stable
Br.– Thomas D. Taggart (Ky)
Tr.– J.H Johnson

Lifetime record: 44 19 7 6 $48,825

Race	Cond	Dist	Times	Race	PP St 1C 2C Str Fin	Jockey	Wt	Odds	Spd	Top finishers	Comment	Field
14Feb39- 6SA	fst	1	:223 :453 1:102 1:353	4↑ Alw 1900	3 2 31¾ 37 39 38¼	Dotter R	113wb	6.60	93-06	Today1042¼Seabiscuit1286Marica113	Tired	3
				Trained in 1938 by H. Oots & H. Wells								
28Sep38- 5HdG	fst	1⅛	:472 1:122 1:372 1:50	3↑ Havre de Grace H 11k	5 4 43 56½ 711 712½	Dotter R	124wb	14.00	86-16	Seabiscuit1282½SavageBeauty1031Mnow1201½	Close quarters	8
3Sep38- 5Nar	fst	1 3/16	:472 1:122 1:363 1:561	3↑ Nar Spl 33k	10 5 31¼ 32½ 1011 1019	Dotter R	128wb	3.30	75-09	Stagehand1191Bull Lea1133Cravat1084	Tired	10
22Aug38- 5Sar	fst	1	:23 :463 1:12 1:38	3↑ ⒻHandicap 1240	4 3 23 11 11½ 12	Gilbert J	128wb	*.65	91-15	Marica1282Idle Miss1125Rust1095	Easily	4
3Aug38- 5Nar	fst	1 70	:233 :472 1:114 1:422	3↑ ⒻMary Dyer H 6.7k	2 6 1hd 11½ 12½ 12	Dotter R	129wb	*.50	93-14	Marica1292Patty Cake112noFair Stein1142	In hand	10
9Jly38- 6Del	fst	1¼	:48 1:121 1:362 2:033	3↑ Sussex H 11k	1 1 13 13 11½ 1½	Dotter R	125wb	*1.00e	103-08	Marica125½Tatterdemalion1173Isolater116no	Driving	6
18Jun38- 6Del	fst	1 1/16	:25 :484 1:121 1:453	3↑ ⒻNewcastle H 11k	3 1 11½ 11½ 13 11	Dotter R	125wb	1.90	91-10	Marica1251Savage Beauty109½Esposa1203	Eased up	6
				Previously trained by H. Wells								
14Oct37- 6Kee	fst	1¼	:464 1:114 1:38 2:042	3↑ Breeders H 7.4k	2 1 15 14 13 1nk	Dotter R	118wb	1.10	98-08	Marica118nkCount Arthur126	Hard drive	2
11Sep37- 6Haw	gd	1¼	:472 1:121 1:374 2:042	3↑ Haw Gold Cup H 16k	10 6 42½ 54½ 69 67¼	Dotter R	120wb	2.70	79-16	Sahri II110hdInfantry116noDellor1142	Bore over badly	12
4Sep37- 5LF	fst	6f	:23 :461 1:104	3↑ Calumet H 3k	4 1 42 34½ 33½ 2nk	Dotter R	127wb	*.60	98-10	BienFait112nkMaric1272MssDolphn102.54	Getting to winner	7
14Aug37- 6LF	fst	1	:232 :46 1:094 1:352	3↑ F S Peabody Mem H 3.1k	3 5 2½ 1hd 11½ 11½	Dotter R	122wb	*1.40	97-08	Marica1221¼Deliberator118noDellor1103	Speed in reserve	8
7Aug37- 6LF	fst	6f	:221 :444 1:102	3↑ Crete H 3.2k	7 10 64½ 45½ 23 13	Dotter R	117wb	2.20	100-05	Marica1173Bien Fait1142½Main Man1061	Ridden out	11
27Jly37- 5AP	fst	1	:224 :464 1:111 1:36	4↑ Alw 1500	2 3 32½ 2½ 1½ 12	Dotter R	105wb	3.30	92-14	Marica1052Infantry1126Sir Jim James110hd	Easily	5
14Jly37- 6AP	fst	1	:231 :461 1:103 1:354	3↑ Handicap 1200	5 1 11½ 1½ 1hd 2½	Dotter R	112wb	*1.00	92-12	Grand Manitou114½Marica1123Preeminent1181	Bore out	5
3Jly37- 6AP	fst	1	:23 :453 1:101 1:364	3↑ ⒻArl Matron H 6.5k	8 5 42½ 4¾ 22 1hd	Dotter R	122wb	3.10	88-13	Marica122hdShatterproof109¾Schoolmom1051	Willingly	13
17Apr37- 6Kee	fst	6f	:224 :461 1:112	3↑ Phoenix H 4.1k	2 5 43 42 22 2¾	Dotter R	110wb	*1.80	96-06	Preeminent110¾Marica1102Capt. Cal1173	Impeded	10
				Previously owned by H. Oots;previously trained by C. Houbre								
20Mar37- 4OP	fst	5½f	1:08	3↑ Handicap 1000	9 2 73¾ 52½ 21½ 11½	Dotter R	116wb	*1.40	97-05	Marica1161½Cardarrone112hdMiss Ginbar99½	Strong finish	11
22Feb37- 5SA	fst	6f	:221 :452 1:103	3↑ Handicap 1235	2 6 45 43½ 21 1no	Dotter R	104wb	*1.50	97-10	Marica104noSilk Mask107¾Delphinium1102	Just up	7

5Jan37- 6SA	fst	6f	:221 :454 1:104	3↑ ⒻHandicap 1545	1	6	53½	51¾	21	11¼	Dotter R	112wb	4.30	96-15	Marica1121¼Bay Bubble1102Uppermost112½	Going away	8
	Previously trained by H. Wells																
23Oct36- 4Kee	gd	6f	:231 :463 1:114	3↑ Alw 1000	5	2	63¼	66	46½	33½	Dotter R	103wb	*1.40	--	Pelerine1082½Dusty Dawn1201Marica1033	Closed fast	6
20Oct36- 6Kee	sl	6f	:231 :482 1:134	Alw 1000	3	4	35	33	3½	11½	Dotter R	105wb	*.90	--	Marica1051½Pelerine111¾Gleeman1136	Going away	6
15Oct36- 5Kee	fst	6f	:223 :461 1:104	3↑ Keene H 2.4k	5	3	44	45	33	2¾	Dotter R	101wb	3.00	--	Myrtlewood128¾Marica1012Gleeman112¾	Closed well	5
7Oct36- 6LF	fst	6f	:222 :454 1:104	3↑ Handicap 800	9	3	21½	22	11	16	Dotter R	103wb	6.00	98-12	Marica1036PanicRelif1093ColonlEd1101½	Drew away rapidly	11
1Oct36- 6LF	hy	6f	:233 :474 1:152	Alw 1000	6	1	59	511	513	512	Dotter R	107wb	3.40	63-38	Billbo1103Panic Relief1082Kentucky Blues1095	Outrun	6
24Sep36- 5LF	fst	6f	:223 :46 1:11	3↑ ⒻAlw 800	4	7	67½	66	65½	42¾	Dotter R	103wb	6.00	94-09	Kentucky Blues104nkSilverette108½Slim Rosie1102		7
	Stumbled badly start																
9Sep36- 5LF	fst	7f	:23 :461 1:111 1:233	3↑ Handicap 800	7	4	42½	43½	43¼	31	Dotter R	105 w	*1.80	95-07	Colonel Ed108noTracker118.51Marica1051	Closed fast	12
4Sep36- 4Was	sl	6f	:233 :481 1:134	3↑ Handicap 1000	3	6	65½	53½	32	22	Dotter R	105 w	6.70	84-22	Mucho Gusto1152Marica105½Noble Count1011	Closed fast	7
5Aug36- 4Was	gd	7f	:231 :471 1:12 1:25	3↑ Handicap 1100	3	3	31½	31½	56¼	77	Dotter R	105 w	8.30	86-09	Bartering Kate110noReaping1073½Salaam1121½	Quit	8
17Jly36- 5Emp	fst	1 1/16	:241 :48 1:13 1:461	3↑ ⒻHandicap 1220	4	2	2nk	41¼	43¼	45½	Dotter R	105 w	15.00	86-14	Jesting1202Tabitha106½Paradisical1103	No excuse	4
10Jly36- 4Emp	fst	1 70	:233 :47 1:121 1:44	3↑ ⒻHandicap 1230	5	3	36	54¾	510	59	Dotter R	104 w	3.20	81-10	Vicaress1211½Tabitha1071½Pretty Night1101	Quit	5
27Jun36- 6Lat	fst	1⅛	:47 1:124 1:381 1:501	ⒻLat Oaks 5.9k	7	3	21	21	1hd	21	Hanka W	116 w	14.00	92-14	Sparta1161Marica1164Gorgeous Lady116½	Gamely	8
20Jun36- 5Haw	fst	1 1/16	:24 :481 1:134 1:452	3↑ Alw 1000	3	1	11½	12	1½	1hd	Dotter R	92 w	3.70	91-14	Marica92hdSalaam1125Buck Langhorne1091	Just lasted	7
9Jun36- 6Haw	fst	6f	:23 :463 1:121	3↑ ⒻAlw 1000	7	7	52¾	43½	42¼	32	Nolan J	103 w	8.40	90-14	Bird Flower1112Nellie Flag111noMarica1035	Closed well	7
5Jun36- 6Haw	fst	6½f	:23 :471 1:123 1:19	3↑ Alw 1000	2	3	21	21	2½	21½	Nolan J	100 w	3.00	91-16	Where Away1171½Marica1004Money Getter112no	Closed well	7
28May36- 5Haw	fst	6f	:232 :473 1:124	3↑ ⒻAlw 1000	2	4	21½	32½	33¼	33	Nolan J	101 w	6.20	86-13	Forever Yours1081Sandstone992Marica1016	Saved ground	6
16May36- 6CD	fst	1⅛	:473 1:124 1:384 1:523	ⒻKy Oaks 6.3k	9	1	11	1½	32	107¾	Haas L	116 w	10.90f	78-08	Two Bob1164Threadneedle116½Seventh Heaven1161½	Quit	12
13May36- 6CD	my	1	:224 :473 1:14 1:414	ⒻAlw 1000	3	3	1hd	1hd	3nk	31½	Hanka W	107 w	4.10	68-29	Threadneedle109.5½Stepinanna1071Marica1073	Weakened	8
	Previously trained by C. Houbre																
8May36- 6CD	fst	7f	:224 :462 1:114 1:252	ⒻAlw 1000	7	9	108	108½	86¾	77½	Hanka W	108 w	16.00	81-15	Mary Terry108noDora May110½Brendard1102	Closed gap	11
31Aug35- 6Dad	fst	6f	:233 :472 1:12	Handicap 1000	5	1	11½	1½	1½	1½	Mayer J	112 w	4.40	96-07	Marica112½Boston Pal1153Emileo1132	Driving	7
24Aug35- 5Dad	fst	5½f	:23 :463 :59 1:052	Alw 700	6	3	1½	1hd	11	1no	Mayer J	110 w	3.00	99-05	Marica110noBoston Pal113½Emileo110½	Hard drive	7
12Aug35- 5Dad	fst	5f	:232 :471 1:00	Alw 600	4	1	13	13	14	15	Mayer J	109 w	*.90	97-08	Marica1095Insulated106noStepinanna104nk	Eased up	8
9Aug35- 2Dad	fst	5f	:232 :473 1:002	ⒻMd Sp Wt	8	2	11	11½	13	15	Mayer J	115 w	*2.10e	95-08	Marica1155Spectrum1151½Haeheart1153	Eased up	12
	Previously trained by H. Wells																
14May35- 4CD	sly	4½f	:233 :473 :544	Clm 3000	3	10		818	819	817	Hanka W	106 w	110.60	72-11	Bushmaster1042½Glitter Glow1081½Barbara A1076	Outrun	10
9May35- 2CD	fst	4½f	:232 :473 :534	ⒻMd Sp Wt	9	12		1216	912	88	Hanka W	115 w	12.90e	86-06	Out Put1151½Monks Gold1151½Parsley115½	Off slow	12

Menow

dk. b. c. 1935, by Pharamond II (Phalaris)–Alcibiades, by Supremus

Lifetime record: 17 7 3 3 $140,100

Own.– H.P. Headley

Br.– Hal Price Headley (Ky)

Tr.– D.A. Headley

28Sep38- 5HdG	fst	1⅛	:472 1:122 1:372 1:50	3↑ Havre de Grace H 11k	8	1	11½	1½	32½	33½	Haas L	120wb	5.25	95-16	Seabiscuit1282½Savage Beauty1031Menow1201½	Went lame	8
24Sep38- 5HdG	fst	1 1/16	:23 :463 1:122 1:44	Potomac H 11k	9	1	11½	11½	11½	11	Workman R	122wb	3.05	98-10	Menow1221Bull Lea1182Sun Egret112hd	Under drive	9
17Sep38- 5Bel	fst	1	:223 :451 1:11 1:362	Jerome H 6.8k	1	2	24	25	44	46¼	Workman R	126wb	*1.20	87-12	Cravat115nkCan't Wait1164The Chief1192	Stopped	6
23Jly38- 6AP	sl	1¼	:48 1:124 1:382 2:061	Classic 34k	2	1	1½	2½	33	56	Wall N	123wb	2.10	69-26	Nedayr1211Bull Lea1211¼Cravat1233	Tired	8
29Jun38- 6Suf	hy	1⅛	:481 1:132 1:393 1:523	3↑ Mass H 59k	5	1	12	14	13	18	Wall N	107wb	10.40	82-28	Menow1078Busy K.107nkWar Minstrel106no	Easily	6
21May38- 5Bel	fst	1	:23 :462 1:113 1:372	Withers 18k	5	1	1½	14	14	12	Kurtsinger C	118wb	*.60e	88-13	Menow1182Thanksgiving1184Redbreast1182	Eased up	9
14May38- 5Pim	sly	1 3/16	:48 1:132 1:40 1:594	Preakness 68k	3	2	1½	12	23	37	Workman R	126wb	7.20	81-20	Dauber1267Cravat126hdMenow1263	Tired badly	9
7May38- 7CD	fst	1¼	:472 1:122 1:381 2:044	Ky Derby 57k	10	7	12	11½	23	46	Workman R	126wb	8.50	79-16	Lawrin1261Dauber1265Can't Wait126no	Swerved,tired	10
28Apr38- 6Kee	fst	1⅛	:472 1:113 1:363 1:493	Blue Grass 8.3k	4	1	11½	1½	1½	2nk	Robertson A	123wb	1.70e	113-08	Bull Lea121nkMenow1238Redbreast1235	No excuse	4
21Apr38- 5Kee	fst	1 1/16	:24 :48 1:122 1:44	ⒸAlw 1200	3	4	32	33	34	34½	Stevenson C	118wb	*.30	99-10	Bull Lea1123Birthday1081½Menow11830	Off poorly	4
15Apr38- 4Kee	fst	6f	:231 :462 1:112	Handicap 1500	3	3	11½	12	11½	11½	Kurtsinger C	122wb	*.10	97-13	Menow1221½King's Heir1126Sweep Royal1093	Eased up	4
2Oct37- 4Bel	fst	6½f-WC	1:151	Futurity 70k	8	7		11½	12	14	Kurtsinger C	119wb	1.80e	106-00	Menow1194Tiger126hdFighting Fox122nk	Easily best	12
	Geldings not eligible																
18Sep37- 4Bel	fst	6½f-WC	1:171	Champagne 5.2k	6	4		13	14	14	Kurtsinger C	113wb	12.00	96-08	Menow1134Bull Lea1161½Fighting Fox1221	Easily best	9
31Jly37- 5AP	fst	6f	:221 :453 1:114	Arl Futurity 40k	6	7	64½	54½	68	74	Corbett C	117wb	9.10e	84-16	DHTeddy's Comet117DHTiger1221C-Note117½	Outrun	8
26Jun37- 6Was	fst	6f	:222 :453 1:11	Was Futurity 34k	4	5	31½	21½	21½	22	Westrope J	117wb	1.90e	95-10	Tiger1172Menow1172Bourbon King117½	Second best	8
18Jun37- 4Was	hy	5½f	:244 :50 1:033 1:11	ⒸMd Sp Wt	1	1	2hd	1½	1½	1no	Dalaski L	118 w	*1.70	71-37	Menow118noPharacase1186Chatter Wrack1181	Hard drive	7
9Jun37- 3Was	sly	5½f	:232 :481 1:013 1:084	Alw 900	2	2	1½	31½	35½	22	Haas L	111 w	5.40	80-21	Employer1082Menow1111Lillian Roth1132	No excuse	6

Myrtlewood

b. f. 1932, by Blue Larkspur (Black Servant)–Frizeur, by Sweeper

Lifetime record: 22 15 4 2 $40,620

Own.– B. Combs

Br.– Brownell Combs (Ky)

Tr.– R.A. Kindred

24Oct36- 6Kee	fst	6f	:222 :46 1:114	3↑ ⒻMatch Race	1	2	2hd	11	12	13	South G	118 w	*.30	--	Myrtlewood1183Miss Merriment118	Won in hand	2
	No purse																
17Oct36- 5Kee	my	1 1/16	:24 :473 1:131 1:484	3↑ ⒻAshland 2.7k	3	1	16	18	18	112	South G	126 w	*.50	--	Myrtlewood12612Sparta111.54Wise Bessa110	Eased near end	3
15Oct36- 5Kee	fst	6f	:223 :461 1:104	3↑ Keen H 2.4k	2	4	1½	12	12	1¾	South G	128 w	*.50	--	Myrtlewood128¾Marica1012Gleeman112¾	Eased final 1/16	5
5Sep36- 6Det	fst	6f	:223 :452 1:103	3↑ Cadillac H 3.6k	4	3	1hd	2hd	2hd	1hd	Burke JH	128 w	*.80	101-07	Myrtlwood128hdBoldLover110noExhbt111½	Won drawing away	10
22Aug36- 6Det	fst	1 1/16	:24 :47 1:113 1:432	3↑ Motor City H 5.7k	9	2	12	12	12	13	South G	122 w	*.90	103-08	Myrtlewood1223Professor Paul95nkCristate1061	Easily	11
8Aug36- 6Was	fst	1	:222 :452 1:094 1:353	3↑ Lakeside H 6.3k	4	1	11½	14	14	13	South G	120 w	*2.10	100-04	Myrtlewood1203Where Away114nkThreadneedle1061	Easily	11
4Jly36- 6AP	fst	1⅛	:474 1:12 1:371 1:493	3↑ Stars & Stripes H 13k	6	1	1hd	31	31¼	52	Fisher HW	110 w	13.40	97-09	Stand Pat1161½Corinto108noWhopper122no	Impeded	12
13Jun36- 6Haw	fst	6½f	:224 :463 1:113 1:181	3↑ Haw Sprint H 5.9k	1	4	11	11½	14	11	Fisher HW	119 w	*1.10	97-13	Myrtlewood1191Billy Bee115nkBilly Jones114no	Handily	8
30May36- 6Lat	fst	6f	:222 :462 1:112	3↑ Quickstep H 6k	2	5	2hd	11½	13	14	Fisher HW	116 w	*1.70	92-16	Myrtlewood1164Dusty Dawn117½Silk Mask1081½	Easily	9
23May36- 5Lat	fst	6f	:222 :462 1:111	3↑ Handicap 1000	6	2	2hd	2hd	21½	23	Fisher HW	116 w	*.90	90-12	Likewise1083Myrtlewood1162Gilbert Elston103½	Impeded	7
12Oct35- 6CI	fst	6f	:22 :452 1:091	Match Race 3k	2	2	11½	11	1nk	2no	McCoy J	110wb	*.30	105-09	Clang110noMyrtlewood110	Hard drive	2
25Sep35- 0Haw	fst	6f	:224 :46 1:104	Match Race 3k	2	2	2hd	1hd	1hd	1no	McCoy J	110 w	*.40	99-11	Myrtlewood110noClang110	Hard drive	2
7Sep35- 6Haw	fst	6f	:223 :46 1:103	3↑ Haw Sprint H 6.2k	5	3	53	43¾	31½	1nk	McCoy J	115 w	*1.20	100-08	Myrtlewood115nkWest Main114nkClang1121½	Driving	10
24Aug35- 6LF	fst	1 1/16	:23 :464 1:11 1:441	3↑ Lincoln H 6.1k	8	2	1hd	11½	12	2nk	McCoy J	114 w	*1.40	95-11	SwepngLght114nkMrtlwood114hdPrncTorch114nk	Just missed	10
17Aug35- 6LF	fst	1	:23 :454 1:101 1:363	3↑ F S Peabody Mem H 6.4k	3	1	11	11½	12	11½	McCoy J	111 w	*3.50	91-11	Myrtlewood1111½Clang1101½Tearout108no	In hand	13
10Aug35- 6LF	sl	6f	:233 :473 1:152	3↑ Crete H 6.4k	12	5	53	54½	52¾	3nk	South G	112 w	*1.90	75-29	SlimRosie108hdWestMain112hdMyrtlewood1121½	Closed fast	14
22Jly35- 4AP	fst	6f	:22 :45 1:092	ⒻAlw 1000	3	3	1½	11½	12	13	South G	113 w	3.40	104-07	Myrtlewood1133Toro Nancy1103Recovery1061½	Easily	6
16Jly35- 4AP	fst	7f	:222 :45 1:10 1:231	ⒻAlw 1000	1	1	14	14	13	1hd	South G	103 w	6.80	97-10	Myrtlewood103hdBanish Fear1056Toro Nancy1173	Driving	8
27Oct34- 6CD	fst	1	:224 :463 1:112 1:372	Ky Jockey Club 11k	7	2	2hd	31½	33	36½	South G	119 w	8.90	85-13	Nellie Flag1191½Good Flavor1225Myrtlewood1193	Weakened	9
25Oct34- 5CD	gd	6f	:224 :461 1:13	Alw 500	6	2	1½	22	22	11	South G	106 w	*4.10	90-18	Myrtlewood1061¼Grey Streak113¾Upside Down1122½	Driving	10
20Oct34- 5CD	fst	5½f	:23 :463 :593 1:06	Alw 600	1	4	12	11	11½	2¾	Fowler G	105 w	5.20	92-08	Hastinola105¾Myrtlewood105½No Saint1101	Weakened	7
8Jun34- 2Lat	fst	5f	:232 :483 1:012	ⒻMd Sp Wt	8	6	11	11½	11½	11½	Meyer C	115 w	8.90	88-16	Myrtlewood1151½Ruths Hope1152Mary T.1153	Easily	11

Now What

ch. f. 1937, by Chance Play (Fair Play)–That's That, by High Time — Lifetime record: 19 5 4 0 $37,045

Own.– A.G. Vanderbilt
Br.– Three D's Stock Farm (Ky)
Tr.– L. McCoy

Date-Race	Cond	Dist	Fractions	Race	Running line	Jockey	Wt	Odds	Figs	Top finishers	Comment	Field
29Oct40- 5Lrl	gd	6f	:23 :472 1:133	3↑ ⒻAlw 1200	3 7 63¼ 63½ 53 42½	Wall N	103wb	5.20	83-19	ThornAppl102¾OPly1071Soldrtt109¾	Closed ground,no threat	11
30Sep40- 6Bel	fst	6f	:224 :463 1:113	3↑ ⒻAlw 1500	4 4 42¾ 53 63¾ 88	Canning W	104wb	8.85	84-15	Colosseum115¾[D]Dinner Date1102½Rosetown1091¾	Tired	8
23Sep40- 5Bel	fst	6f	:231 :471 1:12	3↑ ⒻAlw 1500	1 6 42½ 42¼ 3¾ 4nk	Longden J	108wb	3.15	90-17	Colosseum111noWar Regalia113nkDinner Date110hd	Good try	7
11Sep40- 5Aqu	fst	6f	:223 :462 1:114	Handicap 1530	4 4 33 36 43¾ 43	Bierman C	110wb	2.95	95-10	Witchlike1141Rosetown1101¼Red Dock122¾	Weakened	6
3Sep40- 5Aqu	fst	6f	:223 :47 1:123	3↑ ⒻAlw 1500	3 4 33½ 21 3nk 24¾	Bierman C	110wb	7.35	89-12	Dotted Swiss1054¾Now What1102One Jest117¾	Weakened	7
19Aug40- 5Sar	sly	6f	:224 :47 1:12	3↑ ⒻAlw 1500	2 5 31 41¾ 63¼ 57	Finnegan J	100wb	*1.20	85-11	Glorious Time1062¼Colosseum1121Rosetown1093¼	Faltered	9
8Aug40- 6Sar	fst	6f	:223 :463 1:11	3↑ ⒻHandicap 1530	5 3 32 32 3¾ 22	James B	113wb	4.60	95-12	Wait for Baby1092Now What113½Redlin1224	Second best	6
2Aug40- 5Sar	fst	7f	:224 :461 1:114 1:242	ⒻTest 3.9k	6 2 23 32½ 53½ 89	Longden J	120wb	21.90	85-13	Piquet123hdFairy Chant1262Inkling1142½	Stopped	10
29Jly40- 6Sar	fst	6f	:223 :461 1:11	3↑ ⒻAlw 1500	7 6 32½ 22 33¼ 711½	James B	112wb	7.75	85-08	Dini1223[DH]Redlin116[DH]Little Risk1152	Tired	9
4May40- 6Pim	sl	1 1/16	:233 :483 1:152 1:494	ⒻPim Oaks 14k	11 4 11 42½ 815 924	Workman R	121 w	4.60	47-31	Fairy Chant1211True Call1214Discerning1211	Tired	13
30Apr40- 6Pim	fst	6f	:223 :461 1:123	Rennert H 3.5k	6 2 1hd 1hd 1hd 61¼	Workman R	121 w	*1.95	90-15	Domkin112noShip Biscuit109½Merry Knight122nk	Faltered	8
19Aug39- 3Sar	sl	6f	:23 :464 1:131	ⒻSpinaway 10k	6 2 11 14 12 1½	Workman R	122wb	4.00	86-19	Now What122½Piquet1131½Jeanne d'Arc1131	Ridden out	9
12Aug39- 3Sar	fst	6f	:223 :461 1:104	Sar Spl 9k	8 1 2nk 21 21½ 44½	Westrope J	119wb	7.00	93-06	Bimelech1223Briar Sharp122½Andy K.1221	Tired	8
15Jly39- 6AP	fst	6f	:23 :47 1:13	ⒻArl Lassie 27k	1 4 11 13 12 1nk	Workman R	122wb	*1.30	82-17	Now What122nkWar Beauty1172Piquet117nk	Just lasted	10
4Jly39- 4Emp	fst	5¾f	:223 :461 1:09	ⒻDemoiselle 4.1k	4 1 14 14 15 16	Workman R	119wb	*1.80	94-06	Now What1196Piquet1135Ponemah1131½	Much best	7
14Jun39- 4Aqu	sly	5f	:581	ⒻAstoria 4.4k	3 2 12 11½ 1½	Workman R	116 w	*.80	96-11	Now What116.5½Us1134Fairy Chant119½	Driving	5
27May39- 4Bel	fst	5f-WC	:574	Juvenile 5.6k	5 3 11 11½ 2nk	Fallon L	113 w	2.00	91-11	Cockerel119nkNow What1133Gannet1164	Tired badly	5
20May39- 3Bel	fst	4½f-WC	:521	ⒻMd Sp Wt	8 4 1½ 1nk 11½	Fallon L	116 w	3.00e	94-10	Now What1161½Rosetown1163Thorn Apple116hd	Going away	15
12May39- 6Pim	fst	5f	:223 :473 1:01	Pim Nursery 6.5k	4 2 11½ 12 1½ 2½	Fallon L	119 w	4.25	95-15	Cockerel122½NowWhat1191½Imprudnt119½	Impeded,good try	6

Omaha

ch. c. 1932, by Gallant Fox (Sir Gallahad III)–Flambino, by Wrack — Lifetime record: 22 9 7 2 $154,755

Own.– Belair Stud Stable
Br.– William Woodward Sr (Ky)
Tr.– Cecil Boyd-Rochfort

Date-Race	Cond	Dist	Fractions	Race	Running line	Jockey	Wt	Odds	Figs	Top finishers	Comment	Field
2Jly36♦ Newmarket(GB)	gd	1½ⓉRH	2:343	3↑ Princess of Wales's Stakes 10000	2nk	Beasley P	134	*.70		Tak Ajbar120nkOmaha1345Esquemelling112	Unruly pre-start,tracked in 3rd,led 3f out to 1f out,came again	6
18Jun36♦ Ascot(GB)	sf	2½ⓉRH	4:332	4↑ Ascot Gold Cup 17500	2no	Beasley P	126	*1.35		Quashed126noOmaha1265Bokbul126	Rated in 4th,bid over 1f out,dueled,just failed	9
30May36♦ Kempton(GB)	fm	2ⓉRH	3:441	4↑ Queen's Plate Hcp2000	1nk	Beasley P	130	*.90		Omaha130nkBobsleigh1236Silverlit113	Tracked very slow pace,dueled 1f out,prevailed	5
9May36♦ Kempton(GB)	gd	1½ⓉRH	2:362	4↑ Victor Wild Stakes Alw4000	11½	Beasley P	129	*.80		Omaha1291½Montrose1265Lobau119	Previously trained by James Fitzsimmons	6
				Previously trained by James Fitzsimmons								
20Jly35- 6AP	fst	1¼	:472 1:122 1:354 2:012	Classic 35k	7 7 88 2½ 11½ 11½	Wright WD	126wb	*.40	102-03	Omaha1261½St. Bernard121hdBloodroot1133	Wide	10
29Jun35- 5Aqu	fst	1⅛	:473 1:114 1:37 1:491	Dwyer 11k	2 2 22 2½ 2hd 11½	Wright WD	126wb	*.70	97-14	Omaha1261½Good Gamble1146Cheshire1165	Easily	5
22Jun35- 5Aqu	fst	1⅛	:461 1:112 1:353 1:481	3↑ Brooklyn H 13k	3 4 411 38½ 35¼ 312	Wright WD	114wb	*1.00	90-13	Discovery1238King Saxon1274Omaha1146	Evenly	6
8Jun35- 5Bel	sly	1½	:482 1:133 2:05 2:303	Belmont 43k	3 5 34½ 43½ 2nk 11½	Saunders W	126wb	*.70e	91-15	Omaha1261½Firethorn1268Rosemont1261	Easily	5
25May35- 4Bel	fst	1	:233 :464 1:11 1:363	Withers 12k	2 7 52¼ 4¾ 32 21½	Saunders W	118wb	*.50	90-13	Rosemont1181½Omaha118½Plat Eye1185	Closed well	9
11May35- 6Pim	fst	1 3/16	:473 1:122 1:38 1:582	Preakness 29k	6 6 69 45 16 16	Saunders W	126wb	*.95	98-16	Omaha1266Firethorn1266Psychic Bid1262	Easily	8
4May35- 6CD	gd	1¼	:473 1:132 1:383 2:05	Ky Derby 49k	10 12 96¼ 12 11½ 11½	Saunders W	126wb	4.00	84-11	Omaha1261½Roman Soldier1264Whiskolo1261½	Easily	18
27Apr35- 4Jam	fst	1 70	:231 :464 1:112 1:424	Wood Memorial 14k	2 11 916 711 54¼ 32	Saunders W	112wb	3.20	90-11	Today1122Plat Eye122noOmaha1123	Closed fast	12
22Apr35- 4Jam	fst	1 70	:234 :482 1:124 1:43	Alw 1000	2 4 31½ 2hd 2½ 12	Saunders W	110wb	*.55	98-10	Omaha1102Black Gift105hdThorson111.58	Easily best	4
29Sep34- 4Aqu	fst	1	:231 :462 1:114 1:363	Jr Champion 5k	3 4 46½ 44¼ 21½ 2hd	Kurtsinger C	111wb	*1.00	97-08	Sailor Beware116hdOmaha1118Abner1111	Game rush	5
15Sep34- 3Bel	my	6½f-WC	1:173	Futurity 92k	13 13 53¼ 54½ 45	Kurtsinger C	122wb	5.00	94-05	Chance Sun1224Balladier122½Plat Eye125½	Closed fast	14
6Sep34- 4Bel	fst	6½f-WC	1:163	Champagne 4.4k	12 10 22 21½ 2no	Humphries L	117wb	*1.00e	104-07	Balladier124noOmaha1173Plat Eye1264	Gaining	12
1Sep34- 3Sar	fst	6½f	:232 :472 1:123 1:184	Hopeful 29k	9 10 73½ 83½ 74 47	Kurtsinger C	117wb	5.00e	84-15	Psychic Bid1224Rosemont1173Esposa114hd	Closed gap	16
22Aug34- 3Sar	fst	6f	:224 :463 1:121	Sanford 3.4k	3 9 77¼ 68¾ 46 22	Humphries L	113wb	4.00	89-12	Psychic Bid1132Omaha1131½Boxthorn122nk	Game rush	9
11Aug34- 3Sar	fst	6f	:23 :47 1:121	Sar Spl 6.7k	1 6 77½ 79¼ 55¼ 42	Malley T	122wb	6.00	89-11	Boxthorn1221Plat Eye122hdToday1221	Late speed	7
4Aug34- 3Sar	fst	6f	:23 :47 1:13	U S Hotel 6.9k	2 9 108¾ 109¼ 77¼ 45¾	Malley T	117wb	8.00	81-17	Balladier1172½Today117nkPolar Flight1153	Late speed	10
23Jun34- 1Aqu	fst	5f	:583	Alw 1200	3 2 41¼ 2hd 1hd	Stout J	110wb	*.90	94-12	Omaha110hdAllen Z.1171Moisson1177	Bore in	5
18Jun34- 1Aqu	fst	5f	1:01	Md Sp Wt	13 4 53 3nk 2no	Stout J	115wb	20.00	82-17	Sir Lamorak115noOmaha115½Nubs1152	Closed fast	14

Pompoon

b. c. 1934, by Pompey (Sun Briar)–Oonagh, by Friar Rock — Lifetime record: 26 10 8 1 $153,060

Own.– J.H. Louchheim
Br.– W.R. Coe (Ky)
Tr.– J. Loftus

Date-Race	Cond	Dist	Fractions	Race	Running line	Jockey	Wt	Odds	Figs	Top finishers	Comment	Field
2Aug39- 5Sar	fst	1	:233 :471 1:114 1:37	3↑ Wilson 4.4k	3 4 47 44 43¼ 24	Arcaro E	126wb	3.00	92-08	Eight Thirty1184Pompoon126nkMain Man1265	Outrun early	4
				Geldings not eligible								
12Jly39- 7Suf	sly	1⅛	:482 1:13 1:391 1:52	3↑ Mass H 68k	1 4 41¾ 2½ 2½ 2½	Eccard R	120wb	10.20	85-19	FightingFox113½Pompoon1203BurningStar1102½	Good effort	12
24Jun39- 5Suf	hy	1 1/16	:252 :50 1:154 1:493	3↑ Handicap 1500	4 4 22 24 24 26	Eccard R	126wb	*1.00	62-36	Pagliacci1096Pompoon1268Silent Witness1072	2nd best	4
30May39- 5Bel	fst	1¼	:474 1:12 1:371 2:024	3↑ Suburban H 24k	2 4 41½ 31 54¾ 43½	Richards H	121wb	6.00	82-20	Cravat1212Thanksgiving1201½Handcuff110hd	Faltered	6
10May39- 6Pim	gd	1 3/16	:473 1:123 1:383 1:583	3↑ Dixie H 28k	5 5 42¼ 3½ 66¾ 88¾	Richards H	125wb	5.65	81-18	Sir Damion1132½Tatterdemalion1111½Jacola1171	Tired	14
3May39- 6Pim	fst	1 1/16	:233 :473 1:13 1:45	3↑ Gittings H 3.3k	2 3 35 41¼ 58¼ 511½	Wright WD	126 w	*.85	83-17	Heelfly1146Aethelwold1103Kenty1121	No mishaps	6
25Jun38- 5Aqu	fst	1⅛	:46 1:104 1:35 1:482	3↑ Brooklyn H 25k	3 8 815 715 613 612½	Woolf G	126 w	3.50	86-12	The Chief1056Stagehand1103Unfailing1062	Sore	10
28May38- 5Bel	fst	1¼	:472 1:113 1:361 2:012	3↑ Suburban H 24k	5 4 52¾ 44½ 32½ 2no	Woolf G	128 w	*.70	93-15	Snark120noPompoon1282Aneroid120nk	Just missed	6
11May38- 5Pim	fst	1 3/16	:472 1:12 1:372 1:564	3↑ Dixie Handicap 26k	7 8 713 58¼ 2hd 14	Woolf G	118 w	*3.05	103-13	Pompoon1184Busy K.110nkMasked General106.5½	Easily	12
5Mar38- 6SA	fst	1¼	:461 1:111 1:364 2:013	3↑ S Anita H 126k	11 10 75¼ 53 45¼ 36	Gilbert J	120 w	4.00	97-12	Stagehand100noSeabiscuit1306Pompoon1202	Closed well	18
19Feb38- 6SA	sl	1 1/16	:233 :474 1:12 1:45	3↑ San Carlos H 6.3k	2 5 4¾ 2hd 1hd 11	Gilbert J	124 w	*.70	89-26	Pompoon1241Star Shadow107½He Did1143	Drew out	10
28Jan38- 6SA	fst	7f	:223 :452 1:101 1:23	4↑ Alw 1500	5 2 21 11 15 15	Gilbert J	120 w	*.40	97-14	Pompoon1205Ligaroti1162½Fairy Hill1206	In hand	8
				Previously trained by C.F. Clarke								
24Jly37- 6AP	sl	1¼	:481 1:133 1:381 2:054	Classic 34k	5 2 21½ 42¼ 56 55½	Wright WD	121 w	*1.20	71-26	Flying Scot123½Eagle Pass1181½Burning Star1182	Tired	7
5Jun37- 5Bel	fst	1½	:48 1:121 2:021 2:283	Belmont 46k	3 3 511 411 511 618	Richards H	126 w	3.50	83-06	War Admiral1263Sceneshifter12610Vamoose1262	No excuse	7
15May37- 6Pim	gd	1 3/16	:47 1:122 1:373 1:582	Preakness 55k	7 3 52½ 21 2hd 2hd	Wright WD	126 w	4.80	98-16	War Admiral126hdPompoon1268Flying Scot1262	Game try	8
8May37- 6CD	fst	1¼	:464 1:122 1:372 2:031	Ky Derby 62k	14 6 54½ 21½ 23 21¾	Richards H	126 w	8.00	91-11	WarAdmirl1261¾Pmpoon1268ReapingRewrd1263	Second best	20
1May37- 5Jam	fst	1 70	:231 :47 1:124 1:424	Wood Memorial 26k	4 6 64¼ 54¼ 55½ 55½	Richards H	120 w	*.60	86-10	Melodist1201Sir Damion1202Jewell Dorsett1151	No mishaps	10
15Apr37- 4Jam	fst	6f	:23 :462 1:11	3↑ Paumonok H 9.9k	4 4 52¼ 21 2½ 1nk	Richards H	116 w	*2.00	97-11	Pompoon116nkTintagel1205Fraidy Cat1151½	Hard drive	10
28Oct36- 6Nar	fst	1 70	:231 :47 1:12 1:413	New England Futurity 45k	6 4 2nk 11 2½ 2nk	Workman R	122 w	*.30	97-13	ReapingReward117nkPompn12220OceanRoll1144	Good effort	7

3Oct36- 4Bel	fst	6½f-WC	1:162	Futurity 72k	11	2		2hd	11½	14	Richards H	127 w	*1.60	101-00	Pompoon1274Privlgd125nkFlyngCross122hd	Speed in reserve	17
12Sep36- 4Aqu	fst	6½f	:232 :471 1:114 1:181	Jr Champion 7.2k	5	5	31¼	2nk	2½	11	Richards H	119 w	*.29	96-11	Pompoon1191FlyingScot11010Tedious1101	Bore in,drew away	5
3Sep36- 4Aqu	fst	6f	:232 :472 1:121	Alw 1000	3	3	2½	11	12	14	Richards H	122 w	*.29	93-13	Pompoon1224Dogaway113¾Talked About1055	Good effort	4
27Aug36- 5Sar	fst	5½f	:233 :47 1:054	[R]Handicap 1245	5	3	2nk	31	2nk	2½	Peters M	130 w	*.60	93-12	No Sir116½Pompoon1304Third Count1191	Good effort	5
	Property of lady owners																
6Jun36- 4Bel	fst	5f-WC	:59	National Stallion 16k	7	4		3½	1hd	11½	Peters M	122 w	*2.50	85-14	Pompoon1221½Fencing1221War Admiral122hd	Drew away	10
29May36- 3Bel	fst	5f-WC	:591	Alw 900	10	4		11	13	14	Peters M	112 w	*1.30	84-20	Pompoon1124Your Honor1155All Agog109hd	Easily	10
29Apr36- 1Pim	fst	4½f	:231 :472 :54	Md Sp Wt	1	1		1½	1hd	12	Peters M	116 w	2.40	97-05	Pompoon1162Sonny Joe1165Banjorine1132	Going away	12

Seabiscuit

b. c. 1933, by Hard Tack (Man o' War)–Swing On, by Whisk Broom II

Own.– C.S. Howard

Br.– Wheatley Stable (Ky)

Tr.– T. Smith

Lifetime record: 89 33 15 13 $437,730

2Mar40- 6SA	fst	1¼	:471 1:111 1:36 2:011	3↑ S Anita H 121k	12	5	21	2hd	1hd	11½	Pollard J	130wb	*.70e	101-11	Seabiscuit1301½Kayak II1291Whichcee1141½		13
	Avoided trouble first turn																
24Feb40- 6SA	fst	1$\frac{1}{16}$	:231 :464 1:111 1:422	3↑ S Antonio H 13k	10	5	2½	2½	1½	12½	Pollard J	124wb	*1.70e	100-07	Seabiscuit1242½Kayak II128½Viscounty1104	Much best	13
17Feb40- 6SA	fst	7f	:223 :453 1:103 1:232	3↑ San Carlos H 12k	1	2	94	85¼	69	66¾	Pollard J	127wb	*.80e	88-14	Specify1151¼Lassator105hdViscounty1093	Close quarters	11
9Feb40- 6SA	fst	7f	:224 :454 1:103 1:23	4↑ Handicap 2000	2	5	52¼	63¾	43¼	33	Pollard J	128wb	*1.00	94-13	Heelfly1181Sun Egret1152Seabiscuit1283	Close quarters	8
14Feb39- 6SA	fst	1	:223 :453 1:102 1:353	4↑ Alw 1900	1	3	2nk	23	23	22¼	Woolf G	128wb	*.20	99-06	Today1042¼Seabiscuit1286Marica113	Went lame	3
1Nov38- 6Pim	fst	1$\frac{3}{16}$	:473 1:114 1:364 1:563	3↑ Pim Spl 15k	2	1	11	1no	1½	14	Woolf G	120wb	2.20	101-08	Seabiscuit1204War Admiral120	Driving,best	2
15Oct38- 5Lrl	fst	1	:231 :472 1:121 1:37	2↑ Laurel 10k	6	8	63½	41¼	21½	22½	Woolf G	126wsb	*.60	98-12	Jacola1022½Seabiscuit1263The Chief1164	Second best	12
28Sep38- 5HdG	fst	1⅛	:472 1:122 1:372 1:50	3↑ Havre de Grace H 11k	6	5	32½	2½	11	12½	Woolf G	128wb	*.55	99-16	Seabiscuit1282½Savage Beauty1031Menow1201½	Going away	8
20Sep38- 5Bel	my	1½	:49 1:14 2:051 2:31	3↑ Manhattan H 6k	4	1	52¾	53½	34¼	33	Woolf G	128wb	*1.20	85-12	Isolater108hdRegal Lily1083Seabiscuit12810	Forced wide	5
12Aug38- 5Dmr	fst	1⅛	:462 1:104 1:361 1:49	3↑ Match Race 25k	1	2	2hd	1hd	1hd	1no	Woolf G	130wb	-	124-02	Seabiscuit130noLigaroti115	Driving	2
16Jly38- 7Hol	fst	1¼	:471 1:112 1:373 2:034	3↑ Hol Gold Cup 55k	7	8	912	48	24	11½	Woolf G	133wb	*.70	- -	Seabiscuit1331½Specify109noWhichcee1145	Going away	10
4Jly38- 6AP	sl	1⅛	:484 1:143 1:41 1:541	3↑ Stars & Stripes H 12k	10	7	97¾	67	42½	23½	Woolf G	130wb	*.90	72-30	WarMinstrel1073½Seabiscut130½Arb'sArrow1114	Closed fast	10
16Apr38- 7BM	fst	1⅛	:474 1:114 1:37 1:49	3↑ Bay Meadows H 16k	7	2	21	2hd	11	13	Woolf G	133wb	*.20e	107-10	Seabiscuit1333Gosum1131¾Today112no	Going away	7
27Mar38- 8AC	fst	1⅛	:47 1:114 1:37 1:502	3↑ Agua Caliente H 13k	1	1	1½	11½	13	12	Rich'son N	130wb	*.30	97-13	Seabiscuit1302Gray Jack103hdLittle Nymph984½	Eased up	8
5Mar38- 6SA	fst	1¼	:461 1:111 1:364 2:013	3↑ S Anita H 126k	12	14	127½	1hd	1hd	2no	Woolf G	130wb	*1.90	103-12	Stagehand100noSeabisct1306Pmpoon1202	Impeded,game try	18
26Feb38- 6SA	fst	1⅛	:47 1:113 1:371 1:50	3↑ San Antonio H 9.2k	5	5	46	42½	3½	2no	Workman R	130wb	*.40e	94-12	Aneroid118noSeabiscuit1301½IndianBroom108hd	Just missed	13
11Nov37- 6Pim	fst	1⅝	:501 1:41 2:062 2:451	3↑ Bowie H 12k	8	3	52¾	41¼	1hd	2no	Pollard J	130wb	*1.25	107-11	Esposa115noSeabiscuit1301¼Burning Star1141	Game try	8
5Nov37- 5Pim	fst	1$\frac{3}{16}$	:47 1:113 1:37 1:572	3↑ Riggs H 12k	11	4	55½	4¾	1½	1nk	Pollard J	130wb	*.40e	103-11	Seabiscuit130nkBurningStar114¾CaballroII116½	Hard drive	11
	Previously owned by Mrs C.S. Howard																
16Oct37- 5Lrl	fst	1	:24 :471 1:121 1:372	2↑ Laurel 9.6k	7	3	2hd	2nk	1hd	11½•	Pollard J	126wb	*.70	99-14	[DH]Seabiscuit126[DH]Heelfly1141½Deliberator1161	Gamely	7
12Oct37- 5Jam	fst	1$\frac{1}{16}$	:24 :48 1:124 1:444	3↑ Continental H 12k	2	1	1hd	1nk	12	15	Pollard J	130wb	*.80	89-20	Seabiscuit1305Caballero II1172Moon Side1121	Easily	12
11Sep37- 5Nar	sly	1$\frac{3}{16}$	:473 1:12 1:38 1:57	3↑ Nar Spl H 33k	5	4	46½	21½	33½	32½	Pollard J	132wb	*.85	87-16	Calumet Dick1151Snark1171½Seabiscuit1324	Weakened	6
7Aug37- 5Suf	fst	1⅛	:47 1:11 1:36 1:49	3↑ Mass H 70k	3	3	22½	21	1nk	11	Pollard J	130wb	*1.00	102-06	Seabiscuit1301CaballeroII1081FairKnghtss1082½	Drove out	13
24Jly37- 5Emp	fst	1$\frac{1}{16}$	:233 :472 1:113 1:441	3↑ Yonkers H 10k	2	2	22	1hd	11½	14	Pollard J	129wb	*1.00	102-12	Seabiscuit1294Jesting1083Corinto1093	Going away	6
10Jly37- 5Emp	fst	1$\frac{3}{16}$	:48 1:12 1:382 1:583	3↑ Butler H 25k	1	2	1½	1½	11½	11½	Pollard J	126wb	*.90	98-08	Seabiscuit1261½Thorson1073Corinto1091	Driving,best	6
26Jun37- 5Aqu	fst	1⅛	:47 1:112 1:37 1:501	3↑ Brooklyn H 25k	1	1	11	1½	1hd	1no	Pollard J	122wb	3.20	90-14	Seabiscuit122noAneroid1225Memory Book1143	Hard drive	9
22May37- 7BM	fst	1$\frac{1}{16}$	:24 :473 1:11 1:443	3↑ Bay Meadows H 11k	8	2	2nk	21	1½	11¼	Pollard J	127wb	*.10e	87-15	Seabiscuit1271¼Exhibit105noWatersplash1031	Going away	8
17Apr37- 6Tan	fst	1⅛	:452 1:103 1:36 1:484	3↑ Marchbank H 11k	7	1	15	12	14	13	Pollard J	124wb	*.40	94-08	Seabiscuit1243Grand Manitou110hdSobriety1095	Easily	7
6Mar37- 6SA	fst	1⅛	:463 1:11 1:361 1:484	3↑ S Juan Capistrano H 12k	2	2	21½	2hd	14	17	Pollard J	120wb	*1.50	103-08	Seabiscuit1207GrandManitou108¾SpecialAgent116nk	Easily	10
27Feb37- 6SA	gd	1¼	:454 1:104 1:364 2:024	3↑ S Anita H 125k	3	9	44½	41½	1hd	2no	Pollard J	114 w	6.40	97-13	Rosemont124noSeabiscuit1141Indian Broom1162½	Nosed out	18
20Feb37- 6SA	fst	1⅛	:464 1:11 1:372 1:501	3↑ San Antonio H 9.4k	11	14	128¾	129¼	98¾	53¾	Pollard J	115wb	2.30	92-11	Rosemnt122¾StarShadow106½SpecialAgent1171	Forced wide	16
9Feb37- 6SA	fst	7f	:224 :452 1:104 1:231	4↑ Handicap 1545	5	1	1½	11	1½	14½	Pollard J	112wb	3.20	96-13	Seabiscuit1124½Sir Emerson104nkTime Supply1185	Easily	6
12Dec36- 7BM	fst	1$\frac{3}{16}$	:47 1:112 1:364 1:554	2↑ World's Fair H 11k	4	3	15	13	13	15	Pollard J	113wb	*1.10	- -	Seabiscuit1135Wildland1012½GiantKiller1071½	Easily best	7
28Nov36- 7BM	fst	1	:232 :464 1:112 1:36	2↑ Bay Bridge H 2.7k	6	8	51¾	22	1hd	15	Pollard J	116wb	*2.20	106-07	Seabiscuit1165Uppermost114½Velociter107nk	Eased up	8
31Oct36- 4Emp	fst	1⅛	:491 1:14 1:392 1:52	3↑ Yorktown H 6.5k	7	6	54	66½	33½	31¾	Pollard J	119wb	8.00	93-11	Thorson112nkPiccolo1071½Seabiscuit1193	Closed fast	8
24Oct36- 4Emp	fst	1 70	:233 :473 1:121 1:44	3↑ Scarsdale H 7.3k	2	7	84¾	88¾	63¾	1no	Pollard J	116wb	12.00e	90-13	Seabiscuit116noJesting112hdPiccolo105.53	Just up	11
17Oct36- 6RD	my	1$\frac{1}{16}$	:26 :51 1:18 1:562	3↑ East Hills H 2.7k	4	2	22	24	23	32½	Pollard J	116wb	3.20	29-59	MuchoGusto1111½SafeandSound1031Sebscut1162½	Closed well	6
3Oct36- 5RD	fst	1$\frac{1}{16}$	:232 :464 1:113 1:44	3↑ Western Hills H 2.8k	7	4	52¼	53½	43½	31½	Pollard J	116wb	4.90	92-10	Marynell100½Cristate1081Seabiscuit1161	Closed fast	8
26Sep36- 6Det	fst	1$\frac{1}{16}$	:243 :483 1:13 1:442	3↑ Hendrie H 2.8k	2	2	2½	11	12	14	Pollard J	115wb	2.10	98-12	Seabiscuit1154Cristate1142½Safe and Sound1083	Easily	6
19Sep36- 6Det	fst	1$\frac{1}{16}$	:243 :483 1:133 1:46	3↑ De La Salle H 2.8k	7	1	11	31	63½	63¾	Pollard J	115wb	*1.60	86-13	Cristate106hdProfessor Paul105hdParadisical1091½	Quit	8
7Sep36- 6Det	fst	1⅛	:47 1:12 1:38 1:504	3↑ Governor's H 5.6k	12	3	2hd	2hd	1½	1nk	Pollard J	109wb	4.90	96-13	Seabiscuit109nkProfessor Paul991½Azucar1123	Driving	12
2Sep36- 6Det	sl	1 70	:243 :484 1:14 1:44	3↑ Handicap 1200	3	1	1hd	41¼	31	3½	Pollard J	114wb	3.90	89-18	ProfessorPaul104noSafeandSound102½Seabsct1142½	Impeded	8
22Aug36- 6Det	fst	1$\frac{1}{16}$	:24 :47 1:113 1:432	3↑ Motor City H 5.7k	3	1	33	78	65	44¼	Pollard J	110wb	13.20	99-08	Myrtlewood1223Professor Paul95nkCristate1061	Tired	11
	Previously owned by Wheatley Stable;previously trained by J. Fitzsimmons																
10Aug36- 6Sar	gd	1⅛	:482 1:132 1:401 1:54	3↑ Handicap 1070	1	1	12	12	13	14	Stout J	112wb	*.90	80-17	Seabiscuit1124Treford110	Easily	2
3Aug36- 5Sar	fst	1	:242 :481 1:124 1:382	3↑ Mohawk Claiming 6k	1	1	11½	11	13	16	Stout J	109wb	4.00	89-15	Seabiscuit1096Ann O'Ruley1122Balkan Land1092	Easily	7
25Jly36- 5Suf	fst	1⅛	:473 1:122 1:381 1:511	Miles Standish H 3k	1	2	24	31¾	33½	44¼	Kopel F	115wb	5.90	87-08	Kearsarge99nkTatterdemalion113.54BrownTop109no	Faltered	7
29Jun36- 4Suf	fst	6f	:224 :453 1:114	Alw 1000	2	8	64¾	62¾	34	11½	Knott K	115wb	12.60	96-11	Seabiscuit1151½Deliberate115½Liberal1153	Handily	12
24Jun36- 5Suf	sl	6f	:234 :48 1:134	Commonwealth H 3.2k	6	13	128	1212	109¼	1010¾	Kopel F	115wb	29.40	75-21	PartySpirit107nkIndomitable1054SpeedtoSpare114½	Outrun	13
1Jun36- 5Bel	fst	1$\frac{1}{16}$	:24 :474 1:13 1:45	3↑ Handicap 1240	5	6	67¼	65½	65	66¼	Hanford I	112wb	*1.60e	80-16	Gallant Prince1161½Brown Twig114hdGillie114nk	Stumbled	6
27May36- 5Rkm	sly	1	:234 :473 1:132 1:411	New Hampshire H 4k	9	11	129	129½	129	129½	Kopel F	116wb	8.40	71-16	Faust103noGallant Gay110.5noParty Spirit1112	Outrun	15
18May36- 5Nar	fst	1$\frac{1}{16}$	:234 :472 1:123 1:441	Alw 1200	7	1	11	1hd	1½	13	Kopel F	111wb	2.60	96-11	Seabiscuit1113Piccolo1063Swamp Angel1113½	Easily	7
13May36- 5Nar	fst	1$\frac{1}{16}$	:234 :472 1:123 1:444	Providence H 3.8k	8	1	12½	21	31¼	42½	Kopel F	115wb	4.20	90-13	Tugboat Frank1102Piccolo108noGallant Gay109½	No excuse	8
8May36- 4Jam	fst	6f	:231 :47 1:12	Alw 1000	4	6	77	77¾	53½	42¾	Stout J	113wb	*2.40	89-14	Gleeman1101½Wha Hae1131Stubbs116nk	Finished fast	7
23Apr36- 4Jam	fst	6f	:233 :471 1:121	Handicap 1220	4	4	48	47½	33½	37	Hanford I	120wb	*.50	84-17	Goldeneye1053Chancer1054Seabiscuit1203	No excuse	4
18Apr36- 3Jam	fst	6f	:224 :462 1:12	Alw 1000	1	1	22	25	21½	21½	Hanford I	105wb	5.00	90-13	Tintagel1181½Seabiscuit1054Hollyrood1188	Good effort	5
11Nov35- 6Pim	my	1$\frac{1}{16}$	:24 :491 1:143 1:494	Walden H 11k	10	7	108¾	1012	915	66	Kopel F	108wb	14.45	65-27	Ned Reigh116½Challephen107hdWise Duke112½	No excuse	10
26Oct35- 5Nar	fst	6f	:223 :451 1:111	Pawtucket H 6k	4	4	43½	44	43¾	2½	Stout J	117wb	*1.85	95-10	Clocks111½Seabiscuit1171½Crossbow II1211	Finished fast	5
23Oct35- 5Emp	fst	5¾f	:23 :47 1:084	Ardsley H 3.7k	4	3	2hd	2hd	11	13	Kopel F	112wb	4.00	95-13	Seabiscuit1123Neap1072Wha Hae115½	Easily	6
16Oct35- 5Agm	fst	6f	:234 :46 1:112	Springfield H 2.8k	8	1	12	11½	11	11	Stout J	109wb	8.00	- -	Seabiscuit1091BrightPlumage117hdInfidox1171½	Ridden out	8
2Oct35- 4Suf	fst	6f	:231 :462 1:121	Constitution H 9.2k	10	10	95½	107	108¼	1010	Woolf G	115wb	21.90	84-08	Infidox110nkClocks110nkSparta109½	Outrun	10
21Sep35- 3Jam	fst	6f	:233 :464 1:12	Remsen H 4.7k	2	11	1115	1014	912	97¾	Horn F	112wb	7.00e	84-12	The Fighter122noTeufel1122Postage Due1241½	Off slowly	11
14Sep35- 4HdG	fst	6f	:232 :474 1:13	Eastern Shore H 14k	6	7	85¼	92½	64½	41½	Rosengarten C	112wb	38.50e	86-11	Postage Due117½Wise Duke115noMaerial1201	Forced wide	14
9Sep35- 6Aqu	fst	6f	:233 :48 1:131	Alw 1000	4	4	11	11½	12	13	Kopel F	115wb	12.00	88-13	Seabiscuit1153Count Morse1095Dark Wizard1122	Easily	8
4Sep35- 3Aqu	sly	6f	:232 :473 1:122	Alw 1000	5	3	46¾	45½	54½	36	Kopel F	110wb	10.00	86-10	PhantomFox106noPullman1146Seabiscuit110nk	Finished well	7
2Sep35- 3Aqu	fst	6f	:241 :49 1:12	Babylon H 4.2k	5	6	511	67	67¾	612	Horn F	112wb	1.50e	82-09	NedReigh116noSpeedtoSpare115noGranville1145	No excuse	6
26Aug35- 4Sar	fst	6f	:23 :47 1:12	Alw 1000	5	8	812	86¼	66	68½	Horn F	112wb	25.00	83-10	BoldVenture1151½GrandSlam1223Valvctorn1152	Dropped back	9

Date / Race	Trk	Dist	Fractions	Time	Race	Running line	Jockey	Wt	Odds	Spd	Top three finishers	Comment	Field
14Aug35- 5Sar	gd	5½f	:231 :473	1:071	Alw 1000	11 13 1313 139¼ 106½ 95¼	Gilbert J	112wb	6.00e	82-14	Maerial1181Lovely Girl1042Speed109no	Off slowly	13
27Jly35- 6Suf	fst	6f	:233 :463	1:122	Bay State 3.7k	4 6 31¼ 52¼ 32½ 43	Stout J	123wb	13.60	- -	BlackHighbrow1113NouveauRiche108noSt.Lous108no	Faltered	7
22Jly35- 3Suf	fst	6f	:231 :454	1:112	Alw 1000	5 5 21 2½ 22½ 21½	Stout J	115wb	*1.70	- -	Black Highbrow1151½Seabiscuit1158Nedvive112½	Gamely	5
15Jly35- 5Suf	fst	6f	:232 :472	1:131	Mayflower 3k	4 8 52¼ 42¼ 62½ 44	Horn F	123wb	15.00	- -	Maerial1232Jair111½Tugboat Frank1111½	No excuse	9
4Jly35- 5Nar	fst	5f	:223 :46	:593	Old Colony 6.7k	3 4 42 45 44¾ 52½	Stout J	117wb	*1.40	101-07	BrightandEarly1141Swashbuckler114½Chllphn1121	No excuse	6
26Jun35- 5Nar	fst	5f	:223 :454	:593	Watch Hill Claiming 5k	6 5 2½ 11½ 11 12	Horn F	108wb	*1.70	104-08	Seabiscuit1082Infidox1081Zowie1022	Easily	8
22Jun35- 2Nar	fst	5f	:231 :464	1:003	Alw 1000	9 5 1½ 12 11½ 12	Stout J	110wb	*2.55	99-12	Seabiscuit1102Ned Reigh1102½Tugboat Frank1151½	Easily	9
11Jun35- 1Rkm	hy	5f	:234 :49	1:02	Md Sp Wt	3 8 1½ 21½ 24 26	Stout J	116wb	*.60	78-18	Jubilee Jim1166Seabiscuit1162½Sky Pirate1162	Gamely	8
8Jun35- 4Rkm	fst	5f	:231 :462	:594	Juvenile H 5.7k	2 8 74¼ 65 31¾ 31¼	Stout J	103wb	30.20	94-12	WinterSport1051PostageDue124nkSeabiscut103½	Good effort	12
1Jun35- 1Rkm	fst	5f	:23 :461	1:011	Md Sp Wt	5 7 21 21½ 23 23	Stout J	116wb	7.75	85-14	Swashbuckler1163Seabiscuit1161½Sobriety1163	Good effort	12
28May35- 1Rkm	fst	5f	:232 :474	1:011	Md Sp Wt	2 11 98¼ 97¾ 34½ 42½	Stout J	116wb	*2.05	85-11	SandyMack1161½Browbeatn1131TugboatFrnk116hd	Closed gap	11
21May35- 2Rkm	fst	5f	:231 :473	1:004	Alw 800	7 9 76¼ 87½ 31¼ 3nk	Stout J	106wb	9.85	90-13	Microbe114nkBlackMistress111noSeabiscut1061	Closed fast	9
4May35- 1Jam	fst	5f	:233 :472	1:002	Md Sp Wt	2 2 57½ 55¼ 64½ 68	Burke JH	115wb	2.00e	83-11	Pullman1151½Knowing115½Royal Fox1155	Shuffled	8
1May35- 4Jam	fst	5f	:231 :473	1:01	Alw 1000	4 6 69¼ 56½ 53¾ 2½	Horn F	110wb	10.00	87-15	Galsac116½Seabiscuit110noTransitLady110no	Finished fast	6
	Previously trained by G. Tappen												
25Apr35- 2HdG	fst	4½f	:232 :473	:542	Clm 4000	5 2 51¾ 44½ 4½	Workman R	114wb	3.50	92-07	Cherry Stone115noHiatus110hdProsy113½	Finished fast	11
22Apr35- 2HdG	fst	4½f	:232 :473	:542	Clm 2500	6 7 89¼ 47½ 33½	Peters M	116wb	11.95	89-07	Hiatus113½Deliberate1143Seabiscuit1161½	Close quarters	13
13Apr35- 3Bow	my	4f	:234	:492	Md Sp Wt	8 7 712 66¼ 35½	Horn F	115wb	7.35	80-13	ParaguayTea1122½PatseyBegone1123Sebscut1151½	Off slowly	9
10Apr35- 4Bow	my	4f	:233	:492	Alw 800	9 10 911 97¾ 87¼	Horn F	110wb	30.35	79-15	VictoriousAnn112hdWinterSport1151½Ste.Louise1121	Outrun	12
4Apr35- 1Bow	sl	4f	:24	:493	©Md Sp Wt	1 1 58½ 35½ 21½	Horn F	115wb	3.80	83-15	Borsa1151½Seabiscuit1153Green Mist1151	Finished gamely	8
	Previously trained by V. Mara												
8Mar35- 1Hia	fst	3f		:344	Alw 1000	12 10 63¼ 43½	Horn F	113wb	4.50f	- -	VctorousAnn1102WllwWood113hdTwoEdgd1131½	Finished fast	14
5Mar35- 1Hia	fst	3f		:343	Alw 800	8 8 83¾ 85	Horn F	109wb	49.50	- -	James City1191½Grand Slam108nkBright Light114hd	Impeded	13
27Feb35- 1Hia	fst	3f		:341	Clm 2500	2 1 73¾ 63	Horn F	108 w	11.35	- -	Black Bess100noTransit110noEdri1051½	No excuse	11
22Jan35- 2Hia	fst	3f		:351	Clm 2500	10 6 53¾ 22	Stout J	110	9.50	- -	ClappingJane1072Seabiscuit110hdSpart107nk	Finished fast	12
19Jan35- 1Hia	fst	3f		:343	Alw 1000	5 6 55¾ 44½	Stout J	110	16.85e	- -	Wha Hae1131Wise Duke1103Blue Donna107½	Good effort	10

Stagehand

b. c. 1935, by Sickle (Phalaris)–Stagecraft, by Fair Play

Own.– Maxwell Howard
Br.– J.E. Widener (Ky)
Tr.– Earl Sande

Lifetime record: 25 9 3 6 $200,110

Date / Race	Trk	Dist	Fractions	Time	Race	Running line	Jockey	Wt	Odds	Spd	Top three finishers	Comment	Field
4Mar39- 6Hia	fst	1¼	:48 1:123 1:361	2:022	3↑ Widener H 60k	3 7 78 55¼ 36 32¾	Stout J	126wb	*.35	94-03	Bull Lea1192½Sir Damion114nkStagehand1265		7
	Slow start,steady late gain												
18Feb39- 5Hia	fst	1⅛	:47 1:104 1:353	1:481	3↑ McLennan Mem H 8.6k	7 9 88 77¼ 34 1nk	Stout J	126wb	*2.05	100-05	Stagehand126nkBull Lea1224Mythical King112½	Just up	9
10Sep38- 5Nar	fst	1⅛	:472 1:112 1:37	1:492	3↑ Governor's H 12k	4 6 66 11½ 15 16	Westrope J	124wb	*.45e	101-07	Stagehand1246Two Bob1001½Thanksgiving1155	Much best	6
3Sep38- 5Nar	fst	1 3/16	:472 1:122 1:363	1:561	3↑ Nar Spl 33k	1 9 97¾ 85½ 2hd 11	Westrope J	119wb	*1.15e	94-09	Stagehand1191Bull Lea1133Cravat1084	Drew out	10
27Aug38- 5Nar	fst	1⅛	:473 1:112 1:362	1:501	J C Thornton Mem H 13k	12 7 75½ 55 44¼ 3nk	Westrope J	126wb	*1.75	97-07	Bull Lea116nkPurple King104hdStagehand1261½	Closed fast	12
13Aug38- 5Sar	gd	1¼	:482 1:132 1:39	2:033	Travers 19k	5 8 713 65 63¾ 45½	Westrope J	127 w	3.50	85-11	Thanksgiving1174Jolly Tar112½Fighting Fox1241	Late foot	9
23Jly38- 6AP	sl	1¼	:48 1:124 1:382	2:061	Classic 34k	5 8 815 512 59 45¼	Westrope J	126 w	*1.30e	70-26	Nedayr1211Bull Lea1211¼Cravat1233	Late foot	8
9Jly38- 5Emp	fst	1⅛	:474 1:123 1:382	1:51	Emp City H 12k	3 8 88 66½ 51 1nk	Westrope J	124 w	*1.60	100-06	Stagehand124nkFighting Fox120½Galapas106hd	Just up	8
25Jun38- 5Aqu	fst	1⅛	:46 1:104 1:35	1:482	3↑ Brooklyn H 25k	2 9 916 917 511 26	Westrope J	110 w	*1.00e	93-12	The Chief1056Stagehand1103Unfailing1062	Closed fast	10
18Jun38- 5Aqu	sly	1⅛	:46 1:11 1:353	1:482	Dwyer 12k	4 3 411 412 47 38	Westrope J	126 w	*.70e	91-08	The Chief1194Mythical King1194Stagehand1264	Went well	4
3May38- 5CD	fst	1	:23 :461 1:103	1:354	Derby Trial 3k	7 6 43 42½ 35 35	Westrope J	118 w	*.50e	95-13	The Chief117hdLawrin1185Stagehand1182	Hung	8
5Mar38- 6SA	fst	1¼	:461 1:111 1:364	2:013	3↑ S Anita H 126k	3 5 95½ 42½ 3nk 1no	Wall N	100 w	3.60e	103-12	Stagehand100noSeabiscuit1306Pompoon1202	Hard drive	18
22Feb38- 6SA	fst	1⅛	:47 1:113 1:374	1:502	SA Derby 59k	13 12 1112 79 41½ 1½	Westrope J	118 w	5.60	92-12	Stagehand118½Dauber118½Sun Egret1185	Hard drive	15
15Feb38- 6SA	sl	1	:234 :48 1:132	1:393	Handicap 1500	1 6 610 67½ 3nk 1no	Westrope J	112 w	2.80	81-25	Stagehand112noCan't Wait1181½Dauber1165	Just up	6
8Jan38- 5SA	fst	1	:224 :464 1:122	1:382	Alw 1200	1 9 816 511 22 12½	Westrope J	116 w	*2.50	87-14	Stagehand1162½Solarium1132½Grim Reaper1131½	Going away	10
5Jan38- 3SA	fst	1	:233 :473 1:123	1:374	Alw 1200	5 5 52 32 1hd 12	Westrope J	111 w	*1.00	90-09	Stagehand1112Basque1125Godspeed1078	Going away	6
1Jan38- 2SA	fst	7f	:231 :463 1:12	1:242	Md Sp Wt	4 9 73¾ 61¾ 32½ 2½	Westrope J	118 w	4.20	89-08	GipsyMinstrel118½Stagehand1184Galltor1181	Strong finish	11
2Oct37- 3Bel	fst	7f	:232 :471 1:132	1:26	Md Sp Wt	5 9 915 97¼ 72½ 31½	Stout J	115wb	8.00	78-15	Alps115½[D]Bonnie Sea1151Stagehand115no	Fast finish	9
	Placed second												
21Sep37- 4Bel	fst	6f-WC		1:114	Alw 1200	1 2 54¼ 68½ 512	Balaski L	108wb	25.00	76-18	Tiger1254Pumpkin1193Great Union1121	Outrun	6
18Sep37- 3Bel	fst	5½f-WC		1:051	©Md Sp Wt	3 8 1711 1710 1715	Balaski L	116wb	8.00	73-08	Dah He1161½Gentle Savage116hdJubal Junior1164	Outrun	19
23Aug37- 4Sar	fst	6f	:231 :471	1:131	©Md Sp Wt	1 1 96¾ 98¾ 76¾ 43½	Balaski L	117 w	12.00	82-15	DanCupid117½GrassCutter1172[D]SturdyDuke1171	Held well	16
	Placed third												
4Aug37- 6Sar	fst	5½f	:233 :473	1:082	©Md Sp Wt	16 14 109¼ 87½ 88¼ 56	Westrope J	117 w	12.00	75-18	Gallery God1171Pit Bull1173Minimum1171	Late foot	17
31Jly37- 4Sar	my	6f	:233 :48	1:143	U S Hotel 9.4k	6 8 811 812 75¾ 77¾	Westrope J	113 w	20.00	71-23	Chaps116nkMountain Ridge116hdRed Glare1131	Outrun	8
28Jly37- 7Sar	fst	5½f	:232 :473	1:074	Alw 1000	4 5 57 69¼ 65½ 32	Peters M	112 w	12.00	82-15	Chaps1172Jack Be Nimble112hdStagehand1121	Belated rush	7
6Jly37- 4Emp	fst	5f	:23 :473	1:012	©Md Sp Wt	4 10 1011 1011 96¾ 94¾	Pollard J	116 w	15.00	86-12	Flying Ariel1161Stephen Jay116hdCal Rainey116hd	Outrun	12

Sun Beau

b. c. 1925, by Sun Briar (Sundridge)–Beautiful Lady, by Fair Play

Own.– W.S. Kilmer
Br.– Mr W.S. Kilmer (Va)
Tr.– J. Whyte

Lifetime record: 74 33 12 10 $376,744

Date / Race	Trk	Dist	Fractions	Time	Race	Running line	Jockey	Wt	Odds	Spd	Top three finishers	Comment	Field
8Oct31- 5Haw	fst	1¼	:483 1:122 1:39	2:05	3↑ Haw Gold Cup 27k	2 4 1hd 11 1½ 11½	Maiben J	126wb	1.53	83-16	Sun Beau1261½Mate1206Plucky Play1264	Handily	4
3Oct31- 6Haw	fst	1 1/16	:25 :484 1:132	1:463	3↑ Mid-West H 5k	5 6 52¼ 42 42 62¼	Maiben J	126wb	*.48	83-18	UncommnGold108½JimDndy1021½Kincsen109no	Wide,weakened	7
5Sep31- 5Sar	sl	1¾	:523 2:083 2:333	3:011	3↑ Sar Cup 9.7k	2 3 24 28 28 210	Phillips C	126wb	2.00	59-21	TwentyGrand11810SunBeau126nkSirAshley118	Under urging	3
	Geldings not eligible												
29Aug31- 5LF	gd	1¼	:47 1:12 1:38	2:05	3↑ Lincoln H 28k	4 8 55½ 31½ 11½ 11½	Phillips C	129wb	*.94	93-15	Sun Beau1291½Plucky Play1141The Nut1096	Brisk hand ride	8
8Aug31- 6Haw	fst	1⅛	:48 1:124 1:371	1:492	3↑ Haw H 30k	7 5 2½ 11 1hd 21½	Phillips C	131wb	*.71	98-14	PluckyPlay1061½SunBeau1314PaulBunyan1074	Tired last ⅛	7
1Aug31- 5AP	fst	1¼	:47 1:114 1:362	2:031	3↑ Arlington H 34k	1 2 32 21½ 2½ 13	Phillips C	128wb	*.63	102-06	Sun Beau1283Satin Spar1052½Plucky Play1091	Easily	7
25Jly31- 5AP	fst	1¼	:472 1:113 1:362	2:014	3↑ Arl Cup 26k	1 3 34½ 1hd 11 13½	Phillips C	126 w	*.94	109-02	Sun Beau1263½Mike Hall1262½Gallant Knight1266	Easily	4
18Jly31- 5AP	fst	1⅛	:47 1:112 1:363	1:492	3↑ Handicap 2000	2 2 11½ 11 11 14	Phillips C	125wb	*.97	100-05	SunBeau1254MikeHll1111½Mrts101no	Challenged turn,easily	5
	Previously trained by A. Schuttinger												
7Jly31- 5AP	fst	1	:223 :454 1:093	1:361	3↑ Handicap 2000	4 3 33½ 34½ 33½ 31¼	Watters E	124wb	*1.58	96-07	Morsel1051BestMan101nkSunBu1243	Finished fastest of all	5
18Apr31- 5HdG	fst	1 1/16	:232 :473 1:13	1:444	3↑ Philadelphia H 12k	1 3 2hd 13 13 11½	Kurtsinger C	129wb	*.30	98-11	Sun Beau1291½Paul Bunyan108½Fortunate Youth1032	Easily	6
15Apr31- 4HdG	fst	1 70	:232 :473 1:122	1:423	4↑ Alw 2000	1 1 13 14 18 16	Kurtsinger C	120wb	*.30	97-11	SunBeau1206WilliamT.1092½Folkng10615	Eased up final ⅛	4
	Previously trained by W.A. Crawford												
22Mar31-12AC	fst	1¼	:464 1:111 1:363	2:03	3↑ Aqua Caliente H 117k	4 8 53 11½ 1½ 56¼	Coltiletti F	129wb	*.60	95-08	MkHll116nkThChoctw922PluckyPly110hd	Blocked early,tired	10
1Mar31- 6AC	fst	1⅛	:47 1:12 1:372	1:502	3↑ Fashion 6.7k	9 4 34 31 2hd 13	Coltiletti F	130wb	*.30e	97-13	Sun Beau1303Pigeon Hole115nkAlexander Pantages1101	easily	11
19Feb31- 5AC	fst	6f	:223 :454	1:11	3↑ Alw 1000	10 7 95½ 31½ 11½ 12½	Coltiletti F	120wb	*2.00e	98-11	Sun Beau1202½Crofton975Nellie Custis1054		11
	Easily,worked additional ¼ mile												

22Nov30- 5Bow	fst	1 1/16	:232 :48 1:123 1:46	3↑ Southern Maryland H 41k	9	9	73	73½	42	11½	Coltiletti F	127wb	*1.90	91-14	Sun Beau1271½Valenciennes1081Lady Broadcast1102		9
	Took lead with rush																
11Nov30- 5Pim	fst	1½	:503 1:153 2:063 2:324	3↑ Bowie H 12k	8	7	21	21	21	31¼	Coltiletti F	130wb	*.90	88-12	Inception1081WilliamT.109nkSunBeu1304	Wide,lacked rally	8
1Nov30- 5Lrl	fst	1¼	:47 1:113 1:363 2:024	3↑ Washington H 31k	3	3	64½	21	2nk	11	Coltiletti F	126wb	*1.75	96-11	Sun Beau1261Vanity1072Hot Toddy1102½	Best in str drive	12
29Oct30- 6Lrl	sl	1 1/16	:233 :48 1:133 1:454	3↑ Handicap 2000	4	4	21	21½	23	21½	Coltiletti F	126wb	*.65	86-18	Vanity1101½Sun Beau1263½Jim Dandy1068	Driving	5
18Oct30- 5Lrl	fst	1	:23 :463 1:111 1:382	2↑ Laurel 14k	8	9	83	41½	43½	41½	Coltiletti F	122wb	2.35	94-12	Conclave1051½The Heathen122hdNed O.108no	Used early	10
11Oct30- 5Haw	fst	1¼	:472 1:124 1:38 2:043	3↑ Haw Gold Cup 30k	8	7	44½	2½	1½	11	Coltiletti F	126wb	*2.03	85-14	SunBeau1261PigeonHole1262½Alcibiades117no	Rated,driving	8
4Oct30- 5HdG	fst	1⅛	:473 1:114 1:38 1:51	3↑ H de Grace Cup H 25k	6	6	44	45	45	24	Coltiletti F	126wb	*1.40	91-14	Spinach1164Sun Beau126hdDr. Freeland1061	All out drive	11
20Sep30- 6OW	fst	1¼	:474 1:132 1:392 2:054	3↑ Toronto Aut Cup 8.1k	6	7	65¾	2½	2nk	11	Coltiletti F	132wb	*1.15	92-12	Sun Beau1321Sandy Ford1114Solace1181	Won in hand	9
13Sep30- 5Bel	fst	1 1/16	:231 :47 1:113 1:43	3↑ Handicap 1555	5	4	2hd	2hd	1hd	1¾	Coltiletti F	126wb	*.25	96-08	Sun Beau126¾William T.1102Folking1053	Speed in reserve	5
4Sep30- 2Bel	gd	1	:24 :48 1:12 1:374	3↑ Alw 1200	4	2	21	2½	11	13	Coltiletti F	120wb	*.90	86-12	Sun Beau1203Sun Edwin1206Titus1091½	Wide,easily	4
	Previously trained by W. Irvine																
26Jly30- 5AP	sly	1¼	:473 1:124 1:392 2:073	3↑ Arlington H 44k	3	6	911	1019	1027	1026	Schaefer L	125wb	*3.15	54-20	Pigeon Hole1051Curate1083The Nut1142½	Disliked going	11
23Jly30- 5AP	fst	1	:233 :47 1:12 1:361	3↑ Alw 2000	1	3	21	2½	2hd	12½	Schaefer L	117wb	*2.63	106-03	Sun Beau1172½Brown Wisdom1084Silverdale110½		6
	Easily,worked add'l furlong																
19Jly30- 5AP	fst	1¼	:48 1:122 1:37 2:034	3↑ Arl Cup 32k	3	4	52¾	43	46	46¼	Schaefer L	126wb	2.82	93-00	BlueLarkspur1263½Petee-Wrack126nkToro1262½	No late gain	5
12Jly30- 6AP	fst	1⅛	:48 1:13 1:374 1:504	3↑ Alw 2000	4	4	2hd	2hd	2hd	1½	Schaefer L	117wb	*.73	98-00	Sun Beau117½Paul Bunyan1101Petee-Wrack1124	Gamely	5
4Jly30- 5AP	fst	1⅛	:472 1:12 1:37 1:492	3↑ Stars & Stripes H 33k	2	3	32	31	31½	3½	Schaefer L	125wb	7.30	104-02	Blue Larkspur121½Misstep124noSun Beau1255	Held well	16
28Jun30- 5Was	fst	1¼	:484 1:133 1:382 2:043	3↑ F S Peabody Mem H 14k	1	1	11	2½	86½	1017	Coltiletti F	126wb	*1.82	81-08	PaulBunyan115noIronsides1061½LadyBrodcst1011	Quit badly	10
21Jun30- 4Aqu	fst	1⅛	:473 1:13 1:373 1:51	3↑ Brookdale H 8.2k	4	4	42	31½	2½	32	Coltiletti F	126wb	4.50	86-15	Jack High123hdSortie1202Sun Beau1264	Wide,tired	5
17Jun30- 4Aqu	fst	1⅛	:494 1:162 1:404 1:521	3↑ Handicap 1260	2	3	31	32½	21	11	Coltiletti F	126wb	*.25	82-16	Sun Beau1261Apple Cart105½Bannerette103	Troubled trip	4
9Jun30- 4Bel	my	1	:231 :47 1:112 1:383	3↑ Alw 1400	1	2	21	21½	24	21½	Coltiletti F	125wb	1.60	80-21	Caruso1101½Sun Beau125	Resolute finish	2
23Nov29- 4Bow	sl	1 1/16	:233 :473 1:124 1:462	2↑ Southern Maryland H 46k	2	2	2nk	2nk	56½	910¾	Coltiletti F	127wb	2.35	78-15	Bateau113noVictorian1221Balko1114	Quit	13
26Oct29- 5Lrl	fst	1¼	:463 1:112 1:37 2:024	3↑ Washington H 31k	7	5	94¼	2hd	1½	12	Coltiletti F	125wb	*2.65	96-12	Sun Beau1252Distraction120hdDisplay120hd	Saved ground	10
22Oct29- 5Lrl	sly	1 1/16	:243 :493 1:16 1:492	3↑ Alw 1800	2	2	1nk	1nk	1½	1hd	Coltiletti F	118wb	*.35	70-26	Sun Beau118hdLativich104	Hand ride	2
7Oct29- 5Haw	fst	1¼	:474 1:113 1:361 2:013	3↑ Haw Gold Cup 28k	2	5	46½	3nk	2hd	11½	Coltiletti F	126wb	7.67	107-11	Sun Beau1261½Misstep1264Diavolo1263	Easily	6
2Oct29- 5HdG	hy	1⅛	:492 1:143 1:413 1:553	3↑ H de Grace Cup H 24k	8	6	32¾	21	1nk	11	Coltiletti F	117wb	4.50	72-27	Sun Beau1171Glen Wild107hdBateau1164	Ridden out	9
28Sep29- 4Aqu	fst	1⅛	:48 1:124 1:372 1:50	3↑ Aqueduct H 7.1k	1	2	21½	22	1nk	11	Coltiletti F	116wb	8.00	93-17	Sun Beau1161Diavolo127¾Live Oak104	Driving	3
	Previously trained by C.W. Carroll																
21Sep29- 5OW	fst	1¼	:492 1:143 1:412 2:061	3↑ Toronto Aut Cup H 10k	9	7	42½	32	34	36½	Coltiletti F	122wb	*1.30	83-19	Gaffsman1122½Saxon1144SunBeu1222	Restrained,tired badly	9
13Sep29- 4Bel	fst	1⅛	:473 1:112 1:354 1:482	3↑ Handicap 1570	7	3	21	2½	21½	22	Coltiletti F	126wb	*1.50	101-03	Hot Toddy1102Sun Beau1264Fair Ball1055	Tired late	7
5Sep29- 5Bel	fst	1	:243 :48 1:12 1:37	3↑ Handicap 1255	4	2	21	2½	21½	1hd	Coltiletti F	126wb	2.20	92-09	Sun Beau126hdCoin Collector1124Soul of Honor1085		4
	Up in final strides;Previously trained by W. Irvine																
20Jly29- 5AP	fst	1⅛	:471 1:12 1:373 1:502	3↑ Arlington H 29k	4	10	108	119½	129¾	129½	Johnson A	118wb	*3.54	92-04	Misstep123hdDisplay1151BuddyBauer1141	Stumbled 1st turn	12
17Jly29- 5AP	fst	1	:244 :484 1:13 1:373	3↑ Handicap 2000	2	7	42½	32½	32	2nk	Legere E	116wb	6.47	109-00	Misstep122nkSunBeau1161½Republc115hd	Wide,finished fast	9
	Previously trained by J.O. Burttschell																
4Jly29- 5AP	fst	1⅛	:471 1:113 1:37 1:503	3↑ Stars & Stripes H 20k	4	5	44	33	33	33	Legere E	120wb	5.76	98-08	Dowagiac1082Misstep1251Sun Beau1202	Traffic,wide	13
	Previously trained by A.G. Blakely																
15Jun29- 4Aqu	fst	1⅛	:462 1:122 1:372 1:503	3↑ Brooklyn H 18k	2	3	53¾	41½	32½	34½	Legere E	124wb	7.00	85-16	Light Carbine971½Diavolo1203Sun Beau124hd	Good try	12
12Jun29- 4Aqu	fst	1 1/16	:232 :471 1:13 1:454	3↑ Handicap 1250	1	3	33½	34½	33	34½	Legere E	126wb	*3.00	81-19	Light Carbine1001½Sepoy1003Sun Beau1264	Tired	6
24Nov28- 4Bow	fst	1 1/16	:232 :473 1:122 1:441	2↑ G D Bryan Mem H 50k	14	11	128½	53½	65½	612¼	Craigmyle J	119wb	4.60	90-07	Misstep114hdVictorian1186Nassak1164	Off slowly,wide	16
16Nov28- 4Bow	fst	1 1/16	:233 :48 1:121 1:452	Prince Georges H 12k	4	3	34	34	34	21½	Craigmyle J	126wb	2.35	94-08	Nassak1161½Sun Beau126½Distraction1062½	Gamely	9
27Oct28- 5Lat	sl	1¾	:484 2:062 2:332 3:003	Lat Championship 33k	2	4	46	22	11½	12½	Craigmyle J	126wb	*.57	70-25	Sun Beau1262½Sortie12615Lawley12620	Easing up at end	4
	Previously trained by W. Short																
20Oct28- 5Lrl	fst	1¼	:463 1:123 1:38 2:051	Maryland H 19k	7	8	75¾	42½	3nk	15	Craigmyle J	116wb	6.15	84-19	Sun Beau1165Sortie110hdPetee-Wrack1161½	Easily	11
11Oct28- 5Haw	fst	1¼	:473 1:12 1:371 2:03	3↑ Haw Gold Cup 26k	9	5	21½	2½	11½	52¼	O'Donell S	120wb	7.89	103-06	Display126noMike Hall1262Crusader126hd	Tired late	9
29Sep28- 5HdG	sly	1⅛	:48 1:131 1:411 1:534	3↑ H de Grace Cup H 24k	4	7	65½	55	44	2½	Maiben J	114wb	8.25	80-19	Osmand121½Sun Beau1142½Crusader1241½	Wide,gaining	8
22Sep28- 4HdG	fst	1 1/16	:23 :472 1:12 1:46	Potomac H 23k	6	6	1hd	11½	11½	11	Craigmyle J	114wb	8.50	93-10	Sun Beau1141Victorian1252½Princess Tina1081		8
	Saved ground,ridden out																
19Sep28- 4HdG	my	1 70	:22 :46 1:122 1:444	3↑ Alw 2500	1	6	611	59	47½	34	Craigmyle J	107wb	13.40	82-19	Victorian1154Crusader117hdSunBeu1075	Just missed second	6
4Aug28- 4Sar	fst	1 3/16	:494 1:15 1:401 1:59	3↑ Miller 6.3k	4	3	21½	21½	42¾	58½	Craigmyle J	115wb	2.60	74-14	Reigh Count1272Gerard1155Penalo1151	Quit	5
30Jly28- 5Sar	gd	1¼	:483 1:13 1:39 2:06	3↑ Saratoga H 9.7k	8	4	43½	41¾	42¼	45	Craigmyle J	109wb	4.50	74-15	Chance Shot1221½Black Maria1152Edith Cavell1061½	Tiring	8
7Jly28- 5LF	fst	1¼	:484 1:13 1:392 2:053	3↑ Lincoln H 32k	12	7	95	51¼	2½	2½	Craigmyle J	111wb	14.10	92-10	Toro115½Sun Beau1114Flat Iron118½	No match	15
30Jun28- 4Aqu	gd	1½	:501 1:16 2:073 2:313	Dwyer 25k	2	1	21½	32¼	32½	26	Craigmyle J	110wb	2.60	84-14	Genie1106Sun Beau1101Ironsides1171	Driving	6
	Geldings not eligible																
27Jun28- 4Aqu	fst	1	:234 :473 1:132 1:382	3↑ Handicap 1285	8	6	41½	2nk	1hd	12	Craigmyle J	126wb	5.00	88-19	SunBeau1262Tantvy1081[D]Byrd1201	Outside move,going away	9
15Jun28- 2Aqu	gd	1	:24 :494 1:14 1:384	3↑ Alw 1000	5	3	3½	3nk	1½	12	Craigmyle J	114wb	5.00	86-16	Sun Beau1142St. Henell113noSocial Mug1213	Going away	7
9Jun28- 5Bel	fst	1½	:481 1:133 2:061 2:331	Belmont 74k	1	1	1hd	1hd	613	616	McAtee L	126wb	10.00	62-23	Vito1263Genie1263Diavolo126hd	Dueled,tired badly	6
1Jun28- 2Bel	fst	1⅛	:463 1:12 1:384 1:531	3↑ Alw 1200	7	1	12	13	11	11	McAtee L	111wb	*2.20	79-22	Sun Beau1111Sepoy118½Danthonia1091½	Saved ground	7
19May28- 5CD	hy	1¼	:493 1:154 1:432 2:102	Ky Derby 65k	18	16	1813	1411	1020	1119	Craigmyle J	126wb	38.42	45-26	Reigh Count1263Misstep1262Toro1264	Never a factor	22
11May28- 4Pim	fst	1 3/16	:472 1:13 1:384 2:001	Preakness 70k	6	10	104¾	43½	53¾	55½	Craigmyle J	126wb	17.85	85-14	Victorian126noToro1262½Solace1263	Wide	18
	Geldings not eligible																
8May28- 5Pim	fst	1 70	:232 :48 1:133 1:453	Alw 1500	6	6	52¼	52¾	63¼	1hd	Craigmyle J	112wb	20.75	83-32	Sun Beau112hdDon Q108hdSolace116½	Up in final strides	6
30Apr28- 5HdG	fst	1 1/16	:233 :473 1:122 1:451	Chesapeake 12k	7	5	52½	52¾	1013	1017¼	Craigmyle J	114 w	17.80f	80-13	Bobashela1104Typhoon1224Sortie1222	Crowded	11
27Apr28- 5HdG	gd	1 70	:24 :482 1:13 1:44	Alw 2000	7	7	73½	65½	610	613¼	Craigmyle J	111wb	7.70	77-19	Strolling Player111noToro1148Solace1145	Began slowly	7
24Apr28- 3HdG	hy	6f	:25 :503 1:172	Alw 1200	1	4	3¾	2hd	11½	13	Craigmyle J	106wb	*.50	68-39	Sun Beau1063Water Lad1081War Whoop1115	Easily	5
21Apr28- 3HdG	fst	6f	:232 :473 1:132	3↑ Handicap 1400	4	5	41¼	2hd	1nk	2hd	Craigmyle J	114wb	5.55	88-19	Contemplate113hdSunBeau1145Montferrt120½	Tired last ⅛	6
	Previously trained by G.E. Phillips																
4Nov27- 5Pim	my	1	:24 :483 1:142 1:414	Pim Futurity 61k	5	15	1312	1212	1112	75½	Craigmyle J	122wb	18.95e	73-24	Glade114hdPetee-Wrack119nk[D]Bateau1161½	No factor	15
	Geldings not eligible																
29Oct27- 4Lrl	fst	1	:231 :472 1:133 1:39	Manor H 15k	7	10	103¾	114½	1111	1011¼	GdwinP	107 w	*1.80e	82-10	Eugene S.1051Toro1153Sun Friar1113	Taken up start	11
27Oct27- 4Lrl	fst	1	:231 :47 1:13 1:384	2↑ Alw 1400	6	2	2nk	1hd	11½	1½	GdwinP	103wb	17.20	94-18	Sun Beau103½Fairy Maiden1091Eugene S.1034	Handily	9
	Previously trained by C.W. Carroll																
21Oct27- 2Lrl	sl	6f	:232 :48 1:144	Md Sp Wt	2	6	63¾	54½	43½	44¼	Craigmyle J	115wb	10.35	79-25	[D]ScotchandSoda115nkBobashela1153BarNon1151	Good effort	7
	Placed third by disqualification																

Top Flight

dk.br. f. 1929, by Dis Donc (Sardanapale)–Flyatit, by Peter Pan — **Lifetime record: 16 12 0 0 $275,900**

Own.– C.V. Whitney
Br.– H.P. Whitney (Ky)
Tr.– T.J. Healy

24Sep32- 5HdG	fst 1 1/16	:23 :47 1:123 1:45	Potomac H 25k	2 3 41¼ 41½ 42 42	Workman R	118wb	*1.90	95-08	DarkSecret1101Osculator110noGallantSir1111	Under urging	12
14Sep32- 4Bel	fst 1	:23 :464 1:114 1:374 2↑	ⒻLadies H 2.9k	5 2 2½ 2hd 11½ 11½	Workman R	126wb	*.80	86-17	Top Flight1261½Parry1145Risque1183	Speed to spare	7
30Aug32- 4Sar	fst 1	:231 :461 1:11 1:374 3↑	Delaware H 4.5k	3 1 11 2nk 32½ 45	Workman R	120wb	3.00	87-11	Flagstone104.51Morfr1233TrdAvon1161	Eased up when tired	4
17Aug32- 4Sar	fst 1¼	:234 :473 1:123 2:062	ⒻAlabama 15k	3 2 23 21 13 14	Workman R	126wb	*.40	77-14	Top Flight1264Parry1166Laughing Queen1214	Drawing away	4
16Jly32- 5AP	fst 1¼	:47 1:11 1:37 2:033	Classic 88k	8 3 11½ 1hd 2hd 57	Workman R	118wb	*1.82	84-08	Gusto1263Stepenfetcht1212Evrgold1212	Little left at end	12
2Jly32- 5AP	fst 1⅛	:473 1:12 1:372 1:504	ⒻArl Oaks 18k	5 1 11 11 12 12	Workman R	121wb	*.84	93-06	Top Flight1212Evening121½Parry118hd	Easily	8
9Jun32- 4Bel	fst 1⅜	:484 1:134 1:412 2:201	ⒻC C A Oaks 18k	9 3 21½ 21 2nk 1¾	Workman R	121wb	*.20	70-21	Top Flight121¾Argosie1141Unique1143	Loafing,just held	10
14May32- 5Bel	fst 1	:23 :47 1:12 1:39	ⒻAcorn 15k	1 1 11 12 14 16	Workman R	121wb	*.80	80-20	Top Flight1216Parry1142Unique1144	Drew away	7
30Apr32- 4Jam	fst 1 70	:231 :473 1:12 1:43	Wood Memorial 13k	3 3 32 35 46¼ 47½	Robertson A	115 w	*.50	83-11	Universe120½Economic1203Curacao1144	Tired badly	10
7Nov31- 4Pim	fst 1 1/16	:232 :471 1:122 1:444	Pim Futurity 64k	9 4 2hd 2hd 1½ 1nk	Workman R	119 w	*1.10	98-07	Top Flight119nkTick On1193Burgoo King119no	Lasted	12
	Geldings not eligible										
19Sep31- 4Bel	fst *7f-WC	1:21	Futurity 107k	10 4 2hd 1nk 12½	Workman R	127 w	*1.20e	90-10	TpFlght1272½MdPursut1221Mrfr1221	Drew off under pressure	12
9Sep31- 3Bel	fst 6f-WC	1:113	ⒻMatron 26k	2 1 1hd 1hd 11½	Workman R	127 w	*.17	89-16	Top Flight1271½Parry1191½Pintail1156	Speed to spare	7
22Aug31- 3Sar	fst 6f	:232 :47 1:123	ⒻSpinaway 10k	5 1 11½ 11½ 13 15	Workman R	127 w	*.55	89-10	TopFlight1275DinnerTime1111½Brocado115no	Speed to spare	8
15Aug31- 4Sar	fst 6f	:23 :462 1:12	Sar Spl 11k	2 7 1½ 11 12 11¼	Workman R	119 w	*.70	92-12	TopFlight1191¼IndianRunnr1222Curco1221	Speed in reserve	7
8Jly31- 4AP	fst 5½f	:221 :453 :583 1:051	ⒻLassie 22k	6 3 1½ 13 14 15	Robertson A	120 w	*1.90	99-09	TopFlight1205ModernQueen113½PrincessCml1171	Easily best	15
17Jun31- 4Aqu	my 5f	:58	ⒻClover 6.7k	6 5 1½ 1½ 11	Robertson A	107 w	*2.50e	97-20	Top Flight1071Polonaise1221Brocado112½	Held	12

Twenty Grand

b. c. 1928, by St. Germans (Swynford)–Bonus, by All Gold — **Lifetime record: 25 14 4 3 $261,790**

Own.– Greentree Stable
Br.– Greentree Stable (Ky)
Tr.– Cecil Boyd-Rochfort

29Oct35♦ Newmarket(GB)	gd 1½ⓉRH	2:35 3↑	Rutland Hcp Hcp1600	-	Childs J	133	20.00		Lobau1081½Pharillon111½Linace115	Never a factor;Exact finish position unavailable	11
18Jun35♦ Ascot(GB)	gd 1ⓉStr	1:44 3↑	Queen Anne Stakes Stk7200	7	Beasy M	124	16.50		Fair Trial1093Solerina992Monico109	Chased leaders throughout;Beaten lengths unavailable,	22
	Previously trained by W. Brennan										
23Feb35- 6SA	fst 1¼	:45 1:10 1:36 2:021 3↑	S Anita H 125k	7 11 910 1415 1311 109¾	Coucci S	126wb	10.30	- -	Azucar1172Ladysman1171Time Supply1182	Never a contender	20
18Feb35- 5SA	fst 1 1/16	:24 :473 1:12 1:432 3↑	Handicap 1200	3 1 11 11 2hd 21	Coucci S	116wb	4.00	- -	DEquipoise1251Twenty Grand1163Sarada1051½		5
	Placed first by disqualification										
25Jan35- 6SA	fst 7f	:224 :453 1:094 1:222 3↑	Handicap 1200	3 2 21½ 22½ 35 33½	Coucci S	122 w	*1.20	- -	High Glee1132Mate1201½Twenty Grand1223½	Lame	4
5Oct32- 5Lrl	sl 1 1/16	:242 :492 1:142 1:483 3↑	Handicap 1200	3 4 2½ 1hd 2½ 21½	Kurtsinger C	126 w	*.65	72-25	Mad Frump1081½Twenty Grand126½War Hero112½		6
	Faltered,pulled up lame										
15Sep32- 4Bel	fst 1	:234 :464 1:113 1:364 3↑	Alw 900	4 3 33 23 21 1½	Kurtsinger C	125 w	*.80	91-10	Twenty Grand125½Masked Knight11820Pin Tail1014	Driving	4
	Previously trained by J. Rowe Jr										
19Sep31- 5Bel	fst 2	:501 2:37 2:562 3:232 3↑	J C Gold Cup 13k	2 2 22 13 15 13	Kurtsinger C	114 w	*.02	92-09	TwntyGrnd1143Blenheim1147Barometr114	Easily,much best	3
12Sep31- 5Bel	fst 1⅝	:48 1:38 2:022 2:411	Lawrence Realizatn 33k	3 4 36 2½ 13 16	Kurtsinger C	126 w	*.07	98-04	TwentyGrand1266SunMeadow1235SirAshley1231	Easily,best	4
5Sep31- 5Sar	sl 1¾	:523 2:083 2:333 3:011 3↑	Sar Cup 9.7k	3 1 14 18 18 110	McAtee L	118 w	*.40	69-21	TwentyGrand11810SunBeau126nkSirAshley118	Easily,best	3
	Geldings not eligible										
22Aug31- 5Sar	fst 1¼	:481 1:13 1:384 2:043	Travers 39k	5 5 56½ 2hd 11½ 11¾	McAtee L	126 w	*.14e	86-10	TwntyGrand1261¾St.Bridux1204SunMdow1205	Easily,in hand	5
	Geldings not eligible										
18Jly31- 4AP	fst 1¼	:471 1:12 1:371 2:022	Classic 85k	7 7 74¾ 44 36½ 34	Kurtsinger C	126 w	*.38e	102-05	Mate1264Spanish Play123noTwenty Grand1265		7
	Came wide,finished fast										
4Jly31- 4Aqu	fst 1½	:512 1:16 2:08 2:342	Dwyer 15k	3 1 22 22 1nk 12	Kurtsinger C	126 w	*.02	76-20	Twenty Grand1262Blenheim1124Barometer110	Easily best	3
13Jun31- 5Bel	fst 1½	:49 1:142 2:03 2:293	Belmont 69k	1 3 33 2hd 13 110	Kurtsinger C	126 w	*.80	96-12	TwentyGrand12610SunMeadow126noJamestown126	Cantered	3
16May31- 5CD	fst 1¼	:472 1:12 1:372 2:014	Ky Derby 58k	5 9 104½ 2½ 11 14	Kurtsinger C	126 w	*.88e	107-02	Twenty Grand1264Sweep All1263Mate1264	Easily	12
9May31- 5Pim	fst 1 3/16	:483 1:132 1:383 1:59	Preakness 58k	1 1 73¾ 51½ 31½ 21½	Kurtsinger C	126 w	*1.75e	95-10	Mate1261½Twenty Grand126nkLadder1261	Impeded	7
	Geldings not eligible										
2May31- 4Jam	fst 1 70	:233 :47 1:122 1:423	Wood Memorial 13k	2 4 58 48 24 1½	Kurtsinger C	120 w	*.60	93-09	Twenty Grand120½Clock Tower1106Camper1106	Driving	6
	Previously trained by T.W. Murphy										
14Nov30- 5Pim	my 1 1/16	:234 :483 1:134 1:474	Walden H 13k	1 5 53½ 42¼ 42 31¼	Walls P	125 w	*.95e	82-22	Mate125¾Sweep All105½Twenty Grand1252½	Finished fast	5
5Nov30- 5Pim	my 1 1/16	:234 :482 1:142 1:483	Pim Futurity 58k	8 6 63 64¾ 42¾ 2½	Kurtsinger C	119 w	3.40	78-26	Equipoise119½Twenty Grand119nkMate1194	Finished fast	8
	Geldings not eligible										
16Oct30- 5CD	fst 1	:231 :464 1:111 1:36	Ky Jockey Club 31k	1 7 43 22 1hd 1no	Kurtsinger C	122 w	2.77	101-13	TwentyGrand122noEquipoise12210Knight'sCall1225	Driving	7
4Oct30- 3Aqu	fst 1	:233 :473 1:13 1:38	Jr Champion 9.8k	7 7 65¼ 53¾ 32½ 11	Kurtsinger C	111 w	7.00	90-15	Twenty Grand1111Equipoise1223Ormesby1168	Driving	7
25Sep30- 4Aqu	fst 6f	:233 :472 1:124	Babylon H 6.8k	5 4 74¼ 53¼ 52¾ 43½	Walls P	111 w	*3.20	86-14	Ormesby112hdRollin In1102Gigantic1071½	No mishaps	13
18Sep30- 5Aqu	fst 5f	1:00	Alw 1000	3 5 42¼ 12 13	Garner M	113 w	5.00	87-17	Twenty Grand1133Laddie116nkCamper1222	Easily	10
11Jly30- 6Emp	fst 5f	:232 :474 1:004	Alw 1000	2 5 58 55 44 21	Robertson A	115 w	1.40e	93-13	Phantom Star1101Twenty Grand115½Jamison1103	Closed fast	9
30Apr30- 5Jam	fst 5f	:24 :482 1:014	Md Sp Wt	7 4 31 2½ 11½ 15	McAtee L	118 w	*.70	84-18	Twenty Grand1185Soarer1151½Black Shirt1182	Easily	11

Unerring

br. f. 1936, by Insco (Sir Gallahad III)–Margaret Lawrence, by Vulcain — **Lifetime record: 57 16 13 7 $31,350**

Own.– Woolford Farm
Br.– Herbert M. Woolf (Kan)
Tr.– R.O. Higdon

17Oct41- 5Emp	fst 1 1/16	:233 :471 1:123 1:453 3↑	Alw 2500	6 7 53¾ 53¾ 43 63½	Strickler W	112 w	3.05	87-12	Spanish Duke1141½Sun Eager1071Lovely Night111½	Faltered	7
13Oct41- 5Jam	fst 6f	:224 :461 1:12 2↑	ⒻCorrection H 8.9k	1 5 65 55½ 43 3½	Strickler W	112 w	12.95	91-16	WiseNiece109nkDevil'sGirl112½Unerrng112nk	Strong finish	9
7Oct41- 6Jam	fst 1 1/16	:242 :481 1:133 1:452 3↑	Handicap 3030	1 1 1hd 21 21 22	Strickler W	104 w	8.10	84-14	Dit1222Unerring104¾Birch Rod118¾	Weakened	5
3Oct41- 6Bel	sly 1 1/16	3↑	Alw 2500	6 1 21 2hd 1hd 1¾	Strickler W	103 w	16.55	- -	Unerring103¾Hypocrite1205Tex Hygro1051	Drew out	7
	Time not taken										
29Sep41- 6Bel	fst 1	:234 :47 1:12 1:364 3↑	Alw 2500	3 1 1hd 1hd 42½ 410½	Strickler W	103 w	14.35	80-12	The Rhymer104½Llanero1044Vintage Port1066	Tired	8
22Sep41- 5Bel	fst 6f	:224 :463 1:113 3↑	ⒻAlw 2000	1 6 97¼ 87 87 74¼	Vedder RL	112 w	*1.05e	88-10	Five to One1031Dark Imp1102Fleetborough1051	Outrun	10
15Sep41- 6Aqu	fst 6f	:224 :464 1:12 3↑	ⒻAlw 2000	5 5 54¾ 55 42 2¾	Strickler W	108 w	10.40	93-16	Oasis116¾Unerring108nkPelisse111no	Closed fast	5
6Aug41- 7Was	fst 6f	:223 :463 1:112 3↑	Handicap 1200	2 4 55 53½ 53 42	Strickler W	113 w	3.70	92-11	Malisco1101Woodsaw112noBoysy1101	No mishaps	7
21May41- 6LF	fst 6f	:233 :473 1:134 3↑	ⒻAlw 1010	1 4 1hd 1hd 11½ 11¼	McCombs K	116 w	4.00	82-25	Unerring1161¼Montsin1111½Shine O'Night111½	Driving	7
12May41- 6CD	fst 7f	:232 :47 1:122 1:253 3↑	Alw 1000	3 1 1hd 1hd 1½ 43¼	McCombs K	111 w	7.00	85-15	Topic1102ValdinaGroom1101DancingLight116nk	Tired badly	7
1May41- 6CD	fst 1	:232 :463 1:113 1:363 3↑	Churchill Downs H 3k	3 6 42 77¾ 711 716½	McCombs K	108wb	8.30	79-14	My Bill1004Potranco1165Betty's Bobby109¾	Shuffled back	8
18Apr41- 4Kee	sl 6f	:23 :472 1:131 3↑	ⒻAlw 1200	2 5 63¾ 58 44¼ 34¾	McCombs K	121wb	3.90	81-21	Laatokka105¾Mattie J.1134Unerring121no	Wide	6

10Apr41- 5Kee	fst 6f	:23 :463	1:121	3↑ Phoenix H 3.6k	3	6	66	69	56	59½	Vedder RL	110wb	8.60	81-18	Cherry Jam111hdSmacked1016Parasang1221½	Outrun 7
28Feb41- 6Hia	fst 1⅛	:463 1:112 1:374	1:503	3↑ ⒻEvening H 6.5k	1	3	21	43	42½	54¼	Vedder RL	114wb	3.50e	84-18	Dorimar115nkJeanne d'Arc1023Silvestra102hd	Weakened 13
8Feb41- 6Hia	gd 7f	:224 :453 1:104	1:232	3↑ ⒻBlack Helen H 6.5k	1	3	35½	55	56½	69½	Vedder RL	121wb	4.60e	86-13	Sweet Willow1164Silvestra1052Up the Hill102½	Tired 13
28Jan41- 6Hia	fst 7f	:231 :47 1:112	1:24	4↑ ⒻAlw 1500	3	1	11½	12	12	1nk	Vedder RL	114wb	*.80	93-11	Unerring114nkPretty Pet1115Harp Weaver1081½	Just lasted 5
22Jan41- 5Hia	fst 6½f	:223 :453 1:10	1:163	3↑ Handicap 1600	2	2	31½	31¾	31½	2hd	Vedder RL	111wb	3.30	96-07	ClydeTolson115hdUnerring111nkSundodger110hd	Just missed 7
14Jan41- 6Hia	fst 6f	:223 :451	1:112	4↑ ⒻAlw 1500	6	4	41¾	36	33½	2¾	Vedder RL	114wb	6.45	91-15	Aerial Bomb108¾Unerring1141½Sassy Lady114½	Closed fast 10
17Sep40- 4Aqu	fst 6f	:223 :464	1:112	3↑ Handicap 2035	6	3	31½	32	32	2hd	Meade D	108wb	3.55e	100-07	Dr. Whinny122hdUnerring108nkVolitant1123	Just missed 7
10Sep40- 5Aqu	fst 6f	:223 :464	1:12	4↑ Handicap 1535	3	4	44	46	46	44½	Roberts P	110wb	1.70e	92-10	Rifted Clouds114noWatch Over122½Archworth1064	No mishap 6
8Aug40- 6Was	fst 6f	:223 :46	1:112	3↑ Handicap 1200	3	5	53½	55½	54½	54½	Eads W	112 w	1.90e	90-10	Float Away105hdTalked About1131½Morcarine1081	Outrun 6
16Jly40- 6AP	fst 7f	:233 :47 1:12	1:253	3↑ Alw 1200	1	1	1hd	2½	21½	2½	Eads W	110 w	*1.10	81-16	Talked About114½Unerring1105Co-Sport1082	Forced back 6
6Jly40- 7AP	fst 1	:234 :472 1:113	1:364	3↑ Alw 1200	4	1	11½	1½	1hd	2½	Richard J	113 w	*.80	87-12	Van109½Unerring11310Olympus1132¼	Weakened 5
29Jun40- 6AP	fst 1	:224 :451 1:10	1:361	3↑ ⒻArl Matron H 9.1k	12	8	73¼	42½	43¾	77¼	Bierman C	118 w	*.90e	84-18	Shine O'Night1033Montsin1101Manie O'Hara1091	Impeded 14
17Apr40- 5Kee	sly 6f	:23 :464	1:122	3↑ Handicap 1500	4	2	43	42¼	11½	13	Vedder RL	117 w	*2.10	90-22	Unerring1173Royal Blue109nkSmart Crack106hd	Going away 5
14Feb40- 5Hia	fst 6½f	:233 :472 1:111	1:172	3↑ Handicap 1500	3	2	1½	2½	35	56¾	Wright WD	116 w	*1.60e	85-12	Many Stings118nkArmor Bearer1095Inscoelda1111½	5
	Swerved final ¼,worked mile in 1:38															
30Jan40- 5Hia	fst 7f	:23 :462 1:103	1:232	4↑ ⒻAlw 1200	7	4	41½	32	31¼	3nk	Ryan P	118 w	*2.05	96-09	Flying Lill115nkDolly Val115hdUnerring118½	Swerved 8
16Jan40- 6Hia	fst 7f	:232 :47 1:112	1:24	4↑ ⒻAlw 1400	3	1	1hd	1½	1½	1nk	Ryan P	115 w	*1.80	93-09	Unerring115nkDolly Val1091One Jest108nk	Hard drive 8
8Nov39- 6Pim	fst 1 1/16	:24 :483 1:14	1:472	3↑ ⒻLady Baltimore H 3.9k	3	4	42	51½	43	76¼	Ryan P	118 w	*1.55e	77-21	Manie O'Hara1084Bala Ormont109½Hostility110½	Tired 12
18Oct39- 5Lrl	fst 1 70	:233 :472 1:133	1:424	3↑ Handicap 1500	3	3	11½	2hd	2hd	2hd	Ryan P	108 w	*1.25	95-14	War Minstrel112hdUnerring1085Pernie107½	Game try 6
23Sep39- 5HdG	fst 1 1/16	:24 :472 1:124	1:444	Potomac H 11k	7	4	42½	41½	43	44¾	Ryan P	114 w	4.25	89-15	ThirdDegree1143Porter'sMite116nkElChico1151½	No mishap 7
9Sep39- 5Aqu	fst 1 1/16	:233 :462 1:103	1:43	3↑ ⒻBeldame H 13k	3	1	1½	1½	11	2no	Ryan P	120 w	7.00	98-03	NellieBly102noUnerring1203BalOrmont115hd	Tired in drive 18
31Aug39- 0Was	fst 1	:23 :46 1:104	1:374	ⒻMatch Race 6.2k	2	2	2nk	1½	12	12	Ryan P	110 w	*.70	89-13	Unerring1102Flying Lill110	Handily 2
26Aug39- 7Was	fst 6f	:224 :464	1:114	3↑ Handicap 1000	5	2	2hd	2hd	11	3½	Ryan P	114 w	*.70e	92-12	Robert L.118nkGrass Cutter111nkUnerring1143	Tired badly 9
	Previously trained by B.A. Jones															
15Jly39- 3AP	fst 1	:233 :47 1:11	1:363	Alw 1500	2	1	11½	12	14	12½	Longden J	109 w	*.80e	89-17	Unerring1092½Technician123hdSun Lover1201½	In hand 7
1Jly39- 5AP	fst 1	:23 :454 1:103	1:363	3↑ ⒻArl Matron H 6.1k	8	3	32½	31	21	2nk	Yarberry W	108 w	*1.90	89-17	FlyingLill107nkUnerring1084LadyMaryland1202	Forced wide 9
26Jun39- 6AP	fst 1	:234 :471 1:113	1:37	Alw 1200	7	1	11½	13	16	19	Caffarella M	102 w	*1.00	87-14	Unerring1029Yale O' Nine1122Chief Onaway1184	Much best 7
19Jun39- 5LF	fst 6f	:23 :462	1:121	Alw 800	3	3	32	1hd	11	11¼	Caffarella M	102 w	*2.20	90-16	Unerring1021¼Olney1101½Carla1095	Handily 8
14Jun39- 5LF	gd 7f	:232 :464 1:123	1:254	Alw 800	2	2	21	31½	22	2nk	Hanke E	103 w	*1.50	85-26	Carla111nkUnerring1034Calexico1163	Just missed 7
17May39- 7CD	fst 6½f	:23 :462 1:113	1:182	Alw 800	5	3	32	2½	1½	12	Dupuy H	102 w	*1.80	89-13	Unerring1022American Byrd112hdOlney1123	Drew out 7
1May39- 5CD	fst 6f	:223 :46	1:12	ⒻAlw 800	8	3	21½	21	31	21½	Hanford I	110 w	*3.70e	91-17	FlyingLill1051½Unerrng110nkBurgooMss112.5hd	Good effort 8
17Oct38- 4Emp	fst 5½f	:223 :47	1:053	ⒻAlw 1000	6	6	65	56	56¼	67½	Baird R	114 w	8.00	90-09	Ciencia111noThrottle Wide1115Red Eye1112	Outrun 6
11Oct38- 4Jam	fst 6f	:23 :473	1:12	ⒻAlw 1000	3	1	33½	57½	58	58½	Baird R	109 w	2.60e	83-13	Smart Crack1091½Matterhorn1143Inscoelda122hd	Outrun 6
3Oct38- 4Jam	fst 6f	:231 :472	1:132	ⒻAlw 1200	1	1	21½	35	34½	36½	Rollins C	115 w	10.00	78-15	Smart Crack1145Red Eye1121½Unerring1158	Weakened 5
30Jly38- 6AP	gd 6f	:231 :463	1:12	Arl Futurity 41k	7	3	31	53½	78	77¾	Perkins C	116 w	4.60e	79-18	Thingumabob1175No Competition1171½Hants117½	Tired 10
16Jly38- 6AP	fst 6f	:223 :454	1:113	ⒻArl Lassie 26k	2	5	76	67½	45	33½	James B	119 w	*.90e	85-07	Inscoelda1171Dinner Date1172½Unerring1195	Closed fast 9
4Jly38- 5Hol	fst 5½f	:232 :471 :593	1:06	Starlet 2.8k	3	1	22½	3½	1hd	11½	Adams J	119 w	*.60	--	Unerring1191½Kenty Miss1132½Valley Lass1162½	Easily 5
30Jun38- 3Hol	fst 5f	:231 :473	1:002	Alw 900	2	3	2hd	1hd	1hd	11½	Adams J	118 w	*.20	--	Unerring1181½Pugknows113nkMorning Breeze1132½	Easily 7
21Jun38- 3Hol	fst 5½f	:232 :474	1:063	Alw 1000	3	3	2hd	2hd	1hd	1¾	Perkins C	117 w	*1.10	--	Unerring117¾Bang1146Kenty Miss1083	Handily 6
30May38- 6CD	fst 5f	:232 :462	:59	Bashford Manor 7.1k	2	1	2½	44	41½	22	Perkins C	119 w	3.10e	98-13	Royal Pam1192Unerring119hdCherry Jam1223	Closed well 11
13May38- 4CD	fst 4½f	:224 :462	:531	Alw 800	6	6		2½	2hd	11½	Perkins C	108 w	*1.60	96-07	Unrrng1081½RangeDust1161½AmericanByrd116hd	Going away 6
10May38- 4CD	fst 4½f	:23 :472	:542	Alw 800	1	2		36	35½	1nk	Perkins C	110 w	3.00	90-11	Unerring110nkSteady Don1181¼Tack Point1131½	Hard drive 6
2Mar38- 1Hia	fst 3f	:221	:342	Alw 800	2	4			43	32	Anderson I	114 w	7.40	--	Selmalad117noThird Degree1172Unerring1141½	Closed fast 7
26Feb38- 1Hia	fst 3f	:22	:34	Alw 800	3	4			52½	41¼	Anderson I	112 w	3.10e	--	CherryJam1151Inscoelda112noSweetPtrc112nk	Strong finish 9
12Feb38- 6Hia	fst 3f	:22	:341	ⒻNursery #2 3.4k	5	4			63¼	53¾	Haas L	116 w	4.10	--	Charlotte Girl119½Sweet Patrice1161¼Throttle Wide116hd	7
	Close quarters															
8Feb38- 1Hia	fst 3f	:221	:343	ⒻMd Sp Wt	11	3			4¾	12	Haas L	116 w	*2.05e	--	Unerring1162Sister Reigh116hdCatechism116no	Going away 12
5Feb38- 1Hia	fst 3f	:22	:334	Alw 800	4	6			67½	46	Haas L	113 w	9.00	--	Hireling1182Sweet Patrice115hdSelmalad1184	Late foot 7

War Admiral

br. c. 1934, by Man o' War (Fair Play)–Brushup, by Sweep

Lifetime record: 26 21 3 1 $273,240

Own.– Glen Riddle Farm Stable

Br.– Samuel D. Riddle (Ky)

Tr.– G. Conway

18Feb39- 6Hia	fst 7f	:233 :464 1:104	1:224	4↑ Alw 1500	2	1	11½	11½	1½	1½	Wright WD	126 w	*.20	99-05	WarAdmrl126½Psturzd11912SndyBoot110	Mild hand ride late 3
12Nov38- 5Nar	fst 1⅛	:472 1:113 1:372	1:512	3↑ Rhode Island H 11k	6	2	1nk	12½	16	12½	Kurtsinger C	127 w	*.20	91-17	War Admiral1272½Mucho Gusto1151Busy K.112no	Eased up 6
1Nov38- 6Pim	fst 1 3/16	:473 1:114 1:364	1:563	3↑ Pim Spl 15k	1	2	21	2no	2½	24	Kurtsinger C	120 w	*.25	97-08	Seabiscuit1204War Admiral120	No excuse 2
1Oct38- 5Bel	fst 2	:522 2:343 2:591	3:244	3↑ J C Gold Cup 7k	2	1	11½	12	12	13	Wright WD	124 w	*.08	85-12	War Admiral1243Magic Hour11710Jolly Tar1173	Galloping 3
	Geldings not eligible															
27Aug38- 5Sar	fst 1¾	:484 2:051 2:302	2:554	3↑ Sar Cup 8.3k	3	1	11½	11½	11½	14	Peters M	126 w	*.33	96-08	War Admiral1264Esposa12110Anaflame111	Easily 3
20Aug38- 5Sar	fst 1¼	:473 1:123 1:38	2:034	3↑ Whitney 3.7k	3	1	13	12	11	11	Wright WD	126 w	*.33	90-11	War Admiral1261Esposa12110Fighting Fox117	Handily 3
	Geldings not eligible															
30Jly38- 5Sar	sl 1¼	:491 1:14 1:39	2:06	3↑ Saratoga H 10k	5	1	12	11	12	1nk	Kurtsinger C	130 w	*.70	79-16	War Admiral130nkEsposa1165Isolater105.54	Under drive 5
27Jly38- 5Sar	my 1	:24 :481 1:13	1:392	3↑ Wilson 3.9k	3	2	1½	11½	13	18	Kurtsinger C	126 w	*.60	84-19	War Admiral1268Fighting Fox1161½Esposa121	Much best 3
	Geldings not eligible															
29Jun38- 6Suf	hy 1⅛	:481 1:132 1:393	1:523	3↑ Mass H 59k	6	4	32½	24	33	48¼	Kurtsinger C	130 w	*.40	74-28	Menow1078Busy K.107nkWar Minstrel106no	Weakened 6
6Jun38- 5Aqu	fst 1	:23 :461 1:112	1:364	3↑ Queens County H 6.1k	1	2	22	21	11½	11	Kurtsinger C	132 w	*.55	96-14	War Admiral1321Snark1267Danger Point1121½	Driving 4
5Mar38- 6Hia	fst 1¼	:471 1:113 1:37	2:034	3↑ Widener H 63k	13	3	11	13	15	11½	Kurtsinger C	130 w	*.35	90-12	War Admiral1301½Zevson104½War Minstrel1111	Eased up 13
19Feb38- 5Hia	fst 7f	:23 :452 1:101	1:234	4↑ Alw 1100	6	3	2nk	11½	14	11½	Kurtsinger C	122	*.30	94-13	WarAdmiral1221½SirOracle1166CaballeroII1102½	Eased up 6
3Nov37- 5Pim	fst 1 3/16	:462 1:112 1:38	1:584	Pim Spl H 8.2k	1	2	31	21½	12	11½	Kurtsinger C	128 w	*.05	96-13	WarAdmrl1281½MaskedGenrl1004WrMnstrl109no	Won driving 4
30Oct37- 5Lrl	gd 1¼	:48 1:13 1:384	2:044	3↑ Washington H 19k	7	3	11	13	11½	11½	Kurtsinger C	126 w	*.65	86-22	War Admiral1261½Heelfly1192Burning Star1183	Easily 7
26Oct37- 5Lrl	fst 1 1/16	:241 :48 1:131	1:46	3↑ Alw 1200	8	1	13	13	14	12½	Kurtsinger C	106 w	*.40	87-21	War Admiral1062½Aneroid1134Floradora107hd	Easily 8
5Jun37- 5Bel	fst 1½	:48 1:121 2:021	2:283	Belmont 46k	7	2	13	14	13	13	Kurtsinger C	126 w	*.90	101-06	War Admiral1263Sceneshifter12610Vamoose1262	Easily best 7
15May37- 6Pim	gd 1 3/16	:47 1:122 1:373	1:582	Preakness 55k	1	2	11	11	1hd	1hd	Kurtsinger C	126 w	*.35	98-16	War Admiral126hdPompoon1268Flying Scot1262	Hard drive 8
8May37- 6CD	fst 1¼	:464 1:122 1:372	2:031	Ky Derby 62k	1	2	11½	11½	13	11¾	Kurtsinger C	126 w	*1.60	93-11	War Admiral1261¾Pompoon1268Reaping Reward1263	In hand 20
24Apr37- 5HdG	fst 1 1/16	:232 :472 1:113	1:45	Chesapeake 11k	3	1	11	12	14	16	Kurtsinger C	119 w	*.65e	93-15	WarAdmiral1196CourtScandal119½OverthTop1142	Easily best 7
14Apr37- 4HdG	fst 6f	:23 :461	1:112	Alw 1000	2	1	1hd	12	13	12½	Kurtsinger C	120 w	*.75	96-16	War Admiral1202½Clingendaal1116Airflame1173	In hand 6
10Oct36- 5Lrl	my 6f	:232 :473	1:123	Richard Johnson H 5k	2	2	1hd	2½	22	21½	Kurtsinger C	124 w	*.80	89-23	BottleCap1191½WarAdmiral1248YellowTulp1141½	Closed well 10
19Sep36- 5HdG	fst 6f	:223 :454	1:11	Eastern Shore H 14k	15	1	11½	14	14	15	Kurtsinger C	118 w	7.85	98-12	War Admiral1185Orientalist116hdRex Flag115hd	Easily 15
1Jly36- 5Aqu	fst 6f	:232 :473	1:123	Great American 5.4k	6	3	1hd	1hd	1hd	21½	Kurtsinger C	115 w	2.00	89-15	Fairy Hill1131½War Admiral1152Maedic115½	Weakened 8
6Jun36- 4Bel	fst 5f-WC		:59	National Stallion 16k	6	2		53½	31½	32½	Westrope J	122 w	3.00	82-14	Pompoon1221½Fencing1221War Admiral122hd	Closed gamely 10
21May36- 3Bel	fst 5f-WC		:584	©Alw 900	6	3		1hd	11	12	Westrope J	113 w	10.00	86-18	War Admiral1132Scintillator1135Papenie1161	Going away 8
25Apr36- 1HdG	fst 4½f	:233 :483	:551	Md Sp Wt	9	4		2hd	2½	1no	Peters M	114 w	7.50	89-11	War Admiral114noSonny Joe1141Ground Oak1142½	Hard drive 10

WAR HORSES

THE 1940'S

by David Grening

TWO OF THE MAJOR themes for Thoroughbred racing in the 1940's were established on September 1, 1939. It was the day trainer Ben A. Jones and his son Jimmy went to work for Warren and Lucille Wright's Calumet Farm. On the same day, German armed forces invaded Poland, essentially kicking off World War II.

The merger of the Joneses and the Wrights helped turn Calumet into the dominant stable of the forties. In a decade that spawned four Triple Crown winners, two – Whirlaway in 1941 and Citation in 1948 – wore the devil's-red and blue silks of Calumet. All told, the farm produced nine champion Thoroughbreds in the forties, garnering 19 titles, including five Horse of the Year trophies. In 7 of the 10 seasons, Calumet was the leading money-winning owner, three times topping the $1 million plateau.

Meanwhile, as the war grew in stature – and America's role in it increased – Thoroughbred racing did its part to aid the effort. In addition to contributing millions of dollars to the cause, the country's racetracks were often used by U.S. armed forces during nonracing periods. Toward the end of the war, in 1945, the government shut down racing for four months. The sport had enjoyed a great renaissance until then, and fans came back in droves when racing resumed that May.

Calumet's Whirlaway and John D. Hertz's Count Fleet, the 1943 Triple Crown winner, whetted fans' appetites in the first half of the decade. In the second half, racing enthusiasts were treated to a pair of Triple Crown winners that included Citation, arguably the top Thoroughbred of all time. The bay son of Bull Lea topped Calumet's

Whirlaway was the first of two Triple Crown winners to fly the Calumet Farm colors in the 1940's. The devil's-red and blue silks were atop nine champions during the decade.

amazing run with a 16-race winning streak that began on April 17, 1948, and lasted through January 11, 1950. Despite an injury that sidelined him a year, Citation became the first million-dollar earner in the sport and set a standard for greatness that few, if any, would ever match.

Warren Wright Sr., heir to the Calumet Baking Powder Company, began racing Thoroughbreds in 1932. Unable to achieve his lofty goals with trainers Bert Williams and Frank Kearns, Wright and his wife, Lucille, summoned Ben and Jimmy Jones, who had paired to win the 1938 Kentucky Derby with Lawrin, to the Drake Hotel in Chicago for a breakfast meeting in July 1939.

"'We want to win the Kentucky Derby,'" Jimmy Jones recalled Lucille Wright saying at the beginning of the discussion. "We said, 'We do, too.'"

The Joneses, who had had a falling-out with their primary owner, Herbert Woolf, accepted the Wrights' offer on the spot and went to work on September 1.

Success came swiftly for the new team. On January 10, 1940, opening day at Hialeah, Ben Jones sent out three winners for Calumet. A week later, he had four straight winners, three in major handicaps. Calumet won 75 races in 1940, second only to the 112 of Mrs. Emil Denemark. Calumet's earnings of $148,470 ranked third behind Charles S. Howard and the Greentree Stable of Mrs. Payne Whitney.

Almost half of that amount belonged to a 2-year-old son of Epsom Derby winner Blenheim II, a prolific yet problematic colt named Whirlaway. Overcoming a tendency to bear out in the stretch, Whirlaway won 7 of 16 starts that year, including the Saratoga Special, the Hopeful, and the Breeders' Futurity. He was denied a championship by Woodvale Farm's Our Boots, who only won 3 of 6 starts but finished ahead of Whirlaway 3 of the 4 times they met.

Despite the success of 1940, the Wright-Jones relationship almost did not make it past the next spring.

Whirlaway had finished first and third in two February allowance races to begin his 3-year-old season. Ben Jones, unhappy with the way Whirlaway had been training, decided to skip the Flamingo Stakes and wait for the Tropical Park meet. On March 28, six days after another third-place finish and five weeks before the Kentucky Derby, he entered the colt in a 5 ½-furlong dash. Wright, who was vacationing in the Florida Keys, was surprised to see Whirlaway's name in the entries for so short a race and rushed to Tropical Park to confront the trainer.

"We sat there and argued with the old man until it was too late to scratch him," Jimmy Jones said. "We won that argument. Then the horse, luckily, got up in the last few strides and won his race. Everybody congratulated [Wright]. He got into the spirit of things, shook hands, and said to us, 'I'm going to tell you fellas, I'm never going to bother you again.' But he did."

In Kentucky, Whirlaway's problems persisted. He bore out in the Blue Grass Stakes and was beaten six lengths by Our Boots. He did it again in the Derby Trial, five days before the Kentucky Derby. In a move that exemplified his greatness, Ben Jones saw fit to make an equipment change.

He decided to use a one-eyed blinker, with the cup on the outside, so that the vision in Whirlaway's right eye would be restricted. It would force the colt to rely more on his jockey, giving the rider added control. On the day before the Derby, Jones tested his experiment with Whirlaway's new rider, Eddie Arcaro. Arcaro, although under contract to Greentree, was available to ride Whirlaway because Greentree had no contender that year. Jones instructed Arcaro to blow Whirlaway out through the Churchill Downs stretch, then sat atop his pony and positioned himself 10 feet off the inside rail. He told Arcaro to bring Whirlaway through the opening.

"I had some doubts," Arcaro was quoted as saying. "But if that old man was game enough to sit there and risk me running him over, I was game enough to go through that narrow opening.

Whirlaway handled it perfectly and I felt we had a great shot in the Derby."

The next day, Whirlaway rallied from far back to win the Kentucky Derby by a record eight lengths in a track-record time of 2:01⅖ for 1¼ miles. A week later, he came from last to take the Preakness before whipping three opponents in the June 7 Belmont Stakes to become the sport's fifth Triple Crown winner. Whirlaway won 13 of 20 starts in 1941 and was voted 3-year-old champion and Horse of the Year. Calumet was the country's leading owner with $475,091, a single-season record the stable would shatter three years later.

In 1942, Whirlaway won 12 of 22 starts, including the Massachusetts Handicap on July 15; that victory pushed his earnings to $454,336 and enabled him to surpass Seabiscuit ($437,730) as the sport's all-time leading money winner. He was voted champion handicap horse and repeated as Horse of the Year despite losing 2 of 3 meetings to Albert Sabath's 3-year-old Alsab, who nosed out Whirlaway in a match race at Narragansett Park in Rhode Island. Alsab, who had compiled a 10-race winning streak in 1941 to be named the champion 2-year-old, was voted the top 3-year-old although Shut Out beat him in both the Kentucky Derby and the Belmont.

On June 28, 1943, two days after Whirlaway pulled up sore in the Equipoise Mile, Wright announced the horse's retirement. He finished his career with 32 wins from 60 starts and earnings of $561,161. Within a week, however, it was clear that Calumet's domination was not about to stop. On June 30, Mar-Kell won her eighth race of the season, the Cinderella Handicap, en route to being named that year's champion handicap mare. Still, there was an even more talented filly in the barn.

Twilight Tear, who won 4 of 6 starts as a 2-year-old in 1943, won 11 consecutive races from March 10 through July 22, 1944, and became the first filly to be awarded Horse of the Year honors. (Busher, owned by Col. Edward R. Bradley's Idle Hour Stock Farm, duplicated the feat the next year.) Her streak culminated with a victory in the Arlington Classic, in which she beat four colts. Among them was her stablemate Pensive, who had given Calumet its second Kentucky Derby trophy earlier that year.

All in all, Twilight Tear won 14 of 17 starts in 1944, highlighted by a six-length victory against two colts in the Pimlico Special. She was beset by bleeding problems throughout her career, according to Jimmy Jones, and when she bled in an allowance race at Washington Park in August 1945, she was retired.

Twilight Tear was among the first crop of Bull Lea, who went on to sire seven Calumet champions of the decade. Bull Lea was purchased by Warren Wright for $14,000 at the Saratoga yearling sales of 1936. Many bidders stayed away from the colt because of his four white feet, which, in those days, were deemed to be a bad sign. Bull Lea went on to bank more than $90,000 and was the leading sire in 5 of the 7 years from 1947 through 1953.

In addition to Twilight Tear, Bull Lea's first crop included a dynamo named Armed. Bad ankles sidelined him as a 2-year-old, and his ornery behavior forced his castration before he ever raced. At one point, Calumet made him a lead pony. But

Twilight Tear won 11 straight races in 1944 en route to becoming the first filly to be voted Horse of the Year.

after a while, he shed his nasty disposition and developed into a champion.

Armed had an unspectacular 3-year-old season, winning 3 of 7 outings. In 1945, he came to hand, winning 10 of 15 starts, but only three stakes. Meanwhile, Mrs. Ethel D. Jacobs's Stymie won eight stakes and outpolled Armed for top handicap horse honors.

Stymie and Armed began a two-year rivalry in 1946, with the Calumet runner defeating Stymie twice. On May 30, a crowd of 60,631 – then a New York record – watched Armed, under 130 pounds and spotting Stymie seven, win the Suburban Handicap decisively. Armed won 11 of 18 starts that year and was voted top handicap horse. The Horse of the Year, however, was Assault, the 3-year-old who had swept the Triple Crown.

Armed returned in 1947 and not only captured his second handicap division title, but also was named Horse of the Year. He won 11 of 17 starts, set two track records, and finished worse than third only once – in the Santa Anita Handicap, when he was flown cross-country from Florida and may not have overcome the trip. The brown gelding, who carried a minimum of 130 pounds in 21 of 35 races over his two championship seasons, proved durable enough to race until the age of 9. His career, which ended on a winning note in an allowance race at Gulfstream, concluded with a record of 41-20-10 from 81 starts and career earnings of $817,475.

The great handicap champion Armed blossomed as a 4-year-old, winning 10 of 15 races. He would go on to win consecutive handicap titles in 1946 and 1947.

"He was probably the best handicap horse of his time," Jimmy Jones said. "But, he wasn't a great horse. To be great, you got to be able to do everything great. Armed couldn't handle off tracks, for instance."

While Armed ruled the handicap ranks in 1947, Calumet had a dynamic pair of 2-year-olds to dominate their respective divisions. A filly named Bewitch and a colt named Citation would be awarded championships as Calumet won 100 races and earned $1,402,436, a mark that stood for 22 years.

Citation was 5 for 5 and Bewitch was 7 for 7 when the two met in the Washington Park Futurity on August 16. Free America, another Calumet colt, was 3 for 4, and the three-ply entry was 1-5 at the windows. Bewitch used her dazzling speed to win by a length, although many believe that had jockey Steve Brooks so desired, he could have gotten Citation home. Free America finished third.

"I told the riders we would split the jocks' fee three ways; whoever is in front, leave them alone," Jones related. "I didn't want them to be beating up these horses. Each of the losing riders said, 'If I could have hit my horse a time or two I would have won.'"

Citation defeated Bewitch in Belmont's Futurity and finished his season with a three-length romp in the Pimlico Futurity. He was a unanimous choice for champion 2-year-old colt. Citation, who was primarily trained by Jimmy Jones, began his 3-year-old career by defeating older horses in his first start. Among his victims in the six-furlong race was Armed, whom he would beat again in the Seminole Handicap nine days later.

Returning to his own division, Citation won two more races, the Everglades and the Flamingo, as he competed four times in 26 days during February. After his victory in the Flamingo, Wright was offered $250,000 for Citation. Upon hearing of the offer, Jimmy Jones was quoted as saying, "Whoever buys this horse has got to buy me too, because I'm going with him."

Citation lost his regular jockey in March when Albert Snider drowned while fishing in the Florida Keys. Jones said Snider "fit Citation better than anybody." Eddie Arcaro, who became Citation's rider, lost the first time he rode him when they were carried wide in the Chesapeake Trial at Havre de Grace and finished second to a colt called Saggy. Citation proved the result a fluke five days later when he beat Saggy by $15\frac{1}{2}$ lengths in the Chesapeake Stakes. Thus began the bay colt's 16-race winning streak, which of course included the 1948 Triple Crown.

In the Derby, Citation followed stablemate Coaltown until the stretch, when Arcaro began a steady hand ride that propelled him past Coaltown and on to a $3\frac{1}{2}$-length victory. Two weeks later, against only three rivals in the Preakness, Citation went wire to wire, winning by $5\frac{1}{2}$ lengths. In need of activity before the Belmont, he set a track record winning the Jersey Stakes at Garden State in a track record of 2:03 for 10 furlongs.

Then came the Belmont. A slight stumble at the start provided the lone anxious moment as Citation again went gate to wire, winning by eight lengths in a gallop that was only three-fifths of a second off the track record. He missed some of the summer with a strained back, but went on to win nine more races that year, including the Jockey Club Gold Cup, which he won under double wraps.

"Truly the best one we ever had," Jimmy Jones said. "I never saw a better one."

His last race of 1948 was the $1\frac{1}{4}$-mile Tanforan Handicap at Tanforan Park in San Francisco. Jimmy Jones was not keen on running Citation there, but was doing a friend a favor. Eugene Mori had taken over the track and wanted to turn San Francisco into a racing center, and there was no better way to do that than have the sport's brightest star shine on your racetrack.

Citation romped in a six-furlong prep on December 3; eight days later, he treated 24,809 fans to a track record of $2{:}02\frac{4}{5}$ in his five-length victory in the Tanforan Handicap, but the race proved to be his undoing. According to Jones, there was concrete on the bottom of the racing strip and Citation injured his ankle. He would never be the same. In the winter of 1949, over Jones's objection, Wright had a veterinarian pin-fire the ankle. It didn't help. Citation would not race that year, and when he came back, he was a mere shell of his former self. While he did win his first start back – his 16th victory in a row – he would only take one of his next 12. Of course, the lone triumph was spectacular, as he set a world record of $1{:}33\frac{3}{5}$ in the Golden Gate Mile.

Determined to make Citation the first equine millionaire, Wright, whose health was failing, opted to keep him in training. The owner died on December 28, 1950, but the quest continued under the direction of his widow, and seven months later Citation topped the million-dollar mark by winning the Hollywood Gold Cup. He promptly was retired with earnings of $1,085,760.

"He would have been better off if he had never run in those races in California," Jones said. "He should never be judged on his races after that injury."

While Citation did not race in 1949, it hardly prevented Calumet from maintaining its status as the nation's leading money-winning owner; the stable had another talented Bull Lea colt in Coaltown, who might have been every bit as good as Citation if not for wind problems.

After living in Citation's shadow during his 3-year-old campaign, Coaltown established his own greatness in 1949 by winning 12 of 15 starts and setting a world record of 1:34 in the one-mile Whirlaway Stakes at Washington Park. While he was not good enough to handle the 3-year-old champion, Capot, he was still named the top handicap horse.

In fact, Calumet ended 1949 with four champions, as Bewitch was named top handicap mare and Two Lea and Wistful shared 3-year-old filly honors.

As the 1940's began, racing was flourishing, with new highs for attendance and handle being established on a regular basis. One of the most signifi-

Considered by some to be the greatest Thoroughbred of all time, Citation had a long list of accomplishments, including winning the Triple Crown in 1948, going a record 16 straight races without defeat, and becoming the first horse to earn $1 million.

cant developments of the decade came at the outset, when New York legalized parimutuel wagering and more than $100,000,000 was bet during that first year, far exceeding expectations. Record crowds were going to Jamaica and Belmont, and records were also being set at tracks in Maryland and Florida.

If World War II threatened to end that prosperity, racing did its best not to let that happen. In March 1942, four months after the bombing of Pearl Harbor resulted in the United States' complete participation in the war, the Thoroughbred Racing Associations was formed "for purpose of aiding government financially and in other ways." From that association, the Turf Committee of America was born, and under the leadership of New York Racing Commissioner Herbert Bayard Swope, a plan for racing to help the war-relief effort was devised.

A goal of $2 million was established, to be obtained in three ways. First, each track would donate a percentage of its profits for certain racing periods. Second, there would be days at each meet when all profits would go to the fund. Third, a self-imposed assessment on per capita attendance would be donated.

Racing contributed $3.19 million to the war effort in 1942 and surpassed that with more than $5 million in 1943. On October 2, 1943, Belmont Park hosted a "Back the Attack" day, with admission to the grandstand by purchase of a $25 war bond, or a $100 bond for clubhouse admission. An estimated $25,000,000 in bonds were sold. Such a response evoked a telegram of praise and appreciation from Henry Morgenthau, secretary of the treasury.

The U.S. armed forces took over several racetracks, including Hialeah, Fair Grounds, and Santa Anita, for varying war-related purposes. Santa Anita was used as an ordnance school, and later as a processing facility for local Japanese Americans, who were then sent to more permanent internment camps. Stalls served as actual living quarters. Tanforan Park, in San Francisco, was used by the Navy as a training base.

Race meetings were consolidated – and in some cases, canceled – as a way to conserve gas and rubber products. The 1943 Arlington meet was held at Washington Park. Belmont Park hosted the Saratoga meet for three years from 1943-45. Ak-Sar-Ben canceled its meeting in order not to interfere with the Army's operations at Ak-Sar-Ben Field.

In 1944, with racetracks still prospering, the sport contributed more than $8 million to the war-relief effort. However, in December, James F. Byrnes, director of War Mobilization and Reconversion, issued a request that racing cease by January 3, 1945. Tropical Park and Fair Grounds, the only tracks in operation at the time, put an end to their meetings. Racing was shut down for more than four months.

On May 12, action resumed at Narragansett Park in Rhode Island and Sportsman's Park in Illinois. Santa Anita, which had not raced since late 1941, opened on May 15 and offered free admission to those who purchased war bonds. On May 30, the track welcomed a record crowd of 76,649. New marks were also established at Jamaica (64,537) and Delaware Park (28,000) that day.

The Triple Crown was run in three successive weeks, with Fred Hooper's Hoop Jr. winning the Kentucky Derby on June 9, Mrs. P. A. B. Widener's Polynesian winning the Preakness on June 16, and Walter Jeffords's Pavot taking the Belmont on June 23.

That fall, with fans still purchasing millions of dollars of war bonds, racing showed it had recovered from the war when in September, Belmont Park established a world record in parimutuel wagering as $5,016,745 was bet on an eight-race card. A single-race record of $763,127 was wagered on the nightcap.

In 1942, the United States initiated a gasoline-rationing program that meant fans could only attend races by streetcar or horse-drawn vehicles. That didn't stop them from coming out to the track, especially on the occasions when Count Fleet raced.

Count Fleet's career only lasted 370 days – from June 1, 1942, through June 5, 1943 – but what a glorious 370 days they were. Never off the board in 21 career starts, the John Hertz-bred and -owned colt won 10 of 15 races as a 2-year-old en route to a divisional title.

Amazingly, Hertz, the rental-car and Yellow Cab magnate, almost sold the son of Reigh Count for $4,500 because of his difficult temperament. Jockey Johnny Longden convinced the owner not to sell. "The colt is dangerous," Hertz said. "I'm afraid he'll do you serious injury." Longden replied, "I'm not afraid of him." Satisfied, Hertz decided to keep Count Fleet.

By the fall of that year, Hertz was glad he had. In late September, while preparing for the Futurity at Belmont, the colt worked six furlongs in 1:08 ⅕, a full second faster than the track record. He would finish third in the Futurity.

Count Fleet made amends a week later with a six-length victory in the Champagne Stakes. He covered a mile in 1:34 ⅘, a world record for a 2-year-old. His stakes record would last for 34 years. After closing out his season with three more dominant victories, Count Fleet was assigned top weight of 132 pounds on the Experimental Free Handicap, still the highest assignment since the handicap's debut in 1933.

With Tropical Park ending its 1943 race meeting on January 8 to aid the government's gasoline-conservation plan, Count Fleet was sent to Oaklawn Park instead, where he trained for six weeks, and then on to Belmont. Trainer Don Cameron did not bring Count Fleet to the races for his 3-year-old

Triple Crown winner Count Fleet was almost sold by owner John D. Hertz for $4,500. The Reigh Count colt would win 16 of 21 starts, including a then-record 25-length victory in the Belmont, the final race of his career.

debut until April 13, when he won an allowance race at Jamaica that served as a prep for the Wood Memorial. He then took the Wood four days later, slicing two seconds off the stakes record, but came out of the race with a gash in his left hind leg and was pulled up bleeding.

Cameron had two weeks to work on the injury, and by the first Saturday in May, Count Fleet was ready to go. Despite the transportation restrictions, a crowd of 61,700 fans showed up at Churchill Downs for what was dubbed the Streetcar Derby. They got what they came for as Count Fleet, at odds of 1-2, soared to a three-length victory. A week later, against only three rivals, he galloped to an eight-length score in the Preakness. With a month before the Belmont, Cameron opted to run Count Fleet in the Withers, and he whipped two opponents by five lengths.

As expected, the Belmont turned into a coronation for Count Fleet. Before a crowd of 19,290, he beat only two rivals by 25 lengths in stakes-record time of 2:28⅕ to become racing's sixth Triple Crown winner. Unfortunately, he came out of the race with an ankle injury. Eventually, Cameron would announce that the tendon was affected as well, and Count Fleet would never race again.

Assault overcame numerous physical problems to win the Triple Crown in 1946 and went on to have a solid season as a handicapper in 1947.

"He was the best horse I ever rode," Longden said. "The best horse I ever saw."

On August 6, 1945, the day the United States dropped an atomic bomb on Hiroshima, Japan, a chestnut colt named Assault burst on the scene with a nose victory at 70-1 in the Flash Stakes, the opening-day feature at the Saratoga-at-Belmont meeting. It was one of only two victories that Assault, the King Ranch-bred and -owned son of 1936 Kentucky Derby and Preakness winner Bold Venture, tallied in his 2-year-old season.

Assault was a colt whose will to win helped him overcome myriad physical problems. As a weanling at Robert J. Kleberg Jr.'s King Ranch in Texas, he stepped on a sharp object that pierced his right front foot. As a result, he developed an unorthodox gait, which made him quite difficult to train. Max Hirsch, who had also handled Bold Venture, once said, "I didn't think he'd train at all. But, he's never shown any sign that it hurts him. When he walks or trots, you'd think he was going to fall down. I think that while the foot still hurt him, he got in the habit of protecting it with an awkward gait, and now he keeps it up. But he gallops true. There isn't a thing wrong with his action when he goes fast."

Assault, whose other injuries included several splints, an unreliable knee, and a wrenched ankle, did not make his 3-year-old debut until April 9, when he won the six-furlong Experimental Handicap at Jamaica. Eleven days later, against a strong headwind that caused some horses trouble, Assault scored by 2¼ lengths in the Wood Memorial. A muddy track may have compromised him when he finished a nonthreatening fourth in the Derby Trial at Churchill on April 30.

Four days later, Assault bounced back and roared to an eight-length victory in the Kentucky Derby. A premature move by jockey Warren Mehrtens nearly cost the colt the Preakness, a race he won by a neck over the traffic-troubled, late-closing Lord Boswell. The Belmont, in which Lord Boswell was favored, was not nearly so close, as Assault bounded clear to a three-length victory over Natchez.

In the fall of his 3-year-old season, after being sidelined for six weeks, Assault met up with another of the walking wounded – Stymie, who at one time was owned by King Ranch. The two began a prolonged rivalry that lasted for the next two years. In 1946, Stymie beat Assault in 2 of 3 meetings. The next year, Assault defeated Stymie 4 of 5 times.

One of those races in 1947 was the Butler Handicap at Jamaica. Assault, who was 4 for 4 for the year and had a six-race winning streak dating back to November 9, 1946, was assigned 135 pounds by racing secretary John Campbell. He was conceding nine pounds to Stymie and 18 to Gallorette, the 1946 champion handicap mare. Assault, who by this time was being ridden by Eddie Arcaro, was moving into contention when Arcaro was forced to take up to avoid a tiring Risolator. Turning for home, Assault was last. In the stretch, Arcaro had him running again, but he was knocked off stride and back to last with a furlong to go. Somehow, he managed a third run, squeezed through horses, and defeated Stymie by a head.

Eleven years later, *Daily Racing Form* columnist Leon Rasmussen wrote, "When a lightly weighted horse gets thrown off stride, it's not too difficult for his rider to get him going again, but when it happens to a highweight, only a superior horse can answer the extra demand successfully. Therefore, when the talk turns to great races, Assault's Butler in 1947 receives my award for the best individual performance by a horse in my time."

With as many ailments as Assault had, it was remarkable that he lasted as long as he did, finally retiring after making three starts in late 1950 off a year layoff. He retired with 18 wins from 42 races and earnings of $675,470. "He was always crippled, and a horse with less determination would have quit," said King Ranch veterinarian Dr. James Northway.

Even in retirement, Assault had physical problems. He was sterile and was never able to produce any offspring. He died at the age of 28 on September 1, 1971.

"I never trained a better horse," said Max Hirsch.

While Stymie was almost as good, it certainly wasn't apparent from the beginning. Few horses were as durable as this one, who raced 131 times in a seven-year career that saw him go from frog to Prince Charming.

Hirsch had turned Stymie's dam, Stop Watch, over to King Ranch, but had not completed the necessary paperwork by the time the foal arrived in 1941, so he was officially credited with being the breeder of the colt. Stymie had a nasty disposition as a young horse and it obviously affected his ability. He had not shown much to his trainer, who put Stymie in claiming races in 2 of his first 3 starts.

On June 2, 1943, Hirsch Jacobs – the leading trainer in number of races won for 9 of the previous 10 years – put in a claim slip and took Stymie for $1,500 for his wife, Ethel. The son of Equestrian needed 10 more tries to finally find the winner's circle. Through his first two years of racing, Stymie had won just 7 of 50 starts, not one of them a stakes event. Thanks mainly to the government's ban on racing in early 1945, Stymie went nearly seven months between his 3-year-old finale and his 4-year-old debut. The rest appeared to do him a world of good.

A rejuvenated Stymie won his first stakes on June 2, 1945, taking the Grey Lag Handicap at Jamaica. He would go on to win seven more stakes that year en route to being named champion handicap horse. Stymie excelled as a 5-year-old as well, winning 8 of 20 starts and finishing out of the money only once. He equaled the track record for nine furlongs at Jamaica and set a track mark for 1⅝ miles there that same season.

In 1947, Stymie won seven stakes races and kept alternating with Assault as the all-time leading money-winning Thoroughbred. Although Assault had his number, defeating him in 4 of 5 meetings, Stymie would finish the year as the leading money earner after winning the Gallant Fox Handicap in October.

In July 1948, Stymie fractured a sesamoid at Monmouth Park with his bankroll at $911,335, the highest of any Thoroughbred. His connections tried to make him the first million-dollar earner, but after five starts in the fall of 1949, it was evident it was not going to happen. He retired with $918,485 in earnings, a figure that would be eclipsed by Citation 15 months later.

The working-class hero Stymie was claimed for $1,500 by Hall of Fame trainer Hirsch Jacobs. At the time of his retirement he was the richest Thoroughbred ever.

In many respects, Stymie may have embodied the sport better than any horse of the decade. A warrior with the utmost courage, Stymie overcame a number of obstacles and not only succeeded, but also flourished. His career interrupted by the war-related ban on racing, Stymie was much better in the second half of the decade than he was in the first.

And despite fears to the contrary, so was racing. Having drawn fans in record numbers – buoyed by the exploits of wartime Triple Crown winners Whirlaway and Count Fleet – racing not only survived, but also prospered following the four-month government shutdown in 1945. Tracks throughout the country continued to boom during the last half of the decade. The success of Calumet Farm, as well as that of King Ranch, helped give full flight to the big-stable era and sent racing into the 1950's as the true Sport of Kings.

CHAMPIONS

PAST PERFORMANCES

THE 1940'S

Year by Year Champions

•1940•
•2-Year-Old Male *Our Boots* •2-Year-Old Filly *Level Best* •3-Year-Old Male *Bimelech*
•Handicap Horse *Challedon* •Handicap Mare *War Plumage*
•**HORSE OF THE YEAR** Challedon

•1941•
•2-Year-Old Male *Alsab* •2-Year-Old Filly *Petrify* •3-Year-Old Male *Whirlaway*
•3-Year-Old Filly *Painted Veil* •Handicap Horse *Mioland* •Handicap Mare *Fairy Chant*
•Steeplechase *Speculate*
•**HORSE OF THE YEAR** Whirlaway

•1942•
•2-Year-Old Male *Count Fleet* •2-Year-Old Filly *Ask Me Now* •3-Year-Old Male *Alsab*
•3-Year-Old Filly *Vagrancy* •Handicap Horse *Whirlaway* •Handicap Mare *Vagrancy* •Steeplechase *Elkridge*
•**HORSE OF THE YEAR** Whirlaway

•1943•
•2-Year-Old Male *Platter* •2-Year-Old Filly *Duranza* •3-Year-Old Male *Count Fleet*
•3-Year-Old Filly *Stefanita* •Handicap Horse *Market Wise, Devil Diver* •Handicap Mare *Mar-Kell*
•Steeplechase *Brother Jones*
•**HORSE OF THE YEAR** Count Fleet

•1944•
•2-Year-Old Male *Pavot* •2-Year-Old Filly *Busher* •3-Year-Old Male *By Jimminy*
•3-Year-Old Filly *Twilight Tear* •Handicap Horse *Devil Diver* •Handicap Mare *Twilight Tear*
•Steeplechase *Rouge Dragon*
•**HORSE OF THE YEAR** Twilight Tear

•1945•
•2-Year-Old Male *Star Pilot* •2-Year-Old Filly *Beaugay* •3-Year-Old Male *Fighting Step*
•3-Year-Old Filly *Busher* •Handicap Horse *Stymie* •Handicap Mare *Busher* •Steeplechase *Mercator*
•**HORSE OF THE YEAR** Busher

•1946•
•2-Year-Old Male *Double Jay* •2-Year-Old Filly *First Flight* •3-Year-Old Male *Assault*
•3-Year-Old Filly *Bridal Flower* •Handicap Horse *Armed* •Handicap Mare *Gallorette* •Steeplechase *Elkridge*
•**HORSE OF THE YEAR** Assault

•1947•
•2-Year-Old Male *Citation* •2-Year-Old Filly *Bewitch* •3-Year-Old Male *Phalanx*
•3-Year-Old Filly *But Why Not* •Handicap Horse *Armed* •Handicap Mare *But Why Not*
•Sprinter *Polynesian* •Steeplechase *War Battle*
•**HORSE OF THE YEAR** Armed

•1948•
•2-Year-Old Male *Blue Peter* •2-Year-Old Filly *Myrtle Charm* •3-Year-Old Male *Citation*
•3-Year-Old Filly *Miss Request* •Handicap Horse *Citation* •Handicap Mare *Conniver*
•Sprinter *Coaltown* •Steeplechase *American Way*
•**HORSE OF THE YEAR** Citation

•1949•
•2-Year-Old Male *Hill Prince* •2-Year-Old Filly *Bed o' Roses* •3-Year-Old Male *Capot*
•3-Year-Old Filly *Two Lea, Wistful* •Handicap Horse *Coaltown* •Handicap Mare *Bewitch*
•Sprinter *Delegate, Royal Governor* •Steeplechase *Trough Hill*
•**HORSE OF THE YEAR** Capot

Alsab

b. c. 1939, by Good Goods (Neddie)–Winds Chant, by Wildair **Lifetime record: 51 25 11 5 $350,015**

Own.– Mrs A. Sabath
Br.– Thomas Piatt (Ky)
Tr.– A. Swenke

13May44- 5Bel	fst 6f	:222 :453 1:103 3↑	Handicap 4085	6 6 67¼ 78¼ 57 44½	Haas L	126wb	11.80	92-10	Bossut1164Adultr112noShtOut132½	Finished well,pulled up sore	7
13Nov43- 6Pim	fst 1 3/16	:484 1:141 1:402 2:00 3↑	Bryan & O'Hara H 19k	6 3 77¾ 77¾ 51½ 2nk	Woolf G	122wb	*1.10	82-31	Stefanita117nkAlsab1223Son of Peace1131	Fast finish	9
8Nov43- 8Pim	sly 1 1/16	:241 :494 1:161 1:494 3↑	Alw 2000	1 2 31 52½ 2nk 13	Woolf G	122wb	*2.30	69-28	Alsab1223Abrasion1172Rascal110nk	In hand late	7
30Oct43- 8Pim	sl 6f	:224 :463 1:13 3↑	Alw 3500	4 9 912 917 915 815¼	Woolf G	123 w	7.15	73-27	QuienEs1162½ReapngGlory107nkPompon113hd	Showed nothing	9
14Aug43- 6Nar	sl 1 1/16	:254 :49 1:14 1:464 3↑	King Philip H 6.5k	6 11 119¾ 77¾ 68¾ 47½	Woolf G	126wb	*.60	75-26	Some Chance1102Eire1042½Air Master1043	No threat	11
9Aug43- 6Nar	fst 6f	:23 :462 1:111 3↑	Pawtucket H 6k	8 7 87 85¼ 63¾ 32¾	Woolf G	124wb	*3.80	92-13	Cherrydale1092½ValdinaAlph115nkAlsb124½	Rapid late gain	8
11Nov42- 5Bel	fst 1¼	:474 1:121 1:372 2:021 3↑	Handicap 10350	2 6 77 52 3nk 1¾	Woolf G	126wb	*.75	89-16	Alsab126¾Boysy113½Bon Jour1022	Pulled up lame	7
31Oct42- 5Emp	fst 1 3/16	:484 1:122 1:374 1:562 3↑	Westchester H 28k	1 4 814 714 55¼ 3nk	Bierman C	124wb	*1.15	98-07	Rvrlnd114nkTolRos108noAlsb1241½	Inside,finished fastest	8
21Oct42- 5Jam	fst 1⅝	:501 1:41 2:06 2:441 3↑	Gallant Fox H 16k	3 4 45 35 21½ 21	Bierman C	124wb	*1.05	93-13	DarkDiscovery1001Alsab1241½Mrrg1215	Wearing down winner	6
10Oct42- 6Bel	fst 2¼	:49 2:292 2:542 3:471 3↑	New York H 30k	10 5 711 31 2hd 1hd	Bierman C	121wb	4.25	99-07	Alsab121hdObash1061¼Whirlaway1305	Driving	12
3Oct42- 6Bel	fst 2	:523 2:32 2:562 3:213 3↑	J C Gold Cup 27k	1 2 2½ 1hd 11½ 2¾	Bierman C	117wb	2.80	95-05	Whirlaway124¾Alsab1178Bolingbroke12415	2nd best	4

Geldings not eligible

29Sep42- 7Bel	fst 1⅝	:484 1:393 2:043 2:42	Lawrence Realizatn 11k	2 2 59 54½ 3¾ 13½	Woolf G	126wb	*.25	94-08	Alsab1263½Vagrancy1153Trrrch110nk	Blocked str,drew away	5
19Sep42- 7Nar	fst 1 3/16	:502 1:141 1:383 1:562 3↑	Match Race 25k	2 1 11½ 12 11 1no	Bierman C	119wb	1.60	93-11	Alsab119noWhirlaway126	Just enough	2
7Sep42- 7Was	fst 1¼	:47 1:11 1:36 2:022 3↑	Wash Park H 32k	6 3 815 63¾ 41¼ 21	Robertson A	121wb	*.90	97-11	Mrrg1141Alsb121nkThumbsUp102nk	Wide,bearing in str,gamely	9
29Aug42- 7Was	sl 1¼	:481 1:132 1:393 2:063	American Derby 78k	4 2 513 53½ 11½ 13½	Woolf G	126wb	*.70	77-25	Alsab1263½With Regards1211½Anticlimax1212	Saved ground	7
20Aug42- 6Was	fst 1	:231 :464 1:113 1:361	Dick Welles H 5.3k	5 3 32½ 3nk 1hd 1½	Woolf G	128wb	*.60	97-12	Alsb128½Kng'sAbby1125SomMn1002½	Lost ground,ridden out	6
15Aug42- 7Was	fst 7f	:223 :454 1:111 1:241 3↑	Handicap 3500	1 7 77¼ 65¼ 2hd 1½	Richard J	120wb	3.40	95-12	Alsab120½Sales Talk1016Air Master111½	Carried out	7
8Aug42- 5Was	fst 6f	:224 :454 1:11 3↑	Handicap 2500	5 3 55 67 43½ 43½	James B	120wb	*1.90	92-15	Defense1081½Sales Talk1061½Woof Woof117¾	Outrun	6
6Jun42- 6Bel	fst 1½	:481 1:123 2:031 2:291	Belmont 53k	1 1 55¼ 21 21½ 22	James B	126wb	*.40	94-09	Shut Out1262Alsab1264Lochinvar1266	No late gain	7

Geldings not eligible

23May42- 6Bel	fst 1	:231 :461 1:11 1:361	Withers 20k	4 7 75¾ 42¾ 1½ 12½	James B	126wb	*.75	94-08	Alsab1262½Lochinvar126noFairaris126½	Easily	9

Geldings not eligible

9May42- 6Pim	fst 1 3/16	:47 1:112 1:371 1:57	Preakness 75k	8 7 97¾ 94¼ 32½ 11	James B	126wb	*2.05	98-06	Alsab1261[DH]Requested126[DH]Sun Again126¾	Driving	10
2May42- 7CD	fst 1¼	:472 1:123 1:39 2:042	Ky Derby 76k	7 5 1011 42½ 42½ 22¼	James B	126wb	5.10	83-09	Shut Out1262¼Alsab126hdValdina Orphan1261½	Just up	15
28Apr42- 4CD	fst 1	:233 :47 1:123 1:364	Derby Trial 3.1k	7 8 65½ 45½ 33 33¾	James B	118wb	*1.60	91-16	Valdina Orphan111nkSun Again1183½Alsab1182½	No rally	8

Worked out nine furlongs in 1:54

18Apr42- 6HdG	fst 1 1/16	:234 :481 1:132 1:463	Chesapeake 18k	3 10 97½ 87¾ 32½ 21	James B	122wb	*.95	84-18	Colchis1161Alsab1221½Requested119hd	Gamely	11
13Apr42- 5HdG	fst 6f	:23 :464 1:122	Chesapeake Trial 3.7k	3 6 69 68¼ 64¼ 2½	Schmidl A	126wb	2.05	90-15	Colchis118½Alsab126½Seamanlike114hd	Away slowly	6
7Mar42- 6Hia	fst 1¼	:47 1:122 1:374 2:051 3↑	Widener H 67k	7 12 88½ 52½ 4¾ 51½	Thompson B	109wb	7.85	81-17	The Rhymer111hdBest Seller112hdOlympus107nk	Hung	17
28Feb42- 6Hia	fst 1⅛	:464 1:12 1:374 1:502	Flamingo 35k	3 10 98¾ 54½ 44 38	Vedder RL	126wb	3.40	81-14	Requested1224Redthorn1164Alsab1263	Outside	16
14Feb42- 4Hia	fst 1	:232 :463 1:104 1:363	Alw 1500	6 6 59 46½ 46½ 46¼	Arcaro E	126wb	*.75	- -	BrightWillie1183SirWar1141¾Incoming1021½	Slow late gain	6
7Feb42- 6Hia	fst 7f	:232 :464 1:114 1:243	Bahamas H 6.2k	9 8 99 95¼ 74¾ 65¼	McCreary C	128wb	*.65	84-13	AmericanWolf1144FirstFiddle115noFggrtout114hd	Wide turn	10
12Nov41- 6Pim	fst 1 1/16	:23 :464 1:11 1:443	Walden 10k	5 2 2hd 2hd 11½ 1nk	Vedder RL	122wb	*.10	97-12	Alsab122nkBlessMe1131¼FairCall1161½	Tired,just held on	6
18Oct41- 5Lrl	fst 1 1/16	:234 :482 1:132 1:454	S Lowe Jenkins 7k	3 3 32 1nk 12 14¼	Vedder RL	124wb	*.10	88-16	Alsab1244¼Colchis1183Sweep Swinger1154	Easily	4
4Oct41- 5Bel	gd 1	:231 :46 1:104 1:352	Champagne 13k	6 4 31½ 2hd 13 17	Bierman C	122wb	*.60	98-11	Alsab1227Requested1162½Flaught110nk	Blocked ½ pole	7
23Sep41- 4Bel	fst 6½f	:231 :462 1:094 1:16	Match Race 10k	2 2 21 21 11½ 13½	Vedder RL	122wb	.85	106-07	Alsab1223½Requested122	Ridden out	2
13Sep41- 6HdG	fst 6f	:224 :462 1:123	Eastern Shore H 13k	7 8 83½ 65½ 32½ 13¼	Vedder RL	126wb	*.60	90-18	[DH]Alsab126[DH]Colchis1173Flaught106½	Fast finish	10
6Sep41- 6Was	gd 6f	:223 :463 1:12	Prairie State 5.8k	6 4 42½ 3nk 12 13¼	Vedder RL	126wb	*.30	91-20	Alsab1263¼MissDogwood1143FirstofAll1171	Speed to spare	6
16Aug41- 6Was	fst 6f	:223 :463 1:11	Wash Park Futurity 42k	2 1 41½ 31½ 1hd 1¾	Vedder RL	119wb	*.50	96-10	Alsab119¾Contradiction1172Valdina Orphan1172½	Handily	9
9Aug41- 5Was	fst 5½f	:221 :453 :582 1:05	Wash Park Juvenile 3.2k	5 7 97¼ 72½ 1hd 1¾	Vedder RL	126wb	*.50	100-07	Alsab126¾Valdina Orphan1171Questvive1141	Driving	11
31Jly41- 6AP	gd 6f	:232 :472 1:124	Hyde Park 6.5k	3 3 41½ 1hd 15 15	Vedder RL	122wb	*.40	83-21	Alsab1225Sweep Swinger117hdValdina Orphan1174	Easily	9
19Jly41- 7Suf	fst 5½f	:23 :46 :582 1:051	Mayflower 21k	6 1 43¼ 31½ 11 12¼	Vedder RL	119wb	*.60	100-11	Alsab1192¼Syl's Jimmy110¾Eternal Bull119¾	handily	7
5Jly41- 7Suf	fst 5f	:22 :453 :583	©Miles Standish 10k	8 8 84¾ 65¼ 43½ 2½	Vedder RL	119wb	*1.00	100-09	Eternal Bull114½Alsab1192¾Bold Question117no		8

Away slowly,getting to winner

25Jun41- 6AP	fst 5½f	:223 :463 :583 1:044	Primer 3.5k	3 5 74¼ 43 1hd 17	Vedder RL	122wb	*1.20	97-12	Alsab1227Valdina Orphan1172Memphis114no		12

Outrun early,speed in reserve

31May41- 6LF	sl 5f	:231 :474 1:01	Joliet 6.5k	4 6 99 69 41½ 15	Pool E	122wb	3.90	90-24	Alsab1225Kirwin122hdValdina Orphan122hd	Blocked	13
21May41- 4LF	fst 5f	:23 :463 1:00	Alw 1010	6 4 56½ 57½ 43½ 2½	Craig A	115 w	*1.50	94-25	Valdina Alpha111½Alsab115nkOmathon1131½	Belated rally	6
10May41- 4CD	fst 5f	:231 :461 :592	Alw 1000	6 6 31½ 22 1½ 12½	Thompson B	110 w	*1.10	98-12	Alsab1102½Alohort1113Bayridge1113	Wide,drifted out	6
8May41- 5CD	sl 4½f	:232 :472 :541	Alw 1000	5 5 43½ 31½ 2no	Thompson B	113 w	2.70	91-12	Omathon112noAlszb1133½Famed1096		5

Slow start,impeded by winner

2May41- 6CD	fst 5f	:223 :463 :593	©Bashford Manor 3.5k	9 6 75¼ 710 46½ 42¾	Marinelli J	122 w	9.70	94-11	Black Raider1271½Omathon1221¼Bayridge117no		10

Lost ground turn,good finish

18Apr41- 5Kee	sl *4f	:47	[R]Sp Wt 1500	6 1 2½ 11½ 12	Marinelli J	115 w	5.50	95-06	Alsab1152Some Chance1153Topnard115½	Speed in reserve	8
8Apr41- 4TrP	gd 4f	:232 :471	Alw 1000	10 10 41½ 73 42	Howell R	116 w	4.35	92-06	MissShopper103½SonIslm1111½Drwby116hd	Wide,gradual gain	10
28Mar41- 1TrP	fst 4f	:233 :472	©Md Sp Wt	1 3 31½ 32½ 11	Howell R	116 w	4.60	93-07	Alsab1161Scotch Broth1161½Ask Me1161	Saved ground	12
21Mar41- 1TrP	sly 4f	:232 :481	©Md Sp Wt	6 9 98 77 31½	Howell R	116 w	74.45	87-11	Patriot116hdAlohort1161½Alsab116hd	Finished fastest	9
25Feb41- 1Hia	sly 3f	:222 :332	©Md Sp Wt	1 13 1419 1415¼	Bodiou A	118 w	72.85	- -	Scotland Light1181Methodical118½Requested118½	Outrun	14

American Way

b. g. 1942, by Gino (Tetratema)–Sunchance, by Chance Shot **Lifetime record: 45 12 10 7 $100,982**

Own.– Rokeby Stable
Br.– Paul Mellon
Tr.– J.T. Skinner

27Jun52- 6Del	fst *2½	S'Chase	4:44 4↑	Indian River H 12k	1 5 523 421 425½ 428	Field T	140ws	8.40	- -	Jam15220Monkey Wrench1342The Mast1616	Trailed	5
11Jun52- 6Bel	fst *2¼	S'Chase	4:163 4↑	Temple Gwathmey H 16k	5 8 83½ 78½ 511 616	Field T	141ws	13.85	- -	The Mast153¾Oedipus1631¼Navy Gun1497	No menace	9
3Jun52- 3Bel	fst *2	S'Chase	3:483 4↑	Alw 4500	6 6 57 510 57½ 43¼	Field T	148ws	12.45	- -	Hot1431½Flaming Comet1401½Gerrymander135½	No mishap	7
4Oct51- 5Bel	fst *2½	S'Chase	4:45 4↑	Brook H 16k	10 9 911 917 924 932	Field T	140ws	11.35	- -	Oedipus1613Palaja1387Lone Fisherman148nk	Jumped poorly	12
25Sep51- 3Bel	sf *2	S'Chase	3:53 3↑	Alw 3500	6 7 63¾ 11 13 11	Field T	146ws	3.20e	- -	American Way1461Eolus1422Syracuse Lad1421	Driving	8
11Oct50- 6Bel	fst *2¼	S'Chase	4:182 4↑	Temple Gwathmey H 11k	2 4 2½ 35½ 311 316	Field T	145ws	6.25	- -	Tourist List13810Oedipus1536American Way1454	Tired	5
6Oct50- 5Bel	fst *3	S'Chase	5:422 4↑	Grand National H 23k	1 7 57½ 618 742 834	McDonald RS	145ws	1.85e	- -	Trough Hill1502¼Oedipus1534Pontius Pilate1502½	Tired	9
28Sep50- 3Bel	fst *2	S'Chase	3:434 4↑	Handicap 4045	6 6 630 637 640 6136	McDonald RS	146ws	2.40e	- -	SeaLegs1433Genancoke1433Sergt.Peace1394	Almost fell 4th	6
1Jun50- 5Bel	sl *2	S'Chase	4:03 4↑	Corinthian H 9.1k	5 2 43½ 48½ 48½ 48¼	Field T	148ws	*1.95	- -	Adaptable1411½Hot1403½Monkey Wrench1353	Dull try	7
25May50- 5Bel	fst *2	S'Chase	3:44 4↑	C L Appleton 9k	4 5 37 35 34 37	Field T	145 w	3.80	- -	Darjeeling1302Hot1355American Way1455½	Even effort	7
17May50- 3Bel	fst *2	S'Chase	3:473 4↑	Handicap 4555	2 6 618 615 516 69	Field T	148 w	4.30	- -	Phiblant1332Hot1392Irish Monkey1391½	Jumped poorly	7
10Nov49- 5Pim	fst *2½	S'Chase	4:482 4↑	Manly H 8.2k	2 4 412 411 314 314	Field T	152ws	*1.20e	- -	His Boots1458Trough Hill1566American Way1526	Bobbled	5

20Oct49- 5Lrl	fst	*2½	S'Chase	4:452	4↑	Chevy Chase H 11k	1	4	44½	31	22	31½	Field T	152	ws	1.60e	--	LockandKey1401¼HisBoots145nkAmericnWay1521½	Went well	6
14Oct49- 3Lrl	fst	*2	S'Chase	3:522	4↑	Alw 5000	5	4	45½	44½	21	22	Field T	153	ws	2.30e	--	LarkyDay1532AmericanWay1532½TouristList1468	Closed well	6
7Oct49- 6Bel	fst	*3	S'Chase	5:483	4↑	Grand National H 22k	1	4	410	51¾	49	513	Field T	154	ws	*1.20e	--	His Boots1412½Trough Hill1588Tourist List1462	No mishap	7
29Sep49- 5Bel	sl	*2½	S'Chase	4:521	4↑	Brook H 15k	1	3	47½	22	21	210	Field T	151	ws	4.35e	--	TroughHill15310AmercnWy1511½HsBoots1429	Finished tiring	8
15Sep49- 5Aqu	fst	*2½	S'Chase	4:563	4↑	Glendale H 11k	2	3	315	319	419	421½	Field T	152	w	*1.00e	--	His Boots13520Rapier130½My Good Man1351	No mishap	7
1Sep49- 4Aqu	sl	*2	S'Chase	3:534	3↑	Harbor Hill H 11k	5	4	412	23	11½	12	Field T	148	w	2.30e	--	American Way1482Repose137¾His Boots13710	Ridden out	8
2Jun49- 4Bel	fst	*2	S'Chase	3:44	4↑	Corinthian H 9.4k	6	6	58½	66¾	23	36	Field T	146	w	4.35e	--	Trough Hill1476Elkridge149hdAmerican Way1463½	Weakened	10
10Nov48- 5Pim	gd	3	S'Chase	6:104	4↑	Manly H 18k	7	3	320	21½	210	215	Marzani D	152	w	*.80e	--	Adaptable14415American Way15215Point Bleu1468	Went well	9
28Oct48- 5Lrl	fst	*2½	S'Chase	4:474	4↑	Chevy Chase H 18k	4	3	317	36	11½	11	Marzani D	148	w	*1.50e	--	American Way1481Sun Bath1354Trough Hill1475	Cleverly	8
14Oct48- 5Lrl	fst	*2	S'Chase	3:531	3↑	Butler H 13k	8	9	68½	39½	37½	39½	Field T	149	w	*2.40e	--	Drift1346The Heir1493½American Way1493	Good effort	12
1Oct48- 5Bel	gd	*3	S'Chase	5:50	4↑	Grand Nat'l H 31k	3	5	79½	711	31½	11	Marzani D	144	w	*2.30e	--	American Way1441Tourist List1502Trough Hill1476	Driving	14
23Sep48- 5Bel	fst	*2½	S'Chase	4:471	4↑	Brook H 19k	10	4	53½	78½	44½	33½	Marzani D	143	w	3.45e	--	Trough Hill1422Elkridge1561½American Way1432	Good try	11
16Jly48- 5Aqu	fst	*2½	S'Chase	4:534	4↑	Hitchcock H 11k	3	5	48¼	33	21½	21	Field T	145	w	2.45	--	SunBath1371AmericanWay1454TouristList1432	Strong finish	6
24Jun48- 5Del	gd	*2	S'Chase	3:50	4↑	Georgetown H 12k	2	4	310	316	21	12½	Marzani D	144	w	3.95e	--	AmericnWay1442½Genancoke145nkFlotngIsl14010	Going away	8
17Jun48- 1Del	sl	*2	S'Chase	3:552	4↑	Alw 4000	1	4	513	413	26	28	Bland W Jr	151	w	*1.65e	--	War Battle1558American Way1516Lieut. Well155¾	Went well	5
12Jun48- 3Bel	fst	*2	S'Chase	3:492	4↑	Alw 4500	4	3	33	23	22	25	Bland W Jr	150	w	*2.20	--	Sun Bath1405American Way1502½Cash1362	Went well	6
12May48- 5Pim	fst	2	S'Chase	3:471	4↑	Jervis Spencer H 12k	5	6	628	-	-	-	Bland W	149	w	*1.10e	--	Lieut. Well1441½Canford13812Adaptable1501½	Fell	7
5May48- 3Pim	hy	2	S'Chase	4:132	4↑	Alw 4500	3	3	317	310	11	12	Bland W	150	w	*.70e	--	American Way1502Genancoke1512Floating Isle1531½	Handily	6
29May47- 5Del	fst	*2	S'Chase	4:03	4↑	Tom Roby 13k	8	6	54½	32	14	112	Bland W Jr	149	w	2.50e	--	AmericanWay14912TouristPride1351½TouristList1462	Easily	10
7May47- 5Pim	gd	*2	S'Chase	3:59	4↑	Jervis Spencer H 17k	3	5	612	514	513	517	Field T	140	w	4.50	--	Lieut.Well1448Fleettown141noFloatingIsle1411	No mishap	7
29Apr47- 3Pim	fst	*2	S'Chase	3:544	4↑	Alw 4000	6	2	212	311	1hd	1¾	Field T	147	w	*1.90	--	American Way147¾Adaptable1431½Allier1351	Driving	7
16Nov46- 5Mid	fst	*2½	S'Chase	4:341	4↑	Handicap 2415	5	4	518	1½	1½	11½	Bland W	150	w	-e	--	American Way1501½Caddie16015Lady Janice14030	Driving	5
8Nov46- 3Pim	fst	2	S'Chase	3:564	3↑	Alw 3500	4	6	55½	31	2½	2hd	Field T	149	w	1.85e	--	NeatPleat146hdAmericanWay14910FrCrystl14720	Just missed	6
4Nov46- 3Pim	fst	2	S'Chase	4:00	4↑	Alw 3500	6	2	22	22	13	11	Field T	142	w	4.30e	--	American Way1421Refugio1474Genancoke146.510	Driving	7
11Oct46- 3Bel	fst	*2	S'Chase	3:521	3↑	Alw 4000	5	5	513	511	25	26	Field T	147	w	*1.40	--	LittleSammie1436AmericnWay1478GalaReigh15215	No threat	5
18Sep46- 5Aqu	fst	*2½	S'Chase	4:512	4↑	Glendale H 11k	6	4	42½	65½	413	411½	Field T	136	w	9.00	--	Chesapeake1361½Nvgt150hdKnght'sQust14710	Speed,faltered	6
10Sep46- 3Aqu	fst	*2	S'Chase	3:46	3↑	Alw 3500	1	4	23	11½	13	13	Field T	138	w	2.05	--	AmericanWay1383FredericII1382½GreekFlag151½	Drew away	5
24Jun46- 2Del	fst	*2	S'Chase	3:502	4↑	Alw 3500	1	3	37	25	22	23½	Field T	135	w	8.65	--	SoldierSong1403½AmericnWy1352Rfugo142¾	Bad landing 13th	5
14Jun46- 2Del	fst	*2	S'Chase	3:591	4↑	Clm 3000	6	5	55¼	57	1hd	11½	Field T	139	w	7.75	--	American Way1391½Strawride1482Ducker1341½	Driving	9
27May46- 3Bel	my	*2	S'Chase	4:16	4↑	Md Sp Wt	2	3	34¼	28	5	5	Bland W	146	w	2.35	--	Tetrol13915Chancefield1427Chen13920		5
	Fell 11th,remounted and finished course																			
9May46- 3Pim	fst	*2	S'Chase	3:574	4↑	Md Sp Wt	6	-	-	-	-	-	Bland W	146	w	1.85e	--	[D]Tetrol1462BigThr14620FuntlroyRun146100	Lost rider 1st	11
3May46- 3Pim	fst	*2	S'Chase	4:023	4↑	Md Sp Wt	1	6	87½	66½	28	2½	Bland W Jr	145	w	4.85	--	Military Man150½American Way14512George Corn14140		9
	Bobbled badly 11th																			
13Apr46- 1Mid	fst	*1½	Hurdles	2:40	3↑	Alw 400	5	1	12	1hd	22½	412¾	Field T	134	ws	8.00	--	Binder1534Equirita1388Nobby138¾	Weakened	7

Armed

br. g. 1941, by Bull Lea (Bull Dog)–Armful, by Chance Shot

Lifetime record: 81 41 20 10 $817,475

Own.– Calumet Farm
Br.– Calumet Farm (Ky)
Tr.– B.A. Jones

22Mar50- 6GP	fst	1 1/16	:23 :461 1:103 1:43	4↑	Alw 3000	4	5	46	31	1hd	11	Scurlock O	117	w	2.05	101-07	Armed1171Stud Poker114noHarbourton116hd	Won easily	6
11Mar50- 6GP	fst	1⅛	:473 1:123 1:374 1:492	3↑	Handicap 7500	2	3	33½	52½	4¾	2hd	Nelson E	111	w	*.40e	97-09	Wynford II112hdArmed111hdBewitch1232½	Held gamely	6
11Feb50- 6Hia	fst	1⅛	:463 1:111 1:37 1:501	3↑	McLennan H 33k	8	10	85	95	86¼	67	Scurlock O	112	w	*.55e	80-17	Three Rings1171Royal Governor1161Coaltown1321	Blocked	11
21Jan50- 6Hia	fst	1⅛	:471 1:113 1:364 1:492	3↑	Royal Palm H 11k	7	3	31½	2½	2½	2¾	Scurlock O	121	w	*1.20	90-18	Three Rings120¾Armed1211Renown II1153	Good effort	7
14Jan50- 7TrP	fst	1 1/16	:243 :482 1:123 1:433	4↑	Alw 2500	2	1	1½	1hd	11	12	Scurlock O	117	w	*.30	94-12	Armed1172Appease Not1176First Nighter117nk	Going away	6
3Jan50- 6TrP	fst	6f	:222 :452 1:101	4↑	Alw 2500	6	5	75½	44½	32	2½	Scurlock O	112	w	1.90e	95-14	Kay Gibson107½Armed1121Too Sunny1053	Gaining fast	9
	Previously trained by H.A. Jones																		
5Sep49- 6Was	sl	1¼	:473 1:122 1:373 2:034	3↑	Wash Park H 52k	4	2	31½	2½	21	2¾	Scurlock O	110	w	*.10e	82-19	Coaltown130¾Armed1101Lithe102.524¼	Raced outside	4
23Jly49- 6AP	gd	1¼	:463 1:11 1:361 2:032	3↑	Arlington H 54k	3	3	48½	36	37	34	Scurlock O	113	w	*.40e	84-19	Coaltown1303Star Reward1161Armed1135	Closed well	6
4Jly49- 6AP	fst	1⅛	:472 1:103 1:352 1:482	3↑	Stars & Stripes H 54k	2	4	42	33	34	21¼	Scurlock O	110	w	*.40e	103-09	Coaltown1301¼Armed110½Star Reward121½	Good effort	6
30Jun49- 6AP	fst	7f	:23 :462 1:111 1:234	4↑	Alw 3500	2	7	51¾	41¼	1½	13	Brooks S	122	w	*1.80	91-09	Armed1223Trixie111noBest Prospect110½	Going away	7
20Jun49- 7AP	fst	6f	:223 :452 1:091	4↑	Alw 5000	6	7	96¾	99¼	810	710	Scurlock O	114	w	*1.00e	91-09	CarraraMarble1046Bewitch1151½StarReward118hd	Raced wide	10
	Previously trained by B.A. Jones																		
21May49- 7CD	gd	7f	:233 :463 1:113 1:25	3↑	Churchill Downs H 11k	2	3	46	44½	33	21¼	Johnson WL	118	w	-e	90-18	Free America1201¼Armed1182¾Phar Mon1081½	Closed well	4
	No wagering																		
5May49- 6CD	fst	1 1/16	:252 :502 1:143 1:451	3↑	Clark H 10k	4	1	12	33	32½	35	Glisson G	120	w	.90e	89-14	Shy Guy123hdFree America1155Armed12012	Weakened	4
2May49- 6CD	fst	6f	:232 :464 1:122	4↑	Alw 2500	6	1	54½	45½	22	13¼	Glisson G	113	w	*.20	91-16	Armed1133¼Best Prospect1161½Pomp's Gal1133	Going away	8
	Previously trained by H.A. Jones																		
19Mar49- 6GP	fst	1¼	:45 1:09 1:341 1:594	3↑	Gulf Park H 20k	7	3	38	312	39	37½	Nelson E	116	w	*.10e	100-06	Coaltown1287Three Rings118½Armed1162½	Went well	9
8Mar49- 7GP	fst	7f	:24 :471 1:112 1:232	4↑	Alw 2500	1	3	2hd	1hd	11½	11¼	Nelson E	117	w	*.60	96-08	Armed1171¼Manna H.117½Control1171½	Easily	8
17Feb49- 4Hia	fst	7f	:232 :461 1:103 1:231	4↑	Alw 3500	5	4	54¼	56½	45¾	32½	Nelson E	119	w	*.70	93-12	Rare Jewel1102½Happy C.112hdArmed1191½	Closed well	7
9Feb49- 5Hia	fst	6f	:223 :454 1:11	4↑	Alw 3500	5	1	74¾	61¾	7¾	32¼	Civitello B	119	w	2.10	91-13	Column1151½Tight Squeeze113¾Armed119nk	Closed well	8
21Feb48- 6Hia	fst	1¼	:47 1:11 1:354 2:01	3↑	Widener H 62k	7	2	64	53	53¾	45½	Snider A	130	w	1.65	97-10	El Mono112hdStud Poker1032½Bug Juice1073	Mild rally	9
14Feb48- 6Hia	fst	1⅛	:463 1:104 1:36 1:482	3↑	McLennan H 31k	9	7	53½	64¾	54	31¾	Dodson D	128	w	*.35	97-10	El Mono112hdRiskolater1121¾Armed1281	Closed fast	9
11Feb48- 6Hia	fst	7f	:232 :46 1:101 1:23	3↑	Seminole H 12k	7	6	55¼	53½	43	31¼	Dodson D	128	w	*.40e	96-16	Citation1121Delegate123nkArmed1282	Closed fast	9
2Feb48- 6Hia	fst	6f	:223 :454 1:102	3↑	Alw 5000	3	3	77	78	76¼	66¼	Dodson D	130	w	*.20e	90-10	Citation1131Kitchen Police1101¾Say Blue1071½	Raced wide	7
15Jan48- 6GP	fst	1¼	:462 1:111 1:362 2:02	3↑	Gulf Park H 27k	3	2	34	21½	21	2no	Dodson D	130	w	*.15	97-17	Rampart108noArmed1302½Incline1102½	Just missed	6
2Jan48- 6GP	fst	6f	:231 :46 1:111	4↑	Alw 3500	2	4	47	38	34	1½	Dodson D	124	w	*.45	94-15	Armed124½Stageboy1072Mangohick1172½	Handily	5
31Oct47- 6Pim	sl	1 3/16	:472 1:122 1:384 1:582	3↑	Pim Spl 25k	2	1	31½	31½	3½	33¼	Dodson D	126	w	*.20e	87-24	Fervent120nkCosmic Bomb1203Armed1267	No excuse	4
9Oct47- 6Bel	fst	1	:232 :461 1:104 1:36	3↑	Sysonby Mile 27k	2	1	2hd	2hd	2nk	11¼	Snider A	126	w	*.35	94-15	Armed1261¼With Pleasure12615Ensueno126	Drew out	3
27Sep47- 6Bel	fst	1¼	:471 1:113 1:363 2:024	3↑	Special 100k	2	1	14	12	13	18	Dodson D	126	w	-	86-10	Armed1268Assault126	Much best	2
22Sep47- 5Bel	sly	6f	:231 :463 1:11	3↑	Alw 6500	4	1	32¼	32	31¾	22½	Dodson D	130	w	1.30	92-14	Polynesian1262½Armed1308Ensueno11430	Finished fast	4
1Sep47- 6Was	fst	1¼	:471 1:114 1:372 2:02	3↑	Wash Park H 55k	5	4	2hd	1hd	11	13½	Dodson D	130	w	*.70	95-12	Armed1303¼Honeymoon1111¼With Pleasure1233	Easily	7
20Aug47- 7Was	fst	1⅛	:483 1:123 1:361 1:483	3↑	Whirlaway 43k	4	2	1hd	12	1½	1½	Dodson D	130	w	*.30	104-08	Armed130½With Pleasure1264Service Pilot110hd	Driving	6
9Aug47- 6Was	fst	1	:23 :454 1:102 1:354	3↑	Sheridan H 33k	5	8	87	44½	34½	22	Dodson D	132	w	*.50	94-08	With Pleasure1242Armed132½Rippey112½	Good effort	10
19Jly47- 6AP	fst	1¼	:471 1:113 1:362 2:022	3↑	Arlington H 55k	7	4	11½	12½	13	11	Dodson D	130	w	*.40	93-12	Armed1301Bridal Flower1112¼Challenge Me1142	Driving	8
4Jly47- 6AP	fst	1⅛	:47 1:113 1:36 1:491	3↑	Stars & Stripes H 55k	1	2	32	21	1½	12	Dodson D	130	w	*.50	101-05	Armed1302With Pleasure1173Mighty Story114nk	In hand	7
28Jun47- 6AP	fst	1	:23 :453 1:093 1:35	3↑	Equipoise Mile H 33k	6	4	46½	33½	21	2nk	Dodson D	130	w	*.20	97-08	With Pleasure116nkArmed1303Mighty Story114¾	Just missed	9
21Jun47- 6AP	fst	6f	:223 :45 1:094	3↑	Domino H 29k	5	12	85½	66	34½	21	Dodson D	132	w	*1.20e	97-11	With Pleasure1141Armed132½Spy Song1207½	Closed fast	14
22Mar47- 6GP	fst	1¼	:451 1:094 1:344 2:012	3↑	Gulf Park H 30k	2	2	22	14	16	11	Dodson D	129	w	*.60e	122-00	Armed1291Pot o' Luck1172Concordian116¾	Eased up	10
1Mar47- 7SA	fst	1¼	:452 1:101 1:351 2:014	3↑	S Anita H 133k	14	4	52¼	2½	21½	52¼	Dodson D	129	w	*1.10	95-09	Olhaverry1161¼Stitch Again112½Pere Time108hd	Impeded	22
22Feb47- 6Hia	fst	1¼	:474 1:112 1:36 2:013	3↑	Widener H 61k	6	3	1hd	13	12½	12	Dodson D	129	w	*.25	101-11	Armed1292Talon1224½Let's Dance1154	Handily	6

Date/Race	Cond	Dist	Fractions	Race	St	1st	2nd	Str	Fin	Jockey	Wt	Odds	Speed-Var	Top three	Comment	Field
15Feb47- 6Hia	gd	1⅛	:46[4] 1:11[1] 1:36[4] 1:50	3↑ McLennan H 31k	8	3	2 hd	2 hd	1 1	1 4	Dodson D	130 w	*.25	91-16	Armed130 4 Eternal Reward118 1½ Westminster120 8	Eased up	8
8Feb47- 3Hia	fst	6f	:22[4] :46[1] 1:10[2]	3↑ Handicap 5000	4	3	5 2¼	4 ¾	3 nk	1 1	Dodson D	130 w	*.80	96-15	Armed130 1 Lets Dance116½ Pujante124 5½	Drew out	5
1Feb47- 3Hia	fst	6f	:22[1] :45[1] 1:10[1]	4↑ Alw 5000	1	5	5 4¼	5 4	3 2½	1 hd	Dodson D	128wb	*1.20	97-08	Armed128 hd Hornbeam116 1½ Shiny Penny116 2½	Just up	5
14Sep46- 6Nar	fst	1 3/16	:46 1:10[2] 1:36 1:54[3]	3↑ Nar Spl 38k	2	3	2 3	2 2	2 2½	3 3¾	Dodson D	130 w	*.50	98-16	Lucky Draw123 3½ Pavot123 nk Armed130 5	Weakened	4
Previously trained by B.A. Jones																
2Sep46- 6Was	fst	1¼	:46[2] 1:11 1:35[3] 2:01	3↑ Wash Park H 56k	1	1	3 2	1 1	1 1½	1 3¾	Dodson D	130 w	*.80e	104-03	Armed130 3¾ Challenge Me112 1 Take Wing110 2	Easily	10
21Aug46- 6Was	sl	1⅛	:48 1:12[2] 1:37[4] 1:51[1]	3↑ Whirlaway 45k	5	3	3 1½	3 1½	2 hd	1 1¼	Dodson D	130 w	*.50e	92-18	Armed130 1¼ Challenge Me120 2 Silvery Moon111 3	Drew out	11
3Aug46- 6Was	fst	1	:22[4] :45 1:09[4] 1:35	3↑ Sheridan H 34k	10	4	5 1¾	4 2¼	1 1	1 4	Pierson NL	130 w	*.60e	103-07	Armed130 4 Brookfield124 ¾ Challenge Me112 ¾	Easily	10
31Jly46- 6Was	gd	6f	:22[3] :46 1:10[4]	3↑ Quick Step 22k	3	5	5 5½	4 6	3 5½	2 2½	Pierson NL	130 w	1.70	93-11	FightingFrank108.5 2½ Armed130 6 ThreeDots124 hd	Closed fast	5
20Jly46- 6AP	fst	1¼	:46[4] 1:11 1:35[3] 2:01	3↑ Arlington H 56k	4	2	4 3½	1 ½	1 ½	2 nk	Dodson D	130 w	*.50	101-09	Historian112 nk Armed130 3 Take Wing111 2½	Game try	9
Previously trained by H.A. Jones																
26Jun46- 6AP	fst	1	:23[1] :46 1:11[2] 1:37[1]	3↑ Equipoise Mile H 34k	11	10	10 6	8 4	7 4¼	3 ¾	Dodson D	132 w	*.70	85-14	Witch Sir110 ¾ Old Kentuck106 hd Armed132 no	Close quarters	12
30May46- 6Bel	fst	1¼	:48[2] 1:12[3] 1:37[3] 2:02	3↑ Suburban H 60k	7	6	5 5	4 1½	2 nk	1 2½	Dodson D	130 w	*1.05	90-16	Armed130 2½ Reply Paid110 no Stymie123 1	Going away	11
10May46- 6Pim	fst	1 3/16	:49[4] 1:14[1] 1:38[4] 1:58[2]	3↑ Dixie H 34k	4	4	2 ¾	1 ½	1 3	1 3½	Dodson D	130 w	*.65	90-23	Armed130 3½ Stymie124 2½ Trymenow117 2	Galloping	6
3May46- 6Pim	fst	6f	:22[2] :46[1] 1:12[3]	3↑ Jennings H 8.9k	6	6	6 6½	6 5½	6 3	4 ¾	Snellings A	132 w	*.95	89-23	New Moon115 nk Brookfield122 nk The Doge117 nk	Off slowly	6
20Apr46- 6HdG	fst	1 1/16	:23[3] :47[3] 1:12 1:43[1]	3↑ Philadelphia H 23k	6	4	3 2	2 1½	2 ½	1 1¼	Dodson D	129 w	*.35	102-11	Armed129 1¼ Ellis115 3½ Bobanet119 3	Ridden out	6
15Apr46- 5HdG	fst	6f	:22[4] :46[1] 1:11[1]	3↑ Harford H 8.7k	4	5	6 7½	6 5	5 2½	2 1¼	Snellings A	129 w	*.60	96-15	Bobanet116 1¼ Armed129 2 Alexs112 1½	Forced wide,closed fast	6
Previously trained by B.A. Jones																
30Mar46- 6TrP	fst	1⅛	:46[2] 1:10[3] 1:36[1] 1:48[3]	3↑ Double Event (2) 21k	4	5	4 2	4 1½	2 nk	1 hd	Dodson D	126 w	*.30	102-10	Armed126 hd Historian108 5 Occupy111 5	Driving	5
23Mar46- 6TrP	fst	1⅛	:46[2] 1:10[2] 1:35[4] 1:48[3]	3↑ Double Event (1) 22k	5	6	5 5¼	2 2½	2 hd	1 1½	Dodson D	126 w	*.45	102-08	Armed126 1½ Occupy111 ¾ Historian108 8	Ridden out	7
2Mar46- 6Hia	gd	1¼	:46[4] 1:11[1] 1:36 2:02[2]	3↑ Widener H 63k	3	2	3 4	1 4	1 5	1 4½	Dodson D	128 w	2.20	97-13	Armed128 4½ Concordian109 4 Reply Paid114 1	Easily	8
16Feb46- 6Hia	fst	1⅛	:46[1] 1:10[3] 1:36 1:48[3]	3↑ McLennan H 32k	6	6	4 3	4 5	3 3	2 5	Dodson D	128 w	*.55	93-14	Concordian116 5 Armed128 3 Bob Mann110 2½	Went well	9
6Feb46- 7Hia	fst	7f	:23[3] :46[3] 1:11 1:23[4]	3↑ Handicap 5000	4	3	2 3½	2 3	2 1½	1 nk	Dodson D	130 w	*.80e	93-17	Armed130 nk Buzfuz130 2½ Pot o' Luck120 4	Driving	6
26Jan46- 3Hia	fst	6f	:23[1] :46[2] 1:10[2]	4↑ Alw 4000	9	1	4 1¾	3 1	1 hd	1 nk	Dodson D	126 w	*.45	97-08	Armed126 nk Nowadays115 5 Trouble Sands112 2	Eased up	10
17Nov45- 6Pim	gd	1 3/16	:49[3] 1:14[2] 1:39[1] 1:58[4]	3↑ Pim Spl 25k	2	2	4 3½	3 1½	1 5	1 4	Dodson D	126 w	*.60e	88-20	Armed126 4 First Fiddle126 2 Stymie126 1¼	Well in hand	7
10Nov45- 5Pim	fst	1⅛	:47[1] 1:11[4] 1:37[3] 1:51[3]	3↑ Handicap 5000	1	3	3 3	2 hd	1 1	1 1¾	Dodson D	128 w	*.60e	97-14	Armed128 1¾ Rampart104 hd Gallorette113 2	Eased up late	5
30Oct45- 6Pim	fst	6f	:22[3] :46 1:11[4]	3↑ Alw 3500	5	6	3 3	2 2	1 hd	1 ½	Dodson D	124 w	*.70	94-19	Armed124 ½ Quarter Moon121 5 Jimmie113 2	In hand late	7
20Oct45- 6Lrl	fst	1¼	:46[4] 1:12 1:38[1] 2:04[2]	3↑ Washington H 29k	2	1	3 6½	2 hd	1 2½	1 3½	Dodson D	124 w	*1.25	88-20	Armed124 3½ Dinner Party106 1¼ Good Morning105 hd	Galloping	9
6Oct45- 6Lrl	sl	1⅛	:47[3] 1:12[3] 1:39[3] 1:52[1]	3↑ Havre de Grace H 17k	4	2	2 2	1 1	1 1	2 ¾	Dodson D	126 w	*1.90	86-23	Gay Bit113 ¾ Armed126 6 Dinner Party109 4	2nd best	9
17Sep45- 6Bel	fst	6f-WC	:22[1] :44[3] 1:08[4]	2↑ Fall Highweight H 10k	2	4		4 3½	4 5	2 1	Dodson D	135 w	1.95	96-03	True North140 1 Armed135 4 Breezing Home120 1½	Driving	4
3Sep45- 7Was	fst	1¼	:46[3] 1:10[3] 1:36[1] 2:01[4]	3↑ Wash Park H 57k	5	7	6 5¼	4 4	2 3	2 1½	Dodson D	120 w	3.30e	99-12	Busher115 1½ Armed120 1 Take Wing112 5	Driving	13
1Sep45- 7Was	sl	6f	:23 :47 1:11[3]	3↑ Chicago H 22k	8	8	5 3½	4 4½	3 6	2 2½	Dodson D	123 w	*1.70	89-21	Three Dots124 2½ Armed123 1 Ariel Lad114 hd	Away slowly	9
18Aug45- 5Was	fst	7f	:22[4] :46[2] 1:10[3] 1:23[3]	3↑ Alw 4000	3	2	2 1½	2 1½	1 1	1 3	Dodson D	119 w	*.40	95-14	Armed119 3 ChallengeMe115 no DailyTroubl119 3	Speed to spare	4
8Aug45- 6Was	fst	7f	:22[2] :46 1:11[1] 1:23[4]	3↑ Sheridan H (Div 2) 16k	1	2	3 2	2 1	2 1	1 8	Dodson D	111 w	*1.40	94-14	Armd111 8 EspinoGold108 hd ThreeDots126 hd	Drew away quickly	8
21Jly45- 6Was	fst	6f	:23 :46 1:11[3]	3↑ Alw 4000	2	4	5 3½	4 4¼	4 3	1 1½	Dodson D	116 w	*2.10	92-12	Armed116 1½ Quick Reward105 2 Legislator108 hd	In hand	6
14Jly45- 5Was	sly	7f	:23[4] :47[3] 1:12 1:25[1]	4↑ Alw 3000	3	2	2 2	2 1	1 4	1 2¼	Dodson D	118 w	*1.10	87-19	Armed118 2¼ Happy Pilot113 3 Miss Lark110.5 ½	In hand late	7
3Jly45- 4Was	fst	7f	:22[4] :46[2] 1:12 1:25[1]	4↑ Alw 2500	1	3	2 3	2 3	1 hd	1 2	Dodson D	118 w	*.50	87-14	Armed118 2 Tawny Lady108 3 Five A.M.111 2	Speed in reserve	10
27Jun45- 5Was	sl	7f	:24 :48[3] 1:15[1] 1:29[2]	4↑ Alw 2500	1	3	3 1½	2 hd	1 5	1 4	Dodson D	117 w	*.70	66-34	Armed117 4 Oberver115 3½ Havaheart110 ¾	In hand	8
2Jun45- 6Jam	sly	6f	:23[1] :46[3] 1:11[3]	3↑ Handicap 3480	9	10	10 10	10 8¾	9 8¼	5 6½	Jemas N	109 w	32.50	87-10	Unchallengd112 2 ComnchePeak118 1½ JeanMircl122 1	No speed	11
4Nov44- 6Pim	fst	6f	:22[2] :46 1:11[4]	2↑ Janney H 6.3k	3	6	6 9½	7 6½	7 5½	6 5	Smith FA	110 w	15.45	89-15	Salto116 hd Challamore121 2 Adroit116 1	No factor	7
26Jun44- 6Was	fst	6f	:22[2] :45[4] 1:10[3]	3↑ Alw 2500	3	6	5 8	6 11	5 14	4 7½	McCreary C	104 w	4.80	90-09	Occupation120 1½ Tellmenow105 3 Bright Willie117 3	Mild gain	6
19Jun44- 5Was	sl	6f	:23[2] :47[4] 1:12[4]	Alw 2500	1	4	1 hd	1 hd	1 1	1 1	McCreary C	111 w	4.20	87-24	Armed111 1 Sirde120 4 Sirius111 1¼	Driving	8
3May44- 6Pim	fst	6f	:22[1] :45[3] 1:11[3]	Rennert H 7k	7	4	3 2	4 3	6 8	8 9¾	Smith FA	118 w	*.40e	85-17	Twilight Tear118 1½ Galactic108 3 Ideal Gift112.5 2	Quit	10
15Apr44- 7Pim	sly	6f	:23 :47[4] 1:15[2]	Alw 3500	1	3	1 1½	1 hd	2 1½	2 2	McCreary C	110 w	2.00	74-32	Director J.E.114 2 Armed110 4 Gramps Image114 4	Faltered str	6
4Mar44- 3Hia	fst	7f	:23 :46[1] 1:12[2] 1:26[2]	Alw 1800	5	3	4 3¼	2 2	2 ½	1 3	McCreary C	118 w	*.25e	80-21	Armed118 3 Herald115 no Ray G.118 3	Easily	7
28Feb44- 2Hia	fst	6f	:23[3] :47[3] 1:12[3]	Md Sp Wt	11	5	3 1½	3 1	1 1½	1 8	Arcaro E	120 w	*1.95	86-26	Armed120 8 Saguaro120 2½ Change Here120 hd	Speed to spare	11

Askmenow

br. f. 1940, by Menow (Pharamond II)–Conclave, by Friar Rock

Lifetime record: 27 8 7 4 $138,135

Own.– H.P. Headley
Br.– Hal Price Headley (Ky)
Tr.– K. Osborne

Date/Race	Cond	Dist	Fractions	Race	St	1st	2nd	Str	Fin	Jockey	Wt	Odds	Speed-Var	Top three	Comment	Field
10Sep43- 6Aqu	fst	1⅛	:47[4] 1:13[2] 1:38[3] 1:51[3]	3↑ (F)Beldame H 28k	11	9	10 7	9 5¾	7 5	6 5	Woolf G	119wb	5.65e	84-14	Mar-Kell126 1 Stefanita116 2 Vagrancy122 ½	Slow to begin	11
28Aug43- 6Was	sl	1¼	:49[1] 1:14[1] 1:41 2:07	American Derby 73k	1	1	2 1½	2 2	1 ½	1 hd	Woolf G	115wb	3.80	75-27	Askmenw115 hd BoldCptn117 12 FmousVctory117 ½	Tiring,lasted	7
21Aug43- 6Was	fst	1⅛	:47[4] 1:11[2] 1:37[4] 1:51	3↑ (F)Beverly H 11k	8	7	5 6½	4 4½	2 2	1 nk	Woolf G	115wb	2.30e	93-11	Askmnw115 nk Mar-Kell125 1¼ Burgoo Maid109 2½	Saved ground	8
4Aug43- 6Bel	fst	1¼	:47[1] 1:12[1] 1:38[1] 2:04[2]	(F)Alabama 17k	1	2	2 1	2 1	2 1½	2 1¾	Woolf G	124wb	1.10	76-15	Stefanita117 1¾ Askmenow124 20 Tack Room114	No match	3
24Jly43- 6Was	fst	1¼	:47[2] 1:12[1] 1:37[1] 2:04[3]	Classic 70k	4	4	3 3½	4 6	4 6	4 10	Bierman C	115wb	5.40e	77-14	Slide Rule120 1 Bourmont117 4 Chop Chop123 5	Faltered	8
19Jly43- 6Was	gd	1⅛	:48[2] 1:14 1:40[3] 1:53[3]	Alw 5000	5	3	3 5¼	2 ½	2 ½	1 ½	Bierman C	113wb	3.30e	80-22	Askmenow113 ½ Occupation118 no Bourmont112.5 10	Driving	7
10Jly43- 6Was	fst	1	:23[2] :46[4] 1:12[3] 1:38[1]	3↑ (F)Arl Matron H 12k	10	5	5 2¼	3 1	1 2	1 nk	Bierman C	109wb	5.30	87-17	Askmenow109 nk Mar-Kell126 2½ Pomayya118 1	Gamely	10
30Jun43- 6Was	fst	7f	:23 :46[4] 1:11[3] 1:24[2]	3↑ (F)Cinderella H 6.3k	2	1	1 ½	1 hd	3 2	3 1¼	Bierman C	110wb	4.50	93-17	Mar-Kell122 ½ Hometown106 ¾ Askmenow110 3		10
Drifted out into str,came on again when straightened																
23Jun43- 6Was	fst	6f	:23[1] :47[1] 1:12[4]	(F)Princess Doreen 6k	3	4	5 5	5 5½	4 3	2 1¼	Bierman C	121wb	3.60	86-16	Valdina Marl115 1¼ Askmenow121 no Wiseasyou109 ¾		8
Lost ground,late rush																
26May43- 6Bel	sly	1½	:48[4] 1:14[2] 2:07[3] 2:35	(F)CCA Oaks 18k	3	1	2 2	2 nk	1 hd	2 3½	Bierman C	121wb	*1. 55e	59-25	TooTimly121 3½ Askmnw121 2½ LaReigh121 7	Drifted out final ⅛	6
19May43- 6Bel	sly	1	:23[2] :47[2] 1:12[1] 1:38[3]	(F)Acorn 14k	7	5	6 5¼	5 5	4 3½	4 4½	Bierman C	121wb	*1.90e	76-20	Nellie L.121 2 La Reigh121 1½ Stefanita121 1	No rally late	13
5May43- 6Pim	fst	1 1/16	:23[1] :47[1] 1:12 1:45[4]	(F)Pim Oaks 13k	10	4	3 2	2 1½	1 ½	1 1	Bierman C	121wb	*2.30e	89-14	Askmenow121 1 Too Timely121 2 Pomrose121 nk	Easily	10
14Apr43- 6CD	sl	6f	:23[2] :47[4] 1:14[1]	(F)Ashland 3.4k	4	5	6 4½	4 3	4 5½	3 5¾	Bierman C	121 w	*.90e	76-27	ValdinaMarl118 ¾ Nppy115 5 Askmnow121 1	Close quarters early	6
24Oct42- 5Lrl	fst	1 1/16	:23[2] :48[1] 1:14[2] 1:46[4]	(F)Selima 25k	5	2	3 1½	2 1	1 1	1 1½	Bierman C	111wb	3.55e	83-20	Askmenow111 1½ Good Morning119 hd TooTimly114 3		9
Forced wide,handily																
3Oct42- 4Bel	fst	6½f-W	:22[2] :44[3] 1:08[3] 1:15[1]	Futurity 69k	8	7	3 3	2 3	2 4	2 5	Bierman C	116wb	27.80	91-04	Occupation126 5 Askmenow116 hd Count Fleet119 1½	Driving	10
Geldings not eligible																
26Sep42- 4Bel	fst	6f-WC	:22[2] :45 1:09[1]	(F)Matron 12k	8	8	6 2¼	2 hd	1 hd	2 1	Haas L	114wb	9.25e	100-00	Good Morning109 1 Askmenow114 1½ Navigating114 2	Gamely	20
21Sep42- 7Bel	fst	6f-WC	:22[4] :46 1:11	(F)Alw 2000	3	5	7 4	3 nk	3 nk	5 3¼	Haas L	115wb	6.70	89-06	Samaritan111 hd Stefanita119 nk Cape May111 1	Inside,blocked	13
15Aug42- 6Sar	fst	6f	:23 :46[4] 1:12[3]	(F)Spinaway 10k	1	2	1 nk	1 1	1 2	2 1	Wright WD	113wb	3.35	88-13	Our Page113 1 Askmenow113 4 Wuskenin113 no	Driving	13
11Aug42- 6Sar	sl	5½f	:23[1] :47[2] 1:00[1] 1:07[2]	(F)Alw 1200	5	2	2 1	2 nk	1 nk	1 6	Arcaro E	115wb	4.85	86-19	Askmenow115 6 Navigating115 no Adventurous114 hd	Easily	8
11Jly42- 6AP	gd	6f	:23 :47[1] 1:13[3]	(F)Arl Lassie 34k	9	1	2 hd	2 ½	2 5	2 6	McCombs K	117wb	11.00e	73-30	Fad117 6 Askmenow117 1 Miss Barbara117 ½	Bore out turn	13
7Jly42- 5AP	fst	5½f	:22[3] :47[2] 1:00[1] 1:06[3]	(F)Alw 1500	2	2	1 ½	1 ½	3 1	5 6	Wright WD	116wb	12.40	82-13	MissBarbara116 3½ EvenStitch116 ¾ BlenheimGirl116 nk	Tired	7
27Jun42- 6Del	my	5f	:22[4] :47[1] 1:01	(F)Polly Drummond 8.4k	6	8	7 9	6 8	7 13	7 11¾	Roberts P	113wb	8.70e	78-19	Fair Weather122 1½ La Reigh122 hd Parachutist113 2	Outrun	8
20Jun42- 7Suf	gd	5f	:23 :47[2] 1:00[2]	(F)Betsy Ross 9.4k	3	2	2 1	1 nk	1 hd	3 2	Howell R	111wb	2.70e	89-14	La Reigh111 hd Tellmenow111 2 Askmenow111 ¾	Weakened	7
10Jun42- 5Aqu	fst	5f	:23[2] :47 1:00	(F)Alw 2000	2	4	3 2½	1 ½	3 ½	4 4½	Zufelt F	118wb	8.45	91-11	The Watch118 3 Witchwater113 1½ Mountain Pass113 no	Tired	6
29Apr42- 4Jam	fst	5f	:23 :46[3] 1:00[3]	(F)Rosedale 7.7k	6	7	6 5	7 7½	7 6¾	7 12	Meade D	115wb	2.85	78-09	Hurriette111 no Optimism115 2 Sonorous112 1	Never close	8
22Apr42- 4Jam	fst	5f	:23[1] :46[3] 1:00	(F)Alw 2000	3	1	1 ½	1 2	1 2	1 1¼	Meade D	109wb	3.40	93-11	Askmenow109 1¼ The Watch116 2 Hurriette108 1¼	In hand	11
18Apr42- 3Jam	fst	5f	:23 :47 1:01[4]	(F)Md Sp Wt	5	5	4 1½	2 2	2 3	3 5¾	Meade D	115wb	*2.25	78-19	Optimism115 3½ Good Morning115 2¼ Askmenow115 1	Faltered	11

Assault

ch. c. 1943, by Bold Venture (St. Germans)–Igual, by Equipoise — Lifetime record: 42 18 6 7 $675,470

Own.– King Ranch
Br.– King Ranch (Tex)
Tr.– W.J. Hirsch

9Dec50- 7Hol fst 1¼ :463 1:101 1:35 1:594 3↑ Hol Gold Cup 137k 5 2 53½ 53¾ 44½ 710¼ Gilbert J 121wb 37.95 91-09 Noor1301Palestinian1223Hill Prince1301 8
Carried wide,rallied,flattened out
1Dec50- 7Hol fst 1⅛ :48 1:114 1:361 1:48 3↑ Alw 5000 1 1 2hd 1½ 23 38 Boland W 112wb 1.90 93-11 Noor1247Palestinian1201Assault1121 Weakened 5
22Nov50- 7Hol fst 7f :222 :451 1:093 1:224 3↑ Alw 4000 1 1 11½ 12½ 14 12 Arcaro E 120wb 2.90 95-16 Assault1202Repeluz1162Bernbrook1131 Easing up 7
Previously trained by M. Hirsch
15Oct49- 6Jam fst 1 1/16 :242 :48 1:124 1:442 3↑ Grey Lag H 29k 10 8 87¼ 85 84¼ 86¼ Arcaro E 123wb 4.75e 85-16 Royal Governor1141Three Rings116hdCapot121nk No rally 12
24Sep49- 6Bel fst 1½ :49 1:13 2:022 2:28 3↑ Manhattan H 29k 7 4 66 611 79¼ 714 Gorman D 126wb *2.15 84-13 Donor118¾My Request1258Stunts114hd Wide,outrun 7
10Sep49- 6Aqu fst 1⅛ :473 1:12 1:37 1:504 3↑ Edgemere H 22k 3 9 916 914 48½ 33¾ Gorman D 124wb *2.50 89-16 My Request1193Stunts115¾Assault124½ Closed fast 9
13Aug49- 7Suf hy 1¼ :482 1:133 1:393 2:043 3↑ Mass H 59k 5 2 21 3¾ 3¾ 43 Gorman D 125wb *.40 87-27 FirstNighter104nkGoingAway103¾MichgnIII1172 Lost ground 5
2Jly49- 6Aqu fst 1¼ :484 1:13 1:372 2:024 3↑ Brooklyn H 58k 7 5 42 2½ 11½ 1¾ Gorman D 122wb *.95e 93-14 Assault122¾Vulcan's Forge129nkFlying Missel117¾ Driving 10
24Jun49- 5Aqu fst 7f :231 :46 1:12 1:262 4↑ Alw 4000 4 2 32 1½ 1hd 2no Boland W 119wb *.35 80-27 Michigan III115noAssault1194Spats1082 Weak ride 5
21Feb48- 6Hia fst 1¼ :47 1:11 1:354 2:01 3↑ Widener H 62k 1 5 85¾ 31 42¼ 57 Arcaro E 130wb *1.15 96-10 El Mono112hdStud Poker1032½Bug Juice1073 Faltered 9
14Feb48- 5Hia fst 7f :233 :47 1:113 1:234 4↑ Alw 5000 1 4 33 21½ 2½ 1hd Mehrtens W 126wb *.40 93-10 Assault128hdRampart1097Star Pilot1169 Not urged 4
27Sep47- 6Bel fst 1¼ :471 1:113 1:363 2:024 3↑ Special 100k 1 2 24 22 23 28 Arcaro E 126wb - 78-10 Armed1268Assault126 Outrun 2
19Jly47- 6Bel sly 1⅝ :483 1:39 2:042 2:423 3↑ Gold Cup 109k 2 2 418 45½ 21½ 34¼ Arcaro E 126wb *.55 87-14 Stymie126nkNatchez1264Assault1261 Swerved,tired 7
Geldings not eligible
12Jly47- 5Jam fst 1 3/16 :49 1:134 1:381 1:563 3↑ Butler H 54k 5 2 45 44½ 51 1hd Arcaro E 135wb *.45 93-09 Assault135hdStymie1261¾Gallorette117nk Hard drive 5
21Jun47- 6Aqu fst 1¼ :472 1:121 1:38 2:033 3↑ Brooklyn H 55k 2 1 414 45½ 2½ 13 Arcaro E 133wb *.45 89-14 Assault1333Stymie1244Larky Day1101 Easily 5
30May47- 6Bel fst 1¼ :472 1:114 1:364 2:014 3↑ Suburban H 57k 2 4 46½ 26 21½ 12 Arcaro E 130wb *1.10 91-09 Assault1302Natchez1207Talon1131 Going away 7
9May47- 6Pim fst 1 3/16 :474 1:122 1:384 1:574 3↑ Dixie H 35k 7 1 56½ 54½ 2hd 1½ Arcaro E 129wb *.40e 93-20 Assault129½Rico Monte1203Talon1152 Hand ride 7
3May47- 5Jam fst 1⅛ :47 1:112 1:363 1:494 3↑ Grey Lag H 46k 2 6 68½ 41½ 4nk 1nk Mehrtens W 128wb *1.25 99-13 Asslt128nkLetsDanc110nkConcdnc1202 Bumped,forced wide 8
Daily Racing Form time,1:49 1/5
9Nov46- 5Jam gd 1 3/16 :472 1:112 1:373 1:562 3↑ Westchester H 56k 4 5 69½ 510 11½ 12 Arcaro E 122wb 1.65 94-17 Assault1222½Lucky Draw1284Lets Dance1041½ Cleverly 6
1Nov46- 6Pim fst 1 3/16 :481 1:132 1:39 1:57 3↑ Pim Spl 25k 3 3 314 39½ 11 16 Arcaro E 120wb 2.80 97-16 Assault1206Stymie1263Bridal Flower117½ Easily 4
26Oct46- 5Jam fst 1⅝ :462 1:373 2:03 2:424 3↑ Gallant Fox H 85k 10 6 57½ 11 35½ 34½ Mehrtens W 114wb 4.90 96-11 Stymie1262½Rico Monte1162Assault1148 Weakened 11
19Oct46- 5Jam fst 1 3/16 :473 1:123 1:39 1:572 Roamer H 31k 7 11 96¾ 75¼ 2nk 2½ Mehrtens W 126wb *1.40 88-13 Bridal Flower118½Assault1261½Risolater109nk Hung 12
25Sep46- 6Bel fst 1½ :493 1:143 2:032 2:292 3↑ Manhattan H 28k 2 3 54¼ 53¾ 44¾ 33¾↓ Mehrtens W 116wb 1.90 87-13 Stymie126¾Pavot1213[DH]Flareback1131 Came on again 8
14Sep46- 5GS fst 1⅛ :472 1:121 1:363 1:491 Jersey H 31k 5 6 65½ 31 2hd 2½ Mehrtens W 126wb *.70 98-09 Mahout114½Assault1263Blue Yonder1131¼ No excuse 7
7Sep46- 6Aqu fst 1⅛ :48 1:123 1:39 1:514 Discovery H 28k 4 8 812 67 57¼ 33½ Mehrtens W 126wb *.70e 84-14 Mighty Story1152½Mahout1121Assault126¾ Forced wide 9
27Jly46- 6AP fst 1¼ :491 1:123 1:364 2:023 Classic 94k 2 2 33½ 48½ 610½ 68¼ Mehrtens W 126wb *.70 85-09 The Dude1191¼Sgt. Spence1192½Mighty Story1222 Sulked 6
15Jun46- 6Aqu fst 1¼ :481 1:14 1:411 2:064 Dwyer 58k 6 4 59¼ 33½ 2nk 14½ Mehrtens W 126wb *.40 73-23 Assault1264½Windfields116½Lord Boswell1211½ Easily 6
1Jun46- 6Bel fst 1½ :493 1:141 2:04 2:304 Belmont 110k 1 7 45¼ 33½ 32 13 Mehrtens W 126wb 1.40 84-13 Assault1263Natchez1262Cable126hd Going away 7
Geldings not eligible
11May46- 6Pim fst 1 3/16 :48 1:13 1:40 2:012 Preakness 131k 5 6 65 3½ 14 1nk Mehrtens W 126wb *1.40 75-20 Assault126nkLord Boswell1263½Hampden1264 Ridden out 10
4May46- 7CD sl 1¼ :48 1:141 1:404 2:063 Ky Derby 113k 2 3 54 32 12½ 18 Mehrtens W 126wb 8.20 74-22 Assault1268Spy Song126hdHampden1261 Drew away 17
30Apr46- 5CD my 1 :223 :463 1:123 1:401 Derby Trial 13k 5 5 410 47½ 47½ 44½ Mehrtens W 118wb 4.50 73-32 Rippey110nkSpy Song1184With Pleasure118nk Closed ground 10
20Apr46- 5Jam fst 1 1/16 :233 :47 1:113 1:463 Wood Memorial 31k 11 3 35 34 2hd 12¼ Mehrtens W 126wb 8.85 80-18 Assault1262¼Hampden126½Marine Victory1261 Going away 14
Daily Racing Form time,1:47 1/5
9Apr46- 5Jam fst 6f :23 :47 1:12 Exp Free H 1 11k 6 6 31½ 1½ 13 14½ Mehrtens W 116wb 9.10 91-17 Assault1164½IslamPrince114½LarkmeadAndy110nk Hand ride 11
8Oct45- 5Jam fst 6f :23 :463 1:12 Alw 5000 4 5 43¼ 31 2hd 23 Mehrtens W 117wb 2.15 89-15 Lord Boswell1173Assault1174Landlord1112½ No match 5
12Sep45- 6Aqu fst 6½f :231 :464 1:122 1:18 Cowdin 31k 8 9 117 88 54½ 44 Mehrtens W 120wsb 34.40 91-14 Knockdown1141½Revokd1261SouthernPrd1201½ Finished well 13
5Sep45- 6Aqu fst 6f :223 :463 1:121 Babylon H 14k 6 6 31¼ 21 21 34 Mehrtens W 119wb 10.90 87-17 Southern Pride1201Tidy Bid1133Assault119nk Hung 9
6Aug45- 4Bel sly 5½f-W :221 :452 1:044 Flash 15k 11 1 2nk 42¾ 1no Mehrtens W 113wb 70.60 90-10 Assault113noMist o' Gold122noMush Mush117hd Driving 12
18Jly45- 5Jam fst 6f :23 :461 1:121 ©East View 12k 1 5 53¾ 45½ 53½ 58½ Mehrtens W 118 w 18.05 82-15 Misto'Gold1221½SouthrnPride1183Degage1222 Saved ground 14
12Jly45- 5Aqu fst 5½f :223 :463 1:072 ©Alw 3000 2 2 1hd 21 2½ 11¼ Mehrtens W 111wb 4.65 87-19 Assault1111¼Happy C.116¾Darby Darius1161¼ 7
Saved ground,ridden out
23Jun45- 2Bel fst 4½f-W :231 :464 :53 ©Md Sp Wt 16 3 11½ 21 23 Mehrtens W 116wb 23.95 87-12 Mist o' Gold1163Assault1161Uncle Mac1161½ No mishap 23
12Jun45- 1Bel fst 4½f-W :251 :471 :533 ©Md Sp Wt 12 4 4¾ 62¾ 51¾ Mehrtens W 116 w 79.25 85-12 Leeway109hdChallenge Play1161½The Heir116hd Early speed 15
4Jun45- 4Bel sly 4½f-W :224 :462 :531 ©Md Sp Wt 13 8 118 1114 1214½ Stout J 116 w 17.30 74-13 Grandpa Max1164The Heir1161½Skylighter1161 Evenly 21

Beaugay

b. f. 1943, by Stimulus (Ultimus)–Risk, by Sir Gallahad III — Lifetime record: 18 9 3 0 $148,070

Own.– Maine Chance Farm
Br.– Arthur B. Hancock Sr (Ky)
Tr.– J.W. Smith

29May48- 5Del fst 6f :223 :46 1:113 3↑ Wilmington H 13k 10 13 115 85½ 95¾ 85¾ Nash R 119 w 5.75 88-09 Itsabet1132½[DH]Phar Mon114[DH]Mity Me1121 14
Slow into stride,no threat
1May48- 5Jam fst 6f :232 :463 1:121 3↑ Interborough H 22k 5 1 2hd 4¾ 3nk 93¾ Nash R 121 w *2.25 86-20 Miss Disco1091Tavistock106nkKitchen Police114nk Quit 9
17Apr48- 5GS fst 6f :23 :463 1:114 3↑ ⒻColonial H 20k 8 1 1hd 1hd 1hd 2no Dodson D 122 w *1.90 90-17 Itsabet110noBeaugay1224½Bogle1151½ Game try 13
11Nov47- 4Jam fst 6f :233 :462 1:113 3↑ Can't Wait H 10k 2 3 1hd 21½ 3½ 44 Dodson D 125 w *.95 89-19 Miss Disco1071½Buzfuz126½Gestapo1082 Gave way 6
29Oct47- 5Jam sly 6f :231 :46 1:112 2↑ New Rochelle H 23k 5 2 11 11 11 11 Dodson D 117 w 6.90 94-17 Beaugay1171With Pleasure1322½Buzfuz1251 Driving 9
15Oct47- 5Jam fst 6f :232 :47 1:12 2↑ ⒻCorrection H 17k 10 3 2nk 1½ 11 21 Adams J 123wb 4.40 90-17 Miss Kimo1261Beaugay1232Miss Disco110hd Held on well 11
22Sep47- 6Bel sly 6f-WC :223 :454 1:104 2↑ Fall Highweight H 30k 10 5 1nk 42 31½ 43¼ Dodson D 124 w 6.55 84-14 Rippey131noPipette1142½Ben Lewis103¾ No mishap 12
7Oct46- 5GS fst 6f :223 :461 1:103 3↑ ⒻColonial H (Div 1) 11k 2 4 2hd 3nk 11½ 12 Guerin E 122 w *.70 98-11 Beaugay1222Forgetmenow1111¼Athene113hd Going away 8
18Sep46- 6Aqu fst 6f :222 :461 1:102 Alw 4500 5 1 21½ 2½ 1nk 11 Guerin E 115 w 2.85 100-16 Beaugay1151High Lea114½Pep Well1222½ Drew out 6
7Aug46- 6Was fst 7f :214 :443 1:10 1:23 ⒻArtful H 27k 5 2 1½ 1½ 2½ 47¾ Adams J 121wb *1.00e 90-09 Athenia1161¼Widow's Peak111½Trixie1056 Gave way 9
22Jun46- 6AP gd 6f :223 :454 1:121 ⒻPrincess Doreen 29k 7 3 1½ 31 2½ 21¼ Brooks S 121 w *.90 85-22 SeaSnack1181¼Beaugay1213½RomanBelle110½ Close quarters 15
Previously trained by T. Smith
29Sep45- 4Bel gd 6½f-W :221 :451 1:103 1:171 Futurity 65k 11 4 1hd 21½ - Dodson D 123 w *.70e - - Star Pilot1261Athene1161Mighty Story1192 Bolted,fell 11
Geldings not eligible
22Sep45- 4Bel fst 6f-WC :221 :443 1:092 ⒻMatron 28k 4 1 2nk 31 1nk Kirkland A 123 w *.70 94-07 Beaugay123nkEnfilade119nkAthene1153 Driving 11
11Aug45- 6Was sl 6f :223 :46 1:13 ⒻPrincess Pat 42k 4 2 1½ 13 15 16 Dodson D 119 w *.40 85-18 Beaugay1196Enfilade1192½Breezy Louise1152 Easing up 6
18Jly45- 6Was fst 6f :222 :462 1:121 ⒻArl Lassie 44k 6 2 2hd 1hd 1½ 11¼ Adams J 119 w *.40 89-10 Beaugay1191¼Enfilade1193Aladear1193 Carried out 9
14Jun45- 6Del fst 5f :222 :453 :58 ⒻPolly Drummond 8.6k 2 1 11 1hd 1hd 12 Adams J 119 w *.20 105-12 Beaugay1192Aladear1143Mamanie1138 Easily best 5
5Jun45- 6Bel gd 4½f-W :221 :452 :514 ⒻFashion 5.9k 3 1 1nk 11½ 13½ Adams J 114 w 1.75 96-10 Beaugay1143½Enfilade11915Datura110 Swerved start,easily 3
22May45- 3Jam fst 5f :23 :47 :594 ⒻMd Sp Wt 8 2 1nk 11½ 14 17 Adams J 115 w 3.95 91-14 Bugy1157Srongrl1151BonnBryl1154 Drew away final furlong 12

Bewitch

br. f. 1945, by Bull Lea (Bull Dog)–Potheen, by Wildair **Lifetime record: 55 20 10 11 $462,605**

Own.– Calumet Farm
Br.– Calumet Farm (Ky)
Tr.– H.A. Jones

Date	Track	Fractions	Race	Running line	Jockey	Wt	Odds	Speed	Top three	Comment	Field
3Sep51- 7Was	fst 1	:222 :443 1:09 1:343	3↑ Wash Park H 159k	16 19 1918 1925 1615 1615¼	Brooks S	113wb	7.30	82-07	Curandero115noOil Capitol1161½County Delight1231½		19
	Auxiliary gate opened over a second after main gate										
29Aug51- 7Was	fst 1	:222 :45 1:094 1:354	3↑ ⒻBeverly H 28k	7 9 99½ 1011 77 55½	Dodson D	124wb	*1.70e	84-13	Wistful1261¼War Talk1141¼Lithe1241	No mishap	10
18Aug51- 6Was	fst 7f	:22 :442 1:09 1:212	3↑ Clang H 22k	3 10 911 1012 913 811	Brooks S	118wb	*1.50e	89-07	Lithe1152Seaward110hdWine List1161	Bore in	10
21Jly51- 7Hol	fst 1⅝	:483 1:383 2:032 2:42	3↑ Sunset H 57k	5 3 33½ 53¼ 711 710	Brooks S	110 w	*1.70	84-10	Alderman112noMocopo1066Stormy Cloud105no	Outrun	10
14Jly51- 7Hol	fst 1¼	:464 1:103 2:01	3↑ Hol Gold Cup 137k	4 7 79½ 54 44 24	Lasswell G	108 w	*.35e	90-10	Citation1204Bewitch108noBe Fleet1221	Good effort	10
7Jly51- 7Hol	fst 1 1/16	:231 :462 1:104 1:424	3↑ ⒻVanity H 28k	3 6 57¾ 35 2½ 1¾	Brooks S	125 w	*.35	94-08	Bewitch125¾Fleet Rings1064Great Dream1081½	Driving	7
4Jly51- 7Hol	fst 1⅛	:464 1:11 1:36 1:482	3↑ American H 56k	8 6 63½ 5¾ 1hd 2½	Lasswell G	106 w	*.75e	97-07	Citation123½Bewitch1062¾Sturdy One112¾	Good effort	8
23Jun51- 7Hol	fst 1 1/16	:224 :454 1:102 1:421	3↑ Inglewood H 29k	7 8 89 74¼ 51¾ 4nk	Smith FA	107 w	3.50e	97-08	Sturdy One109hdAll Blue111noBe Fleet123nk	Closed fast	8
30May51- 7Hol	fst 1 1/16	:222 :45 1:101 1:42	3↑ Argonaut H 30k	4 10 1015 87 46½ 43¾	Brooks S	109 w	*.45e	94-08	Be Fleet1183Citation121nkSturdy One111½	Late foot	10
26May51- 6Hol	fst 7f	:221 :444 1:094 1:222	3↑ Handicap 10000	3 9 99 85¾ 75¾ 11¾	Smith FA	110 w	*.70e	97-10	Bewitch1101¾Be Fleet119¾Special Touch123no	Going away	9
19Apr51- 8BM	fst 1	:234 :471 1:114 1:363	3↑ Handicap 5000	3 5 63¼ 54 53 31	Brooks S	110 w	3.65	96-11	Sturdy One109noAlderman1061Bewitch110no	Held well	6
31Mar51- 8BM	fst 1 1/16	:232 :464 1:11 1:431	3↑ San Fran Country H 30k	3 8 87¾ 88½ 74¼ 73	Brooks S	110wb	*1.55	91-11	BeFleet1191¼BullreighJr.113½VinoFno110nk	Close quarters	10
17Mar51- 8BM	fst 1 1/16	:232 :464 1:111 1:43	3↑ St. Patrick's Day H 29k	3 7 76¾ 64½ 42½ 2no	Brooks S	110wb	2.75	95-12	Manyunk113noBewitch110nkSturdy One109nk	Bold finish	8
3Mar51- 7SA	gd 1¼	:462 1:11 1:364 2:023	3↑ S Anita H 135k	7 3 1315 1111 912 611	Brooks S	111 w	*2.85e	76-24	Moonrush114nkNext Move1162¾Sudan111hd	Slow to settle	14
20Jan51- 7SA	fst 1⅛	:461 1:11 1:361 1:483	3↑ ⒻS Margarita H 60k	5 6 56 33½ 22 21	Brooks S	122 w	3.20e	97-16	SpecialTouch1141Bewitch1221¼Bdo'Ross1251½	Strong finish	8
2Dec50- 7Hol	fst 1⅛	:47 1:111 1:362 1:492	3↑ ⒻVanity H 30k	7 7 76¾ 44½ 33 22¼	Brooks S	124 w	2.65e	92-11	Next Move1282¼Bewitch1241Wistful125½	Bore in	9
18Nov50- 6Hol	fst 1	:223 :454 1:102 1:36	3↑ Handicap 10000	2 5 54½ 53½ 32½ 31¼	Brooks S	115 w	*.75e	96-09	Curandero1151Valquest112nkBewitch1151	Finished strong	9
7Nov50- 7Hol	fst 7f	:221 :444 1:091 1:221	3↑ Premiere H 33k	7 14 94¾ 84¾ 64½ 3nk	Brooks S	114 w	9.30	98-12	Star Fiddle108noYour Host125nkBewitch114nk	Forced wide	14
14Oct50- 6GS	fst 1 1/16	:232 :471 1:112 1:434	3↑ ⒻVineland H 24k	13 11 106¾ 78½ 57½ 32½	Brooks S	122 w	*1.20	91-12	Almahmoud1082Lithe118½Bewitch1221½	Closed fast	14
28Sep50- 6Bel	fst 1 1/16	:232 :463 1:11 1:424	3↑ ⒻHandicap 5060	4 6 53 32 2hd 11	Brooks S	122 w	2.20	97-11	Bewitch1221Night Game1102¼Jazz Baby113nk	Ridden out	8
23Sep50- 7Bel	fst 6f	:224 :463 1:111	3↑ ⒻHandicap 5070	5 9 97 89 66½ 44¾	Brooks S	121 w	3.70	89-15	Sweet Dream118noMiss Highbrow1101¼Ouija1103½	No excuse	10
11Mar50- 6GP	fst 1⅛	:473 1:123 1:374 1:492	3↑ Handicap 7500	4 4 54½ 42 1hd 3nk	Scurlock O	123 w	*.40e	97-09	Wynford II112hdArmed111hdBewitch1232½	Lugged in	6
2Mar50- 6Hia	fst 1⅛	:454 1:103 1:353 1:48	3↑ ⒻBlack Helen H 19k	2 5 34½ 2hd 14 17	Scurlock O	126 w	*.70	98-10	Bewitch1267Roman Candle1092Yoncalla1041½	Impeded,best	10
15Feb50- 6Hia	fst 7f	:224 :451 1:102 1:23	3↑ ⒻColumbiana H 9.6k	6 7 76½ 85¼ 43 2no	Scurlock O	126 w	*1.40	97-13	Fighting Fan118noBewitch126¾Nell K.124¾	Just missed	11
3Feb50- 6Hia	fst 6f	:222 :46 1:104	4↑ ⒻAlw 4000	3 3 35½ 33 2hd 11	Culmone J	119 w	*.45	94-12	[D]Bewitch1191Fighting Fan110hdAllie's Pal1166	Bore in	5
	Disqualified and placed third										
11Jan50- 5TrP	fst 6f	:224 :46 1:103	4↑ ⒻAlw 2000	5 5 44½ 42 32 31	Scurlock O	116 w	*.90	93-13	Fighting Fan114noNo Strings1111Bewitch1161½	Good effort	6
15Oct49- 6GS	fst 1 1/16	:224 :461 1:112 1:443	3↑ ⒻVineland H 24k	6 13 1211 58½ 44½ 1¾	Brooks S	126 w	*1.40	90-16	Bewitch126¾Imacomin111¾Lithe1073	Drew out	14
3Oct49- 6Bel	fst 1½	:482 1:131 2:033 2:294	3↑ ⒻLadies H 35k	8 12 129¾ 64¼ 63¼ 41¾	Brooks S	126 w	*1.95	87-14	Gaffery114noMiss Request119nkAdile1151½	Blocked	12
17Sep49- 6Aqu	fst 1⅛	:48 1:124 1:384 1:524	3↑ ⒻBeldame H 72k	17 15 1316 1213 86½ 52¾	Scurlock O	126 w	*2.45	80-17	MissRequest1131[D]Harmonc1121¼Plundr108hd	Slow to settle	18
	Placed fourth by disqualification										
31Aug49- 6Was	fst 1	:223 :444 1:09 1:342	3↑ ⒻBeverly H 27k	4 7 54½ 41½ 22 1nk	Brooks S	125 w	*1.20	98-13	Bewitch125nkStole1046Evanstep111½	Just up	9
6Aug49- 6Was	fst 7f	:213 :44 1:084 1:222	3↑ ⒻMisty Isle H 28k	10 8 87¾ 34½ 21½ 1½	Brooks S	121 w	*1.40	98-08	Bewitch121½Dandilly1171½Stole107nk	Driving	12
27Jly49- 6AP	gd 1	:232 :462 1:102 1:361	3↑ ⒻArl Matron H 27k	7 2 21 22 22½ 23½	Brooks S	121 w	*1.00	87-20	Lithe1023½Bewitch1216Danada Gift112¾	Went well	8
19Jly49- 6AP	fst 7f	:23 :453 1:102 1:232	3↑ ⒻHandicap 4500	3 4 44 33 2hd 2½	Brooks S	122 w	*.70	92-13	Roman Candle105½Bewitch1221½Brownian1104	Hung	6
2Jly49- 6AP	fst 6f	:222 :45 1:10	3↑ ⒻModesty 28k	2 7 93¾ 85 56 53½	Scurlock O	123 w	*1.40e	93-10	No Strings101½Two Lea1112Dandilly1081	No mishap	10
27Jun49- 6AP	fst 6f	:23 :46 1:104	4↑ ⒻAlw 5000	7 5 54 64¾ 2½ 2½	Brooks S	120 w	*.90	92-17	Loriot108½Bewitch1202Blue Helen108nk	Blocked turn	8
20Jun49- 7AP	fst 6f	:223 :452 1:091	4↑ Alw 5000	5 3 52¼ 51¼ 24 26	Brooks S	115 w	*1.00e	95-09	CarraraMarble1046Bewitch1151½StarReward118hd	Went well	10
	Previously trained by B.A. Jones										
30Apr49- 6CD	fst 6f	:222 :452 1:102	3↑ Inaugural H 10k	5 2 44 23 1hd 14½	Glisson G	115 w	*.40e	101-14	Bewitch1154½Enforcer110noSouthern Pride104hd	Easily	7
19Apr49- 5Kee	fst 6½f	:23 :462 1:112 1:181	3↑ Handicap 3500	1 5 43½ 54½ 32 3nk	McCreary C	113 w	*1.10	- -	Plumper108hdJohns Joy107hdBewitch1135	Strong finish	8
	Previously trained by H.A. Jones										
19Mar49- 5GP	fst 6f	:23 :46 1:102	4↑ Alw 3000	4 3 3½ 41¾ 3nk 3½	Nelson E	105 w	*.80	97-06	Carrara Marble120½High Shine112noBewitch1058	Weakened	9
11Aug48- 7Was	sl 7f	:222 :453 1:102 1:243	ⒻArtful H 27k	3 7 54½ 44½ 11 12	Pierson NL	122 w	*.90e	87-16	Bewitch1222Blue Helen1091Miss Mommy1133	Driving	8
21Jly48- 7AP	fst 1	:233 :46 1:10 1:352	Dick Welles 28k	9 2 42½ 32 31 32¼	Pierson NL	118 w	*.80e	93-14	Papa Redbird117hdShy Guy1202½Bewitch1182¼	No excuse	10
14Jly48- 7AP	fst 1	:23 :46 1:11 1:364	ⒻCleopatra H 28k	5 5 65¼ 52¼ 1½ 14	Pierson NL	122 w	*.70e	88-19	Bewitch1224Alablue110¾Ann's Lee1101¼	Easily,bore in	12
3Jly48- 7AP	fst 6f	:214 :443 1:101	3↑ ⒻModesty 29k	16 15 96¾ 69 32 11¼	Woodhouse H	107 w	*1.40e	96-09	Bewitch1071¼Tre Vit1132Bogle1092¼	Drew out	18
23Jun48- 7AP	my 6f	:224 :453 1:114	ⒻPrincess Doreen 28k	6 3 63 66 65½ 52¾	Pierson NL	121 w	*.90	85-19	Miss Mommy121½Silly Gyp112¾Ann's Lee114nk	No excuse	13
	Previously trained by B.A. Jones										
10Apr48- 6Kee	fst 6f	:223 :462 1:12	ⒻAshland 12k	4 1 21 2½ 1hd 1no	Pierson NL	121 w	*.20	92-14	Bewitch121noSilly Gyp115¾Lea Lark1121½	Strong hand ride	4
	Previously trained by H.A. Jones										
4Oct47- 4Bel	fst 6½f-W	:221 :444 1:092 1:154	Futurity 106k	9 3 53 23 33¼	Westrope J	123 w	*.85e	90-10	Citation1223Whirling Fox114nkBewitch1231	Close quarters	14
	Geldings not eligible										
27Sep47- 4Bel	fst 6f-WC	:222 :451 1:101	ⒻMatron 46k	9 3 3nk 3nk 1nk	Dodson D	123 w	*.35	90-10	[D]Bewitch123nkInheritance1152Vaudeville115hd	Bore in	10
	Disqualified and placed last										
16Aug47- 6Was	fst 6f	:223 :45 1:102	Was Futurity 78k	2 1 1hd 14 14 11	Dodson D	119 w	*.20e	98-07	Bewitch1191Citation118hdFree America1182	Ridden out	10
9Aug47- 7Was	fst 6f	:224 :453 1:11	ⒻPrincess Pat 57k	3 1 1hd 14 13 13	Dodson D	119 w	*.30	95-08	Bewitch1193Boswell Lady1154Shy Katie112½	Easily	6
23Jly47- 7AP	fst 6f	:221 :441 1:104	ⒻArl Lassie 58k	1 2 12 13 15 12¾	Dodson D	119 w	*.30e	93-07	Bewitch1192¾Boswell Lady1192¼Lea Lark1192¼	In hand	9
23Jun47- 6AP	fst 5½f	:22 :45 :572 1:04	ⒻPollyanna 20k	2 1 2½ 1hd 14 15	Dodson D	119 w	*.20e	101-10	Bewitch1195Kandy Comfort1163Whirl Some1162	Easily	13
16Jun47- 6AP	fst 5½f	:224 :463 :59 1:05	Hyde Park 23k	2 2 11 14 15 18	Dodson D	119 w	*.50e	96-16	Bewitch1198Loujac116½May Reward116hd	Easily	12
	Previously trained by B.A. Jones										
30Apr47- 6CD	gd 5f	:23 :47 1:003	ⒻDebutante 13k	6 4 32 12 16 18	Dodson D	119 w	*.70	92-26	Bewitch1198Pelt1142Loriot1192	Easily	7
17Apr47- 5Kee	fst *4f	:46	Sp Wt 3000	4 5 32 2hd 1nk	Dodson D	113 w	*.50	100-01	Bewitch113nkCircus Clown115¾Hilda1126	Hard drive	8
10Apr47- 1Kee	fst *4f	:461	ⒻMd Sp Wt	1 5 11 12½ 16	Dodson D	116 w	2.60	99-01	Bewitch1166Blue Helen1161½Bobalee1164½	Easily	11

Bimelech

b. c. 1937, by Black Toney (Peter Pan)–La Troienne, by Teddy — **Lifetime record: 15 11 2 1 $248,745**

Own.– E.R. Bradley
Br.– Idle Hour Stock Farm (Ky)
Tr.– W. Hurley

1Mar41- 6Hia	fst 1¼	:464 1:111 1:362 2:024 3↑	Widener H 65k	5	1	31½	2hd	1hd	42½	Meade D	126 w	*.75	92-12	BigPebble109hdGetOff1151½Hltl1081	Saved ground,led,hung	14
22Feb41- 5Hia	fst 1⅛	:492 1:132 1:38 1:494 4↑	Sp Wt 2500	1	1	11½	11½	11½	11	Meade D	116 w	*.35	92-08	Bimelech1161Hash1185Shot Put1182	Easily	4
20Jly40- 6AP	fst 1¼	:471 1:114 1:37 2:03	Classic 49k	1	1	21½	33½	39	310	Smith FA	126 w	*.60	81-13	Sirocco1217Gallahadion1263Bimelech1268	Weakened	6
8Jun40- 6Bel	fst 1½	:482 1:134 1:381 2:293	Belmont 42k	1	1	21½	1hd	1½	1¾	Smith FA	126 w	*1.35	94-12	Bimelech126¾Your Choice1261Andy K.1268	Drew out	6
18May40- 6Bel	fst 1	:23 :46 1:112 1:371	Withers 20k	6	4	41¾	21½	21½	21½	Smith FA	118 w	*.20	87-15	Corydon1181½Bimelech118noRoman1188	Hung	8
	Geldings not eligible															
11May40- 6Pim	fst 1 3/16	:47 1:12 1:384 1:583	Preakness 70k	5	1	11	11½	11½	13	Smith FA	126 w	*.90	90-15	Bimelech1263Mioland1261½Gallahadion1262	Going away	9
4May40- 7CD	fst 1¼	:48 1:124 1:383 2:05	Ky Derby 72k	2	1	21½	1hd	1½	21½	Smith FA	126 w	*.40	82-14	Gallahadion1261½Bimelech126noDit1261	Weakened	8
30Apr40- 4CD	gd 1	:224 :462 1:112 1:38	Derby Trial 3k	4	1	11	12	12	12¼	Smith FA	118 w	*.10	89-21	Bimelech1182¼Gallahadion1155Sirocco1126	Easily	8
25Apr40- 6Kee	fst 1⅛	:463 1:113 1:372 1:51	Blue Grass 8.5k	3	1	11½	12	13	12½	Smith FA	123 w	*.10e	92-15	Bimelech1232½Roman1233Bashful Duck121	In hand	3
4Nov39- 6Pim	fst 1 1/16	:231 :474 1:131 1:451	Pim Futurity 38k	5	2	21	2hd	11	14	Smith FA	122 w	*.40	94-12	Bimelech1224Rough Pass1225Straight Lead1227	Going away	7
	Geldings not eligible															
7Oct39- 4Bel	fst 6½f-WC	1:164	Futurity 67k	6	4	1hd	12	12	11½	Smith FA	126 w	*.50	88-12	Bimelech1261½Calory1194Call to Colors1192	In hand	7
	Geldings not eligible															
2Sep39- 5Sar	fst 6½f	:23 :461 1:121 1:184	Hopeful 39k	2	9	65¾	56	42¼	1nk	Smith FA	122 w	*.60e	91-09	Bimelech122nkAndyK.1263BoyAngler119nk	Impeded start,str	9
12Aug39- 3Sar	fst 6f	:223 :461 1:104	Sar Spl 9k	4	2	1nk	11	11½	13	Smith FA	122 w	*1.40	98-06	Bimelech1223Briar Sharp122½Andy K.1221	Going away	8
14Jly39- 4Emp	sl 5½f	:224 :462 1:062	Alw 1000	2	3	1½	11½	13	16	Smith FA	117 w	*.60	94-15	Bimelech1176Last Frontier1122Big Flash1126	Much best	5
28Jun39- 4Suf	fst 5f	:224 :46 :591	Md Sp Wt	5	2	2nk	1hd	11½	13	Smith FA	118 w	*1.80	98-16	Bimelech1183Smart Bet1183½Buenos Suerte1183	Easily	8

Blue Peter

b. c. 1946, by War Admiral (Man o' War)–Carillon, by Case Ace — **Lifetime record: 10 8 0 2 $189,185**

Own.– J.M. Roebling
Br.– Joseph M. Roebling (Ky)
Tr.– A. Schuttinger

25Sep48- 5Bel	fst 6½f-W	:22 :441 1:081 1:143	Futurity 113k	10	1		2hd	11½	1½	Guerin E	126wb	2.40e	99-03	BluPtr126½MrtlChrm1237SportPg118½	Driving	12
	Geldings not eligible															
28Aug48- 6Sar	fst 6½f	:232 :47 1:12 1:191	Hopeful 58k	5	2	11	11½	11½	13	Guerin E	126wb	*1.05e	89-12	Blue Peter1263Sport Page1141Curandero114hd	Easily	7
	Daily Racing Form time,1:19 4/5															
14Aug48- 5Sar	fst 6f	:224 :464 :59 1:13	Sar Spl 11k	1	1	11½	13	13	13½	Guerin E	122wb	*.40	83-17	Blue Peter1223½Sport Page1228Entrust1226	Ridden out	4
28Jly48- 5Mth	fst 6f	:221 :462 1:124	Sapling 14k	4	1	16	16	16	16	Guerin E	122wb	*.30e	84-21	Blue Peter1226Harbourton111½Razzmatazz1116	Galloping	7
31May48- 5GS	sly 5f	:222 :453 :584	Garden State 20k	5	1	2hd	1hd	11½	14½	Wright WD	122wb	*1.20	108-15	Blue Peter1224½Noble Impulse1171Irish Sun1227	Easily	5
22May48- 5GS	fst 5f	:222 :462 :583	©William Penn 14k	9	2	12	12½	1½	1¾	Wright WD	117wb	*1.10	109-17	Blue Peter117¾Noble Impulse11710Eatontown1101	Drew out	9
18May48- 4GS	fst 5f	:224 :464 :591	Alw 3500	6	3	12	11	12	13	Wright WD	117wb	*1.40e	106-19	Blue Peter1173Noble Impulse1151Mr. Jay1151½	Easily	10
1May48- 4Jam	fst 5f	:23 :464 1:002	Youthful 19k	3	6	41¾	3½	41¼	32½	Miller P	117wb	4.40	85-20	Eternal World117hdArise1172½Blue Peter1171	Went well	8
24Apr48- 4GS	fst 4½f	:224 :461 :521	Alw 3500	1	3		1hd	1½	13	Miller P	113wb	6.30	- -	Blue Peter1133Mr. Jay1161½Egretta1134	Ridden out	7
17Apr48- 2GS	fst 4½f	:232 :48 :542	©Md Sp Wt	4	9		2hd	32	35	Miller P	120wb	3.20e	- -	Rookwood1202Deep Fen1203Blue Peter120nk	Weakened	12

Bridal Flower

b. f. 1943, by Challenger II (Swynford)–Big Hurry, by Black Toney — **Lifetime record: 44 13 8 12 $222,055**

Own.– King Ranch
Br.– Idle Hour Stock Farm Co (Ky)
Tr.– W.J. Hirsch

5Mar48- 7SA	fst 1⅛	:464 1:113 1:37 1:493 4↑	Handicap 20000	8	5	75¾	75¾	46	45	Peterson M	110 w	*2.10e	90-11	HnkH.1151Brookfld1254ElLobo109no	Forced wide,closed gamely	10
28Feb48- 7SA	fst 1¼	:464 1:114 1:371 2:032 3↑	S Anita H 139k	12	9	43½	77½	913	99¾	Mehrtens W	111 w	18.20	79-22	Talon122noOn Trust1211¾Double Jay1181¼	Forced wide	14
20Feb48- 7SA	fst 1	:231 :462 1:111 1:372 4↑	Alw 7500	4	4	66½	66	55	31¾	Westrope J	113 w	6.05	89-15	Brabancon1151Hank H.120¾Bridal Flower1131	Closed fast	6
14Feb48- 7SA	fst 1⅛	:461 1:102 1:364 1:492 3↑	San Antonio H 69k	9	14	118	1411	1310	118¼	Lt'berg W	114 w	29.80	88-10	Talon122nkDouble Jay1182¼On Trust126½	No factor	18
	Previously trained by M. Hirsch															
8Nov47- 5Jam	sly 1 3/16	:474 1:121 1:384 1:591 3↑	Westchester H 57k	2	2	55	45½	32	11	Mehrtens W	108 w	5.25	80-22	Bridal Flower1081With Pleasure1301½Donor112hd	Drew out	8
6Nov47- 6Pim	hy 1 1/16	:234 :474 1:13 1:464 3↑	ⒻLady Baltimore H 12k	7	3	35½	31	12	19	Mehrtens W	112 w	3.10	84-31	Bridal Flower1129Irisen114hdEarshot117no	Much the best	7
18Oct47- 6Lrl	fst 1¼	:462 1:113 1:38 2:032 3↑	Washington H 29k	5	3	34	34	37	38½	Kirk C	113 w	5.70e	84-20	LoyalLegion1138BlueYonder113.5½BridlFlowr1134	Weakened	6
11Oct47- 6GS	fst 1⅛	:47 1:104 1:36 1:482 3↑	Trenton H 62k	3	5	56½	57	48½	413½	Mehrtens W	116wb	10.10	89-10	Cosmic Bomb1205Double Jay1188Earshot116½	Close quarters	7
4Oct47- 6GS	fst 1 1/16	:232 :472 1:113 1:423 3↑	ⒻVineland H 31k	1	5	54½	55½	59½	515¾	Mehrtens W	118wb	2.05	84-08	Miss Kimo11710Camargo1141½Letmenow111¾	No factor	7
1Oct47- 6Bel	fst 7f	:232 :464 1:111 1:232 2↑	Vosburgh H 28k	3	5	42¼	41¾	4¾	22½	Arcaro E	114wb	7.00	90-14	With Pleasure1322½Bridal Flower1141½Rabies1053	Swerved	8
26Sep47- 6Bel	fst 1	:231 :463 1:113 1:37 3↑	ⒻHandicap 10115	13	5	53	42¼	4¾	32¼	Arcaro E	122wb	*2.30	87-20	CosmicMissile116nkMissKimo1192BridlFlowr122no	No mishap	13
20Sep47- 7Aqu	fst 1⅛	:483 1:131 1:383 1:514 3↑	ⒻBeldame H (Div 2) 60k	2	1	11	11½	1hd	54	Westrope J	118wb	*1.15e	84-12	But Why Not120noMiss Grillo1262Elpis123hd	Tired	11
13Sep47- 6Aqu	fst 1⅛	:502 1:143 1:392 1:522 3↑	Edgemere H 27k	3	2	21½	3nk	1½	32½	Arcaro E	113wb	6.55	82-13	Elpis1141½Stymie1341Bridal Flower1131½	Tired	4
1Sep47- 6Aqu	fst 1 1/16	:242 :474 1:124 1:442 3↑	Aqueduct H 29k	7	2	24	1hd	1hd	44½	Arcaro E	114wb	6.50	87-13	Stymie132½Gallorette122hdElpis1144	Faltered stretch	11
4Aug47- 6Sar	fst 1	:23 :46 1:10 1:352 3↑	Wilson 23k	5	3	35	36½	42½	45	Mehrtens W	112wb	3.90	99-08	Gallorette1121¼Hornbeam1123King Dorsett112¾	Steadied	5
19Jly47- 6AP	fst 1¼	:471 1:113 1:362 2:022 3↑	Arlington H 55k	8	5	21½	22½	23	21	Mehrtens W	111wb	8.10	92-12	Armed1301Bridal Flower1112¼Challenge Me1142	Second best	8
9Jly47- 5Jam	fst 1 1/16	:233 :471 1:121 1:441 3↑	ⒻComely H 28k	4	9	88¾	76½	56¾	512¼	Mehrtens W	126wb	2.55	80-14	Elpis113hdRisolater1212War Date118nk	No menace	9
7Jun47- 5Del	gd 1 1/16	:23 :473 1:132 1:463 3↑	ⒻNew Castle H 30k	6	8	84¼	64¼	4¾	32¾	Mehrtens W	125wb	*2.00	77-21	Elpis1082Rampart111¾Bridal Flower125nk	Close quarters	11
28May47- 6Bel	fst 1 1/16	:224 :454 1:104 1:433 3↑	ⒻTop Flight H 25k	10	7	64¾	76½	1113	1113½	Mehrtens W	126wb	*1.55	79-18	Rytina1041Miss Grillo123nkBe Faithful1211	Flattened out	12
2May47- 5Jam	gd 1 1/16	:232 :473 1:12 1:451 3↑	ⒻHandicap 10050	2	4	47¼	42½	1hd	11½	Mehrtens W	122wb	*.30	87-17	Bridal Flower1221½Be Faithful1216Aladear1114	Easily	5
24Apr47- 5Jam	fst 6f	:232 :47 1:114 3↑	ⒻHandicap 6025	5	4	53¾	32	31	1no	Mehrtens W	122wb	*.90	92-14	Bridal Flower122noRytina1135Recce1206	Driving	5
	Previously owned by J.R. Bradley;previously trained by J.W. Smith															
1Nov46- 6Pim	fst 1 3/16	:481 1:132 1:39 1:57 3↑	Pim Spl 25k	4	1	12	11½	32½	39	DeLara A	117wb	4.25	88-16	Assault1206Stymie1263Bridal Flower117½	Tired	4
19Oct46- 5Jam	fst 1 3/16	:473 1:123 1:39 1:572	Roamer H 31k	2	2	11½	11	1nk	1½	DeLara A	118wb	3.45	89-13	Bridal Flower118½Assault1261½Risolater109nk	Driving	12
15Oct46- 7Bel	fst 1	:233 :461 1:103 1:363 2↑	Turf & Field H 10k	1	2	33½	35½	24	31	DeLara A	115 w	4.15	90-19	Polynesian126¾Coincidence123nkBridalFlower1158	Good try	4
21Sep46- 7Aqu	sly 1⅛	:471 1:122 1:383 1:521 3↑	ⒻBeldame H (Div 2) 56k	8	5	41¼	32	21	11¼	DeLara A	114wb	*2.45	86-13	BridalFlower1141¼Aladear1062½JupitrLght108no	Going away	10
21Aug46- 6Sar	fst 1¼	:473 1:122 1:38 2:041	ⒻAlabama 28k	5	6	58½	21½	21½	23	DeLara A	124wb	*1.25	85-10	Hypnotic1243Bridal Flower124hdAlma Mater1085	Hung	7
	Previously owned by E.R. Bradley															
9Aug46- 6Sar	fst 7f	:222 :444 1:103 1:232	ⒻTest 9.5k	1	7	77½	75¼	32	3¾	DeLara A	123wb	4.70	98-10	RedShoes123nkUpperLevel111½BridlFlowr1232	Finished fast	11
24Jly46- 5Jam	my 6f	:23 :461 1:11	Handicap 7065	1	2	31½	3nk	2nk	3½	Wright WD	115wb	3.85	95-14	Inroc123noMaster Bid112½Bridal Flower115hd	Hung	9
6Jly46- 5Jam	fst 1 1/16	:24 :47 1:114 1:441 3↑	ⒻComely H 23k	5	2	21½	21	3nk	32¾	DeLara A	116wb	*1.35	89-10	Bonnie Beryl114¾Hypnotic1142Bridal Flower1161½	Weakened	9
29Jun46- 6Del	fst 1 1/16	:232 :47 1:114 1:434 3↑	ⒻNew Castle H 28k	4	2	12	12½	12½	14½	DeLara A	111wb	*1.05	94-13	Bridal Flower1114½Surosa1144Mahmoudess1141¼	Easily	6
20Jun46- 6Aqu	fst 1 1/16	:242 :48 1:13 1:462	ⒻGazelle 23k	2	2	21½	1½	12	16	DeLara A	111wb	12.20	82-23	BridalFlower1116Hypnotic1216BonnBryl1161½	Much the best	6
14Jun46- 6Aqu	fst 1 1/16	:24 :481 1:143 1:47	ⒻAlw 8000	1	3	36	25	23	26	DeLara A	112wb	*1.05	73-22	Hypnotic1186Bridal Flower1126Mush Mush1073	Went well	5
4Jun46- 6Bel	fst 6f	:23 :463 1:103	ⒻAlw 5500	3	3	2nk	2nk	1hd	1no	DeLara A	109wb	*1.30	97-11	Bridal Flower109noAladear1083½Mush Mush1072	Hard drive	5
25May46- 7Bel	fst 6f	:223 :462 1:113	Alw 4500	9	6	31½	21½	2hd	1nk	DeLara A	112wb	*1.25	92-14	BridlFlowr112nkSkylghtr1123½Drbyd'Amour117no	Hard drive	9

11May46- 5Bel	fst	6f	:223 :463	1:114	Alw 4500	2	6	63¼	43½	31½	23½	Jessop JD	113wb	3.25	87-14	LarkmeadAndy1183½BridlFlower1131¼HieHeel1221¼	Went well	10
17Nov45- 5Pim	gd	1 1/16	:233 :481 1:134	1:481	ⒻMarguerite 27k	3	3	33	1hd	31½	21	Dodson D	116wb	8.70	76-20	Challadette1191Bridal Flower116¾Athene1166	Gamely	4
12Nov45- 3Pim	fst	1 1/16	:233 :474 1:131	1:473	ⒻAlw 5000	2	1	14	12	1hd	22½	Dodson D	111.5wb	*.45	77-26	Challadette1132½BridalFlower111.55Dtrb1056	Used in pace	6
25Oct45- 4Pim	gd	6f	:23 :463	1:124	ⒻAlw 2500	7	4	1½	11	11½	15	Young S	118 w	2.60	89-19	BridalFlower1185StellarRol115nkArlSong1184	In hand late	11
13Oct45- 6Lrl	fst	1 1/16	:232 :473 1:143	1:472	ⒻSelima 40k	2	4	31½	23	24	35	Dodson D	111wb	7.75	75-20	Athene1114½Edified111½Bridal Flower1115	No rally	9
28Sep45- 4Bel	sly	6f-WC	:231 :46	1:112	ⒻAlw 5000	4	4		3½	32	46	Arcaro E	114 w	2.45	78-21	Pure Gold1141Datura1142Aladear1143	Even effort	5
18Sep45- 4Bel	sly	6f-WC	:214 :443	1:092	ⒻAlw 2500	2			77½	44½	35	McCreary C	119 w	5.00	89-08	Athene1194Pure Gold1191Bridal Flower1192	Slow start	8
	Start obscured by rain																	
23Aug45- 6Bel	fst	6f-WC	:221 :444	1:091	ⒻSpinaway 20k	7	9		97	64¾	2¾	Lindberg H	109 w	3.45	94-05	Sopranist110¾BridalFlower109nkRedShos1142	Finished well	14
15Aug45- 4Bel	fst	6f-WC	:224 :46	1:111	ⒻAlw 3500	2	4		52½	42¾	1¾	Lindberg H	115 w	*.60	85-13	Bridal Flower115¾Harem1153Rytina1152½	Impeded start	9
8Aug45- 2Bel	gd	5½f-W	:224 :461	1:042	ⒻMd Sp Wt	2	3		52¼	4¾	1¾	Lindberg H	115 w	6.00	92-13	BridalFlower115¾Athenia1155DutchCut1151¼	Impeded early	14

Brother Jones

b. g. 1936, by Petee-Wrack (Wrack)-Maridel, by Durbar II **Lifetime record: 40 10 10 5 $48,200**

Own.- H.E. Talbott

Br.- A.B. Hancock (Va)

Tr.- W.R. Miller

10Aug45- 3Bel	fst	*2	S'Chase	3:491	4↑ Shillelah 6.1k	9	7	86¾	54½	58	48	Mallison W	145 ws	7.90	- -	Raylywn1361RougeDragn1521Merctor1376	Saved ground late	10
6Aug45- 3Bel	hy	*2	S'Chase	4:084	4↑ Alw 3000	8	11	717	65¾	34	1hd	Mallison E	139 ws	4.75	- -	Brother Jones139hdMercator1373Boojum II149nk	Driving	14
27Sep44- 5Bel	fst	*2½	S'Chase	4:552	4↑ Brook H 8.8k	2	4	73¼	44	719	727½	Walker G	159 ws	2.90	- -	RougeDrgn1603BurmaRoad1365GrekFlg1341½	Pulled up lame	9
31May44- 5Bel	fst	*2½	S'Chase	4:52	4↑ Meadow Brook H 7k	4	4	43¼	32	22	23½	Walker G	161 ws	*1.95	- -	Iron Shot1593½Brother Jones1616Knight's Quest1473		6
	Bad landing 14th																	
23May44- 5Bel	fst	*2	S'Chase	3:502	4↑ Corinthian H 4.8k	3	7	52½	41½	33	1hd	Walker G	158 ws	5.30	- -	Brother Jones158hdIron Shot158nkKnight's Quest1482½		7
	Between leaders,driving																	
6Oct43- 3Bel	fst	*3	S'Chase	5:533	4↑ Grand National H 18k	11	4	54¼	42¼	12	16	Walker G	150 ws	*2.85	- -	Brother Jones1506Invader145½[DH]Caddie137	Easily	12
15Sep43- 3Aqu	gd	*2½	S'Chase	5:012	4↑ Glendale H 8.6k	5	4	44	32	1hd	11½	Walker G	146 ws	*2.05	- -	Brother Jones1461½Invader145½Parma1358	Impeded	6
25Aug43- 3Bel	fst	*2½	S'Chase	4:471	4↑ Saratoga H 6.2k	1	5	57¼	25	3¾	2½	O'Neill S	146 ws	10.65	- -	Iron Shot148½Brother Jones1461½Corrigan1497	Fast finish	8
18Aug43- 3Bel	fst	*2	S'Chase	3:463	3↑ Beverwyck H 4.1k	8	8	98¼	89¼	57½	38½	Walker G	147 ws	3.75	- -	RougeDragon145½IronShot1458BrothrJons1471½	Steady gain	10
11Aug43- 3Bel	gd	*2	S'Chase	3:52	3↑ North American H 3.8k	2	4	33½	410	32½	21¼	O'Neill S	146 ws	2.60	- -	Elkridge1511¼Brother Jones1462½Redlands1391		6
	Lost stirrup 9th,recovered																	
23Jun43- 3Aqu	fst	*2½	S'Chase	4:53	4↑ Hitchcock H 6.1k	8	7	514	67	33	23	Walker G	143 ws	4.85	- -	Corrigan1423Brother Jones1432Invader1501½	Fast finish	8
9Jun43- 3Aqu	my	*2	S'Chase	3:511	4↑ Lion Heart H 3.8k	6	4	35½	45	43½	46	Walker G	145 ws	*1.35	- -	Knght'sQust1452Invdr150noIronShot1474	Bothered 1st turn	9
1Jun43- 3Bel	my	*2½	S'Chase	5:181	4↑ Meadow Brook H 6.1k	1	2	21½	2nk	112	112	Walker G	141 ws	*1.90	- -	Brother Jones14112Frederic II1402Cottesmore1501½	Easily	7
25May43- 3Bel	fst	*2	S'Chase	3:521	4↑ Corinthian H 3.9k	4	7	54	52¾	31½	2nk	Walker G	139 ws	11.55	- -	Invader145nkBrother Jones1394Boojum II1385	Inside,hung	8
11May43- 3Bel	fst	*2	S'Chase	3:461	4↑ International H 3.9k	7	5	725	820	48	48½	Walker G	140 ws	13.10	- -	Iron Shot1444Knight's Quest1483Invader1501½	No mishap	9
14Nov42- 6Bel	fst	*2½	S'Chase	5:03	4↑ Temple Gwathmey H 3.4k	3	5	42½	32	31½	2¾	Cruz H	142 ws	3.00	- -	Iron Shot144¾Brother Jones142½Cottesmore1561½		10
	Bothered by riderless horse																	
21Oct42- 3Lrl	sl	*2½	S'Chase	5:313	4↑ Chevy Chase H 6.4k	6	2	2½	21½	112	114	O'Neill S	134 ws	12.55	- -	BrotherJones13414StrollingOn1304Cadd1394	Speed to spare	8
28Aug42- 3Sar	fst	*2½	S'Chase	5:114	4↑ Saratoga H 4.3k	1	5	42¾	44	2hd	31¼	Cruz H	138 ws	5.25	- -	Iron Shot136nkElkridge1491Brother Jones1385	Driving	5
22Aug42- 3Sar	fst	*2	S'Chase	4:202	3↑ Handicap 1200	2	4	35	33	3¾	11½	Cruz H	145 ws	7.30	- -	Brother Jones1451½Good Chance1412½Boojum II144¾		7
	Jumped well,driving																	
15Aug42- 1Sar	fst	*2	S'Chase	4:192	3↑ Alw 1200	1	3	621	3nk	32½	34	Cruz H	149 ws	3.55	- -	FayCottage1422½BoojumII1441½BrothrJons1492	Bid,faltered	6
4Jly42- 6PiR	fst	*2	S'Chase	4:162	4↑ Handicap 1650	6	5	1½	11	11	15	Cruz H	146 ws	*1.50	- -	Brother Jones1465Parma14425Chuckatuck14715	Driving	7
25Jun42- 3Del	fst	*2	S'Chase	3:474	4↑ Alw 4000	5	5	43½	26	25	2½	Cruz H	155 w	4.60	- -	Similar143½Brother Jones1558Caddie142hd	Finished well	8
13Jun42- 1Aqu	gd	*2	S'Chase	3:484	4↑ Alw 1500	3	6	68	33½	-	-	Maier F	137 w	12.25	- -	TheBeak1422½GoodChance1504PcoBlncoII1376	Lost rider 9th	8
15Nov41- 3MTP	fst	*2½	S'Chase	5:49	4↑ Handicap 1285	1	6	510	511	49	412½	Collins W	145 w	5.00e	- -	Corrigan156hdCastletown14710BigRebel1392½	Showed little	6
4Nov41- 5Bel	fst	*2½	S'Chase	4:571	4↑ Temple Gwathmey H 3.1k	3	5	512	49	310	23	Collins W	138 w	9.80	- -	Parma1413BrotherJons138hdErndPrs139	Trailed,good finish	6
22Oct41- 2Lrl	fst	*2½	S'Chase	5:062	4↑ Chevy Chase H 6.3k	5	5	518	517	319	320	Jennings E	138 w	11.40	- -	War Lance13315Fay Cottage1375Brother Jones138	Trailed	5
16Oct41- 2Lrl	fst	*2	S'Chase	3:54	3↑ Alw 1000	6	4	318	317	512	510½	Walker G	149 w	*2.20	- -	Rouge Dragon1356Bagpipe1451Frederic II1433	No rally	6
4Oct41- 1Bel	my	*2	S'Chase	3:573	3↑ Handicap 1500	4	2	21	42½	51¼	2hd	Bauman A	144 w	4.15	- -	National Anthem141hdBrother Jones1441Millrace143hd		9
	Poor landing 10th,late gain																	
27Sep41- 2MBr		*2	S'Chase		4↑ Purse 1440	7	7	76¼	-	-	-	Miller R	145 w	-e	- -	Fay Cottage1443The Beak1355Bagpipe138½	Lost rider	9
	No time taken,no wagering																	
14Jun41- 6PiR	fst	*2	S'Chase	4:21	4↑ Handicap 1725	3	4	32½	32½	18	115	Gayer J	136 w	6.85	- -	Brother Jones13615Kellsboro1405Little Cottage II1433		6
	Rated,speed to spare																	
5Jun41- 1Bel	my	*2	S'Chase	4:042	4↑ Alw 1500	1	3	24	22	15	112	Gayer J	138 w	9.00	- -	BrotherJons13812Smoon1457Kllsboro15010	Speed in reserve	8
26May41- 1Bel	fst	*2	S'Chase	3:481	4↑ Alw 1500	1	4	23	22	23	22	Gayer J	144 w	5.05	- -	West Haddon1522Brother Jones1445Frederic II142100		7
	Gained under urging																	
13May41- 1Bel	fst	2	S'Chase	3:492	4↑ Clm 1500	6	6	515	513	311	310	Gayer J	139 w	33.00	- -	Night Heron1398Coxswain1512Brother Jones13915		6
	No early speed,gained under urging																	
21Jun40- 3Del	fst	*2	S'Chase	3:53	4↑ Sp Wt 1000	7	4	3¾	21½	45½	415	Robey T	144wb	45.05	- -	Deanslaw1511Red Gauntlet14412Scurry Along1522	Tired	8
15Jun40- 6UH	fst	*1¼		2:01	3↑ Alw 500	7	8	108	94¼	94	814	Wing W	145 w	184.00	- -	Torch Song145½Navy1492Roustabout158½	No factor	11
23May40- 4Bel	sly	*2	S'Chase	3:572	4↑ Spring Maiden 4.9k	9	15	1216	1125	712	714¾	Gayer J	138 ws	9.50f	- -	Massa1372Fay Cottage1552Star Bramble1445	Never a threat	16
6May39- 3Jam	fst	1 70	:234 :48 1:13	1:432	3↑ Md Sp Wt	3	6	613	615	611	622¾	Balaski L	115wb	60.00	64-11	Gino Rex1153Generalis115¾Burnup1154	Outrun	6
26Apr39- 5Jam	fst	1 70	:233 :474 1:13	1:43	3↑ Md Sp Wt	3	5	59	69½	612	618	Faust F	113 w	60.00	73-14	Challenge1133Black Demon1134Burnup113hd	Never a factor	6
18Nov38- 1Bow	fst	5½f	:233 :48 1:013	1:082	ⒸMd Sp Wt	5	12	1214	1214	65	63½	Yarberry W	111wb	54.35	80-23	One-Tenth111noSir Mowlee1161½Key Man1161	Broke slowly	12
10Oct38- 4Jam	fst	5½f	:223 :461	1:054	ⒸMd Sp Wt	12	12	1223	1224	1218	1224¼	Pikor A	117wb	40.00	67-15	Hy Camp1175Day Off1174Sky Flier112no	No speed	12

Busher

ch. f. 1942, by War Admiral (Man o' War)-Baby League, by Bubbling Over **Lifetime record: 21 15 3 1 $334,035**

Own.-L.B. Mayer

Br.- Idle Hour Stock Farm Co (Ky)

Tr.- G. Philpot

2Jan47- 7SA	fst	6f	:223 :454	1:10	4↑ ⒻAlw 7500	2	6	63	66	56½	55	Westrope J	118 w	*1.00	92-12	Miss Doreen1142Monsoon1141¼Going With Me1111		6
	Dwelt,under urging at finish,worked seven furlongs;Previously trained by G.M. Odom																	
6Oct45- 7Hol	fst	1 1/16	:23 :463 1:111	1:434	3↑ ⒻVanity H 27k	2	4	49	25	11½	12	Longden J	126 w	*.35e	93-09	Busher1262Canina1144Paula's Lulu113hd	Speed in reserve	9
29Sep45- 7Hol	fst	1⅛	:462 1:11 1:371	1:501	Hol Derby 57k	13	6	64¾	4¾	1½	11½	Longden J	123 w	*.65	94-09	Bushr1231½Mano'Glory1121QuickRewrd1212	Bumped 1st turn	14
15Sep45- 7Hol	fst	1	:223 :46 1:112	1:373	Will Rogers H 30k	1	3	3½	43	3½	2hd	Longden J	123 w	*.35	93-11	Quick Reward112hdBusher123½War Allies1103	Driving	14
3Sep45- 7Was	fst	1¼	:463 1:103 1:361	2:014	3↑ Wash Park H 57k	4	3	33	13	13	11½	Longden J	115 w	*1.40	101-12	Busher1151½Armed1201Take Wing1125	Driving	13
29Aug45- 7Was	gd	1	:23 :453 1:104	1:374	3↑ ⒻMatch Race 25k	1	2	1hd	2nk	1hd	1¾	Longden J	115 w	*.50	89-21	Busher115¾Durazna115	Inside,vigorous ride	2
18Aug45- 7Was	fst	1⅛	:463 1:12 1:373	1:512	3↑ ⒻBeverly H 32k	6	6	57½	34½	32½	33¾	Longden J	128 w	*.40e	87-14	Durazna1162½Letmenow1021¼Busher1284	No threat	8
4Aug45- 7Was	fst	1¼	:491 1:14 1:39	2:034	3↑ Arlington H 54k	2	1	12	11	13	14½	Longden J	113 w	*1.10	91-12	Busher1134½Take Wing110noSirde114no	Speed in reserve	8
25Jly45- 6Was	fst	1	:233 :47 1:112	1:372	ⒻCleopatra H 26k	9	4	2hd	12	12	14½	Bailey W	126 w	*.90	91-18	Busher1264½Twosy1162War Date1222½	Speed in reserve	9

Date	Cond/Dist	Fractions	Race	Running line	Jockey	Wt	Odds	Figs	Top three	Comment	Field
4Jly45- 6SA	fst 1 1/16	:224 :461 1:103 1:43	3↑ ⒻS Margarita H 53k	2 5 56 44 3nk 1½	Longden J	126 w	*.75e	97-09	Busher126 1½Whirlabout123½Canina1172	Easily	10
23Jun45- 6SA	fst 1⅛	:46 1:11 1:372 1:50	S Anita Derby 54k	8 4 32½ 1hd 13 2½	Longden J	121 w	*.55	93-09	Bymeabond119½Busher1211Best Effort1265	Wide turn	8
9Jun45- 6SA	fst 1	:223 :454 1:101 1:363	San Vicente 27k	4 4 43½ 21½ 1hd 11¼	Longden J	121 w	*.60e	95-10	Busher121 1¼Sea Sovereign1217Bismarck Sea1212		8
	Impeded by riderless horse										
2Jun45- 6SA	fst 7f	:23 :454 1:104 1:233	ⒻS Susanna 27k	1 2 2½ 11 16 17	Longden J	121 w	*.15	94-15	Busher1217Mist115½Glory Time1152	As rider pleased	7
26May45- 5SA	fst 6f	:224 :463 1:12	ⒻAlw 4000	6 5 1hd 13 15 15	Longden J	121 w	*.20	89-19	Busher1215Glory Time1154Mist1153½	As rider pleased	8
	Previously owned by E.R. Bradley;previously trained by J.W. Smith										
14Oct44- 6Lrl	sl 1 1/16	:233 :474 1:141 1:493	ⒻSelima 29k	3 4 32 23 11½ 13	Arcaro E	117 w	*.90	69-34	Busher1173Ace Card1192½Gallorette1144	Off slowly	10
23Sep44- 4Bel	fst 6f-WC	:222 :451 1:092	ⒻMatron 27k	12 1 51¾ 1hd 1nk	Arcaro E	119 w	*1.40	94-11	Busher119nkTwosy115 1¼Price Level1234	Driving	12
19Sep44- 5Bel	fst 6f-WC	:222 :443 1:083	ⒻAlw 3500	9 5 42½ 3¼ 2hd	Woolf G	119 w	*1.00e	98-05	Nomadic108hdBusher1192Thine1082½	Fast finish	12
30Aug44- 6Bel	fst 6f-WC	:224 :46 1:113	ⒻAdirondack H 10k	11 4 31½ 31¼ 12	Arcaro E	123 w	*2.20	88-18	Busher1232War Date114½Leslie Grey116nk	Bobbled start	12
16Aug44- 6Bel	fst 6f	:222 :462 1:121	ⒻSpinaway 18k	7 12 1111 96¼ 74¼ 43¾	Zufelt F	114 w	*1.20e	85-12	Price Level1152½Ace Card119nkSafeguard1111	Fast finish	12
2Aug44- 3Bel	fst 5½f-W	:224 :454 1:042	ⒻAlw 3000	7 2 2½ 11 14½	Young S	115 w	8.25	92-09	Bushr1154½ScotchPlns115 1¼Conn'sGrl110¾	Speed in reserve	7
30May44- 2Bel	fst 4½f-W	:23 :463 :524	ⒻMd Sp Wt	12 1 21½ 1hd 1½	Atkinson T	115 w	*2.25e	91-09	Busher115½Pin Up Girl115hdFaint Heart115hd	Driving	13

But Why Not

b. f. 1944, by Blue Larkspur (Black Servant)–Be Like Mom, by Sickle

Lifetime record: 46 12 7 5 $295,155

Own.– King Ranch
Br.– Idle Hour Stock Farm Co (Ky)
Tr.– Max Hirsch

Date	Cond/Dist	Fractions	Race	Running line	Jockey	Wt	Odds	Figs	Top three	Comment	Field
10Apr50- 6Jam	fst 6f	:23 :461 1:111	3↑ ⒻCorrection H 18k	3 6 83½ 85¾ 82¾ 106¼	Boland W	123wb	10.00	89-12	Sweet Dream123½Nell K.1263Fighting Fan121nk	No factor	14
	Previously trained by W.J. Hirsch										
25Feb50- 7SA	fst 1¼	:462 1:11 1:351 2:00	3↑ S Anita H 135k	8 5 54 43½ 56 57	Boland W	111wb	52.00	99-11	Noor110 1¼Citation1321Two Lea113nk	Wide,tired	11
22Feb50- 7SA	fst 7f	:222 :452 1:11 1:231	4↑ Handicap 10000	2 2 21 21½ 2hd 1¾	Boland W	110wb	9.65	93-17	But Why Not110¾Bolero1203Top's Boy1112½	Driving	7
13Feb50- 7SA	fst 1	:232 :471 1:112 1:364	4↑ Handicap 8000	5 3 41¾ 43½ 52½ 51¾	Boland W	110wb	4.35	91-13	Old Rockport118hdMoonrush118hdManyunk1201	No mishap	6
4Feb50- 6SA	fst 1⅛	:471 1:114 1:372 1:501	4↑ Handicap 5000	3 1 1½ 1hd 2hd 3½	Boland W	118wb	5.25	91-14	SafeArrival116½Top'sBoy117noButWhyNot1182½	Hard urged	9
25Jan50- 7SA	fst 1	:223 :461 1:112 1:373	4↑ Handicap 5000	8 5 56½ 55 65 44	Arcaro E	115wb	*2.20	85-17	Fervent120 1¼Knockdown120 1¼Autocrat111 1½	Close quarters	8
14Jan50- 7SA	my 1⅛	:472 1:121 1:393 1:524	3↑ ⒻS Margarita H 59k	4 2 21½ 32½ 31½ 34½	Glisson G	116wb	8.85	74-21	Two Lea1262Gaffery1182½But Why Not1163½	Lost whip	8
29Dec49- 7SA	fst 6f	:232 :47 1:111	3↑ ⒻAlw 5000	5 3 21½ 21½ 22 31½	Boland W	111wb	19.30	89-21	Two Lea119hdSweet Dream116 1½But Why Not1114	Hung	7
	Previously trained by M. Hirsch										
12Nov49- 6Jam	fst 1 3/16	:471 1:113 1:37 1:564	3↑ Westchester H 29k	4 1 43½ 43½ 52½ 66½	Boland W	112wb	21.15	85-17	ThreeRings116nkDelegate120hdRoyalGovernor1235	Weakened	11
29Oct49- 6GS	sly 1⅛	:473 1:123 1:392 1:522	3↑ Trenton H 31k	6 5 79 1327 1330 1336	Gilbert J	116wb	11.60	44-26	Sky Miracle113hdChains1113Three Rings1157	Quit	13
22Oct49- 6Jam	fst 1 1/16	:233 :471 1:121 1:451	3↑ ⒻComely H 29k	6 5 35 34 31½ 21¼	Boland W	116wb	9.05	86-17	Lithe107 1¼But Why Not1162Gaffery116no	Good effort	12
15Oct49- 6GS	fst 1 1/16	:224 :461 1:112 1:443	3↑ ⒻVineland H 24k	5 11 99¼ 911 910 67	Gilbert J	118 w	4.50	83-16	Bewitch126¾Imacomin111¾Lithe1073	No mishap	14
17Sep49- 6Aqu	fst 1⅛	:48 1:124 1:384 1:524	3↑ ⒻBeldame H 72k	18 3 34 43½ 56¼ 108¼	Gorman D	125wb	8.65e	75-17	Miss Request1131[D]Harmonica112 1¼Plunder108hd	Tired	18
10Sep49- 5Aqu	fst 7f	:24 :472 1:12 1:25	3↑ Handicap 4040	4 3 42½ 56 55 44¼	Gorman D	122 w	3.15	83-16	Arise1143Paddleduck112½Young Peter118¾	No mishap	5
16Jly49- 6Jam	fst 1 3/16	:472 1:122 1:372 1:571	3↑ Butler H 58k	10 8 33½ 76¼ 78¼ 77¼	Guerin E	118 w	3.25e	83-14	Conniver112noPalestinian1143Stunts1051	Outrun	10
2Jly49- 6Aqu	fst 1¼	:484 1:13 1:372 2:024	3↑ Brooklyn H 58k	3 1 72¾ 73¾ 75¼ 53¼	Guerin E	120 w	*.95e	90-14	Assault122¾Vulcan'sForge129nkFlyingMissel117¾	No mishap	10
8Jun49- 6Bel	fst 1 1/16	:24 :464 1:112 1:433	3↑ ⒻTop Flight H 16k	3 2 23½ 21 11½ 13½	Gorman D	126 w	*1.10	93-13	ButWhyNot1263½Paddleduck119¾Allie'sPal1141	Going away	5
30May49- 6Bel	fst 1¼	:48 1:123 1:38 2:03	3↑ Suburban H 61k	10 2 11 2hd 22 22½	Gorman D	117 w	3.30e	82-17	Vulcan'sForge1242½BtWhyNot1174FlyingMssl108½	Went well	13
14May49- 6Bel	fst 1	:23 :461 1:11 1:362	3↑ Metropolitan H 30k	9 2 63¼ 75¼ 43½ 31¾	Mehrtens W	119 w	5.35	90-15	LoserWepr105 1½Vulcn'sForg126nkBtWhyNot1191	Closed fast	10
5May49- 6Jam	fst 1 1/16	:25 :484 1:13 1:444	3↑ ⒻFirenze H 28k	1 2 22 22 21 12	Gorman D	116 w	7.80e	89-18	But Why Not1162Allie's Pal111½Conniver1263	Drew out	9
30Apr49- 6Jam	fst 1 3/16	:472 1:112 1:363 1:561	3↑ Gallant Fox H 56k	1 2 32 35 613 613	Mehrtens W	110wb	6.95e	82-13	Coaltown1307Vulcan's Forge1192Three Rings1131	Tired	6
	Daily Racing Form time,1:55 4/5										
27Apr49- 6Jam	fst 6f	:232 :464 1:114	3↑ ⒻCorrection H 17k	4 4 63¾ 76¼ 42½ 53½	Arcaro E	119wb	3.65e	88-15	Ocean Brief117hdAlfoxie110¾Paddleduck1112½	No mishap	10
2Apr49- 5Jam	fst 5½f	:23 :463 1:052	4↑ Alw 5000	4 6 66 67½ 69 34½	Mehrtens W	108wb	6.00	86-16	Tavistock1183LocalBand111 1½ButWhyNot108nk	Closed fast	7
15Nov48- 4Jam	fst 1 1/16	:25 :482 1:142 1:472	3↑ Alw 5000	7 2 1hd 1½ 3nk 21¼	Scurlock O	110wb	2.25	75-25	Mother110 1¼But Why Not110hdRinaldo108hd	Held well	7
30Oct48- 6Jam	fst 1 3/16	:48 1:123 1:38 1:574	3↑ Westchester H 57k	2 3 34¼ 76¾ 812 817	Picou C	117wb	5.75e	70-22	Better Self1191War Trophy110nkPhalanx126no	Quit	8
27Oct48- 6Jam	fst 1 1/16	:242 :48 1:13 1:45	3↑ ⒻComely H 29k	8 2 31¾ 42¼ 97 915	Gorman D	119wb	15.05	73-25	Conniver123 1¼Miss Request1205Carolyn A.1182	Quit	10
22Sep48- 6Bel	fst 7f	:224 :452 1:103 1:234	2↑ Vosburgh H 31k	9 6 64½ 74¼ 64¾ 85	Mehrtens W	118wb	5.85e	86-17	Colosal1181Spy Song1292½First Flight124hd	No factor	14
15May48- 5Jam	fst 1 3/16	:48 1:122 1:373 1:571	3↑ Gallant Fox H 87k	5 5 45½ 63¾ 74½ 88¼	Jessop JD	115wb	8.90	82-15	Faultless118hdFervent125½Gallorette1173½	Tired	10
30Apr48- 5Jam	fst 1 1/16	:25 :49 1:133 1:462	4↑ ⒻHandicap 7540	6 4 35 44 43½ 24	Mehrtens W	121wb	*.80	77-17	Harmonica1124But Why Not121noCarolyn A.113 1½	Stumbled	6
25Oct47- 5Jam	fst 1⅝	:50 1:41 2:053 2:442	3↑ Gallant Fox H 83k	3 2 12 23 44 67½	Mehrtens W	112wb	5.75	84-13	Stymie125 1¾Talon1253½Miss Grillo117no	Tired	9
20Oct47- 5Jam	fst 1 3/16	:473 1:121 1:383 1:581	Roamer H 30k	5 5 21½ 31½ 88¾ 814½	Arcaro E	121wb	3.20	70-17	Cosmic Bomb128nkDouble Jay1201Flashco104 1½	Impeded	10
7Oct47- 6Bel	fst 1½	:473 1:123 2:042 2:293	3↑ ⒻLadies H 60k	7 7 2nk 1½ 21 25	Arcaro E	121wb	2.85e	85-14	Snow Goose1135But Why Not1211Gallorette123hd	Weakened	12
20Sep47- 7Aqu	fst 1⅛	:483 1:131 1:383 1:514	3↑ ⒻBeldame H (Div 2) 60k	11 8 105¼ 72¾ 4½ 1no	Arcaro E	120wb	*1.15e	88-12	But Why Not120noMiss Grillo1262Elpis123hd	Hard drive	11
20Aug47- 6Sar	fst 1¼	:472 1:13 1:384 2:05	ⒻAlabama 25k	8 7 48 22 1hd 1nk	Guerin E	126wb	*.70e	83-16	BtWhyNt126nkCosmicMissile1227BeeAnnMac1124	Hard drive	9
26Jly47- 6AP	fst 1¼	:473 1:12 1:354 2:014	Arl Classic 93k	2 1 11 11½ 11 1¾	Mehrtens W	117wb	5.10	96-06	But Why Not117¾Fervent1221Cosmic Bomb1197½	Held well	7
21Jly47- 7AP	gd 1	:23 :46 1:11 1:373	3↑ ⒻArl Matron H 35k	2 2 32 21 11½ 1½	Mehrtens W	114wb	*1.50	84-15	But Why Not114½Say Blue111nkCamargo1123	In hand	14
5Jly47- 5Jam	fst 1 3/16	:483 1:13 1:39 1:574	Empire City 56k	4 5 41¼ 31¾ 2nk 22¼	Mehrtens W	111 w	5.40	85-15	Phalanx1262¼But Why Not111½Harmonica116hd	Weakened	7
14Jun47- 6Aqu	fst 1¼	:474 1:13 1:391 2:054	Dwyer 58k	5 6 56½ 53¼ 2hd 2nk	Mehrtens W	111 w	6.00	78-16	Phalanx126nkBut Why Not1117Brabancon116 1½	Game try	9
20May47- 6Bel	my 1⅜	:483 1:14 1:40 2:181	ⒻC C A Oaks 65k	12 1 64¾ 33 35 43¼	Mehrtens W	121 w	*.70	77-24	Harmonica121nkCosmicMissile1213SnowGoose121hd	Weakened	14
13May47- 6Bel	fst 1	:223 :454 1:12 1:38	ⒻAcorn 19k	6 4 43½ 41¼ 2nk 12	Mehrtens W	121 w	2.00	84-17	But Why Not1212Harmonica1214Alrenie121hd	Going away	13
9May47- 7Pim	fst 1 1/16	:233 :48 1:133 1:462	ⒻPim Oaks 26k	5 1 11 1½ 1hd 11¼	Mehrtens W	121 w	3.90	86-20	But Why Not121 1¼Cosmic Missile1215Oberod121hd	Drew out	10
28Apr47- 4Jam	fst 6f	:23 :462 1:113	ⒻAlw 4500	4 2 21½ 21 2nk 12½	Mehrtens W	109 w	4.65	93-16	But Why Not1092½By Sea1131Cuisine1094	Driving	5
	Previously owned by J.R. Bradley;previously trained by J.W. Smith										
26Oct46- 2Lrl	sly 6f	:23 :48 1:14	Alw 2500	6 1 2½ 11 1½ 1nk	De Lara A	115 w	*.85	84-25	But Why Not115nkLittle Harp1138Gemsbok113 1¼	Driving	6
19Oct46- 4Jam	fst 6f	:23 :464 1:122	ⒻFrizette 20k	10 8 76¼ 55½ 54¼ 52½	Robertson J	108 w	2.80e	86-13	Bimlette110nkCarolyn A.122½Pipette119nk	Even effort	11
14Oct46- 3Bel	fst 5½f-W	:221 :45 1:032	ⒻMd Sp Wt	12 7 3½ 1½ 11	De Lara A	115 w	4.70	97-06	But Why Not1151Telk112nkMuti115½	Ridden out	20
4Oct46- 6Bel	fst 6f-WC	:224 :46 1:102	ⒻAlw 4000	15 4 61¼ 104¼ 86¾	De Lara A	109 w	47.05	82-11	CosmicMissle119 1¼GracieVe1191ShortRgn1191	Showed speed	15

By Jimminy

br. c. 1941, by Pharamond II (Phalaris)–Buginarug, by Blue Larkspur

Lifetime record: 21 9 4 3 $181,120

Own.– Alfred P. Parker
Br.– Idle Hour Stock Farm Co (Ky)
Tr.– J.W. Smith

Date	Cond/Dist	Fractions	Race	Running line	Jockey	Wt	Odds	Figs	Top three	Comment	Field
26Sep44- 6Bel	fst 1⅝	:492 1:391 2:043 2:431	Lawrence Realizatn 17k	2 1 11½ 12 12 13½	Woolf G	126wb	*.30	88-12	By Jimminy1263½Bounding Home126	Saved ground	2
	Geldings not eligible										
26Aug44- 6Was	fst 1¼	:482 1:123 1:371 2:03	American Derby 79k	2 2 11½ 14 14 16	Woolf G	122 w	*1.20	95-09	ByJmmny1226OldKentuck118nkNlsonDunstn118hd	Ridden out	5
12Aug44- 6Bel	fst 1¼	:471 1:114 1:373 2:032	Travers 30k	1 3 2hd 12 11 11	Arcaro E	126wb	*.75	83-16	By Jimminy1261Free Lance112¾Bounding Home1262	Driving	5
	Geldings not eligible										
8Jly44- 5Jam	fst 1 3/16	:464 1:113 1:37 1:561	Empire City 56k	5 3 22 21½ 33 33	Atkinson T	120wb	*.45	97-10	StirUp120½LuckyDraw1202½ByJimminy1202	Drifted out str	7
24Jun44- 6Aqu	fst 1¼	:463 1:12 1:38 2:032	Dwyer 56k	9 4 1nk 11½ 12 14	Atkinson T	114wb	*.95	90-15	By Jimminy1144Stir Up1205Lucky Draw1201	Ridden out	9
17Jun44- 6Aqu	fst 1 1/16	:24 :474 1:132 1:452	Shevlin 12k	4 1 12 11½ 11½ 14	Atkinson T	116wb	2.15	87-15	By Jimminy1164Stir Up122hdStymie1085	Easily	12

12Jun44- 6Aqu fst 7f :23 :46 1:11 1:224 Handicap 4980 5 2 21 21 2½ 13 Atkinson T 116wb 3.25 98-16 By Jimminy1163Lucky Draw1266Stymie1161½ Easily 5
Daily Racing Form time,1:23 1/5
30May44- 5Bel fst 6f :223 :462 1:112 Handicap 4490 5 5 43½ 43 41½ 41¾ Young S 121wb *1.40 91-16 Rodney Stone121noFreezout1151½Sky Tracer116nk Wide,hung 5
20May44- 6Bel fst 1 :231 :461 1:113 1:38 Withers 21k 3 4 31½ 32 22 23 Young S 126wb 3.85 81-14 WhoGoesThere1263ByJmmny126noBoyKnight126nk No match 13
Geldings not eligible
16May44- 6Bel fst 6f :224 :462 1:111 Handicap 4090 6 6 73 64 43 12 Atkinson T 118wb 4.65 94-15 ByJimminy1182Ravnl1111½Jmm115hd Between leaders,driving 7
15Apr44- 6CD gd 6f :224 :461 1:114 3↑ Phoenix H 6.1k 6 3 54½ 68 55½ 511¼ Adams J 111 w 4.90 83-19 RomanSox1081¼AmbrLight1142CoronaCorona1074 No threat 7
3Nov43- 6Pim my 1$\frac{1}{16}$:232 :48 1:141 1:473 Pim Futurity 38k 6 2 22½ 2½ 1½ 2½ Givens C 119wb 5.20 79-30 Platter119½By Jimminy1198Smolensko1222 Gamely 8
Geldings not eligible
22Oct43- 5Pim fst 6f :223 :463 1:133 Alw 2000 5 5 32¼ 31¾ 3nk 13 Givens C 120wb *1.60 85-24 By Jimminy1203Dustman1171¼Vim1172½ Easily 11
13Oct43- 6Pim fst 6f :224 :463 1:132 Richard Johnson 6.8k 8 4 41¼ 32 43¾ 32½ Young S 122wb 2.15 83-17 DirectorJ.E.1152RoyalPrince115½ByJmmny1221 Wide,driving 8
2Oct43- 4Bel sly 6½f-W :231 :461 1:111 1:174 Futurity 68k 4 7 2½ 32 86½ Young S 122wb 40.90 76-17 Occupy1261¼Rodney Stone1221Platter1142 Early speed 11
Geldings not eligible
25Sep43- 2Bel fst 6f-WC :224 :454 1:10 ©Alw 2300 11 2 3½ 41¾ 25 Young S 119wb 7.75 91-04 Pensive1155By Jimminy1195Great Ripple115hd No match 18
28Aug43- 4Bel gd 6½f :223 :463 1:113 1:182 Hopeful 42k 11 5 31½ 21½ 22 34 Givens C 122wb *1.30e 84-12 Bee Mac1193Boy Knight1221By Jimminy122nk Bid,faltered 12
Previously owned by E.R. Bradley
21Aug43- 4Bel fst 6f :224 :464 1:124 Grand Union Hotel 13k 3 7 83½ 61¼ 3½ 1nk Givens C 112wb 7.05e 86-11 By Jimminy112nkSmolensko1161½Boy Knight1221½ Driving 13
17Aug43- 6Bel fst 6f-WC :231 :464 1:12 Albany H 7.2k 2 3 52 41 23 Young S 110wb 8.45 83-14 Rodney Stone1193ByJimminy110hdTropea1194 Impeded start 6
9Aug43- 6Bel fst 6f :23 :462 1:112 Alw 2500 3 2 77¾ 711 77¾ 57½ Young S 112 w 31.20 85-12 Ravenala1121½Stir Up1124Home Flight1122 No factor 8
29Jly43- 5Bel gd 5½f-W :231 :464 1:054 ©Alw 1800 4 8 115 95¼ 613 Young S 111 w 14.75e 72-16 Home Flight116½Stir Up1161½Hercules1165 No factor 12

Capot

br. c. 1946, by Menow (Pharamond II)–Piquet, by St. Germans **Lifetime record: 28 12 4 7 $345,260**
Own.– Greentree Stable
Br.– Greentree Stud Inc (Ky)
Tr.– J.M. Gaver

5Aug50- 6Sar sly 1¼ :482 1:141 1:403 2:063 3↑ Whitney 23k 3 1 11 2½ 41½ 46¼ Atkinson T 120wb *1.15 69-19 Piet1161Sun Bahram1164Adile1151¼ Bore out,weakened 6
1Aug50- 6Sar fst 1 :233 :464 1:114 1:382 3↑ Wilson 17k 5 1 1hd 1hd 1hd 11 Atkinson T 120wb *.65 85-16 Capot1201Donor110noArise1101 Ridden out 7
5Jly50- 6Jam fst 6f :224 :453 1:092 3↑ Fleetwing H 22k 1 2 43½ 75¼ 56 36 Guerin E 128wb 2.35e 98-06 Sheilas Reward116hdGuillotine1156Capot1281 Closed well 9
28Oct49- 7Pim fst 1$\frac{3}{16}$:461 1:104 1:363 1:564 3↑ Pim Spl 15k 1 1 11 12 16 112 Atkinson T 120wb 1.50 96-13 Capot12012Coaltown126 Easily 2
15Oct49- 6Jam fst 1$\frac{1}{16}$:242 :48 1:124 1:442 3↑ Grey Lag H 29k 2 2 2hd 2hd 3½ 31 Atkinson T 121wb *1.50 90-16 Royal Governor1141Three Rings116hdCapot121nk Hung 12
5Oct49- 6Bel fst 1 :224 :453 1:103 1:353 3↑ Sysonby 23k 2 2 2½ 2½ 1hd 11½ Atkinson T 120wb 3.40 96-13 Capot1201½Coaltown1263Manyunk126 Drew clear 3
21Sep49- 6Bel fst 1 :23 :461 1:111 1:364 Jerome H 24k 2 2 2hd 1½ 2½ 1no Atkinson T 126wb *1.70 90-14 Capot126noArise1162Double Brandy109¾ Hard drive 11
8Aug49- 6Sar fst 7f :224 :452 1:102 1:232 Handicap 4065 2 4 2hd 34 43¼ 37 Atkinson T 126wb *.85 92-11 Halt1101Daiquari1066Capot1263½ No rally 6
30Jly49- 6AP gd 1¼ :461 1:104 1:364 2:031 Arl Classic 87k 2 2 38 56 510 515 Atkinson T 126wb 4.50 74-19 Ponder1263Admiral Lea1193Palestinian1266 Tired 6
9Jly49- 6Jam fst 1$\frac{3}{16}$:474 1:123 1:373 1:571 Emp City H 56k 2 1 2½ 21½ 34 33¾ Atkinson T 130wb *1.15e 86-16 Palestinian1252½Reveille1131¼Capot130nk No excuse 7
2Jly49- 6Del fst 1⅛ :463 1:104 1:36 1:482 Leonard Richards 31k 1 3 32½ 32 32 1½ Atkinson T 126wb *.10e 103-08 [D]Capt126½SunBahrm115½[D]WnLst1195 Saved ground,driving 4
Disqualified and placed third due to inference caused by entrymate
11Jun49- 6Bel fst 1½ :514 1:152 2:043 2:301 Belmont 91k 7 5 11½ 11 11 1½ Atkinson T 126wb 5.60 87-13 Capot126½Ponder126½Palestinian12612 Driving 8
Geldings not eligible
4Jun49- 6Bel fst 1⅛ :453 1:093 1:362 1:492 Peter Pan H 18k 6 2 2½ 3½ 43 710 Atkinson T 128wb *1.15 84-18 Ponder123¾Colonel Mike1136Old Rockport119¾ No excuse 9
14May49- 6Pim fst 1$\frac{3}{16}$:462 1:103 1:363 1:56 Preakness 110k 1 2 22 22 2hd 1hd Atkinson T 126wb 2.50 102-08 Capot126hdPalestinian1263Noble Impulse126no Hard drive 9
7May49- 7CD fst 1¼ :462 1:123 1:383 2:041 Ky Derby 119k 9 5 21½ 21 13 23 Atkinson T 126wb 13.10e 83-15 Ponder1263Capot1264½Palestinian1262 Tired 14
3May49- 6CD fst 1 :222 :452 1:101 1:372 Derby Trial 12k 6 3 44½ 45 37 36¾ Atkinson T 118wb 3.90 85-11 Olympia1181¼Ponder1105½Capot1184 Tired 7
23Apr49- 6Jam sly 1$\frac{1}{16}$:233 :47 1:12 1:45 Wood Memorial 46k 3 2 22½ 32 35 36¼ Atkinson T 126wb 5.40 82-14 Olympia126nkPalestinian1266Capot126¾ Went well 8
16Apr49- 6HdG fst 1$\frac{1}{16}$:231 :471 1:121 1:451 Chesapeake 35k 4 2 2½ 1hd 11 1no Atkinson T 122wb *.70 87-20 Capot122noSlam Bang1161½Swap Out1142 Hard urged 6
7Apr49- 6Jam fst 6f :23 :46 1:114 3↑ Handicap 6530 2 3 32 25 24 25 Atkinson T 114wb *.65 87-21 Buzfuz1225Capot114½Energetic1187 Ridden out 4
6Nov48- 7Pim sl 1$\frac{1}{16}$:23 :464 1:12 1:454 Pim Futurity 57k 7 1 1½ 11 12 13½ Atkinson T 119wb *1.30 89-25 Capot1193½Slam Bang122nkSun Bahram1221½ Easily 9
30Oct48- 4Pim fst 1$\frac{1}{16}$:224 :461 1:103 1:423 Alw 4000 5 2 21½ 21½ 1hd 1½ Atkinson T 122wb *.40 105-00 [D]Capot122½SlamBang1164SunBahrm115.51½ Bumped rival str 5
Disqualified and placed second
20Oct48- 6Jam fst 6f :23 :464 1:121 Wakefield 17k 5 4 43¼ 43 2hd 11 Atkinson T 122wb *.95 90-24 Capot1221Entrust11410Prince Quest1224 Drew out 7
2Oct48- 5Bel fst 1 :23 :46 1:112 1:371 Champagne 33k 6 3 1hd 1hd 1½ 1½ Atkinson T 110wb 3.15 88-09 Capot110½Stone Age111½Flying Disc1074 Driving 9
27Sep48- 7Bel fst 1 :232 :462 1:114 1:372 Alw 5000 6 1 11½ 12 13 17 Atkinson T 111wb *2.60e 87-15 Capot1117Benvenuto1112Dry Fly114nk Easily 11
20Sep48- 5Bel fst 6f-WC :223 :452 1:103 Futurity Trial 10k 1 6 2hd 115¼ 99¼ Atkinson T 118 w 40.00 79-12 Ocean Drive118¾Olympia1183Roman Bout1131 Early foot 17
16Sep48- 4Bel fst 6f-WC :223 :452 1:101 Alw 4000 15 11 71¼ 63¼ 119¼ Atkinson T 118 w 5.30 81-15 Roman Bout1082Whirl Awhile118hdEntrust118hd Tired 20
22May48- 4Bel fst 5f-WC :232 :47 :591 Alw 5000 5 2 1hd 2nk 11½ Atkinson T 111 w 2.95 84-14 Capot1111½Mirabeau1146Amarillo Kid1131½ Drew out 6
18May48- 2Bel sl 4½f-W :232 :48 :543 ©Md Sp Wt 10 7 4¾ 2hd 22 Atkinson T 116 w 19.65 80-16 Mirabeau1162Capot116½Illuminable116hd Weakened 21

Citation

b. c. 1945, by Bull Lea (Bull Dog)–Hydroplane II, by Hyperion **Lifetime record: 45 32 10 2 $1,085,760**
Own.– Calumet Farm
Br.– Calumet Farm (Ky)
Tr.– H.A. Jones

14Jly51- 7Hol fst 1¼ :464 1:103 2:01 3↑ Hol Gold Cup 137k 10 6 33 12 13 14 Brooks S 120 w *.35e 94-10 Citation1204Bewitch108noBe Fleet1221 Ridden out 10
4Jly51- 7Hol fst 1⅛ :464 1:11 1:36 1:482 3↑ American H 56k 5 5 52½ 4nk 2hd 1½ Brooks S 123 w *.75e 98-07 Citation123½Bewitch1062¾Sturdy One112¾ Driving 8
14Jun51- 7Hol fst 1 :232 :463 1:104 1:354 4↑ Handicap 15000 3 3 31 1hd 1½ 1½ Brooks S 120 w *.95 98-10 Citation120½Be Fleet123¾Sturdy One110½ Driving 5
30May51- 7Hol fst 1$\frac{1}{16}$:222 :45 1:101 1:42 3↑ Argonaut H 30k 6 5 59½ 44 24 23 Smith FA 121 w *.45e 95-08 Be Fleet1183Citation121nkSturdy One111½ Closed well 10
11May51- 7Hol fst 6f :221 :452 :573 1:10 3↑ Premiere H 18k 3 8 86¼ 96¼ 84 52¾ Brooks S 120 w *1.15 93-12 SpecilTouch122nkMnyunk1141½BullrghJr.1101 Closed ground 10
26Apr51- 8BM fst 6f :223 :453 1:094 3↑ Alw 3000 2 5 55 43½ 33 32½ Brooks S 120 w *.60 97-10 Pancho Supreme1181¼A Lark1181Citation1203½ No excuse 5
18Apr51- 8BM fst 6f :223 :453 1:094 4↑ Alw 3250 4 3 46 43½ 32 31 Brooks S 120 w *.55 98-13 A Lark109noPancho Supreme1201Citation1202¼ Good effort 6
24Jun50- 8GG fst 1¼ :451 1:091 1:34 1:581 3↑ Golden Gate H 57k 3 2 313 37 34 23 Brooks S 126 w 1.20 105-12 Noor1273Citation1261On Trust1032½ No excuse 5
17Jun50- 8GG fst 1⅛ :463 1:093 1:344 1:464 3↑ Forty-Niners H 10k 3 2 21½ 1hd 1hd 2nk Brooks S 128 w *.50 104-08 Noor123nkCitation1283Roman In1112 Outgamed 5
3Jun50- 8GG fst 1 :221 :441 1:073 1:333 3↑ GG Mile H 23k 6 2 22 2½ 1hd 1¾ Brooks S 128 w *.60 104-08 Citation128¾Bolero1235On Trust116nk Driving 6
17May50- 7GG fst 6f :22 :442 1:082 4↑ Alw 4000 4 5 55 52¾ 21½ 2¾ Glisson G 120 w *.25 99-10 Roman In120¾Citation1201¼Blue Border1173 Forced wide 8
4Mar50- 7SA fst 1¾ :474 2:023 2:271 2:524 3↑ S Juan Capistrano H 64k 8 4 2hd 1hd 1hd 2no Brooks S 130 w *.60 127-06 Noor117noCitation13012½Mocopo107hd Just failed 8
25Feb50- 7SA fst 1¼ :462 1:11 1:351 2:00 3↑ S Anita H 135k 5 7 64 32½ 32 21¼ Arcaro E 132 w *.35e 105-11 Noor1101¼Citation1321Two Lea113nk Close quarters 11
11Feb50- 7SA gd 1⅛ :471 1:113 1:372 1:501 3↑ San Antonio H 60k 7 4 35 22 2½ 21 Arcaro E 130 w *.45e 91-17 Ponder1281Citation130½Noor114¾ Forced wide 9
26Jan50- 7SA fst 6f :223 :46 1:104 4↑ Handicap 6000 4 1 42¼ 31½ 2hd 2nk Brooks S 130 w *.25 93-15 Miche114nkCitation1303½Huon Kid107½ Close quarters 6
11Jan50- 4SA sly 6f :223 :461 1:112 4↑ Alw 5000 3 4 33 31½ 3nk 11½ Brooks S 124 w *.15 90-19 Citation1241½Bold Gallant112nkRoman In1163½ Drew away 4
11Dec48- 7Tan gd 1¼ :48 1:13 1:373 2:024 3↑ Tanforan H 54k 2 2 1½ 11½ 13½ 15 Arcaro E 123 w *.05 103-12 Citation1235Stepfather1102½See-tee-see1172 Easily best 7
3Dec48- 7Tan my 6f :231 :463 1:12 Alw 5000 4 5 21½ 2hd 11½ 11½ Arcaro E 126 w *.10 95-23 Citation1261½Bold Gallant1122Barsard1095 In hand 5
29Oct48- 6Pim fst 1$\frac{3}{16}$:504 1:152 1:421 1:594 3↑ Pim Spl 10k 1 1 1 1 1 1 Arcaro E 120 w 83-11 Citation120 Breezing 1
Walkover

16Oct48-7Bel	fst 1⅝	:48 1:381 2:034 2:424 3↑	Gold Cup 111k	8 3 33 12 14 12	Arcaro E	119 w	*.15	90-19	Citation1192Phalanx1265Carolyn A.1232½	In hand 9
		Geldings not eligible								
2Oct48-6Bel	fst 2	:48 2:294 2:562 3:213 3↑	J C Gold Cup 108k	7 1 15 18 18 17	Arcaro E	117 w	*.30	96-09	Citation1177Phalanx12412Beauchef124hd	Easily 7
		Geldings not eligible								
29Sep48-6Bel	fst 1	:224 :452 1:101 1:36 3↑	Sysonby Mile 29k	6 4 46 12 12 13	Arcaro E	119 w	*.10e	94-14	Citation1193First Flight123nkCoaltown1194	Eased up 6
28Aug48-7Was	fst 1¼	:462 1:10 1:353 2:013	American Derby 88k	1 1 21½ 11½ 1hd 11	Arcaro E	126 w	*.10e	95-10	Citation1261Free America1181Volcanic1182	Driving 5
21Aug48-4Was	fst 6f	:223 :45 1:104	Alw 4000	4 3 22 21 11 12½	Pierson NL	120 w	*.20	93-09	Citation1202½King Rhymer1141¼Speculation1176½	Easily 4
5Jly48-7AP	fst 1⅛	:464 1:104 1:354 1:491 3↑	Stars & Stripes H 56k	6 5 53½ 3½ 11½ 12	Arcaro E	119 w	*.30e	100-07	Citation1192Eternal Reward116nkPellicle106hd	Driving 9
12Jun48-6Bel	fst 1½	:482 1:123 2:023 2:281	Belmont 117k	1 1 1hd 14 15 18	Arcaro E	126 w	*.20	97-10	Citation1268Better Self126½Escadru1265	Much the best 8
		Geldings not eligible								
29May48-6GS	fst 1¼	:47 1:113 1:36 2:03	Jersey 61k	4 4 1hd 13 18 111	Arcaro E	126 w	*.10	108-11	Citation12611Macbeth114¾DBovard114¾	Eased up 5
15May48-6Pim	hy 1 3/16	:502 1:16 1:43 2:022	Preakness 134k	4 1 11½ 12 12½ 15½	Arcaro E	126 w	*.10	70-43	Citation1265½Vulcan's Forge1263½Bovard126nk	Galloping 4
		Previously trained by B.A. Jones								
1May48-7CD	sly 1¼	:463 1:112 1:38 2:052	Ky Derby 111k	1 2 26 2½ 12 13½	Arcaro E	126 w	*.40e	80-22	Citation1263½Coaltown1263My Request1261½	Drew away 6
27Apr48-5CD	fst 1	:23 :46 1:103 1:372	Derby Trial 12k	2 2 2½ 12 11½ 11¼	Arcaro E	118 w	*.10	92-23	Citation1181¼Escadru118½Eagle Look11020	Easily 4
		Previously trained by H.A. Jones								
17Apr48-6HdG	gd 1 1/16	:24 :483 1:132 1:454	Chesapeake 29k	4 3 31 11 13 14½	Arcaro E	122 w	*.20	84-16	Citation1224½Bovard1195Dr. Almac1196	Easily 4
12Apr48-6HdG	my 6f	:233 :47 1:122	Chesapeake Trial 12k	6 1 41¾ 41½ 22 21	Arcaro E	126 w	*.30	88-27	Saggy1221Citation1264Dr. Almac1221½	Carried wide 6
28Feb48-6Hia	fst 1⅛	:462 1:103 1:354 1:484	Flamingo 62k	4 4 1hd 1hd 13 16	Snider A	126 w	*.20	97-09	Citation1266Big Dial1184Saggy1221	Easily 7
18Feb48-6Hia	fst 1⅛	:454 1:10 1:352 1:49	Everglades H 10k	1 2 23 1½ 11 11	Snider A	126 w	*.15	96-11	Citation1261Hypnos1094Silverling112	Easily 3
11Feb48-6Hia	fst 7f	:232 :46 1:101 1:23 3↑	Seminole H 12k	8 2 2hd 2hd 1hd 11	Snider A	112 w	*.40e	97-16	Citation1121Delegate123nkArmed1282	Drew out 9
2Feb48-6Hia	fst 6f	:223 :454 1:102 3↑	Alw 5000	2 7 2hd 2hd 1hd 11	Snider A	113 w	*.20e	96-10	Citation1131Kitchen Police1101¾Say Blue1071½	Handily 7
8Nov47-5Pim	my 1 1/16	:234 :483 1:14 1:484	Pim Futurity 48k	4 2 31½ 2hd 1½ 11½	Dodson D	119 w	*.40	74-41	Citation1191½Better Self1198Ace Admiral1222	Ridden out 5
4Oct47-4Bel	fst 6½f-W	:221 :444 1:092 1:154	Futurity 106k	14 4 31½ 13 13	Snider A	122 w	*.85e	93-10	Citation1223Whirling Fox114nkBewitch1231	Easily 14
		Geldings not eligible								
30Sep47-4Bel	fst 6f-WC	:233 :453 1:11	Futurity Trial 10k	2 9 71 61¼ 11	Snider A	116 w	2.10	86-16	Citation1161Gasparilla116nkUp Beat116hd	Drew away 14
16Aug47-6Was	fst 6f	:223 :45 1:102	Was Futurity 78k	5 3 44 47 36 21	Brooks S	118 w	*.20e	97-07	Bewitch1191Citation118hdFree America1182	Good effort 10
30Jly47-7Was	fst 6f	:224 :453 1:103	Elementary 24k	10 5 21½ 1½ 11 12	Dodson D	122 w	*1.40	97-07	Citation1222Salmagundi110noBillings113nk	Going away 10
24Jly47-5AP	fst 5f	:223 :453 :58	Alw 4000	2 4 42 43½ 32 1½	Dodson D	117 w	2.20	102-12	Citation117½Kandy Comfort1141½Queen Hairan1142	Driving 8
21May47-5HdG	gd 5f	:23 :464 :591	Alw 3500	1 4 22 23 22 11¾	Snider A	119 w	*.40	99-18	Citation1191¾Little Tony1138Grand Entry1163	Going away 6
3May47-4Pim	fst 5f	:231 :481 1:011	Alw 3500	1 1 11 1hd 1½ 13½	Snider A	119 w	*1.00	95-19	Citation1193½Newsweekly1191Still Champ119nk	Going away 6
22Apr47-3HdG	sl 4½f	:23 :482 :542	©Md Sp Wt	2 2 35 33 1½	Snider A	120 w	*1.60	93-07	Citation120½Sunday Beau120nkBrass Band120no	Driving 11

Coaltown

b. c. 1945, by Bull Lea (Bull Dog)–Easy Lass, by Blenheim II

Lifetime record: 39 23 6 3 $415,675

Own.– Calumet Farm
Br.– Calumet Farm (Ky)
Tr.– H.A. Jones

30Jly51-6Was	fst 6f	:221 :452 1:093 3↑	Drexel H 16k	4 3 42½ 54 79 79¼	Brooks S	124wb	*1.80	89-10	JohnsJoy124½WineList1121½Yllmntown1131½	Had little left 7
30May51-7Hol	fst 1 1/16	:222 :45 1:101 1:42 3↑	Argonaut H 30k	1 1 14 11½ 79½ 915	Shoemaker W	125wb	*.45e	83-08	Be Fleet1183Citation121nkSturdy One111½	Stopped 10
26May51-6Hol	fst 7f	:221 :444 1:094 1:222 3↑	Handicap 10000	1 4 11 11 1hd 64½	Brooks S	127wb	*.70e	92-10	Bewitch1101¾Be Fleet119¾Special Touch123no	Tired badly 9
5May51-9BM	gd 6f	:222 :452 1:10 3↑	Children's Hospitl H 29k	6 6 41½ 2hd 1hd 12	Shoemaker W	123wb	*1.10	98-20	Coaltown1232SpecialTouch1242½BullrghJr.109no	Going away 8
7Apr51-9BM	fst 6f	:221 :451 1:094 3↑	Art Sparks H 17k	3 5 1hd 2hd 1hd 1no	Brooks S	121wb	2.45	99-08	Coaltown121noSpecial Touch1242¼Manyunk1151¼	Hard drive 8
24Mar51-8BM	fst 6f	:223 :451 1:10 3↑	Alameda H 18k	7 9 93¾ 85½ 107¼ 95¾	Brooks S	126wb	*1.35	92-08	SpecialTouch1211½KitCrson118¾BullrghJr.118no	Raced wide 12
17Feb51-7SA	fst 1⅛	:453 1:101 1:363 1:492 3↑	San Antonio H 68k	11 8 86¼ 84¾ 1416 1414¾	Brooks S	126wb	*1.55e	79-17	All Blue111¾Sudan109hdNext Move119½	Outrun 16
16Dec50-6Hol	fst 6f	:221 :45 1:091 3↑	Alw 5000	6 1 1hd 1hd 11 12½	Brooks S	124 w	2.35e	100-12	Coaltown1242½Star Fiddle124nkBolero124nk	Ridden out 6
		Previously trained by B.A. Jones								
13Apr50-6Kee	fst 6f	:221 :454 1:104 3↑	Phoenix H 12k	2 5 55 54 55 57	Scurlock O	130 w	*.50	91-12	Mount Marcy115noKing Bay1071Ol' Skipper113no	Outrun 6
25Feb50-6Hia	sl 1¼	:48 1:122 1:382 2:06 3↑	Widener H 61k	1 1 11½ 25 46½ 510	Scurlock O	132 w	*.70	65-27	Royal Governor118nkArise1096Going Away1104	Tired badly 6
11Feb50-6Hia	fst 1⅛	:463 1:111 1:37 1:501 3↑	McLennan H 33k	9 3 31 2hd 2hd 32	Mehrtens W	132 w	*.55e	85-17	Three Rings1171Royal Governor1161Coaltown1321	Tired 11
		Previously trained by H.A. Jones								
28Oct49-7Pim	fst 1 3/16	:461 1:104 1:363 1:564 3↑	Pim Spl 15k	2 2 21 22 26 212	Brooks S	126wb	*.30	84-13	Capot12012Coaltown126	Outrun 2
5Oct49-6Bel	fst 1	:224 :453 1:103 1:353 3↑	Sysonby 23k	1 1 1½ 1½ 2hd 21½	Brooks S	126 w	*.10	94-13	Capot1201½Coaltown1263Manyunk126	Bore out,tired 3
5Sep49-6Was	sl 1¼	:473 1:122 1:373 2:034 3↑	Wash Park H 52k	3 4 2hd 1½ 11 1¾	Brooks S	130 w	*.10e	83-19	Coaltown130¾Armed1101Lithe102.524¼	Handily 4
20Aug49-6Was	fst 1	:222 :451 1:083 1:34 3↑	Whirlaway 32k	5 1 11 13 14 12¼	Brooks S	130 w	*.30e	105-03	Coaltown1302¼Ponder118½Star Reward1143	Easily 5
23Jly49-6AP	gd 1¼	:463 1:11 1:361 2:032 3↑	Arlington H 54k	1 4 12 16 15 13	Brooks S	130 w	*.40e	88-19	Coaltown1303Star Reward1161Armed1135	Easily 6
4Jly49-6AP	fst 1⅛	:472 1:103 1:352 1:482 3↑	Stars & Stripes H 54k	3 1 1hd 1hd 12 11¼	Brooks S	130 w	*.40e	104-09	Coaltown1301¼Armed110½Star Reward121½	Ridden out 6
25Jun49-6AP	fst 1	:222 :442 1:083 1:35 3↑	Equipoise Mile H 27k	2 4 33 32 2hd 23	Brooks S	132 w	*.30e	94-12	Star Reward1163Coaltown1322Carrara Marble112hd	Weakened 8
11Jun49-6Nar	fst 1 3/16	:472 1:111 1:361 1:57 3↑	Roger Williams H 16k	3 3 12 18 115 112	Scurlock O	130 w	*.10	88-14	Coaltown13012GrandEntry104hdFncyFlyr1052¼	Much the best 5
30Apr49-6Jam	fst 1 3/16	:472 1:112 1:363 1:561 3↑	Gallant Fox H 56k	5 3 21 11 15 17	Brooks S	130 w	*.25	95-13	Coaltown1307Vulcan'sForge1192ThreRngs1131	Much the best 6
		Daily Racing Form time, 1:55 4/5								
23Apr49-6HdG	my 1 1/16	:272 :531 1:183 1:521 3↑	Edward Burke H 6.3k	0 0 - - - -	Brooks S	130		--	Coaltown130	Walkover 1
19Mar49-6GP	fst 1¼	:45 1:09 1:341 1:594 3↑	Gulf Park H 20k	6 1 15 110 18 17	Scurlock O	128 w	*.10e	108-06	Coaltown1287Three Rings118½Armed1162½	Much the best 9
26Feb49-7Hia	fst 1¼	:472 1:112 1:363 2:02 3↑	Widener H 60k	5 3 15 13 13½ 12	Atkinson T	123 w	*.05e	95-10	Coaltown1232Shy Guy120½Faultless117¾	Easily 6
19Feb49-6Hia	fst 1⅛	:461 1:093 1:344 1:482 3↑	McLennan H 31k	4 1 14 13 14 14	Atkinson T	124 w	*.10e	96-14	Coaltown1244Faultless115½Shy Guy120¾	Eased up 8
14Feb49-5Hia	fst 1⅛	:454 1:084 1:341 1:473 4↑	Alw 4000	4 1 110 112 112 110	Nelson E	114 w	*.20e	103-14	Coaltown11410Three Rings1161½Free America1081¾	Eased up 6
5Feb49-5Hia	fst 6f	:222 :452 1:101 4↑	Alw 3500	1 8 11 11 11¾ 12½	Pierson NL	120 w	*.20e	97-14	Coaltown1202½Free America106nkTavistock1083½	Easily 8
29Sep48-6Bel	fst 1	:224 :452 1:101 1:36 3↑	Sysonby Mile 29k	3 3 34½ 44½ 34 33¼	Pierson NL	119 w	*.10e	91-14	Citation1193First Flight123nkCoaltown1194	Went well 6
15Sep48-6Bel	fst 1	:223 :454 1:103 1:36	Jerome H 30k	1 2 25 23 12 15	Pierson NL	126 w	*.35e	94-16	Coaltown1265Mount Marcy1151½Free America126hd	Easily 10
25Aug48-7Was	fst 6f	:222 :443 1:091 3↑	Great Western H 23k	4 6 52¼ 21 2hd 2½	Pierson NL	115 w	*1.70	100-11	Tre Vit114½Coaltown115hdPinebloom1063	No excuse 10
19Aug48-7Was	fst 1	:231 :46 1:103 1:361	Drexel H 27k	6 1 11 12 11 11	Pierson NL	120 w	*1.00	94-16	Coaltown1201Shy Guy1161½Papa Redbird121nk	Never headed 8
7Aug48-5Was	fst 6f	:23 :454 1:104	Alw 5000	5 2 32 2½ 11 12½	Pierson NL	124 w	*.60	93-10	Coaltown1242½Hypostyle1165Carrara Marble1141	Easily 5
1Jly48-7AP	fst 6f	:223 :454 1:121	Skokie H 22k	5 3 43 54 51¾ 33¾	Pierson NL	124wb	*.30	82-15	Piet113¾Carrara Marble1133Coaltown1241	No excuse 5
29May48-6Bel	fst 1	:223 :451 1:104 1:372	Withers 29k	1 1 13 13 13 21¾	Pierson NL	126wb	*.15	85-16	Vulcan'sForge1261¾Coaltown126noBttrSlf1262½	Tired badly 4
		Geldings not eligible								
19May48-6Bel	fst 7f	:23 :462 1:104 1:232	Swift 17k	4 2 1hd 12 14 16	Pierson NL	126wb	*.10	93-15	Coaltown1266My Request1263½Salmagundi126½	Easily 6
		Previously trained by B.A. Jones								
1May48-7CD	sly 1¼	:463 1:112 1:38 2:052	Ky Derby 111k	2 1 16 1½ 22 23½	Pierson NL	126wb	*.40e	76-22	Citation1263½Coaltown1263My Request1261½	Hard urged 6
22Apr48-6Kee	fst 1⅛	:454 1:092 1:354 1:491	Blue Grass 18k	5 1 16 16 13 14½	Pierson NL	123wb	*.30	101-12	Coaltown1234½Billings1212½Shy Guy1264	Eased up 6
8Apr48-6Kee	gd 6f	:224 :461 1:12 3↑	Phoenix H 13k	3 2 31½ 32½ 11 12½	Robertson J	108wb	*.20e	92-18	Coaltown1082½George Gains116hdFervent1266	Ridden out 8
		Previously trained by H.A. Jones								
26Feb48-5Hia	fst 6f	:223 :452 1:093	Alw 3000	7 4 1½ 13 14 112	Snider A	122 w	*.30	100-10	Coaltown12212Quebec1193½Howdah1111½	Much the best 11
3Feb48-3Hia	fst 6f	:223 :46 1:112	©Md Sp Wt	5 2 12 18 15 12½	Dodson D	120wb	*1.00	91-15	Coaltown1202½Blackmont1151¾Cas Adams1209½	Galloping 9

Conniver

br. f. 1944, by Discovery (Display)–The Schemer, by Challenger II — Lifetime record: 56 15 3 6 $227,825
Own.– H. La Montagne
Br.– Alfred G. Vanderbilt (Md)
Tr.– W. Post

17Sep49-6Aqu	fst 1⅛	:48 1:124 1:384 1:524	3↑ ⒻBeldame H 72k	5 16 1416 1519 97 63	Dodson D	125 w	4.95	80-17	MissRequest1131[D]Hrmonc1121¼Plundr108hd	Closed gap late	18
3Sep49-6Aqu	fst 1 1/16	:243 :482 1:123 1:46	3↑ Aqueduct H 23k	8 14 1412 1313 105 63½	Kirkland A	115 w	11.30	80-19	WineList114½[D]LoserWeeper114¾RiverIn107½	Close quarters	14
20Aug49-6Sar	fst 1¼	:471 1:114 1:364 2:04	3↑ Saratoga H 30k	10 10 818 1014 1115 1113	Adams J	118wb	6.40	75-13	Donor117nkStunts112½My Request1232	Dull effort	12
30Jly49-6Jam	fst 1 3/16	:474 1:124 1:372 1:574	3↑ Merchants & Cits H 22k	2 7 59 51¼ 32½ 41¾	Kirkland A	118wb	2.65	85-18	Chains106nkMy Request126½High Trend1021	Weakened	7
16Jly49-6Jam	fst 1 3/16	:472 1:122 1:372 1:571	3↑ Butler H 58k	1 6 88½ 86¼ 33 1no	Kirkland A	112wb	16.50	90-14	Conniver112noPalestinian1143Stunts1051	Hard drive	10
8Jly49-6Jam	fst 1⅛	:491 1:133 1:383 1:512	3↑ Handicap 6030	3 3 1½ 12 11 1hd	Arcaro E	122wb	1.70	91-18	Conniver122hdLoser Weeper1171½Bug Juice1139	Just lasted	5
2Jly49-6Aqu	fst 1¼	:484 1:13 1:372 2:024	3↑ Brooklyn H 58k	8 7 52½ 62¾ 54 74½	Glisson G	114wb	11.65	88-14	Assault122¾Vulcan's Forge129nkFlying Missel117¾	Outrun	10
13Jun49-6Aqu	fst 1 1/16	:25 :49 1:134 1:472	3↑ Queens County H 22k	9 6 65½ 56½ 43 24	Arcaro E	114wb	3.00	73-29	Three Rings1104Conniver114nkBug Juice1073	Good effort	9
8Jun49-6Bel	fst 1 1/16	:24 :464 1:112 1:433	3↑ ⒻTop Flight H 16k	1 4 44½ 43½ 44 45¼	Arcaro E	123 w	1.90	88-13	But Why Not1263½Paddleduck119¾Allie's Pal1141	No mishap	5
30May49-6Bel	fst 1¼	:48 1:123 1:38 2:03	3↑ Suburban H 61k	12 6 84¾ 128 1215 1215	James B	120 w	6.80	70-17	Vulcan'sForge1242½ButWhyNot1174FlyingMissel108½	Outrun	13
5May49-6Jam	fst 1 1/16	:25 :484 1:13 1:444	3↑ ⒻFirenze H 28k	6 8 55 66¼ 34 32½	Guerin E	126 w	*1.35	86-18	But Why Not1162Allie's Pal111½Conniver1263	Closed well	9
27Apr49-6Jam	fst 6f	:232 :464 1:114	3↑ ⒻCorrection H 17k	7 9 87¾ 87¾ 106¼ 75½	Howell R	126 w	*2.40e	86-15	OceanBrief117hdAlfoxie110¾Paddlduck1112½	Dwelt at start	10
16Apr49-5Jam	fst 6f	:232 :463 1:13	3↑ ⒻHandicap 6065	3 7 78¾ 47½ 22½ 1¾	Guerin E	122 w	1.80e	86-18	Conniver122¾Itsabet118½Allie's Pal118hd	Drew out	7
13Nov48-6Jam	fst 1 3/16	:484 1:13 1:38 1:58	3↑ Butler H 85k	9 8 814 813 812 817	Guerin E	125 w	3.35	69-20	Donor1171½Phalanx1261Better Self121½	Outrun	9
27Oct48-6Jam	fst 1 1/16	:242 :48 1:13 1:45	3↑ ⒻComely H 29k	10 8 813 85¼ 2½ 11¼	Guerin E	123 w	3.35	88-25	Conniver1231¼Miss Request1205Carolyn A.1182	Drew out	10
12Oct48-6Jam	fst 1 1/16	:24 :471 1:12 1:444	3↑ Questionnaire H 29k	5 10 1012 107 62¾ 53	James B	123 w	6.30	86-18	Donor115noCarolyn A.111½Bug Juice1082	Sluggish	11
2Oct48-6Bel	fst 2	:48 2:294 2:562 3:213	3↑ J C Gold Cup 108k	1 4 411 28 311 521	Dodson D	121 w	13.15	75-09	Citation1177Phalanx12412Beauchef124hd	Stopped	7
Geldings not eligible											
28Sep48-6Bel	fst 1½	:473 1:122 2:04 2:30	3↑ ⒻLadies H 58k	3 9 912 72 611 512	Dodson D	126 w	*1.15	76-14	Miss Request1144Gallorette1211Honeymoon1231	No excuse	9
11Sep48-6Aqu	gd 1⅛	:482 1:131 1:39 1:522	3↑ ⒻBeldame H 68k	11 13 137½ 95¼ 51¼ 13½	Dodson D	121 w	*2.35	85-20	Conniver1213½Harmonica114½Gallorette124nk	Easily	14
31Jly48-5Jam	fst 1 3/16	:483 1:14 1:392 1:59	3↑ Merchants & Cits H 22k	6 6 47 44½ 1½ 2¾	Atkinson T	126 w	*1.00	80-22	Beauchef117¾Conniver1261½Vertigo II1171¾	Weakened	7
17Jly48-6Aqu	fst 1¼	:502 1:16 1:404 2:054	3↑ Brooklyn H 57k	6 4 22 21 1hd 1hd	Atkinson T	114 w	2.00	78-21	Conniver114hdGallorette1193Stymie1302	Hard drive	6
10Jly48-6Aqu	fst 1 1/16	:243 :473 1:114 1:433	3↑ ⒻVagrancy H 29k	3 5 58 43 2nk 15	Atkinson T	121 w	*1.65	96-13	Conniver1215Harmonica1202Casa Camara1051	Easily	8
3Jly48-6Nar	fst 1 70	:23 :462 1:113 1:414	3↑ Governor's H 13k	6 11 99 95¾ 75½ 43¼	Zehr F	122 w	*.60	93-08	Reborn112½Willing Spirit1121Misleader1151¾	Late foot	11
26Jun48-6Aqu	fst 1 1/16	:251 :493 1:133 1:452	3↑ Aqueduct H 28k	2 6 54½ 31¼ 1nk 2hd	Zufelt F	117 w	2.70	87-18	Stymie130hdConniver1173½Double Jay1262½	Game try	7
3Jun48-6Bel	fst 1	:234 :464 1:114 1:371	3↑ ⒻHandicap 7535	3 3 32 11½ 13 16	Zufelt F	119 w	*2.05	88-14	Conniver1196Red Stamp1093½Miss Kimo120hd	Easily	5
28May48-6Bel	fst 1⅛	:463 1:111 1:371 1:503	3↑ ⒻHandicap 7530	2 1 16 15 14 12	Zufelt F	116 w	1.30	88-15	Conniver1162Challe Anne1081¾Miss Grillo1265	In hand	5
21May48-6Bel	fst 1	:241 :472 1:121 1:374	4↑ ⒻHandicap 7350	3 1 11 13 13 11½	James B	110 w	1.85	85-20	Conniver1101½Honeymoon1173½Grillette1083½	Driving	4
6May48-5Jam	fst 1 1/16	:242 :49 1:133 1:452	4↑ Handicap 6530	1 3 2½ 2hd 21 3¾	Jessop JD	111 w	1.55	85-14	Lord Grillo112¾Donor122hdConniver111	Faltered	3
28Apr48-6Jam	fst 1 1/16	:243 :49 1:14 1:464	4↑ Handicap 5565	2 8 66¾ 52¾ 1hd 1¾	Jessop JD	118 w	*.95	79-19	Conniver118¾Dangerous Age1112Master Mind1191	Drew out	10
22Apr48-5Jam	fst 1 1/16	:243 :49 1:14 1:464	3↑ Handicap 5530	4 2 22 2½ 12 15	Jessop JD	114 w	*2.10	79-22	Conniver1145Misleader1202East Light1182	Easily	5
2Apr48-5Jam	my 5½f	:223 :464 1:07	4↑ ⒻAlw 5000	6 6 67¼ 54 34¾ 33¼	Jessop JD	108 w	4.85e	80-26	OceanBrief1172½DarkVenus108¾Conniver1082	Dwelt at start	6
6Nov47-6Jam	sly 1 1/16	:244 :49 1:141 1:473	Alw 4500	6 5 42¾ 42¾ 64 34½	Atkinson T	119 w	2.20	70-19	CleanSlate1151½ShortReign1163Conniver1191½	Closed fast	9
30Oct47-6Jam	sly 1 1/16	:242 :483 1:14 1:474	3↑ ⒻAlw 4500	1 5 43 4nk 1hd 11¼	Atkinson T	108 w	3.50	74-22	Conniver1081¼Short Reign1103Head Smart1122	Drew out	7
24Oct47-4Jam	fst 6f	:233 :47 1:122	Alw 4500	4 5 58¾ 56½ 45½ 33¼	Arcaro E	114 w	3.20e	86-19	By Sea118nkDark Venus1143Conniver1141	Closed fast	5
13Oct47-4Bel	fst 1	:233 :47 1:122 1:383	3↑ Clm 8000	5 5 65¼ 31½ 42¾ 42¾	Renick J	102 w	4.20	78-21	ScotchSecret108½BuffetSupper1112FrindorFo112nk	Faltered	8
7Oct47-7Bel	fst 1	:233 :463 1:12 1:381	Alw 5000	3 6 56½ 75¾ 66 54¼	Allgaier H	115 w	3.75e	79-14	Trilby115¾CaptainDorsett118hdRoyalLover1111½	No mishap	8
30Sep47-7Bel	fst 1	:231 :474 1:121 1:374	ⒻAlw 4000	9 9 83 84 1210 1212½	Allgaier H	117 w	11.80e	72-12	Legendra105hdTrilby1174Dancing Margot1051½	No factor	14
8Sep47-5GS	fst 6f	:224 :461 1:104	Alw 4000	7 8 78 69 59 512	Wilson HB	113wb	19.40	85-13	Danada Capt.113hdWhipsaw1165Eternallea1192	No factor	8
29Aug47-6GS	fst 6f	:224 :471 1:131	ⒻAlw 4000	8 9 97 95¼ 76 54¼	Lynch J	112.5 w	36.65	81-16	IDeclare1092GoingAiry116hdFrantie'sBid109¾	Off slowly	9
25Aug47-8GS	fst 1	:24 :472 1:122 1:381	Alw 4000	8 6 56½ 67 610 611¾	Wilson HB	111wb	49.35	84-06	High Trend114nkEnd of Strife1178Glen Heather1163	Outrun	8
16Aug47-6Sar	sly 6f	:23 :463 1:13	Alw 4000	6 8 811 718 615 613½	Allgaier H	112 w	32.45	69-20	Mangohick1214½Indicate1172½Supper Date1211	Outrun	8
9Aug47-8Sar	fst 1	:234 :474 1:12 1:382	Alw 4000	7 6 5¾ 42½ 78¾ 712½	Allgaier H	114 w	31.00	76-09	Dinner Hour109nkTrapeze1133Daily Dip113hd	No factor	8
18Jly47-6Bel	fst 1	:23 :46 1:12 1:381	ⒻAlw 4500	6 9 87 96 1016 1015¾	Allgaier H	118 w	23.10	67-15	Quarantaine1141½BrightSong112½Bimltt1126	Never a factor	11
25Jun47-4Jam	sly 6f	:233 :461 1:111	Alw 4500	3 5 65½ 42½ 42¼ 57½	Allgaier H	118 w	17.55	87-13	OceanBrief1132Parhelion1234Rinldo1141½	Inside,no menace	7
17Jun47-5Aqu	fst 1 1/16	:244 :482 1:131 1:471	3↑ ⒻHandicap 5020	3 3 33 32¼ 41¼ 42¼	Sneller J	105 w	5.20	76-22	Mahmoudess1131Kay Gibson118nkClover Lea1171	No mishap	4
24May47-8Bel	fst 1	:233 :472 1:132 1:393	Alw 4500	3 3 31 1hd 1hd 54	Allgaier H	117 w	33.60	72-19	Khyber Pass1162Leander119noTrapeze116hd	Speed,quit	7
13May47-6Bel	fst 1	:223 :454 1:12 1:38	ⒻAcorn 19k	13 7 53¾ 52¾ 1113 1118¾	Allgaier H	121 w	143.55	65-17	But Why Not1212Harmonica1214Alrenie121hd	No factor	13
5May47-5Bel	my 1	:233 :473 1:133 1:404	Alw 5000	1 3 2½ 41¼ 47 411½	Allgaier H	114wb	*1.80	58-25	Green Dragon1193Rappahannock1132½Marble Arch1136	Quit	5
23Apr47-6Jam	fst 1 1/16	:242 :482 1:133 1:471	Alw 4000	7 2 1hd 2hd 1hd 1½	Allgaier H	113 w	10.25	77-12	Conniver113½Atom Buster1211½Dorothy B. Jr.11410	Driving	7
16Apr47-2Jam	sly 6f	:24 :48 1:132	ⒻMd Sp Wt	6 4 3½ 1hd 1hd 13	Allgaier H	115 w	6.35	84-16	[DH]Conniver115[DH]AppianVia1153PuffofSmoke110¾	Hung late	6
2Oct46-4Bel	fst 6f-WC	:231 :464 1:122	ⒻMd Sp Wt	3 10 103¾ 104¾ 135¾	Donoso R	115 w	28.10	73-25	Easy Living1151½C'est Tout115nkSnowfall1151	No factor	22
23Sep46-1Bel	fst 5½f-W	:221 :444 1:03	ⒻMd Sp Wt	17 4 41¼ 64 55¼	Donoso R	115 w	19.40	94-02	Valse d'Or1151¼Bimlette1151Muti1153	Raced well	22
28Aug46-1Sar	fst 5½f	:222 :452 :581 1:044	ⒻMd Sp Wt	5 9 87¼ 88½ 611 511	Arcaro E	115 w	9.40	88-05	Blue Eyed Momo115hdMuti1155Mae Agnes1162	No threat	13
6Aug46-2Sar	fst 5½f	:231 :47 :592 1:052	ⒻMd Sp Wt	2 8 66 66½ 76½ 1010½	Guerin E	115 w	7.10	85-12	Tea Olive1156Farfalina115hd[DH]Hat Girl115	Even effort	15
1Jun46-1Bel	fst 5f-WC	:222 :45 :572	ⒻMd Sp Wt	17 3 1hd 31½ 33¼	Permane R	115 w	*1.40f	90-05	DancingMargot1151¼Mother1102Conniver1151½	Faltered late	18
23May46-4Bel	fst 5f-WC	:222 :453 :581	ⒻMd Sp Wt	13 8 72¾ 62¾ 64½	Mehrtens W	115 w	4.15f	84-15	Pipette1151Dancing Margot115noWar Fan1151½	Good try	17

Count Fleet

br. c. 1940, by Reigh Count (Sunreigh)–Quickly, by Haste — Lifetime record: 21 16 4 1 $250,300
Own.– Mrs J. Hertz
Br.– Mrs John D. Hertz (Ky)
Tr.– G.D. Cameron

5Jun43-6Bel	fst 1½	:48 1:123 2:033 2:281	Belmont 42k	2 1 18 120 120 125	Longden J	126wb	*.05	97-12	CountFleet12625FairyManhurst126¾Deseronto126	Galloping	3
Geldings not eligible											
22May43-6Bel	my 1	:23 :462 1:103 1:36	Withers 17k	2 1 11½ 13 12 15	Longden J	126wb	*.05	94-21	Count Fleet1265Slide Rule12612Tip-Toe126	Wide,easily	3
Geldings not eligible											
8May43-6Pim	gd 1 3/16	:472 1:114 1:381 1:572	Preakness 60k	2 1 14 14 15 18	Longden J	126wb	*.15	95-15	Count Fleet1268Blue Swords1265Vincentive12620	Easily	4
1May43-7CD	fst 1¼	:463 1:123 1:373 2:04	Ky Derby 72k	5 1 1hd 12 12 13	Longden J	126wb	*.40	87-12	Count Fleet1263Blue Swords1266Slide Rule1266	Handily	10
17Apr43-5Jam	fst 1 1/16	:232 :464 1:112 1:43	Wood Mem 28k	4 1 14 14 14 13½	Longden J	126wb	*.25	98-06	Count Fleet1263½Blue Swords1267Twoses1212	Much the best	8
13Apr43-5Jam	sly 1 70	:234 :472 1:124 1:424	Alw 3000	8 4 31½ 22 2hd 13½	Longden J	122wb	*.15	90-19	CountFlt1223½Bossut1135Towsr113hd	Forced wide first turn	8
10Nov42-6Pim	gd 1 1/16	:231 :473 1:12 1:444	Walden 12k	3 1 18 115 125 130	Longden J	122 w	*.10	94-14	Count Fleet12230Uncle Billies11315Rough Doc1131	Easily	4
31Oct42-6Pim	fst 1 1/16	:231 :462 1:11 1:433	Pim Futurity 34k	3 2 2hd 1½ 13 15	Longden J	119wb	1.25	100-06	Count Fleet1195Occupation1224Vincentive122		3
Geldings not eligible											
20Oct42-5Jam	fst 1 70	:234 :473 1:13 1:44	Alw 5000	5 5 1hd 14 15 16	Longden J	122wb	*.25	84-16	Count Fleet1226Towser1162½Jack S.L.1133	Easily	8
10Oct42-5Bel	fst 1	:231 :46 1:10 1:344	Champagne 12k	8 1 12 13 13 16	Longden J	116wb	*1.05	101-07	Count Fleet1166Blue Swords1197Attendant1101	Easily	8
3Oct42-4Bel	fst 6½f-W	:222 :443 1:083 1:151	Futurity 69k	7 9 22 34 34 35	Longden J	119wb	*1.55	91-04	Occupation1265Askmenow116hdCount Fleet1191½	Gamely	10
Geldings not eligible											
24Sep42-6Bel	fst 6f-WC	:23 :461 1:103	Alw 2000	9 12 51¾ 53 21 12½	Longden J	122wb	*1.40	94-06	CountFleet1222½BullsEye111nkJackS.L.111hd	Swerved start	13
15Sep42-5Aqu	fst 6f	:224 :462 1:12	Alw 2500	2 1 21½ 33 31 1nk	Longden J	118wb	*.70	92-12	CntFlt118nkVrySnooty1124NoondySun1121½	Bumped,driving	10

15Aug42- 6Was	fst 6f	:222 :454 1:12	Wash Park Futurity 68k	11 9 75 54¼ 22 2nk	Longden J	117wb	4.80	91-12	Occupation122nkCntFleet1175BluSwords117hd	Wide,bumped	11
11Aug42- 6Was	gd 6f	:23 :463 1:13	Alw 1800	6 5 3½ 2½ 1½ 1nk	Longden J	119wb	*.50	86-20	CountFleet119nkBlueSwords1084Hygrohour1223	Forced wide	9
22Jly42- 5Emp	fst 5¾f	:232 :463 1:074	Wakefield 6.8k	4 1 31¼ 11 12 14	Longden J	116wb	*.65	98-10	CountFleet1164Rurales1132GoldShower1229	Speed to spare	4
15Jly42- 5Emp	fst 5¾f	:23 :454 1:08	©East View 7.1k	6 5 52 21½ 22 21	Longden J	116wb	*.50	96-09	Gold Shower1161Count Fleet1167Rurales1122	Gamely	6
4Jly42- 4Emp	fst 5½f	:23 :462 :592 1:054	Alw 2000	5 5 53¾ 42½ 11 15	Longden J	111wb	*1.15	97-07	Count Fleet1115Samhar1143Bullpen114hd	Drew away easily	6
19Jun42- 3Aqu	fst 5½f	:23 :471 1:06	©Md Sp Wt	8 6 3¾ 2½ 3½ 14	Longden J	116wb	*.75	97-08	CountFleet1164SewrdBound1161Crst116nk	Bore out str turn	10
15Jun42- 5Aqu	fst 5½f	:23 :473 1:061	Md Sp Wt	9 8 63 44½ 22 21½	Longden J	116wb	*1.35	94-12	Supermont1161½Count Fleet1163Quiz116nk	Trouble early	14
1Jun42- 5Bel	fst 5f-WC	:572	©Md Sp Wt	13 5 3½ 3½ 32½ 21½	Longden J	116wb	4.10	91-07	DoveShoot1161½CountFlet116noSuprmont116nk	Swerved start	16

Delegate

ch. g. 1944, by Maeda (Pennant)–Brides Veil, by Polymelian **Lifetime record: 134 31 21 26 $277,530**

Own.– Woolford Farm
Br.– Herbert M. Woolf (Kan)
Tr.– W. Stephens

6Apr54- 4Jam	fst 6f	:234 :473 1:123	4↑ Clm 10000	1 6 - - - -	Boland W	113wb	*1.50	- -	DeepRiver122hdRunner-up1154½YllowMst108½	Pulled up lame	6
13Feb54- 3Hia	fst 6f	:222 :453 1:101	4↑ Clm 13000	3 7 713 78 54 35½	Boland W	113wb	*1.10	91-09	Ruthred1092½Dean Cavy1163Delegate113no	Mild rally	7
6Feb54- 9Hia	fst 6f	:223 :454 1:111	4↑ Clm 15000	10 12 129¼ 118¼ 85¼ 3nk	Boland W	111wb	4.45	92-11	Chombro113nkSanfoin108noDelegate111½	Late speed	12
30Jan54- 6Hia	fst 6f	:222 :454 1:11	4↑ Clm 13000	1 10 911 89¼ 56½ 33½	Boland W	115wb	4.05	89-12	Easy Paddy114½Ignition1073Delegate115¾	Closed gamely	10
26Jan54- 7Hia	fst 6f	:223 :454 1:103	4↑ Alw 4500	5 11 109¼ 87¼ 63¾ 52	Boland W	112wb	16.95	93-13	Jet Master1151Judge J.B.112noRush Prince1151	Late rally	11
25Dec53- 7TrP	fst 1⅛	:462 1:11 1:371 1:501	3↑ Christmas H 9.1k	6 10 814 78 79 78½	Madden D	111wsb	33.95	81-11	MarkedGame109hdQuickFire1071GulfStream1102½	No threat	13
12Dec53- 7TrP	fst 1 1/16	:233 :471 1:114 1:443	3↑ Ponce de Leon H 8.8k	10 8 74¾ 52 78 87½	Madden D	113wsb	11.25	81-13	Andre1161Capeador109½Marked Game111½	Tired	12
27Oct53- 4Jam	gd 6f	:224 :461 1:114	4↑ Alw 5000	6 6 613 512 58½ 1no	Boland W	120wsb	*1.55	88-17	Delegate120noMohammedan120¾Rae's Reward113½	Just up	6
19Oct53- 6Jam	fst 6f	:23 :454 1:11	2↑ New Rochelle H 22k	10 10 1015 1015 812 78	McCreary C	106wsb	11.15	84-17	White Skies1282¾Hilarious110½Do Report1132½	No factor	10
12Oct53- 6Jam	fst 6f	:23 :462 1:113	3↑ Interborough H 23k	9 9 914 89¼ 710 62¾	McCreary C	108wsb	17.90	86-20	White Skies126hdDo Report112¾Hilarious1101½	Off slowly	9
25Sep53- 5Bel	fst 6f	:223 :462 1:113	4↑ Alw 5000	2 10 1111 1113 56½ 42¼	McCreary C	118wsb	6.75	88-15	Tea-Makr118noThsSd106hdColdCommnd1182¼	Not enough late	12
11Sep53- 6Aqu	fst 7f	:232 :461 1:111 1:234	3↑ Handicap 6060	4 8 99½ 87¾ 45½ 35½	McCreary C	122wsb	*2.20	85-14	Impasse1135½GameChance115noDelegate1222½	Close quarters	10
3Sep53- 7Aqu	fst 6f	:23 :462 1:12	3↑ Clm 12500	2 7 77 58 44½ 1no	Woodhouse H	117wsb	*1.20	92-17	Delegate117noThis Side1176Fancy Bonnet109nk	Just up	8
18Jly53- 3Jam	fst 5½f	:224 :461 :581 1:043	3↑ Clm 12500	7 8 813 79½ 67½ 31¼	Boland W	119wsb	*1.75	94-12	JessLinthicum117½Reprimand114¾Delegt119nk	Closed gamely	8
2Jly53- 6Aqu	fst 6f	:224 :454 1:111	3↑ Handicap 6040	1 6 611 611 47 33	Boland W	118wsb	4.85	93-15	Contribution1141½Hyphasis1221½Delegate1183¼	Late speed	6
27Jun53- 6Aqu	fst 7f	:22 :443 1:092 1:22	3↑ Carter H 59k	8 9 914 912 914 912	Boland W	110wb	25.75	88-09	Tom Fool1352Squared Away1222¼Eatontown1131¼	Trailed	9
13Jun53- 2Bel	fst 6f	:224 :463 1:114	4↑ OClm 12500	1 2 78 66 2½ 12	Boland W	122wsb	*1.40	90-11	Delegate1222Blinker Light118¾All Is Well126½	Drew out	7
27May53- 6Bel	fst 6f-WC	:214 :443 1:101	3↑ Roseben H 23k	1 9 911 916 97½	Boland W	112wb	17.05	82-09	SquaredAway1241¼DarkPeter1221½Sagittarius115hd	Trailed	9
6May53- 6Bel	gd 6f-WC	:221 :444 1:10	3↑ Toboggan H 30k	9 9 74½ 62¾ 52	Anderson P	113wb	7.15e	89-12	Tuscany122noHyphasis116½Dark Peter122nk	Lost bandage	9
21Apr53- 7Jam	fst 6f	:231 :463 1:114	3↑ Handicap 6055	1 8 816 714 612 44¾	Anderson P	122wb	2.55	83-19	Indian Land119noCount Flame1112½Sun Rene1112¼	Late rush	9
11Apr53- 6Jam	fst 6f	:223 :453 1:11	3↑ Jamaica H 23k	7 9 912 911 95¼ 32	Anderson P	115wsb	11.75	90-15	Sagittarius113hdTuscany1242Delegate115½	Closed fast	9
2Apr53- 3Jam	fst 6f	:233 :47 1:114	4↑ Clm 12500	1 3 58½ 45 4¾ 11	Anderson P	120wsb	*.60	88-16	Delegate1201Dictionary1134Harpes1172	Drew out	5
19Feb53- 7Hia	fst 1⅛	:464 1:11 1:37 1:502	4↑ Alw 5000	1 10 107 76½ 54 21½	McCreary C	122wsb	*1.90	82-13	GreatCaptain1081½Delegate122¾WnnngFlt1112	Closed gamely	10
7Feb53- 3Hia	my 6f	:223 :464 1:124	4↑ Clm 20000	5 5 57½ 55½ 3½ 16	McCreary C	118wsb	2.35	84-34	Delegate1186Roaming116nkWar Phar1181½	Easily	5
28Jan53- 7Hia	fst 7f	:224 :46 1:111 1:242	3↑ Palm Beach H 20k	4 13 1311 1111 1011 77¼	Boland W	111wsb	20.30	81-20	OilCapitol107nkBattlefield123½NimbleFox1141½	No mishap	14
16Jan53- 7Hia	fst 6f	:223 :461 1:11	3↑ Hia Inaugural H 19k	9 12 118½ 911 89¼ 79¼	Anderson P	119wb	7.90e	84-21	Nimble Fox1071¾Sagittarius1181½Starecase120½	No factor	12
3Jan53- 7TrP	gd 1 1/16	:224 :46 1:104 1:44	3↑ Robert E Lee H 30k	11 15 1517 1211 1216 98	Anderson P	117wsb	8.95	84-19	Elixir1103Recline1162Topside108no	No menace	15
27Dec52- 7TrP	fst 6f	:222 :451 1:102	3↑ E R Bradley H 17k	13 10 118½ 108¾ 87½ 42¼	Anderson P	122wsb	19.40	93-15	Sagittarius114nkEatontown1151Starecase1231	Closed fast	13
3Dec52- 7TrP	fst 6f	:223 :452 1:102	3↑ Alligator H 9k	5 14 149 1415 1212 117½	Anderson P	126wsb	7.10	87-18	Jet Fleet119hdCongo King1142Recover110no	Off slowly	14
11Nov52- 6Jam	fst 6f	:223 :454 1:11	2↑ Autumn Day H 22k	4 7 77½ 66¼ 53½ 2¾	Anderson P	119wsb	3.50	91-16	Squared Away119¾Delegate119½Tea-Maker1261½	Gaining	7
20Oct52- 6Jam	fst 6f	:224 :453 1:104	2↑ New Rochelle H 22k	2 9 97¾ 85¾ 63½ 11½	Anderson P	114wsb	3.55e	93-20	Delegate1141½Tea-Maker126¾War King1111½	Going away	9
6Oct52- 6Jam	fst 6f	:23 :46 1:11	2↑ Interborough H 23k	7 11 118¾ 117½ 95½ 41¾	Boland W	114wsb	4.50e	90-15	SquaredAway118½Tea-Maker124noTruePattrn1061¼	Late rally	11
1Oct52- 7Bel	fst 6f	:222 :462 1:113	3↑ Handicap 6070	7 8 89¼ 88½ 65¼ 2no	Boland W	122wsb	4.35	91-15	Jazerant117noDelegate122hdNullify1051¾	Just missed	8
24Sep52- 5Bel	fst 6f	:231 :471 1:114	3↑ Handicap 6045	4 5 53¾ 42¼ 43¼ 33½	Boland W	126wsb	*1.35	86-15	Roman Fair1141Acefull1122½Delegate1261	No rally	6
15Sep52- 6Bel	fst 6f-WC	:22 :441 1:082	2↑ Fall Highweight H 24k	5 15 147¼ 91¼ 62¾	Boland W	132wsb	32.85	96-03	Hitex130½Tea-Maker140½Papoose117nk	Off slowly	15
8Sep52- 6Aqu	fst 7f	:223 :451 1:102 1:24	3↑ Bay Shore H 17k	11 11 118¾ 1111 97 95¾	Boland W	114wsb	16.70	84-20	NextMove1151FirstGlance111nkSquaredAway1202	Slow start	12
29Jly52- 5Jam	fst 1 1/16	:25 :481 1:13 1:444	3↑ Handicap 6535	5 6 69 42 1hd 1hd	Boland W	121wsb	2.75	88-19	Delegate121hdBe Gracious1101Lone Eagle1162½	Driving	6
16Jly52- 6Jam	fst 6f	:23 :454 1:101	3↑ Fleetwing H 21k	6 6 66½ 67 66 55¾	Scurlock O	113wsb	13.75	90-16	Tea-Maker114¾Squared Away1202½Arise1221	Outrun	6
4Jly52- 6Aqu	fst 7f	:221 :443 1:09 1:22	3↑ Carter H 29k	4 10 108½ 108 914 79¾	Errico C	116wsb	13.70	92-09	NorthernStar1152CraftyAdmirl1202½ToMrkt123no	Slow start	10
21Jun52- 5Aqu	fst 6f	:222 :452 1:102	3↑ Handicap 7540	2 4 49½ 410 46½ 35	Boland W	120wsb	2.05	95-11	Squared Away1225Tea-Maker121noDelegate1201½	Late rally	4
13Jun52- 6Aqu	fst 6f	:23 :463 1:112	3↑ Handicap 7530	5 5 56 52¼ 41 1no	Boland W	118wsb	2.35	95-14	Delegate118noSheilasReward1261¼HeapBigChief1052	Just up	5
7Jun52- 5Bel	fst 6f	:223 :461 1:104	3↑ Handicap 7540	3 7 77¼ 76 53½ 2¾	Boland W	113wsb	11.20	94-14	First Glance112¾Delegate113½Tea-Maker121no	Late speed	7
29Apr52- 6Bel	gd 6f-WC	:221 :443 1:091	3↑ Toboggan H 23k	2 8 86¼ 66 67¾	Boland W	118wsb	7.10	87-05	DarkPeter108½CraftyAdmiral1182½Tea-Maker1202	Slow start	8
16Apr52- 6Jam	gd 6f	:23 :46 1:111	3↑ Jamaica H 17k	3 9 97¾ 95¼ 85¼ 32½	Boland W	114wsb	12.85	88-15	Tea-Maker1122½Northern Star115noDelegate1142	Late foot	9
11Apr52- 6Jam	fst 6f	:23 :46 1:113	3↑ Mettlesome H 7.9k	5 8 67½ 55¾ 45¼ 1hd	Boland W	111wsb	4.20	89-21	Delegate111hdBryan G.1261Tea-Maker1153	Just up	8
1Apr52- 6Jam	fst 6f	:222 :453 1:094	3↑ Paumonok H 29k	8 11 108¼ 87¾ 88¾ 65¾	Jemas N	110wsb	18.90	92-13	Woodchuck1193½Squared Away116½[D]Jumbo116¾	Late rally	11
4Mar52- 7GP	fst 6f	:22 :442 1:093	3↑ Inaugural H 8.8k	14 15 149¾ 108¼ 66 32¾	Jemas N	119wsb	8.80e	94-11	Tripoli113¾Eatontown1142Delegate119nk	Off slowly	15
28Feb52- 7Hia	fst 6f	:222 :452 1:103	4↑ Alw 4000	1 5 34 36 58½ 57¾	Jemas N	118wsb	2.35	87-12	Hi Billee1162½Prop118nkSuleiman1123½	Tired	7
16Feb52- 6Hia	fst 7f	:224 :452 1:10 1:232	4↑ Alw 5000	6 9 88 810 711 56¼	Jemas N	118wsb	9.65	89-16	Crafty Admiral119nkYildiz1222½Eatontown1161	Forced wide	10
23Jan52- 7Hia	fst 7f	:223 :444 1:091 1:22	3↑ Palm Beach H 13k	5 5 56 56½ 47 59	Woodhouse H	118wsb	6.30	93-12	CraftyAdmiral1072Woodchuck1163OilCapitol1122	No menace	10
17Jan52- 7Hia	fst 6f	:221 :452 1:10	3↑ Hia Inaugural H 13k	8 13 128¾ 118¼ 77¾ 75¼	Woodhouse H	122wsb	6.70	93-12	Spartan Valor121hdJumbo1182Woodchuck1192½	Raced wide	14
12Nov51- 6Jam	fst 6f	:231 :454 1:111	2↑ Autumn Day H 17k	6 9 98¼ 76¼ 76½ 31¼	McCreary C	120wsb	5.90	90-20	Tea-Maker115½Guillotine126¾Delegate120hd	Closed gamely	9
3Nov51- 7Jam	sly 6f	:222 :452 1:121	3↑ Handicap 5065	3 7 79½ 68½ 65¼ 2no	McCreary C	119wsb	*2.20	86-17	Assignment105noDelegate119½Atalanta104½	Just missed	7
19Oct51- 6Jam	fst 6f	:223 :452 1:101	2↑ New Rochelle H 17k	7 11 117¼ 85¼ 63¼ 21½	Woodhouse H	116wsb	9.80	94-15	Squared Away1151½Delegate116½Guillotine1261½	Late rush	12
10Oct51- 5Bel	fst 5½f-W	:22 :441 1:013	3↑ Handicap 4565	8 7 41 11 13	Woodhouse H	113wsb	5.45	106-00	Delegate1133Guillotine132¾Tea-Maker123nk	Driving	8
24Sep51- 6Bel	fst 6f-WC	:222 :443 1:09	2↑ Fall Highweight H 25k	15 15 167¼ 61 42	Woodhouse H	120wsb	15.50	94-07	Guillotine134noSquared Away1262Ferd128no	Off slowly	18
9Aug51- 7Atl	fst 6f	:222 :452 1:092	4↑ Alw 4500	3 7 53½ 43 36 46¾	Boulmetis S	124wsb	*1.90	91-11	Istan1144Chloe1192Vamanos121¾	Weakened	7
31Jly51- 6Jam	fst 6f	:232 :462 1:111	3↑ Handicap 5040	4 5 55 42½ 42 33¼	Mehrtens W	112wsb	7.85	88-16	Repetoire1232¼Mighty Quest1081Delegate1124	Hung	5
18Jly51- 6Jam	fst 6f	:231 :462 1:112	3↑ Fleetwing H 22k	3 9 85¾ 63¼ 62¼ 53¼	Boland W	112wsb	13.95	87-16	More Sun110hdTea-Maker1221½Arise1301½	No rally	9
4Jly51- 6Aqu	fst 7f	:223 :452 1:101 1:232	3↑ Carter H 23k	2 8 811 88¼ 85¼ 76	Boland W	114wsb	14.05	89-17	Arise1221More Sun1081¼Piet1231	Dull try	9
6Jun51- 6Bel	fst 6f-WC	:222 :444 1:084	3↑ Roseben H 12k	7 9 94½ 3½ 1nk	Boland W	111wsb	9.50	97-04	Delegate111nkMiche116noTea-Maker126¾	Just lasted	10
19May51- 6Bel	fst 1	:23 :453 1:10 1:352	3↑ Metropolitan H 36k	13 9 52¼ 42 65½ 64½	Boland W	110wsb	10.65f	92-06	Casemate115½Piet123½Lights Up1221	Forced wide	13
14May51- 6Bel	fst 6f-WC	:222 :444 1:092	3↑ Toboggan H 24k	13 13 132½ 3nk 42	Scurlock O	111wsb	13.95	92-06	Hyphasis110noTea-Maker1231Casemate1191	Weakened	14
7Apr51- 6Jam	fst 1 1/16	:231 :463 1:111 1:441	3↑ Excelsior H 29k	3 5 51¾ 51¼ 85¾ 64	Scurlock O	114wb	4.65	87-12	Lotowhite116hdFerd123¾Great Circle1191¼	Raced wide	11
2Apr51- 6Jam	fst 6f	:223 :46 1:111	3↑ Paumonok H 29k	8 5 52¾ 31 3¾ 31¼	Scurlock O	114wsb	5.20	90-15	Ferd116¾Casemate119½Delegate1141¼	Held well	11
5Mar51- 7GP	fst 6f	:222 :444 1:101	3↑ Inaugural H 7.5k	1 9 65¾ 66½ 55 2¾	Madden D	118wsb	12.70	93-11	Hyphasis118¾Delegate1181Lextown1201½	Finished fast	10
22Feb51- 7Hia	fst 7f	:224 :453 1:102 1:232	4↑ Alw 4500	3 - - - - -	Batcheller L	118wb	2.25	- -	Hyphasis1196Prop124½Black George1192	Refused to break	8
10Feb51- 7Hia	fst 1⅛	:453 1:103 1:361 1:492	3↑ McLennan H 36k	15 8 74¾ 53½ 34½ 66¼	Atkinson T	114wb	9.80	85-14	Gangway1091¼Mount Marcy114hdSunglow1172½	Faltered	15
24Jan51- 7Hia	fst 7f	:222 :451 1:104 1:234	3↑ Palm Beach H 10k	2 12 86¾ 55¼ 41½ 22	Atkinson T	120wb	*2.90	91-17	AmericanGlory1112Delegate120nkMountMrcy114hd	Off slowly	13

17Jan51- 7Hia	fst	6f	:221 :451 1:103	3↑ Inaugural H (Div 2) 9k	4 8 8¼ 6 6¾ 34 23	Scurlock O	122wb	4.80	92-12	Valpam1213Delegate122noNell K.119½	Closed fast 8
14Nov50- 6Jam	fst	1 1/16	:24 :47 1:113 1:442	3↑ Alw 5000	6 4 43¾ 21½ 11½ 21½	Scurlock O	120wb	*1.55	88-17	Ted M.1061½Delegate1203½Uncle Edgar1201¼	Weakened 7
2Nov50- 6Jam	fst	1 1/16	:234 :47 1:111 1:442	3↑ Handicap 5050	2 6 33 2hd 11 12½	Scurlock O	122wb	3.75	90-15	Delegate1222½Crystal Boot1131Wine List118½	Ridden out 7
25Oct50- 6Jam	gd	6f	:23 :46 1:111	2↑ New Rochelle H 17k	2 12 105 115½ 115¾ 86	Scurlock O	117wb	8.60	85-19	MagicWords1131SheilasReward124¾Tea-Makr1252	No factor 12
12Oct50- 6Jam	sly	6f	:23 :46 1:12	3↑ Interborough H 17k	9 9 97¼ 97¾ 86¼ 62	Atkinson T	119wb	3.80	85-18	SheilasRewrd120¾MgcWords112½WsconsnBoy109nk	Closed gap 10
25Sep50- 6Bel	fst	7f	:223 :453 1:102 1:23	2↑ Vosburgh H 18k	1 10 108½ 118¼ 87 66¼	Scurlock O	118wb	6.95	89-15	Tea-Maker1181¼More Sun106½Piet124nk	Close quarters 12
18Sep50- 6Bel	fst	6f-WC	:221 :443 1:084	2↑ Fall Highweight H 25k	3 9 8¾ 72 22	Scurlock O	128wb	17.90	95-06	Arise1332Delegate128nkRoyal Governor129½	Game effort 14
7Sep50- 6Aqu	fst	6f	:224 :454 1:11	3↑ Handicap 4055	5 8 84½ 73¾ 66 54	Scurlock O	122wb	3.45	93-09	Mangohick1173DarkFavorite1051FrindlyFrnk108no	No excuse 11

Previously trained by J.A. Nerud

20May50- 6Bel	sly	1	:23 :452 1:102 1:363	3↑ Metropolitan H 31k	8 6 43½ 42½ 44 96¾	Scurlock O	117wb	11.25	84-13	Greek Ship106½Piet121¾Cochise1211¼	Tired 11
13May50- 5Bel	fst	7f	:23 :454 1:101 1:23	3↑ Handicap 5050	5 5 64½ 57 49 36	Scurlock O	122wb	3.30	89-11	Cochise1205Three Rings1221Delegate122hd	Sluggish start 7
29Apr50- 6Jam	gd	1 3/16	:473 1:12 1:372 1:57	3↑ Gallant Fox H 60k	4 8 83¾ 65 74¾ 77	Atkinson T	118wb	4.05	84-14	BetterSelf1161¼ChicleII120hdLoserWeeper109nk	No menace 13
8Apr50- 6Jam	fst	1 1/16	:241 :473 1:112 1:434	3↑ Excelsior H 24k	7 8 86 54½ 54 33	Errico C	119wb	3.15	91-10	Arise1161½Olympia1261½Delegate1191	Finished well 10
1Apr50- 6Jam	fst	6f	:222 :461 1:104	3↑ Paumonok H 30k	13 8 54¾ 41½ 53¾ 31¾	Woodhouse H	122 w	3.90	95-14	Olympia1241¼Arise118½Delegate1223	Forced wide 15
20Mar50- 6GP	gd	6f	:223 :451 1:103	4↑ Alw 3000	1 6 53 42 2½ 1½	Stout J	112wb	*.50	97-18	Delegate112½Almenow1192½Appease Not111½	Driving 6
12Nov49- 6Jam	fst	1 3/16	:471 1:113 1:37 1:564	3↑ Westchester H 29k	3 8 88 57½ 31 2nk	Errico C	120wb	6.75	92-17	ThreeRings116nkDelegate120hdRoylGovrnor1235	Just missed 11
2Nov49- 6Jam	sly	6f	:232 :462 1:112	2↑ New Rochelle H 17k	2 7 61¾ 51¾ 13 16	Arcaro E	122wb	*1.25	94-19	Delegate1226Better Self124noLithe109no	Easily 8
12Oct49- 6Jam	fst	6f	:224 :461 1:111	3↑ Interborough H 17k	9 8 84¾ 42½ 31 21	Arcaro E	122wb	*2.25	94-15	Royal Governor1191Delegate122noPipette1121½	Good effort 10
6Sep49- 6Haw	fst	6f	:222 :453 1:101	3↑ Haw Inaugural H 12k	2 8 42 42 1hd 2¾	Brooks S	122wb	*1.70	101-06	Star Reward124¾Delegate122noBlue Helen109no	Good try 10
1Aug49- 6Was	fst	7f	:22 :443 1:09 1:221	3↑ Clang H 23k	11 9 94½ 64½ 32 22¼	Brooks S	121wb	*2.50	97-10	Colosal1102¼Delegate1212¼Carrara Marble118hd	Good try 12
13Jly49- 6AP	fst	6f	:224 :452 1:104	3↑ Myrtlewood H 27k	2 3 42 32 42¼ 77½	Scurlock O	124wb	*1.90	85-17	Dandilly1083½WithPleasur1192¼RoylBlood112no	Forced back 9
4Jly49- 6AP	fst	1⅛	:472 1:103 1:352 1:482	3↑ Stars & Stripes H 54k	5 3 2hd 2hd 22 42¼	Garner W	110wb	6.30	102-09	Coaltown1301¼Armed110½Star Reward121½	Faltered 6
18Jun49- 6Det	hy	1 1/16	:243 :484 1:151 1:48	3↑ Governor's H 23k	5 2 21 2hd 1hd 2½	Nelson E	119wb	3.10	75-35	Vulcan's Forge128½Delegate1191½Syndicate1086	Weakened 6
28May49- 6Was	fst	6½f	:223 :453 1:101 1:171	3↑ Steger H 11k	1 5 51¾ 31½ 1hd 12	Nelson E	125 w	*1.40	98-12	Delegate1252Blue Helen1081¼Enforcer1102½	Going away 10
16May49- 6Was	gd	6f	:224 :46 1:111	3↑ Crete H 10k	4 4 41¼ 12 11½ 12½	Nelson E	122wb	*.70	90-28	Delegate1222½Enforcer110nkWithPleasure120½	Wide,driving 6
9Feb49- 6Hia	fst	7f	:23 :452 1:093 1:223	3↑ Seminole H 11k	1 1 1hd 11 12 1hd	Brooks S	125wb	*1.20	99-13	Delegate125hdBlue Border1161Bug Juice1143	Hard drive 6
26Jan49- 6Hia	fst	7f	:231 :453 1:091 1:23	3↑ Palm Beach H 12k	2 8 74¾ 77 63½ 31	Nelson E	126wb	*1.50	96-12	BlueBorder1131BugJuice110hdDelegate126nk	Strong finish 10
17Jan49- 6Hia	fst	6f	:223 :452 1:104	3↑ Hia Inaugural H 12k	8 5 51¼ 52¼ 21½ 1nk	Nelson E	122wb	*1.45	94-14	Delegate122nkKitchenPolice1102¾CircusClown118½	Just up 9
3Jan49- 6TrP	fst	6f	:214 :442 1:094	4↑ Alw 2500	7 5 54½ 54½ 2hd 17	Nelson E	115wb	*1.55	98-16	Delegate1157Coyote122nkLoriot1121¼	Drew away 8
12Oct48- 7Haw	fst	6½f	:224 :461 1:113 1:182	3↑ Haw Sprint H 22k	9 6 53¼ 21 2hd 1nk	Nelson E	116wb	*3.00	92-25	Delegate116nkCarrara Marble1098Blue Helen1081	Just up 10
2Oct48- 7Haw	fst	1¼	:473 1:123 1:391 2:06	3↑ Haw Gold Cup 57k	5 2 12 12 31½ 66¼	Parnell W	117wb	10.20e	72-20	Billings1221½Sun Herod124hd[D]Happy Issue1101	Tired 12
18Sep48- 7Haw	fst	1 1/16	:241 :473 1:122 1:46	3↑ Haw Autumn H 22k	8 6 32 32 24 35	Skoronski A	118wb	2.90	83-15	Billings1165May Reward113noDelegate118nk	Faltered 11
11Sep48- 7Haw	fst	6f	:221 :453 1:114	3↑ Haw Speed H 24k	6 10 96½ 85 51¼ 41¾	Skoronski A	117wb	*3.20	92-20	Billings111nkCarrara Marble104½Bullish1111	Late drive 17
7Jly48- 7AP	fst	6f	:223 :45 1:103	3↑ Domino H 22k	6 3 34½ 33½ 32 42½	Brooks S	117wb	*1.00	91-15	Preoccupy1101¼Plumper111¾Fighting Frank119½	No excuse 6
26Jun48- 6AP	fst	1	:232 :454 1:094 1:351	3↑ Equipoise Mile H 33k	4 4 31½ 2hd 2hd 42	Keene H	119wb	4.50	94-06	Fervent124noMighty Story109¾Loujac1051¼	Faltered 11
21Jun48- 6AP	fst	6f	:224 :444 1:094	3↑ Handicap 5000	5 3 44 34 23 2hd	Keene H	120wb	*1.30	98-05	Mighty Story112hdDelegate120hdPhar Mon1161	Just missed 8
29May48- 6Was	fst	6½f	:223 :453 1:111 1:174	3↑ Steger H 11k	10 2 64 73½ 2hd 1¾	Skoronski A	118wb	*1.70	95-17	Delegate118¾Eternal Reward1172½Tidy Sum113¾	In hand 10
17May48- 6Was	gd	6f	:23 :462 1:112	3↑ Crete H 11k	1 2 31½ 31½ 73½ 87¼	Skoronski A	121wb	*1.50	83-21	Eternal Reward1122Tre Vit111½Air Rate1092	Tired 13

Previously trained by R.O. Higdon

27Mar48- 6TrP	fst	1⅛	:484 1:122 1:363 1:493	3↑ Double Event H (2) 16k	3 2 2hd 2hd 2hd 2nk	Richard J	119wb	*1.00	93-14	Colosal113nkDelegate1195½Childeric1075	No mishap 4
20Mar48- 6TrP	fst	1⅛	:472 1:112 1:362 1:492	3↑ Double Event H (1) 17k	8 2 11 13 1½ 31	Dodson D	119wb	2.10	93-13	Colosal113hdFervent1251Delegate119½	Swung wide 8
6Mar48- 6TrP	fst	1 1/16	:234 :474 1:113 1:431	3↑ Coral Gables H 11k	2 2 1hd 14 16 15	Dodson D	116wb	*1.00	96-12	Delegate1165Stud Poker115hdRespingo1143	Eased up 4
11Feb48- 6Hia	fst	7f	:232 :46 1:101 1:23	3↑ Seminole H 12k	6 3 1hd 1hd 2hd 21	Atkinson T	123wb	3.90	96-16	Citation1121Delegate123nkArmed1282	Weakened 9
24Jan48- 6Hia	my	7f	:231 :462 1:114 1:242	3↑ Palm Beach H 11k	5 3 4¾ 2hd 1½ 12	Atkinson T	118wb	1.90	90-28	Delegate1182Bug Juice1102½Lets Dance1101½	Going away 6
16Jan48- 5Hia	fst	6f	:224 :453 1:094	3↑ Hia Inaugural H 11k	4 2 31 31 3½ 1nk	Jessop JD	117wb	3.45	99-07	Delegate117nkBuzfuz1271¼El Mono1201	Hard drive 6
10Jan48- 6GP	fst	6f	:232 :462 1:111	3↑ Suwannee River H 11k	8 4 51¼ 3nk 2hd 21	Jessop JD	114wb	6.55	93-15	Buzfuz1221Delegate1143½Gestapo111nk	Raced well 9
1Dec47- 6GP	gd	6f	:231 :472 1:12	3↑ Inaugural H 9.2k	3 9 32 2hd 2hd 1nk	Scurlock D	109wb	6.95	90-24	Delegate109nkNance's Ace1141½Iodine1075	Driving 10
4Oct47- 6Haw	fst	6½f	:223 :451 1:104 1:174	3↑ Haw Sprint H 22k	2 8 52¾ 66 65¼ 65	Jemas N	105wb	10.60	90-17	Fighting Frank122noSpy Song1351Plumper1131½	No factor 9
27Sep47- 6Haw	fst	6f	:224 :462 1:111	3↑ Handicap 4500	4 3 2½ 2½ 2nk 2no	Jemas N	106wb	3.30	97-11	Proud Ruler103noDelegate1064½Education117hd	Game try 5
20Sep47- 5Haw	fst	6f	:224 :461 1:11	3↑ Handicap 4500	6 4 3½ 3nk 12 1no	Jemas N	106wb	*1.00	98-09	Delegate106noLove Sonnet1092Proud Ruler1006	Hard drive 7
13Sep47- 7Haw	gd	6f	:222 :461 1:122	3↑ Haw Speed H 22k	1 5 21 31 33½ 36½	Jemas N	103wb	17.40	84-19	SpySng1323½Educatn1133Dlgt103¾	Saved ground,weakened 8
3Sep47- 6Haw	fst	6f	:221 :452 1:11	3↑ Handicap 4500	2 7 22½ 23 33 35	Jemas N	105wb	*2.40	93-14	Bogle1094Jack S.L.1141Delegate1052	Weakened 9
18Aug47- 7Was	fst	6f	:223 :444 1:092	3↑ Great Western H 27k	3 6 55 66½ 711 713	Jemas N	105wb	16.30	90-07	Rippey1151Spy Song1291½Quick Reward1133½	Outrun 7
28Jly47- 7Was	fst	6f	:223 :452 1:094	3↑ Quick Step 22k	4 4 44 46½ 48½ 68½	Jessop JD	116wb	7.30	92-09	WithPleasure130½SpySong1302½Rippey1274½	Speed,faltered 8
3Jly47- 6AP	fst	6f	:223 :45 1:101	3↑ Alw 5000	3 5 1½ 13 12½ 31	Scurlock O	109wb	3.90	95-08	Quick Reward118½Air Patrol118½Delegate1092	Faltered 6

Previously trained by E. Anspach

17Mar47- 6GP	fst	6f	:222 :451 1:104	Magic City H 5.6k	3 3 31½ 32 11 12½	Watson R	124wb	*.75	99-07	Delegate1242½Imperator1203Secnav1222	Easily 5
12Mar47- 4GP	fst	6f	:222 :453 1:103	Alw 3000	9 3 1hd 12 14 13½	Watson R	120wb	*.65	100-05	Dlgate1203½AtomicPowr1126PnnyRwrd109nk	Speed to spare 10
22Feb47- 5Hia	fst	1⅛	:464 1:113 1:371 1:494	Alw 5000	5 2 2½ 32½ 37 518½	Watson R	117wb	3.95	73-11	BulletProof1091½Faultlss11312Cpt.Ptrck1034¾	Flattened out 5
12Feb47- 5Hia	fst	7f	:224 :452 1:102 1:233	©Alw 4000	4 1 11½ 11½ 1½ 31¼	Watson R	122wb	5.75	93-12	Faultless122nkBullet Proof1131Delegate1227	Gamely 8
17Aug46- 6Was	my	6f	:224 :462 1:121	Wash Park Futurity 79k	11 6 41 2½ 22 35¾	Scurlock O	118wb	13.60	83-21	Education1183½Jett-Jett1182½Delegate1181	Bid,failed 12
3Aug46- 7Was	fst	6f	:222 :452 1:111	Elementary 24k	10 9 64 64½ 42½ 46½	Anderson I	125 w	10.80	87-07	Education122hdColonelO'F1254John'sPrd1202½	Bid,faltered 11
24Jly46- 6AP	fst	6f	:224 :46 1:112	©Primer 23k	1 3 11½ 12 13 11¼	Scurlock O	119 w	11.40	90-14	Delegate1191¼Education122hdJohn's Pride119hd	Driving 11
13Jly46- 6AP	fst	6f	:22 :45 1:104	Arl Futurity 79k	7 14 98¼ 911 96¾ 95	Scurlock O	122 w	14.40	88-09	CosmicBomb122¾JetPilot1223ColonelO'F122no	No response 15
6Jly46- 3AP	fst	5½f	:223 :461 :583 1:044	Alw 4000	1 4 42½ 43½ 34½ 34¾	Anderson I	117 w	4.60	92-09	Educton1232½Twt'sBoy1232½Dlgt117hd	No rally,drifted out 5
26Jun46- 2AP	fst	5f	:23 :462 :591	Alw 3500	7 5 51¼ 53 42 1½	Scurlock O	118 w	4.30	96-14	Delegate118½Springtd1152½Bullsh1182	Bothered repeatedly 10
8Jun46- 3Haw	fst	5f	:23 :473 1:011	Md Sp Wt	5 4 11 13 16 18	Scurlock O	118 w	4.00	89-14	Delegate1188Miniver118hdGrand Fellow1183	Speed to spare 6
1Jun46- 1Haw	my	5f	:241 :491 1:022	Md Sp Wt	2 6 54 54½ 46 45½	Scurlock O	118 w	25.60	77-20	Galloway1184Masico Lad1181½Ranahead115no	Closed well 8

Devil Diver

b. c. 1939, by St. Germans (Swynford)–Dabchick, by Royal Minstrel

Lifetime record: 47 22 12 3 $261,064

Own.– Greentree Stable
Br.– Greentree Farm (Ky)
Tr.– John M. Gaver

4Jly45- 5Bel	fst	1¼	:464 1:104 1:363 2:021	3↑ Brooklyn H 56k	2 5 32 42¼ 2½ 21¼	Arcaro E	132wb	*1.25	88-12	Stymie1161¼Devil Diver1322½Olympic Zenith1102	Held well 9
16Jun45- 6Bel	fst	1¼	:502 1:142 1:39 2:04	3↑ Suburban H 52k	1 1 1½ 11½ 12 12	Arcaro E	132wb	*.50	80-15	DevlDvr1322Stym119nkOlympcZnth1061½	Under pressure late 4
9Jun45- 6Bel	fst	1	:234 :47 1:113 1:362	3↑ Metropolitan H 27k	5 4 31½ 32 11 14	Atkinson T	129wb	*.55	92-12	Devil Diver1294Alex Barth123½Boy Knight112¾	Easily 7
4Jun45- 6Bel	sly	6f-WC	:23 :462 1:11	3↑ Toboggan H 16k	6 1 62¼ 41¼ 23 22½	Arcaro E	135wb	*.85	83-13	Apache1292½Devil Diver1354Mrs. Ames1071	No match 9
24May45- 5Jam	fst	6f	:231 :462 1:104	3↑ Paumonok H 8.3k	3 7 55½ 41¾ 31½ 11¼	Arcaro E	132wb	*1.30	98-12	Devil Diver1321¼Apache1292½Alex Barth121hd	Fast finish 7
1Nov44- 7Pim	fst	1 3/16	:481 1:122 1:372 1:563	3↑ Pim Spl 25k	3 2 23 24 24 26	Arcaro E	126wb	1.55	93-12	Twilight Tear1176Devil Diver12610Megogo120	Mild bid 3
21Oct44- 5Jam	sly	1⅝	:483 1:391 2:051 2:46	3↑ Gallant Fox H 55k	2 1 35 33 55 510	Arcaro E	124wb	*3.00	75-15	Some Chance1161Pyracanth1053Stymie1121	Tired 10
30Sep44- 6Bel	fst	2	:513 2:351 3:01 3:271	3↑ J C Gold Cup 26k	2 2 2½ 2hd 21½ 33	Arcaro E	125wb	*1.45	65-17	Bolingbroke1253Strategic125hdDevil Diver125¾	Tired late 4

Geldings not eligible

23Sep44- 6Bel fst 1½ :553 1:2212:1322:363 3↑ Manhattan H 15k 3 2 3½ 1hd 11½ 11¼ Arcaro E 125wb 2.00 55-17 DevlDvr1251¼Crbou102hdBolngbrok126nk Outsprinted rivals 4
16Sep44- 6Nar fst 1 3/16 :463 1:111 1:364 1:56 3↑ Nar Spl 30k 13 5 74½ 64¼ 75 53½ Arcaro E 130wb *1.30e 91-12 Paperboy1101Alex Barth117hdCastleman1131½ No response 13
26Aug44- 6Bel fst 1 :232 :463 1:111 1:361 3↑ Wilson 17k 5 2 21½ 2½ 1hd 12½ Atkinson T 117wb *.25 93-11 Devil Diver1172½Bull Reigh1121Wait a Bit1124 Drew away 5
19Aug44- 6Bel fst 1¼ :48 1:114 1:37 2:021 3↑ Saratoga H 53k 4 5 51¾ 52¾ 73¼ 67 Arcaro E 135wb *2.45 82-13 Paperboy103hdAlex Barth1161½Bolingbroke1181 Tired 7
15Aug44- 6Bel fst 1¼ :481 1:114 1:364 2:02 3↑ Whitney 16k 4 1 1hd 12 11 1½ Arcaro E 117wb *.25 90-17 DevilDiver117½Princequillo1173½Bolngbrok1172 Ridden out 4
31Jly44- 6Bel fst 7f :234 :463 1:104 1:233 3↑ American Legion H 7.8k 1 2 2nk 1nk 11 12½ Arcaro E 136wb *.25 92-12 Devil Diver1362½Bull Reigh1054Bourmont108 Easily 3
13May44- 6Bel fst 1 :23 :453 1:103 1:354 3↑ Metropolitan H 13k 5 5 54¾ 33 21 11½ Atkinson T 134wb *.50e 95-10 Devil Diver1341½Alquest109¾Boysy1081¼ Driving 7
8May44- 6Bel gd 6f-WC :23 :464 1:123 3↑ Toboggan H 6.7k 2 3 53½ 52 3nk 11¼ Arcaro E 134wb *.70e 83-16 Devil Diver1341¼Signator120hdBrownie1142 Drew away 7
8Apr44- 5Jam gd 6f :223 :461 1:111 3↑ Paumonok H 9.2k 1 4 42¼ 45 34½ 11½ Atkinson T 130wb 3.15 96-16 Devil Diver1301½Apache1301Brownie112¾ Bore over,driving 10
5Jly43- 7Was my 1⅛ :491 1:14 1:401 1:533 3↑ Stars & Stripes H 59k 10 5 43½ 44½ 44¾ 55¾ Woolf G 124wb *1.90 74-31 Rounders1161Thumbs Up113hdMarriage1164 No response 10
26Jun43- 6Aqu fst 1¼ :481 1:132 1:383 2:032 3↑ Brooklyn H 33k 8 5 54 32 1½ 11½ Brooks S 123wb *.95e 90-12 Devil Diver1231½Market Wise128¾Don Bingo1133 Driving 9
12Jun43- 6Aqu fst 7f :23 :461 1:112 1:24 3↑ Carter H 9.7k 6 7 78½ 712 82 1hd Woolf G 126wb *3.55 95-12 Devil Diver126hdMarriage1181Doublrab118nk Driving 10
31May43- 6Bel fst 1¼ :47 1:111 1:361 2:012 3↑ Suburban H 38k 11 1 52¼ 64¾ 63¼ 55½ Gilbert J 121wb *2.45e 87-12 Don Bingo1042[D]Market Wise1282½Attention121hd Bothered 17
15May43- 6Bel fst 1 :23 :463 1:103 1:363 3↑ Metropolitan H 14k 9 5 53½ 33½ 31½ 11¼ Woolf G 117wb *1.60e 91-16 DevlDivr1171¼Mrrg116¾ThumbsUp1172 Outside,drawing away 11
10May43- 6Bel fst 6f-WC 1:10 3↑ Toboggan H 7.4k 6 7 107 72 3nk 11 Woolf G 116wb 2.55e 96-05 Devil Diver1161With Regards118noThumbs Up1161 12
Between horses,drew away
24Apr43- 5Jam fst 1 1/16 :242 :481 1:131 1:442 3↑ Excelsior H 12k 7 8 85¾ 87½ 811 511 Gilbert J 115wb 5.00 80-15 Riverland1245Minee-Mo1082½Marrig121no Outside,no threat 11
17Apr43- 4Jam fst 6f :23 :461 1:111 3↑ Handicap 2530 3 3 42 32½ 34 2nk Gilbert J 121wb *1.75 96-06 Doublrab123nkDevilDivr1213Rqustd1211½ Getting to winner 6
10Apr43- 6Jam fst 6f :224 :454 1:121 3↑ Paumonok H (Div 2) 8.8k 6 8 914 813 78 54 McCreary C 123wb *1.55 87-17 With Regards126hdPompion1143Boysy118hd Outrun,late gain 9
17Oct42- 6Jam fst 1 1/16 :233 :472 1:123 1:443 3↑ Continental H 11k 7 8 98¾ 109 1011 109¾ Haas L 119wb 4.30e 80-14 [D]Riverland121noBoysy1141½Doublrab119½ Never a factor 12
10Oct42- 6Bel fst 7f :23 :461 1:103 1:23 2↑ Vosburgh H 8.9k 1 4 52¼ 51½ 22 21 Haas L 124wb *1.50e 94-08 Parasang1121DvlDvr1246Rostown1121½ Close quarters early 7
25Sep42- 6Bel fst 1 :234 :471 1:111 1:36 Alw 2500 3 2 2hd 1nk 2hd 1½ Haas L 116wb *.45 95-08 DevilDiver116½PrtyBustr1111½ScotlndLght1135 Bumped turn 7
22Sep42- 6Bel fst 1 :233 :464 1:111 1:362 Jerome H 8.9k 2 5 34 34½ 32 3nk Haas L 126wb *1.15 93-11 King'sAbbey112nkBlessMe122noDevlDvr1262½ Inside,driving 7
7Sep42- 5Aqu fst 5½f :224 :461 :583 1:05 3↑ Handicap 3555 1 4 22 33½ 42½ 1½ Arcaro E 140wb *2.10 102-04 Devil Diver140½Dogpatch126noVain Prince1161½ Drew away 5
19May42- 4Bel fst 7f :232 :463 1:111 1:231 Handicap 2530 4 2 21 21 2½ 1hd Arcaro E 126wb *1.45 94-12 Devil Diver126hdDogpatch1156First Fiddle117¾ Hard drive 4
9May42- 6Pim fst 1 3/16 :47 1:112 1:371 1:57 Preakness 75k 1 1 32 52¾ 812 813 Arcaro E 126wb 2.40e 85-06 Alsb1261[DH]Requestd126[DH]SunAgn126¾ Close quarters,tired 10
2May42- 7CD fst 1¼ :472 1:123 1:39 2:042 Ky Derby 76k 5 2 54¼ 53 54½ 67¼ Arcaro E 126wb *1.90e 78-09 Shut Out1262¼Alsab126hdValdina Orphan1261½ Saved ground 15
9Apr42- 5Kee my 6f :234 :48 1:132 3↑ Phoenix H 3.4k 2 1 1hd 1hd 1hd 1hd Arcaro E 113.5 w 1.30 85-26 Devil Diver113.5hdWhirlaway1281½Sun Again1122 Driving 5
1Nov41- 6Pim sly 1 1/16 :242 :474 1:132 1:472 Pim Futurity 38k 8 2 2hd 1hd 23 26 Westrope J 119wb *1.15e 77-26 Contradiction1226DevilDiver1191ChiqutM1191½ Second best 8
Geldings not eligible
18Oct41- 6Kee my 6f :231 :464 1:114 Breeders' Futurity 12k 3 3 32 32½ 21 11 McCreary C 122wb 3.00 93-16 Devil Diver1221Miss Dogwood1143Dogpatch1175 Drew out 4
Geldings not eligible
11Oct41- 4Jam gd 6f :224 :461 1:124 Remsen H 12k 1 1 11 21 21 2½ Robertson A 124wb *.75 87-25 Apache110½Devil Diver1242Contradiction119½ Good effort 9
27Sep41- 7Bel fst 6½f-WC 1:164 Futurity 72k 2 5 11 11½ 1½ 2½ Skelly J 126wb *1.45e 87-12 Some Chance122½Devil Diver1261Caduceus119hd Good effort 14
Geldings not eligible
23Sep41- 5Bel fst 6f-WC 1:10 Fut Trial (Div 1) 5k 8 1 11 12 1hd 21¼ Skelly J 122wb *.70e 96-04 Dogpatch1111¼DevlDvr1221½Contrdcton1221½ Tired,bore out 8
30Aug41- 4Sar fst 6½f :224 :461 1:113 1:183 Hopeful 41k 1 1 12 12 1nk 12 Skelly J 119wb *.40e 92-12 DevilDiver1192ShutOut1221½Amphitheatre1221¼ Going away 8
23Aug41- 5Sar fst 6f :23 :47 1:121 Grand Union Hotel 11k 2 2 11 2nk 31¾ 34½ Meade D 119wb *.65e 86-19 Shut Out1163½Requested1261Devil Diver1192½ Went well 7
13Aug41- 6Sar fst 6f :224 :464 1:124 Sanford 6.6k 2 3 11 2hd 1hd 1¾ Meade D 114wb 3.30 88-14 Devil Diver114¾Ramillies110hdColchis117hd Drew out 10
8Aug41- 3Sar fst 5½f :23 :463 1:053 ©Md Sp Wt 8 1 1hd 12 11½ 12 Meade D 116wb *1.50 95-12 Devil Diver1162Ramillies1164Fair Call1164 Easily 19
4Aug41- 3Sar fst 5½f :232 :472 1:064 ©Md Sp Wt 9 6 1hd 1nk 1½ 2hd Meade D 116wb *1.70 89-14 Nipsickle116hdDevil Diver1161Wishbone1162½ Hung 19
29Jly41- 3Sar gd 5½f :231 :471 1:07 ©Md Sp Wt 8 5 55 62¾ 31½ 2¾ Meade D 116 w *1.50 87-17 Sundial116¾Devil Diver116¾Anytime1161½ Closed fast 12
30May41- 3Bel fst 5f :224 :462 :584 ©Alw 1500 7 4 1hd 1hd 1hd 21½ Arcaro E 111 w *2.00 -- SoldierSong1111½DevilDiver111hdEarlynSmart116½ Weakened 7

Double Jay

dk br. c. 1944, by Balladier (Black Toney)–Broomshot, by Whisk Broom II **Lifetime record: 48 17 9 9 $299,005**

Own.– J.V. Tigani
Br.– John W. Stanley (Ky)
Tr.– W. Molter

26Jan50- 7SA fst 6f :223 :46 1:104 4↑ Handicap 6000 2 6 610 613 69¼ 612½ Gilbert J 116wb 25.95 80-15 Miche114nkCitation1303½Huon Kid107½ 6
Trailed,appeared sore afterward
17Jan50- 7SA gd 6f :223 :461 1:113 4↑ Handicap 6000 3 5 56 58 56 44 Gilbert J 120wb 5.05 85-19 Johns Joy122nkOn Trust118¾Blue Border1163 No mishaps 5
Previously trained by W.L. McCue
16Jly49- 7SA fst 1¼ :461 1:103 1:351 2:011 3↑ Hol Gold Cup H 136k 8 4 21½ 31 36 75¼ Bierman C 116wb 3.85 95-12 Solidarity1151¼Ace Admiral1151½Pretal112¾ Tired 11
4Jly49- 7SA fst 1⅛ :472 1:112 1:361 1:483 3↑ American H 56k 3 3 31½ 21 2½ 11 Bierman C 119wb 5.95 100-11 Double Jay1191Solidarity1172Dinner Gong122nk Driving 8
25Jun49- 7SA fst 1 1/16 :231 :461 1:103 1:424 3↑ Inglewood H 29k 8 7 54 51¾ 5¾ 4nk Bierman C 122wb 3.60 94-10 Ace Admiral124hdPretal110noAmble In112hd Close quarters 9
18Jun49- 6SA fst 7f :22 :444 1:094 1:222 3↑ Alw 10000 4 8 64 51¾ 11 12 Bierman C 113wb 3.40 97-10 Double Jay1132On Trust1223May Reward1071½ In hand 8
30May49- 7SA fst 1 1/16 :232 :463 1:103 1:422 3↑ Argonaut H 29k 7 3 32½ 45 45½ 46¾ Bierman C 120wb 2.25 89-13 AceAdmirl1191½Bymeabnd1101¼DnnrGong1244 Wide,weakened 7
25May49- 7SA fst 7f :221 :444 1:093 1:223 3↑ Handicap 7500 6 5 42 2½ 2hd 12½ Bierman C 120wb 9.20 96-09 Double Jay1202½The Shaker1141Bymeabond115nk Wide 7
21Aug48- 7Nar fst 1 1/16 :242 :483 1:122 1:451 4↑ Alw 3500 4 5 22 21½ 31½ 32¾ Keiper P 120wb *.50 88-12 WrTrophy110nkPrfctBhrm1132½DoublJy1201¾ Bid,drifted out 8
14Aug48- 6Suf fst 1¼ :462 1:111 1:36 2:023 3↑ Mass H 67k 4 8 65¾ 52½ 62¼ 32 Stout J 123wb 7.20 109-13 Beauchef1151¼Harmonica110¾DoubleJay123hd Close quarters 12
Previously trained by Claude Feltner
10Jly48- 5Mth fst 1⅛ :463 1:104 1:371 1:502 3↑ Omnibus H 18k 1 3 32½ 43 45½ 49¼ James B 124wb *1.50 92-16 Flash Burn111nkLucky Draw1246½Faraway1102½ Tired 6
26Jun48- 6Aqu fst 1 1/16 :251 :493 1:133 1:452 3↑ Aqueduct H 28k 4 3 21 1nk 2hd 33½ James B 126wb 6.25 83-18 Stymie130hdConniver1173½Double Jay1262½ Weakened 7
Previously owned by Ridgewood Stable
8May48- 6Pim sl 1 3/16 :49 1:141 1:404 2:013 3↑ Dixie H 31k 5 7 76¾ 85¼ 65¾ 76¼ Gilbert J 124wb 4.40 68-41 Fervent1211½Stymie1272½Incline107no Quit 9
24Apr48- 5GS fst 1⅛ :471 1:112 1:362 1:494 3↑ Trenton H 31k 2 4 33 33 31½ 1½ Gilbert J 124wb *1.10 93-08 Double Jay124½Tide Rips109nkElpis115¾ Driving 9
17Apr48- 5Jam fst 1 1/16 :243 :482 1:132 1:46 3↑ Excelsior H 29k 8 2 21 21 21 2¾ Scurlock O 125wb *1.60 82-20 Knockdown114¾Double Jay1252½Stymie1284 Close quarters 9
9Apr48- 5Jam fst 1 1/16 :252 :49 1:132 1:472 3↑ Handicap 7535 5 2 21 11½ 11½ 13½ Arcaro E 126wb *1.15 76-28 Double Jay1263½Elpis1191¼Lets Dance1151 Easily 5
28Feb48- 7SA fst 1¼ :464 1:114 1:371 2:032 3↑ S Anita H 139k 6 11 75¼ 33 33½ 31¾ Gilbert J 118wb 7.75 87-22 Talon122noOn Trust1211¾Double Jay1181¼ Went well 14
14Feb48- 7SA fst 1⅛ :461 1:102 1:364 1:492 3↑ San Antonio H 69k 1 5 74¼ 31½ 31½ 2nk Gilbert J 118wb 6.90 96-10 Talon122nkDouble Jay1182½On Trust126½ Best of others 8
31Jan48- 7SA fst 1¼ :471 1:113 1:364 2:031 Maturity 130k 11 11 63 53½ 43 31½ Gilbert J 118wb 3.40 88-15 Flashco113nkOn Trust1251¼Double Jay1181¼ Finished well 13
23Jan48- 7SA fst 6f :22 :451 1:103 4↑ Handicap 10000 4 7 68½ 67½ 64¾ 61¼ Gilbert J 122wb *1.30 92-15 Ocean Brief114¾Bogle114noHubble Bubble110nk No excuse 7
15Jan48- 7SA fst 6f :22 :451 1:11 4↑ Handicap 10000 6 7 713 615 48 44 Gilbert J 121wb 4.20 88-12 War Allies116nkBogle1091½Bymeabond1122¾ Late foot 7
Previously trained by Charles Feltner
29Nov47- 6Bow fst 1 3/16 :493 1:133 1:392 1:593 3↑ Bryan & O'Hara H 22k 7 7 2hd 11½ 2hd 3¾ Breen J 123wb 1.50e 88-18 Incline107¾Gallorette124hdDouble Jay123hd Held on well 7
22Nov47- 6Bow fst 1 1/16 :242 :483 1:132 1:46 2↑ Prince George Aut H 11k 3 1 1hd 1hd 1hd 1no Breen J 120wb *.30e 91-20 Double Jay120noMaster Bid1033Incline106nk Hard drive 5
7Nov47- 6Pim gd 1 3/16 :493 1:143 1:411 2:01 3↑ Riggs H 29k 4 3 21 21½ 1½ 12¼ Gilbert J 115wb *1.20 77-29 DoubleJay1152¼FlashBurn1091LoyalLgon1181¼ Rated,driving 5
1Nov47- 5Jam gd 1 1/16 :24 :472 1:121 1:443 3↑ Scarsdale H 30k 9 9 108 75¼ 33½ 32½ Gilbert J 118wb 3.95 87-17 WithPleasure1292Gallorette119½DoubleJay1182 Fast finish 12
20Oct47- 5Jam fst 1 3/16 :473 1:121 1:383 1:581 Roamer H 30k 9 9 74½ 73¾ 2½ 2nk Gilbert J 120wb 9.85 85-17 CosmcBomb128nkDblJy1201Flshco1041½ Steadied,led briefly 10
11Oct47- 6GS fst 1⅛ :47 1:104 1:36 1:482 3↑ Trenton H 62k 2 3 22 21½ 23 25 Gilbert J 118wb *.90 98-10 Cosmic Bomb1205Double Jay1188Earshot116½ Impeded start 7
1Oct47- 6GS fst 6f :223 :453 1:103 Benjamin Franklin H 12k 5 3 42½ 21 1½ 14 Gilbert J 126wb *.80 98-11 DoubleJay1264GlenHeathr1121MstrMnd1121½ Speed to spare 6
20Sep47- 5GS fst 1⅛ :464 1:111 1:363 1:493 Jersey H 36k 5 2 22 2½ 1hd 12½ Gilbert J 114wb 1.80 97-10 Double Jay1142½Fervent1252Lighthouse1097 Handily 5

13Sep47- 6GS	fst 1⅛	:463 1:104 1:373 1:511	Alw 5000	5	2	25	24	22	12½	Gilbert J	118wb	*.65	89-08	Double Jay1182½Lighthouse1123Camargo1182	Worked 1¼	5
6Sep47- 6Aqu	gd 1⅛	:483 1:123 1:38 1:511	Discovery H 28k	6	3	31¾	11½	1nk	2no	Gilbert J	115wb	34.35	91-13	Cosmic Bomb126noDouble Jay1151Phalanx1281	Held well	9
25Aug47- 6GS	fst 6f	:222 :452 1:094 3↑	Camden H 11k	2	6	42	52½	45	46½	Gilbert J	115wb	7.85e	95-06	Polynesian1295Air Patrol123nkThe Doge1191¼	Weakened	6
12Aug47- 7Sar	fst 6f	:23 :462 1:111	Alw 4000	2	4	3½	11½	11	11	Gilbert J	116wb	*.95	92-13	DoubleJay1161Mitym1181½Mr.John1096	Worked mile 1:38 1/5	9
2Aug47- 5Jam	fst 1 1/16	:242 :482 1:132 1:464	Handicap 15275	10	2	1½	1½	31½	62¾	Givens C	121wb	*2.65	76-20	ColonelO'F122hdPickMeUp1041OurTommy1111½	Tired badly	11
26Jly47- 4Jam	fst 6f	:224 :46 1:112 3↑	Handicap 10250	4	5	52¾	42¼	41¾	23	Givens C	114wb	7.35	91-14	Hornbm1243DoublJy114hdKngDorstt120nk	No threat to winner	7
Previously trained by W.L. McCue																
3May47- 7CD	sl 1¼	:49 1:142 1:402 2:064	Ky Derby 109k	2	7	42	1223	1218	1224	Gilbert J	126wb	47.30	49-23	Jet Pilot126hdPhalanx126hdFaultless1261	Pulled up sore	13
29Apr47- 5CD	fst 1	:23 :462 1:114 1:373	Derby Trial 12k	6	1	11	1hd	42½	56½	Gilbert J	119wb	3.60	84-17	Faultless118hdStar Reward1103Cosmic Bomb1183	Gave way	6
26Apr47- 5CD	fst 6f	:224 :462 1:114	Alw 3000	1	6	32½	32	35	33¾	Gilbert J	126wb	*1.00	90-13	King Bay1141¼On Trust1262½Double Jay1261¾		6
Away slowly,worked mile in 1:41																
2Nov46- 6CD	fst 1	:224 :462 1:112 1:37	Ky Jockey Club 31k	1	1	1½	1½	1hd	13	Gilbert J	122wb	2.70	94-11	Double Jay1223Education1227Patmiboy1162½	Going away	8
19Oct46- 6GS	fst 6f	:222 :454 1:11	Garden State 33k	4	8	31½	11	13	11½	Gilbert J	122 w	2.05	96-16	Double Jay1221½World Trade1104Mityme1192	Ridden out	11
28Sep46- 6Nar	fst 6f	:23 :46 1:113	J H Connors Mem 20k	7	2	2½	1nk	11½	11¼	Gilbert J	117wb	5.20	93-12	Double Jay1171¼Miss Kimo119¾Donor1223	Driving	14
18Sep46- 6Nar	fst 6f	:223 :452 1:11	ⒻNewport 9.7k	6	3	1nk	11½	1nk	1no	Gilbert J	113 w	*1.40	96-14	Double Jay113noBastogne1108First Sentry1141½	Hard drive	12
25May46- 5Nar	fst 5f	:23 :462 :591	Nar Nursery 10k	4	5	2hd	2hd	2½	2hd	Keiper P	114 w	4.20e	99-10	Fleet West110hdDouble Jay1141Mel Eppley1143	Just missed	12
11May46- 3Nar	fst 5f	:223 :453 :591	Alw 2500	6	8	21½	2½	1½	1no	Maschek F	115 w	*.60e	99-08	Double Jay115noSilee1151½Gay Pet113½	Hard drive	8
25Apr46- 3Nar	fst 4f	:24 :473	ⒸMd Sp Wt	9	7		31¾	1nk	12½	Maschek F	118 w	*1.30	99-01	Double Jay1182½Gemsbok1181½Noble Cyclops1181	Easily	9
Previously trained by L.J. Schaefer																
4Mar46- 4Hia	fst 3f	:221 :332	Hia Juvenile (Div 1) 13k	5	4			21½	31	Dodson D	114 w	11.75	--	Tweet's Boy1141Transair117hdDouble Jay114½	Sharp effort	10
28Feb46- 1Hia	fst 3f	:222 :34	ⒸMd Sp Wt	13	4			54¼	21½	Wall N	120 w	2.90f	--	Eternal War1201½Double Jay120½Tweet's Boy1201	Good try	14
22Feb46- 1Hia	sl 3f	:223 :342	ⒸMd Sp Wt	7	4			43½	21½•	Wall N	118 w	*2.70	--	Milkwagonjoe1181½DHDbleJay118DHStmulus1181½	Held well	14

Durazna

b. f. 1941, by Bull Lea (Bull Dog)–Myrtlewood, by Blue Larkspur

Lifetime record: 19 9 2 4 $70,201

Own.– Brownell Combs
Br.– Brownell Combs (Ky)
Tr.– J.M. Goode

3Sep45- 7Was	fst 1¼	:463 1:103 1:361 2:014 3↑	Wash Park H 57k	7	2	1hd	54½	1323	1328¼	Thompson B	117 w	17.80	73-12	Busher1151½Armed1201TakeWng1125	Faltered,not ridden out	13
29Aug45- 7Was	gd 1	:23 :453 1:104 1:374 3↑	ⒻMatch Race 25k	2	1	2hd	1nk	2hd	2¾	Woolf G	115 w	1.10	88-21	Busher115¾Durazna115	Tired late	2
18Aug45- 7Was	fst 1⅛	:463 1:12 1:373 1:512 3↑	ⒻBeverly H 32k	7	3	34	23	1½	12½	Woolf G	116 w	11.90	91-14	Durazna1162½Letmenow1021¼Busher1284	Ridden out	8
8Aug45- 5Was	fst 7f	:23 :461 1:111 1:24 3↑	Sheridan H (Div 1) 16k	9	2	11	12	14	17	Woolf G	113 w	4.10	93-14	Durazna1137Challenge Me111½Bolus1111½	Speed in reserve	9
1Aug45- 6Was	my 1	:231 :472 1:123 1:392 3↑	ⒻArl Matron H 27k	9	1	21	2½	2hd	36	Woolf G	117 w	5.30	75-33	War Date1134Whirlabout1202Durazna1172	Tired	9
26Jly45- 6Was	fst 6f	:222 :453 1:104 3↑	Myrtlewood H 17k	10	7	41½	32	34½	66¼	Adams J	119 w	8.20	90-11	Three Dots120½Burgoo Maid1091¼Fighting Don1081	Tired	13
14Jly45- 6Was	sly 1	:233 :473 1:114 1:384 3↑	ⒻModesty H 22k	4	1	11	11	13	32¾	South G	120 w	7.50	81-19	War Date110½Night Shadow1142¼Durazna1201¾	Tired	12
27Jun45- 6Was	sl 6f	:232 :482 1:141 3↑	Clang H 11k	5	2	11	1hd	1½	1no	South G	116 w	4.60	79-34	Durazna116noSigma Kappa1066Daily Trouble1113	Driving	10
15Jun45- 6CD	fst 6f	:224 :461 1:122 4↑	Alw 2000	1	1	1nk	1nk	2½	21½	South G	109.5 w	*.70	89-18	Zacapet1101½Durazna109.51½Busyridge1124	Tired	4
28Jun44- 6Was	fst 6f	:222 :453 1:103	ⒻPrincess Doreen 11k	3	1	31½	34½	32½	47¾	Higley J	118 w	3.20	90-09	Twilight Tear1211½Bell Song1106Harriet Sue114nk	Tired	6
20Jun44- 4Was	fst 6f	:231 :47 1:114	ⒻAlw 3000	5	1	2hd	1hd	1½	11¼	Higley J	117 w	*.50	92-10	Durazna1171¼Harriet Sue1132½Bell Song109.5¾	Handily	5
23Oct43- 6CD	fst 6f	:23 :463 1:113	Breeders' Futurity 14k	2	1	1hd	1hd	1hd	12	Higley J	116 w	*2.00e	95-16	Durazna1162Occupy12217Mr. Rabbit117	In hand	3
25Sep43- 6Haw	gd 6f	:222 :47 1:131	Haw Juv H 6.2k	9	3	66¾	22	1hd	1no	Higley J	120 w	*2.20	87-15	Durazna120noCaptnEdd1121½Zcpt1161	Crowded rivals,lasted	11
13Sep43- 5Haw	sly 6f	:233 :48 1:142	ⒻAlw 1300	6	2	31	1hd	11½	14	Higley J	118 w	*.50	81-24	Durazna1184Harriet Sue1151½Miss Fluff1104	Wide,easily	7
26Aug43- 6Was	sly 6f	:232 :481 1:144	Prairie State 6k	1	1	1hd	1hd	12	15	Higley J	108 w	14.40	77-32	Durazna1085Occupy118½All Bright1111	Ridden out	9
18Aug43- 6Was	fst 6f	:224 :463 1:122	Wash Juveniles 6.2k	7	5	1½	2hd	11½	31	Higley J	105wb	11.60	88-15	Alorter114¾Doggone109nkDurazna105¾	Tired	9
10Aug43- 1Was	fst 5½f	:231 :471 :591 1:062	ⒻMd Sp Wt	9	6	1hd	2nk	1½	13½	Whiting L	115 w	3.30	93-13	Durazna1153½Brown Flame115¾Iron Maiden115½	Easily	12
25Jun43- 1Was	fst 5½f	:224 :473 1:003 1:073	ⒻMd Sp Wt	5	4	32	32	31½	31¾	Whiting L	115 w	5.60	85-17	Twilight Tear115¾Letmenow1151Durazna1153	Saved ground	12
19Jun43- 4Haw	fst 5f	:231 :472 1:001	Md Sp Wt	4	2	1hd	1hd	21½	45	Burns G	113 w	3.60	89-14	American Flyer1162½Zacapet1161½Valdina Clown1161		10
Saved ground,tired																

Elkridge

b. g. 1938, by Mate (Prince Pal)–Best by Test, by Black Toney

Lifetime record: 123 31 18 15 $230,680

Own.– K. Miller
Br.– Joseph F. Flanagan (Md)
Tr.– K. Miller

12Oct51- 5Bel	sf *3	S'Chase	5:501 4↑	Grand National H 24k	8	6	913	733	749	769	Smithwick P	141 w	15.50	--	Oedips1651½NavyGun1402½BannerWvs14045	Bad landing 11th	10
4Oct51- 5Bel	fst *2½	S'Chase	4:45 4↑	Brook H 16k	5	6	77½	515	510	410	Smithwick P	143 w	28.05	--	Oedipus1613Palaja1387Lone Fisherman148nk	No excuse	12
27Sep51- 5Bel	fst *2	S'Chase	3:43 3↑	Broad Hollow H 12k	6	7	615	410	917	825	Harr C	140 w	45.60	--	Oedipus1587Palaja1342Genancoke1412½	Gave way	11
16Aug51- 5Sar	hy *2	S'Chase	4:484 3↑	North American H 6.1k	6	2	411	564	5114	5130	Adams FD	142wb	4.95	--	Cherwell13415Lone Fisherman14710Extra Points14030	Quit	6
12Jly51- 5Aqu	hd *2	S'Chase	3:441 4↑	Hitchcock 11k	2	6	716	725	743	756	Zimmerman J	144wb	10.10	--	Genncoke1352½DLarkyDay147nkSemperEadm140½	Dull effort	7
3Jly51- 3Del	fst *2½	S'Chase	4:471 4↑	Indian River H 11k	3	1	210	215	215	212	Adams FD	147 w	1.80	--	CrooningWind13712Elkridge1471½TouristList140	No mishap	4
27Jun51- 5Del	fst *2	S'Chase	3:404 4↑	Georgetown H 12k	3	6	615	513	523	419	Smithwick P	148 w	3.15	--	Crooning Wind13040Oedipus15812Genancoke1373	Outrun	6
14Jun51- 5Bel	sl *2½	S'Chase	4:56 4↑	Meadow Brook H 11k	4	3	32½	46	312	37½	Smithwick P	150 w	3.15	--	Titien II1401½Lone Fisherman1496Elkridge15012	No excuse	5
7Jun51- 5Bel	fst *2	S'Chase	3:432 4↑	Corinthian H 8.7k	1	2	39	33½	37	312¾	Smithwick P	150 w	3.95	--	Oedipus156¾Lone Fisherman14812Elkridge1501	Tired	4
18May51- 5Bel	fst *2	S'Chase	3:42 4↑	International H 9k	4	4	321	420	38	311	Smithwick P	149 w	7.45	--	Pontius Pilate15240Oedipus1547Elkridge1493½	Closed well	7
22Sep50- 5Bel	sf *2	S'Chase	3:482 3↑	Broad Hollow H 11k	4	6	613	613	22	21¼	Adams FD	152 w	4.85	--	Oedipus1471¼Elkridge1521¼Trough Hill1505	Stout effort	10
25Aug50- 5Sar	fst *2½	S'Chase	5:082 4↑	Saratoga H 11k	3	1	12	12	11	13	Adams FD	150 w	4.35	--	Elkridge1503Lone Fisherman1356Oedipus147nk	Handily	6
18Aug50- 5Sar	fst *2	S'Chase	4:082 3↑	Beverwyck H 9.1k	2	3	37	411	333	328	Adams FD	146 w	7.60	--	Pontius Pilate13815Oedipus14313Elkridge14640	No threat	6
10Aug50- 5Sar	fst *2	S'Chase	4:094 3↑	North American H 6.4k	6	2	32	512	636	636	Adams FD	149 w	*1.75	--	TheHeir143nkHamptonRoads14510Scuttleman1354	Done early	6
30Jun50- 5Del	gd *2½	S'Chase	4:51 4↑	Indian River H 12k	1	1	23	25	11½	19	Adams FD	154 w	2.35	--	Elkridge1549Sun Bath1504Monkey Wrench137	Easily	6
22Jun50- 5Del	fst *2	S'Chase	3:463 4↑	Georgetown H 12k	1	3	35	35	31	1½	Adams FD	148 w	3.75	--	Elkridge148½Darjeeling1502Genancoke1427	Driving	8
8Jun50- 5Bel	fst *2½	S'Chase	4:473 4↑	Meadow Brook H 11k	6	2	24	22½	25	26	Adams FD	145 w	12.65	--	Darjeeling1436Elkridge1455Adaptable148hd	Went well	7
10Nov49- 5Pim	fst *2½	S'Chase	4:482 4↑	Manly H 8.2k	4	1	1hd	1hd	422	420	Adams FD	145 w	9.80	--	His Boots1458Trough Hill1566American Way1526	Tired	5
3Nov49- 5Pim	gd *2	S'Chase	3:554 3↑	Battleship H 8.4k	1	7	743	763	668	664	Ansteatt B	150wb	15.90	--	Trough Hill15410Fleettown14620Luan Casca13910	Distanced	7
11Oct49- 6Bel	fst *2¼	S'Chase	4:191 4↑	Temple Gwathmey H 11k	4	3	49½	619	739	739	Ansteatt B	156wb	7.30	--	Hampton Roads152½Sun Bath1575Lock and Key1437	Tired	7
7Oct49- 5Bel	fst *3	S'Chase	5:483 4↑	Grand National H 22k	2	5	513	2hd	515	620	Ansteatt B	152wb	10.15	--	His Boots1412½Trough Hill1588Tourist List1462	Tired	7
29Sep49- 5Bel	sl *2½	S'Chase	4:521 4↑	Brook H 15k	6	2	24	42½	768	798	Ansteatt B	157wb	5.40	--	Trough Hill15310American Way151½His Boots1429	Quit	8
22Sep49- 4Bel	fst *2	S'Chase	3:44 3↑	Broad Hollow H 11k	5	7	721	727	736	625	Smithwick P	157wb	*1.85	--	Sun Bath1496Hampton Roads141¾Trough Hill1522	Outrun	7
1Jly49- 5Del	fst *2½	S'Chase	4:453 4↑	Indian River H 12k	3	5	422	48	12	13	Smithwick P	156wb	*1.00	--	Elkridge1563Sun Bath1361½Tourist List14820	Ridden out	5
23Jun49- 5Del	fst *2	S'Chase	3:461 4↑	Georgetown H 12k	5	4	37	28	2hd	16	Smithwick P	152wb	2.25	--	Elkridge1526Genancoke1455Sun Bath13725	Handily	5
9Jun49- 4Bel	fst *2½	S'Chase	4:433 4↑	Meadow Brook H 11k	7	2	210	312	25	12	Smithwick P	147wb	7.45	--	Elkridge1472Trough Hill1518Rank1404	Going away	7
2Jun49- 4Bel	fst *2	S'Chase	3:44 4↑	Corinthian H 9.4k	4	2	12	2hd	34½	26	Ansteatt B	149wb	21.85	--	Trough Hill1476Elkridge149hdAmerican Way1463½	Weakened	10
12May49- 5Bel	fst *2	S'Chase	3:504 4↑	International H 9k	1	5	23	21½	417	428	Rich J	149wb	7.50	--	Homogenize1396Fleettown1498Lieut. Well14514	Quit	7
10Nov48- 5Pim	gd 3	S'Chase	6:104 4↑	Manly H 18k	6	9	940	827	533	542	Rich J	150wb	16.80	--	Adaptable14415American Way15215Point Bleu1468	Far back	9
3Nov48- 5Pim	fst 2	S'Chase	3:513 3↑	Battleship H 12k	9	4	99½	813	716	719	Rich J	152wb	7.70	--	Genancoke1403½The Heir147noTourist List1475	Outrun	9

14Oct48- 5Lrl	fst	*2	S'Chase	3:531	3↑ Butler H 13k	12	4	35	-	-	-	Bosley J III	153wb	9.60	- -	Drift1346The Heir1493½American Way1493	Fell 10th	12
1Oct48- 5Bel	gd	*3	S'Chase	5:50	4↑ Grand Nat'l H 31k	12	9	810	611	621	728	Bosley J III	156wb	6.55	- -	AmericanWay1441TouristList1502TroughHill1476	No factor	14
23Sep48- 5Bel	fst	*2½	S'Chase	4:471	4↑ Brook H 19k	7	3	31½	1nk	21½	22	Bosley J III	156 w	3.35	- -	Trough Hill1422Elkridge1561½American Way1432	No excuse	11
16Sep48- 5Bel	fst	*2	S'Chase	3:441	3↑ Broad Hollow H 19k	9	12	1120	1122	56½	46	Rich J	155wb	3.15	- -	The Heir1482Little Sammie1381Genancoke1453	Off slowly	12
27Aug48- 5Sar	fst	*2½	S'Chase	5:11	4↑ Saratoga H 11k	6	6	623	513	21	34¼	Rich J	156wb	*1.90	- -	Tourist List1421¼The Heir1483Elkridge1568	Tired	6
12Aug48- 5Sar	fst	*2	S'Chase	4:141	3↑ North American H 8.9k	4	7	725	514	1nk	11½	Rich J	152wb	*2.55	- -	Elkridge1521½Fleettown151hdThe Heir14620	Driving	7
5Aug48- 5Sar	fst	*2	S'Chase	4:141	4↑ Shillelah 8.7k	2	4	423	37	1	1	Rich J	154wb	*1.90	- -	Elkridge154Sun Bath154Floating Isle150	Galloping	5
	Other finishers remounted after falling or losing rider at final fence																	
9Jly48- 5Aqu	fst	*2	S'Chase	3:444	4↑ Lion Heart H 11k	6	2	21	1½	53¼	514	Bosley J III	153wb	*1.55	- -	The Heir1421½Fleettown15110Genancoke147¾	Bobbled	6
2Jly48- 5Del	fst	*2½	S'Chase	4:522	4↑ Indian River H 12k	3	2	220	220	12	12	Bosley J III	151wb	3.55	- -	Elkridge1512Tourist List1423Floating Isle14110	Driving	7
16Jun48- 6Bel	fst	*2½	S'Chase	4:512	4↑ Temple Gwathmey H 16k	4	2	26	23	2hd	21	Bosley J III	151wb	7.05	- -	Adaptable1501Elkridge1514Floating Isle14012	Good try	7
10Jun48- 5Bel	fst	*2½	S'Chase	4:462	4↑ Meadow Brook H 17k	6	1	13	1½	3½	35	Bosley J III	152wb	3.60	- -	Adaptable1463Canford1422Elkridge1521½	Tired	6
3Jun48- 5Bel	fst	*2	S'Chase	3:471	4↑ Corinthian H 11k	5	3	33½	41½	24	34	Bosley J III	153wb	9.45	- -	Fleettown1473½The Heir142½Elkridge1534	Weakened	8
20May48- 5Bel	fst	*2	S'Chase	3:463	4↑ International H 11k	7	3	39	414	933	940	Bosley J III	154wb	11.25	- -	Fleettown1413½Canford1422½The Heir1382½	Quit	10
4Nov47- 5Pim	hy	2	S'Chase	4:131	3↑ Battleship H 11k	3	5	56½	58	518	521¼	Roberts E	155wb	2.70	- -	GrekFlg1365TourstLst141nkFlotngIsl14515	Bad landing 3rd	5
29Oct47- 5Lrl	gd	*2½	S'Chase	4:542	4↑ Chevy Chase H 18k	6	7	617	614	314	215	McGovern J	154wb	4.50	- -	Sun Bath13915Elkridge154½Trough Hill1478	Closed well	7
17Oct47- 6Lrl	fst	*2	S'Chase	3:52	3↑ Butler H 11k	1	1	11	23	451	452½	Miller R	161wb	1.50	- -	Trough Hill141hdSun Bath1372½Allier13750	Stopped	5
2Oct47- 5Bel	fst	*3	S'Chase	5:413	4↑ Grand National 29k	8	1	22	210	620	621¼	Brown N	162wb	*1.05e	- -	Adaptable147hdWar Battle163nkTrough Hill1394	Quit	8
17Sep47- 5Aqu	fst	*2½	S'Chase	4:571	4↑ Glendale H 11k	6	1	21	11	11	12	Brown N	161wb	4.05	- -	Elkridge1612Trough Hill1392Delhi Dan1385	Ridden out	7
5Sep47- 5Aqu	sl	*2	S'Chase	3:541	3↑ Harbor Hill H 11k	7	1	1½	21	411	49	Brown N	163wb	2.95	- -	Floating Isle1451½Big Sun1321½Genancoke1386	Tired	7
26Jun47- 5Del	fst	*2	S'Chase	3:48	4↑ Georgetown H 13k	10	1	11	1hd	44½	57	Brown N	162wb	2.45	- -	Genancoke135½TouristList1373½FloatingIsle137hd	Weakened	12
5Jun47- 5Aqu	fst	*2	S'Chase	3:441	4↑ Lion Heart H 10k	2	1	12	14	11	11	Brown N	158wb	2.85	- -	Elkridge1581Fleettown1426Floating Isle14420	Jumped well	4
28May47- 5Bel	fst	*2½	S'Chase	4:464	4↑ Meadow Brook 17k	6	4	54¼	624	644	650	People C Jr	158wb	*1.15e	- -	WarBattle15612Flttown14112FlotngIsl147no	Never a factor	6
5Nov46- 5Pim	fst	2	S'Chase	3:512	3↑ Battleship H 11k	3	2	2½	21	611	610¾	Roberts E	159wb	*.90e	- -	Galley Boy1321½War Battle1481¼Tourist List1351	Quit	6
15Oct46- 6Bel	fst	*3	S'Chase	5:422	4↑ Temple Gwathmey H 21k	4	4	427	215	215	230	Roberts E	158wb	*1.35e	- -	War Battle13830Elkridge1582½Chesapeake1403	Next best	5
3Oct46- 5Bel	fst	*3	S'Chase	5:484	4↑ Grand National H 30k	8	5	414	21	12	14	Roberts E	151wb	11.20	- -	Elkridge1514Burma Road1622Refugio1343	Easily	10
26Sep46- 5Bel	fst	*2½	S'Chase	4:494	4↑ Brook H 19k	5	4	32½	53½	819	819	Russell EA	154 w	6.60	- -	Burma Road1562½Caddie142noGreat Flare1385	Lost iron	11
16Aug46- 5Sar	fst	*2	S'Chase	4:154	3↑ North America H 5.4k	3	2	23	21	2hd	15	Adams FD	151 ws	*.85	- -	Elkridge1515Last1354Boojum II142	Easily	4
3Jly46- 3Del	fst	*2½	S'Chase	4:463	4↑ Indian River H 12k	6	4	22	25	37	38	Davis J	149wb	3.00	- -	Rouge Dragon1573½Delhi Dan1374½Elkridge1492½	Went well	6
27Jun46- 3Del	fst	*2	S'Chase	3:483	4↑ Georgetown H 12k	5	3	26	24	23	23½	Davis J	149wb	4.55	- -	Rouge Dragon1523½Elkridge1498Beneksar1366	Went well	6
22Jun46- 3Aqu	fst	*2	S'Chase	3:421	4↑ Handicap 4500	4	1	12	14	11½	1nk	Russell EA	155wb	*1.35e	- -	Elkridge155nkWar Battle1461Lancastrian1402	Just lasted	5
10May46- 5Bel	fst	*2	S'Chase	3:45	4↑ International H 8.6k	6	6	624	622	637	635½	Jennings E	153wb	3.65	- -	Fleettown1351Annotator1362½Mercator1557	Outrun	6
28Nov45- 5Pim	sly	2½	S'Chase	5:252	4↑ Manly H 12k	7	5	715	812	727	744	Adams FD	153wb	2.85e	- -	PursuitPlane1325BurmaRoad13912GekFlg1384	Never a factor	10
21Nov45- 5Pim	sl	*2	S'Chase	3:544	3↑ Battleship H 12k	6	6	515	24	24	1no	Adams FD	146wb	9.65	- -	Elkridge146noNavigate1368Caddie1465	Driving	7
12Oct45- 3Lrl	fst	*2	S'Chase	3:54	3↑ Butler H 6.4k	6	7	718	711	839	845	Adams FD	149wb	3.40	- -	Great Flare1302Floating Isle15115Bill Coffman1334	Tired	9
26Sep45- 5Bel	fst	*2½	S'Chase	4:484	4↑ Brook H 9.3k	4	6	913	35	48½	38	Adams FD	148wb	5.30	- -	Raylywn1376Rouge Dragon1552Elkridge148no	Fast finish	10
20Sep45- 5Bel	gd	*2	S'Chase	3:551	3↑ Broad Hollow H 6.1k	2	7	715	712	79½	715¾	Riles S	150wb	4.15	- -	Boojum II1382Caddie138¾Raylywn137hd	Bad landing 4th	7
11Sep45- 5Aqu	my	*2½	S'Chase	4:511	4↑ Glendale H 8.6k	5	5	34½	45¼	46	410¼	Owen W	153wb	3.75	- -	FloatingIsle150nkMerctor1437SoldrSong1403	Flattened out	5
4Sep45- 5Aqu	fst	*2	S'Chase	3:42	3↑ Harbor Hill H 6k	5	4	414	35½	2hd	2½	Owen W	153wb	4.05	- -	Mercator140½Elkridge1533Floating Isle1512½	Driving	7
31Aug45- 5Bel	fst	*2½	S'Chase	4:51	4↑ Saratoga H 9.1k	5	2	32	21½	510	58¼	Owens W	156wb	*2.75	- -	RougeDrgn152nkSoldierSong139noBurmaRod141hd	No mishap	9
24Aug45- 5Bel	sl	*2	S'Chase	3:494	3↑ Beverwyck H 5.9k	7	7	711	719	514	415	Owen W	158wb	*1.45e	- -	War Battle1352Boojum II1373Floating Isle15210	Late gain	7
17Aug45- 4Bel	fst	*2	S'Chase	3:45	3↑ North American H 16k	6	3	45	56¼	21	3¾	Owen W	158wb	3.85e	- -	FloatingIsle149nkChesapeake136½Elkridg1581	Saved ground	10
10Aug45- 3Bel	fst	*2	S'Chase	3:491	4↑ Shillelah 6.1k	2	10	108½	813	713	611	Harrison JS	158wb	3.05	- -	Raylywn1361Rouge Dragon1521Mercator1376	Outrun	10
3Jly45- 3Del	gd	*2½	S'Chase	5:033	4↑ Indian River H 12k	5	4	510	33½	11½	13½	Harrison JS	157wb	*3.85	- -	Elkridge1573½Royal Archer1461Beneksar1302	Easily	8
27Jun45- 3Del	fst	*2	S'Chase	3:503	4↑ Georgetown H 12k	6	4	45½	56	48½	36½	Harrison JS	159wb	4.55	- -	Iron Shot150½Rouge Dragon1596Elkridge159½	Mild rally	8
23Jun45- 3Bel	fst	*2½	S'Chase	4:56	4↑ Meadow Brook H 8.4k	1	3	48	57	23	22½	Harrison JS	160wb	1.80	- -	Floating Isle1472½Elkridge160hdIron Shot1485	No match	6
	Daily Racing Form time, 4:53 4/5																	
12Jun45- 5Bel	fst	*2	S'Chase	3:49	4↑ CL Appleton 5.7k	3	5	53	41¾	14	1hd	Harrison JS	158wb	2.65	- -	Elkridge158hdFloating Isle1496Mercator13910	Just held	8
6Nov44- 6Bel	fst	*3	S'Chase	5:57	4↑ Temple Gwathmey H 15k	5	3	21	45	-	-	Harrison JS	164wb	4.55	- -	Burma Road1391¾Parma135hdAhmisk143nk	Lost rider 15th	7
18Oct44- 3Lrl	fst	*2	S'Chase	4:002	3↑ Butler H 6.5k	7	7	54¼	65¾	46	45	Harrison JS	166wb	*1.60	- -	Raylywn132hdAhmisk1402Boojum II1403	Impeded by faller	10
4Oct44- 5Bel	fst	*3	S'Chase	5:541	4↑ Grand National H 16k	4	3	54½	54	33½	37	Harrison JS	167wb	*.80	- -	Burma Road136hdRouge Dragon1647Elkridge1678	Faltered	6
20Sep44- 5Bel	fst	*2	S'Chase	3:533	3↑ Broad Hollow H 5.8k	4	3	39	37	2½	13	Harrison JS	161wb	*1.30	- -	Elkridg1613BllCoffmn14012IronShot16010	Speed in reserve	6
1Sep44- 5Bel	fst	*2½	S'Chase	4:491	4↑ Saratoga H 8.5k	5	5	57¼	53¾	14	18	Harrison JS	155wb	*1.25	- -	Elkridge1558Bridlespur1321Invader1404	Easily	5
11Aug44- 5Bel	fst	*2	S'Chase	3:48	4↑ Shillelah 5.7k	6	4	42½	32	11	11½	Harrison JS	146wb	*1.05	- -	Elkridge1461½Mercator1417FloatngIsl13510	Bothered early	7
4Aug44- 3Bel	fst	*2	S'Chase	3:491	4↑ Handicap 3000	7	2	32½	38	2½	11¼	Harrison JS	154wb	4.60	- -	Elkridge1541¼FredercII1401½BurmRod1382	Speed in reserve	10
15Jun44- 7Aqu	fst	1¼	:492 1:143 1:42	2:083	3↑ Md Sp Wt	3	2	610	511	611	614¼	Meade D	121wb	4.90	50-18	General War113nkRanging1207Oceanus1131	No mishap	7
1Nov43- 5Pim	fst	2	S'Chase	3:571	3↑ Battleship H 6.9k	8	4	44¾	68	625	625½	Penrod J	147wb	6.25	- -	Knight's Quest1411Invader144½Mercator1392	Outrun	10
26Oct43- 5Pim	sly	2½	S'Chase	5:181	4↑ Chevy Chase H 9.3k	6	4	616	732	-	-	Penrod J	150wb	*1.60	- -	Uncle Seaweed137¾Caddie13820Invader1453		7
	Outrun,jumped poorly,left course																	
18Oct43- 5Pim	gd	2	S'Chase	3:56	3↑ Gov Ogle H 6.6k	4	5	33½	3½	-	-	Morlan L	150 w	6.65	- -	Rouge Dragon1531Caddie1376Greek Flag1373	Lost rider	9
6Oct43- 3Bel	fst	*3	S'Chase	5:533	4↑ Grand National H 18k	9	3	22	32	44½	36½	Riles S	150wb	12.05	- -	Brother Jones1506Invader145½ DH Caddie137hd	No mishap	12
29Sep43- 3Bel	fst	*2½	S'Chase	4:50	4↑ Brook H 6.6k	6	8	54	1016	1023	1022½	Hayhurst R	153wb	4.50	- -	RougeDrgn1473Knght'sQust140noBnkNot1381	Never a factor	10
22Sep43- 3Bel	fst	*2	S'Chase	3:524	3↑ Broad Hollow H 4k	5	2	21½	21	43½	22	Harrison JS	154wb	3.95	- -	Silver Birch1352Elkridge1543Caddie1391	Belated rally	7
15Sep43- 3Aqu	gd	*2½	S'Chase	5:012	4↑ Glendale H 8.6k	1	2	12	12	529	540	Scott A	156wb	5.30	- -	Brother Jones1461½Invader145½Parma1358	Tired	6
1Sep43- 3Aqu	fst	*2	S'Chase	3:441	3↑ Harbor Hill H 4.9k	4	2	24	22	12	14	Harrison JS	151wb	5.95	- -	Elkridge1514Knight'sQuest1451½BnkNot1396	Speed to spare	6
25Aug43- 3Bel	fst	*2½	S'Chase	4:471	4↑ Saratoga H 6.2k	7	4	34¼	35½	59¾	614	Cruz H	154wb	6.30	- -	Iron Shot148½Brother Jones1461½Corrigan1497	Bobbled	8
18Aug43- 3Bel	fst	*2	S'Chase	3:463	3↑ Beverwyck H 4.1k	10	6	87¼	42½	35	410	Smiley J	155wb	5.15	- -	RougDrgn145½IronShot1458BrothrJns1471½	Bad landing 11th	10
11Aug43- 3Bel	gd	*2	S'Chase	3:52	3↑ North American H 3.8k	3	3	43½	21	11	11¼	Cruz H	151wb	*2.30	- -	Elkridge1511¼Brother Jones1462½Redlands1391	Drifted out	6
4Aug43- 3Bel	fst	*2	S'Chase	3:482	4↑ Shillelah 3.9k	1	8	622	44¾	24	22½	Marzani D	150wb	5.55	- -	Delhi Dan1502½Elkridge1507Speculate1326	Checked	10
25May43- 3Bel	fst	*2	S'Chase	3:521	4↑ Corinthian H 3.9k	1	8	711	811	612	619¼	Owen W	157wb	7.85	- -	Invader145nkBrotherJones1394BoojumII1385	Never a factor	8
18May43- 5Bel	fst	*2	S'Chase	3:494	4↑ CL Appleton 3.9k	1	6	58	36½	45½	48½	Leonard W	161wb	10.55	- -	RougeDragon1443Knight'sQuest1492½Redlands1523	Faltered	8
11May43- 3Bel	fst	*2	S'Chase	3:461	4↑ International H 3.9k	9	6	423	719	718	718	Harrison JS	159wb	5.75	- -	IronShot1444Knight'sQuest1483Invadr1501½	Never a factor	9
5May43- 6Jam	fst	1 1/16	:24 :48 1:123	1:45	3↑ Handicap 2540	1	5	56½	511	59½	612	Givens C	107 w	24.25	76-18	Tip-Toe1103Haile112noPlantagenet1105	No mishap	6
1May43- 4Jam	fst	1 70	:243 :481 1:15	1:461	3↑ Md Sp Wt	7	5	42½	32	33½	35	Lindberg H	122wb	4.50	68-19	Deseronto1134Minefinder1131Elkridge1224	Hard urged	10
19Apr43- 4Jam	gd	6f	:232 :481	1:141	3↑ Md Sp Wt	2	6	53	78¼	711	78	Woolf G	126wb	5.05	73-22	Miracle Kin113½Stargoo113hdCamptown1131½	Evenly	14
9Nov42- 5Pim	gd	2½	S'Chase	5:061	4↑ Manly H 6.7k	3	5	58½	77¾	3nk	11½	Harrison JS	157wb	3.85	- -	Elkridge1571½Nayr132½Iron Shot1406	Jumped well,driving	9
2Nov42- 5Pim	fst	2	S'Chase	4:14	3↑ Battleship H 3.5k	2	2	67½	76	11½	13	Harrison JS	151wb	4.80	- -	Elkrdg1513IronShot139½Rdlnds1373	Outside,speed to spare	8
21Oct42- 3Lrl	sl	*2½	S'Chase	5:313	4↑ Chevy Chase H 6.4k	8	7	711	525	651	654	Harrison JS	153wb	2.15	- -	Brother Jones13414Strolling On1304Caddie1394	Outrun	8
14Oct42- 3Lrl	sl	*2	S'Chase	4:183	3↑ Governor Ogle H 4.4k	4	4	49	12	18	18	Harrison JS	148wb	*1.55	- -	Elkridge1488Redlnds1398StrollngOn13312	Speed in reserve	5
7Oct42- 3Bel	fst	*3	S'Chase	6:051	4↑ Grand National H 17k	8	6	825	-	-	-	Harrison JS	147 w	5.15	- -	Cottesmore1557Cupid13430Iron Shot1391	Fell 12th	9
23Sep42- 3Bel	fst	*2	S'Chase	3:483	3↑ Broad Hollow H 3.9k	3	4	42¾	45¾	1½	13½	Harrison JS	145wb	7.15	- -	Elkridge1453½LovelyNight1525RougeDragon1372½	Ridden out	5
9Sep42- 3Aqu	sl	*2½	S'Chase	6:002	4↑ Glendale H 5.9k	3	3	313	210	517	518	Scott A	148wb	4.20	- -	Mandingham1582Iron Shot1415Parma1346	Bobbled,tired	5
2Sep42- 3Aqu	fst	*2	S'Chase	3:494	3↑ Harbor Hill H 3.7k	3	3	32	35¼	32	2nk	Penrod J	149 w	*1.40	- -	Good Chance136nkElkridge149¾Cottesmore1627	Closed fast	4

28Aug42- 3Sar	fst *2½ S'Chase	5:114	4↑ Saratoga H 4.3k	5 1 1½ 2hd 1hd	2nk	Penrod J	149wb	*1.35	--	IronShot136nkElkridge1491BrotherJones1385	Wide into str	5
21Aug42- 3Sar	fst *2 S'Chase	4:153	3↑ Beverwyck H 3.4k	3 4 37 22 1hd	2no	Penrod J	150wb	*1.05	--	Invader143noElkridge1507Iron Shot1374	Gamely	5
14Aug42- 1Sar	fst *2 S'Chase	4:193	3↑ North American H 3.3k	5 2 25 3nk 15	17	Penrod J	146wb	2.85	--	Elkridge1467TheBeak1431IronShot143100	Drew away easily	5
7Aug42- 1Sar	fst *2 S'Chase	4:14	4↑ Shillelah H 3k	2 1 12 21 -	-	Cruz H	150wb	1.95	--	LovelyNight13825IronShot15012Redlnds147	Lost rider 15th	5
1Jly42- 3Del	fst *2½ S'Chase	4:541	4↑ Indian River H 8k	1 1 13 11½ 12	13	Cruz H	141wb	*.95	--	Elkridge1413Good Chance1415Caddie133		5
Bothered by riderless horse												
24Jun42- 3Del	fst *2 S'Chase	3:47	4↑ Georgetown H 8.6k	2 3 47 25 25	26	Cruz H	142wb	5.90	--	Deanslaw1396Elkridge1426Ossabaw1474	Best of rest	5
11Jun42- 3Aqu	fst *2 S'Chase	3:413	4↑ Hitchcock H 6.3k	7 7 713 719 34¼	35	Clements HW	144wb	9.85	--	Bath155hdMandingham1565Elkridge1446	Finished well	7
2Jun42- 5Bel	fst *2½ S'Chase	4:434	4↑ Meadow Brook H 6.6k	1 2 55¼ 52¼ 2hd	2¾	Cruz H	139wb	8.75	--	Invdr139¾Elkrdg1396StrwBoss1424	Bothered by winner last ⅛	7
23May42- 3Bel	fst *2 S'Chase	3:444	4↑ Handicap 2000	7 6 514 44¼ -	-	Clements HW	145wb	4.75	--	Sussex1552Deanslaw1465Straw Boss1534	Lost rider 11th	7
16May42- 3Bel	fst *2 S'Chase	3:433	4↑ Alw 1500	1 4 513 28 12	14	Clements HW	139wb	26.25	--	Elkridge1394Loughtrea1432Frozen North1435	Drew away	9
12May42- 5Bel	fst *2 S'Chase	3:434	4↑ International H 4.3k	7 2 66½ 715 719	821½	McGovern J	133wb	60.30	--	Cottesmore1574Redlands140½Ossabaw152¾	Outrun	8
1May42- 5Pim	fst 2 S'Chase	3:493	4↑ Jervis Spencer H 3.4k	3 2 48 621 840	750	Brown N	136 w	18.85	--	Bath14110Cottesmore1573Redlands14010	Outrun	8
Previously owned by Thomas Hitchcock;previously trained by P. Green												
24Sep41- 1Bel	fst *2 S'Chase	3:52	3↑ Md Sp Wt	3 3 2hd 11½ 16	17	Scott A	134 w	*1.40	--	Elkridge134.57Pico Blanco II1495Glen-Na-Mona1492		9
Lost ground,in hand												

Fairy Chant

ch. f. 1937, by Chance Shot (Fair Play)–Star Fairy, by The Satrap — **Lifetime record: 42 10 8 8 $81,985**

Own.– Foxcatcher Farm
Br.– William du Pont Jr (Ky)
Tr.– R.E. Handlen

13Sep41- 6Aqu	fst 1⅛	:481 1:122 1:381 1:51	3↑ ⒻBeldame H 19k	13 7 109¼ 86½ 31½	1no	Anderson I	123wb	7.05	97-08	Fairy Chant123noImperatrice1161Rosetown1261		14
Traffic,up in closing strides												
9Sep41- 6Aqu	fst 1 1/16	:242 :482 1:124 1:44	3↑ ⒻAlw 3000	5 5 513 59 34	34	Anderson I	120wb	4.40	90-12	Rostown1163Oss1111FryChnt1203	Slow to start,saved ground	5
26Aug41- 6Sar	my 1⅛	:504 1:153 1:404 1:532	3↑ ⒻDiana H 3.5k	2 3 37 22 33	35¾	James B	126wb	2.35	77-20	Rosetown118¾Dorimar1195Fairy Chant1266	Went well	5
2Aug41- 6Sar	fst 1 3/16	:484 1:132 1:393 1:584	3↑ Merchants & Cits H 6.9k	1 4 47 31¾ 3½	56¾	James B	112wb	4.35	77-19	Fenelon126hdAndy K.1172½Corydon108hd	Stopped	7
29Jly41- 6Sar	gd 1	:24 :48 1:124 1:384	3↑ Wilson 7.1k	2 4 32 32 31½	31¼	Donoso R	112wb	6.25	86-17	Parasang1171Fenelon120nkFairy Chant11215	Good effort	4
12Jly41- 7Suf	sly 1 1/16	:234 :473 1:13 1:46	3↑ ⒻHannah Dustin H 13k	3 8 65 41½ 12½	12¾	James B	120wb	8.00	86-21	FairyChant1202¾UptheHill1062ShineO'Night116hd	Easily	10
5Jly41- 6Del	my 1 1/16	:233 :48 1:141 1:49	3↑ ⒻNew Castle H 13k	11 8 611 47½ 36	34½	James B	126wb	7.45	69-28	DottedSwiss1143BalaOrmont1161½FairyChnt1262	Closed fast	13
28Jun41- 6Del	fst 1 1/16	:233 :473 1:12 1:44	3↑ Handicap 2000	2 6 57½ 42½ 44¼	58½	Peters M	118wb	5.30	90-03	Sailor King1102Busy Morn111noRed Dock1191½	Tired	6
1Mar41- 6SA	sly 1¼	:47 1:121 1:383 2:052	3↑ S Anita H 124k	15 14 1313 1012 1013	910¼	Richards H	112wb	24.60	69-29	Bay View108nkMioland1244Bolingbroke1062	Outrun	16
15Feb41- 6SA	my 1 1/16	:241 :483 1:133 1:471	4↑ ⒻS Margarita 11k	1 7 79½ 66½ 54	43	James B	120wb	*.60	73-29	Omelet116nkAugury1201¼Barrancosa1131½	Poor ride	7
7Feb41- 6SA	my 1 1/16	:234 :482 1:124 1:46	4↑ Handicap 2500	2 5 31½ 13 14	12½	James B	118wb	*.70	82-21	FairyChant1182½DuskyDuke1104JusticeM.1102	Easily best	5
25Jan41- 7SA	sl 1	:234 :471 1:124 1:392	4↑ Alw 2500	4 6 35 33 32	33¾	James B	113wb	6.40	77-25	Vino Puro1203Gen'l Manager112¾Fairy Chant1136	Weakened	7
5Oct40- 7Bel	fst 2¼	:484 2:313 2:571 3:484	3↑ New York H 59k	13 7 911 94 1122	1126½	Anderson I	111wb	16.95	84-09	Shot Put106nkEquitable94¾High Fidelity97nk	Outrun	17
1Oct40- 6Bel	fst 1½	:471 1:124 2:05 2:30	3↑ ⒻLadies H 17k	7 12 1121 96¼ 41½	31½	Anderson I	123wb	*2.85	90-12	Salaminia115½Pretty Pet1141Fairy Chant1232¾	Closed fast	12
21Sep40- 5Aqu	fst 1⅛	:472 1:12 1:372 1:504	3↑ ⒻBeldame H 19k	5 9 88¾ 65½ 3½	11¼	Anderson I	119wb	*3.50	102-02	FairyChant1191¼DottedSwiss1141DollyVal1212½	Going away	16
13Sep40- 5Aqu	fst 1 1/16	:25 :50 1:142 1:45	3↑ ⒻAlw 2000	4 4 45¼ 44½ 32	2no	Anderson I	113wb	3.05	89-09	Little Risk108noFairy Chant1132¾Piquet1083¼	Just missed	5
28Aug40- 5Sar	fst 1⅛	:481 1:131 1:383 1:52	3↑ ⒻDiana H 3.2k	3 6 65¾ 44½ 2hd	2hd	Anderson I	118wb	*1.30	90-13	Piquet116hdFairy Chant1183Rosetown1101	Game try	6
10Aug40- 6Sar	fst 1¼	:49 1:14 1:392 2:044	ⒻAlabama 12k	2 6 611 42½ 2hd	21½	Anderson I	124 w	3.70	83-10	Salaminia1111½Fairy Chant1241Piquet1223¼	Forced wide	6
2Aug40- 5Sar	fst 7f	:224 :461 1:114 1:242	ⒻTest 3.9k	9 4 46 21 12	2hd	James B	126wb	9.45	94-13	Piquet123hdFairy Chant1262Inkling1142½	Tired badly	10
26Jun40- 5Aqu	sly 1 1/16	1:46	ⒻGazelle 6.9k	9 8	15	James B	121wb	7.35	--	Fairy Chant1215Raise Up1093Rosetown112¾	Easily	11
Further information unavailable due to blinding rainstorm												
22Jun40- 6Del	fst 1 1/16	:233 :464 1:113 1:451	3↑ ⒻNewcastle H 13k	12 10 63½ 42 54	54	Peters M	112wb	7.20	89-08	Tedbriar108.5½War Beauty1062Orcades107hd	No mishaps	12
13Jun40- 6Del	fst 1⅛	:484 1:13 1:392 1:522	ⒻDel Oaks 6.1k	6 6 5¾ 41¼ 42½	33	Peters M	119wb	3.85	95-10	Piquet1101Rosetown1132Fairy Chant1191	Closed fast	7
1Jun40- 6Bel	my 1⅜	:481 1:124 1:384 2:19	ⒻC C A Oaks 15k	1 8 21 1nk 57½	713½	Wright WD	121wb	*1.80	62-21	Damaged Goods121hdRosetown1213Dipsy Doodle121hd	Quit	9
22May40- 6Bel	fst 1	:223 :46 1:111 1:37	ⒻAcorn 14k	10 10 1012 84 22	25	Wright WD	121wb	*2.05	85-18	Damaged Goods1215Fairy Chant1214War Beauty1212	Bore in	11
4May40- 6Pim	sl 1 1/16	:233 :483 1:152 1:494	ⒻPim Oaks 14k	10 11 84 21 2nk	11	Neves R	121wb	*2.90	71-31	Fairy Chant1211True Call1214Discerning1211	Drew out	13
29Apr40- 5Pim	fst 1 70	:231 :473 1:124 1:432	ⒻAlw 1500	4 8 42½ 2hd 11	2no	Peters M	115wb	4.75	94-17	True Call112noFairy Chant1156Witchlike112½	Bore out	8
22Feb40- 6SA	fst 1⅛	:463 1:112 1:374 1:513	S Anita Derby 61k	5 7 54¾ 65 716	1110¾	Peters M	115wb	8.60e	75-16	Sweepida1201¼Royal Crusader1201Weigh Anchor120hd	Tired	17
3Feb40- 6SA	my 1 1/16	:24 :474 1:124 1:464	3↑ ⒻS Margarita H 12k	4 1 13 13 15	13½	Dodson D	103 w	14.40	78-26	Fairy Chant1033½Omelet1101½Sweet Nancy1082	In hand	10
27Jan40- 5SA	fst 1	:223 :461 1:112 1:38	Alw 1500	5 7 73 97¾ 910	910	McRoberts R	103wb	7.10	69-12	Mioland1142½Gallahadion1061The Gob108½	Outrun	10
20Jan40- 6SA	fst 7f	:222 :454 1:114 1:251	ⒻS Susana 12k	9 9 94¾ 55 46¼	69¾	Peters M	115 w	2.80	76-14	Augury1214Less Time1123½Wanna Hygro1122	Tired	12
28Oct39- 4Lrl	gd 1	:242 :48 1:144 1:414	ⒻSelima 29k	3 5 53 4¾ 41¾	41¼	Peters M	114 w	*2.30	75-24	WarBeauty114noTedbriar114nkMissFerdinand1221	No excuse	11
16Oct39- 5Lrl	fst 1 70	:241 :483 1:132 1:44	ⒻAlw 1200	6 6 3nk 3nk 2hd	2½	Peters M	114 w	*1.30	88-13	Dewy Dawn108½Fairy Chant1141½Baby Sister1081½	Weakened	7
6Oct39- 5Lrl	fst 6f	:234 :472 1:13	ⒻAlw 1100	9 1 64¼ 41½ 1nk	1nk	Peters M	119 w	12.55	89-18	Fairy Chant119nkYarnith1072Thorn Apple1071	Hard drive	10
23Sep39- 3Bel	fst 6f-WC	1:12	ⒻMatron 17k	6 1 75 78	610	Peters M	115 w	5.00	77-13	Miss Ferdinand1154Piquet115½Thorn Apple1151½	Outrun	10
14Jun39- 4Aqu	sly 5f	:581	ⒻAstoria 4.4k	5 5 55¼ 34½	34½	Peters M	119 w	8.00	91-11	Now What116.5½Us1134Fairy Chant119½	Closed well	5
8Jun39- 3Del	fst 5f	:231 :472 1:004	Alw 1000	3 5 53¼ 31½ 1½	12½	Peters M	117 w	3.20	92-13	Fairy Chant1172½Victory Morn1181Cutter1152	Going away	9
1Jun39- 4Del	sl 5f	:24 :49 1:032	ⒻAlw 1000	5 5 44¼ 44½ 42½	21	Peters M	116 w	2.55	78-26	MadanCapet1161Fairy Chant1163Spanked111½	Closed fast	5
13May39- 4Bel	fst 4½f-WC	:52	ⒻFashion 4.9k	8 8 31 43	55½	Peters M	116 w	12.00	89-05	Perida1163Us1161½Rancho's Girl1161	Tired	10
22Apr39- 4Jam	fst 5f	:223 :471 1:002	ⒻRosedale 4k	6 6 69 611 612	614½	Peters M	119 w	2.20	76-14	Spanked1134Rancho's Girl116½Pilot Biscuit1164	Outrun	6
11Feb39- 4Hia	fst 3f	:222 :341	Everglades 3.7k	6 5 42	1no	Peters M	114 w	11.90	--	Fairy Chant114noDrury Lane116noMaedrew114hd	Just up	10
23Jan39- 1Hia	fst 3f	:221 :34	ⒻMd Sp Wt	13 7 53½	41	Peters M	116 w	2.90f	--	ValdinaBess116½Marandan116hdAnnieAlone116½	Good effort	13
16Jan39- 1Hia	gd 3f	:222 :334	ⒻMd Sp Wt	7 9 105¾	106¾	Peters M	117 w	*2.10	--	FlyngGlee1171HastyTriumph117noDmgdGoods1171½	Bad start	12

Fighting Step

ch. c. 1942, by Fighting Fox (Sir Gallahad III)–Stepinanna, by Misstep — **Lifetime record: 35 13 8 5 $157,715**

Own.– Murlogg Farn
Br.– Mrs R.J. Murphy & Miss Susan E. Kellogg (Ind)
Tr.– C. Norman

20Jly46- 6AP	fst 1¼	:464 1:11 1:353 2:01	3↑ Arlington H 56k	3 1 2½ 44½ 69	710½	South G	119 w	12.50	90-09	Historian112nkArmed1303Take Wing1112½	Early speed	9
4Jly46- 6AP	fst 1⅛	:462 1:113 1:37 1:492	3↑ Stars & Stripes H 57k	2 2 22 22 109½	1012½	South G	122 w	3.10	87-13	WitchSir115noRichmondJac1094½OldKentuck108no	Quit badly	11
26Jun46- 6AP	fst 1	:231 :46 1:112 1:371	3↑ Equipoise Mile H 34k	6 8 84½ 42½ 53¾	51	South G	126 w	6.80	85-14	WitchSr110¾OldKntuck106hdArmd132no	Close quarters drive	12
19Jun46- 6AP	hy 7f	:234 :473 1:133 1:271	3↑ Clang H 23k	9 7 51¾ 31 11	1nk	South G	121 w	*2.70	74-31	FightngStep121nkWalkieTalkie1094SigmaKappa103no	Gamely	12
30May46- 6Bel	fst 1¼	:482 1:123 1:373 2:02	3↑ Suburban H 60k	9 2 11½ 11 1nk	54¾	South G	118 w	21.75	85-16	Armed1302½Reply Paid110noStymie1231	Faltered late	11
20May46- 6Bel	fst 1	:234 :47 1:112 1:364	3↑ Sp Wt 10000	1 1 12 2hd 2hd	12	South G	121 w	1.50	90-20	[DH]FightingStep121[DH]Sirde1222ReplyPaid121	Led,hung late	3
11May46- 6Bel	fst 1	:224 :451 1:104 1:37	3↑ Metropolitan H 31k	7 10 1112 129½ 83¾	51½	Adams J	123 w	3.65	87-14	Gallorette110noSirde124noFirst Fiddle126½	Impeded turn	14
4May46- 5Jam	fst 1⅛	:462 1:12 1:37 1:493	3↑ Grey Lag H 35k	6 2 2½ 2hd 41¼	35½	Adams J	126 w	5.25	94-10	Stymie1272Bounding Home1053½Fighting Step1261¾	Faltered	7
27Apr46- 5Jam	sly 1 1/16	:24 :47 1:114 1:45	3↑ Excelsior H 18k	4 3 32½ 43 21	1½	Adams J	123 w	*.85	88-16	Fighting Step123½King Dorsett1154Lets Dance1111		9
Impeded final turn												
18Apr46- 5Jam	fst 1 1/16	:242 :481 1:12 1:431	4↑ Alw 7500	4 1 12 2hd 21½	22½	Arcaro E	119 w	*.60	94-13	Stymie1142½FightingStep11912OlympicZenith1145¼	No match	4
Daily Racing Form time,1:43 3/5												

Date	Cond	Dist	Fractions	Race	PP	St	1st	2nd	Str	Fin	Jockey	Wt	Eq	Odds	Speed	Top finishers	Comment	Fld
6Apr46- 5Jam	fst	6f	:222 :46 1:104	3↑ Paumonok H 11k	7	7	53½	32	2½	1¾	South G	120	w	4.00	97-12	Fighting Step120¾Buzfuz1262Play Pretty1096	Going away	8
23Feb46- 5FG	fst	5½f	:223 :453 :582 1:051	3↑ WFA 2000	4	4	55½	44½	22½	2¾	South G	126	w	*.70	98-13	Scholrshp126¾FghtngStp1264MnyLnds1263	Getting to winner	7
20Oct45- 6CD	fst	6f	:23 :463 1:123	3↑ Autumn H 6.4k	8	4	31	31	31	1nk	South G	123	w	*.50e	90-22	Fighting Step123nkSirius1141Harriet Sue1071¼	Hard urged	12
15Sep45- 7Haw	sl	1 1/16	:24 :48 1:14 1:462	3↑ Haw Autumn H 12k	1	4	53½	3½	12	14	South G	120	w	*.80	86-22	FightingStep1204SigmaKappa1023½Devlu114½	Speed to spare	13
8Sep45- 8Haw	fst	1 1/16	:241 :472 1:12 1:442	3↑ Handicap 3000	1	1	16	14	14	14	South G	118	w	*.40	96-10	FightingStep1184K.Do-Do1035SunnyJck101nk	Speed to spare	7
25Aug45- 7Was	fst	1¼	:48 1:13 1:37 2:024	American Derby 86k	7	4	11½	12	13	11½	South G	118	w	14.80	96-07	FightngStep1181½WarJp1182½Poto'Luck122hd	Weakened late	9
20Aug45- 6Was	fst	7f	:224 :453 1:094 1:224	3↑ Alw 3500	5	1	1½	1½	1hd	1no	South G	109	w	*1.00	99-12	Fighting Step109noQuick Reward1073Icangetit1115	Driving	6
11Aug45- 7Was	gd	1	:223 :453 1:11 1:38	Dick Welles H 32k	7	6	43	32½	22	33	Bailey W	116	w	2.50e	85-15	AirSailor1181½WarJp1251½FghtngStp116½	Vigorous handling	9
30Jly45- 6Was	sl	1	:224 :473 1:114 1:38	Constitution 20k	3	8	74	54	31½	2½	South G	115	w	5.80	87-21	WarJeep121½FightingStp1154SSwllow1245	Getting to winner	9
23Jly45- 6Was	fst	1	:233 :462 1:111 1:362	Alw 3500	3	1	12	11½	12	2no	South G	118	w	*.90	96-11	Icngtt118noFghtngStp11812ArtRo1181½	Saved ground,gamely	6
14Jly45- 7Was	sly	1¼	:48 1:133 1:39 2:054	Classic 84k	1	2	33½	2½	1hd	33¼	South G	119	w	4.00e	78-19	Poto'Luck1191¼AirSailr1192FightngStp1192	Wide,weakened	7
7Jly45- 7Was	fst	7f	:223 :46 1:12 1:25	Skokie H 22k	6	9	63¼	79	42½	32¾	South G	116	w	6.30	85-18	WarJeep1181½Poto'Lck1191¼FightngStp116nk	Saved ground	11
25Jun45- 3Was	sly	6f	:233 :49 1:143	Alw 2500	2	1	21	11½	15	16	South G	120	w	*.50	77-28	FightingStp1206InthBg112noJstngFox1174	Speed in reserve	5
15Jun45- 5CD	fst	6f	:23 :463 1:12	Alw 1800	4	5	1hd	11	11½	13½	South G	113	w	*.40e	93-18	FightingStep1133½RoiRouge113½Bergolatr1131½	Wide,easily	5
9Jun45- 7CD	my	1¼	:48 1:14 1:41 2:07	Ky Derby 76k	13	11	42	46½	816	818½	South G	126	w	19.80	53-28	HoopJr.1266Poto'Luck126¾DarbyDieppe126nk	Tired,swerved	16
2Jun45- 6CD	gd	1⅛	:49 1:14 1:40 1:532	Blue Grass 13k	3	4	42½	62¾	42½	22¼	South G	123	w	17.10	80-17	Darby Dieppe1212¼Fighting Step123noAir Sailor123¾		10
	Close quarters str																	
22May45- 6CD	fst	7f	:23 :462 1:114 1:252	Alw 2500	4	2	21	21	2nk	2no	South G	115	w	5.80	89-18	AirSailor119noFightingStep115nkJoe'sChoice1051½	Driving	6
2Sep44- 6Det	gd	6f	:231 :47 1:13	©Capt M Britt H 4k	7	5	54½	54¼	35½	24½	Caffarella M	108	w	4.15	78-20	Unconditional1164½Fighting Step108noCrack Reward1124		7
	Strong finish																	
26Aug44- 6Det	fst	6f	:224 :46 1:12	Moslem Temple H 10k	6	4	52½	76	54½	52¾	Mojena C	112	w	61.50	85-15	AirSailor1202DarbyDunedn112noUncondtonl116¾	Good finish	10
19Aug44- 5Det	fst	6f	:23 :461 1:122	Handicap 4000	2	6	31	63¾	65	57¾	Burns G	114	wb	20.80	78-16	Beaucaire1131½Unconditional1162½RegalMaid1113	No factor	7
29Jly44- 6Det	fst	6f	:224 :463 1:122	©Alw 5000	4	7	53	65¾	65¼	59½	Glidewell P	118	w	7.80	76-15	Tiger Man106noAir Sailor1186Good Ground1032½	No threat	7
17Jun44- 5Det	fst	5f	:23 :463 :592	Handicap 3000	7	3	2hd	2hd	1hd	33½	Adams J	115	w	*1.30	90-14	Misweet104½Quintero1153Fighting Step1154	No excuse	7
10Jun44- 4Det	my	4½f	:232 :48 :544	Handicap 3000	6	4		32½	21½	1¾	Adams J	112	w	*1.05	88-12	Fighting Step112¾Quintero116hdAgrarian-U116nk	Just up	8
29May44- 3Det	fst	4½f	:231 :471 :541	Md Sp Wt	10	4		42	2nk	15	Adams J	117	w	*2.00	91-09	Fighting Step1175Crack Reward117½Hi Gallant117nk	Easily	12
13May44- 1CD	fst	5f	:231 :473 1:012	Md Sp Wt	6	4	11½	1hd	2hd	2¾	Adams J	116	w	15.90	87-17	Errard116¾FightingStep1163SeeD.1163	Greenly,drifted out	12

First Flight

b. f. 1944, by Mahmoud (Blenheim II)–Fly Swatter, by Dis Donc — **Lifetime record: 24 11 3 3 $197,965**

Own.– C.V. Whitney
Br.– C.V. Whitney (Ky)
Tr.– S.E. Veitch

Date	Cond	Dist	Fractions	Race	PP	St	1st	2nd	Str	Fin	Jockey	Wt	Eq	Odds	Speed	Top finishers	Comment	Fld
15Nov48- 6Jam	fst	6f	:23 :463 1:123	2↑ New Rochelle H 28k	7	6	41½	2hd	3nk	3nk	Clark S	125	w	*2.35	88-25	MissDisco112noBuzfuz121nkFirstFlght1251	Prominent,tired	7
27Oct48- 6Jam	fst	1 1/16	:242 :48 1:13 1:45	3↑ ⒻComely H 29k	5	6	67¼	63¾	42	812	Clark S	126	w	2.95	76-25	Conniver1231¼Miss Request1205Carolyn A.1182	Quit	10
15Oct48- 6Bel	fst	1	:233 :47 1:114 1:372	3↑ ⒻHandicap 10055	2	4	53¼	42	21	1hd	Clark S	126	w	*.60	87-22	FirstFlight126hdSweetDream1147Paddleduck1094	Hard drive	5
4Oct48- 6Jam	fst	6f	:233 :471 1:121	3↑ Fleetwing H 29k	9	9	95¼	64	82¼	3½	Clark S	126	w	2.75	89-19	Buzfuz115hdRoyalGovrnor106½FrstFlght126no	Finished fast	10
29Sep48- 6Bel	fst	1	:224 :452 1:101 1:36	3↑ Sysonby Mile 29k	4	5	510	55	22	23	Clark S	123	w	7.30	91-14	Citation1193First Flight123nkCoaltown1194	Closed well	6
22Sep48- 6Bel	fst	7f	:224 :452 1:103 1:234	2↑ Vosburgh H 31k	13	13	1214	129¾	106½	33½	Donoso R	124	w	4.15	87-17	Colosal1181Spy Song1292½First Flight124hd	Poor start	14
13Sep48- 6Bel	fst	6f-WC	:22 :442 1:083	2↑ Fall Highweight H 31k	13	2		5¾	61½	11¼	Arcaro E	123	w	3.35e	98-05	First Flight1231¼Big Story1243Blue Border1241	Easily	17
2Aug48- 5Sar	fst	6f	:223 :463 1:122	3↑ ⒻAlw 4500	3	7	76	75¼	73½	41	Clark S	116	wb	*1.70	85-18	GreyFlight114nkSnowGoose121nkWatermill114½	Closed fast	10
22Jly48- 5Jam	fst	5½f	:23 :454 :594 1:044	3↑ Handicap 5555	4	2	32	22	22	1½	Clark S	117	wb	4.25	94-16	First Flight117½Grey Flight112nkMiss Disco1154	Driving	5
19Jun48- 5Del	my	1 1/16	:242 :482 1:141 1:49	3↑ ⒻNew Castle H 29k	3	4	32	52½	69½	617	Clark S	118	wb	6.60	51-31	Miss Grillo1192½Elpis1191¾Rampart1176	Quit	7
9Jun48- 6Bel	fst	1 1/16	:233 :463 1:112 1:43	3↑ ⒻTop Flight H 24k	6	7	65¼	55	43½	57½	Clark S	120	w	*2.05	88-18	Honeymoon124noRed Shoes1085Gallorette126½	Faltered	10
2Jun48- 7Bel	fst	1	:23 :454 1:111 1:38	4↑ Alw 5000	5	3	33½	22	22	12½	Clark S	114	w	2.65	84-22	First Flight1142½Mangohick1222Bullet Proof1143½	Easily	6
15Oct47- 5Jam	fst	6f	:232 :47 1:12	2↑ ⒻCorrection H 17k	6	10	1114	1114	94	43	Guerin E	116	wb	4.00e	88-17	Miss Kimo1261Beaugay1232Miss Disco110hd	Sluggish early	11
24Sep47- 6Bel	fst	1	:231 :46 1:11 1:372	Jerome H 30k	1	2	1nk	21	73¼	78¼	Allgaier H	112	wb	7.75	79-18	Donor115nkCosmic Bomb1261½Cornish Knight1132	Tired	12
15Sep47- 5Aqu	sly	7f	:241 :471 1:121 1:25	3↑ ⒻAlw 6000	2	2	2hd	2hd	1hd	2nk	Donoso R	114	w	*.50	87-16	Quarantaine103nkFirstFlight1141¼LittleAnn1087	Went well	4
8Aug47- 6Sar	fst	7f	:223 :452 1:11 1:242	ⒻTest 10k	3	5	33½	43¼	105	88	Arcaro E	120	w	*.45e	86-11	MissDisco110¾Frantie'sBid112¾OcenBrf1101	Close quarters	15
23Jly47- 6Mth	gd	1 1/16	:231 :471 1:124 1:46	ⒻMth Oaks 13k	1	4	33	11	12½	12½	Arcaro E	117	w	*.55e	92-15	First Flight1172½Frantie's Bid1133½Whipsaw1131½	In hand	11
18Jly47- 4Bel	fst	6f	:222 :461 1:112	Alw 5000	6	2	1hd	11	11½	1no	Arcaro E	121	w	*.45	93-15	First Flight121noColonel O'F1226Nassau1181		7
	Held on,worked seven furlongs																	
5Oct46- 4Bel	fst	6½f-W	:224 :452 1:084 1:151	Futurity 93k	1	6		83¾	2hd	11¾	Arcaro E	123	w	*.85e	96-07	First Flight1231¾I Will126hdJet Pilot1225	Going away	13
	Geldings not eligible																	
28Sep46- 4Bel	fst	6f-WC	:223 :45 1:083	ⒻMatron 44k	3	6		2nk	1hd	12¼	Arcaro E	123	w	*.75e	98-07	First Flight1232¼Pipette1231Quarantaine115½	Drew out	10
24Sep46- 4Bel	sly	5½f-W	:223 :451 1:032	ⒻAlw 4000	5	4		2nk	1hd	1¾	Arcaro E	119	w	*1.55	97-07	FirstFlight119¾TeaOlive1141¼CosmicMissile1145	Drew out	10
8Jun46- 4Bel	fst	5½f-W	:223 :452 1:043	ⒻAstoria 14k	8	1	4½	2nk	11½	13¼	Miller P	119	w	*1.15	91-12	FirstFlight1193¼MissKimo1221DarkVenus115hd	Going away	10
18May46- 4Bel	fst	5f-WC	:222 :45 :573	Juvenile 14k	2	8		71¾	33	23	Kirkland A	119	w	*1.00e	89-06	EternalWr1223FrstFlght1191CornshKnght113no	Inside route	12
7May46- 6Bel	fst	4½f-W	:221 :45 :51	ⒻFashion 14k	10	3		1hd	1½	11¼	Kirkland A	110	w	4.15	100-06	First Flight1101¼Miss Kimo1195Miss Disco1191	Drew out	11

Gallorette

ch. f. 1942, by Challenger II (Swynford)–Gallette, by Sir Gallahad III — **Lifetime record: 72 21 20 13 $445,535**

Own.– Mrs M.A. Moore
Br.– Preston M. Burch (Md)
Tr.– E.A. Christmas

Date	Cond	Dist	Fractions	Race	PP	St	1st	2nd	Str	Fin	Jockey	Wt	Eq	Odds	Speed	Top finishers	Comment	Fld
12Oct48- 6Jam	fst	1 1/16	:24 :471 1:12 1:444	3↑ Questionnaire H 29k	3	4	76¾	96	98¼	99	Kirkland A	121	w	5.90	80-18	Donor115noCarolyn A.111½Bug Juice1082	Couldn't keep up	11
28Sep48- 6Bel	fst	1½	:473 1:122 2:04 2:30	3↑ ⒻLadies H 58k	2	2	56¾	3nk	22	24	Jessop JD	121	w	4.05	84-14	Miss Request1144Gallorette1211Honeymoon1231	Went well	9
22Sep48- 6Bel	fst	7f	:224 :452 1:103 1:234	2↑ Vosburgh H 31k	1	8	107½	106¼	75	64¾	Jessop JD	120	w	6.45	86-17	Colosal1181Spy Song1292½First Flight124hd	Dull effort	14
11Sep48- 6Aqu	gd	1⅛	:482 1:131 1:39 1:522	3↑ ⒻBeldame H 68k	7	9	105¾	74¾	62¾	34	Jessop JD	124	wb	3.20	81-20	Conniver1213½Harmonica114½Gallorette124nk	Closed fast	14
	Previously owned by W.L. Brann																	
21Aug48- 6Sar	fst	1¼	:474 1:12 1:372 2:031	3↑ Saratoga H 29k	1	2	47	45	63¾	55¾	Jessop JD	122	w	3.60	86-13	Loyal Legion1181Bug Juice106nkSnow Goose120½	Tired	7
7Aug48- 6Sar	gd	1¼	:494 1:133 1:391 2:051	3↑ Whitney 22k	2	4	35	33	31¾	1¾	Kirkland A	115	w	*.90	82-27	Gallorette115¾Loyal Legion1128Natchez1142	Drew out	4
3Aug48- 6Sar	fst	1	:231 :462 1:121 1:382	3↑ Wilson 17k	7	8	87¾	76½	3¾	11¼	Jessop JD	115	w	2.90	85-17	Gallorette1151¼Mount Marcy1054Miss Disco1091½	Drew out	10
17Jly48- 6Aqu	fst	1¼	:502 1:16 1:404 2:054	3↑ Brooklyn H 57k	5	2	33	32	2hd	2hd	Jessop JD	119	w	5.50	78-21	Conniver114hdGallorette1193Stymie1302	Game try	6
3Jly48- 6Aqu	fst	7f	:23 :461 1:102 1:232	3↑ Carter H 29k	7	6	64¼	55¼	53½	1hd	Jessop JD	122	w	4.25	95-13	Gallorette122hdRippey1321¼Skylighter1101¼	Hard drive	8
9Jun48- 6Bel	fst	1 1/16	:233 :463 1:112 1:43	3↑ ⒻTop Flight H 24k	2	3	3½	31	31½	35	Arcaro E	126	w	2.10	91-18	Honeymoon124noRed Shoes1085Gallorette126½	Forced back	10
22May48- 6Bel	fst	1	:233 :463 1:112 1:364	3↑ Metropolitan H 30k	8	7	75¼	67¾	45	43¾	Arcaro E	118	w	*2.30	86-14	Stymie126¾Colosal1171½Rippey1241½	No mishap	9
15May48- 5Jam	fst	1 3/16	:48 1:122 1:373 1:571	3↑ Gallant Fox H 87k	1	2	11	11½	2hd	3½	Atkinson T	117	w	10.15	89-15	Faultless118hdFervent125½Gallorette1173½	Close quarters	10
8May48- 5Jam	gd	1 1/16	:243 :483 1:131 1:464	3↑ ⒻFirenze H 28k	2	2	31	2½	31	22½	Jessop JD	126	w	*1.70	76-21	Carolyn A.1142½Gallorette126nkRed Shoes1073	Hung	6
30Apr48- 6Jam	fst	1 1/16	:24 :482 1:13 1:464	4↑ Alw 5000	5	3	23	2hd	11	1¾	Jessop JD	115	w	*.30	79-17	Gallorette115¾Calvados1201½Lets Dance1205	Easily	5
24Apr48- 4Jam	fst	6f	:23 :462 1:114	3↑ Handicap 6570	6	8	53	56¼	31¼	2nk	Jessop JD	120	w	13.55	92-18	Rippey126nkGallorette120nkKitchenPolice1161	Good effort	8
29Nov47- 6Bow	fst	1 3/16	:493 1:133 1:392 1:593	3↑ Bryan & O'Hara H 22k	2	4	41½	43½	1hd	2¾	Kirkland A	124	w	*1.20	88-18	Incline107¾Gallorette124hdDouble Jay123hd	Lacked room	7
8Nov47- 5Jam	sly	1 3/16	:474 1:121 1:384 1:591	3↑ Westchester H 57k	3	4	21½	22	2½	52½	Atkinson T	118	w	5.15	77-22	Bridal Flower1081With Pleasure1301½Donor112hd	Tired	8
1Nov47- 5Jam	gd	1 1/16	:24 :472 1:121 1:443	3↑ Scarsdale H 30k	6	10	97½	43½	23	22	Guerin E	119	w	10.50	88-17	WithPleasure1292Gallorette119½DoubleJay1182	Good effort	12

7Oct47- 6Bel	fst	1½	:473 1:123 2:042 2:293	3↑ ⒻLadies H 60k	10 8 45¾ 3½ 52 36	Jessop JD	123 w	8.60e	84-14	Snow Goose1135But Why Not1211Gallorette123hd	Weakened 12
20Sep47- 6Aqu	fst	1⅛	:483 1:131 1:384 1:52	3↑ ⒻBeldame (Div 1) 59k	1 4 53½ 21 2nk 22½	Jessop JD	126 w	*1.85	84-12	SnowGoose1062½Gallortte1262½Crmrgo1122½	Determined bid 10
13Sep47- 6Aqu	fst	1⅛	:502 1:143 1:392 1:522	3↑ Edgemere H 27k	2 1 11½ 2nk 41¾ 44	Jessop JD	122 w	2.50	81-13	Elpis1141½Stymie1341Bridal Flower1131½	Tired badly 4
1Sep47- 6Aqu	fst	1 1/16	:242 :474 1:124 1:442	3↑ Aqueduct H 29k	5 4 47 3nk 31½ 2½	Jessop JD	122wb	2.45	91-13	Stymie132½Gallorette122hdElpis1144	Held well 11
23Aug47- 6Sar	fst	1¼	:48 1:114 1:37 2:032	3↑ Saratoga H 33k	2 2 11 1nk 1hd 2nk	Guerin E	122 w	*.80	91-11	Rico Monte124nkGallorette12212Boss105	Hung late 3
9Aug47- 6Sar	fst	1¼	:491 1:133 1:393 2:023	3↑ Whitney 27k	3 1 12 1½ 1nk 2hd	Arcaro E	112 w	2.05	95-09	Rico Monte113hdGallorette1121½Stymie126	Held well 3
4Aug47- 6Sar	fst	1	:23 :46 1:10 1:352	3↑ Wilson 23k	3 4 47 48½ 31½ 11¼	Jessop JD	112 w	*1.45	104-08	Gallorette1121¼Hornbeam1123KngDorstt112¾	Steadied early 5
26Jly47- 5Mth	fst	1¼	:473 1:12 1:363 2:011	3↑ Mth Park H 29k	4 2 42½ 32½ 34½ 38½	James B	119 w	*1.35	94-02	Round View1127Talon1121½Gallorette119hd	Flattened out 6
12Jly47- 5Jam	fst	1 3/16	:49 1:134 1:381 1:563	3↑ Butler H 54k	2 4 31 33 4½ 31¾	Guerin E	117 w	9.20	91-09	Assault135hdStymie1261¾Gallorette117nk	Swerved turn 5
3Jly47- 5Jam	fst	1 1/16	:241 :482 1:132 1:452	3↑ ⒻHandicap 7530	4 2 22 21 1½ 11¼	Guerin E	128 w	*.80	86-16	Gallorette1281¼Kay Gibson1082½Elpis1142	Mild urging 4
7Jun47- 6Aqu	sly	7f	:23 :461 1:10 1:23	3↑ Carter H 28k	2 5 56½ 54¾ 52¼ 33¼	James B	123 w	*2.25	94-09	Rippey112nkInroc1183Gallorette1232	Fast finish 8
2Jun47- 6Aqu	fst	1 1/16	:242 :482 1:124 1:452	3↑ Queens County H 21k	5 2 21 2hd 1hd 1nk	Jessop JD	119 w	1.70	87-19	Gallorette119nkStymie128noMangoneo1046	Driving 6
10May47- 6Bel	fst	1	:23 :464 1:112 1:372	3↑ Metropolitan H 30k	7 8 98¼ 89¼ 76¼ 32	Givens C	116 w	8.95	85-15	Stymie1241BrownMogl1131Gllortt1161½	Bumped str,swerved 12
26Apr47- 5Jam	fst	1 1/16	:24 :473 1:114 1:44	3↑ Excelsior H 22k	2 5 64 51¾ 53¾ 58½	Wilson HB	118 w	6.55	84-10	Coincidence1155Polynesian126½Lets Dance1121	No menace 8
19Apr47- 4Jam	fst	6f	:23 :46 1:112	3↑ Handicap 6525	1 3 22 48 45¾ 45	Jessop JD	121 w	6.45	89-10	Polynesin1301¾Buzfuz1201¼TdyBd1032	Worked mile 1:42 3/5 5
9Nov46- 5Jam	gd	1 3/16	:472 1:112 1:373 1:562	3↑ Westchester H 56k	3 4 38 48¼ 66¾ 69	Atkinson T	118 w	8.70	85-17	Assault1222½Lucky Draw1284Lets Dance1041½	No mishap 6
26Oct46- 6GS	sly	1⅛	:464 1:112 1:373 1:503	3↑ Trenton H 64k	12 6 66 55¼ 86 88¾	Jessop JD	121 w	*2.35	83-19	Turbine115nkPolynesian123½Man o' Glory1162	No excuse 12
12Oct46- 4Bel	sly	1	:23 :453 1:102 1:353	3↑ Sysonby 25k	4 3 32½ 23 26 212	Jessop JD	117 w	2.35	84-14	Lucky Draw12012Gallorette1171½War Date1172	Went well 4
21Sep46- 6Aqu	sly	1⅛	:474 1:124 1:382 1:512	3↑ ⒻBeldame H (Div 1) 56k	2 7 41¼ 1hd 1½ 1½	Jessop JD	126 w	*.80	90-13	Gallorette126½War Date1131¼Kay Gibson1056	Ridden out 10
14Sep46- 6Aqu	fst	1⅛	:474 1:13 1:38 1:502	3↑ Edgemere H 28k	1 3 32½ 52¼ 41¾ 21½	Jessop JD	123 w	2.15	93-13	Stymie1211½Gallorette1231¼King Dorsett1156	Closed fast 8
9Sep46- 6Aqu	fst	7f	:223 :45 1:10 1:232	3↑ Bay Shore H 18k	2 4 73¼ 77½ 53¼ 1nk	Jessop JD	124 w	6.20	95-18	Gallorette124nkKing Dorsett1201½Polynesian1301	Just up 9
19Aug46- 6Sar	sly	1	:25 :493 1:14 1:39	3↑ Alw 6650	3 2 22 32 35¼ 35¾	Jessop JD	121 w	*1.30	80-20	King Dorsett119¾Stymie1195Gallorette121	Tired 3
5Aug46- 6Sar	fst	1	:23 :461 1:111 1:363	3↑ Wilson 24k	4 7 79½ 63¼ 53½ 2nk	Wilson HB	121 w	6.65	98-08	Pavot126nkGallorette121nkLarky Day112hd	Just missed 11
13Jly46- 5Jam	fst	1 3/16	:47 1:111 1:361 1:551	3↑ Butler H 57k	3 3 31½ 32½ 1½ 2hd	Jessop JD	116 w	6.15	104-08	Lucky Draw105hdGallorette1161½Stymie126¾	Game try 9
4Jly46- 6Suf	fst	1⅛	:473 1:123 1:373 1:494	3↑ Mass H 66k	11 7 74¼ 51½ 21½ 33¾	Jessop JD	119 w	*2.20	88-13	Pavot1202¼Dinner Party1131½Gallorette1192¾	Weakened 11
22Jun46- 6Aqu	fst	1¼	:48 1:131 1:393 2:05	3↑ Brooklyn H 58k	8 7 43½ 2½ 1½ 1nk	Jessop JD	118 w	3.15	82-24	Gallorette118nkStymie1284½Burning Dream110½	Hard drive 8
15Jun46- 6Del	gd	1¼	:473 1:122 1:38 2:041	3↑ Sussex H 29k	5 3 31½ 33½ 22½ 22	Jessop JD	113 w	3.55	92-16	Pavot1152Gallorette1131Stymie1262	Good effort 8
11Jun46- 6Del	fst	1 1/16	:241 :473 1:111 1:43	4↑ Alw 3500	4 1 11½ 1½ 12 11¼	Jessop JD	120 w	*.70	98-14	Gallorette1201¼War Trophy1146George Case120¾	Easily 4
29May46- 6Bel	fst	1 1/16	:224 :454 1:103 1:431	3↑ ⒻTop Flight H 24k	7 3 32½ 42 31½ 52¾	Jessop JD	128 w	*2.25	92-13	Sicily113nkSurosa1131¼Recce1181	Close quarters 11
24May46- 6Bel	fst	1	:231 :462 1:112 1:372	3↑ ⒻHandicap 8050	6 2 2½ 2hd 11½ 12	Jessop JD	122 w	*.90	87-14	Gallrette1222Mahmoudess109nkDarbyDunedn112hd	Drew away 6
11May46- 6Bel	fst	1	:224 :451 1:104 1:37	3↑ Metropolitan H 31k	6 8 1010 104½ 4½ 1no	Jessop JD	110 w	9.60	89-14	Gallorette110noSirde124noFirst Fiddle126½	Just up 14
4May46- 5Jam	fst	1⅛	:462 1:12 1:37 1:493	3↑ Grey Lag H 35k	7 1 1½ 1hd 3nk 47¼	Donoso R	114 w	14.45	93-10	Stymie1272Bounding Home1053½Fighting Step1261¾	Bore in 7
27Apr46- 5Jam	sly	1 1/16	:24 :47 1:114 1:45	3↑ Excelsior H 18k	1 4 43½ 32½ 33 45½	Kirkland A	116 w	6.15	82-16	Fighting Step123½King Dorsett1154Lets Dance1111	Tired 9
17Nov45- 6Pim	gd	1 3/16	:493 1:142 1:391 1:584	3↑ Pim Spl 25k	7 3 33½ 42½ 55¾ 47¼	Atkinson T	117wb	16.15	81-20	Armed1264First Fiddle1262Stymie1261¼	No rally late 7
10Nov45- 5Pim	fst	1⅛	:471 1:114 1:373 1:513	3↑ Handicap 5000	4 2 22 1hd 21 31¾	Scawthorn K	113 w	2.50	95-14	Armed1281¾Rampart104hdGallorette1132	Outgamed for place 5
3Nov45- 5Jam	fst	1 3/16	:48 1:113 1:371 1:564	3↑ Westchester H 56k	6 2 45½ 34 53½ 44	Haskell L	116 w	22.20	92-10	Stymie125hdBuzfuz1162Olympic Zenith1172	Not enough late 10
27Oct45- 7Pim	fst	1 1/16	:241 :482 1:131 1:453	3↑ Handicap 3500	7 5 54½ 53½ 53¼ 53	McCreary C	124 w	3.25	87-17	Salvo120½Polynesian1262He Rolls115hd	Failed to rally 7
8Sep45- 6Aqu	fst	1⅛	:471 1:113 1:373 1:512	Discovery H 28k	1 3 34 33 2½ 77	Atkinson T	120 w	*2.00	83-13	[D]Bobanet115hdWar Jeep122½Chief Barker1162	Tired 11
25Aug45- 5GS	sl	1⅛	:473 1:122 1:381 1:514	Jersey H 32k	2 5 46 45½ 11 52¾	Permane R	121 w	*.95	83-18	Trymenow118nkBuzfuz1152½Turbine114no	Faltered 8
21Jly45- 5Jam	fst	1 3/16	:472 1:112 1:37 1:564	Empire City 57k	9 4 35½ 32½ 1nk 1¾	Atkinson T	116 w	3.00	96-08	Gallorette116¾Pavot1263Post Graduate1163	Drew away 11
14Jly45- 5Aqu	fst	1¼	:481 1:13 1:393 2:051	Dwyer 56k	1 3 33 21½ 2hd 2no	Kirkland A	116 w	6.65	81-18	Wildlife116noGallorette116½Esteem11610	Bid,just missed 6
28Jun45- 6Del	fst	1⅛	:474 1:124 1:383 1:51	ⒻDel Oaks 13k	4 3 11½ 11 11 13	Arcaro E	119 w	*.60	94-08	Gallorette1193Elpis119½Monsoon11312	Speed to spare 5
16Jun45- 7Pim	fst	1 1/16	:24 :48 1:114 1:442	ⒻPim Oaks 22k	6 3 22 21 2½ 1¾	Woolf G	121 w	*.85	96-08	Gallorette121¾Recce121¾Be Faithful1216	Driving 6
7Jun45- 6Bel	fst	1	:23 :47 1:114 1:38	ⒻAcorn 11k	7 3 22 21½ 11½ 11½	Arcaro E	121 w	1.25	84-21	Gallorette1211½Monsoon1216Recce1212	Swerved,driving 7
30May45- 5Jam	fst	1 1/16	:24 :47 1:12 1:454	Wood Mem (Div 1) 27k	7 4 47 43¾ 1hd 22	Atkinson T	121 w	10.85	82-16	Jeep1262Gallorette1212½Dockstader1261½	Driving 9
22May45- 5Jam	fst	6f	:232 :462 1:123	Alw 4000	11 5 2hd 11 11½ 11¾	Arcaro E	113 w	12.85	89-14	Gallorette1131¾Hitem1171½War Trophy113hd	Driving 14
7Nov44- 5Pim	fst	1 70	:224 :47 1:123 1:442	Alw 2500	3 3 34 23 2hd 23½	Gilbert J	114 w	*.95e	85-17	Brookfield1133½Gallortt1145Mndru1105	Swerved repeatedly 6
3Nov44- 5Pim	fst	6f	:222 :46 1:12	ⒻAlw 3000	4 5 31½ 2½ 1hd 2½	Scawthorn K	116wb	2.85	92-28	Monsoon116½Gallorette1163Connie's Girl1121	Driving 8
14Oct44- 6Lrl	sl	1 1/16	:233 :474 1:141 1:493	ⒻSelima 29k	1 2 22 44 33½ 35½	Woolf G	114 w	3.65	63-34	Busher1173Ace Card1192½Gallorette1144	Held well 10
9Oct44- 4Lrl	sl	1 70	:241 :491 1:164 1:491	ⒻAlw 3000	4 2 21 11 14 15	Dodson D	114 w	3.50	63-37	Gallorette1145Whetstone112nkSweetChms1143	Eased up late 6
4Oct44- 6Lrl	hy	6f	:23 :481 1:151	ⓈMaryland Futurity 6k	1 4 32 22 1hd 2no	Dodson D	110 w	*.60e	78-33	Petee Dee111noGallorette1104Sheltie1111	Just missed 8
28Sep44- 5Lrl	fst	6f	:224 :471 1:14	ⓈAlw 2000	1 3 12 13 13 16	Dodson D	115 w	*.80	84-21	Gallorette1156Run Bud Run1182Abiel1181	Easily 8
20Sep44- 1Lrl	sl	5½f	:233 :484 1:02 1:09	ⒻMd Sp Wt	4 3 12 14 14 12	Dodson D	115 w	*1.30	78-28	Gallorette1152Chronoflit1156FourQuns1151½	Mild pressure 11
14Sep44- 1Lrl	hy	6f	:233 :492 1:173	Md Sp Wt	8 7 42½ 21 1½ 33¼	Dodson D	115 w	46.35	63-44	Director118nkWar Trophy1133Gallorette1151	Tired 12

Level Best

ch. f. 1938, by Equipoise (Pennant)–Speed Boat, by Man o' War

Own.– C. Oglebay

Br.– Samuel D. Riddle (Ky)

Tr.– J.P. Jones

Lifetime record: 28 12 6 3 $64,230

12Oct42- 6Lrl	fst	1⅛	:473 1:122 1:381 1:51	3↑ ⒻQueen Isabella H 6.1k	2 6 619 616 621 623½	Young S	114wb	10.50	69-12	Vgrncy1263Lotopos1022Rostown1224	Fractious,broke in air 6
6Oct42- 6Bel	gd	1½	:481 1:133 2:054 2:311	3↑ ⒻLadies H 16k	10 6 12 11 21 810¾	Meade D	117wb	20.50	75-13	Vagrancy1261½Dark Discovery1081½Loveday1175	Tired 10
19Sep42- 6Aqu	sly	1⅛	:472 1:121 1:373 1:50	3↑ ⒻBeldame H 17k	6 7 77½ 69½ 98¼ 916½	Longden J	120 w	9.20	80-06	[DH]Vagrancy119[DH]Barrancosa1164Rosetown126hd	Outrun 10
12Sep42- 6GS	sl	1 1/16	:25 :494 1:142 1:472	3↑ ⒻVineland H 12k	4 2 2½ 2hd 2½ 2¾	Ensor L	115wb	2.50	--	Rosetown121¾Level Best1153½Dark Discovery1095	Weakened 6
5Sep42- 5GS	fst	6f	:224 :462 1:104	3↑ ⒻColonial H 5.9k	1 5 53½ 31 2½ 21¼	Meade D	121 w	*1.25	--	Zaca Gray1131¼Level Best1215Taunt1121	Weakened 6
11Jly42- 7Suf	gd	1 1/16	:23 :46 1:112 1:444	3↑ ⒻHannah Dustin H 13k	4 4 44 913 915 1021	Gilbert J	118wb	*2.30	71-15	Loveday112½Spiral Pass1021Red Moon1112¼	Weakened 10
4Jly42- 6Del	gd	1 1/16	:234 :482 1:124 1:453	3↑ ⒻNew Castle H 12k	3 1 11 11 2hd 611¾	Meade D	125 w	*1.80	79-09	Monida112nkRosetown1195War Hazard1232	Tired badly 8
23Jun42- 5Del	fst	6f	:223 :461 1:113	4↑ Alw 2080	2 2 32 22 2½ 1hd	Meade D	119 w	*.80	95-07	Level Best119hdThe Finest1212½Madigama1176	Hard drive 5
13Jun42- 6Aqu	fst	7f	:223 :451 1:094 1:23	3↑ Carter H 9.8k	5 3 31½ 56 76½ 912½	Meade D	121 w	2.90	87-08	Doublrab120hdSwing and Sway112¾Whirlaway1301½	Impeded 9
4Jun42- 6Bel	fst	1 1/16	:231 :46 1:104 1:424	3↑ ⒻTop Flight H 7k	8 1 11 11 11½ 11¾	Meade D	123 w	*2.90	97-09	Level Best1231¾Up the Hill1141Transient1121½	In hand 9
30May42- 7Bel	fst	7f	:232 :463 1:112 1:233	3↑ ⒻHandicap 2525	2 1 2hd 2hd 1hd 21½	Meade D	122 w	2.65	90-07	Fleetborough1071½LevelBest122hd[D]Mr-Kll1126	Forced wide 6
4Aug41- 5Sar	fst	1	:231 :464 1:113 1:373	3↑ ⒻHandicap 2030	2 1 16 14 1½ 25	Robertson A	118wb	1.95	88-14	War Hazard1045Level Best118hdRosetown1221	Tired badly 6
5Jly41- 6Del	my	1 1/16	:233 :48 1:141 1:49	3↑ ⒻNew Castle H 13k	5 10 1218 1320 1331 1322	Wall N	114 w	*2.35	52-28	DottedSwiss1143BalaOrmont1161½FairyChant1262	13
			Fractious start,unseated rider,refused to extend								
12Jun41- 6Del	fst	1⅛	:474 1:12 1:372 1:494	ⒻDel Oaks 8.8k	1 2 23 24 25 315	Robertson A	119wb	*1.15	91-08	Tangled1139Misty Isle1196Level Best1194	5
			Fractious start,broke through gate,returned bleeding from mouth								
31May41- 4Bel	fst	1⅜	:49 1:13 1:383 2:173	ⒻC C A Oaks 13k	1 1 11½ 14 12 1nk	Robertson A	121wb	*.45	83-12	Level Best121nkDark Discovery1212Nasca121	Just lasted 3
26May41- 6Bel	fst	1 1/16	:24 :474 1:133 1:444	3↑ ⒻHandicap 2035	4 2 2nk 2hd 13 11½	Hanford I	110wb	*.60	87-16	Level Best1101½Laatokka1046Bala Ormont112½	Easily 5
3May41- 6Pim	fst	1 1/16	:232 :472 1:122 1:453	ⒻPim Oaks 12k	5 2 11 1hd 2hd 31¾	Hanford I	121wb	*.60	90-13	Cis Marion121noDark Discovery1211¾Level Best1213½	Tired 8
2Nov40- 4Emp	hy	5¾f	:224 :463 1:10	ⒻAutumn Day 8.9k	4 5 52½ 41 11 12	Robertson A	119wb	*.40	87-22	Level Best1192Dark Imp1102Strange Device1191¾	Easily 7
12Oct40- 6Kee	fst	6f	:224 :461 1:112	ⒻSpecial Event 6.2k	4 5 11½ 12 1½ 12	Longden J	119wb	*.30	95-10	Level Best1192Valdina Myth1192½Meggy1193	Handily 9
5Oct40- 5Lrl	fst	6f	:223 :463 1:121	Richard Johnson 8.2k	6 2 2½ 1½ 12½ 14	Robertson A	116wb	*1.10	93-19	Level Best1164Madigama113.5¾Misty Isle1191	Going away 9
21Sep40- 4Aqu	fst	6½f	:222 :453 1:101 1:17	Jr Champion 12k	2 2 22 23 22 22¼	Robertson A	115wb	3.95	--	King Cole1182¼Level Best1152Nasca115nk	Second best 7

14Sep40- 5HdG	fst 6f	:231 :47 1:112	Eastern Shore H 13k	8 1 2½ 12½ 1½ 2no	Shelhamer A	122wb	*.90	96-10	LittleBens116noLvlBst1221½Portr'sCp1201¾	Tired in drive	9
2Sep40- 6Nar	sly 6f	:23 :461 1:112	Old Colony 10k	1 4 1hd 1hd 11½ 15	Shelhamer A	114wb	*2.50	94-16	LevelBest1145KingCole114.5nkLittleBens1153¾	Easily best	10
17Aug40- 6Sar	fst 6f	:224 :47 1:12	ⒻSpinaway 10k	1 2 1hd 1hd 11 34½	James B	119wb	*.65	87-09	Nasca1163Tangled1161½Level Best1191½	Faltered	6
6Aug40- 5Sar	fst 5½f	:223 :46 1:051	ⓇSar Sales 2.8k	4 1 2hd 1hd 1hd 11¾	James B	119wb	*.55	95-07	Level Best1191¾Cuantos1222Omission122½	Going away	7
4Jly40- 5Emp	my 5¾f	:223 :462 1:091	ⒻDemoiselle 8.1k	6 5 12 14 15 18¼	James B	115wb	5.40	91-14	Level Best1158¼Strange Device122¾Tangled1192	Much best	13
22Jun40- 4Del	fst 5½f	:224 :463 1:071	Alw 1000	7 3 2½ 1½ 1nk 11	Peters M	112wb	*1.10	96-08	Level Best1121Sky Lane115hdSnarler1182½	Drew out	7
13Jun40- 1Del	fst 5f	:23 :463 1:00	ⒻMd Sp Wt	6 3 32¾ 45 2½ 12	Peters M	116wb	*1.25	96-10	LevelBest1162CisMarion116½GranoSaltis116hd	Going away	12

Mar-Kell

b. f. 1939, by Blenheim II (Blandford)–Nellie Flag, by American Flag
Own.– Calumet Farm
Br.– Calumet Farm (Ky)
Tr.– B.A. Jones

Lifetime record: 53 17 17 3 $84,365

14Nov44- 4Pim	fst 6f	:224 :462 1:113 4↑	Alw 3500	5 5 34 46 34 33¾	Dodson D	116wb	2.05	91-18	Sophocles1163½Charitabl116nkMr-Kll1161½	Unable to close	5
12Oct44- 6Lrl	fst 1⅛	:472 1:123 1:40 1:531 3↑	ⒻQueen Isabella H 11k	1 6 615 715 715 716½	Westrope J	118wb	*.15e	65-23	Twilight Tear1265Good Morning1182Legend Bearer1083½	Broke sluggishly,no rally	8
3Oct44- 6Bel	fst 1½	:491 1:131 2:051 2:311 3↑	ⒻLadies H 16k	1 2 21 31½ 54½ 510¼	Arcaro E	126wb	2.30	72-15	Donitas First1154Letmenow1121½Moon Maiden1134	Tired	5
6Sep44- 6Was	sly 1	:24 :48 1:132 1:392 3↑	ⒻModesty H 16k	1 8 57 610 718 719	Smith FA	117wb	*1.90	62-24	Gold Princess1103Night Shadow1121Happy Issue1126	Gave way suddenly	8
19Aug44- 6Was	fst 1⅛	:462 1:11 1:362 1:501 3↑	ⒻBeverly H 29k	5 12 107¾ 98¾ 53½ 2¾	McCreary C	118wb	*2.80	96-09	TrafficCourt115¾Mar-Kell118½Silvestr1041½	Finished fast	12
28Jly44- 6Was	fst 6f	:23 :461 1:11 3↑	ⒻHandicap 5000	1 3 52¼ 52½ 2hd 2nk	Grohs O	116wb	4.10	96-13	GoldPrincess109nkMar-Kell1163TrafficCourt1161	Held well	7
15Jly44- 5Was	fst 7f	:234 :472 1:111 1:233 3↑	ⒻHandicap 3500	6 4 32 31½ 23 35	Haas L	120wb	4.70	93-11	Burgoo Maid1093Traffic Court1162Mar-Kell120½	Saved ground,faltered	6
8Jly44- 6Was	fst 1	:231 :463 1:113 1:363 3↑	ⒻArl Matron H 16k	6 5 54 54½ 76¾ 610½	Smith FA	122wb	*2.10	84-08	HarrietSue103½TrafficCourt1121½HppyIssu1144	No response	7
24Jun44- 6Was	fst 1	:233 :471 1:113 1:361 3↑	Equipoise Mile H 12k	2 4 52¼ 810 812 816	Smith FA	110wb	*.70e	81-07	Sun Again127¾Georgie Drum113nkAnticlimax1042½	Outrun	9
1Jun44- 6Bel	fst 1$\frac{1}{16}$	:23 :454 1:11 1:432 3↑	ⒻTop Flight H 11k	7 8 86¾ 54¾ 23 2¾	McCreary C	126wb	*1.60	93-10	Boojiana106¾Mar-Kell1263Silvestra112½	Driving	10
22May44- 7Bel	fst 1$\frac{1}{16}$	:463 1:121 1:374 1:443 3↑	ⒻHandicap 4965	4 6 69 66¾ 43½ 2nk	McCreary C	120wb	*.90	88-15	Anthemion108nkMar-Kell1204Moon Maiden1121	Belated rally	8
19May44- 6Bel	fst 6f	:231 :462 1:104 3↑	ⒻHandicap 4390	2 4 52½ 42¼ 44½ 33¾	McCreary C	117wb	9.45	92-14	Bossuet125¾Brownie1133Mar-Kell117nk	Late gain	5
2May44- 5Pim	fst 1$\frac{1}{16}$	:24 :481 1:13 1:452 3↑	Philadelphia H 17k	5 5 54½ 53¼ 52 21	McCreary C	113wb	5.85	90-16	Rounders1201Mar-Kell113nkFour Freedoms119½	Driving	5
27Apr44- 5Pim	my 1$\frac{1}{16}$	:241 :484 1:144 1:482 3↑	Gittings H 8.4k	1 2 2hd 44 45 413½	McCreary C	114wb	*.30e	62-39	Sun Again1241Famous Victory101½Tola Rose10912	Tired	4
20Apr44- 7Pim	gd 1 70	:242 :483 1:141 1:452 4↑	Alw 3000	6 2 1½ 13 13 16	McCreary C	115wb	*.55	84-20	Mar-Kell1156In Question1124Homeward Bound1141	Easily	6
13Apr44- 5Pim	gd 6f	:223 :47 1:132 4↑	Alw 2500	4 4 43½ 34 33 26	Smith FA	117wb	*.75	80-25	Sollure1126Mar-Kell1174Homeward Bound116¾	No match	5
18Mar44- 6TrP	fst 1⅛	:471 1:111 1:363 1:491 3↑	Coral Gables H 5.5k	6 3 32 21½ 21½ 22	McCreary C	115wb	*.60e	97-05	Marriage1202Mar-Kell1153Shot Put1052	Bid,no match	6
6Mar44- 5TrP	fst 6f	:222 :45 1:10 4↑	Alw 2000	3 7 76 43 2nk 1¾	McCreary C	117wb	*.90e	100-11	Mar-Kell117¾Adroit106½Sparkling Maid1021	Saved ground	8
7Feb44- 7Hia	fst 6½f	:232 :471 1:121 1:19 4↑	Alw 3500	5 4 31½ 43 44 45	Thompson B	117wb	*.25e	79-29	Sun Again119½Harvard Square113¾Silvestra1083¾	Evenly	6
27Jan44- 3Hia	fst 7f	:233 :471 1:122 1:254 4↑	ⒻAlw 3000	3 1 1½ 12 13 1½	Thompson B	124wb	*.25	83-24	Mar-Kell124½WisMoss1135FddlrsBt1125	Eased up,urged late	5
22Jan44- 5Hia	fst 7f	:234 :472 1:124 1:26 3↑	ⒻEvening H 5.8k	3 5 52½ 41½ 32 11½	Thompson B	126wb	*1.35	82-20	Mar-Kell1261½Silvestra1121½Pig Tails1101	Impeded turn	7
5Oct43- 6Bel	fst 1½	:483 1:134 2:05 2:314 3↑	ⒻLadies H 16k	3 3 33½ 43½ 46½ 48¾	Thompson B	126wb	*1.35	70-17	Stefanita1161½Vagrancy1236Dark Discovery1061½	No threat	7
18Sep43- 6Aqu	fst 1⅛	:474 1:132 1:383 1:513 3↑	ⒻBeldame H 28k	7 6 74¾ 64 31½ 11	Thompson B	126wb	4.00	89-14	Mar-Kell1261Stefanita1162Vagrancy122½	Driving	11
8Sep43- 6Aqu	sly 1$\frac{1}{16}$	:24 :481 1:132 1:44 3↑	ⒻAlw 5300	1 2 2nk 2nk 2nk 21½	Thompson B	118wb	*.50	92-14	GoodMorning1011½Mar-Kell1182Brttny10110	Bid,drifted out	5
21Aug43- 6Was	fst 1⅛	:474 1:112 1:374 1:51 3↑	ⒻBeverly H 11k	1 5 45 33½ 32¼ 2nk	Smith FA	125wb	*.70	93-11	Askmenow115nkMar-Kell1251¼Burgoo Maid1092½	Wide	8
12Aug43- 6Was	sl 7f	:231 :473 1:131 1:272 3↑	ⒻModesty H 6.2k	2 9 75¾ 56½ 25 2nk	Eads W	125wb	*.90	79-33	Burgoo Maid111nkMar-Kell1256Jerry Lee109nk	Away slowly,wide,just missed	10
31Jly43- 6Was	fst 1¼	:484 1:131 1:374 2:033 3↑	Arlington H 58k	9 7 85¾ 86¼ 78½ 810¼	Eads W	110wb	5.80	82-12	Marriage1201Thumbs Up118noAnticlimax1134	Never a factor	10
10Jly43- 6Was	fst 1	:232 :464 1:123 1:381 3↑	ⒻArl Matron H 12k	7 9 84¾ 85¼ 22 2nk	Eads W	126wb	*.90	87-17	Askmenow109nkMar-Kll1262½Pomayya1181	Getting to winner	10
30Jun43- 6Was	fst 7f	:23 :464 1:113 1:242 3↑	ⒻCinderella H 6.3k	10 8 93½ 51½ 1½ 1½	Eads W	122wb	*.80	94-17	Mar-Kell122½Hometown106¾Askmenow1103	Driving	10
22Jun43- 6Was	gd 1	:241 :474 1:13 1:373 4↑	Alw 2500	2 2 23 2hd 2hd 11½	Smith FA	105wb	*.50e	89-17	Mar-Kell1052½King'sAbbey110¾Whrlwy1221½	Much in reserve	7
3Jun43- 6Bel	fst 1$\frac{1}{16}$	:233 :47 1:12 1:442 3↑	ⒻTop Flight H 6.4k	2 5 54 21 11½ 12	Thompson B	122wb	2.10	89-17	Mar-Kell1222YarrowMaid1102Stefanita1061½	Easing up late	6
29May43- 5Bel	fst 6f-WC	1:104 3↑	Roseben H 6.7k	4 6 63¼ 72¾ 62¼	Eads W	114wb	3.15	90-11	Some Chance105hdMettlesome108½Salto1041½	No mishap	7
14May43- 6Bel	my 1	:232 :47 1:12 1:374 3↑	ⒻAlw 3000	4 4 43½ 22 11 18	Thompson B	110wb	3.35	85-23	Mar-Kell1108Vagrancy1226Opera Singer101nk	Easily	8
10Apr43- 6CD	sl 6f	:234 :473 1:13 3↑	Phoenix H 3.6k	8 1 44½ 43½ 43 21½	Eads W	113wb	*1.40	86-26	MssDogwood1131½Mr-Kll1132ThrClovrs105nk	Driving,no match	8
20Mar43- 4OP	fst 6f	:23 :47 1:12 3↑	Handicap 1500	5 1 36½ 36 3½ 11	Eads W	117wb	*.40	91-17	Mar-Kell1171Chipamink1032Alohort1163	Stumbled start	5
9Mar43- 6FG	fst 6f	:223 :46 1:11 3↑	Mardi Gras H 5k	8 6 74 73¾ 42½ 21¼	Eads W	112wb	3.90	97-16	Riverland1241¼Mar-Kell1121½Signator1202½	Saved ground	8
4Mar43- 6FG	fst 6f	:241 :473 1:121 4↑	ⒻAlw 2500	2 3 2hd 1hd 1hd 1no	Eads W	115wb	*.60	92-12	Mar-Kell115noPig Tails1152½Taunt107¾	Driving	4
22Feb43- 6FG	my 6f	:234 :473 1:13 4↑	Washington's Bday H 5k	8 5 53 42 2½ 1no	Eads W	110wb	*2.20	91-23	Mar-Kell110noPompion1173Marriage115nk	Driving	8
4Feb43- 6FG	fst 6f	:231 :463 1:12 4↑	Alw 1500	5 4 43 42½ 3½ 11½	Eads W	113wb	*1.40e	96-14	Mar-Kell1131½Pig Tails1191½Augury1151¾	Drew away	9
7Nov42- 5Pim	fst 1$\frac{1}{16}$	:234 :473 1:121 1:442 3↑	ⒻHandicap 1300	3 3 21½ 21½ 22 22½	Keiper P	120wb	*1.65	93-13	Star Copy1192½Mar-Kell1203½Night Glow1043½	2nd best	5
29Oct42- 6Pim	fst 1$\frac{1}{16}$	:243 :491 1:124 1:44 3↑	ⒻLady Baltimore H 3.1k	4 4 43½ 43½ 3½ 2nk	Eads W	113wb	3.70	98-12	StarCopy110nkMar-Kell1132NghtGlow1025	Getting to winner	5
23Oct42- 6Lrl	sl 6f	:23 :464 1:132 3↑	Alw 2000	3 6 45 64¾ 55¼ 66¾	Claggett H	103wb	*.65e	80-26	Quien Es115hdJay Jay108½Sassy Lady106.5hd	Saved ground	8
8Oct42- 4Bel	fst 6f	:224 :461 1:11 3↑	ⒻHandicap 2560	7 6 66 55 41½ 21	Woolf G	116wb	2.25e	94-12	Yarrow Maid1121Mar-Kell1164Bostoff1091	Bore in	7
30May42- 7Bel	fst 7f	:232 :463 1:112 1:233 3↑	ⒻHandicap 2525	1 2 1hd 1hd 2hd 31½	Eads W	112wb	3.55	90-07	Fleetborough1071½Level Best122hdⒹMar-Kell1126	Disqualified	6
29Apr42- 5CD	fst 6f	:233 :472 1:124 3↑	Alw 1000	2 4 21 2hd 2½ 1nk	Eads W	109wb	*.70	89-13	Mar-Kell109nkJack Twink1156Sea Tack1112	Impeded str	6
23Apr42- 7Kee	fst 6f	:224 :462 1:122 3↑	Alw 1000	1 5 21 22 23 1no	Eads W	110wb	2.20	90-12	Mar-Kell110noEquator114nkPet109no	Driving	8
20Sep41- 7Bel	fst 6f	:221 :46 1:113	ⒻMatron 20k	15 - - - - -	Eads W	119 w	5.10	- -	Petrify1192Light Lady119noFicklebush110½	Broke from outside stalls,left at post	15
16Aug41- 5Sar	my 6f	:23 :472 1:133	ⒻSpinaway 9.8k	5 4 43½ 33 41½ 11	Eads W	113 w	5.40	84-22	Mar-Kell1131Equipet1131Petrify122½	Driving	8
8Aug41- 6Sar	fst 5½f	:224 :463 1:062	ⒻSchuylerville 6k	1 9 72¾ 75½ 62¾ 22	Roberts P	113 w	*1.65	89-12	RompingHome1132Mr-Kll113½PonyBallt1192	Impeded,gamely	15
6Aug41- 4Sar	fst 5½f	:232 :473 1:063	ⒻMd Sp Wt	2 1 1hd 11 13 16	Roberts P	116 w	4.25	90-13	Mar-Kell1166Waygal1161½Frilled116½	Speed in reserve	14
1Aug41- 4Sar	fst 5½f	:231 :473 1:07	ⒻMd Sp Wt	2 5 21½ 23 33½ 44½	Eads W	116 w	6.60	84-15	Allghny1164Wygl116hdHDddl116nk	Close quarters turn,hung	10
23Jly41- 4AP	sl 5½f	:232 :484 1:014 1:082	Alw 1200	7 7 74¼ 73¼ 76 64¾	Eads W	110 w	10.80	74-23	K. Dorko113¾Emolument1151½Kirwin113½	No threat	7
16Jly41- 4AP	fst 5½f	:231 :471 :593 1:063	ⒻAlw 1200	3 8 77 56 512 511¼	Shelhamer A	113 w	*.90e	77-17	Questvive111noKy. Flash1163Fate116nk	Never a factor	8

Market Wise

b. c. 1938, by Brokers Tip (Black Toney)–On Hand, by On Watch
Own.– Louis Tufano
Br.– Estate of Cary T. Grayson (Va)
Tr.– G.W. Carroll

Lifetime record: 53 19 7 10 $222,140

18Sep43- 6Nar	fst 1$\frac{3}{16}$	:472 1:12 1:372 1:552 3↑	Nar Spl H 32k	9 8 88¼ 85 32¼ 1hd	Longden J	124wb	*3.30	98-15	MarktWise124hdAirMastr1004ThumbsUp1222½	Pulled up lame	9
11Sep43- 6Aqu	fst 1⅛	:48 1:12 1:363 1:492 3↑	Edgemere H 17k	1 5 26 35 33 33½	Longden J	126wb	*2.15	96-11	Apache120½ShutOut1233MarketWise1262	Saved ground,hung	6
10Jly43- 5Jam	fst 1$\frac{3}{16}$	:472 1:12 1:372 1:561 3↑	Butler H 33k	6 9 98½ 99¾ 48 37	Westrope J	127wb	*1.85	99-15	Thumbs Up1163Apache1154Market Wise1271	Belated rally	9
5Jly43- 7Suf	sly 1⅛	:472 1:122 1:383 1:52 3↑	Mass H 58k	3 6 48 46½ 31 11	Nodarse V	126wb	*1.20	81-18	Market Wise1261Salto1031Don Bingo1141½	Driving	6
26Jun43- 6Aqu	fst 1¼	:481 1:132 1:383 2:032 3↑	Brooklyn H 33k	9 7 86 42 31½ 21½	Nodarse V	128wb	3.35	88-12	Devil Diver1231½Market Wise128¾Don Bingo1133	Gamely	9
21Jun43- 6Aqu	fst 1⅛	:483 1:132 1:382 1:51 3↑	Alw 5000	2 3 36 33 21 21½	Nodarse V	123wb	1.70	90-15	Shut Out1221½Market Wise1237Attention114	Bid,hung	3

12Jun43- 6Aqu	fst 7f	:23 :461 1:112 1:24	3↑ Carter H 9.7k	7 9 910 914 92¼ 62¾	Nodarse V	122wb	8.60	92-12	Devil Diver126hdMarriage1181Doublrab118nk	Some gain	10
31May43- 6Bel	fst 1¼	:47 1:111 1:361 2:012	3↑ Suburban H 38k	12 12 155 54¼ 52¼ 22	Eads W	128wb	3.40	91-12	Don Bingo1042[D]Market Wise1282½Attention121hd	Driving	17
	Disqualified for bearing over on rival										
25May43- 6Bel	fst 1⅛	:46 1:10 1:361 1:493	3↑ Handicap 3050	6 6 67½ 65¼ 51 1hd	Grohs O	126wb	5.00	93-14	Market Wise126hdBoysy1121Soldier Song102hd		7
	Between leaders,driving										
15May43- 6Bel	fst 1	:23 :463 1:103 1:363	3↑ Metropolitan H 14k	6 11 1112 1111 1011 78	Nodarse V	126wb	13.85	83-16	Devil Diver1171¼Marriage116¾Thumbs Up1172	Late rush	11
30May42- 6Bel	fst 1¼	:481 1:123 1:371 2:014	3↑ Suburban H 38k	8 7 72 41¼ 11½ 12	James B	124wb	4.20	91-07	Market Wise1242Whirlaway1291½Attention1243	Driving	11
16May42- 6Bel	fst 1	:23 :452 1:103 1:362	3↑ Metropolitan H 14k	3 10 911 97½ 97¼ 31¾	James B	125wb	7.85	91-07	Attention1261½Pictor120nkMarket Wise1251	Fast finish	12
9May42- 5Jam	my 1⅛	:473 1:13 1:39 1:52	3↑ Grey Lag H 18k	5 9 815 85½ 44 23	Zufelt F	125wb	*2.30	85-14	Marriage1093[DH]Market Wise125[DH]Boysy1132	Closed fast	11
7Mar42- 6Hia	fst 1¼	:47 1:122 1:374 2:051	3↑ Widener H 67k	15 16 1512 1314 114¼ 105	Eads W	125wb	2.40	78-17	The Rhymer111hdBest Seller112hdOlympus107nk	Lacked room	17
28Feb42- 5Hia	fst 1⅛	:462 1:112 1:364 1:493	4↑ Sp Wt 2500	4 8 53 31 3½ 11½	Eads W	120wb	3.45	93-14	Market Wise1201½Attention120½War Relic120nk	Ridden out	9
21Feb42- 6Hia	gd 1⅛	:472 1:12 1:38 1:504	3↑ McLennan H 15k	2 11 117¾ 97½ 42½ 1½	Eads W	124wb	4.45e	87-14	Market Wise124½Gramps1141Get Off1161½	Drawing away	15
28Jan42- 6Hia	fst 6½f	:23 :472 1:123 1:192	3↑ Handicap 1600	5 7 714 713 74½ 32½	Eads W	124wb	*2.25	79-21	Zacatine1041½Big Ben1151Market Wise1243	Fast finish	7
	Worked mile in 1:41										
14Jan42- 5Hia	fst 7f	:23 :463 1:113 1:243	4↑ Alw 1500	7 6 611 69 64½ 42¾	Robertson A	117 w	*.85	86-14	Allessandro1141Aboyne109nkLlanero1091½	Outside,gamely	9
13Nov41- 6Pim	fst 1⅝	:48 1:393 2:042 2:431	3↑ Governor Bowie H 12k	8 8 611 35¼ 1nk 11½	Eads W	124wb	*1.30	106-09	MarketWise1241½BestSeller101.51½NelliBly1094	Going away	8
30Oct41- 8Pim	fst 1 3/16	:492 1:14 1:393 1:584	3↑ Pim Spl 10k	1 2 23 23 1hd 1hd	Eads W	120wb	-	89-07	Market Wise120hdHaltal126	Hard drive	2
16Oct41- 5Jam	fst 1⅝	:512 1:424 2:073 2:46	3↑ Gallant Fox H 16k	1 2 32 11½ 14 16	Eads W	119wb	*1.40	85-22	MarktWise1196DarkDiscovr1004ShotPut1222½	Much the best	6
4Oct41- 7Bel	fst 2¼	:483 2:304 2:564 3:47	3↑ New York H 58k	4 1 515 2½ 21 22	James B	118wb	*1.25	107-11	Fenelon1192Market Wise1186Corydon1094	Second best	11
27Sep41- 5Bel	fst 2	:492 2:284 2:55 3:204	3↑ J C Gold Cup 10k	4 3 32½ 32 2hd 1no	James B	114wb	4.45	105-09	Market Wise114noWhirlaway1148Fenelon12512	Hard drive	4
	Geldings not eligible										
20Sep41- 6HdG	fst 1 1/16	:233 :48 1:122 1:454	Potomac H 11k	2 7 56½ 64½ 34 21½	Woolf G	120wb	*1.60	87-18	Boston Man1091½Market Wise1203Cape Cod113½	Closed fast	10
6Sep41- 6Aqu	fst 1⅛	:483 1:123 1:372 1:50	3↑ Edgemere H 11k	4 4 53½ 52 31 11½	Eads W	112wb	5.00	102-07	MarktWise1121½RoyalMan1091½Foxbrough1261¾	Going away	7
1Sep41- 6Aqu	fst 1 1/16	:242 :481 1:122 1:433	3↑ Aqueduct H 11k	5 6 55½ 55½ 42½ 33½	Arcaro E	114wb	3.95	92-12	Ponty1052Foxbrough1261¾Market Wise1142½	Closed well	6
9Aug41- 6Rkm	fst 1⅛	:48 1:122 1:374 1:502	3↑ Rkm Park H 6.2k	2 3 2½ 1nk 1½ 12	Howell R	115wb	*.80	97-16	MrktWise1152WarBeauty1022¾TragicEndng1054½	Going away	5
2Aug41- 6Rkm	fst 1 1/16	:232 :464 1:113 1:44	3↑ Granite State H 6.7k	7 5 54 43½ 3¾ 31¾	Taylor WL	116wb	*2.30	94-14	Tragic Ending102¾CapeCod1091Market Wise1162¾	Weakened	9
16Jly41- 7Suf	fst 1⅛	:463 1:111 1:354 1:483	3↑ Mass H 67k	7 9 74½ 53¾ 44½ 46½	Donoso R	111wb	4.70	94-13	War Relic102¾Foxbrough1223½Royal Man1062½	No mishap	9
4Jly41- 7Suf	fst 1 3/16	:473 1:12 1:38 1:563	Yankee H 31k	9 6 44¾ 52 2hd 21	Donoso R	121wb	*2.30	97-13	OurBoots1221MarktWise1212¾RobertMorris1211¾	Weakened	9
21Jun41- 5Aqu	fst 1¼	:49 1:132 1:383 2:032	Dwyer 11k	2 2 33 32½ 21½ 21¼	James B	122wb	10.60	97-08	Whirlaway1261¼Market Wise1222½Robert Morris11912		4
	Altered course,second best										
17Jun41- 5Aqu	fst 1 1/16	:25 :49 1:132 1:45	3↑ Handicap 2065	4 2 2hd 11½ 11½ 11½	Eads W	115wb	2.80	89-11	Market Wise1151½Choppy Sea110½Devil's Crag109½	Driving	8
23May41- 6Bel	fst 1⅛	:463 1:11 1:362 1:49	Peter Pan H 10k	1 7 79 711 66 511¼	Meade D	119wb	4.95	86-17	RobertMorrs1176BrghtGllnt1105KngCol124hd	Close quarters	7
13May41- 5Bel	fst 7f	:23 :463 1:104 1:242	Alw 2000	2 6 613 67½ 58½ 47½	Meade D	126wb	6.70	80-14	AirBrigade1154SheriffCulkin113½MondyLunch1163	No mishap	6
3May41- 7CD	fst 1¼	:463 1:113 1:372 2:012	Ky Derby 73k	7 5 612 66 53¾ 38¼	Anderson I	126wb	19.10	94-08	Whirlaway1268Staretor126nkMarket Wise1262	Late speed	11
26Apr41- 5Jam	fst 1 1/16	:231 :471 1:123 1:453	Wood Memorial 23k	1 8 76½ 64¾ 31½ 1no	Meade D	120wb	8.30	85-16	MarketWise120noCuriousCoin1201½KingCole1205	Hard drive	9
12Apr41- 4Jam	fst 6f	:232 :47 1:12	Alw 2000	4 4 66½ 56¾ 45¼ 32½	Meade D	113wb	4.00	89-11	Zacatine113hdKansas1132½Market Wise1134	Closed fast	6
5Apr41- 4TrP	gd 6f	:221 :472 1:111	Alw 1000	5 8 89½ 810 87½ 99¾	Eads W	115wb	*2.30	84-14	Silvestra105.51Ponty1154Bad Cold1071	Dull effort	9
20Feb41- 5Hia	fst 7f	:223 :452 1:112 1:242	Alw 1400	5 3 36 24 22 11½	Arcaro E	120wb	*1.55	91-15	Market Wise1201½Blue Lily1061Maepeace1114	Going away	7
13Feb41- 6Hia	gd 1⅛	:472 1:12 1:37 1:503	Alw 1400	5 2 2½ 1½ 15 13	Eads W	113wb	*1.60	88-11	Market Wise1133Jacopus1132Clarksville1082½	In hand	7
1Feb41- 6Hia	fst 7f	:224 :453 1:10 1:222	Bahamas H 7k	6 13 1214 1114 611 513	Anderson I	114wb	13.55	88-09	Dispose1182Curious Coin1105Battle Colors1213	Off slowly	15
17Jan41- 5Hia	my 7f	:231 :463 1:122 1:253	Alw 1400	7 6 54½ 44 33 33½	Eads W	117wb	2.35	81-26	Clarksville113hdBattleColors1113½MrktWs1176	Closed well	7
11Jan41- 6Hia	gd 6f	:23 :462 1:113	Hialeah 6.5k	8 10 119 106 62¼ 31½	Eads W	116wb	6.25	89-18	Zacatine116hdBattleColors1161½MarketWis1165	Closed fast	12
4Jan41- 6TrP	fst 1 70	:23 :471 1:121 1:421	Alw 1000	1 5 51¾ 1½ 13 15	Eads W	111wb	*2.15	98-08	Market Wise1115Version1131Take Wing1114	Going away	10
28Dec40- 4TrP	hy 6f	:23 :471 1:142	Alw 1000	9 1 23 21 14 15	Eads W	116wb	38.80	78-29	Market Wise1165Version1161Ponty116no	Easily	9
20Dec40- 4TrP	fst 6f	:224 :46 1:114	Alw 1000	2 8 89 86¼ 811 89½	Anderson I	114wb	31.95	81-14	Zacatine1141½Isolde1112Cape Cod1171	Outrun	10
25Oct40- 2Emp	fst 1 70	:233 :474 1:133 1:451	Md 1750	8 4 41 22 1nk 11½	Anderson I	114wb	43.55	84-13	Market Wise1141½Kahyrite114¾Port Alibi1144	Going away	13
16Oct40- 1Jam	fst 6f	:231 :47 1:13	©Md 1750	12 10 87¼ 1216 1016 715	Westrope J	114wb	110.15	72-16	Okabbit1181½Rancho's Boy1103¼Dandy Fox1182½	Outrun	14
	Previously owned by Brookmeade Stable;previously trained by H. Fontaine										
19Sep40- 2Aqu	fst 6f	:23 :47 1:121	Md 1500	14 9 116½ 1115 87¾ 1013½	Robertson A	111 w	30.05	82-05	RemoteControl1111GranoSaltis1136CynicMiss1083¼	Outrun	14
13Sep40- 1Aqu	fst 6f	:23 :471 1:14	Md 1500	2 2 96 58 55¼ 64	Robertson A	111 w	61.00	83-09	Battle Won106½Outgo114noCynic Miss108½	No mishap	14
19Aug40- 2Sar	sly 6f	:23 :471 1:13	Clm 2500	16 14 1612 1614 168 1714¼	Robertson A	112 w	*1.30f	73-11	Yankee Party1123½Etruscan112½Family Doc112½	Outrun	18
2Aug40- 4Sar	fst 5½f	:224 :464 1:053	Alw 1200	8 12 1010 109¾ 1112 1312¾	Fels B	112 w	81.45e	82-13	Swing and Sway1163½Neutrality116½Thrift Shop116½	Outrun	13
29Jly40- 2Sar	fst 5½f	:223 :461 1:061	©Md Sp Wt	19 21 2118 2121 2122 2021	Robertson A	117 w	6.80f	71-08	MondyLnch1172Maerunway117½PeepShow1171	Raced greenly	21

Mercator

b. g. 1939, by Annapolis (Man o' War)–Ponova, by Pommern **Lifetime record: 46 11 10 9 $64,957**

Own.– W.H. Lipscomb

Br.– Thomas H. Somerville (Va)

Tr.– W.G. Jones

18Aug49- 3Sar	hy *2 S'Chase	4:292	3↑ Alw 2500	7 1 58½ - - -	Leonard W	146wb	*1.25e	--	Kipper14350Oak Bulger1513Bannock Laddie14415		8
	Tired,bolted off course										
11Jun46- 5Aqu	fst *2½ S'Chase	4:511	4↑ Hitchcock H 11k	3 1 1½ 1nk 32½ 32¼	Leonard W	156wb	*.90	--	Delhi Dan133¾War Battle1391½Mercator15614	Tired	5
4Jun46- 5Bel	fst *2 S'Chase	3:541	4↑ Lion Heart H 9.2k	6 1 14 1hd 21½ 23½	Leonard W	156wb	*1.60	--	Burma Road1523½Mercator1563Floating Isle1492½	Bobbled	8
28May46- 5Bel	hy *2½ S'Chase	4:581	4↑ Meadowbrook H 11k	4 1 110 18 13 13	Leonard W	150wb	2.65	--	Mercator1503Beneksar1347Burma Road1521	In hand	8
22May46- 5Bel	fst *2 S'Chase	3:493	4↑ Corinthian H 9.4k	11 1 11 - - -	Leonard W	154 w	*1.80	--	Burma Road1461Navigate1422War Battle1436	Fell at 8th	12
10May46- 5Bel	fst *2 S'Chase	3:45	4↑ International H 8.6k	5 1 15 11½ 32½ 33½	Leonard W	155wb	*1.65	--	Fleettown1351Annotator1362½Mrctor1557	Bobbled 8th,tired	6
28Nov45- 5Pim	sly 2½ S'Chase	5:252	4↑ Manly H 12k	8 2 23 52½ 515 531	Leonard W	153wb	2.90e	--	PursuitPlane1325BurmaRoad13912GreekFlag1384	Tired badly	10
21Nov45- 5Pim	sl *2 S'Chase	3:544	3↑ Battleship H 12k	5 1 2hd 46 412 518	Leonard W	159wb	*1.25	--	Elkridge146noNavigate1368Cadd1465	Dropped back after 1m	7
14Nov45- 3Pim	fst 2 S'Chase	3:502	3↑ Handicap 5000	6 2 63½ 37 33½ 32¾	Leonard W	160wb	*1.45	--	Cosey130¾Floating Isle1492Mercator1602	Good try	7
6Nov45- 5Bel	fst *3 S'Chase	5:50	4↑ Temple Gwathmey H 15k	1 1 1hd - - -	Leonard W	160wb	*1.05e	--	Caddie1396Refugio1304Floating Isle1493	Fell 12th	8
31Oct45- 5Pim	fst 2 S'Chase	3:501	4↑ J Spencer H (Div 2) 11k	5 1 13 15 13 16	Leonard W	153wb	*1.20	--	Mercator1536Floating Isle1525Lieut. Well1345	Handily	7
17Oct45- 3Lrl	fst *2½ S'Chase	5:001	4↑ Chevy Chase H 8.7k	2 2 12 12 13 16	Leonard W	145wb	*1.75	--	Mercator1456Shotlo1303½Floating Isle15150	Easily	6
12Oct45- 3Lrl	fst *2 S'Chase	3:54	3↑ Butler H 6.4k	4 2 1hd 33 413 421	Leonard W	147wb	*1.35	--	Great Flare1302Floating Isle15115Bill Coffman1334		9
	Bobbled 10th,tired										
3Oct45- 5Bel	fst *3 S'Chase	5:48	4↑ Grand National H 18k	3 1 14 11½ 12 15	Owen W	142wb	2.85e	--	Mercator1425Caddie139¾Raylywn1426	Easily	12
26Sep45- 5Bel	fst *2½ S'Chase	4:484	4↑ Brook H 9.3k	2 2 11 - - -	Leonard W	143wb	*.95e	--	Raylywn1376Rouge Dragon1552Elkridge148no	Fell at 12th	10
11Sep45- 5Aqu	my *2½ S'Chase	4:511	4↑ Glendale H 8.6k	3 1 13 14 2hd 2nk	Leonard W	143wb	2.90	--	FloatingIsle150nkMercator1437SoldrSong1403	Bobbled last	5
4Sep45- 5Aqu	fst *2 S'Chase	3:42	3↑ Harbor Hill H 6k	2 2 110 14 1hd 1½	Leonard W	140wb	3.80	--	Mrctor140½Elkrdg1533FlotngIsl1512½	Bobbled several fences	7
1Sep45- 3Bel	fst *2 S'Chase	3:503	4↑ Alw 3000	3 1 12 16 130 150	Leonard W	152wb	2.45	--	Mercator15250Similar1374Invader137	Speed on flat	5
25Aug45- 3Bel	sl *2 S'Chase	3:542	3↑ Alw 3000	6 1 12 1nk 11 12	Harrison JS	139wb	*1.20	--	Mercator1392Blue Funk1302½Parma1385	Jumped well	9
10Aug45- 3Bel	fst *2 S'Chase	3:491	4↑ Shillelah 6.1k	3 1 32 21½ 33 32	McGovern J	137wb	*1.10e	--	Raylywn1361Rouge Dragon1521Mercator1376	Hung	10
6Aug45- 3Bel	hy *2 S'Chase	4:084	4↑ Alw 3000	14 1 18 1hd 1hd 2hd	McGovern J	137wb	9.10	--	BrothrJons139hdMrctor1373BoojumII149nk	Swerved final ⅛	14
27Jun45- 3Del	fst *2 S'Chase	3:503	4↑ Georgetown H 12k	2 1 11 42 35½ 47	McGovern J	137wb	*1.50e	--	Iron Shot150½Rouge Dragon1596Elkridge159½	Weakened	8

18Jun45- 5Bel fst *2 S'Chase 3:48 4 4↑ Corinthian H 5.7k 5 2 13 1nk 2½ 23 Leonard W 138wb *2.65 - - Floating Isle1423Mercator1387Chesapeake1381 No match 8
12Jun45- 5Bel fst *2 S'Chase 3:49 4↑ CL Appleton 5.7k 6 1 21 3¾ 24 36 Leonard W 139wb 3.10 - - Elkridge158hdFloatingIsl1496Mrctor13910 Bad landing 4th 8
19Aug44- 3Bel fst *2 S'Chase 3:49 3↑ Alw 3000 4 2 - - - - Jennings E 140 w *1.25 - - Gay Venture1382Bill Coffman1474Frederic II1474 Fell 6
11Aug44- 5Bel fst *2 S'Chase 3:48 4↑ Shillelah 5.7k 2 3 11½ 1½ 21 21½ Leonard W 141wb 5.45 - - Elkridge1461½Mercator1417Floating Isle13510 No mishap 7
4Aug44- 3Bel fst *2 S'Chase 3:49 1 4↑ Handicap 3000 8 4 45½ 510 53¾ 54¾ Leonard W 149wb 4.20 - - Elkrdg1541½FrdrcII1401½BurmRod1382 Bad landing 5th,tired 10
28Jun44- 4Del fst *2½ S'Chase 4:50 4 4↑ Indian River H 7.5k 2 3 31½ 58 37½ 39 Harrison JS 141wb 2.90e - - Rouge Dragon1612Caddie1437Mercator14110 Early speed 6
31May44- 5Bel fst *2½ S'Chase 4:52 4↑ Meadow Brook H 7k 1 1 1hd 412 629 644½ Owen W 143wb 7.60 - - Iron Shot1593½Brother Jones1616Knight's Quest1473 6
Bad landing 4th,tired
20May44- 3Bel fst *2 S'Chase 3:49 2 4↑ Alw 2500 1 3 41½ 31½ 22 24 Owen W 150 w *.95 - - Frederic II1544Mercator1501½Simoon1383 Bobbled several 7
10May44- 3Pim fst 2 S'Chase 3:50 2 4↑ Handicap 3000 6 3 21 2½ 21½ 22½ Owen W 157 w *.70 - - Mad Policy1412½Mercator1573Circus13920 Bobbled 6
5May44- 5Pim fst 2 S'Chase 3:51 1 4↑ J Spencer H 12k 1 3 23 21 41 21½ Harrison JS 144 w *1.10e - - Rouge Dragon1571½Mercator144nkCaddie1481½ Gamely 10
20Nov43- 3Mtp fst *2½ S'Chase 5:47 4↑ Noel Laing H 1.4k 7 - - - - - Morlan M 145 w 4.00 - - Iron Shot1544Corrigan155½Bank Note1466 Fell 8
8Nov43- 5Pim my 2½ S'Chase 5:09 3 4↑ Manly H 9.1k 6 1 32¾ 2nk 45½ 315¼ Clements HW 139 w *1.95e - - Iron Shot146nkCaddie13915Mercator1393 No mishap 6
1Nov43- 5Pim fst 2 S'Chase 3:57 1 3↑ Battleship H 6.9k 10 1 1nk 11½ 21 31½ Clements HW 139wb *1.30e - - Knight's Quest1411Invader144½Mercator1392 Driving 10
26Oct43- 5Pim sly 2½ S'Chase 5:18 1 4↑ Chevy Chase H 9.3k 7 2 2hd 21½ 425 423¾ Harrison JS 137 w 3.00 - - Uncle Seaweed137¾Caddie13820Invader1453 Nothing left 7
16Oct43- 3Pim sl 2 S'Chase 4:04 3 3↑ Alw 1500 1 2 22½ 13 112 112 Harrison JS 150 w *1.25 - - Mercator15012Mad Policy14015Parma14620 Driving 5
5Oct43- 3Bel fst *2 S'Chase 3:52 4 3↑ Alw 1800 1 3 32 41¾ 32½ 1hd Harrison JS 144wb *1.80 - - Mercator144hdGreek Flag1484The Beak14620 Driving 5
Previously owned by Mrs W.G. Jones
9Aug43- 3Bel fst *2 S'Chase 3:49 3↑ Sp Wt 1500 2 1 12 11½ 11 11½ Jennings E 147wb *1.50e - - Mercator1471½YankeeChance148nkGrekFlg13720 Drifting out 6
Previously owned by Montpelier
29Jly43- 3Bel gd *2 S'Chase 3:50 4 4↑ Alw 1500 5 1 11½ 32 37 311 Jennings E 147 w 4.40 - - Delhi Dan1538Yankee Chance1483Mercator1472 Tired 6
10Jun43- 3Aqu gd *1½ Hurdles 2:45 3↑ Handicap 1500 12 9 1111 67 813 1028 Owen W 138 w 3.50e - - GuineaClub1364GalleyBoy142½TopMilk143½ Never a factor 12
3Jun43- 3Bel fst *2 S'Chase 4:00 4↑ Alw 1500 2 1 11½ 12 23 24 Harrison JS 139 w 3.60 - - SilverBirch1344Merctor1395Cortsno14720 Bad landing 12th 7
21Nov42- 1Mtp fst *1½ Hurdles 3:03 3 3↑ Alw 500 7 5 2½ 16 110 110 Jennings E 137 w - - - Mercator13710Walloper14315Matsonia1388 Easily 7
12Nov42- 3Bel fst *2 S'Chase 4:09 3↑ OMdClm 1200 6 3 35 - - - Owen W 130 w *.85 - - WoodKing1445Fieldfare1404Ffty-Ffty135150 Lost rider 7th 6
Previously trained by S.L. Burch
5Nov42- 3Bel fst *2 S'Chase 4:03 2 3↑ OClm 1200 4 4 45¾ 2hd 1nk 22 Owen W 130 w 4.20 - - Equirita1422Merctor13010Sfght14015 Bid,bore in,faltered 5
14Jly41- 3Emp fst 5½f :22 3 :46 1 1:06 1 ⒸMd Sp Wt 6 5 57½ 513 611 614½ Schmidl A 116 w 35.80 80-10 Toujour1165Hard Blast116hdYar1163 No mishap 9
Ran under the name Ponap

Mioland

b. c. 1937, by Mio d'Arezzo (Laland)–Iolanda, by Vespasian **Lifetime record: 50 18 10 6 $244,270**

Own.– C.S. Howard
Br.– H.W. Ray (Ore)
Tr.– J.H. Stotler

2Aug43- 6Bel fst 1⅛ :46 4 1:11 2 1:36 4 1:49 4 3↑ Handicap 3080 3 3 21 1½ 1nk 1no Atkinson T 117wb 2.65 92-16 Mioland117noCorydon114nkRoyal Nap1125 Hard pressured 6
Previously trained by T. Smith
14Jly43- 6Jam fst 1⅛ :48 1:13 1:38 3 1:51 3 3↑ Handicap 3550 5 4 47 54¼ 45¼ 33½ Shelhamer A 112wb 8.85 86-15 FirstFiddle1221½Lochinvar1182Mioland112no Belated rally 5
26Jun43- 6Aqu fst 1¼ :48 1 1:13 2 1:38 3 2:03 3 3↑ Brooklyn H 33k 1 2 43 66½ 78¼ 716¼ Atkinson T 112wb 33.80 74-12 Devil Diver1231½Market Wise128¾Don Bingo1133 No mishap 9
14Jun43- 6Aqu fst 1⅛ :48 3 1:13 4 1:39 3 1:52 2 3↑ Handicap 3025 2 4 45½ 45 47 47½ Shelhamer A 117wb 3.40 77-17 Pomayya1122Lochinvr1171½SoldrSong1125 Dropped back,wide 4
31May43- 6Bel fst 1¼ :47 1:11 1 1:36 1 2:01 3 3↑ Suburban H 38k 4 9 168 107 128¾ 1210½ Shelhamer A 119wb 52.75 82-12 DonBingo1042ⒹMarketWis1282½Attnton121hd Never a factor 17
1May43- 6Pim fst 1 3/16 :47 1 1:11 3 1:37 2 1:56 2 3↑ Dixie H 23k 1 4 43½ 56 76¾ 77¼ Wright WD 122wb 8.40 94-13 Riverland123¾Attention123noAnticlimax1134 7
Outrun,unwilling to extend
24Apr43- 5Jam fst 1 1/16 :24 2 :48 1 1:13 1 1:44 2 3↑ Excelsior H 12k 9 9 96¾ 1012 1017 1019¾ Robertson A 121wb 16.75 71-15 Riverland1245Minee-Mo1082½Marriage121no Never a factor 11
27Mar43- 7FG fst 1⅛ :47 2 1:11 4 1:36 4 1:49 3 3↑ American H 10k 4 5 53½ 43½ 21½ 2no Shelhamer A 118wb 3.40e 105-12 Marriage117noMioland1182½Rounders1263 6
Saved ground,getting to winner
13Mar43- 6FG fst 1 1/16 :24 :47 4 1:12 1:44 3↑ Fort Jackson H 5k 2 3 45 43 33 33 Haskell L 119wb 3.00e 96-15 Riverland123noValdina Orphan1253Mioland1194 No excuse 5
27Feb43- 7FG fst 1 1/16 :23 4 :46 2 1:11 2 1:43 4 3↑ New Orleans H 27k 4 9 99¾ 98¼ 910 42¾ Haskell L 120wb 11.20e 99-09 Marriage1151½Rounders124½Moscow II108¾ Fast finish 10
18Feb43- 5FG fst 1 1/16 :25 2 :49 4 1:14 4 1:48 4↑ Alw 1000 2 2 2hd 1hd 1hd 1hd Haskell L 124wb *.30 81-15 ⒹMioland124hdBriton115noPaprboy1106 Bothered rival str 4
Disqualified and placed second
6May42- 6Pim fst 1 3/16 :47 2 1:11 4 1:37 4 1:57 3↑ Dixie H 25k 4 2 67¾ 66¼ 41¼ 31¼ Haas L 126 w 7.95 97-12 Whirlaway128¾Attention124½Mioland126hd Held well 8
25Apr42- 5HdG fst 1 1/16 :24 1 :48 2 1:13 1:45 2 3↑ Philadelphia H 11k 5 5 55 31 1½ 2no Shelhamer A 124wb *1.55 91-21 Challedon122noMolnd1241½CpCod1123 Forced wide,hung late 7
10Apr42- 6TrP fst 1⅛ :47 1:10 4 1:36 1:49 3↑ Tropical H 11k 4 6 31 2½ 2nk 2nk Haas L 129wb *.75e 104-10 Sir Marlboro109nkMioland129½Our Boots1196 Driving 8
21Mar42- 6TrP fst 1⅛ :47 1 1:11 3 1:36 1 1:49 2 3↑ Coral Gables H 8.7k 2 5 31½ 11 14 14 Haas L 125wb *2.25 102-10 Mioland1254Signator1041½Llanero102hd Easily 10
7Mar42- 6Hia fst 1¼ :47 1:12 2 1:37 4 2:05 1 3↑ Widener H 67k 16 8 55½ 31½ 61 83½ Haas L 128wb 6.05e 79-17 The Rhymer111hdBest Seller112hdOlympus107nk Faltered 17
28Feb42- 5Hia fst 1⅛ :46 2 1:11 2 1:36 4 1:49 3 4↑ Sp Wt 2500 2 9 84¾ 62½ 43½ 42¼ Haas L 122 w *2.10e 91-14 Market Wise1201½Attention120½War Relic120nk Forced wide 9
20Feb42- 4Hia sly 1⅛ :47 3 1:12 2 1:38 1:51 1 4↑ Alw 1500 5 3 33 2½ 1½ 11¾ Haas L 124wb 2.35e 85-22 Mioland1241¾Sir Marlboro1123Porter's Cap1221 Drew away 5
26Jly41- 7Hol fst 1⅝ :47 3 1:38 2 2:04 2 2:44 2 3↑ Sunset H 27k 9 3 2½ 13 1hd 2no Haas L 128wb *.60 - - King Torch105noMioland1281Wing and Wing105hd Weakened 9
19Jly41- 7Hol fst 1¼ :46 1:10 4 1:36 1 2:02 3 3↑ Hol Gold Cup 88k 6 5 74¼ 33 34½ 32½ Haas L 130wb *.80e 94-06 BigPbbl119nkPprboy982½Molnd1303½ Strong drive,held well 13
4Jly41- 7Hol fst 1⅛ :46 2 1:10 4 1:36 4 1:49 2 3↑ American H 22k 1 5 54½ 41¼ 11½ 1no Haas L 126wb 5.40 98-09 Mioland126noWoof Woof1141Big Pebble117½ Driving 10
30May41- 6Bel fst 1¼ :47 3 1:12 3 1:37 1 2:02 3 3↑ Suburban H 35k 4 3 52¾ 52½ 2nk 56 Haas L 127wb *1.15 81-16 Your Chance1141¼Hash119nkShot Put1102½ Stopped 9
20May41- 6Bel fst 1 1/16 :23 4 :46 3 1:11 3 1:43 3 3↑ Alw 2500 5 1 23 22 21½ 22½ Haas L 127 w 3.00 91-12 Whirlaway1082½Mioland127nkHash1203 Weakened 5
7May41- 6Pim fst 1 3/16 :48 1 1:12 1 1:38 1 1:58 2 3↑ Dixie H 25k 1 5 42 64 31 2hd Haas L 129wb *.95 91-18 Haltal110hdMioland129¾Dit110no Just missed 10
8Mar41- 6SA fst 1½ :47 1 1:12 1 2:03 2:29 1 3↑ S Juan Capistrano H 61k 16 4 2nk 11 11 13 Haas L 130wb *2.30 106-09 Mioland1303Gen'l Manager1074Barrancosa1063 Easily best 17
1Mar41- 6SA sly 1¼ :47 1:12 1 1:38 3 2:05 2 3↑ S Anita H 124k 11 8 96½ 32½ 21½ 2nk Haas L 124wb *1.00e 79-29 Bay View108nkMioland1244Bolingbroke1062 Just missed 16
22Feb41- 6SA sl 1 1/16 :23 4 :47 3 1:12 1 1:45 2 3↑ San Antonio H 12k 6 6 35 35 34½ 1no Haas L 128wb *1.80 85-23 Mioland128noHysterical1111Bay View1051 Just up 11
8Feb41- 6SA sl 7f :23 :46 3 1:11 3 1:24 2 3↑ San Carlos H 13k 3 6 31½ 33 35 44 Haas L 130wb *.90 86-26 Gen'lManager1104Viscounty116noHysterical118no No mishap 12
11Jan41- 6SA my 1⅛ :47 2 1:12 3 1:38 2 1:51 3 3↑ San Pasqual H 12k 8 8 36 2hd 12 14 Haas L 130wb *1.10 86-22 Mioland1304Gen'lManager1123ValdinaGroom1005 Easily best 9
1Jan41- 6SA hy 1 :23 2 :47 2 1:13 1 1:39 3 3↑ New Year H 12k 4 7 65 3nk 11 1nk Haas L 126wb *1.60 80-31 Mioland126nkGen'l Manager1095Sweepida1192½ Hard drive 8
2Nov40- 5Emp hy 1 3/16 :48 1:13 1:39 3 2:00 1 3↑ Westchester H 22k 1 2 52¾ 35 1nk 1¾ Haas L 119wb *1.05 86-22 Mioland119¾Foxbrough1106Hash1223 Drew out 8
8Oct40- 5Jam fst 1 1/16 :23 4 :47 2 1:12 4 1:45 3 3↑ Handicap 2520 2 5 510 32 1nk 12¾ Arcaro E 126wb *.80 85-13 Mioland1262¾Gen'lManagr1121¼KsrofAudly1074½ Going away 5
26Sep40- 6Bel fst 1 :23 4 :47 4 1:11 3 1:37 1 Jerome H 9k 3 - - - - - Vedder RL 125wb *1.10 - - Roman1212Weigh Anchor112nkTola Rose1164 5
Stumbled after start,lost rider
21Sep40- 5HdG fst 1 1/16 :23 2 :47 2 1:12 2 1:44 4 Potomac H 11k 4 6 51½ 1hd 11½ 14 Bierman C 124wb *.95 94-15 Mioland1244Roncat100¾Guerrilla1081¼ Going away 8
10Aug40- 6Was sly 1¼ :49 3 1:14 3 1:39 4 2:05 4 American Derby 59k 3 3 11½ 11 11 13 Adams J 123wb 6.10 81-29 Mioland1233Sirocco1264Weigh Anchor1183½ Going away 5
20Jly40- 7Hol fst 1¼ :46 2 1:11 2 1:37 4 2:03 3 Hol Derby 27k 2 4 55½ 45 43½ 43¾ Wall N 118wb *1.00 91-08 Big Flash1141¼Weigh Anchor114hdSweepida1222½ No excuse 11
13Jly40- 6Hol fst 1⅛ :46 4 1:11 2 1:38 1 1:51 1 Alw 2500 4 5 46½ 55 3½ 12 Pollard J 126wb *2.10 93-05 Mioland1262Weigh Anchor119¾Woof Woof119½ Going away 7
11May40- 6Pim fst 1 3/16 :47 1:12 1:38 4 1:58 3 Preakness 70k 7 4 79 62¾ 32 23 Balaski L 126wb 9.70 87-15 Bimelech1263Mioland1261½Gallahadion1262 Closed fast 9
4May40- 7CD fst 1¼ :48 1:12 4 1:38 3 2:05 Ky Derby 72k 3 3 53 54¼ 43 42½ Balaski L 126wb 6.40 81-14 Gallahadion1261½Bimelech126noDit1261 No mishap 8
9Mar40- 6SA fst 1 1/16 :22 4 :46 3 1:11 3 1:45 1 S Juan Capistrano H 13k 5 7 76½ 32 22½ 11¼ Adams J 117wb *3.00 86-14 Mioland1171¼Weigh Anchor1152½Sweepida1221 Driving 14
22Feb40- 6SA fst 1⅛ :46 3 1:11 2 1:37 4 1:51 3 S Anita Derby 61k 2 16 1512 99¾ 613½ 42¼ Pollard J 120wb 13.30 84-16 Sweepida1201¼Royal Crusader1201Weigh Anchor120hd 17
Closed strongly

10Feb40- 6SA	fst 1	:222 :462 1:112 1:384	San Vicente H 15k	9 9 86½ 1112 1317 137¼	Adams J	120wb	5.80	77-14	Gallahadion1131Sweepida107hdExarch113½	Outrun 19
	Previously owned by Hawthorn Stable;previously trained by H.C. Fear									
27Jan40- 5SA	fst 1	:223 :461 1:112 1:38	Alw 1500	8 3 2hd 2hd 1hd 12½	Dew E	114wb	10.10	88-12	Mioland1142½Gallahadion1061The Gob108½	Easily best 10
18Jan40- 6SA	fst 6f	:222 :454 1:112	Handicap 2000	5 6 51¼ 55 47 44¾	Dew E	112wb	8.00	87-12	Millfang1081¼Destrer1063½Little Cartago103hd	No mishap 7
1Jan40- 4SA	fst 6f	:221 :454 1:112	Alw 1500	7 1 42 46 55¾ 36	Dew E	112wb	20.00	86-16	Augury108noCamp Verde1166Mioland1124	Closed well 7
28Oct39- 7BM	fst 1	:233 :471 1:12 1:383	Handicap 2000	6 3 31 33 34 1no	Dew E	111wb	12.60e	87-17	Mioland111noBig Ben119¾Sweepida1141	Just up 9
19Oct39- 5BM	fst 6f	:23 :462 1:112	Alw 800	4 3 33 45 36½ 28	Dew E	112wb	*.90e	84-17	Augury1158Mioland1125Wee Toney112¾	Second best 7
10Oct39- 6BM	fst 6f	:23 :464 1:121	Alw 800	8 1 3½ 2hd 1hd 13½	Dew E	114wb	5.40	88-20	Mioland1143½Brother Higher1172Shervill1092	Going away 8
24Aug39- 2Lga	fst 5f	:232 :473 1:00	Md Alw 400	4 3 2½ 1hd 1½ 14	Sena T	116wb	*.50	91-12	Mioland1164Black Haw1032½Lacona1111½	Drew away 8
12Aug39- 4Lga	fst 5f	:231 :471 1:003	Md Alw 500	8 7 44 43½ 32 3hd	Merritt N	113wb	2.40	88-15	HelenI.113noIdaB.110noMiolnd113hd	Greenly,finished fast 9

Miss Request

b. f. 1945, by Requested (Questionnaire)–Throttle Wide, by Flying Heels — **Lifetime record: 56 12 6 5 $202,730**

Own.– Mrs B.F. Whitaker
Br.– B.F. Whitaker (Ky)
Tr.– J.P. Conway

25May50- 7Bel	fst 7f	:23 :461 1:104 1:232	3↑ Handicap 4620	4 13 147 146 1511 1517¾	Guerin E	114wb	18.20	75-07	Navy Chief1141High Trend1131Colosal119½	No factor 15
4Feb50- 6SA	fst 1⅛	:471 1:114 1:372 1:501	4↑ Handicap 5000	7 4 55½ 811 913 919	Brooks S	111wb	12.70	73-14	Safe Arrival116½Top's Boy117noBut Why Not1182½	Tired 9
25Jan50- 7SA	fst 1	:223 :461 1:112 1:373	4↑ Handicap 5000	1 3 67½ 711 711 711	Porch G	113wb	16.05	78-17	Fervent1201¼Knockdown1201¼Autocrat1111½	No factor 8
14Jan50- 7SA	my 1⅛	:472 1:121 1:393 1:524	3↑ ⒻS Margarita H 59k	1 5 55½ 69½ 79 816	Arcaro E	117wb	5.00	63-21	Two Lea1262Gaffery1182½But Why Not1163½	Disliked going 8
5Jan50- 7SA	fst 7f	:224 :46 1:11 1:233	4↑ ⒻHandicap 10000	6 5 53 44½ 65½ 77¼	Porch G	118 w	17.35	84-18	Two Lea122nkGaffery1162Sweet Dream1161½	Tired 10
29Dec49- 7SA	fst 6f	:232 :47 1:111	3↑ ⒻAlw 5000	2 6 55 58½ 69¼ 610	Porch G	119 w	12.10	81-21	Two Lea119hdSweet Dream1161½But Why Not1114	Tired 7
22Oct49- 6Jam	fst 1 1/16	:233 :471 1:121 1:451	3↑ ⒻComely H 29k	5 3 45½ 45 44½ 74¼	Arcaro E	121wb	*1.70	83-17	Lithe1071¼But Why Not1162Gaffery116no	No rally 12
8Oct49- 6Bel	fst 2	:501 2:323 2:573 3:224	3↑ J C Gold Cup 54k	1 4 27 2½ 33 34	Arcaro E	121wb	5.80	86-12	Ponder1172½Flying Missel1241½Miss Request1215	Hung 6
3Oct49- 6Bel	fst 1½	:482 1:131 2:033 2:294	3↑ ⒻLadies H 35k	4 5 53 1½ 11½ 2no	Arcaro E	119wb	3.90	89-14	Gaffery114noMiss Request119nkAdile1151½	Just missed 12
17Sep49- 6Aqu	fst 1⅛	:48 1:124 1:384 1:524	3↑ ⒻBeldame H 72k	14 5 57½ 22 2hd 11	Arcaro E	113 w	6.20	83-17	MissRequest1131DHarmonica1121¼Plunder108hd	Drew clear 18
8Sep49- 6Aqu	sly 1 1/16	:241 :482 1:134 1:463	3↑ ⒻHandicap 4550	4 4 31½ 3½ 2hd 53½	Arcaro E	115 w	*1.35	77-16	Gaffery1162½Loraine108noPail of Water1081	Tired 6
17Aug49- 6Sar	sly 1⅛	:483 1:131 1:392 1:522	3↑ ⒻDiana H 11k	7 2 52¼ 35 44½ 413	Glisson G	115 w	*1.50	75-19	Spats1068Adile115½Gaffery1154	Raced wide,tired 7
9Aug49- 6Sar	fst 1⅛	:482 1:13 1:374 1:502	3↑ Handicap 4070	3 2 21½ 2hd 2hd 2hd	Atkinson T	114 w	6.40	98-11	Stunts120hdMiss Request1141½Arise112no	Game effort 7
16Jly49- 6Jam	fst 1 3/16	:472 1:122 1:372 1:571	3↑ Butler H 58k	3 3 54 52¾ 912 1018	Atkinson T	106 w	15.30	72-14	Conniver112noPalestinian1143Stunts1051	Went wide,quit 10
2Jly49- 6Aqu	fst 1¼	:484 1:13 1:372 2:024	3↑ Brooklyn H 58k	6 4 21 1½ 42½ 95½	Delahoussaye J	108 w	19.15	87-14	Assault122¾Vulcan's Forge129nkFlying Missel117¾	Tired 10
29Jun49- 5Aqu	fst 1 1/16	:244 :49 1:134 1:453	3↑ ⒻHandicap 5025	1 3 32½ 31½ 11 13½	Arcaro E	122 w	*1.45	86-14	Miss Request1223½Quibble1115My Emma115no	Handily 5
18Jun49- 6Del	sly 1 1/16	:241 :483 1:133 1:462	3↑ ⒻNew Castle H 29k	3 2 34 35 35 59	Delahoussaye J	115 w	5.10	72-28	Allie's Pal1143½Paddleduck1194Dobodura1101½	Tired 5
14Jun49- 6Aqu	fst 6f	:231 :472 1:133	3↑ ⒻHandicap 5035	2 3 46½ 33½ 31½ 1½	Atkinson T	120 w	2.55	84-28	Miss Request120½Quibble114hdSweet Dream12614	Driving 4
2Jun49- 6Bel	fst 1	:232 :464 1:121 1:381	3↑ ⒻHandicap 5035	1 1 12 2hd 23 36	Arcaro E	119 w	*1.00	77-16	My Emma1104½Back Talk1061½Miss Request1198	Weakened 5
26May49- 6Bel	fst 1	:231 :463 1:12 1:381	3↑ ⒻHandicap 5060	1 7 65½ 69 56½ 58	Arcaro E	122 w	2.95	75-20	Paddleduck1161½Allie's Pal1164Gay Mood1061½	No factor 7
5May49- 6Jam	fst 1 1/16	:25 :484 1:13 1:444	3↑ ⒻFirenze H 28k	3 5 97¼ 915 916 918	Erickson C	118 w	6.20	71-18	But Why Not1162Allie's Pal111½Conniver1263	Quit 9
1Apr49- 6Jam	fst 6f	:223 :47 1:122	3↑ Paumonok H 21k	4 9 911 77 87¾ 85¾	Scurlock O	116 w	*2.35e	83-20	Rippey1251Energetic1102My Request130¾	No factor 13
12Mar49- 7FG	fst 1 1/16	:233 :47 1:12 1:442	3↑ New Orleans H 29k	10 4 53¼ 67 44 35	Picou C	113 w	*.60e	92-11	My Request1254Isigny1051Miss Request1131	Forced wide 11
5Mar49- 7FG	fst 1⅛	:474 1:12 1:381 1:504	3↑ LeCompte H 11k	3 4 66 812 811 815	Picou C	115 w	*.50e	79-11	DHCaillouRouge105DHMyRequest1236Rabies1151	Done early 8
26Feb49- 7FG	sly 1 1/16	:243 :49 1:17 1:514	3↑ Handicap 3500	3 3 47 813 816 816	Erickson C	120 w	*1.50	44-34	Rabies113hdIsigny1074½Caillou Rouge1062	Quit 9
27Oct48- 6Jam	fst 1 1/16	:242 :48 1:13 1:45	3↑ ⒻComely H 29k	9 4 43¼ 31¼ 1½ 21¼	Atkinson T	120 w	*1.60e	87-25	Conniver1231¼Miss Request1205Carolyn A.1182	Weakened 10
9Oct48- 6Jam	fst 1 3/16	:481 1:121 1:38 1:572	Emp City H 57k	3 3 32½ 21½ 11½ 11	Scurlock O	118 w	3.65	89-14	Miss Request1181Quarter Pole1152Noble Hero1161½	Driving 9
28Sep48- 6Bel	fst 1½	:473 1:122 2:04 2:30	3↑ ⒻLadies H 58k	6 3 21 1nk 12 14	Atkinson T	114 w	7.50	88-14	Miss Request1144Gallorette1211Honeymoon1231	Easily 9
17Sep48- 6Bel	fst 1	:231 :462 1:112 1:364	3↑ ⒻHandicap 10090	5 1 11 1nk 11½ 12	Atkinson T	109 w	*3.45e	90-18	Miss Request1092Inheritance1084Carolyn A.1133	Easily 9
25Aug48- 6Sar	fst 1¼	:481 1:13 1:39 2:06	ⒻAlabama 24k	3 2 46½ 33 4¾ 43¼	Arcaro E	122 w	6.85	75-19	Compliance112nkAlablue1083Play Tag108hd	Hung 11
6Aug48- 6Sar	sly 7f	:232 :471 1:122 1:254	ⒻTest 9.2k	4 7 63 87½ 97 914	LeBlanc C	124 w	9.95	73-23	Alablue1144Paddleduck1111½Mackinaw121hd	Outrun 9
5Jly48- 5Del	fst 1⅛	:484 1:123 1:372 1:502	ⒻDel Oaks 27k	4 1 11 1hd 1hd 1½	LeBlanc C	113 w	10.15	97-06	Miss Request113½Mackinaw1191½Scattered119hd	Driving 6
26Jun48- 5Aqu	fst 1 1/16	:243 :48 1:124 1:46	Handicap 5545	5 2 3¾ 33 31¾ 22½	LeBlanc C	111 w	7.00	81-18	ThreeRings1112½MissRequest1111SafeArrvl1223	Closed fast 6
11Jun48- 6Bel	fst 1 1/16	:23 :46 1:113 1:443	Handicap 5550	6 4 45½ 46½ 34 55¾	LeBlanc C	116 w	*2.30	82-18	Lucky Devil1103The Dervish1191½Ghost Run1131	Tired 7
27May48- 4Bel	gd 1	:231 :461 1:12 1:383	ⒻAlw 5000	6 3 3½ 3½ 1nk 12½	LeBlanc C	114 w	*2.25	81-24	Miss Request1142½White Lady1134Beausy1111	Going away 9
18May48- 5Bel	sly 7f	:23 :472 1:13 1:262	ⒻAlw 6000	10 5 67 77¾ 79 88½	LeBlanc C	110 w	11.75	69-22	Alablue111nkSweet Dream1131½Mackinaw1171	Outrun 11
10May48- 5Jam	fst 1 1/16	:24 :48 1:13 1:47	ⒻAlw 6000	3 3 35½ 33½ 21 31¼	LeBlanc C	111 w	14.70	77-20	Compliance1101¼Scattered110hdMiss Request1112	No mishap 8
28Apr48- 5Jam	fst 6f	:23 :463 1:132	ⒻPrioress 24k	5 7 86¼ 95¼ 87 86	Scurlock O	112 w	38.85	78-19	Itsabet116½Picnic Lunch1162Alablue113½	No factor 14
10Apr48- 3Jam	fst 6f	:232 :472 1:133	ⒻAlw 4500	8 7 52 2hd 1hd 1hd	LeBlanc C	117 w	11.70	83-22	Miss Request117hdAlablue1134Past Eight1131½	Hard drive 9
1Apr48- 4Jam	sly 5½f	:232 :482 1:061	Alw 4500	5 4 33 21½ 1nk 32½	LeBlanc C	117 w	7.40	84-18	Mr. Ace1221Jimikin1221½Miss Request1172	Tired 6
4Mar48- 6FG	hy 6f	:24 :483 1:154	ⒻAlw 1600	6 1 22½ 22½ 2½ 11¼	LeBlanc C	116 w	*.50	74-37	Miss Request1161¼Osculation1132Run Sally1065	Going away 7
20Feb48- 5FG	fst 6f	:23 :46 1:113	Alw 1500	1 4 56 57 59 611	Moon F	114 w	7.10	84-14	Monte's Ace1163Back Talk114¾Riverlane1192	Outrun 8
14Feb48- 5FG	hy 6f	:243 :492 1:162	Alw 1800	6 1 56½ 31½ 21½ 22½	Guerin E	115 w	4.90	68-47	Shy Guy1222½Miss Request115½Dad1191¾	Went well 6
22Jan48- 6FG	hy 6f	:24 :504 1:172	ⒻAlw 1400	5 2 21 2½ 13 16	Guerin E	115 w	3.80	66-48	Miss Request1156Queen Hairan1182Beaukiss1085	Easily 9
10Jan48- 4FG	gd 6f	:223 :463 1:121	Alw 1600	7 6 64 67¾ 64½ 67¼	Guerin E	114wb	26.90	85-17	Cotton Joe1142½Safety First119nkEternal Bomb1192	Outrun 7
6Nov47- 5Jam	sly 6f	:232 :47 1:13	ⒻAlw 4000	5 8 67 64 74½ 58	Wilson HB	116wb	20.05	78-19	Vashti1162½Wicki Wicki1161Sweet Dream1164	No mishaps 9
27Oct47- 4Jam	fst 6f	:23 :463 1:121	ⒻAlw 4000	7 7 52¾ 43½ 65 46¼	Wilson HB	114 w	24.65	84-16	Past Eight1141Vashti1145Wicki Wicki114nk	No mishap 12
15Oct47- 3Jam	fst 6f	:23 :47 1:124	ⒻAlw 4000	7 4 53 54 56¾ 58	Scurlock O	116 w	10.40	79-17	SlumberSong1093PastEight116hdSweetDream1163	No mishap 8
2Oct47- 4Bel	fst 6f-WC	:23 :462 1:12	ⒻAlw 4000	7 3 4½ 62¾ 65¾	Scurlock O	114 w	19.45	75-19	Watermill119½Cunning Miss1141¼Supply Line114½	Tired 9
26Sep47- 5Bel	fst 6f-WC	:224 :453 1:102	Alw 4000	10 19 188¾ 2212 2215½	Arcaro E	114 w	14.70	73-17	Final Touch1171¼Salmagundi111½Frankly1172	Outrun 24
20Sep47- 1Aqu	fst 5½f	:233 :473 :592 1:062	Alw 4000	7 8 41¼ 2½ 2hd 2½	Scurlock O	114 w	6.80	91-12	King'sBowl117½MissRequest1141John'sDate117no	Weakened 8
12Sep47- 4Aqu	fst 5½f	:232 :472 1:001 1:07	ⒻMd Sp Wt	12 5 3½ 1nk 1nk 1hd	Scurlock O	116 w	8.90	89-18	Miss Request116hdNo Fiddling1163Heath Fire1162	Driving 12
12Aug47- 5Sar	fst 5½f	:221 :46 :583 1:063	ⒻMd Sp Wt	2 2 22 24 23 97½	Adams J	115 w	24.05	76-13	Dusty Legs1151Vaudeville1151½Bluehaze1151	Faltered 17
4Aug47- 1Sar	fst 5½f	:223 :462 :593 1:053	ⒻMd Sp Wt	9 3 2nk 22 44¾ 48	Arcaro E	115 w	*2.40	81-08	Inheritance1153½Obedient1152Golden Apple1082½	Stopped 12
22Jly47- 3Jam	sly 5½f	:23 :471 :594 1:064	ⒻMd Sp Wt	12 11 62¾ 67 66¼ 610¾	Arcaro E	115 w	9.30	73-21	One Bell1154In Love115¾Crimson Flash1151½	Slow start 12
16Jly47- 4Jam	sly 5½f	:232 :471 1:071	ⒻMd Sp Wt	3 3 2nk 23 57 67¼	Arcaro E	115 w	4.15	75-16	Hirta1151Sun Tavy1153Swing Trot115hd	Early speed 12

Myrtle Charm

b. f. 1946, by Alsab (Good Goods)–Crepe Myrtle, by Equipoise — **Lifetime record: 8 5 1 0 $81,830**

Own.– Maine Chance Farm
Br.– Brownell & Leslie Combs II (Ky)
Tr.– T. Smith

26Jly50- 6AP	fst 1	:23 :454 1:093 1:344	3↑ ⒻArl Matron H 22k	6 2 11 1½ 35½ 815¾	Lasswell G	124 w	*.80	82-10	Lithe1084Wistful118¾Evanstep1073½	Gave way badly 10
1Jly50- 7AP	fst 6f	:222 :444 1:10	3↑ ⒻModesty 21k	5 5 1hd 12 15 16	Lasswell G	121 w	*.70	96-09	Myrtle Charm1216Alsab's Day121hdFamous Shake102½	Easily 6
24May50- 6Bel	fst 6f-WC	:222 :444 1:09	3↑ Roseben H 12k	4 3 41¾ 4¾ 51½ 51¾	Lasswell G	121 w	*1.25	94-07	Olympia130nkWine List1101Royal Governor122hd	No excuse 9
8May50- 5Bel	fst 6f	:223 :46 1:112	4↑ Alw 4000	8 2 12 13 14 16½	Lasswell G	108 w	*1.40	93-17	Myrtle Charm1086½Magic Words115¾Energetic1105	Easily 8
	Previously trained by J.W. Smith									

25Sep48- 5Bel fst 6½f-W :22 :441 1:081 1:143 Futurity 113k 8 3 4¾ 32 2½ Atkinson T 123 w *.75 98-03 BluePeter126½MyrtleCharm1237SportPage118½ Good effort 12
Geldings not eligible
18Sep48- 5Bel fst 6f-WC :222 :453 1:103 ⒻMatron 49k 6 1 11½ 13 13½ Atkinson T 119 w *.45 88-13 Myrtle Charm1193½Stole1152Lithe1152 Easily 14
17Aug48- 6Sar fst 6f :224 :454 1:113 ⒻSpinaway 20k 12 4 3nk 12 15 112 Skoronski A 111 w *1.50 90-14 Myrtle Charm11112Lady Dorimar1111½Gaffery1152 Easily 12
9Aug48- 3Was fst 5½f :23 :453 :581 1:044 ⒻMd Sp Wt 1 3 13 13 15 18 Skoronski A 119 w *1.70 96-19 Myrtle Charm1198Modernistic1194Patmigirl1196 Easily 12

Our Boots

dk. b. c. 1938, by Bull Dog (Teddy)–Maid of Arches, by Wardenofthemarches **Lifetime record: 32 9 3 7 $126,152**

Own.– Woodvale Farm
Br.– Coldstream Stud (Ky)
Tr.– S. Judge

16Jun43- 8Aqu fst 1⅛ :473 1:131 1:392 1:521 4↑ Handicap 3085 5 4 410 57¾ 33½ 1no McCreary C 122 w *1.20 86-13 OurBoots122noPlantagent1104Wllr1097 Up in final strides 6
31May43- 6Bel fst 1¼ :47 1:111 1:361 2:012 3↑ Suburban H 38k 17 7 41¼ 138½ 138¾ 1314½ Young S 110 w 35.15 78-12 Don Bingo1042[D]Market Wise1282½Attention121hd Tired 17
22May43- 7Bel my 1 1/16 :23 :472 1:122 1:443 3↑ Handicap 3585 7 6 611 65½ 31¼ 11 McCreary C 122 w *2.25 88-21 Our Boots1221Copperman1093Wait a Bit1134 Driving 7
17May43- 6Bel fst 7f :23 :461 1:11 1:241 4↑ Handicap 2110 8 9 95¾ 97 76 31¾ Bierman C 119 w 11.40 87-16 Bright Willie1261Dandy Fox106¾Our Boots119no 12
Bore out far turn,finished well
8May43- 5Jam fst 1⅛ :472 1:121 1:374 1:503 3↑ Grey Lag H 19k 2 8 912 913 813 814 Lindberg H 110 w 25.30 81-12 Boysy114nkAhamo106nkTolaRose1124 Shuffled back 1st turn 11
23Sep42- 6Bel fst 1 1/16 :232 :461 1:104 1:423 3↑ Handicap 2530 2 4 47 44 53 2no Bierman C 122 w *1.80 98-09 Staretor110noOurBoots1221½Paperboy102¾ Outside,driving 6
12Sep42- 6Aqu fst 1⅛ :472 1:113 1:37 1:493 3↑ Edgemere H 11k 1 2 36 42½ 41½ 32 Bierman C 116 w 7.10 97-08 The Rhymer114½Pictor1171½Our Boots116no Driving 6
20Aug42- 5Sar fst 6f :23 :463 1:114 3↑ Alw 1500 1 2 11 1hd 33 34½ Arcaro E 117 w 11.15 88-15 Mettlesome1131½Fairaris1143Our Boots117nk Saved ground 5
30May42- 6Bel fst 1¼ :481 1:123 1:371 2:014 3↑ Suburban H 38k 11 2 2hd 2hd 67½ 812 Wright WD 114 w 34.25 79-07 Market Wise1242Whirlaway1291½Attention1243 Pace,tired 11
22May42- 6Bel fst 6f :222 :454 1:104 3↑ Handicap 2545 1 3 68¼ 68½ 66¼ 54½ Wright WD 121wb 15.55 91-09 Ocean Blue116hdBay View1093Parasing118no Good finish 6
9May42- 5Jam my 1⅛ :473 1:13 1:39 1:52 3↑ Grey Lag H 18k 10 6 614 75¼ 88¼ 917 Robertson A 118 w 7.70 71-14 Marriage1093[DH]Market Wise125[DH]Boysy1132 Outrun 11
10Apr42- 6TrP fst 1⅛ :47 1:104 1:36 1:49 3↑ Tropical H 11k 2 4 52¾ 32½ 3¾ 3¾ Wright WD 119 w 3.60 103-10 Sir Marlboro109nkMioland129½Our Boots1196 Saved ground 8
27Mar42- 6TrP fst 1 70 :231 :464 1:111 1:423 4↑ Alw 1200 1 4 1hd 11½ 13 13 Wright WD 120 w *.70 93-14 Our Boots1203Sir Marlboro1153½Porter's Cap1204 Handily 5
21Mar42- 6TrP fst 1⅛ :471 1:113 1:361 1:492 3↑ Coral Gables H 8.7k 6 10 63 54 66½ 45½ McCreary C 120 w 2.75 96-10 Mioland1254Signator1041½Llanero102hd Away slowly 10
7Mar42- 6Hia fst 1¼ :47 1:122 1:374 2:051 3↑ Widener H 67k 2 3 98¾ 94¾ 92¾ 4½ McCreary C 121 w 12.75 82-17 TheRhymer111hdBestSeller112hdOlympus107nk Strong finish 17
21Feb42- 6Hia gd 1⅛ :472 1:12 1:38 1:504 3↑ McLennan H 15k 6 5 85¾ 87 86¾ 43 McCreary C 121 w 10.75 84-14 Market Wise124½Gramps1141Get Off1161½ Went wide 15
7Feb42- 7Hia fst 7f :231 :463 1:113 1:24 4↑ Alw 1500 3 7 714 615 510 49¼ McCreary C 122 w 11.75 83-13 SheriffCulkin1052Challedon1241¼WarRelic1226 Off slowly 7
1Nov41- 5Emp sly 1 3/16 :474 1:124 1:393 1:594 3↑ Westchester H 28k 4 7 47 32½ 34¼ 43½ McCreary C 115 w *2.05 84-18 Gramps1051¾Tola Rose107nkBoysy1131½ Impeded 8
25Oct41- 4Emp fst 5¾f :224 :461 1:074 2↑ Handicap 2530 3 5 65½ 68 56 45½ McCreary C 126 w *1.95 92-08 NightEditor1121½DailyDelvry1122½FrstFddl1021½ No excuse 6
26Jly41- 6AP fst 1¼ :491 1:132 1:372 2:024 Classic 57k 6 2 11½ 33 69¾ 616 Robertson A 126 w 4.40 76-17 Attention1211½Whirlaway1266Bushwhacker1213½ Tired 6
12Jly41- 5Emp fst 1⅛ :483 1:122 1:372 1:50 Emp City H 12k 2 2 2½ 2nk 2½ 2hd Donoso R 124 w *.55 105-05 SwingandSway114hdOurBoots1245Omission1173 Just missed 8
4Jly41- 7Suf fst 1 3/16 :473 1:12 1:38 1:563 Yankee H 31k 1 1 75¾ 74 3nk 11 McCreary C 122 w 3.60 98-13 OurBoots1221MarketWise1212¾RobertMorris1211¾ Drew out 9
10May41- 6Pim gd 1 3/16 :472 1:123 1:391 1:584 Preakness 66k 8 6 41½ 51¼ 36½ 37½ McCreary C 126 w 3.85 81-12 Whirlaway1265½King Cole1262Our Boots126nk Closed well 8
3May41- 7CD fst 1¼ :463 1:113 1:372 2:012 Ky Derby 73k 10 9 47 79 89½ 814¼ McCreary C 126 w 3.90 88-08 Whirlaway1268Staretor126nkMarket Wise1262 No mishap 11
24Apr41- 6Kee my 1⅛ :474 1:12 1:38 1:511 Blue Grass 15k 4 1 2hd 2hd 12 16 McCreary C 123 w 1.60 91-20 Our Boots1236Whirlaway12315Valdina Paul1213 Ridden out 4
19Apr41- 5Kee fst 6f :23 :462 1:121 Alw 1200 2 4 46½ 45½ 32 11 McCreary C 122 w *.70 91-19 Our Boots1221Smacked1133My Bill1131 Drew out 5
2Nov40- 6Pim hy 1 1/16 :233 :48 1:142 1:494 Pim Futurity 38k 1 2 32½ 31 2hd 2no Bierman C 119 w 4.75 71-33 Bold Irishman122noOur Boots1195Whirlaway1221½ Game try 8
Geldings not eligible
19Oct40- 6Kee fst 6f :223 :454 1:111 Breeders' Futurity 12k 2 2 21 31 41¼ 31 Westrope J 122 w *1.40 95-13 Whirlaway1221BluePair119noOurBoots122hd Close quarters 5
28Sep40- 7Bel fst 6½f-WC 1:153 Futurity 81k 3 3 73¼ 65½ 4¾ 11¾ Arcaro E 119 w 6.10 95-05 Our Boots1191¾King Cole1221½Whirlaway1262½ Going away 14
Geldings not eligible
24Sep40- 6Bel fst 6f-WC 1:103 Alw 1500 2 3 21 52¾ 11 13½ Bierman C 111 w 14.45 94-06 Our Boots1113½Springwood111hdNew World1201 Going away 10
Previously trained by C. Porter
23Jly40- 4AP fst 5½f :231 :462 :584 1:051 ⒸAlw 1000 2 3 33½ 32½ 42 31½ Arcaro E 116 w *1.20 93-15 Swell Chance116nkSwain1111½Our Boots1161 No excuse 7
12Jun40- 4Aqu fst 5f :223 :462 :594 ⒸMd Sp Wt 5 3 2hd 12 12 14 Anderson I 117 w 2.40 - - Our Boots1174Good Turn1171½Poppadeets1171¾ Going away 10

Painted Veil

b. f. 1938, by Blue Larkspur (Black Servant)–Killashandra, by Ambassador IV **Lifetime record: 34 11 6 8 $39,205**

Own.– L.B. Mayer
Br.– L. Combs, Trustee (Ky)
Tr.– G. Philpot

15Jly42- 6AP sly 1 :232 :471 1:122 1:382 3↑ ⒻArl Matron H 13k 11 5 77½ 812 813 813¼ Balaski L 122 w *3.30 67-27 Blue Delight1103Emolument102¾Inscolassie1053 13
Broke down after race
30May42- 6Bel fst 1¼ :481 1:123 1:371 2:014 3↑ Suburban H 38k 2 9 51½ 54¼ 77½ 79 Bierman C 112 w 24.55 82-07 Market Wise1242Whirlaway1291½Attention1243 Outrun 11
25May42- 6Bel fst 1 :234 :472 1:121 1:37 3↑ ⒻHandicap 3070 7 7 85¾ 85½ 51¼ 2hd Westrope J 122 w *1.35e 90-12 War Hazard118hdPainted Veil122¾Rosetown119½ Just missed 11
15May42- 6Bel fst 1 :231 :461 1:12 1:383 3↑ ⒻAlw 3000 7 6 56 55 2hd 12 Westrope J 120 w *1.55e 82-13 Painted Veil1202Pomayya120hdChallomine1092 Going away 12
5May42- 5Jam fst 1 1/16 :25 :491 1:134 1:443 3↑ ⒻHandicap 3020 3 2 23 23 21 1½ Westrope J 121 w *.75 90-14 Painted Veil121½Pomayya1226Loveday1123 Driving 5
28Apr42- 4Jam fst 6f :231 :47 1:122 3↑ ⒻHandicap 2525 4 4 43 42½ 41¾ 1hd Westrope J 116 w 2.80 90-12 PaintedVeil116hdAugury1262½Fleetborough104hd Hard drive 4
17Apr42- 5Jam fst 6f :231 :464 1:114 3↑ ⒻHandicap 2045 8 6 54½ 42½ 33½ 33¼ Westrope J 115 w 7.60 90-14 Augury1223Sun Ginger108nkPainted Veil1152 Good effort 9
19Jly41- 5Hol fst 1 :232 :471 1:12 1:37 Salopian H 5k 1 3 34½ 32 22½ 21¼ Westrope J 116 w *.90 95-06 BuckhornCreek1161¼PaintdVeil1165VanGrov1173½ No excuse 5
12Jly41- 7Hol fst 1¼ :462 1:112 1:364 2:031 Hol Derby 28k 2 3 55½ 62¼ 63¾ 62¼ Westrope J 113 w 5.40 92-07 Staretor1151Porter's Cap122nkPaperboy114no No mishap 8
28Jun41- 7Hol fst 1 1/16 :23 :464 1:112 1:432 3↑ ⒻVanity H 10k 4 4 46 34 3nk 1¾ Westrope J 113 w 3.00e 98-03 Painted Veil113¾Cute Trick1141African Queen109¾ Driving 7
14Jun41- 7Hol fst 7f :222 :452 1:103 1:232 3↑ ⒻSequoia H 10k 5 4 51½ 31 1hd 12½ Westrope J 110 w 1.80e 98-08 Painted Veil1102½Augury1241Omelet1145 Handily 7
31May41- 7Hol fst 7f :224 :454 1:103 1:233 Will Rogers H 11k 6 2 31 43½ 46½ 31½ Westrope J 114 w 4.60 95-07 BattleColors1241½StrongArm113hdPaintdVl1141 Good effort 9
24May41- 4Hol fst 6f :224 :46 1:104 Handicap 2500 1 2 21½ 33 39 35¼ Westrope J 116 w 2.80 92-10 StrongArm111nkBattleColors1225PaintedVl1164 Closed well 8
Previously trained by C. Van Dusen
10Mar41- 6SA fst 1 1/16 :23 :464 1:114 1:443 Allied Charities H 13k 4 3 32 1½ 2hd 1hd Wall N 106 w 7.20 89-14 Painted Veil106hdStaretor1146Valdina Groom1143 10
Strong handling,gamely
4Mar41- 7SA sly 1 :233 :474 1:134 1:403 Alw 1510 1 2 21 11 2½ 21 Wall N 109 w *1.70 74-24 BuckhornCreek1141PaintedVeil1093KantrRun108nk Held well 6
28Feb41- 6SA sly 1 1/16 :234 :481 1:131 1:464 Alw 2510 4 2 1hd 33 35½ 21 Wall N 103 w 4.40 77-19 Staretor1081PaintedVeil103¾ValdinaGroom112¾ Closed fast 6
22Feb41- 5SA sl 6f :223 :464 1:132 Handicap 2510 5 5 36 34½ 34 2hd Neves R 107 w 4.70e 82-23 Madigama118hdPaintedVeil107¾Trnsnt109hd Closed strongly 10
18Feb41- 6SA sl 7f :232 :472 1:14 1:271 Alw 1510 1 2 1hd 1½ 1hd 31 Neves R 109 w 10.60 75-26 ValdinaGroom114¾KantarRun108nkPaintedVeil1096 Held well 6
23Jan41- 5SA gd 6f :224 :464 1:12 Handicap 2500 4 4 23 44½ 45½ 35¼ Wall N 104 w 11.50 84-17 GoodTurn1185CuteTrick113nkPaintedVeil104hd Closed well 5
23Nov40- 7BM fst 1 1/16 :233 :474 1:122 1:453 Salinas H 5.6k 3 2 43½ 59½ 611 58½ Neves R 115 w *.70e 73-20 Rackatack1091¼Isometric1067Beret Basque106nk No excuse 9
14Nov40- 5BM fst 6f :224 :463 1:122 Alw 900 5 3 21½ 21 2½ 13½ Rodriguez E 111 w *.30e 87-19 Painted Veil1113½Wild Oats1121Singida106hd Easily best 7
19Oct40- 7BM fst 6f :224 :462 1:111 Marvelous Marin H 2.2k 2 6 21 31 21½ 25 Neves R 114 w *2.00e 88-17 Appeasement1165Painted Veil1141Ira Pan116hd Second best 8
3Aug40- 4Hol fst 6f :23 :462 1:12 Alw 5000 5 7 62¼ 42½ 55¼ 34 Rodriguez E 115 w 19.30 90-06 LadyBos'n1152½LegendCall1141½PaintedVl115hd Closed fast 7
22Jly40- 4Hol fst 5½f :231 :47 :591 1:054 Alw 1200 6 6 53¾ 53¼ 56 48 Rodriguez E 112 w 4.20 92-09 Strong Arm1181½Over Drive1124½Labeled Win1122 Outrun 7
13Jly40- 3Hol fst 6f :23 :463 1:121 ⒻAlw 1500 3 4 21 21½ 22½ 45 Rodriguez E 115 w *.90 88-05 LadyBos'n1114½PersianHeels108½GoldenChance109no Tired 6
6Jly40- 7Hol fst 6f :224 :454 1:113 Starlet 11k 2 13 106 55½ 68¾ 710 Rodriguez E 115 w 7.00 86-10 FlyingChoice1157LadyBos'n115noTinPanAlley122½ Outrun 16
14Jun40- 5Hol fst 5½f :23 :464 :593 1:06 ⒻAlw 1200 4 2 24 22 21 14 Rodriguez E 114 w *1.50 99-12 Painted Veil1144Tex Hygro1112Rio Macaw1143½ Easily 6
2May40- 6Tan fst 5f :23 :47 1:00 Alw 1000 4 1 2hd 1hd 1½ 11 Merritt N 108 w *1.30e 95-14 PaintedVeil1081LongHouse108hdIraPan111hd Drawing away 7

13Apr40- 6Tan	fst 5f	:232 :481 1:012	A B Spreckels H 3k	10 9 82 55 45 43½	Rodriguez E	110 w	*1.20e	84-16	Rackatack1101Ira Pan112hdStrong Arm1142½	Wide	13
30Mar40- 5Tan	my 4½f	:233 :482 :55	ⒻTan Debutante 2.9k	5 7 78 79½ 3nk	Longden J	113 w	3.90e	91-09	Rackatack107hdDollBaby112hdPantdVl1136	Finished fastest	12
	Previously trained by S. Judge										
28Feb40- 5Hia	fst 3f	:22 :331	Hia Juv Champ 3.5k	5 3 51½ 42	Donoso R	116	3.80	--	Maemante1141½Double Call117noRed Mantilla119½		9
	Traffic,finished fast										
22Feb40- 3Hia	fst 3f	:221 :331	Dinner (Div 1) 1.5k	10 5 33½ 3¾	Donoso R	119 w	3.90	--	Rock Wren116nkDouble Call114½Painted Veil1193	Held well	16
6Feb40- 1Hia	fst 3f	:221 :341	ⒻAlw 800	1 2 2½ 1hd	Donoso R	119 w	1.80	--	PaintdVeil119hdMaegay1221Maemante119½	Impeded,swerved	9
31Jan40- 1Hia	fst 3f	:221 :332	ⒻMd Sp Wt	8 4 3½ 11¼	Donoso R	117 w	16.10	--	Painted Veil1171¼Puro Oro1171½Belmar Arra1171½	Driving	14

Pavot

br. c. 1942, by Case Ace (Teddy)–Coquelicot, by Man o' War **Lifetime record: 32 14 6 2 $373,365**

Own.– Walter M. Jeffords
Br.– Walter M. Jeffords Sr (Ky)
Tr.– O. White

10May47- 6Bel	fst 1	:23 :464 1:112 1:372 3↑	Metropolitan H 30k	4 4 42 44½ 33½ 53¾	Adams J	124 w	3.50	83-15	Stymie1241Brown Mogul1131Gallorette1161½	No mishap	12
24Apr47- 5HdG	fst 6f	:222 :46 1:102 3↑	Alw 5000	4 7 64¼ 45 31½ 24	Snider A	128 w	*.70	96-15	Air Patrol1204Pavot1281Alexis116no	Close quarters	7
26Oct46- 5Jam	fst 1⅝	:462 1:373 2:03 2:424 3↑	Gallant Fox H 85k	2 2 47½ 44 511 618½	Arcaro E	125 w	7.25	82-11	Stymie1262½Rico Monte1162Assault1148	Tired	11
5Oct46- 6Bel	fst 2	:491 2:302 2:543 3:223 3↑	J C Gold Cup 27k	3 1 21 2½ 11 15	Arcaro E	124 w	3.40	91-12	Pavot1245Stymie1245Rico Monte12450	Easily	4
	Geldings not eligible										
25Sep46- 6Bel	fst 1½	:493 1:143 2:032 2:292 3↑	Manhattan H 28k	4 2 2nk 11 2½ 2¾	Arcaro E	121 w	3.20	90-13	Stymie126¾Pavot1213[DH]Flareback1131	Good effort	8
14Sep46- 6Nar	fst 1 3/16	:46 1:102 1:36 1:543 3↑	Nar Spl 38k	3 1 34 33½ 33½ 23½	Arcaro E	123 w	7.30	98-16	Lucky Draw1233½Pavot123nkArmed1305	Went well	4
24Aug46- 6Sar	fst 1¼	:46 1:101 1:362 2:013 3↑	Saratoga H 33k	1 1 38 37 45½ 411¾	Kirkland A	126 w	4.15	89-02	Lucky Draw121¾Polynesian1134Stymie1257	Weakened	5
5Aug46- 6Sar	fst 1	:23 :461 1:111 1:363 3↑	Wilson 24k	10 4 33 31¾ 21 1nk	Kirkland A	126 w	8.70	98-08	Pavot126nkGallorette121nkLarky Day112hd	Hard drive	11
13Jly46- 5Jam	fst 1 3/16	:47 1:111 1:361 1:551 3↑	Butler H 57k	2 1 1hd 1½ 3½ 53¼	Kirkland A	127 w	3.25	101-08	Lucky Draw105hdGallorette1161½Stymie126¾	Tired	9
4Jly46- 6Suf	fst 1⅛	:473 1:123 1:373 1:494 3↑	Mass H 66k	8 5 3nk 2nk 11½ 12¼	Kirkland A	120 w	2.70	92-13	Pavot1202¼Dinner Party1131½Gallorette1192¾	Handily	11
15Jun46- 6Del	gd 1¼	:473 1:122 1:38 2:041 3↑	Sussex H 29k	1 1 1hd 12½ 12½ 12	Snellings A	115 w	5.70e	94-16	Pavot1152Gallorette1131Stymie1262	In hand	8
29May46- 6Del	fst 6f	:223 :46 1:113 3↑	Wilmington H 9.4k	5 7 63½ 41½ 32 41½	Longden J	119wb	*1.50	92-16	Brookfield1231Goodrob107hdHappyBuckie116½	Slow to start	7
22May46- 6Bel	fst 6f-WC	:221 :454 1:084 3↑	Roseben H 12k	6 9 82½ 51¾ 43½ 34	Longden J	118wb	12.15	93-11	Polynesian1264Flood Town106hdPavot118¾	Closed well	9
6May46- 6Bel	fst 6f-WC	:232 :471 1:13 3↑	Toboggan H 16k	4 3 4½ 3¾ 57½ 510	Arcaro E	125 w	3.45	66-22	Polynesian124hdCassis1134King Dorsett1172	No mishap	7
25Apr46- 6HdG	my 6f	:23 :464 1:14 4↑	Alw 3500	1 4 21 22 2½ 12	Snellings A	120wb	*.85	83-36	Pavot1202Quarter Moon1202Hasteville1205	Ridden out	4
	Daily Racing Form time, 1:13 3/5										
22Sep45- 6Bel	fst 1⅝	:471 1:374 2:043 2:433	Lawrence Realizatn 28k	6 3 21½ 11 89¾ 1025	Arcaro E	126wb	*1.55e	61-14	Poto'Luck1261¼ChiefBarker108½Michaelo1082	Stopped badly	11
18Sep45- 6Bel	sly 1	:223 :45 1:094 1:371	Jerome H 18k	7 5 58½ 57¾ 34¼ 34½	Arcaro E	125wb	*2.10	83-20	Buzfuz115½Greek Warrior1144Pavot1251	Steady gain	11
15Aug45- 6Bel	fst 1¼	:491 1:124 1:372 2:021 3↑	Whitney 17k	5 1 21½ 36 23 24	Snider A	117 w	1.55e	85-17	Trymenow1034Pavot1173Stymie1262	No match	6
11Aug45- 6Bel	fst 1¼	:462 1:102 1:361 2:024	Travers 33k	4 3 12 12 1½ 46½	Snider A	126wb	*.85	79-16	Adonis1102BurningDream1104SirFrancis116½	Quit final⅛	7
21Jly45- 5Jam	fst 1 3/16	:472 1:112 1:37 1:564	Empire City 57k	1 1 14 12 2nk 2¾	Snider A	126wb	*2.65e	95-08	Gallorette116¾Pavot1263Post Graduate1163	No mishap	11
14Jly45- 5Aqu	fst 1¼	:481 1:13 1:393 2:051	Dwyer 56k	2 2 11½ 46½ 612 626	Arcaro E	126wb	*.80	55-18	Wildlife116noGallorette116½Esteem11610	Quit after 5f	6
23Jun45- 6Bel	fst 1½	:47 1:122 2:041 2:301	Belmont 70k	7 4 43 12 14 15	Arcaro E	126wb	2.10	87-13	Pavot1265Wildlife1261¾Jeep126½	Driving	8
	Geldings not eligible										
16Jun45- 6Pim	fst 1 3/16	:471 1:122 1:384 1:584	Preakness 83k	1 2 42½ 43 41½ 55	Woolf G	126 w	*1.35	83-08	Polynesin1262½HoopJr.126nkDrbyDpp126nk	Bothered stretch	9
6Jun45- 6Bel	gd 1	:233 :472 1:13 1:394	Withers 27k	5 5 53 32 31¼ 2½	Woolf G	126 w	*.20	74-22	Polynesian126½Pavot1262King Dorsett1261	Led,hung	8
	Geldings not eligible										
30Sep44- 4Bel	fst 6½f-W	:22 :441 1:09 1:153	Futurity 68k	9 1 74¾ 52¼ 12	Woolf G	126 w	*.70	94-04	Pavot1262Alexis119nkErrard1191	Easily	15
	Geldings not eligible										
2Sep44- 4Bel	fst 6½f	:223 :461 1:184	Hopeful 58k	5 5 3nk 1nk 11½ 1½	Woolf G	126 w	*.30	86-15	Pavot126½Esteem122½Great Power1142½	Tired,held	8
19Aug44- 4Bel	fst 6f	:23 :464 1:114	Grand Union Hotel 19k	4 5 31¾ 32 3¾ 12½	Woolf G	126 w	*.25	91-13	Pavot1262½Great Power114nkBymeabond114hd	Bothered str	5
12Aug44- 4Bel	fst 6f-WC	:224 :452 1:093	Sar Spl 4.9k	1 3 3¾ 1½ 11¾	Woolf G	122 w	*.35	98-07	Pavot1221¾Plebiscite1227Jeep1224	Drew away	4
5Aug44- 4Bel	fst 6f	:224 :463 1:121	U S Hotel 20k	8 3 2nk 2nk 1½ 12½	Woolf G	126 w	*.70	89-14	Pavot1262½Esteem122nkWar Jeep1222	Mild restraint late	10
22Jly44- 6Suf	fst 5½f	:23 :453 1:053	Mayflower 35k	4 5 31 2½ 11½ 12½	Woolf G	119 w	*1.70	95-12	Pavot1192½Alabama119noLady's Reward1071	Easily	10
4Jly44- 5Del	fst 5½f	:222 :452 :58 1:042	©Christiana 7.5k	7 4 22 2hd 12 12	Dodson D	116 w	*.60	105-05	Pavot1162Hillyer Court1162Alexis116½	Easily	7
26Jun44- 1Del	fst 5½f	:223 :46 :584 1:051	Md Sp Wt	5 2 22 21 13 18	Knapp L	117 w	*.70	101-08	Pavot1178Brides Biscuit1142Guard Ship1141	Galloping	6

Petrify

ch. f. 1939, by Identity (Man o' War)–Sag Rock, by Rock Man **Lifetime record: 11 6 1 1 $41,085**

Own.– A.G. Vanderbilt
Br.– Alfred G. Vanderbilt (Md)
Tr.– L. McCoy

11Jun43- 5Aqu	fst 7f	:23 :463 1:12 1:25 3↑	ⒻHandicap 2560	2 3 52½ 65¼ 53 77½	Wright WD	118wb	7.10	82-17	Yarrow Maid122no[DH]Night Glow112[DH]War Hazard1163		9
	Shuffled back on turn										
25May43- 5Bel	fst 6f	:223 :454 1:12 4↑	Handicap 2030	4 2 1hd 21 23 68¾	Wright WD	115wb	16.85	81-14	Vain Prince114nkAriel Lad1171½Colchis1143	Quit	7
25Oct41- 5Lrl	fst 1 1/16	:232 :473 1:123 1:471	ⒻSelima 28k	4 10 118 1111 1114 1115¾	Donoso R	122wb	*2.00	65-17	Ficklebush1073½HardBaked114½Vagrncy1142	Showed nothing	11
11Oct41- 6Kee	fst 6f	:224 :463 1:114	ⒻSpecial Event 5.8k	3 3 23 23 23 23	Donoso R	119 w	*.60	90-14	Miss Dogwood1193Petrify1194Sis Baker1192	No threat	6
	Worked mile in 1:41 2/5										
20Sep41- 7Bel	fst 6f	:221 :46 1:113	ⒻMatron 20k	13 3 32½ 32 2½ 12	Donoso R	119 w	3.65	92-13	Petrify1192LightLady119noFicklbush110½	Speed in reserve	15
3Sep41- 6Aqu	fst 6f	:231 :472 1:13	ⒻAlw 3000	7 3 41¾ 56¾ 52 12	Donoso R	122 w	*1.30	89-12	Petrify1222Last Sou110nkTaunt1072	Drifted out	7
16Aug41- 5Sar	my 6f	:23 :472 1:133	ⒻSpinaway 9.8k	2 2 22 43 31½ 32	Donoso R	122 w	*.80	82-22	Mar-Kell1131Equipet1131Petrify122½	Driving	8
	Previously trained by A. Holberg										
5Jly41- 6AP	fst 6f	:232 :47 1:123	ⒻArl Lassie 25k	1 2 11 1½ 12 16	Donoso R	117 w	*1.00	84-19	Petrify1176Lotopoise117noCourt Manners1174		7
	Ridden out,drifting out late;previously trained by L. McCoy										
24Jun41- 3Aqu	fst 5½f	:23 :463 1:054	Alw 1500	1 1 1½ 1nk 2hd 1hd	Donoso R	113 w	3.20	98-12	Petrify113hdBen Gray1162Court Manners109hd	Hard drive	5
11Jan41- 1SA	my 3f	:224 :341	Alw 1500	1 2 13 11½	James B	117 w	*.60	--	Petrify1171½Hooks1203Sagittal117no	Bore in,driving	9
7Jan41- 1SA	fst 3f	:22 :332	ⒻMd Sp Wt	14 1 1½ 12	James B	117 w	*1.30	--	Petrify1172Bold Lucy1173Chiquita Mia1172	Easily	16

Phalanx

b. c. 1944, by Pilate (Friar Rock)–Jacola, by Jacopo **Lifetime record: 41 13 7 10 $409,235**

Own.– C.V. Whitney
Br.– Abram S. Hewitt (Va)
Tr.– S.E. Veitch

2Jly49- 6Aqu	fst 1¼	:484 1:13 1:372 2:024 3↑	Brooklyn H 58k	9 8 85¾ 98 96¼ 63½	Gilbert J	123wb	7.65	89-14	Assault122¾Vulcan'sForge129nkFlyingMissel117¾	No menace	10
25Jun49- 6Del	fst 1¼	:482 1:124 1:373 2:02 3↑	Sussex H 28k	6 6 68¾ 63 66½ 58½	Gilbert J	126 w	*.65	91-10	Flying Missel1105Chains1101Rose Beam1152	Dull effort	6
14Jun49- 6Del	fst 1 1/16	:231 :462 1:12 1:451 4↑	Alw 3500	1 5 48 1hd 1½ 13	Gilbert J	123 w	1.85e	87-15	Phalanx1233Mother1101½Rose Beam1142	Easily	6
13Nov48- 6Jam	fst 1 3/16	:484 1:13 1:38 1:58 3↑	Butler H 85k	1 7 613 77½ 63 21½	Clark S	126wb	*2.50	84-20	Donor1171½Phalanx1261Better Self121½	Closed fast	9
6Nov48- 6Jam	fst 2⅛	:50 2:352 3:023 3:354 3↑	Daingerfield H 29k	4 5 419 418 23 1¾	Clark S	129 w	*.80	88-23	Phalanx129¾Flying Missel1024Donor117½	Drew out	10
30Oct48- 6Jam	fst 1 3/16	:48 1:123 1:38 1:574 3↑	Westchester H 57k	1 8 813 89¾ 54½ 31½	Clark S	126 w	*1.05	86-22	Better Self1191War Trophy110nkPhalanx126no	Closed fast	8

16Oct48-7Bel	fst 1⅝	:48 1:381 2:034 2:424 3↑	Gold Cup 111k	1 6 815 59 34½ 22	Donoso R	126 w	10.80 88-19	Citation1192Phalanx1265Carolyn A.1232½	Closed fast 9
	Geldings not eligible								
12Oct48-6Jam	fst 1 1/16	:24 :471 1:12 1:444 3↑	Questionnaire H 29k	11 8 99 64½ 52½ 64	Clark S	126 w	*3.20 85-18	Donor115noCarolyn A.111½Bug Juice1082	No excuse 11
2Oct48-6Bel	fst 2	:48 2:293 2:562 3:213 3↑	J C Gold Cup 108k	3 5 521 311 28 27	Clark S	124 w	6.35 89-09	Citation1177Phalanx12412Beauchef124hd	Closed well 7
	Geldings not eligible								
21Sep48-6Bel	fst 1 1/16	:232 :463 1:113 1:44 3↑	Alw 7500	2 8 820 816 87¼ 46¾	Clark S	122 w	*1.75e 84-14	ThreeRings1051¼Airosa1021½BrightSword1224	Finished fast 8
11Oct47-6Bel	fst 2¼	:473 2:314 3:482 3↑	New York H 109k	4 6 613 47½ 34¼ 35	Guerin E	116wb	2.55 88-11	Rico Monte126noTalon1225Phalanx1167	Stumbled at start 6
4Oct47-6Bel	fst 2	:494 2:293 2:553 3:213 3↑	J C Gold Cup 26k	2 3 31½ 3nk 2hd 1no	Donoso R	117wb	1.50 96-12	Phalanx117noTalon12412Stymie124	Just up 3
29Sep47-6Bel	fst 1⅝	:482 1:382 2:033 2:424	Lawrence Realizatn 28k	1 4 43 33½ 22 2hd	Donoso R	126wb	*1.40 90-14	Cosmic Bomb114hdPhalanx1262Snow Goose1155	Game try 6
6Sep47-6Aqu	gd 1⅛	:483 1:123 1:38 1:511	Discovery H 28k	3 7 76¾ 76½ 62¾ 31	Donoso R	128wb	*1.60 90-13	Cosmic Bomb126noDouble Jay1151Phalanx1281	Closed fast 9
23Aug47-7Was	fst 1¼	:472 1:111 1:35 2:003	American Derby 93k	2 4 410 36½ 36 36¼	Donoso R	126wb	*.90 96-07	Fervent118nkCosmic Bomb1186Phalanx12610	No excuse 4
16Aug47-5Sar	sly 1¼	:511 1:16 1:411 2:061	Travers 28k	1 2 21½ 21½ 1hd 2no	Donoso R	128wb	*.55 77-20	Young Peter124noPhalanx1282½Colonel O'F122	Game try 3
19Jly47-6Bel	sly 1⅝	:483 1:39 2:042 2:423 3↑	Gold Cup 109k	3 7 724 611 43¾ 45¼	Donoso R	112wb	4.60 86-14	Stymie126nkNatchez1264Assault1261	No mishap 7
	Geldings not eligible								
5Jly47-5Jam	fst 1 3/16	:483 1:13 1:39 1:574	Empire City 56k	7 7 78½ 75¼ 4¾ 12¼	Donoso R	126wb	*.70 87-15	Phalanx1262¼But Why Not111½Harmonica116hd	Going away 7
30Jun47-5Jam	fst 1 1/16	:25 :481 1:123 1:452	Alw 7500	2 5 55¼ 23 2hd 12½	Donoso R	126wb	*.45 86-16	Phalanx1262½Tailspin1171Our Tommy1139	Cleverly 5
14Jun47-6Aqu	fst 1¼	:474 1:13 1:391 2:054	Dwyer 58k	6 9 711 64¾ 31 1nk	Donoso R	126wb	*.85 78-16	Phalanx126nkBut Why Not1117Brabancon1161½	Hard drive 9
31May47-6Bel	fst 1½	:50 1:152 2:051 2:292	Belmont 113k	7 9 74 31¾ 1nk 15	Donoso R	126wb	2.30e 91-09	Phalanx1265Tide Rips1262Tailspin1261½	Easily 9
	Geldings not eligible								
24May47-6Bel	fst 1⅛	:461 1:112 1:371 1:503	Peter Pan H 18k	7 9 73¼ 51 52½ 32	Arcaro E	126wb	*.90 86-19	Tailspin1091Brabancon1171Phalanx126hd	Closed fast 11
10May47-6Pim	fst 1 3/16	:471 1:121 1:391 1:59	Preakness 133k	8 10 97½ 76¼ 55 33¾	Arcaro E	126wb	*1.10 83-20	Faultless1261¼On Trust1262½Phalanx1261¼	Closed fast 11
3May47-7CD	sl 1¼	:49 1:142 1:402 2:064	Ky Derby 109k	8 13 1314 53 52¾ 2hd	Arcaro E	126wb	*2.00 73-23	Jet Pilot126hdPhalanx126hdFaultless1261	Sluggish start 13
19Apr47-5Jam	fst 1 1/16	:23 :47 1:114 1:434	Wood Mem (Div 1) 45k	8 8 73 43½ 21 11½	Arcaro E	126wb	*.95 94-10	Phalanx1261½Carolyn A.1211½Owners Choice1268	Drew out 10
12Apr47-5Jam	fst 1 1/16	:242 :482 1:122 1:444	Exp Free H 21k	3 8 85½ 83½ 54¼ 31¼	Arcaro E	122wb	3.00 88-10	CornishKnight110nkSecnav1061Phalanx122hd	Close quarters 9
13Nov46-6Pim	fst 1 1/16	:232 :471 1:122 1:454	Walden 33k	2 11 107 - - -	Donoso R	119wb	3.10 - -	Fervent116hdFaultless1133Royal Governor1167	11
	Ran up on heels of rival,lost rider								
2Nov46-4Jam	fst 1 70	:233 :473 1:133 1:424	Ardsley H 24k	6 7 72½ 22 21½ 12	Luther T	117wb	*.90e 90-12	Phalanx1172Brabancon1131Nathaniel1094	Ridden out 8
29Oct46-5Jam	fst 1 1/16	:24 :48 1:122 1:454	Remsen H 25k	8 8 86¾ 65¼ 41¼ 1¾	Donoso R	117wb	5.10 84-15	Phalanx117¾Tavistock116hdDonor1266	Lugged in final ⅛ 8
23Oct46-4Jam	fst 1 1/16	:24 :48 1:133 1:454	Alw 5000	5 4 11 11½ 11½ 1nk	Arcaro E	119wb	*.55 84-19	Phalanx119nkDinnrHour1198Lndr1222	Drifted out,just held 5
12Oct46-5Bel	sly 1	:23 :454 1:111 1:372	Champagne 27k	6 9 77¾ 56½ 32¼ 2½	Schmidl A	110wb	6.60e 86-14	Donor116½Phalanx110nkJet Pilot1194	Closed well 11
7Oct46-7Bel	fst 1	:231 :464 1:12 1:374	Alw 5000	6 5 55 53 32½ 31¾	Schmidl A	119 w	1.40 83-16	Flashco116nkTavistock1191¾Phalanx1192	Good finish 9
14Sep46-5Aqu	fst 6½f	:234 :48 1:131 1:194	Cowdin 31k	4 10 96¾ 76¾ 73 42½	Wilson HB	110wb	10.85e 83-13	CosmcBomb126nkColonelO'F122¾Brbncon1171½	Finished well 11
31Aug46-4Sar	fst 6½f	:222 :451 1:101 1:17	Hopeful 57k	7 9 117¼ 1011 56¾ 53½	James B	114wb	9.15e 96-00	BlueBorder122no[D]CsmcBmb1262GrndAdmrl1261	Closed well 11
	Placed fourth through disqualification								
27Aug46-6Sar	fst 6f	:224 :46 1:11	Alw 4000	4 5 54¼ 53¼ 42½ 3nk	James B	111wb	*1.70 97-06	Brabancon116noJohnnyDimick111nkPhlnx1112	Finish fastest 5
17Aug46-4Sar	my 6f	:232 :472 1:132	Sar Spl 6.5k	4 3 55 56¾ 43¼ 43½	James B	122wb	2.95e 81-21	GrandAdmrl1221LoyalLegion1221½KhyberPss1221	No menace 5
20Jly46-5Jam	fst 6f	:23 :463 1:113	©East View 51k	11 9 74½ 61¾ 63 33	Miller P	115wb	9.65 90-11	Grand Admiral1151I Will1192Phalanx115½	Close quarters 11
13Jly46-4Jam	fst 6f	:233 :472 1:113	Alw 5000	1 5 56 56 4¾ 11½	Miller P	106wb	3.75 93-08	Phalanx1061½Brabancon1182Owners Choice1153	Drew away 5
22May46-4Bel	fst 5f-WC	:223 :454 :584	Alw 4000	7 6 73¾ 62 4¾	Kirkland A	116 w	*1.25 85-11	Fiddlers Three116½Our Tommy116nkNathaniel111no	10
	Close quarters early								
18May46-4Bel	fst 5f-WC	:222 :45 :573	Juvenile 14k	6 12 92½ 96 97¾	Givens C	117wb	*1.00e 84-06	EternalWar1223FirstFlight1191CornshKnght113no	No factor 12
4May46-1Jam	fst 5f	:23 :47 1:001	Md Sp Wt	4 4 45¼ 33 22 1¾	Givens C	116 w	9.75 89-10	Phalanx116¾Ben Lewis1162Green Dragon1164	Driving 7

Platter

ch. c. 1941, by Pilate (Friar Rock)–Lets Dine, by Jack High **Lifetime record: 10 2 3 2 $60,930**

Own.– George D. Widener
Br.– George D. Widener (Ky)
Tr.– W.F. Mulholland

3Jun44-6Bel	fst 1½	:48 1:131 2:05 2:321	Belmont 72k	7 7 58 43½ 56½ 513½	Longden J	126wb	1.90e 63-16	Bounding Home126½Pensive1268Bull Dandy1264	7
	Hung,pulled up lame;Geldings not eligible								
13May44-6Pim	fst 1 3/16	:481 1:131 1:392 1:591	Preakness 77k	3 4 21½ 22 2½ 2¾	Longden J	126wb	3.05 85-15	Pensive126¾Platter1262Stir Up1264½	Driving 7
6May44-4Jam	fst 6f	:224 :462 1:112	Alw 4000	3 6 65¼ 47 31½ 21¼	Longden J	126wb	*1.80 94-10	Rodney Stone1161¼Platter1262½Bull Dandy1165	9
	Fast finish,worked mile in 1:41 2/5								
12Nov43-6Pim	fst 1 1/16	:234 :483 1:133 1:483	Walden 13k	4 7 65½ 57¼ 43½ 1½	McCreary C	122wb	*2.20e 75-23	Platter122½Royal Prince119nkDirector J.E.1161	Driving 9
3Nov43-6Pim	my 1 1/16	:232 :48 1:141 1:473	Pim Futurity 38k	8 3 36½ 31 2½ 1½	McCreary C	119wb	*1.85 80-30	Platter119½By Jimminy1198Smolensko1222	Just up 8
	Geldings not eligible								
23Oct43-5Jam	fst 1 70	:243 :482 1:132 1:442	Ardsley H (Div 1) 11k	1 1 21 2½ 21 33	McCreary C	112wb	4.25 79-17	Weyamoke1083Pukka Gin126hdPlatter112no	Bore out 10
9Oct43-4Bel	fst 1	:233 :464 1:12 1:381	Champagne 13k	6 1 2hd 52½ 54½ 57	McCreary C	106wb	4.05 76-17	Pukka Gin1131Pressure1065Pensive1101	Pace,tired 12
2Oct43-4Bel	sly 6½f-W	:231 :461 1:111 1:174	Futurity 68k	2 6 4¾ 63½ 32¼	McCreary C	114wb	9.50 81-17	Occupy1261¼Rodney Stone1221Platter1142	Fast finish 11
	Geldings not eligible								
28Sep43-5Bel	fst 6f-WC	:223 :45 1:10	Alw 5000	15 4 76 46½ 42¾	McCreary C	111wb	3.00e 93-09	Tambo111¾Rodney Stone1191Black Badge1191	Good finish 16
23Sep43-4Bel	fst 6f-WC	:231 :462 1:114	Md Sp Wt	3 2 4nk 33½ 2½	McCreary C	116wb	3.25 86-14	Plasma116½Platter1161½Bounding Home1161	Greenly 13

Polynesian

br. c. 1942, by Unbreakable (Sickle)–Black Polly, by Polymelian **Lifetime record: 58 27 10 10 $310,410**

Own.– Elmendorf Farm
Br.– Elmendorf Farm Inc (Ky)
Tr.– M.H. Dixon

1Nov47-5Pim	fst 6f	:224 :464 1:124 2↑	Janney H 9k	2 4 21½ 2hd 1½ 11	Snider A	134wb	*.40 89-24	Polynesian1341The Doge1222Sea Snack1162	Good effort 5
22Sep47-5Bel	sly 6f	:231 :463 1:11 3↑	Alw 6500	3 4 22 1hd 11½ 12½	Arcaro E	126wb	*.85 95-15	Polynesian1262½Armed1308Ensueno11430	Easily 4
25Aug47-6GS	fst 6f	:222 :452 1:094 3↑	Camden H 11k	5 4 52 2½ 12 15	Balzaretti W	129wb	*.40 102-06	Polynesian1295Air Patrol123nkThe Doge1191¼	Easily 6
26Jly47-5Mth	fst 1¼	:473 1:12 1:363 2:011 3↑	Mth Park H 29k	5 3 21½ 21 23 48½	Wright WD	127wb	2.15 94-02	Round View1127Talon1121½Gallorette119hd	Weakened 6
16Jly47-6Mth	fst 1⅛	:473 1:113 1:373 1:503 3↑	Omnibus H 12k	4 2 2½ 1½ 11 1½	Wright WD	129wb	*1.95 102-11	Polynesian129½Round View1144Flash Burn111nk	Driving 7
28Jun47-6Mth	fst 1 1/16	:242 :472 1:111 1:433 3↑	Long Branch H 12k	6 2 11 11 12 1no	Wright WD	129wb	*.75 104-08	Polynesian129noFlash Burn1093½Jeep1102	Hard drive 6
21Jun47-5Mth	fst 6f	:222 :451 1:102 3↑	Oceanport H 11k	7 6 2hd 12 15 12½	Wright WD	134wb	*.45 99-09	Polynesian1342½Misleader1051Gallant Bull104½	Easily 7
30May47-5Del	fst 6f	:221 :453 1:104 3↑	Wilmington H 11k	2 4 44 3½ 1½ 13	Snider A	132wb	*.80 98-14	Polynesian1323Sea Snack1102Rippey112¾	Going away 5
26May47-5Atl	fst 6f	:223 :46 1:11 3↑	Atl City Inaugural H 12k	4 4 21 4¾ 1½ 12½	Arcaro E	130wb	*.95 91-16	Polynesian1302½AirPatrol120nkLighthouse1051½	Going away 8
21May47-6Bel	my 6f-WC	:22 :45 1:10 3↑	Roseben H 17k	2 6 53¼ 42¼ 46 46	Arcaro E	132wb	*2.10 85-13	Inroc1133½Fighting Frank1251½Brown Mogul1161	Tired 7
5May47-6Bel	my 6f-WC	:221 :451 1:11 3↑	Toboggan H 24k	9 3 42½ 53½ 2nk 31¼	Arcaro E	134wb	*2.45 85-10	Buzfuz121¾Degage114½Polynesian134½	Tired 13
26Apr47-5Jam	fst 1 1/16	:24 :473 1:114 1:44 3↑	Excelsior H 22k	5 3 31 2½ 22 25	Arcaro E	126wb	*.95 88-10	Coincidence1155Polynesian126½Lets Dance1121	Weakened 8
19Apr47-4Jam	fst 6f	:23 :46 1:112 3↑	Handicap 6525	5 5 42¾ 33 3¾ 11¾	Arcaro E	130wb	*.70 94-10	Polynesian1301¾Buzfuz1201¼Tidy Bid1032	Drew out 5
5Apr47-5Jam	sly 6f	:223 :46 1:111 3↑	Paumonok H 22k	5 6 64¾ 41½ 21 2hd	Arcaro E	130wb	*2.00 95-14	FightingFrank125hdPolynesn130¾KngDorstt1202	Just missed 9
	Previously raced in name of Mrs P.A.B. Widener								

8Nov46- 6Pim	fst 1 3/16	:473 1:122 1:391 1:591 3↑ Riggs H 30k	5 5 33½ 31 1hd 1½	Snider A	124wb	*1.45	86-21	Polynesian124½RoundView1111FlshBurn1061½	Under pressure 8		
2Nov46- 5Jam	fst 1 70	:23 :464 1:114 1:421 3↑ Scarsdale H 18k	9 5 45 33¼ 31¼ 11½	Snider A	126wb	3.25	93-12	Polynsn1261½FrstFddl1151Buzfuz1171	Drew clear under urging 10		
26Oct46- 6GS	sly 1⅛	:464 1:112 1:373 1:503 3↑ Trenton H 64k	6 1 11 1hd 2½ 2nk	Snider A	123wb	7.90	92-19	Turbine115nkPolynesian123¾Man o' Glory1162	Gamely 12		
19Oct46- 6Lrl	fst 1¼	:47 1:12 1:381 2:03 3↑ Washington H 28k	1 1 11½ 1hd 2hd 31¾	Kirkland A	119wb	*1.40	93-16	Seven Hearts1191Megogo105¾Polynesian119½	Faltered late 6		
15Oct46- 7Bel	fst 1	:233 :461 1:103 1:363 2↑ Turf & Field H 10k	2 1 11½ 11½ 14 1¾	Arcaro E	126 w	*.95	91-19	Polynesian126¾Coincidence123nkBridlFlowr1158	Ridden out 4		
2Oct46- 6Bel	fst 7f	:224 :461 1:111 1:234 2↑ Vosburgh H 19k	8 3 2hd 1hd 3nk 36½	Arcaro E	130wb	*1.50	84-19	Coincidence1182½Alexis1094Polynesian130½	Faltered 11		
16Sep46- 5Atl	fst 6f	:22 :442 1:091 3↑ Pageant H 11k	2 5 21½ 1hd 11½ 16	Arcaro E	126wb	*.45	108-06	Polynesian1266ThreeDots1181½TheDoge118hd	Speed to spare 6		
9Sep46- 6Aqu	fst 7f	:223 :45 1:10 1:232 3↑ Bay Shore H 18k	4 5 41¼ 21½ 21 31¾	Arcaro E	130wb	*2.10	93-18	Gallorette124nkKing Dorsett1201½Polynesian1301	Hung 9		
24Aug46- 6Sar	fst 1¼	:46 1:101 1:362 2:013 3↑ Saratoga H 33k	3 2 12 13 2½ 2¾	Arcaro E	113wb	4.80	100-02	Lucky Draw121¾Polynesian1134Stymie1257	Gamely 5		
15Aug46- 6Sar	fst 1 3/16	:47 1:112 1:362 1:552 3↑ Merchants & Cits H 18k	1 2 11½ 11½ 2hd 21½	Snider A	112wb	6.30	99-06	Lucky Draw1171½Polynesian1121Trymenow11115	Held well 8		
10Aug46- 6Sar	my 1¼	:50 1:154 1:394 2:072 3↑ Whitney 28k	4 3 21 21 35 414	Wright WD	117wb	4.70	58-22	Stymie1202Mahout1032Trymenow11210	Flattened out 5		
5Aug46- 6Sar	fst 1	:23 :461 1:111 1:363 3↑ Wilson 24k	3 2 21½ 2nk 11 4½	Wright WD	117wb	*2.75	97-08	Pavot126nkGallorette121nkLarky Day112hd	Hung 11		
4Jly46- 6Mth	fst 6f	:221 :444 1:103 3↑ Rumson H 13k	5 8 41½ 31 1½ 11¼	Wright WD	130wb	*1.55	- -	Polynesian1301½Brookfield123½New Moon1143½	Driving 9		
24Jun46- 5Jam	fst 6f	:224 :452 1:102 3↑ Fleetwing H 12k	2 3 53½ 42 31½ 31	Wright WD	132wb	*1.20	98-11	Scholarship1061FloodTown110noPolynesin1323	Traffic,hung 8		
8Jun46- 5Del	fst 6f	:214 :45 1:102 3↑ Handicap 5000	8 5 21½ 2hd 12 12¼	Wright WD	126wb	*2.00	100-11	Polynesian1262½Brookfield1261¼New Moon1165	Ridden out 8		
30May46- 6Bel	fst 1¼	:482 1:123 1:373 2:02 3↑ Suburban H 60k	11 1 21½ 21 53¼ 1015¼	Wright WD	115wb	21.40	75-16	Armed1302½Reply Paid110noStymie1231	Quit badly 11		
22May46- 6Bel	fst 6f-WC	:221 :454 1:084 3↑ Roseben H 12k	9 4 2nk 1hd 11 14	Wright WD	126wb	3.45	97-11	Polynesian1264FloodTown106hdPavot118¾	Drew clear easily 9		
11May46- 6Bel	fst 1	:224 :451 1:104 1:37 3↑ Metropolitan H 31k	8 3 2hd 1½ 1hd 97¼	Wright WD	126 w	16.00	82-14	Gallorette110noSirde124noFirst Fiddle126½	Quit badly 14		
6May46- 6Bel	fst 6f-WC	:232 :471 1:13 3↑ Toboggan H 16k	5 1 1hd 1nk 1½ 1hd	Wright WD	124 w	6.15	76-22	Polynesin124hdCsss1134KngDorstt1172	Drifted out,driving 7		
27Apr46- 4Jam	sly 6f	:23 :46 1:121 3↑ Handicap 6020	3 1 32 33 31½ 33¼	Wright WD	123 w	4.60	87-16	Buzfuz1261½Scholarship1141¾Polynesn12310	Some late gain 4		
17Nov45- 6Pim	gd 1 3/16	:493 1:142 1:391 1:584 3↑ Pim Spl 25k	3 4 12½ 11 25 68½	Wright WD	120 w	12.75	79-20	Armed1264First Fiddle1262Stymie1261¼	Weakened 7		
14Nov45- 5Pim	fst 6f	:223 :464 1:123 3↑ Handicap 5000	3 3 2½ 2hd 1hd 1hd	Wright WD	122 w	*1.40	90-23	Polynesian122hdBritish Buddy113nkFirst Son1094	Driving 5		
6Nov45- 6Bel	fst 1	:23 :454 1:11 1:373 2↑ Turf & Field Cup H 10k	6 5 53¼ 21 12 2no	Jemas N	122 w	2.40	86-20	TexMartin104noPolynesian1223GreekWarrior1211¼	Weak ride 7		
27Oct45- 7Pim	fst 1 1/16	:241 :482 1:131 1:453 3↑ Handicap 3500	6 1 11 1½ 1hd 2½	Jemas N	126 w	*1.65	89-17	Salvo120½Polynesin1262HRolls115hd	Saved ground,2nd best 7		
22Oct45- 6Pim	fst 6f	:221 :453 1:11 3↑ Ritchie H (Div 1) 12k	7 5 55 43¼ 21½ 24½	Young S	123 w	*.95	93-10	New Moon1184½Polynesian1232Kopla116½	No match 9		
17Oct45- 6Lrl	fst 6f	:223 :462 1:121 3↑ Handicap 5000	3 4 33 21½ 11 2no	Gilbert J	122 w	*1.70	93-19	The Doge114noPolynesian1221½New Moon1171	Gave way late 8		
3Oct45- 3Bel	fst 6f-WC	:224 :46 1:121 3↑ Handicap 4970	3 3 11 14 13½	Wright WD	124 w	2.60	80-21	Polynesian1243½Saguaro1052½Occupy1224	Easily 4		
18Sep45- 6Bel	sly 1	:223 :45 1:094 1:371 Jerome H 18k	8 4 36 35¼ 45¼ 913¼	Wright WD	126 w	8.35	75-20	Buzfuz115½Greek Warrior1144Pavot1251	Quit badly 11		
15Aug45- 5Bel	fst 6f-WC	:223 :453 1:102 Saranac H 4.9k	1 2 2hd 4½ 1½ 11¾	Wright WD	126 w	*2.70	89-13	Polynesian1261¾Alabama1231¼Buzfuz1261	Ridden out 6		
10Jly45- 5Aqu	fst 1 1/16	:243 :482 1:132 1:454 Shevlin 11k	3 1 21 32 31¾ 511½	Wright WD	126 w	*1.60	73-16	Wildlife1086Coincidence1112½Trymenow1102	9		
	Eased back when outrun										
16Jun45- 6Pim	fst 1 3/16	:471 1:122 1:384 1:584 Preakness 83k	7 4 11 11½ 1½ 12½	Wright WD	126 w	12.00	88-08	Polynesian1262½HoopJr.126nkDarbyDieppe126nk	Ridden out 9		
6Jun45- 6Bel	gd 1	:233 :472 1:13 1:394 Withers 27k	7 2 21½ 21 2nk 1½	Wright WD	126 w	13.90	75-22	Polynesian126½Pavot1262King Dorsett1261	Came on again 8		
	Geldings not eligible										
30May45- 6Jam	fst 1 1/16	:24 :47 1:113 1:45 Wood Mem (Div 2) 27k	9 3 31½ 22 23 49	Balz'etti W	126 w	5.00	79-16	Hoop Jr.1262½Alexis1261½Sir Francis1265	Hung 9		
21May45- 5Jam	fst 6f	:23 :46 1:113 Exp Free H 8.6k	12 4 32½ 2½ 2½ 33¾	Balz'etti W	119 w	22.65	90-14	Jeep1121¾Greek Warrior1112Polynesian1191½	Faltered 13		
13Nov44- 6Pim	fst 1 70	:23 :471 1:131 1:44 Endurance H (Div 2) 12k	7 2 11½ 11½ 11 2½	Meade D	118 w	*1.25	90-18	HailVictory110½Polynesn1182½Bymbond1135	Drifted out str 7		
6Nov44- 6Pim	fst 6f	:223 :463 1:122 Sagamore (Div 2) 9.4k	1 2 11 11 11 11½	Meade D	113 w	*1.55	91-19	Polynesian1131½Kewey Dee119hdThe Doge116hd	Wide,driving 8		
3Oct44- 4Bel	fst 7f	:231 :47 1:121 1:25 ©Alw 3000	6 1 11 11 1½ 1hd	Meade D	119 w	*1.90	85-15	Polynesian119hdUnconditional1163Wildlife1162	Driving 13		
22Sep44- 6Bel	fst 6f-WC	:231 :462 1:113 Alw 3000	7 4 3½ 2hd 11¼	Meade D	116 w	*1.70	83-20	Polynesian1161¼SpartanNoble116noSolPrt1161	Drawing away 9		
29Aug44- 5Bel	fst 6f	:23 :464 1:122 Alw 3500	8 5 31 3½ 3nk 1hd	Meade D	111 w	2.60	88-13	Polynesian111hdGreatPower1112Chckrhll1191½	Bothered str 12		
22Aug44- 5Bel	fst 6f	:223 :463 1:122 Alw 3000	3 4 43½ 44 32½ 32½	Adair R	111 w	4.45	85-17	Bobanet117hdForward1172½Polynesian1112	Driving 12		
16Aug44- 4Bel	fst 5½f-W	:23 :454 1:041 ©Md Sp Wt	1 8 61½ 31½ 12½	Adair R	116 w	4.30f	93-07	Polynesian1162½Ship Call1164Baron Jack1161	Driving 27		
4May44- 6Pim	fst 4½f	:231 :474 :543 Ral Parr 7.9k	2 5 3½ 31½ 43	Scocca D	114 w	12.20	87-10	Alabama117hdDon Chance1191Flying Bridge1222	Tired 5		
29Apr44- 5Pim	gd 4½f	:234 :482 :543 Alw 2000	3 5 56½ 33 33	Scocca D	112 w	9.65	87-10	Alabama1123KeweyDee111noPolynesn1126	Taken up backstr 7		
25Apr44- 4Pim	hy 4½f	:24 :502 :572 ©Md Sp Wt	4 3 32 31 34	Arduini R	113 w	42.70	72-24	KeweyDee1183Potsey1181Polynsn1131	Close quarters,gamely 12		

Rouge Dragon

ch. g. 1938, by Annapolis (Man o' War)–Pimento II, by Pommern
Own.– M.A. Cushman
Br.– Mrs Marion du Pont Scott (Va)
Tr.– W.G. Jones

Lifetime record: 59 25 9 3 $111,255

30Oct46- 5Bel	fst *3	S'Chase	5:484 4↑ Grand National H 30k	10 2 - - - -	Leonard W	161 w	6.30	- -	Elkridge1514Burma Road1622Refugio1313	Fell at 8th 10
26Sep46- 5Bel	fst *2½	S'Chase	4:494 4↑ Brook H 19k	6 1 2½ 32 1027 925	Leonard W	163 w	2.05	- -	Burma Road1562½Caddie142noGreat Flare1385	Tired badly 11
30Aug46- 5Sar	fst *2½	S'Chase	5:082 4↑ Sar H 8.4k	2 1 115 110 4 4	Leonard W	164 w	*.55	- -	Replica II13710Raylywyn1354Beneksar134	4
	Tired,fell at final fence,remounted and ridden to finish in time limit									
23Aug46- 5Sar	fst *2	S'Chase	4:114 3↑ Beverwyck H 5.7k	1 1 13 11½ 12 11	Leonard W	162 w	*1.10	- -	RougeDragon1621WarBattle1442½BoojumII13912	Ridden out 4
3Jly46- 3Del	fst *2½	S'Chase	4:463 4↑ Indian River H 12k	2 1 12 15 13 13½	Leonard W	157 w	*1.15	- -	Rouge Dragon1573½Delhi Dan1374½Elkridge1492½	Easily 6
27Jun46- 3Del	fst *2	S'Chase	3:483 4↑ Georgetown H 12k	3 1 16 14 13 13½	Leonard W	152 w	*1.35	- -	Rouge Dragon1523½Elkridge1498Beneksar1366	6
	Swerved before last fence									
12Jun46- 2Del	my *2	S'Chase	3:594 4↑ Alw 3500	2 2 26 14 22 24	Leonard W	156 w	*.80	- -	Beneksar1414Rouge Dragon1563Boojum II15650	No match 4
16May46- 5Bel	fst *2	S'Chase	3:524 4↑ C L Appleton 8.8k	5 3 315 34 48¼ 412½	Fife M	149 w	*1.05	- -	BurmaRoad1395FloatingIsl1517WrBttl152½	Slow start,tired 6
8May46- 5Pim	fst *2	S'Chase	3:511 4↑ Jervis Spencer H 11k	2 4 32 35½ 11½ 12	Leonard W	153 w	*1.00	- -	Rouge Dragon1532Delhi Dan1371¼Navigate1438	8
	Bobbled 10th,ridden out									
30Apr46- 3Pim	fst *2	S'Chase	3:513 4↑ Alw 3500	2 2 13 14 18 110	Leonard W	152 w	2.85	- -	Rouge Dragon15210Soldier Song152¾Delhi Dan1436	Easily 10
28Nov45- 5Pim	sly 2½	S'Chase	5:252 4↑ Manly H 12k	10 3 48½ - - -	Passmore F	150wb	2.90e	- -	PursuitPlane1325BurmaRoad13912GkFlg1384	Lost rider 13th 10
6Nov45- 5Bel	fst *3	S'Chase	5:50 4↑ Temple Gwathmey H 15k	8 3 36 11 26 413	Owen W	151wb	*1.05e	- -	Caddie1396Refugio1304FloatingIsl1493	Weakened final ¼ 8
31Oct45- 4Pim	fst 2	S'Chase	3:494 4↑ J Spencer H (Div 1) 11k	8 3 37½ 31½ 36 34½	Leonard W	154 w	*1.30	- -	BoojumII1412Raylywn1442½RougeDragn154½	Bad landing 9th 8
3Oct45- 5Bel	fst *3	S'Chase	5:48 4↑ Grand National H 18k	2 2 35 55½ 625 631¾	Leonard W	153 w	2.85e	- -	Mercator1425Caddie139¾Raylywn1426	12
	Poor landings,not persevered with									
26Sep45- 5Bel	fst *2½	S'Chase	4:484 4↑ Brook H 9.3k	1 1 21 23 24 26	Roberts E	155 w	*.95e	- -	Raylywn1376Rouge Dragon1552Elkridge148no	10
	Bothered by riderless horse									
31Aug45- 5Bel	fst *2½	S'Chase	4:51 4↑ Saratoga H 9.1k	7 3 2hd 11½ 1nk 1nk	Roberts E	152 w	3.20	- -	RougeDragn152nkSoldierSong139noBurmaRoad141hd	Gamely 9
17Aug45- 4Bel	fst *2	S'Chase	3:45 3↑ North American H 16k	2 8 67½ 812 915 812¼	Leonard W	157 w	*2.40	- -	Floating Isle149nkChesapeake136½Elkridge1581	No factor 10
10Aug45- 3Bel	fst *2	S'Chase	3:491 4↑ Shillelah 6.1k	10 2 2hd 11½ 21½ 21	Leonard W	152 w	*1.10e	- -	Raylywn1361Rouge Dragon1521Mercator1376	Driving 10
27Jun45- 3Del	fst *2	S'Chase	3:503 4↑ Georgetown H 12k	4 2 21 11 11½ 2½	Owen W	159 w	*1.50e	- -	Iron Shot150½Rouge Dragon1596Elkridge159½	Held gamely 8
24Nov44- 5Pim	fst 2½	S'Chase	4:56 4↑ Manly H 12k	7 2 23 24 24 2½	Leonard W	160 w	*1.25	- -	Royal Archer138½Rouge Dragon1606Invader1321	Gamely 9
17Nov44- 5Pim	fst 2	S'Chase	3:493 3↑ Battleship H 10k	8 3 36 2hd 2hd 21	Leonard W	162 w	*2.20	- -	Ahmisk1441RougeDragn1627BoojumII1404	Led between calls 9
6Nov44- 6Bel	fst *3	S'Chase	5:57 4↑ Temple Gwathmey H 15k	2 2 37 21 21½ 42	Leonard W	163 w	*1.75	- -	Burma Road1391¾Parma135hdAhmisk143nk	Swerved,faltered 7
4Oct44- 5Bel	fst *3	S'Chase	5:541 4↑ Grand National H 16k	5 2 11½ 12 11½ 2hd	Leonard W	164 w	4.05	- -	BurmaRoad136hdRougeDrgn1647Elkridge1678	Jumped poorly 6
27Sep44- 5Bel	fst *2½	S'Chase	4:552 4↑ Brook H 8.8k	3 1 11½ 11½ 12 13	Leonard W	160 w	*2.35	- -	RougeDrgn1603BurmaRoad1365GrekFlg1341½	Speed to spare 9
1Sep44- 5Bel	fst *2½	S'Chase	4:491 4↑ Saratoga H 8.5k	3 4 43½ 42¾ 410½ 413	Leonard W	164 w	1.95	- -	Elkridge1558Brdlspur1321Invdr1404	Bad landing 9th,tired 5
25Aug44- 5Bel	fst *2	S'Chase	3:481 3↑ Beverwyck H 5.9k	4 3 22 13 11½ 11¼	Leonard W	161 w	3.95	- -	RougeDragon1611¼Knight'sQuest1422½Redlands13715	Driving 7

18Aug44- 3Bel my *2 S'Chase 3:49 3↑ North American H 5.8k 4 3 413 49½ - - Leonard W 162 w *1.45 -- Ossabaw134¾Redlands1361½Knght'sQust1458 Lost rider 11th 7
28Jun44- 4Del fst *2½ S'Chase 4:50⁴ 4↑ Indian River H 7.5k 4 4 45½ 35 11½ 12 Leonard W 161 w 2.90e -- Rouge Dragon1612Caddie1437Mercator14110 Swerved 6
21Jun44- 4Del fst *2 S'Chase 3:51³ 4↑ Georgetown H 7.9k 1 4 33 46½ 32½ 1nk Owen W 158 w 6.45 -- RougeDragon158nkKnight'sQuest1446MadPolicy1382 Driving 6
3Jun44- 3Bel fst *2 Hurdles 3:49⁴ 3↑ Alw 2500 2 6 514 513 726 725¼ Owen W 158 w *1.05 -- Raylywn147nkThe Beak1402Yankee Chance1555 Dull 8
16May44- 5Bel fst *2 S'Chase 3:49³ 4↑ CL Appleton 4.6k 2 4 46 417 414 420 Owen W 161 w *.70 -- IronShot1586GreekFlag1442TheBeak14112 Bad landing 8th 5
5May44- 5Pim fst 2 S'Chase 3:51¹ 4↑ J Spencer H 12k 2 2 34 43 1½ 11½ Owen W 157 w *1.10e -- Rouge Dragon1571½Mercator144nkCaddie1481½ Driving 10
22Apr44- 3Pim fst 2 S'Chase 4:01¹ 4↑ Handicap 2000 5 2 1½ 12 1½ 1¾ Owen W 153 w *.70 -- Rouge Dragon153¾Greek Flag1383Good Chance1425 Driving 5
20Nov43- 5Mtp fst 1¾ Hurdles 3:37⁴ 3↑ Alw 500 2 1 1 14 16 17 Harrison JS 162 w *.30 -- Rouge Dragon1627Rollo1576Sander135 3
8Nov43- 5Pim my 2½ S'Chase 5:09³ 4↑ Manly H 9.1k 2 4 43¾ 614 643 649¾ Harrison JS 154 w *1.95e -- Iron Shot146nkCaddie13915Mercator1393 Showed nothing 6
18Oct43- 5Pim gd 2 S'Chase 3:56 3↑ Gov Ogle H 6.6k 9 4 56 65 25 11 Harrison JS 153 w *1.45 -- RougeDrgon1531Cdd1376GrkFlg1373 Bad landing 6th,driving 9
29Sep43- 3Bel fst *2½ S'Chase 4:50 4↑ Brook H 6.6k 8 1 12 21½ 32½ 13 Harrison JS 147 w *2.65 -- Rouge Dragon1473Knight's Quest140noBank Note1381 Easily 10
28Aug43- 3Bel gd 1½ Hurdles 2:52¹ 3↑ Alw 2300 1 3 31 31 46 47 Harrison JS 153 w *1.25 -- BoojumII153hdGulliverII1383Kennebunk1354 Weak handling 5
18Aug43- 3Bel fst *2 S'Chase 3:46³ 3↑ Beverwyck H 4.1k 1 2 33 1½ 1hd 1½ Harrison JS 145 w 12.30 -- Rouge Dragon145½Iron Shot1458Brother Jones1471½ Gamely 10
31Jly43- 3Bel fst *2 S'Chase 3:46⁴ 4↑ Handicap 2075 5 1 12 21½ 33¼ 34½ Lacy H 149 w 3.75 -- Replica II1421½Iron Shot1523Rouge Dragon1497 Tired 6
3Jly43- 4Det fst *2 S'Chase 4:03² 4↑ Handicap 5000 1 3 21½ 2½ 11 12½ Harrison JS 144 w 2.00e -- RougeDragn1442½Bavarian1373½Ossabaw1386 Speed to spare 6
9Jun43- 3Aqu my *2 S'Chase 3:51¹ 4↑ Lion Heart H 3.8k 2 8 79½ 78 89½ 610½ Harrison JS 145 w 7.00 -- Knight's Quest1452Invader150noIron Shot1474 No mishap 9
25May43- 3Bel fst *2 S'Chase 3:52¹ 4↑ Corinthian H 3.9k 8 2 32 2hd 57½ 514¼ Harrison JS 148 w 4.35 -- Invader145nkBrother Jones1394Boojum II1385 Bore in 3rd 8
18May43- 5Bel fst *2 S'Chase 3:49⁴ 4↑ CL Appleton 3.9k 4 3 36 21½ 11 13 Harrison JS 144 w 3.35 -- Rouge Dragon1443Knight's Quest1492½Redlands1523 8
Swerved at final fence
24Apr43- 3Pim fst 2 S'Chase 4:11¹ 4↑ Alw 1500 3 2 11½ 14 112 112 Harrison JS 146 w 3.45 -- Rouge Dragon14612Ossabaw1483Frederic II1501½ 7
Swerved at several fences,eased up late
19Apr43- 1Pim my 2 S'Chase 4:22⁴ 4↑ Clm 2000 2 1 11½ 15 11½ 15 Harrison JS 146 w 2.80 -- RougeDragon1465Alcadl13515StrollngOn1525 Speed to spare 7
Previously owned by Montpelier
21Nov42- 5Mtp fst 1¾ Hurdles 3:33¹ 3↑ Alw 500 1 3 35 34½ 26 28 Harrison JS 153 w - -- Enterprise1398RougeDragon1538Ossabaw15710 Strong finish 4
14Oct42- 3Lrl sl *2 S'Chase 4:18³ 3↑ Governor Ogle H 4.4k 1 1 1hd 35 424 428 Penrod J 135wb 2.50 -- Elkridge1488Redlands1398Strolling On13312 Tired quickly 5
7Oct42- 3Bel fst *3 S'Chase 6:05¹ 4↑ Grand National H 17k 2 3 32 48¼ 632 666 Penrod J 136 w 11.20 -- Cottsmor1557Cupd13430IronShot1391 Bad landing 15th,tired 9
23Sep42- 3Bel fst *2 S'Chase 3:48³ 3↑ Broad Hollow H 3.9k 2 1 1½ 1nk 31½ 38½ Slate F 137 w 3.65 -- Elkrdg1453½LovlyNght1525RougDrgn1372½ Bobbled 8th,hung 5
29Aug42- 3Sar fst *2 S'Chase 4:16 3↑ Alw 1200 4 4 42 77¾ 2½ 12½ Clements HW 139 w *1.15 -- Rouge Dragon1392½Nayr1391Cortesano1522 7
Shuffled back 10th,easily
1Nov41- 3Pim hy *2 S'Chase 4:10¹ 3↑ Alw 1000 2 3 23 12 110 110 Jennings E 134 w *1.75 -- RougeDragon134.510WarPort1461½Millrac1488 Eased up late 8
16Oct41- 2Lrl fst *2 S'Chase 3:54 3↑ Alw 1000 2 1 18 112 18 16 Jennings E 135 w 2.50 -- Rouge Dragon1356Bagpipe1451Frederic II1433 6
Swerved at several jumps
21Aug41- 1Sar fst *2 S'Chase 4:20² 3↑ Alw 1200 2 1 13 110 16 110 Jennings E 138 w *.65e -- Rouge Dragon13810Pico Blanco II1498Sir Wick135hd Easily 7
9Aug41- 1Sar fst *2 S'Chase 4:18 3↑ Alw 1500 5 1 12 15 11 2hd Jennings E 135 w 2.70 -- Buck Langhorne137hdRouge Dragon1352½Archery136100 6
Bad landing last,recovered
14Jun41- 2PiR fst *1½ Hurdles 3:11³ 3↑ Alw 600 3 1 11½ 14 14 15 Jennings E 135 w 33.60 -- RgeDrgn1355KingCob14510NorthSea13515 Never threatened 8
Previously trained by S.L. Burch
26Jun40- 1Del my 5½f :23² :47¹ 1:08¹ ©Md Sp Wt 1 7 65¾ 79½ 1012 810 Driscoll D 118wb 124.85 81-29 Cavalier118nkZacorel1183Fantastical1181½ No excuse 11
20Jun40- 5Del fst 5½f :23¹ :47² 1:07⁴ Alw 1000 4 5 65¼ 68¾ 69¼ 69¾ Driscoll D 111wb 33.10 83-13 Overdrawn1134Miss Brideaux114nkDon Orlan115½ Trailed 6
8Jun40- 1Del fst 5f :23² :47¹ 1:00³ Md Sp Wt 5 10 1012 1011 1117 1121 Driscoll D 116 w 47.20 72-07 Curious Coin1161½Fitzedward116½Primarily1162½ Outrun 11

Royal Governor

ch. g. 1944, by Pilate (Friar Rock)–Feathers, by John P. Grier **Lifetime record: 135 28 15 18 $360,900**

Own.– Mrs J.R.H. Thouron
Br.– Abram S. Hewitt (Va)
Tr.– J.E. Ryan

8Jun55- 6Del sly 1 1/16 :23³ :47³ 1:13² 1:47 3↑ Alw 5000 3 5 59½ 57 59 58 Westrope J 117 w 11.80 68-22 Resilnt103noRustcBlly1172SnorCot1053 Trailed throughout 5
28May55- 7Del fst 1 1/16 :23³ :47¹ 1:11² 1:43⁴ 4↑ Alw 5000 4 6 64½ 37 38 310 Glassner G 119 w 4.80 82-12 RusticBilly1195Browse1065RoyalGovernor1193 Evenly late 6
26May55- 7Bel hd 1⅜Ⓣ 2:18¹ 3↑ Handicap 7500 3 7 56 44½ 46 33¾ Bailey PJ 116 w 7.25 92-04 AlcibiadesII116nkDeepRvrII1153½RoylGovrnor116nk Rallied 8
17May55- 7Bel fst 1 1/16 :24 :47¹ 1:11³ 1:42³ 4↑ Alw 6000 1 3 38 415 519 516 Westrope J 119 w 18.25 82-13 Chief Fanelli1163Dear Brutus1164Capeador1194 Outrun 6
9Apr55- 7Jam fst 6f :23² :46³ 1:11 3↑ Handicap 6000 8 8 813 815 819 816 Westrope J 113 w 35.20 76-17 Squared Away1222½Cyclotron116¾This Side1137 Trailed 8
3Mar55- 8Hia fm 1⅛Ⓣ 1:51¹ 4↑ Alw 4500 6 6 68 44 41½ 1hd Brooks S 118 w *1.80 93-07 RoyalGovernor118hdSickl'sSound105hdSmBrook109hd Driving 7
25Feb55- 5Hia fm 1 3/16Ⓣ 1:56⁴ 4↑ Alw 7500 5 5 53½ 53½ 54 44 Brooks S 110 w 6.35 89-07 Social Outcast1242Maharajah121hdKaster1212 No menace 5
21Feb55- 7Hia fm 1⅛Ⓣ 1:51³ 4↑ Alw 5000 1 5 44 32 21½ 21¼ Guerin E 116 w 2.75 90-09 Potpourri1151¼Royal Governor116nkDead Duck115¾ Gamely 5
10Feb55- 7Hia fm 1 1/16Ⓣ 1:44¹ 4↑ Alw 6000 1 6 54 53 34 53¼ Atkinson T 109 w 24.35 92-05 Mister Black121¾Kaster1212Abbe Sting118½ Gave way late 12
3Feb55- 8Hia hd 1⅛Ⓣ 1:50² 4↑ Alw 5000 4 12 1112 88 76½ 77¾ Atkinson T 110 w 18.45 89-03 Kaster121½Lebanon Lad1042Assuan110nk Never a menace 12
25Jan55- 7Hia hd 1⅛Ⓣ 1:50² 4↑ Alw 6000 3 9 810 74 44 57½ Nichols J 121 w 16.00 89-03 Cascunez1213½Assuan1121Lebanon Lad1093 No mishap 9
21Jan55- 6Hia fst 7f :23⁴ :47 1:11⁴ 1:24³ 4↑ Alw 4500 1 8 86¾ 75¾ 43½ 43½ Nichols J 121 w 22.70 83-18 Helfast118noFull Flight1241Fife and Drum1212½ Late gain 8
21Oct54- 7Bel fst 1 1/16 :23² :46⁴ 1:11⁴ 1:43⁴ 4↑ Alw 5000 2 4 76¾ 78¼ 79½ 711½ Westrope J 120 w 35.75 80-15 FlyWheel1143SpinningTop110hdDr.Stanley1111 Done early 9
16Oct54- 7Lrl fm *1⅛Ⓣ 1:51 3↑ Turf Cup H 25k 13 2 63¾ 106½ 1113 1117 Scurlock D 112wb 26.80 70-13 Stan1262½News Again1112½Tritium1142 Tired badly 13
8Oct54- 6Bel fm 1⅜Ⓣ 2:18¹ 3↑ Alw 10000 2 3 24 22 32½ 43¾ Westrope J 119 w 7.30 92-04 Blood Test113½Aria Viva1131¾Nitribois1141½ Tired late 8
29Sep54- 6Bel fm 1⅜Ⓣ 2:17⁴ 3↑ Lion d'Or H 15k 10 9 912 711 56½ 69¾ Westrope J 115 w 4.55e 88-02 Kaster122½Cascunuez1081¾Tritium1142 Dropped far back 13
22Sep54- 6Bel gd 6f-WC :22⁴ :46¹ 1:11¹ 2↑ Fall Highweight H 25k 1 14 149¾ 1412 1010 1212 Westrope J 113 w 34.80f 73-21 Pet Bully1361½Dutch Lane1171½Dark Peter125½ No speed 14
15Sep54- 6Atl fm 1⅛Ⓣ :47³ 1:12⁴ 1:38² 1:51 3↑ ⓇAmerican Bred 30k 3 9 96½ 95¾ 79 64½ Westrope J 118 w 7.10e 83-13 Brush Burn122¾Closed Door1221County Clare1221 Rallied 10
Restricted to horses foaled within the continental United States
9Sep54- 6Aqu fst 6f :23¹ :47¹ 1:11⁴ 3↑ Handicap 6045 2 6 88¾ 79¾ 79½ 711 Westrope J 113 w 55.90 82-15 CopperKettle119hdBrdly1222Ruthrd1172 Raced far off pace 8
25Aug54- 7Sar fst 1 :24² :47¹ 1:12² 1:37³ 3↑ Handicap 5050 3 9 67½ 77½ 821 922 Eccard R 111 w 40.05 67-18 Crash Dive1222Trusting1124½Bradley1151 Void of speed 9
12Jun54- 7Bel hd 1⅜Ⓣ 2:17² 3↑ Handicap 15085 11 12 1110 105¾ 108¼ 93½ Westrope J 121 w 9.80 -- Kaster121½Williamsburg107hdPicador116no Never a menace 13
31May54- 6Del fst 1 1/16 :23³ :47¹ 1:11² 1:43² 3↑ Brandywine H 24k 5 8 95¾ 99¾ 812 713 Green B 115 w 7.80 81-17 Cold Command116nkFirst Aid1136Better Goods1091 Outrun 10
22May54- 5Bel sf 1⅜Ⓣ 2:21¹ 3↑ Handicap 10045 4 4 2hd 1hd 11 1nk Westrope J 122 w *1.30 -- RoyalGovernor122nkTurgueneff1111½OutPoint113nk Driving 7
10May54- 7Bel sf 7fⓉ 1:31 3↑ Handicap 7555 3 5 55¼ 54½ 1½ 11½ Westrope J 117 w 5.25 -- RoyalGovernor1171½Kaster1224JamiK.1131½ Increasing lead 8
1May54- 5Bel fm 7fⓉ 1:24² 4↑ Alw 7500 1 8 87¾ 88¼ 43½ 32 Atkinson T 119 w 7.80 -- Kaster1191½Pcdor112½RoylGovrnor1192½ Closed ground fast 10
27Apr54- 6Bel fst 1 :22³ :45⁴ 1:10³ 1:37 3↑ Eight Thirty H 15k 3 14 1512 119¼ 915 117 Westrope J 114 w 33.20 82-19 OpenShow119nkGoldenGloves114¾JamieK.111¾ Never a factor 15
19Apr54- 5Jam fst 1 1/16 :24³ :48³ 1:13³ 1:45² 4↑ Alw 5000 4 6 65¼ 44½ 24 33½ Westrope J 122 w 5.15 81-18 War Command1123Lafourche119½Royal Governor1221½ Hung 7
14Apr54- 5Jam fst 6f :23³ :46⁴ 1:11³ 3↑ Handicap 6045 2 1 66 66 63½ 54¼ Westrope J 113 w 13.90 85-18 ColdCommand1231Hilarious1262½Armageddn115½ Late spurt 7
3Mar54- 7Hia hd 1½Ⓣ 2:28⁴ 3↑ Hia Turf H 64k 10 4 64½ 129¾ 1216 1218 Stout J 114 w 3.90e 82-00 Picador1062½Royal Vale126½Parnassus1202 Done early 12
25Feb54- 7Hia hd 1 3/16Ⓣ 1:56 4↑ Alw 6000 4 3 32½ 2hd 1hd 2½ Westrope J 112 w 4.15 96-03 IcebergII121½RoyalGovernor112½CombatBoots1124 Held well 6
17Feb54- 7Hia hd 1 3/16Ⓣ 1:55² 3↑ Bougainvillea H 33k 7 9 98 86¼ 1213 1113 Westrope J 113 w *2.65e 93-00 Parnassus1113½Picador105½Abbe Sting116½ Dull effort 12
12Feb54- 7Hia hd 1 1/16Ⓣ 1:43¹ 4↑ Alw 6000 1 4 42 32 21 1nk Westrope J 112 w 3.10 100-00 Royal Governor112nkMackville1122Parnassus1163 Driving 10
6Feb54- 5Hia fst 6f :22² :45² 1:10¹ 4↑ Alw 5000 4 7 79¼ 67½ 67¼ 56¾ Westrope J 118 w 19.50 90-11 Hyphasis1183Jet Master112¾Eatontown1131 No mishap 8
30Jan54- 8Hia fst 7f :23 :46² 1:11³ 1:24² 4↑ Alw 4500 3 6 66 53½ 51¾ 63 Stout J 118 w 7.45 85-12 Brown Booter1131½Ceremonious109hdSlim1071 No mishap 7
Previously raced in name of Mrs E. duPont Weir
4Nov53- 6Jam fst 6f :23¹ :46 1:11³ 3↑ Sport Page H 22k 2 1 89½ 98½ 88¼ 86 Westrope J 112 w 15.55 83-21 White Skies1301¼Hilarious114hdJoe Jones107¾ No threat 9
31Oct53- 6Lrl fst *1⅛Ⓣ 1:51¹ 3↑ Turf Cup H (Div 1) 23k 1 5 64¼ 65¼ 32½ 21 Guerin E 120 w 3.90 85-15 Sunglow1141RoyalGovrnr1202FreshMeadow1101 Good effort 10

17Oct53-6Jam	fst 1⅛	:472 1:113 1:37 1:501	3↑ Grey Lag H 62k	5	7	88¾	1516	1529	1531	Westrope J	116	w	23.00	64-21	Find1154Dictar119¾Olympic113no	Dull form	15
7Oct53-7Atl	gd 5½f(T)	:221 :453 1:052	3↑ Absecon Island H 11k	9	7	88¼	72¾	52½	52½	Westrope J	118	w	8.00	90-14	Algasir1182Roaming119½Blue Rhymer113no	Blocked late	10
26Sep53-6Atl	fst 1 3/16(T)	:473 1:12 1:362 1:554	3↑ U Nations H 60k	2	4	45	52½	52½	31½	Stout J	118	w	*.60e	111-00	IcebergII1201¼BrushBrun118nkRoyalGovernor118½	Blocked	8
16Sep53-6Atl	fst 1⅛(T)	:47 1:111 1:364 1:50	3↑ (R)American Bred 30k	8	4	31	11½	11½	1nk	Westrope J	122	w	8.30	93-06	RoyalGovernor122nkTheEagl1221½Potpourr122no	Hard drive	9
		Restricted to horses foaled within the continental United States															
5Sep53-7Atl	fst 1 1/16(T)	:232 :464 1:11 1:433	3↑ Atl City Turf H 23k	9	8	76½	65¾	63	2¾	Stout J	109	w	14.30	101-00	SaddleTramp107¾RoylGovrnor109¾IcbrgII119nk	Sharp effort	10
22Aug53-6Atl	fst 1(T)	:232 :47 1:112 1:371	3↑ Boardwalk H (Div 1) 18k	6	7	72¾	33	3½	45¾	Contreras J	112	w	50.40	89-04	Sunglow1083½Armageddon1211½Potpourri114¾	Weakened	10
14Aug53-5Sar	fst 1⅛	:48 1:123 1:381 1:522	3↑ Alw 4500	2	4	57½	68	614	617	Westrope J	113	w	17.05	71-18	CombatBoots1134Bassanio1105Sickl'sSound109no	Done early	6
4Aug53-7Sar	fst 6f	:23 :461 1:123	3↑ Alw 4000	1	10	1016	1017	914	108¼	Westrope J	113	w	16.25	77-17	Kaster118nkMr. Midnight106¾Caesar Did1103	No threat	11
22Jly53-6Jam	fst 1 1/16	:252 :494 1:14 1:451	4↑ Alw 5000	5	4	44	42½	34	45½	Westrope J	118	w	3.35	80-15	Mully S.1181¼Begorra1183½Dawn Flight113¾	No rally	5
3Jly53-7Del	sl 1 1/16	:234 :474 1:124 1:47	3↑ Alw 5000	1	4	45½	47	410	410	Westrope J	111	wb	3.55	66-25	G.R. Petersen1201½Promptness1086Fred R.1202½	No menace	6
27Jun53-7Del	fst 6f	:223 :461 1:111	4↑ Alw 5000	3	5	46½	42½	42	52½	Westrope J	112	wb	*1.75	86-07	Banta112noPotpourri119nkSteak Bone115¾	No rally	6
16Nov51-7Pim	sl 1 3/16	:472 1:112 1:372 1:572	3↑ Pim Spl 15k	2	4	31½	22	412	419	Bierman C	126	wb	*.80e	74-26	Bryan G.1265County Delight12612Call Over1262¼	No rally	4
12Nov51-6Jam	fst 6f	:231 :454 1:111	2↑ Autumn Day H 17k	5	8	53	42½	54	73¼	Boulmetis S	114	wb	6.35	88-20	Tea-Maker115½Guillotine126¾Delegate120hd	No rally	9
5Nov51-6Jam	fst 1 1/16	:25 :482 1:123 1:443	3↑ Handicap 5065	1	6	44½	52¾	33	43	Guerin E	122	wb	*1.20	86-17	(D)All at Once108hdTed M.1152½Lambent112½	Tired	8
		Placed third through disqualification															
27Oct51-5Jam	fst 5½f	:23 :461 1:044	3↑ Handicap 5040	4	4	72¾	63¾	51¾	11¼	Guerin E	122	wb	5.95	94-15	Royal Governor1221¼Pictus117nkVigorous1181½	Driving	7
17Oct51-5Bel	fst 1	:24 :471 1:112 1:364	3↑ Handicap 5050	2	1	2hd	2½	2hd	3¾	Guerin E	116	wb	4.80	89-15	Nullify106hdMiche122¾Royal Governor1162	Game effort	6
28Sep51-7Atl	fst 6f	:23 :462 1:113	3↑ Alw 4500	7	4	66½	66	65¾	44¾	Servis J	119	w	1.90	82-19	Passemson112¾Mahoon117½Woodford Sir1143½	No rally	8
24Sep51-6Bel	fst 6f-WC	:222 :443 1:09	2↑ Fall Highweight H 25k	3	12		156¼	165	125½	Combest N	128	w	*4.85f	90-07	Guillotine134noSquared Away1262Ferd128no	Outrun	18
3Sep51-7Was	fst 1	:222 :443 1:09 1:343	3↑ Wash Park H 159k	14	7	1211	1212	119¼	117¾	Baird RL	116	w	8.50e	89-07	Curandero115noOilCapitol1161½CountyDlght1231½	No factor	19
25Aug51-7Was	fst 1 3/16(T)	:474 1:364 1:544	3↑ Meadowland H 55k	5	7	57	65	811	910	Gorman D	120	w	4.80	90-07	Volcanic1281½Cuore1131½Mr. Fox111no	No factor	9
8Aug51-6Sar	my 6f	:234 :464 1:113	3↑ Handicap 4035	2	3	33	33½	32½	24½	Servis J	121	w	3.65	85-21	NorthernStar1124½RoylGovrnr121noMgcWords1158	Went well	4
4Jly51-7AP	fst 1⅛(T)	:47 1:112 1:361 1:491	3↑ Stars & Stripes H 60k	7	8	64¾	31½	11	11	Arcaro E	115	w	6.80	100-07	Royal Governor1151Volcanic1243½Miche1162	Driving	17
20Jun51-5Del	fst 1 1/16	:23 :463 1:113 1:442	3↑ Alw 4000	4	6	56½	53½	54	45	Nichols J	122	wb	2.10	86-10	Bit o' Fate1171½Loyal Legion1221Arcave1162½	Tired	6
9Jun51-5Del	fst 1¼	:472 1:12 1:37 2:02	3↑ Sussex H 28k	4	2	1hd	34	47½	511	Nichols J	116	wb	5.75	89-14	Cochise1243½Bit o' Fate1084½Post Card1161	Tired	6
5Jun51-6Del	my 6f	:232 :474 1:13	4↑ Alw 3500	1	2	45	43	32	2½	Nichols J	126	wb	*.80	85-28	LoyalLegion117½RoyalGovrnr1262½LedngHom1125	No excuse	6
29May51-6Del	gd 6f	:224 :462 1:113	3↑ Wilmington H 12k	5	6	610	57½	45	31	Nichols J	115	wb	4.50	92-20	CallOver1151Tea-Maker125hdRoyalGovernor115nk	Late rush	6
24May51-4Bel	gd 6f	:222 :453 1:102	3↑ Handicap 4545	4	5	511	57	55	55¾	Nichols J	122	wb	2.60	91-10	SingingStep119nkAri'sMona1042MghtyQust1171½	Dull effort	6
18May51-7Bel	fst 6f	:222 :451 1:101	4↑ Alw 4500	3	3	63¾	53½	32½	32	Guerin E	115	wb	*1.30	97-05	Sagittrus1141½Extngushr114¾RoylGovrnor1151¼	Closed well	7
3Nov50-6Pim	fst 1 3/16	:493 1:14 1:393 1:583	3↑ Pim Spl 15k	1	2	22	21	44	483	Scurlock O	126	wb	*1.70	78-19	One Hitter1262½Chicle II1261¼Abstract1265	Tired	4
27Oct50-6Lrl	fst 6f	:224 :464 1:113	3↑ Alw 4000	7	2	55¼	43¼	41¾	11	McLean P	122	wb	*1.80	89-19	Royal Governor1221Flying Weather1191Magnet1161	Drew out	7
25Sep50-6Bel	fst 7f	:223 :453 1:102 1:23	2↑ Vosburgh H 18k	2	11	1110	106¾	44½	55¼	Guerin E	118	wb	6.75	90-15	Tea-Maker1181¼More Sun106½Piet124nk	Closed gap	12
18Sep50-6Bel	fst 6f-WC	:221 :443 1:084	2↑ Fall Highweight H 25k	7	14		132½	123	32¼	Guerin E	129	wb	8.85	95-06	Arise1332Delegate128nkRoyal Governor129½	Finished well	14
19Aug50-6Sar	my 1¼	:483 1:132 1:383 2:053	3↑ Saratoga H 29k	4	7	89½	56½	47	69¼	Arcaro E	115	w	5.85	71-21	Better Self1141Greek Ship1101Arise1183½	Tired	9
11Aug50-6Sar	fst 7f	:23 :462 1:11 1:233	3↑ American Legion H 9.5k	13	6	32	23	32	66	McLean P	118	w	8.90	92-13	Arise1152Guillotine118nkLoser Weeper1191½	Faltered	13
15Jly50-6Jam	fst 1 3/16	:473 1:121 1:364 1:55	3↑ Butler H 58k	2	2	811	87¾	43½	32	Boland W	118	w	9.80	99-11	(D)Three Rings1201½Loser Weeper118½Royal Governor118½		10
		Placed second through disqualification															
4Jly50-6Aqu	fst 1¼	:474 1:121 1:371 2:03	3↑ Brooklyn H 59k	10	7	57	56	54¼	43¾	Guerin E	118	w	6.90	88-12	MyRequest1191¼DoublBrandy1151½HypocritII1031	No mishap	10
1Jly50-6Aqu	fst 7f	:224 :453 1:102 1:231	3↑ Carter H 24k	3	9	98¼	98¾	97¾	86¼	Rogers C	121	w	8.00	90-10	Guillotine109¾Noble Impulse1141Hyphasis1081	Dull try	10
17Jun50-5Del	fst 1¼	:474 1:122 1:373 2:03	3↑ Sussex H 30k	3	4	66½	42¼	41½	3¾	Rogers C	118	w	3.90	94-14	Cochise125¾Curandero112hdRoylGovrnor1182	Close quarters	7
14Jun50-5Del	sly 1 1/16	:244 :492 1:142 1:451	3↑ Alw 3000	2	4	43½	3½	11	13	Rogers C	120	w	*.35	87-20	Royal Governor1203Taran1145Algasir1178	Easily	4
24May50-6Bel	fst 6f-WC	:222 :444 1:09	3↑ Roseben H 12k	3	9	97¾	85¼	63	31¼	Guerin E	122	wb	10.35	95-07	Olympia130nkWine List1101Royal Governor122hd	Great rush	9
20May50-6Bel	sly 1	:23 :452 1:102 1:363	3↑ Metropolitan H 31k	1	7	76¾	65¾	64½	64½	Rogers C	119	wb	11.25	86-13	Greek Ship106½Piet121¾Cochise1211¼	No rally	11
13May50-6Pim	fst 1 3/16	:484 1:12 1:364 1:561	3↑ Dixie H 26k	9	1	11½	1½	22	46¼	Rogers C	118	wb	4.20	93-13	Loser Weeper1085Double Brandy110¾Going Away106½	Outrun	9
29Apr50-6Jam	gd 1 3/16	:473 1:12 1:372 1:57	3↑ Gallant Fox H 60k	3	3	41½	43	23	52	Rogers C	120	wb	9.15	89-14	BetterSelf1161¼ChicleII120hdLoserWeeper109nk	Weakened	13
8Apr50-6Jam	fst 1 1/16	:241 :473 1:112 1:434	3↑ Excelsior H 24k	1	6	75¾	74½	75	97½	Rogers C	122	w	4.00	86-10	Arise1161½Olympia1261½Delegate1191	Close quarters	10
1Apr50-6Jam	fst 6f	:222 :461 1:104	3↑ Paumonok H 30k	2	13	139	128¼	84½	98½	Rogers C	126	w	7.30	88-14	Olympia1241½Arise118½Delegate1223	No factor	15
25Feb50-6Hia	sl 1¼	:48 1:122 1:382 2:06	3↑ Widener H 61k	5	2	36½	35	22	1nk	Rogers C	118	w	2.95	75-27	Royal Governor118nkArise1096Going Away1104	Hard drive	6
11Feb50-6Hia	fst 1⅛	:463 1:111 1:37 1:501	3↑ McLennan H 33k	10	8	106¾	64¼	44	21	Rogers C	116	w	14.75	86-17	ThreeRings1171RoyalGovernor1161Coaltown1321	Stout rally	11
3Dec49-6Bow	fst 1 3/16	:48 1:123 1:383 1:582	3↑ Bryan & O'Hara H 21k	6	4	51¾	62¾	1112	1114	Lynch J	124	w	2.50	81-10	Double Brandy1111½Oriole108noSeaward1132½	Dull effort	11
19Nov49-6Bow	fst 1 1/16	:241 :482 1:132 1:452	2↑ T K Lynch Mem H 12k	12	9	109¾	96½	57½	45½	Errico C	125	w	*1.20	88-10	Cochise113½Seaward1135Manchac109no	Forced back	13
12Nov49-6Jam	fst 1 3/16	:471 1:113 1:37 1:564	3↑ Westchester H 29k	8	5	56½	77¾	21	3nk	Scurlock O	123	w	3.20	92-17	ThreeRings116nkDelegate120hdRoyalGovernor1235	Game try	11
26Oct49-6Jam	sly 1 1/16	:243 :48 1:122 1:452	3↑ Questionnaire H 23k	7	6	66½	44	1hd	11	Guerin E	118	w	3.60	86-17	Royal Governor1181Donor120½Vulcan's Forge125¾	Driving	8
15Oct49-6Jam	fst 1 1/16	:242 :48 1:124 1:442	3↑ Grey Lag H 29k	7	5	45	31½	1½	11	Scurlock O	114	w	15.25	91-16	Royal Governor1141Three Rings116hdCapot121nk	Driving	12
12Oct49-6Jam	fst 6f	:224 :461 1:111	3↑ Interborough H 17k	6	9	108	105¾	1½	11	Guerin E	119	w	9.50	95-15	Royal Governor1191Delegate122noPipette1121½	Driving	10
3Oct49-6GS	fst 6f	:222 :453 1:10	3↑ Princeton H 12k	4	6	86	76½	78½	56½	Lynch J	118	w	10.20	91-16	RoyalBlood1165CarraraMarble1181Rippy124½	Close quarters	12
19Sep49-6Bel	fst 6f-WC	:23 :461 1:12	2↑ Fall Highweight H 24k	12	4		73¼	31½	1hd	Guerin E	129	w	8.70	81-16	RoyalGovernor129hdRoyalBlood132nkTea-Maker127¾	Driving	13
3Sep49-6Aqu	fst 1 1/16	:243 :482 1:123 1:46	3↑ Aqueduct H 23k	5	4	42½	42½	52¼	84½	Lynch J	114	w	12.10	79-19	Wine List114½(D)Loser Weeper114¾Riverlane107½	Tired	14
23Aug49-6Sar	fst 6f	:223 :463 1:11	3↑ Handicap 4060	1	7	75½	54	51¼	41	Arcaro E	118	w	3.00	92-11	Wine List115hdBlue Border115nkRoyal Blood114¾	Blocked	10
18Aug49-5Sar	sly 6f	:231 :471 1:122	3↑ Handicap 4035	1	2	32	21	2½	2nk	Glisson G	119	w	3.80	86-21	WhirlingFox112nkRoyalGovrnor1198Mngohck1262	Good effort	5
		Daily Racing Form time,1:11 4/5															
12Aug49-6Sar	sly 7f	:234 :464 1:113 1:252	3↑ American Legion H 9.2k	7	6	75½	67½	44½	43½	McLean P	118	w	5.20	85-18	Manyunk119hdWhirling Fox1102Big If1101½	Raced wide	8
		Daily Racing Form time,1:26 1/5															
18Jun49-6Mth	fst 1	:23 :461 1:111 1:373	3↑ Salvator Mile 13k	2	5	67½	54	32	33	McLean P	119	w	*1.90	104-08	Istan1142High Trend1121Royal Governor1191½	Hung	14
30May49-5Del	fst 1 1/16	:232 :464 1:104 1:424	3↑ Brandywine H 12k	4	3	32	2hd	13	15	McLean P	115	w	2.55	99-14	RoyalGovernor1155Coincidence109nkMarchonsII112hd	Easily	8
28May49-6Del	fst 6f	:222 :452 1:103	3↑ Wilmington H 12k	4	6	62½	52¼	21	1½	McLean P	113	w	3.85	99-12	Royal Governor113½Piet1151Royal Blood1151½	Driving	10
14May49-6GS	fst 6f	:221 :451 1:093	3↑ Camden H 17k	1	8	95½	85¾	52¼	43	McLean P	113	w	10.80	98-08	Ocean Brief120noMacbeth1113Buzfuz121no	Late foot	10
6May49-6Bel	fst 6f-WC	:224 :451 1:092	3↑ Toboggan H 24k	7	5	84¼	41½	31½	52½	Adams J	114	w	6.25	91-05	Rippey1291½Pipette108¾Up Beat120no	Swerved	11
28Apr49-6HdG	fst 1 70	:24 :483 1:134 1:421	4↑ Alw 3500	6	4	45¼	31	11	11¼	McLean P	116	w	*.40	97-13	Royal Governor1161½Hash Night11010Leamour115½	Cleverly	6
20Apr49-6HdG	fst 6f	:224 :46 1:113	3↑ Philadelphia H 12k	8	2	85¾	53¼	31	2nk	McLean P	114	w	*3.10	93-14	PepWell112nkRoyalGovrnor114.5hdFultlss119no	Just missed	10
9Apr49-7Jam	fst 6f	:23 :462 1:121	4↑ Handicap 5055	9	5	69	44½	11½	12	Guerin E	121	w	3.55	90-18	Royal Governor1212Master Mind1134Up Beat1181	Driving	9
1Apr49-6Jam	fst 6f	:223 :47 1:122	3↑ Paumonok H 21k	5	6	88½	66	98¼	96	Guerin E	115	w	13.90	83-20	Rippey1251Energetic1102My Request130¾	Outrun	13
26Feb49-7Hia	fst 1¼	:472 1:112 1:363 2:02	3↑ Widener H 60k	4	5	59	33	64¾	69¾	McLean P	111	w	15.85	85-10	Coaltown1232Shy Guy120½Faultless117¾	Quit	6
21Feb49-5Hia	fst 6f	:22 :45 1:103	4↑ Alw 3500	4	4	66¾	54	41	3½	McLean P	118	w	7.00	94-16	BlueBorder121noLoriot114½RoyalGovernor118hd	Stout rally	8
12Nov48-5Pim	fst 1 1/16	:233 :471 1:112 1:422	3↑ Alw 5000	2	5	54¼	43¾	2½	11½	McLean P	114	w	3.80	106-09	RoyalGovrnr1141½LoserWeeper1034Camargo115nk	Drew out	6
2Nov48-6Pim	fst 6f	:223 :452 1:104	2↑ Janney H 9.2k	2	4	65½	58½	46	44	Basile M	110	w	5.90	93-09	Istan117½Lookout Son1093Lanlast112½	Stumbled	7
16Oct48-5Bel	fst 6f	:23 :464 1:12	3↑ Handicap 6040	4	4	74¾	77¼	75¼	87	Permane R	111	w	5.00	83-19	Buzfuz1221½Blue Border120½Knockdown120½	Outrun	8
4Oct48-6Jam	fst 6f	:233 :471 1:121	3↑ Fleetwing H 29k	3	2	106¾	108¼	5½	2hd	Permane R	106	w	25.75	90-19	Buzfuz115hdRoyalGovernor106½FirstFlght126no	Closed fast	10
29Sep48-5Bel	fst 6f	:23 :464 1:122	4↑ Alw 4500	4	3	41¾	21	3nk	11	Atkinson T	117	w	*.45	88-14	Royal Governor1171Ben Lewis115noSonadora1101½	Drew out	6
3Sep48-7Aqu	fst 6f	:241 :481 1:131	3↑ Alw 4000	1	1	42	43¼	3½	11¼	Guerin E	124	w	*2.90	86-24	Royal Governor1241¼Nassau1181½Dutel1072	Driving	9
12Aug48-7Sar	gd 6f	:24 :472 1:122	4↑ Alw 4000	3	2	41¾	52½	41¼	25	Guerin E	114	w	2.85	81-22	Pipette1085Royal Governor1141¾Repand1131	Inside turn	8
29May48-5Del	fst 6f	:223 :46 1:113	3↑ Wilmington H 13k	9	5	73¼	62½	65	97¼	Allgaier H	110	wb	9.65f	87-09	Itsabet113(DH)Phar Mon1142½(DH)Mity Me1121	Outrun	14

8May48- 5GS	gd 1	:233:47 1:121 1:392 3↑	Valley Forge H 20k	10 5 45½ 88¼ 97¾ 1010	Allgaier H	110 w	21.20	80-18	Rampart109nkRippey121¾Senoril110nk	Quit	10
24Apr48- 6HdG	gd 6f	:224:46 1:113 3↑	Harford H 12k	4 5 57 55 55½ 78	Mora H	110 w	4.10	85-28	Loyal Legion1202Daily Dip104hdLittle Harp1121½	Outrun	8
17Apr48- 5Jam	fst 1 1/16	:243:482 1:132 1:46 3↑	Excelsior H 29k	6 5 65½ 52¾ 42¼ 57¼	Atkinson T	114 w	4.05	76-20	Knockdown114¾Double Jay1252½Stymie1284	No mishap	9
1Apr48- 5Jam	sly 6f	:23 :462 1:114 3↑	Paumonok H 35k	5 2 54 32½ 22 23½	Atkinson T	112 w	6.15	88-18	BetterSlf1123½RoylGovrnor1122LtsDnc113hd	Close quarters	13
17May47- 5HdG	fst 1⅛	:472 1:122 1:373 1:503	Potomac 11k	1 4 43 42 55 511¼	Saunders W	120 w	*.90	85-13	Loyal Legion1176Mityme1172Camargo1123	No excuse	5
6May47- 6Pim	fst 1 1/16	:231:47 1:122 1:471	Survivor 9.8k	2 9 810 64¾ 43 3hd	Saunders W	116 w	*.80	82-20	Mityme116noLoyalLgon113noRoylGovrnor1161½	Strong finish	9
26Apr47- 6HdG	fst 1 1/16	:231:47 1:12 1:444	Chesapeake 38k	12 11 117¼ 43½ 41½ 32¼	Saunders W	119 w	*2.20	90-13	BulletProof115.52Secnav114nkRoylGovrnor1192	Closed fast	14
19Apr47- 5HdG	fst 6f	:224:462 1:103	Chesapeake Trial 12k	5 3 94¾ 85½ 52¾ 11	Saunders W	122 w	4.30	99-08	Royal Governor1221Tavistock1141Mityme1181½	Drew out	10
13Nov46- 6Pim	fst 1 1/16	:232:471 1:122 1:454	Walden 33k	6 8 63¾ 44½ 32½ 33	Atkinson T	116 w	4.40	86-20	Frvnt116hdFultlss1133RoylGovrnor1167	Shuffled first turn	11
5Nov46- 6Pim	fst 6f	:23 :47 1:122	Sagamore 12k	8 4 2½ 21 1hd 1no	Atkinson T	116 w	5.70	91-17	Royal Governor116noBastogne113¾Faultless1141½	Driving	8
23Oct46- 6Lrl	gd 1 1/16	:233:474 1:142 1:472	SL Jenkins 9.8k	5 6 42½ 21 11 11¾	Atkinson T	118 w	*.80	80-22	Royal Governor1181¾Golden Bull1137Lovely Imp115no		10
Impeded,much best											
14Oct46- 5Bel	fst 6f-WC	:224:451 1:094	Handicap 5570	3 1 31½ 3nk 1hd	Atkinson T	122 w	*.95	92-06	Royal Governor122hdMr. John1102Lighthouse113¾	Driving	5
5Oct46- 6Lrl	fst 6f	:23 :471 1:12	Richard Johnson 9.3k	3 6 62¼ 63½ 64 22	Kirk C	122 w	*1.40	92-09	Repand1152RoyalGovernr1221½LovelyImp116hd	Belated rush	8
7Sep46- 4Aqu	fst 6f	:222:462 1:123	Babylon H 12k	2 2 42¼ 43¼ 31½ 11	Guerin E	114 w	3.10	89-14	Royal Governor1141Brabancon1111½Miss Disco109¾	Driving	7
2Sep46- 5GS	fst 6f	:222:461 1:112	©William Penn 13k	7 5 62¼ 44 33½ 43¾	Mehrtens W	119 w	4.05	90-14	Jobstown117hdWar Glance1173½Cellophane117hd	No rally	11
24Aug46- 4Sar	fst 6f	:222:453 1:093	Grand Union Hotel 20k	1 4 51½ 44 42¼ 48	Arcaro E	118 w	21.35	96-02	Blue Border110noI Will1266Grand Admiral1262	Good try	9
20Jly46- 5Jam	fst 6f	:23 :463 1:113	©East View 51k	10 5 41¼ 51¼ 51½ 75½	Lynch J	119 w	12.50	87-11	Grand Admiral1151I Will1192Phalanx115½	Bore over	11
4Jly46- 6Del	fst 5½f	:221:461 1:052	Dover 12k	13 3 41 21½ 24 14	Lynch J	116 w	7.15	95-10	RoylGovrnor1164BnLws116nkBulltProof1161½	Speed to spare	13
22Jun46- 5Del	sl 5½f	:231:481 1:072	©Christiana 11k	3 1 2hd 2hd 2½ 21	Mehrtens W	116 w	*2.15	84-27	Mityme1131Royal Governor11610Vacance116no	Second best	7
8Jun46- 3Del	fst 5f	:221:47 1:001	Alw 3000	1 2 4¾ 23 23 43½	Snider A	112 w	*.50e	86-11	Mesl1142Raol122nkPenny Reward1121	Speed,crowded	7
1Jun46- 1Del	fst 5f	:223:464 :593	©Md Sp Wt	6 2 21 1½ 13 14½	Snellings A	118 w	*1.75	92-10	Royal Governor1184½Stepinthedark1182Big Dub111nk	Easily	9

Speculate

br. g. 1936, by Westwick (Ultimus)–Virginia T., by Royal Canopy

Lifetime record: 18 4 7 1 $22,700

Own.– Bayard Sharp
Br.– P.M. Walker (Va)
Tr.– W. Passmore

4Aug43- 3Bel	fst *2	S'Chase 3:482 4↑	Shillelah 3.9k	6 5 520 55¾ 310 39½	Miller P	132 w	10.40	--	Delhi Dan1502½Elkridge1507Speculate1326	Pulled up lame	10
3Jly43- 4Det	fst *2	S'Chase 4:032 4↑	Handicap 5000	6 5 416 412 415 412	Miller P	140wb	*1.10e	--	Rouge Dragon1442½Bavarian1373½Ossabaw1386		6
Slow start,never a menace,stirrup irons broken after last											
14Aug42- 1Sar	fst *2	S'Chase 4:193 3↑	North American H 3.3k	3 4 313 - - -	Passmore W	145wb	*1.30	--	Elkridge1467The Beak1431Iron Shot143100	Pulled up lame	5
22Oct41- 2Lrl	fst *2½	S'Chase 5:062 4↑	Chevy Chase H 6.3k	4 3 39½ 311 - -	Roby T	147wb	*.65	--	War Lance13315Fay Cottage1375Brother Jones138	Ran out	5
3Oct41- 4Bel	sly *3	S'Chase 5:583 4↑	Grand National H 17k	2 4 310 21½ 14 16	Roby T	142wb	3.70	--	Speculate1426Sussex1481LondonTown15430	As rider pleased	7
26Sep41- 4Bel	fst *2½	S'Chase 4:461 4↑	Brook H 6.3k	5 6 316 38 21½ 21	Roby T	142wb	6.00	--	Sussex1441Speculate14215Corrigan1455	Driving	6
11Sep41- 1Aqu	fst *2½	S'Chase 5:53 4↑	Glendale H 5.8k	4 4 410 49 1hd 2hd	Roby T	140wb	1.30	--	ByDn139hdSpcult1402Sussx14815	Bad landings 16th & 17th	4
4Sep41- 1Aqu	fst *2	S'Chase 3:451 3↑	Harbor Hill H 3.7k	3 4 54¼ 47 22 22½	Roby T	141wb	3.45	--	Bath1332½Speculate1416Sussex1492	Finished well	5
23Aug41- 1Sar	fst *2	S'Chase 4:12 3↑	Alw 1500	1 5 59¼ 52½ 23 24	Roby T	152wb	*1.05	--	Corrigan1424Speculate1528Invader1321½	Bad landing last	7
8Aug41- 1Sar	fst *2	S'Chase 4:132 4↑	Shillelah 3.5k	5 5 45½ 22 13 16	Roby T	143wb	*.75	--	Speclte1436WingedHoofs13015TheBeak1374	Rated,drew away	5
28Jly41- 1Sar	gd *2	S'Chase 4:20 4↑	Alw 1200	2 4 418 22 13 14	Roby T	146wb	*1.70	--	Speculate1464Beach Maiden1324Golden Oak14712		6
Gained rapidly,speed to spare;Previously owned and trained by S.J. Holloway											
7Nov40- 3Pim	fst 2	S'Chase 3:563 3↑	Alw 1000	1 5 45½ 35 - -	Cruz H	138 w	4.50	--	Arch Hero1356Chuckatuck14040Wrackonite140	Fell at 14th	6
21Oct40- 2Lrl	hy *2	S'Chase 4:044 3↑	Sp Wt 1000	9 5 35½ 11 18 18	Cruz H	137 w	*1.80	--	Speculate1378DonRoberto1411½Farford13120	Speed to spare	10
14Oct40- 2Lrl	fst *2	S'Chase 3:542 3↑	Sp Wt 1000	6 8 815 48 24 22½	Zajkowski J	134 w	5.50e	--	Simoon1482½Speculate1344Millrace1446	Good finish	8
3Jun40- 1Bel	fst *2	S'Chase 3:51 4↑	Sp Wt 1200	2 6 514 516 38½ 210	Roby T	142 w	3.40	--	FrozenNorth14910Spculate1424GameRunnr14240	Second best	8
23May40- 4Bel	sly *2	S'Chase 3:572 4↑	Spring Maiden 4.9k	13 11 48½ 34 3½ 49	Clements HW	144 w	4.10e	--	Massa1372Fay Cottage1552Star Bramble1445		16
Sent into contention,quit											
13May40- 2Bel	fst *2	S'Chase 3:503 4↑	Sp Wt 1200	4 4 46 43 21 21½	Walker G	142 w	5.60	--	Kellsboro1471½Speculate1425Game Runner14720		5
Determined effort,no match											
6May40- 3Pim	fst 2	S'Chase 4:013 4↑	Sp Wt 1000	7 - - - - -	Zajkowski J	135 w	3.00e	--	Blanket1404Kosan14910Mr. Chips1542	Lost rider 3rd	9

Star Pilot

br. c. 1943, by Sickle (Phalaris)–Floradora, by Bull Dog

Lifetime record: 17 6 4 2 $187,885

Own.– Maine Chance Farm
Br.– Coldstream Stud (Ky)
Tr.– J.W. Smith

2Mar48- 8Hia	fst 1⅛	:462 1:112 1:372 1:502 4↑	Alw 4000	3 4 53 52½ 57 58¾	Dodson D	120 w	*2.85	80-14	Respingo1261½PtrolPont1091¼FrsAr1013½	Hard ridden,tired	10
18Feb48- 5Hia	fst 6f	:222:454 1:103 4↑	Alw 3500	4 4 65 64¼ 66 59½	Jessop JD	108wb	*1.30	85-11	EagleEye1162½YankeeHill111nkBordeaux1144½	Lacked rally	7
14Feb48- 5Hia	fst 7f	:233:47 1:113 1:234 4↑	Alw 5000	3 2 21½ 31½ 32½ 37	Snider A	116wb	10.30	86-10	Assault128hdRampart1097Star Pilot1169	Weakened	4
23Feb46- 7SA	fst 1⅛	:46 1:111 1:372 1:503	S A Derby 109k	3 4 44 22 22 21¾	Kirkland A	122 w	*.50e	89-08	Knockdown1221¾Star Pilot1223½Honeymoon1172½	Went well	5
15Feb46- 7SA	fst 1	:221:453 1:104 1:37	®Alw 10000	2 3 35½ 35½ 25 26	Kirkland A	122 w	*.40e	87-15	Knockdown1226Star Pilot1223Hie Heel117½	Held well	6
Previously trained by R. Waldron											
24Nov45- 5Pim	gd 1 1/16	:233:481 1:13 1:474	Pim Futurity 43k	4 2 2½ 12 12 11¼	Kirkland A	122 w	2.75e	79-24	StarPilot1221¼BillyBumps119nkColonyBoy1171½	Ridden out	8
Geldings not eligible;Previously trained by T. Smith											
31Oct45- 5Jam	fst 1 70	:233:472 1:122 1:441	Ardsley H 16k	6 1 1hd 2nk 2hd 1hd	Kirkland A	126 w	2.45	83-16	StarPilot126hdMisleader1121¾MarineVctory1245	Hard drive	8
20Oct45- 4Jam	fst 1 1/16	:242:482 1:132 1:454	Alw 7500	5 5 54¾ 43½ 37 38½	Kirkland A	122 w	*.55e	75-13	LordBoswell1195MightyStory1193½StarPilot1221¾	Went well	10
3Oct45- 4Bel	fst 1	:233:47 1:123 1:391	Champagne 20k	10 1 1hd 22 23 25	Kirkland A	122 w	*.80e	73-24	Marine Victory1165Star Pilot1221½Mahout106nk	No match	10
29Sep45- 4Bel	gd 6½f-W	:221:451 1:103 1:171	Futurity 65k	9 1 42 42½ 11	Kirkland A	126 w	*.70e	86-14	Star Pilot1261Athene1161Mighty Story1192	Driving	11
Geldings not eligible											
12Sep45- 6Aqu	fst 6½f	:231:464 1:122 1:18	Cowdin 31k	12 8 73¾ 77¾ 64½ 75¾	Kirkland A	126 w	4.75e	89-14	Knockdown1141½Revoked1261Southern Pride1201½	No threat	13
1Sep45- 4Bel	fst 6½f-W	:223:452 1:101 1:163	Hopeful 62k	10 7 71¾ 31 12¼	Kirkland A	112 w	20.35	89-09	Star Pilot1122¼Inroc1121½Revoked126nk	Drew clear	14
25Aug45- 5Bel	fst 6f-WC	:224:454 1:114	Grand Union Hotel 21k	2 4 73¼ 63¼ 21½	Wright WD	113 w	5.50	80-17	Manipur1121½Star Pilot113nkOur Bully112½	Finished well	9
28Jly45- 6Was	sly 6f	:224:462 1:12	Arl Futurity 70k	11 6 3½ 512 612 68¾	Grohs O	122 w	7.20e	81-19	SpySng1225Knockdown1222½MightyStory122no	Dropped back	11
6Jly45- 5Was	fst 5f	:232:48 1:001	Alw 2500	3 1 12 12 13 14	Adams J	115 w	*.80	95-21	Star Pilot1154Instanter1104Fly Off1151	Saved ground	7
23Jun45- 4Bel	fst 5f-WC	:222:454 :583	Nat'l Stallion 16k	2 4 52¾ 52¾ 510¼	Adams J	122 w	*.70e	77-12	Enfilade119nkHarvey's Pal1227Forgetmenow1192½	Outrun	5
15Jun45- 4Bel	fst 4½f-W	:224:46 :521	©Md Sp Wt	5 1 2½ 12 13	Adams J	116 w	*2.05	94-06	Star Pilot1163Allier116noMist o' Gold1162	Easily	13

Stefanita

b. f. 1940, by Questionnaire (Sting)–Stefana, by Stefan the Great

Lifetime record: 27 8 7 4 $72,360

Own.– G.D. Widener
Br.– George D. Widener (Ky)
Tr.– W.F. Mulholland

1Jly44- 6Aqu	fst 1¼	:483 1:132 1:39 2:024 3↑	Brooklyn H 57k	7 4 11½ 11 55 77½	Longden J	110wb	9.20	85-11	Four Freedoms116nkWait a Bit116noFirst Fiddle1265		9
Daily Racing Form time,2:03 3/5											
16Jun44- 5Aqu	fst 1 1/16	:243:48 1:131 1:464 3↑	®Handicap 4725	2 3 22 22 22 22½	Longden J	126wb	*.60	77-17	Good Morning1072½Stefanita1267Night Glow111		3
Fractious post,no match											

1Jun44- 6Bel	fst 1 1/16	:23 :454 1:11 1:432 3↑	ⒻTop Flight H 11k	2 7 65¼ 64¾ 64¼ 44¼	Longden J	124wb	10.50	90-10	Boojiana106¾Mar-Kell1263Silvestra112½	Evenly 10
22May44- 7Bel	fst 1 1/16	:463 1:121 1:374 1:443 3↑	ⒻHandicap 4965	8 8 89¼ 77¼ 810 811	Longden J	122wb	2.95	77-15	Anthemion108nkMar-Kll1204MoonMaiden1121	Never a factor 8
13Nov43- 6Pim	fst 1 3/16	:484 1:141 1:402 2:00 3↑	Bryan & O'Hara H 19k	8 5 21 22 1½ 1nk	McCreary C	117wb	3.30	82-31	Stefanita117nkAlsab1223Son of Peace1131	Driving 9
5Nov43- 6Pim	fst 1 1/16	:24 :484 1:14 1:47 3↑	ⒻLady Baltimore H 5.9k	3 2 21½ 21 21½ 11¼	McCreary C	120wb	*.40	83-24	Stefanita1201¼Barbara Childs1164Ok Sugar953	Driving 5
5Oct43- 6Bel	fst 1½	:483 1:134 2:05 2:314 3↑	ⒻLadies H 16k	7 2 22 3½ 1½ 11½	McCreary C	116wb	3.40	79-17	Stefanita1161½Vagrancy1236Dark Discovery1061¼	Handily 7
18Sep43- 6Aqu	fst 1⅛	:474 1:132 1:383 1:513 3↑	ⒻBeldame H 28k	4 5 22 21 11 21	McCreary C	116wb	*2.90	88-14	Mar-Kell1261Stefanita1162Vagrancy122½	No match 11
28Aug43- 6Nar	fst 1 1/16	:242 :482 1:133 1:46	ⒻNew England Oaks 11k	3 2 2½ 2nk 1½ 11¼	McCreary C	118wb	*.60	87-15	Stefanita1181¼Anthemion116½Best Risk1148	Ridden out 5
4Aug43- 6Bel	fst 1¼	:471 1:121 1:381 2:042	ⒻAlabama 17k	3 1 11 11 11½ 11¾	McCreary C	117wb	*.95	78-15	Stefanita1171¾Askmenow12420Tack Room114	Driving 3
30Jly43- 6Bel	gd 7f	:23 :464 1:121 1:251	ⒻTest 6.5k	11 8 64 41½ 41½ 12	McCreary C	117wb	5.30	84-16	Stefanita1172Best Risk108hdGood Morning120no	Handily 11
30Jun43- 5Jam	gd 1 1/16	:251 :491 1:134 1:462 3↑	ⒻHandicap 5120	2 2 22 22 22 21½	McCreary C	110wb	2.50	79-22	Night Glow1081½Stefanita1104Vagrancy12810	Belated rally 4
23Jun43- 6Aqu	fst 1 1/16	:242 :492 1:15 1:481	ⒻGazelle 6.5k	6 5 53½ 53½ 62½ 2hd	McCreary C	118wb	2.25	73-19	Anthemion112hdStefanita1181½LegendBrr112no	Impeded turn 10
3Jun43- 6Bel	fst 1 1/16	:233 :47 1:12 1:442 3↑	ⒻTop Flight H 6.4k	4 1 12 11 21½ 34	McCreary C	106wb	9.70	85-17	Mar-Kell1222YarrowMaid1102Stfnt1061½	Saved ground,tired 6
29May43- 7Bel	fst 1	:234 :472 1:131 1:392 3↑	ⒻHandicap 2550	3 5 55 32 31½ 45½	McCreary C	114 w	*1.30	71-21	YarrowMaid1171BestRisk1112½MoonMdn1202	Inside,no threat 10
19May43- 6Bel	sly 1	:232 :472 1:121 1:383	ⒻAcorn 14k	4 9 75¼ 44 33½ 33½	McCreary C	121 w	4.80e	77-20	Nellie L.1212La Reigh1211½Stefanita1211	Impeded early 13
10May43- 5Bel	fst 6f	:223 :46 1:112	ⒻAlw 2000	4 10 105 54¼ 47¼ 21	McCreary C	113 w	8.80	92-10	SparklingMaid1101Stefanita113noDearJudy108½	Fast finish 12
1Oct42- 5Bel	fst 6f-WC	:231 :46 1:111	ⒻAlw 2000	8 8 2½ 51¼ 51¾ 65¾	Breen J	113 w	4.20	85-09	ClacketyClack113½NowMandy1131Navigatng1131½	Speed,tired 9
26Sep42- 4Bel	fst 6f-WC	:222 :45 1:091	ⒻMatron 12k	7 18 138½ 176¼ 1611 1211½	Breen J	119 w	7.55	89-00	GoodMorning1091Askmnow1141½Navigtng1142	Never a factor 20
21Sep42- 7Bel	fst 6f-WC	:224 :46 1:11	ⒻAlw 2000	9 3 41½ 1hd 1hd 2hd	Breen J	119 w	22.85	92-06	Samaritan111hdStefanita119nkCape May1111	Hell well 13
14Sep42- 4HdG	fst 6f	:23 :463 1:123	Alw 1500	4 8 75 42¼ 75¼ 58½	Mann W	112wb	*1.70	81-18	Hasteville1102½RoyalFlush1102BarKeep1154	Wide into str 9
27Jun42- 6Del	my 5f	:224 :471 1:01	ⒻPolly Drummond 8.4k	3 5 57 56½ 55½ 43½	Peters M	122wb	4.30e	86-19	Fair Weather1221½La Reigh122hdParachutist1132	Wide 8
17Jun42- 4Aqu	fst 5½f	:223 :46 1:054	ⒻAstoria 7.4k	2 1 31½ 31½ 3½ 11	Breen J	113wb	*1.10e	98-06	Stefanita1131Shannon1131½Witchwater1132	Driving 7
4Jun42- 5Bel	fst 5f-WC	:581	Alw 1500	6 2 2hd 3nk 31 31½	Breen J	108wb	*.70	87-11	SlideRule1111½TotalVictory111noStefanita1083	No mishap 7
28May42- 4Bel	fst 5f-WC	:583	ⒻAlw 1500	4 2 2½ 2nk 1nk 2½	Breen J	115wb	*.30	86-13	Now Mandy115½Stefanita1154Blois1105	Hung 6
16May42- 1Bel	fst 5f	:23 :471 :591	ⒻMd Sp Wt	2 2 1hd 1hd 11 12½	Breen J	116wb	*1.40	95-07	Stefanita1162½Spartiate116noShannon1163	Going away 9
11May42- 4Bel	fst 4½f-WC	:522	ⒻFashion 9.6k	11 4 3½ 42½ 33½	Breen J	111wb	*3.60e	89-07	Pomrose116½Driven Snow1163Stefanita1111	Went well 12

Stymie

ch. c. 1941, by Equestrian (Equipoise)–Stop Watch, by On Watch **Lifetime record: 131 35 33 28 $918,485**

Own.– Mrs E.D. Jacobs
Br.– Max Hirsch (Tex)
Tr.– Hirsch Jacobs

1Oct49- 6Bel	fst 2¼	:474 2:312 2:58 3:511 3↑	New York H 29k	8 8 814 42½ 21½ 23½	McCreary C	122 w	2.40	75-11	Dnr1263½Stym1222½Chains110hd	Circled field,flattened out late 8
24Sep49- 6Bel	fst 1½	:49 1:13 2:022 2:28 3↑	Manhattan H 29k	6 5 78 712 68¼ 48¾	Woodhouse H	118 w	4.35	89-13	Donor118¾My Request1258Stunts114hd	Blocked 7
19Sep49- 5Bel	fst 1	:242 :474 1:124 1:371 3↑	Alw 5000	3 4 46½ 45 33 32½	McCreary C	126 w	2.75	85-19	Stunts1212Three Rings121½Stymie1265	Some gain 5
15Sep49- 6Aqu	fst 1 1/16	:25 :482 1:123 1:452 3↑	Alw 4000	5 6 66½ 68¼ 54 34	Woodhouse H	122 w	6.35	83-17	Quarter Pole1223Brick1051Stymie122hd	Some gain 8
10Sep49- 6Aqu	fst 1⅛	:473 1:12 1:37 1:504 3↑	Edgemere H 22k	6 7 811 79¾ 914 914	Woodhouse H	119 w	7.10	79-16	My Request1193Stunts115¾Assault124½	No factor 9
24Jly48- 6Mth	gd 1¼	:471 1:121 1:374 2:031 3↑	Monmouth H 29k	6 7 711 65¾ 47 412	Permane R	129 w	*.70	78-19	Tide Rips1086Vertigo II1093½Bug Juice1082	Lame 7
17Jly48- 6Aqu	fst 1¼	:502 1:16 1:404 2:054 3↑	Brooklyn H 57k	4 6 59¼ 46 3¼ 33	Permane R	130 w	*.95	75-21	Conniver114hdGallorette1193Stymie1302	Saved ground,hung 6
3Jly48- 5Del	fst 1¼	:471 1:112 1:361 2:02 3↑	Sussex H 30k	4 7 711 31 1hd 11½	Permane R	130 w	*.70	102-10	Stymie1301½Rampart1131Tide Rips109nk	Very wide 8
26Jun48- 6Aqu	fst 1 1/16	:251 :493 1:133 1:452 3↑	Aqueduct H 28k	3 5 66½ 55¼ 3¾ 1hd	Permane R	130 w	*1.05	87-18	Stymie130hdConniver1173½Double Jay1262½	Driving 7
17Jun48- 6Aqu	fst 1 1/16	:241 :48 1:123 1:443 3↑	Queens County H 22k	3 6 617 69¼ 44 22	Permane R	132 w	*.85	89-16	Knockdown1132Stymie132½Gasparilla1072½	Bore in 6
31May48- 6Bel	sly 1¼	:483 1:13 1:372 2:03 3↑	Suburban H 57k	1 6 611 47½ 35¼ 21¾	McCreary C	128 w	*.90	83-22	Harmonica1091¾Stymie1283Colosal1175	Good finish 6
26May48- 6Bel	sly 1⅛	:491 1:123 1:371 1:494 4↑	Alw 7500	1 3 39½ 33 1nk 12	McCreary C	122 w	*.35	92-21	Stymie1222Vertigo II1141½Tide Rips106	In hand late 3
22May48- 6Bel	fst 1	:233 :463 1:112 1:364 3↑	Metropolitan H 30k	9 9 914 912 65½ 1¾	McCreary C	126 w	5.10	90-14	Stymie126¾Colosal1171½Rippey1241½	Late rush 9
15May48- 5Jam	fst 1 3/16	:48 1:122 1:373 1:571 3↑	Gallant Fox H 87k	10 10 1021 1015 62½ 54½	McCreary C	126 w	*1.40	85-15	Faultless118hdFervent125½Gallorette1173½	Fast finish 10
8May48- 6Pim	sl 1 3/16	:49 1:141 1:404 2:013 3↑	Dixie H 31k	6 9 916 913 33 21½	McCreary C	127 w	3.30	72-41	Fervent1211½Stymie1272½Incline107no	No match 9
17Apr48- 5Jam	fst 1 1/16	:243 :482 1:132 1:46 3↑	Excelsior H 29k	7 6 55¼ 42½ 32 33¼	McCreary C	128 w	2.10e	80-20	Knockdown114¾Double Jay1252½Stymie1284	Faltered 9
1Nov47- 5Jam	gd 1 1/16	:24 :472 1:121 1:443 3↑	Scarsdale H 30k	5 12 1220 128 78½ 67½	McCreary C	130 w	*1.85	82-17	WithPleasure1292Gallorette119½DoubleJy1182	Reared start 12
25Oct47- 5Jam	fst 1⅝	:50 1:41 2:053 2:442 3↑	Gallant Fox H 83k	7 8 915 44 11 11¾	McCreary C	125 w	2.50	92-13	Stymie1251¾Talon1253½Miss Grillo117no	Wide,driving 9
11Oct47- 6Bel	fst 2¼	:473 2:314 3:482 3↑	New York H 109k	2 5 513 57¾ 45¼ 412	McCreary C	125 w	2.10	81-11	Rico Monte126noTalon1225Phalanx1167	Tired badly 6
4Oct47- 6Bel	fst 2	:494 2:293 2:553 3:213 3↑	J C Gold Cup 26k	1 1 1hd 2hd 38 312	McCreary C	124 w	*.65	84-12	Phalanx117noTalon12412Stymie124	Flattened out 3
27Sep47- 7Bel	fst 1½	:494 1:15 2:042 2:294 3↑	Manhattan H 28k	5 5 33 42¼ 21½ 21½	McCreary C	132 w	*.75	87-10	Rico Monte1231½Stymie1322½Talon1166	Finished well 6
13Sep47- 6Aqu	fst 1⅛	:502 1:143 1:392 1:522 3↑	Edgemere H 27k	1 4 46 43¼ 31½ 21½	McCreary C	134 w	*.70	83-13	Elpis1141½Stymie1341Bridal Flower1131½	Finished well 4
1Sep47- 6Aqu	fst 1 1/16	:242 :474 1:124 1:442 3↑	Aqueduct H 29k	11 11 1112 73½ 41¾ 1½	McCreary C	132 w	*2.10	92-13	Stymie132½Gallorette122hdElpis1144	Finished fast 11
9Aug47- 6Sar	fst 1¼	:491 1:133 1:393 2:023 3↑	Whitney 27k	2 3 38 34½ 33¼ 31½	McCreary C	126 w	*.45	93-09	Rico Monte113hdGallorette1121½Stymie126	Late rush 3
30Jly47- 7Suf	fst 1⅛	:47 1:123 1:37 1:50 3↑	Mass H 61k	1 7 713 77 32 11½	McCreary C	128 w	*.30	91-14	Stymie1281½Elpis111nkBlue Yonder1111¾	Drew off easily 7
19Jly47- 6Bel	sly 1⅝	:483 1:39 2:042 2:423 3↑	Gold Cup 109k	4 6 522 58½ 31¾ 1nk	McCreary C	126 w	4.75	91-14	Stymie126nkNatchez1264Assault1261	Fast finish 7
	Geldings not eligible									
12Jly47- 5Jam	fst 1 3/16	:49 1:134 1:381 1:563 3↑	Butler H 54k	4 5 58 57½ 3nk 2hd	Permane R	126 w	2.65	93-09	Assault135hdStymie1261¾Gallorette117nk	Led briefly 5
5Jly47- 6Del	fst 1¼	:473 1:112 1:362 2:022 3↑	Sussex H 29k	3 6 412 36 22 13	McCreary C	128 w	*.65	103-14	Stymie1283Natchez1251½Round View1128	Handily 7
28Jun47- 5Jam	fst 1 1/16	:24 :472 1:12 1:44 3↑	Questionnaire H 27k	5 6 67¼ 4¾ 1½ 12	Permane R	125 w	*1.05	93-12	Stymie1252Brown Mogul1142Concordian113no	Fast finish 6
21Jun47- 6Aqu	fst 1¼	:472 1:121 1:38 2:033 3↑	Brooklyn H 55k	1 3 515 59½ 32 23	James B	124 w	2.60	86-14	Assault1333Stymie1244Larky Day1101	Blocked turn 5
2Jun47- 6Aqu	fst 1 1/16	:242 :482 1:124 1:452 3↑	Queens County H 21k	2 6 57 43½ 2hd 2nk	James B	128 w	*1.20	87-19	Gallorette119nkStymie128noMangoneo1046	Hung 6
30May47- 6Bel	fst 1¼	:472 1:114 1:364 2:014 3↑	Suburban H 57k	3 5 511 48½ 35½ 410	James B	126 w	1.95	81-09	Assault1302Natchez1207Talon1131	Flattened out late 7
10May47- 6Bel	fst 1	:23 :464 1:112 1:372 3↑	Metropolitan H 30k	6 12 1213 1211 86½ 11	James B	124 w	*2.30	87-15	Stymie1241Brown Mogul1131Gallorette1161½	Wide,late rush 12
3May47- 5Jam	fst 1⅛	:47 1:112 1:363 1:494 3↑	Grey Lag H 46k	8 7 78¾ 51¾ 51¼ 42½	James B	126 w	2.20	96-13	Assault128nkLetsDance110nkCoincdnc1202	Forced wide,hung 8
	Daily Racing Form time,1:49 1/5									
30Apr47- 4Jam	fst 6f	:231 :462 1:104 3↑	Handicap 6535	5 7 712 712 78¾ 57½	James B	126 w	3.15	89-14	BrownMogl1143½Inroc118¾FlsMov1123	Left,worked 7f in 1:27 7
1Nov46- 6Pim	fst 1 3/16	:481 1:132 1:39 1:57 3↑	Pim Spl 25k	1 4 418 417 21 26	James B	126 w	*.70	91-16	Assault1206Stymie1263Bridal Flower117½	No match 4
26Oct46- 5Jam	fst 1⅝	:462 1:373 2:03 2:424 3↑	Gallant Fox H 85k	8 10 1015 21 15 12½	James B	126 w	5.15	101-11	Stymie1262½Rico Monte1162Assault1148	In hand late 11
12Oct46- 6Bel	sly 2¼	:493 2:343 2:591 3:511 3↑	New York H 58k	6 5 43¾ 1½ 11 11¼	James B	128 w	*1.10	79-14	Stymie1281¼Rico Monte1212Athenia10910	Ridden out 9
5Oct46- 6Bel	fst 2	:491 2:302 2:543 3:223 3↑	J C Gold Cup 27k	4 4 11 1½ 21 25	James B	124 w	*.30	86-12	Pavot1245Stymie1245Rico Monte12450	No match 4
	Geldings not eligible									
25Sep46- 6Bel	fst 1½	:493 1:143 2:032 2:292 3↑	Manhattan H 28k	6 5 42¾ 21 1½ 1¾	James B	126 w	*1.10	91-13	Stymie126¾Pavot1213 DH Flareback1131	Driving 8
14Sep46- 6Aqu	fst 1⅛	:474 1:13 1:38 1:502 3↑	Edgemere H 28k	2 8 52¾ 31¾ 2hd 11½	James B	121 w	*1.50	95-13	Stymie1211½Gallorett1231¼KngDorstt1156	Drew away easily 8
31Aug46- 6Sar	fst 1¾	:514 2:013 2:381 3:072 3↑	Sar Cup 5.9k	1 1 1 1 1 1	James B	126 w	-	--	Stymie126	Walkover 1
	Geldings not eligible,private time									
24Aug46- 6Sar	fst 1¼	:46 1:101 1:362 2:013 3↑	Saratoga H 33k	2 5 518 48½ 32½ 34¾	James B	125 w	2.15	96-02	Lucky Draw121¾Polynesian1134Stymie1257	No menace 5
19Aug46- 6Sar	sly 1	:25 :493 1:14 1:39 3↑	Alw 6650	2 3 35 22 2nk 2¾	James B	119 w	1.45	85-20	King Dorsett119¾Stymie1195Gallorette121	Driving 3
10Aug46- 6Sar	my 1¼	:50 1:154 1:394 2:072 3↑	Whitney 28k	5 4 45½ 11 13 12	James B	120 w	*.55	72-22	Stymie1202Mahout1032Trymenow11210	Wide 5
5Aug46- 6Sar	fst 1	:23 :461 1:111 1:363 3↑	Wilson 24k	9 8 813 74¼ 64 5¾	Woodhouse H	120 w	5.05	97-08	Pavot126nkGallorette121nkLarky Day112hd	Finished well 11
20Jly46- 6Mth	fst 1¼	:464 1:112 1:361 2:014 3↑	Monmouth H 32k	6 7 714 46 22½ 26	Permane R	126 w	*.75	--	Lucky Draw1116Stymie1262½Aonbarr1006	Second best 8
13Jly46- 5Jam	fst 1 3/16	:47 1:111 1:361 1:551 3↑	Butler H 57k	7 9 914 78½ 51¾ 31½	Permane R	126 w	*1.15	102-08	LuckyDraw105hdGallortt1161½Stym126¾	Blocked,fast finish 9
22Jun46- 6Aqu	fst 1¼	:48 1:131 1:393 2:05 3↑	Brooklyn H 58k	7 8 812 53½ 2½ 2nk	Woodhouse H	128 w	*.65	82-24	Gallorette118nkStymie1284½BurningDream110½	Saved ground 8
15Jun46- 6Del	gd 1¼	:473 1:122 1:38 2:041 3↑	Sussex H 29k	8 8 813 56 45½ 33	Woodhouse H	126 w	*.65	91-16	Pavot1152Gallorette1131Stymie1262	Insufficient rally 8

30May46- 6Bel	fst	1¼	:482 1:123 1:373 2:02	3↑ Suburban H 60k	3 11 1120 97 63¾	32½	Permane R	123 w	3.45	87-16	Armed1302½Reply Paid110noStymie1231	Closed well 11
10May46- 6Pim	fst	1 3/16	:494 1:141 1:384 1:582	3↑ Dixie H 34k	5 5 56¼ 54½ 23	23½	Permane R	124 w	1.85	86-23	Armed1303½Stymie1242½Trymenow1172	No match 6
4May46- 5Jam	fst	1⅛	:462 1:12 1:37 1:493	3↑ Grey Lag H 35k	2 7 614 44 2hd	12	Woodhouse H	127 w	*2.10	100-10	Stymie1272BoundingHom1053½FghtngStp1261¾	Speed to spare 7
23Apr46- 5Jam	fst	1 1/16	:25 :491 1:123 1:431	4↑ Alw 8000	1 4 44 23 22	22½	Permane R	121 w	*.40	94-13	Snow Boots1132½Stymie1215King Dorsett1145	No threat 4
18Apr46- 5Jam	fst	1 1/16	:242 :481 1:12 1:431	4↑ Alw 7500	3 4 35 1hd 11½	12½	Permane R	114 w	1.95	97-13	Stym1142½FghtngStp11912OlympcZnth1145¼	Speed in reserve 4
Daily Racing Form time,1:43 3/5												
30Nov45- 7Pim	hy	2½	:532 2:442 3:394 4:351	3↑ Pim Cup H 28k	4 3 45½ 46 16	18	Permane R	128 w	*1.90	25-53	Stymie1288Poto'Luck1282Trymenow1202½	Drew out last ⅛ 6
24Nov45- 6Pim	gd	1 3/16	:481 1:131 1:401 2:00	3↑ Riggs H 30k	5 10 1017 912 3½	1nk	Permane R	123 w	3.05	83-24	Stymie123nkFirstFiddl1261½BrtshBuddy1151¼	Circled field 10
17Nov45- 6Pim	gd	1 3/16	:493 1:142 1:391 1:584	3↑ Pim Spl 25k	6 7 77¾ 67 35	36	Permane R	126 w	4.10	82-20	Armed1264First Fiddle1262Stymie1261¼	Saved ground 7
3Nov45- 5Jam	fst	1 3/16	:48 1:113 1:371 1:564	3↑ Westchester H 56k	10 10 1014 1012 33	1hd	Permane R	125 w	3.75	96-10	Stym125hdBuzfuz1162OlympcZnth1172	Close quarters str turn 10
13Oct45- 5Jam	fst	1⅝	:49 1:403 2:052 2:443	3↑ Gallant Fox H 56k	3 3 1211 94¾ 64¼	63¾	Permane R	126 w	*1.30	88-14	ReplyPaid1081Trymenow113hdOlympicZenith116nk	No threat 12
6Oct45- 5Jam	sly	1 1/16	:233 :473 1:12 1:432	3↑ Continental H 16k	5 7 712 33 2hd	15	Permane R	122 w	4.65	96-09	Stym1225ChiefBarker1143BoundingHom1122	Speed to spare 7
Daily Racing Form time, 1:44												
27Sep45- 6Bel	fst	2	:541 2:372 3:02 3:272	3↑ J C Gold Cup 27k	2 1 32 58 510	36	Permane R	125 w	2.15	61-18	Pot o' Luck114noEurasian1256Stymie1256	6
Geldings not eligible												
1Sep45- 6Bel	fst	1 3/16	:46 1:113 1:37 1:561	3↑ Merchants & Cits H 17k	2 6 619 520 46	36½	Permane R	126 w	*1.00e	87-13	Coronal110½Olympic Zenith1176Stymie1263	Closed fast 6
25Aug45- 6Bel	fst	1¾	:50 2:072 2:321 2:58	3↑ Sar Cup 27k	2 4 47½ 43¼ 13	13	Longden J	126 w	*.75	93-12	Stymie1263OlympicZnth126hdBnkrupt12612	Speed in reserve 4
Geldings not eligible												
18Aug45- 6Bel	fst	1¼	:463 1:104 1:364 2:024	3↑ Saratoga H 54k	7 10 1025 96 52	66	Permane R	126 w	2.40e	80-13	OlympicZenith1082FirstFiddle124nkArlFlght100¾	No menace 10
15Aug45- 6Bel	fst	1¼	:491 1:124 1:372 2:021	3↑ Whitney 17k	2 6 68½ 513 47½	37	Permane R	126 w	*1.45	82-17	Trymenow1034Pavot1173Stymie1262	Outrun 6
28Jly45- 5Jam	gd	1 3/16	:47 1:122 1:373 1:563	3↑ Butler H 56k	6 9 922 820 2nk	11	Permane R	121 w	2.40e	97-12	Stymie1211First Fiddle1202½Rounders1212	Driving 9
16Jly45- 5Jam	my	1 1/16	:24 :48 1:132 1:432	3↑ Yonkers H 11k	1 5 57 52¼ 31	21¾	Permane R	122wb	3.30	94-15	Wait a Bit1171¾Stymie1221½Olympic Zenith1144	Driving 6
4Jly45- 5Bel	fst	1¼	:464 1:104 1:363 2:021	3↑ Brooklyn H 56k	6 9 912 85¼ 43	11¼	Permane R	116 w	6.40e	89-12	Stymie1161¼Devil Diver1322½Olympic Zenith1102	Drew away 9
25Jun45- 5Aqu	fst	1 1/16	:24 :47 1:122 1:453	3↑ Queens County H 11k	7 7 721 619 47½	22	Arcaro E	120 w	*1.00e	84-17	Olympic Zenith1082Stymie1203Haile1061	No match 7
16Jun45- 6Bel	fst	1¼	:502 1:142 1:39 2:04	3↑ Suburban H 52k	3 3 41¾ 46½ 33½	22	Permane R	119 w	2.90	78-15	DevilDiver1322Stymie119nkOlympicZenith1061½	Fast finish 4
2Jun45- 5Jam	fst	1⅛	:48 1:123 1:383 1:494	3↑ Grey Lag H 15k	4 4 411 46½ 21½	1½	Permane R	121 w	3.40	99-10	Stymie121½Alex Barth1267Bounding Home114½	Fast finish 5
29May45- 5Jam	fst	1 1/16	:232 :473 1:123 1:443	4↑ Handicap 3965	3 4 45½ 42¼ 11½	13½	Adams J	119 w	*.90	90-20	Stymie1193½Transformer1101½Eye for Eye1103	Saved ground 4
22May45- 6Jam	fst	1 1/16	:242 :48 1:13 1:454	4↑ Alw 4000	2 3 36 31¾ 2hd	2nk	Mills B	108wb	2.60	84-14	Great Rush114nkStymie1081¼Rounders114hd	Dwelt at start 4
Daily Racing Form time, 1:46 1/5												
25Nov44- 6Pim	fst	2½	:503 2:371 3:282 4:201	3↑ Pim Cup H 29k	2 5 2hd 41½ 25	311½	Kirkland A	109wb	9.50	145-05	Megogo10810Bolingbroke1261½Stymie109nk	Impeded 7
20Nov44- 6Pim	gd	1 3/16	:49 1:141 1:401 1:584	3↑ Riggs H 28k	5 6 52½ 43 32½	35	Kirkland A	108wb	9.85	84-20	Seven Hearts1262Bon Jour1203Stymie1082	Bid,tired 6
15Nov44- 5Bel	fst	1	:23 :461 1:113 1:381	2↑ Victory H 10k	6 9 99¾ 64½ 41	73½	Wright WD	119wb	6.30	79-17	DoraDear106noGrntRc1141½FrstDrft112no	Saved ground,quit 11
4Nov44- 5Jam	fst	1 3/16	:48 1:132 1:39 1:58	3↑ Westchester H 34k	3 10 1019 1010 41½	34	Permane R	109wb	8.50	86-13	Seven Hearts1243½Good Morning109½Stymie1091	Away poorly 10
28Oct44- 6Lrl	fst	1¼	:484 1:133 1:393 2:06	3↑ Washington H 27k	5 5 45½ 57 56	610¼	Clark S	115wb	7.45	70-25	Megogo1101Bon Jour1262Harford1071¼	Flattened out 6
21Oct44- 5Jam	sly	1⅝	:483 1:391 2:051 2:46	3↑ Gallant Fox H 55k	3 10 1019 44½ 31	34	Wright WD	112wb	11.00	81-15	Some Chance1161Pyracanth1053Stymie1121	Bid,hung 10
16Oct44- 5Jam	fst	1 1/16	:233 :474 1:12 1:44	Handicap 7470	2 8 88¼ 44½ 1½	12	Permane R	114wb	5.60	93-16	Stymie1142Saguaro1105Autocrat1145	Drew away 9
13Oct44- 6Jam	sly	1 1/16	:234 :48 1:123 1:45	Alw 3500	8 6 55½ 45½ 33½	23	Mills B	112wb	2.10	85-18	Alory1123Stym112nkAutocrt1145	Sluggish early,finished well 9
10Oct44- 6Jam	fst	1 1/16	:24 :483 1:124 1:45	Handicap 3500	3 8 52¾ 42 3nk	2½	Wright WD	115wb	*2.35	87-14	Autocrat118½Stymie1152½Go Chicago109½	Closed well 9
2Oct44- 7Bel	fst	1 1/16	:241 :473 1:121 1:434	3↑ Alw 3500	1 4 41½ 32 31½	31½	Mills B	109wb	*1.90	90-14	Victory Drive116½Autocrat1141Stymie1095	Hung 5
28Sep44- 8Bel	fst	1 1/16	:231 :461 1:112 1:441	Alw 3500	4 8 810 66½ 65½	45½	Mills B	115wb	*3.00	84-16	Saguaro1205Markobob116½Paddle109hd	Steady gain 9
18Sep44- 7Bel	fst	1 1/16	:232 :464 1:104 1:423	Alw 3500	5 5 56 58½ 59½	616½	Zufelt F	117wb	4.85	81-12	Good Thing1084Pukka Gin1111½Letmenow1087	Hard urged 7
5Sep44- 5Aqu	fst	6f	:232 :471 1:124	Alw 3500	6 7 78 69½ 65	56¼	Zufelt F	116wb	6.10	82-22	FoxBrownie1121½JeanMiracle1211½SmartSheila1081¼	Evenly 9
24Jun44- 6Aqu	fst	1¼	:463 1:12 1:38 2:032	Dwyer 56k	2 9 820 815 611	816½	Stout J	110wb	13.40	73-15	By Jimminy1144Stir Up1205Lucky Draw1201	Never a factor 9
17Jun44- 6Aqu	fst	1 1/16	:24 :474 1:132 1:452	Shevlin 12k	9 10 98¼ 77¼ 43	34	Stout J	108wb	11.30	83-15	By Jimminy1164Stir Up122hdStymie1085	Swerved str 12
12Jun44- 6Aqu	fst	7f	:23 :46 1:11 1:224	Handicap 4980	3 5 512 512 46½	39	Stout J	116wb	6.45	89-16	By Jimminy1163Lucky Draw1266Stymie1161½	Finished well 5
Daily Racing Form Time,1:23 1/5												
13May44- 6Pim	fst	1 3/16	:481 1:131 1:392 1:591	Preakness 77k	5 7 715 713 65½	612¼	Roberts P	126wb	23.30	74-15	Pensive126¾Platter1262Stir Up1264½	Never a factor 7
29Apr44- 7Pim	gd	1 1/16	:233 :482 1:134 1:461	Chesapeake 31k	6 5 54½ 42 42½	47½	Jemas N	114wb	3.30	79-24	Gramps Image114noPensive1163½Gay Bit1144	Saved ground 8
22Apr44- 5Jam	fst	1 1/16	:24 :482 1:124 1:441	Wood Mem (Div 1) 28k	2 8 78½ 52¾ 22	23	Stout J	126wb	8.45	89-14	Stir Up1263Stymie1261Autocrat1262½	Gamely 8
18Apr44- 5Jam	fst	1 70	:241 :483 1:13 1:433	Alw 5000	1 6 43½ 2hd 13	14	Stout J	113wb	3.55	86-14	Stymie1134Olympic Zenith1203Fire Sticky103nk	Easily 9
11Apr44- 5Jam	fst	1 1/16	:242 :50 1:142 1:46	3↑ Handicap 4970	2 4 42 3¾ 2½	25	Longden J	110wb	*1.10	78-17	Grey Wing1165Stymie1101¼Sugar Ration1026	Hung 4
4Mar44- 7Hia	fst	1⅛	:474 1:131 1:391 1:523	Alw 5000	2 9 98½ 65½ 22	1hd	Adams J	116wb	5.00	78-21	Stym116hdFireSticky1033SideBoy1108	Impeded rivals,just up 9
26Feb44- 5Hia	fst	1⅛	:472 1:12 1:39 1:522	Flamingo 20k	2 9 76½ 46½ 43	35	Atkinson T	118wb	19.80	74-21	Stir Up1181Skytracer1184Stymie1183	Closed well 11
19Feb44- 6Hia	fst	1⅛	:471 1:121 1:39 1:532	Alw 5000	6 6 55¼ 46 36	35¾	Atkinson T	114wb	9.45	68-22	Director J.E.1181¾Good Bid1074Stymie1141	Away slowly 6
3Feb44- 5Hia	fst	7f	:233 :47 1:123 1:26	Alw 3000	7 5 58½ 55½ 42	31¾	Adams J	116wb	5.70	80-27	Black Badge1241½Bud Grey104nkStymie1163	Fast finish 7
29Jan44- 5Hia	fst	7f	:233 :473 1:123 1:253	Bahamas H 6.3k	5 8 73½ 73¾ 76¼	78	Brooks S	118wb	5.10	76-15	Ariel Flight1091½Good Bid122nkFreezout1122	Tired 10
25Jan44- 4Hia	fst	6f	:234 :473 1:131	Alw 3000	5 7 76¾ 77¾ 64¾	65	Permane R	111wb	*1.35	78-25	Jimmie107nkFire Sticky1081½Valdina Malden107nk	Outrun 7
8Jan44- 5Hia	fst	6f	:231 :472 1:133	Hialeah 6.2k	7 8 76 72½ 3nk	42	Atkinson T	120wb	3.00	79-21	Black Badge120hdGood Bid1142Brief Sigh116no	Hung 11
1Jan44- 3TrP	fst	6f	:23 :472 1:123	Alw 1200	4 7 45 34 2½	2¾	Atkinson T	120wb	2.25	86-12	Skytracer112.5¾Stymie1201Aloraye1082	Bid,hung 8
10Nov43- 5Jam	sl	1 1/16	:241 :482 1:133 1:454	Handicap 5190	1 6 76¾ 2hd 14	15	Brooks S	120wb	*2.05	84-21	Stymie1205Peppy Miss1101½Doggone105no	Easily 7
6Nov43- 5Pim	fst	1 70	:232 :471 1:133 1:454	T K Lynch Mem H 10k	3 8 87¾ 31½ 2hd	3nk	Jemas N	112 w	3.80	88-23	Royal Prince120nkThe Man113hdStymie1124	Circled field 10
1Nov43- 5Jam	gd	6f	:23 :462 1:124	Handicap 5240	6 8 813 76 41¼	3nk	Brooks S	115wb	4.10	88-20	SweepingTime116hdArielGame109hdStymie115hd	Wide,gamely 8
23Oct43- 6Jam	fst	1 70	:234 :474 1:13 1:434	Ardsley H (Div 2) 11k	5 8 85¾ 32½ 21	21	Lindberg H	108wb	4.25	84-17	Bel Reigh1111Stymie108hdRodney Stone1226	Bid,2nd best 10
20Oct43- 4Jam	fst	1 70	:241 :48 1:132 1:453	Alw 5000	10 10 54¾ 22 2nk	23	Permane R	106wb	7.75	73-19	Weyanoke1143Stymie1065Broadcloth114½	Hung 14
12Oct43- 4Jam	fst	6f	:231 :471 1:123	Alw 5000	14 13 116½ 109 55	1no	Permane R	106wb	7.40f	89-13	Stymie106noSweeping Time1111Aloraye115hd	Driving 14
7Oct43- 5Bel	fst	1	:234 :472 1:131 1:384	Alw 2500	8 8 85¼ 42 3½	44½	Kirkland A	111wb	6.40	75-17	Broadcloth1162Surrogate1161½Wild Rice1161	Impeded early 12
22Sep43- 5Bel	fst	6f-WC	:223 :452 1:101	©Alw 2500	2 13 136¾ 85½	74¼	Kirkland A	106wb	19.20	91-09	PukkaGin1151½Dustman114hdProfessorLee115hd	Good finish 14
16Sep43- 6Aqu	fst	6f	:23 :463 1:122	©Alw 2300	12 13 105½ 73¾ 42	11½	Kirkland A	111wb	6.95f	90-11	Stymie1111½Tumult1111Spheric1161	Driving 14
11Sep43- 5Aqu	fst	6f	:223 :461 1:12	Alw 2500	6 8 811 66½ 67½	57¼	Brooks S	111wb	18.40	85-11	Que Hora1151½Black Badge1222½Ravenala118¾	Broke slowly 8
1Sep43- 4Aqu	fst	6f	:232 :47 1:122	Clm 5000	5 8 75½ 64¼ 46½	46½	Atkinson T	116wb	2.35	83-11	Peppy Miss1145Seeing Eye119hdReimburseme1131½	8
Broke slowly,bore out badly entering stretch												
28Aug43- 1Bel	gd	6f-WC	:223 :462 1:12	Clm 5000	4 8 64 42	3hd	Brooks S	116wb	*2.25	86-10	WestwoodBelle112hdP.T.Boat108noStymie1163	Broke slowly 9
26Aug43- 5Bel	fst	6f-WC	:224 :454 1:102	Alw 2300	8 7 5¾ 73	77	McCreary C	116wb	10.25	87-10	Messari1131½Stir Up1163Late City1161	Swerved start 14
20Aug43- 1Bel	fst	6f-WC	:224 :462 1:12	Clm 5000	10 3 41¾ 3½	2¾	Brooks S	116wb	*3.35	85-12	Seeing Eye116¾Stymie1161½Plucky Raider119hd	No mishap 10
18Aug43- 1Bel	fst	6f-WC	:232 :472 1:121	©MCl 3000	2 4 32 15	15	McCreary C	115wb	*2.15	85-18	Stymie1155HurricaneYank1121ChangeHr117hd	Speed to spare 14
11Aug43- 4Bel	fst	6f-WC	:23 :462 1:12	Clm 3500	9 5 52 41¼	31½	Brooks S	111wb	5.50	84-14	Plucky Raider1161½Westwood Belle116hdStymie1113	Driving 9
5Aug43- 5Bel	fst	5½f-W	:23 :461 1:051	©Md Sp Wt	12 14 155 126¾	1911½	Brooks S	115wb	11.40	76-11	Smolensko115½Triplicate1151½Good Bid115½	No factor 22
28Jly43- 1Bel	gd	5½f-W	:231 :463 1:054	©MCl 4000	8 11 94 84¾	76¼	Gilbert J	116wb	*2.60	79-14	Late City1161½Super Marines1143Lou-Bre116hd	No menace 19
23Jly43- 3Jam	gd	5½f	:233 :48 1:074	©Md Sp Wt	4 5 99¼ 79¼ 65¼	53¼	Atkinson T	116wb	*1.90	77-19	Clansman1161½ReturnCall111½HayaTnty116no	Close quarters 12
28Jun43- 3Jam	fst	5½f	:23 :463 1:062	©Md Sp Wt	13 7 55 57 42½	44¾	Brooks S	116wb	2.10	83-16	BoyKnight116nkCaptainsAide1161½Stronghold1163	No threat 14
25Jun43- 2Aqu	fst	5½f	:233 :473 1:062	Clm 5000	2 2 23 21 2nk	2nk	Atkinson T	111wb	*1.60	93-16	Sweeping Time116nkStymie1115Shamokin1161	Driving 5
21Jun43- 4Aqu	fst	5½f	:232 :48 1:071	©Md Sp Wt	5 1 53 44½ 31½	21	Brooks S	116wb	1.80	88-15	Morani1161Stymi1162Hoodoo1162	Slow to start,good finish 8

17Jun43- 1Aqu fst 5½f :23³ :47³ 1:07 Clm 5000 7 7 43¼ 32 31½ 24 Atkinson T 111wb 2.80 86-19 Chance Mate1164Stymie1112All Talk116½ Driving 7
12Jun43- 1Aqu fst 5f :23⁴ :48³ 1:01³ Mcl 3500 8 7 66½ 53½ 31½ 2nk Rienzi D 108wb *1.90 88-12 More Wine111nkStymie1082Lady Eli110hd Gamely 10
8Jun43- 1Aqu my 5½f :24 :491 1:021 1:08 Mcl 2000 12 11 2nk 2hd 61¾ 21½ Rienzi D 111wb 8.05 83-13 Powdered Milk1111½Stymie1111½Omaloo1105 12
Rushed up,bore out turn,came on again
2Jun43- 1Bel my 5f-WC 1:02¹ Mcl 1500-c 5 10 91¾ 74 74½ Garza I 116wb 19.25 64-31 Assailant1161Free Dutch116½Little Dottie113½ Evenly 14
Claimed from King Ranch,Trainer M. Hirsch
29May43- 1Bel fst 5f-WC :58³ ⒻMd Sp Wt 1 12 1212 1222 1116½ Garza I 116wb 77.65 70-11 Stir Up116¾Rodney Stone1168Home Flight116hd No factor 12
7May43- 1Jam fst 5f :23³ :48¹ 1:01³ Clm 2500 7 7 55 44 43½ 78 Garza I 111wb 30.95 74-18 Sirlette108½Docdonough1164Magic Heels113hd No threat 9

Trough Hill

b. g. 1942, by Tourist II (Son-in-Law)–Rollicking Princess, by Royal Canopy — **Lifetime record: 40 12 10 8 $106,955**
Own.– Mrs S.C. Clark Jr
Br.– Henry W. Frost Jr (Va)
Tr.– J.T. Skinner

11Nov50- 4Mid fst *2½ S'Chase 4:18³ 4↑ Manly H 4.9k 3 4 42¼ 43½ 44½ 59 Field T 160ws - -- IseeYou1372½BannerWvs1331½HmptonRods1522 Disliked going 6
1Nov50- 5Lrl fst *2 S'Chase 3:55² 4↑ Chevy Chase H 9k 1 6 629 523 412 37 Harris H 153ws *.90e -- Hot1425Monkey Wrench1342Trough Hill153no Belated rally 7
6Oct50- 5Bel fst *3 S'Chase 5:42² 4↑ Grand National H 23k 3 4 31½ 11 2hd 12½ Harris H 150ws 1.85e -- TroughHill1502¼Oedipus1534PontiusPilate1502½ Going away 9
29Sep50- 5Bel fst *2½ S'Chase 4:46 4↑ Brook H 15k 5 3 21 21 22 21½ Harris H 151 w *1.70 -- Oedipus1491½TroughHill1515½TouristList1361 Game effort 8
22Sep50- 5Bel sf *2 S'Chase 3:48² 3↑ Broad Hollow H 11k 1 5 513 510 43½ 32½ Harris H 150ws 5.10e -- Oedipus1471¼Elkridge1521¼Trough Hill1505 Sharp effort 10
11May50- 5Bel fst *2 S'Chase 3:51¹ 4↑ International H 8.7k 5 3 31½ - - - Field T 154ws 2.85 -- The Heir1481Adaptable143¾His Boots1502½ Fell at 9th 5
10Nov49- 5Pim fst *2½ S'Chase 4:48² 4↑ Manly H 8.2k 5 2 2hd 3½ 26 28 Harris H 156ws *1.20e -- HisBoots1458TroughHill1566AmericanWay1526 Bad landing 5
3Nov49- 5Pim gd *2 S'Chase 3:55⁴ 3↑ Battleship H 8.4k 3 5 412 11½ 16 110 Field T 154ws 4.90 -- Trough Hill15410Fleettown14620Luan Casca13910 Easily 7
20Oct49- 5Lrl fst *2½ S'Chase 4:45² 4↑ Chevy Chase H 11k 6 3 34 55 45 43 Adams FD 156ws 1.60e -- LockandKey1401¼HisBoots145nkAmrcnWy1521½ Close quarters 6
7Oct49- 6Bel fst *3 S'Chase 5:48³ 4↑ Grand National H 22k 5 3 36 31½ 23 22½ Molony M 158ws *1.20e -- His Boots1412½Trough Hill1588Tourist List1462 Went well 6
29Sep49- 5Bel sl *2½ S'Chase 4:52¹ 4↑ Brook H 15k 7 6 36 32½ 11 110 Molony M 153ws 4.35e -- TroughHill15310AmericanWay1511½HisBoots1429 Ridden out 8
22Sep49- 4Bel fst *2 S'Chase 3:44 3↑ Broad Hollow H 11k 3 4 314 28 25 36¾ Field T 152ws 3.55e -- Sun Bath1496Hampton Roads141¾Trough Hill1522 Weakened 7
1Jly49- 5Del fst *2½ S'Chase 4:45³ 4↑ Indian River H 12k 4 4 - - - - Field T 153ws 2.10 -- Elkridge1563SunBth1361¼TourstLst14820 Lost rider at 5th 5
9Jun49- 4Bel fst *2½ S'Chase 4:43³ 4↑ Meadow Brook H 11k 5 3 311 21½ 15 22 Field T 151ws *1.25 -- Elkridge1472Trough Hill1518Rank1404 Tired badly 7
2Jun49- 4Bel fst *2 S'Chase 3:44 4↑ Corinthian H 9.4k 5 3 22 1hd 13 16 Harris H 147ws 4.35e -- Trough Hill1476Elkridge149hdAmerican Way1463½ Easily 10
12May49- 5Bel fst *2 S'Chase 3:50⁴ 4↑ International H 9k 6 6 - - - - Field T 147 w 3.60 -- Homogenize1396Fleettown1498Lieut. Well14514 Fell 4th 7
20Nov48- 3Mtp hy *2½ S'Chase 5:04³ 4↑ Noel Laing H 3.2k 1 4 41¾ 31½ 21 21½ Field T 156 w - -- Adaptable1531½TroughHill15610TouristList15550 No excuse 5
13Nov48- 4Mid sl *2½ S'Chase 4:44³ 4↑ Handicap 2335 2 1 15 18 15 15 Field T 157 w -e -- Trough Hill1575Adaptable1561½Gunboats1341 In hand 4
28Oct48- 5Lrl fst *2½ S'Chase 4:47⁴ 4↑ Chevy Chase H 18k 7 5 423 46½ 35½ 35 Field T 147ws *1.50e -- American Way1481Sun Bath1354Trough Hill1475 Went well 8
21Oct48- 5Lrl fst *2 S'Chase 3:55¹ 3↑ Governor Ogle H 12k 7 6 65¼ 57½ 46 46½ Peoples C 147ws 1.70e -- Homogenize1342½Point Bleu1463Genancoke1431 No mishap 7
1Oct48- 5Bel gd *3 S'Chase 5:50 4↑ Grand Nat'l H 31k 1 4 35 2½ 21 33 Field T 147ws *2.30e -- AmericanWay1441TouristList1502TroughHill1476 No mishap 14
23Sep48- 5Bel fst *2½ S'Chase 4:47¹ 4↑ Brook H 19k 11 7 43½ 33¼ 11½ 12 Field T 142ws 3.45e -- Trough Hill1422Elkridge1561½American Way1432 Easily 11
9Sep48- 5Aqu fst *2½ S'Chase 4:54 4↑ Glendale H 11k 1 1 1½ 11 13 17 Field T 139 w 2.35 -- Trough Hill1397Big Wrack1322½Navigate140 Easily 4
2Sep48- 5Aqu fst *2 S'Chase 3:44⁴ 3↑ Harbor Hill H 11k 1 6 55¾ 43½ 53¾ 55¼ Field T 142ws 7.00e -- Tourist List145¾Big Wrack1312½Sun Bath1411 Faltered 9
12May48- 5Pim fst 2 S'Chase 3:47¹ 4↑ Jervis Spencer H 12k 6 4 516 521 520 525 Field T 148ws *1.10e -- Lieut. Well1441½Canford13812Adaptable1501½ No excuse 7
17Apr48- 6War fst *2 S'Chase 4:29³ 4↑ Handicap 1330 2 2 13 18 17 110 Field T 162 w - -- Trough Hill16210Tourist List1412Bail Me Out135 Easily 4
22Nov47- 3Mtp fst *2½ S'Chase 5:53 4↑ Noel Laing H 3.2k 4 3 24 25 25 26 Field T 155 w - -- TouristList1506TroughHill1558Adptbl16310 Best of others 6
15Nov47- 5Mid my *2½ S'Chase 4:45³ 4↑ Handicap 2370 2 2 11½ 21 22 34½ Field T 157 w - -- LittleSammie1462½ChanceBullet1402TroughHll1572 Weakened 5
29Oct47- 5Lrl gd *2½ S'Chase 4:54² 4↑ Chevy Chase H 18k 5 4 34½ 26 210 315½ Field T 147 w *2.00 -- Sun Bath13915Elkridge154½Trough Hill1478 Weakened 7
17Oct47- 6Lrl fst *2 S'Chase 3:52 3↑ Butler H 11k 2 3 39 34 1hd 1hd Field T 141 w *1.30 -- Trough Hill141hdSun Bath1372½Allier13750 Hard drive 5
2Oct47- 5Bel fst *3 S'Chase 5:41³ 4↑ Grand National 29k 4 5 46¼ 311 23 3nk Field T 139 w 3.95 -- Adaptable147hdWar Battle163nkTrough Hill1394 Game try 8
17Sep47- 5Aqu fst *2½ S'Chase 4:57¹ 4↑ Glendale H 11k 7 5 42¼ 21 21 22 Field T 139 w *2.35 -- Elkridge1612Trough Hill1392Delhi Dan1385 Weakened 7
11Sep47- 3Aqu fst *2¼ S'Chase 4:20⁴ 4↑ Handicap 4535 3 2 23 2nk 14 16 Field T 138 w 2.90 -- Trough Hill1366Delhi Dan14120Refugio149 Easily 4
Previously owned by Mrs W. Bromley
29May47- 5Del fst *2 S'Chase 4:03 4↑ Tom Roby 13k 3 7 64¾ 54 58½ 617¾ Field T 157 w 2.50e -- American Way14912Tourist Pride1351½Tourist List1462 10
Never a threat
8May47- 4Pim fst *2 S'Chase 3:58² 4↑ Spring Maiden 7.3k 6 1 21 112 120 125 Field T 148 w 6.80 -- Trough Hill14825Allier13515Lady Janice15040 Easily 9
30Apr47- 3Pim fst *2 S'Chase 3:54 4↑ Alw 3500 1 3 11½ 16 23½ 26 Field T 150wb *.70e -- TheHeir1396TroughHill1503Gnncok14712 Fenced poorly 14th 7
12Apr47- 5Mid fst *2 S'Chase 3.54 4↑ Alw 540 1 1 13½ 15 18 112 Field T 141 w - -- TroughHill14112TouristIndex13025Benevolent143500 Easily 5
16Nov46- 3Mid fst *2 S'Chase 3:54⁴ 3↑ Alw 1010 5 2 23 26 - - Peoples C 134 w - -- Genncoke13712Big Wrack134noCpassRose13530 Lost rider 10th 8
6Nov46- 3Pim fst *2 S'Chase 4:01⁴ 3↑ Md Sp Wt 1 2 31½ 26 11 21½ Bland W 147 w 3.15e -- Boston Boy1481½Trough Hill147hdArmy Power145200 11
Bobbled 11th,tired
10Oct46- 3Bel fst *2 S'Chase 3:59 3↑ Md Sp Wt 5 3 312 314 24 28 Land WD 146 w *1.70e -- Last Rock1468Trough Hill1463Phalanger1436 Outrun 8

Twilight Tear

b. f. 1941, by Bull Lea (Bull Dog)–Lady Lark, by Blue Larkspur — **Lifetime record: 24 18 2 2 $202,165**
Own.– Calumet Farm
Br.– Calumet Farm (Ky)
Tr.– B.A. Jones

28Aug45- 6Was fst 6f :22¹ :45² 1:10² 3↑ Alw 5000 3 1 21½ 24 47½ - Dodson D 117 w 1.80 -- FightingDon1103Occupy1165MyTetRambler1111½ Bled,eased 5
1Nov44- 7Pim fst 1³⁄₁₆ :48¹ 1:12² 1:37² 1:56³ 3↑ Pim Spl 25k 2 1 13 14 14 16 Dodson D 117 w *.65 99-12 Twilight Tear1176Devil Diver12610Megogo120 Galloping 3
21Oct44- 6Lrl my 1¼ :48¹ 1:14 1:41⁴ 2:08³ Maryland H 16k 4 1 11 23 46½ 415½ Dodson D 130 w *.15e 51-40 Dare Me1097Miss Keeneland1102½Aera1066 Quit badly 6
12Oct44- 6Lrl fst 1⅛ :47² 1:12³ 1:40 1:53¹ 3↑ ⒻQueen Isabella H 11k 4 1 16 16 15 15 Dodson D 126 w *.15e 82-23 Twilight Tear1265Good Morning1182Legend Bearer1083½ 8
Never extended
2Oct44- 5Bel fst 5½f-W :22⁴ :45² 1:03² 3↑ ⒻHandicap 3480 3 1 2hd 1½ 12½ Arcaro E 126 w *.40e 97-08 Twilight Tear1262½Tellmenow118¾Cocopet1145 5
Bore out,impeded runner-up str
8Aug44- 6Bel fst 1¼ :47¹ 1:11² 1:37² 2:03³ ⒻAlabama 23k 1 1 1½ 11 11½ 2¾ Haas L 126 w *.05 81-14 Vienna114¾Twilight Tear1265Thread o' Gold1171¼ Faltered 4
22Jly44- 6Was fst 1¼ :48 1:12 1:37² 2:03³ Classic 79k 1 1 11 12 13 12 Haas L 114 w *.10e 92-08 TwlghtTr1142OldKntuck1194½Pnsv1265 Saved ground,handily 5
17Jly44- 3Was fst 1 :23³ :47¹ 1:11² 1:36¹ Alw 5000 2 1 12 12 13 11¼ Haas L 117 w -e 97-11 Twilight Tear1171¼Pensive1222Appleknocker1101 Easily 4
Nonwagering event
6Jly44- 6Was fst 7f :23 :45³ 1:09³ 1:22³ Skokie H 11k 5 2 11 12 13 11½ Haas L 121 w *.30e 103-10 TwilightTear1211½Sirde1142½ChallengM1065 Speed to spare 7
28Jun44- 6Was fst 6f :22² :45³ 1:10³ ⒻPrincess Doreen 11k 1 2 21 22½ 2hd 11½ McCreary C 121 w *.40 98-09 TwilightTear1211½BellSong1106HrrtSu114nk Altered course 6
27May44- 6Bel gd 1⅜ :48¹ 1:13³ 1:40 2:21 ⒻC C A Oaks 17k 1 1 12 13 13 14 McCreary C 121 w *.10 66-27 Twilight Tear1214Dare Me1213Plucky Maud1212 Easily 6
17May44- 6Bel fst 1 :23³ :46⁴ 1:11² 1:37 ⒻAcorn 14k 9 4 42 21 11½ 12½ McCreary C 121 w *.20 89-13 TwilightTear1212½Whirlabout1216Evrgt1211 Speed to spare 10
10May44- 6Pim fst 1¹⁄₁₆ :23⁴ :48 1:12³ 1:45¹ ⒻPim Oaks 18k 5 1 11½ 11 11½ 13 McCreary C 121 w *.30 92-19 Twilight Tear1213Plucky Maud1213Everget1215 In hand 5
3May44- 6Pim fst 6f :22¹ :45³ 1:11³ Rennert H 7k 10 3 22 2½ 13 11½ McCreary C 118 w *.40e 95-17 TwilightTear1181½Glctc1083IdlGft112.52 As rider pleased 10
25Apr44- 6Pim sl 6f :22⁴ :47⁴ 1:14 Alw 4000 3 2 2hd 11 1½ 11¼ McCreary C 117 w *.50e 83-35 TwilghtTr1171¼GrampsImage1145Jimmie1146 Rated,drew away 5
17Mar44- 5TrP sly 6f :22¹ :45³ 1:12² ⒻAlw 1800 5 3 37 36½ 2¼ 13 McCreary C 118 w *.30 88-29 Twilight Tear1183Lassie Sue1201½Cuban Bomb1062 Handily 7
10Mar44- 6TrP fst 6f :23 :46⁴ 1:11⁴ Alw 1800 7 1 11 11 14 12 McCreary C 117 w *.25 91-16 Twilight Tear1172Comenow1192½Surrogate122nk Easily 7

29Feb44- 6Hia	fst 6f	:23 :462 1:121 3↑	Leap Year H 5k	4 5 42¼ 3½ 31 32	Smith FA	101 w	9.00	86-23	Mettlesome1161Adulator1121Twilight Tear101hd	Held well	8
8Nov43- 6Pim	sly 1 70	:241 :49 1:153 1:472	ⒻAlw 5000	4 1 15 12 11 12¼	Thompson B	120 w	*.50e	74-28	Twilight Tear1202¼Miss Keeneland1208Red Wonder11110		5
Speed in reserve											
27Oct43- 6Pim	my 1 1/16	:234 :481 1:14 1:482	ⒻSelima 24k	5 3 11 11½ 1nk 21	Thompson B	119 w	*1.20e	75-27	MissKeeneland1111TwilightTr1191½Whrlbout1226	No match	8
20Oct43- 5Pim	fst 1 70	:241 :49 1:143 1:454	ⒻAlw 2500	6 1 11½ 12 11 12	Thompson B	115 w	*.40e	82-21	TwilightTear1152MissKenlnd1096MyMlch1061	Speed to spare	6
16Oct43- 7Pim	sly 6f	:23 :481 1:153	ⒻAlw 2500	1 4 1nk 2hd 2hd 32½	Smith FA	117 w	*1.05e	72-21	Red Wonder111noCountess Wise1142½Twilight Tear117nk		8
Used in pace,lost ground											
3Jly43- 6Was	fst 6f	:224 :464 1:131	ⒻArl Lassie 34k	3 6 22 22 13 12½	Jemas N	113 w	*1.00e	85-14	TwilightTear1132½MissKeeneland1132MusicHall1104	Easily	15
25Jun43- 1Was	fst 5½f	:224 :473 1:003 1:073	ⒻMd Sp Wt	6 5 68½ 45 21 1¾	Eads W	115 w	*1.60	87-17	Twilight Tear115¾Letmenow1151Durazna1153		12
Slow into stride,drawing clear											

Vagrancy

dk. b. f. 1939, by Sir Gallahad III (Teddy)–Valkyr, by Man o' War

Lifetime record: 42 15 8 8 $102,480

Own.– Belair Stud
Br.– Belair Stud (Ky)
Tr.– J. Fitzsimmons

9Oct43- 6Bel	fst 2¼	:504 2:343 2:594 3:521 3↑	New York H 28k	6 4 45¼ 23 31½ 33	Stout J	112wb	4.85	71-17	Bolngbrok1241½FryMnhurst1161½Vgrncy11212	Challenged,tired	6
5Oct43- 6Bel	fst 1½	:483 1:134 2:05 2:314 3↑	ⒻLadies H 16k	2 4 43½ 2½ 2½ 21½	Stout J	123wb	4.10	77-17	Stefanita1161½Vagrancy1236Dark Discovery1061¼	Driving	7
18Sep43- 6Aqu	fst 1⅛	:474 1:132 1:383 1:513 3↑	ⒻBeldame H 28k	9 7 86¼ 75½ 42½ 33	Gilbert J	122wb	9.10	86-14	Mar-Kell1261Stefanita1162Vagrancy122½	Closed well	11
28Aug43- 6GS	sl 1⅛	:474 1:132 1:391 1:524 3↑	Trenton H 13k	5 5 59½ 47 46 56¾	Stout J	109 w	2.95	78-29	Aonbarr113nkWith Regards1182Boysy1134	No threat	7
25Aug43- 6Bel	fst 1⅛	:463 1:111 1:364 1:50 3↑	ⒻDiana H 5.8k	4 4 44½ 33 41¼ 21	Stout J	126wb	*1.30	90-10	Bonnet Ann1131Vagrancy126nkNight Glow1121	Wide	5
20Aug43- 7Bel	fst 1	:233 :463 1:111 1:36 3↑	Alw 3000	5 2 21 2½ 2hd 21¾	Stout J	108wb	3.65	92-14	FamousVictory1051¾Vagrancy108nkFirstFiddle1201	Bid,hung	7
30Jun43- 5Jam	gd 1 1/16	:251 :491 1:134 1:462 3↑	ⒻHandicap 5120	1 3 33½ 33½ 35 35½	Stout J	128wb	*.95	75-22	Night Glow1081½Stefanita1104Vagrancy12810	Tired	4
26Jun43- 6Aqu	fst 1¼	:481 1:132 1:383 2:032 3↑	Brooklyn H 33k	7 9 911 89¾ 89¾ 819¼	Stout J	110wb	23.30	71-12	DevilDiver1231½MarketWise128¾DonBngo1133	Stumbled start	9
19Jun43- 7Aqu	fst 1⅛	:491 1:132 1:391 1:52 4↑	Handicap 3535	1 4 42¼ 43 31 3½	Stout J	117wb	4.30e	86-12	Lochinvar115hdDon Bingo122½Vagrancy1177	Rated,gamely	5
31May43- 6Bel	fst 1¼	:47 1:111 1:361 2:012 3↑	Suburban H 38k	2 5 103¾ 127½ 107½ 109	Durando C	112wb	34.90	84-12	DonBingo1042[D]MarketWise1282½Attention121hd	No threat	17
24May43- 6Bel	fst 1	:232 :464 1:121 1:374 3↑	ⒻHandicap 3025	3 4 42¼ 11 11½ 12	Longden J	126wb	*.65	85-19	Vagrancy1262Too Timely1072½Waygal1021½	Very wide	5
14May43- 6Bel	my 1	:232 :47 1:12 1:374 3↑	ⒻAlw 3000	5 7 65 44 34 28	Longden J	122wb	*.55	77-23	Mar-Kell1108Vagrancy1226Opera Singer101nk	No match	8
7May43- 5Jam	fst 1 1/16	:241 :474 1:131 1:46 3↑	ⒻHandicap 5025	2 3 31½ 31 2½ 2¾	Malley T	126wb	*1.40	82-18	Pomayya122¾Vagrancy1267What Not981½	Trapped,gamely	6
Previously trained by G. Tappen											
24Oct42- 6Lrl	fst 1¼	:473 1:122 1:383 2:032 3↑	Washington H 19k	9 5 2hd 55 69¾ 714	Stout J	108wb	9.20	79-20	Whirlaway130½Thumbs Up1102Riverland1185	Quit badly	9
17Oct42- 6Lrl	sl 1¼	:474 1:124 1:392 2:062	Maryland H 8.8k	1 2 56 57 46 47½	Stout J	117wb	*.65	70-28	Thumbs Up113hdIncoming1112½Equinox1045	Disliked going	7
12Oct42- 6Lrl	fst 1⅛	:473 1:122 1:381 1:51 3↑	ⒻQueen Isabella H 6.1k	1 4 4¾ 1½ 12 13	Stout J	126wb	*.50	93-12	Vagrancy1263Lotopoise1022Rosetown1224	Much in reserve	6
Previously trained by J. Fitzsimmons											
6Oct42- 6Bel	gd 1½	:481 1:133 2:054 2:311 3↑	ⒻLadies H 16k	4 1 411 21 11 11¼	Stout J	126wb	*1.40	86-13	Vagrancy1261¼Dark Discovery1081¼Loveday1175	Ridden out	10
29Sep42- 7Bel	fst 1⅝	:484 1:393 2:043 2:42	Lawrence Realizatn 11k	1 3 47½ 32¼ 1nk 23½	Stout J	115wb	5.00e	90-08	Alsab1263½Vagrancy1153Trierarch110nk	Bore in final ⅛	5
19Sep42- 6Aqu	sly 1⅛	:472 1:121 1:373 1:50 3↑	ⒻBeldame H 17k	9 2 1½ 14 14 14•	Stout J	119wb	*2.15	97-06	[DH]Vgrncy119[DH]Brrncos1164Rostown126hd	Drifted out,tiring	10
29Aug42- 6Nar	fst 1 1/16	:23 :462 1:12 1:443	ⒻNew England Oaks 12k	1 5 54¼ 44½ 21½ 2¾	Stout J	121wb	*.80	93-14	Spiral Pass116¾Vagrancy1213Ubiquitous1166	In trouble	9
7Aug42- 5Sar	fst 1¼	:473 1:121 1:381 2:051	ⒻAlabama 10k	2 2 24 23 21½ 2½	Stout J	126wb	*.30	82-13	[D]Bonnet Ann114½Vagrancy126hdSmiles114	Impeded	3
Placed first through disqualification											
31Jly42- 5Sar	sly 7f	:231 :471 1:122 1:26	ⒻTest 3.4k	5 4 42 31½ 21 1hd	Stout J	123wb	*.55	86-17	Vagrancy123hdTaunt113¾Smiles1132½	Hard drive	6
11Jly42- 5Emp	fst 1 3/16	:474 1:123 1:364 1:56	Emp City H 28k	2 3 32 42 45½ 45¾	Malley T	114wb	*1.50e	101-07	Apache1143Lochinvar1162½Col. Teddy115nk	No mishap	7
4Jly42- 5Emp	fst 1 3/16	:48 1:122 1:374 1:564 3↑	Butler H 33k	2 4 31½ 31½ 32¼ 43¾	McCreary C	100wb	4.20	99-07	Tola Rose1032½Whirlaway132nkSwing and Sway1121	Faltered	7
24Jun42- 6Aqu	fst 1 1/16	:232 :472 1:124 1:45	ⒻGazelle 6.5k	5 3 35 22 12 14	Stout J	126wb	*.50	89-10	Vagrancy1264Smiles112nkMackerel1121½	Drew away	7
18Jun42- 6Aqu	fst 1 1/16	:242 :48 1:123 1:443	ⒻAlw 3500	3 3 32½ 13 13 15	Stout J	121wb	*1.25	91-09	Vagrancy1215Lotopoise1081Smiles108nk	Much the best	6
11Jun42- 6Del	gd 1⅛	:481 1:13 1:394 1:54	ⒻDel Oaks 10k	4 3 32 23 1hd 1no	Malley T	119wb	1.95	79-19	Vagrancy119noWaygal1104Bostoff1103	Hard drive	6
27May42- 6Bel	fst 1½	:51 1:17 2:071 2:313	ⒻCCA Oaks 20k	6 3 1½ 11½ 11½ 12	Malley T	121wb	*.60	84-11	Vagrancy1212Mackerel1214Copperette1213	In hand	6
20May42- 6Bel	fst 1	:232 :46 1:11 1:381	ⒻAcorn 14k	1 6 44½ 57 56½ 21½	Malley T	121wb	*2.20	82-11	Zaca Rosa1211½Vagrancy121nkBonnet Ann1211	Closed fast	15
15May42- 6Bel	fst 1	:231 :461 1:12 1:383 3↑	ⒻAlw 3000	10 9 66 66 86¾ 76¼	Malley T	108wb	4.30	76-13	Painted Veil1202Pomayya120hdChallomine1092	Outrun	12
2May42- 6Pim	fst 1 1/16	:231 :471 1:121 1:453	ⒻPim Oaks 12k	2 3 31½ 22 2½ 1½	Malley T	121wb	*1.95	92-07	Vagrancy121½Chiquita Mia1217Bonnet Ann1211	Driving	7
25Apr42- 2Jam	fst 6f	:23 :462 1:114	ⒻAlw 1500	2 6 74¾ 42½ 11½ 12½	Malley T	113wb	7.80e	93-10	Vagrancy1132½Smiles1131½Draeh1083½	Going away	13
21Apr42- 5Jam	fst 1 1/16	:232 :471 1:122 1:453	Alw 2500	7 6 611 66½ 48 510	Stout J	108wb	3.60	75-17	Air Current113noK. Dorko1136Blue Gino1082	No mishap	7
15Apr42- 4Jam	fst 6f	:23 :462 1:12	ⒻAlw 2000	3 5 58½ 58½ 48½ 34¾	Stout J	110wb	2.80	87-12	Taunt115¾War Melody1104Vagrancy110hd	Closed fast	5
Previously trained by G. Tappen											
25Oct41- 5Lrl	fst 1 1/16	:232 :473 1:123 1:471	ⒻSelima 28k	10 4 31¼ 32 22 34	Deering J	114wb	2.45e	77-17	Ficklebush1073½Hard Baked114½Vagrancy1142	Tired	11
18Oct41- 4Lrl	fst 1 70	:233 :474 1:132 1:45	ⒻAlw 1200	5 2 11 11 12 12	Deering J	113wb	*1.05	84-16	Vagrancy1132Last Sou1092Umbril10812	Ridden out	6
13Oct41- 4Lrl	fst 1 70	:233 :48 1:134 1:452	ⒻAlw 1500	2 4 42¼ 31½ 1½ 12	Deering J	111wb	2.75	82-19	Vagrancy1112Seaway103noUmbril1065	Going away	8
9Oct41- 4Lrl	fst 6f	:224 :47 1:122	Alw 1200	3 6 44¼ 42 42½ 32	Deering J	111wb	8.65	90-18	Bless Me1141½Tomluta117½Vagrancy1114	Closed well	6
Previously trained by J. Fitzsimmons											
20Sep41- 7Bel	fst 6f	:221 :46 1:113	ⒻMatron 20k	11 11 1311 1212 109½ 911	Stout J	115wb	19.30	81-13	Petrify1192Light Lady119noFicklebush110½	Outrun	15
12Sep41- 5Aqu	fst 6f	:23 :464 1:13	ⒻAlw 1500	8 9 84¾ 63¾ 44 3½	Stout J	116wb	6.00	88-12	Smiles113nkLast Sou113nkVagrancy1161	Strong finish	9
1Sep41- 4Aqu	fst 5½f	:232 :474 1:071	ⒻMd Sp Wt	6 5 31¾ 2½ 21 1½	Stout J	116wb	7.55	91-12	Vagrancy116½Waygal1164Jezara116hd	Driving	7
23Aug41- 3Sar	fst 6f	:231 :472 1:14	ⒻAlw 1200	3 10 109¾ 915 89½ 78	Stout J	110wb	32.65	74-19	Court Manners115noBig Meal1151½Spiral Pass1151	Outrun	10

War Battle

b. g. 1941, by Battleship (Man o' War)–Ponova, by Pommern

Lifetime record: 49 11 10 8 $88,360

Own.– K. Miller
Br.– Leslie B. Gray
Tr.– K. Miller

3Oct51- 4Lig	hd *2	S'Chase 4:101 3↑	Alw 2500	7 4 55¾ 58¾ 511 514	Field K	140wb	-	--	Allflor1472½Politician140½Friese1353	Never a factor	9
27Aug51- 3Sar	fst *2	S'Chase 4:14 3↑	Alw 3500	2 3 326 422 530 533	Carter E	146wb	4.65	--	Fulton14012Patrol14614Short Circuit1401	Jumped poorly	5
22Aug51- 3Sar	sl *2	S'Chase 4:292 3↑	Alw 4000	6 3 24 12 312 323½	Riles S	138wb	19.95	--	Elyacin1331½Phiblant15022War Battle13815	Quit	7
15Aug51- 3Sar	gd *2	S'Chase 4:151 4↑	Clm 3000	1 7 74 45½ 616 622	Carter E	137wb	7.70	--	Kipper1523My Good Man1474Trepid1412½	Tired	9
16Jun49- 4Aqu	fst *2½	S'Chase 4:564 4↑	Hitchcock H 11k	4 4 47 310 620 624	Smithwick P	151wb	3.35	--	Homogenize142½Rank1401Navigate143½	Lame	6
25May49- 5Bel	fst *2	S'Chase 3:531 4↑	Alw 4500	4 4 613 514 412 411	Rich J	150wb	7.50	--	Floating Isle1401½Genancoke1402Galactic1407	No mishap	6
19May49- 4Bel	fst *2	S'Chase 3:434 4↑	C L Appleton 9.5k	11 2 1126 1029 942 976	Rich J	146wb	4.70	--	Navigate138½Point Bleu1422½Galactic1382½	Quit	11
10May49- 3Bel	my *2	S'Chase 4:023 4↑	Alw 4500	2 1 14 1hd 716 725	Rich J	152wb	*1.70	--	Floating Isle1466Navigate1462Point Bleu1461½	Quit	7
Daily Racing Form time,4:05 3/5											
23Jun48- 3Aqu	my *2	S'Chase 4:04 4↑	Alw 4500	3 1 110 110 110 17	Bosley J III	152wb	*1.30	--	War Battle1527Big Wrack13740Fred Havecker134	Easily	5
17Jun48- 1Del	sl *2	S'Chase 3:552 4↑	Alw 4000	4 1 2hd 13 16 18	Bosley J III	155wb	2.15	--	WarBattle1558AmericanWay1516Lieut.Well155¾	Ridden out	5
27May48- 5Bel	gd *2	S'Chase 3:491 4↑	C L Appleton 11k	1 2 31¾ 36½ 38 310	Bosley J III	155wb	2.40	--	TheHeir1352Fleettown1468WarBattle15510	Bad landing 8th	5

23Oct47- 6Lrl fst *2 S'Chase 3:50² 3↑ Governor Ogle H 12k 1 3 410 420 421 415 Miller R 164wb 3.40 -- Genancoke1415Sun Bath139noAdaptable15010 Outrun 6
8Oct47- 5Bel fst *2 S'Chase 3:45 3↑ Broad Hollow H 18k 4 1 12 21 32½ 32½ McGovern J 165wb *.75 -- Hampton Roads1382Genancoke140½War Battle165½ Tired 4
2Oct47- 5Bel fst *3 S'Chase 5:41³ 4↑ Grand National 29k 2 2 12 110 13 2hd McGovern J 163wb *1.05e -- Adaptable147hdWarBattle163nkTroughHill1394 Tired badly 8
25Sep47- 5Bel my *2½ S'Chase 4:52¹ 4↑ Brook H 18k 9 2 13 11½ 311 413 Brown N 164wb *1.55 -- Adaptable1408Delhi Dan1384Floating Isle1501 Weak ride 9
26Jly47- 6Jam fst 1 1/16 :24³ :49¹ 1:14¹ 1:48³ 3↑ Md Sp Wt 6 10 915 812 57½ 43 Wilson HB 120wb 3.40 67-14 DeepTexas1132Capt.Dorsett113hdWinterWndII1131 Late foot 10
12Jun47- 5Aqu fst *2½ S'Chase 4:57³ 4↑ Hitchcock H 10k 3 2 39 11½ 110 115 Brown N 162wb *.65e -- War Battle16215Copper Beech1335Floating Isle140 Easily 4
28May47- 5Bel fst *2½ S'Chase 4:46⁴ 4↑ Meadow Brook 17k 1 1 12 1nk 13 112 Brown N 156wb *1.15e -- War Battle15612Fleettown14112Floating Isle147no Easily 6
22May47- 5Bel sl *2 S'Chase 4:07¹ 4↑ Corinthian H 11k 4 3 34½ 46½ 37 32 Roberts E 156wb 5.70 -- Boojum II1431Raylywn1391War Battle15620 7
Bothered by riderless horse
9May47- 5Bel fst *2 S'Chase 3:50⁴ 4↑ International H 11k 1 1 1nk 1½ 22 26 Passmore WJ 156wb .95 -- Boojum II1386War Battle1561½Hidalgo13720 Saved ground 5
12Nov46- 5Pim fst 2½ S'Chase 4:48² 4↑ Manly H 17k 6 2 26 21½ 12 18 Passmore W 148wb 2.85 -- WarBattle1488GalleyBoy1395TouristList13512 Bobbled 15th 6
5Nov46- 5Pim fst 2 S'Chase 3:51² 3↑ Battleship H 11k 6 4 31 33 3½ 21½ Passmore W 148wb *.90e -- GalleyBoy1321½WarBattle1481¼TouristList1351 Second best 6
15Oct46- 6Bel fst *3 S'Chase 5:42² 4↑ Temple Gwathmey H 21k 1 1 120 115 115 130 Passmore W 138wb *1.35e -- WarBattle13830Elkridge1582½Chesapeak1403 Speed to spare 5
9Oct46- 5Bel fst *2 S'Chase 3:49³ 3↑ Broad Hollow H 11k 5 1 15 11 23 33 Mason G 145wb 4.75 -- Lieut. Well1372Greek Flag1311War Battle1455 7
Bobbled several fences
28Sep46- 3Bel fst *2 S'Chase 3:50² 3↑ Alw 5000 5 3 34 21 21½ 21 Adams FD 143wb *.60 -- Tourist List1441War Battle1435Cosey1464 Hard urged 5
6Sep46- 5Aqu fst *2 S'Chase 3:43² 3↑ Harbor Hill H 11k 5 7 77½ 56 611 613¾ Adams FD 151wb *1.25 -- ⒹChesapeake1321Navigate150nkKnight'sQust1488 No mishap 7
23Aug46- 5Sar fst *2 S'Chase 4:11³ 3↑ Beverwyck H 5.7k 3 3 45½ 32½ 22 21 Adams FD 144wb 2.75 -- RougeDragon1621WarBattle1442½BoojumII13912 Bobbled 1st 4
8Aug46- 5Sar gd *2 S'Chase 4:15 4↑ Shillelah 5.6k 4 2 2½ 11 1½ 2no Bauman A 147wb *1.80 -- Tetrol138noWar Battle14725Beneksar1441½ Bothered early 5
26Jun46- 2Del fst *2 S'Chase 3:51 4↑ Alw 3500 3 4 33½ 33½ 34 36¼ Marzani D 141 w *.90 -- Boojum II1532½Gala Reigh1374War Battle1412½ Bobbled 9th 4
22Jun46- 3Aqu fst *2 S'Chase 3:42¹ 4↑ Handicap 4500 2 4 33½ 37 21½ 2nk Marzani D 146 w *1.35e -- Elkridge155nkWar Battle1461Lancastrian1402 Fast finish 5
11Jun46- 5Aqu fst *2½ S'Chase 4:51¹ 4↑ Hitchcock H 11k 5 3 41 31¼ 21½ 2¾ Bauman A 139 w 6.55 -- Delhi Dan133¾War Battle1391½Mercator15614 Saved ground 5
8Jun46- 3Bel fst *1¾ Hurdles 3:22² 3↑ Alw 4000 7 4 32 32 22 21½ Bauman A 153 w *1.10e -- H Hour1371½War Battle1532Yankee Chance138nk Driving 8
28May46- 5Bel hy *2½ S'Chase 4:58¹ 4↑ Meadowbrook H 11k 3 2 210 314 413 616 Bauman A 142 w 8.10 -- Mercator1503Beneksar1347Burma Road1521 No factor 8
22May46- 5Bel fst *2 S'Chase 3:49³ 4↑ Corinthian H 9.4k 3 7 32 2½ 22 33 Bauman A 143 w 12.15 -- Burma Road1461Navigate1422War Battle1436 Held well 12
16May46- 5Bel fst *2 S'Chase 3:52⁴ 4↑ C L Appleton 8.8k 1 2 1hd 2hd 35¼ 312 Adams FD 152 w 2.40 -- Burma Road1395Floating Isle1517War Battle152½ Tired 6
6May46- 3Bel fst 1½ Hurdles 2:50³ 4↑ Alw 4000 1 2 42½ 32 12 12½ Jennings E 155 w 2.55 -- War Battle1552½Mat1392Gala Reigh1434 Drew away 6
28Nov45- 5Pim sly 2½ S'Chase 5:25² 4↑ Manly H 12k 2 1 13 21 617 632 Banks D 142 w 2.85e -- PursuitPlane1325BurmaRoad13912GeekFlag1384 Speed,tired 10
14Nov45- 3Pim fst 2 S'Chase 3:50² 3↑ Handicap 5000 1 5 21 - - - Adams FD 142wsb 20.95 -- Cosey130¾Floating Isle1492Mercator1602 Lost rider 11th 7
3Oct45- 5Bel fst *3 S'Chase 5:48 4↑ Grand National H 18k 9 - - - - - Adams FD 139wsb 4.30 -- Mercator1425Caddie139¾Raylywn1426 Fell 12
24Aug45- 5Sar sl *2 S'Chase 3:49³ 3↑ Beverwyck H 5.9k 5 1 13 12 1hd 12 Adams FD 135wsb *1.45e -- War Battle1352Boojum II1373Floating Isle15210 Drew away 7
17Aug45- 4Bel fst *2 S'Chase 3:45 3↑ North American H 16k 9 2 21½ 2nk 31¼ 63¼ Adams FD 136wb 3.85e -- FloatingIsle149nkChesapeake136½Elkrdg1581 Bobbled,tired 10
17Nov44- 5Pim fst 2 S'Chase 3:49³ 3↑ Battleship H 10k 6 - - - - - Owen W 135wsb 3.15 -- Ahmisk1441Rouge Dragon1627Boojum II1404 Lost rider 4th 9
1Nov44- 3Pim fst 2 S'Chase 3:58 3↑ Alw 2500 1 1 1½ 16 14 110 Owen W 135wsb *1.15 -- War Battle13510Floating Isle1471Refugio1464 In hand 9
29Sep44- 3Bel fst *1¾ Hurdles 3:27 3↑ Alw 2500 5 3 43¼ 31½ 12 11½ Roberts E 136wsb *1.30 -- War Battle1361½Peat Moss1494Beneksar1472½ Mild drive 5
18Sep44- 3Bel fst *1½ Hurdles 2:53 3↑ Alw 2500 6 6 43 32 2hd 2½ Roberts E 136wb 3.15 -- GreyHood137½WarBattl13612ArrvonTm1462 Bid,faltered late 7
31Aug44- 3Bel fst *1½ Hurdles 2:52² Md Sp Wt 2 6 56 48 12 14 Harrison JS 146 w 9.25 -- War Battle1464Cosey1454Persepolis1453 Easily 7
Previously owned by Petard Stable;previously trained by J. Bosley Jr
21Aug44- 3Bel fst *1½ Hurdles 2:50² 3↑ Md Sp Wt 6 11 1010 915 916 721 Jennings E 135 w 28.50 -- ⒹLongchamp II1516Lieut. Well1352Quonset1384 No factor 12
15Aug44- 3Bel fst *1½ Hurdles 2:49 3↑ OMdClm 2000 7 10 917 621 619½ 515¼ Jennings E 137 w 75.10 -- Nordmeer152½Navigate1374Longchamp II1525 Collided 9th 10
7Aug44- 3Bel fst *1½ Hurdles 2:53 3↑ OMdClm 2000 4 2 615 533 527 628¾ McGovern J 137 w 21.55 -- Wolfberry140¾Nordmeer1525Night Porter1523 No mishap 8

War Plumage

br. f. 1936, by On Watch (Colin)–War Feathers, by Man o' War — **Lifetime record: 16 3 3 1 $48,600**

Own.– J.C. Brady
Br.– Howard Oots (Ky)
Tr.– H. Wells

5Nov40- 6Pim fst 1 3/16 :48¹ 1:12¹ 1:38⁴ 1:59³ 3↑ Riggs H 13k 10 4 65 56½ 64¾ 68 Craig A 110wb 43.40 77-21 Rough Pass1053Burning Star113½War Beauty1011½ 10
Saved ground,faltered
26Oct40- 5Lrl fst 1¼ :47² 1:12⁴ 1:38² 2:05 3↑ Washington H 19k 5 5 78½ 85½ 711 710 Craig A 111 w 11.70 75-24 Can't Wait120½True Call105¾Burning Star113¾ Outrun 8
1Oct40- 6Bel fst 1½ :47¹ 1:12⁴ 2:05 2:30 3↑ ⒻLadies H 17k 1 9 812 53 109½ 1016¾ Wall N 126 w 9.00 75-12 Salaminia115½Pretty Pet1141Fairy Chant123¾ Tired 12
21Sep40- 5Aqu fst 1⅛ :47² 1:12 1:37² 1:50³ 3↑ ⒻBeldame H 19k 10 12 1518 128 109½ 1112 Wall N 126 w 7.35 90-02 Fairy Chant1191¼Dotted Swiss1141Dolly Val1212½ Impeded 16
2Sep40- 6Was fst 1¼ :49¹ 1:14¹ 1:39¹ 2:04 3↑ Wash Park H 31k 3 3 1½ 2½ 1hd 11 Wall N 110 w 6.80e 90-14 War Plumage110¾Viscounty1183Burning Star1094 Hard drive 6
26Aug40- 6Was my 1⅛ :51² 1:16 1:42² 1:56¹ 3↑ Alw 1500 2 3 23 23 47 413 Snider A 113 w *1.10e 56-40 Viscounty1224Shot Put1144Yale O'Nine1145 Close quarters 4
2Mar40- 6SA fst 1¼ :47¹ 1:11¹ 1:36 2:01¹ 3↑ S Anita H 121k 9 7 1110 83 88¾ 54½ Neves R 107 w 26.80 96-11 Seabiscuit1301½Kayak II1291Whichcee1141½ Close quarters 13
3Feb40- 6SA my 1 1/16 :24 :47⁴ 1:12⁴ 1:46³ 4↑ ⒻS Margarita H 12k 5 4 411 48 712 815 Dotter R 122 w *2.30 63-26 Fairy Chant1033½Omelet1101½Sweet Nancy1082 Tired 10
9Sep39- 5Aqu fst 1 1/16 :23³ :46² 1:10³ 1:43 3↑ ⒻBeldame H 13k 17 10 117 159¾ 51¾ 53¼ Wall N 121 w *2.20 95-03 NellieBly102noUnerring1203BalOrmont115hd Close quarters 18
14Aug39- 5Sar gd 1¼ :49 1:13³ 1:39³ 2:05 ⒻAlabama 12k 4 1 42½ 11½ 1hd 11½ Peters M 124 w 3.50 84-19 War Plumage1241½Bass Wood11110Hostility1242 Going away 9
17Jun39- 6Del fst 1⅛ :48² 1:13² 1:39² 1:52³ ⒻDel Oaks 5.4k 3 4 23 21 2hd 22 Dotter R 119 w *.45 95-09 Wise Lady1102War Plumage1193Alms11915 Weakened 5
7Jun39- 5Bel fst 1⅜ :47³ 1:12³ 1:38 2:16⁴ ⒻC C A Oaks 14k 8 2 46½ 2hd 15 17 Wall N 116 w 2.60 87-16 War Plumage1167Hostility121½Wise Lady1212 Easily 9
17Sep38- 5HdG fst 6f :23² :46⁴ 1:12⁴ Eastern Shore H 15k 5 11 128 127½ 98¼ 94¼ Gilbert J 113 w *2.00e 85-14 TimeAlone1091SweetNancy110hdT.M.Dorsett112½ Off slowly 15
17Aug38- 5Nar my 5½f :22³ :46² 1:06⁴ ⒻJeanne d'Arc 7.4k 5 10 94¾ 85¼ 43½ 33½ Dotter R 108 w 10.45 87-24 SmartCrack1073HeatherTime119½WarPlumge1081 Closed fast 13
25Jun38- 4Del fst 5f :22² :47 1:00² ⒻPolly Drummond 7k 3 5 64¾ 65½ 44 2hd Dotter R 110 w 14.00 94-08 Bud'sBell113hdWarPlumage1101Soldierette1131 Just missed 10
18Jun38- 3Del fst 5f :23 :46⁴ 1:00² Alw 1000 7 6 31½ 21 21 22 Dotter R 109 w 11.10 92-10 Post Luck1112War Plumage1092Oak Apple1141½ Swerved 7

Whirlaway

ch. c. 1938, by Blenheim II (Blandford)–Dustwhirl, by Sweep — **Lifetime record: 60 32 15 9 $561,161**

Own.– Calumet Farm
Br.– Calumet Farm (Ky)
Tr.– B.A. Jones

26Jun43- 6Was fst 1 :22¹ :44³ 1:10² 1:37 3↑ Equipoise Mile H 13k 11 12 1015 815 64 55¼ Eads W 126wb *1.30 88-11 Best Seller113hdThumbs Up1131¼Some Chance1093 12
Saved ground,pulled up sore
22Jun43- 6Was gd 1 :24¹ :47⁴ 1:13 1:37³ 4↑ Alw 2500 6 5 611 57½ 45 33¼ Eads W 122wb *.50e 86-17 Mar-Kell1052½King'sAbby110¾Whrlwy1221½ Hand ridden late 7
12Dec42- 7FG sl 1⅛ :49 1:14² 1:40 1:53 3↑ Louisiana H 17k 4 8 86¼ 42½ 31½ 11½ Eads W 130wb *.60 89-18 Whirlaway1301½Heartman1203Riverland124nk Saved ground 8
11Nov42- 6Pim sl 1⅝ :50¹ 1:42¹ 2:07² 2:48¹ 3↑ Governor Bowie H 11k 3 4 43 12 13 13 Eads W 129wb *.35 75-24 Whirlaway1293Dark Discovery106hdEquifox109.58 Easily 4
3Nov42- 6Pim my 1 3/16 :50² 1:15³ 1:41¹ 1:59⁴ 3↑ Riggs H 12k 5 5 44½ 55 32 22½ Woolf G 130wb *.45 81-22 Riverland1162½Whirlaway130¾Pictor109¾ 6
Taken back,lost ground str turn
28Oct42- 7Pim fst 1 3/16 :55¹ 1:20³ 1:46⁴ 2:05² 3↑ Pim Spl 10k 1 1 1 1 1 1 Woolf G 126wb - -- Whirlaway126 Galloping 1
24Oct42- 6Lrl fst 1¼ :47³ 1:12² 1:38³ 2:03² 3↑ Washington H 19k 6 9 813 31½ 2hd 1½ Woolf G 130wb *.65 93-20 Whirlawy130½ThumbsUp1102RvrInd1185 Carried wide,driving 9
10Oct42- 6Bel fst 2¼ :49 2:29² 2:54² 3:47¹ 3↑ New York H 30k 3 8 1½ 11 1hd 31¼ Westrope J 130wb *1.05 98-07 Alsab121hdObash1061¼Whirlaway1305 Tired last ⅛ 12
3Oct42- 6Bel fst 2 :52³ 2:32 2:56² 3:21³ 3↑ J C Gold Cup 27k 2 3 33½ 3nk 21½ 1¾ Woolf G 124wb *.55 96-05 Whirlaway124¾Alsab1178Bolingbroke12415 Drawing away 4
Geldings not eligible

26Sep42- 6Bel fst 1½ :481 1:123 2:023 2:273 3↑ Manhattan H 11k 7 7 813 64 31 21½ Westrope J 132wb *.70 102-04 Bolingbroke1151½Whirlaway1322King's Abbey1112½ Wide 8
19Sep42- 7Nar fst 1 3/16 :502 1:141 1:383 1:562 3↑ Match Race 25k 1 2 21½ 22 21 2no Woolf G 126wb *.30 93-11 Alsab119noWhirlaway126 Wearing down winner 2
12Sep42- 6Nar gd 1 3/16 :462 1:11 1:363 1:562 3↑ Nar Spl H 31k 4 7 717 712 21 12 Woolf G 130wb *.40 93-17 Whirlaway1302Boysy112¾Valdina Orphan1141 Ridden out 7
29Aug42- 6GS fst 1⅛ :483 1:122 1:374 1:504 3↑ Trenton H 12k 2 4 1hd 11 1½ 11 Eads W 130wb *.30 -- Whirlaway1301Rosetown111noAonbarr1176 4
Drifted out turn,drew away when straightened
1Aug42- 6AP sly 1¼ :494 1:133 1:38 2:04 3↑ Arlington H 29k 5 5 43½ 2½ 2½ 23½ Arcaro E 130wb *.30 82-17 Rounders1033½Whirlaway1308Strtor1046 Lost ground,tired 5
15Jly42- 7Suf fst 1⅛ :463 1:112 1:36 1:481 3↑ Mass H 61k 7 7 710 44 1hd 12¼ Woolf G 130wb *1.00 102-11 Whirlaway1302¼Rounders1081Attention1224 Driving 7
4Jly42- 5Emp fst 1 3/16 :48 1:122 1:374 1:564 3↑ Butler H 33k 5 7 713 79 43¼ 22½ Woolf G 132wb *.75 100-07 Tola Rose1032½Whirlaway132nkSwing and Sway1121 7
Blocked start,outside,fast finish
27Jun42- 6Aqu fst 1¼ :49 1:13 1:38 2:022 3↑ Brooklyn H 34k 4 8 76¾ 64¾ 42¾ 11¾ Woolf G 128wb *.45 103-05 Whirlaway1281¾Swing and Sway1101½Attention122hd Driving 8
22Jun42- 6Aqu fst 1⅛ :48 1:13 1:372 1:492 3↑ Alw 3500 1 4 35½ 33 31¾ 1no Woolf G 122 w *.30 103-09 Whirlaway122noAttention1172½Swing and Sway113no 5
Hard drive,drifting out
13Jun42- 6Aqu fst 7f :223 :451 1:094 1:23 3↑ Carter H 9.8k 9 9 917 913 96¾ 3¾ Haas L 130wb *2.30 99-08 Doublrab120hdSwingandSway112¾Whirlaway1301½ Fast finish 9
30May42- 6Bel fst 1¼ :481 1:123 1:371 2:014 3↑ Suburban H 38k 5 11 1112 96¾ 43 22 Arcaro E 129wb *1.00 89-07 Market Wise1242Whirlaway1291½Attention1243 Wide 11
6May42- 6Pim fst 1 3/16 :472 1:114 1:374 1:57 3↑ Dixie H 25k 3 8 817 812 51¾ 1¾ Arcaro E 128 w *1.65 98-12 Whirlaway128¾Attention124½Mioland126hd Drawing clear 8
25Apr42- 6CD fst 1 1/16 :24 :473 1:122 1:444 3↑ Clark H 3k 3 4 37½ 35 23 1hd Eads W 127wb *.10 96-11 Whirlaway127hdAonbarr1158½Fairmond1101¼ Wide 5
15Apr42- 5Kee fst 6f :232 :471 1:121 3↑ Handicap 1500 2 8 76½ 55¾ 53 2½ Craig A 126wb *.50e 90-18 Sun Again109½Whirlaway126nkHarvard Square119hd 8
Drifted out,getting to winner
9Apr42- 5Kee my 6f :234 :48 1:132 3↑ Phoenix H 3.4k 3 4 52½ 53½ 31 2hd Craig A 128wb *.60e 85-26 DevilDivr113.5hdWhrlwy1281½SunAgn1122 Getting to winner 5
27Sep41- 5Bel fst 2 :492 2:284 2:55 3:204 3↑ J C Gold Cup 10k 2 4 21 21 1hd 2no Robertson A 114wb *.35 105-09 MarketWise114noWhirlaway1148Fenelon12512 Clear lead str 4
Geldings not eligible
20Sep41- 5Bel fst 1⅝ :49 1:381 2:034 2:441 Lawrence Realizatn 26k 4 2 2hd 15 16 18 Robertson A 126wb *.20 83-13 Whirlaway1268Alaking1125Time Counts1126 Eased up late 4
Geldings not eligible
13Sep41- 6Nar fst 1 3/16 :501 1:143 1:39 1:571 3↑ Nar Spl H 29k 2 4 46½ 32½ 24 24½ Robertson A 118wb *.40 84-14 War Relic1074½Whirlaway1181Equifox1121½ Driving 4
23Aug41- 7Was fst 1¼ :49 1:13 1:382 2:04 American Derby 59k 4 4 21 11 11½ 12¾ Robertson A 126wb *.20 90-08 Whirlaway1262¾Bushwhacker1213½Delray118¾ Speed to spare 5
16Aug41- 6Sar my 1¼ :49 1:132 1:393 2:054 Travers 21k 1 2 311 38 32½ 13¾ Robertson A 130wb *.15 80-22 Whirlaway1303¾Fairymant1122½Lord Kitchener112 Easily 3
6Aug41- 6Sar fst 1 :24 :48 1:122 1:38 Saranac H 4.8k 4 5 56 41¼ 4½ 1no Robertson A 130wb *.65 91-13 Whirlaway130noWarRlc117¾Omsson1121½ Drifted out,just up 5
26Jly41- 6AP fst 1¼ :491 1:132 1:372 2:024 Classic 57k 4 6 66 2hd 2hd 21½ Shelhamer A 126wb *.40 90-17 Attention1211½Whirlaway1266Bushwhacker1213½ 6
Away slowly,forced wide last ⅛,tired
15Jly41- 6AP fst 1⅛ :492 1:131 1:38 1:503 Special Event 5k 2 2 12 12½ 11 12½ Eads W 120wb *.10 94-13 Whirlaway1202½Daily Trouble1122To a Tee112½ 4
Bore out str turn,drew away when straightened
21Jun41- 5Aqu fst 1¼ :49 1:132 1:383 2:032 Dwyer 11k 3 4 44½ 11½ 11½ 11¼ Arcaro E 126wb *.20 98-08 Whirlaway1261¼Market Wise1222½Robert Morris11912 4
Came over turn,drifted out str,speed to spare
7Jun41- 6Bel fst 1½ :494 1:134 2:05 2:31 Belmont 48k 3 3 31½ 13 12 12½ Arcaro E 126wb *.25 87-15 Whirlwy1262½RobertMorrs1265YnkChnc1265 Speed to spare 4
20May41- 6Bel fst 1 1/16 :234 :463 1:113 1:433 3↑ Alw 2500 3 4 35 42½ 11½ 12¼ Eads W 108wb *.75 93-12 Whirlaway1082¼Miolnd127nkHsh1203 Drifting out final ⅛ 5
10May41- 6Pim gd 1 3/16 :472 1:123 1:391 1:584 Preakness 66k 1 8 89 73 15 15½ Arcaro E 126wb *1.15 89-12 Whirlaway1265½KingCole1262OurBoots126nk Speed to spare 8
3May41- 7CD fst 1¼ :463 1:113 1:372 2:012 Ky Derby 73k 4 6 816 42 13 18 Arcaro E 126wb *2.90 102-08 Whirlaway1268Staretor126nkMarket Wise1262 Blocked early 11
29Apr41- 7CD fst 1 :232 :462 1:111 1:363 Derby Trial 2.9k 6 5 55 1½ 21 2¾ Eads W 118wb *.60 95-12 Blue Pair115¾Whirlaway1188Cadmium1106 6
Worked 10f in 2:07 2/5
24Apr41- 6Kee my 1⅛ :474 1:12 1:38 1:511 Blue Grass 15k 2 2 1hd 1hd 22 26 Eads W 123wb *.50 85-20 OurBoots1236Whirlwy12315VldnPul1213 Bore out turn,tired 4
11Apr41- 5Kee fst 6f :223 :462 1:113 Handicap 1500 1 4 47 35 31 1nk Eads W 120wb *1.00 94-17 Whirlaway120nkBlue Pair1163My Bill1053 Drawing away 5
28Mar41- 5TrP fst 5½f :224 :461 1:043 Alw 1200 4 4 53¾ 44½ 31½ 1nk Vedder RL 118wb 2.50 97-09 Whirlaway118nkZacatn118noBluLly1075 Forced wide,just up 6
22Mar41- 4TrP my 6f :233 :473 1:114 Alw 1200 1 5 46 31½ 2hd 31¾ James B 118wb *.85 89-12 Little Beans1181Ponty118¾Whirlaway1182 Hung 6
18Feb41- 5Hia fst 7f :232 :47 1:112 1:231 Alw 1500 2 4 46 32 31 35 James B 122wb *.30 92-12 Agricole1102Cadmium1103Whirlaway1226 Impeded,hung 5
8Feb41- 4Hia gd 6f :222 :451 1:113 Alw 1500 5 5 57¾ 57½ 33½ 1hd Eads W 117wb *.65 91-13 Whirlaway117hdSignator1103Blue Twink1082 Bore out str 5
14Nov40- 6Pim sly 1 1/16 :232 :483 1:16 1:521 Walden 10k 8 7 31½ 21 13 14 Woolf G 122wb *1.50 59-54 Whirlaway1224Magnificent1132Stimady1162 Easily 8
2Nov40- 6Pim hy 1 1/16 :233 :48 1:142 1:494 Pim Futurity 38k 8 5 53½ 21 32½ 35 Longden J 122wb *1.60 66-33 BoldIrshmn122noOurBts1195Whrlwy1221½ Bore out both turns 8
Geldings not eligible
19Oct40- 6Kee fst 6f :223 :454 1:111 Breeders' Futurity 12k 5 5 53 41½ 2hd 11 Longden J 122wb 1.50 96-13 Whirlaway1221Blue Pair119noOur Boots122hd Drew away 5
8Oct40- 5Kee fst 6f :223 :46 1:111 Alw 1000 2 6 610 66¼ 4nk 12 Longden J 122wb *1.40e 96-10 Whirlaway1222Blue Pair1223Valdina Groom114hd Handily 8
28Sep40- 7Bel fst 6½f-WC 1:153 Futurity 81k 11 5 117¼ 41½ 3nk 33¼ Longden J 126wb 2.85 92-05 Our Boots1191¾King Cole1221½Whirlaway1262½ Blocked str 14
Geldings not eligible
24Sep40- 6Bel fst 6f-WC 1:103 Alw 1500 8 1 97¼ 3nk 53 56 Longden J 123wb *1.30 88-06 Our Boots1113½Springwood111hdNew World1201 10
Swerved,impeded,hung late
31Aug40- 5Sar my 6½f :23 :463 1:114 1:18 Hopeful 43k 3 4 45¾ 44 2½ 11 Longden J 122wb *.65 95-13 Whirlaway1221Attention1265Hy-Cop1161¾ Very wide 4
24Aug40- 5Sar fst 6f :23 :47 1:11 Grand Union Hotel 11k 1 6 65¼ 52¾ 32 21½ Longden J 122wb *1.20 95-09 New World1171½Whirlaway1222¼Hy-Cop1161¼ Close quarters 6
10Aug40- 5Sar fst 6f :222 :46 1:111 Sar Spl 9.7k 4 8 89 89 56 11½ Longden J 122wb *1.95 96-10 Whirlaway1221½New World1223Good Turn1222 8
Close quarters start,wide
3Aug40- 5Sar fst 6f :223 :464 1:114 U S Hotel 12k 7 10 109½ 97 54¼ 2nk Longden J 116wb 14.00 93-09 Attention122nkWhirlaway1164Twnkppy1132 Finished fastest 10
27Jly40- 6AP my 6f :234 :48 1:004 1:134 Arl Futurity 44k 3 12 115 63¼ 41½ 35½ Longden J 117wb 9.40 72-28 Swain1175½ValdinaGroom117noWhirlaway117¾ Close quarters 12
20Jly40- 5AP fst 5½f :23 :461 :584 1:051 Alw 1200 1 7 76½ 56½ 52½ 44 Richard J 117 w 3.90 91-13 MistyIsle1192¼BayouCook1171½FlyingStrk114nk Blocked str 7
6Jly40- 6AP fst 5½f :23 :461 :581 1:044 Hyde Park 7.2k 2 10 1110 1116 89¼ 47½ Clark S 117 w 3.40 89-12 MistyIsl1142½DKlb1172¼Cuntos1173 Closed well when clear 13
2Jly40- 5AP fst 5½f :23 :462 :59 1:052 Alw 1000 10 7 44½ 43 21 11 Clark S 111 w 3.40 94-16 Whirlway1111De Kalb1183½Valdina Groom1161 Drawing away 10
25Jun40- 4AP fst 5½f :222 :454 :583 1:052 ©Alw 1000 5 5 57 311 39 33¾ Clark S 111 w 2.90 90-16 My Bill1163Swain116¾Whirlaway1118 Bold late rally 7
3Jun40- 3LF fst 5f :23 :471 1:014 Md Sp Wt 10 5 31½ 56½ 44½ 1no Richard J 116 w *1.50e 86-20 Whirlaway116noBeauBrannon1161VldnSr113nk Bore out badly 11

Wistful

ch. f. 1946, by Sun Again (Sun Teddy)–Easy Lass, by Blenheim II **Lifetime record: 51 13 6 10 $213,060**
Own.– Calumet Farm
Br.– Calumet Farm (Ky)
Tr.– H.A. Jones

18Oct52- 9BM fst 1 1/16 :234 :471 1:11 1:413 3↑ Children's Hospital H 23k 7 9 912 911 97¼ 85¾ Baird RL 110 w *1.35e 96-09 Two Lea112½Moonrush1151½Grantor1202½ No factor 10
4Oct52- 9BM fst 1 :231 :462 1:104 1:363 3↑ ⒻSan Mateo H 11k 5 6 67½ 612 45½ 3¾ Baird RL 117 w *.85e 96-11 Two Lea127½Danae115nkWistful117½ Wide,closed well 7
1Sep52- 8Dmr fst 1⅛ :454 1:094 1:344 1:472 3↑ Del Mar H 26k 5 8 911 96¼ 54½ 44¾ Moreno H 110wb 10.05 100-05 Grantor1131¾Stormy Cloud1081½Moonrush1171½ Stretch gain 11
20Aug52- 7Dmr fst 6f :223 :454 1:101 3↑ Handicap 4000 7 8 812 713 78½ 66¾ Moreno H 113wb 17.95 90-11 Boner1202Gustaf1091½Bullfighter114nk No factor 8
19Jly52- 7Hol fst 1⅝ :48 1:371 2:03 2:414 3↑ Sunset H 54k 4 5 69 63¼ 52¾ 33¾ Moreno H 112wb 5.80 91-10 Great Circle112nkStormy Cloud1083½Wistful1121¼ Wide 8
12Jly52- 7Hol fst 1¼ :461 1:103 1:351 2:001 3↑ Hol Gold Cup 137k 5 10 1114 1214 1117 1013 Shoemaker W 108wb *1.55e 85-07 Two Lea113½Cyclotron1003Sturdy One1063½ No factor 12
28Jun52- 7Hol fst 1 1/16 :224 :454 1:101 1:421 3↑ Inglewood H 28k 7 6 613 67½ 64¼ 63¾ Pearson B 115wb *1.35e 93-08 SturdyOn1111StormyCloud105nkAdmrlDrk1162 Close quarters 7
14Jun52- 7Hol fst 1 1/16 :231 :461 1:11 1:432 3↑ ⒻVanity H 28k 4 8 79½ 77½ 56 21¼ Shoemaker W 112 w *.35e 90-11 Two Lea1221¼Wistful1121¾Jennie Lee117¾ Driving 8
6Jun52- 7Hol fst 1 :223 :453 1:101 1:361 4↑ ⒻAlw 10000 4 7 513 57 33 1no Moreno H 109wb *.75 94-11 Wistful109nkWorn Out112noMiss Traffic1062¼ Wide 7
31May52- 7Hol fst 7f :222 :45 1:092 1:213 3↑ ⒻMilady H 28k 8 11 116½ 76½ 69 59 Neves R 112wb *.75e 92-10 A Gleam1122½Two Lea1176Spanish Cream124no No factor 11
22May52- 7Hol fst 6f :221 :451 :572 1:094 4↑ Handicap 10000 2 9 912 88½ 86¾ 84¾ Moreno H 109wb 36.85 92-07 Ruth Lily109noLast Round1102Reighs Bull117no No factor 9
3May52- 7GG fst 6f :221 :444 1:093 3↑ Handicap 7500 6 6 610 613 613 610 Pierson NL 112wb 20.00 83-14 Warcos1092AdmirlDrake116nkBridlRngs113¾ Showed nothing 6

16Apr52- 7GG	fst 6f	:22 :44^3 1:09^1	3↑ ⒻHandicap 5000	4	6	6^{20}	6^{19}	6^{14}	67½	Pierson NL	120wb	10.45	87-14	GreatDream111^{hd}RuthLily118^{2}SpeclTouch129^1	Strong finish	6
10Apr52- 7GG	my 6f	:22^3 :45^3 1:11^4	3↑ ⒻAlw 3250	3	9	9^{16}	9^{16}	9^{12}	69½	Pierson NL	120 w	*2.30e	72-25	Frigid115^{2}Great Dream118^{2}Island Lass1182½	Outrun	9
22Sep51- 6Aqu	fst 1⅛	:48^2 1:12^2 1:38^2 1:52	3↑ ⒻBeldame 67k	6	10	85¼	74¾	94¾	9^7	Brooks S	126wb	3.70	78-14	Thelma Burger110^{2}Bed o' Roses124½Kiss Me Kate119^{nk}		14
	Wide,failed to respond															
14Sep51- 6Aqu	fst 1$\frac{1}{16}$	:24^1 :47^4 1:13 1:44^4	3↑ ⒻAlw 5000	5	7	7^{17}	6^{14}	57½	36¼	Brooks S	121wb	2.25	84-16	Red Camelia1101¼Vulcania112^{5}Wistful121^{hd}	Late effort	7
29Aug51- 7Was	fst 1	:22^2 :45 1:09^4 1:35^4	3↑ ⒻBeverly H 28k	6	10	10^{13}	9^{11}	5^4	11¼	Brooks S	126wb	*1.70e	90-13	Wistful1261¼War Talk1141¼Lithe124^1	Driving	10
	Previously trained by B.A. Jones															
11Aug51- 7Was	fst 1⅛	:46^4 1:10^2 1:36 1:48^3	3↑ Whirlaway 27k	6	8	8^{12}	67½	52¼	1¾	Brooks S	111wb	3.80	98-06	Wistful111¾Oil Capitol116^{hd}Curandero1161½	Just up	8
7Aug51- 6Was	hy 7f	:23 :46^3 1:11^4 1:25^3	4↑ Alw 4000	2	6	6^{13}	68½	46½	3^2	Brooks S	119 w	6.00	77-30	Yellmantown1131½Cacomo112½Wistful1191½	Closed fast	7
21Jly51- 5AP	fst 7f	:22^3 :45^2 1:09^2 1:22^4	3↑ ⒻAlw 5000	6	7	7^{14}	7^{13}	6^{11}	57¾	Dodson D	122wb	*1.90e	88-08	Jennie Lee111^{2}Lithe1182¾Countess In112^2	No speed	7
3May51- 7CD	fst 1$\frac{1}{16}$	:24^3 :48^2 1:12^3 1:44	3↑ Clark H 11k	6	6	6^{12}	57½	3^3	1^{hd}	Dodson D	116wb	*2.20	98-11	Wistful116^{hd}Shy Guy113^{no}Johns Joy1201½	Just up	6
28Apr51- 7CD	fst 7f	:22^3 :45^3 1:09^1 1:22^4	3↑ Churchill Downs H 12k	7	8	8^{12}	87¾	77¾	65¾	Dodson D	118wb	*1.70	96-10	Johns Joy118^{hd}Roman Bath1183½Mr. Trouble115¾	No excuse	8
21Apr51- 6Kee	fst 1$\frac{1}{16}$	:23^3 :47^2 1:12^3 1:45	3↑ Ben Ali H 12k	5	5	5^4	1½	1^3	1^6	Dodson D	112wb	2.30	89-18	Wistful112^{6}Counterpoint1053½Little Imp110¾	Easily	5
17Apr51- 5Kee	fst 6½f	:23 :47^1 1:12^4 1:19^4	3↑ Handicap 3500	4	9	9^{12}	9^{12}	86¾	85½	Dodson D	118wb	*1.40e	82-18	Cacomo113^{nk}Lady Alice110½Tidy Sum115^2	Sluggish	9
	Previously trained by H.A. Jones															
20Feb51- 7SA	fst 1	:22^2 :46 1:11^2 1:36^3	4↑ Handicap 6000	3	7	7^9	63½	4^4	2^{nk}	Brooks S	115wb	*2.40	93-15	Precession119^{nk}Wistful115½Renown112^{nk}	Slow start	7
12Feb51- 7SA	fst 7f	:22^1 :45 1:09^3 1:22	4↑ Handicap 7500	11	10	10^{12}	109¾	10^{12}	109¾	Smith FA	111wb	*2.35e	85-10	Bullreigh Jr.121^{1}Be Fleet102^{1}Star Fiddle122½	Outrun	11
1Feb51- 7SA	fst 1$\frac{1}{16}$	:23^4 :47^3 1:11^3 1:42^2	4↑ Handicap 7500	5	4	4^4	53½	4^2	3^1	Brooks S	111wb	7.90	95-10	Vino Fino109½Bullreigh Jr.115½Wistful111^{hd}	Impeded	6
20Jan51- 7SA	fst 1⅛	:46^1 1:11 1:36^1 1:48^3	3↑ ⒻS Margarita H 60k	7	5	67½	7^8	6^{10}	6^{12}	Arcaro E	120 w	3.20e	86-16	Special Touch114^{1}Bewitch1221¼Bed o' Roses1251½	Bore out	8
2Dec50- 7Hol	fst 1⅛	:47 1:11^1 1:36^2 1:49^2	3↑ ⒻVanity H 30k	9	9	9^{11}	86¾	65¼	33¼	Glisson G	125 w	2.65e	91-11	Next Move1282¼Bewitch124^{1}Wistful125½	Off slowly	9
14Nov50- 7Hol	my 1	:24 :48^1 1:13^4 1:40^1	3↑ Alw 4000	2	7	7^{14}	78½	5^9	57¾	Glisson G	111 w	*.60e	68-29	Theory1131¼Terry Bargello108½Ohsodry1062½	No excuse	8
4Oct50- 6Bel	fst 1½	:49^1 1:13^3 2:03^4 2:29^2	3↑ ⒻLadies H 29k	7	8	9^{12}	99½	3^7	35½	Brooks S	124 w	2.35	85-11	Next Move1205½My Celeste106^{hd}Wistful1241¼	Closed well	12
16Sep50- 6Aqu	fst 1⅛	:47^3 1:12 1:37 1:50^1	3↑ ⒻBeldame H 66k	12	11	11^{13}	9^{11}	5^9	33¼	Brooks S	125 w	3.20	91-15	Next Move1162¼September108^{1}Wistful1252¼	Closed fast	12
9Sep50- 6Aqu	fst 1⅛	:47^4 1:11^4 1:36^3 1:49^2	3↑ Edgemere H 23k	2	7	75¼	77¼	45½	22½	Dodson D	114 w	6.60e	95-09	Three Rings1212½Wistful114½My Request126^2	Lost ground	11
30Aug50- 6Was	fst 1⅛	:47^3 1:12 1:37^3 1:50^1	3↑ ⒻBeverly H 27k	5	8	88¼	57¼	3^2	21¾	Brooks S	128 w	*1.20	88-16	Lithe1201¾Wistful1281½Include104^1	No excuse	9
16Aug50- 6Was	fst 7f	:22 :45 1:08^4 1:22	3↑ ⒻMisty Isle H 22k	2	10	107¾	97¼	96¾	5^4	Brooks S	123 w	*1.20	93-09	Miss Highbrow1091¼Stole1032¼Lithe118½	Off slowly	10
9Aug50- 7Was	fst 7f	:22^1 :44^4 1:09^2 1:22	3↑ Clang H 22k	5	9	86¼	97¾	62¾	1^1	Brooks S	113 w	8.10	97-11	Wistful113^{1}Laico1161¼Lithe113^{nk}	Drew out	11
26Jly50- 6AP	fst 1	:23 :45^4 1:09^3 1:34^4	3↑ ⒻArl Matron H 22k	4	9	9^{11}	94¼	55¾	2^4	Brooks S	118 w	5.30	94-10	Lithe108^{4}Wistful118¾Evanstep1073½	Finished fast	10
24Jun50- 6AP	my 6f	:23^2 :47 1:13^1	3↑ Alw 3500	7	3	62¼	55¾	77¾	78¼	Roser G	112 w	9.60	72-22	ShyGuy122½RomanBath1085½WhirlingDough110^{nk}	Went wide	8
20Jly49- 6AP	fst 1	:23 :46 1:10^2 1:37	ⒻCleopatra H 26k	2	6	64¼	5^6	46½	32¼	Scurlock O	121 w	*.60e	85-15	Two Lea122^{2}Lithe108^{nk}Wistful121^2	Closed well	6
28May49- 6Bel	fst 1⅜	:49^1 1:14^4 1:41 2:19^3	ⒻC C A Oaks 66k	2	14	138½	63¾	1½	1½	Brooks S	121 w	*.75	73-18	Wistful121½Adile121^{10}Jazz Baby121^1	Hard drive	14
13May49- 6Pim	fst 1$\frac{1}{16}$	:23 :46^3 1:11^1 1:44^2	ⒻPim Oaks 14k	7	10	10^7	2^2	1^{hd}	1¾	Brooks S	121 w	*1.00	90-16	Wistful121¾Imacomin121^{4}Admired121^{no}	Ridden out	12
	Previously trained by B.A. Jones															
6May49- 6CD	fst 1$\frac{1}{16}$	:24 :48 1:13^3 1:47^2	ⒻKy Oaks 30k	8	8	75¼	53½	1^2	14½	Glisson G	116 w	1.40	83-15	Wistful1164½TheFatLady116^{nk}LadyDorimar116^6	Going away	10
30Apr49- 5CD	fst 1	:22^4 :46^3 1:11^2 1:38	ⒻAlw 2500	4	8	6^5	69½	2^3	11½	Glisson G*	108 w	*1.30	89-14	Wistful1081½Lady Dorimar109^{8}Pella108^5	Drew out	11
16Apr49- 6Kee	gd 6f	:23 :47^3 1:13^3	ⒻAshland 13k	4	9	96¾	98¼	6^6	2^4	LoTurco A	115 w	2.80	80-18	Tall Weeds115^{4}Wistful1153½Warsick115½	Belated speed	10
	Previously trained by H.A. Jones															
14Feb49- 4Hia	fst 7f	:23^2 :46^3 1:11^4 1:24^1	ⒻAlw 3500	2	5	62½	2^1	2^{nk}	1^4	Nelson E	112 w	2.60	91-14	Wistful112^{4}Bea Right1144¼Error109^1	Drew out	6
31Jan49- 4Hia	fst 6f	:22^2 :45^2 1:10^4	ⒻAlw 3500	2	9	86¾	8^6	57¼	3^4	Nelson E	114 w	*1.45e	90-12	Cheesecloth110^{4}Duke's Gal110^{no}Wistful114^2	Slow start	10
27Jan49- 5Hia	fst 7f	:23 :46 1:11^3 1:24^2	ⒻAlw 4000	3	5	41½	3^1	2no	1^2	Nelson E	107 w	4.35	90-13	Wistful107^{2}Solid Trick109^{5}Dizzy Whirl104^2	Going away	9
19Jan49- 5Hia	fst 6f	:22^4 :46 1:11^2	ⒻAlw 3500	8	9	107¾	9^8	9^{11}	7^{14}	Pierson NL	112 w	4.60	77-14	Too Sunny1152¼Sub1077½Solid Trick109^2	Impeded	11
15Jan49- 4TrP	fst 6f	:22^3 :46^2 1:12^3	Alw 2000	8	7	75¾	4^7	4^7	49¼	Pierson NL	115 w	*.75	75-17	Abstract1181¼Winged120^{7}Midchannel111^1	No excuse	9
29Oct48- 2Pim	fst 6f	:23 :47 1:12^2	ⒻMd Sp Wt	10	3	2^{hd}	1^1	1^2	1^6	Pierson NL	118 w	*.60	91-10	Wistful118^{6}Best Blue118^{1}Wily118½	Easily	12
30Sep48- 5Bel	sly 5½f-W	:22^2 :45^4 1:04^4	ⒻMd Sp Wt	11			52¼	6^5	86¼	Woodhouse H	116 w	8.00	84-10	Roguish Mood116½Zana116^{1}Error1161½	No factor	17
	Start obscured by mist															

Ghosts and Legends

The 1950's

by Joe Hirsch

In any consideration of the outstanding Thoroughbred stars of the 1950's, two dates are significant.

The first is May 2, 1953, and the site is Churchill Downs. An arresting gray colt named Native Dancer, the nation's first four-legged television star, comes to the 79th Kentucky Derby undefeated in 11 starts. If he can win the Derby and then complete a sweep of the Triple Crown classics in the Preakness and Belmont Stakes, he will have passed major obstacles on his way to a rare perfect record and will be hailed as a superstar of the century.

The second date is August 31, 1955, and the site is Washington Park in suburban Chicago. Two of the greatest 3-year-olds of the era, Nashua and Swaps, are to meet in one of the most celebrated match races in American history. Swaps upset Nashua in the 81st Kentucky Derby. Nashua won the Preakness and Belmont Stakes, and added the Dwyer and the Arlington Classic to his list of victories. Swaps returned to his native California following the Kentucky Derby and scored brilliantly in three stakes at Hollywood Park: the Will Rogers; the Californian, against older horses; and the Westerner. He then underlined his versatility by capturing the American Derby on the grass at Washington Park.

The nation was divided in its admiration for the two colts, largely along geographical lines, and with each succeeding victory following their Derby confrontation, demands for a match race in the best

Only a terrible trip in the 1953 Kentucky Derby kept the handsome gray Native Dancer from an undefeated career. The head loss to Dark Star was the only blemish on his 22-race record.

traditions of the American turf grew louder. Chicago, in the heart of mid-America, and at that time the home of the best summer racing in the country, was an ideal neutral ground. Ben Lindheimer, chairman of Arlington and Washington Parks, was a willing host and announced the details in mid-July.

Derby Day, 1953, and it appeared there really were 100,000 people at the ancient Downs, as announced each year, regardless of the count. Alfred Gwynne Vanderbilt's Native Dancer, the handsome gray son of Polynesian from Geisha, by Discovery, had been a popular 2-year-old champion, winner of all nine of his starts, including four stakes victories at Saratoga. Coming out at 3, he made light work of a division of the Gotham and the Wood Memorial at Jamaica, and was considered a standout in the Derby, which drew only 11 starters. He and his stablemate, Social Outcast, were hammered down to 7-10.

Second choice was Eddie Arcaro and the horse he happened to be riding, Correspondent, at 3-1. Royal Bay Gem was third choice at 7-1, and among the others, all longshots, was the Cain Hoy Stable colt Dark Star, at almost 25-1. He won 3 of 6 starts at 2 but hadn't done anything noteworthy until he scored in the Derby Trial four days before the Run for the Roses, with the familiar Eric Guerin, Native Dancer's regular rider, in the saddle.

Dark Star, under Henry Moreno, set the pace, the first half-mile in a sensible 47⅗ seconds. Let the footnotes of the chart, as called by *Daily Racing Form*'s senior trackman, Don Fair, tell the rest of the story. "Native Dancer, roughed at the first turn by Money Broker [45-1], was eased back to secure racing room, raced wide during the run to the upper turn, then saved ground entering the stretch and finished strongly, but could not overtake the winner, although probably best."

The margin at the wire was a head.

It was one of the most fateful decisions in the long and colorful history of the Derby, not so much for what occurred at the time as for what followed. Native Dancer picked up where he left off, winning them all. Two weeks after the Derby, he won the Withers Mile at Belmont Park by four lengths. The following weekend he won the Preakness, in which Dark Star bowed a tendon, ending his racing career.

He won the Belmont, the Dwyer, the Arlington Classic by nine lengths, the Travers by 5½, the American Derby. There was great anticipation of a meeting that fall between Native Dancer, king of the 3-year-olds, and the great Tom Fool, undefeated in the handicap ranks and emperor of older horses in the United States. But it wasn't to be. "The Dancer" didn't race at all following his American Derby score on August 22, trainer Bill Winfrey citing a stone bruise as the reason the colt was on the shelf.

On holiday all winter, Native Dancer returned to action as a 4-year-old on May 7, 1954, at Belmont Park. Coming from off the pace, as he did through much of his career, he made light work of the field of crack sprinters, which included the stakes-winning Laffango. That race served as his prep for the Metropolitan Mile, eight days later.

Carrying top weight of 130 pounds, the Dancer knew his finest hour in winning that Met Mile. Conceding 13 pounds to Greentree Stable's Straight Face, he appeared hopelessly beaten at the three-eighths pole. Guerin was asking him to run but was receiving a muted response. But then Native Dancer kicked in, and his final quarter, according to *Daily Racing Form*'s Evan Shipman, was one of the greatest ever seen in this country. As late as the furlong pole, the Dancer was still nearly four lengths behind Straight Face, Ted Atkinson up. Flying now on the outside, he got up in the final stride to score by a neck, to the repeated cheers of the 38,090 on hand.

It was a brilliant piece of racing, and the exact measurements were provided several weeks later when Straight Face came back to win the Suburban. Meanwhile, Winfrey was having problems again with the gray's soundness. The trainer and his staff worked hard, and by mid-August Native Dancer was ready for a seven-furlong overnight handicap at Saratoga. Under 137 pounds, he won easily in what was to have tuned him up for the mile-and-three-quarter Saratoga Cup. His people were considering a trip to France that fall for the Prix de l'Arc de Triomphe.

It wasn't to be. Vanderbilt broke the news a few days later with his terse memorandum: "N D N G." Racing was stunned over the retirement of its greatest star, and the full impact of his glorious record struck a responsive chord. Though he'd made only three starts that season, he was an overwhelming choice as Horse of the Year. He was also acclaimed as one of the greats of his era, and more than a few writers speculated that but for the one unfortunate incident in the Kentucky Derby, "the Gray Ghost of Sagamore" deserved ranking with the best of the best.

Nashua and Swaps, forever linked in racing history like Affirmed and Alydar, were exceptional individuals, and as different from each other as two horses can be.

Nashua, by Nasrullah out of Segula, by Johnstown, may have been the soundest horse ever bred in this country. A big, strapping bay full of muscles, he inherited the fiery disposition of his legendary sire plus the fierce talent associated with that marvelous source of bloodstock. He was 2-year old champion with 6 wins and 2 seconds from 8 starts, and was Horse of the Year as well as champion of his division at 3.

There are many stories illustrating Nashua's physical resources. In preparation for the Arlington Classic, which was to be his last start prior to the match race, jockey Eddie Arcaro flew out to Chicago to work him on a Monday morning. Nashua was full of himself and Arcaro was not at his sharpest that day, for the big colt broke the American record with his ebullient five furlongs in 56⅘. Five days later, his edge somewhat blunted by the severe work, Nashua was forced to a hard drive to beat Traffic Judge. Almost any other horse would have bounced like a flat tire.

Swaps, by Khaled out of Iron Reward, by Beau Pere, was an eye-catching chestnut colt, full of balance and quality and the easy grace we have come to associate with the champion athlete. By training he was highly disciplined, but that did not rein in his remarkable ability. When he retired to stud at the end of the 1956 season, he held five world records. An inauspicious 2-year-old with 2 wins from 5 starts, he blossomed at 3 and reached his best form at 4 when he was handicap champion and Horse of the Year.

Swaps's self-control became a matter of national discussion after his victory in the American Derby at Washington Park, 11 days prior to the match race. A large crowd gathered at trackside as the field left the paddock and walked onto the racing strip. They wanted to see the horse who had won the Kentucky Derby and who would soon have a showdown with the mighty Nashua. As the field paraded, Bill Shoemaker guided Swaps to the outer rail, where a group of children stood with their parents. Swaps walked up to a young girl who, at Shoemaker's invitation, hesitantly stretched out a small hand and stroked the colt's nose. Swaps stood like a statue.

Three or four more times during the post parade, Shoe took Swaps to the rail to interact with the crowd, which had never seen anything like it before, and loved it. When Swaps finally broke

The cantankerous Nashua finally exacted revenge for his Kentucky Derby loss to Swaps by defeating the colt from California by 6 ½ lengths in a celebrated match race at Washington Park.

away in a gallop to warm up for the American Derby, he received a warm ovation. He received another after his successful grass debut in the American Derby. Second in the mile-and-three-sixteenths test was Traffic Judge, who had been second to Nashua in the Arlington Classic.

It was noted earlier that Nashua and Swaps were contrasting individuals. The same was true of their interests.

Investment banker William Woodward Jr., owner of Nashua, was the gracious son of a giant in American racing. His father, William Woodward Sr., was chairman of The Jockey Club for 20 years, raced such outstanding horses as Gallant Fox and Omaha, the Triple Crown winners of 1930 and 1935, and was the breeder of Nashua. Rex Ellsworth, owner of Swaps, built a sizable racing and breeding operation in Chino, California, in part with funds borrowed from the Mormon Church, of which he was a member.

Sunny Jim Fitzsimmons, the trainer of Nashua, was one of the most popular and successful horsemen in the annals of American racing. A one-time jockey and jockey's agent, he saddled his first winner in 1900, and had two Triple Crown winners to his credit, Gallant Fox and Omaha. Meshach Tenney, the trainer of Swaps, had been a close friend and associate of Rex Ellsworth's since boyhood. He assisted Ellsworth in his cattle operation and then became his trainer when Ellsworth began to concentrate on Thoroughbreds.

The Nashua-Swaps match at Washington Park received a formidable publicity campaign, not unlike the ones preceding a heavyweight championship bout. The nation's press responded, covering every detail of the preparations and every comment of the principals.

Almost every detail. Swaps had a chronic foot problem, originally triggered by a stone bruise. The condition flared during the weeks leading up to the Santa Anita Derby, but Tenney, who did his own blacksmith work, cut away a portion of the frog, packed it with medication, and covered the area with a pad. Swaps wasn't at his absolute best for the Santa Anita Derby because Tenney was forced to limit his training. But the competition was moderate and Swaps could and did win on his class.

When the foot problem recurred the week of the match race, Ellsworth and Tenney approached Ben Lindheimer and requested a postponement. Lindheimer explained why this was impossible at such a late hour and an agreement was reached to keep quiet about the foot condition.

Even Bill Shoemaker wasn't told, for fear the news might subconsciously affect his riding of Swaps.

Evan Shipman described the match race in the 1956 edition of The American Racing Manual: "There was nothing complicated about it. As the doors opened, Arcaro, yelling like a banshee and wielding his whip with all his strength, shot Nashua to the front, while Swaps, away on the outside, veered farther out toward the outside rail. Nashua was in front as they passed the stand, and he was to be in front for the entire distance, Swaps making repeated thrusts at him, all of them falling short."

Nashua won by 6½ lengths but it was obvious Shoemaker never asked Swaps for anything during the final furlong, once he saw the cause was lost. The winner's time of 2:04⅕ for 1¼ miles on a "good" track was accomplished with fractions of 23, 46, 1:10⅖, 1:37⅗, and 1:50⅗.

Swaps's connections announced he was through for the rest of the season, but Nashua returned to his base in New York to meet older horses for the first time in the Sysonby Stakes at Belmont Park. Though opposed by the likes of Helioscope, High Gun, and Jet Action, Nashua was the favorite at 65 cents to the dollar.

Rain fell all afternoon and the track was sloppy for the Sysonby. High Gun, who had won the Met Mile and the Brooklyn, and lost the Suburban by a head to Helioscope while carrying 133 pounds, came off the pace under Bill Boland to win by a head in one of the finest performances of his career. Jet Action was second, and Nashua, a trifle dull after his experience in Chicago and the severe preparation that preceded the match race, finished third.

Nashua concluded his memorable 3-year-old season with an easy triumph by five lengths in the two-mile Jockey Club Gold Cup, contested on a sloppy track. Plans were being drawn up for a winter racing campaign when they were interrupted by news of a shocking tragedy.

William Woodward Jr., the owner of Nashua, was accidentally shot to death at his home on Long Island by his wife, who mistook him for a burglar.

A dispersal of the Woodward Thoroughbred holdings by sealed bids was quickly organized and a syndicate headed by Leslie Combs II acquired Nashua on a bid of slightly more than $1,250,000. Combs asked Sunny Jim Fitzsimmons to stay on as trainer and continue his plans for Nashua's 4-year-old campaign.

Nashua was to make his first start of 1956 in Hialeah's prestigious Widener Handicap in mid-February. He hadn't run since mid-October, so he needed some training and he got it. A week before the Widener, "Mr. Fitz" vanned him to Tropical Park and, with Ted Atkinson up – Arcaro was in California – Nashua worked the full Widener distance of a mile and a quarter in 2:01⅗. Under Arcaro, and carrying top weight of 127 pounds, Nashua came back to win the Widener by a head from Social Outcast, timed in 2:02. In other words, he went faster in his workout than in his race.

Nashua ran 10 times that season, at distances from seven furlongs to two miles, winning six. Immensely talented, he was not always the most generous of horses, the inheritance of the willful blood of his sire, Nasrullah. Arcaro wouldn't let him get away with too much, but he outweighed "the Master" by 1,100 pounds and there were times when he had his way.

His best race at 4 may have been the Suburban, in which he carried 128 pounds and ran a mile and a quarter in 2:00⅕, beating as good a handicap horse as Dedicate while spotting him 17 pounds.

Despite numerous physical problems, the game Swaps compiled a long list of records, including world marks at a mile, a mile and 70 yards, and a mile and a sixteenth.

He ended his racing career with a second tally in the Jockey Club Gold Cup, giving him an overall record of 22 wins and 4 seconds from 30 starts. He was some piece of work.

Swaps also raced 10 times at 4 and had a brilliant campaign, cut short by injury.

He set a world record of 1:39⅗ for a mile and 70 yards in winning the Broward Handicap at Gulfstream Park under 130 pounds.

He set a world record of 1:33⅕ for a mile in winning the Argonaut Handicap at Hollywood Park under 128 pounds.

He set a world record of 1:39 for a mile and a sixteenth in winning the Inglewood Handicap at Hollywood, carrying 130 pounds.

He set a track record of 1:58⅗ for a mile and a quarter in winning the Hollywood Gold Cup under 130 pounds.

He set a world record of 2:38⅕ for a mile and five furlongs in winning the Sunset Handicap at Hollywood, carrying 130 pounds.

He set a track record of 1:33⅖ for a mile in winning the Washington Park Handicap under 130 pounds.

He equaled the world record of 1:46⅘ for a mile and an eighth in winning the American Handicap at Hollywood under 130 pounds.

Swaps was flown to Atlantic City for the United Nations Handicap on the grass, but his chronic foot problem arose again and he was scratched the day of the race. Vanned to Garden State Park, he resumed training and his people indicated that he would oppose Nashua again in the Jockey Club Gold Cup. But galloping one morning at the south Jersey track, he fractured a bone in his left hind leg and his life was threatened.

Sunny Jim Fitzsimmons sent a special sling from Belmont Park and Swaps literally hung from a rafter over his stall. He had to be lowered and raised every 45 minutes for circulatory reasons, and trainer Mesh Tenney sat by his side to pull on the ropes for the first 36 hours.

Swaps, a good patient, handled the uncomfortable routine with aplomb and was saved for stud.

■ ■ ■

One of the decade's brightest stars was the great handicap champion and Horse of the Year for 1953, Greentree Stable's Tom Fool. Indeed, his undefeated 4-year-old season, when he went 10 for 10 and won important stakes while carrying as much as 136 pounds, was so brilliant that some respected observers of the racing scene list him as one of the best of his era.

Tom Fool, by Menow out of Gaga, by Bull Dog, was 2-year-old champion of 1951 with a record of 5 victories and 2 seconds from 7 starts. It was his 3-year-old campaign, and his failure to contest the classics, that was the one questionable chapter in his career. Had he been as successful at 3 as he was at 2 and 4, he undoubtedly would be ranked with the superstars of the century.

Trained by John Gaver and ridden in all 30 of his starts by Ted Atkinson, Tom Fool made his debut at Saratoga on August 13, 1951, and as a 2-1 favorite, won smartly by four lengths after coming off the pace.

He then won the Sanford and the Grand Union Stakes but finished second in the Hopeful, the major juvenile feature of the meeting, with Cousin the winner. Later that fall he wrapped up the divisional title with victories in the Futurity at Belmont Park and the East View at Jamaica.

After a restful winter in Aiken, South Carolina, Tom Fool was aimed at the classics. His first start at 3 was in a prep for the Wood Memorial at Jamaica, which he won, beating Primate and Cousin. Favored in the Wood Memorial, he went to the front near the furlong pole but was unable to hold off the strong finish by Master Fiddle, who won by a neck.

In the wake of the Wood Memorial, Tom Fool developed a cough and was sidelined throughout the Triple Crown races.

After a conclusive victory in the Wilson Mile at Saratoga, he was established as a solid favorite for the Travers. He went to the front early, appeared to be comfortable on a sloppy track, but tired in the drive and finished third behind One Count and Armageddon. He concluded the campaign with three races at Jamaica, beating Battlefield by a nose in the Grey Lag, losing to Battlefield by a nose in the Westchester, and winning the Empire City under 128 pounds while conceding 19 pounds to runner-up Marcador.

Tom Fool began his signature season by winning a 5½-furlong sprint at Jamaica in late April. He underlined his high quality by capturing the six-furlong Joe Palmer Handicap under 130 pounds and conceding 16 pounds to the fine sprinter Tea-Maker, who was second. Good as he was in the Joe Palmer, however, he was even better four days later in the Metropolitan Mile. Favored at 1-2, he was always prominent despite top weight of 130 pounds, took command on the turn, and stood a hard drive gamely to win by half a length from the classy Royal Vale, to whom he was conceding three pounds.

A week later, in the traditional Suburban Handicap, Tom Fool went off as a slight favorite at 2-1 over Royal Vale, with a good deal of support showing for the Walter Jeffords entry of One Count, Horse of the Year in 1952, and Kiss Me Kate, 3-year-old filly champion of 1951.

Greentree Stable's Tom Fool raced through one of the great campaigns in Thoroughbred history, winning all 10 of his starts in 1953, including the Handicap Triple Crown, while carrying as much as 136 pounds.

Carrying 128 pounds, Tom Fool went to the front at the start and remained there. Royal Vale, under 124 pounds, tested him severely through the final furlong but missed by a nose after a mile and a quarter in 2:00⅗ that touched off one of the most sustained ovations ever heard at Belmont Park.

From the mile and a quarter of the Suburban, Tom Fool successfully dropped back to the seven furlongs of the Carter Handicap at Aqueduct. Under 135 pounds, the highest weight ever carried to victory in the sprint, he equaled the track record of 1:22 while conceding 13 pounds to the tough old speedster Squared Away.

Two weeks later it was back to 10 furlongs for the Brooklyn Handicap, for which Tom Fool was assigned 136 pounds. Favored at 1-4, he was on the lead most of the way in a paceless race (the half went in 48⅗ seconds), built an advantage of some three lengths, and was eased as he passed the winning post with a margin of a length and a half on Golden Gloves, who carried 110 pounds. Tom Fool became the first horse to sweep the Handicap Triple Crown – the Metropolitan Mile, the Suburban, and the Brooklyn – since Whisk Broom II in 1913.

The Brooklyn victory touched off a nationwide tribute to a great horse in terms significant to racing. In his final four starts he never had more than two opponents, and no wagering was permitted on the Wilson Mile and the Whitney at Saratoga, the Sysonby at Belmont, and the Pimlico Special. He left like the champion he was, winning at Pimlico by eight lengths and setting a track record of 1:55⅘ for the mile and three-sixteenths.

A pair of 3-year-olds who fashioned outstanding records as contemporaries, one on the dirt and the other principally on the grass, were Bold Ruler and Round Table. Bold Ruler has come down history's highway as one of the fastest horses ever to race in America. Round Table is hailed as one of the finest turf horses of the century and a good but not great horse on dirt.

Both Bold Ruler and Round Table were foaled at Claiborne Farm near Paris, Kentucky. Bold Ruler, by Nasrullah out of Miss Disco, by Discovery, was bred and owned by Mrs. Henry Carnegie Phipps's Wheatley Stable, whose trainer was Sunny Jim Fitzsimmons, dean of American horsemen. Round Table was bred and originally owned by A. B. "Bull" Hancock Jr. of Claiborne Farm. The Princequillo colt out of Knight's Daughter, by Sir Cosmo, was raced as a 2-year-old by Claiborne under trainer Moody Jolley. He was sold privately, early in his 3-year-old season, for a reported $175,000 to Travis Kerr, an Oklahoma oilman and brother of United States Senator Robert Kerr of Oklahoma. Kerr's horses were trained by Willie Molter, one of California's most successful horsemen.

Bold Ruler and Round Table were foals of 1954, and with such contemporaries as Gallant Man, Gen. Duke, Iron Liege, and Federal Hill, were involved in what is widely recognized as the finest 3-year-old campaign in American racing history.

Bold Ruler began his glittering career with three victories at Jamaica's spring meeting, including an in-hand tally by more than three lengths in the Youthful Stakes. He also won the Juvenile at Belmont but was "tailed" in the starting gate, wrenching his back severely. While recuperating in his stall, he hit his near hock against a wall, injuring himself to the extent that he could not run at Saratoga.

He resumed racing in September, won the Futurity under Eddie Arcaro, and was the 2-1 favorite in a field of 19 for the Garden State Stakes at Cherry Hill, New Jersey. With Arcaro suspended, Ted Atkinson deputized and stalked the pace-setting outsider, Jaunty John, who promptly stopped leaving the half-mile pole. By the time Bold Ruler got straightened out, the race was over and Barbizon, who raced on the outside most of the way under Bill Hartack, got up to win by a desperate nose over Federal Hill.

Arcaro was back on Bold Ruler for the Remsen at Jamaica but the outcome wasn't much different. The spirited Bold Ruler reared at the break, then was checked on the first turn in heavy traffic. He was done for the day, with the victory going to the stretch-running Ambehaving.

Bold Ruler made his 3-year-old debut in Hialeah's seven-furlong Bahamas on January 30, 1957. With Ted Atkinson aboard, he shot to the front out of the gate, led all the way to win by 4½ lengths, and equaled the track record of 1:22. Gen. Duke, a top Calumet Farm prospect, was second, and Federal Hill was third in a field of 11.

The 3-year-old racing that winter was the most brilliant Florida has known, before or since. Bold Ruler's smashing score in the Bahamas made him a standout choice at 2-5 in the nine-furlong Everglades in mid-February. Once again he went to the front out of the gate. He got the first half-mile in a reasonable 46⅗ seconds, but couldn't quite hold off the acceleration of Gen. Duke, who won by a

Bold Ruler was the best of the class of 1957, possibly the finest 3-year-old crop ever. He capped his Horse of the Year resume by defeating Gallant Man and Round Table in the three-horse Trenton Handicap.

head while in receipt of 12 pounds from the favorite. Gen. Duke, timed in 1:47⅖, missed the track record by a fifth of a second, with Bill Hartack up. Iron Liege, of whom we will hear more, finished third as an entry with the winner.

That set the stage for the Flamingo. Bold Ruler, with Eddie Arcaro on hand from California, was the 1-2 favorite. He was always prominent through a lively half-mile in 45⅗, opened an advantage of two lengths at the furlong pole, and was all out to prevail by a neck over Gen. Duke at level weights, setting a track record of 1:47 for the nine furlongs. Iron Liege was third.

Four weeks after the Flamingo, Gulfstream's Florida Derby drew a field of five, with Bold Ruler favored at 3-5. This was a brilliant piece of racing, as Gen. Duke, a particularly handsome bay colt by Bull Lea out of Wistful, took the track from Bold Ruler, fastest of the fast. Hartack then throttled back to a half-mile in 46⅗ seconds.

This was a match race between two extraordinary colts, and at the furlong pole, after a mile in 1:34⅗, Bold Ruler was in front by a head. But Gen. Duke, named for the Civil War hero, wasn't through. He accelerated, won by a conclusive length and a half, and set a world record for nine furlongs of 1:46⅘. Iron Liege was third again, just a head behind Bold Ruler.

Sent to New York, Bold Ruler continued to train aggressively for Mr. Fitz and ran another corking race in the Wood Memorial at Jamaica. He was favored at 1-2 and went to the front at the start. Arcaro slowed the pace to a half in 48 seconds, virtually assuring himself a victory, but it turned out to be tougher than expected.

Gallant Man, an import who had been seasoned in the 3-year-old racing at Hialeah, put up a whale of a fight through the stretch and Bold Ruler was hard-pressed to score by a nose in a track-record 1:48⅘ for nine furlongs. Promised Land, a stretch-runner, was third.

The 1957 Kentucky Derby, for depth of quality and dramatic nature of its story line, has been called the greatest of all Runs for the Roses. Gen.

Gallant Man was denied the 1957 Kentucky Derby when Bill Shoemaker misjudged the finish line, but gained retribution in the Belmont with an eight-length victory in 2:26 ⅗, an American record for a mile and a half. He also won the Travers during a championship-quality season.

Duke, the Florida Derby winner, raced at Keeneland as a prep and bobbled. He went lame at Churchill Downs during Derby Week and was scratched from the Derby, leaving Calumet represented by Iron Liege at 8-1.

Federal Hill, as usual, set the pace, and it was realistic, with a first half-mile in 47 seconds. Bold Ruler and Iron Liege stalked together, a length and a half back, with Round Table fourth and Gallant Man well back in the field of nine. After a mile in 1:36⅘, Federal Hill was still in front but Iron Liege, showing strength, was at the leader's side. Bold Ruler and Round Table followed closely and Gallant Man was moving rapidly past horses.

Iron Liege took command straightening into the long stretch. Federal Hill, still second, was tiring, while Gallant Man, Round Table, and Bold Ruler were closely grouped. Gallant Man, finishing with determination, took aim at Iron Liege and appeared to be abreast in the final sixteenth when his rider, Bill Shoemaker, misjudged the finish and rose prematurely in the irons. Shoe quickly realized his error and began to ride his horse again, but the chance of a lifetime was lost, Iron Liege prevailing by a nose. Gallant Man was almost three lengths ahead of Round Table, and Bold Ruler was fourth.

Ralph Lowe, owner of Gallant Man, had dreamed that the rider of his horse would stand in the irons prematurely and at dinner, the night before the Derby, related his dream to Shoemaker.

"Well, Ralph, now that we've heard about it, you don't have to worry," Shoe said.

With Gallant Man and Round Table absent, Iron Liege was a narrow favorite in the Preakness over Bold Ruler. However, Bold Ruler's people decided to make use of his speed. He outran Federal Hill for the early lead and then remained in front the rest of the way to win by two lengths from Iron Liege.

Iron Liege passed the Belmont Stakes but Gallant Man returned to action, accompanied by a pacemaker, Bold Nero. Bold Ruler was the slight favorite at 85 cents to the dollar, and repeated his Preakness strategy of going to the front. Prompted by Bold Nero, he went the first six furlongs in 1:10⅖, Gallant Man well back in fourth.

Leaving the half-mile pole, Gallant Man began to move up. He had the lead entering the stretch, gradually drew out, and won by eight lengths, setting an American record for a mile and a half of 2:26⅗. Inside Tract, the runner-up, had four lengths on Bold Ruler, who found the trip beyond his scope.

Given the summer off after a strenuous classics campaign, Bold Ruler prepped smartly and then was an easy six-length winner of the Jerome Mile at Belmont on a sloppy track. He had the lead in the Woodward, found the mile and a quarter too far for him, and finished third. But he came back to beat older horses on a sloppy track in the seven-furlong Vosburgh, just missing a track record with his 1:21⅖.

He also won the Queens County at Jamaica and the Benjamin Franklin at Garden State Park, both at a mile and a sixteenth. He carried 136 pounds in the New Jersey race and won by 12 lengths on a sloppy track he loved.

Bold Ruler concluded his 3-year-old campaign in sensational fashion, beating Gallant Man and Round Table in the three-horse Trenton Handicap at Garden State. He led all the way on an off track, and got the mile and a quarter in 2:01⅗. He was later voted Horse of the Year.

He spent the winter season in Florida but did not race and began his 4-year-old campaign with consecutive victories in Belmont Park's six-furlong Toboggan and seven-furlong Carter, coming off the pace in both races, and carrying 133 and 135 pounds, respectively. He made the pace in the Metropolitan Mile under 135 pounds but tired to finish second to Gallant Man, who carried 130 pounds and won by two lengths.

His next race was the Stymie Handicap at nine furlongs, which he won easily by five lengths under 133 pounds. Bold Ruler ran one of his greatest races to capture Belmont's Suburban Handicap on July 4, 1958. Always well placed under Eddie Arcaro, he carried 134 pounds and stood a long drive with great courage to score by a nose over hard-hitting Clem, who was in receipt of 25 pounds.

Later that month he was shipped to Monmouth Park for another stakes at a mile and a quarter, the Monmouth Handicap. Carrying 134 pounds, he beat Sharpsburg by three-quarters of a length, conceding 21 pounds. One week later, he ran in the Brooklyn Handicap, and despite his top weight of 136 pounds, was favored at 2-5. He had a rough trip and finished seventh in a field of eight.

The next day, trainer Jim Fitzsimmons announced that Bold Ruler had run his last race. Mr. Fitz revealed that Bold Ruler had been bothered all season by a splintered cannon bone, which was now threatening a tendon. Despite the injury, he continued to perform with skill and courage. Fitzsimmons later would say Bold Ruler was one of his three greatest horses, together with Nashua and Gallant Fox.

Round Table's career was remarkable for success and durability. He won 43 races, an incredible achievement, from 66 starts, and finished in the money 56 times.

He began racing in February of his 2-year-old season, going three furlongs at Hialeah. After being bumped at the start, he finished fourth under Steve

Brooks, beaten two lengths. He made 10 starts in all that season, winning five times, and displayed a measure of quality with his tally in the Breeders' Futurity at Keeneland.

As he began his 3-year-old campaign, Round Table came under the scrutiny of several prospective buyers, and in February he was sold to Travis Kerr. Kerr's trainer, Willie Molter, flew Round Table to California for the Santa Anita Derby and he was installed as the 13-10 favorite. With the veteran Johnny Longden up for the first time, Round Table went to the front at the furlong pole but couldn't hold the lead on a slow track. He was beaten a head and a nose by Sir William, with Swirling Abbey second.

Round Table went to San Francisco to win the Bay Meadows Derby and then traveled to Lexington, Kentucky, to post a six-length victory in Keeneland's Blue Grass Stakes, setting a track record of 1:47⅖ for the nine furlongs with Ralph Neves up. Well backed in the Kentucky Derby, he finished third.

Returning to the West Coast, Round Table finished second to Social Climber in the Californian and then won five consecutive stakes at Hollywood Park. Four of the stakes were for 3-year-olds and the competition was moderate. But Round Table made an impression when he beat older horses in the Hollywood Gold Cup. Equaling the track record of 1:58⅗ for the mile and a quarter under Bill Shoemaker, he won by more than three lengths from Porterhouse, who carried 119 pounds and was conceding 10 pounds to the favorite.

Once Hollywood's meeting was completed, Round Table was sent to Washington Park for the American Derby on the turf. He had never raced on grass and a betless exhibition was arranged 11 days prior to the country's oldest derby. Round Table won smoothly from just off the pace, then led all the way, as even-money favorite, to win the American Derby by four lengths from Kentucky Derby winner Iron Liege.

His reputation growing with every race, Round Table headed east for Atlantic City's prestigious United Nations Handicap. Favored at 7-10 despite his assignment of 118 pounds, he stumbled at the start and lost position but gamely gained the lead and battled the classy Tudor Era, prevailing by a nose.

The versatile Round Table won three straight grass titles, and was also handicap champion and Horse of the Year in 1958. He retired in 1959 as the richest Thoroughbred in history.

Round Table returned to Chicago to win the Hawthorne Gold Cup by three lengths. With Bill Harmatz up, and favored at 7-10, he was always prominent under 121 pounds and finished strongly to beat the Midwest ace Swoon's Son, who carried 128 pounds. His outstanding 3-year-old campaign was marred when he finished third in the three-horse field for the Trenton Handicap at Garden State Park.

Resuming at Santa Anita in late December, Round Table raced in top form, running off a string of eight consecutive victories. The highlight was his Santa Anita Handicap triumph under 130 pounds, when he set a track record of 1:59⅘ for the mile and a quarter while beating Terrang and Porterhouse with concessions of 11 and 10 pounds, respectively. Later that month he flew to Florida to win the Gulfstream Park Handicap by four lengths under 130 pounds.

Sword Dancer narrowly lost to Tomy Lee in a controversial running of the Derby, but became the runaway 3-year-old champion and Horse of the Year in 1959 with victories in the Belmont and Travers in his own division, and the Monmouth Handicap, Woodward, and Jockey Club Gold Cup against older horses.

The remainder of his busy 4-year-old campaign had mixed success. Heavily favored in the Californian Stakes at Hollywood Park, for example, he finished second to Seaneen under 130 pounds while conceding 21 pounds to the winner. In a similar race at Arlington Park, he was upset by Bernbergoo in the Warren Wright Memorial, carrying 130 pounds to Bernbergoo's 109. He was also the beaten favorite in the Equipoise Mile, when Swoon's Son beat Bardstown in an outstanding piece of racing.

Round Table captured the Arlington Handicap on the turf, beating Clem while conceding 21 pounds, but in the Washington Park Handicap on the dirt, with the same weight spread, Clem won by more than three lengths. Clem was to prove a troublesome opponent on other occasions as well. He upset Round Table in the United Nations Handicap by half a length with a 17-pound concession, and won the Woodward at level weights when the sloppy track at Belmont proved a problem for Round Table.

He salvaged some glory with a victory in the Hawthorne Gold Cup, setting a track record of 1:59⅗ for the mile and a quarter while beating Swoon's Son, to whom he conceded three pounds.

Round Table's durability was underlined by the 14 starts he made in his final season of 1959. Carrying as much as 134 pounds, he alternated victory and defeat until midsummer when he put together three impressive triumphs in the Arlington Handicap, the Washington Park Handicap, and the United Nations. He set track records in the first two events but was particularly impressive in the United Nations, winning under 136 pounds.

His last victory came that fall in the Manhattan Handicap at Aqueduct when he beat Bald Eagle while spotting that good horse 10 pounds, 132 to 122, at a mile and five furlongs on the grass. Three weeks later he returned for the Jockey Club Gold

Calumet Farm's Tim Tam, winner of the 1958 Kentucky Derby and Preakness, lost his bid to sweep the Triple Crown when he fractured a sesamoid at the quarter pole in the Belmont. Courageously, he carried on to finish second.

Cup at two miles, but was unable to handle the 3-year-old Sword Dancer, who won by seven lengths. Round Table's retirement was announced and he left the racing scene as the world's leading money-winner with earnings of $1,749,869.

Sword Dancer and Tim Tam rose to prominence late in the decade, largely on the basis of what they accomplished as 3-year-olds. Both displayed unusual talent, but Sword Dancer was able to do it over an entire season and was voted Horse of the Year in 1959. Tim Tam, the Kentucky Derby and Preakness winner of 1958, broke down in a Belmont Stakes many believe he would have won, ending his racing career. He was forced to settle for divisional honors.

Sword Dancer, by Sunglow out of Highland Fling, by By Jimminy, was owned and bred by the Brookmeade Stable of auto heiress Isabel Dodge Sloane. He showed promise at 2, winning the Mayflower Stakes at Suffolk Downs and finishing third in the Garden State, but he also disappointed on occasion and was slow to come to hand for trainer Elliott Burch.

Sword Dancer took his time in developing at 3. He didn't race at Hialeah, but his second to Easy Spur in the Florida Derby at Gulfstream earned him a bid at the classics, and in many respects his Kentucky Derby was memorable. He turned into the stretch on even terms with Tomy Lee, who was known for his irregular patterns in the drive.

Through the long stretch at Churchill Downs, Sword Dancer and Tomy Lee bumped, several times, with Sword Dancer the aggressor. Near the finish, Sword Dancer, under Bill Boland, came in again to bump Tomy Lee. The latter, tiring badly because he couldn't change leads, was thrown onto a fresh lead. He accelerated and won by a nose under Bill Shoemaker.

Sword Dancer was sailing along in the Preakness, in excellent position behind the leader, when Royal Orbit came sweeping by to upset. Royal Orbit won by four lengths and is credited with one of the most impressive finishes in classic history. With four weeks between the Preakness and the Belmont, Elliott Burch decided to give Sword Dancer a shot at the Metropolitan Mile. He won easily by 3¼ lengths.

Favored in the Belmont Stakes, Sword Dancer reveled in the sloppy going, and beat Bagdad and Royal Orbit in 2:28⅗ for the mile and a half. After the Belmont, Sword Dancer raced outside his division most of the way. He won the Monmouth Handicap, was second in the Brooklyn, and finished the campaign with three victories that earned him signal honors. He won the Travers at Saratoga to nail down the 3-year-old title and proceeded to beat older horses in a highly competitive Woodward and in the Jockey Club Gold Cup, the latter a tour de force with a winning margin of seven lengths.

Sword Dancer wasn't as effective as a 4-year-old of 1960 but ran two outstanding races toward the end of his career. With only one prep race on the grass, he put in a big effort to finish second to T.V. Lark in the United Nations at Atlantic City while conceding seven pounds. He also won the Woodward for the second time, beating Dotted Swiss and Bald Eagle.

Tim Tam, by champion Tom Fool out of champion Two Lea, owned and bred by Calumet Farm, was one of the most professional racehorses of his time. He never won by big margins but compiled a sparkling record of 10 wins from 14 starts. He was out of the money only once.

A late developer, Tim Tam made only one start as a 2-year-old, finishing fourth on a sloppy track at Garden State Park. Trainer Jimmy Jones had high hopes for him, however, and Tim Tam got a lot of seasoning from that one race.

With Bill Hartack up, he won his first two starts in Miami as he turned 3. He then had a couple of educational outings with the veteran Ovie Scurlock aboard before winning the Everglades at Hialeah with Hartack up. From that race on he was unbeatable.

He won the Flamingo on a celebrated disqualification after being bothered in the drive by Jewel's Reward, then captured the Fountain of Youth and Florida Derby at Gulfstream. He lost his rider at the start of Derby Week at Churchill Downs when Hartack broke a leg in the gate on a fractious 2-year-old, and was replaced by Ismael "Milo" Valenzuela.

The track was exceptionally muddy for the Kentucky Derby but Tim Tam won, beating Lincoln Road in 2:05 for the mile and a quarter. He had an easier time of it winning the Preakness from the same opponent, and looked like a winner in the Belmont when he suddenly swerved in the stretch. Losing momentum, he finished second to Cavan and pulled up lame. It was learned later that he shattered a sesamoid, forcing his retirement.

CHAMPIONS

PAST PERFORMANCES

THE 1950'S

YEAR BY YEAR CHAMPIONS

•1950•
•2-YEAR-OLD MALE *Battlefield* •2-YEAR-OLD FILLY *Aunt Jinny* •3-YEAR-OLD MALE *Hill Prince*
•3-YEAR-OLD FILLY *Next Move* •HANDICAP HORSE *Noor* •HANDICAP MARE *Two Lea*
•SPRINTER *Sheilas Reward* •STEEPLECHASE *Oedipus*
•**HORSE OF THE YEAR** Hill Prince

•1951•
•2-YEAR-OLD MALE *Tom Fool* •2-YEAR-OLD FILLY *Rose Jet* •3-YEAR-OLD MALE *Counterpoint*
•3-YEAR-OLD FILLY *Kiss Me Kate* •HANDICAP HORSE *Hill Prince* •HANDICAP MARE *Bed o' Roses*
•SPRINTER *Sheilas Reward* •STEEPLECHASE *Oedipus*
•**HORSE OF THE YEAR** Counterpoint

•1952•
•2-YEAR-OLD MALE *Native Dancer* •2-YEAR-OLD FILLY *Sweet Patootie* •3-YEAR-OLD MALE *One Count*
•3-YEAR-OLD FILLY *Real Delight* •HANDICAP HORSE *Crafty Admiral* •HANDICAP MARE *Real Delight, Next Move (TRA)*
•SPRINTER *Tea-Maker* •STEEPLECHASE *Jam, Oedipus (TRA)*
•**HORSE OF THE YEAR** One Count, Native Dancer (TRA)

•1953•
•2-YEAR-OLD MALE *Porterhouse* •2-YEAR-OLD FILLY *Evening Out* •3-YEAR-OLD MALE *Native Dancer*
•3-YEAR-OLD FILLY *Grecian Queen* •HANDICAP HORSE *Tom Fool* •HANDICAP MARE *Sickle's Image*
•GRASS HORSE *Iceberg II* •SPRINTER *Tom Fool* •STEEPLECHASE *The Mast*
•**HORSE OF THE YEAR** Tom Fool

•1954•
•2-YEAR-OLD MALE *Nashua* •2-YEAR-OLD FILLY *High Voltage* •3-YEAR-OLD MALE *High Gun*
•3-YEAR-OLD FILLY *Parlo* •HANDICAP HORSE *Native Dancer* •HANDICAP MARE *Parlo, Lavender Hill (TRA)*
•GRASS HORSE *Stan* •SPRINTER *White Skies* •STEEPLECHASE *King Commander*
•**HORSE OF THE YEAR** Native Dancer, Dedicate (TRA)

•1955•
•2-YEAR-OLD MALE *Needles* •2-YEAR-OLD FILLY *Doubledogdare, Nasrina (TRA)* •3-YEAR-OLD MALE *Nashua*
•3-YEAR-OLD FILLY *Misty Morn* •HANDICAP HORSE *High Gun* •HANDICAP MARE *Misty Morn*
•GRASS HORSE *St. Vincent* •SPRINTER *Berseem* •STEEPLECHASE *Neji*
•**HORSE OF THE YEAR** Nashua

•1956•
•2-YEAR-OLD MALE *Barbizon* •2-YEAR-OLD FILLY *Leallah, Romanita (TRA)* •3-YEAR-OLD MALE *Needles*
•3-YEAR-OLD FILLY *Doubledogdare* •HANDICAP HORSE *Swaps* •HANDICAP MARE *Blue Sparkler*
•GRASS HORSE *Career Boy* •SPRINTER *Decathlon* •STEEPLECHASE *Shipboard*
•**HORSE OF THE YEAR** Swaps

•1957•
•2-YEAR-OLD MALE *Nadir, Jewel's Reward (TRA)* •2-YEAR-OLD FILLY *Idun* •3-YEAR-OLD MALE *Bold Ruler*
•3-YEAR-OLD FILLY *Bayou* •HANDICAP HORSE *Dedicate* •HANDICAP MARE *Pucker Up*
•GRASS HORSE *Round Table* •SPRINTER *Decathlon* •STEEPLECHASE *Neji*
•**HORSE OF THE YEAR** Bold Ruler

•1958•
•2-YEAR-OLD MALE *First Landing* •2-YEAR-OLD FILLY *Quill* •3-YEAR-OLD MALE *Tim Tam* •3-YEAR-OLD FILLY *Idun*
•HANDICAP HORSE *Round Table* •HANDICAP MARE *Bornastar* •GRASS HORSE *Round Table*
•SPRINTER *Bold Ruler* •STEEPLECHASE *Neji*
•**HORSE OF THE YEAR** Round Table

•1959•
•2-YEAR-OLD MALE *Warfare* •2-YEAR-OLD FILLY *My Dear Girl* •3-YEAR-OLD MALE *Sword Dancer*
•3-YEAR-OLD FILLY *Royal Native, Silver Spoon (TRA)* •HANDICAP HORSE *Sword Dancer, Round Table (TRA)*
•HANDICAP MARE *Tempted* •GRASS HORSE *Round Table* •SPRINTER *Intentionally* •STEEPLECHASE *Ancestor*
•**HORSE OF THE YEAR** Sword Dancer

Ancestor

b. g. 1949, by Challedon (Challenger II)–Bloodroot, by Blue Larkspur
Own.– Mrs Ogden Phipps
Br.– Ogden Phipps (Ky)
Tr.– D.M. Smithwick

Lifetime record: 101 26 14 13 $237,956

13Oct59- 5Aqu	hd	*2½	S'Chase	4:473	4↑	Brook H 19k	1	1	13	12	13	11½	Smithwick AP	162	s	*.70e	--	Ancestor1621½Sun Dog1371½Fairfax152nk	Driving	7
1Oct59- 5Aqu	fm	*2	S'Chase	3:51	4↑	Broad Hollow H 16k	2	1	12½	1hd	11½	1hd	Smithwick AP	160	sb	4.10e	--	Ancstor160hdDrubn1382SunDog13812	Jumped well,hard drive	9
11Sep59- 6Bel	hd	*2½	S'Chase	4:41	4↑	Temple Gwathmey H 56k	6	3	2½	99¾	949	966	Smithwick AP	168	w	3.40e	--	MuguetII1521¾Darubini134nkIdealView1354	Bad landing 9th	9
3Sep59- 5Bel	sf	*2⅛	S'Chase	4:08	4↑	C L Appleton Mem H 11k	1	1	21	312	38	37	Smithwick AP	166	s	*1.30	--	Policeman Day1504Antonino1373Ancestor1668	Speed,tired	5
21Aug59- 5Sar	hd	*2½	S'Chase	5:03	4↑	Saratoga H 19k	3	1	11	22	416	449	Smithwick AP	161	s	2.45e	--	Independence1619Fairfax14930BasilBee15210	Used up early	5
13Jun58- 5Del	fm	*2	S'Chase	3:394	4↑	Georgetown H 10k	3	1	13	13	12	11½	Smithwick AP	169	w	*.60e	--	Ancestor1691½Arywa149nkCarthage1306	Under steady drive	6
5Jun58- 5Bel	fm	*2½	S'Chase	4:44	4↑	Meadow Brook H 13k	5	1	13	14	11	11½	Smithwick AP	165	w	1.65	--	Ancestor1651½Arywa14712Independenc156nk	Held clear lead	6
27May58- 5Bel	fm	*2⅛	S'Chase	4:043	4↑	International H 11k	2	1	13	22	11	1¾	Smithwick AP	162	w	2.45	--	Ancestor162¾Rythminhm14714PnShot1432½	Under brisk drive	6
16Oct57- 6Bel	fm	*2½	S'Chase	4:422	4↑	Temple Gwathmey H 57k	11	2	1hd	1¾	23	27	Murphy J	160	w	*.80e	--	Neji1737Ancestor1601Shipboard1641½	Used up setting pace	12
26Sep57- 5Bel	fm	*2½	S'Chase	4:451	4↑	Brook H 22k	2	1	11	1½	66	516	Murphy J	161	w	1.65e	--	Neji1642¾Independence15110Rythminhm148no	Set pace,tired	10
19Sep57- 5Bel	fm	*2⅛	S'Chase	4:01	3↑	Broad Hollow H 17k	3	1	78	45½	611	621	Smithwick AP	162	w	2.95	--	Indepndnce1488Morpheus1382½Shipboard1623	Bobbled jump	7
12Sep57- 5Bel	fm	*2⅛	S'Chase	3:573	3↑	Harbor Hill H 17k	7	1	12	12	12	12	Smithwick AP	158	w	*1.65e	--	Ancestor1582Independence1486His Boots131nk	Ridden out	9
29Aug57- 5Sar	fm	*2½	S'Chase	5:121	4↑	Saratoga H 22k	2	1	12	1½	35	310¼	Smithwick AP	157	w	*1.80	--	Shipboard161nkIndependence14610Ancstor15713	Speed,tired	6
15Aug57- 5Sar	fm	*2	S'Chase	4:14	4↑	Beverwyck H 17k	3	1	11	16	110	114	Smithwick AP	152	w	5.85	--	Ancestor15214Shipbord163½Morphus14318	Speed in reserve	6
2Aug57- 5Mth	fm	*2	Hurdles	3:56	3↑	Midsummer H 15k	3	3	33½	77	811	78¼	Smithwick AP	153	w	4.50e	--	Ideal View141½Great Tom1412½Rythminhim148nk	Early speed	10
19Jly57- 3Mth	fm	*1¾	Hurdles	3:194	3↑	Alw 4000	10	3	42½	56½	610	612	Smithwick AP	162	w	4.30	--	Marso1531½MyLastTry1303½MossGreen142hd	Some early foot	11
27Jun57- 3Del	fm	*1¾	Hurdles	3:284	3↑	Alw 4000	1	2	412	39	311	39½	Smithwick AP	157	w	*2.20	--	Fairshot140½IdealView1409Ancstor157½	No apparent mishap	5
Previously trained by G.H. Bostwick																				
17Oct56- 6Bel	fm	*2½	S'Chase	4:42	4↑	Temple Gwathmey H 58k	2	1	1½	11	16	118	Adams FD	149	w	6.05	--	Ancestor14918Shipboard1682Morpheus1422½	Ridden out	12
27Sep56- 5Bel	sf	*2½	S'Chase	4:433	4↑	Brook H 17k	8	2	27	26	520	534	McDonald RS	153	w	*2.10e	--	Morpheus1307Pine Shot1323Sundowner14012	Used up early	9
20Sep56- 5Bel	sf	*2	S'Chase	3:47	3↑	Broad Hollow H 11k	4	4	32	55	58½	611	Adams FD	157	w	*1.50e	--	Shipboard164nkBasilia1301½Bavari1542	Early factor,tired	8
13Sep56- 5Bel	fm	*2	S'Chase	3:433	3↑	Harbor Hill H 11k	8	1	11½	1hd	12	12½	Adams FD	153	w	3.45e	--	Ancestor1532½Bavar153½MghtyMo14413	Hard ridden,drew out	8
30Aug56- 5Sar	sf	*2½	S'Chase	5:162	4↑	Saratoga H 11k	4	3	55½	55½	57½	513	Adams FD	155	w	*2.30	--	Mighty Mo1382¾Carthage1432Basilia130hd	Showed nothing	6
16Aug56- 5Sar	hd	*2	S'Chase	4:111	4↑	Beverwyck H 8.8k	1	3	33½	33	36	311	Adams FD	155	w	3.55	--	Bavaria1469Crthg1372Ancstor1552	Bobbled badly 10th jump	7
29Jly55- 5Mth	fm	*1¾	Hurdles	3:20	3↑	Midsummer H 17k	3	1	41¼	87¼	815	716	Adams FD	149	w	*1.40	--	DearBrutus139noCarafar1511½PrinceRegent157hd	Used early	8
1Jly55- 3Del	fm	*2½	S'Chase	4:422	4↑	Indian River H 10k	1	1	11	1hd	21½	2nk	Adams FD	154	w	*.80	--	Beaupre142nkAncestor154nkBilling Bear13312	Came again	6
24Jun55- 0Del	sf	*2	S'Chase	3:56	4↑	Georgetown H 10k	3	3	36	36	22	1nk	Adams FD	148	w	-	--	Ancestor148nkCovetd1403Shpbord1623½	Jumped well,just up	5
Special event - no wagering																				
14Jun55- 3Aqu	fm	*2	S'Chase	3:481	4↑	Aqu Spring Maiden 9.7k	3	2	3½	32½	47½	48¼	Adams FD	162	w	*.45	--	Bavaria1483BeauSir1384½AnotherHyacinth155¾	Bobbled 7th	5
26May55- 5Bel	hd	*2	S'Chase	3:413	4↑	Bel Spring Maiden 9.7k	3	1	1hd	23	24	2½	Adams FD	162	w	*1.10e	--	Carafar153½Ancestor16240PrinceGloriux1403½	Gaining fast	9
21May55- 6Bel	hd	*2½	S'Chase	4:432	4↑	International 21k	9	2	39	37½	212	215	Adams FD	155	w	3.10e	--	Nej15015Ancstor15518Hyvn15518	Early foot,no late threat	10
5May55- 5Bel	fm	*2	S'Chase	3:412	4↑	C L Appleton Mem 9.1k	8	2	25	24	11	13½	Adams FD	134	w	*1.60	--	Ancestr1343½King Commander1628River Jordan1344	Handily	8
28Apr55- 3Bel	sf	*2	S'Chase	3:47	4↑	Alw 4500	7	1	11	21½	2½	12	Adams FD	137	w	*1.45	--	Ancestor1372PrinceGlorieux13012CammellLaird1425	Driving	8
2Apr55- 7Cam	fm	*1Ⓣ		1:40	3↑	Alw 500	1	1	14	11½	1nk	12½	Hobales J	142	wb	-	--	Ancestor1422½Hardrada1511½Xapcourt1387	Going away	5
21Oct54- 6Bel	fm	*2	Hurdles	3:442	3↑	NY Turf Writers H 11k	2	2	21	2½	11	11½	Adams FD	147	w	2.65	--	Ancestor1471½Khumbaba1361½River Jordan1491½	Drew clear	9
13Oct54- 3Bel	fm	*1¾	Hurdles	3:133	3↑	Alw 4200	3	2	23	23	2hd	11	Hobales J	141	w	4.30	--	Ancestor1411Eole III1411Brechin137½	Under hard drive	5
30Sep54- 5Bel	fm	*2	Hurdles	3:433	3↑	Rouge Dragon H 11k	3	1	1½	11½	14	12½	Adams FD	136	w	3.55e	--	Ancestor1362½Hyvania1471Khumbaba1373	Under a drive	8
24Sep54- 3Bel	fm	*1¾	Hurdles	3:15	3↑	Alw 4000	5	5	49½	49	210	210	Field K	140	ws	*1.45e	--	River Jordan14810Ancestor1402Brechin13110	Mild rally	6
16Jly54- 3Mth	fm	*1¾	Hurdles	3:194	3↑	National Maiden 7.4k	3	3	73¼	53¾	49	416	Field K	159	ws	*.70e	--	Neji1574Rythminhim1498Bombez1324	Done very early	8
6Jly54- 6Aqu	fst	1 1/16		:24 :48 1:13 1:444	4↑	Alw 5000	6	6	78¼	79¼	722	726	Glassner G	113	w	15.65	64-15	Bicarb1161South Point1087Bradley1142½	Never a contender	7
1Jly54- 6Aqu	fst	1 1/16		:242 :48 1:123 1:461	3↑	Handicap 7530	1	1	1½	1hd	21	45¼	Atkinson T	110	w	6.55	78-19	Resilient119½Impulsivo118nkG.R. Petersen1104½	Tired	5
25Jun54- 3Aqu	hd	*1½	Hurdles	2:454	3↑	Alw 3700	6	3	34½	31½	12	12½	Adams FD	152	w	1.70	--	Ancestor1522½BillingBer1421½FourtoGo1426	Fully extended	7
18Jun54- 5Mth	fm	1Ⓣ		1:391	3↑	Alw 5000	12	4	41½	76¼	1116	1015	Hanford I	113	wb	17.80e	75-10	IcebergII1183BobsAlibi109noGoingAway109¾	Gave way early	12
12Jun54- 7Bel	hd	1⅜Ⓣ		2:172	3↑	Handicap 15085	6	2	32	42¼	1210	138¼	Roser G	109	wb	52.30	--	Kaster121½Williamsburg107hdPicdor116no	Early speed,quit	13
4Jun54- 3Bel	fm	*1¾	Hurdles	3:124	3↑	Alw 3700	9	1	1½	3½	38½	315¼	Adams FD	149	wb	3.25	--	Sea Term130nkPar Amour13415Ancestor149¾	Tired gradually	9
17May54- 5Bel	fm	*1¾	Hurdles	3:15	3↑	National Maiden 7.4k	10	1	21	3½	45	514	Adams FD	154	wb	*1.35e	--	Neji1374Rythminhim1502½Corinthian139no	Gave way badly	13
11May54- 3Bel	sf	*1¾	Hurdles	3:24	3↑	Alw 4000	4	3	41½	53	513	511	Adams FD	152	w	*1.35	--	Out Point1474Sea Term131noOneida152¾	Unable to keep up	10
27Apr54- 3Bel	fm	*1½	Hurdles	2:47	3↑	Sp Wt 3700	2	4	41½	2½	11½	12	Adams FD	147	w	*.90	--	Ancestor1472Rythminhim1421Altus1357	Drew out when ready	14
3Apr54- 1Cam	hd	1½	Hurdles	2:424	3↑	Md Sp Wt	3	3	21	1½	1¾	12	Adams FD	148	w	-	--	Ancestor1482Coit1482½Salt1423	Driving	8
24Mar54- 0Aik		5½f		1:093								1					--	AncestorNeji		
Previously owned by O. Phipps;previously trained by J. Fitzsimmons																				
1Oct53- 6Bel	fst	1		:231 :463 1:121 1:374	3↑	Handicap 7575	9	4	64¾	713	712	812	Atkinson T	118	w	6.10	73-19	AgainII1121¾Inseparable109noCommonCause1151	Done early	9
8Sep53- 6Aqu	fst	1 1/16		:242 :48 1:131 1:453	3↑	Handicap 7565	4	4	45½	58	613	610	Wall N	120	wb	2.05	76-18	Timely Reward120¾Nothirdchance108½Chello1064½	Tired	7
3Sep53- 6Aqu	fst	1⅛		:48 1:122 1:381 1:523	3↑	Handicap 7535	5	1	11	1hd	23½	21	Wall N	122	wb	*.90e	81-17	G.R. Petersen1201Ancestor1221Assignment118½	Closed well	7
31Aug53- 6Aqu	fst	1 1/16		:243 :48 1:12 1:443	3↑	Aqueduct H 28k	8	2	22½	43½	56½	45	Wall N	109	wb	15.60	86-17	First Aid109½Combat Boots117½Elixir1134	No mishap	9
25Aug53- 6Sar	fst	1⅛		:481 1:123 1:39 1:522	3↑	Handicap 5030	4	2	21½	2hd	1hd	1nk	Wall N	118	wb	4.30	88-19	Ancestor118nkFreedomBell1104Sckl'sSound1153½	Hard drive	5
20Aug53- 6Sar	fst	1⅛		:483 1:132 1:392 1:532	3↑	Alw 5000	8	2	21½	46	612	66¾	Wall N	117	wb	*1.25e	76-20	G.R. Petersen120noSickle's Sound1052Mameluke1171½	Quit	9
17Aug53- 6Sar	fst	7f		:23 :463 1:12 1:25	3↑	American Legion H 11k	1	5	77½	811	812	89	Atkinson T	112	wb	10.20	81-23	Eatontown1221½Kaster1201½Acefull115hd	No speed	8
27Jun53- 6Aqu	fst	7f		:22 :443 1:092 1:22	3↑	Carter H 59k	3	7	77	710	812	810	Wall N	108	wb	31.90	90-09	Tom Fool1352Squared Away1222¼Eatontown1131¼	No factor	9
20Jun53- 6Aqu	fst	1 1/16		:24 :47 1:112 1:441	3↑	Queens County H 29k	4	1	11½	1½	43	54¼	Wall N	104	wb	16.85	89-11	Flaunt105½Indian Land1142½Count Turf110nk	Used early	10
10Jun53- 7Suf	fst	1¼		:462 1:103 1:35 2:021	3↑	Mass H 61k	1	2	21	3¾	56¾	67¼	Wall N	103	wb	28.80	89-12	Royal Vale125½Larry Ellis1131½Count Turf1071¼	Weakened	11
5Jun53- 6Bel	fst	1⅛		:462 1:112 1:371 1:501	3↑	Handicap 7555	6	1	1½	1½	2½	34¾	Wall N	116	wb	8.00	83-12	Arcave1222¼One Hitter1262½Ancestor1161½	Used up	6
26May53- 7Bel	fst	1		:231 :454 1:104 1:364	4↑	Alw 5000	8	2	21	22½	32½	33½	Atkinson T	122	wb	6.10	86-18	Kaster115½Bryan G.1183Ancestor1224	Hard urged	8
20May53- 7Bel	fst	1⅛		:454 1:104 1:371 1:504	3↑	Handicap 7555	4	1	12	2½	33	35	Guerin E	119	wb	2.50	80-19	Arcave1203½Gloriette1051½Ancestor119nk	Tired in drive	9
14May53- 6Bel	fst	1⅛		:454 1:104 1:37 1:502	3↑	Handicap 7565	4	4	33½	31½	24	23½	Guerin E	119	w	*1.50e	83-16	Arcave1113½Ancestor1192Anchor Man1101	Lacked rally	9
9May53- 7Pim	gd	1⅛		:471 1:123 1:383 1:514	3↑	Dixie H 29k	5	1	13	31½	43	44½	Wall N	105	wb	12.80	90-22	RoyalVale1201¾ColdCommand1152½CraftyAdmrl126nk	Faltered	6
4May53- 6Jam	gd	1⅛		:48 1:121 1:373 1:51	3↑	Handicap 7560	8	2	21½	22½	32½	22½	Atkinson T	116	wb	4.70e	88-16	Swoop1122½Ancestor116¾Anchor Man1112	Good try	9
25Apr53- 7Bow	fst	1 1/16		:233 :473 1:122 1:444	3↑	Bowie H 23k	6	1	11	11	22	22½	Wall N	112	wb	14.10	94-14	Royal Vale1162½Ancestor1121½Post Card1154	Good effort	6
21Apr53- 6Jam	fst	1 1/16		:234 :47 1:12 1:451	3↑	Handicap 10160	4	1	2hd	2½	2hd	74¾	Atkinson T	107	wb	9.65e	81-19	One Count1261¾Assignment111noFlaunt106hd	Quit	11
8Apr53- 5Jam	gd	1 1/16		:24 :48 1:124 1:44	3↑	Handicap 6045	5	2	23	23¾	34¾	47	Guerin E	117	wb	2.35	85-16	Assignment1121½King Jolie1184Royal Vale1201½	Weakened	5
14Feb53- 5Hia	fst	7f		:23 :46 1:111 1:242	4↑	Alw 5000	7	3	21	21	2½	11¼	Atkinson T	122	wb	2.75e	88-14	Ancestor1221¼Golden Gloves122¾True Pattern1181½	Driving	7
10Feb53- 8Hia	fst	7f		:231 :461 1:104 1:234	4↑	Alw 4500	4	4	45½	57	67½	69	Stout J	122	wb	20.00	82-13	BlinkerLight116½ChatNoirII1151½Eatontown1102	Done early	8
28Jan53- 7Hia	fst	7f		:224 :46 1:111 1:242	3↑	Palm Beach H 20k	9	7	75¾	88¾	1213	1211	Roberts P	109	wb	28.85e	77-20	OilCapitol107nkBattlefield123½NimbleFox1141½	No menace	14
30Dec52- 7TrP	fst	1 1/16		:233 :47 1:112 1:434	3↑	Alw 3500	9	4	43½	54½	68½	77½	Cole S	109	wb	*2.50	85-12	Topside1181Blinker Light1173½Lancaster Lady1082½	Tired	9
25Dec52- 7TrP	fst	1⅛		:462 1:11 1:37 1:503	3↑	Christmas H 11k	3	6	68	56½	57	55½	Cole S	112	wb	5.65e	82-18	Crystal Boot1202½Elixir115½Recline119hd	No factor	10
17Dec52- 7TrP	fst	1 1/16		:23 :46 1:104 1:433	3↑	Hurricane H 8.9k	3	2	31½	45½	67	66	Stout J	112	wb	6.60	88-13	Libba113¾Chombro110hdRecline1172	Weakened	11
13Dec52- 6TrP	fst	6f		:224 :453 1:103	3↑	Alw 3000	5	6	74	75¼	98	95½	Stout J	119	wb	2.85	88-13	Elixir115nkWhiffenpoof115½Seaflash1121½	No factor	10

17Sep52- 6Bel	fst 1	:232 :471 1:122 1:37	Jerome H 24k	6 7 63¾ 53½ 813 920	GormanD	113wb	17.20	69-26	Tom Fool1207Marcador111nkMark-Ye-Well1301½	Quit	10
6Sep52- 6Aqu	fst 1⅛	:474 1:121 1:38 1:504	Discovery H 28k	9 1 16 14 13 12½	Atkinson T	107wb	10.00e	91-17	Ancestor1072½Flaunt107nkMarcador1101½	Driving	10
2Sep52- 6Aqu	fst 7f	:231 :46 1:103 1:233	Handicap 7535	4 2 1hd 3½ 63¼ 612	Wall N	113wb	4.75	80-13	Flaunt107nkCold Command114nkWhither1128	Close quarters	6
23Aug52- 7Sar	fst 1	:233 :471 1:123 1:393	Alw 5000	2 1 12 13 12 1½	Wall N	116wb	2.85	79-17	Ancestor116½Cold Command1223Anchor Man113¾	Driving	9
13Aug52- 7Sar	my 1	:233 :471 1:123 1:401 3↑	Alw 4000	4 6 53½ 43 52¼ 76¾	Wall N	118wb	*3.25	69-25	Nilufer110noTop Spring1175½Danger Ahead115nk	Weakened	10
4Aug52- 7Sar	fst 1	:24 :473 1:13 1:393	Alw 4000	2 3 3nk 2½ 12 2nk	Wall N	122wb	3.95	79-20	Cold Commnd122nkAncstr1223Common Cause1221	Held well	7
1Aug52- 6Jam	fst 1 1/16	:25 :483 1:131 1:451 3↑	Alw 5000	1 1 11½ 12 14 17	Wall N	115wb	4.10	86-21	Ancestor1157Flaunt1152Big Print1091¼	Easily	6
25Jly52- 6Jam	fst 1 1/16	:242 :482 1:14 1:454 3↑	Alw 5000	4 4 65 64 65 59¾	Wall N	114wb	4.20	73-21	Turks Cap108¾Begorra1084Roman Law1112	Poor start	6
19Jly52- 7Jam	fst 1 1/16	:24 :473 1:124 1:46 3↑	Alw 4500	7 4 42½ 1hd 21 41½	Nichols J	116wb	*2.15e	80-19	FlamingPrince1161½ClosedSeson113noTurksCp110no	Bore out	12
26Jun52- 6Aqu	fst 6f	:223 :462 1:103	Rippey H 10k	4 6 64 65¾ 74¾ 79	Wall N	104wb	7.30	90-15	Hitex120hdTom Fool1262Duke Fanelli1022	Outrun	8
17Jun52- 5Aqu	fst 6f	:222 :46 1:111	Alw 4000	5 2 42 42½ 31 32½	Gorman D	119wb	*1.45	93-12	Rae's Reward119½Giorgetti1192Ancestor1192	Hung	6
14Jun52- 2Aqu	fst 6f	:231 :46 1:112	Alw 4000	7 1 41¼ 41¾ 2hd 12	Guerin E	120wb	*2.15e	95-11	Ancestor1202Thymus120¾Jet a Dandy1203½	Drew out	11
9Jun52- 5Bel	sly 7f	:221 :454 1:12 1:254	Alw 4000	3 5 55½ 45½ 45 33½	Gorman D	120wb	6.85	77-20	Second Look1153Model Quest115½Ancestor120nk	Went well	12
5Jun52- 7Bel	sly 7f	:224 :46 1:104 1:233	Alw 4000	8 3 33 32½ 33 33	Boland W	117wb	4.55	89-08	Giorgetti1141¾Roaming1171¼Ancestor1173½	No rally	8
20May52- 6Bel	sly 1	:23 :461 1:114 1:373	Handicap 10070	2 1 1hd 1hd 64¾ 813	Stuart K	105wb	40.30	73-20	Quiet Step1113Cold Command1101Old Ironsides1123½	Tired	8
16May52- 7Bel	fst 6f	:224 :464 1:113	Alw 4000	1 4 42½ 42½ 33 33½	Arcaro E	118wb	3.70	87-16	King Jolie1182½Requisition1181Ancestor1182	Lacked rally	8
28Apr52- 5Jam	sly 1 1/16	:24 :49 1:14 1:463	Alw 4500	7 1 11 12 2½ 21¾	Gorman D	117wb	2.90	77-22	Swoop1171¾Ancestor1177Top Bet1171½	Faltered	7
23Apr52- 5Jam	fst 1 1/16	:243 :482 1:132 1:462	Alw 4500	6 4 41¼ 21½ 2hd 43¾	Gorman D	114wb	4.75e	78-19	Roaring Bull113½Flaunt1161¾Referee1131½	Weakened	9
19Apr52- 4Jam	fst 6f	:233 :472 1:121	Alw 4000	2 2 63 65¼ 52¼ 43	Gorman D	117 w	*.65e	83-16	Imurguy1121½Swoop114noColonel Hoop1151½	Held well	13
10Apr52- 4Jam	fst 6f	:23 :47 1:122 3↑	Md Sp Wt	1 1 3nk 3nk 2hd 1¾	Shoemaker W	116wb	*.90	85-14	Ancestor116¾Hypalong1211Runner-Up1162½	Handily	11
5Apr52- 4Jam	sly 6f	:24 :48 1:132 3↑	Md Sp Wt	3 3 2½ 2hd 21 21¼	Shoemaker W	116wb	*1.25	79-18	Armagh1161¼Ancestor1163½Jolie Boy116no	Good effort	5
3Mar52- 1Hia	fst 6f	:222 :452 1:11	©Md Sp Wt	7 7 74¾ 66½ 66½ 55¾	Stuart K	122wb	*2.10	86-08	Suggested1223½StopandThink122nkBobsAlibi1221½	No excuse	11
19Feb52- 3Hia	fst 7f	:232 :464 1:114 1:25	©Md Sp Wt	8 1 12 1hd 2½ 21½	Rodriquez E	122wb	*1.35	83-18	Sandtop1221½Ancestor1223Cellini122nk	No excuse	12
15Feb52- 4Hia	fst 7f	:23 :461 1:122 1:252	Md Sp Wt	5 2 21½ 21½ 11½ 2no	Stuart K	122wb	3.20e	85-17	Top Bet122noAncestor1224Snow Man1222½	Faltered	12
9Feb52- 6Hia	fst 7f	:224 :46 1:112 1:243	Alw 4000	6 4 53¼ 32 23 33	Stuart K	114wb	21.80	86-07	Blue Square1171Dinewisely1122Ancestor1141½	Lacked rally	7
9Oct51- 5Bel	fst 6f-WC	:223 :453 1:104	©Md Sp Wt	4 1 62¾ 66¾ 62¾	Gorman D	118wb	*1.95e	84-13	AncientCity1181DeepRiver118nkGoldenGloves118no	No rally	16
1Oct51- 5Bel	fst 6f-WC	:223 :45 1:092	Sp Wt 5000	13 8 118½ 1313 1317	Stuart K	118 w	25.45f	77-11	Hill Gail1184Tom Fool118nkBaybrook1182	Showed little	16
26Sep51- 5Bel	fst 6f-WC	:222 :45 1:101	©Md Sp Wt	25 11 84 116¾ 84¾	Combest J	118 w	11.75e	85-10	Hitex1183½Point Fortune113noChello118no	Closed ground	27

Aunt Jinny

ch. f. 1948, by Heliopolis (Hyperion)–Gaga, by Bull Dog — **Lifetime record: 30 5 4 3 $106,020**

Own.– D.A. Headley
Br.– Duval A. Headley (Ky)
Tr.– M. Calvert

25Feb52- 7SA	fst 6f	:224 :46 1:11 4↑	ⒻAlw 5000	5 1 96½ 75¼ 64¾ 45	Adams J	111 w	9.55	85-15	Great Dream1141Fleet Rings1092Miss Traffic1112		10
	Dropped back,made up ground										
15Feb52- 6SA	fst 7f	:222 :46 1:103 1:233 4↑	ⒻAlw 5000	2 6 94¾ 99¾ 712 69¾	Adams J	110 w	13.35	77-17	Lyceum1072½Fast Reward1142Dashing By1153	Outrun	12
6Feb52- 7SA	fst 6f	:223 :451 1:103 3↑	ⒻLos Cerritos H 18k	11 2 95 119¼ 1211 1211	Scheih F	108 w	96.85	81-14	Sickle's Image1201½A Gleam1122½Frigid105½	Forced wide	13
26Jan52- 7SA	fst 1⅛	:47 1:114 1:381 1:512 3↑	ⒻS Margarita H 62k	8 11 108½ 108¼ 1417 1415	Trent H	105 w	77.60	69-19	Bed o' Roses1291Next Move1301½Toto105½	No speed	14
11Jan52- 7SA	fst 6f	:221 :45 1:09 4↑	Alw 7500	4 3 68 815 1019 916	York R	112 w	43.65	84-13	To Market1141½Reighs Bull1135Vigorous115¾	Outrun	10
	Previously trained by D.A. Headley										
20Oct51- 7GS	fst 1 1/16	:231 :462 1:113 1:433 3↑	ⒻVineland H 31k	6 15 1514 149½ 1517 1411	Woodhouse H	110 w	34.90	81-15	Bedo'Roses1263½Valadium109noDixieFlyer107½	Slow start	15
26Sep51- 6Bel	fst 1	:23 :46 1:104 1:361	Jerome H 24k	3 4 94½ 99¾ 128½ 129¼	Woodhouse H	107 w	44.05	84-14	Alerted115nkMandingo1023Hall of Fame1281	Quit	12
22Sep51- 6Aqu	fst 1⅛	:482 1:122 1:382 1:52 3↑	ⒻBeldame 67k	5 8 1310 1412 1416 1419	Woodhouse H	111 w	16.20	66-14	Thelma Burger1102Bed o' Roses124½Kiss Me Kate119nk	Quit	14
29Aug51- 6Sar	fst 1¼	:484 1:131 1:382 2:053	ⒻAlabama 22k	5 3 44½ 42½ 34 310	Woodhouse H	122 w	3.60	70-18	Kiss Me Kate1268Vulcania1162Aunt Jinny122no	No rally	5
1Aug51- 6Was	fst 1	:23 :46 1:10 1:35	ⒻMisty Isle H 22k	10 3 21½ 21½ 1½ 11½	Woodhouse H	122 w	4.20	95-06	AuntJinny1221½DickieSue115nkWillYouDance1111½	Driving	10
14Jly51- 7AP	fst 1	:224 :452 1:094 1:361 3↑	ⒻArl Matron H 72k	10 2 2hd 11 12½ 21½	Woodhouse H	107 w	37.10	89-08	Sickle's Image1201½Aunt Jinny1075War Talk109¾	Gave way	13
30Jun51- 7AP	fst 6f	:224 :452 1:104 3↑	ⒻModesty H 24k	7 15 1517 1616 1615 1612	Wall N	111 w	34.20	80-08	Sickle'sImage120¾Asphalt1052½TwoRainbows104nk	No factor	17
20Jun51- 6AP	sl 6f	:224 :454 1:121	ⒻCleopatra 16k	1 2 75¼ 89½ 99¾ 86¾	Wall N	118 w	23.20	78-18	Sickle'sImage1151½JennieLee1151¾Fleeterthan111½	Outrun	10
4May51- 7CD	fst 1 1/16	:24 :482 1:133 1:453	ⒻKy Oaks 31k	6 5 86¾ 119½ 1219 1117	Baird RL	116 w	9.30	73-14	How1162¾Astro1102½Sickle's Image1211½	Tired	14
14Apr51- 6Kee	sl 6f	:234 :494 1:18	ⒻAshland 13k	6 4 79¼ 98 811 821	Baird RL	121 w	3.10	41-31	Sickle'sImage121nkJulitsNurs1181½How1152	Disliked going	9
11Nov50- 6Pim	fst 1 1/16	:223 :464 1:12 1:471	ⒻMarguerite 35k	8 4 21 1hd 11½ 21½	Wall N	116 w	*.90	72-19	CarolinaQueen1191½AuntJnny1162½TwoRnbws114hd	Weakened	8
28Oct50- 6Lrl	fst 1 1/16	:23 :471 1:122 1:462	ⒻSelima 49k	7 3 2hd 1hd 1hd 1hd	Wall N	122 w	*1.30	82-18	Aunt Jinny122hdVulcania119nkRose Fern1192	All out	9
21Oct50- 6Jam	fst 1 1/16	:232 :47 1:121 1:454	ⒻDemoiselle 48k	3 1 1hd 11 15 13	Wall N	116 w	12.65	83-17	Aunt Jinny1163Vulcania1192½Rose Fern1191¼	Easily	9
29Sep50- 6Bel	fst 6f-WC	:22 :443 1:092	ⒻAlw 3500	5 6 73 44 2hd	Brooks S	119 w	10.35	94-10	BettyLamar114hdAuntJinny1192½SweetTalk1191¼	Stout try	12
23Sep50- 5Bel	fst 6f-WC	:222 :453 1:12	ⒻMatron 50k	9 9 911 919 926	Brooks S	119 w	11.95	55-22	Atalanta119¾Ruddy1191Sungari119½	Outrun	9
26Aug50- 3Was	fst 5½f	:222 :454 :581 1:044	ⒻAlw 3000	2 3 2hd 1hd 1½ 1nk	Baird RL	115 w	*1.30	96-07	Aunt Jinny115nkPetasus1153Native Valor115¾	Driving	7
15Aug50- 4Was	fst 5½f	:223 :453 :584 1:044	ⒻMd Sp Wt	6 1 1hd 11 13 14	Baird RL	115 w	10.40	96-08	Aunt Jinny1154Dusty Vixen115nkLittle Cindy1152¼	Easily	12
4Aug50- 5Was	fst 5½f	:223 :46 :574 1:042	ⒻMd Sp Wt	6 4 53 55½ 25 37½	Baird RL	115 w	10.50	90-07	Sickle'sImage1156½TheGhizeh1151AuntJnny1153	Lost ground	12
27Jly50- 6AP	fst 6f	:222 :443 1:104	ⒻPollyanna 18k	12 7 54 56½ 78¼ 811	Baird RL	112.5 w	42.00	81-11	Flyamanita1133¾HastyRequest1132Sckl'sImg1141½	No mishap	14
18Jly50- 5AP	hy 5½f	:232 :483 1:013 1:09	ⒻMd Sp Wt	10 10 85¾ 55½ 76½ 44	Baird RL	115wb	6.60	71-34	RomanMiss1151Fleeterthan1151½Sckl'sImg1151½	Lost ground	12
8Jly50- 7AP	fst 6f	:222 :454 1:12	ⒻArl Lassie 55k	7 5 41½ 52¼ 45½ 47	Baird RL	114wb	69.80	79-18	ShawneeSquaw1193½RedCrss1191¼HastyRqst1192¼	No mishap	11
3Jly50- 4AP	fst 5½f	:222 :461 :592 1:061	ⒻMd Sp Wt	5 7 21 1½ 1hd 33	Baird RL	115wb	11.70	86-11	On Velvet1152¼Kissable115¾Aunt Jinny115no	Drifted out	12
25May50- 6Det	hy 5f	:234 :502 1:041	ⒻCurtain Up 6.2k	8 5 56¼ 66½ 64¼ 410	Combest J	110wb	*1.70e	- -	Sweet Pick1104Copperstone1142½Rule-One1143½	Raced wide	8
19May50- 4CD	fst 5f	:23 :462 :591	ⒻMd Sp Wt	1 2 1½ 1hd 2hd 21¼	Gonzalez MN	115wb	8.40	96-09	Miss Mim Jr1151¼Aunt Jinny1152½Sweet Pick1153¼	Gave way	12
26Apr50- 1Kee	fst *4f	:23 :471	ⒻMd Sp Wt	5 11 1112 119¼ 98¼	Gonzalez MN	115wb	4.50f	84-11	MyMom115nkSweetPick1151½DoubleWing115nk	Raced greenly	12

Barbizon

dkb. c. 1954, by Polynesian (Unbreakable)–Good Blood, by Bull Lea — **Lifetime record: 21 7 4 2 $199,460**

Own.– W.L. Jones Jr
Br.– Calumet Farm (Ky)
Tr.– M. Jolley

17Jan58- 7Hia	fst 6f	:222 :453 1:102 3↑	Royal Poinciana H 25k	13 13 128 108¾ 1012 128½	Martin B	119 w	10.20	84-16	Encore115¾Iron Liege124nkSonny Dan118¾	Broke tardily	13
1Jan58- 7TrP	fst 6f	:22 :443 1:093 3↑	New Year's H 11k	4 8 77 77½ 66½ 43¾	Martin B	120 w	8.95	93-12	Pine Echo119½Sonny Dan1201Missile1162¼	Best stride late	8
	Previously owned by Calumet Farm;previously trained by H.A. Jones										
29Oct57- 6GS	fst 6f	:22 :45 1:102	Alw 5500	6 5 68¼ 46 3½ 2½	Hartack W	122 w	*.90	91-16	Jet Colonel122½Barbizon1222½Joe Price122nk	No excuse	8
18Oct57- 6GS	sly 6f	:222 :453 1:11	Alw 5500	5 6 68 42½ 32 22	Hartack W	122 w	*.60	87-22	Irish Whistler1102Barbizon122½Incaseofire1192½	Hung	7
12Oct57- 4GS	fst 6f	:22 :451 1:102 3↑	Alw 5000	4 7 63 41½ 3nk 12	Cook WM	114 w	*1.70	92-11	Barbizon1142Flight History124½Polly's Jet1141¼	Drew out	7
13Jly57- 8AP	sl 1	:224 :453 1:102 1:363	Arl Classic 151k	7 7 711 79¼ 67¼ 69	Erb D	120 w	*.70e	80-20	Clem1171¾Iron Liege1231¾Mantu117hd	Appeared in poor form	7
29Jun57- 8AP	gd 7f	:23 :452 1:112 1:243	L Armour Mem 22k	2 7 52 63¾ 77¼ 88	Martin RJ	120wb	*1.50e	79-17	Iron Liege126hdGreek Game1232Manteau120no	No mishap	8
20Jun57- 6AP	fst 6f	:222 :443 1:094	Alw 10000	3 3 46 36 33 31½	Hartack W	123wb	3.10	93-09	GreekGame1261¼JetColonel117nkBarbizon1238	Closing fast	4
8Jun57- 7Del	sly 1⅛	:464 1:12 1:383 1:513	Leonard Richards 50k	9 5 42½ 711 77¾ 57¼	Hartack W	119wb	*2.30	75-23	Lucky Dip119nkField of Honor1142Gama1141	No mishaps	9
1Jun57- 7Del	fst 1 1/16	:23 :462 1:111 1:443	Kent 35k	1 1 2½ 32 57 816	Gorman D	126wb	*1.80	72-16	LuckyDip1141¼Inswept120½Assmblymn1124	Early speed,tired	10
25May57- 7GS	fst 1⅛	:462 1:103 1:352 1:48	Jersey 62k	6 9 97¾ 87¾ 911 912	Scurlock O	122 w	*.60e	85-12	IronLiege126noClem1188WeTrust111½	Hard urged,no factor	11

21May57- 6GS	my 1 1/16	:24 :471 1:12 1:45	Alw 10000	1 1 1½ 13 13½ 11½	Scurlock O	121 w	*.30	85-16	Barbizon1211½Gam1182WTrust11412	Taken in hand late part	4
20Mar57- 7GP	sly 1 1/16	:232 :464 1:113 1:44	Fountain of Youth 18k	6 8 75 63½ 56½ 511	Scurlock O	122 w	*.20e	79-16	Gen. Duke1191½Iron Liege1131¼Better Bee113hd	No mishap	10
13Mar57- 7GP	fst 6½f	:223 :451 1:094 1:16	Hutcheson 12k	9 3 3nk 2hd 1hd 2no	Hartack W	122 w	*.45e	99-10	JetColonl119noBrbzon1225WTrust1141¾	Just failed to hold	9
5Mar57- 6GP	fst 6f	:222 :452 1:094	Alw 6000	9 10 108¾ 97¾ 58½ 35¾	Hartack W	126 w	*1.20	90-11	JetColonel1132¾Encore1103Barbizon126no	Best stride late	11
27Oct56- 7GS	gd 1 1/16	:221 :454 1:12 1:444	Garden State 319k	15 12 98¼ 66 35 1no	Hartack W	122 w	6.60e	86-18	Barbizon122noFederal Hill122nkAmarullah1223	Just up	19
20Oct56- 6GS	fst 1 1/16	:232 :461 1:111 1:45	Alw 10000	4 5 58 33½ 21½ 2¾	Hartack W	117 w	*1.20	84-19	Federal Hill120¾Barbizon1171½Clem1226	Made bid,tiring	8
12Oct56- 6GS	fst 1	:222 :452 1:104 1:374	Alw 7500	2 6 68½ 35 1hd 11	Hartack W	117 w	1.60	95-12	Barbizon1171Prince Khaled1174Sonny Dan120hd	Easy score	8
8Oct56- 4Bel	fst 6f-WC	:224 :453 1:103	Alw 4500	3 5 63¼ 51¾ 11½	Arcaro E	119 w	*.90	86-14	Brbzon1191½PopCorn113hdBkht113½	Appeared green,drew out	11
27Sep56- 4Bel	fst 6f	:222 :454 1:12	Alw 4000	5 4 22½ 22½ 11½ 12	Arcaro E	116 w	*.75	89-13	Barbizon1162PopCorn116nkBor1133	Swerved late,easy score	5
15Sep56- 5Bel	fst 6f-WC	:222 :452 1:093	©Md Sp Wt	1 6 73¾ 32 1¾	Arcaro E	118 w	*2.15	91-10	Barbizon118¾FullStage1183½ManPowr1181½	Under hard drive	14

Battlefield

ch. c. 1948, by War Relic (Man o' War)–Dark Display, by Display

Lifetime record: 44 22 14 2 $474,727

Own.– G.D. Widener
Br.– John A. Bell Jr (Ky)
Tr.– W.F. Mulholland

14Mar53- 7GP	fst 1¼	:454 1:10 1:344 2:004	3↑ Gulf Park H 59k	9 8 55½ 32 2½ 2nk	Schmidl A	125wb	2.65	95-14	CraftyAdmiral128nkBattlefield1256Dult1141	Hung in drive	11
7Mar53- 7GP	fst 1⅛	:47 1:112 1:36 1:484	3↑ Appleton H 17k	5 6 65½ 44 3½ 1hd	Schmidl A	122wb	*1.05	100-11	Battlefield122hdGolden Gloves1081½Mandingo1061	Just up	8
21Feb53- 7Hia	fst 1¼	:462 1:103 1:363 2:024	3↑ Widener H 130k	5 4 43 31½ 11 3nk	Schmidl A	123wb	4.10	91-09	Oil Capitol114hdAlerted126hdBattlefield1231½	Held well	8
16Feb53- 6Hia	fst 1⅛	:471 1:112 1:363 1:491	4↑ Alw 6000	2 4 33½ 3½ 2hd 1hd	Schmidl A	122wb	*1.05	90-16	Battlefield122hdAlerted1222½BlinkerLight1063	Ridden out	6
12Feb53- 7Hia	fst 7f	:224 :454 1:104 1:232	4↑ Alw 4500	1 5 55 33½ 2½ 1nk	Schmidl A	124wb	*.50	93-13	Battlefield124nkPost Card1093½Corfel111nk	Ridden out	8
28Jan53- 7Hia	fst 7f	:224 :46 1:111 1:242	3↑ Palm Beach H 20k	3 11 107½ 65¾ 41¼ 2nk	Schmidl A	123wb	*2.10	88-20	OilCapitol107nkBattlefield123½NimblFox1141½	Just missed	14
24Jan53- 6Hia	my 6f	:231 :472 1:13	4↑ Alw 5000	2 1 53½ 21½ 1½ 2nk	Schmidl A	123wb	*1.20	83-32	Ken120nkBattlefield1231½Mandingo1174	Faltered	7
1Nov52- 6Jam	fst 1⅛	:484 1:13 1:374 1:501	3↑ Westchester H 56k	7 3 21 11 1½ 1no	Schmidl A	123wb	3.85	95-18	Battlefield123noTom Fool1251Alerted1251¼	Held gamely	9
18Oct52- 6Jam	fst 1⅛	:471 1:11 1:354 1:492	3↑ Grey Lag H 60k	3 5 31 1hd 2hd 2no	Schmidl A	118wb	10.05	99-16	Tom Fool119noBattlefield118nkAlerted1211¼	Sharp effort	11
11Oct52- 7GS	fst 1⅛	:464 1:113 1:372 1:503	3↑ Quaker City H 29k	1 3 36 43¼ 47½ 57¾	Arcaro E	122wb	*1.20	81-18	General Staff1172½Alerted1223Mandingo1082	Impeded	10
27Sep52- 7Bel	fst 1½	:501 1:144 2:05 2:304	3↑ Manhattan H 34k	6 1 1hd 1hd 33½ 78¾	Arcaro E	120wb	*1.70	75-16	Lone Eagle1073½Combat Boots110½One Hitter1173	Tired	8
20Sep52- 6Bel	sly 1⅛	:452 1:10 1:352 1:482	3↑ New York H 29k	4 4 32½ 31½ 2½ 1hd	Arcaro E	118wb	3.15	97-08	Battlefield118hdGeneralStff1131¼CombtBoots1093½	Driving	7
16Sep52- 5Bel	fst 6f	:231 :471 1:12	4↑ Alw 4000	8 6 42¼ 32 2hd 11½	Green B	120wb	*1.50	89-20	Battlefld1201½Mohammedan1141½Assgnmnt112hd	Drew clear	8
8Sep52- 6Aqu	fst 7f	:223 :451 1:102 1:24	3↑ Bay Shore H 17k	6 6 86 99 107½ 119½	Green B	126 w	8.55	80-20	Next Move1151First Glance111nkSquared Away1202	Outrun	12
15Aug52- 6Sar	sl 7f	:231 :463 1:12 1:253	3↑ American Legion H 9k	5 3 3½ 42 43½ 48¼	Green B	126 w	*1.70	79-25	Tea-Maker118¾FirstGlance1091½NorthernStar1196	Weakened	6
8Aug52- 6Sar	fst 6f	:232 :47 1:114	3↑ Handicap 5035	1 5 57¼ 55½ 45½ 53¼	Green B	126 w	*1.20	86-23	Squared Away1221¼Elixir1071First Glance1101	Poor start	5
30May52- 6Bel	fst 1¼	:463 1:102 1:353 2:02	3↑ Suburban H 60k	1 8 813 47 45¼ 77	Arcaro E	124 w	*1.50	83-12	One Hitter112nkCrafty Admiral1132Mameluke1161	Tired	10
17May52- 6Bel	fst 1	:23 :454 1:104 1:362	3↑ Metropolitan H 36k	11 8 64¼ 5¾ 12 2½	Scurlock O	125 w	*1.50	91-14	Mameluke112½Battlefield1251½One Hitter1131	Weakened	11
6May52- 6Bel	fst 6f	:221 :454 1:10	3↑ Handicap 6055	8 7 65¾ 55½ 2½ 2½	Arcaro E	126 w	*1.40	98-14	FirstGlance109½Bttlfld1262½NorthrnStr1142½	Began slowly	8
8Sep51- 6Aqu	fst 1⅛	:474 1:123 1:371 1:502	Discovery H 22k	1 4 43 21 2hd 2hd	Arcaro E	126 w	*.90	93-17	Alerted114hdBattlefield1263½Vulcania1082	Wide,missed	8
18Aug51- 6Sar	gd 1¼	:492 1:141 1:40 2:061	Travers 22k	1 1 3½ 1hd 1hd 1¾	Arcaro E	123 w	*.20	77-17	Battlefield123¾Yildiz1264½Big Stretch1143½	Driving	4
	Geldings not eligible										
4Aug51- 6Mth	fst 1¼	:48 1:123 1:373 2:032	Choice 28k	4 1 34½ 2hd 11 11¼	Arcaro E	126 w	*.70	89-17	Battlefield1261¼UncleMilti11815GoldnTrnd1145	Ridden out	4
21Jly51- 7AP	fst 1¼	:464 1:111 1:354 2:031	Arl Classic 81k	6 6 54½ 2hd 12 2nk	Arcaro E	123 w	*1.50	89-08	Hall of Fame120nkBattlefield1232Ruhe120nk	Just failed	13
7Jly51- 6Aqu	fst 1¼	:481 1:123 1:383 2:042	Dwyer 57k	10 5 32 1hd 1hd 1½	Arcaro E	121 w	1.60	85-16	Battlefield121½Alerted1112½Hull Down1111½	All out	10
30Jun51- 6Aqu	sly 1 1/16	:242 :481 1:122 1:433	Shevlin 22k	2 2 2hd 1hd 2hd 1no	Scurlock O	123 w	*.70	96-16	Battlefield123noAlerted11210Mully S.1122	Just up	7
16Jun51- 6Bel	fst 1½	:494 1:141 2:031 2:29	Belmont 118k	5 6 83½ 22 22 24	Arcaro E	126 w	*1.85	89-08	Counterpoint1264Battlefield1261½BattlMorn1269	No excuse	9
	Geldings not eligible										
9Jun51- 6Bel	fst 1⅛	:461 1:102 1:351 1:474	Peter Pan H 24k	3 6 66¾ 55 34 22¾	Arcaro E	123 w	*.85	99-10	Counterpoint1142¾Battlefield1232¼HallofFm113¾	No excuse	9
26May51- 6Bel	fst 1	:224 :452 1:094 1:354	Withers 29k	7 4 21 21 2hd 1hd	Arcaro E	126 w	*.70	95-12	Battlefield126hdJumbo1265Nullify1264	All out	7
	Geldings not eligible										
22May51- 5Bel	fst 6f	:223 :454 1:101	Alw 4000	2 7 1hd 1½ 11½ 11	Arcaro E	126 w	*.60	99-15	Battlefield1261Nullify1121¼General Staff1134	Handily	7
16May51- 6Bel	fst 7f	:22 :45 1:093 1:222	Swift 12k	4 4 46 22 21 21¼	Arcaro E	126 w	*.85	97-11	Jumbo1261¼Battlefield1265½Iliad1263½	No excuse	9
9Apr51- 6Jam	fst 6f	:23 :46 1:101	Alw 5000	5 4 33 22½ 31 24½	Arcaro E	123 w	*1.35	91-13	Uncle Miltie1174½Battlefield123½Nullify123nk	No excuse	7
30Sep50- 6Bel	fst 6½f-W	:22 :442 1:09 1:152	Futurity 106k	10 5 61 21 1no	Arcaro E	122wb	*.95	95-05	Battlefld122noBgStrtch1223½Rough'nTumbl122no	Ridden out	14
	Geldings not eligible										
25Sep50- 5Bel	fst 6f-WC	:223 :452 1:104	Sp Wt 5000	10 3 1hd 11 1¾	Arcaro E	118wb	*1.10	87-13	Battlefield110¾Pel Dully118½Rough 'n Tumble1182	Handily	11
26Aug50- 6Sar	fst 6½f	:231 :464 1:114 1:18	Hopeful 58k	2 4 41¼ 41¼ 1½ 11½	Guerin E	122wb	*1.30e	95-11	Battlefield1221½Battle Morn1223½Big Stretch1221	Handily	10
12Aug50- 4Sar	fst 6f	:224 :462 1:111	Sar Spl 11k	2 3 1½ 11½ 11½ 1¾	Arcaro E	122 w	*1.00	92-11	Battlefield122¾NorthernStar1222½BattleMorn1221½	Handily	6
26Jly50- 6Mth	fst 6f	:223 :453 1:104	Sapling 14k	8 1 22 2½ 1½ 11½	Arcaro E	122 w	*1.10	94-10	Battlefield1221½UncleMiltie1151LordPutnm1226	Ridden out	8
12Jly50- 6Jam	sl 6f	:231 :454 1:11	East View 50k	1 1 2hd 3nk 2hd 43	Arcaro E	122 w	*1.15	89-12	Win or Lose117½Nullify1222½Iliad119no	Weakened	9
	Awarded third purse money										
28Jun50- 6Aqu	fst 6f	:224 :461 1:104	Great American 18k	8 2 21½ 21 2½ 2hd	Arcaro E	126 w	*.70	98-15	SilverWings117hdBattlefield1265Nullify117no	Just missed	10
14Jun50- 6Aqu	fst 5½f	:223 :463 1:05	©Tremont 13k	7 2 31½ 2hd 2½ 11½	Arcaro E	126 w	*1.95	99-15	Battlefield1261½Patch1171Nullify117¾	Ridden out	10
17May50- 6Bel	fst 5f-WC	:221 :45 :572	Juvenile 15k	3 4 41 2hd 21½	Arcaro E	122 w	*.60	91-06	Liberty Rab1221½Battlefield1222Remove1191½	No excuse	9
5May50- 6Jam	my 5f	:23 :473 :594	Youthful (Div 2) 12k	8 2 2hd 2½ 1½ 11	Arcaro E	122 w	*.75	91-17	Battlefield1221Count Turf1229Liberty Rab122¾	Drew clear	10
28Apr50- 5Jam	sly 5f	:23 :473 1:003	Alw 4000	6 5 42½ 2hd 1hd 12	Arcaro E	122 w	*.75	87-18	Battlefield1222Faneli'sAlley1162PointChcot116no	Handily	6
1Mar50- 5Hia	fst 3f	:213 :324	Juvenile (Div 1) 15k	3 1 1½ 1½	Picou C	117	2.40	--	Battlefield117½FairSelf1142½KingWilson117no	Hard drive	13
21Feb50- 1Hia	fst 3f	:221 :333	Md Sp Wt	13 2 1½ 1½	Picou C	122 b	*1.30f	--	Battlefield122½Propeller122hdChallcote1223	Ridden out	14

Bayou

ch. f. 1954, by Hill Prince (Princequillo)–Bourtai, by Stimulus

Lifetime record: 32 7 8 4 $143,759

Own.– Claiborne Farm
Br.– Claiborne Farm (Ky)
Tr.– M. Jolley

14Jly58- 7AP	fst 6f	:224 :452 1:102	4↑ Alw 2750	5 2 74¾ 74¾ 44 33	Cook LC	119 w	11.00	89-13	Dark Toga1071¾Arcandy1181¼Bayou1191		8
	Came strongly final furlong										
1Feb58- 4Hia	fst 7f	:232 :464 1:12 1:243	4↑ ⒻAlw 7500	2 5 32½ 32 3nk 2½	Grant H	121 w	*1.25	86-14	Pardala113½Bayou121¾LadyElliott1123	In a bit close late	8
18Jan58- 8Hia	fst 6f	:223 :453 1:102	4↑ ⒻAlw 7500	6 8 8¼ 89 78¼ 48	Ruane J5	116 w	3.75	85-11	Beautillon1124½Amort1183Ambulnc112½	Passed tired horses	12
24Oct57- 6Kee	gd 1⅛	:463 1:111 1:361 1:491	3↑ ⒻSpinster 76k	1 4 46½ 43½ 34 45¼	Ussery R	119 w	4.40	86-12	Bornastar1232½PuckerUp1231¾Serchng1231	Well placed,hung	6
	Open to 3-, 4- and 5-year-olds										
7Oct57- 7Bel	sly 1	:231 :461 1:11 1:37	3↑ ⒻMaskette H 29k	9 3 45½ 33 2½ 1½	Ussery R	118 w	5.75	89-14	Bayou118½Rare Treat116hdPink Velvet1134	Fully extended	9
11Sep57- 7Bel	fst 1 1/16	:232 :462 1:112 1:431	ⒻGazelle H 30k	5 12 117¼ 83¾ 3nk 11½	Arcaro E	120 w	6.95	92-12	Bayou1201½EvningTime118noPinkVlvt116½	Rated,going away	13
28Aug57- 7Sar	fst 1¼	:481 1:134 1:392 2:062	ⒻAlabama 29k	1 1 41¼ 72¼ 51¾ 511	Ussery R	121 w	4.15	65-23	Here and There1133Snow White1133Outer Space1212	Tired	11
14Aug57- 7Sar	fst 7f	:224 :46 1:11 1:242	ⒻTest 23k	5 6 914 88¾ 66 44½	Ussery R	124 w	9.75	88-17	MissBlueJay1181½OuterSpace121hdSnowWhite1153	Late bid	10
27Jly57- 6Mth	fst 1⅛	:48 1:112 1:371 1:501	ⒻMth Oaks 59k	8 7 88 87½ 76¾ 64¼	Anderson P	121 w	*3.10	89-13	Romanita117noEveningTime1211MarketBaskt121nk	No excuse	10
29Jun57- 7Del	fst 1¼	:463 1:11 1:372 2:05	3↑ ⒻDelaware H 164k	3 4 49½ 66 86½ 146½	Nelson E	111 w	10.20	70-22	PrincessTuria119½PuckerUp1171LittlePache119nk	No speed	19
22Jun57- 7Bel	fst 1⅜	:484 1:131 1:381 2:163	ⒻC C A Oaks 70k	7 7 72¾ 41½ 2hd 2¾	Arcaro E	121 w	*.65	87-14	Willamette121¾Bayou1215½Woodlawn1211½	Led between calls	10

15Jun57- 7Del	fst 1⅛	:474 1:114 1:383 1:513	Ⓕ Del Oaks 51k	9 3 32½ 21 1hd	1¾	Hartack W	119 w	*.80	82-18	Bayou119¾PillowTalk1191Mrbll1134½	Drew out,clever score	9
3Jun57- 7Bel	fst 1	:223 :45 1:103 1:37	Ⓕ Acorn 36k	11 6 66¾ 1½ 11½	13	Ussery R	121 w	4.30	89-12	Bayou1213Teleran121nkHereandThere1211	Under mild urging	17
24May57- 7Jam	gd 1 1/16	:233 :464 1:12 1:452	Ⓕ Alw 7500	2 5 34½ 31 11½	12½	Ussery R	113 w	3.40	83-17	Bayou1132½Capelet1172½Willamette1111	Kept to pressure	7
25Apr57- 5Kee	fst 6f	:222 :45 1:094	Alw 3500	4 2 51¾ 41¼ 11½	17	Hartack W	115 w	2.10e	97-02	Byou1157Ezgo1204SlghtGo1141½	Drew far away,mildly urged	7
19Apr57- 6Kee	fst 7f	:224 :46 1:103 1:224	Alw 3500	7 1 31½ 75 54	47	Church K	112 w	8.80	91-06	Manteau1135BooneBlaze1201DixieDoge1201	Fell back early	10
12Feb57- 7Hia	fst 1⅛	:473 1:121 1:372 1:502	Ⓕ Alw 5000	6 5 44 41½ 24	21	Brooks S	112 w	*.85	83-18	TooTooFussy1101Bayou1126RoyalRespect1123½	Closed fast	7
26Jan57- 4Hia	fst 6f	:222 :461 1:113	Ⓕ Alw 4500	2 8 85¼ 67½ 57¼	34	Brooks S	121 w	2.55	83-14	Iberia1213½Adormidr116½Byou1212½	Found best stride late	12
19Jan57- 6Hia	fst 6f	:22 :452 1:103	Ⓕ Alw 6000	11 1 33½ 34 32	2nk	Cook LC	109 w	8.05	92-09	Jerilynn109nkBayou1092MagicSpll1092	Reached lead,necked	12
10Jan57- 6TrP	fst 6f	:222 :454 1:112	Ⓕ Alw 2700	7 5 87¼ 76½ 68	44¾	Brooks S	117 w	2.90	85-10	WorthSaving117nkSandysJoy1151GrannyAnnie1123½	Rallied	12
6Nov56- 4CD	my 6f	:231 :47 1:134	Ⓕ Md Sp Wt	1 3 33½ 32½ 2½	12¼	Brooks S	118 w	*2.20	79-20	Bayou1182¼CityBll1183½Lblch1184½	Going away under drive	12
18Oct56- 4Kee	fst 6f	:224 :46 1:111	Ⓕ Md Sp Wt	9 8 66½ 45½ 33½	26	Brooks S	116 w	1.90	88-04	Miss Fleetwood1166Bayou1162½Can't Tell1163½	Next best	12
13Oct56- 6Kee	fst *7f	1:27	Ⓕ Alcibiades 41k	1 3 21½ 49 59½	510	Broussard R	119 w	3.90e	88-11	Leallah1192½Bluebility119noNantua1194½	Failed to stay	6
7Aug56- 3Was	fst 6f	:223 :462 1:124	Ⓕ Md Sp Wt	3 1 44½ 37 35	22	Brooks S	116wb	2.40	79-17	Susette1162Bayou1162ScotchButy116½	Strong stretch rally	12
31Jly56- 1Was	fst 5½f	:223 :453 :584 1:05	Ⓕ Md Sp Wt	6 2 31½ 45 45	23	Brooks S	116wb	3.00	90-12	PontchieGal1163Bayou116hdStymieDir1112¼	Came again late	12
18Jly56- 3AP	fst 5½f	:232 :472 :594 1:062	Ⓕ Md Sp Wt	5 2 62¾ 44½ 45	43¼	Brooks S	118wb	4.00	83-14	Bluebility118hdWherewuzuat118noTherapy1183¼	Went well	12
12Jly56- 4AP	fst 5½f	:23 :46 :59 1:053	Ⓕ Md Sp Wt	3 2 31½ 34 37½	35	Brooks S	116wb	2.10	85-13	Alabama Charm1162½Marnerleen1162½Bayou1162¼	No excuse	12
28Jun56- 1AP	fst 5½f	:232 :48 1:002 1:07	Ⓕ Md Sp Wt	2 2 1hd 1hd 2hd	2nk	Brooks S	118wb	4.70	83-11	SlaveDancer118nkBayou1181¼PontchiGl1183¼	Very sharp try	12
14Jun56- 4Was	fst 5f	:223 :47 1:002	Ⓕ Md Sp Wt	11 10 66½ 54½ 52¼	41	Brooks S	118wb	3.70	83-14	Jestress118½Ray's Delight118nkPontchie Gal113nk	Rallied	12
21May56- 3Was	fst 5f	:222 :454 :584	Ⓕ Md Sp Wt	3 3 32½ 34½ 47½	410¼	Brooks S	118 w	4.80	82-15	SpringTune1186DaisyCrockett1183½PrincessEllen118¾	Tired	10
28Apr56- 3CD	fst 4½f	:23 :46 :533	Ⓕ Md Sp Wt	12 9 1012 1012	89¾	Brooks S	117 w	3.00	82-08	Piccalilli1172½DuntreathGift1172JenO'F1172½	Forced wide	12
14Apr56- 4Kee	sly *4f	:502	Ⓕ Alw 3500	6 4 65½ 55	35	Brooks S	112 w	3.70	90-05	Lori-El1135Rdruth118hdByou1121	Hard urged,raced greenly	7

Bed o' Roses

b. f. 1947, by Rosemont (The Porter)–Good Thing, by Discovery — **Lifetime record: 46 18 8 6 $383,925**

Own.– Alfred G. Vanderbilt
Br.– Alfred G. Vanderbilt (Cal)
Tr.– W.C. Winfrey

1Mar52- 7SA	my 1¼	:452 1:104 1:354 2:01	3↑ S Anita H 141k	5 8 88 87¼ 67¾	48	Guerin E	114wb	4.30e	87-16	D Intnt1111Mch1154½BFlt1142½	Improved position,no menace	15
16Feb52- 7SA	fst 1⅛	:463 1:104 1:364 1:494	3↑ San Antonio H 29k	2 9 78 88¼ 84¼	31	Shoemaker W	120wb	*2.30	91-16	Phil D.117noIntent1181Bed o' Roses1201	Slow start	11
26Jan52- 7SA	fst 1⅛	:47 1:114 1:381 1:512	3↑ Ⓕ S Margarita H 62k	5 8 75¾ 42½ 22	11	Shoemaker W	129wb	*.90e	84-19	Bed o' Roses1291Next Move1301½Toto105½	Mild urging	14
10Nov51- 6Jam	fst 1 3/16	:474 1:121 1:374 1:564	3↑ Butler H 60k	1 7 97¼ 97¾ 51¾	41¾	Guerin E	115wb	3.40	90-18	OilCapitol1081½ThreeRings114hdCountyDelight124nk	Hung	12
6Nov51- 6Jam	fst 1 1/16	:25 :484 1:133 1:443	3↑ Ⓕ Comely H 28k	7 8 88 41¾ 1½	11½	Guerin E	127wb	*1.25	89-19	Bed o' Roses1271½Nothirdchance1121¾Regal1112	Driving	8
27Oct51- 6Jam	fst 1⅛	:464 1:11 1:361 1:491	3↑ Westchester H 30k	11 9 811 89¾ 610	37¼	Guerin E	116wb	3.75	95-15	BryanG.1175½CountyDelight1241¾Bedo'Ross1161	Forced wide	11
20Oct51- 7GS	fst 1 1/16	:231 :462 1:113 1:433	3↑ Ⓕ Vineland H 31k	3 8 87¼ 72¾ 21½	13½	Guerin E	126wb	*2.40	92-15	Bed o' Roses1263½Valadium109noDixie Flyer107½	Easily	15
10Oct51- 6Bel	fst 1½	:483 1:132 2:04 2:301	3↑ Ⓕ Ladies H 30k	13 14 1314 85¼ 32½	21¼	Guerin E	126wb	5.35	86-15	Marta1111¼Bed o' Roses1263½Kiss Me Kate120½	Good effort	14
22Sep51- 6Aqu	fst 1⅛	:482 1:122 1:382 1:52	3↑ Ⓕ Beldame 67k	4 5 62¾ 42 2hd	22	Guerin E	124wb	6.65	83-14	ThelmaBurger1102Bdo'Roses124½KssMKt119nk	Wide,faltered	14
14Sep51- 6Aqu	fst 1 1/16	:241 :474 1:13 1:444	3↑ Ⓕ Alw 5000	6 6 616 715 712	712	Guerin E	118wb	*1.60	78-16	Red Camelia1101¼Vulcania1125Wistful121hd	Dull effort	7
27Aug51- 5Sar	fst 6f	:23 :464 1:12	4↑ Alw 3500	5 1 33 33½ 1½	1¾	Guerin E	119wb	*1.10	88-22	Bed o' Roses119¾Early Heath1091All at Once1243	Easily	6
3Feb51- 7SA	fst 1¼	:451 1:093 1:351 2:002	Maturity 205k	2 6 57½ 32½ 2½	31¾	Combest N	110wb	*.90e	96-08	GreatCircle1151¾Lotowhit116hdBdo'Ross1103½	Blocked,lame	11
20Jan51- 7SA	fst 1⅛	:461 1:11 1:361 1:483	3↑ Ⓕ S Margarita H 60k	1 8 79½ 56 44	32¼	Combest N	125wb	*.55e	96-16	SpecialTouch1141Bewitch1221¼Bedo'Roses1251½	Closed fast	8
29Dec50- 7SA	fst 7f	:221 :45 1:092 1:213	3↑ Ⓕ Anita Chiquita H 15k	7 6 66½ 45 21	11	Guerin E	123wb	1.45	101-07	Bedo'Roses1231SpecialTouch1213½SomeGal1071½	Ridden out	8
16Dec50- 7Hol	fst 1⅛	:462 1:103 1:36 1:483	3↑ Sunset H 58k	4 7 613 76¼ 54½	63	Combest N	110wb	3.90e	95-12	HillPrince128¾NextMove1141½GreatCircle109nk	Late foot	10
9Dec50- 6Hol	fst 1	:222 :453 1:103 1:353	3↑ Handicap 5000	8 6 66¼ 42 1½	12½	Guerin E	118wb	2.60e	99-09	Bed o' Roses1182½Stone Age1101¼Manyunk1201	Drew out	8
2Dec50- 7Hol	fst 1⅛	:47 1:111 1:362 1:492	3↑ Ⓕ Vanity H 30k	6 8 89¾ 76¾ 45	65¼	Combest N	123wb	*.50e	89-11	Next Move1282¼Bewitch1241Wistful125½	Hung	9
25Nov50- 6Hol	fst 7f	:222 :45 1:092 1:22	3↑ Handicap 7500	9 8 96½ 74½ 54½	52¾	Guerin E	120wb	*.70e	96-07	Manyunk115nkChutney1081½Stone Age112½	Slow start	9
27Sep50- 6Bel	fst 1⅝	:473 1:362 2:023 2:423	Lawrence Realizatn 22k	4 6 69 31 13	14½	Combest N	107wb	3.20	91-12	Bed o' Roses1074½Greek Ship1183Theory1101¼	Easily	7
16Sep50- 6Aqu	fst 1⅛	:473 1:12 1:37 1:501	3↑ Ⓕ Beldame H 66k	7 10 912 67 712	88¼	Guerin E	119 w	*1.20e	86-15	Next Move1162¼September1081Wistful1252¼	Dull effort	12
11Sep50- 6Aqu	sly 6f	:234 :473 1:12	3↑ Ⓕ Alw 4000	4 5 56¼ 54 2hd	12½	Guerin E	118 w	*1.25	92-19	Bed o' Roses1182½Leading Home108nkBaby Comet1034	Easily	5
12Aug50- 6Sar	fst 1¼	:473 1:121 1:374 2:03	Travers 23k	5 2 47 34 31	23	Combest N	109 w	*1.35	90-11	Lights Up1103Bed o' Roses1093Passemson1101	Went well	9
15Jly50- 7AP	fst 1¼	:47 1:112 1:353 2:014	Arl Classic 77k	4 8 67¼ 31½ 2hd	2no	Combest N	110 w	7.40	96-07	Greek Song120noBed o' Roses1101¼Your Host1268	Game try	10
3Jly50- 6Aqu	fst 1 1/16	:232 :47 1:12 1:433	Ⓕ Gazelle 22k	4 6 44½ 22 22	21	Scurlock O	116 w	*.25e	95-11	Next Move1211Bed o' Roses1165Renew112¾	In hand	7
27Jun50- 5Aqu	fst 7f	:241 :482 1:122 1:25	Ⓕ Alw 4000	3 3 33½ 33½ 11	11¼	Guerin E	121 w	*.50	87-16	Bedo'Roses1211¼MissDegree108noOurPatrice1081½	Easily	4
8Nov49- 6Jam	fst 1 1/16	:24 :47 1:12 1:454	Ⓕ Demoiselle 56k	5 7 79 45 2hd	11½	Guerin E	116 w	*.50e	84-19	Bedo'Roses1161½NextMove1195RarePerfume1166	Ridden out	12
29Oct49- 6Pim	my 1 1/16	:231 :47 1:122 1:454	Ⓕ Marguerite 36k	4 5 59 22 2½	14	Guerin E	116 w	*.40	81-20	Bed o' Roses1164Striking1192½Fais Do Do1194	Easily	7
22Oct49- 6Lrl	fst 1 1/16	:23 :473 1:133 1:454	Ⓕ Selima 52k	8 4 32 3nk 13	17	Guerin E	116 w	*.40	88-19	Bed o' Roses1167Striking1191Busanda1191¼	Easily	9
17Oct49- 6Lrl	fst 1 1/16	:231 :474 1:141 1:452	Ⓕ Alw 3500	2 3 21½ 2½ 11	13	Guerin E	122 w	1.90	90-23	Bed o' Roses1223Striking1163½Flying Mane10610	Easily	7
1Oct49- 5Bel	fst 6½f-W	:22 :442 1:09 1:153	Futurity 112k	2 16 1611 1516	117½	Woodhouse H	119 w	8.05e	86-06	Guillotine122¾Theory1222The Diver1222½	Off slowly	17
	Geldings not eligible											
24Sep49- 4Bel	fst 6f-WC	:222 :454 1:111	Ⓕ Matron 52k	3 8 75 3½	1½	Guerin E	119 w	3.75	85-15	Bed o' Roses119½Fais Do Do119nkStriking1194	Driving	9
20Sep49- 5Bel	fst 5½f-W	:23 :462 1:06	Ⓕ Alw 4000	5 9 32½ 33½	3hd	Scurlock O	122 w	1.80e	84-16	Fais Do Do114noNext Move116hdBed o' Roses1223	Game try	13
16Aug49- 6Sar	fst 6f	:224 :453 1:112	Ⓕ Spinaway 19k	1 6 32 31½ 3½	41½	Guerin E	119wb	10.05	89-13	SundayEvening1111Strikng115nkFsDoDo111nk	Dwelt at start	6
10Aug49- 6Sar	fst 5½f	:222 :454 1:052	Ⓕ Schuylerville 10k	1 9 95¾ 84½ 53¼	65	Guerin E	122wb	15.00	85-11	Striking1152½Sunday Evening112½Nazma115½	Off slowly	12
23Jly49- 5Det	fst 6f	:224 :461 1:122	Ⓕ Tomboy 32k	5 7 22½ 43½ 44½	54¾	Gorman D	121wb	*2.10	81-15	Here'sHoping1102½HighFreqncy1152DinhRos109nk	Weakened	12
9Jly49- 6AP	my 6f	:224 :464 1:153	Ⓕ Arl Lassie 56k	12 12 96¾ 76¼ 48	3½	Jessop JD	119wb	6.00	67-34	DuchessPeg119hdBabyComet119½Bdo'Ross1196	Strong finish	13
4Jly49- 6Mth	fst 5½f	:23 :482 1:002 1:072	Ⓕ Colleen (Div 2) 12k	1 2 2hd 11 12	12½	Guerin E	119wb	*1.00	87-14	Bedo'Roses1192½SickleFlight1122½WiseCutie1142	Easily	9
18Jun49- 5Aqu	fst 5½f	:232 :47 1:07	Ⓕ Astoria 13k	2 8 54 45½ 24	24½	Guerin E	122wb	*1.35	84-24	BabyComet1194½Bedo'Roses1222½Dentifrice114nk	Went well	10
4Jun49- 5Del	fst 5f	:222 :462 :583	Ⓕ P Drmmnd (Div 2) 13k	2 4 32 31½ 21½	21¾	Gilbert J	122wb	*.45	95-13	Bridal Shower1131¾Bed o' Roses1228Jaleen1102	No excuse	9
28May49- 5GS	fst 5f	:223 :47 :592	Ⓕ Rancocas 14k	2 3 32½ 32 32½	1nk	Gilbert J	122wb	*1.40	96-12	Bed o' Roses122nkChloe1173½Bridal Shower117no	Drew out	13
25May49- 6Bel	fst 5f-WC	:23 :462 :592	Ⓕ Nat'l Stallion 24k	3 1 15 16	13	Guerin E	119wb	*.85	83-20	Bedo'Roses1193SetAside119½ThreeandTwo114	Ridden out	4
20May49- 5Bel	fst 5f-WC	:222 :453 :582	Ⓕ Alw 4000	2 6 1½ 51¾ 43	42¼	Guerin E	115 w	2.25	86-07	Wise Cutie115¾Puff119hdRare Perfume1151½	No mishap	10
7May49- 4Bel	fst 4½f-W	:214 :451 :512	Ⓕ Fashion 13k	6 1 33 33	2hd	Guerin E	115 w	*1.70	97-09	RarePerfume110hdBdo'Ross115nkHghFrquncy1143	Just missed	7
29Apr49- 3Jam	fst 5f	:232 :472 1:003	Ⓕ Md Sp Wt	6 6 11½ 13 14	13	Guerin E	116 w	*1.95	87-16	Bedo'Roses1163RunningStory1161Stefanella116nk	In hand	12
20Apr49- 6Jam	fst 5f	:223 :47 1:00	Ⓕ Rosedale 13k	11 11 77¾ 510 512	812	Guerin E	115 w	8.75	78-17	Baby Comet1143½Rare Perfume1106Abbie Co114hd	Weakened	11
	Previously trained by L. McCoy											
16Feb49- 1SA	fst 3f	:221 :333	Ⓕ Md Sp Wt	6 12 106¾	56½	Gilbert J	115 w	*1.25	- -	Prince'sBd1152½Bullrmmbr1151½RoylSnt115½	Close quarters	13

Berseem

dkb. c. 1950, by Bernborough (Emborough)–Little Priss, by Sweep All
Own.– A. Hirschberg
Br.– Charles T. Fisher (Ky)
Tr.– R. Cornell

Lifetime record: 60 21 11 5 $189,525

Date	Trk	Cond/Dist	Fractions	Race	Calls	Jockey	Wt	Odds	Spd	Top finishers	Comment	Fld
31May56- 7Hol	fst 6f		:221 :45 :57 1:09	4↑ Handicap 12000	2 2 11 11½ 2½ 42¼	Shoemaker W	122wb	*.90	97-09	Scent118hdOne Ton Tony1142Karim115hd		8
	Saved ground,weakened											
12May56- 4Hol	fst 6f		:222 :45 :57 1:092	4↑ Alw 7500	2 4 11½ 12 11½ 21½	Shoemaker W	117wb	*.65	95-11	Spring Count1121½Berseem1174½Poona II117no		5
	Rushed to front,outrun late											
12Sep55- 7BM	fst 6f		:221 :45 1:094	3↑ Autumn H 11k	4 1 11¼ 11½ 11½ 1¾	Longden J	126wb	2.10	98-14	Berseem126¾MisterGus124nkTheCharactr111¾	Cleverly rated	6
25Jly55- 7Hol	fst 6f		:22 :443 :564 1:091	3↑ Los Angeles H 28k	8 3 31 3nk 1hd 42½	Shoemaker W	126wb	*1.55	95-10	Karim112¾History Book1101¼The Character109½	Weakened	9
25Jun55- 7Hol	fst 1 1/16		:224 :452 1:093 1:404	3↑ Inglewood H 27k	7 3 11 1hd 42 45	Longden J	118wb	6.70	93-06	Determine124hdMisterGus114½Aldon1174½	Set pace,gave way	7
18Jun55- 7Hol	fst 7f		:214 :44 1:082 1:211	3↑ Lakes &Flowers H 28k	8 1 12 14 13 21¾	Shoemaker W	128wb	*1.65	92-09	Porterhouse1161¾Bersem126noAldon119no	Could not hold on	10
13May55- 7Hol	fst 6f		:22 :444 1:09	3↑ Hol Premiere H 28k	7 4 51¾ 31 22 22½	Shoemaker W	128wb	*.95	98-11	El Drag1122½Berseem128½Porterhouse1191	Finished gamely	9
9Mar55- 7SA	fst 1 1/16		:233 :454 1:10 1:42	3↑ S Barbara H 28k	6 1 11 12 12 11½	Longden J	120wb	3.10	94-12	Berseem1201½Joe Jones1174Dawn Lark107½	Going away	10
2Mar55- 7SA	fst 7f		:22 :442 1:091 1:221	3↑ C J Fitzgerald H 22k	6 2 2½ 1½ 11 2hd	Shoemaker W	130wb	*.85	92-13	Karim114hdBerseem130hdFabulist1104¾	Barely missed	7
22Feb55- 5SA	fst 6f		:221 :443 1:091	3↑ Handicap 7500	1 2 1½ 1½ 11 13½	Shoemaker W	128wb	2.35	99-12	Berseem1283½Karim114noHour Regards1192¾	Drew clear	6
12Feb55- 5SA	fst 6f		:222 :444 1:09	4↑ Handicap 6000	1 4 2hd 1hd 1hd 11½	Shoemaker W	125wb	*.70	100-08	Bersm1251½OneTonTony1084½DonMcCoy1103½	Under urging	8
2Feb55- 7SA	fst 7f		:222 :452 1:101 1:222	3↑ San Carlos H 23k	11 2 2½ 32½ 1113 1112	Westrope J	122wb	3.45	79-16	Porterhouse115¾Imbros1301¾Encono1142	Stopped badly	11
28Dec54- 7SA	fst 6f		:22 :442 1:09	3↑ Palos Verdes H 23k	7 2 32 32 32½ 2¾	Shoemaker W	124wb	*1.85	99-08	Imbros128¾Berseem1241¾Hour Regards110no	Game try	13
1Nov54- 7GG	fst 6f		:214 :443 1:09	3↑ Handicap 5000	3 2 31 21½ 21 11¾	Shoemaker W	122wb	1.30	96-15	Berseem1221¾LeftyJms1062¾Imbros1261½	Drew clear handily	5
25Sep54- 8Tan	fst 6f		:223 :452 1:094	3↑ Penninsula H 16k	7 1 11½ 13 1hd 1nk	Longden J	124wb	*1.20	102-08	Berseem124nkDuke's Lea1152½Stranglehold1263½	Hard drive	7
9Sep54-11Sac	fst 1 1/16		:234 :464 1:112 1:422	3↑ Governor's H 16k	2 2 11½ 13 14 14	Shoemaker W	127wb	*.50	100-08	Berseem1274Scotch Port107hdSilverado1192½	Drew out	5
2Sep54-10Sac	fst 1 70		:224 :454 1:111 1:424	3↑ Handicap 5620	3 3 1½ 14 14 22	Phillippi J	125wb	*.45	89-11	Silver Ado1142Berseem1252½Chanlea1133	Gave way	7
27Aug54- 7Dmr	fst 6f		:221 :45 1:092	3↑ Handicap 7500	4 3 2½ 13 12 12½	Shoemaker W	120wb	*1.15	99-09	Berseem1202½Big Noise110¾Gesticulator108¾	Won handily	6
	Previously trained by F.E. Childs											
19Jun54- 7Hol	fst 7f		:214 :441 1:083 1:211	3↑ Lakes &Flowers H 28k	3 7 75½ 74¾ 77½ 98½	Harmatz W	110wb	8.35	92-06	Curragh King107¾Imbros1283By Zeus1153	No factor	10
12Jun54- 7Hol	fst 1 1/16		:224 :453 1:093 1:41	3↑ Californian 121k	6 6 56½ 54½ 49 48¾	Harmatz W	114wb	35.20	94-06	Imbros1181Determine1151¾High Scud1146	Wide	9
26May54- 7Hol	fst 7f		:222 :444 1:091 1:213	3↑ Handicap 15000	5 3 32 31 43 44¼	Scurlock O	114wb	6.60	95-10	High Scud109½Kingly110nkImbros1303½	Held well	7
14May54- 7Hol	fst 6f		:22 :45 :571 1:091	3↑ Hol Premiere H 27k	5 5 63¾ 33 43½ 44¾	Scurlock O	119wb	6.85	95-00	Stranglehold115¾Imbros1323½Big Noise110½	Evenly	7
8May54- 8BM	fst 6f		:214 :442 1:093	3↑ Children's Hospital H 28k	6 2 46 45½ 74¾ 73¾	Harmatz W	122wb	*2.10	95-10	Kingly109½Stranglehold1162¼GoldenAbby109½	Flattened out	9
1May54- 8BM	fst 1⅛		:462 1:104 1:354 1:483	3↑ W P Kyne H 100k	5 2 31½ 63¾ 89½ 79¼	Harmatz W	118wb	7.90	93-10	Imbros127½Fleet Bird1214Trusting109hd	Gave way after 5f	12
24Apr54- 8BM	fst 1		:224 :451 1:094 1:352	3↑ GJ Knight H 23k	8 6 43½ 33½ 47 66½	Harmatz W	121wb	5.30	94-09	Imbros1242½Stranglehold111¾Correspondent113hd	Gave way	11
17Apr54- 7BM	fst 1		:232 :463 1:111 1:354	3↑ Handicap 7500	1 2 31½ 2½ 2½ 1no	Harmatz W	118wb	3.25	99-09	Berseem118noImbros1233½High Scud112¾	Driving	6
27Mar54- 8BM	gd 1 1/16		:233 :471 1:113 1:434	3↑ Bay Meadows H 28k	2 3 32½ 3nk 43 44	Harmatz W	121wb	*1.30	85-18	Dcort'd113noCyclotron1171½Southrlngton1112½	Saved ground	8
3Mar54- 7SA	fst 7f		:221 :45 1:091 1:214	3↑ C J Fitzgerald H 22k	2 5 32 12 14 13½	Harmatz W	123wb	5.65	96-10	Berseem1233½Woodchck1221¼Joe Jones1172½		7
	Saved ground,ridden out											
27Feb54- 7SA	fst 1¼		:453 1:094 1:343 2:003	3↑ S Anita H 140k	4 7 118 1616 1625 1421	Arcaro E	115wb	7.80	76-06	Rejectd1181¼Imbros1202¾Cyclotron1161¾	Taken up 1st turn	17
20Feb54- 6SA	fst 1 1/16		:231 :462 1:102 1:421	4↑ Handicap 10000	7 5 53½ 32 1½ 1no	Harmatz W	114wb	6.50	97-06	Bersem114noCyclotron1152½Lffngo1113	Bore out final turn	9
12Feb54- 7SA	fst 6f		:222 :451 1:092	3↑ Lincoln's Bday H 22k	8 3 73¾ 74¾ 77 42¾	Longden J	120wb	3.60	95-09	Imbros1281Woodchuck122nkCyclotron1211½	Forced wide	8
4Feb54- 7SA	fst 6f		:221 :451 1:09	3↑ Handicap 7500	1 6 42½ 42¼ 31 31½	Shoemaker W	118wb	*1.55	98-07	Imbros1241½Hill Gail120nkBerseem1183½	Broke slowly	6
2Jan54- 7SA	fst 7f		:224 :45 1:084 1:203	Malibu Sequet 28k	5 2 2½ 1hd 1hd 2no	Shoemaker W	114wb	*1.45	102-06	Imbros118noBerseem1144½Joe Jones1151	Just missed	7
29Dec53- 7SA	fst 6f		:222 :443 1:09	Alw 10000	1 9 1½ 12 13 12½	Shoemaker W	114wb	*1.70	100-07	Berseem1142½Ali's Gem1222Chanlea118hd	Handily	11
12Dec53- 9BM	fst 1		:224 :454 1:101 1:362	Children's Hospital H 16k	1 4 43½ 3nk 11½ 11	Harmatz W	120wb	5.00	95-08	Berseem1201Golden Abbey113noResistance1111½	Driving	6
26Nov53- 9BM	sl 6f		:224 :46 1:103	San Jose H 11k	7 1 52¼ 31 1hd 22	Harmatz W	120 w	4.55	92-18	Imbros1222Berseem1203Golden Abbey110no	Weakened	8
23Oct53- 7GG	fst 1 1/16		:231 :461 1:101 1:421	Handicap 3500	3 3 2hd 11½ 15 12¼	Shoemaker W	118wb	2.15	94-14	Berseem1182¼Postillion107noSix Fifteen114nk	Handily	7
17Oct53- 8GG	fst 1 1/16		:224 :454 1:10 1:421	Oakland H 29k	3 1 11 2hd 33½ 56	Shoemaker W	116wb	5.20e	88-12	Rejected116nkHistory Book1115Golden Abbey111½	Gave way	14
10Oct53- 8GG	gd 1		:23 :46 1:104 1:362	3↑ GG Mile H 28k	4 1 11 87¾ 813 821	Pearson B	111wb	14.70	65-20	[D]Fleet Bird1221¼Goose Khal1251¾High Scud1134	Quit	8
28Sep53- 7GG	fst 6f		:222 :444 1:084	3↑ Handicap 6000	3 1 2hd 1½ 13 2nk	York R	113wb	1.55	97-13	Cyclotron119nkBerseem1132½Ali's Gem116nk	Just failed	6
19Sep53- 8GG	fst 6f		:214 :442 1:084	Berkley H 17k	4 3 2½ 2½ 11½ 11½	Shoemaker W	117wb	*.60	97-09	Berseem1171½Karim1132¾Six Fifteen1131¾	Ridden out	8
10Sep53- 7Dmr	fst 1		:231 :462 1:11 1:362	[R]Adios H 11k	4 2 2hd 12 12 12¼	Shoemaker W	115wb	*1.15	94-12	Berseem1152¼Last Wave1081¾Karim1173½	Driving	6
2Sep53- 7Dmr	fst 1		:231 :462 1:103 1:36	Handicap 7500	6 3 41 43¼ 64¼ 64¾	Glisson G	118wb	5.85	91-11	OverandUndr110½SmartBarbara1182¼Krm114nk	Wide,weakened	6
	Previously owned by Dixiana;previously trained by J.C. Hodgins											
11Jly53- 7AP	fst 1		:222 :451 1:084 1:344	Handicap 7500	2 5 41½ 3nk 22 3½	Arcaro E	114wb	4.70	97-06	Precious Stone107½Dr.Stanley113hdBerseem1141	Held well	9
4Jly53- 7AP	fst 7f		:221 :45 1:093 1:22	W Wright Mem 30k	2 9 137 1415 1218 1215	Heckmann J	116 w	8.90e	85-06	Van Crosby1163Sir Mango1205Platan116½	No factor	18
26Jun53- 7AP	gd 6f		:223 :454 1:111	3↑ Alw 5000	5 6 54 55 45 34¾	Erb D	118 w	4.60	85-18	Van Crosby1183½Blaze1101¼Berseem1183	Driving	7
30May53- 7Haw	fst 1⅛		:473 1:122 1:382 1:521	Peabody Mem 57k	5 3 32½ 23 23 65	Heckmann J	121 w	6.50e	80-16	Royal Bay Gem1261Platan121¾Sir Mango1231	Bid,tired	10
2May53- 6CD	fst 7f		:224 :451 1:101 1:231	Alw 6000	7 5 56½ 33½ 2hd 11	Arcaro E	115 w	*1.50	97-09	Berseem1151Platan1153Sir Mango1156		8
28Apr53- 7CD	fst 1		:224 :452 1:101 1:36	Derby Trial 15k	9 7 78 57½ 86 711	Arcaro E	114 w	*2.70e	86-14	Dark Star1154Money Broker1182¾Spy Defense112no	Wide	14
11Apr53- 5Kee	fst 6f		:23 :464 1:12	Alw 3250	8 1 74¼ 31½ 12 14	Arcaro E	117 w	*.60	92-10	Berseem1174Jim Brier1112¼Blenriam114¾	Going away	9
11Feb53- 5FG	fst 6f		:224 :463 1:122	Alw 2500	2 4 33 21½ 11 11	Keene H	116 w	*1.40	91-22	Berseem1161Paytu1196Star Request1131	Driving	9
1Nov52- 6CD	fst 1		:224 :46 1:11 1:372	Ky Jockey Club 47k	5 2 22½ 34 34½ 35½	Heckmann J	116 w	1.30e	84-15	Straight Face1224½Spy Defense1161Berseem1165	Weakened	7
25Oct52- 4Kee	fst 6f		:224 :463 1:112	Alw 3000	8 1 32½ 32 11½ 18	Heckmann J	120 w	*1.70	95-11	Berseem1208Uncle Tom114noBull Skin120nk	Easily	8
22Sep52- 5Haw	fst 6f		:224 :454 1:114	©Alw 4000	4 5 53½ 23 22 22½	Erb D	115 w	*.90	86-17	Scriptwriter1152½Berseem1155New Stream1121¼	Raced wide	9
10Sep52- 1Haw	fst 6f		:223 :454 1:11	©Md Sp Wt	9 5 21 11½ 14 18	Erb D	118 w	*2.30	94-07	Berseem1188Coherence118¾Blended1182	In hand	12
20Aug52- 1Was	gd 6f		:23 :472 1:134	©Md Alw 3500	7 2 45 36½ 38 613	Erb D	118 w	*1.50	64-24	American Pluck118hdRico Vino1188Pipe of Peace1181¾	Quit	10
6Aug52- 1Was	fst 5½f		:224 :462 :583 1:044	©Md Sp Wt	4 3 63½ 22 23 23	Brooks S	118 w	4.30	91-12	Nero Fiddled1183Berseem1181Ricacho1183	Held well	12
30Jly52- 1Was	fst 5½f		:224 :453 :572 1:041	©Md Sp Wt	1 2 44 46 35½ 34	Brooks S	118 w	5.30	93-06	Van Crosby1134Nero Fiddled118hdBerseem1182½	No rally	12
23Jly52- 3AP	hy 5½f		:233 :482 1:022 1:092	©Md Sp Wt	8 6 66¾ 69½ 914 916	Brooks S	118 w	*2.30	57-28	Preposterous118½VanCrosby1183½Sampan1182	Disliked going	10
12Jly52- 1AP	fst 5½f		:224 :464 :584 1:054	Md Sp Wt	3 8 64¼ 75¼ 77¾ 54¾	Brooks S	118 w	5.00	86-16	Bob Away118noTime to Khal1083Hardhack118½	No mishap	10

Blue Sparkler

ch. f. 1952, by Knave High (Jack High)–Blue Tiara, by Opera Hat **Lifetime record: 22 11 7 0 $198,625**
Own.– Woodland Farm
Br.– Woodland Farm (NJ)
Tr.– Harry Wells

22Sep56- 7Bel fst 1⅛ :452 1:101 1:363 1:50 3↑ ⒻBeldame H 66k 11 1 12 12 2½ 4¾ Scurlock O 126wb 4.85 88-13 Levee115½Amoret114hdSerchng123nk Held well under impost 14
8Sep56- 9Ran fst 1⅛ :461 1:094 1:341 1:471 3↑ Buckeye H 46k 7 1 11½ 1½ 1hd 2¾ Scurlock O 120wb 3.30 103-06 Bardstown118¾Blue Sparkler1204Paper Tiger115¾ Gamely 12
25Aug56- 7Atl fst 7f :22 :442 1:084 1:223 3↑ Longport H 24k 4 2 3nk 1½ 2½ 21½ Scurlock O 124wb *2.80 91-18 Bardstown1191½Blue Sparkler1246Skipper Bill122½ Gamely 13
11Aug56- 7Atl fst 1⅛ :48 1:114 1:364 1:494 3↑ Atl City H 100k 1 1 11½ 12 11½ 1½ Boulmetis S 113wb 8.70 89-18 BlueSparkler113½SkipperBill115noFind1194 Roused sharply 7
1Aug56- 7Jam fst 6f :224 :453 1:11 3↑ ⒻChamplain H 23k 5 3 31 2½ 11 12½ Scurlock O 125wb *1.90 92-16 [D]BlueSparkler1252½Gandharva1182BlueBanner122hd Bore in 13
Disqualified and placed second
21Jly56- 7Jam sly 1 1/16 :233 :471 1:12 1:43 3↑ ⒻBellerose H 27k 4 1 12½ 11½ 2½ 22½ Scurlock O 125wb *1.35 94-12 Parlo1212½BlueSprklr1251¾Mnotck119hd Made pace,gave way 7
7Jly56- 6Mth sl 1 1/16 :232 :474 1:114 1:443 3↑ ⒻMolly Pitcher H 28k 1 1 12 16 16 18 Scurlock O 120wb *2.00 92-20 Blue Sparkler1208Rico Reto1171Another World1102½ Easily 9
30Jun56- 7Del fst 1¼ :451 1:101 1:362 2:03 3↑ ⒻDelaware H 156k 13 1 13 2hd 2½ 75¼ Scurlock O 118wb 9.30 82-14 FlowerBowl1122Manotick122¾OpenSesame113hd Speed,tired 15
16Jun56- 6Mth fst 6f :212 :433 1:091 3↑ ⒻRegret H 22k 8 4 1hd 12½ 13 12 Scurlock O 119wb *1.50 99-06 BlueSparklr1192Jimminetty114¾PromptImpulse115¾ Driving 9
22May56- 7GS fst 6f :22 :444 1:093 4↑ ⒻAlw 7500 7 7 31½ 13 13 11 Scurlock O 110wb 4.70 96-10 BlueSprklr1101MizClementn121¾PromptImpuls1191 Handily 9
6Aug55- 6Mth fst 1⅛ :47 1:112 1:371 1:503 ⒻMth Oaks 61k 3 1 15 2hd 2hd 2nk Lasswell G 121wb 12.50 93-18 Misty Morn121nkBlue Sparkler1217Manotick121¾ Sharp try 11
20Jly55- 6Mth fst 6f :212 :441 1:102 ⒻMiss Woodford 25k 4 6 31½ 2hd 1½ 1nk Lasswell G 118wb 7.40 93-13 Blue Sparkler118nkGandharva121½Sometime Thing1211½ Held 13
6Jly55- 6Mth fst 6f :214 :444 1:101 ⒻAlw 6000 6 5 1½ 1½ 13 13 Lasswell G 118wb *1.20 94-13 Blue Sparkler1183Wagon Drill1151½Miss Misty1152 Easily 10
30Jun55- 6Mth fst 6f :213 :443 1:103 Alw 5000 5 2 21½ 2hd 1hd 2½ Lasswell G 119wb 6.60e 91-08 WreckMaster118½BlueSparkler1192Indicative1121½ Faltered 8
30May55- 7GS gd 6f :222 :451 1:103 ⒻBetsy Ross 31k 7 8 74¾ 68½ 812 79 Lasswell G 121 w 13.20 82-17 Gandharva1212Sometime Thing1211½Myrtle's Jet1214 Tired 14
14May55- 7Pim sly 1 1/16 :223 :462 1:114 1:461 ⒻBlack-Eyed Susan 26k 4 4 42½ 55½ 814 916 Lasswell G 121 w 10.00 63-22 HighVoltage1211BlessPat1213HenParty121hd Had early foot 9
5May55- 7GS fst 6f :221 :452 1:113 Alw 5000 5 1 3½ 1½ 12 1½ Lasswell G 117 w *.60 90-14 BlueSparkler117½WindsorKing1121½Ellen'sSpy117¾ Driving 8
27Oct54- 7GS fst 6f :222 :454 1:114 ⓈNJ Breeders' 11k 3 2 42½ 32½ 1hd 11 Lasswell G 119 w 1.70e 89-15 [D]Blue Sparkler1191Bunny's Babe122nkDerry1112½ Bore in 7
Disqualified and placed second
12Oct54- 7GS fst 1 70 :223 :462 1:12 1:442 ⒻWanda 33k 2 1 11½ 12 2hd 2nk Lasswell G 114 w *2.50 82-16 [D]BlueBanner113nkBlueSparklr114½MyBluSky1092½ Game try 15
Placed first through disqualification
29Sep54- 7Atl fst 6f :223 :45 1:094 ⓈHome Bred H 11k 1 8 3½ 22 21 1hd Lasswell G 113 w *1.40e 96-10 Blue Sparkler113hdDecimal1093Sorceress1151½ Hard urged 9
14Sep54- 5Atl fst 6f :221 :45 1:111 ⒻAlw 3500 7 8 77¾ 34½ 23 11¼ Lasswell G 114 w 2.80 89-12 Blue Sparkler1141¼Sue Pat110hdPrincess Kiss119¾ Easily 9
30Aug54- 3Atl fst 6f :23 :46 1:102 ⒻMd Sp Wt 10 10 72¼ 32 33 1¾ Lasswell G 119 w 15.00e 93-09 Blue Sparkler119¾Hello Mom119¾Linda's Dream1196 Driving 12

Bold Ruler

dkb. c. 1954, by Nasrullah (Nearco)–Miss Disco, by Discovery **Lifetime record: 33 23 4 2 $764,204**
Own.– Wheatley Stable
Br.– Wheatley Stable (Ky)
Tr.– J. Fitzsimmons

26Jly58- 6Jam fst 1 3/16 :471 1:114 1:37 1:553 3↑ Brooklyn H 57k 1 3 37½ 51½ 78 715 Arcaro E 136wb *.40 83-15 Cohoes1101[D]Shrpsburg1146½ThrdBrothr110hd Tired,roughed 8
19Jly58- 6Mth fst 1¼ :48 1:12 1:362 2:013 3↑ Monmouth H 110k 1 1 11½ 1hd 1½ 1¾ Arcaro E 134wb *.30 98-20 BoldRuler134¾Sharpsburg1136Bll'sSkyBoy105¾ Well in hand 6
4Jly58- 6Bel fst 1¼ :471 1:103 1:351 2:01 3↑ Suburban H 83k 1 3 3nk 11 12 1no Arcaro E 134wb *.50 95-11 BoldRuler134noClm1091½ThrdBrothr1101¼ Strong drive,held 8
25Jun58- 6Bel fst 1⅛ :473 1:111 1:352 1:482 3↑ Stymie H 28k 3 1 12½ 12½ 16 15 Arcaro E 133wb *.40 94-18 BoldRuler1335AdmiralVee112¾PopCorn1081¼ Speed to spare 7
14Jun58- 7Bel fst 1 :231 :461 1:103 1:353 3↑ Metropolitan H 58k 1 1 12 11 11½ 22 Arcaro E 135wb *.95 94-13 GallantMan1302BoldRuler1351½Clm114nk Tired under impost 10
30May58- 7Bel fst 7f :223 :453 1:101 1:223 3↑ Carter H 58k 3 1 41¼ 31 11½ 11½ Arcaro E 135wb *.80 94-17 BoldRuler1351½TickTock1131½GllntMn128no Briskly handled 9
17May58- 7Bel fst 6f-WC :22 :443 1:09 3↑ Toboggan H 29k 2 2 3nk 2½ 1½ Arcaro E 133wb *.40 94-08 BoldRuler133½Clem1172TickTock1163 Under strong handling 10
9Nov57- 7GS gd 1¼ :471 1:111 1:364 2:013 3↑ Trenton H 82k 1 1 18 13½ 13 12¼ Arcaro E 122wb 1.60 97-14 BoldRuler1222¼GallantMan1248½RoundTable124 Ridden out 3
2Nov57- 7GS sly 1 1/16 :231 :462 1:11 1:441 Benjamin Franklin H 27k 4 1 19 111 114 112 Arcaro E 136wb *.20 89-20 BoldRuler13612Sarno1096JetColonel1132½ Breezing all way 4
19Oct57- 7Jam fst 1 1/16 :234 :463 1:103 1:424 3↑ Queens County H 28k 1 1 14 16 16 12½ Arcaro E 133wb *.25 96-15 Bold Ruler1332½Promised Land1113½Greek Spy114½ Eased up 6
9Oct57- 7Bel sly 7f :223 :45 1:084 1:212 2↑ Vosburgh H 23k 3 1 2hd 11½ 15 19 Arcaro E 130wb *.40 103-09 BoldRulr1309TckTock117½St.AmourII1141¾ Fast pace,in hand 8
28Sep57- 7Bel fst 1¼ :471 1:11 1:36 2:01 3↑ Woodward 106k 2 2 21 11 2½ 33½ Arcaro E 120wb 2.15 91-13 Dedicate1261½GallantMn1202BoldRulr120hd Took lead,tired 4
14Sep57- 7Bel sly 1 :23 :454 1:094 1:35 Jerome H 29k 6 3 3½ 11 13 16 Arcaro E 130wb *.20e 99-07 BoldRuler1306Bureaucracy1131¼WingedMercury1062 In hand 6
9Sep57- 7Bel fst 6f :222 :453 1:101 Handicap 15000 1 2 2hd 1hd 14 15½ Arcaro E 128wb *.85 98-13 BoldRuler1285½GreekGame1215Egotistcl115nk Scored easily 8
15Jun57- 6Bel fst 1½ :464 1:102 2:012 2:263 Belmont 113k 1 1 13 1hd 21½ 312 Arcaro E 126wb *.85 93-07 GallantMan1268InsideTract1264BoldRuler1269 Tired badly 6
18May57- 7Pim fst 1 3/16 :462 1:103 1:363 1:561 Preakness 113k 5 1 11 11½ 12 12 Arcaro E 126wb 1.40 92-13 BoldRuler1262IronLiege126nkInsideTrct1262¼ Well handled 7
13May57- 0Pim fst 1 1/16 :231 :464 1:11 1:433 Alw 6000 3 2 12 1hd 1hd 11 Arcaro E 124wb - 92-16 Bold Ruler1241Inswept12012Convoy117 No difficulty 3
Special event between 7th and 8th races - No wagering
4May57- 7CD fst 1¼ :47 1:112 1:364 2:021 Ky Derby 152k 7 2 32 31½ 51¼ 45¾ Arcaro E 126 w *1.20 90-12 IronLiege126noGallantMan1262¾RoundTable1263 No excuse 9
20Apr57- 7Jam fst 1⅛ :48 1:12 1:361 1:484 Wood Memorial 59k 2 1 1½ 1hd 2hd 1no Arcaro E 126 w *.50 102-10 BoldRuler126noGallantMan1266PromisedLand1262¼ Just up 7
30Mar57- 7GP fst 1⅛ :462 1:102 1:343 1:464 Fla Derby 123k 1 2 21 21 1hd 21½ Arcaro E 122 w *.60 107-06 Gen.Duk1221½BoldRulr122hdIronLg1182¼ Reached lead,tired 5
2Mar57- 7Hia fst 1⅛ :452 1:102 1:342 1:47 Flamingo 131k 2 3 21 11½ 12 1nk Arcaro E 122 w *.50 101-07 BoldRuler122nkGen.Duke1222¾IronLiege12212 Held gamely 7
16Feb57- 7Hia fst 1⅛ :462 1:102 1:343 1:472 Everglades 30k 4 1 11½ 11½ 11 2hd Arcaro E 126 w *.40 99-10 Gen.Duke114hdBoldRuler1266IronLg1171¾ Strong try,headed 7
30Jan57- 7Hia fst 7f :223 :45 1:091 1:22 Bahamas 26k 2 3 12 11½ 14 14½ Atkinson T 126 w 3.85e 100-11 BoldRuler1264½Gen.Duke1142FederalHll1261¼ Scored easily 11
6Nov56- 7Jam fst 1 1/16 :24 :48 1:13 1:453 ©Remsen 96k 5 8 87¼ 89 1019 - Arcaro E 122 w *.60 - - Ambhavng1222½Missle1221½Finlandia122nk Poor start,blocked 11
Geldings not eligible
27Oct56- 7GS gd 1 1/16 :221 :454 1:12 1:444 Garden State 319k 1 3 33 1724 1734 1724 Atkinson T 122 w *2.10 62-18 Barbizon122noFederalHill122nkAmrullh1223 Stumbled early 19
13Oct56- 7Bel fst 6½-WC :214 :442 1:083 1:151 Futurity 124k 8 2 22 13 12¼ Arcaro E 122 w *1.25 96-04 BoldRuler1222¼GreekGame122noAmrullh122nk Under pressure 13
Geldings not eligible
5Oct56- 6Bel fst 6f-WC :22 :442 1:083 Sp Wt 7500 7 4 2hd 1hd 1½ Guerin E 118 w *.90 96-04 BoldRuler118½Missile1182½Mqult118½ Under strong pressure 9
24Sep56- 6Bel sly 6f-WC :223 :453 1:101 Alw 5000 1 3 2hd 2hd 21¼ Arcaro E 122 w *.95e 87-19 Nashville1161¼Bold Ruler1221½Bureaucracy113nk Bore out 6
6Jun56- 7Bel fst 5f-WC :22 :441 :56 Juvenile 33k 1 1 21½ 21½ 11 Arcaro E 122 w *.60e 99-05 Bold Ruler1221King Hairan1225Supernatural1225 In hand 8
24May56- 6Bel fst 5f-WC :221 :451 :571 Alw 5000 7 4 2hd 1½ 1nk Arcaro E 122 w *.55e 93-13 Bold Ruler122nkKing Hairan1227Bureaucracy1195 All out 9
2May56- 7Jam fst 5f :23 :463 :594 ©Youthful 17k 8 6 41 2hd 1hd 13½ Atkinson T 122 w *1.00e 91-19 Bold Ruler1223½Red Cadet1221½Encore1223½ Well in hand 10
19Apr56- 5Jam fst 5f :223 :47 1:00 Alw 4000 4 2 2hd 2hd 2hd 11 Atkinson T 118 w 3.15 90-20 Bold Ruler1181Red Cadet1181¾Missile1181½ Ridden out 8
9Apr56- 4Jam gd 5f :232 :474 1:002 ©Md Sp Wt 2 3 21½ 2hd 11½ 13½ Atkinson T 118 w *1.55 88-15 BoldRuler1183½WolfBadge118½ScotchRoyal1182 Easy score 6

Bornastar

dkb. f. 1953, by Alibhai (Hyperion)–Farmerette, by Sickle **Lifetime record: 43 19 7 2 $270,178**
Own.– J.G. Brown
Br.– Shawnee Farm (Ky)
Tr.– W.G. Sparks

21Sep59- 7Aqu fst 1 :223 :45 1:094 1:36 3↑ ⒻMaskette H 29k 5 6 62¾ 53 33 32¾ Arcaro E 119 8.70 - - Idun1191¼Temptd1261½Bornstr1192 Raced evenly in stretch 10
2Sep59- 7Bel sly 7f :22 :443 1:092 1:223 3↑ ⒻVagrancy H 29k 10 6 75¾ 76¼ 65¾ 47 Church K 122 4.45 87-16 DandyBlitzen1131HoneysGem1185Idun1121 Drifted out turn 12
19Aug59- 5AP fst 7f :224 :453 1:102 1:231 3↑ ⒻAlw 5000 7 2 43½ 32½ 1hd 12½ Church K 111 *.70 92-12 Bornastar1112½LaPlume109¾Aesthetic1115 Under mild drive 7
15Aug59- 8AP my 1⅛ :48 1:123 1:392 1:53 3↑ ⒻArl Matron H 57k 11 9 99 711 715 69¼ Church K 122 3.50 68-19 WiggleII1163HoneysGem1183½BornRich111¾ No real threat 12
25Jly59- 6Del fst 1¼ :462 1:111 1:37 2:033 3↑ ⒻDelaware H 155k 1 5 57 42½ 43 43¾ Church K 124 3.40 80-18 Endine117½Polamby114¾Tempted1192½ Well placed,no rally 11
18Jly59- 6Del fst 1 1/16 :231 :464 1:112 1:433 3↑ ⒻNew Castle 35k 3 3 32½ 21½ 33 22¾ Church K 126 4.90 90-18 Tempted1162¾Bornstr126½Chstos112no Showed a good effort 10

Date/Race	Cond	Dist	Fractions	Race	PP St 1/4 Str Fin	Jockey	Wt	Odds	Figs	Top Finishers / Comment	Field
20Jun59-8Was	fst	1	:22 :442 1:084 1:34	3↑ Ⓕ Beverly H 58k	2 4 63½ 33 43 42¼	Church K	126	*.80	95-05	HoneysGem115hdIndianMd1092MllyK.108hd Lacked room early	14
3Jun59-7Was	fst	6f	:222 :444 1:092	3↑ Ⓕ Alw 4000	4 4 53½ 54½ 21 11¼	Church K	118	*.80	98-05	Bornastar118½Tinkalero116¾Betty Linn1132¼ Won in hand	5
1Nov58-7GS	fst	1⅛	:47 1:113 1:38 1:503	3↑ Ⓕ Vineland H 58k	9 5 53 2½ 1½ 1¾	Church K	124 w	*2.10	84-23	Bornastar124¾RareTreat1121¾AGlittr1213 Under hard drive	10
23Oct58-6Kee	fst	1⅛	:473 1:113 1:361 1:492	3↑ Ⓕ Spinster 73k	3 2 2½ 12 12 15	Church K	123 w	*.30	90-19	Bornstr1235MoonGlory1193¼Woodlwn1231½ Very handy score	8
16Oct58-6Kee	fst	*7f	1:261	3↑ Ⓕ Alw 5000	4 4 33½ 21½ 1hd 11¼	Church K	119 w	*.20	97-13	Bornastr1191¼BugBrush1162HstyDoll1132¼ Very handy score	6
27Sep58-7CD	fst	1 1/16	:24 :473 1:112 1:423	3↑ Alw 6500	1 4 34 1hd 11 12	Church K	119 w	*.60	105-08	Bornastar1192Dru Away1182Praised110¾ Going away	8
20Sep58-8CD	sly	1	:232 :463 1:114 1:371	3↑ Ⓕ Falls City H 22k	8 3 2hd 1½ 14 16	Church K	122 w	*.70	89-16	Bornastar1226LittlPch1131¼Woodlwn1111¼ As rider pleased	9
13Sep58-7CD	fst	6f	:223 :453 1:102	3↑ Ⓕ Alw 5000	6 5 66½ 63¼ 11 12	Church K	118 w	*1.10	96-10	Bornastar1182Gerts Image114¾Woodlawn112nk Easily best	9
26Jly58-6Del	fst	1¼	:464 1:111 1:361 2:03	3↑ Ⓕ Delaware H 160k	1 11 88¼ 89¼ 68 109¾	Church K	121 w	5.70	77-12	Endine111noDottedLn1161Woodlwn1081 Showed a dull effort	16
19Jly58-6Del	fst	1 1/16	:231 :462 1:104 1:441	3↑ Ⓕ New Castle 38k	9 4 32½ 32 45½ 88	Church K	126 w	*1.70	82-17	Alanesian1123Mlle.Dianne112¾Endin112½ Failed to respond	15
10Jly58-6Del	fst	6f	:222 :454 1:11	4↑ Ⓕ Alw 4500	1 5 41½ 42¼ 42 2½	Church K	121 w	*.80	89-15	PuckerUp121½Bornastr1212½Slx118hd Blocked early,rallied	6
7Jun58-8Was	fst	1	:222 :451 1:10 1:354	3↑ Ⓕ Beverly H 58k	14 2 21½ 23 1hd 12½	Church K	121 w	2.80	88-16	Bornastar1212½PuckerUp1221¼Burdett104¾ Under mild drive	14
2Jun58-7Was	sl	6f	:23 :463 1:113	3↑ Ⓕ Alw 5000	5 3 21½ 22 1hd 12	Church K	117 w	5.00	87-29	Bornastar1172PuckerUp1216BonniA.108nk Under hand urging	6
24Oct57-6Kee	gd	1⅛	:463 1:111 1:361 1:491	3↑ Ⓕ Spinster 76k	3 3 35 1½ 12 12½	Church K	123 w	9.40	91-12	Bornastar1232½PuckrUp1231¾Srchng1231 Under steady drive	6
17Oct57-0Kee	sly	*7f	1:272	3↑ Ⓕ Alw 5000	3 2 311 38 24 21½	Borgem'ke R	120 w	-	89-13	Pucker Up1261½Bornastar1204Beautillion117¾ Late speed	4
				Special race - Run between 4th and 5th races. No wagering							
20Oct57-7Haw	fst	6½f	:222 :453 1:11 1:174	3↑ Ⓕ Yo Tambien H 17k	1 6 33 23 21½ 11¼	Hartack W	119 w	*.50	91-15	Bornastar1191¼LadyLarue110hdFightingJury1111 Going away	9
21Aug57-8Was	fst	1⅛	:47 1:112 1:363 1:492	3↑ Ⓕ Beverly H 28k	1 1 2hd 1½ 21 34½	Church K	110 w	2.50	89-12	DottedLine1124½[D]LadySwords108hdBornastar1101¼ Impeded	13
				Placed second through disqualification							
14Aug57-8Was	gd	7f	:221 :45 1:094 1:222	3↑ Ⓕ Alw 7500	5 2 23 21 11½ 15	Hartack W	117 w	2.30	93-15	Bornastar1175Beautillion1173Amoret1154 Drew away easily	9
1Aug57-8Was	fst	6f	:22 :45 1:102	3↑ Ⓕ Alw 4500	7 8 77 76½ 53½ 1nk	Hartack W	118 w	*2.10	93-11	Bornstr118nkFghtngJury107hdGunFly118hd Up in final stride	8
24Jly57-8AP	sl	1	:23 :453 1:103 1:37	3↑ Ⓕ Arl Matron H 57k	6 6 76½ 55¼ 24 22	Church K	111 w	66.10f	85-18	Pucker Up1202Bornastar1114½Lady Swords1084 Strong rally	13
17Jly57-7AP	sf	5½fⓉ	:23 :464 :591 1:052	3↑ Alw 4000	6 4 55½ 54½ 74¾ 55¼	Borgemenke R	115 w	9.90	87-15	Springhead1111Apple Bay1171½Dark Toga117nk No mishap	7
1Jly57-8AP	fm	5½fⓉ	:23 :453 :583 1:044	3↑ Ⓕ Alw 10000	2 8 31½ 31 31 1nk	Heckmann J	116 w	17.80	95-05	Bornastar116nkDale'sDelight113nkViciAdmirl1161½ Just up	8
25Jun57-8AP	fm	5½fⓉ	:221 :451 :573 1:033	3↑ Alw 5000	7 6 76¾ 65½ 66¾ 66¾	Hartack W	113 w	20.80	94-08	Craigwood1132½KingBruceII119½VagabondKing1193¼ No speed	8
29Apr57-7CD	fst	6f	:23 :461 1:112	4↑ Ⓕ Alw 5000	4 7 64 63½ 66½ 57¼	Carstens W	115 w	4.90	84-17	Brujari107¾MryH.1063Commrgo1091½ Never a serious threat	7
25Apr57-7Kee	fst	6f	:22 :444 1:093	4↑ Alw 3750	3 3 2hd 1hd 73¾ 86½	Hartack W	114 w	*2.10	91-02	FirstLap119nkInvalidate1191½Brujari107hd Speed 4f,tired	8
18Apr57-3Kee	gd	6f	:231 :462 1:12	4↑ Ⓕ Alw 5000	5 - - - - -	Hartack W	117 w	*1.30	- -	Windsail1174½Mauvernn1122Attc117hd Stumbled,threw rider	5
14Nov56-7CD	fst	1	:231 :46 1:11 1:373	Alw 7500	8 5 55½ 53½ 3½ 1½	Carstens W	116 w	2.80	87-22	Bornastar116½Greek Sword111nkInvalidate1191½ Hard drive	8
9Nov56-7CD	fst	7f	:231 :46 1:104 1:24	Alw 5000	4 2 3nk 21 22½ 22½	Carstens W	116 w	24.10	90-15	JovialJove1222½Bornastar1163½OurHoliday1191 Closed well	11
3Nov56-4CD	fst	1 1/16	:25 :491 1:141 1:461	Alw 4000	1 7 714 66½ 42 21¼	Brooks S	117 w	4.30	86-14	Mr.BobW.1121¼Bornstr117nkOurHoldy1206 Strong stretch bid	7
29Oct56-4CD	gd	6½f	:232 :473 1:13 1:193	Alw 4000	4 2 32 41½ 2½ 11½	Brooks S	119 w	*.40	83-15	Bornastar1191½Persian Poet1125Draw Near1161½ Drew clear	6
19Oct56-7Kee	fst	6f	:221 :45 1:101	Alw 4000	5 4 53 43½ 55 66½	Brooks S	114 w	8.40	92-05	VayaConDios1173½Outfielder117¾Brujari109no Factor,tired	8
9Oct56-3Kee	fst	*7f	1:27	Alw 4000	1 6 1hd 21½ 2hd 31	Brooks S	114 w	4.60	97-07	Homeplac117nkOutfldr117¾Bornstr1143½ Showed good effort	7
31Aug56-6Was	sl	6f	:224 :454 1:111	Ⓕ Alw 6000	5 5 63½ 43½ 55½ 67¼	Adams J	116 w	9.20	82-23	Little Pache1161Beautillion1165Judy Rullah116nk Tired	7
18Aug56-7Was	sly	7f	:23 :474 1:13 1:261	Alw 4500	7 2 32 21 1hd 12	Hartack W	115 w	4.10	74-23	Bornastar1152Peter Parent1201½Whatitoldyou1205 Driving	7
11Aug56-5Was	fst	6f	:223 :461 1:11	3↑ Alw 4000	6 7 53¾ 31½ 42½ 44	Heckmann J	113 w	*1.50	86-14	GallantRunner121¾Letmego1102HowBlue1181¼ Wide,no rally	7
				Open to 3- and 4-year-olds							
3Aug56-3Was	fst	6f	:223 :46 1:11	Md Sp Wt	5 4 2hd 2hd 1hd 12	Hartack W	115 w	*1.80	90-13	Bornastar1152Summer Breeze1151Flutter1158 Handy score	8
28Jly56-6AP	fst	6f	:23 :453 1:103	Alw 5000	5 7 53 53¼ 510 49½	Popara A	110.5 w	33.40	81-16	Tropic King1173Key Biscayne117½Ambiorun1176 Wide turn	10

Career Boy

dk br. c. 1953, by Phalanx (Pilate)–Swanky, by Mahmoud — Lifetime record: 32 8 5 4 $254,661

Own.– C.V. Whitney
Br.– C.V. Whitney (Ky)
Tr.– S.E. Veitch

Date/Race	Cond	Dist	Fractions	Race	PP St 1/4 Str Fin	Jockey	Wt	Odds	Figs	Top Finishers / Comment	Field
6Oct57♦ Longchamp(Fr)	yl	*1½ⓉRH	2:332	3↑ Prix de l'Arc de Triomphe Stk250000	18	Boulmetis S	132	18.00		Oroso132½Denisy1192½Balbo1224 Toward rear throughout.Tanerko 6th	24
14Sep57-7Atl	fm	1 3/16Ⓣ	:473 1:12 1:372 1:561	3↑ U Nations H 100k	9 7 93¼ 72½ 44½ 44	Boulmetis S	123wb	8.80	94-02	Round Table118noTudor Era1122Find1222 Threat,weakened	11
9Sep57-7Atl	sf	1Ⓣ	:244 :483 1:134 1:402	3↑ Alw 4500	7 7 68½ 58 35½ 31¾	Batchellor L	119wb	*1.30	77-21	Akbar Khan1191½Old Roman117nkCareer Boy1191½	7
				Forced wide first turn							
24Aug57-7Sar	fst	1¼	:48 1:123 1:382 2:043	3↑ Saratoga H 58k	1 6 54 63 31½ 32½	Boulmetis S	118wb	6.20	82-17	Reneged1131RicciTavi1161½CarrBoy1184 No apparent excuse	10
16Aug57-7Sar	fst	7f	:22 :46 1:12 1:25	3↑ American Legion H 26k	1 16 1213 1110 95 76	Boulmetis S	121wb	12.90	81-19	RicciTavi1221Nan'sMink1133½[D]Nashville117hd Off slowly	15
13Jly57-6Mth	fst	1¼	:463 1:104 1:354 2:014	3↑ Monmouth H 113k	3 9 98¾ 67¼ 68½ 67	Boulmetis S	119wb	5.00	90-13	Dedicate1243½ThirdBrother119¾Rockcastl109¾ Bumped start	9
4Jly57-7Bel	fst	1¼	:471 1:11 1:363 2:023	3↑ Suburban H 85k	4 4 46 67 86½ 75¾	Boulmetis S	122wb	7.80	81-13	TrafficJudge124hdLoftyPeak118nkDedicate1262½ No mishap	11
27Jun57-7Bel	fst	1⅛	:462 1:103 1:354 1:484	3↑ Handicap 10000	2 3 35½ 45 57½ 56	Boulmetis S	124wb	*1.85	89-13	BeamRider113noCountrmnd1142Mr.Al L.1142 Early foot,tired	5
7Oct56♦ Longchamp(Fr)	hy	*1½ⓉRH	2:344	3↑ Prix de l'Arc de Triomphe Stk160000	48	Arcaro E	122	21.00e		Ribot1326Talgo1222Tanerko122no Rated in 8th,finished well,just missed 3rd.Oroso 6th	20
15Sep56-7Atl	fm	1 3/16Ⓣ	:472 1:12 1:38 1:561	3↑ U Nations H 100k	7 7 54½ 52½ 52½ 11	Boulmetis S	116wb	4.80e	98-02	CrrBoy1161Fnd117hdMstrGus119hd Well rated,strong finish	9
1Sep56-7Atl	fm	1Ⓣ	:242 :48 1:123 1:39	Ventnor Turf H 31k	2 6 89½ 66 78 53¼	Choquette J	124 w	*2.30	83-14	KingGrail115¾Sol-Hi112hdSunnngdl1132 Closed ground late	10
20Aug56-6Sar	fst	1	:242 :483 1:123 1:38	Handicap 6000	1 5 57½ 33½ 32½ 1hd	Arcaro E	122 w	*.95	87-17	CareerBoy122hdQuarterdeck113hdJeanBaptiste112½ Just up	5
16Jun56-6Bel	fst	1½	:472 1:114 2:024 2:294	Belmont 119k	6 5 514 27 33 2nk	Guerin E	126wb	3.60e	89-12	Needles126nkCrrBoy1261½Fbus126hd Missed in strong rally	8
				Geldings not eligible							
26May56-7GS	fst	1⅛	:471 1:104 1:353 1:484	Jersey 62k	5 10 1012 88½ 65½ 32¼	Guerin E	118wb	5.00	91-14	Fabius1262Kingmakr111nkCrrBoy118hd Strong stretch rally	10
5May56-7CD	fst	1¼	:471 1:113 1:364 2:032	Ky Derby 167k	2 15 1312 109 85 65	Guerin E	126wb	4.90e	85-08	Needles126¾Fabius1261½Come on Red126¾ Sluggish early	17
26Apr56-6Kee	sl	1⅛	:474 1:121 1:363 1:51	Blue Grass 33k	3 6 66½ 43½ 21½ 2¾	Guerin E	126wb	*.40e	89-17	TobyB.121¾CareerBoy1263½ReapingRght126nk Gaining slowly	7
11Apr56-7Jam	fst	1 1/16	:242 :484 1:134 1:453	Gotham 29k	7 9 811 57 32 13	Guerin E	122wb	*1.15	84-21	CareerBoy1223JeanBaptiste122nkNail1265 Drew out handily	9
4Apr56-7Jam	fst	6f	:24 :474 1:12	Alw 6000	3 2 64¾ 65½ 2½ 21½	Guerin E	126wb	*.55	85-16	WillofAllah1141½CareerBoy1263BeauFond1152½ No excuse	7
29Oct55-7GS	fst	1 1/16	:231 :461 1:104 1:423	Garden State 282k	8 10 88¾ 55 21½ 2no	Guerin E	122wb	4.50	97-07	Prince John122noCareer Boy1221Needles1224½ Just missed	12
22Oct55-6GS	fst	1 1/16	:231 :461 1:102 1:423	Alw 10000	4 6 75½ 54 2hd 1½	Guerin E	120wb	2.10e	97-10	CareerBoy120½GunShot112nkEsp1143½ Well rated,hard drive	7
8Oct55-6Bel	sly	6½f-W	:221 :451 1:10 1:164	Futurity 125k	11 12 92¾ 85¼ 64½	Guerin E	122wb	*2.80e	83-12	Nail1221¼HeadMan122¾Polly'sJt1221 Appeared to hang late	15
				Geldings not eligible							
30Sep55-6Bel	fst	6f-WC	:214 :441 1:09	Sp Wt 10000	1 3 78¼ 56 1no	Guerin E	118wb	*1.15e	94-11	CareerBoy118noNoorsaga118¾Polly'sJet1183¾ Strong finish	8
27Aug55-6Sar	fst	6½f	:23 :47 1:12 1:181	Hopeful 71k	7 9 910 85 24 23½	Woodhouse H	122wb	3.15e	90-19	Needles1223½Career Boy1226Jean Baptiste1221 Closed well	9
20Aug55-4Sar	fst	6f	:224 :463 1:122	Grand Union Hotel 26k	7 8 811 86½ 33 11¾	Woodhouse H	122wb	*3.70e	86-19	CareerBoy1221¾Nan'sMink114½HeadMan1221½ Steadily clear	8
13Aug55-4Sar	sly	6f	:23 :46 1:112	Sar Spl 15k	1 3 511 49½ 412 49½	Woodhouse H	122wb	3.15e	81-19	Polly'sJet1221½Reneged1225Noorsag1223 Hard urged,outrun	5
6Aug55-6Sar	fst	6f	:23 :464 1:122	U S Hotel 26k	5 8 99¾ 75½ 54 1½	Woodhouse H	114wb	*1.60e	86-18	CareerBy114½CanadianChamp118hdHeadMan1141¼ Hard drive	10
1Aug55-2Sar	fst	5½f	:233 :473 :594 1:062	©Md Sp Wt	8 8 62¾ 31½ 1hd 13½	Woodhouse H	118wb	*1.60	85-18	CareerBoy1183½Thunderstruck1182½DansChoice118½ Driving	14
6Jly55-6Aqu	fst	6f	:23 :47 1:12	Great American 18k	2 7 58½ 510 510 54¾	Arcaro E	114wb	12.15	87-17	GetthereJck1221½Rngd1141Bob-o-Bob114nk Impeded at start	7
20Jun55-4Aqu	fst	5½f	:24 :472 :594 1:062	©Md Sp Wt	8 9 72½ 86¾ 58 42½	Arcaro E	118 w	3.00	89-15	Wild Chorus1181Inkyank118hdTarquitana1181½ Closed a gap	11
14Jun55-5Aqu	fst	5½f	:233 :474 1:001 1:071	©Md Sp Wt	10 10 96½ 85½ 44½ 41¼	Arcaro E	118 w	*1.90	87-18	Network118nkFoldingMon1181BlackEmperor118no Good rally	12
4Jun55-4Bel	fst	5f-WC	:224 :452 :573	©Md Sp Wt	4 8 82 63¾ 32¼	Picou C	118 w	6.10e	89-09	Pester1181½Born Mighty118¾Career Boy118hd Strong finish	12
20May55-5Bel	fst	4½f-W	:222 :444 :504	©Md Sp Wt	3 10 96¾ 36½ 56	Picou C	118 w	7.25e	89-08	Postal1183Reneged1182FoldingMon118nk Rallied,then tired	14

Counterpoint

ch. c. 1948, by Count Fleet (Reigh Count)-Jabot, by Sickle — **Lifetime record: 21 10 3 1 $284,575**

Own.- C.V. Whitney
Br.- C.V. Whitney (Ky)
Tr.- S.E. Veitch

9Aug52- 6Sar	fst 1¼	:48 1:131 1:39 2:053	3↑ Whitney 23k	2	5	39	2½	12	13½	Gorman D	123 w	*.45	80-19	Counterpoint1233½Mandingo1141One Hitter126½		6
Veered in start,drew away																
29Jly52- 4Mth	fst 1 1/16	:233 :471 1:12 1:45	3↑ Alw 5000	1	2	24	2hd	14	13½	Gorman D	124 w	*.40	92-15	Counterpoint1243½Go Between112noPilaster1242½	Easily	4
2Feb52- 7SA	fst 1¼	:47 1:111 1:362 2:024	Maturity 183k	4	5	47	65½	69½	64¾	Gorman D	126 w	*.50	81-13	Intent113nkGold Capitol1141Black Douglas1131	No excuse	9
19Jan52- 6SA	my 1 1/16	:23 :463 1:114 1:451	San Fernando 23k	2	7	611	57	32½	1no	Gorman D	118 w	*.65	82-21	Counterpoint118noPhil D.1151½Intent1146	Just up	9
3Nov51- 6Jam	sly 1 3/16	:473 1:121 1:381 1:583	Emp City H 59k	13	11	129¾	116	4¾	11½	Gorman D	130 w	*2.45	83-17	Counterpoint1301½HallofFame1241¾Audtng1111	Driving,wide	13
20Oct51- 6Jam	fst 1⅝	:502 1:40 2:044 2:424	3↑ Emp Gold Cup 53k	2	3	44	2hd	1hd	11¼	Gorman D	119 w	2.15	100-14	Counterpoint1191¼HillPrinc1264½HullDown11912	Ridden out	4
Geldings not eligible																
13Oct51- 6Bel	fst 2	:493 2:302 2:56 3:213	3↑ J C Gold Cup 53k	2	3	21½	21	2½	1hd	Gorman D	117 w	4.35	96-11	Counterpoint117hdHillPrince12410KissMeKate1142½	Just up	5
3Oct51- 6Bel	fst 1⅝	:484 1:401 2:051 2:432	Lawrence Realizatn 22k	4	4	31	11	13	11¼	Gorman D	126 w	*1.35	87-13	Counterpoint1261¼Saxony1108Alerted1142	Easily	6
26Sep51- 6Bel	fst 1	:23 :46 1:104 1:361	Jerome H 24k	7	8	52¾	43¼	32	44¼	Gorman D	124 w	8.35	89-14	Alerted115nkMandingo1023Hall of Fame1281	Faltered	12
7Jly51- 6Aqu	fst 1¼	:481 1:123 1:383 2:042	Dwyer 57k	9	9	87½	105	109¼	913	Gorman D	126 w	*1.55	72-16	Battlefield121½Alerted1112½Hull Down1111½	Dull effort	10
16Jun51- 6Bel	fst 1½	:494 1:141 2:031 2:29	Belmont 118k	2	4	2hd	12	12	14	Gorman D	126 w	5.15e	93-08	Counterpoint1264Battlefield1261½BttlMorn1269	Ridden out	9
Geldings not eligible																
9Jun51- 6Bel	fst 1⅛	:461 1:102 1:351 1:474	Peter Pan H 24k	7	3	22	2½	13	12¾	Gorman D	114 w	15.75	102-10	Counterpoint1142¾Battlefield1232¼HallofFame113¾	Handily	9
26May51- 6Bel	fst 1	:224 :452 1:094 1:354	Withers 29k	5	7	77	78½	711	512	Adair R	126wb	10.80	83-12	Battlefield126hdJumbo1265Nullify1264	Dull try	7
Geldings not eligible																
19May51- 6Pim	fst 1 3/16	:474 1:112 1:372 1:562	Preakness 110k	7	6	62¼	52¼	23	27	Adair R	126wb	25.80	91-14	Bold1267Counterpoint126¾Alerted1264	Went well	8
5May51- 7CD	fst 1¼	:472 1:122 1:37 2:023	Ky Derby 126k	2	7	86¾	1212	1114	1112	Gorman D	126 w	5.90e	82-09	Count Turf1264Royal Mustang126hdRuhe1262½	Tired	20
26Apr51- 7Kee	my 1⅛	:49 1:142 1:403 1:541	Blue Grass (Div 2) 29k	4	2	31	42	32½	41¾	Dodson D	121 w	7.70	73-27	[D]Sonic123noRuhe123nkRoyal Mustang1211½	Impeded	6
Placed third through disqualification																
21Apr51- 6Kee	fst 1 1/16	:233 :472 1:123 1:45	3↑ Ben Ali H 12k	1	1	12	2½	23	26	Knapp EJ	105 w	*.50e	83-18	Wistful1126Counterpoint1053½Little Imp110¾	Weakened	5
14Apr51- 7Kee	sl 6f	:243 :502 1:17	Alw 2500	4	4	31	12½	14	18	Church K	112 w	*1.10	67-31	Counterpoint1128Baluster1113Fighting Back1161½	Easily	6
23Mar51- 5GP	fst 6f	:223 :452 1:113	Md Sp Wt	4	8	54	45	51¾	42	Church K	120 w	*1.65	85-11	Hurry-Skurry120¾Kentario1201Changeaway120nk	Off slowly	11
26Sep50- 5Bel	fst 6f-WC	:224 :453 1:104	©Md Sp Wt	5	10		106½	77¼	55¼	Dodson D	118 w	*1.25e	82-14	Heliowise1184Galhampden118½Basically118½	No excuse	14
20Sep50- 5Bel	fst 5½f-W	:222 :45 1:031	©Md Sp Wt	15	6		61¼	4nk	24	Dodson D	118 w	9.15e	94-02	BlueHelmet1184Counterpoint118hdFoxeyLad1183	Closed well	27

Crafty Admiral

b. c. 1948, by Fighting Fox (Sir Gallahad III)-Admiral's Lady, by War Admiral — **Lifetime record: 39 18 6 4 $499,200**

Own.- Charfran Stable
Br.- Harry F. Guggenheim (Ky)
Tr.- R.B. Odom

11Nov53- 7Lrl	sf *1½(T)	2:36	3↑ D C Int'l 65k	9	1	2hd	109½	1022	1028	Boland W	126wb	*2.20	46-29	Worden II1266Iceberg II1263Sunglow126½	Flattened out	10
31Oct53- 6Jam	fst 1⅝	:50 1:404 2:06 2:433	3↑ Gold Cup 80k	5	1	12	12½	16	110	Boland W	126wb	*1.00	96-21	Crafty Admiral12610Common Cause126nkAlerted1261½	Easily	7
24Oct53- 6Jam	fst 1⅛	:471 1:111 1:363 1:493	3↑ Westchester H 56k	3	1	1½	1hd	12	21	Arcaro E	128wb	*1.15	97-17	Cold Command1121CraftyAdmirl1284Jampol1121½	No excuse	8
17Oct53- 7Haw	fst 1¼	:461 1:102 1:343 2:003	3↑ Haw Gold Cup H 106k	6	2	24	24	46½	58½	Arcaro E	128wb	*.50	95-08	Sub Fleet1153Smoke Screen1141Indian Hemp1092	No excuse	7
3Oct53- 7Atl	fst 1⅛	:47 1:112 1:362 1:493	3↑ Olympic H 28k	6	2	22½	22	1hd	11¼	Scurlock D	128wb	*.50	96-11	Crafty Admiral1281¼Tuscany1217Count Cavour1041¼	In hand	7
26Sep53- 7Bel	fst 1⅛	:46 1:102 1:354 1:484	3↑ New York H 29k	5	1	12	11½	14	14	Arcaro E	125wb	2.45	95-15	Crafty Admiral1254Flaunt1051½Jampol113¾	In hand	9
15Aug53- 6Was	fst 7f	:223 :453 1:103 1:231	3↑ Clang H 22k	4	6	41¾	45	69½	810	Church K	125wb	4.10	80-16	Cyclotron1162Van Crosby1102Eljay1121	Done early	12
9May53- 7Pim	gd 1⅛	:471 1:123 1:383 1:514	3↑ Dixie H 29k	4	2	23	2hd	32	34½	Arcaro E	126wb	*1.20	91-22	RoyalVale1201¾ColdCommnd1152½CrftyAdmrl126nk	Gave way	6
2May53- 6Jam	my 1 3/16	:474 1:113 1:362 1:552	3↑ Gallant Fox H 71k	6	1	1½	22½	24	43	Church K	129wb	*1.05	96-14	Royal Vale1151½Cold Command1151½One Count129no	Tired	6
14Mar53- 7GP	fst 1¼	:454 1:10 1:344 2:004	3↑ Gulf Park H 59k	3	2	22	2hd	1½	1nk	Church K	128wb	*1.95	95-14	Crafty Admiral128nkBattlefield1256Dulat1141	Hard drive	11
21Feb53- 7Hia	fst 1¼	:462 1:103 1:363 2:024	3↑ Widener H 130k	3	2	11	1hd	21	65¼	Church K	131wb	3.50	86-09	OilCapitol114hdAlerted126hdBattlefld1231½	Flattened out	8
7Feb53- 7Hia	my 1⅛	:473 1:124 1:391 1:532	3↑ McLennan H 64k	7	1	12	12	13	13½	Church K	129wb	3.30	69-34	Crafty Admiral1293½Oil Capitol115¾Ken1171	Ridden out	7
24Jan53- 7Hia	my 1⅛	:483 1:133 1:40 1:534	3↑ Royal Palm H 17k	3	1	13	11½	12	12½	Church K	126wb	*.35	67-32	Crafty Admiral1262½Gushing Oil10715Topside1062½	Easily	5
15Jan53- 7TrP	fst 1⅛	:464 1:112 1:371 1:492	3↑ Tropical H 65k	8	2	2½	21½	23	33	Church K	128wb	*1.70	91-19	Spartan Valor1261½How1061½Crafty Admiral1282	No excuse	12
4Oct52- 6Bel	fst 2	:514 2:332 2:584 3:241	3↑ J C Gold Cup 79k	2	2	11	34½	311	317	Guerin E	124wb	2.15	66-15	OneCount1172Mark-Ye-Wll11715CrftyAdmrl1245	Tired,sulked	4
Geldings not eligible																
1Sep52- 7Was	sly 1	:231 :462 1:104 1:364	3↑ Wash Park H 172k	4	2	2½	11½	12½	12	Guerin E	128 w	2.70	85-15	CraftyAdmiral1282ToMarket1231Sickle'sImage110nk	Handily	10
16Aug52- 7Was	my 1 3/16	:49 1:141 1:402 1:583	3↑ Whirlaway H 44k	2	1	13	11½	13	13	Arcaro E	126wb	*.70	93-23	Crafty Admiral1263Oil Capitol1168Ruhe1132	Easily	8
2Aug52- 6Jam	sly 1 3/16	:48 1:12 1:38 1:572	3↑ Merchants & Cits H 28k	4	1	11½	1½	11	11½	Guerin E	126wb	*1.65	89-18	CraftyAdmirl1261½CombatBoots1126Mandingo1042½	In hand	8
12Jly52- 6Aqu	fst 1¼	:47 1:113 1:37 2:014	3↑ Brooklyn H 59k	4	1	11	13	14	16	Guerin E	116wb	*2.70	98-14	CraftyAdmirl1166CountyDelight122½ToMarket1194½	In hand	11
4Jly52- 6Aqu	fst 7f	:221 :443 1:09 1:22	3↑ Carter H 29k	3	2	22	22	22	22	Gorman D	120wb	3.05	100-09	NorthernStar1152CraftyAdmiral1202½ToMrkt123no	Held well	10
30May52- 6Bel	fst 1¼	:463 1:102 1:353 2:02	3↑ Suburban H 60k	2	1	14	16	14	2nk	Errico C	113wb	13.75	90-12	One Hitter112nkCrafty Admiral1132Mameluke1161	Tired	10
24May52- 7GS	fst 1⅛	:471 1:12 1:372 1:503	3↑ T J Healey H 24k	2	1	11½	1hd	2hd	2½	Errico C	116wb	4.70	88-13	Alerted116½Crafty Admiral1161½Joey Boy112½	Good effort	9
17May52- 6Bel	fst 1	:23 :454 1:104 1:362	3↑ Metropolitan H 36k	10	4	2hd	1½	32	65	Errico C	117 w	3.30	87-14	Mameluke112½Battlefield1251½One Hitter1131	Weakened	11
29Apr52- 6Bel	gd 6f-WC	:221 :443 1:091	3↑ Toboggan H 23k	5	3		3½	31	2½	Errico C	118wb	*2.05	94-05	DarkPeter108½CraftyAdmiral1182½Tea-Mkr1202	Getting fast	8
8Mar52- 7GP	fst 1¼	:462 1:103 1:35 2:01	3↑ Gulf Park H 28k	5	1	12	12	15	1nk	Errico C	114wb	5.55	94-07	Crafty Admiral114nkAlerted114½Why Not Now1132	Impeded	10
16Feb52- 6Hia	fst 7f	:224 :452 1:10 1:232	4↑ Alw 5000	5	2	2½	1hd	12	1nk	Errico C	119 w	*.75	95-16	CraftyAdmiral119nkYildiz1222½Eatontown1161	Driving hard	10
30Jan52- 6Hia	gd 1⅛	:49 1:14 1:39 1:514	4↑ Alw 4500	2	1	11	12	12	1¾	Errico C	108 w	*1.15	79-25	CraftyAdmrl108¾ToyFox10710WhyNotNow1192	Never headed	6
23Jan52- 7Hia	fst 7f	:223 :444 1:091 1:22	3↑ Palm Beach H 13k	7	2	22	2hd	11	12	Errico C	107 w	10.70	102-12	CraftyAdmiral1072Woodchuck1163OilCapitol1122	Drew clear	10
17Jan52- 7Hia	fst 6f	:221 :452 1:10	3↑ Hia Inaugural H 13k	7	9	63	53¼	65¾	44½	Basile M	109 w	20.85	93-12	Spartan Valor121hdJumbo1182Woodchuck1192½	No mishap	14
2Jan52- 6TrP	fst 6f	:223 :452 1:102	4↑ Alw 3000	5	6	31½	2½	1½	11½	Basile M	110 w	4.15	95-12	CraftyAdmiral1101½BullyBoy120nkTeaneckFlash1102	Driving	10
Previously owned by H.A. Grant;previously trained by H. Hughes																
7Aug51- 5Sar	fst 6f	:231 :464 1:123	Alw 3500	7	6	3nk	3½	63	66¼	Green B	113wb	23.45	79-17	Dulat1131¼Yildiz121nkWho Dini103nk	Gave way	7
Previously trained by B.B. Williams																
14Nov50- 5Jam	fst 6f	:223 :462 1:12	Alw 3500	2	4	42¼	53¾	31½	32	Mehrtens W	116 w	2.05	85-17	Who Dini116noTenure1162Crafty Admiral1163	Went well	7
1Nov50- 6Jam	fst 1 1/16	:24 :472 1:12 1:434	Wakefield H 18k	7	1	11	32	33	511	Mehrtens W	112 w	19.75	82-15	Uncle Miltie1265Oats1061Royal Mustang113nk	Tired	11
18Oct50- 6Jam	fst 6f	:223 :453 1:111	Remsen H 12k	3	3	63	97½	1013	87½	Mehrtens W	119 w	3.60	83-15	Repetoire1121½Rough 'n Tumble120noPictus1182	No menace	12
12Oct50- 5Jam	sly 5½f	:23 :47 1:061	Alw 4000	6	3	12	12	13	13½	Mehrtens W	119 w	*.70	87-18	CraftyAdmiral1193½AllIsWell116½GrayMatter114½	Easily	6
5Aug50- 4Sar	sly 6f	:23 :464 1:13	U S Hotel 19k	5	2	2hd	2hd	2½	2½	Mehrtens W	114 w	2.25	82-19	NorthernStar118½CraftyAdmrl1143½Pltoon1092½	Good effort	5
26Jly50- 6Jam	fst 5½f	:223 :462 1:053	Alw 3000	7	4	13	11	13	14	Mehrtens W	118 w	*1.10	90-16	CraftyAdmiral1184FirstRepeater1151¼BlueSpeed1183	Easily	7
13Jly50- 4Jam	fst 5f	:224 :454 :59	©Md Sp Wt	3	2	21½	21½	2hd	12	Mehrtens W	118 w	4.75	95-12	Crafty Admiral1182Tripoli118nkBob Considine1181	Handily	12
7Jly50- 4Jam	fst 5f	:223 :47 :592	©Md Sp Wt	8	10	74¼	57½	33½	42	Atkinson T	118 w	6.10	91-14	Aware118½Tripoli1181Motif118½	Went well	12

Decathlon

b. c. 1953, by Olympia (Heliopolis)–Dog Blessed, by Bull Dog
Own.– River Divide Farm
Br.– Nuckols Brothers (Ky)
Tr.– R.T. Shepp

Lifetime record: 42 25 8 1 $269,530

30Oct57- 7GS	fst 6f	:214 :441 1:093	3↑ Princeton H 22k	7 1 1½ 13 12½ 1nk	Lawless R	133wb	*.40	96-15	Decathlon133nkNan's Mink1121¼Itobe1162½	Taken in hand 7
5Oct57- 7Suf	fst 6f	:221 :451 1:11	2↑ John Alden H 28k	9 3 2hd 1hd 1½ 14	Hartack W	133wb	*.60	93-21	DH Lord Jeep111 DH Decathln1334Venomous114½	Hung,lasted 10
21Sep57- 7Atl	fst 7f	:22 :434 1:082 1:213	3↑ Longport H 22k	4 1 12 13 13 11½	Lawless R	132wb	*.40	98-09	Decathlon1321½Manteau1132½SkipperBll1153	Stumbled start 4
19Aug57- 7Atl	sf 5½f Ⓣ	:232 :47 :59 1:051	3↑ Alw 4500	5 1 13 15 14 11	Lawless R	113wb	*.40	93-07	Decathlon1131Tudor Era1133½Leap Tide1116	Taken in hand 8
27Jly57- 7Nar	fst 6f	:221 :451 1:103	3↑ Bristol H 20k	2 2 2hd 21½ 21½ 21	Lawless R	134wb	*.30	92-18	Oclirock1061Decathlon1341PineEcho115nk	Hit rail on turn 6
10Jly57- 6Mth	fst 6f	:22 :45 1:092	3↑ Rumson H 16k	1 2 13 14 13 12½	Lawless R	133wb	*.40	98-14	Decathlon1332½Nahoodah1231Nan'sMnk1112½	In hand all way 5
11Jun57- 6Mth	fst 6f	:212 :433 1:082	3↑ Oceanport H 16k	7 1 12 11 11 1¾	Hartack W	130wb	*.60	103-07	Decathlon130¾Itobe1162½Nahodah1225	Under a clever ride 7
17Jan57- 7Hia	fst 6f	:213 :442 1:092	3↑ Hia Inaugural H 27k	12 1 1hd 1½ 1½ 1¾	Hartack W	135wb	*.75	98-09	Decathlon1351¾I Appeal1171½Eiffel Blue112hd	Easily best 16
1Jan57- 7TrP	fst 6f	:214 :443 1:092	3↑ New Years H 11k	5 1 1½ 12 12 11¼	Hartack W	133wb	*.30	100-07	Decathlon1331¼GrayPhantom1131NewTrend1141½	Easily best 8
15Dec56- 7TrP	fst 6f	:22 :443 1:092	3↑ Coral Gables H 11k	5 1 11½ 12 12½ 12½	Hartack W	130wb	*.45	100-13	Decathlon1302½Flight History1134Supreme Joy111nk	Easily 11
28Nov56- 7TrP	fst 5½f	:214 :442 :563 1:031	3↑ Inaugural H (Div 1) 11k	5 3 12½ 13 14 14½	Hartack W	126wb	*.35	100-11	Decathlon1264½Apollo110nkWar Age112¾	Much the best 10
31Oct56- 7GS	sly 6f	:221 :444 1:102	3↑ Princeton H 25k	3 5 3½ 22 2½ 2hd	Martin GR	126wb	*2.20	92-17	Decimal112hdDecathlon1262½Impromptu1182	14
	Stumbled start,steadied									
18Oct56- 7Jam	sly 6f	:224 :453 1:104	2↑ Sport Page H 24k	1 2 12 12 12 2¾	Martin GR	126wb	*2.10	92-15	JoeJones125¾Decathlon126½HistoryBook111nk	Used in pace 13
25Aug56- 7Rkm	fst 6f	:213 :44 1:093	Rkm Spl 15k	4 2 21½ 2hd 1hd 1½	Martin GR	129wb	*.50	100-08	Decathlon129½LordJep1091½Tournur105½	Under strong drive 9
6Aug56- 6Mth	sly 6f	:22 :451 1:101	3↑ Rumson H 17k	2 2 11 2½ 33 45½	Martin GR	121wb	*1.10	88-20	Impromptu113noStar Rover1205Admiral Vee111½	Speed,tired 7
23Jly56- 7Jam	fst 6f	:224 :453 1:103	3↑ Wilson H 23k	3 3 12½ 11½ 12 2no	Martin GR	119wb	*1.60	94-17	Ambrgrs107noDcthlon119noMr.Turf1091½	Set pace,nosed out 10
23Jun56- 6Mth	fst 6f	:212 :44 1:091	Select H 23k	4 1 1½ 12 12 12½	Martin GR	126wb	*1.20	99-07	Dcthlon1262½Itob114noMr.Ptrck119nk	Good lead,ridden out 8
12Jun56- 7Mth	fst 6f	:213 :44 1:092	3↑ Oceanport H (Div 2) 17k	3 3 11 1½ 11 1½	Martin GR	116wb	*.80	98-04	Decathlon116½IAppeal113nkRoyalBrr1081¼	Under long drive 10
29May56- 7GS	fst 6f	:222 :444 1:10	Alw 10000	1 1 11½ 11 11½ 11¼	Martin GR	124wb	*.60	94-13	Decathlon1241¼Itobe111hdManorWis1183½	Under clever ride 6
5May56- 7GS	fst 6f	:213 :441 1:094	Del Valley 30k	8 1 11 1½ 11 21	Martin GR	124wb	*1.40	94-13	Mr.Patrick1151Decathlon1241Nan'sMink115¾	Speed,faltered 10
14Apr56- 7Bow	fst 6f	:224 :46 1:111	Gov Gold Cup 34k	7 1 11 12 1½ 2hd	Martin GR	124wb	*.60	95-15	Besomer112hdDecathln1248Kingmakr1121½	Headed,no excuse 7
17Mar56- 7GP	fst 6½f	:222 :45 1:094 1:154	Alw 6000	4 1 12 13 11½ 1nk	Martin GR	122wb	*.50	100-08	Decathlon122nkReaping Right1225Massai1082	Tiring,lasted 8
7Mar56- 7GP	fst 6½f	:22 :443 1:092 1:16	Hutcheson 12k	4 2 11½ 13 13 15	Martin GR	122wb	*.75	99-11	Decathlon1225Busher Fantasy1222Getthere Jack122½	Easily 6
27Feb56- 7Hia	fst 6f	:22 :442 1:094	Alw 10000	7 1 12 13 14 14	Martin GR	122wb	2.30	98-11	Decathlon1224GetthereJack1221½WhittledyCut1113½	Easily 8
1Feb56- 7Hia	gd 7f	:224 :462 1:112 1:244	Bahamas 27k	15 1 11 2hd 35 411	Martin GR	126wb	12.75	75-31	EiffelBlue1144DarkCharger1187GunShot114hd	Early speed 15
21Jan56- 7Hia	sly 6f	:221 :46 1:122	©Hibiscus 23k	2 3 1hd 13 12 1no	Martin GR	122wb	1.90	85-20	Decathlon122noLibertySun112nkComeonRed1145	Just lasted 6
24Dec55- 7TrP	fst 6f	:221 :444 1:103	Dade County H 8.3k	1 4 11½ 12 13 14	Martin GR	126wb	*.70	94-08	Decathlon1264Dark Toga114noLoose Lip1121	Well in hand 6
3Dec55- 7TrP	fst 5½f	:214 :45 :57 1:033	De Soto H 8.8k	2 4 12 11½ 12 13	Martin GR	122wb	3.25	98-11	Decathlon1223Phar Wind1151½Hoop Band119½	Ridden out 10
22Oct55- 7Suf	fst 1 70	:23 :464 1:123 1:433	Mayflower 30k	3 1 13 11½ 31 85¾	Martin GR	122wb	11.70	81-18	Countermnd116¾CombstonII116noAkboy1161	Much used early 14
8Oct55- 6Bel	sly 6½f-W	:221 :451 1:10 1:164	Futurity 125k	5 5 115¾ 1418 1523	Martin GR	122 w	14.65f	65-12	Nail1221¼Head Man122¾Polly's Jet1221	Dropped back early 15
	Geldings not eligible									
1Oct55- 7Atl	sf 1Ⓣ	:233 :471 1:123 1:392	Abescon Island 31k	8 1 11 1hd 65½ 89½	Martin GR	121 w	20.90	74-16	HappyNewYear110¾CombustionII113¾Espea1131½	Speed,tired 11
22Sep55- 6Atl	fm 5½f Ⓣ	:224 :461 :59 1:05	Alw 4000	6 1 2hd 32 46 37	Hartack W	116wb	*1.80	87-06	Nahodah1162ErrardPrince1145Decathlon116nk	Used up early 8
10Sep55- 7Atl	fst 7f	:213 :441 1:09 1:23	Worlds Playground 30k	6 4 33 53½ 610 815	Martin GR	122wb	11.70	76-11	BusherFantasy110¾Espea112nkNeedls1222½	Brief foot,tired 9
3Sep55- 5Atl	fst 6f	:223 :46 1:12	Alw 4500	7 1 2½ 1hd 2hd 2¾	Culmone J	124wb	1.80	84-18	Pylades112¾Decthlon1243BuFond1165	Tried to bear in late 7
27Aug55- 6Sar	fst 6½f	:23 :47 1:12 1:181	Hopeful 71k	4 6 2hd 2½ 912 919	Martin G	122wb	9.05	75-19	Needles1223½Career Boy1226Jean Baptiste1221	Early speed 9
20Aug55- 4Sar	fst 6f	:224 :463 1:122	Grand Union Hotel 26k	6 6 44½ 32 64½ 64	Martin G	122wb	*1.35	82-19	CareerBoy1221¾Nan'sMink114½HedMn1221½	Stumbled at start 8
8Aug55- 6Mth	gd 6f	:214 :453 1:103	Sapling 37k	1 3 2½ 21½ 3nk 22	Martin GR	124wb	2.70	90-22	Needles1162Decathlon1241¼Polly's Jet1245	Closed well 6
4Jly55- 6Mth	fst 5½f	:213 :451 1:04	©Tyro 21k	5 1 12 12 12 1¾	Martin GR	122wb	2.70	104-11	Decathlon122¾Nan'sMink1152BuFond1151½	Under brisk drive 8
25Jun55- 7Nar	fst 5½f	:233 :462 :59 1:054	Nar Nursery 11k	1 5 1½ 11 1½ 1hd	Martin GR	117wb	*.30	93-17	Decathlon117hdOur Pleasure1122¼Impressed1143½	Held on 5
28May55- 7Suf	fst 5f	:222 :454 :581	Bay State Kindrgrtn 11k	6 1 1hd 11 12 11½	Martin GR	117wb	2.00	101-10	Decathlon1171½DarkCharger1174½GettheréJack1221	Driving 8
14May55- 4Suf	fst 4½f	:224 :462 :523	Alw 3000	5 9 11½ 1hd 1¾	Martin GR	119wb	*.50	102-00	Decathlon119¾The River1193Frosty Mr.1191½	Driving clear 10
5May55- 4Suf	fst 4½f	:23 :462 :532	Md Sp Wt	5 4 11½ 11½ 12	Martin GR	118wb	*1.60	98-02	Decathlon1182Suave1183SpiceRound118½	Scored very easily 8

Dedicate

b. c. 1952, by Princequillo (Prince Rose)–Dini, by John P. Grier
Own.– Jan Burke
Br.– Mrs Edward G. Burke (Ky)
Tr.– G.C. Winfrey

Lifetime record: 43 12 9 5 $533,200

2Nov57- 0GS	sly 1¹⁄₁₆	:242 :481 1:124 1:442	3↑ Alw 5575	2 2 21 1½ 1½ 12	Hartack W	126wb	-	88-20	Dedicate1262OleTravis11610WiseMargin114	Placed to drive 3
	Special race - Run between 6th and 7th races. No wagering									
28Sep57- 7Bel	fst 1¼	:471 1:11 1:36 2:01	3↑ Woodward 106k	1 4 44 42 1½ 11½	Hartack W	126wb	3.80	95-13	Dedicate1261½GallantMan1202BoldRuler120hd	Strong drive 4
18Sep57- 7Bel	fst 1⅛	:463 1:10 1:342 1:471	3↑ Nassau County H 28k	3 2 21 2hd 2½ 2nk	Arcaro E	126wb	3.35	103-11	Gallant Man121nkDedicate1261Reneged121nk	Impeded mildly 7
24Aug57- 7Sar	fst 1¼	:48 1:123 1:382 2:043	3↑ Saratoga H 58k	10 7 77½ 73½ 53 58	Boland W	127wb	*1.20	77-17	Reneged1131RicciTavi1161½CrrBoy1184	Bore out in stretch 10
10Aug57- 7Atl	fst 1³⁄₁₆	:472 1:112 1:361 1:544	3↑ Atl City H 100k	8 4 42 2hd 11½ 13	Arcaro E	126wb	*.60	114-09	D Dedicate1263RoyalBeconII1121½Hlfst112½	Crowded horses 8
	Disqualified and placed last,track record disallowed									
13Jly57- 6Mth	fst 1¼	:463 1:104 1:354 2:014	3↑ Monmouth H 113k	7 3 21½ 2hd 12 13½	Arcaro E	124wb	*.90	97-13	Dedicate1243½Third Brother119¾Rockcastle109¾	Mild drive 9
4Jly57- 7Bel	fst 1¼	:471 1:11 1:363 2:023	3↑ Suburban H 85k	3 3 33½ 33½ 31½ 3nk	Boland W	126wb	*4.15	87-13	TrafficJudge124hdLoftyPeak118nkDedict1262½	Impeded late 11
8Jun57- 7Bel	fst 1	:223 :452 1:103 1:36	3↑ Metropolitan H 62k	9 10 74½ 42½ 2hd 2¾	Boland W	126wb	4.00	93-11	Traffic Judge118¾Dedicate1261Greek Spy1141¼	Led briefly 17
30May57- 7Bel	fst 7f	:221 :452 1:101 1:23	3↑ Carter H 58k	5 7 75¼ 3½ 1½ 2hd	Boland W	126wb	6.40	95-13	Portersville111hdDdct126nkJutlnd1123	Led briefly,headed 11
30Mar57- 7Bow	fst 1¹⁄₁₆	:244 :484 1:123 1:443	3↑ J B Campbell H 111k	6 3 3½ 2hd 11 1no	Boland W	124wb	*1.10	90-18	Dedicate124noThird Brother118¾Akbar Khan111¾	Hard drive 8
16Mar57- 7Bow	fst 1¹⁄₁₆	:242 :481 1:121 1:442	3↑ Bowie H 27k	3 4 41½ 2hd 1½ 2no	Cutshaw O	124wb	*1.40	91-14	ThirdBrother116noDedicate1242½PaperTiger117¾	Held well 7
15Feb57- 7Hia	fst 6f	:224 :454 1:101	4↑ Alw 7500	1 6 52¼ 62¾ 63¼ 63	Guerin E	126wb	6.90	91-12	AdmiralVee114nkCanadianChamp1221SkipprBill118hd	Evenly 7
12Nov56- 7Lrl	sf *1½Ⓣ	2:39	3↑ D C Int'l 100k	4 8 76¼ 77½ 412 517	Boland W	126wb	*2.80	37-40	MasterBoing1225MisterGus1267PrinceCortauld1265	Crowded 10
3Nov56- 7Jam	sly 1⅝	:492 1:382 2:032 2:413	3↑ Gallant Fox H 84k	7 2 1½ 32 32 33	Boland W	126wb	5.25	101-14	Summer Tan1241Midafternoon1182Dedicate1261¼	Held well 10
13Oct56- 8Haw	fst 1¼	:47 1:111 1:362 2:022	3↑ Haw Gold Cup H 129k	6 3 3nk 2hd 1hd 1hd	Boland W	120wb	*1.80	91-16	Dedicate120hdSummerTan1194Fnd1195	Held on in hard drive 8
15Sep56- 7Atl	fm 1³⁄₁₆Ⓣ	:472 1:12 1:38 1:561	3↑ U Nations H 100k	5 3 31½ 31½ 41½ 41¼	Boland W	117wb	3.80	97-02	CareerBoy1161Find117hdMisterGus119hd	In close quarters 9
25Aug56- 6Sar	fst 1¼	:483 1:132 1:383 2:041	3↑ Saratoga H 57k	7 3 31 2hd 11 2hd	Boland W	123wb	*1.00	87-18	PaperTiger109hdDedicat1237Fnd1192½	Bore in badly,headed 9
18Aug56- 6Sar	fst 1⅛	:472 1:112 1:364 1:494	3↑ Whitney 46k	7 4 2hd 1hd 13 14	Boland W	116wb	*2.00	101-14	Dedicate1164Summer Tan1204½Paper Tiger112½	Easy score 8
4Aug56- 7Jam	fst 1³⁄₁₆	:474 1:12 1:37 1:554	3↑ Brooklyn H 55k	4 1 1½ 1hd 3½ 1hd	Arcaro E	114wb	*1.75	97-16	Dedicate114hdMidftrnoon116hdFnd1192½	Came again,just up 8
4Jly56- 7Bel	fst 1¼	:463 1:101 1:35 2:004	3↑ Suburban H 83k	3 1 1hd 1hd 1½ 21¼	Woodhouse H	111wb	18.20	95-10	Nashua1281¼Ddct1112¼Subhdr1125	Bobbled at 1⅛,swerved 8
21May56- 5Bel	fst 6f	:231 :463 1:102	4↑ Alw 5000	2 3 53 31½ 21½ 22½	Boland W	120wb	*1.10	94-12	Blessbull1142½Dedicate1204Dark Peter1171¾	Bore in badly 6
15May56- 6Bel	fst 6f	:224 :461 1:103	4↑ Alw 5000	3 5 66½ 35 36 36	Boland W	120wb	*.65	90-13	Dark Ruler1173½White Knight1202½Dedicate1202	No excuse 7
4May56- 7Jam	fst 6f	:234 :461 1:111	4↑ Alw 5000	7 4 11 11 11 2no	Boland W	124wb	*.85	91-20	White Knight113noDedicate1246Goulash113no	Just failed 9
1Oct55- 6Bel	sly 1⅛	:472 1:12 1:361 1:481	3↑ Woodward H 58k	2 1 12 12 32 34	Boland W	110wb	8.85	94-11	TrafficJudge118hdPaperTigr1074Ddct110hd	Made early pace 7
24Sep55- 7Bel	sly 1	:222 :444 1:093 1:351	Jerome H 30k	8 4 44½ 34 45 44¼	Bailey PJ	122wb	5.70	94-10	Traffic Judge1261½Star Rover121noImpromptu1183	Evenly 13
6Sep55- 6Aqu	fst 6f	:23 :462 1:11	3↑ Alw 5000	8 6 33½ 22½ 11 1nk	Boland W	119wb	*1.10	97-16	D Dedicate119nkCrash Dive1176Brother Tex1132½	Bore out 8
	Disqualified									

16Jly55- 7AP	fst 1	:231 :453 1:093 1:351	Arl Classic 148k	5	4	32½	36	512	68½	Boulmetis S	120wb	7.60	87-10	Nashu126½TrffcJudg1201¼Impromptu1204	Early factor,tired	7
9Jly55- 6AP	hy 7f	:23 :46 1:11 1:234	Alw 7500	4	3	2½	2½	2½	25	Hartack W	124wb	*1.30	86-25	SpeedRouser1185Dedicate124nkHoneysAlibi1245	Tired late	8
14May55- 7GS	fst 1⅛	:454 1:094 1:351 1:481	Jersey 62k	9	3	21	1hd	1hd	1nk	Boulmetis S	118wb	3.20	101-07	Dedict118nkSrtog1186Smmy1131½	Held gamely in long drive	12
7May55- 7GS	fst 6f	:22 :443 1:093	Del Valley 31k	9	1	74¼	45	31	1½	Boulmetis S	115wb	8.20	100-05	Dedicate115½Informant1131½Craigwood1121	Strong finish	12
14Apr55- 6Jam	my 1 1/16	:24 :483 1:133 1:464	Alw 5000	4	3	21	1½	11	11½	Boland W	113wb	2.30	78-18	Dedicate1131½Simmy117nkDoorPriz1153½	Under brisk urging	6
9Apr55- 5Jam	fst 6f	:233 :473 1:114	Alw 4000	10	2	2½	2½	12	14	Boland W	115wb	2.60	88-17	Dedicate1154Dobey Doc115½Taratara1104½	Speed to spare	12
2Apr55- 3Jam	fst 6f	:232 :47 1:133 3↑	Md Sp Wt	7	3	1hd	1½	15	14½	Boland W	114wb	3.60	79-18	Dedicate1144½Reclaim114¾Skysweeper109nk	Easy score	14
2Mar55- 4SA	fst 6f	:222 :453 1:111	Alw 4500	5	9	106¾	118½	109¾	88	Boland W	113wb	7.40	81-13	Bangborough1201¾Nasrulline107½Jungle Art1121¼	Outrun	12
17Feb55- 4SA	my 6f	:224 :47 1:122	Md Sp Wt	8	7	54	33	59	912	Boland W	118wb	2.85	71-24	Bangborough118hdHappy America11810Tonalea113nk	Outrun	12
1Nov54- 4Jam	my 6f	:233 :47 1:14	©Md Sp Wt	2	8	52¾	52¼	11½	4¾	Guerin E	118wb	3.05	76-26	TurkishIsle118hdCavort118nkMahopc118½	Weakened in drive	14
26Oct54- 2Jam	fst 6f	:234 :47 1:131	©Md Sp Wt	7	5	2½	2hd	1hd	31½	Guerin E	118wb	3.05	79-22	EverBest118½OutofReach1181Dedicate1186	Shortened stride	10
9Oct54- 2Bel	fst 7f	:23 :471 1:131 1:262	Md Sp Wt	7	5	62¾	62¼	66	44	Guerin E	118 w	4.25	74-15	FlyingFury1181½GoldenLand1182½War'sHistory116hd	Evenly	14
24Sep54- 4Bel	fst 5½f-W	:224 :46 1:042	©Md Sp Wt	9	3		123¾	4¾	51	Guerin E	117 w	5.25	85-14	Taratara117hdRacingFool117noHerHero117½	Tired slightly	27
18Sep54- 3Aqu	fst 6f	:232 :473 1:123	Md Sp Wt	8	4	75½	77¼	75¼	56½	Guerin E	118 w	3.00	82-10	Minute Parade1182½Silent One115½This Evening1182	Outrun	9
31Aug54- 4Aqu	sly 6f	:231 :47 1:12	©Md Sp Wt	11	8	910	99	68	59	Guerin E	118 w	4.50	83-17	Adam'sApple1182HoneysAlibi1183Mr.Al L.1182	Lacked speed	11
21Aug54- 2Sar	fst 5½f	:233 :472 1:00 1:063	Md Sp Wt	12	7	87	1110	715	69¾	Guerin E	118 w	15.25f	74-17	Decimal1184Mr.Al L.118nkRacingFool1182½	Never a menace	13
14Aug54- 5Sar	fst 5½f	:23 :461 1:073	Md Sp Wt	5	12	108¼	1013	1114	1012	Guerin E	118 w	13.70	67-18	LittleDell118nk[DH]RacingFool118[DH]ModelAce118¾	Outrun	13

Doubledogdare

b. f. 1953, by Double Jay (Balladier)–Flaming Top, by Omaha — **Lifetime record: 25 13 6 1 $258,206**

Own.– Claiborne Farm
Br.– Claiborne Farm (Ky)
Tr.– M. Jolley

3Nov56- 7CD	fst 1	:232 :462 1:104 1:37 3↑	ⓕFalls City H 22k	5	5	58	43	21	1¾	Brooks S	121 w	*1.10	90-14	Doubledogdare121¾Queen Hopeful1225Lycka117½	Driving	8
19Oct56- 6Kee	fst 1⅛	:461 1:103 1:361 1:491 3↑	ⓕSpinster 70k	4	9	88½	77	2hd	11¼	Heckmann J	119 w	*2.60e	99-05	Doubledogdre1191¼QueenHopful1233LdySwords1192½	Driving	14
	Open to 3-, 4- and 5-year-olds															
16Oct56- 4Kee	fst 6f	:221 :444 1:091	Alw 7500	3	3	43½	34	23	21¾	Brooks S	119 w	3.20	102-04	Swoon'sSon1261¾Doubledogdare1191½JovilJov1122	Sharp try	4
10Oct56- 5Kee	fst 6f	:224 :454 1:10 3↑	Alw 7500	5	3	42	31½	2hd	11	Brooks S	120 w	*.40	100-04	Doubledogdare1201LeatherKid1182½FthfulSong113nk	Driving	5
29Aug56- 7Was	fst 1⅛	:47 1:113 1:372 1:493 3↑	ⓕBeverly H 27k	1	5	54½	32	53¾	57½	Brooks S	112wb	2.80	85-13	Amoret113nkLadySwords1071QueenHopefl1205	Well up,tired	9
8Aug56- 7Was	fst 7f	:214 :441 1:093 1:222	ⓕMisty Isle H 22k	8	3	55½	32½	21½	2hd	Brooks S	124wb	*.80e	93-11	PuckrUp116hdDoubldogdare1246CandyDsh1192½	Just missed	9
25Jly56- 7AP	fst 1	:224 :452 1:102 1:364 3↑	ⓕArl Matron H 57k	5	2	22	1hd	11	42¼	Heckmann J	114wb	2.10e	86-16	Delta119noAmoret113¾Queen Hopeful1201½	Took lead,tired	12
14Jly56- 8AP	fst 1	:23 :454 1:103 1:364	Arl Classic 158k	2	1	14	11½	12	31¾	Brooks S	112wb	8.50	86-14	Swoon'sSon1201½BenA.Jones117nkDoubledogdare112nk	Tired	8
27Jun56- 7AP	fst 1	:23 :452 1:093 1:36	ⓕCleopatra H 22k	5	3	31½	42	21	2hd	Brooks S	122 w	1.60	92-14	Princess Turia121hdDoubledogdare122hdSupple1154	Sharp	8
9Jun56- 7Bel	fst 1⅜	:49 1:124 1:381 2:163	ⓕC C A Oaks 59k	1	5	56	44	44	54	Brooks S	121 w	2.90	84-12	Levee121nkPrincessTuria121hdLadySwords1211¾	Taken wide	9
16May56- 8Was	gd 6f	:223 :46 1:11	ⓕCoronet 16k	3	8	53¼	54½	3nk	12	Brooks S	117 w	*.70	90-22	Doubledogdare1172Royal Lark1173¼Miss Ottawa1101	Easily	9
4May56- 7CD	fst 1 1/16	:242 :482 1:133 1:444	ⓕKy Oaks 30k	5	3	37	33	21	2no	Brooks S	121 w	1.60	94-14	PrincessTuria116noDoubledogdare1213½Tournure1162½	Nosed	9
28Apr56- 7CD	fst 6f	:224 :453 1:113	ⓕOaks Prep 13k	5	2	46½	45½	21	1½	Brooks S	121 w	*.40	92-10	Doubledogdare121½Princess Turia1182Ament118nk	Just up	8
19Apr56- 6Kee	fst 6f	:221 :453 1:112	ⓕAshland 19k	5	1	23	21	12	13½	Brooks S	121 w	*.40	93-13	Doubledogdare1213½GuardRail1184½WarningBell1144½	Easily	5
12Apr56- 5Kee	fst 6f	:222 :46 1:11	ⓕAlw 5000	2	5	25	32½	1½	1¾	Brooks S	121 w	*.50	95-11	Doubledogdare121¾Guard Rail1184½Supple121hd	Hard drive	6
15Oct55- 6Kee	fst 7f	:223 :453 1:111 1:241	ⓕAlcibiades 39k	1	2	12	12	13	14	Brooks S	119wb	*.30	91-10	Doubledogdare1194Ament1196½Supple1191	Speed in reserve	4
8Oct55- 6Bel	sly 6½f-W	:221 :451 1:10 1:164	Futurity 125k	12	10		51½	64	96	Arcaro E	119wb	4.85	82-12	Nail1221¼Head Man122¾Polly's Jet1221	Brief early foot	15
	Geldings not eligible															
1Oct55- 4Bel	gd 6f-WC	:222 :451 1:094	ⓕMatron 60k	9	8		43½	33	11	Arcaro E	119wb	*1.30	90-10	Doubledogdare1191Glamour1191Beautillon119¾	Strong drive	18
22Sep55- 4Bel	fst 5½f-W	:223 :451 1:032	ⓕAlw 4500	2	7		5¾	11½	13	Arcaro E	119wb	*1.20	91-09	Doubledogdare1193Glamour1122½Ferocious1111	Handy score	17
22Aug55- 6Sar	fst 6f	:232 :471 1:132	ⓕSpinaway 50k	4	2	3½	1½	21	21	Nichols J	119wb	*1.00	80-22	Register1141Doubledogdare119hdAiming High1192	Gamely	6
2Jly55- 6Mth	fst 5½f	:213 :46 1:051	ⓕColleen 27k	2	14	88¾	55	2hd	13	Nichols J	119wb	*2.00	98-11	Doubledogdare1193DarkCharger1191MissErlen1121½	Driving	14
18May55- 6Bel	fst 5f-WC	:223 :452 :573	ⓕNational Stallion 30k	1	2		21	12	16	Westrope J	119wb	*1.45	91-13	Doubledogdare1196Supple1151½Catchpenny1194½	Easily best	6
27Apr55- 6Bel	sly 4½f-W	:214 :451 :512	ⓕFashion 20k	7	7		21	23½	23	Westrope J	114wb	8.70	89-13	Pretty Plunger1143Doubledogdare1144Tweetsie114no	Gamely	14
14Apr55- 4Kee	fst *4f	:50	Alw 3500	3	5		54	41	1hd	Brooks S	112wb	2.90	97-05	Doubledogdare112hdWaikiki1153All Comers1181¼	Driving	7
23Feb55- 6Hia	fst 3f	:214 :331	Hia Juvenile (Div1) 24k	12	11			96¼	53¾	Brooks S	111 w	13.60	- -	Well Marked115½Bob-o-Bob114¾Roman Whirl1171½	Rallied	17

Evening Out

br. f. 1951, by Shut Out (Equipoise)–Evening Belle, by Eight Thirty — **Lifetime record: 21 11 1 4 $214,360**

Own.– Mrs G.D. Widener
Br.– Mrs George D. Widener (Ky)
Tr.– W.F. Mulholland

11Jly55- 6Jam	fst 6f	:23 :461 1:11 3↑	ⓕChamplain H 16k	8	6	41½	21	24½	36¾	Bailey PJ	126wb	5.70	85-17	OilPainting1216Canadiana122¾EveningOut126no	Early speed	9
25Jun55- 6Del	gd 1 1/16	:232 :471 1:12 1:443 3↑	ⓕNew Castle 39k	9	9	83¼	1212	1112	1213	Westrope J	120wb	10.50	75-17	Clear Dawn1162½Open Sesame1121½Cerise Reine120hd	Outrun	15
18Jun55- 6Mth	fst 6f	:212 :441 1:094 3↑	ⓕRegret H 23k	8	7	42	3½	1½	1½	Boulmetis S	122wb	7.30	96-10	Evening Out122½Gandharva1151Another World116½	Driving	12
8Jun55- 6Bel	fst 1 1/16	:224 :451 1:094 1:414 3↑	ⓕTop Flight H 30k	4	10	108½	97	811	811	McCreary C	121 w	8.00	91-11	Parlo1263Gainsboro Girl114½Spinning Top113nk	Outrun	12
1Jun55- 6Bel	fst 7f	:23 :462 1:111 1:241 3↑	ⓕGolden Annivrsy H 20k	6	5	52¾	53½	32½	4¾	Arcaro E	122 w	2.85	88-14	Dispute114¾Parlo125hdOil Painting107no	Speed,late rally	11
17May55- 6Bel	fst 6f	:224 :461 1:11 3↑	ⓕHandicap 5000	10	5	1hd	11	14	31	Arcaro E	125wb	*1.30	93-13	RosClag112¾MissWeesie110nkEvnngOut1254½	Speedy,faltered	10
5May55- 6Bel	fst 6f	:223 :46 1:113 4↑	ⓕAlw 5000	3	5	3½	1hd	1½	1nk	Arcaro E	120wb	*1.30	91-13	EveningOut120nkDispute1171EverBright1091	Cleverly rated	6
18Aug54- 6Sar	fst 1⅛	:474 1:121 1:38 1:523 3↑	ⓕDiana H 23k	10	4	32	11	14	31½	Arcaro E	116wb	*1.30	85-19	LavenderHill1211½LaCorredora121hdEvenngOut1166	Bore out	10
7Aug54- 6Mth	fst 1⅛	:46 1:101 1:37 1:501	ⓕMth Oaks 63k	7	1	15	14	13	12	Arcaro E	117wb	*1.60	95-12	EveningOut1172ClearDawn1212½JuneFete113½	Never headed	14
28Jly54- 7Mth	fst 6f	:22 :452 1:10	ⓕMiss Woodford 24k	5	7	52½	85½	86	34	Woodhouse H	118 w	*1.10	91-11	ClearDawn1122½Parlo1211½EveningOut118hd	Good late rally	10
5Jly54- 6Del	fst 1¼	:454 1:101 1:361 2:023 3↑	ⓕNew Castle H 138k	6	1	22	24	1617	1822	Arcaro E	114 w	*2.30	67-19	GainsboroGirl1134SunshineNell1262LavenderHill111hd	Quit	20
28Jun54- 6Del	fst 1 1/16	:224 :462 1:112 1:443 3↑	ⓕAlw 10000	10	1	11	13	13	11½	Woodhouse H	104 w	*1.10	88-19	EvningOut1041½GrecianQueen1241½LaCorredora124hd	Easily	12
19Jun54- 6Aqu	fst 1 1/16	:244 :484 1:133 1:463	ⓕGazelle 30k	8	10	106½	87¼	44	21	Arcaro E	113 w	*.40	80-19	On Your Own1131Evening Out1131Fascinator1212½	Gaining	11
14Jun54- 5Aqu	fst 7f	:23 :46 1:104 1:234	ⓕAlw 7500	4	4	44	36½	23½	11	Arcaro E	121 w	*.55	91-10	Evening Out1211On Your Own1141Happy Mood1213½	Driving	10
28Apr54- 5Bel	fst 6f	:23 :461 1:11	ⓕAlw 7500	1	4	1½	1hd	1½	1no	Arcaro E	122 w	*.45	94-12	EvnngOut122noDangrousDame1123½SottoVoce1131½	Just up	4
3Oct53- 5Bel	fst 6½f-W	:221 :451 1:092 1:16	Futurity 117k	13	4		1hd	23	55¾	Scurlock O	119 w	3.70	86-11	Porterhouse1223¼Artismo122½Best Years1221¼	Tired	14
	Geldings not eligible															
26Sep53- 5Bel	fst 6f-WC	:221 :452 1:102	ⓕMatron 53k	2	2		1hd	12½	11¾	Scurlock O	119 w	*.80	89-11	Evening Out1191¾Queen Hopeful1191Clear Dawn119nk	Easily	8
21Aug53- 0Sar	fst 6f	:24 :474 1:133	ⓕSpinaway 51k	2	1	11½	13½	15	18	Scurlock O	123 w	-	80-20	Evening Out1238Alines Pet111	Easily	2
	No wagering															
14Aug53- 6Sar	fst 5½f	:23 :47 :59 1:052	ⓕSchuylerville 13k	3	3	1½	1½	13	14½	Scurlock O	123 w	*1.25	90-18	Evening Out1234½Riant1191Incidentally1233	Easily best	6
20May53- 6Bel	fst 5f-WC	:22 :441 :563	ⓕNational Stallion 29k	5	4		2hd	2hd	1hd	Scurlock O	119 w	*1.25	96-08	Evening Out119hdFascinator1193½Clear Dawn119nk	Driving	10
8May53- 6Bel	fst 4½f-W	:222 :452 :52	ⓕFashion 14k	7	3		21½	2½	12½	Scurlock O	114 w	17.65	89-11	EveningOut1142½WolfGal1191¼SittingDuck1191¾	Ridden out	10

First Landing

b. c. 1956, by Turn-to (Royal Charger)–Hildene, by Bubbling Over — **Lifetime record: 37 19 9 2 $779,577**

Own.– Meadow Stable
Br.– C.T. Chenery (Ky)
Tr.– J.H. Hayes

17Sep60- 7Atl	fm 1 3/16Ⓣ	:463 1:12 1:372 1:57	3↑ U Nations H 100k	4 3 56 76¼ 98¼ 98½	Grant H	123	b	11.10	79-12	T.V.Lark1201¼SwordDancer1271¼BallyAche122hd	Fell back	10
5Sep60- 7Aqu	fst 1	:232 :461 1:102 1:344	3↑ Aqueduct H 56k	4 3 52 45 44½ 43	Arcaro E	122	b	2.75	91-11	Bald Eagle130hdIntentionally125noWarhead1133	Even try	5
30Jly60- 7Aqu	sly 1¼	:471 1:12 1:38 2:03	3↑ Brooklyn H 109k	5 5 67½ 68 610 613	Boulmetis S	123	b	3.95	80-17	On-and-On118hdGrekStr1102Wltz1131¼	Disliked the footing	7
16Jly60- 7Mth	fst 1¼	:47 1:111 1:362 2:024	3↑ Monmouth H 112k	9 3 42½ 44½ 33½ 11¼	Arcaro E	123	b	*1.10	92-19	FirstLanding1231¼ManassaMaulr1171½TlntShow1172½	Driving	9
4Jly60- 7Aqu	fst 1¼	:472 1:111 1:361 2:013	3↑ Suburban H 108k	1 1 1hd 1hd 1hd 2½	Ussery R	122	b	6.90	111-11	SwordDancer125½FirstLanding1221½Waltz1154½	Game effort	6
22Jun60- 8Suf	fst 1¼	:463 1:111 1:37 2:033	3↑ Mass H 56k	1 4 413 67 57½ 44¾	Shoemaker W	124	b	*.70	82-16	TalentShow1171½Polyld1163¼BttlNck107no	Appeared to sulk	7
30May60- 7Aqu	fst 1	:224 :453 1:09 1:333	3↑ Metropolitan H 114k	3 8 41¼ 21½ 21 23½	Boulmetis S	123	b	4.05	104-03	Bald Eagle1283½First Landing123nkTalent Show118¾	Gamely	10
30Apr60- 7Aqu	fst 1⅛	:473 1:114 1:37 1:493	3↑ Grey Lag H 70k	7 2 21½ 22 2½ 2nk	Shoemaker W	124	b	*1.70	96-06	SwordDancer126nkFirstLanding124noWhitley1162	Sharp try	11
9Apr60- 8Lrl	fst 1⅛	:474 1:121 1:371 1:492	Lrl Maturity H 70k	3 1 1½ 1hd 1hd 1hd	Shoemaker W	124	b	1.20	123-05	FirstLandng124hdOn-and-On1226Nimmr116¾	Long,hard drive	5
27Feb60- 7SA	fst 1¼	:462 1:104 1:352 2:003	3↑ S Anita H 145k	9 8 75 72¾ 1112 1113	Arcaro E	123	b	4.10	83-11	Linmold110hdFleet Nasrullah113noAmerigo120nk	No factor	12
13Feb60- 7SA	fst 1⅛	:454 1:102 1:354 1:481	3↑ San Antonio H 57k	6 7 64¾ 51½ 4¾ 22¼	Arcaro E	124	b	*2.10	89-12	Bagdad1232¼FrstLndng1242¼HowNow118no	Finished strongly	11
30Jan60- 7SA	fst 1¼	:461 1:103 1:351 2:003	Maturity 166k	4 5 57 1hd 1hd 1½	Arcaro E	116	b	*2.40	96-13	First Landing116½Bagdad1182½Linmold1172	Drew out slowly	8
16Jan60- 7SA	my 1⅛	:472 1:12 1:374 1:50	San Fernando 55k	5 2 2½ 1hd 1hd 2½	Arcaro E	117	b	*.70	81-24	Kingo'Turf113½FirstLanding1175½CivicPride1135½	Gamely	7
8Jan60- 7SA	fst 1 1/16	:231 :461 1:102 1:421	Handicap 1000	4 3 32 21½ 1hd 1nk	Arcaro E	125	b	*1.00	93-14	FirstLanding125nkCivicPride1148Demobilize114no	Driving	5
7Nov59- 7GS	my 1¼	:461 1:111 1:38 2:053	3↑ Trenton H 87k	8 5 43¼ 43½ 54½ 56¼	Arcaro E	123	b	*2.20	71-27	Greek Star115½Amerigo1211½Talent Show119¾	Well up,tired	9
3Nov59- 7Aqu	fst 1 3/16	:473 1:121 1:374 1:573	Roamer H 57k	5 4 33 3½ 1½ 2no	Arcaro E	123	b	2.50	--	Polylad112noFirst Landing1236½Middle Brother1243	Nosed	9
28Oct59- 4Aqu	sl 1	:24 :471 1:122 1:383	Alw 7500	1 1 1½ 1hd 11½ 11½	Arcaro E	124	b	*.55	--	FirstLanding1241½Polylad112hdTopChargr11220	Brisk drive	5
16Oct59- 6Aqu	fst 6f	:223 :462 1:114	Alw 5000	5 4 33½ 32 1hd 1½	Arcaro E	124	b	*.60	--	FirstLanding124½FightinIndian120¾MoonAgain120½	Driving	7
16May59- 8Pim	fst 1 3/16	:471 1:113 1:374 1:57	Preakness 190k	2 5 34 54¼ 610 916	Arcaro E	126	b	*1.60	72-17	RoyalOrbit1264SwordDancer1263Dunce1262½	Tiring,crowded	11
2May59- 7CD	fst 1¼	:473 1:113 1:36 2:021	Ky Derby 163k	3 7 88½ 44 42¼ 32¼	Arcaro E	126	b	*3.60	94-06	TomyLee126noSwordDancer1262¼FirstLanding1261	Good try	17
28Apr59- 8CD	fst 1	:231 :463 1:10 1:361	Derby Trial (Div 2) 15k	3 2 32 2hd 1hd 11	Arcaro E	122		*.40	94-16	FirstLanding1221JohnBruce116¾Quantrell1161¾	Mild drive	6
18Apr59- 7Jam	fst 1⅛	:461 1:11 1:37 1:493	Wood Memorial 88k	3 2 2hd 1hd 1hd 2¾	Arcaro E	126	b	*.85	92-14	ManassaMauler126¾FirstLanding126¾OurDad1266	No excuse	8
13Apr59- 7Jam	gd 6f	:232 :464 1:101	Alw 7500	5 4 3½ 1hd 1½ 13	Arcaro E	124	b	*.35	96-07	FirstLanding1243Nimmer120¾Hilwn1111¾	Under a mild drive	6
28Feb59- 7Hia	fst 1⅛	:454 1:094 1:352 1:491	Flamingo 135k	7 4 45½ 46 36 34¾	Arcaro E	122	b	*.85	84-11	Troilus1223Open View1221¾First Landing1221¼	No excuses	10
18Feb59- 7Hia	fst 1⅛	:461 1:101 1:36 1:494	Everglades 29k	4 1 1hd 1hd 11 1nk	Arcaro E	126	b	*.20	86-17	FirstLanding126nkMoony117noRareRic120nk	Long,hard drive	7
11Feb59- 6Hia	fst 7f	:224 :452 1:093 1:223	Alw 6000	6 4 41½ 32½ 23 22¾	Arcaro E	124	b	*.35	94-17	Octopus1162¾FirstLndng1242¾Moony1081¾	In close,steadied	9
	Previously raced in the name of C.T. Chenery											
25Oct58- 7GS	sly 1 1/16	:222 :463 1:124 1:462	Garden State 297k	6 8 66½ 23½ 21½ 1hd	Arcaro E	122	wb	*1.50	78-31	FirstLanding122hdTomyLee1222SwordDancer1223	Hard drive	13
18Oct58- 6GS	fst 1 1/16	:232 :463 1:114 1:443	Alw 10000	4 5 36 34½ 21 1¾	Arcaro E	122	wb	*.30	87-17	FirstLanding122¾CraftySkipper1205PenBolro1121½	Cleverly	6
11Oct58- 7Bel	fst 1	:231 :47 1:123 1:392	Champagne 151k	7 7 3nk 1½ 11 1nk	Arcaro E	122	wb	*2.00	77-21	FirstLndng122nk[D]TomyL1223Intntonlly1222	Saddle slipped	10
20Sep58- 7Bel	fst 6½-WC	:214 :443 1:082 1:143	Futurity 114k	5 4 41½ 2hd 21	Arcaro E	122	wb	*.40	98-01	Intentionally1221First Landing122nkDunce1223½	No excuse	8
	Geldings not eligible											
23Aug58- 6Sar	fst 6½f	:23 :463 1:11 1:174	Hopeful 57k	2 1 21½ 1hd 11½ 15½	Arcaro E	122	wb	*.45	96-18	FirstLanding1225½FirstMinstr1221¾ThtLuckyDy1224½	Easily	5
6Aug58- 5Sar	fst 6f	:224 :463 1:124	Sar Spl 14k	2 1 21½ 1hd 11½ 17	Arcaro E	122	wb	*.25	84-24	FirstLandng1227Plot1224½Don'tAlb122no	Much the best	4
23Jly58- 6Jam	fst 5½f	:222 :453 :574 1:04	Great American 33k	1 1 1hd 1hd 1½ 1nk	Arcaro E	122	w	*.20	98-15	FirstLandng122nkAtoll11810JtFul1144½	Best in hard drive	4
17Jly58- 5Jam	fst 5½f	:232 :472 :593 1:054	Alw 5000	1 1 11 1½ 1½ 14	Arcaro E	122	w	*.20	89-23	FirstLanding1224Moony116nkBluevll1161½	Under mild drive	5
2Jun58- 6Bel	fst 5f-WC	:223 :45 :57	Juvenile 35k	10 3 2½ 21½ 11	Arcaro E	117	w	*.90	94-12	First Landing1171Watch Your Step1179Bagdad122nk	Driving	10
23Apr58- 6Jam	sly 5f	:23 :463 :583	Alw 4500	2 4 53 32 32½ 11¾	Arcaro E	118	w	*.65	97-12	First Landing1181¾The Hunter118hdSteverino1189½	Driving	5
14Apr58- 4Jam	fst 5f	:223 :462 :584	©Md Sp Wt	2 4 44½ 21½ 2½ 21	Arcaro E	118	w	*.90	95-14	[D]RestlessWind1181FirstLanding1186SteveW.1186	Bore out	7
	Placed first through disqualification											

Gallant Man (GB)

b. c. 1954, by Migoli (Bois Roussel)–Majideh, by Mahmoud — **Lifetime record: 26 14 4 1 $510,355**

Own.– R. Lowe
Br.– H.H. Aga Khan & Prince Aly Khan (GB)
Tr.– J.A. Nerud

6Sep58- 7Bel	fst 1	:23 :452 1:10 1:35	3↑ Sysonby H 28k	1 7 68½ 52¾ 53¾ 54½	Arcaro E	134	w	*.65	94-14	Cohoes116hdMisterJive1133Rengd124nk	No racing room late	7
22Jly58- 7Hol	fst 1⅝	:464 1:371 2:023 2:41	3↑ Sunset H 107k	5 3 37 2hd 1½ 14	Shoemaker W	132	w	*.50	86-18	GallantMan1324EddieSchmidt1106St.Vincent111nk	Eased up	6
12Jly58- 7Hol	fst 1¼	:461 1:101 1:373 2:013	3↑ Hol Gold Cup H 162k	1 5 55½ 3½ 1hd 1½	Shoemaker W	130	w	*.40	85-18	GallantMan130½EddieSchmidt1101¾Seaneen1181¼	Hard urged	5
14Jun58- 7Bel	fst 1	:231 :461 1:103 1:353	3↑ Metropolitan H 58k	9 9 88¼ 57 42 12	Shoemaker W	130	w	2.95	96-13	GallantMan1302BoldRuler1351½Clm114nk	Drew clear handily	10
30May58- 7Bel	fst 7f	:223 :453 1:101 1:223	3↑ Carter H 58k	2 8 86¾ 75½ 53½ 33	Shoemaker W	128	w	3.60	91-17	BoldRuler1351½TickTock1131½GallantMan128no	Closed well	9
9Nov57- 7GS	gd 1¼	:471 1:111 1:364 2:013	3↑ Trenton H 82k	3 3 311 23½ 23 22¼	Shoemaker W	124	w	*1.40	95-14	BoldRuler1222¼GallantMan1248½RoundTbl124	Gaining slowly	3
12Oct57- 5Bel	fst 2	:50 2:321 2:573 3:23	3↑ J C Gold Cup 80k	3 5 54½ 33 1hd 11	Shoemaker W	119	w	*.30	87-14	Gallant Man1191Third Brother1248Reneged12418	Going away	5
28Sep57- 7Bel	fst 1¼	:471 1:11 1:36 2:01	3↑ Woodward 106k	4 3 33½ 31½ 3½ 21½	Shoemaker W	120	w	*.65	93-13	Dedicate1261½GallantMn1202BoldRulr120hd	Rated,no excuse	4
18Sep57- 7Bel	fst 1⅛	:463 1:10 1:342 1:471	3↑ Nassau County H 28k	1 4 53½ 42¼ 3½ 1nk	Shoemaker W	121	w	*.65	103-11	Gallant Man121nkDedicate1261Reneged121nk	Ridden out	7
17Aug57- 7Sar	fst 1¼	:49 1:14 1:39 2:04	Travers 44k	4 4 44 2hd 1hd 1½	Shoemaker W	126	w	*.15	88-17	GallantMan126½Bureaucracy1167FieldofHonor1127	Handily	5
6Aug57- 7Sar	fst 7f	:23 :454 1:111 1:243	Alw 6000	4 4 611 68½ 1hd 14	Shoemaker W	126	w	*.35	92-23	GallantMan1264LittleHermit1161¾Tenacious1191	Much best	6
15Jun57- 6Bel	fst 1½	:464 1:102 2:012 2:263	Belmont 113k	4 4 23 2hd 11½ 18	Shoemaker W	126	w	.95e	105-07	GallantMan1268InsideTract1264BoldRuler1269	Easily best	6
1Jun57- 7Bel	fst 1⅛	:472 1:113 1:361 1:482	Peter Pan H 28k	3 4 32½ 2hd 1hd 12½	Shoemaker W	124	w	*.45	97-10	GallantMan1242½PromisedLand114¾NahHiss1132½	Mild drive	6
4May57- 7CD	fst 1¼	:47 1:112 1:364 2:021	Ky Derby 152k	4 7 79½ 54 3½ 2no	Shoemaker W	126	w	3.70	96-12	IronLiege126noGllntMn1262¾RoundTbl1263	Misjudged finish	9
20Apr57- 7Jam	fst 1⅛	:48 1:12 1:361 1:484	Wood Memorial 59k	4 3 44½ 2hd 1hd 2no	Choquette J	126	w	8.00	102-10	BoldRuler126noGallantMan1266PromisedLand1262¼	Game try	7
6Apr57- 7Jam	sly 6f	:224 :452 1:11	Swift 23k	6 6 67 54¼ 53¾ 41¾	Choquette J	126	w	2.80	90-15	KingHairan1261¼Missile126½Clm126hd	Best stride too late	7
30Jan57- 7Hia	fst 7f	:223 :45 1:091 1:22	Bahamas 26k	8 5 78 57 58 47¾	Choquette J	123	w	*2.05	92-11	BoldRuler1264½Gen.Duke1142FedrlHll1261¼	Only mild rally	11
19Jan57- 7Hia	fst 6f	:221 :451 1:10	©Hibiscus 26k	10 8 94¼ 64½ 53 1½	Choquette J	117	w	2.60e	95-09	GallantMan117½Missile1221½KingHairan1221½	Strong drive	13
3Jan57- 8TrP	fst 6f	:22 :452 1:092	Alw 2800	2 6 33 11½ 16 16	Choquette J	119	w	*.95	100-09	GallantMan1196Gen.Duke1132Asgard119¾	Drew to long lead	12
25Dec56- 5TrP	fst 6f	:224 :46 1:11	Alw 2800	7 6 54¼ 43½ 43 1nk	Choquette J	117	w	4.05	92-12	GallantMan117nkSundayStar114½Buddy1151¼	Cleverly ridden	9
17Oct56- 5Bel	fst 6f	:221 :454 1:101	Alw 4000	7 5 45 55½ 21½ 1¾	Ussery R	113	w	46.95	98-08	Gallant Man113¾Discernment1158Osceola115hd	Driving hard	12
3Oct56- 6Bel	fst 6f-WC	:223 :453 1:102	Alw 4000	4 7 88 99 910	Choquette J	115	w	60.10	77-13	Asgard1153½Dodger1151JollyJck1151½	Showed sluggish form	12
	Previously trained by G. Bloss											
11Jly56- 3Hol	fst 5½f	:222 :461 :583 1:05	Alw 5500	8 10 117½ 119½ 812 67¼	Rivera A	120	w	18.95	84-13	Golden One120½Lealito111¾Blue Torch120no	Made up ground	12
13Jun56- 1Hol	fst 5f	:223 :46 :583	©Md Sp Wt	7 5 2½ 1hd 1½ 1¾	Rivera A	118	w	48.65	92-10	Gallant Man118¾Four Heels113nkGate Smasher118no	Driving	12
29May56- 2Hol	fst 5f	:22 :454 :582	©Md Sp Wt	11 9 96¼ 1011 811 98¾	Rivera A	118	w	75.70	84-10	Golden Notes1181½Pie Master1182½[DH] Vihiunis118	Outrun	12
18May56- 1Hol	fst 5f	:223 :463 :591	©Md Sp Wt	6 9 108¾ 1015 1015 1011	Trejos R	120	w	31.60	78-13	FuriousProfit120¾Jicky1201¼GoldnNots120nk	Always outrun	11

Grecian Queen

dkb. f. 1950, by Heliopolis (Hyperion)–Qbania, by Questionnaire — Lifetime record: 53 12 8 8 $323,575

Own.– Mrs B.F. Whitaker

Br.– Ben F. Whitaker (Ky)

Tr.– J.P. Conway

Date/Race	Cond	Dist	Fractions	Race	Running line	Jockey	Wt	Odds	Speed	Top finishers	Comment	Field
4Aug55- 3Sar	fst	1	:243:474 1:132 1:392	3↑ (F)Alw 5000	5 3 3½ 21½ 35 39	Atkinson T	113wb	4.05	71-16	BattleWave1133HulaHula1096GrcnQun1136	Failed to respond	6
2Jly55- 6Del	fst	1¼	:462 1:112 1:363 2:022	3↑ (F)Delaware H 151k	5 9 104¾ 1112 1117 1120	Errico C	110wb	27.40f	70-17	Parlo1283Open Sesame1142Clear Dawn1191½	Broke to inside	13
25Jun55- 6Del	gd	1 1/16	:232:471 1:12 1:443	3↑ (F)New Castle 39k	7 11 127½ 1415 1214 1112	Errico C	116wb	34.20	76-17	Clear Dawn1162½Open Sesame1121½Cerise Reine120hd	Outrun	15
16Jun55- 6Aqu	fst	1 1/16	:25 :492 1:13 1:463	3↑ (F)Handicap 7500	1 4 41½ 42½ 35 2nk	Moreno H	112wb	11.40	81-19	OldBaasket113nkGrcnQueen112nkRomanWarbler1126	Necked	7
18May55- 7Bel	fst	1	:234:472 1:123 1:373	4↑ (F)Alw 5000	3 6 77½ 810 819 824	Broussard R	114 w	19.85	62-14	Riverina1115Carry the News1116Sweet Nell117¾	Outrun	9
2May55- 7Bel	fst	7f	:233:474 1:131 1:261	4↑ (F)Alw 4500	7 1 31½ 23 36 46½	Broussard R	112 w	9.10	72-22	Intencion115½Sweet Nell1224½Garb1111½	Speed for 5/8	8
18Apr55- 7Jam	fst	6f	:232:47 1:122	3↑ (F)Correctn H (Div 2) 28k	3 4 78¾ 67½ 717 712	Broussard R	111 w	40.20	73-19	BrazenBrat1191RosClag1106Trsong1161	Never in contention	9
12Apr55- 6Jam	sly	6f	:233:47 1:123	4↑ (F)Alw 4500	1 3 89 89¾ 814 713	Cole S	110 w	18.75	71-19	Crisset1122Sweet Nell121¾Murph's Deb112¾	Never close	9
30Oct54- 6Jam	sly	1⅛	:474 1:131 1:394 1:532	3↑ (F)Firenze H 35k	6 6 79½ 1113 1231 1228	Scurlock D	113 w	21.25	51-28	Parlo1257Rivern115¾SpnnngTop1101¾	Disliked sloppy going	13
12Oct54- 6Bel	fst	1½	:471 1:122 2:044 2:321	3↑ (F)Ladies H 61k	8 9 86¾ 44 712 712	Shuk N	116 w	10.10	65-19	Lavender Hill1221½Ming Yellow1132½Riverina1141½	Tired	15
4Oct54- 6Bel	fst	1	:231:463 1:113 1:373	3↑ (F)Maskette H 26k	4 3 5¾ 11½ 12½ 2¾	Shuk N	113 w	8.65f	85-18	Ballerina106¾Grecian Queen1131½Gay Grecque1121	Tired	16
18Sep54- 6Aqu	fst	1⅛	:48 1:12 1:37 1:494	3↑ (F)Beldame H 64k	6 6 68 67½ 47½ 46½	Shuk N	114 w	12.20	90-10	Parlo1163Open Sesame1101¾Clear Dawn1141½	Lacked a rally	9
7Sep54- 6Aqu	fst	1 1/16	:253:493 1:132 1:46	3↑ (F)Alw 5000	4 1 11 1hd 2hd 33¼	Guerin E	122 w	*1.05	81-18	Valadium118nkPetal1183GrecianQueen1226	Shortened stride	4
18Aug54- 6Sar	fst	1⅛	:474 1:121 1:38 1:523	3↑ (F)Diana H 23k	2 5 57 69½ 1017 1015	Atkinson T	120wb	7.35	72-19	Lavender Hill1211½La Corredora121hdEvening Out1166	Quit	10
6Aug54- 6Sar	gd	1	:234:473 1:123 1:384	3↑ (F)Handicap 5045	3 2 2hd 1hd 2½ 2no	Atkinson T	118wb	3.85	83-20	Petal106noGrecian Queen1183Mab's Choice114hd	Outgamed	8
19Jly54- 6Jam	fst	1 1/16	:241:481 1:13 1:45	3↑ (F)Handicap 7550	8 4 44½ 41½ 53 42¾	Guerin E	122wb	2.85	84-19	LavendrHill119¾MingYellow1161¼Nothrdchnc115¾	No excuse	8
5Jly54- 6Del	fst	1¼	:454 1:101 1:361 2:023	3↑ (F)New Castle H 138k	12 6 78 1011 1416 1617	Green B	124wb	7.80	72-19	GainsboroGirl1134SunshineNell1262LavendrHll111hd	Sulked	20
28Jun54- 6Del	fst	1 1/16	:224:462 1:112 1:443	3↑ (F)Alw 10000	6 4 43 34½ 35 21½	Green B	124wb	19.90	86-19	EvningOut1041½GrecianQueen1241½LaCorredor124hd	Gaining	12
22Jun54- 7Aqu	fst	1 1/16	:25 :481 1:13 1:442	4↑ Alw 5000	7 2 21 22 38 412½	Green B	114wb	23.25	79-17	Crash Dive1145South Point1086Bicarb1161½	Tired	8
14Jun54- 6Mth	fst	6f	:221:451 1:101	3↑ (F)Alw 5000	3 6 87½ 812 814 813	Green B	118 w	11.80e	81-09	Cinda118¾Blue Rhymer1133Centenaire107¾	Never a threat	10
11May54- 5Bel	gd	6f	:23 :471 1:12	4↑ (F)Alw 4500	4 4 912 910 914 911	Boland W	120 w	8.10e	78-22	Petal1081SpeedyWave1091Hadassah116nk	Trailed throughout	9
15Apr54- 5Jam	fst	6f	:233:48 1:123	4↑ (F)Alw 5000	3 4 43¼ 35 45½ 34½	Woodhouse H	119 w	3.60	79-18	Outsmart1172½Petal1172GrecianQun119no	Wide,lacked rally	7
1Mar54- 7Hia	hy	1¼	:492 1:154 1:433 1:574	3↑ (F)Black Helen H 32k	5 6 65½ 78½ 711 712	Atkinson T	123 w	4.95	35-41	GainsboroGirl109¾LavenderHill1084½Emard120½	Dull effort	10
22Feb54- 7Hia	fst	7f	:223:452 1:10 1:23	3↑ (F)Columbiana H 21k	10 7 147¾ 1516 1316 1316	Atkinson T	124 w	8.60	79-13	Fascinator1101Lavender Hill105nkAtalanta1261	No speed	16
1Feb54- 7Hia	fst	6f	:224:46 1:104	4↑ (F)Alw 5000	7 5 74½ 86¾ 68 66	Shuk N	122 w	4.55	88-14	Emardee116noWinningStrd1184Atlnt124hd	Faltered in drive	8
23Jan54- 6Hia	fst	6f	:223:46 1:11	4↑ Alw 5000	3 2 74¾ 85¾ 87½ 84¼	Atkinson T	117 w	3.15	89-09	Emardee105½Blenriam1131¼Armageddon112nk	No threat	10
26Sep53- 6Bel	fst	1	:231:461 1:11 1:364	3↑ Sysonby 54k	3 3 31½ 22½ 36 33½	Guerin E	116 w	-	86-15	Tom Fool1263Alerted126½Grecian Queen116	No excuse	3
19Sep53- 6Aqu	fst	1⅛	:48 1:122 1:383 1:521	3↑ (F)Beldame H 66k	7 3 45½ 711 911 813	Arcaro E	125 w	*1.10	71-18	Atalanta1213Miss Traffic1063La Corredora119hd	No excuse	12
26Aug53- 6Sar	fst	1¼	:492 1:142 1:40 2:06	(F)Alabama 27k	4 2 1hd 12½ 12 2nk	Shuk N	126 w	1.20	78-23	Sabette114nkGrecianQueen1269CherryFizz109nk	Game effort	5
8Aug53- 6Mth	fst	1⅛	:481 1:124 1:38 1:511	(F)Mth Oaks 59k	8 3 31½ 1hd 11½ 11	Shuk N	121 w	*.90	94-15	GrecianQueen1211Sabette1131¼ArabActress1212½	Ridden out	9
4Jly53- 6Del	fst	1¼	:473 1:12 1:37 2:024	3↑ (F)New Castle H 121k	4 2 1hd 1hd 11½ 11	Atkinson T	114 w	*1.50	88-14	GrecianQueen1141Devilkin1201½MyCeleste117hd	Drew clear	10
24Jun53- 6Aqu	fst	1 1/16	:233:471 1:113 1:454	(F)Gazelle 30k	9 4 310 38 22 11½	Guerin E	121 w	2.80	85-17	Grecian Queen1211½Canadiana1211¾Sabette1132¾	Drew clear	10
6Jun53- 6Bel	fst	1⅜	:481 1:132 1:384 2:183	(F)C C A Oaks 63k	8 3 33½ 1hd 13½ 1no	Guerin E	121 w	4.20	78-16	GrecianQueen121noSabette1212½MingYellow1213	Tiring fast	9
30May53- 6Del	sly	1⅛	:47 1:113 1:374 1:503	(F)Del Oaks 42k	5 4 47½ 210 212 313½	Boland W	119 w	5.05	78-19	Cerise Reine11912Script1101½Grecian Queen1192	No rally	8
22May53- 6Bel	fst	1⅛	:471 1:122 1:39 1:52	(F)Alw 6500	9 3 33 33½ 21 13	Woodhouse H	118 w	*1.35	79-24	Grecian Queen1183Sabette1082½Milspal1093½	Easily	10
9May53- 6Bel	gd	1	:231:462 1:123 1:392	(F)Acorn 25k	3 10 96¾ 77 64½ 69¼	Scurlock O	121 w	*.90	68-24	Secret Meeting1211Wings o' Morn1213Tritium1212	Faltered	12
15Apr53- 6Jam	fst	6f	:232:47 1:132	(F)Prioress 24k	12 7 98¼ 87 42½ 12¼	Guerin E	121 w	*1.40e	80-21	GrecianQueen1212¼[D]Flamenco121½Tritium121nk	Ridden out	12
7Apr53- 5Jam	sly	6f	:243:48 1:124	(F)Alw 4000	5 1 3½ 3nk 2hd 1½	Guerin E	120 w	*1.30	83-20	Grecian Queen120½Petal1155½Sabette1102	Hard urged	6
8Nov52- 6Pim	fst	1 1/16	:232:473 1:13 1:48	(F)Marguerite (Div 1) 24k	9 4 54½ 53 53 1nk	Guerin E	118 w	*1.70	70-24	Grecian Queen118nkIs Proud121½Mi-Marigold115¾	Just up	9
29Oct52- 6Jam	fst	1 1/16	:252:491 1:131 1:463	(F)Demoiselle 51k	5 1 11 12 12 12½	Guerin E	119 w	2.00	79-22	Grecian Queen1192½Ballerina119¾Tritium1147	Ridden out	7
8Oct52- 6Jam	fst	6f	:23 :46 1:122	(F)Frizette 17k	8 3 32½ 32 32 31¾	Arcaro E	119 w	3.90	83-17	SweetPatootie1191¼PiedmontLass119½GrcnQn1191½	Impeded	8
20Sep52- 4Bel	sly	6f-WC	:221:45 1:092	(F)Matron 52k	6 8 64 63¼ 33¼	Atkinson T	119 w	14.20	91-08	Is Proud1193Aerolite119nkGrecian Queen1192	Sharp effort	9
6Sep52- 4Aqu	fst	6f	:232:472 1:133	(F)Astarita 12k	10 2 31 41¼ 31 1½	Guerin E	119 w	9.15	84-17	GrecianQueen119½PiedmontLass116½Flirtatous122hd	Driving	11
20Aug52- 6Sar	fst	6f	:233:47 1:131	(F)Spinaway 21k	4 6 54 34½ 25 28	York R	119 w	*2.25e	74-22	Flirtatious1198GrecianQueen1194Loto'Hony115nk	No excuse	9
21Jly52- 6Jam	sly	5½f	1:072	(F)Schuylerville 13k	8 32 1¾	York R	111 w	4.45e	81-19	GrecianQueen111¾ColdHeart114noPiedmontLass1144	Driving	9
Further calls unavailable due to heavy rain												
16Jly52- 5Jam	fst	5½f	:23 :463 1:054	(F)Alw 5000	1 2 72¾ 96¾ 45½ 21½	York R	110 w	*1.55e	87-16	Tiny Request1101½Grecian Queen110hdPiedmont Lass1162		9
Strong finish												
23Jun52- 6Aqu	fst	5½f	:23 :464 :591 1:054	(F)Alw 5000	3 2 2hd 31 2½ 2½	Woodhouse H	114 w	17.85	94-13	ColdHeart114½GrecianQueen1141½Equableu1142	Good effort	7
14May52- 6Bel	fst	5f-WC	:224:462 :591	(F)National Stallion 28k	5 5 63 67 610	Boland W	119 w	30.20	73-19	Home-Made1191Appian1193Flirtatious119no	Tired	9
5May52- 5Bel	fst	4½f-W	:223:453 :514	(F)Alw 4000	1 3 62¼ 55 64	Scurlock O	118 w	4.00e	86-14	Flirtatious1182¼MissNancy115¾PearlDvr118nk	Bumped horse	7
22Apr52- 4Jam	fst	5f	:233:472 1:00	(F)Md Sp Wt	5 3 21 2hd 21 11½	Gorman D	116 w	3.55	90-18	GrecianQueen1161½SilverBlue1163½Arista1162½	Drew clear	10
14Apr52- 6Jam	sly	5f	:23 :463 :592	(F)Rosedale (Div 2) 12k	3 2 79¾ 812 89½ 78½	Boland W	114 w	29.60	84-15	Emardee116hdKitchen Maid1152½Waterline1142½	Impeded	10
4Apr52- 2Jam	fst	5f	:233:472 1:001	(F)Md Sp Wt	3 9 87¼ 68 57½ 34	Gorman D	116 w	3.30	85-15	CountssJane1094SweetGoddess111hdGrcnQn116hd	Went well	10
28Feb52- 5FG	fst	2f	:23	(F)Md Sp Wt	5 8 44½ 43½	Van Hook E	111	*1.10	--	Actuate1162½Ruler's Girl111nkE-Town111¾	Slow start	12

High Gun

br. c. 1951, by Heliopolis (Hyperion)–Rocket Gun, by Brazado — Lifetime record: 24 11 5 4 $486,025

Own.– King Ranch

Br.– K.M. & W.P. Little & C.C. Boshamer (Ky)

Tr.– M. Hirsch

Date/Race	Cond	Dist	Fractions	Race	Running line	Jockey	Wt	Odds	Speed	Top finishers	Comment	Field
24Sep55- 6Bel	sly	1⅛	:451 1:101 1:36 1:491	3↑ Sysonby 106k	3 5 58½ 43¾ 33 1hd	Boland W	126 w	4.50	93-10	HighGun126hdJetActon1261¾Nshu1213½	Just up final stride	5
30Jly55- 7AP	fm	1 3/16 (T)	:48 1:12 1:37 1:543	3↑ Arlington H 161k	4 1 1½ 2½ 31½ 75¼	Arcaro E	130 w	*2.20	101-03	Platan1173Impass110¾Mrk-Y-Wll116nk	Early speed,weakened	15
23Jly55- 6Mth	fst	1¼	:464 1:112 1:362 2:021	3↑ Monmouth H 83k	3 2 21¼ 21½ 22½ 21½	Arcaro E	135 w	*.80	93-14	Helioscope1311½HighGun1356PunkinVn1111	Crowded at break	4
9Jly55- 6Aqu	fst	1¼	:49 1:132 1:373 2:032	3↑ Brooklyn H 56k	5 1 14 14 14½ 13½	Arcaro E	132 w	*.50	90-15	High Gun1323½Paper Tiger107noStraight Face11612	In hand	5
4Jly55- 6Aqu	fst	7f	:222:444 1:10 1:232	3↑ Carter H 61k	3 12 129¾ 97¼ 65¾ 63½	Arcaro E	133 w	*1.60	89-13	BobbyBrocato1161SocialOutcst1231Artsmo111½	Broke in air	14
30May55- 6Bel	fst	1¼	:474 1:113 1:36 2:003	3↑ Suburban H 88k	9 2 2½ 2hd 1hd 2hd	Arcaro E	133 w	*.70	97-11	Helioscope128hdHighGun1334½Subahdar1199	Held stubbornly	9
14May55- 6Bel	fst	1	:231:461 1:104 1:353	3↑ Metropolitan H 36k	9 6 52 2hd 12½ 14½	De Spirito A	130 w	*1.85	96-11	HighGun1304½Artsmo115noJoJons119no	Increasing long lead	9
16Oct54- 6Bel	fst	2	:501 2:342 2:594 3:254	3↑ J C Gold Cup 82k	1 1 12½ 13½ 15 13	Arcaro E	119 w	*.50	75-16	HighGun1193Fisherman1191Bicarb12410	Well rated,eased up	7
Geldings not eligible												
9Oct54- 4Bel	fst	1½	:49 1:134 2:04 2:303	3↑ Manhattan H 35k	4 5 2hd 11½ 12 11¼	Arcaro E	123 w	*.50	85-15	High Gun1231¼Subahdar110hdBicarb1162	Under brisk urging	9
27Sep54- 6Bel	fst	1	:232:463 1:11 1:363	3↑ Sysonby 28k	1 4 1hd 1hd 1½ 12	Arcaro E	121 w	*1.25	91-10	High Gun1212Landlocked1261¼Sir Mango1261¾	Drew out	4
21Aug54- 7Was	fst	1⅛	:47 1:111 1:36 1:494	American Derby 115k	6 7 69 57½ 34½ 22	Shoemaker W	124 w	*1.30	90-13	ErrardKing1242HighGun1243½HastyRod124¾	Gaining steadily	9
17Jly54- 7AP	fst	1	:222:45 1:092 1:35	Arl Classic 161k	4 13 117¾ 76½ 45½ 32½	Guerin E	123 w	4.10	94-08	ErrardKing1202½Hloscop120noHghGun123nk	Closed fast late	13
3Jly54- 6Aqu	fst	1¼	:50 1:15 1:40 2:05	Dwyer 57k	5 2 2½ 2½ 1hd 11	Guerin E	126 w	*.55	82-14	HighGun1261PalmTree1145PaperTgr1146	Drew clear steadily	5
12Jun54- 6Bel	fst	1½	:49 1:14 2:033 2:304	Belmont 125k	5 8 811 56½ 22½ 1nk	Guerin E	126 w	3.45e	84-16	High Gun126nkFisherman1265Limelight1263	Just up	13
Geldings not eligible												
5Jun54- 6Bel	fst	1⅛	:501 1:151 1:40 1:522	Peter Pan H 36k	6 7 76 75¼ 2½ 13	Guerin E	116 w	5.80	77-20	High Gun1163Fisherman1211¾Diving Board1161½	Drew out	7

Date	Cond	Dist	Fractions	Race	Running line	Jockey	Wt	Odds	Spd	Finishers	Comment	Fld
29May54- 7GS	fst	1⅛	:472 1:114 1:372 1:513	Jersey 64k	11 9 77 44½ 44½ 32½	Hanford I	111 w	7.10	81-16	WarofRoses1111½RedHnngn1111HghGn1111½	Crowded at start	12
15May54- 7GS	fst	6f	:221 :452 1:11	Del Valley (Div 2) 35k	4 11 108½ 75¾ 65 42	Hanford I	112 w	7.10	91-15	Brsut115nkDucdFr1211Rvolt121¾	Steadied early,good rally	11
8May54- 4Bel	sly	1	:23 :461 1:111 1:363	Withers 35k	6 11 106¾ 75¾ 34½ 34	Guerin E	126 w	5.85	87-12	JetAction1262Buttevant1262HghGun126½	Slow start,rallied	11
Geldings not eligible												
3May54- 6Bel	sly	1⅛	:462 1:103 1:36 1:492	Alw 5000	2 3 31½ 2½ 22½ 23½	Guerin E	119 w	*.95	88-14	PalmTree1163½HighGun1196PaperTiger1222½	No late rally	6
24Apr54- 6Jam	fst	1⅛	:481 1:13 1:383 1:50	Wood Memorial 122k	8 4 42½ 22 44½ 37½	Guerin E	126 w	18.30	88-16	Correlation1263½Fisherman1264HghGun1263	Rider lost whip	8
Geldings not eligible. Daily Racing Form time, 1:50 4/5												
6Apr54- 5Jam	fst	1 1/16	:24 :482 1:132 1:45	Alw 4000	4 3 3½ 2½ 22 26	Guerin E	116 w	*1.10	81-15	Full Flight1136High Gun1166Pat Thompson1139	Faltered	5
7Nov53- 7Jam	sly	1 1/16	:24 :48 1:14 1:473	Alw 7500	1 4 33½ 1hd 13 13	Guerin E	116 w	3.00	74-19	High Gun1163Hobcaw Sage1123Wise Pop1123	Handily	7
24Oct53- 5GS	fst	1 1/16	:233 :473 1:13 1:464	Alw 10000	3 7 64¾ 63¾ 58½ 58	Williams WB	111 w	4.90	68-21	Passembud1152Red Hannigan1133Road-Star1112	No mishap	13
20Oct53- 4Jam	fst	5½f	:233 :474 1:064	ⒸMd Sp Wt	10 8 45 55 44 11¾	Arcaro E	118 w	5.70	84-19	High Gun1181¾Ashenden1182Surmount1182	Ridden out	11

High Voltage

gr. f. 1952, by Ambiorix (Tourbillon)–Dynamo, by Menow
Own.– Wheatley Stable
Br.– Wheatley Stable (Ky)
Tr.– J. Fitzsimmons

Lifetime record: 45 13 5 7 $362,240

Date	Cond	Dist	Fractions	Race	Running line	Jockey	Wt	Odds	Spd	Finishers	Comment	Fld
1Aug56- 7Jam	fst	6f	:224 :453 1:11	3↑ ⒻChamplain H 23k	9 8 1211 139½ 1112½ 76½	Atkinson T	113 w	7.65e	85-16	[D]BlueSparkler1252½Gandharv1182BluBnnr122hd	Stride late	13
21Jly56- 7Jam	sly	1 1/16	:233 :471 1:12 1:43	3↑ ⒻBellerose H 27k	7 4 34½ 56½ 510 512	Atkinson T	114 w	4.80	85-12	Parlo1212½BluSprklr1251¾Mnotck119hd	Bobbled start,tired	7
16Jly56- 7Jam	fst	6f	:23 :461 1:103	3↑ ⒻHandicap 6000	5 6 64½ 53 33 32½	Cole S	118 w	3.15e	91-12	Blue Banner122hdSorceress1142½High Voltage1182	Rallied	9
7Jly56- 6Mth	sl	1 1/16	:232 :474 1:114 1:443	3↑ ⒻMolly Pitcher H 28k	7 4 32½ 47½ 511 716	Moreno H	116wb	8.00	76-20	Blue Sparkler1208Rico Reto1171Another World1102½	Tired	9
30Jun56- 7Del	fst	1¼	:451 1:101 1:362 2:03	3↑ ⒻDelaware H 156k	8 6 58 1111 1412 1414	Atkinson T	119wb	15.50	73-14	Flower Bowl1122Manotick122¾Open Sesame113hd	Fell back	15
16Jun56- 6Mth	fst	6f	:212 :433 1:091	3↑ ⒻRegret H 22k	7 7 78¼ 714 68 43½	Culmone J	117wb	4.20e	95-06	BlueSparkler1192Jimminetty114¾PromptImpulse115¾	Rallied	9
26May56- 7Bel	fst	1 1/16	:223 :451 1:102 1:423	3↑ ⒻTop Flight H 28k	4 2 33½ 55 1012 814	Arcaro E	118 w	4.40e	82-11	Searching121½Prlo1241½RcoRto107nk	Early speed,fell back	10
17May56- 7Bel	fst	1	:224 :452 1:104 1:364	4↑ ⒻAlw 7500	1 2 22 24 55¾ 57¾	Atkinson T	122 w	8.45	82-18	Gandharva1101½FlowerBowl1031¾RareTreat118½	Early speed	10
9May56- 7Jam	fst	6f	:233 :47 1:113	3↑ ⒻCorrection H 22k	8 8 62¼ 73¼ 87¾ 86¼	Atkinson T	120 w	5.35	83-19	Searching120¾Gandharva1191Up Betimes110nk	Wide all way	8
3May56- 6Jam	fst	6f	:233 :463 1:113	4↑ ⒻAlw 6000	1 2 1hd 2hd 2½ 23	Atkinson T	122 w	*1.20	86-15	Sorceress1113High Voltage122hdManotick1222	Held on well	7
24Apr56- 7Jam	fst	1 1/16	:25 :492 1:14 1:462	3↑ ⒻHandicap 10000	3 3 42 53¾ 57¼ 67¾	Atkinson T	126wb	1.80e	72-21	RareTreat1161EscaLass1055RicoReto1111	Early foot,tired	7
14Apr56- 7Jam	fst	1 1/16	:241 :473 1:121 1:431	3↑ Excelsior H 28k	7 3 34½ 78 713 819	Woodhouse H	112wb	9.50	77-15	Find116nkJoe Jones1193½Fisherman1224	Dropped back early	9
9Apr56- 7Jam	gd	5½f	:23 :46 :59 1:05	3↑ ⒻHandicap 6000	6 5 34 32½ 3nk 11	Atkinson T	121wb	*1.40	93-15	High Voltage1211On the Move1143Tarquilla1072½	Driving	6
21Mar56- 7GP	fst	1 1/16	:232 :47 1:113 1:43	3↑ ⒻSuwannee River H 17k	7 4 53 75¾ 1011 1011	Atkinson T	124wb	*2.25	84-10	Tremor106½FlowerBowl1062QueenHopful116hd	Factor,stopped	10
2Mar56- 7Hia	fst	1⅛	:453 1:10 1:36 1:492	3↑ ⒻBlack Helen H 40k	7 2 23 22 3½ 3¾	Atkinson T	125wb	*1.55e	88-09	Clear Dawn108noMiss Arlette112¾High Voltage125hd	Gamely	12
22Feb56- 7Hia	fst	7f	:223 :451 1:092 1:221	3↑ ⒻColumbiana H 25k	7 4 52¼ 43½ 47 26	Atkinson T	126wb	4.75	93-12	Myrtle'sJet1146HighVoltage126nkSometimThng126no	Rallied	12
16Feb56- 7Hia	fst	6f	:224 :461 1:102	4↑ ⒻAlw 7500	1 4 21½ 31 31½ 33¾	Atkinson T	126wb	3.35	91-16	SometimeThing1213FantineBushr109¾HighVoltag1261½	Tired	7
8Nov55- 6Jam	fst	1⅛	:473 1:113 1:37 1:504	3↑ ⒻFirenze H 35k	1 2 33 53¼ 78½ 79	Arcaro E	121wb	*2.15	83-15	RareTreat112½Searching118noWhiteCross1081¼	Early factor	12
31Oct55- 6Jam	gd	1 1/16	:242 :48 1:122 1:441	ⒻHandicap 10000	4 2 21 2½ 1hd 1no	Arcaro E	126wb	*1.05	91-11	HighVoltage126noTwoStars109nkRareTreat1165	Hard drive	5
22Oct55- 7GS	fst	1⅛	:453 1:10 1:353 1:481	3↑ ⒻVineland H 51k	12 6 3½ 2hd 11 13	Arcaro E	117wb	2.80e	96-10	High Voltage1173Manotick1181Crisset110no	Going away	18
8Oct55- 7GS	my	1 1/16	:243 :492 1:153 1:512	ⒻJersey Belle 29k	6 2 23 21½ 1½ 2½	Higley J	121wb	4.70	52-41	RareTreat115½HighVoltage1213RicoRomance1142½	Faltered	9
3Oct55- 6Bel	fst	1	:232 :461 1:104 1:363	3↑ ⒻMaskette H 25k	2 2 43½ 69 816 914	Arcaro E	117 w	*2.45	77-17	OilPainting119nkMissWeesie1045ClearDawn1161	Brief foot	12
23Sep55- 6Bel	fst	1	:231 :46 1:104 1:364	ⒻHandicap 10000	2 4 52¼ 53 56½ 43	Arcaro E	122wb	*.60e	87-17	MistyMorn124¾RareTreat1122¼SweetMusic106hd	Closed well	7
9Sep55- 6Aqu	fst	1 1/16	:251 :493 1:133 1:462	3↑ ⒻHandicap 10000	5 6 53¼ 42½ 53¼ 74	Arcaro E	122wb	1.95	78-20	Searching1201ClearDawn122noSilentOn108nk	Close quarters	8
24Aug55- 6Sar	gd	1¼	:484 1:142 1:394 2:054	ⒻAlabama 29k	7 4 32 44 712 712	Arcaro E	124wb	*.40e	67-22	RicoReto1133BlueBnnr114nkMstyMorn1211¼	Early foot,tired	8
2Jly55- 6Del	fst	1¼	:462 1:112 1:363 2:022	3↑ ⒻDelaware H 151k	3 8 94¾ 64 57½ 46½	Cole S	116wb	10.80	83-17	Parlo1283Open Sesame1142Clear Dawn1191½	Crowded early	13
27Jun55- 6Aqu	fst	1 1/16	:241 :48 1:123 1:453	ⒻGazelle 30k	7 7 65½ 54¼ 3½ 3nk	Arcaro E	121wb	*.75e	86-15	Mnotck113hdTwoStrs113nkHghVoltg1212	Close quarters early	10
18Jun55- 6Del	fst	1⅛	:463 1:11 1:372 1:503	ⒻDel Oaks 49k	6 6 33½ 22 1hd 1nk	Arcaro E	119wb	*.50	87-13	High Voltage119nkHen Party110½Rico Romance113¾	Driving	10
8Jun55- 6Bel	fst	1 1/16	:224 :451 1:094 1:414	3↑ ⒻTop Flight H 30k	2 6 75 64½ 68 78¾	Arcaro E	117wb	2.60	93-11	Parlo1263Gainsboro Girl114½Spinning Top113nk	No excuse	12
28May55- 6Bel	fst	1⅜	:472 1:114 1:372 2:173	ⒻC C A Oaks 63k	4 9 63¾ 51¼ 11 12½	Atkinson T	121wb	*.60e	83-15	High Voltage1212½Lalun1212Manotick121nk	Driving clear	11
14May55- 7Pim	sly	1 1/16	:223 :462 1:114 1:461	ⒻBlack-Eyed Susan 26k	3 3 32 2½ 2hd 11	Arcaro E	121wb	*1.30	79-22	High Voltage1211Bless Pat1213Hen Party121hd	Ridden out	9
4May55- 6Bel	fst	1	:224 :461 1:121 1:384	ⒻAcorn 31k	5 6 63½ 41 21½ 1¾	Arcaro E	121wb	*2.20	80-13	HighVoltage121¾SometimeThing1211¾HenParty121hd	Driving	14
26Apr55- 5Bel	sly	6f	:221 :453 1:111	ⒻAlw 5000	4 3 43½ 45½ 58 47	Atkinson T	121 w	3.25	86-12	Gandharva1174½Sorceress1141¼TwoStrs1171¼	Evenly all way	9
2Nov54- 6Jam	sly	1 1/16	:242 :482 1:142 1:491	ⒻFrizette 53k	8 7 55½ 32 23 42½	Arcaro E	119 w	*.75	63-27	Myrtle'sJet1192HenParty119nkSorcrss119nk	Bothered,tired	9
23Oct54- 7Lrl	fst	1 1/16	:223 :454 1:113 1:45	ⒻSelima 66k	6 6 48 21 1hd 1¾	Arcaro E	119 w	*.60	89-13	High Voltage119¾Myrtle's Jet1194Misty119¾	Ridden out	8
2Oct54- 4Bel	fst	6f-WC	:213 :443 1:10	ⒻMatron 61k	13 3 93 13 13	Arcaro E	119 w	*2.10	91-09	High Voltage1193Blue Banner1192Lalun119½	Easy score	20
23Sep54- 6Bel	fst	5½f-W	:223 :454 1:041	ⒻAlw 5000	8 4 74½ 31½ 32½	Arcaro E	124 w	*1.35	84-13	BlessPat113½Errasina1162HighVoltage1242	Tired in drive	12
1Sep54- 6Aqu	fst	6f	:223 :463 1:124	ⒻAstarita 18k	9 8 96½ 87¾ 44 2no	Arcaro E	125 w	*1.60	88-14	TwoStars119noHighVoltage1252½MyBlueSky110hd	Nosed out	10
23Aug54- 6Sar	fst	6f	:224 :462 1:124	ⒻSpinaway 59k	1 6 78 77 57½ 32	Arcaro E	123 w	*1.80	82-22	Gandharva1111½My Blue Sky111½High Voltage1231	Gaining	9
3Jly54- 6Mth	fst	5½f	:213 :452 1:051	ⒻColleen 28k	8 6 57 47½ 36 1nk	Arcaro E	119 w	*2.40	98-09	High Voltage119nkMenolene1191½Sue Pat112½	Strong drive	14
19May54- 6Bel	fst	5f-WC	:214 :444 :571	ⒻNational Stallion 31k	9 4 31½ 3nk 1¾	Nichols J	119 w	3.35	93-10	High Voltage119¾Delta1191Sly Vixen119hd	Hard punished	9
28Apr54- 6Bel	fst	4½f-W	:214 :444 :511	ⒻFashion 15k	2 5 52¼ 42¼ 2½	Guerin E	119 w	*1.00	92-08	Sofarsogood114½HighVoltage1191½Chapl114¾	Gaining at end	10
14Apr54- 6Jam	fst	5f	:232 :47 :592	ⒻRosedale 13k	9 6 2½ 2hd 21 12	Higley J	114 w	2.15	93-18	HighVoltage1142Guppie1141RedLetterDay1154½	Ridden out	9
10Apr54- 3Jam	fst	5f	:23 :463 :594	ⒻMd Sp Wt	4 3 31 2hd 2hd 12½	Guerin E	116 w	*1.20e	91-13	HighVoltage1162½BlessPat1163½LadyBrownie116nk	In hand	10
2Apr54- 3Jam	fst	5f	:223 :47 :594	ⒻMd Sp Wt	4 6 58 57½ 34 33	Guerin E	116 w	*2.05	88-15	SweetMusic1162½HiddnShip116½HighVoltag1163½	No excuse	10

Hill Prince

b. c. 1947, by Princequillo (Prince Rose)–Hildene, by Bubbling Over
Own.– C.T. Chenery
Br.– C.T. Chenery (Va)
Tr.– J.H. Hayes

Lifetime record: 30 17 5 4 $422,140

Date	Cond	Dist	Fractions	Race	Running line	Jockey	Wt	Odds	Spd	Finishers	Comment	Fld
1Mar52- 7SA	my	1¼	:452 1:104 1:354 2:01	3↑ S Anita H 141k	4 15 1521 1011 79¾ 58¾	Arcaro E	129wb	*1.25e	86-16	[D]Intent1111Miche1154½Be Fleet1142½		15
Moved up inside,failed to threaten												
9Feb52- 6SA	fst	1	:223 :454 1:103 1:354	3↑ San Marcos H 24k	4 10 812 35 2½ 12	Arcaro E	126wb	*.75e	97-14	Hill Prince1262Bryan G.122noBe Fleet1173½	Easily best	11
3Nov51- 7GS	sly	1⅛	:47 1:113 1:374 1:52	3↑ Trenton H 60k	4 8 814 811 48½ 45¼	Arcaro E	130wb	*.70	77-23	Call Over116hdInseparable108hdPost Card1135	No excuse	8
20Oct51- 6Jam	fst	1⅝	:502 1:40 2:044 2:424	3↑ Emp Gold Cup 53k	1 4 21 1hd 2hd 21¼	Arcaro E	126wb	*.35	99-14	Counterpoint1191¼HillPrince1264½HullDown11912	Gave way	4
Geldings not eligible												
13Oct51- 6Bel	fst	2	:493 2:302 2:56 3:213	3↑ J C Gold Cup 53k	1 1 11½ 11 1½ 2hd	Arcaro E	124wb	*.30	96-11	Counterpoint117hdHillPrince12410KssMKt1142½	Just failed	5
29Sep51- 6Bel	fst	1⅛	:464 1:114 1:363 1:49	3↑ New York H 29k	7 8 43 1½ 15 15	Arcaro E	128wb	*.80	94-15	Hill Prince1285One Hitter1171Sudan1051½	Easily	8
24Sep51- 5Bel	fst	1	:232 :461 1:102 1:352	3↑ Alw 5000	3 3 21 2½ 1hd 1¾	Arcaro E	121wb	*1.05	97-16	HillPrince121¾SheilasReward1218OneHitter1211½	Handily	4
15Sep51- 5Aqu	fst	6f	:23 :46 1:104	3↑ Handicap 4560	5 5 57½ 58 56 35½	Arcaro E	128wb	3.10	92-13	Tea-Maker1211NorthernStar1184½HillPrinc128¾	Closed well	7
16Dec50- 7Hol	fst	1⅛	:462 1:103 1:36 1:483	3↑ Sunset H 58k	6 8 713 54½ 42½ 1¾	Arcaro E	128wb	*.45	98-12	HillPrince128¾NxtMov1141½GrtCrcl109nk	Wide into stretch	10
9Dec50- 7Hol	fst	1¼	:463 1:101 1:35 1:594	3↑ Hol Gold Cup 137k	7 7 67 75¼ 55 34	Arcaro E	130wb	3.70	97-09	Noor1301Palestinian1223Hill Prince1301	Blocked,gamely	8
23Nov50- 7Hol	fst	1 1/16	:233 :47 1:104 1:414	3↑ Thanksgiving Day H 44k	8 6 63½ 53 52½ 3hd	Arcaro E	128wb	*1.05	99-07	Your Host124noPonder124hdHill Prince1282	Poor start	10
7Oct50- 6Bel	fst	2	:494 2:31 2:563 3:232	3↑ J C Gold Cup 54k	3 1 12 11½ 13 14	Arcaro E	117wb	1.25	87-13	Hill Prince1174Noor1247Adile1212	Easily best	5
Geldings not eligible												
20Sep50- 6Bel	fst	1	:224 :452 1:103 1:354	Jerome H 24k	11 13 139¾ 107¼ 41¾ 14	Arcaro E	129 w	*1.70	95-10	Hill Prince1294Greek Ship1221Navy Chief108nk	Easily	13

26Aug50- 7Was	fst	1¼	:472 1:112 1:351 2:011	American Derby 78k	3	9	77	24	21	11½	Arcaro E	126wb	*1.50	96-07	Hill Prince1261½All Blue1144½Your Host126nk	Drew out 9
24Jun50- 6Aqu	fst	1¼	:491 1:13 1:374 2:03	Dwyer 45k	5	5	12	13	11	21½	Arcaro E	121 w	*.90	90-12	Greek Song1161½Hill Prince1216Lights Up1164	No excuse 5
10Jun50- 6Bel	fst	1½	:482 1:123 2:021 2:283	Belmont 91k	2	7	11½	11½	42	74	Arcaro E	126wb	*.85	91-13	Middleground1261Lights Up126½Mr. Trouble126hd	Stopped 9
	Geldings not eligible															
30May50- 6Bel	gd	1¼	:472 1:103 1:361 2:02	3↑ Suburban H 59k	5	6	1hd	2½	32	32¾	Woodhouse H	113wb	*.90	87-14	LoserWeeper115nkMyRqust1192½HllPrnc1133½	Bled 7
20May50- 6Pim	sl	1 3/16	:482 1:132 1:401 1:591	Preakness 75k	1	6	31	13	11	15	Arcaro E	126wb	*.70	84-23	Hill Prince1265Middleground1265Dooly1266	Ridden out 6
13May50- 6Bel	fst	1	:23 :454 1:102 1:354	Withers 29k	2	6	43¼	2hd	1½	11½	Arcaro E	126wb	*1.10	95-11	Hill Prince1261½Middleground1264Ferd1263	Handily 7
6May50- 7CD	fst	1¼	:463 1:112 1:364 2:013	Ky Derby 120k	5	9	89¾	52½	31½	21¼	Arcaro E	126wb	2.50	98-09	Mddlground1261¼HllPrnc126½Mr.Troubl1262¾	Close quarters 14
22Apr50- 6Jam	fst	1 1/16	:24 :472 1:12 1:433	Wood Memorial 49k	5	10	44	42	1½	12	Arcaro E	126wb	*1.50	95-13	Hill Prince1262Middleground1261½Ferd126¾	Going away 11
15Apr50- 6Jam	fst	1 1/16	:23 :46 1:113 1:443	Exp Free H #2 27k	10	10	813	1110	1016	920	Arcaro E	124wb	*.50	70-12	Lotowhit1074½RoylCstl106½SturdyOn1061½	Stumbled,impeded 11
5Apr50- 6Jam	sly	6f	:223 :461 :592 1:12	Exp Free H #1 21k	6	6	611	68	34	11¼	Arcaro E	124wb	*.60	91-18	Hill Prince1241¼Starecase1083Casemate116½	Going away 7
	Daily Racing Form time, 1:11 3/5															
14Sep49- 6Aqu	sly	6½f	:23 :461 1:102 1:163	Cowdin 23k	4	6	66	32½	1½	12½	Arcaro E	122wb	*.30	102-15	Hill Prince1222½Selector1171Suleiman117no	Going away 6
7Sep49- 6Aqu	fst	6f	:23 :463 1:123	Babylon H 13k	2	11	119¾	88½	41½	12	Arcaro E	126wb	*.95	89-17	Hill Prince1262Miss Degree106¾Navy Chief121¾	Drew out 11
13Aug49- 5Atl	sly	6f	:23 :461 1:124	World's Playground 16k	3	8	65	42½	2hd	15	Dodson D	117wb	*.40	82-21	Hill Prince1175Attention Mark1171½Cornwall114hd	Easily 8
3Aug49- 4Mth	sly	6f	:224 :46 1:124	Alw 4000	5	7	32	31	11	11	Dodson D	116 w	*.50	84-22	Hill Prince1161Jersey Queen1054Clean Broom1103	Cleverly 7
27Jly49- 5Mth	fst	6f	:22 :452 1:113	Sapling 13k	4	7	77	33½	23	21	Arcaro E	115 w	*.80	89-12	Casemate1221Hill Prince1154½Thorn113¾	Off poorly 7
9Jly49- 4Mth	fst	5½f	:22 :464 :592 1:062	Alw 4000	3	5	64¾	31½	2hd	12	Dodson D	113 w	2.30	92-17	Hill Prince1132Ferd1223Thorn1161½	Going away 7
2Jly49- 4Aqu	fst	5½f	:23 :473 1:062	Md Sp Wt	6	6	54	44½	21	17	Arcaro E	118 w	3.55	92-14	Hill Prince1187Black Wizard1181½Pontalba113½	Easily 10

Iceberg II (Chi)

b. c. 1948, by Espadin (Full Sail)–Bellagamba, by Statuto

Lifetime record: 56 13 10 11 $165,108

Own.– W.A. Hanger
Br.– L.C. Allende (Chi)
Tr.– Horatio A. Luro

4Jly55- 7AP	fm	1⅛(T)	:462 1:104 1:354 1:482	3↑ Stars & Stripes H 28k	7	6	48	53	74¾	42¾	Gorman D	117wb	14.90	97-06	Mark-Ye-Well114nkRuh1111½BluChor1171	Tight quarters str 10
21Jun55- 6AP	fm	1 1/16(T)	:232 :463 1:12 1:433	4↑ Alw 5000	3	8	53	21½	13	1hd	Gorman D	121wb	1.80e	95-11	Iceberg II121hdKing1151¼Ruhe1121	Clear lead,tiring fast 9
11Jun55- 7Bel	fm	1⅜(T)	2:181	3↑ Handicap 15000	1	5	53½	44½	2½	32¼	Gorman D	119wb	7.60	94-04	PrinceHill1171¾Secant111½IcebergII1191½	Made bid,tired 11
10May55- 6Pim	fm	1 1/16(T)	1:433	4↑ Alw 4000	6	6	56½	58½	58	56	Nelson E	119wb	2.10	103-00	Old Glendale1144Potpourri1191Baroda Boy112¾	Off slowly 6
2Mar55- 7Hia	fm	1½(T)	2:293	3↑ Hia Turf H 63k	6	10	104½	42	32	32	Contreras J	112wb	14.35	94-00	Stan128½Capeador1181½Iceberg II112no	Lacked final rally 11
16Feb55- 7Hia	hd	1 3/16(T)	1:56	3↑ Bougainvillea H 34k	1	6	63¾	3½	3nk	34	Contreras J	115wb	8.20	93-03	Cascanuez1221Kaster1213Iceberg II115½	Tired in drive 12
10Feb55- 7Hia	fm	1 1/16(T)	1:441	4↑ Alw 6000	9	9	106½	64	45	43¼	Contreras J	121wb	24.95	92-05	Mister Black121¾Kaster1212Abbe Sting118½	Rallied mildly 12
19Nov54- 7Pim	fm	1(T)	1:403	3↑ Alw 4000	5	6				45½	Shuk N	122wb	5.10	84-07	Kaster1222Modest Pete1151½Rare Knave1172	Taken up early 7
	Fog prevented other race calls															
11Nov54- 7Pim	fm	1½(T)	2:321	3↑ Exterminator H 10k	8	3	52½	86¼	68½	713	Hartack W	116wb	4.30	- -	Cascanuez1144½Kaster121noBrushBurn1244	Dropped far back 10
16Oct54- 7Lrl	fm	*1⅛(T)	1:51	3↑ Turf Cup H 25k	5	7	84¼	64	66	68½	Contreras J	117wb	4.20	78-13	Stan1262½News Again1112½Tritium1142	Tired in drive 13
25Sep54- 6Atl	fm	1 3/16(T)	:48 1:12 1:372 1:57	3↑ U Nations H 67k	6	5	55½	77¾	78¼	74¼	Contreras J	122wb	4.90	90-06	Closed Door117hdRoyal Vale120½Kaster114¾	Dull effort 8
15Sep54- 7Atl	fm	1⅛(T)	:48 1:38 1:511	3↑ [R]Foreign Bred 29k	1	5	53¾	2hd	11	1¾	Contreras J	118wb	*1.00e	87-13	Iceberg II118¾Royal Vale118nkBlood Test1181	Hard urged 8
	Restricted to horses foaled outside the continental United States															
6Sep54- 7Atl	fm	1 1/16(T)	:231 :464 1:112 1:43	3↑ Atl City Turf H 30k	9	7	64	53½	44	41	Contreras J	124wb	8.00	98-01	Landlocked115hdCounty Clare116noKaster1171	Closed fast 13
31Jly54- 7AP	sf	1 3/16(T)	:462 1:112 1:382 1:57	3↑ Arlington H 156k	9	6	65	52	72¾	107	Contreras J	121wsb	5.40e	87-12	Stan114nkBrushBurn1133½SirMngo1251½	Lacked needed rally 14
12Jly54- 7AP	fst	1⅛	:482 1:113 1:37 1:493	3↑ L Armour Mem H 28k	6	2	2½	1hd	1hd	2nk	Church K	124wb	5.40	94-11	Mister Black111nkIceberg II1242½Ruhe1192	Just failed 10
5Jly54- 8AP	fm	1⅛(T)	:47 1:112 1:363 1:492	3↑ Stars & Stripes H 28k	6	6	64¼	32½	22	23	Church K	123wb	6.60	92-08	Sir Mango1243Iceberg II1231Stan114no	Showed game effort 12
18Jun54- 5Mth	fm	1(T)	1:391	3↑ Alw 5000	2	6	31	1hd	12	13	Gorman D	118wb	*1.30	90-10	IcebergII1183BobsAlibi109noGoingAway109¾	Won eased up 12
5Jun54- 7Bel	fst	1	:24 :481 1:134 1:391	4↑ Alw 4500	3	2	1hd	11	2½	23½	Contreras J	120wb	5.30	74-20	Domquil1133½IcebergII1203Lafourch108no	Couldn't keep up 11
3Mar54- 7Hia	hd	1½(T)	2:284	3↑ Hia Turf H 64k	11	7	86½	75¼	88	810	Contreras J	124wb	*2.70e	90-00	Picador1062½Royal Vale126½Parnassus1202	Raced wide 12
25Feb54- 7Hia	hd	1 3/16(T)	1:56	4↑ Alw 6000	2	5	43½	4¾	3½	1½	Contreras J	121wb	*.75	97-03	IcebergII121½RoyalGovernor112½CombatBoots1124	Cleverly 6
20Feb54- 7Hia	fst	1¼	:473 1:114 1:371 2:031	3↑ Widener H 139k	3	5	63½	54	55½	54	Contreras J	119wb	10.75	85-13	Landlocked116hdQuiet Step1131¼Andre117nk	Lacked rally 14
6Feb54- 7Hia	fst	1⅛	:454 1:102 1:362 1:49	3↑ McLennan H 72k	10	12	138½	107¼	139¼	64	Contreras J	119wb	7.50	87-11	Elixir110½[D]RoyalVale1262WiseMargin108¾	Impeded early 16
	Placed fifth by disqualification															
15Jan54- 7TrP	fst	1⅛	:46 1:102 1:363 1:502	3↑ Tropical H 47k	7	12	1310	116¾	44	33½	Contreras J	123wsb	14.35	85-15	Capeador1121Count Cain1052½Iceberg II123no	Closed well 14
11Nov53- 7Lrl	sf	*1½(T)	2:36	3↑ D C Int'l 65k	4	4	3½	2hd	2hd	26	Contreras J	126wb	7.60	68-29	Worden II1266Iceberg II1263Sunglow126½	Good effort 10
31Oct53- 7Lrl	fst	*1⅛(T)	1:512	3↑ Turf Cup H (Div 2) 23k	1	4	31	2hd	11	21½	Contreras J	126wb	*1.70	83-15	County Clare1051½Iceberg II1262Ruhe119no	Good effort 8
26Sep53- 6Atl	fst	1 3/16(T)	:473 1:12 1:362 1:554	3↑ U Nations H 60k	4	5	58	31½	11½	11¼	Contreras J	120wb	7.10	113-00	IcebergII1201¼BrushBrun118nkRoyalGovrnor118½	Drew clear 8
16Sep53- 7Atl	fst	1⅛(T)	:47 1:112 1:361 1:492	3↑ Foreign Bred 29k	4	4	32½	11½	1½	21¼	Contreras J	122 w	3.80	95-06	Royal Vale1221¼Iceberg II1223Stan1152	Game effort 8
	Restricted to horses foaled outside the continental United States															
5Sep53- 7Atl	fst	1 1/16(T)	:232 :464 1:11 1:433	3↑ Atl City Turf H 23k	7	6	54¼	44½	32	31½	Wilson HB	119wb	5.70	100-00	SaddleTramp107¾RoyalGovernor109¾IcebrgII119nk	Went well 10
28Jly53- 6AP	fst	1⅛	:48 1:112 1:36 1:49	3↑ Handicap 6000	3	3	13	14½	16	16	Contreras J	120wb	4.90	97-15	Iceberg II1206Adams Off Ox1101Brush Burn1112	Easily 7
20Jly53- 6AP	fst	1 1/16(T)	:233 :474 1:123 1:442	3↑ L Armour Mem H 29k	13	8	76	53½	74¾	95¾	Contreras J	120wb	8.20	85-15	Abbe Sting1142½The Eagle114nkBobs Alibi1101	Forced wide 13
4Jly53- 8AP	fst	1⅛(T)	:47 1:11 1:36 1:482	3↑ Stars & Stripes H 28k	9	4	21½	22	21	33¼	Contreras J	122wb	5.20	101-05	AbbeSting110nkArmageddon1183IcebergII122½	Dropped back 10
24Jun53- 7AP	fst	1 1/16(T)	:232 :472 1:114 1:423	4↑ Alw 5000	6	7	83½	51¾	44	42¾	Contreras J	120wb	*2.50	98-05	The Eagle114hdVantage120½Hierarch1142¼	Raced wide 10
30May53- 6Bel	fst	1¼	:471 1:11 1:353 2:003	3↑ Suburban H 58k	7	3	45¼	33½	34	49	Contreras J	109wb	18.15	88-17	Tom Fool128noRoyal Vale1247Cold Command1142	Tired 7
20May53- 7Bel	fst	1⅛	:454 1:104 1:371 1:504	3↑ Handicap 7555	6	3	35	33	22½	45¼	Contreras J	121wb	5.25	80-19	Arcave1203½Gloriette1051½Ancestor119nk	Weakened 9
15May53- 6Bel	sly	7f	:222 :454 1:11 1:241	3↑ Handicap 6070	3	8	811	813	711	612	Contreras J	120wb	11.00	77-22	Hitex1171¼Master Fiddle115nkRae's Reward1103½	No speed 8
1May53- 8CD	fst	1	:232 :471 1:112 1:37	4↑ Alw 3300	2	4	31½	32½	21	1hd	Contreras J	120wb	4.30	92-13	Iceberg II120hdGray Challenge1083¾The Gink1145	Just up 7
14Apr53- 3Kee	fst	7f	:23 :462 1:113 1:241	4↑ Alw 3750	3	6	67	55	43	34	Rogers C	122wb	*2.10	87-10	OldMason1111RoyalMustang1103IcebergII122¾	Strong finish 6
20Mar53- 7GP	fst	1 1/16	:253 :502 1:14 1:464	4↑ Alw 5000	2	4	42	3½	31	31¾	Gorman D	121wb	5.45	74-26	Mandingo1161¼Dry Run114½Iceberg II1215	Lacked rally 8
3Mar53- 7Hia	fst	1½(T)	2:284	3↑ Miami Beach H 31k	5	7	48	32½	43½	34½	Contreras J	122wb	*1.20	96-05	Royal Vale1133Dulat1221½Iceberg II122¾	Tired 10
18Feb53- 7Hia	fst	1 3/16(T)	1:573	3↑ Bougainvillea H 20k	3	9	83¼	51¾	1hd	1¾	Contreras J	119wb	8.55	95-05	Iceberg II119¾Brush Burn123noDulat1222½	Driving 16
13Feb53- 7Hia	fst	1 1/16(T)	1:462	4↑ Alw 4500	6	4	32	11	12	12	Contreras J	112wb	*.70	84-16	IcebergII1122Streaking1086SaddleBags1165	Driving clear 7
5Feb53- 7Hia	sf	1⅛(T)	1:54	4↑ Alw 5000	7	1	12	12	11	21½	Contreras J	112wb	4.30	79-19	Brush Burn1191½Iceberg II112¾Chicle II1122	Sharp effort 7
20Jan53- 7Hia	fst	1⅛(T)	1:522	4↑ Alw 5000	7	9	85¾	64¼	53½	65	Nichols J	113wb	*2.85	84-11	Dulat1073Blue Volt1081½Evicted107hd	Raced wide 12
14Jan53- 7TrP	fst	5½f	:22 :45 :58 1:042	4↑ Alw 3200	3	10	109	913	88¾	64½	Nichols J	114wb	79.10	89-17	DoReport1141Earmarked111nkCircusClown1112	Closed ground 10
	Previously trained by Carlos Munoz Guzman															
9Mar52♦	Valparaiso(Chi) fm	*1 3/16(T)LH	1:542	Clsc Casino Municipal de Vina Stk4500						21	Parodi R	119	-		Paschanillo1191Iceberg II119Armadillo119	13
27Feb52♦	Valparaiso(Chi) fm	*1(T)LH	1:364	Premio Cuerpo de Bomberos Hcp700						11	Poblete A	121	*2.00		Iceberg II1211Huaraculen117½Negrina108	10
20Jan52♦	Valparaiso(Chi) fm	*1½(T)LH	2:293	Chilean Derby Stk75000						4	Flores P	128	-		Fascinado1283Liberty1285Soldado128	7
6Jan52♦	Valparaiso(Chi) fm	*1 3/16(T)LH	1:544	Clasico Juan S. Jackson Stk1700						1½	Parodi R	113	*.60		Iceberg II113½Soldado1135Majestic113	6
18Nov51♦	Hipodromo(Chi) sly	*1¼LH	2:054	Pr Junta Central Beneficencia Hcp1600						37	Flores P	126			Gitanita1067Maretako110hdIceberg II126	16

4Nov51♦ Hipodromo(Chi) sly*1⅛LH 1:532 Premio Rosignol Alw500 11 Flores P 118 *.80 Iceberg II1181Palay1236Gitanita114 7
28Oct51♦ Club Hippico(Chi) fm*1½(T)RH 2:30 Clasico El Ensayo Stk9200 22¼ Parodi R 123 - Liberty1232¼Iceberg II1232½Soldado123 13
30Sep51♦ Club Hippico(Chi) fm*1¼(T)RH 2:022 GP Nacional Ricardo Lyon Stk3000 33 Orellana J 123 - Liberty123½Fascinado1102½Iceberg II123 13
19Aug51♦ Club Hippico(Chi) gd *1 1/16(T)RH 1:45 Polla de Potrillos Stk2500 23 Orellana J 123 - Laconico1233Iceberg II123½Fantasma Gris123 26
Soldado 6th,Liberty 11th
29Jly51♦ Club Hippico(Chi) sf *1(T)RH 1:42 Clasico Alberto Vial Infante Stk2200 11 Sepulveda G 120 - Fascinado1177Parcoy1171½Odin126 16
Laconico 5th
17Jun51♦ Hipodromo(Chi) my*7½fLH 1:33 Clasico Domingo 2nd Herrera Stk2000 14 Giraldez C 119 - Odin1191Maretazo119nkToscano119 17
18Mar51♦ Club Hippico(Chi) fst*5f(T)Str 1:01 Premio Centurion Mdn500 1¾ Caballero H 122 2.70 Iceberg II122¾Singo1222Dashing Lad121 11

Idun

b. f. 1955, by Royal Charger (Nearco)–Tige O'Myheart, by Bull Lea — **Lifetime record: 30 17 4 4 $392,490**
Own.– Josephine B. Paul
Br.– Leslie Combs & John W. Hanes (Ky)
Tr.– S.W. Ward

28Oct59- 7Aqu sl 6f :221 :461 1:121 3↑ (F)Interborough H 27k 7 2 23 23 21 2nk Guerin E 124 *1.45 -- Nushi111nkIdun1242Cobul107½ Led between calls,no excuse 7
3Oct59- 7Aqu fst 1⅛ :474 1:121 1:37 1:501 3↑ (F)Beldame H 67k 1 2 21½ 21½ 21½ 22½ Guerin E 121 4.15 -- Tempted1252½Idun121nkHigh Bid1131 No apparent excuse 14
21Sep59- 7Aqu fst 1 :223 :45 1:094 1:36 3↑ (F)Maskette H 29k 9 3 41¾ 41 2hd 11¼ Guerin E 119 8.75 -- Idun1191¼Tempted1261½Bornastar1192 Under hard drive 10
2Sep59- 7Bel sly 7f :22 :443 1:092 1:223 3↑ (F)Vagrancy H 29k 11 5 53 43 24 36 Ussery R 112 3.60 88-16 Dandy Blitzen1131Honeys Gem1185Idun1121 Mild bid,tired 12
10Aug59- 5Sar fst 1 :23 :461 1:104 1:36 3↑ (F)Handicap 7500 5 1 11 1hd 2½ 35 Ussery R 122 2.00 92-15 Tempted122½Polamby1164½Idun1222½ Tired when challenged 5
18Jly59- 6Del fst 1 1/16 :231 :464 1:112 1:433 3↑ (F)New Castle 35k 7 4 53 32 43½ 53¼ Guerin E 116 4.20 90-18 Tempted1162¾Bornstr126½Chstos112no Well placed,weakened 10
6Jly59- 7Bel fst 6f :222 :454 1:111 3↑ (F)Liberty Belle H 27k 1 5 31½ 31½ 1½ 11¼ Hartack W 124 *.95 92-14 Idun1241¼HappyPrincss1151Polmby113½ Under a brisk drive 7
20Jun59- 7Mth fst 6f :213 :451 1:103 3↑ (F)Regret H 22k 8 4 46 34½ 2hd 2¾ Hartack W 126 *1.00 88-19 Mlle.Dianne116¾Idun1261½SandysJoy116¾ Led between calls 8
25May59- 7Bel fst 7f :221 :453 1:111 1:241 3↑ (F)Distaff H 28k 3 6 33½ 32 31 31½ Erb D 125 *1.30 84-18 HappyPrincess1141½Mlle.Dinn115noIdun1251¼ Made even try 8
16May59- 7GS fst 6f :221 :454 1:12 3↑ (F)Colonial H 28k 8 1 2½ 21½ 21½ 11½ Hartack W 124 *1.30 84-20 Idun1241½DandyBlitzn1201BttyLnn113nk Driving,drew clear 8
3Mar59- 7Hia fst 1⅛ :461 1:104 1:371 1:501 3↑ (F)Black Helen H 40k 9 10 89½ 98 1012 1116 Hartack W 124 *1.45 68-17 Rosewood1162½Happy Princess1102½A Glitter122nk Dull try 12
11Feb59- 7Hia fst 7f :223 :452 1:101 1:231 3↑ (F)Columbia H 26k 3 9 21 1hd 11 1nk Hartack W 123 *1.65 94-17 Idun123nkWoodlawn1111½HappyPrincss115½ Under hard drive 15
Previously raced in the name of Mrs C.U. Bay
8Nov58- 6Jam fst 1 3/16 :471 1:114 1:372 1:564 Roamer H 88k 10 4 55 31½ 41 31¾ Hartack W 119 w *4.00 90-15 Warhead1251GreyMonarch119¾Idun1191 Showed a good effort 14
13Oct58- 6Bel fst 1½ :48 1:121 2:034 2:302 3↑ (F)Ladies H 58k 7 2 24 1½ 1hd 43½ Hartack W 122 w 2.35 77-20 Endine1141¾DottedLine123nkAnnie-Lu-Sn1081½ Used in lead 10
4Oct58- 7Bel fst 1⅛ :453 1:10 1:36 1:492 3↑ (F)Beldame H 70k 3 2 32 31½ 41 51¼ Guerin E 124 w *1.35 88-14 OuterSpace117noAGlitter119hdDottedLine120nk No excuse 17
15Sep58- 6Bel fst 1 1/16 :223 :451 1:101 1:431 (F)Gazelle H 29k 7 4 2½ 11 12 14½ Hartack W 124 w *.80 92-15 Idun1244½Munch122noTmptd116¾ Increasing long lead easily 10
5Sep58- 5Bel fst 1 :23 :453 1:103 1:362 (F)Alw 7500 3 2 21½ 2hd 1½ 14 Guerin E 121 w *.40 92-13 Idun1214DandyBlitzen1185BigFright1122 Speed in reserve 4
12Jly58- 6Del sly 1⅛ :47 1:12 1:39 1:521 (F)Del Oaks 49k 2 1 11 11 2hd 22¼ Hartack W 119 w *.70 77-20 BgEffort1192¼Idun1193½Tmptd119½ Rated in lead,no excuse 9
5Jly58- 7Bel fst 1 1/16 :23 :452 1:094 1:433 (F)Mother Goose 28k 2 2 2½ 11 11½ 13 Hartack W 118 w *.45 90-16 Idun1183Lopar1121½Lea Moon113½ Going away easily 9
27Jun58- 5Bel fst 6f :223 :461 1:11 (F)Alw 5000 3 3 2½ 12 14 13 Hartack W 121 w *.25 93-11 Idun1213CountessMarcy1145CarlynSarah1141½ Taken in hand 6
27May58- 7Bel fst 6f :222 :454 1:11 (F)Alw 7500 4 5 63¼ 64½ 46½ 47½ Erb D 118 w *.25 85-16 AGlitter1182½AnyMorn1152CarlynSarah1133 Very wide turn 7
10May58- 6GS fst 6f :22 :452 1:12 (F)Alw 10000 3 2 2½ 11½ 15 18 Erb D 121 w *.10 84-15 Idun1218Delnita118½Say So109 Drew far out with ease 3
30Oct57- 7Jam fst 1 1/16 :24 :481 1:133 1:464 (F)Frizette 89k 2 1 12½ 12 12½ 11½ Hartack W 119 w *.10 76-20 Idun1191½Lopar119hdBigFrght1191 Scored as rider pleased 7
19Oct57- 7GS my 1 1/16 :231 :463 1:113 1:452 (F)Gardenia 144k 5 1 14 16 16 13½ Hartack W 119 w *1.30 83-16 Idun1193½Craftiness119½MeantWell1193 Long lead,eased up 15
12Oct57- 5GS fst 1 :23 :464 1:112 1:372 (F)Alw 10000 2 2 1hd 2hd 1hd 1no Boulmetis S 121 w *.70 95-11 Idun121noQuigFlame112nkLocustTim112½ Loafed lead,lasted 11
21Sep57- 5Bel fst 6f-WC :221 :45 1:093 (F)Matron 63k 12 6 2hd 1½ 13 Hartack W 119wb 2.75 91-09 Idun1193PolyH1192Armorl1192 Drew clear while ridden out 13
14Sep57- 5Bel sly 6f-WC :214 :45 1:10 (F)Alw 6000 1 5 23 2hd 1hd Guerin E 116 w 3.40 89-13 Idun116hdArmorial1111½Pocahonts1192 Under a brisk drive 8
27Aug57- 5Sar sl 6f :231 :472 1:142 (F)Alw 4500 1 3 12½ 1½ 11½ 1¾ Guerin E 119 w *.65 76-27 Idun119¾Abientot1162½CourtPlantng1161 Little speed left 5
Daily Racing Form time,1:14
16Aug57- 4Sar fst 5½f :223 :47 :594 1:063 (F)Alw 3700 8 4 42¾ 2hd 1½ 13½ Guerin E 119 w *1.70 84-19 Idun1193½Picnicking1196SingleStroke1192 Drew out easily 11
19Jly57- 4Bel fst 5f-WC :223 :452 :582 (F)Md Sp Wt 14 1 2½ 21 2¾ Guerin E 115 w *2.20 86-13 [D]Bridgework110¾Idun115nkLament1153 Bothered repeatedly 18
Placed first by disqualification

Intentionally

blk. c. 1956, by Intent (War Relic)–My Recipe, by Discovery — **Lifetime record: 34 18 7 2 $652,258**
Own.– Tartan Stable
Br.– Brookfield Farms (Ky)
Tr.– J.A. Nerud

10Feb62- 7Hia fst 1⅛ :461 1:102 1:352 1:482 3↑ Seminole H 62k 3 1 1hd 11½ 15 18 Ycaza M 126 b 3.85 93-13 Intentionally1268Carry Back127½Yorky120½ Much the best 10
31Jan62- 7Hia fst 7f :222 :444 1:092 1:223 3↑ Palm Beach H 33k 10 2 34 33½ 22 11¾ Ussery R 126 b *2.60 97-11 Intentionally1261¾CarryBack1242Ambiopoise122nk Drew out 13
24Jan62- 8Hia fm 5½f(T) 1:07 4↑ Alw 6000 8 1 31½ 32½ 23 43 Hinojosa H 118 *1.05 80-23 Winonly121hdGordianKnot1151¾CaptainKiddII1121¼ Bore in 8
Previously owned by Brookfield Farms;previously trained by E.I. Kelly
7Nov61- 7Aqu fst 6f :222 :453 1:10 3↑ Sport Page H 23k 10 1 4nk 3½ 3½ 1hd Ycaza M 129 b *.95 95-14 Intentionally129hdWindy Sands1121¼Gyro1191¼ Bore in,up 12
28Oct61- 7GS fst 1¼ :471 1:112 1:363 2:03 3↑ Trenton H 84k 2 1 1½ 1hd 1hd 2½ Boulmetis S 124 b 4.60 89-13 Carry Back120½Intentionally1241¼Ambiopoise120nk Bumped 8
12Oct61- 7GS fst 1⅛ :481 1:121 1:37 1:493 3↑ Quaker City H 27k 5 1 11½ 12 12 12 Boulmetis S 122 b *1.20 89-16 Intentionally1222MailOrder1162¾ChiefofChifs1198 Driving 5
7Oct61- 5GS fst 6f :22 :444 1:093 3↑ Alw 7500 3 3 21 21½ 21½ 13 Boulmetis S 119 b *.70 97-10 Intentionally1193BeauAdmiral1061½MailOrder1223½ Driving 8
16Sep61- 8Atl fm 1 3/16(T) :463 1:111 1:37 1:56 3↑ U Nations H 100k 4 1 1hd 11 1½ 62¾ Boulmetis S 117 b 16.90 90-07 Oink119noTompion1172ArtMarket116nk Used up setting pace 12
4Sep61- 8AP gd 1 :224 :452 1:093 1:343 3↑ Wash Park H 120k 4 2 21 23 35 57 Hartack W 120 b 5.70 93-08 ChiefofChiefs1124¾TalentShow110nkRunforNurse112¾ Tired 11
28Aug61- 6Bel fst 7f :224 :453 1:092 1:223 3↑ Alw 6500 4 1 12 12 14 13½ Ycaza M 117 b *.55 94-11 Intentionally1173½Trans-Way1191Grwol1144 Speed to spare 6
17Sep60- 7Atl fm 1 3/16(T) :463 1:12 1:372 1:57 3↑ U Nations H 100k 5 1 12 41½ 63¼ 85½ Hartack W 124 b 7.60 82-12 T.V.Lark1201¼SwordDancer1271¼BallyAche122hd Used early 10
5Sep60- 7Aqu fst 1 :232 :461 1:102 1:344 3↑ Aqueduct H 56k 1 2 2hd 12 11 2hd Hartack W 125 b 1.95 94-11 Bald Eagle130hdIntentionally125noWarhead1133 Sharp try 5
16Jly60- 8AP fst 1 :221 :443 1:083 1:342 3↑ Equipoise Mile H 55k 8 4 1hd 13 14 1no Hartack W 126 b *1.40 98-09 Intentionally126noDunce1213½Little Tytus1135 All out 8
29Jun60- 7Bel fst 6f :223 :454 1:103 3↑ Toboggan H 27k 6 2 11½ 12 13 12½ Hartack W 128 b *.60e 94-17 Intentionally1282½RickCity1222½Vendett115nk Easily best 6
16Sep59- 7Aqu fst 1⅛ :471 1:12 1:373 1:503 Discovery H 29k 6 4 53½ 43 34½ 35½ Ycaza M 129 b *.90 -- MiddleBrother1163½Demobilize1172Intentionlly129nk Tired 10
7Sep59- 7Bel fst 1 :224 :451 1:092 1:352 Jerome H 56k 3 1 12 13 16 110 Ycaza M 126 b *.75 97-15 Intentionally12610Atoll1202SevenCorners110hd Easy score 6
25Jly59- 8AP fst 1 :224 :452 1:092 1:35 Arl Classic 140k 5 3 32 22 21½ 32¾ Hartack W 123 b *.40 92-13 Dunce1171½On-and-On115¾Intentionally1232¾ Speed,hung 7
27Jun59- 8Was fst 1 :214 :432 1:073 1:331 W Wright Mem 55k 2 1 1½ 11½ 12½ 12¼ Ycaza M 121 b *.80 101-05 Intentionally1212¼On-and-On115¾LittleTytus1094¾ In hand 7
23May59- 6Bel fst 1 :221 :442 1:091 1:353 Withers 90k 11 2 22 2½ 13 13 Ycaza M 126 b 2.75 96-10 Intentionally1263Manassa Mauler1264½Bagdad1261½ Easily 13
9May59- 7GS fst 6f :222 :452 1:112 Del Valley 29k 1 8 3½ 1hd 11½ 11¾ Hartack W 124 b *.60 87-22 Intentionally1241¾CedrBrook1212½NsrullhSwp1211½ Driving 10
18Apr59- 7Jam fst 1⅛ :461 1:11 1:37 1:493 Wood Memorial 88k 6 3 31½ 31 44 47½ Shoemaker W 126 b 2.70 85-14 Manassa Mauler126¾First Landing126¾Our Dad1266 Tired 8
11Apr59- 7Jam sly 1 1/16 :232 :462 1:111 1:43 Gotham 28k 4 2 2½ 2hd 2½ 2¾ Shoemaker W 122 b *.85 94-10 Atoll122¾Intentionally1225Open View114no No excuses 7
6Apr59- 5Jam fst 6f :224 :462 1:104 Alw 7500 4 1 12½ 13 14 16½ Shoemaker W 124 b *.15 93-17 Intentionally1246½Outgiving1131¼ThatLuckyDay1086 Easily 4

22Nov58- 7Pim	fst 1 1/16		:224:462 1:113 1:46	Pim Futurity 168k	3 2 22 13 14 11¾	Shoemaker W	122wb	*1.30	80-28	Intentionally1221¾RicoTso1223½BlckHlls1223½	Hand ridden 9
	Geldings not eligible										
25Oct58- 7GS	sly 1 1/16		:222:463 1:124 1:462	Garden State 297k	10 4 32 33½ 510 512	Nelson E	122wb	8.50	66-31	FirstLanding122hdTomyLee1222SwordDancer1223	Speed,tired 13
11Oct58- 7Bel	fst 1		:231:47 1:123 1:392	Champagne 151k	8 4 4¾ 2½ 32 33¼	Nelson E	122wb	9.25	74-21	FirstLandng122nk[D]TomyL1223Intntonlly1222	Roughed early 10
20Sep58- 7Bel	fst 6½-WC		:214:443 1:082 1:143	Futurity 114k	2 1 1hd 1hd 11	Shoemaker W	122 w	8.30	99-01	Intentionally1221First Landing122nkDunce1223½	Driving 8
	Geldings not eligible										
10Sep58- 7Atl	fst 7f		:214:441 1:094 1:232	World's Playground 36k	5 1 21 2hd 13 2hd	Culmone J	122wb	5.70	89-16	Demobilize119hdIntentonlly1222½PnBolro110hd	Just failed 15
30Aug58- 8AP	fst 6f		:222:443 1:093	Wash Park Futurity 164k	7 7 62¼ 74¾ 66¼ 45¼	Valenzuela I	119 w	10.70	91-03	RestlssWind122nkWinsomeWinner1161½Demoblz1193½	Rallied 10
13Aug58- 6Sar	fst 6f		:231:472 1:13	Grand Union Hotel 34k	5 1 1hd 1hd 1hd 23¼	Arcaro E	120 w	*1.10	80-19	FirstMinister1203¼Intentionally1202½EastIndn1143½	Tired 7
26Jly58- 6Mth	fst 6f		:213:443 1:103	Sapling 58k	5 6 56 47½ 36 24½	Culmone J	124 w	2.70e	84-22	WatchYourStep1144½Intntonlly124hdRstlssWnd1245½	Rallied 8
25Jun58- 6Mth	fst 5½f		:22 :452 :58 1:05	©Tyro 26k	10 1 2hd 12 13 11½	Culmone J	119 w	*2.00	93-16	Intentionally1191½EasySpur1222RoyalAnthem1221½	In hand 13
14Jun58- 5Mth	sl 5½f		:224:472 1:00 1:063	Alw 5000	1 1 11½ 13½ 15 16	Boulmetis S	122 w	*.80	85-31	Intentionally1226Dark Look1221½Rough Tempo1225	In hand 7
29May58- 4GS	fst 5f		:222:463 :59	Alw 4500	6 2 2hd 12 14 14	Truman J	112 w	11.70	95-14	Intentionally1124WeatherProphet1172½JyJyJr.117no	Easily 10

Jam

b. g. 1947, by Impound (Sun Beau)–Cherry Orchard, by Display **Lifetime record: 76 14 11 8 $69,585**

Own.– J.F. McHugh
Br.– Alfred G. Vanderbilt (Md)
Tr.– M.H. Dixon Jr

22Oct55- 5RB	sf *1¼Ⓣ		2:111 3↑	Alw 400	8 7 74½ 64 63¾ 62½	Phelps E	134wb	-	--	Lethnot130nkMeadow Mint133½Another Hyacinth1581	9
5Oct55- 3Lig	fm *2	Hurdles	4:031 3↑	Alw 2000	4 4 35½ 49½ 44¾ 39	Phelps E	141wb	-	--	Morpheus1321Ring o' Roses1478Jam1413	Driving 6
19Sep55- 3Aqu	hd *1¾	Hurdles	3:263 3↑	Alw 3800	3 7 77½ 79 721 722¼	Phelps E	142wb	17.10	--	Morpheus134noKing Gavin1354Irish Pageant1494	Trailed 7
10Sep55- 5Fai	fm *3	S'Chase	6:061 4↑	Foxcatcher Nat'l 3.1k	5 4 453 4 4 4	Phelps E	148wb	6.95	--	Repose153hdMightyMo15320MnkeyWrnch148	Distanced,eased 5
7Sep55- 3Aqu	fm *2	Hurdles	3:453 3↑	Alw 4000	5 6 612 612 624 623	Phelps E	138wb	31.55	--	King Commander150nkThe Proff1479Good Cards142¾	Trailed 6
23Aug55- 3Sar	sf *1½	Hurdles	3:044 3↑	Alw 3500	1 6 88 83¼ 75 511	McDonald RS	141wb	13.65e	--	Galatian146½Polly Pep1422Irish Pageant1346	Mild rally 11
12Aug55- 3Sar	sf *1¾	Hurdles	3:334 3↑	Alw 3500	2 2 54 74¼ 717 718	Phelps E	142wb	4.95	--	Good Cards1342Irish Pageant1351Antagonizer1422	Outrun 9
6Aug55- 3Sar	hd *1½	Hurdles	2:591 3↑	Alw 3500	1 7 511 513 512 55¾	Glass J10	130wb	*1.45e	--	DearBrutus1475RiverJordan151¾Camee151hd	Never a threat 9
5Jly55- 3Aqu	hd *2	S'Chase	3:46 4↑	Alw 4000	6 3 21 39 320 319½	Phelps E	143wb	9.75	--	Beau Sir1384½Moot13815Jam14310	Jumped poorly throughout 6
16Jun55- 5Aqu	fm *2	S'Chase	3:453 4↑	Hitchcock H 10k	4 7 722 723 728 733	Phelps E	143wb	37.20	--	Fulton1322½Shipbrd1631Rythmnhm1426½	Fenced very poorly 7
2Jun55- 5Bel	fm *2½	S'Chase	4:442 4↑	Meadow Brook H 11k	1 6 647 616 - -	Phelps E	136wb	22.00	--	Shipboard1566CurlyJo13115Nj15630	Bobbled,unseated rider 6
21May55- 6Bel	hd *2½	S'Chase	4:432 4↑	International 21k	8 9 924 829 435 451	Phelps E	155wb	64.50	--	Neji15015Ancestor15518Hyvania15518	Raced far back 10
12May55- 5Bel	hd *2	S'Chase	3:411 4↑	Corinthian H 8.9k	4 2 37 412 520 523	Phelps E	137wb	15.65	--	Shipboard1553Beaupr1363Nj1551½	Early foot,jumped poorly 6
28Apr55- 3Bel	sf *2	S'Chase	3:47 4↑	Alw 4500	5 8 611 611 617 621	Phelps E	137wb	5.60	--	Ancestor1372PrinceGlorieux13012CammellLaird1425	Outrun 8
16Apr55- 3Mid	hd *2	S'Chase	3:551 3↑	Alw 750	3 1 2½ 2½ 2½ 23	Phelps E	145wb	-	--	Prince Glorieux1433Jam1455Virginius1458	Tired in drive 9
19Sep53- 5Fai	hd *2	S'Chase	3:513 4↑	Manly H 3.2k	1 5 74 77¼ 511 512	Phelps E	158wb	*1.90	--	Moot141¾Banner Waves144½Uncle Joe1385	No menace 7
12Sep53- 1Fai	fst *1⅞Ⓣ		3:263 3↑	Alw 800	1 2 22 21 21 23½	Gall'her W	155 w	-	--	Sea Term1273½Jam15515Jack Kent139	Went well 3
26Jun53- 5Del	fst *2	S'Chase	3:464 3↑	Georgetown H 12k	3 4 32½ 21 514 515	Phelps E	158wb	4.50	--	The Mast148½Monkey Wrench1351Hunting Fox13612	Quit 6
19Jun53- 6Bel	fst *2¼	S'Chase	4:121 4↑	Temple Gwathmey H 16k	6 3 41¾ 413 740 740	Phelps E	162wb	9.10	--	Errolford1305½Sea Legs1652Oedipus1645	Outdistanced 7
	Daily Racing Form time,4:16 2/5										
4Jun53- 5Bel	fst *2½	S'Chase	4:421 4↑	Meadow Brook H 11k	6 5 22½ 32 - -	Phelps E	162wb	6.10	--	Sea Legs1575Oedipus1642½His Boots1462½	Hit fence 6
3Oct52- 5Bel	sf *3	S'Chase	5:44 4↑	Grand Nat'l H 28k	5 8 823 64½ 515 414	Phelps E	164wb	3.10	--	Sea Legs1365The Mast1542Oedipus1657	Bobbled at jump 9
25Sep52- 5Bel	fst *2½	S'Chase	4:412 4↑	Brook H 17k	7 8 54¼ 42 1hd 15	Phelps E	156wb	2.60	--	Jam1565Oedipus1631Lone Fisherman1313	Drew away 8
18Sep52- 5Bel	sf *2	S'Chase	3:391 3↑	Broad Hollow H 11k	2 7 412 45 21½ 2hd	Phelps E	154wb	2.40	--	Oedipus160hdJam15420The Creek1386	Just missed 8
11Sep52- 5Aqu	fst *2	S'Chase	3:441 3↑	Harbor Hill H 11k	1 6 44 33½ 36 36½	Phelps E	155wb	4.80	--	Semper Eadem1354Hot1472½Jam1556	Bad landing 4th 6
29Aug52- 5Sar	hd *2½	S'Chase	5:064 4↑	Saratoga H 11k	4 3 38 47½ 410 413	Phelps E	156wb	4.70	--	Banner Waves1362Titien II1473His Boots1518	Bobbled 6
14Aug52- 5Sar	sl *2	S'Chase	4:274 4↑	North Am H 6.3k	3 6 31½ 2½ 33 1½	Phelps E	152wb	2.65	--	Jam152½Navy Gun1471Flaming Comet1367	Driving 7
7Aug52- 5Sar	fst *2	S'Chase	4:11 4↑	Shillelah 5.8k	4 2 31½ 22 47 412	Phelps E	153wb	*1.85	--	Oedipus1622His Boots1405Phiblant1405	Stumbled 5
27Jun52- 6Del	fst *2½	S'Chase	4:44 4↑	Indian River H 12k	3 2 23 112 120 120	Phelps E	152wb	2.55	--	Jam15220Monkey Wrench1342The Mast1616	Easily best 5
20Jun52- 6Del	fst *2	S'Chase	3:431 4↑	Georgetown H 12k	7 5 77¼ 55¼ 47½ 25	Phelps E	151wb	10.40	--	The Mast1575Jam1511½[DH]Crooning Wind1431½	Good effort 8
11Jun52- 6Bel	fst *2¼	S'Chase	4:163 4↑	Temple Gwathmey H 16k	3 9 61¼ 65½ 47 49	Phelps E	153wb	11.40	--	The Mast153¾Oedipus1631¼Navy Gun1497	Swerved 9
29May52- 5Bel	fst *2½	S'Chase	4:431 4↑	Meadow Brook H 11k	4 6 2½ 2hd 521 630	Phelps E	152wb	2.60	--	The Mast1462¼Navy Gun14815Titien II1476	Jumped poorly 8
8May52- 5Bel	fst *2	S'Chase	3:424 4↑	C L Appleton Mem 9k	6 6 69 43½ 2hd 13	Phelps E	139wb	*1.00	--	Jam1393Lone Fisherman139¾The Mast143¾	Handily,drew out 6
1May52- 5Bel	sf *2	S'Chase	3:471 4↑	International H 9.3k	7 8 76 2½ 13 18	Phelps E	141wb	*2.90	--	Jam1418Flaming Comet1371Palaja1418	Easily 11
19Apr52- 4Mid	fst *2	S'Chase	3:522 4↑	Handicap 2420	3 4 33½ - - -	Phelps E	148wb	-	--	[D]High Road1401Proceed1381½Crown Royal1381	Lost rider 8
12Apr52- 3War	fst *2	S'Chase	4:122 4↑	Alw 800	6 1 14½ 19 115 117	Phelps E	142wb	-	--	Jam14217Sundance Kid1441½Trout Brook1429	Easily 7
17Nov51- 6Mtp	gd *1¾		3:08 3↑	Alw 700	2 1 13 15 18 110	Smithwick AP	151wb	-	--	Jam15110McGinty Moore148½Beaupre12922	Easily 5
10Nov51- 7Pim	fst 2½		:511 3:022 4:192 3↑	Pim Cup 29k	5 4 21 48¼ 531 545	Culmone J	124wb	16.80	31-16	Pilaster1247Lone Eagle12415Hull Down1188	Early speed 6
17Oct51- 6Bel	fst *2	Hurdles	3:442 3↑	NY Turf Writers H 7.3k	3 5 1½ 2½ 47½ 57	Phelps E	155 w	5.25e	--	Triomphe1432½Hyvania152½Snob Tourist144½	Tired 8
8Oct51- 3Bel	sf *1¾	Hurdles	3:171 3↑	Handicap 4545	2 3 31 21 1½ 21	Phelps E	152 w	4.20	--	Hyvania1461Jam1527Quiet14712	Gave way 6
2Oct51- 8Bel	fst 1 1/16		:224:46 1:112 1:45 3↑	Alw 4000	4 6 78¾ 66 76 78	Passmore WJ	113 w	15.20	78-14	Guard of Honor1141¼Mirabeau110hdSalaise120¾	Outrun 7
8Sep51- 3Fai	fst *1⅞Ⓣ		3:181 3↑	Alw 800	3 2 12 14 18 117	Phelps E	149 w	-e	--	Jam14917Scotch Wave152nkAdmiral Tan1488	Easily 7
31Aug51- 3Sar	fst *2	Hurdles	3:472 4↑	Alw 3500	4 2 2hd 11 13 12	Phelps E	145 w	2.25	--	Jam1452Salemaker131¾Navy Gun1382	Ridden out 7
18Aug51- 3Sar	sl *2	Hurdles	3:592 3↑	Handicap 5045	2 2 21 21 23 38	Phelps E	146 w	4.65	--	Quiet1426½Navy Gun1451½Jam14612	Bobbled 6
10Aug51- 5Sar	sl *1¾	Hurdles	3:353 3↑	Nat'l Maiden 8.3k	7 7 53½ 63 57½ 59	Phelps E	156 w	5.80	--	Fulton160½Manchon1443½Hyvania1512	Stumbled 9
27Jly51- 5Mth	fst *1¾	Hurdles	3:08 3↑	Alw 4000	7 5 31½ 32½ 65 46½	Phelps E	150 w	8.00	--	Fulton1501Titien II1491½Fonda1424	Weakened 7
20Jly51- 7Jam	fst 1 1/16		:243:482 1:132 1:462 3↑	Alw 4500	6 8 108½ 83¼ 98¼ 99¼	Guerin E	115 w	23.15	71-18	Coveted113noDalpark1131Saxony1133½	Outrun 10
5Jly51- 5Aqu	sf *2	Hurdles	3:403 3↑	Forget H 11k	4 6 73½ 55 612 615	Zimmerman J	144 w	4.45	--	Fulton145hdTitien II160¾Hyvania1412	Tired 7
22Jun51- 5Aqu	fst *1¾	Hurdles	3:09 3↑	Na'l Maiden 7.8k	1 4 22 44 410 414	Phelps E	151 w	2.00	--	Fulton1495Hyvania1499Stunts155nk	Bad landing 6th 4
18Jun51- 3Bel	fst *1¾	Hurdles	3:15 3↑	Handicap 4555	6 10 74¼ 3½ 12 13	Phelps E	140 w	7.85	--	Jam1403Quiet1344½Hyvania130½	Driving 10
28May51- 5Bel	sf *1¾	Hurdles	3:194 3↑	Nat'l Maiden 8.1k	5 6 21 2hd 1½ 16	Phelps E	142 w	2.15	--	Jam1426Fulton14915Tellanrun15010	Driving 7
21May51- 3Bel	fst *1½	Hurdles	2:45 3↑	Sp Wt 3000	8 10 22 32½ 32 33½	Phelps E	137 w	*2.20	--	Hyvania1421El Arabi1482½Jam1372	Bobbled 4th 11
5May51- 6War	my *1¾	Hurdles	2:573 3↑	Alw 600	3 3 2½ 1hd 1no 2½	Smithwick AP	142 w	-	--	Swiggle142½Jam1424Kipper1532½	Hung 6
14Apr51- 1DRn	fst *1½	Hurdles	2:301 3↑	Alw 500	7 6 55 41½ 3nk 1hd	Phelps E	135 w	-	--	Jam135hdIrish Clown1471½Wenham142hd	Hard drive 9
18Nov50- 6Mtp	fst *1¾		3:082 3↑	Alw 700	1 2 2½ 2nk 1½ 12	Cushman C	141 w	-	--	Jam1412Allflor142	Handily 2
10Nov50- 5Pim	fst 1⅛		:474 1:123 1:39 1:521	Alw 3500	6 4 35½ 35 24 36½	Catalano A	108wb	11.90	86-21	Twinkley1163Arcave1193½Jam1083	No rally 7
2Nov50- 6GS	fst 1 1/16		:233:473 1:114 1:46	Alw 4000	7 3 32½ 22 22 43	Saunders W	112wb	*3.20	77-16	Twinkley108hdPendant1132½Mackle108½	Hung 8
27Oct50- 5GS	fst 1 1/16		:233:474 1:123 1:471 3↑	Alw 3000	7 4 34 33 32 2hd	Saunders W	112wb	4.00	74-19	Luremenow117hdJam112noIntrigue110no	Just missed 10
4Jly50- 6Del	fst 1 1/16		:233:471 1:121 1:444 3↑	Alw 3500	5 8 79 67¾ 57½ 512	Passmore WJ	112wb	3.70e	77-14	My Nell109.5½Uncle Don1169High Bracket1222	Off poorly 8
1Jly50- 3Del	fst 1 1/16		:234:482 1:141 1:452 3↑	Alw 3500	2 2 22 31 33 26	Passmore WJ	111wb	*1.40	80-14	Uncle Don1166Jam1111½The Flier1141¼	No excuse 5
	Previously owned by Mam Stable;previously trained by H.H. Goodwin										
8Jun50- 7Bel	fst 1 1/16		:232:462 1:114 1:443	Clm 10000	5 3 36 24 23 21¼	Boland W	114wb	4.10	87-14	Oilomacy1201¼Jam114¾Persist1143½	Game try 6
31May50- 4Bel	fst 1		:232:463 1:121 1:391	Clm 8000-c	6 6 63¾ 32 31½ 3½	Stuart K	106wb	*2.70	77-13	Deflation116noPay Window118½Jam1062	Forced wide 7
	Claimed from Mrs L. Laurin;trainer, L. Laurin										

25May50- 3Bel fst 1 1/16 :232 :471 1:121 1:434 Clm 7000-c 2 1 11 12 2½ 22 Atkinson T 117wb 2.20 90-07 Mr. Willie1192Jam117 5½Beret112 2½ Went wide 7
Claimed from Mam Stable;trainer, H.H. Goodwin
15May50- 7Bel fst 1 :231 :462 1:114 1:383 Clm 8000 3 9 86¾ 83¾ 86¼ 63¼ Boland W 114wb 20.35 78-21 AirMail120noFullMeasure109noEthelTerry116¾ Closed gap 13
Previously owned by A.G. Vanderbilt;previously trained by W.C. Winfrey
13Apr50- 8Jam fst 1 1/16 :24 :483 1:123 1:463 Clm 10000 2 6 54¾ 77¼ 75¾ 56 Guerin E 115 w 5.30 74-17 HappyEast113 2½PeaceMission116noEvnLatr113 2½ No menace 10
7Apr50- 7Jam fst 1 1/16 :24 :48 1:132 1:462 Clm 10000 7 7 85¾ 76 710 710 Guerin E 116 w 3.70 71-20 EthelTerry1141HappyEast116noPecMsson1195 Close quarters 9
1Apr50- 7Jam fst 1 1/16 :243 :49 1:141 1:471 Clm 10000 1 4 53½ 51¾ 43¼ 21 Guerin E 116 w 12.20 76-14 Questus1161Jam116hdHappy East116½ Strong finish 9
3Mar50- 7Hia fst 1⅛ :48 1:124 1:38 1:51 Alw 3500 8 7 103½ 95¾ 77½ 86½ Dodson D 115 w 11.40 76-09 Three and Two110nkNoblest113nkHickory1151 Outrun 11
18Feb50- 3Hia fst 7f :23 :461 1:113 1:242 ©Alw 3500 8 6 75 73 75 52¼ Dodson D 122 w 5.30 88-12 Feefifofum109hdPotent1131Hickory118hd Closed gap 9
15Feb50- 3Hia fst 7f :23 :461 1:121 1:253 ©Md Sp Wt 2 3 33½ 2hd 1½ 13 Dodson D 122 w 20.30 84-17 Jam1223Johns Admiral1171Opinionated122 1½ Ridden out 8
7Feb50- 3Hia fst 7f :233 :47 1:122 1:252 ©Md Sp Wt 12 7 43 56¼ 68 712 Woodhouse H 122 w 55.75 73-14 Roughhouse1222Johns Admiral117noNoblest1223 No mishap 12
15Nov49- 4Pim fst 1 1/16 :241 :472 1:13 1:452 Md Sp Wt 4 7 611 613 514 419½ Martin RJ 122 w 7.60 63-14 Alfadur1158Swyndor12210Opal Blossom122 1½ No mishap 10
27Oct49- 1Jam gd 6f :232 :472 1:14 ©Md 8000 10 12 117½ 1114 1117 109½ Scurlock O 122 w 9.50 71-18 DHDeflation116DHBashful Sun1136Beret113¾ Outrun 14
8Oct49- 3Lrl sl 6f :23 :474 1:134 Md Sp Wt 8 8 88¼ 77 79¾ 715 Martin RJ 120 w 9.60 70-23 PrinceDandy1206Possessive117½MiltntLdy117no Never close 9
5Oct49- 3Lrl fst 6f :233 :483 1:14 ©Md Sp Wt 5 6 96½ 67 510 513 Guerin E 122 w 2.90 71-23 Honors1222Hi-Pilate1227Djinn122 2½ Raced wide 12
28Sep49- 4Lrl fst 6f :232 :482 1:144 ©Md Sp Wt 5 6 66¼ 67½ 56¼ 34¼ Martin RJ 122 w 2.90 76-21 Be Fleet122nkOpal Blossom1224Jam122no Closed fast 8
19Sep49- 4Bel fst 5½f-W :223 :454 1:052 ©Md Sp Wt 11 9 98¾ 814 68 Guerin E 118 w 17.25 79-16 Eternal City118¾Ode118nkWar King1184 Closed ground 19

King Commander

dkb. g. 1949, by Brown King (Nid d'Or)–Guinea Egg, by Cohort **Lifetime record: 67 17 15 6 $100,295**
Own.– Mrs L.R. Troiano
Br.– Mrs Joe W. Brown (Ky)
Tr.– E.E. Weymouth

15Jly58- 3Mth fm *1¾ Hurdles 3:201 4↑ Clm 4000 2 4 48 511 - - KnlsJD5 140 w 3.60 -- Caste15012Mielaison1452Curly Joe1455 Broke down 7
Previously owned by L.R. Troiano
19Sep57- 5Bel fm *2⅛ S'Chase 4:01 3↑ Broad Hollow H 17k 5 2 2hd - - - Cotter J 147 w 8.00 -- Independence1488Morpheus138 2½Shipboard1623 Fell,lame 7
12Sep57- 5Bel fm *2⅛ S'Chase 3:573 3↑ Harbor Hill H 17k 3 2 22 43¾ 47 59 Cotter J 152 w 3.70 -- Ancestor1582Independence1486His Boots131nk Speed,tired 9
30Aug57- 3Sar fm *2 S'Chase 4:162 3↑ Alw 6500 2 1 12 13 12 12½ Cotter J 148 w *1.40 -- King Commander148 2½Billing Bear148 2½Affable14025 Easily 6
Previously trained by M.G. Walsh
7Jun56- 5Bel fm *2½ S'Chase 4:394 4↑ Meadow Brook H 17k 2 1 11½ 12 21½ 39½ Smithwick P 164 w 1.55 -- Neji165 3½Carthage1366KngCmmndr1648 Brushed jumps,lame 5
24May56- 5Bel fm *2 S'Chase 3:434 4↑ International H 11k 3 1 14 13 15 17 Smithwick P 160 w *.50e -- King Commander1607Cap-a-Pie140 3½Hyvania1507 Much best 6
17May56- 5Bel fm *2 S'Chase 3:44 4↑ Corinthian H 11k 3 2 1hd 1½ 1hd 23 Smithwick P 160 w *.40e -- Montadet1373King Commander1606Carthage1404 Bore out 6
7Sep55- 3Aqu fm *2 Hurdles 3:453 3↑ Alw 4000 3 1 11½ 12 11½ 1nk Smithwick P 150 w *.65 -- King Commander150nkThe Proff1479Good Cards142¾ Lasted 6
21May55- 6Bel hd *2½ S'Chase 4:432 4↑ International 21k 7 1 18 15 - - Smithwick P 155 w 2.05e -- Neji15015Ancestor15518Hyvn15518 High speed,fell at 15th 10
5May55- 5Bel fm *2 S'Chase 3:412 4↑ C L Appleton Mem 9.1k 1 4 416 36½ 21 23½ Smithwick P 162 w 2.40e -- Ancestor134 3½KingCommandr1628RiverJordan1344 Swerved 8
22Oct54- 6Bel fm *2½ S'Chase 4:39 4↑ Temple Gwathmey H 16k 4 1 12 12½ 14 1¾ Smithwick P 164 w 3.00 -- King Commander164¾Neji1497Coveted13170 Driving,tiring 6
14Oct54- 5Bel fm *3 S'Chase 5:42 4↑ Grand National H 28k 7 1 11 - - - Smithwick P 164 w 2.75e -- Shipboard152 2¾Coveted13122Curly Joe13310 Bobbled 16th 7
5Oct54- 5Bel fm *2½ S'Chase 4:394 4↑ Brook H 17k 2 2 12 13 13 21½ Smithwick P 161 w *1.40e -- Neji137 1½KingCommndr16116Covtd13115 Tired under weight 9
16Sep54- 3Aqu sf *2 Hurdles 3:452 3↑ Bushwick H 8k 4 6 819 58½ 33 33½ Smithwick P 157 w *.90e -- Carafar1433Khumbaba134½King Commander1573 No rally 8
26Aug54- 5Sar fm *2½ S'Chase 5:002 4↑ Saratoga H 11k 2 1 11½ 11 16 19 Smithwick P 154 w 2.00 -- KingCommndr1549Shpbord14814Covtd1328 Speed in reserve 6
19Aug54- 5Sar fm *2 S'Chase 4:083 4↑ Beverwyck H 8.7k 2 1 11 12½ 16 13 Smithwick P 149 w *1.00 -- King Commndr1493MightyMo13520Imbursed1302 Ridden out 5
12Aug54- 5Sar fm *2 S'Chase 4:13 4↑ North American H 8.6k 4 4 2½ 21 2hd 2no Riles S 145 w 1.00e -- Escargot139noKing Commander1456Sun Shower1602 Hung 5
5Aug54- 5Sar sf *2 S'Chase 4:172 4↑ Shillelah H 8.8k 5 4 1½ 11½ 11½ 22 Riles S 143 w 2.45e -- Shipboard1392King Commander14320Coveted13812 Tired 7
30Jly54- 5Mth hd *1¾ Hurdles 3:19 3↑ Midsummer H 11k 5 6 46½ 32½ 2hd 2hd Riles S 152 w 2.20e -- Escargot143hdKing Commndr1522CammellLaird1457 Gamely 7
28Jun54- 5Del hd *2 S'Chase 3:47 4↑ Spring Maiden 6.8k 3 5 43 43 1½ 2½ Smithwick P 160 w *.60e -- Imbursed130½KingCommandr16012Bavaria14012 Outjumped 6
15Jun54- 5Aqu fm *2 S'Chase 3:493 4↑ Spring Maiden 6.8k 1 4 36 33½ 1hd 2hd Smithwick P 160 w *.40 -- Coveted155hdKingCommandr1602Imbursd13285 Bore in,tired 5
13May54- 5Bel fm *2 S'Chase 3:482 4↑ Spring Maiden 6.8k 3 3 45½ 3½ 110 17 Smithwick P 153 w *.95 -- KingCommnder1537IndianFire140 2½Coveted15015 Easy score 5
6May54- 3Bel fm *2 S'Chase 3:482 4↑ Alw 4000 7 6 21½ 43½ 11½ 14½ Smithwick P 143 w *.55 -- KingCommndr143 4½Coveted1434Carafr135 2½ Handily ridden 8
29Apr54- 3Bel fm *2 S'Chase 3:462 4↑ Sp Wt 4000 10 6 411 49 11 2½ Smithwick P 148 w *1.20 -- Shipboard140½KingCmmndr14812PacificPct148 2½ Weakened 11
10Oct53- 3Lig hd *2 Hurdles 3:582 3↑ Handicap 2000 7 7 79 2nk 13 15 Smithwick AP 149 w - -- King Commander1495Allflor143¾Salemaker137hd Easily 8
5Oct53- 5Bel fst *2 Hurdles 3:45 3↑ Rouge Dragon H 11k 7 5 710 47½ 22½ 2hd Smithwick P 154 w *1.60e -- Williamsburg142hdKingCommndr1543Hyvan1466 Just missed 9
28Sep53- 3Bel fst *1¾ Hurdles 3:132 3↑ Alw 4500 6 6 59½ 33½ 1½ 12½ Smithwick P 149 w 2.75e -- KingCommndr149 2½Wllmsburg1402RvrJordn149 4½ Ridden out 9
17Sep53- 3Aqu fst *2 Hurdles 3:421 3↑ Bushwick H 8k 5 3 327 619 11 11 Smithwick P 148 w 3.60e -- KingCommndr1481Williamsburg1392Antagonzr153 1½ Driving 8
21Aug53- 5Sar hd *2 Hurdles 3:502 3↑ Lovely Night H 6.4k 2 1 11 32 36 23½ Smithwick P 149 w *1.35e -- WarRhodes154 3½KingCmmndr149 2½BattlWv139 2½ Hard urged 8
14Aug53- 3Sar fst *1¾ Hurdles 3:302 3↑ Handicap 4085 4 5 77½ 54½ 33 21½ Smithwick P 149 w 3.35e -- War Rhodes150 1½King Commander1493Knocks Twice144 3½ 10
Close quarters
31Jly53- 5Mth fst *1¾ Hurdles 3:221 3↑ Midsummer H 11k 9 6 33 31½ 21 1no Smithwick P 140 w 7.60e -- KingCommandr140noMackville1485War Rhodes147 2½ Just up 13
28Jly53- 3Mth fst *1½ Hurdles 2:42 3↑ Alw 3500 9 2 22 2½ 1hd 11½ Smithwick P 143 w 3.50 -- KingCommndr143 1½JoeRayJr14310FleurdJo14010 Drew clear 9
2Jly53- 5Aqu fst *2 Hurdles 3:394 4↑ Forget H 11k 3 5 511 516 48 46 Cameron C 141 w 5.95e -- Williamsburg135hdEternalSon1432WarRhodes1484 Late foot 6
25Jun53- 5Aqu fst *1¾ Hurdles 3:104 3↑ Amagansett H 8.9k 5 1 12 2hd 22½ 24½ Cameron C 140 w 3.05e -- WarRhodes142 4½KingCmmndr140½EtrnlSon14418 Hard ridden 6
22Jun53- 3Aqu fst *1½ Hurdles 2:441 3↑ Md Sp Wt 2 3 1½ 12 11½ 11½ Cameron C 145 w *.60 -- KingCommander145 1½Imbursed135 1½WatchDog1356 Driving 6
15Jun53- 3Bel sf *1½ Hurdles 2:444 3↑ Sp Wt 3700 3 9 910 78 46 2¾ Cameron C 142 w 56.55 -- Mackville142¾KngCommandr1425Rythminhim1359 Impeded 12
4Jun53- 3Bel fst 7f :231 :47 1:123 1:254 4↑ Clm 5000 2 12 139½ 1313 1320 1313 Nichols J 113wb 49.20 68-20 Demi-Heure113½Brown Dalton1172Riverlane117nk No speed 13
23May53- 2Bel sly 7f :232 :474 1:124 1:251 4↑ Clm 6500 7 6 88½ 815 822 831 Wallis G 113wb 44.70 53-13 Belton Boy119½Hoplite126 2¼Evans Mountain114hd Far back 8
Previously owned by Mrs M.G. Walsh
14Oct52- 4Jam fst 1 1/16 :244 :483 1:133 1:464 Clm 5000 5 2 2hd 22 32½ 35 Nichols J 122wb 3.25 73-19 Jonskid117 2½Lesliefay117 2½King Commander1221 Weakened 8
9Oct52- 7Jam fst 1 1/16 :234 :48 1:132 1:452 3↑ Clm 6000 4 7 711 75½ 66¼ 45¾ Nichols J 117wb 14.50 79-21 Big Road1142Tape Reader110¾Flying Mane1123 Slow start 7
6Oct52- 7Jam fst 1 1/16 :242 :49 1:133 1:461 Clm 7500 9 7 66 64¼ 64½ 77 Nichols J 116wb 39.60 74-15 Westmeath1172Stone Saucer119nkLegate112nk Outrun 9
23Sep52- 8Bel fst 1⅛ :454 1:112 1:374 1:51 3↑ Clm 6000 5 6 65 32 44½ 511 Ploof H 105wb 8.20 73-12 Kay'sChildren1131FlyingMane114hdAttentionSir119 4½ Tired 8
13Sep52- 8Aqu fst 7f :23 :472 1:133 1:263 Clm 5000-c 4 8 93¼ 97 73¾ 43 Schab H 109wb 3.60 74-17 Westmeath1193GalliesPride114hdBlueFlash108no Slow start 9
Claimed from H.M. Boshamer;trained by J.R. Hastie
4Sep52- 2Aqu fst 7f :233 :472 1:13 1:263 Clm 5000 10 12 127¼ 1210 75¼ 31¾ Anderson P 118wb 13.20 75-17 Service113 1¾Grandad113noKing Commander118 1½ Late rush 13
27Aug52- 8Sar fst 1⅛ :49 1:141 1:401 1:54 Clm 5000 8 5 65½ 45 44¼ 34 Hardinbrook JN 114wb 6.70 76-19 NextStop111 1½WallSt.George113 2½KngCmmndr114¾ No mishap 8
21Aug52- 2Sar fst 7f :232 :47 1:13 1:261 Clm 5000 14 9 63 52¾ 33 44 Hardinbrook JN 115wb 9.90 80-22 Service114½Sea Bob1141Next Stop113 2½ Faltered 14
13Aug52- 2Sar my 7f :23 :464 1:124 1:273 Clm 6500 4 8 98¼ 1014 93 86½ Anderson P 119wb 78.50 70-25 Fancy Bonnet115¾Standee1163Lafourche112nk No factor 11
30Jly52- 7Jam fst 1 1/16 :25 :481 1:14 1:462 Clm 7000 4 8 89 87½ 97¾ 912 Anderson P 115wb 31.55 68-20 Harlem Maid1124La Gaulois108nkDocedoe112 2½ Outrun 9
Previously owned by J.W. Brown;previously trained by J.B. Theall
12Jly52- 7Aqu fst 1 1/16 :24 :49 1:134 1:47 Clm 7000 2 7 88½ 99¼ 55 58¼ Hardinbrook JN 114wb 14.65e 71-14 FirstWing1193WingingAlong119¾HarlemMaid1173 No menace 9
2Jly52- 7Aqu fst 1 1/16 :243 :482 1:141 1:483 Clm 5000 7 4 415 55½ 31 1¾ Hardinbrook JN 111wb 2.25 71-18 KingCommndr111¾Vocabulary1091Drems108no Driving clear 7
28Jun52- 2Aqu fst 7f :233 :471 1:132 1:264 Clm 3500 9 10 106¼ 84 1½ 12½ Hardinbrook JN 109wb *3.05e 78-16 KngCmmandr109 2½FrnchQurtr1091KthyMndl1131 Drew clear 11
26Jun52- 1Aqu fst 6f :231 :47 1:13 Clm 3500 5 9 75½ 89¼ 710 67 Coffman E 113wb 7.20 80-15 Muscidae1131Rachel G.109 3½Query108¾ Raced wide 11
20Jun52- 2Aqu fst 7f :231 :47 1:14 1:273 Clm 3500 11 10 95¾ 96 21 2nk Hardinbrook JN 109wb 4.60 74-15 Tio Tito114nkKing Commander109 2½Camouflet109nk Hung 11
28May52- 4GS fst 6f :223 :454 1:12 Clm 5000 8 7 711 814 89½ 915 Culmone J 115wb 4.20 73-15 Tiger Jay113 6½Lady Like114¾Ambrose1152 Outrun 9

Date	Cond	Dist	Fractions	Race	Running line	Jockey	Wt	Odds	Speed-Var	Top finishers	Comment	Starters
20May52- 2GS	sly	6f	:233 :48 1:143	Clm 5000	1 8 65 67 64½ 32¼	Permane R	115wb	5.50	73-21	UpHigh110nkBigKeis1192KingCommander1151½	Strong finish	9
10May52- 1GS	fst	6f	:221 :452 1:123	Clm 5000	11 12 1214 1112 614 56¾	Coffman E	115wb	49.80	78-11	FlyingPolly112¾BigKs1193½Hollowbrook1122	Sluggish start	12
1Apr52- 2Jam	fst	6f	:23 :47 1:123	Clm 5000	6 14 1413 149¼ 1215 1213	Coffman E	113wb	21.60	71-13	Deep River1171Inezmuch117¾Wolf Bait112nk	Outrun	14
1Mar52- 5FG	fst	6f	:231 :472 1:114	Clm 7000	1 4 54 43 45 45	Coffman E	111wb	6.40	89-11	ArizonaK114½QuickTulip1142½TopBrass1112	Close quarters	7
16Feb52- 8FG	gd	6f	:232 :472 1:124	Clm 7000	2 4 51½ 75½ 55½ 54¾	Coffman E	111wb	46.30	84-15	Mr. Michael S.114nkBalsa112nkDynastic114nk	No mishap	8
16Jan52- 6FG	fst	6f	:23 :47 1:134	Clm 6000	7 5 58 69 911 911	Coffman E	117wb	23.40	73-20	Balsa114nkLegatee1091½Odds Advance1122½	No factor	9
12Jan52- 5FG	fst	1 1/16	:242 :482 1:134 1:482 3↑	Alw 1800	5 6 66½ 45½ 56 58	Coffman E	112 w	3.10e	69-18	Gloriette1153½PointFortune1123FancyGent1121½	No menace	7
12Dec51- 1FG	fst	6f	:233 :473 1:151	Clm 5000	7 9 98 65 31½ 1nk	Coffman E	111wb	71.30	77-19	KingCommandr111nkGeorgeDavie1131½BeutfulJn1112	Just up	12
6Dec51- 7FG	fst	6f	:231 :473 1:141	Clm 6000	2 9 107¾ 1013 712 715	Coffman E	112wb	94.30	67-22	Seasoned1111½Quick Tulip1066Balsa1142	Outrun	10
24Nov51- 5FG	fst	6f	:231 :47 1:131	Alw 2000	3 7 79½ 712 712 714	Chiapetta S	108wb	36.70	73-18	Our Challenge117hdPlunger1146Bold Sab117½	Trailed	7
20Oct51- 4GS	fst	6f	:222 :454 1:121	Alw 4500	3 9 912 911 915 913	LeBlanc C	115wb	95.40	74-15	Star Delight1142½La Gaulois117¾Saddle Tramp1122	Trailed	9
17Oct51- 2Bel	fst	6f	:224 :47 1:131	Clm 7500	14 10 86¼ 129 1321 1211	LeBlanc C	113wb	14.05f	72-15	Vantage107¾Flaunt116¾Our Dorie1131½	Outrun	14
3Oct51- 5Bel	fst	6f-WC	:223 :452 1:10	ⒸMd Sp Wt	2 25 2615 2518 2620	LeBlanc C	118 w	71.90e	71-09	Warpath1182Golden Gloves118hdForelock1181	Outrun	26

Kiss Me Kate

ch. f. 1948, by Count Fleet (Reigh Count)–Irish Nora, by Pharamond II — **Lifetime record: 29 7 4 7 $196,505**

Own.– W.M. Jeffords
Br.– Walter M. Jeffords (Ky)
Tr.– O. White

Date	Cond	Dist	Fractions	Race	Running line	Jockey	Wt	Odds	Speed-Var	Top finishers	Comment	Starters
30May53- 6Bel	fst	1¼	:471 1:11 1:353 2:003 3↑	Suburban H 58k	4 4 35 59½ 711 718	Scurlock O	112wb	2.30e	79-17	Tom Fool128noRoyal Vale1247Cold Command1142	Done early	7
5May53- 6Jam	sly	1⅛	:48 1:123 1:373 1:504 3↑	ⒻFirenze H 35k	6 6 56 41½ 1hd 13	Gorman D	126wb	*2.10	92-19	KssMeKate1263ParadngLady1232½LaCorredora123¾	Drew out	8
23Apr53- 6Jam	fst	1 1/16	:25 :481 1:121 1:443 4↑	Alw 5000	4 5 54 43½ 32 2½	Gorman D	115wb	*.70	88-21	Swoop108½Kiss Me Kate1154Deluge113½	Gaining fast	8
11Nov52- 6Pim	sl	1⅛	:49 1:133 1:394 1:522 3↑	ⒻGallorette 29k	4 6 64 52¼ 32½ 23½	Nash R	123wb	2.50	88-22	La Corredora1123½Kiss Me Kate1231Marta1173	Good effort	9
18Oct52- 7GS	fst	1 1/16	:23 :471 1:112 1:453 3↑	ⒻVineland H 49k	4 12 1214 1010 66½ 2¾	Nash R	118wb	8.00e	81-20	Sickle'sImage120¾KissMeKate118¾LilyWhit111hd	Late speed	17
1Oct52- 6Bel	fst	1½	:483 1:132 2:044 2:312 3↑	ⒻLadies H 59k	6 4 52½ 31½ 35½ 44½	Arcaro E	121wb	3.75e	76-15	How1121¼Marta1222½Enchanted Eve112¾	Faltered	11
13Sep52- 7Aqu	fst	1⅛	:474 1:121 1:38 1:51 3↑	ⒻBeldame H (Div 2) 62k	3 9 910 99¾ 86 44¾	Gorman D	122wb	10.80	85-17	Real Delight126¾Marta117½La Corredora1123½	Late foot	9
28Aug52- 6Sar	fst	1¾	:494 2:07 2:33 2:594 3↑	Sar Cup 16k	2 3 32 45 33½ 35	Guerin E	121wb	*1.05	71-20	Busanda1212½Lone Eagle1262½Kiss Me Kate1212	No rally	5
	Geldings not eligible											
19Aug52- 6Sar	fst	1⅛	:49 1:143 1:412 1:532 3↑	ⒻDiana H 11k	3 4 41½ 53 52¾ 45¾	Nash R	126wb	*.85	77-22	Busanda1111¼Nilufer106½Valadium1154	No rally	5
5Jly52- 5Del	fst	1¼	:462 1:104 1:363 2:023 3↑	ⒻNew Castle H 61k	7 2 1½ 12 13 12½	Nash R	126wb	*2.20	97-14	Kiss Me Kate1262½Renew1231½My Celeste1131½	Cleverly	10
30May52- 6Bel	fst	1¼	:463 1:102 1:353 2:02 3↑	Suburban H 60k	4 10 1015 1013 711 43¼	Woodhouse H	107wb	16.45	87-12	One Hitter112nkCrafty Admiral1132Mameluke1161	Late foot	10
21Apr52- 6Jam	fst	1⅛	:471 1:114 1:372 1:511 3↑	ⒻFirenze H 33k	8 6 67 67 45½ 33¾	Arcaro E	123wb	*2.40	86-18	NxtMove1262ThelmaBurger1101¾KssMeKate123¾	Closed fast	9
7Apr52- 6Lrl	fst	6f	:223 :47 1:114 4↑	Alw 5000	1 4 33½ 44 55 32¼	Nash R	117wb	4.80	86-21	[D]SenatorJoe119nkRockyHeghts1052KssMKt117hd	Closed fast	6
13Oct51- 6Bel	fst	2	:493 2:302 2:56 3:213 3↑	J C Gold Cup 53k	3 4 47½ 414 412 310	Shoemaker W	114wb	9.30	86-11	Counterpoint117hdHillPrince12410KissMKt1142½	Rough trip	5
10Oct51- 6Bel	fst	1½	:483 1:132 2:04 2:301 3↑	ⒻLadies H 30k	8 12 98½ 106 77¼ 34¾	Arcaro E	120wb	*2.45	82-15	Marta1111½Bed o' Roses1263½Kiss Me Kate120½	Late rush	14
22Sep51- 6Aqu	fst	1⅛	:482 1:122 1:382 1:52 3↑	ⒻBeldame 67k	13 4 41¼ 31½ 51¾ 32½	Arcaro E	119wb	*1.70	82-14	ThelmaBurger1102Bedo'Roses124½KssMeKt119nk	Closed well	14
29Aug51- 6Sar	fst	1¼	:484 1:131 1:382 2:053	ⒻAlabama 22k	4 2 23 2½ 13 18	Arcaro E	126wb	*.85	80-18	Kiss Me Kate1268Vulcania1162Aunt Jinny122no	Ridden out	5
11Jly51- 6Aqu	fst	1 1/16	:241 :474 1:122 1:46	ⒻGazelle 28k	9 11 85¼ 94¾ 3½ 11½	Mehrtens W	121wb	6.00	84-14	KissMeKate1211½BootAll1121¼SpanishCream1121	Drew clear	12
30Jun51- 5Del	sly	1¼	:474 1:124 1:383 2:043 3↑	ⒻNew Castle H 60k	2 4 64½ 43 46 59	Mehrtens W	113wb	*1.95e	78-20	Busanda1262¼Leading Home109¾How1155	Tired	9
16Jun51- 5Del	fst	1⅛	:463 1:114 1:381 1:502	ⒻDel Oaks 34k	3 4 42½ 4¾ 2½ 14	Mehrtens W	119wb	*.70	93-11	Kiss Me Kate1194Signal1131Jacodema1164	Ridden out	8
2Jun51- 6Bel	fst	1⅜	:48 1:131 1:39 2:164	ⒻC C A Oaks 64k	5 13 43½ 2hd 33½ 24	Mehrtens W	121wb	*1.95	83-11	How1214Kiss Me Kate1211Jacodema1211¾	No excuse	15
23May51- 6Bel	sly	1	:224 :46 1:11 1:362	ⒻAcorn (Div 1) 24k	11 6 3nk 11½ 16 112	Mehrtens W	121wb	7.70	92-14	Kiss Me Kate12112Wisteria121¾Jacodema1211¼	Easily	12
2Apr51- 3Lrl	my	6f	:232 :482 1:13	Md Sp Wt	8 8 64 3nk 14 112	Culmone J	117wb	*1.80	82-25	Kiss Me Kate11712Baker's Wood1222No Disgrace1171	Easily	11
2Mar51- 3Hia	fst	6f	:223 :463 1:124	Md Sp Wt	3 2 85¼ 88¾ 37 33½	Boulmetis S	116 w	7.30	80-17	SylvanRock1212BleuFeatur1161½KssMKt1164	Closed steadily	11
13Feb51- 8Hia	fst	1⅛	:472 1:12 1:374 1:512	Alw 3500	9 4 76 810 89¼ 45	Boulmetis S	109 w	15.80	76-18	OldRowley115nkChallarian118¾TimelyReward1154	Closed gap	9
30Jan51- 3Hia	fst	6f	:223 :462 1:123	Md Sp Wt	8 7 98¾ 1012 69 44½	Mehrtens W	117 w	47.15	80-20	Arctic Flyer122noDictionary1224Graphic122½	Raced wide	12
31Jly50- 4Sar	fst	5½f	:224 :461 :591 1:06	ⒻMd Sp Wt	8 11 135½ 148¾ 1413 1319	Woodhouse H	116 w	19.40	68-12	Rose Fern1165½Chelsie1161Fleecy Cloud1161½	No factor	14
22Apr50- 3HdG	fst	4½f	:222 :462 :524	Alw 3500	3 6 710 67½ 68¼	Snellings A	111 w	28.80	87-14	Brazen Brat1152½Iswas118½Top Spring1221½	Outrun	7
15Apr50- 3HdG	fst	4½f	:231 :47 :533	Alw 3500	11 11 910 116½ 97¾	Snellings A	111 w	12.20	83-16	Top Spring1181½Stag118nkB Battery1181½	No factor	12

Leallah

br. f. 1954, by Nasrullah (Nearco)–Lea Lark, by Bull Lea — **Lifetime record: 20 10 2 2 $152,784**

Own.– C. Clay
Br.– Charlton Clay (Ky)
Tr.– M. Miller

Date	Cond	Dist	Fractions	Race	Running line	Jockey	Wt	Odds	Speed-Var	Top finishers	Comment	Starters
10Jun58- 6Bel	sly	6f	:222 :461 1:113 3↑	ⒻHandicap 7500	2 2 2hd 2hd 31 35	Arcaro E	119 w	4.40	85-17	Mlle. Dianne1195Miss Blue Jay122hdLeallah11910		4
	Speed for half,weakened											
30May58- 7GS	fst	6f	:22 :444 1:103 3↑	ⒻColonial H 29k	2 7 83¾ 88¾ 69 95¾	Grant H	116 w	4.90	85-16	Venomous123½Fall Wind1091½Romanita116½	Always far back	12
23May58- 6Bel	fst	6f	:223 :454 1:104 4↑	ⒻAlw 5500	2 3 1½ 1½ 1hd 21½	Arcaro E	114 w	2.95	92-12	MissBlueJay1151½Leallah1141½FloralGirl1114	Used in pace	7
2Nov57- 7CD	fst	1	:224 :452 1:101 1:361 3↑	ⒻFalls City H 22k	3 1 1hd 1hd 13 14¼	Erb D	114 w	*.70e	94-10	Leallah1144¼Beautillion118¾LdyLru1112	Increasing margin	8
26Oct57- 7CD	fst	6½f	:223 :453 1:104 1:172 3↑	ⒻAlw 4500	3 7 2hd 2hd 12 13½	Heckmann J	115 w	*.60e	94-11	Leallah1153½Lebkuchen1153I Say No1151½	Increased margin	8
9Oct57- 3Kee	fst	6f	:214 :442 1:09	Alw 3750	1 1 11 13 14 12½	Erb D	117 w	*.30e	101-06	Leallah1172½Resolved120noOn-the-Ready1204	Much the best	7
1Oct57- 7Bel	fst	6f	:231 :471 1:11	ⒻAlw 6000	2 1 11 1hd 1hd 2hd	Shoemaker W	117 w	4.75	94-22	Alanesian117hdLeallah1171½Wan1116	Headed in game effort	7
2Sep57- 7Bel	fst	6f-WC	:223 :45 1:092 2↑	Fall Highweight H 29k	2 8 62¾ 75¾ 85½	Lester W	113 w	23.70	86-08	Itobe1241½Commendation116½GayWarrior117nk	Swerved early	11
21Aug57- 4Sar	fst	6f	:224 :462 1:132	ⒻAlw 4500	1 2 23 25 45 513	Ussery R	118wb	2.30	68-22	Htsu1151MgcForst1211Mrs.Hlln1188	Early factor,tired badly	5
20Jly57- 6Mth	fst	6f	:212 :44 1:101	ⒻMiss Woodford 25k	3 7 2hd 23 25 63½	Shuk N	118wb	6.60	90-15	Mrs.Hellen1121½Light'nLovely112noNilLly112no	Used early	15
15Jly57- 6Bel	fst	6f	:223 :46 1:102 3↑	ⒻAlw 5500	2 1 2½ 2½ 33½ 48½	Anderson P	115wb	3.85	88-13	FancifulMiss1143½Alanesian1153Recherche1182	Forced wide	7
2Jly57- 6Bel	fst	6f	:223 :461 1:111	ⒻAlw 5500	2 2 2½ 2hd 31 32¾	Arcaro E	122 w	1.25	90-12	Miss Blue Jay118¾Alanesian1222Leallah122	No excuse	3
13Oct56- 6Kee	fst	*7f	1:27	ⒻAlcibiades 41k	5 1 11½ 14 13 12½	Boulmetis S	119 w	*.40	98-11	Leallah1192½Bluebility119noNantu1194½	Under mild urging	6
28Sep56- 4Bel	sly	6f-WC	:222 :45 1:093	ⒻAlw 6000	4 1 1hd 11 1½	Arcaro E	124 w	*1.20	91-10	Leallah124½Defilade114hdEvening Time1142½	Ridden out	6
13Aug56- 7Was	hy	6f	:23 :472 1:132	ⒻPrincess Pat 97k	2 4 23 11 2hd 46	Arcaro E	119 w	*.30	72-26	Splendored113hdRomant1163½Blublty1112½	Disliked going	8
18Jly56- 7Jam	fst	5½f	:223 :46 :581 1:043	ⒻAstoria 22k	4 2 12 12 12 1¾	Arcaro E	119 w	*.35	95-15	Leallah119¾Marullah1154MissBlueJay1191	Had to be urged	6
7Jly56- 8AP	fst	6f	:22 :443 1:113	ⒻArl Lassie 95k	2 2 2hd 11 15 14	Hartack W	119 w	*.20	86-10	Leallah1194Splendored1192½Frnk'sFlowr119½	Much the best	7
30Jun56- 6Mth	fst	5½f	:211 :443 1:04	ⒻColleen 25k	9 3 22 2hd 14 14½	Boulmetis S	114 w	*1.90	100-07	Leallah1144½Marullah1142Alpenrose1121½	Speed in reserve	12
19Jun56- 6Bel	fst	5f-WC	:22 :444 :572	Alw 4000	2 1 11½ 14 11¾	Arcaro E	113 w	*.35	92-10	Leallah1131¾Prtshr1161¾Asgrd116nk	Eased through stretch	6
11Jun56- 5Bel	fst	5f-WC	:22 :45 :573	ⒻMd Sp Wt	10 2 1½ 13 11¾	Arcaro E	115 w	*.65e	91-12	Leallah1151¾Gossamer1158Lodestone115¾	Speed in reserve	14

Misty Morn

b. f. 1952, by Princequillo (Prince Rose)–Grey Flight, by Mahmoud — **Lifetime record: 42 11 6 7 $212,575**

Own.– Wheatley Stable
Br.– Wheatley Stable (Ky)
Tr.– J. Fitzsimmons

Date/Race	Cond	Dist	Fractions	Race	PP	St	1st	2nd	Str	Fin	Jockey	Wt	Odds	Sp-Var	Top Finishers	Comment	Field
5Jun56- 7Bel	fst	1	:23 :462 1:112 1:373 4↑	Alw 6000	7	3	52¼	55½	69½	67	Atkinson T	117wb	*.85	79-12	Prince Morvi114noJean's Joe1131¾Chief Fanelli1132	Wide,gave way suddenly	8
26May56- 7Bel	fst	1 1/16	:223 :451 1:102 1:423 3↑	ⒻTop Flight H 28k	3	5	89	75¾	54¼	42¼	Atkinson T	124wb	4.40e	94-11	Searching121½Parlo1241½RcoRto107nk	Best stride too late	10
22May56- 7Bel	fst	1 1/16	:241 :472 1:114 1:423 3↑	Handicap 7500	6	3	56	56½	58½	47¾	Arcaro E	123wb	*2.55	88-12	Midafternoon126½Woodbrook110nkMaharajah1177	Outrun	7
14May56- 6Bel	fst	1	:23 :454 1:103 1:364 4↑	Alw 6000	2	4	34½	32	3nk	42	Arcaro E	117wb	3.00	88-14	FirstAid109½WarPiper113½LittleDell1131	Made bid,tired	7
2Mar56- 7Hia	fst	1⅛	:453 1:10 1:36 1:492 3↑	ⒻBlack Helen H 40k	2	8	1118	1113	109¾	97½	Cole S	126wb	*1.55e	81-09	ClearDawn108noMissArlette112¾HighVoltage125hd	Dull try	12
12Nov55- 6Jam	gd	1⅝	:483 1:383 2:04 2:422 3↑	Gallant Fox H 85k	3	6	814	4½	1½	13	Cole S	113wb	10.65	102-13	Misty Morn1133Cavort1118Thinking Cap1163½	Drew clear	9
5Nov55- 6Jam	sly	1 3/16	:471 1:112 1:372 1:56	Roamer H 58k	7	11	1111	86¼	79	68¾	Nichols J	116wb	10.70	87-17	Sailor1123½Cvort1112Nnc'sLd122nk	No apparent mishap	12
26Oct55- 6Suf	fst	1⅛	:473 1:112 1:371 1:502	Yankee H 58k	11	8	76	76¼	56	54	Atkinson T	115wb	3.00	85-18	Rockcastle1131½Nance's Lad1201Speed Rouser1161½	Blocked	11
22Oct55- 7GS	fst	1⅛	:453 1:10 1:353 1:481 3↑	ⒻVineland H 51k	18	13	169¼	1514	1211	1110	Atkinson T	124wb	2.80e	86-10	High Voltage1173Manotick1181Crisset110no	Never a factor	18
12Oct55- 6Bel	fst	1½	:482 1:132 2:051 2:312 3↑	ⒻLadies H 62k	8	9	76	32	42½	2hd	Atkinson T	124wb	*2.25	81-17	Manotick117hdMisty Morn1241¼Countess Fleet1172	Gaining	15
30Sep55- 7Bel	fst	1⅛	:472 1:12 1:371 1:493	Handicap 10000	6	7	74¾	51¼	3½	3¾	Atkinson T	122wb	*.95	90-12	Cavort113¾ThinkingCap122hdMstyMorn1221	Evenly late part	7
23Sep55- 6Bel	fst	1	:231 :46 1:104 1:364	ⒻHandicap 10000	1	7	64¼	64½	2½	1¾	Atkinson T	124wb	*.60e	90-17	MstyMrn124¾RareTreat1122¼SweetMusic106hd	Won cleverly	7
24Aug55- 6Sar	gd	1¼	:484 1:142 1:394 2:054	ⒻAlabama 29k	2	3	42	33	34½	33¼	Atkinson T	121wb	*.40e	76-22	Rico Reto1133Blue Banner114nkMisty Morn1211¼	No excuse	8
17Aug55- 6Sar	sly	1⅛	:474 1:122 1:38 1:511 3↑	ⒻDiana H 23k	5	4	43½	31½	1½	11½	Atkinson T	115wb	*1.05	94-15	MistyMorn1151½CarrytheNews110½OilPainting11820	Driving	6
6Aug55- 6Mth	fst	1⅛	:47 1:112 1:371 1:503	ⒻMth Oaks 61k	8	2	25	1hd	1hd	1nk	Arcaro E	121wb	*1.10	93-18	MistyMrn121nkBlueSparkler1217Manotick121¾	Held gamely	11
23Jly55- 6Jam	fst	1 1/16	:242 :474 1:123 1:44	Saranac H 29k	3	7	712	57½	38	23½	Woodhouse H	112wb	4.60	88-15	Saratoga1263½MistyMorn112nkNanc'sLd1232	Closed gap late	8
9Jly55- 6Mth	fst	1 1/16	:231 :47 1:114 1:452 3↑	ⒻMolly Pitcher H 30k	9	8	84¼	3nk	1½	1¾	Boulmetis S	112wb	*1.50	88-13	Misty Morn112¾Clear Dawn120noManotick111¾	Held gamely	12
22Jun55- 7Nar	fst	1⅛	:482 1:132 1:39 1:52	Providence 37k	3	3	36	14	1hd	11½	Atkinson T	106wb	2.80	86-19	MistyMorn1061½[D]Saratog1231¾Mr.AlL.1115	Drew out in dr.	4
17Jun55- 6Aqu	fst	7f	:232 :464 1:112 1:242	ⒻAlw 5000	5	6	62¼	3½	21	21	Atkinson T	118wb	*.65	87-14	TwoStrs1181MstyMorn1186Sorcrss1112½	Slow to reach stride	6
1Jun55- 6Bel	fst	7f	:23 :462 1:111 1:241 3↑	ⒻGolden Annivrsy H 20k	8	6	63¾	77	66¼	61	Atkinson T	113wb	*2.25	88-14	Dispute114¾Parlo125hdOilPantng107no	Wide in stretch bid	11
27May55- 6Bel	fst	1 1/16	:232 :46 1:102 1:42 3↑	ⒻHandicap 6000	3	3	34	31½	12½	15	Atkinson T	110wb	1.45	101-13	MistyMorn1105Talora119hdCarrytheNws1144	Drew out easily	5
20May55- 6Bel	fst	1⅛	:473 1:124 1:38 1:504	ⒻAlw 6000	8	6	83¾	6½	1½	1½	Lester W	113wb	3.35e	85-15	MistyMorn113½InReserve1175Lalun1212	Well rated,driving	8
12May55- 7Bel	fst	1 1/16	:234 :473 1:123 1:44	ⒻAlw 4000	6	2	31	2½	11	11¾	Atkinson T	114wb	4.70	91-13	Misty Morn1141¾Elenem117nkManotick1201	Fully extended	7
7May55- 4Bel	fst	1	:232 :461 1:113 1:381	Alw 4000	1	5	58	57	57	55¼	Higley J	113wb	11.20	78-14	Jabneh1192½War and Peace1161Thunder Hole1161½	Outrun	6
5Mar55- 3GP	fst	6f	:221 :464 1:123	ⒻAlw 3500	10	3	52¼	87¾	87¾	87	Atkinson T	115wb	3.00	75-14	Derry1133Miss Energy1121Rare Treat1111½	Quit early	11
28Feb55- 6Hia	fst	6f	:223 :454 1:111	ⒻAlw 4500	8	6	34	44	33½	22	Atkinson T	110wb	9.10	89-15	NimbleDoll1162MistyMorn110noWagonDrill1051	Late rally	8
22Feb55- 5Hia	fst	6f	:224 :462 1:104	ⒻAlw 4500	1	7	83¼	912	911	710	Higley J	118wb	36.05	83-15	MissEnergy110½Vestment118hdSometimeThing1182	Far back	9
28Oct54- 6Jam	fst	6f	:233 :47 1:123	ⒻAlw 4500	3	11	1113	1115	69½	58	Cole S	116wb	11.30	76-21	Fantan110hdHurry By1101Lalun1166	Off sluggishly	11
19Oct54- 4Bel	fst	7f	:23 :472 1:124 1:26	ⒻAlw 4000	1	10	86¼	43	42	1hd	Guerin E	116wb	4.70e	80-19	Misty Morn116hdFantan1112Sweet Music1162½	Strong finish	13
12Oct54- 3Bel	fst	6f-WC	:223 :454 1:102	ⒻAlw 4000	8	4		2½	31½	32¼	Atkinson T	119wb	3.70	87-11	Myrtle'sJet1192SweetMusic119nkMistyMorn1192	Even race	11
27Sep54- 4Bel	fst	6f-WC	:221 :453 1:11	ⒻAlw 4000	1	13		168	98	98½	Cole S	119 w	11.00e	77-14	Lalun114½Minnie Moocher119nkSofarsogood1195	Outrun	18
20Sep54- 5Aqu	sly	6f	:222 :462 1:122	ⒻAlw 4000	2	4	44	45½	54	32¼	Atkinson T	115 w	6.35	88-10	Girl Crazy1081¾Minnie Moocher115½MistyMorn115¾	Impeded	11
3Sep54- 5Aqu	fst	6f	:23 :463 1:131	ⒻAlw 4000	3	7	87¾	76¾	44½	34	Atkinson T	116 w	3.10	82-19	Blue Banner1161½Sabourin1162½Misty Morn116nk	Mild rally	9
25Aug54- 4Sar	fst	6f	:223 :463 1:134	ⒻAlw 3500	3	5	55	67	89¼	79¼	Cole S	116 w	3.65e	70-18	CarelssMiss1163PromptImpulse1121PrincssKss116hd	Outrun	12
15Jly54- 4Jam	fst	5½f	:23 :47 1:00 1:063	ⒻSp Wt 4000	4	3	66½	66	33	22	Higley J	116 w	4.90	83-19	Chapel1162Misty Morn1163Precious Lady116hd	Good try	10
9Jly54- 4Aqu	fst	5½f	:232 :47 1:001 1:071	ⒻMd Sp Wt	8	5	42	2hd	14	13½	Higley J	116 w	*.55e	88-19	MistyMorn1163½Maebliss1165Searching1162½	Mild hand ride	12
1Jly54- 4Aqu	fst	5½f	:231 :463 :594 1:064	ⒻMd Sp Wt	1	1	1½	21	23½	21¼	Higley J	116 w	*.50e	89-19	Precious Lady1161¼Misty Morn1163½Searching1161½	Gaining	8
15Jun54- 4Aqu	fst	5½f	:232 :47 1:00 1:07	ⒻMd Sp Wt	2	4	31½	44	42½	33½	Atkinson T	116 w	1.65e	85-17	BlessPat1162FirstFlower1161½MistyMorn116nk	Mild rally	8
10Jun54- 4Bel	fst	4½f-W	:222 :451 :512	ⒻMd Sp Wt	5	11		113¼	84¼	73¾	Atkinson T	116 w	4.45e	88-10	Trying116½Bright Flash1162½[DH]Blue Banner116	No mishap	15
5Jun54- 3Bel	fst	5f-WC	:232 :464 :593	ⒻMd Sp Wt	4	9		95½	812	912	Cole S	116 w	4.65e	69-19	Long Stretch116¾Audrey Lee116½Two Stars116hd	Outrun	12
20Apr54- 3Jam	fst	5f	:23 :473 1:003	ⒻMd Sp Wt	5	6	75½	55½	610	610	Atkinson T	116 w	3.10	77-20	Sorceress1161½FletsDlt1162½Msty1161½	Outrun all the way	8
15Apr54- 4Jam	fst	5f	:233 :473 1:00	ⒻMd Sp Wt	5	4	64¼	78½	47	39½	Atkinson T	116 w	4.30	80-18	Whitewash1163½Bless Pat1166Misty Morn1161	Close quarters,taken up	8

My Dear Girl

ch. f. 1957, by Rough'n Tumble (Free for All)–Iltis, by War Relic — **Lifetime record: 20 8 4 1 $209,739**

Own.– Mrs F.A. Genter
Br.– Ocala Stud Farms Inc (Fla)
Tr.– M. Calvert

Date/Race	Cond	Dist	Fractions	Race	PP	St	1st	2nd	Str	Fin	Jockey	Wt	Odds	Sp-Var	Top Finishers	Comment	Field
27Apr61- 7Lrl	fst	6f	:23 :47 1:121 4↑	ⒻAlw 4000	5	2	32½	11	14	14	Hinojosa H	115	*.70	94-11	My Dear Girl1154Funny Bone1072½Effie J.112¾	Mild urging	7
12Jan61- 7SA	fst	7f	:222 :451 1:093 1:221 4↑	ⒻS Monica H (Div 2) 17k	5	7	41½	32	33	79¾	Arcaro E	118	*1.60	82-15	SwissRoll1174½WiggleII122¾Tritom112nk	Early speed,tired	9
31Dec60- 6SA	fst	6f	:214 :45 1:101 3↑	ⒻLas Flores H 24k	1	14	117¼	106¼	119	2½	Arcaro E	119	6.50	92-13	Linita116½My Dear Girl119nkSwiss Roll1182¼	Closed fast	15
3Dec60- 8Pim	fst	1⅛	:48 1:123 1:384 1:524 3↑	ⒻGallorette 17k	4	1	14	14	14	3nk	Hinojosa H	117	4.80	87-25	SisterAntoine111hdLoyalLadyII114hdMyDearGirl117hd	Sharp	10
25Nov60- 8Pim	fst	6f	:232 :47 1:123 3↑	ⒻAlw 4000	6	8	54	41½	1½	1¾	Chambers A	115	*.80	87-21	My Dear Girl115¾Punta Gorda1181¼Funny Bone107no	Slow start,driving	8
11Nov60- 7GS	my	1⅛	:464 1:11 1:372 1:504 3↑	ⒻVineland H 58k	5	1	11½	1½	21	45¼	Sellers J	113	10.20	78-19	RoyalNative124½MakeSail118¾WiggleII1194	Used up early	9
24Oct60- 7Aqu	fst	6f	:223 :454 1:103 3↑	ⒻInterborough H 29k	13	2	31½	21	21	22	Shoemaker W	114	9.15	90-17	WiggleII1212MyDearGirl114¾Improve114nk	Made game effort	14
8Oct60- 7GS	fst	1 1/16	:231 :463 1:11 1:433	ⒻJersey Belle 29k	9	5	32	23	26	913	Gonzalez MN	115	6.40	79-15	Undulation1127Sister Antoine1152½Vanairess115½	Tired	13
22Sep60- 8Aqu	fst	6f	:223 :451 1:10 3↑	ⒻAlw 5000	4	2	2½	12	14	11¾	Shoemaker W	108	*1.55	97-11	MyDearGirl1081¾MissCloudy1166AliWing1091½	Scored easily	7
7Sep60- 7Aqu	fst	1	:222 :443 1:084 1:352	ⒻGazelle H (Div 2) 22k	7	4	42½	33½	69	1112	Gonzalez MN	118	3.70	79-11	Sarcastic115½Twinkle Twinkle119½Undulation1122	Stopped	12
30Aug60- 6Aqu	fst	7f	:223 :451 1:094 1:224	ⒻAlw 5000	8	1	11½	12	11	2½	Gonzalez MN	114	3.00	95-10	TwinkleTwinkle114½MyDearGirl1141½SistrAnton1143½	Gamely	8
21May60- 7Aqu	fst	1	:224 :451 1:093 1:354	ⒻAcorn 59k	2	2	31	32½	33½	712	Arcaro E	121	3.85	85-06	Irish Jay121nkAirmans Guide1219Sister Antoine121½	Tired	13
10May60- 7Aqu	fst	6f	:222 :451 1:093	Alw 7500	5	4	2½	21	57	511	Woodhouse H	114	8.20	93-07	Brush Fire1192½Irish Lancer119nkNew Commander1161	Tired	8
7Nov59- 7Aqu	sly	1	:232 :473 1:132 1:401	ⒻFrizette 101k	8	4	31½	2hd	2hd	1no	Gonzalez MN	119	*.55	--	MyDearGirl119noIrishJay1197Sarcstc1192½	Long,hard drive	11
24Oct59- 7GS	sly	1 1/16	:232 :472 1:122 1:463	ⒻGardenia 134k	5	1	12	13	12	15	Gonzalez MN	119	4.00	77-23	MyDearGirl1195BlueCrooner119nkHevnlyBody119¾	Mild drive	10
9Oct59- 6Aqu	sly	7f	:222 :45 1:102 1:24	ⒻAlw 5000	1	2	21½	21	1hd	15	Gonzalez MN	119	1.70	--	MyDearGirl1195EveningGlow1193OurSpecialJet116½	Easily	5
22Jly59- 8AP	fst	6f	:222 :45 1:10	ⒻArl Lassie 101k	5	3	1hd	22	3nk	2nk	Gonzalez MN	119	2.10	94-10	Monarchy119nkMy Dear Girl119nkHeavenly Body1191½	Sharp	12
3Jun59- 4Was	fst	5½f	:222 :45 :57 1:031	ⒻAlw 10000	3	4	21	3½	13	15	Gonzalez MN	120	3.40	102-05	My Dear Girl1205Madam Regel114¾Blue Crooner114½	In hand	9
				Previously trained by G. Seabo													
25Feb59- 7Hia	fst	3f	:223 :341	[S]Fla Breeders 27k	19	1			31	12	Gonzalez MN	117	16.90	--	My Dear Girl1172Niequest120hdAlgenib120½	Going away	25
19Feb59- 4Hia	fst	3f	:22 :333	Alw 4500	12	10			106¼	104¾	Gonzalez MN	112	15.75f	--	Niequest110hdRosofSrro117noCrftyKng120no	Unruly at post	13

Nadir

b. c. 1955, by Nasrullah (Nearco)–Gallita, by Challenger II

Lifetime record: 32 11 7 8 $434,316

Own.– Claiborne Farm
Br.– Claiborne Farm (Ky)
Tr.– M. Jolley

30May59- 6Bel	fst 1	:224 :452 1:101 1:351 3↑	Metropolitan H 115k	11 10 119 1111 - -	Arcaro E	121 b	*2.35	- -	Sword Dancer114¾Jimmer112¼Talent Show115no		11
	Went lame leaving backstretch										
20May59- 7Bel	fst 7f	:222 :45 1:092 1:223 3↑	Carter H 58k	2 9 95½ 65½ 58 33¾	Arcaro E	122 b	*1.75	90-15	Jimmer108¾Tick Tock1223Nadir1221	Finished full of run	9
23Apr59- 5Kee	fst 6f	:224 :451 1:092 4↑	Alw 3250	5 6 35 33 2½ 1¾	Brooks S	122 b	*.70	98-08	Nadir122¾LitteReaper1162½Mr.Fantastic1192	Driving hard	6
18Apr59- 6Kee	sly *7f	1:263 3↑	Ben Ali H 13k	4 8 68 66¼ 46 26	Brooks S	125 b	*.70	89-16	GreekChief1136Nadir125hdGleemn1122½	Rallied for placing	8
21Feb59- 7Hia	fst 1¼	:471 1:111 1:36 2:011 3↑	Widener H 139k	1 5 54½ 2½ 2½ 21¼	Hartack W	120 b	2.95	98-13	Bardstown1241¼Nadr1207DHoopBnd117¾	In close early,hung	13
7Feb59- 7Hia	gd 1⅛	:461 1:103 1:36 1:49 3↑	McLennan H 64k	4 2 1hd 13 21½ 34	Hartack W	118 b	2.95	86-15	Sharpburg1164ADragonKiller114noNadir1183½	Used in pace	8
24Jan59- 7Hia	gd 1⅛	:462 1:103 1:353 1:483 3↑	Royal Palm H 33k	8 4 42½ 2½ 21 32¼	Hartack W	120 b	*.75	90-14	Petare120¾Sharpsburg1161½Nadir1203	Made bid,then tired	12
10Jan59- 8TrP	fst 1⅛	:454 1:103 1:361 1:49 3↑	Trop Park H 67k	4 10 64 3½ 2½ 31¾	Hartack W	122 b	2.55	94-13	Bardstown1261½RccTv113nkNdr1222¼	Sharp speed to stretch	14
27Sep58- 7Bel	sly 1¼	:464 1:104 1:353 2:01 3↑	Woodward 111k	4 3 31½ 2hd 2½ 2½	Boland W	120wb	5.20	94-13	Clem126½Nadir1202Reneged1269	Made a sharp effort	7
17Sep58- 6Bel	fst 1⅛	:454 1:094 1:353 1:481 3↑	Nassau County H 29k	3 3 52½ 43 21½ 2hd	Ycaza M	113wb	4.05	95-17	EddieSchmidt108hdNadir1132½Rengd1192¾	Led between calls	10
1Sep58- 8AP	fst 1	:223 :451 1:091 1:34 3↑	Was Park H 139k	7 5 21½ 21½ 21 33¼	Ycaza M	114wb	4.00	99-02	Clem1103¼RoundTable131noNdr1146	Sharp factor to stretch	9
16Aug58- 8AP	hy 1⅛	:482 1:123 1:382 1:513	American Derby 160k	1 1 11 13 14 13¼	Ycaza M	120wb	*2.00	84-22	Nadir1203¼VictoryMorn1231¼TalentShow1201½	Much the best	11
6Aug58- 8AP	fst 1	:23 :454 1:094 1:343	Alw 10000	7 2 21½ 22 2hd 1½	Ycaza M	120wb	*2.30	99-07	Nadr120½StrongBay1232½Alhambra117½	Under strong urging	11
26Jly58- 8AP	fst 1	:224 :452 1:10 1:362	Arl Classic 146k	3 9 95¼ 76¼ 5¾ 31	Nichols J	120wb	3.40	89-14	ADragonKiller117¾TalntShow117nkNdr120no	Raced wide late	12
19Jly58- 7AP	fst 7f	:23 :454 1:10 1:223	Alw 5000	3 6 64¼ 63¼ 1hd 12½	Meaux C	113wb	3.50	95-13	Nadr1132½Olymr116½PrzHost113nk	Wide stretch turn,easily	7
4Jly58- 8Was	gd 1⅛	:472 1:121 1:372 1:503	Stars & Stripes H 85k	2 8 810 811 614 716	Hartack W	122wb	2.90	72-16	Terra Firma118noLincoln Road1249Judge114½	Very dull try	9
27Jun58- 7Was	gd 7f	:224 :46 1:11 1:242	Alw 4500	4 4 77¾ 710 56 32¾	Heckmann J	122wb	*.80	80-22	Prize Host1221¾Olymar1221Nadir1221¼	Closed full of run	7
14Jun58- 6Mth	sl 6f	:223 :471 1:124	Select H 24k	6 13 97½ 53½ 1hd 1no	Nichols J	126wb	4.60	78-31	Nadir126noStrongRuler1206Hubcap122no	Best in long drive	13
29Apr58- 7CD	sl 1	:23 :463 1:13 1:393	Derby Trial 16k	2 5 65¾ 22 32 43½	Heckmann J	122 w	3.40	73-29	Tim Tam122nkEbony Pearl1161¼Flamingo1122	Well placed	8
18Apr58- 6Kee	fst 7f	:232 :452 1:093 1:221	Alw 4500	4 4 32½ 32 1hd 2½	Heckmann J	119 w	3.80	100-10	TimTam122½Nadir119nkHillsdl113hd	Reached lead,sharp try	8
11Apr58- 0Kee	sly 6f	:224 :453 1:103	©Alw 4500	3 4 47½ 35 34½ 34½	Heckmann J	119 w	-	87-18	Benedicto1162RomanBow1162½Nadir11912	Urged,no rally	4
	Special race run before the first race										
1Mar58- 7Hia	fst 1⅛	:464 1:11 1:361 1:484	Flamingo 135k	9 3 31 2½ 44 47¼	Brooks S	122wb	3.25	84-11	DJewl'sReward122hdTimTam1223¾TalntShow1223½	Faltered	9
22Feb58- 6Hia	fst 1 1/16	:223 :453 1:10 1:424	Alw 7500	8 9 65 53¾ 23 23	Hartack W	126 w	*.80	97-12	SirRobby1093Ndr1262¾NshtAmool117hd	Couldn't reach winner	11
14Feb58- 7Hia	fst 7f	:223 :454 1:104 1:234	Alw 5000	5 8 65½ 43 1hd 12½	Hartack W	124 w	*.50	91-18	Nadir1242½FourFivs114¾Ambtwxt1071½	Drew clear with ease	8
26Oct57- 7GS	fst 1 1/16	:23 :462 1:11 1:441	Garden State 277k	5 3 2hd 13 11 12	Hartack W	122wb	3.90	89-16	Nadir1222TerraFirma122noRosTrlls1221	Well rated,driving	13
19Oct57- 6GS	my 1 1/16	:224 :461 1:111 1:44	Alw 10000	7 5 55 34 31 11¼	Brooks S	117wb	3.40	90-16	DHMusicMnFox120DHNdir1171½Yemen1122	Up for dead-heat	10
12Oct57- 7Bel	fst 1	:231 :461 1:112 1:373	Champagne 156k	12 7 55 66 64½ 56¼	Ussery R	122wb	5.00	80-14	Jewel'sReward122nkMistyFlight1221½RoseTrlls122½	Swerved	12
28Sep57- 5Bel	fst 6½-WC	:222 :444 1:093 1:161	Futurity 114k	5 5 73½ 63¾ 53	Hartack W	122wb	2.25	88-09	Jester1221MstyFlght1221¼Alhmbr122nk	Swerved,lost chance	9
	Geldings not eligible										
16Sep57- 7Bel	fst 6½-WC	:22 :453 1:111 1:173	Cowdin 37k	12 11 87 64¾ 32 2hd	Arcaro E	117wb	*2.45e	92-13	Jewel'sReward124hdNadr1171¼Jstr117½	Headed in sharp try	13
6Sep57- 6Bel	fst 6f	:222 :461 1:12	Alw 6000	3 8 77 65½ 42½ 1hd	Arcaro E	119wb	*1.25	89-12	Nadir119hdFletFt1193UnclRlph115¾	Sluggish start,just up	8
13Aug57- 5Sar	fst 5½f	:231 :464 :594 1:062	Alw 4000	2 3 42 31½ 2½ 1nk	Anderson P	118wb	*.65	85-21	Nadir118nkGrandMogul1121Etok1101½	Under very hard drive	8
5Aug57- 4Sar	gd 5½f	:232 :47 1:01 1:073	©Md Sp Wt	1 2 21½ 22 11½ 16	Anderson P	118wb	2.80	79-22	Nadir1186Surinam118nkLeader118nk	Going away with ease	12

Nashua

b. c. 1952, by Nasrullah (Nearco)–Segula, by Johnstown

Lifetime record: 30 22 4 1 $1,288,565

Own.–Leslie Combs II
Br.– Belair Stud Inc (Ky)
Tr.– J. Fitzsimmons

13Oct56- 6Bel	fst 2	:491 2:282 2:541 3:202 3↑	J C Gold Cup 54k	1 1 1½ 2hd 11½ 12¼	Arcaro E	124wb	*.75	102-09	Nashua1242¼Rily1191¾ThrdBrothr1194	Kept to strong drive	7
29Sep56- 7Bel	gd 1¼	:47 1:112 1:371 2:03 3↑	Woodward 80k	1 2 1hd 3nk 31½ 22½	Arcaro E	126wb	*.30	82-12	Mister Gus1262½Nashua126½Jet Action12620	No excuse	4
14Jly56- 6Mth	my 1¼	:46 1:11 1:364 2:024 3↑	Monmouth H 114k	7 1 14 14 14 13½	Arcaro E	129wb	*.30	92-20	Nashua1293½Mr. First1105Mielleux1071	Speed in reserve	8
4Jly56- 7Bel	fst 1¼	:463 1:101 1:35 2:004 3↑	Suburban H 83k	4 2 2hd 2hd 2½ 1¼	Arcaro E	128wb	*1.20	96-10	Nashua1281¼Dedicat1112¼Subhdr1125	Well rated,going away	8
30Jun56- 7Bel	fst 7f	:221 :452 1:102 1:231 3↑	Carter H 58k	3 6 44½ 65 62¾ 73½	Arcaro E	130 w	*1.10	90-12	Red Hannigan1141½Switch On119½Artismo111¾	Well up,hung	10
30May56- 7Bel	fst 1	:224 :451 1:094 1:35 3↑	Metropolitan H 55k	7 1 32½ 42½ 53 4¾	Arcaro E	130 w	*.65	98-09	Midaftrnoon111hdSwtchOn113½Fnd116nk	Came again too late	7
19May56- 7GS	fst 1⅛	:463 1:111 1:362 1:491 3↑	Camden H 33k	4 1 11 1½ 11 12	Arcaro E	129 w	*.40	91-10	Nashua1292Fisherman1201½Mielleux1102	Very handy score	5
5May56- 7Jam	fst 1⅛	:49 1:13 1:38 1:503 3↑	Grey Lag H 55k	6 3 2hd 1hd 1hd 1hd	Atkinson T	128 w	*.95	93-17	Nashua128hdFind118hdFisherman1201¾	Almost fell at start	7
17Mar56- 8GP	fst 1¼	:47 1:113 1:36 2:003 3↑	Gulf Park H 112k	6 5 43½ 53¼ 56 57	Arcaro E	129 w	*.70	89-08	Sailor1191¾Mielleux1101Find116¾	Wide both turns,tired	7
18Feb56- 8Hia	fst 1¼	:463 1:104 1:353 2:02 3↑	Widener H 129k	9 3 41¾ 2½ 2hd 1hd	Arcaro E	127 w	*.40	95-11	Nashua127hdSocilOutcst121hdSlor119nk	Under strong drive	9
	Previously owned by Belair Stud										
15Oct55- 6Bel	sly 2	:494 2:321 2:583 3:244 3↑	J C Gold Cup 79k	3 2 1½ 11 13½ 15	Arcaro E	119 w	*.25	80-14	Nashua1195Thinking Cap11915Mark's Puzzle1198	Easy score	5
24Sep55- 6Bel	sly 1⅛	:451 1:101 1:36 1:491 3↑	Sysonby 106k	5 1 41½ 3nk 22 31¾	Arcaro E	121 w	*.65	91-10	HighGun126hdJetActn1261¾Nshu1213½	Weakened when urged	5
31Aug55- 7Was	gd 1¼	:46 1:102 1:373 2:041	WP Match 100k	1 1 1½ 11½ 12 16½	Arcaro E	126 w	1.20	81-17	Nashua1266½Swaps126	Drew far out to handy score	2
16Jly55- 7AP	fst 1	:231 :453 1:093 1:351	Arl Classic 148k	2 2 22 24 21 1½	Arcaro E	126 w	*.30	96-10	Nashua126½Traffic Judge1201½Impromptu1204	Under a drive	7
2Jly55- 0Aqu	fst 1¼	:493 1:134 1:382 2:034	Dwyer 55k	3 1 1½ 11½ 11½ 15	Arcaro E	126 w	-	88-15	Nashua1265Saratoga12240Mainlander114	Easing up late	3
	Run as special event with no wagering										
11Jun55- 6Bel	fst 1½	:49 1:133 2:042 2:29	Belmont 119k	5 2 1hd 12½ 16 19	Arcaro E	126 w	*.15	93-12	Nashua1269Blazing Count1265½Portersville1266	A romp	8
	Geldings not eligible										
28May55- 7Pim	fst 1 3/16	:471 1:11 1:353 1:543	Preakness 116k	5 4 42½ 2hd 1hd 11	Arcaro E	126 w	*.30	106-08	Nashua1261Saratoga1267TrafficJudg126nk	Rated,mild drive	8
7May55- 7CD	fst 1¼	:472 1:122 1:37 2:014	Ky Derby 152k	5 3 31 2½ 2½ 21½	Arcaro E	126 w	*1.30	96-12	Swaps1261½Nashua1266½Summer Tan1264	Good bid,no excuse	10
23Apr55- 6Jam	fst 1⅛	:471 1:111 1:363 1:503	Wood Memorial 111k	4 2 21½ 22 21½ 1nk	Atkinson T	126 w	1.10	93-17	Nashua126nkSummer Tan12625Simmy1266	Sensational score	5
26Mar55- 7GP	sly 1⅛	:463 1:122 1:391 1:531	Fla Derby 148k	1 5 56½ 22½ 2½ 1nk	Arcaro E	122 w	*.95	78-26	Nashua122nkBlueLem1132½FirstCabin1131	Unruly,hard urged	9
26Feb55- 7Hia	fst 1⅛	:462 1:113 1:371 1:493	Flamingo 141k	2 2 1hd 1hd 1hd 11½	Arcaro E	122 w	*.70	88-12	Nashua1221½Saratoga1224½CupMan1227	Drifted out in drive	12
21Feb55- 0Hia	fst 1 1/16	:231 :47 1:114 1:441	Alw 7500	2 2 3nk 2hd 1½ 11½	Arcaro E	126wb	-	94-11	Nshua1261½Munchausen1172HappyMemries1142½	Unruly late	4
	Special event run between 2nd and 3rd races - No wagering										
9Oct54- 6Bel	fst 6½f-W	:222 :451 1:092 1:153	Futurity 112k	6 4 21 1½ 1hd	Arcaro E	122wb	*.65	94-06	Nshua122hdSummrTan122¾RoylCoinage1227	Held on gamely	7
	Geldings not eligible										
1Oct54- 6Bel	fst 6f-WC	:22 :442 1:081	Sp Wt 10000	4 2 4¾ 2hd 11	Arcaro E	118wb	*1.05	100-00	Nashua1181Royal Coinage1185Pyrenees1181½	Clever score	7
21Sep54- 6Aqu	fst 6½f	:223 :451 1:092 1:16	Cowdin 30k	9 1 2hd 4¾ 41½ 21½	Arcaro E	124wb	*1.25	101-12	SummerTn1201½Nshua124¾Bunny'sBabe1201½	Mildly impeded	10
28Aug54- 6Sar	fst 6½f	:23 :464 1:111 1:174	Hopeful 78k	4 1 1½ 1hd 11 1nk	Arcaro E	122wb	*.55e	96-18	Nashua122nkSummrTan1221½Pyrens1221½	Well rated,held on	8
21Aug54- 4Sar	fst 6f	:23 :463 :592 1:122	Grand Union Hotel 27k	5 2 23 1hd 12 11¾	Arcaro E	122 w	2.75e	86-17	Nashua1221¾Pyrens1152½ModlAc1143½	Won in clever fashion	6
19May54- 7GS	fst 5f	:221 :454 :583	Cherry Hill 20k	3 5 2½ 22 21½ 2nk	Higley J	119 w	3.80	98-13	RoyalNote122nkNashua1195Menolen1191½	Unruly all the way	11
12May54- 6Bel	fst 5f-WC	:221 :453 :58	Juvenile 15k	1 2 1hd 2½ 1½	Arcaro E	117 w	3.00e	89-18	Nshua117½SummerTn1228Lugh1172	Scored under clever ride	8
5May54- 4Bel	fst 4½f-W	:222 :462 :523	©Md Sp Wt	14 9 8¼ 11½ 13	Higley J	118 w	8.50e	86-14	Nashua1183Retract118½Danger Quest118no	Won in hand	21

Native Dancer

gr. c. 1950, by Polynesian (Unbreakable)–Geisha, by Discovery — Lifetime record: 22 21 1 0 $785,240

Own.– A.G. Vanderbilt
Br.– Alfred G. Vanderbilt (Ky)
Tr.– W.C. Winfrey

16Aug54- 0Sar	sly	7f	:233 :472 1:12 1:244	3↑ Handicap 5025	2	3	22½	22	18	19	Guerin E	137	w	-	91-19	Native Dancer1379First Glance1194½Gigantic107	Easily	3
15May54- 6Bel	fst	1	:231 :46 1:101 1:351	3↑ Metropolitan H 39k	3	8	77¾	57	23½	1nk	Guerin E	130	w	*.25	98-11	Native Dancer130nkStraight Face1176Jamie K.1102	Just up	9
7May54- 6Bel	fst	6f	:224 :463 1:114	3↑ Alw 15000	4	3	42	31	12	11¼	Guerin E	126	w	*.15	90-15	Native Dancer1261¼Laffango121nkImpasse114nk	Easily best	7
22Aug53- 7Was	fst	1⅛	:462 1:103 1:352 1:482	American Derby 112k	4	7	711	45½	41¾	12	Arcaro E	128	w	*.20e	99-11	NativeDancr1282Landlocked1201¼PrecousSton1143	Drew out	8
15Aug53- 6Sar	fst	1¼	:494 1:14 1:393 2:053	Travers 27k	1	3	31	21½	11	15½	Guerin E	126	w	*.05	80-20	NativeDancer1265½Dictar1202½GuardianII1141	Easily best	5
Geldings not eligible																		
18Jly53- 7AP	hy	1	:232 :471 1:114 1:38	Arl Classic 154k	4	6	67	34	13	19	Guerin E	126	w	*.70	82-25	NativeDancer1269SirMango120hdVanCrosby1202	Easily best	8
4Jly53- 6Aqu	fst	1¼	:494 1:14 1:392 2:051	Dwyer 56k	3	4	33½	11½	12½	11¾	Guerin E	126	w	*.05	81-17	NativeDancer1261¾[D]Dictar1142GuardnII1144	Much the best	5
13Jun53- 6Bel	fst	1½	:501 1:15 2:041 2:283	Belmont 118k	5	4	32½	2hd	1hd	1nk	Guerin E	126	w	*.45	95-11	NativeDancr126nkJamieK.12610RoylByGm1264½	Held gamely	6
Geldings not eligible																		
23May53- 7Pim	fst	1 3/16	:47 1:114 1:382 1:574	Preakness 113k	4	3	33	2hd	1hd	1nk	Guerin E	126	w	*.20	91-19	NativeDancer126nkJamieK.1266RoyalBayGem1262	Hard drive	7
16May53- 6Bel	fst	1	:234 :471 1:113 1:361	Withers 32k	3	2	2½	1½	12½	14	Guerin E	126	w	*.05	93-12	Native Dancer1264Invigorator1262½Real Brother126	Easily	3
Geldings not eligible																		
2May53- 7CD	fst	1¼	:474 1:121 1:363 2:02	Ky Derby 118k	6	8	42½	42½	21½	2hd	Guerin E	126	w	*.70e	97-09	DarkStar126hdNativeDancer1265Invgortor1262	Roughed,wide	11
25Apr53- 6Jam	fst	1⅛	:50 1:133 1:371 1:503	Wood Memorial 123k	4	2	31	2hd	1½	14½	Guerin E	126	w	*.10e	93-12	NativeDancer1264½TahitianKing126hdInvigortor1263	Easily	7
Geldings not eligible																		
18Apr53- 6Jam	fst	1 1/16	:242 :49 1:134 1:441	Gotham (Div 1) 35k	8	4	62¾	41¼	2hd	12	Guerin E	120	w	*.15	91-10	NatveDancr1202MagicLmp1203Sckl'sSound1201¼	Ridden out	9
22Oct52- 6Jam	fst	1 1/16	:242 :48 1:123 1:441	©East View 56k	1	4	46	33	1½	11½	Guerin E	122	w	*.20	91-15	Native Dancer1221½Laffango1229Teds Jeep1221½	Ridden out	6
Geldings not eligible																		
27Sep52- 6Bel	fst	6½f-W	:214 :442 1:082 1:142	Futurity 107k	8	6		54	2½	12¼	Guerin E	122	w	*.35	100-05	NativeDancer1222¼TahitianKing1224DarkStr1223	Ridden out	10
Geldings not eligible																		
22Sep52- 5Bel	fst	6f-WC	:22 :443 1:093	Sp Wt 5000	6	6		53	12	11¼	Guerin E	118	w	*.40	93-07	NativeDancer1181¼TahitianKing1182¼Reprimnd118hd	In hand	8
30Aug52- 6Sar	fst	6½f	:233 :48 1:123 1:184	Hopeful 62k	4	1	62¾	52½	2hd	12	Guerin E	122	w	*.25	91-19	Native Dancer1222Tiger Skin1222Platan1221	Handily	7
23Aug52- 4Sar	fst	6f	:224 :462 1:111	Grand Union Hotel 20k	1	2	31	1½	11½	13½	Guerin E	126	w	*.55	92-17	NativeDancer1263½Laffango1222½TahitianKing1225½	In hand	5
16Aug52- 4Sar	sly	6f	:231 :464 1:131	Sar Spl 17k	4	2	42½	42	11	13½	Guerin E	122	w	*.70	82-22	NativeDancr1223½DocWalkr1224SouthPont1223½	Ridden out	8
4Aug52- 6Sar	fst	5½f	:231 :47 :593 1:06	Flash 10k	6	4	31	31	1½	12¼	Guerin E	122	w	*.80	87-20	Native Dancer1222¼Tiger Skin1142Bradley122no	Easily	7
23Apr52- 6Jam	fst	5f	:223 :463 :592	©Youthful 14k	4	2	21	2hd	13	16	Guerin E	117	w	*.90	93-19	NativeDancr1176Tribe1221½[DH]Mr.Mdnght1171	Much the best	12
19Apr52- 2Jam	fst	5f	:23 :47 :593	Md Sp Wt	9	7	42	42	1½	14½	Guerin E	118	w	*1.40	92-16	Native Dancer1184½Putney118nkKhan118hd	Drew out easily	9

Needles

b. c. 1953, by Ponder (Pensive)–Noodle Soup, by Jack High — Lifetime record: 21 11 3 3 $600,355

Own.– D.-H. Stable
Br.– W.E. Leach (Fla)
Tr.– H.L. Fontaine

6Apr57- 7GP	fst	1 1/16	:23 :462 1:102 1:42	3↑ Fort Lauderdale H 28k	5	9	920	88½	45½	12	Erb D	126	w	*.65	100-10	Needles1262Tussle Patch110nkGrand Canyon107½	In hand	9
23Mar57- 7GP	fst	1¼	:464 1:111 1:351 2:002	3↑ Gulf Park H 126k	5	7	66½	63¼	33	31½	Erb D	126	w	1.60	95-09	Bardstown130½Fabius1231Needles1264	Very wide,game try	7
11Mar57- 7GP	fst	6½f	:222 :452 1:094 1:16	4↑ Handicap 6000	8	8	88	61½	41¼	2no	Erb D	126	w	4.15	99-13	Admiral Vee119noNeedles1264Nan's Mink110no	Gaining fast	8
18Aug56- 8Was	sf	1 3/16Ⓣ	:472 1:123 1:394 1:591	American Derby 159k	2	8	812	65	64½	52¾	Erb D	126	w	*1.10	74-23	Swoon'sSon122¾TheWarrior1161¾TobyB.116nk	Disliked grass	8
4Aug56- 7Was	fm	6fⓉ	:221 :444 1:094	3↑ Handicap 10000	8	8	812	814	814	86¼	Erb D	120	w	6.30	95-06	BurntChild1131SuthernAccent110nkHutchson1111½	Late foot	8
16Jun56- 6Bel	fst	1½	:472 1:114 2:024 2:294	Belmont 119k	3	8	717	47½	21½	1nk	Erb D	126	w	*.65	89-12	Needles126nkCareer Boy1261½Fabius126hd	All out to hold	8
Geldings not eligible																		
19May56- 7Pim	fst	1 3/16	:472 1:12 1:38 1:582	Preakness 132k	6	9	914	55½	34	21¾	Erb D	126	w	*.60	79-19	Fabius1261¾Needls1261NoRgrts1265½	Rallied from far back	9
5May56- 7CD	fst	1¼	:471 1:113 1:364 2:032	Ky Derby 167k	1	16	1615	74½	2hd	1¾	Erb D	126	w	*1.60	90-08	Needles126¾Fabius1261½ComeonRed126¾	Going away in drive	17
24Mar56- 8GP	fst	1⅛	:462 1:112 1:353 1:483	Florida Derby 145k	13	13	129¾	95¼	42	1¾	Erb D	117	w	*1.70	101-09	Needles117¾CountChic1191¾PintorL113½	Under strong drive	14
25Feb56- 8Hia	fst	1⅛	:453 1:101 1:362 1:492	Flamingo 148k	3	12	117	74½	1hd	12¾	Erb D	117	w	2.60	89-11	Needles1172¾GolfAce1221¾Fabus1222½	Drew out,mild urging	15
6Feb56- 7Hia	fst	7f	:23 :453 1:094 1:224	Alw 10000	3	6	66¾	66¾	44½	25	Erb D	119	w	3.30	91-17	CallMeLucky1125Needles119nkBeuFond1211½	Strong late bid	6
29Oct55- 7GS	fst	1 1/16	:231 :461 1:104 1:423	Garden State 282k	6	11	1111	76¾	31½	31	Choquette J	122	w	*1.70	96-07	PrinceJohn122noCareerBoy1221Needles1224½	Hung slightly	12
15Oct55- 5GS	sly	1	:223 :46 1:111 1:371	Alw 7500	6	8	711	21½	12½	12	Choquette J	122	w	*.70	101-15	Needles1222Nahodah1151Singer1133	Rated early,easy score	8
10Sep55- 7Atl	fst	7f	:213 :441 1:09 1:23	Worlds Playground 30k	7	7	78	43½	42	31	Arcaro E	122	w	*.40	90-11	BusherFantsy110¾Esp112nkNdls1222½	Raced outside,gaining	9
27Aug55- 6Sar	fst	6½f	:23 :47 1:12 1:181	Hopeful 71k	6	4	77¼	54	14	13½	Choquette J	122	w	3.25	94-19	Needles1223½Career Boy1226Jean Baptiste1221	Mild drive	9
8Aug55- 6Mth	gd	6f	:214 :453 1:103	Sapling 37k	2	5	48	43	1hd	12	Choquette J	116	w	6.80	92-22	Needles1162Decathlon1241¼Polly's Jet1245	Drew clear	6
4Jly55- 6Mth	fst	5½f	:213 :451 1:04	©Tyro 21k	7	7	52¾	42½	45	44¼	Choquette J	115	w	*2.30	100-11	Decathln122¾Nan'sMink1152BeauFond1151½	Impeded on turn	8
22Jun55- 7Mth	fst	5f	:214 :46 :583	Alw 4500	1	5	53¾	43½	2½	11	Choquette J	113	w	*1.20	99-07	Needles1131But First1193Nan's Mink1191	Drew out in hand	9
20Apr55- 4GP	fst	4½f	:222 :454 :522	Alw 4000	5	6		31½	2hd	13	Choquette J	111	w	*.75	101-00	Needles1113Tolna Rose113hdRite-Step1193½		10
Steadied early,speed in reserve																		
5Apr55- 5GP	fst	4½f	:224 :454 :524	GP Juvenile 18k	11	10		98½	56	42¾	Choquette J	113	w	2.25	96-01	GetthereJack1221¼Swoon'sSon110½FlyngTddy1101	Poor start	11
29Mar55- 3GP	fst	4½f	:232 :47 :53	[S]Md Sp Wt	2	2		11	13	15	Choquette J	120	w	*1.15	98-02	Needles1205Game o' Hearts1175Elrusa1173	Scored easily	12

Neji

ch. g. 1950, by Hunters Moon IV (Foxhunter)–Accra, by Annapolis — Lifetime record: 49 17 11 9 $270,834

Own.– Mrs Ogden Phipps
Br.– Mrs Marion duPont Scott (GB)
Tr.– D.M. Smithwick

29Sep60- 5Bel	fm	*2½	S'Chase 4:421	4↑ Brook H 19k	2	7	711	44	520	529	Smithwick AP	159	s	*1.65	--	Benguala1436Independence1593½Cartagena1503½	No excuse	7
15Sep60- 5Aqu	fm	*2	S'Chase 3:531	4↑ Broad Hollow H 16k	1	5	67½	69	44	44¾	Smithwick AP	162	sb	*.55	--	Gridiron1362SunDog148¾Benguala1502	Bad landing 7th,sore	6
1Sep60- 5Aqu	fm	*2	S'Chase 3:493	4↑ Harbor Hill H 10k	2	5	58	43½	23	21½	Smithwick AP	164	sb	*1.35e	--	Cartagena1431½Neji1642BasilB13310	Made game late effort	6
21Feb59♦ Leopardstn(Ire)	yl	*3LH	6:28	6↑ Leopardstown Handicap Chase Hcp3000						6	Smithwick AP	168	b	4.50		Zonda1361¼NicAtkins1335Top Twenty136	Rated in midpack,weakened 4 out	12
5Feb59♦ Hurst Park(GB)	gd	3	6:373	5↑ Morden Handicap Chase Hcp1500						31½	Smithwick AP	175	b	4.00		Lochroe1751Arthur Cox140½Neji17515	Toward rear,midrally when blundered 2 out,gaining late	7
29Jan59♦ Gowran Park(Ire)	fm	*3 1/16RH	7:121	5↑ Thyestes Handicap Chase Hcp2000						5	Smithwick AP	168	b	10.00		Slippery Serpent1436Zonda1334Mr. What157	Toward rear,mild late gain	13
22Oct58- 6Bel	fm	*2½	S'Chase 4:453	4↑ Temple Gwathmey H 55k	6	5	77	67	3½	2hd	Smithwick AP	176	wsb	*.95e	--	Bengual147hdNj1764½Trboots135nk	Led between calls,tired	8
9Oct58- 5Bel	hd	*3⅛	S'Chase 6:06	4↑ Grand National H 28k	5	5	57	56½	1hd	12½	Smithwick AP	173	wsb	*1.15e	--	Neji1732½Rythmnhm1474½Drubn130hd	Bad landings,much best	9
30Sep58- 5Bel	sf	*2½	S'Chase 4:474	4↑ Brook H 14k	7	6	77	45½	32½	33¾	Smithwick AP	175	wsb	*1.30e	--	Beguala1433½Independence154nkNeji17510	In close late	7
31Jly58- 5Mth	fm	*2	Hurdles 3:544	3↑ Midsummer H 22k	1	2	35	34	24	35	Smithwick AP	175	wsb	*.50	--	Cloonroughan1565My Last Try140hdNeji1753½	Swerved,tired	7
18Jly58- 3Mth	fm	*1¾	Hurdles 3:151	3↑ Alw 4000	5	5	68	33½	1½	1½	Smithwick AP	162	wsb	*1.10e	--	Neji162½Cloonroughan1565½Ragtime Cowboy130¾	Driving	11
16Oct57- 6Bel	fm	*2½	S'Chase 4:422	4↑ Temple Gwathmey H 57k	7	6	63	31½	13	17	Smithwick AP	173	wsb	*.80e	--	Neji1737Ancestor1601Shpbord1641½	Jumped superbly,easily	12
8Oct57- 5Bel	sf	*3⅛	S'Chase 6:151	4↑ Grand National H 32k	3	4	416	35	1½	16	Smithwick AP	168	wsb	*.80e	--	Neji1686Independence1501¾His Boots132nk	Ridden out	5

Date	Cond	Dist	Type	Time	Race	PP	St	1st	2nd	Str	Fin	Jockey	Wt	Odds	Fig	Top finishers	Comment	Fld
26Sep57- 5Bel	fm	*2½	S'Chase	4:451	4↑ Brook H 22k	7	7	79	31	1½	12¾	Smithwick AP	164wb	1.65e	--	Neji1642¾Independnc15110Rythmnhm148no	Going away easily	10
12Sep57- 5Bel	fm	*2⅛	S'Chase	3:573	3↑ Harbor Hill H 17k	2	3	43	56½	58½	48¼	Murphy J	163wb	*1.65e	--	Ancestor1582Independence1486HsBoots131nk	Bobbled at 7th	9

Previously trained by G.H. Bostwick

Date	Cond	Dist	Type	Time	Race	PP	St	1st	2nd	Str	Fin	Jockey	Wt	Odds	Fig	Top finishers	Comment	Fld
3Aug56- 5Mth	fm	*2	Hurdles	3:533	3↑ Midsummer H 22k	1	2	25	33½	24	22½	Adams FD	164wsb	*1.00	--	FlyingFury1432½Neji1644PolicemanDay1503	Came back lame	5
20Jly56- 3Mth	fm	*1¾	Hurdles	3:21	3↑ Alw 4000	4	4	33	41	21½	21¼	Adams FD	162ws	*.40e	--	Flying Fury1341¼Neji1622Songai1593½	Showed good effort	10
29Jun56- 7Del	fm	*2½	S'Chase	4:462	4↑ Indian River H 10k	8	7	31	56½	24	1no	Adams FD	168wsb	*1.50e	--	Neji168noCarthag136¾Cst1501	Strongly handled,up in time	11
15Jun56- 7Del	fm	*2	S'Chase	3:37	4↑ Georgetown H 10k	4	6	46	45½	38	33½	Adams FD	169wsb	*.40e	--	Ringo'Roses1432Carafar1521½Nj1692½	Rallied under impost	6
7Jun56- 5Bel	fm	*2½	S'Chase	4:394	4↑ Meadow Brook H 17k	1	3	36½	32½	11½	13½	Adams FD	165wb	*1.00	--	Nji1653½Carthage1366KingCommander1648	Drew out in hand	5
26May56- 3Bel	fm	1⅜Ⓣ		2:173	3↑ Handicap 7500	3	6	79½	66	44	2½	Atkinson T	115wb	3.95	98-01	LovelyWave110½Nj115hdKstr125no	Between horses,sharp try	7
21Oct55- 6Bel	sf	*2½	S'Chase	4:553	4↑ Temple Gwathmey H 57k	6	3	21	53½	24	1¾	Adams FD	167wsb	3.40e	--	Neji167¾Rhythmnhm1497HsBoots1371½	Well rated,going away	11
13Oct55- 5Bel	fm	*3	S'Chase	5:542	4↑ Grand National H 28k	6	4	21	42	2½	1hd	Adams FD	163wsb	2.45e	--	Nj163hdRhythmnhm14615HsBoots1351½	Impeded late,recovered	8
4Oct55- 5Bel	fm	*2½	S'Chase	4:462	4↑ Brook H 17k	4	6	56½	43½	22	12	Adams FD	159wsb	*.85e	--	Neji1592Rythminhim1453Hyvania13620	Drew out when urged	7
22Sep55- 5Bel	fm	*2	S'Chase	3:463	3↑ Broad Hollow H 11k	4	3	42½	44	46	22	Adams FD	157wb	4.10	--	Shipboard1582Nj1571½Rhythmnhm145½	Guided wide,sharp try	4
2Jun55- 5Bel	fm	*2½	S'Chase	4:442	4↑ Meadow Brook H 11k	6	3	432	43¼	324	321	Adams FD	156wb	1.60	--	Shpbord1566CurlyJo13115Nj15630	Rated early,no late foot	6
21May55- 6Bel	hd	*2½	S'Chase	4:432	4↑ International 21k	5	4	28	25	112	115	Schulhofer FS	150wb	3.10e	--	Neji15015Ancestor15518Hyvania15518	Increasing long lead	10
12May55- 5Bel	hd	*2	S'Chase	3:411	4↑ Corinthian H 8.9k	5	4	59	513	412	36	Adams FD	155wb	*.90	--	Shipboard1553Beaupre1363Neji1551½	Some early foot	6
2May55- 3Bel	fm	*1¾	Hurdles	3:153	3↑ Alw 4200	4	4	33½	41	21	1hd	Adams FD	155wb	*1.40	--	Neji155hdPermain1326Secnt13625	Tried to bear in,just up	6
22Oct54- 6Bel	fm	*2½	S'Chase	4:39	4↑ Temple Gwathmey H 16k	6	4	54½	59	24	2¾	Adams FD	149wb	2.25	--	King Commander164¾Neji1497Coveted13170	Gaining fast	6
14Oct54- 5Bel	fm	*3	S'Chase	5:42	4↑ Grand National H 28k	1	-	-	-	-	-	Adams FD	149wb	1.95	--	Shipboard1522½Coveted13122CurlyJo13310	Fell at 8th jump	7
5Oct54- 5Bel	fm	*2½	S'Chase	4:394	4↑ Brook H 17k	8	7	712	68	23	11½	Adams FD	137wb	2.55	--	Neji1371½King Commander16116Coveted13115	Going away	9
23Sep54- 5Bel	fm	*2	S'Chase	3:44	3↑ Broad Hollow H 11k	1	1	32	22½	22	22	Adams FD	137wb	2.70	--	Shipboard1542Nej13718Covtd13645	Unable to menace winner	5
6Sep54- 7Atl	fm	1 1/16Ⓣ		:231 :464 1:112 1:43	3↑ Atl City Turf H 30k	13	10	128½	1212	1216	1213	Passmore WJ	114wb	11.90f	86-01	Landlocked115hdCounty Clare116noKaster1171	No speed	13
20Aug54- 5Sar	fm	*2	Hurdles	3:482	3↑ Lovely Night H 6.5k	2	4	39½	34½	32	33½	Adams FD	152wb	*1.10e	--	Carafar139hdCammell Laird1443½Neji1523	Tired when urged	7
6Aug54- 5Sar	fm	*1¾	Hurdles	3:292	3↑ National Mdn 7.4k	2	4	32½	32	11½	12	Adams FD	161wb	*.60	--	Neji1612Heureux II1554Oneida1552	Gradually drew clear	5
16Jly54- 3Mth	fm	*1¾	Hurdles	3:194	3↑ National Maiden 7.4k	6	7	31	2hd	1hd	14	Adams FD	157wb	*.70e	--	Neji1574Rythminhim1498Bombez1324	Drew out with ease	8
1Jly54- 5Aqu	hd	*2	Hurdles	3:40	4↑ Forget H 11k	1	5	510	45½	21	21	Adams FD	142wb	1.35e	--	Hyvania1501Neji1422½Williamsburg1561½	Good late speed	7
24Jun54- 5Aqu	fm	*1¾	Hurdles	3:13	3↑ Amagansett H 9k	1	3	48	35½	31	32½	Adams FD	144wb	3.15e	--	Williamsburg1511Hyvania1481½Nej14410	Insufficient rally	7
18Jun54- 5Mth	fm	1Ⓣ		1:391	3↑ Alw 5000	10	9	74	86¾	59	43¾	Roser G	109wb	17.80e	86-10	Iceberg II1183Bobs Alibi109noGoing Away109¾	Forced wide	12
10Jun54- 3Bel	hd	*2	Hurdles	3:443	4↑ Handicap 4255	4	5	43½	57	32½	2½	Adams FD	140wb	*.50e	--	Hyvania143½Neji1403½Democles1331	Gaining on winner	8
2Jun54- 6Bel	fm	1⅜Ⓣ		2:172	3↑ Handicap 10050	6	5	48	75	66½	76	Adams J	113wb	4.35	--	Kaster119hdOut Point1163½Bicarb108½	Forced to take up	8
26May54- 3Bel	fm	*1¾	Hurdles	3:134	3↑ Alw 3700	6	5	53½	31½	2½	13½	Adams FD	142wb	*1.20	--	Neji1423½Fulton1482½Sea Term1322	Drew clear in hand	9
17May54- 5Bel	fm	*1¾	Hurdles	3:15	3↑ National Maiden 7.4k	5	3	31	1½	12	14	Field K	137wb	*1.35e	--	Neji1374Rythminhim1502½Corinthian139no	Under mild drive	13
4May54- 3Bel	sf	*1½	Hurdles	2:501	3↑ Sp Wt 3700	3	6	62½	66½	38	23½	Adams FD	142 w	5.05	--	Oneida1473½Neji1421½Cam14725	Reserved early,closed fast	10
29Apr54- 3Bel	fm	*2	S'Chase	3:462	4↑ Sp Wt 4000	1	7	923	838	754	754	Adams FD	140 w	6.75	--	Shipboard140½KingCommndr14812PacificPact1482½	Bobbled	11
3Apr54- 6Cam	hd	*1½	Hurdles	2:382	3↑ Alw 700	3	5	55	44	34¼	32½	Field K	130 w	-	--	Rythminhim1391Fiddlers Choice1491½Neji1308	Mild rally	5
24Mar54- 0Aik		5½f		1:093							2				--	AncestorNeji		
6Nov53- 3Jam	gd	6f		:25 :49 1:161	3↑ Md Sp Wt	4	5	42	34½	48½	410¼	Nichols J	120 w	1.90	56-27	Fleet Count115¾Black Saint1207Quisas1172½	Off slowly	5
24Oct53- 1RB	fst	*6fⓉ		1:22	2↑ Alw 300	1	4	65¾	65¾	55	48½	Mergler M	141 w		--	Tico Tico1633Tommy Tiddler1541½Brushless1514	No mishap	14

Next Move

br. f. 1947, by Bull Lea (Bull Dog)–Now What, by Chance Play
Own.– A.G. Vanderbilt
Br.– Alfred G. Vanderbilt (Md)
Tr.– W.C. Winfrey

Lifetime record: 46 17 11 3 $398,550

Date	Cond	Dist	Fractions	Time	Race	PP	St	1st	2nd	Str	Fin	Jockey	Wt	Odds	Fig	Top finishers	Comment	Fld
18Oct52- 7GS	fst	1 1/16	:23 :471 1:112	1:453	3↑ ⒻVineland H 49k	12	10	1013	89¾	78	62¾	Guerin E	126 w	*2.20	79-20	Sickle's Image120¾Kiss Me Kate118¾Lily White111hd	Closed well,no threat	17
1Oct52- 6Bel	fst	1½	:483 1:132 2:044	2:312	3↑ ⒻLadies H 59k	3	2	2hd	41¾	1014	1121	Guerin E	129 w	*2.10	60-15	How1121¼Marta1222½Enchanted Eve112¾	Quit	11
13Sep52- 6Aqu	fst	1⅛	:48 1:124 1:38	1:51	3↑ ⒻBeldame H (Div 1) 62k	1	4	42	41¾	11	13	Guerin E	125 w	*1.30	90-17	Next Move1253Renew1171½Nilufer106nk	Easily	10
8Sep52- 6Aqu	fst	7f	:223 :451 1:102	1:24	3↑ Bay Shore H 17k	9	9	96¼	77	53¼	11	Guerin E	115 w	4.40e	90-20	NextMove1151FirstGlance111nkSquardAwy1202	Driving clear	12
4Jun52- 6Bel	fst	1 1/16	:221 :45 1:103	1:434	3↑ ⒻTop Flight H 24k	8	3	34	56½	89	814	York R	129wb	2.95	78-15	Renew115¾Valadium1152Blue Moon1111½	Bore in	9
17May52- 6Bel	fst	1	:23 :454 1:104	1:362	3↑ Metropolitan H 36k	1	1	1hd	3½	98½	1011	Guerin E	114 w	20.95	81-14	Mameluke112½Battlefield1251½One Hitter1131	Quit badly	11
26Apr52- 6Jam	my	1 3/16	:461 1:103 1:364	1:561	3↑ Gallant Fox H 69k	3	7	1014	109¾	1018	1020	Guerin E	115wb	10.10	75-18	Spartan Valor1292Alerted1101¾Auditing112¾	Outclassed	10
21Apr52- 6Jam	fst	1⅛	:471 1:114 1:372	1:511	3↑ ⒻFirenze H 33k	1	1	12	11½	14	12	Guerin E	126wb	2.95	90-18	NxtMove1262ThelmaBurgr1101¾KissMeKate123¾	Ridden out	9
1Mar52- 7SA	my	1¼	:452 1:104 1:354	2:01	3↑ S Anita H 141k	11	5	64½	77	1120	1117	Shoemaker W	114wb	4.30e	78-16	[D]Intent1111Miche1154½Be Fleet1142½	Tired	15
22Feb52- 7SA	fst	7f	:222 :444 1:094	1:222	3↑ Wash Birthday H 11k	9	3	31½	53½	89½	87¾	Guerin E	126wb	*2.05	85-15	Pet Bully112¾Interpretation113¾Guillotine126nk	Stopped	9
26Jan52- 7SA	fst	1⅛	:47 1:114 1:381	1:512	3↑ ⒻS Margarita H 62k	3	1	13	12	12	21	Guerin E	130wb	*.90e	83-19	Bed o' Roses1291Next Move1301½Toto105½	Held well	14
12Jan52- 6SA	sly	1	:224 :463 1:121	1:391	3↑ ⒻS Maria H 23k	3	3	22	21½	21½	22½	Guerin E	128wb	*1.25	77-22	Special Touch1212½Next Move1282½Blue Cloth108nk	Impeded	8
28Dec51- 7SA	fst	6f	:221 :451	1:094	3↑ ⒻLas Flores H 18k	10	2	3½	2hd	1hd	11	Guerin E	124wb	2.60	96-08	NextMove1241SpecialTouch122nkSickl'sImg1173½	Ridden out	13
5May51- 6Jam	fst	1⅛	:473 1:12 1:382	1:503	3↑ ⒻFirenze H 34k	9	10	64¼	22	3½	31½	Guerin E	126wb	*.90	93-12	Renew112noThelma Berger1091½Next Move126½	Impeded	12
25Apr51- 6Jam	fst	6f	:223 :46	1:112	3↑ ⒻCorrection H 17k	2	8	63¼	105	74½	42[illegible]	Guerin E	128wb	*1.85	88-12	GrowingUp1101DarkFavorite1121MssDgr111hd	Stumbled early	14
3Mar51- 7SA	gd	1¼	:462 1:11 1:364	2:023	3↑ S Anita H 135k	5	2	32	22	2½	2nk	Guerin E	116wb	4.30	87-24	Moonrush114nkNext Move1162¾Sudan111hd	Just missed	14
17Feb51- 7SA	fst	1⅛	:453 1:101 1:363	1:492	3↑ San Antonio H 68k	2	3	33½	2hd	11	3¾	Guerin E	119wb	4.20	93-17	All Blue111¾Sudan109hdNext Move119½	Weakened	16
3Feb51- 7SA	fst	1¼	:451 1:093 1:351	2:002	Maturity 205k	8	2	21	12	31	67	Guerin E	121wb	*.90e	91-08	Great Circle1151¾Lotowhite116hdBed o' Roses1103½	Tired	11
20Jan51- 7SA	fst	1⅛	:461 1:11 1:361	1:483	3↑ ⒻS Margarita H 60k	2	2	21½	21½	32	43¾	Guerin E	130wb	*.55e	94-16	SpecialTouch1141Bewitch1221¼Bedo'Roses1251½	No excuse	8
16Dec50- 7Hol	fst	1⅛	:462 1:103 1:36	1:483	3↑ Sunset H 58k	3	1	11½	12	11½	2¾	Guerin E	114wb	3.90e	97-12	HillPrince128¾NextMove1141½GreatCircle109nk	Game effort	10
9Dec50- 7Hol	fst	1¼	:463 1:101 1:35	1:594	3↑ Hol Gold Cup 137k	6	3	12	11½	2½	45	Guerin E	116wb	10.35	96-09	Noor1301Palestinian1223Hill Prince1301	Tired	8
2Dec50- 7Hol	fst	1⅛	:47 1:111 1:362	1:492	3↑ ⒻVanity H 30k	3	1	12	12	13	12¼	Guerin E	128wb	*.50e	94-11	Next Move1282¼Bewitch1241Wistful125½	Easing up	9
25Nov50- 7Hol	fst	1 1/16	:224 :46 1:102	1:423	ⒻCinderella 29k	1	2	2hd	11½	12	13	Guerin E	126wb	*.45	95-07	Next Move1263Special Touch1232½Fair Regards1141	Easily	8
11Nov50- 7Hol	fst	1 1/16	:231 :463 1:103	1:423	3↑ ⓈGolden St Brdrs' H 29k	2	2	1hd	2½	22	21¼	Guerin E	118wb	2.35	94-12	Your Host1241¼Next Move118½On Trust1131½	Sharp try	7
4Oct50- 6Bel	fst	1½	:491 1:133 2:034	2:292	3↑ ⒻLadies H 29k	6	4	21	15	16	15½	Guerin E	120wb	*2.15	91-11	Next Move1205½My Celeste106hdWistful1241¼	Easily	12
16Sep50- 6Aqu	fst	1⅛	:473 1:12 1:37	1:501	3↑ ⒻBeldame H 66k	2	1	13	12	15	12¼	Combest N	116wb	*1.20e	94-15	Next Move1162¼September1081Wistful1252¼	Easily	12
28Aug50- 6Aqu	fst	1⅛	:471 1:113 1:353	1:49	Discovery H 22k	6	4	43½	32	56½	513	Guerin E	114wb	*.50	89-08	Sunglow113hdSteel Blue1064Bit o' Fate1047	Tired badly	9
23Aug50- 6Sar	fst	1¼	:483 1:13 1:384	2:042	ⒻAlabama 23k	5	4	2hd	12½	13	2nk	Guerin E	126wb	*.70	86-15	Busanda108nkNext Move126hdAntagonism1083	Weak ride	7
12Jly50- 6AP	fst	1	:222 :442 1:08	1:344	ⒻCleopatra H 22k	3	6	55	56¼	54½	32	Guerin E	126wb	*1.40	96-04	Here's Hoping1151Siama1171Next Move126nk	Closed fast	11
3Jly50- 6Aqu	fst	1 1/16	:232 :47 1:12	1:433	ⒻGazelle 22k	2	2	13	12	12	11	Guerin E	121wb	*.25e	96-11	Next Move1211Bed o' Roses1165Renew112¾	Easily	7
24Jun50- 5Del	fst	1⅛	:463 1:104 1:363	1:492	ⒻDel Oaks 33k	2	4	31½	13	14	15	Guerin E	119wb	*.65	95-08	Next Move1195Busanda1104½Include1101¼	Easily	10
27May50- 6Bel	fst	1⅜	:472 1:112 1:362	2:154	ⒻC C A Oaks 62k	3	6	73¼	55	1hd	11	Guerin E	121wb	*1.30	92-11	Next Move1211Aegina1164Busanda1212½	Handily	8
22May50- 6Bel	fst	1 1/16	:222 :451 1:101	1:44	ⒻAlw 5000	3	1	11	11	13	11	Guerin E	122wb	2.05	91-14	Next Move1221Busanda1105Sunday Evening116½	Ridden out	8
10May50- 6Bel	fst	1	:224 :461 1:113	1:371	ⒻAcorn 18k	6	4	33½	31	2½	21¾	Guerin E	121 w	*.30	86-16	Siama1211¾Next Move1214Honey's Gal121no	Forced wide	8
3May50- 6Jam	sly	6f	:231 :47	1:121	ⒻPrioress 17k	9	8	62	11	13	18	Guerin E	115 w	*.85	90-22	Next Move1158Honey's Gal116nkMiss Degree1121½	Easily	9
22Apr50- 6Jam	fst	1 1/16	:24 :472 1:12	1:433	Wood Memorial 49k	7	1	11	11	2½	44¼	Guerin E	121 w	5.35	91-13	Hill Prince1262Middleground1261½Ferd126¾	Weakened	11
13Apr50- 6Jam	fst	6f	:23 :471	1:122	ⒻAlw 4500	5	3	1hd	11½	14	15½	Guerin E	115 w	*.25	89-17	Next Move1155½Abbie Co1104Navy Bean1103	Easily	8

8Apr50- 5Jam fst 6f :224:461 1:111 ⒻAlw 3500 4 2 11½ 12 13 14 Guerin E 116 w *.55 95-10 Next Move1164Countess Molly1133½La Nappe1137 Easily 7
8Nov49- 6Jam fst 1 1/16 :24 :47 1:12 1:454 ⒻDemoiselle 56k 8 3 34 22½ 3½ 21½ Scurlock O 119 w *.50e 82-19 Bedo'Roses1161½NextMove1195RarePerfume1166 Good effort 12
3Nov49- 5Jam gd 6f :233:471 1:122 ⒻAlw 4000 4 5 31½ 21½ 21½ 2¾ Scurlock O 110 w 2.75 88-15 Rare Perfume122¾Next Move1104[D]Nazma1111½ Sharp effort 8
19Oct49- 6Jam fst 6f :23 :464 1:121 ⒻAutumn Day 12k 11 7 64 33 23 24 Guerin E 115 w 6.80 86-17 Rare Perfume1194Next Move1154½Nazma112½ Went well 13
20Sep49- 5Bel fst 5½f-W :23 :462 1:06 ⒻAlw 4000 13 3 2½ 1½ 2no Guerin E 116 w 1.80e 84-16 Fais Do Do114noNext Move116hdBed o' Roses1223 Game try 13
5Sep49- 4Aqu fst 5½f :23 :474 1:001 1:064 ⒻAlw 3500 1 2 12 13 12 15 Guerin E 116 w *1.20 90-17 Next Move1165Light Upon1162Blue Heart116no Easily 8
5Jly49- 5Jam fst 5f :23 :462 1:01 ⒻMd Sp Wt 10 6 13 15 15 12½ Guerin E 116 w 8.35 85-20 NextMove1162½Sailor'sChoice116noSweeptheSky1164 In hand 12
4Jun49- 2Bel fst 5f-WC :222:451 :58 ⒻMd Sp Wt 8 1 2hd 52½ 66 Guerin E 116 w 4.30 84-09 Mislead1161Sailors Choice1162La Nappe1161 Tired 9
16May49- 4Bel fst 4½f-W :221:45 :511 ⒻMd Sp Wt 7 8 4¾ 45 108½ Guerin E 116 w *2.70 89-03 Fais Do Do1165Light Upon116hdOur Patrice1161 Stopped 17

Noor (Ire)

br. c. 1945, by Nasrullah (Nearco)–Queen of Baghdad, by Bahram **Lifetime record: 31 12 6 6 $394,863**
Own.– Estate of C.S. Howard
Br.– H.H. Aga Khan (Ire)
Tr.– B. Parke

9Dec50- 7Hol fst 1¼ :463 1:101 1:35 1:594 3↑ Hol Gold Cup 137k 8 8 79 64¾ 32½ 11 Longden J 130wb *.70 101-09 Noor1301Palestinian1223HillPrinc1301 Rated,drawing away 8
1Dec50- 7Hol fst 1⅛ :48 1:114 1:361 1:48 3↑ Alw 5000 4 4 42¼ 2½ 13 17 Longden J 124wb *.75 101-11 Noor1247Palestinian1201Assault1121 Much best 5
7Oct50- 6Bel fst 2 :494 2:31 2:563 3:232 3↑ J C Gold Cup 54k 4 2 22 21½ 23 24 Longden J 124wb *.65 83-13 Hill Prince1174Noor1247Adile1212 No excuse 5
Geldings not eligible
23Sep50- 6Bel fst 1½ :473 1:123 2:031 2:291 3↑ Manhattan H 29k 3 10 615 52¾ 2½ 2nk Longden J 128wb *.65 92-15 One Hitter110nkNoor1282Ponder1261¼ Slow start 10
18Sep50- 7Bel fst 1 1/16 :231 :462 1:111 1:424 3↑ Handicap 5035 3 4 45½ 43¼ 43 21¼ Longden J 128wb *.95 96-15 One Hitter1071¼Noor1281½Sky Miracle1022½ Not punished 5
22Jly50- 7Hol fst 1¼ :481 1:122 1:361 2:001 3↑ American H 55k 4 5 59 3nk 3nk 1½ Longden J 132wb *.35 99-05 Noor132½Dharan1004Frankly107no Driving 5
24Jun50- 8GG fst 1¼ :451 1:091 1:34 1:581 3↑ Golden Gate H 57k 4 5 515 27 22 13 Longden J 127wb *.70 108-12 Noor1273Citation1261On Trust1032½ Drew out 5
17Jun50- 8GG fst 1⅛ :463 1:093 1:344 1:464 3↑ Forty-Niners H 10k 4 5 54½ 42¼ 2hd 1nk Longden J 123wb 1.80 104-08 Noor123nkCitation1283Roman In1112 Hard drive 5
Previously raced in name of C.S. Howard
4Mar50- 7SA fst 1¾ :474 2:023 2:271 2:524 3↑ S Juan Capistrano H 64k 4 7 64½ 2hd 2hd 1no Longden J 117wb 3.40 127-06 Noor117noCitation13012½Mocopo107hd Hard drive 8
25Feb50- 7SA fst 1¼ :462 1:11 1:351 2:00 3↑ S Anita H 135k 3 10 96¾ 21 2hd 11¼ Longden J 110wb 6.40 106-11 Noor1101¼Citation1321Two Lea113nk Drew clear 11
11Feb50- 7SA gd 1⅛ :471 1:113 1:372 1:501 3↑ San Antonio H 60k 1 8 79½ 64 42 31½ Longden J 114wb 5.15 90-17 Ponder1281Citation130½Noor114¾ Late rush 9
7Jan50- 7SA fst 1 1/16 :232 :471 1:114 1:434 3↑ San Pasqual H 67k 4 11 107¼ 63¾ 24 21 Longden J 112wb 6.45 88-17 Solidarity1211Noor1123Ponder1253 Off slowly 14
31Dec49- 7SA fst 7f :214 :444 1:102 1:232 3↑ San Carlos H 65k 8 9 69½ 79 75 51¾ Neves R 109wb 21.20 90-19 Manyunk114nkStar Reward1201Miche116hd Late rush 12
17Dec49- 8Tan my 1⅛ :473 1:122 1:39 1:514 3↑ San Francisco H 16k 9 9 89½ 66 31½ 2hd Longden J 115wb 4.40 95-20 Huon Kid107hdNoor115noMocopo1091 Gaining fast 9
3Dec49- 8Tan fst 1¼ :464 1:113 1:362 2:021 3↑ Tanforan H 28k 1 6 611 56 45 34½ James B 115wb 5.35 98-03 Miche1152Johns Joy1202½Noor1151½ Raced wide 9
24Nov49- 8Tan fst 1 1/16 :233 :473 1:12 1:44 3↑ Marchbank H 12k 9 6 53¼ 42¼ 31½ 3½ James B 115wb 4.80 99-09 Oration108hdGolden Glory108½Noor115hd Game effort 11
4Nov49- 7Tan fst 6f :224 :454 1:113 3↑ Alw 3000 4 5 610 59½ 68¼ 42¾ James B 120 w 2.25e 94-12 ThreeRivers1141Frankly1141¼FastandFair117½ Closed fast 7
14Oct49- 6BM fst 6f :223 :454 1:104 3↑ Alw 3000 4 7 36 23 1hd 1no James B 117 w 7.95 94-11 Noor117noFrankly1202¾See-Tee-See1201½ Hard drive 7
Previously trained by Frank Butters
28Sep48♦ Newmarket(GB) fm 1¼Ⓣ Str 2:072 Great Foal Stakes Alw3900 11½ Richards G 133 *.50 Noor1331½Pretexte12110Cotswold119 3
Tracked leader,led 150y out,ridden out
11Sep48♦ Doncaster(GB) fm *1¾Ⓣ LH 3:083 St Leger Stakes Stk94000 8 Richards G 126 8.00 Black Tarquin1261½Alycidon1265Solar Slipper1262 14
Prominent to 3f out,weakened
31Jly48♦ Epsom(GB) fm 1½Ⓣ LH 2:401 3↑ Diomed Stakes Stk16400 16 Richards G 116 *.15 Noor1166Straight Play116 2
Led throughout,drew clear 2f out
16Jly48♦ Sandown(GB) gd 1¼Ⓣ RH 2:101 3↑ Eclipse Stakes Stk40900 3nk Johnstone W 114 *2.50 Petition133noSayajirao136nkNoor114¾ 8
Led to 170y out,came again near line
5Jun48♦ Epsom(GB) gd 1½Ⓣ LH 2:40 Epsom Derby Stk80300 35½ Weston T 126 22.00 My Love1261½Royal Drake1264Noor1261 32
Slowly away,well behind after 4f,midpack 3f out,up for 3rd
28Apr48♦ Newmarket(GB) fm 1Ⓣ Str 1:354 2000 Guineas Stakes Stk86700 9 Beary M 126 50.00 My Babu126hdThe Cobbler1264Pride of India1262 18
Never a factor
12Nov47♦ Windsor(GB) fm 5fⓉ Str 1:001 Riverside Nursery Handicap Hcp3300 7 Richards G 120 *2.00 Red brae100noRossini1171½Hidden Valley110½ 19
Chased leaders,never threatened
3Oct47♦ Newmarket(GB) fm 6fⓉ Str 1:161 Bretby Nursery Handicap Hcp3900 1nk Richards G 125 *3.30 Noor125nkWilliam the Lion113½Nursery Rhyme110nk 11
Slowly away,bumped early,rallied to lead 100y out,driving
13Sep47♦ Doncaster(GB) gd 6fⓉ Str 1:15 Bradgate Park Nursery Handicap Hcp4700 13 Richards G 119 5.50 Noor1193Lake Placid112¾Rodin126¾ 8
Sharp run 2f out,soon led,drew clear final furlong
21Aug47♦ Newmarket(GB) fm 6fⓉ Str 1:163 Elveden Stakes Alw5900 43¾ Richards G 123 12.50 Ottoman128nkMistress Ann1251½Rear Admiral1322 5
Led for 4f,gradually weakened
29Jly47♦ Goodwood(GB) fm 6fⓉ Str 1:134 New Ham Foal Stakes Alw7000 44¼ Johnstone W 114 10.00 Pride of India1141½Ottoman119¾Howdah1192 8
Lost touch 1½f out
4Jun47♦ Epsom(GB) fm 6fⓉ LH 1:10 Woodcote Stakes Alw15500 35 Richards G 116 3.50 Lerins1215Fair Friar116noNoor1164 6
Prominent,faded 1f out.Lerins later renamed My Babu
3May47♦ Birmingham(GB) gd 5fⓉ Str 1:034 Compton Wynyates Plate Alw2100 23 Johnstone W 124 6.00 Minster Lovell1243Noor1245Sicklejas1218 6
Toward rear,finished well without threatening

Oedipus

br. g. 1946, by Blue Larkspur (Black Servant)–Be Like Mom, by Sickle **Lifetime record: 58 14 12 9 $132,405**
Own.– Mrs O. Phipps
Br.– Idle Hour Stock Farm Co (Ky)
Tr.– G.H Bostwick

2Sep54- 3Aqu sf *2 S'Chase 3:523 4↑ Alw 4000 6 3 32 32½ 22 21¾ Adams FD 145 w 2.85 -- MightyMo1481¾Oedips14510MonkeyWrench1455 Second best 6
28Aug54- 3Sar fm *1¾ Hurdles 3:24 3↑ Alw 3500 6 2 2½ 66½ 618 620 Adams FD 145 w 5.20 -- Curly Joe1394Heureux II1492½Cammell Laird144nk Gave way 7
5Aug54- 5Sar sf *2 S'Chase 4:172 4↑ Shillelah H 8.8k 4 2 31 412 429 434 Adams FD 145 w 3.95 -- Shipboard1392King Commander14320Coveted13812 Tired 7
18Jun54- 3Aqu hd *1¾ Hurdles 3:12 4↑ Alw 4000 9 5 21½ 31½ 411 610¾ Adams FD 144 w *1.45 -- Cammell Laird1426Curly Joe1321½Corinthien1322½ Quit 9
29May54- 7Pur fm *6fⓉ 1:15 3↑ Alw 400 5 3 62¾ 62¾ 63¾ 65½ Adams FD 141 w 2.65e -- Nairn1372½Escargot141½Beau Broke131½ Never a menace 7
13Aug53- 5Sar fst *2 S'Chase 4:093 4↑ North Am H 8.8k 2 2 22 25 611 617 Adams FD 159 w 1.95 -- The Mast1444Sundowner1432½Virginius1341½ Quit early 6
6Aug53- 5Sar fst *2 S'Chase 4:10 4↑ Shillelah H 8.9k 6 1 11½ 2½ 33 34 Adams FD 160 w *1.95 -- Sun Shower1321Sundowner1393Oedipus1604 Used early 7
19Jun53- 6Bel fst *2¼ S'Chase 4:121 4↑ Temple Gwathmey H 16k 5 2 21½ 35 35½ 37½ Adams FD 164 w 3.20 -- Errolford1305½Sea Legs1652Oedipus1645 No rally 7
Daily Racing Form time,4:16 2/5
4Jun53- 5Bel fst *2½ S'Chase 4:421 4↑ Meadow Brook H 11k 2 1 12½ 1hd 24 25 Adams FD 164 w *1.20 -- Sea Legs1575Oedipus1642½His Boots1462½ No rally 6
14May53- 5Bel fst *2 S'Chase 3:453 4↑ C L Appleton Mem 8.9k 6 1 14 11 12 11½ Adams FD 158 w 1.90 -- Oedipus1581½His Boots1422The Mast1447 Hard drive 6
3Oct52- 5Bel sf *3 S'Chase 5:44 4↑ Grand Nat'l H 28k 3 3 45½ 33 37 37 Foot A 165 w *2.60 -- Sea Legs1365The Mast1542Oedipus1657 No rally 9
25Sep52- 5Bel fst *2½ S'Chase 4:412 4↑ Brook H 17k 3 3 31 21 31 25 Foot A 163 w *2.50 -- Jam1565Oedipus1631Lone Fisherman1313 Impeded 8
18Sep52- 5Bel sf *2 S'Chase 3:391 3↑ Broad Hollow H 11k 4 3 32 2½ 11½ 1hd Foot A 160 w 2.60 -- Oedipus160hdJam15420The Creek1386 Just lasted 8
11Sep52- 5Aqu fst *2 S'Chase 3:441 3↑ Harbor Hill H 11k 5 2 22 44 49 412½ Foot A 162 w 2.45 -- Semper Eadem1354Hot1472½Jam1556 Bad landing last 6

Date	Cond	Dist	Type / Fractions	Time	Age	Race	PP	St	1C	2C	Str	Fin	Jockey	Wt	Odds	Fig	Top finishers	Comment
21Aug52- 5Sar	fst	*2	S'Chase	4:091	4↑	Beverwyck H 9k	2	3	32	31½	513	514	Foot A	165 w	*1.00e	--	His Boots1448Titien II1451Hot1461½	Tired 7
7Aug52- 5Sar	fst	*2	S'Chase	4:11	4↑	Shillelah 5.8k	2	1	11½	12	12	12	Foot A	162 w	2.05	--	Oedipus1622His Boots1405Phiblant1405	All out 5
3Jly52- 5Aqu	fst	*2	S'Chase	3:461	4↑	Hitchcock H 11k	5	5	55	53½	44	35	Foot A	162 w	*.90	--	Hot1442His Boots1433Oedipus1621½	No excuse 6
20Jun52- 6Del	fst	*2	S'Chase	3:431	4↑	Georgetown H 12k	2	2	21	42¼	35½	58	Foot A	164 w	*1.65e	--	The Mast1575Jam1511½[DH]Crooning Wind1431½	Weakened 8
11Jun52- 6Bel	fst	*2¼	S'Chase	4:163	4↑	Temple Gwathmey H 16k	4	2	2½	11	1hd	2¾	Foot A	163 w	*1.90	--	The Mast153¾Oedipus1631¼Navy Gun1497	Weakened 9
12Oct51- 5Bel	sf	*3	S'Chase	5:501	4↑	Grand National H 24k	2	2	21	2½	11	11½	Foot A	165 w	*1.80	--	Oedipus1651½Navy Gun1402½Banner Waves14045	All out 10
4Oct51- 5Bel	fst	*2½	S'Chase	4:45	4↑	Brook H 16k	1	1	11½	11½	13	13	Foot A	161wb	*2.00	--	Oedipus1613Palaja1387Lone Fisherman148nk	Easily 12
27Sep51- 5Bel	fst	*2	S'Chase	3:43	3↑	Broad Hollow H 12k	11	1	22	24	12	17	Foot A	158 w	3.95	--	Oedipus1587Palaja1342Genancoke1412½	Easily 11
6Sep51- 5Aqu	fst	*2	S'Chase	3:47	3↑	Harbor Hill H 11k	4	4	46	53½	3nk	42¾↓	Smithwick P	159 w	*1.95	--	Boom Boom1452Genancoke140¾Tourist List134hd	Blocked 8
30Aug51- 5Sar	fst	*2½	S'Chase	5:053	4↑	Saratoga H 11k	2	2	2½	21	26	38¼	Adams FD	159 w	*1.50	--	Hampton Roads1408Lone Fisherman147nkOedipus15925	7
			Bad landing 10th															
23Aug51- 5Sar	sf	*2	S'Chase	4:192	3↑	Beverwyck H 8.9k	1	1	13	12	11½	13	Adams FD	155 w	*1.40	--	Oedipus1553Hampton Roads13913Boom Boom1452	Easily 7
9Aug51- 5Sar	sf	*2	S'Chase	4:164	3↑	Shillelah 6.1k	2	1	12	11½	3½	33½	Adams FD	154 w	*1.10	--	Banner Waves1341½Extra Points1372Oedipus1542	Tired 5
12Jly51- 5Aqu	hd	*2	S'Chase	3:441	4↑	Hitchcock 11k	3	2	36	36½	52¾	56	Adams FD	157 w	*1.00	--	Genncoke1352¼[D]Larky Day147nkSemprEadem140½	Impeded 7
			Placed fourth through disqualification															
27Jun51- 5Del	fst	*2	S'Chase	3:404	4↑	Georgetown H 12k	4	3	35½	46½	26	24	Smiley J	158 w	*1.75	--	Crooning Wind1304Oedipus15812Genancoke1373	No rally 6
7Jun51- 5Bel	fst	*2	S'Chase	3:432	4↑	Corinthian H 8.7k	2	1	15	12	11	1¾	Smiley J	156 w	*.85	--	Oedipus156¾Lone Fisherman14812Elkridge1501	Driving 4
18May51- 5Bel	fst	*2	S'Chase	3:42	4↑	International H 9k	7	2	21	11½	1hd	24	Smiley J	154 w	2.40	--	Pontius Pilate1524Oedipus1547Elkridge1493½	Held well 7
11Oct50- 6Bel	fst	*2¼	S'Chase	4:182	4↑	Temple Gwathmey H 11k	3	1	1½	21½	23	210	Molony T	153 w	*.45	--	TouristList13810Oedipus1536AmericanWay1454	Bad landing 5
6Oct50- 5Bel	fst	*3	S'Chase	5:422	4↑	Grand National H 23k	4	3	41½	21	1hd	22¼	Molony T	153 w	3.45	--	Trough Hill1502¼Oedipus1534Pontius Pilate1502½	Weakened 9
29Sep50- 5Bel	fst	*2½	S'Chase	4:46	4↑	Brook H 15k	2	1	11	11	12	11¼	Adams FD	149 w	3.15	--	Oedipus1491¼Trough Hill1515½Tourist List1361	Easily 8
22Sep50- 5Bel	sf	*2	S'Chase	3:482	3↑	Broad Hollow H 11k	9	2	25	23	12	11¼	Williams CH	147 w	17.45	--	Oedipus1471¼Elkridge1521¼Trough Hill1505	Ridden out 10
7Sep50- 5Aqu	fst	*2	Hurdles	3:381	3↑	Bushwick H 11k	1	4	73¾	78½	819	816	McDonald RS	152 w	5.10	--	Scare Play1431½Larky Day1531¼Bengal1324	Close quarters 9
25Aug50- 5Sar	fst	*2½	S'Chase	5:082	4↑	Saratoga H 11k	6	3	33½	43½	36	39	Field T	147 w	3.35	--	Elkridge1503Lone Fisherman1356Oedipus147nk	Fair effort 6
18Aug50- 5Sar	fst	*2	S'Chase	4:082	3↑	Beverwyck H 9.1k	3	1	12	12	28	215	Field T	143 w	3.40	--	Pontius Pilate13815Oedipus14313Elkridge14640	Gave way 6
10Aug50- 5Sar	fst	*2	S'Chase	4:094	3↑	North American H 6.4k	3	1	1½	1hd	47½	414	McDonald RS	143 w	2.40	--	TheHeir143nkHamptnRoads14510Scuttlman1354	Bad landing 6
3Aug50- 5Sar	fst	*2	S'Chase	4:102	3↑	Shillelah 6.6k	2	3	3nk	2hd	15	16	Smiley J	135 w	5.35	--	Oedipus1356His Boots15216Repose136hd	Easily 10
27Jun50- 5Del	fst	*2	S'Chase	3:524	4↑	Spring Maiden 7.3k	8	-	-	-	-	-	Smiley J	154 w	*2.05	--	Port Raider15010Whirl Along1426Tolbiac1506	Fell at 1st 8
19Jun50- 4Aqu	sf	*2	S'Chase	3:422	4↑	Spring Maiden 7.3k	1	1	11½	11½	12	12	Smiley J	147 w	*1.35	--	Oedipus1472PortRaider15035LoneFisherman15025	Ridden out 7
13Jun50- 3Aqu	fst	*2	S'Chase	3:461	4↑	Alw 3500	2	1	13	16	110	120	Smiley J	137 w	2.90	--	Oedipus13720Le Buis Fleuri147nkPort Raider1475½	Easily 7
31May50- 3Bel	fst	*1½	Hurdles	2:463	3↑	3500	10	1	14	14	22	39½	Smiley J	142 w	4.15	--	Enon1504½Proceed1425Oedipus14220	Weakened 12
22May50- 3Bel	fst	*1½	Hurdles	2:454	3↑	Alw 3500	3	6	51¼	33	37¼	512	Smiley J	134 w	5.15e	--	Rialto1561½Uncle Sam13110Macanudo143nk	Tired 11
10May50- 3Bel	fst	*2	S'Chase	3:50	4↑	Sp Wt 3500	8	2	1228	-	-	-	Smiley J	142 w	4.00	--	LoneFishrmn1424SeaLegs14210WhattaKnight1361½	Ran out 14
11Oct49- 3Bel	fst	*1½	Hurdles	2:463	3↑	Alw 3000	9	6	512	25	21½	21½	Smiley J	139 w	9.55	--	Silver Bridge1391½Oedipus139½Half Hour1505	Good effort 14
5Oct49- 3Bel	fst	*1½	Hurdles	2:461	3↑	Alw 3500	3	7	68¼	48½	31½	22	Molony T	132 w	7.90	--	SilverBridge1322Oedipus1322½MonkyWrnch13910	Closed well 11
27Sep49- 3Bel	fst	*2	Hurdles	3:463	3↑	Handicap 4045	4	2	35	11	63½	511	Field T	133 w	*2.05e	--	NewRule1381Skyscraper1502½LeBuisFlur145½	Close quarters 9
			Daily Racing Form time,3:47 4/5															
20Sep49- 4Bel	fst	6f	:232 :473	1:122	3↑	Md Sp Wt	10	12	1111	1111	811	716	Renick J	119 w	24.35	72-17	Challadroit1195GoodEnding1192½HickoryLea124no	No mishap 14
9Sep49- 3Aqu	sl	*1½	Hurdles	2:573	3↑	Alw 3000	1	1	1½	1½	21½	32	Adams FD	136 w	*1.35	--	Monkey Wrench1481Firebet1501Oedipus1364	Close quarters 8
30Aug49- 3Aqu	fst	*1½	Hurdles	2:52	3↑	Md Sp Wt	7	1	11	11½	1hd	11	Adams FD	136 w	*1.35	--	Oedipus1361North Branch1314½Alphabetical1323½	Driving 8
25Aug49- 3Sar	fst	*1½	Hurdles	3:082	3↑	Md Sp Wt	1	2	36	611	32½	22	Smiley J	137 w	11.00	--	Titien II1372Oedipus1371½The Viceroy1502½	Closed well 9
			Previously owned by O. Phipps;previously trained by J. Fitzsimmons															
29Jly48- 3Jam	fst	5½f	:232 :472 :592	1:063		©Md Sp Wt	8	9	109¼	106½	108¾	1015	Combest N	116wb	114.80	70-20	Dry Fly116nkBlue Dart1164Fireagain116nk	Trailed 10
9Jun48- 4Bel	fst	5f-WC	:223 :452	:572		©Md Sp Wt	6	13		156¾	168¾	1511	Guerin E	116wb	42.60e	82-09	Prince Quest116¾Halt116½Kibosh116¾	Outrun 17
22May48- 4Bel	fst	5f-WC	:232 :47	:591		Alw 5000	3	3		64	66¾	612	Jessop JD	111wb	10.00e	72-14	Capot1111½Mirabeau1146Amarillo Kid1131½	Outrun 6
29Apr48- 3Jam	fst	5f	:232 :482	1:012		©Md Sp Wt	6	5	67¼	78	77¾	67½	Guerin E	116wb	33.90	75-21	Transfluent116noSwords Town1162Good Egg116nk	No factor 11
24Apr48- 3Jam	fst	5f	:232 :473	1:01		Md Sp Wt	6	5	811	84½	99¾	913	Guerin E	116 w	31.20	72-18	BlueCounselor1163BlueThanks1161½Dsconsolt1161	No factor 12
19Apr48- 3Jam	fst	5f	:23 :472	1:003		©Md Sp Wt	9	5	56	712	610	814	Guerin E	116 w	5.70e	73-17	Ennobled1164Good Egg1165Blue Thanks116¾	Outrun 10

One Count

dk br. c. 1949, by Count Fleet (Reigh Count)–Ace Card, by Case Ace

Lifetime record: 23 9 3 3 $245,625

Own.– Mrs W.M. Jeffords

Br.– Walter M. Jeffords (Ky)

Tr.– O. White

Date	Cond	Dist	Fractions	Time	Age	Race	PP	St	1C	2C	Str	Fin	Jockey	Wt	Odds	Fig	Top finishers	Comment
27Jun53- 6Del	fst	1¼	:452 1:092 1:344	2:002	3↑	Sussex H 28k	5	5	510	43½	45½	44¼	Gorman D	127 w	2.85e	104-07	Royal Vale130nkPost Card1133Risque Rouge1111	Faltered 5
30May53- 6Bel	fst	1¼	:471 1:11 1:353	2:003	3↑	Suburban H 58k	5	6	56¾	48½	56¼	510	Gorman D	126 w	2.30e	87-17	Tom Fool128noRoyal Vale1247Cold Command1142	Tired 7
2May53- 6Jam	my	1 3/16	:474 1:113 1:362	1:552	3↑	Gallant Fox H 71k	3	4	46	44½	35	33	Gorman D	129 w	2.35	96-14	RoyalVale1151½ColdCommand1151½OneCount129no	No excuse 6
21Apr53- 6Jam	fst	1 1/16	:234 :47 1:12	1:451	3↑	Handicap 10160	7	9	88¾	51¼	31	11¾	Gorman D	126 w	*2.15	86-19	One Count1261¾Assignment111noFlaunt106hd	Driving clear 11
7Feb53- 7Hia	my	1⅛	:473 1:124 1:391	1:532	3↑	McLennan H 64k	1	4	45½	46	68½	613	Gorman D	126 w	3.45	56-34	Crafty Admiral1293½Oil Capitol115¾Ken1171	Tired 7
25Oct52- 6Jam	fst	1⅝	:494 1:401 2:051	2:44	3↑	Gold Cup 79k	4	4	3½	16	18	19	Gorman D	119 w	*.60	94-15	One Count1199Alerted1261½Lafourche1191	Easily 6
			Geldings not eligible															
4Oct52- 6Bel	fst	2	:514 2:332 2:584	3:241	3↑	J C Gold Cup 79k	4	3	21	14	13	12	Gorman D	117 w	3.80	83-15	OneCount1172Mark-Ye-Well11715CraftyAdmiral1245	Driving 4
			Geldings not eligible															
24Sep52- 6Bel	fst	1⅝	:482 1:38 2:031	2:42		Lawrence Realizatn 29k	5	6	55½	31	24	24	Guerin E	126 w	1.60	90-15	Mark-Ye-Well1184One Count1265Marcador1143½	Hard urged 7
16Aug52- 6Sar	sly	1¼	:493 1:144 1:401	2:072		Travers 23k	3	5	54½	43	11	13	Guerin E	126 w	4.10	71-22	One Count1263Armageddon1231Tom Fool114¾	In hand 8
			Geldings not eligible															
7Jun52- 6Bel	fst	1½	:483 1:134 2:042	2:301		Belmont 118k	3	3	2hd	1hd	11½	12½	Arcaro E	126 w	12.80	88-14	OneCnt1262½BlueMan12610Armagddn1266	Swerved,drew out 6
17May52- 6Pim	fst	1 3/16	:472 1:12 1:38	1:572		Preakness 113k	1	4	32½	32½	43	36	Arcaro E	126 w	8.10	87-13	Blue Man1263½Jampol1262½One Count126½	No rally 10
10May52- 6Bel	fst	1	:224 :453 1:11	1:37		Withers 31k	5	7	75¾	64¼	34½	23½	Atkinson T	126 w	2.95	85-14	Armageddon1263½One Count1264Primate126¾	Closed well 9
			Geldings not eligible															
7May52- 5Bel	fst	1 1/16	:231 :464 1:122	1:44		Alw 5000	5	6	53¼	21	13	18	Gorman D	117 w	3.10	91-16	One Count1178Brechin109noGrover B.1221	Easily,drew out 8
15Apr52- 7Lrl	my	1	:232 :47 1:13	1:392		Alw 4000	2	4	32	21	21	21½	Hanford I	119wb	1.80	86-23	ComtedeGrasse1161½OneCnt1197OceanBreeze1104	No excuse 5
29Mar52- 6Lrl	fst	6f	:224 :47	1:122		Cherry Blossom 9k	4	7	84½	77½	79	77	Hanford I	115wb	20.60	78-20	Cinda1163½Pintor118noOrco121hd	No factor 9
1Mar52- 6Hia	fst	1⅛	:462 1:113 1:37	1:50		Flamingo (Div 1) 66k	8	10	104	87½	913	914	Stout J	117wb	8.05	72-09	Blue Man1173½Jampol120¾[D]Top Bet111¾	No factor 11
20Feb52- 7Hia	fst	1⅛	:46 1:11 1:374	1:521		Everglades H 13k	7	7	79	68	65	51	Boulmetis S	114wb	4.45	74-18	OneThrow110nkMasterFiddle123nkCandlWood122hd	Late rush 13
13Feb52- 5Hia	fst	7f	:224 :453 1:11	1:242		Alw 3500	9	2	2hd	2½	2½	1hd	Boulmetis S	122wb	*1.90	90-14	One Count122hdImurguy1111½Blenomar1146	Unruly,up 11
30Jan52- 4Hia	sl	6f	:234 :482	1:15		Alw 3500	3	6	31	21½	21½	3nk	Boulmetis S	122wb	2.45	73-28	Why Not119nkNimble Fox116hdOne Count1223	Closed well 10
22Jan52- 4Hia	fst	7f	:224 :462 1:114	1:244		©Alw 3000	1	3	31½	2½	11	11¼	Boulmetis S	122wb	2.65	88-13	One Count1221¼Sandtop1164½Outback1221½	Drew clear 9
24Oct51- 2GS	fst	1 70	:233 :474 1:131	1:443		Md Sp Wt	12	3	21	1½	11	1½	Boulmetis S	119 w	*2.40	84-16	One Count119½Cobber1195High Petal1163	Driving 12
3Oct51- 5Bel	fst	6f-WC	:223 :452	1:10		©Md Sp Wt	16	13		125¾	65¼	97	Shoemaker W	118 w	8.85f	84-09	Warpath1182Golden Gloves118hdForelock1181	No menace 26
26Sep51- 5Bel	fst	6f-WC	:222 :45	1:101		©Md Sp Wt	19	23		2715	2115	189¼	Guerin E	118 w	27.30	81-10	Hitex1183½Point Fortune113noChello118no	Slow start 27

Parlo

ch. f. 1951, by Heliopolis (Hyperion)–Fairy Palace, by Pilate — **Lifetime record: 34 8 6 3 $309,240**

Own.– Foxcatcher Farms
Br.– William duPont Jr (Va)
Tr.– R.E. Handlen

12Oct56- 7Bel	fst	1½	:473 1:113 2:034 2:294	3↑ ⒻLadies H 58k	11 1 14 41¼ 108¾ 1112	Westrope J	116 w	10.55	77-13	FlowerBowl1161¾DottedLn111hdBrghtstStrt107nk	Used early	12
1Oct56- 7Bel	fst	1	:224 :461 1:112 1:37	3↑ ⒻMaskette H 29k	5 4 41½ 32½ 33½ 43¼	Guerin E	117 w	4.60	86-15	Searching123½HappyPrincess1072PuckerUp112¾	Raced evenly	11
22Sep56- 7Bel	fst	1⅛	:452 1:101 1:363 1:50	3↑ ⒻBeldame H 66k	1 2 22 22 31 73	Guerin E	120 w	9.80	86-13	Levee115½Amoret114hdSearching123nk	Well placed,no rally	14
5Sep56- 7Bel	fst	7f	:222 :452 1:103 1:232	3↑ ⒻVagrancy H 23k	4 7 65¾ 66½ 912 1011	Guerin E	125 w	*2.15	82-11	MizClementine125hdSearching1252½HappyPrincess1103	Dull	10
22Aug56- 6Sar	fst	1⅛	:482 1:13 1:383 1:52	3↑ ⒻDiana H 28k	4 1 11 43½ 914 923	Guerin E	125 w	*1.30	67-18	Searching1222RicoReto113¾BlueBanner1172	Saddle slipped	9
21Jly56- 7Jam	sly	1 1/16	:233 :471 1:12 1:43	3↑ ⒻBellerose H 27k	5 2 22½ 21½ 1½ 12½	Guerin E	121 w	4.25	97-12	Parlo1212½Blue Sparkler1251¾Manotick119hd	Drawing clear	7
30Jun56- 7Del	fst	1¼	:451 1:101 1:362 2:03	3↑ ⒻDelaware H 156k	4 2 23 3nk 105¼ 128½	Anderson P	124 w	7.20	78-14	FlowrBowl1122Mantick122¾OpenSesame113hd	Speed,stopped	15
23Jun56- 7Del	gd	1 1/16	:231 :463 1:113 1:44	3↑ ⒻNew Castle 37k	6 7 88½ 75¼ 1211 1211	Guerin E	120 w	*2.40	80-19	Miz Clementine1162½Searching1201½Myrtle's Jet116½	Tired	12
26May56- 7Bel	fst	1 1/16	:223 :451 1:102 1:423	3↑ ⒻTop Flight H 28k	1 3 22 12 1hd 2½	Anderson P	124 w	6.05	95-11	Searchng121½Prlo1241½RcoRto107nk	Held well under weight	10
15May56- 6Bel	fst	6f	:224 :461 1:103	4↑ Alw 5000	4 6 56 67 610 512	Guerin E	115 w	3.85	84-13	DarkRuler1173½WhiteKnight1202½Dedicate1202	Dull effort	7
8Nov55- 6Jam	fst	1⅛	:473 1:113 1:37 1:504	3↑ ⒻFirenze H 35k	10 3 22 1hd 43 57¾	Guerin E	126 w	3.80	84-15	RareTreat112½Searching118noWhiteCross1081¼	Led briefly	12
22Oct55- 7GS	fst	1⅛	:453 1:10 1:353 1:481	3↑ ⒻVineland H 51k	3 5 1hd 1hd 21 64¾	Guerin E	128 w	*1.90	91-10	HighVoltage1173Manotck1181Crsst110no	Tired under impost	18
3Sep55- 6Aqu	fst	7f	:23 :463 1:112 1:233	3↑ ⒻVagrancy H (Div 1) 28k	5 5 75¾ 64½ 3½ 32½	Bailey PJ	129 w	*1.05	89-16	Searching1111½BluBnnr1141Prlo1291¾	Led briefly,faltered	11
20Aug55- 6Sar	fst	1¼	:491 1:132 1:39 2:042	3↑ Saratoga H 55k	3 1 1½ 3½ 36½ 312	Arcaro E	121 w	*.95e	74-19	Social Outcast1253Red Hannigan1069Parlo1212½	Tired late	5
2Jly55- 6Del	fst	1¼	:462 1:112 1:363 2:022	3↑ ⒻDelaware H 151k	10 5 2½ 1½ 16 13	Guerin E	128 w	*1.00	90-17	Parlo1283Open Sesame1142Clear Dawn1191½	Speed to spare	13
8Jun55- 6Bel	fst	1 1/16	:224 :451 1:094 1:414	3↑ ⒻTop Flight H 30k	9 4 52½ 31½ 11 13	Guerin E	126 w	*2.05	102-11	Parlo1263Gainsboro Girl114½Spinning Top113nk	Drew out	12
1Jun55- 6Bel	fst	7f	:23 :462 1:111 1:241	3↑ ⒻGolden Annivrsy H 20k	1 1 1½ 21½ 2hd 2¾	Guerin E	125 w	4.75	88-14	Dispute114¾Parlo125hdOilPntng107no	Good speed,held well	11
30Oct54- 6Jam	sly	1⅛	:474 1:131 1:394 1:532	3↑ ⒻFirenze H 35k	1 1 12 11 16 17	Atkinson T	125 w	*1.70	79-28	Parlo1257Riverina115¾Spinning Top1101¾	Much the best	13
18Sep54- 6Aqu	fst	1⅛	:48 1:12 1:37 1:494	3↑ ⒻBeldame H 64k	9 2 11 12½ 14 13	Guerin E	116 w	5.00	96-10	Parlo1163Open Sesame1101¾Clear Dawn1141½	Mild hand ride	9
25Aug54- 6Sar	fst	1¼	:481 1:13 1:394 2:06	ⒻAlabama 29k	5 1 15 13 15 11½	Arcaro E	121 w	9.30	78-18	Parlo1211½Moonsight1119Open Sesame1113	Long lead,tiring	10
7Aug54- 6Mth	fst	1⅛	:46 1:101 1:37 1:501	ⒻMth Oaks 63k	6 5 57¼ 610 69½ 910	Nash R	121 w	9.20	85-12	Evening Out1172Clear Dawn1212½June Fete113½	Done early	14
28Jly54- 7Mth	fst	6f	:22 :452 1:10	ⒻMiss Woodford 24k	6 5 63½ 53 32½ 22½	Nash R	121 w	20.10	92-11	ClearDwn1122½Prlo1211½EvnngOut118hd	Rallied for placing	10
5Jly54- 6Del	fst	1¼	:454 1:101 1:361 2:023	3↑ ⒻNew Castle H 138k	8 3 33½ 46 47½ 79¼	Nash R	113 w	18.80	80-19	GainsboroGirl1134SunshineNell1262LavenderHll111hd	Tired	20
26Jun54- 6Del	fst	1⅛	:471 1:114 1:381 1:512	ⒻDel Oaks 47k	5 4 1hd 13 13 1¾	Westrope J	113 w	21.50	83-16	Parlo113¾OpenSesm1135O'Alson119½	Clear lead,held gamely	13
4Jun54- 6Del	fst	6f	:222 :454 1:12	ⒻAlw 4000	5 1 2hd 1½ 1hd 21¼	Westrope J	119wb	*1.60	84-15	Greek Lady1191¼Parlo1191½Level Rippey1161	No excuse	8
12May54- 7GS	gd	6f	:223 :454 1:123	ⒻBetsy Ross 38k	11 4 1hd 13 22 33½	Hartack W	111wb	13.50f	81-19	OnYourOwn1141½Jenjy1212Prlo1111	Set early pace,weakened	16
1May54- 3Bel	fst	6f	:23 :471 1:123	ⒻAlw 4000	6 3 53¾ 42½ 65¼ 41	Catalano A	109wb	*2.70	85-16	GayGreeting109noOldBaaskt1181Indn115no	Rallied too late	9
14Nov53- 7Lrl	fst	1 1/16	:232 :47 1:132 1:462	ⒻSelima 57k	4 1 12 1hd 910 914	Boland W	116wb	3.90	68-22	Small Favor1161Queen Hopeful119hdClear Dawn119½	Quit	11
28Oct53- 6Jam	sly	1 1/16	:24 :48 1:124 1:462	ⒻDemoiselle 72k	2 1 12½ 11 21½ 23½	Boland W	119wb	12.65	76-21	O'Alison1193½Parlo1194½Case Goods1192½	Faltered	12
17Oct53- 4Jam	fst	6f	:24 :473 1:133	ⒻFrizette 19k	11 7 74¾ 106 98½ 45½	Scurlock D	110wb	44.80	73-21	IndianLegend110noCaseGoods1193SmallFavr1152½	No mishap	14
18Sep53- 5Aqu	fst	5½f	:23 :473 1:001 1:071	ⒻMd Sp Wt	10 7 52¼ 11½ 16 16	Guerin E	116wb	*2.00	88-17	Parlo1166Errorless1162½The Tormentil111hd	Easily	12
18Jun53- 4Bel	fst	4½f-W	:222 :453 :514	ⒻMd Sp Wt	6 5 3nk 74¼ 108	Peters M	116wb	*1.55	82-10	Talora116hdSunrise Siren116nkThe Tormentil1161	Tired	17
11Jun53- 4Bel	fst	4½f-W	:222 :452 :513	ⒻMd Sp Wt	11 5 3½ 2hd 21¼	Peters M	116wb	10.10	90-12	Mainsail1161¼Parlo116¾Boda1161¼	Lacked rally	12
3Jun53- 4Bel	fst	4½f-W	:223 :453 :514	ⒻMd Sp Wt	3 10 116 86¾ 87	Peters M	116 w	13.30	83-11	Blue Eyes1162½Bonnie Black116hdBunty B.116nk	No mishap	13

Porterhouse

br. c. 1951, by Endeavour II (British Empire)–Red Stamp, by Bimelech — **Lifetime record: 70 19 8 12 $519,460**

Own.– Llangollen Farm
Br.– Mrs M.E. Person (Ky)
Tr.– Charles Whittingham

4Jly58- 7Hol	fst	1⅛	:471 1:11 1:36 1:482	3↑ American H 54k	7 7 77½ 79¼ 611 57½	Shoemaker W	116wb	*1.80e	84-16	HowNow1221¼Seaneen116¾EddieSchmdt1203	Never a contender	7
21Jun58- 7Hol	fst	1 1/16	:231 :462 1:102 1:413	3↑ Inglewood H 54k	3 8 811 77 68¼ 46½	Shoemaker W	118wb	*1.45e	80-16	EddieSchmidt117noHowNw1223¼SoclClimbr1173¼	No menace	8
31May58- 7Hol	fst	5½f	:22 :454 :572 1:033	3↑ Hol Express H 27k	8 9 912 98½ 78½ 63¾	Longden J	124wb	*2.70	90-15	HowNow1191½BettyRose113noGoldenNotes114hd	Full of run	9
10Mar58- 7SA	fst	1 1/16	:23 :461 1:102 1:42	3↑ San Bernardino H 28k	6 7 76 73 51¼ 2hd	Arcaro E	123wb	*1.75e	94-11	Terrang125hdPorterhouse123½Seann1151¾	Getting to winner	7
1Mar58- 7SA	fst	1¼	:452 1:093 1:343 1:594	3↑ S Anita H 135k	5 7 69 56½ 47½ 36	Arcaro E	120wb	13.95	95-09	RoundTable1302½Terrang1193½Porterhous1202	Mild late bid	9
15Feb58- 7SA	fst	1⅛	:462 1:101 1:343 1:464	3↑ San Antonio H 56k	1 9 99½ 99¾ 78¼ 45½	Arcaro E	118wb	6.90	97-11	RoundTable1303½MysticEye1081½PromisedLand116½	Late bid	9
1Feb58- 6SA	fst	1 1/16	:231 :463 1:11 1:412	3↑ San Pasqual H 27k	2 8 711 41½ 32 3½	Longden J	125wb	*.90e	96-10	Terrang122½Fnd121hdPortrhous1254	Made strong late rally	8
4Jan58- 7SA	fst	7f	:221 :444 1:091 1:221	3↑ San Carlos H 60k	9 14 1410 1410 128 2no	Taniguchi G	126wb	*1.45e	92-11	Seaneen114noPorterhouse126nkMysticEye114½	Closed boldly	14
26Oct57- 6Jam	fst	6f	:232 :47 1:112	3↑ Sheepshead Bay H 15k	4 11 1115 1110 117¾ 99¼	Valenzuela I	126wb	7.85	81-17	ByJeepers107nkBunny'sBabe108½AdmiralVee1211	Dull form	11
28Sep57- 6Bel	fst	6f	:224 :461 1:104	3↑ Handicap 10000	2 9 99¾ 99¾ 98¼ 86½	Arcaro E	130wb	*2.10e	88-13	Hastego1161¼Cohoes1201¾Belmont Breeze111hd	Away slowly	9
23Jly57- 7Hol	fst	1⅝	:473 1:364 2:014 2:40	3↑ Sunset H 112k	8 6 66½ 42¼ 33 33¾	Longden J	122wb	*2.00	87-15	Find119hdEddieSchmidt1093¾Portrhous122nk	Went wide late	10
13Jly57- 7Hol	fst	1¼	:452 1:091 1:334 1:583	3↑ Hol Gold Cup H 162k	11 9 95½ 44 34½ 23¼	Longden J	119wb	4.40	97-15	Round Table1093¼Porterhouse1192Find1187	Best of others	11
26Jun57- 6Hol	fst	7f	:22 :442 1:084 1:211	3↑ Alw 20000	1 4 45½ 31 12 16	Longden J	126wb	*.60	94-17	Porterhouse1266LiberalArt1081¼ElKhobr1187	Drew out fast	4
13Jun57- 7Hol	fst	5½f	:213 :442 :563 1:022	3↑ Hol Express H 23k	9 12 115½ 95¾ 46 12½	Longden J	125wb	3.60e	104-17	Porterhouse1262½FlightHistory1121½LibrlArt1091¼	Driving	12
25May57- 7Hol	fst	1 1/16	:222 :451 1:093 1:402	3↑ Californian 116k	6 12 1012 109 918 817	Longden J	119wb	*1.20e	76-20	SocialClmbr1191½RoundTbl1054½Fnd119nk	Failed to respond	12
18May57- 7Hol	fst	7f	:221 :444 1:09 1:204	3↑ Los Angeles H 55k	3 8 63¼ 41½ 3nk 15	Longden J	123wb	*1.25e	96-12	Porterhouse1235Flight History1101Corn Husker119¾	Easily	9
9May57- 7Hol	fst	6f	:214 :443 :564 1:09	3↑ Hol Premiere H 28k	9 10 108¾ 88½ 53¾ 31½	Longden J	124wb	*2.05e	97-13	Find123¾SocialClimbr118¾Portrhous1242½	Best stride late	10
6Mar57- 7SA	fst	1 1/16	:23 :462 1:103 1:42	3↑ S Barbara H 28k	5 6 69 54½ 44 43½	Arcaro E	123wb	2.95e	90-11	Pylades1072½Terrang124½Duc de Fer120½	Mild late rally	7
27Feb57- 7SA	fst	7f	:22 :444 1:091 1:22	3↑ C J Fitzgerald H 22k	1 10 1012 85¾ 78¼ 67¼	Arcaro E	126wb	3.60	86-14	Duc de Fer1201¾Travertine115noTerrang126½	No mishap	10
5Jan57- 7SA	gd	1 1/16	:232 :47 1:111 1:421	4↑ San Pasqual H 27k	5 6 67¾ 66½ 55 33	Arcaro E	126wb	*2.05	90-14	BattleDance110nkHoneysAlibi1202¾Porterhous1262¼	Rallied	7
26Dec56- 7SA	fst	6f	:224 :45 1:101	3↑ Palos Verdes H 22k	8 8 88½ 85¾ 34 11¼	Arcaro E	125wb	*2.50	94-18	Porterhouse1251¼JohniMk119noScnt1191¾	Under mild urging	8
8Oct56- 7Bel	fst	7f	:224 :462 1:11 1:233	2↑ Vosburgh H 24k	6 12 1210 97¼ 87½ 64¾	Valenzuela I	123wb	19.15	87-16	SummerTan1241½JoeJones121½LeBeauPrince121nk	Late rally	15
15Sep56- 7Bel	fst	1	:224 :453 1:094 1:351	3↑ Sysonby H 28k	2 4 44 51¼ 811 99¼	Valenzuela A	117wb	3.90	89-08	Jet Action114hdAdmiral Vee1091Midafternoon116nk	Tired	10
3Sep56- 7Bel	fst	6f-WC	:22 :442 1:09	2↑ Fall Highweight H 30k	4 16 1411 126¾ 84	Westrope J	137wb	5.30	90-09	Impromptu127½Decimal122nkGayWarrior1141½	Closed ground	16
28Jly56- 8AP	fm	1 3/16 Ⓣ	:463 1:103 1:361 1:541	3↑ Arlington H 154k	1 9 1016 1011 1011 99¼	Erb D	118wb	*2.70e	93-06	Mister Gus1181Summer Tan1221¼Sir Tribal1221	No mishap	12
14Jly56- 8Hol	fst	1¼	:452 1:09 1:331 1:583	3↑ Hol Gold Cup H 162k	2 4 57½ 47 38 33¼	Westrope J	119wb	*5.45e	102-05	Swaps1302MisterGus1171¼Porterhous1192¼	Finished stoutly	7
7Jly56- 7Hol	fst	6f	:222 :451 :571 1:09	3↑ Lakes &Flowers H 27k	7 5 63¼ 53½ 33 11½	Valenzuela I	124wb	*1.70	99-13	Portrhous1241½Scnt120hdMoolhBux1202¼	Driving,drew clear	7
9Jun56- 7Hol	fst	1	:222 :451 1:084 1:331	3↑ Argonaut H 52k	4 4 43 46½ 48 37¼	Valenzuela I	119wb	9.95	101-07	Swaps1281¼BobbyBrocato1236Porterhous1192¾	Finished well	6
26May56- 7Hol	fst	1 1/16	:23 :453 1:092 1:404	3↑ Californian 109k	4 3 34½ 33½ 23 1hd	Valenzuela I	118wb	13.35e	98-11	Porterhous118hdSwps1275MstrGus1181¾	Up in final strides	6
11May56- 7Hol	fst	6f	:22 :444 :57 1:091	3↑ Hol Premiere H 28k	5 11 84 64¾ 53¾ 2½	Longden J	118wb	*2.15e	97-10	Cyclotron112½Porterhouse1181OnTonTony1121¼	Gaining fast	12
7Mar56- 7SA	fst	1 1/16	:224 :46 1:102 1:43	3↑ S Barbara H 27k	4 6 44½ 52½ 32 1¾	Arcaro E	116wb	2.10	89-17	Porterhouse116¾Colonel Mack113½Cyclotron1097	Drew clear	6
29Feb56- 7SA	fst	7f	:221 :444 1:092 1:222	3↑ C J Fitzgerald H 23k	2 9 94½ 115¾ 58½ 33½	Arcaro E	124wb	*2.55	87-14	ColonelMack1131½Cyclotron1122Porterhous124nk	Late rally	11
11Feb56- 7SA	fst	1⅛	:47 1:111 1:363 1:49	3↑ San Antonio H 59k	11 10 1012 911 812 77½	Arcaro E	117wb	4.75e	88-16	MisterGus120nkHoneysAlibi116noBobbyBrocato1246½	Outrun	13
1Feb56- 7SA	fst	7f	:222 :45 1:102 1:224	3↑ San Carlos H 23k	6 3 54¾ 53¾ 42¼ 11	Arcaro E	119wb	*1.80	89-17	Porterhouse1191Karm1102¼HckoryStck109hd	Just up,driving	10
10Jan56- 7SA	fst	6f	:223 :453 1:101	4↑ Alw 7500	3 8 76 65¼ 53¾ 1nk	Arcaro E	124wb	3.05	94-12	Porterhouse124nkDuece Admiral1081¼Steven Mc1131	Just up	8
26Dec55- 7SA	sl	6f	:222 :454 1:104	3↑ Palos Verdes H 23k	3 8 53¾ 68 89¾ 1214	Arcaro E	120 w	6.65	77-15	History Book1131Karim1155Hour Regards1112	Stopped badly	12
16Jly55- 7Hol	fst	1¼	:452 1:092 1:341 1:593	3↑ Hol Gold Cup H 137k	4 3 34 55 611 613	Neves R	122wb	2.50e	88-06	Rejected118noAlidon116¾Determine1264	Done early	6
4Jly55- 8Hol	fst	1⅛	:463 1:10 1:342 1:463	3↑ American H 53k	3 2 21½ 42½ 53 43	Neves R	114wb	1.50e	104-06	Alidon116noMisterGus1141¼Rejectd1181¾	Lacked late rally	6

18Jun55- 7Hol fst 7f :214 :44 1:082 1:211 3↑ Lakes &Flowers H 28k 4 7 43½ 35 23 11¾ Longden J 116wb 3.40 94-09 Porterhouse1161¾Berseem126noAlidon119no Saved ground 10
28May55- 7Hol fst 1 :22 :443 1:093 1:344 3↑ Argonaut H 55k 4 5 58¼ 52¼ 65½ 64¾ Neves R 114wb 3.55e 96-09 Alidon113¾Mister Gus116nkRejected118¾ Gave way 9
21May55- 6Hol fst 7f :222 :443 1:081 1:20 3↑ Handicap 15000 1 3 2½ 32 23 24½ Valenzuela I 115wb 7.35 101-06 ElDrag1154½Porterhouse115hdDetermine1283¾ No late speed 7
13May55- 7Hol fst 6f :22 :444 1:09 3↑ Hol Premiere H 28k 4 7 62¼ 51½ 33 32¾ Neves R 119wb 5.70 97-11 El Drag1122¼Berseem128½Porterhouse1191 Closed ground 9
13Apr55- 7GG fst 6f :223 :452 1:092 3↑ Handicap 5000 4 3 22 22 23 32¼ Longden J 118wb *1.50 92-14 Scent1111¼Poona II1231Porterhouse1181¾ Held on well 5
9Mar55- 7SA fst 1 1/16 :233 :454 1:10 1:42 3↑ S Barbara H 28k 1 10 109 109 79 69½ Boland W 120wb 3.95 84-12 Berseem1201½Joe Jones1174Dawn Lark107½ Dull effort 10
26Feb55- 7SA gd 1¼ :46 1:102 1:363 2:03 3↑ S Anita H 149k 6 2 1hd 1hd 21 33¼ Boland W 112wb 19.80e 82-19 PoonaII1132½JoeJones117¾Porterhouse1121¼ Held on gamely 15
16Feb55- 6SA sly 1 1/16 :233 :472 1:123 1:451 4↑ Alw 7500 2 3 21 2½ 21½ 37½ Boland W 118wb *1.55 70-22 MyChief1124½DoubleReigh1153Porterhouse1183½ Weak rally 7
2Feb55- 7SA fst 7f :222 :452 1:101 1:222 3↑ San Carlos H 23k 4 4 44½ 56 31½ 1¾ Arcaro E 115wb 3.30e 91-16 Porterhouse115¾Imbros1301¾Encono1142 Hard drive 11
25Jan55- 6SA fst 6f :214 :442 1:091 4↑ Alw 5000 7 4 32½ 32 22 2nk Arcaro E 121 w *1.15 99-13 Hour Regards115nkPorterhouse121¾Karim1181½ Game try 8
14Jan55- 6SA fst 6f :22 :443 1:09 4↑ Alw 6000 5 6 31½ 23 21½ 1¾ Arcaro E 114 w *1.00 100-11 Porterhouse114¾Hour Regards1173½Fleet Khal109½ Drew out 12
28Dec54- 7SA fst 6f :22 :442 1:09 3↑ Palos Verdes H 23k 9 9 911 99½ 89 53 Boland W 115 w 13.20 97-08 Imbros128¾Bersm1241¾Hour Regards110no Impeded,bore in 13
27Oct54- 6Jam fst 6f :23 :454 1:114 3↑ Interborough H 30k 9 8 107¼ 1211 1615 1610 Boland W 111 w 21.85 78-23 Laffango116noDark Peter119nkSquared Away120¾ No threat 17
18Oct54- 5Bel fst 1 1/16 :24 :474 1:13 1:443 Alw 5000 2 2 2hd 1hd 1hd 22 Boland W 120 w *.60 86-17 Bill Cane1152Porterhouse1205Dan Giddings1096 Tired 6
11Oct54- 6Bel fst 7f :221 :452 1:11 1:234 2↑ Vosburgh H 25k 7 8 84¼ 75½ 63¼ 42¼ Boland W 112 w 17.15 89-16 JoeJones1162PetBully134nkHyphasis111hd Rallied too late 12
22Sep54- 6Bel gd 6f-WC :224 :461 1:111 2↑ Fall Highweight H 25k 3 10 125¼ 75¼ 64½ 56 Boland W 122 w 8.60 79-21 PetBully1361½DutchLane1171½DarkPeter125½ Lacked a rally 14
10Jly54- 6Mth fst 1 1/16 :231 :461 1:104 1:434 Lamplighter H 25k 11 12 1213 128¾ 127¾ 106¾ Nichols J 122wb 11.40e 89-10 Artismo120nkCoastal Light111nkPelouse105½ Dull effort 12
3Jly54- 6Aqu fst 1¼ :50 1:15 1:40 2:05 Dwyer 57k 4 3 33 45 46½ 412 Boland W 114wb 6.65 70-14 High Gun1261Palm Tree1145Paper Tiger1146 No late foot 5
28Jun54- 5Aqu fst 1 1/16 :24 :481 1:144 1:473 Alw 7500 4 3 43½ 53½ 44 35¾ Boland W 113 w 4.10 70-23 [D]PalmTree1131¾PaperTgr1134Portrhous1132½ No late rally 6
Placed second through disqualification
21Jun54- 6Aqu fst 7f :222 :45 1:102 1:233 Shevlin 31k 2 8 75¾ 44 87¼ 88½ Boland W 116wb *2.05e 83-18 QuickLunch111nkRevolt111½DucdeFr111¾ No apparent mishap 13
12Jun54- 6Bel fst 1½ :49 1:14 2:033 2:304 Belmont 125k 9 2 32½ 33½ 610 917 Boland W 126wb 9.30 67-16 High Gun126nkFisherman1265Limelight1263 Quit badly 13
Geldings not eligible
5Jun54- 6Bel fst 1⅛ :501 1:151 1:40 1:522 Peter Pan H 36k 4 3 31½ 32 64½ 67¼ Boland W 126wb *1.30 70-20 HighGun1163Fisherman1211¾DvngBord1161½ Early foot,tired 7
15May54- 5Bel fst 6f :223 :453 1:111 3↑ Handicap 6070 7 7 54½ 55¾ 43½ 1hd Boland W 114wb *1.40 93-11 Porterhouse114hdHilarious1221¾Caesar Did1131 Just up 9
24Feb54- 5SA fst 6f :214 :443 1:091 Alw 6000 1 6 55 33½ 2hd 13 Boland W 122 w *1.05 99-09 Porterhouse1223Rolyat1113½Musselshell114no Drew clear 8
17Oct53- 6Pim fst 1 1/16 :23 :464 1:104 1:451 Pim Futurity 72k 4 4 37 313 416 524 Boland W 122wb *.40e 60-19 Errard King1228War Doings1226Nirgal Lad1197 Poor start 5
Geldings not eligible
3Oct53- 5Bel fst 6½f-W :221 :451 1:092 1:16 Futurity 117k 14 3 2hd 13 13¼ Boland W 122wb 7.05 92-11 Porterhouse1223¼Artismo122½Best Years1221¼ Easily 14
Geldings not eligible
28Sep53- 5Bel fst 6f-WC :221 :45 1:101 Sp Wt 10000 2 11 43 21½ 1hd Boland W 118wb 9.35 90-10 Porterhouse118hdBy Jeepers1181½Athenian118no Hard drive 13
15Aug53- 4Sar fst 6f :224 :462 1:124 Sar Spl 17k 4 3 31½ 22 11 1½ Guerin E 122 w *1.30 84-20 [D]Porterhouse122½Turn-to1224½Permian1222¼ Bore in 5
Disqualified and placed last
24Jun53- 5Del fst 5½f :214 :46 1:051 ©Christiana 15k 2 5 21½ 23 2½ 11¼ Boland W 125 w 4.75 96-13 Prtrhouse1251¼WarofRoses113noTroyWght1161¼ Drew clear 8
10Jun53- 6Bel fst 5f-WC :222 :451 :574 ©Nat'l Stallion 30k 4 3 22 1hd 1nk Boland W 117wb 5.45 90-11 Porterhouse117nkBest Years122½Catspaw1221 Hard drive 8
Geldings not eligible
2Jun53- 4Bel fst 4½f-W :223 :454 :52 ©Md Sp Wt 14 5 72¾ 1½ 13 Boland W 118 w 3.55f 89-14 Porterhouse1183Affrighted1183First Watch113¾ Drew clear 22
23May53- 4Bel sly 5f-WC :23 :47 1:002 ©Md Sp Wt 7 12 127¾ 1011 75¾ Westrope J 118 w 18.40 71-22 Coreopsis1181½Landscaping118nkBlue Skies118¾ No speed 16

Pucker Up

b. f. 1953, by Olympia (Heliopolis)–Lou Lea, by Bull Lea — **Lifetime record: 32 16 8 4 $304,585**
Own.– Mrs A.L. Rice
Br.– Danada Farm (Ky)
Tr.– J.P. Conway

19Jly58- 6Del fst 1 1/16 :231 :462 1:104 1:441 3↑ ⒻNew Castle 38k 14 3 42½ 44 1313 1413½ Brooks S 126wb 8.50 76-17 Alanesian1123Mlle.Dianne112¾Endin112½ Stopped to a walk 15
10Jly58- 6Del fst 6f :222 :454 1:11 4↑ ⒻAlw 4500 5 6 31 3nk 1hd 1½ Brooks S 121wb 1.50 90-15 PuckerUp121½Bornastar1212½Slx118hd Under a strong drive 6
28Jun58- 7Del fst 6f :221 :45 1:094 4↑ Alw 6000 3 3 12 2hd 22 22½ Brooks S 119wb *1.20 93-13 Besomer1182½Pucker Up1191½Ricci Tavi1241 Went wide late 7
7Jun58- 8Was fst 1 :222 :451 1:10 1:354 3↑ ⒻBeverly H 58k 13 1 11½ 13 2hd 22½ Grant H 122wb *2.10 85-16 Bornastar1212½PuckerUp1221¼Burdett104¾ Clear lead,tired 14
2Jun58- 7Was sl 6f :23 :463 1:113 3↑ ⒻAlw 5000 4 1 11½ 12 2hd 22 Burr C 121wb *.80 85-29 Bornastar1172PuckerUp1216BonnieA.108nk Used up in pace 6
12May58- 7GS fst 6f :222 :454 1:104 4↑ Alw 6000 6 2 1hd 1hd 11½ 12 Grant H 112wb *1.20 90-16 PuckerUp1122Irate1103½SundayPtch107nk Under mild urging 8
5Mar58- 7GP fst 6f :221 :45 1:10 3↑ Armed H 11k 8 4 2hd 1hd 22 53 Erb D 118wb *1.95 92-10 JovialJove114noGrekGm114noAron1142½ Used vying for lead 13
24Feb58- 7Hia fst 6f :221 :452 1:112 4↑ ⒻAlw 7500 5 3 3nk 2½ 1hd 2½ Erb D 118wb *.70 87-14 HappyPrincess115½PuckerUp118¾Scansion1121½ Game effort 8
24Oct57- 6Kee gd 1⅛ :463 1:111 1:361 1:491 3↑ ⒻSpinster 76k 2 2 22 2½ 22 22½ Shoemaker W 123wb *.40e 88-12 Bornastar1232½Pucker Up1231¾Searching1231 No excuse 6
Open to 3-, 4- and 5-year-olds
17Oct57- 0Kee sly *7f 1:272 3↑ ⒻAlw 5000 1 1 16 14 14 11½ Heckmann J 126wb - 91-13 Pucker Up1261½Bornastar1204Beautillion117¾ In hand 4
Special race - Run between 4th and 5th races. No wagering
21Sep57- 7Bel fst 1⅛ :45 1:093 1:36 1:492 3↑ ⒻBeldame H 69k 4 2 22 31½ 21½ 1nk Shoemaker W 125wb *1.90 92-13 PuckerUp125nkPlotter119nkGayLf1041 Wide on turn,just up 16
2Sep57- 8Was fst 1 :222 :45 1:094 1:344 3↑ Wash Park H 117k 8 1 11½ 13 11½ 13 Shoemaker W 111wb 5.10 93-15 Pucker Up1113Find122½Swoon's Son130½ Good lead all way 9
24Jly57- 8AP sl 1 :23 :453 1:103 1:37 3↑ ⒻArl Matron H 57k 13 2 11 15 14 12 Shoemaker W 120wb 1.70 87-18 Pucker Up1202Bornastar1114½Lady Swords1084 Mild urging 13
29Jun57- 7Del fst 1¼ :463 1:11 1:372 2:05 3↑ ⒻDelaware H 164k 1 1 16 12 1½ 2½ Shoemaker W 117wb *3.70 76-22 Princess Turia119½Pucker Up1171Little Pache119nk Gamely 19
6Jun57- 7Hol fst 1 :222 :45 1:091 1:343 3↑ ⒻHandicap 15000 2 1 13 14 16 16 Shoemaker W 122wb *.90 93-13 PuckerUp1226SunnyGal105noTripleJay1162 Speed in reserve 8
21May57- 7Hol fst 6f :221 :444 :563 1:091 3↑ ⒻMilady H 21k 3 2 21½ 21½ 21 2nk Taniguchi G 120wb *.80 98-19 Coverit118nkPucker Up1207Myrtle1071 Very strong finish 6
10May57- 7Hol fst 6f :221 :451 :57 1:084 3↑ ⒻHandicap 12000 6 5 3½ 2½ 2½ 2¾ York R 118wb 2.50e 99-09 MissTodd122¾PuckerUp1186½Beautillion116½ Held on gamely 9
27Mar57- 7GP fst 1 1/16 :232 :464 1:111 1:422 3↑ ⒻSuwannee River H 28k 8 3 1hd 11 31 33¼ Arcaro E 114wb *1.60e 95-12 Estacion1091¾Amort1211½PuckrUp114hd Bore out when urged 9
13Feb57- 7Hia fst 7f :224 :452 1:102 1:231 3↑ ⒻColumbiana H 24k 9 5 11½ 12 2½ 34¼ Atkinson T 119wb *.70e 90-15 Amoret116nkQuenHopful1194PuckrUp119nk Early speed,tired 10
6Feb57- 7Hia fst 6f :214 :45 1:093 4↑ ⒻAlw 7500 6 2 1hd 1hd 12 12½ Atkinson T 109wb 3.60 97-11 PckrUp1092½Amoret1132½SupremJoy112½ Cleared with ease 10
18Jan57- 8Hia fst 6f :222 :454 1:104 4↑ ⒻAlw 10000 6 2 41 31½ 43 74½ Martin RJ 118wb *1.75 86-12 Myrtle'sJet118½Glamour1181¼OlympiaDell118nk Speed,tired 11
12Oct56- 7GS fst 1 1/16 :24 :47 1:102 1:422 ⒻJersey Belle 29k 6 1 13 110 111 112 Anderson P 118wb 6.00 98-12 PuckerUp11812LittlePache115hdPrincessTuria1211 Eased up 8
1Oct56- 7Bel fst 1 :224 :461 1:112 1:37 3↑ ⒻMaskette H 29k 7 3 31½ 21 22 32½ Arcaro E 112wb 5.25 86-15 Searching123½HappyPrincess1072PckrUp112¾ Raced evenly 11
19Sep56- 6Bel fst 6f :222 :46 1:113 3↑ ⒻHandicap 7500 3 3 11½ 13 13 12 Arcaro E 118wb *.90 91-14 PuckerUp1182Tarquilla1162Equableu114no Speed in reserve 11
8Aug56- 7Was fst 7f :214 :441 1:093 1:222 ⒻMisty Isle H 22k 7 1 2½ 2½ 11½ 1hd Erb D 116wb 3.10e 93-11 PuckrUp116hdDoubledogdare1246CandyDsh1192½ Just lasted 9
18Jly56- 6AP fm 5½fⓉ :223 :453 :58 1:042 Alw 6000 1 6 11 2hd 11 1¾• Erb D 113wb 2.00 97-06 [DH]PckrUp113[DH]TobyB.120¾Tommy'sJt1141½ All out to last 7
15Jun56- 6Bel fst 6f :233 :46 1:11 ⒻAlw 4500 6 4 13½ 12 1½ 1½ Arcaro E 119wb *1.30 94-14 PuckerUp119½Recherche115¾Bolette1196 Well rated,driving 7
30May56- 5Bel fst 7f :222 :453 1:104 1:241 ⒻAlw 4000 3 2 12 13 13 11½ Arcaro E 119wb *2.00 89-09 PuckerUp1191½FlyingTrapeze1134½PalaceDancr1141½ Driving 9
18May56- 6Bel fst 6f :223 :461 1:113 ⒻAlw 4000 13 4 1hd 2hd 12 11½ Arcaro E 114wb 2.35 91-13 Pucker Up1141½Flying Trapeze1133½Tweetsie1121 All out 13
10May56- 6Jam fst 6f :23 :463 1:123 ⒻAlw 4000 1 3 2hd 31½ 32½ 34¼ Arcaro E 115wb *1.95 80-21 HideOut116¾EthelWalker1163½PuckerUp1158 Blocked early 8
11Oct55- 5Bel fst 6f-WC :22 :45 1:102 ⒻMd Sp Wt 6 1 12 12½ 17 Guerin E 115wb *1.55 87-13 PuckerUp1157Dupatta115nkStolenHour1152¾ Drew out easily 10
28Sep55- 5Bel sly 6f-WC :224 :46 1:121 ⒻMd Sp Wt 2 5 21 3½ 45¼ Moreno H 115 w 11.15 73-22 Countess Tina115¾Navira1151Tug Boat1153½ Speed,tired 18

Quill

ch. f. 1956, by Princequillo (Prince Rose)–Quick Touch, by Count Fleet — **Lifetime record: 26 14 4 2 $382,041**

Own.– R.N. Webster
Br.– R.N. Webster (Ky)
Tr.– L. Laurin

29Jly61- 6Del	gd	1¼	:46 1:11 1:362 2:022	3↑ ⒻDelaware H 159k	9	8	1011	89¼	714	916	Ussery R	123	b	4.70	74-20	AirmansGuide1213½RoyalNative120nkTrtom1182½	Poor effort	12
22Jly61- 6Del	fst	1 1/16	:231 :47 1:113 1:434	3↑ ⒻNew Castle 38k	11	9	1411	1312	1116	1112	Leonard J	120	b	*2.70	78-21	Airmans Guide1166Tritoma1201¾Mountain Glory1121	Dull	15
8Jly61- 6Aqu	fst	1	:224 :453 1:102 1:354	3↑ ⒻAlw 6500	5	3	51¾	32	2½	1¾	Ussery R	118	b	*1.10	89-13	Quill118¾Rash Statement1184½Stretch Drive1181½	Driving	7
26Jun61- 6Bel	fm	7fⓉ	:232 :47 1:114 1:244	3↑ ⒻAlw 5000	4	7	89	53½	21	1¾	Ussery R	114	b	*2.00	88-14	Quill114¾Shuett106¾Pocosb1151½	Won easily,returned sore	8
14Jun61- 7Bel	fst	7f	:222 :453 1:103 1:233	3↑ ⒻVagrancy H 24k	6	12	65¼	1412	149½	147	Ussery R	123	b	10.25	82-15	Sun Glint116noUndulation116½Refute113hd	Bore out late	14
3Jun61- 6Bel	fst	6f	:222 :454 1:102	4↑ ⒻAlw 10000	8	9	912	913	911	814	Ussery R	123	b	3.05	81-13	Improve1144Refute1143¼Repetitious114nk	Slow start,wide	9
22Aug60- 7Sar	fst	1⅛	:471 1:113 1:374 1:512	3↑ ⒻDiana H 38k	1	3	410	47½	33½	27	Ussery R	128	b	*.55	81-14	Tempted1247Quill1281¾Aesthetic1121	Showed a game effort	5
30Jly60- 6Del	sly	1¼	:461 1:103 1:364 2:022	3↑ ⒻDelaware H 146k	7	4	48½	11½	15	19	Ussery R	125	b	5.90	90-15	Quill1259RoyalNative1291¼GeecheeLou110¾	Drew out easily	8
23Jly60- 6Del	fst	1 1/16	:23 :46 1:102 1:431	3↑ ⒻNew Castle 35k	4	5	47	44½	43½	11¼	Ussery R	120	b	*1.60	95-11	Quill1201¼IndnMd1201¾Tmptd1262¼	Under very strong drive	8
9Jly60- 7Mth	fst	1 1/16	:224 :461 1:11 1:434	3↑ ⒻMolly Pitcher H 28k	6	9	66½	42	43½	24	Ussery R	122	b	3.50	82-17	Royal Native1274Quill1221¾Miss Orestes114½	Held on well	10
2Jly60- 8Mth	fst	1 1/16	:232 :47 1:111 1:434	4↑ Alw 6000	2	2	1½	11	11	13½	Blum W	116	b	*.70	86-15	Quill1163½Ideology1155Alsvider1152	Speed to spare	7
4Jun60- 7Bel	fst	1 1/16	:223 :452 1:102 1:43	3↑ ⒻTop Flight H 56k	2	2	21½	41¾	33	21½	Ycaza M	123	b	3.25	87-15	RoyalNatv1261½Qull123¾BugBrush1202	Showed a game effort	10
16May60- 7Aqu	fst	1	:241 :482 1:134 1:384	4↑ ⒻAlw 7500	8	3	31½	32	1½	13½	Ycaza M	114	b	*.65	82-14	Quill1143½Meticulous1222Starlet Miss1081½	Much the best	8
11Jly59- 6Del	gd	1⅛	:48 1:132 1:383 1:513	ⒻDel Oaks 47k	8	3	44	45½	57	510	Ussery R	119	b	4.20	72-21	Resaca1192SilverSpoon119½IndianMaid1194	Gave way early	9
20Jun59- 6Bel	fst	1¼	:461 1:104 1:363 2:022	ⒻC C A Oaks 91k	7	1	2½	21	22	2½	Bailey PJ	121	b	*.25	87-11	Resaca121½Quill12114Czarina1215	Came again in stretch	8
3Jun59- 7Bel	fst	1⅛	:46 1:103 1:361 1:492	ⒻMother Goose 28k	5	3	33	1hd	13	13½	Bailey PJ	124	b	*.45	89-09	Quill1243½Toluene1181½GeecheeLou112¾	Drew out with ease	8
16May59- 7Bel	fst	1	:231 :463 1:12 1:373	ⒻAcorn 59k	2	5	32½	31	11	16½	Ussery R	121	b	*1.85	86-16	Quill1216½Cobul1211½HopeIsEtrnl121½	Drew away with ease	12
7May59- 7Jam	fst	1 1/16	:241 :482 1:13 1:444	ⒻAlw 1000	5	5	44½	44½	44	44¾	Bailey PJ	120	b	1.60	81-17	ShirleyJones114noCobul114¾HighBid1144	Made even effort	7
18Oct58- 7GS	fst	1 1/16	:224 :463 1:114 1:451	ⒻGardenia 135k	7	7	59	23	1hd	1½	Bailey PJ	119	wb	2.20	84-17	Quill119½Resaca1141¼Ruwenzori119hd	Under light urging	12
11Oct58- 6GS	fst	1	:231 :464 1:131 1:404	ⒻAlw 10000	3	6	32½	32	1½	11½	Bailey PJ	121	wb	*.70	78-23	Quill1211½[D]Canario1141¼JmsonWd114¾	Kept to mild urging	10
13Sep58- 6Bel	fst	6f-WC	:221 :451 1:10	ⒻMatron 64k	9	7		51¾	11½	13¾	Bailey PJ	119	wb	3.60	89-15	Quill1193¾RichTradition1192Lvlx1192¾	Drew out with ease	9
5Sep58- 6Bel	fst	6f-WC	:224 :453 1:092	ⒻAlw 5000	2	8		87	43	11	Bailey PJ	111	wb	11.35	92-13	Quill1111MommyDear1191½Recit1124½	Under strong handling	11
22Aug58- 6Sar	fst	6f	:231 :47 1:124	ⒻSpinaway 43k	7	8	99	87½	53½	33½	Anderson P	119	wb	11.00	80-21	RichTradition1191½Recite1192Quill1191¾	Best stride late	10
4Aug58- 6Sar	fst	5½f	:23 :473 1:004 1:073	ⒻSchuylerville 18k	9	7	54½	76	44½	33¼	Arcaro E	116	wb	*1.70	76-24	RichTradition1162LadyBeGood1221¼Quill1161¼	Forced wide	11
22Jly58- 4Jam	fst	5½f	:23 :471 :59 1:051	ⒻAlw 4200	3	4	32	31½	1½	11¼	Arcaro E	116	wb	2.25	92-14	Quill1161¼SitThisOut1163JimsonWeed119¾	Going away	6
11Jly58- 3Jam	fst	5½f	:231 :471 :591 1:053	ⒻMd Sp Wt	9	4	2½	2½	2½	11½	Raia J	115	wb	58.20	90-15	Quill1151½CalaisDover1159AtS1153	Drew clear under drive	9

Real Delight

b. f. 1949, by Bull Lea (Bull Dog)–Blue Delight, by Blue Larkspur — **Lifetime record: 15 12 1 0 $261,822**

Own.– Calumet Farm
Br.– Calumet Farm (Ky)
Tr.– B.A. Jones

15Aug53- 8Was	fst	1⅛Ⓣ	:482 1:12 1:364 1:493	3↑ Grassland H 28k	11	4	52¼	56¼	1019	1113	Arcaro E	122	w	*1.20	84-13	Stan110½Brush Burn1143Vantage115no	Wide,quit	11
29Jly53- 7AP	fst	1	:23 :453 1:091 1:352	3↑ ⒻArl Matron H 43k	5	5	32½	32½	1hd	11¾	Arcaro E	124	w	*.90	95-13	RealDelight1241¾Fulvous107nkBellaFigura1192	Ridden out	7
18Jly53- 6AP	fst	5½fⓉ	:222 :46 :58 1:043	4↑ Alw 4500	5	9	79½	78½	511	47¾	Arcaro E	114	w	*1.20	90-02	Le Monde112hdJo Pilot1114½Recover1093¼	Off slowly	9
13Sep52- 7Aqu	fst	1⅛	:474 1:121 1:38 1:51	3↑ ⒻBeldame H (Div 2) 62k	8	5	54	43	22	1¾	Arcaro E	126	w	*.60	90-17	Real Delight126¾Marta117½La Corredora1123½	Driving,wide	9
2Aug52- 7Was	fst	1	:221 :452 1:093 1:344	3↑ ⒻBeverly H 27k	6	6	63	42½	21	1hd	Arcaro E	129	w	*.80	95-07	Real Delight129hdAesthete1052Sickle's Image1212	Driving	9
16Jly52- 7AP	fst	1	:23 :454 1:094 1:353	3↑ ⒻModesty H 46k	12	9	85¼	55	2½	1hd	Arcaro E	126	w	*.70	94-08	RealDelight126hdSickle'sImage1173½DickieSu1111½	Just up	12
5Jly52- 7AP	fst	1	:222 :452 1:103 1:363	ⒻArl Matron 52k	7	6	65¼	41½	12	12½	Arcaro E	126	w	*.40	89-13	RealDelight1262½BellaFigura1122½WhirlaLea1133	In hand	8
16Jun52- 6AP	fst	6f	:222 :45 1:101	ⒻCleopatra 17k	7	6	54½	33	22	1¾	Arcaro E	121	w	*.40	95-12	RealDelight121¾Recover1152½BellaFigura1123½	Ridden out	10
24May52- 6Bel	fst	1⅜	:483 1:131 1:384 2:174	ⒻC C A Oaks 63k	4	3	11	12	14	12½	Arcaro E	121	w	*.30	82-17	Real Delight1212½Lily White1211½Sufie1214	Easily	10
10May52- 6Pim	fst	1⅛	:492 1:14 1:391 1:514	ⒻBlack-Eyed Susan 24k	3	1	1½	13	14	14½	Arcaro E	121	w	*.30	95-16	RealDelight1214½Dinewisely121hdParadingLady1216	Easily	5
2May52- 7CD	fst	1 1/16	:232 :473 1:13 1:452	ⒻKy Oaks 31k	5	6	52¾	32½	1½	11¾	Arcaro E	121	w	*.50	91-13	Real Delight1211¾Whirla Lea116¾Big Mo1163	In hand	15
23Apr52- 5Kee	fst	6½f	:223 :454 1:101 1:164	Alw 3000	8	2	52	42	33½	2hd	Devine D	110	w	*.70	99-06	WhiteSkies117hdRealDelight1104½ShagTails117¾	Late speed	10
12Apr52- 7Kee	fst	6f	:231 :464 1:114	ⒻAshland (Div 2) 14k	6	1	22	2½	1½	15	Arcaro E	114	w	*.40	93-12	Real Delight1145Ave1153Level Sands1153	Easily,drew out	7
	Previously trained by H.A .Jones																	
22Feb52- 4SA	fst	1	:232 :471 1:12 1:374	ⒻOClm 7500	2	1	11½	12	14	16	Arcaro E	117	w	*.50	87-15	RealDelight1176NuncaNunca117hdAbbeyGirl1135	Much best	8
8Feb52- 2SA	fst	7f	:223 :454 1:12 1:25	ⒻOMd 7500	9	2	1½	12	14	16	Brooks S	119	w	*2.20	80-16	Real Delight1196Blue Norka1192½Sea Cap1191	Easily best	12

Rose Jet

br. f. 1949, by Jet Pilot (Blenheim II)–Knots of Roses, by War Admiral — **Lifetime record: 11 5 1 2 $132,485**

Own.– Maine Chance Farm
Br.– Maine Chance Farm (Ky)
Tr.– J.H. Hayes

8Aug52- 7Sar	fst	6f	:23 :471 1:124	ⒻAlw 4000	7	2	21	1hd	31½	43½	Woodhouse H	116	w	4.35	80-23	Hadassah111hdNilufer1193Knot Hole109½	Gave way	9
8Jly52- 6Aqu	fst	6f	:224 :453 1:104	3↑ ⒻHandicap 7550	6	4	53	610	612	616	Shuk N	113	w	6.70	82-15	Sunshine Nell114nkJacodema1222½Boot All1143	Outrun	6
	Previously trained by W. Booth																	
12Nov51- 7Pim	fst	1 1/16	:233 :472 1:124 1:464	ⒻMarguerite 36k	1	1	1½	1hd	1hd	35¼	Woodhouse H	116	w	*.40	71-19	No Score1162¼Knot Hole1193Rose Jet116¾	Gave way	7
31Oct51- 6Jam	fst	1 1/16	:241 :481 1:13 1:461	ⒻDemoiselle 50k	7	1	12	11½	1hd	1¾	Woodhouse H	116	w	*1.80	81-19	Rose Jet116¾Papoose1193½No Score1192	Driving	8
13Oct51- 6Lrl	fst	1 1/16	:23 :48 1:141 1:47	ⒻSelima 50k	2	1	1hd	11½	1hd	1hd	Guerin E	115	w	*1.40	79-22	Rose Jet115hdFaberose1194½Knot Hole119nk	All out	8
29Sep51- 4Bel	fst	6f-WC	:223 :453 1:111	ⒻMatron 56k	14	4		21	1½	12½	Woodhouse H	119	w	9.15e	85-15	Rose Jet1192½Knot Hole119no[DH]Landmark119hd	Drew out	17
5Sep51- 6Aqu	fst	6f	:224 :462 1:123	ⒻAstarita 13k	9	2	2hd	31½	2hd	31½	Guerin E	119	w	2.30	87-17	Place Card111½Landmark1101Rose Jet1192	Faltered	13
22Aug51- 6Sar	my	6f	:224 :463 1:131	ⒻSpinaway 21k	2	3	2hd	1hd	11	2nk	Guerin E	119	w	*1.05	82-16	Blue Case119nkRose Jet1192Recess1151	Faltered	7
15Aug51- 6Sar	fst	5½f	:224 :461 :593 1:061	ⒻSchuylerville 11k	1	1	1½	1½	11	13	Guerin E	115	w	9.25	86-18	Rose Jet1153Star-Enfin122noLandmark113hd	Going away	12
9Aug51- 6Sar	gd	5½f	:23 :47 1:002 1:072	ⒻAlw 3500	5	6	73¾	53¼	62¾	63¼	Atkinson T	110	w	2.50	77-18	Level Sands1101¼Strings105hdStar Delight113hd	No menace	8
	Previously trained by M. Parke																	
18Jly51- 5Jam	fst	5f	:23 :461 :594	ⒻMd Sp Wt	10	4	11	11	11½	11½	Guerin E	116	w	8.15	91-16	RoseJet1161½GunMoll1163½DustyDarlin1161½	Driving,wide	10

Round Table

b. c. 1954, by Princequillo (Prince Rose)–Knight's Daughter, by Sir Cosmo **Lifetime record: 66 43 8 5 $1,749,869**

Own.– Kerr Stable
Br.– Claiborne Farm (Ky)
Tr.– W. Molter

31Oct59- 7Aqu	fst	2	:463 2:284 2:55 3:221	3↑	J C Gold Cup 110k	1	2	24	2½	36	27	Bailey PJ	124	b	1.70	- -	Sword Dancr1197RoundTable1241¼Tudor Era1242¼	No match	8
10Oct59- 7Aqu	fst	1⅝	:491 1:392 2:041 2:423	3↑	Manhattan H 58k	4	4	41½	31½	1hd	11	Shoemaker W	132	b	*1.55	- -	RoundTable1321BaldEagle1221½Coloneast1122	Brisk urging	11
26Sep59- 7Aqu	fst	1¼	:491 1:141 1:40 2:042	3↑	Woodward 109k	3	2	2½	2hd	31½	31¾	Shoemaker W	126	b	*.70	- -	SwordDancer120hdHillsdale1261¾RoundTable1265	No excuse	4
19Sep59- 7Atl	fm	1 3/16Ⓣ	:472 1:114 1:363 1:551	3↑	U Nations H 100k	6	2	23	2½	11	11¼	Shoemaker W	136	b	*.80	97-03	RoundTable1361¼Noureddin1173½Li'lFella1201½	Mild urging	10
7Sep59- 8AP	fst	1⅛	:47 1:103 1:35 1:471	3↑	Wash Park H 122k	2	5	56¾	43½	13	16½	Shoemaker W	132	b	*.70	106-04	RoundTable1326½Dunce114¾BelluChf112hd	Under mild urging	6
22Aug59- 8AP	fm	1 3/16Ⓣ	:463 1:102 1:352 1:532	3↑	Arlington H 125k	1	3	34	11	12½	1hd	Shoemaker W	132	b	*.80e	104-02	RndTable132hdManassas112nkNoureddin1092	Strong urging	9
15Aug59- 4AP	sf	1⅛Ⓣ	:484 1:132 1:392 1:514	3↑	Handicap 10000	5	2	21½	21	2hd	1nk	Shoemaker W	132	b	*.80	83-17	RndTable132nkTudorEra1151¾TerraFirma1101½	Hand ridden	5
8Aug59- 8AP	sl	1	:23 :46 1:112 1:37	3↑	Equipoise Mile H 56k	1	7	66¼	68½	36	35	Shoemaker W	132	b	*.90	80-23	BetterBee1151BelleauChief1144RoundTable1322¼	Slow start	10
4Jly59- 8Was	fm	1⅛Ⓣ	:47 1:103 1:35 1:471	3↑	Stars & Stripes H 85k	4	2	22	22	12	13¼	Shoemaker W	132	b	*.70	107-00	RndTable1323¼Noureddn110nkTudorEr117½	Scored cleverly	9
25Jun59- 0Was	fm	1 1/16Ⓣ	:242 :473 1:12 1:423	4↑	Exhibition 4k	3	1	16	110	110	110	Brooks S		b	-	97-07	Round Table010On the Job01Martini II03¼	Speed to spare	4
	Special exhibition purse run between 3rd and 4th races. No weights assigned. No wagering																		
13Jun59- 8Was	fst	1	:222 :444 1:091 1:332	3↑	Citation H 56k	2	4	44	41¼	2hd	1nk	Brooks S	130	b	*.90	100-06	RoundTable130nkEtonian1043¼Charli'sSong1122¼	Bore in,up	11
23Feb59- 7SA	sf	1½Ⓣ	:474 1:132 2:062 2:322	3↑	Wash Birthday H 60k	9	5	2½	97¼	1524	1630	Shoemaker W	134	b	*.50e	35-35	Hakuchikar109nkAnsdo1103¾Aorng1071¼	Cut front left heel	16
24Jan59- 7SA	fm	1¼Ⓣ	:453 1:094 1:334 1:582	3↑	San Marcos H 28k	5	1	12½	12	15	15	Shoemaker W	132	b	*.55e	102-00	RndTable1325EddieSchmidt1161AndrewAln115¾	Won in hand	8
3Jan59- 7SA	fst	7f	:224 :45 1:092 1:214	3↑	San Carlos H 56k	4	5	31	2hd	2½	2hd	Shoemaker W	132	b	*1.80	94-12	Hillsdale115hdRoundTable1322¼EddiSchmdt112¾	Closed fast	10
11Oct58- 8Haw	fst	1¼	:463 1:102 1:352 1:594	3↑	Haw Gold Cup H 123k	6	2	21¼	12	12	12¼	Shoemaker W	126	wb	*.70	102-02	RndTable1262¼Swoon'sSon1232Ekb113nk	Good lead in hand	6
27Sep58- 7Bel	sly	1¼	:464 1:104 1:353 2:01	3↑	Woodward 111k	1	1	2hd	43½	59½	517	Arcaro E	126	wb	*.80	78-13	Clem126½Nadir1202Reneged1269	Had speed 6f,tired	7
13Sep58- 7Atl	fm	1 3/16Ⓣ	:472 1:112 1:362 1:543	3↑	U Nations H 100k	2	4	54	22	21	2½	Valenzuela I	130	wb	*.60	105-00	Clem113½Round Table1303Combustion II115¾	No excuse	12
8Sep58- 7Atl	fm	1 1/16Ⓣ	:231 :461 1:112 1:433	3↑	Alw 5000	4	3	33	21½	1hd	12	Shoemaker W	128	wb	*.30	95-05	RoundTabl1282St.Vncnt113nkRfty115hd	Eased final strides	7
1Sep58- 8AP	fst	1	:223 :451 1:091 1:34	3↑	Was Park H 139k	3	8	74¾	44½	34	23¼	Shoemaker W	131	wb	*2.00e	99-02	Clem1103¼Round Table131noNadir1146	Rallying strongly	9
23Aug58- 8AP	fm	1 3/16Ⓣ	:47 1:11 1:36 1:542	3↑	Arlington H 85k	3	4	43	2hd	1hd	12¼	Shoemaker W	130	wb	*.90	99-09	RoundTable1302¼Clem109¾St.Vincent1111½	Drew away easily	8
9Aug58- 8AP	fst	1	:24 :463 1:101 1:344	3↑	Equipoise Mile H 133k	1	8	87	87¼	88½	54	Shoemaker W	131	wb	*.90	94-11	Swoon'sSon129½Bardstown122½IndianCrk107½	In close early	10
19Jly58- 8AP	fm	1⅛Ⓣ	:481 1:12 1:363 1:482	3↑	Laurance Armour H 87k	1	3	42½	41½	21½	1no	Hartack W	130	wb	*.70e	100-07	RndTable130noClem1103¼HoopBnd1182	Blocked off,just up	10
12Jly58- 8AP	fst	1⅛	:47 1:104 1:354 1:483	3↑	W Wright Mem H 85k	4	5	52¼	1hd	12	2hd	Longden J	130	wb	*.30	99-10	Bernburgoo109hdRoundTable1302¼ShnPc1085	Good lead,tired	8
28Jun58- 8Was	fm	1 3/16Ⓣ	:464 1:104 1:362 1:544	3↑	Arch Ward H 56k	3	3	21½	21	11½	12½	Shoemaker W	129	wb	*.30e	99-01	RoundTable1292½TallChiefII1152¼Aysha1062¼	Scored easily	9
20Jun58- 0Was	fm	1 1/16Ⓣ	:243 :49 1:141 1:464	3↑	Alw 6000	3	3	33	2hd	11½	12	Valenzuela I	122	wb	-	76-31	Round Table1222Bernburgoo1143Black Patch114¾	Easily	5
	Special event run between 3rd and 4th races. No wagering																		
7Jun58- 7Hol	fst	1	:231 :461 1:101 1:343	3↑	Argonaut H 53k	2	5	55½	33	32	1no	Shoemaker W	132	wb	*.70	93-24	Round Table132noHow Now1165¾Seaneen1203	Up in time	6
24May58- 7Hol	fst	1 1/16	:233 :47 1:104 1:41	3↑	Californian 108k	1	3	34½	32	23	24¼	Shoemaker W	130	wb	*.15	86-14	Seaneen1094¼RoundTable1303Terrng1154½	Failed to respond	5
11May58-10AC	gd	1 1/16	:23 :46 1:112 1:411	3↑	Caliente H 51k	2	3	43½	2hd	13½	19¼	Shoemaker W	126	w	*.10	105-15	RoundTable1269¼WarMarshall1051LikeMagic108¾	Easy score	10
22Mar58- 7GP	fst	1¼	:471 1:11 1:352 1:594	3↑	Gulf Park H 110k	4	3	37½	22	1½	14	Shoemaker W	130	wb	*.20	100-12	RoundTable1304Meeting111nkOligrchy1112	Speed in reserve	6
14Mar58- 7GP	fst	1 1/16	:232 :462 1:103 1:413	4↑	Alw 10000	4	3	35	21½	1½	13½	Harmatz W	128	wb	*.25	102-11	RoundTable1283½Meeting11111Bureaucracy1092½	Easily best	6
1Mar58- 7SA	fst	1¼	:452 1:093 1:343 1:594	3↑	S Anita H 135k	9	3	42	2hd	1½	12½	Shoemaker W	130	wb	*.15	101-09	RoundTable1302½Terrang1193½Porterhous1202	Under a drive	9
15Feb58- 7SA	fst	1⅛	:462 1:101 1:343 1:464	3↑	San Antonio H 56k	3	6	42½	1hd	12	13½	Shoemaker W	130	wb	*.45	103-11	Round Table1303½Mystic Eye1081½Promised Land116½	Easily	9
25Jan58- 7SA	fst	1¼	:472 1:113 1:362 2:014		S Anita Maturity 156k	5	1	13	11½	13	14½	Harmatz W	126	wb	*.20	91-18	Rnd Table1264½Seaneen117¾Promised Land1252¾	Easing up	6
11Jan58- 7SA	fst	1 1/16	:24 :471 1:111 1:421		San Fernando 27k	3	1	13	14	16	14¼	Shoemaker W	130	wb	*.25	93-13	RndTable1304¼TheSearcher114½Seaneen124hd	Eased at end	6
28Dec57- 7SA	fst	7f	:231 :454 1:094 1:22		Malibu Sequet 28k	4	6	53	31½	1½	1hd	Shoemaker W	130	wb	*.15e	93-11	RoundTable130hdSeaneen1143¼MystcEy122nk	Brisk hand ride	8
9Nov57- 7GS	gd	1¼	:471 1:111 1:364 2:013	3↑	Trenton H 82k	2	2	28	33½	35	310¾	Harmatz W	124	wb	1.70	86-14	BoldRuler1222¼GallantMan1248½RoundTable124	Tired badly	3
1Nov57- 0GS	sly	1 70	:23 :472 1:123 1:413		Alw 6000	1	2	21½	1½	15	18	Shoemaker W	126	wb	-	89-16	RoundTble1268CommdreCurt11111HoosierHony108	Breezing	3
	Special race run between the 4th and 5th races. No wagering																		
12Oct57- 8Haw	fst	1¼	:461 1:103 1:351 2:001	3↑	Haw Gold Cup H 126k	1	2	21½	2hd	1hd	13	Harmatz W	121	wb	*.70	102-08	RndTbl1213Swoon'sSon1282½Fnd1192½	Drew clear with ease	6
4Oct57- 0Haw	fst	1 1/16	:232 :472 1:114 1:434		Alw 5000	2	1	11½	13	14	17	Shoemaker W	126	wb	-	93-18	Round Table1267Hundred Grand1116Mr. Donmar1111½	Easily	4
	Special race run between the 8th and 9th races. No wagering																		
14Sep57- 7Atl	fm	1 3/16Ⓣ	:473 1:12 1:372 1:561	3↑	U Nations H 100k	11	4	1hd	2hd	1hd	1no	Shoemaker W	118	wb	*.70	98-02	RoundTable118noTudorEra1122Find1222	Stumbled st.,gamely	11
31Aug57- 8Was	fm	1 3/16Ⓣ	:473 1:114 1:37 1:55		American Derby 145k	8	1	11½	13	13	14	Shoemaker W	126	wb	*1.00	98-12	Round Table1264Iron Liege1263½Ekaba1202	Very easy score	8
20Aug57- 0Was	fm	1 1/16Ⓣ	:25 :49 1:13 1:433		Alw 5000	4	1	2½	21½	21	11¼	Shoemaker W	124	wb	-	92-08	RoundTable1241¼Ekaba113.52¼MartiniII11215	An easy score	4
	Exhibition race run before 1st race. No wagering																		
20Jly57- 7Hol	fst	1¼	:454 1:094 1:344 2:003		Westerner 115k	8	5	31	13	15	12	Shoemaker W	129	wb	*.15	90-12	RoundTable1292Irisher110noJoePrice1187	Eased at the end	8
13Jly57- 7Hol	fst	1¼	:452 1:091 1:334 1:583	3↑	Hol Gold Cup H 162k	8	4	2hd	11½	14	13¼	Shoemaker W	109	wb	*1.40	100-15	Round Table1093¼Porterhouse1192Find1187	Drew out	11
6Jly57- 7Hol	fst	1⅛	:461 1:102 1:351 1:474		Cinema H 47k	1	2	1½	1hd	14	14	Shoemaker W	130	wb	*.20	95-14	RoundTable1304JoePrice1142¾Seanen1092¾	Speed in reserve	7
15Jun57- 7Hol	fst	1 1/16	:231 :46 1:10 1:41		El Dorado H 37k	5	3	21	1½	14	17	Taniguchi G	126	wb	*.25	90-16	Round Table1267Joe Price1154Playtown107hd	Easy score	6
30May57- 7Hol	fst	1	:222 :452 1:093 1:342		©Will Rogers 28k	9	1	42½	2hd	13	13½	Neves R	122	wb	*.45	94-11	RoundTable1223½JoePrice1182¾Mqult1111¼	Driving,bore out	9
25May57- 7Hol	fst	1 1/16	:222 :451 1:093 1:402	3↑	Californian 116k	4	4	43½	2hd	2½	21½	Neves R	105	wb	2.85	91-20	SocialClmbr1191½RoundTbl1054½Fnd119nk	Led between calls	12
4May57- 7CD	fst	1¼	:47 1:112 1:364 2:021		Ky Derby 152k	3	4	43½	42	41	32¾	Neves R	126	wb	3.60	93-12	IronLiege126noGallantMan1262¾RoundTable1263	Held well	9
25Apr57- 6Kee	fst	1⅛	:48 1:11 1:343 1:472		Blue Grass 31k	1	1	11½	11½	12½	16	Neves R	126	wb	*1.00	108-02	Round Table1266One-Eyed King1212Manteau1211¼	Much best	6
6Apr57- 8BM	fst	1 1/16	:224 :462 1:102 1:413		BM Derby 52k	3	2	12	11	13	14½	Neves R	122	wb	1.80	96-13	Round Table1224½Swirling Abbey1226Irisher1221¼	Easily	6
11Mar57- 7SA	hy	1 1/16	:241 :484 1:144 1:491		San Bernardino H 28k	9	2	21½	21½	22	50½	Longden J	122	wb	*.65e	49-34	LightningJack112¾MysticEye1113¼RoyalHeir1151	Faltered	9
2Mar57- 7SA	sl	1⅛	:474 1:132 1:414 1:541		S Anita Derby 98k	11	3	33½	22	1hd	3hd	Longden J	118	wb	*1.30e	70-30	SirWilliam118hdSwirlingAbbey118noRoundTabl1182½	Ran out	13
	Previously trained by M. Jolley																		
16Feb57- 8Hia	fst	7f	:224 :451 1:092 1:222		Alw 5000	6	1	14	16	16	16	Brooks S	126	wb	7.05	98-10	Round Table1266Lucky Dip1142½Jet Colonel1235	Much best	9
	Previously owned by Claiborne Farm																		
9Feb57- 5Hia	fst	1 1/16	:232 :47 1:112 1:424		Alw 10000	6	5	64	65¾	68½	611	Brooks S	113	wb	6.45	90-15	IronLiege1142¼Gen.Duke112hdMssl1244	Could not keep pace	7
19Jan57- 7Hia	fst	6f	:221 :451 1:10		©Hibiscus 26k	7	3	3½	118	118	1010	Brooks S	122	w	10.60	85-09	Gallant Man117½Missile1221½King Hairan1221½	Speed,tired	13
3Nov56- 6CD	fst	7f	:232 :464 1:113 1:25		Alw 7500	9	4	127¾	139¾	136¼	87¼	Brooks S	122	w	*1.00	81-14	Charlie'sSong113nkSrPutnm107nkEkb113hd	Wide most of way	14
20Oct56- 6Kee	fst	*7f	1:264		Breeders' Futurity 66k	4	7	75¼	76½	32	1½	Brooks S	122	w	2.50	99-04	RoundTable122½Missile1221Tranquil122¾	Under brisk drive	10
11Oct56- 5Kee	fst	6f	:224 :454 1:101		©Alw 5000	2	1	23	21½	21½	11½	Brooks S	119	w	*.40	99-08	RoundTable1191½DixieDudley1163CardinalSin1161½	Handily	5
6Aug56- 7Was	fst	6f	:222 :452 1:102		George Woolf Mem 18k	6	-	-	-	-	-	Brooks S	120	w	2.10	- -	Smart Phil114hdJet Colonel1175Federal Hill1144		9
	Stumbled leaving gate,lost rider																		
21Jly56- 8AP	sly	6f	:223 :46 1:121		Arl Futurity 140k	3	3	32	44½	410	46½	Brooks S	122	w	6.50	76-30	GreekGame1225JetColonel122¾Etonian117¾	Fell back early	7
4Jly56- 7AP	gd	5½f	:221 :454 :59 1:053		Hyde Park 22k	3	5	45¼	47½	310	25	Brooks S	122	w	2.10	85-19	GreekGame1225RoundTable122nkJetColonel118½	Closed fast	8
28Jun56- 3AP	fst	5f	:222 :454 :583		Alw 3500	1	1	4nk	2hd	11½	12	Brooks S	118	w	*.90	97-11	Round Table1182Jet Colonel1181½Kid Jr.1202	Ridden out	6
25Apr56- 6Kee	fst	*4f	:493		Lafayette 20k	1	1		11	1hd	1½	Brooks S	117	w	3.80	99-02	Round Table117½Jet Colonel117hdChookoss1172	Hard urged	9
14Apr56- 3Kee	sly	*4f	:503		Md Sp Wt	1	1		11	11	12½	Brooks S	118	w	*1.20	94-05	Round Table1182½Pandean1188Yonshu113no	Under mild drive	8
24Feb56- 3Hia	fst	3f	:214 :332		Alw 5000	7	5			43	42	Brooks S	116	w	14.50	- -	Myla111½OlympiaJet119½LuckyMistake1161	Bumped at start	14

Sheilas Reward

b. c. 1947, by Reaping Reward (Sickle)–Smart Sheila, by Jamestown — Lifetime record: 33 13 12 3 $119,020

Own.– Mrs L. Lazare
Br.– Mrs Louis Lazare (Ky)
Tr.– Charles Feltner

Date	Trk	Dist	Fractions	Time	Race	PP	St	1C	2C	Str	Fin	Jockey	Wt	Odds	Sp	Top finishers	Comment	Fld
25Jun52- 6Mth	fst	6f	:223 :46	1:104	3↑ Rumson H 18k	2	7	72½	63½	53¼	43¾	Hanford I	124wb	*1.40	90-16	Northern Star1122½Senator Joe115¾War King105½		7
	Wide into stretch,pulled up lame																	
13Jun52- 6Aqu	fst	6f	:23 :463	1:112	3↑ Handicap 7530	4	3	31	2hd	1½	2no	Gorman D	126wb	*1.10	95-14	Delegate118noSheilas Reward1261¼Heap Big Chief1052		5
	Gave way grudgingly;Previously trained by E. Jacobs																	
29Sep51- 6Bel	fst	1⅛	:464 1:114 1:363	1:49	3↑ New York H 29k	4	1	11	2½	25	47½	Gorman D	119wb	4.20	86-15	Hill Prince1285One Hitter1171Sudan1051½	Weakened	8
24Sep51- 5Bel	fst	1	:232 :461 1:102	1:352	3↑ Alw 5000	2	1	11	1½	2hd	2¾	Gorman D	121wb	1.35	96-16	HillPrince121¾SheilasReward1218OneHitter1211½	Gave way	4
10Sep51- 6Aqu	fst	7f	:222 :451 1:101	1:232	3↑ Bay Shore H 18k	11	6	52½	32	2½	1½	Gorman D	126wb	5.85	95-15	SheilasReward126½Guillotine117¾BrynG.123nk	Driving,wide	12
14Jly51- 6Aqu	fst	1¼	:47 1:112 1:364	2:032	3↑ Brooklyn H 57k	5	1	15	15	11½	21	Gorman D	117wb	15.85	89-12	Palestinian1221SheilasRwrd1171¼CountyDlght1244	Weakened	9
10Jly51- 6Aqu	fst	1 1/16	:24 :473 1:113	1:444	3↑ Alw 7500	5	1	2hd	2½	21	32½	Gorman D	116wb	*1.85	87-13	GreekShip1201¾Palestinian120¾ShelsRwrd116no	Drifted out	6
30Jun51- 6Mth	my	1 1/16	:233 :473 1:123	1:464	3↑ Long Branch H 12k	1	1	12	11½	11½	13	Gorman D	118wb	*.90	83-29	Sheilas Reward1183Chains106½Ferd1181¼	Driving	6
23Jun51- 6Aqu	sly	1 1/16	:234 :47 1:111	1:443	3↑ Queens County H 22k	6	1	14	15	13	12	Scurlock O	113wb	2.60	91-12	Sheilas Reward1132Lights Up1212Piet1223	Driving	7
20Jun51- 6Mth	fst	6f	:22 :443	1:094	4↑ Alw 5000	6	3	1½	13	15	18	Gorman D	124wb	*.90	99-08	Sheilas Reward1248Play Toy115hdThe Pincher1242	Easily	6
16Jun51- 7Mth	gd	6f	:223 :454	1:114	4↑ Alw 5000	6	6	54	41¾	31½	2hd	Fernandez F	124wb	*1.70	89-15	JessLinthicum115hdSheilasRwrd1241T-Mkr1242¼	Just missed	8
14May51- 6Bel	fst	6f-WC	:222 :444	1:092	3↑ Toboggan H 24k	3	8		112	114	94½	Arcaro E	122wb	*2.55	89-06	Hyphasis110noTea-Maker1231Casemate1191	Blocked	14
7May51- 6Jam	fst	6f	:23 :461	1:111	3↑ Jamaica H 17k	4	4	2½	2hd	1hd	31½	Arcaro E	124wb	*1.45	89-15	[D]Tea-Maker121½Piet1241Sheilas Reward1242¼	Weakened	7
	Placed second through disqualification																	
1May51- 6Jam	fst	6f	:23 :462	1:11	3↑ Handicap 5030	1	4	2hd	1hd	2hd	21	Atkinson T	124wb	*.75	91-13	Piet1201Sheilas Reward124hdTea-Maker1216	No excuse	6
25Oct50- 6Jam	gd	6f	:23 :46	1:111	2↑ New Rochelle H 17k	11	9	73¼	51¾	21½	21	Arcaro E	124wb	2.65	90-19	MagicWords1131SheilasRewrd124¾Tea-Mkr1252	Good effort	12
12Oct50- 6Jam	sly	6f	:23 :46	1:12	3↑ Interborough H 17k	2	6	75	75¾	43½	1¾	Arcaro E	120wb	*2.55	87-18	SheilasRwrd120¾MgcWords112½WsconsnBoy109nk	Going away	10
3Oct50- 6GS	fst	6f	:222 :45	1:094	3↑ Alw 5000	3	6	43½	66	33	3¾	Fernandez F	122wb	*.60	98-08	EagleRiver112¾AirAttack116hdShlsRwrd122no	Strong finish	10
25Sep50- 6Bel	fst	7f	:223 :453 1:102	1:23	2↑ Vosburgh H 18k	8	5	61¾	41¾	21½	42	Arcaro E	116wb	*2.20	93-15	Tea-Maker1181¼More Sun106½Piet124nk	Faltered	12
18Sep50- 6Bel	fst	6f-WC	:221 :443	1:084	2↑ Fall Highweight H 25k	11	2		2hd	21	75¼	Combest N	135wb	*2.35	92-06	Arise1332Delegate128nkRoyal Governor129½	Tired	14
13Sep50- 5Aqu	sl	6f	:232 :464	1:114	3↑ Handicap 4k	3	1	21	1½	12	14	Arcaro E	122wb	*.80	93-16	Sheilas Reward1224Scipio1112Jacks Town102hd	Easily	5
5Jly50- 6Jam	fst	6f	:224 :453	1:092	3↑ Fleetwing H 22k	7	5	31½	21	21	1hd	Fernandez F	116wb	4.50	104-06	Sheilas Reward116hdGuillotine1156Capot1281	Just up	9
24Jun50- 6Mth	fst	6f	:222 :45	1:094	Select H 12k	5	5	41¾	41¼	1hd	1¾	Fernandez F	116wb	4.20	99-06	Sheilas Reward116¾Hyphasis1122½Fabricate1123	Going away	7
20Jun50- 6Mth	fst	6f	:222 :453	1:11	Alw 4000	5	4	3nk	12	16	17	Fernandez F	124wb	*.50	93-16	Sheilas Reward1247Call Over1181½East Indies121hd	Easily	8
16Jun50- 6Mth	gd	6f	:22 :444	1:101	Alw 6000	3	5	33	2½	22	21½	Stout J	116wb	*1.70	95-10	Casemate1261½Sheilas Reward1166Tea Deb1211	Drifted wide	9
31May50- 5Bel	fst	6f	:22 :451	1:102	Alw 5000	4	5	43¼	21	21½	2¾	Arcaro E	114wb	*1.05	97-13	Guillotine120¾Sheilas Reward1146Detective1131	No excuse	6
27May50- 5Bel	fst	6f	:221 :452	1:103	Alw 4000	6	6	52¼	4¾	1½	11½	Arcaro E	120wb	*.95	97-11	SheilasReward1201½AdmiralDrake1184½ErlyHth111hd	Handily	7
17May50- 4Bel	fst	7f	:222 :453 1:112	1:25	Alw 4000	3	2	1hd	11½	13	11½	Arcaro E	116wb	*.50	85-17	SheilasReward1161½ThasianHero1164KeepRight111no	Easily	10
8May50- 6Bel	fst	7f	:223 :46 1:114	1:244	Swift 12k	8	3	31½	49½	2hd	22½	Rogers C	126wb	32.90	83-17	Ferd1262½SheilasReward126½AdmiralsPrd126hd	Sharp effort	12
3May50- 4Jam	sly	6f	:232 :472	1:124	©Alw 3500	8	3	2hd	12	15	14	Arcaro E	117wb	*.85	87-22	Sheilas Reward1174Erosion123½Teddies Imp120½	Easily	8
28Apr50- 7Jam	sly	6f	:233 :464	1:114	3↑ Sp Wt 3500	6	6	1½	1½	11	2no	Nichols J	116wb	2.55	92-18	RoyalCastle116noSheilsRwrd1165Promptnss1162	Just missed	7
24Apr50- 5Jam	fst	6f	:23 :461	1:113	Alw 3500	8	5	31	21	21	23½	Nichols J	118wb	7.15	89-15	CurtainRaiser1133½SheilsRwrd1183½CupKng1181	Forced wide	9
	Previously trained by T.H. Heard Jr																	
10Sep49- 6Atl	fst	6f	:231 :462	1:131	Alw 3500	6	2	3nk	21	31	34	J'n WL	120wb	4.20	76-21	ThasianHro1202½Conqurnt1201½ShlsRwrd1202½	Weakened,sore	8
31Aug49- 3Atl	fst	6f	:223 :462	1:143	Md Sp Wt	9	1	14	14	11½	1½	Lewis F	113wb	6.00	73-23	Sheilas Reward113½Invariant1172Bambi Lynne120½	Driving	9

Shipboard

ch. g. 1950, by Battleship (Man o' War)–Sea Borne, by Annapolis — Lifetime record: 41 15 6 4 $151,415

Own.– Montpelier
Br.– Mrs Marion duPont Scott (Ky)
Tr.– R.G. Woolf

Date	Trk	Dist	Type	Time	Race	PP	St	1C	2C	Str	Fin	Jockey	Wt	Odds	Sp	Top finishers	Comment	Fld
6Aug59- 5Sar	fm	*2	S'Chase	4:103	4↑ Beverwyck H 16k	2	6	-	-	-	-	Woolfe RG Jr	152	9.70	--	Frfx1442½Indpndnc1627HghBhn1502	Bad landing at 3rd,fell	6
26Jun59- 5Del	fm	*2½	S'Chase	4:372	4↑ Indian River H 10k	6	7	59	45	-	-	Foot A	153	7.30	--	MugutII14315Goky1332½Drubn141hd	Unseated rider 15th jump	8
12Jun59- 5Del	fm	*2⅛	S'Chase	4:004	4↑ Georgetown H 10k	3	7	419	38	1½	31	Foot A	154	8.20	--	Darubini135noIndependence1631Shipboard1544½	Bore out	7
23May59- 6Pur	fm	*1¾Ⓣ		3:023	3↑ Alw 600	2	2	3½	22½	21	2hd	Land H	149	1.65	--	HighlandLight149hdShipboard1494½CarolinaHlls1498	Missed	4
14May59- 5Bel	sf	*2⅛	S'Chase	4:062	4↑ International H 16k	2	4	616	624	624	626	Foot A	161	6.55	--	BasilBee1514½Independnc162hdChmbourq1407	Jumped poorly	6
5Jun58- 5Bel	fm	*2½	S'Chase	4:44	4↑ Meadow Brook H 13k	1	5	615	615	613	615	Woolfe R Jr	160 w	3.40	--	Ancestor1651½Arywa14712Independnc156nk	Trailed far back	6
27May58- 5Bel	fm	*2⅛	S'Chase	4:043	4↑ International H 11k	4	5	513	-	-	-	Foot A	159wb	*1.50	--	Ancestor162¾Rythminhim14714Pine Shot1432½		6
	Bad landing at 9th,fell																	
21May58- 3Bel	fm	*2⅛	S'Chase	4:151	4↑ Alw 5000	5	5	612	26	-	-	Woolfe RG Jr	158 w	*.85	--	Pine Shot1467Out of Reach143nkBavaria14319		6
	Bad landing at 12th,lost rider																	
16Oct57- 6Bel	fm	*2½	S'Chase	4:422	4↑ Temple Gwathmey H 57k	1	9	31	41½	44	38	Foot A	164wsb	4.05e	--	Neji1737Ancestor1601Shpbord1641½	Showed very good effort	12
8Oct57- 5Bel	sf	*3⅛	S'Chase	6:151	4↑ Grand National H 32k	1	5	519	24	48½	48	Foot A	163 w	2.75	--	Neji1686Independence1501¾His Boots132nk	Made bid,tired	5
19Sep57- 5Bel	fm	*2⅛	S'Chase	4:01	3↑ Broad Hollow H 17k	7	7	46	55½	34	310½	Foot A	162 w	*1.65	--	Independence1488Morpheus1382½Shipboard1623	Lost irons	7
29Aug57- 5Sar	fm	*2½	S'Chase	5:121	4↑ Saratoga H 22k	6	6	56½	33½	23	1nk	Foot A	161 w	2.05	--	Shipboard161nkIndependence14610Ancestor15713	Hard drive	6
15Aug57- 5Sar	fm	*2	S'Chase	4:14	4↑ Beverwyck H 17k	1	5	37	312	210	214	Foot A	163 w	2.10	--	Ancstr15214Shpbrd1633½Morphus14318	Couldn't reach winner	6
28Jun57- 7Del	fm	*2½	S'Chase	4:403	4↑ Indian River H 10k	1	8	624	79	24	23½	Smithwick P	164 w	*3.00e	--	Rhythminhim1423½Shipboard1644½Carafar147½	Game effort	14
14Jun57- 5Del	hd	*2	S'Chase	3:353	4↑ Georgetown H 10k	5	8	814	852	732	736	Foot A	164 w	*1.50	--	Morpheus1393½Carafar1477PineShot1372½	Refused to extend	8
17Oct56- 6Bel	fm	*2½	S'Chase	4:42	4↑ Temple Gwathmey H 58k	9	6	69	69½	417	218	Foot A	168 w	*.90	--	Ancestor14918Shipbord1682Morphus1422½	Passed tired ones	12
8Oct56- 5Bel	fm	*3	S'Chase	5:501	4↑ Grand National H 28k	7	5	415	24	15	112	Foot A	164 w	*1.45	--	Shipboard16412Glencannon13312HisBoots1341	Much the best	8
20Sep56- 5Bel	sf	*2	S'Chase	3:47	3↑ Broad Hollow H 11k	5	6	42	22	12	1nk	Foot A	164 w	2.15e	--	Shipboard164nkBasilia1301½Bavaria1542	Held on gamely	8
21Oct55- 6Bel	sf	*2½	S'Chase	4:553	4↑ Temple Gwathmey H 57k	8	11	85¾	42	-	-	Foot A	166 w	*1.70	--	Neji167¾Rhythminhim1497His Boots1371½		11
	Bobbled at 15th jump,fell																	
13Oct55- 5Bel	fm	*3	S'Chase	5:542	4↑ Grand National H 28k	1	8	66	32	-	-	Foot A	165 w	*1.20	--	Neji163hdRhythminhim14615His Boots1351½		8
	Went through 17th hedge,fell																	
22Sep55- 5Bel	fm	*2	S'Chase	3:463	3↑ Broad Hollow H 11k	1	4	31½	1½	11	12	Foot A	158 w	*.80	--	Shipbrd1582Nj1571½Rhythmnhm145½	Won under mild urging	4
25Aug55- 5Sar	fm	*2½	S'Chase	5:063	4↑ Saratoga H 11k	1	3	35½	23½	12½	12	Foot A	160 w	1.75	--	Shipboard1602Palaja13112½BillingBear132½	Held good lead	5
24Jun55- 0Del	sf	*2	S'Chase	3:56	4↑ Georgetown H 10k	4	5	410	47½	32½	33¼	Foot A	162 w	-	--	Ancestor148nkCoveted1403Shpbord1623½	Tired under impost	5
	Special event - no wagering																	
16Jun55- 5Aqu	fm	*2	S'Chase	3:453	4↑ Hitchcock H 10k	6	5	35	32	33	22½	Foot A	163 w	*.90	--	Fulton1322½Shipboard1631Rythminhim1426½	Very game try	7
2Jun55- 5Bel	fm	*2½	S'Chase	4:442	4↑ Meadow Brook H 11k	5	5	330	3nk	14	16	Foot A	156 w	*.60e	--	Shipboard1566Curly Joe13115Neji15630	Taken in hand	6
21May55- 6Bel	hd	*2½	S'Chase	4:432	4↑ International 21k	4	8	514	48½	-	-	Foot A	150 w	*1.50	--	Neji15015Ancstor15518Hyvn15518	Threw rider at 15th jump	10
12May55- 5Bel	hd	*2	S'Chase	3:411	4↑ Corinthian H 8.9k	1	6	47	33½	11½	13	Foot A	155 w	1.15e	--	Shipboard1553Beaupre1363Nej1551½	Bobbled jump,recovered	6
22Oct54- 6Bel	fm	*2½	S'Chase	4:39	4↑ Temple Gwathmey H 16k	1	5	44	33½	-	-	Foot A	151 w	*1.20e	--	King Commander164¾Neji1497Coveted13170		6
	Stumbled 13th jump,lost rider																	
14Oct54- 5Bel	fm	*3	S'Chase	5:42	4↑ Grand National H 28k	5	6	43	12	13½	12½	Foot A	152 w	*1.25e	--	Shipboard1522¾Covtd13122CurlyJo13310	Under brisk urging	7

23Sep54- 5Bel fm *2 S'Chase 3:44 3↑ Broad Hollow H 11k 4 4 1½ 12½ 12 12 Foot A 154 w 1.80 -- Shipboard1542Neji13718Covtd13645 Held lead under urging 5
26Aug54- 5Sar fm *2½ S'Chase 5:002 4↑ Saratoga H 11k 5 5 49 35 26 29 Foot A 148 w *1.25 -- KingCommndr1549Shpbrd14814Covtd1328 Bobbled 8th jump 6
5Aug54- 5Sar sf *2 S'Chase 4:172 4↑ Shillelah H 8.8k 7 5 2½ 21½ 21½ 12 Foot A 139 w *1.35 -- Shipboard1392King Commander14320Coveted13812 Drew out 7
21Jun54- 5Del hd *2 S'Chase 3:434 4↑ Tom Roby 12k 1 7 55½ 2½ 13 14 Foot A 149 w *2.60 -- Shipboard1494Imbursed130hdCammell Laird1434½ Ridden out 7
21May54- 3Bel sf *2 S'Chase 3:56 4↑ Alw 4000 3 3 11½ 11½ 13 12½ Foot A 145 w *.85 -- Shipboard1452½Cherwell14520Moot14060 Fully extended 6
13May54- 5Bel fm *2 S'Chase 3:482 4↑ Spring Maiden 6.8k 5 4 33 1½ - - Foot A 145 w 1.40 -- KingCommander1537IndianFire1402½Covtd15015 Fell at 11th 5
29Apr54- 3Bel fm *2 S'Chase 3:462 4↑ Sp Wt 4000 8 5 23 22 21 1½ Foot A 140 w 6.20 -- Shipbrd140½KingCommander14812PacificPact1482½ Driving 11
28Sep53- 3Bel fst *1¾ Hurdles 3:132 3↑ Alw 4500 8 9 917 818 719 515 Foot A 132 w 10.10 -- KingCommndr1492½Willimsburg1402RvrJordn1494½ Sluggish 9
25Sep53- 3Bel fst *1½ Hurdles 2:43 3↑ Alw 4000 6 6 43½ - - - Foot A 134 w *2.30e -- BattlWv1423½Allflor145nkIndnFr1343½ Stumbled,lost rider 11
17Jun53- 3Bel fst *1½ Hurdles 2:47 Md 4000 5 8 11 1½ 21 11¾ Woolfe RG Jr 140 w *1.65e -- Shipboard1401¾Indian Fire1453½Watch Dog1351½ Going away 9
4Apr53- 7Cam fst 1Ⓣ 1:42 3↑ Alw 400 4 1 1¾ 1nk 1nk 11 Woolfe RG Jr 134 w - -- Shipboard1341Deadeye1401¾Rewing140nk Wide,driving 4
21Mar53- 1SoP fst *6fⓉ 1:124 3↑ Alw 400 2 4 54¼ 57¼ 59 49½ Woolfe RG Jr 132 w - -- ExtraPoints1433½Escarp1474QueerWednsday1402 No menace 5

Sickle's Image

lt br. f. 1948, by Sickletoy (Sickle)–Ariel Image, by Ariel **Lifetime record: 73 27 13 16 $413,275**
Own.– C. Hartwick
Br.– Clarence Hartwick (Ky)
Tr.– C. Hartwick

1Sep54- 7Was fst 1 :222 :443 1:094 1:352 3↑ ⒻBeverly H 28k 10 5 32 33 1217 1222¾ Swain C 121 w 7.20 69-14 Good Call113noVixen Fixit108noLavender Hill1241½ 12
Appeared slightly lame after pulling up
4Aug54- 7Was fst 7f :231 :463 1:114 1:244 3↑ Clang H 23k 9 3 44 33½ 41 2nk Fisk B 116 w 7.00 82-12 Precious Stone114nkSickle's Image116½Hi Billee112¾ 12
Gamely,forced in late
28Jly54- 7AP gd 1 :222 :453 1:102 1:363 3↑ ⒻArl Matron H 34k 8 7 78¾ 1013 1113 1120 Fisk B 124 w 4.70 69-14 LavenderHill1153½VixenFixit1053RosemaryB.111nk Outrun 12
20Jly54- 6AP fst 7f :232 :464 1:121 1:251 3↑ ⒻAlw 5000 4 3 21 3½ 1hd 52½ Fisk B 122 w *.80 81-16 Intencion111hdLillal1222Mimi Mine114hd Tired suddenly 6
10Jly54- 8AP fst 6f :22 :45 1:10 3↑ ⒻModesty H 23k 5 3 22 2½ 13 12½ Dodson D 118 w 8.30 94-13 Sickle'sImage1182½MimiMine1122½VixenFixit103nk Driving 13
5Jly54- 7Det fst 1 :233 :472 1:123 1:384 3↑ ⒻTomboy 8.5k 1 3 31½ 32 32 32½ Baird RL 122 w *1.60 88-15 Rosemary B.1061¾Eternal Frolic102¾Sickle's Image122¾ 7
Could not rally
26Jun54- 6Det sl 6f :232 :472 1:123 3↑ Alw 2300 4 2 43 46 47 411 Swain C 120 w 2.70 74-25 Epic King1197Fiddle1192½Nocallula1141½ Poor effort 6
19Jun54- 7Det gd 6f :231 :471 1:124 3↑ ⒻRose Leaves 11k 2 5 31 32½ 4¾ 65½ Fisk B 122 w *1.50 78-14 Sharbot110nkSunTanGal1102¼TaskFleet108nk Tired in drive 8
31Oct53- 6CD fst 1 :223 :452 1:114 1:363 3↑ ⒻFalls City H 11k 9 5 67 79 56 912 Fisk B 123 w *1.30 82-13 GalaFete1173Cajole1072¾BelleRebelle1061½ Gave way,sore 15
20Oct53- 5Kee fst 6f :221 :454 1:102 3↑ ⒻAlw 4000 4 5 45 46½ 44 33¼ Fisk B 122 w *1.40 97-08 Flyamanita110nkGalaFete1183Sickle'sImage1222¼ Sluggish 5
7Oct53- 7Haw sl 6½f :231 :461 1:122 1:19 3↑ ⒻYo Tambien H 16k 3 5 24 25 21½ 21 Fisk B 124 w 1.50 84-27 Gala Fete1171Sickle's Image124½Good Call111.51 Weakened 6
14Sep53- 6Haw fst 6½f :231 :462 1:103 1:171 3↑ Martie Flynn H 10k 7 2 2hd 1hd 1hd 1½ Fisk B 119 w *1.50 94-18 Sickle'sImag119½CoffMony1111¼Mon-Phro1133 Driving clear 7
7Sep53- 7Was gd 1 :221 :454 1:104 1:364 3↑ Wash Park H 165k 13 2 42 43½ 13 1½ Cook WM 106 w 24.00 85-16 Sickle's Image106½Ruhe1163¼Indian Hemp1142 Hard drive 13
28Aug53- 7Atl fst 7f :221 :444 1:092 1:23 3↑ Alw 6000 3 1 1hd 2hd 1½ 11½ Headley O 109 w *.90 -- Sickle'sImage1091½Halter121½WinningStrid1104 Ridden out 8
20Aug53- 5Atl fst 6f :223 :461 1:113 3↑ ⒻAlw 5000 4 3 42 2hd 12 15 Headley O 112 w *.60 87-18 Sickl'sImge1125BlueRhymer1174MssShdow115hd Easy score 7
15Aug53- 7Atl fst 7f :221 :452 1:093 1:232 3↑ ⒻMermaid H 18k 2 5 52 53½ 43 43¼ Fisk B 118 w 5.60 -- Atalanta1191¼GayGrecque1191WinningStrd1101 Lacked rally 10
29Jly53- 7AP fst 1 :23 :453 1:091 1:352 3↑ ⒻArl Matron H 43k 7 4 55 46 45 75¼ Fisk B 116 w 6.50 90-13 Real Delight1241¾Fulvous107nkBella Figura1192 Faltered 7
23Jly53- 6AP fst 1 :23 :462 1:102 1:354 3↑ Handicap 10000 1 4 45½ 32½ 33 32½ Church K 110 w 3.60 90-16 SubFleet1201¼Jampol1111¼Sickle'sImag1101 Close quarters 8
15Jly53- 6AP fst 6f :223 :453 1:102 4↑ Alw 4500 3 3 31 44 41½ 1¾ Fisk B 112 w *2.20 92-13 Sickle'sImage112¾Futuramatic120nkAirMail114½ Hard urged 9
8Jly53- 7AP fst 6f :214 :444 1:101 3↑ ⒻModesty H 17k 9 3 88¼ 89¼ 84¾ 75 Fisk B 118 w 7.10 88-13 BellaFigura1172GalaFete116¾Night-Phara109.5hd No threat 12
26Jun53- 6Det sl 6f :231 :471 1:131 3↑ Alw 3000 2 4 23 32 2½ 21¾ Fisk B 117 w 2.30 80-29 BlackBantam1131¾Sckle'sImge1171HotPenny111hd Game try 8
29Nov52- 5Bow fst 6f :23 :463 1:114 2↑ Handicap 6045 8 5 74½ 76 63¾ 32 Gorman D 126 w *1.10 -- Nullify1071Nimble Fox1071Sickle's Image126¾ Closed well 8
11Nov52- 6Pim sl 1⅛ :49 1:133 1:394 1:522 3↑ ⒻGallorette 29k 1 2 2hd 1hd 53½ 913 Fisk B 123 w *2.40 79-22 La Corredora1123½Kiss Me Kate1231Marta1173 Stopped 9
1Nov52- 5Pim fst 6f :221 :453 1:104 3↑ Alw 5000 4 1 31 2½ 2½ 1hd Gorman D 121 w *1.70 97-21 Sickle's Image121hdHi Billee1212¼Prop115½ Cleverly 6
18Oct52- 7GS fst 1 1/16 :23 :471 1:112 1:453 3↑ ⒻVineland H 49k 2 3 33½ 1hd 1hd 1¾ Fisk B 120 w 5.00e 82-20 Sickle'sImage120¾KissMeKate118¾LilyWhit111hd Hard drive 17
13Oct52- 6Jam fst 6f :232 :46 1:111 2↑ ⒻCorrection H 24k 6 6 41¾ 83¼ 53 31½ Fisk B 122 w *1.80e 89-21 QuizSong1101½Landmark116noSickl'sImg122¾ Close quarters 12
8Oct52- 7Haw fst 6½f :222 :452 1:093 1:16 3↑ ⒻRegret H 11k 4 1 42 52¼ 1hd 2no Fisk B 120 w *.50 102-13 RomanMiss114noSickle'sImge1203½OurRequst1121½ Faltered 6
17Sep52- 7Haw fst 6f :222 :451 1:093 3↑ Billings H 11k 5 3 52¼ 54½ 44¼ 24½ Adams J 112 w *1.20 96-09 AndyB.W.1194½Sickle'sImage112noUnbridld109¾ Closed fast 7
6Sep52- 7Haw fst 6½f :222 :451 1:092 1:16 3↑ Midwest H 18k 4 6 2½ 42¼ 34 35¼ Fisk B 114 w *2.40 97-09 Sabaean1122½Eljay1143Sickle's Image1141½ No excuse 11
1Sep52- 7Was sly 1 :231 :462 1:104 1:364 3↑ Wash Park H 172k 9 3 53¼ 33½ 22½ 33 Fisk B 110 w 11.90 82-15 CraftyAdmiral1282ToMarket1231Sickle'sImag110nk Faltered 10
26Aug52- 7Was fst 7f :222 :442 1:083 1:211 3↑ Alw 7500 1 2 21½ 31½ 21½ 1hd Church K 108 w 3.30 101-09 Sickle'sImag108hdSprtnVlor1233Cyclotron1112 Held gamely 6
13Aug52- 6Was fst 6f :222 :452 1:093 3↑ Handicap 5000 1 2 4¼ 47½ 45 32 Arcaro E 115 w *.90 96-08 Andy B.W.122½Sun David1171½Sickle's Image115½ No excuse 6
2Aug52- 7Was fst 1 :221 :452 1:093 1:344 3↑ ⒻBeverly H 27k 4 4 31 32 31½ 32 Fisk B 121 w 2.60 93-07 Real Delight129hdAesthete1052Sickle's Image1212 Blocked 9
28Jly52- 4Was fst 6f :221 :453 1:092 3↑ ⒻAlw 4500 6 2 33 23 1hd 11¼ Arcaro E 119 w *.40 99-08 Sickle's Image1191¼Flyamanita1131Gala Fete1072 Driving 6
16Jly52- 7AP fst 1 :23 :454 1:094 1:353 3↑ ⒻModesty H 46k 5 3 33 34 1½ 2hd Fisk B 117 w 8.80 94-08 RealDelight126hdSickle'sImg1173½DckSu1111½ Sharp effort 12
2Jly52- 6Aqu fst 6f :23 :461 1:111 3↑ ⒻBridal Flower H 10k 8 5 105 74¾ 53 32 Fisk B 122 w *2.15e 94-18 Jacodema1151½SunshinNll110½Sckl'sImg122nk Strong finish 13
28Jun52- 6Aqu fst 1 1/16 :25 :49 1:131 1:45 3↑ ⒻVagrancy H 28k 1 1 3nk 22 1½ 42¼ Fisk B 115 w 4.95 87-16 Marta117noRenew118¾Valadium1151½ Weakened 8
21Jun52- 7Mth fst 6f :214 :451 1:112 3↑ ⒻRegret H (Div 2) 17k 2 1 22 21½ 2hd 21 Fisk B 122 w 3.10 90-16 DixieFlyer1131Sickle'sImag1221Bob'sBtty1102 Good effort 9
7Jun52- 7Det fst 6f :23 :462 1:11 3↑ Alw 5000 2 3 31½ 42½ 31 22¼ Armstrong S 121 w *.40 91-14 Pur Sang1202¼Sickle's Image1211¼Radical1132 Good effort 5
30May52- 7Det fst 6f :224 :46 1:104 3↑ F M Alger Mem 7.5k 4 3 1hd 11 12 12 Fisk B 115 w *1.10 94-15 Sickle's Image1152Dixie Flyer113nkBully Boy1101 Driving 8
23May52- 7Det my 6f :242 :48 1:142 3↑ Alw 3500 1 4 1½ 21 2hd 35¼ Fisk B 115 w *1.50 71-30 DixieFlyer1121¾BatedBreath1143½Sickle'sImg1152 Faltered 7
22Feb52- 7SA fst 7f :222 :444 1:094 1:222 3↑ Wash Birthday H 11k 4 7 64¼ 74¾ 43 62¾ Arcaro E 113 w 3.90 90-15 PetBully112¾Interpretation113¾Guillotn126nk Even effort 9
12Feb52- 7SA fst 6f :22 :443 1:094 3↑ Lincoln's BD H 17k 8 3 43 45 33 2no Westrope J 112 w 6.35 96-17 Guillotine126noSickle'sImg112nkRghsBull1211½ Raced wide 8
6Feb52- 7SA fst 6f :223 :451 1:103 3↑ ⒻLos Cerritos H 18k 3 4 3nk 2hd 13 11½ Arcaro E 120 w 2.15 92-14 Sickle's Image1201½A Gleam1122½Frigid105½ Handily 13
12Jan52- 6SA sly 1 :224 :463 1:121 1:391 3↑ ⒻS Maria H 23k 6 5 56 33½ 34½ 58¾ Fisk B 116 w 5.50 71-22 Special Touch1212½Next Move1282½Blue Cloth108nk Tired 8
5Jan52- 7SA fst 7f :221 :45 1:101 1:23 Malibu Sequet 30k 15 2 2hd 64¼ 72¾ 96½ Fisk B 114 w 15.40 83-14 Phil D.118noIntent1152Black Douglas110½ Tired 15
28Dec51- 7SA fst 6f :221 :451 1:094 3↑ ⒻLas Flores H 18k 2 9 62¾ 41¾ 31½ 31¼ Fisk B 117 w 5.55 95-08 NextMove1241SpeclTouch122nkSckl'sImg1173½ Good effort 13
17Nov51- 5CD gd 6f :223 :453 1:111 3↑ Alw 2500 2 5 31½ 34¼ 44 35 Fisk B 115 w *1.00 89-16 DixieFlyer1084Ari'sMona1121Sickle'sImage115no No rally 10
8Aug51- 6HP fst 6f :223 :461 1:114 Alw 3000 7 1 53 11 11 12 Fisk B 121 w *.40 97-13 Sickle'sImage1212Badger1141½Ted Yochum114nk Going away 7
14Jly51- 7AP fst 1 :224 :452 1:094 1:361 3↑ ⒻArl Matron H 72k 8 9 64½ 43 22½ 11½ Fisk B 120 w 3.80 91-08 Sickle'sImage1201½Aunt Jinny1075WarTalk109¾ Drew away 13
30Jun51- 7AP fst 6f :224 :452 1:104 3↑ ⒻModesty H 24k 14 6 89 65 33½ 1¾ Swain C 120 w 6.10 92-08 Sickle'sImge120¾Asphalt1052½TwoRanbows104nk Hard drive 17
27Jun51- 6AP fst 7f :23 :452 1:11 1:24 Warren Wright Mem 24k 12 5 55 58 23 43¼ Fisk B 113 w 6.50 87-13 Jumbo114¾Ruhe1182½Bernwood114hd Good effort 17
20Jun51- 6AP sl 6f :224 :454 1:121 ⒻCleopatra 16k 7 4 4¾ 43 11½ 11½ Fisk B 115 w *3.10 85-18 Sickle'sImage1151½JennieLee1151¾Fleeterthan111½ Driving 10
13Jun51- 7Was fst 6f :222 :452 1:104 ⒻAlw 5000 2 1 31½ 21½ 13 11¾ Swain C 121 w *1.80 92-13 Sickle'sImage1211¼LadyIndian1091½RomanMiss1091 Driving 10
19May51- 7CD fst 6½f :232 :464 1:113 1:174 ⒻAlw 5000 3 4 42 41½ 3nk 21¼ Swain C 121 w *1.10 91-12 Jennie Lee1171¼Sickle's Image1212½Lyceum109no No excuse 7
4May51- 7CD fst 1 1/16 :24 :482 1:133 1:453 ⒻKy Oaks 31k 8 3 32 32½ 43½ 35¼ Fisk B 121 w 5.70 85-14 How1162¾Astro1102½Sickle's Image1211½ Went well 14
28Apr51- 6CD fst 6½f :223 :453 1:10 1:163 ⒻAlw 2500 2 3 44 33½ 1hd 1nk Swain C 121 w *1.10 98-10 Sickle's Image121nkRuddy1183½Biddy Bid1151½ All out 7
14Apr51- 6Kee sl 6f :234 :494 1:18 ⒻAshland 13k 3 1 2hd 21 11½ 1nk Fisk B 121 w *2.00 62-31 Sickle's Image121nkJuliets Nurse1181½How1152 All out 9
6Apr51- 5Jam fst 5½f :222 :452 1:043 ⒻAlw 4500 7 3 2½ 2hd 12½ 12 Fisk B 115 w *1.80 95-13 Sickle'sImage1152FairSelf115nkSweetTalk115½ Ridden out 7
31Mar51- 6LD gd 5f :224 :464 1:001 3↑ Alw 1800 8 2 1hd 11 1½ 11 Spinale J 104 w *.30 90-17 Sickle's Image1041Klimie112noBeaming Light115½ Driving 9
10Feb51- 7SA fst 7f :223 :451 1:103 1:232 ⒻS Susana 65k 11 2 1hd 12½ 1hd 31½ Fisk B 121 w *1.80 86-15 ⒹSweetTlk115noRuthLly1151½Sckl'sImg121½ Close quarters 11
Placed second through disqualification

Date	Cond/Dist	Fractions / Time	Race	PP St 1c 2c Str Fin	Jockey	Wt	Odds	Spd	Top three	Comment	Field
19Jan51- 7SA	gd 6f	:222 :453 1:103	Alw 5000	2 3 2hd 2hd 1hd 22	Smith FA	117 w	2.65	92-19	Phil D.1222Sickle's Image117½Rough'n Tumble118¾	Hung	8
24Nov50- 7Hol	fst 6f	:221 :45 1:10	Ⓕ Lassie 33k	9 11 11 11¼	Fisk B	112 w	*.90	96-10	Sickle's Image1121¼Ruth Lily1073½Worn Out1083	Driving	10
	Fog prevented other calls										
17Nov50- 7Hol	fst 6f	:223 :454 1:103	Ⓕ Alw 5000	3 3 1½ 12 12 12½	Fisk B	116 w	3.55	93-13	Sickle'sImage1162½WornOut1164½HaughtyMiss112nk	In hand	10
23Sep50- 6Nar	fst 6f	:221 :451 1:12	J H Connors Mem 9.3k	2 3 1nk 1½ 11½ 1¾	Fisk B	112 w	*1.40	91-16	Sickle's Image112¾Loridale1092½Fair Game115½	Driving	8
16Sep50- 4Nar	fst 6f	:222 :452 1:113	Alw 2600	7 3 11 12 12 11½	Fisk B	112 w	3.70	93-12	Sickle's Image1121½Blue Roxy1071½Swift Swiv1224	Driving	8
9Sep50- 6Nar	fst 6f	:222 :452 1:111	Ⓕ Jeanne D'Arc 6.7k	5 10 1010 811 79½ 78	Fisk B	111 w	4.40	87-09	Jacodema1162½BettyLamr1051½DollFoot1071½	Sluggish start	11
30Aug50- 6Aqu	fst 6f	:23 :462 1:12	Ⓕ Astarita 12k	4 2 2hd 2hd 31½ 69	Fisk B	113 w	3.50	83-11	Jacodema113½Self Assurance116noRuddy1161	Close quarters	11
24Aug50- 7Sar	fst 5½f	:222 :453 :59 1:054	Ⓕ Alw 3000	6 3 1hd 1hd 11 14½	Fisk B	113 w	2.65	88-12	Sickle's Image1134½Tides1131¼Toto113no	Easily	8
10Aug50- 6HP	fst 6f	:234 :471 1:122	Alw 2200	8 4 1hd 1hd 21½ 23½	Arcaro E	117 w	*.60	92-09	PurSang1173½Sickle'sImage1171½PsychicLad1116	Weakened	8
4Aug50- 5Was	fst 5½f	:223 :46 :574 1:042	Ⓕ Md Sp Wt	10 6 2hd 13 15 16½	MacAndrew D	115 w	*1.00	98-07	Sickle's Image1156½The Ghizeh1151Aunt Jinny1153	Easily	12
27Jly50- 6AP	fst 6f	:222 :443 1:104	Ⓕ Pollyanna 18k	13 2 11 21 23 35¾	MacAndrew D	114 w	5.60	86-11	Flyamanita1133¾HastyRequest1132Sckl'sImg1141½	Weakened	14
18Jly50- 5AP	hy 5½f	:232 :483 1:013 1:09	Ⓕ Md Sp Wt	12 6 2hd 12 15 32½	MacAndrew D	115 w	4.60	72-34	RomanMiss1151Fleeterthan1151½Sickle'sImg1151½	Gave way	12

Silver Spoon

ch. f. 1956, by Citation (Bull Lea)–Silver Fog, by Mahmoud

Lifetime record: 27 13 3 4 $313,930

Own.– C.V. Whitney
Br.– C.V. Whitney (Ky)
Tr.– J.J. Greely Jr

Date	Cond/Dist	Fractions / Time	Race	PP St 1c 2c Str Fin	Jockey	Wt	Odds	Spd	Top three	Comment	Field
14Oct60- 6Kee	fst *7f	1:26	3↑ Ⓕ Alw 7500	5 2 31 3nk 42 57	Rotz JL	121	5.50	90-11	Indian Maid118¾Royal Native1212¼Chance Gauge1061½	Tired	8
	Open to 3-, 4- and 5-year-olds										
1Oct60- 7Bel	fst 1⅛	:461 1:11 1:362 1:492	3↑ Ⓕ Beldame 91k	1 5 41¾ 62¾ 45 46	Shoemaker W	123	4.25	83-16	Berlo1192Royal Native1231Make Sail1193	In close on turn	9
	Previously trained by R.L. Wheeler										
13Aug60- 8AP	fst 1⅛	:48 1:12 1:371 1:502	3↑ Ⓕ Arl Matron H 56k	2 5 54 52½ 21 31½	Shoemaker W	128	*1.40	82-07	RoyalNative128hdWoodlawn1101½SlvrSpoon1281	Reared start	11
5Aug60- 5AP	sl 1	:223 :463 1:124 1:393	3↑ Ⓕ Alw 5000	5 4 32½ 22 22 2no	Shoemaker W	128	*.50	72-30	WeeFleet111noSilverSpoon1283¾Isk1082¼	Getting to winner	6
2Jly60- 7Hol	fst 1⅛	:454 1:094 1:354 1:49	3↑ Ⓕ Vanity H 38k	5 3 2hd 13 12 1¾	Longden J	130	*.70	89-13	SilvrSpoon130¾Tritoma1072¾HonysGm118nk	Wide,hard drive	6
16Jun60- 7Hol	fst 1	:22 :444 1:092 1:344	3↑ Ⓕ Milady H 22k	2 2 24 2hd 12 12¾	Shoemaker W	126	*.70	92-10	SilverSpn1262¾HoneysGem1204LPlum110¾	Drew out handily	7
28May60- 7Hol	fst 1 1/16	:23 :454 1:092 1:403	3↑ Californian 111k	4 4 21½ 23 32½ 45¾	Valenzuela I	118	5.40	86-10	FleetNsrullah1192½EddieSchmidt1131¾Bagdd1231½	Weakened	7
24May60- 7Hol	fst 6f	:212 :434 :56 1:082	3↑ Ⓕ Sequoia H 16k	6 7 65½ 65½ 34 23¼	Shoemaker W	127	*.60	98-09	LiberalLady1173¼SilverSpoon127½SweetJune1093¼	Rallied	9
18May60- 6Hol	fst 6f	:222 :452 :571 1:091	4↑ Alw 10000	1 5 3½ 32½ 34 32¼	Shoemaker W	117	*.90	94-12	Revel113¾LittlMoon1221½SlvrSpoon1176½	In close,steadied	5
27Feb60- 7SA	fst 1¼	:462 1:104 1:352 2:003	3↑ S Anita H 145k	11 3 42½ 41¼ 54 52½	Valenzuela I	120	5.10	93-11	Linmold110hdFleet Nasrullah113noAmerigo120nk	Evenly	12
6Feb60- 7SA	fst 1⅛	:463 1:102 1:36 1:484	4↑ Ⓕ S Margarita H 57k	10 4 3½ 1½ 11 11¾	Arcaro E	130	*.90	88-12	Silver Spoon1301¾Indian Maid1162Narva1131	Under urging	12
21Jan60- 7SA	fst 1 1/16	:23 :46 1:103 1:423	4↑ Ⓕ S Maria H 28k	10 3 1hd 1½ 1½ 11¾	Arcaro E	127	*.90	91-12	SilverSpoon1271¾LaPlume111nkIndianMaid1161½	Drew clear	10
12Jan60- 7SA	gd 7f	:23 :454 1:103 1:23	4↑ Ⓕ S Monica H 22k	5 2 41½ 3nk 3nk 12	Arcaro E	124	*1.40	88-22	Silver Spoon1242Margaretta121¾Indian Maid120nk	Driving	8
1Jan60- 6SA	fst 6f	:22 :444 1:093	4↑ Ⓕ Las Flores H 23k	5 3 84 64½ 67 44¾	Arcaro E	125	*.80	91-11	Margaretta1172½Khalita115noIndian Maid1202¼	Lacked room	9
18Aug59- 6Sar	fst 7f	:221 :45 1:102 1:24	Ⓕ Alw 5000	4 4 47 47 57 511	Boland W	124	1.90	84-17	MommyDear1155MissBlueGem1121Recite1213	Lacked response	5
1Aug59- 7Mth	fst 1⅛	:471 1:111 1:37 1:503	Ⓕ Mth Oaks 55k	3 3 22 33½ 35½ 36	Boland W	121	*.40	85-18	RoyalNative1133½IndianMaid1172½SilverSpoon1214½	Tired	6
24Jly59- 6Mth	gd 1 1/16	:233 :474 1:121 1:444	Ⓕ Alw 7500	5 3 32½ 3nk 2hd 11	Boland W	126	*.70	81-25	SilverSpoon1261IndianMaid118¾RoyalNative1121½	Driving	5
11Jly59- 6Del	gd 1⅛	:48 1:132 1:383 1:513	Ⓕ Del Oaks 47k	5 2 22 1hd 1hd 22	Boland W	119	*.40	80-21	Resaca1192Silver Spoon119½Indian Maid1194	No excuse	9
13Jun59- 7Hol	fst 1⅛	:453 1:092 1:344 1:473	Cinema H 52k	4 5 53 21½ 12¼ 14¾	Boland W	120	2.20	96-08	Silver Spoon1204¾Friar Roach1112¼Civic Pride105½	Easily	8
2May59- 7CD	fst 1¼	:473 1:113 1:36 2:021	Ky Derby 163k	4 9 99 32 32 53¼	York R	121	10.80	93-06	TomyLee126noSwordDancer1262¼FirstLanding1261	Bid,tired	17
25Apr59- 7CD	fst 7f	:23 :452 1:094 1:221	Alw 5000	4 3 3nk 2hd 3½ 32½	York R	117	*1.20	96-14	Sword Dancer1221Easy Spur1221½Silver Spoon1172	In close	5
7Mar59- 7SA	fst 1⅛	:453 1:092 1:354 1:49	S Anita Derby 147k	6 3 31 21 1hd 12½	York R	113	*1.50	89-14	SilverSpoon1132½RoyalOrbit1182½FightinIndn118hd	Driving	10
18Feb59- 7SA	fst 1 1/16	:23 :462 1:11 1:414	Ⓕ S Susana 22k	5 2 2hd 1½ 15 110½	York R	117	*.65	95-13	Silver Spoon11710½Miss Uppity1172Bitter Feud110½	Easily	9
28Jan59- 7SA	fst 6½f	:22 :45 1:102 1:17	Ⓕ S Ynez 17k	11 4 42 41½ 1hd 11¼	York R	116	*.80	93-15	SilverSpoon1161¼GunBox116¾PardalLassie113¾	Handy score	13
7Jan59- 7SA	fst 6½f	:22 :45 1:102 1:17	Ⓕ La Centinela 18k	2 7 53 32½ 12 12¼	York R	119	*.70	93-16	SilverSpoon1192¼BitterFeud1191¾SybilBrand119hd	Easily	14
30Dec58- 5SA	fst 6f	:221 :45 1:093	Ⓕ Alw 4500	10 5 21½ 23 2hd 13¼	York R	115 w	3.80	97-12	SilverSpoon1153¼Satina1152PardalLassie1153½	Easily best	12
	Previously trained by S.E. Veitch										
23Sep58- 3Bel	fst 6f-WC	:223 :454 1:10	Ⓕ Md 8000	11 3 2½ 2½ 16	Nelson E	118 w	18.35	89-11	SilverSpoon1186LynchMary113nkBasqu1121½	Drew out easily	28

St. Vincent (GB)

ch. g. 1951, by Ocean Swell (Blue Peter)–Light of Day, by Hyperion

Lifetime record: 72 17 7 6 $228,280

Own.– J. Gheen
Br.– Lady Irwin (GB)
Tr.– B.R. Roberts

Date	Cond/Dist	Fractions / Time	Race	PP St 1c 2c Str Fin	Jockey	Wt	Odds	Spd	Top three	Comment	Field
10Sep60- 7Dmr	fm 1Ⓣ	:24 :48 1:13 1:382	3↑ Handicap 4000	6 6 63¼ 52¾ 3nk 1no	Lanoway G	113	*1.40	--	St.Vincent113noBalsarrochBoy1091½Queen'sWy1041½	Driving	6
27Aug60- 9Dmr	fm 7½fⓉ	1:324	3↑ Clm 5000-c	2 5 53 52½ 42 2nk	Lanoway G	122	*.80	--	PurePitch114nkSt.Vincent122¾BigJak1141½	Strong late bid	7
	Claimed from Mr & Mrs A.T. Cattani;trainer, J. Nicholson										
22Aug60- 4Dmr	fst 1Ⓣ	:24 :483 1:133 1:40	3↑ Clm 4000	1 5 53½ 42 1hd 12	Lanoway G	120	*.70	--	St.Vincent1202SanDiego1121¾Lesur1171½	Wide into stretch	7
10Aug60- 9Dmr	fm 7½fⓉ	1:33	3↑ Clm 5000	5 6 66 41¼ 31½ 1nk	Lanoway G	119	5.40	--	St. Vincent119nkNet Man1112¼April1091¼	Driving	8
5Aug60- 8Dmr	fst 1 1/16	:233 :473 1:114 1:43	3↑ Clm 3500	6 7 715 78¼ 64¾ 33½	Burns E	117	4.60	82-00	Amarillo Speed112¾Peter Potter1122¾St. Vincent1171¼		7
	Closed ground outside										
29Jly60- 8Dmr	fst 1 1/16	:24 :474 1:113 1:424	3↑ Clm 4000	1 7 611 68 69 69	Neves R	120	4.30	78-08	Baccarat1122¼Tribal Chief112noAmblingorix1204	No threat	7
23Jly60- 8Hol	fst 1 1/16	1:44	4↑ Clm 4000	10 11 1110 97¼ 3nk 1no	Neves R	117	23.90	75-15	St. Vincent117noNoration120¾Paint Brush1142½	Just up	12
9Jly60- 4Hol	fst 1¼	:471 1:12 1:363 2:021	4↑ Clm 4000	3 8 79¾ 64¼ 48½ 56¾	Burns E	117	5.80	75-12	Talktalk1141½Tribal Chief1141Easy Four1204½	Hung	8
4Jly60- 2Hol	fst 1 1/16	:234 :464 1:112 1:432	4↑ Clm 6000	5 7 76 64¾ 62½ 54½	Lanoway G	119	12.40	73-13	Butcher Boy1161¼Blue G.116nkAsombroso1081½	No factor	7
23Jun60- 8Hol	fst 1½	:474 1:131 2:04 2:30	4↑ Clm-c 2500	2 7 69½ 12 12 13¼	Longden J	114	2.70	95-11	St.Vincent1143¼LookOutII117¾NightHawk1111½	Going away	8
	Claimed from Mr & Mrs R. Godfrey,trainer V. Longden										
11Jun60- 3Hol	12 1⅛	:47 1:114 1:364 1:494	4↑ Clm 3000	5 9 107½ 84½ 711 711	Longden J	116	6.20	74-09	Telyar1195½Good Start1162High Drawer119½	No factor	12
27May60- 8Hol	fst 1⅛	:472 1:12 1:374 1:502	4↑ Clm 4000	4 12 1215 77 53 44½	Longden J	117	16.10	77-13	Sassy Sea109½Sayacieux114½Phantom Ace1143½		12
20May60- 8Hol	fst 1 1/16	:233 :47 1:111 1:42	4↑ Clm 7000	2 6 710 613 617 619	Longden J	116	12.70	66-00	Hello Junedear1141¼Tranquilizer1165Selling Fast1223¾		7
10Mar60- 7SA	fm *1¾Ⓣ	2:474	3↑ S Juan Capistrano H 119k	10 17 1514 1617 1312 1115	Trejos R	108	17.00f	73-14	Amerigo122noKing o' Turf1156½Aorangi109no	No factor	17
3Mar60- 8SA	sf *1¾Ⓣ	2:57	4↑ Handicap 10000	2 12 1216 1217 107¼ 44½	Shoemaker W	126	*3.10	47-48	NiteShift1171¾LeBeau114nkLastRow1212½	Best stride late	13
18Feb60- 6SA	fm 1½Ⓣ	:46 1:102 2:033 2:282	4↑ Handicap 7500	13 14 1312 31½ 2½ 13½	Shoemaker W	120	*1.80	85-15	St.Vincent1203½Castlestone117½LockOutII1112½	Going away	14
4Feb60- 4SA	sf 1½Ⓣ	:473 1:14 2:071 2:352	4↑ Handicap 6000	11 10 108¾ 31 31½ 73	Longden J	119	*2.80	47-50	GoodStart112½LastRow119¾TheSands1121½	Bold rally,tired	14
22Jan60- 8SA	fst 1⅛	:463 1:114 1:38 1:504	4↑ Clm 5000	3 10 85 62¾ 52 3½	Longden J	117	5.20	77-16	Flagg'sBandit115½OverdrivII115hdSt.Vncnt1172	Slow start	11
9Jan60- 8SA	fst 1⅛	:471 1:113 1:37 1:50	4↑ OClm 8000	4 10 1012 67 712 611	Longden J	116	9.60	71-11	LandofHope114¾WearandTr1163¼FlyingSouth1161½	No speed	10
	Previously owned by Alberta Ranches Ltd-Gardiner										
21Feb59- 5SA	sly 1 1/16	:234 :472 1:12 1:441	4↑ Alw 10000	6 7 66¼ 54½ 55½ 56¼	Longden J	120	14.20	77-12	Solid Son113nkNew Shift1133½Prophetic1111½	No factor	7
10Feb59- 7SA	sf 1½Ⓣ	:48 1:133 2:06 2:314	3↑ San Luis Rey H 28k	9 10 1011 1115 1129 1128	Longden J	113 b	11.30	40-32	Infntry1133LookoutPont1122¼Whttoldyou118¾	Disliked going	11
28Jan59- 6SA	fm 1¼Ⓣ	:453 1:103 1:353 2:011	4↑ OClm 12500	2 10 99¾ 62 2hd 1no	Longden J	113	*1.40	88-12	St.Vincent113noAorangi1223LookoutPoint113nk	Hard drive	12
16Jan59- 7SA	fm 1¼Ⓣ	:463 1:114 1:36 2:004	4↑ Alw 10000	4 9 89¼ 84¼ 52½ 54½	Longden J	113	9.45	85-10	Andrew Alan1181¾Hakuchikara113noMacBern1181¼	Bid,tired	12
1Jan59- 7SA	fm 1¼Ⓣ	:462 1:112 1:351 2:002	4↑ San Gabriel H 28k	9 8 87 65 89 710	Longden J	122 w	4.10	82-08	MacBern1132¼Andrew Alan1161Hakuchikara1191¼	No factor	9
26Dec58- 6SA	fm 1⅛Ⓣ	:464 1:104 1:354 1:474	3↑ Alw 7500	10 10 914 97¾ 65¼ 55¾	Longden J	113 w	3.30e	92-02	AnxiousMomnt1162¾Hakuchikara1133TllChfII119hd	Good try	10

25Oct58- 7WO sf 1⅝Ⓣ 2:462 3↑ Can Championship 60k 8 10 1118 1222 1226 1226 Contrada G 126 w 14.40 -- JackKetch126hdMahan1264AndrwAln121hd Showed very little 12
20Sep58- 6Bel sf 1⅜Ⓣ :50 1:152 1:401 2:182 3↑ Handicap 10000 8 4 44 55½ 64¼ 65 Ycaza M 120 w 6.15 84-11 LangtonBreeze117¾Sam1111Rfty122no Raced without mishap 10
13Sep58- 7Atl fm 1 3/16Ⓣ :472 1:112 1:362 1:543 3↑ U Nations H 100k 7 12 1211 105½ 813 88 Harmatz W 114 w 13.20 98-00 Clem113½RoundTabl1303CombustonII115¾ Failed to threaten 12
8Sep58- 7Atl fm 1 1/16Ⓣ :231 :461 1:112 1:433 3↑ Alw 5000 5 7 714 69½ 65¼ 22 Ycaza M 113 w 7.40 93-05 RoundTable1282St.Vncnt113nkRfty115hd Strong stretch bid 7
23Aug58- 8AP fm 1 3/16Ⓣ :47 1:11 1:36 1:542 3↑ Arlington H 85k 7 7 710 76¼ 55½ 33 Longden J 111 w 32.80 96-09 RoundTable1302¼Clm109¾St.Vncnt1111½ Off slowly,game try 8
22Jly58- 7Hol fst 1⅝ :464 1:371 2:023 2:41 3↑ Sunset H 107k 3 4 415 47¼ 37½ 310 Longden J 111 w 13.65 76-18 GallantMan1324EddieSchmidt1106St.Vncnt111nk Never close 6
16Jly58- 7Hol fst 1 1/16 :232 :464 1:113 1:44 4↑ Alw 10000 7 8 712 54½ 47 43¾ Longden J 112 w 1.85 71-19 Timloch1121¾FathersRisk1121¼LglCrss115¾ Slow start,wide 8
8Jly58- 5Hol fst 1 :23 :462 1:111 1:363 4↑ Alw 10000 7 8 78½ 66¼ 56½ 53¾ Longden J 112 w 10.45 79-19 Barely Nothing1121½Timloch112¾Khliesas1101¼ No factor 9
2Jly58- 7Hol fst 1 1/16 :233 :472 1:12 1:434 4↑ Alw 7500 2 9 911 86½ 815 815 Longden J 114 w 10.55 61-20 Cino114noRevolt120¾LightnngJck114nk Raced far off pace 9
27Jly57- 8AP fm 1 3/16Ⓣ :481 1:122 1:373 1:552 3↑ Arlington H 125k 7 11 84¾ 72¾ 44 34½ Longden J 120 w 14.80 89-04 Manasss1212Swoon'sSon1282½St.Vncnt120no Stride too late 14
1Jun57- 8Was sf 1⅛Ⓣ :473 1:122 1:39 1:512 3↑ Continental Turf H 28k 3 10 1114 1213 1110 1010 Gilligan L 121 w 4.10 76-14 Bernburgoo1091½Sunningdale112nkBlue Choir113¾ Weak try 13
11May57- 7Pim hd 1⅜Ⓣ :49 1:143 1:393 2:161 3↑ Dixie H 28k 5 10 53½ 52¾ 52¼ 43 Longden J 125 w *1.50 93-04 Akbar Khan1131¼Jabneh1201½Blue Choir116½ Made bid,hung 10
27Apr57- 8BM fst 1⅛ :454 1:101 1:353 1:48 3↑ W P Kyne Mem H 115k 2 14 1416 1313 77 73 Longden J 118 w 5.55 96-10 PibeCarlos110hdEddieSchmidt112½CountChic115no Rallied 15
9Mar57- 7SA sf *1¾Ⓣ :452 2:03 2:29 2:55 3↑ S Juan Capistrano H 115k 4 9 85¾ 4nk 42¼ 68¼ Longden J 125 w *2.20 51-41 Corn Husker116hdSpinney1142½Infantry1111¼ Bid,weakened 13
22Feb57- 7SA fm 1½Ⓣ :47 1:111 2:004 2:261 3↑ Wash Birthday H 29k 7 10 69 42½ 12 14½ Longden J 121 w *2.40 96-04 St.Vincent1214½PrinceofGreine1111½MastrBong124¾ Handily 13
12Feb57- 7SA fm 1½Ⓣ :484 1:123 2:03 2:273 4↑ San Luis Rey H 28k 8 9 64¼ 31½ 57 44 Longden J 122 w 3.70 85-11 Posadas113nkInfantry1141½Prince of Greine1102¼ Bore out 11
2Feb57- 5SA fst 7f :22 :444 1:092 1:221 4↑ Alw 6000 7 6 818 812 816 711 Longden J 113 w 5.55 81-12 Starover1152¼HowNow113noMizban1131½ Never close to pace 8

30May55- 6Bel fst 1¼ :474 1:113 1:36 2:003 3↑ Suburban H 88k 4 7 610 712 717 718 Longden J 126 w 13.70 79-11 Helioscope128hdHighGun1334½Subahdr1199 Never formidable 9
21May55- 7Pim fm 1⅜Ⓣ 2:152 3↑ Dixie H 31k 6 7 78 2hd 13 12½ James B 126 w *1.10 125-00 St. Vincent1262½Kaster120noMaharajah1131 Ridden out 8
16May55- 6Pim fm 1 1/16Ⓣ 1:434 3↑ Alw 4500 5 5 56 22 2hd 1½ James B 124 w 1.60 108-00 St.Vincent124½OldGlendale1133Martha'sWave1073 Driving 6
2Apr55- 7GP fst 1 1/16 :243 :48 1:112 1:432 3↑ Fort Lauderdale H 7.5k 9 9 913 87¾ 84¾ 21¼ Adams J 121 w *1.45 92-12 TwoFisted1091¼St.Vincent1211BadConduct110nk Closed fast 9
5Mar55- 7SA fm *1¾Ⓣ 2:464 3↑ S Juan Capistrano H 115k 13 8 52¼ 41½ 31½ 1½ Longden J 123 w *2.60 127-00 St. Vincent123½Determine126½Gigantic1103¼ Hard drive 13
22Feb55- 7SA fm 1½Ⓣ :463 1:11 2:01 2:252 3↑ Wash Birthday H 29k 4 11 93½ 4¾ 3nk 13½ Longden J 122 w *2.55e 103-00 St. Vincent1223½Alidon1133Kings Mutiny1083½ Going away 13
19Feb55- 5SA fm *6½fⓉ 1:16 4↑ Alw 7500 10 7 74½ 73½ 2½ 41¼ Longden J 121 w 5.55 93-06 Allied118½Pajone113nkScent122½ Hung 11
29Jan55- 6SA fm 1¼Ⓣ :454 1:101 1:344 2:00 4↑ San Gabriel H 31k 5 14 85¼ 74½ 45½ 1hd Longden J 116 w 7.25 100-00 St.Vincent116hdStaroftheForest122noNovrullh119¾ Just up 19
22Jan55- 7SA sf 1¼Ⓣ 2:034 4↑ San Marcos H 29k 6 5 65½ 53½ 41½ 73¾ Longden J 113 w 12.90 77-19 Great Captain1102½Poona II124noHigh Scud115nk Taken up 10
29Dec54- 6SA fm 1⅛Ⓣ :45 1:09 1:344 1:472 3↑ Alw 10000 12 11 1016 912 58½ 36½ Pearson B 110 w 22.65 101-00 PoonaII1083BlueTrumpeter1093½St.Vincnt1101½ Closed fast 12
24Nov54- 6GG fst 1 :23 :462 1:112 1:364 Alw 3500 5 5 62¼ 52¼ 1hd 12¼ Taniguchi G 110 w 8.70 84-18 St.Vincent1102¼KingsMutiny1145ShowMeFirst1201 Driving 7
13Nov54- 6GG my 6f :233 :48 1:131 Alw 3000 6 7 64¼ 63¾ 56 58 Longden J 114 w 3.75 67-39 DoubleReigh1192½TheHoop1142Toro-San109hd Lacked speed 7
27Oct54- 6Tan fst 6f :223 :452 1:094 3↑ Alw 3000 1 6 68¼ 47½ 35 25 Longden J 113 w 9.10 97-06 Sahib1195St. Vincent1131½Swell109½ Wide,good finish 6
20Oct54- 7Tan fst 6f :224 :454 1:102 Alw 3000 4 8 74 54 56½ 54¼ Longden J 114 w 13.65 95-08 MajrSpeed116½TheCharactr1222½TheHoop109½ Broke slowly 8
20Jly54- 7Hol fst 1 1/16 :232 :463 1:11 1:422 El Dorado H 22k 6 8 75 76½ 611 67¾ Longden J 111 w 21.35 88-08 WarTryst1161½HobcawSag1093MusslshII1122½ Never a factor 9
10Jly54- 5Hol fst 1 :231 :463 1:104 1:353 Alw 10000 5 5 31½ 3nk 45 46¼ Longden J 113 w 8.60 91-08 MusselshII114hdWrTryst119¾IndnRd1172¼ Bid turn,weakened 7
5Jly54- 6Hol fst 1 1/16 :234 :472 1:113 1:422 Alw 6000 9 9 82¾ 83 99¼ 912 Longden J 114 w 9.10 84-08 MusselshelI109hdHobcawSge1143½SprngCount120no No factor 9
29Jun54- 6Hol fst 6f :22 :451 :572 1:101 3↑ Alw 7500 2 5 46½ 44½ 43½ 52¾ Neves R 111 w 15.95 92-08 ZePippin1171¼Endorser1221½Ove'randUnder122no No factor 6
1May54- 6BM fst 1 :232 :463 1:113 1:37 Handicap 4000 6 3 2hd 2½ 44 55 Longden J 120 w *.85 88-10 Bright Liberty1131Tchaikowski109½Larks Music1162 6
Flattened out drive
10Apr54- 7BM fst 1 :23 :46 1:111 1:364 Handicap 5000 5 7 67½ 64½ 41¼ 21¼ Longden J 113 w 15.40 93-11 Indian Red1101¼St. Vincent1132½Leterna105¾ Closed well 8
27Mar54- 6BM gd 6f :223 :462 1:11 Alw 4000 3 8 63 87¼ 811 813 Balaski L 114 w *1.45e 79-18 Arrogate119nkBrighterDays1082½ZeBull1133 Showed nothing 8
6Mar54- 4SA fst 6f :222 :452 1:101 Alw 6000 5 6 85¼ 88¾ 811 88¼ Longden J 114 w 3.60e 86-07 Affrighted111½Knockmealdown112noZee Bull1141¼ No factor 8
Previously trained by George Colling
24Oct53♦ Doncaster(GB) gd 7fⓉStr 1:282 Allendale Plate Alw1700 14 Smith D 133 *1.85 St. Vincent1334By Thunder!126½Potential1192 23
Tracked leaders,led over 1f out,quickly clear
7Oct53♦ York(GB) fm6fⓉStr 1:144 Leyburn Stakes Alw2600 44 Smith D 133 *1.00 Swallow Dive1173Byzantium124noComatose 11
Whipped round start,trailed,finished well
12Sep53♦ Doncaster(GB) yl 1ⓉStr 1:394 Prince of Wales's Nursery Hcp Hcp9400 16 Smith D 111 4.50 St. Vincent1116No Worry118¾No Peace1103 20
Prominent,led 1½f out,drew clear 1f out
5Aug53♦ Yarmouth(GB) yl 6fⓉStr 1:13 Cliff Park Stakes Alw2300 67¼ Smith D 130 12.00 Sea Swan1353Carrion1202Birikorus123hd 22
Raced in midpack,evenly late;Race for maidens at time of entry
25Jly53♦ Doncaster(GB) gd 6fⓉStr 1:161 Cantley Plate Alw1700 11½ Smith D 119 2.00 St. Vincent1191½Joe's Ginger1192Sensitive1194 15
Close up,led 1f out,driving;Race for maidens at time of entry
27Jun53♦ Doncaster(GB) fm5fⓉStr :592 Lonsdale Foal Stakes Alw6900 2nk Smith D 115 4.50 Holiday Date127nkSt. Vincent1153Gondola112 4
Tracked leaders,bid 1f out,always held by winner
12Jun53♦ Thirsk(GB) gd 5fⓉStr 1:021 Carlton Miniott Maiden Stakes Mdn1400 21½ Smith D 123 2.50 Brittle1231½St. Vincent123¾Don Quixote1231 21
Prominent,bid 1f out,not good enough
16Apr53♦ Newmarket(GB) gd 5fⓉStr 1:022 Bartlow Stakes Alw2300 Unp Brown LG5 121 16.50 Sybil's Niece1231½Sir Vincent1261½Princely Gift1264
Never a factor;Race for maidens at time of entry

Stan (GB)

b. g. 1950, by Kingsway (Fairway)–Final Sweep, by Brumeaux — Lifetime record: 40 18 2 4 $248,989

Own.– Hasty House Farms
Br.– J. Sharp (GB)
Tr.– H. Trotsek

13Feb61- 9Hia fm 1 1/16Ⓣ 1:431 4↑ Clm 12000 1 12 1226 1112 99¼ 713 Adams JR 115 *2.60 86-04 Mozart1161¼FranciscoII1164¾RhinIndr1115 Pulled up lame 12
1Feb61- 4Hia fm 1 1/16Ⓣ 1:45 4↑ Clm 9000 2 12 1219 810 46½ 11¼ Adams JR 114 8.15 90-10 Stan1141¼Billy Bluejay117noSunningdale1144½ Going away 12
2Nov60- 7WO sf 1 1/16Ⓣ :244 :484 1:152 1:483 3↑ Clm 6000 7 6 65 53½ 2nk 13 Adams JR 115 *.85 69-31 Stan1153Detan1182½West Four11010¾ Drew out with ease 7
20Oct60- 8WO fm 1 1/16Ⓣ :231 :461 1:114 1:434 3↑ Clm 7500 7 9 88¼ 65¾ 31 4nk Adams JR 115 *1.15 93-07 Mr.Rooster113noRoyalBorder112noPercyYats114hd No excuse 9
13Oct60- 7WO fm 1Ⓣ :224 :461 1:122 1:364 3↑ Clm 6000 10 11 108 64½ 2½ 2no Adams JR 115 4.65 95-05 BrownPanther110noStan1153¼Culpepper120½ Strong late bid 12
22Oct59- 7WO fm 1Ⓣ 1:373 3↑ Clm 7500 4 7 89½ 54 2hd 1no Anyon E 120 *1.20 107-00 Stan120noSwallowswift111½John Berry1172¼ Hard drive 12
14Sep59- 6Haw fm 1Ⓣ 1:374 4↑ OClm 5000 4 6 65½ 21 11½ 13 Sellers J 117 *.70 87-13 Stan1173Painted Porch1142Last Impulse114no Easily 7
1Sep59- 9AP fm 1 1/16Ⓣ :233 :471 1:123 1:434 3↑ Clm 5000 9 7 59 32½ 12 13½ Sellers J 109 *1.90 90-16 Stan1093½Last Impulse111hdIrish Spark105nk Easily 9
8Aug59- 4AP sf 1 1/16Ⓣ :232 :472 1:132 1:463 3↑ Clm 8000 1 7 613 68 55½ 33¾ Sellers J 113 *1.30 72-21 Amy's Pet1141½Iskai1142¼Stan1132 Best stride too late 7
21Jly59- 8AP fm 1 1/16Ⓣ :24 :48 1:123 1:442 3↑ Clm 14500 3 7 712 78½ 65½ 41¾ Sellers J 111 *1.90 85-13 Yunlay114hdPripoly1091Camlbck114¾ Going strongly at end 8
14Jly59- 9AP fm 5½fⓉ :223 :46 :58 1:05 4↑ Clm 8500 4 10 910 911 99½ 62½ Sellers J 114 18.90 90-06 O'McSmith114nkMusicSuprme114½RessaBob102nk Closed gap 10

2Mar55- 7Hia fm 1½Ⓣ 2:293 3↑ Hia Turf H 63k 3 10 1112 96¾ 63¼ 1½ Adams J 128 w 7.45 96-00 Stan128½Capeador1181½Iceberg II112no Circled field 11
19Feb55- 7Hia fst 1¼ :48 1:12 1:363 2:022 3↑ Widener H 132k 1 7 76½ 78¼ 67 55¼ Nelson E 116 w 2.95e 88-12 Hasty Road122nkCapeador1192¾Social Outcast126¾ No rally 10
12Feb55- 6Hia fst 1⅛ :463 1:111 1:363 1:494 4↑ Alw 7500 10 10 1016 1014 78¼ 67½ Nelson E 123 w *1.00e 79-15 HastyRoad1201½CeriseReine115½Mahrjh117hd Sluggish early 10
5Feb55- 3Hia fst 7f :224 :454 1:111 1:241 4↑ Alw 4500 4 7 714 77½ 23 11½ Nelson E 124 w 10.85 89-14 Stan1241½King'sEvidenc1095PmpsButy106¾ Impressive score 7
16Oct54- 7Lrl fm *1⅛Ⓣ 1:51 3↑ Turf Cup H 25k 6 12 119 95¾ 41 12½ Nelson E 126 w *2.00 87-13 Stan1262½News Again1112½Tritium1142 Easily,drew out 13
28Aug54- 7Was sf 1 3/16Ⓣ :482 1:132 1:412 2:002 3↑ Meadowland H 55k 2 7 711 611 24 15 Nelson E 120 w *1.70e 72-38 Stan1205CountyClare1111BrushBurn118½ Drew clear easily 10
31Jly54- 7AP sf 1 3/16Ⓣ :462 1:112 1:382 1:57 3↑ Arlington H 156k 2 10 1011 76½ 61¼ 1nk Nelson E 114 w 5.40e 94-12 Stan114nkBrush Burn1133½Sir Mango1251½ 14
Saved ground,going away

5Jly54- 8AP	fm 1⅛Ⓣ	:47 1:112 1:363 1:492	3↑ Stars & Stripes H 28k	9 10 1212 1211 1012	34	Nelson E	114 w	10.90e	91-08	SirMango1243IcebergII1231Stan114no	Closed fast in drive	12
25Jun54- 7AP	fm 1 1/16Ⓣ	:242 :483 1:12 1:434	4↑ Alw 5000	3 6 710 613 513	54¼	Adams J	111 w	2.70	90-12	TheEagle114¾BlueDar1171¼Lordl120¾	Outrun early,rallied	8
17Feb54- 7Hia	hd 1 3/16Ⓣ	1:552	3↑ Bougainvillea H 33k	4 10 119½ 106½ 58	56	Adams J	113 w	7.65	100-00	Parnassus1113½Picador105½Abbe Sting116½	Late rally	12
10Feb54- 6Hia	hd 1 1/16Ⓣ	1:44	4↑ Alw 5000	6 9 99¾ 66¾ 45½	31	Adams J	114 w	4.70	95-04	Brown Booter114½Picador101½Stan114no	Closed gamely	12
22Jan54- 7Hia	fst 7f	:231 :46 1:103 1:232	4↑ Alw 5000	10 7 88¼ 912 917	814	Rotz J	111 w	18.20e	79-18	Hyphasis1182Impasse114¾Brown Booter1104	Outrun	10
31Oct53- 6Lrl	fst *1⅛Ⓣ	1:511	3↑ Turf Cup H (Div 1) 23k	10 8 109½ 1011 711	55	Adams J	111 w	8.50	81-15	Sunglow1141RoyalGovernor1202FreshMeadow1101	Mild rally	10
26Oct53- 7Lrl	fst 1	:24 :472 1:132 1:392	Alw 5000	2 1 31 68 715	817	Adams J	122 w	3.30	71-16	Smart Choice1161County Clare1104Tattletown1192	Stopped	9
26Sep53- 6Atl	fst 1 3/16Ⓣ	:473 1:12 1:362 1:554	3↑ U Nations H 60k	3 6 612 66½ 74½	77¾	Adams J	112 w	9.80	105-00	IcebergII1201½BrushBrun118nkRoyalGovernor118½	Crowded	8
16Sep53- 7Atl	fst 1⅛Ⓣ	:47 1:112 1:361 1:492	3↑ Foreign Bred 29k	2 3 43½ 44 34½	34¼	Adams J	115 w	4.90	92-06	Royal Vale1221¼Iceberg II1223Stan1152	No rally	8
	Restricted to horses foaled outside the continental United States											
29Aug53- 7Was	fst 1 3/16Ⓣ	:473 1:121 1:381 1:57	3↑ Meadowland H 57k	3 8 89½ 97 96¼	42	Arcaro E	118 w	*1.50e	87-16	Brush Burn118hdRuhe121½Jampol1181½	Late speed	13
22Aug53- 7Was	fst 1⅛	:462 1:103 1:352 1:482	American Derby 112k	5 8 610 610 68	58¾	Adams J	117 w	7.40e	90-11	NativeDancr1282Landlocked1201¼PrcousSton1143	No factor	8
15Aug53- 8Was	fst 1⅛Ⓣ	:482 1:12 1:364 1:493	3↑ Grassland H 28k	7 6 73¾ 77¾ 57	1½	Adams J	110 w	7.50	97-13	Stan110½Brush Burn1143Vantage115no	Driving clear	11
27Jly53- 6AP	fst 1 1/16Ⓣ	:224 :46 1:11 1:432	Handicap 10000	4 4 46 33½ 1hd	2½	Adams J	120 w	*1.80e	95-08	Guy109½Stan1201¼Dubuque109nk	Held well	9
16Jly53- 6AP	fst 5½fⓉ	:222 :462 :583 1:044	Alw 4500	9 10 83¼ 64¾ 53¼	1nk	Adams J	110 w	8.70	97-12	Stan110nkDHSmackover120DHWarless1101¼	Just up	10
	Previously trained by Willie Stephenson											
14Oct52♦ Newmarket(GB)	gd 6fⓉStr	1:15	2↑ Challenge Stakes Stk3400		46	Parnell R	105	4.00		Agitator1291Lady Sophia1265Fleeting Storm116hd	Trailed throughout	4
21Aug52♦ York(GB)	fm6fⓉStr	1:112	Gimcrack Stakes Stk16800		49½	Parnell R	126	8.00		Bebe Grande1231½Whistler1264Libator1234	Outrun early,mild late gain	10
25Jly52♦ Hurst Park(GB)	gd 6fⓉStr	1:143	Greensleeves Stakes Alw2200		11½	Parnell R	123	*1.50		Stan1231½Brolly125¾My Brazil116nk	Toward rear,rallied to lead 1f out,driving	10
11Jun52♦ Beverley(GB)	fm5fⓉStr	1:043	Bishop Burton Stakes Alw1400		15	Parnell R5	131	*.15		Stan1315Full Blown1196Lindy119½	Rated in last,rallied to lead over 1f out,quickly clear	5
30May52♦ Stockton(GB)	fm6fⓉStr	1:16	Summer Stakes Alw1700		14	Parnell R5	129	*.15		Stan1294Swallow Falls1195Monocello119		4
24May52♦ Beverley(GB)	fm5fⓉStr	1:033	Leconfield Stakes Alw1600		15	Parnell R5	126	*.90		Stan1265Jetty1264Knuckles136		9
20May52♦ Wolvrhmptn(GB)	gd 5fⓉStr	1:023	Ironbridge Plate Alw1700		11½	Parnell R	129	*1.60		Stan1291½Khandi Star1193Persian Sound119		9
15Apr52♦ Newmarket(GB)	gd 5fⓉStr	1:023	Ashley Stakes Alw2300		15	Parnell R5	118	8.00		Stan1185Sediment1203Amsheer122	Open to maidens at time of entry	21

Swaps

ch. c. 1952, by Khaled (Hyperion)–Iron Reward, by Beau Pere **Lifetime record: 25 19 2 2 $848,900**

Own.– R.C. Ellsworth
Br.– Rex C. Ellsworth (Cal)
Tr.– M.A. Tenney

3Sep56- 8Was	fst 1	:221 :441 1:074 1:332	3↑ Wash Park H 142k	5 3 22 1½ 13	12	Shoemaker W	130 w	*.40	102-13	Swaps1302Summer Tan1152Sea o Erin1123	Well in hand late	6
25Aug56- 8Was	fm 1 3/16Ⓣ	:47 1:103 1:362 1:55	3↑ Arch Ward Mem H 54k	7 2 3½ 2hd 31	76¼	Shoemaker W	130 w	*.30	92-02	Mahan114½SirTribal1161¾PrincMorv113hd	Well up,no excuse	8
25Jly56- 7Hol	fst 1⅝	:463 1:361 2:003 2:381	3↑ Sunset H 110k	5 1 11½ 11½ 16	14¼	Shoemaker W	130 w	*.10	112-08	Swaps1304¼Honeys Alibi1081Blue Volt1083	Eased up late	9
14Jly56- 8Hol	fst 1¼	:452 1:09 1:331 1:583	3↑ Hol Gold Cup H 162k	3 1 22 1hd 14	12	Shoemaker W	130 w	*.15	105-05	Swaps1302MisterGus1171¼Porterhouse1192¼	Eased at finish	7
4Jly56- 8Hol	fst 1⅛	:462 1:092 1:34 1:464	3↑ American H 103k	3 3 34½ 3nk 13	11¾	Shoemaker W	130 w	*.20	100-12	Swaps1301¾MstrGus1116BobbyBrocto1158	Eased final stages	5
23Jun56- 7Hol	fst 1 1/16	:231 :46 1:09 1:39	3↑ Inglewood H 52k	5 3 21½ 1hd 13	12¾	Shoemaker W	130 w	*.30	107-06	Swaps1302¾MisterGus1152BobbyBrocto1217	Eased final 16th	7
9Jun56- 7Hol	fst 1	:222 :451 1:084 1:331	3↑ Argonaut H 52k	1 1 11 1½ 12	11¼	Shoemaker W	128 w	*.20	108-07	Swaps1281¼Bobby Brocato1236Porterhouse1192¾	In hand	6
26May56- 7Hol	fst 1 1/16	:23 :453 1:092 1:404	3↑ Californian 109k	6 4 21½ 1½ 13	2hd	Shoemaker W	127 w	*.35	98-11	Porterhse118hdSwaps1275MistrGus1181¾	Eased by mistake	6
14Apr56- 7GP	fst 1 70	:23 :453 1:092 1:393	3↑ Broward H 25k	4 2 22 11½ 13	12¼	Shoemaker W	130 w	*.30	105-09	Swaps1302¼Gldr1055OurGob114no	Never to a drive,eased up	8
17Feb56- 7SA	fst 1 1/16	:224 :462 1:103 1:43	4↑ Handicap 15000	7 4 42 1hd 1hd	11¾	Shoemaker W	127 w	*.70	89-15	Swaps1271¾Bobby Brocato124nkArrogate1159	Strong finish	7
31Aug55- 7Was	gd 1¼	:46 1:102 1:373 2:041	WP Match 100k	2 2 21 21½ 22	26½	Shoemaker W	126 w	*.30	74-17	Nashua1266½Swaps126	Wide on stretch turn,tired,swerved	2
20Aug55- 7Was	fm 1 3/16Ⓣ	:472 1:114 1:354 1:543	American Derby 146k	5 1 11 11½ 13	11	Shoemaker W	126 w	*.20	101-05	Swaps1261Traffic Judge1194Parador1131½	Very handy score	6
9Jly55- 7Hol	fst 1¼	:463 1:102 1:344 2:003	Westerner 57k	1 1 11½ 12 110	16	Shoemaker W	126 w	*.05	96-11	Swaps1266Fabulous Vegas1171Jean's Joe1203½	Eased up	5
11Jun55- 7Hol	fst 1 1/16	:231 :46 1:10 1:402	3↑ Californian 109k	1 1 22 21 11	11¼	Erb D	115 w	*.65	103-06	Swaps1151¼Detrmine126½MistrGus1173	In hand throughout	6
30May55- 6Hol	fst 1	:222 :452 1:101 1:35	ⓒWill Rogers 27k	3 3 21½ 1hd 13	112	Shoemaker W	126 w	*.15e	100-07	Swaps12612Dequeath122noMr.Sullivan1187	Drew out in hand	6
7May55- 7CD	fst 1¼	:472 1:122 1:37 2:014	Ky Derby 152k	8 1 11 1½ 1½	11½	Shoemaker W	126 w	2.80	98-12	Swps1261½Nshua1266½SummrTn1264	Drew clear when urged	10
30Apr55- 6CD	fst 6f	:23 :462 1:101	Alw 5000	1 3 12½ 12 14	18½	Shoemaker W	123 w	*.30	99-13	Swaps1238½TrimDestiny115¾Styrunnr1104½	Speed in reserve	5
19Feb55- 7SA	fst 1⅛	:454 1:103 1:37 1:50	SA Derby 137k	12 3 31 13 11	1½	Longden J	118 w	3.60e	91-14	Swaps118½Jean'sJoe1183½BlueRuler1183	Went wide,driving	14
19Jan55- 7SA	my 7f	:214 :45 1:103 1:24	San Vicente 22k	1 5 56½ 21 12	13½	Shoemaker W	116 w	4.40e	83-25	Swaps1163½Trentonian120hdJean'sJoe1146	Speed in reserve	8
30Dec54- 6SA	fst 6f	:221 :451 1:10	Alw 6000	5 5 2hd 21 2hd	1no	Shoemaker W	118 w	5.25	95-11	Swaps118noBeau Busher1131¾Battle Dance118½	Strong drive	12
8Jly54- 6Hol	fst 5½f	:221 :453 :581 1:044	ⓒCS Howard 29k	1 5 63½ 65¼ 58	58¾	Burton J	118 w	9.95e	85-12	ColonlMack114¾Mr.Sullivan1221BackHo1181	Showed nothing	6
22Jun54- 7Hol	fst 5f	:221 :454 :582	ⓒHaggin 24k	9 7 83¾ 73 31½	32	Burton J	122 w	6.40e	92-13	Mr. Sullivan114½Back Hoe1221½Swaps1221¾	Good effort	10
10Jun54- 7Hol	fst 5f	:221 :46 :582	ⓒJune Juv 16k	5 5 42½ 32 1½	12½	Burton J	116 w	4.70	94-10	Swaps1162½Trentonian1192Noir116nk	Drew out	7
3Jun54- 7Hol	fst 5f	:221 :452 :58	Westchester 16k	2 5 42½ 53½ 51¾	32¼	Burton J	116 w	7.25	94-11	Back Hoe1191¼Trentonian1191Swaps116½	Failed to rally	7
20May54- 2Hol	fst 5f	:222 :454 :582	ⓒMd Sp Wt	9 5 2hd 2hd 1hd	13	Burton J	120 w	12.60	94-12	Swaps1203Irish Cheer1203½Battle Dance1201½	Won handily	11

Sweet Patootie

dkb. f. 1950, by Alquest (Questionnaire)–Sweet Woman, by Roman **Lifetime record: 21 8 4 1 $64,327**

Own.– Mrs E.E.D. Shaffer
Br.– Coldstream Stud Inc (Ky)
Tr.– H.H. Battle

28Jan54- 6Hia	fst 6f	:23 :463 1:11	4↑ ⒻAlw 4500	4 1 1½ 1½ 2hd	54¾	Erb D	117 w	1.95	88-19	Missou1111¼La Perouse1072Centenaire1101½	Faltered	10
22Jan54- 6Hia	fst 6f	:222 :46 1:112	4↑ ⒻAlw 4500	6 3 2½ 11 11	51¾	Rotz J	109 w	5.30	89-18	Pampas Beauty110nkMissou1111Fulvous114no	Faltered	11
20Jun53- 7Det	fst 6f	:222 :451 1:103	3↑ ⒻRose Leaves 11k	13 1 44½ 68 57	1311	Madden D	110 w	12.70	84-09	Lilly Valenti1111Peu-a-Peu1111½Amabala981	Outrun	13
12Jun53- 6Det	fst 6f	:222 :453 1:103	3↑ Alw 3500	9 2 2½ 3½ 43½	45¼	Madden D	110 w	2.50	90-14	ShagTails1111BlackBantam1112ElaineRuth1062¼	No mishap	10
2May53- 6CD	fst 7f	:224 :451 1:101 1:231	Alw 6000	1 2 32 45½ 76½	616	Madden D	118 w	3.20	81-09	Berseem1151Platan1153Sir Mango1156	Sore	8
15Apr53- 6Kee	fst 6f	:224 :47 1:121	ⒻAshland 22k	4 3 12 12 12	31¼	Madden D	121 w	8.60	90-14	CeriseReine1151Bubbley118nkSweetPatootie1212½	Faltered	10
9Apr53- 5Kee	fst 6f	:222 :452 1:11	ⒻAlw 4000	7 4 1½ 3nk 34	89	Madden D	121 w	4.70	88-10	Task Fleet1152½Bubbley1213Cerise Reine115¾	Early foot	10
4Feb53- 7Hia	sl 7f	:233 :481 1:143 1:282	3↑ ⒻColumbiana H 20k	7 3 21 22 32½	712	Atkinson T	106 w	3.10	56-40	Sunny Dale114¾Emardee1057La Corredora122¾	Tired,swerved	15
21Jan53- 7Hia	fst 6f	:222 :46 1:11	ⒻJasmine 19k	5 2 2hd 42¼ 68¼	1013	Atkinson T	121 w	*.90	80-19	Emardee1183GoodCall1132BiddyJane121½	Stumbled at start	13
18Oct52- 6Kee	fst 7f	:223 :46 1:112 1:233	ⒻAlcibiades 27k	4 1 11½ 12 11½	12	Armstrong S	119 w	*1.10	94-12	Sweet Patootie1192Good Call1193Aerolite119hd	Driving	12
8Oct52- 6Jam	fst 6f	:23 :46 1:122	ⒻFrizette 17k	5 2 2½ 1hd 11	11¼	Atkinson T	119 w	*1.50	85-17	SweetPatootie1191¼PiedmontLass119½GrecnQn1191½	All out	8
17Sep52- 7Atl	fst 6f	:221 :451 1:114	ⒻMargate H 11k	6 7 32 1hd 1½	2no	Armstrong S	127 w	*.70	86-17	PiedmontLass111noSweetPatoot1272½RtsBst1111	Just failed	9
1Sep52- 6Nar	fst 6f	:222 :453 1:113	ⒻJeanne D'Arc 11k	7 1 1½ 13 19	17	Armstrong S	116 w	*.50	93-13	Sweet Patootie1167Air Town105½I'm Marie111¾	Easily best	8
23Aug52- 7Atl	fst 6f	:224 :46 1:121	Longport H 12k	10 1 11½ 13 15	14	Armstrong S	117 w	*.70	84-17	Sweet Patootie1174Prince Dare113½Late Model1091	Easily	11
16Aug52- 3Atl	sly 6f	:222 :45 1:113	Alw 4500	1 1 12 13 14	15	Armstrong S	113 w	3.50	87-20	Sweet Patootie1135Dinner Winner116½Mr. Jones1101	Easily	8

12Jly52- 7Det	fst 5f	:222 :461 :583	ⒻAlw 7500	6 1 12 12½ 13 14	Sisto R	113 w	2.70	100-11	Sweet Patootie1134Task Fleet1081Pegnpat1132¼	Easily	6
7Jun52- 7Haw	fst 5f	:224 :454 :59	ⒻMiss America 12k	3 1 1hd 2hd 2hd 22½	Johnson WL	119 w	4.90	97-13	BiddyJane1222½SwtPatootie1193ArabActress1191¼	Impeded	13
31May52- 4Det	fst 4½f	:23 :473 :534	Alw 2000	6 1 13 14 16	Cook LC	114 w	*.70	92-14	Sweet Patootie1146Full Circle1091¼Caboose1172	Easily	7
29Apr52- 3CD	fst 4½f	:23 :462 :53	Alw 2000	4 4 52¾ 31½ 2hd	Garner W	115 w	3.30	95-14	CelticPlay115hdSweetPtoot115¾Suprm'sBub1183	Just missed	7
2Apr52- 4GP	fst 3f	:213 :324	Alw 2600	5 2 2½ 21	Scurlock D	109 w	*1.70	--	AriGold1041SweetPatootie1094CountTwenty107½	No excuse	8
25Mar52- 3GP	fst 3f	:222 :34	ⒻMd Sp Wt	4 4 2hd 12	Scurlock D	118 w	3.55	--	Sweet Patootie1182Eddie Sue1182½Nalaca1141	Drew away	14

Sword Dancer

ch. c. 1956, by Sunglow (Sun Again)–Highland Fling, by By Jimminy — **Lifetime record: 39 15 7 4 $829,610**

Own.– Brookmeade Stable
Br.– Brookmeade Stable (Va)
Tr.– E. Burch

22Oct60- 7Bel	sf 1½Ⓣ	:50 1:162 2:08 2:331	3↑ Man o' War 110k	8 6 711 53½ 55 36¼	Arcaro E	126 b	*1.40	74-20	Harmonizing1262¼Bald Eagle1264Sword Dancer126nk	Bore in	8
24Sep60- 7Aqu	fst 1¼	:472 1:111 1:354 2:011	3↑ Woodward 112k	2 6 68 53½ 3½ 11½	Arcaro E	126 b	3.15	102-08	SwordDancer1261½DottedSwiss1262½BaldEagle1261	Driving	7
17Sep60- 7Atl	fm 1 3/16Ⓣ	:463 1:12 1:372 1:57	3↑ U Nations H 100k	1 10 1015 87¼ 73¼ 21¼	Arcaro E	127 b	4.40	87-12	T.V.Lark1201¼SwordDancer1271¼BallyAche122hd	Strong bid	10
20Aug60- 8AP	sf 1 3/16Ⓣ	:482 1:132 1:39 1:583	3↑ Arlington H 55k	8 5 67½ 87¼ 64¼ 63	Arcaro E	126 b	3.20	71-26	One-EyedKing1181KingGrail109hdMartiniII109no	Late foot	8
30Jly60- 7Aqu	sly 1¼	:471 1:12 1:38 2:03	3↑ Brooklyn H 109k	3 7 711 56 55¼ 55¾	Arcaro E	127 b	2.00	87-17	On-and-On118hdGreek Star1102Waltz1131¼	Began sluggishly	7
4Jly60- 7Aqu	fst 1¼	:472 1:111 1:361 2:013	3↑ Suburban H 108k	5 6 65¾ 43 3½ 1½	Arcaro E	125 b	2.95	112-11	SwordDancr125½FirstLanding1221½Wltz1154½	Crowded early	6
30May60- 7Aqu	fst 1	:224 :453 1:09 1:333	3↑ Metropolitan H 114k	2 10 106¼ 85½ 78¼ 44½	Arcaro E	127 b	3.35	103-03	BaldEagle1283½FirstLanding123nkTalentShow118¾	Rallied	10
30Apr60- 7Aqu	fst 1⅛	:473 1:114 1:37 1:493	3↑ Grey Lag H 70k	9 10 107¾ 53¼ 1½ 1nk	Arcaro E	126 b	2.65	96-06	SwordDancer126nkFirstLanding124noWhitley1162	Hard drive	11
19Mar60- 7GP	gd 1¼	:473 1:122 1:362 2:011	3↑ Gulf Park H 112k	8 8 89½ 56 56½ 45¾	Arcaro E	127 b	2.55	87-05	Bald Eagle126¾Amerigo1233On-and-On1212	Had no mishaps	8
5Mar60- 6GP	fst 1 1/16	:231 :454 1:103 1:414	Alw 4000	2 6 35 11 12½ 12¼	Hartack W	117 b	*.35	99-08	SwordDancer1172¼Don'tAlibi1114½SixShooter1111½	In hand	8
20Feb60- 7Hia	fst 1¼	:464 1:101 1:351 1:593	3↑ Widener H 126k	8 5 56½ 83¼ 77½ 78¾	Arcaro E	129 b	1.95e	98-07	Bald Eagle123¾On-and-On1191½Talent Show118½	Dull effort	8
1Feb60- 6Hia	fst 7f	:232 :46 1:103 1:231	4↑ Alw 5000	6 5 56 58 45½ 43¾	Arcaro E	126 b	*.25e	90-15	Petare112noMaster Palynch1122½Big Effort1071¼	No mishap	6
	Previously trained by J.E. Burch										
31Oct59- 7Aqu	fst 2	:463 2:284 2:55 3:221	3↑ J C Gold Cup 110k	8 4 47 31½ 13 17	Arcaro E	119 b	*1.25	--	SwordDancr1197RoundTable1241¼TudorEra1242¼	Easy score	8
26Sep59- 7Aqu	fst 1¼	:491 1:141 1:40 2:042	3↑ Woodward 109k	4 3 33 31 2hd 1hd	Arcaro E	120 b	2.90	--	SwordDancer120hdHillsdale1261¾RoundTable1265	Hard drive	4
22Aug59- 6Sar	fst 1¼	:48 1:121 1:372 2:041	Travers 81k	2 4 47 32 31 1½	Ycaza M	126 b	*.95	87-18	Sword Dancer126½Middle Brother1121¾Nimmer1124	Driving	5
1Aug59- 6Jam	fst 1 3/16	:473 1:122 1:374 1:562	3↑ Brooklyn H 113k	4 5 613 83¾ 51¼ 2¾	Shoemaker W	124 b	*1.05	93-15	Babu112¾Sword Dancer124hdAmerigo1173		10
	Unruly post,swerved start										
25Jly59- 7Mth	sl 1¼	:471 1:123 1:391 2:05	3↑ Monmouth H 113k	4 7 67½ 61¼ 1hd 12	Shoemaker W	120 b	*.60	81-32	SwordDancer1202Amerigo1161½Talent Show1242½	Drew clear	10
13Jun59- 7Bel	sly 1½	:463 1:104 2:024 2:282	Belmont 145k	8 7 715 21 2hd 1¾	Shoemaker W	126 b	*1.65	91-10	Sword Dancer126¾Bagdad12612Royal Orbit12615	Brisk drive	9
30May59- 6Bel	fst 1	:224 :452 1:101 1:351	3↑ Metropolitan H 115k	5 9 75 42 21 13¼	Shoemaker W	114 b	2.50e	98-12	SwordDncr1143¼Jimmer1122¼TlntShow115no	Speed to spare	11
16May59- 8Pim	fst 1 3/16	:471 1:113 1:374 1:57	Preakness 190k	7 6 56 2hd 22 24	Shoemaker W	126 b	1.70	84-17	RoyalOrbit1264SwordDancer1263Dunce1262½	Best of others	11
2May59- 7CD	fst 1¼	:473 1:113 1:36 2:021	Ky Derby 163k	14 4 43 1½ 1hd 2no	Boland W	126 b	8.80	96-06	Tomy Lee126noSword Dancer1262¼First Landing1261	Bore in	17
25Apr59- 7CD	fst 7f	:23 :452 1:094 1:221	Alw 5000	1 5 1hd 1hd 1½ 11	Shoemaker W	122 b	3.60	99-14	Sword Dancer1221Easy Spur1221½Silver Spoon1172	Driving	5
4Apr59- 7GP	fst 1⅛	:463 1:094 1:344 1:471	Florida Derby 116k	9 2 2½ 13 12 2¾	Boulmetis S	122 b	3.90	97-10	Easy Spur122¾SwordDancer1229Master Palynch1221	Gamely	9
24Mar59- 7GP	fst 1 70	:233 :472 1:112 1:41	Alw 3800	3 3 2½ 1½ 13 12	Boulmetis S	118 b	1.70	93-14	SwordDancer1182NobleSel1083Dunce1142½	Speed in reserve	8
11Mar59- 7GP	fst 6½f	:221 :443 1:093 1:16	Hutcheson 12k	5 9 76¾ 56 54½ 54	Boulmetis S	122	5.25	91-14	Easy Spur1222½Pointer114½Octopus122nk	In close in drive	9
11Nov58- 6Jam	fst 1 1/16	:24 :472 1:12 1:443	Remsen 28k	4 5 75 73 74¾ 46½	Guerin E	117wb	*1.00	80-21	Atoll1174½RicoTso114hdDrrck1142	In close on backstretch	7
25Oct58- 7GS	sly 1 1/16	:222 :463 1:124 1:462	Garden State 297k	2 9 87¼ 47 33½ 32	Guerin E	122wb	11.40	76-31	First Landing122hdTomyLee1222SwordDancer1223	Game try	13
18Oct58- 8Suf	fst 1 70	:221 :451 1:114 1:424	Mayflower 30k	14 11 1113 65 11½ 14½	Mercier N	116wb	13.00	91-19	SwordDancer1164½Atoll1191¾OpenView1191½	Speed to spare	14
7Oct58- 5Bel	fst 6f	:223 :463 1:122	Alw 4200	2 3 31½ 21 21 1nk	Kay M5	112wb	3.55	86-20	SwordDancer112nkSirSalonga1155Principality1171½	Just up	14
27Sep58- 3Bel	sly 7f	:222 :453 1:111 1:241	Alw 4200	2 4 43¼ 54 32 32¼	Nelson E	118wb	5.30	84-13	Hoist Away118nkMatinal1152Sword Dancer118¾	Held on well	13
10Sep58- 7Atl	fst 7f	:214 :441 1:094 1:232	World's Playground 36k	3 10 83½ 107 77 42¾	Choquette J	111wb	82.70	86-16	Demobilize119hdIntentionlly1222½PnBolro110hd	Closed gap	15
23Aug58- 2Sar	fst 6f	:231 :474 1:133	©Md Sp Wt	4 5 52½ 53 2½ 11¾	Boland W	118wb	*1.15	80-18	Sword Dancer1181¾Time Off1182½Nimmer1183½	Going away	12
15Aug58- 4Sar	fst 5½f	:23 :472 1:001 1:064	©Md Sp Wt	2 3 22½ 21½ 22 21½	Nelson E	118wb	2.20	81-22	Landing1181½SwordDancer11812TimOff1181½	Easily 2nd best	9
26Jly58- 4Del	fst 5½f	:22 :462 :582 1:053	Md Sp Wt	4 7 54½ 45½ 34½ 21½	Grant H	119wb	*3.40	92-12	CarolinaJoy1191½SwordDancer1192Harlegh1192½	Fast finish	13
12Jly58- 4Del	fst 5½f	:222 :47 :592 1:052	©Md Sp Wt	5 3 21 21 21 32½	Anderson P	119wb	4.20	92-12	Genian1192½Troilus119hdSwordDancr1196	Forced pace,tired	8
4Jly58- 4Bel	fst 5½f	:23 :471 1:00 1:062	©Md Sp Wt	9 9 64½ 72¾ 43½ 43	Boulmetis S	118wb	6.25	87-11	Matinal118¾MoonAge118nkLakeErie1182	Forced wide on turn	10
23Jun58- 3Bel	fst 5f-WC	:223 :45 :57	©Md Sp Wt	9 10 1013 109 67	Lovato F	118wb	7.85f	87-06	Benbecul118nkJtFul1184½Occultd115nk	Slow finding stride	20
10Jun58- 7Bel	sly 5f-WC	:222 :443 :57	©Md Sp Wt	11 10 1014 1012 1020	Kay M5	113 w	38.20	74-08	RestlssWind1186TroubldTms1181½BostonTprty118½	No speed	11
28Feb58- 3Hia	fst 3f	:223 :333	©Md Sp Wt	8 5 77¼ 46½	Boulmetis S	120 w	12.35	--	Wizardo'Waxah1202JerseyAdmiral1204½JetEra120no	Rallied	14

Tea-Maker

dkb. g. 1943, by Only One (Lucullite)–Tea Leaves, by Pharamond II — **Lifetime record: 115 29 23 16 $211,530**

Own.– F.A. Clark
Br.– Mrs F. A. Clark (Ky)
Tr.– J.D. Byers

25Sep53- 5Bel	fst 6f	:223 :462 1:113	4↑ Alw 5000	5 2 1½ 1hd 1hd 1no	Gorman D	118 w	*2.30	91-15	Tea-Makr118noThisSd106hdColdCmmnd1182¼	Held on gamely	12
7Sep53- 6Aqu	fst 7f	:224 :454 1:11 1:234	3↑ Bay Shore H 22k	2 2 24 48½ 619 717	Hanford I	120 w	7.10	74-17	Squared Away1302Eatontown1203Elixir1122½	Done early	9
2Sep53- 5Aqu	fst 6f	:224 :46 1:11	3↑ Fayette H 10k	1 1 56 56¾ 44 33	Woodhouse H	121 w	4.35	94-14	DarkPeter1221½WheatState1071½Tea-Makr1214½	Closed well	7
24Aug53- 6Sar	fst 6f	:23 :472 1:121	3↑ Handicap 4575	6 2 23½ 2½ 1½ 2hd	Green B	123 w	*2.55	87-21	Hilarious118hdTea-Maker1232Sandtop116nk	Held gamely	10
15Jly53- 6Jam	fst 6f	:231 :462 1:11	3↑ Fleetwing H 22k	6 2 32½ 21½ 22 2nk	Woodhouse H	117 w	4.40	92-15	Eatntown118nkTea-Makr117hdSquaredAwy1304½	Just missed	7
27Jun53- 6Aqu	fst 6f	:22 :443 1:092 1:22	3↑ Carter H 59k	2 2 44½ 35 55½ 66¼	Woodhouse H	117 w	19.55	94-09	Tom Fool1352Squared Away1222¼Eatontown1131¼	Tired	9
20Jun53- 5Aqu	fst 6f	:224 :461 1:11	3↑ Handicap 7545	5 3 34½ 35½ 33½ 43¾	Woodhouse H	123 w	2.95	93-11	Eatontown114½DarkPeter1211½FrstGlnc1181¾	Tired in drive	7
10Jun53- 5Bel	fst 6f	:23 :463 1:104	4↑ Alw 4500	7 1 41¾ 4¾ 1hd 1¾	O'Brien C	121 w	*1.20	95-19	Tea-Maker121¾Primate1134½Bit o' Fate108½	Drew out	7
2Jun53- 6Del	gd 6f	:224 :462 1:123	4↑ Alw 4000	5 4 32½ 31½ 1hd 1nk	Boman D	121 w	*.40	82-24	Tea-Maker121nkRuthred1212Yildiz126hd	Cleverly	5
27May53- 6Bel	fst 6f-WC	:214 :443 1:101	3↑ Roseben H 23k	3 8 62¾ 66 42¾	Woodhouse H	119 w	6.05	87-09	SquaredAway1241¼DarkPeter1221½Sagittarius115hd	Swerved	9
19May53- 6Bel	fst 6f	:223 :462 1:113	3↑ Joe Palmer H 15k	6 4 32 41¾ 33 21½	Woodhouse H	114 w	7.30	89-27	Tom Fool1301½Tea-Makr1141½Dark Peter121¾	Closed gamely	7
6May53- 6Bel	gd 6f-WC	:221 :444 1:10	3↑ Toboggan H 30k	1 1 96½ 88¼ 74½	Woodhouse H	118 w	7.70	86-12	Tuscany122noHyphasis116½Dark Peter122nk	No menace	9
25Apr53- 5Jam	fst 5½f	:23 :461 :582 1:041	3↑ Handicap 7560	4 5 43½ 44 48 47¾	Woodhouse H	123 w	4.70	89-12	Tom Fool1282½Do Report1162¼Earmarked1143	Raced wide	5
11Nov52- 6Jam	fst 6f	:223 :454 1:11	2↑ Autumn Day H 22k	5 3 32 44 42½ 31¼	Woodhouse H	126 w	*1.95	91-16	Squared Away119¾Delegate119½Tea-Maker1261½	Closed well	7
20Oct52- 6Jam	fst 6f	:224 :453 1:104	2↑ New Rochelle H 22k	4 4 42 42¼ 32 21½	Woodhouse H	126 w	*2.75	91-20	Delegate1141½Tea-Maker126¾War King1111½	Good effort	9
6Oct52- 6Jam	fst 6f	:23 :46 1:11	2↑ Interborough H 23k	2 2 73¾ 85 53¼ 2½	Gorman D	124 w	3.80	91-15	Squared Away118½Tea-Makr124noTrue Pattern1061¼	Gaining	11
27Sep52- 4Bel	fst 5½f-W	:22 :444 1:032	2↑ Handicap 6045	8 7 63¾ 4nk 1no	Woodhouse H	130 w	*1.15	91-05	Tea-Maker130noTruePattern115hdTwoRainbows1062	Just up	9
22Sep52- 6Bel	fst 7f	:223 :454 1:111 1:234	2↑ Vosburgh H 23k	6 6 61¾ 4¾ 1hd 21½	Woodhouse H	123 w	4.05	89-19	Parading Lady1051½Tea-Maker1232Cyclotron110nk	Held well	8
15Sep52- 6Bel	fst 6f-WC	:22 :441 1:082	2↑ Fall Highweight H 24k	10 8 4nk 2hd 2½	Woodhouse H	140 w	13.00	98-03	Hitex130½Tea-Maker140½Papoose117nk	Good effort	15
8Sep52- 6Aqu	fst 7f	:223 :451 1:102 1:24	3↑ Bay Shore H 17k	10 5 33 34 23 53¼	Woodhouse H	123 w	6.65	87-20	NextMove1151FirstGlance111nkSquaredAway1202	No excuse	12
23Aug52- 5Sar	fst 5½f	:23 :46 :582 1:051	3↑ Handicap 5045	6 1 2½ 21½ 2½ 11	Woodhouse H	122 w	4.10	91-17	Tea-Makr1221FirstGlance111½SquardAway126hd	Drew clear	7
15Aug52- 6Sar	sl 7f	:231 :463 1:12 1:253	3↑ American Legion H 9k	4 1 1½ 1hd 1½ 1¾	Woodhouse H	118 w	4.60	87-25	Tea-Maker118¾First Glance1091½Northern Star1196	Driving	6
8Aug52- 6Sar	fst 6f	:232 :47 1:114	3↑ Handicap 5035	2 1 41¼ 45 56 43¼	Woodhouse H	119 w	4.65	86-23	Squared Away1221¼Elixir1071First Glance1101	Raced wide	5
16Jly52- 6Jam	fst 6f	:23 :454 1:101	3↑ Fleetwing H 21k	5 1 21 21 21 1¾	Woodhouse H	114 w	8.45	96-16	Tea-Maker114¾Squared Away1202½Arise1221	Driving	6

4Jly52- 6Aqu fst 7f :221 :443 1:09 1:22 3↑ Carter H 29k 7 9 97½ 97½ 1016 1013 Scurlock O 115 w 15.90 89-09 NorthernStar1152CraftyAdmiral1202½ToMarket123no Outrun 10
21Jun52- 5Aqu fst 6f :222 :452 1:102 3↑ Handicap 7540 3 2 34½ 36 25 25 Gorman D 121 w 3.45 95-11 Squared Away1225Tea-Maker121noDelegate1201½ Impeded 4
14Jun52- 6Mth fst 6f :221 :45 1:112 3↑ Oceanport H 17k 8 5 41¼ 75¼ 76¾ 77¾ Gorman D 120 w *2.30 83-21 GeneralStaff1122HiBillee112nkNorthernStar113hd Faltered 8
7Jun52- 5Bel fst 6f :223 :461 1:104 3↑ Handicap 7540 2 2 3nk 3½ 2½ 31¼ Gorman D 121 w 3.05 94-14 First Glance112¾Delegate113½Tea-Maker121no Held well 7
29May52- 5Del fst 6f :222 :453 1:103 3↑ Wilmington H 12k 5 2 2hd 1hd 13 13 Gorman D 121 w 6.00 98-11 Tea-Maker1213Jet Master113hdSenator Joe119½ Ridden out 8
21May52- 6Bel sl 6f-WC :223 :462 1:124 3↑ Roseben H 17k 1 1 32½ 76¼ 67¾ Gorman D 120 w 6.40 69-23 DarkPeter1133NorthernStar112noSquaredAwy118½ Quit early 7
29Apr52- 6Bel gd 6f-WC :221 :443 1:091 3↑ Toboggan H 23k 8 1 2hd 21 33 Gorman D 120 w 5.10 92-05 Dark Peter108½Crafty Admiral1182½Tea-Maker1202 Faltered 8
16Apr52- 6Jam gd 6f :23 :46 1:111 3↑ Jamaica H 17k 4 1 1½ 1hd 13 12½ Woodhouse H 112 w 10.20 91-15 Tea-Maker1122½Northern Star115noDelegate1142 In hand 9
11Apr52- 6Jam fst 6f :23 :46 1:113 3↑ Mettlesome H 7.9k 6 2 1½ 2hd 2hd 31 Gorman D 115 w 4.20 88-21 Delegate111hdBryan G.1261Tea-Maker1153 Held well 8
1Apr52- 6Jam fst 6f :222 :453 1:094 3↑ Paumonok H 29k 9 3 41¾ 63½ 46¼ 88¾ Gorman D 116 w 11.55 89-13 Woodchuck1193½Squared Away116½[D]Jumbo116¾ Tired 11
12Nov51- 6Jam fst 6f :231 :454 1:111 2↑ Autumn Day H 17k 2 1 31½ 32 32 1½ Porch G 115 w 10.45 91-20 Tea-Maker115½Guillotine126¾Delegate120hd Driving 9
3Nov51- 7Jam sly 6f :222 :452 1:121 3↑ Handicap 5065 6 4 45 34½ 33½ 41 Scurlock O 117 w 4.90 85-17 Assignment105noDelegate119½Atalanta104½ No excuse 7
19Oct51- 6Jam fst 6f :223 :452 1:101 2↑ New Rochelle H 17k 6 2 31½ 31 42 43½ Gorman D 118 w 6.15 92-15 Squared Away1151½Delegate116½Guillotine1261½ Faltered 12
10Oct51- 5Bel fst 5½f-W :22 :441 1:013 3↑ Handicap 4565 2 2 51½ 32 33¾ Gorman D 123 w 6.85 102-00 Delegate1133Guillotine132¾Tea-Maker123nk No mishap 8
1Oct51- 6Bel fst 7f :221 :453 1:103 1:231 2↑ Vosburgh H 18k 13 4 42 3nk 1½ 53 Gorman D 120 w 15.20 91-17 [D]Miche109½War King108¾Bryan G.122nk Faltered 13
Placed fourth through disqualification
24Sep51- 6Bel fst 6f-WC :222 :443 1:09 2↑ Fall Highweight H 25k 9 16 134¼ 113¼ 115¼ Riles S 134 w 13.45 91-07 Guillotine134noSquared Away1262Ferd128no Showed little 18
15Sep51- 5Aqu fst 6f :23 :46 1:104 3↑ Handicap 4560 3 3 11 11½ 11½ 11 Gorman D 121 w 2.70 98-13 Tea-Maker1211Northern Star1184½Hill Prince128¾ All out 7
10Sep51- 6Aqu fst 7f :222 :451 1:101 1:232 3↑ Bay Shore H 18k 9 7 96¼ 74½ 72¼ 63½ Mehrtens W 121 w 7.05 91-15 Sheilas Reward126½Guillotine117¾Bryan G.123nk No mishap 12
17Aug51- 6Sar my 7f :231 :461 1:114 1:252 3↑ American Legion H 9.3k 8 2 2hd 2hd 2½ 2¾ Mehrtens W 120 w 6.45 87-19 [D]War King109¾Tea-Maker1201[D]More Sun113hd Impeded 10
Placed first through disqualification
6Aug51- 7Sar fst 1 :241 :48 1:13 1:384 3↑ Alw 4000 3 5 42 3½ 3nk 41½ Passmore WJ 119 w 2.45 81-18 Blue Hills113½Combat Boots1051Charleston113no Weakened 6
18Jly51- 6Jam fst 6f :231 :462 1:112 3↑ Fleetwing H 22k 7 6 41½ 41¼ 1hd 2hd Mehrtens W 122 w 6.75 90-16 More Sun110hdTea-Maker1221½Arise1301½ Just failed 9
11Jly51- 7Aqu fst 6f :224 :454 1:111 3↑ Handicap 5035 3 6 51¾ 63¼ 42¾ 42¼ Mehrtens W 126 w 4.40 94-14 Repetoire118hdJessLinthcum1182¼MghtyQust112no No mishap 6
4Jly51- 6Aqu fst 7f :223 :452 1:101 1:232 3↑ Carter H 23k 9 7 79 66½ 43½ 64½ Scurlock O 122 w 4.75 90-17 Arise1221More Sun1081¼Piet1231 Stumbled at start 9
29Jun51- 6Aqu sly 6f :23 :461 1:104 3↑ Handicap 5050 4 2 32 32 32 32¾ Mehrtens W 124 w 4.15 95-14 Bryan G.1182½Magic Words116nkTea-Maker1241 Mild rally 6
16Jun51- 7Mth gd 6f :223 :454 1:114 4↑ Alw 5000 8 5 44 51¾ 43 31 Flutie E 124 w 2.00 88-15 JessLinthicum115hdSheilasRwrd1241T-Mkr1242¼ Good effort 8
6Jun51- 6Bel fst 6f-WC :222 :444 1:084 3↑ Roseben H 12k 4 8 73¾ 2½ 3nk Arcaro E 126 w *1.70 97-04 Delegate111nkMiche116noTea-Maker126¾ Crowded early 10
29May51- 6Del gd 6f :224 :462 1:113 3↑ Wilmington H 12k 2 5 42½ 3½ 32 21 Arcaro E 125 w *.95 92-20 CallOver1151Tea-Maker125hdRoyalGovrnor115nk Forced wide 6
14May51- 6Bel fst 6f-WC :222 :444 1:092 3↑ Toboggan H 24k 11 2 2hd 1hd 2no Mehrtens W 123 w 3.45 94-06 Hyphasis110noTea-Maker1231Casemate1191 Just missed 14
7May51- 6Jam fst 6f :23 :461 1:111 3↑ Jamaica H 17k 6 2 42½ 4¾ 2hd 1½ Mehrtens W 121 w 5.35 91-15 [D]Tea-Maker121½Piet1241SheilasRwrd1242¼ Driving,bore in 7
Disqualified
1May51- 6Jam fst 6f :23 :462 1:11 3↑ Handicap 5030 5 2 1hd 2hd 1hd 31 Mehrtens W 121 w 2.90 91-13 Piet1201Sheilas Reward124hdTea-Maker1216 Good effort 6
Previously owned by Mrs S.C. Clark Jr
25Oct50- 6Jam gd 6f :23 :46 1:111 2↑ New Rochelle H 17k 5 10 116 94½ 52½ 31¾ Mehrtens W 125 w 4.20 89-19 MagicWords1131SheilasRewrd124¾Tea-Makr1252 Closed fast 12
12Oct50- 6Jam sly 6f :23 :46 1:12 3↑ Interborough H 17k 6 2 65 65¾ 55 51½ Robertson J 126 w 4.10 85-18 SheilsRwrd120¾MgcWords112½WsconsnBoy109nk Forced wide 10
Previously owned by Mrs F.A. Clark
25Sep50- 6Bel fst 7f :223 :453 1:102 1:23 2↑ Vosburgh H 18k 5 2 11 11½ 11½ 11¼ Robertson J 118 w 6.60 95-15 Tea-Maker1181¼More Sun106½Piet124nk Easily 12
18Sep50- 6Bel fst 6f-WC :221 :443 1:084 2↑ Fall Highweight H 25k 2 11 112 102¼ 42¾ Robertson J 134 w 6.25 94-06 Arise1332Delegate128nkRoyal Governor129½ Finished well 14
2Sep50- 6Aqu fst 7f :224 :452 1:10 1:231 3↑ Bay Shore H 18k 2 2 2hd 21 11 21 Mehrtens W 117 w *2.25e 95-09 Piet1201Tea-Maker1171¼Arise1211½ No excuse 14
15Aug50- 5Sar fst 6f :223 :453 1:101 3↑ Handicap 3565 7 4 41¼ 62¾ 3½ 11 Woodhouse H 122 w *1.60 97-09 Tea-Maker1221Sagittarius1172½Marabout113nk Driving 9
7Aug50- 6Sar fst 1 :241 :481 1:13 1:38 4↑ Alw 4000 6 2 2½ 2hd 2hd 31½ Guerin E 116 w *.75 85-17 The Mater108½Pibroch1131Tea-Maker1164½ No rally 6
3Aug50- 4Sar fst 6f :23 :461 1:111 3↑ Handicap 4050 1 1 11 11½ 11 13 Guerin E 120 w *1.55 92-13 Tea-Maker1203Marabout1163Mount Marcy1231½ Going away 6
15Jly50- 5Jam fst 6f :231 :462 1:11 3↑ Handicap 4565 7 6 51¾ 42 31 1hd Guerin E 122 w 2.55 92-11 Tea-Maker122hdSagittarius118nkWhirling Fox1151 Just up 10
28Jun50- 6Del fst 6f :223 :453 1:11 3↑ Alw 4000 2 4 3nk 11 13 13 Robertson J 117 w *.60 96-09 Tea-Maker1173Rare Mineral115hdLittle Harp1171 Easily 7
17Jun50- 6Del fst 6f :224 :462 1:112 4↑ Alw 4000 2 4 2hd 1hd 11 11½ Culmone J 114 w *1.80 94-14 [D]Tea-Maker1141½Larn1171½LttlHrp1141½ Impeded rival str 6
Disqualified
13Jun50- 6Del fst 6f :224 :454 1:102 4↑ Alw 3000 5 1 1½ 1½ 11 11 Robertson J 116 w 4.25 99-13 Tea-Maker1161Fleeting Star120nkLaran1191 Driving 6
9Jun50- 5Del fst 1 1/16 :234 :473 1:12 1:433 4↑ Alw 3500 1 1 12 1hd 21 23 Culmone J 115 w 2.60 92-12 Curandero1193Tea-Maker115hdSlam Bang1163½ Weakened 7
30May50- 4Del sl 6f :23 :471 1:132 4↑ Alw 3500 3 4 32 21 1½ 1¾ Culmone J 112 w 3.30 84-19 Tea-Maker112¾Lucky Ned115¾Noble Impulse1243 Driving 5
2Nov49- 6Jam sly 6f :232 :462 1:112 2↑ New Rochelle H 17k 1 1 73¾ 85¼ 76½ 66¼ Passmore WJ 110 w 15.70 88-19 Delegate1226Better Self124noLithe109no Never close 8
26Oct49- 6Jam sly 1 1/16 :243 :40 1:122 1:452 3↑ Questionnaire H 23k 6 1 15 67½ 810 814 Passmore WJ 109 w 10.70 72-17 Royal Governor1181Donor120½Vulcan's Forge125¾ Tired 8
20Oct49- 6Jam fst 1 1/16 :244 :48 1:122 1:443 3↑ Handicap 5030 2 3 33½ 46½ 49 59½ Passmore WJ 122 w 4.10 80-16 Our John Wm.1163Dart By1161½Wine List1193½ Tired 6
1Oct49- 6Lrl fst 1 1/16 :232 :474 1:134 1:462 2↑ Laurel 8.6k 1 2 22 2hd 2hd 2nk Passmore WJ 114 w *.60e 85-18 Alfoxie108nkTea-Maker1141Gasparilla1152 Game try 7
24Sep49- 6Lrl fst 6f :224 :463 1:112 3↑ Capitol H 8.7k 9 2 42¼ 31½ 32½ 2no Passmore WJ 117 w *2.60 97-17 Irisen115noTea-Maker117½Big Story1092 Just missed 9
19Sep49- 6Bel fst 6f-WC :23 :461 1:12 2↑ Fall Highweight H 24k 8 3 1hd 2hd 3nk Passmore WJ 127 w 16.05 81-16 RoyalGovernr129hdRoyalBlood132nkTea-Makr127¾ Lost iron 13
15Sep49- 6Aqu fst 1 1/16 :25 :482 1:123 1:452 3↑ Alw 4000 6 2 31 21 31 54¾ Passmore WJ 117 w 3.55 82-17 Quarter Pole1223Brick1051Stymie122hd Weakened 8
5Sep49- 5Aqu fst 6f :231 :462 1:111 3↑ Handicap 4045 5 4 65½ 67½ 34½ 34¼ Passmore WJ 116 w 3.20 92-17 Royal Blood1154Mangohick122nkTea-Maker1164 Faltered 7
29Aug49- 6Aqu sly 7f :233 :47 1:121 1:25 3↑ Bay Shore H 18k 13 7 107 106¾ 52¼ 2½ Passmore WJ 113 w 19.65 86-17 Loser Weeper116½Tea-Maker1131½Rippey121nk Held gamely 15
23Aug49- 6Sar fst 6f :223 :463 1:11 3↑ Handicap 4060 7 4 63½ 74¼ 62¾ 52 Passmore WJ 114 w 5.70 91-11 WineList115hdBlueBorder115nkRoyalBlood114¾ Raced wide 10
12Aug49- 6Sar sly 7f :234 :464 1:113 1:252 3↑ American Legion H 9.2k 4 7 65 56 55 55½ Passmore WJ 116 w 8.20 83-18 Manyunk119hdWhirling Fox1102Big If1101½ Even effort 8
Daily Racing Form time,1:26 1/5
9Aug49- 5Sar fst 6f :223 :453 1:111 4↑ Handicap 3565 4 3 53¾ 54½ 2hd 1hd Passmore WJ 120 w 4.55 92-11 Tea-Maker120hdPipette1162Our John Wm.115nk Hard drive 8
4Aug49- 6Sar gd 6f :23 :464 1:12 3↑ Handicap 4045 3 3 32 22 2hd 2¾ Passmore WJ 119 w *1.30e 87-18 Arise113¾Tea-Maker1192Algasir1084 Weakened 5
21Jly49- 6Jam fst 1⅛ :481 1:13 1:392 1:522 3↑ Handicap 4535 1 2 21 2½ 21 24½ Passmore WJ 122 w 2.10 81-20 Stunts1144½Tea-Maker1222½Prefect1191½ Forced wide 5
16Jly49- 5Jam fst 6f :232 :462 1:112 3↑ Handicap 5050 1 1 55 55¼ 56½ 41½ Passmore WJ 115 w 2.60 92-14 EagleEye111hdMyRequest1261¼BluBordr112hd Closed stoutly 5
9Jly49- 5Jam fst 6f :232 :46 1:112 3↑ Handicap 5065 10 8 43½ 41¼ 1hd 11¼ Passmore WJ 111 w 5.80 94-16 Tea-Maker1111¼Stunts1041My Request126½ Drew out 10
4Jly49- 5Jam fst 1 1/16 :241 :48 1:123 1:454 3↑ Handicap 5040 5 4 31½ 32 3½ 2nk Passmore WJ 119 w 2.50 84-17 Prefect112nkTea-Maker1191¼Coincidence112hd Just missed 6
25Jun49- 5Aqu fst 7f :231 :462 1:12 1:251 3↑ Carter H 29k 5 4 56 43½ 41½ 41½ Passmore WJ 111 w 19.05 84-26 Better Self126nkRippey123½High Trend107¾ No mishap 9
18Jun49- 6Mth fst 1 :23 :461 1:111 1:373 3↑ Salvator Mile 13k 14 6 46 43½ 65 87¾ Passmore WJ 112 w 8.50 99-08 Istan1142High Trend1121Royal Governor1191½ Faltered 14
7Jun49- 6Bel fst 7f :231 :47 1:114 1:241 4↑ Alw 4500 7 2 1hd 1hd 1½ 2hd Passmore WJ 122 w *1.20 89-19 Bug Juice117hdTea-Maker1226Hyblaze115¾ Game try 8
3Jun49- 6Bel fst 6f :22 :452 1:11 4↑ Alw 4000 5 4 34 23 1hd 16 Passmore WJ 113 w 3.50 95-14 Tea-Maker1136Thwarted114nkEagle Eye113½ Easily 11
30May49- 6Bel fst 1¼ :48 1:123 1:38 2:03 3↑ Suburban H 61k 3 7 21 42½ 68 711 Passmore WJ 106 w 23.80 74-17 Vulcan'sForge1242½ButWhyNot1174FlyingMissel108½ Quit 13
20May49- 7Bel sly 1 :222 :453 1:104 1:384 4↑ Alw 4000 5 2 23 23 23 1hd Passmore WJ 114 w 3.60 80-19 Tea-Maker114hdUp Beat122hdThwarted114½ Hard drive 10
14May49- 6Bel fst 1 :23 :461 1:11 1:362 3↑ Metropolitan H 30k 8 6 53 42¼ 22 42¾ Passmore WJ 107 w 10.95 89-15 LosrWeepr1051½Vulcan'sForg126nkBtWhyNt1191 Weakened 10
6May49- 6Bel fst 6f-WC :224 :451 1:092 3↑ Toboggan H 24k 6 8 54 84¾ 86¼ 73 Passmore WJ 110 w 17.30 91-05 Rippey1291½Pipette108¾Up Beat120no No factor 11
30Apr49- 5Jam fst 6f :23 :46 1:112 3↑ Handicap 5040 2 3 34½ 37 25 34¾ Arcaro E 117 w 3.95 89-13 Up Beat1224½Make-Up Man108nkTea-Maker117¾ Went well 7
12Nov48- 6Jam fst 1 1/16 :243 :483 1:143 1:452 3↑ Handicap 5035 7 2 2hd 2½ 2nk 2½ Rustia W 122 w *2.20 85-25 Caifero111½Tea-Maker1223Rinaldo107½ Weakened 7
5Nov48- 6Pim my 2 1/16 :53 2:402 3:061 3:392 3↑ Exterminator H 11k 4 2 45 411 413 426 Passmore WJ 114 w 10.40 83-30 Pilaster126nkPetrol Point1026Miss Grillo12020 Outrun 4
30Oct48- 7Pim fst 1¾ :473 2:033 2:291 2:553 3↑ Governor Bowie H 12k 3 2 36 3½ 38 311 Passmore WJ 120 w 2.60 119-00 Pilaster1242½Natural1048Tea-Maker1204 Went well 7
23Oct48- 5Jam fst 5½f :231 :47 1:052 3↑ Handicap 6030 5 5 44 32½ 33 21¼ Passmore WJ 111 w 4.60 90-22 Grey Flight1151¼Tea-Maker1111½Buzfuz1262 Good effort 5
19Oct48- 6Jam fst 6f :232 :471 1:121 3↑ Handicap 4565 8 8 74 52¼ 4½ 11 Passmore WJ 120 w 11.05 90-22 Tea-Maker1201Energetic114hdNathaniel1211 Driving 9

14Oct48- 7Jam	fst	1 1/16	:244 :483 1:134 1:464	4↑ Alw 5000	3	6	52½	52	1hd	1nk	Passmore WJ	118 w	3.55	79-22	Tea-Maker118nkCencerro1121¼Ned Luck112½	Driving	9
9Oct48- 7Jam	fst	1⅛	:483 1:131 1:382 1:512	3↑ Handicap 5055	3	3	3nk	11	2½	44¼	Anderson P	114 w	6.30	87-14	Bright Sword1211¼Campos1131Frere Jacques1222	Faltered	10
6Oct48- 5Jam	fst	6f	:24 :481 1:13	4↑ Alw 4000	6	2	2hd	1nk	11	11½	Rustia W	119 w	30.85	86-22	Tea-Makr1191½Flying Weather1221Winter Wheat1152	Easily	12
1Oct48- 6Bel	sly	1½	:494 1:151 2:06 2:313	3↑ Handicap 6055	7	3	54	74½	812	818	James B	118 w	5.75	62-22	Frere Jacques122noMy Emma111hdCampos1141½	No mishap	8
21Sep48- 7Bel	fst	1⅛	:472 1:12 1:37 1:494	3↑ Handicap 5080	3	3	21	41¼	2hd	43½	Passmore WJ	108 w	16.20	88-14	War Trophy115hdQuarter Pole1153Star Reward126½	Hung	8
16Sep48- 8Bel	fst	1½	:481 1:124 2:04 2:313	3↑ Alw 5000	1	4	511	33	2½	11	Passmore WJ	109 w	6.20	80-14	Tea-Maker1091Happiness106¾Ready Jack1064	Driving	8
8Sep48- 5Aqu	fst	7f	:25 :483 1:142 1:273	4↑ Alw 4000	3	5	42½	43	31	11¼	Passmore WJ	106 w	17.70	74-31	Tea-Maker1061¼Liberty Road111hdNed Luck1111	Driving	7
30Aug48- 3Aqu	fst	*1¾	Hurdles 3:104	3↑ Alw 4000	7	4	416	523	628	641	Mong'o T	130 ws	11.80e	--	Deep Sea Tale1393Coeur1316Frere Markette1441½	Impeded	7
11Aug48- 5Sar	fst	7f	:233 :47 1:123 1:27	3↑ Md Sp Wt	10	3	52¼	42¼	21	11	Passmore WJ	117 w	50.65	81-21	Tea-Maker1171Brass Band1173½Harbor1173	Driving	10
6Aug48- 5Sar	sl	*1¾	Hurdles 3:332	3↑ National Maiden 7.8k	3	2	25	210	240	250	Mong'o T	143 ws	4.65	--	Lock and Key14650Tea-Maker14330Jordan1301½	Outrun	5
7Jly48- 3Aqu	gd	*1½	Hurdles 2:473	3↑ Md Sp Wt	11	4	67½	911	720	728	Mon'lo T	141 ws	28.40	--	DeepSeaTale1325LionRampant1483½TopKnot137nk	No factor	11
28Jun48- 5Del	fst	*1¾	Hurdles 3:051	3↑ National Maiden 7.9k	6	4	-	-	-	-	Peoples C	150 ws	12.55	--	Lock and Key1437Rank1567Charioteer1352		6

Broken equipment,pulled up

22Jun48- 1Del	fst	*1¾	Hurdles 3:084	3↑ Alw 3500	1	13	79¾	79	718	822	Peoples C	145 ws	7.20	--	Lock and Key1301½Todmorden1371¼Mr. Man1426	Outrun	13
19Jun48- 8Del	my	6f	:231 :481 1:142	4↑ Alw 5000	4	5	54¼	42	55	46½	Passmore WJ	110 w	32.10	73-31	Tacaro Briar1202½Meetmenow1101½Pujante1202½	No mishap	7
27Mar48- 7Cam	fst	*1½	Hurdles 2:45	3↑ Alw 800	2	5	55½	-	-	-	Dodson S	140 w	-	--	GoldenRsk156hdNghtLgnd148hdEscondrjo1344	Lost rider 6th	6
13Mar48- 2Cam	fst	*1½	Hurdles 2:414	4↑ Alw	5	7	713	-	-	-	Seidler W	136 w	-	--	NightLegend153hdDeferment1364TheBoyn1466	Lost rider 4th	8

Tempted

ch. f. 1955, by Half Crown (Hyperion)–Enchanted Eve, by Lovely Night

Lifetime record: 45 18 4 9 $330,760

Own.– Mooring Stable
Br.– Christiana Stables (Ky)
Tr.– H.S. Clark

29Oct60- 8Nar	fst	1 3/16	:463 1:12 1:38 1:572	3↑ Nar Spl H 29k	2	2	22	11	1hd	33	Nelson E	114	5.20	83-25	Reinzi1111½Polylad1191½Tempted1142	Set fast pace,tired	12
12Oct60- 7Bel	fst	1½	:471 1:114 2:042 2:303	3↑ Ⓕ Ladies H 59k	4	1	13	11½	23	86¼	Nelson E	121	6.05	74-15	Berlo1242½Woodlawn112½Who's Ahead105½	Used in pace	13
1Oct60- 7Bel	fst	1⅛	:461 1:11 1:362 1:492	3↑ Ⓕ Beldame 91k	8	1	3nk	31½	88	88¾	Nelson E	123	*2.50	80-16	Berlo1192RoyalNative1231MakeSal1193	Early speed,stopped	9
21Sep60- 7Aqu	fst	1	:23 :453 1:102 1:353	3↑ Ⓕ Maskette H 30k	1	6	64¼	53¼	5¾	1nk	Nelson E	126	*2.20	90-13	Tempted126nkMakeSail118½Craftinss108no	Swerved start,up	12
22Aug60- 7Sar	fst	1⅛	:471 1:113 1:374 1:512	3↑ Ⓕ Diana H 38k	3	2	23	21½	11½	17	Nelson E	124	3.75	88-14	Tempted1247Quill1281¾Aesthetc1121	Going away easily	5
12Aug60- 7Sar	fst	7f	:222 :45 1:102 1:231	3↑ Handicap 1000	10	1	33½	88	106½	108	Nelson E	118	9.35	90-15	Four Lane117½Seven Corners116½Tick Tock1204	Brief speed	10
30Jly60- 6Del	sly	1¼	:461 1:103 1:364 2:022	3↑ Ⓕ Delaware H 146k	2	1	15	31½	59	716	Nelson E	125	5.00	74-15	Quill1259RoyalNative1291¼GeecheLou110¾	Early foot,tired	8
23Jly60- 6Del	fst	1 1/16	:23 :46 1:102 1:431	3↑ Ⓕ New Castle 35k	8	1	12	1½	21	33	Nelson E	126	3.30e	92-11	Quill1201¼IndianMad1201¾Tmptd1262¼	Set pace,tired badly	8
9Jly60- 7Mth	fst	1 1/16	:224 :461 1:11 1:434	3↑ Ⓕ Molly Pitcher H 28k	3	2	2hd	2hd	33½	46¼	Nelson E	127	4.80	80-17	RoyalNative1274Quill1221¾MissOrestes114½	Well up,tired	10
2Jly60- 7Mth	fst	6f	:213 :443 1:10	3↑ Rumson H 28k	8	2	67	65¾	54½	35½	Nelson E	119	*2.10	86-15	Alhambra1183¼SevenCornrs1122¼Temptd119¾	Wide last turn	8
30May60- 4Del	fst	6f	:222 :454 1:104	4↑ Ⓕ Alw 6500	2	1	1hd	13	13	12½	Nelson E	123	*.30	91-13	Tempted1232½Wedlock1142NoraDars1146	Scored well in hand	6
17May60- 7GS	fst	6f	:22 :451 1:11	4↑ Ⓕ Alw 7500	1	1	33	36½	33	22	Nelson E	115	*.30	87-17	WindRose1212Tmptd1151½MissRoyl115½	Wide upper stretch	6
12Oct59- 7Aqu	fst	1 5/16	:472 1:111 1:362 2:09	3↑ Ⓕ Ladies H 57k	5	1	11½	12	12	12¾	Nelson E	128	*.85e	--	Tempted1282¾High Bid1121Big Effort1151½	Saved ground	8
3Oct59- 7Aqu	fst	1⅛	:474 1:121 1:37 1:501	3↑ Ⓕ Beldame H 67k	3	1	11½	11½	11½	12½	Nelson E	125	*1.75e	--	Tempted1252½Idun121nkHigh Bid1131	Drew away,mild urging	14
21Sep59- 7Aqu	fst	1	:223 :45 1:094 1:36	3↑ Ⓕ Maskette H 29k	1	4	3nk	2hd	1hd	21¼	Bailey PJ	126	*2.20	--	Idun1191¼Temptd1261½Bornstr1192	Off sluggishly,game try	10
17Aug59- 6Sar	fst	1⅛	:471 1:111 1:364 1:502	3↑ Ⓕ Diana H 56k	2	1	11	12	13	15½	Nelson E	122	*2.30	97-15	Tempted1225½Polamby1162½SparMaid110hd	Speed in reserve	9
10Aug59- 5Sar	fst	1	:23 :461 1:104 1:36	3↑ Ⓕ Handicap 7500	1	2	21	2hd	1½	1½	Nelson E	122	*.90e	97-15	Temptd122½Polamby1164½Idun1222½	Forced pace,hard drive	5
25Jly59- 6Del	fst	1¼	:462 1:111 1:37 2:033	3↑ Ⓕ Delaware H 155k	5	2	21½	11	2½	31¼	Nelson E	119	*3.20e	83-18	Endine117½Polamby114¾Tmptd1192½	Made very game effort	11
18Jly59- 6Del	fst	1 1/16	:231 :464 1:112 1:433	3↑ Ⓕ New Castle 35k	2	1	12	11½	11½	12¾	Nelson E	116	4.50e	93-18	Tempted1162¾Bornastar126½Chstos112no	Under a mild drive	10
11Jly59- 5Del	gd	1 1/16	:232 :47 1:121 1:443	3↑ Ⓕ Alw 10000	2	1	13	13	13	12	Ussery R	115	*.90e	88-21	Tempted1152Chistosa1132½MissOrsts118¾	Well rated,easily	9
30Jun59- 7Del	fst	6f	:222 :453 1:111	4↑ Alw 6000	5	3	33½	33½	4¾	11¼	Batcheller L	117	*.40	89-17	Tempted1171¼Amplitud112nkStyrunnr122no	Under mild drive	6
8Jun59- 7Bel	fst	1 1/16	:223 :451 1:102 1:424	3↑ Ⓕ Top Flight H 27k	2	2	1½	1½	23	37	Ussery R	118	2.40e	87-13	Big Effort1235½Endine1181½Tempted1181½	Tired badly	7
25May59- 7Bel	fst	7f	:221 :453 1:111 1:241	3↑ Ⓕ Distaff H 28k	1	2	22½	22	21	42¾	Nelson E	120	2.85	83-18	HappyPrincess1141½Mlle.Dianne115noIdun1251¼	Speed,tired	8
13May59- 5GS	sly	6f	:224 :463 1:112	4↑ Ⓕ Alw 5500	3	5	2hd	1hd	12	18	Kirk J5	111	*.70	87-21	Tempted1118DanceCard1183½BonnieA.110nk	Drew out easily	7
5May59- 7GS	fst	6f	:223 :462 1:12	4↑ Ⓕ Alw 6000	11	2	3nk	21½	2½	11½	Kirk J5	110	4.50	84-22	Tempted1101½BattleHill1182½MissOrestes115hd	Drew clear	12
4Nov58- 7GS	sl	1 1/16	:24 :474 1:112 1:45	Ⓕ Jersey Belle 28k	1	1	1hd	1½	11½	1¾	Nelson E	121 w	6.70	85-24	Tempted121¾Lopar115noPointPleasant112hd	Long,hard drive	9
13Oct58- 6Bel	fst	1½	:48 1:121 2:034 2:302	3↑ Ⓕ Ladies H 58k	8	1	14	2½	611	714	Ussery R	114 w	7.35e	67-20	Endine1141¾Dotted Line123nkAnnie-Lu-San1081½	Led,tired	10
4Oct58- 7Bel	fst	1⅛	:453 1:10 1:36 1:492	3↑ Ⓕ Beldame H 70k	2	1	11½	11	3½	61½	Ussery R	114 w	7.90e	87-14	OuterSpace117noAGlitter119hdDottedLin120nk	Used in pace	17
24Sep58- 6Bel	fst	1	:222 :452 1:102 1:363	3↑ Ⓕ Maskette H 29k	11	2	2½	11½	12	12½	Ussery R	113 w	5.10e	91-19	Tempted1132½Alanesian1231¾Annie-Lu-San1112	Ridden out	12
15Sep58- 6Bel	fst	1 1/16	:223 :451 1:101 1:431	Ⓕ Gazelle H 29k	2	1	1½	21	22	34½	Nelson E	116 w	11.55	87-15	Idun1244½Munch122noTempted116¾	Led pace for 4f,tired	10
27Aug58- 6Sar	fst	1¼	:474 1:13 1:384 2:054	Ⓕ Alabama 29k	9	1	12	1hd	1hd	11½	Ussery R	113 w	6.50	79-24	Temptd1131½SprMd1133Lopr1141	Drew clear in strong drive	11
20Aug58- 4Sar	fst	1⅛	:473 1:123 1:383 1:531	Ⓕ Alw 5000	4	1	1½	1½	1½	2nk	Nelson E	116 w	3.65	83-20	A Glitter122nkTempted1165Daumay1192	Made a sharp effort	5
15Aug58- 6Sar	fst	7f	:224 :454 1:113 1:254	Ⓕ Test 25k	13	7	84¼	87½	1013	79	Nelson E	115 w	*4.00	77-22	AnyMorn1151¾DandyBlitzen115¾Armorial1151½	Bore out late	17
26Jly58- 6Del	fst	1¼	:464 1:111 1:361 2:03	3↑ Ⓕ Delaware H 160k	10	2	21	12	1hd	42	Chambers A	106 w	11.00e	85-12	Endine111noDotted Line1161Woodlawn1081	Speed to stretch	16
12Jly58- 6Del	sly	1⅛	:47 1:12 1:39 1:521	Ⓕ Del Oaks 49k	8	2	21	21	34	35¾	Nelson E	119 w	11.50	73-20	Big Effort1192¼Idun1193½Tempted119½	Forced pace,tired	9
30Jun58- 5Del	fst	1	:24 :472 1:112 1:371	Ⓕ Alw 4000	2	3	2hd	1hd	13	13½	Nelson E	118 w	*.70	100-11	Tempted1183½Locust Time1153Bokaris1104	Speed in reserve	5
21Jun58- 7Bel	sly	1⅜	:48 1:124 1:393 2:20	Ⓕ C C A Oaks 71k	2	6	53½	63¼	811	818	Nelson E	121 w	9.90	53-21	A Glitter121½Spar Maid1219Craftiness1214	Speed,stopped	12
12Jun58- 6Bel	fst	1⅛	:461 1:111 1:374 1:511	Ⓕ Alw 10000	6	2	1½	21	21	2½	Nelson E	114 w	18.90	79-17	AGlitter117½Tempted1141¾Lopr1113	Coming again at finish	13
31May58 8Del	fst	6f	:22 :451 1:112	3↑ Ⓕ Alw 5000	5	10	47½	410	48½	32	Nelson E	114 w	*2.80e	86-12	Mumtaz1182TooHasty118noTemptd1141½	Best stride too late	12
14May58- 7Pim	fst	1 1/16	:233 :473 1:123 1:463	Ⓕ Black-Eyed Susan 23k	1	2	21	54½	53¾	54½	Nelson E	121 w	6.10	72-22	Daumay121hdMovitave1213½StaySmooch121¾	Early foot,tired	8
5May58- 6Pim	sly	6f	:223 :47 1:133	Alw 4000	8	6	42	34	31½	32¾	Kirkland A	119 w	*1.60e	79-23	Staysail1121½Alstar1181¼Tmptd1191¼	Raced without mishap	8
23Nov57- 5Pim	gd	1 70	:23 :463 1:114 1:441	Alw 4500	7	5	58½	58¾	59½	56¼	Nelson E	116 w	2.20	82-15	FrankZero1131¼PoliceCll1161½CountDown110hd	Lacked rally	9
9Nov57- 7Nar	gd	1 1/16	:234 :474 1:123 1:474	Ⓕ Jeanne d'Arc 16k	5	4	45½	21	11	13½	Nelson E	109 w	7.00	72-23	Tmptd1093½TwoCentStamp105½Slon116½	Under light urging	9
16Oct57- 4Bel	fst	7f	:224 :472 1:141 1:271	Ⓕ Md Sp Wt	6	11	53½	41	2hd	14½	Nelson E	115 w	4.25e	74-18	Tempted1154½Colic1151½Redone1154½	Kept to mild pressure	14
10Oct57- 5Bel	gd	6f-WC	:23 :47 1:132	Ⓕ Md Sp Wt	18	14		72¾	71¾	157¼	Nelson E	115 w	5.85e	65-28	Doricharger115nkIntent One1151Beguiling115hd	Fell back	21

The Mast

blk. g. 1947, by Annapolis (Man o' War)–Claddagh, by Alcazar

Lifetime record: 36 10 4 7 $103,400

Own.– Mrs J.R.H. Thouron
Br.– Mrs James E. Ryan (Pa)
Tr.– J.E. Ryan

25Jun54- 6Del	hd	*2	S'Chase 3:45	4↑ Georgetown H 12k	1	-	-	-	-	-	McDonald RS	153wsb	*.60	--	SunShower1555Sundowner1403½TouristList1345	Fell at 1st	6
17Jun54- 5Aqu	hd	*2	S'Chase 3:471	4↑ Hitchcock H 11k	5	1	12½	12½	18	112	McDonald RS	150wsb	*1.20	--	ThMast15012SunShower1572BannrWaves1321½	Scored easily	5
3Jun54- 5Bel	hd	*2½	S'Chase 4:391	4↑ Meadow Brook H 11k	5	2	22	15	-	-	McDonald RS	154wsb	2.65	--	Sun Shower1551½Beaupre1324Sundowner14425		7

Bobbled last jump,fell

27May54- 5Bel	fm	*2	S'Chase 3:412	4↑ Corinthian H 8.9k	5	6	68½	56	314	314¾	McDonald RS	156wsb	2.65	--	ExtraPoints1622¾SunShower15212TheMast1563	Lacked rally	7
8May54- 6Bel	sf	*2	S'Chase 3:562	4↑ International 22k	3	4	32½	22	210	218	McDonald RS	153wsb	*2.25	--	ExtraPoints15318TheMast15320HisBoots1531¾	Bobbled badly	13
26Apr54- 3Bel	fm	*2	S'Chase 3:432	4↑ Alw 4500	4	3	42½	23	24	27	McDonald RS	157 w	*2.25e	--	ExtraPoints1397ThMst1575Sundownr1451	Weakened in drive	10

Previously raced in name of Mrs E. duPont Weir

9Oct53- 5Bel	fst	*3	S'Chase 5:451	4↑ Grand Nat'l H 29k	3	4	35½	24½	23	22½	McDonald RS	160wsb	2.30	--	His Boots1412½The Mast16018Mighty Mo1325	Good effort	11

1Oct53- 5Bel	fst	*2½	S'Chase	4:46^{3}	4↑	Brook H 17k	4	3	$3^{4\frac{1}{2}}$	$3^{2\frac{1}{2}}$	1^{3}	1^{hd}	McDonald RS	157	wsb	*2.50	--	The Mast157^{hd}His Boots140^{12}Sundowner151^{1}	Just lasted	9
24Sep53- 5Bel	fst	*2	S'Chase	3:45^{4}	3↑	Broad Hollow H 11k	5	1	$2^{2\frac{1}{2}}$	$2^{\frac{1}{2}}$	$2^{\frac{1}{2}}$	1^{hd}	McDonald RS	155	wsb	3.10	--	The Mast155^{hd}Sundowner150$^{2\frac{1}{2}}$Mighty Mo131^{2}	Just up	7
13Aug53- 5Sar	fst	*2	S'Chase	4:09^{3}	4↑	North Am H 8.8k	3	1	3^{6}	4^{9}	$1^{1\frac{1}{2}}$	1^{4}	McDonald RS	144	wsb	10.85	--	The Mast144^{4}Sundowner143$^{2\frac{1}{2}}$Virginius134$^{1\frac{1}{2}}$	Handily	6
6Aug53- 5Sar	fst	*2	S'Chase	4:10	4↑	Shillelah H 8.9k	4	4	7^{14}	7^{17}	7^{28}	7^{27}	McDonald RS	148	w	4.40	--	Sun Shower132^{1}Sundowner139^{3}Oedipus160^{4}	Quit early	7
3Jly53- 5Del	fst	*2½	S'Chase	4:51^{2}	4↑	Indian River H 12k	4	4	3^{2}	$4^{8\frac{1}{2}}$	4^{5}	4^{7}	McDonald RS	151	w	*1.75	--	Monkey Wrench135^{1}Tourist List136^{hd}Cherwell134^{6}	No rally	5
26Jun53- 5Del	fst	*2	S'Chase	3:46^{4}	3↑	Georgetown H 12k	5	2	$2^{1\frac{1}{2}}$	3^{3}	1^{2}	$1^{\frac{1}{2}}$	McDonald RS	148	w	3.95	--	TheMast148$^{\frac{1}{2}}$MonkeyWrench135^{1}HuntingFox136^{12}	Hard drive	6
19Jun53- 6Bel	fst	*2¼	S'Chase	4:12^{1}	4↑	Temple Gwathmey H 16k	7	6	$6^{9\frac{1}{4}}$	5^{13}	4^{14}	5^{15}	McDonald RS	155	w	22.75	--	Errolford130$^{5\frac{1}{2}}$Sea Legs165^{2}Oedipus164^{5}	No factor	7
	Daily Racing Form time,4:16 2/5																			
4Jun53- 5Bel	fst	*2½	S'Chase	4:42^{1}	4↑	Meadow Brook H 11k	5	3	5^{5}	-	-	-	McDonald RS	154	w	9.45	--	SeaLegs157^{5}Oedipus164$^{2\frac{1}{2}}$HisBoots146$^{2\frac{1}{2}}$	Hit obstacle,fell	6
21May53- 5Bel	fst	*2	S'Chase	3:47^{1}	4↑	Corinthian H 8.8k	2	3	5^{12}	5^{13}	-	-	McDonald RS	156	w	2.80	--	Sea Legs149$^{\frac{1}{2}}$Hot144^{5}His Boots146^{25}	Bobbled,fell	5
14May53- 5Bel	fst	*2	S'Chase	3:45^{3}	4↑	C L Appleton Mem 8.9k	4	4	$4^{7\frac{1}{2}}$	$3^{2\frac{1}{2}}$	$3^{4\frac{1}{2}}$	$3^{3\frac{1}{2}}$	Garr'anT	144	w	*1.20e	--	Oedipus158$^{1\frac{1}{2}}$His Boots142^{2}The Mast144^{7}	No excuse	6
7May53- 5Bel	sl	*2	S'Chase	3:58^{1}	4↑	Int'l H 8.8k	5	5	5^{18}	7^{10}	$3^{6\frac{1}{2}}$	$3^{3\frac{1}{4}}$	McDonald RS	156	w	2.10	--	Sea Legs144$^{2\frac{1}{2}}$Hunting Fox133$^{\frac{3}{4}}$The Mast156^{13}	Closed fast	7
3Oct52- 5Bel	sf	*3	S'Chase	5:44	4↑	Grand Nat'l H 28k	7	5	5^{14}	$4^{3\frac{1}{2}}$	2^{3}	2^{5}	Smithwick P	154	w	3.15	--	Sea Legs136^{5}The Mast154^{2}Oedipus165^{7}	Faltered	9
11Sep52- 5Aqu	fst	*2	S'Chase	3:44^{1}	3↑	Harbor Hill H 11k	2	5	$6^{4\frac{1}{4}}$	$6^{5\frac{1}{2}}$	5^{10}	5^{14}	Smithwick P	157	w	3.70	--	Semper Eadem135^{4}Hot147$^{2\frac{1}{2}}$Jam155^{6}	No factor	6
29Aug52- 5Sar	hd	*2½	S'Chase	5:06^{4}	4↑	Saratoga H 11k	2	4	5^{12}	5^{12}	5^{14}	5^{18}	Smithwick P	158	w	2.55	--	Banner Waves136^{2}Titien II147^{3}His Boots151^{8}	No factor	6
27Jun52- 6Del	fst	*2½	S'Chase	4:44	4↑	Indian River H 12k	2	1	1^{3}	3^{18}	3^{22}	3^{22}	Smithwick P	161	w	*.55e	--	Jam152^{20}Monkey Wrench134^{2}The Mast161^{6}	Fenced poorly	5
20Jun52- 6Del	fst	*2	S'Chase	3:43^{1}	4↑	Georgetown H 12k	5	4	$5^{1\frac{3}{4}}$	3^{2}	1^{5}	1^{5}	Smithwick P	157	w	3.20	--	The Mast157^{5}Jam151$^{1\frac{1}{2}}$[DH]Crooning Wind143$^{1\frac{1}{2}}$	Easily	8
11Jun52- 6Bel	fst	*2¼	S'Chase	4:16^{3}	4↑	Temple Gwathmey H 16k	9	4	$4^{\frac{3}{4}}$	3^{1}	2^{hd}	$1^{\frac{3}{4}}$	Smithwick P	153	w	3.00	--	The Mast153$^{\frac{3}{4}}$Oedipus163$^{1\frac{1}{4}}$Navy Gun149^{7}	Hard urged	9
29May52- 5Bel	fst	*2½	S'Chase	4:43^{1}	4↑	Meadow Brook H 11k	3	8	$6^{7\frac{1}{2}}$	4^{7}	1^{1}	$1^{2\frac{1}{4}}$	Smithwick P	146	w	8.50	--	The Mast146$^{2\frac{1}{4}}$Navy Gun148^{15}Titien II147^{6}	All out	8
8May52- 5Bel	fst	*2	S'Chase	3:42^{4}	4↑	C L Appleton Mem 9k	1	4	$2^{1\frac{1}{2}}$	$3^{2\frac{1}{2}}$	$4^{3\frac{1}{2}}$	$3^{3\frac{3}{4}}$	Smithwick P	143	w	3.10	--	Jam139^{3}Lone Fisherman139$^{\frac{3}{4}}$The Mast143$^{\frac{3}{4}}$	Jumped poorly	6
1May52- 5Bel	sf	*2	S'Chase	3:47^{1}	4↑	International H 9.3k	5	7	-	-	-	-	Smithwick P	144	w	3.50	--	Jam141^{8}Flaming Comet137^{1}Palaja141^{8}	Fell	11
18Jun51- 6Del	fst	*2	S'Chase	3:45^{3}	4↑	Tom Roby 14k	4	4	3^{1}	1^{6}	1^{8}	1^{15}	Snyder J	133	w	4.95	--	The Mast133^{15}Proceed148^{4}Extra Points148^{6}	Driving	10
31May51- 5Bel	fst	*2	S'Chase	3:44^{3}	4↑	Spring Maiden 7.2k	7	5	3^{2}	-	-	-	Snyder J	133	w	3.60e	--	Boom Boom150$^{\frac{3}{4}}$Cicas140^{15}Night Patrol140^{14}	Fell	13
25May51- 3Bel	fst	*2	S'Chase	3:48^{4}	4↑	Alw 4000	1	1	1^{5}	1^{hd}	2^{1}	$3^{2\frac{1}{4}}$	Snyder J	130	w	2.60	--	IrishEaster149$^{1\frac{1}{4}}$SyracuseLad133^{1}TheMst130^{12}	Bobbled last	13
21Jun50- 1Del	gd	*1¾	Hurdles	3:05^{1}	3↑	Alw 3000	1	1	1^{4}	1^{4}	-	-	Snyder J	130	w	1.95	--	Spleen130^{2}Easter Vigil141^{10}Alphabetical135^{10}		7
	Rank early,left course																			
13Jun50- 1Del	fst	*1¾	Hurdles	3:01^{2}	3↑	Alw 3000	6	3	$3^{5\frac{1}{2}}$	2^{hd}	2^{hd}	1^{2}	Coleman R	131.5	w	2.10e	--	The Mast131.5^{2}Sauchiehall130^{10}Easter Vigil142^{15}	Handily	6
2Jun50- 2Del	fst	6f	:23 :47^{1}	1:14^{2}		Md Sp Wt	2	11	$9^{3\frac{1}{2}}$	7^{7}	7^{8}	$6^{5\frac{1}{2}}$	Rogers C	120	wb	23.45	73-22	Hindi120^{1}Extra Early120$^{1\frac{1}{2}}$Dr. Cricket120^{no}	Rough trip	14
24May50- 7Bel	fst	1	:23^{3} :47 1:12^{2}	1:38^{1}	3↑	Md Sp Wt	9	4	$4^{1\frac{3}{4}}$	6^{6}	8^{18}	9^{22}	Hettinger G	115	wb	19.75	61-15	Demon115$^{\frac{3}{4}}$Hyvania115^{6}On the Mark112$^{1\frac{1}{2}}$	Done early	10
9May50- 3Bel	fst	*1½	Hurdles	2:48^{1}	3↑	Sp Wt 3000	10	11	$11^{7\frac{3}{4}}$	$7^{8\frac{1}{2}}$	5^{4}	$4^{4\frac{1}{2}}$	Snyder J	130	w	28.35	--	Wunderprinz145^{hd}Boom Boom150$^{2\frac{1}{2}}$Rialto150^{2}	Finished well	14
14Jun49- 1Del	fst	5½f	:22^{3} :47^{1}	1:06^{4}		Md 6500	4	7	$7^{3\frac{3}{4}}$	$7^{5\frac{1}{2}}$	$4^{6\frac{1}{2}}$	$3^{5\frac{1}{2}}$	Snyder J	111	wb	7.85	82-15	Icy Stare115$^{3\frac{1}{2}}$Make Hay116^{2}The Mast111^{hd}	Closed fast	14

Tim Tam

dkb. c. 1955, by Tom Fool (Menow)–Two Lea, by Bull Lea

Lifetime record: 14 10 1 2 $467,475

Own.– Calumet Farm
Br.– Calumet Farm (Ky)
Tr.– H.A. Jones

7Jun58- 7Bel	fst	1½	:48^{2} 1:13^{3} 2:04^{1}	2:30^{1}		Belmont 114k	7	7	$6^{9\frac{1}{2}}$	2^{1}	$2^{1\frac{1}{2}}$	2^{6}	Valenzuela I	126	w	*.15	76-17	Cavan126^{6}TimTam126$^{5\frac{1}{2}}$Flamingo126$^{\frac{3}{4}}$		8
	Swerved often,finished lame																			
17May58- 8Pim	fst	$1\frac{3}{16}$	:46^{4} 1:11^{3} 1:37^{4}	1:57^{1}		Preakness 133k	8	9	7^{10}	$2^{1\frac{1}{2}}$	$1^{\frac{1}{2}}$	$1^{1\frac{1}{2}}$	Valenzuela I	126	w	*1.10	87-15	TimTam126$^{1\frac{1}{2}}$LincolnRoad126$^{3\frac{1}{2}}$GoneFishin'126no	Ridden out	12
3May58- 7CD	my	1¼	:47^{3} 1:13^{1} 1:38^{2}	2:05		Ky Derby 160k	2	8	8^{11}	$4^{5\frac{1}{2}}$	2^{2}	$1^{\frac{1}{2}}$	Valenzuela I	126	w	2.10	82-17	Tim Tam126$^{\frac{1}{2}}$Lincoln Road126$^{\frac{1}{2}}$Noureddin126^{6}	Fully extended	14
29Apr58- 7CD	sl	1	:23 :46^{3} 1:13	1:39^{3}		Derby Trial 16k	1	6	$5^{5\frac{1}{2}}$	$6^{5\frac{1}{4}}$	$5^{2\frac{1}{2}}$	1^{nk}	Valenzuela I	122	w	*.60	77-29	Tim Tam122^{nk}Ebony Pearl116$^{1\frac{1}{4}}$Flamingo112^{2}	Forced wide	8
18Apr58- 6Kee	fst	7f	:23^{2} :45^{2} 1:09^{3}	1:22^{1}		Alw 4500	8	3	4^{4}	$4^{3\frac{1}{2}}$	3^{nk}	$1^{\frac{1}{2}}$	Hartack W	122	wb	*.60	101-10	TimTam122$^{\frac{1}{2}}$Nadr119^{nk}Hllsdl113^{hd}	Under confident handling	8
29Mar58- 7GP	fst	1⅛	:46^{3} 1:11^{3} 1:36^{2}	1:49^{1}		Florida Derby 119k	5	7	$4^{7\frac{1}{2}}$	3^{6}	2^{2}	$1^{\frac{1}{2}}$	Hartack W	122	w	*.35	88-16	TimTam122$^{\frac{1}{2}}$LincolnRoad118^{7}GreyMonarch122$^{1\frac{1}{2}}$	Strong drive	11
19Mar58- 7GP	fst	$1\frac{1}{16}$	:23^{3} :46^{3} 1:10^{4}	1:42^{4}		Fountain of Youth 16k	2	9	$6^{5\frac{3}{4}}$	5^{5}	2^{hd}	1^{2}	Hartack W	122	w	*.65	96-10	TimTam122^{2}GreyMonarch119^{hd}Li'lFella122^{1}	Speed to spare	10
1Mar58- 7Hia	fst	1⅛	:46^{4} 1:11 1:36^{1}	1:48^{4}		Flamingo 135k	6	6	$5^{2\frac{1}{2}}$	$5^{1\frac{1}{2}}$	2^{hd}	2^{hd}	Hartack W	122	w	*1.50	91-11	[D]Jewel'sRewrd122^{hd}TmTam122$^{3\frac{3}{4}}$TalentShow122$^{3\frac{1}{2}}$	Bumped	9
	Placed first through disqualification																			
15Feb58- 7Hia	gd	1⅛	:45^{4} 1:11^{2} 1:36^{4}	1:51^{2}		Everglades 31k	1	8	6^{7}	4^{3}	1^{hd}	$1^{1\frac{1}{4}}$	Hartack W	114	w	*.70e	78-20	Tim Tam114$^{1\frac{1}{4}}$Kentucky Pride117^{6}Liberty Ruler114$^{\frac{3}{4}}$	Easily	9
5Feb58- 7Hia	fst	7f	:22 :44^{3} 1:09^{1}	1:22^{4}		Bahamas 25k	11	7	9^{13}	7^{9}	$5^{4\frac{1}{2}}$	$3^{\frac{1}{2}}$	Scurlock O	114	w	*.50e	95-10	Olymar123$^{\frac{1}{2}}$KntuckyPride117^{no}TmTm114$^{\frac{1}{2}}$	Rallied on outside	11
28Jan58- 7Hia	fst	6f	:22^{2} :45^{2}	1:10^{4}		Alw 5000	8	7	7^{11}	6^{11}	3^{8}	$3^{5\frac{1}{4}}$	Scurlock O	119	w	*.25e	86-19	KntuckyPride119$^{2\frac{1}{2}}$Yemen116$^{2\frac{3}{4}}$TmTm119^{5}	Strong in stretch	10
22Jan58- 8Hia	my	7f	:23^{4} :47 1:12	1:25^{1}		Alw 5000	6	4	$3^{1\frac{1}{2}}$	3^{2}	$1^{\frac{1}{2}}$	$1^{\frac{1}{2}}$	Hartack W	122	w	*.45	84-24	TimTm122$^{\frac{1}{2}}$BeauDaumier114$^{2\frac{1}{2}}$BigFreeze117^{5}	Stout restraint	9
17Jan58- 6Hia	fst	6f	:22^{3} :45^{4}	1:11^{1}		Alw 5000	6	3	2^{hd}	$1^{\frac{1}{2}}$	1^{2}	$1^{2\frac{3}{4}}$	Hartack W	112	w	*.65	89-16	Tim Tam112$^{2\frac{3}{4}}$Field Trophy110$^{\frac{1}{2}}$Best of Show106$^{1\frac{3}{4}}$	Easily	8
18Oct57- 3GS	sly	6f	:22^{2} :46^{2}	1:12^{2}		Md Sp Wt	8	12	8^{10}	$7^{4\frac{3}{4}}$	$4^{4\frac{1}{2}}$	$4^{4\frac{1}{4}}$	Hartack W	118	w	*.80	78-22	Royal Warrior118$^{1\frac{1}{4}}$Vengeance110^{3}Wait for It110^{hd}		12
	Broke slowly,made up ground																			

Tom Fool

b. c. 1949, by Menow (Pharamond II)–Gaga, by Bull Dog

Lifetime record: 30 21 7 1 $570,165

Own.– Greentree Stable
Br.– Duval A. Headley (Ky)
Tr.– J.M. Gaver

24Oct53- 7Pim	fst	$1\frac{3}{16}$	:47^{4} 1:11^{4} 1:37^{1}	1:55^{4}	3↑	Pim Spl 50k	1	1	1^{3}	1^{5}	1^{6}	1^{8}	Atkinson T	126	w	-	101-20	Tom Fool126^{8}Navy Page120^{no}Alerted126	Much the best	3
	No wagering																			
26Sep53- 6Bel	fst	1	:23^{1} :46^{1} 1:11	1:36^{4}	3↑	Sysonby 54k	2	1	1^{1}	$1^{2\frac{1}{2}}$	1^{6}	1^{3}	Atkinson T	126	w	-	90-15	Tom Fool126^{3}Alerted126$^{\frac{1}{2}}$Grecian Queen116	Under restraint	3
	No wagering																			
8Aug53- 7Sar	fst	1¼	:49 1:13 1:38^{2}	2:05^{2}	3↑	Whitney 27k	1	2	2^{2}	1^{2}	1^{4}	$1^{3\frac{1}{2}}$	Atkinson T	126	w	-	81-20	Tom Fool126$^{3\frac{1}{2}}$Combat Boots114	Very much the best	2
	No wagering																			
4Aug53- 6Sar	fst	1	:23^{2} :46^{2} 1:11^{1}	1:37^{1}	3↑	Wilson 16k	1	1	1^{1}	$1^{2\frac{1}{2}}$	1^{6}	1^{8}	Atkinson T	126	w	-	91-17	Tom Fool126^{8}Indian Land117	No competition here	2
	No wagering																			
11Jly53- 6Aqu	fst	1¼	:48^{3} 1:13^{2} 1:38	2:04^{2}	3↑	Brooklyn H 56k	3	2	2^{hd}	$1^{3\frac{1}{2}}$	1^{3}	$1^{1\frac{1}{2}}$	Atkinson T	136	w	*.25	85-13	Tom Fool136$^{1\frac{1}{2}}$Golden Gloves110^{7}High Scud109^{no}	Easing up	5
27Jun53- 6Aqu	fst	7f	:22 :44^{3} 1:09^{2}	1:22	3↑	Carter H 59k	5	5	5^{6}	4^{5}	$2^{1\frac{1}{2}}$	1^{2}	Atkinson T	135	w	*.65	100-09	Tom Fool135^{2}Squared Away122$^{2\frac{1}{4}}$Eatontown113$^{1\frac{1}{4}}$	Easily best	9
30May53- 6Bel	fst	1¼	:47^{1} 1:11 1:35^{3}	2:00^{3}	3↑	Suburban H 58k	1	1	1^{3}	1^{3}	1^{1}	1no	Atkinson T	128	w	*2.05	97-17	Tom Fool128^{no}Royal Vale124^{7}Cold Command114^{2}	Hard drive	7
23May53- 6Bel	gd	1	:22^{3} :46 1:11^{1}	1:35^{4}	3↑	Metropolitan H 36k	3	2	$2^{2\frac{1}{2}}$	$1^{\frac{1}{2}}$	$1^{1\frac{1}{2}}$	$1^{\frac{1}{2}}$	Atkinson T	130	w	*.50	95-13	Tom Fool130$^{\frac{1}{2}}$Royal Vale127$^{8\frac{1}{2}}$Intent125$^{1\frac{1}{2}}$	Driving,bore in	7
19May53- 6Bel	fst	6f	:22^{3} :46^{2}	1:11^{3}	3↑	Joe Palmer H 15k	4	3	$2^{1\frac{1}{2}}$	2^{hd}	$1^{2\frac{1}{2}}$	$1^{1\frac{1}{2}}$	Atkinson T	130	w	*.70	91-27	Tom Fool130$^{1\frac{1}{2}}$Tea-Maker114$^{1\frac{1}{2}}$Dark Peter121$^{\frac{3}{4}}$	Eased up	7
25Apr53- 5Jam	fst	5½f	:23 :46^{1} :58^{2}	1:04^{1}	3↑	Handicap 7560	1	1	3^{3}	$3^{3\frac{1}{2}}$	$2^{\frac{1}{2}}$	$1^{2\frac{1}{2}}$	Atkinson T	128	w	*.95	97-12	Tom Fool128$^{2\frac{1}{2}}$Do Report116$^{2\frac{1}{4}}$Earmarked114^{3}	Ridden out	5
8Nov52- 6Jam	fst	$1\frac{3}{16}$	:47 1:11^{2} 1:38^{1}	1:58		Empire City H 55k	4	1	$1^{\frac{1}{2}}$	1^{hd}	$1^{\frac{1}{2}}$	1^{hd}	Atkinson T	128	w	*.65	86-23	Tom Fool128^{hd}Marcador109^{2}Roaring Bull105$^{1\frac{1}{2}}$	Hard drive	8
1Nov52- 6Jam	fst	1⅛	:48^{4} 1:13 1:37^{4}	1:50^{1}	3↑	Westchester H 56k	3	2	3^{1}	3^{1}	$2^{\frac{1}{2}}$	2no	Atkinson T	125	w	*1.75	95-18	Battlefield123^{no}TomFool125^{1}Alerted125$^{1\frac{1}{4}}$	Blocked,gaining	9
18Oct52- 6Jam	fst	1⅛	:47^{1} 1:11 1:35^{4}	1:49^{2}	3↑	Grey Lag H 60k	10	2	1^{hd}	2^{hd}	1^{hd}	1no	Atkinson T	119	wb	*1.40e	99-16	Tom Fool119^{no}Battlefield118^{nk}Alerted121$^{1\frac{1}{4}}$	Hard drive	11
11Oct52- 6Jam	fst	$1\frac{3}{16}$	:47^{2} 1:11 1:36^{1}	1:55^{4}		Roamer H 47k	7	5	4^{2}	$3^{1\frac{1}{2}}$	2^{1}	2^{2}	Atkinson T	126	w	*.75	95-14	Quiet Step111^{2}Tom Fool126^{1}Risque Rouge105$^{\frac{3}{4}}$	No excuse	9
30Sep52- 6Bel	fst	1	:23^{2} :46^{3} 1:11^{4}	1:36^{2}	3↑	Sysonby H 15k	7	3	$3^{1\frac{1}{2}}$	$3^{\frac{1}{2}}$	1^{2}	$1^{1\frac{1}{4}}$	Atkinson T	126	w	*1.10	92-18	Tom Fool126$^{1\frac{1}{4}}$Alerted118^{3}Greek Ship118$^{1\frac{1}{4}}$	Easily	8
17Sep52- 6Bel	fst	1	:23^{2} :47^{1} 1:12^{2}	1:37		Jerome H 24k	5	2	$2^{1\frac{1}{2}}$	$2^{1\frac{1}{2}}$	1^{4}	1^{7}	Atkinson T	120	w	2.80	89-26	Tom Fool120^{7}Marcador111^{nk}Mark-Ye-Well130$^{1\frac{1}{2}}$	Hard drive	10
16Aug52- 6Sar	sly	1¼	:49^{3} 1:14^{4} 1:40^{1}	2:07^{2}		Travers 23k	4	1	1^{1}	$1^{1\frac{1}{2}}$	2^{1}	3^{4}	Atkinson T	114	w	*1.55	67-22	OneCount126^{3}Armageddon123^{1}TomFl114$^{\frac{3}{4}}$	Wide,weakened	8
	Geldings not eligible																			
11Aug52- 6Sar	sl	1⅛	:48^{2} 1:13 1:38^{3}	1:53^{2}		Alw 5000	3	2	2^{1}	$2^{\frac{1}{2}}$	1^{hd}	2no	Atkinson T	117	w	*.80	83-22	CountFlame117^{no}TomFool117$^{\frac{1}{2}}$GoldnGloves117$^{\frac{1}{2}}$	Just missed	7

5Aug52- 6Sar	sly	1	:232 :47 1:123 1:392	3↑ Wilson 16k	1	3	37	22	12	14½	Atkinson T	106	w	*.25e	80-25	TomFool1064½NorthernStar1201ColonyDate1148	Drew clear	4
14Jly52- 6AP	fst	7f	:232 :452 1:10 1:223	Alw 6000	4	1	2hd	31	33½	44	Atkinson T	124	w	*.90	93-11	High Scud118½Mark-Ye-Well118½Eljay1183	Weakened	5
26Jun52- 6Aqu	fst	6f	:223 :462 1:103	Rippey H 10k	3	4	41½	52¾	2hd	2hd	Atkinson T	126	w	*1.00	99-15	Hitex120hdTom Fool1262Duke Fanelli1022	Hung	8
19Apr52- 6Jam	fst	1⅛	:48 1:12 1:383 1:522	Wood Memorial 63k	2	1	2hd	22½	1hd	2nk	Atkinson T	126	w	*1.65	84-16	Master Fiddle126nkTom Fool126½Pintor126½	Just failed	14
7Apr52- 6Jam	fst	6f	:232 :464 1:121	Alw 10000	1	5	1½	1hd	11	1nk	Atkinson T	120	w	*.80	86-20	Tom Fool120nkPrimate117nkCousin1202	Won cleverly	6
24Oct51- 6Jam	sly	1 1/16	:242 :48 1:131 1:451	©East View 53k	4	3	45½	42	1hd	1nk	Atkinson T	122	w	*.65	86-15	Tom Fool122nkPut Out122nkRisque Rouge122¾	Hard drive	6
6Oct51- 6Bel	fst	6½f-W	:221 :451 1:101 1:171	Futurity 111k	7	4		41¼	1nk	11¾	Atkinson T	122	w	5.75	86-14	Tom Fool1221¾Primate1221Jet's Date122hd	Driving	10
	Geldings not eligible																	
1Oct51- 5Bel	fst	6f-WC	:223 :45 1:092	Sp Wt 5000	3	1		31½	31½	24	Atkinson T	118	w	*1.90	90-11	Hill Gail1184Tom Fool118nkBaybrook1182	Bothered early	16
1Sep51- 6Sar	gd	6½f	:233 :472 1:123 1:191	Hopeful 62k	2	4	31	1hd	1hd	21¼	Atkinson T	122	w	*.75e	88-20	Cousin1221¼Tom Fool122nkHannibal12212	No excuse	6
25Aug51- 4Sar	fst	6f	:224 :463 1:114	Grand Union Hotel 21k	4	3	32	32	1hd	11	Atkinson T	122	w	2.05	89-16	Tom Fool1221Cousin126¾Jet Master1261¼	Driving	5
20Aug51- 6Sar	fst	6f	:231 :47 1:123	Sanford 11k	6	3	21	21	1½	12¼	Atkinson T	113	w	*.90	85-18	Tom Fool1132¼First Refusal1163½Secant1082½	Easily	8
13Aug51- 5Sar	fst	5½f	:232 :47 :593 1:062	©Md Sp Wt	8	7	52	43½	11	14	Atkinson T	118	w	*2.00	85-17	Tom Fool1184Handsome Teddy1181Warpath1181	Easily	12

Two Lea

b. f. 1946, by Bull Lea (Bull Dog)–Two Bob, by The Porter

Lifetime record: 26 15 6 3 $309,250

Own.– Calumet Farm
Br.– Calumet Farm (Ky)
Tr.– H.A. Jones

25Oct52- 9BM	fst	1¼	:474 1:111 1:36 2:013	3↑ Bay Meadows H 56k	1	2	45½	42½	31	2½	Moreno H	126	w	*.70	114-04	Moonrush115½Two Lea1261Grantor118hd	Finished gamely	8
18Oct52- 9BM	fst	1 1/16	:234 :471 1:11 1:413	3↑ Children's Hospitl H 23k	4	5	55½	43½	1½	1½	Moreno H	122	w	*1.35e	102-09	Two Lea122½Moonrush1151½Grantor1202½	Wide,driving	10
4Oct52- 9BM	fst	1	:231 :462 1:104 1:363	3↑ ⒻSan Mateo H 11k	7	4	33½	34	1hd	1½	Moreno H	127	w	*.85e	97-11	Two Lea127½Danae115nkWistful117½	Saved ground	7
12Jly52- 7Hol	fst	1¼	:461 1:103 1:351 2:001	3↑ Hol Gold Cup 137k	7	2	43	21	1hd	1½	Moreno H	113	w	*1.55e	98-07	Two Lea113½Cyclotron1003Sturdy One1083½	Driving	12
5Jly52- 6Hol	fst	6f	:222 :452 :574 1:10	3↑ ⒻRamona H 22k	8	3	83	83	41½	11	Moreno H	125	w	*2.25e	96-07	TwoLea1251[DH]PrincessLygia113[DH]RuthLly1141	Wide into str	8
28Jun52- 7Hol	fst	1 1/16	:224 :454 1:101 1:421	3↑ Inglewood H 28k	4	4	46	43½	23	43¼	Moreno H	122	w	*1.35e	94-08	SturdyOne1111StormyCloud105nkAdmrlDrk1162	Saved ground	7
14Jun52- 7Hol	fst	1 1/16	:231 :461 1:11 1:432	3↑ ⒻVanity H 28k	5	4	34½	32½	13	11¼	Moreno H	122	w	*.35e	91-11	Two Lea1221¼Wistful1121¾Jennie Lee117¾	Saved ground	8
31May52- 7Hol	fst	7f	:222 :45 1:092 1:213	3↑ ⒻMilady H 28k	10	6	53¾	53¼	21	22½	Moreno H	117	w	*.75e	98-10	A Gleam1122½Two Lea1176Spanish Cream124no	Second best	11
24May52- 4Hol	fst	6f	:222 :453 :574 1:10	4↑ Alw 5000	1	5	53½	62¼	2hd	2nk	Moreno H	113	w	*.75e	96-07	Jennie Lee108nkTwo Lea1132½Akimbo1182	Closed well	7
14May52- 7Hol	fst	6f	:22 :444 :572 1:102	4↑ ⒻAlw 10000	1	6	66¾	66¾	32	11¼	Shoemaker W	112	w	*.90	94-09	Two Lea1121¼La Franza106nkJennie Lee113hd	Wide,bore in	8
2May52- 7GG	fst	6f	:222 :444 1:092	3↑ Alw 4000	7	6	53	53½	74½	55¼	Pierson NL	112	w	*1.35e	89-13	Mohammedan1193Witch-English1221Jennie Lee109¾		9
	Close quarters																	
15Jly50- 6AP	fst	6f	:224 :45 1:094	3↑ Handicap 4000	5	4	44	32½	22	2½	Brooks S	122	w	*.80e	96-07	Porter'sBroom115½TwoLea1225OceanDrive1171	Forced wide	6
25Feb50- 7SA	fst	1¼	:462 1:11 1:351 2:00	3↑ S Anita H 135k	1	2	11½	11	1hd	32¼	Gilbert J	113	w	*.35e	104-11	Noor1101¼Citation1321Two Lea113nk	Game try	11
28Jan50- 7SA	fst	1¼	:472 1:122 1:37 2:022	Maturity 122k	4	2	11	1½	1hd	21	Arcaro E	116	w	*.50e	93-10	Ponder1261Two Lea1165Mocopo1121½	Easing up	9
14Jan50- 7SA	my	1⅛	:472 1:121 1:393 1:524	3↑ ⒻS Margarita H 59k	2	4	32	2½	11	12	Brooks S	126	w	*1.75	79-21	Two Lea1262Gaffery1182½But Why Not1163½	Driving	8
5Jan50- 7SA	fst	7f	:224 :46 1:11 1:233	4↑ ⒻHandicap 10000	1	2	31	21½	1hd	1nk	Brooks S	122	w	*.55	91-18	Two Lea122nkGaffery1162Sweet Dream1161½	Held gamely	10
29Dec49- 7SA	fst	6f	:232 :47 1:111	3↑ ⒻAlw 5000	6	5	44	33½	32	1hd	Brooks S	119	w	*.85	91-21	Two Lea119hdSweet Dream1161½But Why Not1114	Just up	7
17Aug49- 6Was	fst	7f	:212 :443 1:083 1:214	ⒻArtful 22k	4	7	72¾	23	2½	11½	Brooks S	124	w	*.50	101-07	Two Lea1241½Imacomin1121½Stole1071½	Drew out	7
20Jly49- 6AP	fst	1	:23 :46 1:102 1:37	ⒻCleopatra H 26k	1	1	11	14	15	12	Brooks S	122	w	*.60e	87-15	Two Lea1222Lithe108nkWistful1212	Eased up	6
2Jly49- 6AP	fst	6f	:222 :45 1:10	3↑ ⒻModesty 28k	6	6	41½	43¼	33½	2½	Brooks S	111	w	*1.40e	96-10	No Strings101½Two Lea1112Dandilly1081	Strong finish	10
22Jun49- 6AP	fst	6f	:223 :452 1:094	ⒻPrincess Doreen 23k	2	8	31	31	2hd	11¼	Brooks S	111	w	3.30	98-11	Two Lea1111¼No Strings1118Alsab's Day1211	Driving	11
28May49- 4Bel	fst	6f	:231 :471 1:12	ⒻAlw 4000	1	3	42	31½	1½	1¾	Brooks S	113	w	*1.10	90-18	Two Lea113¾Lady Dorimar1134Black Chiffon1103	Drew out	11
20Apr49- 5HdG	fst	6f	:231 :462 1:122	Alw 3000	6	8	63½	51¾	32	1no	Brooks S	114	w	*1.40	89-14	Two Lea114noGambler1142Magna Charta117hd	Hard drive	10
17Sep48- 4Bel	fst	6f-WC	:222 :453 1:102	ⒻMd Sp Wt	12	5		21	2hd	14	Pierson NL	116	w	*.80e	89-12	Two Lea1164Ochita1161½Boomdeay1164	Easily	15
13Sep48- 4Bel	fst	5½f-W	:224 :454 1:043	ⒻMd Sp Wt	13	8		125	51¾	3¾	Pierson NL	116	w	*2.15	90-05	Wild Pitch116nkParting Shot111½Two Lea1161½	Bore out	26
25Aug48- 3Was	fst	5½f	:23 :463 :594 1:064	ⒻMd Sp Wt	6	9	1011	108¼	65½	31	Pierson NL	116	w	*1.50	85-11	Top Hope1161Pella116hdTwo Lea1162	No excuse	12

Warfare

gr. c. 1957, by Determine (Alibhai)–War Whisk, by War Glory

Lifetime record: 16 7 2 4 $414,445

Own.– Bellehurst Stable
Br.– C.H. Jones & Sons (Cal)
Tr.– W.C. Winfrey

26Mar60- 7Aqu	fst	6f	:221 :451 1:093	Swift 27k	5	1	63½	54	2½	11½	Arcaro E	126	b	*.40	104-03	Warfare1261½Francis S.126¾Greek Page126nk	Mild urging	8
	Previously trained by H. Ross																	
6Jan60- 6SA	fst	6f	:223 :46 1:101	Alw 10000	8	3	41½	21	2hd	2nk	Valenzuela I	124	b	*.90	93-13	T.V. Lark124nkWarfare1241½Tompion120¾	Made game effort	8
31Oct59- 7GS	sly	1 1/16	:23 :46 1:10 1:424	Garden State 283k	2	5	41¾	21	2hd	1½	Valenzuela I	122	b	*1.20	96-15	Warfare122½BllyAch1224Tompon122hd	Best under hard drive	10
17Oct59- 7Aqu	fst	1	:223 :451 1:094 1:351	Champagne 230k	8	4	31½	3½	1½	11	Valenzuela I	122	b	2.05	--	Wrfare1221Tompon1225½BllyAch1224	Well rated,going away	10
5Oct59- 7Aqu	fst	7f	:222 :451 1:10 1:223	Cowdin 70k	6	5	43½	42½	11	12½	Valenzuela I	117	b	10.50	--	Warfare1172½VitalForc124nkBllyAch1241¾	Under mild drive	12
28Sep59- 7Aqu	fst	6½f	:221 :451 1:104 1:173	Alw 5000	4	6	43¼	33½	32½	21½	Bauer R	119	b	5.00	--	Four Lane1161½Warfare1193Ira Eaker1161½	Sharp effort	12
12Sep59- 7Dmr	fst	6f	:221 :442 1:093	Dmr Futurity 86k	6	9	84¼	84¾	57½	3¾	Valenzuela I	119	b	*1.90e	95-10	Azure'sOrphan116¾Salatom116noWarfr119hd	Gaining rapidly	11
4Sep59- 7Dmr	fst	6f	:222 :45 1:093	Alw 7500	5	2	41¾	41¼	11½	11	Valenzuela I	122	b	*2.20	96-09	Warfare1221Noble Noor1223¼Fay's Night Out1192¾	Driving	8
22Aug59- 8Dmr	fst	6f	:214 :444 1:092	Alw 5000	9	1	76	88¼	89¼	88	Campas R	112	b	*1.80	89-11	BrightTiny1161¼Fay'sNightOut119½Azure'sOrphan122½	Wide	9
18Jly59- 7Hol	fst	6f	:214 :444 :571 1:10	Hol Juv Champ 163k	12	3	84½	84	53¾	31½	Maese A	122	b	5.30e	91-11	NobleNoor113½Tompion1161Wrfare122nk	Strong stretch bid	15
9Jly59- 7Hol	fst	5½f	:221 :444 :57 1:03	©C S Howard H 30k	8	1	63¼	53½	22	1½	Maese A	114	b	20.10	97-09	Wrfare114½NewPolicy1142¾Hdmstr1142¼	Under strong drive	9
18Jun59- 7Hol	fst	5f	:22 :45 :57	©Haggin 23k	5	7	76¾	87¾	67	65¾	Maese A	119		12.20	92-14	Psyche's First1224½T.V. Lark119noTompion122nk	No excuse	8
4Jun59- 7Hol	fst	5f	:221 :453 :573	©Westchester 18k	1	1	3½	22	21½	31½	Valenzuela I	122		4.25	93-15	BritishRoman122¾NewPolicy122¾Wrfar1223½	Held on gamely	9
23May59- 1Hol	fst	5f	:221 :453 :573	Md Sp Wt	6	2	2hd	1hd	11	13¾	Shoemaker W	120		*1.70	95-09	Warfare1203¾Pierica120¾Jimbo Rose120¾	Drew out easily	10
16May59- 1Hol	fst	5f	:222 :453 :574	Md Sp Wt	6	6	43¼	35	37	37	Neves R	118		3.25	87-14	Temple1182Noble Noor1185Warfare1182	Evenly in drive	10
9May59- 2Hol	fst	5f	:221 :454 :582	Md Sp Wt	8	6	55	56½	42	41¼	Taniguchi G	118		13.05	90-11	Nagea118¾British Roman118½Temple118hd	Some late foot	12

White Skies

ch. c. 1949, by Sun Again (Sun Teddy)–Milk Dipper, by Milkman
Own.– W.M. Wickham
Br.– Charles Nuckols & Sons (Ky)
Tr.– T. Root

Lifetime record: 37 20 8 4 $246,025

25Apr55- 6Bel	fst 6f-WC	:22^{1}	:44^{3}		1:08^{4}	3↑ Toboggan H 28k	1	1		5$^{1\frac{1}{4}}$	2$^{\frac{1}{2}}$	3^{nk}	Guerin E	132wb	*.85	95-08	Sailor106^{no}Bobby Brocato116^{hd}White Skies132^{6}		7
	Failed to respond sufficiently																		
1Apr55- 6Jam	fst 6f	:22^{4}	:46		1:10^{3}	3↑ Paumonok H 29k	8	5	4$^{\frac{3}{4}}$	2^{hd}	1^{hd}	3^{1}	Arcaro E	130wb	*.70	93-19	BobbyBrocato113^{1}Blessbull119^{no}WhiteSkies130$^{8\frac{1}{2}}$	Faltered	12
5Jly54- 6Aqu	fst 7f	:22^{3}	:45^{2}	1:09^{3}	1:23^{3}	3↑ Carter H 62k	6	3	3^{1}	1$^{\frac{1}{2}}$	1$^{2\frac{1}{2}}$	1$^{1\frac{1}{2}}$	Stout J	133wb	*1.85	92-17	White Skies133$^{1\frac{1}{2}}$First Aid115^{nk}Royal Vale126$^{\frac{1}{2}}$	Driving	13
12Jun54- 6Mth	fst 6f	:21^{3}	:44^{2}		1:09	3↑ Oceanport H 18k	7	3	3^{3}	2^{2}	2^{2}	2$^{2\frac{1}{2}}$	Stout J	136wb	*.60	100-06	Master Ace106$^{2\frac{1}{2}}$White Skies136$^{1\frac{3}{4}}$Eatontown113^{3}	Hung late	9
22May54- 6Bel	fst 7f	:22^{2}	:45^{2}	1:09^{4}	1:22^{2}	3↑ Roseben H 34k	12	2	2^{hd}	1^{2}	1^{3}	1$^{\frac{1}{2}}$	Stout J	135wb	*1.15	98-13	WhiteSkies135$^{\frac{1}{2}}$[DH]Impasse115[DH]FirstAid113$^{4\frac{1}{2}}$	Tiring,lasted	13
26Apr54- 6Bel	fst 6f-WC	:22^{2}	:45^{1}		1:09^{1}	3↑ Toboggan H 30k	2	1		1^{hd}	2^{hd}	1$^{2\frac{1}{4}}$	Arcaro E	132wb	*.85	95-07	WhiteSkies132$^{2\frac{1}{4}}$CaesarDid109^{hd}Hilarious120^{1}	Handy score	8
1Apr54- 6Jam	fst 6f	:23	:45^{3}		1:10^{4}	3↑ Paumonok H 30k	2	1	1$^{\frac{1}{2}}$	1$^{1\frac{1}{2}}$	1^{hd}	1no	Arcaro E	130wb	*.75	93-16	WhiteSks130^{no}Laffango115$^{2\frac{1}{2}}$ColdCommand116$^{\frac{3}{4}}$	Just lasted	10
	Daily Racing Form time, 1:10 1/5																		
10Mar54- 5GP	my 5$\frac{1}{2}$f	:23	:47	1:00	1:06^{3}	4↑ Handicap 5000	4	6	4^{2}	3^{1}	1^{2}	1^{4}	Stout J	128wb	*1.50	84-33	WhiteSkies128^{4}Ruthred114$^{1\frac{1}{2}}$HeartFlash107$^{1\frac{1}{4}}$	Much the best	7
4Nov53- 6Jam	fst 6f	:23^{1}	:46		1:11^{3}	3↑ Sport Page H 22k	3	3	2$^{\frac{1}{2}}$	2^{hd}	1$^{\frac{1}{2}}$	1$^{1\frac{1}{4}}$	Stout J	130wb	*1.60	89-21	White Skies130$^{1\frac{1}{4}}$Hilarious114^{hd}Joe Jones107$^{\frac{3}{4}}$	Drew clear	9
24Oct53- 7GS	fst 6f	:22^{1}	:45^{2}		1:11^{2}	3↑ Princeton H 23k	2	5	4^{2}	4^{1}	3^{3}	4$^{4\frac{1}{4}}$	Stout J	128wb	*.50	87-21	[DH]Hyphsis110[DH][D]CandlWood118$^{3\frac{1}{2}}$SkipprBll111$^{\frac{3}{4}}$	Weakened	6
19Oct53- 6Jam	fst 6f	:23	:45^{4}		1:11	2↑ New Rochelle H 22k	6	3	1$^{\frac{1}{2}}$	1$^{2\frac{1}{2}}$	1$^{2\frac{1}{2}}$	1$^{2\frac{3}{4}}$	Stout J	128wb	*2.15	92-17	White Skies128$^{2\frac{3}{4}}$Hilarious110$^{\frac{1}{2}}$Do Report113$^{2\frac{1}{2}}$	Ridden out	10
12Oct53- 6Jam	fst 6f	:23	:46^{2}		1:11^{3}	3↑ Interborough H 23k	1	1	1$^{1\frac{1}{2}}$	1^{hd}	1^{1}	1^{hd}	Stout J	126wb	*1.25	89-20	White Skies126^{hd}Do Report112$^{\frac{3}{4}}$Hilarious110$^{1\frac{1}{2}}$	Just lasted	9
25Sep53- 6Atl	fst 7f	:22^{1}	:44^{4}	1:09^{3}	1:23	4↑ T.R.A. 21k	1	1	1$^{1\frac{1}{2}}$	1^{5}	1^{5}	1^{5}	Boulmetis S	118wb	1.80	98-18	White Skies118^{5}Tuscany126$^{1\frac{1}{2}}$Candle Wood110$^{2\frac{1}{2}}$	Easily	5
19Sep53- 4Atl	fst 7f	:22^{2}	:45^{2}	1:10	1:22^{3}	3↑ Alw 4500	1	1	1^{2}	1^{4}	1^{6}	1^{9}	Stout J	122wb	*.60	- -	WhitSkies122^{9}BrazenBrat119$^{\frac{1}{2}}$Mohammedan119^{5}	Easily best	6
10Sep53- 7Atl	fst 6f	:22^{1}	:45^{2}		1:10^{1}	3↑ King Neptune H 17k	5	7	6$^{4\frac{1}{4}}$	4$^{3\frac{1}{2}}$	4^{3}	3$^{2\frac{1}{2}}$	Stout J	116wb	*1.10	91-15	BlueRhymr104$^{1\frac{1}{2}}$Roaming119^{1}WhiteSkies116$^{\frac{3}{4}}$	Unruly in gate	7
31Aug53- 5Atl	fst 6f	:22^{2}	:45^{2}		1:10^{1}	3↑ Alw 5000	4	2	3$^{2\frac{1}{2}}$	1^{1}	1^{6}	1^{5}	Wilson HB	109wb	*.40	94-16	White Skies109^{5}Topside109$^{1\frac{1}{2}}$Influence118^{4}	Easily	6
26Aug53- 6Atl	fst 6f	:22^{1}	:45^{2}		1:11	3↑ Alw 5000	11	7	5^{6}	3$^{3\frac{1}{2}}$	3$^{1\frac{1}{2}}$	2$^{1\frac{1}{4}}$	LeBlanc R	111wb	2.60	89-21	LateModl112$^{1\frac{1}{4}}$WhteSkies111^{nk}CongoKing116$^{1\frac{1}{2}}$	Forced wide	11
1Nov52- 7GS	fst 6f	:22	:44^{4}		1:10^{4}	3↑ Princeton H 22k	3	2	2$^{1\frac{1}{2}}$	2$^{1\frac{1}{2}}$	1^{hd}	1$^{\frac{3}{4}}$	Stout J	116wb	3.80	94-21	White Skies116$^{\frac{3}{4}}$General Staff124^{hd}Pet Bully120^{nk}	Driving	6
24Oct52- 7GS	fst 6f	:22^{1}	:45^{1}		1:11	3↑ Alw 5000	7	2	2^{2}	2^{hd}	1^{2}	2no	Wilson HB	118wb	2.90	93-20	Pet Bully122^{no}White Skies118$^{\frac{3}{4}}$Occupancy112^{2}	Just missed	7
7Oct52- 6GS	fst 6f	:22^{1}	:45^{2}		1:11	3↑ Fall Inaugural 7.5k	7	2	2$^{1\frac{1}{2}}$	3^{2}	3$^{\frac{1}{2}}$	2^{2}	Stout J	115wb	*1.40	91-17	Mohammedn111^{2}White Skies115^{nk}Pet Bully124^{1}	Good effort	7
10Sep52- 7Atl	fst 6f	:22^{1}	:45		1:09^{1}	3↑ Boardwalk H 16k	3	5	2^{1}	2$^{\frac{1}{2}}$	2$^{\frac{1}{2}}$	2$^{\frac{1}{2}}$	Stout J	117wb	*1.40e	98-12	Dominave100$^{\frac{1}{2}}$White Skies117^{1}Senator Joe120^{hd}	Good effort	7
6Sep52- 7Atl	fst 1Ⓣ	:23	:46^{2}	1:11^{2}	1:37^{2}	Philadelphia Turf H 18k	9	5	5^{3}	2^{hd}	2^{hd}	4$^{2\frac{1}{2}}$	Culmone J	121wb	*2.00	102-00	Faga-La104^{no}Decapolis108^{no}HandsmeTeddy121$^{2\frac{1}{2}}$	Weakened	11
30Aug52- 6Atl	fst 1Ⓣ	:23^{2}	:46^{2}	1:11^{1}	1:36^{1}	Alw 5000	3	1	2^{hd}	1^{1}	1^{1}	2no	Stout J	121wb	*.90	111-00	BobsAlibi114^{no}WhiteSks121^{nk}HndsomTddy124^{hd}	Just missed	10
11Aug52- 6Atl	gd 6f	:22^{3}	:45^{3}		1:11^{4}	Pageant H 11k	4	3	3^{nk}	1^{hd}	1^{3}	1$^{2\frac{1}{2}}$	Stout J	118wb	*.90	86-25	WhiteSks118$^{2\frac{1}{2}}$HandsomeTeddy111^{1}Hannbl126^{4}	Clever score	7
4Aug52- 6Mth	fst 6f	:22^{3}	:45^{3}		1:10^{4}	Alw 5000	3	2	2^{2}	1$^{\frac{1}{2}}$	1^{3}	1^{7}	Stout J	121wb	*.60	94-21	White Skies121^{7}Jeannie C.119$^{4\frac{1}{2}}$Congo King121^{2}	Easily	8
19Jly52- 3Mth	fst 6f	:22^{3}	:45^{3}		1:11^{1}	3↑ Alw 5000	5	3	2^{hd}	1^{1}	1^{3}	1^{1}	Roberts P	105wb	*1.70	92-16	White Skies105^{1}Blue Kay110$^{\frac{1}{2}}$Whiffenpoof115$^{\frac{3}{4}}$	Driving	5
15Jly52- 6Jam	fst 6f	:22^{4}	:45^{4}		1:11^{2}	Handicap 10045	1	2	4$^{2\frac{1}{2}}$	4^{2}	2$^{1\frac{1}{2}}$	2$^{1\frac{1}{4}}$	Rodriguez E	120wb	3.60	89-15	TruePattern107$^{1\frac{1}{4}}$WhiteSkies120^{2}HeapBigChf114^{nk}	Held well	7
5Jly52- 6Mth	fst 6f	:23	:46^{1}		1:12^{2}	Select H 20k	5	9	9$^{5\frac{3}{4}}$	7^{6}	4$^{1\frac{3}{4}}$	3$^{\frac{3}{4}}$	Stout J	114wb	2.40e	85-15	Hannibal122$^{\frac{1}{2}}$Congo King105^{nk}White Skies114^{nk}	Closed well	14
24Jun52- 7Mth	gd 6f	:22^{3}	:45^{3}		1:11^{3}	Alw 5000	5	5	2$^{\frac{1}{2}}$	1$^{1\frac{1}{2}}$	1^{4}	1^{5}	Stout J	115wb	*1.50	90-17	White Skies115^{5}Rae's Reward115^{hd}Thymus115^{3}	Ridden out	8
23Apr52- 5Kee	fst 6$\frac{1}{2}$f	:22^{3}	:45^{4}	1:10^{1}	1:16^{4}	Alw 3000	2	6	2$^{\frac{1}{2}}$	1^{1}	1^{3}	1^{hd}	Porch G	117wb	3.80	99-06	White Skies117^{hd}Real Delight110$^{4\frac{1}{2}}$Shag Tails117$^{\frac{3}{4}}$	Driving	10
18Apr52- 5Kee	fst 7f	:22^{3}	:45^{3}	1:10^{4}	1:24	Alw 5000	2	5	4$^{1\frac{1}{2}}$	2$^{1\frac{1}{2}}$	2^{2}	5$^{4\frac{3}{4}}$	Grohs O	111wb	9.70e	87-19	ColdCommand110^{hd}HillGail121^{nk}GushingOil118$^{1\frac{1}{2}}$	Weakened	8
10Apr52- 5Kee	fst 6f	:22^{3}	:46^{2}		1:11^{3}	Alw 3000	3	5	4^{2}	3$^{\frac{1}{2}}$	1^{3}	1^{5}	Porch G	116wb	*1.40	94-13	White Skies116^{5}Eljay120$^{1\frac{1}{2}}$Cullerton115^{1}	Easily	7
31Mar52- 7GP	fst 7f	:23^{2}	:47	1:11	1:24^{3}	Alw 3000	10	2	2$^{\frac{1}{2}}$	2^{hd}	1$^{\frac{1}{2}}$	2$^{\frac{1}{2}}$	Rodriquez E	119wb	3.20e	89-14	ShortSupply111$^{\frac{1}{2}}$WhiteSkies119^{nk}Fg-L102^{4}	Shortened stride	10
19Mar52- 5GP	fst 6f	:22^{3}	:45^{3}		1:11^{1}	Alw 2600	5	6	2$^{1\frac{1}{2}}$	2$^{1\frac{1}{2}}$	2$^{\frac{1}{2}}$	1^{3}	Rodriquez E	117wb	8.30e	89-16	White Skies117^{3}San-Jo112$^{1\frac{1}{2}}$Colonel Hoop117^{2}	Driving	12
2Nov51- 2Pim	sly 6f	:22^{3}	:47		1:14^{2}	ⒸMd Sp Wt	1	2	2^{hd}	1^{2}	1^{3}	1$^{\frac{3}{4}}$	Richardson HL	110wb	*2.30	79-26	White Skies110$^{\frac{3}{4}}$Charles117^{2}Bit o' Whiz117$^{3\frac{1}{2}}$	Driving	11
7Jly51- 2AP	fst 5$\frac{1}{2}$f	:22^{2}	:45^{3}	:58^{2}	1:04^{4}	Md Sp Wt	6	5	4^{3}	3$^{3\frac{1}{2}}$	3^{3}	8$^{9\frac{1}{2}}$	Richardson HL	111wb	46.70	86-06	Seasn'sBest115$^{3\frac{1}{2}}$Espino'sImage118^{1}GushngOl118^{4}	Gave way	12
27Jun51- 2AP	fst 5f	:22^{4}	:46^{3}		1:00^{2}	ⒸMd Sp Wt	5	11	8$^{8\frac{3}{4}}$	8^{6}	8$^{4\frac{1}{4}}$	7$^{6\frac{3}{4}}$	Richardson HL	111 w	27.90	81-13	QuickSolution118^{3}AceCaptain118^{hd}OldPat118$^{1\frac{1}{2}}$	No threat	11

BOOM TIME

THE 1960'S

by Dave Litfin

THOROUGHBRED RACING ROARED into the 1960's gaining in popularity with every stride, as large and enthusiastic crowds poured themselves and their considerable betting dollars into racetracks from coast to coast.

Aqueduct, which had been completely rebuilt in 1959, reopened to an eager crowd of 42,473 that wagered $3.4 million, and the place was jammed with a record 73,435 fans when Gun Bow won the Metropolitan Handicap on Memorial Day in 1964. Monmouth Park, the picturesque track near the Jersey shore, closed its record-breaking 1962 meeting with a throng of 43,591. Arlington Park regularly drew 30,000 to 40,000 people on weekends. In the West, Santa Anita and Hollywood Park hosted midweek crowds of 25,000, a figure that often doubled on Saturdays.

Racing's inexorable rise to prominence in the landscape of American sports was the synergistic by-product of three fortuitous geographical and economic factors. First, Nevada was the only state that offered casino gambling, and a trip to that remote desert locale, even in the dawn of the space age, remained highly impractical for the great majority of Americans with an inclination to bet their money. Second, there was no such thing as off-track betting, except through illegal bookmakers, many of whom were under close scrutiny in the aftermath of the Kefauver hearings on organized crime. And third, other states were slow to follow New Hampshire's lead when, in 1964, it became the first state in modern times to institute a lottery.

In short, racing was pretty much the only game in town, and it responded to this idyllic state of affairs with steady year-to-year gains on all fronts.

In 1963, total wagering handle rocketed past the $3 billion mark for the first time, as 38,093,417 fans filled the stands and a total of $99,553,769 was distributed in purses. This represented gains of 4 percent in crowds, 5 percent in handle, and 7 percent in purses over 1962 – which had been a record-breaking year as well.

"He would be a brash prophet who would suggest Thoroughbred racing has realized its maximum potential volume of business," wrote *Daily Racing Form* columnist Charles Hatton in his "Review of 1963 Races" for The American Racing Manual. "It continues to grow in public favor, and the trend is toward ever-lengthening seasons in the 24 racing states."

But above and beyond its favorable economic circumstances and convenient access to the nation's

$2 bettors, racing prospered through the 1960's thanks to an improbable sequence of captivating champions who stretched from one end of the decade to the other.

From his appearance and early racing record, few could have guessed that an insignificant-looking gelding bred and owned by Mrs. Richard C. duPont's Bohemia Stable would come to epitomize the qualities of courage and consistency universally admired by horsemen and horseplayers.

Kelso, whom Mrs. duPont named after her friend Kelso Everett, was a dark bay with no conspicuous markings except for a small patch of white hair on his right jowl, where he was bitten as a yearling. Although he was by no means imposing in stature at just over 15 hands as a 3-year-old, and slightly over 16 hands when fully mature, "Kelly" possessed extraordinary propulsive muscling across his hips and hindquarters ("These are outsize and recall a souped-up Ford," Hatton described), and had an efficient low-to-the-ground stride that gave him enough speed to win at six furlongs as well as the stamina to win at two miles. His one Achilles' heel was a trick stifle, which made his connections reluctant to start him on yielding turf.

Kelso's record of five consecutive Horse of the Year titles, from 1960 through 1964, may never be broken. Despite the inflation in purses following his retirement, the gelding's earnings record of $1,977,896 would stand for 15 years.

Kelso's sire was Your Host, a California speedball who was beaten as the heavy favorite in the 1950 Kentucky Derby. Following an accident in which he suffered a broken shoulder and crushed femur, injuries that nearly cost him his life (and would have, had his insurer, Lloyds of London, not insisted on trying to save him for stud duty), Your Host had a decent career as a stallion, but he would have been all but forgotten were it not for Kelso, whose dam was the stakes-placed Maid of Flight.

"Maid of Flight was a nice filly," recalled Mrs. duPont, whose 900-acre Woodstock Farm is located along the banks of the Bohemia River in Chesapeake City, Maryland. "I owned a few shares in Your Host. I'd seen him race and was very fond of him. Since I had a few seasons to him and since he was close by in New Jersey, I decided to send Maid of Flight to him for her first breeding." The foal Maid of Flight dropped in April 1957 at Claiborne Farm near Paris, Kentucky, was Kelso.

Depending on which reference source is consulted, Kelso was either gelded as a yearling by the farm manager, or as a 2-year-old by Dr. John Lee, who trained him for the first three races of his career in September 1959, or the following winter by Carl Hanford, who handled him for the 60 subsequent starts that are now part of racing lore. Whatever the circumstances, it proved to be a fortuitous decision. In 1960 the late-blooming gelding captured the first of his unbelievable five straight Horse of the Year titles, despite the fact that he did not make his debut as a 3-year-old until two weeks after the Triple Crown races were over.

After winning a pair of allowance events by a combined 22 lengths, Kelso was a nonthreatening eighth making his stakes debut in the Arlington Classic. Two races after that, however, he teamed up with Eddie Arcaro, and the duo did not lose again for more than a year. Underneath "The Master," Kelso won the Choice, the Jerome, the Discovery Handicap, the Hawthorne Gold Cup, and the Jockey Club Gold Cup, a streak that made him the first horse in 37 years to be named 3-year-old champion without winning a Triple Crown race.

Kelso returned as a 4-year-old with an allowance win at Aqueduct on May 19, 1961, and 11 days later he carried 130 pounds in the Metropolitan Handicap. Things didn't look good for the even-money favorite as he lagged behind in the early going and remained far back in seventh position at the quarter pole.

"He had absolutely no shot at the head of the stretch, and I didn't give him too much chance at the eighth pole," Hanford told *Daily Racing Form*'s Joe Hirsch on the eve of Kelso's retirement several years later. "But he bulled his way between horses somehow, and got up to win under 130 pounds. I'll never forget it as long as I live."

Kelso completed a sweep of the 1961 Handicap Triple Crown by winning the Suburban and Brooklyn Handicaps in July, and overwhelmed his opposition that autumn winning the Woodward and the Jockey Club Gold Cup by a combined 13 lengths. He closed out his second straight Horse of the Year campaign with a runner-up finish in the Washington, D.C., International, in which he made his grass debut and was finally caught by the year's champion turf horse, T. V. Lark , after setting all the pace.

That would be the first of Kelso's three straight seconds in the D.C. International – he finally won it in 1964 – and it would also be his last race under an aging Arcaro.

After going without a stakes victory through the first eight months of 1962, Kelso received a switch from the soft-handed Bill Shoemaker to the incredibly strong Ismael "Milo" Valenzuela, who, it was said, could hold a starving elephant an inch away from a bale of hay. They went together like hand and glove. Valenzuela rode Kelso 35 times and the pair came away with 22 victories, none more electrifying than the Aqueduct Handicap on Labor Day, September 7, 1964, when Kelso beat his archrival, Gun Bow, by three-quarters of a length.

"The weather was salubrious, a confection of clear skies and 75 degrees, and an enthusiastic throng of 65,066 New Yorkers came out to the Jamaica Bay course to see the sport," Hatton described. "They saw one of the most exciting and dramatic races ever witnessed at any of the three Aqueducts . . . There have been richer events but artistically it has rarely if ever been surpassed within the memory of the oldest racing man."

Gun Bow was the heavy favorite at 55 cents to the dollar, and Kelso was 2-1, having been defeated in five previous stakes starts as a 7-year-old. Gun Bow broke from the rail and went right to the lead, with Kelso stalking close behind. At the quarter pole Kelso began to inch nearer, and many of those who had bet against him suddenly switched allegiances and began shouting, "Come on, Kelso! Go get him, Kelly!"

"The din reverberated, rocking and crashing throughout all five levels of the immense Big A stands and lawns," Hatton continued. "It was like the brink of Niagara, deafening and almost terrifying. Go get him Kelso did . . . The sirocco of sound continued unabated as the field pulled up and Kelso jogged casually back to unsaddle. Perfect strangers thumped one another on the back . . . and there was a continuous roar of applause that did not end until Kelso disappeared from view."

Old-timers recall that ovation as perhaps the longest and loudest ever at a New York track, where the hard-boiled railbirds are not known to dispense their appreciation casually. The New York fans had grown to adore Kelso like no other horse before or since, and Kelso loved them back.

"Whenever we went onto the track he would always walk with the outrider," remembered Valenzuela. "But he would always stop in front of the grandstand and let the other horses keep going. He would stand by himself and look up into the grandstand. It seemed like he wanted to salute the people. He'd stick his ears up, like he knew the applause was for him."

Never before had a horse been so good for so many seasons. Kelso retired with 39 wins from 63 starts, and set an earnings record of $1,977,896 that stood for 15 years. All told, he won 30 stakes races, 13 of them while carrying at least 130 pounds, and set seven track or course records, including a phenomenal clocking of 2:23⅘ for 1½ miles in the 1964 running of the D.C. International. Along that long and winding road, it is safe to say that Kelso beat more good horses than any other Thoroughbred of the 20th century, a list that includes the likes of Gun Bow, Carry Back, Bald Eagle, Tompion, Never Bend, Beau Purple, Quadrangle, and Roman Brother, to name just a few.

Kelso retired to a life of hunting and hacking through the woods on his owner's farm, and made occasional appearances for racing research and charities. A couple of days after leading the post parade for the 1983 Jockey Club Gold Cup along with two other venerable geldings, Forego and John Henry, Kelso died of colic at Woodstock Farm at the age of 26.

Of all the hallowed prose written about Kelso over the course of his distinguished career, no one summed things up more appropriately or more succinctly than Joe Hirsch when he wrote, "Once upon a time there was a horse named Kelso. But only once."

Though Kelso dominated the sport for five straight years, the first half of the 1960's was graced with a number of other exceptionally talented Thoroughbreds who staged many memorable events.

The champion 3-year-old of 1961 was Carry Back, a colt of unlikely lineage who for two seasons did more to merchandise and promote racing to the masses than any horse since Native Dancer.

"The People's Horse," as Carry Back was known, was bred, owned, and trained by the irrepressible Jack Price, a former manufacturer of jet-engine parts in Cleveland, who was in the process of blowing his retirement nest egg in racing until this once-in-a-lifetime stroke of outrageous fortune came along.

As legend has it, Price took over the ownership of an obscure mare named Joppy for $150 as partial payment for an overdue board bill at his small Ohio farm, and kicked in another $150 to close the deal. Then, for a modest $400 fee, he bred his new acquisition to the equally obscure Saggy – a horse who had been the only colt to beat Citation at 3 – and the

Lowdown on French Trainers; Price Hails Diligent Blacksmith

The following report is written exclusively for The Morning Telegraph by Jack Price, owner-trainer-breeder of Carry Back, America's hope in the Arc de Triomphe at Longchamp on October 7.

by **Jack Price**

PARIS, Oct. 3.—I suppose you are wondering why, after I ended my last column with "finis," you are hearing from me again. The reason is when J. S. P. arrived here Monday, he asked me to continue. As an added inducement he increased my pay check by two zeros. So here goes.

Monday evening we went to a cocktail party given by the Bert Taylors at the Tour d'Argent. Everyone important connected with the French turf was invited. We met many owners and public trainers. Their problems are about what they are at home. It is easier to make a profit on the operation of a racing stable here. A public trainer will charge between $5 and $7 per day per horse. All shipping expenses are paid by the Jockey Club. The purses for an average card are high in relationship to the cost of operation. They can do this because of off the course betting. It was an interesting evening, because it gave us a chance to get the views not only of the Calumets and Cain Hoys of Europe but also the views of the trainers and owners of small stables.

Tuesday morning CB galloped about two miles and acted wonderful. Promptly at 9 that morning, the Jockey Club vet and a blacksmith arrived to make CB's shoes conform to French style. They couldn't speak English and as our interpreter, Whitney Tower, was not there, it was very hard to communicate. When the blacksmith tried to file the toes off Carry Back's shoes it was impossible, as the tips were steel and his rasp made no impression.

Used Set of Shoes Brought from States

They suggested pulling his shoes off and grinding down the toes on a wheel. An alternative would be to put on a new set of French plates on him. We objected because I was reluctant for a strange blacksmith to work on him. Things were at an impasse. Finally I decided to take a chance with their blacksmith, but instead of reworking our old shoes, we used a set of new ones which we had brought along with us. The toes were ground off and the blocks behind were rounded under our supervision. The old shoes were then removed and the new ones were tacked on.

The blacksmith was good and as he worked my doubts about his ability to do this job vanished. When he was through the horse was taken out of his stall and walked around for a few minutes. I was completely satisfied. Now the question was—how could he handle the turf Wednesday morning in shoes with no toes?

Tuesday night it rained hard for hours and the turf was soft. Wednesday morning at 7.30 CB walked on the track, galloped perfectly and blew out a quarter of a mile in preparation for his final three-quarter work on Thursday. Mike said he went as good as he ever did. Tomorrow, his work will be timed by the Teletimer from the 1,200-meter pole. This is approximately three quarters of a mile.

With all our doubts about his shoes dissipated and his condition, in my opinion, as good as it ever was, the only question in my mind is: will he be able to negotiate the 1 1-2 miles distance.

PADDOCK PATTER: Saw a horse run in bell boots in front at St. Cloud here. The stands were built in 1955. They have a glass-enclosed dining room and a board in the infield that gives the results and mutuels, but no odds . . . Blacksmith's here clip off the clinched nail ends on a horse's hoof and pull every nail they then can pry off the shoe with a thin flat tool. Blacksmiths in America jerk the shoe off with nippers without bothering to remove the nails . . . Our rooting section is beginning to arrive in force, and Joe Hirsch will take over in that department.

The modestly bred Carry Back was "the People's Horse" and reigned during the 1961 classics, winning the Kentucky Derby and Preakness. His owner, Jack Price, kept a journal — published in Daily Racing Form *— chronicling Carry Back's trip to Paris for the Prix de l'Arc de Triomphe.*

mysterious forces of nature somehow combined to create this uncommonly tough competitor.

"He changed the whole course of my life," admitted Price, who campaigned the stretch-running Carry Back through an ambitious 3-year-old schedule of 16 starts, which included hard-fought wins in the Kentucky Derby and the Preakness from out of the clouds, and photo-finish victories in the Flamingo, the Florida Derby, and the Jerome.

As a 4-year-old, Carry Back became just the fourth millionaire in American racing – joining Round Table, Nashua, and Citation – when he won the Metropolitan Handicap at the expense of, among others, Kelso, who would eventually surpass them all atop the earnings list.

Jack and Katherine Price were nothing if not sporting, and in the fall of 1962 they traveled to Paris with Carry Back to take a shot in the Prix de l'Arc de Triomphe. This was an extremely rare and bold move in those days, when transatlantic shipping was a daunting challenge for even the most experienced and well-heeled owner.

Their quixotic quest captured the imagination of Carry Back fans everywhere, and Price was enlisted by *Daily Racing Form* to write a daily diary during the trip. After Carry Back finished a very respectable 10th in the 24-horse field, beaten less than six lengths for all the marbles, Price was philosophical in his final entry: "Are we sorry we came? No. We set out to prove that a good American horse could compete favorably with the best in Europe on their own grounds and on their own terms . . . We didn't get the money, but we proved our point."

The 3-year-olds of 1962 were not an outstanding crop per se, but there was an element of high drama to their class, with photo finishes determining the winners of the Wood Memorial, Jersey Derby, Florida Derby, Preakness, Belmont Stakes, and, most notably, the Travers.

The Travers pitted Jaipur, winner of the Gotham, Withers, and Belmont, against the well-traveled Ridan, who was the pride of the West Coast.

On some afternoons Jaipur didn't have it, but on others he responded like a genuine champion. Such was the case on August 16, 1962, when he hooked up with Ridan in a gut-wrenching struggle through every desperate yard of the prestigious 1¼-mile Travers.

Jaipur prevailed by a nose to cement his 3-year-old championship, but proved no match for Kelso when next tried against older handicap horses in the Woodward. He never won another race.

Somewhat surprisingly, neither Kelso nor Carry Back was the richest American horse of 1962. That distinction went to the 2-year-old champion colt, Never Bend, trained by Woody Stephens. Never Bend reeled off consecutive wins in the Futurity, the Cowdin, and the Champagne Stakes en route to amassing a bankroll of $402,969 for Capt. Harry F. Guggenheim's Cain Hoy Stable.

Guggenheim, who had secured Stephens as his private trainer toward the end of 1956, customarily sent a couple of yearlings to Europe each year, and they were trained in England by Cecil Boyd-Rochfort, who also had horses for Queen Elizabeth. The best of them was Bald Eagle, who showed flashes of ability marked by inconsistency at Epsom and Ascot. In despair, Boyd-Rochfort sent him back to America in the fall of his 3-year-old season with the comment "Not very genuine."

Stephens and Guggenheim gave Bald Eagle almost a full year to acclimate, and their patience was rewarded with nine stakes wins, including back-to-back runnings of the Washington, D.C., International, and the title of handicap champion in 1960. At Christmas that year, Captain Guggenheim sent Stephens a turkey, and a bonus check for $75,000.

While Kelso was in the process of becoming the world's richest Thoroughbred, a bay filly named Cicada won championships at ages 2, 3 and 4, accumulating total earnings of $783,674, a record among females at the time. Cicada won 23 of 42 lifetime starts, and was trained and raced harder than the average filly, to prevent her from kicking down the proverbial barn for want of something to do.

Shortly after World War II, Bull Lea, who topped the list of leading stallions in the United States five

Northern Dancer won the Kentucky Derby in record time and then took the Preakness, but couldn't stay the mile-and-a-half distance of the Belmont. The diminutive bay went on to become one of the most influential sires of all time.

times, would have been the choice as Sire of the Century, and years later, both Nasrullah and his son Bold Ruler were immensely influential at stud.

But as the millennium approached, Northern Dancer was widely regarded as the most productive and important sire of the 20th century. And to think that Edward P. Taylor's Canadian homebred was passed over when offered for $25,000 at a Windfields Farm yearling sale!

Taylor had a unique method of convincing buyers that he was not keeping his best yearlings for himself: He placed what he considered a fair price on each member of his yearling crop, then held a private sale at the farm. Each horse was offered at the price until half of the yearlings had been sold. Taylor retained those unsold, and in 1962 that group included Northern Dancer.

It is easy to understand the lack of enthusiasm among yearling buyers, because Northern Dancer was a late foal and a bit of a runt, standing barely over 15 hands when fully grown. But he did have a 73-inch girth, comparable to that of a much larger horse, and that ample girth gave him plenty of heart and lung room. Northern Dancer also had exceptional balance, and these qualities may have been the catalysts for his relatively brief but brilliant 10-month tenure on the racetrack.

"He has a stride that looks two sizes too big for him, but it is perfectly controlled, like something they do at the Bolshoi Ballet," Hatton noted.

As a 2-year-old, Northern Dancer won 5 of 7 starts in Canada to establish himself as the best of his division there, and then invaded Aqueduct in November, where he dismantled Futurity Stakes winner Bupers in an allowance race. Northern Dancer concluded his campaign with an easy wire-to-wire triumph in the Remsen just nine days later, but had developed a quarter crack.

The standard procedure at the time was to cut out the crack, send the colt to the farm for the winter, and bring him back to the races in the spring after the crack had finally grown out. Such a course of action would have meant missing the Kentucky Derby, however. Northern Dancer's trainer, Horatio Luro, had read about the work of California-based blacksmith Bill Bane, who had developed a vulcanized patch for quarter cracks. Luro persuaded E. P. Taylor to let him try the patch, and Northern Dancer went to Florida that winter for training and racing.

After winning the Flamingo and the Florida Derby, the small but feisty Northern Dancer went to Keeneland for the Blue Grass, which he won by a well-measured half-length. This set him up perfectly to run the race of his life in the 1964 renewal of the Kentucky Derby, which was exactly what it took to repel the hulking Hill Rise by a neck in the record time of two minutes flat.

Northern Dancer then took the Preakness by 2¼ lengths, but failed in his bid to become the first Triple Crown winner since Citation, fading to third as the 4-5 favorite in the Belmont Stakes behind Quadrangle and Roman Brother (who, a year later, would become the first horse other than Kelso to be named Horse of the Year in the 1960's).

"He fought on gallantly but just couldn't handle that mile and a half," remarked Bill Hartack, who rode Northern Dancer in his final five races. "In fact, I think the most unusual thing about Northern Dancer was that he got a mile and a quarter."

Just two weeks after the Belmont, Northern Dancer returned to Canada and rebounded to win the Queen's Plate easily, but he bowed a tendon shortly thereafter and was retired. In a prescient observation in The American Racing Manual, Charles Hatton wrote of the 3-year-old champion, "It will be disappointing if racing's loss does not prove the stud's gain, as he is a colt of impeccable breeding and demonstrable class."

Of Northern Dancer's racing career, Luro said he most remembered the bay colt's gameness. "He never needed the whip to give his best, just the simple encouragement of a little tap on his shoulder," explained the Argentinean known as the Grand Senor.

"He refused to be punished. Once, in a prep for the Kentucky Derby, the jockey disobeyed my orders and whipped him. To show his disapproval, Northern Dancer wouldn't let me take him to the track for a week. How intelligent he was!" (Northern Dancer's personal preference aside, the Derby was still the Derby, and the chart says that the colt "prevailed under strong left-handed whipping" by Hartack.)

Initially, Northern Dancer's stud fee was $10,000. From his seven sales yearlings in 1967, his first crop, there were seven starters, seven winners, and five stakes winners. In all, there were 21 foals in Northern Dancer's first crop, with 18 starters, 16 winners, and 10 stakes winners.

Stamped with an impeccable pedigree, 1966 Horse of the Year Buckpasser was a star in a stellar era that included Dr. Fager and Damascus.

By 1980, those fortunate enough to send a mare to Northern Dancer paid upward of $100,000 . . . without a guarantee. By 1982 he commanded a stud fee of $250,000, and breeders were rumored during the boom years of the mid-1980's to have paid as much as $1 million to send him their mares.

Unlike Bull Lea, Nasrullah, and Bold Ruler, who were kept under tight control by their owners, Northern Dancer was commercially available, and so he was the first dominant sire with plenty of offspring out there for anyone with enough money to buy them. At the 1983 Keeneland summer yearling sale, a colt by Northern Dancer sent shock waves through the industry when he was sold for $10,200,000. At that time, the Keeneland auction board had only seven numbers. An eighth digit was added after that sale, in order to accommodate the unprecedented demand from buyers around the world.

In 1981, when Northern Dancer was 20, an offer of $40 million was made for his purchase. It was turned down by the 32-person syndicate that stood the horse at Windfields Farm in Maryland.

As successful as his progeny were as racehorses – he sired 146 stakes winners – Northern Dancer's most indelible mark on the breed was his potency as a sire of great sires, such as Lyphard, Nijinsky II, Nureyev, Danzig, The Minstrel, Sadler's Wells, Storm Bird, Vice Regent, and Be My Guest.

Charles Taylor, who took over the Windfields operation in 1981, was interviewed shortly after Northern Dancer was put down in November 1990 at the age of 29.

"Of all my father's accomplishments in racing and breeding, I believe he was most proud of having established the Northern Dancer sire line," Taylor said. "Everyone talks about him being small and stocky, which was true, but to me it was the intelligence through the eye – the look of eagles and all that – that is the thing that remains, the way he carried himself like a champion. I only really remember Northern Dancer as the stallion in the paddock, when he thought all the mares arriving were for him."

Ogden Phipps will surely go down as one of the greatest breeders of the 20th century. Phipps bred and raced more than 100 stakes winners, beginning with 1936 Withers winner White Cockade, and he campaigned such luminaries as Easy Goer and the undefeated Personal Ensign. But many students of the turf feel that Buckpasser was infinitely the best horse ever bred by the former chairman of The Jockey Club.

By 1953 Horse of the Year Tom Fool and out of Busanda, Buckpasser was a great-grandson of the immortal broodmare La Troienne, and wasted little time running roughshod over the 2-year-old class of 1965 for trainer Bill Winfrey.

Winfrey retired after guiding Buckpasser to 9 wins from 11 starts, and record 2-year-old earnings of $568,096. After racing greenly and finishing a fast-closing fourth in his career debut at Aqueduct on May 13, Buckpasser did not lose again until the Futurity, when he finished second on an off track.

Winfrey, who had succeeded one of the sport's legends, Sunny Jim Fitzsimmons, as the Phippses' trainer, noted that Buckpasser was "a bit of a loafer at times, especially in the mornings, but he is determined in the afternoons."

Buckpasser was given over to Eddie Neloy and put away for the year after winning the Champagne, in order to prepare for the 3-year-old classics. He was held in such high regard during the winter of 1966 that Hialeah management, fearing a huge minus pool, refused to allow betting when he ran in the Flamingo, which in that era was the most prestigious of all the stakes races on the path to the Kentucky Derby. Despite drawing a fairly large nine-horse field, the race was run as a betless exhibition and dubbed by the press as the

Damascus clinched the 1967 Horse of the Year award with a powerhouse 10-length victory over Buckpasser and Dr. Fager in the Woodward.

"Chicken Flamingo," with Buckpasser coming again in deep stretch to prevail by a nose.

While training toward the Florida Derby, Buckpasser developed a quarter crack that kept him out of the Triple Crown events. He returned to win an allowance sprint at Aqueduct in early June, and then ran the table, winning nine straight stakes to secure titles as champion 3-year-old, champion handicap horse, and Horse of the Year in 1966. In so doing, Buckpasser – who regularly ran coupled with a "rabbit" in order to ensure sufficient early pace for his late run – set a world record for a mile, winning the Arlington Classic in 1:32⅗. He became the youngest millionaire in racing history, with earnings of $1,218,874 after two seasons of racing.

Recurring quarter cracks and the onset of arthritis in his right fore hoof and pastern compromised Buckpasser's effectiveness as a 4-year-old in 1967, but he still managed victories in the San Fernando Stakes, the Metropolitan Handicap, and the Suburban Handicap. In the latter, he shouldered 133 pounds and appeared beaten in midstretch when fourth, still four lengths from the leaders, but responded to Braulio Baeza's insistent urging and was up in the final strides to edge Ring Twice, while conceding 22 pounds to that rival.

After being upset by the Allen Jerkens-trained Handsome Boy in the Brooklyn Handicap 18 days later, Buckpasser was sidelined for two months due to his infirmities, and it was uncertain whether he would make the Woodward Stakes, in which he would face the crack 3-year-olds Damascus and Dr. Fager.

The 14th running of the Woodward Stakes on September 30, 1967, aroused more interest than any race since the match between Swaps and Nashua a dozen years earlier, and represented a changing of the guard.

Defending Horse of the Year Buckpasser had been out of action since midsummer, but he was installed as the slight favorite at 8-5 over Damascus and Dr. Fager, who were co-second choices at 9-5. Buckpasser and Damascus brought along their respective rabbits, Great Power and Hedevar, to go after the speedy but headstrong Dr. Fager through the opening fractions.

Tom Ainslie, the dean of handicapping authors, recounted the Woodward in The Handicapper's Handbook: "Dr. Fager wilted after running the legs off Hedevar. Meanwhile, Shoemaker let Damascus dawdle twelve to fifteen lengths behind the pace. And when he asked the colt for some run, he got the most sensational burst of speed I have ever seen. Poor Buckpasser tried to come on in the stretch but was not the Buckpasser of old and had all he could do to beat the fading Dr. Fager for second money. The old Buckpasser would have made it close, but under today's weights would have been by no means a cinch to win. The Damascus of the late summer of 1967 was a horse for the ages."

The Woodward was Buckpasser's final race. He was syndicated for stud duty at the unprecedented rate of $4,800,000 for 32 shares, and would eventually become one of the most influential broodmare sires of all time.

While the Woodward marked the end of Buckpasser's career, it put the stamp of greatness on Damascus, who was a unanimous choice as 1967 Horse of the Year after also taking the Preakness, Belmont, Dwyer, American Derby, Travers, and Jockey Club Gold Cup, and finishing second by a nose when tried on turf in the D.C. International.

All in all, Damascus made 16 starts as a 3-year-old and won a dozen times, amassing what was then a single-season earnings record of $817,941.

Damascus is on most lists of all-time greats, but his star might have burned brighter still had he not finished third as the favorite in the Kentucky Derby. Under humid conditions, Damascus washed out and became a nervous wreck while being saddled.

"When he started pinning his ears and kicking his back legs up, I knew we were in trouble," said Bill Shoemaker, who was aboard for 17 of the colt's 21 career wins. "I went to work on him like crazy, but he was completely out of sorts. That was absolutely the most disappointed I have ever been in the outcome of a race."

Damascus atoned, however, coming within two noses of winning 11 straight to close out the year, including an incredible 22-length tour de force in

Dr. Fager closed out his career with a track-record-setting performance in the Vosburgh under 139 pounds. Two starts back, he had set a world record for a flat mile that would last for 29 years.

the Travers. A crowd of 28,576, at the time the second-largest gathering in Saratoga's history, saw the race, which was run in the slop after overnight rains and another downpour that fell just before post time.

The crowd would have been larger had the weather been better – and if Dr. Fager had been running. He had been pointing for the Travers, but a viral infection two weeks earlier had briefly forced him out of training.

The rivalry between Damascus and Dr. Fager began in the Gotham Stakes on April 15, 1967, when 50,522 screaming fans filled Aqueduct to the rafters.

Dr. Fager had won 4 of 5 starts as a 2-year-old, his only loss coming to divisional champion Successor when he was rank early and unable to hold on to a three-length lead in midstretch of the Champagne. The Gotham marked his seasonal debut, while Damascus, who was riding a five-race winning streak, had already taken both his starts at 3, including an impressive score in the Bay Shore three weeks earlier.

"I did want to give him a prep before the Gotham but I couldn't get one," explained John Nerud, who trained the Tartan Farm homebred. "Everyone said I was crazy to run against Damascus first time out, but I just told them to come to the races." At the finish, it was Dr. Fager by a half-length.

As 4-year-olds, Damascus and Dr. Fager met twice more. They first hooked up in the Suburban at Aqueduct on July 4, 1968, and 54,336 fans turned out to watch Dr. Fager, under 132 pounds, repulse every challenge from Damascus. He drew away to a two-length victory over Bold Hour, equaling the track record of 1:59⅗ for 1¼ miles, as Damascus finished third. Sixteen days later, they were back at it in the Brooklyn, in which Dr. Fager carried 135 pounds to Damascus's 130. More importantly, Hedevar was also in the race. Damascus was able to sit back and then unleash a powerful move that carried him to a 2½-length victory in 1:59⅕, breaking the track record equaled by Dr. Fager in the Suburban.

Damascus won twice more that summer, but suffered a career-ending bowed tendon as the favorite in the Jockey Club Gold Cup and was retired to stud by his owner and breeder, Mrs. Edith W. Bancroft.

Following the Brooklyn, in which he had been somewhat rank under rating tactics behind Damascus's rabbit, Dr. Fager was given a looser rein by Braulio Baeza and responded to win the Whitney by eight lengths under 132 pounds. Next, he broke Buckpasser's world record for a mile, winning the Washington Park Handicap at Arlington in 1:32⅕ while carrying 134 pounds. To show his versatility, Dr. Fager then spotted the formidable turf runner Advocator 22 pounds and outdueled him through the stretch when tried on grass for the first (and only) time in the United Nations Handicap at Atlantic City.

Dr. Fager's final race came in the Vosburgh Handicap on November 2, 1968. In an awe-inspiring exhibition of sheer unbridled speed, Dr. Fager,

Native Diver was a headstrong sprinter early in his career, but added another dimension later on, winning the 10-furlong Hollywood Gold Cup from 1965 through 1967. He died of enterotoxemia just nine days after winning the 1967 Del Mar Handicap.

as Bill Nack later wrote in Sports Illustrated, "blew around Aqueduct like a malevolent wind" and stormed through the seven furlongs in a track-record 1:20⅕ while carrying a staggering 139 pounds. The time would remain the benchmark at that track for more than three decades.

After that phenomenal performance, Nerud observed, "He is the best horse I've ever been around . . . He has gone a distance, sprinted, been on the grass and carried weight. Any horse who looks him in the eye is dead. No one horse ever beat Dr. Fager doing anything."

As the story goes, the office staff of William L. McKnight's Tartan Farm chipped in to buy a cheap claimer as a birthday present for the boss. After failing to get their first choice, their alternative gift selection was a mare named Aspidistra, who had managed just two wins from 14 starts, and who could not, in the words of Charles Hatton, "beat a fat man kicking a barrel up a hill."

Nevertheless, Aspidistra produced a pair of champions for Tartan: the freakishly fast and hot-blooded speed demon Dr. Fager, and Ta Wee, who was the sprint champion of 1969 and 1970.

After losing the first two legs of the Triple Crown to Majestic Prince, Arts and Letters was dominant the remainder of the 1969 season, taking the Belmont, Jim Dandy, Travers, Woodward, and Jockey Club Gold Cup.

Ta Wee (Sioux for "beautiful girl") won 13 of 17 starts during her two-season run as the top sprinter in the land, including back-to-back renewals of the Fall Highweight. A tremendous weight carrier, she had a massive set of hips and hindquarters that enabled her to successfully carry 142 pounds in her final race, the Interborough Handicap.

In terms of the dynamically and often violently changing American culture, the 1960's didn't really become "the sixties" until the latter half of the decade, and during those turbulent times racing, too, had to deal with the tragic and untimely losses of some of its leading figures.

Trained by Buster Millerick, Native Diver was as revered on the West Coast as his Eastern counterpart, Kelso, had been in New York. The gritty gelding won 3 of 5 races as a 2-year-old in 1961, and then ran at least 10 times during each of the next six years, winning 37 of 81 starts all told.

Native Diver first came to prominence as a headstrong sprinter with a tendency to bear out around the turn, and tied a world record by running seven furlongs in 1:20 flat in the Los Angeles Handicap. He proved to be more than a one-dimensional sprinter with maturity, winning three straight Hollywood Gold Cups from 1965-67. The 1967 Gold Cup was his penultimate outing, and pushed the 8-year-old's earnings past the $1 million plateau.

Native Diver went out a winner in the Del Mar Handicap on September 4, 1967, but died suddenly just nine days later from enterotoxemia, a breakdown of the intestinal tract. The beloved warhorse was buried at Hollywood Park, which had been the stage for so many of his triumphs.

Like Carry Back, the filly Dark Mirage came from humble beginnings. Obtained for the paltry sum of $6,000 at a Keeneland yearling sale by Lloyd Miller, she was a relative pipsqueak, standing slightly over 14 hands and weighing a bit more than 700 pounds soaking wet.

During her 2-year-old campaign, anyone who thought Dark Mirage would become the first filly to sweep New York's Filly Triple Crown must have kept it to himself for fear of being laughed off the track, because she won just twice from 15 starts. But by the end of her 3-year-old season in 1968, it was obvious there wasn't another in the division who could so much as warm her up.

After a fourth-place finish in her seasonal debut, Dark Mirage ripped off nine straight wins, including the Acorn, Mother Goose, and Coaching Club American Oaks by an aggregate 28 lengths.

Dark Mirage won the Delaware Oaks at the end of July, but was sidelined the remainder of the year by a foot injury that kept her out of the Alabama, as well as preventing a possible confrontation with colts in the fall. Said rival trainer Max Hirsch at the time, "I'm not at all sure that little filly can't beat any of them – Dr. Fager, Damascus, any of them – at a mile and a half, scale weights."

Dark Mirage returned in February 1969 to win her 10th consecutive race, carrying 126 pounds in the Santa Maria Handicap at Santa Anita. In her next start, she carried 130 pounds in the Santa Margarita. Bumped hard at the break, Dark Mirage hesitated and then jumped a cellophane wrapper that had blown onto the track. She was retired after it was discovered she had dislocated a sesamoid in the right front ankle, near the area of her original injury the preceding year.

She never recovered. Her left foreleg wobbled from the additional weight while her right leg was in a cast. After emergency surgery in July 1970, the "Tiny Tigress" with the big heart was put down.

Dr. Timothy Leary encouraged America's youth to turn on, tune in, and drop out in the sixties, and Thoroughbred racing endured a major drug scandal of its own when Dancer's Image finished first in the 1968 Kentucky Derby by a length and a half over Forward Pass. Three days later, a public announcement was made that postrace testing of Dancer's Image had come up positive for the then-prohibited analgesic Butazolidin.

A long legal battle ensued. The stewards awarded the winner's share to Forward Pass, but did not technically disqualify Dancer's Image, because Kentucky racing rules at the time stated only that any horse showing up positive for a derivative of phenylbutazone "shall not participate in the purse distribution."

Later in 1968, a two-week hearing by the Kentucky State Racing Commission upheld the stewards' ruling. At Churchill Downs, Forward Pass's name came down as the Derby winner, and later the names of both horses went up. The purse-distribution decision was appealed by Peter Fuller, owner of Dancer's Image, and nearly two years later the commission's ruling was overturned. The racing commission, in turn, then appealed to the Kentucky Court of Appeals, which awarded first-place money to Forward Pass on April 28, 1972 – nearly four years after the disputed Run for the Roses.

In the May 8, 1972, issue of The Blood-Horse magazine, Kent Hollingsworth wrote, "The purse finally having been distributed, there remains of the Dancer's Image case an unresolved quiddity . . . which will forever plague quiz-show contestants and anyone else ever asked: Who won the 1968 Kentucky Derby? Dancer's Image finished first, was never disqualified from first, but was denied any part of the purse; Forward Pass finished second, has never been declared the official winner but received first money."

In terms of total domination, few campaigns can match that of Arts and Letters in 1969. After being beaten in photo finishes by Majestic Prince in the Kentucky Derby and the Preakness, Paul Mellon's homebred chestnut ruined that rival's bid to become the first undefeated Triple Crown winner, easily thrashing him in the Belmont Stakes by 5 ½ lengths.

The Rokeby Stable colt towered over his opposition during the remainder of the year, winning the Jim Dandy by 10 lengths, the Travers by 6½, the Woodward by two, and the two-mile Jockey Club Gold Cup by 14.

Arts and Letters was on the smallish side at just over 15 hands, and although he was not a flashy horse to look at, he ran with the kind of grim determination that gave credence to famed breeder Federico Tesio's assertion that "a horse runs with his legs and resists with his heart."

As the 1960's came to a close, America scarcely resembled what it had been at the beginning of the decade. A fledgling space program had developed to the point where Neil Armstrong and Buzz Aldrin set foot on the moon in July 1969. A few months later, a hapless expansion team that had established a record for futility by losing 120 games in its debut season of 1962 became the Miracle Mets, after a thoroughly implausible World Series victory over the heavily favored Baltimore Orioles.

By the autumn of 1969, political assassinations, race riots, and anti-Vietnam War protests had exacted a heavy toll on the American psyche, inexorably wearing off the last remaining vestiges of the nation's innocence.

Significant upheaval loomed on the horizon for racing as well. As a new decade of uncertainty dawned, offtrack betting, lotteries, and casinos would provide increasingly sterner competition for America's betting dollar.

The game, and all its many players, would never again be quite the same.

Champions

Past Performances

THE 1960'S

YEAR BY YEAR CHAMPIONS

•1960•
•2-YEAR-OLD MALE *Hail to Reason* •2-YEAR-OLD FILLY *Bowl of Flowers* •3-YEAR-OLD MALE *Kelso*
•3-YEAR-OLD FILLY *Berlo* •HANDICAP HORSE *Bald Eagle* •HANDICAP MARE *Royal Native* •STEEPLECHASE *Benguala*
•**HORSE OF THE YEAR** Kelso

•1961•
•2-YEAR-OLD MALE *Crimson Satan* •2-YEAR-OLD FILLY *Cicada* •3-YEAR-OLD MALE *Carry Back*
•3-YEAR-OLD FILLY *Bowl of Flowers* •HANDICAP HORSE *Kelso* •HANDICAP MARE *Airmans Guide*
•GRASS HORSE *T.V. Lark* •STEEPLECHASE *Peal*
•**HORSE OF THE YEAR** Kelso

•1962•
•2-YEAR-OLD MALE *Never Bend* •2-YEAR-OLD FILLY *Smart Deb* •3-YEAR-OLD MALE *Jaipur*
•3-YEAR-OLD FILLY *Cicada* •HANDICAP HORSE *Kelso* •HANDICAP MARE *Primonetta* •STEEPLECHASE *Barnabys Bluff*
•**HORSE OF THE YEAR** Kelso

•1963•
•2-YEAR-OLD MALE *Hurry to Market* •2-YEAR-OLD FILLY *Tosmah, Castle Forbes (TRA)* •3-YEAR-OLD MALE *Chateaugay*
•3-YEAR-OLD FILLY *Lamb Chop* •HANDICAP HORSE *Kelso* •HANDICAP MARE *Cicada*
•GRASS HORSE *Mongo* •STEEPLECHASE *Amber Diver*
•**HORSE OF THE YEAR** Kelso

•1964•
•2-YEAR-OLD MALE *Bold Lad* •2-YEAR-OLD FILLY *Queen Empress* •3-YEAR-OLD MALE *Northern Dancer*
•3-YEAR-OLD FILLY *Tosmah* •HANDICAP HORSE *Kelso* •HANDICAP MARE *Tosmah, Old Hat (TRA)*
•STEEPLECHASE *Bel Nouvel*
•**HORSE OF THE YEAR** Kelso

•1965•
•2-YEAR-OLD MALE *Buckpasser* •2-YEAR-OLD FILLY *Moccasin* •3-YEAR-OLD MALE *Tom Rolfe*
•3-YEAR-OLD FILLY *What a Treat* •HANDICAP HORSE *Roman Brother* •HANDICAP MARE *Old Hat* •GRASS HORSE *Parka*
•SPRINTER *Affectionately* •STEEPLECHASE *Bon Nouvel*
•**HORSE OF THE YEAR** Roman Brother, Moccasin (TRA)

•1966•
•2-YEAR-OLD MALE *Successor* •2-YEAR-OLD FILLY *Regal Gleam* •3-YEAR-OLD MALE *Buckpasser*
•3-YEAR-OLD FILLY *Lady Pitt* •HANDICAP HORSE *Buckpasser Bold Bidder (TRA)*
•HANDICAP MARE *Open Fire, Summer Scandal (TRA)* •GRASS HORSE *Assagai* •SPRINTER *Impressive*
•STEEPLECHASE *Mako, Tuscalee (TRA)*
•**HORSE OF THE YEAR** Buckpasser

•1967•
•2-YEAR-OLD MALE *Vitriolic* •2-YEAR-OLD FILLY *Queen of the Stage* •3-YEAR-OLD MALE *Damascus*
•3-YEAR-OLD FILLY *Furl Sail, Gamely (TRA)* •HANDICAP HORSE *Damascus, Buckpasser (TRA)*
•HANDICAP MARE *Straight Deal* •GRASS HORSE *Fort Marcy* •SPRINTER *Dr. Fager* •STEEPLECHASE *Quick Pitch*
•**HORSE OF THE YEAR** Damascus

•1968•
•2-YEAR-OLD MALE *Top Knight* •2-YEAR-OLD FILLY *Gallant Bloom, Process Shot (TRA)*
•3-YEAR-OLD MALE *Stage Door Johnny* •3-YEAR-OLD FILLY *Dark Mirage* •HANDICAP HORSE *Dr. Fager*
•HANDICAP MARE *Gamely* •GRASS HORSE *Dr. Fager* •SPRINTER *Dr. Fager* •STEEPLECHASE *Bon Nouvel*
•**HORSE OF THE YEAR** Dr. Fager

•1969•
•2-YEAR-OLD MALE *Silent Screen* •2-YEAR-OLD FILLY *Fast Attack, Tudor Queen (TRA)*
•3-YEAR-OLD MALE *Arts and Letters* •3-YEAR-OLD FILLY *Gallant Bloom*
•HANDICAP HORSE *Arts and Letters, Nodouble (TRA)* •HANDICAP MARE *Gallant Bloom, Gamely (TRA)*
•GRASS HORSE *Hawaii* •SPRINTER *Ta Wee* •STEEPLECHASE *L'Escargot*
•**HORSE OF THE YEAR** Arts and Letters

Affectionately

dkb. f. 1960, by Swaps (Khaled)–Searching, by War Admiral — Lifetime record: 52 28 8 6 $546,660

Own.– Mrs E.D. Jacobs
Br.– Bieber–Jacobs Stable (Ky)
Tr.– H. Jacobs

Date/Race	Cond	Dist	Fractions	Race	Running line	Jockey	Wt	Eq	Odds	Figs	Finishers	Comment	Field
1Nov65- 7Aqu	fst	6f	:224 :453 1:102	3↑ Sport Page H 28k	6 1 2hd 1hd 1½ 2¾	Blum W	127	b	*1.10	90-21	Ornamento112¾Affectionately127¾R. Thomas119no	Gamely	8
14Oct65- 6Kee	fst	*7f	1:27	3↑ ⒻAlw 10000	2 2 1hd 1hd 2hd 1¾	Blum W	121	b	-	88-16	Affectionately121¾Star Maggie11512Basking11811	Driving	4
27Sep65- 7Aqu	fst	1⅛	:463 1:104 1:36 1:491	3↑ ⒻBeldame 82k	1 1 1½ 1hd 31½ 53	Blum W	123	b	2.10e	87-19	WhataTreat118noSteeplJll123½StrghtDl1181½	Swerved start	6
20Sep65- 7Aqu	fst	1	:223 :444 1:084 1:351	3↑ ⒻMaskette H 28k	8 1 1½ 1hd 1hd 2no	Blum W	128	b	2.90e	92-16	Tosmah128noAffectionately1283Straight Deal113½	Sharp	9
5Jly65- 7Aqu	fst	1¼	:463 1:111 1:36 2:01	3↑ Suburban H 108k	7 3 42½ 46½ 512 625	Valenzuela I	119	b	8.95	68-14	Pia Star1171½Smart1198Tenacle1144	Drifted out late	7
26Jun65- 7Aqu	fst	7f	:221 :443 1:091 1:23	3↑ ⒻVagrancy H 58k	1 1 1½ 12 16 1hd	Blum W	137	b	*1.05e	91-13	Affectionately137hdSoughtAftr1113½FcthFcts1191½	All out	13
9Jun65- 7Aqu	fst	6f	:214 :442 1:092	3↑ ⒻLiberty Belle H 28k	4 1 11½ 13 16 16	Blum W	132	b	*.50	96-15	Affectionately1326Songster1123Petite Rouge109½	Easily	8
31May65- 7Aqu	fst	1	:222 :442 1:081 1:342	3↑ Metropolitan H 111k	5 1 11 11 2hd 33¼	Valenzuela I	121	b	4.55	93-16	GunBow130nkChieftain1173Affectionately1214½	Game effort	8
22May65- 7Aqu	fst	1⅛	:47 1:111 1:362 1:494	3↑ ⒻTop Flight H 57k	5 1 13 13 15 18	Blum W	120	b	3.90e	87-20	Affectionately1208Steeple Jill123½Old Hat127¾	Easily	10
19May65- 7Aqu	fst	7f	:221 :441 1:084 1:222	3↑ Roseben H 28k	2 2 1½ 23 23 34½	Blum W	127	b	*.60	89-17	National1162Chieftain1222½Affectionately1272½	Bid,tired	7
21Apr65- 7Aqu	fst	6f	:22 :442 1:092	3↑ Toboggan H 27k	3 1 1½ 13 16 15	Blum W	124	b	*1.45	96-16	Affectionately1245Chieftain1263½ExclusivNshu1152	Easily	8
14Apr65- 7Aqu	fst	7f	:231 :461 1:103 1:24	3↑ ⒻDistaff H 27k	7 1 1½ 12½ 14 13	Blum W	128	b	*.70	86-21	Affectionately1283Treachery115hdPetticoat113hd	Easily	7
31Mar65- 7Aqu	fst	6f	:23 :461 1:11	3↑ ⒻCorrection H 27k	7 1 12 12 13 12	Baeza B	125	b	*.75	88-24	Affectionately1252FacetheFacts123¾ChopHouse122nk	Easily	7
23Jan65- 7SA	fst	1 1/16	:231 :46 1:102 1:424	4↑ ⒻS Maria H 29k	8 1 1½ 1hd 1hd 21	Shoemaker W	122	b	3.40e	88-11	Batteur1191Affectionately1221½CuriousClover118no	Gamely	9
12Jan65- 8SA	fst	7f	:222 :451 1:093 1:222	4↑ ⒻS Monica H (Div 2) 19k	1 4 2hd 21 24 23½	Shoemaker W	126	b	*1.20e	87-16	Chop House1203½Affectionately126nkBatteur118hd	Gamely	10
31Dec64- 8SA	fst	6f	:221 :451 :573 1:10	3↑ ⒻLas Flores H 24k	4 2 2½ 1hd 1hd 1Ꭵ	Shoemaker W	125	b	*.90	92-17	[DH]Affectiontly125[DH]ChopHous1193CurousClovr120½	Driving	10
11Nov64- 7Aqu	fst	7f	:221 :45 1:091 1:22	3↑ Vosburgh H 28k	7 5 22 2½ 13 11	Grant H	120	b	*2.05e	96-17	Affectionately1201RdGr1132Bonjour114nk	Strongly handled	9
2Nov64- 7Aqu	fst	6f	:222 :451 1:102	3↑ Sport Page H 28k	8 3 1½ 1hd 12 11½	Shoemaker W	117	b	*1.75e	91-16	Affectionately1171½Red Gar1132Macedonia1162½	Easily	11
21Oct64- 7Aqu	gd	6f	:214 :45 1:103	3↑ ⒻInterborough H 27k	4 2 32 21½ 1½ 12	Shoemaker W	124	b	*1.60	90-16	Affectionately1242Ballet Rose110¾Charspiv1164	Easily	6
13Oct64- 7Aqu	fst	6f	:221 :451 1:094	3↑ ⒻAlw 10000	5 1 22 2hd 11 12	Shoemaker W	123	b	*.35	94-14	Affectionately1232Gold Frame1083Steeple Jill1142	Easily	5
30Jly64- 7Aqu	fst	6f	:222 :452 1:10	3↑ ⒻHandicap 10000	1 2 11½ 11 12½ 11½	Chambers W	124	b	3.60	93-18	Affectionately1241½ChopHouse120½LookMa1133	Brisk drive	6
1Jly64- 7Aqu	fst	6f	:213 :443 1:101	3↑ ⒻLiberty Belle H 27k	2 3 3nk 32½ 812 815	Ussery R	123	b	4.65	77-17	Tosmah1202LookMa1101½LizzieTsh111no	Early speed,stopped	8
10Jun64- 7Aqu	fst	7f	:221 :443 1:101 1:234	3↑ ⒻVagrancy H 28k	7 2 12 1½ 1½ 41¼	Chambers W	122	b	6.20	86-18	NoResisting112nkOilRoyalty1251LookMa110no	Used in pace	10
2Jun64- 7Aqu	fst	6f	:222 :452 1:102	3↑ ⒻHandicap 8500	3 1 12 13 13 12	Chambers W	122	b	*.90	91-16	Affectionately1222SparklingSiren113nkPmsEgo1215	Handily	8
29May64- 7Aqu	fst	7f	:223 :453 1:103 1:232	3↑ ⒻAlw 10000	3 3 12 12 12 22	Venezia M7	116	b	*1.05	87-17	Colonia1162Affectionately1162No Resisting1161	Gamely	10
16May64- 7GS	fst	6f	:214 :443 1:101	3↑ ⒻColonial H 29k	6 5 1hd 21½ 45 44¾	Grimm PI	123	b	3.30	88-18	Tosmah1151½LookMa1103LatinWalk111nk	Tired under impost	11
1Apr64- 7Aqu	fst	6f	:221 :453 1:104	3↑ ⒻCorrection H 29k	2 2 11 12½ 11½ 12½	Chambers W	121	b	4.25	89-19	Affectionately1212½DecimalCoinag111noChrspv1204	Driving	12
24Feb64- 7SA	fst	7f	:214 :443 1:093 1:224	4↑ ⒻS Monica H 24k	7 5 1½ 1½ 32 125¾	Ycaza M	118	b	*3.40	83-14	ChopHouse116hdSundayDoll1111½JazzQueen112¾	Early foot	16
17Feb64- 6SA	fst	6f	:22 :45 :57 1:093	4↑ ⒻAlw 7500	3 3 21 2½ 21 21	Valenzuela I	120	b	*1.90	95-13	Kea1171Affectionately1201½Sunday Doll1172½	Game effort	8
17Jan64- 7SA	fst	6f	:221 :451 :574 1:103	4↑ ⒻAlw 10000	5 2 2hd 1hd 31 75½	Valenzuela I	120	b	*1.60	85-17	Hi Rated120¾Bloomer Girl1131Savaii1141	Used up early	11
5Nov63- 7Aqu	fst	6f	:214 :442 1:10	3↑ ⒻInterborough H 23k	9 1 2hd 21 1½ 11½	Valenzuela I	116	b	*2.15	93-16	Affectionately1161½Charspiv114½[D]Smart Deb1211	Driving	12
17Oct63- 6Aqu	fst	6½f	:221 :444 1:101 1:17	3↑ ⒻAlw 7500	6 1 1½ 14 14 12	Valenzuela I	114	b	*.70e	95-17	Affectionately1142Speedwell111¾GrenupTm114hd	Mild drive	9
7Oct63- 6Aqu	fst	6f	:221 :452 1:102	3↑ ⒻAlw 7500	5 1 12 11½ 13 2hd	Valenzuela I	114	b	*1.70	91-15	Tamarona116hdAffectionately1142Royal Babs1141	Sharp	6
29Jly63- 6Sar	fst	6f	:214 :451 1:101	3↑ ⒻAlw 6000	9 1 12½ 11½ 11 31¼	Gomez A	114	b	*2.15	96-11	Sailor'sHunch113½WindyMiss120¾Affectionately1142	Tired	9
29Jun63- 7Aqu	sly	6f	:22 :452 1:103	3↑ ⒻLiberty Belle H 27k	2 3 31½ 32½ 65¾ 612	Ycaza M	112	b	3.45	80-13	MahMoola1125Bramalea120¾King'sStory112¾	Bore out,tired	6
24May63- 7Aqu	fm	1 1/16Ⓣ	1:424	3↑ ⒻAlw 10000	1 1 11½ 1hd 2½ 53¾	Adams L	111		4.90	90-06	Errcountess1181¼Speedwell1102My Portrait121hd	Tired	8
18May63- 7Aqu	sly	1	:222 :453 1:111 1:371	ⒻAcorn 60k	3 1 2½ 2hd 914 1125	Adams L	121		6.15	57-17	SpicyLiving1213½Nalee121½LambChop1213	Early speed,tired	12
25Apr63- 7Aqu	fst	6f	:23 :47 1:113	3↑ ⒻAlw 10000	2 1 11 11 12 11½	Shoemaker W	105		*.65	87-17	Affectionately1051½Windy Miss122noSome Song1221½	Easily	8
19Apr63- 6Aqu	fst	6f	:221 :453 1:104	3↑ ⒻAlw 7500	2 3 21½ 11 11½ 11½	Valenzuela I	114		*.30	91-15	Affectiontly1141½RumBottlBy1112Wlson'sB.W.116no	Driving	7
19Oct62- 7GS	fst	1	:223 :454 1:104 1:372	ⒻAlw 10000	10 1 12½ 1½ 21 37	Baeza B	121	b	4.20e	88-20	Wise Nurse1122Smart Deb1215Affectionately1212½	Tired	11
6Oct62- 7Bel	sly	1	:223 :453 1:111 1:38	ⒻFrizette 110k	7 2 2hd 2hd 2hd 33¼	Valenzuela I	119	b	3.20e	81-15	PamsEgo1191½Fool'sPlay1191¾Affectionately1194	Weakened	10
8Sep62- 7Aqu	fst	6f	:213 :442 1:094	ⒻMatron 102k	6 2 2hd 2hd 22½ 35½	Valenzuela I	119	b	*.65	90-11	SmartDeb1191½FashionVerdict1194Affectionately1193	Tired	9
22Aug62- 7Sar	fst	6f	:221 :45 1:102	ⒻSpinaway 79k	8 1 11½ 11½ 11½ 11¼	Valenzuela I	119	b	*.30	96-12	Affectionately1191¼Nalee1192½Rare Exchange1192	Driving	9
28Jly62- 8Mth	fst	6f	:212 :441 1:10	ⒻSorority 100k	9 1 12 15 14 15	Valenzuela I	119	b	*.30	92-16	Affectionately1195Fashion Verdict119¾Nalee1192½	Easily	9
16Jly62- 7Aqu	fst	5½f	:22 :451 1:043	ⒻAstoria 28k	6 1 1½ 12 13 12½	Baeza B	123	b	*.65	96-10	Affectionatly1232½NoRsstng120¾Kng'sStory1172	Mild drive	9
27Jun62- 7Mth	fst	5½f	:213 :462 1:051	ⒻColleen 23k	2 7 51¼ 53¼ 3½ 22½	Baeza B	119		*.60	88-20	NoResisting1122½Affectiontly1195Nl1122	Blocked ⅛ pole	11
18Jun62- 5Bel	fst	5½f	:221 :461 1:051	ⒻNational Stallion 37k	2 2 32 21 1½ 13	Baeza B	119		*.15	95-15	Affectionately1193Charspiv1142½No Resisting119¾	Easily	5
2Jun62 5Del	fst	6f	:221 :463 :59	ⒻPolly Drummond 23k	8 1 1hd 2hd 1hd 11	Valenzuela I	122		*.70	94-22	Affectionately1221Bold Princess1131Nalee1091¼	Driving	9
16May62- 7Aqu	fst	5f	:22 :454 :584	ⒻFashion 22k	2 2 1½ 1½ 12 12	Baeza B	116		*.35	96-16	Affectionately1162FashonVrdct116nkPrncssBbu116½	Handily	7
9May62- 5Aqu	fst	5f	:23 :463 :583	ⒻAlw 5000	5 3 43 21½ 11½ 12½	Baeza B	120		*.75	97-12	Affectionately1202½FashionVerdct1201½PmsEgo1172½	Easily	6
28Apr62- 4Aqu	fst	5f	:22 :462 :591	ⒻAlw 4500	1 1 11 11 11½ 17	Baeza B	117		*1.30	94-10	Affectionately1177Mardoll115noTamanrasset1201½	Easily	7
17Jan62- 3SA	fst	3f	:22 :331	ⒻMd Sp Wt	1 3 13 11½	Baeza B	115		4.30	- -	Affectionately1151½Snickersnee115noDelhiMad1152	Driving	14

Airmans Guide

b. f. 1957, by One Count (Count Fleet)–Navigating, by Hard Tack — Lifetime record: 20 13 2 2 $315,673

Own.– H.A. Grant
Br.– W.P. Little (Ky)
Tr.– B.B. Williams

Date/Race	Cond	Dist	Fractions	Race	Running line	Jockey	Wt	Eq	Odds	Figs	Finishers	Comment	Field
19Oct61- 6Kee	sly	1⅛	:464 1:103 1:36 1:491	3↑ ⒻSpinster 84k	1 1 1½ 2½ 22 42¾	Grant H	123	b	*.70	88-11	BowlofFlowers119¾Primonetta1191TimesTwo1191	No excuse	7
12Oct61- 6Kee	fst	*7f	1:25	3↑ ⒻAlw 7500	3 2 21½ 31½ 2hd 12	Grant H	121	b	*.40	102-09	Airmans Guide1212Indian Maid115¾Flavia1093½	In hand	5
23Sep61- 7Bel	fst	1⅛	:463 1:11 1:361 1:492	3↑ ⒻBeldame 96k	5 2 21 2½ 1½ 1¾	Grant H	123	b	3.65	89-18	Airmans Guide123¾Craftiness1232½Primonetta1185½	Driving	12
29Jly61- 6Del	gd	1¼	:46 1:11 1:362 2:022	3↑ ⒻDelaware H 159k	10 2 23 14 14 13½	Grant H	121	b	*2.40	90-20	Airmans Guide1213½Royal Native120nkTritoma1182½	Easily	12
22Jly61- 6Del	fst	1 1/16	:231 :47 1:113 1:434	3↑ ⒻNew Castle 38k	6 1 1hd 11½ 16 16	Grant H	116	b	10.90	90-21	Airmans Guide1166Tritoma1201¾Mountain Glory1121	Easily	15
8Jly61- 7Mth	fst	1 1/16	:23 :454 1:102 1:431	3↑ ⒻMolly Pitcher H 30k	9 1 11½ 2hd 3½ 105¾	Blum W	124	b	*2.20	83-12	ShirleyJones1212¼SecretHonor114noChalvedele112nk	Tired	16
21Jun61- 7Mth	fst	6f	:213 :44 1:094	3↑ ⒻRegret H 24k	11 2 5¾ 1hd 11½ 11¼	Blum W	121	b	*2.30	93-12	Airmans Guide1211¼Craftiness1121½Staretta1221¼	Cleverly	12
20May61- 7GS	fst	6f	:22 :451 1:104	3↑ ⒻColonial H 28k	2 4 31 42 21½ 3hd	Blum W	119	b	*1.80	90-15	Staretta117hdCoupd'etat117noAirmansGuide1191½	Sharp try	9
29Mar61- 7GP	fst	7f	:221 :45 1:092 1:222	3↑ ⒻSuwannee River H 16k	8 2 41 3nk 11½ 11¾	Hartack W	120	b	*1.15	101-13	AirmansGuide1201¾ShirleyJones1193¼IndianMd119hd	In hand	8
22Mar61- 6GP	gd	6f	:224 :453 1:104	3↑ ⒻAlw 5000	2 3 32 32 12 14½	Hartack W	113	b	*1.65	90-17	AirmansGuide1134½PrimFlower1171½Coupd'etat1232	Easily	8
21May60- 7Aqu	fst	1	:224 :451 1:093 1:354	ⒻAcorn 59k	1 1 11 11½ 1½ 2nk	Blum W	121	b	6.25	97-06	IrishJay121nkAirmansGuide1219SisterAntoine121½	Bore out	13
14May60- 8Pim	gd	1 1/16	:241 :474 1:13 1:461	ⒻBlack-Eyed Susan 23k	2 1 11½ 1hd 2hd 1¾	Harmatz W	121	b	1.70	79-20	Airmans Guide121¾Chalvedele1213Warlike12112	Driving	4
6May60- 7CD	fst	1 1/16	:231 :464 1:12 1:441	ⒻKy Oaks 40k	2 1 1hd 1hd 3nk 33¼	Hartack W	116	b	*1.40	89-15	Make Sail116nkQuaze1163Airmans Guide1162½	Used in pace	8
16Apr60- 6Kee	fst	6f	:222 :453 1:101	ⒻAshland 26k	10 6 11 11½ 11 21	Hartack W	121	b	*1.90	93-10	Tingle1121AirmansGuide1211MakeSail118nk	Held on gamely	12
26Nov59- 8Pim	gd	1 1/16	:233 :472 1:122 1:463	ⒻMarguerite 39k	8 1 11½ 12 11½ 13½	Hartack W	119	b	*.30	77-29	AirmansGuide1193½[D]Improve119nkFlowerBonnet1196	Easily	8
21Nov59- 6Pim	fst	1 1/16	:244 :482 1:131 1:461	Alw 3500	6 1 14 11½ 12 13	Nichols J	117	b	4.40	79-17	AirmnsGuide1173WiseShip1142½CountChuck1151¼	Mild drive	7
23Oct59- 4Kee	fst	6½f	:222 :45 1:093 1:162	ⒻAlw 4000	1 6 1hd 11½ 12 11¼	Hartack W	119	b	2.70	100-13	AirmansGuide1191¼Bolerita1165½HastyDancer1164½	Driving	6
26Aug59- 8AP	fst	6f	:22 :444 1:094	ⒻPrincess Pat 104k	3 11 75½ 88¼ 711 714	Nichols J	116	b	4.80	81-11	HeavenlyBody1161¾Pierpontella1162RashStatmnt1161½	Tired	11
2May59- 5CD	fst	5f	:222 :452 :583	ⒻDebutante 14k	4 5 2hd 2hd 13 12	Gross E	119		4.40	99-06	AirmansGuide1192GreekTop1192¼Sandy'sSisW.1192	Driving	10
18Apr59- 4Kee	sly	*4f	:492	Md Sp Wt	10 4 1½ 16 16	Gross E	115		12.20	95-06	Airmans Guide1156April Five1155Natural Bid1181	Easily	12

Amber Diver

b. g. 1954, by Ambiorix (Tourbillon)–Marapania, by Devil Diver
Own.– Mrs S.C. Clark Jr
Br.– Belair Stud (Ky)
Tr.– S. Watters Jr

Lifetime record: 103 27 23 18 $240,725

30Oct64- 6Aqu fm 3 S'Chase 5:394 4↑ Temple Gwathmey H 55k 4 2 21 1½ 110 120 Aitcheson J 157 4.35 -- Amber Diver15720Aquitania1351Bon Nouvel162½ In hand 7
20Oct64- 5Aqu sf 3 S'Chase 5:401 4↑ Grand National H 28k 6 3 26 28 220 220 Aitcheson J 156 2.75 -- BonNouvl15620AmbrDiver1566BamptonCastle140hd Bobbled 8
17Sep64- 5Aqu fm 2 S'Chase 3:402 4↑ Broad Hollow H 16k 6 3 23 24 - - Murphy J 158 *1.95 -- BonNouvl1462Tuscror149 2½Nutlus1465 Stumbled at 12th,fell 6
27Aug64- 5Sar hd 2½ S'Chase 4:364 4↑ Saratoga H 19k 4 - - - - - Murphy J 158 *.75 -- Nautilus13512Tuscarora15060Rao Raja142 Bobbled 3rd jump 4
7Aug64- 5Sar hd 2 1/16 S'Chase 3:48 4↑ Beverwyck H 16k 7 2 32 1hd 1hd 2½ Murphy J 160 *1.55 -- Nautilus131½Amber Diver16020Tuscarora154no Just failed 7
11Jun64- 5Aqu fm 2½ S'Chase 4:343 4↑ Meadow Brook H 19k 1 3 39 34 2½ 22½ Murphy J 164 1.80 -- RaoRaja1382½AmberDiver16440StrollingSquar13110 2nd best 5
25Oct63- 6Aqu hd *3 S'Chase 5:373 4↑ Temple Gwathmey H 55k 4 2 21½ 11 12 12¼ Aitcheson J 164 *1.60 -- AmberDiver1642¼TheSport158nkTuscarora16330 Brisk urging 7
15Oct63- 5Aqu hd *3 S'Chase 5:371 4↑ Grand National H 27k 3 1 11½ 1hd 31¼ 22 Murphy J 163 *.95e -- Tuscarora1602AmbrDiver163nkThSport15810 Bothered often 8
1Oct63- 5Aqu fm *2½ S'Chase 4:371 4↑ Brook H 20k 8 2 24 23 112 120 Murphy J 155 12.55e -- AmberDiver15520TheSport1583½Tuscror161nk Speed to spare 9
12Sep63- 5Aqu fm *2 S'Chase 3:421 4↑ Broad Hollow H 16k 5 4 46½ 49 414 318¼↓ Murphy J 160 3.35 -- TheSport1453½BrnabysBluff16015[DH]BadgeofHonor151 Tired 5
22Aug63- 5Sar fm 2½ S'Chase 4:38 4↑ Sar H 19k 1 4 36 42¼ 37 410¼ Murphy J 161 3.50 -- Tuscarora1518BadgeofHonr1482Shntyboat145nk Bobbled 10th 5
2Aug63- 5Sar sf 2 1/16 S'Chase 3:473 4↑ Beverwyck H 17k 1 2 26 2½ 21½ 23 Murphy J 161 3.20 -- BadgeofHonor1433AmbrDvr1612½BarnbysBluff16430 Gamely 6
5Jly63- 3Del fm *2½ S'Chase 4:361 4↑ Indian River H 10k 5 1 12 11 13 13½ Murphy J 152 2.30e -- AmbrDiver1523½BarnabysBluff16310BeckysShip1402 Handily 6
25Jun63- 3Del fm *2⅛ S'Chase 4:01 4↑ Georgetown H 10k 1 3 13 12 13 12½ Murphy J 148 4.10 -- AmberDiver1482½BarnabysBluff1641BeckysShip1414 Easily 7
17Jun63- 3Del fm *2⅛ S'Chase 4:032 4↑ Tom Roby 10k 2 5 2½ 13 12 11 Murphy J 143 *1.40 -- Amber Diver1431Red Circle1454Shantyboat13810 Driving 5
23May63- 5Aqu fm *2 S'Chase 3:47 4↑ Hitchcock 11k 4 5 21 2hd 31½ 36 Murphy J 155 2.65 -- Bimeland1314½Kampina1511½AmberDiver1552½ Bold bid,tired 5
4May63- 3War hd *2 S'Chase 4:33 4↑ Alw 3000 4 3 2nk 1hd 1nk 1½ Murphy J 158 - -- Amber Diver158½Welstead1435Bampton Castle1522½ Driving 5
20Apr63- 3Mid fm *2 S'Chase 3:50 4↑ Handicap 2000 2 2 21 1½ 12 12 Murphy J 157 - -- Amber Diver1572Royal Vision1484Half Baked1331 Driving 4
13Apr63- 3Mid fm *2 S'Chase 3:50 4↑ Langley Mem Cup 2k 4 4 32 2½ 12 1¾ Murphy J 148 - -- Amber Diver148¾Royal Vision151½Hustle15110 Driving hard 6
10Nov62- 4Mid sf *2½ S'Chase 4:292 4↑ Alw 1200 7 4 46¼ - - - Murphy J 154 - -- BamptonCastle1568BugleCallII1627HlfBkd1403 Bobbled,fell 9

Previously owned by F.A. Clark; previously trained by F.T. Bellhouse

27Oct62- 7Lrl fm 1Ⓣ 1:373 3↑ Alw 10000 6 6 54½ 98¼ 95¾ 96½ Church K 112 26.60 78-18 Parka111nkGaelicLad1181½CalltheWitness116hd Fell back 10
18Oct62- 3Bel hd *1⅞ Hurdles 3:24 3↑ Alw 4200 4 4 33¼ 31½ 57½ 59½ Cartwright R 144 *2.20 -- Kantikoy135¾Shantyboat1524Ramshorn Creek137¾ Tired 7
11Oct62- 5Bel sf *2½ Hurdles 4:392 4↑ Rouge Dragon H 11k 9 5 611 610 1020 1030 Cartwright R 160 4.95 -- BabyPrince1402½EstecoII1404½Palladio148hd Far off pace 10
1Oct62- 6Bel fm 7fⓉ :23 :461 1:10 1:221 3↑ Alw 7500 5 2 2hd 1hd 2hd 54½ Nelson E 114 21.80 95-00 ShieldBearer1241¼TheAxeII1141CalltheWitness1141½ Tired 9
12Jun62- 5Bel sf *2½ S'Chase 4:47 4↑ Meadow Brook H 19k 6 4 48½ 43 210 214 Cartwright R 152 *2.05 -- Blackmail15014Amber Diver152½Brannagh1394½ No excuse 6
1Jun62- 7Bel hd 7fⓉ 1:222 3↑ Alw 10000 6 8 55½ 54½ 52¼ 53 Adams L 117 6.35 96-01 ShieldBearr1191Narokan1171¼Chich114nk Even performance 10
26May62- 4Pur fm *1Ⓣ 1:443 3↑ Alw 500 4 2 11 1½ 11½ 11½ Foot A 158 *.95 -- AmberDiver1581½PierCapponi145nkNavalTreaty1401½ Handily 9
26Apr62- 8Lrl fst 7f :231 :463 1:113 1:24 4↑ Alw 4000 2 4 42½ 33 22 22½ Church K 119 *2.10 99-09 Klinkhouse1122½Amber Diver1193Maniquest112½ Game try 7
13Apr62- 8Lrl my 7f :224 :462 1:124 1:26 4↑ Alw 4000 4 5 61¾ 51¾ 3nk 1hd Church K 113 16.10 92-17 AmberDiver113hdPolynesinBully1151½RosTrlls1132½ Driving 8
27Oct61- 6Aqu hd *2½ S'Chase 4:354 4↑ Temple Gwathmey H 55k 3 3 3½ - - - Foot A 149 3.95 -- Peal16114NavalTreaty1392Chufquen1413 Bobbled,lost rider 8
19Oct61- 3Aqu hd *2 S'Chase 3:482 4↑ Alw 4200 1 1 1½ 1½ 1hd 13½ Foot A 148 *1.80 -- AmberDiver1483½Negocio1511½BasilBe1418 Under mild drive 7
10Oct61- 5Aqu fm *2½ Hurdles 4:343 4↑ Rouge Dragon H 11k 6 4 2½ 11½ 11 1¾ Foot A 156 4.60 -- Amber Diver156¾Blackmail1354Pocosaba1496 Hard ridden 7
4Oct61- 4Lig fm *2 S'Chase 4:10 4↑ Alw 3000 8 4 1hd 25 36 311 Jackson E 145 - -- Seroul1396Sir Patsy1454½Amber Diver14515 Well up,tired 8
7Sep61- 3Bel hd *1⅞ Hurdles 3:20 3↑ Handicap 5000 2 3 22 45 413 532 Cartwright R 155 2.10 -- Swing Fever1484Seroul14520Gallant Tonto1146 Bobbled 6th 5
24Aug61- 5Sar sf 2 1/16 Hurdles 3:444 4↑ Lovely Night H 11k 4 2 22 21½ 11½ 15 Cartwright R 150 2.10 -- Amber Diver1505Gallant Tonto1452½Seroul1518 Drew out 6
11Aug61- 5Sar hd *2 Hurdles 3:351 4↑ Sar Natl Hurdle 11k 3 2 25 1hd 12 12½ Cartwright R 154 *2.05 -- AmberDiver1542½Seroul16215Blackml15020 Under mild drive 5
5Aug61- 3Sar fm *1⅞ Hurdles 3:212 3↑ Alw 4200 4 3 22 22½ 34½ 49 Schulhofer F 140 *1.25 -- GallantTonto140nkGreekBrother1505¾AfterSupper1373 Tired 6
27May61- 3Pur sf *2 Hurdles 4:24 4↑ Handicap 1500 1 3 3¾ 21 24 26 Foot A 155 *1.05 -- December1396Amber Diver15515Gridiron15015 Made good try 5
2May61- 3Lrl fm *1¾ Hurdles 3:112 4↑ Handicap 4000 6 2 44½ 24 51½ 43½ Cartwright R 154 2.30 -- Palladio153nkMoon Rock140nkMe Broke1363 No excuse 8
21Apr61- 3Lrl fm *1⅝ Hurdles 3:002 3↑ Alw 3500 8 3 22 1hd 2hd 2½ Cartwright R 152 *1.00 -- Praesepe140½Amber Diver1524Me Broke14010 Wide,bumped 11
1Apr61- 5Cam fm *2 S'Chase 3:244 4↑ Springdale Cup 1.2k 2 2 2¾ 11½ 2nk 1no Cartwright R 142 - -- AmbrDvr142noRomo15415Antonno1482 Lost lead,came again 4
10Nov60- 8Lrl sly 6f :223 :464 1:113 3↑ Alw 3500 2 5 65 63¼ 63¾ 56 Korte K 116 b 6.90 91-14 SevnCornrs1131¾Bonus1191¼ColdCut117hd No serious threat 6
2Nov60- 8Lrl gd 6f :224 :47 1:114 4↑ Alw 4000 4 4 34 2hd 1hd 1no Korte K 110 b *2.20 96-11 Amber Diver110noOld Timer110noEastern Hobo1162 All out 6
11Oct60- 6Bel hd 7fⓉ :233 :473 1:114 1:242 3↑ Alw 5000 1 7 42½ 65 54½ 66½ Arcaro E 114 b 5.90 83-11 [DH]Pilot119[DH]CalltheWitness1141CivicGuard1184½ Tired 14
3Oct60- 8Bel fm 7fⓉ :234 :463 1:103 1:232 3↑ Handicap 6000 1 5 55½ 58 1210 1212 Arcaro E 114 b 8.45 83-05 ShieldBearer117½Eurasia1161½Alhambra1172½ Fell far back 12
18Aug60- 7Sar fst 1 :231 :463 1:11 1:372 3↑ Alw 6000 5 3 32 31½ 41 43 Arcaro E 113 b 3.65 87-16 Best Brother1161¾Careless John101¾Lone Wolf113½ Tired 8
1Aug60- 8Sar fst 1 :23 :46 1:101 1:354 3↑ Alw 6000 10 1 11½ 13 21½ 34½ Moreno H 113 b 3.50 93-12 Warhead1164½Derrick116noAmberDivr113½ Used setting pace 10
25Jun60- 5Bel fm 7fⓉ :233 :463 1:111 1:234 3↑ Handicap 6000 1 10 52¼ 32 41½ 43¼ Moreno H 119 4.95 92-05 MysticII124nkVendetta119noEurs1163 Well placed,no rally 10
18Jun60- 5Bel fst 6f :221 :45 1:104 3↑ Alw 5000 6 6 46 46 33 3hd Woodhouse H 114 12.40 93-09 Bumpy Road114hdOutgiving117noAmber Diver114¾ Sharp try 8
6Jun60- 6Bel fm 7fⓉ :232 :463 1:101 1:222 3↑ Handicap 6000 5 3 42½ 54 55 43 Arcaro E 119 3.70 99-00 Shield Bearer119¾Dunce124nkGeneral Arthur1162 Even race 8
26May60- 7Aqu fst 1⅛ :49 1:133 1:391 1:513 4↑ Alw 7500 2 2 2½ 1hd 41 46 Boulmetis S 113 2.95 80-09 Derrick1141½Nasomo1193½Prnc'sGm1131 Swerved in at break 6
7May60- 8Pim fm 1⅛Ⓣ :474 1:114 1:364 1:501 3↑ Riggs H 17k 8 3 3½ 31½ 2½ 3nk Korte K 116 7.60 100-03 Troubadour II108hdCrasher109hdAmber Diver116¾ Held well 12
26Apr60- 8Lrl fst 1 :23 :47 1:114 1:372 4↑ Alw 4000 5 4 43½ 32 31 1no Korte K 113 *1.70 109-02 AmbrDvr113no[DH]CyprianCat116[DH]LordGregor115hd Driving 8
19Nov59- 7Pim fst 1 1/16 :242 :48 1:121 1:451 3↑ Alw 4000 6 1 13 15 16 13½ Korte K 113 *1.00 84-20 AmberDiver1133½WiseGuy113hdPrincipado1112 Scored easily 7
2Nov59- 7Lrl fst 6f :23 :464 1:122 3↑ Alw 4000 7 3 31½ 21 2½ 21 Nichols J 116 *1.40 -- Eastern Hobo1161Amber Diver1163Liberty Sun1111¼ Gamely 7
24Oct59 4Aqu sly 6f :22? :453 1:104 3↑ Handicap 5000 3 2 53½ 55½ 53½ 52¾ Boland W 123 4.40 -- Saci114hdMissile1182Commndton112¾ Bore out into stretch 7
9Oct59- 7Aqu sly 6f :222 :452 1:102 3↑ Handicap 7500 2 5 56 56½ 43¼ 31½ Burr C 109 24.60 -- TickTock124hdDiscard1151½AmberDiver109½ Best foot late 7
25Sep59- 7Aqu fst 1⅛ :481 1:124 1:38 1:504 3↑ Handicap 7500 5 3 33½ 32 44½ 68½ Boland W 113 13.20 -- Demobilize1161½Reinzi1103GreekStr1161 Well placed,tired 6
11Sep59- 7Bel hd 7fⓉ :231 :461 1:11 1:23 3↑ Handicap 7500 11 6 85¾ 75½ 41 2nk Arcaro E 121 5.20 99-01 ShieldBearer122nkAmberDiver121hdVegeo112½ Sharp effort 12
19Aug59- 5Sar fst 1 :24 :471 1:114 1:371 3↑ Handicap 6000 5 3 31½ 21 21½ 23½ Arcaro E 122 2.30 87-16 ShieldBearer1133½AmberDiver122¾Nivrag117hd Held gamely 5
8Aug59- 6Sar fst 1⅛ :481 1:13 1:393 1:53 4↑ Whitney H 58k 5 2 2½ 2½ 3½ 54¾ Nelson E 110 16.05 79-23 Plon114hdAmrgo1122½VllgIdot112hd Forced wide turn,tired 10
3Aug59- 7Sar fst 1 :24 :482 1:131 1:383 3↑ Alw 6000 1 1 1hd 13 12½ 1¾ Arcaro E 114 4.20 84-21 AmberDiver114¾Ambehaving1133½Plion1221 Under hard drive 6
4Jly59- 7Mth fm 1Ⓣ :231 :474 1:114 1:374 3↑ Longfellow H 24k 2 4 32 33 25 36¼ Cook WM 118 33.90 91-03 Li'l Fella1216Fairfield113nkAmber Diver118no No excuse 11
24Jun59- 7Bel fm 1⅜Ⓣ :483 1:123 1:37 2:143 3↑ Bowling Green H 29k 2 2 1hd 54¾ 88¼ 1013 Sorrentino M 117 7.10 91-00 BllHop116nkKngGrl1093½PopCorn1204 Lost whip after break 11
13Jun59- 6Bel sf 7fⓉ :234 :47 1:123 1:254 3↑ Handicap 10000 3 3 44 44¼ 46 34½ Arcaro E 118 *1.80 80-15 CombustionII1191BaldEagle1153½AmberDiver1182 Bore out 6
3Jun59- 6Bel fst 7f :224 :454 1:102 1:23 3↑ Alw 6000 4 2 21 2hd 1hd 2nk Arcaro E 117 *1.55 92-09 CombustionII117nkAmbrDivr1171LittleHermt1175½ Brushed 6
26May59- 7Bel fm 7fⓉ :23 :462 1:102 1:224 3↑ Alw 6000 6 3 2½ 21½ 3½ 42 Nelson E 117 7.95 98-00 Pantene114hdTenacious124noAmbergris1172 Speed,tired 12
9May59- 8Pim fm 1⅜Ⓣ :482 1:143 1:39 2:152 3↑ Dixie H 29k 9 6 53 915 913 918 Nelson E 118 13.00 82-00 One-EyedKing12010Olgrchy1162½MystcII110¾ Fell back early 9
27Apr59- 7Jam fst 6f :224 :453 1:101 4↑ Alw 10000 3 6 68¼ 67 59 56¾ Nelson E 117 32.75 89-15 TickTock120noWarhead124hdItob113¾ Never a strong factor 7
1Nov58- 7Lrl fm *1⅛Ⓣ 1:474 3↑ Turf Cup 24k 2 1 2hd 3nk 4nk 64½ Guerin E 114 w 6.40 92-09 TudorEra1222¼Mahan118hdPntn1141½ Speed to stretch,tired 12
4Oct58- 6Bel fm 7fⓉ :231 :47 1:113 1:242 3↑ Handicap 6000 5 2 2½ 2hd 2½ 11 Valenzuela A 121 w 5.65 93-07 Amber Diver1211St. Amour121¾Pantene1171½ Driving clear 10
20Sep58- 6Bel sf 1⅜Ⓣ :50 1:152 1:401 2:182 3↑ Handicap 10000 7 5 55 2½ 32 43¼ Valenzuela A 121 w 4.70 86-11 LangtonBreeze1172½Saim1111Rfty122no Made bold bid,tired 10
8Sep58- 6Bel sf 1⅜Ⓣ :48 1:141 1:40 2:172 3↑ Handicap 10000 1 6 64 2hd 1½ 1nk Valenzuela A 119 w 4.35 94-06 Amber Diver119nkPop Corn1181Jabneh116¾ Fully extended 10
30Aug58- 7Atl sf 1⅛Ⓣ :483 1:131 1:39 1:522 3↑ Olympic H 28k 3 3 21½ 21 21½ 23 Valenzuela A 114 w 8.10 78-19 Tudor Era1173Amber Diver1146One-Eyed King114¾ Good try 8
16Aug58- 4Sar fst 1 :24 :473 1:13 1:394 3↑ Handicap 5000 3 3 43½ 21 4¾ 32¾ Arcaro E 118 w *1.00 75-22 Tenacious1141¾Ambergris1171Amber Diver1182 Bid,tired 6
9Aug58- 7Sar gd 1⅛ :483 1:133 1:392 1:524 3↑ Handicap 6000 4 2 21 2½ 1½ 11¾ Boland W 114 w 3.15 85-20 Amber Diver1141¾Go Lightly1225Tenacious115¾ Going away 6

16Jly58- 5Jam	fst 1 1/16	:25 :49 1:124 1:442	4↑ Alw 6000	4 2 22 23 23 21½	Arcaro E	113 w	5.20	86-17	Cohoes1101½Amber Diver113½Ambergris1082½	Closing fast	6
4Jly58- 7Bel	fm 7f(T)	:23 :464 1:112 1:24	3↑ Alw 5000	10 3 43 41 2½ 14	Arcaro E	115 w	5.15	--	Amber Diver1154Saci1182½Gray Phantom1181½	Ridden out	10
14Jun58- 6Bel	fst 6f	:224 :462 1:104	4↑ Alw 6000	6 6 54 44½ 47 46¾	Arcaro E	116 w	3.15	87-13	Commendation1162¼GayWarrior1161Craigwood1203½	No rally	7
31May58- 6Bel	fm 7f(T)	:23 :46 1:111 1:231	4↑ Alw 5500	8 3 36 33 3nk 34	Arcaro E	114 w	*1.90	--	CombustionII1171Cavort1173AmbrDivr1141½	Stumbled late	8
28Apr58- 7Jam	sly 6f	:232 :462 1:103	3↑ Alw 7500	4 5 2½ 2½ 21½ 22¼	Woodhouse H	111 w	9.95	92-12	Hastego1222¼Amber Diver1112¾Pylades109nk	Good effort	6
21Nov57- 7Jam	fst 1 1/16	:243 :482 1:13 1:443	Alw 7500	3 2 2½ 3nk 21½ 36½	Atkinson T	111 w	*2.85	80-20	RoscoeManey1125MondayMrning1061½AmbrDivr111nk	Tired	7
9Nov57- 8Jam	sly 1 1/16	:241 :473 1:12 1:441	Alw 5500	7 5 54 31 21½ 34¾	Atkinson T	113 w	*1.20	84-17	FourFathoms1224½TheHorseFar116nkAmbrDvr1133½	Poor start	7
29Oct57- 7Jam	fst 6f	:223 :454 1:112	Alw 6000	2 4 47½ 47 46½ 2nk	Arcaro E	117 w	4.60	90-21	Missile117nkAmber Diver1172Red Cadet1173	Sharp try	9
15Oct57- 7Bel	fst 1	:232 :462 1:114 1:37	3↑ Alw 5000	1 2 23 21 1½ 23	Atkinson T	115wb	*1.60	86-17	JazzAge1153AmberDiver1155CannonFir1122½	Late lead,tired	6
7Oct57- 5Bel	sly 7f	:23 :46 1:111 1:241	Alw 4500	4 3 2½ 1½ 12 12	Arcaro E	117 w	*1.20	89-14	AmbrDivr1172MondayMorning1081½Salor'sKnot1142	Driving	7
28Sep57- 4Bel	fst 1	:24 :471 1:122 1:372	3↑ Alw 5000	5 4 3½ 41½ 31 3nk	Woodhouse H	118 w	*1.60	87-13	JazzAge115noSausg106nkAmbrDvr1181½	Drifted wide on turn	7
31Aug57- 6Sar	fst 1	:234 :474 1:13 1:384	Alw 5000	2 2 1hd 11½ 11½ 2no	Woodhouse H	120 w	*1.95	83-17	PrinceWilly113noAmberDiver1204CannonFire113½	Nosed out	6
24Aug57- 8Sar	fst 1	:233 :471 1:122 1:383	3↑ Alw 4500	4 3 32 22 2hd 24	Woodhouse H	112wb	*2.55	80-17	Patlarkit1224Amber Diver1123Sid's Gambol1121½	No excuse	8
12Aug57- 5Sar	fst 1	:232 :47 1:122 1:383	Alw 4200	1 2 2hd 1hd 11 11½	Woodhouse H	114 w	2.35	84-20	AmberDiver1141½PrinceWilly1092Trac1142½	Drew clear late	7
27Jly57- 6Bel	fst 1 1/16	:231 :46 1:104 1:43	3↑ Alw 5000	6 4 42½ 54 23 3½	Atkinson T	108wb	7.30	93-11	Jesper110nkPromethean115nkAmber Diver1086	Late foot	7
17Jly57- 3Bel	fst 6f	:23 :471 1:13	Md Sp Wt	8 9 85 41 2hd 11	Woodhouse H	120 w	4.90	84-12	Amber Divr1201Avenge1151Winged Mercury1206	Going away	14
2Jly57- 2Bel	fst 6f	:224 :47 1:123	3↑ Md Sp Wt	10 6 56½ 55½ 43 45¼	Broussard R	118 w	*2.60	81-12	BetterBeGay1184½Avenge118¾IndinTruc124hd	Made bid,tired	11
12Jun57- 5Bel	fst 7f	:23 :464 1:123 1:254	3↑ Md Sp Wt	1 4 31½ 33½ 54½ 44¼	Woodhouse H	116 w	*.95	77-12	Charlies Alibi116hdHung Up111hdApostle1164	Dull effort	9
	Previously trained by G.H. Bostwick										
16Oct56- 2Bel	fst 6f	:222 :461 1:112	©Md Sp Wt	12 9 54 45 47 35½	Woodhouse H	118 w	4.75	86-11	Slaipner1184Teno'Clock1181½AmberDiver118½	Closing well	14
4Oct56- 6Bel	sly 6f-WC	:22 :453 1:101	©Md Sp Wt	9 5 64¾ 32½ 32	Woodhouse H	118 w	5.55	86-12	Double X.1182Tenacious118noAmber Diver1181½	Good effort	23
25Aug56- 5Sar	fst 6f	:23 :464 1:123	Sanford 17k	8 10 119¾ 1111 1011 812	Westrope J	111 w	35.50	73-18	Thin Ice116nkClem1165Bora116hd	Far off pace	12
20Aug56- 4Sar	fst 5½f	:232 :47 :592 1:06	©Md Sp Wt	3 4 12 11½ 2hd 34	Arcaro E	118wb	3.20	83-17	Lucky Dip1182Miquelet1182Amber Diver1183	Set pace,tired	14
6Aug56- 2Sar	fst 5½f	:232 :474 :591 1:06	©Md Sp Wt	12 7 41½ 33 24 411	Arcaro E	118wb	*2.65	76-18	Discernment1186AlmondHill118½LuckyDip1184½	Speed,tired	13
16Jun56- 3Bel	fst 5f-WC	:222 :452 :574	Md Sp Wt	11 5 41½ 2½ 2hd	Arcaro E	118 w	*.70	90-10	Gavel113hdAmbrDvr1183Plytown1181½	Wearing down winner	15
7Jun56- 6Bel	fst 5f-WC	:221 :451 :571	©Md Sp Wt	19 3 21½ 2½ 21½	Woodhouse H	118 w	3.30	91-11	Dodger1181½AmberDiver118nkIrishWhistler1186	Held gamely	
30May56- 3Bel	fst 5f-WC	:222 :453 :58	©Md Sp Wt	4 6 33 23 21¼	Woodhouse H	118 w	15.65	88-11	FourFathoms1181¼AmberDiver1182½Easy1182	Very sharp try	13
17May56- 4Bel	fst 4½-WC	:223 :453 :514	©Md Sp Wt	15 5 64½ 812 712	Arcaro E	118 w	5.35	78-10	Roommate1181½Dodger118nkThinIc1187	Fell back very early	16

Arts and Letters

ch. c. 1966, by Ribot (Tenerani)–All Beautiful, by Battlefield **Lifetime record: 23 11 6 1 $632,404**

Own.– Rokeby Stable
Br.– Paul Mellon (Va)
Tr.– Elliott Burch

16May70- 8Hol	fst 1 1/16	:232 :462 1:101 1:401	3↑ Californian 112k	2 7 78½ 76½ 69½ 610	Baeza B	124	*.60	84-12	Baffle1135Figonero1241¼Nodouble130hd	Steadied	8
25Apr70- 7Aqu	fst 1⅛	:46 1:10 1:352 1:482	3↑ Grey Lag H 84k	2 6 711 56½ 35 1½	Baeza B	128	*1.10	94-18	ArtsandLetters128½NeverBow1192GaelicDancer117nk	Driving	9
28Mar70- 7Aqu	fst 1	:223 :444 1:084 1:341	4↑ Westchester 57k	2 5 514 68½ 47 47¼	Baeza B	130	*.30	89-19	Dewan119¾Gaelic Dancer1146Gleaming Light117½	No excuses	7
25Oct69- 7Aqu	fst 2	:511 2:293 2:544 3:222	3↑ J C Gold Cup 106k	1 3 2hd 18 110 114	Baeza B	119	*.30	84-14	Arts and Letters11914Nodouble1249Harem Lady121	Easily	4
27Sep69- 7Bel	fst 1¼	:481 1:121 1:363 2:01	3↑ Woodward 106k	1 4 32 21 1½ 12	Baeza B	120	*.30	95-17	ArtsandLetters1202Nodouble1261½Verbatim1268	Ridden out	4
16Aug69- 6Sar	fst 1¼	:48 1:113 1:364 2:013	Travers 106k	5 4 43½ 31 12 16½	Baeza B	126	*.20	100-06	Arts and Letters1266½Dike120¾Distray114nk	Easy score	5
8Aug69- 7Sar	fst 1	:241 :47 1:113 1:36	Jim Dandy 27k	1 3 33 11 14 110	Baeza B	126	*.10	94-13	ArtsandLetters12610GleamingLight1191½Mr.Mag1145	Easily	4
7Jun69- 8Bel	fst 1½	:51 1:161 2:042 2:284	Belmont 147k	1 2 23 11½ 13 15½	Baeza B	126	1.70	89-12	ArtsandLetters1265½MajesticPrince1262Dike1263½	Easily	6
30May69- 7Aqu	fst 1	:224 :453 1:10 1:34	3↑ Metropolitan H 116k	8 10 88 33½ 1hd 12½	Cruguet J	111	*1.50	97-22	ArtsandLetters1112½Nodouble1293½Promise1191	Mild drive	11
17May69- 8Pim	fst 1 3/16	:464 1:112 1:37 1:553	Preakness 182k	6 6 68¾ 53½ 21 2hd	Baeza B	126	5.00	95-17	MajesticPrinc126hdArtsndLttrs1264JyRy1264	Brushed start	8
3May69- 8CD	fst 1¼	:48 1:122 1:373 2:014	Ky Derby 155k	3 2 42½ 1½ 2½ 2nk	Baeza B	126	4.40	91-11	MajesticPrince126nkArtsandLetters126½Dike12610	Gamely	8
24Apr69- 6Kee	fst 1⅛	:48 1:112 1:353 1:474	Blue Grass 31k	6 2 13 17 18 115	Shoemaker W	126	*.30	98-17	ArtsandLetters12615TrafficMark1262Mr.Concdnc1233	Easily	6
29Mar69- 9GP	fst 1⅛	:482 1:12 1:361 1:482	Florida Derby 121k	5 4 43 4¾ 23 25	Shoemaker W	122	3.10	87-13	Top Knight1225Arts and Letters1222½Al Hattab1221	Gamely	5
19Mar69- 9GP	fst 1 1/16	:243 :484 1:122 1:423	Fountain of Youth 22k	5 5 56 34½ 33½ 22	Shoemaker W	119	*.50	93-17	AlHattab1222ArtsandLetters119¾AdMajora1224	Slow early	5
4Mar69- 8Hia	fst 1⅛	:462 1:103 1:352 1:474	Flamingo 146k	2 2 22 1hd 1hd 22	Cruguet J	122	2.10	94-15	TopKnight1222ArtsandLetters122½BeauBrummel122¾	Gamely	12
19Feb69- 8Hia	fst 1⅛	:47 1:114 1:363 1:493	Everglades 32k	11 8 77¼ 33 13 13	Cruguet J	112	9.00	87-21	Arts and Letters1123Top Knight1222Al Hattab119½	Driving	12
25Jan69- 6Hia	fst 7f	:224 :453 1:093 1:223	©Alw 5500	4 6 54½ 45 36 36	Cruguet J	119	3.50	89-16	Ack Ack1173Distinctive1193Arts and Letters1193	Evenly	9
2Nov68- 8Lrl	fst 1 1/16	:233 :464 1:12 1:44	Pim Lrl Futurity 182k	7 4 34 22 32 41¼	Velasquez J	122	2.80	96-11	King Emperor122hdDike1221Mr. Leader122nk	Lacked rally	8
15Oct68- 6Bel	fst 1	:232 :47 1:114 1:362	Alw 7500	9 2 2½ 12 13 12½	Velasquez J	122	*1.90	92-18	Arts and Letters1222½Hydrologist1222½King of the Castle122¾	Easily	9
25Sep68- 5Bel	fst 7f	:224 :461 1:113 1:241	Md Sp Wt	9 8 63 33 1hd 13½	Velasquez J	122	*3.00	86-19	ArtsandLetters1223½Hydrologist122½WldctHlls1223	In hand	12
18Sep68- 1Bel	fst 6f	:221 :453 1:111	Md Sp Wt	2 3 33 21½ 2½ 23	Velasquez J	122	3.70	86-13	KingoftheSea1223ArtsandLettrs122½ElephntWlk122¾	Gamely	14
11Sep68- 4Aqu	sly 6f	:22 :452 1:122	©Md Sp Wt	6 9 57½ 57 45½ 44¾	Turcotte R	122	*2.00	76-21	Royal Tom122¾Full of Gin1192½Izaak1221½	Mild late rally	12
9Aug68- 5Sar	fst 5½f	:222 :461 :583 1:044	©Md Sp Wt	1 4 3½ 21 33½ 47	Pincay L Jr	122	5.10	86-09	DixieGus122hdCharlestonHarbor1222BeauBrummel1225	Tired	12

Assagai

dkbbr. c. 1963, by Warfare (Determine)–Primary II, by Petition **Lifetime record: 31 11 7 2 $357,074**

Own.– Cragwood Stable
Br.– Robin F. Scully (Ky)
Tr.– M. Miller

21Oct67- 7Aqu	fm 1⅝(T)	2:424	3↑ Man o' War 116k	8 11 913 75¼ 65½ 43	Shoemaker W	126 b	*1.10e	77-20	RuffledFeathrs121hdFortMarcy121noHndsomBoy1263	Rallied	13
2Oct67- 7Aqu	fm 1⅜(T)	1:544	3↑ Long Island H (Div 2) 23k	3 2 21½ 3½ 3nk 1¾	Baeza B	126	*.80	96-04	Assagai126¾Fast Count1091½Kentucky Kin113½	Driving	9
20Sep67- 8Atl	fm 1 3/16(T)	1:54	3↑ U Nations H 100k	4 6 55½ 66½ 54 2nk	Baeza B	122 b	*2.40	102-05	Flit-To110nkAssagai122no(D)MundenPont115hd	Strong finish	8
25Aug67- 7Sar	fm 1⅝(T)	2:392	3↑ Seneca H 29k	1 1 1½ 12 1hd 2nk	Baeza B	126 b	*1.40	96-07	Paoluccio109nkAssagai126¾Isokh1111½	Gamely under impost	11
9Aug67- 7Sar	fm 1 1/16(T)	1:402	3↑ B Baruch H (Div 2) 23k	7 4 33 32 3nk 2¾	Rotz JL	126 b	2.10	97-02	Fort Marcy117¾Assagai1263Paoluccio1121	Finished gamely	7
24Jly67- 8Hol	fm 1½(T)	:494 1:142 2:031 2:274	3↑ Sunset H 108k	1 5 56½ 53½ 56 56¼	Adams L	126	4.00	--	Hill Clown109¾Pretense1293Niarkos121½	Wide on turns	6
2Jly67♦ Saint-Cloud(Fr)	fm*1 9/16(T)LH	2:423	3↑ Grand Prix de Saint-Cloud Stk180000	44½	Baeza B	134	9.00		Taneb134noNelcius1342½Taj Dewan1192	Led,soon well clear,headed 2f out,one-paced late	8
17Jun67- 7Aqu	hd 1⅝(T)	2:412	3↑ Bowling Green H 55k	4 3 23 23 24 21½	Adams L	127	2.10	85-13	Poker1121½Assagai1273Buckpasser135½	Best of others	5
30May67- 8AP	sf 1⅛(T)	:49 1:14 1:39 1:512	3↑ Round Table H 43k	8 6 67 54½ 42¼ 1½	Adams L	124	*.50	84-23	Assagai124½Auteuil1111Voluntario III113hd	Up in time	8
20May67- 8Aqu	fm 1 1/16(T)	1:421	3↑ Alw 15000	6 6 68¼ 66 4¾ 1nk	Adams L	123	2.40	95-05	Assagai123nkIrish Rebellion1002Flit-To120¾	In close,up	10
26Nov66- 7Aqu	fst 1⅝	:474 1:382 2:034 2:423	3↑ Gallant Fox H 58k	11 4 4¾ 814 815 817	Adams L	119	5.40	75-20	Munden Point1132¾Yonder1124Moontrip114½	Tired	11
11Nov66- 7Lrl	fm 1½(T)	:494 1:142 2:284	3↑ D C Int'l 150k	6 2 23 2½ 21½ 33½	Adams L	120	*1.70	71-18	Behistoun1202¼Aniline1271¼Assagai1201	Game try,weakened	10
22Oct66- 7Aqu	fm 1⅝(T)	2:443	3↑ Man o' War 112k	7 2 2½ 21 2hd 1¾	Adams L	121	*1.90	71-29	Assagai121¾Gallup Poll1215Knightly Manner126nk	All out	9
17Sep66- 8Atl	fm 1 3/16(T)	1:583	3↑ U Nations H 100k	9 6 72¾ 74¼ 43 1hd	Adams L	118	*2.30	79-24	Assagai118hdGingerFizz1141¼Toulore118¾	Up final strides	12
3Sep66- 8Atl	fm 1⅛(T)	1:482	3↑ Kelly-Olympic H 35k	10 4 31 41¾ 2hd 2no	Adams L	120	*1.20	93-13	Ginger Fizz115noAssagai1201¼Imasmartee123¾	In close	12
10Aug66- 7Sar	fm 1 1/16(T)	1:40	3↑ Bernard Baruch H 30k	6 5 511 53½ 3½ 13	Adams L	115	*3.10	105-00	Assagai1153GingerFizz114¾NorthernDeamon113no	Mild drive	10
30Jly66- 7Aqu	fm 1⅛(T)	1:49	3↑ Tidal H 59k	8 4 43 52¾ 33 1½	Adams L	109	4.40	90-15	Assagai109½Canal1132½Moontrip1151½	Up in final yards	11
29Jun66- 8Mth	fm 1(T)	1:381	Long Branch 23k	9 9 85½ 52½ 31½ 14	Brumfield D	116	7.70	94-13	Assagai1164Social Song120½Tequillo1181½	Mild drive	13

14Jun66- 8Mth fst 1 1/16⊗ :233 :472 1:12 1:442 Alw 6000 4 2 33 44 34 43½ Brumfield D 119 4.10 79-18 Deck Hand119½Arabian Spy1173Tequillo116no Lacked rally 7
2Jun66- 6Aqu fm 1 1/16(T) 1:413 3↑ Alw 6500 8 2 25 22 12 13½ Blum W 113 12.30 98-02 Assagai1133½SeaCastle1145Hnbj1201½ Drew clear with ease 10
25May66- 8Aqu fst 1⅛ :461 1:103 1:362 1:493 3↑ Alw 6500 5 3 46½ 56½ 46 59 Blum W 113 11.10 79-13 Highest Honors113½Buffle1123½Bushfighter1132½ No mishap 7
7May66- 6Aqu fst 6f :22 :453 1:112 3↑ Alw 5500 6 6 87¼ 65½ 52¾ 1nk Blum W 113 6.30e 86-17 Assagai113nkPitchMan106hdDey Sovereign113nk Up in time 11
13Apr66- 5Kee sly 6f :222 :463 1:122 ©Md Sp Wt 4 3 3½ 1½ 13 12 Adams L 122 3.80 81-18 Assagai1222Puppeteer1177Dominar1222 Under pressure 10
27Nov65- 4Aqu sly 1 :224 :463 1:121 1:39 Md Sp Wt 10 3 3nk 1½ 11½ 2¾ Venezia M 122 4.20e 72-25 HighestHonors122¾Assagai1223½ProspectStret117½ 2nd best 11
20Nov65- 1Aqu fst 1 :233 :464 1:122 1:401 ©Md Sp Wt 5 3 41½ 32 23 44¾ Blum W 122 b 4.00 62-20 Tequillo1171½Squadron E.1222½Paddyland122¾ Speed,tired 10
13Nov65- 3Aqu fst 1 :233 :472 1:13 1:391 ©Md Sp Wt 8 5 62¼ 63 44 31¾ Venezia M 122 b 5.90 70-22 Earldom122¾Mask of Play1221Assagai1221 Finished fast 9
6Nov65- 4Aqu fst 1 :233 :463 1:113 1:374 Md Sp Wt 5 8 76½ 62¾ 51¾ 42¾ Sellers J 122 b 10.20 76-17 Poker122noEarldom1222AmeriPlot122¾ Only mild late rally 12
2Nov65- 4Aqu fst 6f :231 :464 1:12 ©Md Sp Wt 3 8 78½ 711 511 28 Blum W 122 b 7.20 75-18 Nashwood1228Assagai1221Exhibitionist122½ Closed well 14
26Oct65- 5Aqu fst 6f :223 :454 1:13 Md Sp Wt 7 9 109¾ 1016 1015 1115 Blum W 122 b 3.00 63-18 Draeh's Folly122nkNashwood1226Pilot Major122½ Bore out 14
19Oct65- 1Aqu fst 6f :223 :463 1:123 ©Md Sp Wt 8 9 86¼ 85¾ 55 43 Blum W 122 4.70 77-18 Clarinetist122nkSpaceCitation122¾Draeh'sFolly1222 Wide 10
12Jly65- 4Aqu fst 5½f :223 :46 :581 1:043 ©Md Sp Wt 5 7 78½ 69 56 55¾ Boland W 122 48.90 84-10 Amberoid1221Draeh's Folly1221Bobillard1223 No mishap 12

Bald Eagle

b. c. 1955, by Nasrullah (Nearco)–Siama, by Tiger **Lifetime record: 29 12 5 4 $692,922**

Own.– Cain Hoy Stable
Br.– Harry F. Guggenheim (Ky)
Tr.– Woodford C. Stephens

11Nov60- 7Lrl fm 1½(T) :473 1:113 2:33 3↑ D C Int'l 100k 2 1 15 110 16 12 Ycaza M 126 *1.70 75-25 BaldEagle1262Harmonizing1261Zabeg1251¼ Under mild drive 11
29Oct60- 7Aqu sly 2 :472 2:29 2:54 3:192 3↑ J C Gold Cup 109k 4 7 717 43½ 37 313½ Ycaza M 124 2.50e 100-16 Kelso1193½DonPoggio12410BldEgl12415 Lacked needed rally 8
22Oct60- 7Bel sf 1½(T) :50 1:162 2:08 2:331 3↑ Man o' War 110k 7 3 35½ 43 23 22¼ Ycaza M 126 *1.40e 78-20 Harmonizing1262¼BaldEagle1264SwordDancer126nk In close 8
24Sep60- 7Aqu fst 1¼ :472 1:111 1:354 2:011 3↑ Woodward 112k 6 5 31½ 22 42 33 Ycaza M 126 b *.90 99-08 Sword Dancer1261½Dotted Swiss1262½Bald Eagle1261 Hung 7
5Sep60- 7Aqu fst 1 :232 :461 1:102 1:344 3↑ Aqueduct H 56k 3 4 41½ 22 31½ 1hd Ycaza M 130 *1.30 94-11 Bald Eagle130hdIntentionally125noWarhead1133 Just up 5
30Jly60- 7Aqu sly 1¼ :471 1:12 1:38 2:03 3↑ Brooklyn H 109k 2 6 56½ 43 43¼ 43¼ Ycaza M 130 *1.65 90-17 On-and-On118hdGreekStar1102Waltz1131¼ Failed to respond 7
4Jly60- 7Aqu fst 1¼ :472 1:111 1:361 2:013 3↑ Suburban H 108k 4 5 53¾ 33 44½ 46½ Hartack W 133 *.70 105-11 SwordDancer125½FirstLandng1221½Wltz1154½ Impeded early 6
30May60- 7Aqu fst 1 :224 :453 1:09 1:333 3↑ Metropolitan H 114k 8 4 62¾ 32½ 11 13½ Ycaza M 128 *1.95 108-03 Bald Eagle1283½First Landing123nkTalent Show118¾ Easily 10
19Mar60- 7GP gd 1¼ :473 1:122 1:362 2:011 3↑ Gulf Park H 112k 1 6 78 44 32½ 1¾ Ycaza M 126 *1.25 93-05 Bald Eagle126¾Amerigo1233On-and-On1212 Blocked,driving 8
20Feb60- 7Hia fst 1¼ :464 1:101 1:351 1:593 3↑ Widener H 126k 2 6 66¾ 42¼ 1½ 1¾ Ycaza M 123 *1.35 107-07 Bald Eagle123¾On-and-On1191½Talent Show118½ Mild urging 8
6Feb60- 7Hia gd 1⅛ :46 1:101 1:354 1:484 3↑ McLennan H 64k 4 7 74¾ 65¼ 32 2nk Ycaza M 124 *1.55 91-12 On-and-On120nkBldEgl1243TudorEr1201¼ Hung final strides 9
21Nov59- 7Aqu fst 1⅝ :484 1:383 2:033 2:41 3↑ Gallant Fox H 85k 4 6 64¼ 31½ 1hd 11¾ Ycaza M 126 *1.15 -- BaldEagl1261¾Whodunt1123½Whtly114no In close,mild drive 10
11Nov59- 7Lrl fm 1½(T) :47 1:113 2:014 2:28 3↑ D C Int'l 100k 6 2 21 15 14 12½ Ycaza M 126 3.60 -- BaldEagle1262½MidnightSun1224½TudorEra1268 Easily best 12
24Oct59- 6Aqu sf 1½(T) :51 1:182 2:102 2:404 3↑ Man o' War (Div 1) 112k 1 6 64½ 33¼ 35 42¼ Ycaza M 126 2.25 -- Dotted Line1111¼Amerigo121¾Prince Willy112nk No mishaps 10
10Oct59- 7Aqu fst 1⅝ :491 1:392 2:041 2:423 3↑ Manhattan H 58k 3 7 64½ 43½ 41¾ 21 Ycaza M 122 2.45 -- RndTable1321BaldEagle1221½Coloneast1122 Closed gamely 11
14Sep59- 7Aqu fst 1 :23 :46 1:111 1:362 3↑ Aqueduct H 59k 6 9 84 83¾ 41¼ 2¾ Ycaza M 122 5.75 -- Hillsdale132¾BaldEagle1221TickTock119nk In close,sharp 12
15Aug59- 6Sar fst 1¼ :473 1:113 1:361 2:03 3↑ Saratoga H 57k 2 3 33½ 42½ 42½ 1nk Ycaza M 120 *1.40 93-12 BaldEagle120nkGreyMonarch1111¾Amerigo1142 Taken out,up 7
1Aug59- 6Jam fst 1 3/16 :473 1:122 1:374 1:562 3↑ Brooklyn H 113k 6 6 59½ 41½ 41¼ 43¾ Ycaza M 123 4.05 90-15 Babu112¾SwordDncr124hdAmrgo1173 In close,turn & drive 10
4Jly59- 6Bel fst 1¼ :463 1:101 1:354 2:013 3↑ Suburban H 111k 5 9 67½ 53 3nk 11½ Ycaza M 119 3.95 92-13 BaldEgl1191½TIntShow1255½Plon1191 Taken wide,mild drive 10
24Jun59- 8Suf fst 1¼ :473 1:123 1:37 2:022 3↑ Mass H 84k 4 6 54 74¾ 42 31 Ycaza M 112 10.60 92-17 [D]DayCourt115nkAirPilot116¾BldEgl1121¾ Impeded in drive 8
13Jun59- 6Bel sf 7f(T) :234 :47 1:123 1:254 3↑ Handicap 10000 4 5 13 13 12 21 Ycaza M 115 3.30 84-15 CombustionII1191BaldEagle1153½AmberDiver1182 No excuse 6
17Feb59- 9Hia fm 1 1/16(T) 1:443 4↑ Alw 5000 4 6 45 46½ 47 46 Anderson P 124 *3.15 87-09 Little Hermit124hdSaferris1153Royal Float1103 No excuse 9
15Oct58- 6Bel fm 7f(T) :23 :462 1:111 1:24 Handicap 7500 5 10 66 64 73 76 Shoemaker W 124wb *2.00 90-04 Phaeton120½Washington109½Rickover109nk Sluggish start 10
Previously trained by Cecil Boyd-Rochfort
17Jun58♦ Ascot(GB) fm 1(T)RH 1:432 St. James Palace Stakes Stk24100 33 Carr W 126 3.30 Major Portion1262Guersillus1261Bald Eagle1262 5
Tracked in 4th,lacked rally
4Jun58♦ Epsom(GB) gd 1½(T)LH 2:411 Epsom Derby Stk95600 12 Carr W 126 7.00 Hard Ridden1265Paddy's Point1261½Nagami126hd
Sweating,tracked in 4th,weakened over 3f out
21May58♦ York(GB) gd *1 5/16(T)LH 2:234 Dante Stakes Stk15200 11½ Carr W 126 *1.10 Bald Eagle1261½Carbon Copy1262The Mongoose126nk 7
Rated in 5th,led over 1f out,ridden out
30Apr58♦ Newmarket(GB) gd 1(T)Str 1:392 2000 Guineas Stakes Stk65200 79 Carr WH 126 *1.75 Pall Mall126½Major Portion1263Nagami126hd 14
In touch to halfway,ridden and faded 2f out
17Apr58♦ Newmarket(GB) gd 1(T)Str 1:43 Craven Stakes Stk3400 11 Carr WH 130 3.50 Bald Eagle1301Nagami1303Pinched1304 6
Led 2f out,hard ridden to maintain edge
11Oct57♦ Ascot(GB) gd 6f(T)Str 1:181 Duke of Edinburgh Stakes Mdn8000 11 Carr W 119 *1.20 Bald Eagle1191Barleycroft129½Teynham1206 8
Rated toward rear,rallied to lead 150y out,handily;For maidens at closing,three weeks previous

Barnabys Bluff

b. g. 1958, by Cyclotron (Pensive)–Ophelia Rose, by Pavot **Lifetime record: 28 11 7 2 $124,346**

Own.– G.H. Bostwick
Br.– G.H. Bostwick (Ky)
Tr.– G.H. Bostwick

1Oct63- 5Aqu fm *2½ S'Chase 4:371 4↑ Brook H 20k 6 4 37 37 - - McDonald RS 160 sb *1.30e -- AmbrDvr15520ThSport1583½Tuscror161nk Fell 14th,destroyed 9
12Sep63- 5Aqu fm *2 S'Chase 3:421 4↑ Broad Hollow H 16k 1 1 21½ 33 21½ 23¼ Walsh T 160 sb 2.45 -- TheSport1453½BarnabysBluff16015[DH]BadgeofHnr151 Gamely 5
5Sep63- 3Aqu hd *2 Hurdles 3:35 3↑ Handicap 6000 1 4 48 412 417 423 Walsh T 162 *1.30 -- ExhbtA.1544ThSport1431Knghtsboro14718 Tired under impost 5
2Aug63- 5Sar sf 2 1/16 S'Chase 3:473 4↑ Beverwyck H 17k 5 5 59½ 34½ 34½ 35½ Walsh T 164 2.35 -- Badge of Honor1433Amber Diver1612½Barnabys Bluff16430 6
Bad landing 1st
5Jly63- 3Del fm *2½ S'Chase 4:361 4↑ Indian River H 10k 2 3 34 21 23 23½ Walsh T 163 *.90 -- AmbrDivr1523½BarnabysBluff16310BeckysShip1402 Bobbled 6
25Jun63- 3Del fm *2⅛ S'Chase 4:01 4↑ Georgetown H 10k 5 6 43½ 33 33½ 22½ Walsh T 164 *1.50 -- AmberDiver1482½BarnabysBluff1641BeckysShip1414 Gamely 7
26Oct62- 6Bel sf *2½ S'Chase 4:503 4↑ Temple Gwathmey H 55k 4 2 22 11 11 110 Walsh T 157 *1.05 -- BarnabysBluff15710BugleCallII1363½PocktRockt1366 Easily 7
16Oct62- 5Bel fm *3⅛ S'Chase 5:523 4↑ Grand National H 28k 6 3 35 21½ 11½ 11¾ Walsh T 153 *1.70 -- BarnbysBluff1531¾PocketRocket1328BeckysShp1422 Driving 9
4Oct62- 5Bel fm *2½ S'Chase 4:371 4↑ Brook H 19k 5 3 46 2½ 12 16 Walsh T 148 2.95 -- Barnabys Bluff1486Kampina1461Blackmail1575 Easily 5
20Sep62- 5Aqu fm *2 S'Chase 3:453 4↑ C L Appleton Mem H 11k 2 3 36 34 34½ 23 Walsh T 152 2.95 -- Kampina1403Barnabys Bluff1526Beckys Ship1478 Bobbled 6
18Aug62- 3Sar fm 2 1/16 Hurdles 3:474 4↑ Handicap 6000 8 6 65¼ 34 43½ 36¾ Cartwright R 154 3.05e -- GuardianAngel153¾BabyPrince1396BrnbysBlff154no Bobbled 8
11Aug62- 3Sar sf *2 1/16 S'Chase 3:55 4↑ Handicap 6000 5 5 44½ - - - Schulhofer F 151 *1.00 -- Naval Treaty1451¾Julep Time1365Bugle Call II1374 7
Bobbled,lost rider
31Jly62- 3Sar sf 2 1/16 S'Chase 3:512 4↑ OClm 7000 1 4 2½ 11 13 17 Schulhofer F 138 *1.05 -- Barnabys Bluff1387Shantyboat1431½Julep Time14510 Easily 7
25Jly62- 5Mth sf *2 Hurdles 4:094 3↑ Midsummer H 22k 1 - - - - - Thompson J 150 5.80 -- Hunter's Rock1445Miracle Moose1497The Sport14720 8
Ran out,left course
18Jly62- 3Mth fm *1¾ Hurdles 3:20 3↑ Alw 4000 9 3 37½ 1½ 1hd 2½ Thompson JW 147 *2.20 -- Gem Ruby147½BarnbysBluff1472Miracle Moose1471¼ Gamely 9
22Jun62- 4Del sf 1(T) 1:411 3↑ Md Sp Wt 3 3 23 22 2½ 1¾ Shuk N 122 *1.10 76-27 BarnabysBluff122¾PeaceJohn1121Grape1141½ Strong urging 10
7Jun62- 5Bel fm *2 Hurdles 3:43 4↑ Bushwick H 11k 5 3 2hd 21½ 56 59¼ Cartwright R 151 *1.65 -- The Sport1391¼Prince Fearless1302½Hunter's Rock1481½ 6
Saddle slipped
27Oct61- 3Aqu hd *1⅞ Hurdles 3:213 LE Stoddard Jr 11k 4 2 31½ 11 12 1nk Schulhofer F 145 *.65 -- BarnabysBluff145nkHunter'sRock1405½Shntybot1404 Driving 7

28Sep61- 5Bel	fm	*1⅞	Hurdles 3:212	Elkridge 16k	1	2	34½	1hd	11½	11¼	Schulhofer F	145	*1.00	--	BarnabysBluff1451¼Hunter'sRock14010Shntybot1366	Driving 6
17Aug61- 5Sar	hd	*1⅝	Hurdles 2:514	Promise 13k	5	6	43½	2½	1½	11½	Cartwright R	145	2.20	--	Barnabys Bluff1451½Hunter's Rock142½Nizam13818	Drew out 6
26Jly61- 5Mth	fm	*2	Hurdles 3:533	3↑ Midsummer H 22k	1	2	11½	31½	35	-	Cartwright R	136	2.50	--	LandoftheFree149nkNala15510BeModrt149nk	Lost rider last 9
14Jly61- 3Mth	sf	*1¾	Hurdles 3:231	3↑ Alw 4000	4	2	2hd	1½	13	16	Cartwright R	135	2.50	--	BarnbysBlff1356BeModerate1515½GrekBrothr1474½	Handily 7
27Jun61- 4Bel	fst	1⅛	:472 1:12 1:37 1:494	3↑ Md Sp Wt	5	2	2½	2½	21½	23½	Arcaro E	115	*1.80	83-12	Narwhal1233½Barnabys Bluff1154Del Wells1157	Speed,tired 8
15Jun61- 5Bel	fm	*1½	Hurdles 2:442	Annapolis 11k	5	2	1½	1hd	12	15	Cartwright R	145	*.45	--	BarnabysBluff1455AndNow1371¼BlackChallenger1451	Easily 8
2Jun61- 7Del	fm	1Ⓣ	1:383	Alw 4500	3	4	53¾	54	25	21½	Shuk N	110	4.20	87-11	MicheLea1141½BarnabysBluff1104RebelFire117nk	Slow start 9
23May61- 3Aqu	fm	*1½	Hurdles 2:432	Md Sp Wt	6	2	1hd	1hd	110	125	Cartwright R	145	*1.80	--	BarnabysBlff14525BlackChallengr1451¼AndNow145no	Easily 9
8May61- 3Aqu	sf	*1⅝	Hurdles 2:56	3↑ Sp Wt 3700	8	9	912	815	69	47½	Cartwright R	133	39.45	--	Ben Arthur1521Kampina1372½Mantegna1524	Some late foot 11
7Jly60- 6Aqu	fst	5½f	:223 :464 :592 1:064	ⒸMd Sp Wt	1	5	98½	917	915	914	Leonard J	118	10.65	71-16	Jet Request118noRudolph1182MainMark1181½	Raced greenly 9

Benguala

b. g. 1954, by Annapolis (Man o' War)–Bennu, by Heliopolis **Lifetime record: 26 9 1 4 $133,775**

Own.– Montpelier
Br.– Mrs Marion duPont Scott (Va)
Tr.– R.G. Woolf

3Aug61- 5Sar	fm	2 1/16	S'Chase 2:50	4↑ Beverwyck H 16k	7	4	419	69	-	-	Foot A	154	2.45	--	Tuscarora1487Bugle Call II130¾Negocio139hd	Fell at 11th 7
13Jun61- 5Bel	hd	*2½	S'Chase 4:39	4↑ Meadow Brook H 18k	1	6	69	53½	35	35½	Foot A	161	2.95	--	Muguet II163noTuscarora1445½Benguala1618	Bobbled 12th 6
1Jun61- 5Bel	hd	*2⅛	S'Chase 3:561	4↑ International H 16k	4	6	615	617	613	413	Woolf R Jr	160	2.70e	--	Nala155hdMuguet II1606Peal1427	Never a threat 6
21Oct60- 6Bel	sf	*2½	S'Chase 4:462	4↑ Temple Gwathmey H 56k	4	5	530	43	21½	13	Foot A	160	3.35	--	Benguala1603Chufquen13810Sun Dog1603	Going away 9
11Oct60- 5Bel	hd	*3⅛	S'Chase 5:541	4↑ Grand National H 27k	5	5	46	36	315	323	Foot A	156	*1.15	--	Sun Dog14515Cartagena1458Benguala15650	Well up,tired 5
29Sep60- 5Bel	fm	*2½	S'Chase 4:421	4↑ Brook H 19k	4	5	48	32½	12	16	Foot A	148	5.40	--	Benguala1486Independence1593½Cartagena1503½	Easily best 7
15Sep60- 5Aqu	fm	*2	S'Chase 3:531	4↑ Broad Hollow H 16k	5	6	56½	58½	33½	32¾	Foot A	150	8.00	--	Gridiron1362Sun Dog148¾Benguala1502	Swerved,late rally 6
19Aug60- 5Sar	hd	*2⅝	S'Chase 5:054	4↑ Saratoga H 19k	6	6	410	33½	46	46½	Mahoney J	151	11.45	--	MuguetII1605Hustle1431½Indepndnc160hd	Bobbled 1st hedge 7
4Aug60- 5Sar	fm	*2½	S'Chase 4:094	4↑ Beverwyck H 16k	2	4	58½	33	416	422	Foot A	151	*1.60	--	Muguet II1555Sun Dog14714Basil Bee1343	Bad landing 10th 7
30Jun60- 5Bel	hd	*2½	S'Chase 4:414	4↑ Meadow Brook H 19k	7	7	77½	23	1½	1no	Foot A	148	7.35	--	Benguala148noChambourg15530NarcissusII1366	Swerved late 8
16Jun60- 5Bel	sf	*2⅛	S'Chase 3:57	4↑ International H 17k	3	6	811	513	717	728	Foot A	155	6.80	--	Chambourg1478Amateur1468Fairfax152hd	No serious threat 11
6Jun60- 3Bel	fm	*2⅛	S'Chase 3:582	4↑ Alw 5000	8	8	711	54¼	31½	1¾	Foot A	140	*1.35	--	Benguala140¾Hunter's Lad1323½Fairfax1601	Briskly urged 8
13Oct59- 5Aqu	hd	*2½	S'Chase 4:473	4↑ Brook H 19k	6	3	64	45	45	43¼	Foot A	156	7.00	--	Ancestor1621½Sun Dog1371½Fairfax152nk	Even effort 7
1Oct59- 5Aqu	fm	*2	S'Chase 3:51	4↑ Broad Hollow H 16k	6	7	711	69¾	615	622	Foot A	162	4.25	--	Ancestor160hdDarubini1382Sun Dog13812	Never a contender 9
11Sep59- 6Bel	hd	*2½	S'Chase 4:41	4↑ Temple Gwathmey H 56k	9	1	1½	77¾	846	863	Foot A	158	3.10	--	MuguetII1521¾Darubini134nkIdealView1354	Much used early 9
22Oct58- 6Bel	fm	*2½	S'Chase 4:453	4↑ Temple Gwathmey H 55k	4	2	21	21½	1½	1hd	Foot A	147 w	2.30	--	Benguala147hdNeji1764½Trboots135nk	Lost lead,came again 8
30Sep58- 5Bel	sf	*2½	S'Chase 4:474	4↑ Brook H 14k	2	1	12½	11	12	13½	Foot A	143 w	10.15	--	Beguala1433½Independence154nkNeji17510	Speed in reserve 7
21Aug58- 5Sar	fm	*2½	S'Chase 5:161	4↑ Saratoga H 14k	2	3	24	26	2hd	12½	Foot A	139 w	5.55	--	Benguala1392½Carthage133hdDarubin1408	Well rated,easily 5
8Aug58- 3Sar	sf	*2	S'Chase 4:18	4↑ Alw 5000	6	4	48½	2½	24	28	Foot A	139 w	3.50	--	Rythminhim1458Benguala1391½Tremere1409	Best of others 7
31Jly58- 3Sar	fm	*2	S'Chase 4:153	4↑ Alw 4200	4	3	37	35	11½	13	Foot A	136 w	2.70	--	Benguala1363Eastcor1503½Darubini14810	Mild drive 6
20Jun58- 5Del	sf	*2	S'Chase 3:422	4↑ Spring Maiden 9.8k	2	4	24	516	520	420	Foot A	142 w	6.10	--	Arywa1582Blen More1533Prince Nam15115	Bad landing 6th 6
9Oct57- 3Bel	sf	*1½	Hurdles 2:47	Alw 5000	6	4	47½	48½	513	521	Foot A	135 w	4.60e	--	My Last Try1351Sun Dog1308Tombigbee1322	Fell back early 8
3Oct57- 3Bel	fm	*1⅞	Hurdles 3:233	3↑ Alw 5500	6	5	513	623	631	653	Foot A	131wb	6.05	--	Nizam'sPet1387BestGift1438PatrickBegorra1353	No speed 6
8Aug57- 5Sar	fm	*1⅝	Hurdles 3:084	Promise 11k	3	3	2hd	21	33	33½	Foot A	140wb	*1.20e	--	PatrickBegorra1352MyLastTry1301½Benguala1408	No excuse 10
11Jly57- 3Mth	fm	*1½	Hurdles 2:464	Md Sp Wt	2	3	21½	21	1hd	1½	Foot A	145 w	1.80e	--	Benguala145½RomanRequest14010SeaChart1384	Strong drive 6
30Mar57- 7Cam	fm	*1Ⓣ	1:401	3↑ Alw 500	2	4	43¾	42	43	56½	Foot A	132 w	-	--	MuguetII1382SquareDanceII1452½BarodaBoy1481½	No excuse 6

Berlo

br. f. 1957, by Heliopolis (Hyperion)–Faberose, by Rosemont **Lifetime record: 14 8 0 2 $208,186**

Own.– Foxcatcher Farm
Br.– W. duPont Jr (Ky)
Tr.– E.A. Christmas

23Sep61- 7Bel	fst	1⅛	:463 1:11 1:361 1:492	3↑ ⒻBeldame 96k	2	12	1211	115¾	67	48¾	Guerin E	123	3.20	80-18	AirmansGuide123¾Craftiness1232½Primontt1185½	Slow start 12
6Sep61- 7Bel	fst	1	:222 :45 1:092 1:361	3↑ ⒻMaskette H 28k	7	9	913	89	86¾	44½	Guerin E	126	*1.10	88-13	Teacation1161Shimmy Dancer1061½Craftiness1202	No excuse 9
29Aug61- 7Bel	fst	7f	:23 :462 1:11 1:24	3↑ ⒻAlw 10000	8	7	810	87¼	75¼	41½	Guerin E	123	*.60	85-15	Staretta109nkGreatDame112nkMssCloudy1141	Swerved in dr. 8
Previously trained by R.E. Handlen																
12Oct60 7Bel	fst	1½	:471 1:111 2:013 2:303	3↑ ⒻLadies H 59k	9	9	716	33½	13	13½	Guerin E	124	*1.05	00-15	Berlo1242½Woodlawn112½Who's Ahead105½	Speed to spare 13
1Oct60- 7Bel	fst	1⅛	:461 1:11 1:362 1:492	3↑ ⒻBeldame 91k	6	9	96¾	73¼	12	12	Guerin E	119	4.05	89-16	Berlo1192Royal Native1231Make Sail1193	Slow start,clear 9
7Sep60- 6Aqu	fst	1	:221 :442 1:10 1:354	ⒻGazelle H (Div 1) 22k	12	12	1111	72¾	13	12½	Guerin E	122	*1.80	89-11	Berlo1222½SisterAntoin1131FunnyBon109hd	Drew out easily 12
23Jly60- 7Mth	fst	1⅛	:472 1:112 1:364 1:492	ⒻMth Oaks 57k	7	8	87½	95¾	65¾	46¼	Guerin E	121	*1.20	91-14	Teacation1131¼Refute1172Rash Statement1213	No mishap 9
16Jly60- 6Del	fst	1⅛	:471 1:113 1:38 1:503	ⒻDel Oaks 64k	7	10	75½	64¼	31½	32	Guerin E	121	*.70	85-14	Rash Statement1212Sarcastic115noBerlo1212	Wide bid,hung 12
25Jun60- 7Bel	fst	1¼	:483 1:132 1:383 2:041	ⒻC C A Oaks 86k	4	7	3nk	21	1½	1¾	Guerin E	121	*.45	79-13	Berlo121¾Sarcastic1213½Rash Statement1212½	Brisk urging 8
8Jun60- 7Bel	fst	1⅛	:452 1:102 1:364 1:50	ⒻMother Goose 29k	9	7	84¼	41½	1hd	13½	Guerin E	114	2.20	86-17	Berlo1143½Chalvedele1112½MakeSal1212	Had speed to spare 11
2Jun60- 7Bel	fst	6f	:223 :461 1:113	ⒻAlw 5000	3	8	109½	53½	3½	16	Guerin E	115	*2.00	89-14	Berlo1156All Wing115nkRash Statement121½	Speed to spare 12
18May60- 6Aqu	gd	6f	:231 :47 1:114	ⒻAlw 4500	3	5	43½	32½	11	11¼	Guerin E	116	1.95	93-11	Berlo1161¼Princess Rousse;1201Holly Beach1204	Handily 5
15Oct59- 6Aqu	gd	6f	:231 :481 1:141	ⒻMd Sp Wt	4	9	64½	41½	12	12½	Guerin E	115	*1.10	--	Brlo1152½CtchM115nkHulLou115¾	Bumped stretch,mild drive 9
8Oct59- 6Aqu	fst	7f	:23 :462 1:12 1:252	ⒻMd Sp Wt	1	11	42¼	42½	22	31½	Guerin E	115	3.60	--	Kathy Kim115¾Four Cent Stamp115¾Berlo1152½	Off poorly 11

Bold Lad

ch. c. 1962, by Bold Ruler (Nasrullah)–Misty Morn, by Princequillo **Lifetime record: 19 14 2 1 $516,465**

Own.– Wheatley Stable
Br.– Wheatley Stable (Ky)
Tr.– E.A. Neloy

4Jly66- 7Aqu	fst	1¼	:474 1:114 1:37 2:02	3↑ Suburban H 110k	1	1	3nk	45½	56½	610	Baeza B	135 b	*1.40	78-21	Buffle1103Pluck1132Paoluccio1081½	Tired under impost 9
30May66- 7Aqu	fst	1	:221 :44 1:08 1:341	3↑ Metropolitan H 115k	2	6	44	34	22	12½	Baeza B	132 b	*.70e	97-13	Bold Lad1322½Hedevar1132½Tio Viejo115no	Going away 11
18May66- 7Aqu	fst	7f	:221 :444 1:092 1:214	3↑ Roseben H 28k	3	6	44½	43½	1hd	13	Baeza B	126 b	*.50	97-15	Bold Lad1263Davis II118hdHoist Bar117¾	Drew out easily 7
6May66- 7Aqu	fst	7f	:223 :444 1:09 1:221	4↑ Alw 10000	5	1	15	16	16	14	Knapp K	119 b	*.50	95-18	Bold Lad1194A. Deck1195Off the Top117½	Easily the best 7
30Apr66- 7GS	sly	6f	:224 :464 1:123	4↑ Alw 6500	3	2	2hd	1½	1½	1hd	Knapp K	113 b	*.40	81-32	BoldLad113hdBugler11312Cosmo122hd	Under long,hard drive 6
Previously trained by W.C. Winfrey																
1May65- 7CD	fst	1¼	:471 1:114 1:37 2:011	Ky Derby 154k	3	5	65	54	1012	1012	Hartack W	126 b	*2.00	82-05	Lucky Debonair126nkDapper Dan1262Tom Rolfe1261	Tired 11
27Apr65- 7CD	fst	1	:223 :454 1:10 1:351	Derby Trial 15k	2	2	21	13	14	14	Hartack W	122 b	*.30	97-16	Bold Lad1224Carpenter's Rule1166Bugler1164	Well in hand 5
17Apr65- 7Aqu	fst	1⅛	:454 1:093 1:36 1:501	Wood Memorial 92k	7	2	24	24	22½	31¼	Ycaza M	126 b	*.50e	84-18	FlagRasr126nkHltoAll1261BoldLd126½	Lacked late response 11
3Apr65- 6Aqu	fst	6f	:224 :462 1:103	3↑ Alw 8500	3	3	31½	3½	1½	13	Baeza B	114 b	*.25	90-19	BoldLad1143PackTrip1152½ExclusiveNashu1242½	Easily best 5
17Oct64- 7Aqu	sly	1	:224 :461 1:11 1:362	Champagne 176k	1	2	21½	11½	16	17	Baeza B	122 b	*.25	86-21	BoldLad1227Royal Gunner1224½Philately122½	Easy score 6
26Sep64- 7Aqu	fst	6½f	:22 :45 1:093 1:16	Futurity 138k	5	4	44½	42	1hd	11¼	Baeza B	122 b	*.20	100-10	BoldLad1221¼NativeCharger1222¼TomRolfe1225½	Drew clear 5
29Aug64- 6Sar	fst	6½f	:222 :451 1:091 1:153	Hopeful 111k	4	2	22	12	14	17	Baeza B	122 b	*.30e	102-07	Bold Lad1227Native Charger1222Time Tested1223½	Easily 5
8Aug64- 8Mth	fst	6f	:214 :443 1:092	Sapling 102k	8	2	42	41	1hd	1½	Baeza B	122 b	*.70e	95-15	BoldLad122½NativeCharger1223Sadair1228	Long,hard drive 9

1Aug64- 6Mth fst 6f :22 :444 1:093 Alw 6000 3 4 23 24 2½ 12 Baeza B 122 b *.70 94-15 BoldLad1222NativeCharger1222½Sadr12210 Shown whip,clear 6
8Jly64- 7Aqu sly 5½f :222 :46 :592 1:061 Tremont 37k 5 4 42½ 43½ 32½ 1½ Ycaza M 122 b 2.70 82-23 Bold Lad122½Joust1142Turn to Reason114no Brisk handling 9
22Jun64- 7Aqu fst 5½f :22 :45 :572 1:04 ©National Stallion 28k 2 4 32½ 22 21½ 1½ Baeza B 122 b 2.45 93-16 BoldLad122½Tanistair1172TurntoReason1175 Strong urging 4
16Jun64- 6Aqu fst 5f :223 :462 :584 Alw 5000 2 5 41½ 43 33 21½ Baeza B 122 b 5.55 89-19 Groton1221½BoldLad1222½OnHolidy122²½ Drifted final turn 6
8Jun64- 4Aqu sly 5f :222 :464 1:00 ©Md Sp Wt 8 5 33½ 33½ 21½ 1¾ Ussery R 122 *.85 85-19 Bold Lad122¾Casque1224The Jouster1225 Strong handling 8
26May64- 4Aqu fst 5f :223 :464 :594 ©Md Sp Wt 9 7 86¼ 53½ 22 21 Ussery R 122 *2.70 85-16 IndiaInk1221BoldLad122¾Egocentrical1222 Extremely wide 10

Bon Nouvel

b. g. 1960, by Duc de Fer (Spy Song)–Good News, by Happy Argo
Own.– Mrs Theodora A. Randolph
Br.– Dr Archibald C. Randolph (Va)
Tr.– D.M. Smithwick

Lifetime record: 51 16 11 7 $176,149

25Oct68- 6Bel sf 3⅛ S'Chase 6:02 4↑ Temple Gwathmey H 55k 8 1 15 34½ 628 - Aitcheson J Jr 161 *.80e - - China Run1401½Apollon1462Gentle Boy13620 Lame,eased 8
15Oct68- 5Bel fm 2½ S'Chase 4:421 4↑ Brook H 19k 7 1 120 11 1½ 2hd Aitcheson J Jr 161 *1.90e - - Roublet153hdBonNouvel16113ChinaRun13714 Failed to last 8
1Oct68- 5Bel hd 2⅛ S'Chase 3:533 4↑ Broad Hollow H 16k 6 1 15 13 12 21 Aitcheson J Jr 162 b *1.20e - - Exhibit A.1451Bon Nouvel16218Flying Artist1462½ Gamely 6
14Sep68- 4Fai fm *1¼Ⓣ 2:084 3↑ Alw 1200 11 1 1nk 1½ 2¾ 411 Aitcheson J Jr 140 b *1.00 - - Charlie Wright133½Molterer1401½Aiken Road1409 No excuse 11
22Aug68- 5Sar sf 2½ S'Chase 4:421 4↑ Saratoga H 21k 1 1 15 16 1hd 24 Aitcheson J Jr 165 2.00 - - Apollon1444Bon Nouvel1654Roublet155nk Poor landing 16th 4
2Aug68- 5Sar fm 2$\frac{1}{16}$ S'Chase 3:513 4↑ Beverwyck H 16k 2 1 11½ 12 13 12½ Aitcheson J Jr 154 *.30 - - Bon Nouvel1542½Sky Epic13514Appollon1491½ Ridden out 4
29Jly68- 3Sar sf 2$\frac{1}{16}$ S'Chase 3:564 4↑ OClm 10000 7 1 13 14 18 118 Aitcheson J 155 *.70 - - Bon Nouvel15518Atamisqui143¾China Run1321 Easily best 8
28Jun68♦ Auteuil(Fr) fm*2⅝ 5:04 5↑ Prix des Drags Steeplechase Stk17000 26 Robinson W 132 15.00 Vin Sec1326Bon Nouvel1326Pontage1322
Led,soon well clear,headed approaching last,second best
23Jun68♦ Auteuil(Fr) sf *4$\frac{1}{16}$ 7:59 5↑ Grand Steeple-Chase d'Paris Stk68000 - Small D Jr 141 19.00e Haroue1418Parandero14120Philae1412½ 14
With leaders,fell at 6th
31May68- 5Bel fm 2⅛ S'Chase 4:024 4↑ Hitchcock H 11k 4 2 2½ 14 12 33 Aitcheson J Jr 159 *.70e - - Roublet152½Teana1412½Bon Nouvel15940 Fenced poorly 7
23May68- 5Bel fm 2½ S'Chase 4:471 4↑ Meadow Brook H 18k 4 1 14 - - - Aitcheson J 157 *.40e - - Sun Game1412½Irish Hammer146 Overjumped 6th 5
4May68- 4War fm *2 S'Chase 4:401 4↑ Alw 2200 6 5 210 16 115 120 Aitcheson J Jr 154 - - - Bon Nouvel15420Greek Myth1421½Enquest1353 Handily 7
20Apr68- 5Mid hd *2 S'Chase 3:481 4↑ Clark Cup 5.5k 3 2 2¾ 1½ 2hd 2½ Aitcheson J 140 - - - Tuscalee160½Bon Nouvel140noGaddo1404½ Held on willingly 7
13Apr68- 3Mid fm *2 S'Chase 4:492 4↑ W C Langly Mem Cup 2.2k 6 4 2nk 12 11 12 Aitcheson J 142 - - - Bon Nouvel1422Gaddo1379Hustle1421½ Steady drive 6
6Apr68- 3DRn fm *1⅝ Hurdles 2:443 3↑ Alw 1000 5 3 31½ 3¾ 3¾ 1½ Aitcheson J Jr 143 - - - Bon Nouvel143½Lucent147¾Shod Over1381½ Driving 5
7May66- 7War fm *1¼Ⓣ 2:343 3↑ Alw 500 3 2 12 12 12½ 14½ Smithwick AP 147 s - - - Bon Nouvel1474½Aquitania140½Brandon Hill1303 Mild drive 10
23Apr66- 6Mid sf *1¼Ⓣ 2:173 3↑ Alw 200 7 - 813 Walsh T 149 s - - - PrinceBective1391½LazyRiver1381½EarlyFind1434 No threat 12
Dense fog
29Oct65- 6Aqu hd 3 S'Chase 5:334 4↑ Temple Gwathmey H 54k 3 1 16 16 120 130 Walsh T 170 s *.30e - - Bon Nouvel17030Lucentaur13415Mako14650 Outclassed field 6
5Oct65- 5Aqu hd 2½ S'Chase 4:363 4↑ Brook H 20k 2 1 13 15 12 11 Walsh T 169 s *.30e - - Bon Nouvel1691Mako1423Sun Game14350 Good handling 5
16Sep65- 5Aqu hd 2$\frac{1}{16}$ S'Chase 3:432 4↑ Broad Hollow H 16k 6 1 13 15 16 18 Walsh T 162 s *.90e - - Bon Nouvel1628The Sport15410Impeach137¾ Much the best 6
26Aug65- 5Sar fm 2½ S'Chase 4:333 4↑ Saratoga H 22k 2 1 18 12 1½ 22 Walsh T 160 s 2.20e - - TheSport1482BonNouvel1605SunGame1463 Bobbled,2nd best 6
21Aug65- 3Sar fm 2$\frac{1}{16}$ S'Chase 3:411 4↑ Handicap 7500 6 1 12 23 47 419½ Smithwick AP 156 s *1.40e - - Nashandy1465Magic Technique1452½Niksar13712 Used up 7
5Aug65- 8Sar fm 1⅛Ⓣ 1:483 3↑ Alw 6000 1 1 1½ 33 89 1116 Blum W 115 13.50 74-00 Lancastrian1102Winklepicker1124Ali Baba II115½ Used up 14
17Jly65- 5Del hd 1$\frac{1}{16}$Ⓣ 1:453 3↑ Alw 4000 6 5 65½ 77¼ 76¾ 78¾ Turcotte R 122 *2.60e 67-24 ⒹScambio122nkIsland Stream1093½Cannelton1101 Steadied 9
30Oct64- 6Aqu fm 3 S'Chase 5:394 4↑ Temple Gwathmey H 55k 7 1 11 2½ 210 321 Smithwick AP 162 s *.30e - - Amber Diver15720Aquitania1351Bon Nouvel162½ Gave way 7
20Oct64- 5Aqu sf 3 S'Chase 5:401 4↑ Grand National H 28k 3 1 16 18 120 120 Smithwick AP 156 s *.70e - - BonNouvel15620AmberDiver1566BamptonCastle140hd Easily 8
6Oct64- 5Aqu fm 2½ S'Chase 4:401 4↑ Brook H 19k 7 1 16 115 120 112 Smithwick AP 152 s *1.15e - - Bon Nouvel15212Tuscarora1562Pocket Rocket137¾ Easily 8
17Sep64- 5Aqu fm 2 S'Chase 3:402 4↑ Broad Hollow H 16k 4 1 13 14 14 12 Smithwick AP 146 s *1.95 - - Bon Nouvel1462Tuscarora1492½Nautilus1465 Ridden out 6
3Sep64- 5Aqu fm 2 S'Chase 3:43 4↑ Harbor Hill H 11k 7 2 18 112 112 112 Smithwick AP 148 s *1.15 - - Bon Nouvel14812Arctic Flow1352Hustle1491 Easily best 8
26Aug64- 3Sar hd 2$\frac{1}{16}$ S'Chase 3:46 4↑ Alw 5000 3 2 1½ 16 18 125 Hruska J 135 s *1.10e - - Bon Nouvel13525Half Baked1365El Moro1504 Easily best 8
8Aug64- 3Sar hd 1⅞ Hurdles 3:211 3↑ Alw 5500 8 1 11 12 1hd 23 Smithwick AP 143 s 4.25 - - Our Jeep1483Bon Nouvel143hdLumiere1341 Game try 9
29Jly64- 5Mth fm *2 Hurdles 3:544 3↑ Midsummer H 17k 11 5 23 21½ 23 36¼ Smithwick AP 142 s 20.10 - - IntheCloset152nkExhibitA.1656BonNouvel142no Game try 11
17Jly64- 3Mth fm *1¾ Hurdles 3:263 3↑ Alw 4000 2 6 23 12 2hd 24 Smithwick AP 143 s 9.80e - - Rapidan1474Bon Nouvel14310Hermod1482 Set pace,gamely 10
20May64- 3Aqu hd 1⅝ Hurdles 2:521 3↑ Alw 5000 6 5 610 614 719 725 Smithwick AP 143 s 12.20 - - AtomCloud1504PrinceBective1442IntheCloset1478 No speed 8
7May64- 5Aqu fm 2 S'Chase 3:484 4↑ Aqu Spring 14k 10 - - - - - Smithwick AP 143 s 20.20 - - RamshornCreek1483RapidPlay1414Mildor14314 In close,fell 11
18Apr64- 4Mid fm *2 S'Chase 3:52 4↑ Piedmont Cup H 2.3k 6 6 21 22 34½ 38½ Hruska J 137 b - - - War Union II1478Fortification135½Bon Nouvel137¾ Tired 8
11Apr64- 3Mid fm *2 S'Chase 3:581 4↑ WC Langley Mem Cup 2.1k 2 3 11 311 38 212 Hruska J 141 sb - - - Cher Man13812Bon Nouvel141½Seroval151 Set pace,gamely 3
30Nov63- 5Pim sl 6f :24 :481 1:01 1:134 Alw 4000 7 2 21 31½ 54½ 66¾ Turcotte R 119 2.90 74-25 Romay1161½North Channel116½Evil Dick1161 Speed,tired 8
23Nov63- 7Pim sly 6f :231 :47 1:002 1:143 Alw 4000 8 2 52¼ 44½ 34 22 Torres O 113 4.30 75-23 Big Little Man1142Bon Nouvel113¾Evil Dick1165 Gamely 9
14Nov63- 5Pim fst 6f :24 :48 1:01 1:141 Md Sp Wt 11 2 31 11 11½ 11½ Torres O 120 5.10 79-19 Bon Nouvel1201½Turning Point1201Mono Boy120nk All out 12
9Nov63- 5Lrl gd 6f :231 :474 1:133 3↑ Alw 4000 1 5 96½ 919 919 926 Torres O 110 14.00 61-24 LansingLane1227SecondMortgage1151FnfnlTulp1221½ Trailed 9
17Oct63- 3Aqu sf *1⅝ Hurdles 2:583 3↑ O Clm 7500 8 6 23 11 13 1¾ Smithwick AP 147 s 2.80e - - BonNvl147¾HoistHimAboard142¾ⒹAtomCloud1572½ Driving 8
11Oct63- 3Aqu hd 1⅝ Hurdles 2:512 3↑ O Clm 5000 9 6 23 1½ 311 323 Smithwick AP 145 s *2.40e - - Fort Riley1408Cassorbit14015Bon Nouvel145½ Used in lead 11
13Sep63- 3Aqu sf *1⅝ Hurdles 2:571 O Md 7500 2 1 1½ 21 1hd 36½ Smithwick AP 145 s *2.20 - - EarlyFind137½Roi-a-Dan1386BonNouvl14512 Used up in pace 8
30Aug63- 3Aqu fm *1⅝ Hurdles 2:503 O Md 7500 2 4 46 42 31½ 2¾ Smithwick AP 145 s 9.85 - - Lumiere145¾BonNouvl1451JohnCano1452½ Finished strongly 10
7Aug63- 1Sar fst 1⅛ :472 1:124 1:392 1:524 3↑ Md Sp Wt 7 2 64¾ 97 76½ 815 Gustines H 117 54.00 66-13 War Lord1171¾Nacelle1172Mac Brathar117¾ Fell back early 9
30Jly63- 8Sar gd 1⅛ :481 1:134 1:403 1:534 3↑ Md Sp Wt 10 10 119¾ 1111 1112 1019 Sorrentino M 115 13.05 57-20 Watch Word1152½Deer Falls110nkMacBrathar1153½ Far back 11
2Jly63- 3Del fm 1$\frac{1}{16}$Ⓣ 1:434 3↑ Md Sp Wt 7 1 11½ 42 47½ 49¾ Cox N 114 16.50 83-05 GallantChiefII1134SidlingSam1084RockyThumb1131¾ Tired 12
21Jun63- 8Aqu fst 6f :224 :471 1:12 Md Sp Wt 2 9 910 98½ 911 911 Cox N 122 25.95 74-14 BrownJay122noFriendlyPeople1221½SeekndFnd1221 No factor 10
8Jun63- 2Del sly 6f :224 :463 1:13 3↑ Md Sp Wt 7 8 118 96¾ 68¾ 35 Cox N 114 7.80 75-17 Hallatnan1133½Procrastination1081½BonNouvl114hd Rallied 12
25May63- 7Pur fm *7fⓉ 1:29 3↑ Alw 400 3 5 57½ 514 59 44½ Cox N 133 s *1.70e - - AngusBear148noPeacockThroneII1484½Sagvel143hd No excuse 6

Bowl of Flowers

ch. f. 1958, by Sailor (Eight Thirty)–Flower Bowl, by Alibhai — Lifetime record: 16 10 3 3 $398,504

Own.– Brookmeade Stable
Br.– Brookmeade Stable (Ky)
Tr.– E. Burch

11Nov61- 7Aqu	fst	1 3/16	:48 1:121 1:371 1:564	Roamer H 56k	6	5	53	33½	32½	3hd	Rotz JL	121	b	3.45	95-13	Sherluck126noHittingAway120noBowlofFlowers1212¼	Gamely	9
19Oct61- 6Kee	sly	1⅛	:464 1:103 1:36 1:491 3↑	Ⓕ Spinster 84k	3	7	57½	54	32½	1¾	Arcaro E	119	b	4.40	91-11	Bowl of Flowers119¾Primonetta1191Times Two1191	Driving	7
	Open to 3-,4- and 5-year-olds																	
26Sep61- 7Bel	fst	1 1/16	:231 :47 1:114 1:434 3↑	Ⓕ Alw 7500	6	9	88¼	67	34½	32¾	Arcaro E	115		*.65	82-22	RoseO'Neill1132Siesta118¾BowlofFlowrs1155	Returned sore	10
5Aug61- 6Sar	fst	1¼	:481 1:121 1:371 2:031	Ⓕ Alabama 54k	5	5	57½	65	52½	36	Arcaro E	124		*.55	86-10	Primonetta1215MightyFair1141BowlofFlowers124hd	Bore out	6
24Jun61- 7Bel	fst	1¼	:483 1:124 1:374 2:031	Ⓕ C C A Oaks 116k	1	6	4¾	2hd	12	15½	Arcaro E	121		*.45	84-13	BowlofFlowers1215½Funloving1215MightyFair1212¼	Easily	6
10Jun61- 7Bel	fst	1⅛	:473 1:122 1:373 1:503	Ⓕ Mother Goose 87k	5	7	67	42½	23	2hd	Arcaro E	121		*.80	83-18	Funloving117hdBowlofFlowers1211¼MightyFair1171¼	Gaining	8
20May61- 7Aqu	fst	1	:233 :47 1:112 1:372	Ⓕ Acorn 57k	3	7	54	42½	41½	1¾	Arcaro E	121		*.25	81-18	BowlofFlowers121¾BlackDarter121noSevnThrty121nk	Driving	7
4May61- 7Aqu	fst	7f	:231 :462 1:104 1:232	Handicap 10000	1	1	43	31	1½	12	Arcaro E	121		*.30	93-12	BowlofFlowers1212UpScope1172¼BraveAlly1132¾	Easily best	5
12Nov60- 7Aqu	fst	1	:222 :444 1:094 1:353	Ⓕ Frizette 106k	4	10	97	85½	1½	13	Arcaro E	119		*.70e	90-13	BowlofFlowers1193CounterCall1191¾GoodMove1192	Easily	12
22Oct60- 7GS	fst	1 1/16	:23 :464 1:114 1:46	Ⓕ Gardenia 153k	4	13	1116	99¼	53½	1½	Shoemaker W	119		*.70e	80-19	BowlofFlowrs119½AnglSpeed1191PromnntLdy1191½	Taken up	13
15Oct60- 6GS	fst	1	:224 :462 1:12 1:381	Ⓕ Alw 10000	7	7	65¼	1½	11½	13½	Boulmetis S	121		*1.70	91-16	BowlofFlowers1213½AngelSpeed1162½MyPortrait1181	Easily	11
7Oct60- 7Bel	fst	7f	:231 :472 1:123 1:251	Ⓕ Alw 15000	10	6	910	76¾	2½	15	Arcaro E	116		*.80	81-24	Bowl of Flowers1165Dewali116nkMaggie James107nk	Easily	11
29Sep60- 6Bel	fst	6f	:222 :462 1:114	Ⓕ Alw 4500	4	12	1211	76	32½	2hd	Arcaro E	119		*1.60	88-16	Dewali116hdBowlofFlowers119nkPlayTm1166	Slow start,wide	13
20Jun60- 7Bel	fst	5½f	:222 :46 :58 1:041	Ⓕ National Stallion 37k	7	8	56½	44	21½	1no	Ycaza M	114		2.70	101-11	BowlofFlowers114noShuette1148EasternPrincss119½	Driving	8
26May60- 6Aqu	fst	5f	:224 :464 :592	Ⓕ Md Sp Wt	6	8	54½	32½	11	13	Arcaro E	115		*1.05	- -	Bowl of Flowers1153Chuckaway1155Cargreen1153	Easily	9
13May60- 3Aqu	fst	5f	:224 :463 :59	Ⓕ Md Sp Wt	4	7	98½	911	610	26	Arcaro E	115		6.50	- -	Shuette1156BowlofFlowers1151BlesstheBride115½	Greenly	9

Buckpasser

b. c. 1963, by Tom Fool (Menow)–Busanda, by War Admiral — Lifetime record: 31 25 4 1 $1,462,014

Own.– O. Phipps
Br.– Ogden Phipps (Ky)
Tr.– E.A. Neloy

30Sep67- 7Aqu	fst	1¼	:451 1:091 1:353 2:003 3↑	Woodward 107k	6	6	614	33½	38	210	Baeza B	126	b	*1.60e	85-15	Damascus12010Buckpasser126½Dr. Fager12013	Good try	6
22Jly67- 7Aqu	fst	1¼	:462 1:094 1:342 2:001 3↑	Brooklyn H 106k	3	3	33	23	25	28	Baeza B	136	b	*.70	89-11	Handsome Boy1168Bckpassr1364½Mr. Right1133½	No excuse	5
4Jly67- 7Aqu	fst	1¼	:474 1:114 1:363 2:021 3↑	Suburban H 109k	1	5	65	44	44	1½	Baeza B	133	b	*.50	87-17	Buckpasser133½RingTwice1112½Yondr1091½	Up final strides	7
17Jun67- 7Aqu	hd	1⅝Ⓣ	2:412 3↑	Bowling Green H 55k	3	4	47½	46½	35	34½	Baeza B	135	b	*.40e	82-13	Poker1121½Assagai1273Buckpasser135½	Failed to respond	5
30May67- 7Aqu	fst	1	:232 :454 1:10 1:343 3↑	Metropolitan H 109k	5	3	32	34½	21	11¼	Baeza B	130	b	*.30	95-13	Buckpasser1301¼Yonder1084½Impressive1131	Scored easily	6
14Jan67- 8SA	fst	1⅛	:462 1:103 1:354 1:481	San Fernando 56k	3	3	37½	44½	32½	11½	Baeza B	124	b	*.30	91-12	Buckpasser1241½FleetHost121¾Pretens118hd	With authority	6
31Dec66- 6SA	fst	7f	:223 :451 1:093 1:22	Malibu 29k	2	9	76½	54½	21	1¾	Baeza B	126	b	*.40	93-15	Buckpasser126¾Drin1201KingsFvor1171½	Slow start,driving	9
29Oct66- 7Aqu	fst	2	:494 2:333 3:261 3↑	J C Gold Cup 110k	1	4	44½	1hd	11	11¾	Baeza B	119	b	*.30e	65-21	Buckpasser1191¾Niarkos124½O'Hara1248	Drew out handling	7
19Oct66- 7Aqu	sly	1⅝	:492 1:423 2:071 2:441	Lawrence Realizatn 54k	4	5	44½	33½	32½	12½	Baeza B	126	b	*.20e	84-19	Buckpasser1262½Ring Twice116½Poker11612	Going away	5
1Oct66- 7Aqu	sly	1¼	:47 1:114 1:373 2:024 3↑	Woodward 112k	4	6	64½	31½	1hd	1¾	Baeza B	121	b	*.90e	84-24	Buckpasser121¾Royal Gunner126¾Buffle1215	Ridden out	9
20Aug66- 6Sar	fst	1¼	:472 1:112 1:362 2:013	Travers 82k	6	5	512	43½	21	1¾	Baeza B	126	b	*.30e	100-10	Buckpssr126¾Ambrod1233½Buffl120no	Under strong handling	6
6Aug66- 8AP	fst	1⅛	:464 1:103 1:354 1:47	American Derby 129k	9	5	59½	68	42	1nk	Baeza B	128	b	*.60e	101-09	Buckpasser128nkJolly Jet1161Advocator1163	Driving	9
23Jly66- 7Aqu	fst	1¼	:483 1:122 1:364 2:014 3↑	Brooklyn H 107k	2	2	22½	21½	1hd	1hd	Baeza B	120	b	*.60	89-16	Buckpasser120hdBuffle1135Pluck1132	Faltered,came again	5
9Jly66- 8AP	fst	1⅛	:473 1:112 1:363 1:491	Chicagoan 103k	3	3	33	2½	1hd	1¾	Baeza B	123	b	*.30	90-18	Buckpasser123¾Whisper Jet114nkAbe's Hope1167	Mild drive	5
25Jun66- 8AP	fst	1	:221 :433 1:064 1:323	Arl Classic H 108k	4	6	79	59	34	1¾	Baeza B	125	b	*.70e	103-04	Buckpasser1251¾CremeDelaCreme123¾HeJr.116nk	Ridden out	8
18Jun66- 8Del	fst	1⅛	:463 1:10 1:364 1:492	Leonard Richards 41k	2	4	47	48½	2hd	1¾	Baeza B	126	b	*.30e	90-14	Buckpasser126¾Buffle114¾Deck Hand1144	Under hand urging	6
4Jun66- 6Aqu	fst	6f	:222 :451 1:091 3↑	Alw 8500	5	3	22	1hd	1hd	12	Baeza B	115	b	*.40	97-14	Buckpasser1152Tim'sStingry1152Undrstudy121nk	Mild drive	7
3Mar66- 0Hia	fst	1⅛	:462 1:104 1:363 1:50	Flamingo 136k	4	3	34	32	2½	1no	Shoemaker W	122	b	-	85-18	Buckpasser122noAbe'sHope1222¼BlueSkyer1222½	Came again	9
	Run between 7th and 8th races. No wagering																	
23Feb66- 8Hia	fst	1⅛	:452 1:09 1:343 1:474	Everglades 30k	6	2	23	21	2hd	1hd	Shoemaker W	122	b	*.20e	96-12	Buckpasser122hdStupendous115¾Abe's Hope1154	Swerved	8
14Feb66- 0Hia	fst	7f	:224 :45 1:084 1:214	Alw 5000	1	5	514	512	46	24½	Shoemaker W	124	b	-e	95-13	Impressive1224½Buckpasser1241½Stupendous113nk	Rallied	5
	Exhibition race run between 7th and 8th races. No wagering;Previously trained by W.C. Winfrey																	
16Oct65- 7Aqu	fst	1	:223 :453 1:104 1:362	Champagne 223k	1	7	54½	54½	1½	14	Baeza B	122	b	*.90e	86-20	Buckpasser1224Our Michael122½Advocator1221½	Easily	9
25Sep65- 7Aqu	gd	6½f	:23 :462 1:104 1:171	Futurity 151k	7	6	41¾	21	21	2½	Baeza B	122	b	*.70	93-20	PricelessGem119½Buckpassr12210 D Advoctor1223	No excuse	9
11Sep65- 8AP	fst	7f	:223 :452 1:102 1:23	Arl-Wash Futurity 335k	8	8	66½	56¼	14	1½	Baeza B	122	b	*.80	92-15	Buckpasser122½Fathers Image1222Flame Tree122no	Driving	10
28Aug65- 6Sar	fst	6½f	:22 :444 1:093 1:16	Hopeful 110k	7	7	42½	31½	3nk	12½	Baeza B	122	b	*.30e	98-08	Buckpasser1222½Impressive122¾Indulto1222½	Going away	7
7Aug65- 8Mth	fst	6f	:22 :45 1:103	Sapling 112k	1	7	63¾	33½	33	1½	Baeza B	122	b	1.90	89-21	Buckpasser122½Quinta1221½OurMichael1225	Left at post,up	7
30Jly65- 7Mth	fst	5½f	:221 :454 1:04	Alw 5000	3	5	42	33	11	17	Baeza B	122	b	*.90	97-19	Buckpasser1227Model Fool116¾Gary Dear1193	Drew far out	6
7Jly65- 7Aqu	fst	5½f	:221 :45 :572 1:034	Tremont 34k	3	6	66½	42½	2½	1nk	Baeza B	118	b	*.70	94-13	Buckpasser118nkSpringDouble1182½Hospitalty118no	Driving	6
28Jun65- 7Aqu	fst	5½f	:222 :452 :58 1:043	Ⓒ National Stallion 32k	3	5	59	47	34	15♦	Baeza B	122	b	*1.00	90-15	DH Hospitality117 DH Buckpassr1225KentuckyKn117no	Just up	6
8Jun65- 6Aqu	fst	5½f	:223 :461 :583 1:05	Alw 5500	7	5	55	52½	2½	11½	Baeza B	122		*1.90	88-21	Buckpassr1221½KentuckyKin1222½BanderaBeau1194	Driving	9
29May65- 3Aqu	sly	5f	:23 :471 1:00	Ⓒ Md Sp Wt	7	5	43	42	2½	12	Baeza B	122		*1.25	85-20	Buckpasser1222Exhibitionist1222½Clique1224	Easy score	8
13May65- 4Aqu	fst	5½f	:231 :482 1:003 1:07	Ⓒ Md Sp Wt	8	10	66	57	55	41¼	Baeza B	122		5.30	77-26	LonelyGambler122½HndsmeBy122noMaskofPlay117¾	Greenly	10

Carry Back

br. c. 1958, by Saggy (Swing and Sway)–Joppy, by Star Blen — Lifetime record: 61 21 11 11 $1,241,165

Own.– Dorchester Farm Stable
Br.– J.A. Price (Fla)
Tr.– J.A. Price

2Nov63- 8GS	my	1¼	:464 1:111 1:361 2:014 3↑	Trenton H 59k	2	6	44½	12	12	12½	Sellers J	119		7.00	96-22	Carry Back1192½Mongo1242Smart1166	Kept to brisk drive	10
9Oct63- 7Aqu	fst	1½	:47 1:114 2:024 2:28 3↑	Manhattan H 58k	7	9	810	64½	1116	1116	Rotz JL	125		5.50	95-18	Smart1142½Will I Rule112noGarwol1112	Made move,stopped	12
28Sep63- 7Aqu	fst	1¼	:473 1:114 1:362 2:004 3↑	Woodward 108k	4	4	45½	45½	49½	411	Rotz JL	126		8.75	85-13	Kelso1263½Never Bend1201½Crimson Satan1266	Even effort	5
14Sep63- 8Atl	fm	1 3/16Ⓣ	1:551 3↑	U Nations H 125k	10	6	53½	42	51¼	32¾	Grant H	127		*2.60	94-03	Mongo1242Never Bend118¾Carry Back1271½	Made fair try	10
	Daily Racing Form time,1:54 2/5																	
7Sep63- 6Atl	fm	1 1/16Ⓣ	1:423 3↑	Alw 7500	2	3	2hd	1½	14	16	Grant H	116		*1.80	98-02	CarryBack1166PrinceO'Pilsen1183FatCat1141½	Ridden out	7
17Aug63- 7Ran	fst	1⅛	:471 1:113 1:364 1:49 3↑	Buckeye H 33k	2	3	26	25	23	25	Rotz JL	126		*1.80	86-13	Gushing Wind1145CarryBack1262¾Loyal Son1161½	Wide,hung	8
12Nov62- 7Lrl	sf	1½Ⓣ	:471 1:112 2:031 2:281 3↑	D C Int'l 125k	6	4	42	21	31½	36	Rotz JL	126		4.50	84-20	MatchII1281½Kelso1264½CarryBck1265	Good early bid,tired	13
3Nov62- 7GS	sly	1¼	:471 1:121 1:382 2:053 3↑	Trenton H 86k	3	8	712	34	22	2no	Rotz JL	129		*1.20	77-29	Mongo118noCarryBck1294½Snstvo116¾	Impeded st.,sharp try	8
27Oct62- 7Bel	sf	1½Ⓣ	2:283 3↑	Man o' War 114k	5	8	77	43	57½	512	Rotz JL	126		9.25	91-11	BeauPurple1262Kelso1266½TheAxII1261¼	Early bid,weakened	12
7Oct62♦ Longchamp(Fr)	fm	*1½ⓉRH	2:304 3↑	Prix de l'Arc de Triomphe Stk285000						105¾	Breasley A	132		5.50		Soltikoff1221Monade119nkVal de Loir122no		24
																Wide throughout in midpack,one-paced last quarter.Exbury 6th		
3Sep62- 7Aqu	fst	1⅛	:473 1:111 1:36 1:484 3↑	Aqueduct 106k	2	3	31	2hd	3½	41	Rotz JL	128		*.75	97-09	Crozier114½Guadalcanal114hdRidan123½	Speed,hung late	4
28Aug62- 5Aqu	sly	1	:231 :463 1:114 1:373 3↑	Handicap 10000	4	2	1hd	13	18	18	Rotz JL	133		1.00	80-23	CarryBack1338NickelBoy1151Djeddar11610	As rider pleased	4
4Aug62- 6Sar	fst	1⅛	:47 1:11 1:36 1:50 4↑	Whitney 57k	1	5	58½	45	2hd	12	Sellers J	130		*1.60	95-09	Carry Back1302Crozier1114Garwol110no	Under brisk urging	10
21Jly62- 7Aqu	fst	1¼	:471 1:10 1:342 2:00 3↑	Brooklyn H 109k	4	8	811	66	66¼	45	Rotz JL	127		*.85	101-05	BuPurpl1163½Grwol106noPolyld1141½	In close,loose band's	8
14Jly62- 8Mth	fst	1¼	:46 1:10 1:344 2:002 3↑	Monmouth H 109k	4	6	67	33	1hd	13	Rotz JL	124		3.50	104-14	Carry Back1243Kelso130¾Beau Purple117½	Kept to drive	6

4Jly62- 7Aqu	fst 1¼	:484 1:124 1:363 2:003	3↑ Suburban H 105k	3	4	47½	45	45½	47¼	Rotz JL	126	1.85	96-08	BeauPurple1152½Klso1323½Grwol1091¼	Bore in late,checked	4
30May62- 7Aqu	fst 1	:221 :44 1:08 1:333	3↑ Metropolitan H 111k	3	7	79½	77¼	35	12½	Rotz JL	123	4.90	100-08	CarryBack1232½MerryRuler120½RullahRed1114½	Easily best	9
28Apr62- 7Aqu	fst 1⅛	:463 1:101 1:36 1:49	3↑ Grey Lag H 85k	10	8	816	89½	53½	22½	Ycaza M	125	*1.10	94-10	Ambiopoise1152½Carry Back125½Beau Prince115nk	Game try	10
20Apr62- 7Aqu	fst 1	:224 :454 1:102 1:351	4↑ Alw 10000	2	7	77¾	54	11½	15	Ycaza M	126	*.70	92-13	CarryBack1265Garwol117nkGuadalcanal1171¼	Speed to spare	8
17Mar62- 7GP	fst 1¼	:454 1:101 1:36 2:013	3↑ Gulf Park H 112k	3	9	815	53¾	43½	32	Ycaza M	126	*1.25	89-13	[D]Yorky121nkJayFox1121¾CarryBack1261	Wide late,gaining	9
3Mar62- 9FG	fst 1⅛	:47 1:113 1:374 1:503	3↑ New Orleans H 64k	8	9	912	67	52½	33¼	Sellers J	129	*.70	91-14	Yorktown1131½Hillsborough1131¾Carry Back1293½	Late bid	12
24Feb62- 7Hia	fst 1¼	:46 1:101 1:36 2:02	3↑ Widener H 134k	7	10	1015	99¾	55	2nk	Sellers J	127	*1.10	88-12	Yorky120nkCarryBack1273Ambopos121nk	Blocked,fast finish	12
10Feb62- 7Hia	fst 1⅛	:461 1:102 1:352 1:482	3↑ Seminole H 62k	9	7	812	711	56¼	28	Sellers J	127	*.75	85-13	Intentionally1268Carry Back127½Yorky120½	Closed gamely	10
31Jan62- 7Hia	fst 7f	:222 :444 1:092 1:223	3↑ Palm Beach H 33k	12	6	1113	1014	68½	21¾	Sellers J	124	3.15	95-11	Intentionally1261¾CarryBack1242Ambiopois122nk	Sharp try	13
28Oct61- 7GS	fst 1¼	:471 1:112 1:363 2:03	3↑ Trenton H 84k	8	6	67	41¾	31	1½	Sellers J	120	*3.00	90-13	Carry Back120½Intentionally1241¼Ambiopoise120nk	Driving	8
11Oct61- 7Aqu	fst 1⅝	:471 1:38 2:04 2:434	Lawrence Realizatn 54k	1	4	46	33	36	39¼	Sellers J	123	*.55	82-18	Sherlck1231¼Ambiopoise1208CarryBck1234½	Came back sore	6
30Sep61- 7Bel	fst 1¼	:461 1:10 1:344 2:00	3↑ Woodward 109k	1	5	56	43½	47	38½	Sellers J	120	4.00	91-13	Klso1268DivineComedy126½CarryBck120nk	Raced on outside	5
16Sep61- 8Atl	fm 1 3/16Ⓣ	:463 1:111 1:37 1:56	3↑ U Nations H 100k	5	10	910	74¼	65	73¾	Sellers J	123	*1.20	89-07	Oink119noTompion1172Art Market116nk	No apparent excuse	12
2Sep61- 7Bel	fst 1	:223 :451 1:094 1:36	Jerome H 57k	9	7	88	87¼	61¾	1hd	Sellers J	128	*1.95	94-15	CarryBack128hdGarwol111hdBeauPrnc126nk	Up final strides	9
26Aug61- 7Atl	my 7f	:224 :453 1:11 1:243	3↑ Alw 6000	4	7	78	56¼	53¼	1nk	Sellers J	117	*1.00	80-21	CarryBack117nkRareRice114noAbatn1072	Needed mild urging	7
3Jun61- 7Bel	fst 1½	:483 1:133 2:041 2:291	Belmont 148k	2	6	77	77½	713	715	Sellers J	126	*.45	72-13	Sherluck1262¼Globemaster1262½Guadlcnl1264	Returned sore	9
20May61- 8Pim	fst 1 3/16	:481 1:121 1:38 1:573	Preakness 178k	4	8	915	66	24	1¾	Sellers J	126	*1.00	85-22	CarryBack126¾Globemaster1264Crozir126½	Under hard drive	9
6May61- 7CD	gd 1¼	:473 1:112 1:361 2:04	Ky Derby 163k	14	11	1118	613	44½	1¾	Sellers J	126	*2.50	87-14	CarryBack126¾Crozier1262BassClf1262¼	Under strong drive	15
22Apr61- 7Aqu	fst 1⅛	:47 1:112 1:364 1:501	Wood Memorial 86k	6	6	610	47	34	23¼	Sellers J	126	*.95	88-16	Globemaster1263¼Carry Back1266Ambiopoise126hd	Rallied	7
1Apr61- 7GP	sly 1⅛	:462 1:102 1:361 1:484	Florida Derby 115k	5	7	713	41½	32	1hd	Sellers J	122	*1.60	90-16	CarryBack122hdCrozier1223¼BeauPrinc1224	Brushed,driving	8
22Mar61- 7GP	gd 1 1/16	:234 :473 1:113 1:431	Fountain of Youth 17k	1	6	712	59	36	33	Sellers J	122	*1.50	89-17	BeauPrince114noCrozier1223CrryBck1223	Wide late,rallied	7
25Feb61- 7Hia	fst 1⅛	:463 1:113 1:372 1:503	Flamingo 129k	3	5	44	32	21½	1hd	Sellers J	122	*.65	82-19	Carry Back122hdCrozier1228Your Bill1221¾	Forced wide	7
15Feb61- 7Hia	fst 1⅛	:46 1:104 1:37 1:503	Everglades 32k	5	8	711	65¼	43	1½	Sellers J	126	*.65	82-17	CarryBack116½Sherluck114hd[D]Crozier126¾	Bore in,driving	11
8Feb61- 6Hia	fst 1 1/16	:223 :461 1:112 1:443	Alw 7500	3	5	57½	21½	14	12	Sellers J	124	*.90	80-21	CarryBack1242TryCash1103Bookcliffe1103½	Speed to spare	10
1Feb61- 7Hia	fst 7f	:224 :453 1:102 1:234	Bahamas 29k	3	8	74¼	66	64½	45¼	Sellers J	126	2.75	86-19	Vapor Whirl117nkCrozier1263½Nashua Blue1141½	In close	8
8Nov60- 7Aqu	fst 1	:222 :443 1:094 1:362	Remsen 35k	5	8	99¾	77	54½	1½	Sellers J	120	*1.35	86-16	CarryBack120½VaporWhirl111nkAmbiopoise1132½	Hard drive	13
29Oct60- 7GS	sly 1 1/16	:23 :464 1:124 1:462	Garden State 287k	5	14	1010	73¼	12½	13½	Sellers J	122	8.20	78-23	Carry Back1223½Ambiopoise1221¼Guadalcanal1221¼	Easily	15
22Oct60- 6GS	fst 1 1/16	:234 :47 1:114 1:452	Alw 10000	7	9	89¼	67½	55	5¾	Sellers J	120	7.80	82-19	Intensive115noItsaGreatDay120hdGuadalcanl111hd	Bore out	10
15Oct60- 7Bel	fst 1	:223 :454 1:102 1:353	Champagne 183k	1	8	810	89½	811	913	Hartack W	122	*1.95	83-12	RovingMinstrel122noGarwol1222Bronzrullh122no	Poor start	9
3Oct60- 7Bel	fst 7f	:222 :46 1:111 1:24	Cowdin 96k	6	7	76¾	65	33½	11½	Hartack W	114	6.30	87-17	Carry Back1141½Globemaster117nkGarwol114½	Brisk urging	14
10Sep60- 7Atl	fst 7f	:222 :45 1:101 1:223	Worlds Playground 135k	6	9	109	73½	63¾	44½	Culmone J	122	32.90	85-13	HailtoReason1224½ItsaGreatDay122noRossSea122no	Bumped	13
31Aug60- 7Atl	fst 6f	:22 :451 1:101	Seashore 26k	5	4	107	95¾	85¾	56½	Lawless R	114	4.00	87-12	Itsa Great Day1223½Inbalance111¾Cross King114nk	Rallied	15
6Aug60- 7Mth	fst 6f	:214 :444 1:102	Sapling 136k	2	15	127¾	85¾	65	33	Lawless R	122	26.70	87-17	HailtoReason122½He'saPistol1222½CarryBack122nk	Game try	18
30Jly60- 5Del	sly 5½f	:212 :452 :58 1:042	Dover 24k	11	7	53¾	45½	34	21¾	Lawless R	116	*2.90	98-15	KiscoKid1161¾CarryBack1161¾NashuaBlue1163	Closed well	12
20Jly60- 7Aqu	fst 5½f	:23 :464 :59 1:05	Great American 29k	3	3	1hd	3nk	21½	32	Lawless R	117	6.60	92-15	HailtoReason1242Bronzerullah117hdCarryBck117hd	Bore out	12
4Jly60- 5Del	fst 5½f	:214 :453 :573 1:041	©Christiana 23k	4	4	1hd	1hd	11	2½	Lawless R	116	8.00	100-10	ItsaGreatDay125½CarryBack116½CoveredBridge1163	Sharp	9
22Jun60- 7Mth	fst 5½f	:214 :451 :574 1:043	©Tyro 26k	11	7	86¾	65¾	32½	33	Lawless R	115	24.00f	92-12	Chinchilla111½Song of Wine1152½Carry Back1151¾	Game try	14
10Jun60- 6Mth	fst 5½f	:23 :464 :593 1:053	Alw 5000	4	7	73	61¾	76½	56½	Blum W	122	4.90	83-14	Globemaster1222NobleMaestro114½GoldenSixts1221	Bore out	8
18May60- 7GS	sly 5f	:224 :473 :594	Cherry Hill 19k	4	10	107½	88½	78¾	1019	Hartack W	116	*1.90	72-23	IronRail11310SongofWine1132½Reltv114hd	Very dull effort	15
18Apr60- 5GP	fst 5f	:222 :452 :573	Alw 5000	4	2	2hd	1hd	1hd	1½	Hartack W	114	*2.35	107-07	CarryBack114½[D]IronRail1183SongofWn1161½	Fully extended	8
13Apr60- 3GP	fst 4½f	:221 :452 :513	Alw 3000	1	10		65	65	21¼	Hartack W	114	*1.50	100-00	Editorialist1161¼Carry Back1141Glad116hd	Off slowly	12
17Mar60- 5GP	fst 3f	:214 :332	Alw 5000	9	9			44½	42½	Thornburg B	113	40.40	--	Opus115hdIronRail1151[D]LittleTumbler1121½	Mild late bid	14
	Placed third through disqualification															
24Feb60- 7Hia	gd 3f	:22 :334	ⓈHialeah Breeders 24k	17	6			62¼	21¾	Hartack W	120	7.05	--	MyOldFlame1171¾CarryBack120hdJultt117hd	Finished gamely	18
10Feb60- 3Hia	fst 3f	:221 :334	Alw 3500	4	3			34	43½	Layton JR	114	15.85	--	Fading Sky1152New Pepi118¾Mt. Hope118¾	No late response	8
3Feb60- 3Hia	fst 3f	:221 :34	ⓈMd Sp Wt	14	2			21	1nk	Layton JR	118	*1.75f	--	CarryBack118nkKalmia1151½Milndr118½	Under a brisk drive	14
29Jan60- 3Hia	fst 3f	:221 :333	©Md Sp Wt	6	12			89	109¼	Layton JR	114	4.10	--	Opus1184Agapanthus1183Milander113nk	Crowded back early	12

Chateaugay

ch. c. 1960, by Swaps (Khaled)–Banquet Bell, by Polynesian

Lifetime record: 24 11 4 2 $360,722

Own.– Darby Dan Farm

Br.– John W. Galbreath (Ky)

Tr.– J.P. Conway

20Feb65- 8Hia	fst 1¼	:464 1:111 1:371 2:033	3↑ Widener H 135k	11	7	914	109¾	712	716	Baeza B	120	7.40	64-15	PrimordialII118½HotDust1124YourAlibha1131	Showed little	12
6Feb65- 8Hia	fst 1⅛	:471 1:113 1:372 1:504	3↑ Seminole H 65k	4	2	49	69	55	87¾	Baeza B	124	3.80	73-22	Sunstruck119noPiave114nkPointduJour1161½	Fell far back	13
23Jan65- 8Hia	fst 7f	:23 :453 1:101 1:231	3↑ Royal Palm H 30k	5	7	78	77¾	66¼	58½	Broussard R	126	*1.40	84-19	Sunstruck1185Rainy Lake1181¾Morry E.116½	Carried wide	8
16Jan65- 9Hia	fst 7f	:233 :462 1:11 1:234	4↑ Alw 6500	2	9	43½	45	33	1nk	Baeza B	117	*.80	90-20	Chateaugy117nkKnightlyMannr117¾Bbngton119no	Hand ride	9
6Aug64- 6Sar	fst 7f	:23 :46 1:104 1:231	3↑ Alw 8500	1	5	68	67	33	11	Baeza B	124	*1.00e	94-14	Chateaugay1241Decidedly124nkMatch Wits1086	Handy score	7
20May64- 7Aqu	fst 7f	:231 :464 1:113 1:242	3↑ Roseben H 29k	6	4	95¼	96¾	44	2¾	Baeza B	124	*3.10	83-25	Bonjour112¾Chateaugay1242½Red Gar112¾	Wide,game effort	10
2May64- 7Aqu	fst 7f	:223 :451 1:09 1:213	3↑ Carter H 57k	11	1	109½	913	813	812	Baeza B	126	3.65	86-13	Ahoy1332Red Gar112½Gun Bow1261	Never a serious threat	11
16Oct63- 9Suf	fst 1⅛	:464 1:103 1:36 1:49	Yankee H 58k	7	7	815	8711	57	44¾	Baeza B	127	2.30	91-13	NeverBend1264DeanCarl123½QuestLink117nk	Mild late bid	9
2Oct63- 7Aqu	fst 1⅝	:491 1:401 2:04 2:42	Lawrence Realizatn 56k	2	2	43	57½	411	410	Baeza B	126	*.70	85-13	DeanCarl1203¾B.Major120nkMasterDennis1166	No excuse	9
14Sep63- 7Aqu	fst 1	:233 :47 1:113 1:36	Jerome H 57k	7	5	42½	21	21	1½	Baeza B	128	*1.35	88-13	Chateaugay128½Accordant117½Outing Class123½	Driving	7
5Sep63- 7Aqu	fst 7f	:234 :47 1:111 1:232	Handicap 10000	5	2	53	54¾	41½	11	Baeza B	130	*.40	89-18	Chateaugay1301Tropical Breeze1152½Time Step1111	Easily	5
17Aug63- 6Sar	fst 1¼	:472 1:111 1:36 2:022	Travers 81k	4	5	56	44	43½	32½	Baeza B	126	1.75	93-08	Crewman1201½Hot Dust1141Chateaugay1262½	Bore in stretch	6
13Jly63- 7Aqu	fst 1¼	:47 1:111 1:354 2:013	Dwyer H 85k	9	8	814	75¾	55½	31½	Baeza B	129	*.80e	90-08	Outing Class1221Tenacle108½Chateaugay129no	Closed fast	10
8Jun63- 7Aqu	fst 1½	:492 1:143 2:044 2:301	Belmont 145k	5	4	45	32½	1½	12½	Baeza B	126	4.50	--	Chateaugay1262½Candy Spots1261Choker1264	Scored easily	7
18May63- 8Pim	fst 1 3/16	:472 1:113 1:37 1:561	Preakness 180k	4	6	68½	43	21½	23½	Baeza B	126	2.90	88-12	Candy Spots1263½Chteaugay1264½NeverBend1262¼	Game try	8
4May63- 7CD	fst 1¼	:462 1:10 1:352 2:014	Ky Derby 151k	1	6	610	43	11	11¼	Baeza B	126	9.40	93-08	Chateaugay1261¼Never Bend126nkCandy Spots1264¾	Driving	9
25Apr63- 6Kee	fst 1⅛	:462 1:103 1:353 1:48	Blue Grass 30k	1	2	32½	42	1hd	1hd	Baeza B	121	*1.30	97-12	Chateaugay121hdGet Around1213½Lemon Twist121½		10
	Overcame trouble															
10Apr63- 7Kee	fst 1 1/16	:234 :472 1:111 1:431	Alw 4500	5	1	12	12	11	1¾	Ycaza M	120	*.30	98-08	Chateaugay120¾Sleuth Hound1122½Bowl Along11411	Easily	5
23Feb63- 5Hia	fst 7f	:231 :46 1:103 1:233	Alw 5000	6	3	34	22½	11	1¾	Grant H	115	2.90	91-18	Chateaugay115¾Pack Trip1153½Bally Squire1154	All out	9
24Nov62- 8Pim	gd 1 1/16	:251 :494 1:144 1:47	Pim Futurity 117k	7	9	72	1hd	2½	41¼	Grant H	122	5.80	74-22	RightProud122nkDeltaJudge122nkMastrDennis122¾	Swerved	9
17Nov62- 6Pim	fst 6f	:232 :47 :592 1:114	Alw 4000	8	4	21	2hd	1hd	1hd	Ferraro R5	113	*.70	91-20	Chateaugy113hdSirGay1185TheSmoochr1113	Strong urging	11
3Nov62- 5Aqu	sly 1	:24 :48 1:123 1:373	Alw 5000	1	1	11	1hd	21	21½	Shoemaker W	122	*.60	78-18	RoylAscot1191½Chateaugay12214RaritanValley1192½	Gamely	6
25Oct62- 4Bel	fst 7f	:224 :461 1:11 1:234	©Md Sp Wt	11	2	12	11½	12½	16	Baeza B	122	*.90	88-16	Chateaugy1226HoistHimAboard1226½FredmFghtr1222	Easily	14
17Oct62- 1Bel	fst 6f	:224 :462 1:111	©Md Sp Wt	6	5	53½	42	24	22½	Baeza B	122	*1.20	88-11	Might and Main1222½Chateaugay1221¾RunningBowline1221½		14
	Gamely															

Cicada

b. f. 1959, by Bryan G. (Blenheim II)–Satsuma, by Bossuet — **Lifetime record: 42 23 8 6 $783,674**

Own.– Meadow Stable
Br.– Meadow Stud Inc (Ky)
Tr.– J.H. Hayes

15Oct64- 8GS	fst	6f	:221 :451 1:10	3↑ Alw 5000	6	8	76¼	65½	52½	43¼	Shoemaker W	110	*.90	91-12	Relative113 1½Ed'sScholr113nkRhwn122 1½	No stretch threat	8
27Jly63- 7Del	fst	1¼	:464 1:131 1:374 2:04	3↑ ⒻDelaware H 172k	5	7	74½	54	31½	2½	Shoemaker W	128	*1.80	81-20	Waltz Song116½Cicada128noTable Mate123 1¼	Saddle slipped	10
6Jly63- 7Aqu	fm	1 1/16Ⓣ	1:422	3↑ ⒻSheepshead Bay H 28k	3	6	2½	11	12½	1nk	Adams L	128	*1.45	96-04	Cicada128nkNubile1091DollIn117 1½	Hard drive,just lasted	7
12Jun63- 7Aqu	fst	7f	:224 :461 1:101 1:224	3↑ ⒻVagrancy H 21k	2	5	32½	2hd	12	13½	Adams L	127	*.70	92-13	Cicada127 3½Bramalea120½My Portrait1144	Speed to spare	5
25May63- 7Aqu	fst	1⅛	:473 1:111 1:354 1:483	3↑ ⒻTop Flight H 55k	4	3	32	3nk	34½	37	Adams L	128	*1.45	91-09	FirmPolicy125 4½Tamarona111 2½Cicd128¾	Drifted out,tiring	7
17Apr63- 7Aqu	fst	7f	:221 :442 1:09 1:213	3↑ ⒻDistaff H 22k	7	1	34½	34	1½	14	Shoemaker W	125	*.85	98-10	Cicada1254Pocosaba119½Royal Patrice120nk	Ridden out	7
27Mar63- 8GP	fst	7f	:224 :46 1:102 1:231	3↑ ⒻSuwannee River H 16k	4	6	68¼	33½	22½	21¼	Shoemaker W	126	*.50	95-18	OldHat117 1¼Cicad126 4½Coupd'Ett111 1½	In close early,wide	6
27Feb63- 8Hia	fst	1⅛	:464 1:111 1:362 1:492	4↑ ⒻBlack Helen H 47k	4	4	46	33½	34½	58½	Rotz JL	126	*.45	79-14	Pocosaba117hdOldHat1155MissMarcela114 2¾	Pulled up sore	8
13Feb63- 8Hia	gd	7f	:23 :453 1:104 1:234	3↑ ⒻColumbiana H 30k	6	4	45	33½	1½	11¾	Rotz JL	125	*1.30	90-16	Cicada125 1¾RoyalPatrice121½OldHt115 1½	Drew clear easily	7
3Nov62- 7Aqu	sly	1 5/16	:47 1:122 1:383 2:103	3↑ ⒻLadies H 57k	2	1	11½	13	2½	54¾	Shoemaker W	122	*1.80	87-18	Royal Patrice1141Waltz Song115 2¾Oil Royalty1131	Tired	10
20Oct62- 7GS	fst	1⅛	:491 1:132 1:383 1:504	3↑ ⒻVineland H 57k	4	4	31½	41¼	51¼	44¾	Shoemaker W	123	*.70	78-15	Tamarona110hdShirlyJones126 2¼LincolnCntr112 2½	Stumbled	7
13Oct62- 7GS	fst	1 1/16	:234 :474 1:121 1:451	ⒻJersey Belle 27k	1	3	3½	2¼	11	15½	Valenzuela I	121	*.30	84-20	Cicada121 5½LincolnCenter112hdRareStamp115 3½	Clear score	6
22Sep62- 7Aqu	fst	1⅛	:463 1:103 1:354 1:481	3↑ ⒻBeldame 87k	5	9	62¼	41½	11	11½	Shoemaker W	118	3.95	101-06	Cicada118 1½ShirlyJons123 2¼FrmPolcy118 1½	Strong pressure	13
18Aug62- 6Sar	fst	1¼	:472 1:11 1:352 2:013	Travers 82k	5	5	45¼	53¾	64¼	76¾	Ussery R	118	10.05	93-07	Jaipur126noRidan1261Military Plume114¾	Bore in at start	7
11Aug62- 6Sar	my	1¼	:48 1:13 1:384 2:06	ⒻAlabama 57k	8	2	1½	11	2½	35¼	Ussery R	124	*.80	73-21	Firm Policy121 1¾Lincoln Center114 3½Cicada124nk	Gave way	9
28Jly62- 6Del	fst	1¼	:474 1:113 1:363 2:023	3↑ ⒻDelaware H 141k	2	2	2½	13	11	2hd	Shoemaker W	114	3.80	89-21	Seven Thirty120hdCicada1147Bramalea115 1¼	Failed to last	9
14Jly62- 6Del	fst	1⅛	:472 1:121 1:391 1:52	ⒻDel Oaks 57k	1	2	1hd	1hd	32½	34	Baeza B	121	*.50	73-20	NorthSouthGal118 1½Bramalea121 2½Cicada121 2¼	Speed,tired	4
23Jun62- 7Bel	fst	1¼	:471 1:111 1:362 2:023	ⒻC C A Oaks 120k	4	3	3½	3nk	2hd	2½	Shoemaker W	121	*.45	86-13	Bramalea121½Cicad121noFrmPolcy1212	Hung final sixteenth	9
2Jun62- 7Bel	fst	1⅛	:462 1:111 1:37 1:50	ⒻMother Goose 86k	6	1	15	14	11	11	Shoemaker W	121	*.85	86-15	Cicada1211FirmPolicy1214RoyalPatrice121½	Briskly ridden	6
19May62- 7Aqu	fst	1	:223 :443 1:094 1:353	ⒻAcorn 58k	5	3	33	1hd	11	11½	Shoemaker W	121	*.25	90-10	Cicada121 1½Tamarona121½Upswpt121½	Drifted in,ridden out	8
4May62- 8CD	sly	1 1/16	:234 :47 1:114 1:443	ⒻKy Oaks 42k	1	4	4¾	11	13	13	Shoemaker W	121	*.10	89-18	Cicada1213Flaming Page116 2¾Fortunate Isle1166	Easily	6
28Apr62- 8CD	fst	7f	:222 :45 1:092 1:221	ⒻOaks Prep 16k	5	8	64¼	43	1hd	14	Shoemaker W	121	*.30	99-09	Cicada1214Dinner Partner1153Summer Sea118nk	Handy score	12
31Mar62- 7GP	fst	1⅛	:463 1:104 1:37 1:502	Florida Derby 125k	1	2	11	14	2½	2no	Shoemaker W	117	2.45	82-17	Ridan122noCicada1176Admiral'sVoyag122hd	Bore out,gamely	11
20Mar62- 7GP	fst	6f	:221 :452 1:101	3↑ ⒻAlw 4000	3	4	56	31½	11	13½	Shoemaker W	113	*.35	93-13	Ccada113 3½Coupd'Etat117½PrimFlower117 2½	Speed to spare	7
14Feb62- 7Hia	fst	7f	:224 :451 1:094 1:23	3↑ ⒻColumbiana H 33k	8	7	54¼	32½	23	23	Valenzuela I	112	*.65	92-12	Smashing Gail1163Cicada112 1½Seven Thirty1152	Game try	13
7Feb62- 6Hia	fst	6f	:22 :45 1:101	3↑ ⒻAlw 5500	2	9	53½	54	21½	12¾	Shoemaker W	108	*.75	94-13	Cicada108 2¾SevnThirty115¾DreamOn114nk	Stumbled,in hand	11
21Oct61- 7GS	sly	1 1/16	:23 :471 1:13 1:444	ⒻGardenia 161k	7	6	51¼	16	16	110	Shoemaker W	122	*1.00	86-20	Cicada12210Narola119 1¼Tamarona1198	Drew clear,eased up	8
7Oct61- 7Aqu	fst	1	:233 :462 1:111 1:364	ⒻFrizette 121k	6	3	3½	2hd	12	1½	Shoemaker W	119	*.65e	84-17	Cicada119½FirmPolicy119 3½JazzQueen1192	Under hard drive	7
25Sep61- 7Bel	fst	7f	:223 :461 1:112 1:242	ⒻAstarita 30k	6	10	85¼	83½	4¾	1hd	Shoemaker W	122	*.85	85-18	Cicada122hdFirmPolicy1162JzzQun112hd	Slow start,driving	12
9Sep61- 7Bel	fst	6f	:223 :46 1:103	ⒻMatron 98k	3	3	31½	3nk	1½	13½	Shoemaker W	119	*1.35	94-14	Cicada119 3½Jazz Queen1191Pontivy1193	Drew out with ease	9
23Aug61- 7Sar	fst	6f	:231 :463 1:12	ⒻSpinaway 80k	6	5	52	52½	1½	1nk	Valenzuela I	119	*.60e	88-12	Cicada119nkPontivy1193JazzQuen119¾	Saved ground,driving	8
7Aug61- 7Sar	fst	6f	:222 :452 1:11	ⒻSchuylerville 29k	6	4	44	2½	12	11½	Adams L	119	6.15	93-07	Cicada119 1½BatterUp1222Bramale116¾	Kept to brisk urging	10
17Jly61- 7Aqu	fst	5½f	:214 :451 :572 1:034	ⒻAstoria 27k	4	3	33½	32	22	34½	Valenzuela I	123	2.85	95-12	Polylady117 4½BatterUp123noCicad1231	Made bid,then tired	6
28Jun61- 7Mth	fst	5½f	:213 :451 :574 1:04	ⒻColleen 24k	7	5	63	42	2hd	21	Valenzuela I	119	*1.30	97-18	BatterUp1191Cicada1196Pontivy114 2¾	Bold rally,hung late	11
19Jun61- 7Bel	fst	5½f	:223 :461 :583 1:052	ⒻNat'l Stallion 30k	3	3	21	21	2hd	11½	Valenzuela I	119	4.75e	94-20	Cicada119 1½BatterUp1194JazzQueen1191	Going away,driving	8
10Jun61- 5Del	gd	5f	:22 :462 :591	ⒻPolly Drummond 24k	3	1	1hd	1hd	2hd	21¾	Corle RE	122	2.80	91-21	Broadway113 1¾Cicada122¾Miss Summer Time113 1¼	Game try	9
30May61- 5Del	fst	5f	:221 :463 :593	ⒻBlue Hen 11k	1	4	1hd	11	14	15½	Nelson E	116	3.90	91-22	Ccada116 5½DodgeM114noFlshbck110 1½	Going away with ease	12
25May61- 6Aqu	fst	5f	:23 :47 :594	ⒻAlw 5000	5	4	2½	2hd	11	13	Valenzuela I	116	*.35	91-19	Cicada1163Fingerling112 1½Go on Green1125	Speed to spare	7
17May61- 7Aqu	fst	5f	:224 :462 :584	ⒻFashion 24k	3	4	31½	21½	32	33¾	Valenzuela I	116	4.70	92-15	LaurelMae116 3½StrBolt116nkCcd116 1¾	Swerved late,brushed	9
17Mar61- 3GP	fst	3f	:22 :332	Alw 5000	8	5			2hd	1no	Hinojosa H	112	6.45	- -	Cicada112noPryann115nkPortofMecc1121	Best in hard drive	14
10Mar61- 3GP	fst	3f	:213 :324	Alw 3000	5	3			2½	3¾	Ussery R	117	*1.90	- -	Mlle.Tessa112½GutterBall117nkCcd1173	Hung final strides	14
23Feb61- 3Hia	fst	3f	:222 :34	ⒻMd Sp Wt	13	6			1½	14¼	Ussery R	117	*1.15f	- -	Cicada117 4¼AthensMiss117noSecretPort117¾	Bumped,in hand	14

Crimson Satan

ch. c. 1959, by Spy Song (Balladier)–Papila, by Requiebro — **Lifetime record: 58 18 9 9 $796,077**

Own.– Crimson King Farm
Br.– Crimson King Farm (Ky)
Tr. G.R. Pottor

24Oct64- 8Haw	fst	1¼	:472 1:112 1:363 2:013	3↑ Gold Cup H 126k	4	9	86¾	99¼	913	813	Gargan D	120	b	10.30	75-13	GoingAbroad120 2½Interceptd118½OldnTimes123 1¾	No speed	9
3Oct64- 6Kee	fst	1 1/16	:233 :464 1:103 1:42	3↑ Fayette H 28k	4	9	98¼	78¾	814	821	Hinojosa H	120		3.90	75-12	Swoonen113½City Line1194Lemon Twist116¾	Raced far back	10
19Sep64- 8Det	sly	1 1/16	:23 :471 1:14 1:49	3↑ Mich 1 1/16 H 72k	4	12	1221	1113	1023	1122	Hinojosa H	125	b	*2.80	36-34	[DH]GoingAbroad120[DH]Tibaldo112nkCloseBy115 2½	Fractious	12
12Sep64- 9Det	fst	1 1/16	:23 :464 1:112 1:442	3↑ Handicap 15000	7	10	1021	913	-	-	Hinojosa H	126	b	*.60	- -	CityLine121¾Swoonen115½Tibaldo114 1½	Unruly gate,bore in	10
	Sulked																	
5Sep64- 9Det	fst	6f	:213 :442 1:092	3↑ Handicap 7500	6	7	712	66	42½	12½	Hinojosa H	122	b	*.70	99-10	CrimsnSatan122 2½YouLookCute109nkRedEff1205	Easy score	7
19Aug64- 7Det	fst	6f	:22 :444 1:103	3↑ Alw 3000	1	9	54	21	2hd	34½	Gargan D	122	b	*1.50	88-16	MissMaru109 1½LoriJ.1103CrimsonSatan122½	Bold bid,tired	9
21Jan64- 7SA	gd	1 1/16	:231 :464 1:114 1:442	4↑ San Pasqual H 28k	6	7	55	52½	52¾	55	Pierce D	126	b	*1.60	77-26	OldenTimes120¾DocJocoy118hdDonutKing1134	Wide on turn	8
15Jan64- 7SA	fst	1 1/16	:231 :462 1:104 1:422	4↑ Alw 10000	8	7	43	2hd	1hd	12	Pierce D	124	b	*2.20	92-11	Crimson Satan1242Pirate Cove121¾Aldershot118½	Driving	8
4Jan64- 8SA	fst	7f	:221 :444 1:092 1:22	4↑ San Carlos H 59k	6	8	75	42	63¾	811	Chambers W	123	b	11.10	82-14	Admiral'sVoyage1242Cyrano126¾NativeDiver125½	Fell back	8
2Nov63- 8GS	my	1¼	:464 1:111 1:361 2:014	3↑ Trenton H 59k	10	10	108¼	54¼	49	513	Shoemaker W	122	b	*3.30	83-22	Carry Back119 2½Mongo1242Smart1166	Bold bid,weakened	10
19Oct63- 8Haw	sl	1¼	:463 1:11 1:373 2:034	3↑ Haw Gold Cup H 127k	8	9	913	75½	78½	67	Shoemaker W	120	b	*1.10	70-17	AdmiralVic122 1½DonutKing115½Pipr'sSon1103	Dismal effort	10
28Sep63- 7Aqu	fst	1¼	:473 1:114 1:362 2:004	3↑ Woodward 108k	1	5	56½	32½	33½	35	Hinojosa H	126	b	10.00	91-13	Kelso126 3½NeverBend120 1½CrimsonSatan1266	Bold bid,hung	5
14Sep63- 8Atl	fm	1 3/16Ⓣ	1:551	3↑ U Nations H 125k	5	10	109¼	96¼	94½	87	Hinojosa H	125	b	9.30	90-03	Mongo1242Never Bend118¾Carry Back127 1½	Failed to rally	10
	Daily Racing Form time,1:54 2/5																	
2Sep63- 7Aqu	fst	1⅛	:49 1:124 1:371 1:494	3↑ Aqueduct 110k	3	8	89	66½	45	25½	Hinojosa H	129	b	6.00	86-17	Kelso134 5½Crimson Satan129hdGarwol116no	Finished gamely	8
24Aug63- 8AP	my	1⅛	:47 1:111 1:364 1:493	3↑ Wash Park H 113k	6	10	1016	911	33	12	Hinojosa H	126	b	*2.40	88-19	CrimsonSatan1262Piper'sSon110nkB.Major117 4¼	Dwelt,wide	10
13Jly63- 8Hol	fst	1¼	:45 1:09 1:333 1:593	3↑ Hol Gold Cup H 162k	3	9	914	62¼	99¼	1016	Hinojosa H	125	b	*.80	79-14	Cadz111 1½Aldrshot1103OlympdKng111¾	Appeared unruly turn	10
22Jun63- 9Det	fst	1 1/16	:224 :453 1:103 1:403	3↑ Mich 1 1/16 H 58k	9	10	96½	61¼	1½	15½	Hinojosa H	128	b	*2.30	106-09	Crimson Satan128 5½Decidedly117nkGreek Money1143	Easily	10
5Jun63- 9Suf	fst	1¼	:461 1:101 1:351 2:011	3↑ Mass H 59k	1	10	914	11	1½	12½	Hinojosa H	124	b	*2.10	99-12	CrimsnSatn124 2½Admrl'sVoyg1253SunrsCounty120no	Driving	11
30May63- 7Aqu	fst	1	:223 :451 1:10 1:35	3↑ Metropolitan H 115k	3	11	118¾	86½	55	44	Hinojosa H	123	b	4.30	89-10	Cyrano113 1½George Barton1142Sunrise County121½	Bore in	12
27Apr63- 7Aqu	fst	1⅛	:482 1:111 1:361 1:50	3↑ Grey Lag H 84k	4	6	42	1hd	12	21¼	Gomez A	123	b	3.25	90-18	SunriseCounty118 1¼CrimsnSatan123 1½Decidedly120¾	Sulked	9
23Mar63- 8Bow	fst	1 1/16	:242 :481 1:12 1:43	3↑ J B Campbell H 109k	1	6	69½	57¾	34½	2¾	Hinojosa H	124	b	6.70	97-15	Kelso131¾Crimson Satan124hdGushing Wind1166	Late rush	6
9Mar63- 7SA	fm	*1¾Ⓣ	2:481	3↑ S Juan Capistrano H 115k	6	4	11½	2hd	89½	1217	Hinojosa H	125	b	*2.90	69-15	Pardao119nkJuanro114nkRablero119½	Early speed,stopped	13
23Feb63- 7SA	fst	1¼	:462 1:103 1:352 2:004	3↑ S Anita H 145k	9	11	106½	32	34½	25½•	Hinojosa H	125	b	*.90	89-13	Crozier122 5½[DH]Game108[DH]CrimsonSatan125 3¼	Evenly late	14
9Feb63- 7SA	sly	1⅛	:472 1:114 1:374 1:51	4↑ San Antonio H 58k	2	5	51¾	12	13	21	Hinojosa H	127	b	*1.30	76-21	Physician1171CrimsonSatan127 9¼Gam107 2½	Clear lead,tired	6
26Jan63- 7SA	fst	1¼	:464 1:113 1:352 2:003	C H Strub 137k	6	14	147½	13	18	15¾	Hinojosa H	118	b	*.70	96-10	CrimsonSatan118 5¾PirateCove1142Dr.Kacy112nk	Easily best	16
12Jan63- 7SA	fst	1⅛	:453 1:093 1:344 1:471	San Fernando 58k	12	7	49½	2½	2½	1nk	Hinojosa H	117	b	1.70	96-12	CrimsonSatan117nkNativeDiver12010PirateCove1142	Driving	14
5Jan63- 7SA	fst	7f	:214 :442 1:084 1:211	4↑ San Carlos H 61k	4	10	911	97¾	87¾	46	Hinojosa H	121	b	20.60	91-12	Crozier124 1¼OldenTimes125noNativeDiver125 4¾	Mild rally	10
17Nov62- 8CD	gd	1⅛	:482 1:13 1:372 1:50	3↑ Clark H 27k	3	7	64½	55	1½	11¼	Hinojosa H	121	b	*1.80	92-18	CrimsonSatan121 1¼TumbleTurbie116hdBassClef1173	Driving	8

10Sep62- 8AP	sf	1 3/16 (T)	:484 1:121 1:382 1:583	3↑ Arlington H 57k	10	11	89	75¾	73¾	21	Gomez A	122	b	*1.40	73-24	El Bandito1151Crimson Satan122nkRablero109no	Slow start	13
1Sep62- 8AP	fm	1 1/16 (T)	:231 :463 1:11 1:42	Laurance Armour H 33k	6	7	52¼	2hd	12	12½	Gomez A	123	b	3.40	99-04	CrimsnSatn1232½TumbleTurbi1091½GshngWnd122¼	Driving	10
18Aug62- 8Tdn	fst	1⅛	:461 1:102 1:351 1:48	3↑ Buckeye H 29k	10	9	88	51	32½	36¼	Baldwin R	121	b	*1.20	94-10	GushngWind1181½BlackBeard1114¾CrmsnStn1213	No excuse	10
11Aug62- 8Tdn	fst	1 1/16	:232 :47 1:112 1:423	3↑ Handicap 7500	3	6	59	32½	31½	1nk	Baldwin R	119	b	*1.10	102-12	Crimson Satan119nkMysticMountain1092¼Touch Bar112½	Bore in,up	6
1Aug62- 8Mth	fst	1 1/16	:232 :472 1:104 1:42	Choice 56k	3	5	53½	54	44½	35¼	Ycaza M	118	b	2.90	90-16	Jaipur1264½Cyane126¾Crimson Satan118¾	Forced wide late	8
14Jly62- 7Aqu	fst	1¼	:471 1:104 1:36 2:013	Dwyer H 84k	1	6	32	11½	3½	47½	Gilligan L	125	b	*1.30	90-11	Cyane116¾Flying Johnnie1114Noble Jay1192¾	Bore out turn	9
23Jun62- 6Del	fst	1⅛	:473 1:112 1:374 1:504	Leonard Richards 42k	1	5	32½	2hd	12	11¼	Gilligan L	122	b	*.80	83-20	Crimson Satan1221¼Noble Jay1193½Cyane1194½	Handy score	6
			Disqualified from purse money															
9Jun62- 7Bel	fst	1½	:482 1:121 2:021 2:284	Belmont 153k	1	4	33	31	3½	31¼	Ycaza M	126	b	3.80	88-11	Jaipur126noAdmiral'sVoyage1261¼CrimsonSatn1266½	Bore in	8
30May62- 8GS	fst	1⅛	:47 1:102 1:354 1:49	Jersey Derby 130k	6	6	52	3nk	1hd	1no	Gilligan L	126	b	10.10	92-14	[D]CrimsonSatan126noJaipur126noAdmiral'sVoyg1261	Bore in	12
			Disqualified and placed third															
19May62- 8Pim	fst	1 3/16	:474 1:114 1:37 1:561	Preakness 188k	7	6	63¾	62¼	58	712	Phelps B	126	b	13.80	80-13	Greek Money126noRidan1265¼RomanLine1261¾	No mishap	11
5May62- 7CD	fst	1¼	:454 1:101 1:351 2:002	Ky Derby 162k	11	14	1418	1012	64¾	66¼	Phelps B	126	b	21.50	99-06	Decidedly1262¼RomanLin126nkRdn126nk	Bumped at the start	15
26Apr62- 6Kee	fst	1⅛	:473 1:111 1:354 1:473	Blue Grass 33k	6	8	68	54¼	42½	58½	Phelps B	126	b	2.50	90-10	Ridan1264Decidedly1212¼Roman Line1262¼	Wide stretch bid	9
7Apr62- 7Kee	fst	6f	:222 :453 1:102	Alw 5000	4	7	57	22½	12	15	Phelps B	122	b	*.70	92-14	CrimsnSatan1225LeeTown1192¼LoilRoil1163	Scored handily	8
3Mar62- 7Hia	fst	1⅛	:452 1:094 1:353 1:49	Flamingo 136k	10	10	1019	1015	912	715	Shoemaker W	122	b	2.80	75-09	[D]SunriseCounty1221½Prego122nkRidan1224½	Showed nothing	10
21Feb62- 7Hia	fst	1⅛	:46 1:101 1:353 1:482	Everglades 30k	8	9	914	78	614	516	Shoemaker W	122	b	2.30	77-14	SirGaylord1264¾Decidedly1143[D]Ridan126½	Stumbled start	9
7Feb62- 7Hia	fst	7f	:223 :452 1:092 1:22	Bahamas 30k	3	8	813	78¾	34½	35	Shoemaker W	126	b	3.80	95-13	SirGaylord1261¾Ridan1263¼CrimsonSatan1266	Bold bid,hung	8
30Jan62- 7Hia	fst	6f	:223 :453 1:092	Alw 6000	7	9	75¾	32	2hd	2¾	Gilligan L	122	b	3.50	97-14	SirGaylord122¾CrimsonSatan1221½FloridnBy1107	Mild drive	11
18Nov61- 8Pim	gd	1 1/16	:24 :474 1:13 1:462	Pim Futurity 116k	7	7	75¼	2½	12	15	Shoemaker W	122	b	*.30	78-21	CrimsonSatan1225GreenTicket122nkEndymion1221	Mild drive	7
4Nov61- 7GS	fst	1 1/16	:232 :47 1:112 1:441	Garden State 301k	5	11	85¾	43½	13	12½	Shoemaker W	122	b	*1.30	89-15	CrimsnSatn1222½DonutKng122noOby1228	Under brisk drive	11
28Oct61- 5GS	fst	1 1/16	:242 :48 1:121 1:441	Alw 10000	2	4	31½	31	1hd	17	Shoemaker W	122	b	*1.10	89-13	Crimson Satan1227Pinsetter112nkDecidedly1123	Easy score	12
14Oct61- 7Aqu	fst	1	:231 :462 1:111 1:36	Champagne 206k	8	10	8¾	54	43½	42	Phelps B	122	b	6.85	85-16	DonutKing122hdJaipur1222SirGaylord122no	Stride too late	10
7Oct61- 8Haw	fst	1 1/16	:224 :46 1:111 1:431	Haw Juv (Div 2) 18k	3	9	713	45	15	16	Phelps B	114	b	*.90	91-13	Crimson Satan1146Treasury Note1141½Affray1145	Easily	9
30Sep61- 7Haw	sly	1 1/16	:231 :472 1:132 1:472	Alw 5000	10	8	56	2hd	16	16	Phelps B	113	b	4.30	70-25	Crimson Satan1136Dogeola1137Neck Bones113nk	Hard urged	11
22Sep61- 6Haw	fst	6½f	:222 :451 1:101 1:172	Alw 6000	1	9	43½	33½	2½	2nk	Carstens W	114	b	*1.20	87-21	Renade113nkCrimsonSatn114noCraftyActor1131½	Slow start	9
13Sep61- 8Haw	sl	6f	:222 :462 1:13	©Alw 10000	3	8	64	32	31	22	Carstens W	122	b	7.20	80-26	LoilRoil1132CrimsonSatan1221PutOff116¾	Game effort	8
21Jun61- 8AP	fst	5½f	:223 :46 :581 1:042	Hyde Park 17k	8	6	51¼	3½	46	69¼	Carstens W	122	b	28.20	86-16	Ridan1226GreenHornet119noPortofMecca119no	Well up,tired	8
14Jun61- 6Was	fst	5½f	:222 :451 :572 1:032	Alw 5000	5	6	52¾	21½	33½	38	Carstens W	122	b	5.40	90-13	Ridan1176Obey1142Crimson Satan1223	Well placed,tired	7
26Apr61- 6Kee	fst	*4f	:49	Lafayette 15k	6	7		42½	1½	11¾	Carstens W	117	b	2.10	97-07	CrimsnSatn1171¾MikeG.1176JettingHome117hd	Handy score	7
18Apr61- 3Kee	gd	*4f	:492	Md Sp Wt	4	3		33½	22	1¾	Carstens W	120	b	*1.40	95-06	Crimson Satan120¾Tom Turkey1205Dusty Guy1207	Driving	7
11Apr61- 2Kee	gd	*4f	:50	©Md Sp Wt	3	5		3nk	21½	3¾	Carstens W	119	b	*2.00	91-09	I'mforMore119¾Uppercut119hdCrimsonSatan1193½	Game try	12

Damascus

b. c. 1964, by Sword Dancer (Sunglow)–Kerala, by My Babu

Lifetime record: 32 21 7 3 $1,176,781

Own.– Mrs Edith W. Bancroft
Br.– Mrs Thomas Bancroft (Ky)
Tr.– F.Y. Whiteley Jr

26Oct68- 7Bel	gd	2	:502 2:313 3:224	3↑ J C Gold Cup 109k	1	3	48	612	624	637	Adams L	124	*1.30	48-16	QuickenTree1241¼FunnyFllow1193½Chmpon1193	Bowed tendon	6
28Sep68- 7Bel	fst	1¼	:472 1:113 1:37 2:03	3↑ Woodward 106k	3	2	1hd	1hd	1hd	2no	Baeza B	126	*.10	85-16	Mr. Right126noDamascus1267Grace Born12616	Just failed	4
14Sep68- 9Det	fst	1⅛	:471 1:111 1:361 1:49	3↑ Mich 1⅛ H 123k	1	9	1014	79½	66¾	22¾	Baeza B	133	*.30e	93-19	Nodouble1112¾Dmscs133hdMstyRun1092¼	Very wide stretch	12
2Sep68- 7Aqu	fst	1⅛	:47 1:11 1:354 1:482	3↑ Aqueduct 108k	4	3	35	33	2½	11½	Baeza B	134	*.40	94-13	Damascus1341½More Scents1148Fort Drum1143	Going away	6
10Aug68- 8Del	fst	1 1/16	:24 :484 1:123 1:433	3↑ W Du Pont H 53k	4	5	31	2hd	1hd	12	Baeza B	134	*.20	91-20	Damascus1342BigRockCandy113¾CharlesElliott11010	Driving	5
20Jly68- 7Aqu	fst	1¼	:454 1:092 1:343 1:591	3↑ Brooklyn H 109k	2	5	511	2½	1½	12½	Ycaza M	130	1.40e	102-13	Damascus1302½Dr. Fager1353Mr. Right114hd	Won going away	7
13Jly68- 8Mth	fst	1¼	:48 1:121 1:371 2:03	3↑ AL Haskell H 111k	6	6	68	33	21	31½	Ycaza M	131	*.60	85-16	BoldHour1161¼Mr.Rght114nkDmscus1315	Stumbled after start	8
4Jly68- 7Aqu	fst	1¼	:482 1:11 1:343 1:593	3↑ Suburban H 107k	1	2	2½	2hd	22	35	Ycaza M	133	1.40	95-11	Dr. Fager1322Bold Hour1163Damascus1333½	Failed to rally	5
17Jun68- 5Del	fst	1 70	:234 :473 1:114 1:402	4↑ Alw 10000	3	3	24	2hd	11	13¾	Ycaza M	124	*.10	98-16	Damascus1243¾LighttheFuse1196ClassicWork120nk	Handily	5
10Feb68- 8SA	sl	1¼	:482 1:131 1:382 2:04	C H Strub 118k	1	5	57	1½	1hd	2hd	Turcotte R	126	*.20	78-22	Most Host114hdDamscs12610Ruken117½	Gave way gradually	6
20Jan68- 6SA	fst	1⅛	:49 1:13 1:371 1:484	San Fernando 56k	4	2	2½	1hd	11	12	Shoemaker W	126	*.10	88-12	Damascs1262Most Host113hdRuken1204½	Won drawing clear	6
6Jan68- 8SA	fst	7f	:223 :45 1:09 1:211	Malibu 45k	4	1	32½	3½	1½	12½	Shoemaker W	126	*.40	97-15	Damascus1262½Rising Market120nkRuken1231	Handily	8
11Nov67- 7Lrl	fm	1½ (T)	:491 1:14 2:03 2:27	3↑ D C Int'l 150k	2	4	43½	3½	2hd	2no	Shoemaker W	120	*.60	84-13	FortMarcy120noDmascus1202½TobinBronze1272½	Just failed	9
28Oct67- 7Aqu	fst	2	:494 2:302 2:554 3:201	3↑ J C Gold Cup 106k	1	2	22	2hd	14	14½	Shoemaker W	119	*.30	95-12	Dmascus1194½HandsomBoy1247½Successr1196½	Handy score	4
30Sep67- 7Aqu	fst	1¼	:451 1:091 1:353 2:003	3↑ Woodward 107k	5	5	512	1½	15	110	Shoemaker W	120	1.80e	95-15	Damascus12010Buckpasser126½Dr. Fager12013	Easy score	6
4Sep67- 7Aqu	fst	1⅛	:482 1:121 1:361 1:481	3↑ Aqueduct 106k	3	3	34	32	1hd	12	Shoemaker W	125	*.30	95-14	Damascus1252Ring Twice119½Straight Deal1166	Handily	5
19Aug67- 6Sar	sly	1¼	:454 1:11 1:364 2:013	Travers 80k	4	3	316	16	110	122	Shoemaker W	126	*.20	100-10	Damascus12622Reason to Hail1207Tumiga1175	Won eased up	4
5Aug67- 8AP	fst	1⅛	:46 1:101 1:343 1:464	American Derby 120k	2	6	612	66¼	14	17	Shoemaker W	126	*.80	101-16	Damascus1267InReality1203FavorableTurn1121½	Ridden out	7
15Jly67- 7Aqu	sly	1¼	:473 1:12 1:374 2:03	Dwyer H 83k	6	9	912	21	1hd	1¾	Shoemaker W	128	*.50	83-18	Damascus128¾FavorableTurn1122½BlastingChrg116hd	Driving	9
8Jly67- 8Del	fst	1 1/16	:234 :471 1:104 1:421	3↑ W Du Pont Jr H 54k	4	5	58	43	21	2no	Shoemaker W	121	*.20	98-12	Exceedingly113noDamascus1214Flag Raiser1145	Hung	5
17Jun67- 8Del	fst	1⅛	:47 1:113 1:37 1:491	Leonard Richards 41k	4	4	32½	1½	1hd	13¼	Turcotte R	126	*.10	91-13	Damascus1263¼Misty Cloud1191½Favorable Turn1192½	Easily	6
3Jun67- 8Aqu	fst	1½	:47 1:122 2:023 2:284	Belmont 148k	1	6	59½	31	2hd	12½	Shoemaker W	126	*.80	87-15	Dmscus1262½CoolReception126½GentlmanJams1261	In hand	9
20May67- 8Pim	fst	1 3/16	:462 1:104 1:364 1:551	Preakness 194k	2	9	811	88	13½	12¼	Shoemaker W	126	*1.80e	97-11	Damascus1262¼In Reality1264Proud Clarion126¾	Ridden out	10
6May67- 7CD	fst	1¼	:463 1:104 1:36 2:003	Ky Derby 162k	2	6	44	41½	32	34	Shoemaker W	126	*1.70	93-07	ProudClarion1261BarbsDelight1263Damascus1261¼	Bid,hung	14
22Apr67- 7Aqu	fst	1⅛	:462 1:104 1:363 1:493	Wood Memorial 112k	4	3	45	42	11	16	Shoemaker W	126	*.70	88-16	Damascus1266Gala Performance1263Dawn Glory1261½	Easily	9
15Apr67- 7Aqu	fst	1	:233 :461 1:102 1:351	Gotham 57k	9	2	23	2hd	1hd	2½	Shoemaker W	122	*1.30	91-14	Dr. Fager122½Damascus1225Reason to Hail1147	Game try	9
25Mar67- 7Aqu	my	7f	:224 :464 1:124 1:254	Bay Shore 28k	1	4	46	45½	22	12½	Shoemaker W	115	2.40	77-35	Damascus1152½Disciplinarian1171½Nhoc'sBullt1103	Driving	7
11Mar67- 7Pim	fst	6f	:233 :472 1:121	Alw 5000	8	3	31½	42	53¼	1hd	Shuk N	122	*.60	89-16	Dmascus122hdSolar Bomb1221¼Last Cry119½	Bumped late,up	8
30Nov66- 7Aqu	gd	1	:231 :46 1:112 1:37	Remsen 30k	2	3	2hd	32	4¾	11½	Shoemaker W	117	*1.30	83-22	Damascus1171½NativeGuile117½ReflectedGlory119¾	Driving	14
29Oct66- 3Lrl	fst	7f	:224 :462 1:121 1:251	©Alw 4000	2	1	1½	12	19	112	Shoemaker W	119	*.40	93-16	Damascus11912Joxer1153½Roman Away1172½	Scored in hand	7
12Oct66- 5Aqu	fst	7f	:23 :462 1:12 1:243	©Md Sp Wt	8	1	11	11	14	18	Shoemaker W	122	*.90	83-18	Damascus1228Winslow Homer1225Gun Mount1221	Easily	14
28Sep66- 4Aqu	fst	7f	:223 :46 1:113 1:243	©Md Sp Wt	11	9	76	77½	32½	22½	Shoemaker W	122	*2.60	80-19	Comprador1222½Damascus122¾Air Rights1221	Game try	14

Dark Mirage

dkbbr. f. 1965, by Persian Road II (Persian Gulf)–Home by Dark, by Hill Prince — Lifetime record: 27 12 3 2 $362,788

Own.– L.I. Miller
Br.– Duval A. Headley (Ky)
Tr.– E.W. King

Date/Race	Cond	Dist	Fractions	Race	Running line	Jockey	Wt	Eq	Odds	Speed	Finishers	Comment	Fld
1Mar69- 8SA	sl	1⅛	:482 1:131 1:393 1:53 4↑	ⒻS Margarita H 100k	5 5 - - - -	Belmonte E	130		*.70	- -	Princessnesian125noGuest Room1161¾Sinking Spring113¾		9
	Roughed at start,ducked out turn,broke down												
12Feb69- 8SA	fst	1 1/16	:232 :47 1:111 1:43 4↑	ⒻS Maria H 33k	2 3 41¾ 51¾ 4¾ 1nk	Belmonte E	126		*1.00	88-17	DarkMirage126nkDesertLaw115noSinkingSpring1122	Driving	7
27Jly68- 0Del	fst	1⅛	:473 1:114 1:374 1:502	ⒻDel Oaks 57k	2 3 36 22½ 2hd 12	Ycaza M	121		-	85-20	Dark Mirage1212Sale Day1148Singing Rain1172	Mild drive	4
	Exhibition race,run between 7th and 8th races - No wagering												
4Jly68- 8Mth	fst	1⅛	:471 1:121 1:382 1:512	ⒻMth Oaks 54k	3 4 43 2hd 1½ 14	Ycaza M	121		*.20	87-22	Dark Mirage1214Singing Rain1185Guest Room117hd	Easily	6
22Jun68- 7Bel	fst	1¼	:482 1:121 1:364 2:014	ⒻC C A Oaks 116k	4 3 21 13 16 112	Ycaza M	121		*.10	91-15	Dark Mirage12112Gay Matelda1216Syrian Sea1211¼	Easily	6
8Jun68- 7Bel	fst	1⅛	:452 1:101 1:36 1:492	ⒻMother Goose 85k	5 5 55½ 41½ 12½ 110	Ycaza M	121		*.20	89-15	Dark Mirage12110Guest Room121nkParida1211	Easy score	6
25May68- 7Bel	fst	1	:224 :46 1:102 1:344	ⒻAcorn 60k	2 4 42 21 1½ 16	Ycaza M	121		*1.30	100-11	Dark Mirage1216Another Nell121nkGay Matelda1212½	Easily	12
3May68- 8CD	fst	1 1/16	:243 :48 1:123 1:443	ⒻKy Oaks 63k	4 9 86½ 54¼ 2½ 14½	Ycaza M	121		*1.20	89-17	DarkMirge1214½MissRibot121½LadyTramp1213½	Handy score	14
27Apr68- 8CD	fst	7f	:23 :463 1:114 1:243	ⒻLa Troienne 16k	10 8 68 55 21 13	Ycaza M	121		2.70	84-18	Dark Mirage1213Lady Tramp1211Yes Sir1182	Ridden out	12
3Apr68- 7Aqu	fst	6f	:221 :451 1:104	ⒻPrioress 27k	5 3 66 42 21½ 11	Cordero A Jr	121		6.00	89-17	Dark Mirage1211Guest Room121nkPleasantness1213	Driving	6
22Mar68- 6Aqu	fst	1	:233 :47 1:11 1:362 3↑	ⒻAlw 12000	7 1 11½ 13 16 19	Turcotte R	112		*1.00	86-23	Dark Mirage1129Castaneye1118Wild Beauty1132	Easily best	7
15Mar68- 7Aqu	gd	6f	:224 :46 1:104	ⒻAlw 15000	1 5 55½ 55 46½ 47½	Turcotte R	114		13.60	81-21	Pleasantness1184CockeyMiss1182LucretiBor1181½	No threat	5
7Dec67- 7Aqu	fst	7f	:233 :471 1:122 1:252	ⒻAlw 15000	6 3 63¾ 43 21 2½	Turcotte R	116		3.30	78-25	APleasantSort115½DarkMirage116¾Teddy'sTrue1192	Sharp	8
30Nov67- 7Aqu	fst	6f	:222 :453 1:101	ⒻAlw 15000	9 10 1011 1014 914 611	Ycaza M	116		4.70	81-18	GuestRoom1166½Teddy'sTrue1161½TwiceCited1161	No speed	11
22Nov67- 7Aqu	fst	1	:233 :47 1:121 1:38	ⒻAlw 15000	2 5 52¾ 3nk 1hd 2hd	Ycaza M	115		5.60	78-22	Good Game116hdDark Mirage115nkA Pleasant Sort1129	Sharp	6
11Nov67- 8GS	fst	1 1/16	:234 :472 1:12 1:454	ⒻGardenia 187k	8 11 1012 88¾ 65½ 52½	Gavidia W	119		112.70	73-21	Gay Matelda119noGo Go Windy119noPleasantness1191½	Wide	11
1Nov67- 7GS	fst	1 70	:224 :482 1:112 1:423	ⒻAlw 10000	2 6 65¼ 813 88¼ 57½	Ycaza M	115		13.00	73-23	Pleasantness112noObeah1137Amadancer112hd	Showed little	8
25Oct67- 6Aqu	fst	7f	:221 :45 1:101 1:231	ⒻAlw 10000	4 8 66 65 44½ 34	Ruane J	114	b	18.20	86-12	Yes Sir1163Allie's Serenade1121Dark Mirage1141½	Rallied	8
14Oct67- 6Kee	fst	*7f	1:28	ⒻAlcibiades 50k	2 9 33½ 45 1118 1118	Grubb L	119	b	34.60	65-19	Lady Tramp1195Sweet Tooth119¾Walk My Lady1191¼	Tired	12
27Sep67- 7Aqu	fst	7f	:214 :44 1:093 1:223	ⒻAstarita 29k	7 3 44½ 33 77½ 712	Ruane J	116	b	18.00	81-13	SyrianSea1194GoodGame116½DawnofTomorrw1121¾	Fell back	10
16Sep67- 8CD	fst	7f	:223 :454 1:104 1:234	ⒻGolden Rod 62k	13 7 910 46 43½ 43¾	Ruane J	113		22.80	84-13	Shenow1191Moss1131¼Lady Tramp1161½	Stride late	13
9Sep67- 7Aqu	fst	6f	:221 :452 1:10	ⒻMatron 104k	1 7 63¾ 67 67½ 612	Ruane J	119		16.50	81-16	QueenoftheStag1194GayMatlda119¾SyrianSea1193	No threat	7
12Aug67- 4Sar	fst	6f	:22 :453 1:121	ⒻAlw 7000	2 12 54 56 31 11	Ruane J	119		4.30	87-11	Dark Mirage1191Someday109½Sassy Piece113nk	Drew clear	12
2Aug67- 6Sar	fst	5½f	:223 :461 :582 1:043	ⒻMd Sp Wt	7 3 31 2½ 1½ 14	Ruane J	119		5.20	94-08	Dark Mirage1194Chenille119noBest in Show1191	Easy score	11
26Jly67- 3Aqu	gd	5½f	:222 :454 :581 1:044	ⒻMd Sp Wt	10 7 66¾ 611 36½ 36¾	Caceres A	119		4.20	82-15	Ave Valeque1196Terri Tyker119¾Dark Mirage1196	Fair try	12
19Jly67- 3Aqu	fst	5½f	:221 :46 :584 1:052	ⒻMd Sp Wt	7 11 73¼ 64½ 64¾ 22½	Caceres A	119		101.00	83-13	FullofLaughs1092½DarkMirage1192½EsteNoche119hd	Sharp	12
14Jly67- 4Mth	fst	5½f	:222 :462 :593 1:063	ⒻMd Sp Wt	5 6 77 69 57 67¼	Brumfield D	117		21.50	77-19	TwiceCitd1171½WalkMyLdy1171BwamznLdy1173½	No threat	11

Dr. Fager

b. c. 1964, by Rough'n Tumble (Free for All)–Aspidistra, by Better Self — Lifetime record: 22 18 2 1 $1,002,642

Own.– Tartan Stable
Br.– Tartan Farms (Fla)
Tr.– John A. Nerud

Date/Race	Cond	Dist	Fractions	Race	Running line	Jockey	Wt	Eq	Odds	Speed	Finishers	Comment	Fld
2Nov68- 7Aqu	fst	7f	:221 :434 1:074 1:201 3↑	Vosburgh H 57k	3 4 1hd 1hd 13 16	Baeza B	139		*.30	105-12	Dr.Fager1396Kissin'George1276JmJ.125hd	Under mild drive	7
11Sep68- 8Atl	fm	1 3/16(T)	:484 1:123 1:364 1:551 3↑	U Nations H 100k	6 1 1hd 2hd 1hd 1nk	Baeza B	134		*.80	94-10	Dr.Fgr134nkAdvoctor1121¼FortMrcy1181¼	Under stiff drive	9
24Aug68- 8AP	fst	1	:224 :44 1:073 1:321 3↑	Washington Park H 112k	9 6 2hd 1½ 13 110	Baeza B	134		*.30	102-10	Dr. Fager13410Racing Room1161½Info1121	Easily best	10
3Aug68- 6Sar	fst	1⅛	:471 1:113 1:363 1:484 3↑	Whitney 53k	2 1 1½ 13 13 18	Baeza B	132		*.05	97-12	Dr. Fager1328Spoon Bait1141Fort Drum11415	Much the best	4
20Jly68- 7Aqu	fst	1¼	:454 1:092 1:343 1:591 3↑	Brooklyn H 109k	3 2 21½ 1½ 2½ 22½	Baeza B	135		*.60	99-13	Damascus1302½Dr.Fager1353Mr.Right114hd	Rank early going	7
4Jly68- 7Aqu	fst	1¼	:482 1:11 1:343 1:593 3↑	Suburban H 107k	3 1 1½ 1hd 12 12	Baeza B	132		*.80	100-11	Dr.Fager1322BoldHour1163Damascus1333½	Under mild drive	5
18May68- 8Hol	fst	1 1/16	:222 :45 1:083 1:404 3↑	Californian 119k	11 4 2½ 1½ 14 13	Baeza B	130		*1.20	91-13	Dr. Fager1303Gamely1161Rising Market1211½	Much the best	14
4May68- 7Aqu	fst	7f	:222 :45 1:084 1:212 3↑	Roseben H 54k	5 1 1½ 11 13 13	Rotz JL	130		*.20	99-17	Dr. Fager1303Tumiga1213Diplomat Way121¾	Won eased up	5
7Nov67- 7Aqu	fst	7f	:222 :451 1:093 1:213 3↑	Vosburgh H 57k	6 8 52½ 2hd 1hd 14½	Baeza B	128		*.20e	98-16	Dr. Fager1284½Jim J.1151½R. Thomas1223	Wide,easily best	9
21Oct67- 8Haw	fst	1¼	:461 1:101 1:351 2:011 3↑	Haw Gold Cup H 121k	1 1 1½ 1hd 11½ 12½	Baeza B	123		*.30	90-12	Dr.Fagr1232½WhisprJt1141¼Pontmnow1081¼	Without urging	7
30Sep67- 7Aqu	fst	1¼	:451 1:091 1:353 2:003 3↑	Woodward 107k	2 1 1hd 2½ 25 310½	Boland W	120		1.80	84-15	Damascus12010Buckpasser126½Dr. Fager12013	Faltered	6
2Sep67- 8Rkm	fst	1¼	:463 1:11 1:351 1:594	NH Sweep Classic 265k	1 1 1½ 2hd 2hd 11¼	Baeza B	120		*.20	115-17	Dr.Fager1201¼InReality1269BarbsDelight1152¾	Mild drive	5
15Jly67- 9Rkm	fst	1⅛	:462 1:101 1:353 1:481	Rkm Spl 85k	5 1 16½ 13½ 13½ 14¼	Baeza B	124		*.10	105-15	Dr.Fager1244¼ReasontoHail1214¾JackofAllTrds1128¼	Easily	7
24Jun67- 8AP	sly	1	:224 :45 1:102 1:36	AP Classic 106k	1 3 3nk 13 16 110	Baeza B	120		*.40	83-25	Dr.Fagr12010LightningOrphan1161¾DiplomatWay1187	Easily	6
30May67- 7GS	fst	1⅛	:47 1:103 1:353 1:48	Jersey Derby 119k	4 1 1½ 12 13 16½	Ycaza M	126		*.30	97-14	[D]Dr.Fager1266½InReality1268AirRghts12612	Crowded field	4
	Disqualified and placed fourth												
13May67- 7Aqu	fst	1	:223 :441 1:08 1:334	Withers 58k	8 4 21 2hd 11½ 16	Baeza B	126		*.80	99-16	Dr. Fager1266Tumiga1265Reason to Hail1265	Easy score	8
15Apr67- 7Aqu	fst	1	:233 :461 1:102 1:351	Gotham 57k	5 4 33 3nk 2hd 1½	Ycaza M	122		*1.30e	92-14	Dr. Fager122½Damascus1225Reason to Hail1147	Driving	9
15Oct66- 7Aqu	fst	1	:222 :444 1:092 1:35	Champagne 208k	7 4 3½ 1hd 13 21	Shoemaker W	122		*1.00	92-14	Successor1221Dr. Fager1224Proviso1224	Rank early,failed	10
5Oct66- 7Aqu	gd	7f	:224 :46 1:113 1:244	Cowdin 88k	1 10 31 32 21½ 1¾	Shoemaker W	117		*.80	82-22	Dr.Fager117¾InRlty1171½Succssor1172½	Slow start,driving	10
10Sep66- 8Atl	fst	7f	:223 :452 1:103 1:231	World's Playground 28k	3 6 1hd 1½ 14 112	Ycaza M	115		*.90	87-24	Dr. Fager11512Glengary1153½Pointsman115hd	Much the best	11
13Aug66- 4Sar	fst	6f	:223 :462 1:102	Alw 5500	5 5 21½ 22 12 18	Hidalgo D5	117		*.90	96-09	Dr. Fager1178Bandera Road1172Quaker City1152	Easily	8
15Jly66- 3Aqu	fst	5½f	:224 :464 :59 1:05	©Md Sp Wt	8 8 83 21 11½ 17	Hidalgo D5	117		10.80	88-20	Dr. Fager1177Lift Off1224Rising Market122½	Easily best	11

Fast Attack

b. f. 1967, by Your Alibhai (Alibhai)–Fusilade, by Phalanx — Lifetime record: 29 7 4 5 $184,205

Own.– Har–Bar Ranch
Br.– Elcee–H Breeding Farms Inc (Ky)
Tr.– Harry Wells

Date/Race	Cond	Dist	Fractions	Race	Running line	Jockey	Wt	Eq	Odds	Speed	Finishers	Comment	Fld
11Nov70- 8GS	sly	1 1/16	:232 :463 1:112 1:444	ⒻJersey Belle H 29k	2 5 43½ 26 32 2½	Blum W	118	b	5.10	80-21	Predictabl115½FstAttck1183I'mforMm1104	Rallied,no match	10
3Nov70- 8GS	fst	1 70	:222 :452 1:102 1:411	ⒻPrinceton H (Div 2) 24k	2 5 34 33 32 22	Blum W	120	b	*1.00	86-23	PeacefulUnion1122FastAttack120hdI'mforMama1105	Gamely	10
26Oct70- 7GS	fst	1 70	:23 :463 1:112 1:412	ⒻAlw 8000	2 2 2hd 13 14 17	Blum W	118	b	*.70	87-17	Fast Attack1187Imsodear112½Private Parking113no	Easily	9
19Oct70- 8GS	fst	1⅛	:462 1:103 1:362 1:491 3↑	ⒻVineland H 59k	2 4 33 74½ 73¼ 73½	Blum W	113		11.20	87-12	CathyHoney113¾DarkEmerld1111DedictdtoSu116no	No mishap	10
3Oct70- 8Atl	fst	1 3/16	:47 1:111 1:364 1:562 3↑	ⒻMatchmaker 50k	5 7 67¾ 68 78½ 69½	Patterson G	114		6.10e	84-15	Dedicated toSue1131½ColdComfort1085[D]HelenJennings115no		10
	No factor												
23Sep70- 8Atl	fst	1⅛	:484 1:13 1:381 1:503 3↑	ⒻAlw 8000	4 7 64 41¾ 32½ 21¾	Patterson G	109		2.40e	83-20	OfficeQueen1191¾FastAttack1091HelenJennings1233	Gamely	9
5Sep70- 7Bel	fst	1⅛	:471 1:121 1:374 1:504	ⒻGazelle H 58k	7 7 65¼ 55½ 65¼ 53	Vasquez J	117		11.40	77-14	MissileBelle120nkPredictable114nkFnfrluch1221	No mishap	10
28Aug70- 8Atl	fst	1 1/16	:233 :472 1:113 1:441 3↑	ⒻAlw 8000	5 6 33 3½ 1hd 1nk	Blum W	112		*.70	86-19	FastAttack112nkDeb'sDarling113nkPrizeStudnt1136	Driving	8
15Aug70- 6Sar	fst	1¼	:481 1:122 1:373 2:034	ⒻAlabama 59k	2 8 88½ 66½ 55½ 43¾	Thornburg B	118		11.10	85-10	Fanfreluche1181¼Hunnemannia1142Office Queen124½	Rallied	12
8Aug70- 7Lib	fst	1 1/16	:232 :464 1:112 1:44	ⒻCotillion H 57k	2 6 52½ 41¼ 21½ 31	Hole M	116		8.10	85-07	Office Queen123½Ellen Girl117½Fast Attack1162½	Good try	10
27Jly70- 8Mth	fst	6f	:214 :444 1:103 3↑	ⒻAlw 10000	4 7 67 65¾ 55¾ 66	Thornburg B	114		3.10	83-13	PrizeStudent1141½Destny'sTwst115hdFnulHll1154	No threat	7
29May70- 7Bel	fst	1⅛	:444 1:101 1:361 1:494	ⒻMother Goose 119k	5 7 65 73½ 65½ 47¾	Thornburg B	121	b	22.80	79-14	OfficeQueen121¾CathyHoney1212MissileBelle1215	No threat	16
16May70- 7Aqu	fst	1	:224 :453 1:101 1:36	ⒻAcorn (Div 2) 56k	2 5 43 41½ 23 34	Thornburg B	121	b	3.70	83-14	CathyHoney1212MissileBelle1212FastAttack121½	Weakened	12
7May70- 7Aqu	fst	7f	:23 :463 1:112 1:233 3↑	ⒻAlw 15000	3 4 32 21½ 3nk 2nk	Thornburg B	113	b	*1.80	83-22	Native Partner123nkFast Attack113½Meritus1084	Sharp	8

29Apr70- 8GS	fst	6f	:22 :444 1:104	ⒻAlw 12000	5 5 45½ 45 42½ 31	Thornburg B	118	b	2.10	89-15	BoxtheCompass115hdLadySadie1181FastAttack1184	Gamely	6
8Nov69- 8GS	gd	1 1/16	:231 :474 1:124 1:461	ⒻGardenia 200k	10 5 52½ 32 41½ 1hd	Thornburg B	119	b	7.90	74-26	Fast Attack119hdSunny Sal119hdOffice Queen119hd	Driving	11
29Oct69- 8GS	fst	1 70	:23 :464 1:122 1:43	ⒻAlw 10000	3 4 46½ 32½ 2hd 1nk	Thornburg B	114	b	12.00	79-22	Fast Attack114nkMeritus1155Hail Hail1121½	Up in time	10
20Oct69- 7GS	fst	6f	:221 :453 1:12	ⒻAlw 6500	10 1 32 34½ 2hd 1½	Thornburg B	113	b	5.90	84-20	FastAttack113½LostLagoon1123ExclusiveDancer1124	Driving	12
1Oct69- 6Atl	fst	7f	:223 :453 1:103 1:233	ⒻAlw 4500	4 7 63 52¼ 1hd 1nk	Cardone E	114	b	5.10	85-17	Fast Attack114nkSweet Mist1162Bundestag118hd	Driving	10
24Sep69- 7Atl	fst	6f	:222 :453 1:11	ⒻAlw 4500	5 9 62¼ 77½ 43¼ 33	Cardone E	114	b	16.60	84-16	Out in Space116noSweet Mist1163Fast Attack1143	Rallied	11
17Sep69- 5Atl	fst	6f	:214 :45 1:112	ⒻAlw 4500	10 4 53 74¼ 54¾ 42¼	Cardone E	114		24.70	83-16	CleverWitch112hdVirginiaCrckr118¾NotNotc1161½	No mishap	11
27Aug69- 7Atl	fst	6f	:222 :454 1:113	ⒻAlw 5000	9 8 97½ 69¼ 68¾ 512	Maple E	114		8.30	72-16	Craim Check1181Canaveral1148Lost Lagoon116¾	No factor	12
13Aug69- 6Atl	fst	6f	:222 :454 1:113	ⒻAlw 5000	3 6 51½ 55½ 54¾ 44¾	Maple E	114		18.50	79-20	Scamtan1203½Office Queen120¾Sure to Show114½	Even race	8
6Aug69- 6Mth	fst	5½f	:222 :463 :592 1:061	ⒻAlw 7000	4 6 55½ 56½ 57 55½	Maple E	114		22.40	80-19	Dowitcher1162¾Sure to Show1161½Stepolina1161	No threat	8
30Jly69- 4Mth	gd	5½f	:224 :47 1:00 1:063	ⒻAlw 7000	3 7 711 714 66 57	Cardone E	114		19.40	77-17	VelocityQueen1162½CutiePaula116¾CramChck1162¾	No factor	7

Previously trained by W. Gateman

22Mar69- 3FG	fst	4½f	:233 :482 :55	Alw 2600	9 7 41¼ 54½ 32¼	Mora G	117		7.00	86-12	GoTwistGo117¾MissDuplicate1171½FastAttack1171	Rallied	9
12Mar69- 9FG	gd	4½f	:232 :481 :55	ⒻDebutante (Div 2) 7.1k	3 3 54½ 33½ 42½	Nichols J	119		3.90	85-12	Guadarequest1191½MissDuplicate119noNobleIntrgu1191	Hung	10
22Feb69- 3FG	sl	3f	:231 :35	Alw 2800	5 9 67½ 53¼	Nichols J	117		3.20	- -	Mr.MikeM.117½Guadarequest117nkMudBnkSlly1142½	Late foot	10
12Feb69- 3FG	fst	3f	:232 :344	Md Sp Wt	1 1 11½ 12	Suire L	115		*1.50	- -	Fast Attack1152Skylight Star115½Arky Twist118nk	Driving	10

Furl Sail

b. f. 1964, by Revoked (Blue Larkspur)–Windsail, by Count Fleet

Lifetime record: 34 17 2 3 $273,759

Own.– Mrs E.K. Thomas
Br.– Mrs E.K. Thomas (Ky)
Tr.– J. Winans

22Aug68- 8Atl	fst	7f	:221 :443 1:092 1:222 3↑	ⒻAlw 7000	6 3 63 51¼ 43 42¼	Broussard R	119		2.90	89-15	Gay Sailorette118nkRegal Hostess117¾Telepathy1171¼		7

Nothing for drive

9Aug68- 8Atl	fst	6f⊗	:22 :442 1:10 3↑	Kng Nptune H (Div 2) 14k	2 5 33 59½ 57 57¾	Cusimano G	115		5.40	84-16	Chicot1153½Kaskaskia1141Bowler King115nk	Through early	7
20Jly68- 8Del	fst	1 1/16	:232 :472 1:112 1:44 3↑	ⒻNew Castle 38k	3 1 2hd 22 67¾ 1012	Phelps B	117		12.40	77-24	PluckyPan1144SereneQueen1201LadyDiplomat1141½	Used up	12
10Jly68- 8Del	fm	1Ⓣ	1:382 3↑	ⒻAlw 7000	1 1 52¼ 86 710 712	Goldberg L5	116		*1.90	71-15	Inge109nkRhubarb1212I Be Dandy1111½	Bolted first turn	8
24Jun68- 7Bel	fst	7f	:222 :451 1:10 1:223 3↑	ⒻVagrancy H 28k	4 2 41¼ 21 58 512	Rotz JL	123		12.60	82-15	Mac'sSparkler121nkPluckyPan1122½AmerigoLady1218	Tired	7
12Jun68- 8Mth	sly	6f	:213 :443 1:102 3↑	ⒻRegret H 22k	3 3 51¾ 53 43½ 54¼	Passmore WJ	125		2.40	86-16	Codorniz1181¼JustKidding115hdRglHostss1121½	No response	7
22May68- 7Bel	fst	6f	:222 :453 1:10 3↑	ⒻLiberty Belle H 28k	7 5 11 1hd 1hd 1hd	Ycaza M	123		3.40	97-14	FurlSail123hdJustKidding115noMac'sSparkler122¾	Driving	8
4May68- 8GS	fst	6f	:22 :454 1:103 3↑	ⒻColonial H 28k	2 6 32 64 54½ 56¾	Vasquez J	126		*.60	84-19	Telepathy1111PluckyPan112nkGreenGlad1122½	Showed little	7
11Apr68- 6Kee	fst	6f	:213 :444 :57 1:10 3↑	ⒻAlw 7500	4 5 23 22 13 13	Brumfield D	121		*.60	93-11	Furl Sail1213La Contessa1123½Edswinner1101	Easy score	8
15Nov67- 8GS	fst	1 1/16	:234 :474 1:123 1:453	ⒻJersey Belle H 29k	5 1 2hd 23 34 35	Velasquez J	124		*.70	72-27	Sumtex115hdTreacherous1125FurlSl1244	Bore in repeatedly	9
26Oct67- 6Kee	fst	1⅛	:474 1:114 1:37 1:491 3↑	ⒻSpinster 61k	5 1 11 1hd 3nk 34¼	Richard D	119		1.70	87-18	StraightDeal123nk[D]Amerigo'sLady1194FurlSal1193	Impeded	6

Placed second through disqualification

19Oct67- 6Kee	fst	*7f	1:262 3↑	ⒻAlw 10000	1 3 1½ 2hd 12 15	Richard D	118		*.50	91-19	FurlSail1185FineThanks112½LadySwaps1182½	Scored handily	6
10Oct67- 7Kee	fst	6f	:221 :453 :573 1:10 3↑	ⒻAlw 7500	2 1 11½ 11½ 12 13	Richard D	120		*.60	93-17	Furl Sail1203Lady Swaps1232Silver Bright1212½	Handily	5
23Sep67- 8CD	fst	1	:221 :443 1:094 1:36 3↑	ⒻFalls City H 29k	5 1 11½ 12 34½ 711	Knapp K	120		*.70	82-12	Amerigo Lady1165Gusher113½Likely Swap113¾	Used in lead	13
12Jly67- 8Del	gd	1 70	:231 :462 1:12 1:431	ⒻRosenna 18k	5 1 2hd 2½ 41¾ 37	Broussard R	121		*.40	77-18	[D]Lewiston1114½IBeDandy1142½FurlSal1212½	Had no excuses	5
24Jun67- 7Aqu	gd	1¼	:473 1:121 1:374 2:032	ⒻC C A Oaks 131k	7 1 1½ 2hd 34 416	Vasquez J	121		*.70	65-18	Quillo Queen1217Muse1211½Pepperwood1217½	Hard used,sore	10
10Jun67- 7Aqu	fst	1⅛	:47 1:104 1:361 1:493	ⒻMother Goose 97k	7 1 14 14 15 13	Vasquez J	121		*.70	88-12	Furl Sail1213Quillo Queen121noMuse1214½	Speed to spare	11
27May67- 7Aqu	fst	1	:22 :442 1:091 1:353	ⒻAcorn 68k	5 3 2½ 12 16 13	Vasquez J	121		*3.00	90-15	Furl Sail1213Quillo Queen121½Pepperwood1213	Mild drive	17
20May67- 8GS	gd	6f	:214 :452 1:113	ⒻBetsy Ross H 29k	9 1 64¼ 31½ 31½ 11½	Velasquez J	124		3.40	86-20	Furl Sail1241½Rhubarb1241½Lori Mac1155	Going away	10
5May67- 8CD	fst	1 1/16	:234 :464 1:113 1:44	ⒻKy Oaks 60k	2 3 33 33 2hd 32¾	Shoemaker W	121		*.70	89-14	NancyJr.1211¼GaySailorette1211½FurlSail1212	No excuse	8
29Apr67- 8CD	fst	7f	:224 :454 1:10 1:232	ⒻLa Troienne 16k	7 1 32½ 21½ 12 14	Shoemaker W	121		*.40	90-12	Furl Sail1214Overstreet1181¼Gay Sailorette1151	Handily	8
15Apr67- 6Kee	fst	6f	:214 :444 :57 1:092	ⒻAshland 29k	7 1 41 2hd 1½ 2½	Brumfield D	118		2.70	95-12	Dun-Cee115½Furl Sail1184½Woozem1214	Made game effort	7
8Apr67- 7Kee	fst	6f	:221 :453 :58 1:102	ⒻAlw 10000	6 2 31 2hd 11½ 13	Brumfield D	118		*1.10	91-15	Furl Sail1183Fish House1213Dun-Cee1151½	Driving clear	8
11Mar67- 9FG	fst	1 1/16	:233 :464 1:122 1:451	ⒻFG Oaks 17k	3 2 2½ 1½ 13 14	Lopez JR	121	b	*.30	89-12	Furl Sail1214Nancy Jr.1183Filly Folly1153	Mild drive	7
3Mar67- 9FG	fst	1 40	:23 :461 1:122 1:414	ⒻAlw 5000	5 3 21½ 2½ 13 18	Lopez JR	122		*.40	86-13	Furl Sail1228Needle Cushion112noPlessis112nk	Easily	7
4Feb67- 9FG	fst	6f	:221 :463 1:113	ⒻThelma 13k	5 2 21 1½ 13 14½	Lopez JR	119		*1.10	93-13	FurlSail1194½Shenan1173½SunelsGirl112½	Drew out easily	11
6Jly66- 8Mth	fst	5½f	:221 :452 :581 1:044	ⒻColleen 18k	11 8 62¼ 86¾ 67¾ 69¼	Nichols J	119		5.30	84-18	Rhubarb1146Momma Pierre1141½Betoken119hd	No late rally	14
20Jun66- 3AP	fst	5½f	:212 :442 :57 1:034	ⒻMademoiselle 21k	1 3 1hd 2hd 2½ 12	Nichols J	119		5.50	98-06	FurlSail1192Techr'sArt113¾Woozm11910	Vigorously handled	4
7May66- 5CD	fst	5f	:23 :461 :591	ⒻDebutante 19k	2 1 11 1hd 11½ 12	Shoemaker W	122		2.50	94-09	FurlSail1222PoppingMary119½YourIt114hd	Under pressure	7
26Apr66- 6Kee	sly	4½f	:224 :461 :523	ⒻBewitch (Div 2) 12k	2 2 2hd 1hd 12	Fires E	114		*1.60	96-03	Furl Sail1142Idle Dreamer1197Ritanita1141¼	Drew clear	7
16Apr66- 4Kee	fst	4½f	:224 :46 :521	Alw 4500	3 1 11½ 13 16	Fires E	112		13.50	98-06	Furl Sail1126Crimson Beau119hdHe's Bowin1195	Ridden out	8
2Mar66- 8FG	fst	4f	:234 :482	ⒻDebutante 9.2k	3 7 87½ 119½ 129	Holmes D	119		*2.50	81-10	MissMaryM.1221½RomanWick119noPrimPrime119¾	Dull effort	13
21Feb66- 6FG	fst	4f	:234 :483	ⒻAlw 2800	6 6 41½ 42 42½♦	Holmes D	119		*.90	86-11	MissMaryM.115nkRomanWick1171½WeepingHeart106¾	Wide	9
2Feb66- 3FG	hy	4f	:241 :504	ⒻMd Alw 2000	1 1 11½ 13 14½	Holmes D	120		*.60	78-22	Furl Sail1204½Jo-L-Liz1202½Traveling Light1202	Easily	7

Gallant Bloom

b. f. 1966, by Gallant Man (Migoli)–Multiflora, by Beau Max

Lifetime record: 22 16 1 1 $535,739

Own.– King Ranch
Br.– King Ranch (Ky)
Tr.– W.J. Hirsch

4Jly70- 7Aqu	fst	1¼	:482 1:12 1:361 2:011 3↑	Suburban H 110k	2 6 42½ 42½ 711 711	Rotz JL	119	b	3.50	79-12	Barometer1112½Verbatim1163Hitchcock1133	Fell back	8
22Jun70- 7Bel	sly	1⅛	:46 1:10 1:344 1:464 3↑	Nassau County 27k	5 4 52¼ 31½ 47½ 316	Rotz JL	121	b	2.10	86-15	Reviewer1144Dewan12312Gallant Bloom121nk	In close	5
28Feb70- 8SA	sly	1⅛	:47 1:112 1:371 1:503 4↑	ⒻS Margrta Inv'l H 100k	7 4 32 2hd 11½ 12	Rotz JL	129	b	*.80	79-17	GallntBloom1292Commissary1176TippingTime1172½	Handily	8
17Feb70- 8SA	fst	1 1/16	:231 :463 1:111 1:421 4↑	ⒻS Maria H 34k	8 4 43 2½ 1hd 1no	Rotz JL	126	b	*.50	92-11	GallntBloom126noCommissry1165½LuzDlSol1141¼	Hard drive	8
24Oct69- 0Kee	fst	1⅛	:483 1:12 1:37 1:484 3↑	ⒻSpinster 57k	2 2 32½ 22 13 12	Rotz JL	119	b	-	93-17	GallantBloom1192MissRibot1232½SaleDay123nk	Well in hand	4

Exhibition race,no wagering

4Oct69- 8Atl	fst	1 3/16	:48 1:112 1:363 1:552 3↑	ⒻMatchmaker 50k	7 3 31½ 11½ 14 17	Rotz JL	117	b	1.60	99-15	Gallant Bloom1177Gamely1231½Singing Rain1183	Easily	7
30Aug69- 7Bel	fst	1⅛	:462 1:102 1:352 1:49	ⒻGazelle H 53k	2 4 32 21½ 12 13½	Rotz JL	127	b	1.50	91-12	Gallant Bloom1273½Pit Bunny1163Shuvee1271½	Going away	5
26Jly69- 8Del	gd	1⅛	:464 1:122 1:384 1:511	ⒻDel Oaks 59k	4 3 44 21 2hd 21¼	Rotz JL	121	b	*.70	81-23	[D]PitBunny1121¼GallntBlm12112WhiteXmass1113¼	Impeded	7

Placed first through disqualification

19Jly69- 8Mth	fst	1⅛	:472 1:121 1:38 1:504	ⒻMonmouth Oaks 54k	4 2 21½ 1½ 13 112	Baeza B	121	b	*1.40	90-16	GallantBloom12112HailtoPatsy1183AroundthHorn111½	Easily	6
4Jly69- 8Mth	fst	1 70	:223 :454 1:101 1:42	ⒻPost-Deb 27k	1 2 21 1hd 1hd 1½	Rotz JL	117	b	1.50	91-12	Gallant Bloom117½Process Shot117½Golden Or1172½	Driving	6
25Jun69- 5Mth	sly	1 70	:231 :474 1:131 1:431	ⒻAlw 12000	3 2 32 2hd 1hd 12	Rotz JL	119	b	*.30	85-22	Gallant Bloom1192Golden Or1144½Excited11312	Easily	5
28May69- 7Aqu	fst	6f	:212 :443 1:102 3↑	ⒻLiberty Belle H 28k	1 1 11½ 13 15 1no	Belmonte E	114	b	*1.70	91-13	GallntBlm114noClmsFryGold1164Incommuncdo115nk	Driving	8

Previously trained by M. Hirsch

9Nov68- 8GS	sl	1 1/16	:23 :474 1:13 1:454	ⒻGardenia 183k	3 4 31 1hd 11½ 11¼	Rotz JL	119	b	1.90	76-28	GallantBloom1191¼Shuvee11915Let'sBeGay119nk	Hard drive	7
30Oct68- 8GS	fst	1 70	:221 :452 1:102 1:432	ⒻAlw 10000	4 6 66¾ 42¼ 3½ 12¼	Rotz JL	112	b	*.50	77-22	GallantBloom1122¼DeartoAll112nkHailtoYou1121½	Drew out	8
5Oct68- 7Bel	fst	1	:23 :463 1:112 1:37	ⒻFrizette 130k	11 1 13 13 13 2nk	Rotz JL	119	b	*.80	89-13	Shuvee119nkGallantBloom1193Dihl1194	Just failed to last	11
7Sep68- 7Aqu	fst	6f	:23 :453 1:102	ⒻMatron 100k	2 1 13 14 18 19	Belmonte E	119	b	4.40	91-18	Gallant Bloom1199Irradiate1192Queen's Double119¾	Easily	6
30Aug68- 6Aqu	fst	6f	:222 :46 1:112	ⒻAlw 12000	3 1 2hd 12 15 13	Carmean C10	106	b	7.50	86-20	Gallant Bloom1063Shuvee1143Prefer1161	Something left	7

21Aug68- 7Sar gd 6f :214 :454 1:112 ⒻSpinaway 80k 1 3 1½ 2½ 813 818 Toro F 119 b 32.40 73-10 Queen's Double1191¾Show Off119½Fillypasser1194 Stopped 10
20Jly68- 8Mth fst 6f :22 :453 1:11 ⒻSorority 100k 8 1 52 813 820 823 Rotz JL 119 b 6.60 64-17 Big Advance11910Alert Princess119¾White Xmass1193 Tired 8
10Jly68- 4Mth fst 5½f :224 :462 :583 1:05 ⒻAlw 6000 5 1 22 21½ 25 511 Rotz JL 121 *.40 81-15 Big Advance1198Li'l Puss117noGolden Or1212½ Tired badly 5
26Jun68- 7Bel fst 5½f :224 :462 :581 1:041 ⒻNational Stallion 36k 1 2 11½ 11½ 1½ 11¼ Rotz JL 119 *.60 100-12 Gallant Bloom1191¼Golden Or1143Tatallah1198 Hard urged 4
19Jun68- 5Bel fst 5½f :223 :462 :584 1:051 ⒻMd Sp Wt 4 5 21 1½ 13 19 Toro F 119 2.00 95-17 GallntBlm1199WithThisRing1192Repercusson1191½ Easily 10
2Mar68- 0Pal fst 2f :25 ⒻTrial - - 11 - - - Gallant Bloom1Rasberry SherbethdTurned Onhd 5
Palmetto trials,Columbia S.C. No purse,no wagering

Gamely

b. f. 1964, by Bold Ruler (Nasrullah)–Gambetta, by My Babu — **Lifetime record: 41 16 9 6 $574,961**

Own.– W.H. Perry
Br.– Claiborne Farm (Ky)
Tr.– J.W. Maloney

1Nov69- 7Aqu fst 7f :221 :442 1:083 1:213 3↑ Vosburgh H 58k 7 7 95½ 96¾ 95½ 82½ Belmonte E 119 6.60 90-13 Ta Wee123hd[DH]Plucky Lucky116[DH]Rising Market120½ Wide 11
4Oct69- 8Atl fst 1 3/16 :48 1:112 1:363 1:552 3↑ ⒻMatchmaker 50k 3 1 1hd 21½ 24 27 Pincay L Jr 123 *1.10 92-15 Gallant Bloom1177Gamely1231½Singing Rain1183 Gamely 7
13Sep69- 7Bel fst 1⅛ :462 1:103 1:36 1:491 3↑ ⒻBeldame 81k 4 2 11½ 13 13 13 Pincay L Jr 123 *.40 90-16 Gamely1233Amerigo Lady1233½Shuvee1182 Under mild drive 5
18Aug69- 7Sar fst 1⅛ :474 1:114 1:364 1:493 3↑ ⒻDiana H 44k 1 1 13 11½ 13 12½ Belmonte E 127 *.40e 93-14 Gamely1272½Obeah118½Amerigo Lady1231½ Under mild drive 5
7Aug69- 7Sar fst 1 :24 :472 1:121 1:373 3↑ Alw 15000 5 1 11 11½ 11½ 12½ Velasquez J 111 *.50 86-14 Gamely1112½Prevailing1095EneasII1183 Won without urging 6
28Jun69- 8Hol fst 1⅛ :464 1:103 1:354 1:481 3↑ ⒻVanity H 81k 8 8 84¾ 52½ 3nk 21½ Harris W 128 *.90e 89-17 DesrtLaw1191½Gmly128noAmrgoLdy1253¼ Mate won,held on 11
7Jun69- 8Hol fst 1⅛ :463 1:101 1:341 1:463 3↑ Inglewood H 55k 4 4 33 21 34 44 Harris W 117 2.20e 95-13 RisingMarkt1202½Dwn1141½Rvt114hd Made bold bid,weakened 9
17May69- 8Hol fst 1 1/16 :23 :454 1:094 1:402 3↑ Californian 120k 7 8 98¼ 63½ 65½ 87¼ Harris W 119 *3.20e 86-07 Nodoubl1272½RisngMarket1211LondonJet112¾ Checked turn 14
29Apr69- 8Hol fst 7f :223 :45 1:084 1:21 3↑ ⒻWilshire H 22k 3 4 32 32 22 1¾ Harris W 128 *.50e 95-14 Gamely128¾TimetoLeave1232¾IndianLoveCall1201½ Driving 6
20Mar69- 8SA fm 1¼Ⓣ :451 1:09 1:332 1:581 4↑ ⒻS Barbara H 57k 12 3 33 22½ 25 39½ Harris W 129 *.80e 91-00 Pink Pigeon1236Desert Law1173½Gamely1292 Bid,tired 12
8Mar69- 8SA fst 1¼ :46 1:10 1:351 2:014 4↑ S Anita H 145k 14 7 75½ 63 22 21½ Harris W 122 7.00e 87-13 Nodouble1221½Gamely122noQuicken Tree1261 Game effort 16
8Feb69- 8SA sl 1 1/16 :234 :472 1:123 1:453 4↑ San Pasqual H 46k 5 5 44 52¾ 74 67½ Harris W 125 *2.10 67-28 KingsFavr1162½MostHost1181½JimmyPeanuts112no Weakened 8
21Jan69- 8SA my 7f :223 :452 1:102 1:233 4↑ ⒻS Monica H 22k 5 3 21½ 22 2½ 1¾ Harris W 127 *.70e 85-26 Gamely127¾Time to Leave1246Guest Room1152½ Ridden out 5
29Oct68- 8GS fst 1 1/16 :241 :472 1:113 1:431 3↑ Alw 8000 4 3 23 34½ 45 43 Grant H 119 *1.10 86-19 BigRockCandy114hdKing'sPalace114½PetitDuc1152½ No rally 9
14Sep68- 7Aqu fst 1⅛ :473 1:121 1:371 1:493 3↑ ⒻBeldame 81k 2 1 14 11½ 2hd 1no Pincay L Jr 123 *.70 88-14 Gamely123noPolitely123nkAmrgoLdy1235 Came again,just up 5
19Aug68- 7Sar fst 1⅛ :471 1:113 1:37 1:493 3↑ ⒻDiana H 28k 7 4 26 23 11 1nk Belmonte E 130 3.30e 93-14 [D]Gamely130nkGreen Glade1102Mount Regina118¾ Swerved 10
Disqualified and placed second
12Aug68- 6Sar fst 1 :23 :451 1:10 1:361 3↑ ⒻHandicap 15000 2 3 44 31 14 1½ Belmonte E 132 1.70e 93-12 Gamely132½Green Glade1121½Swiss Cheese1139 Driving 8
13Jly68- 8Hol fst 1¼ :45 1:09 1:343 1:594 3↑ Gold Cup H 162k 8 4 49 52½ 75½ 72¾ Harris W 120 *.90e 91-11 Princssnesian117nkRacngRoom1121QucknTr119hd No excuse 11
29Jun68- 8Hol fst 1⅛ :464 1:103 1:351 1:473 3↑ ⒻVanity H 79k 8 5 11½ 11 12½ 1¾ Harris W 131 *.30e 94-08 Gamely131¾Princessnesian1282DsrtLw1151 Drifted out,held 7
8Jun68- 8Hol fst 1⅛ :464 1:101 1:35 1:471 3↑ Inglewood H 57k 3 1 42 2½ 1hd 1no Harris W 119 2.90 96-04 Gamely119noRisingMarket1202HillShn1181 Under hard drive 12
18May68- 8Hol fst 1 1/16 :222 :45 1:083 1:404 3↑ Californian 119k 3 9 67 53½ 24 23 Harris W 116 10.80 88-13 Dr.Fager1303Gamely1161RisingMrkt1211½ Rallied well late 14
1May68- 8Hol fst 7f :222 :443 1:084 1:21 3↑ ⒻWilshire H 23k 6 2 31½ 31½ 1hd 13½ Harris W 125 *1.00e 95-10 Gmly1253½Romanticism119hdNevadMrg1143 Drew out easily 8
2Apr68- 8SA yl 1⅛Ⓣ :481 1:114 1:362 1:49 4↑ San Bernardino H 28k 4 4 31 11½ 1hd 33¼ Lambert J 118 b 2.00 85-12 Tiltable113nkModel Fool1193Gamely1182 Led,tired 6
2Mar68- 6SA fm *1¼Ⓣ :471 1:13 1:374 2:022 4↑ ⒻS Barbara H (Div 1) 42k 6 7 76 2hd 1½ 21½ Ycaza M 128 b *1.80 - - Amerigo'sFancy1181½Gmely1285LadyPitt1151½ Wide,bore in 9
17Feb68- 8SA fst 1⅛ :463 1:104 1:354 1:49 4↑ ⒻS Margarita H 100k 6 6 44½ 21½ 1½ 1no Ycaza M 125 b *1.30e 87-11 Gmly125noPrincessnesian1203AmergoLdy123hd Bore out,up 12
27Jan68- 8SA gd 1 1/16 :223 :46 1:112 1:434 4↑ ⒻS Maria H 36k 4 6 53 3½ 1½ 1¾ Ycaza M 122 b *1.40e 84-14 Gamely122¾Princessnesian117noMoog1102 Hard drive 12
9Jan68- 8SA fst 7f :22 :443 1:102 1:23 4↑ ⒻS Monica H 25k 7 12 99½ 86½ 54½ 33 Shoemaker W 122 b *2.00e 85-20 Amerigo Lady1182Amerigo's Fancy1171Gamely1223 Rallied 13
14Oct67- 8GS fst 1⅛ :482 1:123 1:384 1:511 3↑ ⒻVineland H 56k 1 2 21½ 21 1hd 33¼ Shoemaker W 117 b 2.60 78-23 StraightDeal122nkPolitly1203Gmly1173½ Steadied,weakened 7
30Sep67- 8Atl fst 1 3/16 :46 1:101 1:341 1:551 3↑ ⒻMatchmaker 50k 5 2 23 1hd 1½ 3¾ Velasquez J 114 b 4.80 104-15 Politely118¾StraightDel123hdGmly1143 Propped under whip 13
16Sep67- 7Aqu fst 1⅛ :49 1:132 1:372 1:494 3↑ ⒻBeldame 81k 1 6 54½ 54¾ 45 32¾ Ycaza M 118 b 4.50 84-16 Mac'sSparkler123nkTripleBrook1232½Gamely1182½ In close 6
2Sep67- 7Aqu fst 1⅛ :49 1:124 1:381 1:502 ⒻGazelle H 59k 1 3 52½ 31½ 3nk 43¼ Shoemaker W 123 b *.80 81-16 Sweet Folly1122½Treacherous116¾Swiss Cheese115hd Hung 13
12Aug67- 6Sar fst 1¼ :47 1:113 1:373 2:031 ⒻAlabama 60k 9 5 23 2½ 1hd 12 Shoemaker W 118 b *.90e 92-11 Gamely1182Treacherous1144Muse1141½ Under mild drive 13
3Aug67- 7Sar fst 7f :223 :452 1:093 1:214 ⒻTest (Div 1) 23k 7 3 53 41½ 1½ 16 Belmonte E 121 b 4.80 101-07 Gamely1216Wageko1153Just Kidding121¾ Drew out easily 8
20Jly67- 8Hol fst 1⅛ :463 1:101 1:354 1:491 ⒻHol Oaks 55k 2 2 2½ 1½ 11½ 2½ Shoemaker W 121 b 2.50e 85-15 Amerigo Lady112½Gamely1211½Princessnesian113no Bore out 10
3Jly67- 8Hol fst 1 1/16 :23 :454 1:10 1:422 ⒻPrincess 33k 8 5 53 21 12½ 12¼ Shoemaker W 112 b 2.70 83-13 Gamely1122¼Forgiving1213¼Fish House118hd Kept to drive 9
23Jun67- 6Hol fst 7f :222 :444 1:093 1:222 ⒻAlw 10000 4 8 73¼ 41½ 65 42½ Lambert J 113 b *2.00 85-16 Amerigo Lady115½Fish House1131Francine M.1151 Bad start 8
13Jun67- 8Hol fst 1 :223 :46 1:104 1:363 ⒻHoneymoon 28k 9 8 87¼ 52½ 52¾ 52¾ Blum W 114 3.10e 80-18 SpinnngAround1121½AmrigoLdy114hdNatveHoney118¾ Hung 11
25May67- 8Hol fst 7f :214 :441 1:092 1:221 ⒻRailbird 29k 10 9 62¾ 4¾ 32 21½ Blum W 113 3.00 87-14 Forgiving1181½Gamely113½FrncnM.113hd Finished willingly 14
11May67- 8Hol fst 6f :22 :451 :574 1:103 ⒻGoose Girl 23k 3 7 63¼ 62¾ 21½ 51¾ Blum W 113 *1.00e 80-18 Forgiving118nkLouisador115¾Ellen Gruder115no Bid,hung 11
9Mar67- 4SA fst 1 1/16 :231 :463 1:112 1:434 ⒻMd Sp Wt 8 4 32½ 22 2hd 1nk Shoemaker W 115 *.80 84-13 Gamely115nkScoop Time1155Deerfleet1155 Up in time 11
23Feb67- 2SA fst 6f :22 :451 :573 1:101 ⒻMd Sp Wt 11 10 53 33½ 23 23¼ Shoemaker W 115 *1.20 88-11 Pooncarie1153¼Gamely1151½Partheny115½ Off slowly,gamely 12

Gun Bow

b. c. 1960, by Gun Shot (Hyperion)–Ribbons and Bows, by War Admiral — **Lifetime record: 42 17 8 4 $798,722**

Own.– Gedney Farm
Br.– Maine Chance Farm (Ky)
Tr.– E.A. Neloy

5Jly65- 7Aqu fst 1¼ :463 1:111 1:36 2:01 3↑ Suburban H 108k 1 7 717 715 618 522 Blum W 131 b *1.10 71-14 Pia Star1171½Smart1198Tenacle1144 Attempted to bear out 7
23Jun65- 9Suf fst 1¼ :471 1:112 1:362 2:013 3↑ Mass H 55k 2 2 1hd 1hd 2hd 2no Blum W 131 b *.30 97-17 Smart117noGun Bow1315Tenacle1174½ Held on determinedly 6
31May65- 7Aqu fst 1 :222 :442 1:081 1:342 3↑ Metropolitan H 111k 8 2 31 41 31 1nk Blum W 130 b *.90 96-16 GunBow130nkChieftain1173Affctontly1214½ Strong handling 8
24May65- 6Aqu fst 6f :222 :452 1:102 3↑ Alw 10000 6 4 53½ 54½ 52 2hd Blum W 119 b *.35 91-19 Malicious119hdGun Bow1191Dark King119nk Trapped,gaining 7
27Mar65- 9GP fst 1¼ :47 1:112 1:372 2:042 3↑ Gulf Park H 111k 8 1 1½ 21½ 2½ 31½ Blum W 130 b *.60 75-15 Ampose112¾Tronado112¾GnBow130hd Held well under impost 8
13Mar65- 9GP fst 1⅛ :473 1:112 1:37 1:50 3↑ Donn H 56k 4 1 11 1½ 12 13 Blum W 127 b *.70 84-18 Gun Bow1273Temper108½Lt. Stevens119¾ Wide turn,driving 6
27Feb65- 8SA fst 1¼ :453 1:093 1:351 2:003 3↑ S Anita H 145k 1 1 1hd 2hd 56¼ 47½ Ycaza M 131 b *1.00 88-10 HillRise1201½CandySpots127hdGeorgeRoyal1146 Used early 8
13Feb65- 8SA fst 1⅛ :453 1:093 1:35 1:474 4↑ San Antonio H 57k 4 1 12 11 11 1¾ Ycaza M 129 b 2.30 93-11 Gun Bow129¾Candy Spots127nkGeorge Royal1132 Mild urging 8
11Nov64- 7Lrl hd 1½Ⓣ :464 1:102 2:00 2:234 3↑ D C Int'l 150k 1 1 14 2½ 23 24½ Blum W 126 b 1.50 107-00 Kelso1264½Gun Bow1269Aniline1223½ Tried to bear out 8
24Oct64- 7Aqu fm 1⅝Ⓣ 2:424 3↑ Man o' War 111k 7 2 1hd 1hd 21½ 2¾ Blum W 126 *.75 85-14 TurboJetII126¾GunBow1262½KnightlyManner1211 Game try 9
3Oct64- 7Aqu gd 1¼ :481 1:121 1:371 2:022 3↑ Woodward 108k 2 1 11½ 1hd 2hd 1no Blum W 126 b 1.45 86-22 GnBow126noKlso1264Quadrangle12125 Extreme hand urging 5
7Sep64- 7Aqu fst 1⅛ :463 1:104 1:353 1:483 3↑ Aqueduct 107k 5 1 15 11½ 2½ 2¾ Blum W 128 b *.55 97-16 Kelso128¾Gun Bow1286Saidam1194½ Clear lead,second best 5
22Aug64- 8AP sly 1⅛ :463 1:104 1:373 1:51 3↑ Washington H 114k 1 1 12 12½ 1hd 12 Blum W 132 b *.70 81-16 GunBow1322LemonTwist111hdGoingAbroad1141½ Ridden out 12
8Aug64- 6Sar fst 1⅛ :471 1:104 1:361 1:491 4↑ Whitney 54k 4 1 12 12½ 13 110 Blum W 130 b *.90 99-10 Gun Bow13010Mongo1303Delta Judge1113½ Speed in reserve 4
25Jly64- 7Aqu fst 1¼ :461 1:101 1:35 1:593 3↑ Brooklyn H 110k 3 1 12 12 14 112 Blum W 122 b 11.30 102-12 Gun Bow12212Olden Times122noSunrise Flight113hd Easily 8
18Jly64- 8Mth fst 1¼ :451 1:101 1:353 2:014 3↑ Monmouth H 107k 2 1 14 1hd 2½ 34¾ Blum W 124 b 4.90 88-17 Mongo127nkKelso1304½Gun Bow12418 Set fast pace,hung 5
2May64- 7Aqu fst 7f :223 :451 1:09 1:213 3↑ Carter H 57k 1 9 32½ 32½ 32½ 32½ Guerin E 126 b 3.35e 95-13 Ahoy1332Red Gar112½Gun Bow1261 Well placed,game finish 11
25Apr64- 7Aqu fst 1⅛ :463 1:102 1:352 1:482 3↑ Grey Lag H 82k 6 2 3nk 21 44½ 58 Shoemaker W 128 b *1.65 91-16 Saidam1144Mongo128½Bonjour1122½ Well up,tired 7
21Mar64- 9GP sly 1¼ :454 1:101 1:354 2:014 3↑ Gulf Park H 116k 5 2 1½ 13 13 11¼ Shoemaker W 125 b *.80 90-15 GunBow1251¼[D]AdmiralVic1244½Garwol1131 Fully extended 11
7Mar64- 8Bow fst 1 1/16 :24 :473 1:122 1:444 3↑ J B Campbell H 109k 5 1 12 2¼ 2¼ 2no Shoemaker W 126 b *1.30 89-20 Mongo126noGun Bow1261Uppercut1145 Nosed in sharp effort 7
22Feb64- 7SA fst 1¼ :443 1:091 1:351 2:01 3↑ S Anita H 147k 18 4 32½ 21½ 58 79 Shoemaker W 130 b *1.10 85-10 Mr.Consistency120¾DocJocoy1171½Cyrano1251 Steadied late 18
8Feb64- 7SA fst 1⅛ :452 1:092 1:342 1:472 4↑ San Antonio H 58k 5 2 21 12 14 14 Shoemaker W 125 b *.90 95-12 Gun Bow1254Cyrano1243Quita Dude114no Scored easily 7
25Jan64- 7SA fst 1¼ :451 1:091 1:34 1:594 C H Strub 132k 1 2 21 110 115 112 Shoemaker W 117 b *2.00 100-10 Gun Bow11712Rocky Link114noWin-Em-All11310 Easily best 13

15Jan64- 8SA	fst	1⅛	:46 1:10 1:35 1:474	S Fernando (Div 2) 43k	3	1	11½	13	13	15½	Shoemaker W	114	b	9.50	93-11	GnBow1145½LambChop1153Win-Em-All111hd	Much the best	9
	Previously owned byMaine Chance Farm;previously trained by A. Scotti																	
30Nov63- 7Aqu	my	1	:222 :442 1:094 1:352	3↑ Queens County H 29k	4	1	11	41½	711	714	Brooks S	113	b	*1.60e	77-22	Uppercut1142½Tropical Breeze1111½Get Around1212½	Tired	11
16Nov63- 7Aqu	fst	1⅝	:471 1:382 2:033 2:43	3↑ Gallant Fox H 87k	3	2	2½	2hd	107¼	1114	Guerin E	115	b	17.65	76-15	SunriseFlight112noB.Major1151½MasterDennis1123	Stopped	12
8Nov63- 7Nar	my	1 3/16	:473 1:123 1:393 1:584	3↑ Nar Spl H 26k	2	1	12¼	12	14¼	113	Brooks S	114	b	*2.20	79-35	GnBow11413GridIronHero1119HalfBreed1135	Scored in hand	6
30Oct63- 8GS	fst	1 1/16	:233 :47 1:113 1:443	B Franklin H 28k	2	1	1¼	11¼	1hd	2nk	Brooks S	114	b	10.60	87-22	BigRaff113nkGunBow1141QuestLnk1161½	Just failed to last	8
26Oct63- 5GS	fst	6f	:223 :46 1:112	3↑ Alw 6000	4	5	1hd	3¼	2hd	11	Shoemaker W	119	b	3.70	87-14	GnBow1191JetsPat115½Outriggr115¾	Came again,hard drive	7
9Oct63- 9Suf	fst	6f	:22 :442 1:093	Suf Downs 28k	5	8	74¼	76¼	1115	119	Boland W	115	b	14.60	89-11	Rockity1171¾Indian Relic115½Time Step117¾	Fell far back	11
20Sep63- 8Aqu	fst	7f	:223 :452 1:102 1:232	3↑ Alw 6500	5	1	1hd	1hd	12	12	Sellers J	113	b	*1.30	89-17	GunBow1132FlyingSniper1135½MannJack1031	Kept to drive	6
10Sep63- 8Aqu	fst	1	:223 :45 1:093 1:352	Alw 7500	4	1	1hd	1¼	21	26	Sellers J	115	b	10.00	85-15	Going Around1156Gun Bow1152½President Jim1221½	Gamely	7
	Previously trained by G.T. Poole																	
23Aug63- 5Sar	fst	6f	:221 :451 1:094	Handicap 6500	1	5	21	31¼	46	56½	Ussery R	114	b	*1.65	92-10	BigEnd1163Ornamnto1222Chshr1121½	Prompted pace,used up	5
10Aug63- 4Sar	fst	6f	:223 :454 1:104	3↑ Alw 4500	2	3	21	2hd	13	15	Baeza B	114	b	17.00	94-11	GnBow1145DoubleDouble1191½MannJack1142	Much the best	9
2Jly63- 8Aqu	fst	1⅛	:462 1:111 1:363 1:493	Alw 6500	6	3	33	66	613	614	Ycaza M	117	b	5.65	79-11	Cabelery1172DareSay115¾Tenacle1151	Speed for 4 furlongs	6
22Jun63- 7Tdn	fst	1 1/16	:223 :461 1:112 1:442	Ohio Derby 31k	3	4	76	1319	1311	1320	Boulmetis S	111	b	5.20	71-15	LemonTwist120¾TheBaron110hdGrandStand1132	Never close	15
30May63- 6GS	gd	6f	:224 :461 1:104	3↑ Alw 5000	1	5	2hd	14	16	110	Shoemaker W	111	b	1.50	90-14	GnBw11110Kiboko1142½LadyPonderos1153	As rider pleased	7
24May63- 6Aqu	fst	7f	:224 :453 1:10 1:224	Alw 5000	9	7	73	21	53	44¾	Rotz JL	122	b	19.60	87-11	Going Around122¾Tenacle1192½Much Motion1171½	Bid,tired	9
9May63- 6Aqu	fst	7f	:224 :452 1:094 1:221	Alw 4500	4	5	43½	21½	44½	410½	Rotz JL	122	b	13.60	84-09	Jimmy Cannon1173Going Around122½Tenacle1197	Used up	8
25Mar63- 3GP	fst	1 1/16	:243 :483 1:131 1:454	3↑ Md Sp Wt	3	2	12	13	12	13	Blum W	113	b	2.10	79-19	Gun Bow1133Salt Box113¾New Democracy1138	Ridden out	8
7Mar63- 4GP	fst	7f	:232 :471 1:123 1:254	Md Alw 3000	3	5	52¼	45	36	36	Rotz JL	121		2.70	77-21	Brenner Pass1183Lotus Petal1163Gun Bow12117	Evenly late	10
27Feb63- 3Hia	fst	6f	:222 :453 1:11	©Md Sp Wt	5	10	45	47	58½	411	Hartack W	119		5.45	78-14	Dancing Dervish1194¾Brenner Pass1193½Royal Jay1192¾		11
	Sluggish start																	

Hail to Reason

br. c. 1958, by Turn-to (Royal Charger)–Nothirdchance, by Blue Swords **Lifetime record: 18 9 2 2 $328,434**

Own.– Patrice Jacobs
Br.– Bieber-Jacobs Stable (Ky)
Tr.– H. Jacobs

10Sep60- 7Atl	fst	7f	:222 :45 1:101 1:223	Worlds Playground 135k	3	8	85	62½	12	14½	Ussery R	122	b	*.90	90-13	HailtoReason1224½ItsaGreatDay122noRossSea122no	Easily	13
27Aug60- 6Sar	fst	6½f	:221 :45 1:092 1:16	Hopeful 119k	11	1	54	31½	14	110	Ussery R	122	b	*1.30	104-08	HailtoReason12210Bronzerullah1222½Chinchill1222½	Easily	11
17Aug60- 7Sar	fst	6f	:223 :454 1:113	Sar Spl 35k	7	8	63½	43½	44½	67½	Ussery R	126	b	*1.10	82-15	Bronzerullah1164Ambiopoise116nkChinchilla1191	Bore out	11
6Aug60- 7Mth	fst	6f	:214 :444 1:102	Sapling 136k	7	9	73¾	53½	2½	1½	Ussery R	122	b	*1.50	90-17	HailtoReason122½He'saPistol1222½CarryBack122nk	Driving	18
1Aug60- 7Sar	fst	6f	:224 :46 1:11	Sanford 36k	1	3	21½	11½	14	16	Ussery R	124	b	*.45	93-12	Hail to Reason1246Busher's Beauty1146½Apple114no	Easily	7
20Jly60- 7Aqu	fst	5½f	:23 :464 :59 1:05	Great American 29k	9	6	41	1hd	11½	12	Ussery R	124	b	*1.75	94-15	HailtoReason1242Bronzerullah117hdCarryBack117hd	Driving	12
6Jly60- 7Aqu	fst	5½f	:222 :46 :582 1:05	Tremont 37k	7	9	54	1hd	13	13	Ussery R	118	b	3.75	94-17	HailtoReason1183Bronzerullh1182¾NshuBlu114hd	Mild drive	10
22Jun60- 7Mth	fst	5½f	:214 :451 :574 1:043	©Tyro 26k	2	12	107¾	98¾	64	55½	Ussery R	122	b	5.10	89-12	Chinchilla111½Song of Wine1152½Carry Back1151¾	Mild bid	14
25May60- 7Aqu	sly	5f	:222 :452 :58	Juvenile 37k	8	7	53½	65¼	33½	32½	Ussery R	122	b	5.50	- -	Iron Rail1221½Globemaster1171Hail to Reason1221½	Wide	9
11May60- 7Aqu	fst	5f	:223 :46 :583	Youthful 17k	2	1	42½	42½	31½	1¾	Ussery R	122	b	*1.65	- -	HailtoReason122¾Garwol1221½Opus1222	Under a hard drive	9
3May60- 5Aqu	fst	5f	:221 :46 :584	Alw 4500	2	1	11½	12	14	15	Ycaza M	118	b	*1.00	- -	Hail to Reason1185Stan the Man118¾Ambiopoise1182	Easily	8
15Apr60- 6Aqu	fst	5f	:224 :46 :581	Alw 4500	4	5	31½	3½	31	31¾	Shoemaker W	118	b	*.40	- -	King's Song118noGarwol1181¾Hail to Reason1189	No excuse	7
4Apr60- 5Aqu	fst	5f	:223 :453 :581	©Md Sp Wt	3	-			16	19	Ussery R	118	b	*.50	- -	Hail to Reason1189Mixed Deal1184½Right Note118½	Easily	6
	Foggy																	
31Mar60- 5Aqu	my	5f	:223 :462 :591	©Md Sp Wt	10	9	52¼	3½	21½	21¾	York R	118	b	*1.20e	- -	No Dance1181¾Hail to Reason118nkCumatara1181	Slow start	10
26Mar60- 4Aqu	fst	5f	:223 :462 :584	©Md Sp Wt	2	3	33	21	22	22	Woodhouse H	118	b	7.00	- -	Stan the Man1182Hail to Reason1184Meison1184	Game try	7
21Mar60- 5Aqu	fst	5f	:231 :474 1:001	©Md Sp Wt	7	6	77¾	79½	79¾	68½	Shoemaker W	118		5.00	- -	Garwol1181Stan the Man1181No Dance1184	Raced greenly	9
11Feb60- 1SA	fst	3f	:222 :333	©Md Sp Wt	7	12			137¼	138¼	Shoemaker W	118		10.50	- -	Hi-Daddy-O118hdHustlBubbl1181¾TranqulVc1181½	No speed	14
21Jan60- 1SA	fst	3f	:221 :333	©Md Sp Wt	7	10			1212	1213	Harmatz W	118		22.80	- -	DouglasC.118hdMr.Turk118½RodeoHand118hd	Always far back	14

Hawaii (SAf)

b. c. 1964, by Utrillo II (Toulouse Lautrec)–Ethane, by Mehrali **Lifetime record: 28 21 2 3 $326,963**

Own.– Cragwood Stable
Br.– A.L. Dell (SAf)
Tr.– M. Miller

11Nov69- 7Lrl	fm	1½Ⓣ	:50 1:141 2:27	3↑ D C Int'l 150k	5	4	42½	2½	31½	21¼	Velasquez J	127		*1.20	83-16	Karabas1271¼Hawaii127½Czar Alexander12712	Game try	7
18Oct69- 7Bel	fm	1½Ⓣ	2:271	3↑ Man o' War 113k	6	4	411	31½	3nk	12¼	Velasquez J	126		*1.10	101-11	Hawaii1262¼North Flight1211¼Fort Marcy1261¼	Going away	9
20Sep69- 8Atl	hd	1½Ⓣ	:472 1:123 2:03 2:274	3↑ Sunrise H 55k	5	5	516	53¾	1½	11¼	Velasquez J	126		*.70	97-09	Hawaii1261¼Ruffled Feathers1154Balustrade114no	Drew out	8
10Sep69- 8Atl	sf	1 3/16Ⓣ	:493 1:144 1:41 2:003	3↑ U Nations H Inv'l 125k	9	8	64¾	23	21½	1½	Velasquez J	124		*1.70	67-33	Hawaii124½North Flight1177Fort Marcy1303	Hard drive	10
30Aug69- 8Atl	hd	1⅛Ⓣ	:501 1:14 1:38 1:501	3↑ Kelly-Olympic H 34k	9	9	97¼	105¼	85¾	3¾	Baeza B	124		*2.30	84-19	Fort Marcy128½Balustrade116nkHawaii124¾	No excuse	10
6Aug69- 7Sar	fm	1 1/16Ⓣ	1:42	3↑ B Baruch H (Div 2) 23k	7	5	45½	3½	2hd	14	Ycaza M	122		*1.00	90-10	Hawaii1224Rhinelander II113hdMara Lark1131	Easily	8
26Jly69- 7Aqu	sf	1⅛Ⓣ	1:551	3↑ Tidal H 58k	4	5	64¼	65½	33	31½	Baeza B	123		*1.20	57-47	Fort Marcy126½Baitman1101Hawaii1233	Lacked final rally	8
4Jly69- 8AP	fm	1⅛Ⓣ	:484 1:122 1:372 1:494	3↑ Stars & Stripes H 57k	4	3	43½	53½	44	1¾	Ycaza M	118		*1.50	92-11	Hawaii118¾Great Cohoes1144Quilche1121¼	Under drive	15
17Jun69- 7Bel	fst	1	:233 :47 1:12 1:363	3↑ Alw 15000	7	8	86½	73	63¾	66¾	Ycaza M	117		*.70	84-20	Sly Bird1171Mr. Right119nkTrade In1171	Trapped,no rally	8
3Jun69- 7Bel	sf	7fⓉ	1:234	3↑ Alw 15000	2	9	72¾	32	12	17	Ycaza M	115		*1.90	89-20	Hawaii1157Baitman1152½Rixdal119no	Speed to spare	10
	Previously trained by George Azzie																	
10Oct68♦ Turffontein(SAf)	hy	6½fⓉRH	1:25	3↑ Spring Champion Stakes Stk3700						12½	Rhodes R	126		*.15		Hawaii1262½Cuff Link1281½Villan128½		9
14Aug68♦ Greyville(SAf)	hy	1¼ⓉRH	2:141	3↑ Champion Stakes Stk1500						2nk	Rhodes R	125		*.60		William Penn130nkHawaii1254½Smash and Grab1304		4
27Jly68♦ Clairwood(SAf)	fm	1⅛ⓉLH	1:494	3↑ Winter Handicap Stk9000						12½	Rhodes R	123		*1.25		Hawaii1232½Peter Beware1201½Anglesea1031		12
6Jly68♦ Greyville(SAf)	gd	1 5/16ⓉRH	2:094	3↑ Rothmans July Handicap Stk15000						43	Rhodes R	122		*1.50		Chimboreaa106½William Penn1321½Smash and Grab1221		19
8Jun68♦ Greyville(SAf)	fm	1ⓉRH	1:374	South African Guineas Stk9000						12¾	Rhodes R	126		*.25		Hawaii1262¾Westra126½Tarma1212¼		9
25May68♦ Clairwood(SAf)	fm	6fⓉLH	1:102	Clairwood Anniversary Plate Alw2100						13¾	Rhodes R	132		*.20		Hawaii1323¾Double Eagle1201¾Fountainhead120hd		10
3Feb68♦ Milnerton(SAf)	sf	1ⓉLH	1:39	Cape Mellow-Wood Guineas Stk Alw14000						12	Rhodes R	126		*.50		Hawaii1262Syracuse1261½Tarma123nk		10
20Jan68♦ Kenilworth(SAf)	sf	7fⓉLH	1:284	Guineas Trial Stakes Stk Alw1200						12½	Rhodes R	128		*.40		Hawaii1282½Luna Base1232Master Bidder128hd		7
2Dec67♦ Benoni(SAf)	sf	1ⓉLH	1:42	Royal Reserve Guineas Stk2500						1	Rhodes R	117				Hawaii117Court CraftSend Me		
25Nov67♦ Turffontein(SAf)	sf	5½fⓉStr	1:082	3↑ Chairmans Handicap Stk4500						1	Rhodes R	106				Hawaii106King's MenPat Me Quick		

10Oct67♦ Turffontein(SAf)	yl 1ⓉRH	1:401	Derby Trial Stakes Stk1200	1	Rhodes R	126	Hawaii126Star Flame126Bill Bailey126
30Sep67♦ Turffontein(SAf)	sf 5½fⓉStr	1:08	Turffontein Sprint Alw800	1	Rhodes R	127	Hawaii127EnjoymentKarroo Dust
22Jly67♦ Clairwood(SAf)	fm6fⓉLH	1:103	Margate Handicap Hcp1000	1	Rhodes R	120	Hawaii120IntenseifYoung David
5Jly67♦ Greyville(SAf)	gd 7fⓉRH	1:252	Champion Nursery Stakes Stk1200	3	Rhodes R	121	Master Builder121Macaw121Hawaii121
27May67♦ Greyville(SAf)	gd 6fⓉRH	1:131	African Breeders Plate Stk3000	1	Rhodes R	124	Hawaii124MacawSend Me
28Jan67♦ Benoni(SAf)	fm5fⓉStr	:573	East Rand Juvenile Stakes Stk1200	1	Rhodes R	119	Hawaii119EdmundoEnjoyment
26Dec66♦Turffontein(SAf)	gd 5½fⓉStr	1:083	Pepsi-Cola Cup Stk2100	1	Rhodes R	126	Hawaii126Prussian PrideLobito
12Nov66♦ Benoni(SAf)	fm4fⓉStr	:47	Maiden Juvenile Plate Mdn600	1	Rhodes R	119	Hawaii119Court Craft119Off Parade119

Hurry to Market

b. c. 1961, by To Market (Market Wise)–Hasty Girl, by Princequillo **Lifetime record: 7 3 2 2 $204,129**

Own.– Wilson & Mrs Hull Jr
Br.– Miss Louise Clements (Ky)
Tr.– D. Erb

8Feb65- 8FG	hy 6f	:231 :474 1:133 4↑	Alw 3000	5 4	41½	21	21	2¾	Heckmann J	115 b	*.40	82-23	Little Lu108¾Hurry to Market1151¼Morning Cast114¾		5
	Bid,tired,stumbled repeatedly final furlong														
9Nov63- 8GS	my 1$\frac{1}{16}$	:232 :471 1:12 1:451	Garden State 317k	3 3	2½	1hd	1hd	11	Cook WM	122 b	9.20	84-21	HrrytoMarket1221RomnBrothr1223¼Ishkoodah1221	Driving	14
1Nov63- 8GS	sly 1	:23 :462 1:114 1:384	Alw 10000	3 2	2hd	11½	11½	11½	Cook WM	113 b	25.60	88-21	HrrytoMarkt1131½RomanBrothr120½Susn'sGnt1203	Driving	8
5Oct63- 8Haw	fst 1$\frac{1}{16}$	:224 :462 1:11 1:434	Haw Juvenile 30k	2 9	83¾	34½	44½	37¾	Brumfield D	112	3.70	80-12	CountTario114¾Ishkoodah1107HurrytoMarket1121	Even try	14
27Sep63- 8Haw	fst 6f	:22 :451 1:101	©Alw 10000	3 2	44½	46½	33½	21	Brumfield D	110	8.40	95-12	Flamisan1191HrrytoMrkt1101¼CountTro116½	Gaining at end	7
19Sep63- 6Haw	fst 6f	:223 :461 1:121	Alw 3800	4 6	51½	42	31½	31½	Brumfield D	121	*2.30	84-17	MyPridenJoy1111½Ivalinda118noHrrytoMrkt1212¼	No excuse	8
10Sep63- 3Haw	fst 6f	:222 :461 1:114	Md Sp Wt	7 6	44	32	11	11½	Brumfield D	120	*2.00	88-09	HrrytoMrkt1201½MyPridnJoy1211MssDwnUndr1173	Driving	12

Impressive

dkbbr. c. 1963, by Court Martial (Fair Trial)–High Voltage, by Ambiorix **Lifetime record: 41 13 6 5 $266,346**

Own.– Little M. Farm
Br.– Ogden Phipps & Wheatley Stable (Ky)
Tr.– W.A. Kelley

21Oct67- 6Aqu	fst 6f	:221 :453 1:103 3↑	Alw 15000	7 2	3nk	3½	54	68	Turcotte R	117 b	*1.50	82-16	Wyoming Wildcat1213Hoist Bar1172½Alslad121¾	Weakened	8
7Oct67- 8Atl	fst 7f	:221 :443 1:091 1:21 3↑	Atl City H 28k	8 1	4¾	55½	52¾	712	Broussard R	120 b	*3.60	86-15	FlagRaiser1233SpringDouble1197FullofFun119nk	No rally	10
3Oct67- 8Atl	fst 6f	:22 :442 1:091 3↑	Alw 5500	1 3	1hd	11½	13	15	Broussard R	122 b	*.80	96-15	Impressive1225Fearless Lee1222½Swoonland119½	Easily	8
16Sep67- 6Aqu	fst 6f	:222 :46 1:102 3↑	Alw 15000	3 3	31½	33	41¾	34	Turcotte R	115 b	*1.30	87-16	Successor1133GoldenButtons1191Impressive115hd	No excuse	8
12Jly67- 8Mth	fst 6f	:214 :443 1:101 3↑	Rumson H 23k	3 2	21	31½	32½	105¼	Knapp K	123 b	2.60	86-17	In Reality1173½Country Friend118½Quinta118no	Weakened	13
3Jun67- 7Aqu	fst 6f	:223 :453 1:094 3↑	Alw 15000	5 1	2hd	2½	2½	2no	Turcotte R	124 b	*1.10	94-15	BuzOn115noImpressiv124½Aforthought1192	Brushed in drive	9
30May67- 7Aqu	fst 1	:232 :454 1:10 1:343 3↑	Metropolitan H 109k	4 1	1½	11½	11	35¾	Turcotte R	113 b	15.40	89-13	Buckpasser1301¼Yonder1084½Impressive1131	Used in pace	6
17May67- 7Aqu	fst 7f	:221 :441 1:09 1:221 3↑	Roseben H 27k	6 1	2½	1hd	2½	33¼	Turcotte R	121 b	3.20	92-16	Indulto113¾Our Michael1192½Impressive121no	Drifted out	7
22Apr67- 8GS	fst 6f	:214 :45 1:102 3↑	Cherry Hill H 28k	8 6	43	3nk	3½	53	Turcotte R	124 b	3.10	89-20	OurMichael118noCanHeRun1121¾Irongate1111	Lacked rally	8
12Apr67- 7Aqu	fst 6f	:223 :454 1:101 3↑	Toboggan H 28k	1 1	1½	1hd	1hd	44	Turcotte R	126 b	*2.60	88-21	Advocator1182½BoldandBrv117noBupy1121½	Faltered stretch	9
11Mar67- 8Pim	gd 6f	:224 :461 1:111 3↑	Old Line H 27k	1 3	1hd	3½	33½	67¾	Turcotte R	126 b	*.70	86-14	SubCall1174½HansomHarve120noFaultlssLight1132½	Stopped	7
18Feb67- 9Hia	fst 6f	:213 :441 1:093 4↑	Alw 8000	8 1	1hd	1hd	12	11¼	Knapp K	124 b	2.30	96-09	Impressive1241¼FleetAdmiral112¾CountryFrind113½	Driving	8
25Jan67- 8Hia	fst 7f	:221 :443 1:10 1:231 3↑	Royal Palm H 31k	2 3	1hd	32½	1021	1027	Turcotte R	126 b	4.30	66-15	Bold and Brave116nkBold Tactics1141Quinta116no	Tired	10
11Nov66- 7Aqu	sly 7f	:223 :452 1:10 1:224 3↑	Vosburgh H 57k	9 1	41½	43½	1020	1034	Turcotte R	127 b	5.50	58-17	GallntRomeo1233DavisII1222½FlagRasr121nk	Stopped badly	10
31Oct66- 7Aqu	fst 6f	:221 :444 1:094 3↑	Sport Page H 27k	1 2	1½	1½	11	1½	Turcotte R	126 b	*1.20	94-17	Impressive126½Vitencamps1102Hoist Bar1131½	Driving	8
12Oct66- 8GS	fst 6f	:214 :444 1:093	Quaker City H 29k	7 1	2hd	2½	1½	11¾	Ussery R	126 b	3.10	96-16	Impressive1261¾Our Michael117½Pretense1131	Drew out	11
16Sep66 7Aqu	gd 1	:222 :464 1:12 1:38	Jerome H 68k	6 1	11	2½	914	928	Blum W	117 b	3.50	50-30	BldandBrave1151½Understandng1078OurMichl1101½	Stopped	9
5Sep66- 8Atl	hd 1Ⓣ	1:352	Ventnor H 30k	7 3	1hd	1hd	11½	63½	Knapp K	117 b	*1.30	90-08	Poker113nkWarCensor116¾SpringDouble1142	Tired suddenly	13
29Aug66- 7Aqu	fst 6f	:222 :444 1:102 3↑	Fall Highweight H 28k	2 1	1½	14	16	13	Knapp K	132 b	*2.80	91-13	Impressive1323Brooklyn Bridge128noHoist Bar1232½	Easily	10
12Aug66- 7Sar	gd 1	:232 :46 1:11 1:37	Jim Dandy 28k	2 1	11	21½	44	58	Baeza B	117 b	*1.00	81-16	Indulto1192½Imam114½Federalist Boy1143½	Gave way badly	7
23Jly66- 8Mth	fst 1$\frac{1}{16}$	:233 :464 1:104 1:442	Choice 57k	6 2	11	11½	11½	2no	Knapp K	122 b	*1.40	83-17	Tequillo111noImpressive122nkTurnforHom111hd	Just failed	10
	Previously owned by O. Phipps;previously trained by E.A. Neloy														
25Jun66- 8AP	fst 1	:221 :433 1:064 1:323	Arl Classic H 108k	8 1	12	14	12½	42¾	Knapp K	120 b	*.70e	100-04	Buckpassr1251¾Creme DelaCreme123¾He Jr.116nk	Mate won	8
17Jun66- 8AP	fst 7f	:22 :44 1:081 1:211	Handicap 25000	1 7	41½	22	12	14½	Knapp K	124 b	*1.00	99-08	Impressive1244½JungleBoy1121¼BetterSea1162¼	Handy score	9
23Apr66- 7Aqu	fst 1⅛	:464 1:104 1:362 1:493	Wood Memorial 114k	9 2	1hd	1hd	76½	1116	Knapp K	126 b	*2.20	72-14	Amberoid1262Advocator126noBuffle1262½	Stumbled late	11
16Apr66- 7Aqu	fst 1	:224 :451 1:084 1:343	Gotham 59k	1 3	1½	1½	11½	2¾	Knapp K	118 b	1.90e	94-14	Stupendous114¾Impressive118¾Handsome Boy118hd	2nd best	11
26Mar66- 7Aqu	fst 7f	:223 :444 1:09 1:224	Bay Shore 28k	5 1	2hd	1hd	2hd	23	Knapp K	128 b	*.60	89-19	Quinta1143Impressive128noBuffle1132½	Crowded,held on	8
14Mar66- 7Aqu	fst 6f	:221 :452 1:102	Swift 28k	2 2	31½	1½	14½	17	Knapp K	126 b	*.50	91-21	Impressive1267Quinta126noKeenKuttr1261½	Easily the best	8
26Feb66- 8Pim	sly 6f	:23 :462 1:123	Pimlico H 27k	6 2	2hd	1hd	11½	13	Knapp K	126 b	*.70	87-24	Impressive1263Quinta120½Sandoval115½	Much the best	8
14Feb66- 0Hia	fst 7f	:224 :45 1:084 1:214	Alw 5000	2 2	13	12	14	14½	Knapp K	122 b	-e	100-13	Impressive1224½Buckpasser1241½Stupendous113nk	Driving	5
	Exhibition race run between 6th and 7th races. No wagering														
2Feb66- 8Hia	fst 7f	:224 :453 1:103 1:233	Bahamas 29k	6 3	12	13	1½	24	Knapp K	118 b	3.80	87-18	Graustark1204Impressive1184½Fleet Admiral1161	2nd best	7
22Jan66- 8Hia	fst 7f	:223 :452 1:111 1:244	Hibiscus 33k	3 2	2½	11	13	12¾	Knapp K	117 b	7.20	85-25	Impressive1172¾Needle Him115hdGunflint1152½	Easily best	14
	Previously trained by W.C. Winfrey														
16Oct65- 7Aqu	fst 1	:223 :453 1:104 1:362	Champagne 223k	9 1	11½	1hd	75¼	713	Ycaza M	122 b	*.90e	73-20	Buckpasser1224Our Michael122½Advocator1221½	Used up	9
6Oct65- 7Aqu	fst 7f	:221 :444 1:102 1:233	Cowdin 78k	6 5	53	52¾	32½	41¾	Baeza B	117 b	8.50	86-22	Advocator114hdFathers Image116¾Our Michael1241	Good try	12
29Sep65- 5Aqu	fst 7f	:224 :451 1:102 1:233	Alw 10000	7 2	3nk	1hd	1hd	43¼	Baeza B	124 b	2.20	85-16	FrancisU.119noHospitality1223FlameTree124nk	Wide,tired	7
28Aug65- 6Sar	fst 6½f	:22 :444 1:093 1:16	Hopeful 110k	6 2	2hd	1½	1hd	22½	Ussery R	122 b	*.30e	95-08	Buckpasser1222½Impressive122¾Indulto1222½	Held gamely	7
16Aug65- 7Sar	fst 6f	:221 :453 1:101	Sar Spl 35k	2 3	21	31	11½	11½	Baeza B	114 b	2.60e	97-11	Impressive1141½Flame Tree1245½Irish Ruler1141	Driving	8
9Aug65- 7Sar	my 5½f	:221 :454 :581 1:043	Sanford 36875	2 1	11	1hd	3nk	32¾	Baeza B	115 b	2.50e	91-12	Flame Tree120¾Spring Double1152Impressive115nk	Fair try	8
2Aug65- 7Sar	fst 5½f	:22 :453 :572 1:033	Flash 25k	3 11	84½	52	2½	34	Baeza B	116 b	*1.60	95-09	Indulto1164Amberoid113hdImpressive1161½	Bold bid,hung	12
19Jun65- 4Aqu	fst 5½f	:222 :454 :574 1:041	Alw 5500	2 3	1hd	11½	13	13½	Baeza B	122 b	2.25	92-16	Impressive1223½Francis U.1224Bandera Beau1192	Easily	9
10Jun65- 3Aqu	fst 5f	:223 :463 :591	©Md Sp Wt	10 6	2½	11	1½	14	Baeza B	122 b	10.45	89-18	Impressive1224Total Talent122½Hospitality1223	Easily	10
1Jun65- 4Aqu	fst 5f	:224 :463 :592	©Md Sp Wt	9 10	99½	98	910	911	Baeza B	122	12.40	77-21	RingingAppeal1152Devil'sTattoo122¾TotalTlnt1223	Greenly	10

Jaipur

dkb. c. 1959, by Nasrullah (Nearco)–Rare Perfume, by Eight Thirty

Lifetime record: 19 10 6 0 $618,926

Own.– G.D. Widener
Br.– Erdenheim Farms Co (Ky)
Tr.– W.F. Mulholland

9Feb63-7Hia	fst	1⅛	:462 1:104 1:354 1:484	3↑	Seminole H 58k	2	2	2hd	1½	33½	48¾	Adams L	127		4.90	82-19	Kelso1282¾Ridan1292½Sensitivo1153½	Bumped at start,used	6
30Jan63-8Hia	fst	7f	:233 :46 1:101 1:224	3↑	Palm Beach H 29k	3	3	1hd	21	31½	23¾	Sellers J	127		4.70	91-16	Ridan1273¾Jaipur127¾MerryRulr1171	Attempted to bear out	5
10Nov62-7Aqu	sly	1 3/16	:48 1:12 1:371 1:561		Roamer H 57k	8	2	11	2hd	2hd	21	Valenzuela I	126		*.95	97-13	DeadAhead1171Jaipur1262¼SunriseFlight112nk	Held gamely	9
12Oct62-7Bel	fst	1½	:464 1:122 2:023 2:282	3↑	Manhattan H 58k	5	1	2hd	43	57	611	Shoemaker W	122	b	*.80	80-16	Tutankhamen1112Sensitivo115¾Windy Sands1161	Fell back	9
29Sep62-7Aqu	gd	1¼	:471 1:113 1:37 2:031	3↑	Woodward 115k	7	2	26	34	23	24½	Shoemaker W	120	b	2.45	79-17	Kelso1264½Jaipur1206½Guadalcnl1261½	Swerved in at start	8
18Aug62-6Sar	fst	1¼	:472 1:11 1:352 2:013		Travers 82k	2	2	2hd	1hd	1hd	1no	Shoemaker W	126	b	*.65	100-07	Jaipur126noRidan1261Military Plume114¾	Under hard drive	7
1Aug62-8Mth	fst	1 1/16	:232 :472 1:104 1:42		Choice 56k	6	2	21	21½	1½	14½	Shoemaker W	126	b	*.90	95-16	Jaipur1264½Cyane126¾Crimson Satan118¾	Drew out easily	8
9Jun62-7Bel	fst	1½	:482 1:121 2:021 2:284		Belmont 153k	4	2	22	2½	2½	1no	Shoemaker W	126	b	*2.85	89-11	Jaipur126noAdmiral's Voyage1261¼CrimsonSatn1266½	Just up	8
30May62-8GS	fst	1⅛	:47 1:102 1:354 1:49		Jersey Derby 130k	11	1	1hd	1hd	2hd	2no	Adams L	126	b	3.10	92-14	[D]CrimsnSatn126noJaipur126noAdmiral'sVoyg1261	Impeded	12
	Placed first through disqualification																		
19May62-8Pim	fst	1 3/16	:474 1:114 1:37 1:561		Preakness 188k	3	1	1hd	72¾	913	1019	Ussery R	126		*2.70	73-13	GreekMoney126noRidan1265½RomnLine1261¾	Speed,stopped	11
12May62-7Aqu	fst	1	:223 :454 1:10 1:353		Withers 58k	2	2	21½	22	2hd	11	Shoemaker W	126		*.75	90-13	Jaipur1261GreenTicket126¾Cyrano126no	Well rated,in hand	7
7Apr62-7Aqu	sly	1	:22 :442 1:092 1:37		Gotham 58k	8	4	43	31	1hd	11½	Shoemaker W	122		*1.15	83-20	Jaipur1221½SunriseCounty1182½Sdluck1142	Easily the best	8
14Oct61-7Aqu	fst	1	:231 :462 1:111 1:36		Champagne 206k	2	2	1hd	1hd	1hd	2hd	Arcaro E	122		*1.10e	88-16	DonutKing122hdJaipur1222SirGaylord122no	Held on gamely	10
2Oct61-7Bel	fst	7f	:221 :451 1:10 1:223		Cowdin 80k	11	6	62¼	62½	31½	1½	Arcaro E	124		*1.05e	94-12	Jaipur124½Obey117nkSirGylord1241½	Up in final sixteenth	12
16Sep61-7Bel	fst	6½f	:222 :452 1:103 1:171		Futurity 138k	1	2	1½	1hd	2hd	2nk	Arcaro E	122	b	1.30	94-16	Cyane122nkJaipur122hdSirGaylord1226	Made a sharp effort	5
26Aug61-6Sar	sly	6½f	:22 :45 1:094 1:162		Hopeful 117k	7	3	33½	2½	11	16	Arcaro E	122	b	3.10	98-14	Jaipur1226SuKaWa1225SirGylord1223½	Speed in reserve	9
16Aug61-7Sar	fst	6f	:223 :454 1:10		Sar Spl 38k	5	2	21	2hd	21	22	Arcaro E	120		*.90	96-12	Battle Joined1142Jaipur1206Cavalanche1144	Game try	6
31Jly61-7Sar	sly	5½f	:222 :451 :58 1:041		Flash 29k	7	6	1hd	1½	12½	13¾	Arcaro E	113		*.75e	96-09	Jaipur1133¾SunriseCounty1193½SeaSprt119nk	Scored easily	10
19Jly61-5Aqu	fst	5½f	:224 :461 :581 1:043		©Md Sp Wt	4	2	1½	1hd	14	16	Arcaro E	118		*.90	96-10	Jaipur1186RoyalLevee1183BreezyLane1182	Drew out easily	10

Kelso

dkbbr. g. 1957, by Your Host (Alibhai)–Maid of Flight, by Count Fleet

Lifetime record: 63 39 12 2 $1,977,896

Own.– Bohemia Stable
Br.– Mrs Richard C. duPont (Ky)
Tr.– C.H. Hanford

2Mar66-9Hia	fst	6f	:222 :444 1:10	4↑	Alw 10000	8	3	87¾	89¾	77¾	44½	Boland W	113		3.30	89-13	DavusII119hdTimeTested1191CountryFrind1133½	Closed well	8
22Sep65-7Aqu	fst	1¼	:473 1:12 1:364 2:024	3↑	Stymie H 27k	6	4	45½	1½	16	18	Valenzuela I	128		*.30	84-17	Kelso1288[D]O'Har107¾Ky.Ponr110¾	With complete authority	6
6Sep65-7Aqu	fst	1⅛	:481 1:121 1:363 1:49	3↑	Aqueduct 108k	7	5	510	56	48	49	Valenzuela I	130		*1.00	82-14	Malicious1163Pluck116noRmnBrothr1216	Lacked any response	7
7Aug65-6Sar	fst	1⅛	:471 1:111 1:364 1:494	4↑	Whitney 54k	3	4	44	45	22½	1no	Valenzuela I	130		*1.20	96-08	Kelso130noMalicious1146PiaStar127nk	Up in final strides	5
24Jly65-7Aqu	fst	1¼	:47 1:102 1:35 2:003	3↑	Brooklyn H 107k	1	5	56½	43½	33½	34	Valenzuela I	132		*1.20	91-10	PiaStar1212RomnBrothr1212Kelso1321½	Hung under impost	5
10Jly65-8Del	fst	1 1/16	:241 :482 1:122 1:422	3↑	Diamond State H 21k	2	2	21½	2½	1½	13¼	Valenzuela I	130		*.30	97-13	Kelso1303¼Kilmoray1093Big Brigade114no	Going away	4
29Jun65-8Mth	fst	6f	:222 :454 1:111	4↑	Alw 5000	8	3	56	86¾	54¼	3½	Boland W	122		*.50	85-23	Cachto117noCommunqu122½Klso122hd	Showed strong late bid	8
11Nov64-7Lrl	hd	1½Ⓣ	:464 1:102 2:00 2:234	3↑	D C Int'l 150k	5	2	24	1½	13	14½	Valenzuela I	126		*1.20	112-00	Kelso1264½Gun Bow1269Aniline1223½	Drew out handily	8
31Oct64-7Aqu	fst	2	:484 2:533 3:191	3↑	J C Gold Cup 108k	2	5	43	11½	14	15½	Valenzuela I	124		*.45	101-14	Kelso1245½Roman Brother1196Quadrangle11916	Easy score	6
3Oct64-7Aqu	gd	1¼	:481 1:121 1:371 2:022	3↑	Woodward 108k	3	2	21½	2hd	1hd	2no	Valenzuela I	126		*.95	86-22	Gun Bow126noKelso1264Quadrangle12125	Bore in slightly	5
7Sep64-7Aqu	fst	1⅛	:463 1:104 1:353 1:483	3↑	Aqueduct 107k	3	2	25	21½	1½	1¾	Valenzuela I	128		2.20	98-16	Klso128¾GnBow1286Sadm1194½	Responded to strong urging	5
27Aug64-7Sar	hd	1⅛Ⓣ	1:463	3↑	Alw 9500	4	2	22½	2hd	1½	12½	Valenzuela I	118		*.30	102-00	Klso1182½Knghtsboro1161½RockyThumb1205	Scored in hand	8
25Jly64-7Aqu	fst	1¼	:461 1:101 1:35 1:593	3↑	Brooklyn H 110k	5	6	69	58½	610	514	Valenzuela I	130		*.85	88-12	GnBow12212OldnTimes122noSunriseFlght113hd	Bumped gate	8
18Jly64-8Mth	fst	1¼	:451 1:101 1:353 2:014	3↑	Monmouth H 107k	1	5	56	43¼	3½	2nk	Valenzuela I	130		*.60	93-17	Mngo127nkKlso1304½GunBow12418	Hung through late stages	5
4Jly64-7Aqu	fst	1¼	:472 1:112 1:364 2:014	3↑	Suburban H 110k	6	4	34	32	31½	2hd	Valenzuela I	131		*1.35	91-17	Iron Peg116hdKelso1314Olden Times128¾	Getting to winner	8
25Jun64-7Aqu	fst	1⅛	:483 1:124 1:371 1:50	3↑	Handicap 15000	5	4	43½	21½	11½	11¼	Valenzuela I	136		*.55	91-15	Kelso1361¼TropicalBreeze114½SunrisFlght12110	Mild drive	5
6Jun64-8Hol	fst	1 1/16	:224 :461 1:102 1:413	3↑	Californian 115k	3	5	65	75¼	78¾	68	Valenzuela I	127		*1.40	79-14	Mustard Plaster1111½Mr. Consistency1231½ColordoKing1232½		10
	Impeded																		
23May64-8Hol	fst	7f	:214 :44 1:084 1:212	3↑	Los Angeles H 55k	9	1	713	98½	913	89¼	Valenzuela I	130		*1.70	84-13	Cyrano124hdQuitaDude1142Admiral'sVoyag121no	Dull effort	9
11Nov63-7Lrl	fm	1½Ⓣ	:483 1:133 2:033 2:272	3↑	D C Int'l 150k	8	4	41½	21	2½	2½	Valenzuela I	126		*.50	93-14	Mongo126½Klso12612Nyrcos1223	Sluggish start,game effort	10
19Oct63-7Aqu	fst	2	:482 2:30 2:551 3:22	3↑	J C Gold Cup 108k	1	4	2hd	12	16	14	Valenzuela I	124		*.15	87-14	Kelso1244Guadalcanal1245Garwol1243½	Speed in reserve	7
28Sep63-7Aqu	fst	1¼	:473 1:114 1:362 2:004	3↑	Woodward 108k	2	3	34	2½	1½	13½	Valenzuela I	126		*.25	96-13	Kelso1263½NeverBend1201½CrimsonSatn1266	Speed to spare	5
2Sep63-7Aqu	fst	1⅛	:49 1:124 1:371 1:494	3↑	Aqueduct 110k	7	3	41½	31	12	15½	Valenzuela I	134		*.70	92-17	Kelso1345½CrimsonSatan129hdGrwol116no	Under mild urging	8
3Aug63-6Sar	fst	1⅛	:48 1:12 1:372 1:502	4↑	Whitney 55k	2	4	42½	42½	11	12½	Valenzuela I	130		*.35	93-14	Kelso1302½Saidam1111Sunrise County117hd	Easily the best	7
4Jly63-7Aqu	fst	1¼	:484 1:131 1:381 2:014	3↑	Suburban H 108k	7	3	33	31½	11½	11¼	Valenzuela I	133		*.45	91-13	Kelso1331¼Saidam1111½Garwol1121	Retained a safe margin	7
19Jun63-7Aqu	fst	1⅛	:474 1:113 1:36 1:484	3↑	Nassau County 27k	3	3	31½	31	12	11½	Valenzuela I	132		*.30	97-07	Kelso1321½Lnvn114noPolyld1143	Cleverly rated,easy score	5
23Mar63-8Bow	fst	1 1/16	:242 :481 1:12 1:43	3↑	J B Campbell H 109k	5	5	44½	33	21½	1¾	Valenzuela I	131		*.80	98-15	Kelso131¾Crimson Satan124hdGushing Wind1166	Hard drive	6
16Mar63-8GP	fst	1¼	:482 1:121 1:372 2:031	3↑	Gulf Park H 110k	2	2	1½	12	12	13¼	Valenzuela I	130		*.20	83-20	Kelso1303¼Sensitivo1129Jay Fox113½	Speed in reserve	6
23Feb63-7Hia	fst	1¼	:483 1:122 1:364 2:014	3↑	Widener H 128k	5	3	54½	42½	23	22¼	Valenzuela I	131		*.45	87-18	Beau Purple1252¼Kelso1313Heroshogala1104	Best of others	9
9Feb63-7Hia	fst	1⅛	:462 1:104 1:354 1:484	3↑	Seminole H 58k	1	4	47½	42	12	12¾	Valenzuela I	128		2.35	91-19	Kelso1282¾Ridan1292½Senstvo1153½	Rallied wide,drew away	6
30Jan63-8Hia	fst	7f	:233 :46 1:101 1:224	3↑	Palm Beach H 29k	4	2	2hd	32	43½	45½	Valenzuela I	128		2.45	89-16	Ridan1273¾Jaipur127¾MerryRulr1171	Broke in stride,tired	5
1Dec62-8GS	fst	1½	:493 1:15 2:051 2:301	3↑	Gov's Plate 54k	2	1	1hd	13	13	15	Valenzuela I	129		*.40	105-20	Kelso1295Bass Clef1175Polylad1178	Drew away wlth ease	5
12Nov62-7Lrl	sf	1½Ⓣ	:471 1:112 2:031 2:281	3↑	D C Int'l 125k	3	2	2hd	11	1hd	21½	Valenzuela I	126		2.10	88-20	MatchII1281½Kelso1264½CarryBack1265	Easily best of rest	13
27Oct62-7Bel	sf	1½Ⓣ	2:283	3↑	Man o' War 114k	12	5	43	21½	22	22	Valenzuela I	126		*1.05	101-11	BeauPurple1262Klso1266½ThAxII1261¼	Finished very gamely	12
20Oct62-7Bel	fst	2	:483 2:282 2:532 3:194	3↑	J C Gold Cup 108k	3	2	32	12	18	110	Valenzuela I	124		*.25	103-08	Kelso12410Guadalcanal1242Nickel Boy1241½	Easily best	6
29Sep62-7Aqu	gd	1¼	:471 1:113 1:37 2:031	3↑	Woodward 115k	5	3	38½	13	13	14½	Valenzuela I	126		*.90	84-17	Kelso1264½Jaipur1206½Guadlcnl1261½	Won as rider pleased	8
19Sep62-7Aqu	fst	1¼	:48 1:12 1:362 2:004	3↑	Stymie H 29k	2	3	34½	11½	13	12½	Valenzuela I	128		*1.25	96-14	Klso1282½Plyld114hdTutnkhmn110hd	With complete authority	11
8Sep62-7Atl	fm	1 1/16Ⓣ	1:431	3↑	Alw 6000	2	1	2hd	11½	1½	41¾	Pierce D	113		*.40	93-05	CalltheWitness113nkArtMarket113hdWindySands1131½	Tired	7
22Aug62-6Sar	fm	1 1/16Ⓣ	1:414	3↑	Alw 5000	3	4	41¾	2½	1½	11½	Valenzuela I	124		*.25	97-03	Kelso1241½CalltheWitness1175FountainHill1172	Mild drive	7
14Jly62-8Mth	fst	1¼	:46 1:10 1:344 2:002	3↑	Monmouth H 109k	5	4	45½	44	42½	23	Shoemaker W	130		*.80	101-14	Carry Back1243Kelso130¾Beau Purple117½	In close turn	6
4Jly62-7Aqu	fst	1¼	:484 1:124 1:363 2:003	3↑	Suburban H 105k	4	3	36	22	22	22½	Shoemaker W	132		*.65	100-08	BeauPurpl1152½Klso1323½Grwol1091¼	Couldn't reach winner	4
16Jun62-3Bel	fst	1	:241 :472 1:113 1:353	3↑	Alw 7500	2	4	42	22	2hd	12¼	Shoemaker W	117		*.25	96-14	Klso1172¼Grwol1153½RosNt117½	Rated early,drew out easily	6
30May62-7Aqu	fst	1	:221 :44 1:08 1:333	3↑	Metropolitan H 111k	2	6	69	56½	510	68¼	Shoemaker W	133		*.60	92-08	CarryBack1232½MerryRuler120½RullahRed1114½	Dull effort	9
11Nov61-7Lrl	fm	1½Ⓣ	:483 2:013 2:261	3↑	D C Int'l 100k	6	1	1½	1hd	2hd	2¾	Arcaro E	126		*.40	108-01	T.V.Lrk126¾Klso12612Prnupcl12610	Made very sharp effort	8
21Oct61-7Aqu	fst	2	:494 2:35 3:004 3:254	3↑	J C Gold Cup 105k	3	2	22	13	14	15	Arcaro E	124		*.10	68-25	Kelso1245Hillsborough1248Peace Isle12430	Easily best	4
30Sep61-7Bel	fst	1¼	:461 1:10 1:344 2:00	3↑	Woodward 109k	5	3	21½	2hd	13	18	Arcaro E	126		*.50	100-13	Kelso1268Divine Comedy126½Carry Back120nk	Much the best	5
4Sep61-8AP	gd	1	:224 :452 1:093 1:343	3↑	Wash Park H 120k	8	9	106½	67	47	45¾	Arcaro E	132		*.70	94-08	ChiefofChiefs1124¾TalentShow110nkRunforNurse112¾	Boxed	11
22Jly61-7Aqu	fst	1¼	:462 1:101 1:36 2:013	3↑	Brooklyn H 112k	7	4	316	35½	31½	11¼	Arcaro E	136		*.50	98-10	Klso1361¼DvnComdy118noYorky122hd	Under strong handling	10
4Jly61-7Aqu	fst	1¼	:482 1:122 1:373 2:02	3↑	Suburban H 111k	7	4	43½	3nk	12	15	Arcaro E	133		*.60	96-13	Kelso1335NickelBoy112nkTalentShow110hd	Speed in reserve	10
17Jun61-7Bel	fst	1⅛	:454 1:102 1:351 1:48	4↑	Whitney 56k	5	3	33½	11	2hd	2hd	Arcaro E	130		*.45	96-12	[D]Our Hope111hdKelso1305Reinzi114hd	Roughed repeatedly	7
	Placed first through disqualification																		
30May61-7Aqu	fst	1	:23 :46 1:102 1:353	3↑	Metropolitan H 114k	9	8	85¼	76¼	44	1nk	Arcaro E	130		*1.05	90-16	Kelso130nkAllHands1173SweetWillim1084	Altered course,up	10

19May61- 7Aqu	fst	7f	:23 :461 1:11 1:24	4↑ Alw 10000	7 6	54½	31½	2hd	11½	Arcaro E	124	*.35	90-17	Kelso1241½Gyro115nkLongGoneJohn121½ Drew out with ease	8
29Oct60- 7Aqu	sly	2	:472 2:29 2:54 3:192	3↑ J C Gold Cup 109k	8 3	313	2½	11	13½	Arcaro E	119	*.80	114-16	Kelso1193½Don Poggio12410Bald Eagle12415 Speed to spare	8
15Oct60- 8Haw	my	1¼	:464 1:113 1:364 2:02	3↑ Haw Gold Cup H 144k	4 6	41½	12	13	16	Arcaro E	117	*2.20	86-21	Kelso1176Heroshogala119½On-and-On1221¾ Speed to spare	9
28Sep60- 7Bel	fst	1⅝	:472 1:372 2:021 2:404	Lawrence Realizatn 56k	1 4	42½	11	14	14½	Arcaro E	120	*.50	100-14	Kelso1204½Tompion1231½ToothandNal1165½ Speed in reserve	8
14Sep60- 7Aqu	fst	1⅛	:463 1:102 1:354 1:482	Discovery H 28k	2 6	43½	42	1½	11¼	Arcaro E	124	*1.20	102-14	Kelso1241¼CarelssJohn1161½CountAmbr116½ Swerved,driving	8
3Sep60- 7Aqu	fst	1	:223 :452 1:10 1:344	Jerome H 59k	7 9	95¼	53	32½	1hd	Arcaro E	121	2.65	94-13	Kelso121hdCarelessJohn1162½FourLan1192½ Long,hard drive	13
3Aug60- 7Mth	fst	1 1/16	:224 :46 1:093 1:411	Choice 56k	7 2	21	11	16	17	Hartack W	114	3.90	99-18	Klso1147CarelessJohn114¾CountAmber1143½ Speed to spare	8
23Jly60- 8AP	fst	1	:223 :452 1:103 1:361	Arl Classic 135k	5 10	75¼	97¾	77½	87½	Brooks S	117	3.90	81-13	T.V. Lark120¾John William1232½Venetian Way1231 Dull try	12
16Jly60- 5Aqu	fst	1	:23 :451 1:09 1:341	Alw 4500	4 1	1½	13	110	112	Blum W	117	*1.30	97-10	Kelso11712DoubleDly120noAugustSun109nk As rider pleased	8
22Jun60- 5Mth	fst	6f	:214 :45 1:10	Alw 4500	6 3	43½	31	13	110	Hartack W	117	*1.00	92-12	Kelso11710Burnt Clover1172½Gordian Knot1171½ Ridden out	8
	Previously trained by J.M. Lee														
23Sep59- 3Atl	fst	7f	:22 :442 1:093 1:23	©Alw 3600	3 5	2hd	1hd	2hd	2¾	Blum W	117	*1.90	87-11	WindySands117¾Klso1172WeGuarantee1172½ Made good try	8
14Sep59- 4Atl	fst	6f	:231 :462 1:112	©Alw 3400	6 4	42¼	42½	43½	21½	Block J	117	4.40	86-18	DressUp1201½Kelso1171¾DuskyRam117nk Rallied for placing	7
4Sep59- 2Atl	gd	6f	:232 :471 1:134	©Md Sp Wt	7 8	72¼	66	45	11¼	Block J	120	6.00	76-23	Kelso1201¼Crafty Master120¾Adapt1201 Under a hard drive	12

Lady Pitt

ch. f. 1963, by Sword Dancer (Sunglow)–Rock Drill, by Whirlaway
Own.– Golden Triangle Stable
Br.– John W. Greathouse (Ky)
Tr.– S. DiMauro

Lifetime record: 47 10 14 5 $413,382

19Mar68- 8SA	fst	1 1/16	:24 :472 1:113 1:43	4↑ ⒻOneonta H (Div 2) 15k	5 6	611	610	611	614	Ycaza M	120 b	3.30	74-13	Lucky Spot1165Sculptured115noCourageously1201	6
	Steadied at break,lame														
2Mar68- 6SA	fm	*1¼	:471 1:13 1:374 2:022	4↑ ⒻS Barbara H (Div 1) 42k	1 3	32½	1hd	32½	36½	Pincay L Jr	115 b	9.00	--	Amerigo'sFancy1181½Gamely1285LadyPitt1151½ Speed,tired	9
17Feb68- 8SA	fst	1⅛	:463 1:104 1:354 1:49	4↑ ⒻS Margarita H 100k	3 10	1212	119	79	812	Sellers J	116	8.90	75-11	Gamely125noPrincessnesian1203Amerigo Lady123hd No speed	12
9Feb68- 8SA	sly	7f	:222 :454 1:113 1:244	4↑ ⒻS Paula H 24k	9 6	910	87½	64	21½	Ycaza M	116	14.70	77-23	Sharp Curve1151½Lady Pitt1161¼My Thel108½ Closed fast	10
27Jan68- 8SA	gd	1 1/16	:223 :46 1:112 1:434	4↑ ⒻS Maria H 36k	7 10	1114	72¾	98	912	Lambert J	117	12.10	72-14	Gamely122¾Princessnesian117noMoog1102 Never close	12
28Dec67- 8SA	fst	6f	:22 :45 :571 1:093	3↑ ⒻLas Flores H 24k	4 9	920	917	917	816	Blum W	118	10.00	78-14	SharpCurve1143NevadaMarga118hdPggy'sWorld1092½ Dull try	9
23Nov67- 7Aqu	sly	1⅛	:473 1:13 1:394 1:53	3↑ ⒻFirenze H 57k	4 7	917	1019	1028	1034	Blum W	115	10.80	37-32	Politely1216GreenGlade1141¼Princessnesian1112 No threat	10
9Nov67- 7Aqu	fst	1	:231 :461 1:11 1:363	3↑ ⒻAlw 15000	6 4	33	21½	1½	1¾	Cordero A Jr	118	*.80	85-19	Lady Pitt118¾Narova1091Regal Gleam1201 Long hard drive	7
4Nov67- 7Aqu	my	1¼	:493 1:141 1:393 2:043	3↑ ⒻLadies H 58k	10 2	21½	3½	43	97¾	Cordero A Jr	116	7.00	67-22	SweetFolly1142½HaremLady1081½Muse106nk Speed to stretch	12
24Oct67- 7Aqu	fst	1	:233 :461 1:101 1:352	3↑ ⒻAlw 15000	7 3	32	31	3½	1nk	Cordero A Jr	116	4.40	91-17	Lady Pitt116nkRomanticism118¾Encanta118½ Up in time	8
14Oct67- 8GS	fst	1⅛	:482 1:123 1:384 1:511	3↑ ⒻVineland H 56k	7 3	36½	46½	66¼	614	Baltazar C	116 b	14.00	67-23	Straight Deal122nkPolitely1203Gamely1173½ Factor,tired	7
30Sep67- 8Atl	fst	1 3/16	:46 1:101 1:341 1:551	3↑ ⒻMatchmaker 50k	11 8	911	1013	1019	925	Woodhouse H	118 b	8.70e	80-15	Politely118¾StraightDeal123hdGamely1143 Not a contender	13
16Sep67- 7Aqu	fst	1⅛	:49 1:132 1:372 1:494	3↑ ⒻBeldame 81k	2 3	33	33	34	55¼	Ussery R	123 b	5.20	82-16	Mac'sSparklr123nkTripleBrook1232½Gamely1182½ Weakened	6
6Sep67- 7Aqu	fst	1	:23 :453 1:10 1:353	3↑ ⒻMaskette H 28k	8 6	68½	68	57	33¾	Baeza B	115 b	3.70	86-18	Politely115¾Triple Brook1173Lady Pitt115nk Closed well	9
21Aug67- 7Sar	gd	1⅛	:474 1:123 1:37 1:493	3↑ ⒻDiana H 28k	5 3	33	2½	33½	45¾	Baeza B	118 b	3.00	90-11	PridesProfile114nkStraightDeal1273Malhoa1112½ Bid,tired	9
7Aug67- 6Sar	fst	1	:232 :46 1:103 1:362	3↑ ⒻAlw 15000	8 3	42	42	3nk	23	Rotz JL	114 b	4.10	89-15	ReluctantPearl1163LadyPitt1143BelledeNuit120nk Gamely	9
29Jly67- 6Aqu	fst	1	:222 :443 1:09 1:344	3↑ Alw 15000	5 2	37	45	67½	68¼	Rotz JL	113 b	5.30	86-14	Command Performer109nkAczay108¾Beau Apple113nk Tired	7
5Nov66- 7Aqu	fst	1¼	:481 1:122 1:371 2:022	3↑ ⒻLadies H 56k	7 7	711	76½	67½	54½	Broussard R	120 b	*1.70	81-13	Destro115noStraightDeal1183MissDickey109hd Dull effort	8
15Oct66- 8GS	fst	1⅛	:474 1:112 1:361 1:49	3↑ ⒻVineland H 58k	11 6	66¾	44½	44½	1¾	Broussard R	118 b	3.20	92-15	Lady Pitt118¾Juanita1122½Mac's Sparkler112no Hard drive	11
17Sep66- 7Aqu	fst	1⅛	:47 1:111 1:361 1:492	3↑ ⒻBeldame 85k	2 3	36	36	25	38½	Rotz JL	118 b	3.60	80-18	Summer Scandal1238Straight Deal123½Lady Pitt1182 Hung	10
3Sep66- 7Aqu	fst	1⅛	:473 1:131 1:39 1:522	ⒻGazelle H 55k	1 3	34½	3½	13	2nk	Blum W	124 b	*1.20	74-22	PridesProfile113nkLadyPitt1246SwingingMood1204 Missed	7
13Aug66- 6Sar	fst	1¼	:472 1:12 1:38 2:041	ⒻAlabama 56k	4 5	34	1½	1½	1nk	Blum W	124 b	*1.20	87-09	[D]LadyPitt124nkNatashka1216PridesProfile1141½ Bore in	6
	Disqualified and placed second														
23Jly66- 8Del	fst	1⅛	:463 1:103 1:364 1:494	ⒻDel Oaks 63k	1 2	23½	2hd	13	15	Blum W	121 b	*1.70	88-14	LadyPitt1215HlponWy114hdMssSpn114no Drifted out,handily	11
4Jly66- 8Mth	fst	1⅛	:462 1:111 1:374 1:512	ⒻMth Oaks 57k	5 11	1116	1011	84½	42½	Blum W	121 b	*1.90	84-15	Natashka1161½Indian Sunlite118¾Justakiss118nk Late rush	11
25Jun66- 7Aqu	fst	1¼	:472 1:12 1:382 2:05	ⒻC C A Oaks 119k	5 5	57½	1hd	1hd	1¾	Blum W	121 b	*1.70	73-17	LadyPitt121¾[D]GentleRain121nkPridesProfile1218 Driving	10
11Jun66- 7Aqu	fst	1⅛	:472 1:12 1:371 1:502	ⒻMother Goose 87k	9 5	44½	43¼	1½	11¼	Blum W	121 b	7.20	84-15	LadyPitt1211¼MarkingTime121½PridesProfile1212½ Driving	9
28May66- 7Aqu	sly	1	:224 :452 1:102 1:36	ⒻAcorn 59k	2 7	55	47	63	45	Blum W	121 b	9.50	83-18	MarkngTime1212½AroundtheRoses1212Moccasin121½ No rally	11
6May66- 8CD	fst	1 1/16	:234 :472 1:121 1:444	ⒻKy Oaks 60k	9 1	715	712	76¾	31½	Baeza B	121 b	*2.00	86-14	NativeStreet121hd[D]Justakiss1211½LadyPitt121nk Rallied	10
	Placed second through disqualification														
15Apr66- 7Aqu	fst	1	:223 :45 1:092 1:352	ⒻAlw 10000	5 5	510	32½	2½	12	Baeza B	114 b	*1.10	91-15	Lady Pitt1142Ego Twist1186Be Suspicious1151½ Going away	6
9Mar66- 9GP	fst	1 1/16	:241 :482 1:123 1:432	ⒻOrchid 16k	1 4	43½	44½	22½	2hd	Baeza B	114 b	2.00	91-12	Chalina114hdLady Pitt1141¼Native Street1185 Fast finish	6
26Feb66- 5Hia	fst	1⅛	:48 1:123 1:384 1:514	ⒻAlw 6000	7 6	55½	42	2hd	2½	Adams L	113 b	*.90	75-22	Boiseana115½Lady Pitt1132¼Our Dear Ruth1074 Just failed	8
9Feb66- 8Hia	fst	7f	:224 :452 1:10 1:23	ⒻMimosa 35k	8 7	811	88¼	68	48	Adams L	114	3.60	86-15	Destro1127MyBossLady112hdNativeStreet1211 Broke slowly	8
19Jan66- 7Hia	fst	6f	:221 :454 1:113	ⒻJasmine (Div 1) 20k	2 7	87¼	78½	68½	22	Adams L	116	3.40	84-22	IndianSunlite1162LadyPitt116nkOurDearRuth1121½ Rallied	9
27Nov65- 8Pim	gd	1 1/16	:233 :471 1:113 1:454	ⒻMarguerite 73k	5 8	76¼	54¼	55½	45½	Blum W	119	*1.20	75-18	SwiftLady119¾PridesProfile1193½IndianSunlite1191¼ Wide	8
17Nov65- 7Aqu	fst	1	:224 :454 1:112 1:381	ⒻDemoiselle 30k	5 5	63	44	23	2nk	Velasquez J	116	*1.40	77-27	IndianSunlite114nkLadyPitt1162¾PridesProfile1161 Sharp	12
6Nov65- 8GS	fst	1 1/16	:234 :471 1:121 1:442	ⒻGardenia 183k	6 5	510	55¼	32	22½	Velasquez J	119	10.60	80-21	Moccasin1192½Lady Pitt119½Prides Profile119nk Good try	9
9Oct65- 7Aqu	fst	1	:224 :461 1:103 1:36	ⒻFrizette 122k	1 6	32	23	23	21½	Turcotte R	119	6.90	86-17	Priceless Gem1191½Lady Pitt1195Swift Lady1191 Game try	7
29Sep65- 7Aqu	fst	7f	:222 :45 1:10 1:23	ⒻAstarita (Div 2) 23k	4 9	912	711	33	15	Turcotte R	116	8.20	91-16	[DH] Prides Profile119[DH] Lady Pitt1165Destro1164 Driving	9
21Sep65- 7Aqu	fst	6f	:221 :45 1:094	ⒻAlw 10000	1 8	85½	46	39	310	Turcotte R	116	17.30	84-18	PricelessGem1168LadyDiplomat1192LadyPitt1164 No threat	12
2Sep65- 7Aqu	fst	6f	:224 :47 1:121	ⒻAlw 10000	7 6	64½	32	2½	21¾	Blum W	116	3.70	80-26	Hula Girl1191¾Lady Pitt116¾My Boss Lady1145 Good effort	8
18Aug65- 7Sar	gd	6f	:221 :454 1:113	ⒻAdirondack 25k	14 11	116¾	108¾	73½	64½	Ussery R	114	7.20	85-13	LadyDulcinea114nkLovelyGypsy1201½PridesProfile1232 Wide	14
4Aug65- 6Sar	fst	5½f	:22 :454 :582 1:05	ⒻSchuylrville (Div 1) 23k	3 2	65¾	65	33½	24½	Blum W	116	2.40	87-13	PridesProfile1164½LadyPitt1161½NeverinPrs1194 Wide late	7
31Jly65- 8Mth	fst	6f	:212 :45 1:102	ⒻSorority 124k	10 10	1112	1113	912	918	Blum W	119	8.10	72-17	NatveStrt1196ShimmrngGold1147LovlyGypsy119¾ No speed	15
14Jly65- 7Aqu	fst	5½f	:213 :444 :572 1:041	ⒻAstoria 30k	2 8	86¼	87½	56½	33½	Blum W	117	8.10	88-16	Native Street1172½Lyvette1171Lady Pitt1171 Late rush	10
21Jun65- 6Aqu	fst	5½f	:221 :46 :591 1:06	ⒻAlw 5500	2 3	41½	41	2hd	13	Blum W	119	*.90	83-17	Lady Pitt1193Amerala1192Sweety Kid119¾ Drew out easily	7
5Jun65- 4Aqu	fst	5f	:222 :454 :583	ⒻAlw 5500	1 2	1hd	1½	2hd	2no	Turcotte R	119	*2.75	92-13	ChokePont115noLdyPtt11910Aurous1142 Showed sharp effort	8
14May65- 4Aqu	fst	5f	:231 :474 1:003	ⒻMd Sp Wt	3 9	915	79	32	13½	Blum W	119	3.70	82-21	Lady Pitt1193½Zatullah119hdBoiseana119nk Going away	9

Lamb Chop

ch. f. 1960, by Bold Ruler (Nasrullah)–Sheepsfoot, by Count Fleet — **Lifetime record: 23 12 5 4 $324,032**

Own.– W.H. Perry
Br.– Claiborne Farm (Ky)
Tr.– J.W. Maloney

25Jan64- 7SA	fst 1¼	:45¹ 1:09¹ 1:34 1:59⁴		C H Strub 132k	2 11 12¹¹ - - -	Ycaza M	120	2.40	- -	Gun Bow117¹²Rocky Link114ⁿᵒWin-Em-All113¹⁰		13
	Broke down,destroyed											
15Jan64- 8SA	fst 1⅛	:46 1:10 1:35 1:47⁴		S Fernando (Div 2) 43k	4 4 21½ 2³ 2³ 25½	Ycaza M	115	*.90	87-11	GnBow1145½LmbChop115³Win-Em-All111ʰᵈ	Held on gamely	9
28Nov63- 7Aqu	fst 1⅛	:46³ 1:11⁴ 1:36⁴ 1:49⁴	3↑	Ⓕ Firenze H 27k	1 2 2⁶ 1½ 1³ 1²	Ycaza M	126	*.30	92-14	LambChop126²WaltzSong123⁴DupageLady108⁴	Handy score	6
5Nov63- 8GS	fst 1 1/16	:23 :46² 1:10² 1:41³		Ⓕ Jersey Belle 29k	6 2 2⁵ 1⁵ 1⁸ 1¹²	Ycaza M	123	*.50	102-14	LmbChp123¹²ProdanaNeviesta114ʰᵈGoofed121¾	Easy score	9
17Oct63- 6Kee	fst 1⅛	:48⁴ 1:12² 1:36² 1:48²	3↑	Ⓕ Spinster 69k	5 2 2¹ 12½ 1⁵ 1¹¹	Ycaza M	119	-	95-09	LambChop119¹¹ElevenKeys1192½LaughingBreeze119³	Easily	5
	Open to 3-, 4- and 5-year-olds											
10Oct63- 6Kee	fst *7f	:21³ :44² 1:08² 1:24³	3↑	Ⓕ Alw 10000	5 3 34½ 32½ 1½ 12½	Ycaza M	118	*.50	102-12	LambChop1182½Abrogate112³Bonnie'sGrl1063½	Kept to drive	5
19Sep63- 7Aqu	gd 1⅛	:49¹ 1:13² 1:38³ 1:51	3↑	Ⓕ Beldame 87k	12 5 5² 6³ 2ʰᵈ 2ⁿᵒ	Baeza B	118	*1.15	86-17	Oil Royalty123ⁿᵒLambChop118²SmartDeb1182½	Nosed,sharp	13
11Sep63- 7Aqu	fst 1⅛	:47⁴ 1:11³ 1:37 1:50		Ⓕ Gazelle H 29k	12 6 6³ 5² 1½ 11¾	Baeza B	125	3.35	91-13	LmbChop1251¾DelhiMaid119ⁿᵏSmartDb1232½	Clear under dr.	12
10Aug63- 6Sar	fst 1¼	:47² 1:11³ 1:38 2:04¹		Ⓕ Alabama 57k	5 6 64¾ 62¼ 21½ 2ⁿᵒ	Baeza B	124	*.45e	87-11	Tona114ⁿᵒLmbChop1242½ProdanaNeviesta1144½	Forced wide	9
1Aug63- 7Sar	sly 7f	:22² :46 1:11⁴ 1:25		Ⓕ Test (Div 2) 17k	7 3 6⁶ 64½ 3¹ 2¹	Ycaza M	124	*1.50	84-21	Barbwolf115¹Lamb Chop124⁴No Resisting121½	Bore out late	8
6Jly63- 8Mth	fst 1⅛	:48 1:12² 1:37³ 1:51³		Ⓕ Mth Oaks 56k	1 7 52½ 3¹ 1ʰᵈ 1ʰᵈ	Grant H	118	*2.30	86-16	Lamb Chop118ʰᵈSpicy Living121¹Smart Deb118³	Hard drive	8
22Jun63- 7Aqu	fst 1¼	:47² 1:11¹ 1:37 2:02⁴		Ⓕ C C A Oaks 120k	2 3 4³ 2ʰᵈ 1½ 13½	Gustines H	121	4.15	86-12	LambChop1213½SpicyLiving1211½SmartDeb121¾	Ridden out	10
1Jun63- 7Aqu	fst 1⅛	:48¹ 1:12³ 1:37² 1:50²		Ⓕ Mother Goose 91k	11 10 97½ 95¼ 44½ 32½	Rotz JL	121	4.30e	86-11	SpicyLiving121ⁿᵒSmartDeb1212½LambChop121ⁿᵏ	Closed fast	14
18May63- 7Aqu	sly 1	:22² :45³ 1:11¹ 1:37¹		Ⓕ Acorn 60k	10 7 84¼ 52¼ 33½ 3⁴	Rotz JL	121	4.10	78-17	SpicyLiving1213½Nalee121½LambChop121³	Finished gamely	12
24Apr63- 7Aqu	fst 7f	:23² :46⁴ 1:11³ 1:24²		Ⓕ Comely (Div 2) 17k	4 2 3ⁿᵏ 3² 1ʰᵈ 11½	Baeza B	118	4.30	84-17	LambChop1181½SpicyLivng112¹Fool'sPly1151¼	Driving clear	7
14Feb63- 7SA	my 1 1/16	:22⁴ :46² 1:12² 1:46²		Ⓕ S Susana 27k	5 7 4⁶ 41½ 3² 1½	Ycaza M	115	2.20	72-24	LmbChp115½Nalee115½CurousClovr1144¾	Vigorous handling	7
24Jan63- 7SA	fst 6½f	:22¹ :45³ 1:10¹ 1:16²		Ⓕ S Ynez 22k	5 9 72¾ 82½ 77½ 2⁵	Ycaza M	117	*2.00	90-12	Nalee117⁵LambChop117ⁿᵒDelhiMad111ⁿᵏ	Rallied for placing	9
3Jan63- 7SA	fst 6½f	:22¹ :45 1:10 1:16²		Ⓕ Ⓡ La Centinela 18k	12 9 10⁴ 95¾ 3⁵ 11¼	Ycaza M	119	*2.50	95-15	LmbChp1191¼JoLarTay119ⁿᵒCuriousClover1195½	Hard drive	14
28Dec62- 7SA	fst 6f	:22³ :45⁴ 1:11		Ⓕ Alw 10000	12 1 73¼ 63¾ 62¼ 31¾	Ycaza M	113	*1.30	87-15	DH Lanabu115 DH Nalee1151¾Lamb Chop113½	Slow to settle	12
10Nov62- 8Lrl	sly 1 1/16	:23¹ :47³ 1:13 1:46⁴		Ⓕ Selima 55k	3 4 1ʰᵈ 43½ 55½ 55¾	Hartack W	119	3.30	79-17	Fool's Play119¹Gay Serenade119⁴Smart Deb119½	Fell back	5
2Nov62- 6Aqu	fst 7f	:22⁴ :45⁴ 1:10² 1:23²		Ⓕ Alw 5000	6 2 35½ 36½ 3² 3¹	Shoemaker W	116	*1.15	88-19	Charspiv116½PortofCall114½LmbChp116ⁿᵏ	Wide backstretch	7
1Sep62- 6Aqu	fst 6f	:22¹ :45² 1:11		Ⓕ Alw 4500	1 4 41½ 31½ 3¹ 1½	Ycaza M	119	2.50	90-11	Lamb Chop119½Rare Exchange119½Main Swap112⁵	Hand ride	10
21Aug62- 5Sar	fst 6f	:22³ :46 1:11³		Ⓕ Md Sp Wt	10 4 3⁴ 31½ 1³ 11½	Sellers J	118	*1.00	90-10	Lamb Chop1181½Wise Nurse1184½Blue Blur1184½	Ridden out	10

L'Escargot (GB)

ch. g. 1963, by Escart III (Turmoil II)–What a Daisy, by Grand Inquisitor — **Lifetime record: 57 14 15 7 $212,214**

Own.– Powhatan
Br.– Mrs B. O'Neill (GB)
Tr.– Dan L. Moore

23Sep75♦	Listowel(Ire)	gd 3LH	6:08¹	6↑	Kerry National Hcp Chase Hcp4000	2ʰᵈ	Carberry T	168	12.00	Black Mac145ʰᵈL'Escargot168⁴Double 'Em1331½	11
5Apr75♦	Aintree(GB)	gd 4½LH	9:31	7↑	Grand National Handicap Chase Stk105000	1¹⁵	Carberry T	157	6.50	L'Escargot157¹⁵Red Rum168⁸Spanish Steps143¹² Blundered at 7th,dueled 4 out,led after last	31
12Mar75♦	Cheltenham(GB)	hy 2LH	4:16³	6↑	Two Mile Champion Chase Stk12500	5²³	Carberry T	168	20.00	Lough Inagh168³Royal Relief168⁷Skymas168⁶ Never a factor	8
22Feb75♦	Leopardstwn(Ire)	hy 3LH	6:39³	6↑	Leopardstown Handicap Chase Hcp7500	8	Ennis M	144	16.00	Highway View1331½Lean Forward153²Argent148⁵	9
7Nov74♦	Thurles(Ire)	gd 3RH	6:30²	6↑	Morlony Cup Chase Hcp1900	6	Carberry P	170	5.00	Our Albert133³Mr Baggins1422½Gothic Arch129⁴	8
24Oct74♦	Punchstwn(Ire)	yl 2½RH	5:50³	7↑	Free Handicap Chase Hcp2500	39½♦	Carberry T	151	6.00	Lough Inagh1441½Hillhead IV134⁸ DH Argent146 Finished in dead-heat for 3rd	7
15Apr74♦	Fairyhouse(Ire)	gd 3½RH	7:50	6↑	Irish Grand National Hcp Chase Stk25000	2⁵	Carberry T	148	4.00	Colebridge156⁵L'Escargot148ⁿᵒHighway View134⁸	10
30Mar74♦	Aintree(GB)	gd 4½LH	9:20¹	7↑	Grand National Handicap Chase Stk78000	2⁷	Carberry T	167	8.50	Red Rum168⁷L'Escargot167ⁿᵒCharles Dickens140⁸ 6th halfway,bid 2 out,held by winner	42
14Mar74♦	Cheltenham(GB)	sf 2LH	4:21⁴	6↑	Cathcart Challenge Cup Chase Alw5000	2⁴	Carberry T	157	10.00	Soothsayer157⁴L'Escargot157⁶Clever Scot157² Tracked leaders,bid 3 out,held by winner	7
23Feb74♦	Leopardstwn(Ire)	sf 3LH	6:41¹	6↑	Leopardstown Handicap Chase Hcp7200	6	Carberry T	160	16.00	Lean Forward155¾Ormond King147⁶Inkslinger169⁶	8
1Feb74♦	Sandown(GB)	yl 3 1/16RH	6:33¹	6↑	Gainsborough Chase Alw4500	45½	Carberry T	154	*2.50	Kilvulgan149³Titus Oates149ʰᵈInto View1632½ Tracked leaders,one-paced from 2 out	6
29Dec73♦	Punchstwn(Ire)	hy 2½RH	5:58	4↑	Morgiana Hurdle Alw4200	3⁸	Carberry T	158	3.00	Yenisei168ⁿᵒFlashy Boy163⁸L'Escargot1581½	6
25Sep73♦	Listowel(Ire)	yl 3LH	6:29¹	6↑	Kerry National Hcp Chase Hcp2500	-	Carberry T	168	*1.75	Pearl of Montreal133³Cottage Time126⁴Rough Silk133 Fell	5
23Apr73♦	Fairyhouse(Ire)	fm 3¼RH	6:54¹	6↑	Irish Grand National Hcp Chase Stk27000	8	Moore ALT	163	9.00	Tartan Ace133⁸Skymas143¹⁰Sea Brief160½	14
31Mar73♦	Aintree(GB)	fm 4½LH	9:01⁴	7↑	Grand National Hcp Chase Stk80000	325¾	Carberry T	168	11.00	Red Rum145¾Crisp168²⁵L'Escargot168¹² 17th halfway,13th 7 out,3rd 3 out,no chance with first two	38
15Mar73♦	Cheltenham(GB)	gd *3¼LH	6:37¹	6↑	Cheltenham Gold Cup Chase Stk45000	4¹¹	Carberry T	168	20.00	The Dikler168ⁿᵒPendil168⁶Charlie Potheen168⁵ Progress 5 out,weakened 2 out	8
17Feb73♦	Leopardstwn(Ire)	sf 3LH	6:28¹	6↑	Leopardstown Handicap Chase Hcp7800	7	Carberry T	168	6.00	Sea Brief155⁴Lockyersleigh1332½Argent165²	8
30Dec72♦	Punchstwn(Ire)	sf 2½RH	5:17²	4↑	Morgiana Hurdle Alw2700	2ⁿᵒ	Carberry T	151	*2.50	Lockyersleigh151ⁿᵒL'Escargot151⁴Cart It144⁸	13
29Nov72♦	Haydock(GB)	gd 3LH	6:14¹	6↑	Sundew Chase Alw3900	1ⁿᵒ	Carberry T	161	*.90	L'Escargot161ⁿᵒSpanish Steps161³⁰The Laird166 With leader to 3 out,dueled 1 out,led near line	4
8Nov72♦	Punchstwn(Ire)	gd 3RH	6:40³	6↑	Donaghmore Handicap Chase Hcp1900	2⁴	Carberry T	172	2.00	Sea Brief152⁴L'Escargot172⁵Highway View145¹⁰	5
28Oct72♦	Aintree(GB)	fm 2 15/16LH	5:57¹	6↑	Grand National Trial Hcp Chase Stk15000	2¹²	Carberry T	171	*4.50	Glenkiln140¹²L'Escargot171⁴Gyleburn1491½ Unhurried in 8th,progress under pressure 3 out,second best	11
26Sep72♦	Listowel(Ire)	fm 3LH	7:16²	6↑	Kerry National Hcp Chase Hcp3000	2½	Carberry T	175	*2.50	Culla Hill127½L'Escargot175½Clover Prince133⁵	5
27Apr72♦	Punchstwn(Ire)	fm 3 1/16RH	6:23¹	6↑	Guinness Handicap Chase Hcp5000	-	Moore ALT	169	8.00	Alaska Fort141²Colebridge152⁴Beggar's Way133⁶ Pulled up	11
8Apr72♦	Aintree(GB)	sf 4½LH	10:08²	7↑	Grand National Hcp Chase Stk75000	5⁷	Carberry T	168	*8.50	Well to Do141²Gay Trip163³ DH Black Secret156	42

16Mar72♦ Cheltenham(GB) sf *3¼LH 7:18 6↑ Cheltenham Gold Cup Chase Stk35000 | 47¾ | Carberry T | 168 | 4.00 | Glencaraig Lady168¾Royal Toss168hdThe Dikler1687 12
Prominent,balked and hit 3rd,one-paced from 2 out
5Feb72♦ Leopardstwn(Ire) hy 3LH 6:151 6↑ Foxrock Cup Hcp Chase Hcp2000 | 24 | Carberry T | 175 | *.80 | Esban1344L'Escargot175 3
27Dec71♦ Kempton(GB) gd 3RH 6:124 6↑ King George VI Chase Stk11800 | 48 | Carberry T | 168 | 6.00 | The Dikler161½Spanish Steps1687Titus Oakes168½ 10
Progress at 10th,one-paced from 2 out
27Nov71♦ Newbury(GB) gd *3¼LH 6:372 6↑ Hennessy Gold Cup Hcp Chase Stk19000 | 638 | Carberry T | 175 | 10.00 | Bighorn1516Young Ash Leaf1562Saggart's Choice14225 13
Blundered at 4th,always well behind
3Nov71♦ Fairyhouse(Ire) gd 3RH 7:071 6↑ Donaghmore Handicap Chase Hcp2000 | - | Carberry T | 175 | 6.00 | Veuve1395Proud Tarquin1602Alectryon133 5
Fell
12Apr71♦ Fairyhouse(Ire) gd 3½RH 7:191 6↑ Irish Grand National Hcp Chase Stk29000 | 32¼ | Carberry T | 175 | 8.00 | King's Sprite1391½Proud Tarquin155¾L'Escargot175 19
18Mar71♦ Cheltenham(GB) hy *3¼LH 8:003 6↑ Cheltenham Gold Cup Chase Stk25000 | 110 | Carberry T | 168 | *3.50 | L'Escargot16810Leap Frog16815The Dikler168 8
Chased leader from 12th,left in lead 21st,all out
20Feb71♦ Leopardstwn(Ire) yl 3LH 6:29 6↑ Leopardstown Handicap Chase Hcp6700 | 34 | Carberry T | 170 | 12.00 | Macroney1336King's Sprite1373L'Escargot170 10
9Jan71♦ Punchstwn(Ire) sf 3RH 7:053 6↑ Rathside Chase Alw2700 | - | Carberry T | 168 | *1.75 | French Tan16412No Other1605Proud Tarquin160 6
Lost rider
28Dec70♦ Fairyhouse(Ire) hy 2RH 4:084 4↑ Sweeps Hurdle Stk31000 | 4 | Carberry T | 162 | 4.00 | Persian War1688Lockyersleigh1626Inishmaan160 11
14Nov70- 4Cam sf 2 13/16 S'Chase 5:20 4↑ Colonial Cup 100k - 11 1010 41½ 47½ | 49 | Carberry T | 160 | - -- | Top Bid1601½Shadow Brook1601½Jaunty1586 22
19Mar70♦ Cheltenham(GB) gd *3¼LH 6:472 6↑ Cheltenham Gold Cup Chase Stk25300 | 11½ | Carberry T | 168 | 33.00 | L'Escargot1681½French Tan16810Spanish Steps1686 12
Progress from 6 out,led run-in,all out
21Feb70♦ Navan(Ire) hy 3LH 6:362 6↑ Leopardstown Hcp Chase Hcp8200 | 215 | Carberry T | 167 | *1.50 | King Vulgan14515L'Escargot1671Plume1425 9
17Jan70♦ Haydock(GB) sf 2½LH 5:053 6↑ World Premier Chase Final Stk14000 | 12 | Carberry T | 154 | *2.25 | L'Escargot1542East Bound159nkYoung Ash Leaf15415 17
Always close up,led 1 out,ridden out
26Dec69♦ Fairyhouse(Ire) yl 2¼RH 4:494 5↑ Paddock Handicap Chase Hcp2000 | 13 | Carberry T | 171 | 2.75 | L'Escargot1713Garrynagree16212Dead Beat1336 6
15Nov69♦ Punchstwn(Ire) gd 2½RH 5:244 5↑ Sandymount Chase Alw3200 | 210 | Carberry T | 164 | *.80 | East Bound14310L'Escargot16420Arthur McAlinden15910 11
17Oct69- 6Bel fm 3 S'Chase 5:403 4↑ Temple Gwathmey H 58k 10 5 35 23 2½ | 33 | Carberry T | 152 | *2.30 -- | Somaten1323LakeDelaware148noL'Escargot1521 Bobbled 18th 12
3Jun69- 5Bel sf 2½ S'Chase 4:523 4↑ Meadow Brook H 23k 4 6 44½ 21½ 2hd | 1hd | Carberry T | 148 | 5.40 -- | L'Escargot148hdRural Riot139½Wanderlure1478 Driving 12
12May69♦ Leopardstwn(Ire) sf 2¼LH 4:531 5↑ Woodbine Chase Alw2000 | 18 | Carberry T | 166 | *.50 | L'Escargot1668Twigairy16320Struell Park16610 5
1May69♦ Punchstwn(Ire) gd 2RH 4:17 5↑ Colliers Chase Alw2200 | 16 | Carberry T | 158 | *.65 | L'Escargot1586Twigairy1638Devon Fair1536 5
7Apr69♦ Fairyhouse(Ire) gd 2¼RH 4:45 5↑ Power Gold Cup Chase Alw3600 | 210 | Coonan R | 159 | 3.00 | Kinloch Brae17110L'Escargot15912Straight Fort1714 8
19Mar69♦ Cheltenham(GB) hy 2⅛LH 4:414 5↑ Champion Hurdle Stk25000 | 410½ | Carberry T | 168 | 6.50 | Persian War1684Drumikill1382½Privy Seal1664 17
Chased leader from 4th,one-paced after 7th
22Feb69♦ Leopardstwn(Ire) hy 2LH 4:332 5↑ Scalp Hurdle Alw2800 | 112 | Carberry T | 168 | 4.50 | L'Escargot16812Muir1688Caro Bello1654 10
11Jan69♦ Leopardstwn(Ire) hy 2LH 4:304 5↑ Ticknock Handicap Hurdle Hcp1200 | 34¼ | Carberry T | 166 | 3.00 | French Excuse1424Casque131nkL'Escargot1661½ 8
28Dec68♦ Leopardstwn(Ire) sf 2⅜LH 5:014 5↑ Tower Handicap Hurdle Hcp2600 | 6 | Carberry T | 168 | 5.00 | San-Feliu1452½Shan La1283Ladyfort1488 8
22May68♦ Down Royal(Ire) gd 2RH 3:443 4↑ Carling Black Label Novice Hurdle Alw1700 | 21½ | Carberry T | 167 | *.80 | Ispahan1411½L'Escargot167hdFrench Alliance1492½ 9
30Apr68♦ Punchstwn(Ire) yl 2RH 3:564 5↑ Irish Champion Novice Hurdle Stk4000 | 412 | Carberry T | 167 | 3.00 | Ebony King1572King Candy1534French Tan1686 12
19Mar68♦ Cheltenham(GB) fm 2⅛LH 4:091 5↑ Gloucestershire Hurdle Alw4000 | 16 | Carberry T | 172 | | L'Escargot1726Pick Me Up16415King Penny174½ 11
Led throughout,ridden out
2Mar68♦ Naas(Ire) gd 2⅛LH 4:221 4↑ Oberstown Hurdle Alw3200 | 14 | Carberry P | 152 | 10.00 | L'Escargot1524Golden Scene1473Murpep1452 13
14Oct67♦ Naas(Ire) sf 2⅛ⓉLH 4:262 4↑ Rathangan INH Flat Race (Amateurs) Alw1600 | 12 | Hanbury B | 170 | 3.50 | L'Escargot1702Honest Injun1702½DPlutarch1701 17
27Apr67♦ Punchstwn(Ire) gd 2ⓉRH 3:412 4↑ Cooltrim Plate Alw1600 | 23 | Hanbury B | 167 | 2.50 | Garrynagree1623L'Escargot1676Fulmar1703 13
25Mar67♦ PhoenixPark(Ire) gd 2ⓉRH 3:473 4↑ Ashbourne INH Flat Race (Amateurs) Alw1200 | 21 | Hanbury B | 165 | 6.00 | Irish National1551L'Escargot1653Chamac165½ 16
15Feb67♦ Navan(Ire) sf 2ⓉLH 4:182 Grattan Cup (Amateur Riders) Mdn700 | 15 | Hanbury B5 | 156 | 14.30 | L'Escargot1565Garrynagree15615Nostra1616 22

Mako

dkb. g. 1960, by Tulyar (Tehran)–Puccoon, by Bull Lea **Lifetime record: 75 18 13 12 $162,373**
Own.– Mrs Ogden Phipps
Br.– Ogden Phipps & Wheatley Stable (Ky)
Tr.– D.M. Smithwick

25Oct68- 6Bel sf 3⅛ S'Chase 6:02 4↑ Temple Gwathmey H 55k 6 3 39 710 - - Mahoney J 155 s *.80e -- ChinRun1401½Apollon1462GntlBoy13620 Unseated rider 17th 8
15Oct68- 5Bel fm 2½ S'Chase 4:421 4↑ Brook H 19k 2 2 625 614 425 530 Mahoney J 159 s *1.90e -- Roublet153hdBonNouvel16113ChinaRun13714 Far off leaders 8
1Oct68- 5Bel hd 2⅛ S'Chase 3:533 4↑ Broad Hollow H 16k 3 2 25 34 616 632 Armstrong R 162 s *1.20e -- Exhibit A.1451Bon Nouvel16218Flying Artist1462½ Tired 6
14Sep68- 7Fai fm *1⅞ Hurdles 3:243 3↑ Handicap 3000 5 5 46¼ 59¾ 519 524 Aitcheson J Jr 165 *1.30 -- Farmers Lot1485Bold Beggar1486Shod Over1408 Dull 5
7Sep68- 4Fai fm *1¼Ⓣ 2:09 3↑ Alw 1200 5 3 36 35¾ 33¼ 1¾ O'Brien L 142 *1.70e -- Mako142¾Gaelic Prince1422Semaforo1392½ Driving 17
27Oct67- 6Aqu sf 3 S'Chase 5:463 4↑ Temple Gwathmey H 55k 4 4 44½ 48 429 429 Aitcheson J Jr 168 s *.80e -- Bampton Castle14717Lumiere1357Irish Hammer1425 Evenly 7
17Oct67- 5Aqu fm 2½ S'Chase 4:403 4↑ Brook H 19k 1 3 310 319 33 34¼ Aitcheson J 170 s *.60e -- BragadoII1393½IrishHammer139¾Mko1704½ Poor landing last 5
3Oct67- 5Aqu fm 2 1/16 S'Chase 3:472 4↑ Broad Hollow H 16k 5 3 32½ 39 1hd 13 Aitcheson J 166 s *.30e -- Mako1663Golpista1523¾Irish Hammer138½ Drew out easily 5
25Sep67- 3Aqu fm 2 1/16 S'Chase 3:481 4↑ Harbor Hill H 10k 2 3 34 21 14 112 Aitcheson J 164 s 2.10e -- Mako16412HoistHimAboard1461½BragadoII1401½ Easily best 7
9Sep67- 2Fai fm *1 1/16Ⓣ 2:004 3↑ Alw 1200 17 8 77 65½ 52 2nk Aitcheson J Jr 141 s *1.00e -- Mighty Stroke143nkMako141hdKyrenia1381 Strong late rush 17
24Aug67- 5Sar fm 2½ S'Chase 4:464 4↑ Saratoga H 20k 1 1 15 18 33½ 313½ Aitcheson J 163 s *1.00 -- Spooky Joe1494½Lumiere1369Mako163 Long lead,weakened 4
4Aug67- 5Sar gd 2 1/16 S'Chase 3:493 4↑ Beverwyck H 16k 2 2 1hd 13 1½ 22½ Aitcheson J Jr 165 s *1.00 -- Spooky Joe1442½Mako16510Lumiere142hd Tired under impost 5
2Jun67- 5Aqu fm 3 S'Chase 5:392 4↑ Grand National H 39k 5 - - - - - O'Brien L 164 s *.70e -- Golpista1466General Tingle143hdBampton Castle1463 8
Bobbled 2nd,lost rider

18May67- 5Aqu fm 2½ S'Chase 4:391 4↑ Meadow Brook H 22k 2 5 33 33 14 18 O'Brien L 160 *1.50e -- Mako1608Golpista1443Tuscalee160nk Speed to spare 10
13May67- 1Mal fm *1¾Ⓣ 3:202 4↑ Alw 1000 9 7 55½ 31½ 3½ 2¾ Aitcheson J Jr 149 s -e -- Pardor149¾Mako149½Tout Royal149½ Showed game effort 10
22Apr67- 6Mid hd *1¼Ⓣ 2:152 3↑ Alw 200 2 4 1hd 1hd 33½ 54½ O'Brien L 152 -e -- Double Easter149½Irish Hammer146¾Taut Ship1502 Tired 12
28Oct66- 6Aqu fm 3 S'Chase 5:424 4↑ Temple Gwathmey H 54k 3 1 16 110 21 39 Walsh T 168 s *.50e -- Lumiere1338Bampton Castle1471Mako1687 Fenced poorly 6
4Oct66- 5Aqu sf 2½ S'Chase 4:451 4↑ Brook H 20k 6 2 23 23 310 415 Walsh T 171 *.70e -- General Tingle1497Tails1322Hoist Him Aboard1506 Bobbled 8
25Aug66- 5Sar fm 2½ S'Chase 4:373 4↑ Saratoga H 21k 1 1 31 13 13 18 Walsh T 166 s *.60 -- Mako1668RuralRiot13514GeneralTingle155 Drew out easily 4
5Aug66- 5Sar fm 2 1/16 S'Chase 3:463 4↑ Beverwyck H 16k 2 1 23 23 11½ 13 Walsh T 163 s *.80 -- Mako1633SurugaBay1431½KingsCreek149 Drew out easily flat 5
6Jun66- 5Aqu fm 2½ S'Chase 4:403 4↑ Meadow Brook H 21k 2 1 1hd 11 14 18 Walsh T 158 s *.80e -- Mako1588Tails13410Gramatam1352½ Speed to spare 5
28May66- 5Pur sf *1⅛Ⓣ 2:092 3↑ Alw 600 5 1 12½ 18 16 18 Smithwick AP 148 s *.60e -- Mko1488MarchKing1571½CombinedOperation1531 Under drive 6
11May66- 3Aqu fm 2 1/16 S'Chase 3:512 4↑ Alw 7500 6 5 618 511 38 39½ Walsh T 158 s *.60e -- The Sport1586Lucentaur1433½Mako15810 Fair effort 7
3May66- 9Pim gd 1 1/16 :242 :484 1:134 1:474 4↑ Alw 7000 2 4 44 78 716 812 Lee T 113 3.70e 59-15 Protected112¾RainSong1121½DarkRuana111¾ Fell back early 11
23Apr66- 6Mid sf *1¼Ⓣ 2:173 3↑ Alw 200 12 - 710 Smithwick AP 152 -e -- PrinceBective1391½LazyRiver1381½EarlyFind1434 No threat 12
Dense fog
16Apr66- 5Mid fm *6fⓉ 1:15 3↑ Alw 200 15 11 108¾ 1010 98 89 Smithwick AP 155 s -e -- Win'sStar1431IntheePrime139½BigTulyar155½ Raced far back 15
29Oct65- 6Aqu hd 3 S'Chase 5:334 4↑ Temple Gwathmey H 54k 5 4 312 314 330 345 Smithwick AP 146 s *.30e -- Bon Nouvel17030Lucentaur13415Mako14650 Mate to winner 6
19Oct65- 5Aqu hd 3 S'Chase 5:383 4↑ Grand National H 27k 1 3 2½ 1½ 15 14 Walsh T 142 s *.50e -- Mako1424Lucentaur13315The Sport159½ Kept under urging 6
5Oct65- 5Aqu hd 2½ S'Chase 4:363 4↑ Brook H 20k 3 2 23 25 22 21 Smithwick AP 142 s *.30e -- Bon Nouvel1691Mako1423Sun Game14350 Bad landing 11th 5
18Sep65- 5Fai hd *2 S'Chase 3:573 3↑ Manly H 10k 3 2 2nk 2¾ 2½ 22½ Smithwick AP 153 s *1.00 -- Lucentaur1442½Mako1534½Navy Blue14210 Best of others 6
2Sep65- 5Aqu fm 2 1/16 S'Chase 3:49 4↑ Harbor Hill H 11k 5 5 53 21½ 12 14 Smithwick AP 145 s *1.90e -- Mako1454Risky1434Lucentaur1404 Won with something left 7
23Aug65- 3Sar fm 2 1/16 S'Chase 3:464 4↑ O Clm 6500 1 3 32 23 11½ 13½ Smithwick AP 147 s 5.30 -- Mako1473½Risky1478Sea Smoke1436 Fenced well,easily best 9
14Aug65- 3Sar sf 1⅞ Hurdles 3:24 3↑ Alw 5500 1 3 2½ 2½ 39 422½ Smithwick AP 148 sb 9.30 -- Risky15516SummitSlep1432½OldStr1324 Prominent until 9th 8
28Jly65- 5Mth fm *2 Hurdles 4:07 3↑ Midsummer H 17k 9 1 1hd - - - Smithwick AP 141 sb 15.30 -- Gentles Pride150½Sacred River1422½My Passion1474 10
Used early,outdistanced
19Jly65- 5Del fm 1 1/16Ⓣ 1:442 3↑ Clm 14000 5 4 31½ 52¼ 44½ 56¾ Valenzuela A 114 b 21.20 75-16 Triumvirate112¾Ali Baba II1111½Local Gossip1184½ Tired 6
9Jly65- 3Mth fm *1¾ Hurdles 3:22 3↑ Alw 4000 5 3 2½ 23 4¾ 313½ Smithwick AP 148 sb 3.20e -- Tuscalee15412JumpingJuptr1421½Mko1482½ Held for placing 11
5Jly65- 7Del fst 6f :224 :462 1:112 3↑ Alw 4500 3 7 711 814 812 814 Valenzuela A 112 b 42.10 74-18 Snow House1193½Communique122hdHelioroad108½ No speed 8
2Jun65- 3Aqu fm 2 1/16 S'Chase 3:544 4↑ Alw 5500 2 3 35 35 511 514 Smithwick AP 147 sb 2.90e -- KingsCreek1483½OrkhanBoy1392½Lucentur1301½ Poor landing 8
20May65- 5Aqu fm 2 S'Chase 3:411 4↑ Hitchcock H 11k 3 1 2hd 53 628 635 Smithwick AP 155 sb 1.90e -- Golpista1514RaoRaja1543½NavyBlu154no Landed poorly late 7
6May65- 5Aqu fm 2 S'Chase 3:431 4↑ Aqu Spring 14k 6 1 14 12 1hd 2nk Smithwick AP 151 5.20 -- Gramatam148nkMako1512Navy Blue1542 Bobbled,missed 9
30Apr65- 9Pim fm 1 1/16Ⓣ :243 :481 1:123 1:443 4↑ Alw 5000 1 1 31 613 813 819 Corle RE 119 27.80 73-08 Hyperborean113¾Triumvirate1154Zapata1192½ Tired 9
17Apr65- 6Mid fm *1¼Ⓣ 2:19 3↑ Alw 200 9 1 11 1nk 12 11½ Smithwick AP 149 s -e -- Mako1491½Bonus Pot152½Sun Game146¾ Kept to drive 11
7Nov64- 4Mtp fm *2 S'Chase 3:573 3↑ Alw 1200 2 1 1¾ 2½ 2no 1no Smithwick AP 149 s -e -- Mako149noPocketRocket143nkSkyJinks1394 Up final strides 7
29Oct64- 6Aqu fm 2½ S'Chase 4:34 4↑ NY Turf Writers H 18k 1 2 38 21½ 39½ 218 Smithwick AP 145 s 14.60e -- Sun Game13918Mako1451½Exhibit A.1606 Bad landing 11th 9
23Oct64- 3Aqu sf 1⅝ Hurdles 2:534 3↑ Alw 6000 1 4 31½ 2½ 11 21½ Smithwick AP 151 s 13.60 -- Navy Blue1511½Mako1511Sun Game1512 Game effort 9
15Oct64- 5Aqu hd 2½ S'Chase 4:313 4↑ Rouge Dragon H 11k 1 6 68½ 613 624 634 Smithwick AP 144 sb 10.35 -- Gramatam1391MonarcaII145hdExhibitA.1635 Never a factor 8
24Sep64- 5Aqu hd 2 S'Chase 3:431 4↑ C L Appleton Mem H 11k 8 4 415 23 53½ 66¼ Smithwick AP 145 sb 2.65e -- BeModerate1442Hustle1531RedCircle139¾ Poor landing last 8
19Sep64- 3Fai hd *2 S'Chase 4:023 3↑ Handicap 3000 1 5 56¼ 2hd 13 13½ Smithwick AP 148 s *1.30 -- Mako1433½Half Baked144½Greek King II137¾ Ridden out 5
12Sep64- 2Fai hd 1 1/16Ⓣ 1:483 3↑ Alw 1200 9 6 42¾ 42¾ 42¼ 45¾ Smithwick AP 148 s 2.30e -- LightofDevon1483KingsWild141hdPocketRocket1482¾ Evenly 14
2May64- 5War sf *2 S'Chase 5:143 4↑ Sp Wt 800 4 2 2hd 11 16 12½ Smithwick AP 144 s -e -- Mako1442½What a Boy15330Eugarie148 Kept to hard drive 5
24Oct63- 3Aqu hd *1⅞ Hurdles 3:22 L E Stoddard Jr H 14k 2 5 59½ 52 74¾ 66 Smithwick AP 147 s 3.80e -- Fort Riley139hdTask Force1453½Vesuvius1371 Rough trip 9
4Oct63- 3Aqu fm *1⅝ Hurdles 2:543 Alw 4500 1 4 2hd 11 11½ 22 Smithwick AP 145 sb *.50e -- Marigny1452Mako1452Vesuvius1457 Clear lead,tired 8
26Sep63- 5Aqu fm *1⅞ Hurdles 3:223 Elkridge H 13k 5 4 34½ 3½ 1hd 3nk Smithwick AP 148 sb 2.20 -- Citizenship137hdLumiere136hdMako1482½ Led,gamely 7
16Sep63- 3Aqu sf *1⅝ Hurdles 2:554 3↑ Alw 4300 7 2 32 31½ 1½ 21 Smithwick AP 143 s 2.35 -- Task Force1381Mako1431Prosecutor153¾ Used reaching lead 7
15Aug63- 5Sar fm 1⅝ Hurdles 2:51 Promise H 13k 4 4 48½ 24 24 28 Smithwick AP 143 s 3.65 -- WillIRule1498Mko1436TskForc13712 Bad landing 3rd,gamely 7
3Aug63- 8Sar fm 1 1/16Ⓣ 1:414 3↑ Alw 4700 3 7 87½ 86 55 46 Combest J 111 35.80 91-03 UnclePercy1153½TeleJr.111½SyltII1192 Failed to threaten 11
23Jly63- 3Mth fm *1½ Hurdles 2:46 3↑ Alw 3500 2 3 42 32 33 34¾ Smithwick AP 142 s *1.90 -- RapidAddition1433RamshornCreek1481¾Mko1427 No excuse 8
3Jly63- 3Del fm *1½ Hurdles 2:474 O Md 5000 5 6 44 1hd 1½ 11½ Smithwick AP 145 s *.70 -- Mako1451½Task Force1453½Miller Street14510 Easily best 8
18Jun63- 5Aqu fm *1⅝ Hurdles 2:483 Annapolis 11k 5 6 57½ 25 22 23 Smithwick AP 140 s 18.95 -- Will I Rule1453Mako1408Lumiere1378 Bore in 5th 7
8Jun63- 6Aqu sf 1 1/16Ⓣ 1:451 Handicap 7500 4 3 33½ 79 715 723 Sorrentino M 112 b 2.60e 59-18 TheIbex1243MarlinBay1181Cabelry113nk Dropped back early 7
29May63- 7Aqu sly 1 :223 :454 1:113 1:39 3↑ Alw 7500 5 6 69 65½ 55 57¼ Errico C 107 23.35 66-18 FirstBreak1081¼JimmyCannon112noAncientAttc1161 No speed 6
23May63- 6Aqu fst 6f :223 :454 1:102 Alw 5000 1 7 108¾ 811 617 616 Boland W 117 89.70 77-13 MatchWits1177½MarlinBay117noWaterTwister122½ No speed 10
23Apr63- 7Lrl fst 6f :224 :464 1:113 Alw 4500 4 2 66¾ 613 618 619 Chambers W 112 3.10 77-07 Fairfab1122½Cycloreen1073Short Nail1124 Couldn't stay 7
29Nov62- 7Pim fst 1 1/16 :243 :482 1:134 1:471 Alw 3500 3 4 46 24 1hd 12 Chambers W 122 7.80 74-23 Mako1222Knocklofty122nkPrinceo'Pilsen1223 Kept driving 8
17Nov62- 6Pim fst 6f :232 :47 :592 1:114 Alw 4000 10 9 105 1012 711 711 Broussard R 122 9.80 80-20 Chateaugay113hdSirGay1185TheSmoochr1113 Showed nothing 11
5Nov62- 1Lrl sly 7f :233 :49 1:153 1:283 Md Sp Wt 8 5 52½ 31 1hd 1nk Broussard R 118 3.40 77-18 Mako118nkTeleJr.1182½Scopelk118nk Kept under hard drive 11
Previously owned by O. Phipps; previously trained by J. Fitzsimmons
9Oct62- 6Bel fst 6f :22 :45 1:11 ⒸMd Sp Wt 8 8 610 613 617 610 Ruane J 122 10.40 82-13 Crewman1225Might and Main1222½Rolling Sea1221 Far back 10
4Oct62- 4Bel fst 6f :221 :46 1:104 ⒸMd Sp Wt 6 5 56 64¾ 76½ 812 Sellers J 122 b 4.15 81-15 NoRobbery1226PartyDancer1221¾JohnCanoe122nk Fell back 9
29Sep62- 4Aqu gd 7f :224 :462 1:111 1:243 Md Sp Wt 14 3 63½ 44 37 616 Shoemaker W 122 b *3.00 68-17 CoolPrince1228Dowdeley-Dow1221½Reap theWind1226 Tired 14
21Sep62- 6Aqu fst 7f :223 :46 1:111 1:24 ⒸMd Sp Wt 3 12 64¼ 65¼ 36 37½ Sellers J 122 b 3.50 79-12 SirGay1222½Macedonia1225Mako1222 Rallied insufficiently 14
15Sep62- 1Aqu fst 7f :233 :471 1:123 1:253 Md Sp Wt 7 6 2hd 2hd 2hd 3¾ Sellers J 122 b *3.10 78-13 HonorBlue117½Tempr122nkMko1225½ Forced pace,weakened 14
15Jun62- 4Bel gd 5½f :234 :48 1:07 ⒸMd Sp Wt 4 5 2hd 2hd 2hd 21½ Woodhouse H 122 b *2.25 84-18 MonsieurDavid1221½Mako1221HonorBlu122no Held lead,tired 10
23Apr62- 3Aqu fst 5f :232 :474 1:001 ⒸMd Sp Wt 2 9 44 42½ 35½ 39¼ Woodhouse H 122 3.35 80-22 Cheshire1221¼RoyalTurn1228Mako122¾ Well placed,no rally 10
17Apr62- 3Aqu fst 5f :224 :474 1:011 ⒸMd Sp Wt 10 9 811 611 54 32¼ Woodhouse H 122 8.00 82-26 President Jim1221Prosperous1221¼Mako122¾ Good late bid 10
9Apr62- 3Aqu gd 5f :223 :463 :592 ⒸMd Sp Wt 2 4 95¾ 44 55½ 55¼ Woodhouse H 122 *2.40 88-16 The Beadle1222½Prosperous1222Marching Song122½ Green 10

Moccasin

ch. f. 1963, by Nantallah (Nasrullah)–Rough Shod II, by Gold Bridge **Lifetime record: 21 11 2 4 $388,075**

Own.– Claiborne Farm
Br.– Claiborne Farm (Ky)
Tr.– H. Trotsek

17Jun67- 9AP sly 1 :222 :451 1:103 1:37 3↑ Equipose Mile 43k 2 4 47½ 44¼ 69 59½ Fires E 115 2.20 68-29 Renewed Vigor1111½Estreno II1111½Errante II1144½ 7
Flattened out in drive
24May67- 8AP fst 7f :231 :46 1:103 1:23 3↑ ⒻFour Winds H 21k 4 6 45 67¼ 45½ 31 Fires E 121 b *1.10 89-17 MssMoon120hdMstySwords1111Mccsn1215 Wide,strong finish 7
22Apr67- 6Kee fst 1 1/16 :241 :473 1:114 1:45 3↑ Ben Ali H 23k 3 2 21½ 2hd 32 31¼ Fires E 116 b *1.30 80-17 FrancisU.119nkSwiftRuler1201Moccsn1161½ Lacked response 6
8Apr67- 6Kee fst 6f :213 :451 :571 1:093 3↑ Phoenix H 23k 1 6 43½ 22 2hd 11 Knapp K 114 b 3.30 95-15 Mccsn1141CountryFrnd1144¾GlbrtB.114hd Wore down leader 7
25Feb67- 8Bow fst 7f :223 :442 1:084 1:214 3↑ ⒻBarbara Fritchie H 59k 5 8 4nk 32 3½ 2nk Broussard R 120 b *.60 104-05 Holly-O117nkMccsn1202½LdyDplmt1112¾ Bobbled leaving gate 13
15Feb67- 8Hia fst 7f :23 :452 1:10 1:23 3↑ ⒻColumbiana H 33k 4 3 1½ 15 13 2hd Hartack W 117 b *2.40 94-16 Mac'sSparkler115hdMoccasin1171½StraightDeal122½ Failed 14
6Feb67- 9Hia fst 6f :22 :444 1:103 4↑ Alw 5500 3 8 52¼ 65¼ 46 31¾ Baeza B 114 b *1.00 89-14 FleetAdmiral116¾GoldenButtons1131Moccasin114¾ Steadied 12
4Aug66- 8Sar fst 7f :223 :45 1:10 1:232 ⒻTest (Div 2) 24k 8 2 2hd 23 22 11½ Baeza B 118 b *.90 93-13 Moccasin1181½Native Street1242Politely112¾ Going away 10
25Jun66- 7Aqu fst 1¼ :472 1:12 1:382 2:05 ⒻC C A Oaks 119k 2 2 22 42½ 55 59¼ Broussard R 121 b 2.40 64-17 LadyPitt121¾DGentleRain121nkPridesProfile1218 Weakened 10
28May66- 7Aqu sly 1 :224 :452 1:102 1:36 ⒻAcorn 59k 7 4 22 21 2hd 34½ Broussard R 121 b *1.40 83-18 Marking Time1212½Around the Roses1212Moccasin121½ Tired 11

17May66- 7Aqu	fst 6f	:222 :453 1:102	Alw 10000	5 5 21½ 21 1hd 11½	Baeza B	112 b	*1.10	91-19	Moccasin1121½Imam1151Bold Tactics115nk	Bore out,handily	6
16Apr66- 6Kee	fst 6f	:213 :45 1:10	Ⓕ Ashland 30k	3 9 54½ 66½ 66½ 66¼	Adams L	121	*.30	87-12	Justakiss121nkPridsProfl1211½ChmpgnWomn1182	Away slowly	9
9Apr66- 7Kee	fst 6f	:214 :452 1:101	Ⓕ Alw 10000	6 5 67½ 66½ 55 41¾	Adams L	121	*.20	90-14	Stealaway115¾Dutch Maid110hdJustakiss1211		6
	In close entering stretch										
6Nov65- 8GS	fst 1 1/16	:234 :471 1:121 1:442	Ⓕ Gardenia 183k	7 3 35 31 11½ 12½	Adams L	119	*.30	83-21	Moccasin1192½Lady Pitt119½Prides Profile119nk	Cleverly	9
23Oct65- 0Lrl	fst 1 1/16	:244 :491 1:144 1:454	Ⓕ Selima 93k	1 1 12 13 14½ 15	Adams L	119	-	88-15	Moccasin1195SwiftLady119½Drryll114¾	Scored well in hand	5
	Run between 6th and 7th races. No wagering										
16Oct65- 6Kee	fst *7f	1:254	Ⓕ Alcibiades 37k	2 3 1½ 14 18 115	Adams L	119	-	94-16	Moccasin11915Chalina119noHurry Star11920	Speed to spare	4
	No wagering										
9Oct65- 4Kee	fst 6½f	:23 :463 1:113 1:18	Ⓕ Alw 7500	1 7 76 43¼ 1hd 13	Adams L	119	*.10	88-14	Moccasin1193Fanrullah1074½Strawshy1071½	Drew out easily	7
11Sep65- 7Aqu	fst 6f	:223 :464 1:113	Ⓕ Matron 108k	3 2 2½ 2hd 14 16	Adams L	119	*.40	85-20	Moccasin1196Lyvette1192Shimmering Gold1191	Easily	12
25Aug65- 7Sar	fst 6f	:22 :451 1:11	Ⓕ Spinaway 76k	7 1 2hd 11 14 13½	Adams L	119	*.30	93-10	Moccasin1193½Swift Lady119noForefoot119hd	Much the best	7
17Aug65- 6Sar	fst 5½f	:214 :452 :573 1:04	Ⓕ Alw 5500	1 3 1½ 11 15 18	Adams L	119	*.30	97-11	Moccasin1198IndianSunlite1196RoyalTantrm1193½	Galloping	7
6Aug65- 4Sar	fst 5½f	:221 :46 :58 1:042	Ⓕ Md Sp Wt	9 2 11½ 11½ 14 18	Adams L	119	7.90	95-13	Moccasin1198Lady Dulcinea1196Ultra Quest1192	Easily	12

Mongo

ch. c. 1959, by Royal Charger (Nearco)–Accra, by Annapolis — **Lifetime record: 46 22 10 4 $820,766**

Own.– Montpelier
Br.– Mrs Marion duPont Scott (Va)
Tr.– F.A. Bonsal

11Nov64- 8GS	fst 1¼	:464 1:11 1:352 2:00	3↑ Trenton H 59k	6 6 66½ 2hd 1hd 1½	Chambers W	125	3.00e	105-10	Mongo125½Drill Site112½Sunrise Flight1171¼	Hard drive	8
29Oct64- 5GS	fst 1 1/16	:241 :474 1:111 1:421	4↑ Alw 5500	1 2 22 2½ 1hd 1hd	Chambers W	116	*.70	97-13	Mongo116hdDrill Site113nkSunrise Flight1166	All out	6
10Oct64- 7Atl	fm 1 1/16Ⓣ	1:444	3↑ Boardwalk H 29k	3 5 52¾ 64½ 67¼ 49	Chambers W	127	*.70e	78-18	Turbo Jet II1181½Cool Prince1133Indoctrinate1154½	Tired	7
19Sep64- 8Atl	sf 1 3/16Ⓣ	1:574	3↑ U Nations H 125k	7 6 53½ 75½ 99 96¾	Chambers W	130	*1.90e	77-21	WesternWarrior114¾Parka121hdTurboJetII116nk	Fell back	10
22Aug64- 8Atl	fst 1 3/16	:484 1:122 1:373 1:561	3↑ Atl City H 33k	4 4 44 48 513 522	Chambers W	133	*.90	78-16	Inbalance1146Cool Prince1136Invigor113½	Sluggish,wide	6
8Aug64- 6Sar	fst 1⅛	:471 1:104 1:361 1:491	4↑ Whitney 54k	2 4 33 43½ 33½ 210	Chambers W	130	2.05	89-10	Gun Bow13010Mongo1303Delta Judge1113½	Bested the others	4
18Jly64- 8Mth	fst 1¼	:451 1:101 1:353 2:014	3↑ Monmouth H 107k	5 4 46 2hd 1½ 1nk	Chambers W	127	5.40	93-17	Mongo127nkKelso1304½Gun Bow12418	Drifted out slightly	5
27Jun64- 0Del	fst 1 1/16	:242 :474 1:114 1:434	3↑ Diamond State H 22k	4 2 22½ 2hd 11½ 11½	Chambers W	127	-	90-17	Mngo1271½BoldCmmndr1107ShootLuke1091½	Much the best	4
	Special event run between 7th and 8th races - No wagering										
25Apr64- 7Aqu	fst 1⅛	:463 1:102 1:352 1:482	3↑ Grey Lag H 82k	5 4 45¼ 43½ 24 24	Chambers W	128	3.20	95-16	Saidam1144Mongo128½Bonjour1122½	Finished willingly	7
11Apr64- 7Aqu	fst 1⅛	:48 1:12 1:371 1:50	3↑ Excelsior H 27k	1 2 23 31 53 53¾	Chambers W	129	*1.20	87-17	Uppercut1123Rocky Link116hdMorry E.115nk	In close,tired	6
7Mar64- 8Bow	fst 1 1/16	:24 :473 1:122 1:444	3↑ J B Campbell H 109k	2 6 53¼ 1½ 1½ 1no	Rotz JL	126	*1.30	89-20	Mongo126noGun Bow1261Uppercut1145	Drifted wide,lasted	7
22Feb64- 8Hia	sly 1¼	:47 1:111 1:363 2:011	3↑ Widener H 130k	2 3 46½ 11 11 1hd	Chambers W	125	*2.80	92-18	Mongo125hdSunriseFlight1192AdmrlVc1255	In close,driving	10
8Feb64- 8Hia	sl 1⅛	:464 1:113 1:364 1:494	3↑ Seminole H 61k	8 4 54¼ 31½ 22 53	Chambers W	125	*1.20	83-20	[DH]TopGallnt112[DH]AdmirlVic1241SunrsFlght1191¾	Bold bid	9
1Feb64- 0Hia	fst 7f	:233 :463 1:224	Sp Wt	1 1 11½ 12 11 12½	Chambers W	118	-	--	Mongo1182½DoctorHank1153½Tollwy1156	Drifted out,in hand	4
	Exhibition race - No purse,no wagering. Not to be considered as a race start										
11Nov63- 7Lrl	fm 1½Ⓣ	:483 1:133 2:033 2:272	3↑ D C Int'l 150k	9 1 1hd 11 1½ 1½	Chambers W	126	3.80	94-14	Mongo126½Kelso12612Nyrcos1223	Under long,hard drive	10
2Nov63- 8GS	my 1¼	:464 1:111 1:361 2:014	3↑ Trenton H 59k	4 3 34½ 22 22 22½	Chambers W	124	3.60	93-22	Carry Back1192½Mongo1242Smart1166	Showed good effort	10
19Oct63- 8GS	fst 1 1/16	:233 :47 1:112 1:424	3↑ Quaker City H 27k	3 3 34½ 33 33 34¼	Hartack W	127	*.80	92-14	Saidam1131Inbalance1143¼Mongo127nk	Lacked late response	5
14Sep63- 8Atl	fm 1 3/16Ⓣ	1:551	3↑ U Nations H 125k	2 2 43 31 2hd 12	Chambers W	124	4.90	97-03	Mngo1242NeverBnd118¾CarryBack1271½	Came outside,clear	10
	Daily Racing Form time,1:54 2/5										
31Aug63- 8Atl	fm 1⅛Ⓣ	1:48	3↑ Kelly-Olympic H 35k	10 3 42 43 43¼ 1no	Chambers W	124	*2.50	103-00	Mongo124noBronze Babu1201½Parka116¾	Up in final strides	10
17Aug63- 8Atl	fst 1⅛	:471 1:11 1:352 1:481	3↑ Atl City H 28k	3 5 514 36½ 33½ 32¾	Chambers W	125	*.90	94-12	DnCrl1092Inblnc113¾Mongo1259	Lacked sufficient response	7
20Jly63- 7Aqu	sly 1¼	:472 1:111 1:354 2:013	3↑ Brooklyn H 112k	3 4 33 32 31½ 52¼	Burr C	126	2.75	90-11	Cyrano113noSunrise County1161¼Lanvin108½	In close,tired	10
13Jly63- 8Mth	fst 1¼	:473 1:12 1:363 2:02	3↑ Monmouth H 111k	2 4 42½ 32 1hd 21½	Gilligan L	126	*2.30	90-16	Decidedly1201½Mongo1262½Guadalcanl113¾	Short lead,tired	9
29Jun63- 7Del	fst 1 1/16	:233 :47 1:113 1:431	3↑ Diamond State H 22k	5 4 43 32 2hd 1¾	Gilligan L	126	*.70	93-20	Mongo126¾FortheRoad1142½Polylad115nk	Under a mild drive	6
12Jun63- 8Mth	fst 1	:233 :464 1:113 1:364	3↑ Salvator Mile 17k	2 3 2½ 2hd 1hd 2nk	Gilligan L	126	*.50	89-17	Dedimoud118nkMngo1263½Narokn1144	Stumbled start,failed	6
25May63- 8GS	fst 1⅛	:482 1:121 1:371 1:501	3↑ Camden H 28k	2 1 11 11½ 13 12½	Gilligan L	126	*.90	86-14	Mongo1262½Military Plume1111¾Endymion1133	Mild urging	6
11May63- 7GS	gd 1 70	:223 :461 1:113 1:43	3↑ Valley Forge H 27k	1 2 23 22½ 21 3½	Gilligan L	127	*.50	81-22	Manassa Mauler113½Guadalcanal113hdMongo127¾	No excuse	6
23Mar63- 8Bow	fst 1 1/16	:242 :481 1:12 1:43	3↑ J B Campbell H 109k	6 3 34 47½ 49½ 46¾	Burr C	128	1.60	91-15	Kelso131¾Crimson Satan124hdGushing Wind1166	Forced up	6
9Mar63- 8Bow	fst 1 1/16	:241 :483 1:13 1:444	3↑ Bowie H 26k	5 2 2¾ 2hd 1hd 13½	Burr C	126	*.30	89-23	Mngo1263½WarCouncil1154½FruitShppr106½	Drew out easily	5
22Nov62- 7GS	my 1⅛	:474 1:121 1:381 1:512	3↑ Pilgrim H 55k	1 1 1½ 12½ 13 15	Burr C	120	*.90	80-29	Mongo1205Garwol1096Dedimoud1143	Going away with ease	6
3Nov62- 7GS	sly 1¼	:471 1:121 1:382 2:053	3↑ Trenton H 86k	6 2 2½ 13 12 1no	Burr C	118	5.40	77-29	Mongo118noCarryBck1294½Snstvo116¾	Best under hard drive	8
17Oct62- 7Bel	hd 1⅜Ⓣ	2:131	3↑ Knickerbocker H 30k	5 3 32 31½ 11 2¾	Burr C	120	5.45	103-00	TheAxeII120¾Mongo1201½IrishDandy112½	Clear lead,tired	12
15Sep62- 8Atl	fm 1 3/16Ⓣ	1:563	3↑ U Nations H 100k	5 6 41¾ 1hd 1hd 1nk	Burr C	117	8.70	90-10	Mongo117nkT.V.Lark123½WiseShip1232	Hard ridden to hold	12
1Sep62- 7Aqu	fst 1	:224 :453 1:09 1:343	Jerome H 58k	8 4 42 41¾ 45 65½	Burr C	121	*2.70	89-11	Black Beard1143Fauve109½Dedimoud116½	Well up,tired	12
11Aug62- 8Atl	sf 1 1/16Ⓣ	1:441	Ventnor Turf H 30k	13 2 21½ 12 18 110	Burr C	122	8.30	90-10	Mngo12210NobleJy122hdOurTwg1141	Scored with great ease	14
25Jly62- 7Aqu	fst 1	:224 :443 1:082 1:341	Lexington H 29k	5 2 32 31½ 11 1nk	Burr C	118	3.05	97-10	Mngo118nkDedmoud1172½InForc1172	Drifted out,hard drive	8
7Jly62- 7Del	fst 1	:234 :47 1:112 1:37	Alw 6500	4 2 12 13 15 18	Burr C	114	3.20	91-17	Mongo1148Cyane120¾Water Hole114nk	Long lead,easily best	7
18Jun62- 7Del	fst 6f	:224 :462 1:114	Alw 5000	1 3 32 53 33 23	Burr C	116	2.80	83-25	FortheRoad1163Mngo1161WaterHol1161½	Shuffled back turn	9
23Apr62- 7Lrl	fst 6f	:23 :472 1:122	Alw 4000	2 2 46 43½ 2hd 1¾	Chambers A	120	1.70	93-17	Mongo120¾In Force1173Nemrac1172½	Under strong handling	6
6Apr62- 7Lrl	fst 6f	:23 :47 1:113	Alw 4000	5 8 62¾ 53 22 11	Korte K	112	3.10	97-16	Mongo1121Bullfinch1191Nip o' Brandy1226	Won going away	9
4Nov61- 4Lrl	fst 7f	:231 :464 1:122 1:243	Alw 3200	5 3 52 4¾ 22 23	Lee T	114	*2.20	96-09	WillofIron1123Mngo1142¼DicksPet1145	Showed good effort	7
27Oct61- 7Lrl	fst 6f	:224 :48 1:133	Alw 3000	4 6 74¼ 61¾ 31½ 1¾	Lee T	113	*.80	87-15	Mngo113¾Astounded1132GetSomeMre1143½	Long,hard drive	10
14Oct61- 3GS	sly 6f	:23 :47 1:121	Alw 4000	4 3 51¾ 43 23 23½	Lee T	113	*1.60	79-20	PaddedCll1173½Mngo1135Dck'sPt1173½	Rallied,then evenly	8
27Sep61- 5Atl	fst 7f	:223 :452 1:10 1:222	Alw 3600	7 5 2½ 21 23 31¾	Lee T	109	*1.40	89-10	BrownBulldog116¾Nipo'Brndy1151Mongo109nk	Lacked a rally	8
12Sep61- 5Atl	fst 6f	:221 :45 1:094	Alw 3800	3 5 56¼ 56 34½ 43¾	Lee T	110	*1.50	92-12	SweetEvenin'1132LadyDame1161¼InForce119½	Mild bid,hung	7
2Sep61- 4Atl	fst 6f	:221 :453 1:102	Alw 3600	5 1 31½ 2½ 2nk	Lee T	119	4.10	93-07	Senator119nkMongo1191¼Proud Fox1143	Very sharp effort	8
31May61- 5Del	fst 5f	:22 :463 :592	Alw 4000	8 6 53¾ 68 57½ 55¾	Lee T	120	*.50	86-23	Princegret1201PostExchange1201GetSomeMor1201¾	No excuse	8
18May61- 5Pim	fst 5f	:23 :471 1:00	Md Sp Wt	4 3 11 14 16 110	Lee T	118	*.60	95-18	Mongo11810Reinav1182½Black Blazer118nk	Easily best	6

Native Diver

br. g. 1959, by Imbros (Polynesian)–Fleet Diver, by Devil Diver **Lifetime record: 81 37 7 12 $1,026,500**

Own.– Mr & Mrs L.K. Shapiro
Br.– Mr & Mrs L.K. Shapiro (Cal)
Tr.– M.E. Millerick

Date	Cond	Dist	Fractions	Race	Calls	Jockey	Wt	Odds	Spd	Top finishers	Comment	Fld
4Sep67- 8Dmr	fst	1⅛	:452 1:092 1:342 1:463	3↑ Del Mar H 43k	3 1 12 12 13 13½	Lambert J	130	*.50	100-14	NativeDiver1303½SharpDecline1093½QuickenTre117½	Handily	9
15Jly67- 8Hol	fst	1¼	:454 1:092 1:34 1:584	3↑ Hol Gold Cup H 162k	2 1 14 11 12 15	Lambert J	123	4.80	99-17	Native Diver1235Pretense131¾Biggs1174	Drew out easily	5
4Jly67- 8Hol	fst	1⅛	:452 1:093 1:341 1:47	3↑ American H 54k	6 1 13 11½ 23½ 24¼	Lambert J	123	3.90	93-15	Pretense1314¼Native Diver123¾Biggs1171¾	Held on gamely	8
17Jun67- 8Hol	fm	1 1/16Ⓣ	:221 :46 1:093 1:394	3↑ Inglewood H (Div 2) 44k	6 2 2hd 68½ 715 722	Lambert J	124	2.90	- -	Pretense1284½Biggs1171½AureliusII1114	Early speed,tired	7
3Jun67- 8Hol	fst	1 1/16	:23 :453 1:093 1:413	3↑ Californian 119k	12 4 43 87½ 1313 1317	Pierce D	127	*1.90	70-14	Biggs112¾Make Money1123¾Pretense130hd	Raced wide	14
20May67- 8Hol	fst	7f	:221 :442 1:084 1:21	3↑ Los Angeles H 54k	8 1 11½ 11 1½ 11½	Lambert J	128	*.90	95-16	NativeDivr1281½Shbson1112¼Chclro1142	Under steady drive	8
10May67- 8Hol	fst	6f	:22 :444 :564 1:091	3↑ Premiere H 27k	7 1 31½ 32 43½ 33¾	Lambert J	131	*1.30	91-10	FleetDiscovery1102Chiclero1151¾NativeDivr1312½	No rally	7
18Mar67- 8GG	fst	1	:224 :45 1:094 1:351	3↑ San Fran Mile H 16k	7 1 11½ 1½ 1½ 1hd	Lambert J	133	*.60	92-15	NativeDiver133hdPerris1134½TrplTux113no	Strong handling	8
11Mar67- 8GG	sly	6f	:214 :442 :57 1:092	3↑ Albany H 11k	2 4 1½ 1½ 1½ 11½	Lambert J	130	*.40	92-19	NativeDiver1301½TripleTux113hdChclro117hd	Driving clear	8
25Feb67- 8SA	fst	1¼	:454 1:10 1:352 2:004	3↑ S Anita H 145k	4 1 13½ 2hd 22 23	Pierce D	125	4.70	91-11	Pretense1183Native Diver125¾O'Hara1131½	Held gamely	9
11Feb67- 8SA	fst	1⅛	:45 1:092 1:351 1:483	4↑ San Antonio H 57k	2 1 12 1hd 23 35¼	Lambert J	128	*1.00	84-12	Pretense1212Drin1193¼NatvDvr1282	Set pace on loose rein	8
26Jan67- 8SA	gd	1 1/16	:23 :46 1:103 1:43	4↑ San Pasqual H 27k	3 1 1hd 2hd 32½ 34	Lambert J	132	*.70	84-21	Pretense1184Aurelius II114hdNative Diver1322	No excuse	5
7Jan67- 8SA	fst	7f	:22 :442 1:091 1:22	4↑ San Carlos H 62k	5 1 12 12½ 14 14	Lambert J	128	*2.20	93-15	NativeDiver1284HoistBar1152Pretense118½	Speed to spare	13
25Jly66- 8Hol	fst	1⅝	:454 1:361 2:022 2:402	3↑ Sunset H 85k	6 1 14 32 59 619	Lambert J	130	*1.60	70-16	O'Hara1132Rehabilitate1061½SilkHt1093	Set pace 6f,tired	11
16Jly66- 8Hol	fst	1¼	:451 1:091 1:341 2:00	3↑ Hol Gold Cup H 162k	7 1 12 13 15 14¾	Lambert J	126	*1.40	93-19	NativeDiver1264¾O'Hara112nkTravelOrb1188	Speed to spare	10
4Jly66- 8Hol	fst	1⅛	:452 1:092 1:35 1:474	3↑ American H 56k	7 1 12 13 11 2¾	Mahorney W	128	*1.10	92-16	TravelOrb118¾NativeDiver1284RealGoodDeal1122½	Stubborn	12
18Jun66- 8Hol	fst	1 1/16	:223 :452 1:094 1:413	3↑ Inglewood H 58k	2 1 12 12 13½ 16	Lambert J	125	*2.00	87-18	Native Diver1256Sledge1151Tronado113¾	Under mild drive	14
4Jun66- 8Hol	fst	1 1/16	:223 :453 1:094 1:414	3↑ Californian 120k	7 5 129¾ 1411 1412 1415	Lambert J	127	2.50	71-14	Travel Orb1121Make Money1121½Sledge1121¼	Bore out turns	14
21May66- 8Hol	fst	7f	:214 :44 1:084 1:213	3↑ Los Angeles H 54k	6 3 3½ 31 41½ 41½	Lambert J	128	*.80	90-15	Nasharco1131Pelegrn116nkAurlusII111nk	Hung under impost	8
11May66- 8Hol	fst	6f	:221 :45 :571 1:101	3↑ Premiere H 28k	7 1 41¼ 63 78½ 74¼	Lambert J	130	*.60	86-20	Sledg115noChclro110nkRlGoodDl116½	Forced wide,no chance	9
9Mar66- 7SA	fst	1 1/16	:224 :453 1:093 1:403	3↑ San Bernardino H 27k	5 1 12½ 11½ 11½ 12½	Lambert J	130	*.50e	100-10	Native Diver1302½Real Good Deal1169Prairie Schooner1141	Mild drive	5
26Feb66- 8SA	fst	1¼	:452 1:094 1:35 2:001	3↑ S Anita H 145k	2 1 12 2½ 3nk 32	Lambert J	126	6.10	96-12	Lucky Debonair1241Cupid1171Native Diver126nk	Gamely	13
12Feb66- 8SA	fst	1⅛	:452 1:092 1:343 1:47	4↑ San Antonio H 56k	5 1 12 1hd 43 45	Lambert J	128	2.20	92-14	HillRise125½Terry'sSecret1222½BoldBidder1252	Weakened	6
25Jan66- 8SA	fst	1 1/16	:224 :453 1:094 1:41	4↑ San Pasqual H 28k	3 1 14 11½ 11½ 1hd	Lambert J	128	*1.60	98-15	NativeDiver128hdCupid118nkIsleofGrc1191¼	Lasted,driving	10
8Jan66- 8SA	fst	7f	:22 :443 1:091 1:22	4↑ San Carlos H 61k	7 6 2½ 44½ 1010 109½	Lambert J	132	*1.20	83-15	Cupid1152HillRise126noQuitDud115no	Lost action,bore out	12
28Dec65- 7SA	fst	6f	:213 :442 :563 1:09	3↑ Palos Verdes H 22k	6 1 1½ 11 1½ 1nk	Lambert J	129	*.50	97-13	Native Diver129nkIsle of Greece1141Sledge1211	Driving	6
6Sep65- 8AP	fst	1	:223 :451 1:094 1:351	3↑ Wash Park H 113k	8 1 2hd 33 32½ 62½	Lambert J	128	*2.00	90-11	Take Over110noChieftain126noGallant Romeo1201	Weakened	11
7Aug65- 7Dmr	fst	1 1/16	:221 :45 1:09 1:40	3↑ San Diego H 22k	4 1 13 11½ 12 13½	Lambert J	131	*.30	100-11	NativeDiver1313½NearcoBlue1104½Carang111¾	Much the best	8
17Jly65- 8Hol	fst	1¼	:444 1:084 1:341 2:001	3↑ Hol Gold Cup H 162k	3 1 16 13 14 15	Lambert J	124	*1.20	92-13	NativeDiver1245Babington1141½HllRs1212	As rider pleased	7
5Jly65- 8Hol	fst	1⅛	:45 1:09 1:342 1:471	3↑ American H 53k	1 1 16 12 14 12	Lambert J	125	3.90	96-11	NativeDiver1252Trondo1181¼HllRs122¾	Scored well in hand	6
22May65- 8Hol	fst	7f	:221 :44 1:074 1:20	3↑ Los Angeles H 55k	3 3 11½ 1hd 1hd 1nk	Lambert J	126	1.90	100-13	NativeDiver126nkVikngSprt1266Trondo115¾	Long,hard drive	9
12May65- 8Hol	fst	6f	:214 :441 :561 1:082	3↑ Premiere H 27k	6 3 3nk 2½ 31½ 34	Lambert J	127	*1.40	95-10	VikingSpirit1233Perris1131NtvDvr127hd	Forced pace,tired	8
27Mar65- 8GG	my	1	:222 :453 1:104 1:364	3↑ San Fran Mile H 15k	1 1 13 1½ 1hd 22½	Lambert J	128	*.50	81-24	Viking Spirit1192½Native Diver1286Honored Sir113½	Bore out stretch	5
13Mar65- 8GG	my	6f	:214 :453 :58 1:11	3↑ Albany H 10k	2 4 33½ 2hd 2½ 1hd	Lambert J	129	*.50	85-26	NativeDivr129hdWarHelmt1162Emphl'sLodg1174½	Hard drive	6
9Jan65- 8SA	fst	7f	:214 :44 1:084 1:212	4↑ San Carlos H 58k	5 1 14 13 12 13½	Lambert J	126	1.90	96-12	Native Diver1263½Candy Spots125½Bonjour1144	Mild urging	9
26Dec64- 6SA	gd	6f	:22 :451 :573 1:101	3↑ Palos Verdes H 23k	1 3 12 11½ 11½ 12½	Lambert J	125	2.40	91-25	NativeDiver1252½VikingSpirit1202Sledge125nk	Mild drive	7
7Nov64- 8BM	fst	6f	:22 :442 :563 1:083	3↑ Redwood City H 10k	2 3 12 13 13 15	Lambert J	127	*1.00	99-12	Native Diver1275Testum1233¾Clavo114no	Drew out at will	7
8Aug64- 8Dmr	fst	1 1/16	:22 :443 1:09 1:414	3↑ San Diego H 22k	5 2 11½ 13 13 14	Lambert J	122	*.70	91-15	NativeDiver1224FinalCommand1094½DrillSite117no	Easily	8
18Jly64- 8Hol	fst	1¼	:443 1:084 1:342 2:002	3↑ Hol Gold Cup H 162k	9 1 15 11 2hd 32	Lambert J	117	28.50	89-13	ColoradoKing1182MustardPlastr119hdNtvDvr1174	Weakened	11
4Jly64- 8Hol	fst	1⅛	:451 1:093 1:342 1:462	3↑ American H 55k	5 1 11 2hd 34½ 513	Lambert J	120	6.70	88-15	ColoradoKing1198MustardPlaster1202VikingSpirt1112½	Used	9
20Jun64- 8Hol	fst	1 1/16	:23 :453 1:093 1:413	3↑ Inglewood H 55k	6 1 13 12 13 1¾	Lambert J	116	12.40	87-15	NativeDiver116¾MustrdPlstr1181½Mr.Consstncy1242	Driving	9
6Jun64- 8Hol	fst	1 1/16	:224 :461 1:102 1:413	3↑ Californian 115k	8 1 11½ 1hd 31½ 811	Moreno P	115	11.70	76-14	Mustard Plaster1111½Mr. Consistency1231½ColordoKing1232½	Took up final ⅛	10
18May64- 8GG	fst	1⅛	:46 1:10 1:353 1:481	3↑ Oakland H 29k	6 2 11½ 11½ 11 1nk	Valenzuela I	122	*.40	93-16	NativeDiver122nkEscadal1055½Jim'sPurchase1111	Hand ride	7
25Apr64- 8GG	fst	1 1/16	:224 :452 1:092 1:421	3↑ W G Gilmore H 22k	9 1 12 11½ 13 1nk	Lambert J	120	*1.60	93-15	Native Diver120nkUpper Half1112½Drill Site116¾	Driving	10
11Apr64- 8GG	fst	6f	:22 :444 :571 1:092	3↑ Sacramento H 10k	4 3 2½ 23 23 31	Lambert J	123	*1.10	92-17	Mustard Plaster119nkDouble Lea119¾Native Diver1231	Not enough late	5
28Mar64- 8GG	fst	1	:222 :444 1:09 1:344	3↑ S Fran Mile H (Div 2) 12k	6 2 2½ 2hd 11½ 3½	Lambert J	123	*1.40	93-11	MustardPlaster115nkUpperHlf110nkNtvDvr1233	Used in pace	8
14Mar64- 8GG	fst	6f	:213 :44 :561 1:084	3↑ Albany H 10k	5 4 41½ 45½ 57½ 43¾	Lambert J	126	*1.30	92-14	Double Lea1192½Clavo1111¼Sledge123no	Wide,fast finish	5
8Feb64- 7SA	fst	1⅛	:452 1:092 1:342 1:472	4↑ San Antonio H 58k	7 1 11 37 410 613	Longden J	119	13.80	82-12	Gun Bow1254Cyrano1243Quita Dude114no	Gave way	7
21Jan64- 7SA	gd	1 1/16	:231 :464 1:114 1:442	4↑ San Pasqual H 28k	8 1 13 11 3½ 65½	Church K	123	3.70	76-26	OldenTimes120¾DocJocoy118hdDonutKing1134	In close late	8
4Jan64- 8SA	fst	7f	:221 :444 1:092 1:22	4↑ San Carlos H 59k	5 5 11 1hd 2hd 32¾	Pierce D	125	6.60	90-14	Admiral's Voyage1242Cyrano126¾Native Diver125½	Weakened	8
21Dec63- 8GG	my	1 1/16	:231 :463 1:112 1:444	3↑ Golden Gate H 21k	1 1 16 16 16 11¾	Shoemaker W	130	*.60	80-35	NativeDiver1301¾FriendlyFried1124¾Ol'Bleu104¾	In hand	6
7Dec63- 8GG	fst	1	:23 :46 1:093 1:351	3↑ San Fran Mile H 15k	5 2 11½ 12 14 14½	Shoemaker W	125	*.60	92-20	NativeDiver1254½MoreMegaton1181¼Aroflnt1153½	Easy score	8
26Oct63- 8Tan	fst	1 1/16	:221 :444 1:093 1:42	3↑ Tanforan H 22k	5 3 1hd 1hd 2½ 65½	Volzke M	126	*.40	95-10	Mill'sTurk109nkIc1132RoylTowr1081½	Tired last sixteenth	9
5Oct63- 8Tan	fst	1 1/16	:224 :453 1:092 1:413	3↑ Westlake H 10k	5 1 11½ 15 18 112	Lambert J	123	*1.20	103-14	NativeDivr12312Four-and-Twnty124noMll'sTurk1111½	Easily	7
2Sep63- 8Dmr	fst	1⅛	:443 1:083 1:341 1:47	3↑ Del Mar H 33k	10 1 1½ 32 46½ 77	Neves R	124	*3.20	91-12	Mr.Consistency116hdRapido1162Mr.Wag1131½	Speed 6f,tired	11
17Aug63- 7Dmr	fst	6f	:213 :441 :562 1:083	3↑ Bing Crosby H 15k	5 6 64½ 64¼ 66½ 67¾	Neves R	125	*.90	88-13	Sledge117½Testum1191GallntHost1145	Showed a dull effort	6
3Aug63- 7Dmr	fst	1 1/16	:223 :453 1:092 1:403	3↑ San Diego H 22k	4 1 11½ 11½ 12 11½	Neves R	123	*1.20	97-13	NativeDiver1231½RobRoyIII117½PirateCove119½	Handy score	8
13Jly63- 8Hol	fst	1¼	:45 1:09 1:333 1:593	3↑ Hol Gold Cup H 162k	1 1 11½ 1½ 1hd 45¼	Neves R	121	7.30	90-14	Cadiz1111½Aldrshot1103OlympdKng111¾	Made all pace,tired	10
4Jly63- 8Hol	fst	1⅛	:451 1:093 1:351 1:481	3↑ American H 57k	3 1 1hd 21½ 33½ 75¼	Neves R	122	*1.90	87-12	Dr. Kacy114½Admiral's Voyage1231½[DH]Mr. Consistency1131¼	No excuse	12
15Jun63- 8Hol	fst	1 1/16	:224 :453 1:094 1:421	3↑ Inglewood H 54k	3 1 11 11½ 14 14¼	Neves R	121	3.50	84-12	NativeDiver1214¼PiratCov1153¼Aldrshot1141	Much the best	8
6Jun63- 8Hol	fst	6f	:214 :442 :563 1:084	3↑ Coronado H 16k	4 6 52¼ 44 33½ 23¾	Neves R	124	3.30	93-13	WindySea1193¾NativDvr124hdMr.Wg115½	Altered course turn	7
9May63- 8Hol	fst	6f	:214 :442 :564 1:092	3↑ Hol Premiere H 22k	8 6 52¼ 65¼ 76¾ 66	Neves R	125	*.70	88-13	Winonly1211¾Kisco Kid112½Double Lea115½	Very wide turn	8
29Jan63- 7SA	fst	1 1/16	:223 :453 1:101 1:421	4↑ San Pasqual H 27k	3 1 12 1½ 22 22¾	Neves R	125	*.90	90-15	OldenTimes1252¾NativeDiver1251½Physicn117nk	Held gamely	6
12Jan63- 7SA	fst	1⅛	:453 1:093 1:344 1:471	San Fernando 58k	13 4 18 1½ 1½ 2nk	Shoemaker W	120	*1.40	96-12	CrimsonSatan117nkNativeDiver12010PirateCove1142	Gamely	14
5Jan63- 7SA	fst	7f	:214 :442 1:084 1:211	4↑ San Carlos H 61k	10 1 12 11½ 11 31¼	Neves R	125	*2.40	96-12	Crozier1241¼Olden Times125noNative Diver1254¾	Weakened	10
29Dec62- 6SA	fst	7f	:22 :443 1:09 1:213	Malibu 29k	12 2 13 16 15 16¼	Neves R	117	*.70	95-15	NativeDvr1176¼GrdIronHro1214½Humoso1141½	Speed to spare	13
8Dec62- 8BM	fst	1 1/16	:222 :451 1:092 1:42	San Jose H 16k	1 1 11½ 11 13 12	Neves R	122	*1.10	94-15	NativeDiver1222Raiko112nkRoyalAttack124hd	Scored easily	8
10Nov62- 8BM	fst	6f	:214 :442 :562 1:083	3↑ Salinas H 10k	6 3 11 12 13 15	Neves R	119 b	*.80	100-16	NativeDiver1195Aeroflint118hdMr.Wag1184	Set pace,easily	7
3Nov62- 8BM	fst	6f	:214 :44 1:082	Hillsdale H 10k	7 1 11 12 13 15½	Neves R	120	*1.30	101-15	NativeDiver1205½BoldCorporal1195Jesse'sInvdr114½	Easily	8
11Aug62- 6Dmr	fst	5½f	:22 :45 :564 1:024	3↑ Handicap 5000	5 2 41¾ 41½ 66 57½	Spraker L	114	2.70	97-08	Henrijan115¾Ann's Knight1181½Rob Bob1121¼	Well up,tired	7
28Jly62- 7Dmr	fst	6f	:214 :442 :563 1:09	Oceanside H 16k	5 3 31½ 43 46 43¾	Neves R	123	2.10	93-06	Doc Jocoy126nkTestum120¾Private World1172¾	Raced evenly	8
19Jly62- 7Hol	fst	6f	:214 :443 :563 1:084	3↑ Lakes & Flowers H 27k	5 2 1hd 31 45½ 34¾	Neves R	113	4.00	92-11	WalletLifter1112¾Ann'sKnight1192NativeDvr113½	Wide turn	9

6Jly62- 7Hol	fst 6f	:214:443 :563 1:09 3↑	Alw 12000	2 3 2hd 31½ 44½ 53¼	Neves R	115		*1.60	93-14	CrazyKid1131½LittleJuan116¾Testum112¾ Bore out,weakened 7
8Jun62- 6Hol	fst 7f	:22 :441 1:09 1:214	Alw 8500	8 2 12 1½ 13 14½	Neves R	120		*2.40e	91-14	NativeDiver1204½CalgryBrook114hdWldy1112½ Much the best 12
30May62- 7Hol	fst 1	:222:451 1:093 1:343	©Will Rogers (Div 2) 27k	6 1 1½ 2½ 67½ 614	Neves R	120		6.90	79-11	PrinceofPlnty1142RoyalAttack126½DocJocoy1234½ Gave way 8
12May62- 7Hol	fst 6f	:214:442 :563 1:091	©Debonair 29k	5 5 1hd 1hd 2hd 1no	Neves R	112		*1.40	95-13	Native Diver112noPrince of Plenty1123Black Sheep116hd 12
	Led again late									
30Dec61- 7SA	fst 1$\frac{1}{16}$	:23 :462 1:113 1:443	[S]Cal Br Champ 64k	5 2 21 21½ 47 49¾	Neves R	118		1.60	71-14	Najin1182½BoldCorporl1181¾IndnBlood1185½ Wide,weakened 6
16Dec61- 8Tan	fst 1$\frac{1}{16}$	:224:46 1:102 1:433	San Bruno H 16k	7 2 21 24 23 36¼	Neves R	122		*.30	87-16	Indian Blood1202½Poland China1133¾Native Diver1222½ 7
	Weakened final ⅛									
25Nov61- 8Tan	sly 6f	:222:45 :573 1:102	El Camino H 10k	7 6 11½ 14 18 16¼	Volzke M	120		*.30	94-19	NativeDiver1206¼Turalea1131¼IndianBlood1222 Plenty left 8
7Nov61- 8Tan	fst 6f	:221:443 :571 1:10	Alw 2500	7 3 13 18 112 110	Neves R	114		*.20	96-18	NativeDiver11410NightsGlory1103½Nov'sBoo1144½ In hand 7
27Sep61- 4BM	fst 6f	:221:451 :572 1:094	Md Sp Wt	7 2 12 11½ 15 17½	Neves R	118		*1.50	94-13	Native Diver1187½El Peco1183½Crafty Pupil118hd Easily 9

Never Bend

dkb. c. 1960, by Nasrullah (Nearco)–Lalun, by Djeddah — **Lifetime record: 23 13 4 4 $641,524**

Own.– Cain Hoy Stable
Br.– Harry F. Guggenheim (Ky)
Tr.– W.C. Stephens

2Nov63- 7Aqu	sf 1⅝Ⓣ	2:453 3↑	Man o' War 113k	8 1 12 36 716 1030	Ycaza M	122		4.00	42-28	TheAxeII1265WillIRule1222½Guadalcanal1262½ Speed,tired 11
16Oct63- 9Suf	fst 1⅛	:464 1:103 1:36 1:49	Yankee H 58k	9 1 11 11 12 14	Ycaza M	126		*2.20	96-13	NeverBend1264DeanCarl123½QuestLink117nk Kept to drive 9
7Oct63- 7Aqu	fm 1$\frac{3}{16}$Ⓣ	1:543 3↑	Long Island H 29k	3 2 2½ 2hd 1hd 32¼	Ycaza M	120		*1.10	95-03	DavidK.113nkTheAxeII1262NeverBend1202 Short lead,tired 10
28Sep63- 7Aqu	fst 1¼	:473 1:114 1:362 2:004 3↑	Woodward 108k	3 1 13 1½ 2½ 23½	Shoemaker W	120		4.85	92-13	Kelso1263½Never Bend1201½Crimson Satan1266 Game effort 5
14Sep63- 8Atl	fm 1$\frac{3}{16}$Ⓣ	1:551 3↑	U Nations H 125k	3 1 11 11 1hd 22	Ycaza M	118		5.70	95-03	Mongo1242Never Bend118¾Carry Back1271½ Set pace,gamely 10
	Daily Racing Form time,1:54 2/5									
27Aug63- 7Aqu	fst 1	:231:461 1:102 1:35	Handicap 10000	6 4 41½ 3½ 12 13½	Ycaza M	130		*.50	93-20	NeverBend1303½MasterDennis1152½RollingSe110½ Mild drive 6
17Aug63- 6Sar	fst 1¼	:472 1:111 1:36 2:022	Travers 81k	2 1 11 1hd 33 611	Ycaza M	126		2.95	85-08	Crewmn1201½HotDust1141Chateaugy1262½ Used setting pace 6
2Aug63- 7Sar	my 1	:234:471 1:12 1:373	Alw 7500	2 1 11 11 12 11¾	Ycaza M	126		*.40	89-18	NevrBnd1261¾HenrytheEighth114noMasterDnns1141½ Easily 5
18May63- 8Pim	fst 1$\frac{3}{16}$	:472 1:113 1:37 1:561	Preakness 180k	5 1 11½ 1½ 33 38	Ycaza M	126		1.80	84-12	CandySpots1263½Chateaugay1264½NevrBnd1262¼ Weakened 8
4May63- 7CD	fst 1¼	:462 1:10 1:352 2:014	Ky Derby 151k	6 1 11 11 21 21¼	Ycaza M	126		3.10	92-08	Chateaugay1261¼NeverBend126nkCandySpots1264¾ Gamely 9
26Apr63- 8CD	fst 7f	:23 :453 1:094 1:222	Alw 7500	2 2 1hd 13 14 18	Ycaza M	122		-	98-16	Never Bend1228Space Skates1193½Book Full1101 Ridden out 4
	Nonwagering event									
19Apr63- 6Kee	fst 7f	:222:451 1:10 1:224	Alw 10000	3 5 55 43½ 11 11	Ycaza M	122		-e	94-09	NeverBnd1221BlazeStarr110nkRunnngBowln1132¼ Mild drive 5
	Nonwagering event									
2Mar63- 7Hia	fst 1⅛	:47 1:11 1:36 1:492	Flamingo 135k	5 1 13 12 14 15	Ycaza M	122		*.35	88-16	NeverBnd1225KingToots1222RoylAscot1221¼ Kept to urging 10
18Feb63- 0Hia	my 7f	:233:464 1:241	Special Weight	4 1 1hd 11 15 114	Ycaza M	122			88-17	NevrBnd12214MyCount1105½Dog'sFool1104 Drew out easily 4
	Exhibition. Run between 6th and 7th races. No purse,no wagering. Not to be considered as a race start									
10Nov62- 7GS	sly 1$\frac{1}{16}$	:24 :48 1:122 1:44	Garden State 273k	3 2 21½ 42 33 39	Ycaza M	122		*.50	81-23	Crewmn1226InthePocket1223NverBnd122¾ Lacked response 7
2Nov62- 7GS	fst 1$\frac{1}{16}$	:232:472 1:122 1:441	Alw 10000	2 3 41½ 31½ 13 15	Ycaza M	122		*.40	89-23	Never Bend1225Right Proud112noIn the Pocket1132½ Easily 14
13Oct62- 7Bel	fst 1	:232:461 1:11 1:354	Champagne 189k	4 1 1½ 11½ 14 18	Ycaza M	122		*.45	95-15	Never Bend1228Master Dennis122¾Outing Class122hd Easily 7
1Oct62- 7Bel	fst 7f	:221:453 1:103 1:231	Cowdin 71k	8 12 86½ 64 1hd 13	Ycaza M	124		*.90	91-13	NeverBend1243ValiantSkol1171¼RockyLnk1142 Reared,easily 13
15Sep62- 7Aqu	fst 6½f	:221:452 1:103 1:171	Futurity 152k	9 7 41¾ 31½ 1½ 11¾	Shoemaker W	122		*1.15	97-13	NeverBnd1221¾OutingClss1222½PckTrp122hd Scored handily 13
8Sep62- 8AP	fst 7f	:221:443 1:093 1:214	Arl-Wash Futurity 357k	3 3 42½ 33 1hd 2½	Ycaza M	122		*1.10	97-09	Candy Spots122½Never Bend1226Rash Prince122½ Bore in 13
31Aug62- 8AP	fst 6f	:22 :443 1:092	Alw 10000	7 9 54 54½ 32½ 11½	Ycaza M	115		*.80	97-08	NeverBend1151½AimnFire1152½RashPrince120½ Clear at end 10
4Aug62- 8Mth	fst 6f	:211:44 1:103	Sapling 108k	1 4 1hd 2hd 1hd 31	Ycaza M	122		*.90	88-14	DeltaJudge122½Bonjour122½NeverBend1225 Hard used,tired 9
16Jly62- 8Mth	fst 6f	:213:444 1:101	Alw 4500	4 2 13 15 18 18	Ycaza M	120		*.30	91-21	NevrBnd1208SumDumKid120½MonsieurDavid1209 Mild drive 7
30Jun62- 3Bel	fst 5½f	:224:454 1:043	Md Sp Wt	3 3 11½ 13 16 18	Ycaza M	122		*.95	98-12	Never Bend1228Master Dennis1225Dare Say122nk Easy score 9

Nodouble

ch. c. 1965, by Noholme II (Star Kingdom)–Abla-Jay, by Double Jay — **Lifetime record: 42 13 11 5 $846,749**

Own.– Verna Lea Farm
Br.– Gene Goff (Ark)
Tr.– J.B. Sonnier

24Oct70- 7Aqu	fst 7f	:222:443 1:09 1:212 3↑	Vosburgh H 59k	6 6 63¾ 74¾ 74 52¼	Tejeira J	126		3.30	92-15	Best Turn115hdTrue North115noOcean Bar1132 Lacked rally 11
20Jun70- 9Det	fst 1⅛	:46 1:092 1:344 1:472 3↑	Mich 1⅛ 126k	1 1 47½ 49 69½ 57½	Tejeira J	127		*1.10	92-19	FastHilarious116noFigonero1192½PleasurSkr1115 No excuse 9
30May70- 7Bel	fst 1	:223:45 1:092 1:343 3↑	Metropolitan H 114k	1 3 33 31½ 31½ 1hd	Tejeira J	126		5.80	101-11	Nodouble126hdReviewer1233Dewan122¾ Last strides 10
16May70- 8Hol	fst 1$\frac{1}{16}$	:232:462 1:101 1:401 3↑	Californian 112k	5 4 44 31 46 36½	Pineda A	130		5.00	88-12	Baffle1135Figonero1241½Nodouble130hd No rally 8
21Mar70- 9GP	fst 1¼	:48 1:123 1:38 2:04 3↑	Gulf Park H 123k	3 6 76¾ 2hd 46 58½	Tejeira J	127		2.30	70-17	Snow Sporting1182½Twogundan1152½Al Hattab1142 Bumped 9
7Mar70- 8SA	fst 1¼	:451 1:092 1:341 1:593 4↑	S Anita H 145k	3 5 88½ 94¾ 95¾ 87¾	Tejeira J	132		*1.20	92-05	QuickenTree118¾FiddleIsle1193½FieldMstr1141¾ No excuse 12
7Feb70- 8SA	fst 1$\frac{1}{16}$	:222:451 1:092 1:402 4↑	San Pasqual H 46k	5 5 57½ 2½ 1½ 12	Tejeira J	128		*.70	101-07	Nodouble1282Field Master116¾Dewan120hd Drew clear 9
25Oct69- 7Aqu	fst 2	:511 2:293 2:544 3:222 3↑	J C Gold Cup 106k	2 2 1hd 28 210 214	Belmonte E	124		2.90	70-14	Arts and Letters11914Nodouble1249Harem Lady121 Gamely 4
18Oct69- 8Haw	fst 1¼	:462 1:102 1:351 1:594 3↑	Haw Gold Cup H 123k	5 3 47½ 2½ 11½ 14	Belmonte E	125		*.90	97-07	Nodouble1254Vif111hdVerbatim1241¼ Mild drive 7
27Sep69- 7Bel	fst 1¼	:481 1:121 1:363 2:01 3↑	Woodward 106k	4 1 11 11 2½ 22	Belmonte E	126		2.60	93-17	ArtsandLetters1202Nodouble1261½Verbatim1268 Drifted out 4
1Sep69- 7Bel	fst 1⅛	:464 1:103 1:353 1:482 3↑	Governor Nicolls 109k	4 3 21½ 21½ 31½ 43½	Belmonte E	126		*.50	90-17	Verbatim121½Rising Market1171Tropic King II1142 Tired 7
19Jly69- 7Aqu	fst 1¼	:464 1:103 1:353 2:002 3↑	Brooklyn H 109k	7 2 1½ 12 11 11½	Belmonte E	127		*1.50	94-14	Nodouble1271½Verbatim1201Dike114hd Drifted,going away 7
12Jly69- 8Hol	fst 1¼	:462 1:101 1:341 1:584 3↑	Hol Gold Cup H 162k	4 4 34 32 41¾ 21	Belmonte E	129		*.90	98-12	Figonero1151Nodouble129hdPoleax118hd Held on willingly 6
30May69- 7Aqu	fst 1	:224:453 1:10 1:34 3↑	Metropolitan H 116k	6 4 56 54½ 32 22½	Belmonte E	129		8.80	94-22	Arts and Letters1112½Nodouble1293½Promise1191 Gamely 11
17May69- 8Hol	fst 1$\frac{1}{16}$	:23 :454 1:094 1:402 3↑	Californian 120k	12 6 45½ 41 1½ 12½	Belmonte E	127		4.00	93-08	Nodouble1272½RisingMarkt1211LondonJt112¾ Drawing clear 14
22Mar69- 9GP	fst 1¼	:471 1:113 1:36 2:012 3↑	Gulfstream H 126k	9 1 1½ 11 1½ 2no	Belmonte E	125		2.70	92-10	CourtRecess108noNodbl1252¼TropcKngII1162¾ Raced wide 9
8Mar69- 8SA	fst 1¼	:46 1:10 1:351 2:014 4↑	S Anita H 145k	12 6 43 1½ 12 11½	Belmonte E	122		4.30	89-13	Nodouble1221½Gamely122noQuicken Tree1261 Drew clear 16
1Feb69- 8SA	fst 1¼	:46 1:104 1:362 2:02	C H Strub 126k	3 7 65¾ 1½ 1½ 1no	Pincay L Jr	123		3.10	88-15	[D]Nodouble123noDignitas1159½Cavamore1173½ Drifted out 10
	Disqualified and placed second									
18Jan69- 8SA	sl 1⅛	:46 1:10 1:353 1:49	San Fernando 59k	1 3 55 57 511 514	Pincay L Jr	123		*2.40	73-17	Cavamore1134½Dignitas117hdDewan1204½ In close,tired 10
9Nov68- 7Aqu	fst 1$\frac{3}{16}$	:474 1:114 1:37 1:553	Roamer H 56k	7 7 97¾ 89½ 819 826	Heath M	125		3.90e	71-17	Funny Fellow120nkDraft Card1152Iron Ruler1262 Bled 9
19Oct68- 8Haw	fst 1¼	:472 1:103 1:352 1:591 3↑	Gold Cup H 132k	3 2 21½ 3½ 1hd 11	Heath M	117		4.40	100-07	Nodouble1171Cabildo120noIrish Dude112no Under pressure 10
14Sep68- 9Det	fst 1⅛	:471 1:111 1:361 1:49 3↑	Mich 1⅛ H 123k	11 3 35 22 1½ 12¾	Heath M	111		17.60	96-19	Nodouble1112¾Damascus133hdMisty Run1092¼ Clear at end 12
3Aug68- 8AP	fst 1⅛	:473 1:11 1:36 1:484	American Derby 115k	4 1 12 1½ 2hd 24½	Pincay L Jr	116	b	17.20	85-08	ForwardPass1234½Ndouble116noPoleax1201½ Bore out badly 6
6Jly68- 8AP	fm 1Ⓣ	:232:461 1:113 1:372	Nashua H 34k	9 2 21 21 22 43½	Marquez CH	117	b	6.50	88-09	TeVega1162PaintRock110nkRelntlssPursuit1131¼ Weakened 11
22Jun68- 8AP	fst 1	:23 :454 1:103 1:36	Arl Classic 108k	2 5 2hd 41½ 45 47¾	Blum W	118		13.00	75-16	ExclusivNativ113¾IronRulr1162GoodInvstmnt1165 Weakened 8
30May68- 8GS	fst 1⅛	:471 1:11 1:362 1:49	Jersey Derby 134k	7 3 34 46 57½ 712	Grant H	126		7.40	80-18	OutoftheWay1262½Captain'sGig126nkIronRuler1264 Swerved 10
18May68- 8Pim	fst 1$\frac{3}{16}$	:471 1:11 1:373 1:564	Preakness 195k	1 2 2½ 1hd 35 48	McKeever W	126		16.80	81-15	ForwrdPass1266OutoftheWay126hd[D]Dncr'sImg1262 Impeded 10
	Placed third through disqualification									
6Apr68- 9OP	fst 1⅛	:462 1:103 1:373 1:50	Ark Derby 58k	6 5 43 33 2hd 11	McKeever W	116		*2.50e	93-16	Nodouble1161Te Vega1191½Etony1191½ Strong drive 10
25Mar68- 8OP	fst 1 70	:232:463 1:12 1:411	Alw 7500	6 2 32 2½ 1½ 1½	McKeever W5	112		*2.10e	90-15	Nodouble112½TeVega1225SailorsSong1162 Under hard drive 9
4Mar68- 7OP	fst 6f	:22 :46 1:111	[S]Alw 6000	9 1 65½ 44½ 2hd 1½	McKeever W5	114		*.60e	89-16	Nodouble114½Loud Singer1196Pass 'Em Up1163 Driving hard 9
30Oct67- 8Spt	sly 6½f	:221:453 1:112 1:183	Land of Lincoln 22k	6 3 611 46 45½ 52¼	Fleming W	116		6.80	83-19	Felony118noForeign Comet1141¼Gadget Man1201 No mishap 10

14Oct67- 9Det	fst	1 70	:221 :454 1:102 1:413	Graduation 21k	5 3 2hd 1½ 33 34¾	Maple E	110		4.10e	86-18	Strate Stuff1221¾Mial Spencer1193Nodouble1105	Weakened	10
29Sep67- 8Haw	sl	6½f	:224 :47 1:123 1:193	©To Market (Div 2) 11k	3 2 2hd 2hd 32 33¼	Lopez JR	110		4.70	73-24	Irish Chief111nkLifelike1223Nodouble1101½	Speed,tired	7
9Sep67- 7AP	fst	7f	:224 :46 1:112 1:234	Futurity (Div 1) 185k	7 1 11½ 1hd 67½ 715	Whited D	122	b	38.00	71-22	T.V. Commercial1223¾Gin-Rob1224¼Royal Cap122¾	Used up	9
1Sep67- 7Det	fst	6f	:224 :46 1:112	Alw 3000	7 1 15 16 16 18	Whited DE	115	b	*.90	83-27	Nodouble1158GateCrasher1181CompanyMan1152	Ridden out	7
12Aug67- 6Det	fst	6f	:231 :46 1:113	Alw 3000	8 1 33 22 22 22½	Anderson JR	116	b	3.10	79-17	KeyRulla1202½Nodoubl1166RoyalHrbor1202¼	Held on gamely	8
15Jly67- 8HP	fst	6½f	:221 :47 1:131 1:194	Freshman Derby 22k	4 8 77¾ 75 52½ 22¼	Green FF	111	b	32.80	80-21	MialSpencer1122¼Nodoubl111nkCarbbnLn117hd	Gaining fast	9
8Jly67- 7HP	fst	6f	:233 :47 1:131	Freshman Trial 11k	6 5 2½ 2½ 23 44½	Lawless R	113	b	4.90	83-20	KntuckySherry1122¼RoyalHrbor1121PortDggr1121¼	Weakened	6
23Jun67- 4HP	gd	6f	:24 :481 1:153	Alw 3200	7 4 42½ 31½ 21½ 21¼	Lawless R	118		*1.40	75-27	DandyDodo1151¼Nodouble1181¾GreekBaron1184	Held gamely	10
3Jun67- 6Tdn	fst	5½f	:22 :46 :59 1:053	©Heritage 7.7k	5 3 32½ 32 21½ 32¼	Rincon R	110		2.30	89-15	BeaucoupD'Argent110¾CaribbeanLin1141½Nodoubl1105	Gamely	5
24May67- 5HP	fst	4f	:223 :464	Alw 3600	8 1 31½ 21½ 2nk	Zakoor W	117		5.20	94-11	CaribbeanLine122nkNodouble1173HarkthHrld1222½	Sharp try	8
4May67- 3HP	sl	4f	:25 :524	Md 7500	3 10 42½ 45½ 13½	Rincon R	118		8.30	64-26	Nodouble1183½Gold Rags115noFiela1151¼	Drew clear at end	10

Northern Dancer

b. c. 1961, by Nearctic (Nearco)–Natalma, by Native Dancer **Lifetime record: 18 14 2 2 $580,806**

Own.– Windfields Farm
Br.– E.P. Taylor (Can)
Tr.– H.A. Luro

20Jun64- 7WO	fst	1¼	:474 1:123 1:364 2:021	ⓇQueen's Plate 74k	1 7 85 1½ 14 17½	Hartack W	126	b	*.15	98-08	NorthernDancer1267½Langcrest1264½GrandGrcon1261¼	Easily	8
6Jun64- 7Aqu	fst	1½	:49 1:144 2:04 2:282	Belmont 154k	2 5 52¾ 31 2½ 36	Hartack W	126	b	*.80	92-10	Quadrangle1262RomanBrothr1264NorthrnDncr126½	Bid,tired	8
16May64- 8Pim	fst	1 3/16	:482 1:122 1:373 1:564	Preakness 176k	4 3 33 1½ 13 12¼	Hartack W	126	b	2.10	89-14	NorthernDancer1262¼TheScoundrel126hdHillRis126½	Driving	6
2May64- 7CD	fst	1¼	:46 1:103 1:36 2:00	Ky Derby 156k	7 7 64½ 1hd 12 1nk	Hartack W	126	b	3.40	102-05	NorthernDancer126nkHillRise1263¼ThScoundrl126no	Driving	12
23Apr64- 6Kee	fst	1⅛	:501 1:141 1:382 1:494	Blue Grass 29k	5 2 2hd 2hd 1hd 1½	Hartack W	126	b	*.20	88-11	NorthernDncr126½AllnAdr1214½RoylShuck121nk	Well in hand	5
4Apr64- 8GP	fst	1⅛	:473 1:121 1:38 1:504	Florida Derby 116k	1 2 23 22 1½ 11	Shoemaker W	122	b	*.30	80-16	NorthrnDancr1221ThScoundrl1222½DndyK.1222¼	Ridden out	8
28Mar64- 7GP	fst	7f	:22 :443 1:093 1:222	Alw 6000	2 5 31½ 2hd 13 14	Ycaza M	122	b	*.40	100-14	NorthrnDancr1224ThScoundrl1142¾TroyOurBoy1203	Handily	7
3Mar64- 8Hia	fst	1⅛	:453 1:092 1:343 1:474	Flamingo 138k	9 2 21½ 21 11 12	Shoemaker W	122	b	*1.00	96-16	NorthrnDncr1222Mr.Brck1228Qudrngl1226	Lugged in,driving	11
24Feb64- 0Hia	gd	7f	:231 :461 1:104 1:232	Sp Wt	1 3 1½ 1½ 13 17	Shoemaker W	118	b	-	92-17	Northern Dancer1187Chieftain1182½Trader118		3
	Exhibition event,no purse,no wagering												
10Feb64- 7Hia	fst	6f	:224 :453 1:102	Alw 7000	2 7 55½ 32½ 31½ 32	Ussery R	122	b	1.40	90-17	Chieftan122hdMom'sRqust1132NrthrnDncr1225	Bumped start	7
27Nov63- 7Aqu	fst	1	:233 :461 1:102 1:353	Remsen 28k	3 1 11½ 11½ 13 12	Ycaza M	124	b	*.25	90-17	Northern Dancer1242Lord Date1123Repeating1171	Handily	6
18Nov63- 7Aqu	fst	1	:23 :451 1:103 1:36	Alw 10000	5 4 45½ 41½ 14 18	Ycaza M	124	b	2.60	88-16	NorthernDancer1248Bupers1241½SaVet1164½	Easily the best	6
6Nov63- 7Grd	my	7f	:231 :472 1:141 1:273	ⓇCarleton 8.7k	2 3 21 2hd 1nk 12½	Fitzsimmons J	122	b	*.30	84-28	NorthrnDancr1222½NorthernFlght1151Wnk113hd	Going away	6
12Oct63- 6WO	fst	1⅛	:464 1:112 1:383 1:51	ⓇCoronation Fut 46k	10 7 41¼ 11½ 13 16¼	Turcotte R	122	b	*1.00e	88-16	NorthernDancr1226¼JammdLovly122½Prlou1222¼	Easily best	15
7Oct63- 5WO	fst	1 70	:224 :461 1:11 1:42	ⓇAlw 2900	4 2 35½ 2½ 1hd 11	Turcotte R	122	b	*.45	95-18	Northern Dancer1221Northern Flight11726Fast Answer1123¼		6
	Mild drive												
28Sep63- 6WO	fm	1 1/16Ⓣ	:224 :464 1:12 1:453	ⓇCup & Saucer 42k	5 1 2hd 1hd 2hd 2¾	Turcotte R	124	b	*1.60e	84-13	GrandGarcon113¾NrthrnDncr1241JammdLovly1191½	Gamely	16
	Previously trained by T.P. Fleming												
24Aug63- 6FE	sf	1Ⓣ	:24 :482 1:142 1:432	Summer 20k	1 1 1hd 13 12½ 11¼	Bohenko P	115	b	*1.65e	66-27	NorthrnDancr1151¼SlitherngSm1153½Wndlshm112no	Driving	7
17Aug63- 6FE	fst	6½f	:231 :464 1:122 1:19	Vandal 9.6k	5 3 2hd 12½ 2nk 24	Bohenko P	108	b	6.55	84-12	RamblinRod1224NrthrnDncr1092½BrocktonBoy1151¼	2nd best	11
2Aug63- 3FE	fst	5½f	:231 :472 1:061	ⓇMd Sp Wt	7 2 21 1nk 11 16¾	Turcotte R5	113		*.95	92-13	NorthernDncr1136¾Ncub1187½Fbson1182	Drawing away easily	8

Old Hat

b. f. 1959, by Boston Doge (The Doge)–Fine Feathers, by Double Jay **Lifetime record: 80 35 18 9 $556,401**

Own.– S. Conrad
Br.– W.A. Nelson (Ky)
Tr.– C.C. Norman

2Dec66- 9TrP	fst	6f	:221 :451 1:09	4↑ Alw 5000	1 1 22½ 2½ 11½ 14¾	Sellers J	116		1.80	97-11	Old Hat1164¾Yucatan1193¼Valiant Bull1224½	Mild drive	8
27Oct66- 6Kee	fst	1⅛	:464 1:103 1:371 1:502	3↑ ⒻSpinster 58k	4 2 2hd 32 2hd 21¼	Church K	123		4.60	84-21	OpenFire1231¼OldHat1231¼SummerScandal1236	Game effort	5
20Oct66- 6Kee	sl	*7f	:222 :453 1:101 1:263	3↑ ⒻAlw 10000	3 1 21½ 23 21½ 24¾	Church K	121		1.70	85-27	SummrScandal1214¾OldHat1211½Maestrina1099	Second best	5
1Oct66- 8Det	gd	1 1/16	:24 :472 1:113 1:443	3↑ ⒻSweet Patootie 27k	1 2 2½ 2hd 1½ 11½	Church K	118		*1.10	80-21	Old Hat1181½Out Talk1071½Treasure Chest1154	Game effort	8
24Sep66- 8CD	fst	1	:23 :454 1:101 1:35	3↑ ⒻFalls City H 27k	8 1 1hd 1hd 2½ 1nk	Church K	116		3.80	98-14	OldHat116nkⒹMac'sSparklr1172½NaidniDm1102¾	Came again	9
17Sep66- 7CD	fst	7f	:23 :454 1:10 1:224	3↑ ⒻAlw 5000	2 2 21 32 2¼ 21¼	Church K	111		3.50	92-12	MarrythePrince1211¼OldHat1117TurfTalk1143½	Game effort	7
7Sep66- 8AP	fst	1	:223 :452 1:103 1:353	3↑ ⒻBewitch H 20k	7 8 66 56 58½ 310	Valenzuela I	118		*2.70	78-13	Marry the Prince1201Cologne1129Old Hat1181¼	Rallied	11
20Aug66- 8AP	fm	1⅛Ⓣ	:472 1:113 1:362 1:483	3↑ ⒻMatron H 55k	7 2 2½ 42¾ 69½ 912	Brumfield D	122		5.10	86-11	Swinging Mood1126Margarethen1241Amerivan114nk	Stopped	9
5Aug66- 7AP	fst	6f	:221 :451 1:094	3↑ ⒻAlw 6000	6 6 45½ 55½ 56½ 66	Fires E	113		*.80	88-17	Codorniz1222May's Guide1221¼Country Maid119hd	Dull try	7
23Jly66- 6Del	fst	6f	:221 :452 1:111	3↑ ⒻAlw 5000	6 2 63¾ 68 56½ 3¾	Leonard J	121		*.70	88-14	TurfTalk113¾FlaminHat121noOldHt121no	Made strong finish	7
21Oct65- 6Kee	sly	1⅛	:462 1:102 1:362 1:501	3↑ ⒻSpinster 58k	3 4 49 39 36 43	Gallimore R	123		*.40	83-23	StarMaggie1233Swoonalong123hdFairwayFun119no	No excuse	5
9Oct65- 6Kee	fst	1 1/16	:24 :481 1:114 1:424	3↑ Fayette H 28k	2 1 51¾ 52¾ 41½ 1nk	Gallimore R	119		*1.30	92-14	OldHat119nkLt.Stevens122hdBigBrgd116nk	Up final strides	9
18Sep65- 8Det	fst	1⅛	:471 1:113 1:364 1:492	3↑ Mich 1⅛ H 91k	5 6 73¾ 31 1hd 1½	Gallimore R	115		5.50	94-18	OldHat115½RomanBrother118¾TakeOver114½	Long,hard drive	11
21Aug65- 8AP	fst	1⅛	:482 1:12 1:372 1:494	3↑ ⒻMatron H 78k	2 3 46½ 46½ 24 1¾	Gallimore R	126		1.90	87-17	Old Hat126¾Swoonalong1222¼Miss Cavandish125¾	Just up	6
12Aug65- 8AP	fst	1	:231 :452 1:092 1:343	3↑ ⒻHandicap 15000	5 2 22 2½ 13 21	Gallimore R	124		*.50	95-12	Miss Cavandish1211Old Hat1246Yes Please115½	Failed	5
8Jun65- 7Del	fst	6f	:221 :453 1:101	4↑ ⒻAlw 6000	7 1 32½ 1hd 13 16	Thornburg B	121		*.40	94-10	Old Hat1216Crown Silver1181Jeune Occupy115no	Easily	7
22May65- 7Aqu	fst	1⅛	:47 1:111 1:362 1:494	3↑ ⒻTop Flight H 57k	4 2 23 23 35½ 38½	Brumfield D	127		*2.55	78-20	Affectionately1208SteepleJill123½OldHat127¾	No response	10
6May65- 7CD	fst	7f	:23 :452 1:092 1:22	4↑ ⒻAlw 4500	6 1 22 21½ 1½ 12	Gallimore R	123		*.30	97-14	Old Hat1232Abrogate1185Alecee1182½	Scored well in hand	7
31Mar65- 9GP	fst	7f	:221 :444 1:101 1:23	3↑ ⒻSuwannee River H 21k	3 3 44½ 31 11½ 13¼	Brumfield D	125		*.40	97-15	OldHat1253¼Abrogate1121½MoneytoBurn1101¼	Much the best	6
20Mar65- 9GP	fst	7f	:222 :45 1:103 1:234	3↑ Appleton H 16k	1 5 45½ 47 2hd 2nk	Thornburg B	122		*1.10	93-14	Ampose115nkOld Hat1221¼Editorialist115nk	Gave sharp try	7
24Feb65- 8Hia	fst	1⅛	:473 1:113 1:364 1:494	3↑ ⒻBlack Helen H 60k	5 5 52¼ 32 11 1¾	Brumfield D	125		*.90	86-10	Old Hat125¾Steeple Jill116½Windsor Lady1133	Brisk drive	9
27Jan65- 8Hia	fst	7f	:232 :46 1:104 1:24	3↑ ⒻColumbiana H 31k	10 1 41½ 53½ 22 1¾	Brumfield D	124		5.30	89-19	Old Hat124¾Miami Mood1111½Steeple Jill118½	Up in time	10
7Nov64- 8CD	fst	1	:223 :45 1:094 1:353	3↑ ⒻFalls City H 29k	13 3 33½ 31 2hd 1¾	Brumfield D	128		*.60	95-15	Old Hat128¾De Cathy113¾Abrogate1173	Under hard drive	13
2Nov64- 7CD	fst	7f	:231 :46 1:10 1:222	3↑ ⒻAlw 7500	1 4 31½ 32 12½ 12½	Brumfield D	124		*.30	95-16	Old Hat1242½Godessa116½Tirata1163¼	Easily best	8
15Oct64- 6Kee	fst	1⅛	:474 1:113 1:361 1:482	3↑ ⒻSpinster 58k	5 2 21 21 1½ 11	Brumfield D	123		1.40	95-15	Old Hat1231Miss Cavandish119nkTime for Bed1192½	Driving	5
8Oct64- 6Kee	fst	*7f	1:263	3↑ ⒻAlw 10000	4 1 3½ 22 12 12¼	Brumfield D	118		*.50	90-17	Old Hat1182¼Oil Royalty121nkBatteur1182½	Scored in hand	8
26Sep64- 7Atl	fm	1 1/16Ⓣ	1:432	3↑ ⒻMargate H (Div 1) 29k	9 3 34 108¾ 105¾ 44¼	Thornburg B	119		*3.10	90-04	Snow Scene II1152Batteur112nkIsaduchess1162	Came again	11
5Sep64- 7Aqu	fst	1	:23 :454 1:103 1:363	3↑ ⒻMaskette H 30k	2 3 33½ 35 36 26	Thornburg B	117		4.90	79-21	Tosmah1236Old Hat1172Snow Scene II1132	Finished gamely	13
15Aug64- 8AP	fst	1⅛	:47 1:11 1:362 1:492	3↑ ⒻMatron H 81k	1 4 45 47 23 2½	Thornburg B	116		3.70	88-14	Tosmah117½Old Hat116½Nubile111½	Finished full of run	10
1Aug64- 7Del	fst	1¼	:48 1:124 1:381 2:04	3↑ ⒻDelaware H 121k	1 1 11 2hd 12¼ 11¼	Thornburg B	113		17.00	82-20	Old Hat1131¼Miss Cavandish1151¼Waltz Song116¾	Driving	12
18Jly64- 7Del	fst	1 1/16	:233 :472 1:114 1:442	3↑ ⒻNew Castle 37k	1 1 11½ 13 13 21¼	Thornburg B	110		4.90	86-24	Snow Scene II1071¼Old Hat1102½Spicy Living1242	Game try	9
11Jly64- 6Del	fst	1	:231 :462 1:114 1:383	4↑ ⒻAlw 7500	1 1 13½ 15 15 13	Thornburg B	112		*.90	83-21	Old Hat1123Tona1182½Colonia1158	Bobbled,handily	7
1Jly64- 8Mth	fst	1 1/16	:224 :46 1:102 1:431	3↑ ⒻMolly Pitcher H 29k	12 2 32 2½ 11 32	Zakoor W	119		10.20	87-16	SpicyLiving124noSnowSceneII1122OldHat119½	Used in lead	13
13Jun64- 7Mth	fst	6f	:222 :452 1:101	3↑ ⒻAlw 7500	8 1 4¾ 21 21 11¼	Chambers W	121		3.40	91-13	Old Hat1211¼Cyclopavia1155½Fair Summer1211	Going away	8
7May64- 7CD	sl	6f	:22 :451 1:111	4↑ Alw 5000	2 1 2½ 1½ 12 11	Brumfield D	112		*.70	90-18	Old Hat1121Ambarmar1202Boone Co.1101½	Kept to pressure	7
27Apr64- 6CD	my	6f	:22 :46 1:13	3↑ ⒻAlw 5000	6 4 52½ 41¼ 31¼ 2hd	Brumfield D	114		*.30	81-24	Maiden'sLove113hdOldHat114¾Godessa1112	Missed,sharp try	6
1Apr64- 9GP	fst	7f	:222 :45 1:10 1:23	3↑ ⒻSuwannee River H 16k	1 1 2½ 32½ 46 54½	Brumfield D	118		2.60	92-17	Smart Deb1232Lady Karachi1161Yes Please1111½	Tired	8
26Mar64- 7GP	fst	6f	:222 :452 1:11	4↑ ⒻAlw 4200	2 1 1hd 11½ 12 11½	Brumfield D	113		*.80	89-17	OldHat1131½Suntanned1161LuckyViola1151½	Scored in hand	7

6Jly63-8AP	fst 1	:23 :452 1:10 1:361	3↑ ⒻBeverly H 32k	5	4	44½	44½	55½	66	Hartack W	123	*1.00	82-12	Patrol Woman117½Hushaby118½My Portrait1163½	No excuse	7
31May63-8Was	fst 6f	:214 :444 1:093	4↑ ⒻFour Winds 16k	7	1	32	22	1½	13	Grant H	118	*.60	97-07	Old Hat1183Hushaby1152¼Alecee1151¾	Drew clear in hand	7
16May63-7CD	sly 6f	:23 :462 1:104	4↑ ⒻAlw 4000	2	2	2½	11½	13	17	Vasquez J	121	*.40	92-22	OldHat1217Venture118¾Cynthia'sReward114hd	Scored easily	7
27Mar63-8GP	fst 7f	:224 :46 1:102 1:231	3↑ ⒻSuwannee River H 16k	1	1	22	2½	12½	11¼	Grant H	117	3.35	96-18	OldHat1171¼Cicad1264½Coupd'Ett1111½	Wide,fully extended	6
16Mar63-7GP	fst 6f	:224 :461 1:114	4↑ ⒻAlw 4200	4	1	41	43½	31½	11	Grant H	118	*.65	85-20	OldHat1181Retirement116noCoupd'Etat1143	Long,hard drive	6
27Feb63-8Hia	fst 1⅛	:464 1:111 1:362 1:492	4↑ ⒻBlack Helen H 47k	2	1	13	12	1½	2hd	Grant H	115	8.85	88-14	Pocosaba117hdOldHat1155MissMarcela1142¾	Failed to last	8
13Feb63-8Hia	gd 7f	:23 :453 1:104 1:234	3↑ ⒻColumbiana H 30k	4	3	55½	711	53½	32¼	Grant H	115	5.75	88-16	Cicada1251¾RoyalPatrice121½OldHat1151½	Closed very well	7
7Feb63-8Hia	gd 6f	:222 :454 1:104	4↑ ⒻAlw 5500	7	3	32	21	11½	13¾	Hartack W	119	*1.15	90-18	OldHat1193¾LuckyViola1151½Hushaby1172½	Speed in reserve	10
22Jan63-8Hia	fst 6f	:221 :451 1:10	4↑ ⒻAlw 6000	1	4	33	33½	43	43½	Rotz JL	112	8.45	90-17	PatrolWoman1111¾Coupd'Etat1181¾RedBll112no	Fairly eveny	9
15Nov62-7CD	fst 7f	:221 :443 1:092 1:222	3↑ ⒻAlw 5000	3	4	54	43½	11	2½	Nono R	114	*1.70	97-10	Fortunate Isle114½Old Hat114¾Myway1082	Clear lead,tired	8
3Nov62-8CD	fst 1	:224 :451 1:094 1:353	3↑ ⒻFalls City H 22k	7	3	55½	36	22	22	Nono R	113	16.50	93-12	Primonetta12620ld Hat1131½Fortunate Isle1103	Game try	9
29Oct62-7CD	sly 6f	:224 :464 1:114	ⒻAlw 5000	3	3	43	41½	2½	1¾	Miller S5	111	*.80	87-25	OldHat111¾RecklessDriver1194½Babyo'Mine1083½	Driving	7
19Oct62-8Haw	fst 6f	:222 :451 1:101	3↑ ⒻAlw 4500	6	2	31	22	1hd	11¾	Hartack W	116	*1.20	96-12	OldHat1161¾Cynthia'sReward1123½MissOffset107hd	Driving	8
10Oct62-8Haw	fst 6½f	:221 :453 1:103 1:164	3↑ ⒻYo Tambien H 18k	7	1	22	11	2½	2½	Moreno H	116	5.20	89-20	NarkiSong114½OldHat1166FoolishYouth1161½	Sharp effort	10
3Oct62-8Haw	gd 6½f	:222 :452 1:113 1:164	Handicap 10000	6	1	32½	35	34	34½	Skoronski A	115	4.00	85-22	Boston Sailor114½Mighty Fennec1194Old Hat1156	No rally	7
29Sep62-7Haw	fst 6f	:221 :452 1:111	ⒻAlw 5000	1	3	32½	42¼	41½	31	Hartack W	116	*1.20	90-14	Becky Ann106hdCherry Laurel1151Old Hat116nk	No excuses	11
21Sep62-7Haw	fst 6½f	:221 :451 1:093 1:161	3↑ ⒻAlw 4500	2	4	43½	2½	3nk	31	Burton J	115	*1.60	92-13	Gerts Image114nkFoolish Image108¾Old Hat1152½	Bid,tired	6
13Sep62-8Haw	fst 6f	:221 :451 1:094	3↑ ⒻAlw 4500	7	1	21	1hd	2½	2¾	Skoronski A	111	2.60	97-10	Gerts Image111¾Old Hat1115Cherry Laurel113nk	Game try	7
29Aug62-6AP	fst 6½f	:224 :453 1:101 1:163	ⒻAlw 5000	7	3	22	2hd	2½	1no	Skoronski A	116	2.90	93-08	OldHat116noCherryDear1183½CherryLaurel1182	Up in time	8
25Aug62-7AP	my 6½f	:232 :464 1:113 1:18	Alw 4500	6	2	22	11	14	14¾	Burton J	108	8.30	86-24	OldHat1084¾MghtyFnnc1172½BostonSlor1172¼	Speed to spare	8
11Aug62-8AP	fst 1⅛	:462 1:11 1:36 1:484	ⒻPucker Up 61k	4	3	33½	31½	45	57¾	Phelps B	112	27.20	84-07	RoyalPatrice1121Polylady1143¼DnnrPrtnr1153¼	No response	10
2Aug62-8AP	fst 1	:224 :453 1:11 1:363	ⒻAlw 6000	7	2	1hd	2hd	2hd	2¾	Phelps B	114	23.00	85-13	Venture111¾Old Hat114noHushaby1141¾	Gamely	8
26Jly62-7AP	fst 6f	:22 :451 1:101	3↑ ⒻAlw 4500	8	5	56½	55¾	68	56½	Ruybali J	105	4.00	86-13	Windy Miss1081¾Star Bolt1151½Foolish Youth115nk	Outrun	9
7Jly62-8AP	fst 1	:224 :454 1:103 1:372	ⒻMisty Isle 27k	6	6	98	69	712	59¾	Phelps B	113	17.60	73-16	DinnerPartnr1143¼ChrryLurl1131RodMd1103½	Never a factor	9
21Jun62-8AP	fst 6f	:22 :452 1:103	ⒻAlw 5000	2	4	34	32½	4nk	21	Phelps B	115	4.40	90-10	Rudoma1131Old Hat115½Painful1151	Finished strongly	7
6Jun62-8Was	fst 7f	:221 :444 1:094 1:224	ⒻCleopatra 17k	6	4	34½	36	35	45¼	Phelps B	113	15.70	86-12	CherryLaurel1094Venture109nkDinnerPartner1181	No excuse	12
23May62-8Was	fst 6f	:221 :453 1:101	ⒻCinderella 17k	4	3	4¾	41½	52¾	73¾	Sorenson B	112	9.00	88-16	Dinner Partner114hdRudoma115¾Venture109½	Used in pace	9
5May62-4CD	fst 6f	:221 :45 1:101	Alw 3500	6	1	2hd	12	12	12	Lucas WD	108	4.30	95-06	Old Hat1082Overton Lane1132¼Prince Dale1112½	Drew clear	7
21Apr62-7Kee	fst 6½f	:223 :454 1:102 1:164	ⒻAlw 3750	1	5	33	33	2hd	11½	Grant H	116	*1.60	94-08	OldHt1161½Narola1192½NoCommnt119¾	Brushed,going away	9
11Apr62-7Kee	my 6f	:223 :462 1:104	ⒻAlw 3500	3	3	21	21	2hd	1no	Grant H	116	*1.50	90-14	Old Hat116noPrincess Revoked1167Hushaby1164	Up in time	6
16Mar62-7OP	fst 6f	:221 :464 1:121	Alw 3000	4	9	1014	65¼	32	22½	Campbell RJ	112	6.80	85-20	PrncssBng1092½OldHt112nkDurndl111½	Crowded leaving gate	12
5Mar62-7OP	fst 6f	:223 :463 1:113	Alw 3200	6	3	42½	69	715	714	Cook WM	109	9.30	77-14	Battle Ground114nkThe Nutts111nkNice W.1071¼		8
Taken up repeatedly;Previously owned by Breckenridge Stable																
6Nov61-6CD	gd 6f	:224 :463 1:112	ⒻAlw 3200	8	1	2½	1½	21½	22¼	Phelps B	113	*2.30	87-18	Venture1102¼Old Hat1132½Dinner Partner1101¼	Gamely	9
30Oct61-4CD	fst 6f	:221 :452 1:112	ⒻAlw 3000	1	1	11½	12	1hd	1½	Phelps B	116	6.60	89-16	OldHat116½Venture1093½LuckyViola116¾	Under strong ride	7
20Oct61-6Haw	hy 6f	:222 :464 1:132	Alw 3200	1	1	15	13	1½	11	Phelps B	115	15.30	80-29	Old Hat1151Times Roman1187Wa-Wa Cy1165	Kept to drive	8
18Sep61-5Haw	fst 6f	:222 :461 1:12	ⒻAlw 3500	6	7	43	54	33½	31	Gilligan L	117	10.20	86-16	[D]Narola108nkJet Strauss106¾[D]Old Hat117hd	Bore out	12
Disqualified and placed fifth																
8Sep61-6Haw	fst 6f	:222 :46 1:112	ⒻAlw 4000	8	1	1hd	42½	53	45¼	Chambers W	111	18.10	85-11	Lucky Viola109¾Dorark1092Saba Saba1122½	Used early	8
23Aug61-3AP	fst 6f	:224 :453 1:103	ⒻAlw 4000	1	3	51¼	68½	69½	39¼	Heckmann J	118	16.90	82-11	WindyMiss1187OurJosi1182¼OldHt118nk	Passed tired horses	8
15Aug61-4AP	fst 6f	:23 :451 1:114	ⒻMd Sp Wt	12	1	1½	13	13	1hd	Heckmann J	115	22.70	85-11	OldHat115hdHushaby1154Cynthia'sReward115nk	Just lasted	12
10Aug61-5AP	fst 6f	:232 :46 1:104	ⒻMd Sp Wt	5	10	128¾	1111	815	615	Heckmann J	117	33.90	75-09	Matsu1173Dulaturee1172½Salvia1173½	Never in contention	12
20May61-1CD	fst 5f	:231 :464 :594	ⒻMd Sp Wt	9	8	78	73	75¼	86¼	Cook WM	117	10.40	87-09	Imply117½Lady Oil C.117noPurple Star117¾	No factor	12
13May61-2CD	fst 5f	:224 :463 :594	ⒻMd Sp Wt	1	5	67½	710	68	88½	Cook WM	117	4.70	84-06	Mc Mc Lake1171¾Shot Rock1171½Princess Bang1121		12
Never in contention																

Open Fire

ro. f. 1961, by Cochise (Boswell)–Lucy Lufton, by Nimbus **Lifetime record: 30 13 6 5 $227,329**

Own.– Brandywine Stable

Br.– Renappi Corp. (Va)

Tr.– V.W. Raines

27Oct66-6Kee	fst 1⅛	:464 1:103 1:371 1:502	3↑ ⒻSpinster 58k	1	1	1hd	2½	3nk	11¼	Baeza B	123	1.90	85-21	OpnFire1231¼OldHat1231¼SummerScandl1236	Drawing clear	5
10Oct66-7Kee	fst 6f	:22 :451 :572 1:103	3↑ ⒻAlw 7500	1	5	57	45	22½	11½	Brumfield D	123	*1.00	90-19	OpenFire1231½BearGrass115¾MarrythePrinc1212½	Mild drive	5
17Sep66-7Aqu	fst 1⅛	:47 1:111 1:361 1:492	3↑ ⒻBeldame 85k	5	4	48	49	46½	411	Baeza B	123	*1.50	78-18	SummerScandal1238StraightDeal123½LadyPitt1182	No rally	10
22Aug66-7Sar	sly 1⅛	:471 1:11 1:354 1:484	3↑ ⒻDiana H 28k	4	2	1hd	14	14	110	Lovato F	117	*1.40	101-17	OpenFire11710ReluctantPearl1081¾Mac'sSparklr1131	Easily	8
30Jly66-8Del	fst 1¼	:462 1:102 1:351 2:002	3↑ ⒻDelaware H 122k	4	4	45	13½	14½	15	Lovato F	110	4.30	100-15	Open Fire1105Treachery1102Discipline1193½	Handy score	13
16Jly66-8Del	fst 1 1/16	:234 :472 1:104 1:423	3↑ ⒻNew Castle 36k	5	3	31	12½	13	14	Lovato F	107	7.90	96-15	Open Fire1074Queen Empress1131Ho Ho108¾	Hand urging	9
29Jun66-8Del	fst 1 70	:233 :462 1:12 1:424	3↑ ⒻAlw 4500	1	3	3½	12½	2hd	2nk	Rogers C	121	*1.30	86-19	HoHo112nkOpnFire1211½PeakPerformance1154	Game effort	7
7Jun66-8Del	fst 6f	:222 :46 1:113	3↑ ⒻAlw 6000	8	1	1hd	1½	11½	12½	Rogers C	121	*.80	87-17	Open Fire1212½Shiralee112hdHo Ho1111	Under mild urging	8
21May66-8GS	fst 6f	:22 :453 1:10	3↑ ⒻColonial H 28k	3	1	52	73½	74¼	74¼	Rogers C	112	34.90	90-18	Tosmah1251½Wild Note1161Cohasset114no	Never a threat	8
19Apr66-8Bow	fst 6f	:231 :471 1:123	4↑ ⒻAlw 5500	7	2	63½	42¼	41	12	Rogers C	112	*1.00e	84-20	Open Fire1122Sharon Market112noUpturn112nk	Handy score	8
20Nov65-8Pim	fst 1⅛	:473 1:123 1:394 1:531	3↑ ⒻGallorette 30k	9	5	54½	32	33½	45¾	Ruane J	117	5.10	79-19	Gold Digger1142½Gallarush1113Lovejoy114nk	Well up,tired	14
12Nov65-4Aqu	fst 1	:223 :461 1:111 1:374	3↑ ⒻAlw 7500	3	3	31½	21	23	31¾	Ruane J	119	9.40	77-21	BalletRose1191½SkyWonder119nkOpenFir1191½	No excuse	5
18Oct65-7Aqu	fst 6f	:22 :451 1:103	3↑ ⒻInterborough H 27k	6	6	55	54	23	24	Rotz JL	112	6.60	86-19	Ballet Rose1144Open Fire1132Good Jane114hd	Held gamely	8
9Oct65-8Atl	fst 7f	:222 :45 1:10 1:233	3↑ ⒻParkway H 24k	2	4	21½	46	46½	47½	Valenzuela A	114	7.10	77-13	Juanita1155Mighty Happy1152½Lovejoy114no	Well up,tired	11
28Sep65-7Aqu	fst 7f	:222 :45 1:092 1:231	3↑ ⒻAlw 10000	3	5	31	2½	11	13	Rotz JL	121	3.70	90-17	Open Fire1213Good Jane121¾Crown Silver1161	Ridden out	7
20Sep65-7Aqu	fst 1	:223 :444 1:084 1:351	3↑ ⒻMaskette H 28k	2	5	56½	59	711	89¾	Rotz JL	113	25.80	82-16	Tosmah128noAffectionately1283Straight Deal113½	Tired	9
6Sep65-3Aqu	fst 7f	:224 :46 1:111 1:241	3↑ ⒻAlw 8500	3	4	2hd	11½	11½	1no	Rotz JL	120	*1.20	85-14	OpenFire120noSceree1092½HemandHaw1163	Long,hard drive	6
28Aug65-8Sar	fst 6f	:222 :454 1:104	3↑ ⒻAlw 7500	1	2	1hd	1½	2hd	22½	Rotz JL	120	*1.90	91-08	Silwall1182½OpenFire1201HmndHw1163½	Set fast pace,tired	6
19Aug65-6Sar	sly 7f	:23 :462 1:114 1:243	3↑ ⒻAlw 6500	5	4	53	31½	1hd	12	Rotz JL	121	*1.70	87-15	OpnFire1162½GeeJudge118nkMissDicky1186	Drew clear wide	7
10Jly65-6Del	fst 6f	:222 :454 1:11	3↑ ⒻAlw 4200	4	5	76	54½	45	23½	Nelson E	121	4.40	86-13	MakeaWish1123½OpenFire121nkSouthsideMiss1084	Rallied	8
14Nov64-8Pim	fst 1⅛	:471 1:112 1:374 1:511	3↑ ⒻGallorette 29k	6	2	21	12½	2hd	2no	Ruane J	111	19.40	95-16	Gay Serenade117noOpenFire1112MyCard117½	Made game try	11
31Oct64-8GS	fst 1 1/16	:231 :461 1:10 1:414	ⒻJersey Belle 28k	4	3	55	510	68¼	39¾	Chambers W	112	10.50	89-14	Tosmah1241¾SteepleJill1148OpenFire112hd	No real threat	7
23Oct64-8GS	fst 1 70	:223 :461 1:11 1:41	ⒻAlw 5500	3	4	43	811	713	613	Grant H	120	*2.70	79-16	MyCard1123GoldnHostss112½Lovjoy1183	Impeded backstr	8
6Oct64-6Aqu	fst 7f	:222 :451 1:10 1:231	3↑ ⒻAlw 6500	7	3	42	33	33	33¾	Rotz JL	117	*.65	86-17	Gold Frame108¾Hilly1113Open Fire117¾	Forced out early	7
21Sep64-6Aqu	fst 6f	:224 :454 1:104	3↑ ⒻAlw 8500	2	4	3nk	43½	33½	21	Rotz JL	114	2.30	88-16	Songster1081OpenFire114hdPetiteRouge1133	Finished well	6
8Sep64-6Aqu	fst 1	:233 :464 1:114 1:374	3↑ ⒻAlw 6500	6	3	3½	3½	11	11	Rotz JL	114	*.25	79-20	Open Fire1141Kisco Gal107½Sun Tartan1122	Strong urging	6
27Aug64-6Sar	fst 7f	:223 :451 1:093 1:222	3↑ ⒻAlw 5500	10	1	2½	11½	14	110	Rotz JL	113	*1.00	98-11	OpnFire11310SnugglUp1124[DH]KnwnQuantty117½	Easy score	10
19Aug64-6Sar	fst 6f	:222 :454 1:12	3↑ ⒻAlw 5000	4	3	43	34½	42½	31½	Pierce D	113	2.45	86-13	Tudor Emblem118½Snuggle Up1110Open Fire1131	Closed well	9
2Jly63-5Del	fst 5½f	:222 :464 1:051	ⒻMd Sp Wt	8	1	21	11½	16	110	Ward D5	112	*1.20	95-17	OpnFire11210Ambering1171LakeCampo1171¾	Drew out easily	12
19Jun63-5Del	fst 5f	:224 :47 :59	ⒻMd Sp Wt	10	7	5¾	3nk	32	31¾	Ward D5	112	*2.20	92-14	MyCard1171½Ambring117nkOpnFr1125	Lacked late response	12

Parka

br. g. 1958, by Arctic Prince (Prince Chevalier)–Manchon, by Blenheim II

Own.– Pelican Stable

Br.– Mrs Marion duPont Scott (Va)

Tr.– W.A. Croll Jr

Lifetime record: 93 27 14 18 $446,236

Date	Cond	Dist	Fractions	Time	Race	PP	St	1st	2nd	Str	Fin	Jockey	Wt	Eq	Odds	Fig	Top three	Comment	Fld
4Oct65- 7Aqu	hd	1 3/16Ⓣ		1:54^3	3↑ Long Island H 29k	10	3	2^1	1½	1½	1^1	Blum W	125		*1.40	97-03	Parka125^1Or et Argent116^½Polar Sea120^1½	Long,hard drive	10
18Sep65- 8Atl	fm	1 3/16Ⓣ		1:54^2	3↑ U Nations H 125k	1	5	6^2	5^1¼	4^¾	1^nk	Blum W	119		*1.80	101-06	Parka119^nkHillRis118^5Chftn122^no	Blocked,driving outside	10
4Sep65- 8Atl	hd	1⅛Ⓣ		1:47^3	3↑ Kelly-Olympic H 35k	3	4	3^1	2^2	2^2	1^3	Blum W	118		*1.50	98-05	Parka118^3Indoctrinate114^1Twice as Gay114^3½	Drew out	10
21Aug65- 8Atl	fm	1 1/16Ⓣ		1:41^3	3↑ Philadelphia Turf H 29k	4	5	5^4½	3^2½	2^4	2^3½	Patterson G	119		3.00	95-08	TurboJetII124^3½Parka119^¾TwiceasGay114^4½	Best of others	7
14Aug65- 7Atl	fm	1Ⓣ		1:35	3↑ Alw 4500	7	6	6^7½	6^2¼	3^3½	2^2	Witmer R^5	114		4.50	94-05	TurboJetII121^2Parka114^½Baitman123^1¼	Finished very fast	7
27Feb65- 8Hia	fm	1½Ⓣ		2:29^1	3↑ Hia Turf Cup H 97k	6	6	7^8	4^1½	4^6	6^3¼	Rotz JL	123		*1.90	90-06	HotDust114^hdYourAlibhai113^nkKnightlyMnnr115^2½	Weakened	12
19Feb65- 8Hia	fm	1 1/16Ⓣ		1:43^2	4↑ Alw 7000	2	4	5^3¼	4^4	1^hd	1^hd	Rotz JL	122		*1.50	88-12	Parka122^hdSuspicous119^3½ChfGronmo113^nk	Under hard drive	9
30Jan65- 8Hia	fm	1 3/16Ⓣ		1:53^4	3↑ Bougainvillea H 34k	3	6	6^8	4^3½	2^hd	1^¾	Rotz JL	122		*1.90	100-04	Parka122^¾Western Warrior118^¾Your Alibhai112^1½	Driving	14
22Jan65- 8Hia	fm	1 1/16Ⓣ		1:41^3	4↑ Alw 7500	11	4	5^10	4^7	4^11	3^6	Rotz JL	119		*1.70	91-08	Lucky Turn116^3Your Alibhai113^3Parka119^2	Even effort	11
3Nov64- 7Aqu	fm	1 3/16Ⓣ		1:56^1	3↑ Knickerbocker H 29k	10	3	3^1½	4^2½	4^2	4^2½	Blum W	124		*2.40	86-11	ThirdMartini115^nkGrandApplause108^nkWillIRule116^2	Wide	11
24Oct64- 7Aqu	fm	1⅝Ⓣ		2:42^4	3↑ Man o' War 111k	8	4	4^6	4^1½	7^8	8^13¾	Rotz JL	126		6.95	72-14	TurboJetII126^¾GunBow126^2½KnightlyManner121^1	Bid,tired	9
7Oct64- 7Aqu	fm	1 3/16Ⓣ		1:54^4	3↑ Long Island H 28k	4	3	3^6	3^3	1½	1^2½	Blum W	123		3.25	96-04	Parka123^2½CedarKey126^1WillIRule112^nk	Drew clear easily	7
19Sep64- 8Atl	sf	1 3/16Ⓣ		1:57^4	3↑ U Nations H 125k	3	9	7^4	6^4½	5^5½	2^¾	Blum W	121		10.10	83-21	WesternWarrior114^¾Parka121^hdTurboJetII116^nk	Fast finish	10
5Sep64- 8Atl	fm	1⅛Ⓣ		1:47^1	3↑ Kelly-Olympic H 35k	6	4	4^5	4^8	6^6	7^4	French D	122		5.70	100-01	TurboJetII111^¾Indoctinate110^1¼ColoradoKing126^nk	Tired	9
15Aug64- 8Atl	fm	1 1/16Ⓣ		1:42	3↑ Philadelphia Turf H 29k	2	4	4^1	4^1½	5^2¼	1^¾	Blum W	121		3.30	101-04	Parka121^¾CoolPrince113^noTurboJetII112^no	Long,hard drive	9
1Aug64- 8AP	fm	1 3/16Ⓣ	:47^4 1:12 1:37^3	1:55^4	3↑ Arlington H 56k	5	3	3^3	3^1½	1^1	2^hd	Blum W	118		4.70	88-07	MasterDennis112^hdParka118^1¼Carteret116^4½	Failed to last	10
4Jly64- 8AP	fm	1⅛Ⓣ	:47^1 1:11^1 1:36^2	1:48^3	3↑ Stars & Stripes H 46k	7	6	6^5½	6^4¾	4^5	4^1¾	DeSpirito A	119		*3.10	96-04	SpanishFort112^1¼IrishDandy110^½RobRoyIII106^hd	Rallied	13
27Jun64- 8Mth	fm	1 1/16Ⓣ		1:43^2	3↑ Longfellow H 22k	5	4	5^5¼	5^6	3^2½	1no	DeSpirito A	120		*2.10	98-04	Parka120^noWesternWarrior121^¾RedDog112^hd	Up final stride	7
20Jun64- 7Mth	fm	1Ⓣ		1:37^2	3↑ Alw 7500	3	5	7^16	7^8	7^4¾	2^¾	DeSpirito A	124		*.90e	97-03	Jalico110^¾Parka124^3Jet Clipper110^hd	Wide for the drive	9
10Jun64- 7Mth	fm	1Ⓣ		1:38^4	3↑ Tercentnry H (Div 1) 17k	5	6	5^3¼	2^3	3^3	2no	DeSpirito A	119		*1.00	91-17	Lucky Turn114^noParka119^3Fan Jet111^5	Getting to winner	9
30May64- 7Del	fm	1 1/16Ⓣ		1:40^4	3↑ Brandywine H (Div 2) 18k	8	8	8^8¾	6^5½	3^3½	2^2½	Culmone J	119		*2.00	97-03	Red Dog108^2½Parka119^nkGreek Money115^2	Closed very fast	8
16May64- 9Suf	fm	*1 1/16Ⓣ		1:45^3	3↑ B Tckrmn Jr H (Div 2) 17k	3	6	6^3¾	7^3¼	5^3½	3^1	Nelson E	120		2.70	95-04	WesternWarrior119^noMarlinBay119^1Parka120^nk	Wide stretch	9
2May64- 8Pim	sf	1 1/16Ⓣ	:25^3 :50^3 1:16^3	1:50	3↑ Riggs H 18k	6	6	7^5¼	6^3¼	4^2½	4^2	Turcotte R	120		*1.40	63-35	Mr. Steu114^noDedimoud112^1Grand Applause108^1	Closed fast	11
28Mar64- 9GP	fm	1½Ⓣ	:47 1:11 2:00^4	2:26	3↑ Donn H 59k	7	6	7^13	3^2½	2^3	2^2¼	Chambers W	119		3.70e	97-05	CedarKey122^2¼Parka119^noSuspicious115^1¼	Held for placing	13
18Mar64- 9GP	fm	1 1/16Ⓣ	:22^1 :45^4 1:10^1	1:41^2	3↑ Green Valley H 17k	7	8	9^17	10^10	9^9½	5^2¼	Chambers W	120		*1.50	96-03	PolarSea112^hdCaptain's Cross113^¾Molino115^nk	Settled late	10
29Feb64- 8Hia	fm	1½Ⓣ		2:28^3	3↑ Hia Turf Cup H 98k	7	6	4^3½	5^3	6^6½	8^13	Chambers W	121		*1.60	83-07	Cartert115^3½RoylAscot113^1¼HotDust114^1¼	Early foot,tired	13
20Feb64- 8Hia	fm	1⅛Ⓣ		1:48^4	4↑ Alw 7500	8	7	7^15	8^11	5^6	2^hd	Chambers W	121		3.60	103-04	IrishDandy112^hdParka121^no[D]Finklehoffe115^1¼	Wide,missed	9
1Feb64- 8Hia	fm	1 3/16Ⓣ		1:53^4	3↑ Bougainvillea H 34k	1	7	8^17	8^9½	6^3¼	1^nk	Chambers W	120		6.50	107-00	Parka120^nkSunrise Flight120^1½Hot Dust120^nk	Up near wire	14
24Jan64- 7Hia	fm	1 1/16Ⓣ		1:42^1	4↑ Alw 10000	4	5	5^9	6^9¼	4^7	4^2	Adams L	115		*2.00	98-04	Charablanc112^1¼WldCard112^hdHrdRockMn112^¾	Finished well	11
17Jan64- 7Hia	fm	1 1/16Ⓣ		1:43^2	4↑ Alw 7000	8	9	7^7½	3^3	2^½	1^1¾	Adams L	119		4.70	94-09	Prka119^1¾WesternWarrior115^2½HardRockMn115^1	With ease	12
28Nov63- 8Pim	fm	1½Ⓣ	:47^3 1:13^1 2:04^4	2:32^1	3↑ Dixie H 62k	2	6	6^11	5^7	4^6	3^1	Chambers W	119		3.20	93-14	CedarKey110^1Mr.Steu112^noParka119^4	Finished full of run	12
2Nov63- 8Lrl	sf	1⅛Ⓣ		1:51	3↑ Lrl Turf Cup H 24k	12	8	9^7½	7^3¼	3^nk	2no	Blum W	117		2.50	82-18	[D]Intercepted116^noParka117^1SalesmanPrior109^nk	Bothered	13
	Placed first through disqualification																		
23Oct63- 5Aqu	fm	1 3/16Ⓣ		1:55^1	3↑ Knickerbckr H (Div 1) 21k	7	2	2^2	2^2	2^2	1½	Shoemaker W	110		*2.20	94-03	Parka110^½CedarKy112^2½Thygold110^1½	Under strong handling	8
18Oct63- 7GS	fst	1 1/16	:23^4 :48 1:12	1:43^1	3↑ Alw 5500	5	7	7^3¾	6^7	7^12	7^14	Adams L	119		8.10	80-16	GypsyBaron118^nkWhyLie119^2MorryE.115^8	Never a contender	7
7Oct63- 7Aqu	fm	1 3/16Ⓣ		1:54^3	3↑ Long Island H 29k	7	7	8^8	7^5½	7^5¼	5^5¾	Nelson E	112		13.80	91-03	DavidK.113^nkTheAxeII126^2NeverBend120^2	Never prominent	10
21Sep63- 8Atl	sf	1 1/16Ⓣ		1:47^2	3↑ Boardwalk H 29k	1	4	4^3½	4^3½	3^4	3^3¾	Grant H	116		3.60	70-26	Bronze Babu120^¾Marlin Bay113^3Parka116^2	Lacked a rally	7
31Aug63- 8Atl	fm	1⅛Ⓣ		1:48	3↑ Kelly-Olympic H 35k	6	5	5^2½	5^3½	6^4¾	3^1½	Grant H	116		7.80	101-00	Mngo124^noBronzeBabu120^1½Parka116^¾	Lacked sufficient bid	10
24Aug63- 8Atl	sf	1 1/16Ⓣ		1:45	3↑ Philadelphia Turf H 30k	4	7	8^13	8^12	8^8¼	6^6¼	Grant H	118		*3.20	80-14	Sunrise County116^hdDedimoud115^1¼Hitting Away113^2	Dull	10
12Aug63- 7Atl	fm	1 1/16Ⓣ		1:43	4↑ Alw 6000	7	4	5^11	4^4	4^1½	1^2	Grant H	122		*1.00	96-04	Parka122^2Fat Cat122^½Dedimoud118^2	Kept to mild drive	7
31Jly63- 8Mth	fm	1 1/16Ⓣ		1:44^2	3↑ Longfellow H 34k	1	6	6^11	5^6	4^6	1^2	Grant H	116		5.80	93-07	Parka116^2Inbalance114^1¼Charabanc110^¾	Clear under drive	9
4Jly63- 7Del	fm	1Ⓣ		1:35^4	3↑ Alw 10000	7	7	7^9	7^5	5^5	3^2¼	Culmone J	117		3.50	101-02	Bronze Babu124^1¼Charabanc110^1Parka117^1½	Wide in rally	8
21Jun63- 7Aqu	fm	1 1/16Ⓣ		1:41^4	3↑ Alw 10000	6	6	5^3½	3^2	3^hd	2^½	Adams L	120		5.55	98-01	TheAxeII123^½Parka120^2½MarlinBay111^hd	Stretch bid,hung	8
31May63- 7Mth	fm	1 1/16Ⓣ		1:46^3	4↑ Alw 10000	5	10	8^10	6^6	2^hd	1^1¼	Monacelli E	116		3.90	82-20	Parka116^1¼Pollingfold112^2General Arthur114^1	Drew out	12
17May63- 8GS	fst	1 1/16	:24^1 :48^1 1:12^2	1:44^4	4↑ Alw 6500	1	6	4^1½	7^6¼	8^9¼	7^8½	Monacelli E	117		6.10	77-19	Inbalance119^½Military Plume113^2¾Fat Cat117^1	Fell back	8
4May63- 8Pim	fm	1 1/16Ⓣ	:25^3 :49^1 1:13	1:44^2	3↑ Riggs H 16k	5	4	3^1½	4^2½	4^2½	4^4¼	Monacelli E	111		4.80	89-12	BronzeBabu126^nkShieldBearer118^1½WarCouncil118^2½	Tired	5
17Apr63- 8GP	fm	1 1/16Ⓣ	:23 :46^4 1:11^1	1:42^2	4↑ Alw 4000	6	3	3^2½	1^hd	1^1	1^2	Monacelli E	114		*1.70	93-07	Prka114^2ErinVale114^3WiseCommand116^2¼	Drew out handily	11
6Apr63- 7GP	fm	1Ⓣ	:23^2 :47^2 1:11^2	1:36^4	4↑ Alw 4000	3	4	6^5	8^5¾	4^3¼	2^¾	Grant H	116		*.70	93-13	Tinte109^¾Parka116^1½Bewildroom114^2	Getting to winner	9
23Mar63- 8GP	fm	1½Ⓣ	:48^1 1:12 2:01^2	2:26	3↑ Donn H 41k	3	4	4^1	2^1	2^2	3^4¼	Grant H	115		13.55	95-00	Tutankhamen124^2½ElLoco112^1¾Park115^1¼	Extended bid,tired	12
13Mar63- 8GP	fm	1 1/16Ⓣ	:23^1 :46^2 1:10^1	1:41^1	3↑ Green Valley H 17k	8	3	4^8½	5^6½	4^5	4^5	Grant H	116		5.80	94-06	Tutankhamen122^½El Loco111^2½Carteret116^2	Lacked a rally	9
2Mar63- 8Hia	fm	1 1/16Ⓣ		1:43^1	4↑ Alw 6500	2	6	7^11	8^7¾	5^4	3^3¼	Grant H	117		*1.75	92-05	Moderado108^2AugustSun115^1¼Prk117^1¾	Best stride too late	10
18Feb63- 8Hia	my	1⅛⊗	:46^3 1:11^4 1:37^2	1:50	4↑ Alw 6000	5	6	6^16	5^9	5^5½	4^9¾	Grant H	117		3.30	75-17	JayFox116^½BelowDeck114^8FilisteoII117^1¼	Never prominent	7
31Jan63- 8Hia	fm	5½fⓉ		1:05^2	4↑ Alw 6000	12	9	11^9	10^11	7^8¾	4^2¼	Grant H	124		10.60	88-14	[D]SwiftSands119^nkAlwaysAlive109^1¼ByInvitton119^¾	Rallied	12
3Nov62- 8Lrl	sf	1⅛Ⓣ		1:55^2	3↑ Lrl Turf Cup H 23k	9	8	8^7¾	8^4¼	7^6¾	3^2½	Ferraro R	116		13.10	59-38	BronzeBabu119^1¼WiseShip124^1¼Prk116^1½	Best foot too late	10
27Oct62- 7Lrl	fm	1Ⓣ		1:37^3	3↑ Alw 10000	1	5	4^3	3^1½	3^nk	1^nk	Ferraro R^5	111		5.20	85-18	Parka111^nkGaelicLad118^1½CalltheWitness116^hd	Up in time	10
20Oct62- 6GS	fst	6f	:22^2 :45^2	1:09^4	4↑ Alw 7000	4	7	7^10	7^13	7^10	5^11	Grant H	119		9.10	84-15	Tilmar119^4½St.Tropez119^3½Intervener122^nk	Never a factor	8
22Sep62- 8Atl	fst	1 1/16	:23^3 :46^3 1:10^3	1:41^4	3↑ Boardwalk H 28k	3	4	4^¾	4^3¼	5^7	6^8	Lynch J	111		32.30	90-13	Ambiopoise116^½Hellenic Hero113^¾Towson111^nk	Tired	8
15Sep62- 6Atl	fst	7f	:23 :45^1 1:09^2	1:21^4	3↑ Alw 4500	3	2 4	4^4	8^½	4^6	4^7½	Lynch J	113		6.40	86-15	HellenicHero122^noTilmar116^1½NobleJay118^6	Lacked a rally	6
1Sep62- 8Atl	fm	1⅛Ⓣ		1:50	3↑ Kelly-Olympic H 35k	8	4	4^3¼	3^3½	3^4½	3^2	Lynch J	111		25.60	91-07	WiseShip124^½HittingAway124^1½Park111^½	Finished willingly	11
25Aug62- 8Atl	fm	1 1/16Ⓣ		1:42^2	3↑ Philadelphia Turf H 29k	1	7	6^9½	6^8	7^4¼	5^6¼	Brooks S	113		7.00	93-01	T.V.Lark120^2HellenicHero111^¾LoyalLadyII108^½	In close	8
	Placed fourth through disqualification																		
8Aug62- 7Sar	sf	1 1/16Ⓣ		1:42^1	3↑ Bernard Baruch H 28k	2	5	5^9½	6^6	4^3	5^3¼	Grant H	118		7.25	92-15	HittingAway122^1¼WiseShip126^nkNiksar111^nk	Mild bid,tired	7
7Jly62- 8Mth	fm	1Ⓣ		1:39^1	3↑ Longfellow H 29k	6	5	5^5	5^¾	2^1½	2^1½	Gilligan L	118		9.80	87-11	RoyalRecord115^1½Parka118^1¾Inbalance117^no	Held on gamely	11
27Jun62- 6Mth	sf	1 1/16Ⓣ		1:49^1	3↑ Alw 6000	5	4	3^3½	2^2	2^hd	1^hd	Gilligan L	117		7.70	69-35	Parka117^hdInblnc117^noMrryRulr122^7	Best under hard drive	6
16Jun62- 6Mth	sf	1Ⓣ		1:41^1	3↑ Alw 6000	1	6	6^3	5^3¼	3^½	1^¾	Grant H	116		*2.20	79-29	Parka116^¾August Sun124^7Green Hornet113^1¼	Strong drive	8
6Jun62- 5Mth	fm	1Ⓣ		1:37^2	4↑ Alw 5000	2	7	6^7¼	4^4	4^1¾	3^1	Barrow T	119		4.90	97-04	Li'lFella122^1RoyalRaton115^noPrk119^no	Blocked midstretch	7
22May62- 7GS	fst	1 1/16	:24^2 :48 1:12^2	1:44^2	4↑ Alw 10000	6	4	5^6½	4^2¼	5^3½	5^5¾	Grant H	119		2.70	82-15	TryCash116^2½Fngo116^½L'lBuddy110^2½	Showed an even effort	8
8May62- 7GS	fst	1 1/16	:24 :47^3 1:11^3	1:43^4	4↑ Alw 10000	5	5	5^2¼	5^4¾	2^3	2^1½	Grant H	122		5.10	89-15	Snow Dune122^1½Parka122^noClaret II116^1¼	Gaining at end	8
24Apr62- 7GP	fm	1 1/16Ⓣ	:23 :46^2 1:10^3	1:41^4	4↑ Alw 3800	9	4	3^3½	4^2	2^hd	3^2	Scurlock O	118		*1.70	94-10	HisLegend116^1¼HyPrince115^¾Parka118^2	Bold bid,then tired	9
14Apr62- 7GP	fst	1⅛	:46^3 1:12^2 1:38^3	1:51^1	3↑ Pan American H 20k	5	5	3^4	3^nk	2^2	5^7¾	Hartack W	115	b	8.20	70-15	Shirley Jones121^2½Aeroflint118^3Deton109^1½	Well up,tired	10
7Apr62- 7GP	fst	1 1/16	:24 :47^2 1:11^4	1:44^3	3↑ Fort Lauderdale H 15k	6	3	2^hd	3^½	5^3	5^6¾	Monacelli E	113	b	6.85	78-19	Cactus Tom119^1Aeroflint118^¾Trans-Way122^1	Speed,tired	8
14Mar62- 7GP	fm	1 1/16Ⓣ	:22^3 :45^4 1:09^4	1:41	3↑ Green Valley H 17k	4	3	3^3	3^3	1^hd	3^¾	Monacelli E	109	b	12.95	99-00	Eurasia122^hdNasomo112^¾Parka109^no	Stretch lead,weakened	9
8Mar62- 8GP	fm	1Ⓣ	:23^1 :47 1:11^4	1:36^4	3↑ Alw 4200	5	2	4^1½	3^nk	1^½	1^nk	Grant H	118	b	2.70	94-06	Parka118^nkWise Command120^¾Tapis122^1	Under hard drive	10
12Feb62- 7Hia	fm	1 1/16Ⓣ		1:45^1	4↑ Alw 5000	8	6	6^4½	3^2½	1^hd	1^1½	Grant H	116	b	3.55	85-15	Parka116^1½MissJ.G.107^½RoylRdrss112^1¾	Driving,drew clear	12
30Jan62- 8Hia	fst	7f	:23^1 :46 1:10^3	1:23^2	4↑ Alw 5000	11	2	9^7	9^9½	5^7	5^2¾	Grant H	120	b	5.20	90-14	The Tongan116^½Whitechapel114^1¾Misty Day118^½	Late gain	12
6Jan62- 8TrP	fst	1 1/16	:23^1 :46 1:09^4	1:42^3	3↑ Orange Bwl H (Div 2) 15k	7	4	4^3	4^3	3^2	4^2½	Monacelli E	111	b	7.95	86-14	Eurasia119^½BeauPrince124^2Trans-Wy114^no	Made even effort	9
25Dec61- 8TrP	fst	1 1/16	:22^4 :46 1:10^4	1:44	3↑ Christmas H 11k	4	5	5^4	5^3	4^1½	5^¾	Monacelli E	111	b	64.15	81-27	Humane Leader113^½Eurasia120^noLevel Flight114^nk	Evenly	11
2Dec61- 8TrP	fst	1 70	:22^1 :45^3 1:11^2	1:42	3↑ City of Miami H 11k	8	7	7^6¼	5^5½	5^6	6^6¼	Monacelli E	112	b	9.40	81-13	Eurasia118^1½Pointer114^1½ImWilling113^no	Made even effort	14

25Nov61- 5TrP	fst	6f	:221 :454	1:104	Alw 3000	4	8	89	66	45	42	Grant H	122	b	*1.25	86-21	Cyclobob113¾CountRose1191¼Troa116no	Passed tired horses	10
10Nov61- 7GS	fst	1 70	:232 :471 1:122	1:43	Alw 6000	4	7	52½	42½	42	33	Grant H	122	b	3.80	79-26	Earful111noSho Lea1163Parka122¾	Dwelt at the start	8
26Oct61- 7GS	fst	1	:24 :48 1:13	1:373	Alw 10000	7	5	42	3nk	13	12	Grant H	119	b	2.90	94-24	Parka1192Sho Lea1197Sunshine Cake1111½	Kept to pressure	7
19Oct61- 7GS	fst	1 70	:23 :463 1:12	1:43	Alw 10000	9	5	53	85½	1010	1010	Sellers J	116	b	*2.70	72-16	JayFox1221½Earful1122NobleTurn1141¼	Made a dull effort	11
13Oct61- 7GS	fst	1	:231 :461 1:104	1:374	Alw 10000	9	2	11½	11	12	2no	Sellers J	116	b	*2.50	93-17	HellenicHero119noParka116nkNobleTurn1094	Failed to last	12
26Sep61- 6Atl	fst	7f	:222 :45 1:092	1:214	Clm 13000	3	2	12	13	16	18	Sellers J	120	b	*1.70	94-11	Parka1208GoldenSixties1182¼EnglishSole115no	Mild drive	8
11Sep61- 6Atl	fst	6f	:221 :444	1:092	Clm c-10000	4	2	32	32	31	1hd	Lee T	116	b	*2.10	98-08	Parka116hdLangleyFiver1141½PhlLppy1144	Up final strides	7
	Claimed from W.A. Leiser,F.A. Bonsal trainer																		
19Aug61- 7Atl	fst	7f	:223 :45 1:092	1:22	Alw 4500	8	5	31	54	54½	65½	Lee T	114	b	35.40	87-11	Relative121hdCovered Bridge1141¼Somali Bird1143½	Tired	9
12Aug61- 6Atl	fst	6f	:214 :451	1:102	Alw 4200	1	7	59	67½	76	76	Lee T	116	b	19.20	87-11	Relative1161St. Tropez116[DH]Long Distance1102	No factor	8
27Jly61- 8Del	fm	1 1/16Ⓣ		1:443	3↑ Alw 5000	1	2	2hd	1hd	2hd	11¾	Lee T	114	b	1.50	89-11	Parka1141¾Why Lie1224Almitra117¾	Under long,hard drive	7
13Jly61- 4Del	sly	1 1/16	:234 :474 1:121	1:461	Alw 4000	2	1	1hd	11	2hd	31¼	Lee T	116	b	7.40	77-20	BraxtonBragg116¾RainDance116½Park116no	Drifted out late	6
7Jly61- 4Del	fst	6f	:224 :462	1:112	Alw 5000	5	3	53½	54½	59	57½	Lee T	108		8.80	80-21	RestlessCloud1171¼BraxtonBragg1121¼GlencoeKid1175	Tired	7
14Jun61- 5Del	fm	1Ⓣ		1:391	Alw 5000	2	2	25	37	35½	33¼	Lee T	116		4.50	83-14	World Record1162½Kowtow116¾Parka1162½	Mild late rally	9
6Jun61- 5Del	fst	6f	:221 :454	1:113	Alw 4500	8	4	53½	55	31	31½	Lee T	122		6.40	85-19	Arstar122nkAffectiont1171¼Prk122nk	Best stride too late	12
20May61- 6Pim	fst	6f	:233 :472	1:133	Alw 3000	6	2	43½	33½	1hd	13	Lee T	116		*1.40	82-22	Parka1163Mart1163FndM1131½	Mildly urged,increasing lead	7
16May61- 7Pim	fst	6f	:233 :463	1:13	Alw 4000	4	3	31½	38	36	33	Choquette J	113		2.90	82-22	PhilLippy1131¾LookofEagles1081¼Park1136	Stride too late	7
2May61- 5Lrl	gd	6f	:23 :473	1:133	©Md Sp Wt	7	1	1hd	1½	11½	11½	Choquette J	118		*1.80e	87-12	Parka1181½[DH]Initiator118[DH]Wait Again1184	Kept driving	9

Peal

b. g. 1956, by Hunters Moon IV (Foxhunter)–Golden Bells, by Swing and Sway **Lifetime record: 12 4 5 2 $73,707**

Own.– H.A. Love

Br.– Harry A. Love (Md)

Tr.– C.V.B. Cushman Jr

27Oct61- 6Aqu	hd	*2½	S'Chase	4:354	4↑ Temple Gwathmey H 55k	1	2	2½	38½	18	114	Aitcheson J Jr	161		*1.55	- -	Peal16114NavalTreaty1392Chufquen1413	Had speed to spare	8
17Oct61- 5Aqu	hd	*3	S'Chase	5:402	4↑ Grand National H 28k	2	2	22	1½	2½	2½	Aitcheson J Jr	159		*2.20	- -	Independence138½Peal1598Naval Treaty1386	Jumped well	8
3Oct61- 5Bel	sf	*2½	S'Chase	4:484	4↑ Brook H 19k	6	3	35	43½	21	2¾	Aitcheson J Jr	158		2.95	- -	NavalTreaty133¾Peal1588Chufqun1412	Bore out final drive	7
14Sep61- 5Bel	hd	*2⅛	S'Chase	3:52	4↑ Broad Hollow H 16k	5	2	23	23	11	14½	Aitcheson J Jr	147		2.90	- -	Peal1474½Negocio13210Hustl13418	Going away,mildly urged	6
7Jly61- 3Del	fm	*2½	S'Chase	4:403	4↑ Indian River H 10k	4	1	1½	12	15	17	Aitcheson J Jr	146		*.70e	- -	Peal1467Arywa138noBugleCIIII1427	Well rated,easily best	7
19Jun61- 3Del	fm	*2⅛	S'Chase	4:014	4↑ Tom Roby 10k	5	3	411	2hd	21½	12½	Aitcheson J Jr	141		5.40	- -	Pl1412½Juvntus1334BuglCIII14612	Fenced well,drew clear	7
1Jun61- 5Bel	hd	*2⅛	S'Chase	3:561	4↑ International H 16k	2	1	23	33	36	36	Aitcheson J Jr	142		5.05	- -	Nala155hdMuguet II1606Peal1427	Forced to check slightly	6
22May61- 3Aqu	fm	*2	S'Chase	3:54	4↑ Alw 4500	1	7	2½	23	23	2½	Aitcheson J Jr	137		*1.15e	- -	RealFncy147½Pl137½BslB14230	Slow start,bad landing 12th	8
9May61- 3Aqu	sf	*2	S'Chase	3:53	4↑ Sp Wt 4200	6	5	53½	34½	11½	21	Riles S	152		27.55	- -	OurJeep1431Peal152hdNavalTrety1438	Led briefly,game try	9
9Jun60- 5Bel	fm	*2⅛	S'Chase	3:57	4↑ Bel Spring 13k	4	1	12	-	-	-	Walsh T	142		18.55	- -	Hustle151hdAmateur15614Cartagena1461½		8
	Stumbled 8th fence,lost rider																		
1Jun60- 3Bel	hd	*2⅛	S'Chase	3:563	4↑ Sp Wt 4500	9	1	11½	2½	37½	312	Walsh T	145		7.55e	- -	Amateur1547Black Andy1455Peal1456	Set early pace,tired	9
23Apr60- 5Mid	hd	*2	S'Chase	3:51	4↑ Alw 600	2	4	411	2½	22	28	Aitcheson J Jr	139		-	- -	Doural1438Peal13910Rhythm Master141	Made game try	5

Primonetta

ch. f. 1958, by Swaps (Khaled)–Banquet Bell, by Polynesian **Lifetime record: 25 17 2 2 $306,690**

Own.– Darby Dan Farm

Br.– John W. Galbreath (Ky)

Tr.– J.P. Conway

3Nov62- 8CD	fst	1	:224 :451 1:094	1:353	3↑ ⒻFalls City H 22k	4	2	23	22	12	12	Baird RL	126		*.60	95-12	Primonetta1262Old Hat1131¼Fortunate Isle1103	Easy score	9
18Oct62- 6Kee	fst	1⅛	:46 1:101 1:36	1:482	3↑ ⒻSpinster 73k	6	3	34	21	11	11	Shoemaker W	123		*.60e	95-12	Primonetta1231Royal Patrice119hdFirm Policy1191	Driving	7
	Open to 3-, 4- and 5-year-olds																		
11Oct62- 6Kee	fst	*7f		1:251	3↑ ⒻAlw 10000	2	1	32½	24	2hd	13½	Lynch J	118		*.90	99-13	Primonetta1183½Times Two112nkCyclopavia1046	Easily best	4
22Sep62- 7Aqu	fst	1⅛	:463 1:103 1:354	1:481	3↑ ⒻBeldame 87k	2	1	1hd	1hd	21	45¼	Baeza B	123		*2.80e	96-06	Cicada1181½ShirleyJones1232¼FirmPolcy1181½	Used in pace	13
10Sep62- 7Aqu	fst	6f	:22 :444	1:094	3↑ ⒻHandicap 10000	1	4	41¾	43½	3nk	11½	Valenzuela I	125		*1.35	96-10	Primonetta1251½Staretta119nkReally Sumthin1121½	Easily	8
29Aug62- 7Aqu	my	6½f	:224 :461 1:111	1:174	3↑ ⒻHandicap 10000	6	2	1hd	2½	22	35¼	Valenzuela I	126		*.90	89-19	Play Time1204Linita1231¼Primonetta126½	Used up early	7
28Jly62- 6Del	fst	1¼	:474 1:113 1:363	2:023	3↑ ⒻDelaware H 141k	4	1	1½	33½	36	48¼	Baeza B	124		*1.50e	81-21	SevenThirty120hdCicada1147Bramalea1151¼	Hard used early	9
4Jly62- 8Mth	fst	1 1/16	:232 :463 1:103	1:422	3↑ ⒻMolly Pitcher H 27k	5	1	11	11	11	12	Baeza B	126		*.50	93-11	Primonetta1262Shirley Jones123½Dremflowr1124½	Mild drive	6
20Jun62- 7Mth	fst	6f	:22 :444	1:091	3↑ ⒻRegret H 22k	4	1	1hd	1hd	11½	12½	Baeza B	124		*.40	96-13	Primonetta1242½Coup d'etat1131¼Cup of Tea112¾	In hand	5
12Jun62- 7Bel	sly	6f	:222 :452	1:094	3↑ ⒻAlw 6500	3	1	11½	13	16	110	Baeza B	114		*.25	98-16	Primonetta11410Shuett118¾Whspy1145	Long lead,easy score	4
23Nov61- 7Aqu	fst	1	:223 :453 1:11	1:363	3↑ ⒻFirenze H 28k	5	2	2½	1hd	42	66½	Ycaza M	123		*.80	78-18	Oil Royalty109¾Frimanaha113¾Seven Thirty1164	Used up	8
19Oct61- 6Kee	sly	1⅛	:464 1:103 1:36	1:491	3↑ ⒻSpinster 84k	7	2	2½	1½	12	2¾	Shoemaker W	119		4.30	90-11	Bowl of Flowers119¾Primonetta1191Times Two1191	Gamely	7
	Open to 3-,4- and 5-year-olds																		
23Sep61- 7Bel	fst	1⅛	:463 1:11 1:361	1:492	3↑ ⒻBeldame 96k	4	1	11	1½	2½	33¼	Shoemaker W	118		*3.10	86-18	Airmans Guide123¾Craftiness1232½Primonetta1185½	Tired	12
13Sep61- 7Bel	fst	1⅛	:463 1:11 1:361	1:49	ⒻGazelle H 28k	2	4	2hd	1hd	53¼	59½	Shoemaker W	126		*.55	81-16	Shimmy Dancer1122½My Portrait120noFunloving1226	Tired	11
5Aug61- 6Sar	fst	1¼	:481 1:121 1:371	2:031	ⒻAlabama 54k	2	1	11	11½	1½	15	Shoemaker W	121		2.45	92-10	Primonetta1215MightyFar1141BowlofFlowrs124hd	Mild drive	6
22Jly61- 6Mth	fst	1⅛	:474 1:111 1:361	1:484	ⒻMth Oaks 56k	3	2	1hd	1hd	1hd	2nk	Rogers C	121		*.70	100-15	My Portrait121nkPrimonetta1217Funloving1212	Sharp try	9
15Jly61- 6Del	gd	1⅛	:48 1:123 1:383	1:511	ⒻDel Oaks 59k	3	1	12	11	1½	1no	Shoemaker W	121		*.50	81-27	Primonetta121noMighty Fair1214Funloving1214	All out	6
3Jly61- 7Mth	fst	6f	:221 :451	1:101	ⒻMiss Woodford 22k	5	2	13	13	13	14½	Grant H	121		*.40	91-15	Primonetta1214½HighlandLass112nkAnglSpd1131¾	Mild drive	7
12Jun61- 7Mth	fst	6f	:211 :434	1:082	3↑ ⒻAlw 6000	4	2	34	34	13	13½	Grant H	115		*.70	100-12	Primonetta1153½ShirleyJones1157GrenTrunk1153	Mild drive	7
12Apr61- 7Aqu	fst	6f	:22 :451	1:103	ⒻPrioress 24k	8	2	31½	21½	11	11½	Hartack W	121		*.35	92-12	Primonetta1211½Apatontheback1211¼MightyFair1211	Handily	10
4Apr61- 7Aqu	fst	6f	:23 :47	1:12	ⒻAlw 10000	3	3	1hd	11	113	13¼	Hartack W	123		*.30	85-20	Primonetta1233¼Apatontheback1233½Vivandiere1121	Easily	5
26Nov60- 8Pim	fst	1 1/16	:251 :483 1:124	1:462	ⒻMarguerite 37k	3	1	12	13	14	15	Hartack W	119		*1.00	78-27	Primonetta1195Plum Cake11910Rice Shower1195	Easy score	5
15Nov60- 7Aqu	fst	6f	:222 :46	1:112	ⒻAlw 5000	4	1	11	11½	12	11	Hartack W	119		*.35	88-19	Primnetta1191Marwol1125Short Span1154	Was kept driving	5
28Oct60- 6Aqu	fst	6f	:224 :47	1:113	ⒻAlw 4500	6	1	1hd	1hd	11	12½	Arcaro E	119		*1.10	87-20	Primonetta1192½Shimmy Dancer1161M'selle Mill1162	Easily	13
13Sep60- 4Aqu	fst	6f	:221 :454	1:111	ⒻMd Sp Wt	4	1	11½	12	11½	1¾	Arcaro E	115		4.70	91-12	Primonetta115¾TinyRoyal1152CounterCall115nk	Brisk ride	10

Queen Empress

b. f. 1962, by Bold Ruler (Nasrullah)–Irish Jay, by Double Jay **Lifetime record: 33 15 10 4 $431,419**

Own.– Wheatley Stable
Br.– Wheatley Stable (Ky)
Tr.– E.A. Neloy

26Oct66- 7Aqu	fm	1 1/16Ⓣ				1:44	3↑	ⒻNew York H (Div 2) 23k	7	3	3nk	22	920	935½	Baeza B	120	b	5.70	50-13	Swinging Mood1192Short Fall112noWhat a Treat121¾		9
	Early speed,sulked																					
17Oct66- 7Aqu	fst	6f	:222	:453		1:102	3↑	ⒻInterborough H 27k	2	3	64	64	44½	25	Baeza B	123	b	6.00	86-19	NativeStreet1185QueenEmpress1232Codorniz1181½	In close	6
16Jly66- 8Del	fst	1 1/16	:234	:472	1:104	1:423	3↑	ⒻNew Castle 36k	1	2	2hd	22½	23	24	Baeza B	113	b	*1.10	92-15	Open Fire1074Queen Empress1131Ho Ho108¾	No excuse	9
29Jun66- 7Aqu	fst	7f	:232	:46	1:102	1:231	3↑	ⒻVagrancy H 27k	2	2	1hd	1½	12	12½	Baeza B	123	b	*.20	90-17	QnEmpress1232½PetiteRouge1133½MountRegina113½	Easily	4
8Jun66- 7Aqu	fst	6f	:221	:444		1:093	3↑	ⒻLiberty Belle H 27k	6	4	43	32½	21	2no	Baeza B	122	b	*1.50	95-12	TripleBrook113noQnEmprss1225Cohsst115¾	Altered course	8
21May66- 8GS	fst	6f	:22	:453		1:10	3↑	ⒻColonial H 28k	4	4	41	41½	5¾	42½	Knapp K	122	b	3.70	91-18	Tosmah1251½WildNote1161Cohsst114no	Lacked late response	8
27Apr66- 7Aqu	fst	1	:24	:464	1:11	1:354	3↑	ⒻBed o' Roses H 27k	1	1	1½	1hd	2hd	33	Blum W	123	b	3.20	86-18	StraightDeal1171½WhtaTreat1261½QnEmprss123nk	Weakened	7
18Apr66- 7Aqu	fst	7f	:223	:452	1:094	1:222	3↑	ⒻDistaff H 27k	6	2	33	21½	1hd	2nk	Baeza B	123	b	*.60	94-17	SailorPrincess111nkQueenEmprss1232½Pttcot112no	Bore out	7
9Apr66- 8Bow	fst	7f	:223	:45	1:102	1:232	3↑	ⒻBarbara Fritchie H 59k	3	5	31½	31½	2hd	21	Knapp K	123	b	3.30	95-14	Tosmah1211Queen Emprss1231½Privileged111nk	Game effort	12
30Mar66- 7Aqu	fst	6f	:221	:453		1:111	3↑	ⒻCorrection H 28k	3	4	52¼	32	2hd	12	Knapp K	122	b	*.80	87-20	QnEmpress1222Adorable1122½Admrng1151¾	Loafing,roused	8
2Mar66- 8Hia	fst	1⅛	:47	1:11	1:372	1:502	3↑	ⒻBlack Helen H 62k	5	1	1½	11	32	42¾	Baeza B	117	b	8.00	80-13	WhataTreat1201¾AlondraII110hdTosmah1151	Set pace,tired	11
16Feb66- 8Hia	fst	7f	:231	:453	1:103	1:231	3↑	ⒻColumbiana H 30k	4	1	1½	1½	1hd	33	Baeza B	120	b	2.20e	90-17	Gold Digger112½Tosmah1172½Queen Empress1201	Lead,tired	9
8Feb66- 8Hia	fst	7f	:232	:454	1:101	1:232	4↑	ⒻAlw 8000	7	1	2½	2½	21½	1no	Baeza B	113	b	*.90	92-13	Queen Empress113noTosmah113nkWhat a Treat1193	Driving	7
1Feb66- 8Hia	fst	6f	:221	:46		1:113	4↑	ⒻAlw 6000	6	1	31	1½	12	12½	Baeza B	115	b	*.40	86-23	QueenEmpress1152½MeetMeLater112¾DeCathy113hd	In hand	7
	Previously trained by W.C. Winfrey																					
14Aug65- 6Sar	fst	1¼	:471	1:112	1:364	2:033		ⒻAlabama 63k	13	4	31	75	1726	1736	Baeza B	118	b	6.20e	54-06	WhataTreat118nk[D]Discipline1182Terentia114½	Brief speed	18
12Aug65- 7Sar	fst	7f	:221	:443	1:094	1:231		ⒻHandicap 10000	2	5	23	22	2hd	1no	Baeza B	123	b	*.90	94-12	QnEmprss123noTwoofAkind114½ValiantQueen121no	Lasted	8
5Aug65- 7Sar	fst	7f	:222	:45	1:094	1:23		ⒻTest (Div 2) 23k	1	4	21½	2½	1½	21½	Baeza B	118	b	*.70	93-12	Cestrum1121½Queen Empress118½Ground Control1212	Failed	9
26Jly65- 7Aqu	fst	6f	:214	:45		1:10	3↑	ⒻAlw 10000	1	2	21	21½	1hd	13	Baeza B	111	b	*.70	93-13	Queen Empress1113Petite Rouge1161Ballet Rose1204	Easily	4
20Jly65- 8Mth	fst	6f	:22	:45		1:112		ⒻAlw 5000	6	3	1½	13	11	1½	Grant H	121	b	*.60	85-19	Queen Empress121½Bacasiwo1137Street Show118no	Driving	8
7Nov64- 8GS	fst	1 1/16	:232	:47	1:112	1:44		ⒻGardenia 188k	2	1	11	1½	3nk	1nk	Shoemaker W	119	b	*1.00e	88-13	Queen Empress119nkMarshua119noDiscipline1191¾	Driving	13
24Oct64- 8Lrl	fst	1 1/16	:232	:464	1:122	1:441		ⒻSelima 96k	5	3	21	21	21	2nk	Shoemaker W	122	b	*.40e	96-10	Marshua119nkQueen Empress122nkDiscipline1194½	Failed	7
10Oct64- 7Aqu	fst	1	:224	:453	1:11	1:372		ⒻFrizette 124k	3	3	36½	24½	1½	11	Shoemaker W	119	b	*.90e	81-18	QueenEmpress1191[D]Marshua119¾MoneytoBurn1192½	Easily	8
30Sep64- 7Aqu	my	7f	:224	:462	1:124	1:263		ⒻAstarita 30k	9	4	3½	11½	1hd	1no	Valenzuela I	122		*2.20	73-31	[D]QueenEmpress122noIDeceive1192½Admiring1222	Bore out	12
	Disqualified and placed second																					
23Sep64- 6Aqu	fst	6½f	:222	:452	1:102	1:17		ⒻAlw 9500	2	3	31	32½	21	2hd	Shoemaker W	122	b	*.85	95-13	LayAft116hdQueenEmpress122noMarshua1225	Steadied,sharp	6
26Aug64- 7Sar	fst	6f	:213	:442		1:104		ⒻSpinaway 81k	4	4	32½	22½	24	31	Ycaza M	119	b	*1.05	93-08	Candalita1191Marshua119hdQnEmprss1191	Swerved backstr.	6
19Aug64- 7Sar	fst	6f	:22	:45		1:104		ⒻAdirondack 24k	1	8	21½	22	23	22½	Ycaza M	123	b	*.90	91-13	Candalita1142½Queen Empress1233Marshua123¾	No excuse	9
1Aug64- 8Mth	fst	6f	:22	:443		1:093		ⒻSorority 100k	2	3	42	41	32	34½	Baeza B	119	b	*1.20	89-15	BoldExperience1192½Rhodie1192QnEmpress1195	No excuse	7
15Jly64- 8Mth	fst	5½f	:213	:45		1:04		ⒻColleen 17k	2	5	32	2hd	11½	1¾	Baeza B	119	b	1.30	97-15	QueenEmprss119¾BoldExperience1198Centrvll114nk	Driving	9
29Jun64- 7Aqu	fst	5½f	:222	:453	:574	1:041		ⒻAstoria 28k	7	4	32½	31½	21½	1hd	Baeza B	123	b	*.55	92-16	Queen Empress123hdMarshua1175First Offence1173½	Driving	8
15Jun64- 7Aqu	fst	5½f	:223	:461	:584	1:054		ⒻNational Stallion 26k	4	4	3½	31½	13	12	Baeza B	119		*.35	84-17	QueenEmpress1192Adorabl1142ClrRock1191	Tried to bear in	5
13May64- 7Aqu	fst	5f	:22	:453		:581		ⒻFashion 23k	6	6	45½	46½	33½	1nk	Baeza B	116		4.05	94-18	QueenEmpress116nkBoldExperience1166Privilgd1122	Driving	7
5May64- 6Aqu	fst	5f	:224	:461		:583		ⒻAlw 7500	7	7	45	43½	31	1½	Baeza B	116		*.75e	92-15	QueenEmpress116½Discipline1162½NativPrncss1161½	Driving	8
29Apr64- 3Aqu	sly	5f	:23	:471		:593		ⒻMd Sp Wt	6	3	2hd	1hd	12	1¾	Ussery R	119		2.70e	87-25	Queen Empress119¾Privileged1195½Small Voice1192	Easily	10

Queen of the Stage

b. f. 1965, by Bold Ruler (Nasrullah)–Broadway, by Hasty Road **Lifetime record: 14 9 2 1 $316,515**

Own.– O. Phipps
Br.– Ogden Phipps (Ky)
Tr.– E.A. Neloy

21Jan69- 8Hia	fst	6f	:22	:45		1:092	4↑	ⒻAlw 7000	1	5	1½	2½	24	37¾	Baeza B	118		*.60	89-15	TooBald1157ClemsFairyGold121¾QnoftheStg118¾	Gave way	9
24Oct68- 7Bel	fst	6f	:23	:46		1:101	3↑	ⒻAlw 15000	3	2	11	1hd	13	11¼	Baeza B	120		*.20	94-16	QnoftheStge1201¼QueenVkng1132½GustRoom1133½	Handily	8
14Oct68- 7Bel	fst	6f	:22	:443		1:094	3↑	ⒻInterborough H 27k	1	3	11½	14	12	2nk	Baeza B	119	b	*2.20	96-16	Romanticism117nkQnoftheStg1192½JustKddng1175	Gamely	7
5Oct68- 8Atl	fst	1 3/16	:472	1:111	1:364	1:551	3↑	ⒻMatchmaker 50k	1	1	1hd	1hd	33½	815	Baeza B	114		*2.90	85-12	Politely1234½GreenGlade115¾AmerigoLady1182	Used in pace	11
25Sep68- 8Atl	fst	1 1/16	:233	:464	1:102	1:42	3↑	Alw 7500	4	1	11½	11	1hd	1hd	Baltazar C	111		*.90	97-11	[D]QueenoftheStage111hdBig Rock Candy1135NavyAdmirl114nk		8
	Disqualified and placed second																					
13Sep68- 7Aqu	fst	6f	:223	:462		1:104	3↑	ⒻAlw 15000	7	1	11½	12	12	11½	Baeza B	112		*.90	89-19	Queen of the Stage1121½Just Kidding1164Indian LoveCall116½		7
	Driving																					
28Oct67- 8Lrl	fst	1 1/16	:232	:463	1:124	1:442		ⒻSelima 109k	5	3	43	44½	411	418¼	Baeza B	122		*.40	77-17	SyrianSea1192GayMatelda1193¼SingingRain11913	No excuse	6
7Oct67- 7Aqu	fst	1	:23	:454	1:101	1:352		ⒻFrizette 114k	7	2	2hd	2½	1½	1¾	Baeza B	119		*.40e	91-12	Queen of the Stage119¾Gay Matelda1191Obeah119½	Driving	7
9Sep67- 7Aqu	fst	6f	:221	:452		1:10		ⒻMatron 104k	4	1	21	21	12	14	Baeza B	119		*.30	93-16	QueenoftheStage1194GayMatelda119¾SyrianSea1193	Easily	7
23Aug67- 7Sar	fst	6f	:222	:453		1:101		ⒻSpinaway 80k	9	1	1hd	1½	1½	1½	Baeza B	119		*.80	97-11	QueenoftheStg119½DreamPath1194½GayMtelda119no	Driving	9
29Jly67- 8Mth	fst	6f	:221	:45		1:10		ⒻSorority 103k	2	2	1½	11	1½	1½	Baeza B	119		*.30	92-17	QnoftheStge119½CockeyMiss119noGayMatelda1196	Driving	7
12Jly67- 7Aqu	fst	5½f	:222	:453	:572	1:033		ⒻAstoria 27k	2	1	1½	11½	13	16	Baeza B	117		*.30	95-13	QueenoftheStag1176GayMatelda120½Zoomalong1172	Easily	4
5Jly67- 6Aqu	gd	5½f	:223	:463	:583	1:05		ⒻAlw 10000	7	7	3nk	11½	14	17	Baeza B	116		*.50	88-21	QueenoftheStge1167CopperCanyon107noWiggins1166	Easily	7
10May67- 5Aqu	fst	5f	:224	:464		:59		ⒻMd Sp Wt	2	1	1hd	1hd	12	19	Baeza B	119		*1.70	90-21	QueenoftheStge1199MickBQuick119½FunnyMiss1193½	Easily	10

Quick Pitch

ch. g. 1960, by Charlevoix (Princequillo)–The Ghizeh, by Questionnaire **Lifetime record: 66 23 13 6 $229,217**

Own.– F.P. Ryan
Br.– F.P. Ryan (Ky)
Tr.– E.B. Ryan

24Oct68- 6Bel	fm	2½	Hurdles			4:351	4↑	NY Turf Writers Cup 19k	5	1	1hd	1hd	512	621	Mahoney J	164		*.90	- -	LeCerisier1381½BoldBeggar1564LakeDelawar1455	Done early	9
11Oct68- 3Bel	fm	2⅛	Hurdles			3:53	4↑	Alw 10000	7	1	13	1½	2½	22	Mahoney J	155		*.90	- -	BoldBeggar1512QuickPitch1558NationalAnthem1434	Gamely	7
14Sep67- 5Aqu	hd	2½	Hurdles			4:302	4↑	Rouge Dragon H 11k	5	1	13	13	112	116	Mahoney J	172		*.40	- -	Quick Pitch17216Gay Sparkle1372Brandon Hill131hd	Easily	6
18Aug67- 3Sar	hd	2 1/16	Hurdles			3:382	4↑	Lovely Night H 12k	3	1	11	15	110	118	Mahoney J	170		1.40	- -	QuickPitch17018Roublet15025Lumiere1363	As rider pleased	7
26Jly67- 5Mth	fm	*2	Hurdles			4:033	3↑	Midsummer H 16k	6	1	1hd	12	13	13	Mahoney JA	166		*.80	- -	Quick Pitch1663Amble Up138¾My Chap1489	Kept to urging	9
27Jun67- 3Del	fm	*1¾	Hurdles			3:31	3↑	Holly Tree H 7.9k	3	1	13	125	18	16	Armstrong RO	164		*.60	- -	Quick Pitch1646My Chap15317Calanthe1336	Easily the best	6
1Jun67- 5Aqu	fm	2 1/16	Hurdles			3:402	4↑	Bushwick H 11k	1	1	16	16	16	13	Armstrong R	157		*1.10	- -	Quick Pitch1573Bowzen1442Sandhill Flight148no	Easily	10
24May67- 3Aqu	fm	2 1/16	Hurdles			3:374	4↑	Land Boy H 8.5k	3	2	21½	16	18	12	Armstrong R	151		2.00	- -	Quick Pitch1512Market Center1333Go Lloyd Go1466	Easily	9
15May67- 3Aqu	fm	1⅞	Hurdles			3:224	4↑	Alw 7000	3	2	22	2hd	33½	38	Armstrong R	151		3.10	- -	SandhillFlight1445BoldBeggr1513QuickPtch15110	Weakened	8
27Oct66- 6Aqu	fm	2½	Hurdles			4:341	4↑	NY Turf Writers H 18k	2	6	22	21½	21	32	Biger P	154		2.20	- -	Spooky Joe151noMy Chap1542Quick Pitch1542½	Hung at end	10
10Oct66- 3Aqu	fm	1⅞	Hurdles			3:254	3↑	OClm 7500	4	2	2½	2½	16	13½	Biger P	155		*1.20	- -	Quick Pitch1553½Iambic1454Arenque1401	Scored in hand	9
12Sep66- 7Aqu	fm	1⅝Ⓣ				2:412	3↑	Brighton Beach H 30k	1	1	1½	1118	1128	1138	Combest J	117	b	*2.00	49-13	KnightlyManner116¾GallupPoll110noFastCount1137	Stopped	11
3Sep66- 7FE	sf	1⅜Ⓣ	:513	1:182	1:433	2:234	3↑	Niagara H 29k	2	1	11½	1nk	21	21¾	Combest J	123	b	*.50	64-34	Orbiter1181¾QuckPtch123nkBluSol11025	No apparent excuse	4
26Aug66- 7Sar	fm	1⅝Ⓣ				2:411	3↑	Seneca H 29k	5	1	13	11	1hd	24½	Combest J	125	b	4.70	82-17	Paoluccio1124½QuickPitch1253Dunderhd105nk	Couldn't last	8
19Aug66- 7Sar	fm	1⅛Ⓣ				1:474	3↑	Alw 10000	2	1	13	12	13	11½	Combest J	123	b	5.20	94-06	Quick Pitch1231½Ginger Fizz1182Imam1114	Ridden out	6

10Aug66- 7Sar	fm	1 1/16(T)		1:40	3↑ Bernard Baruch H 30k	5 4 45 2½ 2hd	43¾	Combest J	115	b	16.70	101-00	Assagai1153Ginger Fizz114¾Northern Deamon113no	Faltered	10
30Jly66- 7FE	fm	1(T)	:233 :471 1:114	1:372	3↑ Fair Play 12k	7 6 32½ 1nk 12½	1½	McComb S	119	b	2.25	96-07	QuickPitch119½VictorianEra1234¾GoodOldMort1182¾	Driving	8
19Jly66- 8Mth	fm	1 1/16(T)		1:45	4↑ Alw 6000	5 2 1hd 11½ 2hd	1no	Brumfield D	113	b	3.40	90-10	Quick Pitch113noLeonine1061½Silverado II1132	Hard drive	8
12Jly66- 7Aqu	hd	1⅛(T)		1:474	3↑ Handicap 10000	2 3 41 35 411	417½	Combest J	119	b	8.80	78-04	Flag1174½Canal11810Bonny Star1073	Early speed,tired	6
2Jly66- 8Del	hd	1⅜(T)		2:133	3↑ Sussex H 30k	6 1 11½ 24 49	717	Combest J	117	b	12.00	77-12	Portsmouth1162½Knightly Manner1173½Prolijo1143½	Used up	13
20Jun66- 8Del	fm	1 1/16(T)		1:441	4↑ Alw 5000	7 1 2½ 43¼ 510	517	Combest J	122	b	*.70	66-21	Rucapequen113¾DoubleWarrnt1133Brochazo1145½	No excuse	7
11Jun66- 7Del	sf	1 1/16(T)		1:441	3↑ Alw 7500	4 3 34½ 22 2½	2¾	Rogers C	119	b	4.80	82-25	Lucky Tom119¾Quick Pitch1192Portsmouth1196	Sharp	7
4Jun66- 6Aqu	fst	6f	:222 :451	1:091	3↑ Alw 8500	2 6 58 58 511	713	Combest J	117	b	55.80	84-14	Buckpasser1152Tim'sStingray1152Understudy121nk	No speed	7
23Oct65- 7WO	sf	1⅝(T)	:523 1:514	3:052	3↑ Can Championship 60k	7 2 2½ 611 516	535	Combest J	126	b	2.00	- -	GeorgeRoyal123½BraveLad1265¾Ribot'sFling1218¾	Stopped	11
11Oct65- 7WO	sf	1¼(T)	:503 1:171 1:432	2:111	3↑ Jockey Club Cup H 18k	7 1 11 11 11	12¼	Combest J	126	b	*1.85	58-49	QuickPitch1262¼Bandangn1152BluSol112hd	Kept to pressure	8
25Sep65- 8Aqu	sf	1⅛(T)		1:501	3↑ Handicap 10000	1 1 1½ 1hd 2½	33	Combest J	124	b	5.60	81-16	Master Dennis115noKentucky Jug1143Quick Pitch1244	Tired	7
15Sep65- 7Aqu	fm	1⅝(T)		2:434	3↑ Brighton Beach H 28k	4 3 1½ 2hd 22	36	Combest J	120	b	3.30	75-19	KnightlyMannr1146BraveLad110noQckPtch1204½	Weakened	8
4Sep65- 7FE	fm	1⅜(T)	:473 1:13 1:392	2:20	3↑ Niagara H 30k	2 1 1nk 14 14	1hd	Combest J	120	b	*.60	85-15	QuckPtch120hdBluSol1113¾UnclBlu1133¼	Rated early,lasted	9
27Aug65- 7Sar	fm	1⅝(T)		2:40	3↑ Seneca H 28k	8 1 13 14 1½	2hd	Combest J	119	b	8.60	93-06	Nashandy115hdQuickPitch1198Flg1191	Set pace,held gamely	8
11Aug65- 7Sar	sf	1 1/16(T)		1:423	3↑ Bernard Baruch H 29k	10 3 2hd 12 11½	1no	Combest J	111	b	8.00	92-08	Quick Pitch111noFlag1142Circus1131	Hard ridden to last	10
31Jly65- 7Aqu	fm	1⅛(T)		1:492	3↑ Tidal H 58k	9 5 35 21 2½	42¾	Valenzuela A	113	b	10.60	85-16	OretArgent115nkPursr1122TurboJtII130½	Bold bid,weakened	9
21Jly65- 8Del	fm	1(T)		1:362	3↑ Alw 4500	6 4 46 52¾ 32	35	Combest J	122	b	*1.50	89-09	Captain's Cross1222Uncle Perry1223Quick Pitch1222	Hung	8
3Jly65- 8Del	hd	1⅜(T)		2:122	3↑ Sussex H 29k	9 3 32 11½ 12	21¾	Combest J	115	b	17.60	105-07	CoolPrince1141¾QuickPitch1158Captain'sCross1121	Sharp	11
21Jun65- 7Del	hd	1 1/16(T)		1:423	4↑ Alw 5000	6 2 2hd 2hd 21½	46¾	Lee T	122	b	3.00	84-09	Captain'sCross1164FederlMan1132Sorpsso113¾	Forced wide	7
8Jun65- 8Del	fm	1(T)		1:38	4↑ Alw 4500	5 2 1½ 13 13½	13½	Lee T	119	b	*.80	86-18	Quick Pitch1193½Henbaj1134Bray Head1132½	Easy score	6
29May65- 8Del	fm	1 1/16(T)		1:423	3↑ Brandywine H 24k	4 1 21½ 33 58	813	Combest J	116	b	12.00	78-09	Baitman1153Western Warrior123½Lucky Turn1155	Crowded	10
15May65- 6Aqu	fst	6f	:222 :452	1:104	3↑ Alw 8500	1 7 67¼ 811 813	817	Combest J	117	b	34.50	72-20	CornishPrince107noExclusiveNashu1212½Chokr1174	Far back	8
31Oct64- 8Lrl	fm	1(T)	:223 :452 1:094	1:342	3↑ Maryland H 23k	7 2 21 2hd 42½	54	Grant H	117		3.20	97-05	TwiceasGay113noCoolPrince112hdCachito1112	Speed,tired	11
27Oct64- 7Aqu	fm	1 1/16(T)		1:424	3↑ Handicap 10000	9 2 2hd 11 13	2nk	Ycaza M	122	b	*2.55	92-08	YourAlibhai113nkQuickPitch1221GrandApplause1164	Failed	9
17Oct64- 8Aqu	sf	1⅛(T)		1:532	3↑ Handicap 10000	7 2 1½ 11 75¼	815	Ycaza M	119	b	6.10	53-32	WillIRule1171TomCat1171MeanCold111½	Early speed,tired	9
29Sep64- 7Aqu	sly	1⅛(X)	:47 1:13 1:401	1:542	3↑ Handicap 12000	3 1 14 14½ 32½	58¾	Ycaza M	122	b	*1.25e	60-27	Polizonte1181RockyThmb118nkBraveLad1126	Bore out badly	6
14Sep64- 7Aqu	sf	1⅝(T)		2:433	3↑ Brighton Beach H 28k	2 2 2½ 21 711	721	Grant H	122	b	2.20	61-18	Jalico1123Endymion1152½Weatherbeaten107½	Speed,stopped	8
28Aug64- 7Sar	hd	1⅝(T)		2:383	3↑ Seneca H 29k	7 1 13 12½ 1½	1nk	Grant H	117	b	2.95	106-00	[D]QuickPitch117nkTheIbex1105WillIRul1143	Swerved inside	8
	Disqualified and placed second														
12Aug64- 7Sar	fm	1 1/16(T)		1:422	3↑ Bernard Baruch H 30k	5 3 35½ 32½ 22	23	Grant H	117	b	5.05	91-06	Western Warrior1193Quick Pitch117¾Endymion1092	Gamely	12
4Aug64- 7Sar	hd	1 1/16(T)		1:41	3↑ Alw 10000	10 3 33½ 31½ 2½	1nk	Grant H	120	b	2.40e	101-00	QuckPtch120nkTomCt120hdEndymon1141½	Up in final strides	11
18Jly64- 6Del	fm	1(T)		1:353	3↑ Handicap 10000	2 3 1½ 12 12½	13	Thornburg B	122	b	*2.60	101-07	QuickPitch1223GreekForm113hdBlueThor1101	Scored easily	8
11Jly64- 7Del	fm	1⅜(T)		2:134	3↑ Sussex H 27k	1 1 11½ 12 33	57¾	Thornburg B	118	b	5.80	92-00	RedDog1112¼[D]GrkForm1101½LaughAloud1112	Used up early	7
30Jun64- 7Del	fm	1 1/16(T)		1:42	4↑ Alw 6000	3 1 15 14½ 14	12½	Lee T	116	b	2.50	94-06	Quick Pitch1162½Egg Hunt1034Blue Thor1061	Much the best	8
16Jun64- 7Del	fm	1 1/16(T)		1:424	4↑ Alw 5000	1 2 2½ 1½ 1½	1nk	Lee T	110		4.40	90-10	QuickPitch110nkChicoco110hdInterven114¾	Long,hard drive	7
8Jun64- 7Del	fst	1	:24 :481 1:133	1:392	4↑ Alw 6000	2 1 12 34½ 47	510¾	Turcotte R	124		9.90	68-23	GreekMoney1241¾Mi Rey110¾GypsyBaron1178	Used up early	8
23May64- 6Aqu	fst	6f	:223 :454	1:111	3↑ Alw 7500	5 5 33½ 42½ 68	611	Combest J	115		15.35	76-14	Narokan117½Humorismo115hdMacedonia1212	Well up,tired	6
30Oct63- 7Aqu	hd	1 1/16(T)		1:431	3↑ Handicap 10000	3 1 21½ 2½ 65½	611	Sellers J	119	b	2.45	79-10	WesternWarrior1221JetClipper1131MarlinBay117hd	Stopped	6
19Oct63- 7WO	fm	1⅝(T)	:484 1:374	2:41	3↑ Can Champ 60k	3 1 1hd 78¼ 822	828	Ycaza M	121		5.10	78-00	TheAxeII1264¼HardRockMn1263½BronzeBabu1265¾	Bore out	9
2Oct63- 7Aqu	fst	1⅝	:491 1:401 2:04	2:42	Lawrence Realizatn 56k	7 4 32 35 816	817	Hartack W	120		18.45	78-13	DeanCarl1203¾B.Major120nkMastrDnns1166	Early foot,tired	9
9Sep63- 7Aqu	fm	1⅝(T)		2:40	3↑ Brighton Beach H 28k	6 1 1hd 2½ 12	1nk	Ycaza M	113		4.85	100-00	QuickPitch113nkDavidK.1142½WillIRule111½	All out,lasted	9
23Aug63- 7Sar	fm	1⅝(T)		2:394	3↑ Sar Cup 28k	1 2 22 1hd 11	2nk	Sellers J	110	b	*2.65	106-00	WillIRule107nkQuickPitch1101DavidK.1193	Failed to last	9
15Aug63- 7Sar	fm	1⅛(T)		1:474	3↑ Handicap 7500	2 3 34 31 1½	2nk	Gilligan L	111		5.20	96-04	TheAxeII129nkQuickPitch1113DavdK.1151½	Clearly 2nd best	6
8Aug63- 8Sar	gd	1	:234 :464 1:113	1:374	3↑ Alw 5000	4 2 21 2hd 1hd	11½	Gilligan L	111		2.90	88-12	QuickPitch1111½LuckyTurn1143DoctorHankK.115¾	Handily	7
1Aug63- 8Sar	sly	1(X)	:234 :471 1:12	1:383	3↑ Alw 5000	3 2 22 21 21	21½	Adams L	112		4.90	82-21	Cabelry1121½QckPitch1125TomCat1143	Showed game effort	7
24Jly63- 7Del	fm	1(T)		1:354	Handicap 7500	1 4 41½ 43 32	2hd	Carrozzella M	110		9.80	103-00	WildCard119hdQckPtch1103InWar1173½	Lacked room,sharp	7
5Jly63- 6Del	fst	6f	:23 :463	1:12	Alw 4500	5 3 31½ 21½ 2hd	13½	Vasquez J	118		*1.70	85-24	QuickPitch1183½ShiftyShekl1183¾Frnk'sNod113¾	Mild drive	7
24Jun63- 6Del	fst	6f	:223 :46	1:121	Alw 4500	3 7 81½ 73½ 77¼	62½	Nelson E	122		*1.20	81-21	Aesop'sAble1151¼Redgauntlet1181ShiftyShkl122hd	In close	8
23May63- 6Aqu	fst	6f	:223 :454	1:102	Alw 5000	8 10 96¾ 911 814	819	Ycaza M	117		*1.05	74-13	MatchWits1177½MarlinBay117noWatrTwister122½	Slow start	10
8May63- 6Aqu	fst	6f	:221 :45	1:101	Alw 5000	6 2 21½ 22 42¾	33½	Ycaza M	115		5.75	90-08	Stearic11710'Calaway1152½QuickPtch1152	Drifted out turn	8
20Oct62- 5Kee	fst	6½f	:224 :46 1:102	1:164	Alw 3250	8 4 11 12 13	12½	Nichols J	119		*.70	94-11	QuickPitch1192½NeverWrong1191½BigJoe1193½	Mild urging	9
13Oct62- 3Kee	fst	7f	:231 :461 1:11	1:233	©Md Sp Wt	9 5 41½ 1hd 13	18	Nichols J	120		8.10	90-12	Quick Pitch1208Telethon120¾Putoquill120¾	Easy score	10

Regal Gleam

dkbbr. f. 1964, by Hail to Reason (Turn-to)–Miz Carol, by Stymie

Lifetime record: 32 8 2 4 $246,793

Own.– Patrice Jacobs

Br.– Bieber–Jacobs Stable (Ky)

Tr.– Hirsch Jacobs

9Nov67- 7Aqu	fst	1	:231 :461 1:11	1:363	3↑ (F)Alw 15000	2 1 11 11½ 2½	31¾	Belmonte E	120	b	3.70	83-19	Lady Pitt118¾Narova1091Regal Gleam1201	Led,weakened	7
4Nov67- 8GS	gd	1 70	:23 :483 1:114	1:434	(F)Princeton H 30k	3 5 3nk 41½ 77	99¾	Blum W	115	b	5.50	65-24	GreenGlade113¾Sumtex116½FarestNan1121½	Early bid,tired	12
27Oct67- 7Aqu	fst	6f	:222 :451	1:104	3↑ (F)Alw 15000	2 3 34 23 1hd	11	Belmonte E	117	b	2.70	89-15	Regal Gleam1171Cestrum123¾Fennel1182½	Drew clear	9
16Oct67- 7Aqu	fst	6f	:22 :444	1:093	3↑ (F)Interborough H 28k	5 5 57 78¼ 79½	46¼	Belmonte E	113	b	7.10	89-16	Recall113nkCodorniz1173Romanticism1233	Changed course	9
29Sep67- 7Aqu	sly	6f	:22 :45	1:11	3↑ (F)Alw 15000	6 5 43½ 34½ 23	11¾•	Belmonte E	114	b	2.40	88-20	[DH]RegalGleam114[DH]AmeriBll1161¾CourtCrcut1124½	Driving	8
21Sep67- 7Aqu	hd	1 1/16(T)		1:424	3↑ (F)Alw 15000	7 4 3nk 2hd 31	76	Shoemaker W	111	b	*2.10	86-08	SwimtoMe1161½I'mAllReady116noSpire1111½	Well up,tired	9
15Sep67- 7Aqu	fst	6f	:232 :471	1:114	3↑ (F)Alw 15000	10 4 51½ 2½ 1hd	11½	Belmonte E	111	b	*2.10	84-19	Regal Gleam1111½Cestrum120noAmeri Belle114nk	Drew clear	10
6Sep67- 7Aqu	fst	1	:23 :453 1:10	1:353	3↑ (F)Maskette H 28k	4 2 2½ 2hd 21½	44•	Belmonte E	110	b	16.40	86-18	Politely115¾Triple Brook1173Lady Pitt115nk	Weakened	9
19Aug67- 5Sar	sly	6f	:221 :452	1:102	(F)Alw 15000	4 7 66¾ 54 45	36¼	Ycaza M	115	b	7.70	90-10	PlumPlum1145½Wageko114¾ReglGleam1151½	Evenly in drive	7
20Jly67- 8Hol	fst	1⅛	:463 1:101 1:354	1:491	(F)Hol Oaks 55k	5 3 31 32½ 79	68	Pineda A	115	b	7.20	78-15	AmerigoLady112½Gamely1211½Princssnesn113no	Speed,tired	10
10Jly67- 7Aqu	fm	1 1/16(T)		1:434	3↑ (F)Alw 15000	7 2 2hd 2hd 2½	41¾	Belmonte E	114	b	*2.30	85-13	Encanta116½Bubbles O'Tudor118¾Fatal Step118½	Weakened	7
5Jly67- 7Aqu	gd	6f	:222 :461	1:112	(F)Handicap 15000	7 1 64½ 63¾ 45½	32	Belmonte E	116	b	8.70	84-21	Abifaith1161Rhubarb1241Regal Gleam116hd	Wide turn	7
17Jun67- 8Mth	fst	1 70	:231 :463 1:113	1:432	(F)Post-Deb 29k	7 5 66¼ 912 914	611	Knapp K	118	b	*2.00	73-18	T.V.'sPrincss1121¾Amhrst1122¼FortyMrry's1121¼	No threat	10
10Jun67- 7Aqu	fst	1⅛	:47 1:104 1:361	1:493	(F)Mother Goose 97k	1 2 24 24 25	47½	Cordero A Jr	121	b	23.20	80-12	FurlSail1213QuilloQueen121noMuse1214½	Well placed,tired	11
27May67- 7Aqu	fst	1	:22 :442 1:091	1:353	(F)Acorn 68k	14 4 55 35 57	88½	Cardone E	121	b	19.40	81-15	Furl Sail1213Quillo Queen121½Pepperwood1213	Tired	17
10May67- 7Aqu	fst	7f	:222 :454 1:111	1:25	(F)Comely 29k	7 8 76 711 813	88¼	Cordero A Jr	121	b	8.40	73-21	Gala Honors113¾Just Kidding118nkLake Chelan1161	Tired	11
26Apr67- 7Aqu	fst	6f	:221 :451	1:103	(F)Prioress 28k	5 4 64½ 78½ 713	613	Ycaza M	121	b	*1.30	77-17	Just Kidding1214Great Era121½Lake Chelan121nk	Wide	7
13Apr67- 7Aqu	fst	6f	:224 :46	1:111	(F)Handicap 12000	6 4 42½ 42 2hd	2no	Ussery R	124	b	7.50	87-16	Recall118noRegal Gleam1242½Lake Chelan113nk	Just missed	8
18Jan67- 8Hia	fst	6f	:214 :444	1:094	(F)Jasmine 32k	8 4 65½ 710 815	814	Ycaza M	121	b	13.00	81-12	Woozem1166Quillo Queen115nkIrish County116nk	Far back	10
5Nov66- 8Lrl	fst	1 1/16	:232 :472 1:131	1:452	(F)Selima 125k	9 3 42 42¼ 31½	1½	Ycaza M	122	b	5.30	90-14	Regal Gleam122½Quillo Queen1192Thong1191	Hard drive	14
22Oct66- 8GS	fst	1 1/16	:231 :461 1:103	1:443	(F)Gardenia 196k	7 5 65 58½ 87¾	75½	Cordero A Jr	119	b	12.20	76-20	Pepperwood119hdFish House1191¾Woozem119¾	No mishap	14
8Oct66- 7Aqu	fst	1	:224 :452 1:102	1:372	(F)Frizette 132k	8 2 1½ 11½ 1hd	1hd	Ycaza M	119	b	16.10	81-17	RglGleam119hdIrishCounty1194½Pepprwood1192	Came again	8
28Sep66- 7Aqu	fst	7f	:221 :451 1:11	1:242	(F)Astarita 29k	4 7 811 99 87½	66	Shoemaker W	119		6.40	78-19	IrishCounty1161Pepperwood116nkGreenGlade1164	No speed	10
10Sep66- 7Aqu	fst	6f	:224 :462	1:124	(F)Matron 110k	3 4 21½ 22½ 23	3hd	Cardone E	119		8.00e	79-23	Swiss Cheese119hdGreat Era119noRegal Gleam1198	Game try	9

24Aug66- 7Sar	gd 6f	:221 :454 1:12	ⒻSpinaway 78k	5 1 44 77 613 612	Knapp K	119	6.30	76-17	Silver True119¾Great Era119½Shirley Heights119no Wide 7
6Jly66- 8Mth	fst 5½f	:221 :452 :581 1:044	ⒻColleen 18k	6 1 83¼ 76¾ 89¾ 811	Thornburg B	119	9.00	82-18	Rhubarb1146Momma Pierre1141½Betoken119hd Not a factor 14
25Jun66- 8Del	fst 5½f	:213 :462 1:053	ⒻBlue Hen 24k	6 2 43½ 51¾ 2hd 1no	Thornburg B	119	15.30	92-18	RegalGleam119noFamilyGallry1112½NorthstTrds1112 Just up 11
30May66- 8Del	fst 6f	:221 :47 1:001	ⒻP Drummnd (Div 2) 18k	8 7 64½ 73½ 78½ 74¾	Valenzuela A	116	6.40	83-22	Tota Nell113¾Sentica113nkIntriguing113½ Never close 9
17May66- 5Aqu	fst 5f	:23 :463 :59	ⒻAlw 5500	5 3 33 31½ 1½ 13	Blum W	119	3.00	90-19	Regal Gleam1193Tainted Lady1196Effayeff119no With ease 6
11May66- 5Aqu	fst 5f	:223 :471 1:003	ⒻMd Sp Wt	2 1 32½ 33½ 3nk 11½	Blum W	119	3.60e	82-19	Regal Gleam1191½Henrietta1192½Euphorbia1191 Driving 10
20Apr66- 3Aqu	fst 5f	:224 :464 :59	ⒻMd Sp Wt	2 2 2hd 31 77½ 714	Knapp K	119	3.00	76-16	GreatEra1198GreekSong'sGet119noCurrentEvent119hd Tired 10
13Apr66- 3Aqu	fst 5f	:23 :463 :591	ⒻMd Sp Wt	2 4 44 34½ 34 2¾	Knapp K	119	4.10	88-16	Lake Chelan119¾Regal Gleam1195Euphorbia1192½ Game try 10

Roman Brother

b. g. 1961, by Third Brother (Princequillo)–Roman Zephyr, by Roman — **Lifetime record: 42 16 10 5 $943,473**

Own.– Harbor View Farm
Br.– Ocala Stud Farms Inc (Fla)
Tr.– B. Parke

5Feb66- 8Hia	fst 1⅛	:472 1:112 1:37 1:50	3↑Seminole H 61k	9 7 711 712 58 45¾	Baeza B	126	*.50	79-23	Convex1164½Selari112½Pia Star1181 Mild rally,no threat 9
25Jan66- 8Hia	fst 7f	:23 :46 1:113 1:241	4↑Alw 8000	7 1 58½ 35½ 2hd 1½	Baeza B	123	*.70	88-18	Roman Brother123½Selari1145Sunstruck1142 Mild urging 7
11Nov65- 7Lrl	fm 1½Ⓣ	:493 1:134 2:281	3↑D C Int'l 150k	1 1 2hd 1½ 2hd 31¼	Baeza B	127	*1.40	77-16	Diatome120noCarvin II1201¼Roman Brother127no Held well 7
30Oct65- 7Aqu	fst 2	:47 2:293 2:554 3:223	3↑J C Gold Cup 110k	2 4 33½ 12 16 15	Baeza B	124	*.20	83-21	Roman Brother1245Barenjenal1244Brave Lad1243 Easily 7
12Oct65- 7Aqu	gd 1⅝	:48 1:381 2:431	3↑Manhattan H 56k	2 3 34 13 15 18	Baeza B	125	*.60	89-16	RomanBrother1258HillRise119¾KnightlyManner1144 Easily 8
2Oct65- 7Aqu	fst 1¼	:46 1:104 1:363 2:014	3↑Woodward 109k	5 4 36 11 15 110	Baeza B	126	*1.80	89-18	Roman Brother12610Royal Gunner1211½Malicious126½ Easily 6
18Sep65- 8Det	fst 1⅛	:471 1:113 1:364 1:492	3↑Mich 1⅛ H 91k	2 5 43 83¾ 43 2½	Baeza B	118	*1.80	93-18	OldHat115½RomanBrother118¾TakeOver114½ Gaining at end 11
6Sep65- 7Aqu	fst 1⅛	:481 1:121 1:363 1:49	3↑Aqueduct 108k	3 3 35 32½ 33 33	Baeza B	121	3.10	88-14	Malicious1163Pluck116noRoman Brother1216 Bore out turn 7
23Aug65- 8Sar	fst 1	:232 :461 1:111 1:36	3↑Alw 8500	2 3 34½ 2½ 11½ 16	Baeza B	123	*.30	97-12	Roman Brother1236Reely Beeg1162Spoon Bait1131½ Easily 5
11Aug65- 7Sar	sf 1 1/16Ⓣ	1:423	3↑Bernard Baruch H 29k	4 5 55½ 43½ 55½ 55	Baeza B	123	*1.60	87-08	Quick Pitch111noFlag1142Circus1131 No apparent excuse 10
24Jly65- 7Aqu	fst 1¼	:47 1:102 1:35 2:003	3↑Brooklyn H 107k	4 4 43½ 33 23 22	Baeza B	121	2.80	93-10	PiaStar1212RomanBrother1212Kelso1321½ Game,drifted out 5
10Jly65- 6Aqu	fst 1	:224 :451 1:092 1:342	3↑Alw 10000	1 4 35 11½ 13 15	Baeza B	115	*.80	96-13	Roman Brother1155Riot Squad1172½Africanus119¾ Easily 6
26Jun65- 6Aqu	fst 6f	:222 :453 1:101	3↑Alw 8500	6 4 66 62¾ 43½ 42¾	Baeza B	121	*3.00	89-13	Near Man117½Kilmoray1112R. Thomas117nk Mild late bid 8
6Feb65- 8Hia	fst 1⅛	:471 1:113 1:372 1:504	3↑Seminole H 65k	9 7 712 59 76¾ 74¾	Rotz JL	124	4.30	76-22	Sunstruck119noPiave114nkPointduJour1161½ No late rally 13
16Jan65- 8SA	fst 1⅛	:47 1:11 1:36 1:482	San Fernando 61k	4 8 86½ 94¾ 1012 911	Ycaza M	126	3.50e	79-14	Hill Rise1232Pelegrin114½Canadian B.113no No mishap 12
2Jan65- 8SA	fst 7f	:221 :442 1:092 1:22	Malibu 30k	9 1 96½ 96½ 93½ 105	Ycaza M	126	*1.80	88-09	PowerofDestiny112½Maker'sMark113noHillRis122hd Dull try 10
31Oct64- 7Aqu	fst 2	:484 2:533 3:191	3↑J C Gold Cup 108k	6 3 31½ 21½ 24 25½	Shoemaker W	119	3.35	95-14	Kelso1245½Roman Brother1196Quadrangle11916 Went well 6
14Oct64- 7Aqu	fst 1⅝	:53 1:443 2:083 2:45	Lawrence Realizatn 54k	4 5 54½ 21 42 2nk	Alvarez F	123	2.05	80-18	Quadrangl126nkRomnBrothr123¾KnightlyMnnr1161 Checked 5
28Sep64- 7Aqu	fst 1⅛	:481 1:122 1:364 1:49	Discovery H 27k	3 3 3nk 42 42½ 1no	Alvarez F	125	*1.25	96-13	RomanBrother125noLt.Stevens113¾TwiceasGay109¾ Driving 6
12Sep64- 9Rkm	fst 1 3/16	:462 1:102 1:362 1:554	N H Sweepstakes 144k	9 10 99 65½ 21 1½	Alvarez F	122	*.90	106-12	RomanBrother123½KnightlyManner1161¼Purser114nk Driving 11
29Aug64- 8AP	fst 1¼	:473 1:114 1:364 2:012	American Derby 134k	10 7 76½ 41½ 2hd 11	Alvarez F	122	*2.30	97-15	Roman Brother1221Lt. Stevens1165Close By1205 Drew out 10
8Aug64- 8AP	fst 1	:23 :454 1:104 1:361	Arl Classic 114k	8 9 96¾ 55½ 44½ 43¾	Alvarez F	122	*2.00	84-19	Tosmah1152½Lt. Stevens118noClose By1201¼ No excuse 10
11Jly64- 7Aqu	fst 1¼	:474 1:111 1:36 2:012	Dwyer H 81k	4 4 47 33½ 34 36¼	Alvarez F	124	3.60	87-12	Quadrangle126nkMalicious1206RomanBrother1246 Even race 6
27Jun64- 8AP	fst 1⅛	:454 1:094 1:352 1:48	Chicagoan 115k	9 5 55½ 31 21½ 23	Alvarez F	123	*.80	93-13	DandyK.1143RomanBrother1238CapSize120hd No excuse 11
6Jun64- 7Aqu	fst 1½	:49 1:144 2:04 2:282	Belmont 154k	7 6 63¾ 31 31 22	Alvarez F	126	8.35	96-10	Quadrangle1262RomnBrothr1264NorthrnDancr126½ Gamely 8
30May64- 7GS	fst 1⅛	:473 1:114 1:37 1:493	Jersey Derby 125k	8 5 42½ 11 12 13	Alvarez F	126	3.30	89-20	Roman Brother1263Mr. Brick1263National1261½ Hard drive 8
16May64- 8Pim	fst 1 3/16	:482 1:122 1:373 1:564	Preakness 176k	2 6 64 56 56¼ 55¾	Chambers W	126	25.40	83-14	NorthernDancr1262¼TheScoundrel126hdHllRs126½ No factor 6
2May64- 7CD	fst 1¼	:46 1:103 1:36 2:00	Ky Derby 156k	12 9 98¼ 63¾ 45½ 43½	Chambers W	126	30.60	98-05	NorthernDancer126nkHillRis1263¼ThScoundrl126no In close 12
28Apr64- 7CD	gd 1	:23 :452 1:10 1:351	Derby Trial 16k	3 5 34½ 32½ 1½ 22¼	Chambers W	122	3.70	95-14	HillRise1222¼RomanBrother1222¼ⒹHe'saGem1223 Led,tired 7
18Apr64- 7Aqu	fst 1⅛	:463 1:111 1:362 1:491	Wood Memorial 89k	5 5 56 43 31½ 32¼	Chambers W	126	4.30	93-15	Quadrangle126½Mr. Brick1261¾Roman Brother1264½ Evenly 9
4Apr64- 8GP	fst 1⅛	:473 1:121 1:38 1:504	Florida Derby 116k	3 4 45½ 44½ 43¼ 45¾	Ycaza M	122	7.30	74-16	NorthernDancer1221TheScoundrel1222½DandyK.1222¼ Evenly 8
25Mar64- 9GP	fst 1 1/16	:232 :464 1:112 1:444	Fountain of Youth 18k	1 4 45 33 11 21	Ycaza M	122	*.70	83-17	Dandy K.1121Roman Brother1222½Saltville1111 Held well 9
3Mar64- 8Hia	fst 1⅛	:453 1:092 1:343 1:474	Flamingo 138k	3 7 717 614 613 516	Ussery R	122	2.30	80-16	Northern Dancer1222Mr. Brick1228Quadrangle1226 In close 11
19Feb64- 8Hia	gd 1⅛	:47 1:114 1:381 1:514	Everglades 30k	6 6 611 44½ 23 1hd	Ycaza M	122	*.50	76-25	RomanBrother122hdMr.Brick1226Journalist1193 Bore in,up 8
5Feb64- 8Hia	fst 7f	:224 :451 1:102 1:231	Bahamas 34k	11 2 76¼ 55½ 11½ 13½	Ycaza M	123	*1.80	93-18	RomanBrother1233½ⒹMr.Brick123¾Journlst1201½ Mild drive 13
29Jan64- 7Hia	fst 7f	:224 :452 1:101 1:232	Alw 7000	2 7 57½ 35 34 32¾	Ycaza M	122	*.40	89-11	Delirium1172¼High Finance114½Roman Brother1222 Rallied 8
9Nov63- 8GS	my 1 1/16	:232 :471 1:12 1:451	Garden State 317k	1 4 41½ 3nk 2hd 21	Rotz JL	122	*1.50	83-21	HurrytoMarkt1221RomanBrothr1223¼Ishkoodah1221 Bore in 14
1Nov63- 8GS	sly 1	:23 :462 1:114 1:384	Alw 10000	8 6 44½ 33 21½ 21½	Rotz JL	120	*.80	86-21	HurrytoMarkt1131½RomnBrthr120½Susn'sGnt1203 Poor start 8
12Oct63- 7Aqu	fst 1	:23 :46 1:121 1:38	Champagne 212k	9 7 54¼ 31½ 12 14½	Rotz JL	122	*.95e	78-18	Roman Brother1224½Traffic1221Bupers122½ Drew out easily 11
7Oct63- 5Aqu	fst 7f	:222 :444 1:092 1:223	Alw 7500	3 2 23 21 1½ 13	Rotz JL	115	*.65e	93-15	Roman Brother1153Prexy1154Irvkup115nk Speed in reserve 7
28Sep63- 5Aqu	fst 6½f	:222 :46 1:111 1:173	Alw 5000	3 10 107½ 96¾ 31½ 13½	Rotz JL	117	*3.50	92-13	RomanBrothr1173½ShadyPlanet117½ScotchTune115nk Easily 14
25Jly63- 5Aqu	fst 5½f	:223 :462 :583 1:044	ⒸMd Sp Wt	9 8 76½ 54 2½ 1hd	Rotz JL	122	5.35	95-12	Roman Brother122hdMartyr1225Emblematic1224 Driving 10

Royal Native

ch. f. 1956, by Royal Charger (Nearco)–Native Gal, by Sir Gallahad III — **Lifetime record: 49 18 13 3 $422,769**

Own.– W.B McDonald Jr
Br.– R.W. McIlvain (Ky)
Tr.– P.F. Gacicia

23Sep61- 7Bel	fst 1⅛	:463 1:11 1:361 1:492	3↑ⒻBeldame 96k	1 11 1111 128¼ 1011 812	Boland W	123	33.70	77-18	AirmansGuide123¾Craftinss1232½Prmontt1185½ Broke slowly 12
11Sep61- 8Atl	fm 1⅛Ⓣ	:464 1:102 1:351 1:483	3↑ⒻMiss America H 29k	10 3 34 45 611 99½	Boland W	119	7.20	90-00	Sarcastic120nkLoyalLadyII1111¾ShirleyJones1262½ Stopped 10
23Aug61- 8AP	fst 1⅛	:463 1:103 1:354 1:48	3↑ⒻArl Matron H 46k	8 11 1110 1111 911 89½	Hartack W	120	6.80	87-11	ShirleyJones1241½CallCard1103Equifun111nk Impeded early 11
7Aug61- 8Atl	fm 1 1/16Ⓣ	:24 :473 1:12 1:43	3↑ⒻMargate H 23k	4 6 67 31½ 31 21	Grant H	119	*2.00	95-04	Sarcastic1151RoyalNative1193½Lint1162½ Made game effort 12
29Jly61- 6Del	gd 1¼	:46 1:11 1:362 2:022	3↑ⒻDelaware H 159k	3 10 810 46 24 23½	Adams L	120	9.20	86-20	AirmansGuide1213½RoyalNative120nkTritoma1182½ Game try 12
22Jly61- 6Del	fst 1 1/16	:231 :47 1:113 1:434	3↑ⒻNew Castle 38k	9 13 119 87¼ 713 59½	Adams L	120	14.50	80-21	AirmansGuide1166Tritoma1201¾MountainGlory1121 Sluggish 15
13Jly61- 6Del	sly 1	:231 :462 1:113 1:374	3↑ⒻAlw 7500	3 5 512 713 69¾ 68	Adams L	121	*1.70	79-20	Perizade1212½Tritoma1181Solid Thought1151 Dull effort 8
30Jun61- 7Mth	fst 1 70	:222 :454 1:104 1:401	3↑ⒻAlw 10000	2 4 56 56 57 46¾	Korte K	111 b	*1.30	106-11	ShirleyJones1155DottyKirsten1121LoylLdyII115¾ No factor 8
14Jun61- 7Bel	fst 7f	:222 :453 1:103 1:233	3↑ⒻVagrancy H 24k	2 13 129¼ 96¾ 32½ 4½	Adams L	123	10.50	88-15	SunGlint116noUndulation116½Refute113hd Closed very well 14
3Jun61- 6Bel	fst 6f	:222 :454 1:102	4↑ⒻAlw 10000	7 6 56½ 79 78 612	Rotz JL	123	*3.00	83-13	Improve1144Refute1143½Repetitious114nk Wide on turn 9
20May61- 7GS	fst 6f	:22 :451 1:104	3↑ⒻColonial H 28k	4 9 97½ 87¾ 79¾ 66¾	Korte K	126	4.10	83-15	Staretta117hdCoupd'etat117noAirmansGuide1191½ No mishap 9
11Nov60- 7GS	my 1⅛	:464 1:11 1:372 1:504	3↑ⒻVineland H 58k	3 6 67 34½ 33½ 1½	Hartack W	124	*1.70	83-19	Royal Native124½Make Sail118¾Wiggle II1194 Up in time 9
21Oct60- 6Kee	fst 1⅛	:482 1:13 1:371 1:493	3↑ⒻSpinster 87k	4 2 2hd 2hd 3½ 33	Hartack W	123	*.40	86-24	RashStatement119¾IndianMaid1232¼RoyalNative1234 Tired 6
	Open to 3-, 4- and 5-year-olds								
14Oct60- 6Kee	fst *7f	1:26	3↑ⒻAlw 7500	6 3 52½ 41¾ 21 2¾	Hartack W	121	*.50	96-11	IndianMaid118¾RoyalNative1212¼ChanceGauge1061½ Rallied 8
	Open to 3-, 4- and 5-year-olds								
1Oct60- 7Bel	fst 1⅛	:461 1:11 1:362 1:492	3↑ⒻBeldame 91k	3 3 2hd 11½ 22 22	Hartack W	123	2.70	87-16	Berlo1192RoyalNative1231MakeSal1193 Used vying for lead 9
17Sep60- 7Atl	fm 1 3/16Ⓣ	:463 1:12 1:372 1:57	3↑U Nations H 100k	8 5 66¼ 107¾ 1011 1013	Harmatz W	118	10.30	75-12	T.V.Lark1201¼SwordDancer1271¼BallyAche122hd Fell back 10
10Sep60- 0Atl	sf 1 1/16Ⓣ	:232 :481 1:131 1:454	3↑Alw 5000	1 4 41 2½ 2½ 2½	Hartack W	118	-	81-18	Bally Ache116½Royal Native1188Exaltado1182 In close 4
	Exhibition race - run between 5th and 6th races. No wagering								
13Aug60- 8AP	fst 1⅛	:48 1:12 1:371 1:502	3↑ⒻArl Matron H 56k	10 4 31½ 21 11 1hd	Hartack W	128	2.20	84-07	Royal Native128hdWoodlawn1101½Silver Spoon1281 Driving 11

30Jly60-6Del	sly	1¼	:461 1:103 1:364 2:022	3↑ ⒻDelaware H 146k	6 3 36½ 21½ 25 29	Hartack W	129		*.90	81-15	Quill1259Royal Native1291¼Geechee Lou110¾ Had no mishap 8
9Jly60-7Mth	fst	1 1/16	:224 :461 1:11 1:434	3↑ ⒻMolly Pitcher H 28k	2 5 42½ 31 13 14	Hartack W	127		*1.00	86-17	RoyalNative1274Quill1221¾MissOrestes114½ Much the best 10
4Jun60-7Bel	fst	1 1/16	:223 :452 1:102 1:43	3↑ ⒻTop Flight H 56k	7 7 62¾ 21½ 1hd 11½	Hartack W	126		*1.45	89-15	RoyalNative1261½Quill123¾BugBrush1202 Drew clear in hand 10
28May60-7GS	fst	6f	:221 :452 1:102	3↑ ⒻColonial H 27k	6 5 55 54 5¾ 11½	Hartack W	126		*.70	92-13	RoyalNative1261½BugBrush1231¼Tinkalero118nk Drew clear 6
7May60-7Aqu	fst	1	:234 :463 1:11 1:362	3↑ ⒻBed o' Roses H 27k	7 2 1½ 1½ 11 2nk	Moreno H	128		1.60	94-08	Chistosa106nkRoyal Native1281½Craftiness110¾ Game try 7
30Mar60-7GP	fst	1 1/16	:233 :462 1:101 1:42	3↑ ⒻSuwannee River H 16k	1 2 1hd 13 13 13	Hartack W	130		*.25	98-11	RoylNative1303MeadowsMiss1071½Woodlawn1102 Easy score 6
Previously owned by P.L. Grissom; previously trained by K. Noe Sr											
2Mar60-7Hia	fst	1⅛	:461 1:101 1:36 1:49	3↑ ⒻBlack Helen H 47k	1 3 33 2½ 11½ 13¾	Hartack W	126		*.55	90-15	RoyalNative1263¾HappyPrincess1123½Woodlawn1101¾ Easily 9
24Feb60-6Hia	gd	7f	:223 :444 1:09 1:222	4↑ ⒻAlw 6000	5 4 510 511 49½ 27	Brooks S	124		*.45	91-16	MommyDear1127RoylNative124½StarletMiss1111½ No excuse 6
10Feb60-7Hia	fst	7f	:223 :444 1:10 1:224	3↑ ⒻColumbiana H 25k	2 9 63¼ 51¼ 2½ 14½	Hartack W	122		*1.95	96-12	Royal Native1224½Starlet Miss110¾Mommy Dear1181¾ Easily 12
2Feb60-8Hia	fm	5½fⓉ	1:051	4↑ Alw 5000	1 7 53½ 710 66½ 54	Hartack W	116		*.70	88-09	UpandComingII112½Alarullah1121¼WarEagle1182 Rough trip 8
22Jan60-7Hia	fst	6f	:224 :46 1:10	4↑ Alw 6000	1 3 2hd 1½ 2hd 1nk	Hartack W	116		4.45	95-18	RoylNatve116nkKentuckyPride1152½TalntShow1185 Gamely 6
3Nov59-7GS	fst	1 1/16	:234 :47 1:103 1:423	ⒻJersey Belle 27k	5 2 1hd 1½ 21 25	Hartack W	121		*.90	92-17	HighBid1215RoylNative1212½GeecheLou115nk Impeded,tired 7
23Oct59-6Kee	fst	1⅛	:47 1:11 1:362 1:492	3↑ ⒻSpinster 81k	5 2 2½ 11 11 11	Hartack W	119		*.30	90-13	Royal Native1191Aesthetic119½Tacking119nk Under drive 6
Open to 3-, 4- and 5-year-olds											
16Oct59-6Kee	fst	*7f	1:254	3↑ ⒻAlw 7500	4 4 21 1hd 1½ 11¼	Hartack W	117		*.40	99-16	RoyalNative1171¼Lindaway1061Natal106nk Drew away easily 7
Open to 3-, 4- and 5-year-olds											
26Sep59-7Atl	fm	1 1/16Ⓣ	:231 :472 1:122 1:45	ⒻPageant H 30k	15 2 1hd 12 15 11¼	Hartack W	122		*.70	88-12	RoyalNative1221¼SunsetGlow1133LoyalLadyII1112 Cleverly 15
21Sep59-7Atl	fm	1Ⓣ	:234 :472 1:112 1:362	ⒻAlw 4500	1 1 12 13 16 16	Hartack W	118		*.30	99-01	RylNative1186[DH]SybilBrand118[DH]DanceandPly1052½ Easily 6
9Sep59-6Bel	fst	1	:223 :451 1:10 1:364	ⒻGazelle (Div 1) 22k	4 1 1½ 1½ 1½ 21	Culmone J	121		*.90	89-14	SunsetGlow1081RoyalNative121¾HighBid1182½ Just missed 10
31Aug59-7Atl	fst	7f	:223 :443 1:092 1:221	ⒻAlw 4500	5 2 2hd 1½ 1½ 12	Hartack W	121		*.60	92-17	RoyalNative1212Kit'sPet1142SybilBrand1194½ Easy score 8
1Aug59-7Mth	fst	1⅛	:471 1:111 1:37 1:503	ⒻMth Oaks 55k	5 1 12 12 12½ 13½	Culmone J	113		6.70	91-18	RoyalNative1133½IndianMaid1172½SilverSpoon1214½ Driving 6
24Jly59-6Mth	gd	1 1/16	:233 :474 1:121 1:444	ⒻAlw 7500	2 1 11½ 1hd 3nk 31¾	Boulmetis S	112		3.70	79-25	Silver Spoon1261Indian Maid118¾Royal Native1121½ Tiring 5
14Jly59-5Mth	sly	6f	:22 :452 1:103	ⒻAlw 5000	5 2 1½ 13 13 110	Culmone J	115		*.60	89-22	RoyalNative11510RulingBeauty114½TimetoSell1124 Easily 5
8Jly59-7Mth	fst	6f	:214 :44 1:09	ⒻMiss Woodford 24k	3 4 31½ 23 26 25	Culmone J	114		10.90	92-17	Recite1155RoyalNative1147½MissQuick1152 Best of others 11
27Jun59-5Mth	fst	6f	:221 :454 1:114	ⒻAlw 5000	2 5 41½ 33 11 16	Culmone J	117		*1.30	83-18	Royal Native1176Portulaca1143½Heliotrope II114no Easily 8
23Jun59-7Mth	fst	6f	:222 :461 1:11	ⒻAlw 6000	3 3 21 1½ 11 2½	Hartack W	121		2.30	86-18	Lastborn118½RoyalNative1213Starn'Garter1189 No excuse 6
17Jun59-6Mth	fst	6f	:221 :454 1:113	Alw 5000	9 5 57½ 610 57 46	Gilligan L	117		5.50	78-21	MinstrelShowII1221½RoyalHome1222JohnDoe1222½ Rallied 10
28May59-6GS	fst	6f	:222 :46 1:122	ⒻAlw 4000	4 6 54 45 44½ 35¾	Boulmetis S	110		*.60	76-16	RomanRevel1105PatsyKelly114¾RoyalNative110nk No excuse 9
20May59-6GS	fst	6f	:22 :45 1:113	ⒻAlw 10000	9 1 22 25 25 46¼	Gilligan L	110		19.00	80-18	MissQuick1041¼MissRoyal1213½MerryHll1211½ Used up early 9
Previously owned by Walmac Farm; previously trained by M.M. Greene											
30Jly58-7Mth	sl	6f	:214 :454 1:132	ⒻSorority 23k	2 8 78½ 69 58 23½	Culmone J	114	w	37.90	71-31	MommyDear1123½RoyalNative114nkFlyingJosie1142 Rallied 9
5Jly58-6Mth	fst	5½f	:221 :462 :592 1:053	ⒻColleen 24k	2 5 54½ 58 79½ 66½	Culmone J	114	w	35.40	83-19	LadyBeGood119¾LawdyClaudy1192SybilBrand112¾ No excuse 10
9Jun58-6Bel	sly	5f-WC	:222 :45 :572	ⒻNational Stallion 30k	2 6 911 78 55¾	Hartack W	119	w	11.35	86-11	LadyBeGood1191Aesthetic1191½SitThisOut1143 Late foot 11
13May58-5GS	fst	5f	:231 :48 1:003	ⒻMd Sp Wt	8 7 21½ 21½ 1hd 11½	Grant H	115	w	*2.30	87-20	RoyalNative1151½AnniePie1151½PalmLeaves115nk Handily 10

Silent Screen

ch. c. 1967, by Prince John (Princequillo)–Prayer Bell, by Better Self

Lifetime record: 18 7 2 4 $514,388

Own.– Elberon Farm
Br.– D.R. Noviello & A. Vespo (NY)
Tr.– J.B. Bond

10Mar71-7GP	fst	6f	:214 :44 1:09	4↑ Alw 7000	5 5 23 32½ 34 33	Vasquez J	112	b	*.70	96-08	Royal Comedian113½Insubordination1222½Silent Screen1122 9
Failed to respond											
27Feb71-7Hia	fst	6f	:221 :45 1:101	4↑ Alw 10000	9 5 44 33 42½ 41½	Rotz JL	122	b	*2.40	91-21	HardWork116noBestTurn122hdSmellingSalts1191½ No rally 10
16Jan71-8Hia	fst	6f	:222 :452 1:10	3↑ Super Bowl H 31k	10 10 57½ 35 47 64	Rotz JL	122	b	1.90	90-10	LionSleeps1241½TrueNorth111nkSpottdLn1142 Swerved start 10
1Aug70-7Lib	gd	1 1/16	:241 :472 1:11 1:424	Minuteman H 55k	4 6 54 24 514 618	Rotz JL	123	b	*.50	74-11	WellMannerd1208Rollckng1192TumblnHll1113½ Bobbled start 6
27Jun70-7Bel	sly	1	:23 :461 1:104 1:36	Saranac H 56k	3 3 33 21 11½ 13½	Rotz JL	123	b	*1.40	94-15	Silent Screen1233½Aggressively112½Naskra117hd Handily 6
30May70-8GS	fst	1⅛	:462 1:102 1:352 1:481	Jersey Derby 128k	8 3 31½ 1½ 1hd 33¾	Rotz JL	126	b	3.20	92-10	Prsonality1261¼CornofftheCob1262½SlntScrn1262¾ Weakened 8
16May70-8Pim	fst	1 3/16	:464 1:104 1:363 1:561	Preakness 203k	3 3 11 11½ 1hd 33¼	Rotz JL	126	b	4.20	89-16	Personality126nkMyDadGeorge1263SlntScrn1262 Weakened 14
2May70-9CD	gd	1¼	:464 1:12 1:372 2:032	Ky Derby 170k	6 6 37 11 21½ 56½	Rotz JL	126		5.70	76-16	DustCmmndr1265MyDdGrg126½HghEchln126hd Bumped start 17
18Apr70-7Aqu	fst	1⅛	:472 1:114 1:364 1:492	Wood Memorial 117k	10 2 2½ 2hd 2hd 2¾	Shoemaker W	126		*1.10	88-19	Personality126¾SilentScreen126hdDelawarChf1262 Steadied 14
4Apr70-7Aqu	fst	1	:23 :453 1:101 1:361	Gotham 58k	1 2 2½ 2hd 31 3¾	Rotz JL	126		1.70	85-20	NativeRoyalty114hdDelawareChif114¾SlntScrn1262 No rally 8
3Mar70-8Hia	fst	1⅛	:452 1:093 1:353 1:483	Flamingo 161k	5 3 33 31½ 57½ 812	Rotz JL	122		*.60	80-14	MyDadGrge122noCornofftheCob1223BurdAln1222 Unruly turn 13
4Feb70-8Hia	fst	7f	:232 :461 1:101 1:23	Bahamas 32k	8 4 43 22 23 1hd	Rotz JL	122		*1.90	93-16	SilentScreen122hdGeorgeLewis1224½RstlssRtrt1151 Driving 10
5Nov69-8GS	fst	1 70	:233 :481 1:131 1:431	Alw 15000	8 2 2½ 1hd 1hd 1½	Rotz JL	120		*.40	78-25	Silent Screen120½My Dad George1121Forum1122 Tight hold 8
11Oct69-7Bel	fst	1	:23 :454 1:104 1:371	Champagne 188k	11 6 4¾ 3nk 11 11	Rotz JL	122		*.90	88-19	Silent Screen1221Brave Emperor1221Toasted1221½ Driving 11
1Oct69-7Bel	fst	7f	:222 :454 1:104 1:234	Cowdin 77k	1 6 33 3½ 11 1½	Rotz JL	124		*.40	88-16	SilentScreen124½WigOut114hdInsubordination1241½ Driving 8
6Sep69-8AP	fst	7f	:221 :45 1:094 1:223	Arl Wash Futurity 366k	7 6 42½ 11½ 14 18	Rotz JL	122		4.20	89-21	SilentScreen1228Insubordination1221½WindyTid122¾ Easily 12
8Aug69-4Sar	fst	6f	:222 :454 1:103	ⒸMd Sp Wt	3 1 13 13 16 114	Rotz JL	122		3.10	95-13	SilentScreen12214BraveEmperor1222½PrinceTurn122½ Easily 12
1Aug69-4Sar	fst	6f	:224 :471 1:121	ⒸMd Sp Wt	8 6 54 44 2hd 21	Turcotte R	122		5.40	86-13	Sun Cross1221Silent Screen1221Many Pinnacles1224 Gamely 12

Smart Deb

b. f. 1960, by Dedicate (Princequillo)–Demree, by Revoked

Lifetime record: 37 16 4 8 $383,766

Own.– Mrs R.L. Reineman
Br.– Russell L. Reineman (Ky)
Tr.– A.N. Winick

15Aug64-8AP	fst	1⅛	:47 1:11 1:362 1:492	3↑ ⒻMatron H 81k	5 3 33 35 46½ 56½	Hartack W	119		3.90	82-14	Tosmah117½Old Hat116½Nubile1111½ Could not keep pace 10
29Jly64-8AP	fst	1	:232 :464 1:121 1:374	3↑ ⒻBeverly H 22k	1 4 32 31½ 2hd 2¾	Hartack W	124		*2.30	79-22	StarMaggie119¾SmartDeb1241½Alc1192¼ Carried wide stretch 11
10Jun64-7Aqu	fst	7f	:221 :443 1:101 1:234	3↑ ⒻVagrancy H 28k	3 4 22 32½ 56 74¼	Ussery R	124		*1.95	83-18	NoResisting112nkOilRoyalty1251LookMa110no Speed,tired 10
23May64-7Aqu	fst	1⅛	:473 1:12 1:373 1:504	3↑ ⒻTop Flight H 57k	9 1 14 12 11 31	Ussery R	122		4.05	86-14	Oil Royalty122½Tona114½Smart Deb1221 Set pace,weakened 10
29Apr64-7Aqu	sly	1	:231 :464 1:114 1:374	3↑ ⒻBd o'Ross H (Div 2) 21k	7 2 1hd 1hd 3½ 33¼	Hartack W	127		*2.20	76-25	Beauful1102PamsEgo1221¼SmrtDb1274 Used up setting pace 7
15Apr64-7Aqu	my	7f	:224 :46 1:114 1:251	3↑ ⒻDistaff H (Div 2) 21k	7 1 31 31 1hd 1¾	Hartack W	125		*1.60	80-22	SmrtDb125¾PamsEgo1211½DecimalCoinage1102½ Hard drive 7
1Apr64-9GP	fst	7f	:222 :45 1:10 1:23	3↑ ⒻSuwannee River H 16k	3 3 3½ 1½ 11½ 12	Blum W	123		*.90	97-17	Smart Deb1232Lady Karachi1161Yes Please1111½ In hand 8
26Feb64-8Hia	fst	1⅛	:473 1:12 1:372 1:503	3↑ ⒻBlack Helen H 60k	4 3 32 42¾ 43½ 46	Hartack W	122		*1.70	76-18	PrincessArle1121PatrolWoman1132½Tona1152½ Well up,tired 9
29Jan64-8Hia	fst	7f	:224 :452 1:101 1:232	3↑ ⒻColumbiana H 31k	9 1 33 21½ 1hd 1no	Hartack W	123		*.90	92-11	SmartDeb123noYesPlease1122½LatinWlk113nk Fully extended 10
21Jan64-8Hia	fst	6f	:221 :451 1:094	4↑ ⒻAlw 10000	1 3 2½ 1½ 13 13½	Hartack W	119		*.60	95-13	SmartDeb1193½Alecee1152LuckyViola113¾ Drew out handily 7
5Nov63-7Aqu	fst	6f	:214 :442 1:10	3↑ ⒻInterborough H 23k	2 4 75¼ 76½ 44½ 32	Hartack W	121		3.30	91-16	Affectionately1161½Charspiv114½[D]SmartDeb1211 Bore out 12
Disqualified and placed last											
12Oct63-8GS	fst	1⅛	:481 1:122 1:381 1:51	3↑ ⒻVineland H 58k	2 2 32 3nk 1hd 42¾	Hartack W	121		*2.00	79-20	Oil Royalty118noMy Portrait1122¾Tamarona110no Led,tired 10
5Oct63-7GS	fst	1 1/16	:241 :48 1:123 1:444	3↑ ⒻAlw 6000	2 2 1hd 1hd 11 1nk	Hartack W	116		*.70	86-13	Smart Deb116nkTona1131½Suiti113¾ Lost whip,hand ride 9
19Sep63-7Aqu	gd	1⅛	:491 1:132 1:383 1:51	3↑ ⒻBeldame 87k	10 4 31 3½ 1hd 32	Hartack W	116		6.85	84-17	Oil Royalty123noLamb Chop1182Smart Deb1182½ Led,tired 13
11Sep63-7Aqu	fst	1⅛	:474 1:113 1:37 1:50	ⒻGazelle H 29k	11 5 41½ 3½ 3½ 32	Hartack W	123		4.70	89-13	LambChop1251¾DelhiMaid119nkSmartDeb1232½ Hung in drive 12
17Aug63-8AP	fst	1⅛	:462 1:104 1:364 1:50	3↑ ⒻArl Matron H 83k	1 1 32 3½ 12 1nk	Hartack W	116		4.60	86-16	Smart Deb116nkSolabar1131½Nubile1142 Fully extended 14
7Aug63-8AP	fst	7f	:223 :454 1:111 1:234	3↑ ⒻBeaugay H 17k	2 6 43 22 1hd 1½	Hartack W	118		3.00	88-18	SmartDeb118½Nubile1111¾OilRoyalty113½ Kept to pressure 11

31Jly63- 8AP	fst	1⅛	:463 1:112 1:364 1:494	ⒻPucker Up H 56k	1	2	41½	42½	69	613	Ussery R	126		*2.00	74-15	VitaminShot110nkDelhiMd1193Solbr1143½	Early speed,tired	11
6Jly63- 8Mth	fst	1⅛	:48 1:122 1:373 1:513	ⒻMth Oaks 56k	3	2	2½	2hd	2hd	31	Ussery R	118		3.90	85-16	Lamb Chop118hdSpicy Living1211Smart Deb1183	Speed,tired	8
22Jun63- 7Aqu	fst	1¼	:472 1:111 1:37 2:024	ⒻC C A Oaks 120k	1	1	11½	1hd	31	35	Ussery R	121		3.30	81-12	LambChop1213½SpicyLiving1211½SmartDeb121¾	Drifted out	10
1Jun63- 7Aqu	fst	1⅛	:481 1:123 1:372 1:502	ⒻMother Goose 91k	12	1	1½	11½	21	2no	Baeza B	121		3.75	89-11	SpicyLiving121noSmartDeb1212½LambChop121nk	Came again	14
18May63- 7Aqu	sly	1	:222 :453 1:111 1:371	ⒻAcorn 60k	4	3	31½	63¾	1116	1023	Ussery R	121	b	*2.50	59-17	SpicyLiving1213½Nalee121½LambChop1213	Early speed,tired	12
10May63- 7Aqu	fst	7f	:222 :453 1:101 1:23	ⒻAlw 10000	4	3	31	11	1½	12	Ussery R	121		*.65	91-09	SmartDeb1212FashionVerdict1161½Fool'sPlay1181½	In hand	6
5Apr63- 7GP	fst	6f	:222 :452 1:10	Alw 3800	3	2	32	11½	14	18	Grant H	115		*.30	94-15	Smart Deb1158The Baron1161Rustlin Raymond108¾		8
	Bolted to outside rail final furlong,pulled up																	
17Nov62- 8Pim	fst	1 1/16	:241 :481 1:131 1:453	ⒻMarguerite 44k	6	2	1hd	1½	21	33¾	Ussery R	119		*1.10	78-20	WiseNurse1193½Nalee119nkSmrtDb1192	Well rated,weakened	8
10Nov62- 8Lrl	sly	1 1/16	:231 :473 1:13 1:464	ⒻSelima 55k	2	1	3nk	21½	33	35	Ussery R	119		*1.20	80-17	Fool's Play1191Gay Serenade1194Smart Deb119½	No excuse	5
27Oct62- 7GS	gd	1 1/16	:242 :482 1:123 1:462	ⒻGardenia 159k	3	1	12	11½	2½	2½	Ycaza M	119		*1.20	77-24	MainSwap119½SmartDeb1193Nale1195	Bolted to outside turn	9
19Oct62- 7GS	fst	1	:223 :454 1:104 1:372	ⒻAlw 10000	7	2	22½	2½	11	22	Shoemaker W	121	b	*2.10e	93-20	Wise Nurse1222Smart Deb1215Affectionately1212½	Propped	11
6Oct62- 7Bel	sly	1	:223 :453 1:111 1:38	ⒻFrizette 110k	5	1	1hd	1hd	32	68	Shoemaker W	119		*.70e	76-15	PamsEgo1191½Fool'sPlay1191¾Affectionately1194	Gave way	10
26Sep62- 7Aqu	fst	7f	:221 :444 1:094 1:23	ⒻAstarita 29k	1	4	1½	1hd	11	13	Shoemaker W	122		*.50	92-11	[D]SmrtDb1223MainSwap112nkPamsEgo1193	Bore out badly	10
	Disqualified and placed last																	
8Sep62- 7Aqu	fst	6f	:213 :442 1:094	ⒻMatron 102k	2	1	1hd	1hd	12½	11½	Ussery R	119		2.80	96-11	SmartDeb1191½FashionVerdict1194Affectiontly1193	In hand	9
29Aug62- 8AP	fst	6½f	:222 :45 1:094 1:161	ⒻArl Lassie 67k	6	2	12	12	12	13¼	Ycaza M	119		*1.10e	95-08	Smart Deb1193¼Honey Bunny119¾Fast Luck1192½	Ridden out	10
15Aug62- 8AP	fst	6f	:214 :443 1:091	ⒻPrincess Pat 25k	9	1	1hd	1hd	3nk	1nk	Ycaza M	119		1.80e	98-13	SmartDeb119nkPoonetta1071½HoneyBunny1191½	Came again	11
18Jly62- 8AP	sl	5½f	:231 :471 1:002 1:073	ⒻMademoiselle 17k	9	3	2hd	1hd	13	1nk	Hartack W	119		*.50	79-28	Smart Deb119nkVitamin Shot1162½Eleven Keys1101½	All out	10
27Jun62- 8AP	fst	5½f	:224 :452 :58 1:042	ⒻMiss Chicago 17k	2	1	1hd	1½	1½	14	Hartack W	116		*.60	95-12	SmrtDb1164RoyalEscapade113hdVitmnShot116no	Mild drive	9
5Jun62- 5Was	fst	5f	:221 :45 :574	ⒻAlw 4000	4	4	3hd	11	14	13	Hartack W	119		*1.20	97-10	SmartDeb1193Burnsy119hdQuickChange119nk	Speed to spare	6
19Jan62- 3Hia	fst	3f	:22 :331	ⒻMd Sp Wt	4	3			21	1hd	Blum W	115		7.05	- -	Smart Deb115hdEnglish Nannie1152Speedwell115½	Driving	14

Stage Door Johnny

ch. c. 1965, by Prince John (Princequillo)–Peroxide Blonde, by Ballymoss **Lifetime record: 8 5 2 1 $223,965**

Own.– Greentree Stable
Br.– Greentree Stud Inc (Ky)
Tr.– J.M. Gaver

13Jly68- 7Aqu	fst	1¼	:494 1:13 1:37 2:013	Dwyer H 81k	6	6	43	43¼	2hd	12	Gustines H	129		*.40	90-09	StgeDoorJhnny1292OutoftheWy123noChompion110½	Driving	6
29Jun68- 7Bel	fst	1	:23 :454 1:102 1:352	Saranac H 55k	2	4	44½	43½	2½	11¼	Gustines H	126		*.70	97-15	StgeDoorJhnny1261¼OutofthWy1242½IronRulr1221½	Driving	5
1Jun68- 8Bel	fst	1½	:482 1:122 2:022 2:271	Belmont 161k	7	7	67½	21½	1hd	11¼	Gustines H	126		4.40	97-10	StgeDoorJhnny1261¼ForwardPss12612CllMPrnc1265	Driving	9
23May68- 7Bel	fst	1⅛	:463 1:111 1:361 1:482	Alw 15000	3	5	53½	11	11	14	Gustines H	116		2.10	94-17	StgeDoorJhnny1164DraftCard1181Ardoise118no	Ridden out	8
8May68- 1Aqu	fst	1	:23 :453 1:102 1:351	3↑ Md Sp Wt	3	7	53	64¾	1½	16	Gustines H	114		*.50	92-11	StgeDoorJohnny1146Nageire1146SpaceCowboy115¾	Driving	9
17Apr68- 1Aqu	fst	1	:23 :46 1:104 1:37	Md Sp Wt	2	8			31½	34½	Gustines H	122		3.50	78-17	JadeAmicol1222OakSpring1222½StagDoorJhnny1223	In close	9
6Sep67- 5Aqu	fst	6f	:224 :47 1:123	ⒸMd Sp Wt	9	10	118½	86¼	53	2½	Gustines H	122		*1.50	79-18	Grimaldi122½Stage Door Johnny122¾Forever122hd	Rallied	14
22Aug67- 1Sar	fst	5½f	:221 :461 :591 1:061	ⒸMd Sp Wt	9	11	76	55¼	23	21	Gustines H	122		*2.10	85-13	DreamLanding1221StgeDoorJhnny1225Esteban122½	Greenly	12

Straight Deal

b. f. 1962, by Hail to Reason (Turn-to)–No Fiddling, by King Cole **Lifetime record: 99 21 21 9 $733,020**

Own.– Mrs Ethel D. Jacobs
Br.– Bieber-Jacobs Stable (Ky)
Tr.– H. Jacobs

5Feb69- 6Hia	fm	1 1/16Ⓣ	1:424	4↑ ⒻAlw 7500	9	10	1117	1215	1216	1011¼	Ussery R	118	b	3.10	80-08	Crystal Palace115½Spire1122½Treacherous1121	Outrun	12
27Jan69- 8Hia	fst	7f⊗	:224 :444 1:091 1:221	4↑ ⒻAlw 7000	2	8	819	825	518	211	Ussery R	119	b	4.00	86-18	TooBald11311StraightDeal1193Femtastc1163	Best of others	8
23Jan69- 8Hia	fm	1 1/16Ⓣ	1:444	4↑ ⒻAlw 7500	3	6	68½	57	43	22½	Ussery R	116	b	3.20	78-18	KlassyPoppy1122½StraightDeal1162Mrs.Petrkn1122½	Rallied	9
28Nov68- 7Aqu	fst	1⅛	:472 1:121 1:363 1:493	3↑ ⒻFirenze H 58k	9	6	78¾	54½	54¾	42½	Pincay L Jr	112	b	4.80e	85-16	Politely1312½Obeah112noSerene Queen114no	Bold bid,hung	11
20Nov68- 7Aqu	fst	1	:241 :472 1:122 1:371	3↑ ⒻAlw 15000	3	3	31	2½	1hd	12½	Velasquez J	118	b	2.10	81-21	StraightDeal1182½GuestRoom1201WildBeauty115¾	Mild drive	6
2Nov68- 8GS	fst	1⅛	:47 1:111 1:371 1:494	3↑ ⒻVineland H 58k	5	9	99¾	35	52¾	42	Kallai P	113	b	15.00	86-22	Politely1261½Serene Queen116½Another Nell116no	Rallied	10
17Oct68- 7Bel	fst	1	:224 :453 1:103 1:362	3↑ ⒻAlw 15000	6	6	69½	56	34½	3¾	Velasquez J	116	b	2.20	91-11	NatureII116nkClemsFairyGold116½StraightDeal116½	Wide	7
27Sep68- 7Bel	fst	1	:233 :464 1:11 1:354	3↑ Alw 15000	11	10	87¼	912	712	711	Velasquez J	115	b	12.60	84-19	Trade In116¾Verbatim111½Misty Run113¾	No factor	11
20Sep68- 7Bel	fm	1⅜Ⓣ	2:151	3↑ ⒻAlw 15000	3	4	31	31½	32½	56½	Rotz JL	123	b	6.70	83-10	Harem Lady1232Gay Matelda118½Raison D'Etre1162½	Tired	9
14Sep68- 7Aqu	fst	1⅛	:473 1:121 1:371 1:493	3↑ ⒻBeldame 81k	4	5	410	44	53¾	45¼	Vasquez J	123	b	12.80	83-14	Gamely123noPolitely123nkAmerigo Lady1235	Lacked a rally	5
4Sep68- 7Aqu	fst	1	:223 :452 1:102 1:362	3↑ ⒻMaskette H 29k	7	9	89¾	98¼	76	44½	Toro F	115	b	4.90	80-22	AmergoLdy120noSereneQueen1142GreenGlade1122½	In close	10
16Aug68- 8Sar	fst	1	:231 :463 1:111 1:364	3↑ ⒻAlw 15000	1	7	66½	54	32½	11½	Toro F	116	b	2.30	90-11	StraightDeal1161½TwiceCited113hdSyrianSea1113	Driving	8
3Aug68- 8Del	fst	1¼	:471 1:112 1:37 2:024	3↑ ⒻDelaware H 117k	4	9	910	46	48	47¼	Toro F	116	b	8.50	81-19	Politely1262¾PluckyPan1171½Treacherous1133	Rallied,hung	9
20Jly68- 8Del	fst	1 1/16	:232 :472 1:112 1:44	3↑ ⒻNew Castle 38k	11	11	1012	1013	78¾	67	Cruguet J	117	b	8.60	82-24	Plucky Pan1144Serene Queen1201Lady Diplomat1141½	Hung	12
6Jly68- 7Aqu	fm	1 3/16Ⓣ	1:552	3↑ ⒻShpshdBay H(Div 2) 46k	6	2	11½	1½	45	67¾	Ussery R	118	b	6.90	85-09	Politely125noMount Regina1153Treacherous1142	Tired	9
29Jun68- 8Mth	fst	1 1/16	:232 :47 1:12 1:45	3↑ ⒻMolly Pitcher H 39k	7	9	916	79¼	59	52	Grant H	120	b	3.60	78-21	Politely1221¼Mac'sSparkler123¾GreenGlade114no	Late foot	9
19Jun68- 5Mth	fst	1 70	:233 :473 1:124 1:432	3↑ ⒻAlw 15000	2	6	611	51¼	3nk	2no	Grant H	118	b	*1.00	84-18	SereneQueen118noStraightDeal1182½LaContss1162	No excuse	6
18May68- 7Aqu	fst	1⅛	:471 1:112 1:364 1:49	3↑ ⒻTop Flight H 58k	9	7	710	86½	74¾	76¾	Belmonte E	122	b	5.30	84-11	AmerigoLady119nk[D]Politely1212SereneQueen1111½	No rally	11
4May68- 8Pim	fst	1 1/16	:233 :472 1:121 1:444	3↑ ⒻGallorette H 33k	5	8	87¾	75½	52½	2½	Marquez CH	122	b	*1.30	85-18	Serene Queen109½Straight Deal122½Politely1221	Wide turn	8
27Apr68- 7Aqu	fst	1⅛	:461 1:101 1:354 1:484	3↑ Grey Lag H 85k	1	9	1011	87½	62¾	53½	Marquez CH	113	b	13.30	88-14	BoldHour113¾[D]DiplomatWay1222FortMarcy118no	Late bid	10
20Apr68- 8Bow	fst	1 1/16	:231 :464 1:11 1:42	3↑ J B Campbell H 111k	6	7	74¼	66¼	55¼	54½	Blum W	115	b	7.70	98-08	In Reality1221Barbs Delight117½Peter Piper1172	No rally	7
6Apr68- 7Aqu	fst	1⅛	:453 1:093 1:35 1:48	3↑ Excelsior H 55k	5	6	617	69½	36½	26½	Belmonte E	115	b	2.60	89-14	Peter Piper1126½Straight Deal1154Grace Born1124	Rallied	7
30Mar68- 8Bow	fst	7f	:224 :451 1:09 1:214	3↑ ⒻBarbara Fritchie H 58k	10	9	1014	916	57½	26	Belmonte E	122	b	8.40	90-12	Too Bald1186Straight Deal122¾Treacherous121¾	Rallied	10
13Mar68- 9GP	fm	1Ⓣ	:224 :461 1:111 1:354	3↑ ⒻOrchid H 23k	2	14	1425	1418	1420	1414	Grant H	124	b	*1.80	80-09	Chriscinca109nkRing Francis1093Farest Nan1133	No speed	14
2Mar68- 5Hia	fst	7f	:224 :451 1:092 1:22	4↑ Alw 10000	4	8	816	812	89¼	36¼	Belmonte E	112	b	7.20	93-11	Jim J.1191¼Bold Tactics1165Straight Deal1122	Rallied	8
4Nov67- 7Aqu	my	1¼	:493 1:141 1:393 2:043	3↑ ⒻLadies H 58k	5	3	32	41½	73¾	55¼	Grant H	126	b	*2.30	70-22	SweetFolly1142½HaremLdy1081½Muse106nk	Lacked room late	12
26Oct67- 6Kee	fst	1⅛	:474 1:114 1:37 1:491	3↑ ⒻSpinster 61k	1	6	68½	66	2hd	1nk	Grant H	123	b	*.80	91-18	StraightDel123nk[D]Amrgo'sLdy1194FurlSl1193	Reared start	6
14Oct67- 8GS	fst	1⅛	:482 1:123 1:384 1:511	3↑ ⒻVineland H 56k	6	7	714	57	3nk	1nk	Grant H	122	b	*1.60	81-23	Straight Deal122nkPolitely1203Gamely1173½	Stiff drive	7
30Sep67- 8Atl	fst	1 3/16	:46 1:101 1:341 1:551	3↑ ⒻMatchmaker 50k	1	10	811	57¾	46½	2¾	Cordero A Jr	123	b	*2.00	104-15	Politely118¾StraightDeal123hdGmly1143	Hung under impost	13
16Sep67- 7Aqu	fst	1⅛	:49 1:132 1:372 1:494	3↑ ⒻBeldame 81k	5	4	44½	44½	56½	45¼	Cordero A Jr	123	b	*.70	82-16	Mac'sSparkler123nkTripleBrook1232½Gamely1182½	No excuse	6
4Sep67- 7Aqu	fst	1⅛	:482 1:121 1:361 1:481	3↑ Aqueduct 106k	5	4	47	45	31½	32½	Cordero A Jr	116	b	6.30	92-14	Damascus1252Ring Twice119½Straight Deal1166	Bore out	5
21Aug67- 7Sar	gd	1⅛	:474 1:123 1:37 1:493	3↑ ⒻDiana H 28k	3	5	56½	52¼	23	2nk	Ussery R	127	b	*1.30	96-11	Prides Profile114nkStraight Deal1273Malhoa1112½	Brushed	9
5Aug67- 6Sar	fst	1⅛	:47 1:11 1:352 1:481	4↑ Whitney 56k	7	7	814	78	33	31	Ussery R	116	b	3.80e	102-06	Stupendous114nkRing Twice114¾Straight Deal1164	Rallied	8
29Jly67- 8Del	fst	1¼	:471 1:114 1:37 2:021	3↑ ⒻDelaware H 118k	4	4	46½	2hd	12	11¾	Ussery R	125	b	*2.60	91-20	Straight Deal1251¾Malhoa112¾Miss Spin1141½	Mild drive	10
8Jly67- 7Aqu	fm	1 3/16Ⓣ	1:544	3↑ ⒻSheepshead Bay H 57k	3	7	65½	63¼	52	55	Ussery R	124	b	2.70	91-04	Indian Sunlite1183½Mount Regina117nkAmerivan1191	Hung	10
1Jly67- 8Mth	fst	1 1/16	:234 :471 1:114 1:444	3↑ ⒻMolly Pitcher H 38k	2	6	710	73¾	63¾	22¾	Ussery R	126	b	*1.00	78-17	Politely1152¾StraightDeal1261IndianSunlite1173½	Gaining	7
21Jun67- 7Aqu	gd	7f	:222 :451 1:101 1:234	3↑ ⒻVagrancy H 27k	3	6	619	622	616	611	Ussery R	127	b	2.60	76-21	Triple Brook116½Mac's Sparkler1213Cestrum1112½	Impeded	6
7Jun67- 7Aqu	hd	1 3/16Ⓣ	1:55	3↑ Edgemere H 30k	10	5	58	76¼	45	73¾	Ussery R	115	b	3.80	91-05	GingerFizz117nkChinatowner1143HandsomeBoy111no	In close	14
20May67- 7Aqu	fst	1⅛	:48 1:114 1:37 1:493	3↑ ⒻTop Flight H 55k	2	4	42½	53	1hd	1¾	Cordero A Jr	126	b	2.40	88-14	Straight Deal126¾Mac's Sparkler1224Malhoa112¾	Driving	7
12May67- 7Aqu	sl	1	:234 :471 1:121 1:371	3↑ ⒻHandicap 15000	4	6	65	44½	1½	1¾	Ussery R	126	b	*1.70	82-26	StraightDeal126¾Mac'sSparklr1234ShmmrngGold1133	Driving	8
6May67- 8Pim	fst	1 1/16	:233 :472 1:113 1:423	3↑ ⒻGallorette H 33k	3	8	88¼	78½	56	24	Nelson E	126	b	*2.10	93-14	LadyDiplomat1124StraightDeal126hdIndnSunlt117nk	Rallied	9
25Apr67- 7Aqu	sl	1	:241 :474 1:124 1:373	3↑ ⒻBed o' Roses H 28k	1	8	811	42½	4¾	12½	Ussery R	122	b	3.30	80-28	StraightDeal1222½IndianSunlite116hdKerens110hd	Drew out	9

17Apr67- 7Aqu	sly 7f	:233 :464 1:113 1:241	3↑ ⒻDistaff H 27k	3 3 710 715 711 59	Ussery R	123	b	2.00	76-23	Cologne1131Lady Diplomat1142Miss Moona1226	Far back 7
15Mar67- 9GP	fm 1Ⓣ	:232 :464 1:111 1:351	3↑ ⒻOrchid H (Div 2) 22k	4 9 78¾ 32 21 1½	Velasquez J	122		*.50	98-03	Straight Deal122½Cologne1116Pollen1172½	Up in time 10
1Mar67- 8Hia	fst 1⅛	:47 1:11 1:36 1:483	3↑ ⒻBlack Helen H 65k	10 6 53½ 22 2hd 2hd	Ussery R	122	b	*1.20	92-13	Mac's Sparkler117hdStraight Deal1222Malhoa1162¾	Gamely 13
15Feb67- 8Hia	fst 7f	:23 :452 1:10 1:23	3↑ ⒻColumbiana H 33k	5 12 1314 1216 78¼ 31½	Ussery R	122	b	3.50	92-16	Mac'sSparkler115hdMoccasin1171½StraightDeal122½	Rallied 14
20Jan67- 8Hia	sl 7f⊗	:241 :481 1:131 1:253	4↑ ⒻAlw 7000	7 3 89 75½ 45 1¾	Ussery R	118	b	*1.10	81-19	StraightDeal118¾TradeMrk1151Srols1121¾	Up final strides 8
24Nov66- 7Aqu	fst 1⅛	:473 1:114 1:37 1:493	3↑ ⒻFirenze H 56k	7 8 813 89½ 34 12¼	Ussery R	118	b	3.30	88-21	StraightDeal1182¼Mac'sSparkler113¾BelldNut1121½	Driving 8
5Nov66- 7Aqu	fst 1¼	:481 1:122 1:371 2:022	3↑ ⒻLadies H 56k	5 4 23 2½ 1½ 2no	Ussery R	118	b	4.40	86-13	Destro115noStraightDeal1183MissDickey109hd	Sharp,missed 8
26Oct66- 5Aqu	fm 1 3/16Ⓣ	1:432	3↑ ⒻNew York H (Div 1) 23k	4 6 45½ 46½ 46½ 45¼	Ussery R	122	b	3.10	84-13	IndianSunlite115nkNativeStret119noMountRgn1205	Bore out 9
15Oct66- 8GS	fst 1⅛	:474 1:112 1:361 1:49	3↑ ⒻVineland H 58k	6 7 88¾ 67 56½ 43¼	Ussery R	121	b	*2.00	89-15	LadyPitt118¾Juanita1122½Mac'sSparklr112no	Belated rally 11
17Sep66- 7Aqu	fst 1⅛	:47 1:111 1:361 1:492	3↑ ⒻBeldame 85k	8 7 713 613 57 28	Ussery R	123	b	11.30	81-18	SummerScandal1238StraightDeal123½LadyPitt1182	Rallied 10
7Sep66- 7Aqu	fst 1	:233 :463 1:114 1:374	3↑ ⒻMaskette H 28k	7 6 56 23 26 26	Ussery R	119	b	3.80	73-30	SummerScandal1236StraightDeal119noTrechry1112½	Fair try 9
9Jly66- 7Aqu	hd 1 3/16Ⓣ	1:552	3↑ ⒻSheepshead Bay H 57k	5 3 31½ 32 1hd 1½	Blum W	122	b	*3.40e	93-13	StraightDeal122½MountRegina120hdTreachery111hd	Driving 10
2Jly66- 8Mth	fst 1 1/16	:233 :47 1:112 1:433	3↑ ⒻMolly Pitcher H 38k	5 6 55½ 43½ 24 2nk	Brumfield D	120	b	6.20	87-15	Discipline117nkStraight Deal1203½Lovejoy1122	Sharp try 8
18Jun66- 7Aqu	hd 1⅝Ⓣ	2:384	3↑ Bowling Green H 59k	11 8 1117 1211 1113 1115	Ussery R	115	b	19.30	91-00	Moontrip112hdFlag113½Knightly Manner116¾	Unruly post 12
11Jun66- 8Aqu	fm 1 3/16Ⓣ	1:543	3↑ Handicap 8500	8 4 33½ 43 52¼ 53	Shoemaker W	116	b	4.40	94-03	ChosunVictory113¾WhiteBearLake1131Rochefort112½	Tired 11
21May66- 7Aqu	fst 1⅛	:472 1:112 1:361 1:492	3↑ ⒻTop Flight H 55k	1 2 25 23 26 310	Ussery R	119	b	*1.70e	79-15	Summer Scandal1175Malhoa1135Straight Deal119¾	Tired 7
27Apr66- 7Aqu	fst 1	:24 :464 1:11 1:354	3↑ ⒻBed o' Roses H 27k	2 3 33½ 31½ 3½ 11½	Ussery R	117	b	4.90e	89-18	StraightDeal1171½WhataTreat1261½QuenEmprss123nk	Driving 7
18Apr66- 7Aqu	fst 7f	:223 :452 1:094 1:222	3↑ ⒻDistaff H 27k	2 6 611 77½ 63½ 42¾	Shoemaker W	119	b	3.90e	91-17	SailorPrincess111nkQueenEmprss1232½Pttcot112no	Bore out 7
9Apr66- 8Bow	fst 7f	:223 :45 1:102 1:232	3↑ ⒻBarbara Fritchie H 59k	11 2 85¼ 66¾ 53¼ 42¾	Sellers J	120	b	7.00e	93-14	Tosmah1211Queen Empress1231½Privileged111nk	Stride late 12
12Mar66- 8SA	fm *1¾Ⓣ	2:484	3↑ S Juan Capistrano H 125k	3 5 47 73½ 74½ 68	Gustines H	116	b	17.80	75-17	George Royal118noPlaque115½Tom Cat1141½	Well up,tired 9
24Feb66- 8SA	fm 1¼Ⓣ	:444 1:091 1:34 1:584	4↑ ⒻS Barbara H 46k	13 8 89½ 31 11½ 12½	Shoemaker W	122	b	4.80e	98-02	StraightDeal1222½MissRincon1071½Petticoat113no	Driving 13
16Feb66- 8SA	fm 1⅛Ⓣ	:472 1:12 1:37 1:491	4↑ ⒻHandicap 15000	6 9 812 811 810 89	Shoemaker W	125	b	4.80	78-13	Curious Clover1162Pollen1202½Miss Rincon108½	Wide 12
5Feb66- 8SA	fst 1⅛	:47 1:11 1:361 1:483	4↑ ⒻS Margarita H 61k	9 6 75½ 32½ 32½ 1nk	Shoemaker W	121	b	2.50e	89-12	StraightDeal121nkPollen1192Batteur124no	Long,hard drive 12
22Jan66- 7SA	fst 1 1/16	:223 :45 1:10 1:422	4↑ ⒻS Maria H 31k	7 8 816 85½ 52 2½	Shoemaker W	121	b	3.40e	90-11	PoonaQueen119½StraightDeal121nkGallarush112hd	Sharp try 14
11Jan66- 8SA	fst 7f	:22 :443 1:10 1:223	4↑ ⒻS Monica H 26k	14 9 912 915 1010 55¼	Shoemaker W	112	b	3.70e	85-15	Batteur1231½Terentia1193½Jalousie II117hd	Mild bid 14
28Dec65- 8SA	fst 6f	:221 :451 :573 1:10	3↑ ⒻLas Flores H 26k	3 13 137¾ 129¼ 78 74	Church K	122	b	*2.40e	88-13	Poona Queen117¾Respected116nkFairway Fun116nk	No threat 14
25Nov65- 7Aqu	gd 1⅛	:48 1:124 1:384 1:521	3↑ ⒻFirenze H 55k	3 4 43 2hd 1½ 21¾	Sellers J	118	b	*.70e	73-26	SailorPrincess1111¾StrghtDl118nkPttcot1143½	Second best 7
6Nov65- 7Aqu	fst 1¼	:49 1:132 1:381 2:033	3↑ ⒻLadies H 55k	3 6 55½ 41 11 13	Sellers J	114	b	4.20	80-17	StraightDeal1143SteepleJill1262½YesPles109no	Mild drive 7
27Oct65- 7Aqu	fm 1 1/16Ⓣ	1:423	3↑ ⒻNew York H (Div 2) 23k	2 3 31½ 32 33 34½	Sellers J	116	b	4.40	88-07	Batteur123½GoodJane1104StraightDeal1161½	Held on gamely 9
16Oct65- 8GS	fst 1⅛	:48 1:12 1:371 1:494	3↑ ⒻVineland H 56k	3 2 24 43 44½ 43½	Velasquez J	115	b	9.20	84-21	Steeple Jill1232Cordially113½Tosmah1221	Even race 8
7Oct65- 7Aqu	fst 1	:231 :461 1:104 1:364	ⒻAlw 10000	4 5 54½ 54 21 11½	Sellers J	118	b	1.50	84-20	StraightDeal1181½Terentia1181EdieB.M.1202	Slightly best 6
27Sep65- 7Aqu	fst 1⅛	:463 1:104 1:36 1:491	3↑ ⒻBeldame 82k	6 4 44 52¾ 42 3½	Sellers J	118	b	2.10e	89-19	WhataTreat118noSteepleJill123½StraightDeal1181½	Blocked 6
20Sep65- 7Aqu	fst 1	:223 :444 1:084 1:351	3↑ ⒻMaskette H 28k	1 6 46 35 33 33	Sellers J	113	b	2.90e	89-16	Tosmah128noAffectionately1283Straight Deal113½	Gamely 9
4Sep65- 7Aqu	fst 1⅛	:473 1:122 1:381 1:512	ⒻGazelle H 59k	1 6 77 74¾ 41½ 42½	Cordero A	117	b	4.80	76-20	WhataTreat123½Terentia118½Discipline1181½	In close,hung 13
23Aug65- 7Sar	fst 1⅛	:464 1:11 1:364 1:493	3↑ ⒻDiana H 28k	1 3 33 21 1hd 2hd	Sellers J	113	b	18.50	97-12	SteepleJill126hdStraightDel113½HoHo109no	Very sharp try 8
14Aug65- 6Sar	fst 1¼	:471 1:112 1:364 2:033	ⒻAlabama 63k	9 11 116 96 85½ 78	Sellers S	121	b	20.70	82-06	WhataTreat118nkⒹDiscipline1182Terentia114½	No mishap 18
22Jly65- 8Hol	fst 1⅛	:47 1:11 1:37 1:494	ⒻHol Oaks 56k	6 9 97 52¼ 31½ 12½	Sellers J	112	b	12.30	83-16	StraightDeal1122½SeaEagle1122½GalaHost1183¼	Handy score 11
5Jly65- 8Mth	fst 1⅛	:464 1:11 1:372 1:503	ⒻMth Oaks 57k	4 9 813 815 79¾ 69½	Vasquez J	112	b	13.90	81-19	Summer Scandal1126Terentia116¾Marshua118¾	Slow start 10
23Jun65- 8Mth	fst 1 70	:223 :461 1:114 1:433	ⒻPost-Deb (Div 2) 23k	9 7 78¼ 64¼ 43½ 2no	Turcotte R	112	b	13.90	83-19	Desert Love118noStraight Deal1121Cestrum1123	Sharp try 12
12Jun65- 7Aqu	fst 1¼	:481 1:121 1:37 2:023	ⒻC C A Oaks 129k	7 10 99½ 96¼ 811 817	Boland W	121	b	26.60	68-14	Marshua1212½What a Treat1216Terentia1212½	Never close 10
29May65- 7Aqu	sly 1⅛	:482 1:123 1:513	ⒻMother Goose 97k	10 6 53 54½ 45 44	Belmonte E	121	b	24.50f	74-20	Cordially121noWhat a Treat1211Up Oars1213	No late rally 12
25May65- 6Aqu	fst 6f	:221 :453 1:12	3↑ ⒻAlw 6500	11 8 87 76 51¾ 2no	Boland W	115	b	12.45	83-19	Think Quick112noStraight Deal115½Ruth Fogel118½	Gaining 12
15May65- 7Aqu	fst 1	:222 :45 1:101 1:371	ⒻAcorn 58k	2 5 55½ 45½ 57½ 68¼	Blum W	121	b	65.55	74-20	GroundControl121nkMarshua121noUpOars1213	Wide final ⅜ 10
22Apr65- 8Aqu	fst 6f	:231 :463 1:113	3↑ ⒻAlw 6500	1 6 52 43½ 55 45½	Blum W	113	b	8.10	79-18	Png113½IcCrnvl1151½RuthFogl1153½	Crowded early,no rally 8
16Apr65- 8Aqu	gd 7f	:233 :471 1:122 1:243	3↑ ⒻAlw 6000	6 6 62 51¼ 2½ 1nk	Blum W	112	b	6.80	83-23	StraightDeal112nkGroundControl1134RingaBell1101	Driving 7
8Apr65- 7Aqu	fst 6f	:223 :454 1:111	3↑ ⒻAlw 7500	4 6 63¾ 53½ 66½ 54½	Alvarez F	110	b	11.95	82-20	Self-Supporting118hdIceCrnvl1201½SpnshBrz1131½	In close 9
27Jan65- 7Hia	fst 7f	:23 :46 1:113 1:253	ⒻAlw 6000	5 6 66¼ 49 48½ 55½	Turcotte R	116	b	3.00	75-19	Taunoa1083½LovelyHanna113hdSpecialT.113½	Never a factor 7
20Jan65- 9Hia	fst 6f	:223 :461 1:11	ⒻJasmine (Div 2) 20k	8 8 97 76¾ 67 56	Turcotte R	112	b	8.10	83-15	OpenHearing1123¾SpecialT.113hdMagcRy1142	Sluggish start 9
4Jan65- 8TrP	fst 6f	:222 :453 1:11	ⒻAlw 3200	11 2 33 64½ 88 97¼	Ussery R	121	b	3.50	79-14	Amerivan116hdSpecialT.1211SuzanneMarie121hd	Raced wide 11
10Dec64- 7Aqu	fst 7f	:223 :452 1:101 1:23	Alw 10000	5 1 55½ 33 24 2½	Venezia M5	109	b	2.05	90-14	WazaOurs122½StraightDl1095Mr.Kish1173	Finished gamely 5
23Nov64- 6Aqu	fst 6f	:222 :461 1:12	ⒻAlw 5500	2 6 52 63¼ 2hd 12	Turcotte R	116	b	6.10	83-24	StraightDeal1192½Respected1191½WellHeeld1162	Mild drive 9
18Nov64- 7Aqu	fst 1	:234 :471 1:132 1:391	ⒻDemoiselle 28k	8 1 11 1hd 63¼ 77½	Gustines H	112	b	19.65e	64-26	Discipline1132Lay Aft115¾Cordially1121	Used up early 8
12Oct64- 5Aqu	fst 6½f	:221 :443 1:094 1:163	ⒻAlw 5000	1 6 66½ 77½ 68 57¼	Valenzuela I	119		9.00	90-07	TwoofAkind119½LuckyFlight1142Equiria113¾	Raced evenly 7
7Oct64- 5Aqu	fst 6f	:231 :471 1:12	ⒻMd Sp Wt	5 6 62¾ 43½ 2½ 13	Turcotte R	119	b	13.50f	83-17	Straight Deal1193Holli Dawn119¾Wee Lassie1192½	Driving 14
2Oct64- 4Aqu	sly 7f	:224 :471 1:142 1:284	ⒻMd Sp Wt	7 9 85¾ 812 711 78¼	Alvarez F	119	b	55.90	54-31	EncoreUne119½CmpassRose119½SheetHome119nk	No threat 11
25Sep64- 5Aqu	fst 6f	:223 :463 1:12	ⒻMd Sp Wt	13 8 115 1415 1421 1422	Connolley R	119		72.15f	61-18	Bebopper1191½Up Oars1196Mount Regina119½	Far off pace 14
8Sep64- 5Aqu	fst 6f	:223 :46 1:111	ⒻMd Sp Wt	9 13 139¾ 1219 1020 820	Tartaglia J10	109		11.40e	67-20	Meripats1198Titania1192Be Reasonable114hd	Slow start 14

Successor

b. c. 1964, by Bold Ruler (Nasrullah)–Misty Morn, by Princequillo

Lifetime record: 25 7 6 6 $532,254

Own.– Wheatley Stable
Br.– Wheatley Stable (Ky)
Tr.– E.A. Neloy

3Feb68- 8Hia	fst 1⅛	:454 1:092 1:342 1:471	3↑ Seminole H 65k	5 7 713 715 511 511¾	Baeza B	117	b	2.60	87-14	Favorable Turn1118Rixdal1112In Reality121nk	Outrun 12
26Jan68- 9Hia	fst 7f	:234 :463 1:104 1:231	4↑ Alw 7000	3 6 64½ 45 42¼ 11½	Baeza B	119	b	*.70	93-17	Successor1191½Angelico114¾Gaylord'sFeather113nk	Driving 9
20Jan68- 9Hia	fst 7f	:231 :463 1:111 1:233	4↑ Alw 6500	2 5 46 54½ 53½ 41¼	Baeza B	119	b	*.50	90-14	JohnJacob113½RenewedVigor113nkRoyalSpeed113½	In close 12
18Nov67- 7Aqu	fst 1⅛	:463 1:103 1:361 1:493	3↑ Queens County H 55k	3 6 610 67 46½ 31½	Shoemaker W	116	b	2.30	86-14	Mr. Right115½Proud Clarion1251Successor1161	Bore in 6
11Nov67- 7Aqu	fst 1 3/16	:471 1:11 1:36 1:55	Roamer H 56k	5 6 2hd 1½ 1hd 24	Boland W	118	b	3.00	100-11	Proud Clarion1224Successor1183½Royal Speed1123	Faltered 8
28Oct67- 7Aqu	fst 2	:494 2:302 2:554 3:201	3↑ J C Gold Cup 106k	4 3 35 34 34 312	Boland W	119	b	6.60	83-12	Damascus1194½Handsome Boy1247½Sccssr1196½	No mishap 4
18Oct67- 7Aqu	sly 1⅝	:48 1:402 2:061 2:443	Lawrence Realizatn 54k	6 2 22½ 11½ 1hd 1nk	Baeza B	116	b	*.70	82-23	Successr116nkGentlemnJms1169IrshRbllon11610	Hard urged 6
9Oct67- 7Aqu	fst 1⅛	:464 1:104 1:353 1:483	Discovery H 28k	8 7 75¾ 66½ 33 2¾	Baeza B	119	b	*1.00	92-16	BoldHour119¾Successr1192½GalaPrformnc11810	Closed fast 9
26Sep67- 7Aqu	fst 1	:223 :444 1:083 1:343	3↑ Alw 15000	7 6 64¾ 64 52¾ 31½	Baeza B	112		*.80	93-11	Indulto1201½Flag Raiser123nkSuccessor112hd	Closed fast 8
16Sep67- 6Aqu	fst 6f	:222 :46 1:102	3↑ Alw 15000	1 7 53¾ 54 3nk 13	Boland W	113		1.50	91-16	Successor1133Golden Buttons1191Impressive115hd	Easily 8
4Sep67- 6Aqu	fst 6f	:22 :45 1:093	3↑ Alw 15000	1 6 611 69 39½ 35¾	Baeza B	113		3.10	89-14	Jim J.115¾Mr. Washington1205Successor11310	Stride late 6
20May67- 6Aqu	fst 6f	:221 :452 1:093	3↑ Alw 12000	8 6 74½ 65½ 67½ 67½	Ycaza M	116	b	1.70	87-14	Aforthought1151½BrooklynBrdg1153Voygr105no	No response 8
6May67- 7CD	fst 1¼	:463 1:104 1:36 2:003	Ky Derby 162k	6 10 1013 1213 68¼ 68	Baeza B	126	b	4.60	89-07	ProudClarion1261BarbsDelight1263Dmascs1261¼	No mishap 14
27Apr67- 6Kee	fst 1⅛	:472 1:111 1:363 1:493	Blue Grass 31k	1 5 64¾ 68½ 57 48¼	Broussard R	126	b	*.60	81-17	DiplomatWy1261½ProudClrion1216GentlmnJms126¾	In close 9
15Apr67- 7Kee	fst 7f	:224 :451 1:10 1:22	Alw 7500	6 1 42½ 35 32½ 2no	Baeza B	126	b	*.70	98-12	Ruken122noSuccessor1226Balouf113no	Bold late rally 7
13Mar67- 7Aqu	fst 6f	:222 :452 1:092	Swift 27k	2 4 45½ 58½ 48½ 47¾	Baeza B	126	b	*.50	88-18	SoloLanding1265½SunGala126¾FlyingTackle1261½	No excuse 5
12Nov66- 8GS	sly 1 1/16	:232 :472 1:121 1:441	Garden State 314k	1 5 56 45 31½ 13	Baeza B	122	b	*2.30	84-29	Successor1223Bold Hour1226Proviso122¾	Scored easily 12
29Oct66- 8Lrl	fst 1 1/16	:232 :472 1:133 1:454	Pim Futurity 194k	6 3 43 43½ 21½ 2nk	Shoemaker W	122	b	*.50e	88-16	In Reality122nkSuccessor1222Proviso1224	Bore in,gaining 9
15Oct66- 7Aqu	fst 1	:222 :444 1:092 1:35	Champagne 208k	6 6 54½ 42¼ 23 11	Baeza B	122	b	3.10e	93-14	Successor1221Dr. Fager1224Proviso1224	Won going away 10

5Oct66- 7Aqu	gd 7f	:224 :46 1:113 1:244	Cowdin 88k	4 7 94¾ 87¾ 44 32¼	Baeza B	117	b	2.30	80-22	Dr.Fager117¾InRealty1171½Succssor1172½	In close,rallied	10
24Sep66- 7Aqu	fst 6½f	:224 :46 1:11 1:173	Futurity 147k	7 7 75¼ 74¼ 34 2½	Baeza B	122	b	1.50e	91-18	Bold Hour122½Successor1223½Pinnacle1222	Finished fast	7
20Jly66- 7Aqu	fst 5½f	:231 :463 :582 1:042	Great American 27k	3 1 51¼ 42½ 33 3¾	Baeza B	124	b	*.70	90-23	Native Prince124nkHermogenes120½Successor1246	Bore in	6
6Jly66- 7Aqu	fst 5½f	:221 :452 :574 1:041	Tremont 36k	4 3 42 42 3nk 1nk	Baeza B	114	b	*.90	92-20	Successor114nkBold Hour1143Favorable Turn1141½	Driving	6
24Jun66- 3Aqu	fst 5½f	:233 :471 :592 1:06	©Md Sp Wt	2 1 1½ 13 16 16	Baeza B	122	b	*.10	83-21	Successor1226Richroband1222½Celebration1222	Easily	9
10Jun66- 5Aqu	fst 5f	:222 :454 :58	Md Sp Wt	5 6 34 33 31 2nk	Baeza B	122	b	*.90	95-16	Bold Hour122nkSuccessor1228Bracer122no	Gave sharp try	8

T.V. Lark

b. c. 1957, by Indian Hemp (Nasrullah)–Miss Larksfly, by Heelfly **Lifetime record: 72 19 13 6 $902,194**

Own.– P.W. Madden
Br.– Dr W.D. Lucas (Cal)
Tr.– P.K. Parker

22Nov62- 8Pim	sf 1½Ⓣ	:504 1:183 2:141 2:422	3↑ Dixie H 63k	12 13 1519 1216 912 811¼	Sellers J	122		7.00	32-57	WiseShip123¾SunshineCak1081¼ElBnddo118nk	Never a factor	15
27Oct62- 7Bel	sf 1½Ⓣ	2:283	3↑ Man o' War 114k	6 6 87½ 89¼ 719 822	Sellers J	126		6.70	81-11	Beau Purple1262Kelso1266½The Axe II1261¼		12
	Failed to respond in drive											
17Oct62- 7Bel	hd 1⅜Ⓣ	2:131	3↑ Knickerbocker H 30k	1 6 66½ 95¼ 63¼ 63¼	Ycaza M	123		*1.55	101-00	TheAxeII120¾Mngo1201½IrishDandy112½	No apparent excuse	12
8Oct62- 5Bel	fm 1⅜Ⓣ	2:153	3↑ Long Island H (Div 1) 22k	5 4 21½ 43 32 2¾	Gomez A	124		2.95	91-09	TheAxeII117¾T.V.Lark1242½ShieldBearer1181	Game effort	10
29Sep62- 7Aqu	gd 1¼	:471 1:113 1:37 2:031	3↑ Woodward 115k	3 4 616 815 816 816	Gomez A	126		18.60	68-17	Kelso1264½Jaipur1206½Guadlcnl1261½	Dropped far off pace	8
15Sep62- 8Atl	fm 1 3/16Ⓣ	1:563	3↑ U Nations H 100k	1 10 85¼ 83½ 62¼ 2nk	Gomez A	123		7.00	90-10	Mongo117nkT.V.Lark123½WiseShip1232	Fast finish outside	12
1Sep62- 8Atl	fm 1⅛Ⓣ	1:50	3↑ Kelly-Olympic H 35k	4 9 109¾ 108½ 810 85¼	Longden J	124		*1.70	88-07	WiseShip124½HittngAwy1241½Parka111½	No apparent mishap	11
25Aug62- 8Atl	fm 1 1/16Ⓣ	1:422	3↑ Philadelphia Turf H 29k	2 6 813 78 43¼ 12	Grant H	120		*1.90	99-01	T.V.Lark1202HellenicHero111¾LoyalLadyII108½	Cleverly	8
23Jly62- 7Hol	fst 1⅝	:464 1:361 2:012 2:393	3↑ Sunset H 88k	2 11 108¾ 75¼ 45½ 47¾	Valenzuela A	120		7.10	85-12	ProveIt129noWindySnds1126NotblII1071¾	Lacked room,wide	14
14Jly62- 8Hol	fst 1¼	:45 1:093 1:344 2:00	3↑ Hol Gold Cup H 162k	11 12 1216 95¼ 79 712	Neves R	125		5.50	81-14	Prove It1253¼Windy Sands111½Cadiz1175		12
	Failed to threaten seriously											
4Jly62- 8Hol	fst 1⅛	:46 1:092 1:342 1:473	3↑ American H 55k	9 6 812 78¾ 87¾ 54¾	Sellers J	123		3.10	90-16	ProveIt124nkWindySands1131¼Harpi1103¼	Wide stretch turn	9
16Jun62- 7Hol	fst 1 1/16	:223 :451 1:09 1:41	3↑ Inglewood H 55k	1 8 79¼ 77 76½ 65	Longden J	126		4.50	85-14	ProveIt122¾SeOrbt112nkRblro109no	Saved ground,late gain	10
30May62- 8Was	fm 1 1/16Ⓣ	:24 :472 1:112 1:431	3↑ Round Table H 32k	5 8 714 712 45 21¼	Ycaza M	126		1.90	93-11	PorvenirII1161¼T.V.Lark1261¼RunforNurse118nk	Wide bid	8
10May62- 7Aqu	fst 1⅛	:464 1:112 1:364 1:492	3↑ Sun Forward H 20k	4 5 512 510 48½ 610	Sellers J	127		2.45	85-18	BeauPurple1181½Eurasia1156RuffWeather1081½	Never close	7
1May62- 7Aqu	sf 1 1/16Ⓣ	1:501	3↑ Alw 10000	3 1 21 21½ 2hd 1¾	Sellers J	124		*.65	57-39	T.V. Lark124¾Juanro1141½John William1196	Hard ridden	8
21Apr62- 8Lrl	fm 1⅛Ⓣ	1:474	3↑ Laurel H 28k	3 2 31½ 31½ 34 24½	Longden J	127		*.40	97-00	BronzBbu1174½T.V.Lrk127¾Polrty109nk	Evenly through stretch	9
30Jan62- 7SA	fst 1⅛	:462 1:104 1:361 1:482	4↑ ⓈS Catalina H 27k	3 7 73¼ 72¼ 23 2no	Longden J	127		*1.10	90-12	New Policy118noT.V. Lark12710Dress Up1142¾	Just missed	7
11Nov61- 7Lrl	fm 1½Ⓣ	:483 2:013 2:261	3↑ D C Int'l 100k	4 2 2½ 2hd 1hd 1¾	Longden J	126		3.60	109-01	T.V.Lark126¾Klso12612Prnupcl12610	Under long,hard drive	8
25Oct61- 7Aqu	hd 1⅝Ⓣ	2:40	3↑ Knickerbocker H 29k	10 7 77½ 43 31½ 1no	Longden J	119		6.45	110-00	T.V.Lark119noNasomo113¾WiseShip120¾	Up in final stride	11
14Oct61- 8Haw	gd 1¼	:471 1:112 1:372 2:023	3↑ Haw Gold Cup H 127k	9 6 68 1½ 11½ 1½	Longden J	113	b	7.90	83-17	T.V.Lark113½Heroshogala1097RunforNurse119no	Hard drive	9
29Sep61- 7Haw	sf 1 3/16Ⓣ	:483 1:143 1:402 2:013	3↑ Handicap 10000	5 3 36 42½ 33½ 33	Meaux C	112		2.60	79-25	Tudorich1213GetLucky107hdT.V.Lrk112hd	Raced wide,evenly	9
	Previously owned by C.R. Mac Stable Inc											
9Sep61- 8Haw	fm 1Ⓣ	:23 :47 1:112 1:371	3↑ Chicago H 30k	2 8 109 1014 714 57¾	Meaux C	112		13.80	82-17	Tudorich1122¾NoholmeII1144RunforNurse116nk	Mild rally	13
4Sep61- 8AP	gd 1	:224 :452 1:093 1:343	3↑ Wash Park H 120k	6 11 1115 1115 1117 1115	Solomone M	114		21.60	85-08	ChiefofChiefs1124¾TlntShow110nkRunforNurs112¾	No factor	11
24Aug61- 8AP	fst 1	:232 :46 1:10 1:343	3↑ Wash Park Preview H 15k	6 9 97¼ 108¼ 99¼ 78¾	Shoemaker W	120		*1.20	91-11	Currock1151RomanColonel1141¼WillYe1151¾	Showed dull try	11
9Aug61- 8AP	fst 6½f	:223 :444 1:084 1:151	3↑ Myrtlewood H 16k	8 7 118¾ 1111 1010 88¼	Shoemaker W	120		5.50	91-09	JohnWilliam1121½VitalForce1142RunforNurs1221¼	No factor	11
27May61- 7Hol	fst 1 1/16	:231 :461 1:094 1:402	3↑ Californian 112k	7 8 75½ 75½ 66 47	Longden J	123		2.10	86-12	First Balcony1154½Prove It1271½Sea Orbit1151¼	Dull try	8
20May61- 7Hol	fst 7f	:22 :441 1:083 1:211	3↑ Los Angeles H 55k	5 8 86¾ 75½ 53¼ 1nk	Longden J	121		*2.30	94-11	T.V.Lark121nkNewPolicy117nkFirstBalcony1113	Up in time	9
10May61- 7Hol	fst 6f	:22 :443 :562 1:084	3↑ Hol Premiere H 22k	9 10 97½ 95¾ 85¼ 42½	Longden J	125		10.40	94-13	Revel1261¼Finnegan118½Henrijan117¾	Best stride too late	10
11Mar61- 7SA	fm *1¾Ⓣ	2:48	3↑ S Juan Capistrano H 113k	4 9 108¾ 71¾ 62¾ 44	Arcaro E	122		4.00	83-11	Don'tAlibi118noPrinceBlessed116½NotableII1063½	Mild bid	11
22Feb61- 7SA	fm 1½Ⓣ	:462 1:10 2:002 2:26	3↑ Wash Birthday H 45k	4 5 58 51¾ 41¾ 32¼	Arcaro E	124		*2.40	95-03	GeecheeLou1171½Don'tAlibi120¾T.V.Lrk124no	Good late bid	9
11Feb61- 7SA	fst 1⅛	:452 1:092 1:353 1:483	3↑ San Antonio H 57k	2 10 1115 1112 117¾ 96	Arcaro E	124		5.40	83-12	AmericanComet113½HowNow1161½GreyEagle113½	Dull effort	11
2Feb61- 7SA	fst 1⅛	:461 1:104 1:361 1:49	4↑ ⓈS Catalina H 27k	5 5 56 53½ 44 1¾	Arcaro E	124		*1.20	87-15	T.V.Lark124¾AmericanComet1142FreeCopy1131¾	Hard urged	6
28Jan61- 7SA	fst 1¼	:461 1:103 1:353 2:01	Maturity 167k	4 7 76½ 52½ 52¾ 67¼	Arcaro E	126		3.30	87-13	Prove It1164½Prince Blessed113noGrey Eagle113½	No rally	7
14Jan61- 7SA	fst 1⅛	:464 1:11 1:354 1:473	San Fernando 54k	6 6 54½ 63¼ 44½ 58½	Sellers J	126		1.90	85-11	ProveIt113½Tmpion1236PrinceBlssd1131¼	Appeared to hang	6
7Jan61- 7SA	fst 7f	:22 :443 1:092 1:221	4↑ San Carlos H 58k	12 5 1210 107¾ 85¾ 21	Sellers J	125		*1.60	91-11	FirstBalcony1111T.V.Lark125nkOleFols120¾	Strong finish	12
26Dec60- 7SA	fst 6f	:214 :442 1:092	3↑ Palos Verdes H 23k	6 12 148¼ 95¾ 73½ 41¾	Sellers J	123		4.70	95-10	Ole Fols117nkHenrijan114¾Finnegan118¾	Best stride late	14
15Oct60- 8Haw	my 1¼	:464 1:113 1:364 2:02	3↑ Haw Gold Cup H 144k	5 9 911 913 815 827	Sellers J	121		3.00	59-21	Kelso1176Heroshogala119½On-and-On1221¾	Disliked footing	9
8Oct60- 8Haw	fst 1⅛	:473 1:113 1:352 1:48	3↑ Handicap 10000	2 3 52¼ 64¼ 3½ 2no	Sellers J	123		1.80	98-06	Hymnt115noT.V.Lrk1235RgolttoII110no	Bore in through drive	6
24Sep60- 7Aqu	fst 1¼	:472 1:111 1:354 2:011	3↑ Woodward 112k	7 7 710 75½ 79 615	Sellers J	120		4.35	87-08	SwordDancer1261½DottedSwiss1262½BaldEagle1261	Dull try	7
17Sep60- 7Atl	fm 1 3/16Ⓣ	:463 1:12 1:372 1:57	3↑ U Nations H 100k	10 9 913 66 41½ 11¼	Sellers J	120		8.30	88-12	T.V.Lark1201¼SwordDancer1271¼BllyAch122hd	Driving clear	10
5Sep60- 8AP	fst 1	:23 :452 1:092 1:341	3↑ Wash Park H 122k	1 8 98½ 74½ 52¾ 1hd	Sellers J	116		*2.30	99-05	T.V.Lark116hdDottedSwiss1231¼TalentShow1181½	Up in time	9
27Aug60- 8AP	fst 1⅛	:461 1:102 1:35 1:471	American Derby 118k	8 4 33 2hd 11½ 13½	Sellers J	123		*1.60	100-05	T.V. Lark1233½New Policy1202Heroshogala1111½	Ridden out	8
15Aug60- 7AP	fst 1	:23 :452 1:094 1:344	Alw 1000	2 4 44½ 31½ 1hd 1nk	Sellers J	126		2.30	96-09	T.V.Lark126nkNewPolicy1233BoldLrk1134½	Very handy score	7
23Jly60- 8AP	fst 1	:223 :452 1:103 1:361	Arl Classic 135k	12 3 32 42¼ 1hd 1¾	Sellers J	120		16.70	89-13	T.V. Lark120¾John William1232½Venetian Way1231	Driving	12
9Jly60- 7Hol	fst 1¼	:444 1:084 1:344 2:012	Hol Derby 114k	8 9 97¾ 73 41½ 22	Harmatz W	122		2.20	84-12	Tempstuous1102T.V.Lrk1222BlankCheck1111	Much trouble	9
25Jun60- 7Hol	fst 1⅛	:46 1:093 1:341 1:463	Cinema H 57k	12 11 104¾ 85¾ 59½ 38	Harmatz W	126		*1.80	93-06	NewPolicy1231½Tmpstuous1136½T.V.Lrk126½	From far back	13
11Jun60- 7Hol	fst 1 1/16	:231 :454 1:093 1:411	Argonaut 38k	10 7 76½ 53½ 4nk 11¾	Harmatz W	126		4.60e	89-09	T.V.Lrk1201¾Henrijan114¾NewPolcy123¾	Under mild urging	10
21May60- 8Pim	fst 1 3/16	:484 1:132 1:382 1:573	Preakness 175k	2 6 56 69¼ 69 69½	Harmatz W	126		15.30	75-22	BallyAche1264VictoriaPark1261¾CelticAsh1262¼	No factor	6
14May60- 7Pim	gd 1 1/16	:233 :463 1:111 1:442	Alw 5000	2 7 612 59½ 58½ 48	Harmatz W	122		5.60	80-20	BallyAche1224DivineComedy112hdCelticAsh1104	No factor	7
23Apr60- 8BM	fst 1⅛	:464 1:112 1:362 1:49	Cal Derby 44k	1 3 61¼ 52¼ 46 53¾	Maese A	120		*.70	90-13	NobleNoor120hdHenrjn113¾GntGuy1122½	Bore out in stretch	8
	Previously trained by W. Molter											
2Apr60- 8BM	fst 1 1/16	:224 :452 1:094 1:412	Tropicana 22k	6 6 79 32 1hd 11½	Maese A	118		2.90	97-08	T.V.Lark1181½FlowLine1183½FirstBalcony1143¼	Ridden out	7
25Mar60- 7BM	fst 1 1/16	:224 :454 1:101 1:432	Alw 5000	3 1 59½ 33 21 1½	Maese A	118		2.00e	87-15	T.V.Lrk118½FlowLin1224Tmpstuous1102	Impeded,going away	6
5Mar60- 7SA	fst 1⅛	:453 1:10 1:351 1:474	S Anita Derby 130k	4 6 45½ 52¼ 46 57¾	Barrow T	118		8.60e	85-13	Tompion1184John William1183¼Eagle Admiral118½	Evenly	9
20Feb60- 7SA	fst 1 1/16	:223 :461 1:101 1:422	San Felipe H 58k	10 8 63½ 78½ 45½ 23½	Barrow T	120		13.00e	88-13	FlowLine1183½T.V.Lrk120½JohnWllm1211¼	Finished strongly	13
12Feb60- 7SA	fst 1 1/16	:244 :473 1:113 1:422	ⓈCal Br Champ 67k	1 2 1hd 2hd 21½ 32¾	Valenzuela I	118		3.30	89-13	NwPolcy1181½NoblNoor1181¼T.V.Lrk118no	Weakened slightly	5
27Jan60- 7SA	fst 7f	:221 :45 1:093 1:22	San Vicente H 23k	7 3 61¼ 52½ 43½ 31	Longden J	120		8.70	92-13	JohnWilliam114½NewPolicy120½T.V.Lrk1201½	Gained ground	9
14Jan60- 7SA	sly 6½f	:222 :451 1:093 1:154	San Miguel 22k	5 2 2hd 2hd 23 34¾	Longden J	126		2.80	94-14	NewPolicy118nkTompion1264½T.V.Lark126hd	Held on gamely	5
6Jan60- 6SA	fst 6f	:223 :46 1:101	Alw 10000	2 4 31½ 42½ 3½ 1nk	Longden J	124		5.50	93-13	T.V. Lark124nkWarfare1241½Tompion120¾	Up final strides	8
26Dec59- 7SA	fst 7f	:223 :452 1:094 1:224	ⓈCal Breeders' Trial 27k	1 1 3nk 2hd 1hd 1¾	Shoemaker W	118		4.30	89-13	T.V. Lark118¾Noble Noor1183¼Fighting Hodge1181¼	Driving	5
	Previously trained by P.F. Miller											
31Oct59- 7GS	sly 1 1/16	:23 :46 1:10 1:424	Garden State 283k	9 7 77¼ 76½ 79¼ 712	Maese A	122	b	44.70	84-15	Warfare122½BallyAche1224Tompon122hd	Never close to pace	10
24Oct59- 5GS	sly 1 1/16	:233 :481 1:132 1:471	Alw 10000	5 3 2hd 21½ 23 27	Maese A	120	b	10.80	67-23	BourbonPrince1137T.V.Lark120noKeenation1106½	Went well	7
10Oct59- 8Haw	hy 1 1/16	:231 :471 1:132 1:503	Haw Juvenile H 42k	2 2 11 11 22 47	Maese A	120	b	5.80	52-41	JiveMusic114hdTonyGrff1131Ntgo1226	Set early pace,tired	13
29Sep59- 7Haw	hy 6f	:231 :464 1:134	Alw 3200	2 3 2½ 2½ 2hd 2½	Maese A	120	b	*1.30	77-33	GoodJoy116½T.V.Lark12010GrandTotal1132	Wide,sharp try	8
5Sep59- 8AP	fst 6½f	:222 :443 1:092 1:154	Wash Park Futurity 184k	1 7 56½ 610 77 99	Maese A	122		18.90	92-09	Venetian Way119½Bally Ache1193Lurullah119¾	Fell back	12
24Aug59- 8AP	sl 6f	:223 :462 1:114	Prairie State 18k	5 11 69 712 915 914	Maese A	122		6.10	71-26	VenetianWay1164Winonly116¾Lurullh116¾	Forced back early	11
1Aug59- 8AP	gd 6f	:222 :46 1:122	Arl Futurity 212k	2 6 32½ 46½ 45 1nk	Maese A	122		33.00f	82-22	T.V.Lark122nkBallyAche122noLurullh1221¼	Up final stride	20

18Jly59- 7Hol	fst 6f	:214 :444 :571 1:10	Hol Juv Champ 163k	1 10 9 5½ 12 9½ 14 14	13 10	Pederson G	113	32.20	83-11	NobleNoor113½Tompion1161Warfare122nk	Raced far off pace 15
9Jly59- 7Hol	fst 5½f	:221 :444 :57 1:03	©C S Howard H 30k	7 2 1hd 21 3 3½	4 5½	Pederson G	114	5.80	91-09	Warfare114½NwPolicy114¾Hedmstr1142¼	Weakened in drive 9
18Jun59- 7Hol	fst 5f	:22 :45 :57	©Haggin 23k	8 4 3 2½ 3 4½ 4 5½	2 4½	Pederson G	119	10.05	93-14	Psyche'sFirst1224½T.V.Lark119noTompion122nk	Raced wide 8
4Jun59- 7Hol	fst 5f	:221 :453 :573	©Westchester 18k	3 5 5 3¾ 6 3¼ 45	45	Boland W	122	9.85	90-15	BritishRoman122¾NewPolicy122¾Warfar1223½	Even effort 9
4Mar59- 1SA	fst 3f	:22 :332	©Ⓢ Md Sp Wt	6 1 1½	1¾	Longden J	118	*1.20	- -	T.V.Lark118¾Azure'sOrphan118noFay'sNghtOut118no	Driving 14
20Feb59- 1SA	fst 3f	:212 :322	©Ⓢ Md Sp Wt	6 8 3 6½	2 5½	Longden J	118	8.75	- -	Truly Truckle1185½T.V. Lark118½College Boy1185	Good try 14

Tom Rolfe

b. c. 1962, by Ribot (Tenerani)–Pocahontas, by Roman — **Lifetime record: 32 16 5 5 $671,297**

Own.– Powhatan
Br.– R. Guest (Ky)
Tr.– F.Y. Whiteley Jr

11Nov66- 7Lrl	fm 1½Ⓣ	:494 1:142 2:284	3↑ D C Int'l 150k	5 6 7 8½ 8 8½ 7 8½	6 8¾	Shoemaker W	127	4.30	66-18	Behistoun1202½Aniline1271¼Assagai1201	No serious threat 10
29Oct66- 7Lrl	fm *1⅛Ⓣ	1:54	3↑ Alw 6500	5 7 5 5½ 44 2½	1½	Shoemaker W	123	*.30	86-17	TomRolfe123½AlSirat1121FanJet1131½	Bobbled,hard ridden 7
1Oct66- 7Aqu	sly 1¼	:47 1:114 1:373 2:024	3↑ Woodward 112k	2 8 8 9¼ 6 6¼ 58	4 6½	Shoemaker W	126	4.20	77-24	Buckpasser121¾Royal Gunner126¾Buffle1215	Mild bid 9
17Sep66- 8Det	fst 1⅛	:461 1:103 1:373 1:49	3↑ Mich 1⅛ H 114k	1 8 7 7¼ 6 1¼ 31	2 3½	Shoemaker W	127	*.70	92-13	Stanislas1093½TomRolfe1271¾Selari1101½	In close,brushed 11
5Sep66- 7Aqu	fst 1⅛	:474 1:124 1:384 1:521	3↑ Aqueduct H 114k	8 10 10 12 10 8½ 6 11	1nk	Shoemaker W	127	*2.40	75-25	TomRolf127nkPluck114½BgRockCndy110hd	Up in final strides 11
27Aug66- 8AP	fst 1	:224 :442 1:08 1:324	3↑ Was Park H 109k	2 6 7 13 7 9 57	2 3½	Shoemaker W	128	*.50	98-07	BoldBidder1203½TomRolfe128hdTronado117nk	Sluggish start 7
17Aug66- 0AP	fst 7f	:23 :452 1:09 1:21	3↑ Alw 3000	2 2 21 21 1hd	1 1½	Shoemaker W	123	-	100-09	Tom Rolfe1231½Tronado123	With complete authority 2
	Exhibition race run between 5th and 6th races. No wagering										
3Aug66- 8Mth	fst 1	:242 :472 1:111 1:37	3↑ Salvator Mile H 27k	4 6 6 4¾ 6 5½ 5 4¼	1¾	Shoemaker W	126	*.40	88-19	Tom Rolfe126¾Steel Pike113nkTwin Teddy1121	Mild drive 6
23Jly66- 7Mth	fst 6f	:213 :442 1:10	4↑ Alw 6000	3 7 8 11 6 11 5 5¾	2 1¼	Shuk N	119	2.20e	91-17	VagabondPrinc1131¼TomRolf1192½Pollux119nk	Strong finish 9
3Oct65♦ Longchamp(Fr)	gd *1½ⓉRH	2:352	3↑ Prix de l'Arc de Triomphe Stk325000		6 16¾	Shoemaker W	122	8.00		Sea Bird1226Reliance1225Diatome122nk	20
										7th early,4th halfway,weakened 2f out.Anilin 5th	
13Sep65- 8AP	fst 1¼	:48 1:112 1:361 2:003	American Derby 128k	1 2 1½ 1 1½ 1½	1 2½	Shoemaker W	126	*.40	101-09	TomRlfe1262½RoyalGunner1121¾Mr.Pak1123¼	Scored in hand 5
28Aug65- 8AP	fst 1	:232 :453 1:101 1:344	Arl Classic 107k	2 6 6 12 58 3½	1nk	Shoemaker W	124	*.30	95-13	Tom Rolfe124nkRoyal Gunner1183¾Sum Up1181½	Driving 7
7Aug65- 8AP	fst 1⅛	:47 1:104 1:35 1:472	Chicagoan 110k	3 2 25 1½ 12	14	Shoemaker W	123	*.30	99-07	TomRlfe1234Gummo1205PreciousGift11410	Drew out easily 6
17Jly65- 8AP	gd 1	:224 :454 1:111 1:361	Citation H 53k	5 6 6 12 3 2½ 1 1½	1 3½	Shoemaker W	126	*.50	85-16	TmRlfe1263½Mr.Clown110½PassthWord1165	Drew out easily 6
5Jun65- 7Aqu	fst 1½	:473 1:132 2:032 2:282	Belmont 147k	7 4 46 32 2½	2nk	Turcotte R	126	2.05	89-13	Hail to All126nkTom Rolfe1261First Family126¾	Game try 8
15May65- 8Pim	fst 1 3/16	:46 1:103 1:37 1:561	Preakness 180k	6 5 59 5 2¾ 1 1½	1nk	Turcotte R	126	3.60	92-15	TomRlfe126nkDapperDan1264HaltoAll126nk	Long,hard drive 9
1May65- 7CD	fst 1¼	:471 1:114 1:37 2:011	Ky Derby 154k	9 7 54 4 2½ 33	3 2¼	Turcotte R	126	5.60	92-05	Lucky Debonair126nkDapperDan1262TomRolfe1261	Game try 11
24Apr65- 7CD	fst 7f	:224 :46 1:10 1:224	Alw 6000	6 4 6 6½ 3½ 1 1½	1 1¾	Turcotte R	122	2.50	93-13	Tom Rolfe1221¾Native Charger1221¼Narushua1131	In hand 7
10Apr65- 9Lrl	gd 1 1/16	:231 :471 1:131 1:45	Chesapeake 34k	2 8 8 5½ 3 2½ 2½	1¾	Turcotte R	119	*1.20	92-16	TomRlfe119¾IsleofGreece1193RepublcnWy1131½	Mild drive 8
3Apr65- 8Lrl	fst 1	:231 :463 1:122 1:383	Alw 7500	4 7 5 2½ 2hd 1½	11	Ferraro R	121	*1.10	90-16	TomRolfe1211UncleWillieM.1182AppleCore1122½	Mild drive 7
24Mar65- 7Aqu	gd 7f	:223 :453 1:102 1:233	Bay Shore 29k	1 7 7 6¼ 55 49	3 9½	Shoemaker W	120	*1.20	78-24	FlagRaiser1145½TurntoRson1114TomRolf1202	Sluggish start 7
3Mar65- 7Bow	fst 6f	:23 :47 1:122	Alw 6000	7 4 4 3½ 5 5½ 3 1½	1nk	Turcotte R	122	*.40	85-22	TomRolfe122nkIndeedIDo1191¼GreySpot1161¼	Clever score 7
5Oct64- 7Aqu	fst 7f	:224 :46 1:11 1:234	Cowdin 67k	8 5 6 3¾ 62 1hd	1 2½	Turcotte R	114	12.80	87-21	TomRolfe1142½Sadair1241RoyalGunnr1176	Wide into stretch 8
26Sep64- 7Aqu	fst 6½f	:22 :45 1:093 1:16	Futurity 138k	4 5 56 56 4 4½	3 3½	Shoemaker W	122	18.90	96-10	BoldLad1221½NativeCharger1222¼TomRolfe1225½	Late rally 5
12Sep64- 8AP	fst 7f	:223 :452 1:103 1:232	Arl-Wash Futurity 349k	7 12 12 8¾ 11 13 6 11	5 8½	Turcotte R	122	10.50	81-12	Sadair1222½Umbrella Fella1222¾Royal Gunner1222½	Wide 14
26Aug64- 8AP	fst 6½f	:224 :453 1:104 1:171	©Fut Trial 56k	7 8 9 11 8 11 6 6½	44	Turcotte R	114	24.80e	86-15	RoyalGunner116nkI'mNashville1162½UmbrllFll1201¼	Rallied 10
15Aug64- 4AP	fst 6f	:221 :46 1:104	Alw 5000	1 5 3 5½ 36 35	47	Turcotte R	119	3.20	82-14	Hempen1163½Olympia Tiger1163½My Lark111hd	Well up,tired 7
27Jun64- 3Del	fst 5½f	:224 :474 1:064	Alw 4000	6 4 6 2¼ 75 5 2¾	1 1½	Turcotte R	115	*.70	87-17	TomRolfe1151½EvilWeevil1151WazaOurs1151½	Clear at wire 8
13Jun64- 7Del	fst 5½f	:22 :454 1:043	©Christiana 25k	11 10 8 6¾ 57 511	3 5½	Turcotte R	116	5.50e	92-15	Shannon Run116½Time Tested1195Tom Rolfe1163½	Late bid 11
6Jun64- 3Del	fst 5f	:231 :48 1:002	Md Sp Wt	6 4 44 42 2 2½	13	Turcotte R	120	*2.30	87-21	TomRolfe1203ReasonablyFair1201½Amiri1204	Scored easily 8
12May64- 3Pim	fst 5f	:234 :474 1:01	©Md Sp Wt	2 3 5 1¼ 5 11 37	22	Carrozella M	120	*1.40	88-24	ArtTheft1202TomRolfe1201BigRockCandy1204	Closed fast 9
27Apr64- 3Pim	fst 5f	:242 :483 1:013	©Md Sp Wt	11 8 6 3½ 4 7½ 3 4½	3 1¾	Ferraro R	120	*1.70	85-18	Cosimo1201Art Theft120¾Tom Rolfe1202	Finished very fast 11

Top Knight

ch. c. 1966, by Vertex (The Rhymer)–Ran–Tan, by Summer Tan — **Lifetime record: 46 11 6 8 $545,685**

Own.– Ardwin Farm
Br.– Steven B. Wilson (Fla)
Tr.– G.W. Taylor

9Aug75- 8Nar	fst 6f	:222 :453 1:11	3↑ Alw 4800	5 3 42 48 411	5 11½	Lapensee M	120 b	9.00	79-21	El Arish119½Admiral's Notion1098Sadye's Reveler1141		5
4Aug75- 8Nar	fst 5½f	:224 :453 :573 1:041	3↑ Alw 4800	5 7 6 14 6 14½ 7 15	79	Thomason WC	116 b	9.20	92-11	Measurator112cDivorce Trial110hdMore Cricket118½		7
4Jly75- 11Suf	fst 1 70	:23 :462 1:113 1:43	4↑ Alw 7000	4 3 48 5 7½ 5 7¾	45	Greco T	111 b	16.90	80-21	Megotreat1161Brilliant Mist116noAm Siam1224	No threat	8
14Jun75- 7LD	sly 1	:223 :472 1:133 1:421	3↑ Handicap 7500	8 5 5 10 5 12 5 7½	59	Greco T	108 b	12.40	64-26	BarleyLane112nkCountofWinloc123nkHarpyEgl1158	No factor	8
31May75- 8LD	fst 7f	:233 :474 1:14 1:272	3↑ Alw 5000	5 3 5 7½ 67 6 4¼	3 2¾	Greco T5	111 b	*1.60	75-17	DocHoss114nkPunchoutCowboy1092½TopKnight111nk	Rallied	6
24May75- 8LD	fst 7f	:233 :47 1:131 1:261	3↑ Alw 5000	5 4 5 10 6 13 4 10	46	Greco T5	111 b	*1.10	78-21	Megotreat1143Misty Plumage122½Motor Ting1142½	Dull	6
10May75- 7LD	fst 7f	:233 :472 1:132 1:264	3↑ Alw 4800	2 1 33 32 12	17	Greco T5	109 b	5.20	81-26	TpKnight1097EarlyRythm116¾KentuckyTip1191½	Drew clear	9
23Apr75- 8Suf	fst 1 70	:24 :474 1:124 1:44	4↑ Alw 5500	4 4 5 7½ 5 9½ 48	4 7¾	Marchese P	114 b	9.40	72-25	JimmyMcDaniel1222¾TakonII1121¾NygeiaRoad1123¼	No mishap	6
10Mar75- 8Suf	fst 6f	:222 :451 1:103	4↑ Alw 5000	2 7 7 12 7 13 7 11	67	Marchese P	113 b	9.80	81-23	Bobby More1131½Grey Corner119½Spicer Brook1161¼	Outrun	7
20Feb75- 8LD	fst 7f	:251 :50 1:184 1:33	4↑ Alw 3700	3 2 3½ 4 6½ 5 5¾	3½	Marchese P	114 b	*2.00	49-45	MommaPhenie114½Lacewood114noTpKnight114nk	Closed well	6
1Feb75- 8LD	fst 7½f	:222 :483 1:154 1:364	4↑ Alw 3700	4 5 5 13 59 4 6½	3 13	Marchese P	114 b	*1.20	56-33	Harpy Eagle119½Bold Kip11912Top Knight1147	No threat	6
17Jan75- 8LD	fr 7f	:23 :462 1:124 1:263	4↑ Alw 3800	6 2 47 4 14 34	21	Marchese P	114 b	2.00	81-21	Megotreat1221Top Knight114nkBold Kip1152	Gamely	6
7Dec74- 8LD	fst 7½f	:224 :481 1:15 1:37	3↑ Alw 3500	4 5 6 16 7 14 5 8¾	3 3½	Marchese P	114 b	*1.50	65-33	Motor Ting114¾Dennis Beau1142½Top Knight1142¼	Rallied	7
29Nov74- 7LD	fst 5f	:224 :473 1:003	3↑ Alw 3800	5 10 10 10 10 14 9 11	8 5½	Marchese P	114 b	4.70	79-24	Hi Ole Man1131¾ⒹSir Eagle1101½Pooja115½	No factor	10
	Previously owned by Estate of S.B. Wilson											
3Jun73- 9Suf	fst 6f	:221 :443 1:102	3↑ Handicap 9000	3 7 7 7½ 7 10 5 11	45	Capalbo P	114 b	12.90	84-15	ReneDepot1203LatestThing1121¾CashonDelivry113nk	Rallied	7
19May73- 7LD	fst 1	:224 :463 1:114 1:394	3↑ Handicap 7500	2 3 4 5½ 4 7½ 47	5 4½	Martin RJ	115 b	2.10	80-24	ImmediateJoy1121RiskyAlibhai120½RunningBear1241	Tired	7
5May73- 7LD	fst 7½f	:223 :463 1:121 1:33	3↑ Handicap 7500	6 4 21 2hd 1hd	31	Martin RJ	116 b	3.00	87-22	Ahira113¾Running Bear124nkTop Knight1161¼	Weakened	7
28Apr73- 7LD	sly 1	:231 :473 1:123 1:403	3↑ Alw 5000	5 2 2 3½ 24 4 6½	5 22	Martin RJ	116 b	*1.00	59-30	ImmediateJoy114hdMotorTing1148CircusFle1147	Early speed	6
3Mar73- 7Bow	fst 1 1/16	:231 :463 1:104 1:424	3↑ J B Cmpbll H (Div 1)-G2	10 9 9 11 9 11 11 16	11 21	Martin RJ	112 b	13.70	73-16	Vertee1163¾Amber Hawk112½Favorecidian1152½	Far back	12
24Feb73- 7Bow	fst 7f	:231 :46 1:11 1:242	4↑ Alw 10000	7 3 54 56 5 6½	6 2½	Martin RJ	119 b	3.50	80-24	Mister Diz112¾ⒹStomp and Go119hdSunny Lad119¾	Wide	8
10Feb73- 6Bow	fst 1 1/16	:233 :47 1:112 1:431	3↑ Handicap 12000	7 4 3 1½ 2hd 14	1 3½	Martin RJ	113 b	6.80	92-16	TopKnight1133½HighTrapper1072¾JetaBit1072¾	Ridden out	7
27Jan73- 6Bow	sly 1 1/16	:234 :471 1:114 1:434	4↑ Alw 12000	4 3 24 24 25	4 8¼	Martin RJ	114 b	4.00	81-22	Delay1198Festive Mood117nkNative Heir119no	Tired	7
20Jan73- 7Bow	gd 1 1/16	:244 :49 1:141 1:473	4↑ Alw 12000	4 5 2hd 2½ 1½	3 1¾	Martin RJ	119 b	2.60	68-28	EllensReason1191MajstcRod119¾TpKnght1191¼	Drifted wide	9
2Jan73- 6Bow	gd 6f	:223 :461 1:12	3↑ S Maryland H (Div 1) 16k	5 5 59 6 4½ 5 2½	4 2¼	DeSpirito A	114 b	4.40	80-30	Penholder114hdSunny Lad1111Burning On1101½	Evenly	6
2Dec72- 8LD	gd 7f	:24 :481 1:152 1:29	3↑ Alw 4000	6 5 5 13 5 11 4 5½	1 1½	DeSpirito A	116 b	*.30	70-36	Top Knight1161½Mediate122hdEd n Mert1161½	Driving	6
23Nov72- 8LD	fst 7f	:241 :48 1:132 1:263	3↑ Alw 4000	6 3 1 1½ 1 2½ 15	1 9½	DeSpirito A	114 b	*.80	82-23	Top Knight1149½Mediate1222Hard Joe1143	Ridden out	7
10Nov72- 7LD	fst 5f	:223 :464 :592	3↑ Alw 4000	5 3 35 38 36	24	DeSpirito A	114 b	*1.50	86-27	Dream Bar1134Top Knight1142Hannibob1162	Gamely	7
9Jly72- 7Suf	fst 6f	:222 :451 1:102	3↑ Alw 4000	4 5 5 7½ 7 11 8 13	8 9¼	Miller W	114 b	*.40	80-18	GoodProfit1142WindonTid1171½NorthrnPrd1142½	Dull effort	8
2Jly72- 7Suf	fst 6f	:22 :451 1:104	4↑ Alw 4200	2 2 33 2hd 1hd	21	Miller W	115 b	2.10	86-14	Black Pond1191Top Knight1155Funbun Star1121½	Gamely	6
3Jun72- 7Suf	fst 6f	:22 :442 1:10	4↑ Alw 4500	5 7 5 5½ 5 6½ 48	6 10	Carrozella M	112 b	*1.20	81-14	Black Pond122¾Not Boistrous1224½Last Dance1221½	Bled	8
	Previously trained by R. Metcalf											

5Jly69- 8Mth fst 1 1/16 :234 :472 1:111 1:42 Lamplighter H 27k 4 6 69½ 611 67½ 411 Ycaza M 125 b *.90 84-22 AlHattab1244PrimeFool113noMr.Leadr1137 Dull performance 7
17May69- 8Pim fst 1 3/16 :464 1:112 1:37 1:553 Preakness 182k 1 3 44¼ 31 44 48 Ycaza M 126 b 2.90 87-17 Majestic Prince126hdArts and Letters1264Jay Ray1264 8
Bore out start
3May69- 8CD fst 1¼ :48 1:122 1:373 2:014 Ky Derby 155k 1 3 22 45½ 511 513 Ycaza M 126 b 2.30 78-11 MajesticPrince126nkArtsandLetters126½Dike12610 Gave way 8
29Mar69- 9GP fst 1⅛ :482 1:12 1:361 1:482 Florida Derby 121k 1 2 2½ 2hd 13 15 Ycaza M 122 b *1.10 92-13 TopKnight1225ArtsandLetters1222½AlHattab1221 Handily 5
Previously owned by S.B. Wilson
4Mar69- 8Hia fst 1⅛ :462 1:103 1:352 1:474 Flamingo 146k 5 3 32½ 31 2hd 12 Ycaza M 122 b *1.40 96-15 TpKnight1222ArtsandLetters122½BeauBrummel122¾ Driving 12
19Feb69- 8Hia fst 1⅛ :47 1:114 1:363 1:493 Everglades 32k 4 4 43¼ 43½ 34½ 23 Rotz JL 122 b *1.50 84-21 ArtsandLettrs1123TpKnight1222AlHattab119½ Ducked out 12
5Feb69- 8Hia fst 7f :223 :452 1:102 1:224 Bahamas (Div 2) 25k 1 8 69½ 610 32½ 1½ Ycaza M 122 b 2.20 94-14 [D]Top Knight122½Fast Hilarious1173King of the Castle113hd 9
Disqualified and placed third
16Nov68- 8GS fst 1 1/16 :233 :473 1:12 1:443 Garden State 312k 3 6 66¼ 66¼ 45½ 31¾ Ycaza M 122 b *.40 80-20 BeauBrumml1221¾Stretchapoint122noTpKnight1222 Rallied 10
12Oct68- 7Bel fst 1 :23 :46 1:102 1:351 Champagne 170k 2 2 22 1hd 11 13½ Ycaza M 122 b .80 98-14 TpKnight1223½BeauBrumml1221½KngEmprr12220 Mild drive 4
21Sep68- 7Bel fst 6½f :23 :461 1:10 1:161 Futurity 142k 1 6 41½ 31 12 16 Ycaza M 122 b *.60 99-14 Top Knight1226True North122½Never Confuse1223½ Easily 6
24Aug68- 6Sar fst 6½f :23 :453 1:094 1:16 Hopeful 123k 11 4 42 53 2hd 12½ Ycaza M 122 b 2.90 98-06 TopKnight1222½Reviewer1224Bushido1221½ Won going away 11
10Aug68- 2Sar fst 5½f :222 :453 :573 1:034 Alw 7000 4 1 31 1hd 13 16 Ycaza M 119 b *1.90 98-07 Top Knight1196Flagstaff1221½Never Confuse122no Easily 11
27Jly68- 8Mth fst 6f :214 :444 1:102 Sapling 114k 6 10 1013 1014 85¾ 65¾ Gustines H 122 b 3.40 84-15 Reviewer1222Night Invader122noAl Hattab122nk No threat 10
1Jly68- 7Aqu fst 5½f :221 :453 :572 1:031 Tremont 33k 3 3 42½ 31½ 21½ 2no Baeza B 114 b 1.60 97-08 Buck Run114noTop Knight1148Virginia Delegate114¾ Sharp 5
14Jun68- 4Bel sly 5½f :224 :46 :574 1:04 ©Md Sp Wt 8 5 12 13 16 115 Gustines H 122 b *2.70 101-10 TopKnight12215BorninaTrunk1221VirginiaDelgt1222½ Easily 10
3Jun68- 5Mth fst 5f :231 :473 1:00 ©Md Sp Wt 8 11 1010 65¾ 55 22½ Kassen D 118 b 7.80 87-14 Dot Ed's Bluesky1182½Top Knight118hdFunny Business1182½ 12
Gamely

Tosmah

b. f. 1961, by Tim Tam (Tom Fool)–Cosmah, by Cosmic Bomb **Lifetime record: 39 23 6 2 $612,591**

Own.– Briardale Farm
Br.– Eugene Mori (Ky)
Tr.– J.W. Mergler

2Jly66- 8Mth fst 1 1/16 :233 :47 1:112 1:433 3↑ Ⓕ Molly Pitcher H 38k 3 3 31½ 31½ 34½ 68¾ Boulmetis S 127 b *.80 78-15 Discipline117nkStraightDeal1203½Lovejoy1122 Lost action 8
18Jun66- 8AP fst 1 :223 :443 1:081 1:331 3↑ Equipoise Mile H 55k 5 2 22 23 22½ 2¾ Boulmetis S 119 b 4.40 99-11 Hedevar116¾Tosmah1192¼Bold Bidder12410 Wide in rally 11
30May66- 7Aqu fst 1 :221 :44 1:08 1:341 3↑ Metropolitan H 115k 5 5 55 56½ 88 89½ Boulmetis S 121 b 6.60 87-13 Bold Lad1322½Hedevar1132½Tio Viejo115no Never a threat 11
21May66- 8GS fst 6f :22 :453 1:10 3↑ Ⓕ Colonial H 28k 5 8 86¾ 63 2hd 11½ Boulmetis S 125 b *.90 94-18 Tosmah1251½WildNote1161Cohasst114no With something left 8
16Apr66- 8Bow fst 1 1/16 :24 :482 1:123 1:442 3↑ J B Campbell H 114k 5 2 2½ 2hd 2hd 1no Boulmetis S 118 b 9.10 91-20 Tsmh118noJustAbout1161¼Trondo1161¾ Well ridden to prevail 10
9Apr66- 8Bow fst 7f :223 :45 1:102 1:232 3↑ Ⓕ Barbara Fritchie H 59k 10 1 41½ 41½ 3nk 11 Boulmetis S 121 b 4.10 96-14 Tosmah1211Queen Empress1231½Privileged111nk Handily 12
2Mar66- 8Hia fst 1⅛ :47 1:11 1:372 1:502 3↑ Ⓕ Black Helen H 62k 9 7 76½ 64 21½ 31¾ Ussery R 115 b 2.80 81-13 WhataTreat1201¾AlondraII110hdTosmah1151 Hung in drive 11
16Feb66- 8Hia fst 7f :231 :453 1:103 1:231 3↑ Ⓕ Columbiana H 30k 5 4 63½ 53½ 2hd 2½ Ussery R 117 b *1.50 92-17 Gold Digger112½Tosmah1172½Queen Empress1201 Game try 9
8Feb66- 8Hia fst 7f :232 :454 1:101 1:232 4↑ Ⓕ Alw 8000 2 4 1½ 1½ 11½ 2no Boulmetis S 113 b 2.40 92-13 Queen Empress113noTosmah113nkWhat a Treat1193 Game try 7
17Jan66- 9Hia fst 6f :221 :452 1:103 3↑ RylPnciana H (Div 2) 20k 5 7 75¾ 56 611 88¼ Boulmetis S 120 b 2.80 83-18 TimeTested121noBayPhantom1174SkyWonder113no Dull 9
6Nov65- 6GS fst 6f :224 :452 1:10 4↑ Alw 5500 3 3 1hd 1hd 11½ 14 Boulmetis S 119 b *.40 94-21 Tosmh1194Receptiv113¾Communqu1162½ Handy winner 6
16Oct65- 8GS fst 1⅛ :48 1:12 1:371 1:494 3↑ Ⓕ Vineland H 56k 4 1 14 12 1½ 32½ Boulmetis S 122 b 2.00 85-21 Steeple Jill1232Cordially113½Tosmah1221 Weakened late 8
9Oct65- 8Atl fst 7f :222 :45 1:10 1:233 3↑ Ⓕ Parkway H 24k 5 10 911 912 610 57½ Boulmetis S 134 b *1.10 77-13 Juanita1155Mighty Happy1152½Lovejoy114no Dwelt at start 11
27Sep65- 7Aqu fst 1⅛ :463 1:104 1:36 1:491 3↑ Ⓕ Beldame 82k 2 3 31 2hd 52½ 65 Boulmetis S 123 b *1.10 85-19 What a Treat118noSteeple Jill123½Straight Deal1181½ 6
Bumped start,rushed up wide,tired,swerved stretch
20Sep65- 7Aqu fst 1 :223 :444 1:084 1:351 3↑ Ⓕ Maskette H 28k 3 2 2½ 2hd 2hd 1no Boulmetis S 128 b *.80 92-16 Tosmah128noAffectionately1283Straight Deal113½ All out 9
9Sep65- 8Atl fst 7f :222 :451 1:092 1:22 3↑ Ⓕ Alw 4000 4 4 11½ 15 18 19 Boulmetis S 117 b *.40 93-16 Tosmah1179I Deceive1132Road to Romance1173½ Eased up 8
27Jan65- 8Hia fst 7f :232 :46 1:104 1:24 3↑ Ⓕ Columbiana H 31k 8 6 31 22 44½ 65½ Boulmetis S 128 b *.80 83-19 OldHat124¾MiamiMood1111½SteeplJll118½ Gave way stretch 10
31Oct64- 8GS fst 1 1/16 :231 :461 1:10 1:414 Ⓕ Jersey Belle 28k 1 1 12 14 12 11¾ Boulmetis S 124 b *.30 99-14 Tosmah1241¾SteepleJill1148OpenFire112hd Cleverly ridden 7
17Oct64- 8GS sly 1⅛ :472 1:121 1:39 1:523 3↑ Ⓕ Vineland H 57k 2 1 13 14 14 2hd Boulmetis S 126 b *.40 74-32 Tona113hdTosmah1264Star Maggie1152½ Tired under impost 7
12Oct64- 8GS fst 6f :213 :441 1:084 Quaker City H 30k 12 11 95 54 1½ 12¾ Boulmetis S 124 b *1.10 100-04 Tosmah1242¾Reely Beeg115hdVastland1101¾ Ridden out 14
16Sep64- 7Aqu fst 1⅛ :474 1:112 1:361 1:493 3↑ Ⓕ Beldame 80k 2 2 11 16 16 14 Boulmetis S 118 b *.50 93-13 Tosmah1184Miss Cavandish11810Castle Forbes1182½ Easily 5
5Sep64- 7Aqu fst 1 :23 :454 1:103 1:363 3↑ Ⓕ Maskette H 30k 8 2 2½ 2hd 13 16 Boulmetis S 123 b *.75 85-21 Tosmah1236Old Hat1172Snow Scene II1132 Speed in reserve 13
15Aug64- 8AP fst 1⅛ :47 1:11 1:362 1:492 3↑ Ⓕ Matron H 81k 10 2 2hd 13 13 1½ Boulmetis S 117 b *2.40 89-14 Tosmah117½Old Hat116½Nubile111½ Kept to a hard drive 10
8Aug64- 8AP fst 1 :23 :454 1:104 1:361 Arl Classic 114k 5 1 3nk 14 14 12½ Boulmetis S 115 b 7.90 88-19 Tosmah1152½Lt.Stevens118noCloseBy1201¼ Drew out easily 10
25Jly64- 8AP sl 7f :224 :46 1:12 1:244 Warren Wright H 34k 2 6 1hd 1½ 2hd 21¼ Boulmetis S 118 b *1.60 82-24 Cap Size1241¼Tosmah1183Pollux1143½ Set pace,game effort 11
1Jly64- 7Aqu fst 6f :213 :443 1:101 3↑ Ⓕ Liberty Belle H 27k 3 4 2hd 11 13 12 Boulmetis S 120 b *.35 92-17 Tosmah1202Look Ma1101½Lizzie Tish111no Was ridden out 8
24Jun64- 8Mth sly 6f :22 :45 1:102 Ⓕ Miss Woodford 16k 6 1 1hd 12 14 14½ Boulmetis S 121 b *.30 90-20 Tosmah1214½FlaminHat1182Silwall1154 Long lead,galloping 6
17Jun64- 7Mth fst 6f :221 :444 1:091 Ⓕ Alw 7500 6 1 11 12 16 110 Boulmetis S 124 b *.50 96-16 Tosmah12410Redpoll1214Flamin Hat121nk Eased up at end 6
16May64- 7GS fst 6f :214 :443 1:101 3↑ Ⓕ Colonial H 29k 4 7 3nk 11½ 13 11½ Boulmetis S 115 b *1.70 93-18 Tosmah1151½LookMa1103LatinWalk111nk Under a mild drive 11
2May64- 8GS fst 6f :22 :45 1:103 Ⓕ Betsy Ross 29k 6 4 2hd 12½ 11 2½ Boulmetis S 121 b *1.20 90-18 Nilene Wonder116½Tosmah121¾Ironshire1161½ Game effort 11
25Apr64- 6GS fst 6f :222 :452 1:11 Ⓕ Alw 5500 4 4 2hd 1hd 2½ 41½ Boulmetis S 121 b *.40 87-13 Grey Sibling121½Silwall113noRedpoll1211 Used up in lead 7
26Oct63- 8GS fst 1 1/16 :231 :463 1:111 1:452 Ⓕ Gardenia 168k 9 5 1hd 1hd 21½ 86½ Boulmetis S 122 b *1.60 76-14 CastlForbs119hdBlueNorthr119noMssCvndsh119hd Impeded 15
18Oct63- 8GS fst 1 :223 :452 1:10 1:363 Ⓕ Alw 10000 4 1 14 12 1½ 1hd Boulmetis S 119 b *.50 99-16 Tosmah119hdBlueNorther1172¾CastlForbs116¾ Kept to drive 9
5Oct63- 7Aqu fst 1 :222 :444 1:091 1:36 Ⓕ Frizette 119k 3 1 12½ 13 14 11 Boulmetis 119 b *.45 88-13 Tosmah1191Beautiful Day119hdCastle Forbes1192½ Driving 10
25Sep63- 7Aqu fst 7f :22 :442 1:091 1:23 Ⓕ Astarita (Div 2) 22k 8 2 2hd 1½ 16 15 Boulmetis S 119 b *1.40 91-12 Tosmah1195Beautiful Day119hdTeo Pepi1162 Bore in,easily 9
18Sep63- 8Atl sly 6f :223 :462 1:123 Ⓕ Mermaid 17k 9 1 1hd 15 14 110 Boulmetis S 116 b *.40 79-33 Tosmah11610MyCard113¾LaughingJudy1101 Speed in reserve 9
27Aug63- 5Atl fst 6f :221 :452 1:104 Ⓕ Alw 4500 5 2 1½ 14 14 15 Boulmetis S 117 b *.90 88-18 Tsmh1175First Orbit117½Wendy's Watch1194 Won eased up 6
8Aug63- 5Atl fst 6f :222 :454 1:114 Ⓕ Alw 4000 4 6 2½ 14 15 13 Boulmetis S 121 b *.90 83-22 Tosmah1213Cadabra1178Really Trying1171¼ Scored eased up 9
26Jly63- 5Mth fst 5½f :22 :452 1:054 Ⓕ Md Sp Wt 5 4 1hd 11½ 14 13½ Boulmetis S 117 b *1.50 88-14 Tosmah1173½Lovejoy1171½Isaduchess1172 Speed in reserve 9

Vitriolic

b. c. 1965, by Bold Ruler (Nasrullah)–Sarcastic, by Ambiorix **Lifetime record: 21 9 4 2 $453,558**

Own.– O. Phipps
Br.– Ogden Phipps (Ky)
Tr.– E.A. Neloy

30May69- 7Aqu fst 1 :224 :453 1:10 1:34 3↑ Metropolitan H 116k 10 7 99 86½ 79 711½ Baeza B 119 b 3.70 85-22 Arts and Letters1112½Nodouble1293½Promise1191 11
In close,no response
13May69- 7Aqu fst 1 :233 :461 1:103 1:353 3↑ Alw 15000 7 8 75½ 42 13 12 Belmonte E 117 b *1.00 89-15 Vitriolic1172Best Turn1092Virginia Delegate1093 Driving 8
7May69- 6Aqu fst 6f :221 :454 1:102 3↑ Alw 12000 6 6 69 45½ 3½ 12 Belmonte E 119 b 3.50 91-13 Vitriolic1192VelvetFlash1191½Call a Cop1211½ Handy score 8
20Feb69- 8Hia fst 1⅛ :483 1:122 1:372 1:494 4↑ Alw 7000 5 2 42½ 45 35 68½ Baeza B 113 b *1.70 77-19 San Roque1137Futura Bold116noSubpet1171 Finished early 8
4Feb69- 7Hia fst 6f :222 :452 1:094 4↑ Alw 8000 5 7 812 79½ 711 66¼ Baeza B 113 b *1.50 89-17 Advance Party1123More Scents112noAir King II1141½ 8
Finished well,worked extra ¼
25Jan69- 9Hia fst 7f :231 :452 1:10 1:223 4↑ Alw 7500 9 3 75¼ 68 55½ 44½ Baeza B 115 b *1.30 90-16 PalaisdeGlace115hdPerfectTan1173Mr.Brogann1151½ Rallied 10
21Feb68- 8Hia fst 1⅛ :452 1:091 1:351 1:49 Everglades 30k 3 7 718 713 58 43¼ Baeza B 122 b *.60 87-14 ForwrdPass117hdWiseExchang112nkMastrBold1153 Bumped 8
12Feb68- 8Hia fst 7f :224 :45 1:093 1:222 Alw 6500 3 7 78¾ 68 21½ 11 Baeza B 122 b *1.10 97-07 Vitriolic1221Master Bold119nkIron Ruler1193½ Going away 8
4Nov67- 8Lrl gd 1 1/16 :231 :463 1:124 1:451 Pim-Lrl Futurity 180k 4 6 78¾ 65½ 1hd 13 Baeza B 122 b *.60e 91-15 Vitriolic1223T.V.Commercil1222[D]FmlyFun1222½ Mild drive 7
14Oct67- 7Aqu fst 1 :231 :451 1:09 1:343 Champagne 179k 5 5 511 57½ 34½ 12 Baeza B 122 b 1.50 95-11 Vitriolic1222Iron Ruler1224½Captain's Gig1222½ In hand 5
5Oct67- 7Aqu fst 7f :224 :452 1:092 1:213 Cowdin 71k 1 6 52½ 53¼ 32 23 Baeza B 124 b *.80 95-14 Iron Ruler1173Vitriolic1241¾Family Fun1141 No excuse 6

23Sep67- 7Aqu	fst 6½f	:223 :454 1:093 1:154	Futurity 146k	3 6 54½ 55 33½ 23	Baeza B	122	*.70	98-13	Captain'sGig1223Vitriolic122¾ExclusiveNatv1225½	Rallied	6
9Sep67- 8AP	fst 7f	:224 :454 1:112 1:24	Arl Wash Fut (Div 2) 185k	7 8 817 810 1hd 13½	Shoemaker W	122	*1.30	85-22	Vitriolic1223½ExclusvNtv1224½[D]CourtRcss1221	Ridden out	9
30Aug67- 8AP	fst 6½f	:232 :471 1:123 1:184	©Fut Trial (Div 2) 21k	5 9 812 74¾ 21½ 1½	Ussery R	122	*1.70	81-22	Vitriolic122½Frosty Dear1135Royal Cap113nk	Cleverly	9
16Aug67- 7Sar	fst 6f	:221 :45 1:102	Sar Spl 35k	3 7 813 66 42½ 1no	Baeza B	114	5.30	96-08	Vitriolic114noExclusiveNative122nkPappaStev1143	Driving	9
7Aug67- 7Sar	fst 5½f	:221 :45 :571 1:033	Sanford 34k	5 6 57 36 34½ 24	Ussery R	116	2.50	95-15	ExclusiveNative1154Vitriolic116¾ForwardPss12010	Rallied	6
31Jly67- 7Sar	fst 5½f	:222 :453 :574 1:041	Flash 23k	4 4 55 53½ 42 31½	Gustines H	113	3.10	94-12	ForwardPass114noPappaSteve1151½Vitriolc1131	Closed fast	7
22Jly67- 3Aqu	fst 5½f	:222 :46 :582 1:05	©Md Sp Wt	3 4 58 43½ 21 15	Gustines H	122	*.70	88-11	Vitriolic1225ChathamCenter1221½MaterilWtnss112no	Easily	11
17Jly67- 5Aqu	gd 5f	:224 :463 :593	Md Sp Wt	7 8 85½ 77 52¾ 2½	Baeza B	122	*1.50	86-15	NotBoistrous112½Vitriolic122hdArmorBearer1224½	In close	10
27Jun67- 3Aqu	fst 5½f	:222 :462 :59 1:053	©Md Sp Wt	2 11 119½ 98½ 43 31	Belmonte E	122	8.00	84-18	Skookum122½Noted Scholar122½Vitriolic1222½	Closed well	12
13May67- 3Aqu	fst 5f	:224 :464 :592	Md Sp Wt	2 9 98¾ 1014 813 713	Baeza B	122	*2.60	75-16	Ben Ben122nkFavorable Path1222½Count Flip1223	Greenly	10

What a Treat

dkb. f. 1962, by Tudor Minstrel (Owen Tudor)–Rare Treat, by Stymie

Lifetime record: 30 11 5 4 $321,608

Own.– G.D. Widener

Br.– Erdenheim Farms Co (Ky)

Tr.– S.E. Veitch

24Nov66- 7Aqu	fst 1⅛	:473 1:114 1:37 1:493 3↑	ⒻFirenze H 56k	1 4 35 44 44 54½	Rotz JL	118	2.70e	83-21	StraightDeal1182¼Mac'sSparkler113¾BlldNut1121½	No rally	8
5Nov66- 7Aqu	fst 1¼	:481 1:122 1:371 2:022 3↑	ⒻLadies H 56k	2 1 13 1½ 2½ 43	Rotz JL	121	4.40e	83-13	Destro115noStraightDeal1183MissDcky109hd	Tired abruptly	8
26Oct66- 7Aqu	fm 1 1/16 Ⓣ	1:44 3↑	ⒻNew York H (Div 2) 23k	5 6 76¼ 86¼ 53½ 32	Rotz JL	121	*1.10e	84-13	SwingingMood1192ShortFall112noWhataTreat121¾	Rallied	9
7Sep66- 7Aqu	fst 1	:233 :463 1:114 1:374 3↑	ⒻMaskette H 28k	3 3 35 36 714 715	Rotz JL	123	2.90	64-30	SummerScandal1236StraightDeal119noTreachery1112½	Tired	9
22Aug66- 7Sar	sly 1⅛	:471 1:11 1:354 1:484 3↑	ⒻDiana H 28k	7 3 32 45 57½ 513	Rotz JL	124	3.00	88-17	OpenFire11710ReluctantPearl1081¾Mac'sSparkler1131	Tired	8
1Aug66- 8Sar	fm 1 1/16 Ⓣ	1:403 3↑	Alw 8500	9 5 511 23 12 11½	Rotz JL	113	2.80	102-00	What a Treat1131½Sky Wonder1051½Berry II1152½	Forced very wide,driving	10
20Jly66- 7Mth	fst 1 1/16	:233 :474 1:123 1:444 4↑	ⒻAlw 6000	4 4 41½ 31 1hd 32½	Rotz JL	122	1.70	78-19	MissDickey1151½Lovejoy1151WhataTreat1223½	Raced outside	6
27Apr66- 7Aqu	fst 1	:24 :464 1:11 1:354 3↑	ⒻBed o' Roses H 27k	5 2 2½ 2hd 1hd 21½	Rotz JL	126	*1.60e	87-18	StraightDeal1171½WhataTreat1261½QunEmprss123nk	2nd best	7
14Apr66- 7Aqu	fst 6f	:222 :452 1:102 4↑	ⒻAlw 10000	2 7 76 62¾ 2hd 11	Rotz JL	118	*.80	91-17	WhataTrt1181Samarta116noTheonia1163	Going away at end	8
2Mar66- 8Hia	fst 1⅛	:47 1:11 1:372 1:502 3↑	ⒻBlack Helen H 62k	6 4 43 32 11½ 11¾	Rotz JL	120	*1.60e	83-13	WhataTreat1201¾AlondraII110hdTosmh1151	Drew off readily	11
16Feb66- 8Hia	fst 7f	:231 :453 1:103 1:231 3↑	ⒻColumbiana H 30k	8 3 41½ 3½ 3nk 44	Rotz JL	120	2.10	89-17	Gold Digger112½Tosmah1172½QueenEmprss1201	Speed,tired	9
8Feb66- 8Hia	fst 7f	:232 :454 1:101 1:232 4↑	ⒻAlw 8000	6 3 42½ 33 32 3nk	Rotz JL	119	3.90	92-13	Queen Empress113noTosmah113nkWhat a Treat1193	Gaining	7
26Jan66- 9Hia	sly 7f	:23 :454 1:104 1:232 4↑	ⒻAlw 8000	1 6 32 44½ 67¼ 712	Rotz JL	119	*1.60	80-17	Discipline1131¾Silwall1132½Sailor Princess1112	Gave way	8
27Sep65- 7Aqu	fst 1⅛	:463 1:104 1:36 1:491 3↑	ⒻBeldame 82k	3 2 2½ 3nk 11 1no	Rotz JL	118	2.30e	90-19	WhataTreat118noSteepleJill123½StraightDeal1181½	Driving	6
4Sep65- 7Aqu	fst 1⅛	:473 1:122 1:381 1:512	ⒻGazelle H 59k	8 7 56½ 42½ 1½ 1½	Rotz JL	123	*3.50e	79-20	WhataTreat123½Terentia118½Discipline1181½	Strong drive	13
14Aug65- 6Sar	fst 1¼	:471 1:112 1:364 2:033	ⒻAlabama 63k	4 10 106 32 3½ 1nk	Rotz JL	118	*2.80e	90-06	What a Treat118nk[D]Discipline1182Terentia114½	Driving	18
5Aug65- 7Sar	fst 7f	:222 :45 1:094 1:23	ⒻTest (Div 2) 23k	2 6 52¾ 53¾ 43 44	Rotz JL	124	4.30	91-12	Cestrum1121½QnEmprss118½GroundControl1212	No response	9
12Jun65- 7Aqu	fst 1¼	:481 1:121 1:37 2:023	ⒻC C A Oaks 129k	1 4 43½ 21½ 21 22½	Rotz JL	121	3.50	82-14	Marshua1212½WhataTreat1216Terenti1212½	Clearly 2nd best	10
29May65- 7Aqu	sly 1⅛	:482 1:123 1:513	ⒻMother Goose 97k	7 4 42½ 2hd 11 2no	Rotz JL	121	4.50	78-20	Cordially121noWhataTreat1211UpOars1213	Held on gamely	12
15May65- 7Aqu	fst 1	:222 :45 1:101 1:371	ⒻAcorn 58k	8 7 811 56½ 32 43¼	Baeza B	121	*.95	79-20	GroundControl121nkMarshua121noUpOars1213	Bold bid,hung	10
16Apr65- 7Aqu	gd 7f	:232 :47 1:114 1:243	ⒻComely 27k	1 3 2½ 1½ 12 12	Rotz JL	118	*.35	83-23	What a Treat1182Equiria1135Adorable112¾	Easily the best	5
7Apr65- 7Aqu	fst 6f	:222 :46 1:102	ⒻPrioress 27k	1 4 31½ 32 12 16	Rotz JL	121	2.95	91-17	WhataTreat1216Admiring1213Adorabl1216	Going away easily	6
10Feb65- 8Hia	fst 1⅛	:471 1:122 1:39 1:531	ⒻMimosa 35k	4 4 44½ 22 14 11	Rotz JL	112	*.60	69-21	WhataTreat1121VassarGrad1124¾Amerivan1144½	Mild drive	9
27Jan65- 6Hia	fst 6f	:221 :454 1:121	ⒻAlw 4500	6 8 911 811 65¼ 11½	Freed M5	111	*.90	83-19	WhataTreat1111½CanoeBrook116½NativPrincss1162	Cleverly	11
20Jan65- 8Hia	fst 6f	:222 :46 1:113	ⒻJasmine (Div 1) 20k	1 8 63½ 42 32 2½	Rotz JL	112	4.90	85-15	WildNote114½WhataTreat1121¾FourUnits1123	Closed fast	10
29Sep64- 5Aqu	sly 7f	:224 :463 1:113 1:243	ⒻAlw 5500	8 4 31½ 21½ 23 25	Sorrentino M	119	2.60	78-27	Privileged1145WhtaTreat11910Ping1111½	Made game effort	8
12Sep64- 7Aqu	sl 6f	:222 :46 1:13	ⒻMatron 102k	10 6 45½ 48 58½ 55¾	Sorrentino M	119	13.00	72-27	Candalita1191Admiring1192½Gold Digger119nk	No mishap	10
2Sep64- 5Aqu	fst 6f	:223 :463 1:123	ⒻMd Sp Wt	2 3 42½ 44 22½ 1nk	Sorrentino M	119	*1.25	80-23	What a Treat119nkMerispats1195Titania1192½	Driving hard	13
19Aug64- 7Sar	fst 6f	:22 :45 1:104	ⒻAdirondack 24k	2 9 54 46 58½ 58¼	Ruane J	111	12.95	86-13	Candalita1142½QueenEmpress1233Marshu123¾	Off sluggishly	9
5Aug64- 7Sar	fst 5½f	:222 :461 :581 1:044	ⒻSchuylerville 30k	2 5 62¼ 75 45½ 34½	Ruane J	112	12.40	88-13	Marshua1162Candalita1162½What a Treat1121	Mild late bid	12

Return of the Crown

The 1970's

by Jay Hovdey

It couldn't have been the culture. Nothing worth a damn could have come from a world oozing with the evil juju spawned by Vietnam, Watergate, gas lines, and disco. Big, bad hair was everywhere. The attorney general was going to jail. And forget about what passed as fashion. Polyester was the fabric of choice.

The sporting scene was just as much to blame. There were the quaintly anarchic Oakland A's, with their handlebar mustaches and wretched color schemes. Too weird, you say? Then take the fascist Dodgers or the autocratic Yanks, or shift gears completely and lie down with the dull Steelers, saved only by the occasional diving Swann.

These were the 1970's in America. Forgive us those trespasses. If honesty were the only policy, a rational mind would draw a line through the entire decade and pretend it all happened in a bad dream, induced by constant exposure to Bob Hope specials and the Fonz.

But there was a silver lining. There was a saving grace. With very few exceptions, through nearly every month of every year for 10 solid calendars, there was something extraordinary going on in the world of Thoroughbred racing. It was a giddy era of excess and excellence, the likes of which never will be seen again.

Okay, sure, the sixties were swell with that gang of Dr. Fager, Damascus, Buckpasser, and Kelso. And the fifties were worth a swoon or two over Native Dancer, Tom Fool, Swaps, and Nashua. But then came the morning of January 1, 1980, when the survivors of the 1970's awoke with thick tongues, heads throbbing, and still dizzy from the residue of guilty pleasures. A decade was born, a decade had died, and they looked back in wonder at what had just transpired.

"Whoa. What was that?"

It was nothing less than amazing.

The natural world pays very little attention to the artificial confines of the Roman calendar. Just because it was January did not mean that something was on the boil. In fact, the first organic moment of transcendent significance during the decade occurred just past midnight on March 30, 1970, when a chestnut colt by Bold Ruler emerged from the womb of Princequillo's daughter Somethingroyal at The Meadow, owned by Christopher Chenery, near the northern Virginia town of Doswell.

The birth of Secretariat at decade's dawn set the theme. It would require something very special to penetrate the consciousness to follow. Mere champions and run-of-the-mill classic winners need not apply. Older horses had Forego for inspiration. Young fillies could dream of growing up like Ruffian. And if young colts were intimidated by Secretariat's lofty image, they were no less daunted by the public works of Seattle Slew, Affirmed, and Spectacular Bid.

To that end, the artistic climax of the 1970's came on October 6, 1979, when the 4-year-old Affirmed defeated the 3-year-old Spectacular Bid in the Jockey Club Gold Cup at Belmont Park. The race was the perfect summation, as Affirmed handled his younger opponent by three-quarters of a length and then handed him the torch. The decade closed as it had opened, with a chestnut champion leading the way, his white beacon of a star and stripe illuminating the best parts of the game.

Affirmed, thankfully, was allowed to do what Secretariat was not: enhance his reputation beyond his accomplishments as a 3-year-old. The death of Christopher Chenery in January 1973 forced his heirs, led by Penny Chenery Tweedy, to syndicate Secretariat as a stallion in order to pay estate taxes. They were committed to his retirement at the end of the year. As a result, Uncle Sam was paid off, and history was cheated out of a 4-year-old Secretariat roaming the land, raising the bar higher and higher with each indelible stride.

Of course, by the time Secretariat completed his two seasons of 21 starts, 16 wins, three seconds, one third, $1,316,808 in earnings, the 1973 Triple Crown, and Horse of the Year in both 1972 and 1973, it was safe to say that he had nothing left to prove.

The argument was true, but it was also beside the point.

"There was an unwritten guarantee of high drama whenever he sported the blue and white

In a moment etched in time, jockey Ron Turcotte turns to the infield Teletimer to see that Secretariat has shattered the world record for a mile and a half, winning the 1973 Belmont Stakes by 31 lengths in 2:24.

Chenery blocks," wrote Charles Hatton in the 1973 edition of *The American Racing Manual.*

The Nielson ratings of Secretariat's 1973 Kentucky Derby – accomplished in a race-record 1:59⅖ by 2½ lengths over the relentless Sham – was a 16.5. The Preakness earned a 14.9, and Secretariat rewarded his loyal viewers with a move on the first turn that redefined explosive Thoroughbred power. For the Belmont, as Secretariat attempted to become the first Triple Crown winner since Citation in 1948, the ratings jumped to 17.5, representing more than 11 million homes.

Each giddy, festive atmosphere of a Secretariat appearance was laced with the tensions surrounding an animal who had been syndicated for a world-record amount of $6,080,000 at the beginning of his 3-year-old season. When Secretariat ran, *Time, Newsweek,* and *Sports Illustrated* paid serious attention, as they did with cover stories the week before he went forth to win the Belmont Stakes by 31 lengths.

The date was June 9, 1973, a bright spring day on Long Island, when Secretariat utterly justified every superlative ever hurled his way, every gallon of ink spilled in his praise, every roll of newsprint that recorded his story. He ran his first of 12 furlongs in 12⅕ seconds, accompanied by his shadow, Sham. They ran the next furlong in 11⅗, banking around the long Belmont turn. After a half-mile in 46⅕ – insane by all standards – Sham was done and Secretariat was in a race of his own.

By the time the Big Horse was over a dozen lengths clear around the final turn, the mellow tenor of Belmont announcer Chic Anderson had reached a fevered aria pitch. "He is moving like a tremendous machine!" Anderson proclaimed, unable to hide his glee. The machine continued unabated, a runaway train, and did not stop until Ron Turcotte stood in the irons to admire the final time on the infield tote board: a mile and one-half in 2:24, a world record on dirt.

It may be hard to believe, but there was no anticlimax to Secretariat. The end of his time on stage was marked by two surprising defeats – in the Whitney Stakes at Saratoga (he had a temperature) and the Woodward Stakes at Belmont (he was undertrained). But those blips retreated under the bright glare of his victory in the inaugural Marlboro Cup over his accomplished stablemate, Riva Ridge. And they disappeared completely when Secretariat concluded his career by racing on the grass and winning both the Man o' War Stakes at Belmont and then, as a tribute to trainer Lucien Laurin's homeland, the Canadian International Championship at Woodbine in Toronto.

As the Secretariat story rose and crested, the greatest sportswriters of the age weighed in. There was Red Smith, Jim Murray, Hatton, of course, and Bill Nack, whose biography, *Big Red of Meadow Stable,* told the tale from foal to finish.

Writing in *Newsweek* magazine, as Secretariat stood on the threshold of his Triple Crown, Pete Axthelm captured both the moment and the meaning in a simple handful of words: "If there is urgency in every 26-foot stride that Secretariat takes," Axthelm wrote, "there is also a rich, meandering history behind him; it is a tale of hope and vision, painstaking work and superb performance under pressure – all the elements that contribute to the fascination and beauty of the sport of racing."

In the wake of Secretariat's retirement, the game was threatened with a dire letdown. It could have been 1965 all over again, when the five-year reign of Kelso ended with a dull thud, and nothing of consequence emerged to fill the void.

But then, toward the end of 1973, a giant gelding won both the Roamer and Discovery Handicaps at Aqueduct. At the beginning of 1974, he took the Donn, the Gulfstream Park, and the Widener Handicaps in a sunny procession. A white puff of smoke appeared from the rooftop of the game. The line of succession would hold.

Forego was from the outstanding 1970 crop of 24,361 North American foals registered by The Jockey Club. In addition to Secretariat, Sham, and Forego, they grew up to be Dahlia (champion grass horse of 1975), Desert Vixen (champion 3-year-old filly of 1973 and older female of 1974), Cafe Prince (champion steeplechase horse of 1977 and '78), Shecky Greene (champion sprinter as a 3-year-old in

1973), Allez France (European champion and winner of the Prix de l'Arc de Triomphe), Ancient Title (winner of the Hollywood Gold Cup, the Whitney Handicap, and 18 other stakes), and Mr. Prospector, who enhanced his brief, brilliant career on the track by leaving an everlasting mark as a stallion.

Born on April 30, 1970, at Claiborne Farm in Kentucky, Forego was the son of the Argentine superstar Forli and the 12-year-old mare Lady Golconda, a daughter of 1954 Preakness Stakes winner Hasty Road. To stem the tide of his inordinate growth, he was gelded; and good thing, too, because his chronically troubled left front ankle was not designed to hold up under Forego's tremendous size. How big was he? In the fall of 1974, William H. Rudy of *The Blood-Horse* asked Dr. Manuel Gilman of the New York Racing Association to compare the dimensions of Forego and Secretariat.

"I can't compare him to anything," Gilman said of Forego. "No other good horse that I've ever seen has such measurements."

According to Gilman, Forego girthed 77 inches. Secretariat girthed 76. From his withers to the point

Three-time Horse of the Year Forego won Grade 1 races from 7 furlongs to 1½ miles. The oversized gelding was a champion at 7 despite numerous nagging injuries, and retired in 1978 as the second-leading money earner of all time.

of the shoulder, Forego was 31 inches, while Secretariat was 28½. In terms of length, from point of shoulder to buttocks, Gilman's tape stretched 74 inches – more than six feet! Secretariat was 69½ inches. And on the scale, Forego weighed 1,225 pounds. Secretariat, at the end of his career, weighed 1,154.

Of course, size does not matter in a racehorse unless he can pick it up and move it quickly. Though he was slow to assemble his act at age 3, Forego eventually flourished into a versatile entertainer, winning major races at 7, 8, 8½, 9, 9½, 10, and 12 furlongs. Between his victory in the Donn at the beginning of 1974 at Gulfstream Park, through the Marlboro Cup on October 2, 1976, at Belmont Park, Forego raced 30 times. He won 20, finished second four times, third four times, and fourth in the other two. There were 24 handicaps during that stretch; Forego's average assignment was 131 pounds. Of the eight handicaps he lost, he conceded 24, 22, 20, and 15 pounds to four of the horses who beat him.

Accordingly, Forego was voted Horse of the Year in 1974, 1975, and 1976. In 40 years of keeping track, only Kelso was honored more than twice. The comparisons were predictable and received with modesty by Martha Gerry, Forego's owner, and Sherrill Ward, who trained the champion during his first three campaigns.

"I don't say he's a better horse than Secretariat or Man o' War or Citation," Ward told writer Ed Comerford for *The Horseman's Journal* at the end of the 1975 season. "I can't say he's as good a gelding as Kelso, because he hasn't had the length of time to express that. But outside of Kelso, I'd measure him up to any gelding that I ever saw. I have to wonder what he would have been if he'd been sound."

Forego's unsoundness was legendary, and well documented. The enlarged sesamoid on the outside of his front left ankle created problems both fore and aft. In early 1975 he was temporarily stopped by a filling in his right hind ankle. Toward the end of 1975 the left hind flared up, but he raced on, winning the Woodward Stakes over champion Wajima and Belmont Stakes winner Avatar. Not

Nearly coal-black and more physically imposing than most colts, Ruffian was peerless and unrelenting on the racetrack.

long after that race, the left front ankle filled. His season was finished.

Ward retired at the end of 1975, suffering from a bad heart and an arthritic hip. Eddie Hayward, the trainer who beat Native Dancer with Dark Star in the 1953 Kentucky Derby, had been helping Ward with the stable. But Mrs. Gerry decided to place Forego and the rest of her small string in the hands of Frank Whiteley, the man who had trained Damascus, Tom Rolfe, and Ruffian.

Getting Forego was a mixed blessing. Whiteley could hardly do better than Ward, but he could certainly do worse.

"I just got hardheaded and thought I'd give it a try," Whiteley said. "I had nothing to lose. But when I got him he didn't have but one sound leg."

Somehow, Whiteley held Forego together through another 2½ years, 17 starts, and 11 wins. How did he do it?

"The grace of the good Lord and three hours a day on that hose," Whiteley said.

Without a doubt, Forego's best race during the Whiteley years was the 1976 Marlboro Cup, in which he carried 137 pounds on a sloppy, slippery Belmont main track before getting up to beat Honest Pleasure, winner of the '76 Travers and champion 2-year-old colt of 1975. The margin was a very short head.

There was another race, however, that defined the impact of Forego in equally vivid terms. It was an unassuming seven-furlong allowance race designed to comfortably launch his 1977 season on May 23 at Belmont Park. Of course, he won. Bill Shoemaker was riding Forego by then, and he remembered the moment in an interview with William Leggett of *Sports Illustrated*.

"There was no betting allowed at the track that day because of a mutuel clerks' strike," Shoemaker said. "But 7,500 people showed up. It seemed everyone was down by the walking ring before the race looking at Forego. The clapping was tremendous. They just seemed to want to say thanks for all the great races he's given them."

By the summer of 1978, Forego had developed ringbone in his right hind ankle. After watching her champion beat one horse in the Suburban Handicap on July 4 at Belmont, Mrs. Gerry announced his retirement. And while his earnings of $1,938,957 fell just short of Kelso's all-time mark, on the day he retired, Forego would have won in a close ballot for the title of America's greatest gelding, with additional apologies to Old Rosebud, Exterminator, and Armed.

■ ■ ■

As the Forego saga unfolded, a filly appeared in a parallel universe.

When Ruffian was first displayed for public consideration on May 22, 1974, her purpose on this earth quickly became apparent. She was meant to reveal, once and for all, how big, how beautiful, and how fast a Thoroughbred racehorse could be, and how the combination could be deadly when taken to Ruffian's physical extremes.

The daughter of Reviewer was nearly coal black and larger than most colts. The source of her power was obvious, emanating from large hindquarters, an Olympian reach, and a chest that housed two huge, fuel-injected lungs. Her speed, however, came from a pure, natural-born action of such honeyed grace that she made even the violence of racing seem balletic and civilized.

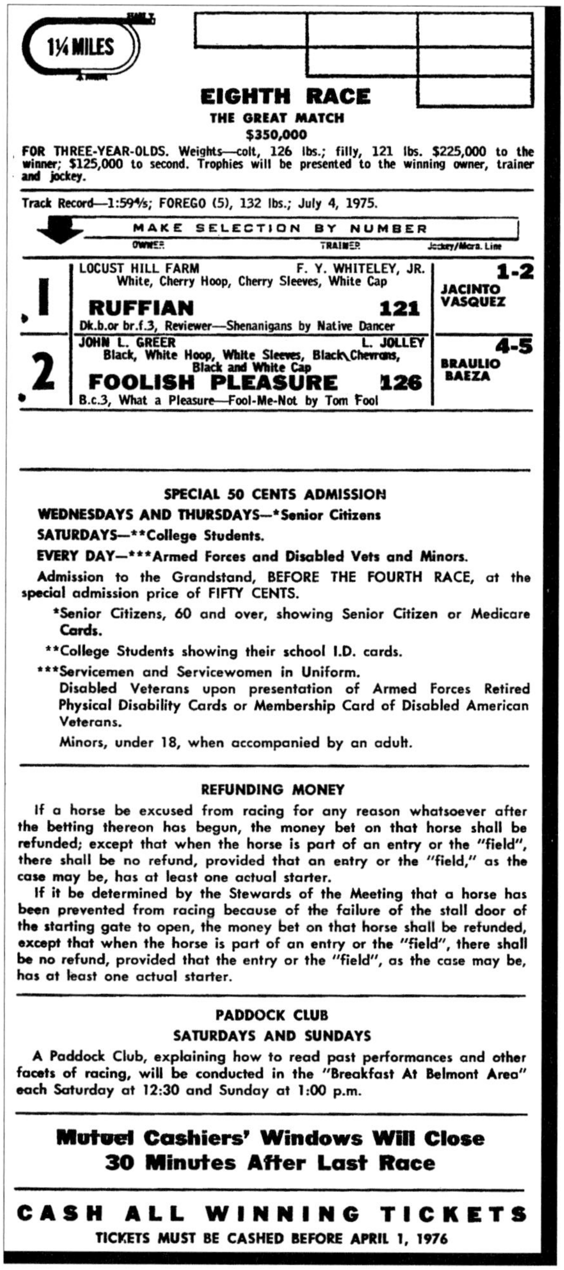

1¼ MILES

EIGHTH RACE

THE GREAT MATCH

$350,000

FOR THREE-YEAR-OLDS. Weights—colt, 126 lbs.; filly, 121 lbs. $225,000 to the winner; $125,000 to second. Trophies will be presented to the winning owner, trainer and jockey.

Track Record—1:59⅘s; FOREGO (5), 132 lbs.; July 4, 1975.

MAKE SELECTION BY NUMBER

	OWNER	TRAINER	Jockey/Mcra. Line
1	LOCUST HILL FARM White, Cherry Hoop, Cherry Sleeves, White Cap **RUFFIAN** 121 Dk.b.or br.f.3, Reviewer—Shenanigans by Native Dancer	F. Y. WHITELEY, JR.	1-2 JACINTO VASQUEZ
2	JOHN L. GREER Black, White Hoop, White Sleeves, Black Chevrons, Black and White Cap **FOOLISH PLEASURE** 126 B.c.3, What a Pleasure—Fool-Me-Not by Tom Fool	L. JOLLEY	4-5 BRAULIO BAEZA

SPECIAL 50 CENTS ADMISSION

WEDNESDAYS AND THURSDAYS—*Senior Citizens

SATURDAYS—**College Students.

EVERY DAY—***Armed Forces and Disabled Vets and Minors.

Admission to the Grandstand, BEFORE THE FOURTH RACE, at the special admission price of FIFTY CENTS.

*Senior Citizens, 60 and over, showing Senior Citizen or Medicare Cards.

**College Students showing their school I.D. cards.

***Servicemen and Servicewomen in Uniform.
Disabled Veterans upon presentation of Armed Forces Retired Physical Disability Cards or Membership Card of Disabled American Veterans.
Minors, under 18, when accompanied by an adult.

REFUNDING MONEY

If a horse be excused from racing for any reason whatsoever after the betting thereon has begun, the money bet on that horse shall be refunded; except that when the horse is part of an entry or the "field", there shall be no refund, provided that an entry or the "field," as the case may be, has at least one actual starter.

If it be determined by the Stewards of the Meeting that a horse has been prevented from racing because of the failure of the stall door of the starting gate to open, the money bet on that horse shall be refunded, except that when the horse is part of an entry or the "field", there shall be no refund, provided that the entry or the "field", as the case may be, has at least one actual starter.

PADDOCK CLUB

SATURDAYS AND SUNDAYS

A Paddock Club, explaining how to read past performances and other facets of racing, will be conducted in the "Breakfast At Belmont Area" each Saturday at 12:30 and Sunday at 1:00 p.m.

Mutuel Cashiers' Windows Will Close 30 Minutes After Last Race

CASH ALL WINNING TICKETS

TICKETS MUST BE CASHED BEFORE APRIL 1, 1976

The Great Match Race between Ruffian and Kentucky Derby winner Foolish Pleasure was a spectacle replete with campaign-style buttons for the filly and the colt.

During 1974, Ruffian sliced through her 2-year-old filly rivals with merciless ease. It was five starts, five wins, and the only horse who was within earshot at the end of a race was Hot n Nasty, Dan Lasater's little flash, in the Sorority Stakes at Monmouth Park. Ruffian won the Spinaway Stakes at Saratoga by nearly 13 lengths, and she was preparing for the same type of assault on the September 26 Frizette Stakes when a hairline fracture was detected in her right hind leg. Were it not for Forego, Ruffian might have been the 1974 Horse of the Year.

In 1975, Ruffian picked up where she left off for trainer Frank Whiteley and the Locust Hill Farm of Mr. and Mrs. Stuart Janney. After an allowance win at Aqueduct in April, she won the Comely Stakes and the Acorn Stakes, then the Mother Goose and the Coaching Club American Oaks. There was really nothing left for her to do, at least among her own age and sex.

Then came the match race with Kentucky Derby winner Foolish Pleasure on July 6, 1975, an event partly inspired by the corny hype over the Billie Jean King-Bobby Riggs "Battle of the Sexes" in tennis, not to mention the nascent movement for women's rights and the success of Virginia Slims cigarettes ("You've come a long way, baby").

On July 4, at the start of that unforgettable holiday weekend, Forego carried 132 pounds to win the Brooklyn Handicap at a mile and one-quarter in a Belmont track record of 1:59⅘. Then the old champ stepped aside to make way for the match, which by then had become a media phenomenon, complete with campaign buttons, a network broadcast, and a Belmont Park crowd of 50,764.

Amid all this, there was still a testing 1¼-mile race to run. Leading up to the match, Foolish Pleasure was trained for speed by LeRoy Jolley. The tough little colt responded by seizing the lead at the start. Ruffian reacted almost too quickly to the challenge. She ducked inward slightly, straightened her course, and then rushed up to thrust her head in front. They went the first quarter, brushing against each other, in 22⅕ seconds.

The mad pace continued into the second quarter-mile, with the filly on the inside. It was at about the three-furlong mark that her right front ankle gave way, shattering the sesamoids and rupturing the supporting soft tissue structure of tendons and ligaments. By the time her jockey, Jacinto Vasquez, could get reined to a stop, she had driven the tip of the splintered cannon bone into the sandy Belmont ground.

The Ogden Phipps-owned Numbered Account was freakishly fast as a 2-year-old, easily winning the division title in 1971.

Ruffian died as she had lived, wild-eyed and slave to no man. She survived the surgery, but in thrashing around during postoperative recovery she ripped loose the cast on her lower leg and spoiled the work of the surgeons. In later years, there would be recovery systems that might have saved her. History is full of such regrets. It was early on the morning of July 7 that Stuart Janney told the attending veterinarians that the great filly should suffer no more. Ruffian was euthanized, and with her a corner of racing was darkened forever.

Ruffian rendered the decade's other champion 3-year-old fillies pale and wan. Those who came before were quickly forgotten. Those who came after could never hope to meet such expectations. Still, they tried.

Office Queen, the champion 3-year-old filly of 1970, started 19 times that year, earning her title for persistence as much as for her victories in the Black-Eyed Susan and Mother Goose. The daughter of Fair Ruler cost just $8,500 as a 2-year-old, and she is usually lost in the shuffle, barely a scene-setter for a procession of vibrant divisional champs that included Turkish Trousers (1971), Susan's Girl (1972), Desert Vixen (1973), and Chris Evert (1974) before Ruffian.

Revidere, coming along in 1976, was certainly no slouch, and there was something comforting in the fact that she was by Reviewer and trained by Frank Whiteley's son, David.

Yet Revidere was very much her own filly. She was a tall, lanky chestnut whose debut was delayed until the spring of her 3-year-old season by growth spurts and tender ankles. Wasting no time, she promptly won her first seven starts before finishing second to that year's older female champion, Proud Delta, in the Beldame Stakes.

Revidere's next race was her best. And, for those who like their racing laced with sweet irony, it occurred in the first running of the Ruffian Stakes at Belmont Park on October 9, 1976. Revidere won by 14 lengths with Jacinto Vasquez in the saddle.

For the remainder of the decade, the 3-year-old scene was colored primarily in the devil's-red and blue of Calumet Farm and the fawn brown of the Galbreath family's Darby Dan Farm.

Calumet's Our Mims, a daughter of Herbager, won all the right races for trainer John Veitch in 1977, taking the Fantasy Stakes, the Coaching Club American Oaks, the Alabama Stakes, and finally the Delaware Handicap by a nose over the older filly Mississippi Mud. She outpolled Darby Dan's Cum Laude Laurie, who beat older mares in the fall but lost twice to Our Mims.

Calumet took a brief intermission in 1978 while Tempest Queen took charge for Darby Dan and trainer Lou Rondinello. The daughter of Graustark raced 13 times, from January to October, and clinched the championship by beating her elders in the Spinster Stakes at Keeneland.

Two days after Tempest Queen won the Spinster, John Veitch unveiled a 2-year-old Calumet filly named Davona Dale in a maiden race at Belmont Park. Over the next nine months the daughter of Best Turn established herself as the breakaway leader of the division, winning 8 of her first 10 starts, including the Kentucky Oaks, the Black-Eyed Susan, and the trio of major springtime races for 3-year-old fillies in New York – the Acorn, Mother Goose, and Coaching Club American Oaks.

The specter of Ruffian hung over the 2-year-old filly division as well as the 3-year-olds. As good as they were, none could ever hope to match her blinding speed and raw power.

Of the 2-year-old filly champions who came before Ruffian, Forward Gal (1970) won 7 of 13 starts, Numbered Account (1971) was the fastest by far, and the Canadian La Prevoyante (1972) was a national heroine. All three of them won the Frizette at Belmont Park. Talking Picture (1973) lost the Frizette, but by then she was already the queen of Saratoga, having become the first to sweep the Schuylerville, Adirondack, and Spinaway Stakes at the upstate New York track.

Dearly Precious, by Dr. Fager, did her best to follow Ruffian's example by winning eight straight races and the championship in 1975. Sensational started quietly for trainer Woody Stephens in 1976, then came on like a champ to win the Frizette and the Selima Stakes at the end of the season. To her credit, Sensational did not wear out until she had made 44 starts over three full campaigns.

Lakeville Miss could have been claimed for $25,000 at Belmont in June 1977, but there were no takers. Safely back home in the stable of Jose Martin, the big, rawboned filly got the message and developed into a monster, eventually running off four straight major stakes at the end of the year to take the championship.

The decade ended democratically for the best of the 2-year-old fillies. Candy Eclair, a graceful gray daughter of Northern Jove, dominated so-so company on the mid-Atlantic circuit in a perfect 1978 season of five starts. Eclipse Award voters allowed her a share of the championship with It's in the Air, a daughter of Mr. Prospector who had five wins and three seconds in eight starts, with stakes victories in Chicago and Los Angeles. There was a suspicion, however, that the best of the bunch might have been the Secretariat filly Terlingua, who defeated males in California and won more money than either of the co-champions.

Smart Angle did nearly everything right in 1979, winning 6 of 9 starts and the Spinaway, Matron, Frizette, and Selima Stakes along the way for Woody Stephens. Waiting in the wings, however, were her undefeated classmates, Genuine Risk and Bold 'n Determined, both poised to take the generation into a new decade.

There were certain races in the 1970's that spoke for the entire era. They were contests of immediate consequence and lasting significance. The memory cheats, plays tricks, and teases with time, but the following events were foolproof:

San Juan Capistrano Handicap, April 4, 1970, at Santa Anita Park

Fort Marcy straddled the decades like that grumpy old man who never left the neighborhood. He was there in the 1960's, defeating Damascus in a thriller at the 1967 Washington, D.C., International, and he was still there at the dawn of the 1970's, winning his second grass championship and his first and only title as Horse of the Year.

Although he was once offered for $77,000 in a paddock sale, by the age of 6 in 1970 Fort Marcy had become an indispensable mercenary. There was nowhere he would not ship for trainer Elliott Burch to carry the colors of his owner and breeder, Paul Mellon. As the 1970 season began, the gelded son of Amerigo had started 54 times at 10 different tracks. His best was yet to come.

Fort Marcy's Horse of the Year campaign started in balmy Florida, detoured through a snowy New York spring, and concluded on a damp autumn afternoon at Laurel when he won his second D.C. International to wrap up the year on three straight major wins. He was playing in a tough division, too, full of old pros and fellow travelers, among them Hitchcock, Red Reality, Vent du Nord, and the great filly Drumtop. And to win the ultimate honor, he had to outpoll the Preakness winner, Personality, whose 18 starts for the Hirsch Jacobs family also included victories in the Woodward Stakes, Jersey Derby, Jim Dandy, and Wood Memorial.

Out west, where Fort Marcy appreciated the firm Southern California ground, the competition was just as rough. All the heavy hitters were present and accounted for in the 1970 San Juan Capistrano, and the result may have been the best grass race of the entire decade.

At the end of the 1¾ miles, Fiddle Isle, under 125 pounds, and Quicken Tree, carrying 124, finished in a dead heat. Fort Marcy, at 124, finished a nose behind those two (it was more like an eyelash), while Hitchcock was only a neck farther back in fourth.

For Fort Marcy, it was one of the best races of a career that finally ended on September 4, 1971, in his 75th start, with 21 wins and earnings of $1,109,791. On that day he finished third in the Kelly-Olympic Handicap at Atlantic City, beaten less than a length by his stablemate Run the Gantlet. Perhaps inspired by such proximity to the old king of the Mellon shed row, Run the Gantlet proceeded to win the United Nations Handicap, the Man o' War Stakes, and the Washington, D.C., International to claim a grass championship of his own.

Match Race, June 17, 1972, at Hollywood Park

It can be argued, without fear of serious contradiction, that the early part of the 1970's produced the century's greatest collection of fillies and mares.

The champions of the era included Shuvee ("massive in all directions," wrote Charles Hatton), twice the winner of the Jockey Club Gold Cup and champion in 1970 and 1971; Numbered Account, a freak at age 2 in 1971 and still one of the best at 3; the petite Chou Croute, the weight-packing sprint champ of 1972 who was dangerous going long; Susan's Girl, the durable three-time champion who retired as the richest member of her sex; Turkish Trousers, so good she did not need to leave California to win her title in 1971; and Desert Vixen, the two-time champ who equaled the Belmont record of 1:46⅕ for nine furlongs in the 1973 Beldame Stakes.

Desert Vixen was upstaged less than an hour later by Secretariat's world-record clocking of 1:45⅗ in the inaugural Marlboro Cup. And while the Marlboro had the effect of rendering the Beldame but a footnote to history, Desert Vixen's victory over a field that included Susan's Girl, Poker Night, Summer Guest, and Convenience was perhaps the finest moment of a career that could brag of 13 wins in 28 starts, including eight in a row in 1973, all by daylight margins.

In terms of sheer depth of quality, the West Coast counterpart to the '73 Beldame was the 1972 Santa Margarita Invitational. Turkish Trousers, the reigning champ of her generation, defeated her fellow 4-year-old Convenience by a head, with the older Typecast just a neck behind in third and Street Dancer a head back in fourth. Manta and Minstrel Miss – both major stakes winners on grass – came home fifth and sixth, certainly no embarrassment under the circumstances.

These mares clawed at each other all through 1972. But the two that emerged at the top were Typecast, a classically constructed daughter of Prince John who was owned by Fletcher Jones, and Convenience, Leonard Lavin's daughter of Fleet Nasrullah who was built like a powerful flying wedge.

Convenience was the speed, Typecast the stayer – even though she had defeated Turkish Trousers at seven furlongs in January 1972. When Convenience beat Typecast by a half-length while getting five pounds in the Vanity Handicap at Hollywood Park on June 3, Jones thought his mare got the worst of the trip and the weights. After a week's worth of negotiations, Jones and Lavin each put up $100,000 (with a $50,000 sweetener from the track) for a nine-furlong match race at level weights on June 17. At a quarter of a million dollars, it was at the time the richest match in history.

Shoemaker rode Typecast for trainer Tommy Doyle, but it was Jerry Lambert and Convenience who carried out the strategy of trainer W. L. Proctor to perfection. They took the lead and then drifted wide, forcing Shoemaker to make his run inside through the stretch with Typecast. Convenience, who battled with a sinus infection in the days before the race, ran with an extended right blinker. With Typecast on the inside, Convenience could not be ambushed. Typecast closed furiously through the last 50 yards, but to no avail. Convenience won by a head.

One week after the match race, Typecast defeated males in Hollywood's Invitational Turf Handicap. She later added the Sunset Handicap and the Man o' War Stakes, also against the boys, to secure honors as the best older female of 1972.

Cougar II, with his high action and distinctive long tail, was a star for trainer Charlie Whittingham on both grass and dirt. His greatest moment on the main track came in his victory in the 1973 Big 'Cap.

Santa Anita Handicap, March 10, 1973, at Santa Anita Park

Charlie Whittingham had so many good older male horses in the 1970's it was almost unfair. There were plenty of times he would saddle two, three, even four horses in major stakes. He liked to say, with a twinkle in his eye and a dash of military flair, "We've got 'em surrounded."

Two of his older boys were champions – Ack Ack and Cougar II – and several others could have been were it not for the presence of their stablemates. In 1970, Whittingham won six grass stakes with Fiddle Isle. In 1971, he won seven races with Ack Ack, ranging from 5½ to 10 furlongs, on both dirt and turf, which was good enough for the Eclipse

Award voters to choose him as their Horse of the Year, best older male, and champion sprinter.

Quack, a big, backward young horse, blossomed by the summer of 1972 to beat his elders in the Hollywood Gold Cup and equaled the world record for 1¼ miles in the process. Kennedy Road also won a Hollywood Gold Cup, plus three other stakes and the honor of Canadian Horse of the Year. And then there was Cougar II, the high-stepping, long-tailed Chilean owned by Mary Jones, who won six stakes in 1971, four in 1972, when he was North American grass champion, and three more stakes in 1973.

For all his zeal on the grass, Cougar's name remains strongly linked to the main track through the 1973 Santa Anita Handicap. He had just turned 7. He had not run since November 11, a period of four months. He would be carrying top weight of 126 pounds and switching to Laffit Pincay Jr., since Bill Shoemaker had broken a bone in his hand that winter.

Whittingham put the miles to Cougar, working him long and hard. "I'd rather run a horse than work 'em, because they can get sour, and you can get one hurt just as easy working as running," Whittingham said. "But I didn't want the racing secretary piling the weight on this horse. The only thing I could do was work him up to the Handicap."

The race played out under gray skies to a crowd of 59,625. Kennedy Road got loose in the stretch and nearly stole the show. But Cougar, knees reaching to the clouds and long tail flying, thrust home to win by a nose, survived a claim of foul for drifting in, and topped the one-two finish for Whittingham.

Kentucky Derby, May 4, 1974, at Churchill Downs

Whitney Tower, witness to a considerable amount of racing history, described the scene of 163,628 people at the 100th Kentucky Derby as something that sounded like a cross between Woodstock and the 1968 Democratic Convention.

Canonero II, the mystery horse and winner of the 1971 Kentucky Derby, drew 82,694 fans to fill cavernous Belmont Park, where he failed in his bid to win the Triple Crown. Not at his physical best, he finished fourth to Pass Catcher in the Belmont Stakes.

"Police were helpless to prevent the mob from breaking through barriers and crowding against the rails," Tower wrote in *Sports Illustrated,* "and an effort to remove an army of stripped-to-the-waist youths from the top of one of the tote boards ended in abashed failure. Bands played, streakers streaked, one of them to the point of such exhaustion that she finished the day by jumping into an infield fountain, and nearly everyone had a good time."

Angel Cordero Jr. and Woody Stephens had a very good time, as it turned out, when the record field of 23 parted like the Red Sea for John Olin's Cannonade to put them forever in the heart of Derby lore. But the centennial Derby was less a legitimate horse race than a gaudy festival of American excess. It was not necessary for Cannonade to do anything else for the rest of his life. He would always be the answer to the question, Who won the 100th Derby?

As it turned out, Cannonade was soon upstaged by Darby Dan Farm's Little Current. The chestnut son of Sea-Bird finished fifth in the rough-and-tumble Derby, coming from far, far back (he actually got the magic "23" in *Daily Racing Form's* first point of call).

In the more sensible 13-horse Preakness field and nine-horse Belmont field, however, Little

Current's powerful stretch kick was unobstructed. He won both races by seven lengths, with Cannonade finishing third in each. Little Current's two legs of the Triple Crown were enough to earn the 3-year-old championship of 1974, despite the fact that he lost his next three races and was retired with a chipped ankle.

The voters were not nearly so kind to Riva Ridge. In 1972, before Secretariat was a household name, Riva Ridge carried the colors of Meadow Stable to victories in the Blue Grass Stakes, Kentucky Derby, and Belmont Stakes and then traveled to California to win the Hollywood Derby under 129 pounds, giving 14 to the runner-up, Bicker.

By the time the Hollywood race was run, the son of First Landing had been a star for a solid year. At age 2 he won 7 of 9 races to be acclaimed champion among males. His first six months of 1972 were every bit as impressive, with the exception of his fourth-place finish on a sloppy track in the Preakness.

In the meantime, Paul Mellon's Key to the Mint overcame an injured stifle during his winter in Florida to finish third in the Preakness and fourth in the Belmont. The son of Graustark then unfurled a remarkable three months, defeating the older Autobiography in the Brooklyn Handicap, the Whitney Handicap, and the Woodward Stakes, and handling the remnants of his 3-year-old peers in the Travers.

Even though Autobiography later put the Mellon colt in his place, winning the Jockey Club Gold Cup by 15 lengths, Key to the Mint's late-season display was enough to erase the memory of Riva Ridge in the minds of the voters.

It should be noted that in Autobiography, Key to the Mint was not facing one of the better older champions of the decade. The son of Sky High II was, however, a horse of some drama. Owned by Sigmund Sommer and trained by Frank "Pancho" Martin, Autobiography started 19 times as a 4-year-old in 1972 at six different tracks. His record included only four outright wins, a dead heat in the San Fernando Stakes at Santa Anita, and a disqualification from victory in the Gallant Fox Handicap at the end of the year. His reputation for durability proved ephemeral, however, when he suffered a fatal breakdown at Santa Anita the following winter.

Canonero II and Bold Forbes injected welcome Latin American flair into the 3-year-old adventures of the 1970's. They both nearly seized the Triple Crown, failed gallantly, and were later rewarded with divisional championships.

Canonero was the mystery horse of 1971, arriving at Churchill Downs with an odd batch of past-performance lines from Venezuela, a couple of losses the previous summer at Del Mar, and connections who were hard-pressed to communicate in English, let alone the local Kentucky patois. So Canonero did all the talking, winning the Derby by 3¾ lengths and then the Preakness by a length and a half. A crowd of 82,694 crammed Belmont Park for a chance to watch Canonero win the Triple Crown, but he was not in the best physical shape for the race and trailed home a sad fourth to Pass Catcher.

Bold Forbes, owned by Esteban Tizol of Puerto Rico and trained by Lazaro Sosa Barrera, led Honest Pleasure and seven others on a wild chase in the 1976 Kentucky Derby to win by a length. In the subsequent Preakness, Honest Pleasure was sent after Bold Forbes from the start. After six furlongs neither colt had much left to resist the finishing kick of Elocutionist, but at least Bold Forbes stuck around for third.

Honest Pleasure wisely stayed home for the Belmont, which gave Bold Forbes and Angel Cordero free rein. While the son of Irish Castle was far from a classic stayer, he had the courage to lead all the way and win by a rapidly diminishing neck in a three-way photo finish with longshots MacKenzie Bridge and Great Contractor.

National Thoroughbred Championship, November 1, 1975, at Santa Anita Park

Forego was supposed to headline the field of major stakes winners gathering at the Oak Tree meet for a $350,000 purse and a juicy spot on network TV. Sadly, Forego's ankles flared up to bring his season to an end.

That left Charlie Whittingham licking his chops. He won the 1¼-mile main-track race with the Argentine mare Dulcia, who closed from last place to beat Royal Glint (winner of the 1976 Santa Anita Handicap), Tizna (two-time winner of the Santa Margarita), and such also-rans as Holding Pattern (the Travers winner), L'Enjoleur (the Queen's Plate winner), Ancient Title (at the peak of his game), and Forceten, who defeated Belmont Stakes winner Avatar in the Swaps Stakes that summer. Allez France, the queen of Europe, also made the race but shipped poorly and finished an uncharacteristic last.

Still, it was a treat for Americans just to see a mare like Allez France under silks. The National Thoroughbred Championship lasted only one more running (Whittingham won it again) and then disappeared. Nine years later the concept was resurrected under a different name, but the inspiration was the same. In 1984, they called it the Breeders' Cup Classic.

Suburban Handicap, July 5, 1976, at Belmont Park

Foolish Pleasure spent the last half of his career living in the shadow of his match race with Ruffian, as if it were his fault.

In fact, the streamlined son of What a Pleasure had been a credit to his generation from the start, when he reeled off nine straight wins and 11 victories in his first 12 races. He was the overwhelming choice as champion 2-year-old of 1974. At age 3 in 1975 he won the Flamingo, the Wood Memorial, and the Kentucky Derby, and suffered second by just a length in the Preakness and by a neck in the Belmont. Furthermore, LeRoy Jolley had him ready to run the race of his life on the day Ruffian broke down.

That same year, Bold Ruler's son Wajima came along late to take the Monmouth Invitational and the Travers, and then shaded Foolish Pleasure by a head in the Governor Stakes at Belmont Park while getting 10 pounds. In the subsequent Marlboro Cup, Foolish Pleasure ran the first bad race of his life and finished a distant fifth. Up ahead, it was Wajima again, this time defeating Forego by a head (while getting 10 pounds). The coffin was nailed shut. Wajima was voted champion 3-year-old over Foolish Pleasure.

As a 4-year-old, Foolish Pleasure won 4 of 8 starts, including the Donn Handicap under 129 pounds. But he was never better than he was for the 1976 Suburban Handicap at Belmont Park.

There were only four in the field for that 90th Suburban. The bad news was obvious. One of them

The pint-sized Ta Wee not only was able to beat males, but also did it carrying a heavy load. The two-time sprint champ won the 1970 Fall Highweight Handicap under 140 pounds.

was Forego, age 6 and fresh from victories in the Metropolitan and the Nassau County Handicaps. Foolish Pleasure got nine pounds from the old champ, 134 to 125. His rider, Eddie Maple, tried to steal away and slow things down. Forego stayed close, though, and so did Lord Rebeau, winner of the Roseben Handicap. They came together at the finish, with Foolish Pleasure obscured on the inside but a nose in front of the mountainous Forego. Between them, in a champion sandwich, Lord Rebeau was a nose behind Forego.

Hollywood Gold Cup, June 18, 1977, at Hollywood Park

Walter Vosburgh, the legendary racing secretary and weight lifter, once got caught saying, "When the fillies can beat the colts, depend upon it – the colts are a bad lot." Of course, he died long before the man-bashers of the 1970's came along.

More appropriate to the spirit of the era was this from Angel Penna Sr., by way of writer Patrick Robinson from *Decade of Champions*: "Most women are a lot braver than most men in terms of pain, which a racehorse endures at the height of battle," Penna said. "They are innately more stoic than we. The secret is to make them want to do their best for you. A great one will not let you down."

Cascapedia was a great one in a grand decade for the success of mares against males. And even though she never beat the colts, she certainly put the fear of God in them. Laffit Pincay had to ride Crystal Water like a demon to edge Don Pierce and Cascapedia by a neck in the 1977 Hollywood Gold Cup. With turf star Caucasus lapped on in third, the Gold Cup was considered the best race of the year.

The daughter of Chieftain, owned by B. J. Ridder, also finished third to Ancient Title in the Del Mar Handicap (ahead of Crystal Water and Pay Tribute) to give her final 1977 record a championship sheen for trainer Gordon Campbell.

Before Cascapedia, Shuvee set the tone for her sisters of the seventies with her twin killing in the Jockey Club Gold Cups of 1970 and '71 – four miles in total. While Shuvee enjoyed long strolls, blink and you missed the best of the female sprinters. They were particularly anti-male, and no less than four of them were champions in open competition:

Ta Wee, a two-time sprint champ, was the rapid yin to Shuvee's slow-burning yang. Nearing the end of her career, she carried 140 pounds to beat Distinctive in the 1970 Fall Highweight Handicap, her second straight win in the Belmont event. She actually picked up two pounds for her next race, the Interborough, and won.

Chou Croute ("sauerkraut" in French, or "inedible cabbage" in English) beat the boys in the 1972 Fall Highweight and the Fayette Handicap en route to her title. When not otherwise occupied, she dusted fillies for fun.

My Juliet, as fast as her old man, Gallant Romeo, won 24 races in 36 starts and the 1976 sprint title. To clinch her championship she beat Bold Forbes wire to wire and on the square in the premier sprint of the New York fall season, the – what's this! – Vosburgh Stakes.

What a Summer picked up where My Juliet left off, winning her 1977 sprint championship by taking the Fall Highweight under 134 pounds. The daughter of What Luck also won in California and nearly bagged the 10-furlong Beldame, losing to Cum Laude Laurie by three-quarters of a length.

Mr. Vosburgh's philosophy was strained further by the exploits of fillies and mares in mixed grass competition during the decade, with the imported Dahlia, Waya, and Trillion leading the way.

Dahlia was a Kentucky-bred daughter of Vaguely Noble, trained by Maurice Zilber and owned by Nelson Bunker Hunt. Author Patrick Robinson called her "a capricious little hussy" who lost far more often than she won. Robinson was fair, however, pointing out that "she tended to make her biggest efforts when the stakes were highest."

Dahlia first descended upon North America as a 3-year-old in 1973 to win the Washington, D.C., International. Back in Europe the following year, she continued to thrash top males like On My Way, Highclere, and Snow Knight (later an American grass champion) in the Coronation Cup, King

Affirmed and Alydar's memorable series of battles reached its zenith in the 1978 Belmont, with Affirmed (inside) desperately getting a head in front at the wire to complete his sweep of the Triple Crown.

George VI and Queen Elizabeth Diamond Stakes, and Benson and Hedges Gold Cup.

In the fall of 1974, Dahlia returned to North America to win the Man o' War Stakes and the Canadian International Championship. She could not be denied the title.

(Two years later, Hunt and Zilber won the North American grass championship again with their 3-year-old colt Youth, a son of Ack Ack who won the Prix du Jockey-Club in France and then crossed the pond to take the Canadian International and Washington, D.C., International.)

Waya, a French filly trained by Angel Penna for Daniel Wildenstein, was arguably the best grass horse of either sex in North America in 1978 when she won the Diana and Flower Bowl Handicaps against mares and the Man o' War and Turf Classic against males. She split two decisions with Mac Diarmida, a 3-year-old colt trained by Scotty Schulhofer who began the year as a maiden and ended up winning the Canadian International and Washington, D.C., International. He was voted champion.

But the Eclipse Award committee felt a pang of guilt. Without admitting it directly, they were thinking of Waya when they created a new category for a female grass champion in 1979.

At the end of 1978, Waya was sold to Peter Brant for $1 million (Wildenstein was, after all, in the business of moving fine art) and went to work for David Whiteley. She never missed a beat, winning two major races on the Santa Anita grass to open the 1979 campaign. After that, Whiteley expanded Waya's horizons to the dirt and was rewarded with four stakes wins, including the Saratoga Cup over the previous year's female champion, Late Bloomer, and assorted males.

By the end of the season, there were championships to go all around. Bowl Game, Greentree Stable's male version of Late Bloomer, got the male grass award after beating Waya 2 out of 3. Trillion, a stalwart of the European scene, finished second in four major North American fall races and was given the female grass title. And Waya herself was honored with the best older filly or mare title, when everyone knew she had been that all along.

Triple Crown winner Seattle Slew (LEFT) *may have given his finest effort in defeat, nearly coming back to beat Exceller in the 1978 Jockey Club Gold Cup despite setting a blistering early pace.*

BELMONT STAKES, JUNE 10, 1978, AT BELMONT PARK

The final plot line of the 1970's began to unspool in June 1977. By the middle of the month, the cast was established and the drama was set in motion. Only the various endings remained in doubt.

On June 2, 1977, over the historic downs at Epsom, England, Nelson Bunker Hunt's Exceller won the Coronation Cup to mark the first victory of his 4-year-old campaign.

On June 11, Seattle Slew won the 109th Belmont Stakes by four lengths to sweep the Triple Crown and remain undefeated in nine starts.

On June 15, also at Belmont Park, a bright chestnut colt named Affirmed won the Youthful Stakes at 5½ furlongs in his second start, with a dark chestnut colt named Alydar finishing fifth making his debut. Alydar had been favored at 9-5.

During the ensuing 12 months, Affirmed and Alydar would face each other eight more times.

The older, more seasoned Affirmed (LEFT) *was not quite ready to abdicate his position as the reigning star of Thoroughbred racing when he met 3-year-old sensation Spectacular Bid* (CENTER) *in the 1979 Jockey Club Gold Cup. In a battle for Horse of the Year, Affirmed defeated his younger rival by three-quarters of a length.*

Each time, the stakes were higher. And each time the two chestnuts came away with a larger piece of the historical pie. Woody Stephens, who tried to beat them with Believe It, called Affirmed and Alydar "the greatest act horse racing has ever had," then added, "I hope it never ends."

Affirmed was bred and owned by Louis and Patrice Wolfson's Harbor View Farm and trained by Lazaro Barrera. Alydar was bred and owned by Admiral and Mrs. Gene Markey's Calumet Farm. He was trained by John Veitch, the son of Hall of Famer Sylvester Veitch.

In their six meetings in 1977, Affirmed beat Alydar four times. Still, the 2-year-old title went right down to the wire in the Laurel Futurity on October 29. They banged away at each other for the last half of the 1⅟₁₆ miles before Affirmed finally won by a neck. Star de Naskra, a fine colt who went on to be sprint champion of 1979, finished 10 lengths behind the feuding chestnuts in third.

The Laurel Futurity was a vivid preview of the 1978 Triple Crown. Affirmed beat Alydar by 1½ lengths in the Kentucky Derby on a day that Alydar protested the texture of the track. Apparently, Pimlico was more to his taste, but the result was the same – Affirmed by a neck. The only thing that stood between Affirmed and the Triple Crown was the mile and one-half of the Belmont Stakes. And Alydar.

Veitch decided to take the blinkers off his colt for the Belmont and told Jorge Velasquez to take the race to Affirmed. Barrera was worried that Affirmed had lost weight, but he was confident his champion could sustain one more round against Alydar. Steve Cauthen, Affirmed's 18-year-old jockey, remained cool and calm in the face of the Triple Crown fuss.

"I knew that Alydar would come up and we would fight it out," Cauthen told William Leggett of *Sports Illustrated*. "I didn't think we'd have to fight it out for a mile, but with Affirmed and Alydar it always seems to turn out that they fight for every inch."

In fact, the Belmont came down to just a few of those precious inches. Locked together, eight red legs churning as if attached to a single desperate beast, Affirmed and Alydar hit the wire as one . . . almost. Alydar ran a better race without those blinkers, but it was Cauthen's surprising left-handed whip applied to Affirmed's side deep in the stretch that might have made the difference. The difference was a head.

Jockey Club Gold Cup, October 14, 1978, at Belmont Park

While Affirmed and Alydar tested each other to the brink and left no lingering questions of their quality, Seattle Slew labored in a comparative vacuum. There was nothing for him to be measured against.

At age 2 in 1976, the son of Bold Reasoning was left dangling without competition in three dazzling starts, climaxed by a 9¾-length win in the Champagne Stakes. Other 2-year-old male champions had more extensive records – Rockhill Native won three major New York stakes in 1979 and was disqualified from a fourth, while Protagonist won the Champagne, the Laurel Futurity, and a division of the Cowdin in 1973 – but few had Seattle Slew's knack for the dramatic.

Indeed, if he had an antecedent, it was Hoist the Flag, the 2-year-old male champ of 1970. Under the guidance of Sid Watters, Hoist the Flag ran four times between September 11 and October 10 and finished first by daylight on each occasion, although he lost the Champagne Stakes in the stewards' stand. Voters ignored the decision.

Hoist the Flag fractured an ankle after winning his first two races at age 3. Thank goodness, Seattle Slew remained sound through his memorable Triple Crown, which turned out to be a textbook piece of training by the young William Turner Jr. in his first crack at the classics. Ridden by Jean Cruguet, Seattle Slew won the Derby by 1¾ lengths after a flat-footed start, then took the Preakness by a geared-down length and a quarter before his coronation in the Belmont. He was the first horse to emerge undefeated from the Triple Crown.

Events off the track were almost as interesting as on, given the cast of characters that included Washington lumberman Mickey Taylor; his wife, Karen; and Jim and Sally Hill of New York and Kentucky. Jim Hill was a practicing racetrack vet.

Hill's hidden ownership got the "Slew Crew" in dutch later on, when both Dr. Hill and Seattle Slew were barred from racing for six months at the end of 1977. At that point it was moot, since Seattle Slew had been put away for the year after his first defeat, a fourth-place finish to J.O. Tobin in the Swaps Stakes at Hollywood Park. At the end of 1977, Turner was fired and Doug Peterson was hired to train Seattle Slew at age 4. But before he had the pleasure of saddling the champion, Peterson had to nurse the tempestuous colt through a viral infection and high fever that nearly spelled the end of the fairy tale.

Seattle Slew returned in May 1978 with a cautious win in allowance company (among the beaten that day was Gallant Bob, the nearly forgotten sprint champion of 1975). Seattle Slew was given another soft allowance spot in August, after which he was tested in the Paterson Handicap at The Meadowlands. His narrow loss to Dr. Patches looked better down the road, when Dr. Patches was accorded a share of the 1978 sprint championship with the same J.O. Tobin who had beaten Seattle Slew in the Swaps.

In the meantime, Exceller had long since ended his stellar European career and was a full-fledged member of Charlie Whittingham's California stable. He won five stakes out west, including the Hollywood Gold Cup over Santa Anita Handicap winner Vigors. Whittingham thought he had the Horse of the Year in the making, so he packed up Exceller and Bill Shoemaker and took the show on the road.

Seattle Slew proved he was back in top form by dusting off the younger Affirmed in the Marlboro Cup on September 16, just 11 days after the Paterson. It was the first time two Triple Crown winners had met. Two weeks later, Seattle Slew was introduced to Exceller in the Woodward Stakes and paid him very little mind, winning by four while controlling all the pace.

The deciding race would be the Jockey Club

Gold Cup on October 14: Affirmed, Seattle Slew, and Exceller for all the marbles. It was a testing mile and a half, played out in mud and cold rain. Seattle Slew set off with the lead, but he was surprisingly joined by Affirmed, who was out of Cauthen's control. It was the wrong day for the saddle to slip.

Affirmed did not last long, but he pressed Seattle Slew hard enough to give Shoemaker hope. Starting from far back, smeared with Belmont mud, Shoemaker and Exceller began to eat into Seattle Slew's long lead. They caught him on the turn, and with a furlong to go Exceller was clearly ahead on all cards. Then, from deep within his unforgiving soul, Seattle Slew fought back under Angel Cordero to make it a contest to the finish. Exceller won by a nose, but Seattle Slew got all the headlines.

Jockey Club Gold Cup, October 6, 1979, at Belmont Park

The precedent had been set by Seattle Slew. Triple Crown winners should be Horse of the Year. The voters agreed in 1978 and anointed Affirmed with the honor. Seattle Slew was given the older male title for his late-season heroics, which seemingly left the grass championship to Exceller as a fitting consolation prize. Five of his seven 1978 stakes victories were on the California turf.

But when the ballots were counted, the grass title went to Mac Diarmida.

"Dumbest thing I ever heard of," said Whittingham, almost, since a few expletives required careful deletion.

Seattle Slew was retired and neither Alydar nor Exceller was ever the same, leaving the 1979 season a sitting duck for bigger, stronger, and apparently more cagey Affirmed, who was freshly syndicated for $14.4 million. After two uninspired January losses under Cauthen, however, Barrera bounced his young rider and added Laffit Pincay to the mix.

Affirmed responded by winning the Strub Stakes (before a crowd of 50,220), the Santa Anita Handicap (66,477 came out), the Californian, and the Hollywood Gold Cup (48,884 in the house), then continued uninterrupted in New York to take a little allowance prep for the Marlboro Cup.

Barrera drew a line in the sand at 131 pounds for Affirmed's Marlboro Cup assignment. Belmont's racing secretary, Lenny Hale, responded with 133. Barrera, exercising both his option and his sense of indignation, announced that Affirmed would pass the race to await the weight-for-age Woodward Stakes, which he won without serious bother.

In Affirmed's absence, Spectacular Bid stepped up to beat fellow 3-year-olds General Assembly and Coastal with arrogant ease. General Assembly had won the Travers by 15 lengths; Coastal had spoiled Spectacular Bid's attempt to win the Triple Crown in June. The score between them would never be even, but the Marlboro helped.

Laboring in the long shadow of Affirmed, Spectacular Bid possessed enough presence to hold his own. His motormouth trainer, the Maryland kingpin Buddy Delp, proclaimed his "Bid" the best horse ever to look through a bridle. Spectacular Bid did his best to back that up with a run of 12 straight wins from September 1978 through his powerful Preakness triumph by 5½ lengths. He won the Derby by 2¾.

Still, the jury was out – and leaning toward conviction – unless Spectacular Bid could beat Affirmed on the square, under weights determined by age, not the handicapper. He got his chance in the Jockey Club Gold Cup on October 6, 1979. A Belmont Park crowd of 36,187 came for the show. No one went home disappointed.

Affirmed and Pincay set the tone of the race and the pace from the start. Spectacular Bid and Shoemaker pressed them down the long Belmont backstretch, while Coastal and Gallant Best stayed out of the way. Suddenly, Spectacular Bid lost his concentration. Shoemaker said the colt spit the bit. Affirmed and Coastal moved to the quarter pole on nearly even terms, yet spread far apart. Pincay, on the outside, was still in control.

That's when something clicked in Spectacular Bid, and the race was on again. The great 3-year-old tested the great 4-year-old through the final three-sixteenths of a mile. Affirmed held the advantage, but Spectacular Bid refused to yield. The wire approached.

"The gray colt got his head inside Affirmed's flanks, perhaps to the girth," Joe Hirsch wrote in his *American Racing Manual* review. "But no one passes Affirmed in the stretch, as Alydar had discovered the season before. Spectacular Bid kept trying and Affirmed produced enough effort to hold him safe." Safe by three-quarters of a length.

"He lost fair and square," Barrera said of the vanquished. "Spectacular Bid had his chance with Affirmed. He got five pounds. He got Shoemaker. And he got beat."

And so the decade ended, though certainly not with a whimper. Affirmed retired with his second straight title as Horse of the Year. Spectacular Bid went to California to follow in the footsteps of the handsome red colt from Harbor View Farm. The calendar turned, but the memories have lingered, paying frequent visits to those 10 unforgettable years.

Champions

Past Performances

The 1970's

Year by year Champions

•1970•
•2-Year-Old Male *Hoist the Flag* •2-Year-Old Filly *Forward Gal* •3-Year-Old Male *Personality*
•3-Year-Old Filly *Office Queen, Fanfreluche (TRA)* •Handicap Horse *Fort Marcy, Nodouble (TRA)*
•Handicap Mare *Shuvee* Grass •Horse *Fort Marcy* •Sprinter *Ta Wee* •Steeplechase *Top Bid*
•HORSE OF THE YEAR Fort Marcy, Personality (TRA)

•1971•
•2-Year-Old Male *Riva Ridge* •2-Year-Old Filly *Numbered Account* •3-Year-Old Male *Canonero II*
•3-Year-Old Filly *Turkish Trousers* •Handicap Horse *Ack Ack* •Handicap Mare *Shuvee* Grass
•Horse *Run the Gauntlet* •Sprinter *Ack Ack* •Steeplechase *Shadow Brook*
•HORSE OF THE YEAR Ack Ack

•1972•
•2-Year-Old Male *Secretariat* •2-Year-Old Filly *La Prevoyante* •3-Year-Old Male *Key to the Mint*
•3-Year-Old Filly *Susan's Girl* •Handicap Horse *Autobiography* •Handicap Mare *Typecast*
•Grass Horse *Cougar II* •Sprinter *Chou Croute* •Steeplechase *Soothsayer*
•HORSE OF THE YEAR Secretariat

•1973•
•2-Year-Old Male *Protagonist* •2-Year-Old Filly *Talking Picture* •3-Year-Old Male *Secretariat*
•3-Year-Old Filly *Desert Vixen* •Handicap Horse *Riva Ridge* •Handicap Mare *Susan's Girl*
•Grass Horse *Secretariat* •Sprinter *Shecky Greene* •Steeplechase *Athenian Idol*
•HORSE OF THE YEAR Secretariat

•1974•
•2-Year-Old Male *Foolish Pleasure* •2-Year-Old Filly *Ruffian* •3-Year-Old Male *Little Current*
•3-Year-Old Filly *Chris Evert* •Handicap Horse *Forego* •Handicap Mare *Desert Vixen* •Grass Horse *Dahlia*
•Sprinter *Forego* •Steeplechase *Gran Kan*
•HORSE OF THE YEAR Forego

•1975•
•2-Year-Old Male *Honest Pleasure* •2-Year-Old Filly *Dearly Precious* •3-Year-Old Male *Wajima*
•3-Year-Old Filly *Ruffian* •Handicap Horse *Forego* •Handicap Mare *Susan's Girl* •Grass Horse *Snow Knight*
•Sprinter *Gallant Bob* •Steeplechase *Life's Illusion*
•HORSE OF THE YEAR Forego

•1976•
•2-Year-Old Male *Seattle Slew* •2-Year-Old Filly *Sensational* •3-Year-Old Male *Bold Forbes*
•3-Year-Old Filly *Revidere* •Handicap Horse *Forego* •Handicap Mare *Proud Delta* •Grass Horse *Youth*
•Sprinter *My Juliet* •Steeplechase *Straight and True*
•HORSE OF THE YEAR Forego

•1977•
•2-Year-Old Male *Affirmed* •2-Year-Old Filly *Lakeville Miss* •3-Year-Old Male *Seattle Slew*
•3-Year-Old Filly *Our Mims* •Handicap Horse *Forego* •Handicap Mare *Cascapedia* •Grass Horse *Johnny D.*
•Sprinter *What a Summer* •Steeplechase *Cafe Prince*
•HORSE OF THE YEAR Seattle Slew

•1978•
•2-Year-Old Male *Spectacular Bid* •2-Year-Old Filly *Candy Eclair, It's in the Air* •3-Year-Old Male *Affirmed*
•3-Year-Old Filly *Tempest Queen* •Handicap Horse *Seattle Slew* •Handicap Mare *Late Bloomer*
•Grass Horse *Mac Diarmida* •Sprinter *Dr. Patches, J.O. Tobin* •Steeplechase *Cafe Prince*
•HORSE OF THE YEAR Affirmed

•1979•
•2-Year-Old Male *Rockhill Native* •2-Year-Old Filly *Smart Angle* •3-Year-Old Male *Spectacular Bid*
•3-Year-Old Filly *Davona Dale* •Handicap Horse *Affirmed* •Handicap Mare *Waya*
•Grass Horse *Bowl Game (M) Trillion (F)* •Sprinter *Star de Naskra* •Steeplechase *Martie's Anger*
•HORSE OF THE YEAR Affirmed

Ack Ack

b. c. 1966, by Battle Joined (Armageddon)–Fast Turn, by Turn–to — **Lifetime record: 27 19 6 0 $636,641**

Own.– Forked Lightning Ranch
Br.– H.F. Guggenheim (Ky)
Tr.– Charles Whittingham

17Jly71- 8Hol	fst 1¼	:452 1:09 1:341 1:594	3↑ Gold Cup Inv'l H 175k	7	1	13	14	16	13¾	Shoemaker W	134	*.30	94-10	Ack Ack1343¾Comtal1111Manta1172	Ridden out	8
5Jly71- 8Hol	fm 1⅛Ⓣ	:463 1:103 1:35 1:471	3↑ American H 79k	5	1	11½	11½	15	14	Shoemaker W	130	*.60	101-09	Ack Ack1304Divide and Rule1216Figonero1191	Easily	7
17Jun71- 8Hol	fst 5½f	:22 :443 :562 1:023	3↑ Hol Express H 33k	2	5	32½	32	2½	13	Shoemaker W	130	*.40	99-14	Ack Ack1303Pitching Wedge109noGalea Pass113nk	Easily	7
13Mar71- 8SA	sl 1¼	:464 1:111 1:37 2:03	4↑ S Anita H 145k	3	1	1hd	14	16	11½	Shoemaker W	130	*.80	83-22	Ack Ack1301½Cougar II1254The Field1091¼	Driving	10
27Feb71- 8SA	fst 1⅛	:46 1:093 1:342 1:47	4↑ San Antonio 88k	8	1	12½	12½	14	13¼	Shoemaker W	124	*1.00	97-11	Ack Ack1243¼Good Manners1151½Hanalei Bay1171½	Handily	11
6Feb71- 8SA	fst 1 1/16	:224 :453 1:093 1:412	4↑ San Pasqual H 55k	5	1	14	14	12	1¾	Shoemaker W	129	*.90	95-07	AckAck129¾DelawareChief118¾Figonro121½	Stumbled,driving	8
	Previously owned by Cain Hoy Stable															
16Jan71- 8SA	gd 7f	:222 :443 1:082 1:21	4↑ San Carlos H 56k	6	2	2½	21	12	11¾	Shoemaker W	126	*1.20	98-13	AckAck1261¾JungleSavage1208KingofCricket119hd	Driving	7
2Jan71- 8SA	gd 6f	:213 :44 :561 1:083	3↑ Palos Verdes H 32k	1	4	1hd	22	31	23½	Shoemaker W	129	*.80	95-11	JungleSavage1173½AckAck129¾KingofCricket1196	Held well	5
6Oct70- 6SA	fm *6½fⓉ	:223 :45 1:064 1:13	2↑ Autumn Days H 21k	2	1	11½	12	13½	11½	Shoemaker W	128	*.30	94-06	AckAck1281½FleetSurprise11710BargainDay11512	Mild drive	4
12Sep70- 6Dmr	fst 5½f	:213 :442 1:021	3↑ Alw 8500	1	4	1½	13	14	15	Shoemaker W	124	*.70	103-12	Ack Ack1245Fleet Surprise116¾Derby Day Boy1143	Driving	6
2May70- 8Hol	fst 7f	:221 :441 1:081 1:203	3↑ Los Angeles H 53k	6	5	1½	1hd	1½	2no	Pierce D	126	*.60	97-11	[D]RightorWrong114noAckAck1264½Baffle1231	Impeded late	6
	Placed first through disqualification															
24Apr70- 8Hol	fst 6f	:214 :441 :561 1:083	4↑ Handicap 15000	2	8	2hd	1½	12½	12	Shoemaker W	123	*.70	98-13	Ack Ack1232First Mate122noFleet Surprise117½	Driving	8
10Apr70- 8Hol	fst 6f	:22 :443 :563 1:084	3↑ Premiere H 33k	1	4	31½	42	41½	43¼	Shoemaker W	124	2.30	94-11	First Mate1182¾Right or Wrong114nkBaffle124nk	Blocked	7
	Previously trained by F.A. Bonsal															
21Jun69- 8AP	fst 1	:223 :45 1:092 1:342	Arl Classic 111k	7	3	33	1hd	14	14½	Baeza B	120	*1.60	89-15	AckAck1204½KingoftheCastl1201¼FstHlrous120nk	Mild drive	10
30May69- 8GS	fst 1⅛	:454 1:094 1:352 1:48	Jersey Derby 137k	6	2	1hd	1hd	1hd	22½	Ycaza M	126	*3.30	94-16	Al Hattab1262½Ack Ack126½Rooney's Shield1261½	Weakened	10
21May69- 8GS	fst 1 1/16	:233 :471 1:112 1:433	Alw 12000	3	3	31½	21	23	2½	Ycaza M	122	*.50	86-19	Night Invader119½Ack Ack122¾Ad Majora1193½	Game effort	6
10May69- 7Aqu	fst 1	:223 :45 1:09 1:344	Withers 58k	8	3	31	2hd	2hd	2¾	Ycaza M	126	*.50	92-14	[D]GleamingLight126¾AckAck126hdTyrant126nk	Bothered late	8
	Placed first through disqualification															
29Apr69- 8CD	fst 1	:221 :45 1:09 1:342	Derby Trial 16k	4	3	33	13	15	17	Ycaza M	122	*.30	101-16	Ack Ack1227Indian Emerald122½Fleet Allied1223	Handily	7
18Apr69- 6Kee	sly 7f	:224 :452 1:10 1:224	Alw 10000	1	2	1½	13	16	112	Ycaza M	121	*.30	94-20	Ack Ack12112Tripsville1122¾Sheik of Bagdad11211	Handily	4
5Apr69- 7Kee	fst 6f	:22 :444 :572 1:101	Alw 7500	6	5	21½	1hd	12	2¾	Brumfield D	119	*.60	91-14	WalkingStick115¾AckAck1192¼Viceregal1225	Couldn't last	7
19Feb69- 8Hia	fst 1⅛	:47 1:114 1:363 1:493	Everglades 32k	3	2	3nk	12	23	45½	Ycaza M	115	7.30	81-21	Arts and Letters1123Top Knight1222Al Hattab119½	Tired	12
5Feb69- 7Hia	fst 7f	:233 :46 1:101 1:223	Bahamas (Div 1) 24k	7	3	21	2½	1hd	1hd	Ycaza M	115	*.80	95-14	Ack Ack115hdAl Hattab1192Curette117nk	Bore out,lasted	8
25Jan69- 6Hia	fst 7f	:224 :453 1:093 1:223	©Alw 5500	6	3	31	2hd	12	13	Ycaza M	117	*.70	95-16	Ack Ack1173Distinctive1193Arts and Letters1193	Handily	9
17Jan69- 5Hia	fst 6f	:22 :45 1:093	©Alw 5000	2	3	13	12	13	16	Ycaza M	119	3.30	96-15	Ack Ack1196Next Beauty1161¾Banquet Circuit1194	Driving	12
	Previously trained by W.W. Stephens															
23Oct68- 5Bel	fst 7f	:231 :463 1:111 1:24	Alw 7000	2	4	11½	11	11½	2hd	Rotz JL	122	3.10	87-13	IFoundGold115hdAckAck122noKingoftheCastle122½	Missed	8
10Oct68- 5Bel	fst 6f	:222 :46 1:112	©Md Sp Wt	12	7	41	3nk	1hd	1no	Ycaza M	122	*1.50	88-17	Ack Ack122noIzaak1222½Alaskan Reindeer1225	Hard drive	14
2Oct68- 3Bel	fst 6f	:222 :454 1:11	©Md Sp Wt	12	6	31½	31½	2hd	2¾	Ycaza M	122	*2.50	89-13	Nephew122¾Ack Ack1221½Banquet Circuit1221½	Good effort	14

Affirmed

ch. c. 1975, by Exclusive Native (Raise a Native)–Won't Tell You, by Crafty Admiral — **Lifetime record: 29 22 5 1 $2,393,818**

Own.– Harbor View Farm
Br.– Harbor View Farm (Fla)
Tr.– Lazaro S. Barrera

6Oct79- 8Bel	fst 1½	:49 1:131 2:022 2:272	3↑ J C Gold Cup-G1	3	2	1½	1hd	1½	1¾	Pincay L Jr	126	*.60	83-21	Affirmed126¾Spectacular Bid1213Coastal12131	Driving	4
22Sep79- 8Bel	sly 1¼	:473 1:114 1:361 2:013	3↑ Woodward-G1	2	2	24	1½	13	12½	Pincay L Jr	126	*.40	92-15	Affirmed1262½Coastal1203¾Czaravich1208½	Ridden out	5
29Aug79- 0Bel	sly 1	:222 :45 1:092 1:34	3↑ Alw 30000	3	1	1½	11	12	16	Pincay L Jr	122	-	98-15	Affirmed1226Island Sultan11514Prefontaine117	Ridden out	3
	No wagering. Exhibition race run between 7th and 8th races															
24Jun79- 8Hol	fst 1¼	:453 1:093 1:341 1:582	3↑ Hol Gold Cup-G1	1	2	1hd	1hd	1hd	1¾	Pincay L Jr	132	*.30	99-13	Affirmed132¾Sirlad1204Text1195	Driving	10
20May79- 8Hol	fst 1 1/16	:222 :444 1:091 1:411	3↑ Californian-G1	2	1	11	11	12	15	Pincay L Jr	130	*.30	89-16	Affirmed1305Syncopate1144Harry's Love117¾	Driving	8
4Mar79- 8SA	fst 1¼	:462 1:101 1:341 1:583	4↑ S Anita H-G1	3	2	21	11½	14	14½	Pincay L Jr	128	*1.30	103-09	Affirmed1284½Tiller1273[DH]PaintedWagon115	Speed to spare	8
4Feb79- 8SA	gd 1¼	:47 1:104 1:353 2:01	C H Strub-G1	8	2	31	11	12	110	Pincay L Jr	126	*.90	91-17	Affirmed12610Johnny's Image1154Quip1157	Handily	9
20Jan79- 8SA	gd 1⅛	:453 1:093 1:35 1:48	San Fernando-G2	4	3	49½	57½	33½	22¾	Cauthen S	126	*.50	88-14	Radar Ahead1232¾Affirmed126nkLittle Reb1204	Drifted out	8
7Jan79- 8SA	fst 7f	:222 :45 1:083 1:21	Malibu-G2	2	1	32	32½	32½	32¼	Cauthen S	126	*.30	96-13	LittleReb1202¼RadarAhed123hdAffrmd1263	Hemmed in to str	5
14Oct78- 8Bel	sly 1½	:451 1:092 2:014 2:271	3↑ J C Gold Cup-G1	2	2	2hd	37	415	518¾	Cauthen S	121	2.20e	65-13	Exceller126noSeattle Slew12614Great Contractor1264¾		6
	Saddle slipped															
16Sep78- 8Bel	fst 1⅛	:47 1:101 1:333 1:454	3↑ Marlboro Cup H-G1	1	2	22½	22½	23	23	Cauthen S	124	*.50	95-12	SeattleSlew1283Affirmed1245NastyandBold1184	No excuse	6
19Aug78- 8Sar	fst 1¼	:48 1:113 1:364 2:02	Travers-G1	3	2	2hd	11½	12	11¾	Pincay L Jr	126	*.70	91-14	[D]Affirmed1261¾Alydar1263¾NastyandBold12615	Came over	4
	Disqualified and placed second															
8Aug78- 8Sar	gd 1⅛	:463 1:101 1:35 1:474	Jim Dandy-G3	4	2	28	27	24	1½	Cauthen S	128	*.05	96-04	Affirmed128½SensitivePrince11920Addison1146½	Going away	5
10Jun78- 8Bel	fst 1½	:50 1:14 2:013 2:264	Belmont-G1	3	1	11	1hd	1hd	1hd	Cauthen S	126	*.60	86-11	Affirmed126hdAlydar12613Darby Creek Road1267¾	Driving	5
20May78- 8Pim	fst 1 3/16	:473 1:114 1:361 1:542	Preakness-G1	6	2	11	11	1½	1nk	Cauthen S	126	*.50	98-12	Affirmed126nkAlydar1267½Believe It1262½	Brisk handling	7
6May78- 8CD	fst 1¼	:453 1:104 1:354 2:011	Ky Derby-G1	2	2	35½	2hd	12	11½	Cauthen S	126	1.80	91-12	Affirmed1261½Alydar1261¼Believe It1264¼	Fully extended	11
16Apr78- 8Hol	fst 1⅛	:45 1:092 1:35 1:481	Hol Derby-G1	2	1	1hd	11	12½	12	Cauthen S	122	*.30	91-17	Affirmed1222Think Snow1223Radar Ahead1222	Driving	9
2Apr78- 8SA	fst 1⅛	:454 1:094 1:353 1:48	S Anita Derby-G1	7	2	11	11½	13½	18	Pincay L Jr	120	*.30	92-16	Affirmed1208Balzac1201Think Snow1202½	Handily	12
18Mar78- 8SA	fst 1 1/16	:241 :482 1:12 1:423	San Felipe-G2	4	2	21	2hd	1hd	12	Cauthen S	126	*.30	89-17	Affirmed1262Chance Dancer1176Tampoy1181½	Driving	6
8Mar78- 6SA	fst 6½f	:213 :442 1:09 1:153	Alw 30000	4	1	43½	11½	14	15	Cauthen S	124	*.20	92-16	Affirmed1245Spotted Charger114½Don F.114hd	Easily	5
29Oct77- 8Lrl	fst 1 1/16	:24 :484 1:133 1:441	Lrl Futurity-G1	3	2	21	2hd	1hd	1nk	Cauthen S	122	1.40	92-27	Affirmed122nkAlydar12210StardeNskr12227	Long,hard drive	4
15Oct77- 6Bel	my 1	:242 :481 1:122 1:363	Champagne-G1	5	3	32	1hd	1½	21¼	Cauthen S	122	*1.20	84-17	Alydar1221¼Affirmed1221¼Darby Creek Road1221½	2nd best	6
10Sep77- 8Bel	gd 7f	:233 :463 1:094 1:213	Futurity-G1	2	2	2½	1hd	2hd	1no	Cauthen S	122	*1.20	94-10	Affirmed122noAlydar12211NastyandBold122hd	Strong drive	5
27Aug77- 8Sar	fst 6½f	:224 :451 1:091 1:152	Hopeful-G1	4	1	32	2hd	1hd	1½	Cauthen S	122	2.30	98-11	Affirmed122½Alydar1222½RegalandRoyal122hd	Good handling	5
17Aug77- 8Sar	fst 6f	:214 :443 1:093	Sanford-G2	3	2	35½	43	2½	12¾	Cauthen S	124	*1.30	92-15	Affirmed1242¾TltUp122hdJtDplomcy124nk	Driving,very wide	6
23Jly77- 5Hol	fst 6f	:213 :442 :562 1:091	Juv Champ (Div 1) 104k	6	3	1hd	1½	14	17	Pincay L Jr	122	*.40	93-15	Affirmed1227He's Dewan1226Esops Foibles122¾	Easily	8
6Jly77- 8Bel	fst 5½f	:222 :454 :572 1:033	Great American 36k	1	1	11	2hd	21½	23½	Cordero A Jr	122	4.60	93-16	Alydar1173½Affirmed1222Going Investor1224	No match	7
15Jun77- 8Bel	fst 5½f	:222 :453 :582 1:05	©Youthful 37k	1	1	2½	2½	1hd	1nk	Cordero A Jr	119	3.40	90-17	Affirmed119nkWood Native119½Sensitive Nose1192½	Driving	11
24May77- 4Bel	fst 5½f	:23 :472 :593 1:06	Md Sp Wt	10	1	1½	11½	12	14½	Gonzalez B	117	14.30	85-21	Affirmed1174½Innocuous1223½Gymnast1222	Ridden out	10

Alydar

ch. c. 1975, by Raise a Native (Native Dancer)–Sweet Tooth, by On-and-On — **Lifetime record: 26 14 9 1 $957,195**

Own.– Calumet Farm
Br.– Calumet Farm (Ky)
Tr.– John M. Veitch

4Jly79- 8Bel	fst 1¼	:492 1:133 1:371 2:013 3↑	Suburban H-G1	4 3 36½ 2hd 3½ 31¼	Fell J	126		*.60	91-16	StateDinner118½MistrBr120¾Alydr126½	Weakened 5
17Jun79- 8Bel	sly 1⅛	:46 1:09 1:333 1:463 3↑	Nassau County H-G3	1 2 21½ 2½ 11½ 13¾	Fell J	124		*.40	94-06	Alydar1243¾Nasty and Bold11614Sorry Lookin113	In hand 3
28May79- 8Bel	fst 1	:224 :45 1:091 1:34 3↑	Metropolitan H-G1	9 3 3½ 32 66½ 612	Velasquez J	126		*.40	86-16	State Dinner1153Dr. Patches1183¼Sorry Lookin1131½	Tired 9
5May79- 8Aqu	fst 7f	:224 :451 1:091 1:214 3↑	Carter H-G2	2 3 35½ 38½ 36 2nk	Velasquez J	126		1.50	92-25	StardeNaskra122nkAlydr1263¾SnstvPrnc1266¾	Finished fast 6
13Apr79- 9OP	fst 1 1/16	:241 :481 1:13 1:433 4↑	Oaklawn H-G2	2 5 3nk 2½ 3½ 2no	Velasquez J	127		*.30	90-19	SanJuanHill114noAlydar127¾ALettrtoHrry1257	Lost the nod 7
31Mar79- 5Hia	fst 7f	:233 :462 1:103 1:222 4↑	Alw 13000	5 2 31½ 3½ 12 17	Velasquez J	114		*.10	91-17	Alydar1147Fort Prevel1224Jachal II1091¼	Much the best 6
19Aug78- 8Sar	fst 1¼	:48 1:113 1:364 2:02	Travers-G1	4 4 32 21½ 22 21¾	Velaquez J	126		1.00	89-14	[D]Affirmed1261¾Alydar1263¾Nasty and Bold12615	Taken up 4
	Placed first through disqualification										
5Aug78- 8Sar	fst 1⅛	:463 1:102 1:351 1:472 3↑	Whitney H-G2	9 7 613 45½ 14 110	Velasquez J	123		*.70	98-09	Alydar12310Buckaroo112hdFather Hogan114nk	Hand ride 9
22Jly78- 8AP	fst 1¼	:474 1:111 1:353 2:002	Arl Classic-G2	3 3 23½ 15 18 113	Fell J	126		*.05	95-19	Alydar12613ChiefofDixieland1141GordieH.1145	Much best 5
10Jun78- 8Bel	fst 1½	:50 1:14 2:013 2:264	Belmont-G1	2 3 21 2hd 2hd 2hd	Velasquez J	126		1.10	86-11	Affirmed126hdAlydar12613Darby Creek Road1267¾	Game try 5
20May78- 8Pim	fst 1 3/16	:473 1:114 1:361 1:542	Preakness-G1	3 6 65½ 42 2½ 2nk	Velasquez J	126	b	1.80	98-12	Affirmed126nkAlydar1267½Believe It1262½	Game effort 7
6May78- 8CD	fst 1¼	:453 1:104 1:354 2:011	Ky Derby-G1	10 9 917 44½ 34 21½	Velasquez J	126	b	*1.20	89-12	Affirmed1261½Alydar1261¼Believe It1264¼	Closed fast 11
27Apr78- 7Kee	gd 1⅛	:471 1:112 1:372 1:493	Blue Grass-G1	9 6 611 47 16 113	Velasquez J	121	b	*.10	89-19	Alydar12113Raymond Earl121noGo Forth1211¾	Ridden out 9
1Apr78- 9GP	fst 1⅛	:471 1:111 1:352 1:47	Florida Derby-G1	6 4 21 1½ 1hd 12	Velasquez J	122	b	*.20	99-10	Alydar1222Believe It1227½Dr. Valeri122nk	Handily 7
4Mar78- 9Hia	fst 1⅛	:453 1:094 1:35 1:47	Flamingo-G1	6 6 65 31 12 14½	Velasquez J	122	b	*.90e	97-05	Alydar1224½NoonTimeSpender1221Dr.Valeri122nk	Ridden out 8
11Feb78- 5Hia	fst 7f	:234 :464 1:103 1:221	Alw 14000	5 8 54 53½ 2hd 12	Velasquez J	122	b	*.30	92-13	Alydr1222NoonTimeSpendr1195½LaVoyagus109nk	Ridden out 8
26Nov77- 8Aqu	sly 1⅛	:471 1:112 1:351 1:474	Remsen-G2	5 4 49 45½ 35 22	Velasquez J	122	b	*.60	94-13	Believe It1222Alydar1221¼Quadratic1166	2nd best 5
29Oct77- 8Lrl	fst 1 1/16	:24 :484 1:133 1:441	Lrl Futurity-G1	1 3 31 1hd 2hd 2nk	Velasquez J	122	b	*.40	92-27	Affirmed122nkAlydr12210StrdNskr12227	Steadied,sharp try 4
15Oct77- 6Bel	my 1	:242 :481 1:122 1:363	Champagne-G1	1 5 42 52¾ 41½ 11¼	Velasquez J	122	b	1.50	85-17	Alydar1221¼Affirmed1221¼DarbyCreekRoad1221½	Ridden out 6
10Sep77- 8Bel	gd 7f	:233 :463 1:094 1:213	Futurity-G1	1 5 32½ 2hd 1hd 2no	Maple E	122	b	1.50	94-10	Affirmd122noAlydr12211NstyndBold122hd	Short lead,missed 5
27Aug77- 8Sar	fst 6½f	:224 :451 1:091 1:152	Hopeful-G1	1 4 44 4¾ 2hd 2½	Maple E	122	b	*1.00	97-11	Affirmed122½Alydar1222½RegalandRoyl122hd	Steadied early 5
13Aug77- 8Mth	sly 6f	:222 :453 1:103	Sapling-G1	4 5 34 23 2hd 12½	Maple E	122	b	*.60	87-17	Alydr1222½NoonTimeSpendr1224½DominantRulr122no	Easily 5
27Jly77- 8Bel	fst 6f	:23 :454 1:10	Tremont 36k	4 4 33 31½ 11 11¼	Maple E	124		*.40	92-16	Alydar1241¼Believe It1173¾Jet Diplomacy1245½	Ridden out 5
6Jly77- 8Bel	fst 5½f	:222 :454 :572 1:033	Great American 36k	7 7 42½ 1hd 11½ 13½	Maple E	117		*.80	97-16	Alydar1173½Affirmed1222Going Investor1224	Ridden out 7
24Jun77- 4Bel	fst 5½f	:224 :461 :581 1:041	Md Sp Wt	9 8 63¾ 1hd 12 16¾	Maple E	122		*2.10	94-20	Alydar1226¾Believe It1221Sauce Boat1173½	Handily 10
15Jun77- 8Bel	fst 5½f	:222 :453 :582 1:05	©Youthful 37k	7 9 912 911 510 55	Maple E	115		*1.80	85-17	Affirmed119nkWoodNative119½SenstvNos1192½	In close turn 11

Ancient Title

dkbbr. g. 1970, by Gummo (Fleet Nasrullah)–Hi Little Gal, by Bar le Duc — **Lifetime record: 57 24 11 9 $1,252,791**

Own.– Kirkland Stable
Br.– Mr & Mrs William Kirkland (Cal)
Tr.– Keith L. Stucki

19Aug78- 8Dmr	fst 1 1/16	:224 :461 1:101 1:401 3↑	San Diego H 43k	6 2 21 55½ 512 -	Shoemaker W	125	b	*.30	- -	Vic's Magic1167Mr. Redoy1197Clout1172½	Lame 6
30Jly78- 7Dmr	fst 6f	:214 :441 :56 1:081 3↑	Alw 17000	2 4 32½ 2½ 1hd 12½	Shoemaker W	117	b	*.40	97-11	AncientTitle1172½SeLeTe1148StainedGlass1144	Drew out 6
19Feb78- 8SA	fst 1⅛	:453 1:093 1:342 1:461 4↑	San Antonio-G1	2 2 2½ 1½ 21½ 27	Shoemaker W	120	b	2.20	94-12	Vigors1217Ancient Title1203½Double Discount1167	7
	No match for winner										
29Jan78- 8SA	fst 1 1/16	:231 :461 1:094 1:401 4↑	San Pasqual H-G2	4 1 12½ 11 1½ 11½	McHargue DG	124	b	1.80	101-09	Ancient Title1241½Mark's Place120nkDouble Discount12017	4
	Broke slowly										
23Oct77- 8SA	fm 1½Ⓣ	:471 1:113 2:013 2:262 3↑	Oak Tree Inv'l-G1	3 2 11 2hd 2hd 3nk	McHargue DG	126	b	6.30	83-17	Crystal Water126nkVigors126noAncient Title1261½	Gamely 10
9Oct77- 8SA	fm 1¼Ⓣ	:444 1:084 1:332 1:572 3↑	C F Burke H-G2	3 2 2½ 1hd 22 56¼	McHargue DG	127	b	*1.80	95-00	DoubleDiscount1161NoTurning118¾Vigors1204	Faltered late 8
5Sep77- 8Dmr	fst *1¼	:443 1:081 1:323 1:552 3↑	Del Mar H-G2	7 1 12½ 13 15 15	McHargue DG	123	b	8.50	106-08	AncientTitle1235PaintedWagon1183Cascapedia1171	In hand 9
29Aug77- 8Dmr	fm 1Ⓣ	:233 :473 1:114 1:36 3↑	Alw 12000	4 1 1½ 1hd 11½ 12½	Pierce D	120	b	*.70	95-06	Ancient Title1202½Chindo117noChil the Kite1202	Handily 6
17Jly77- 8Hol	fst 1 1/16	:223 :454 1:092 1:41 3↑	Citation H 82k	1 4 41½ 42 53½ 42½	Hawley S	124	b	*.90	87-16	PaintdWagon1171¼LegndrioIII114½PayTribute118¾	Bore out 7
18Jun77- 8Hol	fst 1¼	:451 1:09 1:334 2:00 3↑	Hol Gold Cup H-G1	10 7 52¾ 44 44 45¼	Hawley S	125	b	6.50	86-13	CrystalWater129nkCascapedia116noCaucasus1245	Wide,hung 12
5Jun77- 8Hol	fst 1⅛	:46 1:093 1:344 1:473 3↑	Bel Air H-G2	5 3 1hd 2hd 2hd 1no	Hawley S	124	b	*1.10	94-14	Ancient Title124noRajab1146Legendario III115no	Hard drive 6
22May77- 8Hol	fst 1 1/16	:222 :452 1:091 1:41 3↑	Californian-G1	3 6 64½ 33 34 32¼	Hawley S	123	b	5.30	88-14	CrystalWater128hdMark'sPlc1212¼AncntTtl1238	Evenly late 6
6Mar77- 8SA	fst 1¼	:452 1:093 1:341 1:591 4↑	S Anita H-G1	2 7 76½ 76 1112 1113	Hawley S	125	b	3.90	89-09	CrystalWater122hdFaliraki1144¼KingPellnor1305¼	No speed 13
20Feb77- 8SA	fst 1⅛	:463 1:101 1:35 1:474 4↑	San Antonio-G1	2 2 1hd 1½ 2½ 11	Hawley S	119	b	*2.80	93-14	AncntTtle1191DoubleDiscnt1151¾Propernts1143	Going away 10
29Jan77- 8SA	fst 1 1/16	:231 :462 1:101 1:41 4↑	San Pasqual H-G2	6 4 2½ 53 63¾ 56¼	Hawley S	125		*2.10	91-12	Uniformity117¾Distant Land1161Pisistrato117¾	8
	Weakened final quarter										
28Dec76- 8SA	fst 6f	:214 :441 :56 1:083 2↑	Palos Verdes H 47k	11 3 63½ 33½ 34 33½	Cordero A Jr	126		3.00	92-12	Maheras119½Sure Fire1163Ancient Title1263½	Mild rally 13
4Jly76- 8Hol	fm 1⅛Ⓣ	:474 1:113 1:352 1:48 3↑	American H-G2	2 4 45 43 41½ 53½	Hawley S	126	b	2.60	92-09	KingPellinore121¾RiotinParis123¾Caucasus120hd	Weakened 7
20Jun76- 8Hol	fst 1¼	:454 1:10 1:343 1:584 3↑	Hol Gold Cup H-G1	5 6 79½ 52½ 65 69¼	Hawley S	127	b	*1.70	88-09	Pay Tribute1173¼Avatar1232Riot in Paris123¾	8
	Little speed,lacked rally										
23May76- 8Hol	fst 1 1/16	:231 :464 1:09 1:411 3↑	Californian-G1	1 5 55½ 42 32 1hd	Hawley S	127	b	*.80	89-14	AncientTitle127hdPayTrbut1174AustnMttlr116no	Off slowly 6
8May76- 8Hol	fst 1	:23 :454 1:094 1:343 3↑	Caballero H-G3	1 5 55 41¾ 2hd 1½	Hawley S	128	b	1.40	93-15	AncientTitle128½BigDestiny1183½PayTribut1203	Wide rally 5
7Mar76- 8SA	fst 1¼	:452 1:093 1:342 2:002 4↑	S Anita H-G1	9 3 74 43 21½ 2no	Hawley S	124	b	9.30	96-11	Royal Glint124noAncient Title1241¼Lightning Mandate1206½	15
	Just missed										
22Feb76- 8SA	fst 1⅛	:471 1:111 1:353 1:481 4↑	San Antonio-G1	10 5 66 54½ 1010 1010	Hawley S	126	b	3.90	81-13	LightningMandate1182DancingPapa117½MessngrofSong1222¾	10
	Fractious in gate,bore out on turn										
1Nov75- 5SA	fst 1¼	:462 1:102 1:35 2:01 3↑	Nat'l Champ Inv'l 350k	5 5 75½ 32 74¾ 75¾	Pincay L Jr	124	b	*2.20	87-15	Dulcia117nkRoyal Glint1202¼Tizna118½	Wide,tired 11
13Sep75- 8Bel	fst 1¼	:472 1:104 1:352 2:00 3↑	Marlboro Cup Inv'l H-G1	2 4 21½ 11½ 32 37½	Pincay L Jr	126	b	9.00	91-11	Wajima119hdForego1297½Ancient Title126¾	Tired 7
1Sep75- 8Bel	fst 1⅛	:452 1:09 1:341 1:471 3↑	Governor-G1	5 3 34½ 23 21 32	Hawley S	130	b	10.30	89-18	Wajima115hdFoolish Pleasure1252Ancient Title130¾	10
	Long drive,weakened										
2Aug75- 8Sar	fst 1⅛	:462 1:101 1:352 1:481 3↑	Whitney H-G2	6 1 1½ 1½ 1hd 1nk	Hawley S	128	b	3.50	94-07	Ancient Title128nkGroup Plan1153Arbees Boy1184	Best 7
4Jly75- 8Hol	fm 1⅛Ⓣ	:50 1:134 1:373 1:493 3↑	American H (Div 2)-G2	6 2 21 3nk 21½ 31	Pincay L Jr	128	b	*1.50	87-11	Montmartre1151TopCrowd115hdAncntTtl128hd	Broke slowly 9
21Jun75- 8Hol	fst 1¼	:47 1:103 1:344 1:591 3↑	Hol Gold Cup Inv'l H-G1	4 1 11½ 12½ 14 14½	Pincay L Jr	125	b	*1.40	95-15	Ancient Title1254½Big Band115nkEl Tarta1152¾	Much best 7
26May75- 8Hol	fst 1 1/16	:231 :461 1:092 1:401 3↑	Californian-G1	5 2 32 2½ 1hd 1hd	Pincay L Jr	126	b	*1.30	94-16	AncientTitle126hdBigBand1174½Century'sEnvoy1173	Driving 10
10May75- 8Hol	fst 1	:222 :45 1:083 1:334 3↑	Caballero H 55k	6 6 74 21 22½ 23¼	Pincay L Jr	126	b	*1.20	94-10	June's Love1163¼Ancient Title126½Big Band1193	Hung 9
23Feb75- 8SA	fst 1⅛	:454 1:09 1:34 1:464 4↑	San Antonio-G1	1 3 34 33 32½ 32¼	Pincay L Jr	128	b	*1.60	96-10	Cheriepe1202FirstBack117nkAncientTitle1282	No excuse 9
19Jan75- 8SA	fst 7f	:212 :432 1:08 1:211 4↑	San Carlos H-G2	1 8 44½ 31½ 1½ 1¾	Pincay L Jr	128	b	*1.00	97-12	AncientTitl128¾[DH]HudsnCounty116[DH]BhKy117nk	Off slowly 12
26Dec74- 8SA	fst 6f	:221 :444 :562 1:084 2↑	Palos Verdes H-G3	4 4 21½ 2hd 1½ 11½	Pincay L Jr	126	b	*1.10	95-15	Ancient Title1261½Princely Native1161½King of theBlues113hd	8
	Drew clear under urging										
23Jun74- 8Hol	fst 1¼	:471 1:112 1:353 1:594 3↑	Hol Gold Cup Inv'l H-G1	7 3 34 1hd 21½ 22½	Pincay L Jr	125	b	1.50	89-14	TreeofKnowldge1152½AncntTtl125hdWrHm114¾	Bid,weakened 10
27May74- 8Hol	fst 1 1/16	:231 :462 1:092 1:401 3↑	Californian-G1	8 3 22 2hd 1½ 21¼	Grant H	126	b	*1.80	93-16	Quack1261¼Ancient Title126¾Woodland Pines120hd	No match 9
11May74- 8Hol	fst 7f	:222 :45 1:082 1:202 3↑	Los Angeles H-G2	8 2 22 2hd 12½ 1nk	Pincay L Jr	126	b	*2.00	97-14	AncientTtl126nkWoodlndPns1182SoftVctory118nk	Hard urged 8
14Apr74- 8Hol	fm 1 1/16Ⓣ	:223 :464 1:102 1:404 3↑	Lakeside H-G2	6 2 2½ 2½ 54 52¼	Pincay L Jr	126	b	*1.40	93-06	Matun120hdVisualizer1151Dancing Papa1161	Rank,faltered 7

10Mar74- 8SA	sl 1¼	:473 1:12 1:372 2:033 4↑	S Anita H-G1	1 3 2½ 21 23 24½	Pincay L Jr	125	b	2.60	75-26	PrinceDantan1194½AncientTitle125½BigSpruce1225	Good try	11
9Feb74- 8SA	fst 1¼	:464 1:111 1:352 2:004	C H Strub-G1	7 1 11½ 12 13½ 13	Pincay L Jr	121	b	1.40	94-15	AncientTitle1213DancngPp1161PrncDntn1151	In full stride	9
26Jan74- 8SA	fst 1⅛	:464 1:102 1:344 1:473	San Fernando-G2	6 1 12½ 13½ 16 13½	Pincay L Jr	120	b	4.30	94-14	Ancient Title1203½Linda's Chief1233½Mariache II114½		7
	Ridden out											
12Jan74- 8SA	gd 7f	:221 :443 1:093 1:224	Malibu-G2	2 2 1hd 13½ 16 13	Toro F	120	b	2.20	89-15	Ancient Title1203Linda's Chief126½Dancing Papa1204		7
	Opened lead on turn											
27Dec73- 8SA	fst 6f	:214 :442 :563 1:09 2↑	Palos Verdes H-G3	1 5 32½ 41½ 3½ 33	Pincay L Jr	122	b	*1.20	93-13	Woodland Pines1151Tragic Isle1172Ancient Title1222	Hung	8
19May73- 8Hol	fm 1Ⓣ	:222 :46 1:102 1:353	©Will Rogers H-G2	2 3 35 44½ 11 21¾	Toro F	124	b	3.10	90-11	Groshawk1231¾AncntTtl124nk[DH]MugPntr1131¾	Led,no match	10
28Apr73- 8Hol	fst 7f	:214 :434 1:08 1:21	Inglewood-G2	8 1 33 2½ 1½ 1hd	Toro F	122	b	*1.10	94-13	Ancient Title122hdGroshawk1223¾Pontoise1146	Driving	8
31Mar73- 8SA	fst 1⅛	:46 1:094 1:343 1:47	S Anita Derby-G1	4 2 1hd 11½ 33 48	Toro F	120	b	13.60	89-12	Sham1202½Linda'sChief1202¼OutoftheEast1203¼	Wide,tired	6
17Mar73- 8SA	fst 1 1/16	:224 :46 1:10 1:414	San Felipe H-G2	1 1 12 11 2½ 23	Toro F	120	b	15.50	90-13	Linda'sChief1263AncientTitl1201¾OutofthEst1153	No match	9
1Mar73- 8SA	fst 1	:223 :451 1:092 1:334	San Jacinto-G2	3 1 2hd 1hd 21 25	Toro F	122	b	2.30	96-12	Linda'sChief1225AncientTitle1221¼Aljamin1155½	No match	7
1Feb73- 8SA	fst 7f	:22 :442 1:083 1:21	San Vicente-G3	3 4 12 12 1½ 1nk	Toro F	122	b	2.70	98-16	Ancient Title122nkLinda's Chief1227Out of the East114hd		9
	Going away											
18Jan73- 8SA	sly 6f	:214 :451 :581 1:112	San Miguel-G3	3 6 42 41 2hd 23½	Toro F	120	b	2.20	80-24	Linda'sChief1203½AncientTtl1201PlntyofStyl117½	No match	7
30Dec72- 8SA	fst 7f	:214 :441 1:091 1:222	[S]Cal Br Champ 61k	5 2 3½ 1½ 11½ 14¾	Toro F	117	b	1.50	91-10	AncientTitle1174¾RiverLad114¾PlentyofStyle115nk	Handily	8
18Oct72- 8SA	fst 7f	:214 :434 1:074 1:204	Sunny Slope 28k	3 3 2hd 11 12½ 13	Grant H	121	b	7.40	99-14	Ancient Title1213Groshawk1241¼Autry1192½	In full stride	9
25Aug72- 7Dmr	fst 6f	:214 :442 :563 1:09	De Anza 20k	4 2 2hd 2hd 22½ 32½	Harris W	117	b	3.00	91-10	Lucky Mike1192Bottle Brush115½Ancient Title1172½	Tired	5
11Aug72- 7Dmr	fst 6f	:214 :441 :563 1:091	[S]CTBA 16k	2 5 1½ 13½ 13½ 18	Harris W	116	b	1.50	93-14	AncientTitle1168BoldBlcony116noRsHgh1211¾	Much the best	7
22Jly72- 8Hol	fst 6f	:212 :434 :561 1:092	Hol Juv Ch 140k	7 6 53 44½ 55 84½	Valenzuela I	122	b	8.70	87-11	BoldLiz1191DocMarcus122¾[D]LuckyMike122hd	Speed,tired	11
14Jly72- 7Hol	fst 5½f	:211 :442 :564 1:03	Alw 6500	4 7 34 3nk 1½ 15	Grant H	120	b	7.30	97-14	Ancient Title1205Crocation1201Rotarian120¾	Going away	10
7Jly72- 3Hol	fst 5½f	:22 :452 :573 1:04	©Md Sp Wt	3 6 2hd 1hd 21 1hd	Pincay L Jr	118	b	*.60	92-12	AncntTtl118hdSpnLghtnng1187Nbu118nk	Up in final strides	12
15Jun72- 3Hol	fst 5f	:22 :45 :571	©Md Sp Wt	7 3 31 2½ 23 26	Palomino J	118	b	9.20	91-15	Lucky Mike1186Ancient Title1182½Nabu1184	Bid turn,hung	12

Athenian Idol

ch. g. 1968, by Alcibiades II (Alycidon)–Dottys Dream, by Francis S.

Lifetime record: 22 6 2 4 $36,530

Own.– W.L. Pape
Br.– Harbor View Farm (Ky)
Tr.– J. Sheppard

30Mar74- 4Cam	fm *2	S'Chase	4:191 4↑	Carolina Cup 10k	4 4 - - - -	O'Brien M	155		-e	--	Breaking Dawn1391Metello1535½Winigo15099	Fell	6
16Mar74- 4AtH	fm *2	S'Chase	3:522 4↑	Alw 10000	1 5 510 43½ 21 31¼	O'Brien M	154		-	--	Metello147¾Juac Hollow157½Athenian Idol1546		5
17Nov73- 2Cam	fm 2 3/16	S'Chase	5:214 4↑	Colonial Cup 50k	2 12 1115 1112 921 41¼	Fishback J	147		-e	--	LuckyBoyIII149noSoothsayr162noDremMgc1531¼	Closed fast	15
27Oct73- 6FH	fm *2Ⓣ		3:414 3↑	Alw 1000	3 4 53¼ 24 2½ 15	Sheppard J	168		-	--	Athenian Idol1685Minaccia1654Noble Spirit1632	Drew out	7
6Oct73- 4Lig	fm *2½	S'Chase	5:032 4↑	Temple Gwathmey H 25k	1 8 88½ 86½ 3¾ 11¼	Fishback J	140		-e	--	Athenian Idol1401¼Soothsayer1628Top Bid1572	Driving	8
23Aug73- 9Sar	fm 2 1/16	Hurdles	3:424 4↑	Handicap 10000	7 6 57 58½ 16 110	Fishback J	140		5.00	--	Athenian Idol14010Jive145nkManchu Prince1395	Ridden out	8
15Aug73- 9Sar	gd 2 1/16	Hurdles	3:532 4↑	Alw 7500	3 3 53½ 57 38½ 27½	Fishback J	145		2.50	--	Jive1427½Athenian Idol1451¼Hipocampo1481	Second best	6
9Aug73- 9Sar	fm 1⅞	Hurdles	3:24 4↑	Clm 7000	5 5 45½ 2½ 18 110	Fishback J	138		*1.50	--	Athenian Idol13810Star of Vertex1381½Christmas Cheer1419		6
	Ridden out												
1Aug73- 9Sar	fm 1⅞	Hurdles	3:24 4↑	Clm 7000	7 6 512 26 22 43	O'Brien M	150		*3.30e	--	Tater Pie1441Manchu Prince1411¼Seven Trips156¾	Tired	9
11Jly73- 6Del	sly 5f	:222 :463	:584 4↑	Clm 7500	3 4 67½ 79¼ 611 68½	Lee T	114	b	17.60	86-17	Harbor King1143¼Gray Idol1172½Joes Battlecry1121	Outrun	8
6Jun73- 4Del	fm *1½	Hurdles	2:411 3↑	Clm 8000	2 7 913 94½ 44½ 57¼	Achuff W5	148		*2.40	--	Seven Trips150¾Antigua Star1474¾Star of Vertex137hd		10
	Bobbled third jump												
9May73- 5Fai	fm *1⅞	Hurdles	3:211 4↑	Alw 3000	5 4 45 22½ 314 322	O'Brien L	155	s	2.90	--	Babamist14710CastlebarII15212AthenianIdol155¾	Weakened	5
21Apr73- 3Clm	fm *1¾	Hurdles	3:26 3↑	Alw 4000	5 4 41¾ 1¾ 21½ 32¼	Brittle C III	148	s	-	--	Monsieur Ledocteur1482BreakingDawn148nkAthenian Idl1481½		6
	Weakened												
7Apr73- 2Try	sf *1½	Hurdles	2:401 3↑	Alw 1800	4 3 32½ 22½ 12 11½	O'Brien M	155	s	-	--	AthenianIdl1551½PineyCreek136MonsiurLdoctur150	Driving	4
24Mar73- 1Aik	fm *1½	Hurdles	2:41 3↑	Alw 2500	1 9 64½ 32½ 21 24	O'Brien M	155	s		--	Monsieur Ledocteur1504Athenian Idol1551½Jay's Trouble1368		9
	Game try												
17Mar73- 2AtH	gd *1½	Hurdles	3:062 3↑	Alw 1750	6 6 54 1½ 12 12	O'Brien M	155	s		--	Athenian Idol1552Mr. Moody1456Cup Hunt1483	Driving	7
	Previously owned by J. Sheppard												
23Sep71- 3Bel	sf 1⅞	Hurdles	3:284	Elkridge H 19k	7 11 - - - -	Skiffington T Jr	135		41.60	--	Winigo1508JuacHollow1404ManchuPrince1414	Poor landing	11
27Aug71- 9Sar	sf 1⅝	Hurdles	3:082 3↑	Alw 6500	10 9 98½ 63¾ 711 97¾	O'Brien M	141		*2.30	--	ManchuPrince141½BrkngDwn141½GlrousCmbt1421¼	Bobbled	10
12Aug71- 9Sar	fm 1⅝	Hurdles	2:574 3↑	Alw 6500	7 6 77½ 1hd 11 1hd	Skiffington T Jr5	136		14.90	--	[D]AthnnIdl136hdArmyHtch1414½GlorousCombt1452	Bore out	8
	Disqualified and placed third												
28Jun71- 3Del	fm 1 1/16Ⓣ	:231 :471 1:123	1:453 3↑	Md Sp Wt	4 7 65½ 75¾ 68 510	Lee T	113		38.60	66-25	IrishTenor1242¾Chrisaway113nkForwardDrive1135	No factor	9
31May71- 4Del	my 6f	:223 :46	1:123 3↑	Md 7000	11 10 79 1015 1014 99¾	Lee T	110		47.30	72-18	SummrPlanning1101Villad'Est108¾NoonFlowr109½	No factor	12
17Nov70- 1Lrl	gd 7f	:232 :483 1:153	1:282	Md 5000	9 11 84¾ 66 813 821	Lee T	120		9.90	48-24	CallAssistant1129TedsGlow117½SharpDoer1202½	No factor	12

Autobiography

ch. c. 1968, by Sky High II (Star Kingdom)–King's Story, by Bold Ruler

Lifetime record: 36 10 11 4 $385,909

Own.– S. Sommer
Br.– Wheatley Stable (Ky)
Tr.– F. Martin

19Feb73- 8SA	fst 1½	:471 1:121 2:012 2:271 4↑	San Luis Obispo H-G2	3 7 712 - - -	Belmonte E	126	b	*.70e	--	Queen'sHustlr1127ChinaSilk1151¼RvrBuoy1171½	Broke down	9
3Feb73- 8SA	sly 1 1/16	:234 :464 1:102 1:414 4↑	San Pasqual H-G2	1 6 611½ 57 48½ 39¼	Belmonte E	125	b	*1.50	84-12	Single Agent1193½Kennedy Road1195¾Autobiography1252		6
	Passed tired horses											
2Dec72- 7Aqu	fst 1⅝	:463 1:37 2:022 2:41 3↑	Gallant Fox H 56k	2 5 510 31 12½ 1¾	Cordero A Jr	128	b	*.60	100-10	[D]Autobiography128¾CraftyKhal117nkRulbyRson1139	Bore in	7
	Disqualified and placed second											
28Oct72- 7Aqu	fst 2	:474 2:281 2:541 3:212 3↑	J C Gold Cup 113k	7 1 12 110 114 115	Cordero A Jr	124	b	2.10e	89-17	Autobiography12415KeytotheMnt1193RivaRidge11910	Easily	7
20Oct72- 7Aqu	my 1⅛	:48 1:123 1:372 1:494 3↑	Alw 15000	2 4 34 2hd 1hd 12	Cordero A Jr	119	b	1.50	87-20	Autbiography1192CnonroII119nkRulbyRson1163½	Ridden out	6
30Sep72- 7Bel	sly 1½	:47 1:112 2:012 2:282 3↑	Woodward 115k	8 10 1012 49 410 34¼	Cordero A Jr	126	b	6.10e	87-14	Key to the Mint1191¼[D]Summer Guest1163Autobiography1262		10
	Placed second through disqualification											
16Sep72- 7Det	fst 1⅛	:47 1:11 1:36 1:491 3↑	Mich 1⅛ H (Div 1) 78k	4 5 79 78¾ 45 34¼	Cordero A Jr	119	b	*1.20	87-16	King's Bishop116¾Figonero1103½Autobiography1194	Rallied	9
4Sep72- 7Bel	fst 1⅛	:47 1:111 1:354 1:481 3↑	Governor 118k	4 5 31½ 11 11½ 2hd	Cordero A Jr	120	b	4.30e	93-12	Loud114hdAutobiography1202Hitchcock120½	Sharp	12
26Aug72- 8Lib	sly 1¼	:471 1:114 1:371 2:024 3↑	Hobson H 100k	7 2 32 23 22 24¼	Cordero A Jr	121	b	*1.10e	91-20	West Coast Scout1204¼Autbiogrphy1213StaroftheNorth1131¼		7
	Gamely											
5Aug72- 7Sar	fst 1⅛	:474 1:112 1:362 1:491 3↑	Whitney 57k	8 7 75¼ 42 45 45¾	Belmonte E	120	b	5.20	89-12	Key to the Mint1132Tunex1173Loud117¾	Rallied	8
22Jly72- 7Aqu	fst 1¼	:472 1:102 1:35 2:00 3↑	Suburban H 113k	8 7 65 74½ 53½ 42¾	Velasquez J	126	b	*1.50e	93-10	Hitchcock1132WestCoastScout120nkNaskra110½	Raced wide	8
8Jly72- 7Aqu	fst 1 3/16	:484 1:12 1:362 1:544 3↑	Brooklyn H 118k	1 7 95 74½ 33 22	Cordero A Jr	122	b	5.30	98-09	Key to the Mint1122Autobiography1223WestCoastScout1141½		12
	Closed well											
28Jun72- 7Aqu	fst 7f	:223 :443 1:084 1:211 3↑	Nassau County H 28k	6 4 44 45 52 51½	Cordero A Jr	121	b	3.00	93-11	TowzieTyke114¾WstCoastScout116hdSilverMllt116½	Impeded	8
	Placed fourth through disqualification											
19Jun72- 7Aqu	sly 6f	:221 :451 1:091 3↑	Gravesend H 27k	3 5 59 58½ 58½ 57¼	Cordero A Jr	123	b	2.20	90-09	SilverMallet115nkCloseDcson1112½Rollckng1212½	No factor	5

15Apr72- 7Aqu fst 1⅛ :49 1:124 1:364 1:49 3↑ Excelsior H 58k 10 4 21 3nk 1hd 11½ Cordero A Jr 123 b *2.80e 91-10 Autobiogrphy1231½NatvRoylty115hdUrgntMssg119hd Driving 11
1Apr72- 7Aqu fst 1 :223 :442 1:083 1:341 3↑ Westchester H 57k 2 7 67¼ 54 1hd 11 Cordero A Jr 119 b 3.90e 96-15 Autobiography1191Tunx1192NtvRoylty118nk Bore in,driving 11
12Feb72- 8SA fst 1¼ :451 1:091 1:343 2:002 C H Strub 130k 10 7 69½ 52¾ 54 65¾ Belmonte E 118 b 4.00e 90-11 Unconscious121½TriplBnd118¾GoodCounsl116nk Lacked rally 11
29Jan72- 8SA fst 1⅛ :46 1:094 1:344 1:471 San Fernando 89k 1 6 66½ 53 31 1nk♦ Belmonte E 117 b 4.40e 96-07 [DH]Autobiography117[DH]Triple Bend117nkGood Counsel117no 12
Bumped,driving
19Jan72- 8SA fst 1 1/16 :241 :481 1:113 1:414 4↑ Alw 15000 1 6 65½ 66 55 34¼ Pincay L Jr 120 b *.90 89-13 TripleBnd1223¾GoodCounsl117½Autobogrphy120nk Late rally 6
8Jan72- 6SA fst 7f :213 :433 1:082 1:21 Malibu (Div 1) 46k 4 7 55½ 58½ 33 2no Pincay L Jr 117 b *1.40 98-08 KfarTov115noAutbiogrphy1177DplomtcAgnt117½ Just missed 7
1Jan72- 4SA fst 6f :212 :44 :562 1:091 Alw 15000 5 5 65¾ 69¼ 46½ 42¼ Pincay L Jr 122 b *2.00 93-10 Wing Out122½Kfar Tov118nkSingle Agent1181½ Wide turn 6
1Dec71- 7Aqu fst 1⅛ :473 1:124 1:381 1:502 Discovery H 34k 1 9 95 52½ 1hd 14½ Pincay L Jr 115 b 2.30 84-27 Autobiogrphy1154½Minsky1142BoonetheGret1093 Ridden out 11
23Nov71- 7Aqu fst 1⅛ :474 1:122 1:373 1:50 3↑ Alw 10000 6 6 612 57 2½ 1hd Ussery R 115 b *1.00 86-26 Autobiography115hdNight Patrol1137Fair Test113½ Driving 6
2Nov71- 5Aqu fst 6f :224 :461 1:093 3↑ Alw 9000 1 7 76½ 61 2hd 14 Ussery R 117 b *.80e 95-11 Autobiography1174LittleDixBay117¾Accohick1173½ Driving 7
18Oct71- 6Aqu fst 6f :224 :46 1:10 3↑ Alw 12000 7 4 63¾ 4¾ 31 2no Ussery R 117 b 6.50 93-18 Smelling Salts115noAutobiography117hdEver On1213 Sharp 8
Previously owned by O.M. Phipps;previously trained by R. Laurin
3Sep71- 7Bel fst 1⅛ :48 1:12 1:364 1:491 3↑ Alw 14000 2 4 44½ 55¼ 56¾ 56½ Baltazar C 112 6.70 81-17 Joans Bo113nkShadyside111noLaminate1161¼ No rally 7
26Aug71- 6Sar fst 7f :233 :462 1:103 1:223 3↑ Alw 10000 5 5 86¾ 86½ 87¼ 68½ Baltazar C 119 b 5.80 87-12 Riot1191½Bell Bird1192½Arctarus1143½ No threat 8
7Aug71- 4Sar fst 7f :224 :461 1:11 1:233 3↑ Alw 10000 5 5 76½ 83¼ 63½ 64¾ Cruguet J 119 b *2.90 86-11 Wig Out1192Bazoom124hdShadyside116½ No excuse 9
21Jly71- 5Aqu fst 7f :221 :451 1:101 1:224 3↑ Alw 10000 8 7 46 41 2hd 1hd Baltazar C 114 b *.90 87-15 Autobiography114hdSilverShield1122½AdobeEd1121 Driving 10
5Jly71- 5Aqu fst 6f :221 :453 1:102 3↑ Alw 10000 5 9 712 76 44½ 2½ Cruguet J 114 b 6.30 90-17 Ellen'sVoyage105½Autobiogrphy1141SlThrough117nk Gamely 9
10Jun71- 6Bel fst 1 :232 :464 1:113 1:363 3↑ Alw 10000 3 8 66½ 63½ 32½ 22 Baeza B 113 b *2.10 88-19 BoldCrusadr1142Autobiogrphy1132TrnqultyBs114nk Gaining 10
3Jun71- 7Bel fst 1 1/16 :241 :48 1:131 1:451 3↑ Alw 13000 4 5 3nk 41¾ 33 31½ Baeza B 113 b *1.00 76-22 Spread the Word112¾Tranquility Base114¾Autobiography1133 8
Wide turn;Previously trained by E.A. Neloy
18May71- 6Aqu fst 1⅛ :474 1:12 1:38 1:503 3↑ Alw 14000 3 8 87 65¾ 42 22½ Venezia M 108 b 4.90 80-19 EpicJourney1132½Autbiogrphy1081¼PncumRpns1185 Blocked 9
11May71- 8Aqu yl 1 1/16 [T] 1:452 3↑ Alw 13000 10 8 98½ 710 68 54 Baeza B 113 b *.80 80-19 Miannus110½Rough Place110¾Bulgari1132 No excuse 10
28Apr71- 1Aqu fst 7f :223 :461 1:121 1:251 3↑ Md Sp Wt 5 7 813 88¾ 42½ 13½ Baeza B 113 b *.90 75-23 Autobiography1133½Buckner112nkT.V.Replay1122 Mild drive 9
Previously owned by Wheatley Stable
5Jun70- 5Bel sly 5½f :233 :481 1:003 1:07 Md Sp Wt 3 3 54 32½ 33 22 Baeza B 122 b 5.00 83-18 AmberDuke1222Autobiography122hdGreatQuest1225 Gamely 9

Bold Forbes

dkbbr. c. 1973, by Irish Castle (Bold Ruler)–Comely Nell, by Commodore M. **Lifetime record: 18 13 1 4 $523,035**

Own.– E.R. Tizol
Br.– Eaton Farms Inc & Red Bull Stable (Ky)
Tr.– Lazaro S. Barrera

30Oct76- 8Aqu fst 7f :223 :443 1:083 1:214 3↑ Vosburgh H-G2 4 3 2½ 21 23½ 22 Cordero A Jr 126 b *.50 90-16 MyJuliet1202[D]BoldForbes1261It'sFrezng1132½ Bore in,out 6
Disqualified and placed third
19Oct76- 8Bel fst 6f :221 :444 1:092 3↑ Alw 30000 4 3 2½ 2hd 11 11½ Cordero A Jr 119 b *.40 95-14 BoldForbes1191½QuietLittlTbl119¾McCorkl117no Ridden out 6
5Jun76- 7Bel fst 1½ :47 1:111 2:014 2:29 Belmont-G1 8 1 16 16 16 1nk Cordero A Jr 126 b *.90 75-15 Bold Forbes126nkMcKenzieBridge126nkGreatContractor1268½ 10
Bore out,lasted
15May76- 8Pim fst 1 3/16 :45 1:09 1:351 1:55 Preakness-G1 4 1 12 12 2hd 34 Cordero A Jr 126 b 1.10e 91-11 Elocutonst1263½PlythRd126½BoldForbs1263 Drifted,swerved 6
1May76- 8CD fst 1¼ :454 1:102 1:353 2:013 Ky Derby-G1 2 1 15 1½ 1½ 11 Cordero A Jr 126 b 3.00 89-11 Bold Forbes1261Honest Pleasure1263¼Elocutionist1261¼ 9
Drifted,driving
17Apr76- 8Aqu fst 1⅛ :46 1:094 1:342 1:472 Wood Memorial-G1 5 2 13 11½ 14 14¾ Cordero A Jr 126 b *.40 98-11 BoldForbes1264¾OntheSly126nkSonkisser1261½ Ridden out 7
20Mar76- 8Aqu fst 7f :221 :44 1:081 1:204 Bay Shore-G3 7 2 2hd 12 17 17¾ Cordero A Jr 119 b 1.70 97-17 Bold Forbes1197¾Eustace121½Full Out1241½ Kept driving 8
28Feb76- 8SA fst 1 :223 :453 1:093 1:35 San Jacinto-G2 5 1 12 12 14 13 Pincay L Jr 117 b 2.10 94-12 BoldForbes1173Grandaries114¾StainedGlss122nk Mild drive 7
14Feb76- 8SA fst 7f :22 :443 1:09 1:214 San Vicente-G3 7 3 1hd 3½ 12½ 3¾ Pincay L Jr 119 b *1.70 93-11 ThermalEnergy117½StaindGlss122nkBoldForbs119½ Wide turn 7
24Jan76- 8SA fst 6f :221 :45 :57 1:093 San Miguel 33k 2 4 2½ 22 2½ 2no Pincay L Jr 120 b *1.30 91-12 SureFire114noBoldForbes120½RestlessRestless122nk Gamely 6
31Dec75- 4SA fst 5½f :214 :442 1:03 ©Alw 16000 1 3 1½ 2½ 2hd 35 Pincay L Jr 122 b *.30 94-14 Sure Fire114noBeau Talent1145Bold Forbes122hd Weakened 5
3Aug75- 8Sar fst 6f :224 :441 1:094 Sar Spl-G2 5 1 12 18 110 18 Velasquez J 120 b *.10 91-13 BoldForbes1208FamilyDoctor117hdGentleKng1203 Mild drive 5
23Jly75- 8Bel fst 6f :222 :452 1:092 Tremont 26k 2 2 1½ 12 14 15 Pincay L Jr 120 b 1.70 96-16 BoldForbes1205IronBit1149PeerlessMcGrath1141¾ Handily 5
Previously trained by R. Cruz
15Jun75- 7PR fst 6f :222 :443 1:103 Dia Padres 2 2 12 14 15 113 Hiraldo JF 118 b *.15 101-17 Bold Forbes11813Lovely Jay1183El Gallo1183¾ Easily 4
4Jun75- 4PR fst 6f :23 :453 1:112 Alw 3 1 12 13½ 15 18 Hiraldo JF 114 b *.25e 97-11 BoldForbes1148LovelyJay1167¼AnotherBeauty113hd Easily 10
25Apr75- 1PR fst 5f :22 :453 :591 Alw 3 1 14 15 16 18½ Hiraldo JF 116 b *.15 95-20 BoldForbes1168½LovelyJay1136½AnotherBeauty1137 Easily 5
11Apr75- 1PR fst 5f :22 :453 :584 Alw 4 1 15 15 15 15 Hiraldo JF 115 b *.30 97-20 Bold Forbes1155Lovely Jay11611Eternal Day1156½ Easily 5
12Mar75- 1PR fst 5f :22 :454 :592 Md Sp Wt 2 1 15 16 18 117 Hiraldo JF 116 b 35.00 94-20 BoldForbes11617MyDad'sBrandy1162½RubenJ.1161¼ Easily 8

Bowl Game

b. g. 1974, by Tom Rolfe (Ribot)–Around the Roses, by Round Table **Lifetime record: 23 11 6 5 $907,083**

Own.– Greentree Stable
Br.– Greentree Stud Inc (Ky)
Tr.– John M. Gaver Jr

15Jun80- 7Bel fm 1 1/16 Ⓣ :222 :45 1:082 1:40 3↑ Alw 35000 7 7 718 615½ 68¾ 25½ Velasquez J 122 *1.10 90-10 Told1175½BowlGame122hdScythnGold119no Finished strongly 7
10Nov79- 8Lrl sf 1½ Ⓣ :573 1:252 2:232 2:51 3↑ D C Int'l-G1 7 3 21½ 21 2hd 1¾ Velasquez J 127 3.60 -- Bowl Game127¾Trillion124noLe Marmot1208 Driving 8
27Oct79- 8Aqu fm 1½ Ⓣ :481 1:14 2:044 2:281 3↑ Turf Classic-G1 2 3 312 22 22½ 1nk Velasquez J 126 2.80 120-00 Bowl Game126nkTrillion123nkNative Courier1264¾ Driving 7
8Oct79- 8Bel sf 1⅜ Ⓣ :512 1:17 1:42 2:19 3↑ Man o' War-G1 3 3 36 32½ 24 1hd Velasquez J 126 2.60 67-38 Bowl Game126hdNative Courier12611Czaravich1212¾ Driving 4
1Sep79- 8AP fm 1½ Ⓣ :48 1:13 2:061 2:321 3↑ Arlington H-G2 2 9 1024 47 1½ 14½ Velasquez J 124 *.70 78-28 BowlGme1244½YoungBob1108Liveinthesunshine105½ Drew out 14
21Jly79- 8Bel fst 1½ :503 1:15 2:033 2:284 3↑ Brooklyn H-G1 2 3 42½ 34½ 31½ 2¾ Velasquez J 119 5.10 75-24 TheLiberlMember114¾BwlGme119hdStateDinnr1232¾ Gamely 5
1Jly79- 8Bel fm 1⅜ [T] :483 1:133 1:374 2:131 3↑ Tidal H-G2 2 2 2hd 3nk 11 2hd Velasquez J 125 *.70 103-11 Gldn Rsve109hdBowl Game125nkScthn Gold1101¾ Didn't last 5
16Jun79- 8Bel fm 1⅜ [T] :48 1:12 1:352 2:112 3↑ Bowling Green H-G2 3 4 49½ 67¼ 22½ 34 Velasquez J 123 5.20 108-01 Overskate1174Waya125hdBowl Game1231¾ Gave way 7
14Apr79-11Hia hd 1½ Ⓣ 2:263 3↑ Hia Turf Cup H-G2 7 6 64½ 3½ 2½ 1¾ Cordero A Jr 122 2.90 98-10 BowlGame122¾NobleDancerII1305GreatSound111hd Driving 7
4Apr79- 9Hia fm *1⅛ Ⓣ 1:462 4↑ Alw 20000 5 5 58½ 53½ 43½ 35½ Velasquez J 114 *1.20 97-08 That's a Nice1144½Fed Funds1141Bowl Game114½ Bumped 7
22Mar79- 9Hia fst 6f :23 :462 1:103 4↑ Alw 13000 1 8 74¾ 76½ 57½ 510 Velasquez J 114 *.80 80-18 NorthCourse1194GetPermsson1221½Robb'sChrm1194½ Slow st. 8
17Jun78- 8Bel fm 1⅜ Ⓣ :482 1:121 1:361 2:122 3↑ Bowling Green H-G2 2 7 711 76¼ 53 33¾ Velasquez J 124 *1.20 97-10 Tiller1172½Proud Arion1111½Bowl Game124¾ Rallied 10
29May78- 8Hol fm 1½ Ⓣ :472 1:112 2:012 2:254 3↑ Hol Inv'l H-G1 10 8 1011 42 32½ 22½ Velasquez J 123 3.00 96-04 Exceller1272½Bowl Game123½Noble Dancer II1263½ Rallied 12
13May78- 8Pim sf 1½ Ⓣ :48 1:144 2:072 2:332 3↑ Dixie H (Div 2)-G2 6 4 58 42 12 16 Velasquez J 120 *.40 70-29 Bowl Game1206Oilfield110¾Trumpeter Swan110hd Handily 9
15Apr78- 9GP fm 1½ Ⓣ :494 1:152 2:061 2:301 3↑ Pan American H-G2 7 7 66 96 2hd 11½ Velasquez J 117 *1.00 73-22 Bowl Game1171½That's a Nice116½Court Open112¾ Driving 10
25Mar78- 9GP fst 1¼ :46 1:101 1:354 2:003 3↑ Gulf Park H-G1 9 7 810 31 2hd 12 Velasquez J 112 4.10 94-21 BowlGme1122TrueStatement1081½SilverSers1265 Drew clear 11
4Mar78- 8Hia fst 1⅛ :473 1:113 1:362 1:483 4↑ Alw 11000 6 8 86¼ 53¾ 12 15½ Velasquez J 114 *.40 89-05 Bowl Game1145½Roy Roy1229Turra Murra1194½ Easily 8
24Feb78- 8Hia yl *1⅛ Ⓣ 1:52 4↑ Alw 9000 3 10 109¾ 85¾ 42½ 13 Velasquez J 114 *.70 75-30 Bowl Game1143Tabatex1141½In All Sincerity1141½ Handily 10
15Feb78- 3Hia fst 7f :232 :462 1:113 1:241 Md Sp Wt 5 11 1011 89 31 13 Velasquez J 122 *.40 82-20 BowlGme1223Czar'sRansom1222½Yestertime1221 Drew clear 11
3Feb78- 3Hia fst 6f :224 :461 1:11 Md Sp Wt 3 10 1111 810 56 2½ Velasquez J 122 *.30 87-18 Darkest Hour122½Bowl Game1223½Dr. Joe F.1221 Gaining 12
19Jan78- 3Hia sly 6f :214 :45 1:092 Md Sp Wt 4 7 1011 710 46 24 Velasquez J 122 *2.30 92-14 NorthernDictatr1224BowlGame1222DressExtra1226 2nd best 12
Previously trained by John M. Gaver
20Aug77- 1Sar fst 6f :221 :454 1:104 3↑ Md Sp Wt 1 9 65½ 77 67 39 Cauthen S 117 4.70 77-10 Roger W.1176¼Sun Flame1172¾Bowl Game117½ Raced wide 9
11Aug77- 1Sar sly 6f :22 :444 1:10 3↑ Md Sp Wt 8 5 45 411 48 39½ Cauthen S 117 3.90e 80-12 ThePrnc'sPants1228¼CmAwyWthMe1171¼BwlGme1171½Evenly 8

Cafe Prince

b. g. 1970, by Creme Dela Creme (Olympia)–Princess Blair, by Blue Prince — Lifetime record: 52 18 5 4 $228,238
Own.– Augustin Stable
Br.– Verne H. Winchell (Cal)
Tr.– Jonathan E. Sheppard

1Nov80- 3Mtp fm *2½ S'Chase 4:41 4↑ Noel Laing H 5.4k 2 4 41¾ 35 518 633¾ Cushman J 157 - -- Owhata Chief1588½Down First15715Pala Mountain1456 6
18Oct80- 5RB fm *2 S'Chase 3:44 3↑ Metcalf Mem 7k 1 5 3¾ 1nk 11 11¾ Cushman J 158 -e -- Cafe Prince1581¾Quixotic1461Wasted Trip140½ Driving 7
9Oct80- 6Bel fm 2 S'Chase 3:554 3↑ Alw 25000 2 4 512 512 417 420¼ Cushman J 157 3.00 -- Cookie1412½CocontCreek14913PalMountn1424¾ Outrun early 7
27Sep80- 5Fx fm *2⅝ S'Chase 5:034 4↑ Handicap 20000 2 2 2¾ 11½ 1¾ 21 Cushman J 155 - -- Down First1531Cafe Prince1556Blue Nearco1349 4
13Sep80- 6Lig hd *2Ⓣ 3:40 3↑ Alw 2500 8 1 18 112 14 112 Sheppard J 168 - -- CafePrince16812WaterTable16216PrivateGry1688 Ridden out 9
22Aug80- 6Sar fm 2 1/16 S'Chase 3:422 3↑ Handicap 25000 1 4 - - - - Champion R 158 7.90 -- Popular Hero1381Too Few Stripes130¾Romeo Lima1452½ Fell 7
14Aug80- 6Sar fm 2⅜ S'Chase 4:141 4↑ NY Turf Writers H 43k 6 5 11½ 734 - - Champion R 161 1.20e -- Zaccio1571¼Running Comment1422¼Leaping Frog1522¼ Eased 7
1Aug80- 8Del fm 1 1/16Ⓣ :234 :48 1:122 1:46 3↑ Alw 7000 9 7 711 812 69½ 512 Dufton E 117 7.20 62-30 Lightning Lead1176½Freon1152Dr. Williams1053 No factor 9
10Nov79- 6Uni yl *2Ⓣ 3:45 3↑ Alw 1000 2 2 34½ 415 46 424 Strawbridge G Jr 168 - -- Town and Country1685Quixotic1644Ruysch16815 Tired 9
3Oct79- 6Lig sf *2 S'Chase 4:321 4↑ Rolling Rock Cup 17k 1 2 2½ - - - Small D Jr 166 - -- HappyIntellctual1492½FirControl15010Beauhill138 Pulled up 5
23Aug79- 6Sar fm 2⅜ S'Chase 4:174 4↑ NY Turf Writers H 21k 2 4 47½ 64½ 615 636 Quanbeck A Jr 167 *.40e -- Leaping Frog1598¾Tan Jay1506½Canadian Regent143hd Tired 6
3Aug79- 6Sar fm 2 1/16 S'Chase 3:411 4↑ Lovely Night H 21k 3 3 23 13 11½ 12¾ Fishback J 164 *.40e -- CafePrince1642¾LeapingFrog1613¾Mrt'sAngr1555 Ridden out 7
13Jly79- 3Del fm *2¼ S'Chase 4:162 4↑ Handicap 10000 1 5 - - - - Fishback J 165 *1.20 -- Martie'sAnger1521¼DeuxCoup159½StraightandTrue1457 Fell 5
12May79- 7Fai fm *2 3/16 S'Chase 4:112 4↑ Handicap 10000 1 - - - - - Fishback J 164 *1.10 -- DeuxCoup1552¾StraightandTrue1481LoveIn1425 Lost rider 7
28Apr79- 5Fx gd *1Ⓣ 1:473 3↑ Alw 2000 6 9 924 718 1nk 1nk Fishback J 145 - -- CafePrince145nkDeuxCoup1442StatelyPrince137nk Driving 11
18Nov78- 4Cam fm 2¾ S'Chase 5:102 4↑ Colonial Cup 100k 1 7 513 28 2¾ 32 Fishback J 162 - -- GrandCnyon1622DeuxCoup155hdCfePrnc16217 Bid,weakened 10
20Oct78- 6Bel fm 2⅝ S'Chase 4:52 4↑ Temple Gwathmey H 36k 2 1 1½ 2hd 1½ 24 Fishback J 167 *.70 -- FireControl1464CafePrince167noPopularHero1398¾ 2nd best 6
7Oct78- 4Lig yl *2½ S'Chase 5:224 4↑ Int'l Gold Cup H 25k 2 1 14 110 112 114 Fishback J 163 - -- CafePrince16314Crg'sCornr14315PopulrHro14112 Ridden out 6
23Sep78- 7Fai fm *2½ S'Chase 4:574 4↑ Grand National H 10k 1 1 11 1½ 14 13 Fishback J 158 *.70 -- CafePrince1583LeapingFrog155hdHappyIntllctul155 In hand 5
16Sep78- 4Fai fm *1 5/16Ⓣ 2:173 3↑ Alw 1000 2 8 88½ 712 51½ 32¾ Fishback J 145 *1.60 -- PopularHero152noHappyIntellectul1412¾CfPrnc1455 Rallied 10
26Nov77- 4Cam fm 2¾ S'Chase 5:223 4↑ Colonial Cup 100k 1 6 66¾ 36 21½ 15½ Fishback J 162 -e -- Cafe Prince1625½Bel Iman1518Leaping Frog1464½ Handily 12
29Oct77- 6FH yl *2 5/16 S'Chase 5:19 4↑ Handicap 10000 2 7 52¼ 33 1½ 1hd Fishback J 155 -e -- Cafe Prince155hdBel Iman1451Fire Control143½ Lasted 8
14Oct77- 6Bel sf 2⅝ S'Chase 5:161 4↑ Temple Gwathmey H 36k 2 6 32½ 2½ 622 629 Fishback J 159 *1.00 -- Bel Iman14010Deux Coup1493¾Leaping Frog1428 Stopped 6
8Oct77- 4Lig sf *2½ S'Chase 5:311 4↑ Int'l Gold Cup H 25k 1 7 512 115 112 118 Fishback J 155 - -- CafePrnce15518ItsGoodforYou1377MichaelsMad13710 Easily 8
5Oct77- 7Lig yl *7fⓉ 1:361 3↑ Alw 2500 2 8 83½ 63¾ 3¾ 2½ Fishback J 143 -e -- Down First155½Cafe Prince1431½Jacasaba140¾ Rallied 13
25Aug77- 6Sar fm 2⅜ S'Chase 4:184 4↑ NY Turf Writers H 21k 8 4 421 65 33½ 58 Fishback J 158 3.10 -- HappyIntellectual152¾NvlPrson143hdCsmyor1505½ Bid,tired 8
15Aug77- 4Sar fm 2 1/16 S'Chase 3:453 4↑ Alw 12500 2 5 37 31½ 11½ 15 Fishback J 156 *.90e -- CafePrince1565SunnyIce1302¾LeapingFrog14510 Ridden out 9
5Aug77- 6Sar fm 2 1/16 S'Chase 3:441 4↑ Lovely Night H 21k 6 3 411 511 45½ 46¾ Fishback J 157 3.40 -- Life'sIlluson1603¼Csmyor149½HppyIntllctul1543 No mishap 6
23Jly77- 3Del fm 2⅜ S'Chase 4:38 4↑ Indian River H 13k 7 7 73¼ 65¼ 35 36½ Fishback J 158 *.80e -- Jacasaba1422½Salvo1414Cafe Prince158½ Rallied 7
16Jly77- 4Del fm 1 1/16Ⓣ :233 :471 1:12 1:431 3↑ Clm 40000 2 3 34 34½ 45½ 414 Castaneda K 119 2.40 74-10 Famous Jim1177Ensilage117¾Jamison1176 Lacked rally 4

15Nov75- 4Cam fm 2 13/16 S'Chase 5:301 4↑ Colonial Cup 50k 7 7 125¾ 67 41 13 Washer D 160 -e -- Cafe Prince1603Augustus Bay162½Soothsayer162½ Handily 18
25Oct75- 6FH sf *2 5/16 S'Chase 4:45 4↑ Handicap 10000 4 8 712 77½ 3½ 21½ Fishback J 160 -e -- Life'sIllusion1511½CafePrinc160½TllAwrd150½ Closed well 8
4Oct75- 4Lig yl *2½ S'Chase 5:211 4↑ Temple Gwathmey 25k 3 5 53 38½ 36 315¾ Fishback J 151 -e -- HappyIntellectual149¾SpeedKills14715CafePrinc1516 Tired 7
13Sep75- 5Fai fm *2 3/16 S'Chase 4:07 3↑ Handicap 3500 9 8 57½ 33 1½ 11½ Fishback J 158 *.90e -- Cafe Prince1581½County Wicklow1402Winigo143¾ Driving 10

2Aug74- 6Sar fm 2 1/16 S'Chase 3:443 4↑ Lovely Night H 22k 4 9 78 11 16 12¾ Fishback J 145 9.70e -- CfePrince1452¾GranKan1603JuacHollow1548 Speed to spare 10
18Jly74- 6Del fm 1 1/16Ⓣ :233 :463 1:103 1:432 4↑ Alw 5500 3 5 412 47½ 45 5½ McCarron G 119 5.00 86-15 MistrYouEssay113nkBuffloRun112nkJucHollow107hd Closing 6
10Jly74- 4Mth fm 1 1/16Ⓣ :24 :482 1:123 1:431 3↑ Alw 7500 8 3 54 42 57½ 616 Tichenor W 120 14.30 77-11 PamperedJabneh124noMr.Darby12011FlyngWedge124½ Tired 8
25Jun74- 4Del fst 1 1/16 :231 :472 1:122 1:442 4↑ Alw 5500 7 5 510 511 615 718 McCarron G 119 7.00 69-18 PlayEveryDay1125MistrYouEssy1143½CryStrt1071½ No factor 8
8Jun74- 8Del fm *2½ S'Chase 4:323 4↑ Indian River H 13k 11 7 65 43 64¾ 822 Fishback J 146 4.60 -- Gran Kan1581Metello153hdLucky Boy III1552¾ Tired 11
25May74- 5Del fm 1Ⓣ :234 :481 1:134 1:391 3↑ Md Sp Wt 12 5 53½ 32½ 11½ 15 McCarron G 122 4.10e 79-24 Cafe Prince1225Bronze Image122noIdle Gossip1155 Handily 12
11May74- 1Fai fm *7fⓉ 1:262 3↑ Alw 1000 5 2 28 210 412 618 O'Brien L 149 *1.40e -- SunMeeting15213CitizenX.155nkUnexpectedVstor1552½ Tired 15
17Nov73- 4Cam fm *2 Hurdles 3:463 3↑ Handicap 5000 2 6 55 2½ 1½ 12½ O'Brien M 150 - -- Cafe Prince1502½Gun Gold142½Plumsted1391½ Easily 6
27Oct73- 4FH fm *2 Hurdles 4:051 3↑ SK Martin H 10k 1 3 1½ 16 11½ 11½ O'Brien M 136 s - -- CafePrince1361½JuacHollow1623½SummerCrop14210 Driving 6
6Oct73- 1Lig fm *1¾ Hurdles 3:181 3↑ Alw 4000 4 5 119¾ 45½ 21 14 O'Brien M 143 - -- Cafe Prince1434Remagen145½Jacasaba1524½ Drew out 13
17Sep73- 2Bel fst 1⅛⊗ :47 1:111 1:371 1:504 3↑ Md Sp Wt 5 7 77 712 715 716 Maple E 116 13.60 61-14 Walther F.1161Tonk1161½Vehement116hd No factor 7
14Aug73- 9Sar fm 1⅝ Hurdles 2:552 3↑ Md 10000 4 4 54 26 1½ 16½ Fishback J 139 *1.50 -- Cafe Prince1396½Tarrative1363National Park15316 Handily 8
7Aug73- 9Sar fm 1⅞ Hurdles 3:222 3↑ Md Sp Wt 5 5 78½ 25 24 26½ Fishback J 138 5.00e -- Bailar1546½CafePrince1388½NationalPark1542½ Second best 8
16May73- 1Pim fst 6f :231 :471 1:132 3↑ Md 10500 9 7 105½ 85¾ 75¼ 65¼ Lee T 115 20.00 74-10 FeudingClan1152PassingFlight115noPittrnsh1171¼ No threat 12
2May73- 3Pim fst 6f :232 :47 1:122 3↑ Md Sp Wt 4 7 75¼ 95 76¼ 58¾ Black AS 114 b 19.90 75-17 Gallant Hitter1141¾Impressive Imp1143Raza114½ Outrun 12
16Apr73- 2Pim fst 6f :231 :472 1:14 3↑ Md 10500 1 5 43½ 33 2½ 84¼ Lee T 114 b 11.70 72-24 Robert'sDay117noRathcool1142¼VillirsLd114no Speed,tired 11
1Dec72- 3Lrl my 6f :221 :454 1:112 Md Sp Wt 8 8 812 814 822 819 Lee T 120 b 7.90 74-14 DoublEdgeSword1203Startahemp120½ThEqulzr1205 No factor 8
10Aug72- 3Del fst 5½f :224 :473 1:001 1:063 Md Sp Wt 2 5 53 64¼ 615 615 Lee T 120 5.20 70-19 SecurityGuard1201¼CosmicTraffic1203VllrsLd1204 No speed 6

Candy Eclair

gr. f. 1976, by Northern Jove (Northern Dancer)–Candy's Best, by Candy Spots — Lifetime record: 23 15 4 1 $403,845
Own.– Mrs H.D. Paxson
Br.– Mrs Henry D. Paxson (Ky)
Tr.– Mary Edens

3Dec80- 8Aqu fst 6f[•] :223 :462 1:111 3↑ ⒻPetrify H 56k 9 2 51½ 2½ 32 31 Solomone M 124 *1.20 87-21 SoftColrs1141TheWheelTurns113noCndyEclr124nk Weakened 9
11Nov80- 8Aqu fst 7f :24 :482 1:131 1:253 3↑ ⒻFirst Flight H 56k 5 3 1hd 1½ 4¾ 53¾ Brumfield D 126 *.90 69-30 SamartaDancer1121½Jedina1151½Damask Fan112¾ Weakened 9
18Oct80- 8Aqu fst 7f :223 :443 1:084 1:212 3↑ Vosburgh-G1 8 1 2½ 2½ 53½ 86¼ Bailey JD 123 13.90 88-12 PluggdNickle123½JaklinKlugman1231Dav'sFrnd126¾ Used up 9
8Oct80- 8Bel fst 6f :221 :452 1:103 3↑ Boojum H 57k 8 7 31 31½ 52 22¼ Bailey JD 124 10.40 87-22 Double Zeus1202¼Candy Eclair124hdKing's Fashion123no 9
Altered course
24Sep80- 8Bel fst 6f :223 :453 1:103 3↑ ⒻGrey Flight H 55k 5 1 2hd 3nk 11 12¾ Bailey JD 125 *1.30 89-20 Candy Eclair1252¾[D]The Wheel Turns113nkMongo Queen114¾ 8
Ridden out
10Aug80- 9Del fst 6f :213 :44 1:094 3↑ ⒻEndine H 45k 1 5 1hd 2½ 1hd 1¾ Bailey JD 126 *.50 96-10 CndyEclr126¾[D]SheCan'tMiss112¾WondrousMe108no Driving 9
23Jly80- 8Bel my 7f :221 :451 1:10 1:223 3↑ ⒻImperatrice H 55k 5 3 2hd 1hd 21½ 23½ Bailey JD 124 *1.70 85-22 Alada1173½Candy Eclair1242Pradera1153 2nd best 6
2Jly80- 8Mth fm 5fⓉ :22 :444 :571 3↑ ⒻAlw 16000 7 1 4nk 1hd 11 15 Bailey JD 122 *.40 97-03 CndyEclair1225CavyCakes1151½ThalieDncr115no Ridden out 8
15Jun80- 5Bel fst 6f :232 :471 1:11 3↑ ⒻAlw 32000 2 1 11 11 13 11 Bailey JD 119 *.40 87-17 CandyEclair1191Pradera1191¾SpanishFake1192½ Ridden out 5
31May80- 8Mth fst 6f :214 :441 1:093 3↑ ⒻRegret H 33k 6 2 1hd 1½ 11½ 11½ Bailey JD 125 *.40 92-13 CndyEclr1251½GrcnVctry1121¼CornshQueen1163 Ridden out 7
23May80- 7Mth fst 6f :213 :442 1:10 4↑ ⒻAlw 16000 6 1 2hd 1hd 11½ 15 Bailey JD 122 *.70 90-16 Candy Eclair1225Cornish Queen1221¼Hill Billy Dancer118½ 7
Ridden out
1Apr80- 8GP sly 6f :222 :453 1:102 4↑ ⒻAlw 14000 7 2 12 11½ 11 11¼ Solomone M 114 *.40 87-20 Candy Eclair1141¼Guimauve1171¼Dungarven1191 In hand 8
2Jun79- 8Mth fst 6f :212 :441 1:094 ⒻMiss Woodford 27k 2 5 1½ 1½ 1½ 21 Black AS 123 *.60 90-20 DropMeANote1151CndyEclr123¾Restanbegon1192 No excuse 7
4May79- 8CD sly 1 1/16 :241 :48 1:134 1:471 ⒻKy Oaks-G1 6 1 14 11 2hd 47 Black AS 121 3.00 65-30 Davona Dale1214½Himalayan1212Prize Spot121½ Wide,tired 6
21Apr79- 7Kee fst *7f 1:27 ⒻAshland-G2 3 4 11 1½ 1hd 11½ Black AS 121 *.30 88-13 CndyEclr1211½Hmlyn1141¼CountssNorth1151¾ Bumped,driving 7
Previously trained by S. Allen King Jr
28Feb79- 0GP fst 7f :221 :442 1:083 1:21 ⒻBonnie Miss 27k 4 2 11½ 1½ 1½ 2¾ Black AS 122 - 98-17 DavonaDale122¾CandyEclair12220ProveMeSpecial1142 Failed 4
Run between 7th and 8th races - No wagering

14Feb79- 9GP	fst 6f	:22 :441 1:083	ⒻShirley Jones 28k	4	1	14	15	14	11¾	Black AS	122		*.50	96-16	CandyEclair1221¾DavonaDale1228DropMeaNote1141	Handily	4
3Feb79- 9GP	fst 6f	:213 :441 1:101	ⒻAlw 20000	5	2	11½	13	14	12½	Black AS	117		*.10	88-10	CndyEclair1172½PrecociousLss1141¼FeuD'Artfc114nk	Easily	6
21Oct78- 8Lrl	fst 1 1/16	:233 :471 1:13 1:453	ⒻSelima-G1	4	1	11	11½	11½	11½	Black AS	119		2.10	85-24	CndyEclr1191½WhisprFleet1191½DropMeANote11913	Driving	7
30Sep78- 8Atl	fst 7f	:214 :442 1:101 1:221	ⒻMermaid 75k	2	2	11½	12	13	12	Black AS	117		*.90e	91-16	Candy Eclair1172Salem Ho113nkWhisper Fleet1211½	Easily	7
2Sep78- 6Atl	fst 6f	:213 :442 1:10	ⒻBrigantine 21k	4	4	1½	11	12	16	Black AS	113		2.10e	92-19	CandyEclair1136[D]SalemHo113½MaybetheBest114no	Easily	11
23Aug78- 6Mth	fst 6f	:221 :452 1:104	ⒻAlw 9000	1	3	11	1½	12½	15	Black AS	117		*1.30	86-17	Candy Eclair1175Bedtime Toy1171Gentle Touch117¾	Easily	6
5Jly78- 5Mth	fst 5f	:221 :462 :592	ⒻMd Sp Wt	7	4	42½	32	32½	1nk	Black AS	117		7.40	89-23	CandyEclair117nkDropMeANote1175OurRuler117nk	Just up	8

Canonero II

b. c. 1968, by Pretendre (Doutelle)–Dixieland II, by Nantallah

Lifetime record: 23 9 3 4 $361,006

Own.– King Ranch
Br.– Edward B. Benjamin (Ky)
Tr.– W.J. Hirsch

20Oct72- 7Aqu	my 1⅛	:48 1:123 1:372 1:494	3↑ Alw 15000	3	2	22	1hd	2hd	22	Avila G	119	b	*.90	85-20	Autobiogrphy1192CnonroII119nkRulbyRson1163½	Held place	6
20Sep72- 7Bel	fst 1⅛	:461 1:093 1:332 1:461	3↑ Stymie H 28k	5	3	32	2hd	1½	15	Avila G	110	b	5.50	103-07	Canonero II1105Riva Ridge1236Loud115½	Brisk handling	5
1Sep72- 6Bel	fst 1 1/16	:231 :452 1:091 1:412	3↑ Alw 12000	8	2	11	15	1½	55¼	Avila G	114		*1.50	91-12	HolyLand115¾RulebyReason1201½UrgentMessage1201½	Tired	9
12Aug72- 5Sar	fst 7f	:224 :452 1:092 1:222	3↑ Alw 15000	2	6	68	35	36½	26	Gustines H	115		2.80	89-11	Onion1106Canonero II115½Sportique1161½	Gamely	6
29Jly72- 7Aqu	hd 1 3/16Ⓣ	:48 1:112 1:353 1:54	3↑ Tidal H 59k	4	7	79	74¾	1011	99	Rotz JL	117	b	7.10	91-02	Droll Role1211½Twist the Axe111½Tentam108¾	No factor	10
19Jly72- 6Aqu	fm 1 1/16Ⓣ	:234 :471 1:103 1:412	3↑ Alw 15000	3	5	44½	42½	84¼	66	Rotz JL	113		5.00	90-06	Maraschino II1121½Apollo Nine1121Gleaming121hd	Gave way	8
29May72- 7Bel	fst 1	:224 :451 1:094 1:352	3↑ Metropolitan H 118k	7	8	95¼	108¼	1010	89½	Rotz JL	123		2.70	85-13	Executionr119nkBoldReasoning1231¼PecCorps113½	In close	11
20May72- 7Bel	sly 7f	:22 :442 1:091 1:222	3↑ Carter H 57k	5	7	814	711	46½	24¾	Rotz JL	121		4.20	90-09	Leematt1164¾CanoneroII121¾NativeRoylty121¾	Wide,rallied	8
	Previously owned by E. de Caibet;previously trained by J. Arias																
5Jun71- 8Bel	fst 1½	:481 1:122 2:03 2:302	Belmont 162k	7	1	12½	21½	25	44½	Avila G	126		*.70	76-15	PassCatchr126¾JimFrench1263½BoldReason126nk	Weakened	13
15May71- 8Pim	fst 1 3/16	:47 1:102 1:35 1:54	Preakness 189k	9	2	2hd	2hd	1hd	11½	Avila G	126		*3.40	103-09	CanoneroII1261½EasternFleet1264½JimFrench126no	Driving	11
1May71- 9CD	fst 1¼	:464 1:113 1:361 2:031	Ky Derby 188k	12	16	1820	42½	13	13¾	Avila G	126		8.70f	84-13	CanoneroII1263¾JimFrench1262BoldReason126nk	Ridden out	20
10Apr71♦ Rinconada(Ven)	fst*1⅛LH	1:544	3↑ Free Hcp (Series 4a-5a) Hcp3500						33¾	Guzman RD	112		*.40		Mon Chanson1122¼Golden Flake1191½Canonero II1121¾	Tracked in 3rd,lacked rally	11
4Apr71♦ Rinconada(Ven)	fst6½fLH	1:171	3↑ Free Hcp (Series 5a) Hcp3300						16½	Guzman RD	110		*.80		Canonero II1106½Fast Track1102¼Mi Rebano106½	Well placed in 3rd,led 1½ f out,easily	14
21Mar71♦ Rinconada(Ven)	fst*6½fLH	1:164	Free Hcp (Series 6a) Hcp3200						1½	Avila G	126		*1.20		Canonero II126½Latour1083½Carven1102	Midpack,strong late run,led near line	11
14Mar71♦ Rinconada(Ven)	fst* 6½fLH	1:174	Free Hcp (Series 6a) Hcp3200						35	Avila G	126		4.20		Mi Rebano1153King River1172Canonero II126hd	Rated in 7th,finished well	12
7Mar71♦ Rinconada(Ven)	fst*1¼LH	2:032	Free Hcp (Series 8a) Hcp2800						12½	Avila G	115		*1.40		Canonero II1152½Neverest1103½Paupero1081¼	Led final furlong,quickly clear	14
14Feb71♦ Rinconada(Ven)	fst*1LH	1:411	Free Hcp (Series 6a) Hcp3200						34¼	Contreras JE	112				Rienda Suelta1144¼Harmattan114hdCanonero II1121¼	Tracked leader,weakened late	12
7Feb71♦ Rinconada(Ven)	fst*1¼LH	2:061	Clasico Prensa Nacional Stk15800						11	Cruz JE	105				Yves114nkEjemplo127nkOutsville1234¾	Never a factor	12
9Jan71♦ Rinconada(Ven)	my*7fLH	1:262	Free Hcp (Series 7a) Hcp3000						15¼	Contreras JE	110				Canonero II1105¼Silver Spray1163Fast Track1103¼	Always close up,led 2f out,easily clear	14
17Dec70♦ Rinconada(Ven)	fst*6fLH	1:124	Free Hcp (Series 8a) Hcp2800						11	Contreras JE	112				Canonero II1101Grass Paddock1102¼Florencio1123¼	Tracked in 3rd,led 1f out,ridden out	14
12Sep70- 7Dmr	fst 6f	:213 :441 :561 1:084	Dmr Futurity 108k	5	5	64	77	77	57¾	Ferrer I	116		10.90	87-12	June Darling1192Kfar Tov1193Bold Joey1162	Not a factor	9
5Sep70- 6Dmr	fst 6f	:214 :444 :572 1:10	©Alw 5500	3	9	89¼	84½	44	31½	Ferrer I	120		21.50	87-14	King Cross1171½Serenader114hdCanonero II1203	Rallied	9
8Aug70♦ Rinconada(Ven)	fst*6fLH	1:13	Free Hcp (Series 9a) Hcp2600						16½	Contreras JE	110		12.60e		Canonero II1106½Comenve106½Gramal115½	Rallied to lead 1f out,drew clear final 16th	13

Cascapedia

b. f. 1973, by Chieftain (Bold Ruler)–Princess Ribot, by Ribot

Lifetime record: 19 10 4 2 $324,921

Own.– Bernard J. Ridder
Br.– Raymond R. Guest (Ky)
Tr.– Gordon C. Campbell

24Sep77- 8Bel	sly 1⅛	:46 1:111 1:374 1:521	31 ⒻRuffian H-G1	11	2	43	31½	2hd	31	Hawley S	128	b	3.90	65-25	CumLaudeLaurie114½MssissippMd123½Cscpd1281¼	Very wide	12
5Sep77- 8Dmr	fst *1¼	:443 1:081 1:323 1:552	3↑ Del Mar H-G2	6	7	711	56½	37½	38	Hawley S	117	b	3.00	98-08	AncientTitle1235PaintedWagon1183Cascapedia1171	Rallied	9
10Jly77- 8Hol	fst 1⅛	:463 1:103 1:35 1:473	3↑ ⒻVanity H-G1	6	5	55	43	3½	1no	Hawley S	129	b	*1.10	94-17	Cascapedia129noBastonera II1221¼Swingtime1174	Driving	9
18Jun77- 8Hol	fst 1¼	:451 1:09 1:334 2:00	3↑ Hol Gold Cup H-G1	8	10	98¼	33	21	2nk	Pierce D	116	b	3.80	91-13	CrystalWater129nkCascapedia116noCaucasus1245	Forced out	12
4Jun77- 8Hol	fst 1 1/16	:224 :461 1:10 1:404	3↑ ⒻMilady H-G2	3	5	44	31	1½	13	Hawley S	126	b	*1.50	91-15	Cascapedia1263Rocky Trip1152Just a Kick1182	Easily	6
21May77- 8Hol	fm 1 1/16Ⓣ	:221 :451 1:102 1:404	3↑ ⒻHawthorne H 44k	8	3	312	1hd	1½	12¾	Hawley S	123	b	*1.40e	95-07	Cascapedia1232¾BastoneraII124¾StarBall121nk	Mild drive	10
12May77- 8Hol	gd 1⅛	:471 1:111 1:361 1:483	4↑ ⒻAlw 30000	4	3	2½	1hd	12	15	Hawley S	117	b	*.70	89-21	Cascapedia1175Woodsome114nkUp to Juliet1196	Easily	5
29Apr77- 6Hol	fm 1 1/16Ⓣ	:233 :48 1:114 1:42	4↑ ⒻAlw 25000	5	5	31	3½	11	12½	Hawley S	114	b	*.70	89-13	Cascapedia1142½Katonka1152Mia Amore122nk	Handily	5
16Apr77- 8Hol	fm 1⅛Ⓣ	:492 1:141 1:382 1:493	3↑ ⒻGamely H-G2	1	6	65½	41½	31½	2nk	Hawley S	118	b	4.40	88-15	HailHilarious123nkCascapedia1183Swingtim119no	Wide turn	6
10Apr77- 6SA	fst 1	:223 :452 1:093 1:352	4↑ Alw 30000	6	7	79½	66½	67½	43½	Hawley S	109	b	*2.60	88-14	Branford Court116noThe Keed Himself1141½Announcer1182	Rallied	7
25Mar77- 8SA	sl 6½f⊗	:214 :444 1:10 1:163	4↑ ⒻAlw 20000	7	2	55	54	23½	12¾	Hawley S	114	b	*2.10	90-22	Cascapedia1142¾DearRita1145SassyGaelic1223¾	Drew clear	7
26Jun76- 8Hol	fst 1⅛	:474 1:114 1:36 1:482	ⒻHol Oaks-G2	1	7	84¾	95½	66	54¼	Shoemaker W	121	b	4.00	86-14	Answer1211¼Franmari1162I Going115¾	Blocked,no late run	9
12Jun76- 8Hol	fst 1 1/16	:231 :462 1:104 1:413	ⒻPrincess-G3	1	2	2hd	2½	31	56¾	Shoemaker W	122	b	1.40	80-16	HalHlrous1191½Answr1193GoMrch1162	Stumbled start,rushed	7
29May76- 8Hol	fm 1 1/16Ⓣ	:23 :47 1:113 1:421	ⒻHoneymoon H-G3	8	3	2½	1½	12	12½	Shoemaker W	121	b	*.80e	88-14	Cascapedia1212½GoMarch117¾DreamofSprng118no	Full stride	10
13May76- 7Hol	fst 1 1/16	:233 :464 1:111 1:421	ⒻAlw 15000	3	2	2½	1hd	12	12½	Lambert J	116	b	*.40	84-15	Cascapedia1162½Go March1182Franmari12112	Driving	7
28Apr76- 8Hol	fm 1Ⓣ	:23 :471 1:113 1:354	ⒻSenorita 34k	5	7	107½	106¾	55	2½	Lambert J	115	b	2.60	90-20	NowPending117½Cscapdia1153QueentoB119no	Troubled trip	11
6Apr76- 8SA	fm *6½fⓉ	:212 :44 1:071 1:133	ⒻLa Habra 34k	9	2	42	66½	35	23½	Lambert J	115	b	*1.90	87-11	Dancing Femme1143½Cascapedia115nkDoc Shah's Siren1176	No threat to winner	9
26Mar76- 7SA	fst 6f	:221 :452 :574 1:10	ⒻAlw 14000	3	8	31	42	22	1½	Lambert J	120	b	*1.00	89-19	Cascapedia120½Grecian Honey1145Spyjara118hd	Slow strt,saved ground	9
7Mar76- 3SA	fst 6f	:22 :452 :58 1:103	ⒻMd Sp Wt	4	6	21½	2hd	1½	13	Lambert J	117	b	*.70	86-11	Cascapedia1173Jaunting1171Shamar1173½	Slow start,easily	8

Chou Croute

b. f. 1968, by Lt. Stevens (Nantallah)–Witherite, by Ky. Colonel
Own.– Folsom Farm and Jones Jr
Br.– E.V. Benjamin III & William G. Clark (Ky)
Tr.– B. Dunham

Lifetime record: 28 18 2 3 $284,661

3Mar73- 8SA	fst 1⅛	:463 1:101 1:352 1:474	4↑ ⒻS Margarita Inv'l H-G1	7 1 1½ 21 77½ 717¾	Rotz JL	123		4.90	75-11	Susan'sGirl1273Convenience1232¾MinstrlMss115½	Gave way	8
17Feb73- 8SA	fst 1 1/16	:234 :473 1:114 1:42	4↑ ⒻS Maria H-G2	6 1 11 1½ 4¾ 68½	Rotz JL	128		*1.10	83-11	Susan'sGirl125½Conveninc1233HllCrcus119hd	Faltered late	6
16Jan73- 8SA	sly 7f	:221 :444 1:101 1:233	4↑ ⒻS Monica H-G2	2 1 2hd 11 16 114	Rotz JL	128		*1.00	85-25	Chou Croute12814Generous Portion114nkMinstrel Miss1155		7
Won as rider pleased												
28Dec72- 8SA	fst 6f	:221 :452 :571 1:091	2↑ ⒻLas Flores H 35k	3 4 41¾ 51¼ 22½ 1¾	Rotz JL	126		*.80	95-19	Chou Croute126¾Generous Portion1151¼Minstrel Miss1145		10
Relaxed late,going away												
27Oct72- 6Kee	fst 1⅛	:452 1:101 1:35 1:472	3↑ ⒻSpinster 59k	7 3 35 1½ 12 22¼	Rotz JL	123		*.90e	98-15	NumbrdAccnt1192¼ChouCrout1231½BrlyEvn1198	2nd best	7
7Oct72- 6Kee	fst 1 1/16	:231 :461 1:103 1:44	3↑ Fayette H 29k	9 8 79¼ 33 21 1nk	Rotz JL	123		*.70	86-16	ChouCroute123nkSensitiveMusic1171½Chateuvr114nk	Just up	12
9Sep72- 7Bel	fst 1⅛	:46 1:102 1:35 1:472	3↑ ⒻBeldame 112k	8 5 44½ 21 11 32	Rotz JL	123		4.40	95-06	Susan's Girl1181Summer Guest1181Chou Croute1233¼		9
Weakened late												
28Aug72- 7Bel	fst 6f	:223 :454 1:10	3↑ Fall Highweight 28k	1 3 63 73¾ 31 12	Rotz JL	131		9.80	94-12	ChouCroute1312Icecapade135nk[DH]SaxnyWarrr1321½	Driving	10
13Aug72- 8Del	fst 1¼	:464 1:104 1:352 2:003	3↑ ⒻDelaware H 114k	4 2 22½ 54½ 47½ 48	Kotenko R	126		3.80	91-09	BlessingAngelica1143¼Grafitt113¾NumbrdAccount1154	Tired	8
5Aug72- 8Lib	fst 1 1/16	:231 :462 1:104 1:431	3↑ ⒻSusquehanna H 55k	5 2 22 13 14 18	Kotenko R	124		2.30	90-18	ChouCroute1248Grafitti1152½AlmaNorth1175	Crowded,easily	6
22Jly72- 8Mth	fm 1⅛Ⓣ	:46 1:10 1:36 1:483	3↑ ⒻMargate H (Div 2) 35k	1 3 34 54½ 68 718	Kotenko R	123		2.40	79-04	Tanagra114nkSydneys Nurse1167Ziba Blue112nk	Tired	7
8Jly72- 8Mth	fst 1 1/16	:224 :454 1:103 1:434	3↑ ⒻMolly Pitcher H 45k	6 3 34 2½ 11½ 2½	Kotenko R	124		*1.90	85-18	OutinSpace113½ChouCroute1244½SecrtRetreat1122½	Gamely	10
28Jun72- 8Mth	fst 6f	:214 :443 1:102	3↑ ⒻRegret H 28k	8 3 1hd 1hd 3nk 33¾	Kotenko R	128		*1.00	86-20	Lucky Traveler1103Secret Retreat111¾Chou Croute1281¼		8
Stumbled start												
29May72- 7Bel	fst 1	:224 :451 1:094 1:352	3↑ Metropolitan H 118k	1 3 31½ 2½ 75¼ 910	Kotenko R	114		8.80	85-13	Executionr119nkBoldReasoning1231¼PeacCorps113½	Used up	11
15May72- 7Bel	fst 7f	:222 :444 1:09 1:222	3↑ ⒻVagrancy H 29k	7 1 1hd 11 13 14	Kotenko R	124		*1.30	95-08	Chou Croute1244Cyamome1141¼Wire Chief113¾	Easily	10
5May72- 7Aqu	fst 6f	:231 :47 1:102	4↑ ⒻAlw 15000	7 3 52¼ 2hd 1hd 1no	Kotenko R	121		*.40	91-19	Chou Croute121noSea Saga1213Royal Signal1214	Driving	7
19Apr72- 6Kee	fst 6½f	:223 :454 1:103 1:172	4↑ ⒻAlw 6500	4 2 1½ 16 17 17	Kotenko R	121		*.10	91-21	ChouCroute1217PickaNurse117½Jessie'sGirl1142½	Easily	6
1Jan72- 9TrP	fst 6f	:22 :442 1:09	3↑ ⒻNew Years H 30k	9 6 21½ 2½ 1½ 12	Kotenko R	123		*1.10	93-20	Chou Croute1232Magnabid1181Royal Signal1201¼	Easily	14
16Dec71- 8FG	fst 6f	:214 :451 1:101	Alw 4500	6 5 43 32 31½ 11½	Kotenko R	116		*.40e	97-13	Chou Croute1161½Honey Jay1222Ronnie1096	Ridden out	9
29Oct71- 6Kee	fst 1⅛	:463 1:102 1:354 1:49	3↑ ⒻSpinster 63k	1 1 11 12 11 12½	Kotenko R	119		4.00	92-18	Chou Croute1192½Viewpoise119½Alma North119½	Driving	9
22Oct71- 6Kee	fst *7f	1:27	3↑ ⒻAlw 10000	3 3 1½ 11 12 11½	Kotenko R	110		*.30	88-19	Chou Croute1101½Viewpoise1136Secret Retreat1126	Driving	5
13Oct71- 6Kee	fst 6f	:222 :453 :57 1:084	ⒻAlw 7500	3 4 12 12 14 110	Kotenko R	118		*.90	98-15	Chou Croute11810Misty Gem1211Family Way121hd	Easily	10
4Sep71- 6Rkm	fst 6f	:22 :443 1:10	3↑ ⒻAlw 7500	7 3 2hd 14 14½ 16	Kotenko R	111		*.70	94-12	ChouCroute1116MusicalAnnie1153¾FlemishPrncss1151	Easily	9
19May71- 6Aks	my 5½f	:232 :462 :59 1:054	ⒻAlw 6000	7 5 32½ 3½ 1½ 14	Jones K	112		*1.40	81-20	Chou Croute1124Cornish Sister11515Pelani1202	Easily	8
27Jan71- 8Hia	fst 6f	:222 :46 1:112	ⒻJasmine (Div 1) 25k	7 3 42½ 21½ 22½ 33	Kassen D	114		2.90	84-18	Pas de Nom1142½You All112¼Chou Croute114½	Bid,bled	8
18Jan71- 6Hia	fst 6f	:221 :462 1:101	ⒻAlw 10000	1 6 32½ 1½ 11½ 11½	Tauzin L	112		*1.80	93-12	[DH]ChouCrout112[DH]RosemntBw1181½WireChief1121	Driving	9
29Dec70- 9FG	sly 6f	:224 :462 1:104	Alw 2800	6 1 11½ 12 15 111	Tauzin L	116		3.20	95-20	ChouCroute11611ToelessTom1193½TaniasMagic111nk	Easily	8
17Dec70- 6FG	fst 6f	:214 :46 1:121	ⒻAlw 3000	3 8 13 12½ 12 1nk	Tauzin L	113		*.70e	88-13	ChouCroute113nkTaniasMagic110nkCruline115¾	Just lasted	9

Chris Evert

ch. f. 1971, by Swoon's Son (The Doge)–Miss Carmie, by T.V. Lark
Own.– C. Rosen
Br.– Echo Valley Horse Farm (Ky)
Tr.– J.A. Trovato

Lifetime record: 15 10 2 2 $679,475

1Mar75- 8SA	fst 1⅛	:454 1:103 1:36 1:483	4↑ ⒻS Margarita H-G1	5 3 33 31 85 87¼	Velasquez J	127	b	*1.40	82-13	Tizna1201½Susan'sGirl123½GayStyle125no	Faded gradually	12
1Feb75- 8SA	fst 1 1/16	:23 :46 1:094 1:41	ⒻLa Canada 57k	2 3 1½ 1hd 1½ 1no	Velasquez J	128	b	*1.30	97-09	Chris Evert128noMercy Dee1161¾Lucky Spell1196	Driving	7
31Dec74- 8Aqu	fst 6f	:222 :45 1:102	ⒻConniver 25k	2 2 45 55½ 55½ 1½	Velasquez J	122	b	*.90	91-12	ChrisEvert122½Superstitious1161¼Knny'sChoc1131¼	Wide,up	5
17Aug74- 8Sar	sly 1¼	:473 1:12 1:382 2:051	Travers-G1	6 3 2hd 1½ 21 34½	Velasquez J	121	b	1.90	74-16	HoldingPattrn121hdLttlCurrnt1264½ChrsEvrt1212½	Weakened	11
10Aug74- 8Sar	fst 1¼	:474 1:114 1:363 2:023	ⒻAlabama-G1	3 2 21 21½ 21½ 2nk	Velasquez J	121	b	*.50	92-14	QuazeQuilt121nkChrisEvert1215FiestaLibre1152½	Game try	8
20Jly74- 6Hol	fst 1¼	:443 1:084 1:35 2:02	ⒻMatch Race 350k	2 1 1½ 112 125 150	Velasquez J	121	b	.70	81-11	Chris Evert12150Miss Musket121	Galloping	2
22Jun74- 8Bel	fst 1½	:484 1:133 2:032 2:284	ⒻC C A Oaks-G1	1 2 1½ 1hd 11½ 13½	Velasquez J	121	b	*.90	76-16	ChrisEvert1213½FiestaLibre121¾MaudMullr12110	Going away	10
1Jun74- 8Bel	sly 1⅛	:454 1:102 1:353 1:483	ⒻMother Goose-G1	14 3 32 21½ 1hd 1½	Velasquez J	121	b	2.80	84-13	Chris Evert121½Maud Muller1215Quaze Quilt1211¾	Driving	14
11May74- 8Aqu	fst 1	:23 :452 1:093 1:36	ⒻAcorn (Div 2)-G1	1 2 52¼ 43 31½ 1¾	Velasquez J	121	b	*1.80	87-17	Chris Evert121¾Clear Copy1211Fiesta Libre121hd	Driving	9
1May74- 8Aqu	fst 7f	:224 :46 1:111 1:242	ⒻComely-G3	10 4 74¾ 66¼ 67½ 34½	Velasquez J	118	b	*2.00	74-22	Clear Copy113hdShy Dawn1184½Chris Evert1181	Rallied	10
14Nov73- 8Aqu	fst 1	:232 :462 1:11 1:362	ⒻDemoiselle-G3	11 2 2hd 2hd 11 11¼	Pincay L Jr	121	b	*.90	85-18	Chris Evert1211¼Ambalero1161¼Khaled's Kaper1162	Driving	11
3Nov73- 8CD	fst 7f	:231 :464 1:124 1:251	ⒻGolden Rod-G3	2 9 911 913 43½ 11¼	Pincay L Jr	116	b	*1.30e	81-27	Chris Evert1161¼Bundler1198Kiss Me Darlin1168	Driving	13
6Oct73- 7Bel	fst 1	:232 :464 1:112 1:362	ⒻFrizette-G1	11 9 72¾ 31½ 41 2½	Castaneda M	121	b	6.20	85-13	Bundler121½ChrisEvert121nkI'maPleasure1211	Reared start	14
2Oct73- 6Bel	fst 6f	:222 :452 1:101	ⒻAlw 9000	10 7 52½ 44½ 3½ 12¾	Pincay L Jr	120	b	3.10	92-15	ChrisEvert1202¾[D]Sympathetc120½FlshngLdy118½	Ridden out	10
Previously owned by Robish Stable												
14Sep73- 3Bel	fst 6f	:223 :454 1:11	ⒻMd Sp Wt	10 6 31½ 32 2½ 11¾	Pincay L Jr	120	b	3.50	88-11	ChrisEvert1201¾MaudMuller1202½MamaKali1201½	Ridden out	13

Cougar II (Chi)

dkbbr. c. 1966, by Tale of Two Cities (Tehran)–Cindy Lou, by Madara
Own.– Mary F. Jones
Br.– Haras General Cruz (Chi)
Tr.– Charles Whittingham

Lifetime record: 50 20 7 17 $1,162,725

29Sep73- 7Bel	sly 1½	:50 1:132 2:014 2:254	3↑ Woodward-G1	4 5 55 44½ 49½ 315½	Shoemaker W	126		2.90	75-15	Prove Out1264½Secretariat11911Cougar II126½	Even try	5
15Sep73- 7Bel	fst 1⅛	:453 1:091 1:33 1:452	3↑ Marlboro Cup Inv'l H 250k	2 7 79¼ 78¾ 38 35½	Shoemaker W	126		4.00e	98-07	Secretariat1243½RivaRidg1272CougrII1266½	Altered course	7
23Jly73- 8Hol	fm 1½Ⓣ	:484 1:123 2:012 2:26	3↑ Sunset H-G1	4 5 56¼ 21 2hd 11	Shoemaker W	128		*.90e	98-08	Cougar II1281Life Cycle1201½Rock Bath114½	Ridden out	7
24Jun73- 8Hol	fst 1¼	:451 1:09 1:341 1:592	3↑ Hol Gold Cup Inv'l-G1	4 6 617 613 56 35	Pincay L Jr	128		*1.30	89-16	Kennedy Road120noQuack1275Cougar II1281¾	Rallied	6
27May73- 8Hol	fm 1½Ⓣ	:474 1:121 2:004 2:253	3↑ Hol Inv'l H-G1	2 7 713 64½ 34½ 31½	Shoemaker W	130		*.80	98-05	Life Cycle1151½Wing Out118nkCougar II1303½	Late bid	10
5May73- 8Hol	fm 1⅜Ⓣ	2:132	3↑ Century H-G1	3 7 74½ 42 11 13½	Shoemaker W	127		*1.00	91-11	Cougar II1273½Wing Out1183¼Life Cycle1171	Handily	11
7Apr73- 8SA	fm 1¾Ⓣ	:483 2:011 2:241 2:462	4↑ S Juan Capistrano H-G1	6 7 77 66 55¼ 3¾	Shoemaker W	127		*.60	95-08	Queen's Hustler115hdBig Spruce119¾Cougar II1272	Rallied	7
24Mar73- 8SA	yl 1½Ⓣ	:474 1:123 2:03 2:273	4↑ San Luis Rey-G1	5 4 33 75½ 56½ 313	Pincay L Jr	126		*.30	64-23	BgSpruc12610Ccro'sCourt1263CougrII126nk	Disliked footing	10
10Mar73- 8SA	fst 1¼	:462 1:101 1:35 2:00	4↑ S Anita H-G1	10 8 65½ 31 2½ 1no	Pincay L Jr	126		*1.50	98-11	Cougar II126noKennedy Road1194Cabin110nk	Drifted in,up	10
1Nov72- 8SA	fm 1½Ⓣ	:494 1:142 2:023 2:271	3↑ Oak Tree Inv'l 100k	7 8 86½ 44 31 12	Shoemaker W	126		*.30	79-21	Cougar II1262Queen's Hustler122nkBicker122¾	Driving	10
14Oct72- 8SA	fm 1¼Ⓣ	:464 1:104 1:351 2:001	3↑ C F Burke H 57k	5 10 1017 72 31 11¼	Pierce D	128		*.80	89-11	Cougar II1281¼Kentuckian1103Tetrack114nk	Handy score	11
24Jun72- 8Hol	fm 1½Ⓣ	:481 1:113 2:012 2:254	3↑ Inv'l Turf H 125k	2 7 76¾ 2hd 1½ 31½	Shoemaker W	129		*.40	97-08	Typecast117nkViolonor1101¼Cougar II1296½	Drifted in	9
20May72- 8Hol	fst 1 1/16	:224 :444 1:081 1:391	3↑ Californian 133k	6 6 616 47 31½ 12¾	Shoemaker W	127		*.40	99-12	CougarII1272¾KennedyRoad1198MilesTyson1182¼	Going away	6
29Apr72- 8Hol	fm 1⅜Ⓣ	2:11	3↑ Century H 106k	1 5 59 42 14 14¾	Shoemaker W	126		*.90	103-09	Cougar II1264¾Unconscious1231¾Star Envoy118no	Driving	8
8Apr72- 8SA	fm *1¾Ⓣ	:48 1:594 2:231 2:453	4↑ S Juan Capistrano H 125k	9 7 510 1hd 11 2¾	Shoemaker W	127		*.60	98-03	Practicante118¾Cougar II1273¼Nor II1201¼	No excuse	9
11Mar72- 8SA	fst 1¼	:47 1:10 1:343 2:00	4↑ S Anita H 170k	2 4 47 34 31½ 2hd	Shoemaker W	126		*.90	98-10	Triple Bend119hdCougar II1261¼Unconscious1277	Sharp	7
26Feb72- 8SA	fst 1⅛	:46 1:101 1:351 1:472	4↑ San Antonio 86k	3 8 613 67¼ 44 35	Shoemaker W	128		*.60	90-11	Unconscious123noTriple Bend1175Cougar II1281	Mild rally	9
5Feb72- 8SA	fst 1 1/16	:232 :462 1:102 1:411	4↑ San Pasqual H 57k	8 7 68 64¾ 54½ 21½	Shoemaker W	128	b	*.50	94-08	Western Welcome1151½Cougar II128noStar of Kuwait1141½		8
Blocked,rallied												

31Oct71- 8SA fm 1½Ⓣ :451 1:091 1:592 2:243 3↑ Oak Tree Inv'l 100k 8 9 813 12½ 15 15 Shoemaker W 126 *.40 92-08 CougarII1265VgsVc1214¼Mnt1238 Wide rally,hand ride late 10
2Oct71- 7Bel fst 1¼ :461 1:10 1:35 2:002 3↑ Woodward 113k 6 5 48 22 13 15 Shoemaker W 126 4.10 98-13 ⒹCougarII1265WestCoastScout121nkTinajro121no Ducked in 10
Disqualified and placed third
18Sep71- 8Atl sf 1 3/16Ⓣ :492 1:151 1:423 2:02 3↑ U Nations H 100k 10 11 1120 1018 1013 621 Shoemaker W 126 *2.50 39-48 RuntheGantlet117½TwicWorthy1184½Chompon1166 Taken back 11
26Jly71- 8Hol fm 2Ⓣ :48 2:29 2:54 3:191 3↑ Sunset H 138k 5 9 714 1hd 11 2½ Shoemaker W 130 *.70 93-12 OvertheCounter114½CougarII1301Typecast1102½ Lugged in 12
26Jun71- 8Hol fm 1½Ⓣ :471 1:11 2:012 2:262 3↑ Inv'l Turf H 125k 5 7 719 59 34 1nk Shoemaker W 127 *1.30 96-12 CougarII127nkFortMarcy1251½DivideandRule1215 Driving 8
22May71- 8Hol fst 1 1/16 :224 :454 1:094 1:411 3↑ Californian 138k 9 10 1012 65½ 22½ 11¼ Shoemaker W 124 *1.10 89-17 CougarII1241¼MasterHand1124¾FleetSurprise1182½ Driving 11
1May71- 8Hol fm 1⅜Ⓣ 2:132 3↑ Century H 108k 2 8 812 53½ 54 41 Shoemaker W 128 *.60 90-13 Big Shot II111hdⒹThe Field113¾Drumtop117nk Rallied 11
Placed third through disqualification
10Apr71- 8SA fm *1¾Ⓣ :481 2:012 2:241 2:461 4↑ S Juan Capistrano H 125k 2 6 610 53¼ 3½ 13 Shoemaker W 126 1.90 96-07 Cougar II1263ⒹFort Marcy1273¼Try Sheep1142¾ Driving 7
13Mar71- 8SA sl 1¼ :464 1:111 1:37 2:03 4↑ S Anita H 145k 1 5 69½ 78½ 46½ 21½ Pincay L Jr 125 3.80 81-22 Ack Ack1301½Cougar II1254The Field1091¼ Gamely 10
20Feb71- 8SA yl 1½Ⓣ :49 1:133 2:024 2:291 4↑ San Luis Obispo H 65k 5 2 21 31 2hd 2½ Shoemaker W 127 4.00 68-22 Daryl's Joy128½Cougar II127noOnandaga1103 Gamely 7
23Jan71- 8SA fm 1¼Ⓣ :474 1:133 1:374 2:02 4↑ San Marcos H 43k 3 1 1½ 11½ 14 16 Shoemaker W 124 *.90 80-17 CougarII1246StaunchEagle1151½SuertealCobre114hd Handily 7
1Jan71- 8SA yl 1⅛Ⓣ :482 1:131 1:384 1:523 4↑ San Gabriel H 34k 3 8 84½ 77 51¾ 11¼ Shoemaker W 120 *2.30 66-34 CougrII1201¼SurtlCobr111¾TryShp112hd Hard urged,gamely 10
31Oct70- 8SA fm 1½Ⓣ :493 1:144 2:032 2:261 3↑ Oak Tree 108k 2 5 54 42 52¾ 34¼ Toro F 126 b *.30 84-14 Daryl's Joy126nkFiddle Isle1264Cougar II126½ Outside 6
17Oct70- 7Bel sf 1½Ⓣ 2:334 3↑ Man o' War 116k 9 5 54 1016 1027 1025 Shoemaker W 126 6.50 39-40 Fort Marcy1261¾Loud1214½Drumtop123nk Disliked going 10
7Oct70- 7Bel fm 1⅜Ⓣ 2:143 3↑ Manhattan H 62k 4 2 2½ 32 33½ 3¾ Shoemaker W 119 2.10 92-09 ShelterBay113½Loud115nkCougrII1191¼ Saved ground,gamely 13
7Sep70- 7Dmr fm 1⅜Ⓣ :491 1:151 1:391 2:152 3↑ Del Mar H 55k 6 4 45½ 33 32 2hd Toro F 120 5.10 117-02 Daryl's Joy123hdCougar II120noContratodos1103 6
Checked,finished well;Previously owned by Perla de Chico Stud;previously trained by G.A. Riley
22Aug70- 7Dmr fst *1¼ :452 1:10 1:35 1:58 3↑ Cabrillo H 21k 4 5 54¼ 42 1hd 1no Toro F 117 5.40e - - Cougar II117noQuicken Tree124¾Over the Counter1171½ 7
Between horses
8Aug70- 7Dmr fm 1⅛Ⓣ :483 1:123 1:363 1:49 3↑ Escondido H 22k 8 3 32 42½ 2hd 11¾ Toro F 114 6.80e 102-04 Cougar II1141¾Neurologo120½California114nk Drew away 8
1Aug70- 6Dmr fm 1 1/16Ⓣ :221 :461 1:11 1:421 3↑ Alw 8000 5 5 56 41 52¼ 44 Ramos W 112 16.30 98-03 Over the Counter1203Fleet Surprise1201Neurologo117no 6
Lost ground on turn
25Jly70- 6Dmr fst 6f :22 :45 :573 1:10 3↑ Alw 6000 8 6 87 88¼ 85½ 66½ Ramos W 113 35.90 82-09 GrecoTime113½SandCanyon113nkTraffcBt113¾ Never a factor 8
Previously trained by Alvaro Breque
23May70♦ Hipodromo(Chi) fst*1½LH 2:292 Chilean St. Leger Stk7500 4 Azocar S 123 - Burnakoff1232½Exotico1232Morro de Avico123 6
9May70♦ Hipodromo(Chi) gd *1¼LH 2:042 3↑ Clsc Republica del Paraguay-Hcp Stk2000 1¾ Azocar S 128 4.90 Cougar II128¾Antupillan107hdPimpolla1122½ 12
29Mar70♦ Valparaiso(Chi) fm*1 3/16ⓉLH 1:542 3↑ Cl Municipal de Vina del Mar-Hcp Stk5000 11½ Salinas J 117 3.00 Cougar II1171½Sisal119nkGuantanamera1281 12
Burnakoff (108) 4th
8Mar70♦ Valparaiso(Chi) fm*1 3/16ⓉLH 1:552 Clasico Thompson Matthews Stk2000 11½ Astorga C 114 *.90 Cougar II1141½Camotillo1172Burnakoff119½ 5
1Feb70♦ Valparaiso(Chi) fm*1½ⓉLH 2:29 Chilean Derby Stk10000 3 Salinas J 128 - Exotico128Burnakoff128Cougar II128 17
Pimentero 5th,Sisal 7th
11Jan70♦ Valparaiso(Chi) fm*1 3/16ⓉLH 1:564 Clasico Juan S. Jackson Stk5000 31¼ Salinas J 112 - Trinera112½Campomar112¾Cougar II112¾ 12
Sisal 4th,Burnakoff 7th,Gran Kan 11th
13Dec69♦ Hipodromo(Chi) gd *1 3/16LH 1:58 3↑ Pr Inst Nacl Hipodrm Venezuela Hcp2000 33¾ Salinas J 106 - Le Petit Navire1143½Huinche119nkCougar II1063 7
29Nov69♦ Hipodromo(Chi) gd *1 3/18LH 2:172 3↑ Gran Premio Hipodromo Chile Stk2900 52½ Azocar S 115 - A Go Go115hdAlifar128½Sisal115¾ 16
Burnakoff 4th,Huinche 6th,Pimentero 7th
1Nov69♦ Hipodromo(Chi) fst*7½fLH 1:302 3↑ Premio Sabella Hcp700 17 Salinas J 112 *1.50 Cougar II1127Economist115hdPuerte Varas110¾ 15
22Jun69♦ Club Hippico(Chi) sf *1ⓉRH 1:411 Premio Zanzibar Mdn650 12½ Salinas J 121 7.40 Cougar II1212½Crepuicuio1212Exotico121¾ 10
Pimentero 6th
4Jun69♦ Club Hippico(Chi) fm*6½fⓉRH 1:17 Premio Ujiji Mdn650 31¾ Salinas J 121 - Sabrosito1221¾Que Pasa121hdCougar II1211 14
11May69♦ Club Hippico(Chi) sf *5½fⓉStr 1:101 Premio Oropel Mdn650 34½ Azocar S 121 - Napotigre1211½Abaneio1213Cougar II121no 15

Dahlia

ch. f. 1970, by Vaguely Noble (Vienna)–Charming Alibi, by Honeys Alibi **Lifetime record: 48 15 3 7 $1,543,139**
Own.– N.B. Hunt
Br.– N.B. Hunt (Ky)
Tr.– Charles Whittingham

30Oct76- 8SA fm 1⅛Ⓣ :474 1:122 1:362 1:483 3↑ ⒻLas Palmas H-G3 1 12 1216 128½ 96¼ 73½ Castaneda M 124 6.90 82-14 Vagabonda118¾Bastonera II1221¼Accra II115hd Outrun 12
24Oct76- 8SA sf 1½Ⓣ :482 1:134 2:061 2:312 3↑ Oak Tree Inv'l-G1 9 3 13 75 715 727 Pincay L Jr 123 *.50e 31-42 KingPellinore126nkRoyalDerbyII126nkL'Heureux121hd Wide 9
11Oct76- 8Bel sf 1½Ⓣ :493 1:153 2:05 2:311 3↑ Man o' War-G1 10 5 53½ 95¼ 85½ 83 Shoemaker W 123 4.80 65-33 Effervescing1211¼Banghi121hdⒹCrackle121no No excuse 13
26Jly76- 8Hol fm 1½Ⓣ :483 1:122 2:014 2:262 3↑ Sunset H-G1 10 2 12 2hd 75½ 713 Shoemaker W 121 *.70e 83-14 Caucasus121noKingPellinore1243½RiotinPars1231¾ Faltered 10
11Jly76- 8Hol fst 1⅛ :463 1:104 1:354 1:48 3↑ ⒻVanity H-G1 11 8 43 62¾ 74½ 55¾ Shoemaker W 127 *3.00 86-11 MissToshiba120hdBastoneraII1213½BoldBaby1152 Slow start 11
20Jun76- 8Hol fst 1¼ :454 1:10 1:343 1:584 3↑ Hol Gold Cup H-G1 4 2 24 2hd 42 46 Shoemaker W 121 2.40e 91-09 Pay Tribute1173¼Avatar1232Riot in Paris123¾ Weakened 8
31May76- 8Hol fm 1½Ⓣ :491 1:132 2:014 2:264 3↑ Hol Inv'l H-G1 2 6 42½ 12 1½ 1½ Shoemaker W 117 *4.30 94-11 Dahlia117½Caucasus1194PasstheGlass121hd Bumped,driving 12
13May76- 8Hol fm 1⅛Ⓣ :481 1:12 1:37 1:492 4↑ Alw 25000 3 8 912 75½ 51½ 1½ Shoemaker W 111 *1.00 89-14 Dahlia111½Caucasus1161Ameri Flyer121nk Driving 10
25Apr76- 8Hol fm 1⅜Ⓣ :481 1:132 1:374 2:143 3↑ Century H-G1 3 5 75 98¾ 74¾ 31 Lambert J 117 8.50 81-16 Winds of Thought115hdPass the Glass1191Dahlia117no 9
Blocked,taken up
10Apr76- 8Hol fm 1⅛Ⓣ :50 1:141 1:38 1:502 3↑ ⒻGamely H 53k 5 5 57 57 46 44 Hawley S 123 4.90 80-15 Katonka1213Fascinating Girl117noTizna1261 No mishap 5
21Mar76- 8SA fm 1½Ⓣ :462 1:11 2:001 2:244 4↑ San Luis Rey-G1 4 5 54 64½ 76¼ 78¾ Hawley S 121 4.70 82-08 Avatar126hdⒹGa Hai126¾Top Crowd1261 Showed nothing 7
7Mar76- 8SA fst 1¼ :452 1:093 1:342 2:002 4↑ S Anita H-G1 1 14 1212 1420 1012 913 Grant H 120 19.10 83-11 RoyalGlint124noAncientTtl1241¼LghtnngMndt1206½ Dull try 15
31Jan76- 8SA fst 1 1/16 :241 :474 1:113 1:412 4↑ ⒻS Maria H-G2 4 4 32½ 43½ 43½ 47½ Shoemaker W 126 3.70 87-14 GayStyle127noRaiseYourSkirts1206Tizna1271½ Drifted out 9
Previously trained by Maurice Zilber
8Nov75- 7Lrl yl 1½Ⓣ :494 1:152 2:062 2:311 3↑ D C Int'l-G1 7 6 38½ 815 821 827 Saint-Martin Y 124 2.50e 36-37 Nobiliary117¾ComtessedeLoir1243OnMyWayII1272 Bid,tired 9
26Oct75- 7WO fm 1⅝Ⓣ :501 1:392 2:431 3↑ Can Int'l-G1 4 10 911 84½ 54 42 Hawley S 123 *1.95 82-16 Snow Knight126½Comtesse de Loir1231½Crny's Point126hd 11
Wide late
5Oct75♦ Longchamp(Fr) sf 1½ⓉRH 2:333 3↑ Prix de l'Arc de Triomphe-G1 Stk380000 15 Navarro N 129 8.70e Star Appeal1323On My Way1322½Comtesse de Loir1291½ 24
Midpack,heels clipped from behind 3f out,never recovered
21Sep75♦ Longchamp(Fr) sf *1¼ⓉRH 2:092 3↑ Prix du Prince d'Orange-G3 Stk35200 3¾ Navarro N 129 *2.20 Kasteel118½Ramirez132nkDahlia1291½ 10
Rated toward rear,bid 1½f out,hung
31Aug75♦ Deauville(Fr) gd *1 11/16ⓉRH 2:57 3↑ Grand Prix de Deauville-G2 Stk85000 31¾ Piggott L 131 3.00 ⒹDuke of Marmalade1261½L'Ensorceleur131nkDahlia1312 18
Rated in 10th,bid 2f out,3rd 1f out.Placed 2nd via DQ
19Aug75♦ York(GB) gd *1 5/16ⓉLH 2:092 3↑ Benson & Hedges Gold Cup-G1 Stk140000 11½ Piggott L 130 3.50 Dahlia1301½Card King1335Star Appeal1334 6
Led throughout,met challenge 2f out,held well
26Jly75♦ Ascot(GB) gd 1½ⓉRH 2:264 3↑ King George VI & Queen Eliz Stakes-G1 Stk265000 35½ Piggott L 130 6.00 Grundy119½Bustino1305Dahlia1301½ 11
Tracked in 4th,one-paced last quarter

Date/Track	Cond	Dist	Fractions/Time	Age	Race	Calls	Fin	Jockey	Wt	Odds	Spd	Top Finishers	Comment	Field
6Jly75♦ Saint-Cloud(Fr)	gd	*1½ⓉLH	2:38	3↑	Grand Prix de Saint-Cloud-G1 Stk204000		56¾	Piggott L	133	6.00		Un Kopeck134½Ashmore134nkOn My Way1363	Unhurried in 7th,bid 2f out,one-paced last quarter	11
15Jun75♦ San Siro(Ity)	fm	*1½ⓉRH	2:273	3↑	Gran Premio di Milano-G1 Stk124000		64¼	Navarro N	131	1.70e		Star Appeal132¾Duke of Marmalade132¾ⒹUn Kopeck132¾	Never a factor	11
19May75♦ Saint-Cloud(Fr)	gd	*1½ⓉLH	2:331	3↑	Prix Jean de Chaudenay-G2 Stk85500		911	Lequeux A	133	4.20		Ashmore1302Battle Song128½Un Kopeck1341½	Raced in midpack,outfinished	15
4May75♦ Longchamp(Fr)	gd	*1 5/16ⓉRH	2:12	4↑	Prix Ganay-G1 Stk136000		68½	Piggott L	124	6.00		Allez France1244Card King1281½Comtesse de Loir1241	Toward rear throughout	6
9Nov74-5Lrl	fm	1½Ⓣ	:514 1:171 2:062 2:293	3↑	D C Int'l-G1	3 7 87¾ 67 53½	31½	Piggott L	124	*.60	69-29	Admetus127¾Desert Vixen124¾Dahlia1241¾	Rallied,wide	9
27Oct74-7WO	fm	1⅝Ⓣ	:471 1:373 2:40	3↑	Can Int'l-G2	9 7 721 64¾ 1hd	11	Piggott L	123	*.45	105-05	Dahlia1231Big Spruce1261½Carney's Point126hd	Ridden out	9
12Oct74-8Bel	fm	1½Ⓣ	:484 1:134 2:024 2:263	3↑	Man o' War-G1	5 7 78 52¼ 12	12	Turcotte R	123	*2.40	91-10	Dhlia1232CraftyKhale126hdLondnCompany126no	Ridden out	13
15Sep74♦ Longchamp(Fr)	gd	*1¼ⓉRH	2:052	3↑	Prix de Prince d'Orange-G3 Stk27000		3½	Piggott L	129	*.30		On My Way126nkToujours Pret126nkDahlia1272	Rated at rear,bid 2f out,hung	7
20Aug74♦ York(GB)	gd	*1 5/16ⓉLH	2:092	3↑	Benson & Hedges Gold Cup-G1 Stk120000		12½	Piggott L	130	*.50		Dahlia1302½Imperial Prince1221½Snow Knight122nk	Rated in 6th,rallied to lead over 1f out,drew clear	9
27Jly74♦ Ascot(GB)	gd	1½ⓉRH	2:33	3↑	King George VI & Queen Eliz Stakes-G1 Stk258000		12½	Piggott L	130	*1.85		Dahlia1301½Highclere1261Dankaro129	Tracked in 5th,led over 1f out,quickly clear	10
7Jly74♦ Saint-Cloud(Fr)	gd	*1 9/16ⓉLH	2:392	3↑	Grand Prix de Saint-Cloud-G1 Stk152000		1nk	St. Martin Y	129	*2.60		Dahlia129nkOn My Way134nkDirect Flight1361	Led virtually throughout,met challenge 1f out,gamely	11
6Jun74♦ Epsom(GB)	gd	1½ⓉLH	2:362	4↑	Coronation Cup-G1 Stk36000		34½	Pyers WB	123	*1.50		Buoy1261½Tennyson1263Dahlia1235	Raced in last,mild bid 3f out,one-paced last quarter	5
5May74♦ Longchamp(Fr)	hy	*1 5/16ⓉRH	2:231	4↑	Prix Ganay-G1 Stk105000		515	Pyers WB	124	3.70		Allez France1245Tennyson1284Gombos1284	Trailed to 2f out,passed tired ones	10
15Apr74♦ Longchamp(Fr)	fm	*1¼ⓉRH	2:113	4↑	Prix d'Harcourt-G2 Stk51300		46½	Pyers WB	127	3.20		Allez France1273Ksar1261½Mister Sic Top1302	Unhurried in last,mild late gain	9
10Nov73-7Lrl	yl	1½Ⓣ	:511 1:164 2:073 2:314	3↑	D C Int'l-G1	4 8 88½ 53½ 42	13¼	Pyers W	118	4.60	60-40	Dahlia1183¼BigSpruce1271ScottishRifle1271¾	Brisk urging	8
5Oct73♦ Longchamp(Fr)	yl	*1½ⓉRH	2:354	3↑	Prix de l'Arc de Triomphe-G1 Stk306000		1619	Pyers WB	119	8.00		Rheingold1322½Allez France1194Hard to Beat1322	Progress 4f out,soon weakened.San San 12th	27
23Sep73♦ Longchamp(Fr)	sf	*1½ⓉRH	2:432		ⒻPrix Vermeille-G1 Stk153000		56½	Pyers WB	128	*.90		Allez France1282Hurry Harriet1282½El Mina1282	Rated in 6th,brief bid 2f out,returned lame	13
9Sep73♦ Longchamp(Fr)	gd	*1⅜ⓉRH	2:282		Prix Niel-G3 Stk30600		1½	Pyers WB	127	*.90		Dahlia127½Tennyson130¾Dom Luc1235	Well placed in 3rd,led 1f out,driving	5
28Jly73♦ Ascot(GB)	gd	1½ⓉRH	2:302	3↑	King George & Queen Elizabeth Stakes-G1 Stk253000		16	Pyers WB	116	10.00		Dahlia1166Rheingold1332Our Mirage133nk	Rated in 6th,rallied to lead 1½f out,easily clear	12
21Jly73♦ TheCurragh(Ire)	gd	1½ⓉRH	2:434		ⒻIrish Oaks-G1 Stk70000		13	Pyers WB	126	8.00		Dahlia1263Mysterious1264Hurry Harriet126hd	Rated in midpack,rallied to lead 1f out,drew clear	12
10Jun73♦ Chantilly(Fr)	yl	*1 5/16ⓉRH	2:072		ⒻPrix de Diane (French Oaks)-G1 Stk178000		22½	Pyers WB	128	4.50		Allez France1282½Dahlia1284Virunga128hd	Rated in midpack,finished well without threatening	25
20May73♦ Longchamp(Fr)	sf	*1¼ⓉRH	2:102		ⒻPrix Saint-Alary-G1 Stk89200		11½	Pyers WB	123	5.40		Dahlia1231½Virunga1231½Kashara1231	Rated in 7th,rallied to lead 100y out,going away	11
29Apr73♦ Longchamp(Fr)	sf	*1ⓉRH	1:443		ⒻPoule d'Essai des Pouliches-G1 Stk76500		32¾	Pyers WB	128	6.50		Allez France1282½Princess Arjumand128nkDahlia128nk	Tracked in 4th,mild bid 2f out,outfinished	11
8Apr73♦ Longchamp(Fr)	fm	*1ⓉRH	1:401		ⒻPrix de la Grotte-G3 Stk25500		1¾	Pyers WB	128	7.30		Dahlia128¾Gay Style128nkMidou1282½	Rated toward rear,rallied to lead near line	11
26Oct72♦ Longchamp(Fr)	gd	*1ⓉRH	1:443		ⒻPrix des Reservoirs Stk22400		21	Piggott L	126	15.00		Begara1231Dahlia1262Calba1231	Rated in 5th,rallied to lead over 1f out,headed 100y out	11
10Sep72♦ Longchamp(Fr)	sf	*5fⓉStr	1:024		Prix d'Arenberg-G3 Stk32000		55	Piggott L	121			Enitram1282Senantes1211Challenge1211½	Tracked in 4th,lacked rally	6
22Aug72♦ Deauville(Fr)	yl	*6½fⓉStr	1:184		ⒻPrix du Calvados Stk20000		58	Piggott L	126			Fiery Diplomat1261½Cannabis1213Sorata1212	Rated toward rear,passed tired ones	9
6Aug72♦ Deauville(Fr)	sf	*5fⓉStr	:591		Prix Yacowlef (for first-time strs) Stk22300		12	Piggott L	120			Dahlia1202Challenge1232Ruling1231½	Rated in 5th,rallied to lead 150y out,quickly clear	7

Davona Dale

b. f. 1976, by Best Turn (Turn-to)–Royal Entrance, by Tim Tam
Own.– Calumet Farm
Br.– Calumet Farm (Ky)
Tr.– John M. Veitch

Lifetime record: 18 11 2 1 $641,612

Date/Track	Cond	Dist	Fractions/Time	Age	Race	Calls	Fin	Jockey	Wt	Odds	Spd	Top Finishers	Comment	Field
10Sep80-8Bel	fst	1	:232 :461 1:104 1:352	3↑	ⒻMaskette-G1	3 3 33 41¼ 44½	47¼	Velasquez J	123	*1.20	84-22	Bold'nDetrmind122noGnuineRsk1186¾LovSgn120½	Weakened	5
8Aug80-8Sar	fst	7f	:22 :441 1:091 1:221	3↑	ⒻBallerina-G3	2 4 44 3nk 4¾	11	Velasquez J	119	1.80	91-15	DavonaDale1191MistyGallor124noIt'snthAr1191¾	Ridden out	4
26Jly80-5Bel	fst	6f	:224 :46 1:101	3↑	ⒻAlw 32000	5 4 32½ 32½ 32½	31¾	Velasquez J	122	*.70	89-16	Cornish Queen1151½Damask Fan109nkDavona Dale1226	Wide	7
12Sep79-8Bel	fst	1	:23 :453 1:093 1:344	3↑	ⒻMaskette-G2	3 2 31 41½ 44½	43½	Velasquez J	122	2.30	90-20	Blitey112nkIt'sintheAir122noPearlNecklace1253¼	Weakened	5
18Aug79-8Sar	sly	1¼	:473 1:111 1:354 2:00		Travers-G1	5 4 32½ 514 517	428¾	Velasquez J	121	*2.70	72-16	GeneralAssembly12615Smarten12611PrivtAccount1262¾	Tired	7
11Aug79-8Sar	fst	1¼	:49 1:124 1:364 2:012		ⒻAlabama-G1	2 2 2½ 21½ 23	21½	Velasquez J	121	*.30	92-13	It'sintheAir1211½DvnaDale1213¾MairzyDoates1212¼	Gamely	5
30Jun79-8Bel	fst	1½	:491 1:133 2:034 2:30		ⒻC C A Oaks-G1	5 5 31½ 11½ 16	18	Velasquez J	121	*.10	70-24	Davona Dale1218Plankton121½Croquis12114	Ridden out	5
10Jun79-8Bel	fst	1⅛	:453 1:10 1:354 1:484		ⒻMother Goose-G1	5 3 11 11½ 14	110	Velasquez J	121	*.20	83-23	Davona Dale12110Eloquent1214¾Plankton1211	Ridden out	6
26May79-8Bel	fst	1	:223 :452 1:102 1:36		ⒻAcorn-G1	6 3 42½ 2hd 1hd	12¼	Velasquez J	121	*.30	88-25	Davona Dale1212¼Eloquent1217¾Plankton1212¼	Ridden out	8
18May79-8Pim	fst	1 1/16	:231 :464 1:113 1:423		ⒻBlack-Eyed Susan-G2	2 1 11 11 12½	14¼	Velasquez J	121	*.10	92-21	DvonaDale1214¼Phoebe'sDonky1183½Plnkton1214	Ridden out	6
4May79-8CD	sly	1 1/16	:241 :48 1:134 1:471		ⒻKy Oaks-G1	5 5 45½ 31½ 1hd	14½	Velasquez J	121	*.40	72-30	Davona Dale1214½Himalayan1212Prize Spot121½	Ridden out	6
7Apr79-9OP	fst	1 1/16	:231 :463 1:113 1:442		ⒻFantasy-G1	3 5 45 2hd 1hd	12½	Velasquez J	121	*1.10	86-21	Davona Dale1212½Cline1213½Very Special Lady1106	Stumbled st.,clear	7
17Mar79-9FG	fst	1 1/16	:24 :48 1:133 1:45		ⒻDebutante 59k	3 3 2½ 2hd 11½	17	Velasquez J	121	*.30	87-21	DvonaDale1217JustaReflcton118nkOthrSho1152¼	Ridden out	11
28Feb79-0GP	fst	7f	:221 :442 1:083 1:21		ⒻBonnie Miss 27k	3 4 21½ 2½ 2½	1¾	Velasquez J	122	-	99-17	DavonaDale122¾CandyEclair12220ProveMeSpecil1142	Driving; Run between 7th and 8th races - No wagering	4
14Feb79-9GP	fst	6f	:22 :441 1:083		ⒻShirley Jones 28k	2 3 34½ 25 24	21¾	Velasquez J	122	2.70	94-16	CandyEclair1221¾DavonaDale1228DropMeANote1141	Gamely	4
13Jan79-9Crc	fst	1 1/16	:232 :48 1:124 1:441		Trop Park Derby-G3	12 5 52¼ 44 46	45	Velasquez J	114	*1.30	93-12	Bishop's Choice111½Lot o' Gold1192Smarten1192½	No rally	12
30Nov78-6Med	sly	6f	:22 :453 1:111		ⒻHolly 54k	7 7 84¾ 43½ 1hd	11½	Velasquez J	115	*1.10	89-22	Davona Dale1151½Wondrous Me1183Aunt Hattie1123	Driving	11
23Oct78-9Bel	fst	6f	:232 :461 1:102		ⒻMd Sp Wt	8 12 63 31½ 2½	11¼	Velasquez J	119	*1.50	90-14	DavonaDale1191¼Clfd'Argnt11910ConstntTlk1191	Ridden out	12

Dearly Precious

dkbbr. f. 1973, by Dr. Fager (Rough'n Tumble)–Imsodear, by Chieftain — Lifetime record: 16 12 2 0 $370,465

Own.– R.E. Bailey
Br.– Mrs Jean R. Pancoast (Fla)
Tr.– S. DiMauro

Date	Track/Dist	Fractions	Race	Calls	Jockey	Wt	Odds	Fig	Finishers / Comment	Fld
11Jly76- 8Aqu	fst 6f	:214 :442 1:091	(F)Dark Mirage 42k	3 3 31½ 1hd 11½ 12½	Maple E	116	*.40	97-11	Dearly Precious1162½Doc Shah's Siren1141Old Goat1143¾	5
	Pulled up lame									
4Jun76- 8Bel	fst 1⅛	:442 1:084 1:351 1:484	(F)Mother Goose-G1	1 1 1½ 22 512 522	Velasquez J	121	1.20	61-16	GirlinLove1211¼OptimisticGl12111AncntFbls1216¾ Bore out	5
22May76- 8Bel	fst 1	:24 :47 1:111 1:354	(F)Acorn-G1	4 1 11 11½ 12 12¼	Velasquez J	121	2.20	89-15	Dearly Precious1212¼Optimistic Gal121nkTell Me All121nk	8
	Ridden out									
14May76- 8Pim	fst 1$\frac{1}{16}$	:234 :464 1:104 1:422	(F)Black-Eyed Susan-G2	4 2 22 1hd 2hd 2no	Velasquez J	121	*.80	93-14	WhatSmmr111noDrlyPrcous1215Artfully1141 Bore out early	10
5May76- 8Bel	fst 7f	:223 :453 1:101 1:231	(F)Comely-G3	3 1 1½ 11 1hd 2½	Baeza B	121	*.30	85-24	TellMeAll113½DearlyPrecious1215¾Worthyan11310 No excuse	5
26Apr76- 8Aqu	fst 6f	:233 :454 1:094	(F)Prioress 36k	2 1 11½ 11½ 11 12	Baeza B	121	*.20	94-14	Dearly Precious1212Old Goat1188¼Answer1181¼ Handy score	4
3Apr76- 8Pim	fst 6f	:231 :462 1:112	(F)Flirtation 28k	4 1 1½ 14 14 112	Hole M	119	*.20	89-20	Dearly Precious11912NineThrills116½Dad's Thrill113½	8
	Swerved,handily									
6Sep75- 8AP	fst 6f	:22 :451 :574 1:111	(F)Arl Wash Lassie-G3	10 1 32½ 12 13½ 14	Hole M	119	*.40	87-21	Dearly Precious1194Free Journey1192Head Spy119no Easily	12
22Aug75- 8Sar	fst 6f	:233 :454 1:103	(F)Spinaway-G1	4 4 1½ 12 12 11	Hole M	120	*.50	87-17	Dearly Precious1201Optimistic Gal1201¾Quintas Vicki120½	6
	Ridden out									
26Jly75- 8Mth	fst 6f	:221 :452 1:102	(F)Sorority-G1	2 2 2hd 1½ 11 12¼	Hole M	119	*1.10	88-17	Dearly Precious1192¼Optimistic Gal1197Totie Fields1193½	6
	Drew clear									
13Jly75- 8Bel	sly 5½f	:222 :452 :574 1:041	(F)Astoria 27k	3 1 1hd 1hd 11½ 12¾	Hole M	118	*1.00	94-15	DearlyPrcious1182¾OldGoat115½FreJournty115no Ridden out	7
28Jun75- 8Mth	fst 5½f	:22 :451 :573 1:041	(F)Colleen 27k	1 4 33½ 3nk 11½ 14	Hole M	121	1.40	96-18	DearlyPrecious12140ldGoat1174BellsandBlades1177 Driving	7
15Jun75- 8Bel	fst 5½f	:222 :454 :582 1:052	(F)Fashion 28k	6 3 1½ 1½ 11½ 12½	Hole M	117	*.90	88-13	DrlyPrecious1172½HoneyPot117nkQuntsVck1172 Ridden out	8
25May75- 8Del	fst 5½f	:224 :473 1:002 1:064	(F)Polly Drummond 23k	4 3 21 12 11 13	Hole M	115	1.70	84-26	DrlyPrecious1153HayPatcher1152½MimiRos1152 Ridden out	5
22Apr75- 4Aqu	fst 5f	:223 :453 :573	(F)Md Sp Wt	1 1 11½ 11½ 16 19½	Hole M	115	11.80	97-13	DrlyPrcs1159½Angl'sCommnd115½Htton'sRos1102½ Handily	6
15Apr75- 4Aqu	fst 5f	:221 :46 :59	(F)Md Sp Wt	5 5 512 512 513 58¼	Baeza B	115	6.40	82-16	Pleasant Tune1151½Xalapa Sunrise1151½Artful Woman1101¾	5
	Broke slowly									

Desert Vixen

dkbbr. f. 1970, by In Reality (Intentionally)–Desert Trial, by Moslem Chief — Lifetime record: 28 13 6 3 $421,538

Own.– H.T. Mangurian Jr
Br.– Mrs Vanderbilt Adams (Fla)
Tr.– T.F. Root Sr

Date	Track/Dist	Fractions	Race	Calls	Jockey	Wt	Odds	Fig	Finishers / Comment	Fld
21Jan75- 9Hia	fst 6f	:221 :452 1:093 4↑	(F)Alw 10000	2 12 83¾ 96 77 65¼	Long JS7	114	*.80	90-15	BirdIsland1121¼Clandenita1212WingedWishs1141½ No threat	12
9Nov74- 5Lrl	fm 1½(T)	:514 1:171 2:062 2:293 3↑	D C Int'l-G1	6 1 12½ 12½ 12 2¾	Turcotte R	124	5.50	70-29	Admetus127¾Desert Vixen124¾Dahlia1241¾ Gamely	9
26Oct74- 7Kee	fst 1⅛	:48 1:113 1:36 1:482 3↑	(F)Spinster-G1	5 2 2hd 3½ 2½ 2hd	Pincay L Jr	123	*.40	95-17	Summer Guest123hdDesert Vixen1231½Coraggioso1231½ Hung	5
14Oct74- 8Atl	fst 1$\frac{3}{16}$	:482 1:121 1:364 1:551 3↑	(F)Matchmaker-G1	7 4 21 2hd 13 13¾	Pincay L Jr	123	*.30	100-10	Desert Vixen1233¾Coraggioso115hdTwixt1231¾ Handily	9
21Sep74- 8Bel	sly 1⅛	:452 1:093 1:341 1:463 3↑	(F)Beldame-G1	3 1 1½ 1½ 14 112	Pincay L Jr	123	*1.30	94-11	Desert Vixen12312Poker Night1236Tizna1232 Ridden out	9
11Sep74- 8Bel	fst 1	:223 :444 1:094 1:343 3↑	(F)Maskette H-G2	1 3 23 2½ 1½ 11¼	Pincay L Jr	120	6.80	95-13	DesertVixn1201¼PonteVecchio118½PokrNght1163½ Hard drive	12
	Disqualified from purse money									
29Aug74- 8Bel	fst 6½f	:223 :451 1:091 1:152 3↑	(F)Alw 20000	6 1 1hd 21 3½ 21¾	Long JS7	115	*.70	97-06	Full of Hope1161¾Desert Vixen1153North of Venus1134½	6
	Best of others									
22Aug74- 6Sar	fst 6f	:214 :443 1:094 3↑	Alw 20000	1 3 45½ 45 42 11¼	Long JS	103	*2.60	91-15	Desert Vixen1031¼Tambac114nkTarboosh1131¾ Going away	8
15Jun74- 6Bel	fst 6f	:222 :451 1:102 3↑	(F)Alw 25000	3 1 21½ 24 47½ 48	Velasquez J	114	*1.80	83-14	IEncompass1141½HonorableMiss1144¾SongTitle1142¼ Tired	6
30May74- 8Bel	fst 7f	:224 :453 1:094 1:223 3↑	(F)Alw 25000	5 1 22 42 69 614	Velasquez J	124	*1.40	75-14	PonteVcchio1151Flo'sPleasure112½LadyLove1181¾ Gave way	7
23May74- 8Bel	fst 7f	:222 :45 1:091 1:214 4↑	(F)Alw 15000	1 3 22 23 32 34	Velasquez J	118	*.40	89-13	Flightoletti1123½IEncompss107½DsrtVxn11813 Lacked rally	5
13May74- 8Bel	fst 7f	:222 :45 1:094 1:222 3↑	(F)Vagrancy H-G3	7 6 63¾ 118¼ 1313 129¼	Velasquez J	129	*1.40	81-14	Coraggioso119noPonte Vecchio114no(D)Wanda112½ Dull try	14
	Placed 11th through disqualification									
15Sep73- 6Bel	fst 1⅛	:462 1:10 1:34 1:461 3↑	(F)Beldame-G1	5 1 11½ 12 16 18½	Velasquez J	118	*.80	100-07	DesertVixen1188½PokerNight1183Susan'sGrl123¾ Ridden out	7
3Sep73- 7Bel	fst 1⅛	:454 1:094 1:344 1:472	(F)Gazelle H-G2	3 1 11 11½ 16 16	Velasquez J	126	*.90	94-10	DesertVixen1266BagofTunes1171¼PokerNight1204½ In hand	7
11Aug73- 7Sar	sly 1¼	:47 1:113 1:373 2:041	(F)Alabama-G1	7 2 12½ 110 18 18	Velasquez J	119	*.50	84-18	DesrtVixn1198BagofTunes1197½SummerFestvl1167½ Handily	9
1Aug73- 7Sar	fst 7f	:223 :451 1:10 1:23	(F)Test (Div 1)-G2	1 3 21½ 21 13 12½	Velasquez J	121	*1.00	92-13	DesertVixen1212½FullofHope118¾Clandenita1184 Ridden out	5
15Jly73- 8Del	sly 1⅛	:462 1:111 1:371 1:491	(F)Del Oaks-G1	6 2 1hd 11 13 16	Velasquez J	121	*.90	91-17	DsertVixn1216BagofTunes1212¼LadiesAgremnt1126 Driving	10
4Jly73- 8Mth	fst 1⅛	:481 1:112 1:361 1:49	(F)Mth Oaks-G1	3 1 2hd 11½ 12 16	Hole M	114	2.80	95-10	DesertVixn1146LadiesAgreement1114LadyLove111hd Driving	11
23Jun73- 8Mth	gd 1 70	:46 1:102 1:401	(F)Post-Deb (Div 2)-G3	4 2 2½ 14 13 12	Hole M	113	*2.20	100-13	Desert Vixen1132Lilac Hill1159Lady Barbizon1136 Driving	10
14Jun73- 6Bel	fst 6f	:223 :452 1:084 3↑	(F)Alw 10000	5 2 1hd 1½ 13 16	Velasquez J	114	*.70	100-04	DesertVixen1146FullofHope1142Hairbrush1101½ Ridden out	7
4Jun73- 8Mth	fst 6f	:214 :451 1:10	(F)Miss Woodford-G3	6 4 56 33½ 34½ 2¾	Velasquez J	115	*1.70	91-13	ShakeaLeg119¾DesertVixen1155NaturalSound121¾ Gaining	9
25May73- 6Bel	sly 6f	:222 :46 1:10 3↑	(F)Alw 9000	5 4 1½ 12 15 18	Velasquez J	112	*.70	94-16	DesertVixen1128MagcStory11210Proptously113no Ridden out	8
	Previously owned by T.F. Root Sr;previously trained by T.F. Root Jr									
15May73- 6Bel	fst 6f	:221 :443 1:093	(F)Alw 8500	1 5 44 46 33½ 2¾	Velasquez J	118	3.00	95-04	Mulready118¾Desert Vixen118hdFull of Hope1213 Gamely	8
	Previously owned by H.T. Mangurian Jr									
23Nov72- 7Aqu	fst 1	:223 :452 1:102 1:373	(F)Demoiselle 30k	11 8 67 58½ 410 43½	Velasquez J	114	4.30	75-26	Protest114¾Flightoletti1161¼Rose Chapeau1151½ Rallied	14
14Nov72- 5Aqu	sly 7f	:224 :464 1:122 1:254	(F)Alw 10000	6 3 65½ 86½ 66¾ 34	Velasquez J	112	2.60	68-22	Yalobi112noFamous Tale1174Desert Vixen112hd Rallied	8
27Oct72- 2Aqu	fst 6½f	:221 :46 1:112 1:18	(F)Md Sp Wt	12 2 76 42½ 11½ 16	Velasquez J	120	*1.10	88-20	Desert Vixen1206Sumba1201Effeffvee1203 Ridden out	14
19Oct72- 3Aqu	sly 6f	:223 :464 1:121	(F)Md Sp Wt	9 6 68 79 57½ 34½	Pincay L Jr	120	*2.20	77-20	NorthBroadwy1152GlamourPard1202½DsrtVxn1203 Mild rally	14
28Sep72- 3Bel	fst 6f	:222 :46 1:113	(F)Md Sp Wt	9 10 109½ 78 45 2nk	Pincay L Jr	119	2.80	86-15	Flightoletti119nkDsrtVxn1191½GlmourPrd1192½ Lacked room	12

Dr. Patches

ch. g. 1974, by Dr. Fager (Rough'n Tumble)–Expectancy, by Intentionally — Lifetime record: 47 17 14 3 $737,612

Own.– Tartan Stable
Br.– Tartan Farms (Fla)
Tr.– Jan H. Nerud

Date	Track/Dist	Fractions	Race	Calls	Jockey	Wt	Odds	Fig	Finishers / Comment	Fld
13May82- 8Aqu	fst 1	:23 :451 1:091 1:343 4↑	Alw 35000	2 4 34 32½ 31½ 1½	Cordero A Jr	115	3.70	93-17	Dr.Patches115½AndMore1153¼ManStm1101½ Wide into stretch	6
3May82- 7Aqu	fst 6f	:231 :461 1:103 4↑	Alw 32000	4 5 54¾ 56½ 67½ 66¼	Cordero A Jr	115	3.80	82-24	Birthday Song119nkAnd More1152Waj. Jr.1192¾ Raced wide	7
17Apr82- 7Aqu	fst 6f	:22 :443 1:101 4↑	Alw 32000	6 5 510 612 68¾ 55¼	Cordero A Jr	115	4.90	85-23	Gratification1152¼FeathersLad1151½BrthdySong117¾ Outrun	7
30May81- 6Bel	fst 7f	:232 :46 1:10 1:222 3↑	Handicap 32000	4 5 32½ 32 33 33¾	Cordero A Jr	118	3.00	86-17	Rise Jim1222½Ring of Light1201¼Dr. Patches118nk Evenly	6
15May81- 8Bel	fst 7f	:231 :462 1:102 1:233 4↑	Alw 32000	3 5 65 54 59½ 67½	Cordero A Jr	122	2.40e	76-19	Rivalero122¾Winter's Tale122hdTax Holiday1053 Outrun	6
1Nov80- 8Aqu	fst 1⅛	:483 1:131 1:372 1:501 3↑	Stuyvesant H-G3	5 5 42 32 27 26	Cordero A Jr	115	1.80	78-25	PluggedNickle1226Dr.Patches1152¾RngofLght116hd 2nd best	10
16Oct80- 5Med	fst 1¼	:471 1:11 1:352 2:002 3↑	Med Cup H-G2	4 4 42½ 22½ 26 26	Cordero A Jr	116	3.50	98-12	Tunerup1176Dr.Patches1168DewanKeys115no Best of others	12
24Sep80- 7Med	fst 1$\frac{1}{16}$	:24 :472 1:114 1:431 3↑	Alw 25000	4 5 54½ 31½ 2hd 11	Cordero A Jr	115	*.20	93-18	Dr.Patches1151RoylHrrchy1123Mjsty'sWorld1159 Ridden out	7
27Aug80- 8Bel	fst 1	:224 :452 1:10 1:35 3↑	Forego H 85k	2 2 1hd 1½ 2hd 2½	Cordero A Jr	114	*.50	92-17	Tanthem114½Dr. Patches1146¾Hold Your Tricks116¾ Gamely	7
2Aug80- 8Sar	fst 1⅛	:46 1:093 1:351 1:481 3↑	Whitney-G1	1 4 43½ 31½ 2hd 2½	Cordero A Jr	114	4.40	93-10	State Dinner120½Dr. Patches114½Czaravich1232½ Gamely	8
20Jly80- 8Bel	fst 7f	:23 :453 1:092 1:221 3↑	Tom Fool-G3	2 4 33½ 44½ 33½ 23	Hernandez R	119	4.30	88-16	PluggedNickle1213Dr.Patches1191½Isell1191¼ Gained place	6
5Jly80- 7Bel	fst 1⅛	:461 1:101 1:35 1:48 3↑	Alw 35000	3 6 63¾ 2½ 11½ 1hd	Cordero A Jr	115	*.70	87-17	Dr.Patches115hdBigBulldozer1152¼ThinSlice119nk Driving	7

16Jun80- 5Bel fst 6f :223 :452 1:092 3↑ Alw 32000 2 2 44 45 43½ 42¾ Cordero A Jr 122 *.90 92-15 J.P.Brother109¾NiceCtch112½DoublZus115½ Altered course 6
30May80- 8Bel fst 7f :23 :461 1:10 1:221 3↑ Alw 32000 5 1 21 2½ 11 11¾ Cordero A Jr 117 *1.10 91-20 Dr. Patches1171¾Frejus121nkTanthem11710 Ridden out 5
16May80- 8Aqu fst 6f :222 :443 1:092 4↑ Alw 32000 5 6 42½ 43½ 33 31¾ Cordero A Jr 119 1.70 94-16 King'sFashion1191¾PrinceAndrew119noDr.Ptches1192½ Wide 6
3Nov79- 8Aqu sly 1⅛ :474 1:122 1:372 1:502 3↑ Stuyvesant H-G3 4 3 42 41 45¼ 53¼ Cordero A Jr 122 *1.30 80-23 MusicofTime114noWhataGent111hdDewanKys1122 Lacked rally 6
27Oct79- 7Aqu fst 1 :224 :454 1:104 1:36 3↑ Alw 27000 5 3 33 11 14 16½ Cordero A Jr 115 *.40 86-22 Dr.Patches1156½DewanKeys115hdTimtheTiger1142 Ridden out 6
20Oct79- 8Aqu fst 7f :223 :444 1:083 1:21 3↑ Vosburgh-G1 2 3 52 53¼ 41½ 22 Cordero A Jr 126 11.90 94-15 GeneralAssmbly1232Dr.Ptchs126¾Syncopt1262¼ Wide stretch 6
10Oct79- 8Bel sly 6f :221 :451 1:101 3↑ Boojum H 53k 4 4 44½ 69 68½ 410¾ Cordero A Jr 118 1.90 80-26 Syncopate1183¾King's Fashion1197Tilt Up116no No threat 6
19Sep79- 6Med fst 6f :224 :462 1:111 3↑ Alw 25000 5 3 43 32 1hd 12½ Cordero A Jr 115 *.40 89-23 Dr.Patches1152½Wm.Withers117noNoHouseCll1173 Ridden out 7
20Jun79- 6Bel fst 7f :222 :444 1:09 1:22 3↑ Celanese Cup H 80k 3 3 22 22 44½ 35¼ Cordero A Jr 118 *1.10 87-17 [D]StardeNaskra1264NorthCourse1121¼Dr.Ptchs118½ Weakened 4
Placed second through disqualification
28May79- 8Bel fst 1 :224 :45 1:091 1:34 3↑ Metropolitan H-G1 3 1 1½ 11½ 12 23 Cordero A Jr 118 6.60 95-16 State Dinner1153Dr. Patches1183½Sorry Lookin1131½ Tired 9
19May79- 8Aqu sly 7f :222 :45 1:09 1:214 3↑ Roseben H 54k 2 4 32½ 33½ 55¼ 54½ Venezia M 120 4.80 87-14 NiceCatch1141¼RomanMissile1142½Kng'sFshon115nk Weakened 9
5May79- 8Aqu fst 7f :224 :451 1:091 1:214 3↑ Carter H-G2 5 2 67½ 515 622 619 Venezia M 122 9.60 73-25 StardeNaskra122nkAlydar1263¾SensitivePrince1266¾ Outrun 6
Previously trained by John A. Nerud
2Nov78- 6Med fst 1¼ :482 1:12 1:362 2:013 3↑ Med Cup H-G2 7 3 3½ 1½ 11½ 14 Cordero A Jr 119 *.40 105-12 Dr.Patches1194DoTellGeorge1146Niteange1155 Kept driving 7
22Oct78- 8Bel fst 7f :221 :442 1:082 1:21 3↑ Vosburgh H-G2 2 5 43½ 42½ 2½ 1¾ Cordero A Jr 117 *1.30 97-13 Dr.Patches117¾WhataSummer1243¾SorryLookin1095 Driving 8
22Sep78- 6Bel fst 7f :223 :45 1:084 1:211 3↑ Celanese Cup H 52k 2 2 1½ 2hd 2hd 2no Cordero A Jr 117 *.50 96-15 Buckfinder119noDr.Patches1172¾WarmFront113 Just missed 3
5Sep78- 6Med fst 1⅛ :46 1:094 1:35 1:48 3↑ Paterson H-G3 9 2 23½ 21½ 2½ 1nk Cordero A Jr 114 4.70 93-13 Dr.Patches114nkSeattleSlew1282¼It'sFreezing1125 Driving 10
Previously trained by D. Wayne Lukas
26Aug78- 7Sar fst 6f :223 :452 1:083 3↑ Alw 25000 4 3 1½ 11½ 13 16½ Cordero A Jr 122 *1.10 97-12 Dr.Patches1226½Bartendr'sPrd115½SorryLookn1141¾ Driving 7
23Jly78- 7Hol fst 1 :223 :451 1:092 1:341 3↑ Alw 30000 5 4 48½ 43½ 1hd 13 Pincay L Jr 120 *.40 95-11 Dr. Patches1203Transcription1141Farnesio1141½ Easily 6
9Jly78- 8Hol fst 1$\frac{1}{16}$:223 :451 1:092 1:401 3↑ Citation H-G3 1 3 35½ 3½ 1hd 2¾ Cordero A Jr 116 4.10 93-14 Effervescing120¾Dr. Patches1161½Text1222¾ Swerved early 6
Previously trained by John A. Nerud
19Jun78- 8Bel fst 7f :233 :462 1:094 1:213 3↑ Alw 25000 3 1 1hd 1hd 11 2nk Cordero A Jr 122 1.80 94-12 Forego122nkDr. Patches1227Gabe Benzur1152 Held gamely 4
1Jun78- 8Bel fst 1 :224 :45 1:09 1:333 3↑ Alw 25000 7 6 44 41½ 21½ 1nk Cordero A Jr 117 2.60 100-11 Dr. Patches117nkVencedor1193½It's Freezing1195¼ Driving 7
12May78- 8Aqu gd 1$\frac{1}{16}$Ⓣ :232 :48 1:122 1:433 4↑ Handicap 25000 4 5 56 67½ 69½ 613 Venezia M 111 8.70 75-12 Cinteelo1181½True Colors118½All the More113hd Outrun 6
1May78- 8Aqu fst 6f :224 :462 1:104 4↑ Alw 25000 3 1 2hd 43 46 38 Vasquez J 122 3.00 81-24 Prefontaine1221GabeBenzur1227Dr.Patches122hd Weakened 5
26Oct77- 7Aqu fst 1 :233 :463 1:103 1:341 3↑ Alw 20000 1 3 1hd 1½ 1½ 1½ Cordero A Jr 114 1.40 95-17 Dr.Ptchs114½Buckfndr1149¾LghtnngBob1177¼ Strong handling 5
17Oct77- 7Aqu sly 1⊗ :232 :46 1:101 1:343 3↑ Alw 18000 2 3 2½ 2½ 2hd 12 Cordero A Jr 114 *1.80 93-18 Dr. Patches1142Bold Palette1141¼Liberal1177 Ridden out 6
5Oct77- 6Bel fst 6f :221 :452 1:104 3↑ Alw 13000 4 7 53 44½ 24 1¾ Cordero A Jr 119 *.80 88-14 Dr. Patches119¾Super Pleasure1163Tiresome1191 Driving 8
13Sep77- 6Bel fst 6f :224 :454 1:101 3↑ Alw 11000 4 2 2½ 2½ 2hd 12 Cordero A Jr 113 1.60 91-14 Dr. Patches1132Topsider1132¾Jungle Jim1156¼ Drew clear 8
25Aug77- 7Sar fst 6f :22 :451 1:101 3↑ Alw 11000 4 3 41½ 54 52½ 47¼ Vasquez J 112 *1.20 82-21 PeakTop1122¼JungleJim1144¾IroquoisTribe117nk No excuse 9
27Jun77- 8Bel fst 1 :23 :452 1:101 1:351 Saranac-G2 8 5 31½ 3nk 2hd 42 Vasquez J 114 9.60 90-17 Bailjumper1141¼LynnDavis114¾GiftofKings114no Weakened 9
20Jun77- 6Bel fst 6f :224 :462 1:101 3↑ Alw 12000 8 4 2½ 21 2hd 2no Vasquez J 111 *1.10e 91-18 Doctr'sOrdrs114noDr.Ptchs1112½PumpknMoonshn1144¾ Sharp 11
3Jun77- 7Bel fst 6f :224 :46 1:101 3↑ Alw 12000 7 3 32 32½ 32½ 2nk Vasquez J 112 *1.40 91-20 Intercontinent114nkDr. Patches1122Preferred Position1111¾ 7
Finished well
19May77- 6Aqu sly 1 :231 :461 1:103 1:362 Alw 13000 6 2 2½ 25 47½ 48 Venezia M 115 7.50 76-12 LeadngScorer1102½LynnDavis122hdJhnnyD.1155½ Weakened 8
2May77- 6Aqu fst 6f :223 :454 1:102 3↑ Alw 12000 1 5 43 43 52¼ 52 Vasquez J 112 *2.00e 89-15 Solly114hdBartender'sPride104¾HostilePlanet119hd Tired 7
23Apr77- 4Aqu fst 6f[•] :222 :454 1:101 3↑ Md Sp Wt 10 2 33 2hd 1hd 12¾ Vasquez J 112 *.90 96-05 Dr.Patches1122¾LeadingScorer1077¼SunFlame113hd Driving 12
11Apr77- 4Aqu fst 6f[•] :222 :46 1:111 3↑ Md Sp Wt 8 3 1hd 21½ 22½ 23 Vasquez J 112 5.50 88-13 Spirit Level1123Dr. Patches1121First Gang1125 Gamely 11

Exceller

b. c. 1973, by Vaguely Noble (Vienna)–Too Bald, by Bald Eagle
Own.– Belair Stud & Hunt
Br.– Mrs Charles W. Engelhard (Ky)
Tr.– Charles Whittingham

Lifetime record: 33 15 5 6 $1,654,003

29Apr79- 8Hol fm 1⅜Ⓣ :481 1:13 1:371 2:132 3↑ Century H-G1 6 10 1011 53 33½ 33 Hawley S 127 *.70 85-10 StateDinner1122StarSpngld1221Excllr1271¼ Pulled up lame 10
8Apr79- 8SA fm *1¾Ⓣ :48 2:03 2:273 2:48 4↑ S Juan Capistrano H-G1 6 7 716 42 1½ 2¾ Shoemaker W 127 1.50 86-12 Tiller126¾Exceller127¾Noble Dancer II1281½ Weakened 11
18Mar79- 8SA gd 1½Ⓣ :484 1:152 2:08 2:343 4↑ San Luis Rey-G1 2 7 715 76½ 614 629 Shoemaker W 126 *.90 -- NobleDancrII1262½Tllr1264GoodLord1261¾ Disliked footing 7
4Mar79- 8SA fst 1¼ :462 1:101 1:341 1:583 4↑ S Anita H-G1 4 8 812 710 47½ 37½♦ Shoemaker W 127 2.40 95-09 Affirmed1284½Tiller1273[DH]PaintedWgon115 Blocked,rallied 8
Previously owned by N.B. Hunt
5Nov78- 8SA fm 1½Ⓣ :472 1:104 1:591 2:243 3↑ Oak Tree Inv'l-G1 6 7 615 310 35½ 11 Shoemaker W 126 *.30 92-11 Exceller1261StarofErinII1263¾[DH]GoodLord126 Going away 9
14Oct78- 8Bel sly 1½ :451 1:092 2:014 2:271 3↑ J C Gold Cup-G1 5 5 522 2hd 1½ 1no Shoemaker W 126 3.80 84-13 Exceller126noSeattle Slew12614Great Contractor1264¾ 6
Drifted,lasted
30Sep78- 8Bel fst 1¼ :473 1:104 1:351 2:00 3↑ Woodward-G1 3 3 22 22½ 22½ 24 Shoemaker W 126 1.90 105-12 SeattleSlew1264Exceller1266¾It'sFreezing126no No match 5
24Jly78- 8Hol fm 1½Ⓣ :492 1:14 2:03 2:27 3↑ Sunset H-G1 2 7 79 32 2½ 11¼ Shoemaker W 130 *.40e 93-13 Exceller1301¼Diagramatic1221¾Effervescing1221½ Driving 8
25Jun78- 8Hol fst 1¼ :452 1:091 1:333 1:591 3↑ Hol Gold Cup H-G1 7 7 716 611 43½ 1nk Shoemaker W 128 1.20e 95-16 Exceller128nkText118hdVigors1294 Just up 7
29May78- 8Hol fm 1½Ⓣ :472 1:112 2:012 2:254 3↑ Hol Inv'l H-G1 7 12 1213 2hd 11½ 12½ Shoemaker W 127 *2.40 99-04 Exceller1272½Bowl Game123½Noble Dancer II1263½ In hand 12
30Apr78- 8Hol fm 1⅜Ⓣ :482 1:133 1:372 2:13 3↑ Century H-G1 4 9 64¼ 41 35 53¼ Pierce D 128 *1.20 87-08 Landscapr115hdStrSpngld1171½NoTurnng1161½ Wide all way 9
9Apr78- 8SA sf *1¾Ⓣ :472 2:031 2:282 2:51 4↑ S Juan Capistrano H-G1 11 6 54½ 32 32 1nk Shoemaker W 126 *1.30 72-28 Exceller126nkNoble Dancer II1251½Xmas Box115nk Driving 11
19Mar78- 8SA fm 1½Ⓣ :463 1:104 1:593 2:24 4↑ San Luis Rey-G1 7 6 611 64¼ 41½ 41 Shoemaker W 126 *1.40 94-11 Noble Dancer II126nkProperantes126¾Text126hd Blocked 7
8Mar78- 8SA fst 1¼ :473 1:112 1:36 2:011 4↑ Arcadia H-G3 5 5 36 2½ 11½ 11¼ Shoemaker W 126 *1.60 90-16 Exceller1261¼Soldier's Lark1131¼Tacitus1154 Much best 6
Previously trained by Maurice Zilber
19Nov77- 8Aqu sf 1½Ⓣ :51 1:154 2:06 2:331 3↑ Turf Classic 200k 1 1 1hd 58 711 722 Piggott L 126 3.00 -- JohnnyD.1223¾MajesticLight126¾Crow126nk Finished early 9
5Nov77- 8Lrl sf 1½Ⓣ :553 1:204 2:154 2:42 3↑ D C Int'l-G1 6 7 87¾ 47½ 311 316½ Cordero A Jr 127 *1.50 42-41 Johnny D.1202½Majestic Light12714Exceller1273 No threat 8
23Oct77- 7WO sf 1⅝Ⓣ :511 1:443 2:522 3↑ Can Int'l-G1 8 10 812 53¼ 31½ 11 Cordero A Jr 126 *1.20e 38-44 Exceller1261Majestic Light1263½Johnny D.1183 Ridden out 12
8Oct77- 8Bel gd 1½Ⓣ :474 1:121 2:031 2:273 3↑ Man o' War-G1 3 9 914 42½ 52¼ 24½ Cordero A Jr 126 *1.60e 81-13 MjstcLght1264½Excllr126noJohnnyD.121¾ Brushed,alt course 11
23Jly77♦ Ascot(GB) gd 1½ⓉRH 2:302 3↑ King George & Queen Eliz-G1 Stk230000 31½ Head F 133 5.50 The Minstrel120noOrange Bay1331½Exceller1333 11
Raced in midpack,finished well but held by first two
3Jly77♦ Saint-Cloud(Fr) gd *1$\frac{9}{16}$ⓉLH 2:324 3↑ Grand Prix de St Cloud-G1 Stk230000 1nk Head F 134 *1.20e Exceller134nkRiboboy134½Iron Duke1342 10
Trailed to 2f out,sharp run to lead late.Crow 4th,Tip Moss 6th
2Jun77♦ Epsom(GB) gd 1½ⓉLH 2:364 4↑ Coronation Cup-G1 Stk47600 1nk Dubroeucq G 126 *1.60 Exceller126nkQuiet Fling1233Smuggler1266 6
Well placed in 4th,bid 1½f out,up near line
1May77♦ Longchamp(Fr) gd *1$\frac{5}{16}$ⓉRH 2:11 4↑ Prix Ganay-G1 Stk122000 2½ Dubroeucq G 128 6.20 Arctic Tern128½Exceller128nkInfra Green124½ 12
Rated in 9th,late run,up for 2nd.Tip Moss 4th,Crow 7th
17Mar77♦ Saint-Cloud(Fr) hy *1¼ⓉLH 2:172 4↑ Prix Exbury-G3 Stk31000 48¾ Dubroeucq G 130 *1.50 Cheraw126¾Citoyen1302Kasteel1306 7
Never a factor.Far North 6th
3Oct76♦ Longchamp(Fr) hy *1½ⓉRH 2:392 3↑ Prix de l'Arc de Triomphe-G1 Stk412000 19 Dubroeucq G 123 *2.00e Ivanjica1272Crow1233Youth123nk 20
Tracked in 5th,weakened 2f out.Noble Dancer 4th,Pawneese 11th
12Sep76♦ Longchamp(Fr) sf *1$\frac{15}{16}$ⓉRH 3:334 Prix Royal-Oak-G1 Stk191000 14 Dubroeucq G 128 *.20 Exceller1284Sir Montaya128½Adam van Vianen1285 7
Well placed in 3rd,led 2½f out,drew clear in hand
27Jun76♦ Longchamp(Fr) gd *1$\frac{15}{16}$ⓉRH 3:202 Grand Prix de Paris-G1 Stk340000 14 St Martin Y 123 *.40 Exceller1234Secret Man1231½Caron1234 9
Unhurried in 5th,rallied to lead 1f out,going away

6Jun76♦ Chantilly(Fr)	yl	*1½ⓉRH	2:284	Prix du Lys-G3 Stk43500	16	Dubroeucq G	128	*1.90	Exceller1286Brouhaha128nkCaron1281½ Well placed in 3rd,led 1½f out,drew clear	8
19May76♦ Evry(Fr)	sf	*1¼ⓉLH	2:074	Prix Matchem (Listed) Stk23400	12½	Dubroeucq G	124	*.40	Exceller1242½Lithidan1211½Dauphin du Roi124½ Close up,led 3f out,held well	6
2May76♦ Longchamp(Fr)	gd	*1 5/16ⓉRH	2:132	Prix de Suresnes (Listed) Stk23400	21	Dubroeucq G	121	*2.00	Malacate1261Exceller1212Bizantus121hd Tracked in 4th,bid 1½f out,outfinished	8
19Oct75♦ Longchamp(Fr)	sf	*1¼ⓉRH	2:151	Prix de Conde-G3 Stk42500	32¾	St Martin Y	123	*1.75	French Friend1232½Djeban123nkExceller1236 Tracked in 4th,brief bid 2f out,one-paced final furlong	9
1Oct75♦ Evry(Fr)	sf	*1ⓉLH	1:473	Prix Herod (Listed) Stk17600	1hd	Navarro N	128	*2.00	[D]Exceller128hdHappy Tim1211½Chateau Country1215 Bid 2f out,drifted in 1f out,dueled,prevailed Disqualified and placed third for impeding Chateau Country	7
15Sep75♦ Evry(Fr)	yl	*1⅛ⓉLH	1:532	Prix de Blois Mdn11700	1nk	Navarro N	128	4.50	Exceller128nkAppassionato1286Skylab1281½ Rated in 6th,rallied to lead near line	12
10Aug75♦ Deauville(Fr)	gd	*7½fⓉRH	1:312	Prix de Touques Mdn13600	88	Navarro N	123	6.00	Malacate1232½Carvello123nkSalud1231½ Never a factor	12

Foolish Pleasure

b. c. 1972, by What a Pleasure (Bold Ruler)–Fool-Me-Not, by Tom Fool — **Lifetime record: 26 16 4 3 $1,216,705**

Own.– J.L. Greer
Br.– Waldemar Farms Inc (Fla)
Tr.– Leroy Jolley

7Aug76-8AP	fst	1⅛	:452 1:092 1:344 1:473 3↑	Golden Inv'l H 125k	4 2 21 2½ 12 13½	Fires E	125	*.30	96-19	FoolishPleasr1253½Proponnt1082½FstvMood1152	Going away	6
24Jly76-8Aqu	fst	1¼	:464 1:111 1:362 2:011 3↑	Brooklyn H-G1	3 3 43 34½ 34 36½	Maple E	126	3.70	83-14	Forego1342Lord Rebeau1144½Foolish Pleasure126no	Bore in	8
5Jly76-8Aqu	fst	1 3/16	:474 1:112 1:361 1:552 3↑	Suburban H-G1	4 1 11½ 11½ 11 1no	Maple E	125	2.80	85-15	Foolish Pleasure125noForego134noLord Rebeau1164¼	Lasted	4
20Jun76-8Hol	fst	1¼	:454 1:10 1:343 1:584 3↑	Hol Gold Cup H-G1	1 7 69½ 74½ 76 56½	Pincay L Jr	126	1.80	90-09	Pay Tribute1173¼Avatar1232Riot in Paris123¾	Checked	8
6Jun76-8Hol	fst	1⅛	:462 1:102 1:35 1:471 3↑	Bel Air H-G2	2 4 33 42½ 42 33¾	Pincay L Jr	128	*.70	92-13	Riot in Paris122¾Pay Tribute1183Foolish Pleasure1282	Altered course	5
27Mar76-9GP	fm	1 1/16Ⓣ	:231 :464 1:094 1:401 3↑	Can Turf H-G3	3 3 21½ 22 32½ 84¼	Baeza B	129	*.60	99-02	StepForwrd117¾LordHenham112hdConesaba1131½	No excuse	9
6Mar76-9GP	fst	7f	:22 :443 1:091 1:212 3↑	Donn H-G2	2 7 43 63¾ 1½ 13½	Baeza B	129	*.30	97-17	FoolishPlsre1293½PackerCaptain114¾HomJrom112¾	Easily	10
4Feb76-7Hia	fst	7f	:23 :454 1:101 1:222 4↑	Alw 10000	4 3 42½ 43 1hd 17	Baeza B	119	*.30	93-16	Foolish Pleasure1197Dashboard1171Orders117nk	Easy score	7
10Oct75-8Bel	fst	1 1/16	:24 :464 1:11 1:413 3↑	Alw 20000	6 2 21½ 11½ 1hd 2no	Cordero A Jr	120	*.20	94-21	Stonewalk126noFoolishPlsur12010FrstSlc117no	Just missed	6
13Sep75-8Bel	fst	1¼	:472 1:104 1:352 2:00 3↑	Marlboro Cup Inv'l H-G1	4 5 54 66½ 66¼ 510	Cordero A Jr	121	2.80	89-11	Wajima119hdForego1297½Ancient Title126¾	No response	7
1Sep75-8Bel	fst	1⅛	:452 1:09 1:341 1:471 3↑	Governor-G1	6 4 45½ 33 11 2hd	Cordero A Jr	125	3.60	91-18	Wajima115hdFoolishPlsur1252AncntTtl130¾	Held stubbornly	10
6Jly75-8Bel	fst	1¼	:443 1:083 1:352 2:024	Match Race 350k	2 2 1 1 1 1	Baeza B	126	.90	86-11	Foolish Pleasure126	Galloping	2
7Jun75-7Bel	fst	1½	:48 1:122 2:02 2:281	Belmont-G1	2 6 67 43½ 32½ 2nk	Vasquez J	126	*1.30	79-18	Avatar126nkFoolishPleasure1263½MstrDrby1264	Closed fast	9
17May75-8Pim	fst	1 3/16	:471 1:113 1:361 1:562	Preakness-G1	4 7 76 52¾ 23 21	Vasquez J	126	*1.20	87-18	MasterDerby1261FoolshPlsur1261Dbolo1261½	Altered course	10
3May75-8CD	fst	1¼	:452 1:103 1:36 2:02	Ky Derby-G1	3 11 812 43½ 2½ 11¾	Vasquez J	126	*1.90	87-11	Foolish Pleasure1261¾Avatar1262½Diabolo1262½	Ridden out	15
19Apr75-8Aqu	fst	1⅛	:463 1:103 1:352 1:484	Wood Memorial-G1	15 4 43½ 31½ 22 1hd	Vasquez J	126	*.50	91-12	Foolish Pleasure126hdBombay Duck1261Media1264¾	Driving	15
29Mar75-9GP	fst	1⅛	:472 1:12 1:38 1:502	Florida Derby-G1	2 3 33½ 31 2½ 33½	Vasquez J	122	*.20	78-17	PrinceThouArt1183½SylvnPlace118nkFoolishPlsur1227	Hung	9
1Mar75-9Hia	fst	1⅛	:462 1:104 1:361 1:482	Flamingo-G1	2 7 64¼ 43½ 12 11¾	Vasquez J	122	*.40	90-13	FoolishPleasre1221¾PrinceThouArt1223Somethngfblous1222½	Bore in,clear	10
12Feb75-0Hia	fst	7f	:231 :453 1:092 1:212	Alw 7600	2 2 24 25 11 14¼	Vasquez J	122	-	98-15	FoolishPleasure1224¼Ambassador'sImage114½CircleHme119	Exhibition race - no wagering	3
5Oct74-8Bel	fst	1	:233 :463 1:11 1:36	Champagne-G1	9 3 31½ 13 17 16	Vasquez J	122	*.30	88-12	FlishPleasre1226HarvardMn1221¾Rmhorn1221¾	Ridden out	9
25Sep74-8Bel	fst	7f	:23 :462 1:102 1:223	Cowdin-G2	7 6 42½ 31½ 12 16½	Vasquez J	121	*.90	89-14	Foolish Pleasure1216½Our Talisman1135¾CardinalGeorge1131¼	Ridden out	11
24Aug74-8Sar	fst	6½f	:214 :442 1:092 1:16	Hopeful (Div 2)-G1	1 5 32½ 32 2½ 13¾	Baeza B	121	*1.10	96-13	FoolishPleasr1213¾GrkAnswr1211¾OurTlsmn121½	Drew clear	8
10Aug74-8Mth	gd	6f	:22 :45 1:102	Sapling-G1	13 3 43½ 42½ 1hd 11¾	Vasquez J	122	*2.30	88-19	Foolish Pleasure1221¾The BagelPrince1224½BombayDuck1222	Drew clear	15
24Jly74-8Aqu	fst	6f	:221 :453 1:104	Tremont-G3	4 5 22½ 21½ 2hd 1nk	Baltazar C	120	*1.10	89-12	FoolishPlsre120nkWhataSktch1141¼RcksJt115½	Bumped,up	9
27May74-6Del	gd	5½f	:223 :471 :593 1:053	Dover (Div 1)-G3	5 4 3nk 12 15 110	Baltazar C	116	*1.00	90-24	FoolishPleasre11610Jimbosanda1122[D]Ramahorn1161	Easily	7
4Apr74-3Hia	fst	5f	:223 :461 :59	©Md Sp Wt	8 9 42 11½ 13 14½	Baltazar C	120	*1.40	94-18	FoolishPlsure1204½SwingLbrSwng120hdTrKng1201½	Handily	11

Forego

b. g. 1970, by Forli (Aristophanes)–Lady Golconda, by Hasty Road — **Lifetime record: 57 34 9 7 $1,938,957**

Own.– Lazy F Ranch
Br.– Lazy F Ranch (Ky)
Tr.– Frank Y. Whiteley Jr

4Jly78-8Bel	sly	1¼	:483 1:123 1:37 2:014 3↑	Suburban H-G1	3 5 43½ 68½ 611 514	Shoemaker W	132	*.90	89-13	Upper Nile1131½Nearly on Time1092¼Great Contractor1143	Tired after ¾	6
19Jun78-8Bel	fst	7f	:233 :462 1:094 1:213 3↑	Alw 25000	4 4 41½ 31½ 31½ 1nk	Shoemaker W	122	*.30	94-12	Forego122nkDr. Patches1227Gabe Benzur1152	Ridden out	4
17Sep77-8Bel	sly	1⅛	:453 1:101 1:352 1:48 3↑	Woodward H-G1	3 8 79½ 44 4¾ 11½	Shoemaker W	133	*1.90	87-18	Forego1331½SilverSeries114nkGrtContrctor115nk	Ridden out	10
6Aug77-8Sar	sly	1⅛	:463 1:103 1:361 1:492 3↑	Whitney H-G2	7 6 712 716 716 718	Shoemaker W	136	*.80	70-16	Nearly on Time1034½American History1124¾Dancing Gun112¾	Disliked going	7
23Jly77-8Bel	fst	1½	:49 1:124 2:023 2:261 3↑	Brooklyn H-G1	12 6 2hd 21½ 25 211	Shoemaker W	137	*.70	78-17	GreatContractr11211Forego137nkAmrcnHstory112¾	Held 2nd	13
4Jly77-8Bel	fst	1¼	:472 1:113 1:373 2:03 3↑	Suburban H-G1	4 3 36½ 45 42 2nk	Shoemaker W	138	*.30	84-16	QuietLittleTable114nkForego138nkNearlyonTm104¾	Bore out	6
13Jun77-8Bel	fst	1⅛	:471 1:111 1:354 1:481 3↑	Nassau County H-G3	3 5 54 51¼ 4¾ 1½	Shoemaker W	136	*.05	86-21	Forego136½Co Host110nkNorcliffe117½	Easily	7
30May77-8Bel	fst	1	:23 :451 1:101 1:344 3↑	Metropolitan H-G1	10 10 1014 86½ 2hd 12	Shoemaker W	133	*.50	94-14	Forego1332Co Host1112Full Out1151½	Handily	12
23May77-6Bel	fst	7f	:242 :47 1:11 1:224 4↑	Alw 25000	2 3 31 32 2hd 1½	Shoemaker W	122	*.05	88-17	Forego122½Dance Spell1147Sawbones1092	Ridden out	5
2Oct76-8Bel	sly	1¼	:472 1:104 1:35 2:00 3↑	Marlboro Cup H-G1	10 4 86¼ 67½ 44 1hd	Shoemaker W	137	*1.10	99-11	Forego137hdHonestPleasure1191FthrHogn1102¾	Wide,just up	11
18Sep76-8Bel	fst	1⅛	:453 1:091 1:332 1:454 3↑	Woodward H-G1	2 7 76 76½ 42½ 11¼	Shoemaker W	135	*1.10	98-10	Forgo1351¼DanceSpell1152¾[DH]HonstPleasur121	Ridden out	10
21Aug76-8Mth	fst	1¼	:472 1:112 1:354 2:003 3↑	AL Haskell H-G1	7 5 33 22 21 31	Vasquez J	136	*.60	98-12	Hatchet Man1121Intrepid Hero119hdForego1366	Forced wide	8
24Jly76-8Aqu	fst	1¼	:464 1:111 1:362 2:011 3↑	Brooklyn H-G1	4 6 68½ 21½ 2hd 12	Gustines H	134	*.70	90-14	Forego1342LordRebeau1144½FoolishPleasur126no	Ridden out	8
5Jly76-8Aqu	fst	1 3/16	:474 1:112 1:361 1:552 3↑	Suburban H-G1	2 3 32½ 21½ 31½ 2no	Gustines H	134	*.40	85-15	Foolish Pleasure125noForego134noLord Rebeau1164¼	Gamely	4
13Jun76-8Bel	fst	1⅛	:472 1:112 1:362 1:483 3↑	Nassau County H-G3	1 4 42½ 32 1hd 12¾	Vasquez J	132	*.80	84-22	Forego1322¾El Pitirre1152¾Hatchet Man1142	Easily	5
31May76-8Bel	fst	1	:231 :453 1:092 1:344 3↑	Metropolitan H-G1	4 5 54½ 44 41½ 1hd	Gustines H	130	*1.10	94-16	Forego130hdMaster Derby1261½Lord Rebeau1192¼	Sluggish,just up	6
20May76-8Bel	fst	7f	:234 :464 1:10 1:22 4↑	Alw 25000	2 2 41½ 3½ 1hd 11¼	Gustines H	126	*.30	92-18	Forego1261¼Wishing Stone1196½Tiempazo III119½	Easily	4
Previously trained by S.W. Ward												
27Sep75-8Bel	fst	1½	:493 1:132 2:023 2:271 3↑	Woodward-G1	6 3 3½ 1hd 1hd 11¾	Gustines H	126	*.90	84-19	Forego1261¾Wajima11911Group Plan126¾	Drew clear	6
13Sep75-8Bel	fst	1¼	:472 1:104 1:352 2:00 3↑	Marlboro Cup Inv'l H-G1	3 7 76 32 1hd 2hd	Gustines H	129	*1.40	99-11	Wajima119hdForego1297½Ancient Title126¾	Bore out,missed	7
1Sep75-8Bel	fst	1⅛	:452 1:09 1:341 1:471 3↑	Governor-G1	8 8 710 88¾ 54½ 42¾	Gustines H	134	*2.00	88-18	Wajima115hdFoolishPleasure1252AncntTtl130¾	Wide stretch	10
19Jly75-8Bel	fst	1½	:484 1:132 2:024 2:274 3↑	Suburban H-G1	3 6 69½ 42½ 3½ 1hd	Gustines H	134	*.60	81-18	Forego134hdArbees Boy1182¼Loud1147	Just up	7

4Jly75- 8Bel	fst 1¼	:463 1:101 1:344 1:594	3↑ Brooklyn H-G1	2 5	412	31½	1hd	11½	Gustines H	132	*.70	101-07	Frgo1321½MonetryPrncpl109noStopthMusc1215¾	Ridden out	8
26May75- 8Aqu	fst 1	:231 :453 1:084 1:333	3↑ Metropolitan H-G1	3 7	75¼	64¾	34	31	Gustines H	136	*.90	97-11	GoldandMyrrh121¾StoptheMusic124nkForego1363½	Rallied	7
17May75- 8Aqu	fst 7f	:223 :444 1:091 1:213	3↑ Carter H-G2	5 10	811	87¾	22	1hd	Gustines H	134	*.90	93-11	Forego134hdStop the Music1232½Orders1141¼	Brisk drive	10
15Feb75- 9Hia	fst 1¼	:463 1:102 1:35 2:014	3↑ Widener H-G1	5 9	813	45½	1hd	11¼	Gustines H	131	*.70	89-11	Forego1311¼Hat Full1111¼Gold and Myrrh115nk	Ridden out	9
1Feb75- 9Hia	fst 1⅛	:47 1:103 1:343 1:471	3↑ Seminole H-G2	5 8	85	32	2½	1¾	Gustines H	129	*.80	96-09	Forego129¾Mr. Door1151Lord Rebeau1152½	Ridden out	8
9Nov74- 8Aqu	fst 2	:493 2:304 2:56 3:211	3↑ J C Gold Cup-G1	2 8	42½	1hd	12½	12½	Gustines H	124	*.70	90-15	Forego1242½Copte124¾Group Plan1243¼	Ridden out	8
19Oct74- 8Aqu	fst 7f	:223 :452 1:094 1:213	3↑ Vosburgh H-G2	4 10	99½	77½	21	13½	Gustines H	131	*2.20	93-10	Forgo1313½StoptheMusic118noPrinceDantn1191¾	Ridden out	12
28Sep74- 8Bel	fst 1½	:49 1:132 2:022 2:272	3↑ Woodward-G1	5 10	1017	84½	42	1nk	Gustines H	126	*2.30	83-13	Forego126nkArbees Boy1261¾Group Plan1262½	Driving	11
14Sep74- 8Bel	sly 1⅛	:46 1:102 1:343 1:463	3↑ Marlboro Cup H 250k	2 9	810	72¾	34½	34	Gustines H	126	2.70	90-12	Big Spruce1202¾Arbees Boy1191½Forego126½	No final rally	10
2Sep74- 8Bel	fst 1⅛	:452 1:092 1:34 1:461	3↑ Governor-G1	10 8	812	65	57	45¼	Gustines H	128	*1.60	91-09	Big Spruce1182½Arbees Boy1211½Plunk1211¼	Wide	10
20Jly74- 8Aqu	fst 1¼	:472 1:111 1:361 2:012	3↑ Suburban H-G1	6 6	512	46½	44½	31½	Gustines H	131	*1.40	87-12	True Knight1271½Plunk114hdForego1312½	Rallied	10
4Jly74- 8Aqu	fst 1 3/16	:463 1:102 1:354 1:544	3↑ Brooklyn H-G1	6 6	615	48	2hd	1¾	Gustines H	129	*.40	88-14	Forego129¾BillyComeLately1142ArbeesBoy1166	Ridden out	7
26Jun74- 8Aqu	fst 7f	:223 :444 1:084 1:211	3↑ Nassau County H-G3	2 6	612	612	56½	2½	Gustines H	132	*.70	94-10	Timeless Moment112½Forego132½North Sea1142½	Fast finish	6
27May74- 8Bel	fst 1	:222 :443 1:09 1:342	3↑ Metropolitan H-G1	2 6	47½	2hd	11½	22	Gustines H	134	*1.30	94-11	Arbees Boy1122Forego134½Timeless Moment109hd	Gamely	8
18May74- 8Bel	fst 7f	:221 :45 1:092 1:221	3↑ Carter H-G2	7 8	89	63½	11½	12¼	Gustines H	129	*1.40	91-13	Forego1292¼Mr.Prospector1241TimelessMoment1132¾	Easily	8
23Mar74- 9Hia	fst 1¼	:471 1:11 1:354 2:011	3↑ Widener H-G1	5 5	58½	1½	11½	11	Gustines H	129	*.80	92-12	Forego1291True Knight1242Play the Field114no	Driving	7
23Feb74- 9GP	fst 1¼	:464 1:104 1:354 1:594	3↑ Gulf Park H-G2	2 4	413	22	1hd	1½	Gustines H	127	1.40	98-14	Forego127½True Knight1236Golden Don1183	Ridden out	6
9Feb74- 9GP	fst 1⅛	:471 1:112 1:362 1:483	3↑ Donn H-G3	2 4	35	32½	21	1no	Gustines H	125	*.70	91-19	Forego125noTrue Knight123½Proud and Bold122nk	Just up	5
8Dec73- 8Aqu	fst 1⅛	:454 1:10 1:35 1:471	Discovery H-G3	6 5	37	34	11½	1¾	Gustines H	127	*.60	100-13	Forego127¾MyGallant1225[D]KeytotheKingdom1131	Driving	7
24Nov73- 8Aqu	fst 1 3/16	:462 1:11 1:36 1:543	Roamer H-G2	9 4	514	32½	13	15	Gustines H	123	*2.10	89-13	Forego1235My Gallant1212½Twice a Prince1141	Handily	10
10Nov73- 6Aqu	fst 7f	:233 :463 1:102 1:223	3↑ Alw 12000	2 5	35½	36	34	34	Gustines H	122	*.90	84-22	North Sea1152¾Tap the Tree1141½Forego1223½	Evenly	5
20Oct73- 8Aqu	fst 1	:233 :46 1:094 1:34	Jerome H-G2	7 6	63½	32½	2hd	2hd	Gustines H	124	2.20	97-14	Step Nicely118hdForego1243Linda's Chief1261¾	Gamely	10
8Oct73- 5Bel	fst 1	:234 :461 1:093 1:333	3↑ Alw 20000	3 3	31	1½	12½	15½	Gustines H	120	*1.60	100-07	Forego1205½Rule by Reason114noRoyal Owl12010	Ridden out	5
15Sep73- 8Bel	fst 1 1/16	:232 :462 1:102 1:402	Alw 20000	6 4	41½	1hd	13	12½	Gustines H	116	2.10	101-07	Forego1162½Arbees Boy1132Matinee Idol1133	Driving	8
1Sep73- 4Bel	fst 7f	:214 :442 1:091 1:221	Alw 20000	1 6	49½	25	13	1hd	Gustines H	113	*.60	91-10	Forego113hdCutlass113¾Jazziness116nk	Driving	6
24Aug73- 5Sar	fst 7f	:224 :451 1:083 1:21	3↑ Alw 12000	5 4	56½	56	47½	37¼	Anderson P	116	*.60	95-10	Prove Out1126½Cutlass109¾Forego1161¼	No excuse	6
9Jun73- 7Bel	fst 1 1/16	:232 :46 1:101 1:404	Alw 20000	4 5	53¼	12	17	19	Gustines H	111	*1.00	99-05	Forego1119AdaptiveAce114noIllberightbck114no	Ridden out	10
30May73- 7Bel	fst 1	:231 :45 1:091 1:344	Withers-G2	3 5	56	45	43½	35	Anderson P	126	8.00	93-17	Lnda'sChief1263StoptheMusc1262Forgo126½	Between horses	6
5May73- 9CD	fst 1¼	:472 1:114 1:361 1:592	Ky Derby-G1	9 9	912	66	46½	411	Anderson P	126	28.60	92-10	Secretariat1262½Sham1268OurNative126½	Hit rail far turn	13
26Apr73- 6Kee	fst 1⅛	:463 1:11 1:37 1:493	Blue Grass-G1	5 6	611	52½	52¾	55	Anderson P	117	*2.60	84-18	My Gallant117hdOur Native1233½[DH]Warbucks117	No rally	9
31Mar73- 9GP	fst 1⅛	:471 1:102 1:342 1:472	Florida Derby-G1	6 4	56	33	23	23	Anderson P	118	*2.30	94-06	Royal and Regal1222Forego1181¼Restless Jet122hd	Gamely	8
24Mar73- 3GP	fst 7f	:221 :444 1:092 1:213	Alw 6500	1 8	65	53	11	12	Anderson P	119	*.30	96-12	Forego1192Cades Cove114noMalicious Music1143½	Driving	8
7Mar73- 9GP	fst 7f	:221 :443 1:082 1:204	Hutcheson-G3	1 7	56¾	37	24	23¼	Anderson P	116	2.40	97-10	Shecky Greene1223¼Forego1169Leo's Pisces1124½	Away sluggishly	7
10Feb73- 4Hia	fst 6f	:214 :452 1:094	Alw 6500	5 4	45½	32½	11	12½	Anderson P	122	*.60	95-18	Forego1222½Borage1152½Paternity1174	Easily	8
29Jan73- 1Hia	fst 6f	:222 :46 1:102	©Md Sp Wt	4 1	22	1hd	1½	18	Anderson P	122	*1.30	92-16	Forego1228Jonata1222Barclay Jet122½	Easily	11
17Jan73- 1Hia	fst 7f	:232 :461 1:11 1:233	©Md Sp Wt	9 11	97¼	89	79½	47	Anderson P	122	10.30	82-04	BuffaloLark1223¾TwoHarbrs1222CommandrLiz1221¼	Bumped	12

Fort Marcy

b. g. 1964, by Amerigo (Nearco)–Key Bridge, by Princequillo **Lifetime record: 75 21 18 14 $1,109,791**

Own.– Rokeby Stable
Br.– Paul Mellon (Va)
Tr.– E. Burch

4Sep71- 8Atl	fm 1⅛Ⓣ	:492 1:121 1:362 1:483	3↑ Kelly-Olympic H 33k	8 6	68	56	53½	3¾	Velasquez J	126 b	*1.30e	92-11	Run the Gantlet115¾Charlie's Luck110noFort Marcy126hd	Strong finish	8
5Jly71- 7Aqu	fst 1¼	:48 1:121 1:371 2:021	3↑ Suburban H 115k	3 9	88¾	127½	109¾	1010	Velasquez J	120 b	8.10	75-17	Twice Worthy116½Ejemplo1143Tunex117hd	No factor	13
26Jun71- 8Hol	fm 1½Ⓣ	:471 1:11 2:012 2:262	3↑ Inv'l Turf H 125k	6 4	414	25	22	2nk	Lambert J	125 b	4.20	101-12	CougarII127nkFortMarcy1251½DvdndRul1215	Drifted,rallied	8
12Jun71- 7Bel	hd 1½Ⓣ		2:252 3↑ Bowling Green H 56k	5 4	55½	31	3nk	21¾	Turcotte R	128 b	*1.50	104-00	Drumtop1241¾Fort Marcy128noPracticante1151½	Bore in	7
8May71- 8Pim	sf 1½Ⓣ	:501 1:17 2:083 2:341	3↑ Dixie H 56k	4 3	35	22	15	16	Turcotte R	126 b	*.70	66-34	[D]FortMarcy1266Chompion1193½TudorReward1143½	Brushed; Disqualified and placed fourth	5
10Apr71- 8SA	fm *1¾Ⓣ	:481 2:012 2:241 2:461	4↑ S Juan Capistrano H 125k	4 5	59	3nk	1½	23	Velasquez J	127 b	*1.00	93-07	Cougar II1263[D]Fort Marcy1273¼Try Sheep1142¾	Bore out; Disqualified and placed sixth	7
27Feb71- 8Hia	hd 1½Ⓣ		2:264 3↑ Hia Turf Cup H 143k	8 1	1hd	11½	1hd	31¾	Velasquez J	128 b	*.70	100-03	Drumtop119hdThe Pruner1131¾Fort Marcy128¾	Drifted badly	13
13Feb71- 8Hia	hd 1 3/16Ⓣ		1:54 3↑ Bougnvillea H (Div 1) 48k	3 4	414	57½	23	2hd	Velasquez J	126 b	*1.10	99-01	Shelter Bay117hdFort Marcy1262Stop Time1111½	Gamely	10
11Nov70- 7Lrl	sf 1½Ⓣ	:511 1:172 2:151 2:424	3↑ Wash Int'l Inv'l 150k	9 4	41	12	1½	11	Velasquez J	127 b	*1.10	- -	Fort Marcy1271Miss Dan II1175Bacuco127no	Fully extended	10
17Oct70- 7Bel	sf 1½Ⓣ		2:334 3↑ Man o' War 116k	5 4	43	11½	15	11¾	Velasquez J	126 b	*.70	64-40	Fort Marcy1261¾Loud1214½Drumtop123nk	Mild drive	10
16Sep70- 8Atl	fm 1 3/16Ⓣ	:473 1:121 1:374 1:56	3↑ U Nations Inv'l H 125k	7 5	58	42	11½	15	Velasquez J	125 b	*1.50	90-10	Fort Marcy1255Fiddle Isle1271Mr. Leader119nk	Mild drive	10
5Sep70- 8Atl	fm 1⅛Ⓣ	:474 1:112 1:36 1:482	3↑ Kelly-Olympic H 41k	13 11	108¾	95¼	43½	2no	Velasquez J	126 b	*2.10	94-09	Red Reality115noFort Marcy1261Mister Diz1163	Missed	13
21Aug70- 7Sar	fst 1	:24 :464 1:104 1:351	3↑ Alw 15000	5 2	21½	31	31½	31½	Velasquez J	120 b	6.10	96-08	True North116nkMaster Hand1161¼Fort Marcy1201	Good try	7
20Jun70- 8Hol	fm 1½Ⓣ	:481 1:121 2:013 2:253	3↑ Hol Inv'l H 100k	5 3	35	32½	21½	2nk	Velasquez J	126 b	*1.60e	105-10	FiddleIsle128nkFortMrcy1263Govrnor'sPrty1121¼	Sharp try	9
13Jun70- 7Bel	fm 1½Ⓣ		2:263 3↑ Bowling Green H 57k	5 2	28	25	11	1½	Velasquez J	127 b	*1.50	103-13	Fort Marcy127½Drumtop1201½Hitchcock118¾	Driving	7
9May70- 8Pim	fm 1½Ⓣ	:483 1:134 2:022 2:272	3↑ Dixie H 57k	6 4	45	32	2hd	13½	Velasquez J	124 b	*1.30	108-01	FortMarcy1243½WarCensor112½JungleCove114nk	Mild drive	10
25Apr70- 8Hol	fm 1⅜Ⓣ		2:113 3↑ Century H 80k	2 5	54½	53	32½	2no	Velasquez J	123 b	3.70	108-08	Quilche115noFort Marcy123½Pinjara1201¼	Hemmed in	9
4Apr70- 8SA	fm *1¾Ⓣ	:471 2:001 2:24 2:462	4↑ S Juan Capistrano H 125k	3 4	46½	53	3½	3no	Velasquez J	124 b	8.50	95-05	[DH] Fiddle Isle125[DH] Quicken Tree124noFort Marcy124nk	Squeezed	11
18Mar70- 7Aqu	fst 1	:233 :463 1:103 1:351	4↑ Alw 15000	8 4			2½	2no	Velasquez J	116 b	6.90	91-17	Hydrologist120noFortMarcy116noSpiralStaircas1183½	Sharp; View of race obscured by snow	9
14Feb70- 9Hia	fm 1 3/16Ⓣ		1:534 3↑ Bougnvillea H (Div 2) 46k	6 8	713	55½	54½	43¾	Marquez CH	123 b	3.20	96-05	Vent du Nord122noHitchcock1151¼Jungle Cove1142½	Rallied	10
21Jan70- 9Hia	fm 1 1/16Ⓣ		1:424 4↑ Alw 8000	11 8	78¼	53	65½	74¾	Ycaza M	116 b	*1.10	86-07	[D]HighHat113¾ElegantHeir1131½VirginiaBron108¾	No threat	12
29Nov69- 7Aqu	fst 1	:223 :443 1:084 1:342	3↑ Stuyvesant H 60k	5 11	1115	1112	1012	65	Velasquez J	120 b	15.50	90-14	King Emperor1162½Dewan1161¼Jaikyl112nk	No early foot	11
18Oct69- 7Bel	fm 1½Ⓣ		2:271 3↑ Man o' War 113k	2 3	36½	51¾	41¼	33½	Ycaza M	126 b	2.30	97-11	Hawaii1262¼North Flight1211¼Fort Marcy1261¼	Hung under impost	9
10Sep69- 8Atl	sf 1 3/16Ⓣ	:493 1:144 1:41 2:003	3↑ U Nations H Inv'l 125k	7 7	74¾	76½	35½	37½	Ycaza M	130 b	2.30	59-33	Hawaii124½North Flight1177Fort Marcy1303	Close quarters	10
30Aug69- 8Atl	hd 1⅛Ⓣ	:501 1:14 1:38 1:501	3↑ Kelly-Olympic H 34k	7 7	74¾	31½	31½	1½	Ycaza M	128 b	*2.30	85-19	Fort Marcy128½Balustrade116nkHawaii124¾	Driving	10
26Jly69- 7Aqu	sf 1⅛Ⓣ		1:551 3↑ Tidal H 58k	3 6	53¼	32	2hd	1½	Ycaza M	126 b	2.60	59-47	Fort Marcy126½Baitman1101Hawaii1233	Under hard drive	8
4Jly69- 7Aqu	gd 1¼	:512 1:161 1:404 2:044	3↑ Suburban H 107k	5 5	42½	53½	56½	511	Velasquez J	121 b	7.10	61-31	Mr. Right117hdDike114nkChompion1113	Off sluggishly	5
21Jun69- 8Hol	fm 1½Ⓣ	:47 1:12 2:022 2:271	3↑ Hol Turf Inv'l H 100k	7 7	99	2½	11½	1no	Ycaza M	124 b	*1.20	97-11	FortMrcy124noPoleax1173CourtFool115hd	Lasted under drive	12
2Jun69- 7Bel	yl 1⅜Ⓣ		2:19 3↑ Edgemere H 29k	3 3	33½	1hd	2½	32	Ycaza M	126 b	*2.20	69-29	Majetta1142Liaison114hdFort Marcy1261	In close stretch	8
5Apr69- 8SA	fm *1¾Ⓣ	:464 1:593 2:251 2:472	4↑ S Juan Capistrano H 125k	10 4	512	42½	21½	22¾	Ycaza M	124 b	5.10	87-07	Petrone1222¾FortMarcy1241½Rivet115nk	Finished willingly	10
22Mar69- 9GP	fst 1¼	:471 1:113 1:36 2:012	3↑ Gulfstream H 126k	8 7	714	711	79	45	Maple E	121 b	13.90	87-10	CourtRcss108noNodoubl1252¼TropcKngII1162¾	Not a threat	9
22Feb69- 8Hia	fst 1¼	:482 1:12 1:37 2:031	3↑ Widener H 137k	9 8	79½	66¾	68½	63¼	Cruguet J	124 b	5.80	79-26	Yumbel112hdFunnyFellw121noMr.Brognn113¾	Never a threat	11
15Feb69- 8Hia	sf 1 3/16Ⓣ		2:03 3↑ Bougainvillea H 68k	3 4	44½	21½	2hd	1hd	Ycaza M	124 b	3.20	54-46	Fort Marcy124hdTaneb115¾Blanquette II1164	Just up	14

4Feb69- 8Hia	fm 1⅛Ⓣ	1:491	4↑ Alw 8000	6 3 22 13 12 11¼	Ycaza M	119 b	*.80	94-10	FortMarcy1191¼Taneb1133Hibernin113hd	Complete authority 8
11Nov68- 7Lrl	sf 1½Ⓣ	:521 1:18 2:122 2:371	3↑ D C Int'l 150k	8 3 3½ 1hd 2hd 3¾	Ycaza M	127 b	3.80	32-59	Sir Ivor120¾Czar Alexander120noFort Marcy1271¼	Tired 8
19Oct68- 7Bel	sf 1½Ⓣ	2:304	3↑ Man o' War 116k	6 6 66½ 1½ 2½ 23½	Ycaza M	126 b	3.10	85-11	Czar Alexander1213½Fort Marcy1264½Advocator1284½	Gamely 12
30Sep68- 5Bel	hd 1⅜Ⓣ	2:144	3↑ Long Island H (Div 1) 23k	2 7 52 31 55 69	Velasquez J	125 b	*1.10	83-15	Ruth'sRullah112¾RffledFethrs1183CzrAlxndr1152½	Roughed 9
11Sep68- 8Atl	fm 1 3/16Ⓣ	:484 1:123 1:364 1:551	3↑ U Nations H 100k	2 4 55¼ 54¼ 33 31½	Velasquez J	118 b	3.20	92-10	Dr.Fgr134nkAdvoctor1121¼FortMrcy1181¼	Finished willingly 9
31Aug68- 8Atl	hd 1⅛Ⓣ	:474 1:111 1:34 1:48	3↑ Kelly-Olympic H 33k	2 6 65 2hd 1hd 2nk	Velasquez J	124 b	*.60	96-04	ShootingChant112nkFortMarcy1242½Advocator1162	Bumped 6
22Jly68- 8Hol	fm 1½Ⓣ	:472 1:103 2:013 2:263	3↑ Sunset H 118k	6 5 58¼ 2hd 12 1no	Pincay L Jr	122 b	*3.40	106-11	Fort Marcy122noQuicken Tree122½Fiddle Isle1085	Lasted 15
4Jly68- 8AP	fm 1⅛Ⓣ	:48 1:114 1:37 1:503	3↑ Strs & Strps H (Div 2) 44k	3 3 36 14 14 11	Marquez CH	119 b	*1.00	88-13	FortMarcy1191TheKnackII1105NashuaPilot1141¼	Hard drive 7
19Jun68- 8Suf	fst 1¼	:473 1:112 1:362 2:024	3↑ Mass H 61k	6 6 66 54½ 53¾ 41¼	Ycaza M	116 b	*2.20	90-17	Out of the Way112½Big Rock Candy114noKing's Palace114¾	11
Checked										
12Jun68- 7Bel	sly 1⅛	:472 1:114 1:362 1:49	3↑ Nassau County 27k	4 3 33½ 32½ 2½ 2¾	Ycaza M	114 b	*.50	90-14	Primo Richard103¾Fort Marcy1142½Ardoise1054	Game effort 5
27Apr68- 7Aqu	fst 1⅛	:461 1:101 1:354 1:484	3↑ Grey Lag H 85k	10 5 56 44 73¾ 32¾	Velasquez J	118 b	*3.20	89-14	BoldHour113¾[D]DiplomatWay1222FortMarcy118no	Impeded 10
Placed second through disqualification										
6Apr68- 6Aqu	fst 1	:224 :453 1:094 1:352	4↑ Alw 15000	9 9 79 65 3nk 11¾	Velasquez J	116 b	2.20	91-14	Fort Marcy1161¾Rogo111nkBeaupy116hd	Drew out easily 11
23Mar68- 8GP	fm 1Ⓣ	:24 :474 1:112 1:351	4↑ Alw 4500	2 2 22½ 23 23 21¼	Baeza B	122 b	*.60	96-13	QuiteanAccent1091¼FortMarcy1224Hardihood1194½	Gaining 8
14Mar68- 9GP	fm 1 1/16Ⓣ	:23 :471 1:113 1:42	4↑ Alw 5000	6 7 75 33 32 2no	Velasquez J	119	*.50	94-13	New SongII113noFort Marcy1192½Tequillo1197	7
Steadied,just missed										
11Nov67- 7Lrl	fm 1½Ⓣ	:491 1:14 2:03 2:27	3↑ D C Int'l 150k	6 3 33 1hd 1hd 1no	Ycaza M	120 b	8.20	84-13	FortMrcy120noDamascus1202½TobinBronze1272½	Hard drive 9
21Oct67- 7Aqu	fm 1⅝Ⓣ	2:424	3↑ Man o' War 116k	10 4 46½ 53¼ 2hd 2hd	Pincay L Jr	121 b	4.10	80-20	RuffledFeathrs121hdFortMrcy121noHandsmeBoy1263	Sharp 13
7Oct67- 8Aqu	fm 1 1/16Ⓣ	1:414	3↑ Alw 15000	4 4 410 44½ 31 3½	Turcotte R	119 b	*.80	96-03	Mystic Lad118nkFlag118nkFort Marcy1193	Wide,closed fast 10
20Sep67- 8Atl	fm 1 3/16Ⓣ	1:54	3↑ U Nations H 100k	1 3 45 33½ 21 4nk	Velasquez J	115 b	4.70	102-05	Flit-To110nkAssagai122no[D]MundnPont115hd	Checked sharply 8
Placed third through disqualification										
4Sep67- 8AP	fm 1 3/16Ⓣ	:462 1:104 1:364 1:55	3↑ B Lindheimer H 118k	15 12 1118 1110 89¾ 66¼	Turcotte R	119 b	3.10	86-09	FusilierBoy1144½Ramsinga110noCarteret1101¼	In close early 15
9Aug67- 7Sar	fm 1 1/16Ⓣ	1:402	3↑ B Baruch H (Div 2) 23k	2 6 66 55½ 2hd 1¾	Turcotte R	117 b	*1.30	98-02	FortMarcy117¾Assagai1263Paoluccio1121	Under brisk drive 7
29Jly67- 7Aqu	sf 1⅛Ⓣ	1:521	3↑ Tidal H 57k	8 4 41½ 2hd 1hd 13	Turcotte R	111 b	2.50	74-27	Fort Marcy1113Dunderhead1102Flit-To113nk	Mild drive 9
8Jly67- 8AP	fm 1 1/16Ⓣ	:231 :461 1:103 1:414	Nashua H 54k	9 3 37 311 11 14½	Pincay L Jr	118 b	4.60	100-05	FrtMrcy1184½DiplomatWay1192BlastingCharg122nk	In hand 11
28Jun67- 8Mth	fm 1Ⓣ	1:373	Long Branch H (Div 2) 22k	2 4 52 51¼ 31 12	Velasquez J	116 b	3.40	97-07	FortMarcy1162RoyalMalabar124hdJean-Pierre118no	Driving 9
10Jun67- 7Mth	fm 1Ⓣ	:23 :471 1:11 1:362	3↑ Spring H (Div 1) 23k	3 10 1010 1016 913 69	Velasquez J	110 b	6.80	94-00	Lucky Turn118noModel Fool1156Green Felt1162	Hit hedge 10
3Jun67- 6Aqu	hd 1 1/16Ⓣ	1:412	3↑ Alw 9000	5 8 816 74½ 21½ 13	Cordero A Jr	109 b	*1.80	99-01	FortMarcy1093RoyalComedian1143Vis-a-Vis1231	Ridden out 10
25May67- 6Aqu	sl 1⅛	:492 1:141 1:383 1:51	3↑ Alw 9000	1 3 66½ 67 37 34½	Cordero A Jr	110 b	4.40	76-24	Prinkipo1132½Royal Comedian1132Fort Marcy1102	Rallied 8
30Mar67- 7Aqu	sl 1	:234 :472 1:122 1:382	3↑ Alw 7000	4 3 32½ 23 23 32½	Gustines H	110 b	4.70	73-33	Primo Theo1152Tom Poker121½Fort Marcy1107	Held well 6
25Mar67- 8Aqu	my 6f	:231 :482 1:14	3↑ Alw 6500	4 4 57½ 511 410 45½	Ycaza M	115 b	3.60	67-35	MisterPitt'sKid1132½DandySteal1123Disembark121no	Wide 7
3Mar67- 7Hia	fm 1 1/16Ⓣ	1:43	Alw 6000	11 6 710 75½ 33 2hd	Ycaza M	114 b	40.20	90-14	Royal Malabar118hdFort Marcy114½More Skies1123½	Sharp 11
15Feb67- 7Hia	fm *1 1/16Ⓣ	1:444	Alw 7000	2 6 64 1011 915 913	Ycaza M	112	12.40	73-20	High Hat1132Royal Malabar118nkRoyal Esteem1121	Tired 11
4Feb67- 3Hia	fst 7f	:231 :462 1:121 1:251	©Alw 4500	7 4 64¾ 43½ 41½ 11	Ycaza M	118	3.30	83-13	Fort Marcy1181Sun Stream1181½Keene Terra1181½	Driving 12
17Jan67- 4Hia	gd 6f	:221 :453 1:103	©Alw 4500	7 3 66½ 69¾ 48½ 49¼	Ycaza M	118	23.50	82-13	Balouf1166Bold Monarch1181¼Wedgedale1162	No mishap 10
26Nov66- 5Aqu	gd 6f	:222 :47 1:114	Alw 5500	2 7 910 87 811 815	Blum W	119 b	6.30	69-20	Light the Fuse122noMisty Cloud1152½Osage1223	Far back 9
5Nov66- 5Aqu	fst 6f	:213 :443 1:111	Alw 5500	4 7 78¾ 611 66½ 73½	Fires E	119 b	34.60	83-13	Flying Tackle1221½Comfrey115noFort Drum115½	No factor 10
8Oct66- 6Aqu	fst 7f	:224 :453 1:111 1:241	Alw 5500	4 9 119¾ 1111 85¾ 811	Blum W	122 b	9.00	74-17	Major Art1223Unexpected117¾Proviso1223½	Never close 14
1Oct66- 5Aqu	sly 7f	:231 :47 1:131 1:261	Alw 5500	12 1 79½ 77¾ 79¼ 24	Blum W	122 b	3.80	71-24	IrishRebellion1174FortMarcy122noGalaPrformnc122½	Gamely 12
21Sep66- 4Aqu	sly 6f	:231 :472 1:13	Md Sp Wt	4 3 52¼ 41¼ 11½ 14	Blum W	122 b	*1.50	78-24	Fort Marcy1224Quiet Town1221½George Arnold122½	Easily 8
7Sep66- 5Aqu	fst 6f	:224 :48 1:132	Md Sp Wt	14 1 24 21 21 45¾	Blum W	122 b	*1.80e	70-30	Proviso1222½DownatMory's122nkIrishRebellion1223	Tired 14
27Aug66- 1Sar	fst 6f	:224 :471 1:132	Md Sp Wt	3 9 84¾ 107½ 1115 1116	Baeza B	122	7.10	65-08	Twist of Time1224½Prime Motive1221½Court Service122hd	14
Roughed										
29Jly66- 4Aqu	fst 5½f	:23 :471 :592 1:054	©Md Sp Wt	10 6 84¾ 41½ 23 25	Belmonte E	122	3.20	79-17	OneGem1225FortMarcy1221RisingMarket122½	Wide stretch 11
22Jly66- 5Aqu	fst 5½f	:222 :46 :59 1:054	©Md Sp Wt	4 6 108¾ 1010 68 34½	Belmonte E	122	19.80	79-19	Monitor1224½Duke Cannon122hdFort Marcy122½	Stride late 12
14May66- 4Aqu	fst 5f	:223 :462 :59	©Md Sp Wt	2 7 716 78¾ 712 716	Gustines H	122	26.30	74-13	GreatPower1223½BoldAmbition122¾BeauApple1226	Far back 8

Forward Gal

ch. f. 1968, by Native Charger (Native Dancer)–Forward Thrust, by Jet Action

Own.– Aisco Stable

Br.– A.I. Savin (Fla)

Tr.– W.A. Croll Jr

Lifetime record: 26 12 4 6 $439,933

19Oct71- 8GS	fm 1Ⓣ	1:38	ⒻPrinceton H (Div 2) 23k	1 1 11 11½ 21 21¾	Rotz JL	126 b	*1.20	81-15	CanterburyTale1151¾ForwardGal126noWireChif1125	Faltered 7
19Sep71- 8Del	gd 1⅛	:461 1:103 1:373 1:504	ⒻDel Oaks 59k	8 2 22 21 3nk 32¼	Hole M	121 b	2.60	81-20	Lauries Dancer1212¼Secret Retreat114hdForward Gal121nk	8
Lacked rally										
4Sep71- 7Bel	fst 1⅛	:463 1:102 1:352 1:483	ⒻGazelle H 56k	3 1 1hd 1½ 14 13	Hole M	122 b	2.60	91-12	ForwrdGl1223OurCherAmour1181½AlmNorth1232½	Mild drive 8
14Aug71- 7Sar	fst 1¼	:474 1:12 1:371 2:03	ⒻAlabama 53k	3 3 25 23 31½ 36	Hole M	121 b	*2.60	84-05	LauriesDancer1183AlmaNorth1183FrwrdGl1211½	Weakened 11
5Aug71- 7Sar	gd 7f	:221 :45 1:11 1:234	ⒻTest 35k	3 6 41½ 52½ 42½ 32½	Hole M	124 b	*1.40	87-20	Lucky Traveler1152Tibb115½Forward Gal1241½	Lacked rally 12
17Jly71- 8Lib	fst 1 1/16	:224 :454 1:102 1:433	ⒻCotillion H 55k	7 2 33 33½ 32½ 21	Hole M	123 b	*.90	87-17	Alma North1161Forward Gal1234Miss Pat R.110no	Gaining 7
5Jly71- 8Mth	fst 1⅛	:463 1:104 1:361 1:491	ⒻMth Oaks 57k	1 2 2hd 11½ 13 14¾	Hole M	119 b	5.20	96-08	ForwardGl1194¾AlmaNorth1141ForNoReason112½	Mild drive 11
26Jun71- 8Mth	fst 1 70	:224 :46 1:102 1:404	ⒻPost-Deb (Div 2) 22k	1 3 51¾ 65½ 56½ 42¾	Hole M	117 b	*1.10	94-12	Cyamome117¾Isafloridan113noSilent Beauty1192	In close 8
29May71- 7Bel	fst 1⅛	:454 1:102 1:364 1:501	ⒻMother Goose 89k	4 4 31½ 3½ 11 33¼	Velasquez J	121 b	*1.50	80-19	Deceit121¾Grafitti1212½Forward Gal1213	Weakened 9
15May71- 7Aqu	fst 1	:232 :463 1:11 1:363	ⒻAcorn 64k	8 2 2½ 1½ 21 3¾	Hole M	121 b	*.40	83-22	Deceit121½Sea Saga121nkForward Gal1212	No excuses 9
5May71- 7Aqu	fst 7f	:224 :454 1:101 1:232	ⒻComely 34k	7 1 21 1½ 13 14	Hole M	121 b	*.40	84-25	Forward Gal1214Sea Saga1182Deceit115½	Mild drive 8
24Apr71- 8GS	fst 6f	:22 :45 1:102	ⒻBetsy Ross H 29k	7 1 63½ 41¾ 1½ 12½	Hole M	126 b	*.40	92-14	Forward Gal1262½Sea Saga1202Alma North1121	Driving 10
17Apr71- 4GS	fst 6f	:22 :452 1:101	ⒻAlw 12000	6 1 2hd 12 15 16	Hole M	121 b	*.30	93-13	ForwrdGal1216AlmaNorth1151½SwoonsSymbol1135	Handily 6
7Nov70- 8GS	fst 1 1/16	:234 :473 1:114 1:45	ⒻGardenia 188k	6 2 2hd 1hd 1½ 31	Ianelli F	119 b	*1.50	79-15	Eggy119¾Rosemont Bow119nkForward Gal1193	Weakened 9
12Oct70- 7Bel	fst 1	:222 :45 1:10 1:363	ⒻFrizette 125k	3 2 21 14 16 13½	Velasquez J	119 b	*.80	90-16	ForwrdGal1193½Isafloridan1197MakeMLugh119hd	Mild drive 11
5Oct70- 5Bel	fst 6½f	:221 :454 1:102 1:17	ⒻAlw 15000	3 3 2½ 1hd 13 13	Velasquez J	122 b	*1.00	95-10	ForwardGal1223BlessingAngelic1161¼Exorbtnt11610	Handily 9
26Aug70- 7Sar	fst 6f	:221 :453 1:104	ⒻSpinaway 84k	6 2 1hd 1hd 1hd 11	Ianelli F	119 b	2.80	92-14	Forward Gal1191Patelin1192½Deceit119¾	Mild drive 11
17Aug70- 7Sar	fst 6f	:22 :453 1:104	ⒻAdirondack 29k	2 3 2½ 2½ 2½ 21½	Ianelli F	122 b	2.60	90-16	Dutiful1141½Forward Gal122½Patelin1224½	Game try 9
25Jly70- 8Mth	fst 6f	:213 :443 1:113	ⒻSorority 105k	1 6 42¼ 34½ 34½ 12	Ianelli F	119 b	12.00	84-22	Forward Gal1192Unity Hall1191Deceit1192	Driving 12
18Jly70- 6Lib	fst 5½f	:213 :452 1:04	ⒻSchuykill (Div 1) 22k	9 8 65½ 33½ 32 1½	Ianelli F	115 b	*1.80	100-05	Forward Gal115½Hot Gravey1154Native Game1136	Driving 9
24Jun70- 7Bel	fst 5½f	:224 :462 :583 1:05	ⒻNational Stallion 31k	3 4 33 32½ 46½ 48	Blum W	119 b	5.10	87-14	UnityHall1193½BidHigh1194½CarolineG.114hd	Factor,tired 7
10Jun70- 8Mth	fst 5½f	:22 :454 :59 1:054	ⒻColleen 24k	8 7 74¾ 32 35 23	Ianelli F	114 b	5.80	85-17	Deceit1193Forward Gal114nkCaroline G.1133	Gamely 12
3Jun70- 6Mth	fst 5f	:221 :454 :583	ⒻAlw 6000	3 9 1½ 11½ 15 19	Blum W	116 b	18.30	97-13	ForwardGl1169TigerCoed1161½SchoolBoard114no	Ridden out 11
29Apr70- 4GS	fst 5f	:222 :463 :594	ⒻMd Sp Wt	7 1 2½ 23 21 1¾	Blum W	115 b	*1.50	89-15	Forward Gal115¾Lady Herald1151½Reunion1151	Driving 12
22Apr70- 3GS	fst 5f	:222 :471 :592	ⒻMd Sp Wt	2 5 2hd 1hd 2hd 45	Blum W	115 b	3.00	86-17	MurielsDream115hdTelly1153WindsofDestiny1152	Weakened 9
26Mar70- 3GP	sly 5f	:222 :471 1:00	Md Sp Wt	3 4 2hd 32 48 511	Blum W	118	3.30	77-16	HarrodsGreek1115QueenofArts1083LadiesAuxiliry118½	Tired 12

Gallant Bob

dkbbr. g. 1972, by Gallant Romeo (Gallant Man)–Wisp O'Will, by New Policy — **Lifetime record: 77 23 11 8 $489,992**

Own.– R.P. Horton
Br.– J.L. Homan (Ky)
Tr.– Floyd M. Tolle

2Dec79- 7Pen	fst 6f	:223 :462 :582 1:122	3↑ Alw 7200	7 5 63½ 52½ 53½ 41	Lloyd JS	113		8.10	81-25	Musical Mickey115½Jiva Coolit113½Coastal Call116hd		9
Not enough final furlong												
16Nov79- 8Key	fst 6f	:224 :462 1:122	3↑ Alw 12000	6 3 54¾ 79 78½ 76¾	Zook DJ	115		16.90	73-31	BoldPhantm116¾LuckyFling1131RedWhitenGreen1142	Outrun	7
4Nov79- 7Pen	sf 1Ⓣ	1:393	3↑ Alw 7800	7 1 12 11 1hd 23½	Lloyd JS	113		10.50	68-32	Confort1083½GallantBob113nkFrostyHonor1132	Second best	7
29Sep79- 8Tim	fst 4f	:222 :463	3↑ Handicap 8000	1 6 66½ 69 63	Hernandez RZ	110		12.60	90-07	Bee Country113½B.F.'s Sailingman1151Elbuort122no	Outrun	6
1Sep79- 7Tim	fst 4f	:224 :462	3↑ Alw 6500	6 4 43½ 45 54¾	Torre MJ	113		8.20	89-09	Bold and Lucky122¾Light Tiger1131Royal Re Re1162	Tired	6
Previously trained by D. Michael Smithwick												
9Aug79- 4Sar	fm 2 1/16	S'Chase 3:47	3↑ Md Sp Wt	9 1 32 - - -	Aitcheson J Jr	156	s	2.90	--	BronzeCelt1519¾AcademicFreedom1491½Mozambique1492	Fell	11
Previously trained by J.D. Marquette												
17Mar79- 7Key	fst 6f	:224 :462 1:103	4↑ Alw 12000	1 3 1½ 42 714 715	Ruane J	112	b	13.10	74-23	Spunky112¾No No Jim118noPegasus Pete1183½	Tired	7
25Feb79- 7Key	my 7f	:232 :464 1:124 1:26	4↑ Alw 12000	5 2 1hd 54 816 821	Walford J	113		10.10	56-30	GreatCombnation114noPgasusPete1181½NevrRetreat1051½	Tired	9
19Jan79- 8Key	fst 6f	:222 :453 1:103	4↑ Alw 12000	2 6 64½ 54¼ 76 74¼	Solomon G	116		8.80	85-17	DoubleCraps115½Spunky115½GreatCombinaton117hd	No factor	7
29Dec78- 8Key	fst 7f	:222 :45 1:102 1:232	3↑ Alw 12000	2 6 32½ 34 44¼ 65¾	Walford J	116		10.00	84-17	Eastern Monarch1161½Hickory Cap1154Spunky117no	Tired	9
17Dec78- 7Key	fst 6f	:23 :474 1:132	3↑ Alw 12000	7 8 87 88 76¼ 57¼	Black AS	114		4.70	68-31	Ornithologist1133Ten Ten110hdGovernor's Pardon1143½		9
Sluggish early												
3Dec78- 8Key	fst 6f	:224 :46 1:111	3↑ Alw 12000	3 6 55½ 57½ 69½ 510	Pagano SR	112		4.70	76-25	PistolWhite1132EightDominoes1227FloatingPrm113nk	Evenly	8
24Jly78- 8Bel	fst 1	:23 :452 1:092 1:334	3↑ Handicap 25000	5 1 1hd 55 915 917	Velez RI	109		29.80	82-09	Vencedor1163¼Proud Arion1131¼Life's Hope1223½	Used up	9
6Jly78- 8Bel	fst 6f	:222 :452 1:092	3↑ Alw 25000	6 4 45 56½ 58 58¾	Turcotte R	119		16.90	86-19	Buckfinder1192½Myriad1193¾Dan Black115¾	No excuse	6
3Jun78- 7Mth	fst 6f	:214 :443 1:092	4↑ Alw 12000	1 4 1hd 33 49 612	MacBeth D	113		6.50	81-24	White Rammer1173Taylor's Falls1172Buena Shore1224	Tired	7
23May78- 8Key	fst 6f	:222 :451 1:093	4↑ Alw 15000	2 6 41¼ 31½ 21½ 21¼	Mucciolo J	117		*1.50	93-13	BearerBond1121¼GllntBb1172Tmothy'sChmp112hd	Slow start	6
Disqualified from purse money												
14May78- 7Aqu	sly 7f	:224 :453 1:101 1:224	4↑ Alw 25000	6 1 1½ 21½ 412 414½	Borden DA	115		14.00	72-26	Seattle Slew1228¾Proud Arion1191¼Capulet's Song1155		6
Used up												
29Apr78- 7Key	fst 6f	:222 :453 1:093	4↑ Alw 15000	8 4 86¾ 65¼ 99¾ 913	Tejeira J	121		2.90	81-12	Loaded or Busted121½Thunder O'Shay115½Big Z.1154	Outrun	9
9Apr78- 7Key	fst 6f	:223 :463 1:112	4↑ Alw 16000	4 4 65½ 52 54 54	Tejeira J	119		*2.20	81-24	CruiseonIn122hdKohoutek119¾TripleRevers1143	Lacked room	6
25Mar78- 7Key	fst 6f	:23 :462 1:112	4↑ Alw 14000	4 1 41½ 21 21 12½	Black AS	113		*1.60	85-31	Gallant Bob1132½Insubordinate Lad1161½Mighty Steve1154		5
Driving												
10Mar78- 8Key	fst 6f	:224 :461 1:111	4↑ Alw 14000	4 4 1hd 31 44½ 57	Edwards JW	114		3.60	79-29	Mug Hunter1164Kohoutek119hdJiva Coolit1191½	Tired	6
26Feb78- 8Key	fst 6f	:231 :47 1:13	4↑ Alw 13000	2 7 52½ 62¾ 75¾ 53½	Edwards JW	114		5.10	73-34	Kohoutek1191¼Ragtime Cowboy Joe1121Insubordinate Lad114nk		7
Off slowly												
4Oct77- 6Med	fst 6f	:224 :454 1:11	3↑ Alw 25000	6 3 41¼ 66¾ 79 78¾	Black AS	119		*1.00	81-19	Kohoutek1172Godolphin122noThird World1152	Brief speed	7
10Sep77- 8Key	fst 7f	:224 :451 1:102 1:232	3↑ Independence H 27k	1 2 11 2hd 21½ 2½	Black AS	115		2.20	91-23	Ferrous114½GallantBob1155RagtimeCowboyJoe113hd	Gamely	6
1Sep77- 8Mth	fst 6f	:213 :44 1:091	3↑ Handicap 25000	3 2 1hd 32½ 33 33¼	MacBeth D	119		2.90	91-17	SeetheU.S.A.1182½Godolphin108¾GallantBob1192	Held show	6
30Jly77- 5Mth	my 6f	:224 :462 1:102	3↑ Handicap 15000	3 4 3½ 31½ 21½ 22	MacBeth D	120		*1.50	86-23	SeetheU.S.A.1152GallantBb1208ChfTmnco11920	Second best	4
16Jly77- 8Key	fst 6½f	:22 :442 1:081 1:143	3↑ Neshaminy H 27k	4 3 2½ 31½ 45½ 47½	Tejeira J	117		3.80	96-16	My Juliet1211½Raise a King1193½Silver Hope1202½	Tired	4
6Jly77- 8Key	fst 6f	:221 :451 1:093	3↑ Alw 10000	4 5 32 2hd 1hd 1½	Tejeira J	119		2.00	94-15	GallantBb119½ChiefTamanaco1193½WingSouth1161¾	Driving	6
18Jun77- 8Bow	fst 6f	:221 :44 :57 1:09	3↑ Terrapin H 27k	5 6 54 35½ 45½ 34¾	Edwards JW	117		4.60	90-14	Raise a King1163½Whatsyourpleasure1171¼Gallant Bob117no		7
Steadied												
9Jun77- 8Bel	sly 1⊗	:23 :454 1:11 1:363	3↑ Alw 25000	5 1 13 2hd 33 46	Edwards JW	117		2.30	79-23	Star of the Sea1151½El Pitirre110½Dan Black1174	Tired	5
1Jun77- 8Key	fst 6f	:22 :443 1:094	3↑ Garrison H 27k	1 4 2hd 42½ 57½ 59¾	Edwards JW	118		*.40	83-23	ChiefTamanaco114½Bereber1122½RealTerror1135¼	Done early	5
7May77- 8Aqu	fst 7f	:221 :45 1:093 1:221	3↑ Carter H (Div 2)-G2	2 4 21½ 21½ 42¼ 33¼	Edwards JW	116		6.50	87-17	SoyNumeroUno1262½Barrera119¾GallantBob116hd	Weakened	6
20Apr77- 8Aqu	fst 6f⊡	:221 :452 1:102	4↑ Alw 25000	4 2 2½ 2½ 1hd 2½	Edwards JW	122		*1.00	94-14	QuietLittleTable122½GallantBob122½Dr.Emil1151¼	Weakened	6
12Apr77- 8GS	fst 6f	:221 :451 1:102	4↑ Alw 15000	2 3 2hd 2hd 12 11	Edwards JW	119		2.70	91-22	GallantBob1191MovingCloud1191½DeltaLegacy1121¼	Driving	8
6Oct76- 8Bel	fst 6f	:224 :453 1:083	3↑ Boojum H 38k	7 7 2hd 4nk 96½ 98	Arellano J	122		8.70	91-08	SoyNumeroUno1182½It'sFreezing1121¼QueenCityLd112¾	Tired	9
25Sep76- 8Atl	fst 7f	:22 :44 1:074 1:202	3↑ Atl City H 31k	5 3 1hd 2hd 69 612	Arellano J	124		*1.30	89-01	Our Hero1204½Packer Captain115noMexican General115hd		8
Squeezed back												
17Sep76- 8Bel	sly 1	:222 :444 1:093 1:353	3↑ Alw 25000	2 1 11½ 2hd 2hd 2nk	Arellano J	115		*1.10	90-15	Nalees Knight122nkGallant Bob115½Blue Times1191¼		6
Sharp effort												
7Sep76- 8Bel	fst 6f	:224 :451 1:084	3↑ Alw 30000	8 4 11 11 11 11¼	Arellano J	115		3.60	98-12	Gallant Bob1151¼It's Freezing1192¼Relent122no	Driving	8
30Aug76- 8Bel	fst 6f	:223 :454 1:10	3↑ Fall Hwt H (Div 2)-G2	6 8 86¾ 1010 910 813	Gallitano G	140		13.50	79-18	HonorableMiss1301¼Lachesis1261¾RushingMan129nk	Dull try	10
11Aug76- 7Mth	fst 6f	:213 :44 1:082	3↑ Alw 11000	2 3 2½ 21½ 31½ 43	Arellano J	122		*.70	95-13	See the U.S.A.119¾That Wing117nkPompini1222	Weakened	5
18Jly76- 8Del	fst 6f	:214 :444 1:094	3↑ Hannibal H 28k	3 4 1hd 3½ 42 75½	Arellano J	125		*1.90	90-20	SilverHope119½NorthCall119nkNoteofVictory1171½	Gave way	11
3May76- 8Haw	fst 6f	:212 :441 1:082	3↑ Midwest H 45k	3 5 41½ 22½ 33½ 410	Gallitano G	128		*.70	94-08	Marluel'sTroy1108NativeDrone113noSilvrDoctor1122¼	Tired	7
16Apr76- 8Aqu	fst 6f	:22 :45 1:094	3↑ Gravesend H 44k	1 5 1hd 1hd 2½ 31	Brumfield D	128		*2.50	93-18	Christopher R.131¾Mac Corkle115nkGallant Bob128nk	Tired	8
3Apr76- 7Kee	fst 6f	:22 :443 :564 1:082	3↑ Phoenix H 28k	7 3 22 22 1½ 15	Brumfield D	126		*1.10	100-18	Gallant Bob1265Real Value120¾Americo1152½	Drew clear	12
27Mar76- 8Pim	fst 6f	:231 :453 1:104	3↑ J E Hoover H 27k	2 5 2½ 2hd 22½ 2½	Edwards JW	128		2.90	91-20	ChristopherR.130½GallntBob128¾NorthCll1222¾	Drifted out	5
13Mar76- 8Aqu	sly 6f	:213 :452 1:101	3↑ Toboggan H 57k	1 11 3½ 2hd 3nk 36¾	Gallitano G	129		3.50	85-19	Due Diligence1114¾Pompini1132Gallant Bob129¾	Bothered	11
16Feb76- 8Aqu	fst 7f	:222 :451 1:093 1:223	3↑ Sporting Plate H 38k	6 2 1hd 1hd 3½ 83¼	Gallitano G	130		*1.90	85-25	ChristophrR.124½NorthCll110hdDoublEdgSword115hd	Stopped	8
10Jan76- 8Key	fst 6f	:214 :443 1:084	4↑ Bensalem H 27k	2 6 32 33½ 35 37	Gallitano G	131		*.60	91-14	DukeTom1157Rosinate110noGallantBob131no	Stumbled badly	6
3Jan76- 8Aqu	sly 6f	:22 :451 1:104	3↑ Paumonok H-G3	5 3 1hd 1hd 1hd 1hd	Gallitano G	129		*2.00	89-18	GallantBob129hdOurHero1133½HoleinthePants113no	Driving	8
27Dec75- 8Key	my 6f	:224 :462 1:114	3↑ Squires H 27k	1 3 1½ 1½ 1½ 1½	Gallitano G	127		*.70	83-31	Gallant Bob127½Admiral Jim1124½Plain Pete1163½	Driving	7
1Dec75- 8Aqu	fst 6f	:222 :452 1:093	Sword Dancer H 46k	6 1 1hd 2hd 2½ 1hd	Gallitano G	126		*1.80	95-14	GallantBob126hdOurHero1132DueDilgnc113¾	Long,hard drive	9
22Nov75- 8Key	gd 6f	:221 :451 1:094	Flintlock 27k	3 2 2½ 1½ 1½ 11½	Gallitano G	119		*.60	93-20	GallntBb1191½BearerBond112¾BumpyLndng112¾	Drew clear	8
4Oct75- 8Key	fst 6½f	:22 :444 1:10 1:163	Penn Treaty 27k	3 1 3½ 21 11½ 12	Gallitano G	119		*.40	94-14	Gallant Bob1192Talc1192Real Value1174	Ridden out	6
6Sep75- 8Key	fst 7f	:214 :441 1:103 1:24	Philmont H 27k	7 2 31 32 2hd 13	Gallitano G	129		*1.20	89-22	Gallant Bob1293Talc1181¼Ascetic118½	Drew clear	9
13Aug75- 8Mth	fst 6f	:204 :434 1:092	Select H 27k	5 2 27 23½ 2½ 11¼	Gallitano G	129		*2.00	93-17	Gallant Bob1291¼Talc1202Red Cross1173	Driving	7
5Jly75- 8Bow	fst 6f	:223 :454 1:102	Annapolis H 27k	5 3 2hd 11½ 13 13½	Gallitano G	127		*.40	91-17	Gallant Bob1273½French Whistler1141¼Starta Victory1082¼		6
Ridden out												
21Jun75- 8AP	fst 7f	:22 :443 1:10 1:232	Olympia H 33k	5 1 1hd 1½ 12 11	Gallitano G	124		4.40	85-21	Gallant Bob1241Doug118noCountry Boy Jim1211	Driving	11
1Jun75- 8Del	fst 1 1/16	:23 :462 1:12 1:461	Rosemont 29k	5 1 1hd 1hd 56 512	Gallitano G	117		*1.50	66-19	Grey Beret1126Dr's Enjoy Dollars114¾Resound112nk	Tired	10
24May75- 8Del	fst 6f	:214 :45 1:111	Kelso H 27k	4 2 2hd 2hd 2hd 1½	Gallitano G	124		*.90	89-21	Gallant Bob124½Bold Gun121nkReal Value1211½	All out	7
22Mar75- 8Pim	fst 6f	:224 :461 :584 1:111	Hirsch Jacobs 28k	8 3 3½ 2hd 11 2hd	Gallitano G	122		*1.10	90-15	Bombay Duck122hdGallant Bob1224Ben S.116nk	Just missed	9
15Mar75- 8Aqu	sly 7f	:223 :453 1:104 1:234	Bay Shore (Div 2)-G3	8 1 2hd 2hd 1½ 3¾	Gallitano G	119		*2.70	81-21	Lefty113noTass113¾Gallant Bob119nk	Weakened	8
1Mar75- 8Aqu	fst 6f	:214 :452 1:094	Swift-G3	9 2 1hd 11 2½ 33½	Gallitano G	117		3.00	90-16	Singh1143½Laramie Trail114noGallant Bob117¾	Weakened	10
22Feb75- 8Key	fst 7f	:221 :45 1:11 1:253	Patriot-G3	1 3 13 16 18 110	Gallitano G	119		*.40	81-29	GallntBb11910WickdPark1172½Methdioxya1221½	Ridden out	11
15Feb75- 8GS	gd 6f	:221 :454 1:11	Zev 26k	6 1 1hd 13 15 19	Gallitano G	122		*.40	88-30	GallantBob1229LuckyLeaf1161½FamousTrial1161	Ridden out	7
1Feb75- 8Bow	gd 6f	:224 :463 1:12	W P Burch 27k	6 3 13 15 15 14½	Gallitano G	124		*.90	83-28	GallntBob1244½PendulumSam1163KingofFools1161¼	Driving	6

25Jan75- 8Key	sly 6f		:222 :461	1:132	Sentinel 27k	6 1 1½ 1hd 1½	12	Gallitano G	119		*.90	75-33	Gallant Bob1192Sgt. Hunt1176Sneaky Win1121¾	Ridden out	7
1Jan75- 8GS	sly 6f		:222 :46	1:11	Fairmount Park 26k	4 3 11 14 15	19	Gallitano G	122		5.10	88-38	GallantBob1229Sgt.Hunt1222OnPoundStrlng117nk	Ridden out	10
14Dec74- 8Key	fst 1 1/16		:23 :463 1:111	1:421	Heritage-G3	7 2 3nk 1hd 45	513	Gallitano G	118		20.80	- -	Circle Home1243Singh1154Master Derby1213	Tired	10
28Nov74- 8GS	fst 6f		:23 :471	1:131	Autumn Harvest 26k	6 5 2hd 1½ 1hd	2nk	Gallitano G	122		11.20	77-34	Sgt. Hunt118nkGallant Bob1221Impatient Fool1166½	Gamely	12
15Nov74- 8Key	fst 6f		:22 :452	1:112	Alw 7000	1 5 32 55 56	58	Knapp K	119		1.50	- -	Dr. Frank B.1112¼North Call1193½Go Super116nk	Tired	5
6Nov74- 8CD	sly 7f		:224 :46 1:114	1:252	Alw 12500	8 4 1hd 13 22	78½	Gallitano G	117		5.50	71-29	MasterDerby1221¾WaywardRed114¾Ruggle'sFerry115hd	Tired	11
19Oct74- 8Bow	fst 7f		:222 :45 1:104	1:244	©Marlboro Nursery 30k	10 3 12½ 12 2hd	1¾	Gallitano G	113		8.40	81-24	GallntBb113¾GreekAnswer1192¾ParvaHasta1133	Hard drive	10
9Oct74- 7Kee	fst 6f		:221 :443 :564	1:093	Alw 6500	3 1 11 12 11	21½	Melancon L	115		2.30	92-12	RugglesFerry1151½GallntBb1152PackerCaptain1181	Gamely	6
31Aug74- 8Lib	fst 6f		:213 :444	1:114	Kindergarten-G3	11 2 12 13 14	2½	Melancon L	112		5.10	85-19	Master Derby121½Gallant Bob112noTalc113½	Gamely	14
22Aug74- 8Lib	sly 6f		:224 :461	1:112	Alw 5500	6 3 11 13 16	110	Melancon L	112		2.40	88-25	Gallant Bob11210Go Super1152½Spanish Indian1162	Easily	7
6Aug74- 6Lib	fst 5½f		:222 :462	1:051	Alw 5500	2 3 1½ 2hd 2hd	22	Brumfield D	115		13.10	92-19	BuddyBoots1152GllntBb11510WhataFiasco1153	Second best	6
15Jly74- 3Lib	fst 5½f		:224 :481	1:08	Md Clm 12500	10 6 2hd 11½ 1½	11¼	Fantini P	120		46.40	80-25	Gallant Bob1201¼Lil Fairy1202½Shiney Walker1205	Driving	11

Gran Kan (Chi)

dkbbr. c. 1966, by Licencioso (L'Oriflamme)–Klapp, by Espace Vital
Own.– Mrs F. Ambrose Clark
Br.– Haras El Huerton (Chi)
Tr.– C. Furr

Lifetime record: 43 16 5 8 $103,650

15Nov75- 4Cam	fm 2 13/16	S'Chase	5:301 4↑	Colonial Cup 50k	17 17 158 78½ 911	613	O'Brien L	162		-	- -	CafePrince1603AugustusBay162½Soothsayr162½	Never close	18
1Nov75- 3Mtp	fm *2½	S'Chase	4:413 4↑	Noel Laing H 5.6k	10 9 97½ 84¾ 42	34	O'Brien L	155		-	- -	Soothsayer158hdAugustus Bay1514Gran Kan1551½		10
13Sep75- 7Fai	fm *2½	S'Chase	5:02 4↑	Grand National H 12k	3 9 84 3nk 21½	25½	O'Brien L	155		6.10	- -	Augustus Bay1475½Gran Kan1551½Happy Intellectual1465		9
21Aug75- 4Sar	fm 2⅜	S'Chase	4:201 4↑	NY Turf Writers H 22k	8 4 2hd 25 33½	46¼	O'Brien L	158		*1.70	- -	Life'sIllusion145nkSoothsayr160½ArcticJoe1485½	Gave way	9
1Aug75- 6Sar	fm 2 1/16	S'Chase	3:401 4↑	Lovely Night H 22k	6 2 26 26 23	2½	O'Brien L	158		2.70	- -	Life'sIllusion143½GranKan15810Anthropologst1388¾	Gamely	8
15Jly75- 8Bow	my 1 1/16	:232 :472 1:13	1:452 3↑	Alw 7000	1 6 618 614 510	59¼	Stone C	118		12.50	72-18	Fantastex1113½SealedLips1182¼LandofRhythm1212½	Outrun	6
16Nov74- 4Cam	fm 2 13/16	S'Chase	5:24 4↑	Colonial Cup 50k	1 3 63¼ 51¾ 53¼	515	Twyman N	162		-	- -	Augustus Bay1428Tarratine1432John U1535	Fell back	11
2Nov74- 3Mtp	fm *2½	S'Chase	4:353 4↑	Noel Laing H 5.3k	5 2 21½ 22 2½	32½	O'Brien L	163		-	- -	Speed Kills1502John U151½Gran Kan1638	Weakened	5
5Oct74- 4Lig	sf *2½	S'Chase	5:212 4↑	Gold Cup H 25k	7 7 46 55¼ 22	28	O'Brien L	166		-	- -	Arctic Joe1398Gran Kan1664Breaking Dawn1371	Went well	8
14Sep74- 7Fai	sf *2½	S'Chase	5:203 4↑	Grand National H 12k	1 2 42 1½ 12½	13½	O'Brien L	162		*.80	- -	Gran Kan1623½Tall Award140nkJohn U1523½	Driving	5
2Aug74- 6Sar	fm 2 1/16	S'Chase	3:443 4↑	Lovely Night H 22k	10 4 43½ 21 26	22¾	O'Brien L	160		*1.70	- -	Cafe Prince1452¾Gran Kan1603Juac Hollow1548	Gamely	10
8Jun74- 8Del	fm *2½	S'Chase	4:323 4↑	Indian River H 13k	2 4 54 21½ 2hd	11	O'Brien L	158		*1.70	- -	Gran Kan1581Metello153hdLucky Boy III1552¾	Driving	11
4May74- 3War	fm *2	S'Chase	4:212 4↑	Handicap 10000	2 2 22½ 11½ 12	14½	O'Brien L	153	s	-	- -	Gran Kan1534½Wustenchef1563Metello1572½	Ridden out	6
	Previously trained by S. Watters Jr													
21Apr74- 7Mid	fm *1¼Ⓣ		2:171 3↑	Alw 1000	1 1 12 12 11½	1½	O'Brien L	145		-	- -	Gran Kan145½Machu Picchu1292Mod Man1451½	Driving	16
16Sep72- 5Fai	fm *2½	Hurdles	4:514 4↑	Handicap 10000	3 4 64½ 22 1nk	12½	Skiffington T	158		*2.00	- -	Gran Kan1582½Perigo14216Speed Kills1413	Drew clear	8
9Sep72- 2Fai	fm *1 5/16Ⓣ		2:074 3↑	Alw 1200	2 7 78¼ 69½ 410	38	Watters E3	153		*1.00	- -	Jaunty1426Mystic's Desire1422Gran Kan153no	Rallied	9
23Aug72- 7Sar	hd 1⅝Ⓣ	:482 1:363 2:01	2:374 3↑	Seneca H 30k	4 12 1221 1011 89½	810	Ruane J	111		6.80e	94-04	Red Reality113¾Acclimitization114¾ⒹLarceny Kid1133		12
	Steadied at start													
17Aug72- 3Sar	fm 2 1/16	Hurdles	3:421 4↑	Lovely Night H 22k	1 5 2½ 2hd 32½	33¼	O'Brien M	157	s	*.50e	- -	ShadowBrook163¾Dream Magic1522½GrnKan1574	Weakened	8
11Jly72- 4Mth	fm *2 1/16	Hurdles	4:094 4↑	Midsummer H 16k	3 1 1½ 2hd 22	18	O'Brien L	158		2.40	- -	Gran Kan1588Dream Magic1446Ghost Charger145hd	Driving	10
9Jun72- 9Del	fm *2½	Hurdles	4:291 4↑	Indian River H 13k	1 3 34 2hd 14	14	O'Brien M	148	b	2.70e	- -	Gran Kan1484Dualamar1415El Martirio1403½	Ridden out	9
3Jun72- 2Mid	hd *1¼Ⓣ		2:131 3↑	Sp Wt 600	11 9 97½ 63½ 3¾	15	Watters E	158		-	- -	Gran Kan1585Still in All1432½Favori1451½	In hand	11
27May72- 3Mid	fm *1Ⓣ		1:342 3↑	Alw 500	5 2 1nk 1hd 2nk	12½	Watters E	152		-	- -	Gran Kan1522½Port Manech1423La Strega1524	Driving	11
20Nov71- 5Cam	fm *2	S'Chase	3:41 4↑	Alw 5000	1 3 36 2½ 1hd	11½	Skiffington T Jr	155		-	- -	Gran Kan1551½Dualamar140hdTuscalee1511	Driving	14
6Nov71- 4Mtp	sf *2	S'Chase	4:122 3↑	Alw 2000	6 4 32¼ 31½ 45½	48¼	Skiffington T Jr	155		-	- -	Inkslinger1492½Bookbinder140¾Dream Magic1455	Weakened	12
14Oct71- 5Bel	sf 2⅝	Hurdles	4:554 4↑	NY Turf Writers H 33k	6 4 64 53 721	717	Skiffington T Jr	150	s	9.40	- -	Soothsayer1533Predominio1413Wustenchef1623½	Bobbled	8
7Oct71- 9Bel	fm 1⅞	Hurdles	3:212 4↑	Alw 9500	6 4 34½ 32 2½	11½	Skiffington T Jr5	147	s	6.70	- -	Gran Kan1471½John U1423Persian Honour1464	Driving	9
23Aug71- 9Sar	fm 2 1/16	Hurdles	3:441 4↑	Alw 9500	7 3 36 1hd 2hd	31	Skiffington T Jr5	149	s	4.80	- -	Shadow II132¾Dream Magic137nkGran Kan1494	Good try	8
11Aug71- 9Sar	fm 2 1/16	Hurdles	4:454 4↑	Alw 7000	4 2 21½ 17 18	112	Skiffington T Jr5	143	s	8.90	- -	GranKan14312PortManech147nkDuchessofMalfi1353½	Easily	11
12Jly71- 9Aqu	fm 1⅞	Hurdles	3:222 4↑	Sp Wt 6800	7 3 31½ 41½ 611	613	Skiffington T Jr5	147	s	2.80	- -	Blue Runner1452½Big Red Rocket152½Jive1456	Tired	8
29Jun71- 3Aqu	fm 1⅞	Hurdles	3:232 4↑	Alw 7000	2 4 21½ 1½ 23	32¼	Skiffington T Jr5	142	s	*.80e	- -	Jus' Behaving1471Blue Runner1401¼Gran Kan1429	Held well	10
21Jun71- 4Mth	fm *1¾	Hurdles	3:26 4↑	Alw 5500	7 5 42½ 53½ 512	311½	Skiffington T Jr5	147	s	5.40e	- -	Misty Forsome1476½Flying Bee1475Gran Kan1471	Driving	10
	Previously trained by Guillermo Sarmiento													
5Jun70♦	Hipodromo(Chi) fst*1¼LH		2:034 3↑	Clsc Universidad Catolica-Hcp Stk1200		9	Toro L	119		-		Love Me1101¾Good Look1281¼Mariscal1191¼		10
21May70♦	Club Hippico(Chi) fm*1ⓉRH		1:362 3↑	Premio Your Highness Hcp1000		11½	Toro L	112		7.20		Gran Kan1121½Barthou1071½Droguel1191½		7
25Apr70♦	Hipodromo(Chi) gd *7½fLH		1:31 3↑	Premio Jockey Club de Arequipa Hcp1100		12¼	Jorquera G	121		7.20		Gran Kan1212¼Germinal1062½Equino1194		13
19Apr70♦	Club Hippico(Chi) fm*6½fⓉRH		1:163 3↑	Premio Quemarropa Hcp1500		6	Sepulveda C	119		-		Zante106hdPercal114½Meritorio112hd		12
1Feb70♦	Valparaiso(Chi) fm*1ⓉLH		1:38 3↑	Premio Andres G. Scott Hcp1500		8	Astorga C	116		-		Notable114hdParlas126noPuro Oro1142½		8
11Jan70♦	Valparaiso(Chi) fm*1 3/16ⓉLH		1:564	Clasico Juan S. Jackson Stk5000		11	Azocar S	112		-		Trinera112½Campomar112¾Cougar II112¾		12
26Oct69♦	Club Hippico(Chi) fm*1½ⓉRH		2:261	Clasico El Ensayo Stk5000		54¾	Munoz D	123		-		Vagabundo1231Aristocratico123¾Exotico1232½	Good Look 6th	11
31Aug69♦	Club Hippico(Chi) fm*1 1/16ⓉRH		1:404	Polla de Potrillos Stk6000		85¾	Salinas J	123		-		Vagabundo123½Bien Machito1231Aristocratico1232½	Exotico 4th	19
10Aug69♦	Club Hippico(Chi) sf *1ⓉRH		1:401	Clasico Alberto Vial Infante Stk3500		32¾	Astorga C	121		-		Pimentero121¾Oro Es Triunfo1212Gran Kan121½		15
29Jun69♦	Hipodromo(Chi) gd *7½fLH		1:34	Premio All Serene Alw1200		23	Ulloa P	121		-		Aristocratico1123Gran Kan121hdTribuno113¾		10
27Apr69♦	Club Hippico(Chi) fm*6½fⓉRH		1:18	Premio Japon Alw1200		1hd	Astorga C	115		6.40		Gran Kan115hdBriquet1131Dagafiante1122½		9
5Apr69♦	Club Hippico(Chi) fm*5fⓉStr		1:00	Premio Fez Mdn600		1nk	Astorga C	121		9.80		Gran Kan121nkCamaro1172Dagafiante1172		10

Hoist the Flag

b. c. 1968, by Tom Rolfe (Ribot)–Wavy Navy, by War Admiral **Lifetime record: 6 5 0 0 $78,145**
Own.– Mrs S.C. Clark Jr
Br.– John M. Schiff (Ky)
Tr.– S. Watters Jr

20Mar71- 7Aqu fst 7f :22 :443 1:09 1:21 Bay Shore 34k 6 3 21 2½ 14 17 Cruguet J 126 *.30 96-17 Hoist the Flag1267Droll Role117nkJim French1211½ Easily 9
12Mar71- 8Bow fst 6f :232 :471 1:103 Alw 9500 2 4 11 13 16 115 Cruguet J 122 *.10 93-05 HoisttheFlag12215TotheMan1191½Backslidng1191 Drew clear 5
10Oct70- 7Bel fst 1 :22 :443 1:092 1:352 Champagne 205k 10 3 33 1½ 12 13 Cruguet J 122 *.80 96-13 [D]HoisttheFlag1223LimttoRson1223Arctrus1221¼ Caused jam 16
Disqualified and placed last
1Oct70- 7Bel fst 7f :221 :451 1:10 1:222 Cowdin 65k 12 12 99 51½ 21½ 11¾ Cruguet J 115 *1.70 95-13 HoisttheFlag1151¾LimittoReason1154Executonr117¾ Handily 12
23Sep70- 6Bel fst 6½f :223 :461 1:102 1:162 Alw 8500 2 9 1½ 1hd 11½ 15 Cruguet J 122 *.70 98-12 HoisttheFlag1225BoldSkipper1137EastrnFlt1221 Mild drive 9
11Sep70- 2Bel gd 6f :224 :461 1:11 Md Sp Wt 7 11 53½ 21 1hd 12½ Cruguet J 122 3.20 90-14 HoisttheFlag1222½Ogontz122¾SitintheCorner1226 Driving 11

Honest Pleasure

dkbbr. c. 1973, by What a Pleasure (Bold Ruler)–Tularia, by Tulyar **Lifetime record: 25 12 6 2 $839,997**
Own.– B.R. Firestone
Br.– Waldemar Farms Inc (Fla)
Tr.– Leroy Jolley

20Aug77- 8Mth fst 1¼ :47 1:11 1:352 2:002 3↑ AL Haskell H-G1 2 1 1½ 54 58½ 615½ Solomone M 123 2.30 84-19 Majestic Light1248Capital Idea1084½Peppy Addy1162¼ 6
Done after a mile
3Aug77- 5Sar fst 7f :223 :442 1:09 1:22 3↑ Alw 25000 5 2 2½ 1hd 1½ 2½ Vasquez J 117 *.40 94-13 El Portugues119½Honest Pleasure1171¾Piamem119¾ Gamely 6
16Apr77- 7Kee fst 1 1/16 :23 :452 1:093 1:422 3↑ Ben Ali H-G3 1 1 12 14½ 12 1½ Perret C 124 *.60 94-16 HonestPleasure124½IncaRoca1182PackerCaptan113no Driving 9
23Mar77- 9Hia fm 1 1/16Ⓣ 1:402 4↑ Alw 10000 1 2 2hd 2½ 23 55¼ Perret C 122 *.80 91-09 AllFriends1221Improviser1222½QuickDecision1171 Faltered 11
6Nov76- 8SA fst 1¼ :454 1:094 1:35 2:00 3↑ Champions Inv'l H 350k 2 1 11½ 1hd 33 87¾ Perret C 121 2.30 90-09 KngPellinore126noL'Heureux1181¾FestivMood1154 Weakened 10
25Oct76- 8Aqu fst 1 :223 :45 1:084 1:34 Jamaica H 55k 6 3 31½ 21½ 42½ 43¼ Perret C 125 *.60 93-13 Dance Spell119¾Cojak119½Quiet Little Table1142 Weakened 9
2Oct76- 8Bel sly 1¼ :472 1:104 1:35 2:00 3↑ Marlboro Cup H-G1 4 1 11½ 12½ 11½ 2hd Perret C 119 2.80 99-11 Forego137hdHonestPlesur1191FthrHogn1102¾ Failed to last 11
18Sep76- 8Bel fst 1⅛ :453 1:091 1:332 1:454 3↑ Woodward H-G1 1 1 11½ 11 3½ 34 Perret C 121 2.10 94-10 Forego1351¼DanceSpell1152¾[DH]HnstPleasre121 Weakened 10
21Aug76- 6Sar fst 1¼ :463 1:102 1:35 2:001 Travers-G1 4 1 16 12 13 14 Perret C 126 2.10 104-12 HonestPleasure1264Romeo1261½DanceSpell1263 Ridden out 8
7Aug76- 8Mth fst 1⅛ :46 1:10 1:343 1:47 Mth Inv'l H-G1 4 2 21½ 11½ 2½ 36 Perret C 126 *1.10 99-08 MajesticLight1226Appassionato113noHonestPlesr126½ Hung 10
27Jly76- 8Mth fst 1 1/16 :232 :46 1:10 1:411 3↑ Alw 13000 1 1 13½ 11½ 2hd 21½ Baeza B 115 *.10 97-13 Peppy Addy1191½Honest Pleasure1157Lee Gary1171½ Hung 6
15May76- 8Pim fst 1 3/16 :45 1:09 1:351 1:55 Preakness-G1 6 2 22 22 42 57¼ Baeza B 126 *.90 88-11 Elocutionist1263½Play the Red126½Bold Forbes1263 6
Brushed,drifted in
1May76- 8CD fst 1¼ :454 1:102 1:353 2:013 Ky Derby-G1 5 2 25 2½ 2½ 21 Baeza B 126 *.40 88-11 BoldForbes1261HonestPlsr1263¼Elocutonst1261¼ No excuse 9
22Apr76- 7Kee fst 1⅛ :48 1:123 1:372 1:492 Blue Grass-G1 2 1 14 15 12 11½ Baeza B 121 *.10 90-15 HnstPleasre1211½CertanRomo1213IncRoc1212¼ Ridden out 7
3Apr76- 9GP fst 1⅛ :464 1:103 1:351 1:474 Florida Derby-G1 3 1 13 13 13 13 Baeza B 122 *.05 95-14 Honest Pleasure1223Great Contractor1222½Proud Birdie1222 6
Speed in reserve
28Feb76- 9Hia fst 1⅛ :454 1:09 1:334 1:464 Flamingo-G1 7 1 12 18 18 111 Baeza B 122 *.30 98-06 HonestPleasre12211IncaRoca122no[D]Togus1221½ Easy score 8
11Feb76- 0Hia fst 7f :23 :452 1:093 1:222 Alw 10000 4 2 11 14 110 114 Baeza B 122 - 93-18 HonestPleasure12214ParcForillon115½ImprovIt11516 Easily 4
Exhibition race - No wagering
1Nov75- 8Lrl fst 1 1/16 :23 :454 1:103 1:424 Lrl Futurity-G1 3 1 11 13 11½ 12½ Baeza B 122 *.20 99-14 Honest Pleasure1222½Whatsyourpleasure1223½DanceSpll1228 7
Ridden out
18Oct75- 8Bel sly 1 :222 :45 1:101 1:362 Champagne-G1 9 2 1½ 11½ 15 17 Baeza B 122 *1.20 86-17 Honest Pleasure1227Dance Spell1222½Whatsyourpleasure122½ 14
Ridden out
8Oct75- 8Bel fst 7f :224 :452 1:094 1:223 Cowdin-G2 7 1 13 14 15 18 Baeza B 121 2.80 89-18 Honest Pleasure1218Whatsyourpleasure116hdUncle Gene1132 7
Mild drive
13Sep75- 8AP fst 6½f :222 :452 1:113 1:182 ©Arl Wash Futurity-G1 4 8 85½ 72½ 2hd 1nk McHargue DG 122 5.00 83-21 Honest Pleasure122nkKhyber King122nkRule The Ridge1221½ 19
Hard drive
3Sep75- 5Bel fst 6f :23 :462 1:101 Alw 9000 3 2 11 12 12½ 16 Baeza B 120 *.20 91-17 Honest Pleasure1206Pastry1205¾Bakor1204 Ridden out 7
25Aug75- 5Bel fst 6f :223 :46 1:101 Alw 9000 2 3 31 2½ 1½ 2¾ Baeza B 120 *1.20 90-12 TurnandCount120¾HonstPleasre1204BeauTalnt120no Gamely 8
21Jun75- 3Bel fst 5½f :223 :46 :574 1:04 ©Md Sp Wt 6 7 23 2½ 12 15½ Vasquez J 118 *.80 95-12 HonestPlsure1185½DanceSpell118¾TtonRng118¾ Ridden out 10
4Jun75- 3Bel fst 5½f :224 :461 :581 1:042 ©Md Sp Wt 2 4 2hd 2hd 2½ 2½ Vasquez J 118 *.90 92-11 RomanticLead118½HonstPlsur118nkFmlyDoctr1185½ Gamely 10

It's In the Air

b. f. 1976, by Mr. Prospector (Raise a Native)–A Wind Is Rising, by Francis S. **Lifetime record: 43 16 9 6 $892,339**
Own.– Due Process Stable
Br.– Happy Valley Farm (Fla)
Tr.– Reynaldo H. Nobles

11Oct81- 9Suf fst 1 1/16 :233 :472 1:12 1:442 3↑ ⒻHannah Dustin H 52k 2 1 2½ 76 715 722½ Skinner K 123 10.90 64-26 WeberCityMiss1266AngeGal114½WaterDance1162½ Brief speed 8
30Sep81- 6Med fst 6f :221 :45 1:102 3↑ ⒻHandicap 25000 4 6 78¾ 712 715 510 Lopez C 121 3.00 81-20 Delta Crisis1123Larla120noFavorite Prospect1124½ 7
Outrun,worked mile in 1:40 3/5
4Jly81- 9Mth sly 1 1/16 :234 :471 1:112 1:44 3↑ ⒻMolly Pitcher H-G2 6 3 23 47½ 617 626 Tejeira J 114 8.60 59-24 Weber City Miss1192Jameela1186Wistful1212 Tired 6
24Jun81- 8Mth fst 1 1/16 :241 :474 1:12 1:46 3↑ ⒻAlw 17000 1 1 1½ 11 12 1½ Tejeira J 124 *1.40 75-20 It'sintheAir124½DanceTroupe1181¼ReallyMean1185 Driving 6
7Jun81- 8Bel fst 1⅛ :464 1:112 1:363 1:494 3↑ ⒻHempstead H-G2 5 5 52¾ 45¼ 410 417¾ Asmussen CB 115 5.30 60-20 Wistful119hdChain Bracelet1195¾Love Sign11512 Tired 5
25May81- 8Mth fm 1Ⓣ :234 :47 1:112 1:37 3↑ ⒻAlw 17000 7 5 44 21½ 21½ 11½ Velez JA Jr7 110 *1.00 90-10 It'sintheAir1101½LadyLobbyist1155Earlham108½ Drew clear 7
7May81- 8Mth fst 1 :242 :482 1:124 1:374 3↑ ⒻAlw 16000 3 3 32 11 12½ 15¼ Velez JA Jr7 110 *.30 84-16 It'sintheAir1105¼SistrRosmund115¾FlshDoubl108hd Driving 5
26Apr81- 8Aqu fst 1⅛ :461 1:102 1:362 1:493 3↑ ⒻTop Flight H-G1 5 3 36½ 37 48½ 49¾ Asmussen CB 118 4.90 77-23 ChainBracelet1151¾LadyOakley1155WbrCtyMss1183 No threat 5
8Apr81- 9OP fst 1 1/16 :233 :462 1:111 1:441 4↑ ⒻApple Blossom H-G2 4 2 2½ 42¼ 69 69¾ Lopez C 120 7.00 77-20 Bold 'n Determined124hdLa Bonzo1113¼Karla's Enough1193½ 7
Early speed
21Mar81- 8Aqu fst 7f :232 :47 1:123 1:252 3↑ ⒻDistaff H-G3 8 1 53 31 21½ 2hd Asmussen CB 120 *2.30 74-35 LadyOakley114hdIt'sintheAir1205½Lovin'Lass1102 Gamely 8
7Mar81- 9Bow fst 7f :222 :443 1:093 1:23 3↑ ⒻBarbara Fritchie H-G3 4 7 74¾ 76¾ 79½ 611 Lopez C 123 *1.40 79-24 Skipat1247½Whispy'sLass114¾SecretEmotion113hd No mishap 8
Previously owned by Harbor View Farm;previously trained by Lazaro Barrera
11Jan81- 7SA fst 6f :213 :441 :564 1:093 4↑ ⒻAlw 32000 3 7 54 55¼ 31 1nk Pincay L Jr 121 *.90 91-17 It'sintheAir121nkBackatTwo1135½ProudestBee1132¼ Just up 7
8Nov80- 8Aqu fst 1¼ :474 1:114 1:372 2:03 3↑ ⒻLadies H-G1 4 3 21½ 42½ 42 46 Pincay L Jr 118 1.60 75-22 Planktn119noSugarandSpice114noWebrCtyMss1196 Gave way 6
11Oct80- 8Bel fst 1¼ :47 1:114 1:37 2:024 3↑ ⒻBeldame-G1 1 1 2hd 35½ 39 310½ Pincay L Jr 123 3.20 75-17 LoveSign1184MistyGallore1236½It'sintheAir1238½ Tired 4
27Sep80- 8Bel fst 1⅛ :48 1:122 1:364 1:491 3↑ ⒻRuffian H-G1 5 1 1½ 1½ 3nk 3nk Fell J 118 4.00e 81-19 GenuineRisk118noMistyGllor124nkIt'snthAr1185¾ Held well 6
2Sep80- 6Med sly 1⅛ :46 1:103 1:362 1:493 3↑ ⒻLong Look H-G2 1 2 22 2½ 21 22 Fell J 119 2.60 83-18 MistyGallore1232It'sintheAir1195Poppycock112¾ Steadied 6
8Aug80- 8Sar fst 7f :22 :441 1:091 1:221 3↑ ⒻBallerina-G3 4 1 31 1hd 3½ 31 McHargue DG 119 *1.30 90-15 DavonaDale1191MistyGallore124noIt'sinthAr1191¾ Weakened 4
13Jly80- 8Hol fst 1⅛ :453 1:091 1:341 1:47 3↑ ⒻVanity H-G1 6 6 66½ 31½ 3½ 13¾ Pincay L Jr 120 *2.10 97-12 It's in the Air1203¾Conveniently111nkImage of Reality119nk 7
Drew clear
31May80- 8Hol fst 1 1/16 :224 :453 1:091 1:401 3↑ ⒻMilady H-G2 5 4 42½ 35 23 23¼ Pincay L Jr 122 *1.10 91-14 Image of Reality1173¼It's in the Air1221¼Fondre1137 5
Best of others
14May80- 8Hol fst 7f :212 :432 1:071 1:193 3↑ ⒻSilver Spoon H 54k 5 7 85¼ 76¼ 68¼ 45½ Pincay L Jr 123 *1.30 95-14 Splendid Girl1174½Fondre115½Celine114½ Mild bid 9
24Feb80- 8SA fst 1⅛ :462 1:103 1:36 1:482 4↑ ⒻS Margarita H-G1 1 5 42½ 52¼ 3½ 44 Pincay L Jr 124 *1.90 83-11 Glorious Song1202The Very One116noKankam1252 Checked 11
10Feb80- 8SA fst 1⅛ :452 1:093 1:35 1:473 ⒻLa Canada-G1 6 4 45½ 42 44½ 35¾ Pincay L Jr 125 *.80 85-09 GloriousSong1181¾PrizSpot1194It'snthAr1251 Trapped late 7

26Jan80- 8SA fst 1 1/16 :224 :453 1:093 1:411 ⒻEl Encino-G3	7 6 66½ 63¾ 52½ 11¼	Pincay L Jr	124	*2.60	95-09	It'sintheAir1241¼PrizeSpot1211¼[D]Terlingua1211¼	Driving	8
16Jan80- 8SA gd 1 1/8 :472 1:12 1:372 1:50 4↑ⒻSan Gorgonio H 66k	7 3 2hd 2½ 611 724	Pincay L Jr	125	*1.30	55-23	Miss Magnetic11115Maytide1121¼Persona113½	Tired	9
13Oct79- 8Bel sly 1¼ :473 1:124 1:39 2:061 3↑ⒻBeldame-G1	4 1 21 78¼ 59 511	Pincay L Jr	118	*.40	58-27	Waya1233Fourdrinier1184Kit's Double1231¼	Tired	7
29Sep79- 8Bel fst 1 1/8 :474 1:12 1:351 1:472 3↑ⒻRuffian H-G1	4 1 11 12½ 12½ 14	Pincay L Jr	122	3.00	90-12	It's in the Air1224Blitey1135Waya126	Ridden out	4
12Sep79- 8Bel fst 1 :23 :453 1:093 1:344 3↑ⒻMaskette-G2	5 1 1½ 2hd 2hd 2nk	Shoemaker W	122	2.40	94-20	Blitey112nkIt'sintheAir122noPearlNecklace1253¼	Game try	5
26Aug79- 9Del gd 1 1/8 :482 1:122 1:372 1:492 ⒻDel Oaks-G1	1 1 1½ 2hd 11½ 15	Shoemaker W	122	*.30	90-14	It's in the Air1225Jameela1151Himalayan114½	In hand	6
11Aug79- 8Sar fst 1¼ :49 1:124 1:364 2:012 ⒻAlabama-G1	4 1 1½ 11½ 13 11½	Fell J	121	3.10	94-13	It'sintheAir1211½DavonaDale1213¾MairzyDots1212¼	Driving	5
4Aug79- 5Sar fst 6f :221 :45 1:091 3↑ⒻAlw 27000	5 2 11 13 15 18	Fell J	117	*.40	94-12	It'sintheAir1178EnglishTrifle108¾LucyBelle1052¾	Handily	7
15Jly79- 8Hol fst 1 1/8 :453 1:094 1:344 1:472 3↑ⒻVanity H-G1	1 2 22½ 1hd 1½ 1nk	Shoemaker W	113	*.90	95-12	It'sintheAir113nkCountryQueen121hdInnuendo1169	Driving	8
7Jly79- 8Hol fst 1 1/8 :454 1:101 1:353 1:481 ⒻHol Oaks-G1	2 3 21 21 2hd 2hd	Shoemaker W	121	*1.10	91-14	PrizeSpot121hdIt'sintheAir1216VarietyQueen1241	Sharp	7
2Jun79- 8Hol fst 1 1/16 :221 :443 1:092 1:411 3↑ⒻMilady H-G2	4 2 23½ 2hd 1½ 2½	Shoemaker W	112	2.30	88-14	Innuendo115½It'sintheAir112½CountryQueen1213½	Failed	9
11Mar79- 8SA fst 1 1/16 :222 :451 1:092 1:413 ⒻS Susana-G1	7 4 43 32 35½ 39	Pincay L Jr	117	1.90e	84-12	Caline1151Terlingua1158It's in the Air117hd	Checked	8
24Feb79- 8SA fst 7f :22 :442 1:082 1:211 ⒻS Ynez-G3	4 5 44 21½ 33½ 36	Delahoussaye E	121	*1.20	91-12	Terlingua1214Caline1192It's in the Air1213¼	Weakened	5
22Oct78- 8SA fst 1 1/16 :223 :461 1:101 1:411 ⒻOak Leaf-G2	1 2 21½ 2½ 2hd 11½	Delahoussaye E	115	1.60	95-11	It's in the Air1151½Caline11512Spiffy Laree115¾	Handily	8
2Oct78- 8Bel fst 1 :23 :452 1:094 1:352 ⒻFrizette-G1	4 5 62¼ 43 22½ 25	Delahoussaye E	119	6.80	86-14	Golferette1195It'sintheAr1197½TrIngu119¾	Best of others	7
Previously owned by J. Frankel;previously trained by Lou Goldfine								
9Sep78- 8AP fst 6f :221 :451 :571 1:093 ⒻArl-Wash Lassie-G2	8 1 73¾ 63¾ 1hd 14	Delahoussaye E	119	5.40	95-06	It'sintheAir1194AngelIsland119¾Bequa1191¼	Ridden out	8
9Aug78- 8AP fst 6f :221 :464 :582 1:104 ⒻMademoiselle 22k	8 8 65½ 44¼ 1½ 13	Delahoussaye E	115	4.60	89-18	It'sintheAir1153SplittheTab1156AngelIsland122hd	Handily	10
19Jly78- 7AP fst 5½f :222 :453 :573 1:04 ⒻAlw 7500	3 3 31 11 14 17	Sibille R	117	*1.30	95-15	It'sintheAir1177Buddy'sAngel117nkMiniWig1202	Easily	6
26Jun78- 5AP sly 5f :22 :453 :582 ⒻAlw 8500	6 4 47 45½ 33 21½	Sibille R	117	*1.20	92-16	JustaReflection1171½It'sintheAir1172GrdnGlovs1177	Gamely	6
20Jun78- 6AP gd 5f :23 :47 :593 ⒻMd Sp Wt	6 2 1½ 1½ 11 17	Sibille R	118	*.40	88-24	It'sintheAir1187DancingChant1189KlipKlop1182	Ridden out	6
12Jun78- 3AP fst 5f :231 :47 :593 ⒻMd Sp Wt	9 7 31 2hd 2hd 2hd	Sibille R	119	2.70	88-22	Justa Reflection119hdIt's in the Air1197Bye119nk	Gamely	9

J.O. Tobin

dkbbr. c. 1974, by Never Bend (Nasrullah)–Hill Shade, by Hillary

Lifetime record: 21 12 2 2 $659,416

Own.– G.A. Pope Jr
Br.– George A. Pope Jr (Md)
Tr.– Lazaro S. Barrera

8Sep78- 8Bel fm 7f(T) :223 :451 1:093 1:22 3↑ Alw 30000	3 5 2hd 2hd 23½ 47¼	Cauthen S	122	*.40	87-11	Tiller122hdArachnoid122hdQuick Card1157	Broke in air	5
5Aug78- 8Sar fst 1 1/8 :463 1:102 1:351 1:472 3↑ Whitney H-G2	8 4 34½ 2hd 35½ 611	Fell J	128	2.80	87-09	Alydar12310Buckaroo112hdFathrHogn114nk	Squeezed,drifted	9
23Jly78- 8Bel fst 7f :221 :443 1:08 1:204 3↑ Tom Fool H 43k	8 5 11½ 12 14 16½	Fell J	129	*1.30	98-15	J.O.Tobin1296½WhiteRammer119noIt'sFreezing116½	Handily	8
25Jun78- 8Hol fst 1¼ :452 1:091 1:333 1:591 3↑ Hol Gold Cup H-G1	1 1 13½ 16 11½ 44¼	Cauthen S	128	1.20e	91-16	Exceller128nkText118hdVigors1294	Drifted out,turn	7
14May78- 8Hol fst 1 1/16 :222 :452 1:092 1:41 3↑ Californian-G1	4 3 32½ 1½ 11½ 12½	Cauthen S	126	*.50	90-20	J.O.Tobin1262½Replant1201½Cox'sRidge1271¼	Steady drive	6
22Apr78- 8Hol fst 7f :214 :451 1:083 1:212 3↑ Los Angeles H-G2	3 3 21½ 1½ 11½ 13½	Cauthen S	130	*.30	92-17	J.O. Tobin1303½Maheras125½Drapier1215	Going away	4
12Apr78- 8Hol fst 1 1/16 :224 :452 1:091 1:412 3↑ Premiere H 53k	3 1 12½ 14 16 17	Cauthen S	125	*1.10	88-16	J.O. Tobin1257Mr. Redoy1211Miami Sun115¾	Speed to spare	5
25Mar78- 8SA fm 1 1/8(T) :462 1:102 1:344 1:474 4↑ San Bernardino H-G2	2 2 21½ 1½ 1hd 1¾	Cauthen S	123	*.50	88-12	J.O. Tobin123¾Henschel1151½Riot in Paris1194	Driving	6
5Feb78- 8SA sl 1¼ :454 1:093 1:343 2:01 C H Strub-G1	8 1 12½ 14 12 34½	Cauthen S	122	*1.00	86-14	Mr. Redoy1162½Text1212J.O. Tobin1223	Drifted out	9
15Jan78- 8SA sl 1 1/8 :453 1:10 1:353 1:492 San Fernando-G2	4 1 12 13 21 22	Cauthen S	123	*.30	83-17	Text1202J.O. Tobin123¾Centennial Pride1141	Drifted out	5
1Jan78- 8SA sl 7f :221 :444 1:092 1:23 Malibu-G2	5 2 12 13 14 15½	Cauthen S	123	*.70	88-29	J.O. Tobin1235½Bad 'n Big1206Eagle Ki1142	Easily	9
Previously trained by John H. Adams								
17Sep77- 8Bel sly 1 1/8 :453 1:101 1:352 1:48 3↑ Woodward H-G1	2 1 21 2½ 53¾ 58½	McHargue DG	121	2.60	78-18	Forego1331½SilverSeries114nkGreatContractor115nk	Tired	10
3Jly77- 8Hol fst 1¼ :452 1:091 1:333 1:583 Swaps-G1	4 1 11½ 15 18 18	Shoemaker W	120	3.10	98-11	J.O. Tobin1208Affiliate117noText1208	Scored in hand	7
25Jun77- 6Hol fm 1 1/8(T) :47 1:11 1:344 1:47 3↑ Alw 22000	6 2 22 11 12 13	Shoemaker W	107	*.30	101-15	J.O. Tobin1073Riverside Sam1183½Niebo1172	Handily	6
21May77- 8Pim fst 1 3/16 :453 1:094 1:344 1:542 Preakness-G1	6 7 812 57 45½ 55½	Shoemaker W	126	6.50	92-10	Seattle Slew1261½Iron Constitution1262Run Dusty Run1261¼		9
Broke in air								
30Apr77- 8Hol fm 1(T) :232 :463 1:103 1:342 Coronado H 44k	3 4 34 32 21 12	Shoemaker W	124	*.80	98-05	J.O.Tobin1242Bad'nBig1172HighlandLight1182	Mild drive	8
17Mar77- 0SA gd 6f :214 :443 :571 1:10 Alw 20000	1 4 33½ 21 2½ 2¾	Shoemaker W	122	-	88-16	Incredibly Lucky115¾J.O. Tobin1223Important Reason11720		4
Off poorly;Exhibition race - No wagering. Previously trained by Noel Murless								
10Oct76♦ Longchamp(Fr) sf *1(T)RH 1:443 Gran Criterium-G1 Stk182000	34	Piggott L	123	1.20		Blushing Groom1234Amyntor123hdJ.O. Tobin1233	Progress into 2nd 1½f out,lost 2nd near line	10
8Sep76♦ Doncaster(GB) gd 7f(T)Str 1:274 Champagne Stakes-G2 Stk28500	14	Piggott L	126	*.45		J.O. Tobin1264Durtal1237Ampulla1232½	Rated at rear,sharp run to lead 1f out,quickly clear	6
28Jly76♦ Goodwood(GB) fm6f(T)Str 1:122 Richmond Stakes-G2 Stk39500	11½	Piggott L	123	*.70		J.O. Tobin1231½Prior's Walk123hdTchypous1235	Rated in 5th,smooth progress to lead 1½f out,handily	5
8Jly76♦ Newmarket(GB) gd6f(T)Str 1:141 Fulbourn Maiden Stakes Mdn5400	12½	Piggott L	126	*1.50		J.O. Tobin1262½Chain of Reasoning1264Daring March126¾	Rallied to lead 1½f out,easily	14

Johnny D.

b. g. 1974, by Stage Door Johnny (Prince John)–Dusk, by Olden Times

Lifetime record: 18 7 2 6 $371,256

Own.– Dana S. Bray Jr
Br.– Peggy Augustus (Va)
Tr.– Michael Kay

3Aug81 7Sar fm 1(T) :242 :483 1:122 1:362 3↑ Alw 35000	3 8 52½ 41½ 74¾ 97¼	Hernandez R	115	*2.40	87-10	NatvCourr1151¼Gttor115hdMortlFrnds115¾	No late response	9
19Nov77- 8Aqu sf 1½(T) :51 1:154 2:06 2:331 3↑ Turf Classic 200k	4 2 2hd 1hd 1½ 13¾	Cauthen S	122	3.60	--	Johnny D.1223¾Majestic Light126¾Crow126nk	Drew out	9
5Nov77- 8Lrl sf 1½(T) :553 1:204 2:154 2:32 3↑ D C Int'l-G1	5 6 1hd 16 15 12½	Cauthen S	122	10.00	59-41	JohnnyD.1202½MajesticLight12714Exceller1273	Ridden out	8
23Oct77- 7WO sf 1 5/8(T) :511 1:443 2:522 3↑ Can Int'l-G1	6 4 53½ 2hd 21 34½	Velasquez J	118	14.30	33-44	Exceller1261Majestic Light1263½Johnny D.1183	Weakened	12
8Oct77- 8Bel gd 1½(T) :474 1:121 2:031 2:273 3↑ Man o' War-G1	2 8 811 31½ 41¾ 34½	Velasquez J	121	5.40	81-13	Majestic Light1264½Exceller126noJohnny D.121¾	Good try	11
17Sep77- 6Bel sly 1½⊗ :48 1:131 2:034 2:291 Lawrence Realization-G2	3 5 42½ 33½ 310 314	Cordero A Jr	117	*1.20	60-18	Zinov11711Poor Man's Bluff1172½Johnny D.1171	Rallied	8
16Aug77- 8Sar fm 1 1/16(T) :241 :474 1:114 1:42 3↑ Handicap 25000	3 4 33 21½ 2hd 1½	Cordero A Jr	112	*.50	87-11	Johnny D.112½Dominion116nkRuthie's Native1132¼	Driving	7
30Jly77- 8Bel fm 1 1/16(T) :231 :461 1:103 1:41 Lexington H (Div 2)-G2	4 3 32½ 11½ 16 19½	Cordero A Jr	113	*1.40	95-05	JohnnyD.1139½[D]TrueColors117nkForwardChrgr1171¼	Handily	6
4Jly77- 7Bel fm 1 1/16(T) :231 :464 1:102 1:41 3↑ Alw 15000	7 5 2½ 1hd 12 15	Cordero A Jr	115	*.70	95-05	JohnnyD.1155WinterWind1121¾KendallDrive119½	Ridden out	8
22Jun77- 7Bel fm 1 1/16(T) :232 :473 1:11 1:412 3↑ Alw 13000	2 6 2½ 2½ 2hd 1½	Velasquez J	114	*2.30	93-07	JohnnyD.114½ShowtheFlag1129½HonorableGuest113no	Driving	9
1Jun77- 8Bel fst 1 1/8 :471 1:12 1:364 1:491 Peter Pan 54k	8 4 51¾ 3½ 67 69	Montoya D	114	14.10	72-27	Spirit Level114hdSanhedrin1142Lynn Davis1141¼	Bid,tired	9
19May77- 6Aqu sly 1 :231 :461 1:103 1:362 Alw 13000	3 8 85½ 67¾ 37 32½	Velasquez J	115	*1.70	81-12	LeadingScorer1102½LynnDavis122hdJohnnyD.1155½	Rallied	8
2May77- 6Aqu fst 6f :223 :454 1:102 3↑ Alw 12000	2 6 77½ 66½ 63¼ 41	Velasquez J	112	3.50	90-15	Solly114hdBartender's Pride104¾Hostile Planet119hd	Wide	7
Previously owned by Dana S. Bray;previously trained by Thomas J. Kelly								
12Feb77- 7GP fst 1 1/16 :234 :482 1:121 1:443 Alw 7000	7 8 2hd 11½ 2hd 21	Perret C	122	3.70	82-17	Coined Silver1171Johnny D.1224½Court Open1171	Gamely	12
5Feb77- 7GP fst 1 1/16 :234 :474 1:121 1:431 Alw 7000	2 9 95½ 85¾ 56¼ 35½	Perret C	122	4.80	80-18	Baldski114¾Cornucopian1144½Johnny D.1222	Rallied	11
Previously trained by M. Kay								
20Dec76- 6Aqu fst 1 70[•] :242 :49 1:142 1:443 ©Md Sp Wt	1 3 34 2hd 11 15	Velasquez J	122	*.70	--	JohnnyD.1225SeetheWorld1224Portraiture1172	Ridden out	7
11Dec76- 4Aqu fst 6f[•] :232 :472 1:121 ©Md Sp Wt	3 4 41½ 44½ 24 22½	Velasquez J	122	2.90	--	Coffee1222¼Johnny D.1224¾Portraiture1221¼	Gamely	7
Previously trained by Mack Miller								
25Nov76- 3Aqu fst 6f :22 :461 1:114 ©Md 40000	6 7 711 710 45 32	Velasquez J	122	2.70	82-18	DewanndOnly118½PpBrownng1201½JhnnyD.122½	Finished fast	10

Key to the Mint

b. c. 1969, by Graustark (Ribot)–Key Bridge, by Princequillo — Lifetime record: 29 14 4 3 $576,016

Own.– Rokeby Stable
Br.– Paul Mellon (Va)
Tr.– Elliott Burch

27Sep73- 8Atl fm 1 3/16 Ⓣ :473 1:111 1:36 1:543 3↑ U Nations H-G1 6 3 2hd 31 43 1110¼ Baeza B 124 b 3.30 87-08 Tentam1234StarEnvoy1161¼ReturntoRlty113hd Stopped badly 12
15Sep73- 7Bel fst 1⅛ :453 1:091 1:33 1:452 3↑ Marl Cup Inv'l H 250k 1 6 65¼ 67¾ 713 717 Baeza B 126 b 3.50 87-07 Secretariat1243½Riva Ridge1272Cougar II1266½ Dull try 7
21Jly73- 7Aqu sly 1¼ :462 1:10 1:351 2:004 3↑ Suburban H-G1 1 1 1½ 13 16 11¾ Baeza B 126 b *.70 92-16 KeytotheMint1261¾TrueKnight1186CloudyDawn113hd Driving 6
4Jly73- 7Aqu fst 1 3/16 :462 1:092 1:333 1:522 3↑ Brooklyn H-G1 6 2 2½ 2hd 31 45½ Baeza B 128 b *1.60 104-07 Riva Ridge127hdTrue Knight1172Tentam1193½ Hard to rate 7
22Jun73- 7Aqu sly 1⅛ :464 1:111 1:36 1:484 3↑ Alw 20000 2 2 1hd 11½ 12½ 12 Baeza B 126 b *.20 92-16 KytotheMnt1262RulebyReason112hdCloudyDawn1149 Easily 4
28May73- 7Bel sly 1 :223 :444 1:091 1:35 3↑ Metropolitan-G1 8 4 32½ 32 31½ 21¼ Vasquez J 127 b *1.40 92-16 Tentam1161¼KeytotheMint127hdKing'sBishop1186 Wide 8
14Apr73- 7Aqu fst 1⅛ :462 1:093 1:342 1:474 3↑ Excelsior H-G2 1 1 2hd 1hd 11 12 Turcotte R 126 b *.90 97-13 KeytotheMint1262King'sBishop115hdNorthSe1207 Ridden out 5
28Oct72- 7Aqu fst 2 :474 2:281 2:541 3:212 3↑ J C Gold Cup 113k 1 4 22 210 214 215 Baeza B 119 b *1.00 74-17 Autobiography12415KeytotheMnt1193RvRdg11910 2nd best 7
30Sep72- 7Bel sly 1½ :47 1:112 2:012 2:282 3↑ Woodward 115k 3 1 2½ 1hd 13 11¼ Baeza B 119 b 1.70e 91-14 KytothMnt1191¼ⒹSummrGust1163Autobogrphy1262 Driving 10
19Aug72- 7Sar fst 1¼ :453 1:093 1:352 2:011 Travers 111k 6 3 35 23 2hd 11 Baeza B 117 b *.50 99-07 KeytotheMint1171Tentam114½TrueKnight1145 Brisk urging 7
5Aug72- 7Sar fst 1⅛ :474 1:112 1:362 1:491 3↑ Whitney 57k 1 3 1½ 1½ 13 12 Baeza B 113 b *.80 95-12 Key to the Mint1132Tunex1173Loud117¾ Ridden out 8
8Jly72- 7Aqu fst 1 3/16 :484 1:12 1:362 1:544 3↑ Brooklyn H 118k 11 1 1½ 1½ 13 12 Baeza B 112 b 5.20 100-09 Key to the Mint1122Autobiography1223WestCoastScout1141½ 12
Hard drive
10Jun72- 8Bel fst 1½ :48 1:12 2:021 2:28 Belmont 155k 6 4 3½ 23 48 412¾ Baeza B 126 b 3.80 80-08 RivaRidge1267Ruritn126¾CloudyDwn1265 Brushed first turn 10
31May72- 7Bel fst 1 :231 :46 1:10 1:344 Withers 59k 2 4 42 1½ 11½ 11 Baeza B 126 b *1.70 98-16 Key to the Mint1261Icecapade1265½Zulu Tom126¾ Driving 10
20May72- 8Pim sly 1 3/16 :47 1:11 1:362 1:553 Preakness 187k 3 3 21½ 32 34½ 35¾ Baeza B 126 b 4.20 86-18 BeeBeeBee1261¼NoLeHace1264½KytotheMnt126nk Weakened 7
13May72- 6Pim fst 1 1/16 :233 :47 1:11 1:424 Alw 12000 3 4 41 41 13 12½ Woodhouse R 119 b 1.30 96-13 KeytotheMint1192½Ladiga1141½SmilingJack1121½ Driving 5
2May72- 8CD gd 1 :23 :454 1:102 1:361 Derby Trial 22k 3 2 21 12 15 12½ Baeza B 122 b 2.30e 88-20 KeytotheMint1222½NoLeHace1227Dr.Neale1162½ Driving 12
15Mar72- 8Hia fst 6f :214 :442 1:10 Alw 8000 5 12 1230 1244 1242 1242 Baeza B 122 b *1.60 52-18 Over Arranged1156Second Bar1156Nose for Money1152 12
Went down behind at start,came back sore
3Mar72- 9Hia fst 7f :214 :434 1:082 1:212 Bahamas 34k 6 4 54¼ 57 48 410½ Baeza B 115 *1.20e 90-12 NewProspct112hdHldYourPeace11910SecndBar115½ Bumped 10
26Nov71- 7Aqu gd 1 :22 :443 1:103 1:363 Remsen 35k 10 8 76¼ 61¾ 2hd 1½ Baeza B 119 b *.80 84-19 KytotheMint119½DetermindCosmc1193½TrffcCp1173 Driving 12
13Nov71- 8GS fst 1 1/16 :232 :47 1:113 1:433 Garden State 293k 3 2 23 2½ 2hd 32¾ Rotz JL 122 b 5.20 84-19 RivaRidge1222½Freetex122nkKeytotheMint1221¾ Swerved in 8
6Nov71- 5Aqu fst 7f :22 :442 1:093 1:223 Alw 8500 5 2 33 32½ 12½ 12 Rotz JL 119 b *.60 88-16 KytotheMnt1192NoLeHace1223FollwtheLeadr117hd Handily 8
20Oct71- 7GS fst 1 70 :224 :464 1:113 1:424 Alw 6500 7 7 5¾ 1hd 11 1nk Rotz JL 118 *.60 80-18 ⒹKeytotheMnt118nkDeterminedCsmc118½AndrewFeeney118½ 8
Disqualified and placed fourth
29Sep71- 7Bel fst 7f :222 :453 1:111 1:241 Cowdin 68k 4 2 62½ 22 2½ 2no Rotz JL 115 8.70 86-20 Loquacious Don115noKey to the Mint1152Mr. Paul B.1153 9
Carried wide
18Sep71- 7Bel sly 6½f :22 :451 1:094 1:163 Futurity 153k 3 3 21½ 1hd 44 55½ Rotz JL 122 13.10 91-11 RivaRdge1221½ChvrnFlight122½HldYourPeace1222 Gave way 8
4Sep71- 5Bel fst 6f :23 :47 1:114 Alw 9500 2 4 11 1½ 11 1½ Turcotte R 119 3.20 86-12 KytotheMint119½SearchforGold1172PrinceAdgo1173 Driving 12
17Jly71- 6Aqu fst 5½f :221 :454 :583 1:05 Alw 10000 5 4 32½ 1hd 1½ 32½ Rotz JL 122 *1.20 85-15 BeeBeeBee1191LuckyBidder1221½KytothMnt1223 Weakened 11
7Jly71- 5Aqu fst 5½f :222 :461 :583 1:05 ⒸMd Sp Wt 5 4 32 1½ 11 12 Rotz JL 122 *1.30 88-16 KeytotheMint1222FloorShow1221½DrumFire1224 Mild drive 10
23Jun71- 2Bel fst 5½f :223 :461 :582 1:05 ⒸMd Sp Wt 5 1 2½ 1hd 22 25½ Rotz JL 122 *.90 89-15 RivaRdge1225½KeytotheMint1223½Cndyvll122hd Second best 8

La Prevoyante

b. f. 1970, by Buckpasser (Tom Fool)–Arctic Dancer, by Nearctic — Lifetime record: 39 25 5 3 $572,417

Own.– J.L. Levesque
Br.– J. Louis Levesque (Can)
Tr.– J. Starr

28Dec74- 9Crc fm 1 1/16 Ⓣ :224 :463 1:103 1:43 3↑ ⒻMiss Florida H 30k 5 1 17 14 2hd 85¾ Rogers C 121 b *1.30 87-05 Tommy's Girl115noⒹGems and Roses1161Lizabeth Action113¾ 11
Faltered
7Dec74- 8Crc fst 6f :224 :462 1:13 3↑ ⒻAlw 7500 1 2 1hd 1hd 2½ 2¾ Rogers C 122 b *.80 87-20 Tastybit122¾La Prevoyante1221½La Noticia104½ Gamely 7
14Oct74- 7WO sly 6f :22 :451 1:111 3↑ Nearctic H 17k 4 3 3½ 43½ 43 44¼ Leblanc JB 123 b *.95 82-20 HnryTudr1212DontAskMeThat118hdParkRomeo1132½ No rally 6
11Sep74- 8Bel fst 1 :223 :444 1:094 1:343 3↑ ⒻMaskette H-G2 4 1 13 1½ 914 1126 Turcotte R 121 b 3.20 69-13 DesertVixen1201½PonteVecchio118½PokerNight1163½ Tired 12
17Aug74- 7Sar sly 6f :214 :444 1:103 3↑ Alw 25000 5 4 2hd 1hd 1hd 1nk Turcotte R 116 b *.80 87-16 La Prevoyante116nkLonetree1185Piamem114hd Driving 8
8Aug74- 8Sar fst 6f :221 :443 1:09 3↑ ⒻAlw 25000 1 2 1½ 1½ 14 17 Turcotte R 112 b *.30 95-12 LaPrevoyante1127Clandent120noSpclGoddss109no Ridden out 5
1Aug74- 7Sar fst 6f :22 :443 1:082 3↑ ⒻAlw 20000 5 1 1½ 14 15 17¾ Turcotte R 115 b *.60 98-12 LaPrevoyante1157¾FullofHope1175½JavaMoon1214½ Handily 6
30Jun74- 7WO sf 1 1/16 Ⓣ :241 :492 1:152 1:514 3↑ ⒻⓇCanadian 17k 6 1 14½ 13 1hd 36 Castaneda M 124 b *.60 39-52 Hildesheim1174½MusketeerMiss1241½LaPrvynt1242 Gave way 6
22Jun74- 9WO sl 7f :23 :454 1:111 1:242 3↑ ⒻAlw 5000 3 2 1½ 13½ 17 111½ Hawley S 121 b *.20 88-25 LaPrevoyante12111½TwoRings1171¼Victoriancttc1112 Easily 7
12Jun74- 7WO fm *1Ⓣ :233 :474 1:121 1:392 3↑ ⒻHandicap 7500 6 2 12 15 13½ 13 Hawley S 123 b *.85 76-00 LaPrevoynte1233LeveeLuck117noHildeshem1161½ Mild drive 10
26May74- 6WO fst 7f :232 :453 1:094 1:22 3↑ ⒻSeaway 17k 7 2 1hd 12½ 11 22½ Leblanc JB 121 b 1.30 97-11 MissRebound1242½LaPrevoyante1216Hildshm114½ 2nd best 8
13May74- 8Bel fst 7f :222 :45 1:094 1:222 3↑ ⒻVagrancy H-G3 12 1 2hd 2hd 1212 1311 Turcotte R 124 b 3.50 79-14 Coraggioso119noPonte Vecchio114noⒹWanda112½ Stopped 14
Placed 12th through disqualification
19Apr74- 9Hia fst 6f :222 :45 1:09 4↑ ⒻAlw 6000 6 1 1hd 13 15 19 Rivera MA 122 b *.80 98-18 La Prevoyante1229True Pitch1222½Aloha Miss1131 Easily 7
31Oct73- 6Lrl gd 6f :223 :454 1:102 ⒻAlw 7500 5 2 2hd 2hd 1hd 11¼ Leblanc JB 122 b *.20 97-13 LaPrevoynte1221¼ReginaMars1222NturlSound1193 Hand ride 5
20Oct73- 6WO fst 6f :221 :453 1:10 ⒻAlw 5100 1 4 2hd 11 11½ 14 Leblanc JB 119 *.20 95-16 LaPrvoyant1194GlamourPrd1175EmrldLndng121½ Ridden out 5
6Oct73- 7WO fm 1¼Ⓣ :462 1:124 1:401 2:072 ⒻⓇWonder Where 22k 8 1 1½ 56 613 624 Grubb R 123 b *1.25 46-22 ⒹSquareAngel123noMusketeerMss1135½SharpQull118¾ Tired 8
28Sep73- 9WO fm *1 1/16 Ⓣ :23 :484 1:133 1:473 ⒻAlw 5300 4 1 11 12½ 12½ 2no Leblanc JB 121 b *1.30 75-12 LadyShooter116noLaPrvoynt1212¾Vctorntt1166½ Just missed 6
14Sep73- 6WO fst 6f :223 :462 1:094 ⒻAlw 4800 2 3 1hd 13 15 16½ Leblanc JB 118 b *.35 96-16 LaPrvyante1186½GlamourParade1164LadyShootr120½ Easily 6
21Jly73- 7FE fst 6½f :221 :443 1:101 1:164 Friar Rock 11k 8 3 31 22 31 31¾ Leblanc JB 119 b *.55 93-16 Symmetric1181¼ShakeaLeg121½LaPrvoynte1192½ Weakened 8
30Jun73- 6WO sl 1¼ :471 1:131 1:41 2:08 ⓇQueen's Plate 124k 15 2 2hd 2hd 23 810 Leblanc JB 121 b *1.40 56-31 RoyalChocolte1265½Sinister Purpose126nkMyArchieBald1261 17
No excuse
23Jun73- 7WO fst 1⅛ :453 1:092 1:484 ⒻⓇCanadian Oaks 60k 5 1 19 112 2hd 32 LeBlanc JB 121 b *.05 97-13 Square Angel1211½Impressive Lady121½La Prevoyante12112 9
Speed,tired
16Jun73- 8BB sly 1⅛ :47 1:133 1:402 1:54 ⓇQuebec Derby 50k 4 1 15 11½ 1½ 12½ LeBlanc JB 121 b *.25e 79-34 La Prevoyante1212½Victorian Prince1265LeesandDregges1265 6
Driving
27May73- 8BB fst 6f :23 :46 1:104 ⒻVille-Marie 11k 1 4 1½ 11½ 12½ 18 LeBlanc JO 122 b *.05 100-13 LaPrevoyante1228JamRuler1153EmeraldLanding1172 Easily 5
4May73- 8CD fst 1 1/16 :24 :471 1:113 1:441 ⒻKy Oaks-G2 2 1 13 14 11½ 25 LeBlanc JO 121 b *.80 82-15 BagofTunes1215LaPrevoyante1211½Coraggso121hd No excuse 13
28Apr73- 8CD fst 7f :23 :454 1:103 1:234 ⒻLa Troienne 21k 5 3 14 15 11 1no LeBlanc JO 121 b *.20 88-16 La Prevoyante121hdOld Goldie1151½Coraggioso1182½ Lasted 8
7Apr73- 7Kee sly 6f :22 :451 :574 1:103 ⒻAlw 10000 3 8 32 2hd 1hd 13½ LeBlanc JO 124 b *.20 89-21 LaPrvoyante1243½ALittleLovin1121DancingBnd1141 Handily 10
5Mar73- 5GP fst 6f :22 :442 1:084 ⒻAlw 8500 6 5 33 21½ 22 23 LeBlanc JO 122 b *.20 97-07 BoldMemory1173LaPrvynte1222½OperFn107¾ Brushed start 8
11Nov72- 8GS fst 1 1/16 :23 :462 1:114 1:472 ⒻGardenia 190k 5 1 15 18 18 11¾ LeBlanc JO 119 b *.30 68-26 LaPrevoynte1191¾NorthBroadwy119hdFnTunng1191½ Driving 11
28Oct72- 6Lrl sly 1 1/16 :23 :46 1:121 1:462 ⒻSelima 121k 2 2 1½ 15 110 114 LeBlanc JO 122 b *.10 81-14 LaPrvoynte12214Naive1193FamousTale1193½ Much the best 4
Run on Selima-Futurity course
7Oct72- 7Bel sly 1 :222 :453 1:104 1:372 ⒻFrizette 114k 8 1 13 15 15 12 LeBlanc JO 121 b *.30 85-14 LaPrevynte1212CamAxe1212½FineTuning1212 Never headed 8
23Sep72- 7Bel fst 7f :222 :451 1:101 1:233 ⒻMatron 104k 4 1 2hd 11 19 17½ LeBlanc JO 119 b *.20 89-13 LaPrvoyant1197½UpAbov1198½Corggoso119hd Speed to spare 4
9Sep72- 7WO sl 1 1/16 :232 :464 1:114 1:472 ⒻⓇPrin Elizabeth 24k 4 1 12½ 110 17 17½ LeBlanc JO 119 b *.20 75-28 La Prevoyante1197½Cailey Jane1195Buh Buh Buh Bold1197 8
Much the best

25Aug72- 7Sar	gd	6f	:214 :451 1:104	(F)Spinaway 58k	8 3 41 11½ 14 13	LeBlanc JO	120	b	*.40	92-08	LaPrvoyant1203PrincessDoubleday1201Behrm120nk	Handily	10
2Aug72- 7Sar	fst	6f	:222 :46 1:112	(F)Schuylerville 29k	6 2 2hd 12 15 15½	LeBlanc JO	119	b	*1.90	89-14	LaPrvoyante1195½Sparkalark1163½SwetSop1161½	Ridden out	12
22Jly72- 7FE	fst	6½f	:223 :454 1:111 1:174	[R]Colin 12k	4 6 31½ 2hd 14 15	LeBlanc JO	121	b	*.55	90-14	LaPrevoyante1215ZacaSpirt114nkQun'sSplndour1174¼	Easily	10
9Jly72- 0BB	fst	6f	:231 :461 1:112	[R]Fleur de Lys 14k	1 2 12 15 15 19¾	LeBlanc JO	117	b	-	97-16	La Prevoyante1179¾First I Like112	Easily	2
	No wagering												
2Jly72- 7WO	fst	6f	:221 :461 1:111	(F)My Dear 12k	5 1 1hd 12 12 11¼	LeBlanc JO	112	b	*.45	89-17	LaPrevoyante1121¼LadyShooter11510SeaAria1092	Mild drive	7
10Jun72- 4WO	fm	5f(T)	:221 :47 1:00	[R]Alw 4000	2 2 2hd 2hd 1hd 13	LeBlanc JO	119	b	*.50	--	La Prevoyante1193Queen's Splendour1223½Dr. Rowland12210		6
	Ridden out												
31May72- 2WO	gd	5½f	:23 :464 1:062	(F)[R]Md Sp Wt	2 5 14 17 17 18½	LeBlanc JO	119	b	*.80e	88-22	LaPrevoyante1198½CaileyJane1191½NewProvider1191¼	Easily	9

Lakeville Miss

dkbbr. f. 1975, by Rainy Lake (Royal Charger)–Hew, by Blue Prince — **Lifetime record: 14 7 4 1 $371,582**

Own.– Randolph Weinsler
Br.– Randolph Weinsler (Ky)
Tr.– Jose Martin

1Jly78- 8Bel	fst	1½	:464 1:112 2:023 2:292	(F)C C A Oaks-G1	2 3 36½ 2½ 1½ 16	Hernandez R	121	4.60	73-16	LakvilleMss1216Caesar'sWsh1214TmpstQn1215	Ridden out	5
11Jun78- 8Bel	fst	1⅛	:451 1:09 1:342 1:473	(F)Mother Goose-G1	8 5 58 35 2½ 22	Hernandez R	121	8.80	87-15	Caesr'sWsh1212LakvlleMss1211½TempstQueen121hd	Gamely	8
27May78- 8Bel	fst	1	:224 :45 1:094 1:352	(F)Acorn-G1	5 5 56 2hd 21½ 21¾	Hernandez R	121	4.40	89-17	Tempest Queen1211¾Lakeville Miss121nkWhite Star Line1211¾		6
	Game try											
5May78- 8CD	gd	1 1/16	:24 :463 1:113 1:451	(F)Ky Oaks-G1	7 9 88¼ 73¾ 57 68¼	Hernandez R	121	3.50	74-15	WhiteStarLine1212Grnzn1212½BoldRndzvous1212¼	Slow early	11
15Apr78- 8Key	fst	7f	:234 :472 1:131 1:26	(F)Constitution 58k	2 12 87½ 73½ 11½ 14	Hernandez R	121	*.50	79-25	LakevilleMiss1214Paradigmatic112¾LaNijinska1125	Easily	12
1Apr78- 8Pim	fst	6f	:233 :463 :584 1:12	(F)Flirtation 32k	4 5 52½ 34 34 2¾	Hernandez R	119	*.40	85-19	Dance of the Grebe116¾LakevlleMiss1191½Marston's Mill1132		5
	Steadied											
19Nov77- 6Aqu	fst	1⅛	:471 1:114 1:38 1:503	(F)Demoiselle-G2	2 6 44 32½ 24 26¾	Hernandez R	121	*.80	75-18	Caesar'sWish1166¾LakevillMss1212¾IslndKss1141¾	2nd best	7
22Oct77- 8Lrl	fst	1 1/16	:233 :464 1:12 1:452	(F)Selima-G1	4 7 46½ 33 2½ 11	Hernandez R	122	*.50	86-16	Lakeville Miss1221L'Alezane1222¼[D]La Voyageuse1191¼		7
	Steadied,dr.											
1Oct77- 6Bel	fst	1	:233 :45 1:101 1:361	(F)Frizette-G1	5 6 45½ 1½ 13 15	Hernandez R	119	*1.30	87-14	Lakeville Miss1195Misgivings1192Itsamaza119¾	Ridden out	8
21Sep77- 8Bel	my	7f	:23 :46 1:101 1:224	(F)Matron-G1	5 5 84¾ 55 21 1nk	Hernandez R	119	2.60	88-21	Lakeville Miss119nkStub1196¾Akita119¾	Driving	10
5Sep77- 6Bel	fst	6½f	:223 :461 1:112 1:174	(F)Astarita-G3	1 5 43½ 53 1hd 1¾	Hernandez R	112	5.90	87-17	LakvlleMss112¾Sherry Peppers1163¾Temperamental Pet112nk		6
	Driving											
26Aug77- 8Sar	fst	6f	:222 :454 1:104	(F)Spinaway-G1	6 3 1hd 3½ 52 54¼	Hernandez R	119	9.80	82-15	Sherry Peppers119½Akita119noStub1192¾	Used early	8
1Aug77- 8Sar	fst	6f	:223 :461 1:114	(F)Schuylerville-G3	4 7 73½ 63¼ 43½ 3nk	Hernandez R	114	18.80	81-20	L'Alezane121noAkita121nkLakevilleMss1143½	Strong finish	8
30Jun77- 4Bel	fst	5½f	:23 :47 :593 1:061	(F)Md 25000	5 7 33 22 1½ 14	Hernandez R	119	2.40	84-19	Lakeville Miss1194Irish Rising1126¾Hypsipyle119¾	Easily	9

Late Bloomer

b. f. 1974, by Stage Door Johnny (Prince John)–Dunce Cap II, by Tom Fool — **Lifetime record: 24 11 5 5 $512,040**

Own.– Greentree Stable
Br.– Greentree Stud Inc (Ky)
Tr.– John M. Gaver Jr

28Jly79- 8Bel	fm	1¼[T]	:491 1:13 1:373 2:013	3↑ (F)Sheepshead Bay H-G2	4 7 711 84¼ 41 2no	Velasquez J	123	4.50	86-09	Terpsichorist117noLate Bloomer1232¾Warfever110nk	Missed	10
23Jun79- 8Bel	fm	1 1/16(T)	:234 :472 1:104 1:411	3↑ (F)New York H-G3	4 4 42½ 64 64 51½	Velasquez J	124	*.80	88-07	LaSoufriere111½NavajoPrincss118hdEmrldHll120¾	No excuse	8
3Jun79- 6Bel	sly	1¼	:494 1:14 1:391 2:041	3↑ Sar Cup H 109k	6 3 31½ 21 2hd 2no	Velasquez J	119	1.20	76-30	Waya125noLate Bloomer1194¾Sten1101¼	Missed	6
21Apr79-11Hia	fst	1⅛	:464 1:113 1:371 1:502	3↑ (F)Black Helen H-G2	3 4 38 26 2hd 1½	Velasquez J	123	*.20	80-22	LateBloomr123½TimeforPlesur11510Exctbl11216	Ridden out	5
11Apr79- 9OP	my	1 70	:232 :464 1:121 1:43	4↑ (F)Apple Blossom H-G2	5 7 99¾ 77¾ 54½ 42¾	Velasquez J	124	*.50	78-27	MissBaja1131¾Kit'sDouble114noNavajoPrincss1211	No rally	10
30Mar79- 9Hia	fst	7f	:231 :461 1:112 1:241	4↑ (F)Alw 13000	5 7 63½ 55¼ 1hd 17½	Velasquez J	114	*.40	82-23	LateBloomer1147½HuggleDuggle114nkIrishAgate1223½	Easily	7
9Oct78- 8Bel	fst	1¼	:49 1:131 1:374 2:021	3↑ (F)Beldame-G1	3 3 21½ 2½ 1hd 11¼	Velasquez J	123	*.90	89-15	LateBlmr1231¼PearlNcklace1234CmLdLaurie12312	Handily	4
23Sep78- 8Bel	fst	1⅛	:462 1:094 1:343 1:47	3↑ (F)Ruffian H-G1	5 7 64¼ 45 2hd 11½	Velasquez J	122	3.10	92-15	LateBlmr1221½PearlNecklc1244TmpstQueen1172½	Ridden out	9
3Sep78- 9Del	fst	1¼	:483 1:13 1:371 2:021	3↑ (F)Delaware H-G1	7 5 43½ 41¼ 1hd 1no	Velasquez J	119	*2.30	91-12	LateBlmr119noDottie'sDoll1171CmLaudLaurie119no	Driving	9
15Jly78- 8Bel	gd	1¼[T]	:471 1:113 1:354 2:01	3↑ (F)Sheepshead Bay H-G2	8 10 1017 89½ 55 1hd	Velasquez J	118	*2.10	89-11	Late Bloomer118hdWaya115nkPearl Necklace1241¼	Driving	11
24Jun78- 8Bel	fm	1 1/16(T)	:243 :474 1:11 1:411	3↑ (F)New York H (Div 2)-G3	5 6 54 53½ 4¾ 12¾	Velasquez J	115	2.50	90-09	Late Bloomer1152¾Island Kiss1081¼Fia1131½	Drew clear	9
30May78- 8Bel	fm	1 1/16(T)	:241 :473 1:111 1:413	3↑ (F)Garden City H 58k	5 4 54 53½ 21½ 1½	Velasquez J	113	*1.90	88-10	LateBlmr113½PearlNcklc1212HugglDuggl114hd	Ridden out	11
10May78- 8Aqu	gd	1	:24 :47 1:12 1:374	4↑ (F)Handicap 25000	4 3 32 3½ 11 12	Maple E	115	*.80	77-19	[D]LateBloomer1152Nanticious1135GypsyClown113no	Bore in	5
	Disqualified and placed second											
8Apr78- 9GP	fm	1 1/16(T)	:224 :453 1:091 1:41	3↑ (F)Orchid H-G3	10 4 47½ 42½ 52¼ 2½	Maple E	113	3.20	95-03	TimeforPleasure115½LateBloomr113nkRichSoil116½	Gamely	11
15Mar78- 9GP	fm	1(T)	:233 :47 1:11 1:353	3↑ (F)Suwannee River H 32k	3 5 64¼ 64¼ 42¼ 3½	Maple E	113	4.80	91-11	Len'sDetermined119nkWhataSummr122nkLtBlmr1131	Rallied	9
3Mar78- 7Hia	sly	6f	:223 :452 1:091	4↑ (F)Alw 12000	8 2 54¾ 45½ 43½ 34	Maple E	114	*1.90	93-16	Gladiolus1141Dear Paris1123Late Bloomer1141½	Fair try	8
	Previously trained by John M. Gaver											
15Oct77- 2Bel	sly	1 1/16⊗	:241 :482 1:133 1:444	3↑ (F)Alw 15000	7 2 21½ 2hd 12½ 14½	Cauthen S	119	*2.00	78-17	LatBloomr1194½AlphaDelta1193½EqulHonor114¾	Ridden out	7
4Oct77- 5Bel	yl	1 1/16(T)	:244 :491 1:143 1:453	3↑ (F)Alw 13000	2 4 54 31 12½ 14	Cauthen S	114	*2.20	68-28	Late Bloomer1144La Fabelle1147¾Swiss114nk	Handily	8
2Sep77- 7Bel	fst	7f	:23 :461 1:103 1:231	3↑ (F)Alw 11000	4 6 56 46½ 47½ 36¾	Cauthen S	118	*1.80	79-21	CarryItHigh1131¾MenageaTrois1155LateBloomer118nk	Wide	8
23Aug77- 9Sar	fst	7f	:223 :454 1:104 1:232	3↑ (F)Md Sp Wt	9 2 65 73¼ 3½ 13¾	Cauthen S	117	*1.20	88-13	LateBloomr1173¾Misconduct1172¼ConGame117¾	Ridden out	12
4Aug77- 1Sar	fst	6f	:22 :451 1:10	3↑ (F)Md Sp Wt	11 2 74½ 118¼ 78½ 34	Gonzalez B	117	4.80	86-13	MenageaTrois1173¼ConGame117¾LateBlmr117hd	Closed well	14
25Sep76- 4Bel	fst	6f	:222 :452 1:102	(F)Md Sp Wt	5 3 55½ 47 33½ 32¼	Gustines H	119	2.90	88-12	SmileEvenThrough1192¼Flying Buttress119hdLate Blmr1192½		7
	Rallied											
11Sep76- 3Bel	fst	6f	:223 :46 1:11	(F)Md Sp Wt	1 2 3nk 1hd 1½ 2½	Gustines H	119	4.70	86-14	Splendid Size119½Late Bloomer119½Kennelot1191¼	Gamely	11
17Aug76- 1Sar	fst	6f	:23 :47 1:113	(F)Md Sp Wt	6 5 52½ 43½ 46½ 49	Gustines H	119	*2.20	73-14	Shufleur1193½RomanGroundr1191½FlyngAbov1194	No response	7

Life's Illusion

b. f. 1971, by Mystic II (Relic)–Dark Mile, by Black Tarquin — **Lifetime record: 34 13 6 1 $96,828**

Own.– Mrs Virginia G. Van Alen
Br.– Virginia Guest (Md)
Tr.– P.R. Fout

25Aug77- 6Sar	fm	2⅜	S'Chase	4:184	4↑ NY Turf Writers Cup H 21k	3 7 624 86 714 714¾	Quanbeck A Jr	163	*1.20	--	HappyIntellectual152¾NvlPrson143hdCsmyor1505½	Bid,tired	8
5Aug77- 6Sar	fm	2 1/16	S'Chase	3:441	4↑ Lovely Night H 21k	3 2 15 15 13 13¼	Quanbeck A Jr	160	*1.50	--	Life'sIllusion1603¼Casamyor149½HppyIntllctul1543	Easily	6
7Jly77- 4Bel	fm	2	S'Chase	3:38	4↑ Handicap 10000	6 1 116 114 14 14½	Quanbeck A Jr	157	4.50	--	Life's Magic1574½Casamayor149½Down First1385	Easily	7
22Jun77- 5Mth	fm	*2¼	S'Chase	4:224	4↑ Midsummer H 16k	2 1 3nk - - -	Fout DP	158	4.80	--	TallAwrd142½BreakngDawn1391¼Casamayor1502	Left course	8
4Jun77- 7Fai	hd	*2½	S'Chase	5:051	4↑ Handicap 10000	5 3 - - - -	Fout DP	157	5.10	--	TanJay1544¾HappyIntellectual1603BrkngDwn14020	Pulled up	5
30May77- 8Fai	hd	*1 5/16(T)		2:133	3↑ Alw 1000	4 6 620 52¾ 42¾ 47	Fout DP3	138	*1.20	--	Germanicus1531Sun Meeting1465½Plumsted146½	No rally	8
27Nov76- 4Cam	fm	2¾	S'Chase	5:122	4↑ Colonial Cup 100k	12 1 14 2½ 76¼ 710	Fout DP7	150	-	--	GrandCnyon162½FireControl1622½Crag'sCornr160no	Used up	16
28Sep76- 4Mth	fm	*2¼	S'Chase	4:262	4↑ Midsummer H 15k	1 2 2½ 12½ 13 13¾	Skiffington T Jr	160	1.90	--	Life's Illusion1603¾Montpellier139noCrag's Corner1433½		6
	Unruly,driving												
18Sep76- 7Fai	fm	*2½	S'Chase	4:571	4↑ Grand National H 15k	7 4 52 1½ 32 36¼	Skiffington T Jr	161	2.80	--	StraightandTrue1546¼HappyIntellectual157hdLfe'sIllusn1612¾		7
	Tired												
26Aug76- 6Sar	fm	2⅜	S'Chase	4:192	4↑ NY Turf Writers Cup H 22k	6 2 2½ 11½ 2½ 2¾	Skiffington T Jr	160	*1.50	--	Happy Intellectual152¾Life's Illusn1602½StraightandTrue155½		7
	Gamely												

17Jly76- 7Del fm *2⅜ S'Chase 4:342 4↑ Indian River 13k 8 - - - - - - Fout DP 160 *1.60 -- StraightandTrue1512¾Crag'sCorner1362CloverOver1354 Fell 8
25Jun76- 4Del fm *2 1/16 S'Chase 3:564 4↑ Handicap 8000 1 2 11 14 11½ 12 Fout DP 156 3.20 -- Life's Illusion1562Straight and True1527[DH]Deux Coup145 9
Ridden out
16Jun76- 7Bel fm 1 1/16Ⓣ :231 :462 1:103 1:411 3↑ ⒻAlw 12000 7 6 73½ 76¾ 78 79½ Maple E 119 10.10 85-11 StudentLeadr1154½Fiddling122¾PlaceDuphn1151½ No factor 8
6Jun76- 7Del gd 1 1/16Ⓣ :241 :482 1:132 1:463 4↑ Alw 6500 1 6 53 53¾ 46 22 Pilar H 107 3.00 69-29 PimmsCup1122Lif'sIlluson1072BlznWondr1126 Bobbled start 6
15May76- 4Mal hd *2 S'Chase 3:422 4↑ Handicap 7500 4 5 12 - - - Fishback J 158 -- [DH]Castlebar II142[DH][D]Tall Award145hdJuggernaut II1438 5
Left course
8May76- 6Fai fm *2⅛ S'Chase 4:094 4↑ Handicap 7500 4 1 13 14 2hd 21¾ Fishback J 158 - -- LondonGrove1481¾Life'sIllusion1584½AgesAgo14733 Tired 5
15Nov75- 4Cam fm 2 13/16 S'Chase 5:301 4↑ Colonial Cup 50k 2 15 136¼ 1419 104½ 824 Quanbeck A Jr 148 -e -- Cafe Prince1603Augustus Bay162½Soothsayer162½ Outrun 18
Previously raced in name of Virginia Guest
25Oct75- 6FH sf *2 5/16 S'Chase 4:45 4↑ Handicap 10000 2 3 24 21½ 1½ 11½ Quanbeck A Jr 151 -e -- Life'sIllusion1511½CafePrince160½TallAward150½ Driving 8
1Oct75- 7Lig yl *7fⓉ 1:352 3↑ Alw 2500 7 7 107¾ 77¾ 42¼ 1hd Quanbeck A Jr 145 - -- Life'sIllusion145hdTor'sRib145nkRdGrsshoppr149½ Driving 19
13Sep75- 7Fai fm *2½ S'Chase 5:02 4↑ Grand National H 12k 7 6 62¾ 61 66 617 Quanbeck A Jr 148 2.90e -- AugustusBay1475½GranKan1551½HppyIntllctul1465 No threat 9
21Aug75- 4Sar fm 2⅜ S'Chase 4:201 4↑ NY Turf Writers Cup H 22k 5 5 42 15 11½ 1nk Quanbeck A Jr 145 2.50e -- Life'sIllusion145nkSoothsayer160½ArcticJoe1485½ Driving 9
1Aug75- 6Sar fm 2 1/16 S'Chase 3:401 4↑ Lovely Night H 22k 8 1 16 16 13 1½ Quanbeck A Jr 143 *1.80e -- Life'sIllusion143½GranKn15810Anthropologst1388¾ Driving 8
24Jun75- 4Mth fm *2⅛ S'Chase 4:221 4↑ Midsummer H 16k 5 3 34½ 919 - - Quanbeck A Jr 145 4.30e -- Chrisaway14810ArcticJo154nkJzbll'sMn1504 Saddle slipped 9
17May75- 4Mal fm *2 S'Chase 3:532 4↑ Handicap 6000 6 2 12 12½ 12 13 Quanbeck A Jr 148 - -- Life'sIllusion1483CastlebarII1554Shameca1428 Ridden out 6
3May75- 3War fm *2 S'Chase 4:36 4↑ Handicap 10000 5 1 11½ 14 21½ 25 Quanbeck A Jr 144 - -- Jezabell'sMan1435Life'sIllusion1448BlueShore1543 Tired 7
19Apr75- 4Clm fm *2 S'Chase 3:431 4↑ Handicap 10000 7 2 18 110 115 112 Quanbeck A Jr 138 - -- Life'sIllusion13812Afilador145½AlvaroII1478 Ridden out 7
29Mar75- 2Cam fm 7fⓉ 1:332 3↑ Md Sp Wt 4 6 53 43 2½ 12 Quanbeck A Jr5 145 - -- Life's Illusion1452Paulgail1331Kasai1503 Driving 9
22Mar75- 4Aik gd *1⅞ S'Chase 3:40 4↑ Handicap 7500 1 5 2½ 2hd 41½ 65 Quanbeck A Jr 142 - -- Tall Award155½Ballet Master1483Sun Sign1441 Tired 7
16Dec74- 7Aqu sly 1⅛ :49 1:142 1:382 1:504 3↑ Alw 15000 8 6 68½ 718 822 722 Smith RC 109 13.90 59-21 All Our Hopes117½Dicey1172Crag's Corner1176 Outrun 8
16Nov74- 2Cam fm *2 S'Chase 3:462 Handicap 5000 6 3 1½ 1hd 2hd 1hd Quanbeck A Jr 142 b -- Life'sIllusion142hdEarlCardign1446Fortssmo1522½ Just up 8
20Oct74- 1Lig sf *1⅝ S'Chase 3:352 3↑ Md Sp Wt 3 - 16 Quanbeck A Jr7 130 -- Life'sIllusion1306CountyFrost1334SunMeeting148½ Handily 14
Further race positions unavailable due to weather conditions
21Sep74- 2Mid fm *1⅞ S'Chase 3:364 3↑ Md Sp Wt 4 5 22 32½ 32¼ 22 Quanbeck A Jr7 136 -e -- Muller1432Life's Illusion136½Dunshaughlin153¾ Sharp 14
7Sep74- 5Fai sf *1¾ S'Chase 3:314 3↑ Md Sp Wt 12 9 75½ 62¾ 41¾ 23 Quanbeck A Jr5 132 8.00f -- Fortissimo1403Life's Illusion1321Gumersindo1532½ Gamely 14
19Aug74- 4Sar gd 1⅝ S'Chase 2:572 3↑ Md Sp Wt 3 7 67 734 648 447 Quanbeck A 135 16.10 -- MachuPicchu13815UpLikeThunder13822Darnley13810 Rallied 7

Little Current

ch. c. 1971, by Sea-Bird (Dan Cupid)–Luiana, by My Babu **Lifetime record: 16 4 3 1 $354,704**
Own.– Darby Dan Farm
Br.– John W. Galbreath (Ky)
Tr.– T.L. Rondinello

31Aug74- 8Bel sf 1½Ⓣ :49 1:153 2:084 2:35 Lawrence Realizatn-G2 1 4 55 611 613 619 Rivera MA 126 *.60 30-51 Prod1173½PrinceofReason1171½TheScotsmn117nk No excuse 7
17Aug74- 8Sar sly 1¼ :473 1:12 1:382 2:051 Travers-G1 8 10 913 76½ 44 2hd Rivera MA 126 *1.00 79-16 Holding Pattern121hdLittle Current1264½Chris Evert1212½ 11
Just missed
3Aug74- 8Mth fst 1⅛ :463 1:103 1:361 1:494 Mth Inv'l H-G1 6 9 918 813 34½ 2no Rivera MA 127 *1.00 91-11 Holding Pattern117noLittle Current1273Better Arbitor119¾ 10
Just missed
8Jun74- 8Bel fst 1½ :493 1:14 2:041 2:291 Belmont-G1 2 8 812 45 11 17 Rivera MA 126 *1.50 74-11 LittleCurrent1267JollyJohu126noCannonade126¾ Drew clear 9
18May74- 8Pim gd 1 3/16 :47 1:103 1:362 1:543 Preakness-G1 2 12 1211 105 31 17 Rivera MA 126 13.10 97-09 LittleCurrent1267NeapolitnWy1261Cnnond126¾ Steady drive 13
4May74- 8CD fst 1¼ :463 1:114 1:383 2:04 Ky Derby-G1 10 23 2122 1718 713 56½ Ussery R 126 22.60 70-15 Cannonade1262¼Hudson County1263¼Agitate126¾ Closed gap 23
25Apr74- 6Kee fst 1⅛ :463 1:103 1:363 1:491 Blue Grass-G1 7 13 1213 43 42¼ 44¼ Rivera MA 114 5.40 87-15 Judger1234Big Latch117hdGold and Myrrh114hd Rallied 14
30Mar74- 9Hia fst 1⅛ :472 1:11 1:362 1:49 Flamingo-G1 2 9 910 69½ 77¾ 44½ Cordero A Jr 122 6.30e 82-16 Bushongo1222¼Hasty Flyer1221Judger1221¼ Lacked room 10
20Mar74- 9Hia fst 1⅛ :46 1:101 1:36 1:491 Everglades-G2 9 9 912 69 31 1½ Cordero A Jr 113 3.50 86-17 Little Current113½Bushongo112hdHasty Flyer1172 Driving 11
4Mar74- 9GP fst 1⅛ :462 1:111 1:361 1:49 Florida Derby-G1 12 14 1523 1311 711 56¾ Cordero A Jr 118 11.80 82-11 Judger118¾Cannonade1225Buck's Bid118nk Bumped 16
20Feb74- 9GP fst 1 1/16 :23 :453 1:094 1:422 Fountain of Youth-G3 1 14 1425 1117 1111 64¼ Cordero A Jr 113 8.70 85-18 GreenGambados112¾Judger115¾Eric'sChamp112½ Stride late 15
6Feb74- 9GP fst 7f :221 :443 1:093 1:222 Hutcheson-G3 6 13 1317 1216 75¼ 42¾ Cordero A Jr 112 21.10 89-16 Frankie Adams1142¾[DH]Judger110[DH]Training Table113hd 13
Belated rally
5Dec73- 3Aqu fst 7f :224 :453 1:10 1:223 Md Sp Wt 11 2 107¼ 64¾ 3½ 11¾ Cordero A Jr 122 *1.70 88-11 LittleCurrnt1221¾Rube the Great1222SplittingHeadache122hd 12
Drew out
24Nov73- 2Aqu fst 6f :222 :453 1:11 ©Md Sp Wt 10 11 87¼ 67 45 22¾ Cordero A Jr 122 5.40 85-13 Nile Delta1222¾Little Current1224Whoa Boy1221 Bore in 14
8Aug73- 2Sar fst 5½f :223 :462 :592 1:061 ©Md Sp Wt 1 5 21½ 22 44½ 54¾ Cordero A Jr 119 b *2.20 81-13 Ding Dong Bell119nkLea's Pass119nkBuck Hill1191¼ Tired 9
21Jly73- 2Aqu fst 6f :23 :461 1:112 ©Md Sp Wt 4 9 1½ 11½ 11 3½ Cordero A Jr 118 b 3.00 85-14 Monsieur Lafitte118½Third Cavalry118noLittle Current118nk 10
Weakened

Mac Diarmida

dkbbr. c. 1975, by Minnesota Mac (Rough'n Tumble)–Flying Tammie, by Tim Tam **Lifetime record: 16 12 0 2 $503,184**
Own.– J.M. Torsney
Br.– John H. Hartigan (Fla)
Tr.– Flint Schulhofer

4Nov78- 8Lrl fm 1½Ⓣ :50 1:141 2:033 2:27 3↑ D C Int'l-G1 7 6 53½ 42 2hd 1hd Cruguet J 120 4.90 84-16 Mac Diarmida120hdTiller1273Waya1241½ Poor start 8
22Oct78- 7WO fm 1⅝Ⓣ :494 1:391 2:411 3↑ Can Int'l-G1 8 3 22½ 2½ 12 11½ Cruguet J 118 *1.25 94-05 Mac Diarmida1181½Dom Alaric126½Amazer1152¼ Drew clear 10
7Oct78- 8Bel yl 1⅜Ⓣ :492 1:14 1:382 2:161 3↑ Man o' War-G1 5 2 2½ 1½ 2½ 34½ Cruguet J 121 2.00 76-19 Waya1231¾Tiller1262¾Mac Diarmida1214 Used reaching lead 5
17Sep78- 8Bel gd 1½Ⓣ :483 1:131 2:012 2:271 Lawrence Realizatn-G2 7 2 21 2½ 1½ 13½ Cruguet J 123 *.50 88-11 MacDiarmida1233½NatveCourier1146½Robn'sSong1143 Easily 9
4Sep78- 8AP fm 1½Ⓣ :484 1:142 2:05 2:294 Secretariat-G2 1 4 3½ 11 12 13 Cruguet J 120 *.60 90-10 MacDiarmda1203AprilAxe1204½TheLiberalMmbr1144½ In hand 11
29Jly78- 8Bel fm 1 1/16Ⓣ :233 :46 1:103 1:41 Lexington H-G2 4 4 33 22 21 1hd Cruguet J 126 *1.00 91-11 Mac Diarmida126hdJohn Henry1124¼Ashikaga110hd In time 9
16Jly78- 9Del fm 1 1/16Ⓣ :234 :48 1:133 1:464 Leonard Richards-G3 7 7 56 31½ 1½ 13 Cruguet J 122 *.30 70-30 McDiarmda1223PrinceMisko122½StrngProposl1131¼ Handily 10
29May78- 8Mth sf 1Ⓣ :244 :493 1:153 1:421 Long Branch-G3 6 6 46 3nk 13 15 Cruguet J 124 *.50 64-36 MacDrmida1245NoonTimeSpender1182½MorningFrolic116no 8
In hand
22May78- 8Mth fm 1Ⓣ :243 :48 1:131 1:384 3↑ Alw 15000 9 8 55 22½ 1hd 13½ Cruguet J 122 *.60 81-19 Mac Diarmida1223½Prince Misko1174Silent Cal1145 Handily 9
22Apr78- 9GP fm 1 1/16Ⓣ :231 :47 1:11 1:412 Golden Grass H 32k 9 6 63 52½ 11 13½ Cruguet J 121 *1.50 94-08 MacDiarmida1213½DoubleAl1181½PrinceMisko118nk Handily 9
17Mar78- 5GP fm *1 1/16Ⓣ 1:451 Alw 8500 5 5 43½ 31 11½ 12 Cruguet J 112 *.70 81-22 Mac Diarmida1122Rough Sea1143½Fidelius11411 Easily 7
15Feb78- 7Hia fm *1⅛Ⓣ 1:491 Alw 9000 3 4 41½ 22 14 12½ Cruguet J 114 *.90 89-16 Mac Drmida1142½HurricaneDennis1144ContinentalCousin1172 10
Handily
1Feb78- 3Hia fm *1⅛Ⓣ 1:49 Md Sp Wt 2 8 65 52¼ 1hd 15 Cruguet J 120 5.80 90-05 MacDrmda1205FreetheSpirit1203½NovelNotion1202 Handily 10
18Jan78- 3Hia fst 6f :22 :45 1:092 Md Sp Wt 7 9 86¾ 811 711 815 Fell J 120 5.20 81-13 GrayWillowsAce1202WindThmUp1202SilntSunrise1204 Outrun 12
15Oct77- 3Bel sly 6f :23 :462 1:103 Md Sp Wt 8 4 43½ 47 49½ 615 Adams L 122 3.30 74-17 Shindig1224¼Bold Voyager1228Reason Not1222¼ Tired 9
1Oct77- 3Bel fst 6f :221 :461 1:122 ©Md Sp Wt 10 7 46½ 46 33 32 Adams L 122 18.80 78-14 CloudForest122hdCalligraphy1222MacDiarmida1224 Good try 12

Martie's Anger

b. g. 1975, by Spring Double (Double Jay)–Martie's Mad, by Martins Rullah — Lifetime record: 49 15 8 9 $196,990

Own.– W.L. Pape
Br.– Pape & Sheppard (Pa)
Tr.– Jonathan E. Sheppard

17Sep83- 5Lig	fm	*2½	S'Chase	5:19^4	4↑ Int'l Gold Cup 30k	1	3	2^{½}	7^{27}	-	-	Cushman J	149		-	--	SugarBee145^{1}FabulousTim149^{4}SpoutngCrqu142^5	Outrun,eased	7
14Sep83- 6Lig	fm	*7f(T)		1:32^4	3↑ Alw 1000	10	11	7^3	7^{4½}	6^3	6^8	Cushman J	144		-	--	Joe Mac142^{½}Mysterious Arthur151^{1½}Mc Adam142^{2½}		12
28May83- 5Pro	gd	*3	Hurdles	5:58^3	4↑ Hard Scuffle H 30k	2	3	4^{7½}	-	-	-	Houghton B	151		-	--	Double Reefed154^{1¾}Census148^{4}The Hall of Famer140^5	Eased	7
30Apr83- 5Fx	fm	*2¼	S'Chase	4:06^1	3↑ Alw 10000	6	4	4^{4¼}	1^{hd}	2^{nk}	2^{2½}	Cushman J	154		-	--	StoneyCreekBoy138^{2½}Martie'sAnger154^{nk}BalkanChief142^{¾}		6
16Apr83- 6SoP	fm	*1(T)		1:45	3↑ Alw 1000	5	9	8^{6½}	5^2	5^{6¾}	5^6	Cushman J	142		-	--	Caraquet142^{¾}Mc Adam142^{nk}No Picnic142^3		10
2Apr83- 5Cam	gd	*2⅛	S'Chase	4:22^3	4↑ Carolina Cup H 16k	2	4	4^{8½}	4^{11}	4^{3¼}	3^{8¾}	Stickley M	149		-	--	Hypertrophic135^{6}Turtle Head144^{2¾}Martie's Anger149^{10}		4
22Jly81- 8Del	fm	5f(T)		:22^2 :46^1 :58^3	3↑ Alw 11000	2	7	7^{11}	7^{12}	7^{11}	7^{7½}	Dufton E	117	b	6.40e	86-15	Galaxy Road112^{½}[D]Ambitious Ruler112^{1½}Never Rome117^{2½}		8
	Previously trained by Tim Forster																		
17Mar81♦ Cheltenham(GB)	hy	2LH		4:11^2	5↑ Champion Hurdle Stk87500						11	Davies BR	168		100.00		Sea Pigeon168^{1½}Pollardstown168^{nk}Daring Run168^7	Progress from 5th,bid 6th,weakened 2 out	13
26Feb81♦ Wincanton(GB)	yl	2RH		3:48^2	5↑ Kingwell Pattern Hurdle Stk11500						5^{14}	Davies BR	156		25.00		Jugador161^{hd}Gay George166^{hd}Heighlin166^4	Chased leader from third last,weakened approaching last	11
Previously trained by Jonathan Sheppard																			
16Nov80- 4Cam	fm	2¾	S'Chase	5:32^2	4↑ Colonial Cup Int 50k	2	5	3^{2½}	1^{¾}	1^{nk}	3^{½}	Quanbeck A Jr	160		-	--	Sailor'sClue151^{no}CorribChieftain162^{½}Martie'sAnger160^{1¼}		9
4Nov80- 8Aqu	sf	1⅜(T)		:51 1:18 1:44 2:23^3	3↑ Knickrbckr H (Div 2)-G3	5	2	2^1	1^{hd}	2^{hd}	4^5	Hernandez R	114	b	5.90	48-43	LobsangII111^{3}MatchtheHatch115^{2}KingCrimson111^{no}	Weakened	7
10Oct80- 6Bel	fm	2⅝	S'Chase	4:54^4	4↑ Temple Gwathmey H 43k	3	1	2^{hd}	2^{½}	2^{hd}	2^{1½}	Quanbeck A Jr	158		4.20e	--	LeapingFrog148^{1½}Martie'sAnger158^{1½}BlueNrco133^{1½}	Bobbled	7
13Sep80- 4Lig	hd	*2½	S'Chase	5:04^1	4↑ Gold Cup H 30k	2	2	3^{2¾}	3^4	1^1	1^1	Quanbeck A Jr	156		-	--	Martie's Anger156^{1}Leaping Frog150^{6}Running Comment144^8		5
14Aug80- 6Sar	fm	2⅜	S'Chase	4:14^1	4↑ NY Turf Writers H 43k	3	6	6^{10}	3^9	4^4	4^{5¾}	Quanbeck A Jr	159		1.20e	--	Zaccio157^{1¼}Running Comment142^{2¼}Leaping Frog152^{2¼}		7
1Aug80- 6Sar	gd	2$\frac{1}{16}$	S'Chase	3:45^1	4↑ Lovely Night H 43k	1	3	1^{½}	1^{½}	1^{½}	2^{1¾}	Quanbeck A Jr	160		1.60e	--	Zaccio155^{1¾}Martie'sAnger160^{1¾}LeapingFrog153^{1¼}	Bothered	8
3Jly80- 8Bel	fm	1½(T)		:50 1:16 2:05^4 2:30^3	3↑ Handicap 25000	8	4	4^{1½}	1^3	1^{½}	1^{1½}	Hernandez R	124	b	*.90e	71-24	Martie'sAngr124^{1½}PopularHero115^{6}McAdam118^{3¾}	Ridden out	9
12Jun80- 6Atl	fm	*1$\frac{1}{16}$(T)		:24^3 :49^4 1:13^3 1:46	3↑ Alw 8000	4	3	3^{nk}	1^{2½}	1^{2½}	1^2	Dufton E	114	b	*1.30	87-13	Martie's Anger114^{2}Millden114^{2½}Second Paw114^4	Driving	6
24May80- 5Pro	gd	*3	S'Chase	5:51^4	4↑ Hard Scuffle 20k	3	1	1^{½}	1^{½}	1^1	1^{1¼}	Quanbeck A Jr	151		-	--	Martie's Anger151^{1¼}Zaccio140^{5}Leaping Frog156^{16}	Driving	5
17May80- 4Mal	fm	*2	S'Chase	3:44	4↑ National Hunt Cup 7.5k	3	1	1^{½}	1^1	1^{nk}	1^{nk}	Quanbeck A Jr	159		-	--	Martie's Anger159^{nk}Obstacle147^{¾}Popular Hero145^{12}		4
27Apr80- 4Lex	yl	*2½	S'Chase	5:12^1	4↑ Pillar 17k	3	-	-	-	-	-	Quanbeck A Jr	160		-	--	Zacco148^{hd}DddyDumplng150^{18}Schollr154^{12}	Refused to break	5
12Apr80- 3SoP	fm	*2¼	S'Chase	4:21^1	4↑ Sandhills Cup 15k	1	2	2^{nk}	2^1	4^{¾}	2^1	Quanbeck A Jr	158		-e	--	Archange d'Or143^{1}Martie's Anger158^{no}Zaccio155^{¾}	Sharp	7
5Apr80- 3AtH	fm	*2	S'Chase	3:50^1	4↑ Atlanta Cup 15k	1	3	3^8	2^1	2^{½}	2no	Quanbeck A Jr	159		-	--	Winigo139^{no}Martie's Anger159^{1½}Archange d'Or140	Sharp	3
29Mar80- 4Cam	gd	*2⅛	S'Chase	4:10^4	4↑ Handicap 12500	3	7	7^9	7^{11}	4^{6½}	4^{8½}	Quanbeck A Jr	160		-	--	Zaccio152^{6}Popular Hero144^{1}Tan Jay158^{1½}	No menace	7
18Nov79- 4Cam	fm	2¾	S'Chase	5:21^4	4↑ Colonial Cup 50k	4	6	6^5	3^2	3^{½}	1^{½}	Quanbeck A Jr	151		-	--	Martie'sAnger151^{½}LeapingFrog162^{1¼}Quixotic151^{1¼}	Driving	9
27Oct79- 5FH	gd	*2$\frac{5}{16}$	S'Chase	5:08^2	4↑ Handicap 12000	6	4	3^3	2^1	3^{½}	2^{½}	Quanbeck A Jr	152		-	--	Parson'sWaiting140^{½}Mrt'sAngr152^{¾}DownFrst155^{15}	Sharp try	6
12Oct79- 6Bel	sf	2⅝	S'Chase	5:12	4↑ Temple Gwathmey H 36k	3	7	6^{7½}	5^{9½}	3^{10}	3^{13¼}	Quanbeck A Jr	152		*.90e	--	DownFirst147^{13}Parson'sWatng137^{nk}Mrt'sAngr152^{3½}	Mild bid	7
20Sep79- 8Med	fm	1$\frac{1}{16}$(T)		:23^1 :46^4 1:10^2 1:42	3↑ Alw 16000	8	8	8^{13}	7^{6¾}	4^5	1^{1½}	Hernandez R	122	b	*2.70	92-05	Martie'sAnger122^{1½}AgateBay113^{½}Mr.KnowItAll112^{½}	Driving	9
27Aug79- 2Sar	sf	1$\frac{1}{16}$(T)		:23^4 :48^1 1:13^4 1:46	3↑ Alw 17000	1	6	5^{2½}	4^2	1^{½}	1^6	Hernandez R	117	b	20.60	67-29	Mrtie'sAngr117^{6}Slammer117^{2¾}NorthernTrt112^1	Ridden out	10
20Aug79- 1Sar	gd	1½[T]		:49 1:13^2 2:04^1 2:29^1	3↑ Alw 17000	4	3	3^5	4^5	3^3	3^{6½}	Venezia M	117	b	10.30	--	BeauJohnny117^{½}Mr.Justice117^{6}Mrtie'sAngr117^{8¼}	Weakened	8
3Aug79- 6Sar	fm	2$\frac{1}{16}$	S'Chase	3:41^1	4↑ Lovely Night H 21k	2	5	5^{5½}	3^3	3^2	3^{6½}	Quanbeck A Jr	155		*.40e	--	CfePrince164^{2¾}LeapingFrog161^{3¾}Marti'sAngr155^5	Weakened	7
13Jly79- 3Del	fm	*2¼	S'Chase	4:16^2	4↑ Handicap 10000	5	3	3^6	2^4	2^2	1^{1¼}	Quanbeck A Jr	152		4.10	--	Martie'sAngr152^{1¼}DeuxCoup159^{½}StraightndTru145^7	Driving	5
7Jly79- 1Atl	fst	6f		:22^3 :46^1 1:11^3	3↑ Alw 6500	3	6	8^{15}	8^{13}	8^{13}	7^{16}	Walford J	120	b	5.00	68-19	Tom's Luck120^{5}Capt. Ridiculous114^{2}Satan's Reign116^2		8
	Altered course																		
26May79- 2Pro	fm	*2	S'Chase	3:31^4	4↑ Alw 15000	2	4	4^1	1^{nk}	1^1	1^{½}	Quanbeck A Jr	155		-	--	Martie's Anger155^{½}Winigo142^{4}Tall Award163^{nk}	Driving	9
7Apr79- 4AtH	fm	*2	S'Chase	3:51	4↑ Atlanta Cup H 12k	2	5	5^7	3^{4¼}	2^{nk}	1^{hd}	Quanbeck A Jr	149		-	--	Martie'sAngr149^{hd}Winigo138^{2½}DaddyDumpling135^{10}	Just up	5
31Mar79- 3Cam	fm	*2	S'Chase	3:41^2	4↑ Alw 6000	2	2	3^{2¼}	1^{2½}	1^{nk}	1^{2½}	Quanbeck A Jr	146		-	--	Martie'sAngr146^{2½}Underhanded150^{6}Prson'sWtng144	Driving	4
18Nov78- 1Cam	fm	*2	S'Chase	3:42^1	Handicap 7500	5	4	3^{5½}	1^{nk}	1^{nk}	1^{1¼}	Quanbeck A Jr	152		-	--	Martie'sAnger152^{1¼}BananaSplit145^{4½}LoveIn150^{13}	Driving	8
28Oct78- 3FH	fm	*2$\frac{1}{16}$	S'Chase	3:55^4	3↑ Alw 5000	1	9	8^{9½}	5^{14}	-	-	Carrier RN Jr	138		-	--	BitterEnder145^{no}Parson'sWatng144^{2}PumpknP156^{½}	Lost rider	9
4Oct78- 2Lig	gd	*1⅞	S'Chase	3:40	3↑ Md Sp Wt	4	5	5^{2½}	2^1	1^{1½}	1^5	Quanbeck A Jr	140		-	--	Martie'sAngr140^{5}Curazao155^{5}BroadwayReviwr153^{30}	In hand	7
21Sep78- 7Atl	fst	6f		:22 :45^1 1:10^1	3↑ Alw 6500	3	6	6^{5½}	4^{3½}	3^4	3^{3½}	Castaneda K	118	b	*1.80	87-18	Familyholdback115^{3}Pokeberry119^{½}Martie'sAngr118^7	Rallied	6
9Sep78- 6Atl	fm	5½f(T)		:22^2 :46^2 1:04^1	3↑ Alw 6500	2	6	6^6	5^{1¾}	4^{1¾}	2^1	Castaneda K	116	b	10.70	91-07	I Am Sure118^{1}Martie's Anger116^{7}Pokeberry120^4	Gamely	7
4Sep78- 9Bel	fm	1$\frac{1}{16}$(T)		:23^2 :46^2 1:10^4 1:42	3↑ Alw 15000	3	4	4^{3½}	6^{4¼}	9^{12}	9^{16}	Santiago A	113	b	39.20	70-12	CapePlayhous113^{6}Robin'sSong118^{nk}OneCutAbove117^{2¾}	Tired	10
22Aug78- 6Sar	fst	6f		:22^1 :45^2 1:10^3	3↑ Alw 13000	2	3	4^{8½}	4^{9½}	4^{10}	3^{9½}	Santiago A	113	b	11.20	77-20	King's Fashion114^{3½}Alra117^{6}Martie's Anger113^2	Evenly	5
14Aug78- 5Sar	fst	7f		:22^1 :44^4 1:09^3 1:23^1	3↑ Alw 13000	10	8	9^8	8^8	6^{7¼}	3^{4½}	Santiago A	117	b	36.40	84-13	WayStation117^{1½}Williamstown117^{3}Marti'sAngr117^{nk}	Rallied	11
8Aug78- 5Sar	my	1⅛		:47^2 1:12 1:37^4 1:50^3	3↑ Alw 14000	4	3	3^2	2^{hd}	4^{1½}	5^{6¾}	Santiago A	113	b	10.50	75-18	SilverThrone117^{hd}MightHaveBn112^{2¾}SuddnThw113^{1½}	Weakened	8
28Jly78- 7Atl	fst	6f		:22 :45^2 1:10^3	3↑ Alw 6500	2	8	8^{10}	8^{7¼}	6^{7¼}	2^{1¼}	Castaneda K	114	b	4.30	88-16	Holiday Crossing116^{1¼}Martie's Anger114^{4½}Tom's Luck114^{hd}		9
	Wide stretch																		
7Jly78- 1Atl	fst	6f		:22^1 :45^3 1:12^1	3↑ Md Sp Wt	3	5	6^{6½}	6^{7½}	6^{6½}	1^{½}	Pilar H	116	b	4.70	81-24	Martie's Anger116^{½}TV Pruner116^{½}Reshone116^{½}	Driving	9
21Jun78- 2Atl	fm	1(T)		:23^2 :47^1 1:11^1 1:37^2	3↑ Md Sp Wt	7	8	9^{7½}	6^{7½}	5^{12}	5^{7½}	Castaneda K	115		*2.60	76-23	Oil Barrel115^{1}Million122^{1½}Jack Frost122^3	Wide	11
10Jun78- 2Atl	fst	6f		:22^1 :46^2 1:12^2	3↑ Md Sp Wt	4	7	7^{7¾}	7^7	4^{6½}	3^3	Castaneda K	116		27.70	77-20	BayPhoto116^{2½}Richiejim111^{½}Marti'sAngr116^3	Belated rally	10
29May78- 1Fai	fm	*7f(T)		1:25^3	3↑ Md Sp Wt	10	11	13^{9½}	8^{3¼}	6^{4½}	4^{9½}	Quanbeck A Jr	142		11.20	--	Little Catworth155^{1½}Mystan142^{5}Loveable Fizz147^3	Rallied	15

My Juliet

dkbbr. f. 1972, by Gallant Romeo (Gallant Man)–My Bupers, by Bupers — Lifetime record: 36 24 4 2 $548,859

Own.– G. Weasel Jr
Br.– J.R. Bettersworth (Ky)
Tr.– Eugene Euster

24Sep77- 8Bel	sly	1⅛	:46 1:11^1 1:37^4 1:52^1	3↑ ⒻRuffian H-G1	12	1	1^{hd}	1^1	3^{½}	6^{5½}	Black AS	127		*3.50	60-25	CumLaudeLaurie114^{½}MississippiMd123^{½}Cscpd128^{1¼}	Gave way	12
3Sep77-10Det	fst	1⅛	:46 1:10^2 1:36^1 1:48^2	3↑ Mich 1⅛ H-G2	1	1	1^2	1^{1½}	1^2	1^{¾}	Black AS	112		5.20	95-26	My Juliet112^{¾}Strike Me Lucky110^{2½}On the Sly116^2	Driving	10
7Aug77- 8Del	fst	6f	:22 :44^2 1:09^3	3↑ ⒻEndine H 27k	2	2	2^1	1^1	1^{1½}	1^{1¾}	Black AS	127		*.20	97-12	My Juliet127^{1¾}Debby's Turn115^{1¾}Catabias113^5	Easily	4
16Jly77- 8Key	fst	6½f	:22 :44^2 1:08^1 1:14^3	3↑ Neshaminy H 27k	1	1	1^{½}	1^{1½}	1^2	1^{1½}	Black AS	104		*.80	104-16	My Juliet121^{1½}Raise a King119^{3½}Silver Hope120^{2½}	Driving	4
21Jun77- 8Bel	fst	6f	:22^2 :45^4 1:09^4	3↑ ⒻAlw 25000	1	4	1^1	1^2	1^2	1^{½}	Black AS	117		*.40	93-16	My Juliet117^{½}Ivory Wand115^{7}Artfully110^1	Mild drive	6
5Feb77- 8SA	fst	1$\frac{1}{16}$	:23^1 :46^2 1:10^2 1:42	4↑ ⒻS Maria H-G2	1	1	1^2	1^1	1^{1½}	5^{4¼}	Black AS	123		5.20	88-12	HailHilarious122^{hd}Swingtime120^{1¼}BastonrII126^{2¾}	Bore out	10
16Jan77- 8SA	fst	7f	:22 :44^1 1:08^2 1:21^3	4↑ San Carlos H-G2	1	4	3^{1½}	2^{½}	1^1	2^2	Black AS	123		*1.30	93-11	Uniformity115^{2}MyJulit123^{nk}MssngrofSong122^{2¾}	Drifted out	7
1Jan77- 8SA	gd	6f	:21^4 :44^3 :57 1:10^1	4↑ ⒻLas Flores H 44k	5	1	1^{hd}	1^{½}	1^{½}	1^1	Black AS	128		*.90	88-17	My Juliet128^{1}Just a Kick121^{½}Juliana F.115^{nk}	Driving	7
30Oct76- 8Aqu	fst	7f	:22^3 :44^3 1:08^3 1:21^4	3↑ Vosburgh H-G2	5	1	1^{½}	1^1	1^{3½}	1^2	Black AS	120		9.10	92-16	MyJuliet120^2[D]BoldForbes126^{1}It'sFreezng113^{2½}	Ridden out	6
23Oct76- 8Key	fst	6½f	:22^2 :45^1 1:09^4 1:16^3	3↑ ⒻDoylestown H 27k	1	1	1^1	1^2	1^6	1^2	Black AS	125		*.30	94-19	My Juliet125^{2}Kudara111^{4}Point of Balance108^2	Easily	5
11Oct76- 8Mth	fst	6f	:22^1 :45^2 1:10^3	3↑ ⒻTa Wee H 28k	9	1	1^1	1^2	1^4	1^{2¼}	Black AS	127		*.90	87-24	My Juliet127^{2¼}Regal Rumor117^{1¼}Four Bells114^2	In hand	9
1Oct76- 8Key	sly	6f	:22^2 :45^3 1:10^2	3↑ ⒻAlw 9500	2	5	1^{½}	1^{1½}	1^{1½}	1^{½}	Black AS	122		*.50	90-22	My Juliet122^{½}Foxy J.G.115^{9}Boss of the House117^{nk}	Easily	6
3May76- 8Bel	fst	7f	:22^3 :45^2 1:09^3 1:22	3↑ ⒻVagrancy H-G3	1	3	2^1	2^1	1^1	1^{1¼}	Velasquez J	127		*.70	92-17	My Juliet127^{1¼}Shy Dawn119^{1¾}Kudara116^{1¾}	Drew clear	5
17Apr76- 8Pim	fm	1$\frac{1}{16}$(T)	:24 :47^3 1:11^2 1:42^1	3↑ ⒻGallorette H (Div 2)-G3	2	1	2^{hd}	6^4	8^{13}	8^{30}	Passmore WJ	127		*2.60	70-00	Deesse du Val119^{nk}Summertime Promise117^{3½}Jbot114^{nk}		9
	Bobbled																	
31Mar76- 8Aqu	fst	7f	:23^1 :46 1:09^3 1:21^4	4↑ ⒻHandicap 25000	4	1	1^{1½}	1^2	1^2	1^{1½}	Velasquez J	126		*.50	92-15	My Juliet126^{1½}Let Me Linger116^{1¼}Land Girl114^{2¾}	Easily	5
10Jan76- 8SA	fst	7f	:22 :44^3 1:08^3 1:21^1	Malibu-G2	1	4	1^{½}	1^{½}	1^{2½}	3^3	McHargue DG	115		6.10	94-15	Forceten123^{1¼}MssengrofSong120^{1¾}MyJuliet115^3	Weakened	8

Date	Cond	Dist	Fractions	Race	Running line	Jockey	Wt	Odds	Spd	Finishers	Comment	Field
10Dec75- 8Aqu	my	1	:224 :453 1:103 1:353	(F)Next Move H 56k	3 1 1hd 1½ 13 1¾	McHargue DG	125	*1.50	88-19	MyJuliet125¾Channelett117nkSprngIsHr1136¼	Brisk urging	7
15Nov75- 8Lrl	fst	1	:23 :454 1:111 1:364	(F)Anne Arundel H 33k	5 1 11 12 12 1½	McHargue DG	123	*.70	89-20	My Juliet123½Funny Cat114½Gala Lil1191½	Driving	6
1Nov75- 8Mth	fst	1 70	:231 :46 1:101 1:402	(F)Sea Bright H 28k	2 1 24 2hd 11 42½	Turcotte R L	125	*.80	93-16	Funny Cat1111Vivacious Meg115¾Jolly Song114¾	Weakened	10
18Oct75- 8Mth	sly	6f	:214 :444 1:104	(F)Fair Haven H 27k	1 1 11 1½ 13½ 1½	Turcotte RL	123	*.80	86-24	MyJuliet1231½-ingMiss1152BeyondReasoning1162	Easily	7
Previously trained by L.G. Ripley												
16Aug75- 8Key	sly	1 1/16	:224 :454 1:103 1:433	(F)Cotillion-G2	3 2 25 1½ 12 1nk	Brumfield D	116	*2.00	86-18	My Juliet116nkHot n Nasty1164¼Gala Lil1182	Driving	7
30Jly75- 8Sar	fst	7f	:223 :451 1:091 1:22	(F)Test (Div 2)-G3	5 1 11½ 11½ 12 12½	Velasquez J	116	*1.20	95-14	MyJuliet1162½SlipScreen113hd[D]FltVctrss113nk	Ridden out	7
Previously trained by S.A. Long												
28Jun75- 7Aks	fst	1 1/16	:223 :46 1:102 1:43	Omaha Gold Cup 106k	11 1 1½ 11 1hd 22	Hill A	119	7.50	89-12	Gray Bar1142My Juliet119nkMaster Derby1261	Game try	11
20Jun75- 7Aks	fst	6f	:212 :443 1:111	(F)Princess 20k	5 1 2½ 22 2hd 11½	Hill A	121	*.70	81-24	My Juliet1211½The Rage1182Bold and Modest1181½	Driving	6
7Jun75- 8CD	fst	7f	:23 :454 1:104 1:24	(F)Dogwood 23k	6 1 11½ 11½ 11½ 12½	Hill A	121	*.80	87-14	My Juliet1212½Snow Doll1181¾Hope She Does1184¼	In hand	9
29May75- 8Mth	fst	6f	:203 :43 1:09	(F)Miss Woodford 28k	12 1 1hd 13½ 1hd 54	Hill A	121	*2.00	91-08	Stulcer119hdA Charm115noStream Across1192	Hard used	12
16May75- 8Pim	fst	1 1/16	:234 :473 1:123 1:44	(F)Black-Eyed Susan-G3	5 1 13 12 14 14	Hill A	116	14.10	85-24	My Juliet1164Gala Lil1141¾Funalon1213	In hand	6
2May75- 8CD	fst	1 1/16	:232 :463 1:12 1:443	(F)Ky Oaks-G2	10 2 13 12 1½ 45¼	Hill A	121	29.10	80-20	Sun and Snow121nkFunalon1214½Funny Cat121½	Weakened	11
26Apr75- 8CD	fst	7f	:233 :463 1:114 1:253	(F)La Troienne 21k	2 2 12 11 21½ 34	Hill A	121	1.70	75-21	High Estimate121½Hoso1213½My Juliet1211½	Weakened	6
12Apr75- 7Kee	fst	*7f	1:263	(F)Ashland-G3	6 1 12 11 11½ 2hd	Hill A	116	*1.30	90-17	SunandSnow116hdMyJuliet1163½RedCross1143	Just failed	8
5Apr75- 6Kee	fst	6f	:211 :433 :563 1:103	(F)Alw 12500	1 3 11½ 12 11½ 12	Hill A	123	3.20	89-17	My Juliet1232Red Cross1142½Sun and Snow1203½	Hard drive	8
28Nov74- 8CD	fst	7f	:231 :461 1:104 1:233	(F)Pocahontas 24k	9 1 13 11 1½ 1¾	Hill A	121	*1.10	89-21	My Juliet121¾Channelette1158Yale Coed1213½	Handily	12
Previously owned by R.R. Ladd												
20Nov74- 8CD	fst	6f	:214 :452 :572 1:111	(F)Alw 10000	1 2 14 13 14 14	Hill A	116	4.30	90-20	My Juliet1164Miss Cabildo1161¼Yale Coed119nk	Easily	7
23Oct74- 7Spt	fst	6f	:224 :464 1:124	Alw 7500	4 4 13½ 11½ 12 13	Hill A	112	*1.40	87-15	MyJuliet1123TudorPoint1132¾GeneralDiplomat119hd	Driving	7
16Oct74- 3Haw	fst	6f	:222 :46 1:102	Md Sp Wt	7 3 11½ 13 13 16	Hill A	120	14.80	94-13	My Juliet1206Pink Paint120noSherburne1207	Easily	9
Previously trained by R.R. Ladd												
2Apr74- 3Fon	fst	4f	:473	(F)Md Sp Wt	5 3 1½ 1hd 2hd	Orona W	115	9.40	91-09	Bold and Modest115hdMy Juliet1152Political Party1187½		10

Numbered Account

b. f. 1969, by Buckpasser (Tom Fool)–Intriguing, by Swaps **Lifetime record: 22 14 3 2 $607,048**

Own.– O. Phipps
Br.– Ogden Phipps (Ky)
Tr.– R. Laurin

Date	Cond	Dist	Fractions	Race	Running line	Jockey	Wt	Odds	Spd	Finishers	Comment	Field
14May73- 7Bel	fst	7f	:23 :462 1:101 1:223	3↑ (F)Vagrancy H-G3	7 8 52¾ 62¼ 2hd 2nk	Vasquez J	120 b	*1.20	94-08	Krislin113nkNumbered Account120½Fairway Flyer115nk		8
Bold finish,just missed												
28Apr73- 7Aqu	gd	1⅛	:473 1:111 1:354 1:481	3↑ (F)Top Flight H-G1	5 5 53 53¾ 48½ 48½	Pincay L Jr	121 b	1.90	86-14	Poker Night1104Summer Guest123hdRoba Bella1134½	Tired	7
18Apr73- 7Aqu	fst	1	:232 :452 1:10 1:352	3↑ (F)Bed o' Roses H-G2	3 5 611 56½ 34 21½	Pincay L Jr	123 b	*.30	88-15	PokerNight1081½NumberedAccount123½Ferly1144	No excuse	6
6Apr73- 7Aqu	fst	6f	:222 :454 1:094	3↑ (F)Alw 15000	3 2 45½ 32 12 16	Vasquez J	121 b	*.30	94-16	NumbrdAccnt1216PasdNom112noPop'sPck113hd	Ridden out	6
27Oct72- 6Kee	fst	1⅛	:452 1:101 1:35 1:472	3↑ (F)Spinster 59k	2 5 511 55½ 22 12¼	Pincay L Jr	119 b	2.50	100-15	NumberedAccnt1192¼ChouCroute1231½BarlyEvn1198	Handily	7
9Oct72- 8Atl	fst	1 3/16	:464 1:104 1:373 1:573	3↑ (F)Matchmaker 50k	8 8 611 58½ 31½ 2½	Pincay L Jr	115 b	*1.70	87-22	[D]AlmaNrth115½NumbrdAccount115½Honstous1105	In close	8
Placed first through disqualification												
9Sep72- 7Bel	fst	1⅛	:46 1:102 1:35 1:472	3↑ (F)Beldame 112k	2 6 66¼ 31½ 42½ 55¼	Cordero A Jr	118 b	3.90	92-06	Susan'sGirl1181SummerGust1181ChouCrout1233¼	Speed,tired	9
30Aug72- 7Bel	fst	1	:23 :454 1:10 1:353	3↑ (F)Maskette H 27k	3 4 32½ 11 13½ 1¾	Cordero A Jr	115 b	*.50	94-11	NumbrdAccnt115¾Mnt1121Aldncr114½	Stumbled start,driving	4
13Aug72- 8Del	fst	1¼	:464 1:104 1:352 2:003	3↑ (F)Delaware H 114k	7 3 33 21½ 23 34	Cordero A Jr	115 b	*.90	95-09	BlessngAnglica1143¼Grftt113¾NumbrdAccnt1154	Weakened	8
31Jly72- 7Sar	fst	7f	:232 :461 1:103 1:234	(F)Test 27k	3 3 34½ 2½ 1½ 11	Vasquez J	121 b	*.60	88-13	Numbered Account1211LightHearted118¾CandidCathrne1211½		6
Driving												
3May72- 7Aqu	fst	7f	:23 :452 1:09 1:213	(F)Comely 27k	2 5 57½ 57½ 35 2no	Baeza B	121 b	*.20	93-15	Staceyd'Ette115noNumberedAccnt1211¼CandidCathrne1184½		5
Bore in												
19Apr72- 7Aqu	fst	6f	:22 :451 1:10	(F)Prioress 27k	2 4 54 11 13 12½	Baeza B	121 b	*.10	93-14	NumbrdAccount1212½MindyMalone121¾IMove1211½	Handily	6
13Nov71- 8GS	fst	1 1/16	:232 :47 1:113 1:433	Garden State 293k	4 7 44½ 46½ 42 44½	Baeza B	119 b	2.30	82-19	Riva Ridge122½Freetex122nkKey to the Mint1221¾	Evenly	8
6Nov71- 8GS	gd	1 1/16	:234 :474 1:13 1:454	(F)Gardenia 184k	7 7 76 25 2hd 12¾	Baeza B	119 b	*.30	76-28	Numbered Account1192¾Susan'sGirl1196CatmousamRoad1196		11
Ridden out												
23Oct71- 0Lrl	fst	1 1/16	:24 :481 1:13 1:442	(F)Selima 124k	4 3 2hd 1½ 14 16	Baeza B	122 b	-e	91-17	NumberedAccount1226Susceptible119noFarwyFlyr1199	Easily	5
No wagering												
11Oct71- 7Bel	fst	1	:231 :461 1:104 1:353	(F)Frizette 135k	1 4 41 13 16 17	Baeza B	119 b	*.40	95-16	NumbrdAccount1197Susan'sGirl1195BarlyEvn11920	Handily	4
25Sep71- 7Bel	fst	6f	:222 :46 1:102	(F)Matron 105k	2 6 44 21 13 16½	Baeza B	119 b	*.20e	95-10	NumbrdAccnt1196½SteppingHigh119½Informtv119nk	Mild drive	8
25Aug71- 7Sar	fst	6f	:221 :451 1:094	(F)Spinaway 87k	3 5 35½ 32½ 21½ 12½	Baltazar C	119	*1.10	97-12	Numbrd Account1192½Rondeau1191½Debby Deb1192	Driving	7
16Aug71- 7Sar	fst	6f	:222 :454 1:101	(F)Adirondack 34k	8 6 62½ 3nk 31 31½	Baltazar C	122	*.90	93-12	DebbyDeb1141½DancePartner114noNmberdAccnt122nk	Wide	9
4Aug71- 7Sar	my	6f	:22 :462 1:123	(F)Schuylerville 33k	3 3 35 32½ 2½ 11	Baeza B	119	*.20	83-17	Numbered Account1191Bendara1145Vichy1146	Mild drive	4
Previously trained by E.A. Neloy												
19May71- 7Aqu	fst	5f	:22 :452 :572	(F)Fashion 33k	1 5 59½ 57½ 34 13	Baeza B	116	*.60	98-15	Numbered Account1163Rondeau116hdBendara1168	Driving	7
14May71- 3Aqu	fst	5f	:23 :461 :581	(F)Md Sp Wt	1 2 21½ 2½ 14 110	Baeza B	119	*.30e	94-24	NumbrdAccnt11910BrendaBeauty1191MdmRoyl119½	Handily	9

Office Queen

dkbbr. f. 1967, by Fair Ruler (Nasrullah)–Determine Gal, by Determine **Lifetime record: 39 16 6 8 $385,689**

Own.– S.A. Calder
Br.– Ocala Stud Farms Inc (Fla)
Tr.– B. Lepman

Date	Cond	Dist	Fractions	Race	Running line	Jockey	Wt	Odds	Spd	Finishers	Comment	Field
10Jly71- 8Mth	fst	1 1/16	:23 :454 1:102 1:424	3↑ (F)Molly Pitcher 46k	2 5 57½ 45½ 46½ 513	Baltazar C	123	*2.30e	78-16	DoubleDlta1218½CathyHoney118noPeacfulUnon1132	No rally	13
26Jun71- 6Lib	fst	1	:224 :462 1:103 1:36	3↑ (F)Whtemrsh H (Div 1) 22k	1 1 1hd 21 33½ 35	Rivera M	126	*1.40	93-12	DoubleDelta1181½Glenary1143½Office Queen1262	Weakened	9
4Jun71- 8Mth	fm	1 1/16(T)	:232 :47 1:113 1:432	4↑ (F)Alw 12000	5 2 2hd 1½ 13 32	Blum W	122	*1.10	95-08	Evening Bag1172Ziba Blue117hdOffice Queen122¾	Weakened	10
22May71- 7Aqu	fst	1⅛	:471 1:122 1:37 1:493	3↑ (F)Top Flight H 53k	1 2 2hd 3½ 21 32	Baltazar C	127	3.40	86-17	Shuvee127¾Cathy Honey1181¼Office Queen1277	No mishap	5
28Apr71- 7Aqu	fst	1	:232 :464 1:113 1:364	3↑ (F)Bed o' Roses H 32k	3 1 1½ 1½ 11½ 12	Baltazar C	125	6.30	83-23	Office Queen1252Shuvee1273Royal Fillet1103½	Handily	6
17Apr71- 8Bow	fst	7f	:23 :46 1:11 1:233	3↑ (F)Barbara Fritchie H 59k	4 6 72¾ 85½ 75¼ 65½	Broussard R	126	*1.20e	81-23	Cold Comfort1142½Take Warning110½Double Delta117nk	Dull	10
10Apr71- 7Bow	fst	6f	:221 :451 1:112	3↑ (F)Alw 10000	9 1 53 52 3nk 11½	Broussard R	123	2.90	89-23	OfficeQueen1231½ProcessShot1232Sally'sTruce1161	Driving	9
24Mar71- 9GP	fm	1 1/16(T)	:223 :453 1:094 1:413	3↑ (F)Orchid H 46k	10 3 34½ 31½ 1hd 64¼	Cordero A Jr	124	*2.10	92-10	Swoon'sFlowr1152½StolnBase115¾ToterBack1121	Weakened	10
3Mar71- 7Hia	hd	1⅛(T)	1:482	4↑ (F)Alw 12000	5 1 11 1hd 2½ 1½	Baltazar C	121	2.80	96-06	OfficeQn121½TopRound1182½SignoftheTimes112no	Driving	8
9Feb71- 8Hia	fst	6f	:222 :461 1:103	4↑ (F)Alw 10000	2 3 41½ 22 2½ 1¾	Baltazar C	113	*1.00	91-17	OfficeQn113¾RomanConsort113½DorothyJon1131½	Cleverly	8
19Oct70- 8GS	fst	1⅛	:462 1:103 1:362 1:491	3↑ (F)Vineland H 59k	9 3 43½ 31 3nk 62½	Baltazar C	119	3.80	88-12	CathyHney113¾DarkEmrld1111DedicatdtoSu116no	Weakened	10
3Oct70- 8Atl	fst	1 3/16	:47 1:111 1:364 1:562	3↑ (F)Matchmaker 50k	2 4 46½ 55 45 46½	Baltazar C	121	*2.70	87-15	DedicatedtoSue1131½ColdComfort1085[D]Helen Jennings115no		10
Placed third through disqualification												
23Sep70- 8Atl	fst	1⅛	:484 1:13 1:381 1:503	3↑ (F)Alw 8000	6 3 3½ 2hd 1½ 11¾	Baltazar C	119	*1.00	85-20	OfficeQueen1191¾FastAttack1091HelenJennings1233	Handily	9
29Aug70- 8Atl	fm	1 1/16(T)	:24 :481 1:123 1:444	(F)Pageant H (Div 2) 22k	8 4 3½ 2hd 1hd 4nk	Blum W	123	*1.40	82-17	ApplePrincess112noToterBack111noSweetMist115hd	Faltered	8
15Aug70- 6Sar	fst	1¼	:481 1:122 1:373 2:034	(F)Alabama 59k	7 4 44½ 32 23 33¼	Rotz JL	124	4.10	86-10	Fanfrelche1181¼Hunnemannia1142OfficeQn124½	Weakened	12
8Aug70- 7Lib	fst	1 1/16	:232 :464 1:112 1:44	(F)Cotillion H 57k	1 2 21 11 11½ 1½	Rotz JL	123	*1.00	86-07	Office Queen123½Ellen Girl117½Fast Attack1162½	Driving	10
25Jly70- 8Del	fst	1⅛	:453 1:10 1:363 1:494	(F)Del Oaks 60k	11 7 78 85½ 62½ 21¾	Marquez CH	121	*1.00	86-11	VirgniaCrackr1111¾OffcQn121½LumnousLgoon1111	Roughed	12
11Jly70- 8Mth	fst	1⅛	:464 1:111 1:37 1:502	(F)Mth Oaks 57k	7 4 65¼ 31 1hd 31½	Marquez CH	121	*2.30	90-17	Kilts n Kapers116½Sweet Mist1141Office Queen1214	Wide	9

Date	Trk	Dist	Fractions	Race	PP	St	1C	2C	Str	Fin	Jockey	Wt	Eq	Odds	Spd	Top finishers	Comment	Fld
27Jun70-8Mth	gd	1 70	:24 :482 1:124 1:422	ⒻPost-Deb (Div 2) 22k	2	2	1½	13	13	12	Marquez CH	119		*.50	89-20	OfficeQn1192PowdrMountn1136Shp'sChnnl113½	Mild drive	8
20Jun70-7Bel	fst	1¼	:463 1:113 1:38 2:034	ⒻC C A Oaks 133k	7	1	18	13	34	410	Marquez CH	121		2.60	71-17	MissileBelle1211CathyHoney1217KiltsnKprs1212	Rank early	7
29May70-7Bel	fst	1⅛	:444 1:101 1:361 1:494	ⒻMother Goose 119k	3	2	21	1½	12	1¾	Marquez CH	121		6.30	87-14	OfficeQueen121¾CathyHoney1212MissileBelle1215	Driving	16
15May70-8Pim	fst	1 1/16	:232 :47 1:111 1:434	ⒻBlack-Eyed Susan 34k	9	2	21½	2½	2hd	1hd	Marquez CH	118		*2.70	91-11	OfficQun118hdPrncssRoycrft1162½ArtstsProof1161½	Just up	11
6May70-7Aqu	fst	7f	:224 :461 1:11 1:24	ⒻComely (Div 2) 23k	6	1	1hd	2hd	21	21	Marquez CH	118		*1.40	80-17	Royal Signal1181Office Queen1181½Luci Tee1123½	Gamely	8
20Apr70-8GS	sly	6f	:224 :46 1:111	ⒻB Ross H (Div 2) 22k	5	2	2hd	32½	31½	1hd	Marquez CH	124		*1.00	88-17	OfficeQueen124hdLadySadie1153DelayedDelvry113no	Driving	7
7Apr70-6GP	fst	6f	:223 :461 1:114	ⒻAlw 7500	2	2	1hd	11½	13	13	Perret C	122		*.50e	85-19	Office Queen1223Dorothy Jean1071Lady Sadie117no	Handily	7
12Mar70-8SA	fst	1 1/16	:231 :463 1:103 1:421	ⒻS Susana 45k	5	3	42½	42¼	44½	56¾	Rotz JL	115		3.00	85-12	OpenngBd1153½CthyHny1153¼Turn'nTurnAbt115½	No mishap	11
23Feb70-8Hia	fst	7f	:232 :462 1:103 1:24	ⓈFla Breeders H 31k	5	3	32½	32½	32	2no	Rotz JL	122		*1.30	88-12	Joe Namath110noOffice Queen122nkIron Warrior118¾	Missed	9
28Jan70-8Hia	fst	7f	:23 :453 1:104 1:234	ⒻMimosa 35k	4	6	2hd	1½	13	18	Rotz JL	116		*1.40e	89-18	Office Queen1168Devilish Angel114¾Tsip115nk	In hand	16
17Jan70-8Hia	sly	6f	:223 :46 1:111	ⒻJasmine (Div 2) 25k	6	5	31½	31	1½	12	Rotz JL	116		*2.00	88-14	OfficeQueen1162Attil'sHony114hdDvlshAngl114no	Lost whip	8
8Nov69-8GS	gd	1 1/16	:231 :474 1:124 1:461	ⒻGardenia 200k	4	1	1hd	1hd	2hd	3nk	Baltazar C	119		11.90	74-26	Fast Attack119hdSunny Sal119hdOffice Queen119hd	Gamely	11
25Oct69-8Lrl	fst	1 1/16	:23 :462 1:114 1:431	ⒻSelima 122k	9	1	1hd	1hd	1½	24	Baltazar C	119		3.40	94-09	Predictable1194Office Queen119½Sweet Mist1191½	Weakened	10
11Oct69-8Atl	fst	7f	:222 :452 1:104 1:241	ⒻMermaid 29k	6	5	1hd	1hd	11½	12	Marquez CH	114		4.50e	82-18	Office Queen1142Sweet Mist113hdBundestag112¾	Driving	11
20Aug69-5Atl	sly	6f	:223 :463 1:114	ⒻAlw 5000	4	3	1hd	1hd	14	17	Marquez CH	120		*1.10	83-22	OfficeQn1207Boatswain'sMate118½PromisYou114hd	Easily	9
13Aug69-6Atl	fst	6f	:222 :454 1:113	ⒻAlw 5000	5	4	31	42½	23	23½	Broussard R	120		*1.00e	80-20	Scamtan1203½OfficeQueen120¾SuretoShow114½	Held gamely	8
6Aug69-6Mth	fst	5½f	:222 :463 :592 1:061	ⒻAlw 7000	7	3	32½	33	32	45¼	Marquez CH	119		*.80	81-19	Dowitcher1162¾Sure to Show1161½Stepolina1161	Tired	8
25Jly69-5Mth	gd	5½f	:223 :462 :593 1:061	ⒻMd Sp Wt	4	1	3nk	34	21½	14½	Marquez CH	117		1.90	86-24	OfficeQn1174½PleasureGame1176RoughJad1172	Ridden out	9
		Previously trained by R.N. Guerini																
28Feb69-3Hia	fst	3f	:223 :341	ⒻMd Sp Wt	3	4			1½	21	Saumell F	116		8.10	- -	Bushel Basket1161Office Queen1161¼Karen H.116no	Gamely	14
18Feb69-3Hia	fst	3f	:22 :331	ⒻMd Sp Wt	1	6			21½	33¼	Saumell F	116		26.30	- -	Canaveral1161¼Sun Lover1162Office Queen116no	Gamely	14
13Feb69-3Hia	fst	3f	:221 :333	ⒻMd Sp Wt	7	7			77¼	64¼	Saumell F	116		24.90	- -	Bzz-Bzz1161Karen H.116nkMulberry Bush1161	No mishaps	13

Our Mims

b. f. 1974, by Herbager (Vandale)–Sweet Tooth, by On-and-On

Lifetime record: 18 6 6 1 $368,034

Own.– Calumet Farm
Br.– Calumet Farm (Ky)
Tr.– John M. Veitch

Date	Trk	Dist	Fractions	Race	PP	St	1C	2C	Str	Fin	Jockey	Wt	Eq	Odds	Spd	Top finishers	Comment	Fld
4Jly78-7Bel	sly	7f	:224 :46 1:113 1:25	3↑ⒻAlw 30000	3	4	32½	36	21	12¾	Velasquez J	122		*.30	77-13	Our Mims1222¾Mimi Rose115½Sans Arc1152¾	Drew off	5
4Sep77-8Del	fst	1¼	:482 1:122 1:37 2:01	3↑ⒻDelaware H-G1	3	5	58	32½	32	1no	Velasquez J	117		*1.60	97-12	OurMims117noMississippiMud1242¼Dottie'sDoll1188	Driving	5
13Aug77-8Sar	fst	1¼	:492 1:132 1:372 2:03	ⒻAlabama-G1	11	4	33	21	2hd	1nk	Velasquez J	121		5.70	86-13	OurMms121nkSensationl1211¾CumLaudeLaurie121hd	Driving	11
23Jly77-8Bel	fst	1½	:49 1:124 2:023 2:261	3↑Brooklyn H-G1	7	7	1hd	76½	612	618	Velasquez J	110		8.80	71-17	GreatContractr1121Forego137nkAmrcnHstory112¾	Weakened	13
2Jly77-8Bel	fst	1½	:474 1:114 2:033 2:292	ⒻC C A Oaks-G1	3	7	715	1½	13	12½	Velasquez J	121		8.80	73-18	Our Mims1212½Road Princess121½Fia121hd	Driving	12
11Jun77-6Bel	my	1⅛	:461 1:11 1:361 1:484	ⒻMother Goose-G1	2	5	53½	33	65½	68¼	Vasquez J	121	b	14.80	75-17	RoadPrncss1211¾Mrs.Wrrn1212¾CmLdLaurie121nk	Weakened	16
28May77-8Bel	fst	1	:231 :462 1:112 1:364	ⒻAcorn-G1	3	3	31½	42	33½	44¾	Vasquez J	121	b	9.00	79-22	BringouttheBand1213½YourPlaceorMine1211¼Mrs.Warrn121no	Weakened	11
6May77-8CD	fst	1 1/16	:233 :464 1:11 1:433	ⒻKy Oaks-G2	1	7	66½	54	65½	22½	Turcotte R	121	b	6.70	87-17	SweetAlliance1212½OurMms1211Mrs.Wrrn1211¼	Finished well	12
23Apr77-7Kee	sly	*7f	1:264	ⒻAshland-G3	6	5	34	35½	44	38½	Turcotte R	118	b	4.30	80-19	SoundofSummer1184½Mrs.Warren1214OurMims1183	Evenly	9
26Mar77-9OP	fst	1 1/16	:23 :463 1:12 1:45	ⒻFantasy-G2	15	4	33	32½	21	1nk	Brumfield D	112	b	8.60	83-20	OurMims112nkSweetAlliance118hdMeteorDancer1106	Driving	15
10Mar77-8Hia	sly	7f	:233 :462 1:101 1:223	ⒻAlw 5500	7	11	61½	3½	1hd	14	Brumfield D	114	b	*2.10	92-14	OurMims1144[D]LikelyExchange1142½LaLonja114¾	Mild drive	12
20Nov76-8Aqu	fst	1⅛	:464 1:12 1:374 1:504	ⒻDemoiselle-G2	7	4	43½	41	21½	2no	Maple E	113		12.80	81-17	BringouttheBand116noOurMims113nkRoadPrincss112nk	Sharp	12
8Nov76-8Aqu	fst	1	:241 :481 1:132 1:393	ⒻTempted 37k	6	3	43½	33½	24	23	Maple E	113		17.10	65-27	PearlNcklace1143OurMims1133RoadPrncss113no	Second best	10
23Oct76-1Bel	fst	6f	:231 :472 1:123	ⒻMd Sp Wt	3	5	33	44	35	25	Vasquez J	119		*.60	74-18	Bagiorix1195OurMms1191½AffctionateOne119no	Second best	7
16Jun76-8Bel	fst	5½f	:223 :462 :59 1:054	ⒻFashion 38k	1	5	66	56	45	33	Vasquez J	113		5.90	83-21	Drama Critic1132¾Sly Grin119nkOur Mims113nk	Rallied	7
		Disqualified from purse money																
4Jun76-3Bel	fst	5½f	:231 :454 :583 1:052	ⒻMd Sp Wt	9	7	52¼	44	43½	2¾	Turcotte R	119		7.10	87-16	Tickle My Toes119¾OurMims1191½BonnieEmpress1191½	Wide	10
17May76-4Bel	fst	5½f	:23 :463 :59 1:051	ⒻMd Sp Wt	4	5	42½	54½	44¼	45	Velasquez J	119		*2.20	84-14	Miss Medurable1191Din1191¾Spontaneous1192¼	Weakened	8
		Previously trained by R. Cornell																
9Apr76-3GP	fst	5f	:231 :481 1:01	ⒻMd Sp Wt	4	11	95	88¼	76¼	2¾	Castaneda M	119		3.00	80-25	SaxonyMiss119¾OurMims119noBrookward119½	Sluggish early	11

Personality

b. c. 1967, by Hail to Reason (Turn-to)–Affectionately, by Swaps

Lifetime record: 25 8 4 2 $462,603

Own.– Ethel D. Jacobs
Br.– Bieber–Jacobs Stable (Ky)
Tr.– J.W. Jacobs

Date	Trk	Dist	Fractions	Race	PP	St	1C	2C	Str	Fin	Jockey	Wt	Eq	Odds	Spd	Top finishers	Comment	Fld
31May71-7Bel	fst	1	:221 :443 1:092 1:354	3↑Metropolitan H 121k	15	7	88¼	1217	1113	1111¼	Woodhouse R	125	b	7.90	83-10	Tunex113noProtanto1121KnightnArmor114hd	Fell back early	17
22May71-6Aqu	fst	6f	:222 :453 1:094	3↑Alw 15000	1	8	812¼	213¼	815	59½	Belmonte E	117	b	2.20	84-17	Duck Dance1157Prize Silver1191½Happy Harmony115hd		8
		Passed tired horses																
10Apr71-7Aqu	fst	1⅛	:454 1:111 1:38 1:504	3↑Excelsior H 57k	5	5	59¾	51¼	2hd	21½	Belmonte E	126	b	*2.30	80-23	Loud1161½Personality126noKnight in Armor1103	No match	9
3Apr71-8Bow	fst	1 1/16	:232 :471 1:121 1:443	3↑J B Campbell H 115k	8	6	109	911	811	68½	Belmonte E	125	b	*1.10	76-24	Bushido1141½Never Bow1201½True North1205	Brushed	10
13Mar71-7Aqu	fst	6f	:221 :45 1:094	3↑Paumonok H 33k	2	7	67¾	65¾	52½	3nk	Belmonte E	125	b	*2.10	94-17	Forum112noEstimator Dave111nkPersonality1251¼	Wide	8
29Jan71-8Hia	fst	7f	:233 :462 1:104 1:232	4↑Alw 10000	7	3	23	23	22	2¾	Belmonte E	122	b	*.60	90-17	GleamingLight119¾Personality1221CoaltownCt119½	Bore out	8
30Oct70-7Bel	fst	1¼	:462 1:101 1:353 2:014	3↑Woodward 109k	4	1	11	1½	11½	1nk	Belmonte E	121	b	*1.20	91-08	Personlity121nk[DH]Hydrologist126[DH]Twogundn1264½	Driving	7
21Sep70-7Bel	fst	1¼	:464 1:103 1:353 2:004	3↑Stymie H 27k	4	2	23	1hd	1½	2½	Belmonte E	120	b	2.60	95-12	Hydrologist118½Personality1201Judgable1171	Gamely	5
7Sep70-7Bel	fst	1⅛	:452 1:091 1:343 1:48	3↑Gov Nicolls 116k	4	8	98½	107¼	66½	52¼	Belmonte E	123	b	*2.90	92-09	Distinctive119½Hydrologist117½Plymouth110no	No threat	13
22Aug70-6Sar	fst	1¼	:47 1:103 1:354 2:01	Travers 112k	2	3	21½	21½	31	42	Pincay L Jr	126	b	2.10e	101-07	Loud114nkJudgable1171¾Plymouth114hd	Weakened	9
14Aug70-7Sar	fst	1	:23 :453 1:102 1:354	Jim Dandy 30k	1	2	1½	11½	1hd	1hd	Pincay L Jr	126	b	*.70	95-11	Personality126hdLoud1143Plymouth1144	Driving	8
24Jly70-7Aqu	fst	7f	:223 :442 1:09 1:222	3↑Alw 15000	4	2	23	26	24	2nk	Belmonte E	117	b	*.80	89-15	BoldFavorite119nkPrsonlty117hdBllBolnd107nk	Just missed	5
30May70-8GS	fst	1⅛	:462 1:102 1:352 1:481	Jersey Derby 128k	4	5	51¾	3½	3nk	11½	Belmonte E	126		*1.20e	96-10	Personality1261¼CornofftheCob1262½SlntScrn1262¾	Driving	8
16May70-8Pim	fst	1 3/16	:464 1:104 1:363 1:561	Preakness 203k	2	5	65	21½	2hd	1nk	Belmonte E	126	b	4.50e	92-16	Personality126nkMyDadGeorge1263SilentScreen1262	Driving	14
2May70-9CD	gd	1¼	:464 1:12 1:372 2:032	Ky Derby 170k	16	7	914	98½	814	812	Belmonte E	126	b	4.90e	71-16	DustCommanr1265MyDadGrg126½HghEchln126hd	No threat	17
18Apr70-7Aqu	fst	1⅛	:472 1:114 1:364 1:492	Wood Memorial 117k	8	5	31	3nk	1hd	1¾	Belmonte E	126	b	3.10e	89-19	Personality126¾SilentScreen126hdDelawareChf1262	Driving	14
11Apr70-6Aqu	fst	7f	:223 :452 1:103 1:231	Alw 9000	9	9	811	64½	12	15	Belmonte E	122	b	*2.30	85-18	Personality1225TallFellow108nkPrimeVenture117nk	Easily	10
4Apr70-7Aqu	fst	1	:23 :453 1:101 1:361	Gotham 58k	5	3	31½	31	44	42¾	Belmonte E	114	b	4.40e	83-20	NativeRoyalty114hdDelawareChief114¾SilentScrn1262	Tired	8
21Mar70-7Aqu	gd	7f	:232 :464 1:12 1:241	Bay Shore 29k	1	9	106¾	95¼	65½	49½	Belmonte E	112	b	3.00	70-25	SunnyTim1174NativeRoyalty1103DelawareChif1112½	In close	10
3Mar70-8Hia	fst	1⅛	:452 1:093 1:353 1:483	Flamingo 161k	13	4	410	55½	45½	45	Belmonte E	122		4.60e	87-14	My Dad George122noCorn off the Cob1223Burd Alane1222		13
		Finished well																
18Feb70-8Hia	fst	1⅛	:463 1:11 1:361 1:484	Everglades 33k	4	10	1116	1012	66	45¾	Belmonte E	113		3.00	85-15	Naskra1154Burd Alane112nkMy Dad George1171½	In close	13
9Feb70-7Hia	fst	7f	:224 :453 1:11 1:241	Alw 6000	6	8	813	912	33	13½	Belmonte E	122		*1.50	87-16	Personality1223½Grandiose122hdBell Bird117no	Handily	9
3Feb70-4Hia	sly	6f	:222 :461 1:11	©Md Sp Wt	5	3	2½	2hd	14	16	Belmonte E	119		*1.20	89-15	Personality1196Air Song1194Bird of Thoria1191	Easily	10
		Previously trained by H. Jacobs																
26Jan70-4Hia	fst	6f	:221 :453 1:11	©Md Sp Wt	3	7	78½	79	57½	33½	Cordero A Jr	119		4.40	85-13	Summer Air1192Elated Prince1191½Personality1194	Rallied	12
31Oct69-1Aqu	fst	6f	:222 :453 1:102	Md Sp Wt	3	8	96¾	88¼	812	913	Venezia M	122		5.60	78-14	KeepitfrmGeorge1176BonniTm122hdHtHolmr1221½	Off slowly	14

Protagonist

ch. c. 1971, by Prince John (Princequillo)–Hornpipe II, by Hornbeam — Lifetime record: 10 4 1 0 $203,995

Own.– Elmendorf Farm

Br.– Elmendorf Farm (Ky)

Tr.– J.P. Campo

27Apr74- 7CD	fst	7f	:22^3 :45^3 1:11^1 1:23^4	Stepping Stone Purse 10k	10	9	10^{17}	11^{18}	12^{25}	12^{20}	Santiago A	122	b	6.40	68-22	Cannonade122^{2}J.R.'s Pet122½Destroyer122^4	Outrun	13
6Apr74- 8Aqu	sly	1	:23^2 :45^4 1:10^3 1:35^1	Gotham (Div 2)-G2	6	8	8^{11}	8^{9}¼	7^{12}	8^{16}	Santiago A	124	b	*1.50	75-15	Rube the Great119^{4}½Hosiery116^{nk}Cumulo Nimbus116½		8
	Disliked slop																	
16Mar74- 8Aqu	sly	7f	:22 :44^1 1:09 1:22^3	Bay Shore-G3	2	11	11^{15}	10^{15}	8^{13}	4^{8}¼	Santiago A	124	b	*1.90	80-11	HdsnCounty113^{1}¾FrankiAdms119^{5}¾InstdofRoss116¾	Rallied	11
3Nov73- 8Lrl	fst	1 1/16	:23^2 :46^2 1:12 1:43^1	Lrl Futurity-G1	5	4	4^{10}	4^3	1^2	1^3	Santiago A	122	b	*.70	97-12	Protagnist122^{3}HastyFlyer122^{3}½PrncofRson122¾	Going away	5
13Oct73- 8Bel	fst	1	:23^2 :46^4 1:11^1 1:36	Champagne (Div 2)-G1	4	6	7^{3}¼	7^{1}¾	5^{2}¼	1^{nk}	Santiago A	122	b	2.70	88-15	Protagonist122^{nk}PrinceofReason122^{1}Cannonad122^{hd}	Driving	10
26Sep73- 6Bel	fst	7f	:22^3 :45^2 1:10^1 1:23	Cowdin (Div 1)-G2	10	10	11^{11}	10^{9}¾	5^3	1^{1}¼	Santiago A	113	b	3.50	87-11	Protagonist113^{1}¼Hosiery113½Stonewalk113^{2}¼	Going away	12
12Sep73- 7Bel	fst	6½f	:23 :46^2 1:10^3 1:17	Futurity-G1	3	9	10^{9}¼	7^{5}¾	5^{3}½	3^3	Santiago A	122	b	7.40e	88-10	Wedge Shot122^3[D]Judger122^{hd}Protagonist122^1	Bumped	10
	Placed second by disqualification																	
24Aug73- 3Sar	fst	7f	:23^1 :46^1 1:11^1 1:23^4	ⒸMd Sp Wt	2	6	6^{7}½	5^6	2^3	1^2	Santiago A	119	b	5.70	88-10	Protgonist119^{2}DeterminedKing119¾TheScotsmn119^3	Driving	6
11Aug73- 2Sar	fst	6f	:22^3 :46 1:11	ⒸMd Sp Wt	8	3	5^{2}¼	4^{3}¼	4^{4}½	4^{6}½	Santiago A	119	b	5.70	78-12	Take By Storm119^{6}½Hilo119^{no}The Scotsman119^{hd}	Evenly	12
31Jly73- 1Sar	fst	6f	:23 :47 1:11^3	ⒸMd Sp Wt	2	11	8^{6}¼	8^7	6^8	6^{7}¾	Santiago A	119		12.10	74-16	PrinceofReasn119^{nk}TakebyStorm119^{nk}L'sPss119^3	No factor	11

Proud Delta

dkbbr. f. 1972, by Delta Judge (Traffic Judge)–Loving Sister, by Olympia — Lifetime record: 31 12 6 1 $387,761

Own.– Montpelier

Br.– Danada Farm (Ky)

Tr.– Peter M. Howe

4Jly77- 8Mth	fst	1 1/16	:23 :46^1 1:09^4 1:41^4	3↑ ⒻMolly Pitcher H-G2	11	4	5^{3}¼	2^3	3^4	2^4	Velasquez J	123		*2.40	92-09	Dottie'sDoll113^{4}ProudDelta123¾MississippiMud115¾	Gamely	11
4Jun77- 8Bel	fst	1⅛	:47^2 1:12 1:36^3 1:49^1	3↑ ⒻHempstead H-G2	4	1	1½	3^{nk}	3^{3}½	5^{7}¾	Cordero A Jr	124		*1.30	73-18	Pacific Princess112¾Mississippi Mud114^{2}¾Fleet Victress113^{nk}		10
	No excuse																	
30Apr77- 8Aqu	fst	1⅛	:47 1:11 1:36^3 1:49^4	3↑ ⒻTop Flight H-G1	3	4	4^{3}½	2^{hd}	2^{hd}	2no	Velasquez J	124		*.70	86-13	Shawi111^{no}Proud Delta124^{hd}Mississippi Mud114^{no}	Missed	9
8Apr77- 8Aqu	fst	1 1/16⊡	:23 :47^3 1:13 1:45^4	3↑ ⒻBed o' Roses H-G3	1	2	1½	1^{hd}	2^{hd}	2^{1}¾	Maple E	125		*1.30	87-19	Shawi109^{1}¾Proud Delta125^{no}Secret Lanvin111^1	Gamely	8
13Nov76- 8Aqu	fst	1¼	:48^2 1:12^3 1:37^1 2:01^2	3↑ ⒻLadies H-G1	3	1	1^{1}½	1½	1^{hd}	2no	Velasquez J	125		*1.50	89-19	Bastonera II122^{no}Proud Delta125^{7}Sugar Plum Time114¾		9
	Stumbled start																	
9Oct76- 8Bel	sly	1¼	:46^2 1:10 1:35^3 2:01	3↑ ⒻRuffian 132k	1	3	3^{1}½	4^{14}	5^{19}	5^{28}	Velasquez J	123		3.00	66-17	Revidere118^{14}BastonrII123^{2}OptmstcGl118^{2}½	Disliked going	5
25Sep76- 8Bel	fst	1⅛	:46^1 1:10^1 1:34^1 1:46^4	3↑ ⒻBeldame-G1	8	1	1^1	1^1	1^{2}½	1^3	Velasquez J	123		5.50	93-12	ProudDelta123^{3}Revidere118½BastoneraII123^{hd}	Never headed	8
15Sep76- 8Bel	fst	1	:22^4 :45 1:09^1 1:34	3↑ ⒻMaskette H (Div 2)-G2	1	4	2^{hd}	3^1	3½	4^3	Velasquez J	124		3.30	95-10	Sugar Plum Time111½Pacific Princess110^{no}FleetVictrss115^{2}½		9
	Weakened																	
11Jly76- 8Hol	fst	1⅛	:46^3 1:10^4 1:35^4 1:48	3↑ ⒻVanity H-G1	7	2	2^1	10^{12}	10^{21}	10^{26}	Grant H	122		6.40	66-11	Miss Toshiba120^{hd}Bastonera II121^{3}½Bold Baby115^2	Stopped	11
3Jly76- 8Mth	sly	1 1/16	:23^2 :47^2 1:13 1:46	3↑ ⒻMolly Pitcher H-G2	2	1	1½	2^{1}½	7^{4}¼	7^{8}½	Velasquez J	126		*1.30	66-30	GardnVerse112¾SpringIsHere111¾VodkaTm112^{1}¼	Speed,tired	8
29May76- 8Bel	fst	1⅛	:45^3 1:09^4 1:35^1 1:48^2	3↑ ⒻHempstead H-G2	3	1	1^{1}½	1½	1^{1}½	1¾	Velasquez J	124		*1.20	85-19	ProudDelta124¾GardenVerse111^{5}¼LetMeLinger114^{2}½	Driving	8
16May76- 8Bel	fst	1	:23 :45^2 1:09^3 1:35	3↑ ⒻShuvee H 56k	5	-		1½	1^3	1^{4}¼	Velasquez J	122		3.70	93-17	Proud Delta122^{4}¼Snooze108^{hd}Let Me Linger115^4	Mild drive	8
	Obscured by fog																	
24Apr76- 8Aqu	fst	1⅛	:47 1:11^1 1:36 1:49	3↑ ⒻTop Flight H-G1	4	3	3^{2}½	3^1	3½	1¾	Velasquez J	120		5.00	90-13	ProudDelta120¾LetMeLinger116^{hd}SpringIsHere108¾	Driving	7
7Apr76- 8Aqu	fst	1	:24 :47^2 1:11^2 1:35^2	3↑ ⒻBed o' Roses H-G3	3	4	1^{hd}	3^{2}½	5^{4}¾	5^{8}½	Gustines H	122		5.80	80-17	Imminence115^{2}Spring Is Here108^{1}¼Land Girl114^{nk}	Gave way	9
28Feb76- 8Aqu	fst	1⅛	:47^3 1:12^2 1:36^4 1:49^2	3↑ ⒻNext Move H 80k	8	2	2^{1}½	2^3	2^{10}	4^{13}	Velasquez J	124		*2.30	75-22	YesDearMaggy119^{13}Pass aGlance115^{hd}MaryQueenofscts119^{nk}		8
	Weakened																	
11Feb76- 8Aqu	fst	1⅛	:48^3 1:13 1:38 1:50^3	3↑ ⒻRare Treat H 37k	2	1	1^2	1^{hd}	1^3	1^{2}¾	Velasquez J	121		*1.20	82-24	ProudDelta121^{2}¾MaryQueenofscots120^{1}¼PettLuc111^{nk}	Easily	6
24Jan76- 8Aqu	fst	1	:24 :47^3 1:12^3 1:37^2	3↑ ⒻAffectionately H 57k	6	4	3^{1}½	2^{hd}	1^3	1^{1}¾	Velasquez J	114		6.30	79-21	PrdDlta114^{1}¾MaryQueenofscots119^{no}ShyDawn119¾	Driving	10
10Jan76- 8Aqu	fst	6f	:22^1 :46^1 1:11^4	3↑ ⒻInterborough H 57k	5	8	4^{3}½	6^{2}¼	5^{3}½	7^{3}½	Cordero A Jr	114		4.30	80-21	Donetta115^{nk}Foolish Polly118^{1}¼Misinform113½	Impeded	10
	Placed sixth through disqualification																	
15Nov75- 8Aqu	fst	1¼	:50^3 1:14^2 1:38^3 2:03^3	3↑ ⒻLadies H-G1	2	4	3^{1}½	5^{2}¾	5^{6}½	6^{5}½	Gustines H	114		15.30	72-15	Tizna124^{nk}Pass a Glance113^{nk}Susan's Girl126^2	Tired	8
30Oct75- 8Bel	fst	1 1/16	:23^3 :46^2 1:11^1 1:42^4	3↑ ⒻAlw 12000	2	1	1^{hd}	1^{hd}	1^{hd}	1½	Gustines H	118		*1.90	88-17	PrdDlt118½SpunkyPrncss116^{no}Immnnc118^4	Long,hard drive	7
	Previously owned by Ada Rice;previously trained by F. Catrone																	
5Oct75- 8Bel	fst	1	:23^1 :45^1 1:10^2 1:35^4	ⒻⓇSuffolk County H 46k	9	10	11^{11}	7^{7}¾	2^3	1½	Bracciale V Jr	112		8.20	89-19	ProudDelta112½SlipScreen115^{7}¾Imminence112^{nk}	Hard drive	11
8Sep75- 8Bel	fst	7f	:22^4 :45^4 1:10^2 1:23	3↑ ⒻAlw 20000	3	5	5^5	4^4	2^2	2^{hd}	Velasquez J	111		2.00	87-19	FleetVictress113^{hd}ProudDelta111^{15}Remd109^2	Strong finish	5
17Aug75- 5Sar	fst	6½f	:22^3 :45^3 1:10^1 1:16^4	3↑ ⒻAlw 20000	7	1	6^{4}½	4^{3}½	3^{4}½	2^4	Velasquez J	114		5.00	87-17	A Charm107^{4}Proud Delta114¾Land Girl116^{5}½	Wide turn	7
1Aug75- 8Sar	fst	6f	:22^2 :45^2 1:10^1	3↑ ⒻAlw 15000	2	4	4^3	3^{1}½	2^{hd}	1^{nk}	Velasquez J	112		6.90	89-14	Proud Delta112^{nk}Lady Portia114^{6}Lisa A. J.116¾	Driving	5
20Jly75- 5Bel	fm	1 1/16Ⓣ	:23^1 :46^4 1:10^3 1:42^1	3↑ ⒻAlw 15000	10	7	10^{7}¼	10^{7}¾	10^{16}	10^{16}	Shoemaker W	111		12.60	74-11	FleetVictress113^{2}¼HighestTrump112¾TallyRound116¾	Outrun	10
28Jun75- 7Bel	fst	6f	:22^3 :45^4 1:10^2	3↑ ⒻAlw 15000	2	2	5^3	5^3	5^{2}½	5^{2}½	Baeza B	114		2.80	88-11	Misinform112^{no}InnrCommnd116^{nk}FletVctrss116^2	No mishap	7
13Jun75- 7Bel	fst	1⅛	:46^1 1:10^2 1:35^3 1:48^3	3↑ ⒻAlw 15000	3	2	2^{1}½	4^{1}¼	4^{4}½	3^{8}½	Baeza B	113		2.60	75-11	Land Girl113^{no}Footsie111^{8}½Proud Delta113^{1}½	Weakened	6
27May75- 7Aqu	fst	6f	:22^2 :45^3 1:10^4	ⒻAlw 11000	7	7	6^4	4^3	2½	1¾	Baeza B	114		*2.10	89-14	Proud Delta114¾Illiterate106^{3}Piece of Luck113¾	Driving	7
30Apr75- 8Aqu	fst	7f	:22^4 :45 1:08^4 1:21^1	ⒻComely-G3	2	4	3^{2}½	3^4	3^8	4^{12}	Maple E	113		25.30	83-16	Ruffian113^{7}¾Aunt Jin113^{2}½Point in Time113^2	Tired	5
9Apr75- 6Aqu	fst	1	:24^1 :47^3 1:12^1 1:37^4	ⒻAlw 10000	6	5	5^{3}¼	2^3	2^2	1^{3}¼	Maple E	119		4.10	77-20	ProudDlta119^{3}¼RoamngFancy114^{6}½Decantr119^{4}½	Ridden out	6
24Mar75- 4Aqu	fst	6f	:23 :46^3 1:11^3	ⒻMd Sp Wt	5	4	3^2	3^2	2^{hd}	1no	Maple E	121		4.00	85-13	ProudDlta121^{no}Imminence116^{1}½Barny'sBby121^{1}¼	Hard drive	5

Revidere

ch. f. 1973, by Reviewer (Bold Ruler)–Quillesian, by Princequillo — Lifetime record: 11 8 2 1 $330,019

Own.– W. Haggin Perry

Br.– Claiborne Farm (Ky)

Tr.– David A. Whiteley

4Jly77- 6Bel	fst	7f	:23^1 :46^3 1:11^1 1:23^2	3↑ Alw 25000	2	6	1^{1}½	1^{hd}	1^{hd}	2½	Cordero A Jr	117		*.60	84-16	WisePhilip117½Revidere112^{1}¼AmericanHistory117^{2}¼	Gamely	7
23Oct76- 8Bel	fst	1½	:50^1 1:14^2 2:04 2:28^4	3↑ J C Gold Cup-G1	1	1	1^{1}½	1^1	2½	3^{2}¾	Vasquez J	118		*.90	73-18	GreatCntractr121^{1}¼Appassionato121^{1}½Rvdr118^{3}¾	Weakened	10
9Oct76- 8Bel	sly	1¼	:46^2 1:10 1:35^3 2:01	3↑ ⒻRuffian 132k	3	2	2½	1^4	1^9	1^{14}	Vasquez J	118		*1.70	94-17	Revidere118^{14}Bastonera II123^{2}Optimistic Gal118^{2}½	Urging	5
25Sep76- 8Bel	fst	1⅛	:46^1 1:10^1 1:34^1 1:46^4	3↑ ⒻBeldame-G1	3	4	2^1	3^1	3^{3}½	2^3	Shoemaker W	118		*.90	90-12	ProudDelta123^{3}Revidere118½BastonerII123^{hd}	Finished well	8
4Sep76- 8Bel	fst	1⅛	:46^3 1:10^1 1:35 1:47^4	ⒻGazelle H-G2	1	2	2^3	2^3	2^2	1^{1}½	Cordero A Jr	124		*.60	88-15	Revidere124^{1}½PacificPrncss112^{9}AncntFbls112^{15}	Ridden out	5
5Jly76- 8Mth	fst	1⅛	:48 1:12^2 1:37^4 1:50^3	ⒻMth Oaks-G1	7	2	2^1	1½	2^{hd}	1^{hd}	Vasquez J	121		*.60	87-17	Revidere121^{hd}Javamine112^{6}Quacker114^{nk}	Came again	8
26Jun76- 7Bel	fst	1½	:48^2 1:13^3 2:03^1 2:28^2	ⒻC C A Oaks-G1	5	2	2½	1½	2^{hd}	1½	Vasquez J	121		2.40	78-13	Revidere121½OptimisticGal121^{8}½NoDuplicat121½	Came again	10
12Jun76- 8Key	fst	1 1/16	:23^1 :47^4 1:12^2 1:44	ⒻCotillion-G2	3	2	1^{hd}	1^{hd}	1^{1}½	1^4	Vasquez J	118		*.60	84-18	Revidere118^{4}Critical Miss116^{1}½Hay Patcher116^1	Handily	8
11May76- 7Bel	fst	1 1/16	:23^1 :46 1:10^4 1:43^1	3↑ ⒻAlw 15000	7	1	2½	1^{hd}	1^2	1^3	Vasquez J	114		1.20	86-20	Revidere114^{3}Cohabitation114^{nk}Amata119^{1}¼	Brisk drive	7
22Apr76- 7Aqu	fst	1	:22^4 :46 1:10^3 1:35^1	ⒻAlw 15000	7	2	2½	1^2	1^{1}½	1^{2}¾	Vasquez J	114		*1.20	90-14	Revidere114^{2}¾Perl114^{4}Ten Cents a Dance109^5	Mild drive	7
5Apr76- 3Aqu	fst	7f	:23^2 :47^1 1:12^2 1:25	3↑ ⒻMd Sp Wt	8	5	2^1	2½	1^{1}½	1^{7}½	Vasquez J	112		*.50	76-18	Revidere112^{7}½HowPleasing113^{2}YoungatHeart112^7	Ridden out	8

Riva Ridge

b. c. 1969, by First Landing (Turn-to)–Iberia, by Heliopolis — Lifetime record: 30 17 3 1 $1,111,347

Own.– Meadow Stable
Br.– Meadow Stud Inc (Ky)
Tr.– Lucien Laurin

27Oct73- 7Aqu fst 2 :472 2:293 2:551 3:20 3↑ J C Gold Cup-G1 3 2 21½ 611 627 633 Maple E 124 b *.50 63-18 Prove Out1244¾Loud12413Twice a Prince119½ Gave way 6
15Oct73- 8Aqu fst 1⅛ :471 1:102 1:342 1:47 3↑ Stuyvesant H-G2 8 3 43 21½ 13 13 Maple E 130 b *.70 101-09 Riva Ridge1303Forage1161¾True Knight122no Drew clear 9
15Sep73- 7Bel fst 1⅛ :453 1:091 1:33 1:452 3↑ Marl Cup Inv'l H 250k 6 2 2hd 1½ 22 23½ Maple E 127 b *.40e 100-07 Secretariat1243½RivaRidge1272CougarII1266½ Held gamely 7
21Aug73- 7Sar fst 1⅛ :461 1:10 1:354 1:491 3↑ Alw 15000 4 2 21½ 1½ 14 1½ Turcotte R 126 b *.20 95-16 Riva Ridge126½Halo1126Rule by Reason112¾ All out 6
1Aug73- 5Sar fm 1 1/16Ⓣ :232 :463 1:094 1:40 3↑ Alw 15000 1 1 2hd 2hd 11 21¼ Turcotte R 124 b *.50 96-06 WichitaOil1131¼RivaRidge124nkGlemng124no Held for place 7
4Jly73- 7Aqu fst 1 3/16 :462 1:092 1:333 1:522 3↑ Brooklyn H-G1 3 3 33½ 33 1hd 1hd Turcotte R 127 b 1.80 110-07 Riva Ridge127hdTrue Knight1172Tentam1193½ Driving 7
17Jun73- 9Suf fst 1⅛ :473 1:11 1:36 1:481 3↑ Mass H-G2 5 1 11 12½ 13 13¾ Turcotte R 125 b *.40 100-14 Riva Ridge1253¾Crafty Khale1121½Loud1131 Ridden out 7
28May73- 7Bel sly 1 :223 :444 1:091 1:35 3↑ Metropolitan-G1 2 5 58 58½ 511 716¾ Turcotte R 127 b 2.30 80-16 Tentam1161¼Key to the Mint127hdKing's Bishop1186 Wide 8
12May73- 3Aqu fst 6f :222 :452 1:084 4↑ Alw 12000 1 4 21½ 12 14 14 Turcotte R 121 b *.30 99-09 RivaRidge1214DreamofKings1142SilverMallt1122 Ridden out 5
11Nov72- 7Lrl sf 1½Ⓣ :484 1:152 2:121 2:384 3↑ International 150k 8 1 2hd 519 626 638 Velasquez J 120 b 4.20 -- Droll Role1274Parnell1279Steel Pulse1201 Bobbled early 9
28Oct72- 7Aqu fst 2 :474 2:281 2:541 3:212 3↑ J C Gold Cup 113k 3 3 32 317 320 318 Velasquez J 119 b 2.10 71-17 Autobiography12415KeytotheMint1193RivaRidge11910 Tired 7
30Sep72- 7Bel sly 1½ :47 1:112 2:012 2:282 3↑ Woodward 115k 5 2 1½ 2hd 23 46¼ Turcotte R 119 b *1.40 85-14 KytotheMnt1191¼DSmmrGst1163Autobogrphy1262 Gave way 10
20Sep72- 7Bel fst 1⅛ :461 1:093 1:332 1:461 3↑ Stymie H 28k 1 1 1½ 1hd 2½ 25 Turcotte R 123 b *.70 98-07 Canonero II1105Riva Ridge1236Loud115½ Held willingly 5
5Aug72- 8Mth fst 1⅛ :474 1:113 1:364 1:50 Mth Inv'l H 100k 3 3 2hd 2hd 23 46 Turcotte R 126 b *.30 84-16 Freetex1171¼King's Bishop1153½Cloudy Dawn1171¼ Bid,hung 8
1Jly72- 8Hol fst 1¼ :462 1:102 1:342 1:593 Hol Derby 109k 4 1 11½ 1hd 11½ 1nk Turcotte R 129 b *.60 95-16 Riva Ridge129nkBicker114½Finalista120½ Driving 8
10Jun72- 8Bel fst 1½ :48 1:12 2:021 2:28 Belmont 155k 1 1 1½ 13 17 17 Turcotte R 126 b *1.60 93-08 Riva Ridge1267Ruritania126¾Cloudy Dawn1265 Handy score 10
20May72- 8Pim sly 1 3/16 :47 1:11 1:362 1:553 Preakness 187k 2 4 42½ 22 24 46 Turcotte R 126 b *.30 86-18 BeeBeeBee1261¼NoLeHace1264½KytotheMnt126nk No excuse 7
6May72- 9CD fst 1¼ :473 1:114 1:36 2:014 Ky Derby 182k 9 1 11½ 11½ 13 13¼ Turcotte R 126 b *1.50 91-11 RvaRdge1263¼NoLeHc1263½HldYourPc1263½ Scored in hand 16
27Apr72- 6Kee fst 1⅛ :461 1:111 1:364 1:493 Blue Grass 49k 11 3 33 11 1hd 14 Turcotte R 126 b *.30 89-21 RivaRidge1264SensitiveMusc1213ThurloSqur121¾ Mild drive 11
1Apr72- 9Hia sly 1⅛ :453 1:10 1:362 1:494 Everglades 66k 1 3 33 31 41¾ 45¾ Turcotte R 122 b *.70 80-15 Head of the River112¾Hold Your Peace1224New Prospect1191 6
Checked final eighth
22Mar72- 9Hia fst 7f :224 :444 1:093 1:224 Hibiscus 33k 6 2 42½ 22 11 12¼ Turcotte R 122 b *.60 94-26 Riva Ridge1222¼New Prospect115nkSecond Bar1154½ In hand 8
13Nov71- 8GS fst 1 1/16 :232 :47 1:113 1:433 Garden State 293k 5 4 34 32½ 1hd 12½ Turcotte R 122 b *1.00 87-19 Riva Ridge1222½Freetex122nkKey to the Mint1221¾ Driving 8
30Oct71- 6Lrl fst 1 1/16 :231 :462 1:114 1:432 Pim-Lrl Futurity 144k 3 4 33 22 15 111 Turcotte R 122 b *.10 96-24 Riva Ridge12211Festive Mood122¾Drum Fire1222 Handily 5
9Oct71- 7Bel fst 1 :231 :452 1:10 1:362 Champagne 195k 7 1 11 11½ 14 17 Turcotte R 122 b *1.40 91-20 Riva Ridge1227Chevron Flight1223½Head of the River1221½ 7
Ridden out
18Sep71- 7Bel sly 6½f :22 :451 1:094 1:163 Futurity 153k 8 2 31½ 2hd 12 11½ Turcotte R 122 b 3.60 97-11 RvaRidge1221½ChevronFlght122½HoldYourPc1222 Mild drive 8
2Aug71- 7Sar gd 6f :214 :453 1:094 Flash 34k 6 3 21 1½ 13 12½ Turcotte R 116 b 4.50 97-14 RvaRidge1162½LoquacousDon1135RstYourCs1192½ Mild drive 9
21Jly71- 7Aqu fst 5½f :213 :451 :574 1:042 Great American 35k 3 1 2hd 44½ 54½ 86¾ Baltazar C 117 b *1.30 84-15 Chevron Flight120¾Plum Bold1244Chauffeur124no Steadied 10
9Jly71- 6Aqu fst 5½f :214 :451 :573 1:041 Alw 10000 3 1 1hd 1hd 11½ 14 Baltazar C 122 b *2.20 92-17 RivaRidge1224BigBluffer1221LuckyBidder1222 Mild drive 8
23Jun71- 2Bel fst 5½f :223 :461 :582 1:05 ©Md Sp Wt 2 2 1½ 2hd 12 15½ Baltazar C 122 b 2.00 95-15 RivaRidge1225½KeytotheMint1223½Candyvll122hd Mild drive 8
9Jun71- 4Bel fst 5½f :231 :464 :584 1:05 ©Md Sp Wt 7 8 86½ 811 815 716 Baltazar C 122 2.30 79-12 SearchforGld1227TheGenerl1223½CryingtoRun1222 Bumped 10

Rockhill Native

ch. g. 1977, by Our Native (Exclusive Native)–Beanery, by Cavan — Lifetime record: 17 10 2 3 $465,382

Own.– H.A. Oak
Br.– Dr E.W. Thomas & Carolaine Farm (Ky)
Tr.– Herbert K. Stevens

7Jun80- 8Bel my 1½ :501 1:151 2:04 2:294 Belmont-G1 7 6 2hd 1½ 3½ 33½ Oldham J 126 12.80 67-17 TemprnceHll1262GenuinRsk1211½RockhllNtv1262 Weakened 10
3May80- 8CD fst 1¼ :48 1:124 1:373 2:02 Ky Derby-G1 6 2 11½ 21½ 46½ 56 Oldham J 126 *2.10 81-11 GnuineRsk1211Rumbo1261JakInKlgmn1264 Swerved,checked 13
24Apr80- 7Kee fst 1⅛ :473 1:111 1:363 1:50 Blue Grass-G1 4 1 11½ 11½ 12 12 Oldham J 121 *.50 87-18 RockhillNtive1212SuprMomnt121nkGoldStg121nk Ridden out 11
15Apr80- 7Kee gd 1 1/16 :241 :483 1:123 1:432 Alw 24860 1 1 11 13½ 15 16¾ Oldham J 118 *.30 89-19 RckhillNative1186¾HzrdDuk112hdRy'sWord121nk Ridden out 6
5Mar80-10Hia fst 1⅛ :454 1:104 1:37 1:511 Flamingo-G1 8 4 49½ 43½ 24 36 Oldham J 122 *1.40 70-26 Suprbity1226KoluctooBy122noRockhllNtv1223½ Forced wide 10
20Feb80- 9Hia fst 1⅛ :451 1:092 1:351 1:49 Everglades 49k 5 3 35 32 1½ 11¼ Oldham J 122 3.30 87-16 RockhillNative1221¼IrishTowr1142½InlndVoygr112½ Driving 8
6Feb80- 9Hia fst 7f :23 :451 1:092 1:223 Bahamas 36k 5 2 3½ 33 26 312 Oldham J 122 *.30 78-20 IrishTowr11712Ry'sWord117nkRockhllNtv1223 Brushed early 6
23Jan80- 5Hia fst 6f :222 :46 1:11 Alw 15000 6 3 34 2hd 12 11¼ Oldham J 122 *.10 88-21 RockhillNative1221¼SpeedyProspct1155SlvrShrs1151 Easily 6
14Oct79- 8Bel my 1 :23 :463 1:122 1:381 Champagne-G1 6 2 11 12 11½ 21¾ Oldham J 122 *.20 75-25 Joanie'sChief1221¾RockhllNtv1222Googolplx1224¼ Weakened 8
30Sep79- 8Bel sly 7f :223 :461 1:101 1:233 Cowdin-G2 5 4 45½ 21 14 16 Oldham J 122 *.30 84-24 RckhillNtv1226KoluctooBy115noSonofDodo1172 Ridden out 6
15Sep79- 8Bel fst 7f :222 :451 1:092 1:22 Futurity-G1 7 1 21½ 22 14 14 Oldham J 122 *.20 92-11 Rockhill Native1224Sportful1224¼Gold Stage1221½ Handily 8
25Aug79- 8Sar fst 6½f :221 :444 1:093 1:161 Hopeful-G1 2 9 22 2hd 12 16½ Oldham J 122 *1.10 94-12 DRockhillNatv1226½J.P.Brothr122¾GoldStg1221¼ Came over 12
Disqualified and placed sixth
11Aug79- 9Mth fst 6f :214 :443 1:084 Sapling-G1 7 2 32 21 1½ 13 Oldham J 122 2.70 96-10 RockhillNative1223AntiqueGold1227GoldStg1223 Ridden out 7
31Jly79- 9Mth fst 5½f :221 :45 1:03 Tyro 26k 2 3 33 37½ 36½ 22 Oldham J 122 6.30 100-11 AntiqueGold1182RockhillNativ1225½IrshTowr122nk 2nd best 4
30Jun79- 8CD fst 5½f :223 :463 :59 1:051 Jefferson Cup 29k 2 6 44 3nk 11 12 Oldham J 122 *.50 97-10 RockhillNative1222EarlofOdss1225½Egg'sDynmt122½ Driving 9
19Jun79- 7CD fst 5f :224 :46 :582 Alw 10860 4 4 2½ 2hd 1½ 13 Oldham J 122 *.90 97-15 Rockhill Native1223Varga115hdEgg's Dynamite1153 Easily 7
2Jun79- 3CD fst 5f :231 :463 :591 Md Sp Wt 6 5 11 11 12 14 Oldham J 122 *2.50 93-15 Rockhill Native1224Real Emperor122hdBoom Boom Billy1224 7
Ridden out

Ruffian

dkbbr. f. 1972, by Reviewer (Bold Ruler)–Shenanigans, by Native Dancer — Lifetime record: 11 10 0 0 $313,429

Own.– Locust Hill Farm
Br.– Mr & Mrs Stuart S. Janney Jr (Ky)
Tr.– F.Y. Whiteley Jr

6Jly75- 8Bel fst 1¼ :443 1:083 1:352 2:024 Match Race 350k 1 1 - - - - Vasquez J 121 *.40 -- Foolish Pleasure126 Broke down 2
21Jun75- 8Bel fst 1½ :49 1:132 2:031 2:274 ⒻC C A Oaks-G1 5 1 14 11½ 13 12¾ Vasquez J 121 *.05 81-12 Ruffn1212¾EqulChng1219LtMLngr1212¼ Confidently ridden 7
31May75- 8Aqu fst 1⅛ :473 1:113 1:353 1:474 ⒻMother Goose-G1 6 1 11¾ 12 18 113½ Vasquez J 121 *.10 96-07 Rffian12113½SweetOldGirl1212SunandSnow1212½ Easy score 7
10May75- 8Aqu fst 1 :232 :453 1:093 1:342 ⒻAcorn-G1 3 1 11 13 17 18¼ Vasquez J 121 *.10 94-08 Ruffian1218¼Somethingregal121noGallantTrial1211 In hand 7
30Apr75- 8Aqu fst 7f :224 :45 1:084 1:211 ⒻComely-G3 3 5 11 11½ 16 17¾ Vasquez J 113 *.05 95-16 Ruffian1137¾AuntJin1132½PointnTm1132 Slow start,handily 5
14Apr75- 8Aqu fst 6f :23 :454 1:092 ⒻAlw 20000 2 3 11 1½ 12 14¾ Vasquez J 122 *.10 96-17 Ruffian1224¾SirIvor'sSorrow113hdChannelette1132 Easily 5
23Aug74- 8Sar fst 6f :221 :444 1:083 ⒻSpinaway-G1 2 1 12 13 17 112¾ Bracciale V Jr 120 *.20 97-10 Ruffian12012¾LaughingBridge1201½ScottshMlody1205 Easily 4
27Jly74- 8Mth fst 6f :213 :441 1:09 ⒻSorority-G1 3 3 1½ 1hd 1½ 12¼ Vasquez J 119 *.30 95-15 Ruffian1192¼Hot n Nasty11922Stream Across1194 Driving 4
10Jly74- 8Aqu fst 5½f :214 :442 :562 1:024 ⒻAstoria-G3 2 2 11 13 16 19 Bracciale V Jr 118 *.10 99-15 Ruffian1189Laughing Bridge11512Our Dancing Girl1153¼ 4
Speed to spare
12Jun74- 8Bel fst 5½f :222 :451 :57 1:03 ⒻFashion-G3 3 4 11½ 11½ 14 16¾ Vasquez J 117 *.40 100-12 Ruffian1176¾Copernica11713Jan Verzal117nk Ridden out 6
22May74- 3Bel fst 5½f :221 :45 :57 1:03 ⒻMd Sp Wt 9 8 13 15 18 115 Vasquez J 116 4.20 100-15 Ruffian11615Suzest1135Garden Quad116½ Ridden out 10

Run the Gantlet

b. c. 1968, by Tom Rolfe (Ribot)–First Feather, by First Landing

Lifetime record: 21 9 4 1 $559,079

Own.– Rokeby Stable
Br.– Paul Mellon (Va)
Tr.– Elliott Burch

3Jun72- 7Bel	fm 1½Ⓣ	:491 1:134 2:022 2:274	3↑ Bowling Green H 56k	4 4 46 31 12 13	Woodhouse R	121 b	2.20	88-08	Run the Gantlet1213Kling Kling112noOnandaga114½	Driving 7
13May72- 8Pim	yl 1½Ⓣ	:502 1:153 2:043 2:30	3↑ Dixie H 59k	1 5 42½ 33 37½ 47½	Woodhouse R	123 b	*1.10	79-16	Onandaga1103Star Envoy1164New Alibhai112½	Lacked rally 9
25Mar72- 9Hia	fst 1¼	:461 1:103 1:362 2:022	3↑ Widener H 144k	2 9 713 1115 1015 910	Woodhouse R	123 b	4.90e	76-16	GoodCounsl111noHisMajesty1146UrgntMssg121nk	No speed 13
18Mar72- 9Hia	fm 1 3/16Ⓣ	1:523	3↑ Bougainvillea H 73k	9 10 1013 119¾ 119¾ 109¼	Woodhouse R	125 b	*1.60	95-01	Star Envoy1112Bagdads Rocket107nkDouble Entry113no	Dull 14
25Oct71- 7Lrl	sf 1½Ⓣ	:532 1:214 2:204 2:503	3↑ D C Int'l 150k	2 3 2½ 12 14 16	Woodhouse R	120 b	*.80	--	RuntheGantlet1206IrishBall1209Chompion12716	Ridden out 9
16Oct71- 7Bel	sf 1½Ⓣ	:513 1:172 2:064 2:331	3↑ Man o' War 112k	1 4 46 3½ 1hd 12¼	Woodhouse R	121 b	*.90	61-39	RntheGantlet1212¼Gleaming121hdPractcnt126hd	Ridden out 8
18Sep71- 8Atl	sf 1 3/16Ⓣ	:492 1:151 1:423 2:02	3↑ U Nations H 100k	4 6 57½ 34 1½ 11½	Woodhouse R	117 b	3.20	60-48	RntheGantlet1171½TwiceWorthy1184½Chompion1166	Driving 11
4Sep71- 8Atl	fm 1⅛Ⓣ	:492 1:121 1:362 1:483	3↑ Kelly-Olympic H 33k	5 2 43 43 31 1¾	Woodhouse R	115 b	*1.30e	93-11	RuntheGantlet115¾Charli'sLuck110noFortMrcy126hd	Driving 8
31Jly71- 7Aqu	sf 1⅛Ⓣ	:474 1:124 1:383 1:513	3↑ Tidal H 61k	2 7 64½ 45½ 23 14	Woodhouse R	109 b	10.00	77-23	RuntheGntlt1094RoylHrmony110hdOnthTrck1122	Drew clear 11
13Jly71- 7Aqu	fm 1 1/16Ⓣ	:232 :472 1:113 1:432	3↑ Alw 13000	8 6 612 53 41 2nk	Rotz JL	113 b	*1.30	86-15	Hope Eternal115nkRun the Gantlet113nkEvasive Action118hd	8
	Slow start									
26Jun71- 7Bel	fst 1	:232 :461 1:102 1:344	Saranac 56k	2 6 65 41½ 54¾ 56½	Rotz JL	121	2.30e	92-08	Salem121nkFarewell Party1175½Highbinder114½	Bid,tired 7
5Jun71- 7Bel	fm 1 1/16Ⓣ	1:404	3↑ Alw 15000	1 8 86¼ 54¾ 52½ 25½	Rotz J	113 b	3.10	92-06	Gleaming1135½RntheGantlt1132RoughPlace113hd	Wide turn 9
20May71- 7Aqu	fst 1	:231 :461 1:104 1:361	3↑ Alw 15000	7 4 43½ 22 61¼ 76¼	Rotz J	113 b	*.60	80-21	SoleMio1132SilverMallet110hdBoldSkipper110½	Bid,tired 9
10May71- 6Aqu	gd 6f	:222 :454 1:103	3↑ Alw 11000	5 6 65½ 43¼ 3½ 13	Rotz JL	113 b	4.30	90-16	RuntheGantlet1133Plotting1101RsYourGlss110nk	Mild drive 7
14Nov70- 8GS	gd 1 1/16	:224 :463 1:113 1:45	Garden State 352k	9 8 85½ 51¼ 21 1hd	Rotz JL	122 b	9.40	80-21	Run the Gantlet122hdExecutioner122½Ruffinal1221	Driving 15
4Nov70- 5GS	my 1 70	:231 :47 1:122 1:422	Alw 8000	7 8 76¼ 32½ 2hd 2nk	Rotz JL	116 b	*2.30	82-26	Ruffinal116nkRuntheGantlet1167BigBarracuda114½	Gamely 9
26Oct70- 2Aqu	fst 1	:24 :472 1:113 1:36	Md Sp Wt	9 5 42 2½ 1hd 11½	Tejeira J	122 b	3.40	87-15	RntheGantlt1221½FareYouWell1222HeadMt122nk	Mild drive 11
17Oct70- 1Bel	gd 1	:232 :464 1:122 1:382	Md Sp Wt	12 5 54 22 23 22	Tejeira J	122 b	6.20e	79-15	DrollRol1172RunthGntlt1227Woodchoppr'sBll122no	2nd best 13
14Aug70- 1Sar	fst 6f	:223 :46 1:112	Md Sp Wt	13 7 710 1010 812 88½	Pincay L Jr	122	12.90	80-11	Raja Baba1222Sound Thinking1222Gran Bid1222	Rank 13
17Jly70- 3Aqu	fst 5½f	:231 :474 :593 1:052	Md Sp Wt	6 7 74 64¼ 34 37½	Ussery R	122	6.40	78-15	GreatGuffaw1224HardyLife1223½RuntheGantlet122no	Wide 11
8May70- 3Aqu	fst 5f	:231 :47 :592	Md Sp Wt	5 8 1011 89 613 49¼	Velasquez J	122	15.00	79-16	Good Behaving122nkTinsel Time1228Poppadums1221	Greenly 10

Seattle Slew

dkbbr. c. 1974, by Bold Reasoning (Boldnesian)–My Charmer, by Poker

Lifetime record: 17 14 2 0 $1,208,726

Own.– Tayhill Stable
Br.– B.S. Castleman (Ky)
Tr.– Douglas Peterson

11Nov78- 8Aqu	fst 1⅛	:464 1:10 1:342 1:472	3↑ Stuyvesant H-G3	1 1 11½ 13 13 13¼	Cordero A Jr	134	*.10	98-12	SeattleSlew1343¼JumpingHill1152¾WisePhlp113½	Ridden out 5
14Oct78- 8Bel	sly 1½	:451 1:092 2:014 2:271	3↑ J C Gold Cup-G1	1 1 1hd 1hd 2½ 2no	Cordero A Jr	126	*.60	84-13	Exceller126noSeattleSlew12614GrtContrctor1264¾	Bore out 6
30Sep78- 8Bel	fst 1¼	:473 1:104 1:351 2:00	3↑ Woodward-G1	5 1 12 12½ 12½ 14	Cordero A Jr	126	*.30	109-12	SeattleSlew1264Exceller1266¾It'sFreezng126no	Ridden out 5
16Sep78- 8Bel	fst 1⅛	:47 1:101 1:333 1:454	3↑ Marlboro Cup H-G1	4 1 12½ 12½ 13 13	Cordero A Jr	128	2.10	98-12	Seattle Slew1283Affirmed1245Nasty and Bold1184	Driving 6
	Previously owned by Karen L. Taylor									
5Sep78- 6Med	fst 1⅛	:46 1:094 1:35 1:48	3↑ Paterson H-G3	10 1 13½ 11½ 1½ 2nk	Cruguet J	128	*.20	93-13	Dr.Patches114nkSeattleSlew1282¼It'sFrzng1125	Drifted in 10
12Aug78- 7Sar	sly 7f	:22 :444 1:091 1:213	3↑ Alw 25000	5 2 11 15 14 16	Cruguet J	119	*.10	97-18	SeattleSlew1196ProudBirdie1152¾CapitalIdea11516	Handily 5
14May78- 7Aqu	sly 7f	:224 :453 1:101 1:224	4↑ Alw 25000	3 3 2½ 11½ 17 18¼	Cruguet J	122	*.10	87-26	SeattleSlew1228¼ProudArion1191¼Capult'sSong1155	Handily 6
	Previously trained by William Turner Jr									
3Jly77- 8Hol	fst 1¼	:452 1:091 1:333 1:583	Swaps-G1	2 2 32 36 411 416	Cruguet J	126	*.20	82-11	J.O. Tobin1208Affiliate117noText1208	Steadied,bore in 7
11Jun77- 8Bel	my 1½	:482 1:14 2:034 2:293	Belmont-G1	5 1 1½ 14 13½ 14	Cruguet J	126	*.40	72-17	SeattleSlw1264RunDstyRun1262Sanhedrn1262¼	Handy score 8
21May77- 8Pim	fst 1 3/16	:453 1:094 1:344 1:542	Preakness-G1	8 2 1hd 2½ 13 11½	Cruguet J	126	*.40	98-10	Seattle Slew1261½Iron Constitution1262Run Dusty Run1261¼	9
	Drew clear									
7May77- 8CD	fst 1¼	:454 1:103 1:36 2:021	Ky Derby-G1	4 2 2hd 1hd 13 11¾	Cruguet J	126	*.50	86-12	SeattleSlew1261¾RunDstyRn126nkSanhdrn1263¼	Ridden out 15
23Apr77- 8Aqu	fst 1⅛	:474 1:121 1:363 1:493	Wood Memorial-G1	6 1 1hd 11½ 16 13¼	Cruguet J	126	*.10	87-13	Seattle Slew1263¼Sanhedrin1264½Catalan126hd	Handily 7
26Mar77- 9Hia	fst 1⅛	:451 1:09 1:34 1:472	Flamingo-G1	4 1 11½ 16 16 14	Cruguet J	122	*.20	95-15	SeattleSlew1224Gboul122nkFortPrvl1224½	Speed in reserve 13
9Mar77- 9Hia	fst 7f	:221 :44 1:08 1:203	Alw 7000	2 6 1hd 12 14 19	Cruguet J	117	*.10	102-10	SeattleSlw1179WhitRammr1223½SmashingNatv1192½	Easily 8
16Oct76- 8Bel	fst 1	:232 :46 1:10 1:342	Champagne-G1	3 1 12 12 13 19¾	Cruguet J	122	*1.30	96-13	SeattleSlw1229¾FortheMoment1221¼SltoRom1223	Easy score 10
5Oct76- 7Bel	fst 7f	:223 :454 1:092 1:22	Alw 11000	1 8 11½ 11 13 13½	Cruguet J	122	*.40	92-13	SeattleSlew1223½CruiseonIn1196Lancer'sPrid1172¼	Handily 8
20Sep76- 5Bel	fst 6f	:222 :452 1:101	Md Sp Wt	8 10 1½ 12 15 15	Cruguet J	122	*2.60	91-12	Seattle Slew1225Proud Arion122½Prince Andrew1222	Easily 12

Secretariat

ch. c. 1970, by Bold Ruler (Nasrullah)–Somethingroyal, by Princequillo

Lifetime record: 21 16 3 1 $1,316,808

Own.– Meadow Stable
Br.– Meadow Stud Inc (Va)
Tr.– L. Laurin

28Oct73- 8WO	fm 1⅝Ⓣ	:472 1:373 2:414	3↑ Can Int'l-G2	12 2 21½ 15 112 16½	Maple E	117 b	*.20	96-04	Secretariat1176½BigSpruce1261½GoldenDon117¾	Ridden out 12
8Oct73- 7Bel	fm 1½Ⓣ	:47 1:113 2:00 2:244	3↑ Man o' War-G1	3 1 13 11½ 13 15	Turcotte R	121 b	*.50	103-01	Secretariat1215Tentam1267½Big Spruce126½	Ridden out 7
29Sep73- 7Bel	sly 1½	:50 1:132 2:014 2:254	3↑ Woodward-G1	5 2 2½ 1hd 21½ 24½	Turcotte R	119 b	*.30	86-15	ProveOut1264½Secretariat11911CougarII126½	Best of rest 5
15Sep73- 7Bel	fst 1⅛	:453 1:091 1:33 1:452	3↑ Marl Cup Inv'l H 250k	7 5 51¼ 3½ 12 13½	Turcotte R	124 b	*.40e	104-07	Secretariat1243½Riva Ridge1272Cougar II1266½	Ridden out 7
4Aug73- 7Sar	fst 1⅛	:474 1:11 1:36 1:491	3↑ Whitney H-G2	3 4 31 2½ 2hd 21	Turcotte R	119 b	*.10	94-15	Onion1191Secretariat119½Rule by Reason1192	Weakened 5
30Jun73- 8AP	fst 1⅛	:48 1:111 1:35 1:47	Invitational 125k	4 1 13 12½ 16 19	Turcotte R	126 b	*.05	99-17	Secretariat1269My Gallant120nkOur Native12017	Easily 4
9Jun73- 8Bel	fst 1½	:461 1:094 1:59 2:24	Belmont-G1	1 1 1hd 120 128 131	Turcotte R	126 b	*.10	113-05	Secretariat12631TwiceaPrince126½MyGllnt12613	Ridden out 5
19May73- 8Pim	fst 1 3/16	:481 1:112 1:353 1:542	Preakness-G1	3 4 1½ 12½ 12½ 12½	Turcotte R	126 b	*.30	98-13	Secretariat1262½Sham1268Our Native1261	Handily 6
	Daily Racing Form time 1:53 2/5									
5May73- 9CD	fst 1¼	:472 1:114 1:361 1:592	Ky Derby-G1	10 11 69½ 2½ 1½ 12½	Turcotte R	126 b	*1.50e	103-10	Secretariat1262½Sham1268Our Native126½	Handily 13
21Apr73- 7Aqu	fst 1⅛	:481 1:121 1:364 1:494	Wood Memorial-G1	6 7 66 55½ 45½ 34	Turcotte R	126 b	*.30e	83-17	Angle Light126hdSham1264Secretariat126½	Wide,hung 8
7Apr73- 7Aqu	fst 1	:231 :451 1:083 1:332	Gotham-G2	3 3 1hd 12 1½ 13	Turcotte R	126 b	*.10	100-08	Secretariat1263ChampagneCharl11710Flush1172½	Ridden out 6
17Mar73- 7Aqu	sly 7f	:221 :444 1:10 1:231	Bay Shore-G3	4 5 56 53 1hd 14½	Turcotte R	126 b	*.20	85-17	Secretarit1264½ChmpgnChrl1182½Impcunous126no	Mild drive 6
18Nov72- 8GS	fst 1 1/16	:241 :472 1:12 1:442	Garden State 298k	6 6 46¼ 33 11½ 13½	Turcotte R	122 b	*.10e	83-23	Secretariat1223½Angle Light122½Step Nicely122¾	Handily 6
28Oct72- 7Lrl	sly 1 1/16	:224 :454 1:112 1:424	Lrl Futurity 133k	5 6 510 53 15 18	Turcotte R	122 b	*.10e	99-14	Secretariat1228Stop the Music1228Angle Light1221	Easily 6
14Oct72- 7Bel	fst 1	:224 :451 1:094 1:35	Champagne 146k	4 11 98½ 53½ 1½ 12	Turcotte R	122 b	*.70e	97-12	[D]Secretariat1222StoptheMusic1222StepNicly1221½	Bore in 12
	Disqualified and placed second									
16Sep72- 7Bel	fst 6½f	:223 :453 1:10 1:162	Futurity 144k	4 5 65½ 53½ 12 11¾	Turcotte R	122 b	*.20	98-09	Secretariat1221¾StoptheMusic1225SwiftCourr1222½	Handily 7
26Aug72- 7Sar	fst 6½f	:224 :463 1:094 1:161	Hopeful 86k	8 8 96½ 1hd 14 15	Turcotte R	121 b	*.30	97-12	Secretariat1215FlighttoGlory121nkStopthMusc1212	Handily 9
16Aug72- 7Sar	fst 6f	:224 :461 1:10	Sanford 27k	2 5 54 41 1½ 13	Turcotte R	121 b	1.50	96-14	Secretariat1213Lnd'sChf1216NorthstrDncr1213½	Ridden out 5
31Jly72- 4Sar	fst 6f	:231 :462 1:104	Alw 9000	4 7 73¾ 3½ 1hd 11½	Turcotte R	118 b	*.40	92-13	Secretariat1181½Russ Miron1187Joe Iz1182½	Ridden out 7
15Jly72- 4Aqu	fst 6f	:221 :452 1:103	©Md Sp Wt	8 11 66½ 43 1½ 16	Feliciano P5	113 b	*1.30	90-14	Secretariat1136Master Achiever118¾Be on It1184	Handily 11
4Jly72- 2Aqu	fst 5½f	:222 :461 :584 1:05	©Md Sp Wt	2 11 107 108¾ 75½ 41¼	Feliciano P5	113 b	*3.10	87-11	Herbull118nkMaster Achiever1181Fleet 'n Royal118no	12
	Impeded,rallied									

Sensational

dkbbr. f. 1974, by Hoist the Flag (Tom Rolfe)–Meritus, by Bold Ruler

Lifetime record: 44 9 9 9 $496,395

Own.– Mill House
Br.– Mill House (Ky)
Tr.– Woodford C. Stephens

Date/Race	Cond	Dist	Fractions	Race	Running line	Jockey	Wt	Odds	Figs	Result / Comment
15Nov78- 8Aqu	fst	1	:23⁴ :47¹ 1:12 1:37²	3↑ ⒻAlw 30000	8 6 6²½ 8⁹½ 8⁷¾ 5⁶	Cauthen S	115 b	7.70	73-23	Casquette115½Negotiator110⁴TgrHrt122no No late response 9
4Nov78- 8Aqu	fst	1¼	:46¹ 1:11 1:36³ 2:02³	3↑ ⒻLadies H-G1	2 4 4¹⁰ 10¹⁵ 10¹⁹ 10¹⁶	Venezia M	113 b	25.60	68-18	IdaDelia114²½WaterMalone122¹¼CumLaudLur115¹¼ Early foot 11
24Oct78- 6Med	fst	1 1/16	:24² :47⁴ 1:11² 1:42³	3↑ ⒻLong Look H 54k	11 9 9⁷ 9⁸¼ 8¹² 7¹⁴	Venezia M	115 b	3.50e	84-13	WaterMalone120hdQueenLib120⁸TigerHeart115² Stumbled st. 11
1Oct78- 8Bel	fm	1⅜Ⓣ	:48² 1:12 1:37 2:00³	3↑ ⒻFlower Bowl H 54k	3 1 1½ 3² 5⁶ 5⁸½	Velasquez J	113 b	3.90	82-10	Waya120¾Magnificence108⁴¾Leave Me Alone108¹ Used up 7
23Sep78- 8Bel	fst	1⅛	:46² 1:09⁴ 1:34³ 1:47	3↑ ⒻRuffian H-G1	4 3 3³ 3⁴½ 4⁷ 6¹¹	Cauthen S	115 b	10.90	81-15	LateBloomr122¹½PearlNecklace124⁴TempestQueen117²½ Tired 9
10Sep78- 8Bel	fst	1	:23 :45³ 1:09² 1:33⁴	3↑ ⒻMaskette H-G2	5 3 4⁵½ 3⁶ 3⁹ 3⁷¾	Cauthen S	117 b	2.90	91-17	Pearl Necklace123¾Ida Delia113⁷Sensational117hd Wide 5
3Jun78- 8Hol	fst	1 1/16	:22⁴ :46 1:10² 1:41⁴	3↑ ⒻMilady H-G2	7 3 2¹ 3¹ 3² 3²	Pincay L Jr	121 b	3.50	84-18	TaisezVous127¹¾DramaCritiz118nkSensational121nk Evenly 8
20May78- 8Hol	fm	1 1/16Ⓣ	:22¹ :45⁴ 1:10¹ 1:41⁴	3↑ ⒻHawthorne H 45k	4 4 3¹ 1hd 1¹ 1½	Pincay L Jr	119 b	2.80	90-09	Sensational119½Up to Juliet114²½Grand Luxe117² Driving 10
11May78- 7Hol	fm	1 1/16Ⓣ	:22³ :47 1:11 1:42¹	4↑ ⒻAlw 35000	6 4 3¹ 3²½ 2³ 3½	Pincay L Jr	116 b	*1.00	87-14	DramaCrtc116nkSoundofSmmr118nkSnstonl116no Good effort 6
27Apr78- 8Hol	fm	1 1/16Ⓣ	:23³ :48 1:11³ 1:41⁴	4↑ ⒻAlw 30000	4 2 2½ 2½ 2¹ 2hd	McCarron CJ	114 b	*1.40	90-10	Glenaris114hdSensational114½UptoJuliet119hd Just missed 7
15Apr78- 6Hol	sly	1⅛	:46⁴ 1:10³ 1:35¹ 1:48¹	3↑ ⒻGamely H (Div 1)-G2	3 4 4³ 4¹½ 4¹½ 2hd	Cauthen S	120 b	*1.20	91-12	Lucie Manet119hdSensational120²Glenaris113¹ Bumped 7
26Mar78- 8SA	fm	1¼Ⓣ	:47¹ 1:11⁴ 1:36 2:00³	4↑ ⒻS Barbara H-G1	4 2 2¹½ 2¹½ 3¹½ 3¹	Cauthen S	120 b	3.70	83-15	Kittyluck116¹Countess Fager117noSensational120no Hung 9
16Mar78- 8SA	fm	1⅛Ⓣ	:47³ 1:11¹ 1:35² 1:47⁴	4↑ ⒻAlw 35000	1 1 1² 1½ 1² 1no	Cauthen S	119 b	*1.40	88-12	ⒹSensational119noUptoJuliet112²½Glenrs112¹ Drifted out 6
Disqualified and placed second										
26Feb78- 8SA	fst	1⅛	:46 1:10² 1:35⁴ 1:49	4↑ ⒻS Margarita Inv H-G1	5 5 2⁴ 2¹ 2¹ 2¹½	Cauthen S	118 b	8.10	85-16	TaisezVous120¹½Sensational118²MerryLdyIII114⁴½ Good try 11
16Feb78- 8SA	fst	1 1/16	:23 :46² 1:10¹ 1:41⁴	4↑ ⒻAlw 35000	4 3 3³ 2² 2² 2¹¼	Cauthen S	117 b	*.70	92-14	SoundofSummer115¹¼Senstnl117⁴MrryLdyIII114⁸ No excuse 5
10Feb78- 8SA	my	6½f	:22¹ :45⁴ 1:11¹ 1:17³	4↑ ⒻAlw 25000	8 5 5⁵ 4⁴ 3²½ 1¾	Cauthen S	116 b	*1.50	82-25	Sensational116¾Don's Music113²Tumble Along119½ Handily 8
19Nov77- 6Med	fst	1¼	:49⁴ 1:14² 1:38⁴ 2:03⁴	3↑ ⒻLong Look H 105k	1 1 1¹ 1½ 2½ 2⁵	Venezia M	114 b	*1.40	89-19	Dottie's Doll114⁵Sensational114⁴¾Charming Story115³½ 6
Faltered late										
5Nov77- 8Aqu	fst	1¼	:47³ 1:12² 1:37³ 2:02⁴	3↑ ⒻLadies H-G1	8 6 5⁷ 2½ 1¹ 1²¾	Venezia M	110 b	12.90	82-14	Sensatonl110²¾Dott'sDoll114¾ChrmngStory116no Ridden out 8
24Oct77- 8Aqu	gd	1 1/16⊗	:23⁴ :48¹ 1:12¹ 1:43⁴	3↑ ⒻLong Island H-G3	6 4 2¹½ 2¹½ 6⁵½ 7⁷¾	Venezia M	113 b	8.90	79-13	PearlNecklace123¹¼Javamine121hdLeaveMeAlone113¾ Tired 7
15Oct77- 5Bel	my	1⊗	:23¹ :46² 1:11 1:36³	3↑ ⒻGallant Bloom H 25k	4 3 2¹½ 3¹ 3⁴½ 3⁴	Venezia M	118 b	5.80	81-17	Pearl Necklace121²¾Nijana122¹¼Sensational118nk Evenly 6
7Oct77- 6Med	fm	1 1/16Ⓣ	:23¹ :47¹ 1:12 1:44¹	3↑ ⒻAlw 25000	2 5 5²¼ 6²¾ 4³ 5³½	Wallis T	111 b	*1.20	87-09	MascaradaII115nkLikelyDouble115³Becky'sHoney115nk Tired 9
24Sep77- 8Bel	sly	1⅛	:46 1:11¹ 1:37⁴ 1:52¹	3↑ ⒻRuffian H-G1	8 6 5⁷ 6¹¹ 9¹⁶ 9¹⁵	Maple E	115 b	12.00	51-25	CumLaudeLaurie114½MississippiMud123½Cascaped128¹¼ Tired 12
3Sep77- 8Bel	my	1⅛	:46⁴ 1:11 1:35² 1:48	ⒻGazelle H-G2	4 2 2² 2¹ 2³½ 2²¾	Wallis T	120 b	*1.60	84-14	PearlNecklace111²¾Sensational120½RoadPrincss118¾ Gamely 5
13Aug77- 8Sar	fst	1¼	:49² 1:13² 1:37² 2:03	ⒻAlabama-G1	1 1 1² 1¹ 1hd 2nk	Wallis T	121 b	29.70	86-13	OurMims121nkSensatnl121¹¾CumLaudeLaurie121hd Gamely 11
3Aug77- 8Sar	fst	7f	:22¹ :45¹ 1:09² 1:22²	ⒻTest (Div 2)-G3	7 1 6⁸½ 6⁵½ 4⁸ 4⁵¼	Wallis T	121 b	3.80	88-13	NorthernSea121¾Northernette121²FlyngAbov114²½ No mishap 8
16Jly77- 8Mth	fst	1⅛	:46⁴ 1:10³ 1:36 1:49³	ⒻMth Oaks-G1	4 - - - - -	Wallis T	119 b	*2.20	- -	Small Raja121⁴¾Herecomesthebride117¹¼Suede Shoe114² 8
Stumbled start,lost rider										
2Jly77- 8Bel	fst	1½	:47⁴ 1:11⁴ 2:03³ 2:29²	ⒻC C A Oaks-G1	4 9 9¹⁷ 11⁸½ 9¹⁰ 7¹²	Wallis T	121 b	9.80	61-18	Our Mims121²½Road Princess121½Fia121hd Bumped,wide 12
25Jun77- 8Mth	fst	1 70	:22¹ :45² 1:10⁴ 1:43	ⒻPost-Deb-G3	3 6 6⁸½ 4³½ 2¹ 1⁵½	Wallis T	117 b	3.40	83-19	Sensational117⁵½Raise Old Glory113⁵Hagany113nk Easily 6
11Jun77- 6Bel	my	1⅛	:46¹ 1:11 1:36¹ 1:48⁴	ⒻMother Goose-G1	14 13 15¹¹ 14¹² 12¹⁴ 11¹⁵	Velasquez J	121	14.20	68-17	RoadPrincess121¹¾Mrs.Warren121²¾CumLaudeLur121nk Outrun 16
6May77- 8CD	fst	1 1/16	:23³ :46⁴ 1:11 1:43³	ⒻKy Oaks-G2	2 4 4³½ 3² 3³ 6⁷¼	Velasquez J	121 b	2.60e	83-17	SweetAlliance121²½OurMims121¹Mrs.Warrn121¹¼ Weakened 12
23Apr77- 7Kee	sly	*7f	1:26⁴	ⒻAshland-G3	1 4 7⁸ 6¹² 5⁷ 4¹¹½	Velasquez J	121 b	3.70e	77-19	SoundofSummer118⁴½Mrs.Warren121⁴OurMims118³ No rally 9
30Mar77- 9Hia	fst	7f	:22² :45 1:09³ 1:23	ⒻHibiscus 30k	3 8 8⁶¾ 6⁸ 4⁵½ 3¹	Velasquez J	122 b	*.80	87-17	NeedaDime114½GrandLuxe114½Sensational122² Belated rally 8
19Mar77- 3Hia	fst	6f	:22 :44⁴ 1:10¹	ⒻAlw 10000	5 3 4⁶ 4⁵½ 4³½ 3¹	Wallis T	121 b	*.80	91-14	GrandLuxe118hdNoble Madame118¹Sensationl121no Gaining 7
23Oct76- 8Lrl	fst	1 1/16	:22⁴ :45² 1:11 1:43⁴	ⒻSelima-G1	4 5 5⁷ 4² 1hd 1³½	Velasquez J	122 b	*.90	94-13	Sensationl122³½NorthernSe119²Dbby'sTurn119¹ Ridden out 6
4Oct76- 8Bel	fst	1	:22⁴ :45³ 1:10¹ 1:36¹	ⒻFrizette-G1	2 4 2¹½ 2¹½ 2½ 1¹½	Velasquez J	119 b	10.40	87-18	Sensational119¹½Northern Sea119³Mrs. Warren119⁸ Driving 7
22Sep76- 8Bel	fst	7f	:23² :47² 1:12¹ 1:24³	ⒻMatron-G1	7 1 7⁴½ 6²¾ 6¹³ 5¹⁶	Shoemaker W	119 b	3.50	63-17	Mrs. Warren119⁶½Negotiator119³½Resolver119½ No mishap 7
6Sep76- 6Bel	fst	6½f	:23¹ :46³ 1:11 1:17²	ⒻAstarita-G3	3 4 4²½ 4¾ 1hd 1¹¼	Cordero A Jr	112 b	*1.50	89-14	Sensational112¹¼TickleMyToes112³¾SpyFlg112²½ Ridden out 7
27Aug76- 8Sar	fst	6f	:22 :45 1:10²	ⒻSpinaway-G1	5 5 6⁵½ 6⁵½ 3³½ 3³½	Cordero A Jr	119 b	4.60e	84-10	Mrs. Warren119³Exerene119½Sensational119² Rallied 10
16Aug76- 8Sar	fst	6f	:22¹ :45³ 1:11¹	ⒻAdirondack-G3	2 2 4²½ 4²½ 5⁶½ 5⁷¾	Wallis T	116 b	*.90e	76-18	HarvestGirl114²BonnieEmpress114½DramaCritic119¹¼ Tired 7
31Jly76- 8Mth	fst	6f	:21³ :44⁴ 1:10⁴	ⒻSorority-G1	10 1 7⁵½ 4⁵½ 4²½ 2¹¼	Wallis T	119 b	15.50	85-17	Squander119¹¼Sensational119¾Miss Cigarette119nk Wide 11
7Jly76- 8Mth	sly	5½f	:22² :47³ 1:01² 1:09	ⒻColleen (Div 2) 22k	5 8 8¹¹ 7⁹ 5⁶½ 1½	Wallis T	115 b	5.10	72-35	Sensational115½Intrepid Way115½Drama Critic121² Driving 8
28Jun76- 4Bel	fst	5½f	:22³ :46² :58⁴ 1:05¹	ⒻMd Sp Wt	4 2 5²¾ 5²½ 1½ 1¹½	Wallis T	119 b	5.50	89-12	Snsationl119¹½SpyFlag119³¾YourPlcorMn114¹¾ Ridden out 9
13Jun76- 4Bel	fst	5½f	:22⁴ :46⁴ :59³ 1:06¹	ⒻMd Sp Wt	4 2 4³ 4³¼ 4³½ 3¹½	Maple E	119	3.70	82-22	Squander119¾Harvest Girl119¾Sensational119nk Hung 10
4Jun76- 5Bel	fst	5½f	:23 :46³ :59 1:05³	ⒻMd Sp Wt	4 4 5³¼ 7⁶¾ 7⁶½ 4⁵¼	Maple E	119	*1.30	82-16	Din119hdDrama Critic119¹¾Squander119³½ No excuse 10

Shadow Brook

b. g. 1964, by Cohoes (Mahmoud)–Chanteur Star, by Chanteur II

Lifetime record: 78 20 13 15 $307,057

Own.– S.C.Clark Jr
Br.– Elmendorf Farm (Ky)
Tr.– S. Watters Jr

Date/Race	Cond	Dist	Fractions	Race	Running line	Jockey	Wt	Odds	Figs	Result / Comment
3Aug73- 5Sar	gd	2 1/16	Hurdles 3:44	4↑ Lovely Night H 22k	6 5 5¹¹ 4⁴½ 4¹⁷ 4¹³½	O'Brien L	156 s	2.00	- -	JuacHollow150⁴Wustenchef155⁸½StillinAll140¹ No factor 7
26Jun73- 4Mth	fm	*2 1/16	Hurdles 4:13	4↑ Mid Summer H 16k	2 3 3⁷½ 4⁴½ 3⁶½ 3⁷	O'Brien L	161 s	*1.20	- -	DreamMagic152¹JuacHollow148⁶ShadowBrook161¹⁸ No rally 8
9Jun73-10Del	fm	*2⅛	Hurdles 4:33²	4↑ Indian River H 13k	3 4 5⁴¾ 2¹½ 1⁵ 2no	O'Brien L	160	*1.10	- -	Breaking Dawn138noShadow Brook160¹²Master Irish II141⁸ 7
Just missed										
30May73- 6Bel	fst	7f	:22³ :45³ 1:10¹ 1:22³	3↑ Alw 15000	4 1 5⁴½ 7⁸½ 7¹⁴ 6¹⁸	Vasquez J	112 b	27.60	76-17	DndeeMrmalad118³½ZuluTm118⁴CurousCours118² No factor 7
18Nov72- 3Cam	fm	2⅜	S'Chase 5:23⁴	4↑ Colonial Cup 100k	- 4 3¹½ 3¹½ 3¾ 3²¾	O'Brien L	160	-	- -	Soothsayer158²½InkslInger158¼Shadow Brook160nk 16
4Nov72- 5Lrl	gd	1 1/16⊗	:23² :47¹ 1:13² 1:45⁴	3↑ Alw 7000	1 3 3² 4¹½ 4⁶ 5⁶½	Passmore WJ	117 b	*1.60	- -	ConvoyII112³¼MajesticRoad109²¾BurdosII112no Early speed 7
7Oct72- 4Lig	sf	*2½	S'Chase 5:19²	4↑ Temple Gwathmey H 30k	7 5 3³¾ 3⁴¾ 2³ 3⁷¾	O'Brien L	163 s	-	- -	Soothsayer162⁷Speed Kills143¾Shadow Brook163¹⁰ Evenly 12
20Sep72- 5Bel	gd	1 1/16	:24² :48 1:12¹ 1:44	3↑ Alw 15000	1 1 1½ 3½ 2½ 2⁵	Rotz JL	114 b	3.80	77-18	Rocky Mount116⁵Shadow Brook114nkExotico113⁹ Gamely 6
23Aug72- 7Sar	hd	1⅝Ⓣ	:48² 1:36³ 2:01 2:37⁴	3↑ Seneca H 30k	1 1 1¹½ 3³ 5⁷ 9¹²	Rotz JL	114 b	6.80e	92-04	RedReality113¾Acclimitization114¾ⒹLarcnyKd113³ Used up 12
17Aug72- 3Sar	fm	2 1/16	Hurdles 3:42¹	4↑ Lovely Night H 22k	6 2 1½ 1hd 1¹ 1¾	O'Brien L	163 s	*.50e	- -	Shadow Brook163¾Dream Magic152²½Gran Kan157⁴ Driving 8
9Aug72- 8Sar	fm	1 1/16Ⓣ	:23¹ :45⁴ 1:09² 1:40	3↑ Clm 50000	2 4 6⁵ 7⁷ 4⁶ 2⁷	Cordero A Jr	116 b	4.70	90-05	Nevado116⁷Shadow Brook116nkJogging118½ Gamely 10
20Nov71- 2Cam	fm	2⅜	S'Chase 5:17	4↑ Colonial Cup 10k	4 6 8⁶¾ 5⁹ 5⁵ 4¹¹¼	O'Brien L	160 s	-	- -	Inkslinger149nkSoothsayer149⁸Top Bid160³ Evenly 15
5Nov71- 7Aqu	sf	1 1/16Ⓣ	:23⁴ :49⁴ 1:15 1:48²	3↑ Alw 11000	9 2 2½ 2hd 2½ 3hd	Rotz JL	118 b	*2.10	69-31	Chartino116hdHeyGoodLookin116noShadowBrook118¹ Sharp 10
15Oct71- 3Bel	yl	3	S'Chase 5:47	4↑ Gwathmey H 55k	3 7 3³ 3³ 1⁶ 1⁵½	Fishback J	163 s	*.80e	- -	Shadow Brook163⁵½Amerind141⁴½Top Bid160¾ Handily 9
28Sep71- 3Bel	yl	2⅝	S'Chase 4:57¹	4↑ Brook H 33k	2 3 2⁴ 2² 1³ 1²¼	O'Brien L	159 s	*.70e	- -	Shadow Brook159²¼Amarind135nkTingle Creek153⁶ Driving 8
26Aug71- 3Sar	fm	2½	S'Chase 4:37²	4↑ Grand National H 40k	2 1 3⁷ 2½ 1³ 1¹²	O'Brien L	155 s	*1.10e	- -	Shadow Brook155¹²Top Bid163⁵Madagascar142¹ Driving 7
12Aug71- 3Sar	fm	2 1/16	Hurdles 3:43³	4↑ Lovely Night H 22k	2 2 2¹½ 1½ 1½ 1nk	O'Brien L	156 s	1.50e	- -	Shadow Brook156nkSoothsayer139⁸Inkslinger150²½ Driving 7
22Jly71- 3Aqu	fm	2½	Hurdles 4:35¹	4↑ Meadow Brook 22k	4 1 4⁵½ 3⁴½ 2³ 2³	O'Brien L	154 s	1.60e	- -	Wustenchef154³ShadwBrk154⁴Madagascr140²⁰ Second best 7
17Jly71- 8Aqu	fm	1 1/16Ⓣ	:23³ :46² 1:10³ 1:42³	3↑ Alw 20000	2 2 2½ 2½ 1hd 1¹	Rotz J	114 b	5.60	91-07	ShdwBrk114¹PasstheDrink114nkHandsomeKd118³½ Driving 6
5Jly71- 6Aqu	fm	1 1/16Ⓣ	:23 :46¹ 1:10³ 1:42³	3↑ Alw 20000	7 10 10¹⁶ 10¹¹ 10⁷ 9⁴½	Cruguet J	116 b	14.90	85-14	Elephant Walk116nkOur Cadet120½Naskra111no Reared 11
11Jun71- 7Bel	fst	7f	:22⁴ :45³ 1:10² 1:23	3↑ Alw 20000	4 5 7¹¹ 6¹² 6¹⁵ 6²²	Cruguet J	119 b	11.50	70-15	TwiceWorthy119¹½PrizeSilver121⁴LimttoRsn112⁸½ No speed 7
4Jun71- 5Bel	fm	7fⓉ	1:22³	3↑ Alw 15000	1 5 3² 5⁵½ 4² 3²¼	Cruguet J	117 b	5.70	94-09	Shah Abbas117¹½Decies II117¹Shadow Brook117¾ Rallied 9
25May71- 5Bel	fm	7fⓉ	1:22³	3↑ Alw 15000	10 1 6⁵ 5⁵½ 5⁴½ 4⁴	Cruguet J	117 b	11.50	92-08	Our Cadet119¹Shah Abbas117³Wilkinson121no Steadied turn 10
14Nov70- 4Cam	sf	*2⅜	S'Chase 5:20	4↑ Colonial Cup 100k	- 10 9⁹½ 3¾ 1² 2¹½	O'Brien L	160 s	-e	- -	Top Bid160¹½Shadow Brook160¹½Jaunty158⁶ Gamely 22
29Oct70- 7Aqu	yl	1 1/16Ⓣ	1:46¹	3↑ Alw 15000	3 2 4² 4¹½ 5¹¼ 4³½	Cruguet J	116 b	5.50	68-28	Tampa Trouble116²½Perplejo116½Perpetual II116½ Blocked 7

15Oct70- 5Bel	sf	2½	Hurdles	4:491	4↑ NY Trf Writrs Cup H 24k	7	2	32½	55½	414	310	O'Brien L	155	s	2.30e	--	ElMartirio139noWustenchef15110ShadowBrook1551	Fair try 10
6Oct70- 3Bel	fm	1⅞	Hurdles	3:261	3↑ Handicap 14000	4	1	31½	2½	11½	11½	O'Brien L	153	s	*1.30	--	ShadowBrk1531½Wustenchef1497Hipocampo1384½	Mild drive 6
21Sep70- 3Bel	fm	2 1/16	Hurdles	3:414	4↑ Alw 10000	1	1	1½	2½	1½	12½	O'Brien L	153	s	*.60	--	Shadow Brook1532½Taku1506Amarind14414	Under drive 7
10Sep70- 4Bel	sf	2½	Hurdles	4:414	4↑ Rouge Dragon H 17k	5	5	54½	2½	26	29	O'Brien L	152	s	*.80	--	Wustenchef1439ShadowBrk152¾StarofVertex13018	2nd best 7
3Sep70- 3Bel	hd	1⅞	Hurdles	3:20	4↑ Sp Wt 7200	9	3	38	2hd	112	120	O'Brien L	152	s	2.50	--	ShadowBrk15220ShotandShell1458Jus'Behaving145¾	Easily 10
12Aug70- 6Sar	hd	1 1/16Ⓣ		1:392	3↑ B Baruch H (Div 1) 24k	7	2	43	66½	714	716	Cruguet J	109	b	26.60	87-02	BigShotII111¾ShelterBay111¾PleasantHarbour112hd	Tired 9
30Jly70- 7Aqu	fm	1 1/16Ⓣ		1:45	3↑ Alw 15000	2	3	44	54	57½	55	Cruguet J	120	b	7.70	73-22	NeverConfuse116¾Mr.Clinch123nkRhinelanderII1202½	Tired 6
9Jly70- 7Aqu	fm	1 1/16Ⓣ		1:432	3↑ Alw 15000	6	4	55	52½	53	54½	Cruguet J	123	b	7.30	81-14	Red Reality120nkSailstone1092½Thai Silk113nk	No threat 8
4Jly70- 5Aqu	fst	7f	:22 :442 1:084	1:212	3↑ Alw 15000	6	1	811	916	918	916	Gustines H	121	b	31.90	78-12	TrueNrth1212¼TowzieTyke1153½GleamngLght119no	Far back 9
25Jun70- 7Bel	fm	1 1/16Ⓣ		1:422	3↑ Alw 15000	4	4	58	75¼	54¾	58¼	Cruguet J	120	b	9.30	82-13	Mr. Leader120nkZarco123noRed Reality1204½	No room 8
6Jun70- 6Bel	sly	7f	:23 :463 1:112	1:241	3↑ Alw 15000	6	1	63	76	55½	69	Cruguet J	119	b	16.20	77-20	Buck Run119hdBarometer1192½Noble Victory1195	No mishap 8
30May70- 8Bel	fm	1 1/16Ⓣ		1:422	3↑ Alw 15000	2	2	2½	22	2½	1nk	Cruguet J	116	b	8.70	90-16	Shadow Brook116nkJungle Cove1181Afan1131½	Driving 7
23May70- 3Aqu	fst	6f	:223 :451	1:10	3↑ Alw 15000	1	4	55	57½	47	47♦	Cruguet J	119	b	28.70	86-13	Verbatim117noPrize Silver1041Grey Slacks1136	No mishap 6
22Nov69- 7Aqu	fst	1⅝	:494 1:40 2:05	2:423	3↑ Gallant Fox H 59k	5	5	88	1113	1127	1129	Cruguet J	112	b	60.70	63-16	ShipLeave111noHydrologist117hdQuickenTree1163	Far back 11
13Nov69- 7Aqu	gd	1	:232 :461 1:11	1:354	3↑ Alw 15000	6	2	53¼	41¼	32	33¾	Cruguet J	118	b	12.80	84-20	Barometer1161¾Rixdal1142Shadow Brook118½	Weakened late 7
28Oct69- 7Aqu	fst	1	:233 :463 1:112	1:351	3↑ Alw 15000	5	3	47	65¾	67	512	Cordero A Jr	123	b	12.40	79-22	Hydrologist1195Rixdal116hdFlagstaff1123	Fell back 9
18Oct69- 6Bel	fst	1 1/16	:242 :48 1:123	1:43	3↑ Alw 15000	3	2	11	1hd	2hd	1hd	Cruguet J	118	b	4.10	89-17	Shadow Brook118hdRixdal116½Flagstaff1124	Driving 7
30Sep69- 7Bel	fst	1 1/16	:233 :463 1:111	1:423	3↑ Alw 15000	1	1	11	1½	1½	2no	Turcotte R	118	b	19.80	91-19	FourFingers118noShadowBrook1185BoldHour116hd	Sharp try 8
20Sep69- 6Bel	hd	1 1/16Ⓣ		1:402	3↑ Alw 15000	6	4	43	75¼	76	65½	Cruguet J	118	b	3.60	--	Loiret II116¾Dike1111½Rhinelander II120hd	Brief factor 8
13Sep69- 8Bel	fm	1 1/16Ⓣ		1:43	3↑ Alw 15000	8	1	21½	2hd	1hd	2no	Cruguet J	118	b	5.10	--	Swoonland118noShadw Brook1183Hydronaut116½	Nosed out 8
22Aug69- 7Sar	hd	1⅝Ⓣ		2:401	3↑ Seneca H 29k	6	6	46	89½	810	714	Cruguet J	112	b	14.20	78-12	Harem Lady1126Larceny Kid116nkNashandy1121½	Fell back 10
7Aug69- 9Sar	fm	1 1/16Ⓣ		1:422	3↑ Alw 15000	6	4	48	48½	44½	37	Cruguet J	123	b	*1.90	81-12	Tradesman116noLoiretII1187ShadwBrook1231½	No response 6
29Jly69- 7Sar	sf	1 1/16Ⓣ		1:434	3↑ Alw 15000	4	2	24	22	31	2no	Cruguet J	118	b	*1.40	81-18	BurningBridges110noShadwBrook1183RobotIII116¾	Gaining 6
11Jly69- 7Aqu	sf	1⅛Ⓣ		1:542	3↑ Alw 15000	3	2	21½	22	2½	1nk	Cruguet J	116	b	*1.20	63-37	Shadow Brook116nkLoiret II118½[D]Mara Lark1202	Driving 4
28Jun69- 5Bel	fm	7fⓉ		1:222	3↑ Alw 15000	2	3	22	21½	2½	1nk	Cruguet J	117	b	4.60	96-16	ShdowBrook117nkBaitman119nkPasstheBrandy1191½	Driving 7
20Jun69- 6Bel	yl	7fⓉ		1:23	3↑ Alw 15000	2	4	42½	34	11	11½	Cruguet J	117	b	4.00	93-06	Shadow Brook1171½Util1172½Brunch1071	Brisk urging 6
14Jun69- 6Bel	hd	7fⓉ		1:222	3↑ Alw 15000	11	1	3nk	1½	4¾	63¾	Cruguet J	117	b	5.10	92-08	Otomano II1171½Hespero117hdHigh Tribute117½	Speed,tired 12
30May69- 6Aqu	fm	1 1/16Ⓣ		1:423	3↑ Alw 15000	6	5	57	54	52½	32	Cruguet J	117	b	5.30	88-12	Rhinelander II1171Denegri1171Shadow Brook1172	Rallied 8
19May69- 6Aqu	fst	7f	:22 :441 1:10	1:234	3↑ Alw 15000	2	5	26	48	55½	52	Cruguet J	118	b	18.70	80-14	AlleyFighter118noCallaCop1181FlyingTackle118nk	In close 8
8Jun68- 7Del	fm	1 1/16Ⓣ		1:422	3↑ Alw 10000	2	2	24	32	33½	31½	Passmore WJ	119	b	*2.40	90-08	Robot III113½Lucky Turn1191Shadow Brook119½	No excuses 6
1Jun68- 8Del	sf	1 1/16Ⓣ		1:45	3↑ Brandywine H 30k	6	4	66½	33	51¾	74¾	Passmore WJ	112	b	7.60	74-21	Birthday Card1091¾Spoon Bait1121¼Tornum1121	Tired 13
11May68- 7Pim	fst	6f	:231 :462	1:113	3↑ Alw 8500	7	3	45½	44	1hd	2no	Cordero A Jr	112	b	3.20	92-17	BigRockCandy115noShdwBrk1121¼GreatWhitWy122½	Gamely 7
29Apr68- 7Pim	sf	5fⓉ	:223 :461	:584	4↑ Alw 7500	3	4	65	510	48	32½	Passmore WJ	117	b	7.00e	92-15	Road at Sea1171¼Sikkim1171¼Shadow Brook1172	Stride late 9
25Nov67- 7Lrl	fm	1 1/16Ⓣ		1:424	3↑ Laurel H (Div 1) 17k	4	3	42	42½	3nk	1hd	Passmore WJ	111	b	7.70	92-07	ShadowBrook111hdGreenFelt115noAttheHelm1081½	Driving 8
16Nov67- 8Lrl	fst	1	:233 :473 1:122	1:371	3↑ Alw 6000	6	4	3½	2½	1hd	1¾	Passmore WJ	112	b	4.60	95-17	ShadowBrook112¾LighttheFuse1125GayFlight1121½	Driving 8
8Nov67- 8Lrl	fm	*1Ⓣ	:234 :472 1:131	1:394	Alw 6000	4	5	43½	32	1½	11½	Passmore WJ	112	b	*2.40	91-09	ShadowBrk1121½EnglishMuffn1221Mystc'sDsr115hd	Driving 8
11Oct67- 6Aqu	my	1⊗	:232 :463 1:112	1:362	3↑ Alw 12000	2	1	2hd	2½	49	34¾	Turcotte R	112	b	*1.70	81-19	Ski Lift123¾Hornbeam1124Shadow Brook1124½	Used early 7
27Sep67- 8Aqu	fm	1 1/16Ⓣ		1:431	3↑ Alw 12000	3	4	31¼	32	62	43¾	Turcotte R	111	b	7.80	86-10	RoyalComedian113¾RoylConcert1181Hornbeam1132	In close 8
18Sep67- 7Aqu	fst	7f	:224 :453 1:10	1:23	3↑ Alw 15000	8	1	64½	68½	78½	55¼	Turcotte R	115	b	19.60	86-15	Prinkipo113¾FirstandFinest1201¾MajorArt1132	No threat 9
17Aug67- 8Sar	fst	7f	:223 :451 1:091	1:214	3↑ Alw 10000	2	5	68¼	69	45¼	511	Cordero A Jr	116	b	2.70	90-09	PeterPiper1178MisterPitt'sKid1122MjorArt112nk	No threat 6
31Jly67- 6Sar	fst	7f	:222 :453 1:104	1:233	3↑ Alw 10000	4	6	612	54½	43	23½	Cordero A Jr	117	b	17.30	88-12	High Tribute1173½Shadow Brook1173Tanrackin1124	Rallied 8
22Jly67- 6Del	fst	6f	:22 :45	1:104	3↑ Alw 5000	6	8	88¼	78½	710	78¾	Lee T	111	b	4.90	82-18	VikingDancer1111¾LittltoDo111nkLghtthFus1142½	No factor 8
12Jly67- 7Del	gd	6f	:22 :453	1:114	3↑ Alw 4500	9	7	65¾	66	54¼	1½	Lee T	108	b	3.00	86-18	ShadowBrook108½CrownedKing112noGayFlight1122½	Driving 9
21Jun67- 7Del	sf	1Ⓣ		1:382	3↑ Alw 5500	3	2	2½	1hd	2½	2hd	Lee T	114	b	*2.50	83-17	Mystic'sDesire114hdShadowBrook1141¼BleVert124nk	Gamely 9
30May67- 5Del	fst	6f	:222 :463	1:121	Alw 4500	3	6	67¼	43	3nk	11	Lee T	122	b	*1.30e	84-19	Shadow Brook1221Stitches1193Tangelo122no	Drew clear 8
12May67- 7Pim	fst	5f⊗	:224 :464	:591	3↑ Alw 5000	8	7	87½	75¼	62¼	31½	Lee T	113	b	2.70	96-15	LittletoDo1081ComeonGeorge112½ShadwBrk1131½	Gaining 12
25Nov66- 7Lrl	fst	7f	:222 :461 1:121	1:254	Alw 5000	8	2	37	25	23	3hd	Cruguet J	117	b	7.30	90-18	GalaPerformance122noIrishStil122noShdwBrook1173	Gamely 9
18Nov66- 7Lrl	fm	*1Ⓣ	:232 :471 1:14	1:41	Alw 5500	3	4	49	35½	33	21½	Cruguet J	117	b	5.80	83-15	ShootingChant1171½ShdwBrk117½GalaPerfrmnc1224	Game 12
7Nov66- 4Lrl	fst	6f	:232 :48	1:134	©Md Sp Wt	10	5	52¾	44½	32	12½♦	Cruguet J	118	b	*1.20	83-18	[DH]ShdwBrook118[DH]GrandTodd1182½TigersTune1181	Driving 12
12Oct66- 3Aqu	fst	7f	:23 :463 1:13	1:252	©Md Sp Wt	8	3	63¾	56½	33½	33½	Turcotte R	122	b	4.10	75-18	Shah1221½Quiet Town1222Shadow Brook1224	Made fair try 14
28Sep66- 4Aqu	fst	7f	:223 :46 1:113	1:243	©Md Sp Wt	4	3	64½	56½	43	44¼	Turcotte R	122	b	30.10	79-19	Comprador1222½Damascus122¾Air Rights1221	Even race 14
14Sep66- 4Aqu	gd	6f	:223 :464	1:123	©Md Sp Wt	3	7	66	78½	75½	612	Blum W	122		28.50	68-23	Hornbeam1226Quaich1221½Court Service122hd	Showed little 10
27Aug66- 1Sar	fst	6f	:224 :471	1:132	Md Sp Wt	12	4	32	84½	812	812	Turcotte R	122		42.70	69-08	TwistofTime1224½PrimeMotive1221½CourtServc122hd	Swerved 14

Shecky Greene

b. c. 1970, by Noholme II (Star Kingdom)–Lester's Pride, by Model Cadet

Lifetime record: 29 15 4 1 $317,654

Own.– J. Kellman
Br.– Joseph Kellman (Fla)
Tr.– L.M. Goldfine

26Jun74- 8Aqu	fst	7f	:223 :444 1:084	1:211	3↑ Nassau County H-G3	5	3	2hd	22	46	69½	Perret C	126	b	9.20	85-10	Timeless Moment112½Forego132½North Sea1142½	Gave way 6
20Jun74- 8Mth	fm	1 1/16Ⓣ	:243 :482 1:114	1:423	4↑ Alw 12000	1	1	2½	2hd	2hd	41¼	Perret C	115	b	*1.20	95-08	DownAmng118hdBigRedL.1131BldStatemnt113nk	Weakened 6
8Jun74- 7Mth	fst	6f	:221 :443	1:092	3↑ Alw 10000	2	2	1hd	12	12	1¾	Perret C	124	b	*.80	93-17	Shecky Greene124¾Alehouse114noHome Jerome114¾	Driving 8
1Jun74- 7Mth	gd	6f	:222 :452	1:104	4↑ Alw 10000	6	2	2hd	1hd	1hd	33¾	Perret C	119	b	*.40	85-26	ProprBostonian116¾TwinTime119noShckyGrn1191¼	Bore out 8
16Feb74- 5GP	fst	6f	:213 :44	1:092	4↑ Alw 10000	8	1	22	11½	12	12	Turcotte R	122	b	*.30	92-16	ShckyGrn1222HomeJerome1122TrggrHppy112hd	Ridden out 8
2Feb74- 0GP	fst	7f	:222 :442 1:091	1:222	3↑ Sprint Champ H 41k	3	2	2½	1hd	1hd	22	Cordero A Jr	127	b	-	90-17	Cheriepe1152SheckyGreen1273GyPrr1127	Tired under impost 4
	Exhibition race run between 5th and 6th races - No wagering																	
19Jan74- 9GP	fst	6f	:214 :443	1:091	3↑ Renaissance H 31k	5	1	42	32	22	2¾	Cordero A Jr	129	b	*.90	92-17	Lonetree119¾ShckyGreene129½Cherip1162	Bumped after st. 8
22Oct73- 8Aqu	fst	7f	:223 :444 1:084	1:211	3↑ Vosburgh H-G2	5	2	1hd	1½	21½	44¼	Baeza B	126	b	*1.40	91-16	Aljamin118noHighbinder1153TimelsMomnt1121¼	No excuse 8
3Oct73- 7Bel	fst	6f	:223 :451	1:092	3↑ Fall Highweight H-G3	9	3	83	64½	31½	21¼	Perret C	137	b	3.80	95-12	King's Bishop1291¼Shecky Greene137noAljamin1253	Wide 10
15Sep73- 8Bow	gd	6f	:23 :453	1:102	3↑ Patuxent H 28k	5	2	11	11	12	11¼	Perret C	126	b	*1.00	91-17	SheckyGreene1261¼King'sBshop1181¼PlsurCstl1082¼	Driving 9
5Aug73- 8Del	fst	6f	:443	1:094	Kelso H-G3	7	1	33	31½	3½	11¾	Perret C	128	b	*.70	96-14	ShckyGreene1281¾CarCounty1161½LttlBgChf1193	Drew clear 7
28Jly73- 8Haw	fst	6½f	:22 :451 1:092	1:161	3↑ Midwest H 28k	7	1	31	3½	12	14½	Perret C	119	b	*.40	92-11	Shecky Greene1194½Iterate1132Makambo115¾	Easily 8
18Jly73- 8Mth	fst	6f	:214 :44	1:084	Select H-G3	5	2	3nk	2hd	1hd	1½	Perret C	126	b	*1.60	96-14	SheckyGrne126½TimelessMoment1201¼BigBand1154	Driving 7
16Jun73- 9Tdn	gd	1⅛	:461 1:103 1:364	1:501	Ohio Derby-G3	8	4	35½	34	1116	1122	Perret C	122	b	7.80	67-14	OurNative1221½HeartsofLttuc1123ArbsBoy115nk	Speed,tired 12
30May73- 7Bel	fst	1	:231 :45 1:091	1:344	Withers-G2	4	2	21	21½	21½	45½	Cordero A Jr	126	b	7.30	92-17	Linda'sChief1263StopthMusc1262Forgo126½	Bore in on turn 6
5May73- 9CD	fst	1¼	:472 1:114 1:361	1:592	Ky Derby-G1	11	1	13	32	57	616	Adams L	126	b	5.70e	87-10	Secretariat1262½Sham1268Our Native126½	Used in pace 13
28Apr73- 7CD	fst	7f	:224 :444 1:092	1:23	Alw 10000	6	2	12	12½	12½	15	Blum W	122	b	*.50	92-16	SheckyGreene1225RestlessJet122nkCrCounty1194	Mild drive 7
7Apr73- 9OP	gd	1⅛	:462 1:11 1:372	1:493	Ark Derby-G2	7	2	2½	3nk	88¼	1016	Baeza B	126	b	*.90	79-13	Impecunious1262Vodk1231¾Wrbucks1233½	Brushed first turn 10
21Mar73- 9GP	sl	1 1/16	:242 :48 1:114	1:434	Fountain of Youth-G3	3	2	23	21	11	11	Baeza B	122	b	*1.10	84-23	SheckyGreene1221TwiceaPrince117½MyGallant1122½	Driving 6
7Mar73- 9GP	fst	7f	:221 :443 1:082	1:204	Hutcheson-G3	2	3	3½	12	14	13¼	Baeza B	122	b	*.30	100-10	Shecky Greene1223¼Forego1169Leo's Pisces1124½	Easily 7
21Feb73- 9Hia	fst	7f	:231 :46 1:10	1:223	[S]Fla Breeders' H 30k	6	2	12	11½	12½	11¾	Baeza B	127		*.70	94-14	SheckyGrne1271¾StepNicely1164½JmDuncn115no	Ridden out 6
14Feb73- 7Hia	fst	6f	:214 :442	1:083	Alw 8000	1	2	2hd	11½	15	18	Baeza B	122		*2.10	101-13	SheckyGreene1228AssagaiJr115¾StepNicely1153	Ridden out 8
18Nov72- 8CD	fst	1	:223 :451 1:104	1:353	Ky Jockey Club 59k	5	2	21	62¼	818	831	Marquez C	122	b	1.90e	60-20	Puntilla1169Golden Don116nkAnnihilate 'Em1228	Tired 8
8Nov72- 8CD	sl	7f	:223 :45 1:10	1:234	Alw 10000	4	2	1½	11	11½	2nk	Marquez C	122	b	*.50	88-22	Annihilate'Em112nkShckyGreen1229TonitheCt1133	Swerved 10

4Oct72- 7Bel	fst 7f	:221 :444 1:093 1:223	Cowdin 54k	3 5 52¼ 64¾ 54½ 56¼	Marquez C H	121 b	3.80	88-11	StepNicely1152StoptheMusic1212Linda'sChief1151½	Checked	12
12Aug72- 8AP	fst 6f	:223 :46 :58 1:102	Futurity 186k	10 2 43 1½ 15 19	Marquez C	122 b	*.40e	91-16	SheckyGrn1229SunnySouth1221¼Slor'sNghtOut1224	In hand	12
26Jly72- 8AP	sly 5½f	:222 :462 :584 1:051	©Arch Ward 28k	3 5 42 32 13 12	Marquez C	117 b	*1.00	89-26	ShckyGreene1172DeadlyDream1155SunnySouth122½	Driving	12
8Jly72- 6AP	fst 5½f	:222 :444 :564 1:031	Alw 5400	6 1 3½ 18 17 19	Marquez C	115 b	*.30	99-09	SheckyGreene1159StrongSide118hdBacktoJack1152¼	Easily	8
15Jun72- 7AP	fst 5f	:22 :453 :571	Md Sp Wt	6 2 14 15 17 111	Marquez C	118 b	5.90	100-15	SheckyGrne11811HandsomDplomt1185IrshDoubt118hd	Easily	8

Shuvee

ch. f. 1966, by Nashua (Nasrullah)–Levee, by Hill Prince

Lifetime record: 44 16 10 6 $890,445

Own.– Mrs W. Stone
Br.– Whitney Stone (Va)
Tr.– W.C. Freeman

30Oct71- 7Aqu	fst 2	:482 2:30 2:552 3:202	3↑ J C Gold Cup 111k	6 4 2½ 11½ 15 17	Velasquez J	121	*1.30	94-16	Shuvee1217Paraje1242Loud1248	Ridden out	7
11Oct71- 8Atl	gd 1⅜	:482 1:113 1:364 1:564	3↑ ⒻMatchmaker 50k	6 5 45½ 56½ 31 4¾	Turcotte R	118	*1.30	91-12	Deceit113hdSea Saga114hdDouble Delta125½	No excuse	8
2Oct71- 7Bel	fst 1¼	:461 1:10 1:35 2:002	3↑ Woodward 113k	7 4 510 69 69 69	Turcotte R	123	3.70	89-13	ⒹCougarII1265WestCoastScout121nkTinajro121no	No threat	10
11Sep71- 7Bel	sly 1⅛	:453 1:093 1:351 1:483	3↑ ⒻBeldame 82k	2 6 46½ 26 24 2½	Baeza B	123	*.70	90-12	Double Delta123½Shuvee12310Cathy Honey1231½	Second best	7
23Aug71- 7Sar	fst 1⅛	:50 1:141 1:382 1:503	3↑ ⒻDiana H 44k	5 3 31½ 21 21 1nk	Turcotte R	128	*1.10	88-11	Shuvee128nkDouble Delta1265½Cathy Honey116nk	Hard drive	5
7Aug71- 7Sar	fst 1⅛	:473 1:114 1:364 1:492	3↑ Whitney 60k	13 9 108¾ 116¼ 66 33	Turcotte R	116	*4.10	91-11	Protanto117hdPeace Corps1143Shuvee116nk	Rallied wide	14
22May71- 7Aqu	fst 1⅛	:471 1:122 1:37 1:493	3↑ ⒻTop Flight H 53k	5 3 31½ 1½ 11 1¾	Turcotte R	127	*.70e	88-17	Shuvee127¾Cathy Honey1181¼Office Queen1277	Driving	5
28Apr71- 7Aqu	fst 1	:232 :464 1:113 1:364	3↑ ⒻBed o' Roses H 32k	2 4 42½ 42 21½ 22	Turcotte R	127	*.60	81-23	Office Queen1252Shuvee1273Royal Fillet1103½	Gamely	6
15Apr71- 7Aqu	fst 6f	:23 :462 1:103	3↑ Alw 20000	6 1 53½ 67 68 25	Baeza B	116	*1.60e	85-25	SummerAir1195Shvee116nkPrimeVenture1211½	Finished well	9
31Oct70- 7Aqu	fst 2	:503 2:302 2:554 3:213	3↑ J C Gold Cup 108k	4 1 1½ 1hd 12½ 12	Turcotte R	121	2.90	88-16	Shuvee1212Loud1191¼Hydrologist1243¾	Mild urging	5
3Oct70- 7Bel	fst 1¼	:462 1:101 1:353 2:014	3↑ Woodward 109k	2 4 46 41½ 55½ 57¾	Turcotte R	123	7.70	83-08	Personality121nk[DH]Hydrologst126[DH]Twogundn1264½	Hit rail	7
12Sep70- 7Bel	fst 1⅛	:454 1:10 1:351 1:48	3↑ ⒻBeldame 83k	2 2 25 23 11 11	Turcotte R	123	*1.30e	94-14	Shuvee1231Obeah1231¼Cold Comfort1182½	Brisk drive	7
24Aug70- 7Sar	sly 1⅛	:464 1:112 1:371 1:493	3↑ ⒻDiana H 49k	4 6 76¾ 43 21 1no	Turcotte R	120	3.50	93-15	Shuvee120noDark Emerald1094Native Partner1121	Driving	12
8Jly70- 8Mth	fst 1 1/16	:232 :463 1:111 1:44	3↑ ⒻMolly Pitcher 44k	4 3 58¼ 67½ 66½ 56	Baeza B	123	*.70	79-13	DoublRippl112¾WhataDream1151Deb'sDarlng1144	No excuse	9
10Jun70- 7Bel	fst 7f	:222 :452 1:102 1:234	3↑ ⒻVagrancy H 28k	2 4 511 611 611 510	Baeza B	123	2.00	78-15	Process Shot1272½Powder Mountain104¾Native Partner1106		6
	No response										
23May70- 7Aqu	fst 1⅛	:481 1:114 1:362 1:483	3↑ ⒻTop Flight H 57k	2 1 1hd 1½ 1½ 14	Baeza B	120	2.40	93-13	Shuvee1204Singing Rain1227Swiss Cheese110¾	Handily	10
2May70- 8Pim	fst 1 1/16	:233 :464 1:11 1:433	3↑ ⒻGallorette H 32k	5 6 67 56½ 27 28	Davidson J	122	*1.20	84-13	SingingRain1198Shuvee1223½MissFallRiver1091½	No excuse	7
25Apr70- 8Aqu	fst 1	:24 :464 1:11 1:352	3↑ Alw 15000	6 5 75¼ 53 42 43¼	Davidson J	113	*3.30	87-18	GleamngSword1161¾ShinngSword1181½Bromtr120hd	No rally	9
8Apr70- 7Aqu	fst 7f	:23 :452 1:10 1:224	3↑ ⒻDistaff H 27k	2 5 510 512 613 615	Davidson J	123	7.50	72-20	ProcssShot1261¾TaWee1342DedctdtoSu115hd	Never a factor	6
27Nov69- 7Aqu	fst 1⅛	:492 1:134 1:381 1:50	3↑ ⒻFirenze H 56k	1 1 2½ 42 21 2¾	Davidson J	122	*1.40	85-19	Amerigo Lady121¾Shuvee1221½Obeah120½	Finished willingly	8
11Nov69- 7Aqu	gd 1¼	:473 1:121 1:38 2:03	3↑ ⒻLadies H 58k	7 3 612 43 3½ 11¼	Davidson J	117	*2.80	81-22	Shuvee1171¼AmrigoLdy1211¼Obeh1212½	Blocked,hard drive	11
1Nov69- 7Aqu	fst 7f	:221 :442 1:083 1:213	3↑ Vosburgh H 58k	3 10 119 1012 85½ 61¾	Turcotte R	114	14.90	91-13	TaWee123hd[DH]PlckyLucky116[DH]RisingMarkt120½	Late bid	11
13Sep69- 7Bel	fst 1⅛	:462 1:103 1:36 1:491	3↑ ⒻBeldame 81k	3 4 48½ 46 37 36½	Davidson J	118	3.00	83-16	Gamely1233Amerigo Lady1233½Shuvee1182	Finished willing	5
30Aug69- 7Bel	fst 1⅛	:462 1:102 1:352 1:49	ⒻGazelle H 53k	1 5 57 56½ 47 36½	Davidson J	127	*1.10	84-12	Gallant Bloom1273½Pit Bunny1163Shuvee1271½	No excuse	5
9Aug69- 6Sar	gd 1¼	:483 1:131 1:392 2:062	ⒻAlabama 54k	2 4 46 31½ 11½ 14	Davidson J	124	*1.00	76-15	Shuvee1244PitBunny114½HailtoPatsy1182	Easily the best	5
26Jly69- 8Del	gd 1⅛	:464 1:122 1:384 1:511	ⒻDel Oaks 59k	7 5 68½ 56½ 411 417	Davidson J	121	1.60	64-23	ⒹPitBunny1121¼GallantBlm12112WhitXmss1113¼	No excuse	7
12Jly69- 7Lib	fst 1 1/16	:231 :47 1:104 1:431	ⒻCotillion H 55k	3 6 54¾ 53¼ 3½ 1nk	Davidson J	124	*.40	--	Shuvee124nkClass Is Out1133Secret Verdict1142	Just up	7
21Jun69- 7Bel	fst 1¼	:462 1:103 1:363 2:031	ⒻC C A Oaks 119k	4 5 511 44½ 1hd 13	Davidson J	121	*.30	84-17	Shuvee1213Hail to Patsy1211½Secret Verdict1211½	Easily	7
31May69- 7Aqu	fst 1⅛	:474 1:123 1:38 1:501	ⒻMother Goose 87k	1 4 511 55½ 22 12½	Davidson J	121	*1.10	85-17	Shuvee1212½HailtoPatsy1212½RestlssTorndo1214	Ridden out	6
17May69- 7Aqu	fst 1	:223 :443 1:091 1:353	ⒻAcorn 59k	7 5 58½ 36 2hd 1¾	Davidson J	121	*.80	89-14	Shuvee121¾Hail to Patsy1213Big Advance121nk	Mild drive	9
7May69- 7Aqu	fst 7f	:222 :451 1:092 1:223	ⒻComely 28k	3 6 66 45 23 2hd	Davidson J	121	2.90	88-13	TaWee118hdShuvee1215HastyHitter118hd	Getting to winner	6
9Nov68- 8GS	sl 1 1/16	:23 :474 1:13 1:454	ⒻGardenia 183k	5 7 52½ 2hd 21½ 21¼	Davidson J	119	*1.00	75-28	Gallant Bloom1191¼Shuvee11915Let's Be Gay119nk	Game try	7
26Oct68- 0Lrl	fst 1 1/16	:23 :463 1:123 1:444	ⒻSelima 108k	4 5 47 23½ 2hd 1nk	Turcotte R	122	-	93-17	Shuvee122nkProcess Shot1196Queen's Double11940	Driving	5
	Exhibition race run between 7th and 8th races-No wagering										
5Oct68- 7Bel	fst 1	:23 :463 1:112 1:37	ⒻFrizette 130k	7 8 99½ 76 23 1nk	Davidson J	119	4.50e	89-13	Shuvee119nkGallant Bloom1193Dihela1194	Up final strides	11
23Sep68- 7Bel	fst 7f	:223 :46 1:104 1:241	ⒻAstarita (Div 2) 23k	3 6 56½ 65½ 74¾ 31¼	Davidson J	112	10.80	85-17	Dihela1121Imbibe116nkShuvee1122	Found stride late	8
14Sep68- 4Aqu	fst 6f	:223 :461 1:114	ⒻAlw 7000	3 10 107½ 97 64¼ 21¼	Davidson J	119	*2.70	83-14	Gunite1081¼Shuvee119¾Plane119hd	In close,rallied	12
30Aug68- 6Aqu	fst 6f	:222 :46 1:112	ⒻAlw 12000	1 7 711 69½ 25 23	Baeza B	114	6.40	83-20	Gallant Bloom1063Shuvee1143Prefer1161	Finished strongly	7
20Aug68- 5Sar	fst 6f	:221 :462 1:114	ⒻMd Sp Wt	13 11 98 98¼ 2½ 14	Baeza B	119	3.70	89-09	Shuvee1194Table D'Hote119½Ambranded1192½	Easily best	14
13Aug68- 5Sar	fst 5½f	:221 :454 :573 1:04	ⒻMd Sp Wt	4 7 87¼ 1012 613 512	Gustines H	119	4.20	85-11	Ta Wee1196Drip Spring1192Socializing1192½	No mishap	12
3Aug68- 1Sar	fst 5½f	:224 :471 :592 1:054	ⒻMd Sp Wt	7 4 41½ 52¾ 31½ 31½	Baeza B	119 b	*1.40	86-12	Pashamin119noElizabeth'sDancr1161½Shuvee1195	No mishap	10
25Jly68- 5Aqu	gd 5½f	:222 :462 :584 1:051	ⒻMd Sp Wt	8 8 63½ 74¾ 33½ 23	Baeza B	119 b	*2.50	84-18	French Bread1193Shuvee1194Keep a Secret1191	Rallied	9
5Jun68- 4Bel	fst 5½f	:231 :47 :591 1:053	ⒻMd Sp Wt	9 8 52 52 43½ 35¾	Davidson J	119 b	*1.70	87-15	Golden Or119¾Go to Bed1195Shuvee119¾	Raced wide late	10
22May68- 4Bel	fst 5½f	:23 :462 :584 1:052	ⒻMd Sp Wt	4 7 34 33 45 42¼	Davidson J	119	*2.50	92-14	Fillypasser119hdFoolish Miss119nkTudor Home1192	Hung	10
8May68- 4Aqu	fst 5f	:222 :461 :59	ⒻMd Sp Wt	5 8 87¾ 69½ 56½ 47¾	Davidson J	119	*1.90	82-11	Gunite1194Miss Georgene119¾Most Welcome1193	No threat	10

Smart Angle

b. f. 1977, by Quadrangle (Cohoes)–Smartaire, by Quibu

Lifetime record: 17 7 4 1 $414,217

Own.– Ryehill Farm
Br.– Ryehill Farm (Md)
Tr.– Woodford C. Stephens

24Jan81- 8GP	sly 6f	:221 :454 1:11	4↑ ⒻAlw 20000	3 2 1½ 1hd 3½ 59¼	Maple E	115 b	*2.30	75-20	Lacey1175Nice and Sharp1172Sober Jig1151	Faltered	10
12Jan81- 9GP	fm *1Ⓣ	1:373	4↑ ⒻAlw 25000	7 1 13 2½ 57½ 713	Maple E	115	*2.40	80-19	SoloHaina1177LaSoufriere119hdDoingItMyWy122½	Gave way	8
18Dec80- 8Crc	fst 6f	:222 :46 1:113	3↑ ⒻAlw 13000	9 1 42 44½ 811 914	Maple E	118	*.80	80-16	Migdalia C.1133Lacey118nkClassy Witch1146½	Fell back	9
16May80- 8Pim	fst 1 1/16	:232 :464 1:111 1:442	ⒻBlack-Eyed Susan-G2	7 2 22 31½ 34 65	Maple S	121	*.90	78-17	WeberCityMiss1182¼Bishop'sRing1111ChampagnStr114½	Tired	8
5Apr80- 9OP	fst 1 1/16	:231 :464 1:114 1:451	ⒻFantasy-G1	7 4 52¼ 34½ 513 728	Maple S	121	1.40	54-20	Bold 'nDetermind1212½Satin Ribera1154Honest and True1187		7
	Gave way										
22Mar80- 9FG	fst 1 1/16	:241 :473 1:121 1:442	ⒻFG Oaks 56k	7 1 11½ 11½ 11½ 2hd	Maple S	121	*.20	90-15	Honest and True118hdSmartAngle121½LadyTaurianPeace1184		8
	Just failed										
3Mar80- 9Hia	fst 1⅛	:474 1:122 1:38 1:51	ⒻPoinsettia-G3	1 1 16 17 16 17	Maple S	122	*.40	77-23	SrtAngle1227SweetAudrey114½BrownSt.Belle11414	Easily	5
13Feb80- 9Hia	fst 7f	:231 :454 1:103 1:24	ⒻHibiscus 36k	4 2 1hd 2½ 1½ 2no	Maple S	122	*.40	83-14	BrownSt.Belle112noSmrtAngle1222½SweetAudry1172½	Failed	6
17Nov79- 8Aqu	fst 1⅛	:481 1:131 1:383 1:511	ⒻDemoiselle-G2	2 3 51¼ 61¾ 1hd 2no	Maple S	121	*1.10	79-21	GenuineRisk116noSmartAngle1216¾SprucePine1123¾	Bore in	7
20Oct79- 9Pim	fst 1 1/16	:232 :471 1:114 1:451	ⒻSelima-G1	4 2 23 22 11½ 12	Maple S	122	*.50	79-18	SmartAngle1222ParExcellance122½StretBllt1193	Ridden out	6
7Oct79- 8Bel	fst 1	:233 :47 1:123 1:381	ⒻFrizette-G1	8 4 32 11 1hd 11¾	Maple S	119	2.90	77-20	Smart Angle1191¾Royal Suite11911Hardship1195	Driving	11
24Sep79- 8Bel	fst 7f	:231 :462 1:103 1:234	ⒻMatron-G1	3 1 1hd 11 1hd 1½	Maple S	119	8.00	83-22	SmartAngle119½RoyalSuite1193¾NuitD'Amour1193¾	Driving	5
10Sep79- 8Bel	fst 6½f	:224 :461 1:104 1:171	ⒻAstarita-G3	6 1 3½ 3½ 21½ 33¼	Maple S	116	*1.40	87-20	Royal Suite1142¾Andrea F.112½Smart Angle1161½	Weakened	6
26Aug79- 8Sar	fst 6f	:213 :45 1:103	ⒻSpinaway-G1	1 2 24 2½ 12 11½	Maple S	119	*.80	87-12	SmrtAngle1191½JetRating1193½MarthonGrl119hd	Ridden out	6
13Aug79- 8Sar	my 6f	:214 :452 1:11	ⒻAdirondack-G3	1 3 2hd 1hd 1hd 1nk	Maple S	119	3.90	85-14	Smart Angle119nkLucky My Way1141½Andrea F.1142	Driving	9
28Jly79- 7Bow	fst 5½f	:214 :452 :581 1:05	ⒻⓈLuck Penny 32k	4 4 33 36½ 33½ 1nk	Maple S	114	1.30	94-17	Smart Angle114nkHail to Ambition1153Salem's Nymph1229		5
	Driving										
12Jly79- 4Bel	fst 5½f	:22 :453 :582 1:051	ⒻMd Sp Wt	4 2 1hd 1hd 1hd 2hd	Maple E	117	2.00	89-14	RioRita117hdSmartAngle1171¾DamaskFan1171	Stubborn try	10

Snow Knight (GB)

ch. c. 1971, by Firestreak (Pardal)–Snow Blossom, by Flush Royal **Lifetime record: 22 9 5 2 $532,427**
Own.– Windfields Farm
Br.– J.A.C. Lilley (GB)
Tr.– M. Miller

8Nov75- 7Lrl yl 1½Ⓣ :494 1:152 2:062 2:311 3↑ D C Int'l-G1 5 3 59½ 52¾ 611 612 Velasquez J 127 *2.10 51-37 Nobiliary117¾Comtesse de Loir1243On My Way II1272 9
Bobbled backstretch
26Oct75- 7WO fm 1⅝Ⓣ :501 1:392 2:431 3↑ Can Int'l-G1 11 6 66 31 12 1½ Velasquez J 126 3.70 84-16 Snow Knight126½Comtesse de Loir1231½Carney's Point126hd 11
Ridden out
11Oct75- 8Bel gd 1½Ⓣ :493 1:15 2:05 2:291 3↑ Man o' War-G1 8 5 53½ 31½ 3½ 21¾ Velasquez J 126 *1.00 76-22 ⒹOneontheAisle1211¾SnowKnight1261Drollry126nk Bothered 8
Placed first through disqualification
1Oct75- 8Bel gd 1⅜Ⓣ :483 1:133 1:38 2:161 3↑ Manhattan H (Div 2)-G2 5 7 74¾ 4¾ 1hd 1¾ Velasquez J 123 *1.00e 84-17 Snow Knight123¾Shady Character1131¼One on the Aisle1142½ 8
Driving
17Sep75- 8Bel fm 1¼Ⓣ :48 1:121 1:364 2:01 3↑ Brightn Bch H (Div 2) 43k 5 2 32½ 1½ 13 11¼ Baeza B 121 *1.80e 95-08 Snow Knight1211¼Drollery111nkGolden Don1262½ Driving 9
20Aug75- 8Sar fm 1⅝Ⓣ 2:42 3↑ Seneca H-G3 6 1 11 1½ 12 11½ Velasquez J 118 *2.00e 79-21 Snow Knight1181½Golden Don126½Drollery1113 Mild drive 8
26Jly75- 7Atl gd 1³⁄₁₆Ⓣ :49 1:13 1:392 1:57 3↑ U Nations H-G1 7 6 713 912 914 915 Barrera C 118 3.80 70-26 RoyalGlint1203½Stonewalk1205½R.TomCan116hd Unruly start 9
10Jly75- 6Bel gd 1¹⁄₁₆Ⓣ :24 :464 1:11 1:424 3↑ Alw 20000 2 6 68½ 53½ 42½ 2no Velasquez J 122 *1.00 87-13 Harbor Pilot116noSnow Knight1221¾Branford Court1161 7
Circled horses
18Jun75- 6Bel gd 1¹⁄₁₆Ⓣ :233 :471 1:114 1:433 3↑ Alw 15000 4 3 33 32½ 1½ 11 Velasquez J 116 *.90 83-17 SnowKnight1161TelexNumber1132¾Ladd113hd Blocked,easily 6
Previously trained by J. Bentley
27Oct74- 7WO fm 1⅝Ⓣ :471 1:373 2:40 3↑ Can Int'l-G2 5 1 18 12 64¼ 810 Hawley S 117 b 12.90 95-05 Dahlia1231Big Spruce1261½Carney's Point126hd Used early 9
19Oct74- 7WO fm 1¼Ⓣ :48 1:124 1:38 2:03 3↑ Jockey Club Cup H 17k 8 3 21 2hd 3nk 65½ Rogers C 123 *.90 86-09 Carney's Point120noGood Port1142½Olmedo112¾ Tired 8
12Oct74- 6WO fm *1¹⁄₁₆Ⓣ :251 :51 1:161 1:463 3↑ Alw 6500 3 1 11½ 11½ 1hd 2no Hawley S 117 *.65 71-22 Carney's Point126noSnow Knight1172¾Good Port123¾ Missed 5
Previously trained by P. Nelson
20Aug74♦ York(GB) gd *1⁵⁄₁₆ⓉLH 2:092 3↑ Benson & Hedges Gold Cup-G1 34 Taylor B 122 14.00 Dahlia1302½Imperial Prince1221½Snow Knight122nk 9
Stk120000 Tracked in 3rd,one-paced last quarter
27Jly74♦ Ascot(GB) gd 1½ⓉRH 2:33 3↑ King George VI & Queen Eliz 69 Taylor B 119 5.50 Dahlia1302½Highclere1161Dankaro119 10
Stk245000 Tracked leader,led over 2f out,weakened 1½f out
5Jun74♦ Epsom(GB) fm 1½ⓉLH 2:35 Epsom Derby 12 Taylor B 126 50.00 Snow Knight1262Imperial Prince1261Giacometti126nk 18
Stk267000 Led over 6f out,held well
11May74♦ Lingfield(GB) gd 1½ⓉLH 2:394 Derby Trial Stakes 32½ Taylor B 126 2.25 Bustino1261Sin y Sin1261½Snow Knight1262½ 7
Stk23200 Trailed to 4f out,bid 2f out,one-paced final furlong
27Apr74♦ Sandown(GB) gd 1¼ⓉRH 2:094 Classic Trial Stakes 2½ Taylor B 126 *1.75 Bustino121½Snow Knight126¾Understudy1261½ 9
Stk8700 Led,hard ridden over 1f out,headed 100y out,gamely
27Oct73♦ Doncaster(GB) yl 1ⓉLH 1:432 Observer Gold Cup 821 Hide E 126 8.00 Apalachee1262Mississipian12610Alpine Nephew126¾ 10
Stk90000 Tracked in 5th,weakened 3f out
12Sep73♦ Doncaster(GB) gd 7fⓉStr 1:28 Champagne Stakes 2no Taylor B 126 10.00 Giacometti126noSnow Knight1262Pitcairn1262½ 8
Stk22000 Drifted throughout,rallied 1f out,just missed
14Jly73♦ Newbury(GB) gd 7fⓉStr 1:313 Donnington Castle Stakes 15 Taylor B 123 *1.10 Snow Knight1235Red Trooper1191Teasing1191½ 13
Alw4000 Led 2½f out,drew clear final furlong
5Jly73♦ Newmarket(GB) gd 7fⓉStr 1:31 Limekilns Plate 2¾ Moore G 123 *.50 Meon Hill119¾0Snow Knight1232½Charente1191½ 8
Alw2900 Led to 100y out,gave way grudgingly
1Jun73♦ Kempton(GB) gd 6fⓉStr 1:141 Rivermead Maiden Plate 11½ Moore G 126 16.00 Snow Knight1261½Galindo1265Ballylickey120½ 16
Mdn1700 Led over 2f out,driving

Soothsayer

dkbbr. g. 1967, by Mystic II (Relic)–Sagoma, by Saratoga **Lifetime record: 36 13 13 3 $217,119**
Own.– Montpelier
Br.– Mrs Marion duPont Scott (Va)
Tr.– Toby Balding

11Nov76♦ Wincanton(GB) gd 2⅝RH 5:211 6↑ Badger Beer Handicap Chase 318 Linley R 174 12.00 Zeta's Son1616Go-Over16112Soothsayer1741½ 14
Hcp5400 Behind to 12th,bid 2 out,finished well
23Oct76♦ Newbury(GB) yl 2½LH 5:123 6↑ Hermitage Chase 4 Linley R 160 6.50 Game Spirit1601Bula164Lean Forward1608 4
Alw6700 Chased in 3rd,behind from 13th,distanced
Previously trained by P.M. Howe
15Nov75- 4Cam fm 2³⁄₁₆ S'Chase 5:301 4↑ Colonial Cup 50k 9 11 105¼ 89½ 51½ 33½ Aitcheson J Jr 162 -e -- Cafe Prince1603Augustus Bay162½Soothsayer162½ Rallied 18
1Nov75- 3Mtp fm *2½ S'Chase 4:413 4↑ Noel Laing H 5.6k 9 5 75½ 72¾ 1½ 1hd Aitcheson J Jr 158 s -- Soothsayer158hdAugustus Bay1514Gran Kan1551½ All out 10
13Sep75- 7Fai fm *2½ S'Chase 5:02 4↑ Grand National H 12k 2 3 31½ 5¾ 42½ 412 Aitcheson J Jr 161 *1.20 -- AugustusBay1475½GranKan1551½HappyIntellectual1465 Tired 9
21Aug75- 4Sar fm 2⅜ S'Chase 4:201 4↑ NY Trf Wrtrs Cup H 22k 7 6 65½ 310 21½ 2nk Aitcheson J Jr 160 s 3.20 -- Life's Illusion145nkSoothsayer160½Arctic Joe1485½ Sharp 9
Previously trained by Fred Winter
13Mar75♦ Cheltenhm(GB) hy *3¼LH 7:512 7↑ Cheltenham Gold Cup Chase 26 Pitman R 168 28.00 Ten Up1686Soothsayer168½Bula16812 8
Stk54000 Progress 13th,bid 2 out,mistake last,up for 2nd
12Feb75♦ Ascot(GB) hy 3RH 6:503 7↑ Whitbread Trial Hcp Chase 225 Francome J 167 6.50 Ten Up16025Soothsayer167¾Glanford Brigg1615 8
Hcp9300 Tracked leaders,led 16th and 17th,mistakes and weakened 18th
16Jan75♦ Wincanton(GB) sf 2⅝RH 5:514 7↑ John Bull Chase 130 Francome J 168 *.55 Soothsayer16830Game Spirit168 2
Alw3400 Jumped well,led throughout,left clear 14th
26Dec74♦ Kempton(GB) sf 3RH 6:212 7↑ King George VI Chase 38¾ Francome J 157 4.50 Captain Christy1688Pendil168¾Soothsayer15710 6
Stk21000 Tracked leaders,ones paced from 3 out
30Nov74♦ Sandown(GB) yl 2RH 4:00 6↑ Benson & Hedges Gold Cup Chase - Francome J 162 *1.35 Dorless1444Tingle Creek174½Amarind1541½ 10
Stk13000 3rd when fell at 6th
9Nov74♦ Cheltenhm(GB) yl 2½LH 5:15 6↑ Mackeson Gold Cup Hcp Chase 28 Francome J 168 6.00 Bruslee1478Soothsayer1682½High Ken1495 11
Stk14700 Progress from 11th,led 2 out,headed after last,one-paced
30Oct74♦ Ascot(GB) gd 2RH 4:01 6↑ Dunkirk Handicap Chase 21½ Francome J 169 *1.00 Golden Sol1471½Soothsayer1691¾Well Oiled1476 6
Hcp3700 Rated toward rear,bid approaching last,finished well
14Mar74♦ Cheltenhm(GB) sf 2LH 4:214 6↑ Cathcart Challenge Cup Chase 14 Pitman R 157 *1.35 Soothsayer1574L'Escargot1576Clever Scot1572 7
Stk5000 Led approaching second last,comfortably
Previously trained by P.M. Howe
17Nov73- 2Cam fm 2³⁄₁₆ S'Chase 5:214 4↑ Colonial Cup 50k 14 5 68 67 33 2no Aitcheson J Jr 162 s - -- LuckyBoyIII149noSthsayr162noDremMgc1531¼ Just missed 15
3Nov73- 3Mtp fm 2½ S'Chase 4:44 4↑ Noel Laing H 5k 3 7 55¼ 63¼ 2nk 21½ Aitcheson J Jr 165 s - -- LuckyBoyIII1471½Sthsayer16510BrkngDwn140¾ Second best 7
6Oct73- 4Lig fm *2½ S'Chase 5:032 4↑ Temple Gwathmey H 25k 5 7 77½ 42 2nk 21¼ Aitcheson J Jr 162 - -- Athenian Idol1401½Soothsayer1628Top Bid1572 Sharp try 8
3Oct73- 7Lig gd *7fⓉ 1:304 3↑ Alw 2000 14 14 119½ 98 95½ 109 Aitcheson J Jr 155 - -- Loch Lomond II1582Mod Man1431½Dot to Dot131nk No factor 15
18Nov72- 3Cam fm 2³⁄₁₆ S'Chase 5:234 4↑ Colonial Cup 100k 4 14 85¼ 21 1½ 12½ Aitcheson J Jr 158 -e -- Soothsayer1582½Inkslinger158¾Shadow Brook160nk Driving 16
7Oct72- 4Lig sf *2½ S'Chase 5:192 4↑ Temple Gwathmey H 30k 3 10 911 78¾ 13 17 Aitcheson J Jr 162 -e -- Soothsayr1627SpeedKills143¾ShadwBrook16310 Ridden out 12

4Oct72- 6Lig fm *7f(T) 1:34 3↑ Alw 8 7 53 32¾ 1nk 12 Aitcheson J Jr 155 s -e -- Soothsayer1552Jaunty146 1½Emerald Isle145nk Driving 12
16Sep72- 1Fai fm *7f(T) 1:251 3↑ Alw 1000 2 2 75½ 62½ 43 1no Aitcheson J Jr 152 s *1.30 -- Soothsayer152noDetangle1376Tudor Winds1491 Hard drive 14
20Nov71- 2Cam fm 2 13/16 S'Chase 5:17 4↑ Colonial Cup 10k 2 5 53¼ 713 2½ 2nk Fishback J 149 -e -- Inkslinger149nkSoothsayer1498Top Bid1603 Unruly early 15
6Nov71- 2Mtp fst *1 1:352 3↑ Alw 600 5 5 31¼ 2½ 1¾ 11½ Fishback J 149 -e -- Soothsayer149 1½Sail Master1423Eagle's Top142 1¾ Drew out 11
14Oct71- 5Bel sf 2⅝ Hurdles 4:554 4↑ NY Trf Wrtrs Cup H 33k 5 6 32 21½ 16 13 Fishback J 153 2.10 -- Soothsayer1533Predominio1413Wustenchef162 3½ Easily 8
14Sep71- 3Bel sf 2⅝ Hurdles 5:034 4↑ Broad Hollow H 22k 4 5 36½ 15 118 117 Fishback J 143 *1.40e -- Soothsayer14317Inkslinger15116DremMgc1388 With authority 6
12Aug71- 3Sar fm 2 1/16 Hurdles 3:433 4↑ Lovely Night H 22k 5 7 54½ 2½ 2½ 2nk Brittle C III 139 8.60 -- Shadow Brook156nkSoothsayer1398Inkslinger150 2½ 2nd best 7
5Aug71- 9Sar fm 1⅞ Hurdles 3:242 4↑ Alw 12000 7 8 716 22 1½ 12½ Brittle C III 144 *1.60e -- Soothsayer144 2½Shadow II135noDream Magic1411 Driving 8
2Jun71- 4Del yl *2⅛ Hurdles 3:544 4↑ Tom Roby 10k 4 11 107 68¾ 57¼ 510 Brittle C III 133 11.70 -- ExplodeII142¾Balustrd143 2½PortMnch133¾ Poor landing 9th 13
22May71- 7Fai fm *1⅞ Hurdles 3:402 4↑ Alw 1800 1 6 86½ 64¼ 64½ 63½ Brittle C III 145 2.90e -- Alegar131noProfile144 2½Uldimeo141¾ No threat 13
14Nov70- 3Cam fm *2 Hurdles 2:413 Governors H 10k - 8 65½ 41 32 22 Brittle C III 137 -e -- Inkslinger1492Soothsayer137 4½Shadow II1324 Gamely 8
15Oct70- 3Bel sf 2 Hurdles 3:474 LE Stoddard Jr H 17k 1 9 813 42½ 21 23 Brittle C III 139 5.60e -- Inkslinger1483Soothsayer139 4½EasternPromise135 1½ Gamely 9
30Sep70- 3Bel yl 1⅞ Hurdles 3:264 3↑ Sp Wt 7500 6 10 911 34½ 1½ 12½ Brittle C III 134 4.80e -- Soothsayer134 2½TresurHuntIII1544BluRunnr1342 Mild drive 12
19Sep70- 5Fai hd *1¾ Hurdles 3:101 3↑ Md Sp Wt 5 1 53 31¼ 14 112 Brittle C III5 133 s *1.10 -- Soothsayer13312Favori15215Marine Band1428 Handily 7
11Sep70- 3Bel sf 1¾ Hurdles 3:133 OClm 10000 8 8 710 36 23 26 Brittle C III5 140 12.50e -- Summer Crop1456Soothsayr1409Colosso You13818 Steadied 10
23May70- 9Fai sf *7f(T) 1:28 3↑ Md Sp Wt 10 10 64¾ 69¾ 65¾ 510 Brittle C III 140 3.00 -- Dream Magic1362Othello1402Troponi1541 No threat 13

Spectacular Bid

gr. c. 1976, by Bold Bidder (Bold Ruler)–Spectacular, by Promised Land **Lifetime record: 30 26 2 1 $2,781,608**

Own.– Hawksworth Farm
Br.– Mmes Gilmour & Jason (Ky)
Tr.– Grover G. Delp

20Sep80- 0Bel fst 1¼ :502 1:141 1:381 2:022 3↑ Woodward-G1 1 1 1 1 1 1 Shoemaker W 126 88-21 Spectacular Bid126 In hand 1
Walkover,run between 7th and 8th race - Walkover,no wagering
16Aug80- 9Mth fst 1⅛ :464 1:111 1:353 1:48 3↑ AL Haskell H-G1 5 7 65½ 5¾ 1½ 11¾ Shoemaker W 132 *.10 95-15 SpectcularBd132 1¾Glorious Song117 1¼The Cool Virginian1124 8
Ridden out
19Jly80- 8AP fst 1⅛ :461 1:094 1:34 1:461 3↑ Wash Park-G3 4 4 44 2hd 14 110 Shoemaker W 130 *.05 103-17 SpectacularBid13010HoldYourTrcks1198Archtct119 1½ Easily 6
8Jun80- 8Hol fst 1⅛ :45 1:084 1:331 1:454 3↑ Californian-G1 3 3 31½ 11 16 14¼ Shoemaker W 130 *.05 103-05 SpectaculrBid130 4¼PaintKng115 3¾CroBmbno1188 Easy score 7
18May80- 8Hol fst 1 1/16 :223 :452 1:084 1:402 3↑ Mervyn LeRoy H-G2 1 5 42 2hd 13½ 17 Shoemaker W 132 *.20 93-18 SpectaculrBd1327Peregrintor119¾Beau'sEgl1212 Ridden out 6
2Mar80- 8SA sly 1¼ :483 1:122 1:364 2:003 4↑ S Anita H-G1 5 2 22½ 1hd 12½ 15 Shoemaker W 130 *.30 90-18 SpctaclarBid1305FlyingPstr1238Beau'sEgl12214 Ridden out 5
3Feb80- 8SA fst 1¼ :443 1:082 1:324 1:574 C H Strub-G1 3 4 29 2hd 13 13¼ Shoemaker W 126 *.30 104-08 SpectacularBid126 3¼FlyingPaster1219Vldz122½ Handy score 4
19Jan80- 8SA gd 1⅛ :462 1:11 1:353 1:48 San Fernando-G2 1 3 33½ 1hd 1½ 11½ Shoemaker W 126 *.05 89-19 SpectacularBid126 1½FlyngPstr12615Rlunch12033 Drew clear 4
5Jan80- 8SA fst 7f :221 :442 1:08 1:20 Malibu-G2 3 4 52½ 41 1½ 15 Shoemaker W 126 *.30 103-10 SpectacularBid1265FlyingPastr123 1½Ros'sSvll117no Easily 5
18Oct79- 6Med fst 1¼ :474 1:12 1:362 2:011 3↑ Med Cup H-G2 1 3 33 1½ 11½ 13 Shoemaker W 126 *.10 102-14 Spectacular Bid1263Smarten120hdValdez12111 Drew out 5
6Oct79- 8Bel fst 1½ :49 1:131 2:022 2:272 3↑ J C Gold Cup-G1 2 3 2½ 31 2½ 2¾ Shoemaker W 121 1.40 82-21 Affirmed126¾Spectacular Bid1213Coastal12131 Gamely 4
8Sep79- 8Bel fst 1⅛ :472 1:11 1:341 1:463 3↑ Marlboro Cup H-G1 5 3 1hd 1½ 13 15 Shoemaker W 124 *.50 94-17 SpectacularBid1245GenrlAssmbly120 1¼Costl122½ Ridden out 6
26Aug79- 7Del gd 1 1/16 :23 :463 1:111 1:413 Alw 18000 3 3 21½ 16 112 117 Shoemaker W 122 *.05 101-14 SpectacularBd12217ArmadaStrik1127NotSoProud1126 Easily 5
9Jun79- 8Bel fst 1½ :473 1:111 2:022 2:283 Belmont-G1 3 2 2½ 13 2½ 33½ Franklin RJ 126 *.30 73-17 Coastal126 3¼Golden Act126nkSpectacular Bid126 9½ Tired 8
19May79- 8Pim gd 1 3/16 :464 1:103 1:35 1:541 Preakness-G1 2 4 45 1hd 16 15½ Franklin RJ 126 *.10 99-09 SpctacularBd126 5½GoldenAct1264ScrnKng126 1½ Ridden out 5
5May79- 8CD fst 1¼ :472 1:122 1:373 2:022 Ky Derby-G1 3 7 610 2hd 11½ 12¾ Franklin RJ 126 *.60 85-14 SpectacularBid126 2¾GnrlAssmbly1263GoldnAct126 1¾ Driving 10
26Apr79- 7Kee fst 1⅛ :463 1:103 1:361 1:50 Blue Grass-G1 4 4 1hd 12 15½ 17 Franklin RJ 121 *.05 87-20 Spectacular Bid1217Lot o' Gold1218Bishop's Choice12110 4
Easily best
24Mar79-10Hia fst 1⅛ :46 1:093 1:351 1:482 Flamingo-G1 8 3 1½ 18 110 112 Franklin RJ 122 *.05 90-16 Spectacular Bid12212Strike the Min1183Sir Ivor Again122hd 8
Ridden out
6Mar79-11GP fst 1⅛ :474 1:114 1:363 1:484 Florida Derby-G1 5 5 47½ 3½ 11½ 14½ Franklin RJ 122 *.05 90-14 Spectacular Bid122 4½Lot o' Gold122¾Fantasy 'n Reality1223 7
Four wide,clear
19Feb79- 9GP fst 1 1/16 :24 :472 1:104 1:411 Fountain of Youth-G3 2 3 1hd 13 14 18½ Franklin RJ 122 *.10 95-12 Spectacular Bid122 8½Lot o'Gold1171Bishop's Choice1221 6
Ridden out
7Feb79- 9GP fst 7f :224 :444 1:084 1:212 Hutcheson 28k 1 2 2hd 22 13 13¾ Franklin RJ 122 *.05 97-22 SpectcularBid122 3¾Lot o' Gold114 7½Northern Prospect114 3½ 4
In hand
11Nov78- 8Key fst 1 1/16 :224 :462 1:103 1:42 Heritage-G2 6 5 55 1hd 13 16 Franklin RJ 122 *.10 94-13 SpctacularBid1226SunWatcher112 3¼TerrfcSon117no Handily 7
28Oct78- 8Lrl fst 1 1/16 :234 :464 1:11 1:413 Lrl Futurity-G1 2 1 11½ 1½ 14 18½ Franklin RJ 122 *.90 105-14 SpectacularBd122 8½General Assembly12212Clever Trick122 3½ 4
Driving
19Oct78- 6Med fst 1 1/16 :232 :462 1:111 1:431 Young America-G1 5 3 2hd 2½ 2hd 1nk Velasquez J 122 *.30 95-14 SpectclrBid122nkStrikeYourColrs119hdInstrumntLanding1134 9
Driving
8Oct78- 8Bel fst 1 :231 :46 1:101 1:344 Champagne-G1 1 2 11 12½ 14 12¾ Velasquez J 122 2.40 94-19 SpectclrBid122 2¾GeneralAssembly122 5½Crest of theWave122¾ 6
Ridden out
23Sep78- 8Atl gd 7f :22 :443 1:09 1:204 World's Playground-G3 3 3 1½ 12 16 115 Franklin RJ 114 5.20 98-25 SpctaculrBid11415CrstofthWv124 1¼GrotonHgh118½ Driving 7
20Aug78- 9Del fst 6f :222 :46 :58 1:104 Dover 34k 2 4 43 53¾ 44 22½ Franklin RJ 112 *1.00 88-13 StrikeYourColors112 2½SpectacularBid112 5½Spy Charger1221 7
2nd best
2Aug78- 8Mth sly 5½f :224 :461 :59 1:044 Tyro (Div 2) 27k 6 8 816 812 610 46¾ Franklin RJ 118 *1.70 86-22 GrotonHigh122 2½GreatBoon116nkOurGry1164 Very wide early 8
22Jly78- 5Pim fst 5½f :223 :461 :581 1:041 Alw 6500 3 4 31 1hd 13 18 Franklin RJ5 115 *.30 100-17 SpectacularBid1158SilentNative1209DoublePrd1141 Driving 5
30Jun78- 3Pim fst 5½f :223 :463 :582 1:043 Md Sp Wt 5 4 1½ 11½ 12½ 13¼ Franklin RJ5 115 6.30 98-15 Spectacular Bid115 3¼Strike Your Colors1204Instant Love1124 11
Drew out

Star de Naskra

dkbbr. c. 1975, by Naskra (Nasram)–Candle Star, by Clandestine **Lifetime record: 36 15 10 4 $587,391**

Own.– C.J. Lancaster
Br.– Carlyle J. Lancaster (Md)
Tr.– Richard D. Ferris

20Oct79- 8Aqu fst 7f :223 :444 1:083 1:21 3↑ Vosburgh-G1 6 5 41½ 1hd 21 45 Fell J 126 2.80 91-15 GeneralAssmbly1232Dr.Patches126¾Syncopat126 2¼ Gave way 6
8Sep79- 8Bel fst 1⅛ :472 1:11 1:341 1:463 3↑ Marlboro Cup H-G1 4 1 41 43½ 65¾ 68 Fell J 124 8.60 86-17 SpctaculrBid1245GeneralAssmbly120 1¼Costl122½ Weakened 6
4Aug79- 8Sar fst 1⅛ :481 1:104 1:35 1:473 3↑ Whitney-G2 2 1 1½ 1hd 1hd 1¾ Fell J 120 *1.10 97-12 StardeNskra120¾Cos'xRidge117½TheLiberlMmbr120½ Driving 6
14Jly79- 8Aks fst 1⅛ :47 1:111 1:351 1:482 3↑ Cornhusker H 164k 4 4 42 1½ 14 18½ Fell J 125 *1.80 95-14 Star de Naskra125 8½Prince Majestic119 1½Quiet Jay117nk 13
Bumped,easily
20Jun79- 6Bel fst 7f :222 :444 1:09 1:22 3↑ Celanese Cup H 80k 1 2 32½ 32 11½ 14 Fell J 126 1.40 92-17 [D]StardeNaskr1264NorthCours112 1¼Dr.Ptchs118½ Drifted in 4
Disqualified and placed fourth
9Jun79- 5Bel fst 1 :234 :463 1:103 1:343 3↑ Alw 27000 2 2 1½ 1hd 13 16¼ Fell J 115 *.90 95-17 StardeNaskra115 6¼DarbyCreekRoad1154QuietLittleTable1179 6
Ridden out
5May79- 8Aqu fst 7f :224 :451 1:091 1:214 3↑ Carter H-G2 3 4 1½ 1½ 15 1nk Fell J 122 7.70 92-25 StardeNaskra122nkAlydar126 3¾SensitivePrince126 6¾ Lasted 6
22Apr79- 8Aqu fst 6f :213 :45 1:091 3↑ Bold Ruler 80k 5 1 42¾ 11 15 15 Fell J 119 *1.70 97-11 StrdeNaskra1195Vencdor126 1¾BgJohnTylor119 1¼ Ridden out 8
31Mar79- 7Bow fst 6f :22 :442 :553 1:084 4↑ Alw 19000 1 4 22 2hd 11 12¾ Miceli M 112 *.60 96-18 StardeNaskra112 2¾IronDerby112 4½Parnis11212 Ridden out 6
1Jan79- 8Bow sly 1 1/16 :233 :472 1:122 1:434 3↑ Resolution H 55k 4 5 37 51¾ 43½ 47 Passmore WJ 122 2.40 80-22 Frejus109hdCortan114 2½Chati124 4½ No mishap 6

7Dec78- 6Med gd 1 1/16 :234 :471 1:112 1:434 Winter Quarters H 53k 7 7 75½ 52¼ 33½ 21¼ Maple E 121 *2.10 91-19 SilentCal1181½StrdNskr1211¼MornngFrolc1151¼ Drifted out 7
18Nov78- 8Lrl fst 1 :224 :453 1:11 1:373 Japan Racing Assn H 44k 5 2 31½ 2hd 2hd 22 Kupfer T 122 b *.80 83-20 Silent Cal1152Star de Naskra1225Morning Frolic1143 Wide 6
1Nov78- 8Aqu fst 6f :23 :453 1:092 3↑ Alw 30000 1 2 1hd 1hd 1½ 1½ Maple E 120 b 7.30 96-14 StrdeNskra120½WarmFront1193NearlyOnTime1154¾ Driving 5
7Oct78- 8Bow fst 1⅛ :472 1:11 1:362 1:50 Governor's Cup H 108k 5 3 3½ 31½ 37 312½ Moyers L 118 b 11.50 82-21 NastyandBld1232½Dave'sFriend12010StardeNskr11820 Tired 5
16Sep78- 6Bow fst 1 1/16 :242 :492 1:141 1:45 3↑ Alw 16000 6 3 2½ 2½ 1½ 1¾ Kupfer T5 107 *.20 81-26 Star de Naskra107¾Gala Forecast1144Combat Patrol1174 6
Ridden out
4Sep78- 8Del fst 1 1/16 :233 :471 1:112 1:432 Rosemont 33k 5 4 43¼ 31 23 24½ Passmore WJ 122 *.50 87-17 SilentCal1124½StardeNaskra1222Fredd'sFlsh1123 No excuse 8
5Aug78- 8Mth sly 1⅛ :47 1:123 1:393 1:531 Mth Inv'l H-G1 1 4 55½ 43½ 66½ 67 Moyers L 116 3.20 62-31 DeltaFlag112¾Dave'sFriend1202½SpecialHonr1182¾ No rally 7
22Jly78- 8Pim fst 1⅛ :46 1:101 1:352 1:482 Marylander H 56k 5 3 35½ 35 21½ 21 Moyers L 119 3.70 101-17 Dave'sFriend1171StardeNaskra1196SensitvPrnc1225 Brushed 5
1Jly78- 8AP sly 1¼ :462 1:111 1:364 2:032 American Derby-G2 13 8 41½ 22 21½ 25 Moyers L 114 *1.90 75-29 NastyandBold1145StrdeNskra1147BeauSham1147 Second best 13
18Jun78- 10Tdn fst 1⅛ :46 1:10 1:351 1:474 Ohio Derby-G2 5 3 4¾ 4¾ 41¾ 31½ Moyers L 120 8.60 99-04 SpecialHonor115½Batonnier1221StardeNaskra1201 Rallied 10
28May78- 8Bel fst 1⅛ :451 1:092 1:35 1:48 Peter Pan-G3 8 5 44 42½ 46 38½ Moyers L 123 3.90 78-16 Bckaroo1143½DarbyCreekRoad1175StrdeNskr123nk Mild bid 8
14May78- 8Aqu sly 1 :23 :46 1:11 1:364 Withers-G2 3 4 32 22 24 24¾ Moyers L 126 *1.60 77-26 Junction1264¾StardeNaskra1261½Buckaroo126½ Second best 8
24Apr78- 8Aqu fst 1 :234 :462 1:104 1:363 Alw 25000 5 5 42 41 1½ 15½ Moyers L 122 *1.30 83-20 StardeNaskra1225½ShelterHalf1221¾NeverMind1193 In hand 5
8Apr78- 8Key fst 6f :232 :464 1:11 Penn Treaty 27k 3 4 31½ 3nk 1½ 12 Moyers L 122 *.90 87-27 Star de Naskra1222Pirateer1221¼Al Battah1228 Driving 6
25Mar78- 8Pim fst 6f :231 :461 :58 1:11 Hirsch Jacobs 33k 8 9 62½ 34½ 34½ 22½ Moyers L 122 3.30 88-18 ShelterHalf1192½StardeNskr1222¼GamePrnc1161½ 2nd best 9
10Dec77- 6Med fst 6f :223 :453 1:094 Giant Step 53k 8 3 2hd 2hd 31½ 45½ Turcotte RL 122 *1.80 90-06 MomboJumbo1193JustRightClassi1152AlBattah119½ Gave way 8
11Nov77- 8Lrl gd 7f :231 :47 1:122 1:251 Ⓢ Senatorial 30k 6 1 2hd 2½ 22 21 Bracciale V Jr 122 *.30 84-29 TenTen1171StardeNaskra1228M.A.'sDate122nk Carried wide 6
29Oct77- 8Lrl fst 1 1/16 :24 :484 1:133 1:441 Lrl Futurity-G1 4 1 11 3½ 35 310 Bracciale V Jr 122 11.90 82-27 Affirmed122nkAlydar12210Star de Naskra12227 Speed,tired 4
15Oct77- 8Bow fst 7f :224 :452 1:102 1:241 ©Marl Nursery 28k 2 6 5¾ 3½ 11 11 Bracciale V Jr 122 *.60 84-22 StardeNaskra1221PeacefulCountry113½Isella1137 Driving 7
24Sep77- 8AP sly 6½f :221 :444 1:10 1:163 ©Arl Wash Futurity-G1 14 1 42½ 43½ 65 56¾ Bracciale V Jr 122 6.60 85-18 Sauce Boat1222Gonquin1223½Forever Casting122¾ Wide 14
3Sep77- 8Tim fst *6½f :224 :47 1:124 1:173 Tim Futurity 58k 1 2 1hd 2hd 11 14¾ Turcotte RL 122 2.00 96-12 StrdeNaskra1224¾ForeverCastng1227MsWrrnt1192 Drew away 4
21Aug77- 9Del fst 6f :221 :454 1:111 Dover 30k 5 2 41½ 2hd 12 12¾ Bracciale V Jr 114 *1.30 89-15 StrdeNskr1142¾MomboJumbo113¾ⒹFmousCzr1121¾ Ridden out 8
11Aug77- 7Del fst 6f :214 :453 1:103 Alw 12000 3 7 55½ 52¼ 1hd 2hd Bracciale V Jr 120 2.30 92-14 ForevrCasting120hdStrdeNskr1207BombyExprss1151¼ Sharp 7
16Jly77- 8Bow fst 5½f :223 :461 :581 1:041 Ⓢ Playpen 27k 7 5 2½ 2½ 1hd 2¾ Bracciale V Jr 115 *.70 97-20 Quadratic113¾StardeNaskra1154SilkorSatin1133½ Gamely 7
29Jun77- 7Bow fst 5f :224 :462 :584 Ⓢ Alw 9000 6 1 13½ 11½ 12½ 13 Kurtz J 120 *1.20 96-21 StrdeNskra1203MarineCorpTom1172½TenTn1202½ Ridden out 6
14Jun77- 3Bow fst 5f :231 :463 :59 Ⓢ Md Sp Wt 1 6 21 1hd 2½ 13½ Bracciale V Jr 120 6.30 95-18 Star de Naskra1203½Silk or Satin1201Combat Fatigue113hd 8
Handily

Straight and True

dkbbr. g. 1970, by Never Bend (Nasrullah)–Polly Girl, by Prince Bio **Lifetime record: 74 12 9 9 $78,689**
Own.– Mrs O. Phipps
Br.– Mrs Ogden Phipps (Ky)
Tr.– D.M. Smithwick

13Aug79- 4Sar yl 2 1/16 S'Chase 3:463 3↑ Alw 12500 1 3 31 - - - Martin W 151 b 10.70 -- PopulrHero1454¾CanadianRegent1484TanJy15122 Broke down 7
3Aug79- 6Sar fm 2 1/16 S'Chase 3:411 4↑ Lovely Night H 21k 1 1 13 54¼ 619 632 Martin W 144 sb 6.80 -- CafePrince1642¾LeapingFrog1613¾Martie'sAnger1555 Tired 7
13Jly79- 3Del fm *2¼ S'Chase 4:162 4↑ Handicap 10000 4 1 16 14 12 31¾ Martin WS 145 sb 13.20 -- Martie'sAnger1521¼DeuxCoup159½StrghtndTru1457 Lost iron 5
25Jun79- 4Atl fm *1Ⓣ :24 :481 1:131 1:391 3↑ Alw 7500 10 2 21 1011 1015 916 Moseley JW 119 b 28.40 75-14 Great Cloud114hdBeau Rascal119½New Look119¾ Stopped 10
2Jun79- 7Fai gd *2 3/16 S'Chase 4:14 4↑ Handicap 6000 4 4 2¾ 74¼ 613 522¼ Martin W 150 sb 1.60 -- Beauhill142nkPopular Hero1497½Orotund14611 Tired 8
26May79- 2Pro fm *2 S'Chase 3:314 4↑ Alw 15000 3 3 62½ 63 65¾ 513 Martin W 158 b - -- Martie's Anger155½Winigo1424Tall Award163nk No rally 9
12May79- 7Fai fm *2 3/16 S'Chase 4:112 4↑ Handicap 10000 6 2 15 1nk 31½ 22¾ Martin W 148 sb 5.60 -- Deux Coup1552¾Straight and True1481Love In1425 Sharp 7
5May79- 3War fm *2⅛ S'Chase 4:421 4↑ Alw 6000 3 2 22 24 2¾ 1no Martin W 153 sb - -- StraightandTrue153noElVientoII1392½Saramyst131 Just up 3
28Apr79- 4Fx gd *2¼ S'Chase 4:274 4↑ Foxfield Cup H 12k 4 3 2½ 39 220 225 Martin W 154 sb - -- Tall Award15825Straight and True154 Tired 4
22Apr79- 4Mid fm *2 S'Chase 4:02 4↑ Alw 8500 4 1 11¾ 12½ 2hd 2nk Martin W 156 sb - -- FireControl156nkStraightandTrue156hdOwhatChf15920 Sharp 4
4Nov78- 3Mtp fm *2½ S'Chase 4:394 4↑ N Laing H 5.4k 5 1 13 32½ 49½ 514 Quanbeck A Jr 146 - -- Deux Coup153nkFire Control1553Curazao14510 Tired 7
20Oct78- 6Bel fm 2⅝ S'Chase 4:52 4↑ Temple Gwathmey H 36k 4 3 42 615 634 636 Cushman J 147 7.30e -- FireControl1464CafePrince167noPopulrHro1398¾ Done early 6
4Oct78- 6Lig gd *2 S'Chase 4:142 4↑ Handicap 12500 1 3 32¾ - - - Martin WS 149 - -- Owhata Chief153¾Leaping Frog15914Don Panta150 Fell 4
16Sep78- 7Fai fm *2 3/16 S'Chase 4:102 4↑ Handicap 5000 4 3 32 31½ 310 315½ Martin WS 152 sb *1.60 -- OwhtaChief1483½DonPanta14912StrghtndTru15210 No excuse 6
9Sep78- 4Fx hd *2¼ S'Chase 4:133 3↑ Alw 7500 3 2 1½ 13 1nk 2nk Martin WS5 148 sb - -- Leaping Frog156nkStraight and True14812Don Panta156½ 5
14Aug78- 4Sar gd 2⅛ S'Chase 3:572 4↑ Alw 12500 1 3 2hd 53½ 59 517 Martin WS5 150 sb *1.10 -- Emory Jay1402Jive1526½Jacasaba1553¾ Tired after 7th 5
4Aug78- 6Sar sf 2 1/16 S'Chase 3:524 4↑ Lovely Night H 21k 1 3 33 33½ 33½ 32¾ Martin WS 147 b 3.70 -- LeapingFrog1532¾UnAdios137noStrghtndTru1476¼ No mishap 6
22Jly78- 3Del fm 2¼ S'Chase 4:184 4↑ Alw 10000 5 1 13 1hd 1½ 2½ Martin WS5 147 b 2.70 -- LeapingFrog152½StraightandTrue1473½Jacasaba1436 Gamely 6
10Jly78- 6Atl sly 1 1/16 :23 :46 1:104 1:44 3↑ Alw 7500 3 6 815 818 617 519 Pagano SR 112 b 9.60 66-27 ThouFool1071½RoamFree1194WilmingtonFlask1196 No rally 8
21Jun78- 4Mth gd *2¼ S'Chase 4:291 4↑ Midsummer H 15k 6 4 39 23 31 5¾ Martin W 147 sb *1.60 -- Deux Coup153noDon Panta146nkLeaping Frog148no Hung 7
10Jun78- 7Fai fm *2 3/16 S'Chase 4:122 4↑ Handicap 7500 4 3 43¾ 41 2nk 1¾ Martin W 144 sb 1.70 -- Straight and True144¾Deux Coup1547¾Tall Award1462 6
29May78- 7Fai fm *2 3/16 S'Chase 4:144 4↑ Alw 6000 6 3 16 11½ 11 13½ Martin W7 146 sb 2.40 -- StraightandTrue1463½CanadianRegent14711Slvo1504¼ Easily 6
20May78- 4Mal sf *2 S'Chase 3:554 4↑ Handicap 7500 3 3 45½ 44¼ 35½ 2hd Martin B 138 sb - -- ⒹTallAward145hdStraightandTrue1382ElVientoII1446 Sharp 4
Placed first through disqualification
6May78- 6War yl *2⅛ S'Chase 4:403 4↑ Alw 2500 7 1 14 12 215 222 Smithwick D 163 sb - -- ElVientoII16322StraightandTrue1632½Mr.Jam1656 Tired 8
29Apr78- 4SH fm *1⅞ S'Chase 3:423 4↑ Alw 3500 2 2 35 3½ 311 34½ Martin W10 134 sb - -- CanadianRegent1474ElVientoII137½StraightndTru1345 Tired 5
23Apr78- 4Mid fm *2 S'Chase 3:593 4↑ Alw 3500 4 1 22 212 315 312 Martin W10 138 sb - -- FrenchHollow1568FireControl1504StraightndTru13815 Tired 6
15Oct77- 4Mid gd *2½ S'Chase 4:383 4↑ Alw 1500 8 4 75¼ 814 825 733 Aitcheson J Jr 158 b - -- DonPanta1561½ManchuPrinc1382½SunSign143½ Fell far back 9
8Oct77- 4Lig sf *2½ S'Chase 5:311 4↑ Int'l Gold Cup H 25k 3 1 18 830 659 678 Martin W 157 b -e -- CafePrince15518ItsGoodforYou1377MichaelsMd13710 Stopped 8
1Oct77- 4Fax fm *2¼ S'Chase 4:221 3↑ Alw 2500 1 4 413 37 310 414 Aitcheson J Jr 155 b - -- Afilador1562Aunt Sheila15010Orotund1482 4
17Sep77- 5Fai fm *1 5/16Ⓣ 2:15 3↑ Alw 1000 3 4 56 52½ 88½ 916 Skiffington T Jr 150 b 3.10 -- Farnisky1505Corning Day1401¾Michael's Mad140½ No speed 10
10Sep77- 4Fai fm *1 5/16 S'Chase 2:19 3↑ Alw 1000 2 7 64¾ 52 44¾ 48 Aitcheson J Jr 147 s 2.70 -- Deux Coup1402½Corning Day1403½Winigo1372 10
24Aug77- 8Del gd 1 1/16⊗ :24 :481 1:131 1:454 3↑ Alw 7000 3 4 68½ 722 731 736¾ Canessa J 117 b 21.30 43-21 HafPro1172¼JohnAlden1135Admiral'sPppy1137 Through early 7
2Aug77- 8Tim fst 1 1/16 :24 :48 1:141 1:463 3↑ Alw 4200 1 2 41¾ 57½ 513 520 Passmore WJ 114 b 5.30 68-11 Sport News114½Uncle Baby1141½Hey Look1096 Tired 5
3Jly77- 5Pen fst 6f :224 :464 1:094 4↑ Alw 5000 1 6 612 622 623 631 Smith DD 113 b 6.90 66-13 HickoryCap1197½Peggy'sPrince1131½AvalonBech1133½ Outrun 6
27Nov76- 4Cam fm 2¾ S'Chase 5:124 4↑ Colonial Cup 100k 1 14 1226 - - - Fishback J 162 -e -- GrandCanyon162½FireControl1622½Crag'sCorner160no Bled 16
6Nov76- 3Uni fm *2Ⓣ 3:35 3↑ Alw 1000 7 2 43½ 3nk 31½ - McKnight HT Jr 173 - -- Paginai15526DnMiguelII1681OneDy'sFrdom1611 Left course 15
22Oct76- 6Bel sf 2⅝ S'Chase 5:023 4↑ Temple Gwathmey H 36k 1 2 23 31 612 712 Fishback J 162 b *1.00e -- FireControl144hdCrag'sCorner1412¼ArcticJoe1514 Stopped 7
6Oct76- 6Lig gd *2 S'Chase 4:15 4↑ Rolling Rock Hunt H 12k 1 1 11½ 2½ 1½ 11½ Fishback J 162 -e -- StrghtandTrue1621½ManchuPrinc135hdTllAwrd142½ Driving 7
18Sep76- 7Fai fm *2½ S'Chase 4:571 4↑ Grand National H 15k 4 6 2½ 3½ 11 16¼ Fishback J 154 b *1.30e -- StrghtndTrue1546¼HappyIntellectual157hdLife'sIllusion1612¾ 7
In hand
11Sep76- 8Fai hd *1 1/16Ⓣ 2:134 3↑ Alw 1200 2 2 22½ 11 1nk 13½ Rowland J 147 b *.40 -- StraightandTrue1473½RulngLine149noGermncus1423 In hand 8
26Aug76- 6Sar fm 2⅜ S'Chase 4:192 4↑ NY Turf Writers H 22k 5 3 42½ 46 35½ 33¼ Fishback J 155 b 1.70e -- HappyIntellectual152¾Life'sIllusion1602½Strght andTrue155½ 7
Evenly
6Aug76- 6Sar fm 2 1/16 S'Chase 3:49 4↑ Lovely Night H 22k 2 6 65½ 32 33 45 Fishback J 158 b *.90e -- Crag'sCorner1401¼Deux Coup1421¼Casamayor1482½ Bobbled 7
30Jly76- 8Tim fst 1 :24 :474 1:132 1:403 3↑ Alw 4400 5 4 610 512 512 59¼ Rowland J 112 b 2.30 79-15 JohnnieScott1121¾Prdful1123½Bully'sBunny1121½ No factor 6
17Jly76- 7Del fm *2⅜ S'Chase 4:342 4↑ Indian River H 13k 7 4 2hd 12 110 12¾ Fishback J 151 b 2.90 -- StraightandTrue1512¾Crag'sCornr1362ClovrOvr1354 Handily 8
8Jly76- 9Del fst 1 70 :243 :49 1:133 1:43 3↑ Alw 6000 2 1 11½ 2hd 31 31¾ Rowland J 118 b 13.00 80-14 RoyalJete112¾Exploring1201StraightandTrue1183 Weakened 7
25Jun76- 4Del fm *2 1/16 S'Chase 3:564 4↑ Handicap 8000 9 1 21 24 21½ 22 Fishback J 152 b 2.30 -- Life's Illusion1562Straight and True1527ⒹⒽDeux Coup145 9

Second best

Date/Race	Cond/Dist	Fractions	Race	Running line	Jockey	Wt	Odds	Speed	Finishers	Comment
23Jun76- 8Pim	fst 5f	:22 :45 :571	4↑ Clm 30000	6 6 613 613 622 619	Rowland J	114 b	53.60	80-17	Kintla'sFolly1141JivaCoolt114noOxfordFlght1194½	Trailed 6
11Jun76- 4Del	fm *2 1/16 S'Chase	3:504	4↑ Alw 7000	6 5 35½ 32 23 22¼	Fishback J	160 b	2.80	- -	DeuxCoup1402¼StrghtndTru1607JuggrnutII14812	Swerved in 7
30May76- 4Del	yl *2⅛ S'Chase	3:461	4↑ Alw 7000	1 2 22 2½ 15 14¾	Fishback J	155 b	11.50	- -	StrghtndTru1554¾DuxCoup1437JuggrnutII1501¼	Ridden out 8
8May76- 6Fai	fm *2⅛ S'Chase	4:094	4↑ Handicap 7500	2 4 514 412 517 542	Aitcheson J Jr	138 sb	-	- -	LondonGrove1481¾Life'sIlluson1584½AgsAgo14733	No threat 5
26Apr76- 8Pim	fm 1 1/16 Ⓣ	:234 :464 1:113 1:443	4↑ Alw 8000	2 8 1023 1028 1022 1019	Rowland J	115 b	17.50	69-11	Romus119hdRoyal Romany115noLast Hail119 2¾	Outrun 10
11Apr76- 6Mid	fm *1¼Ⓣ	2:174	3↑ Alw 500	2 7 66 38 41¾ 32	Aitcheson J Jr	155 b	-	- -	SpittinImage155hdBabeen1502StraightandTrue155½	Evenly 10
15Nov75- 4Cam	fm 2 1/8 S'Chase	5:301	4↑ Colonial Cup 50k	4 18 167½ 1621 147¼ 1544	Carberry T	160	-e	- -	Cafe Prince1603Augustus Bay162½Soothsayer162½	Outrun 18
1Nov75- 4Mtp	fm *2 S'Chase	4:251	3↑ Alw 2000	9 9 86½ 74½ 32 24	Elser C	156	-e	- -	Tor'sLib1364StraightandTrue156½Afilador156¾	Closed well 19
18Oct75- 4RB	sf *2 S'Chase	5:374	3↑ Alw 3500	3 5 47 310 - -	Elser C	155	-	- -	CltcSongIII15512Jy'sTroubl14210StrtchII15518	Pulled up 6
11Oct75- 5Mid	yl *1½Ⓣ	2:302	3↑ Alw 250	4 6 73 12 11½ 1¾	Rowland JP	141 sb	-e	- -	Straight and True141¾Bacara1506Sabinus159½	Driving 10
4Oct75- 6Lig	yl *7fⓉ	1:351	3↑ Alw 2500	12 12 84 78½ 710 410½	Rowland J	136 b	-	- -	Fortissimo1436Gumersindo1431½Pilot Himself1463	Late bid 14
1Oct75- 7Lig	yl *7fⓉ	1:352	3↑ Alw 2500	2 2 149½ 1110 106 72½	Rowland JP7	136	-e	- -	Life's Illusion145hdTor's Rib145nkRed Grasshopper149½	19

Previously trained by Pierre Head

Date/Race	Cond/Dist	Time	Race	Finish	Jockey	Wt	Odds	Finishers	Comment	Field
22Jun75♦ Auteuil(Fr)	hy *2⅛	4:22	5↑ Prix Arthur O'Connor Chase Alw15700	-	Chirol M	139	19.00	Mister Magoo132½Lift1348Bergerac1392	Fell at 2nd.Tingle Creek 7th	15
27May75♦ Enghien(Fr)	gd *2¼	4:341	5↑ Prix du Puy-de-Dome Chase Alw21700	79¾	Chirol M	136 b	25.00	Celtic Air1364Tofano136½Romati1411½	Well placed in 4th,weakened approaching second last	9
4May75♦ Compiegne(Fr)	gd *2 3/16 LH	4:50	5↑ Prix de la Heronniere Chase Alw4600	1½	Chirol M	136	3.10	Straight and True136½Rayure15020Fort d'Ivry14120	Tracked in 3rd,dueled 1 out,gamely prevailed	5
13Apr75♦ Strasbourg(Fr)	sf *2⅛RH	-	5↑ Prix de l'Ami Fritz Chase Alw3000	11	Bonni F	141	*.80	Straight and True1411Donner141½Vickywyn141	Always close up,led at last,held well.Time not taken	10
22Oct74♦ Enghien(Fr)	hy *1 15/16 LH	3:49	Prix de la Scarpe Hurdle Hcp11600	10	Lautier R	136	5.50	Voldic145nkKamarjaan1568Typhor1413	Never a factor	15
12Aug74♦ Clairefntaine(Fr)	gd *1⅞RH	3:401	4↑ Prix du Golf Hurdle Alw9400	514½	Lautier R	136	3.50	Lord David1454Debil1362½Dark Lessly1366	Tracked in 4th,faded from 2 out	11
23Jly74♦ Evry(Fr)	gd *1⅛ⓉLH	1:533	4↑ Prix Incertitude (Div 2) Hcp5100	76	Gibert A	133	-	Dark Lessly1211Flabel1222Golden Calf127½	Raced in mid-pack throughout	15
22Jun74♦ Saint-Cloud(Fr)	gd *1¼ⓉLH	2:094	4↑ Prix de Castillon Hcp7700	5¾	Gibert A	113	-	Les Capucins120nkA Cappella112nkExpertease123hd	Rated toward rear,gaining late	16
26May74♦ Longchamp(Fr)	gd *1 5/16 ⓉRH	2:143	4↑ Prix des Batignolles Hcp7700	12	Gibert A	110	-	Tetouan114nkNovart117hdBrio Khan1213	Never a factor	13
31Mar74♦ Auteuil(Fr)	hy *1⅞LH	4:02	Prix Santo Pietro Hurdle Mdn (FT)11600	325	Lautier R	136	6.00	Way Away13720The Kid1365Straight and True1362½	Settled in 5th,bid after 3rd last,no chance with first two	9
7Nov73♦ Saint-Cloud(Fr)	hy *1¼ⓉLH	2:202	Prix de Lude Mdn8500	9	Gibert A	123	-	Lourenco Marques1233Bayazid1231½Miribi1233	Toward rear throughout	9
11Oct73♦ Evry(Fr)	sf *1½ⓉLH	2:382	Prix d'Annency Hcp10200	42¼	Gibert A	113	-	Gingko Biloba1161Verine1011Grand Canal123nk	Wide 7th,finished well without threatening	14
24Sep73♦ Maisns-Lfftte(Fr)	sf *1ⓉRH	1:434	Prix du Tage Hcp7600	8	Florin A	117	-	Penrod120nkScarlet Sun100nkMeriadeck1161	Never a factor	15
23Jly73♦ Maisns-Lfftte(Fr)	sf *1 5/16 ⓉRH sf	2:224	Prix Montmartin Mdn7600	10	Gibert A	123	-	Copper1232Extravagant123hdCantador1234	Toward rear throughout	11
7Jun73♦ Chantilly(Fr)	gd *1⅜ⓉRH	2:184	Prix de Montgeroult Mdn7600	52¾	Gibert A	123	-	Veld123nkRibot Lad1162Winterthur117no	Rated in 10th,mild late gain	19
14May73♦ Saint-Cloud(Fr)	sf *1 5/16 ⓉLH	2:222	Prix Isard II Mdn (FT)7600	9	Gibert A	123	-	Florapal1213Valaze123nkNoumay123nk	Never a factor	14

Susan's Girl

b. f. 1969, by Quadrangle (Cohoes)–Quaze, by Quibu

Own.– F.W. Hooper Jr

Br.– F.W. Hooper Jr (Fla)

Tr.– L.R. Fenstermaker

Lifetime record: 63 29 14 11 $1,251,667

Date/Race	Cond/Dist	Fractions	Race	Running line	Jockey	Wt	Odds	Speed	Finishers	Comment
24Nov75- 8Aqu	fst 1	:234 :473 1:122 1:37	3↑ ⒻBerlo H 59k	2 2 21 1hd 1hd 32	Baeza B	126	*1.20	79-16	CostlyDream1151¾LandGirl113nkSusan'sGirl1261	Weakened 11
15Nov75- 8Aqu	fst 1¼	:503 1:142 1:383 2:033	3↑ ⒻLadies H-G1	8 1 21 22 33 3½	Pincay L Jr	126	*1.40	77-15	Tizna124nkPass a Glance113nkSusan's Girl1262	Weakened 8
25Oct75- 7Kee	fst 1⅛	:474 1:12 1:37 1:494	3↑ ⒻSpinster-G1	7 2 2hd 1hd 1hd 1½	Pincay L Jr	123	*.30e	88-15	Susan'sGirl123½FlamaArdient119¾CostlyDrm1234	Hard drive 7
16Oct75- 7Kee	gd *7f	1:282	3↑ ⒻAlw 15000	7 2 22½ 33½ 32 1nk	Nichols J	122	*.30e	81-18	Susan'sGirl122nkCostlyDream114¾MoonGlitter1118	Driving 7
20Sep75- 8Bel	sly 1⅛	:464 1:111 1:36 1:482	3↑ ⒻBeldame-G1	9 1 1½ 1hd 1hd 1nk	Baeza B	123	*.70	85-14	Susan'sGirl123nkTizna1231¾PssGlnc1234	Lost lead,driving 9
10Sep75- 8Bel	fst 1	:233 :462 1:103 1:351	3↑ ⒻMaskette H-G2	1 3 3½ 32 33 33½	Broussard R	128	*1.60	88-18	LetMeLinger117noHonorblMss1213½Ssn'sGrl1285½	No excuse 8
10Aug75- 8Del	fst 1¼	:49 1:13 1:372 2:014	3↑ ⒻDelaware H-G1	5 2 21 11½ 11½ 12¾	Broussard R	125	*.40	93-16	Susan's Girl1252¾Pass a Glance116noRaisela1171½	Handily 6
28Jly75- 8Atl	fst 1 3/16	:473 1:103 1:351 1:541	3↑ ⒻMatchmaker-G1	4 2 41½ 32½ 11 13¼	Broussard R	121	*2.30	105-05	Susan'sGirl1213¼AuntJin1145½PinkTights114¾	Ridden out 6
Previously trained by R.L. Smith										
6Jly75- 8Hol	fst 1⅛	:46 1:094 1:344 1:472	3↑ ⒻVanity H-G1	1 1 2½ 2hd 1½ 2¾	Pincay L Jr	123	*2.60	94-12	Dulcia118¾Susan's Girl1232½La Zanzara120½	Gamely 11
22Jun75- 8Hol	fm 1⅛Ⓣ	:471 1:111 1:36 1:483	3↑ ⒻWilshire H-G3	6 6 75½ 52¼ 31½ 2hd	Pincay L Jr	123	*1.50e	93-12	Tizna123hdSusan's Girl1231½Dulcia1201¼	Gamely 10
31May75- 8Hol	fst 1 1/16	:233 :47 1:104 1:42	3↑ ⒻMilady H-G2	4 2 2½ 3½ 53 43½	Pincay L Jr	125	*1.80	81-11	Modus Vivendi121¾Tizna124nkMercy Dee1112½	Lacked rally 6
10May75- 8Hol	fst 1	:222 :45 1:083 1:334	3↑ Caballero H 55k	7 8 95¼ 85½ 611 613	Toro F	116	6.00	84-10	June's Love1163¼Ancient Title126½Big Band1193	Dull try 9
26Apr75- 8Hol	fm 1⅛Ⓣ	:46 1:102 1:352 1:48	3↑ ⒻLong Beach H-G2	3 4 46½ 32½ 1hd 1½	Tejeira J	124	2.20	96-05	Susan's Girl124½Bold Ballet1183Dulcia1211¼	Driving 6
Previously trained by J.L. Newman										
2Apr75- 8OP	fst 170	:221 :461 1:114 1:422	4↑ ⒻApple Blossom H 61k	12 4 32 1½ 12½ 13½	Nichols J	124	*.90	84-22	Susan's Girl1243½Truchas116nkMatuta1141½	Handily 12
Previously trained by R.L. Smith										
1Mar75- 8SA	fst 1⅛	:454 1:103 1:36 1:483	4↑ ⒻS Margarita H-G1	9 4 44½ 51¾ 21 21½	Pincay L Jr	123	3.50e	87-13	Tizna1201½Susan's Girl123½Gay Style125no	Good try 12
16Feb75- 8SA	fst 1 1/16	:241 :481 1:121 1:42	4↑ ⒻS Maria H-G2	1 1 31½ 3½ 32½ 32	Hawley S	124	3.00e	90-14	Gay Style122¾Tizna1201¼Susan's Girl1242	Weakened 8
18Jan75- 8SA	fst 7f	:22 :442 1:084 1:212	4↑ ⒻS Monica H-G2	1 1 75½ 65 54¼ 2½	Hawley S	125	4.40e	95-12	SisterFleet115½Susan'sGirl125nkModusVivendi123½	Gamely 13
27Dec74- 8SA	fst 1	:241 :472 1:111 1:353	3↑ Alw 20000	1 1 31 34 34½ 35¼	Pincay L Jr	117	1.40	86-15	Nantwice119nkTreeofKnowledge1155Ssn'sGrl1172	Bad start 4
Previously trained by T.W. Kelley										
9Nov74- 8CD	fst 1	:233 :472 1:123 1:372	3↑ ⒻFalls City H-G3	8 2 23½ 2hd 11½ 1no	Gavidia W	126	*.70e	82-19	Susan'sGirl126noCrystalStone114¾EnchntdNtv1121½	All out 9
30Oct74- 8CD	fst 7f	:232 :463 1:11 1:241	3↑ ⒻAlw 12500	8 3 33½ 34 2hd 1½	Gavidia W	114	*1.10	86-22	Susan'sGirl114½GallantDvll1212½DogtoothVolt1213	Driving 9
Previously trained by C.R. Parke										
16Feb74- 8SA	fst 1 1/16	:232 :464 1:111 1:424	4↑ ⒻS Maria H-G2	1 3 44½ 65½ 56 52¾	Baeza B	128	*.80	85-14	Convenience1211½Tizna117nkTallahto119½	Mild bid 8
2Feb74- 8SA	fst 1 1/16	:233 :471 1:104 1:412	4↑ San Pasqual H-G2	1 1 2½ 42 3½ 33	Baeza B	119	*1.30e	92-12	Tri Jet121hdForage1213Susan's Girl1193	Weakened 10
19Jan74- 8SA	gd 7f	:222 :453 1:103 1:24	4↑ ⒻS Monica H-G2	1 1 44 56 45 2½	Baeza B	127	*2.30	82-28	Tizna116½Susan's Girl1271½Impressive Style1181½	Gamely 7
27Oct73- 6Kee	fst 1⅛	:47 1:103 1:36 1:484	3↑ ⒻSpinster-G1	2 2 21½ 21 1½ 11	Baeza B	123	*.70	93-13	Susan's Girl1231Light Hearted1231Coraggioso1194	Driving 6
8Oct73- 8Atl	fst 1 3/16	:47 1:11 1:361 1:551	3↑ ⒻMatchmaker-G1	5 3 37 55½ 43 31¼	Baeza B	125	*1.20	99-13	AlmaNorth1181¼LightHearted121noSusan'sGirl1252	Good try 9
15Sep73- 6Bel	fst 1⅛	:462 1:10 1:34 1:461	3↑ ⒻBeldame-G1	2 3 42½ 56½ 49½ 312	Pincay L Jr	123	2.60	88-07	Desert Vixen1188½Poker Night1183Susan's Girl123¾	7
Passed tired ones;Previously trained by J.W. Russell										

12Aug73- 8Del	fst 1¼	:463 1:104 1:354 2:003	3↑ ⒻDelaware H-G1	6	5	514	44	21	1nk	Pincay L Jr	127		*1.40	99-10	Susn'sGirl127nkSummrGuest1225½LightHeartd1254	Driving	6
4Aug73- 8Lib	fst 1 1/16	:232 :47 1:113 1:433	3↑ ⒻSusquehanna H-G2	5	5	47	44	1hd	13½	Pincay L Jr	125		*.50	88-24	Susan's Girl1253½Twixt1184½Knightly Belle1131¼	Handily	6
7Jly73- 8Hol	fst 1⅛	:454 1:094 1:35 1:474	3↑ ⒻVanity H-G1	1	3	34½	35½	42½	31¾	Pincay L Jr	127		1.40	91-09	Convenience121½MinstrelMiss1211¼Susan'sGrl127½	Bid,hung	8
2Jun73- 8Hol	fst 1 1/16	:231 :464 1:11 1:414	3↑ ⒻMilady H-G2	6	4	2½	1½	2½	21	Pincay L Jr	128		*.90e	85-17	Minstrel Miss1181Susan's Girl1281Pallisima1153	Gamely	6
5May73- 8Hol	fm 1⅜Ⓣ	2:132	3↑ Century H-G1	9	1	11½	1½	21	47¾	Rotz JL	119		5.10	80-11	Cougar II1273½Wing Out1183¼Life Cycle1171	Weakened	11
21Apr73- 8Hol	fm 1⅛Ⓣ	:46 1:10 1:344 1:473	3↑ ⒻLong Beach H-G2	8	6	612	69½	54	2hd	Pincay L Jr	130		*1.70	98-05	BirdBoots115hdSusan'sGirl130¾HillCrcus1201½	Just missed	9
22Mar73- 8SA	fst 1¼⊗	:502 1:15 1:393 2:033	4↑ ⒻS Barbara H-G1	1	1	11½	11½	12	14¾	Pincay L Jr	129		*.30	80-15	Susan'sGirl1294¾VeiledDesire1102½GrayMirag1124½	Driving	5
3Mar73- 8SA	fst 1⅛	:463 1:101 1:352 1:474	4↑ ⒻS Margarita Inv'l H-G1	8	2	32	44	31½	13	Pincay L Jr	127		2.50	93-11	Susan'sGirl1273Convenience1232¾MnstrlMss115½	Drew clear	8
17Feb73- 8SA	fst 1 1/16	:234 :473 1:114 1:42	4↑ ⒻS Maria H-G2	2	2	21	2½	2hd	1½	Pincay L Jr	125		2.60	92-11	Susan'sGirl125½Convnnc1233HllCrcus119hd	Swerved,driving	6
27Jan73- 8SA	fst 1⅛	:453 1:094 1:352 1:481	San Fernando-G2	3	5	55½	54	56	54¼	Tejada V	118		2.80e	87-12	Bicker1201½Royal Owl1201½Commoner114¾	No rally	14
6Jan73- 8SA	fst 7f	:214 :442 1:084 1:212	Malibu-G2	1	1	64½	64	51¼	55	Tejada V	121		*1.10e	91-11	Bicker117hdRoyal Owl120½Tri Jet1171½	In close	13
9Sep72- 7Bel	fst 1⅛	:46 1:102 1:35 1:472	3↑ ⒻBeldame 112k	3	4	24	42	21	11	Pincay L Jr	118		3.30	97-06	Susan's Girl1181Summer Guest1181Chou Croute1233¼	Bore out,driving	9
2Sep72- 7Bel	fst 1⅛	:461 1:10 1:351 1:48	ⒻGazelle H 55k	1	2	25	25	1hd	11½	Pincay L Jr	124		*1.10	94-09	Susan's Girl1241½Honestous1125Light Hearted1215	Driving	7
29Jly72- 8Lib	fst 1 1/16	:231 :464 1:113 1:441	ⒻCotillion H 59k	5	3	31½	21½	11	14½	Tejada V	125		*1.10	85-22	Susan'sGirl1254½GrotonMiss1193Honestous1154	Ridden out	13
20Jly72- 8Hol	fst 1⅛	:462 1:102 1:353 1:483	ⒻHol Oaks 64k	2	4	55½	41¾	33	31¾	Tejeira J	124		*.40	87-15	Pallsm1121¼Brt'sTryst112½Susn'sGrl1243½	Checked,rallied	7
29Jun72- 8Hol	fm 1 1/16Ⓣ	:241 :483 1:14 1:433	ⒻPrincess 33k	2	2	24	2hd	31	2hd	Tejada V	121		*1.10	81-19	Le Cle121hdSusan's Girl121¾Ground Song1171¼	Just missed	7
17Jun72- 7Bel	sly 1½	:491 1:132 2:031 2:292	ⒻC C A Oaks 110k	3	1	1hd	32	34½	38	Tejada V	121	b	*.90	78-09	Summer Guest1214Wanda1214Susan's Girl1216	Gave way	8
27May72- 7Bel	fst 1⅛	:462 1:102 1:353 1:482	ⒻMother Goose 84k	4	3	22	21½	21	2nk	Tejada V	121	b	*.40	92-10	Wanda121nkSusan's Girl1216Summer Guest1211½	Sharp	8
13May72- 7Aqu	fst 1	:232 :454 1:093 1:343	ⒻAcorn 56k	2	2	21½	1½	12	12½	Tejada V	121	b	*.70	94-11	Susan's Girl1212½Wanda1213Stacey d'Ette1213	Handily	7
5May72- 8CD	fst 1 1/16	:241 :481 1:122 1:441	ⒻKy Oaks 61k	7	4	31½	1½	13	11	Tejada V	121	b	*.30	87-16	Susan'sGirl1211BarelyEven1211¾FairwayFlyer1212½	Handily	7
29Apr72- 8CD	fst 7f	:224 :46 1:104 1:234	ⒻLa Troienne 21k	8	2	44½	42½	11	11¾	Tejada V	121	b	*1.10	88-17	Susan'sGirl1211¾BarelyEven1216HempensSong121hd	Easily	8
9Mar72- 8SA	fst 1 1/16	:23 :46 1:102 1:43	ⒻS Susana 54k	3	3	31	1hd	1½	13	Tejada V	115	b	*.30	87-15	Susan'sGirl1153½Dumpty'sDream1156Chargerett115¾	Handily	7
24Feb72- 8SA	fst 7f	:22 :443 1:091 1:214	ⒻS Ynez 47k	5	1	53½	21½	21	13¼	Tejada V	118	b	*1.10	94-13	Susan'sGirl1183¼Foreseer115noImpressiveStyle1186	Easily	10
20Jan72- 8SA	fst 6f	:214 :443 :562 1:083	ⒻPasadena 34k	7	2	32½	3½	1½	1¾	Tejada V	118	b	*1.60e	98-10	Susan's Girl118¾Sumatra113noBrenda Beauty1212½	Driving	7
25Nov71- 8Lib	sly 1 70	:23 :473 1:134 1:434	ⒻVillager 27k	2	1	11½	12½	14	18	Hinojosa H	119	b	*.70	86-27	Susan'sGirl1198RoyalKin11412TurbulentMiss1125	Handily	7
17Nov71- 7Aqu	fst 1	:231 :452 1:10 1:354	ⒻDemoiselle 36k	2	4	34	34½	25	22	Pincay L Jr	119	b	*.50	86-16	DresdenDoll1142Susan'sGrl1194BrndButy1221	Belated rally	14
6Nov71- 8GS	gd 1 1/16	:234 :474 1:13 1:454	ⒻGardenia 184k	2	2	21	15	1hd	22¾	Blum W	119	b	7.70	73-28	NumberedAccnt1192¾Susan'sGirl1196Catmousam Road1196	Second best	11
27Oct71- 7GS	my 1 70	:232 :48 1:131 1:441	ⒻAlw 10000	3	6	53½	32	23	22½	Velasquez J	112	b	*.50	70-33	BoldRoyal1132½Susan'sGirl1123TurbulentMss1142	Willingly	9
11Oct71- 7Bel	fst 1	:231 :461 1:104 1:353	ⒻFrizette 135k	2	3	3½	23	26	27	Velasquez J	119	b	4.70	88-16	NmberdAccnt1197Susan'sGirl1195BarelyEvn11920	Gamely	4
4Oct71- 3Bel	fst 7f	:222 :454 1:104 1:24	ⒻAlw 12000	7	1	32½	2hd	14	15	Velasquez J	123	b	2.40e	87-18	Susan'sGirl1235BoldRoyal116hdBrendaButy1234½	Mild drive	8
15Sep71- 7Bel	fst 7f	:221 :452 1:104 1:232	ⒻAstarita 35k	7	2	1111	106	72¾	43¼	Velasquez J	122		4.30	87-12	BarelyEven1193MissGunflint116noBrdgtO'Brck112nk	Rallied	11
	Previously trained by J.E. Picou																
16Aug71- 7Sar	fst 6f	:222 :454 1:101	ⒻAdirondack 34k	3	2	76½	41¾	41½	52	Velasquez J	122	b	8.60	93-12	DebbyDeb1141½DancePrtnr114noNumbrdAccnt122nk	No rally	9
7Aug71- 8Lib	fst 6f	:221 :46 1:113	ⒻSignature 58k	2	8	75¾	63¾	2hd	15	Brumfield D	118	b	*.90e	87-16	Susan'sGirl1185HempensSong1183CastleFlower1121	Driving	8
24Jly71- 6Aqu	fst 5½f	:22 :46 :582 1:044	ⒻAlw 10000	5	3	42	42	1½	15	Velasquez J	119	b	*1.20	89-15	Susan'sGirl1195RoyalStatut119¾Stcyd'Ett114hd	Mild drive	10
9Jly71- 4Aqu	fst 5½f	:22 :461 :583 1:044	ⒻMd Sp Wt	3	1	62¾	63¾	2hd	14	Velasquez J	119	b	4.20	89-17	Susan'sGirl1194EarlyTide119nkPlsntFlght1191½	Mild drive	8
18Jun71- 3Bel	fst 5½f	:223 :47 :592 1:061	ⒻMd Sp Wt	4	2	33½	34½	23	2½	Velasquez J	119	b	21.40	88-20	Bold Example119½Susan's Girl1194Dandy Duchess1191½	Rallied,finished strongly	10
4Jun71- 2Bel	fst 5½f	:233 :474 :593 1:054	ⒻMd Sp Wt	3	1	31	77	69	410¼	Velasquez J	119		8.80	81-15	BrendaBeauty119nkChildofGrace1198SingleLine1192	Tired	8

Ta Wee

dkbbr. f. 1966, by Intentionally (Intent)–Aspidistra, by Better Self **Lifetime record: 21 15 2 1 $284,941**

Own.– Tartan Stable
Br.– Tartan Farms (Fla)
Tr.– F.S. Schulhofer

5Oct70- 7Bel	fst 6f	:221 :451 1:10	3↑ ⒻInterborough H 21k	2	3	1½	11	15	1¾	Rotz JL	142	*.60	95-10	Ta Wee142¾Hasty Hitter1132½Kushka1121	Handily	5
31Aug70- 7Bel	fst 6f	:231 :461 1:102	3↑ Fall Highweight H 28k	3	3	32	31½	1hd	1nk	Rotz JL	140	*1.50e	93-19	Ta Wee140nkTowzie Tyke121nkDistinctive1344	Safe margin	9
29Jly70- 7Aqu	fst 6f	:22 :443 1:084	3↑ Gravesend H 28k	6	5	64¼	23	23	24	Rotz JL	134	*2.10	95-12	Distinctive1144Ta Wee134hdTyrant121nk	Gamely	9
17Jun70- 8Mth	fst 6f	:213 :443 1:10	3↑ ⒻRegret H 28k	2	5	2hd	1½	12	1½	Rotz JL	136	*.60	92-15	Ta Wee136½Golden Or1133Deb's Darling114½	Driving	8
1Jun70- 7Bel	fst 6f	:221 :444 1:10	3↑ ⒻHempstead H 28k	5	3	2hd	11½	13	13½	Rotz JL	132	*1.20	95-11	Ta Wee1323½Process Shot1271Grey Slacks1112	Easy score	8
8Apr70- 7Aqu	fst 7f	:23 :452 1:10 1:224	3↑ ⒻDistaff H 27k	4	3	21	2hd	1½	21¾	Rotz JL	134	*1.40	85-20	ProcssSht1261¾TaWee1342DedicatdtoSu115hd	Tired-impost	6
27Mar70- 7Aqu	gd 6f	:223 :462 1:112	3↑ ⒻCorrection H 27k	1	5	1½	11½	13	1nk	Rotz JL	131	*.50	86-26	Ta Wee131nkTaken Aback1144Dedicated to Sue1171	Lasted	7
1Nov69- 7Aqu	fst 7f	:221 :442 1:083 1:213	3↑ Vosburgh H 58k	6	5	31	1hd	1hd	1hd	Rotz JL	123	*1.70	93-13	TaWee123hd[DH]PluckyLucky116[DH]RisingMarket120½	Driving	11
15Oct69- 7Bel	fst 6f	:222 :46 1:093	3↑ ⒻInterborough H 27k	5	4	21	11	12	13½	Rotz JL	124	*.50	97-16	Ta Wee1243½Dedicated to Sue1144½Grey Slacks118nk	Easily	7
11Sep69- 7Bel	yl 1 1/16Ⓣ	1:45	3↑ ⒻAlw 15000	2	2	23	21	11½	42¾	Rotz JL	119	1.60	- -	PersianIntrigue118¾DesertLaw1182OlympianIdle116hd	Tired	8
25Aug69- 7Bel	fst 6f	:213 :454 1:101	3↑ Fall Highweight H 28k	9	5	4¾	2½	1hd	1¾	Rotz JL	130	*1.50e	94-17	TaWee130¾KngEmperr1311Gaylord'sFeathr1292½	Hard drive	9
	Previously trained by J.A. Nerud															
31Jly69- 7Sar	fst 7f	:223 :444 1:111 1:233	ⒻTest 27k	1	3	12	16	13	11	Belmonte E	124	*.30	91-16	Ta Wee1241French Bread1158½Bold Tribute1121½	Driving	6
31May69- 8Mth	fst 6f	:212 :434 1:083	ⒻMiss Woodford 29k	11	8	1½	12	15	17	Belmonte E	121	*.60	99-13	Ta Wee1217Imbibe1156Script Girl115hd	As rider pleased	12
7May69- 7Aqu	fst 7f	:222 :451 1:092 1:223	ⒻComely 28k	2	5	32½	1½	13	1hd	Belmonte E	118	*.40	88-13	TaWee118hdShuvee1215HstyHttr118hd	Stumbled start,lasted	6
3Apr69- 7Aqu	fst 6f	:221 :444 1:092	ⒻPrioress 28k	1	9	22	22	2hd	13	Rotz JL	121	2.90	96-15	Ta Wee1213Frances Flower1214Juliet121½	Handy score	9
29Jan69- 8Hia	fst 7f	:224 :453 1:102 1:232	ⒻMimosa 34k	13	8	54¼	43½	22	33½	Rotz JL	114	*1.30	87-15	NuttyDonut1122Queen'sDouble1211½TaWee114hd	Weakened	13
18Jan69- 8Hia	fst 6f	:221 :451 1:102	ⒻJasmine (Div 2) 27k	2	4	11	1½	11½	13	Rotz JL	113	3.40	92-12	Ta Wee1133Spring Sunshine1215Imbibe1121½	Scored handily	12
7Sep68- 4Aqu	fst 6f	:231 :471 1:121	ⒻAlw 7000	9	9	43½	22	1½	12	Rotz JL	119	*1.50	82-18	TaWee1192Dihela1131½DorisWhite1166	Scored well in hand	10
21Aug68- 7Sar	gd 6f	:214 :454 1:112	ⒻSpinaway 80k	7	2	21½	11½	1hd	46¼	Rotz JL	119	*1.10	85-10	Queen's Double1191¾Show Off119½Fillypasser1194	Tired	10
13Aug68- 5Sar	fst 5½f	:221 :454 :573 1:04	ⒻMd Sp Wt	2	10	1½	13	16	16	Rotz JL	119	*.80	97-11	Ta Wee1196Drip Spring1192Socializing1192½	Easily best	12
30Jly68- 4Sar	fst 5½f	:221 :461 :584 1:052	ⒻMd Sp Wt	1	10	13	11	2½	44	Rotz JL	119	*1.90	86-17	Queen's Double1193Hasty Hitter119noIrradiate1191	Tired	12

Talking Picture

dkbbr. f. 1971, by Speak John (Prince John)–Poster Girl, by Nasrullah **Lifetime record: 15 6 2 3 $178,643**

Own.– Elmendorf Farm
Br.– Elmendorf Farm (Ky)
Tr.– J.P. Campo

11May74- 8Aqu	fst 1	:23 :452 1:093 1:36	ⒻAcorn (Div 2)-G1	9	8	85½	67½	64	52¾	Turcotte R	121	2.60	84-17	ChrisEvert121¾ClearCopy1211FiestaLibre121hd	Mild rally	9
22Apr74- 8Aqu	fst 6f	:222 :444 1:101	ⒻPrioress-G3	3	9	98¾	67½	45½	3¾	Turcotte R	115	3.90	91-14	Clear Copy115noHeartful118¾Talking Picture1153¼	Rallied	12
18Feb74- 9GP	fst 7f	:221 :45 1:093 1:223	ⒻBonnie Miss 35k	3	10	1010	1111	1111	94¾	Turcotte R	122	*1.90	86-17	City Girl112¾Maud Muller112½Double Bend1121	No factor	12
30Jan74- 9GP	fst 6f	:221 :453 1:11	ⒻPromise (Div 2) 26k	10	2	89½	55	22	1½	Turcotte R	119	*1.10	84-22	TalkingPicture119½CityGirl1122½DoubleBend1122	Driving	10
27Oct73- 8Lrl	fst 1 1/16	:231 :461 1:111 1:424	ⒻSelima-G1	6	7	68	55	33	33	Venezia M	119	*1.20	96-12	Dancealot119¾I'maPleasure1192¼TlkngPctur1193½	No excuse	9
6Oct73- 7Bel	fst 1	:232 :464 1:112 1:362	ⒻFrizette-G1	2	11	84¾	83¾	74½	53¾	Turcotte R	121	*1.80	82-13	Bundler121½Chris Evert121nkI'm a Pleasure1211	Rallied	14
19Sep73- 7Bel	fst 7f	:224 :46 1:104 1:231	ⒻMatron-G1	2	6	87	83¾	31½	1hd	Turcotte R	119	*.70	86-11	Talking Picture119hdDancealot119nkRaisela119nk	Driving	9
24Aug73- 7Sar	fst 6f	:223 :461 1:10	ⒻSpinaway-G1	6	8	94¾	52½	1½	12½	Turcotte R	120	*1.90e	90-10	TalkingPicture1202½SpecialTeam1203Raisela1202½	Driving	10
13Aug73- 7Sar	fst 6f	:22 :452 1:11	ⒻAdirondack-G2	5	8	86¾	65¼	25	1hd	Baeza B	120	5.80	85-15	TalkingPicture120hdInHotPursuit1204½Bedknob1202	Driving	10

30Jly73- 7Sar fst 6f :221 :453 1:104 ⒻSchuylerville-G2 9 1 74½ 55 43½ 1no Baeza B 116 4.50 86-14 Talking Picture116noImajoy1162Celestial Lights1192 Driving 10
14Jly73- 8Hol fst 6f :22 :444 :57 1:093 ⒻLassie-G2 8 13 115¾ 87¾ 89½ 88 Rotz JL 119 3.20 83-14 Special Goddess1191Calaki119¾Fleet Peach119nk Dull try 13
3Jly73- 3Aqu fst 5½f :221 :444 :564 1:03 ⒻAlw 9500 4 3 43½ 35½ 26 24½ Baeza B 118 *.80 93-11 What Brilliance1184½Talking Picture1188I'm a Pleasure1182 5
Second best
13Jun73- 7Bel sly 5½f :221 :451 :571 1:031 ⒻFashion-G3 5 8 713 711 511 311¼ Baeza B 117 3.50e 88-09 InHotPursuit11710Provincial1171¼TlkngPctur1172½ Rallied 8
4Jun73- 5Bel fst 5½f :23 :462 :58 1:04 ⒻAlw 10000 1 6 85½ 63½ 33½ 22 Baeza B 117 2.70 97-07 In Hot Pursuit1172Talking Picture117¾Nice to Have1174½ 8
Second best
15May73- 3Bel fst 5½f :23 :462 :582 1:043 ⒻMd Sp Wt 5 7 62½ 41 2½ 14 Baeza B 116 *2.60 96-04 Talking Picture1164Shy Dawn1162Graziella1161 Ridden out 10

Tempest Queen

b. f. 1975, by Graustark (Ribot)–Queen's Paradise, by Summer Tan **Lifetime record: 19 8 3 4 $289,219**
Own.– Darby Dan Farm
Br.– Mrs J.W. Galbreath (Ky)
Tr.– Thomas Rondinello

21Mar79-11Hia fst 7f :213 :441 1:091 1:221 3↑ ⒻPoinciana H 32k 3 6 35½ 79 911 913½ Velasquez J 123 *.80 78-18 FrostySkater1192¼NavajoPrincess1221Excitabl1124 Stopped 9
7Mar79-10Hia fst 7f :23 :452 1:101 1:23 4↑ ⒻAlw 15000 8 2 31½ 33 3½ 11¼ Velasquez J 122 *.90 88-14 TempestQn1221¼IrishAgate119½Whatsupbaby114nk Driving 10
17Feb79- 9GP fst 7f :221 :444 1:09 1:211 4↑ ⒻAlw 20000 7 4 52½ 65½ 58½ 611 Velasquez J 122 *.60 87-13 Hagany117noFrostySkater1144½SharpBelle1141 No response 8
21Oct78- 7Kee fst 1⅛ :464 1:103 1:362 1:49 3↑ ⒻSpinster-G1 3 1 11 12 11 11¾ Velasquez J 119 8.40 92-14 TempstQueen1191¾Northerntt123hdLklyExchng123hd Driving 10
23Sep78- 8Bel fst 1⅛ :462 1:094 1:343 1:47 3↑ ⒻRuffian H-G1 6 2 21 2½ 33 35½ Venezia M 117 18.10 86-15 LateBloomr1221½PearlNcklace1244TmpstQn1172½ Weakened 9
2Sep78- 8Bel my 1⅛ :462 1:11 1:364 1:494 ⒻGazelle H-G2 4 1 11½ 11½ 14 15½ Velasquez J 117 1.60 78-21 TmpstQueen1175½Lulubo1164¾Terpschorst1135¾ Ridden out 5
12Aug78- 8Sar sly 1¼ :47 1:121 1:381 2:04 ⒻAlabama-G1 5 2 21 2hd 32½ 310 Velasquez J 121 4.50 71-18 WhiteStarLine1211½SummerFlng1218½TmpstQn1217 Bid,tired 6
2Aug78- 7Sar fst 7f :221 :45 1:092 1:212 ⒻTest (Div 1)-G2 2 6 63¼ 74½ 55 46¾ Velasquez J 124 *2.50 91-10 WhiteStarLine1211½SilknDlght1143¼Zrld1142 No room early 8
1Jly78- 8Bel fst 1½ :464 1:112 2:023 2:292 ⒻC C A Oaks-G1 5 2 21½ 32 35½ 310 Velasquez J 121 4.40 63-16 LakevilleMiss1216Caesar'sWish1214TmpstQn1215 Weakened 5
11Jun78- 8Bel fst 1⅛ :451 1:09 1:342 1:473 ⒻMother Goose-G1 2 2 23 23 32½ 33½ Velasquez J 121 1.90 85-15 Caesar'sWish1212LakevilleMss1211½TmpstQn121hd Weakened 8
27May78- 8Bel fst 1 :224 :45 1:094 1:352 ⒻAcorn-G1 1 1 23 1hd 11½ 11¾ Velasquez J 121 4.90 91-17 TempstQueen1211¾Lakeville Miss121nkWhite Star Line1211¾ 6
Ridden out
13May78- 8Aqu fst 7f :224 :451 1:094 1:23 ⒻComely-G3 3 5 2hd 2hd 21½ 23 Turcotte R 118 *1.40 83-21 Mashteen1133TempstQn1181½Mucchin1133 Altered course 6
30Apr78- 8Aqu fst 6f :23 :464 1:112 ⒻPrioress 42k 1 5 11½ 11½ 13 12½ Velasquez J 118 *.30 86-20 TempestQueen1182½SweetJoyce112nkSilverIce1154½ Handily 5
22Feb78- 9Hia gd 1⅛ :471 1:114 1:37 1:50 ⒻPoinsettia-G3 5 6 32 2hd 11 11½ Velasquez J 113 2.00 82-18 Tempest Queen1131½Jevalin1142L'Alezane122nk Ridden out 9
30Jan78-10Hia fst 7f :223 :46 1:102 1:231 ⒻAlw 8500 1 7 24 21½ 12 12 Velasquez J 114 *.60 87-20 TempestQn1142Mucchina1154½MakeItKnown1173½ Driving 10
17Jan78- 3Hia fst 6f :214 :45 1:094 ⒻMd Sp Wt 11 2 21½ 32 1hd 14 Velasquez J 119 *.90 94-11 TempstQueen1194Marci Lynn1191Ericka Downs1196 In hand 11
2Dec77- 5Aqu sly 6f :222 :46 1:103 ⒻMd Sp Wt 5 1 1½ 1hd 1hd 2nk Cordero A Jr 119 3.50 90-18 IvyRoad119nkTempestQueen1194¾MissBaja1195 Just failed 9
16Nov77- 4Aqu fst 6f :223 :462 1:112 ⒻMd Sp Wt 9 5 2½ 1hd 1hd 2hd Velasquez J 119 5.70 86-19 Idmon112hdTempest Queen1192¾Miss Ivor1194 Gamely 9
1Nov77- 2Aqu fst 6f :224 :462 1:121 ⒻMd Sp Wt 13 14 129¼ 1211 710 66¾ Velasquez J 119 28.20 75-18 AllforAmy1192¾Tara'sTheme119nkMissIvor1192¾ Off slowly 14

Top Bid

b. g. 1964, by Olympia (Heliopolis)–High Bid, by To Market **Lifetime record: 74 25 9 11 $310,128**
Own.– Mrs O. Phipps
Br.– Wheatley Stable (Ky)
Tr.– D.M. Smithwick

17Nov73- 2Cam fm 2 13/16 S'Chase 5:214 4↑ Colonial Cup 50k 5 10 - - - - - McDonald RS 158 -e -- LuckyBoyIII149noSthsyer162noDreamMgc1531¼ Broke down 15
11Nov73- 6Mid fm *1¼Ⓣ 2:19 3↑ Alw 300 9 - 39¾ Brittle C III 153 s -e -- Still In All1438Sabinus1401¾Top Bid1533 Hung 16
Further running positions unavailable due to weather conditions
27Oct73- 5FH fm *1½Ⓣ 2:294 3↑ Alw 1500 7 2 3¾ 35½ 31 11½ Brittle C III 142 s -- Top Bid1421½Tor's Lib149¾Honest Crook1494 Driving 8
6Oct73- 4Lig fm *2½ S'Chase 5:032 4↑ Temple Gwathmey H 25k 4 1 11 1½ 1nk 39¼ Brittle C III 157 -e -- Athenian Idol1401¼Soothsayer1628Top Bid1572 Weakened 8
3Oct73- 6Lig gd *2 S'Chase 4:102 4↑ Handicap 10000 1 3 11½ 12 1½ 33¼ Aitcheson J Jr 162 -- ⒹPerigo150nkJuac Hollow1603Top Bid1622 In close 10
Placed second by disqualification
15Sep73- 6Fai fm *2½ Hurdles 5:211 4↑ Grand National H 12k 2 2 16 13 12½ 11¼ Aitcheson J Jr 152 s 2.70 -- Top Bid1521¼Summer Crop1395Dream Magic1532 Driving 6
8Sep73- 6Fai hd *2⅛ Hurdles 4:133 4↑ Alw 4850 1 2 32½ 1¾ 11 11¼ Aitcheson J Jr 158 s 5.00 -- Top Bid1581¼Wustenchef1585Castlebar II1501 Driving 4
24Aug73- 9Sar fm 1⅞ Hurdles 3:231 4↑ OClm 6000 7 5 55½ 24 21½ 1hd Aitcheson J Jr 154 s *2.20 -- Top Bid154hdTarratine133¾Hipocampo1476 Driving 7
8Aug73- 9Sar fm 2 Hurdles 3:372 4↑ OClm 8000 6 3 322 316 46 - Aitcheson J Jr 155 s 2.60 -- Hipocampo1391¾ManchuPrinc1396FarmrsLot1422 Lost rider 8
3Aug73- 5Sar gd 2 1/16 Hurdles 3:44 4↑ Lovely Night H 22k 3 3 49 611 625 521 Aitcheson J Jr 149 s 6.60e -- Juac Hollow1504Wustenchef1558½Still in All1401 Tired 7
22Jly73- 6Del sf 1Ⓣ :232 :473 1:121 1:39 3↑ Alw 8500 8 4 65¼ 715 716 726 Cooke C 118 24.50 54-31 Mr. Clinch120nkLeematt1224Away Satan1181 Tired 8
18Nov72- 3Cam fm 2 13/16 S'Chase 5:234 4↑ Colonial Cup 100k 7 2 74¾ 3½ 41 43 Brittle C III 160 - -- Soothsayr1582½Inkslinger158¼ShadowBrook160nk Weakened 16
4Nov72- 5Mtp fm *2 Hurdles 4:253 3↑ Alw 1500 3 3 25 2nk 25 26 Brittle C III 143 s -e -- Summer Crop1436Top Bid1432½Arctic Joe15110 Best of rest 8
28Oct72- 4FH sf *2 Hurdles 4:12 3↑ Handicap 10000 9 1 11½ 56¼ 63¾ 58 Brittle C III 157 s - -- Persian Honour145½Americus1391Dream Magic1505 Tired 11
21Oct72- 4RB fm *2 S'Chase 4:093 4↑ Alw 3500 3 2 21½ 23 44¼ 35½ Gregory T 143 -e -- Profile1431½Americus1464Top Bid143¾ Tired 8
7Oct72- 6Lig sf *7fⓉ 1:374 3↑ Alw 1500 12 1 1¾ 1nk 2no 44½ Brittle C III 155 s - -- Perpetual II1581½Dream Magic143½Powdermill1432½ Tired 12
Previously trained by Pierre Head
25Aug72◆ Clairefontaine(Fr) gd *2 11/16 5:14 4↑ Grand Steeple-Chase de Deauville Stk18800 310¼ Lautier R 156 8.00 Mr. So and So145nkBelpic14710Top Bid156½ 20
Tracked leaders,led 2 out,headed 1 out,outfinished
8Aug72◆ Clairefontaine(Fr) gd *2⅜ 4:46 4↑ Prix Leopold d'Orsetti Hcp Hcp15000 11 Lautier R 158 6.00 Kind Tady14315Mini Chief134½Malefine145½ 17
Rated in midpack,bid 3 out,weakened after second last
9Jly72◆ Auteuil(Fr) gd *2 3/16 4:22 5↑ Prix Palamede Alw15400 24 Dreux T 137 *2.20 Pique Puce1454Top Bid1362½Mehryvan1471½ 15
Tracked in 4th,2nd 2 out,outfinished
18Jun72◆ Auteuil(Fr) gd *2⅛ 4:12 5↑ Prix Arthur O'Connor Alw15400 99 Lautier R 154 3.00 Bengalien1362Mistonette1413Franc Ryk1452 13
Rated in 6th,brief effort 3 out,weakened
Previously trained by D.M. Smithwick
27Nov71- 8Lrl gd 1¼⊗ :47 1:121 1:39 2:044 3↑ Lrl Turf Cup 28k 2 1 32½ 617 639 649 Nelson E 115 b 4.50 42-20 CrackRulr1161½FreshAlibha11310SrMtthw1094½ Early speed 6
20Nov71- 2Cam fm 2 13/16 S'Chase 5:17 4↑ Colonial Cup 10k 3 11 75¾ 813 68 38¼ Aitcheson J Jr 160 s -e -- Inkslinger149nkSoothsayer1498Top Bid1603 Rallied 15
6Nov71- 3Mtp sf *2½ S'Chase 4:493 4↑ Noel Laing H 5.6k 4 8 87¼ 811 716 821½ Aitcheson J Jr 165 s - -- TingleCreek1548TheCritter143nkAttribution144nk No factor 9
15Oct71- 3Bel yl 3 S'Chase 5:47 4↑ Gwathmey H 55k 1 4 65½ 43 515 310 Aitcheson J Jr 160 s 4.10 -- Shadow Brook1635½Amerind1414½Top Bid160¾ Bobbled 9
28Sep71- 3Bel yl 2⅝ S'Chase 4:571 4↑ Brook H 33k 5 7 713 59½ 413 513 Aitcheson J Jr 162 s 1.60 -- Shadow Brook1592¼Amarind135nkTingle Creek1536 Bobbled 8
18Sep71- 8Fai fm *1 5/16Ⓣ 2:202 3↑ Alw 1200 8 7 66¾ 55 21 13 Aitcheson J Jr 153 s *.50 -- Top Bid1533Mystic's Desire1476Pelham II1404½ Handily 8
11Sep71- 2Fai fm *1 5/16Ⓣ 2:122 3↑ Alw 1200 2 13 1413 97¼ 87 14 Aitcheson J Jr 142 s *1.00e -- TopBid1424BrandyPrinceII156½Mystic'sDesr142¾ Mild drive 14
26Aug71- 3Sar fm 2½ S'Chase 4:372 4↑ Grand National H 40k 5 4 24 31 23 212 Aitcheson J Jr 163 s 2.40 -- Shadow Brook15512Top Bid1635Madagascar1421 2nd best 7
12Aug71- 3Sar fm 2 1/16 Hurdles 3:433 4↑ Lovely Night H 22k 6 6 64¾ 54 410 511 Aitcheson J Jr 162 s *1.30e -- Shadow Brook156nkSoothsayer1398Inkslinger1502½ Tired 7
14Nov70- 4Cam sf *2 13/16 S'Chase 5:20 4↑ Colonial Cup 100k - 8 66¼ 74 35 11½ Aitcheson J Jr 160 -e -- Top Bid1601½Shadow Brook1601½Jaunty1586 Driving 22
16Oct70- 5Bel sf 3 S'Chase 5:522 4↑ Temple Gwathmey H 55k 6 4 312 31½ 13 14 Aitcheson J Jr 156 2.10 -- Top Bid1564Duke Cannon1329Tingle Creek1467 Handy score 7
17Sep70- 4Bel fm 2½ S'Chase 4:37 4↑ Broad Hollow H 17k 9 3 513 49 21½ 26 Aitcheson J Jr 155 *1.50e -- TingleCreek1396TopBid1554½DukeCannon13215 Bobbled 12th 10
1Sep70- 4Bel fm 2 S'Chase 3:412 4↑ International H 16k 4 4 47 44 1½ 1½ Aitcheson J Jr 152 *.90e -- Top Bid152½Lost Lamb135hdVocalist1429 Hard drive 6
20Aug70- 6Sar hd 2 1/16 S'Chase 3:444 4↑ Saratoga H 18k 4 3 23 2½ 16 19 Aitcheson J Jr 146 s *1.60e -- Top Bid1469The Critter1342½Teana1412 Easy score 7
13Aug70- 6Sar hd 2 1/16 Hurdles 3:434 4↑ Lovely Night H 17k 3 1 1½ 21 1½ 21½ Aitcheson J Jr 150 3.00 -- Metello1411½Top Bid1502½Augustus Bay1482½ Game try 9
29Jly70- 4Mth fm *2 1/16 Hurdles 4:03 4↑ Midsummer H 16k 2 3 42½ 1hd 1hd 53¼ Aitcheson J Jr 150 *2.00 -- Encarnado136nkAtrevido1402Predominio144no Weakened 7
28Aug69- 3Bel fm 2 Hurdles 3:372 3↑ Alw 12000 8 5 33 21½ 3½ 65 Aitcheson J Jr 153 *1.40e -- Lake Delaware156½Bold Beggar150½Attribution153¾ Tired 8

Date	Cond	Dist	Fractions	Time	Race	PP	St	1st	2nd	Str	Fin	Jockey	Wt	Eq	Odds	Fig	Top finishers	Comment	Starters
6Aug69- 3Sar	gd	2 1/16	S'Chase	3:484	4↑ Alw 8500	2	6	46½	1½	11	13	Aitcheson J Jr	143		*.80	--	Top Bid1433Yale Fence14715Brandon Hill1555	Mild drive	9
23Jly69- 5Mth	sf	*2 1/16	Hurdles	4:251	4↑ Midsummer H 16k	1	2	25	28	417	474	Aitcheson J Jr	154		*1.50	--	Nashandy15610CarillonII14116LakeDelaware15548	Poor form	4
3Jly69- 3Del	hd	*2⅛	Hurdles	4:001	3↑ Holly Tree H 10k	2	3	44½	21	24	24½	Aitcheson J Jr	156		*.70	--	Lake Delaware1494½Top Bid156hdBonavena1532¼	Very unruly	6
5Jun69- 5Bel	fm	2 1/16	Hurdles	3:432	4↑ Bushwick H 18k	3	2	34½	34½	15	12	Aitcheson J Jr	149		4.10	--	Top Bid1492National Anthem15412Kurrewa1413	Won in hand	10
26May69- 3Aqu	fm	1⅞	Hurdles	3:232	4↑ Alw 10000	7	3	322	23	53½	511	Aitcheson J Jr	152		*.80	--	Hipocampo146hdLakeDelaware1463½NtionlAnthm1523	Tired	7
10May69- 2Mal	sf	*1¾(T)		3:132	4↑ Alw 1000	9	8	55½	31¾	2nk	13	Aitcheson J Jr	150		-e	--	Top Bid1503Pembroke1431½Astrographer1505	Driving	10
3May69- 5War	hd	*2	S'Chase	4:471	4↑ Sp Wt 1200	6	4	34½	33½	28	210	Aitcheson J Jr	153		-e	--	Vocalist15310Top Bid1536Aiken Road1533	Fair try	7
19Apr69- 7Mid	sf	*1¼(T)		2:203	3↑ Alw 2000	4	6	31½	2½	1½	11	Aitcheson J Jr	149	s	-e	--	Top Bid1491Greek Myth1494Long Valley1551½	Driving	13
8Aug68- 5Sar	sf	2 1/16	Hurdles	3:412	4↑ Sar National 11k	8	6	11½	28	615	642	Aitcheson J Jr	156		*.80	--	NationalAnthem13630YaleFenc158noCountrySttng149no	Tired	8
16Jly68- 3Mth	fm	*1¾	Hurdles	3:244	3↑ Alw 6000	2	5	42½	32½	1hd	33¼	Aitcheson J Jr	147		*.90	--	Tuscalee151¾Mrlgo1482½TopBd1473½	Bad landing final jump	7
4Jun68- 5Bel	fm	2⅛	Hurdles	3:563	4↑ Bushwick H 11k	3	3	31½	11	11	12	Aitcheson J Jr	150		*1.60	--	Top Bid1502Lake Delaware1387Miralgo1542½	Easy score	6
28May68- 3Bel	fm	2⅛	Hurdles	4:021	4↑ Alw 9000	4	2	2½	45	1hd	11	Aitcheson J Jr	142		*1.20	--	Top Bid1421Miralgo1542Crannog1401½	Under hard drive	6
9May68- 5Aqu	fm	1⅞	Hurdles	3:251	4↑ Aqu National 11k	4	3	32½	23	11½	1¾	Aitcheson J Jr	142		*.50	--	TopBid142¾Daufuskie1511½Lucnt1524½	Stumbled 10th,lasted	10
6May68- 3Aqu	fm	1⅞	Hurdles	3:282	4↑ Alw 7500	7	1	11½	12	13	18	Aitcheson J Jr	143		*1.20	--	Top Bid1438Ringling154½Out of Print1543	Easily best	8
13Apr68- 1Mid	fm	*1½	Hurdles	2:471	3↑ Md Sp Wt	11	7	96½	32½	2½	13	Aitcheson J Jr	145		-e	--	Top Bid1453Chippendale1451Arnold W.137½	Drew out easily	14

Previously owned by Wheatley Stable;previously trained by E.A. Neloy

Date	Cond	Dist	Fractions	Time	Race	PP	St	1st	2nd	Str	Fin	Jockey	Wt	Eq	Odds	Fig	Top finishers	Comment	Starters
15Aug67- 7Sar	fst	6f	:224 :452	1:094	Alw 15000	3	4	65½	68½	68	614	Baeza B	118	b	3.50	85-10	JimJ.1143RoadatSea1204½FlyingTackle1141½	Trailed field	6
7Jly67- 7Aqu	fm	1 1/16(T)		1:43	Alw 15000	5	5	66	65	57	57	Baeza B	120	b	2.10	84-09	Irish Rebellion116noMake It116½Fort Drum1164	Wide	6
28Jun67- 7Mth	fm	1(T)		1:381	Long Branch (Div 1) 22k	3	2	1hd	11	3½	21¼	Gustines H	120	b	5.40	93-07	Blasting Charge1201¼Top Bid120nkMake It112hd	Gamely	8
3Jun67- 8Del	fst	1 1/16	:23 :46 1:102	1:424	Kent 31k	12	11	136¼	1313	1314	1215	Nelson E	120	b	10.60	80-17	Galaerfrmance1204Mr.Scipio114½MstyCloud120nk	No speed	14
8May67- 8Pim	gd	1 1/16⊗	:23 :454 1:101	1:44	Woodlawn 29k	4	5	55	44	1hd	1hd	Nelson E	116	b	*3.70	90-18	TopBid116hdCharlsEllott113hdCltcAr116hd	Strong pressure	10
29Apr67- 4Aqu	fst	7f	:232 :471 1:121	1:251	Alw 12000	6	2	1hd	1hd	11	1hd	Belmonte E	120	b	7.30	80-18	Top Bid120hdYorkville1182½Bologna Gellis1183	Hard drive	6
18Mar67- 9FG	fst	1⅛	:474 1:113 1:371	1:50	La Derby 54k	9	6	64	74	61¾	64½	Anderson P	118		3.60	89-07	AsktheFare115hdDiplomtWy126½GrndPremr1202½	No mishap	10
4Mar67- 8SA	fst	1⅛	:453 1:103 1:37	1:494	SA Derby 139k	11	7	54	62¾	53¾	67	Mahorney W	118	b	3.70e	76-16	Ruken1181½Tumble Wind1181½Sand Devil118½	No mishap	13
22Feb67- 8SA	fst	1 1/16	:23 :464 1:11	1:424	San Felipe H 62k	1	8	109¼	76	63½	4nk	Mahorney W	118	b	3.90e	89-12	Rising Market118noRuken117nkField Master113no	Rallied	13
8Feb67- 8SA	fst	1 1/16	:233 :47 1:11	1:423	Alw 10000	5	4	31	1½	11½	1½	Mahorney W	117	b	24.80	90-15	Top Bid117½Dr. Isby1176Ruken120½	Under hard drive	8
2Feb67- 8SA	fst	1 1/16	:224 :461 1:104	1:433	[R]S Catalina 24k	5	1	11½	1hd	42	79½	Blum W	118	b	6.70	75-18	Serve Notice118½[D]Beau Alibi118nkNechako1181½	Used up	9
12Jan67- 5SA	fst	7f	:223 :451 1:10	1:23	Alw 7500	3	7	1hd	11½	13	1nk	Blum W	115	b	*2.40	88-15	TopBid115nkServeNotice1202½GentlemansGame1202½	Lasted	7
26Dec66- 5SA	fst	6f	:221 :453 :573	1:094	Alw 7000	1	12	118½	109¾	97½	912	Baeza B	116	b	3.70	81-14	RisingMarket114noSandDevil1184Bradleyvill116½	No factor	12
17Oct66- 4Aqu	fst	6½f	:23 :462 1:111	1:172	Alw 6000	1	7	74¾	76¼	57½	59	Baeza B	116	b	*.80	84-19	JackofAllTrades1136ReflectedGlory1132StampAct119¾	Wide	7
27Sep66- 7Aqu	fst	6½f	:231 :462 1:11	1:174	Alw 10000	6	2	32½	62	66	68	Baeza B	119	b	3.40	83-21	Wilbur Clark1221½Racing Room1191½Gordorigo1191	In close	6
10Sep66- 8AP	fst	7f	:223 :452 1:101	1:223	Arl-Wash Futurity 367k	4	12	118¾	63½	78¼	917	Adams L	122	b	9.70	75-13	DiplomtWy122hdWilbrClrk1227LghtnngOrphn122¾	Crowded	15
27Aug66- 6Sar	fst	6½f	:222 :453 1:103	1:171	Hopeful 107k	4	3	46	45½	35	31¾	Adams L	122	b	*.10e	90-08	BoldHour1221¾GrtPowr122hdTopBd1226½	Drifted out stretch	5
17Aug66- 7Sar	fst	6f	:221 :451	1:103	Sar Spl 33k	6	5	66	77½	47½	37¾	Baeza B	114	b	9.20	87-14	Favorable Turn1167Bold Hour120¾Top Bid114hd	Rallied	7
8Aug66- 7Sar	fst	5½f	:224 :461 :583	1:05	Sanford 34k	3	4	42	32	33	35	Baeza B	115	b	2.00	87-13	Yorkville1152SrWnzlot1153TopBd115¾	Swerved into stretch	5
13Jly66- 6Aqu	fst	5½f	:22 :454 :582	1:05	Alw 5500	7	5	2hd	2hd	2hd	12	Knapp K	122	b	*.90	88-17	TopBid1222QuakerCity1172½Voyager1192½	Speed in reserve	8
1Jly66- 5Aqu	fst	5½f	:222 :462 :59	1:053	©Md Sp Wt	8	4	21	1hd	13	16	Baeza B	122	b	*.90	85-19	TopBid1226GayLordFlynn122¾Seance117nk	Easily the best	12
17Jun66- 5Aqu	fst	5½f	:221 :46 :584	1:053	©Md Sp Wt	6	7	32½	57	59	312	Baeza B	122		3.30	73-22	FavorableTurn12212LiftOff122noTopBid122no	Bumped rail	12

Trillion

b. f. 1974, by Hail to Reason (Turn-to)–Margarethen, by Tulyar

Lifetime record: 32 9 14 3 $954,672

Own.–Stephenson & Hunt
Br.– N.B. Hunt (Ky)
Tr.– Maurice Zilber

Date	Cond	Dist	Fractions	Time	Race	PP	St	1st	2nd	Str	Fin	Jockey	Wt	Eq	Odds	Fig	Top finishers	Comment	Starters
10Nov79- 8Lrl	sf	1½(T)	:573 1:252 2:232	2:51	3↑ D C Int'l-G1	5	2	32½	51¾	1hd	2¾	Fell J	124		7.70	--	Bowl Game127¾Trillion124noLe Marmot1208	Hung	8
4Nov79- 8SA	fm	1½(T)	:454 1:10 2:011	2:252	3↑ Oak Tree Inv'l-G1	5	4	510	53½	53	21¾	Shoemaker W	123		*.90	86-12	Balzac1261¾Trillion1231Silver Eagle126½	Gamely	9

Previously owned by E. Stephenson

Date	Cond	Dist	Fractions	Time	Race	PP	St	1st	2nd	Str	Fin	Jockey	Wt	Eq	Odds	Fig	Top finishers	Comment	Starters
27Oct79- 8Aqu	fm	1½(T)	:481 1:14 2:044	2:281	3↑ Turf Classic-G1	7	2	27	44	33	2nk	Shoemaker W	123		4.40	120-00	Bowl Game126nkTrillion123nkNative Courier1264¾	Steadied,in close	7
21Oct79- 8WO	sf	1⅝(T)	:493 1:412	2:483	3↑ Can Int'l-G1	7	4	43½	2hd	1hd	2nk	Shoemaker W	123		3.20	57-42	Golden Act118nkTrillion1232½Gain1187	Sharp try	10
7Oct79♦ Longchamp(Fr)	gd	*1½(T)RH		2:284	3↑ Prix de l'Arc de Triomphe-G1 Stk382000						58¼	Piggott L	127		16.00		Three Troikas1203Le Marmot1231Troy123nk	Tracked in 4th,effort 3f out,beaten when bumped 1f out	22
16Sep79♦ Longchamp(Fr)	fm	*1¼(T)RH		2:033	3↑ Prix du Prince d'Orange-G3 Stk44600						2½	Lequeux A	127		2.50		Rusticaro126½Trillion127hdNorthern Baby1212	Tracked leader,slight lead 3f to 1f out,dueled,outgamed	8
9Sep79♦ Longchamp(Fr)	gd	*1½(T)RH		2:354	4↑ Prix Foy-G3 Stk44600						21½	Lequeux A	124		2.50		Pevero1231½Trillion124½Gay Mecene1301	Led for 2f,tracked leader,led again 2f out,headed 100y out	6
15Aug79♦ Deauville(Fr)	fm	*1¼(T)RH		2:01	4↑ Prix Gontaut-Biron-G3 Stk44600						22	Lequeux A	129		*.70		Rusticaro1282Trillion129noStrong Gale1232	Well placed in 3rd,led 2f to 150y out,second best	9
1Jly79♦ Saint-Cloud(Fr)	gd	*1 9/16(T)LH		2:332	3↑ Grand Prix de Saint-Cloud-G1 Stk191000						710½	Lequeux A	131		7.30		Gay Mecene1344Ela-Mana-Mou1211Gain121nk	Rated toward rear,passed tired ones Placed sixth through disqualification	13
24Jun79♦ Longchamp(Fr)	gd	*1⅛(T)RH		1:513	3↑ Prix d'Ispahan-G1 Stk127000						35	Piggott L	129		.90		Irish River1215Opus Dei132hd[D]Trillion1291½	Led,clear 2½f out,headed 1f out,drifted left; Disqualified and placed 5th	8
27May79♦ Longchamp(Fr)	sf	*1 3/16(T)RH		2:103	4↑ Prix Dollar-G2 Stk79000						12½	Piggott L	129		*.60		Trillion1292½Pevero123½Talis Filius123¾	Led throughout,drew clear 2f out,handily.Rusticaro 7th	7
29Apr79♦ Longchamp(Fr)	sf	*1 5/16(T)RH		2:171	4↑ Prix Ganay-G1 Stk127000						21½	Piggott L	124		*.60		Frere Basile1281½Trillion124hdPevero1283	Led for 2f,settled in 4th,lacked room on rail,up for second	8
1Apr79♦ Longchamp(Fr)	hy	*1¼(T)RH		2:194	4↑ Prix d'Harcourt-G2 Stk80000						12	Piggott L	127		*1.10		Trillion1272Fatusael1281Frere Basile1284	Led throughout,finished strongly	11
4Nov78- 8Lrl	fm	1½(T)	:50 1:141 2:033	2:27	3↑ D C Int'l-G1	6	3	31	52¼	73½	44½	Hawley S	124		*1.90	79-16	Mac Diarmida120hdTiller1273Waya1241½	Wide late	8
21Oct78- 8Bel	fm	1½(T)	:49 1:133 2:03	2:264	3↑ Turf Classic-G1	2	2	21½	2½	3nk	3nk	Shoemaker W	123		3.50	90-09	Waya123noTiller126nkTrillion1231¾	Held gamely	6
8Oct78♦ Cologne(Ger)	gd	*1½(T)RH		2:302	3↑ Preis von Europa-G1 Stk260000						32½	Piggott L	128		*1.80		Aden119½Tip Moss1282Trillion128hd	Tracked in 3rd,lacked rally.Strong Gale 4th	14
1Oct78♦ Longchamp(Fr)	sf	*1½(T)RH		2:36	3↑ Prix de l'Arc de Triomphe-G1 Stk382000						22	Shoemaker W	127		16.00		Alleged1302Trillion1272Dancing Maid120¾	Tracked leaders,2nd 2f out,chased winner home.Gay Mecene 8th	18
10Sep78♦ Longchamp(Fr)	gd	*1⅜(T)RH		2:17	4↑ Prix Foy-G3 Stk38200						12	Piggott L	127		*1.80		Trillion1272Monseigneur128noDom Alaric1304	Led throughout,handily	7
22Jly78♦ Ascot(GB)	fm	1½(T)RH		2:302	3↑ King George VI & Queen Eliz-G1 Stk290000						1221	Piggott L	130		7.00		Ile de Bourbon1201½HawaiianSound120nkMountcontour1331½	Never a factor	13
2Jly78♦ Saint-Cloud(Fr)	gd	*1 9/16(T)LH		2:413	3↑ Grand Prix de Saint-Cloud-G1 Stk195000						21	Piggott L	131		*2.00		Guadanini1341Trillion1311½Noir et Or1211	Tracked in 3rd,dueled 1½f out,outfinished	9
25Jun78♦ Longchamp(Fr)	yl	*1⅛(T)RH		1:534	3↑ Prix d'Ispahan-G1 Stk136000						22	Piggott L	129		*1.50		Carwhite1322Trillion129¾Gairloch132nk	Led,clear 1f out,headed 100y out,saved 2nd.Kenmare 6th	10

28May78♦ Longchamp(Fr)	fm *1 3/16(T)RH 1:594 4↑	Prix Dollar-G2 Stk85000	1nk	Piggott L	129	*1.50	Trillion129nkCarwhite129¾Monseigneur129 2½	Led throughout,held gamely.Tip Moss 5th	7
15May78♦ Saint-Cloud(Fr)	sf *1½(T)LH 2:422 3↑	Prix Jean de Chaudenay-G2 Stk85000	3nk	Piggott L	131	*2.00	Guadanini130hdDom Alaric130hdTrillion1312	Tracked leader,led 3f out,dueled 150y out,just failed	11
30Apr78♦ Longchamp(Fr)	sf *1 5/16(T)RH 2:181 4↑	Prix Ganay-G1 Stk131000	13	Piggott L	124	5.90	Trillion1243Monseigneur128¾Sirlad128hd	Led virtually throughout,ridden clear.Carwhite 5th	8
2Apr78♦ Longchamp(Fr)	hy *1¼(T)RH 2:152 4↑	Prix d'Harcourt-G2 Stk65800	2nk	Piggott L	122	*1.30e	Monseigneur128nkTrillion122 2½Carwhite128 2½	Tracked entrymate in 2nd,led halfway,dueled 1½f out,gamely Previously trained by Francois Mathet	8
30Oct77♦ Longchamp(Fr)	sf *1 15/16(T)RH 3:283	Prix Royal-Oak-G1 Stk95600	2 1½	Badel A	124	4.00	Rex Magna128 1½Trillion124½Dunfermline1244	Rated in midpack,rallied to lead 1½f out,headed 100y out	13
9Oct77♦ Longchamp(Fr)	sf *1 9/16(T)RH 2:444	Prix de Royalleiu-G3 Stk40800	14	Badel A	123	*.50	Trillion1234Paix Armee120 2½Proud Event123 1½	Tracked leader,led 2f out,easily clear	9
18Sep77♦ Longchamp(Fr)	fm *1½(T)RH 2:302	(F)Prix Vermeille-G1 Stk204000	6 3½	Dubroeucq G	128	*2.00	Kamicia128 1½Royal Hive128nkFabuleux Jane128hd	Tracked in 5th,led 2f out,drifted left,headed 1f out,faded	18
30Jly77♦ Evry(Fr)	sf *1½(T)LH 2:404	(F)Prix de Minerve-G3 Stk25500	16	Dubroeucq G	126	*.30	Trillion1266Beronaire119nkSwiss1193	Led virtually throughout,clear 2f out,in a canter	7
12Jun77♦ Chantilly(Fr)	sf *1 5/16(T)RH 2:104	(F)Prix de Diane-G1 Stk220000	2hd	Dubroeucq G	128	5.00	Madelia128hdTrillion128 2½Fabuleux Jane128¾	Led or dueled,led 3f to 1f out,came again near line	13
27May77♦ Longchamp(Fr)	gd *1½(T)RH 2:324	(F)Prix des Tuileries Stk20000	15	Dubroeucq G	123	5.70	Trillion1235Lestelle123nkKelso's Niece123nk	Led throughout,unchallenged	13
19Mar77♦ Saint-Cloud(Fr)	hy *1¼(T)LH 2:27	(F)Prix Perruche Bleue Mdn (FT)9900	1¾	Dubroeucq G	123	*1.30	Trillion123¾Angelotte123½Lyanta1238	Tracked leader,led 2f out,held well	7

Turkish Trousers

dkbbr. f. 1968, by Bagdad (Double Jay)–Nas-Mahal, by Nasrullah

Lifetime record: 18 12 1 2 $308,225

Own.– Mrs H.B. Keck
Br.– Howard B. Keck (Ky)
Tr.– Charles Whittingham

3Jun72- 8Hol	fst 1⅛	:464 1:102 1:351 1:472 3↑	(F)Vanity H 105k	8	2	3 1½	31	31	4 1¾	Shoemaker W	123	1.80	93-08	Convenience121½Typecst126¾StreetDncr115½	Weakened late	9
18May72- 8Hol	fst 1	:224 :461 1:094 1:341 3↑	(F)Milady H 44k	7	5	2½	21	3 4½	712	Shoemaker W	125	*1.80	83-16	Typecast1236Balcony's Babe114noConvenience122½	Checked	9
4Mar72- 8SA	fst 1⅛	:461 1:101 1:351 1:474 4↑	(F)(S) Margarita Inv'l 10k	6	4	42	42	31	1hd	Shoemaker W	125	1.70	93-09	TurkishTrousers125hdConvenience118nkTypcst124hd	Driving	12
19Feb72- 8SA	fst 1 1/16	:224 :454 1:094 1:411 4↑	(F)(S) Maria H 57k	8	3	32	32	12½	1½	Shoemaker W	123	2.90	96-10	Turkish Trousers126½Typecast126 4¼Street Dancer123 1¼	Drifted,driving	8
9Feb72- 8SA	fst 7f	:213 :441 1:083 1:211 4↑	(F)(S) Barbara Cy Fair H 20k	2	4	3 2½	3 1½	2 1½	3 5½	Shoemaker W	126	*.60	91-15	Convenince119 2¾StrtDncr123 2¾TurkshTrousrs1264	Mild rally	7
18Jan72- 8SA	fst 7f	:213 :44 1:084 1:212 4↑	(F)(S) Monica H 47k	9	5	2 2½	3 2½	21	23	Shoemaker W	126	*.90	93-10	Typecast1233TurkishTrousrs126¾GoddssSpcl1144	Drifted in	10
25Aug71- 7Dmr	fm 1⅛(T)	:484 1:132 1:374 1:50	(F)Dmr Oaks 26k	3	1	1½	1½	1½	1 1¾	Shoemaker W	124	*.30	95-05	TurkishTrousers124 1¾Aladancr117noShlfTlkr118 1¾	Drew out	5
22Jly71- 8Hol	fst 1⅛	:464 1:103 1:351 1:474	(F)Hol Oaks 64k	8	2	21	2½	2 1½	1nk	Shoemaker W	124	*.40	93-14	TurkishTrousers124nkConvennc1156Blcony'sBb115 3½	Driving	8
2Jly71- 8Hol	fm 1 1/16(T)	:224 :463 1:11 1:414	(F)Princess 33k	8	3	32	3½	2 2½	1¾	Shoemaker W	121	*.60	90-10	TurkishTrousers121¾Conveninc1152Blcony'sBb115 1¼	Driving	10
3Jun71- 8Hol	fst 1 1/16	:231 :461 1:103 1:422	(F)Honeymoon 33k	1	3	2 1½	2hd	1½	13	Shoemaker W	121	*.50	83-14	TurkshTrousrs1213Convenience115noMiaMood114 1½	Driving	9
18May71- 8Hol	fst 7f	:22 :442 1:09 1:214	(F)Railbird 28k	6	4	55	4 3½	23	1¾	Shoemaker W	121	*.70	91-16	TurkshTrousrs121¾Convennc1152CountssMrkt115hd	Driving	9
27Apr71- 8Hol	fm 1(T)	:224 :462 1:103 1:354	(F)Senorita (Div 2) 32k	2	4	45	54	31	12	Shoemaker W	118	*.90	91-12	TurkishTrousers1182Aladancer118hdLadyofRome112nk	Easily	6
11Mar71- 8SA	fst 1 1/16	:234 :472 1:112 1:424	(F)(S) Susana 54k	1	1	2hd	2hd	1hd	1¾	Shoemaker W	115	*.80	88-16	TurkishTrousrs115¾GenrousPorton1156SposSpd1152	Driving	9
18Feb71- 8SA	fst 7f	:213 :443 1:101 1:233	(F)(S) Ynez 33k	5	6	55	3 2½	2½	1 3¾	Shoemaker W	112	*1.40	85-16	TurkishTrousers112 3¾UllaBritta115 1¼SaposSpd1143	Driving	7
9Feb71- 8SA	fst 1 1/16	:24 :484 1:131 1:431	(F)(S) Ysabel 28k	8	3	3½	31	32	3¾	Shoemaker W	116	*.60	85-11	Balcony'sBabe116¾Aldncr116noTrkshTrousrs1162	No excuse	8
22Jan71- 7SA	fst 1	:23 :463 1:103 1:354	(F)Alw 7000	1	4	3½	3 2½	13	15	Rosales R	115	2.20	95-15	Turkish Trousers1155Hollywood Gossip115nkShelfTalker115nk	Handily	10
7Jan71- 8SA	fst 6½f	:22 :451 1:10 1:162	(F)La Centinela 29k	6	8	7 2¼	6 2¼	32	4 1¾	Rosales R	118	*2.50	89-11	CrowningGlory118hdWicked Firy1181Hollywood Gossip113¾	No excuse	11
30Dec70- 5SA	fst 6f	:22 :452 :573 1:094	(F)Md Sp Wt	10	8	6 2¾	2½	2½	1 2½	Shoemaker W	115	3.40	93-11	Turkish Trousers115 2½At Twilight110nkGrecian Times1156	Rushed into contention,won convincingly	12

Typecast

b. f. 1966, by Prince John (Princequillo)–Journalette, by Summer Tan

Lifetime record: 57 21 12 9 $535,567

Own.– Westerly Stud
Br.– Nuckols Bros. (Ky)
Tr.– A.T. Doyle

9Oct72- 7Bel	sf 1½(T)	:48 1:14 2:054 2:314 3↑	Man o' War 117k	1	10	11 9½	2½	1½	1¾	Cordero A Jr	123 b	*2.30	68-33	Typecast123¾Ruritania121 4½Droll Role1261	Driving	11
27Sep72- 6Bel	fm 1⅜(T)	:492 1:134 1:373 2:133 3↑	Manhattan H (Div 1) 46k	5	4	5 4½	4 4½	24	22	Pincay L Jr	122 b	4.60	96-06	Star Envoy1162Typecast122 3½Exotico111½	Raced wide	10
9Sep72- 7Bel	fst 1⅛	:46 1:102 1:35 1:472 3↑	(F)Beldame 112k	1	3	34	5 2½	77	6 8¼	Sellers J	123 b	5.90	89-06	Susn'sGirl1181SummerGust1181ChouCrout123 3¼	Speed,tired	9
24Jly72- 8Hol	fm 2(T)	:481 2:291 2:54 3:203 3↑	Sunset H 135k	4	3	47	5 3½	3 1½	1hd	Sellers J	120 b	3.20	87-16	Typecast120hdOver the Counter112nkViolonor114hd	Driving	10
8Jly72- 8Hol	fm 1⅜(T)	2:131 3↑	(F)Beverly Hills H 64k	8	6	515	55	6 9½	310	Lambert J	127 b	*1.10	79-13	Hill Circus11510Manta116hdTypecast127nk	Rallied	8
24Jun72 8Hol	fm 1½(T)	:481 1:113 2:012 2:254 3↑	Inv'l Turf H 125k	6	6	6 6½	31	2½	1nk	Lambert J	117 b	5.70	99-08	Typecast117nkViolonor110 1¼Cougar II129G½	Driving	9
17Jun72- 7Hol	fst 1⅛	:462 1:10 1:35 1:473 4↑	(F)Match Race 250k	1	2	2nk	2 1½	22	2hd	Shoemaker W	120 b	*.40	94-14	Convenience120hdTypecast120	Closed fast	2
3Jun72- 8Hol	fst 1⅛	:464 1:102 1:351 1:472 3↑	(F)Vanity H 105k	1	5	6 4½	5 2½	4 1½	2½	Tejada V	126 b	*1.40	94-08	Convenience121½Typecast126¾Street Dancer115½	Gamely	9
18May72- 8Hol	fst 1	:224 :461 1:094 1:341 3↑	(F)Milady H 44k	9	7	6 2½	4 1½	2 1½	16	Tejada V	123 b	4.50	95-16	Typecast1236Balcony's Babe114noConvenience122½	Driving	9
22Apr72- 8Hol	fm 1 1/16(T)	:221 :454 1:102 1:411 3↑	(F)Long Beach H 55k	5	6	511	3 2½	2 1½	1¾	Tejada V	122 b	1.90	93-09	Typecast122¾Balcony's Babe1163Manta123 1½	Driving	8
21Mar72- 8SA	fm 1¼(T)	:443 1:082 1:324 1:583 4↑	(F)(S) Barbara H 65k	5	3	312	3 7½	57	-	Belmonte E	124 b	*1.10	- -	Hail the Grey1122Manta1255Street Dancer1181	Bled	7
4Mar72- 8SA	fst 1⅛	:461 1:101 1:351 1:474 4↑	(F)(S) Margarita Inv'l 10k	1	7	75	63	54	3nk	Pincay L Jr	124 b	*1.40e	93-09	TurkishTrousers125hdConvnnc118nkTypcst124hd	Closed fast	12
19Feb72- 8SA	fst 1 1/16	:224 :454 1:094 1:411 4↑	(F)(S) Maria H 57k	1	4	4 4½	5 4½	2 2½	2½	Pincay L Jr	126 b	*1.20	95-10	TurkishTrousers126½Typecast126 4¼StreetDncr123 1¼	Rallied	8
18Jan72- 8SA	fst 7f	:213 :44 1:084 1:212 4↑	(F)(S) Monica H 47k	5	7	99	911	5 4½	13	Pincay L Jr	123 b	3.50	96-10	Typecast1233TurkishTrousers126¾GoddessSpecl1144	Driving	10
25Oct71- 8SA	yl 1⅛(T)	:481 1:124 1:364 1:494 3↑	(F)Las Palmas H 32k	1	5	4 4½	2½	15	16	Shoemaker W	126 b	*.50	80-20	Typecast1266Hail the Grey1161Aladancer119 1½	Easily	6
14Oct71- 7SA	fm 1⅛(T)	:47 1:112 1:352 1:471 3↑	(F)Alw 12000	6	4	45	22	14	16	Shoemaker W	123 b	*.30	93-07	Typecast1236Boughs o' Holly117 2½Dating115 2¼	Easily	6
7Aug71- 7Dmr	fm 1⅛(T)	:483 1:122 1:361 1:484 3↑	(F)Ramona H 27k	9	7	7 8½	67	5 6½	2 1½	Shoemaker W	116 b	2.90	99-02	StreetDancer114 1½Typecst116½Mnt130 1¾	Wide,finished fast	9
26Jly71- 8Hol	fm 2(T)	:48 2:29 2:54 3:191 3↑	Sunset H 138k	7	11	1218	7 4¼	34	3 1½	Alvarez F	110 b	38.60	92-12	Over the Counter114½Cougar II1301Typecast110 2½	Rallied	12
10Jly71- 8Hol	fm 1⅜(T)	2:121 3↑	(F)Beverly Hills H 66k	10	7	5 4½	3 2½	3 3½	2 3½	Shoemaker W	116 b	3.20	94-09	Manta127 3½Typecast116¾Hail the Grey1074	Lacked rally	11
2Jly71- 7Hol	fm 1(T)	:23 :464 1:104 1:351 3↑	(F)Handicap 14000	3	5	5 3½	5 2½	3 1½	1nk	Shoemaker W	120 b	*1.40	94-8	Typecast120nkStreet Dancer116 1½Mizzle1162	Driving	9
19Jun71- 7Hol	fm 1(T)	:231 :463 1:101 1:353 4↑	(F)Alw 12000	7	7	710	6 9½	5 5¼	1½	Shoemaker W	117 b	*2.30	92-13	Typecast117½Hi Q.120 2¼Sallarina120½	Driving Previously trained by M. Lipton	8
17Apr71- 7Hol	fm 1 1/16(T)	:224 :462 1:104 1:423 3↑	(F)Long Bch H (Div 1) 55k	5	9	914	89	53	5 3½	Lambert J	114 b	5.80	82-16	Tipping Time1152Blow Up II110¾Beja117no	Rallied	9
6Apr71- 8SA	fm 1⅛(T)	:473 1:113 1:352 1:481 4↑	(F)(S) Ana H 32k	8	5	5 5½	7 6½	89	8 8¾	Pincay L Jr	121 b	5.30	79-12	Mizzle114 1¼Tipping Time120 1¼Sight to See110½	No speed	8
27Feb71- 8GG	gd 1 1/16	:224 :464 1:12 1:443 3↑	(F)Golden Poppy H 27k	4	8	89	815	716	7 13½	Grant H	123 b	*1.60	67-23	HiQ.117 2¼IrishTryst1101SchatzP111nk	Never in contention	8
2Feb71- 8SA	fst 1 1/16	:231 :462 1:103 1:43 4↑	(F)Oneonta H 29k	11	11	1111	9 6½	3 1½	1¾	Pincay L Jr	122 b	*1.60	87-12	Typecast122¾Belle o' Belgium114 1¾Loved119 3¼	Driving	11

Date-Race	Cond/Dist	Fractions	Race	Running line	Jockey	Wt	Odds	Figs	Top finishers	Comment/Field
22Jan71- 8SA	fm 1⅛Ⓣ	:234 :484 1:132 1:504 4↑	ⒻAlw 12000	1 1 31 52½ 11½ 11¼	Pincay L Jr	120 b	*1.40	75-25	Typecast1201¼SlvrGoblt1164½ThorolyBlu119¾	Outside rally 12
15Jan71- 8SA	hy 1 1/16	:25 :494 1:151 1:48 4↑	ⒻAlw 10000	6 3 21 3½ 1½ 14	Pincay L Jr	120 b	*.90	62-36	Typecast1204DustyEys1151ScrltLrkspur1186	Speed to spare 6
26Nov70- 8BM	my 1 1/16	:232 :471 1:12 1:443 3↑	ⒻThnksgvng Day H 22k	3 10 82¾ 66½ 35 22	Toro F	122 b	*1.30	74-24	TalestoTell1162Typecast1221½ThFrstDy1142¾	Finished fast 11
28Oct70- 8SA	fm 1⅛Ⓣ	:454 1:101 1:341 1:463 3↑	ⒻLas Palmas H 32k	1 3 46½ 53½ 57 56	Sellers J	117 b	4.00	90-04	Manta1254Beja119½Thoroly Blue115½	Hung 8
11Sep70- 7Dmr	fm 1 1/16Ⓣ	:231 :48 1:12 1:432 3↑	ⒻAlw 8500	6 5 43½ 33 41½ 11½	Lambert J	118 b	*.60	96-13	Typecast1181½[D]Dress Me Up111¾Sony Gay1132	6
	Saved ground,checked									
2Sep70- 7Dmr	fm 1 1/16Ⓣ	:224 :462 1:11 1:43 3↑	ⒻOsunitas 16k	4 8 813 88¾ 66½ 3½	Lambert J	118	*.70	97-05	QueenJanine118nkDressMeUp111nkTypcst1182	Finished well 11
24Aug70- 8Dmr	fm 1 1/16Ⓣ	:231 :47 1:111 1:423 3↑	ⒻHandicap 8500	2 6 68¼ 55½ 1½ 18	Lambert J	122 b	*1.70	100-04	Typcst1228MssLrksvll112hdWndyMm117hd	Drew off quickly 6
14Aug70- 6Dmr	fm 1 1/16Ⓣ	:233 :473 1:111 1:423 3↑	ⒻAlw 8000	2 3 23½ 22½ 21½ 12	Lambert J	117 b	5.80	100-01	Typecst1172Chatupv1141¼Boughso'Holly1172½	Bumped start 6
17Jly70- 7Aqu	fst 1	:223 :444 1:092 1:35 3↑	ⒻAlw 15000	3 3 2½ 32½ 913 915	Baltazar C	120 b	9.00	77-15	RoyalFillet1161½TaknAback118½NativePartner1166	Stopped 9
6Jun70- 8GG	fst 1 1/16	:23 :461 1:101 1:431 3↑	ⒻSn Juan Bautista H 21k	6 6 64 41½ 32½ 2¾	Gonzalez JT	118 b	*2.80	87-17	Windy Mama117¾Typecast1181½Flying Dot1161½	Game try 10
26May70- 5Hol	fm 1Ⓣ	:233 :473 1:113 1:363 4↑	ⒻAlw 10000	4 5 61¾ 42½ 31½ 1nk	Pincay L Jr	117 b	3.10	88-10	Typecast117nkBelleo'Belgium1172Lover'sQurrl114½	Driving 7
7May70- 7Hol	fm 1 1/16Ⓣ	:234 :482 1:13 1:431 4↑	ⒻAlw 12000	5 5 55½ 64½ 64½ 56	Pierce D	120 b	6.70	77-17	Luz del Sol1201Fairfleet II1142Hi Q.1171¾	Even try 8
18Apr70- 8Hol	fm 1 1/16Ⓣ	:232 :47 1:102 1:41 3↑	ⒻLong Beach H 46k	8 14 139¾ 137¾ 149¼ 1410	Alvarez F	111 b	17.20	84-08	TippingTime115¾PatteeCnyon120nkSchatziPi1151¼	Far back 15
8Apr70- 5SA	fst 1 1/16	:231 :463 1:11 1:423 4↑	ⒻAlw 15000	4 4 36 32½ 1½ 11	Pincay L Jr	114 b	2.50	90-09	Typecast1141Hi Q.1203Dumptys Lady1162¾	Driving 6
26Mar70- 7SA	fst 1⅛Ⓣ	:473 1:113 1:362 1:481 4↑	ⒻAlw 15000	4 4 41½ 42 22 22½	Pierce D	114 b	4.00	85-12	Boughs o' Holly1162½Typecast1142¾Riva1161¾	Second best 8
18Mar70- 5SA	fst 1 1/16	:232 :47 1:113 1:432 4↑	ⒻAlw 10000	5 4 46 43 43 32	Pierce D	118 b	2.60	84-13	Hi Q.1182I've Bin Spotted120hdTypecast118¾	No rally 6
6Mar70- 7SA	fst 1 1/16	:231 :463 1:104 1:422 4↑	ⒻAlw 9000	6 5 63¾ 63 43½ 33¾	Pierce D	116 b	2.60	87-07	Gay Year120hdDumptys Lady1163¾Typecast1164¼	Closed well 6
28Feb70- 8SA	sly 1⅛	:47 1:112 1:371 1:503 4↑	ⒻS Margrta Inv'l H 100k	2 7 75½ 76½ 615 616	Alvarez F	110 b	29.20	63-17	GallantBlm1292Commissary1176TippingTime1172½	No speed 8
6Feb70- 4SA	fst 1 1/16	:232 :47 1:113 1:434 4↑	ⒻAlw 6500	1 1 13 12½ 1½ 1¾	Pierce D	119 b	1.80	84-12	Typecast119¾Queen Janine1196Make Me Yours1134	Driving 6
17Jly69- 8Hol	fst 1⅛	:463 1:103 1:35 1:472	ⒻHol Oaks 54k	7 8 86 65 57 57½	Pineda A	113 b	8.10	87-11	TippngTime121noCommissary1181¼YnezQn1145	Even effort 8
9Jly69- 7Hol	fm 1Ⓣ	:223 :461 1:111 1:363	ⒻAlw 7500	4 7 79½ 74½ 33 31½	Pineda A	120 b	*1.80	86-13	Sallarina117hdSeric1141½Typcst1204	Best stride too late 7
2Jly69- 8Hol	fm 1 1/16Ⓣ	:231 :461 1:103 1:412	ⒻPrincess 27k	8 9 912 85¼ 54½ 56½	Alvarez F	112 b	5.10	85-08	Tipping Time1155Ynez Queen114hdMarjorie's Theme1211¼	9
	Never a threat									
20Jun69- 4Hol	fm 1 1/16Ⓣ	:232 :481 1:123 1:434	ⒻAlw 7000	3 7 65½ 41¾ 11 13	Lambert J	117 b	*1.70	80-13	Typecast1173Tasu1203Queen Janine1141½	Wide rally 7
3Jun69- 5Hol	fst 1	:223 :453 1:103 1:362	ⒻAlw 7500	4 10 109 56½ 32½ 3½	Lambert J	117 b	4.10	83-17	Caper Mate115noFar Piece117½Typecast1178	Bid,not enough 10
16May69- 6Hol	fst 1 1/16	:231 :462 1:104 1:43	ⒻAlw 7000	1 4 42½ 43 32 23	Rosales R5	115 b	2.90	77-14	Marjorie'sTheme1173Typecst115½FarPiec1204	Saved ground 10
2May69- 5Hol	fst 1 1/16	:23 :462 1:11 1:43	ⒻAlw 7500	7 10 1011 85½ 43½ 23	Rosales R5	115 b	4.20	77-13	TippingTime1203Typecast115¾Mrjor'sThm1173	Outside rally 11
18Apr69- 8Hol	fst 1	:231 :462 1:104 1:362	ⒻAlw 8500	6 8 77½ 74½ 65½ 32½	Pierce D	117 b	5.60	81-18	Marjorie's Girl117½Snap Hance1092Typecast117nk	Wide 8
7Apr69- 4SA	gd 1 1/16	:24 :484 1:14 1:462	ⒻAlw 7500	3 2 22½ 44½ 34 22½	Rosales R5	108	6.70	68-22	Sallarina1162½Typecst1081½MagicCsmnts1154	Saved ground 6
3Apr69- 6SA	fst 6f	:221 :454 :582 1:111	ⒻAlw 6500	8 3 108 109 79½ 68½	Trevino S	118	51.60	77-20	Mrjorie'sGirl115½Marjori'sThm115½TppngTm1183	No factor 12
20Mar69- 2SA	fst 6f	:221 :453 :581 1:112	ⒻAlw 6000	9 2 86½ 910 89 810	Pineda A	118	1.90	75-17	BelleMere118hdMarjorie'sGirl1104Sallrn113½	Lacked speed 9
6Mar69- 2SA	fst 6f	:224 :463 :592 1:12	ⒻAlw 5000	6 12 1011 1011 89 57¼	Pineda A	118	4.90	75-16	HappyMomnt1183HazelA.115¾WindyMama1183	Took up start 12
26Feb69- 4SA	sl 6f	:222 :464 1:00 1:133	ⒻMd Sp Wt	4 9 65 55 23 11¼	Pineda A	116	2.50	74-24	Typecast1161¼DoubleGoGo1151QueenNaleika1154	Slow start 9

Wajima

b. c. 1972, by Bold Ruler (Nasrullah)–Iskra, by Le Haar

Lifetime record: 16 9 5 0 $537,838

Own.– East–West Stable
Br.– Claiborne Farm (Ky)
Tr.– S. DiMauro

Date-Race	Cond/Dist	Fractions	Race	Running line	Jockey	Wt	Odds	Figs	Top finishers	Comment/Field
25Oct75- 8Bel	sly 2	:494 2:32 2:57 3:231 3↑	J C Gold Cup-G1	4 2 2hd 1hd 2hd 2nk	Baeza B	119	*.30	83-15	Group Plan124nkWajima11910Outdoors1241¼	Fought gamely 4
27Sep75- 8Bel	fst 1½	:493 1:132 2:023 2:271 3↑	Woodward-G1	5 2 2½ 2hd 2hd 21¾	Baeza B	119	1.10	82-19	Forego1261¾Wajima11911Group Plan126¾	Steadied late 6
13Sep75- 8Bel	fst 1¼	:472 1:104 1:352 2:00 3↑	Marl Cup Inv'l H-G1	1 6 64½ 42½ 2hd 1hd	Baeza B	119	4.70	99-11	Wajima119hdForego1297½Ancient Title126¾	Bumped,driving 7
1Sep75- 8Bel	fst 1⅛	:452 1:09 1:341 1:471 3↑	Governor-G1	1 5 56½ 55¼ 31½ 1hd	Baeza B	115	2.70	91-18	Wajima115hdFoolishPleasure1252AncientTitle130¾	Driving 10
16Aug75- 7Sar	fst 1¼	:483 1:123 1:37 2:02	Travers-G1	5 2 21½ 11 15 110	Baeza B	126	*.90	95-14	Wajima12610Media1263¾Prince Thou Art1262	Ridden out 5
2Aug75- 8Mth	fst 1⅛	:462 1:102 1:361 1:493	Mth Inv'l H-G1	2 5 64¾ 52½ 32½ 1nk	Baeza B	118	*.70	92-18	Wajima118nkIntrepid Hero1152My Friend Gus1161¼	Driving 8
19Jly75- 8Bow	fst 1⅛	:473 1:114 1:364 1:49	Marylander H 57k	6 2 3½ 11 13 18	Baeza B	116	*.30	102-11	Wajima1168Logical1139Pimms Cup109¾	Brushed,ridden out 7
12Jly75- 8Bel	sly 1⅛	:453 1:093 1:35 1:482	Dwyer H-G2	6 7 63½ 44 35½ 23	Baeza B	118	*.90	82-16	Valid Appeal1103Wajima1184Hunka Papa1163	Raced wide 8
29Jun75- 8Bel	fst 1	:232 :464 1:104 1:344	Saranac-G2	5 4 63 84 42½ 2hd	Baeza B	114	*1.30	94-12	Bravest Roman114hdWajima1143¾Valid Appeal114no	Gaining 9
21Jun75- 6Bel	fst 1	:223 :453 1:10 1:351	Alw 20000	4 2 21½ 3½ 1hd 1½	Baeza B	113	*.80	92-12	Wajima113½Bravest Roman1163Packer Captain1132	Driving 5
11Jun75- 6Bel	fst 6½f	:224 :46 1:101 1:161 3↑	Alw 15000	7 5 53½ 52½ 31 13½	Baeza B	113	2.30	95-17	Wajima1133½Townsand116noSailors Watch1201¼	Ridden out 7
29Jan75- 9Hia	fst 7f	:222 :444 1:09 1:22	Bahamas 33k	2 10 78½ 712 69½ 55	Baeza B	115	*1.10	90-14	Ascetic1151½Ellora1152½Sylvan Place113¾	No excuse 11
2Nov74- 8Lrl	fst 1 1/16	:233 :464 1:114 1:423	Lrl Futurity-G1	3 3 22 32 31½ 21	Baeza B	122	3.60	99-13	L'Enjoleur1221Wajima1221¾Bombay Duck1223¾	Good try 9
19Oct74- 7Kee	fst *7f	1:254	Breeders' Futurity-G3	6 5 76¼ 1011 78¼ 46¼	Baeza B	122	1.80	88-15	PackerCaptain1221½MasterDrby1224RugglesFerry122¾	Wide 11
5Oct74- 5Bel	fst 6f	:224 :462 1:11	Alw 9500	9 8 87½ 54 2½ 13½	Baeza B	121	*.60	88-12	Wajima1213½Pride of Pan Gil1193Doug119nk	Handily 10
	Previously owned by H.I. Snyder									
21Sep74- 3Bel	fst 6f	:223 :462 1:101	ⒸMd Sp Wt	5 5 52¼ 31 2hd 1nk	Baeza B	121	*.60	92-12	Wajima121nkTumeko1215¼Rue de Rivoli1218½	Driving 6

Waya (Fr)

b. f. 1974, by Faraway Son (Ambiopoise)–War Path, by Blue Prince

Lifetime record: 29 14 6 4 $822,816

Own.– P. Brant
Br.– Dayton Ltd (Fr)
Tr.– David A. Whiteley

Date-Race	Cond/Dist	Fractions	Race	Running line	Jockey	Wt	Odds	Figs	Top finishers	Comment/Field
10Nov79- 8Lrl	sf 1½Ⓣ	:573 1:252 2:232 2:51 3↑	D C Int'l-G1	8 7 42½ 64¼ 78¼ 616	Asmussen CB	124	19.30	- -	Bowl Game127¾Trillion124noLe Marmot1208	Tired 8
27Oct79- 8Aqu	fm 1½Ⓣ	:481 1:14 2:044 2:281 3↑	Turf Classic-G1	3 4 618 68½ 69½ 67¾	Asmussen CB	123	4.50	112-00	BowlGame126nkTrillion123nkNativeCourier1264¾	Fell back 7
13Oct79- 8Bel	sly 1¼	:473 1:124 1:39 2:061 3↑	ⒻBeldame-G1	5 7 714 43½ 22 13	Asmussen CB	123	3.00e	69-27	Waya1233Fourdrinier1184Kit's Double1231¼	Ridden out 7
29Sep79- 8Bel	fst 1⅛	:474 1:12 1:351 1:472 3↑	ⒻRuffian H-G1	2 4 35 37½ 311 39	Velasquez J	126	2.30	81-12	It's in the Air1224Blitey1135Waya126	Evenly 4
10Sep79- 7Bel	fm 1 1/16Ⓣ	:24 :47 1:11 1:414 3↑	Alw 30000	1 4 48½ 33 22 32½	Cordero A Jr	119	*.50	84-17	John Henry1172Silent Cal117½Waya119no	Hung 4
28Jly79- 8Bel	fm 1¼[T]	:491 1:13 1:373 2:013 3↑	ⒻSheepshead Bay H-G2	10 10 1013 107¼ 85 74¾	Shoemaker W	130	*2.00	81-09	Terpsichorist117noLate Bloomer1232¾Warfever110nk	Outrun 10
16Jun79- 8Bel	fm 1⅜[T]	:48 1:12 1:352 2:112 3↑	Bowling Green H-G2	4 5 512 57 53½ 24	Cordero A Jr	125	*.80	108-01	Overskate1174Waya125hdBowl Game1231¾	Rallied 7
3Jun79- 6Bel	sly 1¼	:494 1:14 1:391 2:041 3↑	Sar Cup H 109k	5 6 69 31 1hd 1no	Cordero A Jr	125	*.90	76-30	Waya125noLate Bloomer1194¾Sten1101¼	Driving 6
28Apr79- 8Aqu	sly 1⅛	:48 1:122 1:374 1:504 3↑	ⒻTop Flight H-G1	2 8 717 57½ 22 1nk	Cordero A Jr	128	*1.60	81-17	Waya128nkPearl Necklace1207Island Kiss1121	Driving 8
25Mar79- 8SA	yl 1¼Ⓣ	:462 1:104 1:354 2:01 4↑	ⒻS Barbara H-G1	2 7 713 53 31½ 11¼	Cordero A Jr	131	*.70	82-18	Waya1311¼Petron's Love1171Island Kiss1113	Easily 8
14Mar79- 8SA	sf 1⅛Ⓣ	:47 1:11 1:36 1:481 4↑	ⒻSanta Ana H 65k	1 10 1011 86¼ 31 13½	Cordero A Jr	127	*1.00	86-14	Waya1273½Amazer123¾Shua115hd	Easily 10
10Feb79- 8SA	sf 1¼Ⓣ	:484 1:123 1:364 2:033 4↑	Arcadia H-G3	8 7 78¾ 45 32½ 21¾	Cordero A Jr	123	*1.80	67-25	Fluorescent Light1211¾Waya123nkAs de Copas1181	Gamely 9
	Previously owned by D. Wildenstein;previously trained by Angel Penna									
4Nov78- 8Lrl	fm 1½Ⓣ	:50 1:141 2:033 2:27 3↑	D C Int'l-G1	8 8 811 73¼ 51½ 33	Cordero A Jr	124	2.90	81-16	Mac Diarmida120hdTiller1273Waya1241½	Lacked room 8
21Oct78- 8Bel	fm 1½Ⓣ	:49 1:133 2:03 2:264 3↑	Turf Classic-G1	6 5 57 41½ 1hd 1no	Cordero A Jr	123	*1.60	90-09	Waya123noTiller126nkTrillion1231¾	Long hard drive 6
7Oct78- 8Bel	yl 1⅜Ⓣ	:492 1:14 1:382 2:161 3↑	Man o' War-G1	4 4 47 42 31 11¾	Cordero A Jr	123	6.60	81-19	Waya1231¾Tiller1262¾Mac Diarmida1214	Driving clear 5
1Oct78- 8Bel	fm 1¼[T]	:482 1:12 1:37 2:003 3↑	ⒻFlower Bowl H 54k	2 6 78 43 22½ 1¾	Cordero A Jr	120	*.50	91-10	Waya120¾Magnificnce1084¾Leave Me Alone1081	Going away 7
21Aug78- 8Sar	fm 1⅛Ⓣ	:45 1:091 1:332 1:452 3↑	ⒻDiana H-G2	7 8 711 54 1hd 12¾	Cordero A Jr	115	2.40	100-00	Waya1152¾Pearl Necklace1254Fia110½	Ridden out 12
15Jly78- 8Bel	gd 1¼[T]	:471 1:113 1:354 2:01 3↑	ⒻSheepshead Bay H-G2	6 8 711 46 32½ 2hd	Cordero A Jr	115	2.80	89-11	Late Bloomer118hdWaya115nkPearl Necklace1241¼	Sharp 11
24Jun78- 6Bel	fm 1 1/16Ⓣ	:231 :46 1:10 1:40 3↑	ⒻNew York H (Div 1)-G3	3 5 56½ 33½ 25 23	Cordero A Jr	116	*.90	93-09	Pearl Necklace1223Waya116hdDottie's Doll1182	Good try 7

15Jun78- 8Bel fm 1 1/16Ⓣ :23 :454 1:093 1:41 3↑ ⒻAlw 25000 7 6 55 21½ 1½ 12 Velasquez J 117 *.70 91-15 Waya1172Maria's Baby1171½Magnificence117½ Handily 7
7Jun78- 8Bel fm 1 1/16Ⓣ :233 :481 1:12 1:431 3↑ ⒻAlw 20000 1 8 89 73 11½ 12½ Cordero A Jr 117 *1.20 88-08 Waya1172½Milina117nkMake It Known1123¼ Handily 8
2Oct77♦ Longchamp(Fr) gd *1⅛ⓉRH 1:532 3↑ ⒻPrix de l'Opera-G2 Stk63500 1hd St-Martin Y 121 *1.10e Waya121hdBeaune1211Silk Slipper121½ 12
Rated in last,rallied to lead near line

18Sep77♦ Longchamp(Fr) fm*1¼ⓉRH 2:041 3↑ Prix du Prince d'Orange-G3 Stk42000 32 St-Martin Y 119 7.00 Carwhite126hdGairloch1212Waya119nk 11
Trailed to 1½f out,sharp late run,up for 3rd.Tip Moss 6th

4Sep77♦ Longchamp(Fr) gd *1ⓉRH 1:411 3↑ Prix du Rond-Point-G3 Stk42200 62½ St-Martin Y 120 3.00 Pharly128½River Dane122nkMonseigneur1211½ 7
Chased leaders throughout,never threatened

7Aug77♦ Deauville(Fr) gd *1ⓉStr 1:373 3↑ ⒻPrix d'Astarte-G3 Stk42200 42½ St-Martin Y 128 *2.20 Sanedtki128¾Hartebeest1281Silk Slipper121¾ 13
Rated in 6th,mild bid over 1f out,evenly late

13Jly77♦ Evry(Fr) gd *1⅛ⓉLH 1:522 ⒻPrix Chloe-G3 Stk33100 2hd St-Martin Y 128 *.80 Lillan128hdWaya128¾Dekeleia128¾ 11
Rallied toward rear,finished fast,just failed

26Jun77♦ Longchamp(Fr) gd *1¼ⓉRH 2:062 ⒻPrix de Malleret-G3 Stk51000 2hd St-Martin Y 123 *.60 Les Saintes Claires123hdWaya1231½Kamicia123hd 9
Tracked in 5th,led 1f out,dueled late,outgamed

12Jun77♦ Chantilly(Fr) sf *1 5/16ⓉRH 2:111 ⒻPrix de Royaumont-G3 Stk41900 11 St-Martin Y 128 3.30 Waya1281Kalkeen128½Kelso's Niece128¾ 13
Rated at rear,long drive to lead final strides

30May77♦ Saint-Cloud(Fr) gd *1ⓉLH 1:433 ⒻPrix de la Croix St. Jacques Mdn (FT)13000 16 St-Martin Y 123 *1.40 Waya1236Sonabie123½Come Gailly123½ 11
Tracked in 3rd,led over 1f out,easily clear

What a Summer

gr. f. 1973, by What Luck (Bold Ruler)–Summer Classic, by Summer Tan **Lifetime record: 31 18 6 3 $479,161**
Own.– Mrs B.R. Firestone
Br.– Milton Polinger (Md)
Tr.– Leroy Jolley

26Nov78- 8Aqu fst 6f :221 :451 1:101 3↑ Sport Page H 54k 6 1 3nk 31 21½ 2nk Fell J 124 *.70 92-20 Topsider109nkWhat a Summer1241¼Affiliate1182¼ Sharp 6
19Nov78- 8Aqu fst 7f :222 :45 1:091 1:221 3↑ ⒻFirst Flight H 42k 2 3 2hd 11½ 13 11½ Fell J 126 *.50 90-17 WhtaSmmr1261½FlyingAbove1201¾Mrs.Wrrn1132 Ridden out 5
22Oct78- 8Bel fst 7f :221 :442 1:082 1:21 3↑ Vosburgh H-G2 6 3 32 21 1½ 2¾ Fell J 124 5.90 96-13 Dr.Patches117¾WhataSummr1243¾SorryLookin1095 Gamely 8
21Sep78- 6Med fst 6f :221 :46 1:101 3↑ ⒻEgret H 54k 3 6 31 32 22½ 31¾ Cordero A Jr 127 *.70 92-19 Dainty Dotsie127½Gladiolus1161¼What a Summer1271½ Wide 9
28Aug78- 8Bel sly 6f :22 :45 1:092 3↑ Fall Highweight H-G2 5 3 11½ 14 12 11¾ Cordero A Jr 134 *.90 95-14 WhtaSmmr1341¾Buckfindr1298WhiteRmmr1281¼ Ridden out 5
8Jly78- 8Hol fst 6½f :212 :431 1:074 1:141 3↑ ⒻSilver Spoon H 42k 6 1 2½ 1½ 1½ 1¾ Shoemaker W 126 *.50 99-14 What a Summer126¾Eximious1144Dallas Deb1145 Driving 6
17Jun78- 6Bel fst 6f :221 :45 1:09 3↑ ⒻHandicap 30000 3 1 11 11½ 14 16 Cordero A Jr 126 *.50 97-12 What a Summer1266Gladiolus1191½Flying Above1101 Easily 4
29May78- 8Bel fst 1 :223 :45 1:091 1:343 3↑ Metropolitan H-G1 8 6 63 42 41½ 42¾ Perret C 120 12.90 92-16 Cox'sRidge130¾Buckfinder112½QuietLittlTbl1181½ No rally 9
7May78- 8Aqu my 7f :221 :441 1:082 1:214 3↑ ⒻVagrancy H-G3 1 3 32 22½ 22 21¾ Vasquez J 127 *1.60 90-13 Dainty Dotsie1241¾What a Summer1273Navajo Princess110½ 6
No match

8Apr78- 9GP fm 1 1/16Ⓣ :224 :453 1:091 1:41 3↑ ⒻOrchid H-G3 1 1 15 11½ 1hd 41¼ Solomone M 122 *1.20 95-03 TimeforPleasure115½LateBloomr113nkRichSoil116½ Bore out 11
15Mar78- 9GP fm 1Ⓣ :233 :47 1:11 1:353 3↑ ⒻSuwannee River H 32k 2 1 11 1hd 1hd 2nk Solomone M 122 1.90 92-11 Len'sDetermind119nkWhtaSmmr122nkLatBlmr1131 Bore out 9
4Feb78- 7Hia fst 7f :224 :454 1:101 1:221 4↑ ⒻAlw 16000 8 1 11½ 13 12 11½ Solomone M 122 *.60 92-10 WhataSummr1221½CumLaudeLaurie1227Plain and Fancy114¾ 8
Ridden out

22Oct77- 7Kee fst 1⅛ :461 1:102 1:36 1:482 3↑ ⒻSpinster-G1 10 1 11½ 11 2hd 45¼ Vasquez J 123 3.00 90-17 CumLaudeLaurie1191MssissippiMd1233¾IvoryWnd123½ Tired 10
10Oct77- 8Bel gd 1¼ :482 1:131 1:373 2:014 3↑ ⒻBeldame-G1 2 1 12½ 11½ 11 2¾ Vasquez J 123 3.30 89-13 CumLdLaurie118¾WhtaSmmr1231½ChrmngStory118½ Gamely 7
13Sep77- 8Bel fst 1 :24 :47 1:112 1:372 3↑ ⒻMaskette H-G2 7 1 11 1½ 1½ 1hd Vasquez J 126 *.80 81-24 WhataSummer126hdCrabGrass114nkHarvestGirl1113 Lasted 8
29Aug77- 8Bel fst 6f :22 :452 1:10 3↑ Fall Highweight H-G2 12 3 54½ 42 1hd 12 Vasquez J 134 8.00 92-19 What a Summer1342BroadwayForli123½Piamem129nk Driving 12
4Aug77- 8Sar fst 6f :221 :45 1:09 3↑ ⒻHandicap 25000 5 4 52½ 41½ 1hd 13½ Vasquez J 125 *1.60 95-13 WhataSmmr1253½Artfully112½QuintasVicki1121¼ Ridden out 9
9Jly77- 8Hol fst 6½f :214 :441 1:083 1:15 3↑ ⒻSilver Spoon H 43k 5 3 2½ 11½ 12 12 Shoemaker W 122 3.10 95-14 What a Summer1222RegalRumor1242SingBack113nk Driving 7
4Jun77- 8Mth fst 6f :203 :453 1:093 3↑ ⒻRegret H 27k 1 7 12½ 2hd 23½ 36 Perret C 123 b *.90 86-16 Cast the Die1164½IvoryWand1181½What a Summer123½ Wide 8
2May77- 8Aqu fst 6f :214 :451 1:102 3↑ ⒻGrey Flight H 42k 1 4 1½ 1hd 2hd 31¾ Maple E 126 b *.70 89-15 Sylvan'sGirl112¾ShyDawn1201WhataSummr1261¼ Weakened 6
23Apr77- 6Aqu fst 6f⊡ :221 :453 1:104 4↑ ⒻHandicap 25000 1 5 11 14 15 11¾ Black AS 123 b *.70 95-05 What a Summer1231¾Moontee1112Sylvan's Girl114¾ Easily 6
23Mar77- 8Aqu my 6f⊡ :221 :454 1:113 3↑ ⒻDistaff H-G3 1 5 14 17 15 12½ Maple E 118 b *.60 91-15 WhataSummer1182½SecretLanvin112nkShyDawn1204 Driving 5
Previously owned by Estate of M. Polinger;previously trained by Grover G. Delp

27Dec76- 8Lrl fst 1 :222 :444 1:102 1:362 3↑ ⒻⓈAll Brandy H 30k 4 1 14 13 34 97¾ McCarron CJ 123 b *.50 83-16 Gala Lil1222Avum1123Shark's Jaws113½ Saddle slipped 10
Previously owned by M. Polinger

11Dec76- 8Lrl fst 1 :23 :461 1:114 1:381 ⒻAnne Arundel H 27k 2 1 14½ 16 15 13¼ McCarron CJ 122 b *.30 82-22 What a Summer1223¼Turn the Guns1141¼Avum114½ Driving 7
23Nov76- 8Lrl fst 1 :223 :443 1:102 1:361 ⒻⓈAlw 15000 3 1 17 15 17 14¾ McCarron CJ 122 b *.20 92-17 What aSummr1224¾Avum1173Body Snatcher1175 Ridden out 7
30Oct76- 8Key fst 1 1/16 :232 :472 1:112 1:441 ⒻHeirloom 34k 1 1 11½ 2½ 2hd 21¾ McCarron CJ 116 *.80 81-24 Forlana1181¾WhtSmmr1162½MsssppMd1165 Weakened late 9
21Oct76- 8Bow fst 7f :224 :453 1:10 1:23 3↑ ⒻAlw 8500 5 3 11 11½ 13½ 13 McCarron CJ 113 *.50 90-21 WhataSmmr1133ⒹChesapeakeBugeye1191Avum1196 Driving 9
14May76- 8Pim fst 1 1/16 :234 :464 1:104 1:422 ⒻBlack-Eyed Susan-G2 2 1 12 2hd 1hd 1no McCarron CJ 111 3.30e 93-14 WhataSummer111noDearlyPrecious1215Artfully1141 Driving 10
7May76- 5Pim fst 6f :223 :453 1:102 ⒻAlw 7500 1 4 1½ 13 13½ 15 McCarron CJ 117 *.20 94-16 What a Summer1175Avum1171¼Miss Berta1173½ Handily 6
26Apr76- 7Pim fst 6f :231 :463 1:122 ⒻAlw 7000 7 3 3nk 14 16 15 McCarron CJ 112 *.40 84-23 WhataSmmr1125Hillybob1143¾TurntheGuns112¾ Ridden out 8
10Apr76- 9Pim fst 6f :232 :464 1:122 3↑ ⒻMd Sp Wt 7 3 2½ 12 15 18 McCarron CJ 114 *1.40 84-22 What a Summer1148Bold Folly1145Hap's Easter1141 Easily 12

Youth

b. c. 1973, by Ack Ack (Battle Joined)–Gazala II, by Dark Star **Lifetime record: 11 8 1 1 $687,624**
Own.– N.B. Hunt
Br.– N.B. Hunt (Md)
Tr.– Maurice Zilber

6Nov76- 8Lrl sf 1½Ⓣ :531 1:201 2:184 2:461 3↑ D C Int'l-G1 1 5 45 31½ 13 110 Hawley S 120 *1.80 - - Youth12010On My Way II127noIvanjica1246 Ridden out 8
23Oct76- 8WO sf 1⅝Ⓣ :49 1:423 2:48 3↑ Can Int'l-G1 5 8 814 3nk 13 14 Hawley S 117 *.95 60-35 Youth1174Improviser1267Effervscng1171½ As rider pleased 11
3Oct76♦ Longchamp(Fr) sf *1½ⓉRH 2:392 3↑ Arc de Triomphe-G1 Stk412000 35 Pyers WB 123 *2.00e Ivanjica1272Crow1233Youth123nk 20
Well up throughout

5Sep76♦ Longchamp(Fr) gd *1⅜ⓉRH 2:22 Prix Niel-G3 Stk51000 1¾ Piggott L 130 *.80 Youth130¾Arctic Tern1262½Malacate1304 5
Led throughout,met challenge 1f out,held well

24Jly76♦ Ascot(GB) fm 1½ⓉRH 2:291 3↑ K George & Q Elizabeth-G1 Stk290000 911 Head F 120 *1.85 Pawneese1171Bruni133noOrange Bay133¾ 10
Tracked in 4th,wide turn 2½f out,weakened

6Jun76♦ Chantilly(Fr) gd *1½ⓉRH 2:272 Prix du Jockey-Club-G1 Stk386000 13 Head F 128 *1.90e Youth1283Twig Moss128¾Malacate1281½ 18
Tracked in 5th,led 2f out,clear 1f out,driving

16May76♦ Longchamp(Fr) gd *1 5/16ⓉRH 2:133 Prix Lupin-G1 Stk212000 1¾ Head F 128 *.40e Youth128¾Arctic Tern1281Empery1284 12
Well placed in 3rd,led 1½f out,held well

19Apr76♦ Longchamp(Fr) gd *1 5/16ⓉRH 2:094 Prix Daru-G2 Stk85000 14 Head F 128 *1.70 Youth1284Danestic1281½French Scandal128½ 10
Tracked in 4th,led 2f out,drew clear 1f out.Far North 8th

4Apr76♦ Longchamp(Fr) sf *1 5/16ⓉRH 2:203 Prix Greffulhe-G2 Stk86000 11½ Head F 128 4.20 Youth1281½Velino1281½Yule Log1281½ 9
Rated in 5th,strong late run to lead 70y out,going away

4Oct75♦ Longchamp(Fr) sf *1⅛ⓉRH 1:574 Prix Saint Roman-G3 Stk42500 22½ Navarro N 123 3.25 Far North1232½Youth1232½Ydja123¾ 9
Tracked in 4th,bid 2f out,second best

14Sep75♦ Longchamp(Fr) sf *1ⓉRH 1:463 Prix de Fontenoy Mdn (FT)15600 11½ Navarro N 123 5.90 Youth1231½Chateau Country123½Three Hlfs1231½ 7
Tracked in 3rd,led 1½f out,drew clear,handily

The Cup Is Born

The 1980's

by Steven Crist

THERE IS NO ARGUMENT that the last minute of the twentieth century commenced at 11:59 p.m. on December 31, 1999. There can be little more dispute that the last minute of championship racing as practiced in the United States for the bulk of that century commenced at 11:14 a.m., Pacific time, on November 10, 1984.

That was the minute that it took 10 2-year-olds to be loaded into the starting gate at Hollywood Park for the inaugural Breeders' Cup Juvenile, the opener on a card featuring seven rich new races. The revolutionary attempt to create a single showcase day of championship-deciding events was at last a reality, with the nation's top 2-year-olds moving into position and the stars of six other divisions assembled in one barn area for the biggest afternoon ever.

And yet, the moment was surreal. It wasn't just that the 64,254 on hand were rubbing the sleep from their eyes, unaccustomed to being at a racetrack before noon, much less seeing a Grade 1 race with the sun still in the east. The whole proposition of assembling the world's best runners at one track for a single day of title matches even now seemed a fantasy. Would the event really work and last more than a year? Would a sport whose highest awards had for decades been decided in ancient and storied fixtures suddenly convert to a one-day showdown for honors and riches?

The decade's first Horse of the Year was its best.

At the end of the 1970's, Spectacular Bid was ranked below that starry era's foremost champions on the basis of his 3-year-old campaign in 1979. He had been a fine colt, but on the heels of Seattle Slew's and Affirmed's Triple Crowns in the two preceding seasons, his failure to complete the sweep made him the exception rather than the norm. Nor did it help that trainer Bud Delp boasted that "Bid" was "the best horse ever to look through a bridle," and blamed his Belmont Stakes failure on the implausible notion that the colt had stepped on a safety pin.

In 1980, though, Delp gave Spectacular Bid the opportunity to prove he belonged with Affirmed and Seattle Slew, and Bid took it, mounting the most dominant 4-year-old campaign since Tom Fool a quarter-century earlier and achieving more in his post-Triple Crown career than Secretariat, Seattle Slew, or Affirmed.

Spectacular Bid swept the Strub Series at Santa Anita like no horse before him, stretching from a

1¼ MILES

Second Leg Fall Championship—Three-Year-Olds and Upward
THE WOODWARD
(27th RUNNING)
$200,000 ADDED
(Grade I)

FOR THREE-YEAR-OLDS AND UPWARD AT WEIGHT FOR AGE. By Subscription of $500 each, which should accompany the nomination; $1,500 to pass the entry box, with $200,000 added. The added money and all fees to be divided 60% to the winner, 22% to second, 12% to third and 6% to fourth. Weight for age. Three-year-olds, 120 lbs.; older, 126 lbs. Mrs. William Woodward, Sr. has donated a trophy to be presented to the owner of the winner and trophies will also be presented to the winning trainer and jockey and mementoes to the grooms of the first four finishers.

(Closed Wednesday, September 3, 1980 with 23 nominations.)

ONE MILE AND A QUARTER (Starting on Turn)
Track Record—2:00; SEATTLE SLEW (4), 126 lbs.; September 30, 1978.

MAKE SELECTION BY NUMBER

	OWNER / TRAINER	Jockey/Morn. Line
1	HAWKSWORTH FARM — G. G. DELP Blue, Black Cross Sashes, Black Sleeves, Two Blue Hoops, Black Cap **SPECTACULAR BID** 126 Gr.c.4, Bold Bidder—Spectacular by Promised Land	**1-10** **WILLIAM SHOEMAKER**

SCRATCHED—TEMPERENCE HILL, WINTER'S TALE, DR. PATCHES

THIS RACE IS A WALKOVER

THE WOODWARD

Winners since 1975

STAKES RECORD: 2:00 by Kelso in 1961 and by Seattle Slew in 1978.

1975—Lazy F Ranch's Forego, 5 (H. Gustines); 126 lbs.; time, 2:27 1-5; ($64,920); Tr: S. W. Ward.
1976—Lazy F Ranch's Forego, 6 (W. Shoemaker); 135 lbs.; time, 1:45 4-5; ($103,920); Tr: F. Y. Whiteley, Jr.
1977—Lazy F. Ranch's Forego, 7 (W. Shoemaker); 133 lbs.; time, 1:48; ($105,000); Tr: F. Y. Whiteley. Jr.
1978—Tayhill Stable's Seattle Slew, 4 (A. Cordero, Jr.); 126 lbs.; time, 2:00; ($97,800); Tr: D. Peterson.
1979—Harbor View Farm's Affirmed (L. Pincay, Jr.); 126 lbs.; time, 2:01 3-5; ($114,600); Tr: Laz Barrera.

First run in 1954. Run at Aqueduct in 1959, 1960 and from 1962 to 1967. Distance one mile in 1954; a mile and an eighth in 1976 and 1977; a mile and a half from 1972 to 1975, inclusive. Run as a handicap in 1976 and 1977. In 1971 Cougar 2nd finished first but was disqualified and placed third.

THE WOODWARD was named in honor of the late William Woodward, former chairman of The Jockey Club and master of the famed Belair Stud.

SPECIAL GROUPS

Arrangements may be made for Special Groups to attend the races — Service Clubs, Business Groups, Conventions. etc. Write Special Groups, Aqueduct, P. O. Box 90, Jamaica, N. Y. 11417. Phone 641-4700, Ext. 475.

MUTUEL WINDOWS WILL CLOSE
30 MINUTES AFTER LAST RACE

Emblematic of Spectacular Bid's overwhelming dominance of the 1980 racing season was his unopposed victory in the Woodward.

blazing 1:20 for seven furlongs in the Malibu to a record 1:57⅘ for 10 furlongs in the Strub, leaving solid handicap rivals such as Flying Paster in his wake. He then ripped off five straight victories under 130 pounds or more, winning the Santa Anita Handicap and Hollywood's Mervyn LeRoy Handicap and Californian Stakes before heading east to take the Washington Park Stakes at Arlington and the Haskell at Monmouth.

After eight straight victories by a combined 37¾ lengths, he had scared off all comers. On September 20 at Belmont Park, he completed his career with a walkover, racing the mile and a quarter of the Woodward unopposed in 2:02⅘ to the cheers of a crowd acknowledging one of the greatest.

Bid would prove to be the last of his kind in the century, not just in terms of quality, but in form as well. After a decade in which one champion after another had come up through the same ranks – juvenile honors, Triple Crown bids, fall battles at Belmont Park – Spectacular Bid was the last to play strictly by those rules as the eighties spun off into new ways of creating and campaigning for Eclipse Awards. As it turned out, he would be the last 2-year-old male champion in the century to win the Kentucky Derby or the divisional title at 3.

Seven of the 10 Kentucky Derbies in the 1970's were won by the favorite. After Spectacular Bid, favorites lost the century's remaining 20 Derbies, and the 1980 rendition was not even won by a colt or gelding.

Genuine Risk won her first six starts against fillies, then tried colts in the Wood Memorial. She finished third, beaten 1½ lengths by eventual Derby second choice Plugged Nickle. Trainer LeRoy Jolley was not inclined to take on colts again, but owners Bert and Diana Firestone persisted. Sent off at 13-1, Genuine Risk swept to the lead entering the stretch and held off the closers to become the first filly to win the Derby since Regret in 1915.

Her next start turned out to be the decade's most controversial race. Santa Anita Derby victor Codex, who had not been nominated to the Kentucky Derby by his then little-known trainer, D. Wayne Lukas, made a winning move to grab the lead turning for home in the Preakness. His jockey, Angel Cordero Jr., a fierce competitor who took every available edge, forced Genuine Risk wide as she ranged up outside him. Codex was the better horse, and the incident did not affect the race's outcome, but the idea of the storybook filly Derby winner being muscled and intimidated by Cordero and a colt became an inflammatory image, and the Firestones appealed the outcome to the Maryland Racing Commission. After a hearing only slightly less carnivalesque than the Scopes Monkey Trial, the result stood.

Over a muddy track in the Belmont, 50-1 shot Temperence Hill ran down the filly as Codex faded to seventh. Temperence Hill turned out not to be a fluke, winning the Travers, Jockey Club Gold Cup, and Super Derby to take the 3-year-old title. Genuine Risk received 3-year-old filly honors, her Derby outweighing her loss to the higher-weighted Bold 'n Determined in the Maskette.

The runner-up in the Gold Cup that year also received an Eclipse Award. John Henry was the nation's top grass horse that season, and with 53 starts under his girth seemed in the twilight of a remarkable career, but he was just getting warmed up to become the decade's most enduring star.

Obscurely bred (by the Michigan-based sire Ole Bob Bowers), sold three times for pittances early in his career, racing for purses as low as $2,400 at Evangeline Downs, John Henry was seemingly transformed when he made his first start on the grass at Belmont Park in June 1978, winning by 14 lengths under a $35,000 claiming price. Over the next two years the bay gelding became a frequent gutty winner of grass stakes, and reached the level of champion in 1980 with eight victories in graded events, including the San Juan Capistrano and Oak Tree Invitational. An ornery, scrappy sort, John Henry would reign as a blue-collar hero for the first half of the decade, prompting memories of Kelso and Forego as he returned with triumphs at advancing age year after year.

As a 6-year-old in 1981, John Henry took it to the next level, scoring dramatic photo-finish victories

The cantankerous and game John Henry was the pre-eminent horse during the first half of the decade, winning Horse of the Year titles in 1981 and 1984. Early in his career, the gelding raced for purses as low as $2,400.

on both grass and dirt. He notched his first Grade 1 on the dirt when he won the Santa Anita Handicap in March. In August, Arlington Park offered the sport's first seven-digit purse to entice entrants to its new international grass event, the Arlington Million, and John Henry ensured its status as an instant classic with a heart-stopping nose victory. Returning to the dirt, he won the Jockey Club Gold Cup by a head, then switched coasts and footing again to take the Oak Tree Invitational by a neck.

He was an easy selection as champion older horse, grass horse, and Horse of the Year over Pleasant Colony, who won the first two legs of the Triple Crown and the Woodward but sputtered in the Belmont, Travers, and Marlboro.

A filly winning the Derby, an ex-claimer grass gelding winning Horse of the Year – this was not your typical decade of champions. The 1982 season continued the oddball trend. Gato Del Sol, a loping California stretch-runner, won a weak Kentucky Derby at 21-1, then chagrined traditionalists by skipping the Preakness because trainer Eddie Gregson thought his colt was better suited to a longer rest and the longer distance of the Belmont. It seemed that even the Triple Crown was no longer sacred. The Preakness was heisted by wire-to-wire winner Aloma's Ruler, and then a new face appeared on the sophomore scene: Conquistador Cielo, a speedy but somewhat brittle colt who had been withheld from the Derby and Preakness by trainer Woody Stephens, whipped the best older horses around, winning the Metropolitan Mile by 7¼ lengths in a sizzling 1:33.

That was on a Monday and the Belmont was on Saturday, so no one took Stephens too seriously when he said he was thinking about wheeling the colt right back. Stephens loved the way Conquistador bounced out of the race, jogged him the wrong way over the Belmont track the rest of the week, and didn't mind when the weatherman called for rain on the weekend. Breaking from the outside post in a field of 11 over a sloppy track, Conquistador Cielo went to the lead and forgot to stop, swamping Gato Del Sol by 14 widening lengths.

The appearance of dazzling displays of first speed in the Met and then stamina in the Belmont impressed no one more than the breeding community, which snapped up stallion shares over the next sixty days at a record $910,000 apiece. Conquistador Cielo won his next two starts with ease, if not brilliance, taking the Dwyer and the Jim Dandy, then faced Gato Del Sol and Aloma's Ruler in a Travers that seemed like a fourth leg of the Triple Crown. Over a dry track at 10 furlongs, Conquistador – who appeared on the track wearing front bandages for the first time – never shook loose early and then tired late, settling for third behind longshot Runaway Groom and Aloma's Ruler.

Conquistador Cielo never raced again, but he had done enough in a week to be the Horse of the Year. John Henry was back as a 7-year-old but won only 1 of 6 starts, while two horses tried and failed to match his 1981 campaign: Lemhi Gold, the champion older horse, won the Jockey Club Gold Cup and Marlboro Cup on dirt but then ran off the board in the Oak Tree Invitational. Perrault, the grass champion, won the Hollywood Gold Cup and the second Arlington Million but pulled up with a career-ending injury in the Marlboro.

It was a star-crossed year all around. Timely Writer, one of the early favorites for the Kentucky Derby, was euthanized after suffering a fatal injury in the Jockey Club Gold Cup. Landaluce, the champion 2-year-old filly, evoked legitimate com-

Conquistador Cielo had plenty of speed and could carry it over a distance. Just five days after winning the Met Mile in 1:33, he took the Belmont Stakes wire to wire by 14 lengths.

parisons to Ruffian, winning all five of her starts by a combined 46½ lengths, but contracted an infection in November and died in trainer Lukas's arms. Roving Boy, that year's champion 2-year-old, did not race again for 10 months and then broke down past the finish line in his second start back as a 3-year-old.

The 1983 Horse of the Year announcement was one of the few to carry some real suspense. It was a year of brief runs by specialists. The 3-year-olds had taken turns beating one another through the classics, then Slew o' Gold put together a championship campaign in the fall, winning the Woodward and the Jockey Club Gold Cup. Bates Motel had been a runaway leader of the older horses but then lost his last three starts of the year.

It came down to a 2-year-old and a grass filly. Woody Stephens, who had won his second straight Belmont with Caveat, unveiled a gritty son of Seattle Slew named Swale early in the summer, then waited until August to showcase Devil's Bag, a flashy Halo colt with a world of speed. Winner of all five of his starts, Devil's Bag set stakes records of 1:21⅗ in the Cowdin and 1:34⅕ in the Champagne, then stretched out to win the Laurel Futurity in another romp as if he might be racing's next great one. No 2-year-old since Secretariat had been Horse of the Year, but perhaps this was a worthy successor.

After winning the Arc de Triomphe, Europe's most prestigious race, the French filly All Along made a unique run through North America's top fall turf races and was named 1983's Horse of the Year.

When the envelope was opened, though, 1983's top honor went to All Along, whose campaign broke all the rules. The 4-year-old French-bred filly lost her first three starts of the year in France, then began an astounding six-week international run: Victories over males in the Prix de l'Arc de Triomphe in Paris, the Rothmans International at Woodbine in Canada, the Turf Classic at Aqueduct, and the Washington, D.C., International at Laurel.

Critics carped that her three North American victories came over yielding grass in races that were run from 5 to 10 seconds off the course records, but no horse had put together such a transcontinental assault before. Her award illustrated how quickly the sport was changing. Grass racing already was thriving, helped by John Henry and the popularity of the Arlington Million, and All Along's success added an element of international possibilities that would take full flower a year later with the Breeders' Cup.

The 1984 season had more than its share of drama even before that inaugural Cup, most of it provided by Stephens's 3-year-olds. Devil's Bag, whose $36 million syndication had been announced in December, whistled through his season debut in February but then, before a record Hialeah crowd that had gathered for a coronation, tired and finished a shocking fourth in the Flamingo. He won his next two starts around one turn but was never the same and was retired to stud.

In the meantime, Swale proved to be the one who could carry his speed. He alternated victories and losses in seven starts, losing three times at odds-on but winning the Hutcheson, the Florida Derby, and the Kentucky Derby. After dropping the

Preakness to Gate Dancer, he gave Stephens his third straight Belmont Stakes victory. A week later, the trainer was heading off on a fishing vacation when he got a phone call from the stable: While cooling out after a routine gallop, Swale had keeled over, dead from an apparent heart attack.

The summer and fall leading up to the Breeders' Cup belonged to a pair of returning champions. John Henry, as good as ever at 9, wrapped up his fourth grass title, winning all six of his turf starts from May to October including a one-time sponsor's bonus of $500,000 for sweeping the Arlington Million, Turf Classic, and inaugural Ballantine's Classic at The Meadowlands. The only question was which Breeders' Cup race the old man would contest: the $2 million Breeders' Cup Turf or the $3 million Classic on dirt. The latter event would have meant facing Slew o' Gold, who had come back with a vengeance at 4 and swept through the Whitney, Woodward, Marlboro, and Jockey Club Gold Cup.

Shortly after pre-entries were taken, however, a strained ligament sent John Henry to the sidelines, and Slew o' Gold was expected to be the star of the afternoon. As the fields began taking shape for the new races, it seemed that everyone wanted to be a part of history.

The seven races roughly corresponded to the sport's divisions, except that there was no race for 3-year-olds, who by season's end were expected to race their elders anyway. There was the Juvenile for 2-year-old colts and geldings, the Juvenile Fillies for 2-year-old fillies, the Sprint for sprinters, the Distaff for fillies and mares 3 and up, the Turf for grass horses of both sexes, and the Classic for 3-year-olds and up. The oddball event was the Mile, a grass race clearly designed to attract Europeans.

First up was the Juvenile. Chief's Crown, New York's best 2-year-old, had cruised through the traditional Saratoga and Belmont tests but then skipped the Champagne in order to get a race in California under his belt in Santa Anita's Norfolk.

The Breeders' Cup ushered in a new era of racing in the United States. The first day of championship events ended with a rodeo finish, resulting in an upset by 31-1 Wild Again (INSIDE) *in the Classic.*

He proved clearly best in the Juvenile as the 3-5 favorite, winning the race and the 2-year-old title by acclamation. It turned out to be quite a key race: Tank's Prospect, the runner-up, would come back to win the 1985 Preakness for the burgeoning Lukas outfit, while Spend a Buck, who finished third, would win the 1985 Derby as well as turn the sport on its ear. The Breeders' Cup era had begun with a formful and title-making note.

The rest of the afternoon was a scriptwriter's dream, a blend of improbable outsiders and convincing performances that either clearly sealed championships or threw them up for grabs. It all came down to the Classic, where Slew o' Gold found himself playing bumper cars in deep stretch between Gate Dancer and the 31-1 shot Wild Again. Slew o' Gold, who ended up third, was elevated to second on the disqualification of Gate Dancer, and the previously unsung Wild Again had won history's richest race. The outcome was not enough to keep Slew o' Gold from being named champion older male, but in a different photo finish he dropped the Horse of the Year title to John Henry.

While few could summon the bile to be unkind to the ageless and lovable John Henry, Slew o' Gold's backers had every right to feel cheated that the rules had changed. Before the Breeders' Cup, there had been no question that Slew o' Gold was the best horse in training, going undefeated in 1984 despite being troubled by quarter cracks. Had he not run, voters would have been left only with the memory of his perfect season; instead, he was being penalized for contesting the Classic and losing it through no fault of his own. The message was clear: Unless you had a championship utterly and unquestionably sewn up, you were expected to show up for the new Super Bowl – and you had better win.

Racing now had a year-end national event that the sport's promoters hoped could grow in popu-

Spend a Buck ran the field off its feet in the 1985 Kentucky Derby. His connections then broke standard by pursuing a $2 million bonus offered by Garden State Park instead of trying for the Triple Crown.

larity and prestige to match what had been its lone marquee events, the Triple Crown races for 3-year-olds in the spring. Only six months later, though, the hallowed Triple Crown came under assault from an unlikely pair: the third-place finisher in the inaugural Breeders' Cup Juvenile and a maverick securities salesman who had purchased Garden State Park in Cherry Hill, New Jersey.

The 1985 classic season began conventionally enough, as Chief's Crown returned from his Breeders' Cup Juvenile triumph to rip through the Swale Stakes at Gulfstream, the Flamingo at Hialeah, and the Blue Grass at Keeneland. He looked like a legitimate 6-5 shot for the Derby, a race that probably was decided at the start when front-running Wood Memorial winner Eternal Prince broke slowly. That left Spend a Buck loose on the lead over a fast and speed-favoring track. Six in front after six furlongs in 1:09⅗, he just kept going. Chief's Crown tried to make a run at him turning for home but couldn't come close and ended up third behind the rallying Stephan's Odyssey, whom he had beaten in the Flamingo.

Spend a Buck's winning margin was an impressive 5¼ lengths and his time of 2:00⅕ was the third-fastest in history behind Secretariat's 1:59⅖ and Northern Dancer's 2:00. He would have been a heavy Preakness favorite, but for the second time in just four years, the Derby winner was not headed to Pimlico.

Spend a Buck had begun his 3-year-old campaign with a mediocre third in Aqueduct's Bay Shore, then headed away from the top classic prospects to run in two new rich events at Garden State Park, which had just reopened for the first time in eight years after being nearly destroyed by fire. The track had been purchased and transformed into a modern showplace by Robert Brennan, who tried to draw attention to his inaugural meeting's Derby preps by putting up a $2 million bonus for any horse who could take the Cherry Hill Mile and the Garden State Stakes, then win the Kentucky Derby and the $1 million Jersey Derby. That sounded like a 100-1 shot, but now Spend a Buck was three-quarters of the way there.

His connections had already decided their horse was not cut out to handle a mile and a half at Belmont, so they had no Triple Crown to bid for and more than two million reasons to return to Garden State instead of going to Pimlico. Traditionalists wailed, but the Preakness was run in his absence. Chief's Crown was even money and ran well, but was nipped at the wire by Tank's Prospect in track-record time.

Spend a Buck was 1-20 to complete his Garden State bonus nine days later in the Jersey Derby, but he had to gut it out. Never able to get clear early, he barely held off a stretch-long challenge from a Woody Stephens-trained gelding named Creme Fraiche to win by a neck. Twelve days later, with Spend a Buck spending the day in his stall, Creme Fraiche ran down barnmate Stephan's Odyssey to give Stephens an astounding fourth straight Belmont victory as Chief's Crown faded to third as the favorite.

Spend a Buck raced only twice more, staying in New Jersey to run second in the Haskell behind Skip Trial and then scoring his lone victory over older horses, edging Carr de Naskra in the Monmouth Invitational before being retired to stud. In a year filled with strong performers, no one else could put together quite a solid enough second season to unseat him. Chief's Crown regained his winning ways in the Travers and the Marlboro but then ran fourth in the second Breeders' Cup Classic, which was won by fellow 3-year-old Proud Truth. Mom's Command swept the Filly Triple Crown and the Alabama but barely held her own division title as 3-year-old Lady's Secret, who had beaten Mom's Command in the Test, swept her elders in that fall's Maskette, Ruffian, and Beldame. Lady's Secret then finished second to a fellow Lukas trainee, 4-year-old Life's Magic, in the Breeders' Cup Distaff. Vanlandingham took the Suburban and the Jockey Club Gold Cup on dirt and the D.C. International on turf, but failures elsewhere, including the Breeders' Cup Classic, left him with only the older-horse title.

Spend a Buck galloped to an easy Horse of the Year award, meaning that for the second time in as many runnings, a horse who had skipped the Breeders' Cup entirely had won the sport's highest honor. The Cup races, held at Aqueduct, did decide many of that year's titles, however: Eclipse Awards went to the winners of both grass races, Cozzene and the filly Pebbles; Distaff winner Life's Magic; Sprint winner Precisionist; and the 2-year-old Tasso.

Spend a Buck's unorthodox championship season blazed no lasting trails. Within a decade, he had proven a bust at stud, Brennan was out of racing due to securities violations, the Jersey Derby was a grass race, and Garden State offered racing of little importance. His challenge to the Triple Crown, however, galvanized the hosts of those three races to band together, forming Triple Crown Productions to promote and market the series and offer bonus money of its own to keep horses from ever again straying from the classic path.

The 1986 Triple Crown was never in danger of being swept but offered some individual milestones. In the Derby, 73-year-old Hall of Fame trainer Charlie Whittingham and 54-year-old Hall of Fame rider Bill Shoemaker teamed for a last-to-first victory with Ferdinand. In the Preakness, eventual 3-year-old champion Snow Chief rebounded from an 11th-place finish as the Derby favorite to win by four. As for the Belmont, who else? Danzig Connection took to a sloppy track and gave Woody Stephens a fifth consecutive Belmont, a record sure to stand, and to boggle the mind and the odds, for ages.

The 1986 season, however, belonged to a pair of very different 4-year-olds: the front-running gray filly Lady's Secret and the stretch-running brown colt Turkoman. In the end, a record number of Eclipse Award voters, unwilling to compare apples and oranges, split their Horse of the Year ballots.

Lady's Secret gained the nickname Iron Lady as she made 15 starts for Lukas in 1986 from coast to coast. Having run out of fillies to conquer after early-season triumphs in the El Encino, La Canada, Santa Margarita, and Shuvee, she tried males in the Met Mile and ran third. A brief return to her division was followed by three more Grade 1 races against males, and she finished third in the Iselin, second in the Woodward, and won the Whitney. Then she went back to trouncing her own, sweeping the Maskette-Ruffian-Beldame series a second time under weights of up to 129 pounds before winning the Breeders' Cup Distaff under a hand ride.

Turkoman won the Widener, the Oaklawn Handicap, and the Marlboro Cup and was flying at the finish of the races he lost. With a little more luck he might have rounded out his season with two additional victories, but instead ran second to Creme Fraiche in a paceless Jockey Club Gold Cup and second again to Skywalker in the Classic after circling very wide from 16 lengths back over an inside-speed-favoring track. Those decisions tipped the scales to Lady's Secret, who had finished a neck in front of Turkoman when both were beaten in the Met Mile. She became Lukas's first Horse of the Year and joined Twilight Tear in 1944, Busher in 1945, and All Along in 1983 as the only fillies to win that prize.

Lady's Secret became just the fourth female to be elected Horse of the Year after a prolific and highly successful 1986 campaign.

Ferdinand, the 1986 Derby winner, got off to a slow start as a 4-year-old, but finished with a rush, nailing down Horse of the Year with a narrow victory over Alysheba in the Breeders' Cup Classic.

Turkoman was retired at year's end and Lady's Secret came back the worse for wear, winning only a pair of allowances from five starts. In 1987, a 4-year-old again was Horse of the Year, but the power resided in the 3-year-olds, a crop memorable for its talent and for its extreme depth.

After a chaotic spring of confusing prep races, Alysheba came into the Derby with a career record of just 1 for 10, but stormed to a three-quarter-length victory over Bet Twice at 8-1. He edged that same colt by half a length in the Preakness, setting up the first possible Triple Crown since Pleasant Colony's attempt in 1981. Most of the prerace speculation focused not on whether 3-for-12 Alysheba was the next Secretariat, but on drug policy. Alysheba had been racing on the antibleeding medication Lasix, which over the past decade had been legalized in most racing jurisdictions. It was prohibited in New York, however, where concerns lingered over the drug's ability to flush other evidence from a horse's system.

For whatever reason, the Belmont wasn't Alysheba's day. In a stunning reversal, Bet Twice romped to a 14-length triumph while Alysheba finished fourth, beaten a nose and a neck for second by Cryptoclearance and Gulch.

Alysheba and Bet Twice renewed their rivalry in the Haskell, where Bet Twice evened the score with a neck victory. They headed for Saratoga and the Travers, but waiting for them was Java Gold, who had looked like something special winning the Remsen at 2 before missing the classics with a virus. Since returning, he had defeated older horses twice, most recently in Saratoga's Whitney Handicap. The Travers track came up a wet one and Java Gold relished it, circling a field that included eight Grade 1 winners to beat Cryptoclearance by two lengths, with Polish Navy third, Bet Twice fourth, and Alysheba a distant sixth.

Java Gold then took the Marlboro and might have stolen the Horse of the Year title had he won his next start, but he suffered a season-ending broken foot during the Jockey Club Gold Cup, finishing second to 5-year-old Creme Fraiche.

The season came down to a faceoff in the Breeders' Cup Classic between the last two Derby winners. Ferdinand had lost 8 of his first 9 starts after the 1986 Derby but then hit stride halfway through his 4-year-old campaign, winning the Hollywood Gold Cup, Cabrillo, and Goodwood in succession. Alysheba had followed his Travers debacle with an easy victory in the Super Derby at Louisiana Downs.

In a rousing finish that lived up to its billing, Ferdinand got the jump and then held off Alysheba by a nose through a furious drive to win the race and the Horse of the Year and older-horse titles. Alysheba's gallant effort earned him the 3-year-old honors over Java Gold and Bet Twice, and several other Breeders' Cup winners cemented their championships with Cup triumphs: Epitome (2-year-old filly), Sacahuista (3-year-old filly), Theatrical (turf male), and Miesque (turf female).

The Cup was now the final arbiter of titles, and would be again in the 1988 season, an unforgettable year capped by a Breeders' Cup that many still call the most dramatic day of racing they have ever seen.

Forty Niner, a compact chestnut who did enough for trainer Stephens as a 2-year-old in 1987 to win the juvenile championship without running in the Breeders' Cup, was a solid early favorite for the 1988 Triple Crown races. In both the Florida Derby and the Lexington Stakes, however, the Mr. Prospector colt surrendered the lead in the stretch, fueling doubts about his ability to last 10 furlongs. Meanwhile, out west, an unusual rival emerged

In what many consider to be the most thrilling moment in racing history, Personal Ensign (OUTSIDE), *in her 13th and final career start, nips Derby winner Winning Colors at the wire of the 1988 Breeders' Cup Distaff, making her the first major horse in 80 years to retire undefeated.*

from the Lukas stable: Winning Colors, an Amazonian roan filly, clobbered her peers by eight lengths in the Santa Anita Oaks, then handled the boys just as easily, winning the Santa Anita Derby on the lead by 7½.

When the gates opened at Churchill Downs, Winning Colors shot to the lead again with Forty Niner tracking her in second. Turning for home, she was sailing along three in front while Forty Niner, still being conserved for the drive, had fallen back to fifth. He rallied furiously in the stretch, making up almost seven lengths, but fell a neck short of catching the filly. The big Secretariat colt Risen Star, who had run down Forty Niner in the Lexington, was a fast-closing third after a wide trip.

Lukas had his first Derby, and Stephens was determined not to let Winning Colors loose on the lead again. In the Preakness, Forty Niner was hustled to the front and stayed there for six furlongs, with the filly just a head behind. The early battle cost both horses any chance and set the table for Risen Star to come flying to a clear victory as Winning Colors tired to third and Forty Niner faded to seventh. For the Belmont, Forty Niner went to the sidelines, Winning Colors went to the lead but stopped after less than a mile, and Risen Star racked up the fastest time and widest margin since his sire's as he galloped home a 14¾-length winner.

It would be Risen Star's final race, but Forty Niner reemerged in the summer to win the Haskell and Travers in a pair of photos over another Mr. Prospector colt, Seeking the Gold, who represented the resurgent Ogden Phipps stable and its young trainer, Shug McGaughey. The Phippses had begun incorporating more speed influences into their breeding program and in the summer of 1988 saw it come to fruition with Seeking the Gold, the 2-year-old colt Easy Goer, and the 4-year-old filly Personal Ensign.

Easy Goer lost his debut by a neck but then quickly stamped himself as a special 2-year-old. A chestnut son of Alydar and the champion mare Relaxing, he would settle early and then unleash spectacular moves around the turn, a particularly effective style at sweeping Belmont Park, where he scored stunning victories in the Cowdin and the Champagne.

Personal Ensign, by Private Account, won her only two starts at 2, including the Frizette, then fractured a rear pastern shortly before the 1986 Breeders' Cup and was sidelined nearly a year. She returned at 3 with screws in her ankle and won all four of her starts, including the Beldame. When she began her 4-year-old campaign with daylight victories in the Shuvee, Hempstead, and Molly Pitcher, fans noticed she was now 9 for 9 and turf writers began hitting the history books to find the last comparable undefeated racehorse. There had been none since Colin, 15 for 15 in 1907-08.

Personal Ensign made it 10 for 10 trying males, running down Gulch to win a three-horse Whitney. A sterner test came in the Maskette, where a rested Winning Colors opened a clear lead, but Personal Ensign was up in time to win by three-quarters of a length. She then ran her record to 12 for 12 with a romp at 1-10 in the Beldame.

It would have been an outstanding season even without the star of the handicap division. Alysheba was a much better colt at 4 and proved it by winning the Strub and then edging Ferdinand in the Santa Anita Handicap and the San Bernardino. He followed defeats in the Pimlico Special and Hollywood Gold Cup with a rousing score over Bet Twice and Gulch in the Iselin, then came back to New York. His sporting owners, Clarence and Dorothy Scharbauer, decided to silence those who said Alysheba could not win east of the Hudson without his usual Lasix and took him off the medication for the Woodward, where he threaded his way through traffic to nail Forty Niner by a neck.

The 1988 Breeders' Cup was the first held at Churchill Downs, and despite damp and chilly weather drew a crowd of 71,237. They were in for a memorable day. Gulch, so often overshadowed by the strong 3-year-old class of '87, rallied powerfully to win the Sprint, earning that division's title. Miesque became the first repeater in Cup history, again coming over from France to take the Mile with a flourish. Open Mind led a 1-2-3 finish by

With darkness about to fall, Alysheba holds off a late run from Seeking the Gold to win the 1988 Breeders' Cup Classic. The victory put Alysheba at the top of the list of Thoroughbred money winners.

Lukas trainees in the Juvenile Fillies. Easy Goer failed to catch Is It True on a muddy track he never picked up, but would still be champion at year's end.

The day came down to the Distaff and the Classic. In the Maskette rematch everyone had been waiting for, between a Derby-winning filly and an unbeaten 4-year-old making what had been announced as her final career start, Winning Colors came onto the track breathing fire and quickly opened a clear lead; Personal Ensign seemed to be slipping and sliding in the slop and was eight lengths back after six furlongs. Turning for home, her task seemed hopeless. She was still four lengths behind with a furlong to go, but somehow Personal Ensign kicked into high gear and began slashing into the lead, lunging at the wire to remain undefeated by a nose.

The skies were nearly dark when post time arrived for the Classic. Alysheba now had to win to ensure Horse of the Year honors over Personal Ensign, while Forty Niner had one last chance to unseat the retired Risen Star for the 3-year-old title. Waquoit led down the backstretch and Forty Niner made his move but was gunned into the worst going at the rail and fell back after stepping on a soft spot. Alysheba launched his bid on the turn and hauled in Waquoit, but now Seeking the Gold was flying down the center of the track. Those two battled to the wire and Alysheba prevailed by half a length, nailing down top honors and running his bankroll to a record $6,679,242.

The decade ended with a season dominated by its best rivalry. Like Affirmed and Alydar 11 years earlier, Sunday Silence and Easy Goer were not only inches apart, but also miles ahead of their contemporaries.

Easy Goer came back bigger and better at 3, winning the Swale by nearly nine lengths and then roaring to a 13-length Gotham victory with a mile in 1:32⅖, the fastest ever by a 3-year-old. A workmanlike three-length Wood Memorial triumph seemed to prime him perfectly for Kentucky.

On the other coast, a challenger emerged. Having waited 26 years between Derby starters, Charlie Whittingham was back three years after Ferdinand, with a colt named Sunday Silence who came from just off the pace to win the Santa Anita Derby by 11.

The two arrived in Louisville as the favorites and as a study in complementary contrasts. They had grown up eight miles apart in the Bluegrass on the farms of two brothers. Easy Goer, with his regal pedigree, had been foaled at Seth Hancock's Claiborne Farm while Sunday Silence had been born and raised at renegade elder brother Arthur's Stone Farm. Easy Goer had run all but one of his races in New York, while Sunday Silence had not left California. Easy Goer, an enormous chestnut, was the classic pride of the Eastern establishment while the slender, raven-coated Sunday Silence carried the banner of California, which was on a Derby roll with Ferdinand, Alysheba, and Winning Colors.

The epic rivalry between Sunday Silence and Easy Goer was at its most dramatic in the 1989 Preakness. The multi-staged battle ended with Sunday Silence (LEFT) a desperate nose in front.

The Derby looked like Affirmed and Alydar all over again, as the nimbler Sunday Silence sliced to the lead in upper stretch and Easy Goer came with too little too late, barely edging stablemate Awe Inspiring for second. For Easy Goer's downhearted fans, it felt like the previous November, and not just because the Derby Day temperature – the coldest on record – dipped to 43 degrees; for a second time, their champion had seemed not to fire his usual powerful shot over the muddy track. McGaughey wondered whether his colt simply didn't relish Churchill Downs, scene of his only other defeat since his debut.

The Preakness two weeks later ended with a breathtaking stretch duel. This time Easy Goer was sharper, and moved outside the Lukas-trained Houston to seize a brief lead before Sunday Silence joined him. Easy Goer dropped to the inside and seemed sure to blow by, but the two colts matched strides every step of the way, and it was Sunday Silence by a nose at the wire. Had Sunday Silence proved his superiority or had the wide-running Easy Goer fallen into a trap in tight quarters?

Sunday Silence was finally favored in the Belmont, and this time it wasn't close. He made a nice move after a mile to take the lead between calls, but Easy Goer was on his home court and the extra distance was going to work to his advantage. He swept by his nemesis in upper stretch and ran off by himself, scoring by eight lengths in a brilliant 2:26, the second-fastest Belmont ever.

This race seemed like the true bill, and Easy Goer's excuses in the prior two legs suddenly sounded more plausible. Sunday Silence's stock dropped when he lost the Swaps in his next start to the unheralded Prized. Meanwhile, Easy Goer became the toast of racing in the months ahead, running off consecutive victories in the Whitney, Travers, Woodward, and Jockey Club Gold Cup. Sunday Silence returned with an easy but otherwise uninspiring victory in the Super Derby. So despite Sunday Silence's 2-1 lead in matchups, the two colts headed for Breeders' Cup VI at Gulfstream Park in the same roles they had played in the spring classics: Easy Goer the odds-on favorite, Sunday Silence the outsider with something to prove.

Easy Goer broke slowly and fell far behind as Sunday Silence stalked in third behind Slew City Slew and Blushing John, the latter a Pimlico Special and Hollywood Gold Cup winner who would be named champion older horse at year's end. Turning for home, Easy Goer was 4½ lengths back, and was basically no closer when Sunday Silence finally collared Blushing John with a furlong to go. Pat Day, determined to beat Sunday Silence by nailing him with a single rush rather than engaging in a Preakness-like duel, finally turned his colt loose but it was too late. Gaining with every massive stride, Easy Goer fell a neck short and Sunday Silence dug in for his third victory in four meetings.

In the absence of either, the other would have been a dominant Triple Crown winner with only history as a benchmark. Instead, each proved the other's greatness and provided superb drama in the process.

Nine years earlier, on a September afternoon at Belmont Park, Spectacular Bid had capped his career alone and unchallenged. Now that kind of solitary triumph seemed inconceivable. The Breeders' Cup had created a new theater of war, and the last, epic battle between Sunday Silence and Easy Goer was a fitting finale to the decade.

CHAMPIONS

PAST PERFORMANCES

THE 1980's

YEAR BY YEAR CHAMPIONS

•1980•
•2-YEAR-OLD MALE *Lord Avie* •2-YEAR-OLD FILLY *Heavenly Cause* •3-YEAR-OLD MALE *Temperence Hill*
•3-YEAR-OLD FILLY *Genuine Risk* •HANDICAP HORSE *Spectacular Bid* •HANDICAP MARE *Glorious Song*
•GRASS HORSE *John Henry (M) Just a Game II (F)* •SPRINTER *Plugged Nickle* •STEEPLECHASE *Zaccio*
•HORSE OF THE YEAR Spectacular Bid

•1981•
•2-YEAR-OLD MALE *Deputy Minister* •2-YEAR-OLD FILLY *Before Dawn* •3-YEAR-OLD MALE *Pleasant Colony*
•3-YEAR-OLD FILLY *Wayward Lass* •HANDICAP HORSE *John Henry* •HANDICAP MARE *Relaxing*
•GRASS HORSE *John Henry (M) De La Rose (F)* •SPRINTER *Guilty Conscience* •STEEPLECHASE *Zaccio*
•HORSE OF THE YEAR John Henry

•1982•
•2-YEAR-OLD MALE *Roving Boy* •2-YEAR-OLD FILLY *Landaluce* •3-YEAR-OLD MALE *Conquistador Cielo*
•3-YEAR-OLD FILLY *Christmas Past* •HANDICAP HORSE *Lemhi Gold* •HANDICAP MARE *Track Robbery*
•GRASS HORSE *Perrault (M) April Run (F)* •SPRINTER *Gold Beauty* •STEEPLECHASE *Zaccio*
•HORSE OF THE YEAR Conquistador Cielo

•1983•
•2-YEAR-OLD MALE *Devil's Bag* •2-YEAR-OLD FILLY *Althea* •3-YEAR-OLD MALE *Slew o' Gold*
•3-YEAR-OLD FILLY *Heartlight No. One* •HANDICAP HORSE *Bates Motel* •HANDICAP MARE *Ambassador of Luck*
•GRASS HORSE *John Henry (M) All Along (F)* •SPRINTER *Chinook Pass* •STEEPLECHASE *Flatterer*
•HORSE OF THE YEAR All Along

•1984•
•2-YEAR-OLD MALE *Chief's Crown* •2-YEAR-OLD FILLY *Outstandingly* •3-YEAR-OLD MALE *Swale*
•3-YEAR-OLD FILLY *Life's Magic* •HANDICAP HORSE *Slew o' Gold* •HANDICAP MARE *Princess Rooney*
•GRASS HORSE *John Henry (M) Royal Heroine (F)* •SPRINTER *Eillo* •STEEPLECHASE *Flatterer*
•HORSE OF THE YEAR John Henry

•1985•
•2-YEAR-OLD MALE *Tasso* •2-YEAR-OLD FILLY *Family Style* •3-YEAR-OLD MALE *Spend a Buck*
•3-YEAR-OLD FILLY *Mom's Command* •HANDICAP HORSE *Vanlandingham* •HANDICAP MARE *Life's Magic*
•GRASS HORSE *Cozzene (M) Pebbles (F)* •SPRINTER *Precisionist* •STEEPLECHASE *Flatterer*
•HORSE OF THE YEAR Spend a Buck

•1986•
•2-YEAR-OLD MALE *Capote* •2-YEAR-OLD FILLY *Brave Raj* •3-YEAR-OLD MALE *Snow Chief*
•3-YEAR-OLD FILLY *Tiffany Lass* •HANDICAP HORSE *Turkoman* •HANDICAP MARE *Lady's Secret*
•GRASS HORSE *Manila (M) Estrapade (F)* •SPRINTER *Smile* •STEEPLECHASE *Flatterer*
•HORSE OF THE YEAR Lady's Secret

•1987•
•2-YEAR-OLD MALE *Forty Niner* •2-YEAR-OLD FILLY *Epitome* •3-YEAR-OLD MALE *Alysheba*
•3-YEAR-OLD FILLY *Sacahuista* •HANDICAP HORSE *Ferdinand* •HANDICAP MARE *North Sider*
•GRASS HORSE *Theatrical (M) Miesque (F)* •SPRINTER *Groovy* •STEEPLECHASE *Inlander*
•HORSE OF THE YEAR Ferdinand

•1988•
•2-YEAR-OLD MALE *Easy Goer* •2-YEAR-OLD FILLY *Open Mind* •3-YEAR-OLD MALE *Risen Star*
•3-YEAR-OLD FILLY *Winning Colors* •HANDICAP HORSE *Alysheba* •HANDICAP MARE *Personal Ensign*
•GRASS HORSE *Sunshine Forever (M) Miesque (F)* •SPRINTER *Gulch* •STEEPLECHASE *Jimmy Lorenzo*
•HORSE OF THE YEAR Alysheba

•1989•
•2-YEAR-OLD MALE *Rhythm* •2-YEAR-OLD FILLY *Go for Wand* •3-YEAR-OLD MALE *Sunday Silence*
•3-YEAR-OLD FILLY *Open Mind* •HANDICAP HORSE *Blushing John* •HANDICAP MARE *Bayakoa*
•GRASS HORSE *Steinlen (M) Brown Bess (F)* •SPRINTER *Safely Kept* •STEEPLECHASE *Highland Bud*
•HORSE OF THE YEAR Sunday Silence

All Along (Fr)

b. f. 1979, by Targowice (Round Table)–Agujita, by Vieux Manoir — Lifetime record: 21 9 4 2 $3,015,764

Own.– D. Wildenstein
Br.– Dayton Ltd (Fr)
Tr.– Patrick L. Biancone

10Nov84- 6Hol	fm 1½Ⓣ	:491 1:131 2:011 2:251	3↑ BC Turf-G1	7 7 73¼ 1½ 11 2nk	Cordero A Jr	123	3.20	94-00	Lashkari122nkAllAlong123½Ram122½ Failed to hold winner	11
21Oct84- 7WO	gd 1⅝Ⓣ	:491 1:391 2:044 2:424	3↑ Rothmans Int'l-G1	5 8 812 63¾ 34 42¼	Swinburn WR	123	*.75	84-15	Majesty'sPrince1262JckSld126noEsprtduNord126nk Bid,hung	9
7Oct84♦ Longchamp(Fr)	sf *1½ⓉRH	2:39	3↑ Prix de l'Arc de Triomphe-G1 Stk550000	38	Swinburn WR	127	2.90e		Sagace1302Northern Trick1206All Along127¾ Progress into 7th 2½f out,mild late gain.Sadler's Wells 8th	22
22Sep84- 8Bel	fm 1½Ⓣ	:484 1:13 2:013 2:251	3↑ Turf Classic-G1	1 4 43 32½ 33 44¼	Swinburn WR	123	1.80	94-10	JohnHenry126nkWin1264Majesty's Prince126hd Flattened out	6
12Nov83- 8Lrl	yl 1½Ⓣ	:514 1:173 2:084 2:35	3↑ DC Int'l-G1	6 6 52½ 13½ 16 13¼	Swinburn WR	124	*.40	44-56	AllAlong1243¼WelshTerm1272¾Majsty'sPrnc127hd Ridden out	8
29Oct83- 8Aqu	yl 1½Ⓣ	:494 1:144 2:09 2:34	3↑ Turf Classic-G1	10 3 36½ 2hd 14 18¾	Swinburn WR	123	*.90	71-29	AllAlong1238¾ThunderPuddles1261½ErinsIsl1261 Ridden out	10
16Oct83- 9WO	yl 1⅝Ⓣ	:511 1:42 2:45	3↑ Rothmans Int'l-G1	5 10 811 42½ 11½ 12	Swinburn WR	123	*1.65	75-25	AllAlong1232ThundrPuddls126¾Mjsty'sPrnc126nk Drew clear	11
2Oct83♦ Longchamp(Fr)	fm*1½ⓉRH	2:28	3↑ Prix de l'Arc de Triomphe-G1 Stk635000	11	Swinburn WR	127	17.30e		All Along1271Sun Princess120nkLuth Enchantee120no Rated in midpack,rail bid 2f out,led 100y out. Time Charter 4th	26
11Sep83♦ Longchamp(Fr)	sf *1½ⓉRH	2:403	3↑ Prix Foy-G3 Stk39600	2¾	Head F	120	6.00		Time Charter127¾All Along120½Great Substence1262 Rated in 7th,lacked room 2f out,angled out,gaining late	11
3Jly83♦ Saint-Cloud(Fr)	gd *1 9/16ⓉLH	2:344	3↑ Grand Prix de Saint-Cloud-G1 Stk276000	77¾	Starkey G	131	5.75		Diamond Shoal134¾Lancastrian134¾Zalataia129¾ Tracked in 3rd,weakened 1½f out,bled.Lemhi Gold 4th	9
12Jun83♦ Chantilly(Fr)	fm*1½ⓉRH	2:242	4↑ La Coupe-G3 Stk44200	32¾	Starkey G	127	*1.20		Zalataia1242Flower Prince123¾All Along1276 Tracked leader,led 2f out,headed and faded 150y out	8
28Nov82♦ Tokyo(Jpn)	fm*1½ⓉLH	2:27	3↑ Japan Cup-G1 Stk940000	2nk	Moore GW	117	5.20		Half Iced121nkAll Along117nkApril Run1211 Closed well	15
3Oct82♦ Longchamp(Fr)	sf *1½ⓉRH	2:37	3↑ Arc de Triomphe-G1 Stk637000	1521	Starkey G	120	17.00		Akiyda120hdArdross130½Awaasif120hd Raced in midpack to 3f out,weakened quickly	17
12Sep82♦ Longchamp(Fr)	fm*1½ⓉRH	2:293	ⒻPrix Vermeille-G1 Stk191000	11½	Starkey G	128	7.30		All Along1281½Akiyda128hdGrease128¾ Tracked in 3rd,led 2½f out,ridden out.Zalataia 6th	13
14Jly82♦ Saint-Cloud(Fr)	gd *1 9/16ⓉLH	2:463	3↑ Prix Maurice de Nieuil-G2 Stk95600	1½	Gorli S	113	5.20		All Along113½No Attention1283Arc d'Or1282 Close up,led 1f out,held well	12
13Jun82♦ Chantilly(Fr)	sf *1 5/16ⓉRH	2:164	ⒻPrix de Diane-G1 223000	55¾	Gorli S	128	13.00		Harbour1282Akiyda1282Paradise128¾ Tracked in 4th,led briefly 1½f out,weakened 170y out	14
5Jun82♦ Epsom(GB)	fm 1½ⓉLH	2:321	ⒻEnglish Oaks-G1 Stk220000	65¾	St. Martin Y	126			Time Charter1261Slightly Dangerous1261½Last Feather126¾ Toward rear,brief bid 2f out,one-paced late.Awaasif 4th	13
23May82♦ Longchamp(Fr)	sf *1¼ⓉRH	2:20	ⒻPrix Saint-Alary-G1 Stk127000	24	Gorli S	128	*.70		Harbour1284All Along1281½Perlee128nk Well placed in 3rd,led 2f to 1f out,no chance with winner	8
27Mar82♦ Saint-Cloud(Fr)	sf *1 5/16ⓉLH	2:232	ⒻPrix Penelope-G3 Stk51000	14	Gorli S	123			All Along1234Paradise1231Charmer1231 Strong run to lead 1f out,ridden clear	11
27Feb82♦ Saint-Cloud(Fr)	hy *1¼ⓉLH	2:241	ⒻPrix Mirska Alw18800	14	Gorli S	123			All Along1234Zalataia1231Magic and Magic1231 Tracked in 3rd,led 2f out,easily. Previously trained by Maurice Zilber	13
10Nov81♦ Amiens(Fr)	sf *1 50ⓉRH		ⒻPrix d'Hornoy Mdn7200	1nk	Vache S	119			[DH]All Along119[DH]Tarbelissima118nkVitilla1211 Tracked leader,dueled 1f out,gamely.Time not taken	12

Althea

ch. f. 1981, by Alydar (Raise a Native)–Courtly Dee, by Never Bend — Lifetime record: 15 8 4 0 $1,275,255

Own.– Alexander & Aykroyd & Groves
Br.– Groves–Alexander–Aykroyd (Ky)
Tr.– D. Wayne Lukas

27Jun84- 8Hol	fst 7f	:214 :442 1:083 1:211	3↑ ⒻA Gleam 66k	7 2 21 21 34½ 612	Valenzuela PA	116	*1.20	79-19	Lass Trump1161Pleasure Cay1165½Angel Savage1122 Tired	9
5May84- 8CD	fst 1¼	:472 1:114 1:363 2:022	Ky Derby-G1	1 1 11 55 1922 1930¾	McCarron CJ	121	*2.80e	54-19	Swale1263¼Coax Me Chad1262At the Threshold126nk Tired	20
21Apr84- 9OP	fst 1⅛	:463 1:101 1:352 1:464	Ark Derby-G1	10 1 11 1½ 16 17	Valenzuela PA	121	3.00	109-04	Althea1217PineCircle118noGateDancer118no Kept to drive	11
14Apr84- 9OP	fst 1 1/16	:23 :463 1:104 1:411	ⒻFantasy-G1	1 6 52 31½ 1hd 2¾	Pincay L Jr	121	*.60	101-10	MyDarlingOne121¾Alth12110PrsonblLdy118¾ Poor st,drifted	6
11Mar84- 8SA	fst 1 1/16	:232 :472 1:113 1:433	ⒻS Susana-G1	2 3 32 1½ 11 1¾	Pincay L Jr	117	*.60	83-18	Althea117¾PersonableLady115hdLife'sMagc1164 Proved best	5
25Feb84- 8SA	fst 1	:224 :462 1:11 1:37	ⒻLas Virgenes 250k	1 5 51¾ 42 42½ 1no	Pincay L Jr	124	*1.00	83-18	Althea124noVagabondGal117nkMyDarlingOn1143¼ Rough trip	6
18Dec83- 8Hol	fst 1 1/16	:222 :454 1:101 1:413	Hol Futurity-G1	4 2 2½ 1hd 34 611	Pincay L Jr	118	2.80	76-14	FaliTime121½BoldT.Jay1213½Life'sMagic1183 Led,weakened	12
27Nov83- 8Hol	fst 1 1/16	:23 :464 1:112 1:43	ⒻHol Starlet-G2	6 1 11 11 11½ 11½	Pincay L Jr	120	*1.20	80-20	Althea1201½Life's Magic120hdSpring Loose1202½ Driving	6
12Nov83- 8SA	sly 1 1/16	:224 :463 1:113 1:442	ⒻOak Leaf-G1	1 1 11 11½ 1½ 2½	Pincay L Jr	117	*.90	78-23	Life's Magic115½Althea11717Percipient115hd Game try	9
26Oct83- 8SA	fst 7f	:222 :451 1:10 1:231	ⒻAnoakia-G3	2 2 2hd 2hd 2½ 21¼	Pincay L Jr	123	*.10	83-20	Percipient1171¼Althea1231½Personable Lady117½ Bore out	4
14Sep83- 8Dmr	fst 1	:223 :454 1:102 1:344	Dmr Futurity-G2	4 1 11 12½ 16 16½	Pincay L Jr	117	*.30	94-14	Althea1176½Juliet's Pride1154Gumboy1142½ Easy score	5
4Sep83- 8Dmr	fst 1	:223 :453 1:102 1:36	ⒻDebutante-G2	4 1 110 114 114 115	Pincay L Jr	119	*.30	88-17	Althea11915Diachrony1134Victorous Joy113½ Easily	6
23Jly83- 8Hol	fst 6f	:214 :441 :564 1:092	Juv Champ-G2	3 4 2hd 13 17 110	Pincay L Jr	117	2.30	90-21	Althea11710RejectedSuitor1171AutoCommander1171½ Easily	9
9Jly83- 8Hol	fst 6f	:22 :444 :573 1:103	ⒻLandaluce-G2	11 1 2hd 2hd 1hd 22	Pincay L Jr	117	*.40e	82-23	Simple Magic1162Althea11713Reb's Gateau1161½ Game try	11
22Jun83- 6Hol	fst 5f	:214 :443 :57	ⒻMd Sp Wt	10 1 2hd 1½ 12½ 16½	Pincay L Jr	117	*.80	92-19	Althea1176½MissCamouflage116noBigPotential1165½ Driving	10

Alysheba

b. c. 1984, by Alydar (Raise a Native)–Bel Sheba, by Lt. Stevens — Lifetime record: 26 11 8 2 $6,679,242

Own.– Dorothy & Pam Scharbauer
Br.– Preston Madden (Ky)
Tr.– Jack C. Van Berg

5Nov88-10CD	my 1¼	:474 1:122 1:383 2:044	3↑ BC Classic-G1	5 4 48½ 31 1hd 1½	McCarron CJ	126		*1.50	73-20	Alyshb126½SkngthGold1225Wquot126nk Bumped start,driving	9
14Oct88-10Med	fst 1¼	:461 1:092 1:334 1:584	3↑ Med Cup H-G1	3 3 37 21 1hd 1nk	McCarron CJ	127		*.50	108-05	Alysheba127nkSlewCitySlew1166¼PleasntVrgnn114nk Driving	5
17Sep88- 8Bel	fst 1¼	:473 1:111 1:35 1:592	3↑ Woodward H-G1	4 3 31 3½ 3½ 1nk	McCarron CJ	126		*1.80	101-08	Alysheba126nkForty Niner119nkWaquoit1221¼ Driving	8
27Aug88- 9Mth	fst 1⅛	:462 1:094 1:343 1:474	3↑ Iselin H-G1	4 5 511 45 22½ 1¾	McCarron CJ	124		*1.00	95-12	Alysheba124¾Bet Twice1234Gulch1222½ Driving	6
26Jun88- 8Hol	fst 1¼	:454 1:093 1:342 1:592	3↑ Hol Gold Cup H-G1	6 5 58 31½ 24 26½	McCarron CJ	126	b	*1.00	88-07	Cutlass Reality1166½Alysheba1265½Ferdinand1254 2nd best	6
14May88- 8Pim	fst 1 3/16	:462 1:102 1:352 1:541	4↑ Pim Spl H 600k	2 3 32 2½ 44½ 44¼	McCarron CJ	127	b	*.60	92-19	BetTwice124¾LostCode1261Cryptoclearanc1212½ Drifted str	6
17Apr88- 8SA	fst 1⅛	:462 1:094 1:343 1:471	4↑ S Bernardino H-G2	1 2 21½ 1hd 2hd 1no	McCarron CJ	127	b	*.80	93-17	Alysheba127noFerdinand127hdGood Taste1133½ Driving	5
6Mar88- 8SA	fst 1¼	:463 1:10 1:343 1:594	4↑ S Anita H-G1	2 3 33 1½ 11 1½	McCarron CJ	126	b	*1.00	90-13	Alysheba126½Ferdinand1272½Super Diamond1242¼ Driving	4
7Feb88- 8SA	fst 1¼	:453 1:094 1:351 2:002	C H Strub-G1	3 5 58½ 1hd 1hd 13	McCarron CJ	126	b	*.90	87-16	Alysheba1263Candi's Gold1178On the Line1198½ Drew out	6
21Nov87- 7Hol	fst 1¼	:462 1:101 1:352 2:012	3↑ BC Classic-G1	9 9 98¼ 54 41 2no	McCarron CJ	122	b	3.60	85-12	Ferdinand126noAlysheba1221¼JudgAnglucc1261½ Just missed	12
27Sep87-10LaD	fst 1¼	:47 1:112 1:362 2:031	Super Derby-G1	2 7 76½ 32½ 21 1½	McCarron CJ	126	b	*.50	85-19	Alysheba126½Candi'sGold1261½Parochil1263¼ Brushed rival	8
22Aug87- 8Sar	sly 1¼	:461 1:10 1:362 2:02	Travers-G1	6 7 712 78½ 69 620¼	McCarron CJ	126	b	*2.50	70-16	JavaGold1262Cryptoclearance1266¾PolshNvy1261½ No factor	9
1Aug87- 9Mth	fst 1⅛	:463 1:093 1:34 1:47	Haskell Inv'l H-G1	4 2 32½ 21 32½ 2nk	McCarron CJ	126	b	1.50	99-07	BetTwice126nkAlysheba126nkLostCod12412 In close on turn	5
6Jun87- 8Bel	fst 1½	:492 1:134 2:03 2:281	Belmont-G1	3 4 47 47 39 414¼	McCarron CJ	126	b	*.80	65-15	Bet Twice12614Cryptoclearance126noGulch126nk Rough trip	9
16May87- 9Pim	fst 1 3/16	:471 1:113 1:364 1:554	Preakness-G1	6 6 56½ 43 2hd 1½	McCarron CJ	126	b	*2.00	88-18	Alysheba126½Bet Twice1261½Cryptoclearance1263½ Driving	9

2May87- 8CD fst 1¼ :462 1:11 1:364 2:032 Ky Derby-G1 3 14 1312 31½ 21 1¾ McCarron CJ 126 b 8.40 80-09 Alysheba126¾BetTwice1262¼AvisCopy126nk Stumbled midstr 17
23Apr87- 7Kee fst 1⅛ :464 1:102 1:361 1:482 Blue Grass-G1 4 4 32 42½ 2hd 1hd McCarron CJ 121 b *.90 95-13 [D]Alysheba121hdWar121hdLeo Castelli1218 Ducked out 5
Disqualified and placed third
22Mar87- 8SA gd 1 1/16 :224 :462 1:104 1:43 San Felipe H-G1 3 7 76½ 63½ 4¾ 2¾ Day P 120 b 3.30 85-23 ChartheStars116¾Alysheb1202¾TmprtSl1222½ Lugged in str 8
8Mar87- 9SA fst 1 1/16 :231 :464 1:112 1:43 Alw 30000 6 4 44½ 45 44 45 Day P 114 b *.70 81-15 Barb's Relic1172¾Blanco114¾Rakaposhi1141½ No rally 9
14Dec86- 8Hol fst 1 :221 :444 1:093 1:361 Hol Futurity-G1 12 4 41¾ 22½ 2½ 2nk Day P 121 b 6.60e 82-18 TemperateSl121nkAlyshb121nkMstrfulAdvoct1212¼ Sharp try 12
1Nov86- 1SA fst 1 1/16 :222 :454 1:102 1:434 BC Juvenile-G1 4 13 1211 98¾ 77½ 32½ Shoemaker W 122 b 33.40 79-13 Capote1221¼Qualify1221¼Alysheba1222¼ Angled out str 13
10Oct86- 7Kee fst 1 1/16 :234 :473 1:122 1:451 Breeders' Futurity-G2 10 4 41½ 31½ 2hd 2¾ Brumfield D 121 b 4.30 79-18 Orono121¾Alysheba1211¼Pledge Card1211 Wide 10
27Sep86- 9TP gd 1 :213 :45 1:104 1:371 In Memoriam 120k 4 5 33 1½ 2hd 2½ Brumfield D 120 b *2.30 91-07 RainbowEast120½Alysheba12012DavidL.'sRib1206 Game try 11
14Sep86- 3TP fst 1 1/16 :24 :481 1:131 1:462 Md Sp Wt 4 1 1hd 1½ 13 18 Brumfield D 119 b *.30 78-22 Alysheba1198Aerator119½Najor Domo1196 Easily 12
22Aug86- 9AP fst 1 :232 :462 1:111 1:364 Md Sp Wt 9 6 64¾ 34 33 2hd Day P 120 1.80 77-14 GemMaster120hdAlysheba1203¼Contractor'sTun12014 Rallied 10
21Jly86- 4Hol fst 5½f :222 :454 :581 1:05 Md Sp Wt 2 6 46½ 47 56 54¾ Romero RP 118 2.40 84-16 FleetingJet118½BiloxiBlues1181¼SoyAmigo1182¾ No rally 7

Ambassador of Luck

b. f. 1979, by What Luck (Bold Ruler)–Detente, by Dark Ruler **Lifetime record: 23 14 4 3 $489,583**

Own.– Envoy Stable
Br.– C.T. Fuller (Pa)
Tr.– Mitchell C. Preger

14Sep84- 8Bel fst 7f :231 :462 1:103 1:23 3↑ Ⓕ Alw 33000 4 6 21 2hd 11½ 1¾ Graell A 115 *.60 87-18 AmbassadorofLuck115¾QuixoticLady1192¾MadamForbes122¾ 6
Bumped,hand ride
18Aug84- 3Sar fst 6f :221 :451 1:094 3↑ Ⓕ Revidere 55k 1 7 43 31½ 21½ 31½ Graell A 122 *.80 89-15 MadmForbs1171¼OnthBnch117nkAmbssdrofLck122¾ Weakened 7
4Sep83- 8Bel fst 1 :224 :452 1:101 1:362 3↑ Ⓕ Maskette-G1 6 1 11½ 13 14 15 Graell A 116 *.20 83-13 AmbassadorofLuck1165A Kiss forLuck120hdAmCapable1094½ 6
Ridden out
5Aug83- 8Sar fst 7f :23 :461 1:094 1:221 3↑ Ⓕ Ballerina-G3 3 1 21½ 1hd 11½ 11 Graell A 124 *.60 91-14 AmbassadorofLck1241Number1193¾BroomDance1223 Driving 4
Previously owned by S.D. Peskoff
4Jly83- 9Mth fst 1 1/16 :241 :47 1:094 1:411 3↑ Ⓕ Molly Pitcher H-G2 5 2 24 23 1½ 13½ Graell A 117 2.40 99-13 AmbassadorofLuck1173½Kattegat'sPride1221DanceNumber1155 8
Drew off
16Jun83- 8Bel fst 7f :224 :45 1:093 1:221 3↑ Ⓕ Handicap 35000 5 1 34½ 21½ 15 16 Graell A 124 *.90 91-22 AmbassadrofLck1246SproutedRye1212Syrnn1195 Ridden out 5
4Jun83- 7Bel gd 6f :22 :443 1:083 3↑ Ⓕ Alw 35000 5 2 21 1hd 11 14¾ Graell A 117 1.40 99-08 AmbassdrofLck1174¾JonesTimeMachine12211Mrs.Roberts1174¼ 5
Ridden out
12May83- 8Aqu fst 6f :232 :463 1:102 3↑ Ⓕ Handicap 35000 5 2 1hd 11½ 12 11½ Graell A 122 2.60 89-20 AmbassadorofLck1221½VivaSec1172½Mochil11810 Ridden out 5
Previously trained by Flint S. Schulhofer
11Sep82- 8Bel fst 1 :222 :45 1:094 1:344 3↑ Ⓕ Maskette-G1 6 5 41¼ 31 21½ 23½ Graell A 111 15.70 87-12 TooChic1103½AmbassadorofLuck1111AntiLib116¾ No match 8
6Sep82- 3Bel fm 1 1/16 [T] :241 :472 1:113 1:421 3↑ Ⓕ Alw 35000 3 3 32½ 31½ 31½ 31¼ Graell A 115 4.50 89-18 Norsan1121¼MajestcNorth115hdAmbssdorofLck1152 Even try 7
24Aug82- 7Sar fm 1 [T] :24 :473 1:113 1:364 3↑ Ⓕ Alw 35000 6 2 21 1hd 1hd 3nk Graell A 117 *2.50 92-12 Suspcous112noSunwontshn117nkAmbssdrofLck117¾ Weakened 7
5Aug82- 8Sar fst 7f :221 :45 1:094 1:224 Ⓕ Test-G2 7 2 33¼ 21½ 22 21 Graell A 121 29.20 87-16 GoldButy1161AmbssdrofLck1211¾Numbr1141¾ Best of others 12
25Jly82- 9WO fst 7f :221 :443 1:084 1:23 Ⓕ Duchess 56k 1 7 51¾ 31 12 1¾ Graell A 123 *1.75 94-12 AmbassadorofLuck123¾ProudLou1185Aironlass118no Driving 8
3Jly82- 10Suf fst 6f :22 :452 1:103 Ⓕ Pinafore 31k 1 8 73½ 41½ 11 11½ Graell A 122 *1.30 88-16 AmbassdrofLck1221½ASttusSymbol119nkNornd1121½ Driving 10
12Jun82- 10Suf fst 6f :221 :452 1:102 Ⓕ Linda 31k 6 3 2½ 11 13 1¾ Graell A 122 *1.40 89-16 AmbassdorofLck122½HopfulContrct1182Crushm1161¾ Driving 12
Previously owned by Ransom & Peskoff;previously trained by W.M. Carrelli
17Apr82- 7Kee sly 1 1/16 :233 :473 1:121 1:45 Ⓕ Ashland-G2 6 5 67 55 1013 1031 Day P 118 6.40e 50-21 Blush With Pride1182¾Exclusive Love116nkDelicate Ice11311 10
Fell back
7Apr82- 7Kee fst *7f 1:27 Ⓕ Alw 29940 1 4 11 1½ 2½ 45 McKnight J 120 *1.50 83-13 ExclusiveLov112hdNoonBlloon1202½AplchHony1232½ Gave way 7
12Mar82- 9OP fst 6f :213 :452 1:112 Ⓕ Magnolia 64k 9 5 55½ 32½ 31½ 23 Patterson G 121 *.60e 85-23 JasminJul1123AmbssdrofLck121½SnowPlow1213 Second best 12
Previously owned by R. Ransom
15Feb82- 9OP fst 6f :22 :463 1:121 Ⓕ M Washington 58k 6 - 13½ Patterson G 115 *1.40 84-22 AmbssdorofLck1153½Ecoled'Humanite1182ShadMss1122 Fog 8
31Oct81- 8Lrl fst 1 1/16 :23 :464 1:131 1:461 Ⓕ Selima-G1 2 1 12 1hd 11 22¼ Shoemaker W 119 3.90 75-24 SnowPlow1192¼Ambassador ofLuck1191ChillingThought1196 6
Drifted out
17Oct81- 6Key fst 6f :221 :452 1:104 Ⓕ Schuykill (Div 1) 22k 6 1 3nk 1½ 1½ 13¾ Black AS 115 6.00 88-18 AmbassadrofLck1153¾Delicate Ice115hdMarshua's Lady115hd 9
Ridden out
20Sep81- 9Lat fst 6f :223 :461 1:00 1:134 Ⓕ Clipsetta (Div 2) 11k 5 2 2½ 2½ 21 1¾ Sayler B 114 *.40 75-29 AmbassadorofLuck114¾GoldenTry110hdRiddles11312 Driving 7
5Sep81- 5RD fst 5½f :221 :451 :581 1:051 Ⓕ Md Sp Wt 4 1 12 14 18 116 Woods CR Jr 120 *1.10 89-27 AmbassdorofLck12016SummerTimeLass1207BestofQuiz1204 9
Easily

April Run (Ire)

b. f. 1978, by Run the Gantlet (Tom Rolfe)–April Fancy, by No Argument **Lifetime record: 18 8 2 4 $1,092,514**

Own.– Mrs B.R. Firestone
Br.– F. Feeney (Ire)
Tr.– Francois Boutin

28Nov82♦ Tokyo(Jpn) fm*1½Ⓣ LH 2:27 3↑ Japan Cup-G1 3½ Asmussen CB 121 1.80 Half Iced121nkAll Along117nkApril Run1211 15
Stk801000 Always close up,bid 1f out,outfinished.John Henry 13th
6Nov82- 8Lrl yl 1½Ⓣ :483 1:131 2:07 2:31 3↑ D C Int'l-G1 8 7 812 11 12 16½ Asmussen CB 124 *.70 64-36 April Run1246½Majesty's Prince1204½Thunder Puddles1201½ 10
Ridden out
23Oct82- 8Aqu fm 1½Ⓣ :501 1:14 2:052 2:294 3↑ Turf Classic-G1 2 5 46½ 43 11 16½ Asmussen CB 123 *1.30 92-08 AprlRn1236½Naskra'sBreeze1263¼BottldWtr1264¼ Ridden out 7
3Oct82♦ Longchamp(Fr) sf *1½Ⓣ RH 2:37 3↑ Prix de l'Arc de Triomphe-G1 4¾ Asmussen CB 127 15.00 Akiyda120hdArdross130½Awaasif120hd 17
Stk637000 Led briefly,soon lost place,8th 2½f out,gaining late
12Sep82♦ Longchamp(Fr) fm*1½Ⓣ RH 2:321 4↑ Prix Foy-G3 1no Piggott L 120 *.50 April Run120no[D]Mariacho123nkNo Attention1232 7
Stk47800 Led throughout,met challenge 1f out,very game
21Aug82♦ Deauville(Fr) gd *1 11/16Ⓣ RH 3:011 3↑ Ⓕ Prix de Pomone-G2 32 Moore GW 128 3.20 Zalataia119½Akiyda1281¾April Run128¾ 13
Stk63700 Midpack behind slow pace,impeded twice,finished well
2May82♦ Longchamp(Fr) gd *1 5/16Ⓣ RH 2:093 4↑ Prix Ganay-G1 99 Piggott L 124 3.50 Bikala128½Lancastrian1282Al Nasr128nk 10
Stk127000 Never a factor
18Apr82♦ Longchamp(Fr) fm*1½Ⓣ RH 2:322 4↑ Prix d'Hedouville (Listed) 41¼ Piggott L 124 *.70 Gap of Dunloe121nkProtection Racket128nkTwo Step121¾ 8
Stk30600 Toward rear,bid 1f out,finished well
7Nov81- 8Lrl fm 1½Ⓣ :502 1:153 2:064 2:311 3↑ D C Int'l-G1 1 4 42½ 2hd 1½ 21 Paquet P 117 3.20 62-37 ProvidentialII1271AprilRun1173½GalaxyLibra127¾ Lost whip 10
24Oct81- 8Aqu gd 1½Ⓣ :482 1:14 2:061 2:311 3↑ Turf Classic-G1 4 4 42½ 2hd 13½ 1¾ Paquet P 118 2.60 85-15 AprlRn118¾GalxyLibra1263TheVeryOne1235 Bore out,driving 9
4Oct81♦ Longchamp(Fr) yl *1½Ⓣ RH 2:351 3↑ Prix de l'Arc de Triomphe-G1 3¾ Paquet P 120 6.50e Gold River127¾Bikala123noApril Run1202 24
Stk595000 Midpack,checked 1½f out,angled out,held by first two
13Sep81♦ Longchamp(Fr) gd *1½Ⓣ RH 2:324 Ⓕ Prix Vermeille-G1 11½ Paquet P 128 4.80 April Run1281½Leandra128hdMadam Gay1283 10
Stk208000 Tracked in 3rd,led 2f out,driving
22Aug81♦ Deauville(Fr) gd *1 11/16Ⓣ RH 3:014 3↑ Ⓕ Prix de Pomone-G3 15 Paquet P 123 *.50 April Run1235Anitra'sDance123nkTerre Froide1281½ 8
Stk47600 Rated at rear,rallied to lead 1f out,handily
5Jly81♦ Saint-Cloud(Fr) gd *1 9/16Ⓣ LH 2:384 3↑ Grand Prix de Saint-Cloud-G1 43¼ Paquet P 118 13.00 Akarad1212Bikala121½Lancastrian134nk 10
Stk240000 Well placed in 3rd,lacked rally

14Jun81♦ Chantilly(Fr) fm*1 5/16ⓉRH 2:062 ⒻPrix de Diane (French Oaks)-G1 Stk240000 34¼ Starkey G 128 4.70 Madam Gay1284Val d'Erica128nkApril Run128hd 14
Rated in 7th,bid 2f out,up for 3rd

16May81♦ Saint-Cloud(Fr) sf *1 5/16ⓉLH 2:202 ⒻPrix Cleopatre-G3 Stk49300 13 Paquet P 119 2.40 April Run1193Landresse1193Leandra1191½ 9
Led throughout,ridden clear 1f out

28Apr81♦ Saint-Cloud(Fr) gd *1½ⓉLH 2:342 ⒻPrix Dushka Mdn14600 16 Paquet P 126 6.80 April Run1266La Hougue126¾Heliade1202 17
Tracked leader,led 2f out,easily clear

28Mar81♦ Saint-Cloud(Fr) hy *1¼ⓉLH 2:234 ⒻPrix Dorina Mdn (FT)14000 22½ Paquet P 123 4.00 Marie d'Urcel1232½April Run1232Cariziana123nk 11
Tracked in 3rd,bid 2f out,second best

Bates Motel

b. c. 1979, by Sir Ivor (Sir Gaylord)–Sunday Purchase, by T.V. Lark **Lifetime record: 19 9 1 4 $851,050**

Own.– J. Getty Phillips & Riordan
Br.– Mrs G.F. Getty II (Ky)
Tr.– John H.M. Gosden

24Sep83- 8Bel fst 1¼ :472 1:111 1:361 2:011 3↑ Marlboro Cup H-G1 5 6 66½ 23 2½ 3¾ McCarron CJ 124 b *.80 91-17 HighlandBlade117nkSlewo'Gld119½BatesMotel1244 Weakened 9
3Sep83- 8Bel fst 1⅛ :454 1:092 1:34 1:463 3↑ Woodward-G1 5 5 73¾ 42½ 2hd 2no Lipham T 123 b *.60 94-13 Slewo'Gold118noBatesMotel1235SingSing1195 Just missed 10
20Aug83- 9Mth fst 1⅛ :463 1:101 1:343 1:471 3↑ Monmouth H-G1 6 6 67 63½ 12½ 12½ Lipham T 124 b *.90 99-16 BatesMotel1242½IslandWhirl124nkLinkage1152½ Ridden out 9
7Aug83- 8Dmr fst 1 1/16 :23 :46 1:103 1:41 3↑ San Diego H-G3 4 4 42½ 1hd 15 17 Lipham T 122 b *1.10 95-18 BatesMotel1227The Wonder123hdRunaway Groom1173 Easily 6
6Mar83- 8SA fst 1¼ :453 1:093 1:344 1:593 4↑ S Anita H-G1 13 13 911 52½ 11 12½ Lipham T 118 b 3.80 91-17 BatesMotl1182½It'sthOn123noWvrngMonrch1214½ Wide,clear 17
20Feb83- 8SA fst 1⅛ :454 1:093 1:343 1:47 4↑ S Antonio H-G1 7 9 915 78½ 12½ 13½ Lipham T 114 b 6.20 94-13 Bates Motel1143½Time to Explode121noIt's the One1243 10
Jostled,driving
6Feb83- 8SA my 1¼ :473 1:113 1:361 2:02 C H Strub-G1 3 4 43 76¾ 99¾ 1018 Lipham T 115 b 10.40 61-19 Swing Till Dawn1152Wavering Monarch1211Water Bank1172 10
Shuffled back st
1Jan83- 6SA fst 1 1/16 :23 :454 1:093 1:41 4↑ Alw 35000 3 2 21½ 2½ 12 11½ Lipham T 116 2.10 96-11 BatesMotel1161½ExclusiveOne1183FightingFit1166½ Driving 5
25Nov82- 8Hol fst 1 1/16 :224 :453 1:094 1:41 Affirmed H 85k 3 9 99¼ 78¼ 55 31¾ Lipham T 115 b 5.90 88-18 Poley118nkExclusiveEra1151½BatesMotel115hd Bobbled st. 11
17Oct82- 5SA fst 1 1/16 :223 :454 1:094 1:413 3↑ Alw 32000 10 7 83¼ 87¼ 53½ 11 Lipham T 118 b 3.30 93-09 BatesMotel1181Pettrax116nkWestCoastNative1112½ Driving 11
6Oct82- 6SA fst 1 :22 :443 1:092 1:342 Alw 30000 3 6 613 45½ 33½ 33 Lipham T 119 b 4.10 93-15 Jet Travel115hdPoley1173Bates Motel1193½ Lugged in 6
11Sep82-11Bmf fst 1 1/16 :224 :46 1:102 1:413 Sophomore H 21k 4 5 54½ 43 21 1nk Lipham T 114 b *1.20 91-19 Bates Motel114nkPet's Dude1146Top Pole1184 Driving 8
18Aug82- 5Dmr fst 1 1/16 :223 :452 1:101 1:414 Alw 15000 1 3 36 2½ 2hd 14 Lipham T 114 b 15.90 91-21 Bates Motel1144Penngrove1122Royal Serb1182 Driving 6
11Aug82- 5Dmr fst 1 1/16 :224 :461 1:103 1:423 Alw 15000 5 5 64½ 75¼ 78 710 Lipham T 117 b 16.80 77-16 Poley1152Checker's Orphan115nkDurable115hd No factor 8
5Jly82- 9Hol fm 1Ⓣ :232 :462 1:101 1:344 Alw 21000 7 10 1020 1022 1020 1017 McCarron CJ 120 *2.30 78-06 Prosperous115nkSir Pele1202½Salty Creek117no Dull 10
31May82- 6Hol fst 1 1/16 :224 :462 1:11 1:432 3↑ Md Sp Wt 7 3 32 22½ 13½ 18 McCarron CJ 114 b 3.40 78-19 Bates Motel1148Crimson Axe1093The Hague1173½ Easily 11
1May82- 6Hol fst 1 1/16 :231 :464 1:114 1:432 3↑ Md Sp Wt 12 9 1010 64 56½ 43½ Sibille R 115 b 10.60 74-15 Valais114½Bruin County1242½Tree Runner114½ Wide 12
4Apr82- 3SA fst 1 1/16 :222 :453 1:101 1:422 ©Md Sp Wt 10 12 1227 1118 414 39¼ Sibille R 118 b 60.70 80-09 Donbion1183¼Chargeur1186Bates Motel118½ Stumbled start 12
28Feb82- 2SA fst 1 1/16 :23 :462 1:104 1:43 ©Md Sp Wt 8 8 1112 119¼ 612 710 McCarron CJ 118 b 23.50 76-09 Penngrove118noHatamoto1181Seventh Dwarf1184 Wide 12

Before Dawn

b. f. 1979, by Raise a Cup (Raise a Native)–Moonbeam, by Tim Tam **Lifetime record: 14 9 2 1 $432,855**

Own.– Calumet Farm
Br.– Calumet Farm (Ky)
Tr.– John M. Veitch

5Aug82- 8Sar fst 7f :221 :45 1:094 1:224 ⒻTest-G2 8 7 95½ 75½ 1114 913 Vasquez J 121 5.10 75-16 GoldBeauty1161AmbassadrofLck1211¾Numbr1141¾ No factor 12
22May82- 8Bel fst 1 :231 :46 1:093 1:341 ⒻAcorn-G1 1 3 42½ 65 89½ 913 Velasquez J 121 *1.60 82-11 Cupecoy's Joy1212¾Nancy Huang1213½Vestris1212¼ Tired 9
30Apr82- 8CD fst 1⅛ :482 1:131 1:373 1:501 ⒻKy Oaks-G1 7 2 21 1½ 2hd 2¾ Velasquez J 121 *1.30 90-13 Blush With Pride121¾Before Dawn1212¼Flying Partner1216 7
Held gamely
3Apr82- 9OP fst 1 1/16 :234 :481 1:143 1:47 ⒻFantasy-G1 3 2 1hd 1hd 32½ 36 Velasquez J 121 *.40 67-33 FlyingPartner1182¾SkillfulJoy1213¼BforDwn1215½ Weakened 7
27Mar82-10FG fst 1 1/16 :24 :471 1:121 1:452 ⒻFG Oaks-G3 2 4 55 3nk 14 12½ Velasquez J 121 *.30 85-16 Before Dawn1212½Girlie1213½Linda North1181 Poor st.,dr. 7
17Feb82- 9Hia fst 7f :222 :45 1:094 1:23 ⒻHibiscus 36k 2 2 32½ 21½ 11½ 11 Velasquez J 122 *.10 88-21 Before Dawn1221All Manners1174First Flurry1173½ Handily 5
8Feb82- 9Hia fst 6f :22 :45 1:094 ⒻAlw 20000 5 1 2hd 11 14 18 Velasquez J 122 *.30 94-23 BeforeDawn1228FirstFlurry1151ExclusvLov1151¼ Ridden out 7
9Jan82- 9Hia fst 6f :214 :452 1:104 ⒻJasmine 37k 8 3 54 41½ 2½ 1no Velasquez J 122 *.30 89-15 Before Dawn122noIron Queen1171¼Larida1137 Driving 9
10Oct81- 7Bel fst 1 :233 :464 1:111 1:362 Champagne-G1 1 4 1½ 1hd 21 24¾ Velasquez J 119 *.80 81-14 Timely Writer1224¾Before Dawn1193New Discovery122nk 13
Best of others
19Sep81- 7Bel my 7f :231 :462 1:104 1:231 ⒻMatron-G1 2 3 11 11½ 13 16½ Velasquez J 119 *.40 86-13 BefreDwn1196½ArabinDncr1191¼MystclMood119¾ Ridden out 9
3Sep81- 8Bel fst 6½f :224 :453 1:094 1:163 ⒻAstarita-G2 2 2 2½ 11 12½ 12½ Velasquez J 119 *.10 93-19 BeforeDwn1192½BettyMoney1126½TakeLadyAnne1121 Easily 5
23Aug81- 8Sar fst 6f :22 :444 1:092 ⒻSpinaway-G1 7 3 31½ 11½ 15 17¾ McCarron G 119 *.80 93-12 BfreDwn1197¾BettyMoney1192½TakeLadyAnne119no Handily 10
24Jun81- 8Bel fst 5½f :221 :454 :574 1:041 ⒻFashion 55k 3 4 32½ 31½ 13 15¼ Velasquez J 115 *.50 94-19 Before Dawn1155¼Mystical Mood1152½Bold and Joyful1153 7
Ridden out
15Jun81- 6Bel fst 5½f :222 :454 :572 1:033 ⒻMd Sp Wt 5 3 13 13 14 16¾ Velasquez J 117 1.90 97-10 BforeDawn1176¾ChillingThought11710Spell1175 Ridden out 7

Blushing John

ch. c. 1985, by Blushing Groom (Red God)–La Griffe, by Prince John **Lifetime record: 19 9 1 2 $1,524,599**

Own.– Allen E. Paulson
Br.– North Ridge Farm (Ky)
Tr.– Richard J. Lundy

4Nov89-10GP fst 1¼ :461 1:102 1:35 2:001 3↑ BC Classic-G1 7 2 23 11½ 1hd 31¼ Cordero A Jr 126 21.50 106-01 SundaySilnce122nkEasyGoer1221BlshngJohn1269¾ Willingly 8
13Oct89- 9Med fst 1¼ :461 1:102 1:344 2:001 3↑ Med Cup H-G1 6 6 55 64¼ 610 720 Cordero A Jr 124 *.60 73-16 MiSelecto1152MaketheMost1105¾[DH]MasterSpeaker114 Tired 8
9Sep89- 8AP sly 1⅛ :481 1:132 1:384 1:504 3↑ Wash Park H-G2 2 1 21½ 2½ 13 17½ Day P 124 *.40 77-34 Blushing John1247½Grantley112¾Paramount Jet1131¼ Easily 5
12Aug89- 9AP sf 1¼Ⓣ :52 1:173 1:442 2:111 3↑ Arlington H-G1 5 1 2½ 31 519 531¾ Day P 124 *1.20 - - UnknownQuantityII1123FrostytheSnowmn1221¾Delegnt113hd 5
Eased stretch
25Jun89- 8Hol fst 1¼ :472 1:114 1:362 2:002 3↑ Hol Gold Cup H-G1 7 3 23½ 1½ 11 11 Day P 122 *1.30 90-19 Blushing John1221Sabona1163½Payant1161 Much the best 7
4Jun89- 8Hol fst 1⅛ :462 1:101 1:344 1:464 3↑ Californian-G1 1 2 22 21 1hd 21¼ Day P 124 3.00 102-14 Sabona1151¼BlushingJohn1243½LvlyOn1181 Gave way stretch 6
13May89- 9Pim fst 1 3/16 :462 1:10 1:342 1:531 4↑ Pim Spl H 700k 11 4 44¼ 23 2hd 12 Day P 117 7.10 101-10 BlushingJohn1172ProperRlty1181¼Grncus113½ Brushed,clear 12
15Apr89- 6OP fst 1⅛ :47 1:111 1:361 1:49 4↑ Oaklawn H-G1 2 4 42 52¼ 54 42 Day P 119 3.10 86-21 Slew City Slew118½Stalwars113noHomebuilder1151½ Bumped 8
25Mar89- 9OP fst 1 1/16 :243 :492 1:134 1:43 4↑ Razorback H-G2 4 5 41¼ 4nk 2hd 11½ Day P 117 4.20 86-24 Blushing John1171½Lyphard's Ridge1113Proper Reality1234 5
Wide,ridden out
9Mar89- 8OP fst 1 :231 :463 1:112 1:372 4↑ Alw 25000 9 10 711 45 21½ 13 Day P 114 *1.50 85-23 Blushing John1143Flippable114hdZarbyev1146½ Wide 11
Previously trained by Francois Boutin
5Nov88- 7CD gd 1Ⓣ :233 :472 1:123 1:383 3↑ BC Mile-G1 5 8 1012 1215 1123 1030 Day P 123 2.00e 66-04 Miesque1234Steinlen126hdSimply Majestic1261¼ Outrun 12
4Sep88♦ Longchamp(Fr) sf *1ⓉRH 1:403 3↑ Prix du Moulin de Longchamp-G1 Stk243000 49 Mosse G 123 8.50 Soviet Star128hdMiesque1245Gabina1204 7
Rated in 6th,rallied to lead 2f out,headed and weakened 1f out
14Jun88♦ Ascot(GB) gd 1ⓉRH 1:392 St. James's Palace Stakes-G1 Stk290000 43½ Head F 126 7.50 Persian Heights1261½Raykour126½Caerwent1261½ 7
Tracked leader,one-pace through stretch
29May88♦ Longchamp(Fr) sf *1⅛ⓉRH 1:54 Prix Jean Prat-G1 Stk146000 42¼ Head F 128 1.20 Lapierre1281½Fijar Tango128½Triteamtri128nk 9
Rated at rear,7th 2½f out,5th 1f out,evenly late

8May88♦ Longchamp(Fr) fm*1ⓉRH 1:371 Poule d'Essai des Poulains-G1 Stk298000 1no Head F 128 *.60e Blushing John128noFrench Stress1282Tay Wharf1281 10
Trailed,progress 3f out,angled out to lead 1f out,all out
17Apr88♦ Longchamp(Fr) yl *1ⓉRH 1:413 Prix de Fontainebleau-G3 Stk51300 12 Head F 128 *1.40 Blushing John1282Triteamtri128½Soviet Lad128hd 7
Led throughout,quickened 2½f out,clear 1f out,ridden out
11Nov87♦ Saint-Cloud(Fr) sf *1¼ⓉLH 2:203 Criterium de Saint-Cloud-G1 Stk89300 34½ Head F 123 *.70 Waki River123½Hours After1234Blushing John123½ 9
Unhurried in 5th,late gain to take 3rd near line
30Oct87♦ Longchamp(Fr) fm*1⅛ⓉRH 1:511 Prix Saint Roman-G3 Stk47200 14 St Martin Y 123 *.60 Blushing John1234Triteamtri123nkTruly Special1231½ 9
Rated in 4th,led over 1f out,quickly clear,handily
13Sep87♦ Longchamp(Fr) gd *1ⓉRH 1:42 Prix de Villebon Mdn (FT)21300 11 Head F 123 3.60 Blushing John1231Reve Dore1231Lytrump123no 7
Tracked in 3rd,led before halfway,clear over 1f out,ridden out

Bold 'n Determined

b. f. 1977, by Bold and Brave (Bold Ruler)–Pidi, by Determine — **Lifetime record: 20 16 2 0 $949,599**

Own.– Saron Stable
Br.– G.E. Layton (Ky)
Tr.– Neil Drysdale

24Apr81- 7Kee fst 1 1/16 :242:484 1:122 1:434 3↑ ⒻBewitch 58k 2 1 11 1½ 1hd 1nk Delahoussaye E 121 *.30 87-19 Bold'nDtrmind121nkLikely Exchange1136½Save Wild Life1104 5 Driving
8Apr81- 9OP fst 1 1/16 :233:462 1:111 1:441 4↑ ⒻApple Blossom H-G2 3 1 1½ 1hd 1hd 1hd Delahoussaye E 124 *.30 87-20 Bold 'n Determined124hdLa Bonzo1113¼Karla's Enough1193½ 7 Fully extended
30Mar81- 9OP fst 6f :214:452 1:10 4↑ ⒻAlw 30000 4 4 44½ 11 14 16 Maple E 113 *.30 95-20 Bld'nDtrmnd1136RunKy.Run1212½HmpnsSyn1161¼ Ridden out 5
3Jan81- 8SA fst 7f :214:441 1:084 1:212 ⒻLa Brea 54k 4 1 31½ 32 1hd 2no Delahoussaye E 125 *.40 93-10 Dynamite114noBold'nDetermined1256Pachn1142½ Just missed 5
9Nov80- 8SA fm 1¼Ⓣ :452 1:094 1:343 1:591 3↑ ⒻYellow Ribbon Inv-G1 2 2 25 33 31½ 45 Delahoussaye E 119 *1.20 86-09 Kilijaro1233¾Ack'sSecret1231¼QueentoConqur123½ Weakened 10
25Oct80- 7Kee fst 1⅛ :473 1:112 1:362 1:491 3↑ ⒻSpinster-G1 5 2 31 2hd 1hd 1nk Delahoussaye E 119 *.30 91-20 Bold'nDetermind119nkLoveSgn1197½LklyExchng123¾ Driving 6
16Oct80- 7Kee fst *7f 1:261 3↑ ⒻAlw 29750 1 5 1hd 11 12 16¾ Delahoussaye E 120 *.10 92-20 Boldn'Determined1206¾ViteView1201¼Shawn'sGl1204 Handily 6
10Sep80- 8Bel fst 1 :232:461 1:104 1:352 3↑ ⒻMaskette-G1 1 2 22½ 1hd 2hd 1no Delahoussaye E 122 10.40 91-22 Bold'nDetrmined122noGenuineRisk1186¾LovSgn120½ Driving 5
28Jun80- 8Bel fst 1½ :494 1:143 2:062 2:314 ⒻC C A Oaks-G1 2 3 2hd 1hd 3½ 1hd Delahoussaye E 121 *1.20 61-25 Bold 'n Determind121hdErin'sWord121hdFarewell Letter121¼ 7 Driving
8Jun80- 8Bel sly 1⅛ :461 1:111 1:363 1:493 ⒻMother Goose-G1 8 3 33 1½ 2hd 2hd Delahoussaye E 121 *.50 79-23 Sugar and Spice121hdBold'nDetrmind1218¾Erin's Word1213½ 8 Gamely
24May80- 8Bel fst 1 :222:444 1:093 1:364 ⒻAcorn-G1 7 3 2½ 11 12 12¾ Delahoussaye E 121 *.40 84-17 Bold'nDetermind1212¾MiteyLively1211¼Sugar andSpice1213½ 8 Driving
2May80- 8CD fst 1 1/16 :242:483 1:133 1:444 ⒻKy Oaks-G1 2 1 1½ 1hd 11½ 11½ Delahoussaye E 121 *.60 84-18 Bold'nDetermind1211½Mitey Lively121½Honest and True1213 8 Driving
5Apr80- 9OP fst 1 1/16 :231:464 1:114 1:451 ⒻFantasy-G1 3 2 1hd 1½ 11½ 12¼ Delahoussaye E 121 *1.10 82-20 Bold 'nDetermind1212¼Satin Ribera1154Honest and True1187 7 Drew clear
9Mar80- 8SA fst 1 1/16 :222:45 1:093 1:411 ⒻS Susana-G1 6 2 210 22 3½ 1½ Delahoussaye E 115 3.50 95-10 Bold'nDetermined115½StreetBllt115nkTblHnds11512 Just up 7
23Feb80- 8SA fst 7f :213:441 1:092 1:222 ⒻS Ynez-G2 1 6 64¼ 67 44½ 42 Delahoussaye E 121 2.10 89-14 Table Hands124hdStreet Ballet1191¼Hazel R.119¾ Rallied 7
30Jan80- 8SA gd 6f :214:444 :57 1:094 ⒻPasadena 53k 4 1 32 3½ 1hd 12¼ Delahoussaye E 121 *.80 90-21 Bld'nDetrmnd1212¼Thundrt116nkBckAtTwo1154½ Drew clear 5
21Oct79- 8SA gd 1 1/16 :23 :47 1:124 1:461 ⒻOak Leaf-G2 7 5 53¾ 2hd 12½ 13 Cordero A Jr 115 1.80 70-28 Bold'nDetrmined1153HazelR.1151¼ArcadesAmbo1152 Driving 8
12Oct79- 4Bel sly 1 :23 :462 1:114 1:391 ⒻAlw 18000 5 2 21½ 2½ 12 15 Cordero A Jr 115 *1.30 72-24 Bold'nDetermind1155Tell a Secret115½Two Cents Extra11511 5 Driving
1Oct79- 7Med sly 6f :221:454 1:11 ⒻAlw 14000 3 4 45 34 1hd 14 Cordero A Jr 114 2.70 90-16 Bld'nDetrmind1144LoaddGun1179SproutdRy1121½ Drew out 7
3May79- 4Hol fst 5f :22 :453 :572 ⒻMd Sp Wt 6 1 32 31 32 1hd Delahoussaye E 115 3.40 93-14 Bold'nDetrmind115hdOvrdrawnLdy1152½AudaciousFinance115½ 7 Driving

Brave Raj

dkbbr. f. 1984, by Rajab (Jaipur)–Bravest Yet, by Bravo — **Lifetime record: 9 6 1 0 $933,650**

Own.– Dolly Green
Br.– Dr W.S. Karutz (Fla)
Tr.– Melvin F. Stute

14Dec86- 8Hol fst 1 :221:444 1:093 1:361 Hol Futurity-G1 8 5 31½ 33 52½ 53¼ Valenzuela PA 118 *1.70 79-18 TemperateSl121nkAlyshb121nkMstrfulAdvoct1212¼ Lugged in 12
1Nov86- 2SA fst 1 1/16 :221:453 1:101 1:431 ⒻBC Juv Fillies-G1 4 4 46 32 13½ 15½ Valenzuela PA 119 4.00 85-13 Brave Raj1195½Tappiano1193½Saros Brig1191¾ Driving 12
12Oct86- 9Crc fst 1 1/16 :24 :481 1:134 1:481 ⒻⓇMy Dear Girl 400k 3 2 21 14 14 1¾ Valenzuela PA 120 *.50 78-14 BraveRaj120¾AddedElgnc1202½BlusCourt1207 Drifted,lasted 13
21Sep86- 9Crc sly 7f :221:453 1:112 1:25 ⒻⓇSusan's Girl 75k 4 5 2½ 21 14 14½ Valenzuela PA 118 *.50 91-16 BraveRaj1184½CarolsInhertnc1186ApplngOn1189½ Ridden out 9
31Aug86- 8Dmr fst 1 :22 :452 1:102 1:354 ⒻDmr Debutante-G2 1 3 3½ 2½ 11½ 13½ Black CA 117 *1.50 89-12 BraveRaj1173½RoadtoHappiness113noSoftCopy1153½ Easily 7
18Aug86- 8Dmr fst 7f :22 :443 1:092 1:223 ⒻSorrento-G3 5 5 52¼ 42½ 3½ 11¼ Valenzuela PA 117 *1.90 92-14 Brave Raj1171¼Breech1172½Footy1211¾ Lugged in 10
6Aug86- 8Dmr fst 6f :213:444 :564 1:10 ⒻJr Miss 55k 9 9 63 52½ 43½ 2¾ Valenzuela PA 117 *1.60e 87-13 Footy114¾Brave Raj117hdEvil Elaine1142½ Off in tangle 10
4Jly86- 7Hol fst 6f :212:45 :571 1:10 ⒻLandaluce-G3 6 9 76½ 75¾ 58 59¾ Valenzuela PA 116 10.30 84-09 DelicateVin1162AnythngforLov1141½PurduQun1195 No threat 9
Previously owned by Alben Partnership;previously trained by Ben Perkins Jr
22May86- 5GS fst 5f :223:462 :59 ⒻMd Sp Wt 2 1 13 12½ 15 17½ Thomas DB 116 10.00 86-22 BrveRaj1167½Daremightythngs1161½Wondcor1163 Ridden out 7

Brown Bess

dbbr. f. 1982, by Petrone (Prince Taj)–Chickadee, by Windy Sands — **Lifetime record: 36 16 8 6 $1,300,920**

Own.– Calbourne Stable
Br.– Calbourne Farm (Cal)
Tr.– Charles J. Jenda

6Oct90- 8BM fm *1⅛Ⓣ :462 1:104 1:361 1:462 3↑ ⒻCal Jockey Club H-G3 5 3 35 33 12 2nk Kaenel JL LB 120 *.90 98-12 Sweet Roberta115nkBrown Bess1203Oeilladine1144 2nd best 6
18Aug90- 8Dmr fm 1⅛Ⓣ :473 1:114 1:363 1:49 3↑ ⒻRamona H-G1 5 4 43 53 64¼ 55 Kaenel JL LB 122 *2.10 88-10 DoubleWedge114¾RluctntGust1173Nkshk116no 4-wide stretch 8
16Jun90- 8GG fm 1⅜Ⓣ :482 1:131 1:374 2:153 3↑ Golden Gate H-G2 11 5 47½ 33½ 32 43½ Kaenel JL 117 *3.50 89-10 PetiteIle1131½Valdali1141PleasantVrty1161 Brushed drive 11
12May90- 8GG fm 1⅜Ⓣ :483 1:14 1:382 2:153 3↑ ⒻYerba Buena H 150k 3 1 12 1hd 2hd 31¼ Kaenel JL 124 *.70 92-09 Petite Ile118¾Double Wedge112½Brown Bess1244 Set pace 5
31Mar90- 8SA fm 1¼Ⓣ :45 1:10 1:34 1:582 4↑ ⒻS Barbara H-G1 2 3 32 1hd 1½ 1no Kaenel JL 123 *.70 96-09 BrwnBss123noRoyalTouch121hdDoubleWdg1112¾ Game winner 5
11Mar90- 8SA fm 1⅛Ⓣ :48 1:113 1:352 1:474 4↑ ⒻS Ana H-G1 4 2 21 21 1hd 3hd Kaenel JL 123 *1.30 86-15 Annoconnr119hdRoylTouch121noBrwnBss1231 Strong effort 7
12Nov89- 8SA fm 1¼Ⓣ :452 1:091 1:332 1:573 3↑ ⒻYellow Ribbon Inv'l-G1 6 7 64½ 3½ 1hd 11¾ Kaenel JL 123 4.10 108-00 BrownBess1231¾Drby'sDughtr119½ColordoDncr1192 Hand ride 11
7Oct89- 8BM fm *1⅛Ⓣ :471 1:114 1:363 1:47 3↑ ⒻCal Jockey Club H-G3 2 3 32 31½ 1hd 11 Kaenel JL 120 *.90 95-17 Brown Bess1201Nikishka1152Gold Firecracker1134 Driving 5
19Aug89- 8Dmr fm 1⅛Ⓣ :482 1:122 1:364 1:484 3↑ ⒻRamona H-G1 5 2 2½ 2hd 2hd 1nk Kaenel JL 117 5.00 89-11 Brown Bess117nkDaring Doone117½Galunpe1181½ Gamely 7
17Jun89- 8GG fm 1⅜Ⓣ :49 1:132 1:373 2:15 3↑ Golden Gate H-G2 2 1 1½ 12 11½ 32¼ Chapman TM 114 3.40 88-10 FranklyPerfect122nkPleasntVrty1142BrwnBss1142 Weakened 7
13May89- 8GG fm 1⅜Ⓣ :474 1:124 1:373 2:153 3↑ ⒻYerba Buena H-G3 5 4 66½ 52½ 12 12½ Kaenel JL 119 *1.50 87-20 BrownBss1192½Carmanetta1144½FlttrngNws111hd Wide rally 10
15Apr89- 8GG fm 1⅛Ⓣ :491 1:131 1:374 1:501 3↑ ⒻCountess Fager H-G3 1 6 64½ 63¾ 31 11½ Kaenel JL 117 2.40 97-15 Brown Bess1171½Beat1151Daring Doone1131 Forced out 3/16 9
18Mar89- 8GG sly 1 1/16⊗ :232:463 1:101 1:422 3↑ ⒻGolden Poppy H-G3 1 5 73½ 54½ 32 22½ Kaenel JL 117 4.90 84-14 Invited Guest1162½Brown Bess117¾Daloma1163 Gamely 7
11Feb89- 8GG gd 1 :233:473 1:113 1:363 3↑ ⒻPrincessnesian H 55k 5 1 1½ 2hd 23 310 Kaenel JL 118 *1.40 72-27 Novel Sprite1147Lady Annabelle1133Brown Bess1181½ 8 No late response
7Jan89- 8SA fst 1⅛⊗ :47 1:11 1:36 1:484 4↑ ⒻSan Gorgonio H-G2 1 3 32½ 41½ 611 516¾ Kaenel JL 118 6.90 68-14 NoReview117½Annoconnr1222½WhiteMischifII1161¾ Faltered 6

Date/Race	Cond	Dist	Fractions	Race	Running line	Jockey	Wt	Odds	Spd	Top three	Comment	Field
12Nov88-8BM	gd	1⅛(T)	:481 1:12 1:372 1:502	3↑ (F)Hillsborough H-G3	3 2 21½ 21 12 13	Kaenel JL	116	2.90	88-14	BrownBess1163Balbonella1181½Griefnggrvton1142	Hand ride	6
8Oct88-8BM	fm	*1⅛(T)	1:463	3↑ (F)Cal Jockey Club H-G3	10 2 23 22 2hd 1¾	Kaenel JL	115	10.90	102-03	BrownBss115¾JungleDawn1161½Choritzo120½	Strong urging	10
4Sep88-8BM	fm	1 1/16(T)	:234 :49 1:133 1:423	3↑ (F)Tizna H 54k	3 1 1½ 1hd 2hd 2no	Kaenel JL	118	2.70	96-10	Davie'sLamb120noBrwnBss1183HollyDonna1132	Just missed	7
20Aug88-11Bmf	fst	1 1/16	:23 :461 1:094 1:42	3↑ (F)Lady Morvich H 32k	2 3 31½ 2½ 11 11	Kaenel JL	120	3.20	82-16	Brown Bess1201Chanango's Alibi1192Stemware1181		7
Gamely under urging												
4Jly88-11Pln	fst	1 1/16	:244 :484 1:121 1:434	3↑ (F)Alameda County H 32k	2 2 2hd 1½ 12 2½	Kaenel JL	120	*.90	84-16	Stemware115½BrwnBess1203Honeymoon Toast1142	No match	6
4Jun88-8GG	fm	1(T)	:233 :473 1:114 1:362	3↑ (F)Lakes & Flowers H 53k	6 3 32 21 11½ 12	Baze RA	116	*1.40	85-17	Brown Bess1162Chanango's Alibi1151Miss Alto1161	Wide	6
21May88-8GG	fm	1(T)	:232 :474 1:12 1:364	3↑ (F)(R)Star Ball Inv'l H 52k	8 4 31½ 2hd 1½ 12	Baze RA	116	*1.60	83-17	BrwnBess1162Sovereign Answer113¾Griefnaggrevation116no		9
Restricted to horses stabled at Golden Gate Fields												
6Apr88-8GG	fm	1 1/16(T)	:232 :484 1:123 1:441	4↑ (F)Handicap 24000	3 2 22 21 11 1no	Castaneda M	115	2.80	81-19	BrwnBess115noMissMaiTai1161½LurnLgh1151½	Strong urging	5
17Mar88-7GG	fm	1(T)	:231 :464 1:112 1:372	4↑ (F)Handicap 22000	4 1 11½ 1½ 1½ 42½	Castaneda M	115	5.40	77-21	Cruisin' Two Su1161½Lauren Leigh115hdTender Force1171		10
Drifted out ⅛												
31Mar87-8GG	fm	1(T)	:23 :463 1:111 1:36	4↑ (F)Alw 24000	4 5 53¾ 32½ 1hd 11¼	Baze RA	115	*2.60	87-13	BrwnBss1151¼TndrForc1154AbstrctEnrgy1152½	Bumped start	8
12Mar87-8GG	sly	1	:232 :47 1:113 1:384	4↑ (F)Alw 20000	3 3 33 32 23 24	Castaneda M	121	4.00	70-28	Pass All Hope1164Brown Bess1212River Char1211	2nd best	7
8Feb87-8BM	gd	1 1/16(T)	:233 :483 1:134 1:452	4↑ (F)Palo Alto H 55k	1 2 21½ 1hd 2hd 32½	Castaneda M	114	4.20	73-21	RoyalRegatta120½BrigadeSpecial1132BrwnBss1142	Weakened	9
17Jan87-4BM	fm	1 1/16(T)	:233 :481 1:132 1:451	4↑ (F)Int'l Jockey's Cup 17k	7 3 45 12 11½ 12	Eddery P	121	*.80	77-23	Brown Bess1212Mia Rosa117nkGolden Twenties1175	Driving	8
14Dec86-7BM	fst	1 1/16	:224 :46 1:104 1:431	3↑ (F)Alw 17000	2 2 22 21 12 14	Castaneda M	115	3.60	76-17	Brown Bess1154Bramble Dawn113¾Roberts Regal Girl1153		10
Stumbled start												
11Nov86-6BM	fm	1(T)	:234 :474 1:123 1:381	3↑ (F)Alw 20000	3 2 21 1hd 1hd 2no	Campbell BC	114	3.70	89-11	NobHillNative114noBrownBess1142GirlnBlu1144	Just missed	6
22Oct86-8BM	fm	7½f(T)	:232 :48 1:123 1:313	3↑ (F)Alw 19000	1 1 3½ 1hd 1hd 2hd	Campbell BC	114	4.00	86-14	Heartlifter117hdBrown Bess1144Soft Dawn1086	Gamely	9
28Sep86-9BM	gd	7½f(T)	:231 :464 1:114 1:303	3↑ (F)Clm 50000	3 4 42 42½ 1hd 2no	Campbell BC	114	52.60	91-08	GirlinBlue114noBrownBess1141¼J.D.Canyon1091	Just missed	10
10Sep86-11Bmf	fst	1	:224 :461 1:103 1:36	3↑ (F)Alw 17000	10 6 63¾ 54½ 817 918¼	Lamance C	118	13.00	70-22	Heartlifter114hdIcy Run1145Wooly Nan1142½	Outrun	10
29Jly86-7SR	fst	1	:223 :451 1:103 1:371	3↑ (F)Md Sp Wt	7 4 52 32 1hd 11½	Lamance C	121	*1.90	86-17	BrownBess1211½NorthernFey1143½MuffettsSun114½	Driving	8
16Jly86-4Sol	fst	6f	:214 :444 :572 1:102	3↑ (F)Md Sp Wt	8 5 54½ 55½ 34 32½	Lamance C	121	4.90	88-13	Whirling Too116noSwift Victress1162½Brown Bess1211½		10
Bumped start,pinched ⅝												
28Sep85-2BM	fst	6f	:224 :46 :583 1:111	3↑ (F)(S)Md Sp Wt	6 7 75½ 53½ 53½ 45	Lamance C	116	6.70	78-19	Donna's Terne1161Manhattan Magic1161½A Real Gasser1162½		7
Lacked rally												

Capote

dkbbr. c. 1984, by Seattle Slew (Bold Reasoning)–Too Bald, by Bald Eagle **Lifetime record: 10 3 0 1 $714,470**

Own.– Beal & French Jr & Klein
Br.– North Ridge Farm (Ky)
Tr.– D. Wayne Lukas

Date/Race	Cond	Dist	Fractions	Race	Running line	Jockey	Wt	Odds	Spd	Top three	Comment	Field
10Oct87-3SA	fst	6f	:213 :443 :564 1:092	3↑ Alw 34000	5 3 32 33 58 613¼	McCarron CJ	114	*.80	78-17	Decore1141½HotSauceBby115noCaballodOro116hd	Done early	6
2Sep87-3Bel	fst	7f	:223 :452 1:11 1:234	3↑ Alw 31000	1 1 1hd 1½ 1hd 43½	Cordero A Jr	114	*.50	79-16	Mr. Classic1171Landyap1131¼Britton's Mill1171½	Weakened	5
10Aug87-6Sar	sly	7f	:223 :451 1:094 1:224	3↑ Alw 29000	4 2 1hd 1hd 22 36¾	Cordero A Jr	115	*1.70	81-19	Quick Call114¾Leo Castelli1126Capote1157	Weakened	6
2May87-8CD	fst	1¼	:462 1:11 1:364 2:032	Ky Derby-G1	5 2 11½ 105½ 1623 -	Cordero A Jr	126	6.30e	--	Alysheba126¾Bet Twice1262¼Avies Copy126nk	Eased	17
18Apr87-8Aqu	my	1⅛	:47 1:113 1:362 1:49	Wood Memorial Inv'l-G1	5 1 11 11½ 34 47¾	Cordero A Jr	126	*1.30	82-15	Gulch126hdGone West1266Shawklit Won1261¾	Gave way	8
4Apr87-8Aqu	sly	1	:222 :442 1:081 1:343	Gotham-G2	5 1 2hd 22 35½ 49½	Day P	123	*1.40	83-21	Gone West1141Shawklit Won1148½Gulch123hd	Weakened	9
1Nov86-1SA	fst	1 1/16	:222 :454 1:102 1:434	BC Juvenile-G1	3 1 11½ 11 12½ 11¼	Pincay L Jr	122	*2.40	82-13	Capote1221¼Qualify1221¼Alysheba1222¼	Driving	13
11Oct86-8SA	fst	1 1/16	:223 :461 1:11 1:451	Norfolk-G1	3 1 11½ 1½ 11½ 11¾	Pincay L Jr	118	3.70	75-17	Capote1181¾Gulch118¾Gold on Green1182¾	Driving	6
3Oct86-6SA	fst	6f	:214 :443 :563 1:092	Md Sp Wt	1 5 12½ 15 17 111	Pincay L Jr	118	*3.10	91-17	Cpte11811WindwoodLane1183½BooBoo'sBuckroo118hd	Easily	12
1Sep86-6Dmr	fst	6f	:22 :444 :57 1:094	Md Sp Wt	8 4 3½ 35 1116 1121¾	Shoemaker W	118	4.00	67-13	SpecialTrick1185SwordCharger118¾CharlieZee1184	Greenly	12

Chief's Crown

b. c. 1982, by Danzig (Northern Dancer)–Six Crowns, by Secretariat **Lifetime record: 21 12 3 3 $2,191,168**

Own.– Star Crown Stable
Br.– Carl Rosen (Ky)
Tr.– Roger Laurin

Date/Race	Cond	Dist	Fractions	Race	Running line	Jockey	Wt	Odds	Spd	Top three	Comment	Field
2Nov85-7Aqu	fst	1¼	:464 1:11 1:362 2:004	3↑ BC Classic-G1	5 3 44½ 2hd 32½ 49¾	MacBeth D	122	*1.80	82-10	ProudTruth122hdGateDancr1264Trkomn1225¾	Bid,weakened	8
13Oct85-6Bel	gd	1(T)	:231 :46 1:102 1:362	3↑ Handicap 40000	2 4 35 36 34 12½	MacBeth D	125	*.70	83-25	Chief's Crown1252½Intensify1142½Smile11612	Ridden out	5
14Sep85-8Bel	fst	1¼	:47 1:11 1:361 2:011	3↑ Marlboro Cup H-G1	8 5 64 3½ 1½ 1nk	MacBeth D	119	10.50	92-09	Chief'sCrwn119nkGateDancr125¾Vanlandnghm122hd	Driving	9
31Aug85-8Bel	gd	1⅛	:461 1:10 1:341 1:463	3↑ Woodward-G1	3 4 46½ 44½ 35 35½	Pincay L Jr	121	1.90	88-10	TrackBarrn1234Vanlndinghm1231½Chf'sCrwn121½	Weakened	6
17Aug85-8Sar	fst	1¼	:481 1:114 1:361 2:011	Travers-G1	3 4 41½ 31 1½ 12¼	Cordero A Jr	126	*1.20	91-08	Chief's Crown1262¼Turkoman1263Skip Trial126½	Driving	7
3Aug85-5Sar	fm	1(T)	:243 :482 1:122 1:363	Tell 55k	4 3 53 32 2hd 1¾	Cordero A Jr	122	*.70	93-09	[D]Chief'sCrwn122¾ExclusivePartnr1154½ExplosiveDancr115nk		6
Swung out turn;Disqualified and placed fourth												
8Jun85-8Bel	my	1½	:47 1:104 2:012 2:27	Belmont-G1	1 4 42½ 1hd 32 35	Cordero A Jr	126	*2.00	80-12	CremeFrach126½Stphn'sOdyssy1264½Chf'sCrwn1264	Weakened	11
18May85-8Pim	fst	1 3/16	:451 1:092 1:341 1:532	Preakness-G1	3 5 45 21 11 2hd	MacBeth D	126	*1.00	101-10	Tank's Prospect126hdChief's Crown1262¼Eternal Prince1263		11
Just failed												
4May85-8CD	fst	1¼	:454 1:093 1:344 2:001	Ky Derby-G1	2 2 26 26 25 35¾	MacBeth D	126	*1.20	90-08	Spend a Buck1265¼Stephan's Odyssey126½Chief's Crown126nk		13
Lacked rally												
25Apr85-7Kee	fst	1⅛	:482 1:12 1:354 1:473	Blue Grass-G1	2 1 11½ 11 13 15½	MacBeth D	121	*.30	99-16	Chief'sCrwn1215½FloatngRsrv121hdBnnrBob12111	Hand ride	4
30Mar85-11Hia	fst	1⅛	:484 1:122 1:361 1:482	Flamingo-G1	5 1 1hd 11 12½ 11	MacBeth D	122	1.30	90-12	[D]Chief'sCrown1221ProudTruth122nkStephan's Odyssey1223½		8
Disqualified and placed second - reversed by Fla. board												
2Mar85-10GP	fst	7f	:223 :451 1:093 1:222	Swale 51k	9 2 2hd 2hd 11 13¼	MacBeth D	122	*.30	92-15	Chief'sCrwn1223¼CremeFrch1173½ChrokFst113nk	Ridden out	9
10Nov84-1Hol	fst	1	:222 :45 1:10 1:361	(C)BC Juvenile-G1	5 6 64¾ 32½ 21 1¾	MacBeth D	122	*.70	--	Chief'sCrown122¾Tank'sProspect122¾SpndBck1226½	Driving	10
27Oct84-8SA	fst	1 1/16	:231 :463 1:104 1:422	Norfolk-G1	6 2 2½ 1hd 1hd 11	MacBeth D	118	*.30	89-13	Chief'sCrwn1181½MatthewT.Parker1189VivaMx118hd	Driving	6
6Oct84-8Bel	fst	1	:221 :452 1:103 1:363	Cowdin-G1	4 4 21 12 13 16	MacBeth D	122	*.50	82-17	Chief'sCrwn1226BioncLght12212½ScrptOho1221¼	Ridden out	8
15Sep84-5Bel	sly	7f	:224 :46 1:102 1:231	Futurity-G1	5 2 68 64 34 21	MacBeth D	122	*.70	85-18	SpectacularLove1221Chief'sCrown1223½Mugzy's Rullah1222¾		8
Wide str.;Previously owned by A. Rosen												
26Aug84-8Sar	fst	6½f	:214 :444 1:092 1:16	Hopeful-G1	3 4 33½ 3½ 1½ 13¾	MacBeth D	122	*1.10	92-15	Chif'sCrwn1223¾TffnyIc1223¾Mugzy'sRullh122½	Ridden out	9
3Aug84-8Sar	fst	6f	:223 :46 1:101	Sar Spl-G2	4 3 33 2hd 1hd 12¾	MacBeth D	117	*2.10	89-19	Chief's Crown1172¾Do It Again Dan117hdSky Command122¾		6
Ridden out												
5Jly84-6Bel	fst	5½f	:222 :454 :58 1:042	Md Sp Wt	5 1 1hd 2hd 11 15	MacBeth D	118	*1.10	93-15	Chief'sCrown1185DesertWar1182¼TigerBiddr1184	Ridden out	9
22Jun84-4Bel	fst	5½f	:221 :461 :59 1:053	Md Sp Wt	1 1 43½ 46½ 34½ 21	MacBeth D	118	5.20	86-21	SecretaryGeneral1181Chif'sCrown1181¼TffnyIc1189	Rallied	10
13Jun84-4Bel	fst	5f	:224 :462 :584	Md Sp Wt	8 8 46½ 613 513 411½	Cordero A Jr	118	3.10	81-18	Don't Fool With Me1188Attribute118nkMount Reality1183¼		8
Carried out												

Chinook Pass

dkbbr. g. 1979, by Native Born (Native Dancer)–Yu Turn, by Turn-to **Lifetime record: 25 16 4 1 $480,073**

Own.– Hi Yu Stable
Br.– Hi Yu Stable (Wash)
Tr.– Laurie N. Anderson

21Aug83- 9Lga	fst 1	:22 :443 1:093 1:353	3↑ Lga Mile H 182k	6	1	16	15	14	16	Pincay L Jr	125	*1.15	91-25	ChinookPass1256TravellngVctor118noErthquck119nk	In hand	14
31Jly83- 8Dmr	fst 6f	:214 :442 :561 1:083	3↑ Bing Crosby H 54k	5	1	13	15	17	18	Pincay L Jr	125	*.50	95-20	ChnkPss1258VagabondSong1162½HaughtyButNc1152	Easily	7
23Apr83- 8SA	fst 6½f	:211 :434 1:083 1:152	4↑ San Simeon H 66k	7	1	16	15	15	14	Pincay L Jr	124	*1.30	93-16	ChnookPss1244Shanekite1181¼Earthquack121hd	Ridden out	7
13Mar83-11TuP	fst 6f	:21 :431 :56 1:092	3↑ Phoenix Gold Cup-G3	1	4	1hd	1hd	12	53½	Pincay L Jr	126	*.40	85-19	BirthdaySong115½Dave'sFriend1211SonofDodo1151½	Weakened	9
2Mar83- 8SA	sly 6½f	:211 :432 1:074 1:143	4↑ Potrero Grande H 64k	5	1	15	12½	14	13½	Pincay L Jr	123	*.60	97-15	ChnookPass1233½HaughtyButNice1154TheCaptan114no	Easily	5
	Previously trained by Bud Klokstad															
26Jan83- 8SA	gd 6½f	:214 :443 1:094 1:164	4↑ Sierra Madre H 66k	5	1	15	15	12½	1nk	Pincay L Jr	121	*.70	75-22	ChinookPass121nkFightingFt1161½PolcInspctor1202	Driving	7
2Jan83- 8SA	fst 7f	:221 :443 1:082 1:21	Malibu-G2	7	5	11½	1½	45½	616¼	McCarron CJ	120	1.90	79-13	TimetoExplode117nkPrinceSpellbnd1235WaveringMnrch1232		8
	Lunged at start															
26Dec82- 8SA	fst 6f	:21 :431 :544 1:073	2↑ Palos Verdes H 67k	6	2	14	13½	13½	13½	Pincay L Jr	120	*1.60	100-08	ChinookPss1203½GenralJmmy112¾Unprdctbl1222	Ridden out	8
4Dec82- 8Hol	fm 5fⓉ	:221 :441 :56	3↑ Meteor H 54k	4	4	12	12	13	13	Pincay L Jr	117	*.80	100-05	ChinookPss1173Dv'sFrnd1171FortClgry1151	Bumped,driving	7
14Nov82- 9Hol	fst 6f	:213 :441 :56 1:083	3↑ Nat Sprint Ch (Div 2) 114k	2	8	31½	3½	31½	32	Shoemaker W	112	2.90	92-12	Unpredictabl1201½RmmbrJohn120½ChnkPss112hd	Poor start	8
25Oct82-10LA	fst 6f	:21 :443 :571 1:10	3↑ Orange Coast H 26k	5	1	13	1hd	1½	2nk	Davidson JR	114	2.90	95-16	PompeiCourt122nkChnkPss1142ToB.orNot119no	Just missed	6
25Sep82- 9Lga	my 1 1/16	:233 :463 1:122 1:46	Puget Sound H 24k	7	1	14	12	1hd	27	Frazier B	120	*.90	62-32	IronBilly1187ChinookPass120hdBabaAdhem1131½	Little left	7
17Sep82- 9Lga	fst 5f	:212 :432 :551	3↑ Handicap 12000	4	2	12	13	15	16½	Davidson JR	113	*.25	104-14	ChnookPss1136½MyOmen1051½LotoCanada1172	Saved ground	6
22Aug82- 9Lga	fst 1	:221 :451 1:102 1:353	3↑ Lga Mile H-G2	5	1	1½	1	2hd	21½	Davidson JR	113	7.95	89-20	PompeiiCrt1211½ChinookPss113noPolcInspctor1194	Gamely	11
8Aug82- 9Lga	fst 6½f	:211 :434 1:083 1:15	3↑ Governor's H 35k	7	1	14	13	12½	12	Baze G	118	2.15	94-15	ChinookPass1182RoyalHudson114noTilttheBlnc123no	Driving	8
25Jly82- 9Lga	fst 6f	:213 :441 :562 1:091	3↑ Speed H 29k	7	2	11½	1½	12	1½	Baze G	114	*1.75	90-17	ChinookPass114½Foolish Owners1173Che1121½	Saved ground	9
5Jly82- 9Lga	fst 1	:222 :453 1:11 1:371	Seattle Slew H 28k	7	1	1hd	57	-	-	Baze G	123	*2.95	- -	NightCommand121nkFabulsOmen1202SkiRacr1181½	Distanced	14
1May82- 9Lga	fst 5½f	:213 :442 :562 1:022	Alw 12000	5	2	13½	13	13	18	Baze G	116	*.70	100-16	Chinook Pass1168Ski Racer1205½Fabulous Omen11413	Easily	6
10Apr82- 7PM	fst 6f	:221 :46 :581 1:11	Alw 3000	5	2	11	12	11	11	Baze G	120	*.40	92-18	ChinookPss1201LighthouseJim1204½FamilyFox1171½	Handily	7
20Mar82-10PM	fst 6f	:221 :45 :574 1:112	Alw 3000	2	5	13	15	15	12	Taketa J	117	*.30	90-16	ChinookPass1172FamilyFox1202UpYourIncome120½	Driving	6
30Aug81- 9Lga	fst 6½f	:213 :443 1:104 1:172	[S]Gottstein Fut 98k	5	4	1½	12½	1hd	1117	Loseth C	121	*1.20	65-23	Belle of Ranier1181Sarada Spy1213Long Gyland121hd		14
	Broke slowly,rushed up,gave way str															
12Aug81- 9Lga	fst 6f	:212 :443 :57 1:102	Stripling 24k	9	1	13½	13	14	11½	Loseth C	121	*1.30	84-20	ChnookPss1211½LongGylnd117noHotSummrKnght1182½	Driving	9
11Jly81- 9Lga	gd 5½f	:22 :451 :574 1:042	ⒸWash Stallion 26k	8	1	12	12½	14	14	Sorenson D	118	5.70	90-21	ChnookPss1184SrdSpy1202½ChngT1182½	Saved ground,easily	9
27Jun81- 4Lga	fst 5½f	:221 :453 :582 1:051	Ⓒ[S]Md Sp Wt	2	2	11½	12	14	12	Sorenson D	120	1.95	86-18	ChinookPass1202SaradaSpy1204FlashYourWallet1201	Driving	8
20Jun81- 4Lga	sl 5½f	:22 :47 1:003 1:074	Ⓒ[S]Md Sp Wt	1	1	14	12	13	1¾	Baze MB	120	5.95	73-29	[D]ChnkPss120¾TopThought120hdHotSummrKnght120hd	Driving	7
	Disqualified and placed second															

Christmas Past

gr. f. 1979, by Grey Dawn II (Herbager)–Yule Log, by Bold Ruler **Lifetime record: 15 8 2 3 $563,670**

Own.– Cynthia Phipps
Br.– Cynthia Phipps (Ky)
Tr.– Angel Penna Jr

26Feb83-10GP	fst 1¼	:481 1:131 1:373 2:023	3↑ Gulf Park H-G1	11	10	911	63¼	3½	1nk	Velasquez J	117	*1.30	83-19	ChristmasPast117nkCraftyProspctor115¾Rvlro1202½	Driving	12
11Feb83- 9GP	fst 1 1/16	:24 :473 1:113 1:423	4↑ ⒻAlw 25000	8	4	44	31½	11	15	Vasquez J	122	*.30	88-21	ChristmsPst1225Acharmer1159SheCommandum117nk	Handily	8
9Oct82- 8Bel	fst 1½	:473 1:114 2:04 2:311	3↑ J C Gold Cup-G1	7	6	619	34½	25	36½	Vasquez J	118	7.00	57-25	Lemhi Gold1264½Silver Supreme1262Christmas Past11817		10
	Wide,weakened															
26Sep82- 8Bel	fst 1⅛	:461 1:101 1:352 1:483	3↑ ⒻRuffian H-G1	8	7	74¼	1hd	11½	15	Vasquez J	117	2.50	84-19	ChristmsPast1175MadmoslIForl1122¼LovSgn123¾	Ridden out	8
15Sep82- 8Bel	fst 1⅛	:463 1:101 1:344 1:473	ⒻGazelle H-G2	2	6	62¾	21	44½	44¼	Vasquez J	123	*.70	85-14	BroomDance121nkNmbr1232¾MdmoslIForl1141¼	Bid,weakened	7
24Jly82- 9Mth	fst 1⅛	:474 1:112 1:362 1:492	ⒻMonmouth Oaks-G2	9	6	62¼	3½	1½	11¼	Vasquez J	121	*.40	88-14	ChristmasPast1211¼Milingo1191¼MadmoslIForl1121½	Driving	9
26Jun82- 8Bel	fst 1½	:471 1:11 2:021 2:283	ⒻC C A Oaks-G1	1	4	412	1hd	12	16	Vasquez J	121	2.50	77-20	ChristmasPast1216Cupcoy'sJoy121noFlyngPrtnr1213	Driving	10
4Jun82- 8Bel	fst 1⅛	:454 1:094 1:351 1:482	ⒻMother Goose-G1	6	5	59	47	21½	2¾	Vasquez J	121	7.10	84-18	Cpecoy'sJoy121¾ChrstmsPst1213¼BlushWthPrd1214¾	Rallied	12
22May82- 8Bel	fst 1	:231 :46 1:093 1:341	ⒻAcorn-G1	9	5	53	44½	56½	59½	Vasquez J	121	4.30	85-11	Cupecoy's Joy1212¾Nancy Huang1213½Vestris1212¼	Wide	9
24Mar82- 9GP	fst 1 1/16	:241 :474 1:114 1:441	ⒻBonnie Miss-G3	2	6	41¾	31	11½	13	Vasquez J	121	*.40	80-22	Christmas Past1213Norsan1131Our Darling1121½	Ridden out	6
4Mar82- 9Hia	fst 1⅛	:481 1:121 1:363 1:492	ⒻPoinsettia-G3	6	5	31½	21½	11½	16	Vasquez J	113	7.20	85-23	Christmas Past1136Larida1147Smart Heiress112½	Handily	8
1Feb82- 6Hia	fst 1 1/16	:24 :482 1:133 1:451	ⒻMd Sp Wt	6	2	2hd	13	16	111	Vasquez J	120	*.60	77-25	ChristmasPast12011Friedenau12012Saidamzelle1202½	Easily	9
18Jan82- 4Hia	fst 6f	:222 :453 1:104	ⒻMd Sp Wt	9	10	76¼	48½	36½	29	Vasquez J	120	*1.40	80-20	Artic Moss1209Christmas Past120nkPittsy1205	Bore in	12
8Oct81- 9Bel	fst 6f	:223 :461 1:123	ⒻMd Sp Wt	5	7	64¾	53½	34	33¼	Vasquez J	117	*1.60	76-21	Initial Encounter1172¾PushYourLuck117½ChristmasPast117½		12
	Rallied															
23Sep81- 3Bel	fst 6f	:224 :462 1:12	ⒻMd Sp Wt	7	13	109½	87¾	54½	32½	Vasquez J	117	8.20	78-18	Pert112nkBroom Dance1172¼Christmas Past117¾	Rallied	13

Conquistador Cielo

b. c. 1979, by Mr. Prospector (Raise a Native)–K D Princess, by Bold Commander **Lifetime record: 13 9 0 2 $474,328**

Own.– H. DeKwiatkowski
Br.– L.E. Iandoli (Fla)
Tr.– Woodford C. Stephens

21Aug82- 8Sar	fst 1¼	:462 1:103 1:354 2:023	Travers-G1	4	1	21	2hd	1hd	31¼	Maple E	126	*.40	86-14	RunawayGroom126½Aloma's Ruler126¾ConquistdrCielo1265¾		5
	Rank,tired															
8Aug82- 8Sar	fst 1⅛	:463 1:104 1:354 1:483	Jim Dandy-G3	2	1	1½	14	12	11	Maple E	128	*.10	92-14	ConquistadorCielo1281Lejoli11414NoHomeRun11417	Handily	4
5Jly82- 8Bel	fst 1⅛	:451 1:083 1:333 1:464	Dwyer-G2	1	1	11	14	15	14	Maple E	126	*.10	93-13	ConquistadorCielo1264John'sGold1148¾Renvstd1198¼	Easily	6
5Jun82- 8Bel	sly 1½	:471 1:12 2:031 2:281	Belmont-G1	11	2	11½	14	110	114	Pincay L Jr	126	4.10	79-17	Conquistador Cielo12614Gato Del Sol1264Illuminate1263¾		11
	Wide,ridden out															
31May82- 8Bel	fst 1	:224 :45 1:09 1:33	3↑ Metropolitan H-G1	11	1	3nk	12	15	17¼	Maple E	111	*2.00	101-12	Conquistador Cielo1117¼Silver Buck1112½Star Gallant1111¼		14
	Ridden out															
19May82- 7Bel	fst 1	:231 :454 1:094 1:341	3↑ Alw 35000	4	1	1hd	13	17	111	Maple E	113	*.70	95-14	ConquistdorCielo11311Swinging Light119¾Bachelor Boo1243¼		7
	Ridden out															
8May82- 7Pim	fst 1 1/16	:241 :473 1:113 1:441	Alw 27000	3	2	22	21	11½	13	Maple E	112	*.50	84-20	CnquistdrCielo1123DoublNo11510SixSails1122½	Bore in,clear	5
26Feb82- 7Hia	fst 7f	:224 :451 1:094 1:221	Alw 14000	1	7	1½	11½	12½	14	Maple E	116	*.60	92-18	ConquistadorCilo1164Hostg11610MystcSqur116nk	Ridden out	7
16Feb82- 9Hia	fst 7f	:223 :443 1:10 1:23	Alw 14000	1	6	53½	67½	44	47¼	Maple E	116	5.60	81-17	StarGallant1164CutAway1202Rex'sProfile1161¼	No factor	7
12Aug81- 8Sar	gd 6f	:213 :45 1:111	Sanford-G2	2	8	64½	78	54½	4nk	Maple E	122	3.70	84-12	Mayanesian115hdShipping Magnate115noLejoli115no	Bumped	10
3Aug81- 8Sar	fst 6f	:221 :453 1:103	Sar Spl-G2	2	6	63¾	2hd	1hd	1½	Maple E	117	8.20	87-18	ConquistdrCielo117½Herschelwalker1171¼Timely Writer1221¼		10
	Driving															
10Jly81- 6Bel	fst 5½f	:23 :464 :59 1:05	Md Sp Wt	7	3	32	21	13	18	Saumell L	118	*1.60	90-12	Conquistador Cielo1188High Ascent1186Greers' Leader1181½		9
	Ridden out															
29Jun81- 4Bel	fst 5½f	:224 :464 :593 1:062	Md Sp Wt	9	8	44¼	53	23	3¾	Saumell L	118	4.60	82-15	AntiguaBird118¾Commodity118hdConquistdorCilo1181½	Wide	10

Cozzene

gr. c. 1980, by Caro (Fortino II)–Ride the Trails, by Prince John

Lifetime record: 24 10 5 5 $978,152

Own.– J.A. Nerud
Br.– John A. Nerud (Fla)
Tr.– Jan H. Nerud

2Nov85- 4Aqu	fm	1Ⓣ	:224 :462 1:111 1:35	3↑ BC Mile-G1	6 3	32½ 31½ 2½	12¼	Guerra WA	126	3.60	101-00	Cozzene1262¼[D]PalaceMusic126noAlMamoon126no	Drew clear	14
3Oct85- 8Med	sly	1 1/16⊗	:232 :47 1:121 1:45	3↑ Cliff Hanger H-G3	6 4	52½ 55½ 513	616	Guerra WA	123	*1.00	62-25	LateAct117nkSilverSurfer1162½PxNobscum1167	Off sluggish	7
24Aug85- 9Mth	fm	1⅛Ⓣ	:481 1:122 1:362 1:482	3↑ Longfellow H-G2	6 4	38½ 45½ 1hd	12	Guerra WA	122	*.70	98-09	Cozzene1222Zoffany114¾Mourjane1173	Driving	8
11Aug85- 8Sar	fm	1⅛Ⓣ	:474 1:102 1:342 1:47	3↑ B Baruch H-G2	3 5	54 32 2hd	2nk	Guerra WA	120	2.20	92-13	Win124nkCozzene1204½Sitzmark112¾	Bore out	9
13Jly85- 9Mth	fm	1 1/16Ⓣ	:243 :48 1:113 1:422	3↑ Oceanport H-G3	8 3	35 32½ 2hd	13	Guerra WA	121	*1.70	93-14	Cozzene1213StaytheCourse1193½RovingMinstrel1181	Driving	9
8Jun85- 4Bel	sly	6f	:214 :442 1:091	3↑ Jaipur 81k	3 4	35 34 33½	33¼	Cordero A Jr	117	2.40	93-12	Mt. Livermore1192¾Main Top117½Cozzene117¾	Even try	7
27May85- 7Bel	fm	7fⓉ	:223 :45 1:093 1:23	3↑ Wise Ship 56k	2 7	44 24 22½	31¾	Guerra WA	119	*.40e	87-19	Sitzmark1191Red Wing Dream119¾Cozzene1191	Off slowly	7
10May85- 8Bel	fst	6f	:221 :452 1:11	3↑ Alw 36000	7 7	56½ 46 2½	11¼	Guerra WA	124	5.10	87-20	Cozzene1241¼Basket Weave124½Momento II1192½	Driving	7
10Nov84- 4Hol	fm	1Ⓣ	:223 :453 1:084 1:323	3↑ BC Mile-G1	5 3	32½ 3½ 1hd	31¾	Guerra WA	126	3.80	103-01	Royal Heroine1231½Star Choice126nkCzzene126nk	Weakened	10
10Oct84- 8Bel	fm	1Ⓣ	:221 :451 1:092 1:33	3↑ Alw 36000	2 3	32 11½ 14	14	Guerra WA	117	*.90	100-12	Cozzene1174Sitzmark1152¾Alev1152¾	Ridden out	6
21Sep84- 8Med	fm	1 1/16Ⓣ	:233 :47 1:103 1:402	3↑ Cliff Hanger H (Div 2) 73k	6 3	31 2hd 1hd	1½	Guerra WA	115	*1.00	100-06	Cozzene115½Ayman1121¼Pin Puller1144¾	Driving	6
8Sep84- 8Bel	fm	1⅜[T]	:472 1:114 1:36 2:143	3↑ Man o' War-G1	1 4	42½ 31½ 2hd	31¾	Guerra WA	126	10.80	82-16	Majesty's Prince126¾Win1261Cozzene126nk	Weakened	9
12Aug84- 8Sar	fm	1⅛Ⓣ	:473 1:12 1:342 1:472	3↑ B Baruch H-G2	3 3	3½ 3nk 3nk	31	Venezia M	114	3.40	89-07	Win112¾Intensify113nkCozzene114hd	Evenly	9
14Jly84- 8Atl	fm	1 3/16Ⓣ	:481 1:114 1:352 1:54	3↑ U Nations H-G1	8 4	42¼ 31 23½	21½	Venezia M	114	9.70e	92-14	Hero'sHonor1231½Czzene114noWho'sforDinner110hd	Gamely	11
23Jun84- 8Mth	fm	1 1/16Ⓣ	:234 :474 1:11 1:41	3↑ Alw 19000	3 4	41 42½ 3½	1¾	Swatuk B	115	2.70e	106-03	Cozzene115¾Wild Again1192Castle Guard1172	Drew clear	6
9Jun84- 6Bel	fst	6f	:221 :444 1:091	3↑ Jaipur 58k	3 10	64½ 55½ 68	67¾	Cordero A Jr	115	*2.00	88-10	CannnShell1152ChanBalum1152BelievetheQuen1153	In close	12
28May84- 8Bel	fst	1	:223 :444 1:084 1:34	3↑ Metropolitan H-G1	7 6	43 33 36	48¼	Venezia M	114	13.10	87-17	Fit to Fight124hdA Phenomenon1267¼Moro1161	Tired	10
10May84- 8Bel	fst	7f	:23 :454 1:091 1:211	3↑ Alw 33000	5 4	42½ 32½ 24½	27½	Venezia M	119	6.90	88-17	Fit to Fight1247½Cozzene1192Mugatea1191	Wide stretch	7
20Oct83- 8Med	fst	1 1/16	:232 :462 1:102 1:434	Palisades 53k	5 5	43½ 32 21	2hd	Cordero A Jr	113	7.10	90-16	Bet Big114hdCozzene113½Jacque's Tip1191	Just missed	7
9Oct83- 8Bel	fst	1	:231 :46 1:093 1:34	Jamaica H-G3	8 4	53 33½ 57¼	510½	Bailey JD	113	8.10	84-10	Bounding Basque1151½A Phenomenn1203Bet Big1155¾	Tired	8
5Sep83- 7Bel	fst	7f	:223 :452 1:103 1:241	3↑ Alw 27000	1 6	21½ 2½ 11	11¼	Cordero A Jr	115	*1.00	81-20	Cozzene1151¼DavetheDude1172EcstaticPride1131¼	Driving	9
17Aug83- 9Sar	fst	6f	:221 :45 1:093	3↑ Alw 20000	11 9	21½ 2½ 1hd	12¼	Cordero A Jr	112	*1.60	92-11	Czzene1122¼StopCard1145¾CglSprngs112hd	Brushed,driving	12
27Jly83- 7Sar	fst	6f	:214 :444 1:102	3↑ Alw 20000	6 9	65½ 37 34	23¼	Migliore R	111	*1.90	85-13	Big McCoy1063¼Cozzene1112Spring Fever113nk	Raced wide	11
25May83- 6Bel	fst	6f	:223 :46 1:111	3↑ Md Sp Wt	3 11	53½ 21½ 2hd	13	Migliore R	113	*4.10	86-16	Czzene1133GallantMinded113¾BigMcCoy113no	Slow st,clear	12

Dave's Friend

b. g. 1975, by Friend's Choice (Crimson Satan)–Duc's Tina, by Duc de Fer

Lifetime record: 76 35 16 8 $1,079,915

Own.– John Franks
Br.– R.L. Beall (Md)
Tr.– Albert Toups

18Jun86- 9LaD	fst	6f	:222 :454 1:114	3↑ Alw 15000	5 2	52¼ 21 32½	42¼	Trosclair AJ	114	*.70e	81-20	Wendy Tom122nkLittle Slick118hdTexas Delta1122		6
	Unable to sustain bid;Previously trained by Jack C. Van Berg													
26Jan86- 7FG	gd	6f	:224 :47 :591 1:121	4↑ Alw 11500	1 2	11 1½ 2hd	53¾	Snyder L	114	*1.30	80-26	Head Games1141Justto Satisfy You1131½Double Ready121nk		9
	Weakened in stretch													
4Dec85- 7Aqu	fst	6f[•]	:22 :451 1:102	3↑ Alw 36000	2 6	1½ 11½ 11½	23	MacBeth D	115	3.50	89-18	Sonrie Jorge1153Dave's Friend115noDewan for Us1151		6
	Held place gamely;Previously trained by Frank Trosclair													
31May85- 9LaD	fst	6f	:231 :473 1:134	3↑ Alw 14000	5 3	31½ 31½ 1hd	1nk	Snyder L	114	*.80e	73-39	Dave's Friend114nkEstate1152½Safe Cracker1187	Driving	6
	Previously trained by Jack C. Van Berg													
18Apr85- 9OP	fst	6f	:213 :442 1:082	4↑ Count Fleet Sprint H 159k	9 2	21½ 3nk 33	812¼	Patterson G	118	2.60e	86-20	Taylor'sSpecial1235Mt.Livermore1192¼T.H.Bend110no	Tired	10
6Apr85- 8OP	fst	6f	:223 :461 1:103	4↑ Alw 18000	6 3	11½ 1½ 12	21½	Snyder L	112	*1.00	85-18	Wipe'EmOut1121½Dve'sFrnd1121CheyenneChr112½	No match	7
28May84- 9Aks	fst	6f	:222 :45 1:101	3↑ Ak-Sar-Ben H 102k	9 11	1110 1111 1114	1113½	MacBeth D	124	3.60	72-28	TimelessNative1231½FivePrcnt110hdAllSoldOut1151	Trailed	11
3May84- 8CD	sly	7f	:23 :46 1:102 1:23	4↑ Churchill Downs 33k	5 5	41½ 43 46	511½	Delahoussaye E	118	*.60	80-23	Habitonia118½Roman Jamboree1152Euathlos1137	Wide	5
19Apr84- 9OP	fst	6f	:212 :441 1:09	4↑ Count Fleet H 130k	2 7	43¾ 33½ 33	11½	Delahoussaye E	122	4.90	100-12	Dave'sFrind1221½AllSoldOut1143½LuckySlvton113hd	Driving	8
4Apr84- 5SA	fm	*6½fⓉ	:21 :431 1:071 1:14	4↑ Alw 45000	4 3	33½ 32½ 46	57	Pincay L Jr	117	1.70	82-17	Champagne Bid1221¾Famous Star1144Academic1191	Tired	7
21Mar84- 8SA	fst	5½f	:214 :444 :57 1:031	4↑ El Conejo H (Div 2) 50k	5 2	2½ 1hd 12	21¼	Pincay L Jr	120	4.30	94-15	Night Mover1171¼Dave's Friend1201½Bara Lass1173	Gamely	7
13Nov83- 5SA	my	6f	:22 :452 :573 1:102	3↑ Alw 45000	7 1	31 21 1hd	11	McCarron CJ	117	*2.10	86-26	Dave's Friend1171Total Departure1153Hey Rob1177	Driving	7
15Oct83- 8SA	fst	6½f	:212 :441 1:091 1:16	2↑ Morvich H 65k	1 3	32 31 34	33½	Meza RQ	121	6.80	86-17	KangrooCourt119hdShanekite1203½Dave'sFrind121½	Even try	7
24Sep83-10Dar	fm	*6fⓉ	1:07	3↑ Chateaugay 16k	3 4	32 32 24	44¼	McKnight J	118	*.40	101-00	SmrtandShrp1154WndyProspct115hdCmpRobbr115hd	Weakened	6
27Aug83- 8CD	fst	6f	:214 :444 :571 1:102	3↑ Alw 13980	4 5	32 2hd 11½	13	McKnight J	122	*.20	94-11	Dave'sFrind1223RonnyTurcott112noFlynqTrophy1124	Drivinq	5
7Aug83-10Suf	fst	6f	:214 :443 :58 1:093	3↑ Suf Sprint H-G3	1 5	31½ 44 57	58	Snyder L	123	4.80	85-18	All Sold Out110¾Let Burn1151½Gold Beauty1244	Tired	8
4Jly83- 9CD	sly	7f	:233 :462 1:094 1:231	3↑ Firecracker H 44k	2 3	11 1½ 11½	2nk	Snyder L	124	*.70	91-19	ShotN'Missed121nkDave'sFrnd1245Rackensack1185½	Gamely	4
30May83- 9Aks	fst	6f	:221 :443 1:094	3↑ Ak-Sar-Ben H 116k	9 4	3½ 43 32	2½	Snyder L	127	*1.00	87-25	AllSoldOut110½Dave'sFriend1271BoldRuddy112nk	Game try	13
14Apr83- 9OP	fst	6f	:22 :454 1:10	4↑ Count Fleet Sprint H 117k	8 5	31 2hd 12½	15	Snyder L	124	4.60	95-22	Dave's Friend1245General Jimmy117noLiberty Lane113no		9
	Wide,drew clear													
13Mar83-11TuP	fst	6f	:21 :431 :56 1:092	3↑ Phoenix Gold Cup-G3	6 7	56½ 56½ 62¾	2½	Snyder L	121	4.20	88-19	BirthdaySong115½Dave'sFrnd1211SonofaDodo1151½	Gaining	9
26Feb83- 9OP	fst	6f	:22 :46 1:112	4↑ Handicap 50000	6 2	45 43 43	43	Snyder L	128	*.70e	85-23	Rackensack120nkPrcl1102½Sndbggr117nk	Lacked closing bid	7
19Feb83- 9OP	fst	6f	:22 :46 1:111	4↑ Handicap 50000	6 3	2hd 1hd 15	12½	Snyder L	124	*1.30	89-22	Dave'sFriend1242½LuckyPoint116½CircleofStel1164	Driving	7
6Feb83- 7SA	my	1 1/16	:231 :471 1:113 1:43	4↑ Alw 35000	4 2	31 65½ 620	-	Romero RP	115	1.60	--	Red Crescent117¾Mandato1156Sari's Dreamer1115	Eased	6
15Jan83- 8SA	fst	7f	:221 :442 1:082 1:21	4↑ San Carlos H-G2	1 4	1½ 11 12½	2¾	Romero RP	117	*1.50	94-10	KangrooCourt118¾Dav'sFrnd117noShnkt1184	Lacked late run	6
18Dec82- 8Hol	fst	7f	:214 :442 1:083 1:203	3↑ Yuletide H 55k	3 3	2hd 1hd 2hd	22	Romero RP	117	6.10	92-21	Time to Explode1182Dave's Friend1172Travelling Victor1141½		8
	2nd best													
4Dec82- 8Hol	fm	5fⓉ	:221 :441 :56	3↑ Meteor H 54k	2 3	42½ 33 34½	23	Black K	117	3.30	97-05	ChinookPass1173Dave'sFriend1171FortCalgry1151	No threat	7
14Nov82- 8Hol	fst	6f	:212 :433 :553 1:081	3↑ Nat Sprint Ch (Div 1) 115k	7 4	52¾ 33 22	31	Shoemaker W	114	4.70	95-12	Mad Key1161Shanekite120hdDave's Friend114nk		9
	Saved ground,driffted out str													
2Oct82- 8Haw	fst	6½f	:213 :44 1:091 1:153	3↑ Midwest H 31k	4 2	33 32½ 2½	32¼	Jones K	123	*1.20	93-20	Tinsley's Hope119hdGo With the Times1122¼Dave's Frnd1231¾		7
	Wide bid,bled													
5Sep82- 9Tdn	fst	6f	:22 :452 :574 1:102	3↑ George Lewis H 27k	5 1	1hd 12½ 1½	12½	Jones K	127	*.50	92-22	Dave's Friend1272½Silahis1225½Ballacashtal117nk	Driving	6
21Aug82- 9Det	fst	6f	:212 :442 :564 1:091	3↑ Prince 15k	6 1	21 21½ 21½	1½	Jones K	120	*1.00	94-14	Dave'sFriend120½Tinsley'sHope120nkSoloRide1132	All out	7
	Previously trained by Robert E. Holthus													
16Jly82- 8Aks	fst	6f	:212 :432 1:09	3↑ Ak-Sar-Ben H 56k	6 4	2hd 2½ 22	3¾	Jones K	125	*1.70	91-19	Smokite123noMadKey114¾Dave'sFrnd125hd	Lacked response	11
5Jly82- 8Aks	fst	6f	:222 :45 1:101	3↑ Alw 18000	1 4	1½ 1hd 11½	1½	Jones K	122	*.80	86-21	Dave's Friend122½Smokite1222Destroy 'em1161	Driving	5
12Jun82- 9Aks	fst	6f	:212 :434 1:083	3↑ Speed 31k	6 3	1hd 1hd 2½	12•	Jones K	117	*1.10	94-18	[DH]Dave's Friend117[DH]Ogataul1162Daddyal117hd	Driving	8
23May82- 3LaD	fst	6f	:221 :444 1:083	3↑ Alw 14500	3 2	11 11½ 12½	14½	Snyder L	122	*.20	106-03	Dave'sFrnd1224½HiHoBlack1196YstrdysHro1176	Ridden out	5
8May82- 8LaD	fst	6f	:222 :451 1:094	3↑ Alw 14000	4 3	21½ 2hd 1½	17½	Snyder L	114	*.40	100-12	Dave'sFriend1147½SpecialSpecial114nkPartout1141	Driving	10
29Apr82- 8CD	fst	7f	:23 :463 1:102 1:224	3↑ Ch Downs H (Div 2) 35k	5 3	1½ 11½ 22	46¾	Romero RP	121	*2.10	86-15	BayouBlack1193¼VodikaCollins1183½PrincCrmson116hd	Tired	6
	Previously trained by Louis G. Marshall													
3Jly81- 8Bel	my	6f	:221 :45 1:09	3↑ True North H 55k	2 2	42½ 64½ 76¾	79	Black AS	128	2.20	88-16	Joanie's Chief1091¼Proud Appeal117nkGuiltyConscnce1133½		7
	Tired													

7Jun81- 9Suf	fst 6f	:222 :452 1:103	3↑ Suf Downs H 79k	1 5 2½ 21 2½ 2no	Black AS	128	*.80	88-29	RingofLight116noDave'sFriend128¾Triocala112½	Brushed	10
17May81- 8Bel	fst 6f	:223 :453 1:094	3↑ Roseben H 55k	3 2 2½ 1hd 11 42¼	Romero R	132	*1.30	91-22	RingofLight113¾GuiltyConscnce1121Convnnt114½	Weakened	8
Previously trained by Robert L. Beall											
25Apr81- 7Aqu	fst 6f	:221 :451 1:093	3↑ Bold Ruler 80k	3 2 1hd 13 13½ 11½	Black AS	123	*.60	93-23	Dave'sFrnd1231½NaughtyJimmy1191½Fppno1192¾	Drew clear	6
15Apr81- 8Aqu	fst 6f	:22 :452 1:10	4↑ Alw 32000	4 1 1hd 12 14½ 1½	Black AS	122	*.10	91-23	Dave'sFrnd122½HerbWater1172½BoldVoyagr1225	Ridden out	5
Previously owned by Mrs Robert L. Beall											
29Mar81- 8Aqu	fst 6f	:214 :442 1:092	3↑ White Skies H 54k	3 2 11 11 12 13¾	Bracciale V Jr	130	*.30	94-21	Dave'sFriend1303¾GuiltyConscience114½RarePerformer1174½	Handily	4
13Mar81- 8Key	fst 7f	:221 :452 1:092 1:222	4↑ Alw 14000	4 3 34 22 21½ 1no	Bracciale V Jr	119	*.20	95-28	Dave's Friend119noCheating Arthur1227King Bold Reality1197	Bumped st.,driving	5
3Jan81- 9Bow	fst 6f	:221 :45 :564 1:09	3↑ Southern Maryland H 42k	1 1 11 11½ 13 14¾	Bracciale V Jr	129	*.30	95-14	Dave'sFriend1294¾Gasp1132PeaceforPeace111¾	Ridden out	5
20Dec80- 6Lrl	fst 1	:232 :462 1:103 1:35	3↑ Alw 18000	2 1 1½ 1½ 11 12	Bracciale V Jr	122	*.30	98-12	Dave's Friend1222Naughty Jimmy116nkGasp1224½	Ridden out	7
29Nov80- 8Aqu	my 6f	:214 :441 1:081	3↑ Sport Page H 57k	2 2 11 12 14 15	Bracciale V Jr	126	*1.20	102-13	Dave'sFriend1265TiltUp114nkHawkin'sSpecl1142	Ridden out	8
21Nov80- 8Lrl	fst 5f	:222 :444 :57	3↑ Alw 18000	8 3 1hd 1½ 12 15	Bracciale V Jr	119	*.20	101-15	Dave's Friend1195No Scruples1133Right Bank113no	Handily	9
8Nov80- 5Lrl	fst 6f	:223 :462 :58 1:103	3↑ Alw 20000	3 2 11 11 11½ 12	Bracciale V Jr	122	*.40	93-12	Dave's Friend1222Gasp1157Hot Words1131	Driving	7
18Oct80- 8Aqu	fst 7f	:223 :443 1:084 1:212	3↑ Vosburgh-G1	2 4 1½ 1½ 11 31½	Bracciale V Jr	126	4.20	92-12	PluggdNickle123½JaklinKlugmn1231Dv'sFrnd126¾	Weakened	9
8Oct80- 8Bel	fst 6f	:221 :452 1:103	3↑ Boojum H 57k	7 3 1hd 2hd 2½ 52½	Bracciale V Jr	127	4.10	86-22	DoubleZeus1202½CndyEclr124hdKng'sFshon123no	Drifted out	9
21Jun80- 9Bow	fst 6f	:223 :45 :563 1:093	3↑ Terrapin H 27k	2 3 11 11½ 1hd 2½	Bracciale V Jr	128	*.50	91-19	Isella117½Dave's Friend1284Fuzzbuster1121	Drifted out	4
Previously owned by Bel-Mar Stable											
17May80- 8Aqu	fst 6f	:22 :443 1:09	3↑ Roseben H 55k	4 1 11½ 11½ 12 11¼	Bracciale V Jr	126	*1.50	98-16	Dave'sFriend1261¼DoubleZeus118½StateDinner1181¾	Driving	7
20Apr80- 7Aqu	fst 6f	:214 :441 1:094	3↑ Bold Ruler 81k	1 2 11½ 12 12 12¾	Bracciale V Jr	123	4.10	94-16	Dave's Friend1232¾Tilt Up1211½Double Zeus121¾	Driving	6
5Apr80- 7Pim	fst 6f	:23 :453 :574 1:103	3↑ J E Hoover H 31k	4 3 21 26 37½ 312½	Bracciale V Jr	125	*.30	80-19	Isella11611AmbitiousRuler1101½Dave'sFrnd125no	Lugged in	4
22Mar80- 9Pim	fst 1 1/16	:24 :474 1:121 1:44	3↑ [S]Alw 25000	4 1 11 11 1½ 2¾	Bracciale V Jr	124	*.70	84-21	Red Light117¾Dave's Friend124¾T.V. Hill117¾	Weakened	7
18Feb80- 8Aqu	fst 6f[•]	:212 :442 1:093	3↑ Sporting Plate H 55k	5 3 21 1hd 12 12¼	Black AS	122	4.10	96-19	Dave'sFriend1222¼DoublZus1263¼BoldndStormy115no	Driving	6
9Feb80- 8Bow	fst 7f	:23 :46 1:101 1:233	4↑ Alw 20000	2 4 11 1hd 2½ 22¼	Black AS	122	*.90	85-26	PolePosition1222¼Dave'sFrind1223½IslndSultn1222½	Failed	5
12Jan80- 9Bow	gd 6f	:224 :454 :58 1:11	3↑ S Maryland H 43k	4 3 1hd 11 13 12¼	Bracciale V Jr	118	*.90	85-33	Dave's Friend1182¼Isella115¾Shelter Half118¾	Driving	8
25Nov79- 8Aqu	fst 6f	:22 :444 1:092	3↑ Sport Page H 54k	5 3 2hd 1hd 1hd 31¾	Black AS	119	5.10	94-21	Amadevil113nkTanthem1231½Dave's Friend119¾	Weakened	7
11Nov79- 6Aqu	fst 6f	:22 :443 1:093	3↑ Alw 25000	4 2 2hd 2hd 2hd 45	Bracciale V Jr	117	1.90	90-15	Tilt Up1173¼C.J.'s Boy1171Bold and Stormy117¾	Gave way	6
26May79- 8Pim	my 1 1/16	:24 :48 1:114 1:46	3↑ City of Baltimore H 33k	1 1 11 2hd 24 37¾	Bracciale V Jr	124	*.30	67-27	Revivalist1151¾T.V. Hill1146Dave's Friend1244	Bore in	5
14May79- 8Pim	gd 1⅛	:474 1:114 1:371 1:503	[S]Jennings H 56k	5 1 11 1½ 11 2no	Bracciale V Jr	124	*.30	89-13	WhataGent111noDave'sFrnd1242½TakethePledge112hd	Nosed	7
5May79- 6Pim	fst 1 1/16	:233 :47 1:103 1:423	3↑ [S]Alw 25000	1 1 1½ 11 13 13¼	Bracciale V Jr	115	*.30	92-13	Dave'sFriend1153¼GalaForecast1171½BigPunt1155	Handily	5
26Apr79- 8Pim	fst 6f	:231 :454 :57 1:094	4↑ Alw 19000	1 3 11 11½ 12 12½	Bracciale V Jr	119	*.40	97-17	Dave's Friend1192½Tiny Monk107½Bold Road1153	Handily	8
16Nov78- 6Med	fst 6f	:22 :451 1:103	Palisades H 53k	1 6 1½ 1hd 1½ 1no	Bracciale V Jr	126	*.50	92-15	Dave's Friend126noTanthem1142Al Battah119nk	Lasted	9
4Nov78- 7Lrl	fst 6f	:222 :454 :571 1:094	3↑ Handicap 20000	4 3 1½ 1½ 14 14	Bracciale V Jr	125	*.50	97-16	Dave'sFrnd1254Hmpt'sLrk1152¼SportngPowdr115hd	Handily	7
7Oct78- 8Bow	fst 1⅛	:472 1:11 1:362 1:50	Governor's Cup H 108k	4 1 1½ 11½ 21 22½	Bracciale V Jr	120	3.80	92-21	NastyandBold1232½Dave'sFrind12010StrdNskr11820	2nd best	5
16Sep78- 8Bow	fst 1 1/16	:23 :473 1:123 1:441	[S]Chesapeake H 27k	1 1 11½ 11½ 11 1¾	Bracciale V Jr	119	*.10	85-26	Dave'sFriend119¾KingofFools1109PerfectDaddy1143	Driving	4
4Sep78- 8Bel	fst 1	:222 :45 1:093 1:36	Jerome H-G2	5 1 11½ 1½ 1hd 41¼	Bracciale V Jr	119	3.40	87-14	SensitivePrince118nkDarbyCreekRoad122nkSorry Lookin112¾	Ducked in	5
5Aug78- 8Mth	sly 1⅛	:47 1:123 1:393 1:531	Mth Inv'l H-G1	3 1 11 11½ 1½ 2¾	Bracciale V Jr	120	*1.40	68-31	DeltaFlag112¾Dave'sFrnd1202½SpecilHonor1182¾	Weakened	7
22Jly78- 8Pim	fst 1⅛	:46 1:101 1:352 1:482	Marylander H 56k	3 1 11½ 13 11½ 11	Bracciale V Jr	117	*1.00	102-17	Dave's Friend1171Star de Naskra1196Sensitive Prince1225	Bobbled,driving	5
11Jly78- 7Pim	fst 6f	:232 :461 :574 1:094	3↑ Alw 7500	3 3 11½ 11½ 13 18	Bracciale V Jr	117	*.30	97-18	Dave'sFriend1178HellorHeaven110¾Wm.Withers1216	Handily	7
27May78- 8Key	fst 7f	:213 :44 1:082 1:212	Patriot-G3	1 4 11½ 11½ 11½ 12	Bracciale V Jr	117	*1.00	102-13	Dave'sFriend1172FullPartner115noShelterHlf1191½	Driving	4
14May78- 8Key	sly 6½f	:213 :441 1:09 1:154	Alw 20000	1 6 1½ 11 14 18	Bracciale V Jr	114	1.90	94-20	Dave's Friend1148Al Battah122½Bold Conceiver1123	Easily	6
22Apr78- 5Pim	fst 6f	:232 :471 :59 1:112	Alw 6500	7 3 11 1½ 14 110	Bracciale V Jr	120	*.30	89-16	[D]Dave'sFriend12010SeaofDavid107nkBackBayBu1153	Bore in	7
Disqualified and placed seventh											
12Apr78- 2Pim	fst 6f	:233 :463 1:104	3↑ Md Sp Wt	7 2 1½ 11½ 16 112	Bracciale V Jr	115	*1.30	92-19	Dave'sFriend11512BlackBeau1141¼NorthrnStndrd1093	Easily	8

De La Rose

b. f. 1978, by Nijinsky II (Northern Dancer)–Rosetta Stone, by Round Table

Lifetime record: 26 11 6 0 $544,647

Own.– H. DeKwiatkowski

Br.– Dr & Mrs R. Smiser West & Mackenzie Miller (Ky)

Tr.– Woodford C. Stephens

31Mar82- 9GP	fm 1Ⓣ	:24 :472 1:112 1:351	3↑ ⒻS River H (Div 2)-G3	3 6 611 67½ 77¾ 65½	Maple E	123	*.90	88-10	Tchr'sPt1141¼ShrkSong1143½Blush113hd	No apparent excuse	9
5Mar82- 9Hia	fm 1⅛Ⓣ	1:47	3↑ ⒻBlack Helen H-G2	3 7 77 66 43½ 42¼	Maple E	124	*.60	96-09	HoneyFox123¾Endcott1131¼ShrkSong112½	Slow start,bobbled	8
15Feb82- 9Hia	fm 1 1/16Ⓣ	1:423	3↑ ⒻColumbiana H 63k	8 9 98¾ 86¾ 47½ 23¾	Maple E	124	*.90	81-14	HoneyFox1213¾DeLaRose124hdShrkSong113hd	Slow start,wide	10
15Nov81- 8Hol	fm 1⅛Ⓣ	:462 1:11 1:352 1:473	Hol Derby (Div 1)-G1	2 7 79¾ 51¾ 11 1nk	Maple E	119	*.70	92-10	De La Rose119nkHigh Counsel1225Lord Trendy122hd	Slow start,driving	8
17Oct81- 9WO	fm 1¼[T]	:492 1:154 1:411 2:052	3↑ ⒻE P Taylor-G3	4 8 84½ 2hd 13½ 12½	Maple E	118	*.30	80-20	De La Rose118½Sangue118½Sajama1181¼	Handily	9
12Oct81- 8Bel	fm 1¼[T]	:473 1:12 1:364 2:002	ⒻAthenia H-G3	6 8 89¾ 11½ 13 12¾	Maple E	125	*.90	92-11	DeLaRse1252¾NobleDamsel111¾AndoverWay1131	Ridden out	8
30Sep81- 8Bel	fm 1 1/16[T]	:241 :473 1:114 1:42	ⒻLamb Chop H 56k	6 8 76 31 11 11¾	Maple E	123	*.50	86-20	DeLaRose1231¾AndoverWay114nkWingsofGrace113hd	Driving	9
7Sep81- 8Bel	fm 1¼[T]	:472 1:112 1:372 2:013	3↑ ⒻFlower Bowl H-G2	5 5 518 52¾ 22 21¾	Maple E	116	*.40	84-22	Rokeby Rose1141¾De La Rose1161Euphrosyne1104	Wide	6
16Aug81- 8Sar	yl 1⅛Ⓣ	:474 1:124 1:372 1:503	3↑ ⒻDiana H-G2	1 5 46½ 52¼ 2½ 11¾	Maple E	114	*1.10	74-26	DeLaRose1141¾RokebyRose1153Euphrosyne112nk	Ridden out	8
26Jly81- 8Bel	fm 1¼[T]	:473 1:122 1:354 2:001	Lexington-G2	10 10 810 2½ 21½ 21¼	Maple E	121	*.80	92-08	Acaroid1171¼De La Rose1214Wicked Will117nk	2nd best	11
27Jun81- 8Bel	fst 1½	:474 1:114 2:014 2:281	ⒻC C A Oaks-G1	3 6 58½ 616 623 627	Maple E	121	*.40e	52-16	[D]RealPrize1212½WaywardLass1212½BannerGala12113	Outrun	6
13Jun81- 8Mth	fm 1Ⓣ	:24 :472 1:111 1:353	Long Branch-G3	9 7 74¼ 11½ 12½ 18½	Maple E	117	*.30	97-16	DeLaRose1178½CenturyBanker114noVictorinDoubl1143	Easily	9
31May81- 8Bel	fm 1Ⓣ	:23 :454 1:102 1:342	Saranac-G2	1 7 66 31½ 12½ 16½	Maple E	112	*.80e	93-10	DeLaRose1126½StageDoorKey114½ColorBearer1143	Handily	7
23May81- 6Bel	fm 1Ⓣ	:234 :46 1:092 1:331	Alw 35000	1 4 21½ 2½ 1hd 13¾	Maple E	112	*.60	99-11	DeLaRose1123¾ExplosiveBid1158SlvrExprss1101¾	Ridden out	7
1May81- 8CD	fst 1 1/16	:25 :484 1:13 1:434	ⒻKy Oaks-G1	3 6 55½ 53 21½ 2no	Day P	121	1.50e	89-17	HeavnlyCause121noDeLaRse1215WaywrdLss1213	Just missed	6
8Apr81- 7Kee	fst 7f	:231 :461 1:103 1:224	ⒻAlw 25780	6 5 88½ 76½ 43½ 45¾	Day P	118	*.60e	86-17	DameMysterse1212¾Bushmaid1132¼SwetRvng121¾	No factor	9
2Mar81- 9GP	fst 1 1/16	:25 :492 1:133 1:442	ⒻBonnie Miss 87k	3 7 75¼ 47 47 47½	Perret C	114	3.90	71-22	DameMystrieuse1181BannerGala1135HeavnlyCs1211½	Outrun	7
11Feb81- 9GP	fst 7f	:223 :45 1:092 1:221	ⒻForward Gal 43k	7 9 910 89 64½ 42	Perret C	114	9.90	91-18	DameMysterse1181¼HeavnlyCs121¾MstrsDrm113no	Rallied	10
15Nov80- 8Aqu	fst 1⅛	:48 1:123 1:373 1:504	ⒻDemoiselle-G1	4 6 67 64½ 21½ 2hd	Maple E	116	6.80	81-20	RainbowCnnection119hdDeLaRs1166TnTnToo1162¼	Ducked in	6
29Oct80- 8Aqu	gd 1⅛Ⓣ	:48 1:13 1:384 1:512	ⒻMiss Grillo 55k	4 5 57 51¾ 11½ 21	Maple E	121	1.40	86-13	Smilin' Sera1181De La Rose1213¾Seaholme1183¾	Gamely	8
5Oct80- 8Bel	fst 1	:241 :48 1:124 1:38	ⒻFrizette-G1	3 7 52½ 41 43 57½	Venezia M	119	11.70	70-23	HeavenlyCause1191½SweetRevnge1194½Prayrs'nPromiss119hd	Tired	8
22Sep80- 8Bel	fst 7f	:232 :471 1:114 1:243	ⒻMatron-G1	5 6 54½ 43½ 43 43¼	Maple E	119	6.60	76-23	Prayers'nPromises119hdHeavenlyCs1191SwtRvng1192¼	Wide	8
29Aug80- 8Bel	fm 7fⓉ	:23 :46 1:094 1:232	ⒻEvening Out 56k	1 6 65 42 2hd 1hd	Maple E	114	*.50	87-13	DeLaRose114hdBravoNative11210PrimeProspect1132¾	Driving	7
20Aug80- 6Sar	fm 1[T]	:24 :484 1:134 1:381	ⒻAlw 20000	2 6 54½ 1½ 11½ 15	Maple E	114	1.80	88-16	DeLaRose1145PicturePretty109noJanJill114¾	Ridden out	10
30Jly80- 8Sar	fst 6f	:212 :444 1:102	ⒻSchuylerville-G3	10 11 1118 98½ 810 711	Maple E	114	*1.60	77-12	SweetRevnge114nkCompanonshp1143HvnlyCs1143	Poor start	11
11Jly80- 4Bel	fst 6f	:23 :48 1:12	ⒻMd Sp Wt	2 11 911 42½ 1hd 13½	Maple E	117	*.50	82-16	De La Rose1173½Bravo Native1175¾Circle Game117hd	Slow start,ridden out	11

Deputy Minister

dkbbr. c. 1979, by Vice Regent (Northern Dancer)–Mint Copy, by Bunty's Flight — Lifetime record: 22 12 2 2 $696,964

Own.– Due Process Stable
Br.– Centurion Farms (Can)
Tr.– Reynaldo H. Nobles

17Nov83- 8Med fst 1¼ :47 1:104 1:361 2:022 3↑ Med Cup-G1 9 7 76¾ 31 11 2nk MacBeth D 118 5.10 90-18 Slewpy116nkDeputy Minister1181Water Bank117½ Gamely 9
5Nov83- 8Aqu fst 1⅛ :474 1:111 1:361 1:49 3↑ Stuyvesant H-G2 1 4 43 42 22 21¼ MacBeth D 119 2.50 89-22 FittoFight1171¼DeputyMinister119hdSingSing1154 Gamely 7
22Oct83- 8Aqu fst 7f :221 :45 1:083 1:21 3↑ Vosburgh-G1 6 8 74½ 53 44½ 32¼ MacBeth D 126 4.40 94-19 APhenomenon1231¾FittoFight126½DeputyMinister1261 Wide 8
28Sep83- 7Bel fst 1 :232 :454 1:093 1:342 3↑ Alw 40000 4 6 54 42½ 22 32¼ MacBeth D 115 *1.10 91-19 FittoFight1192Reinvested115nkDeputyMinistr1152 Weakened 6
3Sep83- 8Bel fst 1⅛ :454 1:092 1:34 1:463 3↑ Woodward-G1 8 8 84¼ 63½ 69 612½ MacBeth D 121 4.60 81-13 Slew o' Gold118noBates Motel1235Sing Sing1195 No factor 10
30Jly83- 8Sar fst 1⅛ :464 1:104 1:353 1:482 3↑ Whitney H-G1 7 7 64½ 63¾ 64¼ 42¾↓ MacBeth D 126 1.70 90-14 IslandWhirl123noBoldStyl114¾Sunny'sHlo1162 Wide stretch 9
17Jly83- 8Bel fst 7f :224 :453 1:093 1:221 3↑ Tom Fool-G2 5 8 85½ 42¼ 12½ 14¾ MacBeth D 126 3.40 91-13 DeputyMinister1264¾FittoFight119noMudln126hd Ridden out 9
12Feb83- 10GP fst 1⅛ :471 1:11 1:354 1:483 3↑ Donn H-G2 7 7 66½ 31 1hd 11¼ MacBeth D 122 *1.10 89-17 DeputyMinister1221¼KeyCount1133½Rivalro1212½ Ridden out 16
29Jan83- 10GP fst 7f :22 :444 1:10 1:224 3↑ Sprint Champ H 63k 4 9 1113 107 5½ 1½ MacBeth D 122 5.50 90-20 DeputyMinister122½Wipe'EmOut1092½CenterCut118½ Driving 12
Previously owned by Due Process, Centurion Farms & Kinghaven Farms;previously trained by John Tammaro
21Nov82- 8Aqu fst 6f :222 :452 1:092 3↑ Sport Page H 57k 3 9 94¾ 87¼ 87½ 78¼ MacBeth D 124 *1.60 86-24 Maudlin1154[D]King'sFashion117hdTopAvengr115nk No menace 11
Previously trained by Michael Tammaro
28Oct82- 8WO fst 6f :224 :452 1:092 3↑ Alw 16000 6 1 1½ 12½ 16 16½ Platts R 115 *.30 96-19 DeputyMinistr1156½ToutOuRien1231½RddyRodstr1262 Easily 6
Previously trained by John Tammaro
24Feb82- 9Hia fst 7f :232 :46 1:094 1:221 Alw 25000 8 2 31½ 21 44½ 99 MacBeth D 122 4.70 83-19 DistinctivePro1194½D'Accord1192¼CecisLilBandt115¾ Tired 9
27Jan82- 9Hia fst 7f :223 :451 1:094 1:221 Bahamas 38k 5 9 76 57 55½ 59½ MacBeth D 122 *1.10 82-19 Aloma'sRulr117hdDstnctvPro1174LtsDontFght1193 Steadied 9
Previously owned by Centurion Farms & Kinghaven Farms
5Nov81- 6Med fst 1 1/16 :232 :471 1:113 1:443 Young America-G1 7 5 42 11 14 13 MacBeth D 122 *1.90 86-17 DeputyMinister1223LaserLight1191RealTwister1192 Driving 14
24Oct81- 8Lrl gd 1 1/16 :233 :47 1:122 1:443 Lrl Futurity-G1 3 4 42½ 1hd 11½ 1no MacBeth D 122 *1.60 85-18 DeputyMinister122noLaserLght1229[D]CgyCougr122hd Driving 8
10Oct81- 7Bel fst 1 :233 :464 1:111 1:362 Champagne-G1 11 6 52 41¾ 44 48 Cordero A Jr 122 3.50 76-14 TimelyWritr1224¾BeforeDawn1193NewDscovry122nk Weakened 13
Previously trained by Bill Marko
2Aug81- 9WO fst 6f :221 :462 1:111 [R]Bull Page 42k 4 7 52½ 31½ 1½ 12½ Duffy L 122 *.30 87-17 DeputyMinstr1222½FraudSquad1152½MapleCrk1173½ Handily 7
11Jly81- 9WO fst 6f :222 :45 1:103 Colin 27k 2 5 2½ 1hd 1hd 11½ Duffy L 122 *.15 90-15 DeputyMinister1221½RichSaul1151MapleCrk1131¼ Ridden out 6
Previously owned by Centurion Farms
21Jun81- 9WO fst 5½f :221 :454 1:044 [R]Clarendon 32k 6 1 41¾ 31½ 1½ 14¾ Duffy L 122 *.30 93-16 DeputyMinister1224¾RichSaul1151¼RoyalFriesn1153 Handily 6
8Jun81- 8Bel fst 5½f :22 :453 :581 1:044 ©Youthful 56k 6 5 33 31½ 1½ 11¼ Duffy L 122 1.50 91-19 DeputyMinistr1221¼Ringaro1224NwDscovry115hd Ridden out 6
18May81- 9WO fst 5f :22 :451 :571 Victoria 28k 6 1 1½ 1hd 11 13¾ Duffy L 117 *1.20 101-16 DeputyMinistr1173¾Youngship1174½RegalSton1171½ Handily 8
10May81- 4WO fst 5f :23 :471 :592 [R]Md Sp Wt 6 4 11½ 11 14 14 Duffy L 120 2.10 90-17 DeputyMinistr1204BraveRegent1208Pck'sChoc1201¼ Handily 11

Devil's Bag

b. c. 1981, by Halo (Hail to Reason)–Ballade, by Herbager — Lifetime record: 9 8 0 0 $445,860

Own.– Hickory Tree Stable
Br.– E.P. Taylor (Md)
Tr.– Woodford C. Stephens

28Apr84- 8CD fst 1 :232 :46 1:101 1:353 Derby Trial 54k 3 1 11½ 12 11½ 12¼ Maple E 122 *.10 91-16 Devil's Bag1222¼Biloxi Indian1225Secret Prince1222¾ 5
Under steady urging
19Apr84- 7Kee gd 7f :231 :46 1:111 1:233 Alw 25860 3 2 1hd 12½ 15½ 115 Maple E 123 *.10 88-27 Devil'sBag12315SoVague1201½TrplSc1234 Widened with ease 5
3Mar84- 11Hia fst 1⅛ :462 1:093 1:341 1:47 Flamingo-G1 7 1 1hd 1hd 33½ 47¼ Maple E 122 *.30 90-13 Time for a Change122nkDr. Carter1226Rexson's Hope1221 8
Gave way approaching stretch
20Feb84- 10Hia fst 7f :23 :453 1:092 1:213 [R]Flamingo Prep 29k 2 3 22½ 2½ 11½ 17 Maple E 122 *.05 95-16 Devil'sBg1227FrndlyBob1191½Tumblr11511 Strong hand ride 4
29Oct83- 8Lrl fst 1 1/16 :233 :462 1:112 1:421 Lrl Futurity-G1 3 1 1hd 15 14 15¼ Maple E 122 *.05 97-09 Devil'sBag1225¼HailBoldKing1225½Pieda'Tierre1228 Easily 5
15Oct83- 6Bel fst 1 :23 :461 1:094 1:341 Champagne-G1 3 1 11½ 13 15 16 Maple E 122 *.30 94-14 Devil'sBag1226Dr.Carter1223½OurCasey'sBoy1224½ Handily 12
28Sep83- 8Bel fst 7f :223 :451 1:083 1:212 Cowdin-G2 5 3 11½ 12 15 13 Maple E 115 *.50 95-19 Devil'sBag1153Dr.Carter1153ExitFiveB.1153 Ridden out 9
28Aug83- 7Bel sly 6f :22 :452 1:103 Alw 22000 4 3 11½ 14½ 14½ 15¼ Cruguet J 122 *.50 89-16 Devil's Bag1225¼Exit Five B.1195Spender1172½ Handily 6
20Aug83- 6Sar fst 6f :221 :453 1:103 Md Sp Wt 6 1 12 11½ 14 17½ Maple E 118 *1.10 87-16 Devil'sBag1187½ChimesKeeper1187¼FrenchFlame118nk Easily 9

Easy Goer

ch. c. 1986, by Alydar (Raise a Native)–Relaxing, by Buckpasser — Lifetime record: 20 14 5 1 $4,873,770

Own.– Ogden Phipps
Br.– Ogden Phipps (Ky)
Tr.– Claude McGaughey III

4Jly90- 8Bel fst 1¼ :463 1:094 1:352 2:00 3↑ Suburban H-G1 1 2 2½ 11½ 12½ 13¾ Day P 126 *.20 97-12 Easy Goer1263¾De Roche1134¾Montubio1131¾ Ridden out 7
28May90- 8Bel fst 1 :223 :45 1:091 1:342 3↑ Metropolitan H-G1 8 6 55 43½ 33½ 31¾ Day P 127 *.40 95-18 Criminal Type120nkHousebuster1131½Easy Goer1273 9
Wide,mild response
16May90- 8Bel sly 7f :232 :463 1:10 1:221 3↑ Gold Stage 47k 2 2 24 21½ 1½ 17½ Day P 121 *.20 93-14 Easy Goer1217½Hadif11910½Yurtu12129 Ridden out 4
4Nov89- 10GP fst 1¼ :461 1:102 1:35 2:001 3↑ BC Classic-G1 1 6 611 44½ 34 2nk Day P 122 *.50 107-01 Sunday Silence122nkEasy Goer1221Blushing John1269¾ 8
Finished boldly
7Oct89- 8Bel fst 1½ :483 1:134 2:05 2:291 3↑ J C Gold Cup-G1 3 4 35½ 11 12 14 Day P 121 *.10 74-23 EasyGoer1214Cryptoclearnc12619½ForvrSlvr126¾ Ridden out 7
16Sep89- 8Bel my 1¼ :481 1:122 1:361 2:01 3↑ Woodward H-G1 1 4 45½ 43 1hd 12 Day P 122 *.30 92-17 EasyGoer1222ItsAcedemic109¾ForeverSilver1195 Ridden out 5
19Aug89- 8Sar fst 1¼ :464 1:103 1:353 2:004 Travers-G1 5 4 34½ 21 11½ 13 Day P 126 *.20 96-04 EsyGor1263ClvrTrvor1269ShyTom1265¾ Ducked in,ridden out 6
5Aug89- 8Sar fst 1⅛ :481 1:12 1:36 1:472 3↑ Whitney H-G1 1 4 43 42½ 1½ 14½ Day P 119 *.30 98-12 Easy Goer1194½Forever Silver122½Cryptoclearance1224 6
Steadied,easily
10Jun89- 8Bel fst 1½ :47 1:111 2:004 2:26 Belmont-G1 7 5 42½ 11 14½ 18 Day P 126 1.60e 90-13 EasyGoer1268SundaySilnce1261LeVoyageur12612 Ridden out 10
20May89- 10Pim fst 1 3/16 :462 1:093 1:341 1:534 Preakness-G1 2 5 54½ 1hd 2hd 2no Day P 126 *.60 98-10 Sunday Silence126noEasy Goer1265Rock Point1262 8
Broke in air,brushed
6May89- 8CD my 1¼ :463 1:112 1:374 2:05 Ky Derby-G1 13 6 58 52½ 63½ 22½ Day P 126 *.80e 69-28 Sunday Silence1262½Easy Goer126hdAwe Inspiring126¾ 15
Bothered st,rallied
22Apr89- 8Aqu fst 1⅛ :483 1:132 1:382 1:503 Wood Memorial-G1 3 2 2½ 2½ 11 13 Day P 126 *.10 82-29 EasyGoer1263RockPoint126hdTripleBuck12611½ Ridden out 6
8Apr89- 7Aqu fst 1 :222 :441 1:083 1:322 Gotham-G2 5 2 42¼ 21½ 12½ 113 Day P 123 *.05 104-14 EasyGoer12313DiamndDonnie1147¼ExpnsvDcson1187½ Handily 5
4Mar89- 11GP fst 7f :214 :443 1:10 1:221 Swale 57k 1 6 511 310 1½ 18¾ Day P 122 *.30 93-18 Easy Goer1228¾Trion112nkTricky Creek1227½ Handily 6
5Nov88- 8CD my 1 1/16 :233 :471 1:121 1:463 BC Juvenile-G1 9 7 77¾ 66 23 21¼ Day P 122 *.30 74-20 IsItTrue1221¼EasyGor1228Tgl1223 Bumped st,jumped tracks 10
15Oct88- 8Bel fst 1 :224 :453 1:10 1:344 Champagne-G1 1 2 2½ 21½ 11½ 14 Day P 122 *.10 91-17 EasyGoer1224IsItTrue12215½IrishActor1221¼ Ridden out 4
1Oct88- 8Bel fst 7f :222 :453 1:104 1:233 Cowdin-G1 6 5 53½ 21½ 21 13 Day P 122 *.30 84-21 EasyGoer1223WinnersLaugh1221[D]IsItTrue122¾ Ridden out 6
9Sep88- 5Bel fst 6½f :22 :444 1:091 1:152 Alw 27000 2 4 35½ 34½ 11½ 15½ Day P 122 *.60 98-16 Easy Goer1225½Winners Laugh1174½Icy Jr,117¾ Ridden out 6
19Aug88- 5Sar fst 7f :224 :453 1:101 1:223 Md Sp Wt 2 5 32 32 1hd 18½ Day P 118 *.60 89-19 EasyGoer1182½IsItTru1188MgcEgl1183¾ Steadied,ridden out 8
1Aug88- 3Bel fst 6f :23 :463 1:113 Md Sp Wt 4 7 53½ 2½ 2hd 2no Day P 118 *1.70 81-18 Lorenzoni118noEasy Goer1185¼Tiajuana1183 Off slowly 7

Eillo

ch. c. 1980, by Mr. Prospector (Raise a Native)–Barbs Dancer, by Northern Dancer — Lifetime record: 17 12 0 1 $657,670

Own.– Crown Stable
Br.– O.A. Cohen (Fla)
Tr.– Budd Lepman

Date/Race	Track	Dist	Fractions	Race	Running line	Jockey	Wt	Odds	Figs	Top three finishers	Comment	Starters
10Nov84-3Hol	fst	6f	:222 :453 :571 1:101	3↑ BC Sprint-G1	5 2 11½ 11 12½ 1no	Perret C	126	*1.30	--	Eillo126noCommemorate1241½Fighting Fit1262½	Driving	11
6Oct84-8Med	fst	6f	:222 :45 1:094	3↑ Chief Pennekeck H 73k	3 1 11 12½ 14 15	Perret C	124	*.50	93-18	Eillo1245Introspective1122¼RollinonOver114nk	Ridden out	6
11Sep84-8Key	fst	6f	:22 :443 1:084	3↑ Alw 16000	1 3 11½ 12 13 19	Perret C	120	*.20	97-19	Eillo1209Obgyn1202Good Ole Master120¾	Handily	6
21Jly84-5Mth	sly	6f	:221 :444 1:093	3↑ Alw 17000	5 1 11½ 11½ 13 11¼	Perret C	122	*.40	92-16	Eillo1221¼Lordly Love1173¼Her Pal1153	Driving	6
19Apr84-9OP	fst	6f	:212 :441 1:09	4↑ Count Fleet H 130k	8 2 1hd 1hd 21½ 79	Perret C	126	*1.10	91-12	Dave'sFriend1221½AllSoldOut1143½LuckySalvton113hd	Tired	8
31Mar84-9GP	fm	1Ⓣ	:23 :462 1:10 1:35	4↑ Alw 20000	3 1 1hd 21½ 1022 1131	Perret C	115	*.90	64-09	HapesMill1221¼BlueEmmanuelle1151OutofHock122no	Tired	11
5Mar84-9Hia	fst	7f	:231 :453 1:091 1:214	3↑ Sprint Champ H 76k	5 1 1hd 11 13 16	Perret C	125	*.30	94-23	Eillo1256Awesome Count1141Victorious1143½	Ridden out	5
10Feb84-9Hia	fst	7f	:23 :452 1:09 1:211	4↑ Alw 20000	4 1 1½ 1½ 12½ 13	Perret C	122	*.30	97-22	Eillo1223Brother Liam122½Bill Wheeler1225	Handily	6
28Jan84-8Hia	fst	6f	:221 :451 1:084	4↑ Kendall 22k	5 2 11 12 12½ 17	Perret C	122	*.50	99-15	Eillo1227Compo's Tempo1172Fast Reason117nk	Handily	6
9Jan84-9Hia	fst	6f	:22 :442 1:081	3↑ Tallahassee H 37k	3 2 1½ 12½ 12½ 13	Perret C	115	2.10	102-15	Eillo1153Center Cut1165½In the Bucks111½	Drew clear	10
30Nov83-9Crc	sly	6½f	:221 :451 1:104 1:173	3↑ Alw 17000	1 4 1½ 1½ 2½ 46½	Perret C	119	*.80	90-19	ChainLink'sDrm117hdMyMc1173½CourtousMjsty1173	Gave way	6
11Nov83-9Crc	fst	6f	:221 :453 1:111	3↑ Handicap 25000	6 1 1hd 1½ 12 32¾	Perret C	116	*1.40	92-16	Opening Lead1102Center Cut116¾Eillo116½	Weakened	7
8Oct83-8Bel	fst	6f	:221 :453 1:102	3↑ Fall Highweight H-G2	6 4 3½ 2½ 63½ 78	Velasquez J	130	3.80	82-19	Chas Conerly136½Singh Tu124½Let Burn1344	Tired	9
27Sep83-8Med	fst	6f	:22 :45 1:082	3↑ Alw 20000	2 3 2hd 11½ 12 14½	Velasquez J	114	*.70	101-14	Eillo1144½KingBoldReality1106JewelrySale1171	Ridden out	7
17Sep83-7Bel	fst	6f	:222 :454 1:104	3↑ Alw 27000	2 2 1½ 1½ 12½ 1½	Velasquez J	115	*.60	88-17	Eillo115½Nearice1134Big McCoy108no	Driving	7
31Aug83-7Mth	gd	6f	:231 :461 1:10	3↑ Alw 11500	1 4 11½ 12½ 12½ 17	Perret C	114	*.50	90-20	Eillo1147Talc Powder1156Stoneyford106hd	Ridden out	8
26Feb83-6GP	fst	6f	:222 :452 1:101	©Md Sp Wt	3 4 11 14 14 18	Perret C	122	*1.10	88-19	Eillo1228Silent Landing1223U.S. Flag1221	Easily	11

Epitome

b. f. 1985, by Summing (Verbatim)–Honest and True, by Mr. Leader — Lifetime record: 14 5 5 1 $631,755

Own.– J.A. Bell III
Br.– Jessica Bell Nicholson & H. Bennett Bell (Ky)
Tr.– Philip Hauswald

Date/Race	Track	Dist	Fractions	Race	Running line	Jockey	Wt	Odds	Figs	Top three finishers	Comment	Starters
24Nov88-9CD	fst	1⅛	:472 1:122 1:382 1:514	3↑ ⒻFalls City H-G3	14 10 107¼ 107¼ 42½ 22	Day P	116	3.80e	81-20	Top Corsage1212Epitome1163Lawyer Talk111hd	No threat	14
5Nov88-6CD	my	1⅛	:474 1:12 1:381 1:52	3↑ ⒻBC Distaff-G1	1 7 810 816 813 713½	Day P	119	10.30e	68-20	PersonlEnsign123noWinnngColrs119½GoodbyHlo1195	Outrun	9
25Oct88-7Kee	fst	1 1/16	:251 :491 1:14 1:461	3↑ ⒻAlw 28600	1 1 1hd 2½ 1hd 22	Day P	120	*.30	73-24	Stoneleigh'sHope1172Epitome1203DoItaZn112½	Led,weakened	5
8Oct88-6Kee	fst	1 1/16	:25 :491 1:131 1:45	3↑ ⒻAlw 40600	5 5 42½ 31 1hd 11½	Romero RP	113	*.50e	81-21	Epitome1131½StillWaving1141Bstofbothworlds118no	Driving	6
17Sep88-4Bel	fst	6f	:224 :46 1:101	3↑ ⒻAlw 30000	1 4 54½ 45 43½ 1hd	Day P	113	3.80	88-08	Epitome113hdBanbury Fair1153¼Sharpening Up1172	Driving	7
1Apr88-9OP	fst	1 1/16	:231 :47 1:12 1:434	ⒻHoneybee 88k	1 6 76½ 54½ 24 24½	Day P	115	*.80e	77-27	LostKitty1154½Epitome1153Far'sTm1155	Jumped gate tracks	8
21Nov87-2Hol	fst	1	:22 :44 1:09 1:362	ⒻBC Juv Fillies-G1	6 11 1114 89 36 1no	Day P	119	30.40	81-12	Epitme119noJeanneJones1192¾DremTm119hd	Up final stride	12
8Nov87-8CD	fst	1	:221 :451 1:113 1:381	ⒻPocahontas 53k	5 9 98½ 43½ 22 12¼	Day P	114	*1.50	78-19	Epitome1142¼Darien Miss1145Cushion Cut1181¼	Driving	9
24Oct87-8Kee	fst	1 1/16	:224 :462 1:104 1:443	ⒻAlcibiades H-G2	7 6 78¼ 65½ 34½ 22½	Smith ME	118	13.70	80-15	Terra Incognita1182½Epitome118¾Pearlie Gold1187	Rallied	8
13Oct87-3Kee	fst	1 1/16	:233 :474 1:132 1:454	ⒻMd Sp Wt	2 7 44½ 42 11 15	Day P	120	*.90	77-13	Epitome1205Indian Riffle120¾Sincere Foolish1205	Easily	12
7Sep87-6Bel	fst	7f	:221 :46 1:114 1:252	ⒻMd Sp Wt	3 4 54½ 53 32½ 34¾	Migliore R	117	5.00	70-19	Aquaba1171¾Dangerous Type1173Epitome1173¾	Rallied	10
13Aug87-3Sar	fst	7f	:221 :453 1:11 1:241	ⒻMd Sp Wt	8 7 75 66 24 22½	Santos JA	117	6.20e	78-14	WinningColors1172½Epitome1174Bippus1171½	Lugged in late	11
20Jly87-4Bel	my	5½f	:223 :462 :584 1:052	ⒻMd Sp Wt	7 9 79 89¼ 610 511¼	Romero RP	117	3.70	77-15	Truth or Dare1174Missy Valentine1171¾Towering Success1125		10
Slow start,wide												
28Jun87-4Bel	fst	5½f	:23 :464 :592 1:06	ⒻMd Sp Wt	4 9 811 89¼ 58 54¾	Bailey JD	117	37.90	80-19	Joe's Tammie1122¾Heavenly Halo1172Connecting Link117no		9
Raced wide												

Estrapade

ch. f. 1980, by Vaguely Noble (Vienna)–Klepto, by No Robbery — Lifetime record: 30 12 5 5 $1,924,556

Own.– A.E. Paulson
Br.– N.B. Hunt (Ky)
Tr.– Charles Whittingham

Date/Race	Track	Dist	Fractions	Race	Running line	Jockey	Wt	Odds	Figs	Top three finishers	Comment	Starters
7Dec86-8Hol	fm	1½Ⓣ	:474 1:121 2:01 2:254	3↑ Hol Turf Cup Inv'l-G1	8 4 4¾ 54 79½ 612¼	Toro F	123	*1.20e	81-09	Alphabatim126hdDahar126nkTheatrical126½	Weakened	8
1Nov86-6SA	fm	1½Ⓣ	:472 1:111 2:003 2:252	3↑ BC Turf-G1	5 1 12½ 11 2hd 34	Toro F	123	2.70e	84-07	Manila122nkTheatrical1263¾Estrapade1232¾	Weakened	9
12Oct86-8SA	fm	1½Ⓣ	:464 1:111 2:003 2:26	3↑ Oak Tree Inv'l-G1	6 1 11½ 12 12 12¼	Toro F	123	*.40e	85-12	Estrapade1232¼Theatrical1265½Uptown Swell126½	Driving	10
31Aug86-8AP	fm	1¼Ⓣ	:471 1:113 1:371 2:004	3↑ Bud Arl Million-G1	7 6 64½ 1hd 11½ 15	Toro F	122	*2.10e	90-11	Estrapade1225Divulge126hdPennine Walk126½	Driving	14
9Aug86-8Dmr	fm	1Ⓣ	:23 :461 1:104 1:342	3↑ ⒻPalomar H-G2	3 3 32 41 44½ 65¾	Toro F	124	*.90e	94-04	Aberuschka118hdSauna1183½Fran's Valentine119nk	Boxed in	9
29Jun86-8Hol	fm	1¼Ⓣ	:464 1:104 1:341 1:59	3↑ ⒻBeverly Hills H-G2	3 2 25 11½ 11½ 1½	Toro F	122	*.90e	112-02	Estrapade122½Treizieme1151½Sauna1172¼	Driving	7
8Jun86-8Hol	fm	1⅛Ⓣ	:461 1:10 1:334 1:454	3↑ ⒻGamely H-G1	5 3 32 31½ 31 21¾	Shoemaker W	123	*.70	101-00	La Koumia1181¾Estrapade1232¼Tax Dodge1151¼	Steadied	8
25May86-8Hol	fm	1 1/16Ⓣ	:25 :484 1:121 1:413	3↑ ⒻWilshire H-G2	5 3 2½ 2hd 3nk 3nk	Shoemaker W	124	*.60	96-03	Outstandingly117hdLaKoumia118hdEstrapade1243½	Held well	5
30Mar86-8SA	fm	1¼Ⓣ	:481 1:124 1:363 2:01	4↑ ⒻS Barbara H-G1	7 4 41½ 3½ 21½ 2½	Shoemaker W	124	*.80e	81-16	MountainBear119½Estrapade1243½RoyalRegatta1162¼	Gamely	8
24Nov85-8Hol	fm	1⅛Ⓣ	:464 1:104 1:36 1:481	3↑ ⒻMatriarch Inv'l-G1	5 2 21 1hd 1hd 41¾	Shoemaker W	123	*.60e	--	FactFinder1231Tamarinda123noPossibleMate123¾	Weakened	10
Previously owned by Summa Stable (Lessee)												
10Nov85-8SA	fm	1¼Ⓣ	:473 1:114 1:352 2:002	3↑ ⒻYellow Ribbon Inv'l-G1	8 3 31½ 31 11 1¾	Shoemaker W	123	*.80	85-18	Estrapade123¾Alydar's Best118½La Koumia118½	Driving	11
19Oct85-8SA	fm	1⅛Ⓣ	:453 1:094 1:35 1:471	3↑ ⒻLas Palmas H-G2	7 4 42½ 31 13 13½	Shoemaker W	124	*1.00e	91-12	Estrapade1243½L'Attrayante118noJohnica1181¾	Driving	11
2Sep85-8Dmr	fst	*1¼	:461 1:103 1:352 1:58	3↑ Dmr Inv'l H-G2	1 1 11 2hd 21 43¾	Delahoussaye E	117	*2.70	83-15	Barberstown117½My Habitony1181First Norman1142¼	Tired	10
14Jly85-8Hol	fst	1⅛	:453 1:092 1:342 1:474	3↑ ⒻVanity Inv'l H-G1	4 6 611 55½ 34½ 33	Stevens G	119	2.90	107-02	DontstopThemusic118¾SaltSpring1142¼Estrapd1192½	Rallied	7
30Jun85-8Hol	fm	1⅛Ⓣ	:482 1:123 1:362 1:481	3↑ ⒻBeverly Hills H-G2	3 2 21 21 2hd 2no	McCarron CJ	125	*.40	89-09	Johnc115noEstrpd125½L'Attrynt1184	Veered in,bumped start	5
2Jun85-8Hol	fm	1⅛Ⓣ	:471 1:101 1:342 1:463	3↑ ⒻGamely H-G1	1 5 43½ 42 2hd 1¾	McCarron CJ	124	*.80	97-05	Estrapade124¾Johnica115½Possible Mate1162	Driving	6
21Apr85-8SA	fm	*1¾Ⓣ	:461 2:01 2:262 2:474	4↑ S Juan Capistrano H-G1	2 2 11 11 1½ 21½	Toro F	120	1.40e	123-14	Prince True1241½Estrapade120hdSwoon117¾	Gamely	7
16Mar85-8SA	fm	1⅛Ⓣ	:461 1:103 1:35 1:47	4↑ ⒻSanta Ana H-G1	4 3 32½ 31 13 16	Toro F	123	*2.50	92-10	Estrapade1236FactFinder119nkAirDstngu1161¼	Easily	10
24Feb85-8SA	fst	1⅛	:46 1:10 1:35 1:48	4↑ ⒻS Margarita Inv'l H-G1	7 7 54 78½ 819 830	Toro F	123	3.10	59-16	LovlierLinda1193Mitternd1231¾Prcpnt1161½	Showed nothing	8
31Jan85-8SA	fm	1⅛Ⓣ	:472 1:114 1:354 1:473	4↑ ⒻAlw 42000	4 5 41¾ 2hd 12½ 15½	Toro F	118	*.70	89-16	Estrapade1185½Clear Talk1135Linda's Leader1132	In hand	6
Previously trained by Maurice Zilber												
21Oct84-8SA	fm	1¼Ⓣ	:472 1:113 1:354 2:00	3↑ ⒻYellow Ribbon Inv'l-G1	8 6 65 32 33 33½	Lequeux A	123	20.00	83-13	Sabin1232¼Grise Mine1181¼Estrapade123hd	Bid,hung	8
7Oct84♦ Longchamp(Fr)	sf	*1½ⓉRH	2:39	3↑ Arc de Triomphe-G1 Stk550000	1530	Samani H	127	31.00		Sagace1302Northern Trick1206All Along127¾	Chased leaders,weakened halfway.Sadler's Wells 6th	22
27Sep84♦ Maisns-Lffitte(Fr)	sf	*1¼ⓉStr	2:083	3↑ La Coupe de Maisons-Laffitte-G3 Stk63000	14	Lequeux A	122	2.50e		Estrapade1224Palace Music121nkBob Back119nk	In touch,led over 1f out,drew clear 170y out.Seattle Song 4th	11
16Sep84♦ Longchamp(Fr)	sf	*1¼ⓉRH	2:143	3↑ Pr Prince d'Orange-G3 Stk62700	42½	Guignard G	122	5.20		Lovely Dancer1301½Fly Me124½Darly126nk	Midpack,bid over 1f out,gaining late,just missed 3rd	8
16May84♦ Longchamp(Fr)	yl	*1¼ⓉRH	2:152	4↑ ⒻPrix de la Pepiniere (Listed) Stk40000	13	Lequeux A	123	*.60		Estrapade1233Badinage119½Maganyos1273	Led throughout,ridden clear 1f out,going away	5
21Apr84♦ Saint-Cloud(Fr)	yl	*1 5/16ⓉLH	2:24	4↑ ⒻPrix Corrida-G3 Stk62000	34¾	Lequeux A	126	3.00		Fly Me128¾Marie de Litz1284Estrapade1261	Rated toward rear,progress to take 3rd near line	11

24Mar84♦ Saint-Cloud(Fr)	gd *1 5/16 Ⓣ LH 2:233	ⒻPrix Transvaal Alw30500	51¾	Lequeux A	120	*1.00	Sisnel121nkAborigine118½Olindo121½	Rated in 7th,sharp run over 1f out,hung	8
11Sep83♦ Longchamp(Fr)	yl *1½ⓉRH 2:42	ⒻPr Vermeille-G1 Stk268000	22	Piggott L	128	3.20	Sharaya1282Estrapade128nkVosges128nk	Chased winner over 1f out,hard ridden,saved 2nd	12
4Sep83♦ Longchamp(Fr)	gd *1½ⓉRH 2:381 3↑	ⒻPrix des Tourelles Alw29000	13	Piggott L	118	*.80	Estrapade1183Fly Me1184Tinorosa1262	Rated in 6th,rallied to lead over 1f out,soon clear,handily	8
6Aug83♦ Deauville(Fr)	gd *1¼ⓉRH 2:11	ⒻPrix de Dives Mdn24500	1nk	St Martin Y	128	3.00e	Estrapade128nkDear Lorraine1282Allicance128½	Rated at rear,wide bid 3f out,long drive to lead near line	14

Family Style

ch. f. 1983, by State Dinner (Buckpasser)–Sharp Kitty, by Blade **Lifetime record: 35 10 8 7 $1,537,118**

Own.– Mr & Mrs Eugene V. Klein
Br.– Selective Seasons (Ky)
Tr.– D. Wayne Lukas

27Sep87- 8Bel	fst 1⅛	:462 1:092 1:35 1:483 3↑	ⒻRuffian H-G1	11 2 52½ 86¼ 109¼ 116½	Day P	121	*.40e 77-19	ⒹSacahuista114hdCoup de Fusil1171¾Clabber Girl112½		12
	Finished at far turn									
23Aug87- 9AP	fst 1⅛	:464 1:12 1:383 1:521 3↑	ⒻArl Matron-G2	3 1 1½ 11 12½ 11¼	Hawley S	123	*.30 70-30	Family Style1231¼Royal Cielo1132½Tide114hd	Driving	7
2Aug87- 8AP	fst 1	:224 :45 1:094 1:35 3↑	ⒻCleopatra 54k	5 2 22½ 1hd 13 19	Hawley S	123	*.50 86-22	FamilyStyle1239LadyVernl115½MssBd1155	Drifted wide turn	6
18Jly87-10Aks	fst 1⅛	:471 1:113 1:372 1:502 3↑	ⒻQueen's H-G3	6 2 21 2hd 2hd 2hd	Doocy TT	122	*.70 85-25	SocialBusinss111hdFmlyStyl1223½HppyHollowMss117½	Gamely	8
5Jly87-10Aks	fst 1 1/16	:23 :461 1:102 1:442 3↑	ⒻBud BC 133k	4 3 22 23 21 22	Doocy TT	122	*1.00 79-24	Explosive Girl1102Family Style1222Turn and Dance114nk		9
	Saved ground									
30May87- 8Hol	fst 7f	:221 :45 1:101 1:23 3↑	ⒻA Gleam H-G3	1 7 73¾ 54½ 53½ 65½	Stevens GL	120	7.80 83-14	Le L'Argent118¾Sari's Heroine1173½Rare Starlet1151		8
	Off slowly,outrun									
1May87- 7CD	fst 1 1/16	:24 :48 1:113 1:424 3↑	ⒻBud BC H 154k	6 2 21 32 44 56	Stevens GL	119	*.40e 88-12	Queen Alexandra117¾Infinidad1162½I'm Sweets1162¾		6
	Saved ground,gave way									
15Apr87- 9OP	fst 1 1/16	:232 :463 1:101 1:411 4↑	ⒻApple Blossom H-G1	4 3 32½ 33 23 24	Stevens GL	120	*.30 91-18	NorthSider1224FamilyStyle1202QueenAlexndr119½	2nd best	7
1Mar87- 8SA	fst 1⅛	:454 1:103 1:36 1:484 4↑	ⒻS Margarita Inv'l H-G1	3 3 44 51½ 44 64¾	Stevens GL	120	2.40e 80-15	NorthSider117hdWinterTreasure1151¼FrauAltiva117nk	Tired	12
15Feb87- 8SA	my 1⅛	:462 1:103 1:361 1:493	ⒻLa Canada-G1	2 2 22½ 1hd 12 12½	Stevens GL	122	*1.00 81-17	FamilyStyle1222½WinterTreasure1174Sr'sHron1211¾	Driving	6
24Jan87- 8SA	fst 1 1/16	:231 :471 1:114 1:43	ⒻEl Encino-G3	5 4 45 44 44½ 410¼	Stevens GL	122	*.80 76-18	SeldomSeenSue1146Miraculous1171¾TopCorsage1222½	Tired	6
3Jan87- 8SA	fst 7f	:222 :451 1:10 1:223	ⒻLa Brea-G3	1 5 42¾ 41¾ 11 16	Stevens GL	122	*1.70e 87-16	Family Style1226Sari's Heroine119hdWinter Treasure1171¾		6
	Finished strongly									
6Dec86- 8Hol	gd 1⅛	:462 1:112 1:364 1:50 3↑	ⒻSilver Belles H-G2	1 3 31½ 21½ 12 1½	Stevens GL	115	6.70 87-13	Family Style115½Infinidad1149½Waterside1132¼		7
	Drifted out into str,swerved,lugged in,gamely									
31Oct86- 8SA	fst 1 1/16	:231 :463 1:112 1:431	ⒻLinda Vista H-G3	8 8 84¾ 94¾ 99¼ 811¼	Delahoussaye E	121	*1.70 74-16	Marianna'sGirl1141¼WintrTrsur1182½FnKudos1151¾	No rally	9
22Oct86- 8SA	fst 6½f	:221 :452 1:094 1:161 3↑	ⒻCascapedia H 48k	1 5 54 55¼ 54 32	Delahoussaye E	117	10.50 87-23	Winter Treasure117¾Her Royalty1211¼Family Style1173½		5
	5 wide into str									
2Aug86- 9Aks	fst 1⅛	:48 1:12 1:372 1:503	ⒻAks Oaks-G3	3 5 42½ 33½ 58 712¼	Baze RA	120	*.30 72-20	TrickyFingers1174LadyGallnt1114Mrnn'sGrl116hd	No excuse	9
6Jly86- 9Hol	fst 1⅛	:454 1:101 1:344 1:474	ⒻHol Oaks-G1	2 2 22½ 22 37 311	McCarron CJ	121	2.10 87-09	HiddenLight1215AnEmpress1216FamilyStyle12120	Faltered	4
14Jun86- 8Bel	fst 1⅛	:463 1:111 1:362 1:493	ⒻMother Goose-G1	5 4 45½ 31½ 2½ 31	Vasquez J	121	*.80e 78-20	LifeattheTop121½DynamicStar121½FamlyStyl121no	Lugged in	8
26May86- 6GS	fst 1⅛	:464 1:12 1:383 1:512	ⒻJersey Belle 152k	3 3 43 31½ 2hd 2no	Pincay L Jr	121	*.40 72-20	I'm Sweets118noFamily Style1219½True Chompion1186¼		8
	Bumped turn,missed									
16May86- 9Pim	fst 1 1/16	:224 :464 1:111 1:443	ⒻBlack-Eyed Susan-G2	1 2 22 21½ 12 13¼	McCarron CJ	121	*.40 81-22	Family Style1213¼Steel Maiden1211½Firgie's Jule121½		8
	Lugged in,driving									
2May86- 9CD	fst 1⅛	:463 1:11 1:371 1:503	ⒻKy Oaks-G1	10 8 86½ 74¼ 31½ 3nk	McCarron CJ	121	4.40e 89-14	TiffanyLass121hdLifeattheTop121nkFamlyStyl121hd	Rallied	12
19Apr86- 9OP	sly 1⅛	:454 1:101 1:354 1:481	Ark Derby-G1	1 4 42 41¾ 32 34½	Maple S	121	2.90e 88-07	Rampage1181½Wheatly Hall1153Family Style1213	Evenly	14
12Apr86- 9OP	fst 1 1/16	:232 :471 1:113 1:42	ⒻFantasy-G1	7 6 31 31 32½ 44½	McCarron CJ	121	*2.00 86-16	Tiffany Lass1212½Lotka1162Turn and Dance112hd	No rally	8
23Mar86- 8SA	fst 1 1/16	:23 :463 1:112 1:422	ⒻS Anita Oaks-G1	1 4 43 41½ 45 45	Pincay L Jr	117	1.50e 84-17	HiddenLight1171½TwilightRidge1172¼AnEmpress1171¼	Evenly	6
5Mar86- 9GP	fst 1 1/16	:232 :474 1:123 1:451	ⒻBonnie Miss-G3	3 4 33 33 33½ 33¾	Velasquez J	121	3.00 71-27	PatriciaJ.K.1213¼Noranc121½FamilyStyle1214½	Drifted out	11
15Dec85- 8Hol	fst 1	:22 :443 1:09 1:341	Hol Futurity-G1	6 8 75 69 58½ 613¼	Pincay L Jr	118	*2.10 79-09	SnowChief1216½ElectricBlue121noFerdinnd121nk	Wide,tired	10
24Nov85- 8Aqu	fst 1⅛	:491 1:133 1:382 1:501	ⒻDemoiselle-G1	3 5 53½ 52¾ 2hd 2nk	Velasquez J	121	*.40 84-15	I'mSweets121nkFamilyStyle121nkStealKss1124¾	Just missed	8
2Nov85- 2Aqu	fst 1	:223 :452 1:104 1:354	ⒻBC Juv Fillies-G1	1 6 63¾ 32 22½ 21	Pincay L Jr	119	*.60e 86-10	Twilight Ridge1191Family Style1197¼Steal a Kiss1193¼		12
	Bore in start									
14Oct85- 8Bel	fst 1	:224 :46 1:111 1:371	ⒻFrizette-G1	2 3 31 3½ 1½ 11½	Pincay L Jr	119	1.20 79-19	FamilyStyle1191½Funistrada119hdGuadery1196	Brisk urging	7
29Sep85- 8Bel	fst 7f	:23 :464 1:112 1:24	ⒻMatron-G1	1 2 31½ 42½ 23 2nk	Pincay L Jr	119	*.60 82-19	MusicalLark119nkFamilyStyle1192½I'mSweets119no	Game try	5
7Sep85- 8Haw	fst 6½f	:222 :454 1:111 1:18	ⒻArl-Wash Lassie-G1	1 6 53½ 62¾ 2hd 12	Pincay L Jr	119	*.70 83-26	Family Style1192Deep Silver1194Pamela Kay1192	Driving	8
26Aug85- 8Sar	sly 6f	:22 :453 1:12	ⒻSpinaway-G1	5 5 56½ 59½ 45 11	MacBeth D	119	*2.30e 80-21	FamilyStyle1191MusicalLark119hdNervousBaba119nk	Driving	7
15Aug85- 8Sar	fst 6f	:214 :443 1:093	ⒻAdirondack-G2	5 5 22 21½ 22 21¾	MacBeth D	114	2.80e 90-08	NervousBaba1141¾FamilyStyle1144¼StealaKiss114nk	Gamely	8
28Jly85- 6Bel	fst 6f	:223 :462 1:113	ⒻMd Sp Wt	5 2 2hd 11 14 17	Velasquez J	117	*.70 84-16	FmilyStyle1177PasdsTros1171NorthofDnzg1172½	Ridden out	8
7Jly85- 6Bel	fst 5½f	:223 :454 :58 1:042	ⒻMd Sp Wt	1 1 34 35 36½ 37	Velasquez J	117	14.40 86-16	Storm and Sunshine1174¾Patti's Lark1172¼Family Style1172½		9
	Bore out stretch									

Ferdinand

ch. c. 1983, by Nijinsky II (Northern Dancer)–Banja Luka, by Double Jay **Lifetime record: 29 8 9 6 $3,777,978**

Own.– Mrs H.B. Keck
Br.– H.B. Keck (Ky)
Tr.– Charles Whittingham

22Oct88- 8SA	fst 1⅛	:462 1:094 1:342 1:471 3↑	Goodwood H-G3	2 4 54 65¼ 56½ 57	Shoemaker W	125	*1.60 86-12	Cutlass Reality1241¾Lively One1161¼Stylish Winner1133½		8
	Saved ground,no rally									
26Jun88- 8Hol	fst 1¼	:454 1:093 1:342 1:592 3↑	Hol Gold Cup H-G1	4 4 47 41¾ 34½ 312	Shoemaker W	125	2.60 83-07	Cutlass Reality1166½Alysheba1265½Ferdinand1254		6
	Bid,lacked late response									
12Jun88- 8Hol	fst 1⅛	:473 1:104 1:35 1:473 3↑	Californian-G1	3 4 41½ 44 47 49	Shoemaker W	126	*.70 90-09	CutlassRelty1152¾Gulch1264½JudgAnglucc1261¾	No response	4
17Apr88- 8SA	fst 1⅛	:462 1:094 1:343 1:471 4↑	S Bernardino H-G2	3 3 32 2hd 1hd 2no	Shoemaker W	127	1.00 93-17	Alysheba127noFerdinand127hdGood Taste1133½	Just missed	5
6Mar88- 8SA	fst 1¼	:463 1:10 1:343 1:594 4↑	S Anita H-G1	4 4 45½ 2½ 21 2½	Shoemaker W	127	1.70 89-13	Alysheba126½Ferdinnd1272½SuperDmond1242¼	Wide,2nd best	4
14Feb88- 8SA	fst 1⅛	:454 1:102 1:354 1:483 4↑	San Antonio H-G1	1 6 612 56½ 35½ 23½	Shoemaker W	128	*.70 82-20	Judge Angelucci1223½Ferdinand128nkCrimson Slew1152¼		6
	Rallied,2nd best									
21Nov87- 7Hol	fst 1¼	:462 1:101 1:352 2:012 3↑	BC Classic-G1	6 7 64¾ 31½ 3½ 1no	Shoemaker W	126	*1.00 85-12	Ferdinand126noAlysheba1221¼JudgeAngelucc1261½	Prevailed	12
7Nov87- 8SA	my 1⅛	:483 1:131 1:373 1:504 3↑	Goodwood H-G3	4 5 53½ 52 21 11	Shoemaker W	127	1.60 75-26	Ferdinand1271Candi's Gold117¾Skywalker123hd	Driving	5
29Aug87- 8Dmr	fst 1⅛	:453 1:091 1:344 1:472 3↑	Cabrillo H 125k	2 3 21 2hd 1hd 12	Shoemaker W	126	1.50 93-12	Ferdinnd1262SuperDiamond124½Nostalg'sStr116	Ridden out	3
28Jun87- 8Hol	fst 1¼	:46 1:093 1:343 2:003 3↑	Hol Gold Cup H-G1	5 5 42 21 2½ 11¼	Shoemaker W	124	*.40e 89-12	Ferdinand1241¼[DH]Judge Angelucci118[DH]Tasso1154	Driving	11
7Jun87- 8Hol	fst 1⅛	:464 1:104 1:353 1:481 3↑	Californian-G1	1 7 65 53½ 54 43¾	Shoemaker W	126	*1.70 92-17	JudgeAngelucci1181IronEyes115noSnowChief1262¾	No rally	8
10May87- 8Hol	fm 1⅛Ⓣ	:49 1:122 1:353 1:47 3↑	John Henry H-G1	5 2 2½ 2hd 21½ 32¼	Shoemaker W	123	1.90 91-09	Al Mamoon121¾Skip Out Front1141½Ferdinand123no	Tired	5
29Mar87- 8SA	fm 1½Ⓣ	:493 1:143 2:031 2:271 4↑	San Luis Rey-G1	2 1 1½ 2hd 3nk 42¼	Shoemaker W	126	*1.50 77-19	Zoffny126nkLouisLeGrnd126nkLongMick1261¾	Broke stride	5
8Mar87- 8SA	fst 1¼	:454 1:101 1:35 2:003 4↑	S Anita H-G1	9 5 55¾ 1hd 11 2no	Shoemaker W	125	*1.30e 86-15	Broad Brush122noFerdinand1256½Hopeful Word117nk	Sharp	9

8Feb87- 8SA	fst	1¼	:464 1:102 1:343 2:00		C H Strub-G1	4 2 31 2½ 21½	2no	Delahoussaye E	126		*2.00	89-14	SnowChf126noFrdnnd1264½BrodBrush1267	Bumped hard late	8
18Jan87- 8SA	fst	1⅛	:482 1:121 1:363 1:49		San Fernando-G1	1 6 54 55 45	46½	Shoemaker W	123		1.30	77-19	VarietyRoad123nkBroadBrush1262¾SnowChief1263½	Checked	8
26Dec86- 8SA	fst	7f	:222 :444 1:09 1:213		Malibu-G2	11 10 96¼ 75¼ 41¾	11¼	Shoemaker W	123		4.20	92-13	Ferdinand1231¼Snow Chief1261½Don B. Blue1144	Driving	12
7Jun86- 8Bel	sly	1½	:474 1:124 2:04 2:294		Belmont-G1	7 5 33½ 3½ 2½	31½	Shoemaker W	126		3.60	69-16	DanzigConnecton1261¼JohnsTrsur126nkFrdnnd1262¾	Steadied	10
17May86- 8Pim	fst	1 3/16	:472 1:11 1:36 1:544		Preakness-G1	5 6 614 612 24	24	Shoemaker W	126		3.10	89-18	SnowChief1264Ferdinnd1266½BrodBrush126no	Best of others	7
3May86- 8CD	fst	1¼	:451 1:101 1:37 2:024		Ky Derby-G1	1 15 1620 52 11	12¼	Shoemaker W	126		17.70	83-10	Frdnnd1262¼BoldArrngmnt126¾BrodBrush126nk	Bothered start	16
6Apr86- 5SA	fst	1⅛	:471 1:11 1:36 1:483		S Anita Derby-G1	2 6 55 54 54½	37	Shoemaker W	122		5.20	79-15	Snow Chief1226Icy Groom1221Ferdinand122¾	No threat	7
22Feb86- 8SA	fst	1	:223 :453 1:102 1:353		San Rafael-G2	9 7 77¼ 41½ 12	2½	Shoemaker W	116		*1.90	89-16	VarietyRoad116½Ferdinand1166½JettingHom116¾	Just failed	9
29Jan86- 8SA	fst	1 1/16	:23 :462 1:11 1:43		[R]S Catalina 65k	6 7 64¾ 64½ 32	1½	Shoemaker W	114		2.20	86-15	Ferdinand114½VarietyRoad1142¾GrandAlleginc1172½	Driving	8
4Jan86- 8SA	fst	1	:221 :453 1:103 1:361		©[R]Los Feliz 81k	3 4 32½ 3½ 11½	2hd	Shoemaker W	114	b	*.80	87-13	Badger Land117hdFerdinand1146Cut by Glass1161¼	Wide str	7
15Dec85- 8Hol	fst	1	:22 :443 1:09 1:341		Hol Futurity-G1	2 9 95¾ 35½ 35½	36½	Shoemaker W	121	b	34.40	85-09	SnowChief1216½ElectricBlue121noFerdinnd121nk	Off slowly	10
	Previously owned by H.B. Keck														
3Nov85- 1SA	fst	1	:231 :471 1:12 1:372		Md Sp Wt	1 3 32½ 11 11	12¼	Ward WA	117	b	*.40	81-15	Ferdinand1172¼StarRibot1173½ImperiousSpirt1172¾	Driving	6
20Oct85- 6SA	fst	1	:223 :463 1:12 1:373		Md Sp Wt	7 6 53¼ 2½ 2hd	2no	Toro F	117	b	*2.30	80-17	AcksLikaRuler117noFerdinand1174½Frankstrll1171¾	Bumped	10
6Oct85- 6SA	fst	6f	:214 :451 :573 1:101		Md Sp Wt	3 10 96 56¾ 48	311	Shoemaker W	117	b	18.70	76-16	Judge Smells1178½Our Grey Fox1172½Ferdinand1172	Outrun	12
8Sep85- 6Dmr	fst	6f	:223 :46 :581 1:102		Md Sp Wt	5 10 1012 1012 89½	811½	Shoemaker W	118	b	4.30	74-08	Don B. Blue118hdEl Corazon1185½Au Bon Marche1181	Outrun	11

Flatterer

dkbbr. g. 1979, by Mo Bay (Cyane)–Horizontal, by Nade — **Lifetime record: 51 24 7 5 $538,708**

Own.– W.L. Pape
Br.– Pape & Sheppard (Pa)
Tr.– Jonathan E. Sheppard

31Oct87- 5Fai	fm	*2⅝	S'Chase 5:151	3↑	BC Chase 250k	10 2 - - -	-	Dunwoody R	156		*.80	- -	Gacko1568¾Inlander156½Gateshead1563¾	Pulled up	10
17Oct87- 6GrM	fm	*2Ⓣ	3:312	3↑	Alw 1000	2 4 32 22 22	16	Fitzgerald JM	155		-	- -	Flatterer1556FleetingRoy1584WhisperingGrass1551	Handily	13
9May87- 6PW	fm	*3	S'Chase 5:273	4↑	Iroquois Mem 100k	2 3 31¾ 15 16	14	Tomson-Jones T	168		-	- -	Flatterr1684SameEchelon1681¼Eremt1682	Never threatened	9
18Apr87- 5Mid	sf	*2⅛	S'Chase 4:243	4↑	Middleburg H 25k	1 2 22 22 32½	36½	Thompson TL	178		-	- -	Gogong1503½Sailor's Dance1543Flatterer1789	No gain	5
17Mar87♦ Cheltenham(GB)		2LH	3:571	4↑	Champion Hurdle Stk101000		21½	Fishback J	168		10.00		See You Then1681½Flatterer1681Barnbrook Again1686	Outpaced approaching 3 out,rallied 1 out,finished well	18
16Nov86- 4Cam	fm	2¾	S'Chase 5:124	4↑	Colonial Cup Int'l 60k	2 5 64 2hd 15	117	Fishback J	162		-	- -	Flatterer16217TurtleHead1621¼JeanRapier1622¾	Ridden out	9
18Oct86- 5RB	fm	*1½Ⓣ	2:282	3↑	Alw 1000	1 9 97½ 21 13	110	Dufton E	145		-	- -	Flatterer14510Rug Raiser1551Student Dancer1451	Easily	10
27Jun86♦ Auteuil(Fr)	yl	*3 3/16LH	6:09	5↑	Grande Course de Haies d'Auteuil Stk160000		25	Dunwoody R	141		9.50		Le Rheusois1415Flatterer1412Gacko13720	Tracked pacesetting winner,bid 2 out,second best	7
17May86- 6Mal	fm	*2¼	S'Chase 4:182	4↑	Nat'l Hunt Cup H 25k	5 2 32 13½ 16	17	Fishback J	176		-	- -	Flatterer1767Jolly Four1488Kalankoe1505	Driving	5
5Apr86- 4AtH	fm	*2	S'Chase 3:461	4↑	Ath Cup H 53k	6 2 11 13 11	12	Fishback J	173		-	- -	Flatterer1732Steve Canyon1446Chammsky15020	Driving	6
17Nov85- 4Cam	fm	2¾	S'Chase 5:141	4↑	Colonial Cup 60k	2 2 22 21 2nk	12	Fishback J	162		-	- -	Flatterer1622Salute II1629Gateshead16211	Driving	9
19Oct85- 6Bel	fm	2Ⓣ	:522 2:303 2:562 3:214	3↑	NY Turf Writers H 56k	3 4 86 65½ 44	35¾	Cruguet J	118		3.40	87-20	Bobby Burns1123¾Dance Caller1212Flatterer1183½	Rallied	9
11Oct85- 6Bel	fm	2⅝	S'Chase 4:511	4↑	Temple Gwathmey H 55k	2 7 715 1hd 14	12	Fishback J	170		*.60e	- -	Flatterer1702Gateshead1588Chammsky15217	Handily	7
27Jun85- 5Mth	fm	*2¼	S'Chase 4:193	4↑	Midsummer H 21k	2 3 46 2hd 12	21¾	Guessford B	170		*.60e	- -	Chammsky1491¾Flatterer1701¼Huallatiri1436	Second best	7
18Nov84- 4Cam	fm	2¾	S'Chase 5:09	4↑	Colonial Cup 50k	2 5 53¼ 32¼ 2hd	11¼	Fishback J	160		-	- -	Flatterer1601¼Census16218Eremite1518	Up final stride	7
27Oct84- 7FH	yl	*1½Ⓣ	2:402	3↑	Alw 1500	3 4 41¾ 2hd 2hd	16	Fishback J	154		-	- -	Flatterer1546SmokeRise1412HeartoftheDesert140½	Easily	10
21Sep84- 6Bel	fm	2½	S'Chase 4:40	4↑	Brook H 42k	4 1 21½ 13 12½	12	Fishback J	167		*.40e	- -	Flatterer1672Census15621Double Reefed153	Ridden out	4
24Aug84- 6Sar	yl	2⅜	S'Chase 4:22	4↑	NY Turf Writers H 43k	1 2 210 1hd 1hd	11¾	Fishback J	164		*.60e	- -	Flatterer1641¾Census15512½DoubleRefd15818¾	Clearly best	5
17Aug84- 7Sar	fm	1 1/16Ⓣ	:232 :472 1:12 1:424	3↑	Alw 36000	7 7 95½ 83¼ 76¾	78¾	Cruguet J	115		16.30	74-17	Quick Dip1171¼Lost Canyon114nkRoman Bend115½	Outrun	9
26May84- 6Pro	fm	*3	S'Chase 6:081	4↑	Hard Scuffle H 35k	2 2 11 11½ 1nk	2½	Fishback J	164		-	- -	Census154½Flatterer16412Uncle Edwin1448	Failed	6
12May84- 5Clm	fm	*1¼Ⓣ	2:142	3↑	Alw 1000	3 2 2½ 1½ 1½	12	Achuff CW	142		-	- -	Flatterer1422Dellersbeck1445Another Ripple1496	Driving	6
7Apr84- 4AtH	fm	*2	S'Chase 3:522	4↑	Delta Air H 50k	2 1 12 12 14	14	Fishback J	160		-	- -	Flatterer1604Census1522½TheHallofFamr143no	Well in hand	9
24Mar84- 1Aik	fm	*1Ⓣ	1:464	3↑	Alw 1000	8 1 14 13 2hd	43¾	Wiseman B	143		-	- -	Beat a Path1431½Bomb1522Deify146nk		10
20Nov83- 4Cam	gd	*2¾	S'Chase 5:18	4↑	Colonial Cup 50k	1 9 99 41¾ 1nk	13¼	Francome J	151		-	- -	Flatterer1513¼Twas Ever Thus1511¾Census16011	Ridden out	12
14Oct83- 6Bel	sf	2⅝	S'Chase 5:062	4↑	Temple Gwathmey H 43k	8 4 44 22½ 1½	11¼	Francome J	154		*.30e	- -	Flatterer1541¼MysteriousArthur1421¾GivWhrl1454¼	Handily	8
1Oct83- 4Fx	fm	*2¼	S'Chase 4:16	4↑	Grand National H 15k	1 5 2nk 1½ 15	17	Cushman J	150		-	- -	Flatterer1507Mc Adam1405Mysterious Arthur1447	Easily	8
17Sep83- 4Lig	fm	*2	S'Chase 3:551	3↑	Alw 9000	1 4 22 22 11	18	Cushman J	151		-	- -	Flatterer1518Mc Adam141¾Hawaiki156nk	Easily	6
18Aug83- 6Sar	sf	2⅜	S'Chase 4:274	3↑	NY Turf Writers H 43k	5 4 713 43½ 44	410¼	Martin WS	140		*.90e	- -	DoubleReefed1611¼SugarBee135hdCensus1489	Jumped poorly	7
10Aug83- 6Sar	fm	2 1/16	S'Chase 3:442	3↑	Alw 19000	3 3 32 42½ 1hd	11¾	Cushman J	146		*.90	- -	Flatterer1461¾Sugar Bee1498¾Hawaiki1559½	Driving	7
23Jly83- 2Bel	gd	1 1/16[T]	:244 :484 1:13 1:451	4↑	Clm 50000	1 2 45 44½ 34	32¼	Velasquez J	117		3.80	73-23	Millbank1082¼MagnusPater117noFlattrr117nk	Steadied turn	6
13Jly83- 5Bel	fm	1Ⓣ	:24 :473 1:111 1:36	4↑	Clm 70000	2 6 64½ 65½ 58½	57¾	Velasquez J	113		21.30	77-12	Cannon Royal1172Revocation113¼Fan Letter108¾	No factor	9
30Apr83- 3Fx	fm	*2	S'Chase 3:443	3↑	Alw 6000	2 3 3¾ 2nk 2½	2¾	Cushman J	144		-	- -	Bomb149¾Flatterer14415Paddy's Punch1434		8
9Apr83- 1AtH	sf	*2	S'Chase 4:101	3↑	Md Sp Wt	3 2 21½ 11½ 14	18	Cushman J	144		-	- -	Flatterer1448Bomb1497Publisher14810	Easily	6
5Dec82- 5Aqu	gd	1 1/16[•]	:231 :471 1:12 1:453		Clm 45000	3 8 1012 915 917	916	Hernandez R	114		16.90	69-16	Brae Axe117¾Asticou1133¼David K.1133¼	Outrun	10
22Nov82- 1Aqu	yl	1⅛Ⓣ	:49 1:15 1:411 1:543		Clm 45000	4 3 35 21 33½	32¼	Velasquez J	114		*1.60	69-27	Whale'sEye113¾PrideofSatan1171½Flatterr114nk	Lacked bid	7
11Nov82- 3Aqu	fm	1⅛Ⓣ	:503 1:15 1:404 1:532		Clm 45000	6 4 43½ 21 3½	2no	Velasquez J	114		5.30	77-22	FourBases117noFlatterer114noWeThaPeople117¾	Just missed	8
20Oct82- 9Med	fm	1Ⓣ	:233 :471 1:111 1:363		Clm 45000	6 7 67¾ 63½ 64¾	32¾	Gonzalez MA	115		3.90	88-13	Limit Position1151¼Ablantin1161½Flatterer1151¼	Rallied	8
29Sep82- 9Med	fm	1Ⓣ	:233 :471 1:114 1:373		Clm 45000	6 6 66½ 64¾ 22	11¼	Gonzalez MA	112		3.50	86-14	Flatterer1121¼Fair Roger1142½Papal Order113½	Drew clear	7
9Sep82- 8Med	fm	1 1/16Ⓣ	:232 :471 1:112 1:423		Clm 32000	3 6 64 62¼ 22½	2½	Dufton E	116		6.60	88-07	Fire Away112½Flatterer1163Hey Kennedy1122¾	Rallied	9
30Aug82- 1Sar	fm	1[T]	:242 :474 1:122 1:372		Clm 35000	4 4 31½ 41½ 51¼	51¾	Samyn JL	117	b	3.00	87-09	Milieu117¾Mighty Mecca117nkSunset Mark117¾	Hung	10
23Aug82- 2Sar	fm	1 1/16[T]	:224 :472 1:12 1:434		Clm 40000	9 8 53 31 44½	49¾	Samyn JL	117	b	6.10	81-13	[D]Full Concert117¾Current Pride1135¾Lucrative Way1173¼	Off slowly	10
10Aug82- 1Sar	my	1⅛	:481 1:122 1:381 1:512		Clm 50000	1 1 2hd 44 77½	714	Velasquez J	117	b	7.00	64-16	RichButterfly1102DomandJerry107nkAncestry1172¾	Stopped	7
9Jly82- 9Bel	fm	1¼[T]	:493 1:133 1:391 2:041		Clm 35000	2 3 21½ 42½ 73¼	42¼	Samyn JL	113	b	8.40	71-13	SparkyRidge1171IntentionalForce1151¼Whppn115no	Steadied	10
26Jun82- 7Del	fm	1Ⓣ	:231 :462 1:111 1:38	3↑	Alw 10000	5 4 47½ 54 42	54¼	Dufton E	110	b	6.70	81-13	HiddnCapital110½JohnnyKas119¾SwingtheBlade1123	Outrun	6
11Jun82- 8Del	fm	5fⓉ	:224 :464 :59	3↑	Alw 9500	6 6 63¾ 53½ 44	66½	Dufton E	110		7.70	81-15	NobleOcean1192PrincelyRulr1172½Papadopoulos1171	Outrun	7
1May82- 8Key	fst	1 1/16	:232 :474 1:124 1:441		[S]Barberry 27k	6 4 42½ 46½ 517	528	Walford J	117	b	*2.30	55-23	Fabiano1178½Gray Charles1129½Once Twice11310	Tired	8
18Apr82- 7Key	fst	1 70	:224 :47 1:131 1:442		[S]Alw 15000	6 7 711 76¾ 22	1nk	Dufton E	115	b	2.00	78-23	Flatterer115nkOnce Twice1155Sioux Dancer1101¼	Driving	7
2Apr82- 8Key	fst	1 70	:232 :472 1:13 1:442		[S]Alw 13000	2 1 2hd 1½ 11	13	Dufton E	114	b	4.20	78-27	Flatterer1143InGoodTime1132¼SirBrendBoy1141½	Drew clear	7
23Mar82- 5Key	fst	6f	:223 :464 1:133		[S]Md Sp Wt	2 5 44 34½ 1½	13½	Dufton E	120	b	20.50	74-24	Flatterer1203½Frisky Dan120¾Jewel's Gold115hd	Drew off	9
20Feb82- 3Key	gd	6f	:224 :473 1:131		[S]Md Sp Wt	7 7 714 610 512	513	Dufton E	120		5.00	63-25	CarolinaDutchmn1151½LittleSlalom1208½IcyBdg120½	Outrun	8
16Jan82- 6Aqu	fst	6f[•]	:223 :461 1:114		Md Sp Wt	12 14 1416 1418 1314	1216	Miceli M	122		76.80	69-10	Let'EmHum1221IntervenngHero122noIvanLendl1221	Outrun	14

Forty Niner

ch. c. 1985, by Mr. Prospector (Raise a Native)–File, by Tom Rolfe — Lifetime record: 19 11 5 0 $2,726,000

Own.– Claiborne Farm
Br.– Claiborne Farm (Ky)
Tr.– Woodford C. Stephens

Date	Cond/Dist	Fractions	Race	Running line	Jockey	Wt	Odds	Speed	Top three finishers	Comment	Field
5Nov88-10CD	my 1¼	:474 1:122 1:383 2:044 3↑	BC Classic-G1	3 5 511 84¼ 73¾ 45¾	Krone JA	122	3.70	67-20	Alysheba126½Seeking the Gold1225Waquoit126nk	Shied shadow 2nd turn	9
22Oct88-8Aqu	fst 1	:223 :451 1:09 1:34 3↑	NYRA Mile H 567k	5 3 43¾ 3½ 11 1nk	Fox WI Jr	121	*.40	96-18	Forty Niner121nkMawsuff1151¼Precisionist124nk	All out	6
17Sep88-8Bel	fst 1¼	:473 1:111 1:35 1:592 3↑	Woodward H-G1	2 2 2½ 1hd 1hd 2nk	Pincay L Jr	119	2.70	101-08	Alysheba126nkForty Niner119nkWaquoit1221¼	Gamely	8
20Aug88-8Sar	fst 1¼	:483 1:131 1:374 2:012	Travers-G1	5 2 1½ 1½ 12 1no	McCarron CJ	126	2.20	93-09	FortyNiner126noSeekingtheGold126¾Brian'sTm1265½	Driving	6
30Jly88-9Mth	fst 1⅛	:473 1:112 1:352 1:473	Haskell Inv'l H-G1	1 1 21½ 1hd 1hd 1no	Pincay L Jr	126	*.80	96-10	Forty Niner126noSeeking the Gold1254Primal117½	Driving	5
16Jly88-8Mth	fst 1	:231 :452 1:091 1:334 3↑	Alw 30000	4 2 22 21 12½ 17¼	Krone JA	114	*.30	104-09	Forty Niner1147¼Slew City Slew1176Blue Buckaroo1172½	Won eased up	6
21May88-9Pim	gd 1 3/16	:47 1:111 1:363 1:561	Preakness-G1	4 1 1hd 1hd 78 714¼	Day P	126	2.30	72-11	RisenStr1261¼Brn'sTm1261¼WnnngColors1212½	Brushed rival	9
7May88-8CD	fst 1¼	:464 1:112 1:36 2:021	Ky Derby-G1	17 2 34½ 57 34 2nk	Day P	126	4.90e	86-11	WinningColors121nkFortyNiner1263RisnStr126½	Fast finish	17
16Apr88-8Kee	fst 1 1/16	:24 :48 1:122 1:424	Lexington-G2	4 2 31 21½ 1½ 2hd	Day P	121	*.40	92-18	RisnStr118hdFortyNnr12112Stlwrs1182	Steadied st.,gamely	5
8Apr88-8Kee	fst 7f	:23 :452 1:084 1:22	Lafayette 72k	7 2 42½ 3½ 11 15	Day P	121	*.50	96-21	Forty Niner1215Buoy12210Aloha Prospector1215	Ridden out	8
5Mar88-10GP	fst 1⅛	:463 1:104 1:363 1:494	Florida Derby-G1	9 1 1½ 11½ 12 2nk	Maple E	122	3.00	83-16	Brian'sTime118nkFortyNiner1223Notebook122nk	Just missed	10
15Feb88-10GP	fst 1 1/16	:232 :463 1:104 1:431	Fountain of Youth-G2	7 1 1hd 1hd 1hd 1no	Maple E	122	*.80	85-21	Forty Niner122noNotebook1221Buoy1192	Driving	9
3Feb88-9GP	fst 7f	:214 :443 1:094 1:23	Hutcheson-G3	5 2 2hd 2½ 21½ 21	Maple E	122	*.70	88-24	PerfectSpy1141FortyNiner122½Notebook1224	Couldn't gain	7
30Oct87-8Kee	fst 1 1/16	:224 :464 1:11 1:434	Breeders' Futurity-G2	2 1 21 2hd 2hd 1no	Maple E	121	*.40	87-18	Forty Niner121noHey Pat1212½Sea Trek1213	Driving	7
17Oct87-8Bel	fst 1	:23 :464 1:104 1:364	Champagne-G1	7 2 31½ 2hd 11½ 14¼	Maple E	122	3.30	81-20	Forty Niner1224¼Parlay Me1221¼Tejano1225½	Drew away	11
20Sep87-6Bel	gd 7f	:221 :452 1:093 1:223	Futurity-G1	1 2 11½ 11½ 13 13	Maple E	122	4.50	89-14	FortyNinr1223Tsarbaby1222¼CrusaderSword1224	Ridden out	5
19Aug87-8Sar	sly 6f	:214 :443 1:10	Sanford-G2	3 3 22 21½ 1hd 13½	Maple E	115	6.10	90-15	Forty Niner1153½Once Wild1153Velvet Fog1155½	Driving	6
7Aug87-8Sar	fst 6f	:214 :45 1:101	Sar Spl-G2	2 4 1½ 2hd 31 610	Maple E	117	3.40	79-17	Crusader Sword117nkTejano1175½Endurance1194	Tired	8
17Jly87-5Bel	fst 6f	:222 :46 1:113	Md Sp Wt	8 4 1½ 11½ 13 13¼	Maple E	118	*1.40e	82-20	Forty Niner1183¼Dynaformer1182¾Tsarbaby1181½	Ridden out	13

Genuine Risk

ch. f. 1977, by Exclusive Native (Raise a Native)–Virtuous, by Gallant Man — Lifetime record: 15 10 3 2 $646,587

Own.– Mrs B.R. Firestone
Br.– Mrs G.W. Humphrey Jr (Ky)
Tr.– Leroy Jolley

Date	Cond/Dist	Fractions	Race	Running line	Jockey	Wt	Odds	Speed	Top three finishers	Comment	Field
10Aug81-1Sar	fst 7f	:224 :452 1:09 1:212 3↑	ⒻAlw 32000	3 2 1hd 11 16 18¼	Fell J	119	*.10	95-15	Genuine Risk1198¼Clown's Doll117½Samarta Dancer1193¾	Ridden out mile 1:34 3/5	4
25May81-6Bel	fm 1 1/16Ⓣ	:243 :474 1:12 1:42 3↑	ⒻAlw 35000	5 2 31½ 1½ 1hd 32	MacBeth D	121	*.40	84-12	Smilin'Sera1101¾InRhythym117nkGenuineRisk121no	Weakened	6
11Apr81-7Aqu	fst 7f	:224 :453 1:101 1:224 4↑	ⒻAlw 32000	2 4 22½ 2½ 17 19½	Vasquez J	122	*.10	87-22	GnuineRisk1229½BacktoStay1102½Justacam114nk	Ridden out	5
27Sep80-8Bel	fst 1⅛	:48 1:122 1:364 1:491 3↑	ⒻRuffian H-G1	1 5 3½ 31 2hd 1no	Vasquez J	118	*.50	81-19	GenuineRisk118noMistyGallore124nkIt'snthAr1185¾	Driving	6
10Sep80-8Bel	fst 1	:232 :461 1:104 1:352 3↑	ⒻMaskette-G1	2 4 45 31 1hd 2no	Vasquez J	118	*1.20	91-22	Bold'nDetrmind122noGnunRsk1186¾LovSgn120½	Just missed	5
7Jun80-8Bel	my 1½	:501 1:151 2:04 2:294	Belmont-G1	1 5 53 2½ 1hd 22	Vasquez J	121	5.10	69-17	Temperence Hill1262Genuine Risk1211½Rockhill Native1262	Led,gamely	10
17May80-9Pim	fst 1 3/16	:474 1:111 1:36 1:541	Preakness-G1	5 6 44 43¼ 21 24¾	Vasquez J	121	*2.00	94-12	Codex1264¾GnuineRisk1213¼ColonelMorn1267	Bothered turn	8
3May80-8CD	fst 1¼	:48 1:124 1:373 2:02	Ky Derby-G1	10 7 74¼ 11½ 12 11	Vasquez J	121	13.30	87-11	Genuine Risk1211Rumbo1261Jaklin Klugman1264	Driving	13
19Apr80-8Aqu	fst 1⅛	:472 1:113 1:37 1:504	Wood Memorial-G1	3 3 32 31½ 32 31½	Vasquez J	121	8.20	79-17	PluggedNickle1261½ColnlMorn126hdGnunRsk1213¾	Game try	11
5Apr80-7Aqu	gd 1	:233 :464 1:12 1:383	ⒻHandicap 35000	4 4 32 11½ 11 12¼	Vasquez J	124	*.20	73-20	GenuineRisk1242¼TellaSecret1153¼SprucPn11311	Ridden out	4
19Mar80-7GP	fst 7f	:22 :444 1:094 1:223	ⒻAlw 17000	3 5 44 32½ 1½ 12½	Vasquez J	113	*.40	91-20	GenuineRisk1132½SoberJig1123½PeaceBells1151½	Ridden out	6
17Nov79-8Aqu	fst 1⅛	:481 1:131 1:383 1:511	ⒻDemoiselle-G2	6 4 3½ 2hd 2hd 1no	Pincay L Jr	116	1.20	79-21	GenuineRisk116noSmartAngle1216¾SprucePine1123¾	Driving	7
5Nov79-8Aqu	fst 1	:23 :46 1:102 1:36	ⒻTempted-G3	4 5 51½ 11½ 12 13	Vasquez J	114	*.90	86-18	GenuineRisk1143StreetBallet117½TellScrt1144½	Ridden out	9
18Oct79-6Aqu	fst 1	:233 :47 1:114 1:362	ⒻAlw 15000	6 2 21 2hd 12 17¼	Vasquez J	115	*.60	84-18	GenuineRisk1157¼GoingEast1175CintoTora1154½	Ridden out	6
30Sep79-4Bel	sly 6½f	:223 :452 1:112 1:18	ⒻMd Sp Wt	8 11 45 46½ 23 11¾	Vasquez J	118	*3.10	86-24	GenuineRisk1181¾RemoteRuler11813Espadrille1181¾	Driving	11

Glorious Song

b. f. 1976, by Halo (Hail to Reason)–Ballade, by Herbager — Lifetime record: 34 17 9 1 $1,004,534

Own.– Hunt & Stronach
Br.– E.P. Taylor (Can)
Tr.– John Cairns

Date	Cond/Dist	Fractions	Race	Running line	Jockey	Wt	Odds	Speed	Top three finishers	Comment	Field
13Dec81-8Hol	fst 1⅛	:463 1:103 1:361 1:493 3↑	ⒻSilver Belles H 107k	1 4 54 52¼ 33½ 42¾	McCarron CJ	125	*.80	78-21	Happy Guess117hdTrack Robbery1232½Targa112hd	Dull	6
22Nov81-8Hol	fm 1⅛Ⓣ	:473 1:114 1:352 1:47 3↑	ⒻMatriarch 221k	9 4 45½ 43½ 23 22½	McCarron CJ	123	4.90	92-08	Kilijaro1232½Glorious Song123nkBersid120½	Wide	9
31Oct81-7Kee	fst 1⅛	:472 1:113 1:363 1:491 3↑	ⒻSpinster-G1	4 6 41¼ 42 22 1nk	Platts R	123	2.20	91-19	Glorious Song123nkTruly Bound1196Safe Play119¾	Driving	7
11Oct81-8Bel	fst 1¼	:482 1:121 1:37 2:014 3↑	ⒻBeldame-G1	4 7 32 2½ 22½ 27[illegible]	Velasquez J	123	*1.70	84-16	LoveSign1237[DH]Jameela123[DH]GloriousSng1235½	Weakened	7
19Sep81-8Bel	my 1¼	:481 1:114 1:354 2:003 3↑	Marlboro Cup H-G1	7 6 45 34 65½ 79¼	Platts R	118	23.10	88-13	NobleNashua1163¾AmbrPss1201½TmprncHll1271¼	Early speed	8
15Aug81-9Mth	fst 1⅛	:46 1:092 1:342 1:472 3↑	Monmouth H-G1	5 5 66 75¼ 67 78	Platts R	119	3.10	90-09	Amber Pass1172Joanie's Chief1082Ring of Light114no	Unruly before start	10
1Jly81-9WO	fst 1⅛	:463 1:104 1:36 1:48 3↑	Dominion Day H-G3	2 3 31½ 2½ 14½ 15½	Platts R	125	*.35	102-14	GloriousSong1255½DrivingHome1252½ByeByTony112hd	Handily	8
26Apr81-8Hol	fst 1	:224 :461 1:112 1:362 3↑	Mervyn LeRoy H-G2	6 4 53¾ 32 1hd 2nk	Toro F	121	*1.70	84-21	ElevenStitches115nkGloriousSng1212¼SummrTime Guy1145½	Sharp try	8
8Mar81-8SA	fst 1¼	:452 1:092 1:341 1:592 4↑	S Anita H-G1	11 8 89¼ 66½ 57 55½	McHargue DG	119	10.30	86-11	John Henry1281King Go Go1171½Exploded115no	Wide	11
22Feb81-8SA	fst 1⅛	:444 1:084 1:342 1:471 4↑	ⒻS Margarita H-G1	6 4 47 44½ 31 2nk	McCarron CJ	130	*1.10	93-12	PrincessKarenda118nkGlorousSong1301¼Ack'sScrt1222	Sharp	10
31Jan81-8SA	gd 1 1/16	:23 :462 1:104 1:431 4↑	ⒻS Maria H-G2	1 3 32 2hd 12½ 12	McCarron CJ	127	*.50	85-23	Glorious Song1272Track Robbery1175Miss Huntington11310	Eased final yards	4
10Jan81-8SA	fst 7f	:214 :434 1:074 1:201 4↑	San Carlos H-G2	1 7 75½ 63 46 46½	Hawley S	120	4.50	92-10	Flying Paster1243¼To B. or Not1232Double Discount1151½	Flattened out;Previously trained by Gerald W. Belanger Jr	8
6Sep80-7Bel	fst 1⅛	:45 1:092 1:341 1:47 3↑	Marlboro Cup H-G1	4 7 710 63¾ 22 24½	Velasquez J	117	*1.70	87-15	Wintr'sTl1234½GlorousSng117nkJklnKlugmn1183½	Went well	8
16Aug80-9Mth	fst 1⅛	:464 1:111 1:353 1:48 3↑	AL Haskell H-G1	2 5 75¾ 4nk 2½ 21¾	Velasquez J	117	6.70	93-15	Spectacular Bid1321¾GlorsSng1171¼The Cool Virginian1124	Drifted out,brushed	8
12Jly80-9WO	fm 1¼Ⓣ	:453 1:112 1:371 2:013	[R]Maturity H 54k	2 4 35½ 11½ 13 13½	Leblanc JB	121	*.25	99-09	Glorious Song1213½Great State1261Nice Idea1211	Handily	6
1Jly80-7WO	fst 1⅛	:48 1:114 1:364 1:501 3↑	Dominion Day H-G3	2 5 54¾ 3nk 11½ 11	Leblanc JB	123	*.30	91-13	GloriousSng1231MapleGrove1184Knight'sTurn1181½	Handily	8
15Jun80-10Det	fst 1⅛	:471 1:112 1:374 1:50 3↑	Mich Mile H-G2	7 6 54¾ 34 1hd 1no	Leblanc JB	117	3.10	87-25	Glorious Song117noPrince Majestic1154½Uncool1221	Lasted	7
26May80-8AP	fm 1⅛Ⓣ	:484 1:13 1:372 1:501 3↑	Laurance Armour H 117k	3 6 54 44 21 21	Velasquez J	118	2.80	85-16	Overskate1271GlorousSong1183YoungBob114¾	Best of others	7
26Apr80-6Aqu	fst 1⅛	:472 1:114 1:364 1:493 3↑	ⒻTop Flight H-G1	2 4 511 44 1½ 11¾	Velasquez J	123	1.90e	87-19	Glorious Song1231¾Misty Gallore1261¾Blitey1172¾	Driving	7
24Feb80-8SA	fst 1⅛	:462 1:103 1:36 1:482 4↑	ⒻS Margarita H-G1	3 7 75¾ 42 1hd 12	McCarron CJ	120	2.30	87-11	Glorious Song1202The Very One116noKankam1252	Drew off; Previously owned by F. Stronach	11
10Feb80-8SA	fst 1⅛	:452 1:093 1:35 1:473	ⒻLa Canada-G1	2 6 56 31½ 1hd 11¾	McCarron CJ	118	3.30	91-09	GloriousSong1181¾PrizeSpot1194It'sinthAr1251	Drew clear	7
26Jan80-8SA	fst 1 1/16	:224 :453 1:093 1:411	ⒻEl Encino-G3	8 7 55½ 51¾ 31 43¾	McCarron CJ	116	*2.60	91-09	It'sintheAir1241¼PrizeSpot1211¼[D]Terlingua1211¼	Impeded; Placed third through disqualification	8

Date	Cond	Dist	Fractions	Race	PP	St	1st	2nd	Str	Fin	Jockey	Wt	Eq	Odds	Speed	Top three finishers	Comment	Fld
6Jan80- 8SA	fst	7f	:214 :44 1:081 1:204	ⒻLa Brea 52k	3	3	34	32	2½	2½	McCarron CJ	116		6.70	98-11	Terlingua121½Glorious Song1164Prize Spot1217	Gamely	4
Previously trained by F.H. Loschke																		
3Nov79- 7Grd	fst	1¼	:501 1:16 1:411 2:084	3↑ⒻⓇMaple Leaf 34k	1	5	31	11½	11	1¾	Leblanc J	122		*.40e	71-30	GloriousSng122¾SinstrQun1111½DncngDors1091½	Ridden out	8
20Oct79- 8WO	sf	1⅛Ⓣ	:49 1:154 1:422 2:101	3↑ⒻNettie 70k	1	6	54	21	53¾	410¼	Leblanc J	118		2.25	46-44	SenoritaPoquito1182¼Christy'sMnt1242½Liveinthesnshine1245½		10
Weakened																		
6Oct79- 8WO	sf	1⅛Ⓣ	:483 1:154 1:421 2:11	ⒻⓇWonder Where 36k	12	8	84¾	1hd	1½	11½	Leblanc J	120		*1.75	52-48	GloriousSong1201½Fud'Artfc1202½DoublDwn1115½	Ridden out	12
23Sep79- 7WO	fst	1⅛	:483 1:124 1:371 1:50	3↑ⒻⓇBelle Mahone 34k	5	5	54	21½	1hd	12½	Leblanc JB	115		5.30	92-19	GlorsSng1152½LVoygus1258Chrsty'sMount1235½	Drew clear	7
8Sep79- 8WO	fm	6½fⓉ	:223 :453 1:10 1:162	ⒻⓇOnt Damsel 29k	3	2	2hd	2hd	12	1½	Leblanc JB	114		*1.65	98-08	GloriousSong114½Feud'Artifice1201SusieBggr1142½	Driving	8
18Aug79- 8FE	gd	1 1/16	:23 :47 1:113 1:441	ⒻDuchess 28k	8	5	52¾	32	32½	22	Leblanc JB	117		4.60	88-29	Kamar1232GloriousSong117½Feud'Artifc120nk	Finished well	10
10Aug79- 6FE	fst	1 70	:23 :464 1:111 1:421	Ⓕ 10000	8	3	33	1hd	12	1¾	LeBlanc JB	112		8.55	92-18	Glorious Song112¾Feu d'Artifice1181¾[DH]Raise Your Sights1151		8
Ridden out																		
2Aug79- 7FE	sl	6f	:23 :464 1:123	ⒻHandicap 12500	4	3	2½	1hd	42¼	56	LeBlanc JB	119	b	*.70	78-24	Your My Choice114¾Sundae Star120nkRaise Your Sights1201¾		7
Pressed,gave way																		
15Jly79- 5WO	sly	6f	:22 :451 1:11	3↑ⒻAlw 7500	4	3	1hd	22	21½	12	LeBlanc JB	112		*.75	88-17	GloriousSng1122CougarKittn1144½BoogieDancer1152	Wide	7
7Jly79- 6WO	fst	6f	:222 :45 1:094	3↑ⒻAlw 7500	2	5	1hd	12	13½	19	LeBlanc JB	112		2.95	94-09	GloriousSong1129HermnvlI1152AlbonLdy118nk	Bore out turn	9
20Nov78- 1Grd	fst	7f	:23 :463 1:134 1:264	ⒻⓇMd Sp Wt	5	4	2hd	1½	11½	13	Clark D	117		4.45	81-23	GloriousSng1173Look'nLeap117hdWicketLady1172½	Handily	12

Gold Beauty

b. f. 1979, by Mr. Prospector (Raise a Native)–Stick to Beauty, by Illustrious **Lifetime record: 12 8 2 1 $251,901**

Own.– Mrs P.B. Hofmann
Br.– Mr & Mrs P.B. Hofmann (Fla)
Tr.– William Curtis Jr

Date	Cond	Dist	Fractions	Race	PP	St	1st	2nd	Str	Fin	Jockey	Wt	Eq	Odds	Speed	Top three finishers	Comment	Fld
8Oct83- 8Bel	fst	6f	:221 :453 1:102	3↑Fall Highweight H-G2	2	1	1hd	1½	43	57½	Brumfield D	140		5.60	82-19	Chas Conerly136½Singh Tu124½Let Burn1344	Tired	9
11Sep83- 8Bel	fst	6f	:22 :451 1:103	3↑Boojum 55k	1	1	1½	1½	11½	22	Brumfield D	123		*.80	87-22	ChasConerly1182GldBeauty1233¾Shimatoree1202¼	Weakened	4
7Aug83-10Suf	fst	6f	:214 :443 :58 1:093	3↑Suf Sprint H-G3	5	1	2hd	1hd	2½	32¼	Brumfield D	124		*.70	91-18	All Sold Out110¾Let Burn1151½Gold Beauty1244	Weakened	8
26Jun83- 8Bel	fst	6f	:222 :451 1:102	3↑True North H-G3	6	2	2½	14	14	12½	Brumfield D	121		*.70	90-24	GoldBeauty1212½SinghTu1111¼FittoFight1132	Ridden out	8
21May83- 9Mth	fst	6f	:224 :453 1:093	3↑ⒻRegret H 33k	6	1	12½	11½	1½	12¾	Brumfield D	126		*.40	92-17	GldBeauty1262¾PlatnumBll1161¼SproutdRy1181¼	Ridden out	8
16Oct82- 8Aqu	fst	7f	:224 :454 1:104 1:234	3↑Vosburgh-G1	5	1	11	1½	13	31	Brumfield D	120		*.60	81-26	EngneOne126½[D]DukeMitchell123½GldBty1201½	Weakened	6
Placed second through disqualification																		
10Sep82- 8Bel	fst	6f	:222 :45 1:091	3↑Fall Highweight H-G2	5	1	2hd	14	16	16	Brumfield D	126		5.20	96-20	Gold Beauty1266Engine One131nkOsorno1251	Ridden out	9
5Aug82- 8Sar	fst	7f	:221 :45 1:094 1:224	ⒻTest-G2	2	5	11½	11½	12	11	Brumfield D	116		*1.00	88-16	GldBeauty1161AmbassadorofLuck1211¾Number1141¾	Driving	12
17Jly82- 8Key	fst	6f	:22 :444 1:094	3↑ⒻSpring Valley H 28k	1	4	1½	1hd	12	15½	Brumfield D	118		*.20	93-19	GldBty1185½ATearinHerEye1143¾MadamMschf1151½	Easily	8
5Jly82- 8Key	fst	6f	:213 :44 1:10	ⒻRushland 28k	6	1	2½	18	110	110	Tejeira J	114		*.20	92-15	Gold Beauty11410Lady Ann's Key114½Sparkling Savage1181¾		7
Easy score																		
24Jun82- 6Mth	fst	6f	:214 :442 1:082	3↑ⒻAlw 10000	5	1	13	11½	16	112	Brumfield D	114		*.70	98-17	Gold Beauty11412Keys Special1083Satan Gal1134	Easily	7
16Feb82- 4Hia	fst	6f	:214 :444 1:101	ⒻMd Sp Wt	8	4	11½	15	17	112	Brumfield D	120		4.70	92-17	Gold Beauty12012Illiana1202Tracie Elaine120½	Ridden out	12

Groovy

ch. c. 1983, by Norcliffe (Buckpasser)–Tinnitus, by Restless Wind **Lifetime record: 26 12 4 1 $1,346,956**

Own.– Prestonwood Farm
Br.– Marshall T. Robinson (Tex)
Tr.– Jose Martin

Date	Cond	Dist	Fractions	Race	PP	St	1st	2nd	Str	Fin	Jockey	Wt	Eq	Odds	Speed	Top three finishers	Comment	Fld
21Nov87- 1Hol	fst	6f	:211 :44 :554 1:084	3↑BC Sprint-G1	1	3	3½	21½	23½	24	Cordero A Jr	126		*.80	94-12	VerySbtle1214Groovy1261¾ExclusvEnough1241	Pressed pace	13
10Oct87- 7Bel	fst	7f	:224 :451 1:092 1:223	3↑Vosburgh-G1	8	1	11	12½	15	1¾	Cordero A Jr	126		*.30	89-22	Groovy126¾Moment of Hope1263Sun Master1261½	Driving	8
23Aug87- 8Sar	fst	7f	:22 :441 1:084 1:214	3↑Forego H-G2	5	1	11½	11½	12½	11¾	Cordero A Jr	132		*.60	93-14	Groovy1321¾Purple Mountain1131¾Sun Master1182	Driving	6
Previously owned by J.A. Ballis																		
18Jly87- 8Bel	fst	7f	:231 :454 1:092 1:222	3↑Tom Fool-G2	5	1	12	11½	14½	16½	Cordero A Jr	128		*.60	90-20	Groovy1286½Sun Master121nkMoment of Hope1193	Driving	6
5Jly87- 9FL	fst	6f	:221 :444 1:092	3↑Bud BC 156k	3	3	1½	1hd	1½	1hd	Pezua JM	122		*.05	102-11	Groovy122hdPurpleMountn1192½VinnietheVipr1197	Driving	7
21Jun87- 8Bel	my	6f	:22 :44 1:074	3↑True North H-G2	1	1	11½	14	15	15¾	Cordero A Jr	123		*.20	101-10	Groovy1235¾King's Swan120nkSun Master117no	Ridden out	4
6Jun87- 1Bel	fst	6f	:213 :44 1:082	3↑Roseben H-G3	1	1	12½	14	14½	14¼	Cordero A Jr	119		*1.10	98-15	Groovy1194¼Love That Mac1182King's Swan1213½	Drew clear	6
15Nov86- 8Aqu	fst	6f	:213 :441 1:084	3↑Sport Page H-G3	4	1	1½	1hd	3½	46½	Cordero A Jr	122		*.50	90-22	BestbyTest1125King'sSwan118hdSunMaster1171½	Weakened	7
Previously owned by Ballis & Kruckel Jr																		
1Nov86- 3SA	fst	6f	:211 :433 :554 1:082	3↑BC Sprint-G1	9	2	31	31½	32	44¼	Santos JA	124		*.40	92-13	Smile1261¼PineTreeLane1231¾BedsidePrmise1261¼	Weakened	9
15Oct86- 8SA	fst	6f	:212 :434 :554 1:081	3↑Ancient Title H 76k	5	1	11½	13	12½	12	Santos JA	123		*.40	97-18	Groovy1232Rosie's K.T.1171Sun Master114½	Driving	8
1Sep86- 8Bel	fst	1	:22 :44 1:082 1:34	Jerome H-G1	4	1	18	13½	2½	45¼	Velasquez J	124		2.50	90-14	Ogygian126hdMogambo1192Moment of Hope1113¼	Tired	5
17Aug86- 8Sar	my	7f	:214 :441 1:082 1:211	3↑Forego H-G2	1	4	12	14	15	1¾	Santos JA	118		2.00	96-11	Groovy118¾Turkoman1244¾Innamorato110nk	Driving	8
20Jly86- 8Bel	fst	7f	:221 :443 1:084 1:213	3↑Tom Fool-G2	2	2	11½	12½	16	16¼	Santos JA	112		2.50	94-14	Groovy1126¼Phone Trick1266Basket Weave119nk	Drew clear	5
4Jly86- 6Bel	fst	6f	:214 :444 1:09	Firecracker 53k	4	1	11½	12	12½	12¾	Velasquez J	119		*1.20	97-11	Groovy1192¾RoyalPennant1153LandingPlot122hd	Drew clear	8
Previously trained by Howard Crowell																		
7Jun86- 7Bel	sly	7f	:213 :442 1:094 1:232	Riva Ridge 81k	2	1	12½	11	22½	48½	Day P	117	b	2.90	76-16	Ogygian1223½Wayar115hdLanding Plot1225	Weakened	5
17May86- 8Pim	fst	1 3/16	:472 1:11 1:36 1:544	Preakness-G1	4	1	1½	1hd	35½	613¾	Perret C	126		11.10	79-18	SnowChief1264Frdinand1266½BroadBrush126no	Used in pace	7
3May86- 8CD	fst	1¼	:451 1:101 1:37 2:024	Ky Derby-G1	14	1	11	1515	1628	1649¾	Pincay L Jr	126		57.30	33-10	Ferdinnd1262¼BldArrangement126¾BrodBrush126nk	Stopped	16
Previously trained by Petro Peters																		
19Apr86- 8Aqu	fst	1⅛	:472 1:111 1:361 1:503	Wood Memorial-G1	2	1	11	11	21	3¾	Perret C	126		3.80	81-18	Broad Brush126½Mogambo126nkGroovy1261¼	Weakened	7
5Apr86- 8Aqu	fst	1	:222 :444 1:083 1:343	Gotham-G2	8	1	11½	13	13½	2¾	Santos JA	114		8.70	92-18	Mogambo121¾[D]Groovy1141¼Tasso1231	Bore in	9
Disqualified and placed fifth																		
22Mar86- 7Aqu	fst	7f	:223 :451 1:093 1:22	Bay Shore (Div 1)-G2	6	4	21	1hd	2hd	24½	Santos JA	117		5.10	86-25	Zabaleta1144½Groovy1179½Belocolus1142	Best of rest	8
Previously owned by T. Kruckel Jr;previously trained by Kimberly Hardy																		
8Jan86- 9GP	sly	6f	:213 :444 1:114	Spectacular Bid 46k	1	4	1½	12	12½	1¾	Perret C	113	b	*.90	80-21	Groovy113¾Kenny Lane1141¼Limited Practice1131½	Driving	6
Previously trained by John B. Adams																		
2Nov85- 1Aqu	fst	1	:222 :452 1:104 1:361	ⒸBC Juvenile-G1	11	1	11½	31½	1014	1016	Murphy DJ	122	b	22.90	69-10	Tasso122noStormCt1221¾SctDncr122no	Stumbled after start	13
19Oct85- 8Bel	fst	1	:231 :462 1:12 1:371	Champagne-G1	1	1	12	12	23	29¾	MacBeth D	122		10.90	69-17	Mogambo1229¾Groovy122hdMr. Classic1221¾	No match	5
10Oct85- 8Med	fst	1 1/16	:224 :46 1:102 1:433	Young America-G1	10	1	12	1½	43½	57½	MacBeth D	119		*2.00	77-15	StormCat119noDnzigCnnection122nkMogmbo1196	Weakened	12
14Sep85- 6Bel	fst	7f	:222 :453 1:093 1:222	Futurity-G1	6	3	1½	1½	22½	29½	Murphy DJ	122		4.70	80-09	Ogygian1229½Groovy1226[DH]Mr. Classic122	2nd best	6
2Sep85- 8Med	fst	6f	:222 :45 1:103	Forever Casting 28k	9	8	31½	1hd	12½	12½	Murphy DJ	112		7.90	89-10	Groovy1122½Hey Now Harry114nkKruckel1142½	Driving	11

Guilty Conscience

b. c. 1976, by Court Ruling (Traffic Judge)–Gracefully, by Gallant Man — **Lifetime record: 41 14 8 4 $382,805**

Own.– Mrs R. Davison
Br.– Mrs R. Davison (Md)
Tr.– Hubert Hine

Date	Cond	Dist	Fractions	Race	PP	St	1C	2C	Str	Fin	Jockey	Wt	Odds	Sp-Var	Finishers	Comment	Fld
28Nov81- 8Aqu	fst	6f	:23 :462 1:103	3↑ Sport Page H 54k	4	4	42	31½	22½	33¼	Asmussen CB	126	*.90	85-28	WellDecoratd1172¾EnginOn116½GltyConscnc1261¼	Weakened	6
17Oct81- 8Aqu	fst	7f	:224 :454 1:093 1:22	3↑ Vosburgh-G1	6	2	42	4nk	13	13¾	Asmussen CB	126	2.90	91-23	GuiltyConscience1263¾RisJm1261WllDcortd123no	Ridden out	8
7Oct81- 8Bel	fst	6f	:224 :452 1:091	3↑ Boojum H 55k	2	5	76¼	55½	2hd	15	Asmussen CB	115	4.50	96-25	GuiltyCnscnce1155ImperlDlmm112nkMudln115½	Ridden out	8
26Aug81- 8Bel	fst	1	:223 :45 1:084 1:334	3↑ Forego H 83k	2	3	1hd	2hd	32	38¾	Asmussen CB	112	4.30	90-16	Fappiano119¾Herb Water1088Guilty Conscience112nk	Tired	5
29Jly81- 7Sar	sly	7f	:224 :454 1:092 1:221	3↑ Alw 32000	4	2	11½	13	16	16¾	Asmussen CB	117	*.50	91-18	GltyCnscienc1176¾SngSng1092½DynmcMov115nk	Ridden out	6
3Jly81- 8Bel	my	6f	:221 :45 1:09	3↑ True North H 55k	1	3	65	52½	4nk	31½	Asmussen CB	113	5.50	95-16	Joanie's Chief1091¼Proud Appeal117nkGuilty Conscience1133½	Rallied	7
6Jun81- 7Bel	fst	1	:231 :461 1:102 1:353	3↑ Alw 37000	3	3	11	13	15	15	Asmussen CB	115	*1.30	90-14	GuiltyConscience1155Joanie's Chief1171½Prince Crimson115½	Drew clear	10
17May81- 8Bel	fst	6f	:223 :453 1:094	3↑ Roseben H 55k	8	4	32	34	31	2¾	Asmussen CB	112	16.20	92-22	RingofLight113¾GuiltyConscience1121Convennt114½	Rallied	8
2May81- 8Aqu	gd	7f	:222 :451 1:094 1:23	3↑ Carter H-G2	3	3	21½	1hd	12	2½	Lovato F Jr	111	5.60e	85-19	AmberPass114½GltyCnscienc1111Dunhm'sGft1161	Game try	7
4Apr81- 9Pim	fst	6f	:223 :45 :572 1:101	3↑ J E Hoover H 32k	3	3	52¼	44½	43	52½	McCauley WH	114	*1.30	92-19	NaughtyJimmy1131¼Gasp1131RexImperator112hd	No menace	7
29Mar81- 8Aqu	fst	6f	:214 :442 1:092	3↑ White Skies H 54k	1	4	33	32½	32	23¾	Asmussen CB	114	6.30	90-21	Dave'sFriend1303¾GuiltyConscience114½Rare Performer1174½	Gained place	4
14Mar81- 8Aqu	fst	6f[•]	:231 :462 1:111	3↑ Toboggan H 53k	1	1	11½	1hd	2½	22½	Asmussen CB	115	2.50	85-18	Dr.Blum1232½GltyCnscnc115noDunhm'sGft1182¾	Brushed st.	4
16Feb81- 8Aqu	fst	6f[•]	:222 :45 1:091	3↑ Sporting Plate H 55k	4	1	21½	2½	2hd	2nk	Asmussen CB	115	4.30	98-13	Dr.Blum122nkGuiltyConscience115¾RingofLight113¾	Sharp	6
28Jan81- 8Aqu	fst	6f[•]	:221 :444 1:10	4↑ Coaltown 54k	2	4	2hd	2hd	21	43½	Asmussen CB	119	*1.20	90-20	Dr.Blum1211¾Dunham'sGift1231¾TonyMack114hd	Weakened	6
16Jan81- 8Aqu	fst	6f[•]	:223 :453 1:102	4↑ Handicap 32000	1	5	2½	11	14	16	Asmussen CB	116	*1.70	92-24	GuiltyConscience1166BoldVoyager114noSkt1101¾	Ridden out	7
9Dec80- 8Med	fst	6f	:223 :46 1:103	3↑ Alw 25000	1	5	11½	12½	15	14	Asmussen CB	117	*1.20	90-22	GltyCnscience1174AmbtousRulr1175TwoPr110¾	Ridden out	9
28Nov80- 7Aqu	sly	6f	:223 :453 1:101	3↑ Alw 32000	4	4	32	2½	1hd	11¾	Asmussen CB	119	5.30	92-17	GltyConscience1191¾TrckRwrd119nkSpyChrgr1153¾	Driving	6
5Apr80- 7Pim	fst	6f	:23 :453 :574 1:103	3↑ J E Hoover H 31k	1	4	45	49½	49½	412½	Adams JK	110	8.10	80-19	Isella11611AmbitiousRuler1101½Dave'sFriend125no	Trailed	4
26Mar80- 8Pim	fst	1 1/16	:23 :461 1:104 1:434	4↑ Alw 23000	7	3	32	23	511	515	Adams JK	117	2.20	71-23	Dooley's1155Grey Beret1152¼Best Man1152	Tired	7
9Feb80- 9Bow	fst	1 1/16	:233 :473 1:124 1:452	3↑ [S]G L Stryker H 27k	2	3	33	31½	32½	87¼	Adams JK	115	*2.20e	72-26	Skipper'sFriend1131ThCoolVrgnn1191½T.V.Hll1141	Steadied	8
26Jan80- 5Bow	fst	7f	:223 :443 1:093 1:231	4↑ [S]Alw 20000	4	2	21½	31½	43	42½	Adams JK	119	*.70	86-21	Skippr'sFriend1191¼AmbitousRulr119hdGsp1151¼	No excuse	5
22Dec79- 8Lrl	fst	1	:23 :461 1:112 1:372	[S]E T Chewing H 32k	7	2	3nk	1½	12	11	Adams JK	117	1.30e	86-15	GltyConscience1171TheCoolVirginian1231¼DurhamRangr1171¼	Driving	7
10Dec79- 8Lrl	fst	1	:24 :471 1:114 1:362	[S]Alw 20000	5	1	12	12	14	17	Adams JK	113	*.80	91-23	GuiltyConscience1137StormWatch1131FunnyCap1112	Handily	6
23Nov79- 8Lrl	fst	7f	:224 :46 1:094 1:221	Capitol H 46k	10	5	3½	21	2hd	21½	Adams JK	109	54.20	98-17	PolePosition1211½GultyCnscnc1096Buck'sChf112¾	Good try	12
12Nov79- 8Med	gd	6f	:221 :45 1:102	3↑ Alw 20000	1	4	31½	35	34	23½	Adams JK	115	16.40	89-20	Coup de Kas1133½Guilty Conscience1151Klassy Flight110no	Up for place	8
30Oct79- 7Med	fst	6f	:221 :453 1:11	Palisades H (Div 2) 43k	8	5	64¼	64½	53¾	45	Adams JK	109	67.70	85-20	Rise Jim120¾Convenient1154Pianist110nk	No factor; Awarded third purse money	9
19Oct79- 8Med	fst	6f	:23 :454 1:10	3↑ Alw 25000	6	4	61¾	54	48	58	Adams JK	112	17.10	87-19	Amadevil1154Coupon Rate1154Team Captain122no	No threat	8
6Oct79- 6Med	fst	6f	:221 :451 1:111	3↑ Alw 20000	5	1	23	33½	35½	55½	Adams JK	116	5.60	83-17	Bold Bishop1152½Wm. Withers122½Sir Rossel1152	Tired	6
26Sep79- 7Med	fst	6f	:222 :452 1:103	3↑ Clm 32000	7	2	31½	2hd	11½	13	Adams JK	112	19.10	92-19	Guilty Conscience1123Two Pair1162Simplified1112	Driving	8
18Aug79- 8Tim	fst	4f	:222 :453	3↑ [S]Jet H 16k	5	7		96¼	812	86	Sasser B	112	33.60	92-08	Silk or Satin1191¾Great Point1181¼Ten Ten117½	Outrun	10
7Aug79- 8Bow	fst	6f	:224 :454 :572 1:101	Alw 10000	6	4	32	2½	23	22½	Adams JK	115	16.30	86-22	GreatPoint1202½GltyConscience1153RootieToot1122½	Wide	6
25Jly79- 8Bow	fst	7f	:224 :454 1:101 1:231	3↑ [S]Alw 25000	5	4	44	43	45½	56½	Adams JK	115	21.50	82-22	Side Board1173Combat Patrol1221½Great Point1151½	Tired	7
9Jly79- 8Bow	fst	6f	:223 :454 :582 1:12	Alw 9000	4	6	66¼	46	58	68½	Iliescu A	115	7.20	71-26	J.D.May115noAnothergamblr115nkJohnVonWolfgng115¾	Tired	7
21Apr79- 8Pim	fm	1 1/16(T)	:24 :481 1:132 1:454	[S]Survivor 32k	8	1	14½	42	715	823	Adams JK	116	4.20e	59-17	DurhamRangr1167DoubleRefd1221¾Mon110hd	Used early pace	8
7Apr79- 8Pim	fst	6f	:232 :47 :59 1:114	Hirsch Jacobs 33k	1	5	32	42	78½	715	Adams JK	119	3.80	73-18	BreezingOn1222½FearlssMcGuire113¾OurGary1221¼	Bore out	8
28Mar79- 8Bow	fst	7f	:233 :464 1:112 1:242	[S]Alw 20000	6	1	14	13	15	13¼	Adams JK	117	3.20	83-25	GltyConscience1173¼ForLoveandGlory120hdDouble Reefd1171	Driving	6
16Mar79- 6Bow	fst	6f	:23 :463 :592 1:131	Alw 11000	1	3	1½	11½	13	11½	Adams JK	120	2.40	74-37	GltyConscience1201½Watch The Varmint1131Native Ginger1152	Driving	6
10Feb79- 3Bow	fst	6f	:223 :461 :582 1:12	Alw 10000	9	1	21	1hd	11½	13	Adams JK	112	2.50e	80-31	GuiltyConscience1123Ransack1171Buck'sChief1151½	Driving	9
31Jan79- 8Bow	fst	6f	:223 :454 :581 1:12	Alw 10000	8	7	43	2hd	23	55	Adams JK	112	3.00e	75-26	Sugarbuck1083¾Ransack120nkTigger Too1121	Drifted out	10
5Jan79- 5Bow	fst	6f	:224 :461 :581 1:114	Md 25000	7	5	33	31½	1hd	11¾	Adams JK	120	30.90e	81-23	GuiltyConscience1201¾Sugarbuck1151EazySwezy1204	Driving	12
24Oct78- 4Med	fst	6f	:221 :453 1:123	Md Sp Wt	8	11	1113	1116	1122	1123	Kurtz J	120	52.50	59-13	Infusive120nkPonchoSorefoot1203NevrRome1202	No threat	12

Gulch

b. c. 1984, by Mr. Prospector (Raise a Native)–Jameela, by Rambunctious — **Lifetime record: 32 13 8 4 $3,095,521**

Own.– P.M. Brant
Br.– Peter M. Brant (Ky)
Tr.– D. Wayne Lukas

Date	Cond	Dist	Fractions	Race	PP	St	1C	2C	Str	Fin	Jockey	Wt	Odds	Sp-Var	Finishers	Comment	Fld
5Nov88- 4CD	sly	6f	:21 :441 :562 1:102	3↑ BC Sprint-G1	10	5	87¼	67	41¾	1¾	Cordero A Jr	126	5.80e	91-20	Gulch126¾Play the King1261Afleet126½	Driving	13
9Oct88- 7Bel	my	7f	:223 :452 1:094 1:222	3↑ Vosburgh-G1	2	4	42½	32½	22	22¾	Cordero A Jr	126	*.50e	87-24	Mining1262¾Gulch1265½High Brite1264½	Held place	4
27Aug88- 9Mth	fst	1⅛	:462 1:094 1:343 1:474	3↑ Iselin H-G1	2	3	31	31	32½	34¾	Cordero A Jr	122	2.40	90-12	Alysheba124¾Bet Twice1234Gulch1222½	Weakened	6
6Aug88- 8Sar	sly	1⅛	:472 1:113 1:353 1:474	3↑ Whitney H-G1	2	1	11½	11	2hd	21½	Santos JA	124	1.80	94-12	Personal Ensign1171½Gulch12417King's Swan123	Tight turn,drifted out	3
16Jly88- 8Bel	fst	7f	:23 :461 1:101 1:222	3↑ Tom Fool-G2	1	1	2½	2hd	2hd	2¾	Santos JA	128	*.40	89-22	King's Swan128¾Gulch1286Abject1192	Brushed late	4
12Jun88- 8Hol	fst	1⅛	:473 1:104 1:35 1:473	3↑ Californian-G1	4	2	3½	31	21	22¾	Stevens GL	126	4.20	96-09	CutlassReality1152¾Gulch1264½JudgeAnglucc1261¾	2nd best	4
30May88- 8Bel	fst	1	:222 :444 1:084 1:343	3↑ Metropolitan H-G1	4	3	21	2hd	1½	1½	Santos JA	125	1.40e	92-19	Gulch125½Afleet1241½Stacked Pack110¾	Driving	8
7May88- 8Aqu	fst	7f	:223 :444 1:082 1:202	3↑ Carter H-G1	3	3	1½	1hd	1½	11¼	Santos JA	124	2.20	99-13	Gulch1241¼Afleet1242Its Acedemic1081¾	Driving	8
16Apr88- 9OP	gd	1⅛	:463 1:103 1:351 1:47	4↑ Oaklawn H-G1	7	2	42	42¼	22	33¾	Delahoussaye E	120	5.70	94-12	LostCode126¾Cryptoclearnc1223Gulch1204	Lacked solid bid	8
30Mar88- 8SA	fst	6½f	:214 :442 1:083 1:15	4↑ Potrero Grande H 70k	3	1	1½	21	21½	11¼	Delahoussaye E	123	1.20	95-18	Gulch1231¼Very Subtle1202¼Gallant Sailor111	Driving	3
18Mar88- 8SA	fst	6f	:221 :45 :564 1:084	4↑ Alw 55000	6	3	41	2hd	1hd	11¾	Delahoussaye E	116	3.10	94-18	Gulch1161¾Sebrof1183½My Gallant Game1163½	Driving	6
Previously trained by LeRoy Jolley																	
21Nov87- 7Hol	fst	1¼	:462 1:101 1:352 2:012	3↑ BC Classic-G1	11	8	87¾	87½	910	915¼	Santos JA	122	25.20	70-12	Ferdinand126noAlysheba1221¼Judge Angelucci1261½	Outrun	12
21Oct87- 8Aqu	fst	1	:224 :452 1:092 1:344	Jamaica H-G3	1	7	711	65½	33½	2¾	Santos JA	123	*.80	91-19	Stacked Pack110¾Gulch123¾Homebuilder1121¾	Rallied	8
20Sep87- 8Bel	gd	1¼	:482 1:123 1:364 2:01	3↑ Marlboro Cup H-G1	2	4	58	34	32	43¼	Santos JA	117	4.80	90-14	Java Gold1202¼Nostalgia's Star116nkPolish Navy117¾	Hung	5
5Sep87- 8Bel	fst	1⅛	:46 1:091 1:34 1:47	3↑ Woodward-G1	8	6	88¾	68½	33	2¾	Santos JA	118	5.50	91-15	Polish Navy116¾Gulch118nkCreme Fraiche1192¾	Rallied	9
22Aug87- 8Sar	sly	1¼	:461 1:10 1:362 2:02	Travers-G1	4	6	612	44	55	410¼	Santos JA	126	9.90e	80-16	JavaGold1262Cryptoclearnce1266¾PolshNvy1261½	No threat	9
8Aug87- 8Sar	fst	1⅛	:462 1:102 1:351 1:482	3↑ Whitney H-G1	1	6	58	42½	12½	2¾	Santos JA	117	3.40e	92-13	Java Gold113¾Gulch1172¼Broad Brush127no	Drifted out	7
6Jun87- 8Bel	fst	1½	:492 1:134 2:03 2:281	Belmont-G1	9	6	813	816	412	314	Day P	126	7.70e	65-15	Bet Twice12614Cryptoclearance126noGulch126nk	Wide str	9
25May87- 8Bel	fst	1	:223 :442 1:091 1:344	3↑ Metropolitan H-G1	9	9	811	62¼	3nk	1nk	Day P	110	5.80	91-16	Gulch110nkKing's Swan121½Broad Brush1282	Driving	9
16May87- 9Pim	fst	1 3/16	:471 1:113 1:364 1:554	Preakness-G1	7	8	66¾	73¾	43½	45½	Cordero A Jr	126	3.50	82-18	Alysheba126½BetTwice1261½Cryptoclearnce1263½	Weakened	9
2May87- 8CD	fst	1¼	:462 1:11 1:364 2:032	Ky Derby-G1	6	15	1618	126¾	76	64¼	Shoemaker W	126	4.90e	76-09	Alysheba126¾Bet Twice1262¼Avies Copy126nk	Very wide	17

Date/Race	Cond	Dist	Fractions	Race	PP	St	1st call	2nd call	Str	Fin	Jockey	Wt	Eqp	Odds	Speed	Finishers	Comment	Field
18Apr87- 8Aqu	my	1⅛	:47 1:113 1:362 1:49	Wood Memorial Inv'l-G1	1	4	67½	44½	22½	1hd	Santos JA	126		3.60	90-15	Gulch126hdGone West1266Shawklit Won1261¾	Strong urging	8
4Apr87- 8Aqu	sly	1	:222 :442 1:081 1:343	Gotham-G2	4	9	812	612	49½	39½	Vasquez J	123		2.60	83-21	Gone West1141Shawklit Won1148½Gulch123hd	Rallied	9
21Mar87- 8Aqu	fst	7f	:222 :453 1:101 1:231	Bay Shore-G2	3	5	63	52¾	21½	11	Santos JA	123		*.60	85-28	Gulch1231High Brite119nkShawklit Won1145½	Drew clear	9
28Feb87- 9Hia	fst	6f	:222 :451 1:101	Key West 43k	7	4	42	31	53¼	41½	Cordero A Jr	122	b	*.80	87-19	Mr. Zippity Do Dah114½Bet Twice122¾Vlid Prospect112nk	Lunged in air str	9
1Nov86- 1SA	fst	1 1/16	:222 :454 1:102 1:434	BC Juvenile-G1	7	3	31½	21	33	54¾	Cordero A Jr	122		2.60	77-13	Capote1221¼Qualify1221¼Alysheba1222¼	Bid,weakened	13
11Oct86- 8SA	fst	1 1/16	:223 :461 1:11 1:451	Norfolk-G1	4	4	31½	2½	33	21¾	Cordero A Jr	118		*.80	73-17	Capote1181¾Gulch118¾Gold on Green1182¾	Best of rest	6
13Sep86- 7Bel	fst	7f	:23 :454 1:093 1:221	Futurity-G1	7	1	31	1½	15	11¼	Cordero A Jr	122		*.20	91-11	Glch1221¼Demn'sBegone1227½CaptainVald122no	Ridden out	7
23Aug86- 8Sar	fst	6½f	:214 :442 1:094 1:162	Hopeful-G1	3	2	22	21	12	13½	Cordero A Jr	122		*.30	90-10	Gulch1223½Persevered1227½Flying Granville122nk	Driving	4
1Aug86- 8Sar	fst	6f	:222 :452 1:10	Sar Spl-G2	8	3	21	2½	11½	12½	Cordero A Jr	122		*1.00	90-17	Gulch1222½Jazzing Around1174¾Java Gold1171½	Driving	10
13Jly86- 8Bel	my	6f	:22 :444 1:102	Tremont-G3	5	4	32½	1hd	11	13½	Cordero A Jr	115		*1.00	90-15	Gulch1153½Shawklit Won1171½Bucks Best11513	Ridden out	5
2Jun86- 4Bel	fst	5f	:23 :46 :573	Md Sp Wt	5	5	52	41	11½	17¾	Bailey JD	118		*1.10	99-13	Gulch1187¾FlyingGranville1182½JamesOscar1182	Ridden out	7

Heartlight No. One

dkbbr. f. 1980, by Rock Talk (Rasper II)–Icantell, by Tell

Lifetime record: 7 5 1 1 $322,880

Own.– B. Bacharach
Br.– Blue Seas Music Inc (Md)
Tr.– Pedro Marti

Date/Race	Cond	Dist	Fractions	Race	PP	St	1st call	2nd call	Str	Fin	Jockey	Wt	Eqp	Odds	Speed	Finishers	Comment	Field
16Oct83- 8Bel	fst	1¼	:471 1:11 1:352 2:003 3↑	ⒻBeldame-G1	4	1	12½	2½	2½	2hd	Pincay L Jr	118	b	*.50	95-14	DanceNmbr123hdHrtlghtNo.On1188½Mochl1232½	Just missed	7
25Sep83- 8Bel	fst	1⅛	:452 1:09 1:342 1:471 3↑	ⒻRuffian H-G1	5	2	2½	2hd	1½	11	Pincay L Jr	117	b	*1.60	91-15	HrtlightNo.One1171Mochil113½TrySomthngNw1161½	Driving	12
20Aug83- 8Dmr	fm	1⅛Ⓣ	:474 1:12 1:372 1:501	ⒻDmr Oaks-G2	3	5	65½	43	11	13½	Pincay L Jr	122	b	*1.50	87-11	HrtlightNo.One1223½Foggy Moon1151Fabulous Notion1221¼	Rough trip,driving	10
28Jly83- 5Dmr	fm	1Ⓣ	:233 :473 1:114 1:363	ⒻAlw 20000	6	3	2hd	12½	16	16½	Pincay L Jr	120	b	*.30	90-10	HrtlightNo.One1206½GoldenGrand120noSwtDn1203½	Driving	7
10Jly83- 8Hol	fst	1⅛	:454 1:101 1:363 1:494	ⒻHol Oaks-G1	3	1	12½	16	16	112	Pincay L Jr	121	b	3.60	80-21	HeartlightNo.One12112Prcptrss1212½RdyforLuck1212	Easily	7
4Jun83- 6Hol	fst	6f	:221 :443 :572 1:101 3↑	ⒻMd Sp Wt	1	4	2hd	13	16	17	Pincay L Jr	117	b	*1.40	86-20	HeartlightNo.One1177HellionQuen1154½NclyNtv1222½	Easily	11
8Jan83- 4SA	fst	6f	:213 :444 :571 1:094	ⒻMd Sp Wt	5	11	109¼	69	35	35½	Shoemaker W	117	b	*2.30	83-10	Anesthesiologist1173½Taisez Too1172Heartlight No. One117¾	Rallied,hung	12

Heavenly Cause

ro. f. 1978, by Grey Dawn II (Herbager)–Lady Dulcinea, by Nantallah

Lifetime record: 21 9 4 2 $622,481

Own.– Ryehill Farm
Br.– Ryehill Farm (Md)
Tr.– Woodford C. Stephens

Date/Race	Cond	Dist	Fractions	Race	PP	St	1st call	2nd call	Str	Fin	Jockey	Wt	Eqp	Odds	Speed	Finishers	Comment	Field
31Oct81- 7Kee	fst	1⅛	:472 1:113 1:363 1:491 3↑	ⒻSpinster-G1	5	5	62¾	53	66½	612	Day P	119		3.30	79-19	Glorious Song123nkTruly Bound1196Safe Play119¾	Outrun	7
22Oct81- 7Kee	fst	1 1/16	:243 :482 1:12 1:434 3↑	ⒻAlw 26820	1	3	22	11½	13	14½	Day P	120		*.30	87-19	Heavenly Cause1204½Sweetest Chant1177Forever Cordial1151	Ridden out	4
26Sep81- 8Key	fst	1 1/16	:234 :474 1:112 1:424	ⒻCotillion-G3	4	6	42	32½	34	45¾	Saumell L	121		*1.40	84-20	TrulyBound1214½PukkaPrincss118nkDebonrDncr1181	Blocked	8
10Sep81- 8Bel	fst	7f	:222 :451 1:10 1:23 3↑	ⒻAlw 32000	4	5	59	56½	47½	49¼	Venezia M	118		3.30	78-16	Wayward Lass1151Highest Regard1156¾Cherokee Frolic1181½	No factor	5
27Jun81- 8Bel	fst	1½	:474 1:114 2:014 2:281	ⒻC C A Oaks-G1	4	4	42½	45½	412	418	Pincay L Jr	121		*.40e	61-16	[D]RealPrize1212¼WywrdLss1212¼BannerGala12113	Weakened	6
5Jun81- 8Bel	fst	1⅛	:47 1:11 1:354 1:484	ⒻMother Goose-G1	1	5	42½	42	21	2nk	Pincay L Jr	121		*.70e	83-17	WaywrdLss121nkHeavnlyCause1212¾BannerGl1211¾	Bore in	8
23May81- 8Bel	fst	1	:231 :46 1:094 1:351	ⒻAcorn-G1	1	5	2½	11½	12	13¾	Pincay L Jr	121		*.30e	92-13	HeavnlyCause1213¾Dame Mysterieuse1214Autumn Glory121½	Ridden out	7
1May81- 8CD	fst	1 1/16	:25 :484 1:13 1:434	ⒻKy Oaks-G1	4	4	41½	1½	11½	1no	Pincay L Jr	121		1.50e	89-17	HeavnlyCse121noDe La Rose1215WaywardLass1213	Driving	6
25Apr81- 8CD	fst	7f	:234 :473 1:113 1:24	ⒻLa Troienne 26k	6	6	53	1½	11½	15	Day P	121		*.30	87-23	HeavnlyCause1215Fiddleatune1215Roger'sTurn1212	Handily	6
4Apr81- 9OP	fst	1 1/16	:233 :471 1:122 1:434	ⒻFantasy-G1	3	3	42½	1hd	1hd	1hd	Pincay L Jr	121		*1.90	89-19	HeavnlyCause121hdNell's Briquette1215¼Wayward Lass1214½	Prolonged dr	9
2Mar81- 9GP	fst	1 1/16	:25 :492 1:133 1:442	ⒻBonnie Miss 87k	1	3	32	32	34	36	Maple E	121		*.70	73-22	DameMysterieuse1181BannrGala1135HvnlyCs1211½	Weakened	7
11Feb81- 9GP	fst	7f	:223 :45 1:092 1:221	ⒻForward Gal 43k	6	8	42½	53	32	21¼	Maple E	121		*1.20	92-18	DameMystrieuse1181¼HeavnlyCs121¾MstrsDrm113no	Gaining	10
1Nov80- 9Lrl	fst	1 1/16	:234 :472 1:122 1:432	ⒻSelima-G1	4	2	2½	31	11½	12¼	Pincay L Jr	122		1.60	91-14	HvnlyCause1222¼RainbowConnctn1222¼Carolina Command1223½	Ridden out	6
23Oct80- 6Med	fst	1 1/16	:231 :461 1:113 1:443	ⒻGardenia-G3	4	6	59½	34	12½	22	Pincay L Jr	121		*.20	84-15	CarolinaCommnd1182HvnlyCaus1218½StunnngNtv1181	Wide	7
5Oct80- 8Bel	fst	1	:241 :48 1:124 1:38	ⒻFrizette-G1	2	4	32	3½	2hd	11½	Pincay L Jr	119		5.70	78-23	HvnlyCause1191½SweetRevenge1194½Prayers'nPromises119hd	Driving	8
22Sep80- 8Bel	fst	7f	:232 :471 1:114 1:243	ⒻMatron-G1	3	7	34	33	1hd	2hd	Pincay L Jr	119		4.90	79-23	Prayers 'n Promises119hdHeavnlyCause1191Sweet Revenge1192¼	Sharp	8
8Sep80- 7Bow	fst	7f	:233 :471 1:122 1:252	ⒻMarlboro Nursery 43k	5	6	53½	42	1½	15	Maple E	116		2.60	78-25	HeavnlyCause1165Cavort113hdStunningNtv1141½	Drew clear	6
29Aug80- 8Bel	fm	7fⓉ	:23 :46 1:094 1:232	ⒻEvening Out 56k	6	5	54½	52½	47	412¾	Saumell L	113		4.80	74-13	De La Rose114hdBravoNtive11210PrimeProspect1132¾	Wide	7
20Aug80- 6Sar	fm	1[T]	:24 :484 1:134 1:381	ⒻAlw 20000	8	7	87½	65	711	717	Saumell L	114		*1.20	71-16	De La Rose1145Picture Pretty109noJan Jill114¾	Bothered	10
30Jly80- 8Sar	fst	6f	:212 :444 1:102	ⒻSchuylerville-G3	11	2	814	65	44½	33¼	Saumell L	114		6.80	85-12	SweetRevenge114nkCompanionship1143HeavnlyCs1143	Wide	11
23Jly80- 4Bel	sly	7f	:232 :471 1:113 1:242	ⒻMd Sp Wt	7	2	74½	31½	14	19	Saumell L	117		4.70	80-22	HeavnlyCause1179WaywardLass1176Zimbaba1174½	Ridden out	8

Highland Bud

b. g. 1985, by Northern Baby (Northern Dancer)–Fleur d'Or, by Exclusive Native

Lifetime record: 27 10 10 3 $508,269

Own.– Jesse M. Henley Jr
Br.– William Floyd (Ky)
Tr.– Jonathan E. Sheppard

Date/Race	Cond	Dist	Surface	Time	Race	PP	St	1st call	2nd call	Str	Fin	Jockey	Wt	Odds	Speed	Finishers	Comment	Field
14Nov93- 4Cam	fm	*2¾	S'Chase	5:074 4↑	Colonial Cup 100k	8	10	106½	-	-	-	Dunwoody R	162	-	--	DeclareYourWish1622¾Simonov1511¾LnesomeGlry1602	Lame	11
16Oct93-10Bel	sf	2⅝	S'Chase	4:532 3↑	BC Chase 250k	9	8	54½	31	1½	28½	Dunwoody R	156	*.70e	--	Lonesome Glory1568½Highland Bud1565Mistico1564	Sharp try,second best	9
11Sep93- 6Fai	fm	1¼Ⓣ		2:133 3↑	Alw 1000	1	2	31½	31¼	1hd	12¼	Miller B	150	*1.80	--	Highland Bud1502¼Equal Measure1442My Babys Fast1432¾		8
10Oct92- 2Bel	sf	2⅝	S'Chase	4:562 3↑	BC Chase 250k	4	6	51½	51½	1hd	13	Dunwoody R	156	*1.10e	--	Highland Bud1563Mistico1563Sassello1468½	Driving	10
7Sep92-10Mth	fm	*2¼	S'Chase	4:134 3↑	Handicap 20000	3	4	44	32	1½	2no	Miller B	154	5.40	--	Ninepins148noHighlandBud1547SummitPoint1411¼	Game try	7
29Sep91- 2Fx	hd	*2Ⓣ		3:134 3↑	Alw 1000	5	9	918	45	2nk	22	Guessford B	150	-	--	Jive With Five1502Highland Bud1504Tower of Torture150nk	Blocked,driving	11
6Jun91- 4Bel	yl	2	S'Chase	3:37 4↑	Handicap 45000	5	2	42½	44½	619	639	Dunwoody R	156	*.70e	--	WoodyBoyWould1471½MadeNble14613LeSauvage1495½	Tired	7
11May91- 6PW	sf	*3	S'Chase	5:592 4↑	Iroquois H 100k	6	2	53¾	34¾	2½	22	Smithwck DM Jr	168	-	--	VictorianHill1682HghlndBd1687DclrYourWsh16313	Bid,hung	8
21Apr91- 2Due	fm	*2¼	S'Chase	4:16 4↑	Dueling Int'l 250k	5	8	47¾	411	23	29½	Guessford B	154	22.00	--	Victorian Hill1549½Highland Bud1546¾Penascal1543	Tired	8
6Apr91- 4AtH	fm	*2⅛	S'Chase	3:592 4↑	Ath Cup H 100k	3	5	53	32	31¾	33½	Guessford B	160	-	--	DeclreYourWish145noChiefoftheCln1483½[D]HighlndBud1604½	Disqualified and placed sixth;Previously trained by Jonathan E. Sheppard	7
7Apr90- 4AtH	fm	*2⅛	S'Chase	4:022 4↑	Ath Hunt Cup 100k	2	6	63¼	35	21	2hd	Guessford B	162	-	--	PolrPlesur150hd[DH]SmmrColony156[DH]HghlndBd16215	Gamely	6
31Mar90- 6Cam	fm	*1Ⓣ		1:42 3↑	Sp Wt 1000	2	11	1011	86½	48½	46	Guessford B	150	-	--	Morewoods1504Summer Colony1501Chief of the Clan1501		12
19Nov89- 4Cam	fm	*2¾	S'Chase	5:174 4↑	Colonial Cup 60k	1	3	3¾	11½	13	114	Dunwoody R	151	-	--	Highland Bud15114Opacity1602¾Dawson1602¼	Easily	5
28Oct89- 3FH	fm	*2⅝	S'Chase	4:584 3↑	BC Chase 250k	1	3	34½	2hd	17	110	Dunwoody R	146	-	--	HighlandBud14610PolarPleasure15615VctornHll1464	Driving	8

8Oct89- 7Mid	fm *2 1/16	S'Chase	3:54³ 4↑	O Clm 25000	3 10 9 9½ 5⁴ 1½	1 1¼	Guessford B	148	-	Highland Bud148 1¼Yaw147 1Cadent148 1 Driving	10
24Sep89- 3Fx	gd *2Ⓣ		3:15² 3↑	Sp Wt 1000	1 1 2½ 1¹ 1²	2hd	Miller B	150	-	Uranio152hdHighland Bud150²Delivery150³	7
Previously trained by David Nicholson											
27Apr89♦ Punchestwn(Ire)	hy 2RH		4:04³	Irish Champion Hurdle Stk28700		3 10¾	Dunwoody R	163	4.00	Royal Derbi163 10Lunulae155¾Highland Bud163 6 Prominent,bid 2out,never threatened.Ikdam 4th,Vayrua 5th	11
7Apr89♦ Aintree(GB)	sf 2LH		4:24⁴	Glenlivet Anniversary Hurdle Stk60400		2⁵	Dunwoody R	154	*2.25	Vayrua154 5Highland Bud154hdBank View154 15 Rated toward rear,progress at 4th,saved 2nd	9
16Mar89♦ Cheltenham(GB)	hy 2LH		4:18⁴	Triumph Hurdle Stk80500		2 1½	Dunwoody R	154	8.00	Ikdam154 1½Highland Bud154hdDon Valentino154 2½ Tracked leaders,bid over 1f out,finished well.Royal Derbi 4th	27
28Jan89♦ Cheltenham(GB)	yl 2LH		4:14	Food Brokers Hurdle Stk18600		1³	Dunwoody R	157	4.00	Highland Bud157 3Enemy Action161 8Propero154 3 Tracked in 3rd,led approaching last,driving	6
30Dec88♦ Newbury(GB)	gd 2 1/16LH		4:00²	Wickham Hurdle Alw5000		1 10	Dunwoody R	154	*1.85	Highland Bud154 10Victory Gate154 4Durzi154 6 Close up,led at 5th,ridden clear approaching last Previously trained by John Oxx	15
24Sep88♦ Down Royal(Ire)	gd 1¾ⓉRH		- 3↑	Ulster St Leger Alw7000		3⁴	Hogan D	125	*.65	Husaam130 2Dublin's Coq Hardi117 2Highland Bud125 4 Led to 2f out,gradually faded.Time not taken	5
20Aug88♦ Phoenix Park(Ire)	yl 1¾ⓉRH		3:03 3↑	St Leger Trial Alw6900		1³	Quinton R	122	2.50	Highland Bud122 3Ard Countess131 5Allen's Mistake134nk Tracked in 3rd,led over 2f out,drew clear final furlong	7
13Jly88♦ Down Royal(Ire)	gd *1½ⓉRH		-	Ulster Harp Derby Alw14400		1⁴	Quinton R	123	6.00	Highland Bud123 4Magistro128 2Montefiore123 4 Led throughout,drew clear final furlong.Time not taken	4
8Jly88♦ Gowran Park(Ire)	gd 1¼ⓉRH		2:11 3↑	Dunbell Maiden (Div 2) Mdn2900		1¾	Quinton R	126	*.50	Highland Bud126¾Burrow Bard126 4John O'Dreams126 4 Tracked leader,led 1½f out,held well	9
19Sep87♦ Leopardstwn(Ire)	sf 1ⓉLH		1:46⁴	Torquay Maiden Mdn3900		3 4½	Hogan D	126	4.00	Clash of Ideas126 2Law Lord126 2½Highland Bud126 1½ Tracked in 3rd,close 6th on rail over 2f out,3rd 1f out	15
29Aug87♦ The Curragh(Ire)	gd 7fⓉStr		1:28²	Panasonic Copier Maiden Mdn6100		2½	Hogan D	126	14.00	Gold Discovery126½Highland Bud126 1Easter King123 1½ Tracked in 5th,3rd 1½f out,2nd 100y out	17

Inlander (GB)

b. g. 1981, by Ile de Bourbon (Nijinsky II)–Blissful Evening, by Blakeney **Lifetime record: 38 10 8 1 $233,148**

Own.– Dogwood Stable
Br.– Cleaboy Farms Co (GB)
Tr.– Charles Fenwick Jr

9Apr88- 4AtH	fm *2⅛	S'Chase	4:01² 4↑	Atlanta Hunt Cup 100k	4 5 - - -	-	Morris G	158	-	MickeyFree148nkSaffan145noPolarParalll152 1½ Fell at 6th	8
5Dec87- 4Cam	fm *2¾	S'Chase	5:21¹ 4↑	Colonial Cup 60k	1 6 5 4½ 4⁴ 2¹	1 3¼	Morris GL	162	-	Inlander162 3¼Ormus162 3Statesmanship162 2¾ Driving	8
21Nov87- 5Pmt	fm *2⅜	S'Chase	4:04 4↑	Crown Royal H 40k	4 4 6 1½ 4⁵ 3½	1hd	Morris GL	155	-	Inlander155hdStatesmanship152hdMckyFr148 2 Strong urging	7
31Oct87- 5Fai	fm *2⅝	S'Chase	5:15¹ 3↑	BC Chase 250k	4 10 8 8½ 4 3½ 3 4½	2 8¾	Morris GL	156	9.40	Gacko156 8¾Inlander156½Gateshead156 3¾ Strong pressure	10
17Oct87- 5RB	fm *2	S'Chase	3:58³ 4↑	Handicap 50000	1 2 2³ 3² 4²	4⁴	Hendriks R	156	-	PolarParallel153 1¼MickeyFree146 2TheCleverest149¾ Tired	6
Previously trained by Reg Akehurst											
16Jun87♦ Ascot(GB)	gd 2½ⓉRH		4:28³ 4↑	Ascot Handicap Hcp26700		1 10	Adams N	105	5.00	Inlander105 10White Mill110 4El Conquistador136no Tracked in 3rd,bid 2½f out,led 2f out,easily clear	9
30May87♦ Kempton(GB)	gd 2ⓉRH		3:26¹ 4↑	H S Persse Memorial Handicap Hcp6700		1²	Carson W	111	*2.10	Inlander111 2All Is Revealed114 2Ile de Roi131 4 Tracked in 3rd,led 170y out,driving	9
4May87♦ Haydock(GB)	gd 2LH		3:46³ 4↑	Handicap Hurdle Hcp47700		1no	Smith-Eccles S	148	4.00	Inlander148noSantopadre133hdJanus145 6 Rated at rear,rallied to lead on line	8
8Apr87♦ Ascot(GB)	gd 2RH		3:57² 5↑	Kestrel Handicap Hurdle Hcp11000		2¾	McKeown D⁷	157	*1.75	Beat the Retreat161¾Inlander157 25Kescast161 2 Prominent,chasing winner 2 out,finished well	8
21Mar87♦ Lingfield(GB)	sf 2¼LH		4:56¹ 5↑	Bic Razor Gold Cup Hcp Hurdle Hcp33600		3 18	Smith-Eccles S	161	6.50	Tigerwood150 12Mandavi151 6Inlander161 2 Progress into 3rd 2 out,one-paced to line	15
14Mar87♦ Sandown(GB)	gd 2RH		3:50 5↑	Imperial Cup Hcp Hurdle Stk27500		1¹	Smith-Eccles S	143	10.00	Inlander143 1Kescast146 5Timely Star154 1½ Midpack,rallied 2 out,led 1 out,all out	23
Previously trained by Jeff Davies											
4Nov86♦ Fontwell(GB)	gd 2¼LH		4:41¹ 4↑	Veuve Clicquot Hcp Hurdle Hcp7100		6 13½	Heaver G⁷	157	*2.25	Hot Handed154 1The Diplomat140 2½Paris North159 3 Prominent,weakened approaching second last	10
25Oct86♦ Doncaster(GB)	yl 2¼ⓉLH		4:10² 3↑	Elmfield Park Stakes Alw4300		7	Lines R³	114	11.00	Troy Fair126 1½Shah's Choice118 6La Rose Grise114¾ Toward rear,bid to track leaders 4½f out,soon weakened	11
15Mar86♦ Lingfield(GB)	yl 2¼LH		5:02² 5↑	Bic Razor Gold Cup Hcp Hurdle Hcp29000		1²	Woods S⁷	133	*4.50	Inlander133 2Moon Mariner143 8Opening Bars145 2 Led 2 out,swerved badly right last,ridden out	16
8Mar86♦ Sandown(GB)	gd 2RH		3:58 5↑	Imperial Cup Handicap Hurdle Stk27300		4¹	Woods S	133		Insular136¾Hypnosis142nkPeter Martin142no Lost place at 3rd,rallied 2 out,gamely	19
3Feb86♦ Fontwell(GB)	sf 2¼LH		4:58⁴ 5↑	Lyminster Handicap Hurdle Hcp4400		1⁶	Lovejoy J	152	3.30	Inlander152 6Lir142 1Hal's Prince157¾ Led at 5th,quickened clear 6th,ridden out	16
23Jan86♦ Huntingdon(GB)	gd 3RH		6:06 5↑	Sapley Handicap Hurdle Hcp3400		2nk	Lovejoy J	153	10.00	Jennie Pat168nkInlander153 15North West149 3 Midpack,progress after 6th,bid 3 out,gamely	21
15Jan86♦ Windsor(GB)	gd 2		3:53⁴ 5↑	Weir Handicap Hurdle Hcp3000		9	Lovejoy J	161	14.00	Quite a Night156 2Batu162 2Rix Woodcock154 2 Never a factor	24
6Jan86♦ Chepstow(GB)	sf 2LH		4:19² 5↑	Duck Conditional Jockeys Hcp Hurdle Hcp2100		1⁴	Heaver G⁴	146	5.50	Ribobelle146 2Panto Prince148 5Chemist Broker0 3 Toward rear throughout	21
26Dec85♦ Kempton(GB)	sf 2RH		4:11¹ 4↑	Boxing Day Handicap Hurdle Hcp8000		5 30	Lovejoy J	143	12.00	Yabis148 15The Tariahs150 7Dhofar161 4 Never a factor	10
10Dec85♦ Plumpton(GB)	sf 2LH		3:49 4↑	December Handicap Hurdle Hcp3100		5 23	Lovejoy J	154	*2.25	Mr Key152 15Pip143 4Mighty Steel142no Rated at rear,close 3rd 3 out,soon weakened	10
19Oct85♦ Newmarket(GB)	gd 2¼ⓉRH		3:51² 3↑	Cesarewitch Handicap Hcp68400		9 17¾	Still R	105	20.00	Kayudee113 2Jamesmead116hdBourbon Boy120½ Prominent to 4f out,gradually weakened	21
10Sep85♦ Folkestone(GB)	gd *1 15/16ⓉRH		3:24³ 3↑	Windsor Hotel Stakes (Amateurs) Alw3300		2no	Woods S⁵	154	5.00	Careo153noInlander154 3Cheshire House154 4 Toward rear,long drive halfway,strong late run,just missed	17
27Aug85♦ Chepstow(GB)	sf 2ⓉLH		3:57² 3↑	Lysaght Handicap Hcp3700		2no	Bennyworth D⁵	163	*1.85	Carmel State143noInlander163 1½Rocas142 15 Dwelt,far behind,soon midpack,strong late run,just missed	7
10Aug85♦ Lingfield(GB)	hy 2ⓉLH		3:46⁴ 4↑	Gatwick Handicap Hcp3900		2½	Adams J⁷	131	10.00	Neraida107½Inlander131 8New Zealand125nk Midpack,bid 2f out,dueled 170y out,gamely	11
21Jun85♦ Ascot(GB)	gd *2¾ⓉRH		5:13 4↑	Queen Alexandra Stakes (Listed) Stk22000		7	Carson W	114	25.00	Valuable Witness129 2½Ravaro124 12Real Pegus112 3 Tracked in 5th,weakened over 2f out	11
3Jun85♦ Folkestone(GB)	fm *1 15/16ⓉRH		3:20¹ 4↑	Dover Handicap Hcp2600		2hd	Landau G⁷	127	7.50	Forewarn122hdInlander127¾Puget128 2 Tracked leaders,bid 1f out,dueled final 16th,gamely	17
16Apr85♦ Fontwell(GB)	sf 2¼LH		4:43	Amberley Hurdle Alw1200		1⁴	Lovejoy J	156	*3.30	Inlander156 4Ribobelle151 8Bronski150 12 Prominent,led 3 out,all out	13

Date/Track	Cond/Dist	Time	Race	Calls	Fin	Jockey	Wt	Odds	Comp	Finishers / Comment	Field
8Apr85♦ Plumpton(GB)	hy 2LH	4:09^{4}	John Hare Maiden Hurdle Mdn1000		1^{15}	Lovejoy J	152	3.50		Inlander152^{15}Atkins152^{8}Coldharbour Lad148^{10} Led at 6th,clear 2 out,mistake last,handily	8
31Jan85♦ Lingfield(GB)	hy 2LH	4:26^{2} 4↑	Haddon Novices Hurdle Alw1000		-	Jones A^{7}	138	12.00		Pottstown145^{1}Larry-O162^{12}Telephone Numbers157^{10} Always behind,tailed off and eased before 2nd last	7
Previously trained by Henry Candy											
15Oct84♦ Sandown(GB)	yl 1¾ⓉRH	3:10	Leatherhead Stakes Alw3900		4^{3¾}	Williams T^{3}	120	3.50		Widdicombe Fair124¾Recamier120^{2}In the Shade120^{1} Midpack,ridden into lead 2f out,headed 1f out,weakened	11
2Oct84♦ Nottingham(GB)	gd 1¾ⓉLH	3:06^{3}	Nottingham Goose Fair Hcp Hcp6900		6^{14¾}	Williams T^{3}	123	*3.00		Carnet de Danse126^{1½}Whispering Grass133^{3}Chatter103^{3} Pushed along early to keep pace,led 1½f out,soon weakened	9
26Sep84♦ Sandown(GB)	yl 1¾ⓉRH	3:05^{2} 3↑	Autumn Handicap Hcp7200		2no	Williams T^{5}	116	9.00		Vital Boy116^{no}Inlander116½Madam Flutterbye117^{4} Close up,slight lead 1f out,dueled,just missed	9
18Sep84♦ Lingfield(GB)	gd 1½ⓉLH	2:39	Hartfield Stakes Alw5300		5^{6}	Matthias J	123	16.00		Luminate123^{1½}Newsells Park130½Kafouaine130^{1½} Tracked leaders,weakened 2f out	14
3Aug84♦ Newmarket(GB)	gd 1½ⓉRH	2:31^{3}	Running Gap Handicap Hcp10800		4^{9½}	Williams T^{5}	112	16.00		Crazy131^{2½}Rynechra128^{no}Newsells Park117^{7} Tracked leaders,outfinished	9
5May84♦ Newmarket(GB)	fm 1½ⓉRH	2:35^{2}	Culford Stakes Alw8200		6^{18¼}	Eddery Pat	123	5.00		Baynoun133^{4}Face Facts126^{12}Jerry Can133^{nk} Never a factor	14
13Apr84♦ Newbury(GB)	gd 1⅜ⓉLH	2:24^{2}	Spring Maiden Stakes Mdn5900		4^{4½}	Matthias J	126	20.00		Spicy Story126¾Kinski126^{3}Longboat126¾ Tracked in 3rd,dueled briefly 2f out,weakened 1f out	10
18Oct83♦ Leicester(GB)	gd 7fⓉStr	1:25^{1}	Soar Maiden Stakes (Div 2) Mdn2300		5^{12¾}	Curant R	126	14.00		Bold Patriach126¾Raami126^{2}Triple Tower126^{3} Tracked leaders,weakened 2f out	18

Jimmy Lorenzo (GB)

dkbbr. g. 1982, by Our Jimmy (Tom Rolfe)–Love Beach, by Lorenzaccio — **Lifetime record: 37 11 3 9 $248,646**

Own.– Bertram R. Firestone
Br.– J.W. Demestre (GB)
Tr.– Rodney Jenkins

Date/Track	Cond/Dist	Time	Race	Calls	Fin	Jockey	Wt	Odds	Comp	Finishers / Comment	Field
15May93- 4Mgo	gd *2¼ Hurdles	4:08^{2} 4↑	Handicap 15000	6 5 5^{17} 5^{10} 6^{20}	6^{39½}	Newman G	154	-	--	Arctic Circle137^{4}Dangerfield148^{6}Billy King148^{1½}	6
Previously trained by Jonathan E. Sheppard											
7Sep92- 2Fai	gd *1⅜Ⓣ	2:15 3↑	Alw 2500	6 9 9^{17} 5^{5} 5^{11}	4^{19¼}	Neilson S	154	*1.60	--	Lord of Flanders151^{13}Greg147^{3¼}Oslek154^{3} Late rally	9
16Nov91- 3Cam	fm *2¾ S'Chase	5:14 4↑	Colonial Cup 60k	9 6 7^{4¾} 4^{6} 7^{8}	7^{9½}	Smart J	162	-	--	Moonstruck162^{2}Made Noble160^{1¼}Double Bill162^{1½} Bid,hung	10
12Oct91- 3Fai	gd *2⅝ S'Chase	5:10^{3} 3↑	BC Chase 250k	10 10 11^{16} 10^{12} 10^{17}	9^{42¾}	Smart J	156	6.40	--	MorleyStrt156^{9¾}Declare Your Wish156^{15½}CheeringNews146^{hd}	12
Dull effort											
18Aug89- 8Sar	fm 2⅜ S'Chase	4:18^{1} 4↑	NY Turf Writers H 115k	5 7 4^{6} 4^{6} 4^{4}	4^{6¾}	Scudamore P	162	1.40e	--	DoubleBill142^{1½}UptownSwell152^{nk}PolrPlsur149^{5} Rank early	7
9Jun89- 4Bel	sf 2 S'Chase	3:58^{4} 4↑	Alw 40000	3 7 5^{5} 5^{3½} 2^{1}	1^{2}	Scudamore P	155	*.60e	--	JimmyLornzo155^{2}DuelingOak143^{8}BrkCln139^{hd} Bobbled,clear	8
8Apr89- 4AtH	yl *2⅛ S'Chase	4:21^{2} 4↑	Ath Cup H 100k	3 5 5^{9½} 4^{8} -	-	Guessford B	162	-	--	Polar Pleasure148^{1¼}Kesslin150^{8}Limaton138^{10} Lost rider	5
1Apr89- 6Cam	fm *1Ⓣ	1:43 3↑	Sp Wt 1000	1 11 9^{7½} 4^{2½} 1^{2}	1^{10}	Guessford B	150	-	--	Jimmy Lorenzo150^{10}Census150^{1}Tisa Feast150½ Ridden out	11
27Nov88- 4Cam	fm 2¾ S'Chase	5:15^{4} 4↑	Colonial Cup 60k	2 8 8^{12} 8^{14} 4^{1¾}	1^{2¼}	Smart J	162	-	--	Jimmy Lorenzo162^{2¼}Le Sauvage151^{2}Polar Pleasure162^{1}	8
Under hand ride											
29Oct88- 4Fai	fm *2⅝ S'Chase	5:12^{2} 3↑	BC Chase 250k	10 14 11^{7¼} 2^{nk} 1½	1¾	McCourt G	156	8.40	--	JimmyLorenzo156¾Kalankoe153^{1½}PolarPleasure156¾ Driving	14
20Oct88- 6Mid	fm *2 S'Chase	3:52^{3} 4↑	O Clm 25000	9 12 12^{14} 4^{3} 1½	1^{8}	Smart J	152	-	--	Jimmy Lorenzo152^{8}Jet Wave156^{7}Pajarero144^{5} Handily	12
Previously trained by Peter Hedger											
6Apr88♦ Ascot(GB)	gd 2RH	3:46^{3} 5↑	Kestrel Handicap Hurdle Hcp11200		3^{1¼}	Shoemark I^{7}	157	*2.00		Convinced147¾Relekto152½Jimmy Lorenzo157^{6} Rated toward rear,bid 2 out,finished well	8
12Mar88♦ Sandown(GB)	gd 2RH	3:55^{2} 5↑	Imperial Cup Handicap Hurdle Stk57600		4^{6½}	Osborne J	160	20.00		Sprowston Boy151½Jimbalou140^{2}Capa133^{4} Rated toward rear,bid 2 out,finished well	15
25Feb88♦ Wincanton(GB)	gd 2RH	3:42^{3} 5↑	Kingwell Hurdle Alw24100		5^{27½}	Shoemark I	156	11.00		Floyd162^{3}Private Audience156^{2½}Past Glories156^{12} Never a factor	7
1Jan88♦ Windsor(GB)	gd *2	3:59 5↑	New Year's Day Hurdle Stk42100		3^{7}	Richards M	158	4.00		Celtic Shot158^{6}Beech Road158^{1}Jimmy Lorenzo158^{4} Rated in 8th,brief bid 2 out,no late response	10
26Dec87♦ Kempton(GB)	gd 2RH	3:51^{4} 4↑	Royal Garden Htl Hcp Hurdle Hcp9700		1^{10}	Shoemark I^{7}	154	*3.00		JimmyLrnzo154^{10}Chasing the Dragon153½Brookmount152^{nk} Progress 3 out,led 2 out,drew clear in hand	16
8Dec87♦ Fontwell(GB)	gd 2¼LH	4:23^{4} 4↑	Coomes Handicap Hurdle Hcp16100		3^{2¼}	Shoemark I^{7}	152	16.00		Southernair156^{nk}Osric150^{2}Jimmy Lorenzo152^{10} Unhurried,bid over approaching last,outfinished	9
21Nov87♦ Ascot(GB)	yl 2RH	3:55^{2} 5↑	Snow Hill Handicap Hurdle Hcp17600		1^{4}	Shoemark I^{7}	140	3.50		Jimmy Lorenzo140^{4}Beat the Retreat165½Insular150^{20} Rated in 5th,led approaching last,ridden out	6
7Nov87♦ Warwick(GB)	yl 2LH	3:44^{4} 4↑	St Mary's Trial Hurdle Alw9200		4^{3¾}	Shoemark I^{7}	159	7.00		Lashkafdal147^{no}Nebris166¾Rampallion152^{3} Progress 2 out,lacked finishing bid	8
19May87♦ Newtn Abbot(GB)	fm *2 1/16 LH	3:53^{4} 4↑	C Vicary Meml Clng Cup Hcp Hurdle Hcp5900		1½	Shoemark I^{7}	157	4.50		Jimmy Lorenzo157½Bronze Opal144^{25}Come on Gracie153^{12} Rated in last,progress 3 out,dueled 2 out,led last,gamely	7
8May87♦ Newtn Abbot(GB)	fm *2 1/16 LH	3:48 4↑	McEwans Export Handicap Hurdle Hcp6100		2^{3}	Shoemark I^{7}	158	7.00		Bronze Opal142^{3}Jimmy Lorenzo158^{5}Redgrave Girl139^{10} Progress 4 out,2nd approaching last,no match.New course record	10
14Apr87♦ Exeter(GB)	sf 2⅛RH	4:26^{3} 5↑	Handicap Hurdle Hcp7100		1^{3}	Richards M	156	*3.00		Jimmy Lorenzo156^{3}Cons Pal144^{6}Lord Murphy154^{4} Rated toward rear,progress 4th,led on bit 1 out,handily	18
28Mar87♦ Newbury(GB)	hy 2 1/16 LH	4:11^{4} 5↑	Schweppes Handicap Hurdle Hcp16800		3^{11½}	Shoemark I^{7}	133	20.00		Juven Light155^{10}Ra Nova163^{1½}Jimmy Lorenzo133^{3} Toward rear,progress 3 out,ridden without response 2 out	10
5Mar87♦ Lingfield(GB)	sf 2LH	4:09^{4} 5↑	Three Counties Handicap Hurdle Hcp6900		3^{4½}	Richards M	152	*2.50		Rix Woodcock146^{2}Young Nicholas161^{2½}Jimmy Lorenzo152½ Rated in 10th,bid 2 out,held by first two	11
6Feb87♦ Sandown(GB)	gd 2RH	3:59^{1} 5↑	Me & My Girl Handicap Hurdle Hcp6500		7^{10¾}	Richards M	148	14.00		Easter Lee144^{2}How Now144¾Neblin159^{2½} Behind,progress at 3rd,bid 3 out,soon one-paced	16
24Jan87♦ Kempton(GB)	yl 2RH	4:01^{1} 5↑	Lanzarote Handicap Hurdle Hcp20100		9	Richards M	140	8.00		Stray Shot140^{4}Record Harvest152^{no}Cool Strike140^{5} Never a factor	9
26Dec86♦ Kempton(GB)	sf 2RH	4:02^{2} 4↑	Haven Abroad Handicap Hurdle Hcp8000		2^{4}	Richards M	142	7.50		Yabis161^{4}Jimmy Lorenzo142^{1}Welsh Warrior143^{1½} Trailed,progress into 2nd 3 out,always held by winner	13
20Nov86♦ Kempton(GB)	yl 2RH	4:07^{1} 4↑	Fairview Homes Hcp Hurdle Hcp6000		3^{6½}	Richards M	156	10.00		Oryx Minor160½Freemason159^{6}Jimmy Lorenzo156^{10} Progress 3 out,one-paced from second last	10
5Nov86♦ Newbury(GB)	gd 2 3/16 LH	4:58^{1} 4↑	Tom Masson Trophy Hurdle Alw7600		-	Corrigan P	152	33.00		Ibn Majed156^{10}Ten Plus162^{hd}Mrs Muck153^{20} Behind when brought down at 6th	9
19Apr86♦ Stratford(GB)	yl 2LH	4:05^{2}	Tote Hurdle Alw8000		4^{25½}	Richards M	154	*2.00		Heart of Stone150^{12}Bollin Palace150^{12}Avebury154^{1½} Progress from behind halfway,never threatened	12
31Mar86♦ Huntingdon(GB)	sf 2 1/16 RH	4:19^{1} 4↑	EBF Miltons Handicap Hurdle Hcp4000		1^{7}	Richards M	161	*1.75		Jimmy Lorenzo161^{7}Kingholm Quay137¾Deep Trouble138^{12} Rated in last,progress halfway,led over 2 out,handily	5

22Mar86♦ Newbury(GB) gd 2 1/16LH 4:052 Tote Credit Handicap Hurdle Hcp24000 35½ Richards M 151 20.00 My Dominion1492½Wantage1443Jimmy Lorenzo1511 23
Led 2 out,headed last,one-paced to line

15Jan86♦ Windsor(GB) gd 2 3:55 Rays Hurdle Alw2800 22 Richards M 157 20.00 Brunico1502Jimmy Lorenzo1578Crimson Bold150¾ 22
Toward rear,progress 3 out,angled out last,finished well

27Dec85♦ Taunton(GB) hy 2⅛RH 4:192 Holly Tree Hurdle (Div 2) Alw1200 13 Richards M 149 *3.00 Jimmy Lorenzo1493Gibbous Moon14910Sedgewell Lad15220 14
Midpack,progress 4 out,led over 2 out,ridden out

20Dec85♦ Fakenham(GB) gd *2LH 4:09 West Norfolk Hurdle Alw1200 311 Richards M 152 14.00 Boom Patrol1521Northern Hope14710Jimmy Lorenzo1521½ 15
Midpack,gained 3rd out 2 out,never reaching leaders

26Nov85♦ Newtn Abbot(GB) gd 2LH 4:062 St Just Hurdle Alw1700 37½ Richards M 154 25.00 Purple Peak1542½Christo1545Jimmy Lorenzo1546 16
Progress into 2nd before halfway,weakened after 2nd last

11Nov85♦ Plumpton(GB) gd 2LH 3:464 Cuckfield Hurdle Alw1200 619½ Richards M 147 33.00 Courageous Charger1474The Italian1476Nice Business1472 14
Never a factor

John Henry

b. g. 1975, by Ole Bob Bowers (Prince Blessed)–Once Double, by Double Jay **Lifetime record: 83 39 15 9 $6,597,947**

Own.– Dotsam Stable

Br.– Golden Chance Farm Inc (Ky)

Tr.– Ronald McAnally

13Oct84- 8Med fm 1⅜Ⓣ :464 1:11 1:351 2:13 3↑ Ballantine H 900k 4 8 89 53½ 31½ 12¾ McCarron CJ 126 *.60 100-06 JohnHnry1262¾Who'sforDinner115hdWin1201 Came out,clear 12

22Sep84- 8Bel fm 1½Ⓣ :484 1:13 2:013 2:251 3↑ Turf Classic-G1 4 1 11½ 1½ 1½ 1nk McCarron CJ 126 *1.00 98-10 JohnHnry126nkWin1264Majesty'sPrnc126hd Strong handling 6

26Aug84- 9AP fm 1¼Ⓣ :482 1:122 1:372 2:012 3↑ Bud Arl Million-G1 6 4 31½ 32 1hd 11¾ McCarron CJ 126 *1.10 87-15 JohnHenry1261¾RoyalHeroine1223GatodelSol126no Drew out 12

23Jly84- 8Hol fm 1½Ⓣ :471 1:103 1:594 2:244 3↑ Sunset H-G1 7 5 47 32 21 11 McCarron CJ 126 *1.20 96-08 JhnHnry1261LoadtheCannons1181½PairofDeuces113nk Driving 9

24Jun84- 8Hol fst 1¼ :47 1:10 1:35 2:002 3↑ Hol Gold Cup H-G1 4 4 43½ 32 32 22 McCarron CJ 125 2.60 87-20 DesertWine1222JohnHnry1251½Sari'sDreamer114nk Game try 8

28May84- 8Hol fm 1½Ⓣ :49 1:123 2:011 2:25 3↑ Hol Inv'l H-G1 1 2 31½ 31½ 3nk 1½ McCarron CJ 126 *.80 95-08 JohnHnry126½GalantVert1162¾LoadtheCannons1201¼ Driving 9

6May84- 8GG fm 1⅜Ⓣ :472 1:12 1:354 2:13 3↑ Golden Gate H-G3 6 3 34½ 22 1½ 12 McCarron CJ 125 *.50 103-09 John Henry1252Silveyville1176Lucence1166 Slow st.,clear 6

1Apr84- 8SA fm 1½Ⓣ :482 1:132 2:022 2:264 3↑ San Luis Rey-G1 4 2 21 1½ 2½ 3¾ McCarron CJ 126 1.60 80-17 Interco126nkGato del Sol126½John Henry1263½ Weakened 10

4Mar84- 8SA fst 1¼ :453 1:10 1:35 2:003 4↑ S Anita H-G1 10 7 76¼ 45 56 58 McCarron CJ 127 *2.40 78-17 Interco1212¾Journey at Sea1171½Gato del Sol1171¾ 12
Stumble after start

11Dec83- 8Hol gd 1⅜Ⓣ :494 1:153 1:40 2:163 3↑ Hol Turf Cup-G1 4 2 22½ 1½ 2hd 1½ McCarron CJ 126 *1.50 72-27 John Henry126½Zalataia1231½Palikaraki1261¼ Came again 12

13Nov83- 8SA gd 1½Ⓣ :472 1:131 2:034 2:291 3↑ Oak Tree Inv'l-G1 2 5 31 43½ 31 2½ McCarron CJ 126 *.80 68-31 Zalataia123½JohnHnry1261½LoadthCnnons1223½ Held gamely 9

15Oct83- 8Bel fst 1½ :48 1:123 2:01 2:261 3↑ J C Gold Cup-G1 7 6 53 45 55 56¾ McCarron CJ 126 2.90 82-14 Slew o'Gold1213Highland Blade126nkBounding Basque1211½ 11
Weakened

28Aug83- 9AP gd 1¼Ⓣ :503 1:154 1:413 2:042 3↑ Arl Million-G1 13 3 21 2½ 2½ 2nk McCarron CJ 126 *1.40 72-28 Tolomeo118nkJohnHenry126½Nijinsky'sSecret1262 Sharp try 14

4Jly83- 8Hol fm 1⅛Ⓣ :49 1:13 1:363 1:482 3↑ American H-G2 1 3 33 21½ 2½ 11¼ McCarron CJ 127 2.10 88-12 JohnHenry1271¼PrinceFlorimund120½Tonzarun114no Driving 8

28Nov82♦ Tokyo(Jpn) fm*1½ⓉLH 2:27 3↑ Japan Cup-G1 Stk801000 138 Shoemaker W 126 *.90 Half Iced121nkAll Along117nkApril Run1211 15
Prominent to stretch

13Nov82- 6Med gd 1¼ :473 1:121 1:37 2:012 3↑ Med Cup H-G2 2 5 37½ 44¼ 35½ 35¾ Shoemaker W 129 *1.10 89-15 Mehmet1181¼ThirtyEghtPcs1134½JhnHnry1294½ Lacked a bid 9

31Oct82- 8SA fm 1½Ⓣ :472 1:103 1:593 2:24 3↑ Oak Tree Inv'l-G1 6 4 44 21½ 2½ 12½ Shoemaker W 126 1.40 95-05 John Henry1262½Craelius1221½Regalberto1262 Drew clear 7

17Oct82- 8SA fm 1¼Ⓣ :471 1:11 1:343 1:583 3↑ C F Burke H-G2 6 3 31½ 42 42¾ 41½ Shoemaker W 129 *.80 92-06 Mehmet117hdCraelius1141½It's the One124no Evenly 7

28Mar82- 8SA fm 1½Ⓣ :462 1:102 2:00 2:24 4↑ San Luis Rey-G1 3 3 33 33 43½ 34¾ Shoemaker W 126 *.50 90-05 Perrault1263¼Exploded1261½John Henry126no Evenly 5

7Mar82- 8SA fst 1¼ :45 1:09 1:342 1:59 4↑ S Anita H-G1 9 8 913 51¼ 2½ 2no Shoemaker W 130 *1.30 94-07 [D]Perrault126noJhnHenry1303¼It'stheOne123nk Impeded end 11
Placed first by disqualification

6Dec81- 8Hol fm 1½Ⓣ :49 1:13 2:03 2:264 3↑ Hol Turf Cup 550k 5 1 12 11 3½ 42 Shoemaker W 126 *.40 84-11 Providential II126nkQueen to Conquer1231½Goldiko126nk 10
Weakened;Previously trained by Victor J. Nickerson

8Nov81- 8SA fm 1½Ⓣ :472 1:102 1:593 2:232 3↑ Oak Tree Inv'l-G1 4 3 1½ 1½ 2hd 1nk Shoemaker W 126 *.40 98-02 John Henry126nkSpence Bay1264½The Bart126no Driving 7

10Oct81- 8Bel fst 1½ :48 1:123 2:021 2:282 3↑ J C Gold Cup-G1 8 5 42½ 21 11½ 1hd Shoemaker W 126 *3.10 78-14 JohnHenry126hdPeatMoss126¾Relaxing123hd Bore in,driving 11
Previously trained by Ronald McAnally

30Aug81- 6AP sf 1¼Ⓣ :501 1:153 1:422 2:073 3↑ Arl Million 1000k 12 8 86½ 56 31 1no Shoemaker W 126 *1.10e -- John Henry126noThe Bart1262¼Madam Gay117½ Just up 12
Previously trained by Victor J. Nickerson

11Jly81- 8Bel fm 1½Ⓣ :494 1:142 2:03 2:264 3↑ Sword Dancer-G3 3 3 31½ 11 11½ 13½ Shoemaker W 126 *.30 90-13 JohnHnry1263½PassingZone1261¾PeatMoss1261¾ Ridden out 5
Previously trained by Ronald McAnally

14Jun81- 8Hol fst 1¼ :453 1:093 1:344 2:002 3↑ Hol Gold Cup H-G1 7 7 66¼ 65¾ 46½ 42¾ Pincay L Jr 130 *1.20 86-16 [D]Caterman120hdEleven Stitches1222½Super Moment117nk 10
Wide late

17May81- 8Hol fm 1½Ⓣ :511 1:151 2:04 2:274 3↑ Hol Inv'l H-G1 5 2 2½ 2½ 1½ 1¾ Pincay L Jr 130 *.40 01-12 John Henry130¾Caterman122hdGalaxy Libra110nk Driving 7

29Mar81- 8SA fm 1½Ⓣ :46 1:104 2:00 2:251 4↑ San Luis Rey-G1 1 2 21½ 22 1hd 12¼ Pincay L Jr 126 *.20 89-11 John Henry1262¼Obraztsovy1261½Fiestero126hd Easily 6

8Mar81- 8SA fst 1¼ :452 1:092 1:341 1:592 4↑ S Anita H-G1 3 7 65¼ 22 1hd 11 Pincay L Jr 128 1.90 92-11 John Henry1281King Go Go1171¼Exploded115no Driving 11

16Feb81- 8SA fm 1½Ⓣ :474 1:113 1:59 2:24 4↑ San Luis Obispo H-G2 4 1 11 11 12½ 11½ Pincay L Jr 127 *.50 95-05 John Henry1271½Galaxy Libra1195½Zor1151½ Ridden out 6

16Nov80- 8SA fm 1½Ⓣ :454 1:101 1:582 2:232 3↑ Oak Tree Inv-G1 6 5 56½ 66¾ 37½ 11½ Pincay L Jr 126 *1.50 98-02 John Henry1261½Balzac126½Bold Tropic126nk Drew clear 10
Previously trained by Victor J. Nickerson

25Oct80- 8Aqu sf 1½Ⓣ :514 1:192 2:13 2:393 3↑ Turf Classic-G1 4 1 12 23 25 38 Pincay L Jr 126 *2.00 35-57 Anifa1233Golden Act1265John Henry126nk Weakened 8

4Oct80- 8Bel fst 1½ :494 1:15 2:051 2:301 3↑ J C Gold Cup-G1 3 2 21 2½ 23 25½ Cordero A Jr 126 *.70 63-19 Temperence Hill1215½John Henry1262Ivory Hunter1263¼ 7
Best of others

7Sep80- 8Bel fm 1¼[T] :483 1:122 1:362 1:592 3↑ Brighton Beach H-G3 5 1 1hd 11½ 11½ 1nk Cordero A Jr 125 *.40 97-15 John Henry125nkPremier Ministre1174Match the Hatch1133 5
Driving

12Jly80- 8Bel fm 1½Ⓣ :47 1:111 2:01 2:251 3↑ Sword Dancer 161k 2 2 21 1½ 2hd 21¼ McHargue DG 126 *.80 97-15 Tiller1261¼John Henry1265Sten12612 Gamely 4

14Jun80- 8Bel fm 1⅜Ⓣ :473 1:113 1:352 2:131 3↑ Bowling Green H-G2 3 1 1½ 1hd 1½ 2nk McHargue DG 128 *1.80 96-15 Sten117nkJohn Henry1281Lyphard's Wish120nk Brushed 9
Previously trained by Ronald McAnally

26May80- 8Hol fm 1½Ⓣ :483 1:123 2:012 2:252 3↑ Hol Inv'l H-G1 4 1 14 12½ 1½ 1nk McHargue DG 128 *.90 93-09 John Henry128nkBalzac1201½Go West Young Man1172½ 10
Fully extended

6Apr80- 8SA fm *1¾Ⓣ :46 1:594 2:464 4↑ S Juan Capistrano H-G1 3 1 12 11½ 12 11¼ McHargue DG 126 *2.20 93-08 John Henry1261¼Fiestero114nkThe Very One113hd Driving 11

16Mar80- 8SA fm 1½Ⓣ :464 1:104 1:592 2:23 4↑ San Luis Rey-G1 3 2 21 2½ 2½ 11½ McHargue DG 126 6.90 100-00 John Henry1261½Relaunch126noSilver Eagle126no Drew out 7

23Feb80- 10Hia fm 1½Ⓣ 2:292 3↑ Hia Turf Cup H-G2 10 2 31½ 11 11½ 1½ McHargue DG 122 2.30 84-22 JohnHenry122½DancingMaster1135IvoryHunter111hd Driving 10

20Jan80- 8SA fst 1¼ :47 1:113 1:364 2:013 4↑ San Marcos H-G3 2 1 11½ 11 11 12½ McHargue DG 124 *.80 85-17 John Henry1242½El Fantastico1132¼Commemorativo110nk 5
Handily

1Jan80- 8SA gd 1⅛Ⓣ :48 1:121 1:371 1:494 4↑ San Gabriel H-G3 4 2 22 21½ 2½ 1hd McHargue DG 123 *1.70 78-22 John Henry123hdSmasher1115As de Copas1173 Driving 9

8Dec79- 8BM fm 1⅛Ⓣ :471 1:111 1:363 1:493 3↑ Bay Meadows H 114k 7 5 44½ 83¾ 1hd 21¼ McHargue DG 123 2.70 103-00 Leonotis1181¼John Henry1234Capt. Don117½ Held on 14

5Nov79- 8SA fm 1⅛Ⓣ :461 1:102 1:352 1:48 3↑ HP Russell H (Div 2) 45k 5 2 11 11 12 13¼ McHargue DG 122 *.70 87-15 JohnHenry1223¼Rusty Canyon114hdLeonotis1172 Ridden out 8

14Oct79- 8SA fm 1¼Ⓣ :454 1:10 1:343 1:591 3↑ C F Burke H-G2 5 3 21½ 1hd 1hd 21¼ McHargue DG 118 3.40 90-09 Silver Eagle1151¼John Henry118½Shagbark1181¼ Gamely 9
Previously trained by Victor J. Nickerson

10Sep79- 7Bel fm 1 1/16Ⓣ :24 :47 1:11 1:414 3↑ Alw 30000 2 1 13 11½ 12 12 Santiago A 117 1.90 87-17 John Henry1172Silent Cal117½Waya119no Ridden out 4

22Aug79- 7Sar fm 1⅛Ⓣ :462 1:111 1:343 1:462 3↑ Alw 27000 3 1 11½ 11½ 11½ 12½ Santiago A 115 *1.40 95-13 John Henry1152½Told114¾Poison Ivory1224 Driving 7

29Jly79- 7Pen sly 1 1/16 :232 :471 1:114 1:443 3↑ Capital City H 33k 7 5 41½ 31 41¼ 42 Santiago A 113 2.30 81-23 Horatius118nkTanthem1121½Shy Jester115nk Hung 7

14Jly79- 8Bel fm 1 1/16Ⓣ :233 :47 1:104 1:413 3↑ Sword Dancer 57k 2 1 2hd 21 22 22½ Santiago A 119 5.70 85-11 Darby Creek Road1192½John Henry1194Poison Ivory1191¾ 8
Best of others
6Jly79- 6Atl fm 1 1/16Ⓣ :23 :462 1:102 1:411 3↑ Sunrise H 35k 2 2 21½ 1½ 1hd 22¼ McCauley WH 111 *1.50 98-09 Chati1182¼John Henry111½Fed Funds1154 Tired 11
24Jun79-10Suf fst 1⅛ :453 1:10 1:36 1:483 3↑ Mass H-G3 9 4 68¾ 84¼ 96 108½ Borden DA 108 6.90 89-21 Island Sultan110¾Western Front113½Quiet Jay1161½ Tired 13
5Jun79- 8Mth fst 1 :232 :47 1:114 1:373 4↑ Alw 18000 1 3 2hd 13 18 114 McCauley WH 119 *.90 85-23 John Henry11914Thou Fool119noM.A.'s Date1131¾ Driving 7
26May79- 6Mth fst 6f :22 :443 1:104 4↑ Alw 16000 4 4 53½ 41¾ 21½ 2½ McCauley WH 117 6.90 85-19 ReallyandTruly117½JohnHnry1171¼Kintla'sFolly1153 Gamely 7
Previously trained by Robert A. Donato
29Oct78- 6Pen fm 1 1/16Ⓣ 1:412 Chcltetwn H (Div 2) 22k 5 2 21 1½ 12 11 Broussard R 124 *.70 - - John Henry1241Scythian Gold1166½Berlin's Burning1122 7
Ridden out
15Oct78- 5SA fm 1¼Ⓣ :453 1:094 1:342 1:59 3↑ C F Burke H (Div 1)-G2 2 1 1hd 1hd 44 65 Baltazar C 117 2.80 87-08 Star of Erin II113noImproviser1152¾Mr. Redoy1181¼ Tired 9
8Oct78- 8SA fm 1⅛Ⓣ :46 1:102 1:351 1:474 Volante H-G3 6 4 42 41 31½ 3½ Baltazar C 122 *2.30 87-12 WaysideStation117noAprilAxe120½JohnHenry1222 In close 11
16Sep78- 8AP gd 1 1/16Ⓣ :241 :484 1:131 1:454 Round Table H-G3 6 1 11 13 18 112 Amy J 121 *.50 80-30 JhnHnry12112GordieH.109noBringtheMoney111no Ridden out 9
9Sep78- 5Bel fm 7fⓉ :232 :46 1:093 1:22 3↑ Alw 21000 1 1 11½ 11½ 11 11½ Amy J 113 3.60 94-09 John Henry1131½Gab Bag1174Proud Arion1171¼ Hard ridden 8
18Aug78- 7Sar fm 1 1/16Ⓣ :251 :49 1:12 1:41 3↑ Alw 23000 7 2 2½ 2hd 44 47¼ Amy J 112 5.10 85-08 Blue Baron1172¼Quip1141Stir the Embers1194 Weakened 8
8Aug78- 7Sar gd 7f :223 :444 1:081 1:202 3↑ Alw 23000 2 2 31½ 24 38 514 Santiago A 113 2.90 89-04 DarbyCreekRoad11311Liberal117¾GoldenReserve117¾ Tired 6
29Jly78- 8Bel fm 1 1/16Ⓣ :233 :46 1:103 1:41 Lexington H-G2 5 1 12½ 12 11 2hd Santiago A 112 5.90 91-11 Mac Diarmida126hdJohn Henry1124¼Ashikaga110hd Gamely 9
19Jly78- 8Bel fm 1Ⓣ :24 :473 1:104 1:351 Hill Prince H 37k 5 1 2hd 2hd 2½ 21½ Santiago A 111 3.60 92-12 DarbyCreekRd1211½JhnHnry1112ScythianGold1116 Gamely 9
1Jly78- 8Mth fm 1 1/16Ⓣ :232 :47 1:11 1:432 Lamplighter H-G3 4 2 2hd 1hd 1½ 3½ Santiago A 112 *1.50 83-16 North Course112nkHoratius114nkJohnHenry112no Weakened 9
25Jun78- 6Bel hd 1 1/16Ⓣ :232 :47 1:102 1:411 3↑ Alw 18000 2 5 62½ 52 42 1nk Santiago A 112 3.40 90-07 John Henry112nkTurn of Coin1171¾Valinsky1171¾ Driving 9
1Jun78- 7Bel fm 1 1/16Ⓣ :231 :47 1:11 1:413 Clm 35000 1 2 21 1½ 17 114 Santiago A 117 3.30 88-12 JhnHnry11714ContinentalCousin117¾CptnPeter1132¼ Driving 10
21May78- 2Aqu fst 6f :224 :471 1:123 Clm 25000 4 4 32½ 1½ 11 12½ Santiago A 117 12.30 80-27 John Henry1172½Please See Me1171½Orfanik115nk Driving 9
Previously owned and trained by H. Snowden Jr
11Apr78- 7Kee fst 6f :22 :45 :59 1:093 Alw 8500 4 4 47½ 46 48½ 49½ McKnight J 113 6.40 84-15 Johnny Blade1074½Schottis112½Jester Beau1154½ No mishap 6
Previously owned by D. Lingo & C. Madere;previously trained by Phil Marino
22Mar78- 9FG fst 6f :23 :47 1:12 Clm 25000 7 6 78 89 64¾ 34 Copling D 114 25.10 81-16 Kim's Red1142Bunny Wag1122John Henry1141 Rallied 9
22Feb78- 9FG fst 6f :223 :463 1:113 Clm 20000 11 2 98¾ 98¾ 1015 1020 Elmer D 112 b 19.10 67-19 AdriaticEditions1144Bladesville113½Kim'sRed1141 Outrun 11
15Feb78- 6FG fst 6f :22 :462 1:113 Clm 25000 5 5 85¼ 61¼ 63¾ 66¼ Guajardo A 112 b 4.90 81-19 MercrCounty1121½Gen'sLTroy1121AdrtcEdtons1141 No mishap 8
4Feb78- 6FG fst 1 40 :252 :493 1:151 1:43 Alw 7500 2 9 84¾ 83½ 53¼ 55¾ Guajardo A 112 17.10 72-23 HogTown114¾TrafficWarning114hdSmokePole1092½ No mishap 10
23Jan78- 8FG gd 1 40 :241 :473 1:131 1:424 Alw 7500 7 4 42¾ 52¾ 86¾ 86½ Guajardo A 112 22.20 72-24 CabriniGreen117½DayTimeTudor1121As in Elbow112no Tired 9
31Dec77- 9FG fst 6f :22 :46 1:121 Sugar Bowl H 50k 4 12 127¾ 127½ 1210 1114 McKnight J 113 16.80 70-21 CabriniGreen122½CouponRate113¾SpecialHonr1101¼ Outrun 12
17Dec77- 6FG gd 6f :223 :472 1:122 ©Alw 7000 1 6 64¼ 62¾ 53¾ 31¼ McKnight J 113 7.90 82-18 CabriniGreen1201¼CouponRate113hdJohnHenry113hd Rallied 12
3Dec77- 8FG fst 6f :222 :462 1:114 Alw 7000 1 7 75¾ 54 51¾ 43½ McKnight J 120 8.70 82-19 DragonTamer1171½TrafficWarnng1171¼HogTwn117¾ Rallied 11
19Nov77- 9FG fst 6f :221 :464 1:124 ©Sthern Hospitality 19k 8 12 105 63¼ 64¼ 59 Guajardo A 122 9.60 72-22 CbrniGreen1144MajesticSpiral1122½HogTown112hd Late bid 12
5Sep77-11EvD sly 6f :232 :47 1:01 1:142 Lafayette Futurity 86k 1 6 45 32½ 1hd Guajardo A 120 5.10 79-26 JohnHenry120hdLilLizaJayne1171SoundNote1203½ Driving 12
25Aug77- 7EvD gd 6f :223 :462 1:002 1:13 Sp Wt 2700 8 5 33 32 2½ Guajardo A 120 4.10 85-21 Note to Mame117½John Henry1203Tudor Luck117hd 9
6Aug77- 7EvD sly 5f :224 :483 1:001 Alw 2400 4 9 54½ 1hd 13 Guajardo A 120 3.00 82-19 John Henry1203Motor Dude1201½Bell's Chief1174 Driving 12
29Jly77- 8JnD fst *6f :233 :473 1:02 1:152 Handicap 7500 9 9 - - - - Munster L 102 3.90 - - RunLikeHeck1191CapGardnr1072HarktheLedr1102 Lost rider 9
2Jly77- 6JnD sly 5f :23 :481 1:011 Alw 4500 2 5 42 33 23 Spiehler G 116 *2.60 81-19 KindaNughty1133JhnHnry1161MossBluffKd1152 Bid,weakened 7
7Jun77- 8JnD fst 4f :22 :471 Alw 3500 4 6 59 55½ 31 Spiehler G 120 14.60 89-11 DancngMeadw109¾DancingJudge120nkJhnHnry1201 Rallied 8
20May77- 1JnD fst 4f :23 :481 Md Sp Wt 1 7 54½ 34 1no Spiehler G 120 1.70 85-15 JhnHnry120noYouSexyThing1172Ricky'sChoice112¾ Driving 8

Just a Game II (Ire)

dkbbr. f. 1976, by Tarboosh (Bagdad)–Hobby, by Falcon

Lifetime record: 28 14 4 3 $416,069

Own.– P.M. Brant
Br.– Rathvale Stud (Ire)
Tr.– LeRoy Jolley

1Jan82- 9Crc yl *1⅛Ⓣ 1:502 3↑ ⒻLa Prvoynte (Div 2)-G3 3 1 1½ 1hd 12½ 13 Cordero A Jr 123 *.50 71-28 JustaGmeII1233SweetestChnt115nkIrshJoy1143½ Ridden out 9
22Nov81- 8Hol fm 1⅛Ⓣ :473 1:114 1:352 1:47 3↑ ⒻMatriarch 221k 3 3 34½ 23 55 77 Cordero A Jr 123 3.70 88-08 Kilijaro1232½Glorious Song123nkBersid120½ Gave way 9
13Nov81- 8Hol fm 1 1/16Ⓣ :234 :474 1:113 1:404 3↑ ⒻAlw 40000 6 1 11 11 13 11 Cordero A Jr 114 *1.10 95-05 Just a Game II1141Saison1152½Mi Quimera1143 Driving 9
Previously trained by David A. Whiteley
2Nov81- 7Aqu gd 1Ⓣ :234 :48 1:131 1:38 3↑ ⒻAlw 32000 4 1 1½ 32½ 39 316 Cordero A Jr 115 *.80 72-12 Adlibber1225StephanieLeigh12211JustaGameII1159¾ Tired 4
3Oct80- 8Bel fm 1⅜Ⓣ :51 1:15 1:393 2:152 3↑ Man o' War-G1 1 2 21 2½ 1hd 21½ Brumfield D 123 *.90 83-20 FrenchColonial1261½JstaGmeII1233¾GoldnAct126no Gamely 5
1Sep80- 8Bel fm 1¼Ⓣ :474 1:114 1:362 2:004 3↑ ⒻFlower Bowl H-G2 7 1 33½ 1½ 14 12 Brumfield D 124 *2.00 90-12 JustaGmeII1242HeyBabe114noEuphrosyne112nk Ridden out 11
17Aug80- 8Sar fm 1⅛Ⓣ :48 1:124 1:363 1:49 3↑ ⒻDiana H-G2 9 1 11 11 13 1nk Brumfield D 123 *1.60 82-18 JustaGameII123nkTheVeryOne117hdRelaxing1131¼ Driving 9
4Jly80- 8Atl fm 1 3/16Ⓣ :484 1:132 1:38 1:573 3↑ ⒻMatchmaker-G2 3 2 42½ 32½ 12 11 Brumfield D 120 *.60 79-28 JustaGmeII1201LaSoufriere115noRecordAcclam1152 Driving 10
21Jun80- 8Bel fm 1¼Ⓣ :49 1:13 1:363 2:002 3↑ ⒻNew York H-G3 5 1 1½ 11½ 14 11 Brumfield D 121 *1.10 92-11 JstaGameII1211Poppycock112hdPleaseTryHard1132¼ Driving 6
5Jun80- 8Bel fm 1Ⓣ :23 :461 1:104 1:353 3↑ ⒻAlw 35000 2 1 1hd 1½ 15 14 Brumfield D 119 *.50 87-10 Just a Game II1194Chestnut Speester117noKarin Jones115nk 6
Ridden out
5Apr80- 9GP fm 1 1/16Ⓣ :223 :461 1:101 1:402 3↑ ⒻOrchid H-G3 5 3 32½ 21 13 1¾ Brumfield D 119 *.70 99-07 JustaGmeII119¾LaSoufriere1152½LaRouquineII114hd Driving 10
12Mar80- 9GP fm 1Ⓣ :232 :471 1:103 1:351 3↑ ⒻSwnnee Rvr (Div 1) 31k 3 2 2hd 11½ 15 15 Brumfield D 117 *1.70 94-13 JustaGmeII1175LaSoufriere1134½LaVoygus120no Ridden out 10
25Feb80- 9Hia fm 1 1/16Ⓣ 1:423 4↑ ⒻAlw 16000 2 2 21 12 15 16½ Brumfield D 115 4.10 85-17 JustaGameII1156½BallGate115noLaSoufriere1154 Ridden out 7
18Feb80- 7Hia fst 6f :221 :452 1:103 4↑ ⒻAlw 14000 8 6 76½ 77 65¾ 56½ Vasquez J 115 4.40 83-20 Hill Billy Dancer1172Yoka1153Guimauve115½ No mishap 9
29Jan80- 9Hia fst 6f :22 :452 1:103 4↑ ⒻAlw 14500 5 4 31 2½ 2½ 98 Vasquez J 116 4.20 82-25 SilverOaks1161HillBllyDncr1161SstrRosmund116hd Gave way 10
Previously trained by Charles Magnier
9Jun79♦ Epsom(GB) yl 1½ⓉLH 2:433 ⒻEnglish Oaks-G1 Stk140000 1025 Shoemaker W 126 20.00 Scintillate1263Bonnie Isle1261Britannias Rule1264 14
Prominent to halfway,lost place downhill turn,weakened
2Jun79♦ Leopardstwn(Ire) gd 1⅛ⓉLH 1:582 3↑ Kilmacanogue H Hcp6600 2¾ Piggott L 131 4.00 Mississippi133¾Just a Game II131noOisin Dubh1342½ 8
Led to 2f out,dueled briefly,gave ground grudgingly
7Oct78♦ The Curragh(Ire) gd 1ⓉStr 1:424 Beresford Stakes-G2 Stk15000 1hd Carberry T 123 50.00 Just a Game II123hdSandy Creek1264Accomplice126¾ 5
Tracked in 3rd,bid 2f out,led 100y out,gamely
30Sep78♦ Phoenix Park(Ire) gd 5fⓉStr :582 Maher Nursery H Hcp6900 54¼ Coogan B 130 8.00 Feathers Lad126nkLattygar1073Sun's Image102hd 10
Toward rear,mild late gain
9Sep78♦ Phoenix Park(Ire) gd 7fⓉRH 1:21 ⒻPark Stakes-G3 Stk11200 22 Morgan J 126 10.00 Solar1262Just a Game II126hdSister Jinks1162 9
Close up,mild bid 3f out,chased winner home
23Aug78♦ York(GB) gd 6fⓉStr 1:14 ⒻLowther Stakes-G3 Stk24500 9 Carson W 123 12.00 Devon Ditty1261½Eyelet123nkGreenland Park129½ 11
Slow into stride,never a factor
12Aug78♦ Phoenix Park(Ire) gd 6fⓉStr 1:121 Naas Nursery H Hcp3700 1nk Morgan J 115 *1.50 Just a Game II115nkPitora1004Nice Client1098 8
Tracked in 3rd,drifted left 2f out,led 100y out,held gamely
7Aug78♦ Leopardstwn(Ire) gd 5fⓉStr 1:032 Newtonpark Nursery H Hcp3700 31½ Coogan B5 116 *1.35 Meeson Girl105hdConcordia1221½Just a Game II116¾ 10
Missed break,progress halfway,finished well
29Jly78♦ The Curragh(Ire) gd *6fⓉStr 1:18 Railway S-G3 Stk8600 2nk Swinburn WR 122 14.00 Solar119nkJust a Game II1226Cajolery1196 4
Dueled thoughout,very game

19Jly78♦ Naas(Ire)	fm 5f Ⓣ Str	1:001	Clane Nursery H Hcp3600	11	Morgan J	113	8.00	Just a Game II1131Nice Client103noMeeson Girl103½	Tracked in 3rd,led 150y out,driving	7
8Jly78♦ Leopardstown(Ire)	gd 7f Ⓣ LH	1:344	Hennessy VSOP Race Alw3300	77¾	Coogan B5	114	8.00	Five Stars Final122nkHighest Regards122hdSwizzle122½	Tracked in 3rd,weakened 1½f out	9
8Jun78♦ Lmrick Jnctn(Ire)	gd 5f Ⓣ Str	:583	Ballykisteen Maiden Mdn2200	1no	Coogan B5	118	5.00	Just a Game II118noReal Snug1234Saulest1236	Tracked leaders,rallied to lead on line	13
24May78♦ Down Royal(Ire)	fm 5f Ⓣ Str	-	W&R Barnett Ltd Maiden Mdn1300	31¼	Corr J	123	10.00	Mount Oriel126nkDallynot1231Just a Game II1232	Toward rear,finished well without threatening.Time not taken	9

Lady's Secret

gr. f. 1982, by Secretariat (Bold Ruler)–Great Lady M., by Icecapade

Lifetime record: 45 25 9 3 $3,021,425

Own.– Mr & Mrs E.V. Klein

Br.– Robert H. Spreen (Okla)

Tr.– D. Wayne Lukas

10Aug87- 1Sar	sly 1⅛	:471 1:113 1:361 1:492 3↑	Alw 45000	2 - - - - -	McCarron CJ	117	*.30	--	Kamakura11511The Watcher1222¼Jack of Clubs1192½	Bolted	5
21Jly87- 8Mth	fst 1 1/16	:231 :462 1:11 1:432 3↑	ⒻAlw 25000	1 2 1½ 13½ 19 17	McCarron CJ	119	*.10	88-18	Lady'sSecret1197BriefRemarks115nkShaknBy115¾	Easy score	6
4Jly87-10Mth	fst 1 1/16	:231 :461 1:10 1:42 3↑	ⒻMolly Pitcher H-G2	3 2 21½ 2½ 2hd 22	McCarron CJ	125	*.30	93-10	ReelEasy1122Lady'sSecret125¾Cattonc117nk	Best of others	8
13Jun87- 8Mth	sly 6f	:222 :444 1:094 3↑	ⒻAlw 25000	5 1 2hd 1½ 11 13½	Cordero A Jr	122	*.30	91-14	Lady'sSecret1223½Nick'sNag1156BriefRmrks1158	Ridden out	5
14Mar87-10GP	fst 1⅛	:462 1:11 1:361 1:484 3↑	Donn H-G2	2 1 12 43 618 632½	Day P	120	*.80	55-18	LittleBoldJohn111noSkipTrl1186WsTms1174½	Fin. after ½	7
1Nov86- 5SA	fst 1¼	:461 1:10 1:344 2:011 3↑	ⒻBC Distaff-G1	5 1 14 14 14 12½	Day P	123	*.50	83-13	Lady's Secret1232½Fran's Valentine1232Outstandingly123¾		8
	Ridden out										
12Oct86- 8Bel	fst 1¼	:461 1:10 1:352 2:013 3↑	ⒻBeldame-G1	4 1 15 11 1½ 1½	Day P	123	*.05	90-13	Lady's Secret123½Coup de Fusil1231¾Classy Cathy11823½		4
	Drifted,ridden out										
21Sep86- 8Bel	fst 1⅛	:454 1:093 1:341 1:464 3↑	ⒻRuffian H-G1	5 2 1½ 13½ 16 18	Day P	129	*.50	93-12	Lady's Secret1298Steal a Kiss1092¼Endear1196	Handily	6
6Sep86- 8Bel	fst 1	:231 :454 1:094 1:332 3↑	ⒻMaskette-G1	5 1 11 11½ 14½ 17	Day P	125	*.30	98-10	Lady's Secret1257Steal a Kiss1091¾Endear120no	Handily	6
30Aug86- 8Bel	fst 1⅛	:453 1:092 1:334 1:46 3↑	Woodward-G1	4 1 11½ 12½ 2hd 24¾	Cordero A Jr	121	1.40e	92-14	Precisionist1264¾Lady'sScrt1215½PrsonlFlg1105¾	2nd best	5
16Aug86- 9Mth	sly 1⅛	:464 1:103 1:353 1:484 3↑	Iselin H-G1	1 1 11½ 1hd 1hd 33½	Day P	120	*1.20	86-16	Roo Art1172¼Precisionist1251¼Lady's Secret1206	Gave way	5
2Aug86- 8Sar	sly 1⅛	:463 1:104 1:363 1:494 3↑	Whitney H-G1	2 1 12½ 13 12½ 14½	Day P	119	*1.30e	86-22	Lady's Secret1194½Ends Well1163¼Fuzzy110nk	Ridden out	7
5Jly86- 9Mth	fst 1 1/16	:23 :46 1:091 1:411 3↑	ⒻMolly Pitcher H-G2	4 1 1½ 1½ 13½ 16¼	Day P	126	*.20	99-13	Lady's Secret1266¼Chaldea1142¼Key Witness1121½	Easily	8
8Jun86- 8Bel	my 1⅛	:444 1:094 1:353 1:483 3↑	ⒻHempstead H-G1	4 2 1hd 1hd 22½ 26	Day P	128	*.40	78-16	Endear1156Lady's Secret1281½Ride Sally12413	2nd best	5
26May86- 8Bel	fst 1	:232 :454 1:091 1:333 3↑	Metropolitan H-G1	4 1 2hd 1hd 1½ 31¼	Day P	120	5.30	96-11	Garthorn1241¼LoveThatMac117noLady'sSecrt120nk	Held well	8
17May86- 8Bel	fst 1 1/16	:233 :461 1:101 1:414 3↑	ⒻShuvee H-G1	3 1 11 11 13 13½	Day P	126	*.70	93-15	Lady's Secret1263½Endear1156¼Ride Sally1251	Easy score	6
16Apr86- 9OP	fst 1 1/16	:231 :454 1:101 1:402 4↑	ⒻApple Blossom H-G1	4 1 13 1hd 2½ 2nk	Velasquez J	127	*.40	99-16	LoveSmitten119nkLady'sSecret1276Sefa'sBeauty1226	Failed	7
23Feb86- 8SA	fst 1⅛	:462 1:10 1:343 1:47 4↑	ⒻS Margarita H-G1	1 1 11½ 11 11½ 12¾	Velasquez J	125	*1.60	94-11	Lady'sSecret1252¾Johnica1201¼DontstopThemusc1222	Easily	9
9Feb86- 8SA	fst 1⅛	:464 1:11 1:363 1:494	ⒻLa Canada-G1	3 1 1½ 11½ 11½ 11¼	McCarron CJ	126	*.50	80-16	Lady'sSecrt1261¼Shywing1194NorthSider1181¾	Hard ridden	6
18Jan86- 8SA	fst 1 1/16	:222 :452 1:093 1:414	ⒻEl Encino-G3	8 3 1½ 13 12½ 12	McCarron CJ	124	*.80	92-12	Ldy'sScrt1242Shywng1194ShrpAscnt119nk	Lugged into stretch	10
27Dec85- 8SA	fst 7f	:222 :45 1:093 1:222	ⒻLa Brea-G3	1 3 1hd 1½ 2hd 2½	McCarron CJ	124	*.80	87-16	SavannahSlew119½Lady'sScret1243AmbraRidge1142½	Gamely	7
	Previously owned by E.V. Klein										
2Nov85- 5Aqu	fst 1¼	:464 1:112 1:364 2:02 3↑	ⒻBC Distaff-G1	1 1 14 11 21½ 26¼	Velasquez J	119	*.40e	80-10	Life's Magic1236¼Lady's Secret1193Dontstop Themusic1231¼		7
	Ducked out start										
13Oct85- 8Bel	fst 1¼	:454 1:102 1:36 2:033 3↑	ⒻBeldame-G1	4 1 1½ 12 13 12	Velasquez J	118	*.60	80-19	Lady'sSecret1182Isayso1232¾KamikazeRick1182¼	Ridden out	5
22Sep85- 8Bel	fst 1⅛	:462 1:094 1:343 1:472 3↑	ⒻRuffian H-G1	3 1 11½ 14 15 14	Velasquez J	116	*.30e	90-17	Lady's Secret1164Isayso1152¼Sintrillium118hd	Ridden out	6
7Sep85- 8Bel	fst 1	:222 :444 1:091 1:344 3↑	ⒻMaskette-G1	6 1 1½ 11 14 15½	Velasquez J	111	*1.00e	91-14	Lady's Secret1115½Dowery117noMrs. Revere117¾	Ridden out	8
9Aug85- 8Sar	fst 7f	:214 :441 1:091 1:223 3↑	ⒻBallerina-G2	4 3 21½ 2hd 1½ 1no	MacBeth D	117	*.90e	89-19	Lady'sSecret117noMrs.Revere1162¾SolarHalo116¾	Driving	9
1Aug85- 8Sar	gd 7f	:221 :444 1:09 1:213	ⒻTest-G2	9 1 42½ 31½ 1hd 12	Velasquez J	121	10.10	94-13	Lady'sScrt1212Mom'sCommand124nkMjstcFolly118½	Driving	10
6Jly85- 6Bel	fst 6f	:22 :451 1:111 3↑	ⒻThe Rose 54k	6 1 32 3nk 12 14¾	Velasquez J	116	*.40	86-20	Lady'sScrt1164¾FoolishIntentions115¾ProudClarioness115nk		6
	Ridden out										
22Jun85- 9Mth	fst 6f	:221 :443 1:093 3↑	ⒻRegret H 49k	6 1 11½ 11½ 12½ 13½	Antley CW	114	*.40	92-16	Lady'sSecret1143½FurashFolly1182Nck'sNg1202½	Ridden out	6
26May85- 5Bel	fst 6f	:222 :444 1:09	ⒻBowl of Flowers 55k	6 1 1½ 1hd 14 17	Velasquez J	121	*.50	97-13	Lady'sSecrt1217RideSally114nkIndinRomnc1143	Ridden out	7
11May85- 8Bel	fst 7f	:22 :443 1:091 1:221	ⒻComely-G3	1 4 43 45 47½ 411	Cordero A Jr	121	6.30	80-12	Mom'sCommnd1214½MajestcFolly1131¾ClocksScrt1214¾	Tired	9
28Apr85- 8Aqu	fst 6f	:222 :451 1:10	ⒻPrioress-G3	5 1 21 21½ 21½ 21¼	Velasquez J	118	*1.30	90-21	ClocksSecret1151¼Lady'sSecret1185RideSally1122	Gamely	8
16Apr85- 9OP	fst 6f	:214 :45 1:10	ⒻPrima Donna 76k	7 2 32½ 3½ 11½ 15	Velasquez J	123	*.80	90-18	Lady'sSecret1235TakeMyPictur1232Lt.A.J.1121¾	Ridden out	9
23Feb85- 8GG	fst 6f	:213 :442 :573 1:10	ⒻVallejo 43k	1 3 1½ 1½ 1hd 21½	Baze RA	122	1.90	87-16	SavannahSlew1141½Ldy'sScrt1226SprtdMdm1143½	Game try	7
30Jan85- 8SA	fst 7f	:221 :444 1:094 1:232	ⒻS Ynez-G3	6 1 2hd 1hd 2hd 53¾	Valenzuela PA	122	7.40	79-17	Wlsing Up119¾Rascal Lass1222Reigning Countess119¾	Hung	9
12Jan85- 8BM	fst 6f	:222 :444 :572 1:101	Determine 44k	7 1 2½ 1hd 2hd 2nk	Baze RA	115	*1.10	88-21	Bedside Promise113nkLady'sScrt1151½[D]SantaRosaPrince115no		8
	Gamely										
5Jan85- 8BM	fst 6f	:222 :45 :573 1:10	ⒻHail Hilarious 43k	5 3 31½ 1hd 13 14	Baze RA	120	*.70	89-16	Lady's Secret1204Missadoon1125Bloomer Miss115no		7
	Bumped start,wide into str										
9Nov84- 9Hol	fst 6f	:221 :453 :58 1:111	ⒻMoccasin 61k	8 1 1hd 2½ 1½ 1½	McCarron CJ	120	*1.90	--	Lady's Secret120½Neshia1131Lotta Blue1173	Driving	9
20Oct84- 8SA	fst 1 1/16	:224 :454 1:102 1:423	ⒻOak Leaf-G1	6 1 13 1½ 36 516¼	Sibille R	115	7.10	72-13	FolkArt1174½Pirate'sGlow1156½WaywardPirate1153½	Tired	6
8Oct84- 8SA	fst 7f	:22 :443 1:101 1:233	ⒻAnoakia-G3	11 1 12½ 13½ 12 3hd	Black K	120	6.10e	82-16	WaywardPirate120hdPrt'sGlow117noLdy'sScrt1201¼	Weakened	11
8Aug84- 8Dmr	fst 6f	:22 :451 :58 1:111	ⒻJunior Miss 53k	3 1 2hd 1hd 22½ 46	Valenzuela PA	122	3.00e	76-21	Doon's Baby1172½Fiesta Lady1173Trunk117½	Weakened	6
23Jly84- 3Hol	fst 6f	:214 :443 :572 1:11	Ⓕ[R]Wavy Waves 46k	5 1 1½ 12 12 11½	Valenzuela PA	117	2.20	82-18	Lady's Secret1171½Full o Wisdom115½Neshia1172¼	Driving	6
7Jly84- 8Hol	fst 6f	:213 :444 :571 1:10	ⒻLandaluce-G3	13 1 2hd 22½ 25 49	Valenzuela PA	116	21.40e	78-18	WindowSeat1146½RaiseaProspctor1191FulloWsdom1141½	Tired	13
2Jly84- 8Bel	fst 5½f	:214 :454 :583 1:051	ⒻAstoria 75k	4 3 1hd 1hd 21 55½	Cordero A Jr	112	2.60	83-15	Faster Than Fast1103Something113½Queen Breeze1121½		9
	Pace between horses										
21May84- 4Bel	fst 5f	:221 :454 :584	ⒻMd Sp Wt	1 3 11½ 11½ 11½ 11½•	Cordero A Jr	117	*1.40	93-09	[DH]Lady'sScrt117[DH]Bonnie's Axe1171½Launching Shot1172¼		8
	Drifted out										

Landaluce

dkbbr. f. 1980, by Seattle Slew (Bold Reasoning)–Strip Poker, by Bold Bidder

Lifetime record: 5 5 0 0 $372,365

Own.– French & Beal

Br.– Spendthrift Farm & Francis Kernan (Ky)

Tr.– D. Wayne Lukas

23Oct82- 8SA	fst 1 1/16	:223 :454 1:094 1:414	ⒻOak Leaf-G1	6 3 1hd 13 14 12	Pincay L Jr	117	*.05	92-10	Landaluce1172SophisticatedGirl1158GrnjRn115½	Ridden out	7
11Oct82- 8SA	fst 7f	:222 :45 1:09 1:214	ⒻAnoakia-G3	8 2 3nk 12 18 110	Pincay L Jr	123	*.10	91-15	Landaluce12310Rare Thrill1171¼Time of Sale1202½	Easily	8
5Sep82- 8Dmr	fst 1	:223 :46 1:104 1:353	ⒻDmr Debutante-G2	4 2 2½ 1hd 11½ 16½	Pincay L Jr	119	*.30	90-12	Landaluce1196½IssuesN'Answers1164GranjaReina1132	Easily	6
10Jly82- 8Hol	fst 6f	:212 :434 :56 1:08	ⒻHol Lassie-G2	3 2 2½ 11½ 19 121	Pincay L Jr	117	*.30e	97-16	Landaluce11721Bold Out Line1151½Barzell119½	Easy score	5
3Jly82- 4Hol	fst 6f	:22 :443 :562 1:081	ⒻMd Sp Wt	6 2 11½ 13 16 17	Pincay L Jr	117	*.80	96-10	Landaluce1177MidnightRapture1165MissBigWig1161½	Easily	7

Lemhi Gold

ch. c. 1978, by Vaguely Noble (Vienna)–Belle Marie, by Candy Spots — Lifetime record: 22 8 3 1 $1,129,645

Own.– Aaron U. Jones
Br.– Aaron U. Jones (Ky)
Tr.– Olivier Douieb

Date / Track	Cond	Dist	Fractions	Age	Race	PP St 1st 2nd Str Fin	Jockey	Wt	Odds	Speed	Top finishers	Comment	Field
23Jly83♦ Ascot(GB)	gd	1½ⓉRH	2:303	3↑	King George & Queen Eliz-G1 Stk296000	823¾	Head F	133	16.00		Time Charter130¾Diamond Shoal1331Sun Princess1172	Unruly pre-start,dwelt,rushed to lead,headed 4f out,weakened	9
3Jly83♦ Saint-Cloud(Fr)	gd	*1 9/16ⓉLH	2:344	3↑	Grand Prix de Saint-Cloud-G1 Stk276000	42¼	Head F	134	9.00		Diamond Shoal134¾Lancastrian134¾Zalataia129¾	Led to 1f out,faded.All Along 7th	9
29May83♦ Longchamp(Fr)	gd	*1⅛ⓉRH	2:03	4↑	Prix Dollar-G2 Stk69000	79	Head F	129	2.20		Welsh Tern129nkOrofino1291Darly123½	Tracked in 3rd,weakened 1½f out	9
												Previously trained by Lazaro S. Barrera	
31Oct82- 8SA	fm	1½Ⓣ	:472 1:103 1:593 2:24	3↑	Oak Tree Inv'l-G1	4 1 1hd 33½ 43½ 57¼	McCarron CJ	126	*.90	88-05	John Henry1262½Craelius1221½Regalberto1262	Speed,tired	7
9Oct82- 8Bel	fst	1½	:473 1:114 2:04 2:311	3↑	J C Gold Cup-G1	2 3 28 14 15 14½	McCarron CJ	126	2.60	64-25	LmhiGld1264½SilverSuprm1262ChrstmsPst11817	Ridden out	10
18Sep82- 8Bel	fst	1¼	:473 1:113 1:36 2:01	3↑	Marlboro Cup H-G1	2 3 31 11 15 18¾	Vasquez J	115	7.50e	93-17	LmhiGold1158¾SilvrSupreme117¾ParofDucs1169	Ridden out	8
29Aug82- 8AP	fm	1¼Ⓣ	:462 1:101 1:35 1:584	3↑	Bud Million 1000k	5 8 85¾ 52¼ 44½ 45¼	McCarron CJ	126	3.20	120-00	Perrault1262¼Be My Native118nkMotavato1262¾	Rallied	14
7Aug82- 8Sar	fst	1⅛	:472 1:11 1:352 1:474	3↑	Whitney H-G1	1 5 47 45 56¼ 45¾	McCarron CJ	117	5.70	90-14	SilverBuck1151½Wntr'sTl119nkTpShos1134	Broke in the air	6
10Jly82- 8Bel	fm	1½Ⓣ	:491 1:132 2:014 2:26	3↑	Sword Dancer H-G2	2 1 13 1½ 1hd 1nk	McCarron CJ	126	*1.00	94-11	Lemhi Gold126nkErin's Isle1267¾Field Cat1261¾	Driving	5
31May82- 8Hol	fm	1½Ⓣ	:492 1:132 2:013 2:251	3↑	Hol Inv'l H-G1	6 3 32 3½ 1hd 22½	Guerra WA	123	*.60	91-07	Exploded1172½Lemhi Gold123¾The Bart1252½	Game try	6
18Apr82- 8SA	fm	*1¾Ⓣ	:46 1:584 2:453	4↑	San Juan Cap H-G1	4 4 35½ 1hd 12½ 17	Guerra WA	121	3.10	99-06	Lemhi Gold1217Exploded1181¾Perrault1292½	Easy score	9
13Mar82- 8SA	gd	1½Ⓣ	:484 1:13 2:022 2:272	4↑	S Marino H (Div 1) 66k	4 1 12½ 12½ 15 15	Guerra WA	119	2.30	78-29	Lemhi Gold1195Exploded1191½Chancey Bidder1124¼	Easily	8
25Feb82- 8SA	fm	1⅛Ⓣ	:464 1:111 1:353 1:48	4↑	Alw 35000	8 5 42 41½ 1½ 11¼	Guerra WA	113	*1.70	87-13	Lemhi Gold1131¼Fingal's Cave1142½Essenbee1152½	Driving	10
15Feb82- 8SA	fst	1 1/16	:231 :462 1:10 1:41	4↑	ⓇEl Monte 73k	1 5 43 31½ 33½ 31¼	Guerra WA	114	3.40	95-12	Woodland Lad119½Sir Dancer115¾Lemhi Gold1141½	Evenly	10
6Feb82- 6SA	fst	1 1/16	:231 :462 1:094 1:41	4↑	Alw 25000	4 5 53½ 33½ 23½ 25½	Guerra WA	114	*.90	90-09	Shashy1155½Lemhi Gold1143½Call Me Mister117½	No match	7
29Aug81- 8Bel	fst	1	:223 :444 1:082 1:331		Jerome H-G2	11 9 108¼ 913 913 915	Velasquez J	117	11.60	87-09	Noble Nashua1203½Maudlin1123½Sing Sing1091¾	Outrun	11
15Aug81- 8Sar	sly	1¼	:463 1:112 1:372 2:034		Travers-G1	6 7 811 911 923 726	Vasquez J	126	16.80	55-20	WillowHour126hdPleasantColony1261¾LordAvie1264¼	Outrun	10
2Aug81- 8Sar	fst	1⅛	:47 1:103 1:36 1:491		Jim Dandy-G3	6 7 53 33 31½ 2½	Cordero A Jr	117	3.40	88-11	WillowHour117½LemhiGold117½SilverSupreme114¾	Steadied	8
9Jly81- 9Hol	fm	1Ⓣ	:23 :462 1:103 1:35		ⓇWestwood (Div 2) 40k	6 5 44 62¼ 4¾ 1½	McCarron CJ	114	2..50	94-09	Lemhi Gold114½Rock Softly114hdIsland Whirl115hd	Driving	7
28Mar81- 8SA	fst	1 1/16	:223 :46 1:10 1:42		San Felipe H-G2	6 5 57½ 68 711 58	Pincay L Jr	119	*1.50	83-13	Stancharry118nkSplendidSpruce116½FlyingNshu1211¾	Evenly	12
19Mar81- 7SA	fst	1	:223 :452 1:093 1:351		Alw 22000	5 5 44 44½ 46½ 49	Pincay L Jr	120	*.20	84-07	Torso1144Native Tactics1204½El Jebel109½	Lacked rally	5
8Mar81- 4SA	fst	1	:222 :461 1:11 1:353		©Md Sp Wt	6 8 54½ 31½ 14½ 114	Pincay L Jr	118	*.70	91-11	LemhiGold11814HaloReason118½AtYourPleasure1182½	Easily	8

Life's Magic

b. f. 1981, by Cox's Ridge (Best Turn)–Fire Water, by Tom Rolfe — Lifetime record: 32 8 11 6 $2,255,218

Own.– E.V. Klein
Br.– D.C. Parrish III & Mr & Mrs D. Parrish (Ky)
Tr.– D. Wayne Lukas

Date / Track	Cond	Dist	Fractions	Age	Race	PP St 1st 2nd Str Fin	Jockey	Wt	Odds	Speed	Top finishers	Comment	Field
2Nov85- 5Aqu	fst	1¼	:464 1:112 1:364 2:02	3↑	ⒻBC Distaff-G1	6 7 710 21 11½ 16¼	Cordero A Jr	123	*.40e	86-10	Life'sMgc1236¼Ldy'sScrt1193DontstopThmusc1231¼	Drew off	7
12Oct85- 7Kee	fst	1⅛	:48 1:124 1:373 1:502	3↑	ⒻSpinster-G1	2 10 115½ 72 2½ 22½	Velasquez J	123	*2.20	82-19	DonstopThemusic1232½Life'sMgc1231¼Dowery123½	Wide rally	11
22Sep85- 8Bel	fst	1⅛	:462 1:094 1:343 1:472	3↑	ⒻRuffian H-G1	1 6 57 611 47½ 46¼	Pincay L Jr	120	*.30e	84-17	Lady's Secret1164Isayso1152¼Sintrillium118hd	Mild gain	6
24Aug85- 8Sar	fst	1¼	:474 1:113 1:362 2:02	3↑	ⒻDelaware H-G1	5 5 58 53½ 31 33	Velasquez J	122	*.90e	87-13	Basie1101½Heatherten1261½Life's Magic1222	Wide,weakened	5
3Aug85- 8Sar	fst	1⅛	:474 1:112 1:351 1:473	3↑	Whitney H-G1	5 4 45½ 44½ 45½ 46½	Velasquez J	113	7.60	90-11	TrackBarrn124½CarrdeNskr1204¼Vnlndnghm1241¾	No threat	5
20Jly85- 8Bel	fst	1½	:48 1:12 2:022 2:282	3↑	Brooklyn H-G1	7 5 57 32½ 2½ 2½	Velasquez J	114	6.50	77-22	BoundngBasque111½Life'sMgic1143¾PineCircl1151¾	Gamely	10
4Jly85- 8Bel	fst	1¼	:463 1:10 1:342 2:01	3↑	Suburban H-G1	9 7 911 47 46½ 410	Velasquez J	115	10.60	83-17	Vanlandingham1158¾Carr de Naskra120nkDramatic Desire1091	Mild response	9
9Jun85- 8Bel	gd	1⅛	:474 1:12 1:37 1:484	3↑	ⒻHempstead H-G1	4 4 45½ 42½ 21½ 24¼	Velasquez J	122	1.20	79-18	Heatherten1244¼Lif'sMgc1222¼Sf'sButy1205	Best of others	6
18May85- 8Bel	fst	1 1/16	:23 :462 1:112 1:422	3↑	ⒻShuvee H-G2	4 6 54 32 1½ 12	Velasquez J	121	3.10	90-15	Life'sMagic1212Heatherten1266½SomforAll1096¾	Drew clear	7
												Previously owned by Hatley & Klein	
17Apr85- 9OP	fst	1 1/16	:233 :472 1:104 1:421	4↑	ⒻApple Blossom H-G1	4 6 67½ 53 31½ 34	Velasquez J	123	1.80	86-19	Sefa's Beauty120noHeatherten1274Life's Magic1233½	Carried out str	7
16Mar85- 8SA	fm	1⅛Ⓣ	:461 1:103 1:35 1:47	4↑	ⒻSanta Ana H-G1	1 4 55¾ 62¾ 911 812¼	Valenzuela PA	122	4.30	80-10	Estrapade1236Fact Finder119nkAir Distingue1161¼	Tired	10
3Mar85- 8SA	fst	1¼	:454 1:091 1:342 2:003	4↑	S Anita H-G1	3 5 59½ 55½ 57 44	Valenzuela PA	117	22.40	82-14	Lord at War1251¾Greinton1201Gate Dancer1251¼	Evenly	7
10Feb85- 8SA	fst	1⅛	:462 1:102 1:354 1:484		ⒻLa Canada-G1	4 4 35 33 46 35¼	Velasquez J	126	2.00	80-15	Mitterand121¾Percipient1174½Life's Magic126½	Evenly	5
10Nov84- 5Hol	fst	1¼	:471 1:113 1:37 2:022	3↑	ⒻBC Distaff-G1	5 5 56 33 23 27	Velasquez J	119	3.50	- -	PrincessRooney1237Life'sMagic119¾Adored1232	Held place	7
21Oct84- 8Bel	fst	1¼	:473 1:112 1:37 2:031	3↑	ⒻBeldame-G1	4 2 21 1hd 1½ 13¾	Velasquez J	118	1.40	82-21	Life'sMgic1183¾MissOceana1189¾KeyDancr11818	Ridden out	4
1Sep84- 8Bel	fst	1⅛	:47 1:111 1:351 1:473		ⒻGazelle H-G1	1 2 32 41½ 32½ 32¾	Velasquez J	122	*.70	86-13	Miss Oceana1212Sintra117¾Life's Magic122hd	Weakened	5
11Aug84- 8Sar	fst	1¼	:48 1:114 1:363 2:023		ⒻAlabama-G1	2 3 21 2½ 2½ 1hd	Velasquez J	121	*.80e	87-15	Life'sMgc121hdLuckyLuckyLucky12115½ClssPly1213¾	Driving	5
21Jly84- 9Mth	sly	1⅛	:473 1:113 1:371 1:50		ⒻMth Oaks-G2	2 6 74½ 1hd 12 16½	Velasquez J	121	*.50	85-16	Life's Magic1216½Flippers1181Cassowary1124	Driving	10
7Jly84- 8Bel	sly	1½	:50 1:15 2:043 2:294		ⒻC C A Oaks-G1	3 2 24 31 21½ 21½	Velasquez J	121	*.40e	69-16	ClassPlay1211½Life'sMagc1212¼MssOcn12122	Best of others	5
16Jun84- 8Bel	fst	1⅛	:453 1:093 1:352 1:484		ⒻMother Goose-G1	1 5 55 53 11½ 13¼	Velasquez J	121	1.60	83-22	Life's Magic1213¼Miss Oceana121¾Wild Applause1214¼	Off slowly,clear	5
26May84- 8Bel	fst	1	:23 :453 1:102 1:354		ⒻAcorn-G1	3 9 89¼ 54 22½ 2nk	Velasquez J	121	2.70e	86-15	MissOceana121nkLif'sMgc1215½ProudClronss121no	Sharp try	9
5May84- 8CD	fst	1¼	:472 1:114 1:363 2:022		Ky Derby-G1	5 13 138 86¼ 88¼ 88	Brumfield D	121	*2.80e	77-19	Swale1263¼CoaxMeChad1262AttheThreshold126nk	No factor	20
8Apr84- 8SA	fst	1⅛	:452 1:10 1:36 1:49		S A Derby-G1	1 7 714 611 69½ 59	Cordero A Jr	115 b	9.20e	75-16	MightyAdversry1201¼Precisonst120nkPrncTru1202½	Checked	8
												Previously owned M.E. Hatley	
11Mar84- 8SA	fst	1 1/16	:232 :472 1:113 1:433		ⒻS Susana-G1	1 5 43 42 42 3¾	Cordero A Jr	115	2.80	82-18	Althea117¾Personable Lady115hdLife's Magic1154	Rallied	5
16Feb84- 7SA	fst	1	:23 :463 1:114 1:38		ⒻAlw 35000	6 5 53 42½ 22½ 21½	Pincay L Jr	119	*.30	76-23	VagabondGal1171½Life'sMgc1191½Dchrony119no	Wide,bumped	6
18Dec83- 8Hol	fst	1 1/16	:222 :454 1:101 1:413		Hol Futurity-G1	10 9 88½ 71½ 44½ 34	Cordero A Jr	118	10.80	83-14	FaliTime121½BoldT.Jay1213½Life'sMagic1183	Fin. strong	12
27Nov83- 8Hol	fst	1 1/16	:23 :464 1:112 1:43		ⒻHol Starlet-G2	5 5 41¼ 21 32 21½	McCarron CJ	120	2.00	78-20	Althea1201½Life's Magic120hdSpring Loose1202½	Gamely	6
12Nov83- 8SA	sly	1 1/16	:224 :463 1:113 1:442		ⒻOak Leaf-G1	5 7 44½ 21½ 2½ 1½	McCarron CJ	115	1.80	79-23	Life's Magic115½Althea11717Percipient115hd	Driving	9
5Nov83- 8SA	fst	1 1/16	:23 :464 1:113 1:441		Norfolk-G1	8 7 51¾ 42 31 2no	Pincay L Jr	117	2.00	80-20	FaliTime118noLife'sMgc117¾Artchok1182	Wide into stretch	10
10Oct83- 8Bel	fst	1	:224 :454 1:101 1:363		ⒻFrizette-G1	10 9 74¼ 32½ 32½ 2no	Cordero A Jr	119	*1.50e	82-15	Miss Oceana119noLife's Magic1192Lucky Lucky Lucky1198¾	Just missed	10
4Sep83- 8AP	fst	7f	:22 :442 1:094 1:232		ⒻArl-Wash Lassie-G1	5 11 910 812 38 23¾	Shoemaker W	119	3.40	81-22	MissOceana1193¾Life'sMgc1194BottlTop1193	Circled horses	11
25Aug83- 3Dmr	fst	6f	:221 :454 :591 1:121		ⒻAlw 17000	3 7 714 611 44 12	Pincay L Jr	117	4.00	77-22	Life's Magic1172Diachrony1184½Early Quest118¾	Driving	7

Lord Avie

b. c. 1978, by Lord Gaylord (Sir Gaylord)–Avie, by Gallant Man — **Lifetime record: 16 8 4 4 $705,977**

Own.– S K S Stable
Br.– Viking Farms Ltd (Ky)
Tr.– Daniel Perlsweig

15Aug81- 8Sar	sly	1¼	:463 1:112 1:372 2:034	Travers-G1	7	10	1026	68¾	45½	31¾	Velasquez J	126		3.90	79-20	Willow Hour126hdPleasant Colony1261¾Lord Avie1264¼	Wide	10
1Aug81- 8Mth	fst	1⅛	:473 1:104 1:352 1:482	Haskell Inv'l H-G1	5	5	55	21½	23	25	Velasquez J	126		*.50	88-12	FiveStarFlight1195LordAv1265OrnryOdis112½	Best of others	6
14Jly81- 8Mth	fst	1 70	:233 :474 1:122 1:421	3↑ Alw 17000	3	5	513	48	22½	12	Velasquez J	116		*.20	85-27	Lord Avie1162Bold Josh1225Corre Pronto1138	Ridden out	5
6Mar81- 9GP	fst	1⅛	:47 1:111 1:374 1:502	Florida Derby-G1	4	8	916	56¼	1½	14½	McCarron CJ	122		*1.00	80-17	Lord Avie12241½Akureyri122¾Linnleur1186	Ridden out	11
16Feb81- 9GP	fst	1 1/16	:241 :48 1:121 1:442	Fountain of Youth-G3	3	6	711	75¾	41¼	3hd	McCarron CJ	122		*.40	79-23	Akureyri119noPleasant Colony122hdLord Avie1221½	Rallied	9
4Feb81- 9GP	fst	7f	:223 :452 1:101 1:232	Hutcheson 56k	2	5	713	516	45½	1hd	McCarron CJ	122		*.30	87-22	LordAvie122hdSpiritdBoy1141½Lnnlur1142½	Brushed,driving	7
1Nov80- 6Med	fst	1 1/16	:224 :46 1:113 1:443	Young America-G1	2	7	812	76	2½	11½	Velasquez J	122		*.40	86-19	Lord Avie1221½Sezyou1191¼Financial Genius1193	Driving	10
12Oct80- 8Bel	fst	1	:23 :461 1:113 1:371	Champagne-G1	7	9	76¼	64¼	21	12¼	Velasquez J	122		3.40	82-19	Lord Avie1222¼Noble Nashua1224Sezyou1221¾	Ridden out	9
28Sep80- 8Bel	fst	7f	:224 :463 1:111 1:233	Cowdin-G2	3	7	64	21	1hd	12¼	Velasquez J	119		1.80	84-22	LordAvie1192¼Akureyri1153Dasho'Pleasure1151¾	Ridden out	7
6Sep80- 8AP	fst	7f	:221 :444 1:11 1:234	Arl Wash Futurity-G1	12	11	108¾	68	2hd	22	Bailey JD	122	b	*2.80	81-20	WellDecoratd1222LrdAv122noFrwyPhntom122no	Bid,weakened	15
23Aug80- 8Sar	fst	6½f	:222 :453 1:103 1:17	Hopeful-G1	6	9	93¾	72¾	42½	22	Bailey JD	122	b	3.20	85-17	Tap Shoes1222Lord Avie1226Well Decorated122nk	Bore in	9
9Aug80- 9Mth	fst	6f	:22 :45 1:11	Sapling-G1	2	8	76	54¼	25	2¾	Bailey JD	122	b	3.40	84-19	TravellingMusic122¾LordAvie1225½TimelessEvent122hd	Wide	8
21Jly80- 8Bel	fst	6f	:222 :46 1:112	Tremont-G3	4	3	64¾	67¾	55½	31	Bailey JD	122		4.80	84-24	GoldnDerby122hdGretProspctor1151LrdAv1223¾	Raced wide	9
7Jly80- 8Bel	fst	5½f	:224 :461 :582 1:043	Juvenile 53k	1	2	42½	42¼	21½	1½	Bailey JD	115		12.20	92-16	Lord Avie115½Jiggs Alarm1159Mambo1131	Driving	5
25Jun80- 3Mth	fst	5f	:214 :454 :581	Md Sp Wt	6	4	24	22	11	1½	Bailey JD	118		*1.00	95-10	LordAvie118½ClosetheCase1188¼SteelCurtain1181¼	Driving	7
17Jun80- 6Mth	fst	5f	:22 :454 :582	Md Sp Wt	6	3	31½	31	35	32	Bailey JD	118		17.90	92-16	TravllngMusc118noGrtProspctr1182LrdAv1185½	Came again	10

Manila

b. c. 1983, by Lyphard (Northern Dancer)–Dona Ysidra, by Le Fabuleux — **Lifetime record: 18 12 5 0 $2,692,799**

Own.– B.M. Shannon
Br.– E.M. Cojuangco Jr (Ky)
Tr.– Leroy Jolley

6Sep87- 8AP	fm	1¼Ⓣ	:482 1:133 1:383 2:022	3↑ Bud Arl Million-G1	3	4	43	41½	13	11½	Cordero A Jr	126		*1.00	82-27	Manila1261½Sharrood1263¼Theatrical1263¾	Driving	8
16Aug87- 8Sar	fm	1⅛Ⓣ	:48 1:104 1:341 1:472	3↑ Bernard Baruch H-G2	3	2	2½	2hd	1hd	2½	Vasquez J	127		*.30	89-08	Talakeno115½Manila127¾Duluth1142	Just failed	4
15Jly87- 4Atl	sf	1 3/16Ⓣ	:512 1:161 1:411 1:584	3↑ U Nations H-G1	3	2	2½	1½	11	12½	Vasquez J	124		*.10	69-33	Manila1242½Racing Star1153Air Display110no	Ridden out	5
1May87- 8CD	fm	1⅛Ⓣ	:49 1:122 1:363 1:484	4↑ E T Turf Classic 169k	2	2	21	2½	12½	13	Vasquez J	120		*.40	- -	Manila1203Vilzak1121Lieutenant's Lark1202¼	Ridden out	4
14Apr87- 7Kee	fm	1⅛Ⓣ	:461 1:104 1:361 1:482	4↑ Elkhorn 53k	5	4	43	31½	1hd	13	Vasquez J	113		*.40e	115-00	Manila1133Lieutennt'sLrk1127½RoylTrsurr1122¼	Ridden out	7
1Nov86- 6SA	fm	1½Ⓣ	:472 1:111 2:003 2:252	3↑ BC Turf-G1	2	4	43½	32	31½	1nk	Santos JA	122		8.80	88-07	Manila122nkTheatrical1263¾Estrapad1232¾	Checked,just up	9
20Sep86- 8Bel	hd	1½Ⓣ	:511 1:164 2:042 2:274	3↑ Turf Classic-G1	9	3	41½	21	2hd	1no	Santos JA	119		*.90	85-10	Manila119noDamister126nkDanger's Hour1261½	Just up	9
5Sep86- 9Med	yl	1⅜Ⓣ	:484 1:144 1:401 2:184	3↑ Ball Scotch Classic-G3	8	4	45	31	13½	19½	Santos JA	120		*.70	71-29	Manila1209½I'm a Banker1263Fiery Celt1264½	Ridden out	9
9Aug86- 7Atl	fm	1 3/16Ⓣ	:471 1:103 1:343 1:523	3↑ U Nations H-G1	2	4	44	31	21	11¼	Santos JA	114		2.80	101-08	Manila1141¼UptownSwell116hdLieutenant'sLrk1214½	Driving	8
12Jly86- 8Bel	yl	1¼[T]	:494 1:14 1:39 2:031	Lexington-G2	5	5	74¾	34	21½	1no	Santos JA	126		*1.70e	78-22	Manila126noGlow1233¾Dance Card Filled1141½	Long drive	10
7Jun86- 8Hol	fm	1⅛Ⓣ	:474 1:114 1:351 1:47	Cinema H-G2	4	4	44	42	31½	12½	Toro F	117		3.50	97-02	Manl1172½VrnonCstl1202½FullofStrs115no	Blocked,drew out	10
18May86- 8Bel	fm	1Ⓣ	:224 :453 1:093 1:343	Saranac-G2	9	8	911	87½	55	21¾	Velasquez J	114		*.70e	90-13	Glow1141¾Manila114nkPillaster1201¼	Checked st.	11
17Apr86- 7Kee	yl	1 1/16Ⓣ	:234 :484 1:144 1:483	Forerunner 56k	6	9	53	31	22	22½	Velez RI	118		*1.10	84-13	Autobot1122½Manila1183½Glow1124¼	2nd best	10
9Apr86- 7Kee	fm	1 1/16Ⓣ	:233 :504 1:16 1:492	Alw 33510	1	3	22	2½	14	17¼	Velez RI	111		*.90	83-17	Manila1117¼SharpGinistrelli1112½AerialDisply1123	Easily	6
18Mar86-10Hia	fst	1 1/16⊗	:232 :462 1:113 1:431	Md Sp Wt	5	2	21	11	12	18	Velez RI	119		*.40	87-16	Manila1198NudistColony11911CaptainKingwell1191	Driving	9
	Previously owned by E.M. Cojuangco Jr																	
23Oct85- 6Aqu	fst	1	:241 :481 1:124 1:382	Md Sp Wt	1	7	62½	41½	22	21¼	Cordero A Jr	118		2.40	73-17	Fabulous Flight1181¼Manila1182½Man Up118hd	Poor start	8
21Aug85- 6Sar	fst	6f	:222 :461 1:113	Md Sp Wt	3	4	65¼	56	45½	22	Cordero A Jr	118		11.00	80-14	PerfectbyFar1182Manila118½RoyalDoulton1182½	Wide str.	12
3Aug85- 3Sar	fst	6f	:221 :453 1:114	Md Sp Wt	1	13	34	47	79½	78	Cruguet J	118		8.70	73-11	RelCourg1182¼ProudWorld118hdArMco1183½	Slow start,tired	13

Miesque

b. f. 1984, by Nureyev (Northern Dancer)–Pasadoble, by Prove Out — **Lifetime record: 16 12 3 1 $1,987,514**

Own.– Flaxman Holdings Ltd
Br.– Flaxman Holdings Ltd (Ky)
Tr.– Francois Boutin

5Nov88- 7CD	gd	1Ⓣ	:233 :472 1:123 1:383	3↑ B C Mile-G1	8	7	67	32½	2hd	14	Head F	123		2.00e	96-04	Miesque1234Steinlen126hdSimply Majestic1261¼	Driving	12
4Sep88♦ Longchamp(Fr)	sf	*1ⓉRH	1:403	3↑ Prix du Moulin de Longchamp-G1 Stk243000						2hd	Head F	124		*.20e		Soviet Star128hdMiesque1245Gabina1204	Tracked in 4th,rail bid 1½f out,held by winner	7
14Aug88♦ Deauville(Fr)	gd	*1ⓉStr	1:383	3↑ Prix Jacques le Marois-G1 Stk160000						11	Head F	124		*.60		Miesque1241Warning1212Gabina118no	Rated toward rear,rallied to lead 1f out,ridden out	6
29May88♦ Longchamp(Fr)	sf	*1⅛ⓉRH	1:551	4↑ Prix d'Ispahan-G1 Stk131000						1nk	Head F	124		*.20e		Miesque124nkSt Andrews1281½Jalaajel128hd	Rated in 4th,lacked room 1f out,strong run to lead late	6
21Nov87- 4Hol	fm	1Ⓣ	:231 :453 1:09 1:324	3↑ B C Mile-G1	4	5	33½	32	12	13½	Head F	120		3.60	103-00	Miesque1203½Show Dancer126½Sonic Lady1231	Ridden out	14
26Sep87♦ Ascot(GB)	gd	1ⓉRH	1:40	3↑ Queen Elizabeth II Stakes-G1 Stk395000						22½	Cauthen S	120		*.25		Milligram1202½Miesque1205Sonic Lady123	Tracked in 3rd,ridden and drifted left 1f out,second best	5
6Sep87♦ Longchamp(Fr)	yl	*1ⓉRH	1:372	3↑ Prix du Moulin de Longchamp-G1 Stk282000						12½	Head F	120		*.10e		Miesque1202½Soviet Star1231Grecian Urn1202½	Tracked in 4th,3rd 2f out,led 2f out,drew clear 1f out	7
16Aug87♦ Deauville(Fr)	gd	*1ⓉStr	1:35	3↑ Prix Jacques le Marois-G1 Stk190000						13	Head F	118		*.70e		Miesque1183Nashmeel1182½Hadeer128½	Rated at rear,rallied to lead over 1f out,handily	9
14Jun87♦ Chantilly(Fr)	sf	*1 5/16ⓉRH	2:112	ⒻPrix de Diane (French Oaks)-G1 Stk390000						24	Head F	128		1.80e		Indian Skimmer1284Miesque128¾Masmoud1281	Never far away,4th 3f out,2nd 1f out,chased winner home	11
17May87♦ Longchamp(Fr)	sf	*1ⓉRH	1:38	ⒻPoule d'Essai des Pouliches-G1 Stk285000						12½	Head F	128		*.20e		Miesque1282½Sakura Reiko1283Libertine128hd	Rated in last,rallied to lead 150y out,going away	8
30Apr87♦ Newmarket(GB)	gd	1ⓉStr	1:382	Ⓕ1000 Guineas Stakes-G1 Stk229000						11½	Head F	126		*1.85		Miesque1261½Milligram126hdInterval1263	Rated at rear,angled out over 1f out,led 100y out,handily	14
3Apr87♦ Maisns-Lfftte(Fr)	hy	*7fⓉStr	1:332	ⒻPrix Imprudence (Listed) Stk33600						12½	Head F	128		*.30e		Miesque1282½Grecian Urn1282Musimara128nk	Well placed in 3rd,led 150y out,easily	5
5Oct86♦ Longchamp(Fr)	fm	*1ⓉRH	1:372	ⒻPrix Marcel Boussac-G1 Stk107000						1½	Head F	121	b	*1.40e		Miesque121½Milligram121nkSakura Reiko1212	Unhurried in last,strong late run to lead near line	11
21Sep86♦ Longchamp(Fr)	yl	*7fⓉRH	1:252	Prix de la Salamandre-G1 Stk113000						11½	Head F	120	b	3.60e		Miesque1201½Sakura Reiko1203Whakilyric1201	Rated at rear,sharp run to lead 170y out,driving	10
24Aug86♦ Deauville(Fr)	sf	*6fⓉStr	1:142	Prix Morny-G1 Stk95400						31	Head F	120	b	7.20		Sakura Reiko1201Shy Princess120noMiesque1203	Close up,led 150y to 170y out,lost 2nd on line	8
9Aug86♦ Deauville(Fr)	gd	*6fⓉStr	1:143	Prix de Lisieux Mdn (FT)20700						12	Head F	123	b	4.00		Miesque1232Proflare1231Lumen Dei1231	Tracked leader,led 1f out,ridden out	6

Mom's Command

ch. f. 1982, by Top Command (Bold Ruler)–Star Mommy, by Pia Star **Lifetime record: 16 11 2 1 $902,972**

Own.– P. Fuller
Br.– Peter Fuller (Ky)
Tr.– Edward T. Allard

Date	Cond	Dist	Fractions	Race	PP	St	1st	2nd	Str	Fin	Jockey	Wt	Odds	Spd	Top three	Comment	Fld
10Aug85- 8Sar	fst	1¼	:464 1:104 1:363 2:031	ⒻAlabama-G1	2	1	12½	14	14½	14	Fuller A	121	*.60	84-16	Mm'sCmmnd1214Fran'sValntn1213½FoxyDn12114	Ridden out	5
1Aug85- 8Sar	gd	7f	:221 :444 1:09 1:213	ⒻTest-G2	2	5	1hd	2hd	31½	22	Fuller A	124	*.50	92-13	Lady's Secret1212Mom's Command124nkMajestic Folly118½		10
	Gained place																
6Jly85- 8Bel	fst	1½	:461 1:103 2:031 2:32	ⒻC C A Oaks-G1	8	1	12	15	17	12½	Fuller A	121	*.50	60-20	Mom'sCmmnd1212½Bssrbn1214FoxyDn121½	Drifted out,clear	9
15Jun85- 8Bel	fst	1⅛	:45 1:092 1:493	ⒻMother Goose-G1	1	1	12	11½	14½	15½	Fuller A	121	*1.40	79-18	Mm'sCmmnd1215½LL'Argnt121nkWllowyMood1215¼	Ridden out	11
25May85- 8Bel	fst	1	:22 :441 1:09 1:354	ⒻAcorn-G1	8	1	17	16	14	13	Fuller A	121	*.70	86-11	Mm'sCmmnd1213LeL'Argent1219½Diplomette1211¼	Handily	8
11May85- 8Bel	fst	7f	:22 :443 1:091 1:221	ⒻComely-G3	9	1	11½	11	12	14½	Fuller A	121	2.30	91-12	Mom'sCommnd1214½Majestic Folly1131¾Clocks Secret1214¾		9
	Ridden out																
19Apr85- 8GS	fst	1 1/16	:23 :462 1:102 1:413	ⒻCherry Blossom H 117k	8	1	12½	11½	13	14	Fuller A	121	*1.10	- -	Mm'sCmmnd1214GoldenSilenc1136WllowyMood1181¾	Handily	10
11Apr85- 8GS	fst	6f	:212 :433 1:082	ⒻGoldfinch H 66k	1	5	2½	22½	25	22½	Fuller A	123	*.50	- -	ClocksScrt1142½Mm'sCmmnd123nkWllowyMood1205	Drifted out	6
23Mar85- 9Pim	sly	6f	:23 :46 :582 1:104	ⒻFlirtation 32k	5	1	13½	16	18	119	Fuller A	119	*.40	92-21	Mm'sCommnd11919AppealingGirl1192¼ClassyCut1142	Easily	5
2Dec84- 8Hol	fst	1 1/16	:222 :454 1:104 1:44	ⒻHol Starlet-G1	16	3	3nk	1½	1hd	57	Fuller A	120	16.20	- -	Outstndngly1202¾Fran'sValntn1202½WsngUp120nk	Weakened	16
27Oct84- 8Lrl	fst	1 1/16	:224 :454 1:104 1:433	ⒻSelima-G1	4	1	12½	15	16	12¼	McCarron G	119	17.10	90-13	Mom'sCommand1192¼Diplomette119½Soliciting1192	Driving	7
14Oct84- 8Bel	fst	1	:222 :452 1:114 1:39	ⒻFrizette-G1	2	1	13	2½	3½	35¾	Fuller A	119	5.40	64-28	Charleston Rag1195¾Tiltalating119noMom's Command1191¼		6
	Off poorly,weakened																
12Sep84- 8Bel	fst	6½f	:221 :452 1:11 1:174	ⒻAstarita-G2	2	10	11	2hd	12	11¼	Fuller A	116	19.10	87-14	Mom's Command1161¼Self Image1125¾Winter's Love112no		10
	Poor start,clear																
27Aug84- 8Sar	fst	6f	:221 :452 1:11	ⒻSpinaway-G1	2	6	31½	35½	45	46¼	Fuller A	119	15.30	79-16	Tiltalating1191¼Socible Duck1193½Contredance1191½		7
	Steadied at start																
4Aug84-10Suf	fst	6f	:221 :453 :581 1:113	ⒻPriscilla 25k	5	2	2hd	2hd	1hd	1¾	Fuller A	116	3.40	83-21	Mm'sCmmnd116¾SheerIce1168½MyFriendFran1161½	Driving	8
17Jly84- 8Rkm	fst	5f	:221 :464 1:00	ⒻⓇFaneuil Miss 10k	5	11	85	66¼	44	1hd	Carrasco B	113	44.70	84-21	Mm'sCmmnd113hdCircleFoot113nkMyFriendFrn113½	Driving	11

North Sider

dkbbr. f. 1982, by Topsider (Northern Dancer)–Back Ack, by Ack Ack **Lifetime record: 36 15 7 5 $1,126,400**

Own.– Mrs Audrey Reed
Br.– Cisley Stable–Robert P. Levy (Ky)
Tr.– D. Wayne Lukas

Date	Cond	Dist	Fractions	Race	PP	St	1st	2nd	Str	Fin	Jockey	Wt	Odds	Spd	Top three	Comment	Fld
21Nov87- 3Hol	fst	1¼	:471 1:113 1:364 2:024	3↑ ⒻBC Distaff-G1	2	4	54½	67½	614	625½	McCarron CJ	123	7.70	52-12	Sacahuista1192¼Clabber Girl1234Oueee Bebe119hd	Weakened	6
	Previously owned by Paternostro & Lukas																
31Oct87- 8Kee	fst	1⅛	:462 1:101 1:354 1:483	3↑ ⒻSpinster-G1	3	7	62¼	53½	87¾	911½	Perret C	123	*1.40e	82-14	Sacahuista1193Ms. Margi1192½Tall Poppy123no	Tired	13
27Sep87- 8Bel	fst	1⅛	:462 1:092 1:35 1:483	3↑ ⒻRuffian H-G1	7	6	64½	63¼	78	106¼	Pincay L Jr	122	*.40e	78-19	[D]Sacahuista114hdCoupdeFusil1171¾ClabberGirl112½	Tired	12
12Sep87- 8Bel	fst	1	:223 :444 1:092 1:35	3↑ ⒻMaskette-G1	6	3	32	2hd	2hd	1nk	Cordero A Jr	123	1.20e	90-19	NorthSider123nkWisla1163¼Funistrad116nk	Strong handling	7
14Aug87- 8Sar	fst	7f	:213 :44 1:092 1:223	3↑ ⒻBallerina-G2	4	3	34½	33½	3nk	44	Romero RP	122	*.80e	85-21	I'mSweets119¾StormandSunshine1163PineTrLn122nk	Weakened	5
19Jly87- 8Hol	fst	1¼	:453 1:091 1:344 2:003	3↑ ⒻVanity Inv'l H-G1	7	1	11	12	2½	26½	Pincay L Jr	121	2.90	82-07	Infinidad1136½North Sider1212¾Clabber Girl1151¾	Tired	7
28Jun87- 8Bel	fst	7f	:222 :454 1:104 1:241	3↑ ⒻVagrancy H-G3	1	2	31½	31	11	12	Cordero A Jr	121	2.30	81-19	NorthSidr1212StormandSunshine1172¾Funstrd1145½	Driving	6
20Jun87- 9Mth	fst	1 70	:233 :464 1:101 1:393	3↑ ⒻBud Breeders' H 155k	3	1	11	12½	13	12½	Perret C	120	*.90	98-13	NorthSidr1202½BarbicueSauce112nkCoupdeFusl1133	Handily	7
5Jun87- 8Bel	gd	1⅛	:481 1:121 1:37 1:50	3↑ ⒻHempstead H-G1	2	1	12	13	1½	54	Cordero A Jr	120	*.90	73-19	Catatonic116hdMs. Eloise1181Steal a Kiss1111½	Weakened	7
16May87- 8Bel	fst	1 1/16	:224 :453 1:102 1:414	3↑ ⒻShuvee H-G1	10	2	22½	2hd	11½	2no	Day P	120	*1.90	93-18	Ms.Eloise117noNorthSidr1207½Clmnn'sRos1141¾	Just failed	10
1May87- 7CD	fst	1 1/16	:24 :48 1:113 1:424	3↑ ⒻBud BC H 154k	2	3	42½	2½	22½	46	Cordero A Jr	123	*.40e	88-12	QueenAlxandra117¾Infndd1162½I'mSwts1162¾	Flattened out	6
15Apr87- 9OP	fst	1 1/16	:232 :463 1:101 1:411	4↑ ⒻApple Blossom H-G1	1	2	1hd	11	13	14	Cordero A Jr	122	*.30e	95-18	NorthSidr1224FamilyStyle1202QuenAlxndr1192½	Ridden out	7
3Apr87- 9OP	fst	1 1/16	:224 :461 1:111 1:421	3↑ ⒻBud BC H 133k	1	3	33	2hd	12½	14	Cordero A Jr	121	*1.30	90-17	NorthSider1214QueenAlexandra1221¾Ann'sBid1232¼	Easily	8
17Mar87- 8SA	fm	1⅛Ⓣ	:481 1:114 1:36 1:48	4↑ ⒻS Ana H-G1	5	5	52½	43	34½	35½	Cordero A Jr	120	5.80	81-17	Reloy1162Northern Aspen1193½North Sider120½	Evenly	7
1Mar87- 8SA	fst	1⅛	:454 1:103 1:36 1:484	4↑ ⒻS Margarita Inv'l H-G1	5	5	54½	41	11½	1hd	Cordero A Jr	117	2.40e	85-15	NorthSider117hdWinterTreasure1151¼FrauAltv117nk	Driving	12
	Previously owned by Lettuce Farm & Paternostro																
7Feb87- 8SA	fst	1 1/16	:224 :461 1:103 1:423	4↑ ⒻS Maria H-G2	6	2	23	2½	1½	2¾	Delahoussaye E	118	11.70	87-14	Fran's Valentine121¾North Sider1182Infinidad1131	Gamely	8
28Jan87- 7SA	fst	1 1/16	:232 :47 1:113 1:441	4↑ ⒻAlw 45000	3	2	21½	1hd	12½	12	Pincay L Jr	118	*1.90	80-21	North Sider1182Ambra Ridge1141¼Sign Off1151¾	Drew out	8
2Nov86- 8BM	fst	1 1/16	:233 :47 1:111 1:431	3↑ ⒻⓇWatch Wndy H 50k	6	2	1hd	11	11½	13	Baze RA	123	*.90	76-21	NorthSider1233Hertlftr1167GoldnTk1151	Dueled,ridden out	6
	Restricted to horses stabled at Bay Meadows																
12Oct86- 8BM	fst	1 1/16	:241 :473 1:122 1:433	3↑ ⒻTizna H 49k	2	3	31½	31½	2hd	2¾	Baze RA	123	*.70	73-19	Good Zar114¾North Sider123nkPetillante1154	Bid,failed	4
4Oct86- 6BM	fst	1	:231 :47 1:112 1:362	3↑ ⒻⓇBerry Bush H 25k	2	2	2½	1½	1hd	1no	Baze RA	121	*.60	86-16	North Sider121noWine Taster114nkBarbie Karen1145	Gamely	8
23Aug86- 9Aks	fst	1⅛	:494 1:15 1:403 1:55	3↑ ⒻQueen's H-G3	8	5	32	31	1hd	34	Baze RA	115	2.40	58-36	Oriental117Beauty Cream111North Sider115	Bumped start	9
26Jly86- 7Aks	fst	1 1/16	:24 :471 1:114 1:44	3↑ ⒻBud BC 123k	8	2	1hd	13	12	22½	Baze RA	115	2.00	80-23	Oriental1152½North Sider1153½Crystal Pleat1182	No match	9
4Jly86- 5Hol	fm	6fⓉ	:22 :444 1:083	3↑ ⒻHandicap 35000	5	3	1½	11	2½	54½	Delahoussaye E	118	7.40	94-00	Aberuschka1222Loucoum1152½Bold n Special110hd	Weakened	7
20Jun86- 8Hol	fst	6f	:221 :452 :57 1:092	3↑ ⒻAlw 35000	2	5	41¾	42½	67	612¼	McCarron CJ	122	2.10	85-11	BoldNSpcl109½FolkArt1174Conn'sTj117hd	Bumped hard start	6
7Jun86- 5Hol	fm	6fⓉ	:223 :452 :564 1:084	3↑ ⒻHandicap 35000	2	6	41¼	42	42½	43	Valenzuela PA	121	3.40	95-02	Lichi115noLoucoum1152½Regal Ties113½	Steadied break	6
9Feb86- 8SA	fst	1⅛	:464 1:11 1:363 1:494	ⒻLa Canada-G1	2	4	42½	43½	33½	35¼	Delahoussaye E	118	6.80	75-16	Lady'sSecret1261¼Shywing1194NrthSidr1181¾	Bobbled start	6
1Feb86- 8SA	my	1 1/16	:221 :453 1:12 1:443	4↑ ⒻS Maria H-G2	3	5	611	42½	34	35¾	Baze RA	118	5.20	72-24	LoveSmittn1202¼Johnc1213½NorthSdr1186	Wide into stretch	9
15Jan86- 8SA	fst	7f	:221 :44 1:084 1:213	4↑ ⒻS Monica H-G3	4	2	32½	45	33	21¼	Pincay L Jr	119	12.80	91-14	HerRoyalty1201¼NrthSidr1192TkMyPctur117½	Saved ground	8
	Previously owned by Lettuce Farm																
28Dec85- 8BM	fst	1 1/16	:232 :47 1:104 1:414	ⒻBM Deb 51k	1	3	32	31	2½	12½	Baze RA	125	*.40	83-14	NorthSider1252½CementCreek1143½BubbleBite118hd	Handily	8
15Dec85- 8BM	fst	6f	:222 :451 :573 1:092	ⒻFoster City 48k	7	1	21	13	14	14	Baze RA	122	*.40	92-20	NorthSider1224ImpressiveAnnie1171BubbleBite1222	Easily	7
23Nov85- 8BM	fst	1 1/16	:233 :472 1:104 1:413	ⒻSan Jose H 51k	2	5	3nk	1½	15	15	Baze RA	114	*1.50	84-15	NorthSider1145BubbleBite113nkRascalLass1202	Ridden out	7
18Nov85- 8BM	fst	1	:232 :473 1:12 1:362	3↑ ⒻAlw 18000	4	3	31	41½	14	15	Baze RA	114	*.70	86-20	North Sider1145Normira1097Renee's Lark1161	Much best	8
24Oct85- 8BM	fst	6f	:224 :461 :581 1:104	3↑ ⒻAlw 17000	6	8	76½	44½	42¼	23	Baze RA	117	*.60	82-23	Abstract Energy1173North Sider117noPirate Annie117hd		8
	Fractious in gate,broke in a tangle,very wide into stretch																
14Oct85- 4BM	fst	6f	:222 :453 :57 1:092	ⒻAlw 13000	6	4	23	2hd	16	17	Baze RA	120	*.90	92-18	NorthSidr1207Hylnd'sHHop1131½Prsuson1091	Not threatened	7
20Sep85- 1BM	fst	6f	:223 :453 :574 1:101	3↑ ⒻMd Sp Wt	1	2	1hd	1½	14	16	Baze RA	116	*.90	88-17	NrthSidr1166SharpBrd116½MnhttnMgc116no	Not threatened	6
13Sep85- 6Bmf	fst	6f	:224 :453 :581 1:11	3↑ ⒻMd Sp Wt	6	4	1hd	2hd	21½	31¼	Baze RA	117	*.70	81-24	PeggyDee1173NobHillNative117nkNorthSidr117no	Weakened	10

Open Mind

ch. f. 1986, by Deputy Minister (Vice Regent)–Stage Luck, by Stage Door Johnny — Lifetime record: 19 12 2 2 $1,844,372

Own.– K. Makamura
Br.– Due Process Stables (NJ)
Tr.– D. Wayne Lukas

2Sep90- 8Bel	fst 1	:23 :452 1:094 1:353 3↑	(F)Maskette H-G1	2 6 611 611 613 610½	Krone JA	123	2.80e	80-13	Go for Wand118²½Feel the Beat123noMistaurian1164	Outrun	6
10Aug90- 8Sar	fst 7f	:221 :45 1:091 1:22 3↑	(F)Ballerina-G1	3 8 713 812 511 511¼	Stevens GL	119	2.80e	84-13	FeeltheBeat1192FantasticFind1164ProperEvidence1192	Wide	8
Previously owned by E.V. Klein											
4Nov89- 6GP	fst 1⅛	:462 1:111 1:353 1:472 3↑	(F)BC Distaff-G1	9 8 813 87½ 37 33¾	Cordero A Jr	119	5.20e	103-01	Bayakoa1231½Gorgeous1192¼Open Mind1195	Mild rally	10
15Oct89- 8Bel	fst 1¼	:491 1:131 1:383 2:051 3↑	(F)Beldame-G1	6 5 511 66¾ 57½ 57	Cordero A Jr	118	*.80	59-38	Tactile118nkColonialWaters1234½Ros'sCntn123¼	No factor	6
24Sep89- 8Bel	fst 1⅛	:47 1:112 1:36 1:482 3↑	(F)Ruffian H-G1	5 5 56½ 43½ 21½ 33¾	Cordero A Jr	120	2.00	81-24	Bayakoa1253½ColonlWaters118nkOpnMnd1209	Bid,weakened	6
12Aug89- 8Sar	my 1¼	:493 1:15 1:394 2:041	(F)Alabama-G1	4 7 715 55 33½ 1nk	Cordero A Jr	121	*.20e	79-23	OpnMind121nkDearlyLoved1211¾DreamDl1215	Up final yards	7
3Jly89- 8Bel	fst 1½	:483 1:124 2:042 2:322	(F)C C A Oaks-G1	4 3 22 2hd 22 2no	Cordero A Jr	121	*.30	58-21	(D)NiteofFun121noOpnMind12120RoseDiamond1211½	Impeded	6
Placed first through disqualification											
11Jun89- 8Bel	fst 1⅛	:463 1:102 1:344 1:472	(F)Mother Goose-G1	4 5 52 2½ 1hd 1hd	Cordero A Jr	121	*.30	90-19	Open Mind121hdGorgeous12118Nite of Fun1212½	Driving	5
27May89- 8Bel	sly 1	:221 :45 1:101 1:352	(F)Acorn-G1	8 11 98½ 2hd 11 14½	Cordero A Jr	121	*.40e	88-18	Open Mind1214½Hot Novel1214Triple Strike1212	Drew clear	11
5May89- 9CD	sly 1⅛	:48 1:121 1:373 1:503	(F)Ky Oaks-G1	2 4 33½ 24 21 12¼	Cordero A Jr	121	*.30e	89-19	OpnMnd1212¼ImaginaryLady1218Blondeinmotl1216½	Driving	5
1Apr89-11Lrl	fst 1116	:234 :464 1:111 1:43	(F)Pim Oaks 200k	1 7 78 42¾ 31 12	Cordero A Jr	122	*.40	94-19	OpenMind1222Dreamy Mimi122nkSeraglio114½	Brushed,clear	7
5Mar89-10GP	fst 1116	:242 :482 1:123 1:434	(F)Bonnie Miss-G2	2 4 44 42½ 1½ 13	Cordero A Jr	121	*.40	82-20	Open Mind1213Seattle Meteor1211Surging1145¾	Drew clear	6
1Feb89- 9GP	fst 7f	:22 :45 1:104 1:241	(F)Forward Gal-G3	5 8 813 79¼ 23 12	Cordero A Jr	121	*2.30	83-24	OpnMnd1212Surgng114nkGorgsDoctor1189½	Steadied,handily	9
19Nov88- 7Aqu	fst 1⅛	:49 1:131 1:383 1:52	(F)Demoiselle-G1	7 5 65½ 67 42½ 1nk	Cordero A Jr	121	*.40e	75-20	Open Mind121nkDarby's Daughter1191¾Gild121hd	Driving	10
5Nov88- 5CD	my 1116	:232 :47 1:123 1:463	(F)BC Juv Fillies-G1	8 11 1016 108¼ 42 11¾	Cordero A Jr	119	*.70e	75-20	OpnMind1191¾DarbyShuffle119nkLeaLucnd119¾	Driving,best	12
15Oct88- 7Bel	fst 1	:223 :452 1:103 1:364	(F)Frizette-G1	6 4 46 35½ 23 2no	Cordero A Jr	119	*.30e	81-17	SomeRomnce119noOpnMnd1196½Ms.GoldPole1191½	Mate won	7
18Sep88- 3Lrl	fst 7f	:224 :46 1:111 1:24	(F)USFG Lassie 95k	2 4 67½ 68½ 45 24½	McCarron CJ	119	6.10	86-10	Ms.GoldPole1194½OpnMind119½SafelyKpt1191½	Wide,rallied	9
30Aug88- 7Mth	fst 6f	:223 :461 1:11	(S)NJ Breeders 32k	3 5 52¼ 2hd 2½ 1nk	Castaneda M	113	6.80	85-18	Open Mind113nkMs. Gold Pole11610Doc David1153	Driving	7
15Aug88-11Mth	fst 6f	:23 :464 1:124	(S)Md Sp Wt	11 1 42 2½ 11 15	Castaneda M	115	10.90	76-18	OpnMnd1155OperationJonathon1182½RoyalNDr118nk	Driving	11

Outstandingly

b. f. 1982, by Exclusive Native (Raise a Native)–La Mesa, by Round Table — Lifetime record: 28 10 4 3 $1,412,206

Own.– Harbow View Farm
Br.– Harbor View Farm (Ky)
Tr.–Lazaro S. Barrera

19Jan87- 8SA	fm 1⅛(T)	:482 1:124 1:38 1:501 4↑	(F)San Gorgonio H-G2	6 2 21 41½ 31 53½	Stevens GL	120	*1.50	72-29	Frau Altiva1171Auspiciante1221¼Solva1191¼	Tired	7
2Jan87- 8SA	fm 1⅛(T)	:462 1:111 1:362 1:49 4↑	(F)Alw 48000	3 3 35 42½ 11 11¼	Stevens GL	121	*.90	82-18	Outstandingly1211¼Frau Altiva1173New Bruce1142¼	Driving	8
23Nov86- 8Hol	fm 1⅛(T)	:473 1:113 1:354 1:48 3↑	(F)Matriarch Inv'l-G1	7 3 43 43 84¾ 76½	Stevens GL	123	*2.00	81-13	Auspiciante1231½Aberuschka1231Reloy120¾	Tired	12
1Nov86- 5SA	fst 1¼	:461 1:10 1:344 2:011 3↑	(F)BC Distaff-G1	2 4 35 24 24 34½	Stevens GL	123	7.60	78-13	Lady'sSecrt1232½Frn'sVlntn1232Outstndngly123¾	Weakened	8
19Oct86- 8SA	fm 1⅛(T)	:46 1:104 1:351 1:473 3↑	(F)Las Palmas H-G2	4 2 32½ 32 1½ 11½	Stevens GL	118	4.40	89-11	Outstandingly1181½Shywing118noJusticara1181¼	Driving	6
8Oct86- 5SA	fm *6½f(T)	:222 :45 1:081 1:143 3↑	(F)Atmn Dys H (Div 1) 50k	2 5 2½ 31½ 31½ 31¼	Stevens GL	120	2.20	85-14	Lichi115noTax Dodge1191¼Outstandingly1201¼	Evenly	7
Run in divisions											
13Jly86- 9Hol	fst 1¼	:481 1:12 1:364 2:02 3↑	(F)Vanity Inv'l H-G1	4 2 21 31½ 34½ 36¾	Stevens GL	118	6.10	75-15	MagnificntLindy1165DntstopThemusic1241¾Outstndingly1183½		5
Tired											
28Jun86- 8Hol	fst 1⅛	:462 1:11 1:354 1:484 3↑	(F)Milady H-G2	2 4 54½ 63¼ 46½ 46¼	Stevens GL	120	1.60e	87-12	DontstopThmusc1222¼MgnfcntLndy117hdTruffls1104	No rally	7
25May86- 8Hol	fm 1116(T)	:25 :484 1:121 1:413 3↑	(F)Wilshire H-G2	3 1 1½ 1hd 1hd 1hd	Stevens GL	117	2.40	96-03	Outstandingly117hdLa Koumia118hdEstrapade1243½	Driving	5
10May86- 8Hol	fst 7f	:22 :444 1:091 1:214 3↑	(F)A Gleam H-G3	2 1 53½ 53¾ 2hd 11¼	Stevens GL	120	2.80	95-12	Outstandingly1201¼Eloquack110½Shywing1205½	Driving	5
12Apr86- 8SA	fst 1116	:223 :46 1:104 1:432 4↑	(F)(R)S Lucia H 88k	4 5 55½ 33 1½ 14	Pincay L Jr	120	*1.30	84-19	Outstndingly1204LaMimosa116hdPalmReadr1181½	Ridden out	9
30Mar86- 8SA	fm 1¼(T)	:481 1:124 1:363 2:01 4↑	(F)S Barbara H-G1	6 5 66½ 78 77¼ 67½	Stevens GL	116	6.80	74-16	MountainBear119½Estrapade1243½RoylRegatta1162¼	Outrun	8
21Mar86- 8SA	fm 1⅛(T)	:47 1:12 1:363 1:493 4↑	(F)Alw 45000	4 6 69 64¾ 53¼ 1½	Stevens GL	114	*1.30e	79-21	Outstandingly114½Water Crystals1153½Connie's Taj1141¼		6
Driving											
2Mar86- 1SA	fst 6½f	:211 :431 1:081 1:15 4↑	(F)Amerigo Lady H 48k	2 6 710 713 411 24	Stevens GL	116	5.40	91-13	TakeMyPctur1194Outstndngly116hdHrRoylty123¾	Full of run	7
8Feb86- 1SA	fst 6f	:213 :444 :571 1:10 4↑	(F)Alw 45000	7 2 77½ 64 53 21¾	Stevens GL	116	*2.10	86-19	GotYouRunnn1161¾Outstndngly116½CoulBy1192	Sluggish early	7
7Jly85- 8Hol	fst 1⅛	:464 1:104 1:351 1:472	(F)Hol Oaks-G1	2 6 611 610 413 417½	Shoemaker W	121	9.10	94-05	Fran's Valentine121hdMagnificent Lindy1219Deal Price1218½		6
Passed tired horses;Previously trained by Frank Martin											
15Jun85- 8Bel	fst 1⅛	:45 1:092 1:493	(F)Mother Goose-G1	10 11 109 1115 719 718¾	Guerra WA	121	12.00e	60-18	Mom'sCmmnd1215½LeL'Argent121nkWillowyMood1215¼	Outrun	11
25May85- 8Bel	fst 1	:22 :441 1:09 1:354	(F)Acorn-G1	3 8 816 616 512 413¾	Velasquez J	121	8.20	72-11	Mom'sCommand1213LeL'Argent1219½Diplomett1211¼	No factor	8
11May85- 8Bel	fst 7f	:22 :443 1:091 1:221	(F)Comely-G3	2 9 98¾ 912 610 511¾	Velasquez J	121	4.50	79-12	Mom'sCommand1214½Majestic Folly1131¾Clocks Secret1214¾		9
Off slowly											
13Apr85- 9OP	fst 1116	:23 :463 1:104 1:431	(F)Fantasy-G1	9 8 97¾ 97¼ 68½ 712½	Velasquez J	121	*1.80	72-17	Rascal Lass1181½Denver Express1133½Little Biddy Comet1142		11
Bumped second turn											
4Mar85- 9GP	fst 1116	:232 :482 1:124 1:444	(F)Bonnie Miss-G3	3 6 64 86¼ 74½ 22	Bailey JD	121	*.40	75-19	LucyManette1212Outstandingly121nkMickBrckn121hd	Rallied	9
21Feb85- 9GP	fst 7f	:23 :463 1:114 1:243	(F)Alw 30000	4 6 55 42½ 41 11¼	Bailey JD	121	*.30	81-24	Outstandngly1211¼MickBrckn121½Burk'sExprss114¾	Driving	6
16Dec84- 8Hol	gd 1116	:222 :453 1:103 1:432	Hol Futurity-G1	2 10 119 74 79 810¾	Guerra WA	118	9.60	--	Stephan'sOdyssey1211FirstNormn1211½RghtCon121hd	Outrun	13
2Dec84- 8Hol	fst 1116	:222 :454 1:104 1:44	(F)Hol Starlet-G1	13 11 1211 65¼ 3nk 12¾	Guerra WA	120	6.00	--	Outstandingly1202¾Frn'sVlntn1202½WsngUp120nk	Drew clear	16
10Nov84- 2Hol	fst 1	:223 :46 1:112 1:374	(F)BC Juv Fillies-G1	8 9 98¾ 73¾ 41¼ 2½	Guerra WA	119	22.80	--	(D)Fran'sValntn119½Outstndngly1192¼DustyHrt119nk	Rallied	11
Placed first through disqualification											
28Oct84- 3Aqu	gd 7f	:221 :452 1:093 1:223	Alw 20000	3 3 69½ 57 410 410¾	Guerra WA	114	*.90	77-14	YoungMonrch1223¼SunnyCabn1173SntorBrdy1174½	No factor	7
16Aug84- 8Sar	fst 6f	:221 :45 1:102	(F)Adirondack-G2	7 6 65¾ 44 22½ 2¾	Cordero A Jr	114	*1.40	87-21	Contredanc114¾Outstndngly1142¼Orntl1144¾	Wide,ducked in	7
29Jly84- 6Bel	fst 5½f	:223 :454 :574 1:041	(F)Md Sp Wt	4 4 11½ 11½ 15 112	Cordero A Jr	117	2.50	94-15	Outstandingly11712Appealing Sam1175½Alice B. Tobin117no		7
Ridden out											

Pebbles (GB)

ch. f. 1981, by Sharpen Up (Atan)–La Dolce, by Connaught
Own.– Sheikh Mohammed al Maktoum
Br.– Warren Hill Stud–Mimika Financiera (GB)
Tr.– Clive E. Brittain

Lifetime record: 15 8 4 0 $1,457,271

2Nov85- 6Aqu fm 1½Ⓣ :48 1:12² 2:02² 2:27 3↑ B C Turf-G1 13 12 13¹³ 4²½ 11 1nk Eddery P 123 *2.20 106-00 Pebbles123nkStrawberry Road II126¹¼Mourjane126¹ All out 14
19Oct85♦ Newmarket(GB) gd 1¼ⓉStr 2:04³ 3↑ Champion Stakes-G1 Stk205000 13 Eddery Pat 126 4.50 Pebbles126³Slip Anchor122hdPalace Music129¹½ 10
Rated in7th,rallied to lead over 1f out,quickly clear
6Jly85♦ Sandown(GB) gd 1¼ⓉRH 2:07¹ 3↑ Eclipse Stakes-G1 Stk260000 12 Cauthen S 130 3.50 Pebbles130²Rainbow Quest133¹½Bob Back133²⁰ 4
Rated in last,sharp run to lead 3f out,comfortably
18Jun85♦ Ascot(GB) gd 1¼ⓉRH 2:05⁴ 4↑ Prince of Wales's Stakes-G2 Stk72000 2¹½ Cauthen S 130 1.25 Bob Back133¹½Pebbles130noCommanche Run133¹² 4
Tracked leader,dueled 1f out,soon headed,won duel for 2nd
26Apr85♦ Sandown(GB) gd 1ⓉRH 1:42² 4↑ Trusthouse Forte Mile-G2 Stk63400 1¹½ Cauthen S 130 *1.35 Pebbles130¹½Vacarme126½Sarab126²½ 7
Tracked leaders,led 3f out,held well
20Oct84♦ Newmarket(GB) fm 1¼ⓉStr 2:01 3↑ Champion Stakes-G1 Stk206000 2nk Robinson P 119 7.50 Palace Music122nkPebbles119¹½Raft122nk 15
Rank toward rear,sharp late run,gaining late.Tolomeo 9th
20Jun84♦ Ascot(GB) gd 1ⓉRH 1:40³ Ⓕ Coronation Stakes-G1 Stk64400 2¹½ Piggott L 130 *2.75 Katies130¹½Pebbles130⁵So FIne126¾ 10
Tracked leaders,dueled over 2f out,headed 100y out
3May84♦ Newmarket(GB) gd 1ⓉStr 1:38 Ⓕ 1000 Guineas Stakes-G1 Stk197000 13 Robinson P 126 8.00 Pebbles126³Meis El-Reem126nkDesirable126¾ 15
Midpack,lacked room 2f out,led 1f out,drew clear
19Apr84♦ Newmarket(GB) gd 7fⓉStr 1:24³ Ⓕ Nell Gwyn Stakes-G3 Stk28300 11 Robinson P 119 7.00 Pebbles119¹Leipzig119¹½Meis El-Reem119¹ 9
Led 3f out,met challenge 1f out,held gamely
28Sep83♦ Newmarket(GB) gd 6fⓉStr 1:14⁴ Ⓕ Cheveley Park Stakes-G1 Stk93700 2nk Robinson P 123 33.00 Desirable123nkPebbles123noPrickle123¾ 12
Toward rear,bid 2f out,2nd 1f out,dueled late,gamely
26Aug83♦ Goodwood(GB) fm 7fⓉRH 1:28³ Ⓕ Waterford Candelabra Stakes-G3 Stk34700 5⁵¾ Mercer J 121 3.50 Shoot Clear121¹Satinette121³Tapaculo118¹½ 8
Rank in midpack,beaten 2f out
17Aug83♦ York(GB) gd 6fⓉStr 1:12¹ Ⓕ Lowther Stakes-G2 Stk34800 4⁴¼ Robinson P 123 5.50 Prickle123²½Desirable123nkChapel Cottage128¹½ 9
Close up,hard ridden over 1f out,faded late
25Jun83♦ Newmarket(GB) gd 6fⓉStr 1:14¹ Ⓕ Childwick Stud Stakes Alw9100 13 Robinson P 125 3.30 Pebbles125³Sajeda120¾Follow Me Follow125⁵ 13
Tracked leaders,led 1f out,ridden clear
9Jun83♦ Newbury(GB) gd 6fⓉStr 1:16² Ⓕ Kingsclere Stakes Alw10100 14 Robinson P 117 12.00 Pebbles117⁴Refill117¹Valkyrie120³ 7
Rallied to lead over 1f out,drew clear in hand
30May83♦ Sandown(GB) yl 5fⓉStr 1:05 Ⓕ Ann Boleyn Maiden Stakes Mdn5800 14 Robinson P 123 33.00 Sperrin Mist123¹Miss Mint123²Cutlers Corner123² 17
Never a factor

Perrault (GB)

ch. c. 1977, by Djakao (Tanerko)–Innocent Air, by Court Martial
Own.– Baron T. van Zuylen & Fradkoff
Br.– Sasse & Sheed (GB)
Tr.– Charles Whittingham

Lifetime record: 25 9 5 5 $1,489,942

18Sep82- 8Bel fst 1¼ :47³ 1:11³ 1:36 2:01 3↑ Marlboro Cup H-G1 3 2 21 8²⁴ - - Pincay L Jr 128 b 3.70 -- Lemhi Gold115⁸¾Silver Supreme117¾Pair of Deuces116⁹ 8
Pulled up,returned lame
29Aug82- 8AP fm 1¼Ⓣ :46² 1:10¹ 1:35 1:58⁴ 3↑ Bud Million 1000k 7 5 54 3¹½ 11 12¼ Pincay L Jr 126 b *1.30e 125-00 Perrault126²¼Be My Native118nkMotavato126²¾ Drew out 14
15Aug82- 8Dmr fm 1⅛Ⓣ :48⁴ 1:12¹ 1:36² 1:48² 3↑ Eddie Read H-G2 6 3 2½ 11 31 31 Pincay L Jr 129 b *.70 95-06 Wickerr119½SpenceBay122½Perrault129¹¼ Sluggish,bore out 7
13Jun82- 8Hol fst 1¼ :45² 1:09¹ 1:33⁴ 1:59¹ 3↑ Hol Gold Cup H-G1 4 4 43 2hd 1¹½ 11 Pincay L Jr 127 b *.70 95-15 Perrault127¹Erins Isle118½It's the One125² Driving 8
18Apr82- 8SA fm *1¾Ⓣ :46 1:58⁴ 2:45³ 4↑ S Juan Capistrano H-G1 9 2 25 2hd 2²½ 3⁸¾ Pincay L Jr 129 b *.40e 90-06 Lemhi Gold121⁷Exploded118¹¾Perrault129²½ Weakened 9
28Mar82- 8SA fm 1½Ⓣ :46² 1:10² 2:00 2:24 4↑ San Luis Rey-G1 5 1 1¹½ 1¹½ 11 1³¼ Pincay L Jr 126 b 1.70e 95-05 Perrault126³¼Exploded126¹½John Henry126no Ridden out 5
7Mar82- 8SA fst 1¼ :45 1:09 1:34² 1:59 4↑ S Anita H-G1 4 5 57 4¹¼ 1½ 1no Pincay L Jr 126 b 4.20e 94-07 ⒹPerrault126noJohnHenry130³¼It'stheOne120nk Drifted out 11
Disqualified and placed second
10Feb82- 8SA yl 1¼Ⓣ :47³ 1:38¹ 2:04³ 4↑ Arcadia H-G3 7 4 4⁴½ 1½ 1¹½ 15 Pincay L Jr 124 b *1.60 64-36 Perrault124⁵Silveyville117¹¹Le Duc de Bar111⁵ Handily 7
Previously trained by Pierre Pelat
8Nov81- 8SA fm 1½Ⓣ :47² 1:10² 1:59³ 2:23² 3↑ Oak Tree Inv'l-G1 5 5 4²½ 5⁵½ 7¹¹ 7¹⁵ St Martin Y 126 b 7.70e 83-02 John Henry126nkSpence Bay126⁴½The Bart126no Tired 7
4Oct81♦ Longchamp(Fr) yl *1½ⓉRH 2:35¹ 3↑ Prix de l'Arc de Triomphe-G1 Stk591000 4²¾ Samani H 130 b 27.00 Gold River127¾Bikala123noApril Run120² 24
Tracked in 5th,finished well without threatening
30Aug81♦ Deauville(Fr) fm *1 11/16ⓉRH 2:58³ 3↑ Grand Prix de Deauville-G2 Stk112000 1hd St Martin Y 131 b *1.20 Perrault131hdCastle Keep126¾Glenorum131¹½ 11
Rated in 6th,rallied to lead near line
14Jly81♦ Saint-Cloud(Fr) gd *1 9/16ⓉLH 2:38² 3↑ Prix Maurice de Nieuil-G2 Stk112000 1²½ St Martin Y 130 b *1.30 Perrault130²½Roi Guillaume113nkDom Menotti128² 10
Unhurried in 5th,led 1f out,going away
23May81♦ Evry(Fr) sf *1½ⓉLH 2:42³ 4↑ Grand Prix d'Evry-G2 Stk60000 2hd St Martin Y 124 b 6.50 Lancastrian124hdPerrault124¾Kelbomec124²½ 12
Rated in 6th,rallied to lead 1f out,caught final strides
10May81♦ Longchamp(Fr) hy *1½ⓉRH 2:49² 4↑ La Coupe-G3 Stk35300 1hd St Martin Y 123 b *2.60 Perrault123hdSon of Love123hdMonsieur Dagobert123¹ 10
Tracked in 3rd,sharp late run to lead near line
20Apr81♦ Longchamp(Fr) fm *1½ⓉRH 2:33² 4↑ Prix d'Hedouville (Listed) Stk26500 3¹¼ St Martin Y 121 b 2.80 Lancastrian123¾En Calcat126½Perrault121¹½ 10
Rated behind leaders,bid 1f out,twice hit by rival's whip
21Mar81♦ Saint-Cloud(Fr) sf *1¼ⓉLH 2:19¹ 4↑ Prix Exbury-G3 Stk35500 2¹½ Lequeux A 126 b 4.50 Armistice Day128¹½Perrault126²Sabzawar123¹½ 9
Rated behind slow pace,rallied to lead 1f out,headed 100y out
19Oct80♦ Longchamp(Fr) sf *1½ⓉRH 2:41¹ 3↑ Prix du Conseil de Paris-G2 Stk76500 5³¼ Badel A 122 b 7.10 En Calcat126½Lancastrian124²½Satilla117no 14
Rated in 6th,led over 1f out to 170y out,faded
31Aug80♦ Deauville(Fr) gd *1 9/16ⓉRH 2:56 3↑ Grand Prix de Deauville-G2 Stk63700 2³ Badel A 118 b 10.10 Glenorum119³Perrault118nkVincent126¾ 13
Tracked leader,led 2f to 1f out,one-paced to line
4Aug80♦ Vichy(Fr) gd *1½ⓉRH 2:36 3↑ Grand Prix de Vichy-G3 Stk51000 2nk Badel A 114 *3.00 Perouges132nkPerrault114¹½Brousoy117¹ 10
14Jly80♦ Saint-Cloud(Fr) sf *1 9/16ⓉLH 2:47 3↑ Prix Maurice de Nieuil-G2 Stk51000 3³¾ Badel A 114 12.30 Buckpoint128³Proustille113¾Perrault114hd 11
Tracked in 4th,2nd over 1f out,one paced,just saved 3rd
14Jun80♦ Saint-Cloud(Fr) gd *1½ⓉLH 2:46 Prix Sica Boy Alw20100 1½ Badel A 121 2.60 Perrault121½Maiymad126¹½Koreillo120hd 6
15May80♦ Longchamp(Fr) fm *1 5/16ⓉRH 2:16¹ Prix de Nanterre Mdn12500 1½ Badel A 126 21.90 Perrault126½Tajtal126¾Dom Menotti126nk 9
Tracked in 4th,dueled briefly 1f out,led 100y out
5Nov79♦ Maisns-Lffte(Fr) sf *1⅛ⓉStr 2:04⁴ Prix Bagheera Mdn12200 4²½ Lequeux A 123 Vezzani118²Al Ward123½Talk It Over123hd 11
Rated in 6th,brief bid 2f out,one-paced final furlong
5Oct79♦ Saint-Cloud(Fr) gd *1ⓉLH 1:47² Prix Mieuxce Mdn12200 3¹¼ Lequeux A 123 Pedrillo123¾Shakapour123½Perrault123² 11
Rated in 7th, bid 1½ furlong out,held by first two
20Sep79♦ Maisns-Lffte(Fr) gd *7fⓉStr 1:28¹ Prix de l'Yser Mdn (FT)12200 4³½ Lequeux A 123 Arch121½Tarrago123¹Shakapour123² 13
Chased in 6th,mild late gain

Personal Ensign

b. f. 1984, by Private Account (Damascus)–Grecian Banner, by Hoist the Flag — **Lifetime record: 13 13 0 0 $1,679,880**

Own.– Ogden Phipps
Br.– Ogden Phipps (Ky)
Tr.– Claude McGaughey III

5Nov88- 6CD	my 1⅛	:474 1:12 1:381 1:52	3↑ ⒻBC Distaff-G1	6 6 58½ 58 34 1no	Romero RP	123	*.50	82-20	Personal Ensign123noWinning Colors119½Goodbye Halo1195	9
	Tight early,just up									
16Oct88- 8Bel	fst 1¼	:481 1:12 1:362 2:011	3↑ ⒻBeldame-G1	1 3 22 2hd 12 15½	Romero RP	123	*.10	92-16	PersonlEnsign1235½ClassicCrown118½ShmSy1187 Ridden out	5
10Sep88- 8Bel	fst 1	:224 :451 1:09 1:341	3↑ ⒻMaskette-G1	2 3 36 22 2hd 1¾	Romero RP	123	*.30	94-14	PersonalEnsgn123¾WinningColrs1185¼ShmSy11511¼ Driving	4
6Aug88- 8Sar	sly 1⅛	:472 1:113 1:353 1:474	3↑ Whitney H-G1	3 3 33 21 1hd 11½	Romero RP	117	*.80	96-12	PersonalEnsign1171½Gulch12417King'sSwan123 Brisk urging	3
4Jly88- 10Mth	fst 1$\frac{1}{16}$	:24 :472 1:104 1:414	3↑ ⒻMolly Pitcher H-G2	5 3 23 2½ 12½ 18	Romero RP	125	*.40	96-14	Personal Ensign1258Grecian Flight1197Le L'Argent1171	5
	Bumped,forced wide									
11Jun88- 7Bel	fst 1⅛	:471 1:112 1:353 1:473	3↑ ⒻHempstead H-G1	5 3 31½ 31 14 17	Romero RP	123	*.40	89-13	PersonlEnsgn1237HomtwnQun1092ClbbrGrl118nk Ridden out	5
15May88- 8Bel	fst 1$\frac{1}{16}$	:23 :453 1:10 1:413	3↑ ⒻShuvee H-G1	5 3 33 2hd 1½ 11¾	Romero RP	121	*.70	94-15	Personal Ensign1211¾Clabber Girl1183½Bishop's Delight1112¾	6
	Driving									
18Oct87- 8Bel	fst 1¼	:493 1:134 1:382 2:042	3↑ ⒻBeldame-G1	8 2 2½ 13 14 12¼	Romero RP	118	1.30	76-23	PersnlEnsgn1182¼CoupdFusl1232½SlntTurn1183¾ Drew clear	10
10Oct87- 5Bel	fst 1	:223 :454 1:102 1:363	ⒻRare Perfume-G2	2 3 11 15 15 14¾	Romero RP	115	*.80	82-22	PrsnlEnsign1154¾OneFromHevn1183¾KyBd1181½ Ridden out	9
24Sep87- 5Bel	fst 1	:233 :464 1:113 1:361	3↑ ⒻAlw 33000	5 2 12½ 13 15 17¾	Romero RP	113	*.20	84-20	PersonalEnsign1137¾WithaTwist117nkRosaMay1176 Handily	5
6Sep87- 5Bel	fst 7f	:232 :462 1:103 1:231	3↑ ⒻAlw 31000	3 5 43 1hd 11½ 13¾	Bailey JD	113	*.70	86-19	PersonalEnsign1133¾ChicShirine1131¼WithTwst117½ Handily	6
13Oct86- 8Bel	fst 1	:232 :46 1:101 1:362	ⒻFrizette-G1	2 2 2½ 2hd 1hd 1hd	Romero RP	119	*.30	83-16	PersonalEnsign119hdCollins1195½FlyingKatuna119 Driving	3
28Sep86- 6Bel	my 7f	:231 :463 1:103 1:224	ⒻMd Sp Wt	5 7 22½ 11½ 17 112¾	Romero RP	117	*.90	88-15	Personal Ensign11712¾Graceful Darby1172¾Nastique1171½	7
	Hesitated start,clear									

Pleasant Colony

dkbbr. c. 1978, by His Majesty (Ribot)–Sun Colony, by Sunrise Flight — **Lifetime record: 14 6 3 1 $965,383**

Own.– Buckland Farm
Br.– T.M. Evans (Va)
Tr.– John P. Campo

19Sep81- 8Bel	my 1¼	:481 1:114 1:354 2:003	3↑ Marlboro Cup H-G1	5 5 79 66 45 46½	Velasquez J	123	*1.10	90-13	Noble Nashua1163¾Amber Pass1201½Temperence Hill1271¼	8
	Lacked response									
5Sep81- 8Bel	fst 1⅛	:461 1:094 1:343 1:471	3↑ Woodward-G1	7 5 66½ 55¾ 21½ 11¾	Cordero A Jr	123	*1.90	91-14	PleasantClny1231¾AmberPass1261¼HerbWtr1162 Ridden out	9
15Aug81- 8Sar	sly 1¼	:463 1:112 1:372 2:034	Travers-G1	8 5 57½ 2hd 2½ 2hd	Cordero A Jr	126	*1.60e	81-20	WillowHour126hdPleasntColny1261¾LordAvie1264¼ Bore out	10
6Jun81- 8Bel	fst 1½	:482 1:141 2:04 2:29	Belmont-G1	11 11 119½ 34½ 34 31¾	Velasquez J	126	*.80	73-14	Summng126nkHghlndBld1261½PlsntColny12611 Finished well	11
16May81- 9Pim	fst 1$\frac{3}{16}$	:473 1:113 1:362 1:543	Preakness-G1	12 8 77¼ 62¾ 2½ 11	Velasquez J	126	*1.50	97-14	Pleasant Colony1261Bold Ego1262Paristo1265 Driving	13
2May81- 8CD	fst 1¼	:451 1:101 1:36 2:02	Ky Derby-G1	7 17 1618 43 11½ 1¾	Velasquez J	126	3.50	87-12	PleasntColny126¾Woodchopper1263Partez1262¼ Ridden out	21
18Apr81- 9Aqu	fst 1⅛	:454 1:102 1:362 1:493	Wood Memorial-G1	5 3 413 37 13 13	Fell J	126	12.70	87-23	Pleasant Colony1263Highland Blade1265Cure the Blues1266	6
	Handily;Previously trained by Lee P. O'Donnell									
6Mar81- 9GP	fst 1⅛	:47 1:111 1:374 1:502	Florida Derby-G1	6 11 1118 911 57 513	Bracciale V Jr	122	3.90	67-17	Lord Avie1224½Akureyri122¾Linnleur1186 No factor	11
16Feb81- 9GP	fst 1$\frac{1}{16}$	:241 :48 1:121 1:442	Fountain of Youth-G3	8 9 813 86 3nk 2no	Bracciale V Jr	122	16.70	79-23	Akureyri119noPleasant Colony122hdLord Avie1221½ Brushed	9
9Nov80- 8Aqu	fst 1⅛	:474 1:123 1:373 1:501	Remsen-G1	5 6 710 64¾ 32 2½	Bracciale V Jr	116	5.20	83-21	ⒹAkreyri117½PleasntColny1162FoolshTanner1133½ Impeded	8
	Placed first through disqualification									
27Oct80- 8Aqu	sf 1⅛Ⓣ	:484 1:144 1:411 1:544	Pilgrim 58k	12 12 1314 1213 57½ 2¾	Bracciale V Jr	115	42.90	69-30	Akureyri115¾Pleasant Colony1152Jetzier1222¼ Wide	14
13Oct80- 8Bow	fst 7f	:224 :453 1:11 1:25	ⒸMar Nursery (Div 1) 35k	10 4 75 75¼ 74 52¼	Brumfield D	113	6.50	78-23	John'sRoll116nkPantdShld114noMtchngGft119½ Lacked a bid	11
22Sep80- 2Med	fst 1 70	:224 :471 1:132 1:443	Md Sp Wt	8 7 711 49 13 19½	Asmussen CB	118	4.60	78-18	PleasntClny1189½Community Interest1185½Solid Credit1182½	8
	Drew clear									
1Sep80- 4Bel	fst 7f	:223 :461 1:112 1:243	Md Sp Wt	7 3 3½ 42 613 616	Brumfield D	118	27.90	63-21	Summing1185Academy H.1187Bay Ridge118nk Tired	7

Plugged Nickle

b. c. 1977, by Key to the Mint (Graustark)–Toll Booth, by Buckpasser — **Lifetime record: 21 11 3 1 $647,206**

Own.– J.M. Schiff
Br.– J.M. Schiff (Ky)
Tr.– Thomas J. Kelly

2May81- 8Aqu	gd 7f	:222 :451 1:094 1:23	3↑ Carter H-G2	2 5 45½ 54 34 53½	Vasquez J	123	*1.60	82-19	AmbrPass114½GuiltyConscienc1111Dunhm'sGft1161 Weakened	7
24Jan81- 9GP	sly 7f	:221 :444 1:093 1:223	3↑ Sprint Champ H 58k	2 4 31 34 34½ 45¼	Asmussen CB	124	1.90	86-20	King's Fashion1222½Jaklin Klugman1241½Joanie's Chief1081¼	7
	Weakened									
4Jan81- 8SA	fst 7f	:213 :433 1:073 1:202	Malibu (Div 1)-G2	4 5 75¼ 79½ 912 915	Asmussen CB	126	*1.10	83-07	Doonesbury1171¾Roper114hdUnalakleet1146 Dull try	9
1Nov80- 8Aqu	fst 1⅛	:483 1:131 1:372 1:501	3↑ Stuyvesant H-G3	7 1 11 11½ 17 16	Asmussen CB	122 b	*1.60	84-25	PluggdNickle1226Dr.Ptchs1152¾RngofLght116hd Ridden out	10
18Oct80- 8Aqu	fst 7f	:223 :443 1:084 1:212	3↑ Vosburgh-G1	5 2 31 32 21 1½	Asmussen CB	123	5.10	94-12	PluggdNickle123½JaklinKlugman1231Dav'sFrnd126¾ Driving	9
30Aug80- 8Bel	fst 1	:222 :444 1:091 1:341	Jerome H-G2	3 2 2hd 2hd 33 37	Fell J	124	2.30	90-17	JaklinKlugmn122nkFappiano1146¾PlggdNckl1244 Bore out	6
16Aug80- 8Sar	fst 1¼	:454 1:101 1:361 2:024	Travers-G1	5 4 53¼ 43½ 42¼ 48¼	Fell J	126	*1.80	78-13	TemprnceHill1261½FirstAlbrt126noAmbrPss1266¾ Weakened	9
3Aug80- 8Sar	fst 1⅛	:462 1:103 1:361 1:492	Jim Dandy-G3	3 5 45½ 3½ 1½ 1nk	Fell J	128	*.50	88-12	PluggdNckle128nkCurrntLegnd1211¼HerbWatr114½ Driving	8
20Jly80- 8Bel	fst 7f	:23 :453 1:092 1:221	3↑ Tom Fool-G3	6 2 21½ 2hd 12 13	Fell J	121	2.60	91-16	PluggedNickle1213Dr.Patches1191½Isella1191¼ Ridden out	6
3May80- 8CD	fst 1¼	:48 1:124 1:373 2:02	Ky Derby-G1	11 1 31½ 32 68½ 78¼	Thornburg B	126	2.60	79-11	GenuineRisk1211Rumbo1261JaklinKlugman1264 Weakened	13
19Apr80- 8Aqu	fst 1⅛	:472 1:113 1:37 1:504	Wood Memorial-G1	10 1 11 11 11½ 11½	Thornburg B	126	*.50	81-17	PluggdNickle1261½ColonlMoran126hdGnunRsk1213¾ Driving	11
29Mar80- 9GP	fst 1⅛	:473 1:112 1:363 1:501	Florida Derby-G1	8 2 11 12 15 16	Thornburg B	122	*.40	81-19	PluggedNickle1226NakedSky1221½LordGallant1181½ Easily	8
10Mar80- 9GP	fst 7f	:223 :452 1:10 1:223	Hutcheson 29k	2 5 63½ 31½ 12 17	Thornburg B	122	*.80	91-27	PlggdNckle1227Executon'sRson122½OneSon114½ Ridden out	6
26Feb80- 9Hia	fst 6f	:22 :452 1:094	Alw 14000	2 4 34½ 31½ 32 24	Thornburg B	122	2.30	90-22	GoldStage1224PluggdNickle122¾SonofaDodo1154 No match	7
11Nov79- 8Aqu	my 1⅛	:48 1:122 1:372 1:502	Remsen-G2	6 1 11½ 13 15 14¾	Thornburg B	122	*.80	83-24	Plugged Nickle1224¾Googolplex117½Proctor1134¾ Handily	8
27Oct79- 9Pim	fst 1$\frac{1}{16}$	:24 :47 1:112 1:434	Lrl Futurity-G1	4 5 65½ 11 13½ 11¾	Thornburg B	122	4.60	86-14	PluggedNickle1221¾GoldStage1222NewRegent1223½ Driving	8
17Oct79- 3Aqu	fst 1	:234 :461 1:103 1:353	Alw 15000	2 3 31½ 1½ 15 19¼	Vasquez J	115	*1.00	88-17	Plugged Nickle1159¼Buck's Turn1172Self Pressured1153¾	7
	Ridden out									
6Oct79- 5Bel	fst 6f	:223 :453 1:104	Alw 16000	3 3 22 22 24 21½	Rocco J5	110 b	3.00	86-21	Speed City1151½Plugged Nickle1102Imaromeo1151½ Bumped	7
15Sep79- 8Bel	fst 7f	:222 :451 1:092 1:22	Futurity-G1	5 3 11½ 12 37 713	Cordero A Jr	122 b	7.30	79-11	Rockhill Native1224Sportful1224¼Gold Stage1221½ Tired	8
29Aug79- 7Bel	sly 6½f	:223 :46 1:104 1:17	Alw 17000	2 4 1hd 1hd 11½ 21½	Vasquez J	118	*.90	89-15	SonofaDodo1181½PluggedNickle1183½ITakeAll115nk 2nd best	4
4Aug79- 6Sar	fst 6f	:22 :452 1:104	Md Sp Wt	11 6 2hd 1½ 11 11½	Vasquez J	118	8.80	86-12	Plugged Nickle1181½Buck Island1182¾Now and Then1181	12
	Ridden out									

Precisionist

ch. c. 1981, by Crozier (My Babu)–Excellently, by Forli

Lifetime record: 46 20 10 4 $3,485,398

Own.– F.W. Hooper
Br.– F.W. Hooper (Fla)
Tr.– L. William Donovan

24Dec88-10Crc	fst 7f	:222 :45 1:104 1:243	3↑ Sunny Isle H 87k	5 7 3nk 32½ 1215 1212½	Perret C	123	*.70	79-15	PositionLeader1171¼ThRdRolls114noAbovNorml114¾ Faltered	12
Previously trained by John W. Russell										
10Dec88- 8Hol	fst 1⅛	:46 1:102 1:354 1:483	3↑ Native Diver H-G3	7 2 11 11½ 2hd 2hd	McCarron CJ	123	1.90	94-15	CutlassReality124hdPrecisonst1232¾Pynt1162 Sharp effort	7
20Nov88- 8Hol	fm 1⅛Ⓣ	:463 1:101 1:342 1:463	3↑ Citation H-G2	10 1 11½ 11 12½ 2nk	McCarron CJ	121	*2.30	95-10	Forlitano118nkPrcsonst1213½SkpOutFront117¾ Held gamely	11
5Nov88- 4CD	sly 6f	:21 :441 :562 1:102	3↑ BC Sprint-G1	6 6 42¼ 43½ 53¼ 52¼	McCarron CJ	126	7.40	89-20	Gulch126¾PlaytheKing1261Aflet126½ Wide lt.,lacked rally	13
22Oct88- 8Aqu	fst 1	:223 :451 1:09 1:34	3↑ NYRA Mile H 567k	4 1 1½ 1½ 21 31½	Vega A	124	3.20	94-18	Forty Niner121nkMawsuff1151¼Precisionist124nk Weakened	6
10Sep88- 8Dmr	fst 1	:223 :453 1:092 1:343	3↑ Bud BC H 148k	3 1 1½ 1hd 11½ 1¾	McCarron CJ	125	*.30	95-12	Precisionist125¾Lively One1142He's a Saros1161¾ Driving	4
28Aug88- 8Dmr	fst 1⅛	:453 1:093 1:343 1:471	3↑ Cabrillo H-G3	4 1 11½ 11 15 13½	McCarron CJ	122	*.20	94-12	Precisionst1223½ConqurngHro1136CrcusPrnc115½ Ridden out	4
1Aug88- 8Dmr	fst 1	:222 :453 1:091 1:331	3↑ Alw 48000	5 1 12½ 11½ 13½ 14	McCarron CJ	114	*.80	102-12	Precisionist1144Candi'sGold1162½RdAttck1155½ Ridden out	5
16Jly88- 8Bel	fst 7f	:23 :461 1:101 1:222	3↑ Tom Fool-G2	4 3 1½ 1hd 45½ 48¾	McCarron CJ	119	2.40	81-22	King's Swan128¾Gulch1286Abject1192 Set pace,tired	4
29Jun88- 8Hol	fst 1	:224 :45 1:094 1:343	4↑ Alw 55000	6 - - - - -	McCarron CJ	115	*.90	- -	Epidaurus1151RedAttack117nkMidwestKing1161¼ Lost rider	7
Previously trained by L.R. Fenstermaker										
1Nov86- 7SA	fst 1¼	:46 1:101 1:343 2:002	3↑ BC Classic-G1	2 2 21 22 23½ 32½	Stevens GL	126	1.70	84-13	Skywalker1261¼Turkoman1261½Precisionist1261¾ Bumped 7/8	11
13Oct86- 8SA	fst 1⅛	:463 1:102 1:354 1:482	3↑ Yankee Valor H 94k	2 1 1hd 1½ 13½ 14½	Stevens GL	127	*.60	87-19	Precisionist1274½Garthorn1242Tasso1171½ Ridden out	5
13Sep86- 8Bel	fst 1¼	:473 1:11 1:354 2:00	3↑ Marlboro Cup H-G1	1 1 11½ 13 2hd 21½	Velasquez J	127	*1.20	96-11	Turkoman1231½Precisionist1278¾RooArt119½ Best of others	5
30Aug86- 8Bel	fst 1⅛	:453 1:092 1:334 1:46	3↑ Woodward-G1	5 2 21½ 22½ 1hd 14¾	McCarron CJ	126	*1.20	97-14	Precisionst1264¾Ldy'sScrt1215½PrsonlFlg1105¾ Drew clear	5
16Aug86- 9Mth	sly 1⅛	:464 1:103 1:353 1:484	3↑ Iselin H-G1	2 2 21½ 2hd 2hd 22¼	McCarron CJ	125	1.70	88-16	RooArt1172¼Precisionist1251¼Lady'sSecret1206 Held place	5
20Jly86- 9Hol	fst 1¼	:454 1:091 1:343 2:002	3↑ Hol Gold Cup H-G1	1 2 2½ 1hd 2hd 32	McCarron CJ	127	*.90	88-06	SuperDiamond1181½Alphabatim120½Prcisionst1276 Weakened	6
1Jun86- 8Hol	fst 1	:222 :441 1:082 1:333	3↑ Californian-G1	1 2 21½ 11 11½ 1½	McCarron CJ	126	*.50	95-14	Precisionist126½SuperDiamond1173½Skywalker1212½ Driving	7
13Apr86- 8SA	fst 1⅛	:451 1:093 1:35 1:473	4↑ S Bernardino H-G2	1 2 1½ 12½ 1½ 1nk	McCarron CJ	126	*.80	91-15	Precisionist126nkGreinton1268Encolure11614½ Driving	4
2Mar86- 8SA	fst 1¼	:451 1:091 1:34 2:00	4↑ S Anita H-G1	4 2 21 22½ 32½ 63½	McCarron CJ	126	*1.20	86-13	Greinton122¾Herat1122Hatim118nk Tired	13
25Jan86- 8SA	fst 1 1/16	:232 :461 1:094 1:411	4↑ S Pasqual H-G2	5 2 1hd 1½ 13½ 14½	McCarron CJ	126	*.30	95-11	Precisionist1264½BareMinimum113¾MyHabitony1163½ Easily	6
30Nov85- 8Hol	my 6f	:214 :443 :562 1:084	3↑ Nat'l Sprint Champ-G3	5 3 31½ 21 31 42¾	McCarron CJ	124	*.40	97-09	Pancho Villa1221Charging Falls1221½Temerity Prince122nk	6
Wide stretch										
2Nov85- 3Aqu	fst 6f	:22 :444 1:082	3↑ BC Sprint-G1	2 4 31½ 32 3½ 1¾	McCarron CJ	126	3.40	99-10	Precisionist126¾Smile124¾Mt. Livermore1261¼ Driving	14
23Jun85- 8Hol	fst 1¼	:461 1:093 1:342 1:582	3↑ Hol Gold Cup H-G1	6 1 12½ 12 1hd 21¾	McCarron CJ	125	*1.00	118-00	Greinton1201¾Precisionist1251¼Kings Island1125 Weakened	6
9Jun85-10Hol	fst 1	:23 :45 1:083 1:323	3↑ Californian-G1	2 2 2½ 2½ 21½ 22¾	McCarron CJ	126	*.60	107-02	Greinton1192¾Precisionist1263½LordatWar1261¼ No excuse	4
19May85- 8Hol	fst 1	:221 :444 1:083 1:324	3↑ Mervyn LeRoy H-G2	5 1 1hd 12½ 14 14	McCarron CJ	126	*.60	109-08	Precisionist1264Greinton1211My Habitony1151¾ Easily	5
13Apr85- 8SA	fst 1⅛	:45 1:09 1:342 1:47	4↑ San Bernardino H-G2	3 2 21½ 2½ 1½ 2nk	McCarron CJ	127	1.40	94-13	Greinton120nkPrecisionist127hdAl Mamoon11510 Gamely	6
9Mar85- 8SA	fst 6½f	:213 :44 1:084 1:152	4↑ Potrero Grande H 76k	6 5 3½ 21½ 41¾ 63¾	McCarron CJ	128	*.90	89-14	FiftySixinaRow117hdHulaBlaze1201½Coyotero114nk Drifted	6
3Feb85- 8SA	fst 1¼	:453 1:094 1:343 2:001	C H Strub-G1	5 1 12½ 1½ 1hd 1no	McCarron CJ	125	*1.10	88-12	Precisionist125noGrenton117½GtDncr12616 Strong handling	5
19Jan85- 8SA	fst 1⅛	:47 1:103 1:35 1:472	San Fernando-G1	5 1 12½ 11½ 12½ 14	McCarron CJ	126	*1.70	92-16	Precisionist1264Greinton120nkGate Dancer1268½ Handily	7
26Dec84- 8SA	fst 7f	:222 :441 1:083 1:212	Malibu-G2	5 4 31 1hd 11 12¾	McCarron CJ	126	*1.00	93-15	Precisionist1262¾Bunker1173½Milord1154 Ridden out	7
10Nov84- 7Hol	fst 1¼	:453 1:103 1:37 2:032	3↑ BC Classic-G1	7 1 3½ 613 721 727¾	McCarron CJ	122	7.70	- -	Wild Again126hd[D]Gate Dancer122½Slew o' Gold1265 Tired	8
22Sep84-10LaD	fst 1¼	:462 1:102 1:35 2:001	Super Derby-G1	1 2 11½ 13½ 13 2hd	Shoemaker W	126	1.70	107-04	GateDancer126hdPrecisionist12611BgPstol1267 Game effort	8
3Sep84- 8Dmr	fst *1¼	:451 1:09 1:34 1:564	3↑ Del Mar H-G2	10 1 16 13 12½ 11¾	McCarron CJ	116	*1.20	93-18	Precisionist1161¾Pair of Deuces1163Super Diamond1172¾	10
Never headed										
19Aug84- 8Dmr	fm 1⅛Ⓣ	:471 1:112 1:36 1:48	Dmr Derby H-G2	7 2 11½ 1½ 32½ 76½	McCarron CJ	124	*2.70	91-05	TsunamiSlew1193PrinceTrue119noMajesticShore115¾ Tired	12
22Jly84- 8Hol	fst 1¼	:453 1:101 1:35 1:594	Swaps-G1	6 1 11½ 12 17 110	McCarron CJ	123	3.70	92-15	Precisionist12310PrincTru120hdMjstcShor1141½ Ridden out	7
30Jun84- 8Hol	fst 1⅛	:46 1:103 1:354 1:483	Silver Screen H-G2	1 1 11½ 11 3nk 31½	McCarron CJ	121	*1.30	84-20	Tights119noM. Double M.1161½Precisionist1211¼ Weakened	6
5May84- 8Hol	fm 1Ⓣ	:23 :454 1:10 1:341	Spotlight H 67k	1 1 11½ 11½ 34 69¾	Guerra WA	123	*1.10	87-12	Tights1193½Loft1151Prince True1182½ Bumped,bore out	10
8Apr84- 8SA	fst 1⅛	:452 1:10 1:36 1:49	S A Derby-G1	4 1 13 12 13 21¼	McCarron CJ	120	*1.10	83-16	MightyAdversry1201¼Precsonst120nkPrncTru1202½ Game try	8
3Mar84- 8SA	fst 1	:22 :444 1:091 1:35	San Rafael-G2	2 1 12 12½ 12½ 15	McCarron CJ	120	3.00	93-14	Precisionist1205Fali Time1221¼Commemorte118¾ Driving	6
11Feb84- 8SA	fst 7f	:222 :442 1:092 1:224	San Vicente-G3	5 2 2½ 2hd 1½ 2nk	McCarron CJ	122	*.60	86-18	Fortunate Prospect119nkPrecisionist122½Tights1172 Sharp	5
25Jan84- 8SA	fst 6f	:212 :441 :562 1:09	San Miguel 64k	2 3 2hd 1½ 12½ 12	McCarron CJ	122	1.30	93-19	Precisionist1222FortuntProspct1203Commmort1201½ Driving	5
18Dec83- 8Hol	fst 1 1/16	:222 :454 1:101 1:413	Hol Futurity-G1	5 1 1½ 2hd 77¾ 1011½	McCarron CJ	121	*1.90	75-14	FaliTime121½BoldT.Jay1213½Lif'sMgc1183 Checked,weakened	12
25Nov83- 8Hol	gd 1Ⓣ	:233 :473 1:122 1:373	Hoist the Flag (Div 2) 83k	4 1 12 12½ 11 1½	McCarron CJ	116	*.80	80-22	Precisionist116½Fali Time1202½Tights1153 Driving	8
28Oct83- 8SA	fst 6½f	:214 :442 1:094 1:161	Alw 22000	1 1 21½ 1½ 13 14½	McCarron CJ	113	*1.10	89-19	Precsnst1134½DonnrPrty1173½Fortun'sKngdm1173½ Handily	7
23Jly83- 8Hol	fst 6f	:214 :441 :564 1:092	Juv Champ-G2	9 1 53¼ 46½ 510 514½	Lipham T	117	*.60	75-21	Althea11710Rejected Suitor1171Auto Commander1171½	9
Lacked a rally										
13Jly83- 6Hol	fst 6f	:221 :45 :573 1:101	Md Sp Wt	1 3 13 16 16 17½	Lipham T	116	*1.00	86-19	Precisionist1167½TriumphantBanner116noFaliTm1165 Easily	8

Princess Rooney

gr. f. 1980, by Verbatim (Speak John)–Parrish Princess, by Drone

Lifetime record: 21 17 2 1 $1,343,339

Own.– Paula Tucker
Br.– Ben & Tom Roach (Ky)
Tr.– Neil Drysdale

10Nov84- 5Hol	fst 1¼	:471 1:113 1:37 2:022	3↑ ⒻBC Distaff-G1	4 2 2hd 1½ 13 17	Delahoussaye E	123	*.70	- -	Princess Rooney1237Life's Magic119¾Adored1232 Drew off	7
27Oct84- 7Kee	fst 1⅛	:484 1:133 1:382 1:502	3↑ ⒻSpinster-G1	7 3 34 32 11½ 16	Delahoussaye E	123	*.80	85-25	PrncssRny1236LuckyLuckyLucky119½Hthrtn1232 Drew clear	9
9Oct84- 7Kee	fst *7f	1:244	3↑ ⒻAlw 22340	4 3 3nk 1½ 12 14½	Delahoussaye E	123	*.20	99-13	PrincssRooney1234½QunofSong1232½RglVlly1232 Ridden out	6
26Aug84- 8Dmr	fst 1 1/16	:23 :462 1:102 1:402	3↑ ⒻChula Vista H-G3	4 3 21 2½ 12½ 12½	Valenzuela PA	123	*1.00	98-13	PrincessRney1232½FlagdLun1152¼MomnttoBuy1162½ Driving	5
15Jly84- 8Hol	fst 1⅛	:461 1:10 1:341 1:461	3↑ ⒻVanity Inv'l H-G1	1 3 32½ 21 2½ 1hd	Delahoussaye E	120	5.30	98-15	Princess Rooney120hdAdored12010Salt Spring1131½ Driving	7
16Jun84- 8Hol	fst 1 1/16	:23 :46 1:091 1:41	3↑ ⒻMilady H-G2	3 5 65¾ 56½ 37½ 22½	Hawley S	122	4.10	87-16	Adored1192½Princess Rooney1221Lass Trump1173½ Gamely	7
13May84- 0Hol	fst 1 1/16	:23 :462 1:102 1:414	3↑ ⒻHawthorne H-G2	3 4 3½ 2½ 22 34	Delahoussaye E	123	-	82-18	Adored117noHolidayDancr1164PrncssRoony12311 Weakened	4
Exhibition race - No wagering										
30Mar84- 8SA	fst 1	:22 :452 1:101 1:354	4↑ ⒻⓇSusan's Girl 44k	2 2 21 2½ 2hd 1no	Delahoussaye E	122	*1.10	89-18	PrincssRooney122noBaraLss1178½Cpch1193 Brushed,driving	4
Previously trained by Joseph H. Pierce Jr										
14Jan84- 8Hia	fm 1 1/16Ⓣ	1:414	4↑ ⒻBal Harbour 23k	4 2 2hd 1½ 31½ 43	Perret C	117	-	86-14	Aspen Rose1121Pat's Joy1191Jubilous1171 Drifted out	10
No wagering,tote malfunction										
19Dec83- 8Med	fst 6f	:231 :463 1:103	3↑ ⒻAlw 20000	2 5 31½ 1hd 21½ 21	Vasquez J	120	*.30	89-11	PrimDeLaPrim1121PrincssRny1203½Myr'sBst114½ Lost whip	5
Awarded first purse money;Previously trained by Frank Gomez										
28May83- 8Bel	fst 1	:23 :452 1:094 1:35	ⒻAcorn-G1	6 3 21½ 21½ 23 27½	Vasquez J	121	*1.10	82-18	Ski Goggle1217½Princess Rooney121nkThirty Flags1216	9
Altered course										
6May83- 8CD	fst 1⅛	:47 1:12 1:373 1:504	ⒻKy Oaks-G1	1 1 11 11 11½ 11¼	Vasquez J	121	*.20	88-15	PrincssRooney1211¼BrightCrocus1212Bemissed121½ Driving	7
23Apr83- 7Kee	sly 1 1/16	:231 :463 1:113 1:452	ⒻAshland-G2	4 2 1hd 1hd 12½ 19½	Vasquez J	121	*.20	79-24	PrincssRooney1219½Shamivor1149Dcson1167½ Drifted,clear	6
13Apr83- 7Kee	fst *7f	1:272	ⒻAlw 27700	8 1 21 2hd 13 110	Vasquez J	123	*.30	86-21	PrincessRney12310FiestyBelle1143½SlvrdSlk1131 Handily	8
5Mar83- 7GP	fst 7f	:221 :45 1:103 1:234	Alw 30000	2 8 31½ 3½ 1½ 1½	Vasquez J	114	*.20	85-19	PrncssRny114½Morgnmorgnmorgn1152¼Alchs1152¾ Driving	8
23Oct82- 6Med	fst 1 1/16	:234 :471 1:11 1:43	ⒻGardenia-G2	6 1 1½ 12 17 111	Vasquez J	121	*.30	94-11	PrincessRooney12111For Once'nMyLife1183GoldSpruce11812	7
In hand										

10Oct82- 8Bel	fst 1	:223 :461 1:113 1:39	ⒻFrizette-G1	2 1 1hd 11½ 16 18	Fell J	119	*1.30	70-29	PrincessRny1198WinnngTck1193½WkndSurprs119nk	Handily	13
11Sep82- 9Crc	fst 7f	:222 :454 1:102 1:234	ⒻMelaleuca 27k	7 1 11 12½ 18 112	Pennisi FA	116	*.20	97-14	PrincssRooney11612Hiusoanso1144Rina'sMissy1146	Easily	8
1Sep82- 9Crc	fst 7f	:222 :46 1:111 1:251	ⒻAlw 10000	1 2 1½ 11½ 110 118	Pennisi FA	116	*.90	90-18	PrncssRoony11618CourtUnon116nkFlwlssDmond1161¼	Easily	5
7Jun82- 7Crc	fst 5f	:223 :463 :593	ⒻAlw 9500	1 3 1½ 11½ 13 14	Pennisi FA	114	*1.20	94-15	PrincssRny1144Ishudhdtht107noRoyltyMss1176	Ridden out	6
22May82- 3Crc	fst 5f	:224 :47 1:002	ⒻMd Sp Wt	9 8 3nk 1hd 12 13	Pennisi FA	115	*2.10	90-14	Princess Rooney1153Rilia1152Marie V.1151	Driving	9

Relaxing

b. f. 1976, by Buckpasser (Tom Fool)–Marking Time, by To Market — **Lifetime record: 28 13 2 5 $590,030**

Own.– O. Phipps
Br.– O. Phipps (Ky)
Tr.– Angel Penna

10Oct81- 8Bel	fst 1½	:48 1:123 2:021 2:282 3↑	J C Gold Cup-G1	2 10 1011 43 21½ 3¾	Cordero A Jr	123	3.30	77-14	John Henry126hdPeat Moss126¾Relaxing123hd	Wide	11
27Sep81- 8Bel	fst 1⅛	:462 1:102 1:344 1:473 3↑	ⒻRuffian H-G1	2 4 45 3½ 1hd 1¾	Cordero A Jr	123	*.90	89-19	Relaxing123¾Love Sign1205¾Jameela1222	Driving	4
5Sep81- 8Bel	fst 1⅛	:461 1:094 1:343 1:471 3↑	Woodward-G1	6 9 911 88¾ 77½ 45	Velasquez J	120	4.80	86-14	PleasntColny1231¾AmberPass1261¼HerbWater1162	Checked	9
23Aug81- 7Del	fst 1¼	:462 1:102 1:352 2:01 3↑	ⒻDelaware H-G1	3 9 815 42 11 12¾	Cordero A Jr	119	*.60	95-15	Relaxing1192¾Wistful1211Lady of Promise1111	Ridden out	10
11Apr81- 8Aqu	fst 1¼	:472 1:11 1:353 2:004 3↑	Excelsior H-G2	6 4 48½ 318 38 35¼	Cordero A Jr	125	*.40	87-22	Irish Tower1274¾Ring of Light113½Relaxing1251	Late bid	6
14Mar81- 9Bow	fst 1¼	:48 1:122 1:373 2:043 3↑	JB Campbell H-G2	8 6 611 42¼ 1½ 13	Cordero A Jr	123	2.80	97-25	Relaxing1233Irish Tower1282½Peat Moss1121	Easily	9
10Jan81- 8Aqu	fst 1⅛⊡	:483 1:132 1:384 1:514 3↑	Assault H 55k	1 4 31 2hd 15 14	Cordero A Jr	122	*.20	87-24	Relaxing1224StiffSentence1103½LarkOscillaton1095	Easily	5
13Dec80- 8Aqu	fst 1⅝⊡	:484 1:402 2:051 2:422 3↑	Gallant Fox-G2	3 9 913 22 1½ 12	Encinas RI	120	*.50	106-10	Relaxing1202Fool's Prayer11413Dallasite1115½	Ridden out	10
6Dec80- 8Aqu	fst 1⅛⊡	:474 1:12 1:372 1:491 3↑	ⒻFirenze H-G2	7 7 77 63½ 11½ 14½	Velasquez J	118	*.90	100-14	Relaxing1184½SugarandSpice115noPlankton1212	Ridden out	8
27Nov80- 7Aqu	fst 1⅛	:48 1:122 1:362 1:483 3↑	ⒻHandicap 35000	4 6 31½ 12½ 19 112	Cordero A Jr	122	*.70	92-24	Relaxing12212Bien Fait1103General J.1081¼	Handily	6
9Nov80- 7Aqu	gd 1⅜Ⓣ	:50 1:162 1:42 2:182 3↑	ⒻHandicap 35000	4 6 77¼ 2hd 15 16½	Cordero A Jr	118	*1.20	79-21	Relaxng1186½ExactlySo110nk[D]ProudBarbara1144	Ridden out	7
26Oct80- 8Aqu	sf 1½Ⓣ	:514 1:18 2:10 2:351 3↑	ⒻLong Island H-G3	4 3 2½ 21 25 29	Cordero A Jr	113	2.70	56-35	TheVeryOne1209Relaxing113½ProudBarbara11313	Drifted out	5
9Oct80- 6Med	gd 1⅜Ⓣ	:50 1:15 1:393 2:161 3↑	ⒻQueen Charlotte H-G3	5 4 41½ 4¾ 53¼ 43½	Cordero A Jr	113	4.50	80-14	TheVeryOne1191¾HeyBbe115nkRiddle'sReply1141½	Weakened	10
1Sep80- 8Bel	fm 1¼[T]	:474 1:114 1:362 2:004 3↑	ⒻFlower Bowl H-G2	3 8 814 85¼ 78 63½	Vasquez J	112	4.70	86-12	JustaGameII1242HeyBabe114noEuphrosyne112nk	No menace	11
17Aug80- 8Sar	fm 1⅛Ⓣ	:48 1:124 1:363 1:49 3↑	ⒻDiana H-G2	2 7 47½ 42 43¼ 3nk	Vasquez J	113	14.90	82-18	JustaGameII123nkTheVeryOne117hdRelaxing1131¼	Rallied	9
21Jun80- 8Bel	fm 1¼[T]	:49 1:13 1:363 2:002 3↑	ⒻNew York H-G3	6 3 32 21½ 45½ 65¾	Encinas RI	115	2.90	86-11	JustaGmeII1211Poppycock112hdPleasTryHrd1132¼	Bid,tired	6
	Previously trained by Floreano Fernandez										
5Apr80- 8SA	fst 1 1/16	:231 :462 1:10 1:403 4↑	ⒻS Lucia H 55k	7 5 69 69½ 510 37½	Pincay L Jr	120	*2.30	90-10	ImageofReality1187FlamingLeaves121½Relaxng120½	Mild bid	8
23Mar80- 8SA	fm 1¼Ⓣ	:472 1:121 1:36 2:002 4↑	ⒻS Barbara H-G1	4 8 87¾ 43 32 31¼	McHargue DG	118	6.20	84-14	Sisterhood1181Petron'sLove114nkRelxng1181¼	Lacked room	10
13Mar80- 5SA	gd 1⅛Ⓣ	:472 1:12 1:37 1:492 4↑	ⒻAlw 22000	12 7 74¼ 51¾ 41¾ 11¼	Pincay L Jr	117	*1.70	80-20	Relaxing1171¼T.V. Caper1152Island Kitty114nk	Driving	12
	Previously trained by John Dunlop										

10Nov79♦ Doncaster(GB)	sf *1¼ⓉLH	2:214	Armistice Stakes Alw8000	11½	Carson W	129	3.30	Relaxing1291½Tahitian King1354Wrmington1353	Rated at rear,rallied to lead 150y out,driving	4
29Oct79♦ Chepstow(GB)	gd 1½ⓉLH	2:451	Mademoiselle Stakes (Lady Amateurs) Alw2100	11½	Guest E	140	*.65	Relaxing1401½Abielle1357Wingau1472	Progress 4f out,led over 2f out,ridden out	19
13Oct79♦ Ascot(GB)	gd 1½ⓉRH	2:483 3↑	ⒻPrincess Royal Stakes-G3 Stk30000	41½	Starkey G	118	14.00	Alia115¾Crystal Queen115hdOdeon118¾	Toward rear,progress 2f out,hung	11
5Oct79♦ Lingfield(GB)	fm 1¼ⓉLH	2:064	Hartfield Stakes Alw3900	17	Carson W	127	*2.00	Relaxing1277Tantot1172Persian Risk1202½	5th stretch 2½f out,led over 1f out,easily clear	10
22Sep79♦ Ayr(GB)	yl 1¼ⓉLH	2:143	Brodick Alw4500	461¼	Johnson E	128	*1.10	Pinaka1344Pendles Secret128¾Theydon Prince1311½	Trailed,7th 2f out,mild late gain	10
13Sep79♦ Salisbury(GB)	gd 1¼ⓉRH	2:094	ⒻNetheravon Maiden Stakes Mdn2900	18	Starkey G	123	*3.30	Relaxing1238Tantot123noRed Jay1231½	Long drive to lead over 1f out,quickly clear	13
31Aug79♦ Sandown(GB)	gd 1¼ⓉRH	2:111	Autumn Maiden Stakes Mdn3500	76	Carson W	123	7.00	Wearmouth1261½Hay Reef1232Jakaroo126½	Sweating,never a factor	12
18May79♦ Newbury(GB)	gd 1⅜ⓉLH	-	Shaw Maiden Stakes Mdn5000	77¼	Muddle R	123	5.50	Tyrondero1261Beau Reef126hdBalinger1263	Toward rear,some late progress.Time not taken	19
21Apr79♦ Newbury(GB)	gd 7fⓉStr	1:303	Bucklebury Maiden Stakes Mdn (FT)4400	24	Piggott L	123	*1.60	Sandfornia1234Relaxing1231½Hay Reef123nk	Midpack,bid over 1f out,no chance with winner	14

Rhythm

b. c. 1987, by Mr. Prospector (Raise a Native)–Dance Number, by Northern Dancer — **Lifetime record: 20 6 3 4 $1,592,532**

Own.– Ogden Mills Phipps
Br.– Ogden Mills Phipps (Ky)
Tr.– Claude McGaughey III

8Jun91- 7Bel	fst 1⅛	:442 1:084 1:342 1:463 3↑	Nassau County H-G2	4 9 917 78½ 77 713¾	Cordero A Jr	115	6.60e	82-08	Festin1167Gervazy112nkFarma Way1232¼	Flattened out	10
17May91- 8Bel	fst 1	:234 :464 1:11 1:361 3↑	Handicap 47000	5 4 42 32 34 34¾	Cordero A Jr	122	*1.00	84-14	FarewllWv114noSoundofCnnons1164¾Rhythm1225	Lacked rally	5
23Mar91-11GP	fst 1¼	:472 1:11 1:351 2:01 3↑	Gulf Park H-G1	6 7 710 612 614 613¼	Perret C	118	5.30	83-17	Jolie's Halo1193Primal117noChief Honcho1181¼	No rally	8
9Feb91- 9GP	fst 1⅛	:454 1:102 1:35 1:472 3↑	Donn H-G1	3 12 1213 1111 911 814¼	Perret C	121 b	*1.60	86-06	Jolie'sHalo1148SportsView116nkSecretHello116hd	No rally	12
26Jan91-10GP	fst 1 1/16	:242 :481 1:12 1:422 3↑	Creme Fraiche H 75k	5 3 34½ 33 31½ 2nk	Perret C	121 b	*.60	101-10	NewYrkSwll111nkRhythm1211¼MrcdsWon1127	Drifted,missed	5
27Oct90- 9Bel	fst 1¼	:454 1:094 1:353 2:021 3↑	BC Classic-G1	7 11 117¾ 63¾ 811 813½	Perret C	121 b	*2.60	72-15	Unbridled1211IbnBey1261ThirtySixRd121no	Bid,tired badly	14
15Sep90- 8Bel	fst 1⅛	:451 1:083 1:331 1:454 3↑	Woodward H-G1	3 7 612 66½ 64½ 32¾	Perret C	120 b	3.10	102-09	Dispersal1231¼QuietAmercn1171½Rhythm120nk	Belated rally	8
18Aug90- 7Sar	fst 1¼	:472 1:112 1:362 2:023	Travers-G1	3 11 1311 79½ 32½ 13½	Perret C	126 b	6.50	91-09	Rhythm1263½ShtGnSctt126nkSrRchrdLws1263½	Wide,driving	13
28Jly90-10Mth	fst 1⅛	:471 1:111 1:363 1:491	Haskell Inv'l H-G1	5 5 42 3nk 41¾ 32½	Perret C	121 b	2.90	86-10	RstlssCon1182¼BarondVaux117nkRhythm121hd	Lacked fin bid	7
30Jun90- 8Bel	fst 1⅛	:462 1:094 1:343 1:472	Dwyer-G2	3 3 32 21 32½ 21½	Perret C	123	1.30	95-03	Profit Key1231½Rhythm1231¾Graf1142	Bore out,gamely	4
9Jun90- 7Bel	gd 1⅛	:474 1:122 1:363 1:49	Colin-G3	5 5 65½ 62½ 2½ 12¼	Perret C	122	*.60	89-13	Rhythm1222¼Senator to Be1151¾Paradise Found1152½		8
	Wide,good handling										
21May90- 7Bel	gd 7f	:224 :452 1:094 1:222 3↑	Alw 33000	1 5 65 53 21 11¼	Perret C	113	*1.10	92-20	Rhythm1131¼SenatortoBe1122½FarewllWave1195	Going away	7
7Apr90- 8Aqu	gd 1	:22 :441 1:082 1:334	Gotham-G2	1 5 53¾ 65½ 68½ 57¾	Perret C	121	3.60	85-14	ThirtySixRed1141¼SenorPete1213½BurntHlls1141¾	No factor	10
3Mar90-10GP	fst 1 1/16	:232 :473 1:122 1:443	Fountain of Youth-G2	6 3 41½ 54½ 1012 108¼	Perret C	122	2.90	80-24	Shot Gun Scott122½Smelly119noUnbridled117¾	Faltered	13
10Feb90-10GP	fst 7f	:214 :442 1:102 1:242	Hutcheson-G3	9 1 78 77¾ 47½ 78	Perret C	122	*.90	76-18	Housebuster1193Yonder1221Stalker114¾	Tired	11
4Nov89- 8GP	fst 1 1/16	:232 :464 1:111 1:433	BC Juvenile-G1	3 5 52¾ 11 12 12	Perret C	122	2.60e	93-01	Rhythm1222Grand Canyon1221¾Slavic1221	Driving	12
14Oct89- 8Bel	fst 1	:231 :46 1:11 1:373	Champagne-G1	1 4 33½ 1hd 2½ 2nk	Perret C	122	2.30e	77-26	Adjudicating122nkRhythm1223Senor Pete1224¾	Gamely	6
24Sep89- 6Bel	fst 7f	:23 :471 1:13 1:253	Alw 30000	4 6 52¾ 52½ 1½ 14	Cordero A Jr	122	*.50	74-21	Rhythm1224Hot Candy1173¼Give a Buck1172	Ridden out	7
15Sep89- 9Bel	gd 7f	:223 :453 1:103 1:24	Md Sp Wt	3 4 42 2½ 11 13	Perret C	118	2.40	82-18	Rhythm1183ThirtySixRed1182½JamesHarper1189¼	Ridden out	10
11Aug89- 6Sar	fst 5f	:223 :463 :59	Md Sp Wt	1 4 42½ 31½ 34½ 37¾	Perret C	118	*.80	83-19	Three Way Split1187Prone118¾Rhythm118nk	Weakened	8

Risen Star

dkbbr. c. 1985, by Secretariat (Bold Ruler)–Ribbon, by His Majesty — Lifetime record: 11 8 2 1 $2,029,845

Own.– L. Roussel III & Lamarque Stable
Br.– Arthur Hancock III & Leone J. Peters (Ky)
Tr.– Louie J. Roussel III

11Jun88- 8Bel	fst 1½	:471 1:114 2:013 2:262	Belmont-G1	5 2 24 16 110	114¾	Delahoussaye E	126	*2.10	88-13	RisenStar12614¾Kingpost1262Brian'sTime12611¼	Ridden out	6
21May88- 9Pim	gd 1 3/16	:47 1:111 1:363 1:561	Preakness-G1	3 4 31½ 31 12	11¼	Delahoussaye E	126	6.80	86-11	RisenStar1261¼Brian'sTime1261¼WinnngColors1212½	Driving	9
7May88- 8CD	fst 1¼	:464 1:112 1:36 2:021	Ky Derby-G1	1 13 1315 99¼ 67½	33¼	Delahoussaye E	126	5.50	83-11	WinningColors121nkFortyNiner1263RisnStr126½	Very wide	17
16Apr88- 8Kee	fst 1 1/16	:24 :48 1:122 1:424	Lexington-G2	5 5 53½ 53½ 2½	1hd	Vasquez J	118	3.20	92-18	Risen Star118hdForty Niner12112Stalwars1182	Driving	5
13Mar88-11FG	fst 1 1/16	:241 :473 1:12 1:431	La Derby-G3	1 6 67½ 67 42½	11¾	Romero SP	120	2.60	96-14	Risen Star1201¾Word Pirate118¾Pastourelles1181¾	Driving	7
27Feb88-10FG	fst 1 40	:233 :461 1:122 1:40	Derby Trial 23k	11 9 914 55½ 22	11	Romero SP	120	*1.10	93-20	Risen Star1201Pastourelles1153½Jim's Orbit1221	Driving	12
6Feb88-10FG	gd 1 1/16	:24 :473 1:124 1:463	Lecomte H 24k	7 5 55 21 21	21¼	Romero SP	122	*.30e	78-21	Pastourelles1131¼RisenStar1223RunPaulRun1141	Held place	7
2Jan88- 8FG	gd 1 1/16	:24 :49 1:141 1:473	©Alw 9200	5 5 52½ 11 14	110	Romero SP	119	*.30	74-26	Risen Star11910Mr. Buttercup1161Proper Duty1194½	Easily	7
6Dec87- 9FG	fm *7½fⓉ	:241 :481 1:144 1:341	©Alw 8400	10 12 914 65¼ 13	14	Romero SP	120	*.40	78-18	Risen Star1204Quick Bob1174½Jacumlea1201	Easily	12
	Previously owned by L.J. Roussel III;previously trained by Rene Gebbia											
11Oct87-10LaD	fst 7f	:231 :462 1:102 1:223	Sport of Kings Fut 210k	5 3 31½ 32 36	215	Snyder L	121	2.40	80-21	Success Express12115Risen Star1212¾Big Snoz12113	Tired	6
24Sep87- 9LaD	fst 6½f	:222 :453 1:12 1:19	Minstrel 40k	3 9 53½ 66¼ 43½	11	Walker BJ Jr	112	*.90	80-27	RisnStr1121BoldChadr1151½SholSrchr115½	Soundly bumped	9

Roving Boy

b. c. 1980, by Olden Times (Relic)–Black Eyed Lucy, by Prince Royal II — Lifetime record: 9 6 2 0 $843,675

Own.– R.E. Hibbert
Br.– Robert E. Hibbert (Ky)
Tr.– Joseph Manzi

2Nov83- 8SA	fst 1 1/16	:224 :46 1:104 1:433	Alibhai H-G3	6 4 33 43 21½	1no	Delahoussaye E	124	*.40	83-23	Roving Boy124noHula Blaze1102½Lagoon Lover115no		6
	Broke down past finish line											
14Oct83- 8SA	fst 6½f	:213 :444 1:093 1:154 3↑	Alw 30000	2 5 44¼ 34 11½	2hd	Delahoussaye E	115	*.50	91-19	CivicLeader117hdRovingBoy1153ShadyFox1106	Just missed	7
12Dec82- 8Hol	fst 1 1/16	:222 :454 1:101 1:414	Hol Futurity 761k	1 6 41 2hd 1hd	1nk	Delahoussaye E	121	1.70	86-20	RovingBoy121nkDesertWine1212FifthDivision1214	Driving	9
30Oct82- 8SA	fst 1 1/16	:223 :45 1:091 1:413	Norfolk-G2	1 5 34 3nk 11½	14½	Delahoussaye E	118	*1.50	93-10	Roving Boy1184½Desert Wine1183½Aguila1181¼	Easily	9
8Sep82- 8Dmr	sl 1	:222 :461 1:123 1:384	Dmr Futurity-G2	8 5 35½ 2½ 2½	1½	Delahoussaye E	117	*1.60	74-30	Roving Boy117½Desert Wine12011Balboa Native1144	Driving	9
25Aug82- 8Dmr	fst 1	:222 :454 1:094 1:352	Balboa 53k	2 5 43½ 43 32	11½	Delahoussaye E	115	6.90	91-12	RvngBoy1151½Encourgr1152½FullChok1174½	Bobbled,driving	5
13Aug82- 6Dmr	fst 1	:221 :46 1:121 1:372	©Md Sp Wt	7 1 12 12 13	16	Delahoussaye E	117	*2.00	81-17	RvingBoy1176Morry'sChamp1173½DebonairHerc1172	Driving	10
31Jly82- 6Dmr	fst 6f	:22 :453 :584 1:113	©Md Sp Wt	8 5 4¾ 2hd 2hd	2½	Delahoussaye E	118	19.90	79-15	Be a Scholar118½Roving Boy1184Jolly Be First1182½	Sharp	9
21Jly82- 6Dmr	fst 5½f	:22 :453 1:04	©Md Sp Wt	2 10 1116 1121 1123	715	Pincay L Jr	118	7.70	76-17	EchoGrande1181½Mezzo1181¼InflationBeater1186	No threat	11

Royal Heroine (Ire)

dkbbr. f. 1980, by Lypheor (Lyphard)–My Sierra Leone, by Relko — Lifetime record: 21 10 4 2 $1,217,397

Own.– R.E. Sangster
Br.– B.L. Ryan (Ire)
Tr.– John H.M. Gosden

25Nov84- 8Hol	yl 1⅛Ⓣ	:484 1:122 1:361 1:492 3↑	ⒻMatriarch-G1	1 2 2½ 2½ 2hd	11	Toro F	123	*.80	83-17	Royal Heroine1231Reine Mathilde1202Sabin1232¼	Driving	6
10Nov84- 4Hol	fm 1Ⓣ	:223 :453 1:084 1:323 3↑	BC Mile-G1	10 5 63¾ 53 3½	11½	Toro F	123	*1.70e	105-01	Royal Heroine1231½Star Choice126nkCozzene126nk	Driving	10
9Sep84- 8Dmr	fm 1⅛Ⓣ	:484 1:124 1:363 1:482 3↑	ⒻRamona H-G1	7 5 62¾ 61¾ 65¾	22½	Toro F	126	*.60	93-05	Flag de Lune1152½Royal Heroine126hdSalt Spring115¾	Wide	9
26Aug84- 9AP	fm 1¼Ⓣ	:482 1:122 1:372 2:012 3↑	Bud Arl Million-G1	1 1 1½ 1½ 2hd	21¾	Toro F	122	14.70	85-15	JohnHenry1261¾RoyalHeroin1223GtodlSol126no	Best of rest	12
11Aug84- 8Dmr	fm 1Ⓣ	:23 :47 1:113 1:351 3↑	ⒻPalomar H-G3	8 4 33 32 21½	1nk	Toro F	125	*.60e	97-06	ⒹRoyal Heroine125nkMoment to Buy115¾L'Attrayante1203		8
	Drifted in,brushed;Disqualified and placed third											
1Jly84- 8Hol	fm 1⅛Ⓣ	:464 1:104 1:343 1:471 3↑	ⒻBeverly Hills H-G2	8 7 76 63 1hd	11¾	Toro F	123	*.70	94-06	RylHeroine1231¾Adored121nkComedyAct118nk	Bumped,clear	9
17Jun84- 8Hol	fm 1 1/16Ⓣ	:23 :471 1:101 1:401 3↑	Inglewood H-G3	8 6 53¼ 63¾ 41	1½	Toro F	116	4.60	98-06	RoyalHeroine116½BelBolide120½VinStBenet118hd	Driving	13
18Mar84- 8SA	fm 1⅛Ⓣ	:46 1:104 1:351 1:482 4↑	ⒻSanta Ana H-G1	7 5 - - -	-	Toro F	122	2.90	- -	Avigaition1182¾Pride of Rosewood1161¾L'Attrayante122¾		9
	Fell over downed rival											
20Nov83- 6Hol	fm 1⅛Ⓣ	:463 1:113 1:354 1:481	Hol Derby (Div 1)-G1	5 5 57 1hd 11	1¾	Toro F	119	3.70	89-13	RoyalHeroine119¾Interco1223½PacMani1223	Brushed,driving	11
	Previously trained by Michael R. Stoute											
6Nov83- 8SA	fm 1¼Ⓣ	:474 1:134 1:374 2:021 3↑	ⒻYellow Ribbon-G1	9 9 75½ 86¼ 86¾	710	Swinburn WR	119	40.20	66-24	Sangue1231½L'Attrayante1192Infinite119½	Outrun	12
2Oct83♦ Longchamp(Fr)	fm*1⅛ⓉRH	1:50 3↑	ⒻPrix de l'Opera-G2 Stk63700		11½	Swinburn WR	123	*2.40		Royal Heroine1231½Fly With Me121nkLittle Meadow121hd	Rated in 6th,split horses to lead 1f out,ridden out	18
10Sep83♦ Doncaster(GB)	sf 1ⓉLH	1:424 3↑	ⒻSceptre Stakes (Listed) Stk25000		1nk	Swinburn WR	122	*1.10		Royal Heroine122nkFlamenco1181Gaygo Lady119¾	Always close up,led 3f out,held gamely	6
12Aug83♦ Newbury(GB)	gd *7fⓉLH	1:282 3↑	ⒻHungerford Stakes-G3 Stk35900		22½	Swinburn WR	118	4.00		Salieri1232½Royal Heroine1181½Tecorno1212½	Tracked in 5th,bid over 1f out,always held by winner	10
6Jly83♦ Newmarket(GB)	gd 1ⓉStr	1:411 3↑	Child Stakes-G3 Stk13200		12	Swinburn WR	117	*2.00		Royal Heroine1172Flamenco1201½Lindas Fantasy1173	Tracked leader,led 3f out,ridden out.Annie Edge 5th	8
4Jun83♦ Epsom(GB)	sf 1½ⓉLH	2:404	ⒻEnglish Oaks-G1 Stk205000		718¼	Swinburn WR	126	4.50		Sun Princess12612Acclimatise1262½New Coins1261½	Lathered up,rated in 6th,never threatened	15
28Apr83♦ Newmarket(GB)	gd 1ⓉStr	1:413	Ⓕ1000 Guineas-G1 Stk140000		21½	Swinburn WR	126	10.00		Ma Biche1261½ⒹRoyal Heroine126hdFavoridge126½	Led 2f out,faded,back up for 2nd;Disqualified from 2nd place purse	18
14Apr83♦ Newmarket(GB)	gd 7fⓉStr	1:30	ⒻNell Gwyn Stakes-G3 Stk23700		31½	Swinburn WR	119	3.00		Favoridge1191½Annie Edge119hdRoyal Heroine1191	Tracked leaders,bid 1½f out,saved 3rd	9
18Aug82♦ York(GB)	gd 6fⓉStr	1:13	ⒻLowther Stakes-G2 Stk34200		21½	Starkey G	123	*1.75		Habibti1231½Royal Heroine1233Annie Edge123nk	Tracked in 4th,rallied to lead 1f out,soon headed,2nd best; Previously trained by Mick Ryan	8
24Jly82♦ Ascot(GB)	gd 6fⓉStr	1:152	ⒻPrincess Margaret (Listed) Stk9800		12½	Robinson P	123	4.00		Royal Heroine1242½Henry's Secret127noBright Crocus1271½	Tracked leader,led 1f out,drew clear	6
7Jly82♦ Newmarket(GB)	gd 6fⓉStr	1:131	ⒻPrincess Maiden Stakes Mdn7300		13	Robinson P	123	12.00		Royal Heroine1233Montrevie1233The Babe123¾	Tracked leaders,led 1½f out,easily clear	20
26Jun82♦ Doncaster(GB)	yl 6fⓉStr	1:153	ⒻLonsdale Maiden Stakes Mdn1800		43½	Lowe J	123	33.00		Bright Cone123noSuper Entente1233Jumaireh123½	Prominent,bid 2f out,one-paced final furlong	15

Sacahuista

b. f. 1984, by Raja Baba (Bold Ruler)–Nalees Flying Flag, by Hoist the Flag — **Lifetime record: 21 6 7 2 $1,298,842**

Own.– Beal & French Jr
Br.– G. Watts Humphrey Jr & William S. Farish (Ky)
Tr.– D. Wayne Lukas

15Oct88-3Bel	fst 6f	:22^1 :45^1 1:09^4	3↑ⒻAlw 41000	1	2	4^{7½}	4^8	3^5	2^{¾}	Romero RP	115	b	*.60	89-17	Starita115^{¾}Sachust115^{4¾}Poculton115^{6½}	Wide,finished fast	4	
25Sep88-8Bel	fst 1⅛	:47 1:11 1:35^2 1:48	3↑ⒻRuffian H-G1	1	6	7^{3½}	11^{15}	11^{23}	10^{23}	Stevens GL	119	b	*1.50e	64-16	ShamSay113^{¾}ClassicCrwn115^{6}MakeChang114^{nk}	Bobbled start	11	
12Aug88-8Sar	fst 7f	:22^1 :44^2 1:08^4 1:21^3	3↑ⒻBallerina-G1	6	2	4^{1½}	5^3	5^{7½}	5^{7¾}	Santos JA	119	b	3.00	86-08	Cadillacing116^{nk}Thirty Zip116^{hd}Ready Jet Go111^{5½}	Tired	6	
21Nov87-3Hol	fst 1¼	:47^1 1:11^3 1:36^4 2:02^4	3↑ⒻBC Distaff-G1	5	1	1^2	1^{2½}	1^{2½}	1^{2¼}	Romero RP	119	b	2.90	78-12	Sacahuista119^{2¼}Clabber Girl123^{4}Oueee Bebe119^{hd}	Driving	6	
31Oct87-8Kee	fst 1⅛	:46^2 1:10^1 1:35^4 1:48^3	3↑ⒻSpinster-G1	2	1	1^{½}	1^1	1^{2½}	1^3	Romero RP	119	b	*1.40e	94-14	Sacahuista119^{3}Ms. Margi119^{2½}Tall Poppy123^{no}	Ridden out	13	
27Sep87-8Bel	fst 1⅛	:46^2 1:09^2 1:35 1:48^3	3↑ⒻRuffian H-G1	12	1	1^{hd}	1^1	1^{2½}	1^{hd}	Migliore R	114	b	*.40e	84-19	[D]Sacahuista114^{hd}CoupdeFusil117^{1¾}ClbbrGrl112^{½}	Lugged in	12	
	Disqualified and placed third																	
12Sep87-9Pha	fst 1$\frac{1}{16}$	:23^3 :47 1:10^3 1:42^4	ⒻCotillion H-G3	4	1	1^{hd}	1^{½}	1^{½}	1^{nk}	Perret C	119	b	4.30	90-18	[D]Sacahuist119^{nk}SlntTurn118^{7½}SnglBld117^5	Caused bumping	8	
	Disqualified and placed second																	
6Aug87-8Sar	fst 7f	:21^3 :43^3 1:08 1:21	ⒻTest-G2	11	3	5^{3½}	4^{5½}	4^{8½}	5^{9¼}	McCarron CJ	121	b	6.90e	88-14	VerySbtle121^{5¼}UptheApalache121^{3½}SlntTrn121^{hd}	Weakened	14	
19Jly87-8Hol	fst 1¼	:45^3 1:09^1 1:34^4 2:00^3	3↑ⒻVanity Inv'l H-G1	1	4	4^6	5^{5½}	5^{5½}	5^{11¼}	Antley CW	109	b	8.30	78-07	Infinidad113^{6½}NorthSidr121^{2¾}ClbbrGrl115^{1¾}	Wide into str	7	
12Jly87-8Hol	fst 1⅛	:46^1 1:10^1 1:35^4 1:48^3	ⒻHol Oaks-G1	3	2	1^{hd}	2^{hd}	1^{½}	2^{½}	Stevens GL	121	b	*1.60	93-09	PerchancetoDream121^{½}Sachst121^{5}PnBILdy121^2	Outfinished	6	
20Jun87-8Hol	fst 1$\frac{1}{16}$	:22^2 :45^3 1:10^1 1:43	ⒻPrincess-G2	1	4	4^{1½}	3^{1½}	2^{2½}	2^{nk}	Stevens GL	122	b	2.30	94-11	RansomedCaptive116^{nk}Schst122^{1¼}VrySbtl122^2	Saved ground	6	
6Jun87-8Hol	fst 7f	:22 :44^3 1:09^3 1:22^3	ⒻRailbird-G3	3	2	2^{½}	3^2	3^{3½}	3^{6½}	Stevens GL	122	b	1.90	84-17	VerySbtle122^{5½}JoeytheTrp117^{1}Schust122	No late response	4	
30Nov86-8Hol	fst 1	:22^4 :45^4 1:10^1 1:36	ⒻHol Starlet-G1	3	3	2^{½}	2^{1½}	2^{2½}	2^{½}	Pincay L Jr	120	b	*1.20	82-16	Very Subtle120^{½}Sacahuista120^{11}Infringe120^{1¼}		6	
	Bobbled break,lugged out backside,through stretch																	
1Nov86-2SA	fst 1$\frac{1}{16}$	:22^1 :45^3 1:10^1 1:43^1	ⒻBC Juv Fillies-G1	8	5	5^7	7^9	7^{13}	4^{10¾}	Pincay L Jr	119	b	*1.90	74-13	Brave Raj119^{5½}Tappiano119^{3½}Saros Brig119^{1¾}	Rallied	12	
5Oct86-8SA	fst 1$\frac{1}{16}$	:22 :45^3 1:10^2 1:44^3	ⒻOak Leaf-G1	5	3	2^{1½}	2^{½}	1^{½}	1^{2¼}	McCarron CJ	115	b	1.90	78-15	Sacahuista115^{2¼}Silk'sLady115^{nk}DelicatVn115^{nk}	Drew clear	7	
10Sep86-8Dmr	fst 1	:22^2 :45^2 1:10^1 1:35^3	Dmr Futurity-G1	1	1	1^{hd}	2^{½}	1^{hd}	2no	Day P	117	b	4.90	90-11	Qualify114^{no}Sacahuista117^{½}Brevito116^5	Sharp	9	
	Previously owned by L.R. French Jr																	
29Aug86-6AP	fst 7f	:22^1 :45 1:10^1 1:23^2	ⒻArl-Wash Lassie-G1	6	2	2^{½}	2^{hd}	2^{hd}	2^{1¼}	McCarron CJ	122	b	3.20	84-19	DelicateVine122^{1¼}Sacahuista122^{¾}RulingAngl122^{1½}	2nd best	6	
14Aug86-8Sar	fst 6f	:22 :45^2 1:11	ⒻAdirondack-G2	6	1	2^{½}	2^{hd}	1^{hd}	1^1	McCarron CJ	119	b	*.30	85-20	Sacahuista119^{1}Collins114^{4½}Release the Lyd116^2	Driving	7	
30Jly86-8Sar	fst 6f	:22 :45^2 1:10^3	ⒻSchuylerville-G3	5	2	2^1	1^{hd}	1^{2½}	1^{3½}	McCarron CJ	115	b	*2.20	87-13	Sacahuist114^{3½}OurLttlMrg114^{1¾}Collns114^4	Leaned in,clear	9	
11Jly86-6Hol	fst 5½f	:22^2 :45^4 :57^4 1:04^2	ⒻMd Sp Wt	10	1	1^1	1^{hd}	1^4	1^9	McCarron CJ	118	b	9.20	92-14	Sacahuista118^{9}Ninepaytheline113^{nk}AlwysWomn118^{2½}	Easily	11	
5Jun86-5Hol	fst 5f	:22^2 :46^2 :59^3	ⒻMd Sp Wt	3	4	8^{8½}	8^{10}	6^7	5^{6¼}	Valenzuela PA	118		14.90	82-16	PrchncetoDream118^{hd}RomnGem118^{4}QuickMssngr118^1	Outrun	9	

Safely Kept

dkbbr. f. 1986, by Horatius (Proudest Roman)–Safely Home, by Winning Hit — **Lifetime record: 31 24 2 3 $2,194,206**

Own.– Jayeff B Stable & Weisbord
Br.– Mr & Mrs David Hayden (Md)
Tr.– Alan E. Goldberg

4Oct91-9Med	fst 6f	:22 :44^2 1:08^4	3↑ⒻBud BC H-G3	4	2	2^{1½}	2^{½}	1^{hd}	1^2	Stevens GL	L 128	*.40	98-12	SafelyKpt128^{2}BrghtCndls114^{1¾}DvlshTouch115^{2¾}	Ridden out	7	
8Sep91-3Pim	fst 6f	:23 :46^1 :58^2 1:11	3↑ⒻDistaff H 95k	5	4	1^{hd}	1^{hd}	1^{hd}	1^{½}	Stevens GL	L 130	*.30	90-12	Safely Kept130^{½}In the Curl118^{1¾}Wood So112^{nk}	Driving	6	
4Aug91-9Mth	my 1 70	:23 :46^1 1:10^1 1:40	3↑ⒻBud BC H-G3	3	1	1^{½}	3^2	3^3	3^{4¾}	Wilson R	L 123	*.70	91-08	Toffeefee115^{4½}Colonial Waters117^{nk}Safely Kept123^{3¼}		7	
	Not good enough																
20Jly91-9Lrl	fst 6f	:21^3 :43^4 :57 1:08^3	3↑F J DeFrancis 300k	5	6	6^7	3^{2½}	3^{2½}	3^{6¼}	Black CA	L 121	2.50	92-15	Housebuster126^{5}Clever Trevor123^{1¼}Safely Kept121^{3¼}		6	
	Dwelt,not driven late																
30Jun91-8AP	fst 7f	:22^3 :45^3 1:10^1 1:23	3↑ⒻBud BC H 155k	1	4	1^1	1^{1½}	1^{3½}	1^{7½}	Perret C	L 126	*.30	88-17	SaflyKpt126^{7½}NurseDopey118^{4½}TokenDanc114^{2½}	Ridden out	7	
6Jun91-8Bel	fst 6f	:22^3 :45^4 1:10	3↑ⒻGenuine Risk-G2	3	1	1^{1½}	1^{½}	1^{½}	1^2	Perret C	122	*.20	90-12	Safely Kept122^{2}Missy's Mirage109^{3}Token Dance117^3	Easily	5	
11May91-9GS	fst 6f	:21^4 :44^3 1:08^2	3↑ⒻBud BC H-G3	4	2	1^1	1^{½}	1^{½}	1^{1¼}	Black CA	L 128	*.30	101-09	SafelyKept128^{1¼}AvieJane117^{8½}TokenDance115^{9½}	Ridden out	4	
	Previously owned by Jayeff B. Stable & Weisbord																
27Oct90-3Bel	fst 6f	:21^4 :44^2 1:09^3	3↑BC Sprint-G1	4	1	1^1	2^{hd}	1^{hd}	1^{nk}	Perret C	123	12.20	91-11	Safely Kept123^{nk}Dayjur123^{4}Black Tie Affair126^{2¼}		14	
	Saved ground,gamely																
14Oct90-8Bel	fst 6f	:21^4 :44^1 1:08	3↑Boojum H-G3	4	1	2^1	2^1	4^{2½}	4^{2¾}	Perret C	120	*1.60	96-09	Carson City116^{1}Mr. Nickerson121^{1¼}Once Wild118^{½}	Weakened	6	
22Sep90-9Med	sly 6f	:21^3 :44^2 1:09^1	3↑ⒻBud BC-G3	1	5	1^{hd}	2^{hd}	1^{hd}	1^{nk}	Krone JA	L 127	*.50	96-12	Safely Kept127^{nk}Sexy Slew115^{1¾}Diva's Debut120^{2½}	Driving	7	
9Sep90-2Pim	fst 6f	:22^3 :45^4 :57^4 1:11	3↑ⒻDistaff H 95k	6	3	2^{hd}	1^{½}	1^{3½}	1^{1¼}	Krone JA	L 126	*.20	91-14	Safely Kept126^{1¼}Amy Be Good117^{2¼}Run Spot113^{3½}	Easily	6	
18Aug90-8Pim	fst 6f	:22 :44^4 :56^4 1:09	3↑De Francis Dash 350k	5	1	2^{hd}	4^{2½}	5^6	4^{6½}	Antley CW	L 121	*.80	94-08	NorthernWolf120^{2½}Glitterman124^{1½}Sewickly126^{2½}	Willingly	7	
4Jly90-10FL	fst 6f	:21^3 :43^4 1:09^4	3↑Bud BC 183k	1	3	1^{½}	1^{hd}	1^3	1^{2¼}	Perret C	117	*.30	97-15	Safely Kept117^{2¼}Northern Crush113^{4}For Really109^2	Easily	7	
7Jun90-8Bel	fst 6f	:22 :45^1 1:10^1	3↑ⒻGenuine Risk-G2	3	3	1^{½}	1^2	1^{3½}	1^3	Perret C	122	*.20	88-15	SafelyKept122^{3}Div'sDbut119^{13}Lvtton117^8	As rider pleased	4	
12May90-8GS	fst 6f	:22 :45 1:09^2	3↑ⒻBud BC-G3	1	3	1^1	1^1	1^3	1^4	Perret C	125	*.05	96-13	SafelyKept125^{4}MollyBolt111^{3½}ProudEmilia112^{½}	Good effort	6	
18Apr90-8Kee	fst 6f	:22^1 :45^2 1:10^2	3↑ⒻTbred Club of Am-G3	2	4	1^1	1^{1½}	1^{3½}	1^{3½}	Perret C	123	*.20	90-11	SafelyKpt123^{3½}Volterra112^{no}MdcnWomn117^3	Sluggish start	5	
1Mar90-10GP	fst 6f	:21^4 :45^1 1:11	3↑ⒻAlw 24000	3	2	2^{hd}	1^{hd}	1^4	1^{5½}	Perret C	122	*.20	90-19	SafelyKept122^{5½}Cutlasee115^{2¼}SpiritofFighter119^{1¾}	Easily	6	
4Nov89-4GP	fst 6f	:21^4 :44 1:09	3↑BC Sprint-G1	13	1	1^{1½}	1^{½}	1^2	2^{nk}	Perret C	121	6.90	101-04	Dancing Spree126^{nk}Safely Kept121^{nk}Dispersal124^1	Gamely	13	
	Previously owned by B. Weisbord																
8Oct89-10Pim	fst 6f	:23 :46^1 :58^2 1:11^1	ⒻColumbia 100k	5	2	1^1	1^{1½}	1^3	1^{4½}	Perret C	122	*.10	90-18	SafelyKept122^{4½}Cojinx119^{½}KathleentheQueen117^3	Drew off	5	
10Sep89-2Pim	fst 6f	:22^3 :45 :57 1:10	3↑Ⓕ[R]Distaff H 95k	2	1	1^{½}	1^{1½}	1^{3½}	1^{4¾}	Perret C	124	*.10	96-09	SafelyKept124^{4¾}IntheCurl116^{¾}RunSpot110^{1¼}	Bumped,clear	6	
3Aug89-8Sar	fst 7f	:22 :44^2 1:08^1 1:21^2	ⒻTest-G1	3	5	1^1	1^1	1^4	1^{1½}	Perret C	121	2.80	95-14	SafelyKept121^{1½}FntstcFnd114^{6}Cojnx116^{16}	Slow st.,driving	5	
16Jly89-8Bel	fst 6f	:21^3 :45 1:11^3	ⒻPrioress-G2	3	5	2^{2½}	1^3	1^7	1^{3¾}	Cordero A Jr	118	*.30	81-22	SafelyKpt118^{3¾}Cojinx114^{4}TheWayIt'sBinn114^{4½}	Ridden out	5	
4Jly89-3Mth	fst 6f	:20^4 :43^1 1:08^3	3↑ⒻRegret 33k	1	3	1^{2½}	1^3	1^8	1^{5½}	Wilson R	116	*.30	97-13	SafelyKept116^{5½}ReadyJetGo116^{no}FeeltheBeat116^{10½}	Easily	4	
8Jun89-8Bel	gd 6f	:21^4 :44^3 1:09^2	3↑ⒻGenuine Risk-G2	4	1	1^{1½}	1^4	1^5	1^4	Cordero A Jr	114	*.70	92-14	Safely Kept114^{4}Aptostar122^{4}Cagey Exuberance122^3	Driving	4	
6May89-9GS	fst 6f	:21^2 :44 1:08^3	3↑ⒻBud BC H-G3	3	2	1^5	1^5	1^4	1^{2¾}	Vigliotti MJ	108	*2.30	99-16	Safely Kept108^{2¾}Social Pro116^{7}Kerygma117^{hd}	Driving	9	
9Apr89-11Lrl	fst 6f	:22^1 :45^3 :58^2 1:11^3	Ⓕ[S]Politely 60k	7	5	2^{hd}	1^{hd}	1^4	1^4	Wilson R	118	*.40	85-22	SaflyKpt118^{4}NoblestHeart114^{5}SkatngLdy115^{1¾}	Ridden out	11	
	Previously trained by Carlos A. Garcia																
18Sep88-3Lrl	fst 7f	:22^4 :46 1:11^1 1:24	ⒻUSFG Lassie 95k	5	6	2^{hd}	1^{1½}	1^{hd}	3^5	Desormeaux KJ	119	*.40	86-10	Ms.GoldPole119^{4½}OpenMind119^{½}SafelyKept119^{1½}	Weakened	9	
14Aug88-9Pim	fst 6f	:23 :46^2 :58 1:10^3	Ⓕ[S]Smart Angle 50k	1	3	1^2	1^{3½}	1^5	1^{9½}	Desormeaux KJ	114	*.10	93-16	SaflyKpt114^{9½}HardHeadedWoman112^{4}HayRoll110^{6½}	Handily	7	
	Previously owned by Dark Hollow Farm																
24Jly88-9Pim	fst 5½f	:22^2 :46 :58^2 1:05	ⒻPlaypen 54k	3	4	1^2	1^3	1^5	1^{7½}	Desormeaux KJ	110	*.30	96-21	SfelyKpt110^{7½}TruxtonTwo110^{hd}CrclthFloor114^2	Ridden out	7	
21Jun88-4Pim	fst 5f	:22^1 :45^4 :58^3	ⒻMd Sp Wt	6	3	1^3	1^4	1^4	1^{6½}	Desormeaux KJ	119	*.40	92-19	SafelyKept119^{6½}CirclethFloor119^{6¾}PchIsl119^{hd}	Going away	7	
7Jun88-4Pim	fst 5f	:22 :45^2 :58^3	ⒻMd Sp Wt	2	2	1^{hd}	2^{hd}	2^{½}	2^{½}	Sarvis DA	119	*2.20	91-19	BeansBeans119^{½}SafelyKpt119^{2¼}CirclthFloor119^{5½}	Game try	7	

Slew o' Gold

b. c. 1980, by Seattle Slew (Bold Reasoning)–Alluvial, by Buckpasser — Lifetime record: 21 12 5 1 $3,533,534

Own.– Equusequity Stable
Br.– Claiborne Farm (Ky)
Tr.– John O. Hertler

10Nov84- 7Hol	fst	1¼	:453 1:103 1:37 2:032	3↑ BC Classic-G1	4	5	59½	2½	2hd	3½	Cordero A Jr	126	*.60e	--	WildAgain126hd[D]GateDancer122½Slewo'Gold1265	Roughed	8
Placed second through disqualification																	
20Oct84- 8Bel	fst	1½	:493 1:141 2:034 2:284	3↑ J C Gold Cup-G1	5	2	22	12½	14½	19¾	Cordero A Jr	126	*.10	76-17	Slwo'Gld1269¾HalBoldKng1211BoundngBsqu1263	Ridden out	5
29Sep84- 8Bel	fst	1¼	:474 1:113 1:364 2:022	3↑ Marlboro Cup H-G1	6	4	3½	11½	11½	11¾	Cordero A Jr	129	*.80	86-19	Slewo'Gold1291¾CarrdeNskra1192CanadnFctor1142½	Driving	9
15Sep84- 8Bel	sly	1⅛	:451 1:092 1:344 1:474	3↑ Woodward-G1	6	2	3½	21½	21	1½	Cordero A Jr	126	*.70	88-18	Slew o' Gold126½Shifty Sheik1163Bet Big1163¾	Driving	6
4Aug84- 8Sar	fst	1⅛	:464 1:10 1:351 1:483	3↑ Whitney H-G1	1	1	2hd	2hd	1hd	11¾	Cordero A Jr	126	*.40	92-13	Slewo'Gold1261¾TrackBarron11711¼Thumbsucker115	Easily	3
2Jly84- 1Bel	gd	1	:223 :444 1:092 1:342	3↑ Alw 36000	1	2	24	1hd	13	17½	Cordero A Jr	115	*.40	93-15	Slewo'Gld1157½CannonShll1151¾NorthrnIc1083¼	Ridden out	5
Previously trained by Sidney Watters Jr																	
15Oct83- 8Bel	fst	1½	:48 1:123 2:01 2:261	3↑ J C Gold Cup-G1	3	5	63¼	2½	12	13	Cordero A Jr	121	3.00e	89-14	Slwo'Gld1213HighlandBlad126nkBoundngBsqu1211½	Driving	11
24Sep83- 8Bel	fst	1¼	:472 1:111 1:361 2:011	3↑ Marlboro Cup H-G1	2	2	1hd	13	1½	2nk	Cordero A Jr	119	4.80	92-17	HighlandBlade117nkSlewo'Gld119½BtsMotl1244	Wide,missed	9
3Sep83- 8Bel	fst	1⅛	:454 1:092 1:34 1:463	3↑ Woodward-G1	6	7	42	21	1hd	1no	Cordero A Jr	118	4.00e	94-13	Slew o' Gold118noBates Motel1235Sing Sing1195	Driving	10
13Aug83- 8Sar	gd	1¼	:464 1:101 1:352 2:01	Travers-G1	1	2	2½	2hd	2hd	21¾	Cordero A Jr	126	*2.40	93-11	PlayFellow1261¾Slewo'Gold1262¼Hyperborean1262½	Gamely	7
30Jly83- 9Mth	fst	1⅛	:463 1:102 1:36 1:491	Haskell H-G1	5	8	87	44	51¾	64	Cordero A Jr	124	*1.00	85-17	DeputdTstmony124nkBetBig1162Parftmnt116½	Lacked room	10
11Jun83- 8Bel	fst	1½	:472 1:113 1:594 2:274	Belmont-G1	1	3	21½	1½	21	23½	Cordero A Jr	126	*2.50	77-14	Caveat1263½Slewo'Gld1261¾Barberstown126no	Led,weakened	15
29May83- 8Bel	fst	1⅛	:453 1:091 1:334 1:464	Peter Pan-G3	5	4	2½	12½	18	112	Cordero A Jr	126	*.80	93-11	Slew o' Gold12612I Enclose1233¾Foyt1176	Ridden out	5
7May83- 8CD	fst	1¼	:471 1:114 1:364 2:021	Ky Derby-G1	1	7	78	75½	33	43¼	Cordero A Jr	126	10.10	83-10	Sunny'sHalo1262DesrtWine126nkCaveat1261	Bothered start	20
23Apr83- 8Aqu	fst	1⅛	:481 1:121 1:372 1:51	Wood Mem (Div 2)-G1	1	6	52	41¾	1hd	1nk	Maple E	126	*1.30	80-24	Slewo'Gold126nkParfaitement126½HighHonors1269¾	Driving	7
13Apr83- 1Aqu	fst	1⅛	:483 1:123 1:374 1:504	Alw 23000	4	2	1hd	11	16	17¾	Cordero A Jr	117	*1.00	81-19	Slewo'Gold1177¾LawTalk1171¼ElCubanaso117¾	Ridden out	6
19Mar83-10Tam	fst	1 1/16	:24 :48 1:13 1:471	Tampa Derby 100k	2	5	42½	43½	23	2¾	Rivera H Jr	118	2.30	82-21	Morganmorganmorgan118¾Slew o' Gold118¾Quick Dip1186		14
Steadied,checked																	
5Mar83-10Tam	fst	1 1/16	:232 :474 1:132 1:472	Sam F Davis 12k	4	7	86¾	43	32½	33¾	Molina VH	118	*.40	78-23	Saverton1181¾TwoTurnsHome1202Slewo'Gold1181¼	Mild bid	8
13Nov82- 8Aqu	gd	1⅛	:482 1:124 1:374 1:501	Remsen-G1	11	4	52½	53	610	612	Lovato F Jr	115	*1.80e	72-20	PaxinBello1131¾Chummng1158PrimitivePleasre113hd	Tired	11
23Oct82- 9Aqu	fst	1	:233 :47 1:121 1:372	Alw 20000	8	2	2½	1hd	11½	11¾	Lovato F Jr	117	3.70	79-21	Slew o'Gold1171¾LastTurn1172¾Chumming1222¾	Ridden out	9
15Oct82- 3Aqu	fst	6½f	:232 :47 1:121 1:184	Md Sp Wt	8	1	2½	2½	1½	1nk	Cordero A Jr	118	*.60	81-26	Slew o' Gold118nkCountertrade1186Majesty Cove1182½		8
Lugged in,driving																	

Smile

dkbbr. c. 1982, by In Reality (Intentionally)–Sunny Smile, by Boldnesian — Lifetime record: 27 14 4 3 $1,664,027

Own.– Frances A. Genter Stable
Br.– F.A. Genter Stable Inc (Fla)
Tr.– Flint S. Schulhofer

7Mar87-10GP	fst	1 1/16⊗	:234 :473 1:114 1:443	3↑ GP Bud BC H 133k	3	2	2½	1hd	22½	45½	Vasquez J	120	*.90	72-25	BolshoBoy1164ArctcHonymoon1141LttlBoldJohn115½	Gave way	5
24Jan87-10Hia	fst	1⅛	:464 1:104 1:36 1:484	3↑ Seminole H-G2	1	1	2½	1hd	1½	65¼	Vasquez J	121	*1.40	82-17	LaunchaPegass1151½Arctic Honeymn116hdDarnThatAlarm118nk		8
Weakened																	
3Jan87- 7Crc	fst	1 3/16	:483 1:13 1:391 1:593	3↑ Bud BC H 143k	5	2	2½	1hd	12½	21½	Vasquez J	122	*.90	117-14	ArcticHoneymoon1141½Smle1229DrnThtAlrm120no	Gave way	6
1Nov86- 3SA	fst	6f	:211 :433 :554 1:082	3↑ BC Sprint-G1	1	4	2½	1hd	1hd	11¼	Vasquez J	126	11.00	96-13	Smile1261¼PineTreeLane1231¾BedsidePromise1261¼	Driving	9
27Sep86- 8Pha	sly	7f	:212 :44 1:092 1:221	3↑ Bud BC 148k	5	1	33	43¼	44¼	611¾	Cordero A Jr	122	*.90	84-17	LazerShow1128¼IAmtheGame115noPurplMountain114¾	Wide	7
30Aug86- 6AP	fst	1	:222 :443 1:081 1:34	3↑ Equipoise Mile H-G3	4	2	3½	11	13	15	Vasquez J	121	*1.30	91-15	Smile1215Taylor's Special1242Red Attack1143½	Ridden out	7
26Jly86- 9Aks	fst	1⅛	:48 1:112 1:363 1:492	3↑ Cornhusker H-G2	2	1	11	11	1hd	34	Vasquez J	120	*1.10	86-23	Gourami1162½Honor Medal1141½Smile1201	Tired	7
13Jly86- 9Cby	gd	1⅛	:464 1:101 1:35 1:48	3↑ Canterbury Cup H 165k	3	1	11	11	12	1½	Vasquez J	119	*.80e	103-09	Smile119½Dramatic Desire1131¼Forkintheroad1163½	Driving	9
5Jly86- 6Bel	fst	1 1/16	:232 :461 1:102 1:422	3↑ Alw 40000	6	2	11	13½	15	14¼	Vasquez J	115	*.40	90-15	Smile1154¼ValiantLark1153½LittleMissouri1155	Ridden out	6
22Jun86- 8Bel	fst	6f	:221 :443 1:09	3↑ True North H-G2	2	2	21	2hd	2½	44¼	Vasquez J	119	4.30	93-19	PhoneTrck127¾LoveThatMac1173½Cullendale111hd	Weakened	5
26May86- 8Bel	fst	1	:232 :454 1:091 1:333	3↑ Metropolitan H-G1	6	2	31	3nk	53	77½	Vasquez J	121	6.70	89-11	Garthorn1241¼LoveThatMc117noLdy'sScrt120nk	Stumbled st.	8
10May86- 7Bel	fm	6f(T)	:22 :443 1:091	3↑ Alw 36000	12	2	1hd	1½	11½	12	Vasquez J	119	*1.90	94-19	Smile1192[DH]Fortunate Prospect119[DH]Roving Minstrel1191		12
Drew clear																	
16Nov85- 8Aqu	sly	7f	:213 :442 1:09 1:214	3↑ Vosburgh-G1	3	5	25	32	46½	49¾	Vasquez J	124	*.50	82-22	AnothrReef1242¾PanchoVilla1244¾WhoopUp1262¼	Weakened	6
2Nov85- 3Aqu	fst	6f	:22 :444 1:082	3↑ BC Sprint-G1	11	1	21	1hd	1hd	2¾	Vasquez J	124	6.40	98-10	Precisionist126¾Smile124¾Mt. Livermore1261¼	Gamely	14
13Oct85- 6Bel	gd	1(T)	:231 :46 1:102 1:362	3↑ Handicap 40000	1	1	1hd	1hd	2hd	35	Vasquez J	116	3.20	78-25	Chief's Crown1252½Intensify1142½Smile11612	Gave way	5
Previously trained by Carl Nafzger																	
18Aug85- 9Cby	fst	1 70	:231 :462 1:094 1:401	3↑ Alw 20000	3	1	11	11	1hd	22½	Oldham J	120	*.40	104-11	Come Summer1122½Smile1202Ridan Clarion116½	Failed	6
21Jly85- 9FP	fst	1⅛	:464 1:111 1:362 1:49	FP Derby-G3	3	2	11	12	12½	14	Vasquez J	123	*.30	104-18	Smile1234Premier Partner1143Clever Allemont1235¾	Easily	7
Previously trained by Frank Gomez																	
6Jly85- 8AP	fst	1¼	:474 1:112 1:36 2:013	American Derby-G1	5	1	11½	11½	11	31¾	Vasquez J	123	*.70	87-15	Creme Fraiche1231Red Attack114¾Smile1237	Tired	5
15Jun85- 8AP	sly	1⅛	:483 1:13 1:38 1:511	Classic-G1	4	1	11½	12	15	17½	Vasquez J	117	*.90	75-27	Smile1177½RedAttack1141¾CleverAllemont1231¼	Ridden out	6
1Jun85- 8AP	fst	1	:223 :443 1:084 1:343	Sheridan-G2	1	2	26	23	21½	2¾	Vasquez J	124	*.50	87-15	Banner Bob124¾Smile124noClever Allemont1243	Tired	5
18May85- 9Crc	fst	7f	:22 :443 1:101 1:234	Carry Back 68k	1	1	21	11½	16	111½	Vasquez J	123	*.05	97-13	Smile12311½Paravon112nkHickoryHillFlyer114½	Ridden out	7
9May85- 0Crc	fst	7f	:223 :453 1:102 1:233	Alw	4	2	12½	13	19	110¾	Vasquez J	116	-	98-13	Smile11610¾SingleBidder1169¾NowICn1164	Speed in reserve	4
Exhibition race run between 6th and 7th races - No wagering or purse																	
20Oct84- 9Crc	fst	1 1/16	:241 :483 1:131 1:463	[R]In Reality (FSS) 400k	10	1	11	1½	11½	12	St Leon G	120	*.20	86-16	Smle1202EmergencyCall12014½CovertOperaton1201¾	Driving	12
29Sep84- 9Crc	sly	7f	:222 :46 1:111 1:243	[R]Affirmed (FSS) 120k	4	4	22½	1½	15	17	St Leon G	118	*.40	93-18	Smile1187Kejinsky118¾Emergency Call1187	Ridden out	11
25Aug84- 9Crc	fst	6f	:222 :462 1:133	[R]Dr.Fgr(FSS)(Div2) 42k	8	2	11½	12	16	14	St Leon G	116	*.40	83-19	Smile1164Water Gate1162[D]Hickory Hill Flyer116nk	Easily	10
4Aug84- 9Crc	fst	5½f	:223 :47 1:001 1:07	Criterium (Div 2) 40k	1	7	13	12	12½	12½	St Leon G	114	2.60	90-21	Smile1142½Spend a Buck116hdCherokee Fast1164½	Easily	7
Run in divisions																	
16Jun84- 2Crc	sly	5f	:224 :464 1:001	Md Sp Wt	6	4	1hd	1hd	1½	13	St Leon G	115	7.30	91-18	Smile1153Valid Likeness1157Cosmic Dust115hd	Drew clear	10

Snow Chief

dkbbr. c. 1983, by Reflected Glory (Jester)–Miss Snowflake, by Snow Sporting — Lifetime record: 24 13 3 5 $3,383,210

Own.– Grinstead & Rochelle
Br.– Blue Diamond Ranch (Cal)
Tr.– Melvin F. Stute

7Jun87- 8Hol	fst	1⅛	:464 1:104 1:353 1:481	3↑ Californian-G1	2	2	21	2½	21½	31	Solis A	126 b	1.90	95-17	JudgeAnglucc1181IronEys115noSnwChf1262¾	Bobbled start	8
17Apr87- 9OP	fst	1⅛	:463 1:101 1:343 1:463	4↑ Oaklawn H-G2	7	2	1hd	1½	11½	1¾	Solis A	123 b	*.80	101-11	Snow Chief123¾Red Attack112½Vilzak1081½	Driving	7
29Mar87-10GP	fst	1¼	:49 1:134 1:382 2:024	3↑ Gulf Park H-G1	1	1	12	2hd	2½	34¾	Solis A	124 b	*.70	76-24	SkipTrial1184½CremeFraich120nkSnwChf124nk	Taken out st	4
8Mar87- 8SA	fst	1¼	:454 1:101 1:35 2:003	4↑ S Anita H-G1	3	2	2hd	2hd	32½	57	Valenzuela PA	126 b	2.40	79-15	Broad Brush122noFerdinand1256½Hopeful Word117nk		9
Bumped into stretch																	
8Feb87- 8SA	fst	1¼	:464 1:102 1:343 2:00	C H Strub-G1	7	1	11	1½	11½	1no	Valenzuela PA	126 b	2.40	89-14	SnowChf126noFrdnnd1264½BrodBrsh1267	Bumped hard late	8
18Jan87- 8SA	fst	1⅛	:482 1:121 1:363 1:49	San Fernando-G1	5	1	1hd	1hd	2hd	33	Valenzuela PA	126 b	*.90	81-19	VarietyRd123nkBrodBrsh1262¾SnwChf1263½	Stumbled start	8
26Dec86- 8SA	fst	7f	:222 :444 1:09 1:213	Malibu-G2	4	5	31	3nk	11½	21¼	Valenzuela PA	126 b	*1.40	91-13	Ferdinand1231¼SnwChief1261½DonB.Blue1144	Bumped start	12
5Jly86- 8Hol	fst	1	:221 :443 1:08 1:324	Silver Screen H-G2	1	3	21½	35	38½	311	Solis A	127 b	*.60	88-08	Melair1156½Southern Halo1134½Snow Chief127hd	Tired	12

26May86- 9GS	fst 1¼	:47 1:112 1:372 2:03	Jersey Derby-G2	5 1 12½ 1½ 12 12	Solis A	126 b	*.60	89-20	Snow Chief1262Mogambo1261½Tasso1261¼	Kept to drive 10
17May86- 8Pim	fst 1 3/16	:472 1:11 1:36 1:544	Preakness-G1	2 2 2½ 2hd 14 14	Solis A	126 b	2.60	93-18	SnowChief1264Frdnnd1266½BrodBrush126no	Strong handling 7
3May86- 8CD	fst 1¼	:451 1:101 1:37 2:024	Ky Derby-G1	12 4 43 41 911 1119½	Solis A	126 b	*2.10	63-10	Ferdinand1262¼BoldArrangemnt126¾BrdBrush126nk	Gave way 16
6Apr86- 5SA	fst 1⅛	:471 1:11 1:36 1:483	S Anita Derby-G1	3 2 11½ 12 12½ 16	Solis A	122 b	*.30	86-15	Snow Chief1226Icy Groom1221Ferdinand122¾	Ridden out 7
1Mar86- 9GP	fst 1⅛	:464 1:12 1:38 1:514	Florida Derby-G1	12 1 11½ 1½ 12½ 11¾	Solis A	122 b	*1.50	73-29	Snow Chief1221¾Badger Land1225Mogambo122nk	Driving 16
2Feb86- 8BM	sly 1 1/16	:223 :452 1:093 1:423	El Camino Real Derby-G3	2 2 21½ 2hd 1hd 12½	Solis A	120 b	*.70	79-28	Snow Chief1202½Badger Land120½Darby Fair1207	In hand 6
12Jan86- 8SA	fst 7f	:221 :444 1:091 1:213	[S]Cal Br Champ 115k	7 2 52½ 61¾ 11 14	Solis A	126 b	*.40	92-11	SnowChief1264VarietyRoad115nkAirPirate1174½	Ridden out 8
15Dec85- 8Hol	fst 1	:22 :443 1:09 1:341	Hol Futurity-G1	9 5 2hd 13½ 15 16½	Solis A	121 b	2.90	92-09	SnowChief1216½ElectricBlue121noFerdinnd121nk	Ridden out 10
29Nov85- 8Hol	sly 1⊗	:221 :451 1:11 1:37	Hoist the Flag 191k	5 5 66½ 24 24 25	Solis A	120	*1.10	73-20	DarbyFair1205SnowChief1202½AcksLikaRuler114¾	2nd best 6
2Nov85-14SA	fst 1	:232 :473 1:121 1:362	[S]BJ Ridder 108k	4 6 53½ 32 32 1hd	Solis A	122	*.40	86-13	SnwChief122hdVarietyRoad115½RaisedonStag11510½	Driving 7
13Oct85- 8SA	fst 1 1/16	:221 :454 1:103 1:443	Norfolk-G1	2 6 55½ 56 32½ 13	Solis A	118	*1.50	78-17	Snow Chief1183Lord Allison1181¼Darby Fair1181½	Driving 9
2Oct85- 8SA	fst 7f	:221 :451 1:101 1:233	Sunny Slope 76k	5 6 76¾ 54¾ 44 2nk	Solis A	119	*2.30	82-17	LouisianaSlew115nkSnowChief1194½DonB.Blue115¾	Rallied 8
11Sep85- 8Dmr	fst 1	:231 :471 1:113 1:36	Dmr Futurity-G1	5 4 52¼ 41 34½ 32½	Solis A	117	7.80	85-15	Tasso117nkArewehavingfunyet1172¼Snow Chief1173¼	Evenly 6
4Sep85- 8Dmr	fst 6f	:221 :451 :564 1:10	[R]Rancho Santa Fe 54k	7 1 52¾ 25 21½ 11¾	Meza RQ	117	7.20	88-17	SnwChief1171¾LittleRedCloud1172½QuickTwst1141¼	Driving 7
30Jun85- 5Hol	fst 5½f	:212 :433 :562 1:024	Desert Wine 51k	4 9 614 617 614 69½	Meza RQ	115	8.40	--	Hilco Scamper1174½Little Red Cloud1173½Sir Mahmoud116½	9
	In close st									
19Jun85- 5Hol	fst 5f	:224 :452 :573	[S]Md Sp Wt	4 6 2½ 1hd 1hd 12½	Meza RQ	118	2.20	--	SnwChf1182½GloryPath118noWindatHsBck1184½	Ridden out 10

Spend a Buck

b. c. 1982, by Buckaroo (Buckpasser)–Belle de Jour, by Speak John — **Lifetime record: 15 10 3 2 $4,220,689**

Own.– Hunter Farm
Br.– Irish Hill Farm & R.W. Harper (Ky)
Tr.– Cam Gambolati

17Aug85- 9Mth	fst 1⅛	:464 1:094 1:341 1:464 3↑	Monmouth H-G1	3 1 12 11½ 1½ 1no	Pincay L Jr	118	*.50	101-10	SpendaBck118noCarrdeNaskra1209[D]Rumptious1121	Driving 6
27Jly85- 9Mth	fst 1⅛	:47 1:104 1:354 1:483	Haskell Inv'l H-G1	7 1 1½ 1½ 1hd 23¾	Pincay L Jr	127	*.70	88-13	SkipTrial1163¾SpendaBuck1271CremeFraiche1264	Gave way 7
27May85- 9GS	fst 1¼	:452 1:09 1:35 2:023	Jersey Derby-G3	5 1 1hd 1½ 1½ 1nk	Pincay L Jr	126	*.05	--	SpendaBuck126nkCremeFraiche126hdElBasco1264¾	Driving 9
4May85- 8CD	fst 1¼	:454 1:093 1:342 2:001	Ky Derby-G1	10 1 16 16 15 15¼	Cordero A Jr	126	4.10	96-08	SpndaBck1265¼Stphn'sOdyssy126¾Chf'sCrown126nk	Driving 13
20Apr85- 8GS	fst 1⅛	:453 1:092 1:34 1:454	Garden State 304k	2 1 13½ 13 16 19½	Cordero A Jr	122	*.40	--	Spend a Buck1229½I Am the Game1175½Do It Again Dan115nk	9
	Ridden out									
6Apr85- 8GS	fst 1	:223 :452 1:10 1:352	Cherry Hill Mile H 244k	7 1 12½ 12 16 110½	Cordero A Jr	122	1.70	--	SpndaBck12210½IAmtheGme115¾KingBabar1161½	Ridden out 14
23Mar85- 8Aqu	fst 7f	:224 :453 1:093 1:221	Bay Shore-G2	1 6 31 41¼ 34½ 35½	Cordero A Jr	123	*1.40	84-23	Pancho Villa1143¾El Basco1141¾Spend a Buck1232	9
	Weakened under impost									
10Nov84- 1Hol	fst 1	:222 :45 1:10 1:361	©BC Juvenile-G1	3 1 1hd 12½ 11 31½	Cordero A Jr	122	6.40	--	Chief'sCrwn122¾Tank'sPrspct122¾SpndBck1226½	Weakened 10
18Oct85- 8Med	fst 1 1/16	:23 :46 1:111 1:45	Young America-G1	4 1 11½ 11 1½ 2¾	Cordero A Jr	122	*1.00	83-22	ScriptOhio119¾SpendaBck122nkTank'sProspect1192	Gamely 11
22Sep84- 9AP	fst 1	:222 :444 1:10 1:38	Arl Wash Futurity-G1	6 3 21 2hd 1½ 1½	Hussey C	122	2.90	71-24	SpendaBuck122½Dusty'sDarby1222½VivaMaxi1221¾	All out 7
2Sep84-11RD	fst 1 1/16	:234 :473 1:12 1:451	Cradle H 125k	6 2 11 14 18 115	Hussey C	120	*1.20	80-18	SpendaBuck12015GrandNative1206Alex'sGame120nk	Easily 13
16Aug84- 7Crc	fst 6f	:223 :461 1:124	Alw 15000	1 1 11½ 14 16 19½	Hussey C	112	*.50	87-23	SpendaBuck1129½SecretGoal1128½Mr.Introienne1143	Handily 5
4Aug84- 9Crc	fst 5½f	:223 :47 1:001 1:07	Criterium (Div 2) 40k	4 2 23 22 22½ 22½	Hussey C	116	*.60	87-21	Smile1142½SpendaBuck116hdCherokeeFast1164½	Held place 7
25Jly84- 8Crc	fst 5½f	:224 :463 :592 1:06	Alw 11000	3 1 1½ 11½ 13 14	Hussey C	113	2.40	95-20	Spend a Buck1134Mr. Introienne1161½Playing Politics1144½	8
	Ridden out;Previously raced in name of D.W. Diaz									
14Jly84- 2Crc	fst 5½f	:23 :47 1:001 1:071	Md Sp Wt	6 3 11½ 1hd 12 1nk	Hussey C	116	5.50	89-19	SpndaBck116nkHckoryHllFlyr1163SuprbAnswr1163½	Driving 12

Steinlen (GB)

b. c. 1983, by Habitat (Sir Gaylord)–Southern Seas, by Jim French — **Lifetime record: 45 20 10 7 $3,300,100**

Own.– D. Wildenstein
Br.– Allez France Stables Ltd (GB)
Tr.– D. Wayne Lukas

27Oct90- 6Bel	gd 1Ⓣ	:223 :454 1:10 1:351 3↑	BC Mile-G1	11 4 42 63 53 41½	Santos JA	126	4.90	88-15	RoyalAcademy122nkItsallgreektom122¾Prolo122½	Mild rally 13
6Oct90- 8Bel	fst 1¼	:473 1:112 1:352 2:003 3↑	J C Gold Cup-G1	2 3 31½ 67½ 615 625¾	Santos JA	126	14.30	68-11	Flying Continental126nkDe Roche1261¾Izvestia1216¼	Tired 6
2Sep90- 8AP	fm 1¼Ⓣ	:483 1:13 1:364 1:593 3↑	Arl Million-G1	11 2 21½ 22 42½ 36½	Santos JA	L 126	3.30	107-00	GoldenPhesnt1261¼WthApprovl1265¼Stnln126nk	Lacked rally 11
12Aug90- 8Sar	gd 1⅛Ⓣ	:464 1:104 1:353 1:482 3↑	Bernard Baruch H-G2	5 2 2½ 2hd 12 22	Santos JA	126	*.30	86-11	Who'stoPay1102Steinln1263RiverofSn1158	Not good enough 5
21Jly90- 8Atl	fm 1 3/16Ⓣ	:484 1:114 1:354 1:52 3↑	Caesars Int'l H-G2	7 1 11 1½ 11½ 13¾	Santos JA	L 124	*1.60	103-10	Steinlen1243¾Capades1121¼Alwuhush1211	Driving 8
4Jly90- 8Hol	fm 1⅛Ⓣ	:464 1:102 1:351 1:474 3↑	American H-G2	5 2 21 2hd 1½ 2¾	Pincay L Jr	L 125	*1.60	88-16	ClassicFame117¾Steinlen1251¼PleasantVarty1162½	Held 2nd 7
28May90- 8Hol	gd 1¼Ⓣ	:483 1:131 1:374 2:03 3↑	Hol Turf H-G1	3 2 25 21 21 1nk	Pincay L Jr	124	3.80	78-22	Steinlen124nkHawkster1225¼Santangelo110hd	Driving 6
13May90- 8Hol	fm 1⅛Ⓣ	:484 1:121 1:352 1:47 3↑	John Henry H-G2	5 2 21 1hd 2hd 32	Santos JA	126	1.80	91-09	GoldenPheasnt1201¾ClassicFame117nkStnln1261¾	Lost whip 5
8Apr90- 8SA	fm 1Ⓣ	:213 :45 1:09 1:332 4↑	El Rincon H-G2	5 4 42 32½ 21 1hd	Santos JA	125	*1.00	96-05	Steinlen125hdBruho1175Wonder Dancer111¾	Driving 6
4Mar90- 5SA	fm 1Ⓣ	:214 :45 1:09 1:342 4↑	Arcadia H-G3	7 3 48 57¼ 54½ 74¾	Santos JA	126	*1.20	86-18	Prizd1241HappyToss115hdOntheMenu1122¾	Needed response 9
4Nov89- 7GP	gd 1Ⓣ	:232 :472 1:112 1:371 3↑	BC Mile-G1	2 4 52½ 63¼ 21 1¾	Santos JA	126	1.80	88-13	Steinln126¾Sabona126½MostWlcom126nk	Rough trip-driving 11
21Oct89- 8Kee	yl 1⅛Ⓣ	:483 1:132 1:39 1:522 3↑	Bud BC-G3	4 4 53½ 51¾ 1hd 1hd	Santos JA	126	*.30	80-20	Steinlen126hdCrystal Moment1263Posen126nk	Driving 10
3Sep89- 8AP	fm 1¼Ⓣ	:491 1:134 1:391 2:033 3↑	Arl Million-G1	4 2 22 32 3½ 1½	Santos JA	126	5.30	76-25	Steinlen126½LadyinSilver117½YankeeAffair126hd	Driving 13
13Aug89- 8Sar	sf 1⅛Ⓣ	:501 1:14 1:381 1:51 3↑	Bernard Baruch H-G1	6 3 32½ 32½ 1½ 15	Santos JA	121	*1.90	72-28	Steinlen1215Soviet Lad111¾Brian's Time1122	Ridden out 8
2Aug89- 5Sar	fm 1 1/16Ⓣ	:24 :481 1:112 1:41 3↑	Daryl's Joy (Div 1)-G3	8 3 32 11 11½ 12½	Cordero A Jr	122	*.40	92-08	Steinln1222½ExpensvDcson1172SprklngWt1101	Stumbled st. 8
4Jly89- 8Hol	fm 1⅛Ⓣ	:481 1:112 1:344 1:471 3↑	American H-G1	4 2 21½ 2½ 1hd 2no	Stevens GL	121	*.80	92-12	MisterWonderflII115noSteinln121hdPrnk1171½	Bumped start 8
18Jun89- 8Hol	fm 1 1/16Ⓣ	:233 :461 1:093 1:393 3↑	Inglewood H-G2	3 2 23½ 21 11½ 12¼	Stevens GL	120	*1.00	96-10	Steinlen1202½Pasakos1152Mi Preferido117½	Bumped early 7
14May89- 8Hol	fm 1⅛Ⓣ	:462 1:094 1:334 1:461 3↑	John Henry H-G1	3 2 2½ 1hd 1hd 2¾	Stevens GL	121	*2.80	96-08	Peace116¾Steinlen121½Pay the Butler1161½	Held on well 8
30Apr89- 8Hol	fm 1Ⓣ	:231 :46 1:091 1:33 3↑	Premiere H-G3	5 2 2½ 2hd 2hd 21	Stevens GL	121	*1.70	98-06	Peace1151Steinlen121nkPolitical Ambition1222½	Gamely 8
9Apr89- 8SA	fm 1Ⓣ	:234 :473 1:113 1:353 4↑	El Rincon H 107k	3 3 41¾ 42 42 31½	Pincay L Jr	122	*1.50	91-15	Political Ambition121½Patchy Groundfog1181Steinlen122nk	5
	Well up throughout									
9Mar89- 8SA	fm 1Ⓣ	:23 :461 1:093 1:341 4↑	Alw 60000	6 1 11 11 11 1nk	Pincay L Jr	118	*.70	100-00	Steinln118nkPc1165ExclusvPrtnr116¾	Bumped st.,lunged in 6
5Nov88- 7CD	gd 1Ⓣ	:233 :472 1:123 1:383 3↑	BC Mile-G1	3 4 33 43 43 24	Pincay L Jr	126	37.40	92-04	Miesque1234Steinlen126hdSimplyMajestc1261¼	Gained place 12
23Oct88-10Lrl	fm 6fⓉ	:221 :452 :574 1:102 3↑	Lrl Dash 200k	8 4 711 713 64¾ 1no	Pincay L Jr	124	7.60	90-15	Stenln124noMc'sFghtr117½Fourstrdv117½	Lugged in driving 11
8Oct88- 8Bel	sf 1Ⓣ	:24 :484 1:144 1:42 3↑	Kelso H-G3	5 3 3½ 32 57¾ 67¾	Stevens GL	121	*1.70	47-60	San'stheShadow116¾Posen117½Tinchen'sPrince1144¾	Tired 7
27Aug88- 7Sar	gd 1 1/16Ⓣ	:242 :473 1:114 1:432 3↑	Bud BC H-G3	5 1 1½ 1hd 1hd 1nk	Day P	120	*.40	80-23	Steinlen120nkIron Courage1132½Barood1103	Driving 6
14Aug88- 8Sar	fm 1⅛Ⓣ	:47 1:094 1:333 1:464 3↑	Bernard Baruch H-G1	7 1 1½ 1½ 1hd 2½	Day P	120	2.80	92-14	My Big Boy113½Steinlen120nkWanderkin115¾	Held well 9
4Jly88- 8Hol	fm 1⅛Ⓣ	:471 1:104 1:334 1:462 3↑	American H-G1	4 1 11 12 1hd 21	Stevens GL	121	*.70	95-06	SkipOutFront1151Steinlen121hdWorldCourt1131	Held place 4
19Jun88- 8Hol	fm 1 1/16Ⓣ	:24 :47 1:10 1:402 3↑	Inglewood H-G2	4 1 12½ 13½ 15 12½	Stevens GL	119	2.10	92-10	Steinln1192½DeputyGovernor1201¾Galunpe115no	Ridden out 6
15May88- 8Hol	fm 1⅛Ⓣ	:463 1:10 1:34 1:46 3↑	John Henry H-G1	7 1 12½ 11½ 11 22	Stevens GL	120	3.80	96-05	DeputyGovernr1182Stenln120½StopthFghtng115½	Rank early 8
1May88- 8Hol	fm 1Ⓣ	:23 :454 1:091 1:331 3↑	Premiere H-G3	6 4 31½ 11½ 11½ 1hd	Stevens GL	119	*1.90	98-06	Steinlen119hdSiyah Kalem1151Neshad115hd	Bumped start 8
10Apr88- 8SA	fm 1Ⓣ	:222 :454 1:101 1:344 4↑	El Rincon H 147k	1 1 11 1½ 12½ 11¾	Stevens GL	117	4.10	101-12	Steinlen1171¾Political Ambition120hdNeshad1173½	Driving 9
26Mar88- 5SA	fm 1Ⓣ	:23 :463 1:11 1:354 4↑	Alw 54000	3 3 2hd 1hd 13½ 15	Stevens GL	114	4.90	96-12	Steinlen1145Sanam1142¼Le Belvedere1141¾	Ridden out 7
12Mar88- 7SA	fst 1 1/16	:224 :46 1:103 1:431 4↑	Alw 55000	5 6 63½ 51¾ 54½ 75	Stevens GL	114	14.20	80-19	No Marker114hdMasterful Advocate1174Forkintheroad114nk	8
	Bid,faltered									
21Jan88- 8SA	fm 1⅛Ⓣ	:473 1:12 1:372 1:503 4↑	Alw 55000	3 3 31 21½ 33½ 33½	Stevens GL	114	14.30	70-26	Temperate Sil1202¾Ivor's Image115¾Steinlen1141½	12
	Bumped start,lugged in stretch;Previously trained by Robert Frankel									

30Oct87- 8SA	gd	1⅛(T)	:471 1:122 1:37 1:501	3↑ Alw 45000	2 9 1014 1011 78½	76	Delahoussaye E	116	*3.00	70-24	ConquerngHero118hdWrldCourt1091¼GallntArchr1141¼	Wide	10
												Previously trained by Patrick-Louis Biancone	
26Aug87♦ Deauville(Fr)	sf	*1(T)Str	1:413	3↑ Prix Quincey-G3 Stk48200		51¾	Boeuf D	130	11.00		Tobin Lad1201½Pasticcio126noLibertine117nk	Pressed in 3rd,lacked rally,one-paced late	9
18Aug87♦ Deauville(Fr)	sf	*1(T)RH	1:443	3↑ Prix du Cercle Listed28400		31	Mosse G	131	10.00		Ephialtes128¾Dom Valory128nkSteinlen131½	Tracked in 4th,bid 1½f out,lost 2nd near line	10
23Jly87♦ Saint-Cloud(Fr)	sf	*1(T)LH	1:431	4↑ Prix Sir Gallahad Listed34000		33¾	Cruz AS	130	1.50		Ephialtes123nkIstikal1303Steinlen130½	Led to over 1f out,one-paced	4
30May87♦ Saint-Cloud(Fr)	sf	*1(T)LH	1:452	4↑ Prix Lovelace Listed34000		11½	Cruz AS	126	*.10		Steinlen1261½Al Joharah1181½Herald's Voice1192½	Rated in last,dueled 1½f out,led 1f out,handily	4
20Apr87♦ Longchamp(Fr)	fm	*1⅛(T)RH	1:523	4↑ Prix de la Butte Mortemort Listed29000		13	Cruz AS	127	*2.30		Steinlen1273North Verdict127hdMachado130nk	Well placed in 3rd,led 1½f out,drew clear 1f out	9
9Apr87♦ Evry(Fr)	sf	*1⅛(T)LH	2:004	4↑ Prix de Savigny Alw17300		1¾	Cruz AS	128	7.20		Steinlen128¾Simsim1192½Herald's Voice119½	Close up,ridden to lead final 16th,driving	15
27Mar87♦ Maisns-Lfftte(Fr)	hy	*1¼(T)RH	2:183	4↑ Prix Flechois Alw18700		11½	Cruz AS	119	13.50		Steinlen1191½Fabulous Pearl1281½Swedish Princess1212½	Tracked in 4th,led 100y out,ridden out	14
15Jun86♦ Chantilly(Fr)	fm	*1(T)RH	1:363	Prix de Pontarme Listed28000		75	Lequeux A	120	13.00		Thrill Show1231½Majestic Voice123hdStar Maite130hd	Trailed to 1½f out,mild late gain	14
29May86♦ Longchamp(Fr)	fm	*1(T)RH	1:414	Prix du Pre-Catalan Alw22300		2¾	Legrix E	123	8.00		Green Mount123¾Steinlen1231½Shecky Red1182	Rated toward rear,finished well without threatening	8
26Apr86♦ Evry(Fr)	hy	*1(T)LH	1:494	Prix de la Beauce Mdn20500		39	Legrix E	123	2.20		Magical Wonder1235Forbidding1234Steinlen1234	Tracked in 3rd,never threatened,beaten 1½f out	6

Sunday Silence

dkbbr. c. 1986, by Halo (Hail to Reason)–Wishing Well, by Understanding **Lifetime record: 14 9 5 0 $4,968,554**

Own.– Gaillard & Hancock III & Whittingham et al
Br.– Oak Cliff Thoroughbreds Ltd (Ky)
Tr.– Charles Whittingham

24Jun90- 8Hol	fst	1¼	:464 1:101 1:343 1:594	3↑ Hol Gold Cup H-G1	4 4 31½ 2hd 2hd	2hd	Valenzuela PA	126	*.50e	98-09	CriminalType121hdSndaySilnce1263½OpnngVrs1192¾	Gamely	7
3Jun90- 9Hol	fst	1⅛	:471 1:104 1:351 1:48	3↑ Californian-G1	2 1 1½ 1½ 11½	1¾	Valenzuela PA	126	*.10	94-14	Sunday Silence126¾Stylish Winner1153Charlatan III111	Awkward break;Previously owned by Gaillard & Hancock III & Whittingham	3
4Nov89-10GP	fst	1¼	:461 1:102 1:35 2:001	3↑ BC Classic-G1	8 4 35 21½ 2hd	1nk	McCarron CJ	122	2.00	107-01	SndaySlnc122nkEsyGr1221BlushngJohn1269¾	Good handling	8
24Sep89-10LaD	fst	1¼	:471 1:121 1:374 2:031	Super Derby-G1	7 5 42½ 1hd 14	16	Valenzuela PA	126	*.40	85-15	SundaySilence1266BigEarl126hdAweInspiring126nk	Drew out	8
23Jly89- 8Hol	fst	1¼	:473 1:114 1:362 2:014	Swaps-G2	2 1 11½ 12½ 14	2¾	Valenzuela PA	126	*.20	82-18	Prized120¾Sunday Silence12610Endow1231¼	Lugged out late	5
10Jun89- 8Bel	fst	1½	:47 1:111 2:004 2:26	Belmont-G1	6 3 21½ 21 24½	28	Valenzuela PA	126	*.90	82-13	Easy Goer1268Sunday Silence1261Le Vygr12612	Second best	10
20May89-10Pim	fst	1 3/16	:462 1:093 1:341 1:534	Preakness-G1	7 4 33 32 1hd	1no	Valenzuela PA	126	2.10	98-10	Sunday Silence126noEasy Goer1265Rock Point1262	Bumped,steadied,brsh	8
6May89- 8CD	my	1¼	:463 1:112 1:374 2:05	Ky Derby-G1	10 4 46½ 31 11½	12½	Valenzuela PA	126	3.10	72-28	Sunday Silence1262½Easy Goer126hdAwe Inspiring126¾	Steadied st,swerved	15
8Apr89- 5SA	fst	1⅛	:453 1:093 1:344 1:473	S A Derby-G1	4 3 32 2½ 16	111	Valenzuela PA	122	2.40	91-12	Sunday Silence12211Flying Continental122¾Music Merci122½	Jostled start	6
19Mar89- 8SA	fst	1 1/16	:221 :451 1:091 1:423	San Felipe H-G2	5 4 24 24 12	11¾	Valenzuela PA	119	2.90	88-16	SundaySilnce1191¾Flying Continental1183½Music Merci1243½	Broke awkwardly	5
2Mar89- 7SA	sly	6½f	:213 :443 1:084 1:152	Alw 32000	5 2 1hd 11 13½	14½	Valenzuela PA	119	*.90	93-18	SndaySilnce1194½HeroicType119¾MightBRght1193½	Driving	7
3Dec88- 3Hol	fst	6½f	:22 :443 1:094 1:163	Alw 24000	1 5 31½ 1½ 11½	2hd	Gryder AT	120	1.80	92-12	Houston120hdSunday Silence1201¼Three Times Older1172	Lugged out lt	7
13Nov88- 2Hol	fst	6f	:22 :444 :564 1:092	Md Sp Wt	9 2 21½ 1½ 14	110	Valenzuela PA	118	*.70	95-13	SundaySilnce11810Moment of Time118¾Northern Drama1181¼	Veered out st	10
30Oct88- 6SA	fst	6½f	:214 :451 1:102 1:17	Md Sp Wt	11 7 32 2hd 11	2nk	Valenzuela PA	118	*1.50	85-13	CroLover118nkSndaySlnc1187½GrnStorm118hd	Raced greenly	12

Sunshine Forever

b. c. 1985, by Roberto (Hail to Reason)–Outward Sunshine, by Graustark **Lifetime record: 23 8 6 3 $2,084,800**

Own.– Darby Dan Farm
Br.– John W. Galbreath (Ky)
Tr.– John M. Veitch

4Nov89- 9GP	gd	1½(T)	:483 1:132 2:033 2:28	3↑ BC Turf-G1	6 8 1210 1314 1412	1414½	Cordero A Jr	126	18.20	70-13	Prized122hdSierra Roberta1191Star Lift126nk	Outrun	14
22Oct89-11Lrl	sf	1¼(T)	:50 1:153 1:42 2:073	3↑ Bud Int'l-G1	7 2 21½ 78½ 79¾	68	Cordero A Jr	126 b	7.00	51-38	Caltech1221¾YankeeAffair1262½MistrWondrfulII1261¼	Tired	11
14Oct89- 6Bel	fm	1¼[T]	:501 1:141 1:38 2:014	3↑ Handicap 50000	3 3 52 32 24	23	Cordero A Jr	122	*1.20	82-18	Coosaragga1153SnshnForvr1221¾CrystlMomnt1132¼	2nd best	9
30Sep89- 1Bel	gd	1 1/16(T)	:232 :47 1:112 1:424	3↑ Alw 50000	6 4 54½ 65½ 610	57¾	Cordero A Jr	115	*.60	74-27	Maceo115nkPosen1152½Valid Fund1154½	Wide	6
7May89- 8Aqu	sf	1 1/16(T)	:261 :522 1:18 1:501	3↑ Fort Marcy H-G3	3 4 43½ 42½ 43	31½	Cordero A Jr	126	*.20	52-46	Arlene's Vlntn112¾Frstardave113¾SnshineFrvr1263¾	Rallied	5
11Feb89-10GP	fm	1 1/16(T)	:234 :47 1:101 1:41	3↑ Can Turf H-G2	3 5 55½ 53½ 33	23	Cordero A Jr	126	*1.30	92-12	Equalize1263SunshineForever1262¼MiSelecto1162	Steadied	7
5Nov88- 9CD	gd	1½(T)	:513 1:143 2:084 2:351	3↑ BC Turf-G1	2 2 21 3½ 2hd	2½	Cordero A Jr	122	2.10	- -	GreatCommunicatr126½SnshineFrever122¾IndianSkimmr1239	Gamely	10
23Oct88- 7Lrl	fm	1¼(T)	:474 1:122 1:374 2:03	3↑ Bud Int'l-G1	4 3 21 1½ 2hd	1nk	Cordero A Jr	122	*.80	82-15	SunshineForever122nkFranklyPerfct122½Squll1221¼	Driving	14
9Oct88- 8Bel	sf	1½(T)	:521 1:172 2:072 2:334	3↑ Turf Classic-G1	1 1 1½ 11½ 12½	14¾	Cordero A Jr	121	*2.10	55-45	SnshineForvr1214¾MyBigBoy126¾MostWelcom126hd	Driving	9
24Sep88- 8Bel	fm	1⅜[T]	:491 1:142 1:383 2:142	3↑ Man o' War-G1	9 5 42½ 1hd 11½	1½	Cordero A Jr	120	*1.70	85-15	SnshineForevr120½PythButlr1261MyBgBoy1261½	Brushed,drv	9
20Aug88- 7WO	fm	1¼(T)	:472 1:122 1:362 2:00	3↑ Arl Million-G1	8 12 52½ 21½ 32½	31¼	Velasquez J	118	3.95	106-07	MillNative126¾Equaliz126½SunshnForvr1181½	Finished well	14
30Jly88- 8Bel	sf	1½(T)	:503 1:154 2:07 2:321	3↑ Sword Dancer H-G1	2 4 42 43½ 33	21½	Cordero A Jr	114	*1.00	61-37	Anka Germania1171½Sunshine Forever1141¾Carotene1144¾	Finished strong	7
10Jly88- 8Bel	fm	1¼[T]	:50 1:134 1:381 2:03	Lexington-G2	3 3 31½ 1½ 1½	11¾	Cordero A Jr	123	*.60	79-18	SunshineForever1231¾HodgesBay114hdAskNot114nk	Driving	8
24Jun88- 8Bel	fm	1 1/16(T)	:241 :464 1:11 1:411	Hill Prince-G3	5 4 31 1hd 12½	16	Cordero A Jr	114	1.90	90-10	SunshineForever1146Posen1212¾KrisGreen1144	Ridden out	7
8Jun88- 5Bel	fm	1 1/16(T)	:24 :452 1:091 1:401	3↑ Alw 33000	1 4 410 36½ 11	13¼	Cordero A Jr	112	*.60	95-05	SnshineForevr1123¼Hertnc1171TurnngforHom1172¾	Driving	10
22May88- 8Bel	yl	1(T)	:23 :473 1:123 1:382	Saranac-G2	5 6 66¼ 53¼ 23½	2¾	Cordero A Jr	114	4.70	72-27	Posen123¾Sunshine Forever1144½Blew by Em1171	Checked	8
9May88- 5Aqu	gd	1⅛(T)	:494 1:144 1:404 1:53	3↑ Alw 31000	12 5 52½ 41½ 21	11¾	Cordero A Jr	115	*.50	70-25	SnshineForever1151¾SultrySeason1163I'veDoneMyTime112no	Going away	12
25Apr88- 7Aqu	fm	1 1/16(T)	:232 :472 1:12 1:442	3↑ Md Sp Wt	7 6 59½ 46 23	13	Cordero A Jr	115	*1.00	83-18	SnshineForever1153ProfitbyEntry1152OnBorrowdTime1242½	Drew clear	10
17Dec87- 5Hia	fst	1⅛⊗	:491 1:134 1:384 1:512	Md Sp Wt	9 5 44½ 45½ 37½	311½	Guerra WA	119	3.60	62-24	Fancy Hoofer1197Samurai Steel1194½Sunshine Forever1198	Lacked resp	11
16Oct87- 6Bel	fm	1 1/16(T)	:234 :474 1:123 1:452	Md Sp Wt	8 7 56 32 1hd	2hd	Bailey JD	118	2.60	69-26	SmartLad118hdSnshineForevr1185¾RuntoDylght1185	Gamely	11
9Sep87- 6Bel	fst	7f	:224 :461 1:104 1:232	Md Sp Wt	6 5 87½ 710 711	511¾	Bailey JD	118	68.50	73-15	Firery Ensign1182½Cherokee Colony1185Foolish McDuff1183¾	No threat	13
21Aug87- 4Sar	fst	6f	:222 :462 1:12	Md Sp Wt	5 11 1011 911 86¾	79	Bailey JD	118	24.10	71-14	Digress1182Yurtu1181¾Gnome's Treasure1181	No factor	12
12Aug87- 3Sar	gd	7f	:223 :463 1:114 1:243	Md Sp Wt	1 11 54½ 75½ 912	815¾	Bailey JD	118	20.90	63-22	FortRily1186¾John'sConcord118nkForvrSlvr1183½	No factor	12

Swale

dkbbr. c. 1981, by Seattle Slew (Bold Reasoning)–Tuerta, by Forli — Lifetime record: 14 9 2 2 $1,583,660

Own.– Claiborne Farm
Br.– Claiborne Farm (Ky)
Tr.– Woodford C. Stephens

9Jun84- 8Bel	fst 1½	:492 1:133 2:021 2:271	Belmont-G1	6 1 11 11½ 13 14	Pincay L Jr	126	*1.50	84-10	Swale1264Pine Circle1263Morning Bob126hd	Ridden out 11
19May84- 8Pim	fst 1 3/16	:451 1:091 1:342 1:533	Preakness-G1	5 2 22½ 31½ 55½ 76¾	Pincay L Jr	126	*.80	95-07	Gate Dancer1261½Play On1263½Fight Over126¾	Bothered 10
5May84- 8CD	fst 1¼	:472 1:114 1:363 2:022	Ky Derby-G1	15 3 31½ 12 15 13¼	Pincay L Jr	126	3.40	85-19	Swale1263¼CoaxMeChad1262AttheThreshold126nk	Drew off 20
17Apr84- 7Kee	sly 1 1/16	:233 :471 1:112 1:452	Lexington 53k	2 2 32½ 25½ 25 28	Pincay L Jr	123	*.10	71-23	He Is a Great Deal1118Swale1237½Timely Advocate1127½	5
Best of others										
31Mar84-10GP	fst 1⅛	:463 1:101 1:344 1:473	Florida Derby-G1	7 2 2½ 2hd 1½ 1¾	Pincay L Jr	122	2.70	94-14	Swale122¾Dr. Carter1227Darn That Alarm1221	Driving 9
17Mar84- 9GP	fst 1 1/16	:234 :473 1:111 1:43	Fountain of Youth-G2	7 3 2½ 2hd 32 31½	Maple E	122	*.40	84-17	DarnThatAlrm112½CounterftMoney1121Swl122nk	Weakened 8
7Mar84- 9GP	fst 7f	:223 :452 1:093 1:221	Hutcheson-G3	10 3 3nk 2hd 1hd 18	Maple E	122	*1.00	93-21	Swale1228ForHalo1141DarnThatAlarm1122¼	Wide,ridden out 12
5Nov83- 8Med	fst 1 1/16	:224 :461 1:112 1:451	Young America-G1	7 5 47½ 33 22 1no	Maple E	122	2.30	83-20	Swale122noDisastrous Night1193Dr. Carter1196	Driving 16
8Oct83- 7Kee	fst 1 1/16	:232 :471 1:112 1:44	Breeders' Futurity-G2	3 3 2hd 1hd 1hd 1hd	Maple E	121	*1.10	86-14	Swle121hdSpender1212½BackBayBarrister121½	Wide,driving 8
10Sep83- 8Bel	fst 7f	:223 :452 1:103 1:24	Futurity-G1	4 2 1½ 1hd 2½ 1no	Maple E	122	*1.60	82-15	Swale122noShuttle Jet122¾Hail Bold King1225	Driving 5
21Aug83- 8Sar	fst 6½f	:214 :451 1:104 1:172	Hopeful-G1	3 7 32 21½ 1hd 33¼	Maple E	122	3.40	82-23	Capitol South1222¾Don Rickles122½Swale122hd	Weakened 13
1Aug83- 8Sar	my 6f	:221 :46 1:123	Sar Spl-G2	4 5 2hd 12 14 1¾	Maple E	117	2.60	77-24	Swale117¾Shuttle Jet1173¾Big Walt117½	Driving 7
21Jly83- 4Bel	fst 6f	:223 :454 1:112	Md Sp Wt	7 2 12 16 14 11¼	Maple E	118	*.60	85-20	Swale1181¼Capitol South1181¼Legatee1187¾	Driving 7
7Jly83- 4Bel	fst 5f	:223 :454 :58	Md Sp Wt	2 3 1½ 11½ 1½ 22½	Maple E	118	*.70	96-19	Shuttle Jet1182½Swale1186Rowdy Yates1181	Lugged in 8

Tasso

b. c. 1983, by Fappiano (Mr. Prospector)–Ecstacism, by What a Pleasure — Lifetime record: 23 9 4 4 $1,207,884

Own.– Farish & Robins (Lessees)
Br.– G. Robins & T.H. Sams (Fla)
Tr.– Neil Drysdale

13Dec87- 8Hol	fm 1½(T)	:483 1:13 2:022 2:27	3↑ Hol Turf Cup-G1	14 13 1312 108¾ 107¼ 94½	Toro F	126 b	13.90	81-16	Vilzak126nkForlitano1262¼Political Ambition122hd	14
Lacked needed rally										
29Nov87- 8Hol	fm 1⅛(T)	:474 1:11 1:35 1:472	3↑ Citation H-G2	9 7 62¼ 74 52¾ 53	Delahoussaye E	119 b	*2.00	88-11	Forlitano120¾Conquering Hero115nkIfrad115¾	Wide 12
16Nov87- 8SA	fm 1¼(T)	:484 1:14 1:39 2:044	3↑ [R]H P Russell H 84k	11 8 85½ 106¾ 75 3nk	Delahoussaye E	120 b	*1.90	63-34	GllntArchr115noWrldCourt117nkTsso1201½	Wide throughout 11
3Sep87- 8Dmr	fm 1⅛(T)	:48 1:131 1:383 1:51	3↑ Alw 40000	2 4 410 54½ 41½ 1½	Delahoussaye E	116 b	2.30	78-22	Tsso116½HopefulWord117hdQuntllon1161¾	Boxed in stretch 6
8Aug87- 8Dmr	fst 1 1/16	:224 :454 1:10 1:404	3↑ San Diego H-G3	4 6 67 64¼ 54½ 56	Delahoussaye E	117 b	*1.50	90-10	Super Diamond123½Nostalgia's Star1161Good Command1142¾	7
Wide ⅜ turn										
28Jun87- 8Hol	fst 1¼	:46 1:093 1:343 2:003	3↑ Hol Gold Cup H-G1	11 9 96 43 32 21¼↓	McCarron CJ	115 b	4.30	88-12	Ferdinnd1241¼[DH]JudgeAnglucc118[DH]Tsso1154	Wide into str 11
7Jun87- 8Hol	fst 1⅛	:464 1:104 1:353 1:481	3↑ Californian-G1	3 6 55 63½ 65½ 53¾	Pincay L Jr	117 b	5.30	92-17	JudgAngelucc1181IronEys115noSnwChf1262¾	Wide into str 8
14May87- 8Hol	fst 1	:232 :461 1:101 1:35	4↑ Alw 45000	2 6 53¾ 52¾ 42½ 1hd↓	Pincay L Jr	117 b	*1.30	88-13	[DH]Tsso117[DH]Metronomc117hdSouthrnHlo1172½	Wide into str 6
2May87- 8Hol	fst 7f	:213 :434 1:082 1:21	3↑ Triple Bend H 80k	3 5 511 511 56½ 56	Delahoussaye E	120 b	5.30	93-13	BedsidePromise1242Zabaleta1181¾BoldrThanBold1182	Wide 5
13Oct86- 8SA	fst 1⅛	:463 1:102 1:354 1:482	3↑ Yankee Valor H 94k	3 5 46 48 47½ 36½	Pincay L Jr	117 b	4.50	80-19	Precisionist1274½Garthorn1242Tasso1171½	Broke slowly 5
5Sep86- 8Dmr	fst 1 1/16	:222 :454 1:102 1:414	El Cajon 55k	5 6 75½ 31½ 1½ 13	Pincay L Jr	117 b	*1.00	91-16	Tsso1173SouthernHalo114½BrghtTom114½	Wide into stretch 9
26May86- 9GS	fst 1¼	:47 1:112 1:372 2:03	Jersey Derby-G2	3 8 813 66 35½ 33½	Pincay L Jr	126 b	3.40	85-20	Snow Chief1262Mogambo1261½Tasso1261¼	Stride late 10
7May86- 8Aqu	fst 1	:224 :46 1:101 1:353	Withers-G2	5 7 85¾ 85¼ 44½ 22¾	Pincay L Jr	126 b	*.70	85-15	ClearChoic1262¾Tsso1264¾LndngPlot1262¾	Best stride late 10
19Apr86- 8Aqu	fst 1⅛	:472 1:111 1:361 1:503	Wood Memorial-G1	4 3 53 65½ 46 42	Pincay L Jr	126 b	*.80	80-18	Broad Brush126½Mogambo126nkGroovy1261¼	Wide 7
5Apr86- 8Aqu	fst 1	:222 :444 1:083 1:343	Gotham-G2	6 7 811 811 56½ 32	Pincay L Jr	123	2.00	91-18	Mogambo121¾[D]Groovy1141¼Tasso1231	In close after start 9
Placed second through disqualification										
15Mar86- 7Aqu	fst 7f	:231 :461 1:11 1:234	Manassa Mauler 55k	2 8 53½ 31 1hd 13	Maple E	122	*.60	82-23	Tasso1223Lil Tyler122noRiomundo115no	Driving 9
Previously owned by Robins & Waldemar Inc										
2Nov85- 1Aqu	fst 1	:222 :452 1:104 1:361	©BC Juvenile-G1	7 7 85¾ 64½ 33 1no	Pincay L Jr	122 b	5.60	85-10	Tasso122noStorm Cat1221¾Scat Dancer122no	Just up 13
19Oct85- 7Kee	fst 1 1/16	:232 :474 1:121 1:46	Breeders' Futurity-G2	9 4 31 2hd 12½ 16	Pincay L Jr	121 b	*.90	76-24	Tsso1216ReglDreamer1213½ThunderngForc121hd	Ridden out 11
9Oct85- 7Kee	fst *7f	1:272	Alw 33040	1 4 43 65½ 2½ 2¾	Pincay L Jr	121	*.30	85-18	FarawayIsland112¾Tasso1218SonoftheDesert1211½	Rallied 7
11Sep85- 8Dmr	fst 1	:231 :471 1:113 1:36	Dmr Futurity-G1	6 5 31½ 2½ 22 1nk	Pincay L Jr	117	*1.00	88-15	Tasso117nkArewehavingfunyet1172½Snow Chief1173¼	Driving 6
17Aug85- 7Dmr	fst 1	:222 :463 1:114 1:363	Alw 23000	1 4 42 22 2hd 14	Delahoussaye E	118	*.60	85-17	Tasso1184Speedy Shannon1187½Salerno Beach1184½	Easily 6
22Jly85- 3Hol	fst 6f	:222 :46 :582 1:103	Md Sp Wt	5 7 77½ 55¼ 32½ 11	Pincay L Jr	118	2.10	94-07	Tasso1181Bright Tom1187Darby Fair1181¼	Driving 7
31May85- 4Hol	fst 5f	:222 :454 :582	Md Sp Wt	4 8 77½ 69 38½ 36½	Pincay L Jr	118	3.40	- -	MightyTrip1181DarbyFair1185½Tasso1184½	Rank post parade 10

Temperence Hill

b. c. 1977, by Stop the Music (Hail to Reason)–Sister Shannon, by Etonian — Lifetime record: 31 11 4 2 $1,567,650

Own.– Loblolly Stable
Br.– Dr A.F. Polk Jr (Ky)
Tr.– Joseph B. Cantey

12Nov81- 6Med	fst 1¼	:471 1:113 1:363 2:022	3↑ Med Cup H-G2	9 10 64 32½ 34 43½	Maple E	124 b	5.90	86-14	Princelet110¾Niteange114¾Peat Moss1212	Lacked bid 14
10Oct81- 8Bel	fst 1½	:48 1:123 2:021 2:282	3↑ J C Gold Cup-G1	4 9 99¼ 96½ 83¾ 64	Maple E	126 b	6.60	74-14	John Henry126hdPeat Moss126¾Relaxing123hd	Wide 11
19Sep81- 8Bel	my 1¼	:481 1:114 1:354 2:003	3↑ Marlboro Cup H-G1	3 7 68½ 56 34½ 35¼	Maple E	127 b	4.10	92-13	Noble Nashua1163¾Amber Pass1201½Temperence Hill1271¼	8
Lacked response										
5Sep81- 8Bel	fst 1⅛	:461 1:094 1:343 1:471	3↑ Woodward-G1	9 8 87½ 77¼ 56 55¾	Maple E	128 b	11.40	85-14	PleasntClny1231¾AmberPass1261¼HerbWtr1162	Raced wide 9
19Aug81- 1Sar	fm 1 3/16(T)	:484 1:122 1:362 1:552	3↑ Alw 35000	6 5 54½ 53½ 66 55	Maple E	122 b	2.50	84-13	Manguin115noScythianGold1192½TheLibrlMmbr1152	No factor 6
18Jly81- 8Bel	fst 1½	:492 1:134 2:013 2:26	3↑ Brooklyn H-G1	5 6 77 810 713 817	Maple E	128	2.30	73-15	Hechizado1164TheLiberlMembr113¾PeatMoss1113¼	No factor 10
4Jly81- 8Bel	sly 1¼	:473 1:114 1:36 2:02	3↑ Suburban-G1	1 4 49 45 33½ 1hd	MacBeth D	127	3.20	90-20	Temperence Hill127hdRing of Light115¾Highland Blade113nk	8
Brushed,driving										
14Jun81- 8Hol	fst 1¼	:453 1:093 1:344 2:002	3↑ Hol Gold Cup H-G1	2 4 55¼ 75¾ 56¾ 56	Maple E	129	3.20	83-16	[D]Caterman120hdEleven Stitches1222½Super Moment117nk	10
Lacked room										
25May81- 8Hol	fst 1⅛	:452 1:101 1:353 1:482	3↑ Californian-G1	3 4 411 52½ 32½ 2hd	Maple E	130	*1.60	87-15	ElevenStitches122hdTemprnceHill130nkKilijaro1233¾	Sharp 12
10Apr81- 9OP	fst 1 1/16	:232 :464 1:112 1:432	4↑ Oaklawn H-G2	4 5 43 1hd 1½ 12	Maple E	126	*.60	91-18	TemprnceHll1262SunCtchr1231¾Uncool1142½	Brushed,clear 5
28Mar81- 9OP	fst 1 1/16	:244 :49 1:13 1:441	4↑ Razorback H-G2	1 5 56½ 31 2hd 1nk	Maple E	124	*.40	87-21	TemprnceHill124nkBlueEnsign1133Belle'sRulr1124½	Driving 6
25Oct80- 8Aqu	sf 1½(T)	:514 1:192 2:13 2:393	3↑ Turf Classic-G1	5 4 33 68 711 716	Maple E	121	2.40	27-57	Anifa1233Golden Act1265John Henry126nk	Tired 8
18Oct80-10LaD	gd 1¼	:491 1:143 1:393 2:063	Super Derby 500k	3 4 25 1½ 13 15½	Maple E	126	*.50	92-19	TemprnceHill1265½FirstAlbert126½CactusRoad126no	Driving 8
4Oct80- 8Bel	fst 1½	:494 1:15 2:051 2:301	3↑ J C Gold Cup-G1	1 3 43 1½ 13 15½	Maple E	121	2.30	69-19	TemprncHll1215½JohnHnry1262IvoryHuntr1263¼	Ridden out 7
6Sep80- 7Bel	fst 1⅛	:45 1:092 1:341 1:47	3↑ Marlboro Cup H-G1	6 8 811 74½ 55 511¾	Maple E	119	6.20	80-15	Wintr'sTl1234½GlorousSng117nkJkInKlugmn1183½	No factor 8
16Aug80- 8Sar	fst 1¼	:454 1:101 1:361 2:024	Travers-G1	3 9 915 55 3nk 11½	Maple E	126	3.80	86-13	TemperenceHill1261½FirstAlbert126noAmbrPss1266¾	Driving 9
19Jly80- 8Bel	fst 1½	:513 1:163 2:05 2:283	3↑ Brooklyn H-G1	1 2 32 45½ 48 410½	Maple E	114 b	2.10	66-20	Winter'sTale1205StateDinner1213½RingofLight1142	Tired 5
5Jly80- 8Bel	fst 1⅛	:451 1:091 1:353 1:49	Dwyer-G2	7 6 611 57½ 46 21	Maple E	129 b	8.20	81-17	AmberPass1141TempernceHill129hdComptroller1193	Rallied 8
22Jun80- 8Bel	hd 1(T)	:23 :452 1:093 1:334	Saranac-G2	2 10 1210 1211 911 77¾	Maple E	128 b	4.90	88-05	KeytoContent1143CurrentLegnd114½BenFab1233	No threat 13
7Jun80- 8Bel	my 1½	:501 1:151 2:04 2:294	Belmont-G1	3 7 85 3½ 2hd 12	Maple E	126 b	53.40	71-17	Temperence Hill1262Genuine Risk1211½Rockhill Native1262	10
Brisk urging										

31May80- 7Bel fm 1 1/16(T) :224:454 1:10 1:423 3↑ Alw 35000 6 4 512 412 33 31¾ Maple E 113 b 8.10 81-19 FrenchColonial121nkPerceran1171½TemprncHll113no Gaining 6
26May80- 8Key fst 1⅛ :472 1:113 1:362 1:484 Pa Derby-G3 7 7 713 610 612 511¼ Haire D 122 b *.70 80-15 LivelyKing1224Mutineer122nkStutzBlackhawk1224 No rally 7
10May80- 8Aqu fst 1 :232:454 1:091 1:342 Withers-G2 3 7 78¾ 69½ 28 25½ Haire D 126 b 3.30 88-13 ColonlMoran1265½TemperenceHill1264¼J.P.Brothr126½ Wide 7
12Apr80- 9OP fst 1⅛ :462 1:104 1:382 1:503 Ark Derby-G1 8 9 918 89¾ 41¾ 11¼ Haire D 123 b 4.60e 90-21 TemperencHll1231¼Bold'NRullng1173¾SunCtchr120nk Driving 10
29Mar80- 7OP sly 1 70 :234:48 1:124 1:421 Alw 25000 1 3 31½ 33 23 24¾ Maple E 121 b 1.60 80-23 Loto Canada1214¾Temperence Hill1211¾Raise a Kid1122½ 7
2nd best
15Mar80- 9OP fst 1 70 :22 :452 1:112 1:424 Rebel H 64k 3 12 1117 814 44 12¼ Haire D 114 b 16.50 82-22 Temperence Hill1142¼Royal Sporn1112½Be a Prospect123hd 15
Drew out
4Mar80- 8OP fst 1 70 :234:48 1:134 1:434 3↑ Alw 15000 4 3 44 43½ 32½ 1½ Maple S 114 b 3.00 77-24 TemprnceHll114½Tonimarow1142ElGatoGrande1144½ Driving 8
26Feb80- 4OP fst 6f :221:47 1:132 3↑ Md Sp Wt 3 7 611 56½ 25 1¾ Maple S 114 b *.80 78-24 TemprnceHill114¾WrongSurf1156TailbackTodd1148 Driving 8
29Sep79- 4Bel fst 6½f :23 :463 1:103 1:164 Md Sp Wt 7 9 84¼ 96¾ 712 715 Maple S 118 b 16.40 77-12 Inland Voyager1188Preferred List118hdRaise a Crown1181¼ 12
Wide
4Aug79- 2Sar fst 6f :22 :451 1:102 Md Sp Wt 1 9 109¾ 89 78 68½ Maple E 118 5.30 79-12 Dressage1185¼Attengur1182½TrafficBreaker118no No factor 11
22Jly79- 4Bel fst 6f :221:461 1:113 Md Sp Wt 9 6 1112 1114 912 410¾ Maple E 118 11.00 73-18 Fappiano1183½Buck Island1186¾Rectory118½ Late gain 11

Theatrical (Ire)

b. c. 1982, by Nureyev (Northern Dancer)–Tree of Knowledge, by Sassafras **Lifetime record: 22 10 4 2 $2,943,627**
Own.– A.E. Paulson
Br.– Mr & Mrs B.R. Firestone (Ire)
Tr.– William I. Mott

21Nov87- 6Hol fm 1½(T) :471 1:111 2:001 2:242 3↑ BC Turf-G1 12 4 48 11½ 1hd 1½ Day P 126 *1.80e 99-00 Theatrical126½Trempolino1223½VillgStrII126nk Long drive 14
Previously owned by Firestone & Paulson
24Oct87- 8Aqu fm 1⅜(T) :501 1:142 1:382 2:152 3↑ Man o' War-G1 5 2 22 2hd 1hd 12½ Day P 126 *.30 94-07 Theatricl1262½LeGloriux121½MdnghtCousns1266 Ridden out 8
26Sep87- 8Bel sf 1½(T) :491 1:133 2:044 2:291 3↑ Turf Classic-G1 5 2 27 1½ 12 13¾ Day P 126 *1.00 78-25 Theatrical1263¾RiverMemories1164¼Talkno1268¾ Ridden out 6
6Sep87- 8AP fm 1¼(T) :482 1:133 1:383 2:022 3↑ Bud Arl Million-G1 4 3 2½ 11 23 34¾ Day P 126 2.30 77-27 Manila1261½Sharrood1263¼Theatrical1263¾ Tired 8
1Aug87- 8Bel fm 1½(T) :491 1:132 2:024 2:26 3↑ Sword Dancer H-G1 2 1 1hd 21½ 23½ 23 Day P 124 *.40 91-10 [D]Dance of Life1223Theatrical1245½Akabir1144 Checked 4
Placed first through disqualification
13Jun87- 8Bel fm 1⅜[T] :50 1:14 1:381 2:14 3↑ Bowling Green H-G1 1 3 33 33 2hd 11 Day P 123 *1.30 87-24 Theatrical1231Akabir116nkDance of Life121nk Ridden out 10
30May87- 8Bel fm 1¼[T] :481 1:123 1:362 2:004 3↑ Red Smith H-G2 5 3 32 42¼ 31 11¾ Day P 122 2.80 90-24 Theatrical1221¾DanceofLife1221¼Equalize112hd Ridden out 11
21Feb87-10Hia fm 1½(T) 2:283 3↑ Hia Turf Cup H-G1 6 1 1hd 11 1½ 1nk Day P 121 *1.30 87-14 Theatrical121nkLong Mick1151½Creme Fraiche1185 Lasted 8
31Jan87-10Hia fm 1 3/16(T) 1:54 3↑ Bougainvillea H-G2 11 9 85 62¼ 33½ 22 Day P 122 *1.60 85-14 Akabir1132[D]Theatrical122nkFlying Pidgeon1201 Bore in 14
Disqualified and placed 14th;Previously trained by Robert Frankel
7Dec86- 8Hol fm 1½(T) :474 1:121 2:01 2:254 3↑ Hol Turf Cup Inv'l-G1 2 1 2hd 1½ 11 3nk Stevens GL 126 *1.20e 93-09 Alphabatm126hdDahar126nkTheatrcl126½ Rider dropped whip 8
1Nov86- 6SA fm 1½(T) :472 1:111 2:003 2:252 3↑ BC Turf-G1 1 2 22½ 21 1hd 2nk Stevens GL 126 2.70e 88-07 Manila122nkTheatrical1263¾Estrapade1232¾ Gamely 9
12Oct86- 8SA fm 1½(T) :464 1:111 2:003 2:26 3↑ Oak Tree Inv'l-G1 5 5 53½ 22 22 22¼ Stevens GL 126 *.40e 83-12 Estrapade1232¼Theatricl1265½UptownSwll126½ Best of rest 10
Previously trained by Dermot K. Weld
31Aug86- 8AP fm 1¼(T) :471 1:113 1:371 2:004 3↑ Bud Arl Million-G1 14 11 108½ 107 99½ 1010¾ Cauthen S 126 *2.10e 79-11 Estrapade1225Divulge126hdPennine Walk126½ Pinched st. 14
Previously owned by B.R. Firestone
27Jly86♦ Dusseldorf(Ger) gd *1½(T)LH 2:273 3↑ Grosser Preis von Berlin-G1 22 Kinane MJ 132 6.20 Acatenango1322Theatrical1323¼Orfano1171½ 8
Stk80400
Tracked leaders,bid 1½f out,chased winner home
20Jun86♦ Ascot(GB) fm 1½(T)RH 2:291 4↑ Hardwicke Stakes-G2 712 Kinane MJ 124 *2.75 Dihistan121¾St. Hilarion1264Iroko1211 10
Stk73300
Progress 2½f out,drifted badly right,weakened
Previously owned by B.R. Firestone
2Nov85- 6Aqu fm 1½(T) :48 1:122 2:022 2:27 3↑ BC Turf-G1 14 8 810 107¼ 117¼ 117 Piggott L 122 3.80e 99-00 Pebbles123nkStrawberryRoadII1261¼Mourjan1261 Raced wide 14
8Sep85♦ Phoenix Park(Ire) hy 1¼(T)RH 2:091 3↑ Phoenix Champion Stakes-G1 77½ Kinane MJ 123 8.00 Commanche Run1323Bob Back132¾Damister123no 11
Stk564000
Brief progress 4f out,never threatened.Triptych 10th
29Jun85♦ The Curragh(Ire) gd 1½(T)RH 2:294 Irish Derby-G1 2½ Kinane MJ 126 6.00 Law Society126½Theatrical1262½Damister126hd 13
Stk370000
Rallied to lead 2f out,headed 100y out.Triptych 5th
5Jun85♦ Epsom(GB) gd 1½(T)LH 2:361 Epsom Derby-G1 725 Piggott L 126 10.00 Slip Anchor1267Law Society1266Damister126no 14
Stk458000
Tracked in 6th,weakened 3f out,drifted left
11May85♦ Leopardstwn(Ire) yl 1¼(T)LH 2:134 Derrinstown Derby Trial-G2 14 Kinane MJ 123 *1.00 Theatrical1234Northern Plain1262Lord Duke1233 8
Stk51600
Tracked in 4th,led 2f out,soon clear,drifted slightly
27Apr85♦ The Curragh(Ire) gd 1⅜(T)RH 2:252 Ballysax Stakes 12 Piggott L 123 2.50 Theatrical1232Leading Counsel13112Snow Plant123nk 6
Stk11500
Steadied start,5th early,rail bid,angled out,led 1f out
15Oct84♦ Gowran Park(Ire) fm 1 1/16(T)RH 1:372 Kilkenny EBF Maiden 11 Kinane MJ 126 *1.10 Theatrical1261Pala Chief1263Jazz Ballet126no 16
Mdn3200
Tracked in 4th,dueled 1f out,led 100y out,handily

Tiffany Lass

dkbbr. f. 1983, by Bold Forbes (Irish Castle)–Sally Stark, by Graustark **Lifetime record: 10 8 1 1 $534,943**
Own.– A.U. Jones
Br.– Aaron U. Jones (Ky)
Tr.– Lazaro S. Barrera

13Jun87- 8Hol fst 1⅛ :454 1:101 1:351 1:481 3↑ (F)Milady H-G1 4 2 22½ 2½ 22½ 22¾ Stevens GL 120 2.20 93-11 SeldomSeenSue1172¾TiffanyLass1204½FrauAltv115½ 2nd best 7
9May87- 9Hol fst 1 :222:444 1:084 1:333 3↑ (F)Hawthone H-G2 3 2 21 32½ 35½ 38 Stevens GL 123 *.60 87-10 Seldom Seen Sue1144Clabber Girl1164Tiffany Lass1236 5
Lacked response
29Apr87- 8Hol fst 6f :214:444 :564 1:092 3↑ (F)Silver Spoon 62k 4 2 2½ 2½ 1hd 1¾ Stevens GL 123 *1.10 96-13 Tiffany Lass123¾Luisant1182¼Seldom Seen Sue116½ Gamely 4
2May86- 9CD fst 1⅛ :463 1:11 1:371 1:503 (F)Ky Oaks-G1 1 2 32 22 2hd 1hd Stevens GL 121 *1.20 89-14 TiffanyLass121hdLifeattheTop121nkFamlyStyl121hd Driving 12
12Apr86- 9OP fst 1 1/16 :232:471 1:113 1:42 (F)Fantasy-G1 1 1 1hd 1hd 1½ 12½ Stevens GL 121 3.40 91-16 Tiffany Lass1212½Lotka1162Turn and Dance112hd Drew out 8
22Mar86-10FG fst 1 1/16 :23 :462 1:114 1:45 (F)FG Oaks-G3 5 3 34 21 2½ 1¾ Frazier RL 121 *1.00 87-17 TiffanyLass121¾PatriciaJ.K.1211½TurnandDnc1125½ Driving 6
2Mar86-10FG fst 1 1/16 :234:48 1:14 1:46 (F)Davona Dale 38k 9 4 53¾ 53 21½ 13 Frazier RL 122 *.30 82-25 TiffanyLass1223SuperSet1225PortofDeparture117½ Easily 10
15Feb86-10FG fst 6f :214:462 :582 1:11 (F)Thelma 47k 1 4 1hd 2hd 13 19 Frazier RL 112 *.70 90-24 Tiffany Lass1129Best in Class122½My Mafalda1123½ Easily 9
9Jan86- 8FG sl 6f :222:471 :593 1:124 (F)Alw 9000 6 2 32½ 2hd 12 15 Frazier RL 119 *.50 81-32 TiffanyLass1195TwelveMileLimit1148PrttyPlum1191½ Easily 7
24Dec85- 6Hol fst 6f :22 :453 :573 1:10 (F)Md Sp Wt 3 6 31 31 21½ 11 Stevens GL 118 *.80 94-12 TiffanyLass1181Barbarn1184½Bggr'sWllt1183½ Saved ground 11

Track Robbery

ch. f. 1976, by No Robbery (Swaps)–Left at Home, by Run for Nurse **Lifetime record: 59 22 12 7 $1,098,537**

Own.– Summa Stable
Br.– E. Kitchen (Ky)
Tr.– John W. Russell

Date	Cond	Dist	Fractions	Race	PP	St	1st	2nd	Str	Fin	Jockey	Wt	Eq	Odds	Fig	Finishers	Comment	Fld
8Jan83- 8SA	fm	1⅛Ⓣ	:45 1:091 1:333 1:462 4↑	ⒻSan Gorgonio H 84k	4	1	11½	1hd	1110	118	Valenzuela PA	122		6.00	87-05	Castilla1221StarPastures119hdCatGirl115½	Fin. after 6f	11
5Dec82- 8Hol	fm	1⅛Ⓣ	:463 1:104 1:344 1:472 3↑	ⒻMatriarch (Div 2) 172k	2	1	14	13	3nk	42¼	Valenzuela PA	123		4.00	91-08	Castilla120hdSangue1231½Star Pastures123¾	Steadied	9
26Nov82- 6Med	fst	1⅛	:464 1:12 1:383 1:52 3↑	ⒻLong Look H-G2	4	1	13	11½	35½	69½	Valenzuela PA	124		*.70	63-21	LadyDean1212¾Prismatical114nkCleverGuest1093½	Gave way	6
30Oct82- 7Kee	sly	1⅛	:461 1:10 1:35 1:474 3↑	ⒻSpinster-G1	6	1	12	12	16	19	Valenzuela PA	123		4.00	98-08	TrackRbbry1239BlushWthPrd1191½OurDrlng1192¼	Ridden out	9
	Previously trained by Robert L. Wheeler																	
18Aug82- 8Dmr	fst	1 1/16	:223 :452 1:091 1:40 3↑	ⒻChula Vista H 77k	1	2	21½	31½	411	414	Delahoussaye E	123		*1.10	86-21	Matching1166Miss Huntington116noCat Girl1178	Faltered	4
11Jly82- 8Hol	fst	1⅛	:462 1:101 1:352 1:48 3↑	ⒻVanity H-G1	1	1	1½	1½	2hd	21½	Delahoussaye E	123		2.30	87-16	Sangue1201½Track Robbery1231½Cat Girl1172	Game try	7
27Jun82- 8Hol	fst	1 1/16	:231 :461 1:102 1:413 3↑	ⒻMilady H-G2	6	1	11½	11	2hd	22½	Delahoussaye E	124		*1.10	84-12	Cat Girl1142½Track Robbery124noAck's Secret1235	Gamely	6
23May82- 8Hol	fm	1⅛Ⓣ	:461 1:102 1:341 1:464 3↑	ⒻGamely H-G2	8	1	11	1hd	21½	42	Delahoussaye E	125		*1.70	94-05	Ack'sSecrt1221MissHuntington117¾Vocalist114nk	Weakened	9
7Apr82- 9OP	fst	1 1/16	:233 :472 1:123 1:451 4↑	ⒻApple Blossom H-G1	5	1	11	1½	2hd	1no	Delahoussaye E	124		*.90	82-30	Track Robbery124noAndover Way1205½Jameela1231	Driving	6
20Mar82- 8SA	fst	1⅛	:454 1:094 1:344 1:471 4↑	ⒻS Ana H-G2	5	1	11	11½	12½	15¼	Delahoussaye E	123		2.30	93-12	TrackRobbry1235¼Manzanera1171¼Ack'sSecret1231¼	Driving	8
28Feb82- 8SA	fst	1⅛	:453 1:092 1:35 1:473 4↑	ⒻS Margarita H-G1	1	2	2hd	1hd	2hd	22½	Delahoussaye E	123		6.80e	88-09	Ack'sSecrt1182½TrackRobbry1231PstForgttng1222½	Gamely	10
13Feb82- 8SA	fst	1 1/16	:223 :46 1:101 1:42 4↑	ⒻS Maria H-G2	2	4	43½	42½	33	32½	Delahoussaye E	124		2.70e	88-16	Targa1142½Jameela124hdTrack Robbery124¾	Rallied	8
6Jan82- 8SA	hy	1⅛	:474 1:123 1:393 1:523 4↑	ⒻSan Gorgonio H 79k	3	1	1½	11	1½	1½	Delahoussaye E	123		*.80	66-34	TrackRbbry123½RainbowConnection1177Targa11411	Driving	5
13Dec81- 8Hol	fst	1⅛	:463 1:103 1:361 1:493 3↑	ⒻSilver Belles H 107k	3	1	11	1hd	1hd	2hd	Delahoussaye E	123		4.40	81-21	HappyGuess117hdTrackRobbery1232½Targa112hd	Just missed	6
5Dec81- 8BM	yl	1⅛Ⓣ	:474 1:133 1:40 1:542 3↑	ⒻCal Jockey Club H 107k	3	2	22	21½	1hd	1nk	Mena F	124		*1.00	68-24	TrckRbbry124nkBrryBush1201½Tolt111½	Headed str,came back	7
21Nov81- 8BM	sf	1 1/16Ⓣ	:232 :483 1:144 1:502 3↑	ⒻChildren's Hosp H 56k	5	1	11½	11½	1½	1½	Mena F	125		*.90	56-44	Track Robbery125½Tolita112½Noaah1181	Gamely	10
18Oct81- 8SA	fm	1⅛Ⓣ	:451 1:094 1:341 1:47 3↑	ⒻLas Palmas H-G3	4	1	11	2hd	22½	44¾	Valenzuela PA	122		3.60e	87-12	Ack'sSecrt1191¾QntoConqur123nkBrryBush1182¾	No excuse	9
30Aug81- 8Dmr	fm	1⅛Ⓣ	:464 1:104 1:361 1:484 3↑	ⒻRamona H-G2	5	2	2hd	1hd	3½	31½	Valenzuela PA	123		*2.90	92-10	QueentoConqr120½AmbrEver1121TrckRbbry1231½	Weakened	10
19Aug81- 8Dmr	fst	1 1/16	:222 :45 1:093 1:413 3↑	ⒻChula Vista H 81k	6	1	17	13	31	36	Valenzuela PA	125		*1.50	86-17	Save Wild Life118½Princess Karenda1205½TrackRobbery1251¼		6
	Used in pace																	
12Jly81- 8Hol	fst	1⅛	:453 1:091 1:341 1:47 3↑	ⒻVanity Inv'l H-G1	7	1	17	14½	14½	13½	Valenzuela PA	120		3.70	94-14	TrackRbbry1203½Princess Karenda118nkSave Wild Life1173¼		7
	Never threatened																	
13Jun81- 8Hol	fm	1⅛Ⓣ	:46 1:101 1:341 1:464 3↑	ⒻBeverly Hills H-G3	2	1	15	13	12	11¼	Valenzuela PA	120		3.60	96-10	TrackRobbery1201¼PrincessKarenda1214½SaveWildLife1152½		5
	Driving																	
31May81- 8Hol	fm	1 1/16Ⓣ	:231 :463 1:111 1:404 3↑	ⒻWilshire H-G3	6	1	13	1½	12	1¾	Valenzuela PA	118		4.80	95-09	TrackRobbry118¾LuthMusic1151¾SaveWildLife1161½	Driving	6
6May81- 8Hol	fm	1 1/16Ⓣ	:23 :461 1:101 1:41 3↑	ⒻⓇMatinee H(Div1) 43k	3	1	11½	2hd	2hd	33½	Valenzuela PA	122		3.80	90-09	Targa1103Ack's Secret122½Track Robbery1221½	Weakened	6
24Apr81- 8Hol	fm	1⅛Ⓣ	:454 1:11 1:354 1:481 3↑	ⒻGamely H-G2	2	1	11½	11½	1hd	46	Valenzuela PA	118		24.10	83-12	Kilijaro1272½PrincessKrnd1212½WshngWll1221	Used in pace	6
11Apr81- 8SA	fst	1 1/16	:221 :452 1:10 1:414 4↑	ⒻⓇS Lucia H 56k	6	2	21	53½	912	916	Lipham T	124		*2.20	76-15	Finance Charge1135½Si1151¾Swift Bird1182¾	Tired	10
7Mar81- 8SA	fst	1⅛	:46 1:094 1:352 1:48 4↑	ⒻSanta Ana H-G3	2	2	2½	2½	11½	22	Delahoussaye E	119		4.30	87-11	QueentoConquer1212TrckRbbry1195Ack'sScrt1235	No match	7
20Feb81- 8SA	fm	1⅛Ⓣ	:464 1:104 1:351 1:472 4↑	ⒻAlw 40000	1	1	12	12½	11	11½	Pincay L Jr	120		*1.80	90-10	TrackRobbery1201½GrafittiGal1151Hthr'sTurn1131¾	Driving	8
31Jan81- 8SA	gd	1 1/16	:23 :462 1:104 1:431 4↑	ⒻS Maria H-G2	4	1	11½	1hd	22½	22	Pincay L Jr	117		4.10	83-23	GloriousSong1272TrckRbbry1175MssHuntngton11310	Gamely	4
22Jan81- 8SA	fst	1 1/16	:224 :46 1:10 1:411 4↑	ⒻAlw 40000	1	1	11	11½	14	12	Pincay L Jr	117		2.60e	95-14	Track Robbery1172Princess Toby1186Miss Huntington1134		7
	Not threatened																	
16Jan81- 8SA	fst	1 1/16	:231 :463 1:11 1:42 4↑	ⒻAlw 40000	7	2	24	21	2½	31½	Pierce D	119		*1.30e	89-12	Kankm115noPrncssToby1171½TrckRbbry1191½	Bid,not enough	7
4Oct80- 8BM	fm	1 1/16Ⓣ	:231 :47 1:114 1:434 3↑	ⒻTizna H 45k	11	1	15	12	1½	51½	Lipham T	115		8.40	87-09	Fresca121noNoaah114nkLusty Try112nk	Failed to last	11
9Aug80- 8Dmr	fm	1Ⓣ	:231 :462 1:102 1:344 3↑	ⒻPalomar H-G3	1	1	1½	1hd	33	99	Lipham T	113		6.30e	91-05	A Thousand Stars115noWishing Well1212½Devon Ditty120nk		9
	Done after 6f																	
31Jly80- 8Dmr	fm	1 1/16Ⓣ	:24 :483 1:122 1:431 3↑	ⒻAlw 35000	4	1	12½	1½	1½	2¾	Lipham T	116		3.00	92-07	PrincessToby116¾TrackRobbery116¾More So1133	Hung late	6
11Jly80- 8Hol	fm	1 1/16Ⓣ	:23 :463 1:101 1:401 4↑	ⒻAlw 50000	6	2	33	22	32½	44	Lipham T	117		14.70e	94-09	Love You Dear117¾Princess Toby122nkA Thousand Stars1173		8
	Lacked rally																	
28Jun80- 8Hol	fm	1⅛Ⓣ	:471 1:112 1:35 1:472 3↑	ⒻBeverly Hills H-G3	3	3	32½	41¼	32	62¾	Lipham T	113		9.60e	90-12	CountryQueen122noWishngWell122½TheVeryOne117nk	Hung	10
13Jun80- 8Hol	fst	1 1/16	:222 :452 1:084 1:411 4↑	ⒻMarket Basket 50k	2	3	22	33	611	612	Lipham T	117		26.10	77-13	SplendidGrl1151½Picea1124½Canonzton1171¼	Done after 6f	7
1Jun80- 5Hol	fm	1Ⓣ	:23 :461 1:10 1:354 4↑	ⒻAlw 40000	7	2	3½	2½	1hd	1no	Lipham T	114		25.90	90-10	TrackRobbery114noOutremer1143Conveniently1162½	Gamely	7
15May80- 8Hol	fst	6f	:22 :442 :563 1:083 4↑	ⒻAlw 35000	4	4	1½	3nk	62¼	78½	Olivares F	115		34.20	85-13	Canonization117nkDouble Deceit1152Outremer1152½	Tired	7
3May80- 8Hol	fst	6f	:213 :434 :552 1:073 4↑	ⒻAlw 35000	7	1	47	46½	510	69½	Olivares F	115		9.10e	89-13	SplendidGirl1152¾DoublDct1171½ShnHgh1142½	Flattened out	7
	Previously owned by Blue Sky Stable;previously trained by Phil Schvaneveldt																	
16Dec79-10TuP	fst	6½f	:213 :434 1:09 1:164	ⒻMolly Butler H 14k	2	9	41½	42½	89	107½	Kato A	115	b	6.40	84-19	Maurita1122Megabuck112noGaelicGiggl110nk	Done after ½	11
2Dec79-10TuP	fst	6½f	:214 :45 1:094 1:161	Az Republic H 12k	10	2	11½	11½	75¼	1314	Powell JP	115	b	3.60	76-22	Ken'nBold117nkHourLong1151½FullFlm1201	Faltered stretch	14
11Nov79- 8TuP	fst	6f	:214 :442 :562 1:094	Alw 4300	6	3	31	3½	23	2nk	Powell JP	115	b	*.50	88-17	VestdWys113nkTrckRbbry1153½LustyVkng1141	Strong finish	7
4Nov79- 9TuP	fst	5f	:213 :444 :57	Black Canyon H 11k	6	4	44	43½	24	37½↓	Powell JP	117	b	2.90	84-20	Nervous John1233½Full of Flame1194[DH]Track Robbery117		8
	Between horses early																	
22Sep79-11Alb	fst	1	:233 :464 1:12 1:393	Alb Derby H 23k	2	1	12	12	21	21¼	Powell JP	118	b	*1.30	81-23	HappyIrishman1191¼TrackRobbery1183¼TurquoisPrncss1112¼		12
18Aug79- 9Cen	gd	1 1/16	:232 :471 1:122 1:474	ⒻLady & Dove 13k	2	2	13	16	16	12½	Powell JP	116	b	*.30	68-26	Track Robbery1162½Nalees Battle1161½Lady Go Marching1162		8
	Wide,ridden out																	
5Aug79- 9Cen	fst	1⅛	:471 1:122 1:38 1:512	Cen Derby 22k	3	2	2½	11½	21	2hd	Kato A	112	b	*.80	88-16	Keen'n Bold114hdTrack Robbery1122To Erin112hd	Gamely	8
19Jly79- 7Aks	fst	1 70	:224 :461 1:104 1:423	ⒻPrincess 26k	5	3	3nk	31	2½	2hd	Kato A	120	b	2.40	85-19	MerryThought114hdTrackRbbery1204TurquoisePrincess118½		8
	Dueled outside																	
5Jly79- 7Aks	my	6f	:222 :451 1:112	ⒻGood Life 26k	10	5	3½	2hd	1hd	1nk	Kato A	116		3.90	80-25	Track Robbery116nkRappid Action1144Merry Thought114nk		10
	Outside,driving																	
24Jun79- 9Cen	fst	1	:23 :462 1:122 1:392	Turf Club Centre H 6.3k	6	3	3½	11½	12	1nk	Kato A	124	b	*.60	82-14	Track Robbery124nkAiles Sound114½To Erin115½	Lasted	13
10Jun79- 9Cen	my	6f	:212 :44 :563 1:102	Turn of the Cntry H 5.6k	2	2	1½	13	14	16	Kato A	121	b	*.40	88-16	TrackRobbery1216Mr. Moon Babe115¾Tatty Walk1122	Easily	6
28May79- 8Cen	fst	5½f	:22 :45 :572 1:04	Alw 2800	7	4	2hd	1½	13	14	Kato A	112	b	*.60	92-15	Track Robbery1124Gravitational1141Alliance Royal1162		8
	Much the best																	
30Mar79- 9TuP	fst	6f	:214 :443 :57 1:10	Alw 4500	7	1	2½	1½	15	16	Kato A	114	b	3.10	87-26	TrackRbbry1146VestedWays1132ShdyJck114½	Much the best	7
12Nov78-10LA	gd	6f	:213 :45 :584 1:114	ⒻSaddleback 22k	8	4	33	33½	65¾	68¾	Harris W	117	b	9.20	82-13	Sateen115hdScotts Princess1153½Go Zulu Sis1171¼	Tired	10
30Sep78- 8Cen	fst	6f	:222 :451 :573 1:11	Alw 2800	3	6	41	2½	1½	11	Andrews EH	118	b	*.50	85-18	TrackRobbery1181TattyWalk1156Babu'sGlory116nk	Bit wide	6
16Sep78- 6Cen	fst	5½f	:214 :443 :564 1:032	Alw 2600	4	6	42	31	12	15	Lintner K	113	b	*1.80	95-13	TrackRobbery1135TattyWalk1151CaptainNygeia1121½	Easily	8
3Sep78- 9Cen	fst	6f	:212 :441 :563 1:093	Gold Rush Fut (Div 2) 59k	2	4	43½	32½	34½	35¼	Andrews EH	119	b	3.40	87-13	NativoRango122nkTorpedoAlley1195TrckRbbery1198	Evenly	9
29Jly78- 8Cen	fst	6f	:221 :453 :581 1:111	Alw 2400	1	2	1½	12	14	16	Andrews EH	115	b	*1.40	84-18	Track Robbery1156To Erin1132½Rising Rullah1151	Easily	9
2Jly78- 9Cen	fst	5½f	:22 :451 :572 1:041	ⒻM Brown (Div 2) 23k	9	6	2½	31	26	28	Andrews EH	119	b	14.20	83-19	Gazette1198TrackRobbery1193½CallMeDanny116hd	2nd best	12
10Jun78- 5Cen	fst	5f	:222 :474 1:013	ⒻMd Sp Wt	1	10	42½	2½	12	1nk	Kato A	119	b	*1.50	74-25	Track Robbery119nkHoney Lamb1191Top Hop1092	Lasted	10

Turkoman

dkbbr. c. 1982, by Alydar (Raise a Native)–Taba, by Table Play — **Lifetime record: 22 8 8 3 $2,146,924**

Own.– Saron Stable
Br.– Corbin Robertson (Ky)
Tr.– Gary Jones

Date	Track	Fractions	Race	Running line	Jockey	Wt		Odds	Spd	Finish	Comment	Fld
1Nov86-7SA	fst 1¼	:46 1:101 1:343 2:002	3↑ BC Classic-G1	1 9 916 88½ 36½ 21¼	Day P	126		*1.60	86-13	Skywalker1261¼Turkomn1261¼Precisionst1261¾	Wide stretch	11
4Oct86-8Bel	fst 1½	:504 1:16 2:041 2:28	3↑ J C Gold Cup-G1	1 3 42½ 42¾ 32 2hd	McCarron CJ	126		*.50	80-14	CremeFraiche126hdTurkmn1264¾DanzgConnctn1211¼	Gamely	6
13Sep86-8Bel	fst 1¼	:473 1:11 1:354 2:00	3↑ Marlboro Cup H-G1	4 5 59 33 1hd 11½	Stevens GL	123		1.40	98-11	Turkoman1231½Precisionist1278¾Roo Art119½	Driving	5
17Aug86-8Sar	my 7f	:214 :441 1:082 1:211	3↑ Forego H-G2	2 8 815 813 35½ 2¾	McCarron CJ	124		*1.30	95-11	Groovy118¾Turkoman1244¾Innamorato110nk	Rallied	8
26May86-8Bel	fst 1	:232 :454 1:091 1:333	3↑ Metropolitan H-G1	7 8 814 75¾ 64½ 41½	McCarron CJ	125		*1.20	95-11	Garthorn1241¼LoveThatMac117noLady'sSecrt120nk	Five wide	8
18Apr86-9OP	fst 1⅛	:473 1:11 1:354 1:472	4↑ Oaklawn H-G2	2 3 35 21 2hd 11½	McCarron CJ	123		*.80	97-12	Turkoman1231½Gate Dancer123hdRed Attack11424	Driving	4
29Mar86-11Hia	fst 1¼	:471 1:101 1:334 1:583	3↑ Widener H-G1	1 6 613 44 33 1½	McCarron CJ	121		*1.20	105-06	Turkoman121½Darn That Alarm112noGate Dancer1249	Driving	6
7Mar86-9Hia	fst 6f	:21 :433 1:081	3↑ Tallahassee H 39k	8 8 916 915 56½ 12¾	McCarron CJ	120		*1.00	99-16	Turkoman1202¾Beveled1131½Cost Conscious1111	Driving	9
14Dec85-8Hol	fst 1	:221 :444 1:091 1:341	Affirmed H-G3	6 9 911 76 33 11¼	McCarron CJ	121		*1.50	92-14	Turkomn1211¼BannerBob1215½FloatingReserve1171¼	Driving	10
17Nov85-6Hol	fm 1⅛Ⓣ	:47 1:104 1:344 1:464	Hol Derby (Div 1)-G1	8 6 510 47½ 78 79½	McCarron CJ	122		*1.10	- -	CharmingDuke1223½Herat1222¾LaKoumia119½	Lacked response	13
	Run in divisions											
2Nov85-7Aqu	fst 1¼	:464 1:11 1:362 2:004	3↑ BC Classic-G1	3 7 78¾ 63½ 43 34	Vasquez J	122		7.70	88-10	ProudTruth122hdGtDncr1264Trkomn1225¾	Steadied far turn	8
16Oct85-8Bel	fst 7f	:231 :464 1:11 1:222	3↑ Alw 27000	2 6 65¼ 43½ 13½ 110	Vasquez J	114		*.50	90-22	Trkmn11410PurplMountn1141¾AccordngtoLuk1145	Ridden out	6
17Aug85-8Sar	fst 1¼	:481 1:114 1:361 2:011	Travers-G1	2 1 2½ 2½ 2½ 22¼	McHargue DG	126		7.60	92-08	Chief's Crown1262¼Turkoman1263Skip Trial126½	Weakened	7
21Jly85-8Hol	fst 1¼	:47 1:104 1:36 2:012	Swaps-G1	3 8 76½ 63¾ 31 2no	McHargue DG	115		*1.90	105-04	Padua115noTurkomn1153½Don't Say Halo120¾	Fast finish	8
29Jun85-7Hol	fst 1	:222 :444 1:084 1:334	Silver Screen H-G2	2 9 910 89¾ 56¼ 43½	McHargue DG	118		*1.50	100-00	PanchoVilla118½ProudestDoon1182Nostalg'sStr1181	Crowded	9
16Jun85-5Hol	fst 1	:23 :453 1:10 1:341	Alw 32000	3 6 66¼ 33 12½ 13½	McHargue DG	115		*.80	102-02	Turkoman1153½Ascension1164Sapient1142½	Ridden out	7
20Apr85-8GG	fst 1⅛	:474 1:112 1:361 1:483	Cal Derby-G2	9 8 75½ 32 33½ 22½	McHargue DG	115		*1.70	87-13	Hajji'sTreasure1152½Trkomn115noNostlg'sStr1163½	Gamely	10
30Mar85-8GG	fst 1 1/16	:222 :452 1:093 1:411	Gold Rush 56k	10 8 911 85¼ 45 2hd	McHargue DG	115	b	*1.60	97-13	ProtctYourslf117hdTrkomn115nkFullHonr1151½	Just missed	10
3Mar85-6SA	fst 1 1/16	:224 :461 1:102 1:432	©Alw 28000	9 5 42½ 42¼ 64 33	Hawley S	114	b	*1.40	81-14	BoldrThanBold118noAscenson1093Trkomn1141¼	Drifted out	9
30Jan85-9SA	fst 1 1/16	:232 :473 1:114 1:433	Alw 25000	5 6 74½ 64¼ 33 31½	Hawley S	114	b	*.50	81-17	RoyalOlympia1151½RelaunchTun114hdTrkmn1141½	Lugged in	7
13Jan85-4SA	fst 1 1/16	:224 :462 1:112 1:42	©Alw 24000	5 6 63 3½ 2½ 22½	Hawley S	114	b	3.60	88-13	Skywalkr1182½Turkoman1146Royal Olympia115½	Wide turn	7
19Dec84-6Hol	sly 6f	:223 :463 :594 1:123	Md Sp Wt	8 9 99¾ 66¼ 22 1½	Hawley S	118	b	2.80	86-15	Turkoman118½Bloom's Beau1183½Time of the Fox118½		10
	Wide ⅜ turn,drifted in late											

Vanlandingham

b. c. 1981, by Cox's Ridge (Best Turn)–Populi, by Star Envoy — **Lifetime record: 19 10 3 3 $1,409,476**

Own.– Loblolly Stable
Br.– Loblolly Stable (Ky)
Tr.– Claude McGaughey III

Date	Track	Fractions	Race	Running line	Jockey	Wt		Odds	Spd	Finish	Comment	Fld
5Apr86-9OP	fst 1 1/16	:231 :454 1:10 1:42	4↑ Razorback H-G2	9 2 21½ 21 11½ 2½	Day P	125		*.50e	90-16	RedAttack111½Vanlandingham1251½InevitablLdr111hd	Bested	9
2Mar86-8SA	fst 1¼	:451 1:091 1:34 2:00	4↑ S Anita H-G1	11 3 32½ 58 811 812¼	MacBeth D	125		10.60	77-13	Greinton122¾Herat1122Hatim118nk	Tired	13
15Feb86-10GP	fm 1 1/16	:23 :463 1:093 1:40	3↑ Can Turf H (Div 2)-G2	7 2 21 2hd 11½ 1½	MacBeth D	126		*.80	100-02	Vndlandinghm126½EndsWell1155Dr.Schwrtzmn1183¼	Driving	8
8Dec85-8Hol	fm 1½Ⓣ	:492 1:15 2:042 2:282	3↑ Hol Cup Inv'l-G1	11 2 11 11½ 1hd 32¾	MacBeth D	126		8.30	- -	Zoffany1262¼Win126nkVanlandingham1262	Weakened	13
16Nov85-9Lrl	sf 1½Ⓣ	:511 1:171 2:092 2:353	3↑ D C Int'l-G1	4 1 12 12 12 11	MacBeth D	126		7.10	41-55	Vanlandingham1261Yashgan126noJupiterIsland1261¼	Driving	10
2Nov85-7Aqu	fst 1¼	:464 1:11 1:362 2:004	3↑ BC Classic-G1	2 2 2½ 41 77 715	Day P	126		4.50	77-10	Proud Truth122hdGate Dancer1264Turkoman1225¾		8
	Steadied near stretch											
5Oct85-8Bel	my 1½	:492 1:132 2:03 2:27	3↑ J C Gold Cup-G1	1 1 11 12 11½ 12½	Day P	126		3.20	85-19	Vnlndinghm1262½GateDancr1267½CrmFrch1212¼	Ridden out	7
14Sep85-8Bel	fst 1¼	:47 1:11 1:361 2:011	3↑ Marlboro Cup H-G1	7 1 11 1hd 3½ 31	Day P	122		8.80	91-09	Chief'sCrown119nkGateDancr125¾Vnlndnghm122hd	Weakened	9
31Aug85-8Bel	gd 1⅛	:461 1:10 1:341 1:463	3↑ Woodward-G1	2 3 31½ 23 24½ 24	Day P	123		2.40	90-10	Track Brn1234Vanldghm1231½Chf's Crown121½	Best rest	6
3Aug85-8Sar	fst 1⅛	:474 1:112 1:351 1:473	3↑ Whitney H-G1	2 3 32 34½ 35 34¾	Day P	124		*1.10	92-11	TrackBarrn124½CarrdNskr1204¼Vnlndnghm1241¾	Bobbled st.	5
4Jly85-8Bel	fst 1¼	:463 1:10 1:342 2:01	3↑ Suburban H-G1	2 1 11½ 11½ 12 18¾	MacBeth D	115		8.60	93-17	Vanlandingham1158¾Carr de Naskra120nkDramatic Desire1091		9
	Brisk urging											
16Jun85-9CD	fst 1⅛	:473 1:112 1:36 1:484	4↑ Stephen Foster H 56k	1 1 1½ 1½ 1½ 1½	Day P	121		*.10	98-10	Vanlndinghm121½Manantil1121½SovrgnExchng1132½	Driving	7
31May85-8CD	fst 7f	:221 :444 1:092 1:22	4↑ Alw 22490	5 3 12 13 14 16	Woods CR Jr	115		*.30	97-13	Vanlandingham1156Jetabid112¾Another Tom1124	Easily	5
5May84-8CD	fst 1¼	:472 1:114 1:363 2:022	Ky Derby-G1	12 4 63½ 1111 1518 1619	Day P	126		6.00e	66-19	Swale1263¼CoaxMeChd1262AtthThrshold126nk	Returned sore	20
31Mar84-9OP	fst 1 1/16	:214 :444 1:094 1:41	Rebel H 117k	7 4 34 2½ 1½ 11¼	Day P	115		*1.20	103-05	Vnlndinghm1151¼WndFlyr1186½Lvsumdoubl1123	Drew clear	10
2Mar84-8OP	fst 1	:222 :45 1:093 1:351	Alw 17500	4 2 1hd 11 15 110	Day P	121		*.70	- -	Vanlandinghm12110DirtyBirdie1212½SharprThn112½	Handily	7
26Jan84-7Aqu	my 1 1/16⊡	:233 :48 1:123 1:441	Alw 22000	7 1 1½ 1hd 11½ 13	Lovato F Jr	117		3.00	91-10	Vnlndinghm1173Charmed Rook117nkLeroy S.1176	Drew out	9
7Jan84-5Aqu	fst 1 1/16⊡	:24 :49 1:15 1:48	Alw 22000	3 3 31½ 2½ 22 26	Lovato F Jr	117		*1.10	66-24	Lt.Flag1176Vnlndnghm1177½Coopr'sHwk1172½	Best of others	7
26Nov83-1CD	fst 1	:234 :473 1:132 1:382	Md Sp Wt	8 1 12 11 1½ 11½	Day P	117		*.90	77-21	Vanlandingham1171½Pemcor1177Thunder Chick1142	Handily	11

Wayward Lass

dkbbr. f. 1978, by Hail the Pirates (Hail to Reason)–Young Mistress, by Third Martini — **Lifetime record: 25 9 7 6 $435,237**

Own.– Flying Zee Stable
Br.– H.A. Luro (Fla)
Tr.– Jose Martin

Date	Track	Fractions	Race	Running line	Jockey	Wt		Odds	Spd	Finish	Comment	Fld
20Sep81-1Bel	gd 1 1/16	:24 :48 1:131 1:454	3↑ ⒻHandicap 35000	4 2 21 12½ 15 16	Asmussen CB	124		*.20	73-27	WaywrdLass1246Nora'sLass1137SweetMaid1196	Ridden out	4
10Sep81-8Bel	fst 7f	:222 :451 1:10 1:23	3↑ ⒻAlw 32000	1 4 43 32 2½ 11	Asmussen CB	115		4.90	87-16	Wayward Lass1151Highest Regard1156¾Cherokee Frolic1181½		5
	Driving											
27Jun81-8Bel	fst 1½	:474 1:114 2:014 2:281	ⒻC C A Oaks-G1	2 3 31½ 31½ 21½ 22¼	Asmussen CB	121		5.00	77-16	ⒹRealPrize1212¼WaywrdLss1212¼BannerGala12113	Impeded	6
	Placed first through disqualification											
5Jun81-8Bel	fst 1⅛	:47 1:11 1:354 1:484	ⒻMother Goose-G1	2 2 2½ 2½ 11 1nk	Asmussen CB	121		13.10	83-17	WywrdLss121nkHeavnlyCause1212¾BannerGala1211¾	Driving	8
15May81-8Pim	sly 1 1/16	:231 :47 1:113 1:441	ⒻBlack-Eyed Susan-G2	2 2 2½ 42¾ 32½ 23	Asmussen CB	121		3.00	81-18	Dame Mysterieuse1213Wayward Lass121¾Real Prize1211¾		7
	Finished strong											
1May81-8CD	fst 1 1/16	:25 :484 1:13 1:434	ⒻKy Oaks-G1	1 3 3½ 2½ 32½ 35	Asmussen CB	121		8.40	84-17	HeavnlyCause121noDeLaRose1215WaywrdLss1213	Weakened	6
18Apr81-7Kee	fst 1 1/16	:23 :464 1:112 1:44	ⒻAshland-G2	3 4 43½ 32 3½ 2¾	Asmussen CB	121		5.00	85-20	TrulyBound121¾WywrdLss121¾DameMysterieus12110	Gamely	5
4Apr81-9OP	fst 1 1/16	:233 :471 1:122 1:434	ⒻFantasy-G1	4 6 52¾ 42½ 34 35¼	Asmussen CB	121		2.20	84-19	Hvnly Cse121hdNl's Brqte1215¼WywrdLass1214½	Weakened	9
15Mar81-8Aqu	fst 1 1/16⊡	:234 :473 1:112 1:433	ⒻLevel Best 56k	2 2 2hd 13 1½ 31	Asmussen CB	121		*.20	95-10	RealPrize114hdInTrueForm1121WaywardLss1214¼	No excuse	7
15Feb81-8Aqu	fst 1⅛⊡	:473 1:121 1:37 1:50	ⒻRuthless-G3	4 2 21½ 14 18 111	Asmussen CB	121		*.20	96-11	WywrdLss12111RealPrize115½FbulousMusc1124	Ridden out	7
31Jan81-8Aqu	fst 1 1/16⊡	:232 :473 1:122 1:433	ⒻSearching 54k	2 3 1hd 13 18 112	Asmussen CB	118		*.10e	96-11	WywrdLss11812RealPrize1131½FabulousMusic1125¾	Driving	6
17Jan81-7Aqu	fst 1 1/16⊡	:24 :482 1:141 1:453	ⒻBusanda 56k	4 3 32½ 21 14 17	Asmussen CB	116		3.00e	86-23	WywrdLss1167InTruForm1122ExplosvKngdom11210	Drew clear	10
1Jan81-8Aqu	fst 6f⊡	:222 :454 1:112	ⒻRosetown 56k	2 6 2hd 43 44 33¾	Hernandez R	115		*1.00	83-21	Vandanya1122¾InTrueForm1131WywrdLss115nk	Well up,placed	7
7Dec80-8Aqu	fst 6f⊡	:221 :451 1:101	ⒻTreetop 55k	4 2 21½ 22½ 23½ 2¾	Cordero A Jr	122		4.90	92-08	DameMysterieuse122¾WywrdLss1221InTrueForm1157	Gamely	5
18Nov80-7Med	fst 6f	:224 :47 1:121	ⒻAlw 14000	2 5 33 34 36 48½	Wilson R	120		3.20	73-23	Seed the Cld109½Dame Mystrse1208Drop a Gem120hd	Bled	6
1Nov80-8Key	fst 6f	:222 :454 1:113	ⒻSchuykill 28k	3 3 23 24 23 1½	Wilson R	114		6.80	84-21	WaywardLss114½SurePrincess1132½Ruler'sDncr115¾	Driving	9
11Oct80-4Bel	fst 6f	:223 :46 1:11	ⒻMd Sp Wt	1 1 2½ 2hd 1½ 11½	Lovato F Jr5	113		*1.40	87-17	Wayward Lass1131½Sight1182½Banner Gala1183¼	Ridden out	11
29Sep80-4Bel	fst 6f	:222 :46 1:112	ⒻMd Sp Wt	1 1 24 43½ 22 23¾	Lovato F Jr5	112	b	3.50	81-19	Dame Mystrse1173¾Waywd Lass1123¾Real Prize1176	2nd best	10
5Sep80-2Bel	fm 1 1/16Ⓣ	:23 :472 1:124 1:471	ⒻMd Sp Wt	6 1 11½ 1½ 1½ 54	Asmussen CB	117	b	*.90	56-34	Carduel117nkGdynia1171½Fabled Morn1171	Used up	12

29Aug80- 8Bel	fm	7f(T)	:23 :46 1:094 1:232	(F)Evening Out 56k	2 4 2½ 6½ 612 719	Asmussen CB	112 b	9.60	68-13	De La Rse114hdBrvo Ntive11210Prime Prspt1132¾	Brief foot	7
15Aug80- 2Sar	gd	1 1/16[T]	:241 :482 1:13 1:462	(F)Md Sp Wt	6 1 11½ 11 21½ 24½	Cordero A Jr	117 b	*1.20	73-22	Seaholme1174½WywrdLss1172¼Zimbaba1171½	Best of others	10
4Aug80- 6Sar	fm	1[T]	:242 :483 1:133 1:38	(F)Md Sp Wt	6 2 11½ 13 2hd 21¾	Cordero A Jr	117	*1.70	87-12	BravoNative1171¾WaywardLass1172Seaholme1171½	2nd best	9
23Jly80- 4Bel	sly	7f	:232 :471 1:113 1:242	(F)Md Sp Wt	3 4 2½ 2½ 24 29	Cordero A Jr	117	*1.50	71-22	Heavenly Cause1179WaywrdLass1176Zimbaba1174½	2nd best	8
2Jly80- 3Bel	fst	5½f	:222 :454 :583 1:051	(F)Md Sp Wt	8 6 32½ 45½ 47½ 35	Cordero A Jr	117	4.40	84-17	PrimeProspct1171¼QueenDesignate1123¾WywrdLss1171	Wide	9
23Jun80- 4Bel	fst	5½f	:224 :462 :584 1:052	(F)Md Sp Wt	3 8 46 47 37½ 36	Cordero A Jr	117	6.30	82-15	FamousPartner1172Shalomar1174WywardLass1171¼	Rallied	9

Winning Colors

ro. f. 1985, by Caro (Fortino II)–All Rainbows, by Bold Hour **Lifetime record: 19 8 3 1 $1,526,837**

Own.– Eugene V. Klein

Br.– Echo Valley Horse Farm Inc (Ky)

Tr.– D. Wayne Lukas

4Nov89- 6GP	fst	1⅛	:462 1:111 1:353 1:472 3↑	(F)BC Distaff-G1	8 5 55½ 66½ 921 924¼	Stevens GL	123	5.20e	83-01	Bayakoa1231½Gorgeous1192¼Open Mind1195	Tired badly	10
21Oct89- 7Aqu	fst	1⊗	:23 :451 1:091 1:334 3↑	(F)Bud BC H 156k	1 3 2½ 31 43½ 48¼	McCarron CJ	119	*.60	85-05	Wakonda1164Foresta1081½Toll Fee1112¾	Tired	5
30Sep89- 9TP	fst	1 1/16	:233 :471 1:373 1:444 3↑	(F)Bud BC 155k	7 1 1½ 11 13 12	McCarron CJ	115	*.70	86-28	WinningColors1152GrecianFlight1232¼LawyrTlk1234	Driving	7
9Sep89- 8Bel	fst	1	:233 :461 1:101 1:353 3↑	(F)Maskette-G1	1 1 11½ 1½ 34½ 48½	Perret C	123	*.50	78-15	MissBrio1161¼ProperEvidnc1165½Aptostr1231¾	Used in pace	5
26Aug89- 1Sar	fst	6f	:23 :454 1:101 3↑	(F)Alw 41000	5 1 2hd 1hd 1½ 14¼	Day P	115	*.40	89-16	Winning Colors1154¼Royal Rexson1151½Lake Valley1155¼	Stumbled,handily	5
13May89- 8Bel	fst	1 1/16	:224 :444 1:09 1:404 3↑	(F)Shuvee H-G1	2 1 1½ 1hd 78 721¾	Stevens GL	121	1.30	76-16	Bankr'sLady1222¼Rose'sCantn1171¼GrcnFlght1171¼	Stopped	7
29Apr89- 8Hol	fst	7f	:214 :442 1:09 1:213 3↑	(F)A Gleam H-G3	4 4 2hd 1½ 2hd 44½	Stevens GL	123	*.40	91-10	Daloma1151¾Survive1162¾Behind the Scenes116hd	Weakened	7
5Nov88- 6CD	my	1⅛	:474 1:12 1:381 1:52 3↑	(F)BC Distaff-G1	8 1 12½ 12½ 11½ 2no	Stevens GL	119	4.00e	82-20	Personal Ensign123noWinning Colors119½Goodbye Halo1195	Just failed	9
15Oct88- 8Kee	fst	1⅛	:472 1:12 1:372 1:51 3↑	(F)Spinster-G1	2 1 1hd 11½ 32½ 415	Stevens GL	119	*.30	64-24	HailaCab1233WillaontheMove1192Integra12310	Gave way	5
10Sep88- 8Bel	fst	1	:224 :451 1:09 1:341 3↑	(F)Maskette-G1	4 1 15 12 1hd 2¾	Stevens GL	118	2.10	93-14	PersonlEnsign123¾WinningColrs1185¼ShamSy1151¼	Gamely	4
11Jun88- 8Bel	fst	1½	:471 1:114 2:013 2:262	Belmont-G1	3 1 2½ 410 524 641¾	Stevens GL	121	2.20	46-13	Risen Star12614¾Kingpost1262Brian's Time12611¼	Stopped	6
21May88- 9Pim	gd	1 3/16	:47 1:111 1:363 1:561	Preakness-G1	5 2 2hd 2hd 22 32½	Stevens GL	121	*1.90	83-11	Risen Star1261¼Brian's Time1261¼Winning Colors1212½	Brushed,bckstr	9
7May88- 8CD	fst	1¼	:464 1:112 1:36 2:021	Ky Derby-G1	11 1 13½ 13 13½ 1nk	Stevens GL	121	3.40	86-11	WinningColrs121nkFortyNiner1263RsnStr126½	Strong drive	17
9Apr88- 5SA	fst	1⅛	:453 1:092 1:344 1:474	S A Derby-G1	5 1 11½ 12½ 17 17½	Stevens GL	117	*2.60	90-13	WinnngColors1177½LivelyOne1221¼MPrfrdo1222½	Ridden out	9
13Mar88- 8SA	fst	1 1/16	:222 :454 1:10 1:42	(F)S A Oaks-G1	1 1 11 11 15 18	Stevens GL	117	2.10	91-15	WinningClrs1178JeannJons1171¼GoodbyHlo1179	Ridden out	4
20Feb88- 8SA	fst	1	:221 :461 1:11 1:364	(F)Las Virgenes-G1	4 2 12½ 11 1hd 2nk	Stevens GL	119	*.70	84-18	GoodbyeHalo123nkWnnngClrs1198SdB.Fst1157½	Just failed	5
20Jan88- 8SA	fst	1	:22 :454 1:11 1:363	(F)[R]La Centinela 80k	2 1 11½ 12½ 14 16½	Stevens GL	114	*.70	85-22	WinningColrs1146½LittlePssword1143Forwrnng1161	Handily	7
27Dec87- 3SA	fst	6f	:214 :444 :57 1:094	(F)Alw 32000	1 5 12½ 12 13½ 13½	Stevens GL	114	*1.30	89-17	Winning Colors1143½Floral Magic1182¾Constantly Right1161¼	Slow st.,veered in	6
13Aug87- 3Sar	fst	7f	:221 :453 1:11 1:241	(F)Md Sp Wt	9 3 1½ 11½ 14 12½	Romero RP	117	*1.90	81-14	Winning Colors1172½Epitome1174Bippus1171½	Ridden out	11

Zaccio

ch. g. 1976, by Lorenzaccio (Klairon)–Delray Dancer, by Chateaugay **Lifetime record: 42 22 7 3 $288,124**

Own.– Mrs L.C. Murdock

Br.– Blue Bear Stud (Ky)

Tr.– W. Burling Cocks

7Oct84- 6Mid	fm	*1¼(T)	2:172 3↑	Alw 500	6 9 51½ 11½ 11¼ 14	Hendriks R	146	-	--	Zaccio1464Past Glory1425Night Fever1442	Ridden out	10
29Sep84- 6Fx	fm	*1(T)	1:464 3↑	Alw 1000	2 3 1½ 2nk 21½ 21¼	Hendriks R	146	-	--	Local Kid1461¼Zaccio1466Fiddler's Dam1411		5
15Sep84- 8Fai	yl	*1 5/16(T)	2:19 3↑	Alw 1000	4 5 56¾ 31 69 611½	Hendriks R	140	*.80e	--	Yale Key133¾Locust Grove1521½Heart of the Desert1435½		7
21Nov82- 4Cam	fm	*2¾ S'Chase	5:11 4↑	Colonial Cup 50k	9 7 49½ 43¼ 14 18	Hendriks R	162	-	--	Zaccio1628Sailor's Clue16210Double Wrapped1591¼	Easily	13
3Nov82- 8Lrl	yl	1 1/16(T)	:23 :472 1:133 1:461 3↑	Alw 10000	8 3 49 715 817 823	Adams JK	116	3.40	49-33	SunandShine1152½GrayDude116nkDevoir1139	Fin. after ½	8
8Oct82- 6Bel	fm	2⅝ S'Chase	4:523 4↑	Temple Gwathmey H 42k	4 3 32½ 15 13 13¼	Hendriks R	163	*.60	--	Zaccio1633¼Shaban1421½Double Reefed1493¾	Ridden out	5
25Sep82- 6Fai	fm	*1 5/16(T)	2:142 3↑	Alw 1000	5 7 44½ 41¼ 1nk 12¾	Hendriks R	143	1.70e	--	Zaccio1432¾Abelard's Lust1551¼Oh So Choosy1491¼	Driving	13
26Aug82- 8Sar	gd	2⅜ S'Chase	4:19 4↑	NY Turf Writers H 43k	2 3 24 23 11 1nk	Hendriks R	161	*1.40	--	Zaccio161nkGive a Whirl1467¼Running Comment1456	Driving	7
16Aug82- 4Sar	fm	2 1/16 S'Chase	3:451 3↑	Handicap 25000	1 3 2½ 16 110 116	Morris GL	159	*.80	--	Zaccio15916LeapngFrog1401½DoubleReefed1532¾	Easy score	6
6Aug82- 6Sar	fm	2 1/16 S'Chase	3:424 4↑	Lovely Night H 43k	2 5 48 25 1½ 22	Morris GL	159	*1.60	--	Quiet Bay1512Zaccio1594¼Uncle Edwin1558	Gamely	7
29Jly82- 8Del	fm	1 1/16(T)	:24 :48 1:122 1:44 3↑	Alw 8500	10 10 1114 1012 815 612	Smith GP	117	2.30	72-13	Big Curley1225½Going Aground1131Brown Gold1064½	Outrun	12
9Jly82- 6Bel	fm	1⅜(T)	:483 1:134 2:03 2:272 3↑	Handicap 25000	7 5 55 44½ 59 513	Maple E	117	4.30	74-13	Cookie120½Give a Whirl1092Double Reefed121¾	No factor	7
28Jun82- 8Del	fm	1 1/16(T)	:241 :474 1:12 1:441 3↑	Alw 10000	2 4 410 48 45 24½	Smith GP	119	4.70	78-19	GlldedAge1214½Zaccio119hdPhiladelphialwyr1192½	Game try	6
3Apr82- 4AtH	fm	*2 S'Chase	3:50 4↑	Delta Cup H 24k	2 1 1½ 11¼ 2nk 31	Morris GL	159	-	--	Double Reefed146¾Daddy Dumpling146nkZaccio159	Tired	3
27Mar82- 5Cam	fm	*2¼ S'Chase	4:104 4↑	Carolina Cup 15k	1 3 34 21½ 1nk 21½	Morris GL	160	-	--	Quiet Bay1441½Zaccio1609Archange d'Or1442	Gave way	4
22Nov81- 4Cam	gd	2¾ S'Chase	5:143 4↑	Colonial Cup Int'l 50k	4 8 65¾ 45½ 11 111	Morris GL	160	-	--	Zaccio16011Al Arof1513Sailor's Clue160nk	Ridden out	9
7Nov81- 3Mtp	gd	*2½ S'Chase	4:534 4↑	Noel Laing H 4.9k	2 4 44¼ 110 112 115	Morris GL	158	-	--	Zaccio15815Cookie14818Yellow Boy141		4
31Oct81- 6FH	yl	*2 5/16 S'Chase	5:16 4↑	S K Martin H 15k	1 1 1½ 63¼ 69¾ 623	Morris GL	160	-	--	Uncle Edwin142½Al Arof14612Pestamystic1371½		6
17Oct81- 5Fx	hd	*2⅝ S'Chase	4:584 4↑	Grand National H 16k	1 2 12 14 1½ 1nk	Cushman J	159	-	--	Zaccio159nkSailor's Clue154		2
3Oct81- 8Med	fm	1 1/16(T)	:222 :462 1:114 1:432 3↑	Alw 13000	4 9 911 810 89¼ 814	Maple E	118	*2.80	71-15	The Missing Gift1131½Miroslav1142Hasty Tasty1131	Outrun	10
29Aug81- 3AP	sf	*2⅜ S'Chase	4:44 4↑	Arl H 32k	3 4 56 519 546 556	McWade R	161	*.50	--	Double Reefed137nkUncle Edwin13534Snailwell138hd	Tired	5
21Aug81- 4Sar	fm	2 1/16 S'Chase	3:392 3↑	Handicap 25000	1 2 1½ 11½ 2½ 24½	McWade R	164	*1.30e	--	Codicioso1464½Zaccio1646½Triple Try14414	Best of others	8
14Aug81- 7Sar	fm	1 1/16[T]	:234 :482 1:12 1:422 3↑	Alw 21000	1 11 1110 1111 95¾ 96¼	Montoya D	117	11.20	92-10	RedWingPrince1143½Santo'sJoe117¾SpartnMystc112no	Outrun	11
10Oct80- 6Bel	fm	2⅝ S'Chase	4:544 4↑	Temple Gwathmey H 43k	2 4 46 - - -	Small D Jr	160	*.80	--	LeapingFrog1481½Marti'sAngr1581½BluNrco1331½	Lost rider	7
14Aug80- 6Sar	fm	2⅜ S'Chase	4:141 4↑	NY Turf Writers H 43k	1 2 21½ 11 21½ 11¼	McWade R	157	*1.10	--	Zccio1571¼RunningComment1422¼LeapingFrog1522¼	Driving	7
1Aug80- 6Sar	gd	2 1/16 S'Chase	3:451 4↑	Lovely Night H 43k	4 2 2½ 2½ 2½ 11¾	McWade R	155	*1.30	--	Zccio1551¾Martie'sAnger1601¾LeapngFrog1531¼	Ridden out	8
17Jly80- 4Del	fm	2¼ S'Chase	4:224 4↑	Indian River 12k	3 1 12 12 12 14½	McWade R	152	*.60	--	Zaccio1524½Baronial1423¼Leaping Frog1549	Handily	4
18Jun80- 3Mth	fm	*2¼ S'Chase	4:21 4↑	Mid Summer H 15k	4 2 31½ 12½ 14 13	McWade R	153	*.60e	--	Zaccio1533Town and Country1401¼Leaping Frog1582	Driving	6
24May80- 5Pro	gd	*3 S'Chase	5:514 4↑	Hard Scuffle 20k	5 3 31¼ 41¼ 21 21¼	McWade R	140	-	--	Martie's Anger1511¼Zaccio1405Leaping Frog15616		5
27Apr80- 4Lex	yl	*2½ S'Chase	5:121 4↑	Pillar 17k	1 2 11 1nk 1hd 1hd	McWade R	148	-e	--	Zaccio148hdDaddy Dumpling15018Schoeller15412		5
12Apr80- 3SoP	fm	*2¼ S'Chase	4:211 4↑	Sandhills Cup H 15k	3 6 42½ 31¾ 2nk 31	McWade R	155	-e	--	Archanged'Or1431Martie'sAnger158noZaccio155¾	Held well	7
29Mar80- 4Cam	gd	*2⅛ S'Chase	4:104 4↑	Handicap 12500	2 3 22¼ 33¼ 13 16	McWade R	152	-	--	Zaccio1526Popular Hero1441Tan Jay1581½	Ridden out	7
22Mar80- 4Aik	fm	*1⅞ S'Chase	3:53 4↑	Handicap 7500	1 5 46 2nk 13 15	McWade R	149	-	--	Zaccio1495Alizar1324Empty Wallet1465	Handily	5
18Nov79- 1Cam	fm	*2 S'Chase	3:424	Alw 7500	5 6 32½ 14 18 121	Skiffington T Jr	154	-	--	Zccio15421ClassSymbl1442ChanceRomance1463½	Ridden out	7
11Oct79- 4Bel	sf	2 S'Chase	3:531 3↑	Alw 11000	2 5 43 15 11½ 1¾	McWade R5	138	*1.70	--	Zccio138¾AcadmicFreedom13621BillyComLtly1482¼	Driving	7
24Aug79- 4Sar	fm	2 1/16 S'Chase	3:411 3↑	Alw 11000	8 2 23 11½ 11½ 2nk	Skiffington T Jr	139	*.70	--	Parson'sWaiting135nkZaccio13918PumpkinPie1404	Bobbled	8
10Aug79- 4Sar	fm	2 1/16 S'Chase	3:434 3↑	Alw 10000	1 11 106¼ 43½ 1hd 19¼	Skiffington T Jr	137	*1.50	--	Zccio1379¼RunningComment139hdBillyComeLtly1561½	Easily	11
12May79- 2Fai	fm	*1⅞ S'Chase	3:422 3↑	Md Sp Wt	3 2 4¾ 1hd 1½ 12	McWade R7	135	1.80	--	Zaccio1352Odd Man1568Abbots Walk1566	In hand	6
28Apr79- 1Fx	gd	*2 S'Chase	3:42 4↑	Md Sp Wt	3 3 21 11½ - -	McWade R7	132		--	Ventarron15415Royal Greed1568Lochcruin15410	Lost rider	7
21Apr79- 3Clm	fm	*1(T)	1:43 3↑	Alw 1000	4 3 32½ 31¼ 1hd 11	McWade R5	139	-	--	Zaccio1391Cheviot1582½Ten Ducks131½	Driving	8
14Apr79- 2SoP	fm	*7f(T)	1:32 3↑	Md Sp Wt	6 3 31 2nk 1¾ 12½	Skiffington T Jr	132	-	--	Zaccio1322½Sacred Melody1468Elsaik1454	Drew out	6
31Mar79- 2Cam	fm	*7f(T)	1:302 3↑	Md Sp Wt	7 7 1210 78 39 38	Skiffington T Jr	145	-	--	Cheviot1537Sky News1501Zaccio1453	Rallied	13

Going Global

The 1990's

by Jay Privman

Bill Mott sat in the film theater of Belmont Park, a small room hidden in the bowels of the racetrack, just around the corner from the jockeys' room. It was nearly dusk on October 28, 1995, and the trainer was flush with excitement and pride over having just watched his horse Cigar win the Breeders' Cup Classic. It was Cigar's 12th consecutive victory, completed a perfect 10-for-10 campaign that year, and secured for Cigar the titles of both Horse of the Year and champion older horse.

Cigar was 5, an age when many horses with his accomplishments are immediately whisked off to stud. But Allen Paulson, Cigar's owner, got into the sport because he likes to watch his horses run. Cigar in 1995 had raced in Florida, California, Arkansas, Maryland, and Massachusetts. And now Mott and Paulson were looking for new worlds to conquer.

"He'll race next year," Mott said, "but he'll have a different type of campaign."

The face of racing was changing demonstrably in the 1990's, and Cigar came along at the opportune time. Racing always had been an international sport. Horses from the United States often were sent by boat to Great Britain at the beginning of the century. Midway through the century, the Washington, D.C., International laid the groundwork for the Breeders' Cup Turf, a late-season race designed to bring together the world's premier grass horses. The Breeders' Cup, launched in 1984, succeeded in bringing the best of Europe's runners to the United States for a championship event.

But the frequency and ease of international racing skyrocketed in the 1990's. The Japan Cup, in November, and races in Hong Kong in December became increasingly desirable targets. Horses could fly there in less time than it took to travel by van from Kentucky to Florida. Trainer Leo O'Brien sent a New York-bred, Fourstars Allstar, to The Curragh and won the Irish 2000 Guineas. Dr Devious was purchased in Europe for Sid and Jenny Craig by bloodstock agent Murray Friedlander, came to the United States for the Kentucky Derby, then returned to Great Britain and won the Epsom Derby.

In the Middle East, Sheikh Mohammed bin Rashid al-Maktoum audaciously decided to have his best runners winter in Dubai before heading back to Europe. Those horses would race with the stable name Godolphin, named for one of the three founding stallions of the modern Thoroughbred. In

Godolphin's first year of operation, Lammtarra, having spent the winter in Dubai, won the Epsom Derby, a grueling 1½-mile race, in his first start of the year. Godolphin later would send horses to Australia for the Melbourne Cup, and to the United States for the Kentucky Derby. Sheikh Mohammed also organized the Emirates World Championship Series, which linked some of the world's premier races, such as the Japan Cup, Melbourne Cup Breeders' Cup Turf, and Breeders' Cup Classic. Daylami, who raced for Godolphin, won the first Emirates World Series in 1999, when he completed his year with an overpowering victory in the Breeders' Cup Turf.

In 1995, Sheikh Mohammed startled the racing world by announcing his country would play host, beginning the following March, to the Dubai World Cup. The purse would be $4 million, $1 million more than the Breeders' Cup Classic, with a winner's share of $2.4 million, making it the richest race in the world. Having earned the title of Horse of the Year with Cigar, and looking for new challenges, Mott felt the Dubai World Cup was the ideal forum to establish Cigar's place in history.

Cigar was on the verge of proving himself one of the great horses of the century. He had blossomed under Mott's care, but the foundation had been laid years earlier. The Triple Crown, particularly the Kentucky Derby, increasingly became the focal point of owners and trainers during the 1990's. Trainers such as Bob Baffert, D. Wayne Lukas, and Nick Zito focused their entire operations around developing classic runners. And they were amazingly successful. Those three trainers won 7 of the

Two-time Horse of the Year Cigar ushered in a new era of international competition in 1996, when he traveled to the Middle East and won the inaugural running of the Dubai World Cup.

10 Kentucky Derbies run in the 1990's. Frequently, though, they went through a number of horses trying to find the right one. Some runners were pushed early and often to see if they were worthy of going to the Derby, and a number fell by the wayside and never were the same again.

Cigar, however, was not forced to try to make the classics. As a son of grass stakes winner Palace Music, Cigar had a pedigree that indicated he would do better on turf. He never raced at age 2, and did not win his first race – at six furlongs on dirt at Hollywood Park, in only his second start – until May 9, 1993, eight days after that year's Kentucky Derby was won by Sea Hero.

"He had a good-sized frame, but his muscles hadn't filled into that frame," said Alex Hassinger Jr., who trained Cigar for his first nine races. "He seemed like a route horse, and he seemed like a horse who would get better with time. I didn't know if that meant three months, six months, or a year or two, but I felt he'd get better. We also were having trouble with his knees. He wasn't the kind of horse who would hold up well under all those dirt races. That, along with his pedigree, is why we pointed him for the grass. So we raced him on turf. And by going slow, we had a horse for later on."

Cigar needed arthroscopic surgery to remove a chip in a knee at the end of his 3-year-old season. After he recuperated, Paulson decided to switch trainers. He sent Cigar to Mott in New York.

Cigar's first race for Mott was July 8, 1994. He finished fourth in an allowance race on the turf at Belmont Park. Three more losses, all in turf allowance races, followed. On October 28, Mott put Cigar back on the dirt, in a one-turn mile race at Aqueduct. Sent off at 7-2 in a six-horse field, Cigar romped by eight lengths. He was now 3 for 14. Yet that victory was the first step Cigar took on his path to greatness. He came back and won the NYRA Mile to close out 1994, then headed to Florida, where he took over as the best horse in America.

The baton was passed on February 11, 1995. Just as Cigar entered the backstretch and took the lead in the Donn Handicap at Gulfstream Park, the race favorite, Holy Bull, the 1994 Horse of the Year, was pulled up with a career-ending injury. Cigar won by 5 ½ lengths, but few noticed, the attention being focused on Holy Bull. Cigar, though, quickly made a name for himself. He traveled throughout the country and won everywhere he went.

His name, along with the winning streak, helped Cigar break through and capture the consciousness of America's sports fans. He was featured in magazines such as People, Sports Illustrated, Esquire, Newsweek, and Cigar Aficionado. Funny thing was, Cigar was not named for a tobacco product. Paulson, an accomplished pilot who made his fortune first by developing and patenting airplane parts, and then as head of Gulfstream Aerospace, named Cigar for an aviation checkpoint in the Gulf of Mexico, approximately 100 miles west of Tampa, Florida.

Paulson had once stopped in Dubai during a record around-the-world flight. But Cigar had never been out of the country until March 16, 1996, when he boarded a plane bound for Dubai, with a stopover at Shannon Airport in Ireland. "We got to Ireland on the 17th," recalled Tim Jones, Mott's assistant, who accompanied Cigar on the flight. "We couldn't get any gas for the plane. The stopover was supposed to take 45 minutes. But we sat on the tarmac for four hours. No one was around. It was St. Patrick's Day."

The trip alone was daunting. Dubai was 7,000 miles from Florida, where Cigar had spent that winter, and where he had won the Donn Handicap for the second straight year. But Cigar also was fighting a quarter crack and a bruise in his right front hoof. The injuries forced him to miss nearly two weeks of training and a start in the Santa Anita Handicap, and resulted in an accelerated workout schedule in order to prepare him for the World Cup. He also had to adjust to the time change – Dubai is nine hours ahead of Miami – and the desert climate, as well as an unfamiliar surface and racetrack.

Cigar's arrival thrilled Sheikh Mohammed, for Cigar's presence gave instant credibility to the inaugural World Cup. "I had a dream, and now they are all here," Sheikh Mohammed said. "If Cigar wins, he will be champion of the world."

There were 11 horses in the race, but Cigar was clearly the star. Though betting is prohibited in Dubai, he was the race favorite in Great Britain and the United States. His opposition included the top American runner Soul of the Matter, along with Godolphin's main challenger, Halling.

The race was run at night, under the lights of Nad al-Sheba racetrack. Around the world, attention was riveted on the World Cup. Bookmakers' shops in London were filled that afternoon. In Manhattan, the race was broadcast live on New York City's offtrack betting channel. In California, fans crawled out of bed early and headed to Santa Anita, where the race was shown at 7 a.m. local time.

Cigar, with Jerry Bailey riding, stalked the early pacesetters, moved for the lead with a half-mile to go, and took over with a quarter-mile remaining. But in midstretch, Soul of the Matter, ridden by Gary Stevens, came with a furious rush.

"He looked like he was beat," Mott recounted. "The first thing that flashed into my mind was the time we had missed training him. As a result, he had to work three times in eight days and then ship halfway around the world. We put a lot of pressure on him. It was an unusual training schedule. There was nothing nice and smooth and steady about it. When Soul of the Matter ran to him, I thought, 'There's the 13 days we missed.' It was the first time he'd been in a head-to-head battle since the streak started. In the other races, he'd leave everyone for dead with a half-mile to go. He'd run by the pacesetters, and the come-from-behind horses couldn't catch him. We didn't know what would happen when he was challenged."

He responded like a champion. Despite the trip, the missed training, and the sore foot, Cigar fought off Soul of the Matter and won by a half-length. From Dubai to London, to New York and Los Angeles, a collective roar went up. No one had known what to expect, and no one could have expected anything better. "It was pretty awesome," Mott said.

Cigar had now won 14 races in a row, and was closing fast on the record of 16 straight set by Citation nearly 50 years earlier. Cigar returned to the United States and won the Massachusetts Handicap for No. 15, then went to Arlington International Racecourse for a specially designed race, the Arlington Citation Challenge. Despite carrying 130 pounds, breaking from the outside post in a field of 10, and being forced to race wide the whole trip, Cigar won by 3½ lengths to tie Citation.

The attempt to break the record would come in the Pacific Classic at Del Mar on August 10. Cigar was training well, Mott said, but was starting to show some wear and tear, particularly on the inside of his right front foot. "He was developing foot problems," Mott said. "He had a quarter crack with a patch on it. We were dealing with issues we hadn't had the previous year."

Still, Mott was confident Cigar would win. "Every time I went over with him, I felt I had the best horse," he said. "Of course, you had to have racing luck, but you get to the point where you think he's going to repeat the previous 16."

Mott and Bailey feared one opponent, the speedy Siphon. He had won the Hollywood Gold Cup a few weeks earlier, beating Geri, a Mott-trained horse whom Bailey had ridden. "We didn't want Siphon to get an easy lead and steal the race. We wanted to keep him within range," Mott said. "I think the thing that we forgot is that we had Cigar, not Geri."

Cigar followed Siphon into the first turn of the 1¼-mile race, but when Dramatic Gold loomed up outside Cigar around the first turn, Bailey used Cigar to hold his position. Cigar, his competitive juices flowing, then got into a duel with Siphon. They sped through the second quarter in 22⅘ seconds, and the third quarter in 23⅖. They reached the six-furlong mark in 1:09⅕. By the time they hit the quarter pole, having run a mile in 1:33⅗, both Cigar and Siphon were spent.

Dare and Go, like Siphon, was trained by Richard Mandella. He took advantage of the wicked early pace and roared past both Cigar and Siphon, then drew off to a 3½-length victory. Cigar, in a remarkable effort, still finished second, some seven lengths in front of Siphon. He had won the battle, but lost the war. A Del Mar record crowd of 44,181, which had sent Cigar off at 1-10, was stunned into silence. The streak was over.

"It was something we had braced for," Mott said. "If you keeping taking them over, eventually they're going to get beat. But I was pretty grateful for what we had had."

Later that evening at the barn, Mott noticed something he would never forget. Cigar always liked people, and attention. He was attuned to the click of a camera shutter, and the telltale crinkling of a peppermint being unwrapped from cellophane.

"Bailey went over to give him a peppermint, but he wouldn't take it," Mott said. "I know horses don't think like humans, but he acted like he knew something was different, like he knew he got beat. I don't think he was proud. All the other times, he was a proud horse."

Cigar raced just three more times. He won once, and twice lost in photo finishes. He closed his career with a third-place finish in the 1996 Breeders' Cup Classic. But he had done enough earlier in the year, particularly in Dubai, to be rewarded with the Horse of the Year title for the second straight year. He was the only horse to receive that honor twice in the 1990's.

Mott and Bailey rode his coattails. Mott won Eclipse Awards as champion trainer in both 1995 and 1996, and in 1997, at age 45, became the youngest trainer inducted into the National Museum of Racing's Hall of Fame. Bailey won Eclipse Awards as champion jockey in 1995 and 1996, then added a third straight in 1997.

Mott, Paulson, and Paulson's wife, Madeleine, understood Cigar's place in history, and his importance to racing, and thus took him around the country so fans could see him. Cigar's sendoff was equally inspired. One week after his final race, Cigar was paraded before the National Horse Show at Madison Square Garden. Five blocks of Seventh Avenue were cordoned off to accommodate the horse van. Children rushed to the outside of the ring to pet Cigar, who was ridden by Bailey.

Cigar retired with record earnings of $9,999,815, but the streak is his enduring legacy, both for the number of races won and for the breadth and scope of where Cigar ran. He traveled across the country, and then halfway around the world, while winning 16 straight races. His campaign was unprecedented – nine tracks, six states, two continents, and four time zones. No horse had accomplished so much with such an ambitious racing and travel schedule, and that is why Cigar must rank as one of the all-time greats.

Cigar would be remembered only for his racing career, however. There would be no little Cigarettes trying to follow in his footsteps. Cigar was infertile, and eventually was retired to the Kentucky Horse Park. For Mott, it was an oddly perfect ending.

"I'm sure people will criticize me, but I'm satisfied that that's the way it turned out," Mott said. "As great a sire as Secretariat was, people always said he wasn't that good, because they tended to compare his offspring to him. That's not fair. If Cigar had turned out to be a mediocre stallion, I would have had to listen to that, people saying he wasn't that good a stallion because he didn't reproduce himself. So when I heard he was infertile, for me it was less traumatic than when he lost at Del Mar. I had no emotion. I just thought, 'It's over.'"

Cigar's success and popularity fueled a rebirth in interest in American racing. Ideas that had crashed and burned early in the decade were born anew. The American Championship Racing Series, a nationally televised group of races for older horses that ran from 1991-93, died because of infighting among the member tracks. When the series was disbanded, Barry Weisbord, the organizer, said, "I think the ACRS is a martyr, or let's say a wasted opportunity." An attempt to create a centralized national office failed miserably midway through the decade when Thoroughbred Racing Associations member tracks refused to remove the handcuffs from J. Brian McGrath, who was hired as the commissioner. But some of McGrath's core beliefs – organizing licensing and corporate sponsorships

A horse of uncommon gameness, Silver Charm won the Kentucky Derby and Preakness by tight margins, and came back as a 4-year-old to win the Dubai World Cup in another photo.

among the tracks – were cornerstones of the National Thoroughbred Racing Association, which was launched in 1998 and took over from the TRA as the sport's national office.

The NTRA, led by Commissioner Tim Smith, grew out of a concept first proposed by Fred Pope, a Kentucky advertising executive, who created the National Thoroughbred Association as a means for owners to control the financial destiny of the sport. One of the NTRA's first missions was to enhance racing's presence on television. A series of races for older horses trod the same ground as the ACRS pioneers, and an aggressive national advertising campaign was launched, featuring the waiflike actress Lori Petty screaming "Go Baby Go."

The combination of racing's increased television exposure, the emphasis on Triple Crown races, and the success of Cigar in Dubai came together gloriously for Silver Charm and his silver-haired trainer, Bob Baffert. Media savvy, quick with a quip, and possessed of horses who could flat-out run, Baffert became the most recognizable figure in the sport in the late 1990's. He won both the Kentucky Derby and the Preakness Stakes in consecutive years, with Silver Charm and Real Quiet – both of whom won Eclipse Awards as champion 3-year-old – but Silver Charm was the stable's star.

Baffert, like D. Wayne Lukas and Nick Zito, made the Triple Crown, particularly the Derby, the focal point of his training operation. But Baffert's Derby winners had accomplished careers as older horses, too, in part because he gave them lengthy vacations following the classics. After nearly sweeping the Triple Crown in 1997, Silver Charm got a six-month break, then embarked on his 1998 campaign. The main goal was the Santa Anita Handicap. But when Silver Charm came up with a foot bruise on the eve of that race, an audible was called, and plans were made to send him to Dubai.

Had Cigar lost the inaugural Dubai World Cup, the course of history might have changed. But Americans took the first three spots in Dubai the year Cigar won, and then American-based runners finished 2-3 in the second Dubai World Cup. In just two runnings, it had become a premier target, the spring's counterpart to the Breeders' Cup Classic.

Silver Charm was flown to Dubai and, in one of the most courageous performances of the decade, re-rallied after being passed at midstretch – "Silver Charm is coming again. This is incredible," race-caller Derek Thompson exclaimed – to beat Swain in a photo finish.

Baffert had an amazing year. In addition to the Dubai World Cup, he almost won the Triple Crown with Real Quiet, who lost the Belmont Stakes by a nose to Victory Gallop. And Baffert sent out Silverbulletday to a victory in the Breeders' Cup Juvenile Fillies, which secured an Eclipse Award for her. Silverbulletday also was the champion 3-year-old filly of 1999, a year when Baffert received the Eclipse Award as champion trainer for the third straight year.

Baffert started his training career with Quarter Horses before switching to Thoroughbreds. He wore cowboy boots, jeans, and sunglasses, and concentrated on winning Triple Crown races. He was following a path first cleared by Lukas.

By the end of the century, Lukas had won 12 Triple Crown races, including four Kentucky Derbies, three of which were won in the 1990's, and 15 Breeders' Cup races. His horses had won more than $200 million in purses, and nearly two dozen Eclipse Awards. But for Lukas, the 1990's were a tumultuous decade, filled with the highest highs and the lowest lows.

Lukas guided Criminal Type to the Horse of the Year title in 1990, which included victories over Sunday Silence in the Hollywood Gold Cup and over Easy Goer in the Metropolitan Mile. But behind the scenes, Criminal Type's owner, Calumet Farm, was struggling to stay afloat in a financial whirlpool. A number of horses had to be sold, including a 2-year-

Serena's Song was an iron filly for trainer D. Wayne Lukas, setting an earnings record for a North American-based female and defeating males on two occasions.

old named Strike the Gold, who would go on to become the first of two Derby winners for Nick Zito. Calumet's prized stallion, Alydar, the sire of Strike the Gold, died under mysterious circumstances. Calumet was named champion breeder for 1990, and had the Horse of the Year. A year later, the farm, which was run by J. T. Lundy, declared bankruptcy. Creditors like Lukas lost millions.

Calumet's property was saved from developers by Henryk de Kwiatkowski, who purchased the historic farm. Calumet's priceless collection of trophies was kept from being parceled out by an auction house after sufficient funds were raised in an effort spearheaded by James E. Bassett III, chairman of the board of Keeneland Association.

In December 1993, Lukas's son and chief assistant, Jeff, was trampled by the colt Tabasco Cat and suffered severe head injuries. Jeff Lukas fell into a coma and nearly died, and though he survived and returned to work for his father, the injuries left him unable to handle as much responsibility as he had before the accident.

Yet Tabasco Cat got Lukas rolling again. Tabasco Cat won both the Preakness and the Belmont in 1994, the first two of six consecutive Triple Crown race victories for Lukas. In 1994, Lukas led the nation in purse earnings and won the Eclipse Award as champion trainer. He swept the Triple Crown events in 1995 with two different horses, Thunder Gulch (Derby, Belmont) and Timber Country (Preakness), then won the 1996 Derby with Grindstone. None of those horses, however, raced beyond age 3.

In 1999, Lukas was on the verge of wrapping up the Triple Crown. Charismatic, who twice was risked in claiming races, emerged as the best colt of his generation with upset victories in both the Derby and the Preakness. But he finished third in the Belmont, and suffered career-ending fractures to his left front leg. Once again, tragedy raced head-and-head with triumph in the Lukas barn. Lukas's year ended on an upswing, with upset victories in the Breeders' Cup by Cash Run in the Juvenile Fillies and Cat Thief in the Classic, and a Horse of the Year trophy for Charismatic.

Lukas's iron horse was a filly, Serena's Song, who won the Eclipse Award as champion 3-year-old filly in 1995. In three years of racing, she started 38 times, won 18 – including 11 Grade 1 races – and earned $3,283,388, a record for a North American-based female. She beat the boys twice at age 3, in the Haskell Invitational and the Jim Beam Stakes, and just missed at age 4 in the Whitney Handicap.

Serena's Song was owned by Bob and Beverly Lewis, who had a remarkable run of success. They owned Silver Charm and Charismatic, and twice in three years won the Derby and Preakness before suffering crushing losses in the Belmont. The exuberant couple, both in their 70's and married more than 50 years, charmed the sport with their enthusiasm, sportsmanship, and generosity. They were rewarded with the Eclipse Award of Merit in 1997.

Serena's Song was part of a golden era for fillies and mares in the 1990's. Bayakoa, an Argentine import who arrived in this country with a nervous disposition, thrived under the patient care of trainer Ron McAnally. She won 21 of 39 starts – including 12 Grade 1 races in the United States – and earned the second of her two championships in 1990. McAnally then mined the same vein and came up with another Argentine import, Paseana, who also was a two-time Eclipse Award winner. A hearty mare who won graded stakes at age 8, Paseana captured 10 Grade 1 races, including two runnings of Santa Anita's storied Santa Margarita Invitational Handicap. Both Bayakoa and Paseana won the Breeders' Cup Distaff.

Sky Beauty, who would bring tears to the eyes of her trainer, Allen Jerkens, when she won, took 15 of 21 starts, including 10 Grade 1 races. She swept the New York Racing Association's triple crown for 3-year-old fillies in 1993, and got an overdue Eclipse Award the following year. Trainer Charlie Whittingham, in the twilight of his career, brilliantly managed the turf mare Flawlessly, who won three consecutive runnings of both Del Mar's Ramona Handicap and Hollywood Park's Matriarch Stakes. A two-time champion, Flawlessly always needed plenty of rest after her late-season campaigns, and Whittingham always was accommodating.

Two other veteran trainers wrapped themselves in glory in the latter part of their careers: Jimmy Croll, with Housebuster, and Sonny Hine, with Guilty Conscience, had trained champion sprinters, but each of them ended up both training and owning a Horse of the Year in the 1990's. Holy Bull and Skip Away provided bookends around Cigar, and preceded Silver Charm, during an exciting run for 3-year-olds and up during the decade.

Croll acquired Holy Bull when a longtime client, Rachel Carpenter, left the colt to him in her will. Holy Bull won 7 of his first 8 starts, and entered the 1994 Kentucky Derby as the 2-1 favorite. But he trained poorly at Churchill Downs, and ran to those works. He finished 12th. Croll then wisely took Holy Bull off the Triple Crown trail, and mapped out a schedule that resulted in him being named Horse of the Year.

Holy Bull whipped older horses in the Metropolitan Mile, but he earned his greatest respect in his last two starts of the year. In the Travers Stakes, run at the same 1¼-mile distance of the Derby, Holy Bull was forced into fractions of 46⅕ seconds for the first half-mile and 1:10⅖ for six furlongs. The stretch-running Concern seemed poised to take advantage of the crackling pace, and when he roared outside Holy Bull at the top of the stretch, Saratoga's racecaller, Tom Durkin, cleverly announced, "There is cause for Concern." Holy Bull, however, would not be denied. He bravely

Though he floundered as the 2-1 favorite in the Kentucky Derby, the steel-gray Holy Bull buzzed through the competition for the remainder of his 1994 campaign. After a dominating victory over the best older horses in the country in the Woodward, he was named Horse of the Year despite passing the Breeders' Cup.

fought off Concern and won by a neck. It was 17 lengths back to the third horse, Tabasco Cat, who had won the Preakness and Belmont that year.

Holy Bull then closed out his season with a five-length romp against older horses in the Woodward Stakes. He passed the Breeders' Cup Classic but secured Horse of the Year when Concern defeated older horses in the Classic. Holy Bull's 1995 campaign came to a sudden end in his second start of the year, when he suffered a career-ending injury in the Donn Handicap. Cigar won the Donn, and went on to be Horse of the Year. Cigar held the title as best older horse for two years, before relinquishing it to Skip Away.

Sonny Hine and his wife, Carolyn, purchased Skip Away as a 2-year-old in training. Hine trained Skip Away, and Carolyn was listed as the owner, but this was a partnership through and through. Skip, as Carolyn affectionately called him, became a member of the Hine family. They treated him as if he were a son, showering him with love and affection, and sticking up for him when he was not given credit the Hines believed he was due.

Just as Holy Bull passed the baton to Cigar in the 1995 Donn, so Cigar passed the baton to Skip Away in the 1996 Jockey Club Gold Cup. By that point, Skip Away already had won the Blue Grass Stakes and the Haskell Invitational, and had finished second in both the Preakness and the Belmont, but the Jockey Club Gold Cup announced his arrival. Skip Away was named champion 3-year-old and was ready to assert himself as the best older horse in the country.

In 1997, Skip Away won the Jockey Club Gold Cup for the second straight year and completed his season with a runaway six-length score in the Breeders' Cup Classic, a race to which he was supplemented for $480,000. He was the champion older horse, beating out such accomplished runners as Formal Gold, who defeated Skip Away three times that year and earned one of the highest Beyer Speed Figure of the decade, a 125. But Skip Away missed out on Horse of the Year, which went to the unbeaten 2-year-old Favorite Trick. The Hines were crushed, even though Carolyn was rewarded with the Eclipse Award as champion owner.

Determined to prove that Skip Away should have been Horse of the Year, the Hines designed an aggressive 1998 campaign to showcase Skip Away. He won his first seven starts of the year, racing in Florida, Maryland, Massachusetts, California, New Jersey, and New York, earning points like a politician campaigning in primaries. Although Skip Away lost his final two starts, including the Breeders' Cup Classic to Awesome Again, he was named Horse of the Year and, for the second straight year, champion older horse. Skip Away won 18 of 38 starts, including 10 Grade 1 races, and earned $9,616,360, second only to Cigar.

While Holy Bull, Cigar, and Skip Away were succeeding each other, Lonesome Glory was a constant in the steeplechase division. He was the champion at age 4 in 1992, again in 1993, 1995, 1997, and finally at age 11 in 1999, becoming the only five-time Eclipse Award-winning steeplechaser. Lonesome Glory won the Colonial Cup at Camden, South Carolina, three times. He was bred and owned by Kay Jeffords, was trained by Bruce Miller, and was ridden by Miller's daughter Blythe.

Favorite Trick, who beat out Skip Away for Horse of the Year in 1997, became only the second 2-year-old to earn that title, following Secretariat in 1972. Favorite Trick, who won all eight of his starts, was a precocious little fellow, but he proved versatile, too. He won dashing 4 ½ furlongs in April, and completed the year with a 5 ½-length romp going 1$\frac{1}{16}$ miles in the Breeders' Cup Juvenile in November. His trainer, Patrick Byrne, also sent out that year's champion 2-year-old filly, Countess Diana.

Favorite Trick may have been a Horse of the Year, but the most talked-about 2-year-old of the nineties was Arazi. A Kentucky-bred who began his career in France, Arazi won 6 of his first 7 starts, all on turf, before arriving in Kentucky with trainer Francois Boutin for the 1991 Breeders' Cup Juvenile. In one of the most electrifying performances of the decade, Arazi darted through traffic down the backstretch and around the far turn to go

European star Arazi created a stir with his blowout victory in the 1991 Breeders' Cup Juvenile, but surgery on both knees following the race compromised his ability. He was never the same, and finished eighth as the favorite in the Kentucky Derby.

from 13th to second, then roared past Bertrando and drew off to win by 4¾ lengths while being geared down by his jockey, Pat Valenzuela. He was the champion 2-year-old colt, got support for Horse of the Year, and immediately became the future-book favorite for the 1992 Kentucky Derby.

Arazi needed arthroscopic surgery on both knees following the Breeders' Cup, and did not have the proper time to prepare for the Derby. He had one prep race in France before returning to Kentucky. He was rattled by the crowds that pressed against the rail during training hours in the days prior to the race. Despite the obstacles, he was sent off as the 9-10 favorite. Skeptics, though, abounded. The morning of the race, turf writer Dick Jerardi had had enough of the Arazi hype.

"I've decided what Arazi will be good for," Jerardi announced. "Years from now, when another overrated horse comes along, we'll be able to say, 'He's just another Arazi.'" Arazi proved Jerardi prophetic. Arazi made another powerful move on the turn in the Derby, but flattened out and finished eighth.

A.P. Indy, who was scratched with a quarter crack the morning of the 1992 Derby, went on to win the Belmont Stakes and the Breeders' Cup Classic to take that year's titles as Horse of the Year and champion 3-year-old colt. Arazi, six months after the Derby, returned from France and, remarkably, was sent off the 3-2 favorite in the Breeders' Cup Mile. He finished 11th and was retired, but his co-owners, Allen Paulson and Sheikh Mohammed al-Maktoum, had forged a partnership that would later pay off with Cigar's participation in the first Dubai World Cup.

There are disappointments, of which Arazi was surely one, and then there are heartbreaks. There is a difference. With a disappointment, you shrug your shoulders and move on. A heartbreak, though, makes you question and doubt, and curse the fates. And there was no greater heartbreak than the 1990 Breeders' Cup, the darkest day in American racing since Ruffian died as a result of injuries suffered in her 1975 match race against Foolish Pleasure.

It was the first Breeders' Cup run at Belmont Park, and the crisp fall air made it a perfect afternoon for racing. But disaster struck early. Mr. Nickerson and Shaker Knit suffered fatal injuries in the Breeders' Cup Sprint, setting the tone for the day.

That year's Distaff brought together two champions from 1989. Bayakoa and Go for Wand both had won Breeders' Cup races at Gulfstream Park, and they came into the 1990 Distaff atop their respective divisions. The first mile of the 1⅛-mile race was dazzling. Go for Wand, a 3-year-old, and the 6-year-old Bayakoa hooked up from the start, and drew away from their rivals. They were locked together, Go for Wand on the inside, Bayakoa on the outside, the crowd of 51,236 enthralled by the pure desire of both.

And then, without warning, Go for Wand fractured her right front ankle at the sixteenth pole. She nose-dived to the dirt, then her instincts compelled her to stand. The sight of her struggling was horrifying. Go for Wand was euthanized immediately, and was buried the next day at Saratoga. "It should be a victory, but it isn't," said Ron McAnally, Bayakoa's trainer. "They give their lives for our enjoyment."

As dusk began to gather over Belmont Park, Unbridled won the Classic, becoming the first horse to win that race and the Kentucky Derby in the same year. But that feat was overshadowed by the numbing events earlier in the day.

The sport lost others, both human and equine, during the decade. Trainers Laz Barrera, Francois Boutin, Henry Clark, W. Burling Cocks, Buddy Hirsch, Horatio Luro, Jack Price, Willard Proctor, Rodney Rash, Woody Stephens, Mesh Tenney, Harry Trotsek, Bob Wheeler, Charlie Whittingham, and Frank Wright; jockeys Eddie Arcaro and Eric Guerin; cinematographer Joe Burnham; photographer Kathryn Dudek; racetrack owners Edward J. DeBartolo and Robert Strub; racecaller Fred Capossela; steward Keene Daingerfield; sports impresario Sonny Werblin; auctioneer John Finney;

Heatbreak marred the running of the 1990 Breeders' Cup at Belmont Park. Three horses, including the brilliant champion Go for Wand, suffered fatal injuries.

celebrated grooms Clem Brooks and Eddie Sweat; owner breeders Leslie Combs II, Rex Ellsworth, Thomas Mellon Evans, Daniel Galbreath, Frances Genter, Warner Jones, Howard Keck, Gene Klein, Paul Mellon, Stavros Niarchos, Alfred G. Vanderbilt, Frank Whitham, and Zenya Yoshida; and respected writers Pete Axthelm, Jim Bolus, Mary Jane Gallaher, Bob Harding, Kent Hollingsworth, Bill Leggett, Oscar Otis, and Whitney Tower all died.

Racehorses Great Communicator, Izvestia, Pleasant Stage, Prairie Bayou, and Three Ring were taken too soon. Death also claimed the retired horses Ack Ack, Bayakoa, Best Pal, Blushing Groom, Damascus, Easy Goer, Flying Paster, Forego, Grey Dawn II, and Sir Ivor, and three of this century's greatest stallions, Mr. Prospector, Nijinsky II, and Northern Dancer.

Bill Shoemaker retired as a jockey in 1990 with a record 8,833 victories, began training, and one year later was paralyzed in a car accident. Julie Krone, who became the first female jockey to win a classic when she captured the 1993 Belmont with Colonial Affair, retired in 1999. Hall of Fame trainer MacKenzie Miller, long associated with philanthropist Paul Mellon, retired two years after the two gentlemen of the turf won the Kentucky Derby with Sea Hero. Johnny Longden, the only man to both ride and train a Derby winner, stopped training. Trainer Gary Jones and jockeys Steve Cauthen and Sandy Hawley also retired, as did Lester Piggott, after a brief comeback that saw him win the 1990 Breeders' Cup Mile on Royal Academy.

Animal rights became an increasingly important issue. Organizations such as Re-Run, United Pegasus Foundation, and the Thoroughbred Retirement Fund

Michael Dickinson turned in one of the great training feats of all time when he sent out Da Hoss (RIGHT) *to win the 1998 Breeders' Cup Mile off only a minor prep race following a two-year layoff.*

helped to give retired racehorses a dignified way to live out their lives, but the sickening death of Exceller in a Swedish slaughterhouse in July 1997 was a reminder that more needed to be done.

The robust American economy was good for business. Sales prices at the top end of the market boomed. Total sales at the 1999 auctions were a record $1 billion. The average at the benchmark Keeneland July Yearling Sale in 1999 was up 21 percent from the previous year. The economic gains helped American breeders hold on to the best stallions, unlike the early 1990's, when horses such as Forty Niner and Sunday Silence were whisked off to Japan.

Tracks struggled with increased competition from casinos and state-run lotteries. "We have lost our exclusive franchise, and yet we are being regulated as if the old system still applied," said Ogden Mills Phipps, chairman of The Jockey Club. When Arlington International Racecourse could not get additional gambling approved for track grounds, owner Richard Duchossois elected not to race in 1998 or 1999. But some tracks, such as Delaware Park and Prairie Meadows, were able to put slot machines on track grounds, then watched their bottom lines and purses soar. The proliferation of simulcasting also kept purses and revenues high during the decade. But while handle was up, and big events, such as the Breeders' Cup and Triple Crown races, attracted record crowds, ontrack attendance on a daily basis was declining. Full-card simulcasting came to California, Florida, and Kentucky. New York became the last state to allow horses to race on antibleeding medications such as Lasix.

Racetracks became sought-after properties. Frank Stronach's Magna Entertainment purchased Santa Anita, Gulfstream Park, Golden Gate Fields, Remington Park, and Thistledown. Churchill Downs acquired Hollywood Park, Calder Race Course, and Ellis Park, and opened Hoosier Park in Indiana. Lone Star Park opened in Texas and became a raging success, while Sam Houston and Retama Park both rebounded from shaky starts. Fair Grounds was rebuilt after being destroyed by fire. Suffolk Downs reopened to great success. Emerald Downs opened in Washington State to replace longtime fan favorite Longacres. But nothing could save Ak-Sar-Ben or Detroit Race Course, and Atlantic City barely had a pulse.

Laffit Pincay Jr. put an exclamation point on his Hall of Fame career when on Dec. 10, 1999, he rode his 8,834th winner, passing Shoemaker's record for victories by a jockey. But Russell Baze, who won 400 races every year from 1992 through 1998, was on a pace to eventually catch Pincay. Michael Dickinson was trying to bring European-style training methods to the United States. He owned his own facility in Maryland, and used it as the launching pad for a startling comeback by Da Hoss, who won the 1996 Breeders' Cup Mile, was off for nearly two years, then had one prep before a repeat victory in the 1998 Mile.

Racing looked far different from how it did at the beginning of the century. Racetracks were changing hands, with the power being concentrated among a core group of businessmen. The impact of the Internet raised possibilities never before dreamed of for betting and flow of information. New home-wagering ventures were altering how and where fans placed their bets. Sports fans largely were tuning out the droning sameness of racing's weekday cards, but major events sparked record interest, and summertime meets at Del Mar and Saratoga were thriving. Stallions shuttled between Northern and Southern Hemispheres. And trainers and owners were increasingly emboldened to race their horses around the world. These were the trends racing was embracing as the sport dove headlong into the next millennium.

CHAMPIONS

PAST PERFORMANCES

THE 1990'S

YEAR BY YEAR CHAMPIONS

•1990•
•2-YEAR-OLD MALE *Fly So Free* •2-YEAR-OLD FILLY *Meadow Star* •3-YEAR-OLD MALE *Unbridled* •3-YEAR-OLD FILLY *Go for Wand* •HANDICAP HORSE *Criminal Type* •HANDICAP MARE *Bayakoa* •GRASS HORSE *Itsallgreektome (M) Laugh and Be Merry (F)* •SPRINTER *Housebuster* •STEEPLECHASE *Morley Street*
•**HORSE OF THE YEAR** Criminal Type

•1991•
•2-YEAR-OLD MALE *Arazi* •2-YEAR-OLD FILLY *Pleasant Stage* •3-YEAR-OLD MALE *Hansel* •3-YEAR-OLD FILLY *Dance Smartly* •HANDICAP HORSE *Black Tie Affair* •HANDICAP MARE *Queena* •GRASS HORSE *Tight Spot (M) Miss Alleged (F)* •SPRINTER *Housebuster* •STEEPLECHASE *Morley Street*
•**HORSE OF THE YEAR** Black Tie Affair

•1992•
•2-YEAR-OLD MALE *Gilded Time* •2-YEAR-OLD FILLY *Eliza* •3-YEAR-OLD MALE *A.P. Indy* •3-YEAR-OLD FILLY *Saratoga Dew* •HANDICAP HORSE *Pleasant Tap* •HANDICAP MARE *Paseana* •GRASS HORSE *Sky Classic (M) Flawlessly (F)* •SPRINTER *Rubiano* •STEEPLECHASE *Lonesome Glory*
•**HORSE OF THE YEAR** A.P. Indy

•1993•
•2-YEAR-OLD MALE *Dehere* •2-YEAR-OLD FILLY *Phone Chatter* •3-YEAR-OLD MALE *Prairie Bayou* •3-YEAR-OLD FILLY *Hollywood Wildcat* •HANDICAP HORSE *Bertrando* •HANDICAP MARE *Paseana* •GRASS HORSE *Kotashaan (M) Flawlessly (F)* •SPRINTER *Cardmania* •STEEPLECHASE *Lonesome Glory*
•**HORSE OF THE YEAR** Kotashaan

•1994•
•2-YEAR-OLD MALE *Timber Country* •2-YEAR-OLD FILLY *Flanders* •3-YEAR-OLD MALE *Holy Bull* •3-YEAR-OLD FILLY *Heavenly Prize* •HANDICAP HORSE *The Wicked North* •HANDICAP MARE *Sky Beauty* •GRASS HORSE *Paradise Creek (M) Hatoof (F)* •SPRINTER *Cherokee Run* •STEEPLECHASE *Warm Spell*
•**HORSE OF THE YEAR** Holy Bull

•1995•
•2-YEAR-OLD MALE *Maria's Mon* •2-YEAR-OLD FILLY *Golden Attraction* •3-YEAR-OLD MALE *Thunder Gulch* •3-YEAR-OLD FILLY *Serena's Song* •HANDICAP HORSE *Cigar* •HANDICAP MARE *Inside Information* •GRASS HORSE *Northern Spur (M) Possibly Perfect (F)* •SPRINTER *Not Surprising* •STEEPLECHASE *Lonesome Glory*
•**HORSE OF THE YEAR** Cigar

•1996•
•2-YEAR-OLD MALE *Boston Harbor* •2-YEAR-OLD FILLY *Storm Song* •3-YEAR-OLD MALE *Skip Away* •3-YEAR-OLD FILLY *Yanks Music* •HANDICAP HORSE *Cigar* •HANDICAP MARE *Jewel Princess* •GRASS HORSE *Singspiel (M) Wandesta (F)* •SPRINTER *Lit de Justice* •STEEPLECHASE *Coreggio*
•**HORSE OF THE YEAR** Cigar

•1997•
•2-YEAR-OLD MALE *Favorite Trick* •2-YEAR-OLD FILLY *Countess Diana* •3-YEAR-OLD MALE *Silver Charm* •3-YEAR-OLD FILLY *Ajina* •HANDICAP HORSE *Skip Away* •HANDICAP MARE *Hidden Lake* •GRASS HORSE *Chief Bearhart (M) Ryafan (F)* •SPRINTER *Smoke Glacken* •STEEPLECHASE *Lonesome Glory*
•**HORSE OF THE YEAR** Favorite Trick

•1998•
•2-YEAR-OLD MALE *Answer Lively* •2-YEAR-OLD FILLY *Silverbulletday* •3-YEAR-OLD MALE *Real Quiet* •3-YEAR-OLD FILLY *Banshee Breeze* •HANDICAP HORSE *Skip Away* •HANDICAP MARE *Escena* •GRASS HORSE *Buck's Boy (M) Fiji (F)* •SPRINTER *Reraise* •STEEPLECHASE *Flat Top*
•**HORSE OF THE YEAR** Skip Away

•1999•
•2-YEAR-OLD MALE *Anees* •2-YEAR-OLD FILLY *Chilukki* •3-YEAR-OLD MALE *Charismatic* •3-YEAR-OLD FILLY *Silverbulletday* •HANDICAP HORSE *Victory Gallop* •HANDICAP MARE *Beautiful Pleasure* •GRASS HORSE *Daylami (M) Soaring Softly (F)* •SPRINTER *Artax* •STEEPLECHASE *Lonesome Glory*
•**HORSE OF THE YEAR** Charismatic

A.P. Indy
Own: Farish, Goodman, Kilroy & Tsurumaki

Dk. b or b. c. 3 (Mar) KEEJUL90 $2,900,000
Sire: Seattle Slew (Bold Reasoning)
Dam: Weekend Surprise (Secretariat)
Br: W. S. Farish, III & W. S. Kilroy (Ky)
Tr: Drysdale Neil D

Life	11	8	0	1	$2,979,815	114	D.Fst	8	6	0	0	$2,405,185 114
1992	7	5	0	1	$2,622,560	114	Wet(355)	3	2	0	1	$574,630 111
1991	4	3	0	0	$357,255	-	Turf(308)	0	0	0	0	$0 -
	0	0	0	0	$0	-	Dst(0)	0	0	0	0	$0 -

31Oct92-10GP	fst	1¼	:454 1:10 1:35 2:001	3↑BCClasic-G1	114	4	8 3¾	8 3¾	4 2½	2 ½	1 2	Delahoussaye E	121	*2.10	- -	A.P. Indy121 2 Pleasant Tap126 ½ *Jolypha*118 1½	Drew clear,ridden out	14
10Oct92-8Bel	gd	1¼	:461 1:10 1:35 1:584	3↑JkyClbGC-G1	107	5	7 15	7 12	6 2¼	3 3½	3 6¾	Delahoussaye E	121	2.90	- -	Pleasant Tap126 4½ Strike the Gold126 2¼ *A.P. Indy*121 ½	Stumbled badly strt	7
13Sep92-8WO	fst	1⅛	:473 1:122 1:382 1:513	MlsonMil-G2	93	2	3 1	3 2	5 5	6 4¼	5 2½	Delahoussaye E	126	*.70	- -	*Benburb*119 ½ Elated Guy117 ½ Vying Victor119 hd	Lacked late response	7
Previously owned by Tomonori Tsurumaki																		
6Jun92-8Bel	gd	1½	:47 1:114 2:26	Belmont-G1	111	1	4 1¾	4 2	2 hd	2 hd	1 ¾	Delahoussaye E	126	*1.10	- -	A.P. Indy126 ¾ My Memoirs126 nk Pine Bluff126 13¼	Closed strongly,drvng	11
24May92-8Bel	fst	1⅛	:453 1:10 1:351 1:472	PeterPan-G2	108	6	5 2½	5 2½	1 ½	1 2½	1 5½	Delahoussaye E	126	*.50	- -	*A.P. Indy*126 5½ Colony Light114 4¾ Berkley Fitz114 2	Drew off, ridden out	7
4Apr92-5SA	fst	1⅛	:461 1:102 1:361 1:491	SADerby-G1	95	3	4 4	4 2	4 3	3 ½	1 1¾	Delahoussaye E	B122	*.90	- -	*A.P. Indy*122 1¾ Bertrando122 nk Casual Lies122 3½	Rallied, driving	7
29Feb92-8SA	fst	1	:223 :46 1:10 1:352	SnRafael-G2	100	5	3 2	2 1	2 ½	2 2	1 ¾	Delahoussaye E	B121	*.50	- -	*A.P. Indy*121 ¾ Treekster116 9 Prince Wild118 ½	Strong urging,up late	6
22Dec91-5Hol	fst	1 1/16	:23 :464 1:11 1:424	HolFut-G1	–	11	8 6¼	9 5¾	6 3¾	1 ½	1 nk	Delahoussaye E	B121	3.20	- -	*A.P. Indy*121 nk *Dance Floor*121 5½ *Casual Lies*121 2	Bid strongly, driving	14
4Dec91-8BM	fst	1	:23 :464 1:112 1:362	Alw 21000NC	–	1	1 ½	1 hd	1 hd	1 1	1 3	Delahoussaye E	B117	*.20	- -	*A.P. Indy*117 3 Kalookan Boy117 3½ Fabulous Pole117 no	Drew clear, driving	8
27Oct91-6SA	gd	6½f	:214 :453 1:113 1:181	Md Sp Wt 25k	–	4	8	7 6	6 3¼	3 2½	1 4	Delahoussaye E	B117	*1.30	- -	*A.P. Indy*117 4 Dr Pain117 3½ *Hickman Creek*117 2	Blocked, ridden out	9
24Aug91-4Dmr	fst	6f	:221 :451 :572 1:101	Md Sp Wt 29k	–	2	4	5 5	4 5	4 8	4 5½	Delahoussaye E	B117	*2.30	- -	ShrpBndit117 2½ Anonymouslw117 2¾ *RchrdofEnglnd*117 nk	3 wide, mild rally	7

Ajina
Own: Paulson Allen E

Dk. b or b. f. 4 (Apr)
Sire: Strawberry Road*Aus (Whiskey Road)
Dam: Winglet (Alydar)
Br: Allen E. Paulson (Ky)
Tr: Mott William I

Life	17	7	3	2	$1,327,915	108	D.Fst	17	7	3	2	$1,327,915 108
1998	4	1	0	0	$135,300	106	Wet(378)	0	0	0	0	$0 -
1997	9	3	2	2	$979,175	108	Turf(313)	0	0	0	0	$0 -
	0	0	0	0	$0	-	Dst(0)	0	0	0	0	$0 -

26Jly98-8Del	fst	1¼	:473 1:121 1:381 2:041	+3↑ⒻDelH-G3	89	1	1 1	1 1	1 hd	3 ½	6 4¾	Smith M E	120	1.80	83-07	Amarillo110 ¾ Tuxedo Junction115 2¼ Timely Broad110 no	Dueled, gave way	9
20Jun98-8Bel	fst	1 1/16	:222 :444 1:083 1:394	3↑ⒻHmpstedH-G1	94	4	3 1	4 2	5 3	5 6	4 13	Smith M E	122	*1.70	87-12	Mossflower114 12 GlitterWomn120 no *ColonilMinstrl*118 1	Wide,no response	6
16May98-4Pim	fst	1⅛	:462 1:102 1:354 1:483	3↑ⒻPimDstfH-G3	106	2	1 hd	1 ½	1 ½	1 3½	1 3	Bailey J D	120	*.50	97-13	Ajina120 3 NaskrColors112 nk PochosDremGirl113 3½	Rail,vigorous hnd ride	8
11Apr98-6OP	fst	1 1/16	:231 :464 1:114 1:44	4↑ⒻBayakoa40k	69	7	3 2	2 1	3 1½	8 7½	8 11½	Day P	112	*.40	76-10	WaterStreet113 nk ProperBnner116 1 WesternFlick116 nk	Fractious in gate	8
8Nov97-4Hol	fst	1⅛	:454 1:091 1:342 1:471	3↑ⒻBCDistaf-G1	108	1	3 2½	3 1½	3 1½	1 hd	1 2	Smith M E	B120	4.80e	90-06	Ajina120 2 *Sharp Cat*120 3½ Escena123 1	Rail trip, driving	8
19Oct97-9Bel	fst	1⅛	:463 1:103 1:352 1:481	3↑ⒻBeldame-G1	102	8	4 4	3 2½	3 1	2 2½	2 2	Smith M E	119	2.90	87-12	Hidden Lake123 2 *Ajina*119 2 Jewel Princess123 1¼	Spd inside,game fin	8
16Aug97-8Sar	fst	1¼	:48 1:121 1:363 2:021	ⒻAlabama-G1	105	6	1 1½	1 1½	1 hd	2 hd	2 1¼	Smith M E	121	*.75	96-16	Runup the Colors121 1¼ Ajina121 3½ *Tomisue's Delight*121 12	Gamely on rail	6
19Jly97-9Bel	fst	1¼	:48 1:121 1:354 2:002	ⒻCCAOaks-G1	102	3	1 1½	1 2½	1 5	1 6	1 2¼	Smith M E	121	1.15	95-08	Ajina121 2¼ Tomisue's Delight121 8 Key Hunter121 15	Clear,ridden out	5
21Jun97-9Bel	fst	1⅛	:454 1:102 1:353 1:482	ⒻMthrGoos-G1	101	2	2 2½	2 2	2 1½	1 hd	1 1¼	Smith M E	121	18.00	88-13	*Ajina*121 1¼ *Sharp Cat*121 1½ Tomisue's Delight121 11½	Clear after long drive	6
31May97-9Bel	fst	1	:221 :443 1:084 1:342	ⒻAcorn-G1	89	3	5 3	5 3¾	5 5½	3 6	3 7¼	Santos J A	121	23.00	85-14	Sharp Cat121 2½ Dixie Flag121 4¾ *Ajina*121 1¼	Inside trn,good finish	7
1May97-8CD	fst	7f	:222 :45 1:094 1:223	ⒻLaTroienne113k	79	3	7	5 2	4 3¾	5 10	4 11	Bailey J D	121	3.90	84-08	Star ofGoshen115 11 *PearlCity*115 no *FlyingLauren*116 no	Stalked pace, inside	8
6Apr97-9OP	fst	1 1/16	:231 :464 1:114 1:423	ⒻFantasy-G2	85	1	1 hd	2 ½	3 1½	3 6½	3 14	Bailey J D	121	1.90	81-16	*Blushing K. D.*121 6 Valid Bonnet121 8 Ajina121 6	Bore out first turn	5
9Mar97-10GP	fst	1 1/16	:231 :462 1:10 1:431	ⒻBonnieMs-G2	80	2	3 3	3 2½	3 3½	3 6½	4 13	Bailey J D	119	5.70	78-16	*Glitter Woman*117 7¼ Southern Playgirl119 ¾ *DixieFlag*114 5	Chased fast pace	5
30Nov96-7Aqu	fst	1⅛	:493 1:142 1:402 1:533	ⒻDemoisel-G2	83	9	3 2	2 ½	2 hd	1 ½	1 7	Day P	121	*1.05	72-21	Ajina121 7 Hidden Reserve114 4½ Biding Time114 ¾	Drew off,ridden out	9
10Nov96-9Aqu	fst	1	:23 :46 1:111 1:362	ⒻTempted-G3	86	5	4 2	4 2	4 nk	2 hd	1 ½	Bailey J D	112	2.65	88-17	*Ajina*112 ½ Glitter Woman114 7 *Aldiza*114 1	Stdied start,prevailed	7
13Oct96-2Bel	fst	7f	:223 :461 1:104 1:232	ⒻMd Sp Wt 34k	87	5	2	3 ½	3 nk	1 2	1 3	Bailey J D	117	*1.70	84-11	*Ajina*117 3 Recoleta117 5 *Runup the Colors*117 1½	Speed outs,ridden out	11
15Sep96-2Bel	fst	6f	:222 :46 :581 1:103	ⒻMd Sp Wt 34k	75	1	6	2 ½	2 ½	2 1½	2 2½	Bailey J D	116	3.75	86-08	U R Unforgetable116 2½ *Ajina*116 9 Miss Queen116 1	Tried winner 3/16's	10

Anees
Own: The Thoroughbred Corporation

B. c. 3 (Feb) KEESEP98 $330,000
Sire: Unbridled (Fappiano) $200,000
Dam: Ivory Idol (Alydar)
Br: Farfellow Farms, Ltd. (Ky)
Tr: Hassinger A L Jr

Life	7	2	0	2	$699,200	102	D.Fst	7	2	0	2	$699,200 102
2000	3	0	0	1	$90,000	99	Wet(420)	0	0	0	0	$0 -
1999	4	2	0	1	$609,200	102	Turf(300)	0	0	0	0	$0 -
	0	0	0	0	$0	-	Dst(0)	0	0	0	0	$0 -

6May00-8CD	fst	1¼	:454 1:094 1:353 2:01	KyDerby-G1	77	1	16 11	15 8	11 5½	11 9	13 20½	Nakatani C S	L126 b	17.10	84 -	FusichiPegsus126 1½ Aptitude126 4 Impechmnt126 ½	Awkward,swerve start	19
8Apr00-5SA	fst	1⅛	:471 1:112 1:362 1:49	SADerby-G1	99	3	6 8	6 9½	6 8	5 4	4 6	Nakatani C S	LB120 b	4.20	84-16	The Deputy120 1 War Chant120 2 Captain Steve120 3	Improved position	6
19Mar00-7SA	fst	1 1/16	:23 :454 1:101 1:423	SnFelipe-G2	99	1	6 5½	5 7	4 4½	4 3½	3 3¾	Bailey J D	LB119 b	3.90	86-14	*Fusaichi Pegasus*116 ¾ *The Deputy*122 3 Anees119 hd	Saved grd, up for show	7
6Nov99-8GP	fst	1 1/16	:221 :46 1:101 1:421	BCJuven-G1	102	9	14 11	14 8	8 7¾	4 1¾	1 2½	Stevens G L	L122 b	30.30	96 -	Anees122 2½ Chief Seattle122 ¾ High Yield122 2¼	Bumped start,drifted	14
10Oct99-7SA	fst	1	:221 :454 1:094 1:353	Norfolk-G2	95	2	6 7½	6 8½	3 9½	3 5	3 5	Stevens G L	LB118 b	9.50	88-15	Dixie Union118 ½ Forest Camp118 4½ *Anees*118 9½	Inside move,bested rst	6
3Sep99-3Dmr	fst	1	:224 :47 1:12 1:373	Md Sp Wt 48k	82	5	4 5	4 4	4 1¾	1 hd	1 2	Stevens G L	LB118 b	4.90	84-09	Anees118 2 Silver Axe118 2½ Gilty Moment118 1½	4 wide bid, driving	8
21Aug99-3Dmr	fst	5½f	:22 :452 :574 1:042	Md Sp Wt 40k	48	9	6	8 18	8 19	8 14	6 13	Desormeaux K J	LB118	7.70	78-14	*Tavasco*118 3½ Brave Slew118 nk *Valiant Vision*118 ¾	Lugged out start	9

Answer Lively
Own: Franks John

B. c. 3 (Mar)
Sire: Lively One (Halo)
Dam: Twosies Answer (Two's a Plenty)
Br: John Franks (Ky)
Tr: Barnett Bobby C

Life	14	4	4	0	$938,296	103	D.Fst	13	4	4	0	$936,296 103
1999	7	0	3	0	$243,000	103	Wet(320)	1	0	0	0	$2,000 -
1998	7	4	1	0	$695,296	100	Turf(259)	0	0	0	0	$0 -
	0	0	0	0	$0	-	Dst(0)	0	0	0	0	$0 -

2Oct99-8LaD	fst	1¼	:463 1:10 1:353 2:002	SuperDby-G1	89	1	1 2	1 1	1 hd	6 12	6 19	Gonzalez C V	L126	4.10	83-09	Ecton Park126 2 Menifee126 2 Pineaff126 6	Pace, gave way drive	8
5Sep99-8RP	fst	1⅛	:47 1:114 1:364 1:492	RPDerby-G3	100	7	1 3	1 1	1 1	1 1½	2 1½	Gonzalez C V	LB115	1.90	91-07	TemperenceTime119 1½ AnswerLively115 1 StellrBrush124 4¾	Could not last	8
1May99-8CD	fst	1¼	:474 1:122 1:372 2:031	KyDerby-G1	100	7	5 3	4 2	6 4	7 4¾	10 5¾	Perret C	L126	37.00	83-14	*Charismatic*126 nk Menifee126 ¾ Cat Thief126 1¼	Steadied both turns	19
10Apr99-10OP	fst	1⅛	:46 1:101 1:36 1:491	ArkDerby-G2	85	7	3 2	3 2	3 2	4 6	5 9¾	Solis A	L122	2.10	81-16	[D]Valhol118 4½ Certain122 2 Torrid Sand118 1	Stalked 4-wide, empty	7
Placed 4th through disqualification																		
14Mar99-9FG	fst	1 1/16	:24 :48 1:124 1:432	LaDerby-G2	103	7	3 2	3 2	3 ½	2 ½	2 hd	Day P	L122	1.80	94-20	KimberlitePipe122 hd AnswrLivly122 hd EctonPrk122 2¼	3w turn, forced out	8
21Feb99-9FG	fst	1 1/16	:232 :473 1:123 1:444	RisenStar125k	95	1	4 2½	5 2¾	6 4¼	3 2	2 no	Day P	L122	*.70	87-21	Ecton Park114 no Answer Lively122 ½ *Kimberlite Pipe*122 1½	3w, outfinished	12
30Jan99-9FG	fst	1	:223 :453 1:113 1:382	LecomteH100k	71	11	6 6½	6 5¼	4 3	5 4	7 7¼	Albarado R J	L122	*.50	80-20	SomeActor114 no DesertDmon114 1½ SilvrChdr114 ¾	Wide, 6w, 4w, no impct	14
7Nov98-4CD	fst	1 1/16	:231 :463 1:113 1:44	BCJuven-G1	97	4	3 1½	3 3½	3 ½	1 2	1 hd	Bailey J D	L122	*2.70	91-07	Answer Lively122 hd Aly's Alley122 ¾ Cat Thief122 5½	Hard drive	13
18Oct98-8Kee	fst	1 1/16	:223 :454 1:111 1:44	BrdrsFut-G2	97	1	1 1	2 hd	1 2	1 1	2 nk	Gonzalez C V	L121	2.40	88-20	Cat Thief121 nk *Answer Lively*121 3½ Yes It's True121 4½	In bit tight 1st turn	8
3Oct98-5LaD	fst	6½f	:221 :444 1:10 1:163	SprtOKngFt77k	100	10	1	2 ½	2 ½	1 4½	1 9	Gonzalez C V	L120	*.50	91-15	Answer Lively120 9 Kodi Act120 3½ Brassy Wells120 5	Ridden out, sharp	10
20Sep98-1LaD	fst	6f	:222 :46 :573 1:10	Alw 16000N2L	91	6	2	3 1½	2 hd	1 4	1 9	Gonzalez C V	L113	*1.50	94-17	*Answer Lively*113 9 Blue Autumn119 ½ Tricky Mocha119 4	Rated, ridden out	7
19Jly98-9LS	fst	6f	:211 :442 :573 1:111	Middlegrnd153k	54	11	1	1 1	1 2	4 2½	5 6¼	Gonzalez C V	L121 b	3.70	80-13	Wings of Jones121 1 Brassy Wells121 3¼ Lou'sCandi121 1½	Clear lead, faded	11
24Apr98-3Kee	fst	4½f	:221 :461 :523	Md Sp Wt 39k	–	4	1	1 ½		1 2½	1 6½	Albarado R J	L118 b	3.30	93-08	AnswerLively118 6½ *HiddnCity*118 2½ Fntstisch118 2½	Drew clear, ridden out	8
9Apr98-4Kee	my	4½f	:222 :453 :514	Md Sp Wt 39k	–	9	5	3 1½		3 5½	4 13	Albarado R J	L118 b	2.80	84-16	TacticalCat118 7 ShortGo118 5 RokebysChrm118 1	Pressed pace, gave way	10

Arazi

Own: Allen E. Paulson & Sheikh Mohammed Maktoum

Ch. c. 3 (Mar) KEENOV89 $350,000
Sire: Blushing Groom*Fr (Red God)
Dam: Danseur Fabuleux (Northern Dancer)
Br: Ralph C. Wilson Jr. (Ky)
Tr: Boutin Francois

Life	14	9	1	1	$1,212,351	95	D.Fst	2	1	0	0	$520,000	95
1992	6	2	0	1	$113,023	95	Wet(422)	0	0	0	0	$0	–
1991	8	7	1	0	$1,099,328	–	Turf(403)	12	8	1	1	$692,351	92
	0	0	0	0	$0	–	Dst(0)	0	0	0	0	$0	–

31Oct92–7GP fm 1 Ⓣ :224 :454 1:09 1:324 3↑ BCMile-G1 **92** 3 32½ 32½ 42½ 119 119 Valenzuela P A 122 *1.50 - - *Lure*1223 *Paradise Creek*122nk Brief Truce1221½ No excuse, no rally 14
4Oct92 Longchamp (Fr) sf *1 Ⓣ RH 1:44 3↑ Prix du Rond-Point-G2 Stk 141400 14 Cauthen S 123 *.00 Arazi1234 Calling Collect123hd *Alhijaz*1301½ 11
Rated in 5th,sharp run to lead over 1f out,quickly clear
20Sep92 Longchamp (Fr) gd *1¼ Ⓣ RH 2:072 3↑ Prix du Prince d'Orange-G3 Stk 71800 36 Cauthen S 121 *2.50e Arcangues1266 Prince Polino121hd *Arazi*1213 5
Unhurried in last,outside bid 2f out,lost 2nd near line
16Jun92 Ascot (GB) gd 1 Ⓣ RH 1:391 St James's Palace Stakes-G1 Stk 366800 52¼ Cauthen S 126 *1.10 Brief Truce126no Zaahi1261½ Ezzoud126no 8
Rated in 6th,prgrss 2-1/2f out,evenly late.Rodrigo De Triano 4th
2May92–8CD fst 1¼ :474 1:121 1:373 2:03 KyDerby-G1 **95** 17 1610 115½ 21½ 54 88¼ Valenzuela P A **B**126 *.90 - - Lil E. Tee1261 Casual Lies1263¼ Dance Floor1262 Bid, weakened 18
7Apr92 Saint-Cloud (Fr) sf *1 Ⓣ LH 1:48 Prix Omnium II (Listed) Stk 37500 15 Cauthen S 128 *.00e Arazi1285 Supermec1282½ River Majesty128½ 8
Unhurried in 5th,smooth rally to lead 2f out,drew clear in hand
2Nov91–6CD fst 1 1/16 :231 :463 1:12 1:443 BCJuven-G1 – 14 1312 97¼ 22 16 15 Valenzuela P A **B**122 *2.10 - - *Arazi*1225 *Bertrando*1223½ Snappy Landing122hd In hand 14
5Oct91 Longchamp (Fr) gd *1 Ⓣ 1:412 CIGA Grand Criterium-G1 Stk 359000 13 Mosse G 123 *.20 *Arazi*1233 *Rainbow Corner*123hd *Seattle Rhyme*123¾ 6
Tracked leader, ridden & rallied clear, pushed out
8Sep91 Longchamp (Fr) gd *7f Ⓣ 1:204 Prix de la Salamandre-G1 Stk 144000 15 Mosse G 123 - *Arazi*1235 *Made of Gold*123nk Silver Kite123nk 8
3rd straight, rallied to lead 2f out, hung right, easily
18Aug91 Deauville (Fr) gd *6f Ⓣ 1:131 Prix Morny Agence Francaise-G1 Stk 284500 13 Mosse G 123 *.50 *Arazi*1233 Kenbu120¾ Lion Cavern1232 4
Tracked leader, led 2f out, clear 1 1/2f out, ran on well
21Jly91 Maisons-Laffitte (Fr) gd *5½f Ⓣ 1:052 Prix Robert Papin-G2 Stk 103800 11½ Mosse G 123 *.80 *Arazi*1231½ Showbrook1233 *Steinbeck*1232 6
Good headway 2f out, led 1 1/2f out, hard ridden, ran on well
3Jly91 Longchamp (Fr) gd *5f Ⓣ :583 Prix du Bois-G3 Stk 54900 1¾ Mosse G 125 1.40 *Arazi*125¾ Steinbeck121½ *Worldwide*1214 4
Always 2nd, led 1f out, ran on well, comfortably
12Jun91 Evry (Fr) gd *6f Ⓣ 1:141 Prix La Fleche Stk 35500 13 Head F 121 - *Arazi*1213 Tabac1262 Valley Road121hd 7
30May91 Chantilly (Fr) gd *5f Ⓣ :59 Prix d'Orgemont Maiden 29000 22½ Head F 123 - Steinbeck1232½ *Arazi*123nk Gramatique1183 6

Artax

Own: Paraneck Stable

Dk. b or b. c. 4 (Mar) FTKNOV95 $82,000
Sire: Marquetry (Conquistador Cielo) $10,000
Dam: Raging Apalachee (Apalachee)
Br: Vinery & Carondelet Farm (Ky)
Tr: Albertrani Louis

Life	25	7	9	3	$1,685,840	124	D.Fst	25	7	9	3	$1,685,840	124
1999	15	4	5	1	$1,205,920	124	Wet(329)	0	0	0	0	$0	–
1998	7	2	3	1	$362,120	109	Turf(289)	0	0	0	0	$0	–
	0	0	0	0	$0	–	Dst(0)	0	0	0	0	$0	–

6Nov99–6GP fst 6f :22 :44 :554 1:074 3↑ BCSprint-G1 **124** 5 7 2hd 11 11½ 1½ Chavez J F L126 f 3.70 103 - Artax126½ *Kona Gold*1262¾ Big Jag126½ Took over,driv.,lasted 14
16Oct99–9Bel fst 6f :221 :443 :554 1:073 3↑ FrstHlsH-G2 **123** 1 2 11 1hd 14½ 16½ Chavez J F L120 f *1.85 103–11 *Artax*1206½ Good and Tough1181½ *Intidab*116nk Sharp speed,ridden out 7
25Sep99–9Bel fst 7f :221 :443 1:083 1:213 3↑ Vosburgh-G1 **111** 4 6 1hd 1hd 13 13½ Chavez J F L126 f 4.30 94–09 *Artax*1263½ Stormin Fever126hd *Mountain Top*126½ Speed outside, driving 6
6Sep99–9Sar fst 7f :221 :441 1:081 1:211 3↑ ForegoH-G2 **103** 1 9 73¼ 75¼ 44 55¼ Smith M E L117 f 8.50 94–12 Crafty Friend119nk Affirmed Success1191¼ SirBear1192¼ Hustled, no rally 9
11Aug99–9Sar fst 6f :224 :452 :57 1:09 3↑ APhenomH-G2 **116** 2 4 1½ 1hd 2hd 21½ Smith M E L117 f 7.00 94–12 Intidab1131½ Artax1172¾ Yes It's True117½ Set pace inside,gamely 7
31Jly99–9Pha fst 6f :214 :44 :563 1:082 3↑ PhaBCH-G3 **104** 1 9 4¾ 3nk 43½ 21¼ Decarlo C P L119 f *.70 100–09 Loaded Gun1141¼ Artax119¾ *Power by Far*115hd Off very wide 9
4Jly99–8Bel fst 7f :223 :444 1:08 1:203 3↑ TomFoolH-G2 **101** 3 4 31 3½ 33 35¾ Smith M E L117 f 2.45 93–08 *Crafty Friend*116¾ Affirmed Success1195 Artax117hd Speed 3 wide, faded 5
5Jun99–8Bel fst 6f :212 :442 :564 1:093 3↑ TruNrthH-G2 **103** 4 7 65 41¾ 3nk 2¾ Chavez J F L119 f *1.00 92–10 Kashatreya110¾ Artax119¾ *The Trader's Echo*1111 Pinched back, gamely 9
15May99–7Pim fst 6f :231 :453 :571 1:091 3↑ MdBCH-G3 **96** 5 8 52¼ 3nk 23 58½ Chavez J F L116 f - 90–06 *YesItsTrue*1134¾ ThTrdrsEcho109½ PurplPssion114¾ Impeded, checked 1/8 8
2May99–8Aqu fst 7f :223 :444 1:08 1:20 3↑ CarterH-G1 **123** 9 3 2hd 2½ 1½ 13¼ Chavez J F L114 f 5.10 102–11 Artx1143¼ AffirmdSuccss1192½ WstrnBordrs1132½ Speed outside, driving 9
10Apr99–7Aqu fst 6f :213 :433 :551 1:072 3↑ BoldRlrH-G3 **113** 5 2 2hd 2½ 21½ 22½ Chavez J F L115 f 4.00 98–07 Kelly Kip1232½ *Artax*1156¾ Brushed On115nk Speed outside,2nd best 5
21Mar99–8Aqu fst 7f :223 :45 1:093 1:22 4↑ Alw 46000N3X **96** 3 8 1hd 1½ 2hd 2no Velasquez C L115 f *.75 92–15 Iron Will119no Artax1152 Well Noted1151¼ Set pace, gamely 8
Previously trained by Bradshaw Randy 1998: (333 45 49 46 0.14)
3Mar99–6SA fst 1 :223 :454 1:10 1:354 4↑ OC 100k/N$Y -N **94** 5 21 31 43 44½ 56¼ Antley C W **LB**118 3.70 86–19 Klinsman120½ Bold Words1184½ River Keen1181¼ Stalked pace, weakened 5
6Feb99–8SA fst 1⅛ :452 1:092 1:343 1:473 Strub-G2 **79** 5 12½ 15 11½ 68¾ 721¼ Solis A **LB**119 b 6.30 76–12 EvntofthYr1192¾ DrFong1214½ HnmnHghwy1171¾ Speed,inside,gave way 7
16Jan99–7SA fst 1 1/16 :231 :47 1:104 1:41 SnFndoBC-G2 **86** 4 1½ 1hd 2hd 56 716 McCarron C J **LB**120 4.20 82–16 DixiDotCom1164½ *EvntofthYr*1224½ *OldToppr*118½ Dueled,weakened,stdied 8
26Dec98–8SA fst 7f :23 :452 1:09 1:212 Malibu-G1 **104** 3 7 1hd 1½ 2½ 21½ McCarron C J **LB**119 4.00 96–08 Run Man Run1151½ Artax1192 Event of the Year121nk Inside duel 10
20Nov98–4Hol fst 7½f :22 :45 1:09 1:273 3↑ OC 100k/N$Y -N **93** 3 4 1hd 2hd 22 28½ McCarron C J **LB**115 *.80 84–15 Sea of Secrets1168½ Artax1154½ *Emailit*1178 Dueled, second best 5
2May98–8CD fst 1¼ :453 1:103 1:353 2:021 KyDerby-G1 **49** 12 1010 107¾ 1211 1329 1339¼ McCarron C J L126 11.50 55–02 *Real Quiet*126½ Victory Gallop1262¼ Indian Charlie126hd Bid, tired badly 15
4Apr98–5SA fst 1⅛ :46 1:094 1:342 1:47 SADerby-G1 **95** 6 34 33½ 32½ 34½ 39¼ McCarron C J **LB**120 2.60 92–05 Indian Charlie1202¼ *Real Quiet*1207 Artax1206 3 wide, faded stretch 7
14Mar98–8SA fst 1 1/16 :224 :464 1:104 1:413 SnFelipe-G2 **108** 1 11½ 11 1½ 11 1hd McCarron C J **LB**122 *1.20 95–11 Artax122hd Real Quiet1197 Prosperous Bid1166 Off rail, gamely 5
1Feb98–7SA fst 1 1/16 :224 :46 1:101 1:421 StCtlina-G3 **109** 1 11 1hd 1hd 11½ 15½ McCarron C J **LB**114 2.10 92–17 *Artax*1145½ Souvenir Copy1203 Allen's Oop1173½ Fought off rival, drvg 6
2Jan98–6SA fst 1 1/16 :224 :464 1:11 1:424 Alw 46000N$Y **97** 6 2hd 11 12 2hd 2½ Solis A **LB**115 *.40 88–15 Futuristic115½ *Artax*11510 Crafty Flight115no Outgamed, long drive 6
14Dec97–7Hol fst 1 1/16 :223 :454 1:101 1:411 HolFut-G1 **100** 7 52¾ 63¼ 32 3½ 21 McCarron C J **LB**121 3.40 94–11 Real Quiet1211 Artax1211¾ Nationalore1211 Outfinished 11
16Nov97–9Hol fst 1 1/16 :23 :47 1:123 1:451 Md Sp Wt 33k **88** 5 34½ 22 13 17 19 McCarron C J **LB**119 *1.30 75–28 Artax1199 *Availability*1198 Codeact1193 Much the best 7
26Oct97–6SA fst 7f :231 :46 1:104 1:23 Md Sp Wt 33k **67** 1 7 52¼ 61¾ 42½ 37½ McCarron C J **LB**120 4.00 81–14 Classic Cat1206 Crypt de Chine1201½ *Artax*120no Bbld gap,in tight 3/8 8

Banshee Breeze

Own: Tafel James B. and Jayeff B Stables

B. f. 4 (Mar)
Sire: Unbridled (Fappiano)
Dam: Banshee Winds (Known Fact)
Br: James B. Tafel (Ky)
Tr: Nafzger Carl A

Life	18	10	5	2	$2,784,798	115	**D.Fst**	16	9	4	2	$2,584,798 115
1999	7	4	3	0	$1,358,818	114	**Wet(420)**	2	1	1	0	$200,000 109
1998	10	6	2	2	$1,425,980	115	**Turf(288)**	0	0	0	0	$0 –
	0	0	0	0	$0	–	**Dst(0)**	0	0	0	0	$0 –

6Nov99-3GP	fst	1⅛	:462 1:094 1:343 1:472	3↑ⒻBCDistaf-G1	**108**	3	62¼	53	44½	21	2¾	Day P	L123 f	2.20	99 -	BeutifulPlesure123¾ BnshBrz1231¼ *HritgofGold*1231¼	Stdy bkstr, bid, hung	8
16Oct99-6Kee	fst	1⅛	:462 1:102 1:351 1:47	3↑ⒻSpinster-G1	**106**	7	64¼	54½	52¾	41¼	22½	Day P	L123 f	*.30	97-09	KeeperHill1232½ BnshBrz123no ALdyFromDixi1231	5wide trip,bid,2ndbest	9
27Aug99-8Sar	sly	1¼	:47 1:103 1:351 2:022	3↑ⒻPrsnlEnH-G1	**109**	6	47½	44¾	25	23½	22¼	Bailey J D	L124 f	*.70	94-20	*BeutifulPlesure*1132¼ BnsheeBreez1241½ KprHill1182¼	Game finish outside	6
7Aug99-8Sar	fst	1⅛	:48 1:112 1:363 1:494	3↑ⒻGoFWandH-G1	**109**	5	42½	31½	21	1hd	1½	Bailey J D	L124 f	*.65	87-16	BnsheeBreeze124½ *BeutifulPlesur*1138¾ *HritgofGold*1172	Inside trip, driving	5
5Jun99-10CD	fst	1⅛	:482 1:124 1:372 1:50	3↑ⒻFlrDLisH-G3	**110**	4	42	42	3½	1½	1½	Albarado R J	L124 f	*.30	93-12	*BnsheeBreeze*124½ SilntEskimo1144½ MdowVist1098¾	Bid 4w,driftd in 1/8pl	4
9Apr99-9OP	fst	1 1/16	:223 :452 1:094 1:413	4↑ⒻAplBlsmH-G1	**114**	2	57	59	41½	1hd	11¼	Bailey J D	L122 f	*.70	96-11	*Banshee Breeze*1221¼ Sister Act1149¼ *Silent Eskimo*112nk	Bold move, all out	6
28Feb99-10GP	fst	1 1/16	:25 :482 1:114 1:424	3↑ⒻRampartH-G2	**108**	5	32	21½	2½	1½	15½	Bailey J D	L122 f	*.60	93-16	*BnsheeBrez*1225½ GlittrWomn1194 TimlyBrod1143½	Drew away, ridden out	5
7Nov98-8CD	fst	1⅛	:473 1:12 1:37 1:494	3↑ⒻBCDistaf-G1	**105**	4	42½	33½	32	21½	2no	Bailey J D	L120 f	*.80	95-07	Escena123no *Banshee Breeze*1205 Keeper Hill120½	4w 2nd turn, missed	8
17Oct98-9Kee	fst	1⅛	:461 1:103 1:35 1:47	3↑ⒻSpinster-G1	**115**	5	56	53½	31	15½	112	Albarado R J	L119 f	*.80	101-05	BnsheeBreez11912 RunupthColors123½ Aldiz1233½	Bumped st., ridden out	8
22Aug98-8Sar	fst	1¼	:474 1:122 1:374 2:032	ⒻAlabama-G1	**107**	4	53½	41	2hd	12	16	Bailey J D	L121 f	2.35	91-09	*Banshee Breeze*1216 *Lu Ravi*121nk *Manistique*1216½	Quick 4w move,driving	6
25Jly98-8Bel	fst	1½	:491 1:142 2:044 2:312	ⒻCCAOaks-G1	**102**	6	46	31½	1½	1½	1nk	Bailey J D	L121 f	1.90	87-20	*Banshee Breeze*121nk Keeper Hill12117 BestFriendStro12121	3 wide,driving	6
27Jun98-8Bel	fst	1⅛	:454 1:10 1:342 1:473	ⒻMthrGoos-G1	**96**	9	74½	85¼	54	48	34	Davis R G	L121	5.10	88-16	*Jersey Girl*1211 Keeper Hill1213 *Banshee Breeze*1211	Bumpd strt,steadied	11
1May98-9CD	fst	1⅛	:484 1:133 1:384 1:52	ⒻKyOaks-G1	**100**	6	73¼	62	41½	11½	2nk	Bailey J D	L121	4.10	84-14	Keeper Hill121nk BansheeBreeze1213¾ *ReallyPolish*121½	Clear lead, missed	13
4Apr98-8Kee	fst	1 1/16	:232 :47 1:104 1:43	ⒻAshland-G1	**88**	5	42½	41	44	44	34½	Romero R P	L120	2.60	88-12	Well Chosen1151 Let1153½ Banshee Breeze120no	Chased pace evenly	7
16Mar98-11GP	gd	1 1/16	:24 :482 1:134 1:462	ⒻBonnieMs-G2	**89**	4	52½	53½	62¾	2hd	11½	Romero R P	114	*1.90	75-33	BansheeBreeze1141½ Santri1142 CottonHouseBy1142½	Boxed, angled out	8
1Mar98-5GP	fst	7f	:222 :453 1:11 1:242	ⒻAlw 31000N2L	**96**	10	3	62½	3nk	13	18	Romero R P	120	*2.00	78-21	*BnsheeBreeze*1208 Chndelle1204¾ AppelingPrid1205	Much best, ridden out	10
8Feb98-4GP	fst	7f	:224 :462 1:121 1:251	ⒻMd Sp Wt 28k	**86**	11	7	72½	41¼	1½	12¾	Romero R P	120	6.40	74-21	*Banshee Breeze*1202¾ *Coral Sea*120hd *AddedGold*1205½	Outside rally,drew off	12
21Jun97-1CD	fst	5½f	:22 :454 :582 1:051	ⒻMd Sp Wt 42k	**45**	12	11	87½	710	511	79½	Peck B D	119	11.80	84-08	Lolabell1197½ Ghostpasser119no Puddlejump1191	No speed, never close	12

Bayakoa (Arg)

b. f. 1984, by Consultant's Bid (Bold Bidder)–Arlucea, by Good Manners

Lifetime record: 39 21 9 0 $2,817,524

Own.– Mr & Mrs F.E. Whitham
Br.– Haras Principal (Arg)
Tr.– Ronald McAnally

19Apr91-9OP	fst	1 1/16	:222 :451 1:093 1:411	4↑ⒻApple Blossom H-G2	4	5	56	54	69½	614½	Pincay L Jr	**L**	125	*.70	81-14	DegenerateGl1151¼Chron1212FttoScout1165	Four wide early	6
16Feb91-8SA	fst	1⅛	:462 1:101 1:351 1:482	4↑ⒻS Margarita H-G1	2	1	11½	1hd	22	22	Pincay L Jr	**LB**	126	*.80	86-12	Little Brianne1192Bayakoa1261¾A Wild Ride1192¼	Held 2nd	7
2Feb91-8SA	fst	1 1/16	:224 :462 1:104 1:413	4↑ⒻS Maria H-G1	3	1	1hd	2½	45	411	Pincay L Jr	**LB**	128	*.20	84-11	LittleBrianne1172LunElgnt1142½Somthngmrry1146½	Faltered	4
27Oct90-5Bel	fst	1⅛	:462 1:103 1:354 1:491	3↑ⒻBC Distaff-G1	4	2	2½	2hd	2½	16¾	Pincay L Jr		123	1.10	88-15	Bayakoa1236¾ColonialWaters1232½VlyMd119nk	Driving,clear	7
6Oct90-8Kee	fst	1⅛	:47 1:103 1:343 1:47	3↑ⒻSpinster-G1	7	2	2hd	12	13	13	Pincay L Jr	**LB**	123	*.80	99-11	Bayakoa1233Gorgeous1236Luthier's Launch123no	Ridden out	8
1Sep90-8Dmr	fst	1 1/16	:23 :462 1:10 1:403	3↑ⒻChula Vista H-G2	4	1	11	2hd	2hd	1no	Pincay L Jr	**LB**	127	*.40	98-02	Byakoa127noFantasticLook1134½FormdableLdy1121¾	Gamely	5
4Aug90-8Dmr	fst	1 1/16	:231 :463 1:10 1:402	3↑ San Diego H-G3	5	1	1½	1½	22½	22¼	Pincay L Jr	**LB**	122	*.50	97-05	QuietAmericn1152¼Byakoa1223½Bosphorus112½	Second best	6
16Jun90-8Hol	fst	1 1/16	:231 :462 1:10 1:411	3↑ⒻMilady H-G1	2	2	21½	21	2½	12¼	Pincay L Jr		127	*.10	94-08	Bayakoa1272¼Fantastic Look1137½Kelly1108	Ridden out	4
19May90-8Hol	fst	1	:223 :442 1:083 1:34	3↑ⒻHawthorne H-G2	5	4	3½	3½	11	14	Pincay L Jr		125	*.50	94-12	Bayakoa1254StormybutValid1193½FantasticLook1151¼	Wide	5
18Apr90-9OP	gd	1 1/16	:231 :463 1:103 1:402	4↑ⒻApple Blossom H-G2	1	1	12	12	1½	22¾	Pincay L Jr		126	*.10	97-21	Gorgeous1222¾Bayakoa12610½Affirmed Classic11210	Gamely	4
4Mar90-8SA	fst	1¼	:454 1:094 1:344 2:011	4↑ S Anita H-G1	3	3	55½	912	916	1029	Pincay L Jr		122	*1.90	59-18	Ruhlmann1211¾CriminlType119hdFlyingContinentl121½	Wide	10
18Feb90-8SA	sly	1⅛	:463 1:104 1:36 1:482	4↑ⒻS Margarita H-G1	4	2	1hd	12	13½	16	McCarron CJ		127	*.50	94-18	Byakoa1276Gorgeous1255Luthier's Launch1135	Easy winner	4
4Feb90-5SA	gd	1 1/16	:233 :473 1:113 1:43	4↑ⒻS Maria H-G1	2	1	1½	11½	14	13½	McCarron CJ		126	*.30	88-18	Bayakoa1263½Nikishka1172½Carita Tostada1124½	Much best	4
4Nov89-6GP	fst	1⅛	:462 1:111 1:353 1:472	3↑ⒻBC Distaff-G1	1	2	21	11½	12	11½	Pincay L Jr		123	*.70	107-01	Bayakoa1231½Gorgeous1192¼Open Mind1195	Driving	10
14Oct89-8Kee	fst	1⅛	:47 1:104 1:35 1:474	3↑ⒻSpinster-G1	4	1	13	16	17	111½	Pincay L Jr		123	*.40	95-21	Baykoa12311½GoodbyeHalo1231½SharpDance1193	Ridden out	6
24Sep89-8Bel	fst	1⅛	:47 1:112 1:36 1:482	3↑ⒻRuffian H-G1	2	1	11½	12	11½	13½	Pincay L Jr		125	*1.30	85-24	Bayakoa1253½Colonial Waters118nkOpen Mind1209	Driving	6
2Sep89-8Dmr	fst	1 1/16	:221 :451 1:094 1:414	3↑ⒻChula Vista H-G2	2	2	32	31	65¼	615	Pincay L Jr		127	*.70	76-11	Goodbye Halo1201¾Flying Julia1124½Kool Arrival1152¾		6
	Gave way early																	
15Jly89-8Hol	fst	1⅛	:463 1:102 1:343 1:471	3↑ⒻVanity H-G1	5	1	11½	11½	14	15	Pincay L Jr		125	*.70	101-11	Bayakoa1255FlyingJulia1123½GoodbyHlo122no	Rated on lead	6
17Jun89-9Hol	fst	1 1/16	:231 :46 1:101 1:42	3↑ⒻMilady H-G1	1	2	11½	11½	11½	11	Pincay L Jr		124	*.20	90-15	Bayakoa1241FlyingJulia1134½CaritTostd115½	Finished well	5
20May89-8Hol	fst	1	:223 :443 1:081 1:324	3↑ⒻHawthorne H-G2	5	1	1½	12½	13½	14½	Pincay L Jr		122	*.60	99-07	Bayakoa1224½Goodbye Halo1233½Behind the Scenes114½		5
	Clear throughout																	
19Apr89-9OP	fst	1 1/16	:23 :47 1:111 1:413	4↑ⒻApple Blossom H-G1	5	1	11½	11½	14	14	Pincay L Jr		120	1.10	93-22	Bayakoa1204Goodbye Halo1259Invited Guest1163	Wide	6
19Feb89-8SA	fst	1⅛	:461 1:102 1:351 1:482	4↑ⒻS Margarita Inv'l H-G1	7	2	12	13	14	12	Pincay L Jr		118	3.50	87-21	Bykoa1182GoodbyeHalo1255½NoReviw117½	Veered out start	7
28Jan89-8SA	fst	1 1/16	:23 :461 1:101 1:41	4↑ⒻS Maria H-G2	1	1	13½	12½	11½	2¾	Pincay L Jr		118	4.00	95-14	MissBrio119¾Byko1181½Annoconnr1224½	Broke through gate	7
5Jan89-8SA	sly	1	:222 :453 1:101 1:362	4↑ⒻAlw 55000	1	1	11¾	15	110	112	Pincay L Jr		117	*.60	86-17	Bayakoa11712Small Virtue118¾Oueee Bebe116nk	Easily	6
17Dec88-7Hol	gd	7f	:213 :44 1:09 1:22	3↑ⒻAlw 35000	1	5	11	11	12½	22	Gryder AT		117	3.80	92-17	Miss Brio1162Bayakoa1172¾Valdemosa1173½	No match	7
30Oct88-8SA	fm	1Ⓣ	:223 :46 1:093 1:344	3↑ⒻMidwick H 112k	8	2	11	11½	41½	1013¼	Gryder AT		116	8.50	87-13	Balbonella1162¾Choritzo1182½Davie's Lamb1181	Faltered	10
6Oct88-8SA	fm	1Ⓣ	:23 :461 1:101 1:343	3↑ⒻAlw 60000	9	1	11½	1½	21	23	Gryder AT		121	*1.40	98-00	Daloma1093Byko1213½MssAlto1161¼	Lugged out backstretch	10
5Sep88-5Dmr	fst	1	:222 :453 1:094 1:34	3↑Ⓕ[R]June Darling 49k	5	1	11½	12½	16	110	Gryder AT		117	8.00	96-12	Bayakoa11710QueenForbes115½CaritaTostd119¾	In hand late	8
6Aug88-8Dmr	fm	1 1/16Ⓣ	:232 :463 1:102 1:412	3↑Ⓕ[R]Osnitas H (Div 2) 64k	2	1	11½	1½	2hd	53¼	Gryder AT		117	6.10	90-09	Choritzo115nkMy Virginia Reel1201¾Fiara1201¼	Rank early	6
29May88-10Cby	fm	1Ⓣ	:23 :461 1:10 1:343	3↑ⒻLady Canterbry H 150k	11	1	13½	13	12½	66½	Velasquez J		115 b	*2.30	90-04	Balbonella1152Nature'sWay1162½Dv'sLmb118½	Flattened out	12
11May88-8Hol	fm	1Ⓣ	:231 :46 1:10 1:341	4↑ⒻAlw 46000	1	1	11½	11	12½	12¼	Pincay L Jr		117	3.20	93-07	Bayakoa1172¼Quadrada116hdNew Bride1143½	Hand ride	9
	Rank 7/8,vanned off due to heat prostration. Previously trained by Jorge Machado																	
1Nov87♦ Hipodromo(Arg)	my	*1LH	1:343	3↑ Gr Pr Palermo-G1 Stk20200						112	Lezcano M		111	*2.05		Bayakoa11112Laborioso118¾Speeding Light1186	Led throughout,clear 4f out,easily	11
10Oct87♦ San Isidro(Arg)	fm	*1ⓉLH	1:33	3↑ Gr Pr San Isidro-G1 Stk15100						21½	Lezcano M		110	4.70		Cautin1311½Bayakoa1105Gorbot1331½	Tracked leader,led 3f out,headed 1f out	9
23Aug87♦ Hipodromo(Arg)	fst	*1LH	1:344	ⒻPolla de Potrancas-G1 Stk22500						23	Riveiro R		123	34.10		Podeica1233Bayakoa1232Abloom123nk	Led to 2f out,second best;Previously trained by OL Finarelli	17
18Jly87♦ San Isidro(Arg)	fm	*1ⓉLH	1:371	ⒻGr Pr 1000 Guineas-G1 Stk23800						910¼	Riveiro R		123	6.10		Pero Yo Se1232½Fiara1233Ecumenica123¾	Tracked in 3rd,weakened 2f out	14
21Jun87♦ San Isidro(Arg)	fm	*7fⓉLH	1:232	ⒻPr Mas Valente Alw6000						14	Riveiro R		121	6.65		Bayakoa1214Pinuela1213Rumbilla121nk	Pressed pace,led 1½f out,drew clear	11
17May87♦ Hipodromo(Arg)	fst	*7½fLH	1:312	ⒻGr Pr Jorge de Atucha-G1 Stk22900						613¾	Riveiro R		121	6.05		Candila1216Fichada1211Matricule121¾	Led to 2f out,weakened	10
10Apr87♦ Hipodromo(Arg)	fst	*5fStr	:563	ⒻPr Mister Prieto Mdn4000						17	Riveiro R		121	*1.20		Bayakoa1217Cogotuda1212½Fulleria121nk	Wire to wire,drew clear in hand	8
15Feb87♦ Hipodromo(Arg)	fst	*5fStr	:584	ⒻPr Villares Mdn4800						22	Riveiro R		121	3.35		Scherezade1212Bayakoa121¾Mi Cachorra1214	Led to 1f out,dueled briefly,outfinished	11

Beautiful Pleasure

Own: Oxley John C

B. m. 6 (Mar)
Sire: Maudlin (Foolish Pleasure)
Dam: Beautiful Bid (Baldski)
Br: Farnsworth Farm (Fla)
Tr: Ward J T Jr

Life	25	10	5	2	$2,734,078	113	
2001	4	0	1	0	$87,500	104	
2000	7	3	2	0	$730,000	113	
	0	0	0	0	$0	-	
D.Fst	20	7	4	2	$2,022,268	112	
Wet(359)	5	3	1	0	$711,810	113	
Turf(318)	0	0	0	0	$0	-	
Dst(0)	0	0	0	0	$0	-	

6Oct01-8Bel	fst	1⅛	:47	1:111	1:36	1:491	3↑ⒻBeldame-G1	84	1	1hd	12½	2hd	510	615	Chavez J F	L123	4.30	69-21	Exogenous1201¼ Flute120hd Spain1234¾	Drifted out turn	8
24Aug01-8Sar	fst	1¼	:49	1:132	1:382	2:043	3↑ⒻPrsnlEnH-G1	104	1	12½	12	1½	21	21¼	Chavez J F	L117	*2.20	81-21	Pompeii1171¼ BeautifulPleasure1172½ IrvingsBby1171	Drifted out stretch	7
29Jly01-9Sar	fst	1⅛	:464	1:103	1:362	1:493	3↑ⒻGoFWandH-G1	90	6	17	112	110	32	57¼	Chavez J F	L118	*1.30e	86-12	Serra Lake1131¾ *Pompeii*1141¾ March Magic1142¼	Long lead, tired	8
23Jun01-8Bel	fst	1 1/16	:231	:46	1:101	1:42	3↑ⒻHmpstedH-G1	92	6	11½	1½	1½	62¼	77	Chavez J F	L120	*.80e	80-23	Critical Eye115nk Jostle117¾ Apple of Kent1172½	Drifted out stretch	7
4Nov00-3CD	fst	1⅛	:461	1:102	1:344	1:473	3↑ⒻBCDistaf-G1	95	9	22½	33½	21	56½	68	Chavez J F	L123	5.10	90 -	Spain1201½ *Surfside*1201½ *Heritage of Gold*123¾	Drifted turn, tired	9
14Oct00-8Bel	fst	1⅛	:46	1:091	1:331	1:46	3↑ⒻBeldame-G1	112	5	14½	15	12	22	22	Chavez J F	L123	1.50	99-09	Riboletta1232 BeautifulPlesure12314½ Penttonic1232¼	Drifted out stretch	5
25Aug00-8Sar	fst	1¼	:483	1:122	1:371	2:033	3↑ⒻPrsnlEnH-G1	103	2	14½	15	12½	11½	15	Chavez J F	L124	*.90	87-22	BeutifulPlesure1245 [D]BckinShpe114nk HeritgofGold124¾	Drifted stretch	5
30Jly00-8Sar	sly	1⅛	:47	1:11	1:363	1:494	3↑ⒻGoFWandH-G1	105	5	12½	17	15½	1hd	21	Chavez J F	L125	*.35	91-08	HeritageofGold1231 *BeutifulPlesure*1256 RozRobt114½	Pace, clear, gamely	5
24Jun00-8Bel	fst	1 1/16	:23	:453	1:093	1:412	3↑ⒻHmpstedH-G1	109	5	12½	15	16	17	17¼	Chavez J F	L124	*.25	90-16	BeautifulPlesure1247¼ Penttonic1121 RozRobt1153¾	On her own courage	6
20May00-8Bel	sly	1	:232	:462	1:102	1:353	3↑ⒻShuveeH-G2	113	3	12½	14½	12½	14½	16¾	Chavez J F	L122	*.25	87-28	*BeutifulPlesure*1226¾ *BiogiosRose*115no UpWeGo1148¼	Complete authority	5
9Apr00-9OP	fst	1 1/16	:234	:473	1:114	1:421	4↑ⒻAplBlsmH-G1	100	3	68½	68½	66	64	53¾	Chavez J F	L121	*.80	89-25	*Heritage of Gold*1181 *Lu Ravi*1141 Bordelaise113½	Rank early,traffic 1/4	7
6Nov99-3GP	fst	1⅛	:462	1:094	1:343	1:472	3↑ⒻBCDistaf-G1	109	5	2hd	11½	13	11	1¾	Chavez J F	L123	3.00	100 -	BeutifulPlesure123¾ BnsheBrz1231¼ *HritgofGold*1231¼	Drifted late, driving	8
10Oct99-5Bel	sly	1⅛	:453	1:091	1:341	1:473	3↑ⒻBeldame-G1	113	1	13	15	13½	12	14¾	Chavez J F	L123	2.40	93-23	*BeautifulPleasure*1234¾ Silverbulletdy1196 Ctinc1237¾	Strong pace off rail	5
27Aug99-8Sar	sly	1¼	:47	1:103	1:351	2:022	3↑ⒻPrsnlEnH-G1	112	4	15	14½	15	13½	12¼	Chavez J F	L113	4.70	96-20	*BeutifulPlesure*1132¼ BnsheeBreeze1241½ KprHill1182¼	Soon clear, driving	6
7Aug99-8Sar	fst	1⅛	:48	1:112	1:363	1:494	3↑ⒻGoFWandH-G1	108	4	1½	11½	11	2hd	2½	Chavez J F	L113	3.45	86-16	BnsheeBreez124½ *ButifulPlsur*1138¾ *HritgofGold*1172	Speed off rail,gamely	5
19Jun99-8Bel	fst	1 1/16	:231	:461	1:094	1:403	3↑ⒻHmpstedH-G1	111	4	32½	31	2hd	2½	2½	Chavez J F	L112	4.20	93-06	Sister Act117½ Beautiful Pleasure1129¼ Catinca1224¾	Drifted late, gamely	6
22May99-8Bel	fst	1	:223	:45	1:09	1:341	3↑ⒻShuveeH-G2	103	3	2½	21½	2hd	41¾	43¾	Chavez J F	L113	3.40	89-13	Catinca121½ *Sister Act*1171½ Tap to Music1151¾	Speed in hand,weakened	6
23Apr99-7Kee	fst	7f	:222	:442	1:083	1:211	4↑ⒻAlw 48054N$Y	104	1	4	1½	1½	12½	15½	Chavez J F	L115	*.70	96-03	BeautifulPleasure1155½ MyWildRose1182 Qunh120hd	Duck in start,drifted	4
14Nov98-8CD	fst	1	:223	:452	1:093	1:342	3↑ⒻCDDstafH-G2	110	3	96¼	75	52¾	31	33	Chavez J F	L110	3.70	98-11	DremScheme1131½ *SisterAct*1111½ *ButifulPlsur*1108¾	Sluggish start,no gain	9
16Oct98-5Kee	fst	*7f	:223	:453	1:103	1:252	3↑ⒻAlw 39980N2X	93	3	7	52¼	41¾	1hd	16	Chavez J F	L110	*1.00	102-06	BeautifulPlesure1106 CuntoEs115½ Antoniette1132	Lacked room 1/4 pole	11
9Apr98-7Kee	gd	7f	:222	:45	1:102	1:234	ⒻAlw 46460N2X	72	6	3	31	32	55	410	Day P	L119	*1.40	76-15	Flashstorm1192 Aunt Anne1194 Tricky Move1194	Pressed pace, tired	6
8Nov97-2Hol	fst	1 1/16	:224	:46	1:103	1:42	ⒻBCJuvFil-G1	58	13	119¾	65½	52	57½	1020¾	Bailey J D	LB119	7.60	70-06	Countess Diana1198½ Career Collection1194 Primaly1192	Bid 4w, empty	14
11Oct97-8Kee	fst	1 1/16	:23	:454	1:092	1:451	ⒻAlcibiad-G2	80	2	21½	2½	21	23½	32¾	Bailey J D	L118	*.50	79-24	*CountssDin*1182¾ LilyOGold118hd ButifulPlsur118¾	Takn bck angld out trd	6
21Sep97-7Bel	fst	1	:224	:454	1:094	1:353	ⒻMatron-G1	98	2	11	11½	11½	16	14½	Bailey J D	L119	*1.05	86-12	ButfulPlsur1194½ DmondOnthRn1191¾ Crrll11912½	Dictated pce,riddn out	11
25Aug97-4Sar	fst	6½f	:221	:454	1:103	1:172	ⒻMd Sp Wt 34k	89	8	2	3nk	12½	16	15	Bailey J D	L118	*1.10	90-13	*ButfulPlsr*1185 TffyDvnport11810 TllofStrfford1182¾	Drew off, ridden out	8

Bertrando

dkbbr. c. 1989, by Skywalker (Relaunch)–Gentle Hands, by Buffalo Lark

Lifetime record: 24 9 6 2 $3,185,610

Own.– 505 Farms & Nahem
Br.– Ed Nahem (Cal)
Tr.– John Shirreffs

14Jan95-5SA	gd 7f	:221	:442	1:083	1:212	4↑ San Carlos H-G2	92	3	3	1½	32	52¾	65	Stevens GL	LB	120	b	5.70	90-12	Softshoe Sure Shot114½Ferrara115½Subtle Trouble115nk	Rail,gave way	7
2Jan95-8SA	fm 1⅛Ⓣ	:47	1:12	1:364	1:491	4↑ San Gabriel H-G2	82	2	2	21½	21½	44½	69¾	Romero RP	LB	120	b	5.40	63-27	Romarin1191¼Inner City1161Ianomami1161	Stalked,gave way	6
26Nov94-8Aqu	fst 1	:223	:454	1:111	1:36	3↑ NYRA Mile-G1	69	3	1	2½	95½	1018	1024¾	Stevens GL		121	b	5.00	63-28	Cigar1117Devil His Due1242½Punch Line1121	Dueled,tired	12
5Nov94-10CD	fst 1¼	:463	1:111	1:363	2:022	3↑ B C Classic-G1	104	12	1	12	3½	53½	67¼	Stevens GL	L	126	b	8.80	93-07	Concern122nkTabascoCat1221½DramtcGold1221½	Tired,inside	14
15Oct94-5SA	fst 1⅛	:453	1:10	1:341	1:463	3↑ Goodwood H-G2	113	3	1	13½	11½	3nk	1nk	Stevens GL	LB	120	b	3.70	100-13	Bertrando120nkDramaticGold1151Tossofthecoin1157½	Rail,brushed 1/16,came back	6
17Sep94-8Bel	fst 1⅛	:462	1:102	1:343	1:464	3↑ Woodward-G1	96	7	1	11	2½	56¼	512	Valenzuela PA		126	b	23.50	85-10	HolyBull1215DevilHisDue1261½ColonialAffair1263½	Used up	8
13Aug94-4Dmr	fst 1¼	:442	1:083	1:334	1:592	3↑ Pacific Classic-G1	60	3	1	1½	77½	817	834	Valnzuela PA	LB	124	b	*2.40	66-10	TinnersWy1241BstPl1244½DrmtcGold1175½	Rail,dueled,tired	9
28Jly94-8Dmr	fm 1Ⓣ	:23	:47	1:11	1:361	3↑ [R]Wickerr 66k	103	4	1	11½	12	11½	11¼	Valnzuela PA	LB	121	b	*1.50	89-11	Bertrando1211¼Bon Point116noDaros114½	Gamely	6
	Previously trained by Robert Frankel																					
6Nov93-8SA	fst 1¼	:464	1:111	1:36	2:004	3↑ B C Classic-G1	111	7	1	11½	11	11½	22	Stevens GL	LB	126	b	*1.20e	89-10	Arcangues1262Bertrando1261¾Kissin Kris1221¼	Second best	13
18Sep93-8Bel	sly 1⅛	:453	1:094	1:342	1:47	3↑ Woodward-G1	125	4	1	15	12½	17	113½	Stevens GL		126	b	*.90e	94-15	Bertrando12613DevilHisDu1263VllyCrossng126hd	Ridden out	6
21Aug93-3Dmr	fst 1¼	:46	1:094	1:341	1:592	3↑ Pacific Classic-G1	117	1	1	11½	1½	11½	13	Stevens GL	LB	124	b	3.10e	100-00	Bertrando1243MissionaryRidg124¾BstPl1242	Inside,driving	7
24Jly93-11Mth	fst 1⅛	:462	1:103	1:354	1:491	3↑ Iselin H-G1	109	2	1	11½	1½	3½	32½	Solis A	L	119	b	*.90	86-15	ValleyCrossing113hdDevilHisDue1232¼Bertrando1198	Tired	8
3Jly93-3Hol	fst 1¼	:462	1:101	1:35	2:00	3↑ Hol Gold Cup H-G1	113	2	1	11½	11	2½	22½	Solis A	LB	118	b	3.50e	94-05	Best Pal1212½Bertrando1185½Major Impact114nk	Good try	10
31May93-9Bel	fst 1	:221	:441	1:083	1:341	3↑ Metropolitan H-G1	110	7	1	1½	1hd	1hd	21½	Stevens GL		121	b	4.00	95-03	Ibero1191½Bertrando121nkAlydeed1242½	Gamely	9
6Mar93-5SA	fst 1¼	:471	1:11	1:351	2:002	4↑ S Anita H-G1	98	4	1	11	1hd	31½	99¾	McCarron CJ	LB	120	b	2.40e	83-13	SirBufort119noStrRcrut117hdMjorImpct1141¾	Brushed start	11
7Feb93-8SA	fst 1¼	:472	1:114	1:354	2:003	C H Strub-G1	112	1	1	11½	11	1½	21¼	McCarron CJ	LB	122	b	*.30	91-11	SiberianSummr1181¼Brtrndo1222MjorImpct1183	Outfinished	8
16Jan93-8SA	sly 1⅛	:46	1:103	1:364	1:511	San Fernando-G2	109	3	1	11	11½	16	19	McCarron CJ	L	120	b	*1.50e	77-30	Bertrndo1209StarRecruit120¾TheWckdNorth1164	Coasted in	8
26Dec92-8SA	fst 7f	:222	:45	1:081	1:203	Malibu-G2	102	7	1	11	1hd	2hd	3¾	McCarron CJ	LB	120	b	*1.40e	98-09	StaroftheCrop118½TheWckdNrth116nkBrtrndo1205½	Game try	11
	Previously owned by 505 Farms, Headley & Nahem; previously trained by Bruce Headley																					
4Apr92-5SA	fst 1⅛	:461	1:102	1:361	1:491	S Anita Derby-G1	92	1	1	11	11	1½	21¾	Solis A	B	122	b	1.10	82-11	A.P. Indy1221¾Bertrando122nkCasual Lies1223½	Held 2nd	7
15Mar92-8SA	fst 1 1/16	:222	:454	1:101	1:423	San Felipe-G2	97	4	1	1hd	1hd	12½	1¾	Solis A	B	122	b	*.40	90-13	Bertrando122¾Arp1161¾Hickman Creek1161½	Hard drive	6
2Nov91-6CD	fst 1 1/16	:231	:463	1:12	1:443	©B C Juvenile-G1	-	5	1	11½	1hd	25	25	Solis A	B	122	b	2.50	87-09	Arazi1224¾Bertrando1223½Snappy Landing122hd	2nd best	14
13Oct91-8SA	fst 1 1/16	:221	:454	1:102	1:424	Norfolk-G1	-	3	1	11½	11½	14	19	Solis A	B	118	b	*1.50e	89-16	Bertrando1189Zurich118¾Bag118¾	Ridden out	9
	Previously owned by G. Headley																					
11Sep91-8Dmr	fst 1	:214	:45	1:102	1:362	Dmr Futurity-G2	-	4	1	11	11	14	13½	Solis A	B	114	b	8.70	84-18	Bertrando1143½Zurich1144½Star Recruit1152	All out	10
25Aug91-9Dmr	fst 6f	:214	:444	:571	1:101	[S]Md Sp Wt	-	3	3	1½	2hd	1½	12	Solis A	B	117	b	4.00	88-12	Bertrando1172Ebonair1171Simple King1124½	All out	11

Best Pal

b. g. 1988, by Habitony (Habitat)–Ubetshedid, by King Pellinore **Lifetime record: 47 18 11 4 $5,668,245**
Own.– Golden Eagle Farm
Br.– Mr & Mrs John C. Mabee (Cal)
Tr.– Richard Mandella

15Jan96- 8SA fst 1 1/16 :232 :472 1:11 1:413 4↑ San Pasqual H-G2 **84** 5 6 84½ 84½ 87½ 813½ McCarron CJ **LB** 120 2.20 73-16 Alphabet Soup1181¾Luthier Fever1152Cezind1144½ No rally 9
11Nov95- 8SA fst 1⅛ :46 1:102 1:352 1:483 3↑ Ⓢ Cal Cup Classic H 250k **104** 5 6 75¾ 42¾ 22 21¼ McCarron CJ **L** 124 *.80 89-17 LuthierFever1181¼BestPl1242SemiMaar116nk Closed gamely 10
18Oct95- 7SA fst 1 :231 :462 1:10 1:351 3↑ Skywalker 65k **103** 2 4 43 42¼ 41¾ 11 McCarron CJ **L** 120 *1.10 93-16 BstPl1201GeengerMan114¾SlewofDmscus1203½ Determinedly 6
2Jly95- 6Hol fst 1¼ :453 1:092 1:34 1:592 3↑ Hol Gold Cup H-G1 **107** 6 7 712 58 67¾ 57 McCarron CJ **L** 120 8.30 96-04 Cigar1263½TinnersWay118hdTossofthecon118½ Mild late bid 8
11Jun95- 6Hol fst 1⅛ :464 1:103 1:351 1:473 3↑ Californian-G1 **101** 3 6 66¼ 64¼ 42¼ 44¼ McCarron CJ **L** 120 *1.50 91-08 Concern1222¾Tossofthcon118½TnnrsWy1161 4 wide into lane 8
15Apr95- 9OP fst 1⅛ :462 1:104 1:352 1:471 4↑ Oaklawn H-G1 **108** 1 5 57½ 53½ 43½ 47½ McCarron CJ **L** 121 4.00 95-13 Cigar1202½Silver Goblin1194Concern1221 Middle move 7
11Mar95- 5SA wf 1¼ :45 1:091 1:334 1:591 4↑ S Anita H-G1 **113** 10 9 915 66 42½ 2hd McCarron CJ **L** 122 *1.50e 99-12 UrgentRequest116hdBstPl1221DareandGo120hd Strong rally 10
12Feb95- 8SA fst 1⅛ :451 1:093 1:343 1:472 4↑ San Antonio H-G2 **111** 3 7 79 21 11 13 McCarron CJ **L** 121 *1.80 96-12 Best Pal1213Slew of Damascus119½Tossofthecoin1171¾ 10
Big inside move
22Jan95- 8SA fst 1 1/16 :232 :471 1:103 1:411 4↑ San Pasqual H-G2 **102** 5 4 55 44 44 43¼ McCarron CJ **L** 122 *.90 86-15 DelMarDennis1182Slew ofDamascus1201¼Tossofthecoin117no 6
Wide trip
4Dec94- 9Hol fst 1⅛ :462 1:102 1:353 1:482 3↑ Native Diver H-G3 **110** 6 7 74¼ 73¼ 1½ 14 McCarron CJ **L** 121 *1.50 92-10 BstPl1214Tossofthcon1173½RoylChrot1142½ 5 wide 2nd turn 7
5Nov94-10CD fst 1¼ :463 1:111 1:363 2:022 3↑ BC Classic-G1 **110** 6 6 75 83¾ 65 53¼ McCarron CJ **L** 126 5.80e 97-07 Concern122nkTabasco Cat1221½Dramatic Gold1221½ 14
7-wide stretch,no threat
24Sep94- 9TP my 1⅛ :492 1:133 1:374 1:501 3↑ Ky Cup Classic 376k **97** 4 4 41¾ 31 46 33½ McCarron CJ **L** 115 *1.30 78-20 Tabasco Cat1202Mighty Avanti1151½Best Pal1151½ 6
Checked ¼ pole,no late response
13Aug94- 4Dmr fst 1¼ :442 1:083 1:334 1:592 3↑ Pacific Classic-G1 **109** 7 7 810 4½ 2hd 21 McCarron CJ **L** 124 3.90e 99-10 TinnersWay1241BestPl1244½DrmtcGold1175½ 4 wide 2nd turn 9
22Jly94- 3Hol fst 7f :221 :444 1:09 1:211 3↑ Ⓢ Answer Do 61k **102** 2 4 510 59½ 53¼ 12¾ Desormx KJ **LB** 117 *.40e 98-10 BstPl1172¾Marmoe117¾YearsofDrmng1215 Strong hand ride 5
Previously trained by Gary Jones
13Feb94- 8SA fst 1⅛ :464 1:103 1:35 1:472 4↑ San Antonio H-G2 **98** 7 9 87¼ 72¾ 66½ 710¼ Black CA **LB** 121 *1.80 86-14 TheWickedNorth1164½ⒹHillPass116½Region1174½ Raced wide 9
22Jan94- 8SA fst 1 1/16 :231 :47 1:11 1:41 4↑ San Pasqual H-G2 **102** 1 6 75 64 41¼ 21¾ Black CA **LB** 122 2.40 88-12 HillPass1151¾BestPl122¾LottryWnnr116hd 5 wide into lane 7
6Nov93- 8SA fst 1¼ :464 1:111 1:36 2:004 3↑ BC Classic-G1 **98** 4 4 43½ 63½ 98¼ 1010½ Black CA **LB** 126 1.80 80-10 Arcangus1262Brtrndo1261¾KssnKrs1221¼ Drifted out,tiring 13
16Oct93- 8SA fst 1⅛ :451 1:092 1:344 1:48 3↑ Ⓢ Cal Cup Classic H 250k **102** 1 5 512 55¼ 1½ 13½ Black CA **LB** 126 *.30 93-10 Best Pal1263½Native Boundary1161¼Goldigger's Dream1071¼ 7
Wide,handily
21Aug93- 3Dmr fst 1¼ :46 1:094 1:341 1:592 3↑ Pacific Classic-G1 **111** 7 6 42 2½ 21½ 33¾ Black CA **LB** 124 *.40 96-00 Bertrando1243MissionaryRidg124¾BstPl1242 Weakened a bit 7
3Jly93- 3Hol fst 1¼ :462 1:101 1:35 2:00 3↑ Hol Gold Cup H-G1 **117** 5 5 54½ 21 1½ 12½ Black CA **LB** 121 *1.10 97-05 Best Pal1212½Bertrando1185½Major Impact114nk Driving 10
31May93- 8Hol fm 1¼Ⓣ :474 1:112 1:343 1:573 3↑ Hol Turf H-G1 **100** 6 5 32½ 21 32½ 23½ Black CA **LB** 122 7.40 102-00 Bien Bien1193½Best Pal122nkLeger Cat116hd Game for 2nd 8
10Apr93- 8OP fst 1⅛ :464 1:102 1:353 1:483 4↑ Oaklawn H-G1 **107** 2 7 812 710 65 32½ Desormx KJ **L** 123 2.80 90-19 Jovial1171¼LilE.Tee1231¼BestPl1231¼ Lost footing,4 wide 10
6Mar93- 5SA fst 1¼ :471 1:11 1:351 2:002 4↑ S Anita H-G1 **105** 1 8 76½ 73¾ 74¾ 55 Desormx KJ **LB** 124 *1.40 88-13 Sir Beaufort119noStar Recruit117hdMajor Impact1141¾ 11
Wide,climbing,lost shoe
24Jan93- 8SA fst 1 1/16 :234 :47 1:11 1:414 4↑ San Pasqual H-G2 **102** 3 3 33½ 3½ 1hd 22¾ Desormx KJ **LB** 124 *1.00 92-15 Jovl1152¾ⒹBstPl124½Mrqutry118hd Came out,impeded foe ⅝ 7
Disqualified and placed fifth
9May92-10Pim fst 1 3/16 :473 1:112 1:354 1:544 4↑ Pim Spl H-G1 **104** 7 3 31½ 31 22 44¼ Desormx KJ **L** 126 *.60 84-23 StriketheGold114¾FlySoFree1161¼TwlghtAgnd1222¼ Gave way 7
11Apr92- 8OP fst 1⅛ :46 1:094 1:351 1:48 4↑ Oaklawn H-G1 **121** 6 5 55 53¼ 1½ 11½ Desormx KJ **L** 125 *.70 96-20 BestPal1251½SeaCadet120½TwilightAgenda1234 4 wide⅜ 7
7Mar92- 5SA fst 1¼ :46 1:094 1:34 1:59 4↑ S Anita H-G1 **123** 4 5 53¼ 1½ 13 15½ Desormx KJ **LB** 124 *1.70 99-10 Best Pal1245½Twilight Agenda1242¼Defensive Play1153 7
Wide,ridden out
9Feb92- 8SA fst 1¼ :463 1:102 1:35 1:594 C H Strub-G1 **119** 5 3 31 1hd 11½ 11¼ Desormx KJ **LB** 124 *1.20 95-11 Best Pal1241¼Dinard1208Reign Road118¾ Wide,ridden out 8
Four wide backstretch,steadied near 3/8 pole
18Jan92- 8SA fst 1⅛ :47 1:111 1:353 1:481 San Fernando-G2 **121** 4 7 73¾ 4¾ 1½ 13½ Desormx KJ **LB** 122 2.80 89-21 Best Pal1223½Olympio1225½Dinard120½ Wide,ridden out 9
30Nov91- 8Hol fm 1⅛Ⓣ :472 1:111 1:342 1:454 3↑ Citation H (Div 2)-G2 - 5 3 32 42 52¼ 21¾ Desormx KJ **LB** 119 4.80 99-07 Fly Till Dawn1191¾Best Pal119nkWolf1191 Wide trip 8
9Nov91- 8SA fst 1⅛ :471 1:103 1:354 1:49 3↑ Ⓢ Cal Cup Classic H 250k - 2 3 31 2hd 1hd 2hd Valenzuela PA **L** 124 *.40 85-18 Charmonnier112hdBstPl1247ElgntBrgn1172¾ Carried out ¼ 10
22Sep91-10LaD fst 1¼ :462 1:11 1:36 2:004 Super Derby-G1 - 4 3 311 32½ 44 46½ Valenzuela PA **L** 126 *.90 99-02 Free Spirit's Joy1262½Olympio1261Zeeruler1263 Bumped 7
10Aug91- 3Dmr fst 1¼ :454 1:094 1:341 1:594 3↑ Pacific Classic 1000k - 6 5 64 32 22½ 11 Valenzla PA **LB** 116 4.90 -- BstPl1161TwlghtAgnd1242¾Unbrdld1241¼ Wide backstretch 8
7Jly91- 8Hol fst 1¼ :462 1:103 1:353 2:003 Swaps-G2 - 4 3 21½ 21 2hd 14 Valenzla PA **LB** 116 *1.40 94-05 BestPl1164CorportRport114¾ComplngSound1237 Ridden out 4
Previously trained by Ian Jory
16Jun91- 8Hol fst 1⅛ :47 1:103 1:344 1:474 Silver Screen H-G3 - 1 2 21½ 2½ 11½ 2nk Valenzla PA **LB** 123 *.90 95-07 Compelling Sound118nkBest Pal1233½Caliche's Secret1175 5
Edged for win
18May91-10Pim fst 1 3/16 :461 1:101 1:35 1:54 Preakness-G1 - 5 6 54 32½ 35 511 Stevens GL **L** 126 2.70 84-14 Hansl1267CorporateRport1262¾MnMnstr126½ Bid wide,tired 8
4May91- 8CD fst 1¼ :462 1:111 1:372 2:03 Ky Derby-G1 - 15 10 87 72¾ 52½ 21¾ Stevens GL **LB** 126 5.20 93-04 Strike the Gold1261¾Best Pal1261¼Mane Minister126hd 16
Saved ground,2nd best
6Apr91- 5SA fst 1⅛ :462 1:101 1:351 1:48 S Anita Derby-G1 - 5 5 53¾ 41¾ 1½ 2½ Stevens GL **LB** 122 *1.60 89-11 Dinard122½Best Pal1221¾Sea Cadet1222 Wide backstretch 9
3Mar91- 8SA gd 1 :231 :47 1:104 1:354 San Rafael-G2 - 2 3 33½ 2hd 2hd 3½ Stevens GL **LB** 121 2.30 87-13 Dinard118hdApollo118½Best Pal1218 Saved ground 5
9Dec90- 8Hol fst 1 :22 :443 1:094 1:352 Hol Futurity-G1 - 7 8 73¾ 42 1½ 11 Santos JA **LB** 121 *1.10e 87-20 BestPal1211GeneralMeeting121hdReignRoad1215 Wide trip 9
27Oct90- 7Bel fst 1 1/16 :23 :46 1:103 1:432 ©BC Juvenile-G1 - 9 4 62½ 3½ 44½ 65¾ Valenzuela PA 122 1.80 79-15 FlySoFree1223TakMeOut1222LstMountn122hd Bobbled start 11
7Oct90- 8SA fst 1 1/16 :223 :461 1:102 1:424 Norfolk-G1 - 7 2 21 2½ 13 14½ Valnzuela PA **LB** 118 *.50e 89-12 Best Pal1184½Pillaring1181¼Formal Dinner1182 Much best 12
12Sep90- 8Dmr fst 1 :223 :461 1:101 1:352 Dmr Futurity-G2 - 9 2 21 1½ 12 13½ Valnzuela PA **LB** 120 *1.10e 89-14 Best Pal1203½Pillaring116hdGot to Fly1176 Came in early 11
22Aug90- 8Dmr fst 7f :22 :443 1:093 1:221 Balboa-G3 - 4 2 32½ 32½ 11 12 Valnzuela PA **LB** 119 1.60 90-11 Best Pal1192Xray1172¾Sunshine Machine1174½ Driving 7
27Jly90- 8Dmr fst 6f :22 :451 :571 1:09 Ⓢ I'm Smokin 50k - 5 2 21 1hd 13 17 Valnzuela PA **L** 118 *.50 95-11 BestPal1187JustasSwift118hdWarfarePrinc1131¼ Ridden out 5
23Jun90- 8GG fst 5½f :21 :44 :561 1:023 Ladbroke Futurity 100k - 7 6 75¾ 76 35 22½ Hansen RD 117 4.90 97-09 Broadway'sTopGun1202½BestPal1172½Sunshine Machine1173 10
Closed well
18May90- 4Hol fst 5f :214 :45 :573 Md Sp Wt - 5 4 32 31½ 21½ 1½ Valenzuela PA 117 4.80 94-07 Best Pal117½Barrage1177Just as Swift1172½ Driving 10

Black Tie Affair (Ire)

gr. c. 1986, by Miswaki (Mr. Prospector)–Hat Tab Girl, by Al Hattab **Lifetime record: 45 18 9 6 $3,370,694**
Own.– Jeffrey Sullivan
Br.– Stephen D. Peskoff (Ire)
Tr.– Ernie T. Poulos

2Nov91- 8CD fst 1¼ :482 1:123 1:38 2:024 3↑ BC Classic-G1 8 1 11½ 11 11 11¼ Bailey JD **LB** 126 b 4.00 96-09 Black Tie Affair1261¼Twilight Agenda1262½Unbridled126nk 11
Well rated
14Sep91- 8AP sly 1⅛ :463 1:104 1:362 1:492 3↑ Wash Park H-G2 3 1 11 12 13½ 17½ Sellers SJ **LB** 120 b 1.50 87-31 BlackTieAffar1207½SummrSqull11918½ScrtHllo11425 Driving 4
1Sep91-11Mth fst 1⅛ :462 1:102 1:351 1:474 3↑ Iselin H-G1 7 1 1½ 1½ 1hd 1nk Day P **LB** 119 b 4.10 99-03 BlckTieAffr119nkFarmaWy122½ChfHoncho1153¼ Game score 8
11Aug91- 9Aks fst 1⅛ :464 1:103 1:353 1:483 3↑ Cornhusker H-G3 1 1 1½ 11 12 13½ Day P **LB** 124 b *.30 102-10 Black Tie Affair1243½Bedeviled1174Whodam1135 Driving 5
13Jly91- 9Det fst 1⅛ :474 1:12 1:372 1:494 3↑ Mich Mile H-G2 4 1 11 11 11½ 12½ Day P **LB** 122 b *.60 95-16 Black Tie Affair1222½Whiz Along1102Solo Matt113¾ 11
Confidently ridden
22Jun91- 9CD fst 1⅛ :474 1:114 1:362 1:494 3↑ Stephen Foster H-G3 5 1 11 11 12½ 12¾ Diaz JL **LB** 119 b *1.20 99-06 BlackTieAffar1192¾PrvtSchool111noGrydr1153 In hand late 5
27May91- 8Bel fst 1 :22 :441 1:091 1:352 3↑ Metropolitan H-G1 9 2 42 66 99¾ 911 Diaz JL 122 b 14.70 82-16 In Excess1172¼Rubiano1111¾Gervazy1141½ Done early 14
4May91- 8Aqu fst 7f :224 :452 1:084 1:211 3↑ Carter H-G1 2 1 2½ 31½ 23 22¼ Diaz JL 123 b 7.10 94-17 Housebuster1222¼BlackTiAffr1232½Grvzy116no Saved ground 8
12Apr91- 8Kee fst 7f :222 :452 1:09 1:214 3↑ Commonwealth BC-G3 6 2 21½ 21½ 2½ 11 Diaz JL **LB** 124 b 7.10 101-12 BlackTieAffair1241Housebustr1244ExmplryLdr115hd Driving 6

23Mar91- 9OP fst 1 1/16 :233 :472 1:112 1:424 4↑ Razorback H-G2 3 2 21 2hd 1hd 32¼ Diaz JL LB 118 8.80 88-11 Bedeviled1152Din'sDancer117nkBlackTieAffair118hd Gamely 7
24Nov90- 8Haw fst 1¼ :474 1:122 1:374 2:032 3↑ Bud Gold Cup H-G2 5 1 1½ 1½ 11½ 11½ Diaz JL LB 116 b 8.30 84-30 BlackTieAffair1161½MiSelecto115¾SilverTowr1126½ Driving 10
27Oct90- 3Bel fst 6f :214 :442 1:093 3↑ BC Sprint-G1 11 6 89½ 58 47½ 34¼ Pincay L Jr 126 b 53.20 87-11 SafelyKept123nkDayjur1234BlckTAffr1262¼ Wide,mild rally 14
21Sep90- 10LaD fst 7f :222 :45 1:093 1:222 3↑ Island Whirl H 100k 3 4 21½ 32½ 32½ 21½ Velasquez J L 120 b *.80 96-14 Potentiality1131½Black Tie Affair1201Ankles1131 Gamely 8
25Aug90- 9AP fst 1 :221 :444 1:092 1:36 3↑ Equipoise Mile H-G3 3 2 21½ 1hd 11½ 13½ Velasquez J L 119 b *.30 91-16 Black Tie Affair1193½Bio1128New Plymouth1103 Driving 4
11Aug90- 7AP sly 1 :232 :462 1:111 1:354 3↑ Handicap 28000 4 2 1hd 1½ 13 17½ Velasquez J L 121 b *.70 92-18 Black Tie Affair1217½Bio113¾Old Stories112½ Ridden out 6
21Jly90- 10LaD fst 6f :213 :441 1:10 3↑ Bud BC 139k 7 3 64½ 47 45 31¾ Guidry M L 120 b *1.00 95-08 Glitterman118½SilentReflex1161¼BlackTiAffr120nk Rallied 8
17Jun90- 8AP fst 7f :221 :442 1:083 1:211 3↑ Isaac Murphy H 48k 1 4 1hd 2hd 21¼ 24¼ Guidry M 119 b 1.60 100-10 BeauGenius1214¼BlackTieAffr1193Trtmtr1132 Saved ground 5
28May90- 8Bel fst 1 :223 :45 1:091 1:342 3↑ Metropolitan H-G1 9 2 32½ 33 56 610½ Guidry M 117 b 132.90 86-18 Criminal Type120nkHousebuster1131½Easy Goer1273 Tired 9
5May90- 8Aqu my 7f :212 :434 1:091 1:22 3↑ Carter H-G1 2 3 49 66¾ 63 47¾ Guidry M 119 b 11.10 84-17 DancngSpree1232DncngPrtns115hdSwckly1195¾ Lacked rally 7
12Apr90- 8Kee fst 7f :231 :452 1:083 1:22 3↑ Commonwealth BC-G3 5 1 2hd 2hd 1hd 1hd Guidry M 121 b 32.10 99-09 BlackTieAffair121hdShakerKnit1152Momsfurrr118nk Driving 9
24Mar90- 8Spt fst 6f :232 :462 :582 1:111 4↑ J R Johnston Mem 53k 1 1 24 34½ 24 26 Guidry M 124 b 1.50 91-17 DeeLance1246BlackTieAffair124½Brett'sLick1242 2nd best 7
4Nov89- 4GP fst 6f :214 :44 1:09 3↑ BC Sprint-G1 7 9 1112 915 914 913¼ Razo E Jr 124 b 74.60 88-04 Dancing Spree126nkSafely Kept121nkDispersal1241 13
Bumped after start
16Sep89- 9AP fst 1 :232 :461 1:103 1:354 Sheridan-G3 6 1 1hd 1hd 1hd 1½ Razo E Jr 118 b 4.90 82-27 BlackTieAffair118½Bio1201¾AndovrMn1232¼ All out,driving 9
3Sep89- 7AP fst 6f :222 :453 1:094 3↑ Handicap 40000 2 6 1hd 1½ 12½ 2no Razo E Jr 115 b *1.50 91-15 Carborundum115noBlackTieAffr115hdThRdRolls1122¾ Gamely 9
12Aug89- 5AP fst 7f :223 :451 1:103 1:234 3↑ Handicap 35000 7 2 3½ 2½ 1½ 11¼ Razo E Jr 113 b 2.60 83-19 BlackTieAffr1131¼YukonJoey111¾ContactGam1122¾ Driving 7
29Jly89- 6AP fst 6f :223 :451 1:093 3↑ Alw 25000 2 5 1½ 1½ 1½ 1nk Razo E Jr 115 b 4.70 92-12 Black TieAffair115nkThe Red Rolls1222Highland Ruckus1174½ 6
Driving
20Jly89- 8AP sl 1 :233 :47 1:121 1:373 3↑ Alw 31000 1 1 1½ 1½ 11½ 2½ Razo E Jr 113 b 5.30 72-36 Joel115½Black Tie Affair1132¼All Nonesense1133¼ Gamely 7
1Jly89- 9AP fm 1 1/16 Ⓣ :23 :461 1:11 1:431 Arl Heights 56k 2 2 21 22½ 32½ 88¼ Razo E Jr 119 b 18.10 83-15 Ebros1152½Ruszhinka113¾Downtown Davey119hd Tired 8
18Jun89- 9Haw fm 7½f Ⓣ :233 :462 1:104 1:293 Oil Capitol H 52k 7 7 63¼ 42 34 55¾ Razo E Jr 116 b *2.20 87-10 Tex's Zing1201½All Nonesense1182¼J.C.'s Darlin Boy116¾ 11
Bid,weakened
27May89- 7Spt fst 1⅛ :461 1:111 1:364 1:501 Ill Derby-G2 6 7 68 68¾ 511 611¾ Razo E Jr 117 b 55.60 82-18 ⒹNotation119hdMusicMerci1242½Endow124½ Rallied briefly 7
13May89- 7Spt fst 1 1/16 :241 :481 1:132 1:464 T D Nash H 111k 1 3 3½ 2½ 33½ 45½ Razo E Jr 118 b 20.40 74-18 Endow1214Notation117nkⒹNooo Problema1181¼ Weakened 10
Placed third through disqualification
30Apr89- 8Spt fst 6f :231 :463 :584 1:122 3↑ Bud BC H 87k 3 7 67½ 56¼ 54¼ 31¾ Razo E Jr 112 b 2.80 86-21 Daddy Rex116nkWolf Ticket1161½Black Tie Affair1121¼ 7
Drifted wide turn
23Apr89- 8Spt fst 1 :242 :481 1:13 1:392 Bold Favorite H 54k 9 2 2½ 2½ 1hd 1no Razo E Jr 118 b 3.10 83-24 Black Tie Affair118noNooo Problema1194All Nonesense1203½ 9
Brushed with rival;Previously owned by Hudson River Farm;previously trained by Walter C. Reese
24Feb89- 9GS fst 6f :223 :454 1:102 Bold Reasoning 21k 5 5 4¾ 31 34 44 Madrid A Jr 122 b 1.60 86-13 Dim Lights1223O.K. at Cards118noE.E. Express1181 Tired 6
12Feb89- 8Pha fst 1 :224 :453 1:11 1:374 ⓇCupid 21k 4 4 3nk 1hd 11 2hd Petersen JL 116 b 6.40 85-19 Keewatin116hdBlackTieAffr1166½RacingRascal116¾ Bumped 7
4Feb89- 9GS gd 6f :222 :452 1:10 Del Valley 32k 5 3 43¼ 44¼ 46¼ 46½ Madrid A Jr 115 b 2.50 85-17 Cheerfy1193DimLights1152½GreatestProspect1151 Even try 6
14Jan89- 8Pha gd 1 70 :223 :46 1:11 1:421 Philmont 30k 4 3 52¼ 64¾ 55 49¼ Madrid A Jr 119 b *1.60 75-16 A.M. Swinger1155Executive Edition1151¼Racing Rascal1153 11
Steadied turn
30Dec88- 6Med fst 6f :221 :451 1:102 Deputy Minister 40k 7 5 31½ 31½ 31½ 2nk Madrid A Jr 118 b 3.30 90-10 OedipusAppeal114nkBlckTAffr118noWrgod112no Just missed 7
24Dec88- 9Pha sly 6½f :221 :444 1:104 1:173 Allegheny 28k 3 6 53¼ 42½ 3½ 2hd Madrid A Jr 118 b 2.90 85-27 Dixieland Brass114hdBlack Tie Affair1182½Robin's Erik1146 7
Just missed
9Dec88- 7Med fst 1 :234 :471 1:121 1:382 Slewpy 40k 6 5 31½ 51¼ 66 69½ Verge ME 118 b 10.00 73-16 Doc's Leader1202½Heliport115¾Seminole Slewpy116nk Faded 7
28Nov88- 8Med sly 6f :223 :454 1:101 Alw 25000 5 5 52¾ 34½ 48½ 39 Verge ME 119 b *1.50 82-19 Cheerfy1177½Fightin'Buck1171½BlackTieAffr119no Even try 6
6Nov88- 8Pha fst 7f :222 :443 1:10 1:232 Malus 22k 7 2 3nk 32½ 3½ 11½ Verge ME 119 b 4.10 90-22 BlackTieAffr1191½Doc'sLdr1211¾Chrfy119½ Came in,driving 7
29Oct88- 9Pha fst 1 1/16 :224 :462 1:113 1:453 Heritage 69k 4 1 1hd 31½ 55 47¼ Verge ME 117 b *3.00 69-22 Doc'sLeadr1171¼Alydrome1143½SeminolSlwpy1172½ Gave way 11
5Oct88- 8Pha fst 6f :221 :463 1:124 Alw 11500 2 6 44½ 2hd 12½ 17 Verge ME 120 *1.10 77-23 BlackTieAffair1207EltonsAppl1141¾CuttrEx114¾ Drew clear 7
28Sep88- 5Pha fst 6f :222 :462 1:121 Md Sp Wt 6 6 31 1½ 2hd 11 Verge ME 118 4.30 80-21 BlackTieAffair1181Thunder God1185½First Grade Reader1181 10
Driving

Boston Harbor
Own: Overbrook Farm

B. c. 3 (Apr)
Sire: Capote (Seattle Slew)
Dam: Harbor Springs (Vice Regent)
Br: Overbrook Farm (Ky)
Tr: Lukas D. W

Life	8	6	1	0	$1,934,605	99	D.Fst	6	5	0	0	$1,847,325	99
1997	1	0	0	0	$6,000	71	Wet(375)	2	1	1	0	$87,280	90
1996	7	6	1	0	$1,928,605	99	Turf(281)	0	0	0	0	$0	–
	0	0	0	0	$0	–	Dst(0)	0	0	0	0	$0	–

2Feb97- 5SA fst 1 1/16 :222 :451 1:092 1:423 SntCatlnaS105k **71** 6 31 3½ 1hd 33½ 414¾ Bailey J D B123 *.90 75- 09 Hello1201¾ Bagshot1168 Carmen's Baby1205 Pressed pace, tired 8
26Oct96- 8WO fst 1 1/16 :231 :464 1:11 1:432 BCJuven-G1 **99** 2 1½ 11½ 12½ 11 1nk Bailey J D 122 2.40 92- 02 Boston Harbor122nk Acceptable1222½ Ordway1222½ Driving, prevailed 10
11Oct96- 8Kee fst 1 1/16 :24 :474 1:121 1:451 BrdrsFut-G2 **93** 1 11½ 11½ 11½ 11½ 1½ Bailey J D 121 *.20 83- 22 *Boston Harbor*121½ Blazing Sword1212½ Haint1214½ Headed, came again 5
21Sep96- 7TP wf 1 1/16 :224 :461 1:101 1:424 KyCupJuv-G3 **90** 1 12 11½ 11 13½ 17 Barton D M 120 *.40 81- 13 *Boston Harbor*1207 Play Waki for Me1186 Dr. Spine1125½ Drew off, handily 8
1Sep96- 9ElP fst 7f :22 :45 1:094 1:223 ElPJuvenil100k **93** 4 1 1½ 11 15½ 16 Barton D M 121 *.30 100- 11 *Boston Harbor*1216 NeartheBank1132 MountainLion1122 Drew off, handily 6
26Jly96- 7Sar my 6f :213 :45 :571 1:101 Sanford-G3 **80** 1 4 21½ 21½ 24 210½ Bailey J D 118 1.75 79- 12 KellyKip11810½ *BostonHarbor*118nk *SyFloridSndy*1154½ Ins spd,altered crse 8
29Jun96- 9CD fst 6f :213 :451 :572 1:094 BshfdMnr-G3 **97** 3 7 52½ 31½ 12 14 Luzzi M J 115 *1.00e 94- 12 BostonHrbor1154 Priri Junction1151½ NoblTlnt115hd Split foes, drew clear 8
25May96- 1CD fst 5f :231 :47 :59 Md Sp Wt 31k **77** 9 1 11 1½ 14 15 Barton D M 118 4.40 93- 12 *Boston Harbor*1185 Brandon J R1181½ Renewed118no Drew off, handily 9

Buck's Boy
Own: Quarter B. Farm

B. g. 7 (Apr)
Sire: Bucksplasher (Buckpasser) $5,000
Dam: Molly's Colleen (Verbatim)
Br: Irish Acres Farm (Ill)
Tr: Hickey P. N

Life	30	16	5	2	$2,750,148	112	D.Fst	8	5	0	0	$243,458	108
2000	2	1	0	0	$150,000	101	Wet(299)	2	1	0	0	$13,170	84
1999	3	1	1	1	$292,300	110	Turf(324)	20	10	5	2	$2,493,520	112
	0	0	0	0	$0	–	Dst(0)	0	0	0	0	$0	–

4Mar00- 9GP fm 1½ Ⓣ :474 1:122 2:244 3↑ PanAmerH-G2 **101** 3 12 11½ 11½ 1½ 1½ Prado E S L120 *.90 91- 10 Buck's Boy120½ Thesaurus113½ ⒹBeautiful Dancer114nk Fully extended 7
9Jan00- 10GP fm 1⅜ Ⓣ :454 1:10 1:35 2:12 3↑ MDiarmdH-G3 **64** 7 1hd 1hd 1hd 612 718½ Gomez G K L122 *.30 74- 11 UnitesBigRed1131 Thesaurus1121¼ CarpentersHalo1132¾ Dueled, stopped 8
6Nov99- 9GP gd 1½ Ⓣ :47 1:103 2:243 3↑ BCTurf-G1 **110** 5 12 11½ 11 1hd 34½ Gomez G K L126 6.40 89- 09 Daylami1262½ *Royal Anthem*1262 Buck's Boy1261¼ Off hedge, weakened 14
25Sep99- 8WO fm 1⅜ Ⓣ :481 1:12 1:36 2:13 3↑ SkyClscH-G3 **101** 3 12 12 11 2hd 22½ Landry R C L124 *.20 99 - DwsonsLegcy1142½ BucksBoy1242¼ *Thornfild*11612 Faltered upper stretch 5
10Sep99- 7WO gd 1⅛ Ⓣ :463 1:102 1:343 1:47 3↑ Alw 49761N$MY **110** 4 13 13 13 16 110½ Landry R C L122 *.35 95- 11 Buck's Boy12210½ *Cracker's Folly*1226 Sunshine Journey1225 Easily 4
7Nov98- 9CD fm 1½ Ⓣ :491 1:134 2:033 2:283 3↑ BCTurf-G1 **110** 2 12½ 11 12½ 12 11¼ Sellers S J L126 3.60 92- 09 *Buck's Boy*1261¼ Yagli1261¾ Dushyantor126no Steady urging 13
10Oct98- 8Bel sf 1½ Ⓣ :484 1:134 2:06 2:331 3↑ TfClscIv-G1 **112** 2 13 12 11½ 13½ 13 Sellers S J L126 *1.45 70- 30 *Buck's Boy*1263 Cetewayo1266 Lazy Lode1263 Lost whip, ridden out 6
12Sep98- 9Bel fm 1⅜ 🅃 :484 1:134 1:374 2:13 3↑ ManOWar-G1 **109** 5 21½ 2hd 21½ 1hd 21¼ Fires E L126 4.20 93- 12 Daylami1261¼ *Buck's Boy*1262¾ Indy Vidual126hd Speed, clear, gamely 9
26Jly98- 8WO fm 1⅜ Ⓣ :503 1:144 1:384 2:152 3↑ HongKongJC219k **106** 3 11 11 11 13 12¼ Fires E L121 *.85 90- 17 Buck's Boy1212¼ Crown Attorney1191¾ *Terremoto*115nk Driving 6
Previously trained by Pridham Hilary A 1998(as of 7/4): (56 4 6 5 0.07)
4Jly98- 10Lrl fm 1¼ Ⓣ :48 1:113 1:354 2:002 3↑ FtMcHenryH100k **104** 4 21½ 21 2½ 1½ 12 Fires E L118 *.50 91- 16 *Buck's Boy*1182 *Winsox*1161¼ Casey Tibbs1141¾ Snug hold 2w,driving 7
6Jun98- 8Bel fm 1¼ 🅃 :464 1:104 1:342 1:581 3↑ ManhttnH-G1 **106** 3 22½ 2½ 12½ 11½ 32¼ Fires E L117 4.70 99- 02 ChiefBearhrt1221¾ Devonwood113½ *BucksBoy*1171½ Middle move,clr,game 9
23May98- 10Pim fm 1½ Ⓣ :50 1:151 2:04 2:281 3↑ RiggsH75k **103** 3 12½ 11½ 1½ 11½ 11¼ Prado E S L117 *.40 104- 08 Buck's Boy1171¼ *Cetewayo*1121¼ Lord Zada1118¾ Brk in,steady hand rde 8
Previously trained by Hickey P Noel 1998(as of 4/4): (6 1 1 0 0.17)
4Apr98- 10OP fst 1⅛ :464 1:11 1:36 1:481 4↑ OaklawnH-G1 **102** 4 12 12 11½ 31½ 77¼ Fires E L115 7.20 88- 15 Prcocty1141¼ FrskMNow1171½ PhntomOnTr117¾ Gave way upper stretch 7

7Mar98-10GP fm 1½ Ⓣ :472 1:111 2:003 2:232 3↑PanAmerH-G2 108 3 12½ 11½ 11½ 1½ 1¾ Fires E L115 5.00 111 - Buck's Boy115¾ *African Dancer*115¾ RoyalStrand1142½ Fast pace, prevailed 9
14Feb98-10GP fm 1⅜ Ⓣ :474 1:123 1:362 2:122 3↑GPBCH-G2 108 2 13 11½ 13 11½ 2¾ Fires E L115 8.00 93-07 Flag Down120¾ *Buck's Boy*1152 Copy Editor1161½ Set pace, failed late 12
8Nov97-7Hol fm 1½ Ⓣ :471 1:11 1:593 2:234 3↑BCTurf-G1 101 1 11½ 11 11 2½ 45¼ Guidry M LB126 35.40 93-02 Chief Bearhart126¾ Borgia119½ Flag Down1264 Game for 4th 11
Previously trained by Pridham Hilary A 1997(as of 10/11): (185 49 31 23 0.26)
11Oct97-9Haw fst 1¼ :47 1:112 1:361 2:002 3↑HawGldCp-G3 108 7 15 14 12 11 11¼ Guidry M L114 3.10 103-11 BucksBoy1141¼ CairoExpress1154¾ BeboppinBby115hd Gamely, prevailed 7
20Sep97-7AP yl 1 1/16 Ⓣ :233 :461 1:111 1:433 3↑[S]WHBishopH53k 104 5 13 11½ 11½ 13 12¼ Guidry M L117 1.60 88-12 *Buck's Boy*1172¼ *Canyon Run*1224 Chrysalis House1167 Led throughout 5
30Aug97-7AP fm *1 1/16 Ⓣ :232 :46 1:092 1:402 3↑[S]MyTrip31k 96 6 2½ 1½ 11 21 23¼ Guidry M L117 *.90 100 - CanyonRun1193¼ *BucksBoy*1171¾ LemonGrss113no Dueled drew off placed 7
6Aug97-7AP fst *1 1/16 1:454 3↑Alw 31678c 100 2 1½ 11 11½ 11½ 12 Guidry M L119 *.80 110-17 Buck'sBoy1192 *RuggedBugger*1196½ RecouptheCash1162½ Led throughout 5
28Jun97-5AP fm 1 Ⓣ :243 :48 1:113 1:351 3↑Alw 31000c 98 6 21½ 21 1hd 12 12¾ Guidry M L116 4.30 96-03 *Buck's Boy*1162¾ Lord Comet116½ Going Far1161½ Drew clear driving 7
8Jun97-8AP fst 1 :233 :473 1:131 1:38 3↑Alw 29040N3X 100 5 21 21 12 14 113½ Guidry M L116 *.50 86-17 *Buck's Boy*11613½ PolarIceCaps116nk CherokeeSaga119nk As rider pleased 6
Previously trained by Hickey P Noel 1997(as of 4/19): (34 4 6 6 0.12)
19Apr97-11Spt fst 1 1/16 :23 :474 1:124 1:441 3↑[S]MlwkeeAveH65k 90 6 43½ 43½ 43½ 31 67¼ Nolan P M L114 5.20 83-20 PolrExpedition1232½ BboppinBby117¾ MrGorgff1131¼ Bore out first turn 10
Previously trained by Matthews Doug 1997(as of 4/3): (27 5 3 2 0.19)
3Apr97-8OP fst 1 :224 :46 1:104 1:374 4↑Alw 30000N$Y 90 5 66¾ 64½ 31 32 4¾ Nolan P M L116 11.30 89-19 [DH]Truckee116 [DH]OSteven116nk CaptTiffsBeau114½ 3 wide rally,even late 9
Previously trained by Hickey P Noel 1996(as of 9/30): (203 52 35 24 0.26)
30Sep96-8AP gd *1 Ⓣ :234 :471 1:112 1:361 3↑Alw 21402N3X 76 7 35½ 31½ 22 32 66 Gomez G K 114 *1.40 87-08 Going Far114¾ Cosa Diavolo116no Glen Savoye1162½ Faded stretch, bled 10
14Sep96-7AP fm 1 1/16 Ⓣ :233 :474 1:114 1:423 3↑Alw 23042N3X 98 1 66 66 66 32 2¾ Gomez G K 114 5.80 92-09 Jaunatxo114¾ Buck's Boy1145 Glen Savoye116¾ Quick move stretch 9
18Aug96-3AP fst 6f :223 :453 :581 1:111 3↑[S]Alw 18500N2X 85 5 7 21½ 2½ 11 1nk Gomez G K 117 *.90 89-15 Buck's Boy117nk Limitless1142¾ *Slicker*1173¼ All out, gamely 8
27Jly96-7AP wf 1 :23 :46 1:112 1:381 3↑[S]Alw 21000N1X 84 8 2hd 2½ 2½ 12½ 11¼ Gomez G K 114 *1.70 78-22 *Buck's Boy*1141¼ *Soft Shoe*114no Bill's Dusty1133 Driving 10
8Jly96-1AP fst 6f :224 :464 :591 1:12 3↑[S]Md Sp Wt 18k 79 3 1 21 11 14 113 Gomez G K 115 *.80 85-18 *Buck's Boy*11513 Silken Star1158½ Purple Lover1221½ As rider pleased 6
17Jun96-9AP sly 1⅛ ⊗ :484 1:142 1:423 1:562 3↑[S]Md Sp Wt 19k 33 6 32½ 43 33½ 44 514¾ Gomez G K 114 *2.20 47-36 ArnsJhnHnry1142¾ *RcknRbb*113nk BlSksFrbck113nk Lacked late response 9

Cardmania

dkbbr. g. 1986, by Cox's Ridge (Best Turn)–L'Orangerie, by J.O. Tobin
Lifetime record: 77 17 12 20 $1,522,783
Own.– Jean Couvercelle
Br.– Delta Thoroughbreds Inc (Ky)
Tr.– Derek Meredith

28Apr95-7Hol fst 6f :212 :433 :552 1:074 3↑Los Angeles H-G3 102 8 3 99¾ 88½ 67 34 Nakatani CS LB 119 7.20 97-06 ForestGazelle1161LuckyForever1143Cardmani1191 Wide trip 10
14Apr95-8Kee fst 7f :224 :452 1:092 1:22 3↑Commonwealth BC-G2 93 5 2 31 62½ 85 85½ Bailey JD L 113 7.90 86-10 GoldenGear118hdTurkomatic112nkLitdeJustice121nk Tired 8
11Mar95-8SA wf 6½f :213 :441 1:081 1:143 4↑PtroGrande H-G3 96 3 2 43 55 63½ 23½ Dlhoussaye E LB 119 2.70 95-07 LitdeJustice1153½Cardmn119hdPhonRobrto116½ Game for 2nd 6
12Feb95-8SA fst 1⅛ :451 1:093 1:343 1:472 4↑San Antonio H-G2 100 1 5 68 74¾ 68 66½ Dlhoussaye E LB 117 12.40 89-12 BestPal1213SlwofDmscus119½Tossofthcon1171¾ Saved ground 10
28Jan95-8SA fst 6f :21 :433 :56 1:082 4↑Palos Verdes H-G3 102 3 7 910 109 51½ 22 Dlhoussaye E LB 120 *1.80 93-11 D'hllvnt1172Crdmn1202¾SubtlTroubl115hd Best stride late 10
14Jan95-5SA gd 7f :221 :442 1:083 1:212 4↑San Carlos H-G2 100 4 2 41½ 53¾ 42½ 41¼ Dlhoussaye E LB 120 2.10 94-12 Softshoe Sure Shot114½Ferrara115½Subtle Trouble115nk 7
Fell back,late bid
10Dec94-9Hol fst 6f :212 :434 :553 1:081 3↑Underwood BC-G3 103 8 2 86½ 87¼ 74¾ 21½ Dlhoussaye E LB 120 3.10 97-07 WekivaSprings1181½Cardmania120noGundaghi120¾ Wide rally 9
5Nov94-4CD fst 6f :211 :443 :563 1:093 3↑BC Sprint-G1 110 12 8 128 126½ 66 31½ Dlhoussaye E L 126 22.60 97-01 Cherokee Run126hdSoviet Problem1231½Cardmania126no 14
Wide stretch,finished well
15Oct94-4SA fst 6f :213 :442 :564 1:084 3↑Ancient Title BC H-G3 85 1 6 88¼ 88¼ 87½ 46¾ Dlhoussaye E LB 121 4.20 86-08 Saratoga Gambler1133Uncaged Fury114nkConcept Win1173½ 8
Broke through gate
8Jan94-8SA fst 7f :22 :443 1:084 1:211 4↑San Carlos H-G2 106 3 2 54½ 54 42½ 1¾ Dlhoussaye E LB 122 1.90 96-07 Cardmania122¾The Wicked North1172½Portoferraio1151 7
4 wide into lane
6Nov93-2SA ft 6f :21 :434 :56 1:083 3↑BC Sprint-G1 109 5 5 96½ 66½ 54½ 1nk Dlhoussaye E LB 126 5.30 94-04 Cardmania126nkMeafr123½GlddTm1241¼ 5 wide,strong finish 14
17Oct93-5SA fst 6f :212 :434 :56 1:08 3↑Ancient Title H-G3 109 3 4 41¾ 43½ 4½ 12½ Dlhoussaye E LB 116 6.00 97-09 Cardmania1162½Music Merci1172Bahatur114no 4 wide rally 8
18Sep93-4BM fst 6f :221 :442 :562 1:084 3↑BM BC H 155k 101 7 8 87½ 87¾ 34 21½ Baze RA LB 116 3.30 90-14 LuckyForevr1141½Crdmn1162½Schrndo1152½ Rallied far wide 9
21Aug93-8Dmr fst 7f :221 :443 1:083 1:211 3↑O'Brien H 87k 102 6 1 53½ 54 43 3¾ Stevens GL LB 116 6.00 93-09 Slerp117nkPortoferraio114½Cardmania116no Wide trip 7
3Jly93-8Hol fst 7f :213 :434 1:081 1:204 3↑Triple Bend H-G3 108 6 7 78¾ 79 54 2¾ Dlhoussaye E LB 116 7.80 99-09 NowListen116¾Cardmania116½StaroftheCrop1203 Wide trip 10
11Jun93-7Hol fst 5½f :214 :441 :56 1:021 3↑[R]Porterhouse 56k 99 6 6 68½ 610 66½ 35 Dlhoussaye E B 119 2.10 96-09 Knight Prospector1143½Anjiz1161½Cardmania1192 Wide trip 6
16May93-8Hol fst 6f :214 :441 :561 1:083 3↑Los Angeles H-G3 99 6 7 77½ 77¼ 75½ 52½ Black CA B 117 21.10 95-08 StaroftheCrop119nkFabulous Champ116hdWild Harmony1161 7
Awkward start,wide
18Apr93♦ Sha Tin(HK) yl *7fⓉRH 1:221 3↑Hong Kong Int'l Bowl (Listed) 45½ Cruz AS 126 8.60 Glen Kate123noHelene Star1261½Quicken Away1264 14
Stk388000
Tracked leaders in 3rd,lacked rally,faded 1f out
27Mar93-8SA fst 6½f :213 :442 1:083 1:144 4↑Potrero Grande H-G3 106 1 8 73¼ 43 33 25 Dlhoussaye E B 117 8.00 93-09 GraySlewpy1185Crdmnia1172½StaroftheCrop1191 No match 8
21Feb93-10TuP fst 6f :211 :431 :544 1:064 3↑Phoenix Gold Cup H-G3 92 6 2 32½ 22 32½ 33 Hansen RD 121 *1.90 97-09 HonortheHero1132½B.G.'sDrone112½Crdmani1211¼ Late gain 8
30Jan93-4SA fst 6f :213 :44 :561 1:084 4↑Palos Verdes-G3 101 2 4 2hd 1hd 1½ 31¼ McCarron CJ B 117 11.70 92-11 MusicMerci114nkStaroftheCrop1191Crdmn117¾ Good effort 7
9Jan93-8SA my 7f :221 :444 1:092 1:221 4↑San Carlos H-G2 98 1 1 1hd 1hd 21½ 25 Black CA 117 4.80 87-15 Sir Beaufort1205Cardmania117½Excavate114½ Held 2nd 6
12Dec92-8Hol fst 6f :221 :451 :571 1:091 3↑VO Underwood H-G3 109 4 2 2½ 31 33 31½ McCarron CJ 124 10.10 92-15 Gundaghia1161¼GraySlewpy124nkCrdmn1246½ Brushed start 5
27Nov92-8Hol fm 5½fⓉ :214 :442 :554 1:02 3↑Hol Turf Express H 200k 94 4 6 63¼ 63¼ 64 83½ Black CA B 118 25.60 92-05 Answer Do121noRepriced118noGundaghia1171¼ Weakened 11
31Oct92-4GP fst 6f :213 :433 :553 1:081 3↑BC Sprint-G1 87 6 8 74 118 1210 129 McCarron CJ 126 31.70f 93-00 Thirty Slews126nkMeafara1203Rubiano126no Through early 14
12Oct92-8SA fst 6f :21 :433 :553 1:082 3↑Ancient Title BC H-G3 96 6 4 76¾ 55 54½ 42½ McCarron CJ B 119 18.50 91-14 GraySlewpy118nkTrickMe1141¼LightofMorn1171 Wide trip 9
9Aug92♦ Hoppegartn(Ger) gd 6½fⓉRH 1:143 3↑Grosser Preis von Berlin-G3 11 Lequeux A 132 19.20 Mr Brooks132½Monde Bleu1321Dream Talk1323½ 12
Stk231000
Soon pushed along to keep pace,weakened over 2f out
4Jly92♦ Hamburg(Ger) gd *6fⓉStr 1:07 3↑Holsten Trophy-G3 49¼ Badel A 132 4.80 Dream Talk1347Montepulciano1212¼Princess Nana119hd 4
Stk134000
Tracked in 3rd,weakened 1½f out
25May92♦ Sandown(GB) gd *5fⓉStr 1:001 3↑Temple Stakes-G2 53½ Lequeux A 129 12.00 Snaadee1292Blyton Lad129nkMedaille d'Or129nk 9
Stk115000
In touch for a half,lost place entering final furlong
9May92-8Hol fst 6f :22 :443 :563 1:083 3↑Los Angeles H-G3 109 4 4 43½ 43½ 32 11¾ Dlhoussaye E B 118 6.00 97-08 Cardmania1181¾GrySlwpy1193½RobynDncr1192 4 wide stretch 5
Previously trained by Myriam Bollack
12Apr92-8Kee fst 7f :222 :451 1:094 1:222 3↑Commonwealth BC-G3 98 4 2 32 2½ 41¼ 43 Perret C B 121 2.90 94-12 Pleasant Tap1162½To Freedom115noRun on the Bank118½ 6
Carried out pole
22Mar92-8SA sly 6½f :22 :45 1:101 1:17 4↑Potrero Grande H-G3 101 4 2 3½ 2½ 2hd 11 Dlhoussaye E B 117 3.20 85-16 Cardmania1171Frost Free1173½Answer Do1237 Brushed 3½ 4
7Mar92-6SA fst 6½f⊗ :221 :444 1:082 1:144 4↑Zooron H 63k 103 5 6 64 53½ 43 1nk Dlhoussaye E B 116 3.80 96-06 Cardmania116nkFrostFr1181¼Doyouswhts1143 4 wide stretch 10
22Feb92-8SA fst 5½f :213 :441 :554 1:02 4↑El Conejo H 106k 103 2 4 42½ 41¾ 32½ 32¾ McCarron CJ B 116 6.00 102-06 GraySlewpy1141¾FrstFree1191Crdmania1162¾ Always close 5
11Jan92-8SA fst 7f :221 :441 1:082 1:211 4↑San Carlos H-G2 106 7 7 58½ 57½ 56½ 44 McCarron CJ B 116 4.20 93-11 Answer Do1201½Individualist115hdMedia Plan1162½ 7
Stumbled start,wide
14Dec91-8Hol fst 6f :212 :442 :563 1:084 3↑V O Underwood-G3 - 3 6 54½ 53½ 52¾ 31 Badel A B 120 8.90 95-09 Individualist114hdThrtySlws1171Crdmn1203 4 wide stretch 8
29Nov91-8Hol fm 5½fⓉ :214 :44 :551 1:012 3↑Turf Expr H (Div 2) 112k - 5 6 42 32 3½ 31 Guignard G B 116 17.20 - - Answer Do120¾Apollo115nkCardmania116½ Good effort 8
20Oct91♦ San Siro(Ity) hy *5fⓉStr :584 Premio Omenoni-G3 1½ Badel A 119 5.30 Cardmania119½Magrana1193GoldFutures119nk 10
Stk99600
Tracked in 4th,led 170y out,held gamely

17Aug91♦	Deauville(Fr)	yl	*5fⓉStr	:59^3	3↑	Prix Piaget	Hcp51000	1^{hd}	Badel A	121	4.70	Cardmania121^{hd}Tamara's Twinkle113^{1}Merry Hunter121¾	Pressed pace,dueled halfway,led near line,all out	16
3Aug91♦	Deauville(Fr)	yl	*6fⓉStr	1:12^2	3↑	Prix de la Municipalite et du District	Hcp53900	2^{nk}	Badel A	121	8.50	Merry Hunter118^{nk}Cardmania121^{nk}Rangoon121½	Pressed pace,dueled final furlong,outgamed	18
16Jly91♦	Maisns-Lffitte(Fr)	gd	*6fⓉStr	1:11^1	3↑	Prix de la Boe	Hcp34300	1^1	Badel A	121	10.00	Cardmania121^{1}Rechetnikov108^{hd}Ginger Candy130^1	Tracked leader,led 1f out,driving	16
4Jly91♦	Evry(Fr)	gd	*6½fⓉStr	1:17^3	4↑	Prix de Marcoussis (Apprentices)	Clm22600	1^{hd}	Benoist O^5	131	3.40	Cardmania131^{4}Light Moon127¾Cervino111½	Chased clear leader,led 100y out,held gamely	9
25Jun91♦	Saint-Cloud(Fr)	gd	*1ⓉLH	1:42^4	4↑	Prix des Heliotropes	Clm26200	3^{3½}	Benoist O^5	122	24.00	Jet Jeans120^{1½}Radar Limit121^{2}Cardmania122^3	Midpack,progress into 4th 2½f out,one-paced final furlong	16
24Apr91♦	Evry(Fr)	sf	*6fⓉStr	1:13^2	4↑	Prix Teddy	Hcp19200	10^{5½}	Badel A	122	5.00	Light Moon112^{nk}Mill Lady123^{hd}Sharpvite126^{nk}	Tracked in 5th on rail,one paced	18
11Apr91♦	Longchamp(Fr)	gd	*7fⓉRH	1:20^3	4↑	Prix des Gravilliers	Hcp55700	12	Badel A	118	7.00	Idefix127^{nk}Platinum Dancer119¾Positano117¾	Chased in 5th,bumped on rail over 1f out,unable to recover	18
30Mar91♦	Maisns-Lffitte(Fr)	sf	*6fⓉStr	1:14^2	3↑	Prix du Rey	Hcp36900	3^{1¾}	Badel A	123	3.50	Platinum Dancer120^{1½}Heart Noble130^{nk}Cardmania123^{nk}	Dueled early,2nd halfway,lost 2nd near line	17
13Mar91♦	Maisns-Lffitte(Fr)	hy	*6fⓉStr	1:15^2	4↑	Prix Prince Chevalier	Alw21300	2¾	Badel A	126	12.00	Nityo121¾Cardmania126^{hd}Reinstate121½	Tracked in 4th,2nd halfway,held by winner	13
2Nov90♦	Evry(Fr)	sf	*6fⓉStr	1:15^2	3↑	Prix du Lunain	Hcp23700	11	Badel A	128	4.50	Ginger Candy119^{1½}Sulmona134^{2}Nao119^{no}	Dueled to 1½f out,weakened	15
15Oct90♦	Maisns-Lffitte(Fr)	gd	*6fⓉStr	1:11^3	4↑	Prix de Menil-Vicomte	Hcp23900	4¾	Badel A	128	8.50	Graphus126½King of Sun107^{nk}Sharpvite130^{hd}	Rated in 6th,strong run over 1f out,gaining late	12
29Sep90♦	Evry(Fr)	gd	*1ⓉLH	1:38^4	3↑	Prix d'Epernon	Hcp40200	8^{5¾}	Badel A	127	13.00	Graveron133^{no}Jilgueno124^{1½}Blue de Valois136½	Never a factor	17
16Sep90♦	Longchamp(Fr)	gd	*7fⓉRH	1:21^3	4↑	Prix du Pont de Flandre	Hcp22800	9^{7¾}	Badel A	126	6.50	Despatch130^{hd}Brenton110^{2½}Elviss117½	Never a factor	16
8Sep90♦	Evry(Fr)	gd	*6fⓉStr	1:11^1	3↑	Prix Paris-Turf	Hcp39600	3¾	Lawniczak D	121	9.50	Vitola117½Platinum Dancer119^{nk}Cardmania121¾	Tracked in 6th,finished well without threatening	18
29Aug90♦	Deauville(Fr)	gd	*6fⓉStr	1:14^3	3↑	Prix des Entraineurs	Alw14200	1^{2½}	Bollack M	161	*1.60e	Cardmania161^{2½}Pretty Liloy150^{nk}Wise Bird143½	Tracked leaders,led 150y out,going away Race in which all riders are trainers	12
18Aug90♦	Deauville(Fr)	yl	*1ⓉRH	1:48	4↑	Prix de Barfleur	Clm28500	2^{1½}	Badel A	128	*1.70	Prince Florent118^{1½}Cardmania128^{nk}Zingaro116^1	Chased clear leader,led 1½f out to 100y out,second best	9
12Jly90♦	Evry(Fr)	gd	*1ⓉLH	1:36^1	4↑	Handicap de l'Essonne	Hcp57300	6^{3¾}	de Smyter M	119	17.00	Forest Angel131^{1½}Mephistopheles112^{nk}Dom Valory130^{hd}	Well placed in 7th,evenly late	18
27Jun90♦	Longchamp(Fr)	hy	*7fⓉRH	1:27^3	4↑	Prix de la Chaussee	Clm35800	3½	Badel A	128	*.80	Appolino124^{hd}Morgause121½Cardmania128^{1½}	Rated at rear,bid 2f out,finished well	10
18Jun90♦	Longchamp(Fr)	gd	*7fⓉRH	1:22^3	4↑	Prix de Fausses-Reposes	Clm26600	1^2	Badel A	128	*1.90	Cardmania128^{2}Elviss120^{1½}Sumotori122½	Tracked in 3rd,led 1½f out,clear 1f out,handily	10
12Jun90♦	Chantilly(Fr)	yl	*1ⓉRH	1:42^1	4↑	Prix du Bois Saint-Denis	Clm26200	1½	Badel A	128	*1.50	Cardmania128½Morgause123^{2}Millery122^{hd}	Led to halfway,3rd 3f out,came again to lead near line	10
31May90♦	Chantilly(Fr)	gd	*1ⓉRH	1:38^1	4↑	Prix de Chaumont	Clm26200	3^{2½}	Badel A	127	2.50	Normandy Dancer119½Solido127^{2}Cardmania127^2	Tracked leader,effort over 1f out,one-paced late	6
22May90♦	Maisns-Lffitte(Fr)	gd	*1ⓉStr	1:39^4	4↑	Prix de Chatou	Clm22200	1^1	Badel A	130	5.40	Cardmania130^{1}Moknine126¾Armero119½	Tracked leader,led before halfway,ridden out	15
7May90♦	Saint-Cloud(Fr)	gd	*1ⓉLH	1:43^4	4↑	Prix de Grignon	Clm18000	1^{1½}	Badel A	123	4.20	Cardmania123^{1½}Riche Mare128^{hd}Moknine123^{no}	Dueled early,settled in 6th,rallied to lead 1f out,ridden out	20
16Apr90♦	Longchamp(Fr)	sf	*1ⓉRH	1:43^1	4↑	Prix des Bouleaux	Clm17700	14	Badel A	123	14.00	Solido128^{nk}L'Ambitieux123^{nk}[DH]Il Danieli128	Tracked in 6th,weakened 2f out	19
29Mar90♦	Saint-Cloud(Fr)	gd	*1ⓉLH	1:42	4↑	Prix de Bernay	Clm22700	2¾	Badel A	126	8.20	My Genelle122¾Cardmania126^{1½}Rooty126½	Rated in 7th,4th 2f out,2nd 100y out,held by winner	15
15Mar90♦	Evry(Fr)	gd	*1ⓉLH	1:40^4	4↑	Prix de Corbeil	Hcp51800	12	Lawniczak D	117	72.00	Jilgueno103^{nk}Le Scoot114½Arctic Swell108^{nk}	Dueled for a half,4th 3f out,weakened over 1f out	17
2Mar90♦	Maisns-Lffitte(Fr)	hy	*1ⓉStr	1:45^3	4↑	Prix de Conches	Clm19000	14	Badel A	126	8.50	My Genelle124^{no}Bouche d'Aigre114^{2}Carridge126^{no}	Never a factor	18
24Nov89♦	Maisns-Lffitte(Fr)	sf	*7fⓉStr	1:30^4		Prix de Limours	Clm16200	5^{3¼}	Badel A	130	13.00	Jame's Song121^{no}Icy Calm121½Oh Lucky Day119^{1½}	Toward rear,progress 1½f out,finished well	23
31Oct89♦	Maisns-Lffitte(Fr)	sf	*1⅛ⓉStr	1:54^2		Prix de Chanteloup	Clm16800	14	Badel A	128	6.50	Catabell126^{2½}Trickiest116^{1}Swift Legs Dancer119^{hd}	Never a factor	25
23Oct89♦	Saint-Cloud(Fr)	fm	*1ⓉLH	1:42^4		Prix Arreau	Clm15900	3^2	Badel A	128	3.70	Catabell126^{1½}Lyphard's Fire121½Cardmania128^{2½}	Rated in midpack,rail bid 2f out,3rd 1f out; Previously trained by Christiane Head	15
1Oct89♦	Saint-Cloud(Fr)	gd	*1ⓉLH	1:43^1		Prix de Carville	Clm14900	1^{1½}	Guignard G	126	*1.30	Cardmania126^{1½}Off Stage117½Jame's Song113½	Toward rear,sharp run to lead 150y out.Claimed for $18,137	12
26Aug89♦	Deauville(Fr)	sf	*1ⓉRH	1:47^3		Prix Caprice	Clm18100	5^4	Guignard G	130	4.50	Margousier127^{1}Le Scoot124^{nk}Victory Queen118^2	Rated toward rear,finished well without threatening	15
20Jly89♦	Saint-Cloud(Fr)	fm	*1ⓉLH	1:41		Prix de Mantes	Clm24700	3^{4½}	Head F	130	*2.50	My Genelle122^{3}Swift Legs Dancer130^{1½}Cardmania130¾	Rated at rear,10th 2f out,wide run to get up for 3rd	14
17Jun89♦	Saint-Cloud(Fr)	gd	*1ⓉLH	1:44^1		Prix de Giberville	Clm29800	1^2	Guignard G	122	*1.80	Cardmania128^{2}Hercle121^3[DH]Golden Mountains122	Rated in 9th,5th 2f out,led 1f out,ridden clear	13
5Jun89♦	Saint-Cloud(Fr)	sf	*1ⓉLH	1:46		Prix Memorandum	Mdn19000	3^{1½}	Guignard G	123	2.20	Susperregui123^{hd}Boutonnement118^{1½}Cardmania123^{hd}	Tracked in 3rd,bid over 1f out,not good enough	11
26Apr89♦	Evry(Fr)	sf	*1ⓉLH	1:45^2		Prix de la Beauce	Mdn18700	2^{nk}	Mosse G	123	*1.50	Prospector'sImage123^{nk}Cardmnia123¾SilverRiverman123^{1½}	Tracked in 5th,led over 1f out,dueled 170y out,gamely	13
15Nov88♦	Saint-Cloud(Fr)	sf	*7fⓉLH	1:29		Prix Pitchoury	Mdn21400	3^{2½}	Guignard G	123	*1.50	Idefix119^{2}Creator123½Cardmania123¾	Tracked in 3rd,2nd 2f out,outfinished	12
31Oct88♦	Saint-Cloud(Fr)	sf	*7fⓉLH	1:29^2		Prix Samourai	Mdn20900	3^1	Mosse G	123	8.70	Mistralien123^{1}Aliocha123^{hd}Cardmania123^2	Tracked in 5th,2nd 1f out,lost 2nd on line	17
10Oct88♦	Saint-Cloud(Fr)	gd	*1ⓉLH	1:44^3		Prix du Vallon	Mdn (FT)20100	4^{4½}	Moore GW	123	15.00	Forest Guard123½Nursery Slope123^{2½}Strange Alliance123^{1½}	Raced in midpack,mild late gain	13

Charismatic

Own: Lewis Robert B. and Beverly J

Ch. c. 3 (Mar)
Sire: Summer Squall (Storm Bird) $25,000
Dam: Bali Babe (Drone)
Br: Parrish Hill Farm & W. S. Farish (Ky)
Tr: Lukas D. W

Life	17	5	2	4	$2,038,064	108	D.Fst	15	5	2	4	$2,035,934 108
1999	10	4	2	1	$2,007,404	108	Wet(315)	1	0	0	0	$2,130 71
1998	7	1	0	3	$30,660	85	Turf(286)	1	0	0	0	$0 24
	0	0	0	0	$0	-	Dst(0)	0	0	0	0	$0 -

5Jun99- 9Bel	fst	1½	:47^{3} 1:12 2:01^{4} 2:27^{4}	Belmont-G1	**107**	4	2^{hd} 2½ 1^{hd} 2½ 3^{1½}	Antley C W	L126	*1.60	103- 06	LmonDropKid126^{hd} VisionndVrs126^{1½} Chrismtic126^{4¾}	Drifted, vanned off	12
15May99-10Pim	fst	1$\frac{3}{16}$	:45^{1} 1:10^{1} 1:35^{1} 1:55^{1}	Preakness-G1	**107**	6	10^{6} 10^{7¾} 8^{3¾} 1^{3} 1^{1½}	Antley C W	L126	8.40	89- 09	Charismatic126^{1½} Menifee126^{hd} *Badge*126^{2½}	5wd mv,drftd 3/16,drvg	13
1May99- 8CD	fst	1¼	:47^{4} 1:12^{2} 1:37^{2} 2:03^{1}	KyDerby-G1	**108**	16	7^{3½} 7^{2¾} 3^{1½} 2½ 1^{nk}	Antley C W	L126	31.30	89- 14	*Charismatic*126^{nk} Menifee126^{¾} Cat Thief126^{1¼}	5-wide trip,driving	19
18Apr99- 8Kee	fst	1$\frac{1}{16}$	:23^{1} :46^{4} 1:10^{3} 1:41	Lexingtn-G2	**108**	5	6^{5} 4^{2½} 3^{1½} 2^{hd} 1^{2½}	Bailey J D	L115	12.10	103- 07	*Charismatic*115^{2½} YnkeeVictor115^{¾} FindersGold115^{2}	3 wide 2nd turn,drvng	12
3Apr99- 5SA	fst	1⅛	:47^{1} 1:11^{2} 1:36^{1} 1:48^{4}	SADerby-G1	**94**	8	6^{3½} 6^{3¾} 6^{4} 5^{7} 4^{8¼}	Pincay L Jr	LB120	44.30	83- 13	GenrlChllng120^{3½} PrimTimbr120^{3½} DsrtHro120^{1¼}	Improved position some	8
6Mar99- 7BM	fst	1$\frac{1}{16}$	:22^{4} :46 1:10 1:43^{1}	ElCamRlD-G3	**95**	2	6^{7½} 6^{7½} 6^{4¾} 3^{3½} 2^{hd}	Warren R J Jr	LB115	10.60	83- 24	Cliquot115^{hd} Charismatic115^{3½} No Cal Bread117^{¾}	Angled out, rallied	7
19Feb99- 6SA	fst	7f	:21^{4} :43^{4} 1:08^{1} 1:21^{2}	Alw 50000N$Y	**94**	2	4 5^{9½} 5^{9} 3^{6½} 2^{5}	Pincay L Jr	LB117	17.20	93- 08	Apremont119^{5} Charismatic117^{2} *Forestry*119^{7}	Finished willingly	5
11Feb99- 6SA	fst	6½f	:21^{4} :44^{2} 1:10^{2} 1:17^{1}	Clm 62500(62.5-55)	**80**	8	7 8^{6¼} 6^{5} 5^{4} 2^{nk}	McCarron C J	LB117	2.70	82- 17	[D]What Say You110^{nk} Charismatic117^{nk} ValleyDon117^{1}	Bothered near 1/8	9
Placed first through disqualification														
31Jan99- 8SA	gd	1$\frac{1}{16}$	:23^{4} :47^{3} 1:12 1:42^{4}	StCtlina-G2	**71**	2	5^{2½} 5^{4¼} 5^{5} 5^{7½} 5^{13½}	Pincay L Jr	LB117	30.10	75- 15	GeneralChallenge117^{3} BuckTrout120^{1} Brillintly115^{3½}	Bit tight 7/8,wkened	5
16Jan99- 5SA	fst	1$\frac{1}{16}$	:23^{3} :47^{2} 1:11^{4} 1:44	Alw 54000N$Y	**78**	8	7^{3¼} 7^{5¾} 7^{3½} 7^{3¼} 5^{4}	Pincay L Jr	LB117	17.90	79- 16	Mr. Broad Blade116^{hd} Brilliantly116^{1} Outstanding Hero116^{2}	Bit tight 3/4	10
27Dec98- 1SA	fst	6½f	:21^{3} :44^{1} 1:09 1:15^{2}	Alw 50000N$Y	**85**	5	7 7^{8¼} 7^{6¾} 8^{5¼} 3^{4½}	Pincay L Jr	LB117	23.10	87- 06	*BrightValour*116^{4} OutstndingHero116^{½} Chrismtic117^{nk}	Outside,late for 3rd	8
21Nov98- 1Hol	fst	6½f	:22^{2} :45^{3} 1:10^{4} 1:17^{1}	Md 62500(62.5-55)	**83**	3	5 4^{2} 4^{1½} 1^{2} 1^{5}	Pincay L Jr	LB119	*1.30	80- 20	Charismatic119^{5} Wandering119^{2} Pick Up Stixs119^{6}	Rail trip,clearly best	6
17Oct98- 4SA	fm	1 (T)	:23^{2} :47^{2} 1:13 1:38^{1}	Md Sp Wt 35k	**24**	4	1^{1½} 1^{1} 7^{3¾} 8^{12} 9^{25¾}	McCarron C J	LB120 b	3.40	42- 28	LxingtonBch120^{no} DncngMjsty120^{1¼} *CompnyApprovl*120^{3½}	Speed, stopped	9
1Oct98- 1SA	fst	1	:22^{1} :45^{2} 1:10^{4} 1:37	Md Sp Wt 35k	**60**	2	1^{3} 1^{3½} 1^{1} 2^{2} 3^{10¼}	Pincay L Jr	LB120 b	2.10	76- 15	CrownngStorm120^{10} NrthrnAvn120^{nk} Chrsmtc120^{4}	Inside, edged for 2nd	7
23Aug98- 2Dmr	fst	5½f	:22^{3} :46 :58^{3} 1:05	Md Sp Wt 36k	**57**	2	3 3^{½} 3^{nk} 4^{2½} 4^{5}	McCarron C J	LB118 b	*.70	83- 11	Out in Front118^{2} Round Four118^{hd} Kona Coast118^{3}	3 wide, weakened	4
25Jly98- 4Dmr	fst	6f	:22^{2} :45^{4} :58^{2} 1:11^{2}	Md Sp Wt 37k	**66**	2	6 1^{1} 1^{2} 2^{½} 3^{1½}	Nakatani C S	LB118 b	*2.00	80- 12	Prized Demon118^{½} Seayabyebye118^{1} Charismatic118^{6}	Inside, outfinished	8
20Jun98- 3Hol	fst	5f	:22^{2} :45^{3} :57^{4}	Md Sp Wt 37k	**48**	3	4 4^{4¾} 3^{5} 6^{8½} 6^{13¼}	Flores D R	B118	12.20	81- 15	O'Rey Fantasma118^{2½} *Aristotle*118^{2} Buck Trout118^{3½}	Inside, weakened	6

Cherokee Run

Own: Jill E. Robinson

Dk. b or b. h. 5 (Mar)
Sire: Runaway Groom (Blushing Groom*Fr)
Dam: Cherokee Dame (Silver Saber)
Br: George C. Onett (Fla)
Tr: Alexander Frank A

Life	28	13	5	5	$1,531,818	114	D.Fst	22	9	5	4	$1,321,951 114
1995	2	1	0	0	$66,456	114	Wet(356)	6	4	0	1	$209,867 103
1994	9	3	3	3	$943,690	114	Turf(236)	0	0	0	0	$0 -
	0	0	0	0	$0	-	Dst(0)	0	0	0	0	$0 -

17Apr95- 8Aqu	fst	6f	:21^{4} :44^{1} :56^{1} 1:08^{4}	3↑BoldRlrH-G3	**105**	5	4 5^{4½} 4^{4} 4^{2} 4^{2¾}	Smith M E	125	*.65	- -	Rizzi112^{1½} *Lite the Fuse*111^{1} Evil Bear116^{nk}	Rated, rally, no punch	6
10Mar95- 9GP	fst	7f	:22^{2} :45 1:08^{4} 1:21^{3}	3↑GPSprChH100k	**114**	3	4 2^{hd} 2^{hd} 1^{hd} 1^{2½}	Smith M E	L122	1.50	- -	Cherokee Run122^{2½} Waldoboro113^{1½} Evil Bear116^{no}	Fast pace, ridden out	6
5Nov94- 4CD	fst	6f	:21^{1} :44^{3} 1:09^{2}	3↑BCSprnt-G1	**114**	11	2 9^{2¾} 3^{2½} 2^{½} 1^{hd}	Smith M E	L126	*2.80	- -	*Cherokee Run*126^{hd} Soviet Problem123^{1½} Cardmania126^{no}	Rallied, just up	14
17Sep94- 5Bel	fst	7f	:22^{2} :44^{3} 1:09 1:21^{4}	3↑Vosburgh-G1	**105**	7	4 4^{2½} 2^{2½} 1^{1} 3^{1}	Perret C	126	2.40	- -	Harlan126^{½} American Chance126^{½} *Cherokee Run*126^{1}	Led str, outfnshd	10
7Aug94- 8Sar	fst	6f	:22^{2} :45^{1} :56^{3} 1:08^{3}	3↑APhenomH-G3	**112**	7	4 6^{1¾} 4^{¾} 2^{hd} 2^{½}	Perret C	120	*.70	- -	Boundary117^{½} CherokeeRun120^{2½} ICan'tBelieve113^{2}	Dueled str, outfnshd	7
16Jly94- 9Lrl	fst	6f	:21^{4} :44^{4} :56^{3} 1:08^{4}	3↑DeFrncsM-G2	**114**	1	6 5^{3¾} 3^{1} 1^{1} 1^{2¼}	Perret C	114	*1.70	- -	CherokeeRun114^{2¼} BoomTownr119^{½} FuMnSlw107^{½}	Good trip, drove clear	11
26Jun94- 7Bel	fst	7f	:23^{3} :46^{2} 1:10^{1} 1:22^{1}	3↑TomFool-G2	**112**	1	3 1^{hd} 1^{1} 1^{1} 2^{hd}	Perret C	121	*1.80	92- 16	Virginia Rapids124^{hd} *Cherokee Run*121^{1¾} Boundary119^{2¾}	Set pace, missed	5
30May94- 8Bel	fst	1	:22^{4} :45 1:09^{2} 1:33^{4}	3↑MtropltH-G1	**111**	2	5^{2¼} 5^{3½} 2^{½} 2^{2} 2^{5½}	Perret C	118	16.70	- -	*Holy Bull*112^{5½} Cherokee Run118^{no} *Devil His Due*122^{2}	Rallied for place	10
7May94- 9Bel	fst	7f	:22^{3} :45^{1} 1:09^{1} 1:21^{2}	3↑CarterH-G1	**106**	9	2 3^{½} 3^{nk} 1^{½} 3^{1½}	Davis R G	119	*1.90	- -	VirginiRpids118^{1¼} *PunchLine*114^{nk} CherokeeRun119^{3¾}	Dueled, missed 2nd	11
2Apr94- 8Aqu	fst	1	:23^{3} :46 1:09^{2} 1:34^{2}	3↑WschstrH-G3	**106**	7	3^{1½} 3^{2} 2^{1} 1^{hd} 3^{¾}	Perret C	119	*1.00	- -	*Virginia Rapids*116^{½} *Colonial Affair*121^{nk} Cherokee Run119^{2¼}	Lugged in str	7
Previously trained by Gomez Frank 1993: (359 48 56 42 0.13)														
16Mar94- 9GP	fst	7f	:22^{3} :45^{2} 1:09^{4} 1:22	4↑Alw 47600N$Y	**100**	1	5 2^{hd} 1^{½} 1^{1} 1^{2¼}	Perret C	115	*.50	- -	Cherokee Run115^{2¼} Swedaus119^{no} Hold Old Blue115^{1½}	Drew off, easily	6
Previously trained by Alexander Frank A 1993(as of 10/10): (102 14 25 22 0.14)														
10Oct93- 6Bel	fst	1	:23^{1} :45^{4} 1:09^{4} 1:35^{1}	JamaicaH-G2	**97**	2	1^{hd} 2^{hd} 1^{hd} 1^{½} 3^{4½}	McCauley W H	120	4.20	- -	*Mi Cielo*116^{2¾} *Prospector's Flag*113^{1¾} *Cherokee Run*120^{¾}	Dueled, wknd str	8
21Aug93- 7Sar	fst	1¼	:47 1:11^{3} 1:37 2:01^{4}	Travers-G1	**94**	1	3^{1½} 4^{1} 6^{1} 6^{3¼} 7^{10}	Day P	126	7.70e	- -	Sea Hero126^{2} Kissin Kris126^{1} Miner's Mark126^{hd}	Mild bid, wknd	11
1Aug93-11Mth	fst	1⅛	:46^{1} 1:10^{2} 1:36^{1} 1:49^{2}	HsklInvH-G1	**91**	4	2^{1} 3^{1½} 4^{3¾} 3^{5} 4^{10¼}	Day P	123 f	*.80	- -	Kissin Kris118^{2¼} Storm Tower119^{8} Dry Bean113^{hd}	Well placed, empty	7
3Jly93- 8Bel	gd	1⅛	:45^{4} 1:09^{3} 1:34^{4} 1:47^{3}	Dwyer-G2	**102**	6	2^{½} 2^{½} 1^{hd} 1^{2½} 1^{6}	Day P	123	1.70	- -	CherokeeRun123^{6} *MinersMrk*123^{1¼} SilvrofSilvr123^{2¾}	Drew off, ridden out	6
5Jun93- 9Bel	gd	1½	:48^{4} 1:13^{4} 2:29^{4}	Belmont-G1	**88**	1	2^{3} 1^{hd} 1^{2} 5^{4} 6^{13}	Antley C W	126	4.20	- -	Colonial Affair126^{2¼} *Kissin Kris*126^{¾} Wild Gale126^{2}	Led stretch, tired	13
15May93-10Pim	fst	1$\frac{3}{16}$	:46^{4} 1:11^{1} 1:37 1:56^{3}	Preaknes-G1	**97**	12	3^{½} 3^{1} 4^{2} 2^{hd} 2^{½}	Day P	126	9.40	- -	Prairie Bayou126^{½} Cherokee Run126^{7} El Bakan126^{nk}	3-wide,led,game try	12
24Apr93- 9CD	sly	1	:23 :46^{2} 1:11^{3} 1:37^{2}	DerbyTrl-G3	**103**	2	1^{hd} 1^{hd} 1^{1½} 1^{4½} 1^{3}	Day P	L122	*.70	- -	Cherokee Run122^{3} Darien Deacon114^{9} Ground Force117^{2}	Handily	9
6Apr93- 8Kee	fst	7f	:22^{2} :45 1:09^{1} 1:21^{1}	Lafayett-G3	**103**	5	1 2^{½} 2^{½} 1^{½} 1^{3½}	Day P	L118	*1.50	- -	*CherokeeRun*118^{3½} *PovertySlew*112^{3} Willimstown121^{1}	Drew off, ridden out	8
20Mar93- 8GP	sly	7f	:22^{3} :45^{3} 1:10^{1} 1:23^{1}	Swale-G3	**99**	7	4 4^{1½} 4^{1¾} 2^{1½} 3^{nk}	Bailey J D	114	*.90	- -	PrmrExploson114^{hd} DmlootDmshoot113^{nk} *ChrokRn*114^{2¼}	Stalked,gamely	8
Previously trained by Gomez Frank 1992: (371 51 53 39 0.14)														
5Mar93- 7GP	fst	7f	:23^{4} :47^{3} 1:11^{2} 1:23^{1}	Alw 37290NC	**99**	3	2 2^{hd} 1^{½} 1^{3} 1^{5}	Vasquez J	117	*.90	- -	Cherokee Run117^{5} Wild Gale117^{6} Ziao112	Handily	4
26Dec92-10Crc	fst	1$\frac{1}{16}$	:24^{1} :48^{3} 1:14^{1} 1:48^{1}	WhtAPlsr-G3	**85**	6	4^{4} 5^{1¼} 2^{2} 2^{½} 2^{½}	Vasquez J	115	*.60	- -	Virgil Cain115^{½} *Cherokee Run*115^{2¼} Kassec112^{2}	Outfinished	7
16Dec92- 9Crc	fst	1 70	:24^{1} :48^{3} 1:13 1:45^{1}	Alw 21000NC	**89**	3	4^{2} 4^{1} 3^{1} 1^{1} 1^{1½}	Vasquez J	120	*.40	- -	Cherokee Run120^{1½} Ziao112^{1¼} Game Red112^{nk}	Circled drew off	7
22Nov92- 9Crc	gd	7f	:22^{3} :46^{1} 1:11 1:23^{4}	Alw 22500NC	**91**	2	3 3^{4} 3^{2} 1^{1½} 1^{2¾}	Vasquez J	114	*.40	- -	*Cherokee Run*114^{2¾} *Virgil Cain*114^{4} Dr. RosesHope112^{4}	Drew off ridden out	5
27Oct92- 7Crc	fst	6f	:22 :45^{3} 1:11	Alw 17600NC	**93**	6	3 4^{3½} 3^{2} 1^{2½} 1^{5½}	Vasquez J	116	*1.90	- -	*Cherokee Run*116^{5½} *Virgil Cain*116^{2} Wake Me At Noon116^{1}	Drew off	6
12Aug92- 8Crc	fst	6f	:22 :45^{3} 1:12^{1}	Alw 15500NC	**76**	1	7 5^{3} 4^{4} 1^{1} 1^{2½}	Vasquez J	114	3.30	- -	*Cherokee Run*114^{2½} Pride of Burkaan112^{5} Aspen Fortune112^{no}	Drew off	7
16Jly92- 7Crc	fst	5½f	:22^{1} :46 1:06^{2}	Alw 15500NC	**–**	3	3 3^{1} 2^{1} 2^{hd} 5^{8¾}	Vasquez J	116	*1.40	- -	StaceysBird116^{2} Itsalilknownfact116^{no} AspenFortune114^{6½}	In tight, tired	6
27Jun92- 3Crc	sly	5f	:22^{2} :46^{2} :59^{1}	Md Sp Wt 14k	**70**	6	3 2^{1} 2^{½} 1^{2} 1^{1}	Vasquez J	116	9.40	- -	Cherokee Run116^{1} *Vanguard Knight*116^{3} Midnight Cookie111^{2½}	Drew off	8

Chief Bearhart

Own: Sam-Son Farm

Ch. h. 5 (Feb)
Sire: Chief's Crown (Danzig)
Dam: Amelia Bearhart (Bold Hour)
Br: Richard D. Maynard (Ont-C)
Tr: Frostad M(0 0 0 0 .00) 1998:(0 0 .00)

Life	26	12	5	3	$3,381,557	112	D.Fst	4	1	0	1	$54,508 99
1998	9	3	2	1	$909,710	111	Wet(339)	0	0	0	0	$0 –
1997	7	5	2	0	$2,011,259	112	Turf(260)	22	11	5	2	$3,327,049 112
	0	0	0	0	$0	–	Dst(0)	0	0	0	0	$0 –

29Nov98 Tokyo (Jpn)	fm	*1½ Ⓣ LH 2:254		3↑ Japan Cup-G1 Stk 2041500	45	Santos J	126 b	7.60		El Condor Pasa121 2½ Air Groove121½ *Special Week*121 2	Rated in 14th,progress over 2f out,finished well.Maxzene 5th 15
7Nov98-9CD	fm	1½ Ⓣ	:491 1:134 2:033 2:283	3↑ BCTurf-G1	104 8 1313 1210 99½ 58 43	Santos J A	L126 b	6.50	89- 09	*Buck's Boy*126 1¼ Yagli126 1¾ Dushyantor126no	Circled five wide 13
18Oct98-6WO	fm	1½ Ⓣ	:521 1:161 2:043 2:293	3↑ CanIntnl-G1	106 3 64½ 56 42 32½ 22	Santos J A	L126 b	*1.50e	82- 17	Royal Anthem119 2 Chief Bearhart126½ *Parade Ground*119 3	Second best 8
27Sep98-8WO	yl	1⅜ Ⓣ	:491 1:13 1:373 2:153	3↑ SkyClasscH109k	104 3 69½ 68½ 54¾ 13 13¼	Santos J A	L125 b	*.25e	89- 11	Chief Bearhart125 3¼ Green Means Go114 1¾ Desert Waves112 2	Handily 6
5Sep98-8WO	fm	1½ Ⓣ	:51 1:154 2:052 2:30	3↑ NiagaraBCH270k	105 5 411 63½ 41¼ 1½ 12¾	Santos J A	L123 b	*.30e	82- 18	*Chief Bearhart*123 2¾ Green Means Go113 1½ Crown Attorney117½	Driving 6
15Aug98-8Sar	fm	1½ Ⓣ	:523 1:182 2:292	3↑ SwrdDncH-G1	101 6 32 31½ 32 53¾ 53¼	Santos J A	L123 b	*1.20	66- 25	Cetewayo115¾ Val's Prince113nk Dushyantor119 2¼	3 wide each turn 6
11Jly98-8Bel	fm	1⅜ Ⓣ	:503 1:144 1:382 2:132	3↑ BwlnGrnH-G2	98 6 65 67 67½ 64½ 34¼	Santos J A	L124 b	*.30	84- 13	*Cetewayo*112 2 Officious113 2¼ Chief Bearhart124 1½	Hard ridden final turn 6
6Jun98-8Bel	fm	1¼ Ⓣ	:464 1:104 1:342 1:581	3↑ ManhttnH-G1	111 1 913 98½ 87¼ 33 11¾	Santos J A	L122 b	*.65e	101- 02	ChiefBearhart122 1¾ Devonwood113½ *BucksBoy*117 1½	Circld widest,in time 9
22Apr98-8Kee	gd	1½ Ⓣ	:523 1:181 2:074 2:313	4↑ Elkhorn-G3	103 5 43 53 53 53½ 2¾	Santos J A	L122 b	*.70	81- 19	African Dancer114¾ *ChiefBearhart*122 1¼ *Chorwon*114nk	Closed fast, gaining 5
8Nov97-7Hol	fm	1½ Ⓣ	:471 1:11 1:593 2:234	3↑ BCTurf-G1	110 5 810 86¾ 54½ 3½ 1¾	Santos J A	LB126 b	*1.90	98- 02	Chief Bearhart126¾ Borgia119½ Flag Down126 4	Circled 5w, drvng 11
19Oct97-8WO	fm	1½ Ⓣ	:504 1:144 2:043 2:29	3↑ CanIntnl-G1	111 2 69¾ 52¾ 11½ 13 12¼	Santos J A	L126 b	*.65e	83- 11	*Chief Bearhart*126 2¼ *Down the Aisle*126 3½ *Romanov*119 8½	Driving 6
28Sep97-9WO	fm	1⅜ Ⓣ	:492 1:132 1:373 2:132	3↑ SkyClasscH108k	112 1 65 42 2hd 15 16	Santos J A	L123 b	*1.05	100- 05	*Chief Bearhart*123 6 Honor Glide119 5¾ Intheblinkofani111 8½	Ridden out 6
4Jly97-6AP	fm	1½ Ⓣ	:51 1:154 2:292	3↑ StrStBCH-G3	105 2 65½ 63¾ 2hd 2hd 2hd	Santos J A	L119 b	*1.40	99- 11	Lakeshore Road114hd *Chief Bearhart*119 1¾ *Awad*119½	Dueled late drifted 9
14Jun97-3WO	fm	1⅛ Ⓣ	:453 1:091 1:333 1:461	3↑ KngEdBCH-G3	110 1 812 810 75¼ 3½ 13¼	Santos J A	L119 b	*.85e	95- 05	ChiefBearhrt119 3¼ *CrownAttorney*108nk Kiridshi124 1¾	Driving, perfect trip 8
25Apr97-8Kee	fm	1½ Ⓣ	:491 1:141 2:041 2:282	4↑ Elkhorn-G3	104 8 611 66¼ 44½ 31½ 1½	Santos J A	L114 b	1.90	98- 11	*Chief Bearhart*114½ *Snake Eyes*113 3 Lassigny122 1	Wore down rivals 8
11Apr97-8Kee	fm	1 Ⓣ	:23 :462 1:102 1:342	4↑ MakrsMrk-G3	104 5 913 912 812 610 2½	Santos J A	L114 b	6.70	95- 06	*Influent*116½ *Chief Bearhart*114 1 Foolish Pole113 1½	Thru inside, gaining 9
26Oct96-9WO	gd	1½ Ⓣ	:50 1:152 2:054 2:301	3↑ BCTurf-G1	95 14 52¾ 73½ 106¾ 1012 1111	Hawley S	L121 b	20.10	66- 18	Pilsudski126 1¼ *Singspiel*126 1¼ Swain126 2½	Brief factor, tired 14
29Sep96-8WO	sf	1½ Ⓣ	:51 1:162 2:071 2:331	3↑ CanIntnl-G1	111 5 46 43 21 22½ 22	Hawley S	L118 b	7.80	60- 30	Singspiel126 2 Chief Bearhart118 3½ *Mecke*126 3½	Mild rally, 2nd best 7
25Aug96-11WO	fm	1½ Ⓣ	:502 1:151 2:283	ⓇBreeders285k	107 3 74½ 56 2hd 15 19½	Walls M K	L126 b	*1.35e	85- 15	Chief Bearhart126 9½ Firm Dancer126½ Sealaunch126 1¼	Drew off, driving 9
25Jly96-2WO	fm	*1⅜ Ⓣ	2:16	3↑ Alw 27400N2X	98 2 31 32 32½ 12½ 12½	Hawley S	L109 b	*.50	- -	*Chief Bearhart*109 2½ *Set Ablaze*113 2 *Quest for Approval*121 5½	Clear, handily 5
7Jly96-8WO	fst	1¼	:46 1:111 1:37 2:034	ⓇQueensPlt425k	97 2 1314 1212 107¼ 59½ 43¾	Hawley S	L126 b	*2.55	88- 12	Victor Cooley126 1½ *Stephanotis*126¾ Kristy Krunch126 1½	Late gain 13
23Jun96-6WO	fst	1⅛	:454 1:094 1:362 1:50	ⓇPlateTrial111k	99 4 88½ 917 815 55 32	Hawley S	126 b	1.70	94- 12	Northface126½ Firm Dancer126 1½ Chief Bearhart126 1¼	Late rally 9
26May96-5WO	fst	1 1/16	:232 :471 1:132 1:45	Alw 25600N2L	93 9 1010 911 63¼ 13 16¼	Hawley S	115 b	3.85	84- 19	ChifBrhrt115 6¼ BoldDcison118¾ LorrsMnMn115 9½	Handily, much the best 10
13Apr96-4Kee	fm	1 1/16 Ⓣ	:224 :464 1:114 1:42	Alw 41360N2X	81 3 65½ 64½ 53¾ 44½ 36	Romero R P	114 b	8.70	- -	Trail City112 3 Krigeorj's Gold115 3 *Chief Bearhart*114 6	Settled, mild bid 10
23Mar96-6FG	fm	*1 Ⓣ	:242 :49 1:134 1:392	Md Sp Wt 25k	78 9 66 76 43½ 1½ 14	Romero R P	119 b	6.50	- -	Chief Bearhart119 4 Mister Eye119 1½ *Chorwon*119 1½	Drew clear, driving 12
25Jun95-5WO	fst	5f	:223 :453 :58	Md Sp Wt 22k	50 2 5 65 611 411 410	Ramsammy E	115 b	10.75	- -	Frozen Ice120 4½ Rare Admiral120 3½ Island Gladiator115 2	No threat 8

Chilukki

Own: Stonerside Stable LLC

B. f. 4 (Feb) FTFFEB99 $875,000
Sire: Cherokee Run (Runaway Groom) $20,000
Dam: Song of Syria (Damascus)
Br: Dr. & Mrs. R. S. West & Mr. & Mrs. M. Miller (Ky)
Tr: Baffert Bob

Life	17	11	3	0	$1,201,828	110	D.Fst	15	9	3	0	$1,130,588 110
2001	2	1	1	0	$130,000	97	Wet(389)	2	2	0	0	$71,240 109
2000	8	4	1	0	$309,105	110	Turf(252)	0	0	0	0	$0 –
	0	0	0	0	$0	–	Dst(0)	0	0	0	0	$0 –

11Feb01-3SA	fst	1⅛	:474 1:112 1:36 1:493	ⒻLaCanada-G2	90 4 32½ 32½ 3nk 21½ 22	Stevens G L	LB119	*.90	85- 16	Spain122 2 Chilukki119 2½ Letter of Intent116½	Bid 3wd,vied,2nd best 5
21Jan01-3SA	fst	1 1/16	:24 :481 1:114 1:422	ⒻElEncino-G2	97 3 1½ 1½ 1½ 12 12½	Stevens G L	LB119	1.60	92- 13	Chilukki119 2½ *Spain*122½ Queenie Belle119 4	Speed,clear,gamely 4
30Dec00-8SA	fst	7f	:224 :452 1:092 1:221	ⒻLaBrea-G1	94 2 4 43 31 3½ 41½	Stevens G L	LB121	*.70	92- 08	Spain123¾ Cover Gal119nk Serenita115½	Rail trip,bid,gamely 6
4Nov00-1CD	fst	1	:222 :452 1:094 1:332	3↑ⒻCDDstafH-G2	108 9 41½ 21 2½ 2hd 1hd	Stevens G L	L116	*1.70	103 -	Chilukki116hd *Reciclada*113 4 Rose of Zollern114 2¾	3 path, fully extended 10
13Sep00-3Dmr	fst	6f	:221 :443 :563 1:091	3↑ⒻⓇCERFH77k	104 2 2 1hd 1hd 12½ 15	Bailey J D	LB120	*.20	94- 08	*Chilukki*120 5 Sea of Ice115 2½ Trying Ty117 2	Inside, ridden out 4
25Aug00-3Sar	fst	6½f	:221 :444 1:084 1:15	ⒻAlw 50000N$Y	110 2 4 11 1½ 11½ 11¼	Bailey J D	L122	*.55	99- 10	*Chilukki*122 1¼ DtYouMizBlue115 2 KtzMeIfYouCn119 7	Pace, clear, driving 5
29Jly00-8Sar	fst	7f	:214 :44 1:091 1:223	ⒻTest-G1	89 1 11 51¾ 77¼ 74 66¾	Sellers S J	L120	*1.75	85- 11	*DreamSupreme*115 1¼ *BigBambu*118 2¾ FindersFee123¾	Stumbled badly start 11
4Jly00-7Mth	gd	6f	:22 :443 :564 1:092	3↑ⒻRegret75k	107 4 3 2hd 1hd 13½ 15	Nakatani C S	L116	*.20	94- 06	Chilukki116 5 SuperduperMiss113 2¼ Elektrline113 12	Vied,clear,ridden out 6
11Mar00-6FG	fst	1 1/16	:233 :472 1:123 1:444	ⒻFGOaks-G3	45 9 32½ 31 3nk 712 827¼	Albarado R J	L121	*.70	60- 20	Shawnee Country121 2 Eden Lodge121 1¼ Zoftig121 1	3w, asked, stopped 9
19Feb00-9FG	fst	1 1/16	:24 :474 1:122 1:45	ⒻDvonaDal-G3	90 2 21 2hd 1½ 13 2½	Flores D R	L122	*.40	85- 19	*ShwneeCountry*122½ Chilukki122 1 HumbleClrk122 4¾	Tried to get out, wide 9
6Nov99-4GP	fst	1 1/16	:223 :454 1:101 1:431	ⒻBCJuvFil-G1	91 3 32 32½ 1hd 2hd 21¼	Flores D R	L119	*1.50	90 -	Cash Run119 1¼ Chilukki119½ *Surfside*119½	Stalked,led,outfinishd 9
9Oct99-8SA	fst	1	:23 :463 1:104 1:36	ⒻOakLeaf-G1	94 2 21 31 2hd 11 11¼	Flores D R	LB118	*.50	91- 11	Chilukki118 1¼ Abby Girl118 4¼ Spain118½	Drifted in 1/16,drvng 5
29Aug99-7Dmr	fst	7f	:221 :443 1:10 1:232	ⒻDMrDeb-G1	88 1 4 2½ 11 13 11	Flores D R	LB121	*.20	86- 13	*Chilukki*121 1 Spain115 4 *She's Classy*116 5½	Dueled,clear,held dvng 7
7Aug99-8Dmr	fst	6½f	:214 :443 1:094 1:162	ⒻSorrento-G2	98 1 4 1hd 11 14 16	Flores D R	LB121	*.20	89- 11	*Chilukki*121 6 November Slew117 3 She's Classy117 10	Inside,clear,easily 6
26Jun99-7CD	fst	5½f	:222 :453 :572 1:033	ⒻDebutant-G3	98 6 1 11 1hd 13 15¼	Martinez W	L121	*.30	100- 09	*Chilukki*121 5¼ *MissWineshine*112 1¼ CecilisCrown115no	Widened, ridden out 9
31May99-9CD	fst	5½f	:213 :443 :571 1:04	KyBC-G3	93 1 1 1½ 1hd 13 14¾	Albarado R J	L112	*.40	98- 09	*Chilukki*112 4¾ *Barrier*115½ Sky Dweller115 1¾	Pace, hand urging 7
28Apr99-1CD	gd	4½f	:22 :443 :51	ⒻMd Sp Wt 39k	109 3 2 1hd 13 19¼	Flores D R	L118	*1.10	105- 15	*Chilukki*118 9¼ Shattered Heart118 5 Sweet Dixie118 1	Off inside, driving 10

Cigar

Own: Paulson Allen E

B. h. 6 (Apr)
Sire: Palace Music (The Minstrel)
Dam: Solar Slew (Seattle Slew)
Br: Allen E. Paulson (Md)
Tr: Mott William I

Life	33	19	4	5	$9,999,815	121	D.Fst	20	17	2	1	$8,357,800 121
1996	8	5	2	1	$4,910,000	117	Wet(300)	2	1	0	0	$1,560,000 117
1995	10	10	0	0	$4,819,800	121	Turf(269)	11	1	2	4	$82,015 99
	0	0	0	0	$0	–	Dst(0)	0	0	0	0	$0 –

26Oct96-10WO	fst	1¼	:462 1:104 1:352 2:01	3↑ BCClasic-G1	115 7 85¾ 63½ 4nk 4¾ 3hd	Bailey J D	L126	*.65	- -	Alphabet Soup126no *Louis Quatorze*121hd Cigar126½	Bid,hung 13
5Oct96-10Bel	fst	1¼	:473 1:112 1:354 2:003	3↑ JkyClbGC-G1	115 6 34½ 34½ 31 3½ 2hd	Bailey J D	L126	*.20	- -	Skip Away121hd Cigar126 2 Louis Quatorze121 1	Drifted late,game 6
14Sep96-8Bel	fst	1⅛	:461 1:102 1:343 1:47	3↑ Woodward-G1	116 4 42½ 42½ 3½ 11 14	Bailey J D	L126	*.35	- -	Cigar126 4 L'Carriere126½ Golden Larch126¾	Swept wide,ridden out 5
10Aug96-6Dmr	fst	1¼	:454 1:091 1:333 1:594	3↑ PacClasc-G1	111 4 21 2½ 11 2½ 23½	Bailey J D	LB124	*.10	- -	Dare and Go124 3½ *Cigar*124 7 *Siphon*124 8	Stalkd fst pce,2ndbest 6
13Jly96-10AP	fst	1⅛	:464 1:101 1:353 1:481	3↑ CitatnChlg1075k	117 10 63½ 62¾ 31 1½ 13½	Bailey J D	L130	*.30	- -	Cigar130 3½ Dramatic Gold118nk Eltish118 2	Lost ground drew clear 10
1Jun96-10Suf	fst	1⅛	:454 1:093 1:361 1:493	3↑ MassH500k	112 3 46 33 13 14½ 12½	Bailey J D	LB130	*.10	- -	*Cigar*130 2½ Personal Merit111 10½ *Prolanzier*112nk	Handily 6
27Mar96 Nad Al Sheba (UAE)	ft	*1¼	LH 2:034	4↑ Dubai World Cup Stk 4000000	1½	Bailey J	125	-		*Cigar*125½ Soul of the Matter125 8 L'Carriere125¾	5th after 1f,bid 4f out,led 2f out,dueled 1-1/2f out,prevailed 11
10Feb96-10GP	fst	1⅛	:464 1:104 1:353 1:49	3↑ DonnH-G1	117 1 31½ 32 2hd 12½ 12	Bailey J D	L128	*.20	- -	*Cigar*128 2 *Wekiva Springs*117 4 Heavenly Prize115 3	Rated, easily 8
28Oct95-8Bel	my	1¼	:481 1:121 1:353 1:592	3↑ BCClasic-G1	117 10 31 4¾ 11½ 12 12½	Bailey J D	L126	*.70	- -	*Cigar*126 2½ L'Carriere126 1 Unaccounted For126¾	Took over 4w trn,drvng 11
7Oct95-10Bel	fst	1¼	:48 1:112 1:36 2:011	3↑ JkyClbGC-G1	111 6 31 21 21 11½ 11	Bailey J D	L126	*.35	- -	*Cigar*126 1 Unaccounted For126 9¾ Star Standard121 2	Stalked outs,clear 7
16Sep95-9Bel	fst	1⅛	:454 1:093 1:334 1:47	3↑ Woodward-G1	111 5 32½ 34 2hd 14 12¾	Bailey J D	L126	*.10	- -	*Cigar*126 2¾ Star Standard121 3 Golden Larch126¾	Cruised in hand 6
2Jly95-6Hol	fst	1¼	:453 1:092 1:34 1:592	3↑ HolGdCpH-G1	118 1 42 41½ 11 13 13½	Bailey J D	LB126	*.90	- -	*Cigar*126 3½ *Tinners Way*118hd Tossofthecoin118½	Much best, driving 8
3Jun95-10Suf	fst	1⅛	:471 1:102 1:351 1:483	3↑ MassH750k	117 6 33½ 31½ 2½ 13 14	Bailey J D	LB124	*.20	- -	*Cigar*124 4 Poor But Honest107 5½ Double Calvados113nk	4 wide, ridden out 6
13May95-10Pim	fst	1 3/16	:48 1:112 1:351 1:533	4↑ PimSpclH-G1	114 1 11½ 11 11½ 14½ 12¼	Bailey J D	L122	*.40	- -	*Cigar*122 2¼ Devil His Due121 2¾ *Concern*121 4½	Steady hand drive 6
15Apr95-9OP	fst	1⅛	:462 1:104 1:352 1:471	4↑ OaklawnH-G1	121 4 42½ 45½ 42 1hd 12½	Bailey J D	L120	*1.70	- -	*Cigar*120 2½ Silver Goblin119 4 Concern122 1	Rallied, drew clear 7
5Mar95-9GP	fst	1¼	:472 1:114 1:364 2:024	3↑ GPH-G1	116 9 43½ 43½ 3nk 14 17½	Bailey J D	L118	*.50	- -	*Cigar*118 7½ Pride of Burkaan114 1 Mahogany Hall113 2	As rider pleased 11
11Feb95-9GP	fst	1⅛	:462 1:103 1:363 1:493	3↑ DonnH-G1	114 4 11 12 1hd 1½ 15½	Bailey J D	L115	4.00	- -	*Cigar*115 5½ Primitive Hall112 2 Bonus Money112 3½	Dueled, drew off 9

5Mar95- 9GP fst 1¼ :472 1:114 1:364 2:024 3↑ GPH-G1 **116** 9 43½ 43½ 3nk 14 17½ Bailey J D L118 *.50 - - *Cigar*1187½ Pride of Burkaan1141 Mahogany Hall1132 As rider pleased 11

11Feb95- 9GP fst 1⅛ :462 1:103 1:363 1:493 3↑ DonnH-G1 **114** 4 11 12 1hd 1½ 15½ Bailey J D L115 4.00 - - *Cigar*1155½ Primitive Hall1122 Bonus Money1123½ Dueled, drew off 9

22Jan95-10GP fst 1 1/16 :231 :464 1:112 1:431 4↑ Alw 33000N4X **108** 5 1hd 1½ 11 11 12 Bailey J D L122 *.50 - - *Cigar*1222 Upping the Ante1198¾ Chasin Gold1221 Led throughout 8

26Nov94- 8Aqu fst 1 :223 :454 1:111 1:36 3↑ NYRAMiH-G1 **115** 6 41¼ 41 12 15 17 Bailey J D 111 8.90 - - *Cigar*1117 Devil His Due1242½ Punch Line1121 Drew off, rddn out 12

28Oct94- 6Aqu fst 1 :222 :443 1:094 1:353 3↑ Alw 34000N2X **104** 6 2hd 11½ 13 14 18 Smith M E 117 3.50 - - *Cigar*1178 Golden Plover1193½ Gulliviegold1092 Ridden out 6

7Oct94- 8Bel fm 1 1/16 Ⓣ :232 :463 1:104 1:412 3↑ Alw 36000N3X **79** 2 42½ 33½ 2hd 33 38½ Krone J A 117 3.40 - - UnaccountedFor1142½ SameOldWish1196 *Cigr*117½ Mid move, 4 wide turn 6

16Sep94- 7Bel fm 1 ⓣ :23 :452 1:083 1:33 3↑ Alw 34000N2X **76** 10 84¾ 74 46 65½ 78¼ Bailey J D 117 *1.90 - - Jido1082½ Bermuda Cedar1142 Limited War1132 Wide all, no threat 11

8Aug94- 1Sar fm 1⅛ Ⓣ :472 1:12 1:363 1:483 3↑ Alw 34000N3X **86** 1 42½ 43 41½ 41¼ 33 Smith M E 117 3.20 - - My Mogul1191½ Next Endeavor1191½ Cigar117nk In tight, steadied 8

8Jly94- 7Bel fm 1 1/16 Ⓣ :243 :482 1:123 1:43 3↑ Alw 34000N3X **77** 5 2hd 1hd 2hd 41¼ 49 Smith M E 117 *1.70 - - Dancing Hunter117½ *Compadre*1173 I'm Very Irish1125½ Dueled, tired turn 5

Previously trained by Hassinger Alex L Jr 1993(as of 11/20): (111 14 17 14 0.13)

20Nov93- 6Hol fm 1⅛ ⓣ :461 1:102 1:341 1:464 HolDerby-G1 **71** 9 52½ 54½ 41½ 76½ 1114¼ Valenzuela P A LB122 24.80 - - ExplosiveRed1221¼ *JeuneHomme*122nk *ErlofBrking*122½ Bid turn, gave way 14

5Nov93- 8SA fm 1⅛ ⓣ :48 1:121 1:36 1:48 VolanteH-G3 **98** 4 44 42½ 32 21½ 22 Valenzuela P A LB117 7.70 - - Eastern Memories1132 Cigar117nk Snake Eyes120½ Finished well 9

25Sep93- 5BM fm 1 1/16 ⓣ :23 :453 1:10 1:413 AscotH-G3 **99** 1 53¾ 54¾ 41½ 13½ 3nk Valenzuela P A LB117 4.10 - - Siebe115nk *Nonproductiveasset*114hd Cigar1172¼ Room rail, led, wknd 11

3Sep93- 8Dmr fm 1 ⓣ :224 :47 1:11 1:35 3↑ Alw 40000N3L **96** 4 22 22 21 2hd 2½ McCarron C J LB115 3.30 - - Kingdom of Spain119½ Cigar115½ Saturnino1173 Bid 1/8,outfinished 6

18Aug93- 5Dmr fm 1 1/16 ⓣ :231 :472 1:111 1:414 3↑ Alw 36000N$Y **94** 5 43½ 43½ 53½ 1hd 12¾ McCarron C J LB115 *1.90 - - Cigr1152¾ OurMotionGrnted122hd TheBerklyMn1142¼ Quick gain early str 10

12Jun93-10Hol fm 1 1/16 ⓣ :231 :48 1:113 1:412 Alw 39000N2L **84** 10 75 72½ 4¾ 31½ 31¾ Valenzuela P A L117 2.90 - - *Nonproductiveasset*115½ Tossofthecoin1191¼ *Cigar*1172¾ In tight 1/4,rallied 10

23May93- 9Hol fm 1 1/16 ⓣ :232 :471 1:103 1:411 Alw 39000N$Y **85** 11 32 31 2hd 11½ 41¾ Valenzuela P A LB117 3.80 - - *Pleasedontexplain*117½ SttelyWrrior115½ FleetWizrd115¾ Lead 1/8, faltered 12

9May93- 3Hol fst 6f :22 :443 :564 1:092 3↑ Md Sp Wt 32k **93** 3 4 21 1hd 12 12¼ Valenzuela P A 117 5.20 - - Cigar1172¼ *Golden Slewpy*1165½ Famous Fan115hd Off slowly, rushed 6

21Feb93- 6SA gd 6f :214 :452 :58 1:104 Md Sp Wt 28k **53** 9 7 64 75¾ 67 713 Valenzuela P A B118 5.10 - - Demigod118nk *Cardiac*1182 [D]*Sir Hutch*1182½ No factor 9

Correggio (Ire)

b. g. 1991, by Sadler's Wells (Northern Dancer)–Rosa Mundi, by Secretariat **Lifetime record: 15 6 3 2 $274,725**

Own.– William C. Lickle

Br.– Ballydoyle Stud (Ire)

Tr.– Janet E. Elliot

12Jly98- 9Del fm *2¼ Hurdles 4:142 4↑ Midsummer Hurdle 50k 5 1 1hd 1hd 511 621 Kingsley A Jr 160 1.90 -- PrimeLegacy1429SerenityPrayer1521½Teb'sBnd1481 Faltered 8

9May98- 6PW yl *3 Hurdles 5:514 4↑ Iroquois-G1 6 1 12 12 1hd 33¼ Kingsley A Jr 156 - -- RowdyIrishmn156¾Confdnt1562½Crrggo15638 Weakened late 6

18Apr98- 3Mid fm *2½ Hurdles 5:422 4↑ Temple Gwathmey H-G2 5 1 13 12 2½ 29 Kingsley A Jr 162 - -- To Ridley1529Correggio1621¼Smart Jaune1464½ Gamely 5

11Apr98- 4AtH fm *2⅜ Hurdles 4:40 4↑ Atlanta Cup-G1 3 - - - - - Kingsley A Jr 158 - -- Soaringoverseattle1428½SerenityPryr1504PrmLgcy1424 Fell 5

10May97- 6PW fm *3 Hurdles 5:302 4↑ Iroquois-G1 2 1 12¼ 12½ 18 19¼ Kingsley A Jr 156 -- Correggio1569¼Lonesome Glory156½Confidente1563¼ Handily 6

17Nov96- 5Cam fm *2¾ Hurdles 5:092 4↑ Colonial Cup-G1 7 1 11 11½ 12 11 Teter J 160 -- Correggio1601Stop and Listen162¾Mr Yankee162¾ Driving 12

26Oct96- 5FH sf *2⅝ Hurdles 5:104 4↑ BC Grand Nat H-G1 3 1 11¼ 11 12 13 Kingsley A Jr 138 -- Correggio1383Mr Yankee1401½Rowdy Irishman1542½ Driving 10

29Sep96- 4Fx yl *2⅛ Hurdles 4:121 3↑ Alw 12500 9 1 11¼ 15 13 15 Teter J 146 -- Correggio1465Winterton15623Duraznillo152½ In hand 10

16Sep96- 8Pha sf 1⅛ⓣ :503 1:174 1:444 1:59 3↑ Md Sp Wt 11 6 54½ 32 12 13½ Castillo RE 122 3.80 61-35 Correggio1223½Psychothrpy1221¼Pondrously116½ Drew clear 11

13Nov94- 2Cam fm *2¼ Hurdles 3:58 RG Woolfe Mem 25k 8 2 11¼ 1½ 23 28 Miller C 149 -- MacheteRoad1458Corrggio1492½UnitedCongress149½ Gamely 12

Previously trained by Charles O'Brien

19Sep94♦ Listowel(Ire) sf 2LH 4:193 Devon Inn 3YO Hurdle Alw8500 34½ O'Dwyer C 158 5.00 Brief Reunion1543Nun's Island1541½Correggio1583½ 15
Led,clear at 3rd,headed 2 out,brushed 1 out,evenly late

15Sep94♦ Dundalk(Ire) yl 1½ⓣLH 2:403 3↑ Riverstown Maiden Mdn5000 515¾ Roche C 126 *1.25 Father Sky126¾Native Joy1233½Better Style1231½ 16
Tracked leader,led halfway,headed over 2f out,weakened

22Aug94♦ Tralee(Ire) yl 2LH 3:512 Kellihers Electricl 3YO Hurdle Alw8400 12 O'Dwyer C 145 7.00 Correggio1452Celibate1452½Dr Leunt14512 17
Led at 2nd,mistakes 4 and 3 out,won driving

2Jly94♦ Naas(Ire) gd 1¼ⓣLH 2:082 Virginia EBF Maiden Mdn7100 55 Roche C 121 *2.25 Bhavnagar1211½Muzrak121¾Bubbly Prospect1212½ 16
Broke alertly,taken back to 4th,drifted and bumped 1½f out

1Jun94♦ The Curragh(Ire) gd 1¼ⓣStr 2:102 Curragh Bldstk Agency EBF Mdn Mdn5100 2hd Roche C 126 5.00 Better Choice126hdCorreggio1262½Ivory Reef126nk 12
Led to halfway,tracked leader,led again 1f out,caught at line

Countess Diana

Own: Kaster Mr. and Mrs. Richard Propson et al

B. f. 4 (Mar)
Sire: Deerhound (Danzig) $7,500
Dam: T. V. Countess (T. V. Commercial)
Br: Richard S Kaster (Ky)
Tr: Lohmeier Mary J

Life	**14**	**7**	**2**	**0**	**$1,117,185**	**103**	**D.Fst**	**11**	**4**	**2**	**0**	**$932,565**	**99**
1999	**4**	**2**	**0**	**0**	**$64,620**	**103**	**Wet(341)**	**2**	**2**	**0**	**0**	**$153,000**	**103**
1998	**4**	**0**	**1**	**0**	**$32,780**	**95**	**Turf(249)**	**1**	**1**	**0**	**0**	**$31,620**	**93**
	0	**0**	**0**	**0**	**$0**	**–**	**Dst(0)**	**0**	**0**	**0**	**0**	**$0**	**–**

21Oct99- 9Kee fm 1 1/16 ⓣ :23 :47 1:113 1:414 3↑ Ⓕ Alw 51450c **93** 3 11½ 11 12 12 13 Perret C L117 2.80 93- 06 CountssDn1173 TssosMqcRoo1174 Aslwofwht117½ Controlled pace,driviq 9

25Sep99- 9TP fst 1 1/16 :234 :474 1:121 1:444 3↑ Ⓕ TPBC-G3 **72** 3 1½ 1hd 1hd 43½ 714¾ Prado E S L114 f 3.60 64- 24 Ruby Surprise1181 Let1183½ *French Braids*114nk Out in strip, faded 8

22Aug99- 8Sar fst 7f :22 :443 1:092 1:23 3↑ Ⓕ BalrinaH-G1 **66** 5 3 2½ 22 96½ 917 Chavez J F L116 f 4.40 73- 16 Furlough114no *Bourbon Belle*1171½ [DH]*Catinca*121 Tired after a half 10

8Aug99- 6Sar sly 6½f :213 :444 1:10 1:163 3↑ Ⓕ Alw 55000N$Y **103** 5 1 11 11 15 15¾ Chavez J F L117 f *1.00 91- 18 CountessDin1175¾ MemoryCll1141½ CottgGrdn1144¼ Strong pace, handily 6

Previously trained by Mott William I 1998(as of 9/12): (437 107 80 53 0.24)

12Sep98- 8Bel fst 1⅛ :47 1:12 1:371 1:493 Ⓕ GazelleH-G1 **80** 4 2hd 1hd 1hd 5¾ 69½ Sellers S J L117 3.30 72- 25 *Tap to Music*1121¼ Keeper Hill1221 *French Braids*1151 Between rivals, tired 7

27Jun98- 8Bel fst 1⅛ :454 1:10 1:342 1:473 Ⓕ MthrGoos-G1 **95** 5 2hd 1½ 2½ 24 45 Sellers S J L121 6.80 87- 16 *Jersey Girl*1211 Keeper Hill1213 *Banshee Breeze*1211 Stayed well inside 11

7Jun98- 8Bel fst 1 :223 :452 1:101 1:361 Ⓕ Acorn-G1 **77** 4 1hd 31 42¼ 58 511½ Sellers S J L121 *1.00 71- 22 *Jersey Girl*1212¾ Santaria121no Brave Deed1211¾ Spd on rail,tired 10

13May98- 8Bel fst 7f :213 :443 1:091 1:223 Ⓕ NassauCo-G3 **92** 4 1 45½ 44½ 23 22½ Sellers S J L118 *.75 86- 12 *Jersey Girl*1212½ Countess Diana1189 Foil11418 Stumbled strt,rail mve 4

Previously trained by Byrne Patrick B 1997(as of 11/8): (127 46 23 10 0.36)

8Nov97- 2Hol fst 1 1/16 :224 :46 1:103 1:42 Ⓕ BCJuvFil-G1 **95** 8 21½ 2½ 11 12 18½ Sellers S J LB119 *2.00 91- 06 Countess Diana1198½ Career Collection1194 Primaly1192 Led 2w, drvng 14

11Oct97- 8Kee fst 1 1/16 :23 :454 1:092 1:451 Ⓕ Alcibiad-G2 **85** 6 11½ 1½ 11 13½ 12¾ Sellers S J L118 1.70 82- 24 *CountessDin*1182¾ LilyOGold118hd BeutifulPlesur118¾ Drew clear, handily 6

29Aug97- 8Sar gd 7f :222 :454 1:102 1:24 Ⓕ Spinaway-G1 **93** 1 1 1½ 1hd 15 16½ Sellers S J L121 *.85 85- 15 *Countess Diana*1216½ Brac Drifter121hd Aunt Anne1212½ Kept to task 5

23Jly97- 9Sar fst 6f :221 :453 :573 1:101 Ⓕ Schylrvl-G2 **99** 1 3 1½ 1hd 12½ 12 Sellers S J L116 2.30 90- 13 *Countess Diana*1162 Love Lock1195 Sequence1162 Dictd pce,somthng left 6

28Jun97- 7CD fst 5½f :221 :454 :573 1:034 Ⓕ Debutant-G3 **91** 1 1 1½ 2hd 11½ 2½ Sellers S J L115 *1.70 99- 08 Love Lock115½ *Countess Diana*1159 Quick Lap115nk Drew clear, outfinishd 13

Previously trained by Garcia Carlos A 1997(as of 6/6): (110 15 15 17 0.14)

6Jun97- 3Pim fst 4½f :222 :452 :512 Ⓕ Md Sp Wt 16k **96** 5 2 22½ 21 1½ Johnston M T 119 6.20 106- 11 CountessDiana119½ *BracDrifter*11910 *Epistol*119hd Stalked,came wd,drivng 7

Criminal Type

ch. c. 1985, by Alydar (Raise a Native)–Klepto, by No Robbery
Own.– Calumet Farm
Br.– Calumet Farm (Ky)
Tr.– D. Wayne Lukas

Lifetime record: 24 10 5 3 $2,351,817

15Sep90- 8Bel fst 1⅛ :451 1:083 1:331 1:454 3↑ Woodward H-G1 1 4 32 21½ 43½ 64¾ Santos JA 127 *1.00 100-09 Dispersal1231¼Quiet American1171½Rhythm120nk Tired 8
4Aug90- 7Sar fst 1⅛ :484 1:122 1:362 1:483 3↑ Whitney H-G1 1 1 11½ 12 13 11½ Stevens GL 126 *.40 94-06 CriminalType1261½DancingSpree1212½MiSelcto1177¼ Driving 6
24Jun90- 8Hol fst 1¼ :464 1:101 1:343 1:594 3↑ Hol Gold Cup H-G1 2 2 2½ 1hd 1hd 1hd Santos JA 121 2.40 99-09 CriminlType121hdSundaySilence1263½OpnngVrs1192¾ Gamely 7
28May90- 8Bel fst 1 :223 :45 1:091 1:342 3↑ Metropolitan H-G1 6 3 21 21½ 21½ 1nk Santos JA 120 8.40e 97-18 CrimnlTyp120nkHousbustr1131½EsyGor1273 Drifted out late 9
12May90-10Pim fst 1 3/16 :464 1:103 1:342 1:53 4↑ Pim Spl H-G1 8 2 21½ 22 21½ 1nk Santos JA 117 7.70 101-16 CriminlType117nkRuhlmann1241¼DeRoch1141½ Jostled break 10
14Apr90- 8OP fst 1⅛ :462 1:102 1:352 1:471 4↑ Oaklawn H-G1 6 4 32 21 45 47¾ Pincay L Jr 119 1.70 89-17 Opening Verse1182½De Roche1142Silver Survivor1163½ 8
Wide first turn
1Apr90- 8SA fst 1⅛ :46 1:093 1:342 1:471 4↑ San Bernardino H-G2 1 3 32½ 34½ 23 22 Pincay L Jr 119 1.70 98-11 Rhlmnn1232CrmnlTyp1191½StylshWnnr113¾ Winner too tough 6
4Mar90- 8SA fst 1¼ :454 1:094 1:344 2:011 4↑ S Anita H-G1 9 5 77 26 24 21¾ Solis A 119 5.80 86-18 Ruhlmann1211¾Criminal Type119hdFlying Continental121½ 10
Wide into lane
11Feb90- 8SA fst 1⅛ :452 1:094 1:36 1:49 4↑ San Antonio H-G2 2 3 35 33 1½ 11 Solis A 117 4.70 91-14 CrimnlTyp1171StylshWnnr1136½Rhlmnn1224½ Strong effort 7
28Jan90- 8SA fst 1 1/16 :224 :46 1:103 1:422 4↑ San Pasqual H-G2 7 3 32½ 21½ 21 1½ McCarron CJ 114 7.60 91-19 CriminalType114½LivelyOne122½PresentValue1214½ Driving 8
12Jan90- 8SA fst 1 :222 :454 1:102 1:36 4↑ Alw 47000 7 4 42½ 42 3½ 11¼ Pincay L Jr 122 1.40 87-22 Criminal Type1221¼Script1112Lowell1152 Wide final ⅜ 7
17Dec89- 7Hol fst 1 :23 :454 1:10 1:343 3↑ Alw 30000 3 1 2hd 2hd 12 15 Pincay L Jr 118 *1.30 91-14 CriminlType1185GoodDeliverance1163½Chrltn1161¾ Driving 8
18Nov89- 6Hol fst 1 :223 :451 1:093 1:342 3↑ Alw 30000 3 2 31 41¼ 42½ 33¼ Pincay L Jr 121 3.10 89-17 KingTaufan1181¼GoodDeliverance1162CrimnlType1211 Wide 7
2Nov89- 7SA fst 1 :233 :471 1:114 1:353 3↑ Alw 37000 4 1 1hd 2hd 3nk 2no Pincay L Jr 119 *1.20 91-16 Splurgr111noCrmnlTyp119¾Mr.DndyDncr1154½ Bumped start 6
22Oct89- 5SA gd 1⅛⊗ :46 1:10 1:351 1:474 3↑ Alw 37000 4 1 11 11 2hd 2hd Delahoussaye E 119 3.80 96-09 Sepoy117hdCriminlType1197Charlatan117¾ Ducked in,bumped 8
8Oct89- 3SA fst 1 1/16 :233 :47 1:11 1:423 3↑ Alw 34000 7 2 1hd 1hd 1hd 1½ McCarron CJ 118 4.70 88-17 Criminal Type118½Kaboi1143Stephen's Sooner1172¾ 7
Jostled early,driving
13May89- 7Hol fst 1 1/16 :231 :471 1:112 1:433 4↑ Alw 28000 2 5 31 1hd 2hd 31½ McCarron CJ 116 *1.40 80-11 Remar116nkPureExpense1191¼CrmnlTyp1162½ Lacked response 7
24Apr89- 9SA fm 1⅛Ⓣ :463 1:112 1:363 1:493 3↑ Alw 36000 3 6 54 42¾ 54¼ 48¼ McCarron CJ 120 *1.90 71-19 NorthrnDrama112¾OrneryGuest1143ElitRgnt1224½ No mishap 9
12Apr89- 7SA fst 1 1/16 :233 :471 1:11 1:422 4↑ Alw 36000 7 5 4¾ 1½ 2½ 33¼ Pincay L Jr 118 *2.30 86-14 Awesome Bud120¾Elite Regent1202½Criminal Type1181 8
Previously trained by Patrick-Louis Biancone
5Nov88♦ Saint-Cloud(Fr) sf *1½ⓉLH 2:364 Prix Le Fabuleux (Listed) Stk33600 833 Kessas JL 121 33.00 Robore1233Valuable1204Plaza Gizon1261½ 8
Chased in 4th behind clear leader,weakened 2f out
28Sep88♦ Saint-Cloud(Fr) fm*1½ⓉLH 2:343 Prix Sicambre (Listed) Stk31900 57 Legrix E 123 13.00 Hello Calder1232Andaroun1233Opposite Abstract1231 5
Tracked slow pace in 3rd,4th 2f out,weakened final furlong
27Sep87♦ Longchamp(Fr) yl *1ⓉRH 1:442 Prix des Chenes-G3 Stk56000 67 Boeuf D 121 5.00 Harmless Albatross1182½Baranof1212½Titus Groan121hd 9
In touch in 5th,never threatened
24Aug87♦ Deauville(Fr) sf *1ⓉRH 1:464 Prix de Caen Mdn21100 1½ Boeuf D 123 5.20 Criminal Type123½Pintoriccio1231½Antiqua123nk 7
Tracked in 4th,taken wide into stretch 3f out,led 100y out
3Aug87♦ Clairefontaine(Fr) sf *1ⓉRH 1:413 Prix des Tritons Alw13600 2no Boeuf D 119 10.00 Hymen119noCriminal Type119½Le Play1191½ 13
Tracked in 3rd,bid 1½f out,led 170y out,caught on line

Dance Smartly

dkbbr. f. 1988, by Danzig (Northern Dancer)–Classy 'n Smart, by Smarten
Own.– Sam-Son Farms
Br.– Sam-Son Farms (Can)
Tr.– James E. Day

Lifetime record: 17 12 2 3 $3,263,836

5Sep92- 9AP fm 1 3/16Ⓣ :484 1:122 1:361 1:54 3↑ ⒻBeverly D-G1 100 6 2 2½ 2½ 21½ 31¾ Day P L 123 *1.60e 94-08 Kostroma1231½RubyTiger123nkDanceSmartly1232 Mild rally 13
15Aug92- 9AP gd 1 1/16Ⓣ :234 :472 1:12 1:422 3↑ ⒻArl Bud BC H 154k 92 4 2 21½ 21½ 1hd 32 Day P 123 *.20 92-13 Alcando1131¼Explosive Kate112¾Dance Smartly1233 Faded 6
19Jly92- 8WO sf 1⅛Ⓣ :512 1:183 1:444 2:122 ⓇMaturity-G1C 93 5 1 2hd 1½ 11½ 1½ Day P L 121 *.05e 39-61 DnceSmrtly121½SwordDance1262½ShinyKey126nk Ridden out 6
14Jun92- 7WO fm 1⅛Ⓣ :444 1:09 1:34 1:46 3↑ K Edward Gold Cup-G3 100 1 6 66½ 63¾ 2hd 2no Day P L 119 *.40e 97-06 ThundrRegnt113noDncSmrtly1191½TotofRum1193 Just missed 11
2Nov91- 4CD fst 1⅛ :471 1:114 1:374 1:504 3↑ ⒻBC Distaff-G1 - 10 5 65½ 42½ 1hd 11½ Day P LB 120 *.50e 94-09 DnceSmrtly1201½Versailles Treaty1202¾BroughttoMind123½ 13
Driving clear
15Sep91- 9WO fst 1⅛ :482 1:121 1:364 1:491 Molson Million-G2 - 10 3 21 2½ 2hd 12 Day P 116 1.65 106-11 Dance Smartly1162Shudanz1176Majesterian1171 Hand ride 10
18Aug91- 8WO yl 1½Ⓣ :47 1:12 2:054 2:312 ⓇBreeders'-G1C - 6 3 33½ 11½ 14½ 18 Day P 121 *.30e 83-17 Dance Smartly1218Shiny Key126hdJanuary Man1265 Handily 10
28Jly91- 8FE fst 1 3/16 :454 1:10 1:363 1:563 ⓇPrince of Wales-G1C - 5 3 32 32 11½ 12 Day P 121 *.10e 99-03 DnceSmrtly1212ProfssorRbbt1262¾Shudnz1264¾ Ridden out 6
7Jly91- 8WO fst 1¼ :472 1:114 1:371 2:032 ⓇQueens Plate-G1C - 3 4 42 32 11½ 18 Day P 121 *.55e 91-15 DanceSmartly1218WildernessSong1213½Shudanz126½ Easily 9
16Jun91- 8WO fst 1⅛ :48 1:123 1:383 1:511 ⒻⓇCan Oaks-G1C - 3 3 21½ 2½ 1hd 14½ Day P 121 *.05e 96-19 DanceSmrtly1214½Wilderness Song12110Platinum Paws1211½ 8
Hand ride
1Jun91- 9WO fst 1 1/16 :24 :483 1:122 1:433 ⒻSelene-G1C - 6 3 32 32½ 2hd 13¼ Swatuk B 120 *.50e 96-10 DnceSmrtly1203¼ThroughFlight123nkAreydne113hd Handily 9
4May91- 9WO fst 6f :222 :453 1:103 ⒻStar Shoot-G3C - 2 6 42¼ 31 1½ 12½ Swatuk B 120 *.35e 92-14 DanceSmrtly1202½DiamondSyl1164½Areydne1141½ Hand ride 7
27Oct90- 4Bel fst 1 1/16 :223 :454 1:11 1:44 ⒻBC Juv Fillies-G1 - 7 1 1hd 1hd 22 36 Hawley S 119 b 13.50e 76-15 MeadwStr1195PrivatTreasur1191DncSmrtly1194¼ Weakened 13
15Sep90- 7WO yl 1Ⓣ :232 :464 1:114 1:392 ⒻNatalma (Div 1)-G2C - 3 1 1½ 1hd 12 1½ Hawley S 116 b *1.10 77-18 DanceSmrtly116½ⒹLadyBeGreat1144½Malbay1141½ In hand 8
13Aug90- 8FE sly 6f :23 :47 1:131 ⒻⓇOnt Deb-G2C - 7 1 41½ 33 21 22½ Hawley S 116 *.45 81-20 RegalPennant1152½DanceSmrtly1167¼UnrlAffr1161½ Mild bid 8
1Aug90- 8WO fst 5½f :222 :461 1:05 ⒻAlw 23200 - 4 1 2hd 1hd 12½ 14¾ Hawley S 116 *.50 95-10 DanceSmartly1164¾SilentBattle1164Kaydann117nk Hand ride 8
7Jly90- 3WO fst 5½f :224 :461 1:061 ⒻMd Sp Wt - 3 6 43 22 11 13½ Driedger I 114 *.50 89-11 Dance Smartly1143½Kaydanna119¾Chili Lee1192½ Authority 6

Daylami (Ire)

Own: Godolphin Racing Inc

Gr/ro. h. 5 (Apr)
Sire: Doyoun*Ire (Mill Reef) $2,600
Dam: Daltawa*Ire (Miswaki)
Br: His Highness the Aga Khan's Studs S.C. (Ire)
Tr: bin Suroor Saeed

Life	21	11	3	4	$4,614,762	118	D.Fst	1	0	0	0	$150,000 -
1999	7	4	1	0	$3,501,449	118	Wet(294*)	0	0	0	0	$0 -
1998	6	3	0	2	$689,218	111	Turf(309)	20	11	3	4	$4,464,762 118
	0	0	0	0	$0	-	Dst(0)	0	0	0	0	$0 -

6Nov99- 9GP gd 1½Ⓣ :47 1:103 2:243 3↑ BCTurf-G1 118 3 66½ 54½ 33 2hd 12½ Dettori L L126 *1.60 94- 09 Daylami1262½ *Royal Anthem*1262 Buck's Boy1261¼ Drew clear, driving 14
3Oct99 Longchamp (Fr) hy *1½Ⓣ RH 2:382 3↑ Prix de l'Arc de Triomphe-G1 Stk 1144500 923½ Dettori L 131 4.00 Montjeu123½ El Condor Pasa1316 Croco Rouge1315 14
Timeform rating: 106 *Unhurried in 8th,weakened 1-1/2f out*
11Sep99 Leopardstwn (Ire) sf 1¼Ⓣ LH 2:082 3↑ Irish Champion Stakes-G1 Stk 889100 19 Dettori L 130 1.50 Daylami1309 Dazzling Park1202½ Dream Well130½ 7
Timeform rating: 135 *Tracked in 3rd,led over 1-1/2f out,drew clear.Royal Anthem 5th*
24Jly99 Ascot (GB) gd 1½Ⓣ RH 2:291 3↑ King George VI & Queen Eliz St-G1 Stk 946800 15 Dettori L 133 3.00 *Daylami*1335 Nedawi133½ Fruits of Love1332½ 8
Timeform rating: 135 *Rated in 4th,5th 3f out,led 1-1/2f out,drew clear.Oath 7th*
4Jun99 Epsom (GB) yl 1½Ⓣ LH 2:401 4↑ Coronation Cup-G1 Stk 324000 1¾ Dettori L 126 4.50 *Daylami*126¾ Royal Anthem126½ Dream Well1261 7
Timeform rating: 124 *Rated in 4th behind slow pace,long drive to lead 100y out*

Date	Track	Cond	Dist	Course	Time	Age	Race	Spd/Calls	Fin	Jockey	Wt	Odds	Top Finishers	Field
23May99	Curragh (Ire)	gd	1¼ Ⓣ	RH	2:101	4↑	Tattersalls Gold Cup-G1		22½	Dettori L	126	*1.00	Shiva1232½ *Daylami*1261 Make No Mistake126½	6
Timeform rating: 118							Stk 134300						Tracked leader,led 2f out,headed 1f out,second best.Insatiable4th	
28Mar99	Nad Al Sheba (UAE)	ft	*1¼	LH	2:003	4↑	Dubai World Cup-G1		54¼	Velazquez J	126	-	Almutawakel126¾ Malek126¾ *Victory Gallop*1261½	8
Timeform rating: 118+							Stk 5000000						Tracked leaders,bumped after 3f,trailed halfway,mild late gain	
17Oct98	Newmarket (GB)	gd	1¼ Ⓣ	Str	2:033	3↑	Champion Stakes-G1		32¼	Dettori L	128	*1.20	Alborada120nk Insatiable1282 Daylami1281	10
Timeform rating: 120							Stk 680700						Rated in 6th,outpaced 3f out,bid 2f out,briefly 2nd,faded late	
12Sep98-9Bel		fm	1⅜ T		:484 1:134 1:374 2:13	3↑	ManOWar-G1	111 2 55½ 53¾ 65¾ 44	11¼	Bailey J D	L126	*1.25	94-12 Daylami1261¼ *Buck's Boy*1262¾ Indy Vidual126hd Finished fast, clear	9
25Jly98	Ascot (GB)	gd	1½ Ⓣ	RH	2:293	3↑	King George VI & Queen Eliz St-G1		43	Kinane M J	133	6.00	*Swain*1331 High-Rise1211½ *Royal Anthem*121½	8
Timeform rating: 126							Stk 995700						Tracked in 4th,mild bid & drifted right 1-1/2f out,one-paced late	
4Jly98	Sandown Park (GB)	gd	1¼ Ⓣ	RH	2:064	3↑	Eclipse Stakes-G1		1½	Dettori L	133	*1.50	Daylami133½ Faithful Son1336 *Central Park*122½	7
Timeform rating: 125+							Stk 414800						Tracked in 4th,rallied to lead 2f out,ridden out	
16Jun98	Ascot (GB)	yl	1¼ Ⓣ	RH	2:081	3↑	Prince of Wales's Stakes-G2		3½	Dettori L	134	*2.00	Faithful Son129nk *Chester House*118nk *Daylami*1343½	8
Timeform rating: 124+							Stk 198200						Tracked in 3rd,bid & in tight 1-1/2f out,angled out,gaining late	
24May98	Curragh (Ire)	gd	1¼ Ⓣ	RH	2:061	4↑	Tattersalls Gold Cup-G2		11½	Dettori L	130	*1.25	Daylami1301½ Stage Affair1243 *Quws*1277	5
Timeform rating: 126							Stk 107200						Tracked in 3rd,led ovr 1f out,driving.Dr Johnson 4th,Ebadiyla 5th	
Previously trained by Alain De Royer-Dupre														
7Sep97	Longchamp (Fr)	gd	*1 Ⓣ	RH	1:37	3↑	Prix du Moulin de Longchamp-G1		33½	Mosse G	123	3.60	*Spinning World*1283 Helissio128½ *Daylami*123nk	9
							Stk 252300						Rated in 6th,finished well without threatening.Rebecca Sharp 7th	
17Aug97	Deauville (Fr)	gd	*1 Ⓣ	Str	1:342	3↑	Prix Jacques le Marois-G1		22	Mosse G	123	2.50	*Spinning World*1302 Daylami1236 Neuilly1233	6
							Stk 276800						Behind,rallied to lead briefly 1-1/2f out,2nd best.Starborough 4t	
17Jun97	Ascot (GB)	gd	1 Ⓣ	RH	1:39		St James's Palace Stakes-G1		35	Mosse G	126	3.50	Starborough1261 Air Express1264 Daylami126½	8
							Stk 373400						Rated in 6th,angled out 2f out,one-paced late.Desert King 4th	
11May97	Longchamp (Fr)	sf	*1 Ⓣ	RH	1:423		Poule d'Essai des Poulains-G1		12	Mosse G	128	1.60	Daylami1282 Loup Sauvage1282½ Visionary128¾	6
							Stk 298700						Rated in last,sharp run to lead 100y out,driving.Yalaietanee 4th	
20Apr97	Longchamp (Fr)	gd	*1 Ⓣ	RH	1:394		Prix de Fontainebleau-G3		12	Mosse G	128	2.00	*Daylami*1282 Loup Sauvage128½ Fine Fellow1281	6
							Stk 63100						Tracked in 3rd,led 170y out,driving.Majorien 4th	
2Nov96	Saint-Cloud (Fr)	sf	*1¼ Ⓣ	LH	2:154		Criterium de Saint-Cloud-G1		2¾	Mosse G	126	*.80e	Shaka126¾ *Daylami*1262 Sendoro1262½	10
							Stk 132800						Unhurried in 8th,rallied to lead 1f out,soon headed second best	
7Oct96	Evry (Fr)	gd	*1 Ⓣ	LH	1:441		Prix Herod (Listed)		12	Mosse G	128	*.60	Daylami1282 Bartex1282 Herakles128nk	6
							Stk 46800						Tracked leader,led 1f out,easily clear	
19Sep96	Longchamp (Fr)	yl	*1 Ⓣ	RH	1:482		Prix de Fontenoy-EBF		11½	Mosse G	128	*1.60	*Daylami*1281½ *Rate Cut*128nk *Visionary*1282	9
							Maiden 34900						Rated in 6th,led 1f out,not fully extended	

Dehere

Own: Due Process Stable

B. c. 3 (Apr)
Sire: Deputy Minister (Vice Regent)
Dam: Sister Dot (Secretariat)
Br: Due Process Stable (Ky)
Tr: Nobles Reynaldo H

Life	9	6	2	0	$723,712	103	D.Fst	7	5	1	0	$578,280 103
1994	2	1	1	0	$127,800	103	Wet(361)	2	1	1	0	$145,432 102
1993	7	5	1	0	$595,912	102	Turf(313)	0	0	0	0	$0 –
	0	0	0	0	$0	–	Dst(0)	0	0	0	0	$0 –

Date/Race	Cond	Dist	Fractions	Race	Spd	PP	St	1C	2C	Str	Fin	Jockey	Med/Wt	Odds	Pace	Top Finishers	Comment	Field
19Feb94-9GP	gd	1 1/16	:224 :453 1:102 1:443	FntnOYth-G2	**99**	6	57½	58½	53	1hd	1¾	Perret C	L119	2.40e	- -	Dehere119¾ Go for Gin1191¼ Ride the Rails1173¾	Rallied, drew clear	6
5Feb94-1GP	fst	1 1/16	:241 :482 1:124 1:433	Alw 38610N$MY	**103**	1	1½	1½	1hd	1hd	2¾	Smith M E	L115	*.10	- -	RidetheRils115¾ *Dehr*1151 2½ SnorConquistdor1153	Pace, dueled, gave way	4
6Nov93-6SA	fst	1 1/16	:223 :462 1:104 1:424	BCJuven-G1	**75**	7	44½	44	3½	53½	812½	McCarron C J	B122	*.70	- -	Brocco1225 Blumin Affair1221½ *Tabasco Cat*1223	Bid 1/4, flattened out	11
16Oct93-7Bel	fst	1	:231 :463 1:12 1:354	Champagn-G1	**90**	2	23	22½	2½	12	14	McCarron C J	122	*.30	- -	Dehere1224 Crary122¾ Amathos122½	Stalked 3w, ridden out	6
18Sep93-6Bel	sly	7f	:222 :453 1:101 1:231	Futurity-G1	**102**	4	5	41½	33	23	2½	McCarron C J	122	*.40	- -	*Holy Bull*122½ *Dehere*1225 Prenup1228	Bumped start, late bid	6
29Aug93-8Sar	fst	6½f	:222 :453 1:092 1:154	Hopeful-G1	**97**	3	1	1hd	1hd	1½	12½	McCarron C J	122	*.40	- -	Dehere1222½ Slew Gin Fizz1222 Whitney Tower1221¼	Drew off, ridden out	7
13Aug93-8Sar	fst	6f	:221 :454 :581 1:102	Sanford-G3	**90**	2	5	51¼	51¾	1hd	15	McCarron C J	122	*.40	- -	*Dehere*1225 Prenup1155½ *Distinct Reality*1222¾	Angled out 5w, in hand	6
29Jly93-9Sar	fst	6f	:214 :45 :572 1:094	SarSpcl-G2	**89**	1	6	31	4¾	51¾	1nk	Maple E	117	*2.10	- -	*Dehere*117nk Slew GinFizz1172 WhitneyTower1175¾	Angled out 5w, driving	9
30Jun93-5Mth	fst	5f	:222 :463 :59	Md Sp Wt 17k	**77**	1	10	62¾	65	34½	14	Bravo J	118	*.90	- -	*Dehere*1184 *Justinthefastlane*1184¾ Luckie Peri1184	5w rally, ridden out	12

Eliza

Own: Allen E. Paulson

B. f. 4 (Mar)
Sire: Mt. Livermore (Blushing Groom*Fr)
Dam: Daring Bidder (Bold Bidder)
Br: Allen E. Paulson (Ky)
Tr: Hassinger A L Jr

Life	12	5	2	2	$1,095,316	99	D.Fst	11	4	2	2	$960,466 99
1994	3	0	0	1	$16,776	95	Wet(357)	1	1	0	0	$134,850 84
1993	4	1	1	1	$270,540	99	Turf(316)	0	0	0	0	$0 –
	0	0	0	0	$0	–	Dst(0)	0	0	0	0	$0 –

Date/Race	Cond	Dist	Fractions	Race	Spd	PP	St	1C	2C	Str	Fin	Jockey	Med/Wt	Odds	Pace	Top Finishers	Comment	Field
28Dec94-3SA	fst	6½f	:22 :443 1:083 1:15	3↑ⓇMarktBaskt60k	**90**	8	5	52¼	31	43	44½	Stevens G L	LB115	3.00	- -	*Key Phrase*1141 Pirate's Revenge1163½ Velvet Tulip122no	Bid 1/4, empty	8
10Oct94-8SA	fst	1 1/16	:23 :47 1:103 1:403	3↑ⒻLadySecrtH106k	**68**	2	43	41½	31	411	523¾	Antley C W	L119	4.50	- -	HollywoodWldct1242½ Exchng1213 DncngMrg11314	Bid 3-w turn, stopped	5
3Sep94-5Dmr	fst	6½f	:214 :444 1:082 1:144	3↑ⒻⓇJuneDarlH66k	**95**	7	3	1½	13	12	33	Valenzuela P A	LB120	*1.40	- -	*Starolamo*1162¾ Nijivision114nk Eliza120½	Fast pace, weakened	7
19Jun93-8Hol	fst	1 1/16	:223 :452 1:092 1:422	ⒻPrincess-G2	**78**	1	11	12	13	21½	48¼	Valenzuela P A	LB119	*.30	- -	Fit to Lead117hd Swazi's Moment115hd Passing Vice1198	Lost action str	5
30Apr93-9CD	fst	1⅛	:47 1:122 1:383 1:522	ⒻKyOaks-G1	**91**	8	54	55	31	1hd	21¼	Valenzuela P A	L121	*.60	- -	Dispute1211¼ Eliza121nk Quinpool121nk	Dueled, gave way	11
3Apr93-5SA	fst	1⅛	:464 1:101 1:352 1:49	SADerby-G1	**96**	4	21½	2½	1½	2hd	31	Valenzuela P A	LB117	3.20	- -	Personal Hope122¾ Union City122nk Eliza1171½	Quick move,outfinished	7
7Mar93-8SA	fst	1 1/16	:23 :471 1:11 1:424	ⒻSAOaks-G1	**99**	7	31	2½	12	16	12¼	Valenzuela P A	LB117	1.80	- -	Eliza1172¼ Stalcreek1171 Dance for Vanny1171¾	Rapid gain, driving	9
31Oct92-5GP	fst	1 1/16	:231 :47 1:103 1:424	ⒻBCJuvFil-G1	**92**	9	31½	3nk	11	11½	11	Valenzuela P A	L119	*1.20	- -	*Eliza*1191 *Educated Risk*119½ *Boots 'n Jackie*1195½	Drew off, driving	12
17Oct92-8Kee	fst	1 1/16	:223 :461 1:10 1:431	ⒻAlcibiad-G2	**99**	3	22½	21	11½	17	14	Valenzuela P A	LB118	*.80	- -	*Eliza*1184 Avie's Shadow1185 True Affair1184	Much the best, handily	6
19Sep92-10AP	sl	1	:233 :463 1:122 1:392	ⒻArlWaLas-G2	**84**	2	1hd	12	12	17	112	Valenzuela P A	L119	*.90	- -	*Eliza*11912 Banshee Winds1193 Tourney1191½	Stumbled, easily	6
19Aug92-8Dmr	fst	7f	:214 :441 1:092 1:223	ⒻSorrento-G3	**80**	7	5	1½	11½	1½	23½	Valenzuela P A	B117	*1.10	- -	Zoonaqua1173½ *Eliza*1171 Medici Bells117nk	No match for winner	11
9Aug92-6Dmr	fst	5½f	:211 :44 1:03	ⒻMd Sp Wt 29k	**87**	6	7	31	1hd	11½	12½	Stevens G L	117	*1.90	- -	Eliza1172½ *Set Them Free*1175 Nijivision1172	Ridden out	10

Escena

Own: Paulson Allen E

B. m. 5 (May)
Sire: Strawberry Road*Aus (Whiskey Road)
Dam: Claxton's Slew (Seattle Slew)
Br: Allen E. Paulson (Ky)
Tr: Mott William I

Life	29	11	9	3	$2,962,639	114	D.Fst	22	9	7	3	$2,632,645 114
1998	9	5	3	0	$2,032,425	114	Wet(375)	3	0	2	0	$120,000 104
1997	9	2	1	2	$428,514	104	Turf(311)	4	2	0	0	$209,994 103
	0	0	0	0	$0	–	Dst(0)	0	0	0	0	$0 –

Date/Race	Cond	Dist	Fractions	Race	Spd	PP	St	1C	2C	Str	Fin	Jockey	Med/Wt	Odds	Pace	Top Finishers	Comment	Field
7Nov98-8CD	fst	1⅛	:473 1:12 1:37 1:494	3↑ⒻBCDistaf-G1	**105**	7	11	12	12	11½	1no	Stevens G L	L123	3.00	95-07	Escena123no *Banshee Breeze*1205 Keeper Hill120½	Out in strip, driving	8
28Aug98-8Sar	fst	1¼	:474 1:123 1:374 2:04	3↑ⒻPrsnlEnH-G1	**95**	3	1½	12	11	1hd	66	Bailey J D	L123	*.85	82-16	Tomisue's Delight1152 Tuzia114nk One RichLady1141½	Set pace, gave way	8
2Aug98-8Sar	fst	1⅛	:472 1:112 1:361 1:494	3↑ⒻGoFrWndH-G1	**102**	5	1hd	11	1hd	1hd	2no	Bailey J D	L124	*.30	87-16	Aldiza114no Escena1243 *Tomisue's Delight*1162	Dug in determinedly	7
27Jun98-7Hol	fst	1⅛	:481 1:113 1:353 1:48	3↑ⒻVnityIvH-G1	**114**	6	2½	2hd	1hd	1½	12	Bailey J D	LB124	*.40	86-18	Escena1242 Housa Dancer11510 Different119¾	Clear late	7
6Jun98-10CD	fst	1⅛	:482 1:123 1:372 1:50	3↑ⒻFlrDLisH-G3	**113**	3	1½	1½	11	12½	16	Sellers S J	L123	*.60	94-19	*Escena*1236 *One Rich Lady*1131½ Tomisue's Delight1186	Drew off, driving	5
1May98-7CD	fst	1 1/16	:234 :473 1:121 1:444	3↑ⒻLouvlBCH-G2	**104**	3	32½	41½	2hd	13½	14	Bailey J D	L119	*.70	87-14	*Escena*1194 One Rich Lady1133½ Three Fanfares109hd	Rallied, drew clear	10
10Apr98-10OP	fst	1 1/16	:224 :461 1:101 1:404	4↑ⒻAplBlsmH-G1	**113**	7	42	3½	1½	11½	12½	Bailey J D	L117	3.10	104-13	*Escena*1172½ *Glitter Woman*1195 Toda Una Dama1157	Drew off, driving	7
1Mar98-10GP	fst	1 1/16	:241 :474 1:12 1:443	3↑ⒻRampartH-G2	**103**	5	21½	21	2hd	1hd	22	Bailey J D	L119	1.70	82-24	*Dance for Thee*1132 *Escena*119½ Glitter Woman1216¼	Stretch lead,gave way	6
1Feb98-9GP	fst	170	:24 :48 1:114 1:411	3↑ⒻSabinH-G3	**104**	3	42	42	2½	2hd	2hd	Bailey J D	L119	*.70	90-14	Radiant Megan113hd Escena119¾ Biding Time1131½	Late lead,just failed	7

8Nov97–4Hol	fst	1⅛	:454 1:091 1:342 1:471	3↑(F)BCDistaf-G1	99	7	42½	21½	21	31	35½	Bailey J D	LB123	4.80e	84–06	Ajina1202 *Sharp Cat*1203½ Escena1231	Stalked 4w, tired	8
13Oct97–9Bel	fm	1⅛ [T]	:472 1:104 1:344 1:47	3↑(F)AtheniaH-G3	94	3	1hd	1hd	1hd	32	45½	Bailey J D	L119	*.60	99–08	RpidSelction1131¾ Dynsty114nk *Prchrsnightmr*1113½	Argued pace,weakned	6
24Aug97–7AP	gd	1 3/16 (T)	:473 1:114 1:363 1:541	3↑(F)BeverlyD-G1	98	3	21½	21½	21	41½	65¼	Day P	L123	5.40	94–15	MemoriesofSilver123nk Mxzene1233¼ DnceDesign123no	Chased, gave way	6
2Aug97–8Dmr	fm	1⅛ (T)	:50 1:14 1:38 1:494	3↑(F)RamonaH-G1	103	7	2½	2½	2½	1½	1¾	Day P	LB115	6.60	86–16	Escena115¾ Real Connection1151¼ Different121½	Stalked,lead 1/8,drvng	7
28Jun97–9Bel	fst	1 1/16	:223 :452 1:094 1:404	3↑(F)HmpstedH-G1	101	9	52½	42½	31½	45	510	Bailey J D	L115	9.10	85–13	*HiddenLke*1172 *TwicetheVice*1212 JwlPrincss1245¼	Wide move,nothing left	9
24May97–9Bel	fst	1	:222 :443 1:094 1:351	3↑(F)ShuveeH-G2	98	8	2hd	31	3nk	42¼	35	Day P	L116	3.30	83–17	*Hidden Lake*1154 Flat Fleet Feet1201 Escena116¾	3w move,no punch	9
2May97–7CD	fst	1 1/16	:242 :481 1:121 1:423	3↑(F)LouvlBCH-G2	104	4	42½	42½	55½	22½	23½	Day P	L116	3.20	94–05	Halo America1203½ Escena1164 *Rare Blend*116½	Angld out 1/4pole hung	7
11Apr97–9OP	gd	1 1/16	:231 :463 1:104 1:413	4↑(F)AplBlsmH-G1	104	4	42	42½	32	22½	45½	Day P	L116	5.80	94–12	*HaloAmeric*1174 JewelPrincess124hd Different1211½	Mild bid,flattened out	8
12Mar97–10GP	fm	*1 1/16 (T)	:241 :483 1:121 1:42	4↑(F)Alw 39000N4X	93	5	1½	1½	1hd	1hd	11¼	Day P	L116	*.80	91–07	Escena1161¼ *Rebecca Mae*116¾ Chris' Diamond1161½	Set pressured pace	8
8Sep96–9Bel	my	1⅛	:454 1:094 1:35 1:48	(F)GazelleH-G1	96	1	57	44	32½	21	21¼	Day P	L121	2.90	89–16	My Flag1211¼ *Escena*1211¼ Top Secret1172	Inside move turn,game	6
17Aug96–8Sar	gd	1¼	:483 1:131 1:374 2:03	(F)Alabama-G1	98	4	22	22	1hd	2hd	24	Day P	L121	3.75	90–14	*Yanks Music*1214 Escena121½ *My Flag*1213¼	Bid btwn,stayed well	7
27Jly96–8Sar	fst	7f	:212 :431 1:074 1:21	(F)Test-G1	81	1	7	32½	21½	45	511½	Bailey J D	L115	*1.45	89–08	CapoteBelle1152½ *FlatFleetFeet*1153½ JJsdrem1234	Good move turn,empty	8
22Jun96–9Bel	fst	1⅛	:441 1:081 1:341 1:474	(F)MthrGoos-G1	100	3	31	3½	11½	11	2nk	Day P	L121	*1.20	91–12	Yanks Music121nk Escena1215½ Cara Rafaela1216	With pace,clear,dug in	7
3May96–9CD	fst	1⅛	:47 1:112 1:37 1:494	(F)KyOaks-G1	101	1	1hd	11	11	11½	2nk	Day P	L121	3.00	– –	PikePlaceDancer121nk Escena1215½ CaraRafel1212	Drew clear, outfinishd	6
5Apr96–9OP	fst	1 1/16	:232 :471 1:121 1:434	(F)Fantasy-G2	93	7	3½	31	1½	15	17	Day P	117	2.60	– –	Escena1177 Antespend121½ *Ski Trail*117hd	Drew off, handily	7
13Mar96–10GP	fst	1 1/16	:241 :483 1:133 1:453	(F)BonnieMs-G2	97	4	41¼	4¾	31½	2hd	21½	Day P	114	4.00	– –	*My Flag*1171½ *Escena*1147¼ La Rosa1175¾	Lunged, in tight 1/4p	5
24Feb96–6GP	fst	1 1/16	:233 :474 1:122 1:442	(F)Alw 30000N2X	92	6	41½	41¼	1hd	12½	14½	Bailey J D	117	*1.10	– –	Escena1174½ *Bright Time*117¾ Marfa's Finale1174	Stalked pace,riddenout	10
25Nov95–6Aqu	fst	1⅛	:47 1:123 1:383 1:504	(F)Demoisel-G2	76	5	614	53¾	42	24	38¼	Bailey J D	112	2.60	– –	La Rosa1148 Quiet Dance114nk *Escena*11217	Split rivals, wkned	7
26Oct95–7Bel	fst	6f	:222 :46	:584 1:112	(F)Alw 32000N1X	75	4	4	61¾	41¼	11½	12½	Bailey J D	116	*.45	– –	Escena1162½ Echo Echo Echo116¾ Hello Brian118no	Sent thru on rail 1/4p	7
1Oct95–2Bel	fst	6f	:222 :463	:584 1:113	(F)Md Sp Wt 30k	90	6	5	78¾	52¾	12	14½	Perez R B	117	22.30	– –	*Escena*1174½ Carly's Crown1179 Adoradancer1174	6w move 1/4p,clear	10

Favorite Trick

Own: Joseph Lacombe Stable Inc

Dk. b or b. c. 3 (Apr) OBSFEB97 $100,000
Sire: Phone Trick (Clever Trick)
Dam: Evil Elaine (Medieval Man)
Br: Mr. & Mrs. M. L. Wood (Ky)
Tr: Mott William I

Life	16	12	0	1	$1,726,793	109	D.Fst	12	9	0	1	$1,399,116	104
1998	8	4	0	1	$494,795	109	Wet(340)	2	2	0	0	$158,882	97
1997	8	8	0	0	$1,231,998	101	Turf(218)	2	1	0	0	$168,795	109
	0	0	0	0	$0	–	Dst(0)	0	0	0	0	$0	–

7Nov98–7CD	fm	1 (T)	:231 :462 1:104 1:351	3↑BCMile-G1	97	3	11	3½	1hd	32	87½	Day P	L123	*2.60	85–09	Da Hoss126hd Hawksley Hill1264¼ Labeeb1261½	Dueled weakened	14
17Oct98–8Kee	fm	1 (T)	:221 :461 1:104 1:35	3↑KeeBC-G2	109	5	1½	1½	1½	11½	13½	Day P	L123	3.00	93–08	FvoriteTrick1233½ SovietLine126no *WildEvent*1262	Rated early,hand urged	5
29Aug98–7Sar	fst	7f	:22 :442 1:091 1:223	KngsBshp-G2	103	7	1	54½	59	51¾	52	Day P	L124	*1.25	90–12	Secret Firm121¾ Mint121¾ Scatmandu116nk	Traffic inside stretch	8
9Aug98–8Sar	fst	1⅛	:464 1:112 1:363 1:50	JimDandy-G2	103	3	32	32½	42	41¾	1no	Day P	L119	*1.95	86–22	FvoritTrick119no DputyDimond114nk RffsMjsty1141½	Split rivals, got nod	7
19Jly98–9Mth	fst	1 1/16	:232 :47 1:11 1:43	LngBrnchBC100k	101	3	1hd	1hd	1hd	1hd	1hd	Day P	L116	*.20	86–14	*FvortTrck*116hd TomorrwsCt1133½ ArctcSwp1142¼	Long drive pvld outsid	6
2May98–8CD	fst	1¼	:453 1:103 1:353 2:021	KyDerby-G1	89	7	46	54¼	54	710	812¼	Day P	L126	4.40	82–02	*Real Quiet*126½ Victory Gallop1262¼ Indian Charlie126hd	Bid, tired badly	15
11Apr98–9OP	fst	1⅛	:46 1:104 1:372 1:494	ArkDerby-G2	101	8	2hd	1hd	1hd	11	3nk	Day P	L122	*.40	87–10	VctoryGllop122hd HnmnHghwy118hd FvrtTrck1223	Fast pace, outfinished	9
14Mar98–5GP	fst	7f	:221 :444 1:094 1:224	Swale-G3	104	5	3	42¼	42	21½	11¾	Day P	L122	*.30	86–18	FvoritTrick1221¾ GoodndTough114nk DicDncr1132½	Fast pace,split horses	9

Previously trained by Byrne Patrick B 1997(as of 11/8): (127 46 23 10 0.36)

8Nov97–6Hol	fst	1 1/16	:223 :452 1:092 1:412	BCJuv-G1	101	3	31½	31½	21	12	15½	Day P	LB122	*1.20	94–06	*FavoriteTrick*1225½ *DawsonsLegacy*122nk Nationlore122¾	Got thru, drew off	8
18Oct97–8Kee	fst	1 1/16	:232 :463 1:111 1:431	BrdrsFut-G2	100	1	32	33½	32	2½	13	Day P	L121	*.40	92–21	*Favorite Trick*1213 Time Limit121nk Laydown121½	Circld ldrs drew clear	5
30Aug97–8Sar	fst	7f	:214 :45 1:103 1:234	Hopeful-G1	91	4	4	42½	43½	1hd	11½	Day P	L122	*.45	86–12	*Favorite Trick*1221½ K. O. Punch1225 Jess M1227½	4w move,ridden out	7
13Aug97–9Sar	sly	6½f	:213 :444 1:101 1:17	SarSpcl-G2	97	1	4	31	3½	1½	13½	Day P	L122	*.70	92–19	*Favorite Trick*1223½ *Case Dismissed*114nk K. O. Punch1198	Clear path on rail	5
28Jun97–9CD	fst	6f	:21 :444	:571 1:094	BshfdMnr-G3	97	8	3	32½	21½	2½	14½	Day P	L121	*.50	94–08	*FvoriteTrick*1214½ DoublHonor1151½ *CowboyDn*1184	Drew clear, ridden out	8
26May97–9CD	gd	5½f	:223 :462	:583 1:044	KyBC106k	91	8	4	44	32	13½	18½	Day P	L121	*1.40	95–08	*Favorite Trick*1218½ Jess M115nk Cutie Luttie1125	Angld in, handily	8
3May97–3CD	fst	5f	:214 :454	:583	WHAS-11117k	88	9	6	3nk	4¾	2hd	1nk	Day P	L117	7.00	95–05	*Favorite Trick*117nk Cowboy Dan1207 Soldier Field117½	Dueled, prevailed	13
25Apr97–2Kee	fst	4½f	:231 :471	:531	Md Sp Wt 34k	–	2	2	31		11	11½	Day P	118	*1.20	90–16	*FvoriteTrick*1181½ *BrightNov*1187 NorthrnImpct1185	Drew clear, ridden out	8

Fiji (GB)

Own: Newgate Stud Farm LLC

B. m. 5 (Apr)
Sire: Rainbow Quest (Blushing Groom*Fr) $80,765
Dam: Island Jamboree (Explodent)
Br: Newgate Stud Company (GB)
Tr: Drysdale Neil D

Life	12	8	1	2	$894,482	109	D.Fst	0	0	0	0	$0	–
1999	2	0	0	1	$55,850	100	Wet(391*)	0	0	0	0	$0	–
1998	7	6	0	1	$805,560	109	Turf(394)	12	8	1	2	$894,482	109
	0	0	0	0	$0	–	Dst(0)	0	0	0	0	$0	–

15Oct99–8Kee	fm	1 3/16 (T)	:474 1:113 1:363 1:534	3↑(F)VnryFstLdy558k	100	8	85¼	77½	33½	32½	34¼	Bailey J D	L117	*1.40	98 –	*Happyanunoit*1194 Pleasant Temper119nk Fiji1171½	Bid, no late response	9
2Oct99–9SA	fm	1¼ (T)	:47 1:104 1:35 1:592	3↑(F)YlwRibbn-G1	96	1	44½	41¾	41¾	62¾	63½	Bailey J D	LB123	*2.00	87–10	Spanish Fern1231¼ Caffe Latte1181¼ Shabby Chic118½	Chased, no late bid	7
8Nov98–8SA	fm	1¼ (T)	:491 1:142 1:391 2:051	3↑(F)YlwRibbn-G1	108	6	74¼	42	31	1hd	12	Desormeaux K J	LB122	*.80	62–38	Fiji1222 [D]See You Soon1221¾ Sonja's Faith122nk	3 wide bid, driving	10
1Aug98–8Dmr	fm	1⅛ (T)	:49 1:123 1:36 1:472	3↑(F)RamonaH-G1	91	4	75¼	74¼	63¼	43¾	36	Desormeaux K J	LB125	*.40	92–03	See You Soon114½ Sonja's Faith1135½ *Fiji*1251¼	Off bit slow,btwn foes	8
7Jun98–6Hol	fm	1⅛ (T)	:473 1:104 1:343 1:472	3↑(F)GamlyBCH-G1	109	5	67	52¾	31½	1hd	13	Desormeaux K J	LB123	*.60	86–16	Fiji1233 Kool Kat Katie119nk *Squeak*1161¾	Stalked, pulled clear	6
18Apr98–7SA	fm	1¼ (T)	:473 1:12 1:36 2:001	4↑(F)SntBrbrH-G2	107	1	33½	31½	11	14	15½	Desormeaux K J	LB119	*.40	87–18	*Fiji*1195½ Pomona1154 Ecoute1141½	Overpowered rivals	5
21Mar98–8SA	fm	1⅛ (T)	:481 1:143 1:381 1:494	4↑(F)SntaAnaH-G2	106	6	21	2½	2½	1½	14½	Desormeaux K J	LB115	*1.90	80–21	*Fiji*1154½ *Shake the Yoke*1161 Golden Arches120nk	Stalked, drew off	6
19Feb98–2SA	fm	1⅛ (T)	:491 1:131 1:381 1:51	4↑(F)Alw 57000N$Y	103	4	33	2hd	11½	15	19	Desormeaux K J	LB117	*.40	74–30	*Fiji*1179 *Alzora*1155 Miss Universal116nk	Much the best	6
25Jan98–8SA	fm	1 (T)	:244 :482 1:12 1:353	4↑(F)Alw 50000N$Y	99	4	42½	32½	31½	2hd	1½	Desormeaux K J	LB116	*.90	81–23	*Fiji*116½ *Griega*1154 Ava Knowsthecode1151	Held off rival driving	8
27Dec97–3SA	fm	1⅛ (T)	:491 1:124 1:363 1:483	3↑(F)Alw 50200N$Y	97	6	1hd	11	1hd	2hd	2no	Desormeaux K J	LB114	2.10	87–13	*Sixy Saint*115no *Fiji*1147½ Signoretta1161¼	Broke in tangle, game	7

Previously trained by Henry Cecil

25Jly97 Chepstow (GB)	gd	1¼ (T) LH	2:082	3↑(F)Daffodil Stakes (Listed) Stk 30700							1no	Fallon K	119	3.00		Fiji119no Bint Baladee1171¼ Dances With Dreams118½	*Tracked in 4th,rallied to lead 3f out,hard ridden to hold*	8
17Sep96 Sandown Park (GB)	gd	1 (T) RH	1:431	(F)EBF Maiden Stakes Maiden 8400							11¾	Eddery P	123	*.55		*Fiji*1231¾ Alphabet1231½ Listed Account123no	*Led virtually throughout,ridden out*	7

Flanders

Own: Overbrook Farm (William T. Young)

Ch. f. 2 (Apr)
Sire: Seeking the Gold (Mr. Prospector)
Dam: Starlet Storm (Storm Bird)
Br: Overbrook Farm (Ky)
Tr: Lukas D. W

Life	5	4	0	0	$805,000	102	D.Fst	5 4 0 0		$805,000	102
1994	5	4	0	0	$805,000	102	Wet(370)	0 0 0 0		$0	-
1993	0	M	0	0	$0	-	Turf(254)	0 0 0 0		$0	-
	0	0	0	0	$0	-	Dst(0)	0 0 0 0		$0	-

Date	Cond	Dist	Fractions	Race	Spd	PP	St	1C	2C	Str	Fin	Jockey	Wt	Odds	Figs	Top Finishers	Comment	Fld
5Nov94- 5CD	fst	1 1/16	:23 :46^1 1:11^2 1:45^1	ⒻBCJuvFil-G1	**92**	2	2^{hd}	2^{hd}	2^{hd}	2½	1^{hd}	Day P	119	*.40e	- -	Flanders119^{hd} *Serena's Song*119^4 Stormy Blues119½	Gamely, ret. sore	13
8Oct94- 6Bel	fst	1 1/16	:23^1 :46^4 1:12^1 1:43^4	ⒻFrizette-G1	**102**	1	1^{1½}	1^2	1^3	1^7	1^{21}	Day P	119	*.30	- -	*Flanders*119^{21} ChangeForDollr119¾ PrettyDiscreet119^{10}	Drew off, in hand	4
17Sep94- 4Bel	fst	1	:23 :46^2 1:11 1:35	ⒻMatron-G1	**101**	4	1^1	1^{1½}	1½	1^1	1^{3¼}	Day P	119	*.60	- -	[D]*Flanders*119^{3¼} *Stormy Blues*119^{4½} Pretty Discreet119½	Pace, ridden out	6
Disqualified and placed 6th																		
29Aug94- 8Sar	fst	7f	:21^4 :44^4 1:10^1 1:23	ⒻSpinaway-G1	**96**	2	1	1^1	1^1	1^2	1^{4¾}	Day P	119	4.10	- -	Flanders119^{4¾} Sea Breezer119½ *Stormy Blues*119^{nk}	Pace, ridden out	6
10Aug94- 5Sar	fst	5f	:22^3 :46 :58	ⒻMd Sp Wt 25k	**82**	5	5	3^1	1^{hd}	1^1	1^{7½}	Day P	117	*.60	- -	*Flanders*117^{7½} Jovial Joust117^{6½} Share the Fun117¾	Stalked 3w, rddn out	8

Flat Top

dkbbr. g. 1993, by Alleged (Hoist the Flag)–Lady of the Light, by The Minstrel

Lifetime record: 14 6 2 0 $244,450

Own.– Mrs Henry A. Gerry
Br.– Landon Knight (Ky)
Tr.– Janet E. Elliot

Date	Cond	Dist	Fractions	Time	Age	Race	PP	St	1C	2C	Str	Fin	Jockey	Med Wt	Odds	Figs	Top Finishers	Comment	Fld
22Nov98- 5Cam	fm	*2¾	Hurdles	5:11^2	4↑	Colonial Cup 100k	4	2	2^2	2½	2½	1^{5¾}	Ryan CG	L 156	-	- -	Flat Top156^{5¾}Romantic156^{nk}Dictador156^{1¼}	Drew clear	8
24Oct98- 5FH	fm	*2⅝	Hurdles	4:55^2	4↑	Grand Nat'l BC H-G1	5	1	1^1	1½	1½	1^{1¼}	Patterson B	L 156	-	- -	Flat Top156^{1¼}Romantic156¾Mario156^{3½}	Driving	7
4Oct98- 8Cnl	gd	2¼	Hurdles	4:01^4	4↑	Ferguson Mem H-G2	9	1	1^2	2^{hd}	1^{hd}	1½	Patterson B	L 142	6.10	- -	FlatTop142½ApproachingSquall142^{1}Mro150^{1¼}	Dueled,driving	9
7Sep98- 1Sar	yl	*2 1/16	Hurdles	3:46^1	4↑	Handicap 45000	4	3	2^{1½}	1^{hd}	2^{1½}	2^{5½}	Patterson B	L 142	3.55e	- -	Romntc152^{5½}FltTop142^{2}SmnolSprt130^{2½}	Good run final turn	8
12Aug98- 1Sar	sf	*2 1/16	Hurdles	3:44^4	4↑	Alw 40000	5	1	1^{3½}	1^{1½}	2^{hd}	5^{3½}	Kingsley A Jr	L 148	*1.90e	- -	Grenade148^{2½}It's a Giggle146^{no}Dalton River148¾		7
Struggled after last																			
1Nov97- 3Pmt	yl	*2⅜	Hurdles	4:09	3↑	ⓇUS ChSupreme 75k	4	2	1½	1^1	2¾	2^{2½}	Clancy S	L 149	-	- -	Teb's Blend145^{2½}Flat Top149^{2}Willstown145^{27}	Gamely	6
11Oct97- 4Mor	fm	*2¼	Hurdles	4:19	3↑	ⓇArt McCashin 30k	4	1	1^{1¼}	1¾	1^1	1no	Clancy S	L 145	16.30	- -	Flat Top145^{no}Dictador150^{2½}Clearance Code150^{no}	Driving	9
1Jun97- 3Suf	fm	*2¼	Hurdles	4:24^3	4↑	Alw 14700	7	2	2^{2½}	2½	4^{5½}	4^{10¾}	Delozier JW III	LB 146	2.40	- -	Brigade of Guards155^{1¼}Thelightfntistic151^{5}Gliding143^{4½}		7
Chased,stopped																			
17May97- 3Mal	hd	*2¼	Hurdles	4:26	3↑	Alw 20000	6	2	4^{5½}	5^5	4^{4½}	4^{10¾}	Delozier JW III	L 142	-	- -	SmartJaune144^{8}StreetView148^{2½}BrgdofGurds148^{nk}	No excuse	6
17Nov96- 3Cam	fm	*2 5/16	Hurdles	4:15		RG Woolfe Mem 25k	12	1	1¾	1½	1½	1^2	Teter J	L 149	-	- -	Flat Top149^{2}Ratify149^{2}Tomahawk Warrior145^1	Driving	12
Previously owned by Timothy-N-Rye Stable;previously trained by Jeff Teter																			
5Oct96- 6Mid	gd	*2⅛	Hurdles	4:09^3		Md Sp Wt	3	3	5^{20}	2^3	2^{hd}	1^{1½}	Teter J	L 150	-	- -	FlatTop150^{1½}Soaringoversettl150^{6}Hrdhddrshmn150^8	Driving	14
Previously owned by Kenneth L. & Sarah K. Ramsey;previously trained by Niall M. O'Callaghan																			
27May96- 7AP	sly	1	:23^1 :47^2 1:15^1	1:44	3↑	Md 10000	8	4	8^{13}	8^{28}	8^{45}	8^{48}	Gryder AT	113 b	7.30	- -	Skat Kat122^{1¾}Go Big Red108^{4}Longhaul Titus108½		8
Gave way,eased																			
17May96- 4CD	fst	1 1/16	:23^2 :47^1 1:12^1	1:45^1	3↑	Md 15000	11	9	10^{15}	11^{16}	12^{24}	12^{26¾}	Bourque CC	L 114	6.30	58-11	StardustMiner119^{3}LightHeart115^{2½}Andrewsmyman105^{1¼}		12
Never close																			
23Mar96- 6FG	fm	*1Ⓣ	:24^2 :49 1:13^4	1:39^2		Md Sp Wt	2	9	9^{11}	10^{11}	9^{11}	8^{12½}	Emigh CA	119	12.60	72-17	ChiefBerhrt119^{4}MstrEy119^{1½}Chorwon119^{1½}	Lugged out early	12

Flawlessly

b. f. 1988, by Affirmed (Exclusive Native)–La Confidence, by Nijinsky II

Lifetime record: 28 16 4 3 $2,572,536

Own.– Harbor View Farm
Br.– Harbor View Farm (Ky)
Tr.– Charles Whittingham

Date	Cond	Dist	Fractions	Age	Race	Spd	PP	St	1C	2C	Str	Fin	Jockey	Med Wt	Odds	Figs	Top Finishers	Comment	Fld
27Aug94- 6AP	fm	1 3/16Ⓣ	:47^3 1:11^3 1:36^4 1:55^2	3↑	ⒻBeverly D-G1	**103**	8	4	5^5	4^{3½}	2^{1½}	2½	McCarron CJ	L 123	*2.00	89-09	Hatoof123½Flawlessly123½Potridee123½	Prominent late	8
6Aug94- 8Dmr	fm	1⅛Ⓣ	:47^3 1:11^3 1:36^1 1:48^1	3↑	ⒻRamona H-G1	**101**	1	4	4^6	4^1	1^{hd}	1^{hd}	McCarron CJ	LB 124	1.30	95-02	Flwlssly124^{hd}HollywdWldct124^{1¼}Skmbl116^2	4 wide 2nd turn	5
3Jly94- 8Hol	fm	1⅛Ⓣ	:48 1:11^1 1:35 1:47^2	3↑	ⒻBeverly Hills H-G1	**101**	1	4	4^{2½}	4^{1¾}	5^{1¾}	3^{nk}	McCarron CJ	LB 124	1.60	87-14	Corrazona119^{nk}Hollywood Wildcat124^{no}Flawlessly124^1		7
Lacked room on rail ¼-⅛																			
12Jun94- 8Hol	fm	1⅛Ⓣ	:46^4 1:10 1:34^1 1:46^2	3↑	ⒻGamely H-G1	**100**	5	6	6^{5½}	5^{2¼}	3^2	3^5	McCarron CJ	LB 124	*.70	87-10	Hollywood Wildcat122^{2¼}Mz. Zill Bear114^{2¾}Flawlessly124^{nk}		6
Broke slightly in air,5 wide 2nd turn																			
28Nov93- 7Hol	fm	1⅛Ⓣ	:47 1:10^4 1:34^3 1:46^3	3↑	ⒻMatriarch-G1	**102**	2	5	6^{3¾}	5^{1¾}	1½	1^{nk}	McCarron CJ	LB 123	*.90	91-09	Flwlssly123^{nk}Toussud123^{2}Skmbl123^{hd}	Awaited room 2nd turn	7
6Nov93- 5SA	fm	1Ⓣ	:22^3 :45^4 1:09^2 1:33^2	3↑	BC Mile-G1	**90**	4	5	7^{4½}	7^7	9^9	9^{10}	McCarron CJ	LB 123	3.10	88-04	Lure126^{2¼}Ski Paradise120^{1¾}Fourstars Allstar126^{hd}		13
Tight quarters 1st turn																			
28Aug93- 9AP	gd	1 3/16Ⓣ	:49^2 1:13^3 1:38 1:55^3	3↑	ⒻBeverly D-G1	**103**	2	3	2^{1½}	2^1	1^1	2no	McCarron CJ	L 123	*.50	88-11	[D]Let'sElope123^{no}Flawlssly123^{nk}VBorghs123^{no}	Bumped late	7
Placed first through disqualification																			
7Aug93- 8Dmr	fm	1⅛Ⓣ	:47 1:10^4 1:35^4 1:48^1	3↑	ⒻRamona H-G1	**107**	2	2	2^6	3^{3½}	2^{1½}	1^1	McCarron CJ	LB 125	*.90	95-03	Flawlessly125^{1}Heart of Joy114^{1}Let's Elope118½		7
Floated out ¼,brushed 3/16,ridden out																			
27Jun93- 8Hol	fm	1⅛Ⓣ	:48^1 1:11^2 1:35^1 1:47	3↑	ⒻBeverly Hills H-G1	**108**	4	3	3^{1½}	2½	1^{2½}	1^9	McCarron CJ	LB 123	.90	89-11	Flwlssly123^{9}Jolyph121^{no}PrtyCtd117^2	Drew off,kept to task	4
29Nov92- 7Hol	fm	1⅛Ⓣ	:47^1 1:10^4 1:34 1:46	3↑	ⒻMatriarch-G1	**108**	6	5	5^{3½}	5^3	3^{3½}	1^1	McCarron CJ	LB 123	*1.40	94-07	Flawlessly123^{1}Super Staff123^{2}Kostroma123½	Strong finish	9
8Nov92- 8SA	fm	1¼Ⓣ	:47^1 1:11^2 1:35 1:59^1	3↑	ⒻYlwRibIn-G1	**106**	7	4	4^3	2^{1½}	2^1	2no	McCarron CJ	LB 123	*.70	91-09	SuperStaff123^{no}Flawlessly123^{3½}Cmpgnrd123^{hd}	Resolute try	9
18Oct92- 8SA	fm	1⅛Ⓣ	:48^1 1:11^4 1:35 1:46^4	3↑	ⒻLas Palmas H-G2	**104**	4	3	3^{3½}	3^2	2^{1½}	2¾	McCarron CJ	LB 124	*.50	84-22	Super Staff116¾Flawlessly124^{4}Re Toss115½	Boxed in ⅜	7
15Aug92- 8Dmr	fm	1⅛Ⓣ	:51^3 1:15^3 1:38^4 1:50	3↑	ⒻRamona H-G1	**95**	4	1	1½	1½	1^2	1^3	McCarron CJ	LB 123	1.40	86-11	Flwlssly123^{3}RToss115^{hd}Polmc116½	Set slow pace,ridden out	7
28Jun92- 8Hol	fm	1⅛Ⓣ	:49 1:12 1:35 1:47	3↑	ⒻBeverly Hills H-G1	**103**	3	1	1^{hd}	1½	2^{hd}	1^{hd}	McCarron CJ	LB 122	1.90	89-12	Flawlessly122^{hd}Kostroma124^{1¾}Alcando113^1	Ultra game	5
1Dec91- 8Hol	fm	1⅛Ⓣ	:47^1 1:10^4 1:34^4 1:46^3	3↑	ⒻMatriarch-G1	-	3	7	8^{4¾}	7^{2¾}	1^{hd}	1^{1¾}	McCarron CJ	L 120	6.30	97-07	Flawlessly120^{1¾}FirthGroom123½FrtLst123^{no}	5-wide stretch	14
10Nov91- 8SA	fm	1¼Ⓣ	:49^2 1:14^2 1:37^4 2:01	3↑	ⒻYellow Ribbon-G1	-	6	3	3^2	3^1	4^2	2^2	McCarron CJ	LB 119	5.00	81-17	Kostroma123^{2}Flawlessly119½FiretheGroom123^{hd}	Good effort	13
5Oct91- 8SA	fm	1Ⓣ	:22 :45^4 1:10^2 1:33^2		ⒻH C Ramser H 112k	-	10	7	7^{3¼}	2½	2^{hd}	1½	McCarron CJ	LB 123	*.70	96-09	Flawlssly123½Gravieres117^{4½}ZamaHummer117^2	Game effort	10
25Aug91- 8Dmr	fm	1⅛Ⓣ	:48^2 1:13^1 1:37^3 1:49^2		ⒻDmr Oaks-G3	-	2	5	5^4	5^2	2^{hd}	1^2	McCarron CJ	L 120	*.70	91-09	Flawlessly120^{2}SettlSymphony120½Fowd120^{1¼}	Speed to spare	6
10Aug91- 8Dmr	fm	1Ⓣ	:23^1 :46^3 1:10^2 1:34^4		ⒻSan Clemente H 109k	-	8	6	5^4	4¾	1½	1^{1¾}	McCarron CJ	L 120	*1.50	98-04	Flawlessly120^{1¾}GoldFlc114^{2¼}MssHghBld117^2	4-wide stretch	9
5Jly91- 7Hol	fm	1 1/16Ⓣ	:24 :48^2 1:12^4 1:42^2		ⒻⓇStreet Dancer 61k	-	4	3	3^{2½}	3^1	2^{hd}	1^{1¾}	McCarron CJ	L 118	*1.70	83-09	Flwlssly118^{1¾}Jol'sPrncss114^{hd}Sprucory114^{3½}	Strong effort	6
Previously trained by Richard E. Dutrow																			
19Jan91- 7Aqu	fst	1 70⊡	:24^1 :47^2 1:11^1 1:41^4		ⒻBusanda 69k	-	7	3	4^{4½}	-	-	-	Krone JA	121	*1.40	- -	I'maThriller112^{4}WinCraftyLady116^{5}I'mTickldPnk112^{hd}	Bled	7
9Dec90- 8Aqu	fst	1 1/16⊡	:24^1 :48^4 1:13^4 1:46^3		ⒻTempted-G3	-	4	6	5^{1¾}	4^2	3^{nk}	1^{hd}	Bailey JD	121	4.60	75-25	Flawlessly121^{hd}Debutnt'sHlo121^{1½}SlptThruIt114^{1¼}	Driving	12
17Nov90- 8Aqu	gd	1⅛	:50 1:15^3 1:41 1:53^4		ⒻDemoiselle-G2	-	6	1	1½	1^{hd}	2^{hd}	4^{4¼}	Cordero A Jr	119	5.50	63-39	Debutant's Halo116^{2}Private Treasure121^{nk}Slept Thru It112^2		7
Weakened																			
27Oct90- 4Bel	fst	1 1/16	:22^3 :45^4 1:11 1:44		ⒻBC Juv Fillies-G1	-	5	12	12^{10}	10^{8½}	8^{8½}	7^{12¾}	Pincay L Jr	119	46.20	69-15	Meadow Star119^{5}Private Treasure119^{1}Dance Smartly119^{4¼}		13
Improved position																			
6Oct90- 7Bel	fst	1	:22^4 :46^1 1:11 1:35^2		ⒻFrizette-G1	-	1	3	2½	2^1	2^6	3^{14¼}	Bailey JD	119	5.20	78-11	MeadwStr119^{14}ChampagneGlow119^{nk}Flwlssly119^{3¼}	Weakened	5
27Sep90- 9Med	fm	1 1/16Ⓣ	:22^1 :46^1 1:11^1 1:43^3		ⒻGardenia-G3	-	15	7	6^{3½}	4^2	2^{hd}	1^{4½}	Bailey JD	112	7.50	79-21	Flawlessly112^{4½}SweetSarita114^{no}MadamSandie112^{1¾}	Driving	15
14Sep90- 4Bel	fst	6f	:21^4 :45^1 1:11		ⒻMd Sp Wt	-	5	3	3^{3½}	3^1	2^{hd}	1^{1¼}	Bailey JD	117	8.90	84-16	Flawlessly117^{1¼}I'm a Thriller117¾Boots117^3	Driving	6
13Jun90- 4Bel	fst	5f	:22^1 :46 :58^4		ⒻMd Sp Wt	-	6	6	4^{2½}	4^4	4^{4½}	4^{10}	Cordero A Jr	117	8.50	84-20	MeadowStar117^{5¼}WinCrafty Lady117¾My Fantazy117^4	Tired	7

Fly So Free

ch. c. 1988, by Time for a Change (Damascus)–Free to Fly, by Stevward | **Lifetime record: 33 12 5 3 $2,330,954**

Own.– Thomas F. Valando
Br.– Bruce Hundley & Wayne Garrison (Ky)
Tr.– Flint S. Schulhofer

Date	Cond	Dist	Fractions	Race	Fig	PP	St	1c	2c	Str	Fin	Jockey	Wt	Odds	Spd	Top finishers	Comment
6Nov93- 2SA	ft	6f	:21 :434 :56 1:083	3↑ BC Sprint-G1	83	11	8	119	118¾	910	910	Bailey JD	126	8.00	84-04	Cardmania126nkMeafara123½Gilded Time1241¼	5-wide
18Sep93- 4Bel	sly	6f	:222 :451 :57 1:092	3↑ Fall Highweight H-G2	110	8	7	33	31	2½	1½	Bailey JD	135	4.10	93-14	FlySoFree135½DemalootDemashoot1261½TakeMOut1343	Driving
15Aug93- 9Sar	fst	7f	:221 :442 1:084 1:214	3↑ Forego H-G2	97	5	9	76½	75¼	44½	46¼	Bailey JD	116	1.90	90-12	Birdonthewire1171½Harlan1102¼SnorSpdy1172½	Broke in air
10Jly93- 8Bel	fst	7f	:224 :45 1:083 1:204	3↑ Tom Fool-G2	107	2	2	31	43	22	21¾	Krone JA	119	*.90	97-08	Birdonthewire1191¾Fly So Free1192Take Me Out1194	In tight ¼ pole
31May93- 9Bel	fst	1	:221 :441 1:083 1:341	3↑ Metropolitan H-G1	105	6	7	73¾	61¾	41¾	44¼	Krone JA	118	6.20	93-03	Ibero1191½Bertrando121nkAlydeed1242½	Wide trip
6May93- 8Bel	fst	7f	:224 :452 1:084 1:21	3↑ Alw 40000	105	5	1	2½	21	11½	13¼	Krone JA	117	*.30	98-08	Fly So Free1173¼Majesterian1171½Shining Bid1171	Driving
10Apr93- 8Aqu	fst	1	:232 :452 1:084 1:343	3↑ Westchester H-G3	106	10	1	31	32	1hd	2¾	Krone JA	118	*1.20	90-26	Bill of Rights110¾Fly So Free1181¼Loach1133½	Gamely
6Mar93- 8GP	fst	6½f	:214 :442 1:083 1:15	4↑ Alw 31000	101	4	6	66	44	23	24¾	Santos JA	114	2.40	97-09	Alydeed1224¾Fly So Free114noCold Digger1133	Gamely
3Oct92- 6Bel	fst	7f	:223 :452 1:10 1:224	3↑ Vosburgh H-G1	97	5	7	61¾	73½	66	57½	Day P	126	*1.60e	82-17	Rubiano126¾SheikhAlbadou1261¼SaltLk1234¼	No threat,wide
13Sep92- 8Bel	fst	6f	:221 :444 :562 1:09	3↑ Fall Highweight H-G2	99	1	4	53½	43	44½	43¼	Day P	134	2.70	92-12	SaltLake1282½BurnFair126¾BelongtoMe122hd	Rallied wide
8Aug92- 8Mth	fst	1⅛	:453 1:09 1:341 1:464	3↑ Iselin H-G1	82	2	4	44½	55½	76	914½	Krone JA	117	2.90	90-00	Jolie's Halo116hdOut of Place1131Valley Crossing1111½	Flattened out
28Jun92- 7Bel	fst	1 1/16	:233 :463 1:101 1:412	3↑ Alw 47000	108	4	2	2hd	2hd	1½	12	Krone JA	115	*.40	95-14	FlySoFree1152HonestEnsign115½SilverEnding11911¼	Driving
6Jun92- 7Bel	my	1⅛	:444 1:082 1:334 1:463	3↑ Nassau County H-G2	95	8	4	42½	52¼	62½	79¾	Santos JA	116	*2.30	86-08	StrikethGold116nkPlsntTp1191½SltrySong1112¾	Wide,tired
9May92-10Pim	fst	1 3/16	:473 1:112 1:354 1:544	4↑ Pim Spl H-G1	110	5	1	1½	2hd	12	2¾	Santos JA	116	7.40	87-23	StrikethGold114¾FlySoFree1161¼TwilightAgnd1222¼	Gamely
11Apr92- 8OP	fst	1⅛	:46 1:094 1:351 1:48	4↑ Oaklawn H-G1	111	1	4	42	43	44½	56¼	Santos JA	118	6.00	90-20	Best Pal1251½Sea Cadet120½Twilight Agenda1234	Steadied
21Mar92-10OP	fst	1 1/16	:23 :46 1:101 1:424	4↑ Razorback H-G2	101	8	6	68	49	49	45¼	Santos JA	121	*.70	82-15	Tokatee115½On the Edge112nkTotal Assets1104½	Four wide
2Nov91- 8CD	fst	1¼	:482 1:123 1:38 2:024	3↑ BC Classic-G1	-	5	4	54	42½	34	44	Santos JA	B 122	27.70	92-09	BlackTieAffair1261¼TwlghtAgnd1262½Unbrdld126nk	Bid,hung
15Sep91- 9WO	fst	1⅛	:482 1:121 1:364 1:491	Molson Million-G2	-	4	2	32	32	59½	49	Santos JA	126	*1.25	97-11	DanceSmartly1162Shudanz1176Majesterin1171	Couldn't stay
17Aug91- 8Sar	fst	1¼	:472 1:112 1:36 2:011	Travers-G1	-	3	3	32½	31½	32½	32¾	Santos JA	126	4.10	95-06	CorporateReport126nkHansel1262½FlySoFree1263	Willingly
28Jly91- 8Sar	fst	1⅛	:462 1:103 1:354 1:484	Jim Dandy-G2	-	1	3	42	31½	2hd	11¼	Santos JA	126	2.10e	93-08	Fly So Free1261¼Upon My Soul1143Strike the Gold1283	Rank early,drv
7Jly91- 8Bel	fst	1⅛	:454 1:10 1:354 1:491	Dwyer-G2	-	5	1	2hd	21	31½	33½	Bailey JD	126	*.50	79-17	LostMountain1231SmoothPrformnc1142½FlySoFr1267	Weakened
8Jun91- 6Bel	fst	7f	:22 :45 1:10 1:23	Riva Ridge-G3	-	6	10	117¾	84	3½	12	Bailey JD	122	*.50	89-10	Fly So Free1222Formal Dinner1222½Dodge1221¼	Bumped start,six wide,driving
4May91- 8CD	fst	1¼	:462 1:111 1:372 2:03	Ky Derby-G1	-	1	4	42	3½	42	54¼	Santos JA	B 126	3.30	91-04	Strike the Gold1261¾Best Pal1261¾Mane Minister126hd	Came out st,bore in far turn
13Apr91- 8Kee	gd	1⅛	:473 1:12 1:354 1:482	Blue Grass-G2	-	3	2	21	21½	2½	23	Santos JA	B 121	*.30	90-07	StrikethGold1213FlySoFr1213½NoworkAllPly1214½	No excuse
16Mar91-10GP	fst	1⅛	:464 1:113 1:371 1:502	Florida Derby-G1	-	3	4	43	21	12	11	Santos JA	122	*.40	85-13	FlySoFree1221StriketheGold1184Hansel1222¾	Hard drive
23Feb91-10GP	fst	1 1/16	:223 :454 1:101 1:441	Fountain of Youth-G2	-	1	4	4¾	1½	12½	16	Santos JA	122	*.50	92-12	Fly So Free1226Moment of True1171¼Subordinated Debt1134	Hard drive
2Feb91-10GP	fst	7f	:22 :442 1:094 1:231	Hutcheson-G2	-	8	8	52¾	82¾	41¾	11	Santos JA	122	*1.10	90-08	FlySoFree1221ToFredm119noSunnyndPlsnt114nk	Strong race
27Oct90- 7Bel	fst	1 1/16	:23 :46 1:103 1:432	©BC Juvenile-G1	-	3	3	3½	1hd	1½	13	Santos JA	122	*1.40	85-15	FlySoFree1223TakMeOut1222LostMountn122hd	Driving,clear
6Oct90- 6Bel	fst	1	:222 :451 1:101 1:353	Champagne-G1	-	9	6	74¼	67¼	11½	15¼	Santos JA	122	3.70	91-11	FlySoFree1225¼HappyJazzBand122nkSubordinated Debt1221¼	Wide,driving
21Jly90- 7Bel	fst	5½f	:221 :453 :583 1:042	Tremont BC-G3	-	4	7	57½	47	47½	45½	Bailey JD	117	*1.80	91-15	Hansel1153Vermont1152½Stately Wager115hd	Stumbled start
8Jly90- 6Bel	fst	5½f	:222 :454 :573 1:043	Alw 27000	-	2	5	42½	42½	41¾	1¾	Bailey JD	117	1.60	96-10	FlySoFree117¾AlsknFrost1172¼SlfEvdnt1191¼	Strong finish
22Jun90- 5Mth	fst	5½f	:222 :453 :574 1:041	Alw 16500	-	4	4	42½	31	33½	34	Bruin JE	120	*.70	93-12	Fighting Affair1172¼Alaskan Frost1171¾Fly So Free12014	Lacked response
14May90- 4Bel	fst	5f	:222 :453 :574	Md Sp Wt	-	1	2	31½	1hd	14	18¼	Santos JA	118	*1.70	99-11	FlySoFree1188¼StatlyWagr118nkMononghl1182¼	Ridden out

Gilded Time

Own: Milch, Silverman, Silverman, Et Al

Ch. c. 3 (Feb) OBSFEB92 $80,000
Sire: Timeless Moment (Damascus)
Dam: Gilded Lilly (What a Pleasure)
Br: Harry T. Mangurian, Jr. (Fla)
Tr: Vienna Darrell

Life	6	4	0	1	$975,980	107	D.Fst	5	3	0	1	$775,400	107
1993	2	0	0	1	$120,000	107	Wet(319)	1	1	0	0	$200,580	91
1992	4	4	0	0	$855,980	102	Turf(285)	0	0	0	0	$0	-
	0	0	0	0	$0	-	Dst(0)	0	0	0	0	$0	-

Date	Cond	Dist	Fractions	Race	Fig	PP	St	1c	2c	Str	Fin	Jockey	Med/Wt	Odds	Spd	Top finishers	Comment	Field
26Dec93- 8SA	fst	7f	:22 :44 1:084 1:21	Malibu-G2	78	1	4	2hd	1hd	3nk	611¾	McCarron C J	LB116	*.80	- -	Diazo120½ *Concept Win*1162 *Mister Jolie*116no	Fast pace, weakened	8
6Nov93- 2SA	fst	6f	:21 :434 :56 1:083	3↑ BCSprnt-G1	107	2	8	32	21½	21	3¾	McCarron C J	LB124	5.40	- -	*Cardmania*126nk *Meafara*123½ Gilded Time1241¼	Pressed pace, no rally	14
31Oct92- 8GP	fst	1 1/16	:223 :46 1:102 1:432	BCJuven-G1	87	3	55	53	4nk	2hd	1¾	McCarron C J	L122	*2.00	- -	Gilded Time122¾ It'sali'lknownfact122½ *RiverSpecial*1225	Dueled,prevailed	13
26Sep92- 9AP	sly	1	:222 :452 1:103 1:374	ArlWaFut-G2	91	3	2hd	21½	1hd	14	15½	McCarron C J	L121	*1.10	- -	*GildedTime*1215½ Boundlessly1214 Rockmundo121¾	Much the best, handily	6
8Aug92-10Mth	fst	6f	:212 :44 :554 1:074	Sapling-G2	102	5	6	4¾	31	21½	1½	McCarron C J	L122	*1.10	- -	*Gilded Time*122½ Wild Zone1227½ *Great Navigator*1223¼	Driving	8
15Jly92- 4Hol	fst	6f	:221 :452 :573 1:101	Md Sp Wt 28k	79	5	8	55½	21	11½	14	Stevens G L	B117	*.70	- -	*Gilded Time*1174 Chayim1172¼ Gulable1172	Handily	8

Go for Wand

b. f. 1987, by Deputy Minister (Vice Regent)–Obeah, by Cyane | **Lifetime record: 13 10 2 0 $1,373,338**

Own.– Christiana Stable
Br.– Christiana Stables (Pa)
Tr.– William Badgett Jr

Date	Cond	Dist	Fractions	Race	PP	St	1c	2c	Str	Fin	Jockey	Wt	Odds	Spd	Top finishers	Comment	Field
27Oct90- 5Bel	fst	1⅛	:462 1:103 1:354 1:491	3↑ ⒻBC Distaff-G1	2	1	1½	1hd	1½	-	Romero RP	119	*.70	- -	Bayakoa1236¾Colonial Waters1232½Valay Maid119nk	Fell	7
7Oct90- 8Bel	fst	1⅛	:453 1:091 1:331 1:454	3↑ ⒻBeldame-G1	5	2	2½	2½	12	14¾	Romero RP	119	*.10	105-09	GofrWnd1194¾ColonialWtrs1238¾BuythFrm1232¼	Ridden out	5
2Sep90- 8Bel	fst	1	:23 :452 1:094 1:353	3↑ ⒻMaskette H-G1	1	2	21½	2½	11	12½	Romero RP	118	*.30	91-13	GofrWnd1182½FeeltheBeat123noMisturn1164	Good handling	6
11Aug90- 8Sar	gd	1¼	:481 1:112 1:36 2:004	ⒻAlabama-G1	3	1	11	12	12½	17	Romero RP	121	*.50	100-09	Go for Wand1217Charon12148Pampered Star121	Ridden out	3
2Aug90- 8Sar	fst	7f	:221 :443 1:081 1:21	ⒻTest-G1	2	8	2½	2hd	11½	12	Romero RP	124	*1.20	100-05	GoforWnd1242ScreenProspct1182¼TokenDnce1182½	Driving	10
10Jun90- 8Bel	fst	1⅛	:46 1:102 1:353 1:484	ⒻMother Goose-G1	6	2	21	21½	11½	11¼	Romero RP	121	*.80	90-20	GoforWnd1211¼Charon1214¼StellaMadrid1212¾	Wide,driving	6
4May90- 9CD	my	1⅛	:481 1:13 1:39 1:524	ⒻKy Oaks-G1	1	4	42	31½	22	23	Romero RP	121	*.30	81-20	Seaside Attraction1213Go for Wand1213Bright Candles1212½	Flattened out	10
21Apr90- 8Kee	my	1 1/16	:243 :482 1:122 1:433	ⒻAshland-G1	5	3	1½	11½	14	15	Romero RP	121	*.30	88-12	Go for Wand1215Charon1217½Piper Piper1128	Driving	5
10Apr90- 8Kee	my	*7f	1:262	ⒻBeaumont-G3	6	2	32	3nk	14½	18½	Romero RP	122	*.40	95-05	GoforWand1228½Trumpet's Blare119hdSeasideAttraction119½	Ridden out	6
4Nov89- 5GP	fst	1 1/16	:234 :472 1:12 1:441	ⒻBC Juv Fillies-G1	4	5	63½	43½	31	12¾	Romero RP	119	2.50	90-01	GofrWnd1192¾SweetRoberta119½StellaMdrd1192	Drew clear	12
14Oct89- 7Bel	fst	1	:23 :454 1:11 1:384	ⒻFrizette-G1	6	2	21	22	22½	2½	Romero RP	119	*1.00	70-26	StellaMdrd119½GofrWnd1195¼DncColony1191¾	Finished well	7
2Oct89- 2Bel	sly	1	:231 :462 1:114 1:363	ⒻAlw 32000	9	1	11½	13	16	118¼	Romero RP	116	*1.50	82-26	GoforWand11618¼InFullCry116½Jen'sWish1166	Ridden out	9
14Sep89- 2Bel	fst	6f	:221 :452 1:103	ⒻMd Sp Wt	6	3	33	11	12½	14	Romero RP	117	2.40	86-15	Go for Wand1174Nina1171½Worth Avenue117nk	Drew clear	9

Golden Attraction

Own: Overbrook Farm

B. f. 3 (Jan)
Sire: Mr. Prospector (Raise a Native)
Dam: Seaside Attraction (Seattle Slew)
Br: Overbrook Farm (Ky)
Tr: Lukas D. W

Life	11	8	1	1	$911,508	99	D.Fst	8	7	0	0	$545,588	99
1996	3	2	0	0	$235,920	96	Wet(395)	3	1	1	1	$365,920	94
1995	8	6	1	1	$675,588	99	Turf(284)	0	0	0	0	$0	-
	0	0	0	0	$0	-	Dst(0)	0	0	0	0	$0	-

21Sep96-9TP	sly	1 1/16	:23⁴ :46⁴ 1:11 1:42²	3↑ⒻTPBC-G2	94	4	12	12	12	13	11½	Stevens G L	114	1.30e	83-06	GoldnAttrction1141½ BdroomBlus1173 BttyVn1191½	Broke sharply lasted	8
18Aug96-8Sar	fst	7f	:22² :44⁴ 1:09 1:21⁴	3↑ⒻBalrinaH-G1	73	3	2	1½	2hd	33	615½	Bailey J D	116	6.00	81-09	ChposSprings120½ CpoteBelle1171 BrodSmile1144	Pace,gave way mid str	6
8Aug96-7Sar	fst	6f	:21⁴ :45 :57¹ 1:10³	3↑ⒻAlw 50600n1y	96	3	4	11½	12	13	12¼	Bailey J D	115	*.45	88-11	GoldenAttrction1152¼ *LittlBuckls*1224 WildLightning1171	Set strong pace	5
28Oct95-2Bel	gd	1 1/16	:23 :46² 1:11 1:42²	ⒻBCJuvFil-G1	91	3	11	1½	11	1hd	32	Stevens G L	119	*1.10	- -	MyFlag119½ CaraRafel1191½ *GoldenAttrction*11917	Pace in hand,wknd late	8
7Oct95-5Bel	fst	1 1/16	:23 :46 1:11¹ 1:42⁴	ⒻFrizette-G1	99	5	11½	1hd	12½	12½	1¾	Stevens G L	119	*1.80	- -	Golden Attraction119¾ *My Flag*1198½ Flat Fleet Feet11912½	Something left	5
16Sep95-4Bel	fst	1	:22 :44³ 1:09⁴ 1:36¹	ⒻMatron-G1	89	2	24	21½	1hd	1½	1nk	Stevens G L	119	*.45	- -	*Golden Attraction*119nk *Cara Rafaela*1195½ My Flag1192	Dug in,long drive	8
28Aug95-8Sar	fst	7f	:22 :45¹ 1:10¹ 1:23⁴	ⒻSpinaway-G1	93	3	3	1½	11½	12	1¾	Stevens G L	121	*2.30	- -	*GoldenAttrction*121¾ FltFleetFeet1211 WstrnDrmr1213½	Dug in,came again	8
6Aug95-8Mth	sly	6f	:21² :45 :57³ 1:10⁴	ⒻSorority-G3	80	6	1	34½	2½	21½	2¾	Barton D M	119	*.70	- -	CrftyButSwt119¾ *GoldnAttrction*1194½ CrlssHrss1192	No match for winner	6
21Jly95-8Sar	fst	6f	:21³ :44³ :57¹ 1:10⁴	ⒻSchylrvl-G2	90	6	1	2hd	1hd	1hd	12½	Barton D M	121	3.15	- -	GoldnAttrction1212½ DylghtCom112hd WstrnDrmr1213½	Dueled outs,clear	8
2Jly95-10CD	fst	5½f	:22 :45³ 1:04	ⒻDebutante105k	82	2	3	1½	11	13	1½	Barton D M	115	*1.20e	- -	*GoldnAttrction*115½ WstrnDrmr1213½ TipicllyIrsh115¾	Drew off, just lasted	9
4Jun95-2Hol	fst	5f	:22 :46 :58²	ⒻMd Sp Wt 34k	72	7	4	22	21½	12	14½	Stevens G L	B118	*.40	92-10	*GoldnAttrction*1184½ Fillycp118hd Woodyoublivit1183½	Drew off,much best	7

Hansel

b. c. 1988, by Woodman (Mr. Prospector)–Count on Bonnie, by Dancing Count

Lifetime record: 14 7 2 3 $2,936,586

Own.– Lazy Lane Farms Inc
Br.– Marvin Little Jr (Va)
Tr.– Frank L. Brothers

17Aug91-8Sar	fst 1¼	:47² 1:11² 1:36 2:01¹	Travers-G1	2	2	21	2hd	2½	2nk	Bailey JD	126	1.90	98-06	Corporate Report126nkHansel1262½Fly So Free1263		6
	Tore tendon of left foreleg in upper str															
27Jly91-10Mth	gd 1⅛	:46 1:10¹ 1:35¹ 1:48	Haskell H-G1	1	3	3½	22	36½	313	Bailey JD	L 126	*.50	85-15	Lost Mountain118hdCorporate Report12013Hansel1262½		5
	Steadied entering 1st turn,rank briefly															
8Jun91-8Bel	fst 1½	:46³ 1:11³ 2:02 2:28	Belmont-G1	5	3	1hd	11½	12½	1hd	Bailey JD	126	4.10	90-08	Hansel126hdStrike the Gold1263Mane Minister1262½		11
	Drifted late,lasted															
18May91-10Pim	fst 1 3/16	:46¹ 1:10¹ 1:35 1:54	Preakness-G1	4	3	31½	2hd	15	17	Bailey JD	L 126	9.10	95-14	Hansel1267Corporate Report1262¾Mane Minister126½		8
	Drifted out-driving															
4May91-8CD	fst 1¼	:46² 1:11¹ 1:37² 2:03	Ky Derby-G1	6	5	63½	52	74¾	1010¾	Bailey JD	LB 126	*2.50	84-04	Strike the Gold1261¾Best Pal1261¾Mane Minister126hd		16
	Tiring,ducked in															
21Apr91-8Kee	fst 1 1/16	:24² :47⁴ 1:11¹ 1:42³	Lexington-G2	3	2	21½	1½	15	19	Bailey JD	LB 121	*.30	91-09	Hansel1219Shotgun Harry J.1152¾Speedy Cure1183		4
	Jumped tracks late,much the best															
30Mar91-10TP	fst 1⅛	:45³ 1:09³ 1:34¹ 1:46³	Jim Beam-G2	3	3	41¼	31½	1½	12½	Bailey JD	LB 121	4.60	112-00	Hansl1212½Richman1216WilderThnEvr121½	Impressive score	11
16Mar91-10GP	fst 1⅛	:46⁴ 1:11³ 1:37¹ 1:50²	Florida Derby-G1	7	5	54½	32	43½	35	Day P	L 122	4.70	80-13	Fly So Free1221Strike the Gold1184Hansel1222¾	Bore out	8
23Feb91-10GP	fst 1 1/16	:22³ :45⁴ 1:10¹ 1:44¹	Fountain of Youth-G2	2	5	84	68	610	511¼	Day P	119	6.10	81-12	FlySoFree1226MomntofTrue1171¼SbordntdDbt1134	No rally	10
22Sep90-8AP	gd 1	:23 :45² 1:10⁴ 1:36²	Arl-Wash Futurity-G2	1	3	31½	51½	31	1nk	Day P	122	*1.40	89-17	Hansel122nkWalesa1221¼Discover1223¼	Blocked turn	7
25Aug90-8Sar	my 6½f	:22 :44³ 1:09³ 1:16¹	Hopeful-G1	1	6	35½	35½	33½	24½	Day P	122	6.50	95-04	Deposit Ticket1224½Hansel122¾Link122nk	No match	6
11Aug90-10Mth	my 6f	:21³ :44⁴ 1:11	Sapling-G2	1	8	52½	34	35½	35¼	Day P	122	*1.40	81-17	DepostTckt1223¾AlsknFrost1221½Hnsl122no	Green,mild gain	9
21Jly90-7Bel	fst 5½f	:22¹ :45³ :58³ 1:04²	Tremont BC-G3	5	5	32	2½	2½	13	Romero RP	115	3.40	97-15	Hansel1153Vermont1152½Stately Wager115hd	Brisk urging	7
7Jun90-4AP	fst 5f	:22⁴ :46⁴ :59¹	Md Sp Wt	4	6	31	1hd	13	13½	Romero RP	118	*1.10	93-14	Hansel1183½Bandito Barney1184Roman Envoy118½	Handily	10

Hatoof

ch. f. 1989, by Irish River (Riverman)–Cadeaux d'Amie, by Lyphard

Lifetime record: 21 9 4 1 $1,864,063

Own.– Sheikh Maktoum al Maktoum
Br.– Gainsborough Farm Inc (Ky)
Tr.– Christiane Head

5Nov94-9CD	fm 1½Ⓣ	:46⁴ 1:10³ 2:00 2:26²	3↑ B C Turf-G1	109	2	13	107¾	76	41½	21½	Swinburn WR	123	12.70	110-00	Tikkanen1221½Hatoof1231½Paradise Creek126½	14
	Lacked room early,gamely															
15Oct94♦ Newmarket(GB)	gd 1¼ⓉStr	2:05³	3↑ Champion Stakes-G1 Stk468000							5¾	Swinburn WR	127	*1.50		Dernier Empereur130noGrand Lodge124nkMuhtarram130hd Led for a half,tracked leader,outpaced 1½f out,gaining late	8
27Aug94-6AP	fm 1 3/16Ⓣ	:47³ 1:11³ 1:36⁴ 1:55²	3↑ ⒻBeverly D-G1	104	3	7	78	65	42	1½	Swinburn WR	123	2.90	90-09	Hatoof123½Flawlessly123½Potridee123½ Late wide rush	8
31Jly94♦ Deauville(Fr)	yl *1ⓉStr	1:36⁴	3↑ ⒻPrix d'Astarte G2 Stk94500							1¾	Swinburn WR	126	*1.30		Hatoof126¾Ski Paradise130nkLunafairy119? Held up in last,late rally to lead 50y out,driving	8
29May94♦ Longchamp(Fr)	gd *1⅛ⓉRH	1:51³	3↑ Prix d'Ispahan-G1 Stk150000							43¾	Swinburn WR	124	*2.70		Bigstone128nkMuhtarram1281½Marildo1282 Tracked in 4th,bid over 2f out,led 2f to 1½f out,faded	7
6Nov93-7SA	fm 1½Ⓣ	:48³ 1:12² 2:01² 2:25	3↑ B C Turf-G1	104	8	7	85¾	73¾	52½	53¾	Swinburn WR	B 123	15.30	89-04	Kotshn126½BnBn1261¼Luzur126¾ Steadied far turn,weakened	14
16Oct93♦ Newmarket(GB)	gd 1¼ⓉStr	2:06⁴	3↑ Champion Stakes-G1 Stk534000							13	Swinburn WR	126	*2.50		Hatoof1263Ezzoud129noDernier Empereur1242 Toward rear,joined leaders 3f out,led 2f out,ridden clear	12
27Sep93♦ Maisns-Lfftte(Fr)	hy *1¼ⓉStr	2:08	3↑ La Coupe de M-Laffitte-G3 Stk60000							14	Swinburn WR	129	2.50e		Hatoof1294Baya124nkSawasdee1234 Unhurried in 5th,lacked room 3f out,led 2f out,easily clear	9
24Jun93♦ Longchamp(Fr)	fm*1¼ⓉRH	2:07³	4↑ La Coupe-G3 Stk59300							41¾	Swinburn WR	127	*.60		D'Arros1231Marildo130½Diese124nk Trailed to 1f out,outside bid,never threatened	5
30May93♦ Longchamp(Fr)	fm*1⅛ⓉRH	1:50³	4↑ Prix d'Ispahan-G1 Stk158000							43½	Swinburn WR	124	*1.00e		Arcangues1281½Misil128½Shanghai1281½ Trailed for nearly a mile,wide rally 1½f out,hung	7
7May93♦ Saint-Cloud(Fr)	yl *1ⓉLH	1:43³	4↑ Prix du Muguet-G3 Stk95600							1¾	Swinburn WR	127	3.00		Hatoof127¾Shanghai1301½Northern Crystal126½ Tracked leader in 2nd,led final furlong,held well	5
18Oct92-4WO	yl 1¼Ⓣ	:49² 1:16 1:42¹ 2:07⁴	3↑ ⒻE P Taylor-G2	101	5	6	65	53	43	11¼	Swinburn WR	118	*2.00	62-45	Hatoof1181¼Urban Sea1181¼Hero's Love123hd Ridden out	12
4Oct92♦ Longchamp(Fr)	sf *1⅛ⓉRH	2:02²	3↑ ⒻPrix de l'Opera-G2 Stk142000							1½	Swinburn WR	126	*1.80		Hatoof126½La Favorita1211Ruby Tiger128no Behind,9th 2½f out,hard ridden,strong bid 1f out,led near line	12
6Sep92♦ Longchamp(Fr)	sf *1ⓉRH	1:40³	3↑ Prix du Moulin de Longchamp-G1 Stk320000							32½	Mosse G	120	6.20		All at Sea120nkBrief Truce1232½Hatoof1202 Held up in 6th,ridden 2f out,finished well	10
16Aug92♦ Deauville(Fr)	sf *1ⓉStr	1:40⁴	3↑ Prix Jacque le Marois-G1 Stk342000							53½	Swinburn WR	120	16.00		Exit to Nowhere1301Lahib130hdCardoun123nk Never far back,effort over 1f out,one-paced.StarofCozzene 4th	14

Date/Track	Time	Race	Fin	Jockey	Wt	Odds	Top Finishers / Comment	Fld
17May92♦ Longchamp(Fr) gd *1ⓉRH	1:37	ⓕPoule d'Essai des Pouliches-G1 Stk317000	63¾	Swinburn WR	128	*1.70	Culture Vulture128½Hydro Calido128¾Guislaine128nk Tracked in 2nd,outpaced 2f out,evenly late	9
30Apr92♦ Newmarket(GB) gd 1ⓉStr	1:392	ⓕ1000 Guineas-G1 Stk335000	1hd	Swinburn WR	126	5.00	Hatoof126hdMarling126¾Kenbu126½ Well placed,dueled 2f out,drifted left,led 150y out,just held	14
10Apr92♦ Maisns-Lfftte(Fr) yl *7fⓉStr	1:274	ⓕPrix Imprudence (Listed) Stk37800	2nk	Swinburn WR	128	*.60e	Kenbu128nkHatoof1282½Plume Magique1281 5th early,tracked entrymate after 2f,led briefly,outfinished	6
6Oct91♦ Longchamp(Fr) yl *1ⓉRH	1:403	ⓕPrix Marcel Boussac-G1 Stk237000	2nk	Eddery Pat	123	7.50	Culture Vulture123hdHatoof1231Vereine123½ Reserved behind,hampered 3f out,strong late run,just missed	14
18Sep91♦ Longchamp(Fr) gd *1ⓉH	1:401	ⓕPrix d'Aumale-G3 Stk65300	2no	Guignard G	121	4.00	Guislaine121noHatoof1211Lady Normandy125½ Toward rear,wide bid 2f out,finished fast,just missed	12
3Sep91♦ Longchamp(Fr) sf *1ⓉRH	1:464	ⓕPrix de Toutevoie Mdn (FT)31700	11	Guignard	123	2.20	Hatoof1231Eastern Exodus123½Formidable Flight1232 Led to 1½f out,dueled,led again near line	6

Heavenly Prize

Own: Phipps Ogden

B. m. 5 (Feb)
Sire: Seeking the Gold (Mr. Prospector)
Dam: Oh What a Dance (Nijinsky II)
Br: Ogden Phipps (Ky)
Tr: McGaughey III Claude R

Life	18	9	6	3	$1,825,940	111	D.Fst	16	9	5	2	$1,607,940	111
1996	1	0	0	1	$33,000	107	Wet(366)	2	0	1	1	$218,000	99
1995	7	4	3	0	$895,900	111	Turf(306)	0	0	0	0	$0	–
	0	0	0	0	$0	–	Dst(0)	0	0	0	0	$0	–

Date	Cond	Dist	Fractions	Race	Fig	PP	St	1C	2C	Str	Fin	Jockey	Wt	Odds		Top Finishers	Comment	Fld
10Feb96-10GP	fst	1⅛	:464 1:104 1:353 1:49	3↑DonnH-G1	107	4	74¼	73¾	54¾	36	36	Day P	L115	6.50	- -	*Cigar*1282 *Wekiva Springs*1174 Heavenly Prize1153	Steady advance	8
28Oct95-4Bel	my	1⅛	:454 1:092 1:332 1:46	3↑ⓕBCDistaf-G1	96	8	912	912	912	410	213½	Day P	L123	*.80e	- -	InsideInformtion12313½ HevenlyPriz1232¼ *Lkwy*1231	Late advance on rail	10
7Oct95-7Bel	fst	1⅛	:48 1:121 1:361 1:483	3↑ⓕBeldame-G1	103	2	42½	43½	46	23	2¾	Day P	L123	*.65	- -	SerenasSong119¾ HeavenlyPrize1236¾ Lakewy1236¾	Taken wide,game fin.	5
20Aug95-8Sar	fst	1¼	:48 1:124 1:382 2:04	3↑ⓕJAMorisH-G1	106	4	67½	56	31	13	18½	Day P	127	*.15	- -	HevenlyPriz1278½ ForcingBid1082 CinnmonSugr1142	Going away,in hand	8
23Jly95-8Sar	fst	1⅛	:471 1:111 1:371 1:494	3↑ⓕGoFrWand-G1	97	3	47	48½	46½	13	111	Day P	123	*.35	- -	*Heavenly Prize*12311 Forcing Bid1082 Little Buckles1113¾	Ridden out	5
18Jun95-9Bel	fst	1 1/16	:23 :46 1:102 1:431	3↑ⓕHmpstedH-G1	111	4	42	45½	25	21	11¼	Day P	122	1.00	- -	*Heavenly Prize*1221¼ *Little Buckles*11110½ Sky Beauty1243	Advanced, clear	4
21Apr95-9OP	fst	1 1/16	:224 :454 1:103 1:423	4↑ⓕAplBlsmH-G1	104	5	66½	68½	56½	21	11	Day P	120	*1.00	- -	*Heavenly Prize*1201 Halo America1164 *Paseana*1225	Rallied, driving	6
2Apr95-9OP	fst	1 1/16	:232 :47 1:11 1:422	4↑ⓕOPBudBCH148k	102	6	44	34	35	24	23½	Day P	121	*.20	- -	Halo America1153½ *Heavenly Prize*1219 *Biolage*111nk	Rallied, second best	6
5Nov94-6CD	fst	1⅛	:474 1:121 1:373 1:503	3↑ⓕBCDistaf-G1	105	3	64½	21½	23	22	2nk	Day P	120	2.10	- -	OnDrmr123nk HvnlyPriz1201½ MissDominiqu1231¼	Finished determinedly	9
8Oct94-11Bel	fst	1⅛	:463 1:112 1:361 1:484	3↑ⓕBeldame-G1	111	3	45	43½	41½	1½	16	Day P	119	-e	- -	HevenlyPrize1196 *EductdRisk*12310 ClssyMirg12311	Exhibition, ridden out	4
4Sep94-8Bel	fst	1⅛	:461 1:101 1:35 1:471	ⓕGazelleH-G1	106	3	53	53	41½	4¾	16½	Smith M E	123	*.70	- -	*HevnlyPriz*1236½ CinnmonSugr1181¾ *SovrignKitty*1181	Drew off, ridden out	5
13Aug94-8Sar	fst	1¼	:48 1:12 1:372 2:031	ⓕAlabama-G1	111	2	41½	41½	1½	12	17	Smith M E	121	5.20	- -	*HeavenlyPrize*1217 Lakewy12111 SovereignKitty1211¼	Drew off, ridden out	7
23Jly94-9Sar	sly	7f	:221 :442 1:09 1:22	ⓕTest-G1	99	2	8	73¼	76	36	33	Smith M E	121	*1.50	- -	TwistAfleet1141 Penny'sReshoot1182 *HeavenlyPrize*12110¼	Late inside bid	8
18Jun94-7Bel	fst	6f	:221 :452 :57 1:09	ⓕPrioress-G2	95	2	6	54	3½	21½	22¼	Smith M E	121	*.70	- -	PennysReshoot1162¼ HevenlyPrize1216 BeckysShirt1141½	Circled, rallied	6
12Mar94-7GP	fst	6f	:214 :45 :573 1:101	ⓕⓇWhatASummr51k	84	6	12	95¾	74½	54¼	22½	Smith M E	118	*1.00	- -	SwiftandClassy1162½ HevenlyPrize118¾ *ShnniesBet*116no	Midpack, rallied	13
6Nov93-3SA	fst	1 1/16	:232 :472 1:112 1:43	ⓕBCJuvFil-G1	90	4	43	42	42	31	33	Smith M E	119	*1.90	- -	*Phone Chatter*119hd *Sardula*1193 Heavenly Prize119½	Bid 1/8,flattened	8
16Oct93-4Bel	fst	1	:224 :451 1:10 1:352	ⓕFrizette-G1	94	5	62	61½	1½	12	17	Smith M E	119	2.40	- -	HeavenlyPrize1197 FctsofLove1194¾ Footing1192½	Well rated, ridden out	7
15Sep93-5Bel	fst	6f	:224 :462 :583 1:104	ⓕMd Sp Wt 25k	88	4	4	52¾	1½	14	19	Smith M E	117	*1.40	- -	*Heavenly Prize*1179 Amy Be Happy1171¾ Vibelle117nk	Drew off, ridden out	7

Hidden Lake

Own: Clay Robert N. and Farmer, Tracy

B. f. 4 (Apr) KEESEP94 $13,000
Sire: Quiet American (Fappiano)
Dam: Friendly Circle (Round Table)
Br: Charles Nuckols, Jr. & Sons (Ky)
Tr: Kimmel John C

Life	22	7	4	6	$947,489	119	D.Fst	20	6	4	6	$866,589	119
1997	9	4	1	1	$697,600	119	Wet(361)	2	1	0	0	$80,900	101
1996	8	2	1	4	$189,439	102	Turf(294)	0	0	0	0	$0	–
	0	0	0	0	$0	–	Dst(0)	0	0	0	0	$0	–

Date	Cond	Dist	Fractions	Race	Fig	PP	St	1C	2C	Str	Fin	Jockey	Wt	Odds		Top Finishers	Comment	Fld
8Nov97-4Hol	fst	1⅛	:454 1:091 1:342 1:471	3↑ⓕBCDistaf-G1	71	8	65	64¼	67	89¾	722	Migliore R	LB123	1.70	68-06	Ajina1202 *Sharp Cat*1203½ Escena1231	Dull effort	8
19Oct97-9Bel	fst	1⅛	:463 1:103 1:352 1:481	3↑ⓕBeldame-G1	105	1	2½	21	1½	12½	12	Migliore R	L123	*2.30	89-12	Hidden Lake1232 *Ajina*1192 Jewel Princess1231¼	Took over after 3/4's	8
27Jly97-8Sar	fst	1⅛	:473 1:114 1:361 1:493	3↑ⓕGoFrWand-G1	105	6	11½	11½	1½	1hd	1hd	Migliore R	L123	*.70	88-17	*Hidden Lake*123hd Flat FleetFeet1202 *ClearMandate*1133	Came again on rail	7
28Jun97-9Bel	fst	1 1/16	:223 :452 1:094 1:404	3↑ⓕHmpstedH-G1	119	7	31½	21½	2hd	12½	12	Migliore R	L117	4.90	95-13	*HiddenLke*1172 *TwicetheVice*1212 JewlPrincss1245¼	Took over when asked	9
24May97-9Bel	fst	1	:222 :443 1:094 1:351	3↑ⓕShuveeH-G2	107	4	54¾	56	41¼	12	14	Migliore R	L115	8.80	88-17	*Hidden Lake*1154 Flat Fleet Feet1201 Escena116¾	Split foes,drew away	9
Previously trained by Greenman Walter 1997(as of 5/3): (84 15 14 11 0.18)																		
3May97-6CD	fst	7f	:224 :452 1:094 1:221	4↑ⓕHmnaDstH-G3	105	4	7	54	55½	21½	2¾	Desormeaux K J	L115	5.40	96-05	Capote Belle118¾ *Hidden Lake*115nk *J J'sdream*1173½	Closed fast, gaining	8
11Apr97-9OP	gd	1 1/16	:231 :463 1:104 1:413	4↑ⓕAplBlsmH-G1	94	8	53½	54	63¼	67¾	611	Desormeaux K J	L116	18.60	89-12	*HloAmeric*1174 JewelPrincess124hd Diffrnt1211½	Raced outside,weakened	8
9Mar97-7SA	fst	1⅛	:48 1:121 1:364 1:491	4↑ⓕSMrgrtaH-G1	101	6	33	31½	31½	2½	3¾	McCarron C J	LB114	10.40	86-12	Jewel Princess125½ Top Rung116nk Hidden Lake1143	Bid 1/8,good effort	6
16Feb97-8SA	fst	1 1/16	:231 :464 1:101 1:413	4↑ⓕSntMriaH-G1	102	5	67	54	42¾	42½	46½	McCarron C J	LB116	10.80	88-12	*Jewel Princess*1235 Cat's Cradle118½ Top Rung1171	Closed willingly	7
29Dec96-5SA	gd	7f	:222 :443 1:091 1:22	ⓕLaBrea-G2	101	6	5	55½	55	22	11	McCarron C J	LB115	6.60	92-10	HiddenLake1151 *BellesFlag*1193 TiffnyDimond1154½	Slippd thru,strng rlly	7
16Jun96-9CD	fst	1 1/16	:231 :464 1:112 1:431	ⓕDogwood82k	94	6	45½	33	31½	41½	33	Valdivia J Jr	L114	4.00	92-12	Ginny Lynn121½ Everhope1212½ *Hidden Lake*1141½	Bid 5wide gave way	7
25May96-9CD	fst	1	:23 :453 1:101 1:352	ⓕEdgewood83k	93	7	2½	31½	32	22½	23	Day P	L114	*.90	93-09	Everhope1143 Hidden Lake1143 *Mariuka*112no	Settld chasd winner	7
5May96-8Hol	fst	7f	:214 :444 1:093 1:222	ⓕRailbird-G2	83	4	6	65½	64¾	22	43¾	McCarron C J	LB118	2.40	- -	*Supercilious*1211¾ TiffanyDimond1181¾ *RwGold*121nk	Rallied inside,flattnd	6
10Mar96-4SA	fst	1 1/16	:232 :473 1:112 1:43	ⓕSAOaks-G1	90	2	54½	54	33½	34	35¼	McCarron C J	LB117	5.70	- -	Antespend1172¼ Cara Rafaela1173 Hidden Lake1172½	Failed to sustain bid	5
18Feb96-8SA	fst	1	:222 :463 1:104 1:362	ⓕLsVrgnes-G1	89	2	59	56½	53½	34	35	McCarron C J	B116	6.20	- -	*Antespend*1202½ CaraRafaela1222½ HiddenLke1161¾	Awkward strt,rllied w	6
28Jan96-8SA	fst	7f	:222 :453 1:093 1:223	ⓕSntaYnez-G3	87	6	5	44½	43½	34	31½	McCarron C J	B116	*1.20	- -	Raw Gold1211 *Pareja*121½ Hidden Lake1167½	Unhurried,finishd well	6
6Jan96-3SA	fst	6½f	:213 :443 1:091 1:154	ⓕAlw 42000N1x	102	1	6	68½	64	32	1nk	McCarron C J	B117	*1.50	- -	HiddenLk117nk DncingPrism1173½ Bbinthwoods1177	Closed rush, up late	6
18Nov95-6Hol	fst	7f	:222 :452 1:093 1:214	ⓕMakersMark106k	93	3	5	53	44	24	24	McCarron C J	B114	4.10	- -	AdvancingStar1144 *HiddenLake*1143½ SrtogFlower1212½	Strong rally turn	6
18Oct95-8SA	fst	6f	:214 :45 :571 1:093	ⓕAnoakia78k	89	1	7	65	53¾	42½	2½	McCarron C J	B115	9.30	88-12	CntsCrusd115½ HiddnLk115nk Thnkyourluckystr1163½	Strong rally 4-wide	8
27Aug95-8Dmr	fst	7f	:214 :441 1:09 1:222	ⓕDMrDeb-G2	65	9	12	1214	129¾	99¾	810¼	Blanc B	B115	26.40	- -	Batroyale1194 *Proud Dixie*1172 *General Idea*1161	Far back, no threat	12
5Aug95-4Dmr	fst	6f	:22 :45 :574 1:103	ⓕMd Sp Wt 37k	76	4	7	79½	76	64¼	11¼	Blanc B5	B113	3.80	- -	HddnLk1131¼ PssonFlowr118½ TckttoHouston118½	Closed rush very wide	8
16Jly95-4Hol	fst	5f	:221 :453	ⓕMd Sp Wt 34k	73	3	7	76½	512	54	31	McCarron C J	B118	19.80	- -	Blacktie Bid118½ Totally Spellbound118½ *Hidden Lake*118½	Best stride late	9

Hollywood Wildcat

Own: Irving & Marjorie Cowan

Dk. b or b. m. 5 (Feb)
Sire: Kris S. (Roberto)
Dam: Miss Wildcatter (Mr. Prospector)
Br: Irving Cowan & Marjorie Cowan (Fla)
Tr: Drysdale Neil D

Life	21	12	3	3	$1,432,160	111	D.Fst	15	8	1	3	$1,034,580 110
1995	1	1	0	0	$36,250	102	Wet(399)	1	1	0	0	$38,480 79
1994	6	2	2	1	$304,300	111	Turf(346)	5	3	2	0	$359,100 111
	0	0	0	0	$0	-	Dst(0)	0	0	0	0	$0 -

10Feb95-8SA	fst 7f	:224 :454 1:093 1:213	4↑ⒻⓇLtlBrianne65k	102	4 5 31 31 13 14½	Delahoussaye E	LB121	*.70	- -	HollywoodWildct1214½ Nijivision1152 FlyngnthLn1131¼	Quick gain, easily	5
5Nov94-6CD	fst 1⅛	:474 1:121 1:373 1:503	3↑ⒻBCDistaf-G1	92	6 22 43 54¾ 610 68¼	Delahoussaye E	L123	*1.80	- -	OneDremer123nk HvnlyPriz1201½ MissDominiqu1231¼	Close up, flattened	9
10Oct94-8SA	fst 1 1/16	:23 :47 1:103 1:403	3↑ⒻLadySecrtH106k	110	3 11 11 1hd 11 12¼	Delahoussaye E	LB124	*.70	- -	HollywodWldct1242¼ Exchng1213 DncngMrg11314	Drew clear, ridden out	5
6Aug94-8Dmr	fm 1⅛ Ⓣ	:473 1:113 1:361 1:481	3↑ⒻRomanaH-G1	101	5 54 57½ 52½ 43 2hd	Delahoussaye E	LB124	*.80	- -	Flwlessly124hd *HollywoodWildct*1241¼ *Skimble*1162	Angled out,closed rush	5
3Jly94-8Hol	fm 1⅛ Ⓣ	:48 1:111 1:35 1:472	3↑ⒻBevHilsH-G1	101	4 72¼ 74¾ 73¾ 51¾ 2nk	Delahoussaye E	LB124	*1.00	- -	Corrazon119nk HollywoodWildct124no *Flwlessly*1241	Finished well 5-wide	7
12Jun94-8Hol	fm 1⅛ Ⓣ	:464 1:10 1:341 1:462	3↑ⒻGamelyH-G1	111	2 31½ 44 63½ 2½ 12¼	Delahoussaye E	LB122	2.70	- -	HollywoodWildct1222¼ MzZill[illegible]r1142¾ Flwlssly124nk	Strong rally, handily	6
5Feb94-8SA	fst 1⅛	:473 1:112 1:361 1:484	ⒻLaCanada-G2	87	2 11 2hd 23 33½ 35¼	Delahoussaye E	LB122	*.50	- -	Stalcreek119¾ Alyshena1154½ *Hollywood Wildcat*122¾	Wide trip, no rally	4
6Nov93-4SA	fst 1⅛	:464 1:11 1:36 1:481	3↑ⒻBCDistaf-G1	108	6 1hd 22 2hd 1hd 1no	Delahoussaye E	LB120	*1.30	- -	HollywoodWildcat120no Pasean1232½ ReToss1231	Lost whip,held gamely	8
11Oct93-8SA	fst 1 1/16	:224 :461 1:101 1:41	3↑ⒻLadySecrtH106k	106	1 34½ 31½ 2hd 12 12	Delahoussaye E	LB117	*.70	- -	*Hollywood Wildcat*1172 Re Toss1172 WeddingRing1134½	Early gain, handily	5
22Aug93-8Dmr	fm 1⅛ Ⓣ	:472 1:114 1:362 1:481	ⒻDMrIvOks-G2	102	3 43 45½ 43 42 11	Delahoussaye E	LB120	*.80	- -	*HollywoodWildct*1201 *PossblyPrfct*1201¾ *MmSnds*120nk	Closed rush, driving	10
1Aug93-5Dmr	fm 1 Ⓣ	:221 :46 1:102 1:344	ⒻSnClmenteH83k	107	8 66½ 54½ 72¾ 12 14½	Delahoussaye E	LB120	*2.10	- -	*HollywoodWildct*1204½ MimiSnds1161¼ BelStrtBlus1171	6-wide str, handily	10
11Jly93-8Hol	fst 1⅛	:462 1:103 1:353 1:482	ⒻHolOaks-G1	107	4 2½ 21 21 1hd 11¾	Delahoussaye E	LB121	16.60	- -	*HollywoodWildcat*1211¾ FittoLed1216½ Adorydr121no	Well handled, driving	9
Previously trained by Tortora Emanuel 1993(as of 6/19): (258 42 39 36 0.16)												
19Jun93-9Crc	fst 7f	:222 :45 1:10 1:232	ⒻAzaleaH100k	81	4 5 3½ 2½ 41½ 33¼	Coa E M5	L117f	5.30	- -	*Kmscontrydmond*1151¾ Njvsn1131½ *HllywdWldct*117no	Failed to sustain bid	10
9Apr93-9OP	fst 1 1/16	:231 :474 1:124 1:441	ⒻFantasy-G2	77	1 53 51¼ 3½ 65 610	Arguello F A Jr	L121f	11.60	- -	Aztec Hill1215 Adorydar1172 *Stalcreek*117½	Failed to sustain bid	7
20Mar93-10Tam	fst 1 1/16	:233 :48 1:123 1:453	ⒻFlaOaks100k	78	1 105¼118 114¼ 43½ 22	Lopez R D	L121f	*1.70	- -	Star Jolie1112 Hollywood Wildcat121nk *Jacody*111¾	6 wide gaining	11
7Mar93-7GP	fst 6f	:221 :45 :572 1:102	ⒻAlw 31000NC	82	3 1 41¼ 3½ 22 31	Bailey J D	L117	1.30	- -	OurSwetMg113no GtrCoEd1081 HollywoodWildct1173¾	Failed to respond	6
12Sep92-10Crc	fst 7f	:222 :46 1:113 1:25	ⒻⓇFSSsnsGirl125k	54	1 5 52¾ 64¼ 77¾ 614½	Arguello F A Jr	L118	*.50	- -	Boots 'n Jackie1182 Exercising1182½ Sigrun1183	Well placed, faded	8
1Aug92-9Mth	fst 6f	:214 :451 :58 1:104	ⒻSorority-G3	86	3 3 56 34½ 22½ 14	Arguello F A Jr	L119	3.60	- -	HollywoodWldct1194 *FmlyEntrprz*1193¾ DAccrdrss119nk	Drew off driving	6
12Jly92-10Crc	fst 5½f	:221 :462 1:063	ⒻMelalucaH50k	78	2 7 41½ 42 12 12½	Arguello F A Jr	L118	*1.20	- -	*HollywoodWildct*1182½ DebbiesBliss118hd Ⓓ*BootsnJcki*1121	Much the best	12
7Jun92-9CD	gd 5½f	:224 :472 1:06	ⒻDebutante59k	79	1 1 31½ 3½ 11 13	Arguello F A Jr	LB116	7.80	- -	*HollywoodWildcat*1163 CosmicSpeedQueen1181 DixieBand1152	Ridden out	14
15Apr92-3Crc	fst 4½f	:224 :472 :534	ⒻMd Sp Wt 14k	68	3 1 2½ 1½ 15	Douglas R R	116	2.30	- -	*Hollywood Wildcat*1165 ⒹMarti Huizenga116¾ Supah Gem116nk	Drew off	6

Holy Bull

Own: W. A. Croll Jr

Gr. c. 4 (Jan)
Sire: Great Above (Minnesota Mac)
Dam: Sharon Brown (Al Hattab)
Br: Pelican Stable (Fla)
Tr: Croll W A Jr

Life	16	13	0	0	$2,481,760	122	D.Fst	13	12	0	0	$2,412,400 122
1995	2	1	0	0	$51,000	117	Wet(344)	3	1	0	0	$69,360 103
1994	10	8	0	0	$2,095,000	122	Turf(302)	0	0	0	0	$0 -
	0	0	0	0	$0	-	Dst(0)	0	0	0	0	$0 -

11Feb95-9GP	fst 1⅛	:462 1:103 1:363 1:493	3↑DonnH-G1	-	9 21 22 - 922 -	Smith M E	127	*.30	- -	*Cigar*1155½ Primitive Hall1122 Bonus Money1123½	Pulled up in distress	9
22Jan95-9GP	fst 7f	:223 :451 1:093 1:22	3↑OlympicH100k	117	5 3 2½ 2½ 1hd 12½	Smith M E	126	*.40	- -	Holy Bull1262½ Birdonthewire1192¾ Patton115¾	Fast pace, handily	6
17Sep94-8Bel	fst 1⅛	:462 1:102 1:343 1:464	3↑Woodward-G1	116	5 21 21 1½ 12½ 15	Smith M E	121	*.90	- -	*Holy Bull*1215 Devil His Due1261½ *Colonial Affair*1263½	Drew off, ridden out	8
20Aug94-7Sar	fst 1¼	:461 1:102 1:354 2:02	Travers-G1	115	1 2hd 13 14 11 1nk	Smith M E	126	*.80	- -	*Holy Bull*126nk Concern12617 *Tabasco Cat*1261	Dueled gamely, drvng	5
31Jly94-10Mth	fst 1⅛	:472 1:112 1:354 1:481	HsklInvH-G1	115	3 11 12 12 11½ 11¾	Smith M E	126	*.20	- -	*Holy Bull*1261¾ *Meadow Flight*1181¾ Concern1181	Repell foe,confidently	6
3Jly94-8Bel	fst 1 1/16	:222 :451 1:092 1:41	Dwyer-G2	119	1 11 11 11½ 13 16¾	Smith M E	124	*.30	- -	*Holy Bull*1246¾ Twining1225 Bay Street Star1199	Pace, ridden out	4
30May94-8Bel	fst 1	:224 :45 1:092 1:334	3↑MtropltH-G1	122	6 11 11 1½ 12 15½	Smith M E	112	*1.00	- -	*Holy Bull*1125½ Cherokee Run118no *Devil His Due*1222	Drew off, driving	10
7May94-8CD	sly 1¼	:471 1:114 1:373 2:033	KyDerby-G1	85	4 53½ 63¼ 99 1019 1218¼	Smith M E	126	*2.20	- -	Go for Gin1262 Strodes Creek1262½ Blumin Affair126¾	Off slow, gave way	14
16Apr94-9Kee	fst 1⅛	:474 1:123 1:374 1:50	BlueGras-G2	113	1 12 12½ 12½ 12 13½	Smith M E	121	*.60	- -	HolyBull1213½ ValiantNature1215 MahoganyHll1212¼	Drew off, hand ride	7
12Mar94-10GP	fst 1⅛	:46 1:10 1:344 1:473	FlaDerby-G1	115	6 12 12 12 11½ 15¾	Smith M E	122	2.70	- -	*Holy Bull*1225¾ Ride the Rails122no Halo's Image1221	Led, handily	14
19Feb94-9GP	gd 1 1/16	:224 :453 1:102 1:443	FntnOYth-G2	57	4 1hd 1hd 2½ 66¾ 624¼	Smith M E	119	*1.30	- -	Dehere119¾ Go for Gin1191¼ Ride the Rails1173¾	Vied for lead, tired	6
30Jan94-9GP	fst 7f	:213 :44 1:081 1:211	Hutchesn-G2	108	1 3 11½ 11 2hd 1¾	Smith M E	122	*.50	- -	Holy Bull122¾ *Patton*1133 You and I1193	Came again,impressive	5
23Oct93-11Crc	fst 1 1/16	:23 :462 1:113 1:461	ⓇFSInRealty400k	93	9 11½ 11½ 12 14 17½	Smith M E	120	*.50	- -	*Holy Bull*1207½ Rustic Light1201 ForwardtoLead1201½	Handily, convincing	12
18Sep93-6Bel	sly 7f	:222 :453 1:101 1:231	Futurity-G1	103	2 1 11 1½ 13 1½	Smith M E	122	3.10	- -	*Holy Bull*122½ *Dehere*1225 Prenup1228	Set pace, driving	6
2Sep93-7Bel	fst 6½f	:22 :441 1:094 1:17	Alw 28000N1X	91	3 1 1½ 1hd 13½ 17	Smith M E	119	*.90	- -	*Holy Bull*1197 Goodbye Doeny1173 End Sweep119½	Set pace, handily	6
Previously owned by Targan Stables												
14Aug93-7Mth	fst 5½f	:213 :444 :571 1:034	Md Sp Wt 16k	101	1 3 11 11½ 11½ 12½	Rivera L Jr	118	*1.10	- -	*Holy Bull*1182½ Palance1187½ *Hold My Tongue*1189	Super speed,green,drvg	9

Housebuster

dkbbr. c. 1987, by Mt. Livermore (Blushing Groom)–Big Dreams, by Great Above

Lifetime record: 22 15 3 1 $1,229,696

Own.– Robert P. Levy
Br.– Murphy Stable & Blanche P. Levy (Ky)
Tr.– Warren A. Croll Jr

2Nov91-2CD	fst 6f	:21 :442 1:091	3↑ BC Sprint-G1	2 6 22 21 2hd 99	Perret C	B 126	*.40	92-02	Sheikh Albadou1243Pleasant Tap126½Robyn Dancer126nk		11
Bobbled start,bothered by rivals whip str,came back lame											
28Sep91-8Bel	fst 7f	:231 :454 1:094 1:214	3↑ Vosburgh-G1	1 5 31 31 1½ 15½	Perret C	126	*.40	95-14	Housebuster1265½Senator to Be126nkSunshine Jimmy1262½		6
Stumbled start,driving											
25Aug91-8Sar	fst 7f	:214 :434 1:08 1:21	3↑ Forego H-G2	3 4 1hd 1½ 12 1no	Perret C	126	*.60	100-12	Housebuster126noSenorSpeedy1121CleverTrvor1202½	Driving	6
20Jly91-9Lrl	fst 6f	:213 :434 :57 1:083	3↑ F J DeFrancis 300k	2 2 32½ 42½ 21½ 15	Perret C	126	*2.40	98-15	Housebuster1265ClevrTrvor1231¼SflyKpt1213¼	Wide,driving	6
27May91-8Bel	fst 1	:22 :441 1:091 1:352	3↑ Metropolitan H-G1	4 1 11½ 1hd 44½ 810¼	Perret C	124	*.90	83-16	In Excess1172¼Rubiano1111¾Gervazy1141½	Speed,tired	14
4May91-8Aqu	fst 7f	:224 :452 1:084 1:211	3↑ Carter H-G1	1 4 1½ 11 13 12¼	Perret C	122	*1.30	96-17	Housebuster1222¼BlackTieAffair1232½Gervazy116no	Driving	8
12Apr91-8Kee	fst 7f	:222 :452 1:09 1:214	3↑ Commonwealth BC-G3	4 3 11½ 11½ 1½ 21	Perret C	B 124	*.30	100-12	BlackTieAffair1241Housbustr1244ExmplryLdr115hd	2nd best	6
16Mar91-6GP	fst 7f	:22 :442 1:091 1:214	3↑ Deputy Minister H 50k	8 3 3½ 3nk 2hd 23	Perret C	122	*.40	94-07	Unbridled1193Housebuster122noShuttleman1145	Gamely	9
29Sep90-8Bel	fst 7f	:213 :44 1:082 1:21	3↑ Vosburgh-G1	4 5 42 2½ 33½ 615	Perret C	122	*.30	84-11	Sewickley1264½SunshineJmmy122¾Glttrmn1261¾	4-wide,tired	9
3Sep90-8Bel	fst 1	:223 :444 1:084 1:34	Jerome H-G1	5 2 21 1½ 16 113	Perret C	126	*.40	99-10	Housebuster12613Citidancer114¾D'Prrot1122	Good handling	5
18Aug90-8Sar	fst 7f	:213 :441 1:084 1:214	King's Bishop-G3	8 1 33 2½ 15 13¼	Perret C	122	*.30	96-05	Housebstr1223¼Poppiano115nkSunshine Jimmy1155	Handily	9
23Jun90-8AP	fst 1	:23 :452 1:093 1:343	Sheridan-G3	3 1 11 12 13 14½	Perret C	123	*.05	98-13	Housebstr1234½Spanish Drummer11510½Copelan's Game1139½		5
Under wraps											
28May90-8Bel	fst 1	:223 :45 1:091 1:342	3↑ Metropolitan H-G1	3 1 11 11½ 11½ 2nk	Perret C	113	2.40	97-18	CriminalType120nkHousebuster1131½EasyGoer1273	Good try	9
9May90-8Bel	fst 1	:223 :452 1:10 1:344	Withers-G2	6 1 11 1½ 11½ 12	Perret C	126	*.50	95-14	Housebustr1262ProfitKey1264SunnyServe1264½	Ridden out	6
28Apr90-9CD	fst 1	:222 :453 1:111 1:373	Derby Trial-G3	5 2 11 11½ 12 15¼	Perret C	122	*.20	89-26	Housebustr1225¼PrivatSchool119½FllngSky1173	Ridden out	6
11Apr90-0Kee	fst 7f	:22 :45 1:084 1:224	Lafayette-G3	1 1 1hd 12½ 15 111	Perret C	121	-	95-09	Housebstr12111SacraHoxen11427CritclChoc113	Ridden out	3
17Mar90-5GP	fst 7f	:223 :444 1:091 1:221	Swale-G3	2 2 1½ 1½ 12 11	Perret C	122	*.90	95-15	Housebstr1221SummerSquall1226ThirtySixRd1138¾	Handily	6
10Feb90-10GP	fst 7f	:214 :442 1:102 1:242	Hutcheson-G3	5 5 1hd 1hd 14 13	Romero RP	119	1.90	84-18	Housebuster1193Yonder1221Stalker114¾	Driving	11
16Jan90-9GP	fst 6f	:22 :452 1:112	Spectacular Bid 50k	5 5 31 1½ 13½ 12¼	Perret C	114	*1.50	88-20	Housebuster1142¼FitContendr1132½Stalker1145	Ridden out	8
Previously trained by Ronald L. Benshof											
24Nov89-9Med	fst 6f	:213 :442 1:094	Morven BC 48k	3 2 1hd 11 16 17	Madrid A Jr	113	4.00	93-14	Housbstr1137Thoddsonchoc119noBoldHour'sLck1134¾	Easily	8
8Nov89-4Med	sly 6f	:214 :45 1:111	Md Sp Wt	6 3 2hd 1hd 12 12¾	Krone JA	118	*.50	86-17	Housebuster1182¾Mr.MichaelJ.1181BigTedK.118hd	Easily	11
17Oct89-2Med	sly 6f	:212 :443 1:103	Md Sp Wt	8 3 41 1hd 2½ 32¼	Chavez JF	118	3.70	87-14	Stalker1182Canadian Roy118nkHousebuster1181	Weakened	8

Inside Information

Own: Ogden Mills Phipps

B. f. 4 (May)
Sire: Private Account (Damascus)
Dam: Pure Profit (Key to the Mint)
Br: Ogden Mills Phipps (Ky)
Tr: McGaughey III Claude R

Life	17	14	1	2	$1,641,806	119	D.Fst	14 12 0 2	$1,001,806	112
1995	8	7	1	0	$1,160,408	119	Wet(389)	3 2 1 0	$640,000	119
1994	7	6	0	1	$462,798	102	Turf(259)	0 0 0 0	$0	–
	0	0	0	0	$0	–	Dst(0)	0 0 0 0	$0	–

28Oct95–4Bel	my	1⅛	:454 1:092 1:332 1:46	3↑Ⓕ BCDistaf-G1	**119**	1	41	1½	11½	17	113½	Smith M E	123	*.80e	- -	InsideInformation12313½ HeavenlyPrize1232¼ *Lakewy*1231	Brisk hand ride	10
8Oct95–8Kee	fst	1⅛	:48 1:121 1:371 1:50	3↑Ⓕ Spinster-G1	**100**	4	32½	31½	21	1hd	1hd	Smith M E	123	*.50	- -	*InsideInformation*123hd JdeFlush1234 MrihsStorm1233	Fractious, sluggish	4
16Sep95–6Bel	fst	1 1/16	:231 :46 1:092 1:404	3↑Ⓕ RuffianH-G1	**112**	5	2½	1½	15	18	111	Smith M E	125	*.10	- -	*InsdInformton*12511 UnlwflBhvor110no Incnrt1121¼	Widened under wraps	6
13Aug95–8Sar	gd	7f	:224 :46 1:10 1:222	3↑Ⓕ BalrinaH-G1	**98**	3	6	51¾	21½	22½	26	Smith M E	126	*.40	- -	ClssyMirg1196 *InsidInformtion*1264½ *LursPistoltt*1125	Stumbled badly start	6
4Jly95–9Mth	fst	1 1/16	:234 :464 1:101 1:434	3↑Ⓕ MlyPchrH-G2	**106**	3	32	2½	1hd	14	16¾	Smith M E	124	*.30	- -	InsideInformation1246¾ JadeFlush1151¾ *HloAmeric*1184¼	As rider pleased	5
3Jun95–10Mth	fst	170	:224 :462 1:111 1:414	3↑Ⓕ MthBdBCH-G3	**107**	2	35	31	2hd	12½	12¼	Smith M E	123	*.30	- -	*Inside Information*1232¼ Morning Meadow1155 Incinerate11610	Decisively	5
20May95–8Bel	fst	1	:224 :462 1:102 1:35	3↑Ⓕ ShuveeH-G1	**111**	1	2½	2hd	11	13	15½	Santos J A	119	2.25e	- -	*InsidInformton*1195½ SkyButy12616 *RstordHop*1152	Quick move, ridden out	4
26Apr95–7Kee	fst	7f	:224 :453 1:093 1:213	4↑Ⓕ Alw 45590N$Y	**102**	4	2	1½	12½	14	14	Smith M E	118	*.30	- -	*InsideInformtion*1184 TrvrsCity1184½ ScoopthGold114½	Set pace, drew off	6
18Nov94–6Aqu	fst	6½f	:224 :454 1:094 1:16	3↑Ⓕ Alw 42000N$Y	**102**	4	4	2hd	11	13	18	Smith M E	120	*.15	- -	*InsideInformtion*1208 LittlBuckls112hd RchforClvr11710½	Drew off, handily	5
12Jun94–8Bel	fst	1⅛	:451 1:083 1:332 1:462	Ⓕ MthrGoos-G1	**89**	2	1hd	1hd	2hd	33½	310¼	Smith M E	121	*.70	- -	*Lakewy*1214¼ CinnmonSugr1216 *InsideInformtion*121nk	Set pace, gave way	6
8May94–8Bel	my	1	:224 :452 1:093 1:341	Ⓕ Acorn-G1	**96**	3	2hd	11	12½	16	111	Smith M E	121	*.50	- -	InsdInformton12111 CnnmonSgr1211½ *SovrgnKtty*1213¾	Drew off, handily	5
23Apr94–8Kee	fst	1 1/16	:242 :491 1:14 1:464	Ⓕ Ashland-G1	**101**	4	2½	2½	1½	14½	15½	Smith M E	121	*.80	- -	*InsideInformation*1215½ Bunting115nk PrivateStatus1182	Drew off, handily	6
5Mar94–10GP	fst	1 1/16	:231 :462 1:103 1:424	Ⓕ BonnieMs-G2	**93**	6	52½	41	2hd	1hd	12¾	Smith M E	114	3.00	- -	*InsideInformation*1142¾ CinnamonSugr113nk JdeFlush1144	Rated, drew off	10
21Feb94–1GP	fst	1 1/16	:241 :481 1:122 1:431	Ⓕ Alw 29000N2X	**88**	3	11	11½	11	11½	1nk	Smith M E	118	*.60	- -	*InsideInformtion*118nk CinnmonSugr12111 TrubyTwo1185½	Led, just lasted	5
6Feb94–7GP	fst	7f	:224 :453 1:10 1:22	Ⓕ Alw 25000N2L	**95**	7	1	2hd	1hd	11½	17	Smith M E	118	*1.10	- -	*InsdInfrmtn*1187 BlshngBlnd118nk MssPrspctr1215½	Handily, convincingly	9
2Nov93–6Aqu	fst	1	:232 :464 1:121 1:382	Ⓕ Alw 30000N1X	**75**	3	31	3½	2½	31½	33	Smith M E	116	*.80	- -	SovrignKitty116no Bunting1163 *InsidInformtion*1166¾	Bmpd gate,bid, hung	7
15Sep93–3Bel	fst	6f	:223 :462 :584 1:113	Ⓕ Md Sp Wt 25k	**79**	4	3	42½	2½	13	17½	Smith M E	117	1.90	- -	InsidInformton1177½ JdFlush117½ MssApplus1172¾	Circled 4w, ridden out	7

Itsallgreektome

gr. g. 1987, by Sovereign Dancer (Northern Dancer)–Sans Supplement, by Grey Dawn II

Lifetime record: 29 8 10 2 $1,994,618

Own.– Jhayare Stables
Br.– Sugar Maple Farm (Fla)
Tr.– R.B. Hess Jr

26Feb94- 8SA	fm	1¼Ⓣ	:472 1:112 1:36 2:003	4↑ Ⓡ San Marino H 82k	63	5	6	610	64½	79	718	Desormx KJ	**LB** 120	b	2.20	66-16	Semillon1162¼Memento Mori114noAlex the Great1141¾		7
	Very wide into lane																		
17Jan94- 3SA	fm	1Ⓣ	:223 :454 1:093 1:343	4↑ Alw 55000	86	4	6	611	610	56½	22¼	Dlhoussaye E	**LB** 116	b	2.30	90-08	RobberRamble1152¼Itsallgrktom116nkBonPont1151¼	Late bid	6
	Previously trained by Wallace Dollase																		
15Nov92- 8CD	yl	1⅛Ⓣ	:483 1:122 1:364 1:491	3↑ River City H 112k	102	8	8	66	64½	43½	4½	Nakatani CS	**LB** 122	b	*2.10	89-10	Cozzene'sPrince117noLotusPool118½Stgcrft114no	Hung late	8
7Mar92- 8SA	gd	1Ⓣ	:23 :462 1:094 1:343	4↑ Arcadia H-G3	108	5	8	87½	74¾	53¼	2¾	Valenzla PA	**LB** 123		*2.50	89-20	FlyTillDawn120¾Itsallgrktom123½Qthf1151¼	5-wide stretch	11
5Jan92-10Hia	fm	1½Ⓣ	2:281	3↑ Hia Turf Cup H 200k	104	1	2	2½	1½	1hd	2nk	Velasquez J	**L** 124	b	*.40	86-14	CrystalMoment113nkItsallgrktome1241PassagereduSoir1152½		13
	Outfinished																		
15Dec91- 8Hol	fm	1½Ⓣ	:52 1:173 2:064 2:30	3↑ Hol Turf Cup-G1	-	1	3	41¾	52	32	2hd	Desormx KJ	**LB** 126	b	*1.40	73-21	Miss Alleged123hdItsallgreektome1261¼Quest for Fame126¾		7
	Boxed in ¼ out,4-wide into stretch,game try																		
2Nov91- 7CD	fm	1½Ⓣ	:504 1:154 2:062 2:304	3↑ BC Turf-G1	-	8	2	2½	2hd	1hd	2½	Velasquez J	**LB** 126	b	4.70	95-06	MissAllegd123½Itsallgreektom1262QustforFm1262	Game try	13
12Oct91- 8Kee	fm	1⅛Ⓣ	:471 1:111 1:36 1:482	3↑ Keeneland BC-G3	-	6	4	31½	1hd	11	12¼	Velasquez J	**LB** 126	b	1.40	103-00	Itsallgrktome1262¼OpenngVrs1264SuprAbound1261½	Driving	6
1Sep91- 9AP	fm	1¼Ⓣ	:473 1:111 1:354 1:592	3↑ Arl Million-G1	-	5	5	67½	88	88½	76	Sellers SJ	**L** 126		4.90	95-07	Tight Spot126hdAlgenib122nkKartajana123nk	Evenly	10
10Aug91- 3Dmr	fst	1¼	:454 1:094 1:341 1:594	3↑ Pacific Classic 1000k	-	1	6	53½	45	55½	65½	Nakatani CS	**LB** 124		7.80	--	BestPal1161TwilightAgnda1242¾Unbrdld1241¼	Saved ground	8
29Jun91- 4Hol	fst	1¼	:464 1:101 1:341 1:592	3↑ Hol Gold Cup-G1	-	9	6	54	33	34	32¾	Nakatani CS	**LB** 119		8.30	97-00	Mrqutry110hdFrmWy1222¾Itsllgrktom1193½	Wide to far turn	9
27May91- 8Hol	fm	1¼Ⓣ	:481 1:114 1:36 2:00	3↑ Hol Turf H-G1	-	4	5	58½	34½	1hd	2¾	Nakatani CS	**LB** 123		*1.60	92-09	Exbourne119¾Itsallgreektome123½Prized1233½	No mishap	6
3May91- 8CD	fm	1⅛Ⓣ	:48 1:111 1:352 1:471	4↑ ET Turf Classic-G3	-	8	6	66	65¾	4¾	2no	Nakatani CS	**LB** 123	b	*1.40	109-00	Opening Verse116noItsallgreektome1233Pedro the Cool112nk		11
	Crowded early																		
14Apr91- 8Kee	gd	1⅛Ⓣ	:494 1:143 1:384 1:511	4↑ Elkhorn-G2	-	1	2	2hd	2½	11½	1¾	Baze RA	**LB** 123	b	*.60	89-13	Itsallgrktom123¾PrtArmy113¾SprkO'Dn113¾	Fully extended	7
23Mar91- 8GG	yl	1Ⓣ	:241 :483 1:124 1:384	3↑ S F Mile H-G3	-	1	6	68½	65¾	65	42	Nakatani CS	**LB** 124	b	*.90	82-16	Forty Niner Days113nkExbourne1161½Blaze o' Brien116nk		6
	Rallied inside																		
16Dec90- 8Hol	fm	1½Ⓣ	:474 1:123 2:011 2:244	3↑ Hol Turf Cup-G1	-	1	6	86¾	63¼	11	11	Nakatani CS	**LB** 122	b	*2.50	97-04	Itsallgrktom1221Mshkour1262LvthDrm126hd	4-wide stretch	14
11Nov90- 8Hol	fm	1⅛Ⓣ	:464 1:101 1:342 1:463	Hol Derby-G1	-	6	10	107¾	97¼	43	1hd	Nakatani CS	**LB** 122	b	2.80	95-09	Itsallgreektome122hdSeptiemCl1222Anshn1221¾	Bumped 1/16	12
27Oct90- 6Bel	gd	1Ⓣ	:223 :454 1:10 1:351	3↑ BC Mile-G1	-	6	6	53	21	2½	2nk	Natakani CS	122	b	36.90	90-15	RoylAcademy122nkItsallgreektome122¾Prolo122½	Sharp try	13
22Sep90- 8BM	fm	1 1/16Ⓣ	:234 :48 1:114 1:431	Ascot H-G3	-	5	6	63¾	31½	11	11	Nakatani CS	**LB** 122	b	*.70	89-14	Itsallgrektom1221NoblDr.112½ProforSur117hd	Rallied wide	7
19Aug90- 8Dmr	fm	1⅛Ⓣ	:483 1:131 1:371 1:493	Dmr Derby-G2	-	4	8	89	76½	44½	23	Baze RA	**LB** 122	b	4.00	87-08	[D]Tight Spot1223Itsallgreektome1221¾Predecessor122¾		10
	Troubled trip;Placed first by disqualification - ruling rescinded 9/26/90																		
5Aug90- 8Dmr	fm	1 1/16Ⓣ	:241 :48 1:112 1:414	La Jolla H-G3	-	4	4	46½	45¼	32½	2no	Garcia JA	**L** 119	b	*1.80	98-04	Tight Spot118noItsallgreektome1194Music Prospector1181		6
	Just missed																		
10Jun90- 8Hol	fm	1⅛Ⓣ	:474 1:113 1:36 1:474	Cinema H-G2	-	10	9	96¾	85½	2½	31	Nakatani CS	117	b	2.70	88-10	Jovial1151Mehmetori113noItsllgrktom1172½	Nipped for 2nd	10
26May90- 8Hol	fm	1 1/16Ⓣ	:23 :461 1:093 1:401	Will Rogers H-G3	-	2	6	77½	76¼	1½	11¾	Nakatani CS	114	b	13.50	94-06	Itsallgreektome1141¾Warcrft120½BllCov116nk	Broke slowly	9
5May90- 6Hol	fm	1Ⓣ	:23 :454 1:092 1:343	Spotlight BC H 109k	-	8	8	76	64½	2hd	1no	Nakatani CS	112		31.90	91-08	Itsallgreektome112noWarcraft120nkRobyn Dancer115½	Wide	9
4Mar90- 3SA	fst	1 1/16	:24 :483 1:13 1:441	Alw 37000	-	6	5	41½	51¾	46½	47¾	Davis RG	118	b	2.80	74-18	Warcraft1206Apprised120hdOh Wow1201¾	Broke awkwardly	8
9Feb90- 7SA	fst	6f	:213 :443 :57 1:101	Alw 34000	-	1	8	85½	86¾	59	49½	Davis RG	120	b	6.40	75-23	BurntHills120noOneMoreWork1203TalentedPirat1206½	Outrun	8
6Jan90- 5SA	fst	6f	:213 :434 :56 1:084	Alw 34000		2	7	52¼	41¾	42	41¼	Davis RG	120	b	9.40	91-09	PhantomX.120½BurntHills120¾DuetotheKing117no	Evenly	10
21Sep89- 9LaD	fst	7f	:223 :461 1:122 1:26	Super Derby Juv 50k	-	7	7	66½	55½	713	720½	Davis RG	116		*1.40	57-25	CopperKenny1122¼RocketGibralter116½LeCounty1161¼	Dull	8
26Aug89- 6Dmr	fst	6f	:214 :45 :572 1:10	Md Sp Wt	-	6	9	64½	44	33	1nk	Davis RG	117		28.10	88-13	Itsallgreektome117nkDachi's Folly117hdJet West1172		11
	Prevailed in hard drive																		

Jewel Princess

Own: Stephen & Stephen & The Thoroughbred Corp

B. m. 5 (Apr)
Sire: Key to the Mint (Graustark)
Dam: Jewell Ridge (Melyno*Ire)
Br: Farnsworth Farms (Fla)
Tr: Dollase Wallace A

Life	29	13	4	7	$1,904,060	116	D.Fst	19	9	3	5	$1,638,000	116
1997	7	2	1	3	$497,400	114	Wet(293)	3	1	1	1	$107,510	107
1996	9	5	3	1	$1,150,800	116	Turf(247)	7	3	0	1	$158,550	97
	0	0	0	0	$0	-	Dst(0)	0	0	0	0	$0	-

8Nov97- 4Hol fst 1⅛ :454 1:091 1:342 1:471 3↑ⒻBCDistaf-G1 – 4 77½ 88¼ 79½ 55¼ 833 Nakatani C S LB123 *1.00e 57- 06 Ajina1202 *Sharp Cat*1203½ Escena1231 Pulled up near line 8

19Oct97- 9Bel fst 1⅛ :463 1:103 1:352 1:481 3↑ⒻBeldame-G1 98 2 711 67½ 55½ 35 34 Nakatani C S L123 f 2.30 85- 12 Hidden Lake1232 *Ajina*1192 Jewel Princess1231¼ Came wide,game fin 8

20Jly97- 8Hol fst 1⅛ :463 1:101 1:341 1:462 3↑ⒻVanityH-G1 103 1 31½ 34½ 32½ 33½ 34 Nakatani C S LB123 *.90 90- 04 TwicetheVice121hd RlConnction1144 JwlPrincss1236½ Angled out too late 5

28Jun97- 9Bel fst 1$\frac{1}{16}$:223 :452 1:094 1:404 3↑ⒻHmpstedH-G1 112 8 86½ 88½ 76¼ 35 34 Nakatani C S L124 *1.55 91- 13 *HiddenLke*1172 *TwicetheVice*1212 JewelPrincess1245¼ Inside move into str 9

11Apr97- 9OP gd 1$\frac{1}{16}$:231 :463 1:104 1:413 4↑ⒻAplBlsmH-G1 107 3 87¼ 87 74¾ 44½ 24 Nakatani C S L124 *.90 96- 12 *HloAmeric*1174 JewelPrincess124hd Different1211½ Up for place, no match 8

9Mar97- 7SA fst 1⅛ :48 1:121 1:364 1:491 4↑ⒻSMrgrtaH-G1 102 2 43 52½ 54¼ 31 1½ Nakatani C S LB125 *.40 87- 12 Jewel Princess125½ Top Rung116nk HiddenLake1143 Rallied 4w,late surge 6

16Feb97- 8SA fst 1$\frac{1}{16}$:231 :464 1:101 1:413 4↑ⒻSntMriaH-G1 114 4 56 64½ 53¼ 21½ 15 Nakatani C S LB123 *1.00 95- 12 *Jewel Princess*1235 Cat's Cradle118½ Top Rung1171 Quick gain,much best 7

26Oct96- 6WO fst 1⅛ :482 1:123 1:363 1:482 3↑ⒻBCDistaf-G1 114 1 55 55 42½ 2½ 11½ Nakatani C S L123 2.40 - - *Jewel Princess*1231½ Serena'sSong1231¾ Different1235¼ Drew clear, driving 6

6Oct96- 5SA fst 1$\frac{1}{16}$:224 :454 1:094 1:414 3↑ⒻLdyScBCH-G2 106 1 58 59 44 31½ 2½ Nakatani C S LB122 *.60 - - Top Rung116½ *Jewel Princess*1221¾ Sleep Easy1165 Step slow,bid midstr 5

21Jly96- 9Hol fst 1⅛ :464 1:102 1:343 1:47 3↑ⒻVnityIvH-G1 116 2 31 41 1hd 11½ 13 Nakatani C S LB120 2.50 - - Jewel Princess1203 Serena'sSong125¾ TopRung116½ Quick gain inside 3/8 6

23Jun96- 9Hol fst 1$\frac{1}{16}$:224 :461 1:094 1:404 3↑ⒻMladyBCH-G1 112 5 57½ 56½ 43½ 32 2¾ Nakatani C S LB120 1.80 - - Twice the Vice120¾ *Jewel Princess*1201¼ *Urbane*1171 Strong rally wide 5

25May96- 8Hol fst 1$\frac{1}{16}$:233 :464 1:102 1:411 3↑ⒻHawthrnH-G2 104 1 67½ 57 57 31½ 2hd McCarron C J LB120 *.90 - - Borodislew119hd Jewel Princess120½ Urbane1186 Closed rush wide 6

3May96- 7CD fst 1$\frac{1}{16}$:242 :474 1:12 1:422 3↑ⒻLouvlBCH-G2 108 3 54 54½ 32½ 2hd 1nk McCarron C J L118 2.00 - - JewelPrincss118nk *SrnsSong*1237½ *NskrColors*1133½ Dueld gamely, prevaild 6

10Mar96- 7SA fst 1⅛ :48 1:122 1:364 1:492 4↑ⒻSMrgrtaH-G1 100 6 84½ 63¼ 63½ 43½ 3¾ Solis A LB119 2.00 - - *TwicetheVice*117nk SleepEsy115½ *JewelPrincss*1192¾ Wide turn,outfnshd 2d 8

11Feb96- 6SA fst 1⅛ :472 1:112 1:364 1:492 ⒻLaCanada-G2 98 2 64½ 64 51½ 2hd 12½ Solis A LB119 *.90 - - Jewel Princess1192½ Dixie Pearl1161¼ Privity117¾ Impeded strt,best 6

20Jan96- 8SA fst 1$\frac{1}{16}$:233 :472 1:113 1:414 ⒻElEncino-G2 104 2 41½ 41 2hd 2hd 12½ Solis A LB117 2.70 - - *Jewel Princess*1172½ Sleep Easy1193½ Urbane1191¾ Rallied 3-w,riddn out 4

30Dec95- 8SA fst 7f :224 :452 1:084 1:212 ⒻLaBrea-G2 91 2 6 55 64 47 33¾ Nakatani C S LB119 3.20 - - Exotic Wood1192 Evil's Pic1191¾ *Jewel Princess*1191¼ Mild rally wide 6

4Nov95- 8SA fst 1$\frac{1}{16}$:224 :46 1:101 1:412 ⒻLndVsBCH-G3 105 1 46½ 45½ 2½ 13 19 McCarron C J LB118 2.80 88- 17 Jewel Princess1189 *Radu Cool*1153½ Ski Dancer1185 Rapid gain,much best 5

14Oct95- 8SA fm 1 Ⓣ :232 :47 1:112 1:363 ⒻHCRamsrSrH107k 92 1 1011 1012 89¼ 54¼ 3¾ Pincay L Jr LB117 *2.20 - - Ski Dancer117nk Radu Cool114½ *Jewel Princess*1174 Split hrss,strong rlly 10

20Aug95- 8Dmr fm 1⅛ Ⓣ :474 1:123 1:372 1:493 ⒻDMrOaks-G1 91 6 67½ 510 53¾ 54½ 52½ Solis A LB120 7.40 - - Bail Out Becky120no *Sleep Easy*1201¼ Top Ruhl120¾ Best stride late 9

29Jly95- 2Dmr fm 1 Ⓣ :224 :462 1:111 1:36 ⒻSnClmntH-G3 97 6 65¾ 55 41½ 1½ 11 McCarron C J LB115 10.40 - - Jewel Princess1151 Auriette1192 Scratch Paper1192 Strong rally 4-wide 6

20May95- 8Hol fm 1$\frac{1}{16}$ Ⓣ :24 :48 1:12 1:413 ⒻHnymoonH-G3 81 5 53 62¾ 61¾ 33 55¾ Antley C W LB116 15.00 82- 12 Auriette117¾ Artica1193 Top Shape1181¾ Failed to respond 6

30Apr95- 8Hol fm 1 Ⓣ :221 :451 1:10 1:343 ⒻSenrtaBC-G3 84 3 79½ 68 54¼ 53¼ 53½ Antley C W LB118 3.50 - - Top Shape114nk Artica118nk *Auriette*1162¾ No late gain 10

8Apr95- 8BM fm 1 Ⓣ :234 :473 1:123 1:38 ⒻSanJoseBCH69k 90 5 53 42½ 41¾ 21 12 Chapman T M LB115 2.40 - - JewelPrincss1152 SlwDlSiglo1163½ Whtninspirtion1133 4w 2nd trn, ,handy 6

12Mar95- 8SA fst 1$\frac{1}{16}$:233 :473 1:12 1:423 ⒻSAOaks-G1 62 2 54 41½ 53½ 517 525¼ McCarron C J LB117 11.40 - - *Serena's Song*117hd *Urbane*11714 Mari's Sheba117no Showed little 5

22Feb95- 8SA fm 1 Ⓣ :234 :484 1:141 1:39 ⒻAlw 50000c 84 1 44 45 42½ 4¾ 11 Nakatani C S LB114 5.90 - - Jewel Princess1141 Kuda114nk Artica117½ Finished well 4-wide 6

Previously trained by Sherman Lee A 1994(as of 12/4): (125 20 17 18 0.16)

4Dec94- 1Crc fst 1$\frac{1}{16}$:234 :481 1:142 1:503 ⒻAlw 17500n1x 61 5 54¾ 43½ 32 1½ 12½ Castillo H Jr 117 6.50 - - *JewelPrincess*1172½ *WithaPrincess*1201 StceyLcey1173¼ Circled, drew clear 6

13Nov94- 3Crc sly 7f :233 :471 1:132 1:272 ⒻMd 30000 62 5 6 31 22½ 1hd 1¾ Castillo H Jr 117 7.40 - - *JwlPrncss*117¾ ShockngPlsur1199½ Nlgorhythm117nk Poor st, stalked pace 6

27Oct94- 3Crc gd 5½f :222 :47 1:003 1:073 ⒻMd 20000 33 7 7 55¾ 58½ 57 38½ Ramos W S 118 6.50 - - LetsGotoIt1186 Glitterchick1182½ *JewelPrincss*118nk Lacked late response 7

Kotashaan (Fr)

Own: La Presle Farm

Dk. b or b. h. 5 (May)
Sire: Darshaan*GB (Shirley Heights*GB)
Dam: Haute Autorite (Elocutionist)
Br: Wertheimer & Frere (Fr)
Tr: Jarnet T

Life	22	10	5	2	$2,812,114	111	D.Fst	1	0	0	0	$6,250	105
1993	10	6	3	0	$2,622,468	111	Wet(345*)	0	0	0	0	$0	-
1992	4	1	0	0	$39,200	105	Turf(330)	21	10	5	2	$2,805,864	111
	0	0	0	0	$0	-	Dst(0)	0	0	0	0	$0	-

28Nov93 Tokyo (Jpn) fm *1½ Ⓣ LH 2:242 3↑ Japan Cup-G1 Stk 2525600 21¼ Desormeaux K 126 4.20 Legacy World1251¼ Kotashaan125hd Winning Ticket121nk 16

6Nov93- 7SA fm 1½ Ⓣ :483 1:122 2:012 2:25 3↑ BCTurf-G1 111 13 95¾ 95 31 2hd 1½ Desormeaux K J LB126 *1.50 - - Kotashaan126½ *Bien Bien*1261¼ Luazur126¾ Quick gain,long drive 14

10Oct93- 8SA fm 1½ Ⓣ :482 1:121 2:001 2:25 3↑ OakTree-G1 111 4 23 1hd 11½ 13½ 14 Desormeaux K J LB124 *.50 - - *Kotashaan*1244 Luazur1245½ Let's Elope12121 Early gain,ridden out 4

5Sep93- 8Dmr fm 1⅜ Ⓣ :494 1:142 1:384 2:15 3↑ DMrInvH-G2 108 7 44½ 54½ 53 31 2no Desormeaux K J LB123 *.40 - - Luazur116no *Kotashaan*1232¾ Myrakalu1141 Rallied 5 wide stretch 7

8Aug93- 8Dmr fm 1⅛ Ⓣ :481 1:121 1:363 1:482 3↑ EdReadH-G1 109 2 66 63¾ 62¾ 3½ 13 Desormeaux K J LB122 *.90 - - Kotashaan1223 Leger Cat116½ Rainbow Corner114no Circled field,handily 6

18Apr93- 4SA fm *1¾ Ⓣ :473 1:113 2:224 2:45 4↑ SnJnCpoH-G1 108 1 54½ 54 42½ 32 1no Desormeaux K J LB121 *.90 - - *Kotashaan*121no *Bien Bien*1191¼ Fraise12310 Patient ride, just up 5

21Mar93- 8SA fm 1½ Ⓣ :473 1:113 2:00 2:234 4↑ SanLsRey-G1 108 1 43 32 3nk 1½ 11¼ Desormeaux K J LB124 *.80 - - *Kotashaan*1241¼ Bien Bien12413 Fast Cure1247 Rallied 3 wide,driving 4

15Feb93- 8SA yl 1½ Ⓣ :494 1:15 2:052 2:273 4↑ SLsObspH-G2 108 1 77 75 5¾ 12 17 Desormeaux K J LB114 1.80 - - *Kotashaan*1147 CarnivalBby112nk TheNmesJimmy1151¾ Quick gain 5 wide 8

23Jan93- 8SA gd 1¼ Ⓣ :482 1:131 1:371 2:013 4↑ SnMarcsH-G2 105 4 74¼ 51¾ 52¼ 41 21 Desormeaux K J LB116 12.80 - - Star of Cozzene1201 *Kotashaan*1162 CarnivalBaby1121½ Rallied inside turn 7

1Jan93- 8SA gd 1⅛ Ⓣ :474 1:114 1:361 1:481 4↑ SnGabrlH-G3 92 8 85½ 62¾ 74¼ 53½ 46¾ Walls M K LB114 20.10 - - *Star of Cozzene*1183 Bistro Garden1143 *Leger Cat*115¾ Long rally wide 9

19Nov92- 8Hol fm 1$\frac{1}{16}$ Ⓣ :231 :47 1:11 1:412 3↑ Alw 50000nc 84 1 67½ 63¼ 65 65½ 59 McCarron C J B115 2.10 - - *Star of Cozzene*1141¼ Super May1144½ Memo1143 No threat 6

27Apr92- 8SA fm 1¼ Ⓣ :472 1:114 1:353 1:594 4↑ ⓇSJacintoH110k 98 2 32 31½ 32 63½ 44½ McCarron C J B119 *1.50 - - MissionryRidge119¾ FnticBoy1182 LtinAmricn1161¾ Rank early, stumbled 8

4Apr92- 8SA fst 1⅛ :462 1:102 1:35 1:471 4↑ SnBrdnoH-G2 105 3 78 66 64½ 54½ 55¼ McCarron C J LB117 4.50 - - *Another Review*1143 *Defensive Play*1151¼ *Loach*116¾ Blocked 1/4, no rally 11

12Mar92- 8SA fm 1 Ⓣ :231 :463 1:094 1:333 4↑ Alw 44000nc 102 3 65 54½ 52¾ 31 11¼ McCarron C J B121 *1.60 - - Kotashaan1211¼ *Regal Groom*117hd Mujaazif121hd Good trip, driving 9

19Sep91 Maisons-Laffitte (Fr) gd *1¼ Ⓣ 3↑ La Coupe de Maisons-Laffitte-G3 Stk 68000 21½ Guignard 119 - *Tel Quel*1191½ *Kotashaan*1191½ April Night123½ 9

15Aug91 Deauville (Fr) gd *1¼ Ⓣ 2:064 Prix Guillaume d'Ornano-G2 Stk 97500 3nk Guignard 125 - Glity121nk Arcangues127no Kotashaan1252 6

23Jun91 Longchamp (Fr) gd *1¼ Ⓣ 2:051 Grand Prix de Paris Louis Vuitton-G1 Stk 534300 32¼ Guignard 128 - Subotica128nk Sillery1282 Kotashaan128nk 9

19May91 Longchamp (Fr) gd *1¼ Ⓣ 2:062 Prix La Force-G3 Stk 64400 1nk Guignard 123 - Kotashaan123nk Funny Baby1231½ John Balliol1235 6

30Apr91 Longchamp (Fr) sf *1$\frac{5}{16}$ Ⓣ 2:253 Prix de Courcelles Stk 36900 1 Guignard 123 - *Kotashaan*123 Rancher123½ *Malmsey*1232 8

7Apr91 Longchamp (Fr) sf *1⅜ Ⓣ 2:19 Prix Noailles-G2 Stk 88400 510 Guignard 128 - *Pistolet Bleu*1283 Subotica1284 Pigeon Voyageur1283 9

30Nov90 Maisons-Laffitte (Fr) yl *1⅛ Ⓣ Prix Manitou III 28700 11½ Guignard 121 - Kotashaan1211½ *Cudas*1212 Pactolo121no 15

16Nov90 Saint-Cloud (Fr) yl *1 Ⓣ Prix Gardefeu 28700 2no Doleuze 118 - Svetlana120no *Kotashaan*1182½ *La Carene*1202½ 18

Laugh and Be Merry

dbbr. f. 1985, by Erin's Isle (Busted)–Imaflash, by Reviewer
Own.– Pin Oak Stable
Br.– Pin Oak Farm (Ky)
Tr.– Angel Penna Jr

Lifetime record: 26 9 7 3 $482,937

29Sep90- 9Med fm 1⅜Ⓣ :49 1:134 1:381 2:154 3↑ ⒻQueen Charlotte H-G3 4 4 41½ 31½ 1hd 11¼ McCauley WH 118 *.30 92-15 LghandBeMrry1181¼MissUnnameable1131¾MemoriesofPam1134 8 Driving
9Sep90- 8Bel fm 1¼T :473 1:113 1:354 2:001 3↑ ⒻFlower Bowl H-G1 5 3 33 31 1½ 1½ McCauley WH 115 *1.10 99-01 LaughandBeMerry115½Foresta1153GailyGaily117nk Driving 13
28Jly90- 9WO fm *1⅛Ⓣ 1:444 3↑ ⒻBud BC H-G2C 3 6 63¾ 42½ 23 21½ McCauley WH 119 *.85 110-00 Fieldy1241½LaughandBeMrry119½SttlSngu1154½ Lacked rally 8
16Jun90- 8Bel fm 1¼T :471 1:104 1:341 1:582 3↑ ⒻNew York H-G2 5 4 43 32 21 2no McCauley WH 114 *1.60 108-03 Capades119noLaugh and Be Merry1146Key Flyer1091¼ 7 Gamely,just missed
2Jun90- 5Bel fm 1 1/16T :243 :472 1:11 1:404 3↑ ⒻHandicap 47000 5 2 24 21½ 11½ 13¼ McCauley WH 119 *1.80 101-04 LaughandBeMerry1193¼Highland Penny1202½Ann Alleged113nk 6 Hand ride
7Apr90- 9GP fm 1½Ⓣ :472 1:111 1:593 2:241 3↑ ⒻOrchid H-G2 7 3 2hd 2hd 11½ 2hd McCauley WH 113 2.50 104-01 Coolawin112hdLaughandBeMrry1134¼GlyGly1213½ Just failed 10
17Mar90- 7GP hd 1 1/16Ⓣ :231 :463 1:10 1:401 3↑ ⒻBuckram Oak H-G3 2 4 45 43 42½ 1no McCauley WH 112 4.10 100-04 LaughandBeMrry112noSummrSecrtary114noPrincessMora1131¼ 12 Driving
17Feb90- 6GP fm 1Ⓣ :234 :48 1:12 1:352 4↑ ⒻAlw 24000 5 6 64 32 2½ 1½ McCauley WH 119 *1.30 97-03 LghandBeMrry119½Contumelious1177MotlSwng1192 Driving 11
7Nov89- 5Aqu fst 1⅜⊗ :49 1:393 2:174 3↑ ⒻAlw 36000 1 3 46 21½ 15 18¾ McCauley WH 117 *.80 90-18 LaughandBeMerry1178¾Moment of Dare115noD'or Etoile1171 6 Ridden out
22Oct89- 8Aqu fst 1⅜ :483 1:133 1:383 2:142 3↑ ⒻLong Island H-G2 5 4 53 41¼ 55½ 511¾ Samyn JL 112 2.20 96-15 Warfie1111¼River Memories1136½Noble Links1112 Faltered 6
29Sep89- 9Med yl 1⅜Ⓣ :471 1:131 1:382 2:163 3↑ ⒻQueen Charlotte H-G3 12 3 34 2½ 22½ 22¾ Samyn JL 113 5.60 79-24 SpruceFir1172¾LghandBeMrry1134½Epmthus114nk 2nd best 12
16Sep89- 7Bel yl 1¼T :501 1:151 1:41 2:064 3↑ ⒻFlower Bowl H-G1 5 6 54 54 711 816½ Samyn JL 113 8.30 44-40 RiverMemories1121¾Capades1162¼MissUnnameable1161¼ Tired 11
14Aug89- 8Sar gd 1⅛T :484 1:13 1:373 1:501 3↑ ⒻDiana H-G2 4 4 46½ 32½ 43 31¾ Antley CW 114 9.30 87-18 DWooing111nkGlowing Honor1151½Laugh and Be Merry114nk 9 Finished well
2Jly89- 8Bel fm 1⅜T :482 1:124 1:36 2:123 3↑ ⒻSheepshead Bay H-G2 2 5 31½ 32½ 41½ 32¼ Santos JA 112 6.80 92-13 Love You byHeart1181Nastique1171¼LaughandBeMerry112no 10 Lacked room
17Jun89- 8Bel sf 1¼T :503 1:153 1:402 2:054 3↑ ⒻNew York H-G2 5 4 43½ 21½ 22 22½ Santos JA 112 10.80 62-35 MissUnnameable1082½DLghandBeMrry1121¼LoveYoubyHrt119½ 8 Bore in;Disqualified and placed fourth
31May89- 5Bel fm 1¼T :51 1:164 1:403 2:033 3↑ ⒻAlw 33000 8 6 42½ 32 24 22¼ Samyn JL 119 *1.30 74-17 Starofanera1122¼LaughandBeMrry1191¼Highland Penny119½ 9 Held place
1Apr89- 8Hia fm *1⅛Ⓣ 1:503 3↑ ⒻKey Largo 50k 6 6 65¾ 51¾ 32½ 51½ Samyn JL 115 4.70 76-22 Judy'sRedShoes1221FrauleinLieber112noFirstPrediction115½ 11 Weakened
19Feb89-10GP fm 1½Ⓣ :472 1:122 2:023 2:264 3↑ ⒻOrchid H-G2 13 3 56½ 11 2hd 3½ Samyn JL 110 38.20 89-09 GailyGaily110noAnkaGrmania120½LghndBMrry1101 Weakened 13
23Jan89- 8GP fm 1½Ⓣ 1:144 2:044 2:284 4↑ ⒻAlw 19000 3 6 64½ 2½ 1hd 11¼ Samyn JL 119 *1.80 80-14 LghandBeMrry1191¼LadyofMyArt1193½FntGlow1172 Driving 12
1Jan89-10Crc fm 1½Ⓣ :483 1:123 2:012 2:262 3↑ ⒻLa Prev Inv'l H-G2 4 8 87½ 117¼ 95¾ 74½ Samyn JL 110 28.50f 89-06 Judy'sRdShoes120½GailyGly111½BeutyCrm118nk No menace 14
11Dec88- 9Crc fm *1⅛Ⓣ 1:453 3↑ ⒻMy Chrmr H (Div 2) 48k 11 11 125½ 127½ 65¼ 46 Gonzalez MA 111 55.40 84-10 Judy'sRedShoes1173½Orange Motiff1131¼Chores at Dawn1131¼ 13 Late gain
6Nov88- 6Aqu fst 1⅛ :481 1:131 1:394 1:533 3↑ ⒻAlw 31000 2 3 35½ 32½ 14 15 Santos JA 115 2.50 67-26 LaughandBeMerry1155DBlackBeavr115nkFinez1151¾ Driving 6
14Oct88- 5Bel fm 1Ⓣ :232 :471 1:12 1:371 3↑ ⒻAlw 29000 10 6 44 42½ 32 27¼ Santos JA 114 17.30 72-22 TimelyBusiness1147¼LaughandBeMrry114hdCourtaflame114¾ 12 Gained place
19Jun88- 1Bel fst 1 1/16 :231 :46 1:103 1:424 ⒻAlw 29000 5 5 612 615 621 627¾ Santos JA 118 10.30 60-21 Maplejinsky1165½Near1184Bai Shun1163¼ Outrun 6
18May88- 6Bel sly 1 :23 :461 1:12 1:391 ⒻMd Sp Wt 9 4 2½ 2½ 11 1hd Santos JA 121 *2.00 69-19 LaughandBeMrry121hdEdistoLight1213JolScot1215¾ Driving 9
13Jan88- 5GP fst 1 1/16 :234 :483 1:143 1:48 ⒻMd Sp Wt 7 7 62¾ 41½ 22½ 22½ MacKinze HA 121 13.90 58-28 KeytotheStage1212½LaughandBeMrry1212½Words Hurt1211½ 12 2nd best

Lit de Justice

Own: Evergreen Farms

Gr/ro. h. 6 (Jan)
Sire: El Gran Senor (Northern Dancer)
Dam: Kanmary*Fr (Kenmare*Fr)
Br: Swettenham Stud (Ky)
Tr: Sahadi Jenine

Life	36	10	8	6	$1,397,649	114	D.Fst	13	6	0	3	$1,038,215	114
1996	7	4	0	2	$888,100	114	Wet(327)	2	1	0	1	$149,150	101
1995	11	3	3	2	$352,265	113	Turf(327)	21	3	8	2	$210,284	105
	0	0	0	0	$0	-	Dst(0)	0	0	0	0	$0	-

26Oct96- 5WO fst 6f :213 :44 :561 1:083 3↑ BCSprint-G1 114 5 13 1310 108½ 54 11¼ Nakatani C S L126 b *4.00 - - Lit de Justice1261¼ *Paying Dues*126nk Honour and Glory1231¼ Driving 13
17Aug96- 8Dmr fst 7f :214 :44 1:081 1:203 3↑ POBrienH-G3 106 8 8 713 58 54½ 33½ Nakatani C S LB123 b *.80 - - AlphbtSoup1183½ *BoundlssMomnt*116no *LtdJstc*123no Early gain,up for 3rd 8
28Jly96- 8Dmr fst 6f :22 :443 :561 1:08 3↑ BCrsbBCH-G3 113 6 4 68¼ 42½ 2hd 13½ Nakatani C S LB121 b *1.10 - - LitdeJustice1213½ ConcptWin116no GoldLnd1161¾ Strong rally,much best 6
6Apr96- 8SA fst 6½f :221 :444 1:082 1:142 4↑ PtroGrnH-G3 97 6 5 54 42½ 45½ 47¾ Solis A LB122 b 1.80 - - *Abaginone*1156 DramticGold117½ KingdomFound1181¼ Unruly gate,empty 6
2Mar96- 9SA fst 7f :224 :453 1:094 1:221 4↑ SnCrlosH-G2 100 5 8 84½ 73¾ 61¾ 31½ Nakatani C S LB123 b *.70 - - KingdomFound1161¼ LkotBrve114nk LitdJustic123½ Rallied 6-w,flattened 8
4Feb96- 8SA fst 6f :212 :44 :561 1:084 4↑ PlsVrdsH-G3 112 8 8 77½ 77½ 42½ 11½ Delahoussaye E LB122 b *1.10 - - Lit de Justice1221½ *Siphon*119½ Lakota Brave115nk Closed rush,ridden out 9
7Jan96- 8SA fst 5½f :212 :441 :553 1:014 4↑ ElConejoH104k 114 3 6 68 67 11½ 15½ Nakatani C S LB119 b 2.40 - - *Lit de Justice*1195½ A. J. Jett1124 Fu Man Slew116½ Much best,track record 6
17Dec95- 9Hol gd 1 Ⓣ :24 :474 1:12 1:36 3↑ Alw 55000c 99 3 99 99½ 85¼ 51¾ 2no Nakatani C S LB115 b *1.60 83- 17 Bon Point115no *Lit deJustice*1151¼ PolishAdmiral1161¼ Strong rally 6-wide 9
28Oct95- 3Bel gd 6f :213 :442 :562 1:09 3↑ BCSprint-G1 101 5 10 1314 108¾ 65¼ 32¼ Nakatani C S L126 b 14.50e - - DesertStormer123nk MrGreeley1232 LitdeJustic126nk Angled 7w,late rally 13
16Sep95- 7Bel fst 7f :222 :444 1:092 1:222 3↑ Vosburgh-G1 87 3 12 1110 129¾ 1315 138½ Nakatani C S L126 b 4.00 - - Not Surprising126no You and I126no Our Emblem1261 Angled out thru str 13
19Aug95- 8Dmr fst 7f :214 :434 1:08 1:20 3↑ POBrnBCH-G3 113 7 7 711 78¼ 12 16½ Nakatani C S LB118 b 4.50 - - LitdeJustice1186½ DHallevnt1172½ Pembroke1191¼ Closed rush,trck recrd 7
15Jly95- 9Hol fm 5½f Ⓣ :204 :423 :541 1:002 3↑ HolBudBCH153k 105 1 4 410 411 46½ 23 Black C A LB119 b 4.50 - - Pembroke1203 *LitdeJustice*119hd CyrnoStorm1182¾ Roused 1/4,finshd well 5
18Jun95-11Hol gd 1 1/16 Ⓣ :24 :48 1:113 1:413 4↑ Alw 60000N$MY 104 6 64½ 63 31 21 21¾ Nakatani C S LB114 b *1.70 86- 13 *Jahafil*1141¾ Lit de Justice1142¾ *Inner City*1165 Bore out badly str 7
20May95- 3Hol fst 6½f :214 :434 1:07 1:131 3↑ RichCreamH74k 88 3 4 416 413 414 413 Nakatani C S LB121 b *1.10 90- 04 Lucky Forever1185 Blumin Affair1163 D'Hallevant1205 No stride, outrun 4
14Apr95- 8Kee fst 7f :224 :452 1:092 1:22 3↑ CmwlthBC-G2 104 1 6 52½ 43 1hd 3nk Nakatani C S L121 b 2.80 - - Golden Gear118hd Turkomatic112nk Lit deJustice121nk Late rally, gaining 8
11Mar95- 8SA fst 6½f :213 :441 1:081 1:143 4↑ PtroGrnH-G3 104 6 6 67¼ 68½ 11½ 13½ Nakatani C S LB115 b *1.20 - - LitdeJustice1153½ Cardmni119hd PhoneRoberto116½ Strong move,handily 6
18Feb95- 8SA fst 5½f :212 :441 :56 1:021 4↑ ElConejoH110k 95 5 7 79 76½ 3½ 22 Nakatani C S LB115 b *1.10 - - PhoneRoberto1142 D*LitdeJustic*1151 LostPn112¾ Forced way betwn hrses 8
Disqualified and placed 6th
18Jan95- 3SA gd 6½f :212 :441 1:09 1:154 4↑ Alw 53000c 94 1 6 66½ 43 13 12½ Nakatani C S LB118 b *1.40 - - LitdeJustice1182½ VirtuousRegent1172¾ Marmoe1162 Strong rally,handily 6
3Dec94- 7Hol fm 1 Ⓣ :231 :463 1:103 1:351 3↑ Alw 42000N3L 98 8 810 810 41½ 1½ 1½ Nakatani C S LB116 b *1.70 - - *Lit de Justice*116½ *Saltgrass*1142 Pricelessly116¾ Circled field,all out 9
16Oct94- 8SA fm 1 Ⓣ :23 :46 1:091 1:334 3↑ CFKostrH-G2 100 1 43 41¼ 41¾ 42½ 54¼ Desormeaux K J L115 b 6.70 - - Bon Point116½ Journalism1202 Johann Quatz1171¼ No rally 5
27Aug94- 2Dmr fm 1 1/16 Ⓣ :242 :492 1:133 1:433 3↑ Alw 44534N2L 95 2 76½ 77 54 3½ 1nk Nakatani C S L119 *.70 - - Lit deJustice119nk EasternSpirit1221¾ Arinthod122½ Rallied 4-wide,all out 9
30Jly94- 7Dmr fm 1 1/16 Ⓣ :233 :48 1:13 1:441 3↑ Alw 44534N2L 88 4 78¾ 78½ 73¾ 53¼ 2½ Nakatani C S LB119 *1.30 - - Wesnorth119½ *Lit de Justice*1193½ Latin Book119hd Blocked,finished well 10
Previously trained by Alain De Royer-Dupre
12Jun94 Chantilly (Fr) gd *1 Ⓣ RH 1:364 4↑ Prix du Chemin de Fer du Nord-G3 Stk 60400 32¼ Mongil W 123 - Zabar1272 Jeune Homme129nk Lit de Justice1232 6 *Well placed in 3rd, 2nd 2f out, lost 2nd near line*
4Jun94 Maisons-Laffitte (Fr) sf *1 Ⓣ RH 1:423 4↑ Prix Pegase (Prix Durbar) Alw 20500 1¾ Mongil W 123 *.00 Lit de Justice123¾ Djanord127nk *Enjoy Plan*127½ 12 *Settled mid-pack,bid 2f out,dueled 1-1/2f out,prevailed*
29Apr94 Saint-Cloud (Fr) gd *1 Ⓣ LH 1:432 4↑ Prix Prince Chevalier Alw 19900 2hd Mongil W 125 - Reference Lisa118hd *Lit de Justice*125nk Ocean Orbit1211 7 *Unhurried in 5th, strong late run, just missed*
27Nov93 Maisons-Laffitte (Fr) hy *1 Ⓣ Str 1:434 3↑ Prix Tantieme (Listed) Stk 35400 2nk Mongil W 123 - What Katy Did120nk Lit de Justice123¾ Irish Prospector1231½ 7 *Held up towards rear, rallied 1f out, gaining at line*
10Nov93 Evry (Fr) sf *6f Ⓣ Str 1:194 3↑ Prix Contessina (Listed) Stk 35400 21½ Mongil W 123 - Huron Warrior1231½ Lit de Justice123½ Way West1232 11 *Rated in 6th, bid 2f out, finished well*

21Oct93 Maisons-Laffitte (Fr) hy *6f Ⓣ Str 3↑ Prix d'Ecajeul 94 Boeuf D 126 - Raftsong115no Attaris1142½ Palme121 17
Hcp 55400 *Never a factor*

10Oct93 Longchamp (Fr) sf *1 1/16 Ⓣ RH Prix de la Roseraie 55½ Boeuf D 128 - Sacrement128¾ Ilbiri128¾ *Rustic Belle*1251 10
29500 *Reserved in 8th, finished well without threatening*

29Sep93 Evry (Fr) sf *6½f Ⓣ Str 3↑ Prix Aly Khan (Amateur riders) 8 C Asis Trem 146 *.00 Zelda142¾ Illuminator1462¼ Mixmatch1421 9
20000 *Missed break, well behind throughout*

2Apr93 Maisons-Laffitte (Fr) sf *7f Ⓣ Str Prix Bubbles 42 W Mongil 128 - *Matelot*128no Egoiste1281½ Cyrano Storme128½ 6
31300 *Dwelt, soon 4th, bid over 1f out, hung*

18Nov92 Evry (Fr) sf *1 Ⓣ LH Prix des Chenes-G3 66¼ Mongil 123 - Dancienne1201 Dernier Empereur123nk Ranger1232½ 6
Stk 63900 *Behind in 5th, never threatened*

19Sep92 Evry (Fr) gd *6½f Ⓣ Str 1:161 Criterium d'Evry (Listed) 2nk Boeuf 121 - Firm Friend118nk Lit de Justice1211½ Borodislew118nk 8
Stk 44300 *Rated in 6th,dueled 1f out,outgamed*

1Sep92 Evry (Fr) sf *6f Ⓣ Str Prix d'Ommeel-EBF 33½ Mongil 128 - *Firm Friend*1251½ Ski Paradise1202 Lit de Justice128½ 9
29600 *Well placed in 3rd,never catching first two*

22Aug92 Deauville (Fr) sf *7f Ⓣ Str 1:273 Challnge d'Or Piaget(Lst-Rstr) 46¼ Mongil 126 - Master Peace1262½ Top Salse126¾ Marchand de Sable1263 18
Stk 592300 *Rated in 8th,mild late gain*

1Aug92 Deauville (Fr) yl *6f Ⓣ Str 1:133 Prix Yacowlef (Listed-Unraced) 42¼ Boeuf 126 - Wixon122nk Gold Splash122½ Berdansk1261½ 5
Stk 42200 *Led to 1-1/2f out,faded*

Lonesome Glory

ch. g. 1988, by Transworld (Prince John)–Stronghold, by Green Dancer **Lifetime record: 44 24 5 6 $1,400,068**
Own.– Mrs Walter M. Jeffords Jr
Br.– Walter M. Jeffords Jr (Ky)
Tr.– F. Bruce Miller

23Apr99- 9Kee fm *2½ Hurdles 4:36 4↑ E Royal Chase-G1 2 3 33 33 1hd 12 Miller B L 154 *.80 -- Lonesome Glory1542DltonRiver154nkMaster McGrath154hd 7
Stalked pace,driving
27Mar99- 5Cam fm *2¼ Hurdles 4:224 4↑ Carolina Cup-G1 5 6 54½ 32 1hd 16¾ Miller B L 154 - -- Lonesome Glory1546¾Assurance1541¼Romantic15415 Handily 6
22Nov98- 5Cam fm *2¾ Hurdles 5:112 4↑ Colonial Cup 100k 7 6 67 76½ 51½ 59½ Miller C L 156 - -- Flat Top1565¾Romantic156nkDictador1561¼ No threat 8
27Aug98- 9Sar fm *2⅜ Hurdles 4:12 4↑ NY Turf Writers H-G1 4 7 77 76 613 617 Miller B L 162 *1.30 -- Hokan142nkRomantic1433Sundin142hd Lacked response 7
28Jun98-12CD fm *2½ Hurdles 4:282 4↑ Hard Scuffle H-G1 3 3 44 31½ 1½ 11½ Miller B L 158 3.30 -- Lonesome Glory1581½Clearance Code150noNinepins1402½ 8
Inside trip,driving
16Nov97- 4Cam fm *2¾ Hurdles 5:112 4↑ Colonial Cup-G1 4 9 93¼ 82¾ 3nk 1½ Miller B L 156 -- LonsmGlry156½RowdyIrshmn156noMstrMcgrth1567¾ Driving 10
21Aug97- 9Sar sf 2⅜ Hurdles 4:31 4↑ NY Turf Writers H-G1 6 5 58 44 34 34 Miller B L 156 *1.00 -- Bisbalense1422Confidnt1402LonsomGlry156½ Flattened out 6
31Jly97- 9Sar fm 2 1/16 Hurdles 3:421 4↑ AP Smthwck Mem H-G2 3 5 42 42 45 45½ Miller B 160 2.05 -- BrigadeofGuards1442WaterSkippr1402¾Mro156¾ No late bid 6
10May97- 6PW fm *3 Hurdles 5:302 4↑ Iroquois-G1 1 5 55 58¼ 28 29¼ Miller C L 156 -- Correggio1569¼LonesomeGlory156½Confidente1563¼ Held on 6
12Apr97- 5Cam fm *2¼ Hurdles 4:272 4↑ Carolina Cup-G1 3 4 63 22½ 2½ 11½ Miller B L 154 -- LonsmeGlry1541½HudsonBay1569¾PrimeLegcy1547¾ Driving 6
17Nov96- 5Cam fm *2¾ Hurdles 5:092 4↑ Colonial Cup-G1 2 11 106½ 54 512 520 Miller B 162 -- Correggio1601Stop and Listen162¾Mr Yankee162¾ Mild bid 12
26Oct96- 5FH sf *2⅝ Hurdles 5:104 4↑ BC Grand Nat H-G1 6 3 21¼ 55 64¾ 68¼ Miller B 168 f -- Corrggio1383MrYankee1401½RowdyIrshmn1542½ Early speed 10
12Oct96- 2Mor gd *1½Ⓣ 2:544 3↑ Alw 2500 6 7 74¾ 55 2hd 2nk Miller C 165 *1.20 -- Rowdy Irishman165nkLonesome Glory1651½Bisblens165hd 12
Wide,just missed
20Jan96♦ Haydock(GB) sf 3LH 6:214 5↑ Peter Marsh Limited Hcp Chase-G2 413½ Miller B 164 2.25 ScottonBanks160½Smith'sBand14713GarrisonSavannah153hd 6
Stk47100 Tracked leader,mistake 6th,outpaced 5 out,brief bid,one paced late
1Dec95♦ Sandown(GB) gd 2 9/16RH 5:081 5↑ Crowngap Construction Hcp Chas 111 Miller B 140 2.75 LonesomeGlory14011EgyptMillPrince15115KingCredo14014 4
Hcp16200 Rated in 4th,bid 3 out,led last,ridden clear.Remittance Man 4th
12Nov95- 4Cam gd *2¾ S'Chase 5:201 4↑ Colonial Cup 100k 7 8 76½ 52¼ 1½ 11¼ Miller B 162 -- LonesmeGlry1621¼RowdyIrishman1621½Mistco1622¼ Driving 9
17Aug95- 9Sar fm 2⅜ Hurdles 4:124 4↑ NY Turf Writers H 107k 4 5 517 65½ 1½ 1nk Miller B 166 *1.25 -- Lonesome Glory166nkMistico1604½Rowdy Irishman1423 6
Reserved,closed late
27Jly95- 1Sar fm 2 1/16 Hurdles 3:402 4↑ AP Smithwick H 50k 4 5 710 52 2½ 11 Miller B 164 *1.10 -- LonsomGlry1641IrshApproch1461Mstco160½ Wide,drew clear 8
13May95- 8PW gd *3 Hurdles 5:324 4↑ Iroquois 93k 4 3 34 41½ 1hd 12¾ Miller B 156 -- LonesmeGlory1562¾Confdnt15612VctornHll1562¼ Ridden out 5
22Apr95- 3Mid fm *2½ Hurdles 4:372 4↑ Temple Gwathmey H 50k 1 4 411 34½ 22 21 Miller B 164 -- MasterMcGrath1471LonesomeGlory16420IrishApproach14710 5
Lost whip
1Apr95- 6Cam fm *1⅜Ⓣ 2:194 3↑ Alw 2500 4 5 52 41 31 12 Miller B 150 96-14 LonesmeGlry1502HudsonBay1471TheFrugalKing1503 Handily 10
13Nov94- 4Cam fm 2¾ S'Chase 5:081 4↑ Colonial Cup 100k 1 7 41 42¼ 2½ 1hd Miller B 162 -- LonesomeGlory162hdMistico16221VictorianHill162¾ Driving 8
22Oct94- 3FH fm *2⅝ Hurdles 4:58 4↑ BC Grand National 143k 2 4 43 53 3nk 34 Miller B 156 -- WarmSpell1562½MasterMcGarth1561½LonesomGlory1561¼ 6
Bid,hung
18Aug94- 9Sar sf 2⅜ Hurdles 4:30 4↑ NY Turf Writers H 109k 3 7 78 68¼ 46½ 37½ Miller B 168 1.90e -- Mistco1684CheerngNews1423½LonesomGlory168nk Late gain 8
14May94- 7PW gd *3 Hurdles 5:283 4↑ Iroquois 100k 1 6 715 - - - Miller B 168 -- Mistico16815Warm Spell16822Victorian Hill16835 Fell 7
23Apr94- 3Mid fm *2⅝ Hurdles 4:413 4↑ Temple Gwathmey H 50k 2 3 36 35 21½ 1nk Miller B 164 -- LonesmGlry164nkWarmSpell1629CheeringNews1448 Driving 5
2Apr94- 6Cam fm *1⅜Ⓣ 2:21 3↑ Alw 1000 6 3 33¾ 24 21 1nk Miller B 154 -- LonesmGlry154nkMessagePad1516GrenHghlndr1544 Driving 6
14Nov93- 4Cam fm *2¾ S'Chase 5:074 4↑ Colonial Cup 100k 4 9 95½ 95 52¼ 34½ Miller B 160 -- Declare Your Wish1622¾Simonov1511¾LonesomeGlory1602 11
Late rally
16Oct93-10Bel sf 2⅝ S'Chase 4:532 3↑ BC Chase 250k 1 9 97½ 41½ 2½ 18½ Miller B 156 1.80 -- Lonesome Glory1568½Highland Bud1565Mistico1564 Driving 9
26Sep93- 2Fx gd *2Ⓣ 3:31 3↑ Alw 1000 5 2 35 3½ 18 18 Miller B 150 -- Lonesome Glory1508Cheering News150hdFlown1508 Easily 6
22May93- 3Pro gd *3 Hurdles 5:584 4↑ Handicap 25000 2 3 22 32¼ 21¾ 2no Miller B 159 -- Talkin Butter146noLonesome Glory15910Break Clean1435 4
1May93- 6GrM gd *3 Hurdles 5:193 4↑ Handicap 25000 1 4 327 321 22 1hd Miller B 153 -- Lonesome Glory153hdCircuit Bar1508Delessio1466 8
Up in final strides
12Dec92♦ Cheltenham(GB) sf 2 11/16LH 5:414 4↑ Sport of Kings Challenge 1hd Miller B 155 20.00 Lonesome Glory155hdAl Mutahm14725Beebob14210 4
Stk23500 Tracked in 3rd,shaken up approaching last,led near line
7Nov92- 3Pmt gd *2⅜ S'Chase 4:08 4↑ Delta Airline 50k 5 4 39 49½ 32½ 32½ Miller B 153 -- Green Highlander150noMistico1542½Lonesome Glory1534 6
Lacked response
24Oct92- 2FH fm *2½ S'Chase 4:462 4↑ Supreme 50k 2 5 47½ 68½ 2½ 1½ Miller B 149 -- Lonesome Glory149½Hodges Bay1501½Bel Ange153nk Driving 9
9Oct92- 7Bel yl 2½ S'Chase 4:411 4↑ Queen Mother Supr 50k 1 3 43½ 42½ 33 2¾ Lawrence J II 149 2.70 -- BelAnge149¾LonsomGlry1497GrnHghlndr1505¼ Finished well 7
27Sep92- 2Fx yl *2Ⓣ 3:283 3↑ Alw 1000 1 6 52 2hd 1½ 1nk Miller B 150 -- LonesomGlry150nkHero'sHour1476HodgesBay1472½ Driving 10
23May92- 3Pro fm *2½ S'Chase 4:042 3↑ Alw 20000 2 3 3½ 2¾ 12 13½ Lawrence J II 142 -- LonesmGlry1423½Hopscotch147¾RunwyRomnc152 Ridden out 5
9May92- 7PW fm 1½Ⓣ 2:361 3↑ Sp Wt 2000 6 4 415 49 31 1nk Daniels P 145 -- LonesomeGlory145nkFuller'sFolly1507Brdford15010 Driving 9
19Apr92- 4Mid gd *2⅛ S'Chase 3:553 4↑ OClm 15000 10 9 44½ 41½ 42½ 1nk Thornton C 141 -- LonesmeGlry141nkTrulyNolen1445SteadyMoney1445 Driving 10
12Oct91- 5Fai gd *2 1/16 S'Chase 4:023 3↑ Md Sp Wt 4 7 96 41¼ 1hd 12 Thornton C 140 6.60 -- LonesmeGlry1402ParadeMrch13712RuntoCourt1524½ Rallied 10
5Oct91- 3Mid hd *1¼Ⓣ 2:181 3↑ Md Sp Wt 4 7 73¾ 78½ 410 414½ Miller B 145 -- Big Estero1506Rock Eagle1628Starting Game147½ Rallied 12
2Sep91- 8Fai hd *7fⓉ 1:28 3↑ Md Sp Wt 4 9 97½ 41¼ 21 32½ Miller B 147 *2.60 -- Abacus1492¼Rangeless144nkLonesome Glory1472¾ 11
27May91- 1Fai fm *1⅜Ⓣ 2:122 3↑ Md Sp Wt 8 8 96¾ 83½ 77 515½ Miller B 142 5.10 -- Steeple Chaser1521Dawn Attack1371½Phoenix Force1364 9

Lure

Own: Claiborne Farm & Nicole P. Gorman

B. h. 5 (May)
Sire: Danzig (Northern Dancer)
Dam: Endear (Alydar)
Br: Claiborne Farm & The Gamely Corp. (Ky)
Tr: McGaughey III Claude R

Life	25	14	8	0	$2,515,289	115	D.Fst	3	2	0	0	$118,700 106
1994	7	3	3	0	$552,236	112	Wet(433)	4	1	2	0	$47,750 79
1993	8	6	2	0	$1,212,803	115	Turf(392)	18	11	6	0	$2,348,839 115
	0	0	0	0	$0	-	Dst(0)	0	0	0	0	$0 -

Date/Race	Cond	Dist	Surf	Fractions	Race	Fig	PP	St	1C	2C	Str	Fin	Jockey	Wt	Odds		Top finishers	Comment	Fld
5Nov94- 7CD	fm	1	Ⓣ	:231 :461 1:094 1:342	3↑ BCMile-G1	88	14	53½	74¾	53¾	913	99¾	Smith M E	126	*.90	- -	Barathea1263 Johann Quatz126hd Unfinished Symph1231½	Flattened out	14
8Oct94- 5Bel	fm	1	Ⓣ	:23 :453 1:094 1:34	3↑ KelsoH-G3	110	3	34	34½	3½	1½	2no	Smith M E	128	*.30	- -	Nijinsky's Gold114no Lure1282¼ A in Sociology117nk	Led late, missed	7
12Aug94- 8Sar	fm	1⅛	Ⓣ	:481 1:112 1:343 1:46	3↑ BBaruchH-G2	112	4	31	2½	2½	1½	11	Smith M E	125	*1.00	- -	Lure1251 *Paradise Creek*1266 Fourstardave1146	Stalked, ridden out	5
26Jun94- 7Atl	fm	1$\frac{3}{16}$	Ⓣ	:473 1:102 1:341 1:523	3↑ CsrIntlH-G1	107	1	11	1hd	1hd	21	1no	Smith M E	123	*.60	- -	*Lure*123no FourstrsAllstr1171½ StrofCozzen1211½	Jumped shadow, driving	5
20May94-11Pim	fm	1⅛	Ⓣ	:484 1:131 1:364 1:482	3↑ DixieH-G2	100	3	2hd	2hd	2hd	1½	2¾	Smith M E	124	*.50	- -	*Paradise Creek*124¾ *Lure*1245½ Astudillo115½	Bobbled,led 1/4,gamely	5
6May94- 8CD	fm	1⅛	Ⓣ	:47 1:111 1:361 1:481	3↑ TurfClsc-G2	98	3	33	23½	32	22½	24	Smith M E	123	*.30	- -	*Paradise Creek*1184 Lure1232½ Yukon Robbery1162½	Angld inside hung	7
15Apr94- 8Kee	yl	1⅛	Ⓣ	:492 1:151 1:402 1:533	4↑ Elkhorn-G2	109	4	1½	11	1½	15	14	Smith M E	123	*.30	- -	Lure1234 Buckhar1202 Pride of Summer1203	Drew off in hand	5
6Nov93- 5SA	fm	1	Ⓣ	:223 :454 1:092 1:332	3↑ BCMile-G1	112	12	2hd	11	1½	12	12¼	Smith M E	B126	*1.30	- -	*Lure*1262¼ *Ski Paradise*1201¾ Fourstars Allstar126hd	Wide early,well handld	13
16Oct93- 6Bel	sf	1	Ⓣ	:224 :454 1:103 1:354	3↑ KelsoH-G3	111	2	63	42	2hd	11	13¼	Smith M E	125	*.70	- -	*Lure*1253¼ Paradise Creek1205 Daarik112½	Angled out, ridden out	10
30Jly93- 8Sar	fm	1$\frac{1}{16}$	Ⓣ	:24 :471 1:11 1:404	3↑ DarylsJy-G3	108	2	42	43	41½	11	13	Smith M E	122	*.20	- -	*Lure*1223 *Fourstardave*1222 Scott the Great1151¼	Ridden out	6
27Jun93- 5Atl	fm	1$\frac{3}{16}$	Ⓣ	:47 1:104 1:35 1:531	3↑ CsrIntlH-G2	115	1	1½	11½	11½	12½	21	Smith M E	123	*.80	- -	Star of Cozzene1201 *Lure*1239¼ Finder's Choice1132¼	Outfinished	7
6Jun93- 8Bel	gd	1¼	Ⓣ (boxed)	:481 1:12 1:353 1:584	3↑ ETManhtn-G2	114	5	2hd	2hd	2hd	11	2¾	Smith M E	124	*.60	- -	*Star of Cozzene*118¾ Lure1247 Solar Splendor1122¼	Led, outfinished	8
14May93-11Pim	fm	1⅛	Ⓣ	:464 1:104 1:351 1:473	3↑ DixieH-G3	109	8	3½	2½	1hd	13½	11½	Smith M E	124	*.80	- -	Lure1241½ *Star of Cozzene*1192 Binary Light1151¾	Bobbled, well handled	8
30Apr93- 8CD	fm	1⅛	Ⓣ	:47 1:104 1:342 1:461	3↑ TurfClsc-G3	112	4	1½	1½	11	12	1¾	Smith M E	123	*1.10	- -	*Lure*123¾ Star of Cozzene1182 Cleone116no	Led throughout	8
4Apr93- 7Kee	fm	*1	Ⓣ	:23 :454 1:102 1:342	4↑ Alw 27360N$Y	107	7	2hd	1hd	1½	13	14	Smith M E	123	*.50	- -	*Lure*1234 Rocket Fuel118nk Kiri's Clown120½	Much the best	7
31Oct92- 7GP	fm	1	Ⓣ	:224 :454 1:09 1:324	3↑ BCMile-G1	112	1	11½	12	11	13	13	Smith M E	122	5.40	- -	*Lure*1223 *Paradise Creek*122nk Brief Truce1221½	Well rated, driving	14
10Oct92- 5Bel	sf	1	Ⓣ	:222 :46 1:102 1:361	3↑ KelsoH-G3	102	4	21½	31½	21	22	22¾	Smith M E	111	2.70	- -	*Roman Envoy*1172¾ *Lure*1112 Val des Bois1184	Second best	9
14Sep92- 7Bel	fm	1$\frac{1}{16}$	Ⓣ (boxed)	:243 :47 1:104 1:41	3↑ Alw 33000NC	110	7	2½	2hd	12	14	110¼	Smith M E	113	*1.00e	- -	Lure11310¼ Mucho Precious1173¼ *Scuffleburg*115½	Dueled, drew off	9
6Jun92- 6Bel	my	7f		:213 :441 1:222	RivaRidg-G3	79	5	5	43½	44½	78¾	611	Smith M E	122	2.00	- -	Superstrike1151¼ ThreePt1222½ Windundrmywings115nk	Used up stretch	7
21Apr92- 8Kee	my	1$\frac{1}{16}$		:232 :471 1:122 1:44	Lexingtn-G2	–	1	32	31½	11	1hd	2nk	Smith M E	B118	*.40	- -	My Luck Runs North115nk Lure118no Agincourt1151	Outfinished	5
4Apr92- 8Aqu	fst	1		:221 :434 1:081 1:353	Gotham-G2	100	2	4¾	1hd	2hd	2hd	14½	♦Smith M E	114	*.60	- -	DH Lure114 DH *DevilHisDue*1144½ BestDecorted114nk	Swerved, came again	8
15Mar92- 7Aqu	fst	6f		:23 :47 :584 1:111	Alw 27000NC	106	7	2	2hd	2hd	13	18¾	Smith M E	117	*.40	- -	*Lure*1178¾ Courting Pleasure1171 *Winning Force*1172¼	Drew off	9
12Oct91- 8Bel	fst	1		:222 :45 1:102 1:363	Champagn-G1	–	6	83	82½	63¾	88¾	613¾	Bailey J D	122	*1.50	- -	TritoWtch1227½ SnppyLnding1223½ PineBluff122no	Four wide, no excuse	15
25Sep91- 1Bel	sly	7f		:221 :451 1:094 1:232	Alw 27000NC	–	4	3	33	21½	21½	21¼	Bailey J D	117	*.40	- -	Devil On Ice1221¼ Lure11714 Crafty Coventry119hd	Chased outside winner	5
13Jun91- 4Bel	wf	5f		:212 :44 :561	Md Sp Wt 24k	–	8	5	2½	2hd	12	15	Bailey J D	118	*1.00	- -	Lure1185 In a Walk1182¾ Money Run1183	Outside sp, ridden out	8

Maria's Mon

Own: Pin Oak Stable & Mrs Morton Rosenthal

Gr/ro. c. 3 (Apr)
Sire: Wavering Monarch (Majestic Light)
Dam: Carlotta Maria (Caro*Ire)
Br: Morton Rosenthal (Ky)
Tr: Richard Schosberg

Life	7	4	1	1	$507,140	105	D.Fst	7	4	1	1	$507,140 105
1996	2	0	1	0	$8,800	93	Wet(307)	0	0	0	0	$0 -
1995	5	4	0	1	$498,340	105	Turf(303)	0	0	0	0	$0 -
	0	0	0	0	$0	-	Dst(0)	0	0	0	0	$0 -

Date/Race	Cond	Dist	Fractions	Race	Fig	PP	St	1C	2C	Str	Fin	Jockey	Wt	Odds		Top finishers	Comment	Fld
4Aug96- 8Sar	fst	1⅛	:472 1:111 1:35 1:471	JimDandy-G2	73	3	42½	32½	44½	713	627¼	Davis R G	119 f	3.35	74- 19	LouisQutorz124nk *WllsWy*11415 ScrtodEstdo1143	Rated btwn,no response	8
17Jly96- 7Bel	fst	6½f	:223 :453 1:094 1:16	3↑ Alw 44000N$Y	93	5	6	42½	41¼	41	23¼	Davis R G	115 f	*.60	91- 08	MyIInquire1223¼ MrisMon115hd ThrDimonds1141¾	5w move 1/4 pole,game	7
7Oct95- 9Bel	fst	1$\frac{1}{16}$	:223 :451 1:102 1:421	MoetChmp-G1	105	8	35	57½	4¾	11	13¾	Davis R G	122	2.60	- -	Maria's Mon1223¾ Diligence122¾ *Devil's Honor*122¾	Steady adv,ridden out	8
16Sep95- 5Bel	fst	1	:224 :453 1:093 1:35	Futurity-G1	101	6	42	41	1hd	11	12¾	Davis R G	122	3.65	- -	*MrisMon*1222¾ *LouisQutorz*1221¼ *HonourndGlory*1222	Rated,clr when roused	7
27Aug95- 8Sar	fst	7f	:222 :453 1:102 1:232	Hopeful-G1	86	2	7	1hd	1hd	32	36½	Davis R G	122	3.10	- -	Hennessy1223¼ LouisQuatorze1223¼ *MariasMon*1229	Rushed ins,wknd 1/8p	7
21Jly95- 7Sar	fst	6f	:213 :45 :573 1:104	Sanford-G3	90	3	4	2hd	1hd	12½	12¼	Davis R G	115	*1.00	- -	Maria's Mon1152¼ Seeker's Reward1156 Frozen Ice112hd	Battled for lead	11
4Jly95- 2Bel	fst	5½f	:23 :464 :583 1:043	Md Sp Wt 30k	92	7	4	2½	1½	14	110½	Davis R G	116	*1.70	- -	*MrisMon*11610½ D *LouisQutorze*1163¾ ShwklitPower1163½	Drew off, driving	7

Meadow Star

ch. f. 1988, by Meadowlake (Hold Your Peace)–Inreality Star, by In Reality

Lifetime record: 20 11 1 2 $1,445,740

Own.– Carl Icahn
Br.– Jaime S. Carrion (Fla)
Tr.– Leroy Jolley

Date/Race	Cond	Dist	Fractions	Race	Fig	PP	St	1C	2C	Str	Fin	Jockey	Wt	Odds	Speed	Top finishers	Comment
31Oct92- 6GP	fst	1⅛	:47 1:104 1:353 1:48	3↑ ⒻBC Distaff-G1	92	11	13	126½	114½	87¾	77¾	Day P	L 123	37.00	89-03	Paseana1234VersaillesTreaty123½MagicIMaidn1191½	Outrun
11Oct92- 8Kee	fst	1⅛	:48 1:123 1:371 1:494	3↑ ⒻSpinster-G1	92	10	7	74½	74	46	38¼	Day P	LB 123	10.70	78-25	Fowda1232¼Paseana1236Meadow Star1232½	Duck,carried out
20Sep92- 8Bel	fst	1$\frac{1}{16}$	:231 :464 1:10 1:412	3↑ ⒻRuffian H-G1	90	6	4	52	31½	54¼	58¾	Bailey JD	112	4.60	86-15	VersaillesTreaty120½QuickMischief1163Nannerl1192¼	Tired
25May92- 5Bel	fst	6½f	:224 :453 1:094 1:162	3↑ ⒻAlw 41000	93	1	4	31½	2½	33½	32¾	Santos JA	117	*1.10	88-10	MakinFaces1172¼PupptShw119½MdwStr1177½	Altered course
14Apr92- 8Kee	fst	6f	:22 :452 1:093	3↑ ⒻTCA-G3	88	3	8	76	77	74	76¼	Santos JA	B 123	*.80	89-10	Ifyoucouldseemenow120hdHarbourClub1173MadamBear117no	Slow start
21Sep91- 8Bel	fst	1$\frac{1}{16}$	:233 :462 1:103 1:413	3↑ ⒻRuffian H-G1	-	5	4	43	52	64	67½	Bailey JD	117	2.90	86-14	Queen120½ShrpDnc1141¼LdyD'Accord113nk	Drifted badly str
1Sep91- 8Bel	fst	1	:232 :462 1:101 1:344	3↑ ⒻMaskette-G1	-	1	6	67½	65½	55½	47¾	Bailey JD	118	*.80	88-07	Queena123hdFit to Scout123nkScreen Prospect1167½	Broke outward,drifted out
6Jly91- 8Bel	gd	1¼	:462 1:101 1:343 2:002	ⒻC C A Oaks-G1	-	1	2	23½	2½	22	27	Bailey JD	121	1.20	88-05	Lite Light1217Meadow Star1212Car Gal1218¼	2nd best
9Jun91- 8Bel	fst	1⅛	:492 1:132 1:363 1:484	ⒻMother Goose-G1	-	2	1	12	1hd	1hd	1no	Bailey JD	121	.90	85-18	MeadowStr121noLiteLight12115NaleesPn121no	Wide,driving
25May91- 8Bel	fst	1	:231 :462 1:113 1:372	ⒻAcorn-G1	-	3	4	41	1½	12	16	Bailey JD	121	*.60	83-17	Meadow Star1216Versailles Treaty1212½Dazzle Me Jolie1212¾	Drifted,ridden out
20Apr91- 8Aqu	fst	1⅛	:463 1:104 1:354 1:482	Wood Memorial-G1	-	6	4	45½	31½	44½	410¼	Antley CW	121	2.00	84-23	CahillRoad1263LostMountn1266HappyJazzBand1261¼	Tired
30Mar91- 8Aqu	gd	1	:242 :49 1:14 1:38	ⒻComely-G2	-	5	2	2½	2hd	2½	11¾	Antley CW	121	*.30	72-28	MeadowStr1211¾DoItWithStyle1143I'maThrllr1181¾	Driving
16Mar91- 6Aqu	fst	7f	:233 :472 1:111 1:23	ⒻQuofStage 44k	-	5	1	2½	1hd	12½	14¾	Antley CW	121	*.10	87-22	MeadowStr1214¾Nany'sAppeal118½ChristnCzrn1144¼	Driving
27Oct90- 4Bel	fst	1$\frac{1}{16}$	:223 :454 1:11 1:44	ⒻBC Juv Fillies-G1	-	9	8	52½	3½	12	15	Santos JA	119	*.20	82-15	MeadwStar1195PrivatTrsur1191DncSmrtly1194¼	Drifted,drv
6Oct90- 7Bel	fst	1	:224 :461 1:11 1:352	ⒻFrizette-G1	-	4	1	1½	11	16	114	Santos JA	119	*.10	92-11	MeadwStr11914ChampagnGlow119nkFlwlssly1193¼	Drew off
16Sep90- 8Bel	fst	7f	:222 :452 1:101 1:224	ⒻMatron-G1	-	2	3	33½	32	12	16	Santos JA	119	*.20e	90-14	MeadowStr1196Verbasle1193ClarkCottage1192¼	Drew clear
27Aug90- 8Sar	fst	6f	:214 :451 1:101	ⒻSpinaway-G1	-	8	3	43	43	21	12	Santos JA	119	*.70	93-12	MeadwStr1192GardenGal1191GoodPotntl1198½	Wide,driving
1Aug90- 8Sar	fst	6f	:221 :46 1:111	ⒻSchuylerville-G2	-	2	3	43½	42½	2hd	13	Antley CW	119	*1.00	88-08	MeadwStr1193GardnGal1196PryrfulMss1143	Steadied,clear
18Jly90- 8Bel	fst	5½f	:22 :454 1:041	ⒻAstoria BC-G3	-	4	4	36½	33	31½	11¼	Santos JA	113	*1.90	98-16	Meadow Star1131¼Sweet Sarita1146Pay'n and Play'n1122	Strong handling
13Jun90- 4Bel	fst	5f	:221 :46 :584	ⒻMd Sp Wt	-	5	4	2½	1½	1½	15¼	Santos JA	117	2.20	94-20	MeadwStr1175¼WinCraftyLdy117¾MyFntzy1174	Brisk urging

Miss Alleged

b. f. 1987, by Alleged (Hoist the Flag)–Miss Tusculum, by Boldnesian — Lifetime record: 15 5 4 3 $1,746,118
Own.– Fares Farms
Br.– Carl M. Freeman (Ky)
Tr.– Charles Whittingham

26Apr92- 8SA fm *1¾Ⓣ :47 2:00 2:23 4 2:46 2 4↑ San Juan Cap H-G1 98 5 6 6 3¼ 5 4½ 4 6 2 7 McCarron CJ LB 118 *1.20 94-12 Fly Till Dawn121 7 Miss Alleged118¾ Wall Street Dancer114 1¼ 9
Steadied,boxed in backstretch,angled out ⅜,4 wide ⅛
5Apr92- 8SA fm 1¼Ⓣ :48 1:12 1:36 1:59 3 4↑ ⒻS Barbara H-G1 103 1 6 5 4½ 5 3½ 3 2 2 1¼ McCarron CJ LB 124 1.90 88-12 Kostroma121 1¼ MissAllegd124 2½ FreeatLst117½ Saved ground 6
17Feb92- 8SA gd 1½Ⓣ :49 3 1:15 2 2:04 3 2:28 3 4↑ San Luis Obispo H-G3 106 1 6 5 2½ 5 3 5 3½ 3 3 McCarron CJ LB 121 *1.30 68-29 Quest for Fame121 1¾ Cool Gold Mood114 1¼ Miss Alleged121 3 9
4-wide into lane
15Dec91- 8Hol fm 1½Ⓣ :52 1:17 3 2:06 4 2:30 3↑ Hol Turf Cup-G1 - 7 5 3 1½ 3½ 2½ 1 hd McCarron CJ LB 123 2.90 73-21 Miss Alleged123 hd Itsallgreektome126 1¼ Quest for Fame126¾ 7
Game effort;Previously trained by Pascal Bary
2Nov91- 7CD fm 1½Ⓣ :50 4 1:15 4 2:06 2 2:30 4 3↑ BC Turf-G1 - 12 6 8 4¼ 5 2½ 5 2¼ 1½ Legrix E LB 123 42.10f 96-06 MissAlleged123½ Itsallgreektome126 2 QustforFm126 2 Driving 13
19Oct91-11Lrl sf 1¼Ⓣ :49 3 1:14 4 1:41 2 2:06 2 3↑ Bud Int'l-G1 - 10 4 5 4 6 2¾ 7 4½ 5 4¼ Legrix E 123 11.00 70-38 Leariva123 1¾ Sillery122½ Goofalik126 1¼ Needed rally 13
6Oct91♦ Longchamp(Fr) sf *1½ⓉRH 2:31 2 3↑ Arc de Triomphe-G1 Stk1483000 11 11½ Legrix E 127 43.00 Suave Dancer123 2 Magic Night120 1 Pistolet Bleu123 3 14
Toward rear,in tight 2f out,never a factor.Generous 8th
22Sep91♦ Longchamp(Fr) gd *1¼ⓉRH 2:10 2 3↑ Prix Prince d'Orange-G3 Stk59700 2 nk Legrix E 122 1.75 Passing Sale126 nk Miss Alleged122 1½ Glity126 1½ 5
Rallied to lead over 1f out,caught near line.Cudas 5th
30Jun91♦ Saint-Cloud(Fr) gd *1½ⓉLH 2:28 3↑ Grand Prix de Saint-Cloud-G1 Stk41200 4 4½ Legrix E 131 13.00 Epervier Bleu134 3 Rock Hopper134¾ Passing Sale134 1 12
Unhurried in 6th,mild late gain
8Jun91♦ Evry(Fr) sf *1½ⓉLH 2:35 2 4↑ Grand Prix d'Evry-G2 Stk99300 3 3½ Legrix E 122 5.00 Wajd120 2 Epervier Bleu126 1½ Miss Alleged122 nk 7
Tracked leader,outfinished
20May91♦ Saint-Cloud(Fr) gd *1½ⓉLH 2:37 2 4↑ Prix Jean de Chaudenay-G2 Stk86800 3 4 Legrix E 129 1.50 Dear Doctor128 1½ Passing Sale132 2½ Miss Alleged129 nk 6
Tracked in 4th,bid 2f out,hung
16Sep90♦ Longchamp(Fr) gd *1½ⓉRH 2:29 3 ⒻPrix Vermeille-G1 Stk228000 2 nk Boeuf D 128 8.00 Salsabil128 nk Miss Alleged128½ In the Groove128½ 9
Never far away,led briefly 1f out,dueled,outgamed.Wajd 4th
24Jun90♦ Longchamp(Fr) sf *1½ⓉRH 2:41 3 ⒻPrix de Malleret-G2 Stk90400 1 2 Legrix E 128 *1.00 Miss Alleged124 2 Whitehaven121 1 Ruby Tiger121 8 4
Tracked in 4th,rallied to lead 150y out,handily
27May90♦ Longchamp(Fr) gd *1 5/16ⓉRH 2:13 ⒻPrix de Royaumont-G3 Stk54200 1 1 Boeuf D 123 *1.10 Miss Alleged123 1 VueCvlir123 hd SvourusLdy123 3 4
Tracked leader,led 1f out,handily
15May90♦ Longchamp(Fr) gd *1⅜ⓉRH 2:26 3 ⒻPrix de Celles St Cloud Mdn (FT)30300 1 2 Legrix E 123 2.70 Miss Alleged123 2 Passagere du Soir123 1½ Eliush123 1 7
Well placed in 3rd,led over 1f out,drew clear

Morley Street (Ire)

ch. g. 1984, by Deep Run (Pampered King II)–High Board, by High Line — Lifetime record: 47 21 7 3 $888,696
Own.– Michael Jackson
Br.– M. Parkhill (Ire)
Tr.– Toby Balding

16Dec95♦ Ascot(GB) gd 3 3/16RH 6:18 4↑ Long Walk Hurdle-G1 Stk67300 8 McCoy AP 161 11.00 Silver Wedge161 4 Putty Road161 5 Top Spin161 nk 11
Always behind,lost touch 4 out,distanced
17Nov95♦ Ascot(GB) gd 2½RH 4:58 4↑ Ascot Hurdle-G2 Stk36300 3 13½ Bradley G 154 25.00 Large Action154 1½ Atours159 12 Morley Street154 5
Rated in 4th,bid 3 out,weakened approaching last
11Sep94♦ Merano(Ity) sf 2½RH 4↑ Corsa Siepi di Merano Stk103000 4 4¾ Bradley G Vaquero155½ Amazing Feat148¾ Reckless William155 3 7
Rated at rear,mild bid 4 out,evenly late.Time not taken
17Aug94♦ York(GB) gd 1¾ⓉLH 2:56 2 3↑ Ebor Handicap Hcp227000 19 Williams J 133 33.00 Hasten to Add129½ Admiral's Well120 1½ Solartica111 no 21
Always behind.Halkopous 16th
25Jun94♦ Newcastle(GB) fm2ⓉLH 3:24 4 3↑ Northumberland Plate Hcp Hcp170000 4 1¼ Williams J 120 40.00 Quick Ransom120 no Hasten to Add114 1 Tioman Island131 nk 20
Behind,progress 4f out,gaining late.Further Flight(136) 16th
16Jun94♦ Ascot(GB) gd 2½ⓉRH 4:27 3 4↑ Ascot Gold Cup-G1 Stk289000 8 25½ Williams J 128 40.00 Arcadian Heights128¾ Vintage Crop128 7 Sonus128 3½ 9
Never a factor.Oh So Risky 6th
27Apr94♦ Ascot(GB) yl *2ⓉRH 3:35 4 4↑ Sagaro Stakes-G3 Stk61300 11 31¼ Williams J 124 20.00 SafetyinNumbrs120¾ CairoPrince120 1¼ ArcdianHeights124 nk 13
Always behind.Oh So Risky 7th,Flakey Dove 9th
15Mar94♦ Cheltenham(GB) 2 1/16LH 4:02 1 4↑ Champion Hurdle-G1 Stk260000 Bradley G 168 16.00 Flakey Dove163 1½ Oh So Risky168¾ Large Action168 1½ 15
Bumped at 1st,never recovered,tailed off,eased before 3 out
11Dec93♦ Cheltenham(GB) 2⅝LH 5:16 1 5↑ Tripleprint Gold Cup Hcp Chase-G3 Stk80800 7 55½ Frost J 164 14.00 FragrantDawn142 3 YoungHustlr155¾ FreelineFinishing144 20 11
Mistake at 8th,always behind,distanced.Egypt Mill Prince 9th
13Nov93♦ Cheltenham(GB) 2 9/16LH 5:18 4 5↑ Mackeson Gold Cup Hcp Chase-G3 Stk83100 9 54½ Guest R 167 20.00 BradburyStar162 7 EgyptMillPrince143 4 GenrlPershing165 2½ 15
Rated at rear,well behind,brief progress at 11th
29Oct93♦ Newmarket(GB) 2ⓉRH 3:34 3↑ George Stubbs Rated Hcp (Listed) Stk24000 3 4¾ Williams J 133 12.00 My Patriarch127 4 Ritto113¾ Morley Street133 nk 12
Rated at rear,finished well without threatening
3Apr93♦ Aintree(GB) 2LH 3:46 4↑ Aintree Hurdle-G1 Stk76300 1 1½ Bradley G 161 6.00 Morley Street161 1½ Granville Again161 2 Flown161 hd 6
Rated at rear,cruised up after 2nd last,steadied,led late
16Mar93♦ Cheltenham(GB) 2 1/16LH 3:51 2 4↑ Champion Hurdle-G1 Stk213000 12 16½ Bradley G 168 20.00 Granville Again168 1 Royal Derbi168 2½ Halkopous168 3 18
Chased leaders,weakened 2 out.Vintage Crop 6th,Flown 8th
6Feb93♦ Sandown(GB) 2 1/16RH 4:06 3 5↑ AGFA Hurdle Alw22500 5 Dunwoody R 164 1.85 Mole Board149 6 Valfinet154 20 Ruling149 15 5
Rated in 4th,2nd at 5th,weakened quickly over 2 out,distanced
12Dec92♦ Cheltenham(GB) 2⅛LH 4:23 4 4↑ Bula Hurdle-G2 Stk56100 3 16 Dunwoody R 162 1.85 Halkopous156 10 Granville Again162 6 Morley Street162 nk 6
Tracked in 4th,always one-paced.Oh So Risky 4th,Kribensis 5th
20Nov92♦ Ascot(GB) 2½RH 4:54 4 4↑ Ascot Hurdle-G2 Stk36100 2 hd Dunwoody R 164 2.50 Muse154 hd Morley Street164 8 Tyrone Bridge154 2½ 7
Rated at rear,sharp bid 3 out,led after last,caught near line
15Nov92♦ Cheltenham(GB) 2 1/16LH 4:26 3 4↑ Elite Hurdle Alw58800 1 1 Dunwoody R 162 - Morley Street162 1 Granville Again156 2 Oh So Risky159 3 4
Rated in 3rd,bid over 1f out,led after last,held well
23Oct92♦ Doncaster(GB) gd 2 1/16ⓉLH 3:45 2 3↑ Doncaster Writers Stakes Alw8400 1 3½ Williams J 131 2.10 Morley Street131 3½ Jungle Dancer131 hd Glaisdale116 20 5
Rated in 4th,progress 3f out,led 1f out,drew clear
4Apr92♦ Aintree(GB) gd 2½LH 4:46 2 4↑ Aintree Hurdle-G1 Stk78500 ½ Dunwoody R 161 *.80 Morley Street161½ Minorettes Girl156 10 Forest Sun161 10 6
Unhurried,progress halfway,led after 2 out,idled,just held
10Mar92♦ Cheltenham(GB) gd 2LH 3:57 2 4↑ Champion Hurdle-G1 Stk229000 6 7½ Frost J 168 *2.00 Royal Gait168½ Oh So Risky168 no Ruling168 6 16
Settled behind leaders,mild bid 2 out,weakened.Chirkpar 7th
1Feb92♦ Leopardstwn(Ire) yl 2LH 3:51 3 4↑ Irish Champion Hurdle (Listed) Stk78700 2 no Frost J 164 *.70 Chirkpar161 no Morley Street164¾ Minorettes Girl159 4 9
Rated toward rear,rallied to lead 1 out,caught on line
15Nov91♦ Ascot(GB) gd 2½RH 4:52 4 4↑ Ascot Hurdle-G2 Stk46100 1 nk Frost J 164 *.45 Morley Street164 nk King's Curate164 7 Danny Harrold154 7 6
Rated in 5th,mistake 3 out,led run-in,held gamely
12Oct91- 3Fai gd *2⅝ S'Chase 5:10 3 3↑ BC Chase 250k 7 6 4 7¾ 4 3 1 3 1 9¾ Martinez AV 156 *.60 -- MrlyStreet156 9¾ Declare Your Wish156 15½ Cheering News146 hd 12
Ridden out

12Sep91♦ Doncaster(GB)	gd 2¼ⓉLH	3:56 3↑	Doncaster Cup-G3 Stk70800	2no	Williams J	126	33.00	Great Marquess129noMorley Street1264Haitham126hd	Rated in last,rallied 2¼f out,just missed	8
20Aug91♦ York(GB)	gd *2ⓉLH	3:30	Lonsdale Stakes (Listed) Stk38000	435½	Williams J	126	9.00	Supreme Choice1122½Retouch1263Bondstone12630	Rated in 5th,progress halfway,weakened 3f out	7
6Apr91♦ Aintree(GB)	yl 2½LH	4:542 4↑	Aintree Hurdle-G1 Stk92000	16	Frost J	161	*1.35	Morley Street1616Nomadic Way1615Run for Free161no	Jumped well,led on bit after 2nd last,finished strongly	9
12Mar91♦ Cheltenham(GB)	yl 2LH	3:544 4↑	Champion Hurdle-G1 Stk253000	11½	Frost J	168	*4.00	Morley Street1681½Nomadic Way168hdRuling1685	Progress halfway,dueled and hit 3rd last,led 2 out,drifted,all out	24
1Mar91♦ Newbury(GB)	yl $2\frac{9}{16}$LH	5:073 4↑	Berkshire Hurdle-G2 Stk30800	12	Frost J	166	*.70	Morley Street1662Danny Harrold15920Vagador166	Progress 7th,led 2 out,hampered by loose horse over 1 out,driving	6
26Dec90♦ Kempton(GB)	gd 3RH	6:172 5↑	Feltham Novices Chase-G1 Stk73900	-	Frost J	161	*1.60	Sparkling Flame16115Ardbrin161Man on the Line161	Jumped left,not fluent in 3rd,weakened and eased before 3 out	7
15Dec90♦ Ascot(GB)	gd 2½RH	4:541 5↑	Noel Novices Chase-G2 Stk31900	28	Frost J	164	*.50	RemittanceMan1618MorlyStreet16410BraveDefender1573½	Mistake 3rd,jumped left,chased winner 4 out,second best	5
3Dec90♦ Worcestor(GB)	gd 2½LH	5:254 5↑	Fred Rimell Meml Novices Chase Alw11500	12	Frost J	162	*.15	Morley Street1622Popeswood152½Pamber Priory15220	Rated in 2nd,led at 5th,headed briefly at 7th,won under wraps	9
16Nov90♦ Ascot(GB)	gd 2½RH	4:45 4↑	Ascot Hurdle-G2 Stk47000	13	Frost J	164	*.80	Morley Street1643Sabin du Loir15415Brabazon1543	Rated in last,2nd at 7th,led on bit 1 out,won under wraps	5
20Oct90- 2Bel	sf 2⅝ S'Chase	4:531 3↑	BC Chase 250k 11 5 54 42½ 14	111	Martinez AV	156	*2.00 - -	MrlyStrt15611SummrColony1563Moonstruck1561¾	Ridden out	12
6Oct90♦ Goodwood(GB)	*2ⓉB	3:494 3↑	Gatwick South Terminal Stakes Alw12500	1hd	Williams J	125	10.00	Morley Street125hdMichelozzo12510Indian Baba1201½	Rated at rear,long drive to lead near line	9
7Apr90♦ Aintree(GB)	fm2½LH	4:392 4↑	Aintree Hurdle Stk62500	115	Frost J	160	*.80	Morley Street16015Joyful Noise1603Ikdam16015	Confidently ridden,led after 2nd last,quickly clear	6
13Mar90♦ Cheltenham(GB)	gd 2LH	3:503 4↑	Champion Hurdle Stk128000	512¼	Frost J	168	10.00	Kribensis1683Nomadic Way168¾Past Glories168½	Rated in touch,lacked rally	19
23Dec89♦ Chepstow(GB)	sf 2½LH	5:17 4↑	Sport of Kings Challenge Hurdle Alw37700	2¾	Frost J	160	*.60	Propero155¾Morley Street16010Calabrese1554	Rated toward rear,progress halfway,left in lead 3 out,headed late	8
9Dec89♦ Cheltenham(GB)	fm2½LH	5:022 4↑	Sport of Kings Challenge Hurdle Alw37700	17	Frost J	160	*.55	Morley Street1607Deep Sensation1552½Ikdam155½	Rated at rear,long drive to lead 1 out,drew clear	8
25Nov89♦ Newbury(GB)	gd $2\frac{1}{16}$LH	3:482 4↑	Gerry Feilden Hurdle Stk25300	26	Frost J	157	3.50	Cruising Altitude1576Morley Street1574Nomadic Way1541	Progress at 5th,2nd over 2 out,second best.Royal Derbi 6th	8
8Apr89♦ Aintree(GB)	hy 2½LH	5:082 4↑	Mumm Prize Novices Hurdle Stk25400	11½	Frost J	159	3.50	Morley Street1591½Trapper John155¾Undaunted15530	Tracked leaders,lost place 4 out,led last,drifted left,driving	10
15Mar89♦ Cheltenham(GB)	sf 2½LH	5:172 4↑	Sun Alliance Novices Hurdle Stk77400	410½	Frost J	161	5.00	Safar's Lad1615Trapper John1615Knight Oil161½	Smooth progress 4 out,bid over 1 out,weakened run-in	22
8Feb89♦ Ascot(GB)	gd 2RH	3:55 4↑	AF Budge Novices Hurdle Stk16100	13	Frost J	170	*.80	Morley Street1703Penny Forum1642Lalitpour1706	Mistake 4th,led approaching last,ridden out	7
31Dec88♦ Newbury(GB)	gd $2\frac{9}{16}$LH	5:044	Ramsbury Hurdle Alw8500	115	Frost J	157	*1.10	Morley Street15715Cash Is King1526Lapiaffe15210	Rated at rear,sharp run to lead over 1 out,handily	7
2Dec88♦ Sandown(GB)	gd 2RH	4:051	Nat'l Hunt Guide Novices Hurdle Alw7100	12	Frost J	154	2.50	Morley Street1542Pipers Copse1587The Artful Rascal1545	Rallied approaching last,ridden to lead near line	17
5Nov88♦ Sandown(GB)	gd 2ⓉRH	3:554	EBF Marten Julian NH Flat Race Alw5200	11	Charlton A4	158	*.70	Morley Street1581Gaelic River1566Scampered143hd	Toward rear,progress 3f out,led over 1f out,comfortably	22
8Apr88♦ Aintree(GB)	gd 2ⓉLH	4:05 4↑	Supreme Nat'l Hunt Flat Race Alw4000	2½	Charlton A	156	*1.60	Black Mocassin162½Morley Street1566Alekhine1567	Progress 6f out,led 2f out,caught near line	16
12Mar88♦ Sandown(GB)	gd 2ⓉRH	4:02 4↑	Flyers Nat'l Hunt Flat Race Alw3900	112	Charlton A7	147	16.00	Morley Street14712Alekhine154¾Errant Knight1544	Midpack,rallied to lead over 1f out,handily	22

Northern Spur (Ire)

Own: Cella Charles J

B. h. 5 (Apr)
Sire: Sadler's Wells (Northern Dancer)
Dam: Fruition (Rheingold)
Br: Swettenham Stud and Partners (Ire)
Tr: McAnally Ronald L

Life	15	6	4	3	$1,614,425	114	D.Fst	0	0	0	0	$0	-
1996	4	1	1	1	$195,000	107	Wet(280)	0	0	0	0	$0	-
1995	4	2	0	1	$1,265,000	114	Turf(302)	15	6	4	3	$1,614,425	114
	0	0	0	0	$0	-	Dst(0)	0	0	0	0	$0	-

22Jun96- 4Atl	fm $1\frac{3}{16}$ Ⓣ	:501 1:142 1:38 1:553	3↑CsrIntlH-G1	103 6 11 1hd 2hd 31½ 33½	McCarron C J	L122	1.80	81- 18	Sandpit1221¾ Diplomatic Jet1171¾ NorthernSpur122¾	Set pace, weakened	8
27May96- 9Hol	fm 1¼ Ⓣ	:48 1:112 1:353 1:592	3↑HolTurfH-G1	104 5 412 410 44 33 23½	McCarron C J	L123	*1.60	87- 09	*Sandpit*1203½ Northern Spur123¾ Awad1191¾	Long rally for 2nd	6
1May96- 8Hol	fm $1\frac{1}{16}$ Ⓣ	:233 :464 1:102 1:391	4↑Alw 60000N$MY	107 2 22 22½ 21 1½ 11	McCarron C J	L122	*1.30	- -	Northern Spur1221 WavyRun116nk UnusualHeat117½	Angled,finished well	6
19Feb96- 8SA	fm 1½ Ⓣ	:49 1:143 2:05 2:301	4↑SLsObspH-G2	101 5 32½ 2½ 1hd 21½ 43½	McCarron C J	L123	*1.00	- -	*Windsharp*115¾ Wandesta1142¾ Virginia Carnival115hd	Short lead 1/4, tired	6
28Oct95- 7Bel	sf 1½ Ⓣ	:523 1:19 2:134 2:42	3↑BCTurf-G1	114 12 21 21 11½ 1½ 1nk	McCarron C J	L126	3.95	- -	NorthernSpur126nk FreedomCry1262 Crnegie1262½	Prompted,stayed well	13
8Oct95- 8SA	fm 1¼ Ⓣ	:49 1:134 1:374 2:021	3↑OakTree-G1	110 8 2½ 2½ 1hd 12 11½	McCarron C J	L124	4.70	79- 21	*Northern Spur*1241½ Sandpit1243 Royal Chariot1243	Stalked pace, driving	8
27Aug95- 8AP	fm 1¼ Ⓣ	:462 1:103 1:351 1:583	3↑ArlMilln-G1	81 9 67 83¾ 94¼ 108¼ 1014¾	McCarron C J	126	5.60	- -	Awad1262¼ Sandpit126nk The Vid126½	Taken up mid stretch	11
6Aug95- 8Dmr	fm 1⅛ Ⓣ	:491 1:12 1:36 1:482	3↑EdReadH-G1	104 2 89 85¾ 85¼ 33 32¾	McCarron C J	118	5.50	- -	Fastness1151¼ Romarin1191½ Northern Spur1182	Finished well	8

Previously trained by Andre Fabre

1Oct94 Longchamp (Fr)	yl *1⅞Ⓣ RH 3:13	Prix de Lutece-G3 Stk 70500	2½	Jarnet T	128	*.40	The Little Thief121½ Northern Spur1282 Sheshara1185	*Led,dueled final furlong,failed*	6
11Sep94 Longchamp (Fr)	sf *1½Ⓣ RH 2:344	Prix Niel-G2 Stk 126100	21½	Peslier O	128	11.00	*Carnegie*1281½ Northern Spur1281½ *Sunshack*128nk	*Well placed in 3rd,led 1-1/2f out,headed 150y out.Celtic Arms 4th*	10
26Jun94 Longchamp (Fr)	sf *1⅞Ⓣ RH 3:162	Prix Hubert de Chaudenay-G2 Stk 90700	12	Jarnet T	123	*.20	Northern Spur1232 *Bayrika*1204 Party Season1236	*Led to halfway,tracked in 3rd,led again 1f out,driving*	4
30May94 Saint-Cloud (Fr)	gd *1¾Ⓣ LH 3:041	Prix du Lys-G3 Stk 60300	11½	Jarnet T	123	1.40	*Northern Spur*1231½ Sans Ecocide123¾ Cafe Milano1232½	*Wire to wire,met challenege 1f out,driving*	5
12May94 Longchamp (Fr)	gd *1½Ⓣ RH 2:323	Prix de l'Avre (Listed) Stk 37200	31	Mongil W	128	7.50e	Bataillon128hd Cafe Milano1281 *Northern Spur*128¾	*Tracked in 3rd,dueled 1-1/2f out,faded late.The Little Thief 6th*	12
16Nov93 Saint-Cloud (Fr)	hy *1¼Ⓣ LH 2:234	Prix Saraca (Listed) Stk 34400	2¾	Guillot S	123	*.90	*Red Rubin*120¾ Northern Spur1232¾ Exit Line120nk	*Led,repelled first challenge over 1f out,headed 100y out*	4
17Oct93 Compiegne (Fr)	sf *1⅛Ⓣ LH 1:573	Prix du Tremble-EBF 14800	13	Guillot S	123	*1.30	Northern Spur1233 *Stylish Condor*1162 *Kabriz*1281½	*Led throughout,drew clear over 1f out,handily*	12

Not Surprising
Own: Van Worp Robert E

Ch. g. 9 (Feb)
Sire: Medieval Man (Noholme II)
Dam: Tenderly Calling (Always Gallant)
Br: Raven Brook Farm, Inc. (Fla)
Tr: Van Worp Judson

Life	61	23	4	5	$1,112,301	120	D.Fst	43	16	3	4	$752,172 120
1999	1	0	0	0	$129	77	Wet(260)	13	6	0	1	$326,000 114
1998	6	2	1	1	$21,974	96	Turf(174)	5	1	1	0	$34,129 100
	0	0	0	0	$0	-	Dst(0)	0	0	0	0	$0 –

2May99-9Tam	fm	5f Ⓣ	:214 :444 :563	3↑Alw 14600NC	77	9	3	43¾	64½	75	54¼	♦Garcia J J	L114f	*2.10	- -	FlshyLink1141¼ AdorbleRcer1141 *WrittnApprovl*1151½	Well placed, no rally	10
20Jun98-12Crc	fst	6f	:213 :451 :58 1:112	3↑MiamiBchH300k	40	7	7	115	1212	1219	1228½	Rivera J A II	L112	59.80	62- 22	Heckofaralph1151 Thunder Breeze1133 Nicholas Ds1152	Outrun	13
25May98-11Crc	fst	6f	:214 :451 :574 1:111	3↑Alw 25000N$Y	89	6	3	31	31	36	37½	Rivera J A II	L115	6.30	83- 19	NicholsDs1175½ PerfectPremier1152 NotSurprising115¾	Chased fast pace	8
2May98-8Tam	fst	7f	:224 :454 1:104 1:233	3↑Alw 13000NC	91	4	3	32½	32	11½	14	Whitley K	L119	*.70	95- 13	NotSurprising1194 KingWillow1191¼ SilingSin1191	Drew off under press.	10
21Apr98-9Tam	fst	6f	:222 :452 :573 1:103	3↑Alw 12200N2Y	84	3	5	65¼	33	32½	2¾	Henry W T	L119	*.70	98- 14	*BubbaHiggins*119¾ *NotSurprising*1192¾ FlshyLink119no	Finished well, 2nd b.	9
4Apr98-8Hia	fst	6f	:214 :45 :581 1:093	3↑HiaSprChpH50k	82	6	6	65	61¾	54¾	512½	Henry W T	L117	5.90	79- 22	WesternBorders1143½ NicholsDs1161½ Heckofrlph1186¼	Failed to menace	7
24Feb98-9Tam	fst	5½f	:231 :462 1:041	4↑Alw 11400N1Y	96	8	4	43	1hd	1hd	12¼	Henry W T	L116	*.90	100- 15	Not Surprising1162¼ AdorableRacer1194 Threshold116¾	Came in, drew off	8
6Apr97-9Hia	fst	7f	:23 :452 1:094 1:224	3↑HiaSprChH50k	91	7	2	2½	3½	65	79	Henry W T	L116	4.30	83- 21	Stormy Do1123¼ Derivative1111½ Thats Our Buck1131½	Pressed fast pace	11
7Mar97-9GP	sly	6f	:213 :442 :571 1:11	4↑Alw 50000N$Y	91	3	4	25	24	32½	51¾	Davis R G	117	*1.70	83- 22	Sonic Signal117no Stormy Do115½ Tuxedo Landing115no	Chased fast pace	6
16Feb97-10GP	gd	6f	:22 :442 :572 1:093	3↑DepMinstrH75k	87	5	1	63½	41¼	53¼	57¼	Henry W T	116	6.40	85- 10	Templado1132¼ *Sea Emperor*114no *Punch Line*1193½	Middle move	6
5Oct96-7Bel	fm	1 Ⓣ	:233 :463 1:101 1:342	3↑KelsoH-G3	76	10	2½	31	5¾	99¼	913¾	Castillo H Jr	113	30.50	- -	Same Old Wish113hd *Da Hoss*120nk Volochine116hd	Speed 3w,tired str	10
21Sep96-9Bel	fst	7f	:23 :454 1:084 1:211	3↑Vosburgh-G1	103	3	3	41	62¾	67	54½	Davis R G	126	12.60	- -	Lngfuhr1261¼ HonourndGlory122¾ LitethFus1262½	Close up inside,empty	8
2Sep96-9Sar	fst	7f	:22 :442 1:091 1:214	3↑ForegoH-G2	99	7	2	56½	69½	53¼	44½	Davis R G	118	4.50	92- 11	*Langfuhr*110nk Top Account1154 Lite the Fuse121nk	Mild late bid	7
8Aug96-9Sar	fst	6f	:214 :441 :554 1:081	3↑APhenomn-G2	99	2	2	42½	63¼	45	49¼	Davis R G	120	6.50	- -	ProspectBy1131¾ *HonourndGlory*1195 LitthFus1232½	Rail move turn,empty	7
20Jly96-11Lrl	fst	6f	:213 :434 :562 1:084	3↑DeFrncsM-G2	102	2	6	69	76½	54½	45½	Castillo H Jr	117	4.60	- -	LitetheFuse117no MdowMonstr1191¾ *ProspctBy*1143¾	Taken wide, no rally	7
4Jly96-8FL	gd	6f	:22 :451 1:104	3↑FLBC-G3	106	3	6	43	32	23	3½	Castillo H Jr	119	*1.10	- -	ForstWldct119hd *FrndlyLovr*115½ NotSurprsng1197¼	Lacked late response	8
8Jun96-7Bel	fst	6f	:213 :44 :561 1:09	3↑TruNrthH-G2	113	7	8	65¾	64½	32½	11	Davis R G	121	2.80	- -	NotSurprising1211 ProspectBy1132¾ *ForestWildct*114½	Circled 5w 1/4 pole	8
26May96-8Bel	fst	6f	:223 :453 :57 1:091	4↑Hcp 46000	107	6	4	42	3nk	11	13	Castillo H Jr	122	*2.25	- -	*NotSurprising*1223 KingsFiction110hd DistinctRlty111hd	4w to lead 1/4 pole	6
5May96-9Bel	gd	7f	:222 :442 1:082 1:204	3↑CarterH-G1	80	1	6	63¼	54¼	78¾	914	Perret C	121	4.30	- -	LitetheFus121hd FlyingChvron1153 PlcidFund114½	Hustled ins,no impact	10
6Apr96-9Hia	fst	7f	:232 :453 1:094 1:222	3↑HIASpChH50k	107	7	2	72¾	4¾	11	12¾	Perret C	118	*.80	- -	Not Surprising1182¾ Constant Escort1122 *Excelerate*113½	Ridden out	8
24Mar96-8Hia	fst	6f	:221 :443 :57 1:10	3↑DadeCounty28k	69	1	4	2hd	5¾	65½	69¼	Davis R G	119	*.70	- -	CrftyChrs113hd OrExbrntLd1131¾ ConstntEscrt1132	Vied for lead briefly	6
18Feb96-10GP	fst	6f	:213 :443 :571 1:103	3↑DepMinstrH50k	89	4	5	45½	64¾	64½	56¾	Davis R G	123	*.80	- -	Jess C's Whirl1153 Buffalo Dan117nk *Patton*1142½	No speed	6
28Oct95-3Bel	gd	6f	:213 :442 :562 1:09	3↑BCSprint-G1	100	3	1	85¾	52¾	34	42½	Davis R G	126	*3.30	- -	DesertStormer123nk MrGreely1232 LitdJustic126nk	Clear shot str,no kick	13
16Sep95-7Bel	fst	7f	:222 :444 1:092 1:222	3↑Vosburgh-G1	106	10	2	42	42	2hd	1no	Davis R G	126	*3.25	- -	Not Surprising126no You and I126no Our Emblem1261	5w move,long drive	13
23Aug95-9Sar	fst	7f	:223 :45 1:09 1:214	3↑ForegoH-G2	120	4	2	33½	32½	11½	14	Davis R G	121	4.70	- -	*NotSurprising*1214 OurEmblem1135 LitethFus123nk	Rated,quick move 1/4p	4
6Aug95-8Sar	gd	6f	:22 :451 :571 1:093	3↑APhenomH-G2	114	9	1	52¾	41½	21½	12	Davis R G	115	*3.15	- -	*NotSurprising*1152 ChimsBnd1191 MiningBurrh116no	Roused upper str,clr	10
4Jly95-7FL	fst	6f	:212 :442 1:09	3↑FLBudBC-G3	110	2	9	42½	2½	11	11½	Davila J R Jr	113	4.50	- -	*Not Surprising*1131½ Friendly Lover1193 *Schossberg*1159	Driving	9
17Jun95-9Bel	fst	1⅛	:462 1:104 1:354 1:49	3↑BroklynH-G2	91	9	5¾	41	31	56½	813¾	Davis R G	112	9.60	- -	You and I1151 *Key Contender*1121 Slick Horn1137¼	Rated, 4 wide move trn	9
29May95-9Bel	gd	1	:221 :441 1:083 1:343	3↑MtropltH-G1	104	3	73¾	65¾	44	35	45	Davis R G	113	20.80	- -	*You and I*1121 *Lite the Fuse*1132½ Our Emblem1141½	Adv turn, no str bid	9
29Apr95-11Hia	sly	1⅛	:464 1:104 1:35 1:481	3↑SeminoleH50k	105	1	72	21½	11	11½	12½	Castillo H Jr	L117	2.10	- -	NotSurprising1172½ PrideofBurkn1171 Byton1148	Slipped thru,riddenout	9
1Apr95-8Hia	fst	7f	:233 :46 1:093 1:221	3↑HiaSpChpH50k	105	2	6	4¾	31½	3nk	12	Davis R G	L114	12.30	- -	*Not Surprising*1142 Evil Bear118¾ *Turf Star*1121	Fast pace, drew off	10
11Mar95-9GP	fm	1 1/16 Ⓣ	:224 :464 1:104 1:41	3↑FtLdrdlH-G3	93	5	52¾	73¼	95¼	94¼	98¼	Henry W T	L114	28.00	- -	The Vid1203 FlyingAmerican113nk *DJ'sRainbow*1141¼	Good position, faded	12
18Feb95-11Tam	fst	1 1/16	:233 :464 1:111 1:442	3↑TamBudBC77k	99	4	32½	32	31	14	1hd	Henry W T	L114	3.20	- -	Not Surprising114hd Mighty Avanti1135 Boisterous1131½	Just lasted	12
28Jan95-10Tam	fst	7f	:224 :452 1:101 1:231	3↑BCSuper45k	96	8	8	73¼	2½	2hd	32½	Henry W T	L122	*.20	- -	Boisterous1102½ Mr. Tooth116no *Not Surprising*1227½	Circled field hung	9
7Jan95-9Tam	wf	6f	:223 :461 :581 1:104	3↑Pelican28k	105	9	5	55	4¾	16	111½	Henry W T	L113	*.90	- -	NotSrprsng11311½ HonrClny116no RgnngGlry122no	Drew off impressively	12
25Jly94-8Crc	sly	1 1/16	:243 :491 1:133 1:454	3↑Hcp 20000	85	4	63½	51¾	53¾	43¼	58¼	Ramos W S	L117	*.60	- -	Silent Lake1121¼ *Departing Cloud*1132¾ Jack's Hope1124	Squeezed start	6
16Jly94-11Crc	fst	1⅛	:471 1:122 1:384 1:523	3↑SpndABuckH100k	100	5	43	41½	51¼	43¼	54¼	Valles E S	L115	12.30	- -	Daniel'sBoy111¾ It'sali'lknownfact1103 *AggressiveChief*115nk	Circled field	8
25Jun94-11Crc	fst	7f	:232 :462 1:103 1:232	3↑EmDunesH100k	98	6	6	51¾	42	52¾	52½	Henry W T	L116	2.90	- -	Swedaus111nk DHScore a Birdie113 DH*Daniel's Boy*111¾	Middle of pack	7
4Jun94-9Crc	gd	5f Ⓣ	:221 :46 :574	3↑LagoMarH100k	100	1	7	93	72½	41¼	22	Henry W T	L116	6.60	- -	*Cool Air*1182 Not Surprising1161½ Absent Russian112nk	Steady advance	12
14May94-6LaD	fst	1⅛	:482 1:121 1:364 1:492	3↑ArkLaTxH-G3	91	9	42	44	53	710	78¼	Henry W T	L115	5.30	- -	Nelson1162¼ Eequalsmcsqured1151 DixiePokerAce1151	Evenly, weakened	10
23Apr94-10Hia	sly	1⅛	:453 1:102 1:352 1:482	3↑SeminoleH100k	105	7	53¾	52½	21	11	11¾	Henry W T	L113	11.90	- -	NotSurprising1131¾ DDnielsBoy111¾ NorthrnTrnd1161¾	Rallied, drew off	8
3Apr94-9Hia	fst	7f	:223 :444 1:091 1:214	3↑HiaSpChpH50k	101	11	2	3½	2½	3nk	33	Sellers S J	L113	24.10	- -	DJackLivingston110hd DJCat1153 *NotSurprising*1132	Shut off mid stretch	11

Placed second through disqualification

19Feb94-10Tam	fst	1 1/16	:231 :471 1:121 1:441	3↑TamBudBC78k	97	12	63¼	63¼	1hd	12	22	Henry W T	L113	3.70	- -	Pride of Burkaan1132 Not Surprising1132 Repletion1222½	Clear lead hung	12
29Jan94-10Tam	wf	7f	:222 :452 1:11 1:241	3↑BCSuper47k	94	4	4	43	42½	2hd	12	Henry W T	L122	*1.50	97- 13	NotSrprsng1222 PrmrAngl122½ JnkBondKng1132½	Stalked pace drew off	12
8Jan94-10Tam	fst	6f	:221 :451 :58 1:101	3↑Pelican28k	101	3	5	41¾	52¼	11½	13	Henry W T	L116	2.80	- -	*NotSurprising*1163 *OhSoStriking*1153½ BobthHt1181½	Slipped thru.drew off	12

Previously trained by White William P 1993(as of 12/8): (503 75 81 66 0.15)

8Dec93-9Crc	fst	5f	:214 :453 :581	Hcp 22000	85	1	5	62¾	65	32	32¼	Ramos W S	L118f	3.60	- -	Grey Counter116no *Probable Call*1162¼ *Not Surprising*1183	Rallied, hung	9
23Oct93-8Crc	fst	7f	:22 :45 1:092 1:222	3↑MiamiBchH75k	74	7	8	113¼	95½	912	915¼	Lee M A	L112f	35.10	- -	Song of Ambition1163½ *Coolin It*113nk Daniel's Boy1172½	Outrun	12
26Sep93-11Crc	fst	6½f	:221 :443 1:10 1:164	3↑Hcp 20000	89	7	1	4¾	42¼	32½	46¾	Lee M A	L114f	5.70	- -	*SongofAmbtn*116nk DJCt119½ MyLckRnsNrth1126	Stalked pace, gave way	7
1Sep93-9Crc	fm	*5f Ⓣ	:583	Hcp 20000	86	8	1	83¾	87½	64	1¾	Lee M A	L119f	*1.30	- -	NotSurprising119¾ MyBoyCry111½ *SergiosTurn*112no	Circled,up final strds	10
30Jly93-1Crc	fst	7f	:232 :461 1:102 1:224	3↑Hcp 20000	86	3	3	22½	21½	34	46	Lee M A	L112f	4.90	- -	MyLckRnsNorth1111 *Hmbgboo*1162¼ ColorflCrw1132¾	Close up, weakened	5
11Jly93-1Crc	sly	5f	:223 :461 :59	Alw 19900NC	80	4	4	32	32	31½	11	Lee M A	L118f	1.70	- -	Not Surprising1181 Aspen Fortune1162½ Trade Bill116nk	Circled, drew off	5
19Jun93-10Crc	fst	7f	:221 :45 1:093 1:223	CarryBackH100k	82	4	4	53½	53	45½	57	Lee M A	L117f	2.50	- -	*Humbugaboo*1122½ Signoir Valery1124¼ Kassec113hd	Middle of pack	8
6Jun93-10Crc	fst	6f	:213 :444 :57 1:10	Hcp 20000	94	1	3	33	31½	22	11¼	Lee M A	117f	3.80	- -	Not Surprising1171¼ *Humbugaboo*1144 Ships in the Night1102¼	Ridden out	7
17Oct92-11Crc	fst	1 1/16	:233 :473 1:123 1:473	ⓇFSInRealty410k	73	9	116	107	1412	117	710½	Lee M A	120	10.40	- -	*Silver of Silver*1204 Crafty120no Fiery Special1202½	Improved position	15
19Sep92-10Crc	fst	7f	:214 :444 1:104 1:243	ⓇFSAffirmed125k	72	10	10	83¾	74¾	56	56¾	De'Oliveira W G	118	2.90	- -	FierySpecil1182 ShipsintheNight1183½ GentlPtrick118nk	Blocked 1/4 pole	10
6Sep92-10Crc	fst	7f	:23 :461 1:114 1:25	TurnberryI50k	–	3	4	41	2½	1hd	1½	De'Oliveira W G	116	*.70	- -	NotSurprising116½ DucdSligovil1123 Dotsappel1124	Prevailed, long drive	5
22Aug92-11Crc	fst	6f	:212 :444 1:114	ⓇFSDrFager75k	90	5	9	43½	33½	31½	1hd	De'Oliveira W G	116	2.10	- -	*Not Surprising*116hd *Gentle Patrick*116¾ *Fiery Special*1164½	Prevailed	9
9Aug92-11Crc	fst	6f	:213 :451 1:113	Alw 22000NC	78	2	6	66½	54	1½	12	De'Oliveira W G	114	9.80	- -	*Not Surprising*1142 ThatsOurBuck1182½ It'saRunaway116nk	Much the best	6
19Jly92-10Crc	fst	5½f	:221 :454 1:053	Criterium50k	61	8	4	21	2½	32	66¾	De'Oliveira W G	116b	15.60	- -	Thirty Two Slew1184 Summer Set1121 *It's a Runaway*1161	Faded	8
5Jly92-5Crc	fst	5½f	:222 :46 1:053	Alw 15500NC	65	2	9	75¾	65	44	35	Douglas R R	116	7.70	- -	*ThirtyTwoSlew*1163 ItsaRunwy1162 NotSurprising1161	Pinched back start	9
2May92-3Crc	fst	5f	:224 :472 1:003	Md Sp Wt 15k	73	8	8	75¾	55½	4nk	12¾	Lee M A	116	3.50	- -	Not Surprising1162¾ My Max1161¼ Leader of the Law1161½	Drew off	12

Paradise Creek

Own: M.Nishiyama

Dk. b or b. h. 5 (Feb)
Sire: Irish River*Fr (Riverman)
Dam: North Of Eden*Ire (Northfields)
Br: Mr. & Mrs. Bertram R. Firestone (Va)
Tr: Mott W

Life	25	14	7	1	$3,401,416	117		
1994	11	8	2	1	$2,634,774	117		
1993	5	1	2	0	$136,052	106		
	0	0	0	0	$0	–		

D.Fst	1	0	0	0	$12,000	–
Wet(301)	0	0	0	0	$0	–
Turf(311)	24	14	7	1	$3,389,416	117
Dst(0)	0	0	0	0	$0	–

27Nov94 Tokyo (Jpn)	fm	*1½ Ⓣ LH	2:233	3↑ Japan Cup-G1 Stk 3389500							2no	Day P	126	4.00		Marvelous Crown125no Paradise Creek1251¼ Royce and Royce1251¼	*Rated in mid-pack,rallied 2f out,dueled final 16th,just missed*	14
5Nov94- 9CD	fm	1½ Ⓣ	:464 1:103 2:00 2:262	3↑ BCTurf-G1	107	13	43½	1½	1hd	11½	33	Day P	L126	*.80	- -	Tikkanen1221½ Hatoof1231½ Paradise Creek126½	Led, weakened	14
15Oct94-10Lrl	fm	1¼ Ⓣ	:461 1:102 1:353 1:593	3↑ DCIntl-G1	114	6	64	73¾	1hd	1hd	15½	Day P	L126	*.20	- -	Paradise Creek1265½ Redcall126no Beneficial1263¾	4wd trp,confident ride	9
28Aug94-10AP	fm	1¼ Ⓣ	:48 1:112 1:352 1:593	3↑ ArlMilln-G1	111	12	56½	55½	46	22	1¾	Day P	L126	*1.80	- -	*Paradise Creek*126¾ Fanmore1261¾ Muhtarram126½	Well handled, clear	14
12Aug94- 8Sar	fm	1⅛ Ⓣ	:481 1:112 1:343 1:46	3↑ BBaruchH-G2	110	1	42½	31	31½	2½	21	Day P	126	1.10	- -	Lure1251 *Paradise Creek*1266 Fourstardave1146	Bid, 2nd best	5
11Jun94- 7Bel	fm	1¼ [T]	:462 1:10 1:334 1:573	3↑ ETManhtn-G1	117	2	1hd	11	1hd	12½	16¾	Day P	124	*.30	- -	ParadiseCreek1246¾ SolrSplendor112½ RiverMjesty1137	Drew off, driving	7
20May94-11Pim	fm	1⅛ Ⓣ	:484 1:131 1:364 1:482	3↑ DixieH-G2	102	4	31	42¼	42¼	2½	1¾	Day P	L124	1.30	- -	*Paradise Creek*124¾ *Lure*1245½ Astudillo115½	Rated 3wd,bid,driving	5
6May94- 8CD	fm	1⅛ Ⓣ	:47 1:111 1:361 1:481	3↑ TurfClsc-G2	107	6	45½	46½	44½	12½	14	Day P	L118	3.30	- -	*Paradise Creek*1184 Lure1232½ Yukon Robbery1162½	Circld field drew off	7
12Mar94-11GP	fm	1 1/16 Ⓣ	:231 :47 1:102 1:391	3↑ FtLaudrdlH100k	108	4	41	42½	41½	2½	1¾	Smith M E	L125	*.70	- -	*Paradise Creek*125¾ Bidding Proud115¾ *SocialRetiree*1141¼	Slipped through	9
29Jan94- 9GP	fm	1⅛ Ⓣ	:472 1:111 1:343 1:474	3↑ CanTurfH-G2	107	7	32½	32½	21	1hd	13¼	Smith M E	L123	*.40	- -	*PrdiseCrek*1233¼ GlnfiddichLd113¾ NijinskysGold113nk	Well rated, handily	8
8Jan94- 9GP	fm	1 1/16 Ⓣ	:24 :473 1:111 1:402	3↑ AppletnH-G3	106	5	32	41½	3½	1½	13	Smith M E	L121	*1.20	- -	*Paradise Creek*1213 Fourstars Allstar117nk Elite Jeblar111no	Easily	8
28Nov93- 5Hol	fm	1⅛ Ⓣ	:47 1:102 1:334 1:454	3↑ CitatonH-G2	105	3	1½	1hd	1hd	1hd	22¼	Day P	LB120	*2.10	- -	JeuneHomme1142¼ *PardiseCreek*120no JohnnQutz1202	Fast pace, held 2nd	8
6Nov93- 5SA	fm	1 Ⓣ	:223 :454 1:092 1:332	3↑ BCMile-G1	94	6	52¼	42	53½	85½	88	Day P	LB126	8.20	- -	*Lure*1262¼ *Ski Paradise*1201¾ Fourstars Allstar126hd	Well placed, no rally	13
16Oct93- 6Bel	sf	1 Ⓣ	:224 :454 1:103 1:354	3↑ KelsoH-G3	104	10	21	31	3nk	21	23¼	Day P	120	3.00e	- -	*Lure*1253¼ Paradise Creek1205 Daarik112½	Second best	10
30Apr93- 8CD	fm	1⅛ Ⓣ	:47 1:104 1:342 1:461	3↑ TurfClsc-G3	106	1	32	31½	42½	46	42¾	Day P	L123	2.70	- -	*Lure*123¾ Star of Cozzene1182 Cleone116no	Failed to respond	8
31Mar93- 8GP	fm	1 1/16 Ⓣ	:234 :474 1:113 1:414	4↑ Hcp 55000	104	4	21½	31½	33	31½	11	Day P	L122	*.50	- -	Paradise Creek1221 Sylva Honda1131 Flying American1112	Ridden out	7
22Nov92- 8Hol	fm	1⅛ Ⓣ	:453 1:093 1:341 1:471	HolDerby-G1	102	5	31½	2½	1½	1½	1no	Day P	LB122	*1.50	- -	*Paradise Creek*122no *Bien Bien*1221¼ Kitwood122hd	All out, just lasted	12
31Oct92- 7GP	fm	1 Ⓣ	:224 :454 1:09 1:324	3↑ BCMile-G1	105	11	64½	63¼	64	44	23	Day P	122	30.30	- -	*Lure*1223 *Paradise Creek*122nk Brief Truce1221½	Finished well	14
3Oct92- 9Med	fm	1 1/16 Ⓣ	:232 :463 1:101 1:402	PlsdsBCH77k	98	4	21½	21	21	21	21	Smith M E	119	*.40	- -	BiddingProud1161 ParadiseCreek119nk MarylandMoon1142½	Second best	6
7Sep92- 9AP	fm	1¼ Ⓣ	:482 1:13 1:373 2:01	Secretar-G1	97	3	31½	41½	52¼	32½	2½	Smith M E	123	*2.40	- -	Ghazi114½ Paradise Creek1231¾ Tango Charlie117hd	In tight, angled out	10
6Aug92- 8Sar	fm	1⅛ Ⓣ	:47 1:101 1:34 1:463	HallOFme-G2	100	4	21	1½	11	11½	11	Smith M E	115	*1.30	- -	ParadiseCreek1151 SmilingandDancin1191¾ SpectaculrTide122hd	Driving	8
22Jly92- 7Bel	fm	1 1/16 Ⓣ	:234 :463 1:10 1:40	3↑ Alw 31000NC	99	5	21	21	2½	1hd	12¼	Smith M E	113	*.50	- -	*Paradise Creek*1132¼ Victory Cross1176 Timber Cat111hd	Ridden out	9
18Jun92- 7Bel	fm	1 1/16 Ⓣ	:232 :461 1:10 1:402	3↑ Alw 29000NC	97	10	2½	21	1½	13	14	Perret C	112	*1.00	- -	*Paradise Creek*1124 Scuffleburg1146 Alfaares117½	Ridden out	11
24Aug91- 8Sar	fst	6½f	:213 :442 1:103 1:173	Hopeful-G1	–	9	2	74¾	57¼	37½	49¼	Cordero A Jr	122	3.40	- -	Salt Lake1229 Slew's Ghost122hd *Caller I. D.*122hd	Five wide, no rally	9
19Jly91- 5Bel	hd	7f Ⓣ	:224 :454 1:103 1:223	Md Sp Wt 24k	–	2	12	52	41¾	13	111	Smith M E	118	3.00	- -	Paradise Creek11811 Forever Fighting118hd Jay Gee1181¼	Handily	12

Paseana (Arg)

b. f. 1987, by Ahmad (Good Manners)–Pasiflin, by Flintham

Own.– Sidney H. Craig
Br.– Haras Vacacion (Arg)
Tr.– Ronald McAnally

Lifetime record: 36 19 10 2 $3,171,203

23Jly95- 7Hol	fst	1⅛	:461 1:103 1:353 1:481	3↑ Ⓕ Vanity H-G1	89	4	4	46½	32½	47	511½	McCarron CJ	LB 123	*1.30	80-09	Private Persuasion1143Top Rung1162¾Wandesta1194½	Mild bid ⅜,weakened	7
25Jun95- 4Hol	fst	1 1/16	:232 :463 1:101 1:412	3↑ Ⓕ Milady H-G1	100	3	5	59¼	55	33½	23½	McCarron CJ	LB 123	*.80	90-14	Pirate's Revenge1163½Paseana1234Private Persuasion1161¾	Best of others	5
28May95- 9Hol	fst	1 1/16	:223 :452 1:094 1:422	3↑ Ⓕ Hawthorne H-G2	98	4	6	611	63¾	3½	12	McCarron CJ	LB 122	2.10	89-13	Paseana1222Pirate'sRvng117¾TopRung1178	4 wide into lane	7
21Apr95- 9OP	fst	1 1/16	:224 :454 1:103 1:423	4↑ Ⓕ Apple Blossom-G1	95	1	3	36	33½	32½	35	McCarron CJ	L 122	2.00	89-15	HeavnlyPrize1201HaloAmeric1164Psn1225	Mild middle move	6
26Feb95- 8SA	fst	1⅛	:47 1:11 1:36 1:484	4↑ Ⓕ S Margarita H-G1	96	2	3	43	32½	32	22	McCarron CJ	LB 123	1.30	87-16	QueensCourtQn1202Pasna123½KlassyKm1169	Game effort	5
5Feb95- 8SA	fst	1 1/16	:224 :461 1:092 1:413	4↑ Ⓕ S Maria H-G1	95	3	4	52¼	45½	34½	24½	McCarron CJ	LB 123	2.20	82-15	Queens Court Queen1184½Paseana123¾Key Phrase1173½	Closed willingly	5
28Aug94- 8Dmr	fst	1 1/16	:224 :461 1:101 1:402	3↑ Ⓕ Chula Vista H-G2	108	2	3	33½	32½	3½	1no	McCarron CJ	LB 123	*.30e	104-03	Paseana123noExchange120¾MagiclMaidn118nk	Determinedly	4
6Mar94- 8SA	fst	1⅛	:464 1:104 1:36 1:49	4↑ Ⓕ S Margarita H-G1	104	6	5	41½	41¼	1½	12¾	McCarron CJ	LB 123	*1.10	88-18	Paseana1232¾KalitaMelody117hdStalcreek1192	Kept to task	9
12Feb94- 8SA	fst	1 1/16	:231 :471 1:11 1:414	4↑ Ⓕ S Maria H-G1	104	3	4	3½	3½	21½	2no	McCarron CJ	LB 124	*.70	86-14	SupahGem116noPsn124noAlysbll1161½	Drifted out near wire	7
6Nov93- 4SA	fst	1⅛	:464 1:11 1:36 1:481	3↑ Ⓕ BC Distaff-G1	108	3	4	32½	31	2hd	2no	McCarron CJ	LB 123	2.50	89-10	Hollywood Wildcat120noPaseana1232½Re Toss1231	Game try	8
17Oct93- 8Kee	my	1⅛	:463 1:103 1:353 1:482	3↑ Ⓕ Spinster-G1	102	3	4	32	31	21	11	McCarron CJ	L 123	*1.20	92-07	Pasean1231GryCshmr1234Jcody1191	Brushed 3/16,hard drive	9
19Sep93- 8Bel	my	1 1/16	:232 :464 1:103 1:414	3↑ Ⓕ Ruffian H-G1	70	1	3	44½	42	57	520¾	McCarron CJ	125	*1.20	72-16	SharedInterest1142½Dsput1153TrnbckthAlrm1232¼	Gave way	5
18Jly93- 8Hol	fst	1⅛	:472 1:102 1:351 1:474	3↑ Ⓕ Vanity H-G1	102	3	4	51¾	1½	11½	21¼	McCarron CJ	LB 126	*.70	97-10	Re Toss1151¼Paseana1262¼Guiza1143	Clear,overtaken	8
12Jun93- 8Hol	fst	1 1/16	:23 :46 1:094 1:413	3↑ Ⓕ Milady H-G1	107	1	5	42	31	1hd	1½	McCarron CJ	LB 125	*.40	93-13	Paseana125½Bold Windy114½Re Toss1165	Hard drive,gamely	7
16Apr93- 9OP	fst	1 1/16	:23 :461 1:103 1:414	4↑ Ⓕ Apple Blossom H-G1	107	1	4	43	4¾	12½	13½	McCarron CJ	L 124	*.40	92-13	Paseana1243½Looie Capote1154½Luv Me Luv Me Not114nk	4 wide,2nd turn	9
28Feb93- 8SA	fst	1⅛	:481 1:121 1:364 1:492	4↑ Ⓕ S Margarita H-G1	100	2	2	3½	1½	1hd	2hd	McCarron CJ	LB 125	*.40	83-17	Southern Truce115hdPaseana1251¾Guiza1143	Rider dropped rein briefly⅛	9
6Feb93- 8SA	fst	1 1/16	:232 :472 1:104 1:411	4↑ Ⓕ S Maria H-G1	108	3	3	31½	32	21	22¼	McCarron CJ	LB 126	*.70	96-12	Race the Wild Wind1172¼Paseana1261¼Southern Truce1164½	Not enough late	6
31Oct92- 6GP	fst	1⅛	:47 1:104 1:353 1:48	3↑ Ⓕ BC Distaff-G1	105	14	4	3½	1hd	13	14	McCarron CJ	L 123	2.70e	97-03	Paseana1234Versailles Treaty123½Magical Maiden1191½	Strong hand ride	14
11Oct92- 8Kee	fst	1⅛	:48 1:123 1:371 1:494	3↑ Ⓕ Spinster-G1	102	4	5	63	52	22	22¼	McCarron CJ	LB 123	*.50	84-25	Fowda1232¼Paseana1236MeadwStar1232½	Broke awkwardly	10
30Aug92- 4Dmr	fst	1¼	:461 1:102 1:35 2:004	3↑ Pacific Classic 1000k	101	2	2	2½	3½	31½	56¼	McCarron CJ	LB 119	*1.70	89-11	MissionaryRidge1243½DefnsivePlay124nkClrt1242	Weakened	7
19Jly92- 8Hol	fst	1⅛	:47 1:103 1:351 1:48	3↑ Ⓕ Vanity H-G1	98	2	2	2hd	1hd	11½	12	McCarron CJ	LB 127	*.30	94-12	Paseana1272Fowda1181¼Re Toss1153	Driving	6
13Jun92- 8Hol	fst	1 1/16	:223 :454 1:10 1:412	3↑ Ⓕ Milady H-G1	102	7	6	53	4¾	11½	12¾	McCarron CJ	LB 125	*.40	94-12	Paseana1252¾Re Toss115¾Fowda1191¾	Wide,handily	7
17Apr92- 9OP	fst	1 1/16	:233 :464 1:11 1:42	4↑ Ⓕ Apple Blossom H-G1	114	1	4	33	2hd	13	14½	McCarron CJ	L 124	*.40	91-23	Paseana1244½FitforaQueen1213½SldoutFront1092	Ridden out	8
1Mar92- 8SA	fst	1⅛	:461 1:101 1:344 1:472	4↑ Ⓕ S Mrgta Inv'l H-G1	110	1	2	22½	21½	1hd	12¼	McCarron CJ	LB 122	*.40	93-15	Pseana1222¼LaramieMoon1166ColourChart1182½	Ridden out	5
8Feb92- 8SA	fst	1 1/16	:223 :461 1:104 1:414	4↑ Ⓕ S Maria H-G1	104	1	2	1½	1½	11½	12½	McCarron CJ	LB 120	*.80	94-16	Pseana1202½ColourChrt1181¾Campagnarde1171¼	Ridden out	5
5Jan92- 8SA	sly	1⅛⊗	:47 1:123 1:393 1:534	4↑ Ⓕ S Gorgonio H-G2	97	1	2	21½	13	12½	12½	McCarron CJ	LB 118	*.60	91-31	Paseana1182½Laura Ly11216Reluctant Guest11723	Handily	4
23Nov91- 8Hol	fst	1 1/16	:23 :464 1:111 1:423	3↑ Ⓕ Silver Belles H-G2	-	4	2	1hd	2hd	1½	15½	McCarron CJ	117	*1.70	88-18	Pseana1175½Damewood116nkLunaElegante117½	Clear,driving	6
14Oct91- 3SA	fst	1 1/16	:231 :471 1:111 1:422	3↑ Ⓕ Manta H 61k	-	4	3	42½	41	32	22	McCarron CJ	117	2.20	89-16	LaCharlatna1172Pasen1171PmprdStr1131¾	Wide backstretch	6
13Apr91♦ San Isidro(Arg)	fm	*1⅛ⓉLH	1:462	3↑ Ⓕ Clasico Abril-G2 Stk16500							12½	Sarati M	122	*.70		Paseana1222½Inimitable1322½Sereana1321½	Tracked in 3rd,led 2f out,handily	9
30Mar91♦ San Isidro(Arg)	fm	*1⅜ⓉLH	2:142	3↑ Ⓕ Clasico Federico de Alvear-G2 Stk16400							42½	Garcia M	120	2.05		Fail132hdBallesta1202½Teresine132no	Tracked in 3rd,bid 2f out,weakened final 16th	9
8Dec90♦ San Isidro(Arg)	fm	*1¼ⓉLH	2:012	3↑ Ⓕ Copa de Plata-G1 Stk24400							710	Sarati M	119	*1.10		Jewellery119hdFail132nkCampagnarde119nk	Never a factor	12
3Nov90♦ San Isidro(Arg)	gd	*1¼ⓉLH	1:592	Ⓕ Gran Premio Enrique Acebal-G1 Stk34000							14	Sarati M	123	2.15		Paseana1234Pupy Hill123nkJewellery1232½	Tracked in 5th,sharp run to lead over 1f out,quickly clear	10
14Oct90♦ Hipodromo(Arg)	fst	*1¼LH	2:022	Ⓕ Gran Premio Seleccion-G1 Stk47600							38½	Sarati M	123	5.20		Campagnarde1231½Silver Beauty1237Paseana123¾	Tracked in 4th,3rd 4f out,no further response	16

21Sep90♦ Hipodromo(Arg) fst *1⅛LH 1:502 ⒻClasico Francisco J Beazley-G2 Stk15300 1½ Garcia M 123 3.95 Paseana1231½Silver Beauty1246Campagnarde1232½ 11
Rated in 6th,2nd 2f out,led over 1f out,driving
22Aug90♦ San Isidro(Arg) fm *7fⓉLH 1:214 ⒻPremio Baluarte Alw3900 14 Sarati M 123 *.65e Paseana1234Caramel Toss1234Ksteel Mi1238 7
Tracked leader,led 2f out,drew clear
1Aug90♦ San Isidro(Arg) fm *7fⓉLH 1:23 ⒻPremio Cerrito Mdn3000 1½ Sarati M 123 *1.75 Paseana1231½La Calada1234Mining Lark1232 14
Tracked in 3rd,4th halfway,rallied to lead 1f out,handily

Phone Chatter

Own: Sarkowsky Herman

Ch. m. 5 (Feb)
Sire: Phone Trick (Clever Trick)
Dam: Passing My Way (Pass the Glass)
Br: Herman Sarkowsky (Ky)
Tr: Mandella Richard E

Life	15	5	3	1	$838,742	98		D.Fst	12	5	2	1	$820,617	98
1996	1	0	0	0	$4,125	86		Wet(344)	0	0	0	0	$0	–
1995	4	0	1	1	$27,125	92		Turf(238)	3	0	1	0	$18,125	92
	0	0	0	0	$0	–		Dst(0)	0	0	0	0	$0	–

13Jan96-8SA fst 6f :212 :44 :56 1:082 4↑ⒻAlw 55000N$Y **86** 4 5 511 57½ 57 46¾ Pincay L Jr **LB**117 b 6.70 - - *Igotrhythm*1143 Ballerina Gal122¾ Angi Go1223 Showed little 5
15Nov95-8Hol fm 1 Ⓣ :23 :462 1:10 1:341 3↑ⒻⓇFlawlessly61k **84** 7 53 21 31 88½ 76¾ Desormeaux K J L115 b 4.70 - - *TwicetheVice*1201¼ NorcliffeDancer116nk ReauPerrault117½ Early bid wide 8
9Sep95-8Dmr fm 1 1/16 Ⓣ :24 :481 1:114 1:422 3↑ⒻPalomarH-G2 **89** 3 54 55½ 55 76¼ 56¼ Pincay L Jr L117 b 9.50 - - Morgana1181¼ Yearly Tour1181¼ Lady Affirmed117hd No rally 7
19Jly95-8Hol fm 1 Ⓣ :242 :481 1:121 1:354 4↑ⒻMDurslag75k **92** 2 35 32½ 42 41¼ 2½ Pincay L Jr L117 b 4.10 83- 15 Morgn118½ PhoneChtter117½ FondlyRemembrd118¾ Finished well 3-wide 6
8Jun95-8Hol fst 7f :222 :452 1:091 1:21 3↑ⒻAlw 60000 **85** 3 5 55½ 53½ 56½ 37 Black C A **LB**118 2.10 - - PrivtePersusion1164 LunrSpook1173 PhonChttr118½ No speed, mild rally 5
28Dec94-8SA fst 7f :221 :443 1:094 1:214 ⒻLaBrea-G2 **87** 7 7 78½ 76½ 55½ 43¾ Pincay L Jr 117 1.80 - - Top Rung115¾ *Klassy Kim*1191 Twice the Vice1192 Steady rally inside 7
16Oct94-8Kee fst 1⅛ :473 1:113 1:362 1:484 3↑ⒻSpinster-G1 **74** 6 33 64 613 819 823¼ Nakatani C S 119 2.20 - - Dispute1231½ Lets Be Alert1197 Miss Dominique1232½ Stopped, no excuse 8
12Sep94-8Dmr fst 1 :221 :452 1:094 1:344 3↑ⒻVilleVignH66k **94** 1 31½ 32 31 32 2¾ Pincay L Jr 119 *.40 - - MissDominique117¾ PhoneChtter119½ PubRiver11211 Steady rally 3-wide 5
25Aug94-8Dmr fst 6½f :214 :441 1:083 1:15 ⒻⓇCERF60k **94** 6 4 63½ 32 31½ 11 Pincay L Jr 117 *.50 - - Phone Chatter1171 Airistar120½ *Klassy Kim*11510 Rallied 3-w,late surge 6
6Nov93-3SA fst 1 1/16 :232 :472 1:112 1:43 ⒻBCJuvFil-G1 **95** 6 64 53 31½ 2½ 1hd Pincay L Jr **B**119 2.30 - - *Phone Chatter*119hd *Sardula*1193 Heavenly Prize119½ Wore down rivals 8
9Oct93-8SA fst 1 1/16 :222 :462 1:104 1:413 ⒻOakLeaf-G1 **98** 5 34 32½ 2½ 1hd 1½ Pincay L Jr **B**117 5.00 - - *Phone Chatter*117½ Sardula1167½ Tricky Code1153 Drifted str,rallied 6
4Sep93-8Dmr fst 7f :214 :453 1:091 1:213 ⒻDMrDeb-G2 **83** 8 7 76¾ 55½ 47½ 27½ Pincay L Jr **B**119 2.00 - - Sardula1167½ *Phone Chatter*119nk Ballerina Gal1142½ Long rally,up for 2nd 8
14Aug93-8Dmr fst 6½f :214 :443 1:094 1:161 ⒻSorrento-G3 **85** 5 5 56 55¼ 32 12¾ Pincay L Jr **B**117 4.90 - - PhoneChttr1172¾ Rhpsodic121½ Nossmblyrquird1174½ Closed rush 5 wide 6
4Jly93-4Hol fst 5½f :214 :454 :582 1:043 ⒻMd Sp Wt 32k **69** 3 5 65 45½ 31½ 11¾ Pincay L Jr **B**117 2.80 - - *Phone Chatter*1171¾ Strong Colors1172 CocoLuv1173½ Steady rally, driving 8
20Jun93-4Hol fst 5f :214 :443 :571 ⒻMd Sp Wt 32k **66** 5 4 78 810 59½ 66½ Pincay L Jr **B**117 *3.50 - - DanceWithGrace1172 *SmilinIrishEyes*1172¾ MalibuLight1171 Showed little 10

Pleasant Stage

Own: Buckland Farm

B. f. 3 (Mar)
Sire: Pleasant Colony (His Majesty)
Dam: Meteor Stage (Stage Door Johnny)
Br: Mrs. Thomas M. Evans (Ky)
Tr: Speckert Christopher

Life	10	2	3	2	$844,272	94		D.Fst	10	2	3	2	$844,272	94
1992	6	0	2	1	$157,032	94		Wet(346)	0	0	0	0	$0	–
1991	4	2	1	1	$687,240	–		Turf(336)	0	0	0	0	$0	–
	0	0	0	0	$0	–		Dst(0)	0	0	0	0	$0	–

11Jly92-8Bel fst 1¼ :50 1:133 1:38 2:032 ⒻCCAOaks-G1 **88** 2 63½ 52¼ 32 33 32½ Bailey J D 121 2.10 - - Turnback theAlarm1211¼ EasyNow1211¼ PleasantStage1211 Rallied, hung 6
7Jun92-8Bel fst 1⅛ :452 1:093 1:352 1:484 ⒻMthrGoos-G1 **64** 2 79½ 710 79 711 718¾ Delahoussaye E 121 b 1.80 - - *TurnbckthAlrm*1212¼ EsyNow1211¾ QunofTriumph121¾ Outrun, dull effort 7
23May92-8Bel fst 1 :224 :453 1:10 1:35 ⒻAcorn-G1 **94** 6 129¾118 72 32½ 22 Delahoussaye E 121 b 4.30 - - ProspctorsDlit1212 PlsntStg1211½ *TurnbckthAlrm*1215¾ 6 wide turn, rallied 12
1May92-9CD fst 1⅛ :481 1:122 1:38 1:512 ⒻKyOaks-G1 **89** 4 64 66 54 43½ 2½ Delahoussaye E 121 b 3.40 - - *LuvMeLuvMeNot*121½ PlsntStg121½ *ProspctorsDlit*121nk Lugged in, gaining 6
18Apr92-8Kee fst 1 1/16 :23 :464 1:11 1:423 ⒻAshland-G1 **86** 9 1011 99¼ 68 58½ 46½ Delahoussaye E 121 *2.00 - - ProspctorsDlt1212½ SpnnngRond1211 *LvMLvMNt*1213 Middle move, hung 10
8Mar92-8SA fst 1 1/16 :232 :464 1:11 1:431 ⒻSAOaks-G1 **87** 3 77¾ 67½ 75 44 41¾ Delahoussaye E **B**117 *1.90 - - GoldenTrt117no MgicIMidn1171 QunsCourtQun117¾ 3 wide turn mild rally 8
2Nov91-3CD fst 1 1/16 :234 :474 1:124 1:462 ⒻBCJuvFil-G1 – 14 127¼106 116 44½ 1hd Delahoussaye E **B**119 5.80 - - Pleasant Stage119hd *La Spia*1192½ CadillacWomen119nk Trailed,up in time 14
14Oct91-8SA fst 1 1/16 :231 :464 1:112 1:432 ⒻOakLeaf-G2 – 2 56¾ 56 42½ 31 12 Delahoussaye E **B**116 6.50 - - *Pleasant Stage*1162 SovietSojourn1163 LaSpia1155½ Angled out,ridden out 5
6Sep91-6Dmr fst 1 :224 :463 1:113 1:37 ⒻMd Sp Wt 31k – 6 56 55 56 22½ 22 Delahoussaye E **B**116 *1.70 - - QueensCourtQuen1162 *PlsntStg*1169 IllustriousLdy1163½ 3 wide, hung late 7
18Aug91-4Dmr fst 6f :22 :451 :574 1:103 ⒻMd Sp Wt 30k – 1 8 88¾ 68½ 58 36 Ortega L E **B**117 33.50 - - *Captivant*1175½ Praslin117½ Pleasant Stage1172 Off slowly, late rally 8

Pleasant Tap

b. c. 1987, by Pleasant Colony (His Majesty)–Never Knock, by Stage Door Johnny

Lifetime record: 32 9 9 5 $2,721,169

Own.– Buckland Farm
Br.– T.M. Evans (Va)
Tr.– Christopher Speckert

31Oct92-10GP fst 1¼ :454 1:10 1:35 2:001 3↑ BC Classic-G1 111 13 11 106½ 96¼ 31½ 22 Stevens GL 126 2.50 98-03 A.P. Indy1212Pleasant Tap126½Jolypha1181½ Finished well 14
10Oct92-8Bel gd 1¼ :461 1:10 1:35 1:584 3↑ J C Gold Cup-G1 117 6 5 57½ 2hd 12½ 14½ Stevens GL 126 3.40 97-04 PleasantTap1264½StrikthGold1262¼A.P.Indy121½ Going away 7
19Sep92-8Bel fst 1⅛ :463 1:102 1:344 1:47 3↑ Woodward-G1 112 6 4 54 64 42 21¾ Delahoussaye E 126 1.90 92-06 SultrySong1261¾PleasantTap126hdOutofPlc126no Up for 2nd 8
18Jly92-8Bel fst 1¼ :46 1:102 1:352 2:001 3↑ Suburban H-G1 112 2 5 39 32 1hd 11½ Delahoussaye E 119 2.00 90-16 Pleasant Tap1191½Strike the Gold1191¼Defensive Play1155 7
Ducked out,driving
6Jun92-7Bel my 1⅛ :444 1:082 1:334 1:463 3↑ Nassau County H-G2 111 7 8 814 75¼ 51½ 2nk Delahoussaye E 119 5.30 96-08 Strike the Gold116nkPleasant Tap1191½Sultry Song1112¾ 9
Sted,blocked turn
25May92-8Bel fst 1 :222 :444 1:082 1:333 3↑ Metropolitan H-G1 107 10 11 117¼ 87 43 22¼ Delahoussaye E 119 6.70 100-05 DixieBrass1072¼PlesntTp1191¾InExcss121nk Rallied,inside 11
2May92-7CD fst 7f :224 :452 1:094 1:221 4↑ Chl Downs H-G3 104 5 6 82½ 73½ 42 1no Delhoussaye E **B** 120 *.80 99-02 PleasntTap120noTakMOut1202CntrllRod113¾ Brsh wire drvg 9
12Apr92-8Kee fst 7f :222 :451 1:094 1:222 3↑ Cmwlth BC-G3 105 3 6 66½ 64½ 2hd 12½ Delhoussaye E **B** 116 *.90 97-12 PleasntTap1162½ToFreedom115noRunontheBank118½ Driving 6
20Feb92-8SA fst 6f :22 :443 :562 1:084 4↑ Alw 50000 100 3 4 54 55½ 54 21¼● Delhoussaye E **B** 121 *1.80 91-16 Rushmore1151¼DHValiantPete117DHPleasntTap121½ Rallied 5
11Jan92-8SA fst 7f :221 :441 1:082 1:211 4↑ San Carlos H-G2 93 1 6 711 710 69 66¼ Delhoussaye E **B** 119 b *1.90 91-11 AnswerDo1201½Individualist115hdMedPln1162½ Broke slowly 7
30Nov91-8Hol fm 1⅛Ⓣ :472 1:111 1:342 1:454 3↑ Citation H (Div 2)-G2 - 3 6 76½ 73½ 74¼ 85¾ Flores DR 116 b 20.40 95-07 Fly Till Dawn1191¾Best Pal119nkWolf1191 No mishap 8
Run in divisions
2Nov91-2CD fst 6f :21 :442 1:091 3↑ BC Sprint-G1 - 7 8 1113 1110 63¼ 23 Delhoussaye E **B** 126 b 8.80 98-02 Sheikh Albadou1243Pleasant Tap126½Robyn Dancer126nk 11
8-wide stretch,lugged in
12Oct91-8SA fst 1⅛ :47 1:103 1:343 1:474 3↑ Goodwood H-G2 - 2 5 53 43½ 45 34½ Pincay L Jr **B** 117 b 3.70 86-15 The Prime Minister115noMarquetry1194½Pleasant Tap1173½ 6
5-wide stretch
7Sep91-3Dmr fst 6½f :224 :452 1:10 1:161 3↑ Alw 50000 - 5 3 41¾ 42 21½ 11¾ Solis A **B** 121 b 2.80 87-15 PleasntTap1211¾DMediaPlan1171½AsktheMn115nk Wide trip 5
30Mar91-8SA fst 1⅛ :461 1:10 1:342 1:47 4↑ San Bernardino H-G2 - 9 8 75¼ 62¾ 54½ 34 Solis A **B** 116 b 5.80 91-07 Anshan115noLouis Cyphre1124Pleasant Tap116no Wide trip 9
9Mar91-5SA fst 1¼ :46 1:101 1:344 2:001 4↑ S Anita H-G1 - 6 9 98½ 43 23½ 33½ Solis A **B** 115 b 36.20 89-10 Farma Way1202¾Festin115¾Pleasant Tap1155½ 4-wide ⅞ 10
10Feb91-8SA fst 1¼ :461 1:102 1:344 2:004 C H Strub-G1 - 1 7 77 77¾ 67¾ 56¼ Delhoussaye E **B** 116 b 5.30 84-10 DefnsvPly122hdMyBoyAdm1171¼InExcss1214½ Ducked in early 7
19Jan91-8SA fst 1⅛ :462 1:101 1:341 1:463 San Fernando-G2 - 7 9 88 83¾ 67 510 Solis A **B** 120 b 3.10 87-09 In Excess1264Warcraft1202¾Go and Go1231¼ Wide trip 9
26Dec90-8SA fst 7f :22 :441 1:083 1:213 Malibu-G2 - 7 9 1012 99¼ 54½ 11¼ Solis A **B** 117 b 3.70 95-10 PleasntTap1171¼Bedevld1201½DutothKng1171¼ Broke slowly 10
1Dec90-8Hol fst 1⅛ :464 1:103 1:351 1:472 3↑ Native Diver H-G3 - 3 6 66½ 55½ 32½ 2no Solis A **B** 115 b 6.30 97-09 Warcraft117noPleasntTap115nkGoandGo1151¼ Bumped start 7
27Oct90-8Bel gd 1½Ⓣ :494 1:153 2:041 2:293 3↑ BC Turf-G1 - 1 5 74½ 96½ 911 815¾ Bailey JD 121 b 10.40 66-15 IntheWings126½WithApprovl1261½ElSnor1262½ Saved ground 11
4Oct90-8Bel fst 1 1/16 :232 :462 1:104 1:421 3↑ Alw 50000 - 8 4 31½ 1½ 11½ 13¼ Cordero A Jr 113 b 2.60 91-18 PleasantTap1133¼OutofPlace1122IndianToss1154 Drew clear 8
21Sep90-9Med fst 1⅛ :462 1:093 1:343 1:471 Pegasus H-G1 - 6 2 21½ 32½ 64½ 710½ Desormeaux KJ 115 b 7.70 88-01 SilverEnding1192MusicProspectr116½RunwyStrm1131½ Tired 12
5May90-8CD gd 1¼ :46 1:11 1:373 2:02 Ky Derby-G1 - 9 12 1113 44 36 39½ Desormeaux KJ 126 b 40.70 91-00 Unbridled1263½SummerSquall1266PlesntTp1263 In close st. 15
24Apr90-8Kee fst 1 1/16 :231 :464 1:111 1:432 Lexington-G2 - 9 7 63 51¼ 31½ 22 Desormeaux KJ 115 b 11.40 87-11 Home at Last1182Pleasant Tap1155Thirty Slews1162½ 9
Lacked room 5/16 pole

18Mar90- 8SA	fst 1 1/16	:224 :463 1:11 1:42	San Felipe H-G2	-	11 10 96¼ 107½ 99¼	614¾	Delahoussaye E	119 b	*2.70	78-16	RealCash113⁵½Warcrft117¾MuscProspctr117³	Never menaced	12
4Feb90- 9SA	gd 1	:223 :463 1:113 1:38	Alw 37000	-	4 8 43 33 3½	11¼	Delahoussaye E	118 b	*1.00	77-18	PleasantTap1181¼T.V.Rebel118¾VideoRanger116no	Driving	10
25Nov89- 8Hol	fm 1 Ⓣ	:232 :473 1:112 1:353	Hoist the Flag-G2	-	10 6 2½ 2hd 1hd	2no	Delahoussaye E	118 b	4.50	86-13	Single Dawn114noPleasant Tap1182¾Doyouseewhatisee121nk		12
	Rough start												
4Nov89- 8GP	fst 1 1/16	:232 :464 1:111 1:433	BC Juvenile-G1	-	1 12 1211 127¼ 88¼	66½	Delahoussaye E	122	11.30	86-01	Rhythm1222Grand Canyon1221¾Slavic1221	Without speed	12
4Oct89- 8SA	fst 7f	:221 :444 1:10 1:222	Sunny Slope 80k	-	6 6 711 710 31	1¾	Delahoussaye E	116	12.40	88-15	PleasntTp116¾GrandCanyon1154Doyouseewhats1196	Driving	7
9Sep89- 6Dmr	fst 6f	:22 :452 :572 1:091	Md Sp Wt	-	9 6 65½ 63¼ 44	34½	Baze RA	117	19.70	88-11	GrandCanyn1172½JetWest1171¾PleasntTp1174	Troubled trip	9
19Aug89- 4Dmr	fst 6f	:221 :451 :571 1:093	Md Sp Wt	-	2 7 715 715 714	69¾	Delahoussaye E	117	22.00	80-14	Social Jokes117½Profit Key117³Silver Ending117no	Outrun	7

Possibly Perfect

Own: Blue Vista Inc

B. m. 5 (May)
Sire: Northern Baby (Northern Dancer)
Dam: Avasand (Avatar)
Br: Mr. & Mrs. Robert Witt (Ky)
Tr: Frankel Robert J

Life	18	11	2	4	$1,377,634	105	D.Fst	0	0	0	0	$0	-
1995	6	5	1	0	$743,100	105	Wet(309)	0	0	0	0	$0	-
1994	3	2	0	1	$228,800	103	Turf(304)	18	11	2	4	$1,377,634	105
	0	0	0	0	$0	-	Dst(0)	0	0	0	0	$0	-

26Aug95- 6AP	fm 1 3/16 Ⓣ	:484 1:13 1:372 1:544	3↑ⒻBeverlyD-G1	105	7 3½ 2½ 2½ 1hd	1¾	Nakatani C S	123	*.70	- -	Possibly Perfect123¾ Alice Springs123no *Alpride*123hd	Wore down rivals	7
5Aug95- 8Dmr	fm 1⅛ Ⓣ	:491 1:132 1:373 1:494	3↑ⒻRamonaH-G1	104	6 21 31 21 21½	11¼	Nakatani C S	B123	*1.20	- -	*Possibly Perfect*1231¼ *Morgana*115hd Yearly Tour116hd	Late surge, driving	7
2Jly95- 9Hol	fm 1⅛ Ⓣ	:471 1:101 1:342 1:463	3↑ⒻBevHilsH-G1	104	5 4½ 42¼ 42 2½	21¾	Desormeaux K J	B124	*.70	- -	Alpride1151¾ *Possibly Perfect*1241 Wandesta1196½	Bid 1/8, flattened	6
4Jun95- 9Hol	fm 1⅛ Ⓣ	:472 1:112 1:344 1:464	3↑ⒻGamelyH-G1	103	5 1hd 11½ 1½ 12	11¾	Desormeaux K J	B123	*.50	91- 12	PssblyPrfct1231¾ LdAffrmd1141 *DntRdMLps*1141¾	Controlled pace,drivng	6
14May95- 9Hol	fm 1 1/16 Ⓣ	:234 :473 1:103 1:401	3↑ⒻWilshirH-G2	103	5 1½ 1½ 2hd 1½	11¾	Desormeaux K J	B121	*.50	- -	*PossiblyPerfect*1211¾ Morgn116½ AubeIndienne1193½	Fast pace,drew clear	5
2Apr95- 7SA	fm 1 Ⓣ	:232 :481 1:12 1:36	4↑ⒻAlw 60000N$MY	102	3 2½ 31 2½ 13	1½	Nakatani C S	B115	*.90	- -	*PossiblyPerfect*115½ FantasticKim1171¾ Wende115½	Quick gain, ridden out	7
10Apr94- 8SA	fm 1¼ Ⓣ	:472 1:114 1:36 2:002	4↑ⒻSntBrbrH-G1	103	5 22 1½ 1½ 12	1½	Desormeaux K J	B121	*.70	- -	*Possibly Perfect*121½ Pracer1152¾ Waitryst114½	Clear lead 1/8,all out	5
19Mar94- 8SA	yl 1⅛ Ⓣ	:501 1:142 1:382 1:51	4↑ⒻSntaAnaH-G1	103	7 11½ 11 1½ 12	11¾	Desormeaux K J	B119	2.30	- -	*PossiblyPerfct*1191¾ HrosLov1201½ DWitryst115hd	Well rated,held gamely	7
27Feb94- 8SA	fm 1 Ⓣ	:231 :47 1:102 1:344	4↑ⒻBnaVstaH-G3	98	3 32 2½ 3½ 3½	42	Desormeaux K J	B120	*1.30	- -	DLady Blessington119no Skimble1181½ Hero's Love121½	Bid 3w 1/8,empty	9
	Placed third through disqualification												
14Nov93- 8SA	fm 1¼ Ⓣ	:50 1:144 1:382 2:024	3↑ⒻYlwRibIn-G1	101	11 11 1½ 1hd 11½	11¼	Nakatani C S	B118	16.60	- -	PossiblyPerfct1181¼ Tribultion118hd Mituschk122no	Slow pace,well rated	13
30Oct93- 8Kee	yl 1⅛ Ⓣ	:484 1:134 1:403 1:533	ⒻQEIICup-G1	93	5 2½ 21 42½ 21½	32½	Day P	121	2.40	- -	Tribulation1212 MiamiSands121½ *PossiblyPerfect*1213	Boxed, hung stretch	9
2Oct93-11LaD	fm 1 1/16 Ⓣ	:231 :484 1:14 1:444	ⒻDeBartOaks100k	92	4 65 64 62¾ 11	13½	Desormeaux K J	119	*.70	- -	Possibly Perfect1193½ Lady Tasso116½ She's a Little Shy114½	Driving	11
22Aug93- 8Dmr	fm 1⅛ Ⓣ	:472 1:114 1:362 1:481	ⒻDMrIvOks-G2	100	2 11½ 1½ 1½ 11	21	Desormeaux K J	B120	7.20	- -	*HollywoodWldct*1201 *PossblyPrfct*1201¾ *MmSnds*120nk	Led late, outfinished	10
25Jly93- 8Hol	fm 1 1/16 Ⓣ	:232 :461 1:103 1:413	Alw 39000N2L	94	1 22½ 27 22 11½	11¼	Desormeaux K J	B114 b	2.30	- -	Possibly Perfect1141¼ Capel1172 Minjinsky1172¾	Swerved str,drew clear	7
23Jun93- 5Hol	fm 1⅛ Ⓣ	:471 1:111 1:354 1:483	3↑ⒻMd Sp Wt 34k	82	1 3½ 3½ 1½ 13	13½	Desormeaux K J	B115	3.40	- -	*PossiblyPerfect*1153½ StrltMinistr115no *IndioRos*1151¼	Drew off, ridden out	10
	Previously trained by Antonio Spanu												
8Oct92	Evry (Fr) sf *1 Ⓣ LH		ⒻPrix de Saint-Eutrope 29100			51¼	Asmussen	128	-		Hawk Beauty128hd Nakama125¾ Kiruna128½	*Led for 7 furlongs, met challenge gamely, faded near line*	12
21Sep92	Maisons-Laffitte (Fr) sf *1 Ⓣ RH		ⒻPrix Sauge Pourpree 35500			31¼	Jarnet	128	-		Dancienne128½ Mariemma128¾ Possibly Perfect1281½	*Close up in 4th, bid for lead 1-1/2f out, no late foot*	13
3Jly92	Maisons-Laffitte (Fr) sf *6f Ⓣ Str		ⒻPrix de la Marne 32800			32¼	Asmussen	128	-		Myza1281½ Quelle Affaire128¾ Possibly Perfect128½	*Raced in 7th, 4th on rail 1f out, angled out, no further response*	11

Prairie Bayou

Own: Loblolly Stable

Ch. g. 3 (Mar)
Sire: Little Missouri (Cox's Ridge)
Dam: Whiffling (Wavering Monarch)
Br: Loblolly Stable (Ky)
Tr: Bohannan Thomas K

Life	12	7	3	0	$1,450,621	101	D.Fst	9	7	1	0	$1,429,005	101
1993	8	5	2	0	$1,405,521	101	Wet(293)	3	0	2	0	$21,616	90
1992	4	2	1	0	$45,100	85	Turf(178)	0	0	0	0	$0	-
	0	0	0	0	$0	-	Dst(0)	0	0	0	0	$0	-

5Jun93- 9Bel	gd 1½	:484 1:134 2:294	Belmont-G1	-	5 108 - - -	-	Smith M E	126	*2.70	- -	Colonial Affair1262¼ *Kissin Kris*126¾ Wild Gale1262	Broke down	13
15May93-10Pim	fst 1 3/16	:464 1:111 1:37 1:563	Preaknes-G1	98	3 109¾ 97¾ 85¼ 1hd	1½	Smith M E	126	*2.20	- -	PrairieBayou126½ CherokeeRun1267 ElBakn126nk	Angled 5-wide, driving	12
1May93- 8CD	fst 1¼	:463 1:111 1:364 2:022	KyDerby-G1	101	5 1612 168¼ 65 44	22½	Smith M E	126	*4.40	- -	Sea Hero1262½ *Prairie Bayou*126hd Wild Gale126nk	Circled, 6 wide	19
10Apr93- 8Kee	fst 1⅛	:481 1:121 1:37 1:493	BlueGras-G2	96	8 88½ 810 86¾ 2hd	12	Smith M E	121	3.70	- -	Prairie Bayou1212 Wallenda121no Dixieland Heat121¾	Circled 5 wide	9
27Mar93-11TP	fst 1⅛	:472 1:113 1:372 1:504	JimBeam-G2	98	1 811 78½ 53¾ 12	1¾	McCarron C J	121	*1.20	- -	*PrairieByou*121¾ ProudestRomeo1212 *MinersMrk*1215	Circled field, driving	9
20Feb93- 8Aqu	fst 1 1/16 ⊡	:24 :483 1:131 1:451	WhirlawyBC110k	99	4 55½ 2½ 2hd 1hd	13	Smith M E	117	*.40	- -	*Prairie Bayou*1173 Rohwer1143 Slews Gold1147	Dueled, driving	5
24Jan93- 8Aqu	fst 170 ⊡	:243 :48 1:122 1:424	CountFltG368k	93	1 56 54¾ 32 1½	13	Smith M E	117	*.90	- -	*Prairie Bayou*1173 Slews Gold1175½ *Rohwer*1175	Drew off, driving	6
13Jan93- 8Aqu	sly 170 ⊡	:24 :493 1:142 1:433	PRicco52k	90	2 46½ 45 44 22	21¼	Smith M E	117	*1.30	- -	Bert'sBubbleator1171¼ *PrairieBayou*1171 ClassiEnvoy11716	Late inside bid	4
20Dec92-10Lrl	my 1⅛	:484 1:134 1:393 1:524	InnerHarbr50k	84	6 88½ 87¼ 62¾ 2hd	2no	Velazquez J R	122	*1.50e	- -	Jorge of Mexico113no Prairie Bayou1223½ Ozan113¾	5 wide just missed	9
	Previously trained by Reinstedler Anthony 1992(as of 11/18): (137 29 29 21 0.21)												
18Nov92- 7CD	fst 1 1/16	:24 :474 1:132 1:45	Alw 28700NC	85	9 99 109½ 86¾ 1½	13	Bartram B E	B121	*2.40	- -	PrairieBayou1213 EnchntingFuture1184 ColonilMiner1214	Much the best	11
10Nov92- 4CD	fst 1 1/16	:241 :482 1:143 1:461	Md Sp Wt 25k	79	6 1110 911 53 11	11½	Bartram B E	B119	6.60	- -	*Prairie Bayou*1191½ *Union City*1193 Waxahachie1197	Circled field, driving	11
14Oct92- 5Kee	fst 7f	:222 :46 1:112 1:234	Md Sp Wt 18k	61	9 2 86 95¼ 911	710	Miller D A Jr	B119	8.10	- -	TurnOfftheLites1194 CountryEldr119¾ ChrmdHlo119no	Failed to menace	12

Queena

b. f. 1986, by Mr. Prospector (Raise a Native)–Too Chic, by Blushing Groom

Lifetime record: 17 10 2 1 $565,024

Own.– Emory A. Hamiton
Br.– Emory Alexander (Ky)
Tr.– Claude McGaughey III

2Nov91- 4CD	fst 1⅛	:471 1:114 1:374 1:504	3↑ ⒻBC Distaff-G1	13 11 1214 118¼ 85¾	55	Smith ME	123	5.70	89-09	DanceSmrtly1201½VersaillesTreaty1202¾Brought toMind123½		13
	Broke slowly,7-wide into stretch											
21Sep91- 8Bel	fst 1 1/16	:233 :462 1:103 1:413	3↑ ⒻRuffian H-G1	6 5 53½ 31 2½	1½	Cordero A Jr	120	2.10	94-14	Qna120½SharpDance1141½LadyD'Accord113nk	Wide,driving	7
1Sep91- 8Bel	fst 1	:232 :462 1:101 1:344	3↑ ⒻMaskette-G1	6 3 31½ 31½ 21	1hd	Cordero A Jr	123	3.70	96-07	Queena123hdFittoScout123nkScreenProspect1167½	Wide drv	6
4Aug91- 8Sar	fst 7f	:214 :441 1:084 1:22	3↑ ⒻBallerina-G1	3 6 53 43½ 42½	1hd	Smith ME	119	3.00	95-08	Queena119hdMssy'sMrge1112DremTouch1103½	Blocked turn	9
23Jun91- 8Bel	fst 7f	:221 :45 1:091 1:22	3↑ ⒻVagrancy H-G3	7 3 41 2½ 1½	1no	Smith ME	115	*.90	94-07	Queena115noMissy's Mirage1091½Gottagetitdone1112	Driving	10
20May91- 8Bel	fst 7f	:224 :46 1:11 1:241	3↑ ⒻAlw 41000	2 3 1½ 22 1hd	13	Smith ME	119	1.80	83-16	Queena1193Dreamy Mimi1192Token Dance119nk	Going away	5
12Feb91- 9GP	fst 6f	:221 :453	1:101 4↑ ⒻAlw 21000	9 4 37 42½ 32½	32¼	Bailey JD	120	1.90	92-12	Avie Jane1152Ivory Princess115nkQueena1203½	Hung	9
	Previously raced under name of Emory Alexander											
17Jan91- 9GP	gd 6f	:22 :454	1:113 3↑ ⒻFirst Lady H 50k	8 2 53½ 54 54½	52½	Bailey JD	115	3.70	84-22	Spirit of Fighter1182Mistaurian115hdLove's Exchange128hd		9
	Bumped,gaining											
22Nov90- 9Lrl	fst 7f	:232 :463 1:104 1:231	3↑ ⒻStraight Deal H 100k	4 10 21½ 21½ 21½	2½	Smith ME	116	*.90	90-14	Iceycindy113½Queena1163½Thirty Eight Go Go114hd	Hung	10
21Oct90- 9Bel	fst 7f	:222 :444 1:091 1:222	3↑ ⒻFirst Flight H-G2	1 5 3½ 42¾ 3½	12½	Bailey JD	113	5.90	92-18	Queena1132½QuckMischief115¾APennyIsaPnny1222½	Driving	5
22Sep90- 9Med	sly 6f	:213 :442	1:091 3↑ ⒻBud BC-G3	4 6 57¼ 44½ 54½	54½	Smith ME	113	9.10	91-12	SafelyKpt127nkSxySlw1151¾Dv'sDbut1202½	Lacked response	7
23Aug90- 7Sar	fst 7f	:231 :463 1:102 1:224	3↑ ⒻAlw 30000	3 4 1hd 1½ 1½	1nk	Smith ME	119	2.30	91-16	Queena119nkAishah1142¾Moon Drone1124	Long drive	6
4Aug90- 6Sar	fst 6f	:223 :46	1:101 3↑ ⒻAlw 28000	6 2 32 3½ 2hd	1½	Smith ME	114	*1.20	93-04	Queena114½Rumgumption1124LovlyHrss114¾	Strong handling	10
9Jly90- 1Bel	fst 7f	:23 :47	1:114 1:244 3↑ ⒻAlw 27000	1 3 1½ 11 11½	12	Smith ME	122	2.60	80-20	Queena1222Mime113½Unite and Conquer1176	Hand ride	6
21Jun90- 7Bel	fst 6f	:224 :464	1:121 3↑ ⒻMd Sp Wt	5 3 2hd 1½ 13	16	Smith ME	122	*.90e	78-22	Queena1226Timetocheckin1144By Descent1141¼	Brisk urging	9
30Apr90- 4Aqu	my 7f	:23 :471 1:13 1:263	3↑ ⒻMd Sp Wt	2 6 53½ 42½ 44½	43½	Smith ME	124	*.90	65-26	DancinBaba115noIncaLegacy1151½GabrlIP.1152	Lacked rally	7
31Mar90- 1Aqu	sly 6f	:214 :452	1:112 4↑ ⒻMd Sp Wt	1 6 45 45½ 33	22¼	Smith ME	122	4.00	81-18	JustBeLucky1222¼Queena1222FullTill1153	Steadied,green	8

Real Quiet

Own: Pegram Michael E

B. c. 4 (Mar) KEESEP96 $17,000
Sire: Quiet American (Fappiano) $35,000
Dam: Really Blue (Believe It)
Br: Little Hill Farm (Ky)
Tr: Baffert Bob

Life	20	6	5	6	$3,271,802	115	D.Fst	18	6	5	5	$3,268,462	115
1999	5	2	2	1	$1,101,880	115	Wet(364)	2	0	0	1	$3,340	74
1998	6	2	3	0	$1,788,800	111	Turf(248)	0	0	0	0	$0	–
	0	0	0	0	$0	–	Dst(0)	0	0	0	0	$0	–

27Jun99-5Hol	fst	1¼	:47 1:102 1:342 1:593	3↑HolGldCp-G1	115	2	42	41½	41½	31½	1½	Bailey J D	LB124 b	*.90	97-03	Real Quiet124½ Budroyale124nk *Malek*1247	Trapped rail 2nd turn	4
29May99-13Suf	fst	1⅛	:472 1:11 1:36 1:49	3↑MassH-G2	112	2	2½	21	3½	32	33¼	Stevens G L	LB121 b	*.80	88-16	*Behrens*118½ *Running Stag*1132¾ *Real Quiet*1214½	3p, bid 2nd, weakened	6
8May99-6Pim	fst	1 3/16	:47 1:111 1:36 1:541	3↑PimSpclH-G1	113	5	34	32½	33	2hd	1nk	Stevens G L	L120 b	1.90	94-19	RealQuiet120nk FreeHouse1245 FredBearClw1132	Aim 3w,dueled,long drv	5
18Apr99-7LS	fst	1	:24 :471 1:111 1:353	3↑TexsMile-G3	110	5	43½	34½	1½	2½	2nk	Stevens G L	L116 b	*.50	94-15	Littlebitlively116nk *Real Quiet*1161¾ Allen's Oop1134¾	Outfinished	8
7Mar99-8FG	fst	1⅛	:483 1:124 1:364 1:49	4↑NwOrlnsH-G3	102	6	31½	21½	21	2½	2½	Desormeaux K J	L122 b	*.50	94-13	Precocity118½ Real Quiet122nk Allen's Oop108¾	3w, 4w, bid, no match	6
6Jun98-9Bel	fst	1½	:483 1:132 2:29	Belmont-G1	110	7	64	31	1½	14	2no	Desormeaux K J	L126 b	*.80	99-09	Victory Gallop126no Real Quiet1266 *Thomas Jo*1261¼	Clear, bumpd missed	11
16May98-10Pim	fst	1 3/16	:462 1:11 1:354 1:543	Preaknss-G1	111	10	85½	69	51¾	1½	12¼	Desormeaux K J	L126 b	2.50	92-13	Real Quiet1262¼ *Victory Gallop*126¾ Classic Cat1263¾	4-6wd trip,lug in,drvg	10
2May98-8CD	fst	1¼	:453 1:103 1:353 2:021	KyDerby-G1	107	3	68	65¾	11	11½	1½	Desormeaux K J	L126 b	8.40	94-02	*Real Quiet*126½ Victory Gallop1262¼ Indian Charlie126hd	Led mile, lasted	15
4Apr98-5SA	fst	1⅛	:46 1:094 1:342 1:47	SADerby-G1	107	7	66	56½	45	23	22¼	Desormeaux K J	LB120 b	3.00	99-05	Indian Charlie1202¼ *Real Quiet*1207 Artax1206	Slowly gaining	7
14Mar98-8SA	fst	1 1/16	:224 :464 1:104 1:413	SnFelipe-G2	108	5	32½	33	2½	21	2hd	Desormeaux K J	LB119 b	4.10	95-11	Artax122hd Real Quiet1197 Prosperous Bid1166	Gaining late stretch	5
18Jan98-7GG	sly	1 1/16	:222 :461 1:104 1:431	GGDerby200k	59	7	76½	55½	65¾	812	822½	Desormeaux K J	LB120 b	*1.10	63-19	CloverHunter1206½ MantlesStar1201½ AllensOop1204	Gave way btwn foes	8
14Dec97-7Hol	fst	1 1/16	:223 :454 1:101 1:411	HolFut-G1	102	2	42½	41¾	21½	1hd	11	Desormeaux K J	LB121 b	*1.50e	95-11	Real Quiet1211 Artax1211¾ Nationalore1211	Fully extended	11
29Nov97-11CD	fst	1 1/16	:232 :47 1:12 1:434	B&WKyJC-G3	93	6	106½	86¾	62¾	55½	31¾	Flores D R	L116 b	12.40	90-09	*Cape Town*113½ *Time Limit*1191¼ *Real Quiet*1161½	Late bid finished well	11
18Oct97-3SA	fst	1 1/16	:232 :472 1:122 1:441	Md Sp Wt 35k	87	7	63	51½	42	2½	13	Desormeaux K J	LB120 b	1.60	82-19	Real Quiet1203 Opine1207 Sydney Harbour1205	Wide early,strng finsh	7
5Sep97-6Dmr	fst	1	:221 :454 1:104 1:363	Md Sp Wt 39k	78	7	66	78½	55	33½	48	Stevens S A	LB118 f	2.20e	79-13	Old Trieste1182½ *Johnbill*1185½ Just Ruler118no	Mild rally	9
24Aug97-8Sfe	fst	7f	:221 :444 1:10 1:234	IndnNtFtCp571k	68	2	8	95	65¼	34	32¾	Stevens S A	L120 f	4.60	86-12	Grady120nk *General Gem*1202½ Real Quiet1202½	Gaining	12
8Aug97-8Sfe	fst	7f	:22 :442 1:10 1:234	[R]Alw 10000NC	54	1	9	2hd	2hd	25	37½	Stevens S A	L120 f	2.10	81-15	General Gem1207 Thatsaknife120½ Real Quiet1205	Empty	10
19Jly97-7Hol	fst	5½f	:221 :443 :562 1:023	Md Sp Wt 34k	75	4	4	3nk	32	34	36½	Flores D R	LB118	2.30	93-08	MeadowPrayer1184½ KonaWind1132 RelQuiet11813	Lacked late response	6
29Jun97-1CD	my	6f	:212 :451 :572 1:10	Md Sp Wt 41k	74	1	5	34	44½	37	38½	Steiner J J	L118 f	10.70	84-09	*PolishedBrass*1181½ *TropicLightning*1187 RelQuiet1185	Chased pace evenly	10
15Jun97-1CD	fst	5f	:22 :451 :574	Md Sp Wt 36k	57	1	3	45½	48	612	710	Steiner J J	L119 f	5.00	89-12	Dice Dancer1191 *Polished Brass*1195 Da Devil1192½	Close up, faded inside	11

Reraise

Own: Fey,Class Racing Stable, Opas, et al

B. g. 5 (Apr)
Sire: Danzatore (Northern Dancer) $3,000
Dam: Get Us to Paris (Policeman*Fr)
Br: Willard Sergent (Ky)
Tr: Dollase Craig

Life	9	8	1	0	$922,830	119	D.Fst	8	7	1	0	$862,830	119
2000	1	1	0	0	$31,200	103	Wet(279)	1	1	0	0	$60,000	105
1999	2	2	0	0	$135,000	109	Turf(230)	0	0	0	0	$0	–
	0	0	0	0	$0	–	Dst(0)	0	0	0	0	$0	–

12Nov00-3Hol	fst	6f	:22 :444 :57 1:093	3↑Alw 53560N$Y	103	1	3	1hd	11½	11½	11½	Nakatani C S	LB117	*.30	89-15	Rerise1171½ TheMorrisMonro121no SonofPistol1231	Dueled,clear,driving	4
2May99-3GG	gd	6f	:222 :444 :562 1:083	3↑OaklandH98k	105	1	3	11	12½	12½	12½	Nakatani C S	LB125	*.10	97-12	*Reraise*1252½ Early Pioneer113hd Saylo115½	Won as pleased	4
8Apr99-9OP	fst	6f	:21 :434 :554 1:082	4↑CtFltSpH-G3	109	1	4	1hd	1½	13½	12¾	Nakatani C S	L122	*.30	102-12	*Reraise*1222¾ Run Johnny1141¾ E J Harley1151¼	Quick pace, ridden out	6
7Nov98-6CD	fst	6f	:21 :441 :561 1:09	3↑BCSprnt-G1	112	3	3	1½	11	12½	12	Nakatani C S	L124	3.80	98-03	*Reraise*1242 Grand Slam124hd *Kona Gold*1261	Drew clear, driving	14
26Sep98-8TP	fst	6f	:212 :441 :561 1:082	KyCpSpnt-G2	119	1	7	1½	11½	18	112	Nakatani C S	L116	*.70	99-13	*Reraise*11612 Copelan Too114nk Mr Bert1144	Off inside, ridden out	7
20Aug98-6Dmr	fst	7f	:22 :441 1:092 1:221	3↑OC 80k/N$Y -N	93	4	4	11½	11½	11	24½	Delahoussaye E	LB116 b	*.70	84-14	Young At Heart1174½ *Reraise*1162 *Zede*117½	Speed, no match late	5
4Jly98-3Hol	fst	6f	:22 :441 :56 1:082	PlayaDlRey68k	115	6	1	1½	1hd	1½	16	Delahoussaye E	LB116 b	*1.00	95-14	Reraise1166 SouvenirCopy122½ *FullMoonMadness*1183½	Drew clear, driving	6
27May98-7Hol	fst	6f	:221 :45 :571 1:092	3↑Alw 42000N$Y	105	2	4	11½	1hd	1½	13	Delahoussaye E	LB116 b	*1.30	90-18	*Reraise*1163 *Shot Md*1145 Wayne's Choice1163½	Pulled clear, driving	5
Previously trained by Matlow Richard P 1997(as of 10/29): (30 3 3 1 0.10)																		
29Oct97-2SA	fst	6f	:214 :45 :573 1:10	Md 62500(62.5-55)	94	6	7	64½	63½	41¾	12	Delahoussaye E	LB120	6.20	88-16	*Reraise*1202 Lucky Sandman1203 Truely Yours1206	Drew clear, 6 wide	9

Rubiano

ro. c. 1987, by Fappiano (Mr. Prospector)–Ruby Slippers, by Nijinsky II

Lifetime record: 28 13 6 1 $1,273,457

Own.– Centennial Farm
Br.– Third Kirsmith Racing Associates (Va)
Tr.– Flint S. Schulhofer

31Oct92-4GP	fst 6f	:213 :433 :553 1:081	3↑BC Sprint-G1	102	10	1	116¼	85¾	56	33¼	Krone JA	126	*2.10	99-00	Thirty Slews126nk Meafara1203 Rubiano126no	Fin. well	14
3Oct92-6Bel	fst 7f	:223 :452 1:10 1:224	3↑Vosburgh-G1	113	4	4	71¾	31½	31½	1¾	Krone JA	126	*1.60e	90-17	Rubiano126¾ Sheikh Albadou1261¼ Salt Lake1234¼		8
	Blocked,altered course																
16Aug92-8Sar	my 7f	:221 :451 1:10 1:222	3↑Forego H-G2	110	6	1	74¼	52½	2hd	13¼	Krone JA	124	*1.00	93-14	Rubiano1243¼ Drummond Lane1151½ Diablo1144	Wide,driving	8
18Jly92-7Bel	fst 7f	:224 :453 1:092 1:213	3↑Tom Fool-G2	108	2	2	54	43	1½	11	Krone JA	126	*1.70	96-12	Rubiano1261 Take Me Out1191½ Arrowtown1191	Driving	8
25May92-8Bel	fst 1	:222 :444 1:082 1:333	3↑Metropolitan H-G1	89	7	8	107	107¼	78	811¼	Santos JA	120	4.10	91-05	Dixie Brass1072¼ Pleasant Tap1191¾ In Excess121nk	Tired	11
2May92-8Aqu	fst 7f	:22 :441 1:081 1:212	3↑Carter H-G1	108	7	3	76	74½	42½	1hd	Santos JA	118	2.90	98-07	Rubiano118hd Kid Russell112½ In Excess1221¾	Wide driving	9
22Mar92-8Aqu	fst 1	:24 :47 1:103 1:344	3↑Westchester H-G3	107	4	2	2½	2½	11	1no	Santos JA	117	*1.20	88-25	Rubiano117no Out of Place1152 Wild Away1112	All out	6
26Oct91-8Aqu	fst 1	:223 :444 1:083 1:333	3↑NYRA Mile H-G1	-	9	9	104½	104	83¼	1hd	Santos JA	116	5.00	94-08	Rubiano116hd Sultry Song1111 Diablo112nk	Driving	15
2Oct91-8Bel	fst 1	:24 :472 1:11 1:352	3↑Handicap 47000	-	2	4	31	1hd	11½	1no	Santos JA	121	1.80	93-07	Rubiano121no Crackedbell1185 Shots Are Ringing1081¼		5
	Saved ground,driving																
19Sep91-8Bel	fst 1	:233 :462 1:101 1:344	3↑Alw 47000	-	2	4	52½	2½	11	1hd	Santos JA	115	*.90	96-07	Rubino115hd Crckdbll122nk Fftysvnvtt1151¼	Lugged in drive	6
25Aug91-8Sar	fst 7f	:214 :434 1:08 1:21	3↑Forego H-G2	-	5	2	55	64	53¼	43½	Smith ME	116	6.60	96-12	Housebustr126no SenorSpeedy1121 ClvrTrvor1202½	Four wide	6
13Jly91-8Bel	sly 7f	:221 :442 1:083 1:213	3↑Tom Fool-G2	-	2	4	43½	44	23	22½	Bailey JD	121	*.80	93-08	Mr. Nasty1192½ Rubiano1211¼ Senor Speedy11914	2nd best	4
27May91-8Bel	fst 1	:22 :441 1:091 1:352	3↑Metropolitan H-G1	-	13	9	64½	3½	21½	22¼	Bailey JD	111	24.30	91-16	In Excess1172¼ Rubiano1111¾ Gervazy1141½	Rallied wide	14
4May91-8Aqu	fst 7f	:224 :452 1:084 1:211	3↑Carter H-G1	-	4	5	53	42½	46	44¾	Smith ME	113	12.50	91-17	Housebuster1222¼ BlackTiAffr1232½ Grvzy116no	Saved ground	8
29Mar91-8Aqu	gd 1	:231 :46 1:093 1:344	3↑Westchester H-G3	-	2	3	22½	32	21	11¾	Bailey JD	111	7.50	88-17	Rubiano1111¾ Senor Speedy1133 Killer Diller1158¼	Driving	9
2Mar91-10GP	fst 1⅛	:48 1:112 1:354 1:48	3↑Broward H 75k	-	5	7	72¾	54	69	612¾	Castillo H Jr	112	10.90	84-17	ChiefHoncho1164½ NoMarkr1121¼ Barkada1144	Bid,weakened	8
9Feb91-9GP	fst 1⅛	:454 1:102 1:35 1:472	3↑Donn H-G1	-	12	9	98¾	85¼	811	611¼	Santos JA	113	29.50	89-06	Jolie'sHalo1148 SportsView116nk SecretHllo116hd	No threat	12
14Jan91-8GP	fst 1 1/16	:24 :481 1:12 1:432	4↑Alw 25000	-	6	4	44	41	11	11	Bailey JD	112	2.00	96-05	Rubiano1121 Allied Flag1141 Out of Place114nk	Stiff drive	7
3Nov90-8Aqu	fst 1	:223 :453 1:083 1:324	3↑NYRA Mile-G1	-	8	7	62½	1216	1215	1219¼	Santos JA	111	2.70e	79-14	QuietAmricn1164¾ DancingSpre119hd Swckly1242	Done early	12
20Oct90-8Bel	fst 1	:224 :45 1:092 1:353	Jamaica H-G2	-	4	3	31½	11	11½	2nk	Cordero A Jr	112	4.10	91-17	ConfidntialTalk111nk Rbiano112½ SunshinJmmy1142¼	Gamely	7
26Sep90-8Bel	fst 7f	:23 :454 1:092 1:214	3↑Alw 41000	-	2	6	42	41½	41	2nk	Santos JA	113	*1.90	95-12	Six Speed113nk Rubiano113¾ Two Eagles1151¾	Rallied	9
29Aug90-6Bel	fst 6½f	:222 :452 1:101 1:163	3↑Alw 28000	-	6	1	56	44¼	1½	13	Santos JA	113	*2.10	94-14	Rubiano1133 Senor Speedy113hd Dancinwiththedevil1122¼		8
	Saved ground,clear;previously trained by H. Allen Jerkens																
30Jly90-6Bel	fm 1(T)	:23 :454 1:101 1:341	3↑Alw 31000	-	6	6	66½	63½	811	713½	Bailey JD	111 b	*1.90	81-06	GoDtch1123 CommissionrBrt111½ DfnsPolcy117¾	Nothing left	9
20Jly90-6Bel	fst 7f	:221 :45 1:092 1:23	3↑Alw 28000	-	3	4	32	23	27	25	Bailey JD	111 b	2.70	84-19	Carson City1125 Rubiano1118½ Any Minute Man117½	2nd best	6
3Apr90-3GP	fst 7f	:221 :453 1:112 1:25	Alw 19000	-	2	5	2hd	2½	11½	14	Vasquez J	122 b	*.60	81-26	Rubiano1224 Joe's Lad117nk Budd Believes1102½	Drew clear	7
25Mar90-3GP	fst 6f	:213 :444 1:112	Alw 23000	-	1	6	21	22	22½	2½	Smith A Jr	122 b	3.60	87-17	Dr. Jimmy122½ Rubiano122¾ Joe's Lad1179¼	Rallied	6
2Mar90-8GP	fst 7f	:221 :45 1:103 1:24	Alw 19000	-	8	2	3nk	52½	811	812½	Migliore R	122	1.90	73-17	Gervazy122½ HomeatLast122hd ThirtySixRed1222¾	Gave way	10
30Jan90-7GP	fst 6f	:221 :461 1:12	Md Sp Wt	-	2	11	21½	2½	14	14	Migliore R	122	*1.70	85-19	Rubiano1224 FallingSky1225 Thewhlsofjustc122nk	Drew clear	12

Ryafan

Own: Juddmonte Farms Inc

B. f. 3 (Mar)
Sire: Lear Fan (Roberto)
Dam: Carya (Northern Dancer)
Br: Juddmonte Farms (Ky)
Tr: Frankel Robert J

Life	10	7	1	0	$1,342,142	106	D.Fst	0	0	0	0	$0	–
1997	7	5	0	0	$1,135,822	106	Wet(302)	0	0	0	0	$0	–
1996	3	2	1	0	$206,320	–	Turf(379)	10	7	1	0	$1,342,142	106
	0	0	0	0	$0	–	Dst(0)	0	0	0	0	$0	–

30Nov97–6Hol	yl	1¼ Ⓣ	:512 1:162 1:403 2:054	3↑ⒻMatriarc-G1	106	7	21	2½	2½	12	1hd	Solis A	120	*2.00	67– 31	Ryafan120hd *Maxzene*1232¾ Yokama123no	Just lasted, driving	8
Previously trained by Gosden John H M 1997(as of 11/2): (3 2 0 0 0.67)																		
2Nov97–7SA	fm	1¼ Ⓣ	:501 1:15 1:393 2:034	3↑ⒻYlwRibbn-G1	105	7	32½	32½	21	11	11¼	Solis A	B118	2.60	69– 29	*Ryafan*1181¼ Fanjica1221½ Memories of Silver1221	Brushed 3w 1/8, drvng	8
4Oct97–8Kee	fm	1⅛ Ⓣ	:464 1:11 1:35 1:463	ⒻQEIICup-G1	101	3	31	31½	41½	32	11½	Solis A	121	2.80	96– 07	*Ryafan*1211½ Auntie Mame121nk Golden Arches121nk	Thru inside, clear	8

2Aug97	Goodwood (GB)	gd	1¼ Ⓣ RH 2:052	3↑ ⒻNassau Stakes-G2 Stk 139300	12½	Hills M	121	*2.25	*Ryafan*1212½ Entice1182 Papering1273	*Tracked in 3rd,2nd 3f out,led 2f out,ridden out.Last Second 5th*	7
9Jly97	Newmarket (GB)	gd	1 Ⓣ Str 1:382	3↑ ⒻFalmouth Stakes-G2 Stk 99400	1¾	Eddery P	118	4.00	*Ryafan*118¾ Ocean Ridge1186 Theano1272	*Tracked in 3rd,led 150y out,driving.Rebecca Sharp 6th*	7
8Jun97	Chantilly (Fr)	sf	*1 5/16 Ⓣ RH 2:081	ⒻPrix de Diane (French Oaks)-G1 Stk 420900	44	Dettori L	126	12.40	Vereva1261½ Mousse Glacee1262 Brilliance126½	*Led to over 1f out,weakened late.Always Loyal 6th*	12
24May97	Curragh (Ire)	yl	1 Ⓣ Str 1:421	ⒻIrish 1000 Guineas-G1 Stk 228100	43½	Dettori L	126	*3.00	Classic Park1261 Strawberry Roan1262½ Caiseal Ros126no	*Tracked in 4th,3rd 1-1/2f out,no rally.Oh Nellie 5th,Seebe 6th*	10
6Oct96	Longchamp (Fr)	yl	*1 Ⓣ RH 1:394	ⒻPrix Marcel Boussac-G1 Stk 262300	1hd	Dettori L	123	*2.00e	Ryafan123hd Yashmak1232½ Family Tradition1231½	*Well placed in 4th,dueled entrymate 1f out,gamely prevailed*	13
8Sep96	Curragh (Ire)	gd	7f Ⓣ Str 1:261	ⒻMoyglare Stud Stakes-G1 Stk 242800	2½	Eddery P	123	4.50	Bianca Nera123½ *Ryafan*123nk Azra123hd	*Tracked in 3rd,led 3f to 1-1/2f out,faded,back up for 2nd*	10
29Jun96	Doncaster (GB)	gd	7f Ⓣ Str 1:303	ⒻEBF Lonsdale Maiden Stakes Maiden 8400	11¼	Eddery P	123	*1.20	Ryafan1231¼ Ajayib1231¾ Elrayahin1233½	*Led throughout setting modest pace,held well*	7

Saratoga Dew

Own: Engel Charles F

B. f. 3 (Apr) EQUJAN90 $10,000
Sire: Cormorant (His Majesty)
Dam: Super Luna (In Reality)
Br: Mrs. Helen B. Chenery (NY)
Tr: Sciacca Gary

Life	11	8	1	0	$541,580	108	D.Fst	8	6	0	0	$287,580	101
1992	11	8	1	0	$541,580	108	Wet(336)	3	2	1	0	$254,000	108
1991	0	M	0	0	$0	–	Turf(311)	0	0	0	0	$0	–
	0	0	0	0	$0	–	Dst(0)	0	0	0	0	$0	–

31Oct92–6GP	fst	1⅛	:47 1:104 1:353 1:48	3↑ⒻBCDistaf-G1	82	4	1hd	1½	2hd	1212	1213½	McCauley W H	119	*2.00	– –	Paseana1234 Versailles Treaty123½ MagicalMaiden1191½	Gave way readily	14
10Oct92–6Bel	gd	1⅛	:453 1:093 1:341 1:464	3↑ⒻBeldame-G1	108	1	1½	11	11	12½	16	McCauley W H	119	2.00	– –	Saratoga Dew1196 Versailles Treaty1236 Coxwold1236¼	Ridden out	5
2Sep92–8Bel	fst	1⅛	:46 1:101 1:344 1:473	ⒻGazelleH-G1	101	2	22	22½	22	1hd	11¼	McCauley W H	120	*1.00	– –	*Saratoga Dew*1201¼ Vivano1144¼ Tiney Toast113¾	Prevailed, driving	6
15Aug92–8Sar	my	1¼	:471 1:112 1:362 2:023	ⒻAlabama-G1	99	5	11	11	11½	11	2no	McCauley W H	121	6.70	– –	*November Snow*121no *Saratoga Dew*1211¾ *Pacific Squall*121no	Outfinished	7
25Jly92–10FL	gd	1 1/16	:233 :473 1:121 1:45	ⒻⓈNYOaks100k	101	5	21½	21	11½	13½	16½	McCauley W H	112	*.40	– –	SaratogaDew1126½ NoblesHoney10927 ShesQueen112no	Drew off, handily	6
27Jun92–10Mth	fst	170	:221 :454 1:102 1:413	ⒻPostDeb-G2	80	7	119½	98¾	611	610	69¼	McCauley W H	119	2.70	– –	*Diamond Duo*113nk C. C.'s Return1156 Miss Legality121hd	No threat	12
3Jun92–8Bel	fst	7f	:224 :454 1:232	3↑ⒻⓈHydeParkH86k	96	5	4	1hd	2½	1hd	1nk	McCauley W H	114	2.40	– –	SrtogDew114nk MissIronSmoke114¾ BnsMomnt1124½	Long drive, driving	7
28Mar92–8Aqu	fst	1	:23 :462 1:112 1:371	ⒻComely-G2	93	7	2½	21	31	1hd	11	McCauley W H	114	*.80	– –	*Saratoga Dew*1141 CityDance113½ LookingforaWin11410	Up in final strides	7
16Mar92–8Aqu	fst	7f	:224 :462 1:113 1:243	ⒻOverAll54k	93	8	2	2½	2hd	13	14¾	McCauley W H	116	*1.60	– –	*Saratoga Dew*1164¾ Miss CoverGirl116hd GiveNotice1181¼	Drew off,driving	9
8Feb92–6Aqu	fst	6f ⊡	:23 :464 1:114	ⒻⓈAlw 27000NC	91	4	2	1hd	1hd	15	111½	McCauley W H	121	*.70	– –	*Saratoga Dew*12111½ Be Special1161½ Ain't She Nice116¾	Led throughout	6
19Jan92–6Aqu	fst	6f ⊡	:233 :482 1:14	ⒻⓈMd Sp Wt 24k	71	11	9	52½	11½	13½	15¾	McCauley W H	121	8.90	– –	*Saratoga Dew*1215¾ Montana Gal1212 *Kyle's Kreem*1215	Drew off,driving	11

Serena's Song

Own: Lewis Robert B. and Beverly J

B. f. 4 (Apr) KEEJUL93 $150,000
Sire: Rahy (Blushing Groom*Fr)
Dam: Imagining (Northfields)
Br: Dr. Howard Baker (Ky)
Tr: Lukas D. W

Life	38	18	11	3	$3,283,388	114	D.Fst	35	17	11	2	$3,093,388	114
1996	15	5	7	2	$1,161,133	112	Wet(327)	3	1	0	1	$190,000	103
1995	13	9	2	0	$1,524,920	114	Turf(326)	0	0	0	0	$0	–
	0	0	0	0	$0	–	Dst(0)	0	0	0	0	$0	–

9Nov96–8CD	fst	1	:22 :442 1:092 1:362	3↑ⒻCDDstafH-G2	102	6	33½	33½	1½	12½	2¾	Barton D M	125	*.50	– –	FstCtch109¾ SerensSong125no BdroomBlus1126	Backd up when whipped	9
26Oct96–6WO	fst	1⅛	:482 1:123 1:363 1:482	3↑ⒻBCDistaf-G1	112	3	22	22	21	1½	21½	Stevens G L	123	2.70	– –	*Jewel Princess*1231½ Serena's Song1231¾ Different1235¼	Led, second best	6
6Oct96–9Bel	fst	1⅛	:464 1:102 1:342 1:47	3↑ⒻBeldame-G1	110	4	1½	1hd	1½	1½	2¾	Stevens G L	123	*.95	– –	YanksMusic119¾ SerenasSong1233 ClearMandte1231	Pace off rail,gamely	6
14Sep96–9Bel	fst	1 1/16	:233 :471 1:111 1:414	3↑ⒻRuffianH-G1	107	4	2½	1hd	11	1½	2nk	Stevens G L	126	*.75	– –	*YanksMusic*116nk SerenasSong1269 HeadEast108nk	Clear turn,outfinished	6
25Aug96–9Mth	fst	1 1/16	:232 :464 1:103 1:412	3↑PIselinH-G1	109	6	2½	2½	1hd	1hd	33¼	Barton D M	115	*1.60	– –	Smart Strike1152¼ Eltish1161 Serena's Song115½	Stalked led no match	7
3Aug96–8Sar	fst	1⅛	:47 1:102 1:352 1:483	3↑WhitneyH-G1	110	9	12	11	12½	12½	2nk	Bailey J D	116	3.55	– –	MahognyHll113nk SerensSong1161 PeksndVlleys121½	Dictated pace,game	9
21Jly96–9Hol	fst	1⅛	:464 1:102 1:343 1:47	3↑ⒻVnityIvH-G1	111	6	41½	31	31	32	23	Bailey J D	B125	*1.60	– –	JewelPrincess1203 SerenasSong125¾ TopRung116½	Bid 1/4,no match,wide	6
29Jun96–9Bel	fst	1 1/16	:234 :462 1:10 1:413	3↑ⒻHmpstedH-G1	104	5	41	2½	2hd	12	13¾	Bailey J D	125	*.40	– –	SerenasSong1253¾ Shoop115hd RestoredHope114¾	Took over when asked	8
1Jun96–10CD	fst	1⅛	:463 1:11 1:363 1:501	3↑ⒻFlrDLisH-G3	105	8	32½	31	1hd	11	1½	Stevens G L	124	*.60	– –	*Serena's Song*124½ *Halo America*1171¼ Alcovy1176	Clear lead lasted	9
18May96–4Pim	my	1⅛	:47 1:104 1:361 1:493	3↑ⒻPimDstfH-G3	103	2	12	11	11	13	11½	Stevens G L	123	*.30	– –	*Serena's Song*1231½ Shoop1166¼ *ChurchbellChimes*1145½	Off rail, hand drive	4
3May96–7CD	fst	1 1/16	:242 :474 1:12 1:422	3↑ⒻLouvlBCH-G2	108	4	1½	1½	11	1hd	2nk	Stevens G L	123	*.60	– –	JewelPrincess118nk *SerenasSong*1237½ *NskrColors*1133½	Roughd up in gate	6
12Apr96–9OP	sly	1 1/16	:23 :46 1:102 1:413	4↑ⒻAplBlsmH-G1	99	2	22	21½	21	21½	33	Stevens G L	124	*.60	– –	*TwicetheVice*1171½ HaloAmeric1151½ SerensSong1242½	Chased, weakened	7
2Mar96–7SA	fst	1¼	:462 1:102 1:354 2:02	4↑SAH-G1	94	11	51¼	31	2hd	43	712¼	Stevens G L	B114	6.00	– –	Mr Purple1162 Luthier Fever1145 Just Java1143	Bid 1/4, gave way	11
17Feb96–6SA	fst	1 1/16	:234 :473 1:103 1:421	4↑ⒻSntMriaH-G1	105	5	22	3½	2hd	11½	11¼	Stevens G L	B124	*.30	– –	SerensSong1241¼ *TwicetheVice*1183 RlConnction1141¼	Drew clear, driving	5
27Jan96–8SA	fst	7f	:222 :444 1:084 1:212	4↑ⒻSntMncaH-G1	108	1	1	2½	2hd	1½	1½	Stevens G L	B123	*1.10	– –	*SerenasSong*123½ *ExoticWood*1184½ KlassyKim116nk	Drifted str,held gamly	6
28Oct95–4Bel	my	1⅛	:454 1:092 1:332 1:46	3↑ⒻBCDistaf-G1	87	6	3½	32	33	39	518¾	Stevens G L	119	2.50	– –	InsideInformtion12313½ HevnlyPriz1232¼ *Lkwy*1231	Asked late turn,empty	10
7Oct95–7Bel	fst	1⅛	:48 1:121 1:361 1:483	3↑ⒻBeldame-G1	104	4	11	12½	15	13	1¾	Stevens G L	119	2.05	– –	SerenasSong119¾ HeavenlyPrize1236¾ Lakewy1236¾	Easy lead,plenty left	5
23Sep95–9TP	fst	1 1/16	:231 :463 1:103 1:413	3↑ⒻTPBudBC-G2	110	1	31½	32½	2½	21	25½	Stevens G L	119	*.20	– –	Mariah's Storm1175½ *Serena's Song*1194½ Alcovy1177	Drew even, hung	5
3Sep95–8Bel	fst	1⅛	:464 1:101 1:342 1:471	ⒻGazelleH-G1	105	2	2½	2hd	1½	15	17	Stevens G L	124	*.35	– –	SrnsSong1247 MissGoldnCircl113nk GoldnBr1214¼	When ready,ridden out	6
30Jly95–11Mth	fst	1⅛	:46 1:102 1:353 1:484	HsklInvH-G1	110	8	31	2hd	12	15	1¾	Stevens G L	118	*1.50	– –	*Serena's Song*118¾ Pyramid Peak1203½ Citadeed1182	Lasted, driving	11
8Jly95–9Bel	fst	1¼	:474 1:12 1:372 2:034	ⒻCCAOaks-G1	95	4	31	1½	11	1hd	21½	Stevens G L	121	*.20	– –	Golden Bri1211½ *Serena'sSong*1218 ChangeForaDollar1212	Led,outfinished	6
9Jun95–8Bel	fst	1⅛	:463 1:111 1:363 1:501	ⒻMthrGoos-G1	101	6	1½	2hd	1½	13	13	Stevens G L	121	*.05	– –	Serena's Song1213 *Golden Bri*1216 Forested12112	Drew clear, driving	6
19May95–10Pim	fst	1⅛	:47 1:112 1:36 1:482	ⒻBlkEySsn-G2	113	6	21	21½	2½	11	19	Stevens G L	122	*.40	– –	*SrnsSong*1229 Conqstdorss1151¼ RrOpportnty1157	Rated kindly,hand ride	7
6May95–8CD	fst	1¼	:454 1:101 1:353 2:011	KyDerby-G1	91	13	11	11	11	43½	1611½	Nakatani C S	121	*3.40e	– –	ThunderGulch1262¼ TejnoRun126hd *TimbrCountry*126¾	Set pressured pace	19
1Apr95–11TP	fst	1⅛	:463 1:111 1:362 1:493	JimBeam-G2	114	3	1½	1½	11	13	13½	Nakatani C S	116	*.90	– –	Serena's Song1163½ Tejano Run1215 Mecke1214	Set pace, drew off	8
12Mar95–8SA	fst	1 1/16	:233 :473 1:12 1:423	ⒻSAOaks-G1	106	4	21	2½	2hd	13	1hd	Nakatani C S	B117	*.70	– –	*Serena's Song*117hd *Urbane*11714 Mari's Sheba117no	Clear lead,held well	5
19Feb95–8SA	fst	1	:224 :46 1:10 1:352	ⒻLsVrgnes-G1	108	1	1½	2hd	1hd	1½	11¼	Nakatani C S	B122	*.50	– –	*Serena's Song*1221¼ *Cat's Cradle*118nk Urbane1162	Hit rail 3/8,gamely	7
29Jan95–8SA	fst	7f	:223 :444 1:083 1:212	ⒻSntYnzBC-G3	102	5	1	1½	2½	11½	12	Nakatani C S	B123	1.50	– –	*Serena's Song*1232 Cat's Cradle1212 Call Now1214½	Inside trip,ridden out	5
17Dec94–9Hol	fst	1 1/16	:233 :464 1:104 1:414	ⒻHolStrlt-G1	103	5	11	1½	1hd	11½	1no	Nakatani C S	B120	*.40	– –	*Serena's Song*120no Urbane1203½ *Ski Dancer*1204	Prevailed,long drive	5
5Nov94–5CD	fst	1 1/16	:23 :461 1:112 1:451	ⒻBCJuvFil-G1	92	12	3½	1hd	1hd	1½	2hd	Nakatani C S	119	7.00	– –	Flanders119hd *Serena's Song*1194 Stormy Blues119½	Dueled, gamely	13
8Oct94–8SA	fst	1 1/16	:222 :454 1:094 1:414	ⒻOakLeaf-G1	90	1	11	1½	1½	12	12¾	Nakatani C S	B115	3.70	– –	Serena's Song1152¾ *Call Now*1154½ Mama Mucci11511	Fast pace, driving	5
3Sep94–8Dmr	fst	7f	:214 :434 1:081 1:212	ⒻDMrDeb-G2	75	3	6	63¾	54	45½	49¾	Stevens G L	B119	2.90	– –	Call Now1154½ How So Oiseau1191¾ SkiDancer1163½	Bumped start,settled	9
12Aug94–8Dmr	fst	6½f	:213 :443 1:091 1:154	ⒻSorrento-G2	87	6	1	42½	4nk	21	32	Stevens G L	B121	*.60	– –	How So Oiseau1172 SkiDancer117no Serena'sSong1218	Bid 3-w 1/4, empty	8
25Jly94–8Hol	fst	6f	:22 :451 :572 1:10	HolJuvCh-G2	85	4	1	52½	51¼	43	2½	Stevens G L	B117	1.50	– –	Mr Purple117½ Serena's Song1171½ *Cyrano*1171½	Settled, rallied 4-w	7
9Jly94–4Hol	fst	6f	:213 :443 :57 1:10	ⒻLandaluc-G2	86	9	1	31½	2hd	1hd	14½	Stevens G L	B116	*1.20	– –	Serena'sSong1164½ Embroidered1162 *CatsCradle*1162¾	Rallied 3-w,handily	10
25Jun94–3Hol	fst	5f	:22 :45 :572	ⒻMd Sp Wt 32k	88	8	1	1hd	16	17	110	Stevens G L	B118	1.80	– –	*Serena's Song*11810 Valid Attraction118hd Guise1183½	Drew off, handily	8
12Jun94–9CD	fst	5½f	:22 :453 1:051	ⒻDebutante92k	59	1	4	1hd	2hd	44	45½	Barton D M	112	6.50	– –	Chrgedupsycmore1211 PhoneBird1161½ *OurGem*1163	Bumped, lost action	9
28May94–1CD	fst	5f	:223 :46 :59	ⒻMd Sp Wt 20k	54	11	10	89	711	510	56½	Sellers S J	119	3.20	– –	Phone Bird1193 Me My119nk B J Shiny Gold1192	Bid, hung, 5 wide	12

Silver Charm

Own: Lewis Robert B. and Beverly J

Gr/ro. h. 5 (Feb)
Sire: Silver Buck (Buckpasser) $7,500
Dam: Bonnie's Poker (Poker)
Br: Mary Lou Wootton (Fla)
Tr: Baffert Bob

Life	24	12	7	2	$6,944,369	123	D.Fst	23 11 7 2	$6,644,369	123
1999	5	1	0	2	$431,363	118	Wet(310)	1 1 0 0	$300,000	113
1998	9	6	2	0	$4,696,506	123	Turf(233)	0 0 0 0	$0	–
	0	0	0	0	$0	–	Dst(0)	0 0 0 0	$0	–

12Jun99-9CD	fst	1⅛	:464 1:11 1:352 1:471	3↑ SFosterH-G2	104	3	42½	44½	42½	44	48½	Antley C W	L123	1.40	98-03	*VictoryGllop*1205 *NiteDremr*110¾ Littlbitlivly1152¾	Hopped start,weakened	7
28Mar99 Nad Al Sheba (UAE)	ft	*1¼	LH 2:003	4↑ Dubai World Cup-G1							614¼	Stevens G	126	-		Almutawakel126¾ Malek126¾ *Victory Gallop*1261½		8
Timeform rating: 101				Stk 5000000												*Tracked in 5th,weakened over 2f out.Daylami 5th,Running Stag 7th*		
6Mar99-5SA	fst	1¼	:472 1:112 1:352 2:003	4↑ SAH-G1	118	1	31½	41¼	42¼	41½	31	Stevens G L	LB124	*1.00	97-11	FreeHouse123½ EventoftheYer119½ SilvrChrm1243	Came back on outside	6
30Jan99-10GP	fst	1⅛	:463 1:102 1:353 1:481	3↑ DonnH-G1	106	12	99½	99¼	76¾	63½	35¼	Stevens G L	L126	*.80	91-14	Puerto Madero1202¾ *Behrens*1132½ Silver Charm126nk	Mild wide rally	12
10Jan99-8SA	fst	1 1/16	:242 :472 1:104 1:413	4↑ SnPsqalH-G2	109	3	33	38½	36	31	11¼	Stevens G L	LB125	*.30	95-10	Silver Charm1251¼ Malek1193½ Crafty Friend1182	Rallied,good handling	5
27Nov98-11CD	fst	1⅛	:472 1:112 1:361 1:49	3↑ ClarkH-G2	113	2	1hd	1hd	2hd	2½	1hd	Stevens G L	L124	*.30	99-14	*SilverChrm*124hd Littlebitlively1131 WildRush117½	Dueled, headed, gamely	8
7Nov98-10CD	fst	1¼	:473 1:12 1:371 2:02	3↑ BCClasic-G1	115	8	52¼	41	2½	1hd	2¾	Stevens G L	L126	2.50	94-07	Awesome Again126¾ *Silver Charm*126nk Swain126no	Led, drifted late	10
17Oct98-8SA	fst	1⅛	:464 1:101 1:343 1:471	3↑ GdwdBCH-G2	111	5	34½	31½	3½	1hd	12½	Stevens G L	LB124	*.50	100-07	Silver Charm1242½ *Free House*1242½ Score Quick1156	Bid 3 wide, driving	6
26Sep98-10TP	fst	1⅛	:462 1:10 1:343 1:472	3↑ KyCpClH-G3	123	1	32	31	2hd	2hd	117 ↓	Stevens G L	L123	*.50	100-14	DH *SilverCharm*123 DH WildRush11717 Acceptable1175	Long drive, brushed	5
25Jly98-8Dmr	fst	1 1/16	:23 :464 1:102 1:41	3↑ SnDiegoH-G3	63	4	21½	21	31	510	527	Stevens G L	LB125	*.30	72-09	Mud Route1176 Hal's Pal1135½ Benchmark1175½	Stalked,gave way	5
13Jun98-9CD	fst	1⅛	:464 1:11 1:36 1:483	3↑ SFosterH-G2	116	1	35	44	31	1½	21	Stevens G L	L127	*.40	100-07	*AwesomeAgain*1131 SilverCharm1275¼ Semoran1142¼	Drifted, bumped 1/16	7
28Mar98 Nad Al Sheba (UAE)	ft	*1¼	LH 2:041	4↑ Dubai World Cup-G1							1no	Stevens G	126	-		Silver Charm126no Swain1262½ Loup Sauvage126no		9
Timeform rating: 129+				Stk 4000000												*Tracked in 3rd,led over 2f out,repelled challenges,all out*		
7Feb98-8SA	wf	1⅛	:472 1:11 1:344 1:471	Strub-G2	113	3	21	32	3½	12	14	Stevens G L	LB123	*.30	100-07	*Silver Charm*1234 *Mud Route*1172 Bagshot1177	4 wide 2nd turn	6
17Jan98-8SA	fst	1 1/16	:241 :482 1:121 1:414	SnFndoBC-G2	112	1	21½	21½	2½	1hd	11	Stevens G L	LB122	*.20	94-13	*Silver Charm*1221 Mud Route1163 *Lord Grillo*12010	Left handed urging	4
26Dec97-8SA	fst	7f	:222 :45 1:092 1:212	Malibu-G1	109	6	5	51¾	41½	31	2½	Stevens G L	LB123	*.30e	96-13	Lord Grillo119½ *SilverCharm*1233 SwissYodeler1152	Blocked upper stretch	9
7Jun97-9Bel	fst	1½	:491 1:134 2:284	Belmont-G1	109	2	31	2hd	1hd	1hd	2¾	Stevens G L	L126	*1.05	89-14	*Touch Gold*126¾ Silver Charm1261 *FreeHouse*12614	Speed outside,led,game	7
17May97-10Pim	fst	1 3/16	:464 1:102 1:352 1:544	Preaknes-G1	118	7	44½	31½	21	21	1hd	Stevens G L	L126	3.10	93-15	SilverChrm126hd FreeHouse126hd CptinBodgit1261¼	Stalk 3w,all out btwn	10
3May97-8CD	fst	1¼	:472 1:121 1:371 2:022	KyDerby-G1	115	5	42½	41¼	3½	1hd	1hd	Stevens G L	L126	4.00	93-05	*SilverChrm*126hd CptinBodgit1263½ FreeHouse1263	Steadied, brushd lastd	13
5Apr97-6SA	fst	1⅛	:45 1:09 1:342 1:473	SADerby-G1	110	3	2½	2½	2hd	1hd	2hd	Stevens G L	LB120	2.10	95-10	Free House120hd *Silver Charm*1202 Hello120no	Fast pace,just missed	10
16Mar97-7SA	fst	1 1/16	:223 :46 1:101 1:422	SnFelipe-G2	102	6	51¾	54	53¾	32	2¾	McCarron C J	LB122	*1.10e	90-12	*FreeHouse*119¾ SilverCharm1221 KingCrimson116¾	Angled out,finshd well	9
8Feb97-6SA	fst	7f	:222 :444 1:084 1:21	SnVicnte-G3	110	5	5	31	42½	1½	11¾	McCarron C J	LB120	2.60e	99-13	Silver Charm1201¾ *Free House*1202 *Funontherun*114½	Perfect trip, driving	9
11Sep96-8Dmr	fst	7f	:223 :451 1:093 1:224	DMrFut-G2	97	7	3	21	31½	2hd	1hd	Flores D R	LB116	1.60e	86-15	*SilvrChrm*116hd GoldTribut1153½ SwissYodlr1212¾	Wore down entry mate	7
24Aug96-6Dmr	fst	5½f	:214 :444 :57 1:031	Md Sp Wt 37k	95	2	2	1hd	1½	11½	11¼	Flores D R	LB118	*.40e	97-09	*Silver Charm*1181¼ Gold Tribute1188 So Easy1185	Fast pace, driving	8
10Aug96-3Dmr	fst	6f	:214 :444 :572 1:10	Md Sp Wt 37k	77	2	4	1hd	1hd	1½	24	Flores D R	B118 b	2.80e	85-08	DeedsNotWords1184 *SilverChrm*1181 *ConstntDemnd*118¾	Rushed,fast pace	8

Silverbulletday

Own: Pegram Michael E

B. f. 4 (Jan)
Sire: Silver Deputy (Deputy Minister) $75,000
Dam: Rokeby Rose (Tom Rolfe)
Br: Highclere Inc. & Clear Creek (Ky)
Tr: Baffert Bob

Life	23	15	3	1	$3,093,207	115	D.Fst	19 13 1 1	$2,372,187	115
2000	5	1	2	1	$271,457	110	Wet(365)	4 2 2 0	$721,020	110
1999	11	8	1	0	$1,707,640	115	Turf(278)	0 0 0 0	$0	–
	0	0	0	0	$0	–	Dst(0)	0 0 0 0	$0	–

23Jly00-8Del	fst	1¼	:48 1:12 1:363 2:021	3↑ ⒻDelH-G3	103	6	21	2hd	21	21½	33	Sellers S J	L119	*.90	96-09	Lu Ravi1171 Tap to Music1162 Silverbulletday1194½	Bid, weakened	8
4Jly00-9Mth	gd	1 1/16	:24 :474 1:121 1:43	3↑ ⒻMPchrBCH-G2	110	1	31	31	31½	22	2hd	Nakatani C S	L118	*1.00	86-19	*Lu Ravi*116hd Silverbulletday1185¾ *Bella Chiarra*1161¼	Eased out, gamely	7
3Jun00-9CD	fst	1⅛	:472 1:12 1:354 1:481	3↑ ⒻFlrDLisH-G3	109	1	1½	11	1½	21½	24	Nakatani C S	L119	1.70	91-15	*HeritgeofGold*1214 Silverbulltdy1192½ RozRobt115nk	Easy pace, weakened	5
5May00-7CD	fst	1 1/16	:243 :482 1:12 1:424	3↑ ⒻLouvlBCH-G2	101	2	32	41	41¾	42	42¾	Bailey J D	L120	*.90	93-10	*HeritageofGold*1191¼ *RozaRobata*112no BellChirr1161½	Bid, no late response	6
19Apr00-8Kee	fst	1 1/16	:244 :483 1:123 1:433	4↑ ⒻDbldogdare99k	106	2	2hd	2hd	1½	11½	1nk	Bailey J D	L123 f	*.30	87-13	Silverbulletday123nk Roza Robata11615 Pepita Ramoje116	Dueled,driving	3
6Nov99-3GP	fst	1⅛	:462 1:094 1:343 1:472	3↑ ⒻBCDistaf-G1	90	6	52	42½	23	43	611¼	Bailey J D	L120	*1.60	89 -	BeutifulPlesure123¾ BnsheeBreeze1231¼ *HritgofGold*1231¼	Close up, faded	8
10Oct99-5Bel	sly	1⅛	:453 1:091 1:341 1:473	3↑ ⒻBeldame-G1	105	3	23	25	23½	22	24¾	Bailey J D	L119	*.45	88-23	*BeautifulPlesure*1234¾ Silverbulletdy1196 Ctinc1237¾	Rail,lost whip 1/8pole	5
11Sep99-9Bel	fst	1⅛	:453 1:093 1:342 1:473	ⒻGazelleH-G1	100	1	51¾	41	3nk	13½	11¾	Bailey J D	L124	*.20	93-15	Silverbulletdy1241¾ QuensWord1132 AwfulSmrt115¾	3 wide, clear, driving	6
21Aug99-8Sar	fst	1¼	:492 1:134 1:383 2:023	ⒻAlabama-G1	115	6	54	32	2hd	12	19	Bailey J D	L121	*.40	95-13	*Silverbulletday*1219 StrollingBelle1213 Gndri1216½	When asked, ridden out	7
10Jly99-9Mth	fst	1 1/16	:234 :471 1:111 1:43	ⒻMthBCOks-G2	102	4	32	21½	2½	11	15	Bailey J D	L121	*.05	86-14	*Silverbulletday*1215 BoomTownGirl1211 BgLdyJne11612¼	Drew off, handily	4
5Jun99-9Bel	fst	1½	:473 1:12 2:014 2:274	Belmont-G1	96	3	1hd	1½	3nk	53½	710½	Bailey J D	L121	5.10	95-06	LmonDropKid126hd VisionndVrs1261½ Chrismtic1264¾	Set pressured pace	12
14May99-11Pim	fst	1⅛	:47 1:104 1:351 1:474	ⒻBlkEySsn-G2	109	1	1hd	1½	15½	14½	13	Stevens G L	L122	*.10	104-12	Silverbulletdy1223 *DrmsGllore*11716½ VeVStr1157¼	Pace inside,ridden out	7
30Apr99-9CD	fst	1⅛	:473 1:121 1:371 1:494	ⒻKyOaks-G1	107	5	65½	62½	2hd	12½	12	Stevens G L	L121	*.10	94-13	*Silvrbulltdy*1212 DrmsGllor1214¾ SwpingStory1216	Hand urged,clearly bst	7
3Apr99-8Kee	my	1 1/16	:223 :46 1:104 1:413	ⒻAshland-G1	108	6	47½	37½	31½	11½	17	Bailey J D	L123	*.30	100-15	*Silverbulletdy*1237 MrleyVle1154½ GoldFromtheWst1154½	Widened in hand	6
13Mar99-9FG	sly	1 1/16	:24 :484 1:133 1:444	ⒻFGOaks-G3	101	7	64½	42½	31½	1½	13	Stevens G L	L121	*.30	87-27	*Silvrbulltdy*1213 RunwyVnus112no BrushdHlory1141¼	4w, 3w bid, clear late	7
20Feb99-9FG	fst	1 1/16	:242 :482 1:13 1:441	ⒻDvonaDal-G3	100	1	56	45	21½	11½	12¼	Stevens G L	L122	*.10	90-21	*Silvrbulltdy*1222¼ BrushdHlory114nk *OnSopbox*1196¾	Bobbled, inside, drvng	8
28Nov98-9CD	fst	1 1/16	:24 :473 1:121 1:434	ⒻGoldnRod-G3	104	4	43½	32½	11	16	110	Stevens G L	L122	*.10	92-05	*Silverbulletday*12210 Here I Go1133 Lefty's Dollbaby1136¼	3 wide, drew off	6
7Nov98-5CD	fst	1 1/16	:232 :471 1:12 1:433	ⒻBCJuvFil-G1	101	5	55	54	31	12	1½	Stevens G L	L119	*.80	93-07	*Silverbulletdy*119½ *ExcllntMting*1192½ ThrRing119nk	6wide 2nd turn,driving	10
11Oct98-8Kee	fst	1 1/16	:224 :454 1:104 1:421	ⒻAlcibiad-G2	97	2	54¾	56	1hd	11	12½	Stevens G L	L118	*1.00	97 -	*Silverbulletdy*1182½ ExtendedApplause1187 GrndDd1181	4wide, hand urging	11
29Aug98-8Dmr	fst	7f	:214 :441 1:092 1:221	ⒻDMrDeb-G2	81	1	3	2hd	11	21½	47½	Delahoussaye E	LB121	*1.60	81-13	*ExcellentMeeting*1155½ Anthkrn1152 ColordoSong115hd	Dueled, weakened	9
8Aug98-8Dmr	fst	6½f	:214 :443 1:103 1:172	ⒻSorrento-G2	84	4	3	42½	2hd	12	12	Stevens G L	LB121	*.70	84-15	Silverbulltdy1212 *ExcllntMting*117½ ColordoSong1175	3 wide turn, driving	7
27Jun98-7CD	fst	5½f	:214 :451 :574 1:043	ⒻDebutant-G3	87	4	4	3½	2hd	11½	11¾	Martinez W	L115	*.30	96-10	*Silvrbulltdy*1151¾ ThHppyHoppr1153¼ MncrisRos1153¾	4wide, steady drive	9
13Jun98-3CD	fst	5½f	:22 :453 :58 1:043	ⒻMd Sp Wt 45k	86	9	4	31½	2hd	16	111	Sellers S J	L118	*1.00	96-11	*Silverbulletday*11811 *Forever Maisie*118½ Drive Thru Blues1181	Ridden out	12

Singspiel (Ire)

Own: Sheikh Mohammed Bin Rashid Al Maktoum

B. h. 5 (Feb)
Sire: In the Wings*GB (Sadler's Wells)
Dam: Glorious Song (Halo)
Br: Shiekh Mohammed Bin Rashid Al Maktoum (Ire)
Tr: Stoute Sir Michael R

Life	20	9	8	0	$5,952,825	115	D.Fst	1 1 0 0	$2,400,000 –
1997	4	3	0	0	$2,947,330	–	Wet(247)	0 0 0 0	$0 –
1996	7	4	3	0	$2,724,139	115	Turf(334)	19 8 8 0	$3,552,825 115
	0	0	0	0	$0	–	Dst(0)	0 0 0 0	$0 –

Date / Track	Cond	Dist	Time	Race	Fig / Calls	Fin	Jockey	Wt	Odds	Pace	Top Finishers / Comment	Field
19Aug97 York (GB)	gd	1 5/16 Ⓣ	LH 2:12	3↑ Juddmonte International Stakes-G1 Stk 533400		11½	Dettori L	131	4.00		Singspiel1311½ Desert King1231½ Benny the Dip1231¼ *Tracked leader,led over 2f out,handily.Bosra Sham 4th*	4
26Jly97 Ascot (GB)	sf	1½ Ⓣ	RH 2:362	3↑ King George VI & Queen Eliz St-G1 Stk 832500		44¾	Dettori L	133	4.00		Swain1331 *Pilsudski*1331¼ Helissio1332½ *Rated in 5th.4th 3f out.bid 2f out.briefly 3rd.weakened late*	8
6Jun97 Epsom (GB)	gd	1½ Ⓣ	LH 2:373	4↑ Coronation Cup-G1 Stk 314900		15	Dettori L	126	*1.25		Singspiel1265 Dushyantor126½ Le Destin1264 *Led for 5f.tracked leader.led 3-1/2f out.clear 2f out.handily*	5
3Apr97 Nad Al Sheba (UAE)	ft	*1¼	LH 2:014	4↑ Dubai World Cup (Listed) Stk 4000000		11¼	Bailey J	126	-		*Singspiel*1261¼ Siphon1261½ Sandpit1262½ *3rd early.rated in 5th.rail bid to lead 2f out.driving.No betting*	12
24Nov96 Tokyo (Jpn)	fm	*1½ Ⓣ	LH 2:234	3↑ Japan Cup-G1 Stk 2982300		1no	Dettori L	126	6.60		*Singspiel*126no Fabulous La Fouine1171¼ Strategic Choice126nk *Rated in 6th,dueled 2f out,all out,very game.Awad 5th,Pentire 8th*	15
26Oct96-9WO	gd	1½ Ⓣ	:50 1:152 2:0542:301	3↑ BCTurf-G1	113 10 42¼ 2½ 1hd 11	21¼	Stevens G L	L126	*1.10e	76- 18	Pilsudski1261¼ *Singspiel*1261¼ Swain1262½ Led 2nd turn, game	14
29Sep96-8WO	sf	1½ Ⓣ	:51 1:162 2:0712:331	3↑ CanIntnl-G1	115 7 35 21½ 11 12½	12	Stevens G L	L126	*1.90	62- 30	Singspiel1262 Chief Bearhart1183½ *Mecke*1263½ Drew clear, driving	7
14Sep96 Goodwood (GB)	gd	1¼ Ⓣ	RH 2:071	3↑ Select Stakes-G3 Stk 62100		11	Asmussen C	129	*1.10		*Singspiel*1291 *Wall Street*1198 Farasan1192½ *Led throughout,ridden out*	4
9Jly96 Newmarket (GB)	gd	1½ Ⓣ	RH 2:284	3↑ Princess of Wales's Stakes-G2 Stk 98900		21¼	Kinane M	128	1.75		Posidonas1331¼ *Singspiel*1282½ Annus Mirabilis1282½ *Rated in 6th,progress 3-1/2f out,bid 2f out,held by winner*	8
8Jun96 Epsom (GB)	gd	1½ Ⓣ	LH 2:401	4↑ Coronation Cup-G1 Stk 278100		2nk	Kinane M	126	2.25		Swain126nk Singspiel1265 De Quest126no *Tracked leader,bid 2f out,always held by winner*	4
27Apr96 Sandown Park (GB)	gd	1¼ Ⓣ	RH 2:063	4↑ Gordon Richards Stakes-G3 Stk 49900		13	Dettori L	122	*1.10		Singspiel1223 *Pilsudski*122½ Naked Welcome122½ *Tracked in 5th,led 3f out,drew clear.Prince Of Andros 6th*	11
8Sep95 Doncaster (GB)	yl	1½ Ⓣ	LH 2:454	Troy Stakes (Listed) Stk 35500		12½	Kinane M	123	*.30		*Singspiel*1232½ Jumairah Sun1184 Tenorio123 *Tracked leader,led 3f out,met challenge 2f out,won ridden out*	3
15Aug95 York (GB)	gd	1½ Ⓣ	LH 2:294	Great Voltigeur Stakes-G2 Stk 130900		2no	Kinane M	121	2.50		*Pentire*124no *Singspiel*1213½ Luso1264 *Tracked leader,led 2-1/2f out,dueled final furlong,gamely*	4
8Jly95 Sandown Park (GB)	gd	1¼ Ⓣ	RH 2:051	3↑ Eclipse Stakes-G1 Stk 418400		2nk	Kinane M	122	4.50		*Halling*133nk Singspiel1223 Red Bishop1334 *Tracked pacesetting winner,bid 1f out,not good enough.Eltish 5th*	8
25Jun95 Longchamp (Fr)	gd	*1¼ Ⓣ	RH 2:021	Grand Prix de Paris-G1 Stk 411300		2nk	Kinane M	128	4.00e		Valanour128nk Singspiel128½ Diamond Mix1281½ *Wide in 8th,7th 2-1/2f out,rallied 1-1/2f out,gaining late*	10
9May95 Chester (GB)	gd	1 9/16 Ⓣ	LH 2:381	Chester Vase-G3 Stk 80000		44¾	Swinburn W	122	*1.00		*Luso*122hd Court of Honour126¾ Maralinga1224 *Rated towards rear,wide bid over 2f out,one-paced late*	7
29Apr95 Sandown Park (GB)	gd	1¼ Ⓣ	RH 2:072	Thresher Classic Trial-G3 Stk 116700		2nk	Swinburn W	122	8.00		*Pentire*122nk Singspiel1221½ Balliol Boy1223 *Rated in 5th,dueled final 16th,gamely.Luso 4th,Torrential 5th*	8
8Oct94 Ascot (GB)	gd	7f Ⓣ	Str 1:271	Hyperion Conditions Stakes Alw 27900		28	Swinburn W	123	2.25		*Celtic Swing*1238 Singspiel12310 Winners Choice125nk *Rated in last,progress 2-1/2f out,chased winner home*	6
21Sep94 Chester (GB)	yl	7f Ⓣ	LH 1:35	Marford Maiden Stakes Maiden 8800		12½	Dettori L	126	*.70		Singspiel1262½ *Embryonic*1262 Maybe Today1181½ *Chased leading group,pushed along hlfwy,led ovr 1f out,soon clear*	8
6Sep94 Leicester (GB)	gd	7f Ⓣ	Str 1:231	David Millns Maiden Stks(Div1) Maiden 9800		52¾	Reid J	126	5.00		Mandarina121no Shahid1262½ Oakbury126hd *Sluggish start,late progress through last quarter*	16

Skip Away

Own: Hine Carolyn H

Gr/ro. h. 5 (Apr)
Sire: Skip Trial (Bailjumper)
Dam: Ingot Way (Diplomat Way)
Br: Anna Marie Barnhart (Fla)
Tr: Hine Hubert

Life	38	18	10	6	$9,616,360	125	D.Fst	34 16 9 5	$8,615,740 125
1998	9	7	0	1	$2,740,000	121	Wet(333)	3 2 0 1	$994,000 118
1997	11	4	5	2	$4,089,000	125	Turf(261)	1 0 1 0	$6,620 72
	0	0	0	0	$0	–	Dst(0)	0 0 0 0	$0 –

Date-Race	Cond	Dist	Fractions	Race	Fig PP Calls	Fin	Jockey	Wt	Odds	Pace	Top Finishers	Comment	Field
7Nov98-10CD	fst	1¼	:473 1:12 1:3712:02	3↑ BCClasic-G1	110 6 21 2½ 4¾ 63¼	64	Bailey J D	L126 b	*1.90	91- 07	Awesome Again126¾ *Silver Charm*126nk Swain126no	Pressed, empty	10
10Oct98-10Bel	sly	1¼	:462 1:093 1:3412:003	3↑ JkyClbGC-G1	100 4 2hd 2½ 22 34	310¼	Bailey J D	L126 b	*.35	81- 14	Wagon Limit1265½ Gentlemen1264¾ Skip Away1264	Dueled outside, faded	6
19Sep98-9Bel	fst	1⅛	:452 1:09 1:3411:474	3↑ Woodward-G1	119 2 2hd 1½ 11 12	11¾	Bailey J D	L126 b	*1.10	91- 18	Skip Away1261¾ Gentlemen1266 Running Stag1269	About his business	5
30Aug98-11Mth	fst	1⅛	:463 1:10 1:3441:471	3↑ PIselinH-G2	114 4 31 2hd 11 1hd	1no	Bailey J D	L131 b	*.05	102- 09	*Skip Away*131no Stormin Fever1139 ⒹTestafly1142¾	Driving	7
28Jun98-7Hol	fst	1¼	:462 1:093 1:34 2:00	3↑ HolGldCp-G1	117 2 11 1hd 1hd 11	11¾	Bailey J D	LB124 b	*.40	95- 05	*Skip Away*1241¾ Puerto Madero1241 Gentlemen1243	Gamely, kicked clear	8
30May98-9Suf	fst	1⅛	:462 1:101 1:3441:471	3↑ MassH-G3	121 1 1hd 12½ 11½ 12	14¼	Bailey J D	L130 b	*.30	103- 07	*SkipAway*1304¼ PuertoMdero1164¾ KJsAppel1134	Set pace much the best	5
9May98-7Pim	gd	1 3/16	:47 1:112 1:3541:541	3↑ PimSpclH-G1	118 4 12 12½ 12½ 14	13¼	Bailey J D	L128 b	*.20	94- 16	*Skip Away*1283¼ Precocity115nk Hot Brush113¾	Contrlld pce 2w,drivng	5
28Feb98-10GP	fst	1¼	:463 1:101 1:3512:031	3↑ GPH-G1	114 2 21 2hd 11½ 12	12¼	Bailey J D	L127 b	*.10	95- 16	*Skip Away*1272¼ Unruled1121¾ Behrens1141¼	Fast pace, drew off	6
7Feb98-10GP	fst	1⅛	:463 1:104 1:3621:50	3↑ DonnH-G1	109 3 2hd 31 2hd 12½	12¾	Bailey J D	L126 b	*.40	87- 24	*Skip Away*1262¾ Unruled112½ Sir Bear113nk	Angled out, ridden out	10
8Nov97-8Hol	fst	1¼	:461 1:093 1:3341:59	3↑ BCClassc-G1	120 1 31 12½ 15 15	16	Smith M E	L126 b	*1.80	102- 06	*SkipAwy*1266 DputyCommndr122¾ ⒹWhiskyWsdom1263	Drew off, handily	9
18Oct97-9Bel	fst	1¼	:47 1:10 1:3341:584	3↑ JkyClbGC-G1	116 1 2½ 1hd 1hd 16	16½	Bailey J D	L126 b	1.45	103- 04	*SkipAwy*1266½ *InstntFrindship*12610 WgonLimit121¾	Spd on rail,ridden out	7
20Sep97-9Bel	fst	1⅛	:471 1:111 1:35 1:472	3↑ Woodward-G1	116 2 1hd 2hd 33 34½	25½	Sellers S J	L126 b	1.35	87- 15	Formal Gold1265½ *Skip Away*126nk Will's Way12640	Gamely for 2nd	5
23Aug97-9Mth	fst	1 1/16	:224 :452 1:09 1:401	3↑ PIselinH-G2	115 1 44 45 32½ 25	25¼	Sellers S J	L124 b	*.90	101- 07	*FormlGold*1215¼ SkipAwy1242½ DstortdHumor1156	No match 2nd best late	4
2Aug97-8Sar	fst	1⅛	:47 1:104 1:3521:481	3↑ WhitneyH-G1	115 2 33 33 31½ 35	36½	Sellers S J	L125 b	*1.10	88- 25	Will's Way117no *Formal Gold*1206½ Skip Away1259½	3w 2nd turn,no bid	6
4Jly97-9Bel	fst	1¼	:472 1:12 1:3712:021	3↑ SuburbnH-G2	118 1 3½ 41 31 3nk	11½	Sellers S J	L122 b	*1.00	86- 23	Skip Away1221½ *Will's Way*116¾ Formal Gold12015	3w move 1/4 pole	6
31May97-11Suf	fst	1⅛	:471 1:104 1:3511:474	3↑ MassH-G3	122 3 2hd 2½ 1hd 1½	1hd	Sellers S J	L119 b	*.70	104- 01	*Skip Away*119hd *Formal Gold*1143½ Will's Way1142¼	Dueled, prevailed	6
10May97-9Pim	fst	1 3/16	:463 1:10 1:3431:53	4↑ PimSpclH-G1	125 8 41½ 42 32 22	2½	Sellers S J	L119 b	3.30	101- 17	*Gentlemen*122½ *Skip Away*1196½ *Tejano Run*1148	3wd trip,closed gamely	8
20Apr97-7LS	fst	1	:232 :461 1:0931:342	3↑ TexasMile250k	92 5 63 52½ 43½ 34½	37½	Sellers S J	L116 b	*.60	- -	Isitingood1233 *Spiritbound*1164½ Skip Away1162½	4wide 1st turn, dull	7
1Mar97-10GP	fst	1¼	:46 1:104 1:3542:021	3↑ GPH-G1	115 2 2½ 1hd 1hd 2½	22¼	Sellers S J	L122 b	*.40	89- 19	Mt. Sassafras1132¼ Skip Away122nk *Tejano Run*1142	Fast pace, held place	6
8Feb97-10GP	fst	1⅛	:47 1:104 1:35 1:472	3↑ DonnH-G1	112 7 21½ 2½ 21½ 21½	21¼	Sellers S J	L123 b	*.70	100- 04	Formal Gold1131¼ Skip Away1236 Mecke120hd	Stalk fast pace, hung	10
5Oct96-10Bel	fst	1¼	:473 1:112 1:3542:003	3↑ JkyClbGC-G1	115 4 2½ 2½ 2hd 1½	1hd	Sellers S J	L121 b	5.80	94- 10	Skip Away121hd Cigar1262 Louis Quatorze1211	Dug in,prevailed	6
15Sep96-9WO	fst	1⅛	:464 1:103 1:36 1:49	WoMilion-G1	108 1 55½ 55 53¾ 1½	14	Sellers S J	L126 b	*1.15	101- 09	*Skip Away*1264 Victor Cooley119no Stephanotis1193½	Driving, drew clear	7
24Aug96-7Sar	fst	1¼	:461 1:103 1:3612:022	Travers-G1	111 3 31½ 41 3½ 31½	31¾	Santos J A	L126 b	*1.45	95- 03	Will's Way126¾ Louis Quatorze1261 *Skip Away*1263½	Stdied on rail backstr	7
4Aug96-10Mth	fst	1⅛	:461 1:094 1:3421:473	BckHskIH-G1	113 2 43 44 31½ 3½	11	Santos J A	L124 b	*.60	103- 01	Skip Away1241 Dr. Caton1151 Victory Speech1214½	Driving	7
23Jun96-14Tdn	fst	1⅛	:461 1:104 1:3531:474	OhioDrby-G2	110 10 52¾ 52 1½ 13	13½	Santos J A	LB122 b	*.70	103- 08	*SkipAwy*1223½ *VictorySpeech*1189¼ ClshbyNight118nk	Rallied, 5w. riddn out	10
8Jun96-9Bel	fst	1½	:464 1:104 2:02 2:284	Belmont-G1	105 13 63¾ 2hd 11½ 1hd	21	Santos J A	L126 b	8.00	89- 13	Editor's Note1261 *Skip Away*1264 *My Flag*1216	4w move 2nd trn,dug in	14
18May96-10Pim	fst	1 3/16	:461 1:094 1:3421:532	Preaknes-G1	107 11 31 23 22 21	23¼	Sellers S J	L126 b	3.30	98- 10	LouisQuatorze1263¼ SkipAwy1263 *EditorsNote*1262½	Stalked,bid 1/8,2d bst	12
4May96-8CD	fst	1¼	:46 1:10 1:35 2:01	KyDerby-G1	87 16 64½ 84½ 78½ 1216	1216¾	Sellers S J	L126 b	7.70	- -	Grindstone126no Cavonnier1263½ Prince of Thieves126nk	Close up no rally	19
13Apr96-9Kee	wf	1⅛	:462 1:101 1:3441:471	BlueGras-G2	113 5 2½ 1hd 1½ 14	16	Sellers S J	L121 b	4.60	- -	SkipAwy1216 LouisQutorze1211½ EditorsNote1213	Drew clear, ridden out	7
16Mar96-10GP	fst	1⅛	:462 1:094 1:3431:474	FlaDerby-G1	104 3 53 44½ 45½ 23	36¼	Sellers S J	L122 b	7.90	- -	*Unbridled's Song*1225¾ Editor's Note122½ *Skip Away*1222¼	Fast pace, evenly	9
10Feb96-8GP	fst	1 1/16	:233 :474 1:1141:441	Alw 26000N1x	100 4 53½ 31 1½ 16	112	Sellers S J	L117 b	*1.10	- -	SkipAway11712 *Hedge*120no NaturlSelection1201½	Much the best, handily	12
10Jan96-1GP	fst	1 1/16	:23 :463 1:1141:454	Alw 26000N1x	– 1 43½ 53 56¾ -	-	Bailey J D	117	*.40	- -	Blushing Jim1171½ Head Minister1171¼ NightRunner1177¾	Distanced, bled	5
25Nov95-7Aqu	fst	1⅛	:471 1:114 1:3731:501	Remsen-G2	94 1 63½ 43 32 1½	2nk	Bailey J D	112	2.30	- -	Tropicool112nk Skip Away1122 Crafty Friend1133	Led 1/8, 2nd best	11
29Oct95-7Bel	fst	1	:223 :461 1:1131:37	Cowdin-G2	79 7 31½ 31½ 2hd 2hd	2no	Wilson R	122	5.30	- -	Gator Dancer122no Skip Away1223 *In Contention*1224¾	Dueled,led,missed	8
6Oct95-9Med	fst	1 ⊗	:23 :463 1:1041:371	WrldAppeal40k	79 10 67¼ 64 35½ 36	33¼	Wilson R	115	1.80	- -	Spicy Fact1153¼ *Play ItAgainStan*117no SkipAway1159	Quick move, gamely	10
16Aug95-5Mth	fst	1	:24 :474 1:13 1:39	Md Sp Wt 22k	78 2 33 23½ 21½ 110	112¼	Wilson R	118	*.80	- -	Skip Away11812¼ *Clash by Night*1187½ DarnThatErica1134¼	Drew off, easily	8
9Jly95-9Mth	fm	5f Ⓣ	:22 :451 :572	GildedTime33k	72 4 7 79 67 36	21½	Marquez C H Jr	112	5.00	- -	Cold Snap1181½ *Skip Away*1121 Cobb's Creek1211¾	Slow early, rallied	7
16Jun95-5Mth	fst	5f	:22 :462 :584	Md Sp Wt 17k	47 2 10 89¾ 711 514	48¾	Marquez C H Jr	118	*.80e	- -	*Cold Snap*1134¼ Foolspruce1182 *Beau Coup*1182½	Off slowly, rallied	10

Sky Beauty

Own: Georgia E. Hofmann

B. m. 5 (Feb)
Sire: Blushing Groom*Fr (Red God)
Dam: Maplejinsky (Nijinsky II)
Br: Sugar Maple Farm (Ky)
Tr: Jerkens H. A

Life	21	15	2	2	$1,336,000	111		
1995	3	1	1	1	$91,105	101		
1994	6	5	0	0	$438,855	111		
	0	0	0	0	$0	–		
D.Fst	20	14	2	2	$1,288,135	111		
Wet(419)	1	1	0	0	$47,865	100		
Turf(387)	0	0	0	0	$0	–		
Dst(0)	0	0	0	0	$0	–		

Date	Cond	Dist	Fractions	Race	Fig	PP	St	1c	2c	Str	Fin	Jockey	Wt	Odds		Top finishers	Comment	Fld
18Jun95-9Bel	fst	1 1/16	:23 :46 1:102 1:431	3↑ⒻHmpstedH-G1	91	1	2½	25	35	38	311¾	Smith M E	124	*.75	- -	*Heavenly Prize*1221¼ *Little Buckles*11110½ Sky Beauty1243	Chased ins, tired	4
20May95-8Bel	fst	1	:224 :462 1:102 1:35	3↑ⒻShuveeH-G1	101	4	32½	3½	21	23	25½	Krone J A	126	*.35	- -	*InsideInformtion*1195½ SkyBeuty12616 *RestoredHope*1152	Rated 4w, gamely	4
3May95-7Bel	gd	7f	:222 :454 1:091 1:212	3↑ⒻVagrncyH-G3	100	1	4	31½	41¾	11½	14	Smith M E	125	*.35	- -	SkyButy1254 *AlysConqust*1148 ThroughthDoor11019	Going away, rddn out	4
5Nov94-6CD	fst	1⅛	:474 1:121 1:373 1:503	3↑ⒻBCDistaf-G1	85	8	76	74¼	65¾	915	912¼	Smith M E	123	1.90	- -	OneDremer123nk HevenlyPrize1201½ MissDominiqu1231¼	Wide dull effort	9
17Sep94-6Bel	fst	1 1/16	:232 :46 1:101 1:413	3↑ⒻRuffianH-G1	106	3	2hd	2½	1hd	11	11¼	Smith M E	130	*.40	- -	Sky Beauty1301¼ *Dispute*1172¼ Educated Risk114nk	Stalked 3w, driving	5
24Jly94-8Sar	fst	1⅛	:47 1:11 1:363 1:492	3↑ⒻGoFrWand-G1	105	1	1½	1hd	11	13	110½	Smith M E	123	*.10	- -	*Sky Beauty*12310½ *Link River*123no Life Is Delicious1237½	Pace, ridden out	5
19Jun94-8Bel	fst	1⅛	:474 1:113 1:351 1:472	3↑ⒻHmpstedH-G1	107	4	1½	1hd	1hd	1hd	1nk	Smith M E	128	*.30	94-16	*Sky Beauty*128nk *You'd Be Surprised*11812½ Schway Baby Sway1097	Driving	5
21May94-8Bel	fst	1 1/16	:231 :454 1:093 1:403	3↑ⒻShuveeH-G1	111	2	2½	2hd	1hd	14	19½	Smith M E	125	*.30	- -	*Sky Beauty*1259½ For all Seasons1133 Looie Capote112no	Ridden out	4
4May94-8Bel	fst	7f	:222 :451 1:09 1:213	3↑ⒻVagrncyH-G3	105	6	4	42¼	31	1½	13	Smith M E	122	*.40	- -	*Sky Beauty*1223 For all Seasons1147¾ *Pamzig*107¾	Drew off, ridden out	6
6Nov93-4SA	fst	1⅛	:464 1:11 1:36 1:481	3↑ⒻBCDistaf-G1	101	1	53	66	52	32	54¼	Smith M E	120	4.30	- -	Hollywood Wildcat120no Paseana1232½ Re Toss1231	Lost ground 2nd turn	8
10Oct93-7Bel	fst	1	:231 :461 1:103 1:353	ⒻRrPrfume-G2	100	4	2½	21	2hd	1hd	11¾	Smith M E	124	*.30	- -	Sky Beauty1241¾ Fadetta112nk For all Seasons114nk	Prevailed, driving	6
14Aug93-9Sar	fst	1¼	:464 1:112 1:371 2:032	ⒻAlabama-G1	98	3	34	32½	2hd	1½	11½	Smith M E	121	*.70	- -	*Sky Beauty*1211½ Future Pretense1211¾ SilkyFeather1211½	Stalked, driving	8
11Jly93-8Bel	fst	1¼	:47 1:103 1:353 2:012	ⒻCCAOaks-G1	96	5	2½	2hd	1½	11½	1½	Smith M E	121	*.10	- -	*Sky Beauty*121½ Future Pretense1212 Silky Feather1213	Ridden out	5
6Jun93-9Bel	fst	1⅛	:464 1:11 1:361 1:493	ⒻMthrGoos-G1	102	4	2½	21	2½	12	15	Smith M E	121	*.50	- -	*Sky Beauty*1215 Dispute1213½ Silky Feather1215	Drew off, ridden out	4
8May93-8Bel	fst	1	:224 :453 1:101 1:352	ⒻAcorn-G1	107	6	31½	2½	1½	12	15¼	Smith M E	121	*.40	- -	*Sky Beauty*1215¼ Educated Risk1212½ In Her Glory1215¾	In hand	6
13Mar93-10GP	fst	1 1/16	:24 :491 1:14 1:433	ⒻBonnieMs-G2	94	1	21½	21½	2½	2½	2¾	Maple E	114	*1.30	- -	*Dispute*114¾ *Sky Beauty*1143 *Lunar Spook*1174¾	Bid, hung	6
19Sep92-5Bel	fst	7f	:222 :46 1:103 1:231	ⒻMatron-G1	92	2	8	41¾	3½	1½	12¾	Maple E	119	*.40	- -	Sky Beauty1192¾ *Educated Risk*1192¼ Family Enterprize1192¼	Driving	9
31Aug92-8Sar	fst	6f	:22 :45 1:094	ⒻSpinaway-G1	95	1	4	33	3½	1½	11¾	Maple E	119	*.30	- -	[D]*Sky Beauty*1191¾ FamilyEnterprize11910 [D]TryintheSky1192½	Ridden out	5
Disqualified and placed third																		
13Aug92-8Sar	fst	6f	:214 :451 1:10	ⒻAdirondk-G2	96	7	5	46	31	2hd	13½	Maple E	116	1.70	- -	Sky Beauty1163½ *Missed the Storm*1147 Distinct Habit1213	Driving	7
15Jly92-6Bel	fst	5½f	:222 :454 :574 1:041	ⒻAlw 27000NC	89	3	2	2½	31	11	12½	Maple E	121	*1.10	- -	*SkyBeauty*1212½ *TenaciousTiffany*1187 Clarwithaflare116½	Drew off, driving	7
3Jly92-3Bel	fst	5f	:22 :453 :58	ⒻMd Sp Wt 24k	85	3	4	41½	21	11	12	Maple E	117	5.30	- -	*Sky Beauty*1172 *Port of Silver*117¾ Quinpool1174¾	Driving	8

Sky Classic

ch. c. 1987, by Nijinsky II (Northern Dancer)–No Class, by Nodouble

Lifetime record: 29 15 6 1 $3,240,398

Own.– Sam–Son Farm
Br.– Sam–Son Farms (Can)
Tr.– James E. Day

Date	Cond	Dist	Fractions	Race	Fig	PP	St	1c	2c	Str	Fin	Jockey	Med/Wt		Odds	Spd	Top finishers	Comment	Fld
31Oct92-9GP	fm	1½Ⓣ	:474 1:112 2:00 2:24	3↑ BC Turf-G1	110	3	5	31½	31½	1hd	2no	Day P	L 126		*.90	101-00	Fraise126noSky Classic1262Quest for Fame1261	Game try	10
3Oct92-7Bel	fm	1½Ⓣ	:481 1:114 1:594 2:242	3↑ Turf Classic Inv-G1	110	6	3	42	42	1hd	11¾	Day P	126		*1.00	103-06	SkyClassic1261¾Fraise1262½SolarSplendor126nk	Mild drive	6
6Sep92-10AP	fm	1¼Ⓣ	:482 1:114 1:352 1:594	3↑ Arl Million-G1	108	6	4	55½	53½	1½	2hd	Day P	L 126		*1.20	98-03	DearDoctr126hdSkyClssc126nkGoldnPhsnt1262¼	Game 2nd	12
16Aug92-9AP	fm	1¼Ⓣ	:491 1:13 1:371 2:003	3↑ Arlington H-G2	102	3	5	44	53¼	31	11¼	Day P	L 125		*.30	94-09	SkyClassic1251¼[D]PlateDancer115¾Duckaroo112hd	Driving	9
28Jun92-5Atl	fm	1 3/16Ⓣ	:462 1:092 1:334 1:521	3↑ Caesars Int'l H-G2	106	2	8	87½	63¾	33	11¼	Day P	L 123		*.70	99-08	SkyClassic1231¼CheninBlanc1151LotusPool114½	Ridden out	9
7Jun92-7Bel	yl	1¼[T]	:48 1:121 1:371 2:022	3↑ ET Manhattan H-G2	107	8	5	55	31	2½	13	Day P	123		*1.20	78-22	SkyClssc1233RomnEnvoy1111¼LgrCt1161¼	Blocked ¼,driving	11
15May92-10Pim	fm	1⅛Ⓣ	:483 1:122 1:36 1:474	3↑ E T Dixie H-G3	105	8	6	67¼	66	32	1½	Day P	L 122		*1.00	96-11	SkyClassic122½FourstarsAllstar1162SocilRtr1121¾	Driving	10
1May92-8CD	fm	1⅛Ⓣ	:471 1:102 1:342 1:462	3↑ E T Turf Classic-G3	104	4	5	41¼	31½	2hd	2½	Day P	LB 123		*1.60	103-00	Cudas117½SkyClassic1231½FourstarsAllstar118no	2nd best	12
22Apr92-8Kee	fm	1Ⓣ	:233 :464 1:112 1:362	4↑ Fort Harrod-G3	99	3	5	52¼	61¼	64	41½	Day P	B 122		*1.10	95-05	Shudanz114nkTo Freedom113nkCudas1171	No late rally	9
2Nov91-7CD	fm	1½Ⓣ	:504 1:154 2:062 2:304	3↑ BC Turf-G1	-	1	1	1½	1hd	2hd	44½	Day P	B 126		3.30	91-06	Miss Alleged123½Itsallgreektome1262Quest for Fame1262		13
Pace,weakened																			
20Oct91-8WO	fm	1½Ⓣ	:482 1:123 2:03 2:274	3↑ Rothmans Int'l-G1	-	6	3	31½	1½	1hd	11	Day P	126		*.75e	101-05	Sky Classic1261Panoramic1261Tot of Rum126hd	Driving	11
22Sep91-8WO	fm	1¼Ⓣ	:454 1:102 1:352 2:003	3↑ [R]Seagram Cup H-G3C	-	3	6	66	42¼	3½	11¾	Day P	122		*.90	97-06	Sky Classic1221¾[D]Izvestia1252½Karmani1191¼	Hand ride	7
21Jly91-10WO	fm	1¼Ⓣ	:474 1:122 1:36 2:011	[R]Can Maturity-G1C	-	4	4	44½	3½	11½	11½	Walls MK	126		*.05e	94-12	SkyClassic1261½Secret'nClassy1262BrrBush126½	Ridden out	5
16Jun91-9WO	fm	1⅛Ⓣ	:451 1:083 1:333 1:461	3↑ K Edward Gold Cup H-G3	-	7	6	65½	43½	1½	14½	Day P	119		*.45e	93-07	SkyClassic1194½SlewofAngels1111¼Jalaajel116½	Hand ride	7
2Jun91-8WO	fm	1 1/16[T]	:23 :46 1:093 1:411	4↑ [R]Connaught Cup-G3C	-	4	5	56	24½	11½	12½	Day P	115		*.65	98-07	SkyClassic1152½StormyGladitor1191½Grncus1172½	Hand ride	6
1May91-8CD	fm	1⅛Ⓣ	:481 1:122 1:372 1:491	3↑ Alw 27870	-	3	5	53¾	63	2hd	13	Day P	B 116		*1.20	99-01	Sky Classic1163Alaqua118hdSpark O'Dan1182¼		9
Jostled 3/16,ridden out																			
14Apr91-8Kee	gd	1⅛Ⓣ	:494 1:143 1:384 1:511	4↑ Elkhorn-G2	-	6	1	1hd	1½	21½	63	Day P	B 113	b	4.50	86-13	Itsallgreektome123¾Pirate Army113¾Spark O'Dan113¾		7
Shied,misstep 3/16																			
16Mar91-7GP	fst	1 1/16	:232 :473 1:114 1:44	4↑ Alw 30500	-	8	8	84¼	85¾	87½	87¾	Day P	112		5.70	85-13	Gun Deck113¾Rowdy Regl1121½Lucky Tent114½	Wide stretch	8
23Nov90-8CD	gd	1⅛	:474 1:12 1:373 1:503	3↑ Clark-G3	-	7	4	45	44½	54	57½	Swatuk B	LB 113		26.70	87-14	SecretHello1152Din'sDncr1194DRoch1211½	Never threatened	7
27Oct90-8Bel	gd	1½Ⓣ	:494 1:153 2:041 2:293	3↑ BC Turf-G1	-	3	3	2½	109¼	1116	1126¼	Hawley S	121		38.20	56-15	In the Wings126½With Approval1261½El Senor1262½	Used up	11
14Oct90-7WO	sf	1½Ⓣ	:50 1:151 2:082 2:344	3↑ Rothmans Int'l-G1	-	5	2	21½	11	2½	21¼	Hawley S	118		21.95	65-37	FrenchGlory1261¼SkyClassic1183Cozzene'sPrinc1181	Gamely	10
30Sep90-9WO	sf	1¼Ⓣ	:481 1:13 1:383 2:051	3↑ Niagara H-G3	-	9	3	3nk	1hd	1hd	65¼	Hawley S	115	b	3.45	69-26	Hodges Bay117noShellac116noSteady Power1152½	Tired	13
15Sep90-9WO	yl	1[T]	:232 :47 1:112 1:373	Alw 28500	-	4	6	54½	33	32½	31½	Hawley S	119		*.45	84-18	Noble Concorde1141½Viking King115noSky Classic1197½		6
Closed willingly																			
8Oct89-7WO	fst	1 1/16	:231 :47 1:122 1:46	Grey-G3	-	5	5	25	1½	12½	13½	Hawley S	122		*.35	79-21	Sky Classic1223½La Dolce Vita117¾Halo's Honey1133		7
Ducked in,handily																			
24Sep89-8WO	fm	1 1/16Ⓣ	:223 :45 1:101 1:422	[R]Cup & Saucer-G1C	-	11	8	64¼	2hd	16	110	Hawley S	122		*.25	92-15	SkyClassic12210TruthSquad122hdFrenchKing1222½	Handily	11
10Sep89-5WO	fm	1[T]	:23 :471 1:114 1:36	Summer-G3	-	2	9	84¾	4¾	11½	15½	Hawley S	122		*1.20	97-09	SkyClassic1225½D'Parrot1224DestinationMoon122¾	Handily	11
23Aug89-8WO	fm	*7f[T]	:234 :473 1:14 1:261	Md Sp Wt	-	6	3	53¼	52¾	12	15	Hawley S	115		*.35	85-00	SkyClssc1155DestinationMoon120½VikingKng1201¼	Handily	10
22Jly89-10WO	fst	6f	:222 :45 1:101	[R]Vandal-G3C	-	3	6	42	21	21	2hd	Hawley S	115		*.55	92-14	EverSteady122hdSkyClassic1155¾Halo'sHoney115¾	Game try	7
24Jun89-9WO	fst	5½f	:224 :463 :59 1:06	[R]Clarendon-G3C	-	4	7	42	42	32	21¼	Hawley S	115		*.60	86-19	Ever Steady1171¼Sky Classic1152Briar Bush1178	Steadied	7

Smoke Glacken

Own: Karkenny & Levy & Roberts

Gr/ro. c. 3 (Apr) FTKJUL95 $34,000
Sire: Two Punch (Mr. Prospector)
Dam: Majesty's Crown (Magesterial)
Br: Perry M. Rosebrock (Md)
Tr: Carroll Henry L

Life	14	10	2	1	$759,560	117	D.Fst	11	8	1	1	$663,310	117
1997	8	6	1	1	$475,060	117	Wet(385)	3	2	1	0	$96,250	102
1996	6	4	1	0	$284,500	93	Turf(225)	0	0	0	0	$0	-
	0	0	0	0	$0	-	Dst(0)	0	0	0	0	$0	-

19Jly97-10Lrl	fst	6f	:22 :444 :57 1:092	3↑DeFrncsM-G2	110	2	2	1½	13½	12	11½	Perret C	L113	*.40	97-15	SmokeGlacken1131½ WiseDusty112hd *CapoteBelle*110¾	Well off rail, dug in	7
28Jun97-3Mth	fst	6f	:213 :441 :554 1:082	JerShrBC-G3	117	1	3	11	12½	13	12½	Perret C	L122	*.10	100-12	*SmokeGlacken*1222½ PrtnersHero1158¼ KingBuck1157¾	Fast pace decisive	4
7Jun97-7Bel	fst	7f	:224 :453 1:083 1:204	RivaRidg-G3	114	6	1	11½	11½	12½	13¼	Perret C	L123	*.70	97-05	*Smoke Glacken*1233¼ Trafalger1231 Wild Wonder120nk	Kept to task	6
20Apr97-8Kee	fst	1 1/16	:23 :47 1:11 1:431	Lexingtn-G2	91	2	13	1hd	2½	23	28½	Perret C	L118	*.70	83-08	TouchGold1158½ *SmokeGlckn*1183 DdsNotWords112¾	No match for winner	5
16Mar97-9FG	fst	1 1/16	:224 :453 1:101 1:423	LaDerby-G3	97	8	12	13	12	1½	3½	Perret C	L122	*.70	96-17	*CryptoStar*118hd StopWatch118½ SmokeGlcken1223½	Failed to sustain bid	9
1Mar97-9OP	sly	1	:224 :47 1:123 1:383	Southwst-G3	102	6	13	12	12	13	18	Perret C	L117	*.60	86-27	SmkGlckn1178 *PhntmOnTr*1223½ AlwysMyPlc1132½	Unchallenged, handily	8
8Feb97-9OP	my	6f	:22 :461 :591 1:114	MntnValley53k	101	3	1	1hd	13	12½	13½	Perret C	L119	*.10	82-24	*Smoke Glacken*1193½ *Prosong*1161½ Near the Bank1191¼	Held sway, driving	5
12Jan97-9FG	fst	6f	:214 :45 :564 1:092	BlackGoldH37k	102	1	3	23	2½	11	15½	Perret C	L122	*.50	97-10	*Smoke Glacken*1225½ Traufast Slew11414 Auto Be aHero114	Much the best	3
15Sep96-8Bel	fst	1	:222 :45 1:101 1:351	Futurity-G1	72	7	3½	1hd	1hd	32½	514	Perret C	122	*.90	73-13	Traitor1225½ *Night in Reno*1226 Harley Tune122½	Speed 4w,tired late	9
31Aug96-8Sar	fst	7f	:213 :441 1:093 1:233	Hopeful-G1	93	6	2	2hd	11	15	19	Perret C	122	7.00	88-12	Smoke Glacken1229 *Ordway*1222 Gun Fight122¾	Speed outside,in hand	8
17Aug96-11Mth	fst	6f	:211 :44 :563 1:10	Sapling-G2	86	4	5	2½	2hd	12	11¾	Perret C	122	2.50	93-07	*Smoke Glacken*1221¾ Harley Tune1224¾ Country Rainbow122¾	Driving	10
28Jly96-9Mth	fst	5½f	:22 :451 :574 1:043	Tyro40k	84	1	4	21½	2hd	2hd	11	Perret C	116	*.70	96-08	*Smoke Glacken*1161 *Johnny Legit*1162¼ Partner's Hero1163½	Driving	9
12Jly96-8Mth	fst	5½f	:221 :452 :574 1:043	Md Sp Wt 20k	84	3	1	1½	14	19	18½	Mojica R Jr	118	*.80	96-15	*Smoke Glacken*1188½ Mary's Socialite1184½ Fromsilvertogold1181¾	Easily	7
30Jun96-2Mth	sly	5½f	:214 :451 :582 1:052	Md Sp Wt 20k	82	7	1	1hd	1½	2hd	2½	Mojica R Jr	118	9.80	91-12	*Confide*118½ *Smoke Glacken*1184¾ Capture the Gold1185	Gamely	7

Soaring Softly

Own: Phillips Racing Partnership

Ch. f. 4 (Mar)
Sire: Kris S. (Roberto) $75,000
Dam: Wings of Grace (Key to the Mint)
Br: Galbreath/Phillips Racing Partnership (Ky)
Tr: Toner James J

Life	16	9	1	3	$1,270,433	105	D.Fst	6	1	1	2	$54,643	90
1999	8	7	0	0	$1,193,450	105	Wet(378)	2	1	0	1	$22,340	81
1998	6	1	1	2	$54,643	90	Turf(336)	8	7	0	0	$1,193,450	105
	0	0	0	0	$0	-	Dst(0)	0	0	0	0	$0	-

6Nov99-7GP	gd	1⅜ Ⓣ	:491 1:14 1:383 2:134	3↑ⒻBCF&MTrf-G1	105	12	96	87½	83¾	31½	1¾	Bailey J D	L123	*3.60	87-09	Soaring Softly123¾ *Coretta*123hd Zomaradah123hd	4 wide rally, up late	14
30Oct99-6Bel	fm	1¼ Ⓣ	:504 1:15 1:383 2:012	3↑ⒻFlrBlIvH-G1	103	6	62	62½	4nk	3nk	11	Bailey J D	L118	3.05	84-17	*Soaring Softly*1181 Coretta118¾ Mossflower115½	4 wide move, driving	7
5Sep99-9Sar	fm	1⅛ Ⓣ	:473 1:112 1:342 1:454	3↑ⒻDianaH-G1	94	6	74¾	75	53	52¾	53¾	Smith M E	L118	*2.10	97 -	HeritgeofGold1151 *KhumbMel*114nk Mossflower114½	3 wide move 2nd turn	9
17Jly99-8Bel	fm	1¼ Ⓣ	:503 1:151 1:391 2:021	3↑ⒻNewYorkH-G2	102	4	43	42½	2½	1hd	1no	Smith M E	L117	*1.20	80-20	Soaring Softly117no Tampico116¾ Anguilla119hd	3 wide turns, got nod	6
31May99-9Bel	fm	1⅜ Ⓣ	:522 1:16 1:391 2:15	3↑ⒻShpshdBH-G2	101	4	41	44¾	44	14½	15½	Smith M E	L114	2.90	80-20	*SoaringSoftly*1145½ StarryDremer114¾ PinforePrk1133¼	Quick inside move	6
8May99-8GS	fm	*1⅛ Ⓣ	:473 1:123 1:371 1:49	3↑ⒻVinelandH50k	98	3	37	38	33½	2½	13	Smith M E	L115	*1.00	110-10	*SoringSoftly*1153 AbsolutelyQuni1182 *HousVirgin*1122	Control 3w drew off	6
17Apr99-7Kee	fm	1⅛ Ⓣ	:472 1:111 1:353 1:482	4↑ⒻAlw 58500N3X	94	4	89	87¼	810	63½	1½	Sellers S J	L115	3.50	87-18	*Soaring Softly*115½ *Mocha Mocha*1151 Riotous Miss1151	Rail, hand urging	9
1Mar99-8GP	fm	*1⅛ Ⓣ	:503 1:144 1:393 1:511	4↑ⒻAlw 34000N3L	88	8	84¾	73½	75	2hd	11¼	Smith M E	L116	4.10	80-16	*SoringSoftly*1161¼ MomntsofMgic1161¾ GurrEtPx118½	4 wide, edged away	9
5Dec98-6Aqu	fst	1 1/16 ⊡	:233 :482 1:124 1:453	3↑ⒻAlw 43000N2X	77	4	44	51¾	33½	23½	2¾	Gryder A T	L114	2.70	76-21	Light Bail116¾ *Soaring Softly*1141½ Global Star1161¼	Finished strongly	6
20Nov98-7Aqu	fst	1	:233 :47 1:113 1:37	3↑ⒻAlw 43000N2X	76	6	43½	43½	21½	26	39¼	Gryder A T	L114	3.05	75-24	Santaria1148 OneRunBaby1141½ SoringSoftly1144¼	Wide move, weakened	6
1Nov98-6Aqu	fst	1	:243 :481 1:124 1:374	3↑ⒻAlw 43000N2X	83	4	43½	44	31½	43	35	Gryder A T	L114	5.00	75-33	Christmas List1143 *Santaria*1142 Soaring Softly1141	Wide trip, no rally	5
27Jun98-8Bel	fst	1⅛	:454 1:10 1:342 1:473	ⒻMthrGoos-G1	70	3	94¾	75	84½	716	619½	Gryder A T	L121	28.00	72-16	*Jersey Girl*1211 Keeper Hill1213 *Banshee Breeze*1211	Betwn rivals,no rally	11
7Jun98-8Bel	fst	1	:223 :452 1:101 1:361	ⒻAcorn-G1	90	9	72¾	76	74¾	46	44½	Davis R G	L121	38.50	78-22	*Jersey Girl*1212¾ Santaria121no Brave Deed1211¾	Drifted str,gamely	10
24Apr98-5Kee	fst	*7f	:214 :443 1:10 1:263	ⒻAlw 43495N2L	82	3	7	76½	65	2½	12½	Sellers S J	L119	*1.90	96-08	SoringSoftly1192½ JudithLynn119nk *CuntoEs*1221½	Drew clear, ridden out	9
11Nov97-5Aqu	gd	1	:223 :451 1:11 1:374	ⒻMd Sp Wt 31k	81	5	44½	69½	36	12	14	Smith M E	119	*2.10	81-20	*SoringSoftly*1194 NewDirection1144 GretRspct1198½	Drew clear,ridden out	9
18Oct97-1Bel	gd	7f	:223 :453 1:093 1:22	ⒻMd Sp Wt 34k	67	4	5	66	54	35	310	Bravo J	119	5.20e	81-09	Azarba11910 *Pretty Blue*119no *Soaring Softly*1192½	Lost nod for place	7

Storm Song

Own: Dogwood Stable

B. f. 3 (Feb) KEESEP95 $100,000
Sire: Summer Squall (Storm Bird)
Dam: Hum Along (Fappiano)
Br: W. S. Farish & O. M. Phipps (Ky)
Tr: Zito Nicholas P

Life	12	4	1	2	$1,020,050	97	D.Fst	11	4	1	2	$1,017,830	97
1997	5	0	0	2	$121,845	89	Wet(353)	1	0	0	0	$2,220	57
1996	7	4	1	0	$898,205	97	Turf(283)	0	0	0	0	$0	-
	0	0	0	0	$0	-	Dst(0)	0	0	0	0	$0	-

31May97-9Bel	fst	1	:221 :443 1:084 1:342	ⒻAcorn-G1	82	1	32½	31½	33½	47½	711¼	Bravo J	L121	5.90	81-14	Sharp Cat1212½ Dixie Flag1214¾ *Ajina*1211¼	Close up inside,tired	7
2May97-9CD	fst	1⅛	:474 1:114 1:37 1:501	ⒻKyOaks-G1	88	7	86¾	86½	68½	510	49¾	Perret C	L121	18.00	83-05	BlushingKD1212½ TomsusDlght121¾ [D]*ShrpCt*1216½	Bumped start, late bid	9
Placed third through disqualification																		
5Apr97-8Kee	fst	1 1/16	:232 :464 1:112 1:434	ⒻAshland-G1	89	5	43½	37½	37½	39½	38½	Perret C	L121	4.80	80-22	Glitter Woman1216½ Anklet1212 Storm Song1216	Chased pace evenly	6
9Mar97-10GP	fst	1 1/16	:231 :462 1:10 1:431	ⒻBonnieMs-G2	65	1	43	43	47	510	522	Perret C	L122	3.60	69-16	*Glitter Woman*1177½ Southern Playgirl119¾ *Dixie Flag*1145	Outrun	5
9Feb97-10GP	fst	170	:234 :47 1:101 1:391	ⒻDvonaDal-G3	83	4	45	43½	43	46½	513¾	Perret C	L121	1.30	85-08	*Glitter Woman*1194 City Band1214 Southern Playgirl121¾	Faltered	6
26Oct96-4WO	fst	1 1/16	:223 :46 1:104 1:433	ⒻBCJuvFil-G1	97	4	77½	65	53½	11	14½	Perret C	L119	*1.60	91-02	StormSong1194½ LoveThtJzz1193½ CriticlFctor1194½	Perfect trip driving	12
6Oct96-8Bel	fst	1 1/16	:222 :451 1:093 1:422	ⒻFrizette-G1	96	6	36	33	21	11½	14	Perret C	L119	2.85	87-12	*Storm Song*1194 Sharp Cat1196 Aldiza1196½	Wide move trn,drew clr	7
15Sep96-7Bel	fst	1	:224 :452 1:10 1:36	ⒻMatron-G1	88	4	44	36½	31½	32	21	Perret C	119	6.50	82-13	Sharp Cat1191 *Storm Song*1192½ Fabulously Fast1192	Advanced turn,game	6
30Aug96-8Sar	fst	7f	:221 :443 1:10 1:233	ⒻSpinaway-G1	66	6	7	51¼	53	77½	610½	Day P	121	4.50	78-12	Oath121¾ Pearl City121no Fabulously Fast1219	Roused turn,no rally	9
12Aug96-8Sar	fst	6½f	:214 :452 1:104 1:173	ⒻAdirondk-G2	76	9	2	52½	41	1hd	16	Day P	113	6.80	87-10	StormSong1136 LstTwoSttes1131 [DH]Lrkwhistl116	6w bid 1/4p,going away	9
1Aug96-4Sar	sly	6f	:22 :454 :582 1:114	ⒻAlw 38147N2L	57	5	6	31	31½	32½	45¾	Day P	117	*.45e	76-13	Last Two States115¾ Pentelis1174 Carodela1171	5w turn,no rally	6
19Apr96-3Kee	fst	4½f	:222 :453 :513	ⒻMd Sp Wt 33k	–	6	4	42		2hd	14	Day P	117	5.90	- -	StormSong1174 DblosStry1172 NghtynHghty1171¼	Drew clear, ridden out	10

The Wicked North

Own: Philip & Sophie Hersh Trust

Ch. h. 5 (May)
Sire: Far North (Northern Dancer)
Dam: Wicked Witchcraft (Good Behaving)
Br: Edward Zurek (Ky)
Tr: Bernstein David

Life	17	8	4	1	$1,180,750	116	D.Fst	14	7	4	0	$1,095,750	116
1994	6	3	1	0	$921,750	116	Wet(240)	1	0	0	1	$30,000	93
1993	5	2	1	1	$166,200	112	Turf(235)	2	1	0	0	$55,000	104
	0	0	0	0	$0	-	Dst(0)	0	0	0	0	$0	-

2Jly94-3Hol	fst	1¼	:47 1:102 1:35 2:003	3↑HolGdCpH-G1	97	2	31	31½	32	47	48¾	Desormeaux K J	LB122	*.60	- -	SlewofDamascus117¾ *Fnmore*116½ DelMrDennis1167½	Early bid 3-w,empty	5
5Jun94-8Hol	fst	1⅛	:46 1:094 1:334 1:463	3↑Calfrnin-G1	116	1	2hd	21	32	31	1nk	Desormeaux K J	LB120	*.80	- -	ThWckdNorth120nk KngdomFnd1161¾ *SlwfDmscs*1163½	Hard drive,up late	7
16Apr94-10OP	fst	1⅛	:463 1:101 1:352 1:474	4↑OaklawnH-G1	111	5	22½	31	22	1hd	11½	Desormeaux K J	L119	*.90	- -	*TheWickedNorth*1191½ DevilHisDue120hd *BrothrBrown*116½	Rallied, driving	12
5Mar94-5SA	fst	1¼	:472 1:112 1:352 2:00	4↑SAH-G1	111	3	2½	2hd	1½	11½	11½	Desormeaux K J	LB118	*1.80	- -	[D]*The Wicked North*1181½ Stuka1151¼ *Bien Bien*120no	Drifted, drew clear	8
Disqualified and placed 4th																		
13Feb94-8SA	fst	1⅛	:464 1:103 1:35 1:472	4↑SnAntnoH-G2	115	8	2½	1hd	2hd	13	14½	Desormeaux K J	LB116	6.40	- -	The Wicked North1164½ [D]Hill Pass116½ Region1174½	Long lead, driving	9
8Jan94-8SA	fst	7f	:22 :443 1:104 1:211	4↑SnCrlosH-G2	104	6	3	31½	41½	21½	2¾	Solis A	LB117	*1.10	- -	Cardmania122¾ *The Wicked North*1172½ Portoferraio1151	Finished well	7
6Nov93-9SA	fst	7f	:214 :441 1:082 1:204	3↑SmileH100k	105	7	2	32½	32	21	23½	Smith M E	LB117	*2.90	- -	Memo1183½ The Wicked North117hd *Ibero*1201	Bid 1/8, no match	12
23Oct93-9Lrl	yl	1 Ⓣ	:24 :48 1:124 1:38	3↑DCIntl-G1	88	3	1½	1hd	2hd	3½	79	Black C A	L126	3.50	- -	Buckhar1261½ [D]Cleone126no Maryland Moon1262	Steadied,in tight 1/8	8
6Sep93-5BM	fm	1 1/16 Ⓣ	:223 :46 1:101 1:414	3↑SFrncscoH-G3	104	7	21	22	21	11½	12½	Solis A	LB114	3.20	- -	TheWickdNorth1142½ ThTndrTrck1172 *SlwofDmscus*115¾	Stlkd 2w, driving	7
1Aug93-8Dmr	fst	6f	:22 :444 :562 1:082	3↑BCrosbyH-G3	112	5	2	2hd	2hd	2hd	1hd	Black C A	LB116	7.80	- -	*The Wicked North*116hd Thirty Slews1211 BlackJackRoad115½	Held gamely	6
16Jan93-8SA	sly	1⅛	:46 1:103 1:364 1:511	SnFrnndo-G2	93	5	21	21	22	26	39¾	Nakatani C S	L116	2.90	- -	Bertrndo1209 StrRecruit120¾ *ThWickdNorth*1164	Pressed pace, weakened	8
26Dec92-8SA	fst	7f	:222 :45 1:081 1:203	Malibu-G2	103	2	5	21	42	33	2½	Nakatani C S	LB116	4.30	- -	StroftheCrop118½ TheWickedNorth116nk *Bertrndo*1205½	Strong late rally	11
21Nov92-8Hol	fst	1 1/16	:23 :46 1:101 1:41	LBareraH-G3	107	2	11	1hd	1hd	2hd	2nk	Desormeaux K J	LB116	*1.20	- -	*StrRcrt*117nk ThWckdNorth116½ LottryWnnr115no	Fast pace, held gamely	7
8Nov92-7SA	fst	1	:23 :461 1:102 1:354	3↑Alw 36000NC	104	5	1½	2hd	1hd	12	13	Desormeaux K J	LB115	*1.10	- -	TheWickedNorth1153 DoubleoSlew1153½ *DesertSun*1164	Drew off, handily	8
9Oct92-7SA	fst	1	:23 :462 1:101 1:352	Alw 32000NC	104	2	1½	1½	12	13	12½	Desormeaux K J	LB117	2.20	- -	*ThWckdNorth*1172½ SoEvrClvr117¼ TurbulntKrs1201	Well rated ridden out	9
7Sep92-6Dmr	fst	6½f	:214 :443 1:09 1:152	3↑Md Sp Wt 28k	96	3	6	1hd	1½	13½	15	Desormeaux K J	LB118	3.30	- -	*The Wicked North*1185 Pennington1185 Compeii118nk	Dueled ridden out	12
22Dec91-9Hol	fst	6½f	:213 :443 1:10 1:164	Md Sp Wt 28k	–	2	9	814	813	713	65¾	Pincay L Jr	118	15.00	- -	Saron Lake1181¼ Play Ten1181 *Treekster*118nk	Broke slowly	9

Thunder Gulch

Own: Tabor Michael

Ch. c. 3 (May) KEEJUL93 $40,000
Sire: Gulch (Mr. Prospector)
Dam: Line of Thunder (Storm Bird)
Br: Peter M. Brant (Ky)
Tr: Lukas D. W

Life	16	9	2	2	$2,915,086	110	D.Fst	15	9	1	2	$2,890,798	110
1995	10	7	0	1	$2,644,080	110	Wet(348)	1	0	1	0	$24,288	79
1994	6	2	2	1	$271,006	99	Turf(278)	0	0	0	0	$0	–
	0	0	0	0	$0	–	Dst(0)	0	0	0	0	$0	–

7Oct95-10Bel fst 1¼ :48 1:11 2 1:36 2:01 1 3↑ JkyClbGC-G1 **90** 4 21 31 45 49½ 514 Stevens G L 121 b 3.05 - - *Cigar*1261 UnaccountedFor1269¾ StarStandard1212 Hard ridden turn,tired 7
23Sep95-10TP fst 1⅛ :47 3 1:11 4 1:36 4 1:49 2 3↑ KyCpClsscH396k **108** 5 52¾ 43 2½ 2hd 11 Stevens G L 121 b *.20 - - Thunder Gulch1211 *JudgeTC*1121½ BoundbyHonor1138 Raced 4 wide, clear 6
19Aug95-8Sar fst 1¼ :47 1 1:11 2 1:37 1 2:03 3 Travers-G1 **110** 5 41½ 42 1½ 1½ 14½ Stevens G L 126 b *.75 - - *Thunder Gulch*1264½ Pyramid Peak1262 Malthus1262½ Quick outs move 7
23Jly95-8Hol fst 1⅛ :46 2 1:10 1 1:35 3 1:49 Swaps-G2 **101** 4 21 2½ 21 1hd 12 Stevens G L B126 b *.90 - - *Thunder Gulch*1262 *Da Hoss*118¾ *Petionville*120¾ Drew clear, driving 7
10Jun95-9Bel fst 1½ :50 1 1:15 1 2:32 Belmont-G1 **101** 10 31 2½ 2hd 1hd 12 Stevens G L 126 b *1.50 - - *ThunderGulch*1262 StarStandard1263½ Citdeed1261½ Prominent, prevailed 11
20May95-10Pim fst 1 3/16 :47 1 1:10 4 1:35 2 1:54 2 Preaknes-G1 **105** 11 54½ 55 54½ 4¾ 3¾ Stevens G L 126 b 3.80 - - TmbrCountry126½ OlvrsTwst126nk *ThundrGlch*1264 3w advance,outfnshed 11
6May95-8CD fst 1¼ :45 4 1:10 1 1:35 3 2:01 1 KyDerby-G1 **108** 16 53½ 42 21 12 12¼ Stevens G L 126 b 24.50 - - ThundrGulch1262¼ TjnoRun126hd *TimbrCountry*126¾ Drew clear ridden out 19
15Apr95-7Kee fst 1⅛ :49 1:13 1 1:37 2 1:49 1 BlueGras-G2 **101** 4 31½ 31 3½ 42¼ 44½ Day P 121 b *1.30 - - WildSyn1212½ SuveProspect121hd TejnoRun1212 Pressed pace, gave way 6
11Mar95-10GP fst 1⅛ :47 1 1:11 3 1:36 2 1:49 3 FlaDerby-G1 **101** 7 32½ 31½ 2½ 21½ 1no Smith M E 122 b 2.00 - - Thunder Gulch122no Suave Prospect1225 Mecke1222 All out, just up 10
18Feb95-9GP fst 1 1/16 :23 1 :46 4 1:11 1:43 1 FntnOYth-G2 **105** 9 72 62 3nk 1hd 1nk Smith M E 119 b 4.70 - - *ThunderGulch*119nk SuaveProspect1174 JamblyJzz1193½ Dueled, prevailed 12
18Dec94-8Hol fst 1 1/16 :22 4 :46 1:09 3 1:40 3 HolFut-G1 **99** 1 47 47½ 47 25 26½ Nakatani C S B121 b 3.80 - - *Afternoon Deelites*1216½ *Thunder Gulch*12110 A. J. Jett121½ Best of rest 5
26Nov94-7Aqu fst 1⅛ :48 1 1:14 1:40 2 1:53 4 Remsen-G2 **89** 9 75 73¾ 41¼ 21 1nk Stevens G L 115 5.60 - - ThunderGulch115nk WestrnEcho1193 MightyMg114¾ Lugged in str, drvng 10
Previously trained by Kimmel John C 1994(as of 11/11): (180 32 23 28 0.18)
11Nov94-8Aqu fst 1 :23 :46 1 1:11 1 1:37 2 Nashua-G3 **79** 6 42½ 42½ 41½ 42½ 44¾ Bailey J D 112 *1.35 - - Devious Course1142 Mighty Magee1122¾ Old Tascosa122no No threat 7
23Oct94-8Aqu my 7f :22 2 :45 4 1:11 1 1:24 3 Cowdin-G2 **79** 4 7 65 74 35 22½ Velazquez J R 122 4.40 - - Old Tascosa1222½ Thunder Gulch1221½ Adams Trail1222¼ Rallied inside 8
4Oct94-3Bel fst 6f :22 4 :46 3 :58 3 1:11 Md Sp Wt 28k **82** 4 3 73¼ 31 31 1no Velazquez J R 118 *1.00 - - Thunder Gulch118no Porphyry118½ Last Effort1181½ Driving 9
16Sep94-3Bel fst 6f :22 4 :46 3 :58 4 1:11 1 Md Sp Wt 28k **69** 2 3 41¼ 51¼ 31 3nk Velazquez J R 118 6.50 - - Crusader's Story118no Porphyry118nk *Thunder Gulch*1181½ Rough trip 8

Tight Spot

b. c. 1987, by His Majesty (Ribot)–Premium Win, by Lyphard
Own.–Anderson & VHW Stable & Whitham
Br.– Verne H. Winchell (Ky)
Tr.– Ronald McAnally

Lifetime record: 21 12 3 1 $1,566,100

16Aug92-8Dmr fm 1⅛Ⓣ :47 4 1:11 1 1:35 2 1:47 1 3↑ Eddie Read H-G1 103 2 2 1hd 2hd 31 44 Pincay L Jr LB 125 *1.50 96-02 Marquetry118noLuthirEnchntur116hdLgrCt1154 Saved ground 7
21Mar92-8GG fm 1Ⓣ :23 4 :47 1 1:10 4 1:35 2 3↑ S F Mile H-G3 108 1 1 11½ 1½ 1hd 1nk Pincay L Jr LB 125 *.80 101-03 Tight Spot125nkNotorious Pleasure116½Forty Niner Days1161 9
Held gamely
28Feb92-8SA fm 1Ⓣ :23 :45 3 1:09 2 1:33 2 4↑ Alw 55000 106 5 1 11 13 13 11½ Pincay L Jr LB 121 *.60 96-04 Tight Spot1211½Laxey Bay116noEton Lad114¾ Ridden out 6
2Nov91-5CD fm 1Ⓣ :24 :48 1:12 2 1:37 2 3↑ BC Mile-G1 - 12 7 31 2hd 51¼ 96¼ Pincay L Jr LB 126 2.80 91-06 Opening Verse1261¼Val des Bois126noStar of Cozzene1232¼ 14
Dueled,tired
1Sep91-9AP fm 1¼Ⓣ :47 3 1:11 1 1:35 4 1:59 2 3↑ Arl Million-G1 - 7 3 21½ 21 2½ 1hd Pincay L Jr L 126 *1.80 101-07 Tight Spot126hdAlgenib122nkKartajana123nk All out 10
11Aug91-8Dmr fm 1⅛Ⓣ :47 2 1:11 2 1:35 1 1:47 1 3↑ Eddie Read H-G1 - 7 1 13½ 11½ 12½ 13½ Pincay L Jr LB 125 *1.10 102-02 TightSpot1253½ValdesBois115nkMadjaristn116nk Ridden out 7
4Jly91-8Hol fm 1⅛Ⓣ :47 2 1:10 2 1:34 1 1:46 3↑ American H-G2 - 1 1 11½ 11½ 11½ 11 Pincay L Jr LB 123 *1.70 100-08 Tight Spot1231Exbourne1223Super May118½ Ridden out 8
8Jun91-8Hol fm 1 1/16Ⓣ :24 1 :47 3 1:11 1:40 1 3↑ Inglewood H-G2 - 3 1 12½ 13 14 14½ Pincay L Jr LB 121 *.80 94-07 TightSpot1214½Somethingdiffernt116hdRzn114no Ridden out 6
8May91-8Hol fm 1⅛Ⓣ :47 1:10 1 1:33 2 1:44 4 4↑ Alw 50000 - 2 1 11½ 11½ 11 1nk Pincay L Jr LB 117 *1.40 106-01 Tight Spot117nkHigh Rank1155Tarsho1141¼ Held gamely 5
19Aug90-8Dmr fm 1⅛Ⓣ :48 3 1:13 1 1:37 1 1:49 3 Dmr Derby-G2 - 9 1 11½ 11½ 12½ 13 Pincay L Jr LB 122 *1.10e 90-08 ⒹTightSpot1223Itsallgrektom1221¾Prdcssor122¾ Came over 10
Disqualified and placed 10th - ruling rescinded 9/26/90
5Aug90-8Dmr fm 1 1/16Ⓣ :24 1 :48 1:11 2 1:41 4 La Jolla H-G3 - 6 2 2½ 2hd 12 1no Delhoussaye E L 118 2.30 98-04 TightSpot118noItsallgrktom1194MuscProspctor1181 Driving 6
22Jun90-7Hol fm 1 1/16Ⓣ :23 4 :47 2 1:11 2 1:41 3 ⓇStar Dust 79k - 5 1 1½ 1½ 11½ 12 Delahoussaye E 117 2.60 87-15 TightSpot1172Predecessor114hdKeptHisCool112no Driving 7
21Apr90-8GG fst 1⅛ :44 4 1:08 3 1:34 1:46 4 Cal Derby-G3 - 9 4 42 43½ 49½ 413¾ Black CA 115 2.70 77-14 StalwartCharger1152¼MusicPrspectr1178Tsu'sDawning1173½ 12
Evenly
31Mar90-10TP my 1⅛ :46 3 1:11 2 1:37 2 1:49 2 Jim Beam-G2 - 10 3 2hd 2½ 48 518 Black CA 121 4.50 80-20 Summer Squall1212½Bright Again1218Yonder1216 Gave way 10
3Mar90-8SA fst 1 :23 :46 4 1:11 1 1:36 3 San Rafael-G2 - 7 2 21½ 21 22½ 22½ Black CA 115 13.70 81-22 MisterFrisky1152½TightSpot1152LandRsh1156½ Good effort 7
28Jan90-8GG fst 1 :22 2 :45 3 1:09 4 1:34 El Cerrito H 53k - 1 2 3½ 2hd 11 12½ Hansen RD 115 4.70 95-14 TightSpot1152½MuchDivorced116½DragRace1197 Hard ridden 6
17Dec89-3Hol fst 1 1/16 :23 1 :47 2 1:12 1:43 2 Md Sp Wt - 6 1 11 1½ 12½ 17 Delahoussaye E 117 *.70 83-14 TightSpot1177Carrie'sGlory117¾HawaiianPass1171 Easily 7
26Nov89-2Hol gd 1 1/16 :23 3 :47 1 1:11 4 1:43 4 Md Sp Wt - 4 1 1½ 1hd 1hd 24 Delahoussaye E 117 3.80 77-21 AssyrianPirate1174TightSpot117hdRiflemaker1174 Weakened 8
12Nov89-4SA fst 1 1/16 :23 2 :47 1:11 2 1:42 2 Md Sp Wt - 4 1 1½ 2hd 22½ 39½ Baze RA 118 3.30 82-14 Land Rush1184Riflemaker1185½Tight Spot1183 Weakened 6
14Oct89-4SA fst 6½f :22 :45 1 1:10 3 1:17 Md Sp Wt - 2 1 2hd 1hd 2½ 22 Baze RA 117 *1.70 83-15 ElToreo1172TightSpot1174GoodFieldNoHit1175 Held place 6
9Sep89 6Dmr fst 6f :22 :46 2 :57 2 1:09 1 Md Sp Wt - 0 4 21 3½ GC 712½ Solis A 117 10.00 79-11 Grand Canyon1172½Jet West117¾Pleasant Tap1174 Wide 9

Timber Country

Own: Overbrook Farms / Gainesway Stable & Lewis

Ch. c. 3 (Apr) KEEJUL93 $500,000
Sire: Woodman (Mr. Prospector)
Dam: Fall Aspen (Pretense)
Br: Lowquest, Ltd. (Ky)
Tr: Lukas D. W

Life	12	5	1	4	$1,560,400	106	D.Fst	11	5	1	3	$1,537,900	106
1995	5	1	1	2	$631,810	106	Wet(274)	1	0	0	1	$22,500	96
1994	7	4	0	2	$928,590	100	Turf(294)	0	0	0	0	$0	–
	0	0	0	0	$0	–	Dst(0)	0	0	0	0	$0	–

20May95-10Pim fst 1 3/16 :47 1 1:10 4 1:35 2 1:54 2 Preaknes-G1 **106** 7 66 65½ 67½ 3½ 1½ Day P 126 *1.90 - - TimberCountry126½ OlivrsTwist126nk *ThundrGulch*1264 Circled 5w, driving 11
6May95-8CD fst 1¼ :45 4 1:10 1 1:35 3 2:01 1 KyDerby-G1 **104** 15 139¾ 105¾ 106¼ 64¼ 32¼ Day P 126 *3.40e - - ThundrGulch1262¼ TjnoRun126hd *TmbrCountry*126¾ Settled, saved ground 19
8Apr95-5SA fst 1⅛ :46 2 1:10 1:34 4 1:47 4 SADerby-G1 **104** 8 63¼ 64½ 66½ 35 41¼ Day P B122 1.80 - - LrrytheLegnd122hd AftrnoonDlits122nk Jumron1221 Rallied with pressure 8
19Mar95-5SA fst 1 1/16 :23 :46 3 1:10 1 1:42 SnFelipe-G2 **97** 3 44 42 42 32½ 21 Day P B122 2.20 - - AfternoonDeelites1191 TimberCountry1222 LkeGeorg11614 Finished well 4
4Mar95-5SA gd 1 :24 :48 4 1:13 1 1:37 3 SnRafael-G2 **96** 2 54 52½ 52½ 32 32 Day P B121 *.70 - - *LrrythLgnd*1181 FndrlDncr1181 TmbrCountry1213½ Angled out,lost ground 5
5Nov94-8CD fst 1 1/16 :23 1 :47 1:12 3 1:44 2 BCJuven-G1 **100** 7 96¼ 73¾ 31½ 1½ 12 Day P 122 *2.40 - - Timber Country1222 Eltish1223 Tejano Run1221¼ Drew off,driving 13
8Oct94-8Bel fst 1 1/16 :23 2 :46 1 1:11 1 1:44 MoetChmp-G1 **100** 10 1½ 1hd 1hd 1hd 1½ Day P 122 3.70 - - *TimberCountry*122½ SierraDiblo1226½ OnTrget122nk Pace 3w, lasted, drvng 11
14Sep94-8Dmr fst 7f :21 3 :44 1:09 3 1:22 1 DMrFut-G2 **88** 5 7 810 710 32½ 31 Nakatani C S B119 6.00 - - On Target115½ *Supremo*115½ *Timber Country*11910 Finished well 4-wide 9
24Aug94-8Dmr fst 6½f :22 1 :45 1:10 1:16 3 Balboa-G3 **79** 7 4 52½ 54¼ 42¼ 1nk Solis A B117 8.40 - - TimberCountry117nk DesrtMirg115nk Suprmo1174 Lost ground,late surge 7
6Aug94-6Dmr fst 6½f :22 :45 1 1:10 1 1:16 3 Md Sp Wt 35k **78** 5 4 43 32 2hd 1½ Solis A B117 *1.00e - - *TmbrCountry*117½ DngrousScnro1173 TcSqud1172½ Wore down rival inside 9
2Jly94-10CD fst 6f :21 1 :45 1 1:10 1 BshfdMnr-G3 **68** 13 10 95 64¾ 69½ 68¾ Pincay L Jr 117 *1.60e - - *Hyroglyphic*1166 Boone's Mill1161 Hobgoblin116nk Stumbled, hung 13
2Jun94-5Hol fst 5f :22 :45 1 :57 3 Md Sp Wt 32k **61** 4 6 77 77¾ 66½ 36¼ McCarron C J B117 9.90 - - *AponusAll*1171¼ SettleSint1175 TimberCountry117nk Closed wllngly,green 8

Unbridled

b. c. 1987, by Fappiano (Mr. Prospector)–Gana Facil, by Le Fabuleux
Own.– Frances A. Genter Stable Inc
Br.– Tartan Farms Corp (Fla)
Tr.– Carl A. Nafzger

Lifetime record: 24 8 6 6 $4,489,475

Date	Cond/Dist	Fractions	Race	Calls	Jockey	Wt	Odds	Figs	Finishers / Comment	Field
2Nov91- 8CD	fst 1¼	:482 1:123 1:38 2:024	3↑ BC Classic-G1	7 11 1016 85¾ 45½ 33¾	Perret C	LB 126	4.30	92-09	Black Tie Affair1261¼Twilight Agenda1262½Unbridled126nk Mild rally	11
6Oct91- 8Kee	fst 1⅛	:472 1:112 1:36 1:484	3↑ Fayette H-G2	1 5 56½ 43½ 31½ 23	Perret C	LB 122	1.90	88-17	SummrSquall1223Unbridled1222½SecrtHllo1151¾ Veered out	5
10Aug91- 3Dmr	fst 1¼	:454 1:094 1:341 1:594	3↑ Pacific Classic 1000k	8 7 79 56 44½ 33¾	Perret C	LB 124	6.20	--	Best Pal1161Twilight Agenda1242¾Unbridled1241¼ Came on	8
3Aug91- 5AP	fst 7f	:223 :444 1:084 1:21	3↑ Alw 25500	2 6 610 610 25 16½	Day P	L 122	*.40e	98-12	Unbridled1226½SpnshDrummr1191¾Prfcton1174 Strong finish	7
11May91- 9Pim	fst 1 3/16	:464 1:10 1:341 1:522	4↑ Pim Spl H-G1	4 5 510 57½ 610 610	Perret C	L 122	2.40	93-13	FarmaWay1193SmmrSqll1202½Jol'sHlo119nk Weakened,bled	7
13Apr91- 8OP	sly 1⅛	:463 1:104 1:354 1:48	4↑ Oaklawn H-G1	5 8 815 815 75¾ 56	Day P	L 124	2.00	89-03	Festin115¾Primal1153¼Jolie's Halo1201 Belated rally	8
16Mar91- 6GP	fst 7f	:22 :442 1:091 1:214	3↑ Deputy Minister H 50k	4 9 814 814 34 13	Day P	L 119	3.10	97-07	Unbridled1193Housebuster122noShuttleman1145 Ridden out	9
27Oct90- 9Bel	fst 1¼	:454 1:094 1:353 2:021	3↑ BC Classic-G1	14 13 1311 96¾ 32½ 11	Day P	121	6.60e	86-15	Unbridled1211IbnBey1261ThirtySixRed121no Strong drive	14
23Sep90- 10LaD	fst 1¼	:462 1:111 1:361 2:02	Super Derby-G1	9 9 94¾ 32 43½ 23½	Velez JA Jr	L 126	*.90	102-00	HomeatLast1263½Unbridled126nkCee'sTzzy1261 Six wide ⅜	9
3Sep90- 8AP	fm 1¼Ⓣ	:491 1:131 1:372 2:013	Secretariat-G1	4 7 75½ 63¼ 3nk 2¾	Fires E	L 126	*.50e	103-03	SuperAbound114¾Unbridld1261½SuperFan117¾ Brushed start	8
18Aug90- 9AP	fst 1	:224 :451 1:092 1:342	3↑ Alw 23500	1 4 42 21 13 111½	Fires E	L 112	*.30	99-12	Unbridled11211Lampkin Cache116½Remington's Pride1194 Much the best	8
9Jun90- 8Bel	gd 1½	:48 1:121 2:014 2:271	Belmont-G1	5 6 42½ 44½ 46 412¾	Perret C	126	*1.10	81-13	GoandGo1268¼ThirtySixRd1262BrondVux1262½ Bid wide,tired	9
19May90- 10Pim	fst 1 3/16	:47 1:104 1:353 1:533	Preakness-G1	6 9 87½ 54 2hd 22¼	Perret C	126	*1.70	96-12	SmmerSqull1262¼Unbrdld1269MstrFrsky126½ Best of others	9
5May90- 8CD	gd 1¼	:46 1:11 1:373 2:02	Ky Derby-G1	8 11 1214 2½ 11 13½	Perret C	126	10.80	101-00	Unbrdld1263½SummrSqull1266PlsntTp1263 Tight st.,driving	15
14Apr90- 8Kee	my 1⅛	:474 1:121 1:351 1:483	Blue Grass-G2	4 5 52 41¾ 31½ 33¾	Perret C	121	4.10	87-10	SmmerSquall1211¾LandRush1212Unbridld1213 Flattened out	5
17Mar90- 10GP	fst 1⅛	:482 1:123 1:39 1:52	Florida Derby-G1	4 5 42 41¾ 31 14	Day P	122	2.50	77-22	Unbridled1224Slavic122nkRunTurn1221 Brushed str,driving	9
3Mar90- 10GP	fst 1 1/16	:232 :473 1:122 1:443	Fountain of Youth-G2	5 10 127 99¼ 51¾ 3½	Day P	117	7.60e	87-24	Shot Gun Scott122½Smelly119noUnbridled117¾ Lacked room	13
14Jan90- 10Crc	fst 1⅛	:483 1:131 1:384 1:522	Trop Park Derby-G3	4 3 32 32½ 43½ 55¾	Perret C	119	*1.30	91-11	Run Turn1174¼Country Day112hdShot Gun Scott119½ Tired	8
24Dec89- 10Crc	fst 1 1/16	:233 :481 1:131 1:451	What a Pleasure 56k	9 8 85½ 74½ 2hd 15	Velez JA Jr	112	*1.50	96-11	Unbridled1125Fiery Best1172½Alwys Rng115nkBumped,drew clear	10
22Oct89- 10Crc	fst 1 1/16	:25 :494 1:143 1:473	ⓇIn Reality (FSS) 450k	4 10 85¼ 54½ 32 22¾	Velez JA Jr	120	5.20	81-19	Shot Gun Scott1202¾Unbridled120¾Swedaus1203½ Rallied	14
24Sep89- 9Cby	fst 1	:231 :461 1:11 1:371	Cby Juvenile 150k	1 4 74½ 42½ 2½ 2½	Smith ME	120	5.20e	89-15	Appealing Breeze120½Unbridled1204½Table Limit1203½ Hung	7
13Sep89- 8AP	sly 7f	:223 :461 1:112 1:24	Arch Ward 37k	1 5 54½ 54 312 319¾	Smith ME	115	3.30	62-31	Karen'sTom1122¾SecretHello12217Unbridld1157½ No threat	5
23Aug89- 8AP	fst 6½f	:221 :45 1:104 1:171	Waukegan BC 55k	7 7 79½ 613 38½ 37	Smith ME	116	*1.10	82-21	SecretHello1165Karen'sTom1132Unbridld1161¼ Broke inside	8
2Aug89- 4AP	fst 6f	:223 :461 1:113	Md Sp Wt	10 11 64¾ 11½ 17 110½	Smith ME	122	*3.10	82-20	Unbrdld12210½SoundofCannons122½HomeatLast122nk Easily	12

Victory Gallop

Own: Prestonwood Farm LLC

B. c. 4 (May) KEESEP96 $25,000
Sire: Cryptoclearance (Fappiano) $50,000
Dam: Victorious Lil (Vice Regent)
Br: Tall Oaks Farm (Ont-C)
Tr: Walden W. E

Life	17	9	5	1	$3,505,895	118	D.Fst	16	9	4	1	$3,485,895	118
1999	4	3	0	1	$1,399,295	118	Wet(334)	1	0	1	0	$20,000	90
1998	8	3	4	0	$1,981,720	114	Turf(238)	0	0	0	0	$0	-
	0	0	0	0	$0	-	Dst(0)	0	0	0	0	$0	-

Date	Cond/Dist	Fractions	Race	Fig	Calls	Jockey	Wt	Odds	Figs	Finishers / Comment	Field
1Aug99- 9Sar	fst 1⅛	:47 1:104 1:36 1:483	3↑WhitneyH-G1	116	2 710 810 65¾ 2hd 1no	Bailey J D	L123	*.90e	93- 07	Victory Gallop123no Behrens12312 Catienus1133 Quick outside move	8
12Jun99- 9CD	fst 1⅛	:464 1:11 1:352 1:471	3↑SFosterH-G2	118	1 710 711 76¼ 11½ 15	Bailey J D	L120	*1.30e	107- 03	*VictoryGallop*1205 *NiteDreamer*110¾ Littlebitlively1152¾ Hand urging, sharp	7
28Mar99 Nad Al Sheba (UAE)	ft *1¼ LH	2:003	4↑ Dubai World Cup-G1 Stk 5000000		31½	Bailey J	126	-		Almutawakel126¾ Malek126¾ *Victory Gallop*1261½	8
Timeform rating: 123										*Tracked in 4th,wide bid 1-1/2f out,hung.Silver Charm 6th*	
3Mar99- 3GP	fst 1 1/16	:25 :483 1:123 1:434	4↑ Alw 44000c	111	1 55 42½ 41¼ 11 12¾	Bailey J D	L119	*.30	88- 28	Victory Gallop1192¾ Delay ofGame119¾ *DancingGuy*1155¾ Steady hand ride	5
7Nov98-10CD	fst 1¼	:473 1:12 1:371 2:02	3↑BCClasic-G1	114	1 1013 1011 85¼ 51¾ 41	Solis A	L122	7.50	94- 07	Awesome Again126¾ *Silver Charm*126nk Swain126no Strong rally between	10
29Aug98- 9Sar	fst 1¼	:484 1:13 1:372 2:032	Travers-G1	107	7 52½ 52½ 32 31½ 2no	Solis A	L126	*1.20	91- 09	CorondosQust126no VictoryGllop126no RffsMjsty1265 Wide, finished fast	7
9Aug98-11Mth	fst 1⅛	:47 1:104 1:353 1:483	BckHskIH-G1	108	5 57 58½ 45 33 21¼	Stevens G L	L125	1.20	94- 13	*CorondosQust*1241¼ VictoryGllop125½ GrndSlm1188¼ Steadied late, gamely	6
6Jun98- 9Bel	fst 1½	:483 1:132 2:29	Belmont-G1	110	9 108½ 97 57½ 24 1no	Stevens G L	L126	4.50	99- 09	Victory Gallop126no Real Quiet1266 *Thomas Jo*1261½ Bumpd late got nod	11
16May98-10Pim	fst 1 3/16	:462 1:11 1:354 1:543	Preaknss-G1	107	9 74 89¼ 4¾ 2½ 22¼	Stevens G L	L126	*2.00	90- 13	Real Quiet1262¼ *Victory Gallop*126¾ Classic Cat1263¾ 4w 2d turn, gamely	10
2May98- 8CD	fst 1¼	:453 1:103 1:353 2:021	KyDerby-G1	106	13 1516 1411 75½ 33½ 2½	Solis A	L126	14.60	93- 02	*Real Quiet*126½ Victory Gallop1262¼ Indian Charlie126hd Rallied, gaining	15
11Apr98- 9OP	fst 1⅛	:46 1:104 1:372 1:494	ArkDerby-G2	101	5 76½ 87¾ 83¾ 21 1hd	Solis A	L122	7.80	87- 10	VictoryGallop122hd HnumnHighwy118hd FvoriteTrick1223 Driving 3 wide	9
21Mar98- 9OP	fst 1 1/16	:231 :473 1:131 1:443	Rebel-G3	105	7 43½ 51¾ 3½ 1½ 1hd	Coa E M	L119	4.10	85- 24	*VictoryGllop*119hd Robinwould1146 Whtflshyctor114¾ Lost whip, prevailed	10
Previously trained by Eppler Mary E 1997(as of 11/1): (106 18 11 10 0.17)											
1Nov97-10Lrl	sly 1⅛	:49 1:141 1:40 1:533	LrlFut-G3	90	3 46½ 44 44½ 36 21¾	Johnston M T	L122	*1.40	68- 35	*FightforMlady*1221¾ *VictoryGllop*122½ Essentil1229½ 4wd most-trip,gaind 2d	6
11Oct97- 9Cnl	fst 1	:22 :444 1:101 1:364	Chenery100k	85	5 64¾ 64¼ 43 2hd 1¾	Johnston M T	L119	1.80	- -	VictoryGllop119¾ *FightforMldy*1153½ *PersonlFive*1193¼ Drifted in late, prvld	8
1Sep97- 9Cnl	fst 7f	:222 :451 1:093 1:223	NewKent54k	80	3 4 52½ 54¾ 2½ 12	Johnston M T	L114	8.90	- -	*VictoryGllop*1142 UnrelMdnss1205 *LuisitsChoicl*1142½ Strong rally, drew clr	6
2Aug97- 1Lrl	fst 7f	:232 :481 1:141 1:264	Md Sp Wt 20k	60	8 2 1hd 1hd 15½ 18¾	Prado E S	L120	1.90	75- 17	*Victory Gallop*1208¾ *Essential*1205¼ Do I Ever120nk Drew off, mild pressre	8
20Jly97- 1Del	fst 5f	:23 :472 :593	Md Sp Wt 23k	42	8 5 84¾ 76½ 69 59¾	McCarthy M J	118	5.20	76- 20	Carreras1184¾ He's a Charm1184½ Duck Grayson118nk Passed tiring rivals	8

Wandesta (GB)

Own: Juddmonte Farms Inc

Ch. m. 5 (Mar)
Sire: Nashwan (Blushing Groom*Fr)
Dam: De Stael (Nijinsky II)
Br: Juddmonte Farms (GB)
Tr: Frankel Robert J

Life	21	7	3	5	$1,255,145	108	D.Fst	1	0	0	1	$45,000	98
1996	7	3	2	1	$718,250	108	Wet(387*)	0	0	0	0	$0	-
1995	8	3	0	3	$437,400	104	Turf(380)	20	7	3	4	$1,210,145	108
	0	0	0	0	$0	-	Dst(0)	0	0	0	0	$0	-

Date	Cond/Dist	Fractions	Race	Fig	Calls	Jockey	Wt	Odds	Figs	Finishers / Comment	Field
1Dec96- 7Hol	fm 1¼Ⓣ	:49 1:131 1:364 2:00	3↑ⒻMatriarc-G1	107	12 85½ 84¾ 72 41¼ 1½	Nakatani C S	LB123	5.70	88- 10	Wandest123½ Windshrp1231¾ *MemoriesofSilver*120¾ Quick gain 4w,driving	12
3Nov96- 5SA	fm 1¼Ⓣ	:491 1:133 1:364 2:003	3↑ⒻYlwRibbn-G1	100	1 86½ 86 72¾ 62½ 52	Nakatani C S	LB122	*.90	93- 07	Donna Viola122½ Real Connection122hd DixiePearl122nk Blocked 1/4 & 1/8	8
13Oct96- 5SA	fm 1⅛Ⓣ	:48 1:12 1:353 1:463	3↑ⒻLsPlmasH-G2	106	1 44 34 32½ 12½ 12	Nakatani C S	LB120	*1.00	97- 03	Wandesta1202 Real Connection1131¾ Alpride1204½ Quick gain,perfct trip	5
20Apr96- 5SA	fm 1¼Ⓣ	:49 1:14 1:374 2:02	4↑ⒻSntBrbrH-G2	95	4 32½ 42 33 32 35½	Nakatani C S	LB121	*.80	- -	*Auriette*1163½ Angel in MyHeart1192 *Wandesta*1217½ Bumpd strt,steadd 3/8	5
24Mar96- 5SA	fm 1½Ⓣ	:481 1:121 2:023 2:274	4↑SanLsRey-G1	108	2 76½ 74½ 52¾ 1½ 2nk	Nakatani C S	LB117	*2.10	- -	Windsharp117nk Wandesta1172¼ SilverWizrd1224 Bumped str,outfinshed	7
19Feb96- 8SA	fm 1½Ⓣ	:49 1:143 2:05 2:301	4↑SLsObspH-G2	107	4 54½ 31 2hd 11½ 2¾	Nakatani C S	LB114	4.20	- -	*Windsharp*115¾ Wandesta1142¾ VirginiaCrnivl115hd Lead late, outfinished	6
14Jan96- 8SA	fm 1⅛Ⓣ	:484 1:122 1:363 1:49	4↑ⒻSnGrgnoH-G2	106	4 52½ 43 42 1½ 13	Nakatani C S	L119	2.60	- -	Wandesta1193 *Matiara*1182½ *Yearly Tour*1171½ Quick gain 3-wide turn	6
26Nov95- 6Hol	fm 1¼Ⓣ	:493 1:132 1:363 2:001	3↑ⒻMatriarc-G1	102	10 83¾ 103¾ 103½ 61¾ 31¼	Nakatani C S	L123	6.50e	- -	Duda1231 *Angel in My Heart*120nk *Wandesta*123no Strong rally wide	14
12Nov95- 8SA	fm 1¼Ⓣ	:471 1:122 1:372 2:013	3↑ⒻYlwRibbn-G1	95	9 74½ 62 94¾ 53½ 64¼	Nakatani C S	LB122	*2.80e	- -	Alpride122½ Angel in My Heart118hd Bold Ruritana1221¼ No rally	12
23Jly95- 7Hol	fst 1⅛	:461 1:113 1:353 1:481	3↑ⒻVnityIvH-G1	98	1 68 69 55 35½ 35¾	Nakatani C S	LB119	2.00	- -	PrivatePersusion1143 TopRung1162¾ Wndest1194½ Split horses,flattened	7
2Jly95- 9Hol	fm 1⅛Ⓣ	:471 1:101 1:342 1:463	3↑ⒻBevHilsH-G1	102	1 53½ 55¾ 54 42 32¾	Nakatani C S	LB119	3.30	- -	Alpride1151¾ *Possibly Perfect*1241 Wandesta1196½ Closed willingly insde	6
29May95- 9Hol	fm 1¼Ⓣ	:481 1:12 1:354 1:593	3↑HolTurfH-G1	89	6 104½ 104½ 84¾ 86½ 89½	Day P	LB114	6.90	80- 10	Earl of Barking1152¼ *Sandpit*122hd Savinio117¾ No threat	10
9Apr95- 8SA	fm 1¼Ⓣ	:50 1:133 1:374 2:013	4↑ⒻSntBrbrH-G1	104	7 52¼ 53 21½ 2½ 12	Nakatani C S	LB118	*1.10	- -	Wandesta1182 Yearly Tour116no Morgana1164 Split horses,rddn out	7

18Mar95- 8SA fm 1⅛ Ⓣ :491 1:133 1:38 1:50 4↑ⒻSntaAnaH-G1 **104** 5 57 57 42 31 12 Nakatani C S **LB**115 1.90 - - *Wandesta*1152 Yearly Tour116¾ Aube Indienne120nk Found hole,late surge 7
19Feb95- 4SA fm 1⅛ Ⓣ :474 1:13 1:382 1:503 4↑ⒻAlw 46000c **103** 3 31½ 45 42 2½ 1nk Nakatani C S **LB**120 *.50 - - *Wandesta*120nk Ruby Cairo120³½ *Mille Nuits*117½ Blocked str,up late 10
27Nov94- 7Hol gd 1⅛ Ⓣ :484 1:131 1:371 1:492 3↑ⒻMatriarc-G1 **101** 3 75 74 83¾ 41¼ 3½ Nakatani C S **LB**120 10.60 - - Exchange123hd Aube Indienne123½ *Wandesta*1201¼ Quick gain 5-wide str 8
Previously trained by Charlton Roger 1994(as of 11/6): (2 0 0 0 0.00)
6Nov94- 8SA fm 1¼ Ⓣ :47 1:112 1:363 2:021 3↑ⒻYlwRibIn-G1 **62** 1 12 1½ 1hd 56½ 918 Day P **LB**118 *2.20e - - AubeIndienne122½ FondlyRemembered122nk Zoonaqua1221 Rushed, tired 11
Previously trained by Roger Charlton
17Aug94 York (GB) gd 1½ Ⓣ LH 2:28 3↑ ⒻYorkshire Oaks-G1 Stk 214300 622½ Carson W 123 6.00 Only Royale1336 Dancing Bloom133½ State Crystal1233 7
Well placed in 3rd,weakened over 2-1/2f out
7Aug94 Deauville (Fr) gd *1 11/16 Ⓣ RH 2:574 3↑ ⒻPrix de Pomone-G2 Stk 94500 22½ Eddery P 119 - Bright Moon1322½ Wandesta1193 *Molesnes*132no 7
Tracked in 3rd,led 3f out,headed 1f out,no further response
16Jly94 Newmarket (GB) gd 1½ Ⓣ RH 2:31 3↑ ⒻAphrodite Stakes (Listed) Stk 25400 11¾ Dettori L 116 4.50 Wandesta1161¾ Darrery1282 Moon Carnival128no 11
Promiment in 5th,led over 1f out,driving
22Oct93 Doncaster (GB) gd 7f Ⓣ Str EBF Flaxton Maiden Stakes Maiden 11600 614 ↓unknown jockey 121 - Golden Nashwan1263½ Moving Arrow1263 Faal Mario1262½ 15
Tracked in 4th,drifted left 1f out,one-paced.

Warm Spell

ch. g. 1988, by Northern Baby (Northern Dancer)–Smilin' Sera, by Explodent **Lifetime record: 19 12 3 1 $457,964**
Own.– John K. Griggs
Br.– Robert G. Kluener (Ky)
Tr.– John K. Griggs

13Nov94- 4Cam fm 2¾ S'Chase 5:081 4↑ Colonial Cup 100k 3 6 73½ - - - Lawrence J II 162 -- Lonesome Glory162hdMistico16221Victorian Hill162¾ Fell 8
22Oct94- 3FH fm *2⅝ Hurdles 4:58 4↑ B C Grand Nationl 143k 4 3 32¼ 21 1hd 12½ Lawrence J II 156 -- WrmSpll1562½MasterMcGrth1561½LonsmeGlry1561¼ Driving 6
18Aug94- 9Sar sf 2⅜ Hurdles 4:30 4↑ NY Turf Writers H 109k 7 8 811 78¾ 58½ 58 Lawrence J II 168 *1.20 -- Mistico1684Cheering News1423½Lonesome Glory168nk 8
Wide,lacked rally
28Jly94- 1Sar sf 2 1/16 Hurdles 3:474 4↑ Handicap 50000 1 7 712 42¼ 2hd 12½ Lawrence J II 164 2.50 -- Warm Spell1642½Mistico1681¾Cheering News146nk Driving 7
14May94- 7PW gd *3 Hurdles 5:283 4↑ Iroquois 100k 6 4 413 2½ 28 215 Lawrence J II 168 -- Mistico16815Warm Spell16822Victorian Hill16835 7
Bid,outrun by winner
23Apr94- 3Mid fm *2⅝ Hurdles 4:413 4↑ Temple Gwathmy H 50k 1 2 24 23 11½ 2nk Lawrence J II 162 -- LonesomeGlory164nkWarmSpll1629ChrngNws1448 2nd best 5
9Apr94- 3AtH fm *2⅛ Hurdles 3:554 4↑ Rob HumphryCH 100k 4 5 64¾ 33 41 1½ Lawrence J II 164 -- Warm Spell164½Rolling Cart1422Castleworth1446 Driving 7
19Aug93- 9Sar gd 2⅜ Hurdles 4:152 4↑ NY Turf Writers 118k 4 3 68 21½ 11½ 15 Lawrence J II 161 1.80 -- Warm Spell1615Castleworth1422Darby Sky1454 Driving 9
29Jly93- 1Sar fm 2 1/16 Hurdles 3:424 4↑ Handicap 46000 7 8 59½ 31 1hd 1¾ Lawrence J II 158 *1.70 -- Warm Spell158¾Castleworth14012Rolling Cart1451½ Gamely 10
8May93- 7PW gd 3 Hurdles 5:43 4↑ Iroquois 100k 6 1 2nk 21 31½ 22½ Lawrence J II 163 - -- Mistico1682½Warm Spell1633Darby Sky1685 Strong bid 7
18Apr93- 3Mid gd *2⅝ Hurdles 5:08 4↑ Temple Gwathmy H 50k 1 1 12 2hd 13 15 Lawrence J II 156 -- Warm Spell1565Ninepins1542½Woodlast1421¼ Ridden out 7
3Apr93- 4AtH fm *2⅛ Hurdles 4:003 4↑ Ath Cup H 100k 4 6 53 - - - Griggs K 156 -- Ninepins1501½Circuit Bar149hdLexington Ball1385 Fell 8
4Jun92- 4Bel fm 2 S'Chase 3:363 4↑ Handicap 45000 1 2 22½ 2hd 16 17½ Griggs K 148 *.80 -- WarmSpell1487½NordicSurpris142nkWoodlst144nk Mild drive 7
9May92- 9PW fm 3 S'Chase 5:314 4↑ Iroquois 100k 8 2 21 21½ 2¾ 32 Griggs K 158 -- VictorianHill1681¾Mistico168nkWarmSpll1586½ No response 8
26Apr92- 4Lex fm *2½ S'Chase 4↑ Coca Cola H 25k 3 2 33 2¾ 17 17 Lawrence J II 148 -- Warm Spell1487Mistico1423Three Bells for Me1396 Handily 4
Fractional times unavailable
4Apr92- 5AtH fm *2⅛ S'Chase 4:04 4↑ Alw 30000 7 2 2nk 15 11½ 12½ Lawrence J II 145 -- WarmSpell1452½TalkinButter1495[D]Rainlough141hd Driving 7
16Nov91- 5Cam fm *2 S'Chase 3:361 Alw 15000 6 1 11 11½ 1½ 12¼ Griggs K 151 -- Warm Spell1512¼Plusser1481Hero's Hour14815 Driving 13
19Oct91- 4GrM fm *2¼ S'Chase 4:32 Alw 15000 9 7 22½ 12 16 115 Griggs K 150 -- WrmSpll15015WiseOne14512BlackSeaDancr1385 Ridden out 10
21Jly91- 3Sar fm 2 1/16 S'Chase 4:012 3↑ Md Sp Wt 9 7 614 11 14 110 Cooney P 138 -- WamSpell13810Tuniche1556LdsCstl1556 Brilliant first out 9

Yanks Music

Own: Audrey H. Cooper & Michael Fennessy

B. f. 3 (May)
Sire: Air Forbes Won (Bold Forbes)
Dam: Traipsing (Darby Creek Road)
Br: Irish American Bloodhorse Agency ,Ltd. (Ky)
Tr: O'Brien Leo

Life	9	7	2	0	$787,600	111	D.Fst	7	6	1	0	$607,600	111
1996	7	5	2	0	$751,000	111	Wet(330)	2	1	1	0	$180,000	104
1995	2	2	0	0	$36,600	85	Turf(284)	0	0	0	0	$0	–
	0	0	0	0	$0	–	Dst(0)	0	0	0	0	$0	–

6Oct96- 9Bel fst 1⅛ :464 1:102 1:342 1:47 3↑ⒻBeldame-G1 **111** 6 31 31 2½ 2½ 1¾ Velazquez J R 119 2.30 95- 12 Yanks Music119¾ Serena's Song1233 Clear Mandate1231 5w turn,in time 6
14Sep96- 9Bel fst 1 1/16 :233 :471 1:111 1:414 3↑ⒻRuffianH-G1 **107** 2 52½ 41¼ 21 2½ 1nk Velazquez J R 116 2.10 90- 10 *YanksMusic*116nk SerenasSong1269 HeadEst108nk Came wide,came again 6
17Aug96- 8Sar gd 1¼ :483 1:131 1:374 2:03 ⒻAlabama-G1 **104** 3 36 33½ 2hd 1hd 14 Velazquez J R 121 6.30 94- 14 *Yanks Music*1214 Escena121½ *My Flag*1213¼ Advanced outs 2nd turn 7
6Jly96- 8Mth fst 1 1/16 :234 :47 1:103 1:421 ⒻMthBCOks-G2 **96** 4 32½ 41½ 33½ 34 23 Velazquez J R 121 *.30 102 - Top Secret1143 *Yanks Music*1211 Mesabi Maiden1214¾ Finished well 5
22Jun96- 9Bel fst 1⅛ :441 1:081 1:341 1:474 ⒻMthrGoos-G1 **100** 5 56 55 42 21 1nk Velazquez J R 121 2.10 91- 12 Yanks Music121nk Escena1215½ Cara Rafaela1216 7w move trn,long drive 7
18May96 9Bel gd 1 :214 :442 1:091 1:347 ⒻAcorn G1 **95** 3 84¼ 62¼ 82½ 43 2½ Velazquez J R 121 *.00 00- 14 StardeLdyAnn121½ *YnksMusic*1211½ StopTrffic1212 Caught in traffic turn 12
18Apr96- 7Aqu fst 7f :224 :453 1:10 1:221 ⒻAlw 35000NC **103** 3 6 73¾ 61¾ 11½ 15½ Velazquez J R 114 2.15 - - YanksMusic1145½ StopTraffic1161½ ZeeLdy1143 Quick 6w move,rddn out 8
23Nov95- 6Aqu fst 1 :231 :461 1:113 1:373 ⒻAlw 33000N1X **82** 4 32½ 34½ 2hd 12½ 13¾ Migliore R 116 2.00 - - *Yanks Music*1163¾ *Break Through*1132 *Flume*1187 Drifting str,clr late 6
5Nov95- 2Aqu fst 6f :222 :462 :583 1:11 ⒻMd Sp Wt 28k **85** 9 8 66½ 3½ 12 19¾ Velazquez J R 118 2.75 - - *YnksMusc*1189¾ ClstlGlnc1182½ SwtEmmLou118½ Advanced 4w,drew away 9

Two out of Three Ain't Bad

2000–2004

by Jay Privman

There is no more challenging feat in horse racing than sweeping the Triple Crown. To do it, a 3-year-old Thoroughbred must win three races at three different distances at three different tracks in three different states in the space of just five weeks. There is a reason only 11 horses, ranging from Sir Barton in 1919 through Affirmed in 1978, have done it. It takes a truly great horse.

Racing at the end of the 20th century had reached unprecedented heights in terms of international participation, but, much as a free market ebbs and flows, so too did the focus of racing shift back to the home-grown product as the 21st century began to unfold. In three consecutive years, from 2002 through 2004, a horse won the Kentucky Derby at Churchill Downs, came back two weeks later to capture the Preakness Stakes at Pimlico in Maryland, and then bid for a Triple Crown sweep three weeks later in the Belmont Stakes in New York. In all three instances—first with the mercurial War Emblem, then the popular gelding Funny Cide, and then the brilliant Smarty Jones—the quest came up short. But the nation's attention was riveted on horse racing with each successive attempt, was ratcheted up each year, and reached a fever pitch when Smarty Jones took an unbeaten record into the Belmont Stakes.

A record crowd of 120,139 stuffed itself into every nook and cranny of Belmont Park on the chance to see history made. And with a quarter-mile remaining, Smarty Jones was sailing along with a seemingly insurmountable lead. The noise was deafening. Belmont Park, which had seen Secretariat, Seattle Slew, and Affirmed complete Triple Crown bids in the 1970's, literally shook. The crowd was ready to celebrate the end of the longest Triple Crown drought in history, surpassing the fallow years from Citation in 1948 to Secretariat in 1973.

But the champagne went flat. The grind of the Triple Crown, and a fast-paced middle half-mile in the Belmont Stakes, caught up to Smarty Jones in the final furlong of the 1 ½-mile race. Exhausted, yet straining valiantly to hold on, he switched leads in a courageous, desperate effort to stave off Birdstone. But he could not. It was the only time in his career that he failed.

"Since January, everything has gone absolutely right. This one didn't," said John Servis, who trained Smarty Jones.

Someday Farm's Pennsylvania-bred Smarty Jones caught the front-running Lion Heart with a furlong to go and pulled away to score a 2 ¼-length victory in the 130th Kentucky Derby at soggy Churchill Downs.

Smarty Jones picked up the momentum that first gathered with War Emblem, was accentuated by Funny Cide, and was bolstered by the success of a fanciful book and film on the popular 1930's racehorse Seabiscuit. Seemingly overnight, Smarty Jones became a pop-culture phenomenon. His perfect record was alluring from a pure athletic standpoint. And he appealed to the general public in part because his owners, trainer, and jockey—all from the Philadelphia area—were perceived as underdogs and thus were easy to root for.

Roy Chapman, an elderly car dealer hooked to an oxygen tank while suffering from emphysema, and his wife, Pat, bred Smarty Jones in Pennsylvania and kept him to race. Servis, from a racing family that eked out a living in the hard-scrabble Mid-Atlantic region, was a respected trainer who rarely had a horse of national caliber. And jockey Stewart Elliott, a journeyman with a checkered past, had never ridden in the Kentucky Derby until Smarty Jones came along.

The Kentucky Derby marked Smarty Jones's seventh straight victory. It also brought the Chapmans a $5-million bonus from Oaklawn Park, which was celebrating its 100th anniversary and put up a lucrative prize that year for a horse who could sweep the Rebel Stakes and Arkansas Derby at Oaklawn and then add the Kentucky Derby. Mission accomplished.

But two months after the Belmont, and before he could race again, Smarty Jones was retired to stud duty after the Chapmans accepted a lucrative offer from Three Chimneys Farm in Kentucky.

No such fate awaited Funny Cide, because he was a gelding. As with Smarty Jones, the plebian background of both the horse and his connections made Funny Cide a folk hero in the spring of 2003.

It seemed as though Funny Cide had a story from central casting. There was the iconoclastic trainer, the veteran Barclay Tagg, who did not suffer fools gladly and came across as preferring animals to people. There was the misunderstood jockey, Jose Santos, who became a cause celebre after the Kentucky Derby when a careless newspaper article insinuated he had cheated in America's greatest race. And there were his everyman owners, a group of 10 men in their 50's, some of whom had known each other since their high school days in upstate New York and had pooled $75,000 to buy Funny Cide.

Funny Cide was a 12-1 shot in the Derby, but he quickly became a fan favorite and was sent off the betting choice in both the Preakness and Belmont. His notoriety exploded exponentially in the fortnight between the Derby and the Preakness. A report in *The Miami Herald,* accompanied by an oblique still photo, raised the possibility that Santos might have carried an electrical buzzer in his right hand in the Derby. It was a titillating story for news outlets that usually shun racing. For 48 hours, Santos had his credibility unnecessarily questioned, since any cursory examination of the videotape of the stretch run, or any number of other still photos, would have found the report preposterous.

There was an emotional catharsis for Santos and his family when Funny Cide won the Preakness. By the time Funny Cide arrived at the Belmont, only five weeks after he burst into national consciousness in the Derby, he was the most popular horse in racing. More than 100,000 people turned out in a miserable, driving rainstorm to see if Funny Cide could sweep the Triple Crown.

Empire Maker, who had defeated Funny Cide in the Wood Memorial, had been considered the

Funny Cide, with veteran jockey Jose Santos astride, became the first gelding since Clyde Van Dusen back in 1929 to win the Kentucky Derby.

nation's best 3-year-old heading into the Kentucky Derby, for which he was the favorite. But Empire Maker was suffering from a minor foot injury the week of the Derby, which interrupted his training. On Derby Day, he could not catch Funny Cide.

Empire Maker's trainer, Bobby Frankel, was in the midst of a streak that saw him crowned the nation's champion trainer four consecutive years, from 2000 through 2003. Frankel shrewdly held Empire Maker out of the Preakness in order to have his colt at his best for the Belmont. Funny Cide—who did not have the luxury of skipping the Preakness—could not handle a fresh, fit Empire Maker. He finished third.

War Emblem, who began this decade's run of Triple Crown bids in 2002, never attained the level of popularity of Smarty Jones or Funny Cide, even though he too won the Kentucky Derby and Preakness. War Emblem had been owned by octogenarian Russell Reineman, but after a front-running victory in the Illinois Derby four weeks before the Kentucky Derby, Reineman sold War Emblem to The Thoroughbred Corporation of Saudi Arabian Prince Ahmed bin Salman. War Emblem also was transferred from Bobby Springer, a quiet, Midwest-based trainer, to one of racing's most recognizable trainers, the glib Westerner Bob Baffert.

War Emblem gave trainer Bob Baffert his third triumph in America's greatest race.

Perhaps if Reineman had held on to the colt and won the Derby, America would have embraced the War Emblem story. Instead, a not insignificant percentage of racing fans felt as though Baffert and Prince Ahmed had bought the Derby. That resentment also might have been fueled by the tense relationship that had developed between the United States and the Middle East. Only eight months before War Emblem's Derby victory, the twin towers of the World Trade Center were destroyed on September 11, 2001, in an attack linked to Islamic fundamentalists, the majority of whom were from Saudi Arabia.

War Emblem used his wicked early speed to lead from start to finish in both the Derby and the Preakness, much as he did in the Illinois Derby. But in the Belmont Stakes, he stumbled badly at the start of the race, nearly unseating his jockey, Victor Espinoza. Taken out of his usual style, War Emblem was in trouble. War Emblem bravely worked his way into contention, but then faded badly after 1 ¼ miles. A little more than one month later, Prince Ahmed died from what Saudi officials said was a heart attack.

The early-season achievements of War Emblem, Funny Cide, and Smarty Jones in their respective Triple Crown bids carried significant weight. Of the three, only War Emblem—in the Haskell Invitational—won another race at age 3, yet all three received Eclipse Awards for divisional championships at year's end. Such is the power of the Triple Crown.

Belmont Park was the site of those three bids for the Triple Crown, and also played host to the Breeders' Cup only seven weeks after the September 11 attacks. The track is barely 25 miles from where the World Trade Center stood. It was an unnerving, wary time for Americans. The nation was on edge. Security throughout the country—especially at airports—became far more severe and noticeable. Fans attending sporting events and concerts were patted down. And at that year's Breeders' Cup, sharpshooters from local and federal agencies lined the roof of Belmont Park, on the chance that a large crowd just outside Manhattan might attract terrorists.

War Emblem, with Victor Espinoza aboard, used his tactical speed to win an impressive victory in the 128th Kentucky Derby while leading the field from gate to wire. He was the first Derby winner to keep the lead from start to finish since the filly Winning Colors in 1988.

Fortunately, the day went off smoothly, and was punctuated by an unprecedented second straight victory in the Breeders' Cup Classic by Tiznow, who stubbornly held off the foreign-owned Sakhee to win by a nose. Tom Durkin, the track announcer at Belmont Park, exhaled emotionally at the finish of the race when Tiznow prevailed, saying, "Tiznow wins it for America."

Earlier that summer, Tiznow was seemingly done. Not long after winning the Santa Anita Handicap, a troublesome back interrupted his training. He was the defending Horse of the Year, a title he earned in 2000 in large part because of his Breeders' Cup Classic victory at Churchill Downs, but he appeared unlikely to return. His quiet, patient trainer, Jay Robbins, never gave up, though. In July, Tiznow started breezing. Robbins was cautiously optimistic that Tiznow could make it back, but there could be no missteps along the way.

In his first start in five months, Tiznow finished third in the Woodward Stakes at Belmont Park. One month later, Tiznow was sent off the favorite in the Goodwood Breeders' Cup Handicap at Santa Anita's Oak Tree meeting, but he turned in a lethargic effort, finishing third. His health was fine, though, so Robbins pressed on.

Suddenly, about two weeks before the Breeders' Cup, Tiznow started training strongly again. On the day it mattered most, he ran his best race of the year.

Though Tiznow was named champion older horse for 2001, he could not claim Horse of the Year for a second straight year. The 2001 title went to Point Given, a 3-year-old who had been retired two months before the Breeders' Cup. Point Given, however, by then had proven that he was a colt of rare talent.

Point Given was huge, with long legs, a massive torso, and a powerful yet graceful stride. He was

California-bred Tiznow courageously battled back to defeat Prix de l'Arc de Triomphe winner Sakhee in the 2001 Breeders' Cup Classic at Belmont Park, becoming the first two-time Classic winner in history.

awkward early at age 2, but improved sharply in the fall of 2000 and just missed winning the Breeders' Cup Juvenile at Churchill Downs. Although he lost that year's 2-year-old championship to the colt who beat him in the Juvenile, Macho Uno, Point Given was recognized as the Kentucky Derby favorite as the 3-year-old class of 2001 began its early-season preparations.

Point Given won his only two preps for the Kentucky Derby, including the Santa Anita Derby. Baffert, his trainer, was privately admitting he thought Point Given had the talent to sweep the Triple Crown. But on Derby Day, Point Given turned in the worst performance of his career. He was kept close to a scalding pace that was the fastest in Derby history, and had no response in the stretch drive. He wound up fifth, the only time in his career that he finished worse than second.

In the Preakness, though, Point Given avenged his Derby loss to Monarchos, and re-established himself as the division's leader. He was just getting warmed up. In the Belmont, Point Given crushed his rivals, including Monarchos, by more than 12 lengths. It was a bittersweet victory for Baffert and jockey Gary Stevens, who thought the tactics they employed in the Derby might have cost Point Given the Triple Crown. As Point Given came to the wire in the Belmont, Baffert could not fully enjoy the performance. "I started feeling like, 'What a shame,'" he said.

"It'll always be bittersweet with these victories in the Triple Crown without the Derby," Stevens said. "I feel like he's a champion. He should have a Triple Crown next to his name."

Point Given came back later in the summer to win the Haskell Invitational at Monmouth, then again left his West Coast base and, in his final career start, captured the Travers Stakes at Saratoga. He thus became the first horse to win four consecutive races worth $1 million or more.

Participation in the Breeders' Cup Classic was not compulsory for Horse of the Year in 2002 and 2003, either, but those champions, like Point Given, compiled a body of work in their respective years that was difficult to ignore.

Azeri fashioned one of the great careers for a filly or mare in turf history, and not just because she was named Horse of the Year in 2002. She also was a three-time winner as the nation's best older filly or mare, captured Oaklawn Park's Apple Blossom Handicap three straight years, and won 11 Grade 1 races.

In 2002, Azeri won eight times in nine starts, including five Grade 1 races. She clinched Horse of the Year when all the cards fell her way on Breeders' Cup Day at Arlington Park. Azeri won the first Breeders' Cup event of the day, and in the final race, the Breeders' Cup Classic, all the top male contenders for Horse of the Year—including War Emblem—were upset by the longshot Volponi. Many voters decried Azeri's selection, but she was the logical choice.

In addition to helping Azeri, Volponi also inadvertently exposed an attempted betting coup by three larcenous young men who had found holes in the way the pick-six bet was processed and had rigged a computer program to guarantee they would win. The scam was uncovered when they possessed the only winning tickets, and multiples of them, in that year's Breeders' Cup pick six. It would forever be known as the Fix Six.

Laura de Seroux trained Azeri for her first 16 races, which included Horse of the Year and two divisional championships. But de Seroux and Michael Paulson, who oversaw the Allen Paulson Living Trust that owned Azeri, had a disagreement

Point Given, a towering son of Thunder Gulch, became the first horse to win four consecutive races worth $1 million or more after capturing Saratoga's Travers Stakes, the "Midsummer Derby," in 2001.

Azeri became North America's all-time leading female money-winner in 2004. She earned a career total of $4,079,820 while accumulating 17 victories 24 starts. Her best year was 2002, when she was named Horse of the Year after winning eight of her nine starts, including the Breeders' Cup Distaff.

in the fall of 2003 over the management of Azeri. Paulson turned her over to trainer D. Wayne Lukas, who shared Paulson's vision of trying Azeri against males. And though Azeri failed in two such attempts, including the 2004 Breeders' Cup Classic, her record against females brought her a third straight divisional title.

Mineshaft, who began his career in Great Britain, had not even raced in this country when Azeri won her Breeders' Cup race in 2002. But by one year later, Mineshaft had risen to the top of the sport. In 2003, he won seven times in nine starts, with four Grade 1 victories, including the Woodward Stakes and Jockey Club Gold Cup. But Mineshaft's connections always seemed as though they were reluctant to send Mineshaft to that year's Breeders' Cup Classic at Santa Anita, and sure enough, they announced after the Jockey Club Gold Cup that Mineshaft had a career-ending injury. When the longshot Pleasantly Perfect won the Classic, Mineshaft's Horse of the Year title was secured.

In 2004, however, the stars were aligned for the Breeders' Cup Classic. A perfect storm brought together in that year's Classic at Lone Star Park the five leading candidates for Horse of the Year. Azeri was trying to beat the boys. The 3-year-old Birdstone was attempting to add the Classic to victories in the Belmont and Travers. Roses in May had won five straight races, including the Whitney at Saratoga. And Pleasantly Perfect, who had traveled halfway around the world to win the Dubai World Cup earlier in the year, was seeking a second straight victory in the Classic.

But those four horses never had a chance against one of the most brilliant racehorses seen in America in decades. Ghostzapper was the rare sort who was as effective at seven furlongs as he was at 1 ¼ miles. He won the Vosburgh Stakes against older sprinters as a 3-year-old, but it wasn't until his eighth lifetime start, in August of 2004, that Frankel finally stretched him out past seven furlongs.

There was no turning back. Ghostzapper won the Iselin Handicap at Monmouth, then the Woodward at Belmont Park, before leading from start to finish for an overpowering three-length victory in the Breeders' Cup Classic. It was a satisfying ending to the season, with the sport's biggest year-end award settled the way it is supposed to be, on the racetrack.

Ghostzapper was breathtakingly fast. He equaled or set four track records, earned Beyer Speed Figures of 114 or higher in his last six starts, and four times achieved a Beyer Speed Figure of at least 120. Unfortunately, he needed plenty of time between his races, and thus made only 11 starts during a career that began in November 2002 and ended in May 2005. He did not come out often, but when he did, it was a treat.

Longevity was the hallmark of another admired racehorse of this century, one whose career began before the previous century ended. Kona Gold, trained and co-owned by one of America's great horsemen, Bruce Headley, raced from May 1998 through July 2003 and won 14 of 30 starts, all in sprints, including his division's most important race, the Breeders' Cup Sprint. In 17 of his races, Kona Gold earned a Beyer Speed Figure of at least 110, and he reached 115 or more 10 times.

A gelding, Kona Gold finished third in the 1998 Sprint at Churchill Downs, second in the 1999 Sprint at Gulfstream Park, then won in 2000, when the Breeders' Cup returned to Churchill. That gave jockey Alex Solis his first win in a Breeders' Cup race after 31 failures. Solis could not have had a more appropriate partner for that elusive victory, since he rode Kona Gold in 28 of his 30 races.

Kona Gold ran in the Breeders' Cup Sprint twice more, and though he did not win, he became the first horse to run in five Breeders' Cups.

Xtra Heat, the new century's best female sprinter, also put together a remarkable record. Although she never raced beyond seven furlongs after her 2-year-old year, Xtra Heat was such an accomplished sprinter that she won the 3-year-old filly title in 2001, when she finished second to males in the Breeders' Cup Sprint. Xtra Heat was small in stature, but had an intense desire to win. She captured 26 of 35 starts in a career that spanned nearly four seasons. She earned Beyer Speed Figures of 110 or more six times.

The Breeders' Cup continued to attract the elite of Europe. Johannesburg completed an unbeaten 2-year-old campaign with his seventh straight victory in his first start on dirt, in the 2001 Breeders' Cup Juvenile. The globetrotting Fantastic Light, who won Grade or Group 1 races on three continents while racing in England, France, Hong Kong, Ireland, Japan, the United Arab Emirates, and the United States, wrapped up his ambitious career with a victory in the 2001 Breeders' Cup Turf. Ouija Board added the 2004 Breeders' Cup Filly and Mare Turf to victories that year in the English Oaks and Irish Oaks. High Chaparral, the Epsom and Irish Derby winner of 2002, won the Breeders' Cup Turf outright in 2002 at Arlington Park, then dead-heated for the win with Johar in 2003 at Santa Anita.

Johar was one of a record four Breeders' Cup winners that year for trainer Richard Mandella, who also won the Juvenile Fillies with Halfbridled, the Juvenile with Action This Day, and the Classic with Pleasantly Perfect.

Julie Krone, who in 2000 became the first female jockey or trainer inducted into the National Museum of Racing and Hall of Fame, came out of retirement for an encore performance in California in 2003 and won her first Breeders' Cup race with Halfbridled.

Jerry Bailey won the Eclipse Award as champion jockey four straight years, from 2000 through 2003, and set a single-season record for purse earnings in 2003, when his mounts earned $23,354,960. Steve Asmussen in 2004 set a single-season record for training wins with 555, obliterating the mark of 496 set by Jack Van Berg in 1976. Frankel won a record 25 Grade 1 stakes races in 2003.

Two of the sport's greatest jockeys, John Longden and Bill Shoemaker, died. And other great jockeys retired, including Eddie Delahoussaye, Chris McCarron, Laffit Pincay Jr., and, for the second time, Krone. Joe Hirsch, the longtime executive columnist for *Daily Racing Form,* also retired.

Affirmed, Conquistador Cielo, Seattle Slew, Spectacular Bid, and Sunday Silence—all Horses of the Year—passed

Two Hall of Fame trainers—P. G. Johnson and Jimmy Jones—also died. Johnson capped a six-decade career with Volponi's win in the 2002 Breeders' Cup Classic. Jones won the Kentucky Derby twice, and his father, Ben—for whom Jimmy was a long-time assistant—won it six times. They worked for Calumet Farm, which still holds the record for Triple Crown race victories, with 17. That is a mark the modern-day horseman can only dream of achieving. But the dreams and hopes that owners, trainers, and jockeys attach to a young horse, most notably a newly turned 3-year-old embarking on a quest for the Kentucky Derby and the Triple Crown, are what sustain the sport and nourish the soul, year after year.

Champions

Past Performances

2000–2004

•2000•
•2-YEAR-OLD MALE *Macho Uno* •2-YEAR-OLD FILLY *Caressing* •3-YEAR-OLD MALE *Tiznow* •3-YEAR-OLD FILLY *Surfside* •HANDICAP HORSE *Lemon Drop Kid* •HANDICAP MARE *Riboletta* •GRASS HORSE *Kalanisi* (M) *Perfect Sting* (F) •SPRINTER *Kona Gold* •STEEPLECHASE *All Gong*
•**HORSE OF THE YEAR** Tiznow

•2001•
•2-YEAR-OLD MALE *Johannesburg* •2-YEAR-OLD FILLY *Tempera* •3-YEAR-OLD MALE *Point Given* •3-YEAR-OLD FILLY *Xtra Heat* •HANDICAP HORSE *Tiznow* •HANDICAP MARE *Gourmet Girl* •GRASS HORSE *Fantastic Light* (M) *Banks Hill* (F) •SPRINTER *Squirtle Squirt* •STEEPLECHASE *Pompeyo*
•**HORSE OF THE YEAR** Point Given

•2002•
•2-YEAR-OLD MALE *Vindication* •2-YEAR-OLD FILLY *Storm Flag Flying* •3-YEAR-OLD MALE *War Emblem* •3-YEAR-OLD FILLY *Farda Amiga* •HANDICAP HORSE *Left Bank* •HANDICAP MARE *Azeri* •GRASS HORSE *High Chaparral* (M) *Golden Apples* (F) •SPRINTER *Orientate* •STEEPLECHASE *Flat Top*
•**HORSE OF THE YEAR** Azeri

•2003•
•2-YEAR-OLD MALE *Action This Day* •2-YEAR-OLD FILLY *Halfbridled* •3-YEAR-OLD MALE *Funny Cide* •3-YEAR-OLD FILLY *Bird Town* •HANDICAP HORSE *Mineshaft* •HANDICAP MARE *Azeri* •GRASS HORSE *High Chaparral* (M) *Islington* (F) •SPRINTER *Aldebaran* •STEEPLECHASE *McDynamo*
•**HORSE OF THE YEAR** Mineshaft

•2004•
•2-YEAR-OLD MALE *Declan's Moon* •2-YEAR-OLD FILLY *Sweet Catomine* •3-YEAR-OLD MALE *Smarty Jones* •3-YEAR-OLD FILLY *Ashado* •HANDICAP HORSE *Ghostzapper* •HANDICAP MARE *Azeri* •GRASS HORSE *Kitten's Joy* (M) *Ouija Board* (F) •SPRINTER *Speightstown* •STEEPLECHASE *Hirapour*
•**HORSE OF THE YEAR** Ghostzapper

Past performances include races through September 2005.

Action This Day

Own: Hughes B. Wayne

B. c. 4 (Feb) KEEJUL02 $150,000
Sire: Kris S. (Roberto) $150,000
Dam: Najecam (Trempolino)
Br: Jaime S. Carrion, Trustee (Ky)
Tr: Mandella Richard E

Life	9	2	1	0	$822,484	98	D.Fst	7	2	1	0	$822,084 98
2005	1	0	0	0	$0	80	Wet(351)	1	0	0	0	$0 87
2004	5	0	0	0	$5,284	98	Turf(355)	1	0	0	0	$400 80
	0	0	0	0	$0	-	Dst(T)(293)	0	0	0	0	$0 -

```
15Jan05-7SA fst 1 1/16 :224 :461 1:10 1:42 SnFndoBC-G2 80 3 74¾ 83¼ 95 89½ 813¾ Flores D R LB116 8.30 81- 11 Minister Eric116½ Mass Media118³ Skipaslew116hd Saved ground to 1/4 9
26Dec04-5SA fm 1 (T) :23 :474 1:113 1:344 3↑ Alw 72848N2X 80 8 85¾105¼ 97¼ 95¼ 97¼ Flores D R LB117 *3.70 81- 12 RunningFree119no SuprStrut120³ OnthAcorn117hd Saved ground, no rally 11
1May04-10CD sly 1¼ :463 1:114 1:371 2:04 KyDerby-G1 87 4 1813 1893¼ 1412 1210 613¾ Flores D R L126 43.40 65- 21 Smarty Jones1262¾ Lion Heart1263¼ Imperialism1262 Steadied 3/8,mild bid 18
10Apr04-9Kee fst 1⅛ :463 1:11 1:364 1:492 BlueGras-G1 89 1 58¼ 611 77½ 67½ 613½ Flores D R L123 10.30 80- 20 The Cliff's Edge123½ Lion Heart1236 Limehouse1233¾ No factor 8
14Mar04-5SA fst 1 1/16 :231 :464 1:11 1:424 SnFelipe-G2 84 3 43½ 55½ 64½ 76½ 79½ Flores D R LB119 2.60 81- 09 Prechintthebr116no StAveril1224½ HrvrdAvenu1161 Pulled,inside,wkened 9
8Feb04-8SA fst 1⅛ :47 1:11 1:362 1:491 Sham81k 98 7 67½ 67¾ 66 43½ 41½ Flores D R LB123 1.90 87- 13 MasterDavid1161 Borrego120hd Preachinatthebr116hd 5wd into lane,rallied 7
25Oct03-7SA fst 1 1/16 :221 :45 1:094 1:433 BCJuvnle-G1 92 2 1213 1213 106½ 31½ 12½ Flores D R LB122 26.80 86- 07 ActionThisDay1222½ MinisterEric1225 ChpelRoyl122no 4 wide, going away 12
28Sep03-1SA fst 1 1/16 :232 :473 1:12 1:453 Md Sp Wt 45k 79 5 77¾ 712 69½ 52½ 1no Solis A LB117 *1.00 76- 16 ActionThisDy117no NtiveApprovl117½ CourgeousAct1174 Bid btwn,gamely 7
5Sep03-2Dmr fst 1 :224 :463 1:104 1:37 Md Sp Wt 51k 74 5 66 66¾ 57½ 46 27 Solis A LB120 4.10 82- 10 Coldntight1207 ActionThisDay120nk ThtsnOutrge1203 Bit tight 1/16,late 2d 6
```

Aldebaran

Own: Flaxman Holdings Ltd

B. h. 5 (Feb)
Sire: Mr. Prospector (Raise a Native)
Dam: Chimes of Freedom (Private Account)
Br: Flaxman Holdings Ltd (Ky)
Tr: Frankel Robert J

Life	25	8	12	3	$1,739,186	122	D.Fst	12	5	5	1	$965,006 122
2003	8	5	1	1	$1,110,606	122	Wet(405)	3	1	2	0	$574,400 110
2002	8	1	6	0	$428,800	113	Turf(275)	10	2	5	2	$199,780 105
	0	0	0	0	$0	-	Dst(T)(423)	0	0	0	0	$0 -

```
25Oct03-5SA fst 6f :21 :431 :55 1:074 3↑ BCSprint-G1 105 6 12 1312 127 99 65½ Bailey J D LB126 *2.10 93- 05 Cajun Beat1232¼ Bluesthestandard1262 Shake You Down126½ Belated rally 13
31Aug03-10Sar fst 7f :22 :441 1:083 1:211 3↑ ForegoH-G1 122 4 7 79½ 57 1½ 14¾ Bailey J D L123f *1.60 101- 09 Aldebaran1234¾ Najran1141¼ Gygistar1196¾ Clear sailing inside 7
4Jly03-8Bel fst 7f :222 :444 1:093 1:222 3↑ TomFoolH-G2 105 4 6 713 711 2½ 12 Bailey J D L122f *.95 88- 15 Aldebaran1222 Peeping Tom1172½ State City1183¾ Going away on rail 7
14Jun03-10CD fst 1⅛ :464 1:102 1:35 1:472 3↑ SFosterH-G1 101 6 63½ 66 63½ 56½ 39½ Bailey J D L120 3.20 91- 04 Perfect Drift115hd Mineshaft1239½ Aldebaran120½ Improved position 10
26May03-9Bel sly 1 :221 :442 1:083 1:34 3↑ MtropltH-G1 110 6 711 79 51¾ 11½ 1nk Bailey J D L119 4.40 96- 14 Aldebaran119nk Saarland1143 Peeping Tom1143¾ Ducked out stretch 8
3May03-5CD fst 7f :222 :45 1:093 1:214 4↑ CDH-G2 111 5 10 1111 97½ 32 12½ Bailey J D L120 *1.30 93- 08 Aldebaran1202½ Pass Rush117nk Cappuchino115hd Swung 7w, drew off 12
12Apr03-9Aqu my 7f :224 :452 1:091 1:212 3↑ CarterH-G1 108 5 1 58¾ 56½ 35 23½ Bailey J D L118 2.15 92- 13 Congaree1223½ Aldebaran1181¼ Peeping Tom1143¾ Game finish on rail 5
2Mar03-7SA fst 7f :222 :443 1:091 1:212 4↑ SnCrlosH-G1 110 6 2 510 54¾ 1hd 15 Valdivia J Jr LB116 2.40 99- 08 Aldebaran1165 Crafty C. T.116½ Grey Memo1163 5wd into lane,clear 6
30Nov02-9Aqu fst 1 :222 :443 1:081 1:33 3↑ CigarMiH-G1 109 5 52 51¾ 41½ 32½ 25½ Chavez J F L116 4.20 95- 12 Congaree1195½ Aldebaran116nk Crafty C. T.1172¼ 4 wide, held place 8
26Oct02-5AP yl 1 (T) :234 :483 1:124 1:364 3↑ BCMile-G1 85 7 127½148 149 1311 1112¾ Chavez J F L126 14.90 81- 09 Domdrivr126¾ RockofGibrltr122no GoodJournyy1261¼ Check early and 1/4pl 14
21Sep02-9Bel fst 7f :222 :45 1:092 1:221 3↑ Vosburgh-G1 107 6 3 47 48 46 22½ Day P L126 *1.50 89- 16 Bonapaw1262½ Aldebaran1262½ Voodoo1261¼ Game finish outside 6
1Sep02-9Sar fst 6½f :212 :441 1:09 1:153 3↑ ForegoH-G1 111 7 6 710 67 35 22½ Day P L115 1.95 95- 15 Orientate1222¼ Aldebaran1153¾ Multiple Choice1142½ Game finish outside 8
3Aug02-6Sar fst 7f :224 :45 1:094 1:212 3↑ Alw 51000N3X 104 1 7 67 56 42 21¼ Bailey J D L121 *.65 97- 10 Voodoo1211¼ Aldebaran1211¼ Smooth Jazz1191½ Inside move, gamely 7
27May02-9Bel fst 1 :222 :443 1:083 1:331 3↑ MtropltH-G1 113 9 92¾ 84¼ 44 25½ 24¾ Bailey J D L115 4.30 98 - SweptOverboard1174¾ Aldebaran1151½ CraftyC.T.1164½ Good finish inside 10
14Apr02-8Kee sly 7f :213 :442 1:091 1:212 3↑ CmwlthBC-G2 106 6 6 614 610 22 21¼ Desormeaux K J L118 *1.80 96- 12 Orientate1201¼ Aldebaran1184¼ Twilight Road118½ Ck start,bmp 3/16s 7
24Mar02-7SA fst 7f :221 :444 1:092 1:213 4↑ OC 62k/N2x-N 105 1 6 78 76½ 32 13 Desormeaux K J LB118 *1.60 97- 10 Aldebaran1183 Jimmy Z118½ Mo Mon1185 4wd into lane,rallied 8
25Nov01-7Hol yl 1⅛ (T) :473 1:122 1:364 1:491 + HolDerby-G1 100 9 1011 1010 83¾ 53 34 Chavez J F LB122 *1.10e 78- 20 Denon1221 Sligo Bay1223 Aldebaran122hd 4wd 2nd turn,late 3rd 12
28Oct01-8Bel fm 1 (T) :241 :47 1:103 1:333 3↑ NassauH139k 105 5 76¾ 75¾ 52 2½ 13¼ Chavez J F 113 4.80 90- 13 Aldebaran1133¼ Capsized114nk Tubrok1144½ When asked, ridden out 7
  Previously trained by Henry Cecil
4Oct01 Newmarket (GB) yl 1 (T) Str 1:382 3↑ Joel Stakes (Listed) 31½ Quinn T R 123 6.00 Beckett123¾ Priors Lodge127¾ Aldebaran123½ 11
  Timeform rating: 110 Stk 40800 Tracked leaders,bid over 1f out,not good enough.Aunty Rose 8th
14Sep01 Doncaster (GB) yl 1¼ (T) LH 2:11 Joy UK Cndtns Stks(1-1/4m,60y) 21¼ Ryan W 121 6.00 Lagudin1211¼ Aldebaran1211¼ Nooshman128¾ 9
  Timeform rating: 110 Alw 29400 Tracked in 4th,led over 1f out,dueled,headed 70y out
20Jly01 Newbury (GB) gd 7f (T) LH 1:283 3↑ Systems Conditions Stk(7f,64y) 2nk Quinn T R 116 *1.00 Umistim126nk Aldebaran116½ Patsy's Double119¾ 7
  Timeform rating: 109+ Alw 24500 Rated in 5th,3rd 3f out,gaining late
20Jun01 Ascot (GB) gd 7f (T) Str 1:274 Jersey Stakes-G3 2nk Quinn T R 123 10.00 Mozart123nk Aldebaran123¾ Ratio123½ 18
  Timeform rating: 108 Stk 97800 Rated at rear,progress 2f out,strong late bid,held by winner
26May01 Kempton (GB) gd 1 (T) RH 1:38 Heron Stakes (Listed) 21¾ Quinn T R 124 2.00 Dandoun1241¾ Aldebaran124nk Reef Diver1248 6
  Timeform rating: 110 Stk 38200 Tracked leader,led briefly 2f out,dueled 1f out,outfinished
7May01 Doncaster (GB) gd 1 (T) LH 1:382 Doncaster Racecourse Cndtns St 21½ Quinn T R 127 2.75 Dandoun1271½ Aldebaran1275 Dayglow Dancer129¾ 7
  Timeform rating: 108+ Alw 23900 Tracked leader,quickened w/winner 2f out,outfinished
20Oct00 Doncaster (GB) gd 7f (T) Str 1:261 October Maiden Stakes (Div 2) 12 Quinn T R 126 *2.50 Aldebaran1262 Take to Task126½ Polish Off1264 21
  Timeform rating: 100+ Maiden 7700 Dwelt,soon mid-pack,rallied to lead over 1f out,driving
```

All Gong (GB)

Own: Houghland Calvin

Dk. b or b. g. 6 (Feb)
Sire: Kris*GB (Sharpen Up*GB) $24,230
Dam: Bonne Ile*GB (Ile de Bourbon)
Br: The Kris Syndicate and Kirtlington Stud Ltd (GB)
Tr: Miller F. B

Life	30	7	7	6	$461,163	-	D.Fst	0	0	0	0	$0 -
2003	2	0	0	0	$9,231	-	Wet(253)	0	0	0	0	$0 -
2002	5	1	0	3	$98,000	-	Turf(375)	1	0	0	1	$290 -
Aik (T)	0	0	0	0	$0	-	Dst(T)(273)	0	0	0	0	$0 -

```
25Apr03-8Kee fm *2½ (T)Hurdles 4:441 4↑ RylChsHd-G1 - 5 22½ 22 22½ 36½ 412¾ Massey R L158 8.60 - - McDynmo1587½ ShmrockIsle1585 PristhPrinc158nk Chase, tired,collapsed 8
5Apr03-4Stn fm *2¼ (T)Hurdles 3:52 4↑ Alw 25000N$Y - 4 42½ 52 44¼ 44½ 411¾ Miller F B Jr L156 - - - Dynability1441 Baksheesh14410¼ Pelagos156½ Mild bid,even finish 6
17Nov02-5Cam yl *2¾ (T)Hurdles 5:251 4↑ ColonlCp-G1 - 3 31 33½ 310 413 315½ Miller F B Jr L156 - - - Flat Top1566½ Tres Touche1569¼ All Gong156½ Lacked late response 7
19Oct02-4FH sf *2⅝ (T)Hurdles 5:192 4↑ (R)BrCupStp-G1 - 2 33½ 43 35½ 24 33¾ Miller F B Jr L156 - - - Flat Top1563 Tres Touche156¾ All Gong1568¾ Well placed, mild gain 8
28Sep02-4Shw sf *2½ (T)Hurdles 5:024 4↑ LegcyCpHrd30k - 3 69½ 64 45½ 44½ 39 Miller F B Jr L154 - - - Tres Touche1541½ Pelagos1547½ All Gong1542½ No rally 8
11May02-6PW fm *3 (T)Hurdles 5:322 4↑ Iroquois-G1 - 1 23½ 22 32 3nk 1nk Miller Blythe L158 - - - All Gong158nk Praise the Prince1585¼ Flat Top15812½ Gamely 7
13Apr02 Nakayama (Jpn) gd *2⅝ RH 4:504 4↑ Nakayama Grand Jump 1133¾ Miller B 140 28.00 St Steven1401½ Gokai1407 Fusaichi Gold140no 15
  Stk 1151900 Towards rear throughout
18Nov01-5Cam fm *2¾ (T)Hurdles 5:053 4↑ ColonlCp-G1 - 2 921 77 47½ 24 215½ Massey R L156 - - - Lord Zada15615½ All Gong15613¼ Al Skywalker156½ Second best 11
20Oct01-4FH fm *2⅝ (T)Hurdles 4:541 4↑ (R)BrCupStp-G1 - 4 42½ - - - - Miller Blythe L156 - - - Quel Senor1565¾ Lord Zada1561¾ Praise the Prince1562¼ Fell eighth fence 9
29Sep01-5Shw fm *2½ (T)Hurdles 4:424 4↑ LegacyCup30k - 6 67 48 44 3½ 2½ Miller Blythe L158 - - - Darn Tipalarm154½ All Gong1581½ Lord Zada154nk Steady advance 12
12May01-6PW fm *3 (T)Hurdles 5:35 4↑ Iroquois-G1 - 3 55½ 44½ 41¾ 24 29¾ Miller Blythe L158 - - - Rand1589¾ All Gong15815 Electron158 Second best 6
27Apr01-7Kee fm *2½ (T)Hurdles 4:342 4↑ RylChsHd-G1 - 10 31½ 21½ 3½ 23½ 23 Miller Blythe L158 *1.90 - - Pompeyo1583 All Gong1581 Rand1581¼ Inside, no match 10
14Apr01-4Ath fm *2⅝ (T)Hurdles 4:412 4↑ AtlntCup-G1 - 4 42½ 57 56 2½ 2½ Bentley D L158 - - - Electron142½ All Gong1587¾ Masamadas1426¾ Just missed 6
19Nov00-5Cam gd *2¾ (T)Hurdles 5:191 4↑ ColonlCp-G1 - 5 89½ 813 412 43 33 Miller Blythe L156 - - - Romantic1561¼ Campanile1561¾ All Gong1567 No excuse 8
28Oct00-4FH fm *2⅝ (T)Hurdles 4:534 4↑ BrCupStp-G1 - 7 21½ 2½ 1hd 12 13¼ Miller Blythe L156 - - - All Gong1563¼ Popular Gigalo1561¼ Allgrit156¾ Stalked wide, drew off 9
6Oct00-2Cnl fm *2¼ (T)Hurdles 3:591 4↑ FrgsnMHH-G2 - 1 718 715 69¾ 515 414 Miller Blythe L152 2.20e - - Spring Salute1427¾ Al Skywalker140¾ Pompeyo1485½ Passed tiring rivals 9
13May00-6PW fm *3 (T)Hurdles 5:50 4↑ Iroquois-G1 - 5 33½ 2½ 24 2hd 21¼ Miller Blythe L154 - - - Pinkie Swear1541¼ All Gong154nk Greek Hero15414¾ Second best 6
15Apr00-4Ath fm *2⅝ (T)Hurdles 4:423 4↑ AtlntCup-G1 - 2 36 42½ 22 1½ 1½ Miller Blythe L142 - - - All Gong142½ Allan Prell1426½ Darn Tipalarm1514½ All out 5
6Nov99-3Pmt fm *2⅜ (T)Hurdles 4:02 3↑ (R)USChampHur70k - 3 78 54 64 3nk 31½ Miller F B Jr L162 - - - Muscle Car1581½ Darn Tipalarm154no All Gong1623½ Rallied 8
```

9Oct99–2Mor fm *2¼ Ⓣ Hurdles 4:264 3↑ Ⓡ AMcCSupHur29k – 5 32½ 33½ 36½ 35½ 529 Miller F B Jr L162 - - - Little Hurt1502 Darn Tipalarm1548¼ How Goes15418¼ Stumbled 5
Previously trained by Nicky Henderson
15Apr99 Cheltenham (GB) gd 2⅛ Ⓣ LH 4:014 4↑ Endsleigh Insur Novices Hurdle Alw 12700 416½ Fitzgerald M A 162 5.00 Star of Dungannon1625 *Samakaan*1629 Lawahik1622½ 17 *Tracked leader,bid 4 out,with leaders 2 out,weakened after last*
16Mar99 Cheltenham (GB) yl 2 1/16 Ⓣ LH 3:543 4↑ Supreme Novices Hurdle Stk 130300 946¼ Fitzgerald M A 162 25.00 *Hors La Loi III*15417 *Joe Mac*1627 Arctic Fancy162nk 20 *Slowly away,soon in touch,struggling after 5th,beaten 3 out*
29Jan99 Doncaster (GB) gd 2½ Ⓣ LH 4:581 EBF Natl Hunt Novices Hurdle Alw 9600 12½ Fitzgerald M A 164 *1.20 All Gong1642½ Woodfield Gale1611½ Professor Cool154nk 17 *Rated in mid-pack,progress to lead after third last,held well*
18Jan99 Doncaster (GB) yl 2 1/16 Ⓣ LH 4:111 4↑ National Hunt Novices Hurdle Alw 7100 13½ Fitzgerald M A 165 *1.10 *All Gong*1653½ Broadnard1592½ *Knockara Fair*1592½ 18 *Close up traveling well,led on bit 2 out,drew clear,easily*
2Jan99 Newbury (GB) hy 2⅝ Ⓣ LH 5:332 5↑ Challow Novices Hurdle Stk 44000 429 Fitzgerald M A 161 5.00 King's Road1612 Rio's King16118 Storm Of Gold1619 5 *Rated in 4th,clumsy at 2nd,3rd after 6th,weakened 4 out*
11Dec98 Cheltenham (GB) gd 2⅛ Ⓣ LH 4:16 EBF Natl Hunt Novices Hurdle Alw 12500 11½ Fitzgerald M A 154 14.00 All Gong1541½ Beau1598 Rio's King16410 13 *Tracked leaders making occasional mistake,led 1 out,driving*
25May98 Huntingdon (GB) gd 2 1/16 Ⓣ RH 3:384 National Hunt Flat Race Alw 2800 24 Fitzgerald M A 161 1.75 Bay Caster1594 *All Gong*1611 Rocket Man159¾ 8 *Led to over 1f out,held 2nd*
17May98 Fakenham (GB) gd 2 Ⓣ LH 3:532 National Hunt Flat Race Alw 2700 114 Fitzgerald M A 154 *.60 All Gong15414 Dreamington Rovers1496 Arctic Melody159¾ 6 *Led throughout setting easy pace,quickened clear 4f out,handily*
18Apr98 Ayr (GB) gd 2 Ⓣ LH 3:361 National Hunt Flat Race(Div 1) Alw 9400 48½ Fitzgerald M A 152 *3.00 Crazy Horse1583 Market Scan1583½ Three Lakes1522 13 *Mid-pack,progress over 2f out,one-paced late*
20Feb98 Sandown Park (GB) gd 2 1/16 Ⓣ RH 3:564 National Hunt Flat Race Alw 3100 318 Fitzgerald M A 147 *1.40 Boca Boca14411 Steeples Lad1507 All Gong1474 15 *Rated towards rear,progress halfway,one-paced late*

Ashado

Own: Starlight Stables LLC, Saylor, Paul and Martin, Johns

Dk. b or b. f. 4 (Feb) KEESEP02 $170,000
Sire: Saint Ballado (Halo) $125,000
Dam: Goulash (Mari's Book)
Br: Aaron U. Jones & Marie D. Jones (Ky)
Tr: Pletcher Todd A

Life	20	12	4	2	$3,711,440	106	D.Fst	13	7	3	1	$1,796,000	105
2005	6	3	1	0	$841,000	105	Wet(372)	7	5	1	1	$1,915,440	106
2004	8	5	2	1	$2,259,640	106	Turf(312)	0	0	0	0	$0	–
	0	0	0	0	$0	–	DstⓉ(394)	0	0	0	0	$0	–

1Oct05–7Bel fst 1⅛ :473 1:112 1:354 1:484 3↑ⒻBeldame-G1 103 6 2½ 2½ 1hd 12 1½ Velazquez J R L123 *1.70 87–15 Ashdo123½ HppyTicket1232½ SocietySelection1233¼ Speed, clear, gamely 7
26Aug05–9Sar fst 1¼ :464 1:111 1:362 2:02 3↑ⒻPrsnlEns-G1 85 5 26 24½ 41¾ 47½ 414¾ Velazquez J R L122 *.45 79–12 ShdowCst1182¾ PrsonlLgnd1169½ TwoTrlSoux1182½ Close up inside, tired 6
31Jly05–9Sar fst 1⅛ :47 1:112 1:363 1:501 3↑ⒻGoFWandH-G1 105 5 2½ 2½ 2½ 17 19½ Velazquez J R L121 *1.15 84–16 Ashado1219½ Bending Strings1151 Andujar1181¾ Drew away when asked 5
18Jun05–9Bel fst 1 1/16 :241 :473 1:111 1:41 3↑ⒻOPhippsH-G1 101 1 1hd 1½ 1½ 13½ 13 Velazquez J R L120 *.85 95–11 *Ashdo*1203 SocitySlction119¾ BndingStrings1156 Drew clear when roused 5
20May05–9Pim slyS 1 1/16 :241 :484 1:131 1:444 3↑ⒻPmBCDsfH-G3 101 4 11½ 11 11½ 12½ 2¾ Velazquez J R L123 *.30 86–30 Silmaril115¾ *Ashado*1235 Friel's for Real1141½ Pace, 2nd best 4
9Apr05–11OP fst 1 1/16 :233 :47 1:11 1:434 4↑ⒻAplBlsmH-G1 94 5 21½ 2½ 2hd 2½ 52 Velazquez J R L121 *.50 85–17 DreamofSummer117nk StarPrde116½ *ShdowCst*1161¼ Pressd,fell apart late 7
30Oct04–2LS gd 1⅛ :463 1:102 1:352 1:481 3↑ⒻBCDistaf-G1 102 1 31 52 41½ 1½ 11¼ Velazquez J R L119 *2.00 108–02 Ashado1191¼ StormFlagFlying123nk *StellarJyne*1191½ Blocked 1/4,steadied 11
2Oct04–9Pha fst 1 1/16 :234 :473 1:111 1:413 ⒻCotillnH-G2 102 5 21½ 21 2½ 1½ 12¾ Coa E M L124 *.20 107–13 *Ashado*1242¾ Ender's Sister1173½ *My Lordship*1151¼ When ready,drew clear 7
21Aug04–10Sar sly 1¼ :471 1:112 1:362 2:023 ⒻAlabama-G1 103 5 3½ 3nk 1hd 2hd 33 Velazquez J R L121 *.60 91–18 SocietySelection1212½ *StellarJyne*121½ *Ashdo*1215¼ Vied 3 wide, weakened 8
24Jly04–8Bel my 1¼ :483 1:122 1:363 2:022 ⒻCCAOaks-G1 106 4 2½ 2½ 11½ 15 14½ Velazquez J R L121 *.75 85–22 Ashado1214½ StellarJayne1217½ *MagicIllusion*1214 Drew clear when asked 6
26Jun04–9Bel fst 1⅛ :47 1:104 1:352 1:48 ⒻMthrGoos-G1 96 4 1hd 2hd 1hd 2½ 22½ Velazquez J R L121 *.90 88–11 Stellar Jayne1212½ *Ashado*1211¾ Island Sand1215 Stayed on for place 6
30Apr04–10CD my 1⅛ :46 1:094 1:363 1:504 ⒻKyOaks-G1 102 1 33½ 24½ 24 2hd 11¼ Velazquez J R L121 *2.30 83–17 Ashado1211¼ *Island Sand*1211¾ *Madcap Escapade*1211¼ Moved 4w,stiff drive 11
3Apr04–9Kee fst 1 1/16 :24 :472 1:112 1:442 ⒻAshland-G1 97 1 31 32 32 22½ 2½ Velasquez C L123 1.70 89–14 Madcap Escapade118½ *Ashado*1234 Last Song1203 Ck 1st turn,4w bid 4
6Mar04–9FG fst 1 1/16 :234 :473 1:121 1:43 ⒻFGOaks-G2 94 1 32 32½ 31½ 12½ 13¾ Velasquez C L121 *1.10 95–10 Ashado1213¾ *Victory U. S. A.*1211¼ Shadow Cast121½ 3-w bid, clear,driving 6
29Nov03–7Aqu fst 1⅛ :47 1:12 1:382 1:524 ⒻDemoisel-G2 84 5 3½ 31 1hd 1½ 1no Bailey J D L117 *.55 72–19 *Ashado*117no La Reina121½ Dr. Kathy11510 Vied, clear, got nod 7
25Oct03–3SA fst 1 1/16 :224 :464 1:104 1:423 ⒻBCJuvFil-G1 95 5 32½ 31½ 41 31½ 22½ Velazquez J R LB119 13.30 88–07 Halfbridled1192½ *Ashado*119nk *Victory U. S. A.*1199¼ Saved ground, rallied 14
4Oct03–6Bel fst 1 1/16 :231 :471 1:121 1:434 ⒻFrizette-G1 88 3 31½ 42 41¾ 33 34 Santos J A L120 2.80 77–26 SocietySlction1201¼ VictoryUSA1202¾ Ashdo1206¾ Stayed on well stretch 8
29Aug03–8Sar fst 7f :222 :452 1:103 1:24 ⒻSpinaway-G1 84 2 3 2hd 1hd 1½ 11¼ Prado E S L121 3.10 87–10 Ashado1211¼ *Be Gentle*1218¼ Daydreaming1211¾ Bumped start, gamely 6
23Jly03–9Sar sly 6f :22 :452 :582 1:12 ⒻSchylrvl-G2 81 6 5 4¾ 2hd 11½ 13 Prado E S L118 *2.55 82–17 *Ashado*1183 Maple Syrple1222½ Hermione's Magic1181 Quick 3 wide move 7
18Jun03–3Bel sly 5½f :213 :444 :573 1:042 ⒻMd Sp Wt 43k 93 4 4 1½ 1½ 12½ 17 Velazquez J R L118 *1.10 91–19 *Ashdo*1187 PleseTkeMeOut1183¾ Menifeeque118nk When roused, widened 5

Azeri

Own: Allen E. Paulson Living Trust

Ch. m. 6 (May)
Sire: Jade Hunter (Mr. Prospector) $10,000
Dam: Zodiac Miss*Aus (Ahonoora*GB)
Br: Allen E. Paulson (Ky)
Tr: Lukas D. W

Life	24	17	4	0	$4,079,820	112	D.Fst	23	16	4	0	$3,039,820	112
2004	8	3	2	0	$1,035,000	112	Wet(327)	1	1	0	0	$1,040,000	111
2003	5	4	1	0	$817,080	109	Turf(272)	0	0	0	0	$0	–
	0	0	0	0	$0	–	DstⓉ(323)	0	0	0	0	$0	–

30Oct04–9LS fst 1¼ :47 1:111 1:351 1:59 3↑BCClasic-G1 109 3 31 42 73½ 55½ 59¾ Day P L123 15.20 - - *Ghostzapper*1263 RosesinMy1264 PlesntlyPerfect126¾ Broke slow, rail trip 13
10Oct04–8Kee fst 1⅛ :464 1:113 1:37 1:493 3↑ⒻSpinster-G1 108 1 21½ 21½ 2hd 1hd 13 Day P L123 *.40 93–12 Azeri1233 Tamweel123½ Mayo On the Side1233¾ 3-4w,mild hand urging 7
27Aug04–9Sar fst 1¼ :461 1:093 1:354 2:033 3↑ⒻPrsnlEnH-G1 97 2 21½ 2hd 11½ 2hd 21¼ Day P L122 *.60 88–11 StormFlagFlying1161¼ *Azeri*122½ Nevermore1144½ Stalked fast pace game 5
1Aug04–9Sar fst 1⅛ :473 1:104 1:35 1:474 3↑ⒻGoFWandH-G1 106 5 11½ 1½ 1½ 1hd 11¾ Day P L120 2.95 96–14 Azeri1201¾ *Sightseek*1222 *Storm Flag Flying*1177 Pace, resolute, clear 5
19Jun04–9Bel fst 1 1/16 :231 :453 1:10 1:412 3↑ⒻOPhippsH-G1 78 1 1½ 1hd 2½ 410 411¾ Day P L123 *.80 81–20 Sightseek1203¼ Storm Flag Flying1176½ Passing Shot1162 Set pace, tired 4
31May04–9Bel fst 1 :232 :46 1:10 1:352 3↑MtropltH-G1 103 3 32½ 3½ 51¼ 62¾ 86¾ Day P L117 5.80 77–34 PicoCntrl119¾ BowmnsBnd1142¼ StrongHop1191½ Close up inside, empty 9
1May04–8CD fst 7f :222 :45 1:093 1:223 4↑ⒻHmnaDstH-G1 99 2 4 21 21½ 2hd 2hd Smith M E L125 *.70 89–06 Mayo On the Side114hd Azeri1257¼ Randaroo121nk Bid btwn,game rail 4
3Apr04–9OP fst 1 1/16 :231 :463 1:104 1:411 4↑ⒻAplBlsmH-G1 112 1 11 1½ 11½ 12½ 11½ Smith M E L123 2.00 104–09 Azeri1231½ ⒹWild Spirit1191¾ Star Parade1147¼ Pace off rail, driving 6
Previously trained by De Seroux Laura 2003(as of 9/28): (93 14 13 11 0.15)
28Sep03–6SA fst 1 1/16 :232 :471 1:111 1:424 3↑ⒻLdyScBCH-G2 101 5 54½ 53½ 53½ 32 32¼ Smith M E LB128 *.20 88–16 Got Koko118½ ⒹElloluv1161¾ *Azeri*1281 3wd into lane,no bid 6
Placed second through disqualification
10Aug03–8Dmr fst 1 1/16 :231 :47 1:11 1:42 3↑ⒻCLHrschH-G2 100 1 11 1½ 11½ 12½ 13¼ Smith M E LB127 *.30 95–12 Azeri1273¼ *Got Koko*118hd Tropical Blossom1084½ Bit off rail,handily 5
21Jun03–8Hol fst 1⅛ :471 1:103 1:351 1:482 3↑ⒻVanityH-G1 109 6 2½ 1hd 2hd 11 12 Smith M E LB127 *.30 92–14 *Azeri*1272 Sister Girl Blues111½ *Bare Necessities*1184½ Dueled,inched clear 7
24May03–8Hol fst 1 1/16 :23 :461 1:10 1:414 3↑ⒻMladyBCH-G1 109 4 2hd 11 12½ 12½ 13 Smith M E LB125 *.20 95–05 *Azeri*1253 Enjoy1143 Tropical Blossom1111 Speed,met bids,clear 6
5Apr03–8OP fst 1 1/16 :241 :483 1:121 1:43 4↑ⒻAplBlsmH-G1 105 6 32 42 2½ 21½ 1hd Smith M E L123 *.40 95–11 *Azeri*123hd Take ChargeLady1183¼ *Mandy'sGold*1162 Restrained, 4-w, game 7
26Oct02–3AP gd 1⅛ :461 1:093 1:351 1:483 3↑ⒻBCDistaf-G1 111 4 11 11 11 12 15 Smith M E L123f *1.80 105 - *Azeri*1235 Farda Amiga119hd Imperial Gesture1193¼ Off rail, driving 8
2Oct02–8SA fst 1 1/16 :222 :452 1:084 1:41 3↑ⒻLdyScBCH-G2 102 5 1hd 1½ 1hd 12½ 13½ Smith M E LB127 *.30 99–03 *Azeri*1273½ Starrer115hd Mystic Lady1161 Inside,clear,handily 7
11Aug02–8Dmr fst 1 1/16 :233 :471 1:11 1:423 3↑ⒻCLHrschH-G2 101 3 1hd 1½ 11 13 12 Smith M E LB126 *.10 90–15 *Azeri*1262 Angel Gift1142 Se Me Acabo1142½ Pulled,inside,handily 5
22Jun02–3Hol fst 1⅛ :463 1:104 1:354 1:484 3↑ⒻVanityH-G1 107 2 11 11 12½ 13½ 13 Smith M E LB125 *.30 88–10 *Azeri*1253 *Affluent*1193 DHStarrer117 Speed,inside,handily 5
25May02–8Hol fst 1 1/16 :232 :462 1:101 1:42 3↑ⒻMladyBCH-G1 109 2 11 11 12 13½ 13½ Smith M E LB122 *.60 93–09 *Azeri*1223½ Affluent1194 Collect Call1153 Inside,clear,riddn out 6
6Apr02–11OP fst 1 1/16 :232 :472 1:12 1:423 4↑ⒻAplBlsmH-G1 110 1 44 42 2½ 1½ 11¾ Smith M E L117 *1.00 95–15 *Azeri*1171¾ Affluent118¾ Miss Linda1182 Broke in air, drifted 5
10Mar02–8SA fst 1⅛ :471 1:111 1:361 1:49 4↑ⒻSMrgrtaH-G1 110 1 31 42 32½ 2½ 13 Smith M E LB115 2.20 91–16 *Azeri*1153 Spain1181 Printemps1164 3wd bid,clear late 7
9Feb02–8SA fst 1⅛ :481 1:123 1:37 1:491 ⒻLaCanada-G2 105 4 55 54½ 54 31½ 21 Smith M E LB115 2.90 89–11 Summer Colony1191 *Azeri*1151 *Ask MeNoSecrets*1151½ 4wd into lane,rallied 6
12Jan02–3SA fst 1 :233 :464 1:103 1:354 4↑ⒻOC 80k/N2X-N 100 4 42 42 2½ 11½ 13 Smith M E LB117 *.40 92–13 Azeri1173 Elaine's Angel117nk Angel Gift1175 Bid,clear,handily 6
17Dec01–7Hol fst 6½f :22 :443 1:09 1:152 3↑ⒻAlw 39000N1X 103 2 5 53¼ 1hd 11 13 Smith M E LB118 *.50 94–15 *Azeri*1183 Burning Breeze1184½ Pine Lake Lady1181 Bid,clear,handily 7
1Nov01–4SA fst 6f :212 :432 :561 1:084 3↑ⒻMd Sp Wt 38k 94 4 4 2hd 1hd 12½ 16 Smith M E LB120 17.30 95–13 *Azeri*1206 *Southern Oasis*1203½ Blushing Rahy1202½ Rid out,in hand late 9

Banks Hill (GB)

Own: Juddmonte Farms Inc

B. f. 4 (Feb)
Sire: Danehill (Danzig)
Dam: Hasili*Ire (Kahyasi*Ire)
Br: Juddmonte Farms (GB)
Tr: Frankel Robert J

Life	15	5	5	3	$1,824,008	112	D.Fst	0	0	0	0	$0	–
2002	7	1	2	3	$667,077	106	Wet(370)	0	0	0	0	$0	–
2001	7	3	3	0	$1,145,276	112	Turf(412)	15	5	5	3	$1,824,008	112
	0	0	0	0	$0	–	Dst(T)(295)	0	0	0	0	$0	–

1Dec02-4Hol fm 1⅛ (T) :481 1:113 1:354 1:481+3↑ (F)Matriarc-G1 101 2 2hd 2½ 1hd 2hd 41¾ Bailey J D LB123 *1.30 86-17 DrssToThrll120hd GoldnAppls1231½ MgcMssn123no Inside duel,outkicked 6
26Oct02-7AP yl 1¼ (T) :49 1:132 1:382 2:032 3↑ (F)BCF&MTrf-G1 106 5 58½ 56½ 53½ 41½ 21½ Bailey J D L123 3.80 87-09 Starine1231½ Banks Hill123nk Islington118nk 4 wide, move willingly 12
Previously trained by Fabre Andre 2002(as of 10/5): (2 0 0 1 0.00)
5Oct02-8SA fm 1¼ (T) :483 1:132 1:37 1:593 3↑ (F)YlwRibbn-G1 99 5 53¾ 53½ 52 42¼ 34 Nakatani C S 123 *1.00 91-05 GoldenApples1231 VoodooDncer1233 BnksHill1233 Lacked room 5/16-3/16 6
8Sep02 Longchamp (Fr) gd *1 (T) RH 1:391 3↑ Prix du Moulin de Longchamp-G1 Stk 294600 2½ Hughes R 125 2.40 Rock of Gibraltar123½ Banks Hill1251½ Gossamer120nk 7
Timeform rating: 120 — Tracked in 3rd,led over 1f out,headed 100y out
18Aug02 Deauville (Fr) gd *1 (T) Str 1:35 3↑ Prix Jacques le Marois-G1 Stk 344600 11½ Peslier O 127 *1.70 Banks Hill1271½ *Domedriver*1301½ Best of The Bests1301 8
Timeform rating: 126 — Rated in 5th,rallied to lead 150y out,driving.Turtle Bow 4th
19Jun02 Ascot (GB) gd 1¼ (T) RH 2:042 4↑ Prince of Wales's Stakes-G1 Stk 372000 35¾ Peslier O 123 *3.50 Grandera1265 Indian Creek126¾ *Banks Hill*1231½ 12
Timeform rating: 115 — Rated in 6th,mild bid 2f out,hung.Nayef 4th
19May02 Longchamp (Fr) gd *1⅛ (T) RH 1:512 4↑ Prix d'Ispahan (1 1/8m,55y)-G1 Stk 134200 31½ Peslier O 125 *.60 Best of The Bests128½ Poussin1281 Banks Hill1252 4
Timeform rating: 116+ — Tracked pacesetting winner,lost 2nd near line
27Oct01-7Bel fm 1¼ [T] :483 1:132 1:373 2:001 3↑ (F)BCF&MTrf-G1 112 5 42 31½ 2hd 15 15½ Peslier O 119 6.00 90-10 Banks Hill1195½ Spook Express1231¾ Spring Oak119nk Rail trip, drew off 12
9Sep01 Longchamp (Fr) yl *1 (T) RH 1:39 3↑ Prix du Moulin de Longchamp-G1 Stk 217700 23 Hughes R 120 *1.50 *Slickly*1283 *Banks Hill*1201½ Hawkeye123½ 8
Timeform rating: 116+ — Rated towards rear,late gain into 2nd.Vahorimix 6th
19Aug01 Deauville (Fr) sf *1 (T) Str 1:384 3↑ Prix Jacques le Marois-G1 Stk 244800 31¼ Hughes R 121 2.30 Proudwings127½ Vahorimix125¾ Banks Hill121no 9
Timeform rating: 114+ — Midpack,outpaced 2f out,bid 1f out,bumped 60y out.Plcd 2nd via DQ
Placed second through disqualification
22Jun01 Ascot (GB) fm 1 (T) RH 1:393 (F)Coronation Stakes-G1 Stk 381500 11½ Peslier O 126 *4.00 Banks Hill1261½ Crystal Music126½ Tempting Fate126nk 13
Timeform rating: 119+ — Twrds rear,lacked room 2f out,angled out,led 100y out,going away
3Jun01 Chantilly (Fr) gd *1 (T) RH 1:361 (F)Prix de Sandringham-G2 Stk 69800 11½ Peslier O 123 *1.10 *Banks Hill*1231½ Lethals Lady123no Lurina1231 10
Timeform rating: 115 — Rated in 9th,rallied to lead 120y out,handily.Calista 5th
13May01 Longchamp (Fr) gd *1 (T) RH 1:363 (F)Poule d'Essai des Pouliches-G1 Stk 233800 2hd Peslier O 126 3.30 Rose Gypsy126hd *Banks Hill*126hd Lethals Lady126½ 15
Timeform rating: 115+ — Slowly away,soon bumped,steadied 2f out,angled out,finished fast
24Apr01 Chantilly (Fr) hy *1 (T) RH 1:462 (F)Prix d'Angerville (Listed) Stk 35500 43 Soumillon C 123 *3.50 Calista123nk Five Fishes1232 Love and Adventure123¾ 8
Timeform rating: 102 — Trailed to 1-1/2f out,angled out,finished fast.Volga 5th
31Oct00 Maisons-Laffitte (Fr) hy *7f (T) Str 1:282 (F)Prix Pearl Cap-EBF Alw 23300 11½ Peslier O 121 *.60 Banks Hill1211½ *Bermuda Girl*121¾ *Surya*1261½ 5
Timeform rating: 79 — Steadied early,tracked in 4th,led and bumped 1f out,clear in hand

Bird Town

Own: Marylou Whitney Stables

B. f. 3 (Apr)
Sire: Cape Town (Seeking the Gold) $20,000
Dam: Dear Birdie (Storm Bird)
Br: Marylou Whitney Stables (Ky)
Tr: Zito Nicholas P

Life	12	4	6	1	$871,251	101	D.Fst	10	3	5	1	$795,656	101
2003	8	3	4	0	$815,976	101	Wet(395)	2	1	1	0	$75,595	98
2002	4	1	2	1	$55,275	80	Turf(280)	0	0	0	0	$0	–
	0	0	0	0	$0	–	Dst(T)(318)	0	0	0	0	$0	–

4Oct03-9Bel fst 1⅛ :474 1:122 1:363 1:491 3↑ (F)Beldame-G1 100 5 1½ 1½ 1hd 22½ 24½ Gryder A T L120 11.20 79-26 Sightseek1234½ Bird Town1204¾ Buy the Sport120¾ Pace, second best 7
16Aug03-9Sar fst 1¼ :482 1:124 1:374 2:05 (F)Alabama-G1 85 5 33 32 22 57¾ 511 Prado E S L121 1.60 71-14 IslndFshion1216 AwesomeHumor1211 SpoknFur1211¼ Bumped after start 6
26Jly03-9Sar fst 7f :223 :451 1:081 1:204 (F)Test-G1 100 7 1 31 3½ 25½ 24½ Prado E S L122 *1.75 98-08 Lady Tak1224½ Bird Town1221½ *House Party*1221¾ 3 wide, game finish 7
6Jun03-10Bel fst 1 :232 :461 1:102 1:351 (F)Acorn-G1 96 7 2hd 1hd 1½ 11 1hd Prado E S L121 2.65 90-16 Bird Town121hd *Lady Tak*1211 Final Round1213¼ Game while drifting 7
2May03-10CD fst 1⅛ :46 1:10 1:353 1:483 (F)KyOaks-G1 101 5 87 86 74 4nk 13½ Prado E S L121 18.20 95-07 *Bird Town*1213½ Santa Catarina121hd Yell121¾ Stumble start,6w,drv 12
10Apr03-8Kee my *7f :214 :442 1:094 1:264 (F)Beaumont-G2 98 7 1 2hd 11½ 2hd 21¼ Coa E M L118 3.30 91-15 My Boston Gal1201¼ *Bird Town*1184¾ Midnight Cry1184 Dueled, good try 9
23Feb03-5GP fst 7f :214 :444 1:101 1:224 (F)Charon52k 100 5 3 25 22 17 112½ Coa E M L120 3.40 94-13 Bird Town12012½ Crafty Brat1181¼ WesterlyBreeze1223¾ Kept to pressure 6
16Jan03-9GP fst 170 :233 :482 1:132 1:421 (F)Alw 34000N1x 84 6 11 11 1½ 2hd 2nk Day P L119 2.80 90-18 *Yell*121nk *Bird Town*1195½ Marnesia Light1172¼ Inside, gamely 7
14Dec02-10Crc fst 1 1/16 :234 :491 1:143 1:472 (F)ThreeRing100k 76 2 31½ 42 21½ 2hd 31 Coa E M L117 *1.40 74-15 Dakota Light111¾ Never Fail114nk Bird Town1173¾ Dueled str, weakened 8
23Nov02-9CD fst 1 1/16 :242 :482 1:133 1:464 (F)Alw 37940N1x 70 4 53 43½ 42¼ 21 2¾ Day P L122 *.40 73-19 InCseofWind122¾ BirdTown1226 *FemleAccomplice*120hd Hop start,8w lane 7
6Nov02-1CD my 1 1/16 :24 :482 1:134 1:471 (F)Md Sp Wt 40k 80 2 11 11 11 14 16¾ Day P L120 *1.00 72-27 Bird Town1206¾ *Throne*1201¼ Tarnished Halo1202¾ In control,ridden out 10
9Oct02-3Kee fst *7f :223 :463 1:12 1:282 (F)Md Sp Wt 50k 78 5 8 43 33 33 24 Day P L118 8.20 78-23 Star of Atticus1184 *Bird Town*118hd Oyster Bay11810½ 4-5w bid, all out 10

Caressing

Own: Pollard Carl F

Dk. b or b. f. 4 (Apr)
Sire: Honour and Glory (Relaunch) $15,000
Dam: Lovin Touch (Majestic Prince)
Br: Brereton C. Jones (Ky)
Tr: Vance David R

Life	18	5	2	3	$955,998	105	D.Fst	17	5	2	2	$933,360	105
2002	5	0	1	2	$74,588	105	Wet(345)	1	0	0	1	$22,638	87
2001	8	2	0	1	$190,768	94	Turf(267)	0	0	0	0	$0	–
	0	0	0	0	$0	–	Dst(T)(351)	0	0	0	0	$0	–

10Aug02-10EIP fst 1⅛ :48 1:113 1:362 1:493 3↑ (F)GrdeniaH-G3 97 7 22½ 52½ 52¾ 46½ 47¼ Thompson T J L115 fb 3.80 93-13 Minister's Baby1171¾ *Lakenheath*1153¾ Softly1141¾ 4w,empty in lane 8
6Jly02-7PrM fst 1 1/16 :223 :453 1:10 1:414 3↑ (F)IowaDistaf127k 105 1 68 69½ 21½ 2½ 2no Thompson T J LB114 fb 4.10 102-05 *Minister'sBaby*120no Caressing1142 Netherland1142¾ 3 wide bid, led,missed 10
8Jun02-8AP fst 7f :23 :462 1:101 1:224 3↑ (F)ChcgoBCH-G3 86 6 3 32½ 41¼ 45½ 36 Emigh C A L115 f 3.00 85-17 *MandysGold*116hd CatandtheHat1166 Cressing1154¾ No match for top two 6
5Apr02-10OP fst 1 1/16 :232 :462 1:113 1:441 4↑ (F)Bayakoa75k 90 5 43½ 45½ 32 24 32¾ Lopez J L116 f 1.60 84-18 Due to Win112¾ Red n'Gold1182 Caressing1164¾ Not enough late 8
16Mar02-10OP fst 1 1/16 :232 :473 1:122 1:442 3↑ (F)OaklwnBC-G3 88 1 43½ 43 44 45½ 46¾ Lopez J L112 f 5.30 79-20 AskMeNoSecrets1164½ Redn'Gold116hd Descapate1182¼ No late response 5
22Nov01-9CD fst 1⅛ :484 1:131 1:371 1:492 3↑ (F)FallCtyH-G3 94 5 42½ 42½ 31½ 34 64¾ Albarado R J L113 f 29.20 84-18 ForestScrts1131½ Printmps1171 UnbridldElin121½ Loomed 5w,flatten out 7
3Nov01-9CD fst 1 :23 :461 1:102 1:351 3↑ (F)CDDstafH-G2 94 2 43 62¼ 63¼ 54 43½ Douglas R R L115 fb 8.60 87-14 Nasty Storm1151¼ *Forest Secrets*1131 Trip1171¼ No late reponse 8
5Oct01-9Hoo sly 1 1/16 :221 :462 1:112 1:44 (F)InBCOaks-G3 87 1 2hd 1hd 21 34 34¼ Douglas R R LB121 fb *.90 85-25 Scoop1213 Gold Huntress1151¼ Caressing1214 Off rail,forced in 1/8 9
8Sep01-7Bel fst 1⅛ :454 1:093 1:343 1:473 (F)GazelleH-G1 88 3 3½ 4nk 74½ 711 613¼ Douglas R R L118 fb 22.40 79-14 *Exogenous*1183½ TwoItemLimit118no FleetRene1223 Between rivals, tired 8
11Aug01-9AP fst 1⅛ :47 1:123 1:381 1:503 (F)SngprPlt-G3 89 3 42 42½ 3½ 1hd 11 Douglas R R L120 fb *1.30 96-18 Caressing1201 Gal On the Go1203½ *Scoop*1229 3 wide, hard drive 8
21Jly01-8Del fst 1 1/16 :234 :481 1:13 1:451 (F)DelOaks-G3 81 4 73½ 82½ 92½ 74¾ 711 Day P L115 f *1.40 70-20 Zonk1151 Mystic Lady1222½ Lady Andromeda115½ No solid response 11
8Jun01-7Bel fst 1 :223 :452 1:094 1:344 (F)Acorn-G1 68 4 61¾ 65¼ 72 59 513 Day P L121 f 2.90 80-07 ForestSecrets121nk *VictoryRide*121nk RlCozzy121¾ 5 wide run turn, faded 8
3May01-8CD fst 7f :221 :45 1:101 1:224 (F)LaTroien-G3 91 2 9 912 99¼ 52 11 Day P L121 f *1.70 91-08 Caressing1211 SweetNnette121¾ GollyGreeley1161¼ Bmp,sht off strt,10w 9
4Nov00-4CD fst 1 1/16 :23 :462 1:11 1:423 (F)BCJuvFil-G1 92 6 53½ 53½ 52¾ 1hd 1½ Velazquez J R L119 f 47.00 97 - *Caressing*119½ PlatinumTiara1191¾ ShesaDevilDue1191¼ Angled 6w,driving 12
30Sep00-9AP fst 1 :223 :454 1:104 1:364 (F)ArlWaLas-G3 82 4 2½ 2hd 21½ 34½ 22¾ Kuntzweiler G L119 f 3.40 82-16 Thunder Bertie1192¾ *Caressing*119nk Zahwah1193¼ Came back, 2nd best 10
2Sep00-11RD fst 6f :222 :453 :583 1:12 (F)Bassinet100k 79 9 4 42 1hd 13 17 Kuntzweiler G L120 f 3.50 91-16 Caressing1207 The Hess Express120no *Doe Na Wane*1201½ Ridden out 10
9Aug00-5EIP fst 5½f :223 :462 :584 1:052 (F)Md Sp Wt 25k 75 5 4 2hd 2hd 12 11 Kuntzweiler G L119 f 2.20 92-16 *Caressing*1191 Selassie1141 Starry Cat1191½ Forced pace,hand urg 11
2Jly00-5CD fst 5½f :214 :45 :58 1:05 (F)Md Sp Wt 43k 59 1 9 54½ 57 53¾ 41½ Kuntzweiler G5 L114 f 4.00 91-05 MdmFullChrg119hd OnToughCt1191¼ LhsPromis119nk Up rail,lug in 3/16s 10

Declan's Moon

Own: Jay Em Ess Stable

Dk. b or b. g. 3 (Feb) EASSEP03 $125,000
Sire: Malibu Moon (A.P. Indy) $30,000
Dam: Vee Vee Star (Norquestor)
Br: Brice Ridgely (Md)
Tr: Ellis Ronald W

Life	5	5	0	0	$627,300	107	D.Fst	5	5	0	0	$627,300 107
2005	1	1	0	0	$120,000	97	Wet(369)	0	0	0	0	$0 –
2004	4	4	0	0	$507,300	107	Turf(206)	0	0	0	0	$0 –
	0	0	0	0	$0	–	Dst(Ⓣ)(365)	0	0	0	0	$0 –

Date/Race	Cond	Dist	Fractions	Race	Sp	Running line	Jockey	Wt	Odds	Sp-Par	Top finishers	Comment	Field
5Mar05-5SA	fst	1 1/16	:232 :464 1:104 1:422	StCtlina-G2	97	6 31½ 21 3½ 2hd 12	Espinoza V	LB122f	*.80	93-08	DeclnsMoon1222 GoingWild1223 SpnishChstnut1221¼	3wd bid,led past 1/8	6
18Dec04-8Hol	fst	1 1/16	:232 :46 1:10 1:413	HolFut-G1	96	3 21 2½ 1hd 11 11	Espinoza V	LB121	*1.20	93-11	*Declan's Moon*1211 Giacomo121no Wilko1212	Bid,led,held gamely	7
20Nov04-8Hol	fst	7f	:214 :441 1:082 1:213	HolPrevu-G3	98	5 5 32 31 1½ 12	Espinoza V	LB122	*.40	94-11	*Declan's Moon*1222 Bushwacker114hd Seize theDay1172	3wd bid,ridden out	8
8Sep04-8Dmr	fst	7f	:221 :443 1:084 1:211	DMrFut-G2	107	1 3 23½ 24 2½ 1nk	Espinoza V	LB116	6.20	96-11	*DeclansMoon*116nk *RomanRuler*1209½ *SwissLad*1164	Bid btwn,brushed,game	4
31Jly04-3Dmr	fst	5½f	:22 :451 :572 1:033	Md Sp Wt 49k	87	1 2 1hd 1hd 11 15	Flores D R	LB118	14.70	97-09	*Declan's Moon*1185 Currency Trader1182 Cashmula118½	Inside, ridden out	7

Fantastic Light

Own: Godolphin Racing Inc

B. h. 5 (Feb)
Sire: Rahy (Blushing Groom*Fr) $80,000
Dam: Jood (Nijinsky II)
Br: Gainsborough Farm, Inc. (Ky)
Tr: bin Suroor Saeed

Life	25	12	5	3	$8,486,957	117	D.Fst	0	0	0	0	$0 –
2001	6	4	2	0	$3,634,859	117	Wet(323)	0	0	0	0	$0 –
2000	9	3	2	1	$4,525,766	107	Turf(387)	25	12	5	3	$8,486,957 117
	0	0	0	0	$0	–	Dst(Ⓣ)(382)	0	0	0	0	$0 –

Date/Race	Cond	Dist	Fractions/Time	Race	Sp	Running line / Finish	Jockey	Wt	Odds	Sp-Par	Top finishers	Comment	Field
27Oct01-9Bel	fm	1½ Ⓣ	:48 1:121 2:01 2:241	3↑BCTurf-G1	117	2 42½ 41¼ 22 12½ 1¾	Dettori L	L126	*1.40	108 -	Fantastic Light126¾ Milan1215¾ Timboroa126¾	Well placed, driving	11
8Sep01 Leopardstwn (Ire) (Timeform rating: 133)	gd	1¼ Ⓣ	LH 2:014	3↑ Irish Champion Stakes-G1 Stk 949600		1hd	Dettori L	130	2.25		*Fantastic Light*130hd Galileo1236 Bach1304	*Unhurried in 3rd,led 1-1/2f out,dueled over 1f out,very game*	7
28Jly01 Ascot (GB) (Timeform rating: 130+)	gd	1½ Ⓣ	RH 2:273	3↑ King George VI & Queen Eliz St-G1 Stk 1069000		22	Dettori L	133	3.50		Galileo1212 *Fantastic Light*1331 *Hightori*133hd	*Rated in 9th,progress 2f out,strong bid 1f out,outfinished*	12
20Jun01 Ascot (GB) (Timeform rating: 133)	gd	1¼ Ⓣ	RH 2:042	4↑ Prince of Wales's Stakes-G1 Stk 349500		12½	Dettori L	126	3.30		Fantastic Light1262½ Kalanisi126¾ Hightori1261¼	*Rated in 6th,angled out 2f out,led 1f out,driving.Observatory 4th*	9
27May01 Curragh (Ire) (Timeform rating: 128)	yl	1 5/16 Ⓣ	RH 2:132	4↑ Tattersalls Gold Cup-G1 Stk 218600		1nk	Dettori L	126	*1.25		*Fantastic Light*126nk Golden Snake1263 Kalanisi1261	*Tracked in 3rd,4th 3f out,led 1f out,driving.Bach 5th*	6
24Mar01 Nad Al Sheba (UAE) (Timeform rating: 128)	fm	*1½ Ⓣ	LH 2:281	4↑ Dubai Sheema Classic-G2 Stk 2000000		2no	Dettori L	123	-		Stay Gold123no *Fantastic Light*1232 *Silvano*1232½	*Rated in 6th,led over 1f out,headed on line.Endless Hall 4th*	16
17Dec00 Sha Tin (HK) (Timeform rating: 128)	gd	*1¼ Ⓣ	RH 2:021	3↑ Hong Kong Cup-G1 Stk 1794800		11¾	Dettori L	126	*1.90		Fantastic Light1261¾ Greek Dance126no *Jim and Tonic*1261½	*Trckd ldrs,2nd 3f out,led over 1f out,driving.Forbidden Apple 4th*	13
26Nov00 Tokyo (Jpn)	fm	*1½ Ⓣ	LH 2:26	3↑ Japan Cup-G1 Stk 4278300		3nk	Dettori L	126	7.90		*T.M.Opera O*126nk Meisho Doto126no *Fantastic Light*1261¾	*Wide in 11th,bid 1f out,gaining late.Ela Athena4th,John's Call9th*	16
4Nov00-9CD	fm	1½ Ⓣ	:501 1:151 2:033 2:264	3↑BCTurf-G1	107	2 64 64¼ 63 53 52	Dettori L	L126	11.90	107 -	Kalanisi126½ Quiet Resolve126no John's Call126hd	Checked deep stretch	13
7Oct00-9Bel	fm	1½ Ⓣ	:502 1:153 2:034 2:282	3↑TfClscIv-G1	103	1 84½ 53¼ 44 47½ 43½	Dettori L	L126	*1.40	83-18	John's Call126½ Craigsteel1261¾ Ela Athena1231¼	Came wide, stayed on	12
9Sep00-9Bel	fm	1⅜ [T]	:504 1:16 1:41 2:172	3↑ManOWar-G1	106	1 77 73¼ 61¾ 2hd 11	Bailey J D	L126	*.65	68-31	Fantastic Light1261 Ela Athena123nk Drama Critic1262	3 wide move, clear	8
29Jly00 Ascot (GB) (Timeform rating: 128)	gd	1½ Ⓣ	RH 2:294	3↑ King George VI & Queen Eliz St-G1 Stk 1127600		21¾	Reid J	133	12.00		*Montjeu*1331¾ *Fantastic Light*1333½ Daliapour1331	*Rated in 6th,2nd 200y out,no chance with winner.Beat All 4th*	7
8Jly00 Sandown Park (GB) (Timeform rating: 114)	gd	1¼ Ⓣ	RH 2:051	3↑ Eclipse Stakes-G1 Stk 544800		56	Reid J	133	5.00		*Giant's Causeway*122hd Kalanisi1332½ Shiva1301½	*Tracked in 4th,ridden without response 2f out.Sakhee 4th*	8
9Jun00 Epsom (GB) (Timeform rating: 124)	yl	1½ Ⓣ	LH 2:413	4↑ Coronation Cup-G1 Stk 377300		2¾	McCarron C	126	1.75		Daliapour126¾ Fantastic Light126¾ Border Arrow1267	*Trckd in 3rd,2nd hfwy,3rd 2-1/2f out,in tight,regained 2nd 1f out*	4

Previously trained by Michael Stoute

Date/Race	Cond	Dist	Time	Race	Finish	Jockey	Wt	Odds	Top finishers	Comment	Field
25Mar00 Nad Al Sheba (UAE) (Timeform rating: 126)	gd	*1½ Ⓣ	LH 2:273	4↑ Dubai Sheema Classic-G3 Stk 2000000	13	Fallon K	121	-e	Fantastic Light1213 Caitano1242 High-Rise1242	*Rated twrd rear,rallied to lead over 1f out,drifted right,driving*	16
3Oct99 Longchamp (Fr) (Timeform rating: 95)	hy	*1½ Ⓣ	RH 2:382	3↑ Prix de l'Arc de Triomphe-G1 Stk 1144500	1129	Reid J A	123	33.40	Montjeu123½ El Condor Pasa1316 Croco Rouge1315	*Towards rear throughout.Tiger Hill 5th,Borgia 7th,Daylami 9th*	14
19Sep99 Newbury (GB) (Timeform rating: 125)	yl	1⅜ Ⓣ	LH 2:212	3↑ Arc Trial (Listed) Stk 81200	1¾	Fallon K	126	2.25	Fantastic Light126¾ High-Rise1289 Pegnitz1283½	*Trailed,ridden 4f out,dueled 1f out,drftd rght & lft,led 150y out*	6
17Aug99 York (GB) (Timeform rating: 121)	gd	1½ Ⓣ	LH 2:29	Great Voltigeur Stakes-G2 Stk 160400	11¼	Stevens G	121	4.00	*Fantastic Light*1211¼ Bienamado1211½ Glamis1211	*Tracked in 4th,led over 3f out,ridden out.Mutafaweq 4th*	7
3Jly99 Sandown Park (GB) (Timeform rating: 121)	gd	1¼ Ⓣ	RH 2:062	3↑ Eclipse Stakes-G1 Stk 465100	3¾	Stevens G	122	6.00	Compton Admiral122nk Xaar133½ *Fantastic Light*1221½	*Tracked in 5th,bid 1f out,outfinished.Croco Rouge7th,LearSpear8th*	8
15Jun99 Ascot (GB) (Timeform rating: 120)	gd	1¼ Ⓣ	RH 2:041	3↑ Prince of Wales's Stakes-G2 Stk 239100	2hd	Stevens G	117	14.00	Lear Spear129hd Fantastic Light1172½ Xaar1291	*Settled in 6th,bid 1-1/1f out,dueled 1f out,gamely.Shiva 7th*	8
8May99 Lingfield (GB) (Timeform rating: 104)	gd	1 7/16 Ⓣ	LH 2:301	Lingfield Derby Trial-G3 Stk 88900	46¾	Tani K	122	3.00	Lucido1191¼ Daliapour121½ Royal Rebel1195	*4th early,ridden hfwy,drifted left & bumped 3f out,wknd 1f out*	5
24Apr99 Sandown Park (GB) (Timeform rating: 106+)	sf	1¼ Ⓣ	RH 2:153	Thresher Classic Trial-G3 Stk 108600	1no	Holland D	123	6.50	Fantastic Light123no Dehoush1231½ Glamis1232	*Tracked in 4th,led 1f out,rider misjudged finish,just lasted*	7
11Sep98 Goodwood (GB) (Timeform rating: 103)	yl	1 Ⓣ	RH 1:443	Stardom Stakes (Listed) Stk 33500	32½	Cochrane R	123	2.25	*Mutaahab*123½ Glamis1232 *Fantastic Light*123	*Tracked pacesetting winner,outpaced final furlong*	3
22Aug98 Sandown Park (GB) (Timeform rating: 103+)	gd	1 Ⓣ	RH 1:441	Sun Conditions Stakes Alw 11900	1¾	Reid J	126	3.50	Fantastic Light126¾ *Aesops*1232½ Adnaan1232½	*Prominent,2nd halfway,dueled 1f out,led 70y out*	5
2Aug98 Sandown Park (GB) (Timeform rating: 82+)	gd	7f Ⓣ	RH 1:331	Carshalton Novice Stakes Alw 10400	11¾	Reid J	124	8.00	*Fantastic Light*1241¾ *Sicnee*1302 Sampower Star1322	*Dwelt,outpaced 3f out,raced greenly,led 75y out,going away*	5

Farda Amiga

Own: Old Friends, Inc., Winner Silk, Inc. and De Camargo, Jose

B. f. 3 (Feb)
Sire: Broad Brush (Ack Ack) $100,000
Dam: Fly North (Pleasant Colony)
Br: Payson Stud Inc (Ky)
Tr: Lobo Paulo H

Life	8	4	1	0	$1,282,302	103	D.Fst	2	1	0	0	$366,502 103
2002	6	3	1	0	$1,248,902	103	Wet(415)	2	1	1	0	$850,000 103
2001	2	1	0	0	$33,400	78	Turf(333)	4	2	0	0	$65,800 84
	0	0	0	0	$0	–	Dst(Ⓣ)(375)	0	0	0	0	$0 –

Date/Race	Cond	Dist	Fractions	Race	Sp	Running line	Jockey	Wt	Odds	Sp-Par	Top finishers	Comment	Field
26Oct02-3AP	gd	1⅛	:461 1:093 1:351 1:483	3↑ⒻBCDistaf-G1	103	3 45½ 45½ 45 35 25	Day P	L119	4.90	100 -	*Azeri*1235 Farda Amiga119hd Imperial Gesture1193¼	Broke awkwardly	8
17Aug02-9Sar	gd	1¼	:474 1:123 1:381 2:043	ⒻAlabama-G1	100	3 512 57 42 31½ 1¾	Day P	L121	3.35	82-19	Farda Amiga121¾ Allamerican Bertie1212¾ You1214¾	Awkward start	6
3May02-9CD	fst	1⅛	:474 1:121 1:371 1:502	ⒻKyOaks-G1	103	1 75 75¾ 51½ 21½ 11¼	McCarron C J	L121	20.00	84-17	*Farda Amiga*1211¼ *Take Charge Lady*1211¼ Habibti121½	Lean in 3/16s,driving	9
9Mar02-7SA	fst	1 1/16	:23 :462 1:102 1:423	ⒻSAOaks-G1	95	1 911 88¾ 85½ 54 42	McCarron C J	LB117	35.20	89-10	You117½ Habibti1171½ Ile de France117no	4wd into str,missed 3d	9
9Feb02-2SA	fm	1 Ⓣ	:232 :472 1:12 1:364	ⒻOC 80k/n1x-N	84	7 79 88½ 65½ 63¾ 1hd	McCarron C J	LB118	5.20	78-19	Farda Amiga118hd Ile de France1182 *Tempo West*118½	Blocked 3/16-1/8,up	8
9Jan02-7SA	fm	1 Ⓣ	:234 :47 1:11 1:353	ⒻBlueNorthr76k	70	8 53¾ 42 42½ 64¾ 76½	Almeida G F	LB114	6.30	77-14	*Megahertz*1161½ Nunatall1161 *La Martina*1203	3wd 1st turn,no rally	8
23Nov01-5Hol	fm	1 Ⓣ	:244 :49 1:123 1:361	ⒻMiesque-G3	78	9 85 74¾ 85¾ 67¼ 53	Almeida G F	LB118	24.60	80-19	Forty On Line1171 Riskaverse121hd Daisyago1181½	3wd 2nd turn,late bid	10
3Sep01-5Dmr	fm	1 Ⓣ	:222 :471 1:121 1:37	ⒻMd Sp Wt 49k	75	7 713 76¼ 21½ 2hd 12½	Almeida G F	LB118	9.70	80-14	Farda Amiga1182½ PufftheMagic1181½ CastingCall1185	3 wide move,clear	9

Flat Top

Own: Gerry Mrs. Henry A

Dk. b or b. g. 11 (Mar)
Sire: Alleged (Hoist the Flag)
Dam: Lady of the Light (The Minstrel)
Br: Landon Knight (Ky)
Tr: Elliot Janet E

Life	21	9	2	3	$592,306	51	D.Fst	1	0	0	0	$0	22
2004	1	0	0	0	$0	–	Wet(260)	1	0	0	0	$0	–
2002	5	2	0	3	$237,831	–	Turf(337)	1	0	0	0	$0	51
	0	0	0	0	$0	–	Dst(T)(317)	0	0	0	0	$0	–

23Oct04- 5FH fm 2⅝ (T)Hurdles 5:064 4↑BrCupStp-G1 – 1 2½ 2½ 58 - - Massey R L156 - - - McDynamo156½ *Hirapour*156½ Sur La Tete15615½ Tired, pulled up 7
17Nov02- 5Cam yl *2¾ (T)Hurdles 5:251 4↑ColonlCp-G1 – 7 1½ 2½ 1½ 1½ 16¼ Massey R L156 - - - Flat Top1566¼ Tres Touche1569¼ All Gong156½ Drew off, driving 7
19Oct02- 4FH sf *2⅝ (T)Hurdles 5:192 4↑[R]BrCupStp-G1 – 6 12 11 13½ 14 13 Massey R L156 - - - *Flat Top*1563 *Tres Touche*156¾ All Gong1568¾ Led throughout 8
29Aug02- 9Sar sf 2⅜ (T)Hurdles 4:28 4↑NYTurfWH-G1 – 2 63¾ 51¾ 2½ 36 312½ Massey R L150 17.40 - - Zabenz1467¼ Double Leaf1405¼ *Flat Top*1503 Tried winner ninth 8
11May02- 6PW fm *3 (T)Hurdles 5:322 4↑Iroquois-G1 – 5 56½ 44 21 1hd 35½ Ryan C G L158 - - - All Gong158nk Praise the Prince1585¼ Flat Top15812½ Out finished 7
26Apr02- 7Kee fm *2½ (T)Hurdles 4:392 4↑RylChsHd-G1 – 7 67 58½ 64 311 324¼ Massey R L158 3.30 - - It's a Giggle1582 *Al Skywalker*15822½ Flat Top15814½ Not a threat 7
28Apr00- 9Kee fm *2½ (T)Hurdles 4:421 4↑RylChsHd-G1 – 6 43 33 32 12 11½ Miller Blythe L154 2.20 - - Flat Top1541½ Campanile154½ *Pinkie Swear*1548 Stalked,6wide,driving 7
22Nov98- 5Cam fm *2¾ (T)Hurdles 5:112 4↑ColonlCp-G1 – 4 22 21 2½ 2½ 15¾ Ryan C G L156 - - - *Flat Top*1565¾ Romantic156nk Dictador1561¼ Drew clear 8
24Oct98- 5FH fm *2⅝ (T)Hurdles 4:552 4↑BCGrdNat-G1 – 5 11 1½ 1½ 1½ 11¼ Patterson B L156 - - - *Flat Top*1561¼ Romantic156¾ Mario1563½ Driving 7
4Oct98- 8Cnl gd 2¼ (T)Hurdles 4:014 4↑FrgsnMHH-G2 – 9 12 1hd 2hd 1hd 1½ Patterson B L142 6.10 - - *Flat Top*142½ *Approaching Squall*1421 Mario1501¼ Dueled, driving 9
7Sep98- 1Sar yl 2$\frac{1}{16}$ (T)Hurdles 3:461 4↑Hcp ---s – 4 21½ 1½ 1hd 21½ 25½ Patterson B L142 3.55e - - Romantic1525½ *Flat Top*1422 Seminole Spirt1302½ Good run final turn 8
12Aug98- 1Sar sf 2$\frac{1}{16}$ (T)Hurdles 3:444 4↑Alw 40000N2X – 5 13½ 15 11½ 2hd 53¼ Kingsley A Jr L148 *1.90e - - Grenade1482¼ *It's a Giggle*146no *Dalton River*148¾ Struggled after last 7
1Nov97- 3Pmt yl *2⅜ (T)Hurdles 4:093 3↑[R]USChampHur75k – 4 1½ 1½ 11 2½ 22½ Clancy S L149 - - - Teb's Bend1452½ Flat Top1492 Willstown14527¾ Outfinished 6
11Oct97- 6Mor fm *2¼ (T)Hurdles 4:19 3↑[R]AMcCSupHur30k – 3 11½ 1½ 1½ 11 1no Clancy S L145 16.30 - - Flat Top145no Dictador1502½ *Clearance Code*150no Driving 9
1Jun97- 3Suf fm *2¼ (T)Hurdles 4:241 4↑Alw 14700N$Y – 7 25 22½ 21 46½ 410¾ Delozier J W III LB146 2.40 - - *Brigade of Guards*1551¼ Thelightfantistic1515 Gliding1434½ Flattened out 7
17May97- 3Mal hd *2¼ (T)Hurdles 4:26 3↑Alw 20000N3L – 6 46 43 55 44 410¾ Delozier J W III L142 - - - Smart Jaune1448 *Street View*1482½ *Brigade of Guards*148nk No threat 6
17Nov96- 3Cam fm *2$\frac{1}{8}$ (T)Hurdles 4:15 RGWolfeMem25k – 12 11½ 111 1½ 11½ 12 Teter J L149 - - - Flat Top1492 Ratify1522 *Tomahawk Warrior*1451 Well handled 12
3Nov96- 4Uni gd *1¼ (T) 3:111 3↑Alw 20NC – 3 712 66 63½ 32 1hd Moran A K L145 - - - *Flat Top*145hd Talkin Butter1502½ Gatello150½ Up in final strides 10
Non-wagering event Previously trained by Teter Jeff 1996(as of 10/5): (2 1 0 0 0.50)
5Oct96- 6Mid gd *2⅛ (T)Hurdles 4:093 Md Sp Wt 7k – 3 518 36½ 22 12 11½ Teter J L150 - - - *FltTop*1501½ Soringoversttl1506 Hrdhddirishmn1508 Stalked pace, driving 14
Previously trained by O'Callaghan Niall M 1996(as of 5/27): (123 20 18 16 0.16)
27May96- 7AP sly 1 :231 :472 1:151 1:44 3↑Md 10000 –0 8 4¾ 810 823 831 848 Gryder A T 113 b 7.30 01- 45 Skat Kat122 1¾ Go Big Red1084 Longhaul Titus108½ Brief foot far backstr 8
17May96- 4CD fst 1$\frac{1}{16}$:232 :471 1:121 1:451 3↑Md 17500(17.5-15) 22 11 91310 17 1118 1228 1226¾ Bourque C C L110 6.30 58- 11 StrdustMiner1193 LightHert1152½ Andrewsmymn1051¼ No speed, outrun 12
23Mar96- 6FG fm *1 (T) :242 :49 1:134 1:392 Md Sp Wt 25k 51 2 99½ 99½ 1010 98 812¼ Emigh C A 119 12.60 - - Chief Bearhart1194 Mister Eye1191½ *Chorwon*1191½ No rally 12

Funny Cide

Own: Sackatoga Stable

Ch. g. 5 (Apr)
Sire: Distorted Humor (Forty Niner) $60,000
Dam: Belle's Good Cide (Slewacide)
Br: Win Star Farm, LLC (NY)
Tr: Tagg Barclay

Life	24	8	4	5	$3,220,319	114	D.Fst	19	6	3	4	$2,160,319	112
2005	3	0	0	0	$45,834	101	Wet(429)	5	2	1	1	$1,060,000	114
2004	10	3	2	3	$1,075,100	112	Turf(306)	0	0	0	0	$0	–
	0	0	0	0	$0	–	Dst(T)(366)	0	0	0	0	$0	–

2Jly05- 9Bel fst 1¼ :462 1:094 1:343 2:002 3↑SuburbnH-G1 77 5 512 613 711 618 619½ Bailey J D L117 2.95 76- 05 Offlee Wild1161¼ Tap Day115nk Pollard's Vision1182 Wide, no response 8
11Jun05- 9Bel fst 1⅛ :461 1:10 1:341 1:463 3↑BroklynH-G2 94 5 56 65 64½ 58 510½ Santos J A L119 2.55 87- 07 Limehouse1151½ Gygistar1172 [D]Cuba1133½ Steadied into turn 9
Placed 4th through disqualification
20May05-11Pim sly[S] 1$\frac{3}{16}$:462 1:114 1:381 1:58 4↑PimSpclH-G1 101 1 43½ 32 22 45 47½ Santos J A L120 3.80 79- 30 Eddington1165¼ PollrdsVson1171¾ Prsdntlffr115½ Stalked pace, gave way 7
30Oct04- 9LS fst 1¼ :47 1:111 1:351 1:59 3↑BCClasic-G1 102 9 73 63 42½ 88¼ 1014¼ Santos J A L126 7.70 - - *Ghostzapper*1263 RosesinMay1264 PlesntlyPerfect126¾ Traffic early, tired 13
2Oct04-10Bel fst 1¼ :473 1:113 1:362 2:022 3↑JkyClbGC-G1 112 7 2½ 3nk 32 2½ 1¾ Santos J A L126 *2.80 85- 13 FunnyCid126¾ NwfoundlndI1261 ThCliffsEdg1223¾ Gamely between rivals 7
22Aug04- 9Sar fst 1¼ :462 1:104 1:36 2:004 3↑SarBCH-G2 107 5 31½ 41½ 2½ 2½ 25 Prado E S L118 *1.00 98- 11 EveningAttire1155 *FunnyCide*1183¾ BowmnsBnd1161½ 3 wide trip, 2nd best 7
3Jly04- 7Bel fst 1¼ :461 1:091 1:334 1:592 3↑SuburbnH-G1 111 1 31 2½ 2hd 1½ 3nk Santos J A L117 4.10 100 - PeceRules120nk Newfoundlnd114no FunnyCide117¾ Speed on rail, gamely 8
19Jun04-10Suf fst 1⅛ :483 1:122 1:363 1:49 3↑MassH-G2 110 7 21 2½ 2hd 3nk 2hd Santos J A LB117 *2.10 98- 10 OfflWild113hd FunnyCid117hd ThLdysGroom1161½ 2wd thru-out,game fin 9
31May04- 9Bel fst 1 :232 :46 1:10 1:352 3↑MtropltH-G1 106 9 42½ 51¾ 41 52¼ 55¼ Santos J A L118 4.20 79- 34 PicoCentrl119¾ BowmnsBnd1142¼ StrongHope1191½ Between foes, 3 wide 9
3Apr04- 8Aqu my 1⅛ :48 1:12 1:364 1:492 3↑ExlsrBCH-G3 109 3 21½ 2½ 2hd 12 1½ Santos J A L120 *1.30 92- 08 Funny Cide120½ Evening Attire1198 Host114nk Dug in gamely inside 5
29Feb04- 9FG fst 1⅛ :47 1:102 1:352 1:483 4↑NwOrlnsH-G2 108 2 32½ 33 32 43¼ 32¾ Santos J A L118 5.40 98- 05 *Peace Rules*119hd Saint Liam1142¾ *Funny Cide*1181¼ Bumped, game for 3rd 8
7Feb04-10GP fst 1⅛ :471 1:11 1:353 1:473 3↑DonnH-G1 103 5 33 31 31½ 34 38½ Santos J A L119 3.00 92- 09 Medaglia d'Oro1224¾ Seattle Fitz1133¾ Funny Cide1194 3 wide, tired 8
10Jan04-10GP fst 7f :223 :453 1:101 1:224 4↑OC 100k/N$Y-N 102 2 3 4nk 11½ 13 15 Santos J A L118 *.40 88- 20 FunnyCide1185 AmericnStyle1167½ WckyforLov1223 Drew off, ridden out 5
25Oct03- 9SA fst 1¼ :461 1:101 1:341 1:594 3↑BCClasic-G1 97 4 52¼ 65¼ 78 1011 914¾ Krone J A LB121 8.70 91- 07 *PleasantlyPerfect*1261½ *Medagliad'Oro*126¾ *Dynever*121nk Drifted wide, tired 10
3Aug03-11Mth fst 1⅛ :47 1:104 1:36 1:491 HsklInvH-G1 94 5 52½ 54½ 55 47½ 39 Santos J A L123 *1.00 86- 08 Peace Rules1211¾ Sky Mesa1187¼ Funny Cide1231 Outside 1/4,mild bid 7
7Jun03-11Bel sly 1½ :483 1:132 2:023 2:281 Belmont-G1 104 4 11 1hd 21 33 35 Santos J A L126 *1.00 86- 14 EmpireMker126¾ TenMostWnted1264¼ FunnyCid1265¼ Set pace 3w, tired 6
17May03-12Pim gd 1$\frac{3}{16}$:47 1:113 1:362 1:553 Preakness-G1 114 9 32 21 2½ 15 19¾ Santos J A L126 *1.90 95- 12 FunnyCide12693 MidwayRod1262¾ Scrimshw126no Bmpd brk,ratd 3w,clear 10
3May03-10CD fst 1¼ :461 1:102 1:353 2:01 KyDerby-G1 109 5 32 31½ 2½ 1hd 11¾ Santos J A L126 12.80 94- 06 *Funny Cide*1261¾ *EmpireMaker*126hd PeaceRules126hd Bmp start,stiff drive 16
12Apr03- 8Aqu my 1⅛ :471 1:11 1:354 1:483 WoodMem-G1 110 4 21½ 21½ 21 2hd 2½ Santos J A L123 5.20 92- 12 Empire Maker123½ *Funny Cide*1237½ Kissin Saint1231 Bumped after start 8
9Mar03- 9FG fst 1$\frac{1}{16}$:232 :463 1:103 1:423 LaDerby-G2 99 2 11 11½ 1½ 43½ 33¼ Santos J A L122 6.10 94- 17 *Peace Rules*1222¼ [D]Kafwain1221 Funny Cide122½ Came again rail 10
Awarded second purse money
18Jan03-10GP fst 1$\frac{1}{16}$:232 :471 1:112 1:43 HolyBull-G3 87 13 72¼ 41½ 44 44 56½ Santos J A L122 5.30 87- 10 Offlee Wild116hd Powerful Touch1163 Bham1182½ Hit gate, wide, tired 13
19Oct02- 5Bel fst 1 :232 :462 1:114 1:363 [S]SleepyHllo100k 89 2 3½ 31 1hd 1½ 1nk Santos J A L122 *.20 86- 16 FunnyCid122nk SpitthDvil1153 GoRockinRobn1158½ Bumped start, driving 6
29Sep02- 8Bel fst 7f :223 :454 1:102 1:224 [S]BFBongard83k 103 5 4 1hd 1½ 18 19 Santos J A L117 2.95 89- 18 *FunnyCide*1179 SpitethDvil1172 InfinitJustic122nk When asked, ridden out 10
8Sep02- 6Bel fst 6f :223 :462 :584 1:111 [S]Md Sp Wt 43k 96 12 6 3½ 11½ 110 114¾ Santos J A L119 *2.25 82- 18 *FunnyCid*11914¾ HighPricd1191¾ PolishPosh1194½ When asked, ridden out 12

Ghostzapper

Own: Stronach Stables

B. h. 5 (Apr)
Sire: Awesome Again (Deputy Minister) $125,000
Dam: Baby Zip (Relaunch)
Br: Adena Springs (Ky)
Tr: Frankel Robert J

Life	11	9	0	1	$3,446,120	128	D.Fst	9	7	0	1	$3,299,120	124
2005	1	1	0	0	$450,000	122	Wet(428)	2	2	0	0	$147,000	128
2004	4	4	0	0	$2,590,000	128	Turf(287)	0	0	0	0	$0	–
	0	0	0	0	$0	–	Dst(T)(403)	0	0	0	0	$0	–

30May05- 9Bel fst 1 :222 :442 1:082 1:331 3↑MtropltH-G1 122 2 32 31½ 12½ 18 16¼ Castellano J J L123 b *.65 95- 05 Ghostzppr1236¼ SilvrWgon1155 SirShcklton116hd Drew away when asked 6
30Oct04- 9LS fst 1¼ :47 1:111 1:351 1:59 3↑BCClasic-G1 124 1 1½ 1½ 11 12 13 Castellano J J L126 b *2.50 - - *Ghostzapper*1263 Roses in May1264 Pleasantly Perfect126¾ Drew clear late 13
11Sep04-10Bel fst 1⅛ :453 1:083 1:331 1:461 3↑Woodward-G1 114 3 3nk 2½ 2hd 2hd 1nk Castellano J J L126 b *.40 100- 15 *Ghostzapper*126nk *SaintLiam*1269¼ BowmansBnd1267¼ Carried out, bumped 7
21Aug04- 9Mth sly 1⅛ :454 1:093 1:351 1:473 3↑IselnBCH-G3 128 3 21½ 21½ 2½ 12 110¾ Castellano J J L120 b *.40 103- 16 *Ghostzppr*12010¾ Prsidntilffir11721¼ Zoffingr115no Drew out,hand ridden 4
4Jly04- 9Bel fst 7f :222 :443 1:081 1:202 3↑TomFoolH-G2 120 3 2 32 2hd 14½ 14¼ Castellano J J L119 b *1.35 98- 13 *Ghostzppr*1194¼ Aggdn1143½ UnforgettbleMx114½ 4 wide move, hand ride 4
27Sep03- 7Bel fst 6½f :214 :441 1:083 1:143 3↑Vosburgh-G1 116 2 10 1013 79½ 3nk 16½ Castellano J J L123 b 3.10 100- 16 *Ghostzapper*1236½ Aggadan1261¼ Posse1231¾ Quick 4 wide move 10
23Aug03-10Sar fst 7f :213 :433 1:083 1:22 KngsBshp-G1 106 9 5 1011 811 86 3½ Castellano J J L117 b 6.30 96- 07 ValidVideo121nk GreatNotion117nk *Ghostzpper*1171¾ Finished fast outside 13
26Jly03- 7Sar fst 7f :222 :443 1:09 1:213 3↑Alw 49000N2X 99 4 5 32½ 33 1½ 1½ Castellano J J L119 b *.60 99- 08 Ghostzapper119½ *Clock Stopper*1153½ Bold Truth1201½ 3 wide trip, gamely 6
20Jun03- 7Bel my 6f :22 :443 :564 1:091 3↑Alw 45000N1X 102 3 4 612 57½ 44½ 13½ Castellano J J L114 b *.95 93- 14 *Ghostzapper*1143½ *As Wicked*1192 Patriot's Song120nk Rolled home outside 6
26Dec02- 3SA fst 6f :211 :44 :553 1:081 Alw 52000N1X 84 4 7 53¼ 64 57 47½ Valdivia J Jr LB120 *.30 89- 07 Scrimshaw120hd *Zayed*1184½ *Eye of the Tiger*1203 Squeezed bit start 8
16Nov02- 6Hol fst 6½f :22 :442 1:091 1:152 Md Sp Wt 41k 99 6 3 41¼ 3½ 12½ 19 Valdivia J Jr LB120 11.50 94- 12 Ghostzpper1209 BinnysTrick1201 Settlespectculr1202 3wd bid,ridden out 10

Golden Apples (Ire)
Own: Tanaka Gary A

B. m. 5 (Apr)
Sire: Pivotal*GB (Polar Falcon) $71,344
Dam: Loon*Fr (Kaldoun*Fr)
Br: James Egan and David Hanley (Ire)
Tr: Cecil Ben D

Life	16	6	6	2	$1,672,583	108	D.Fst	0	0	0	0	$0	–
2003	1	0	1	0	$50,666	103	Wet(280)	0	0	0	0	$0	–
2002	7	3	3	0	$1,111,680	108	Turf(472)	16	6	6	2	$1,672,583	108
	0	0	0	0	$0	–	DstⓉ(316)	0	0	0	0	$0	–

26Jly03–8Dmr fm 1⅛ Ⓣ :501 1:144 1:373 1:49 3↑ⒻJCMabeeH-G1 103 5 3½ 3½ 3½ 3½ 2½ •Stevens G L LB122 1.90 87–08 Megahertz116½ DH Tates Creek123 DH Dublino1212 3wd bid,willingly 5
1Dec02–4Hol fm 1⅛ Ⓣ :481 1:113 1:354 1:481 +3↑ⒻMatriarc-G1 105 1 31 3½ 3½ 1hd 2hd Valenzuela P A LB123 1.40 88–17 DrssToThrill120hd GoldnAppls123½ MgicMsson123no 3wd,led,caught late 6
26Oct02–7AP yl 1¼ Ⓣ :49 1:132 1:382 2:032 3↑ⒻBCF&MTrf-G1 105 6 1112 1110 115½ 72¼ 42 Valenzuela P A L123 *2.80 87–09 Starine1231½ Banks Hill123nk Islington118nk Steadied sharply early 12
5Oct02–8SA fm 1¼ Ⓣ :483 1:132 1:37 1:593 3↑ⒻYlwRibbn-G1 108 3 32½ 31 3½ 1hd 11 Valenzuela P A LB123 1.40 95–05 Golden Apples1231 Voodoo Dancer1233 BanksHill1233 4wd bid,led,gamely 6
17Aug02–7AP fm 1 3/16 Ⓣ :483 1:114 1:35 1:544 3↑ⒻBeverlyD-G1 108 3 53 43½ 43 2½ 1¾ Valenzuela P A L123 2.40 103–06 *Golden Apples*123¾ Astra123nk England's Legend123½ Broke slowly 6
27Jly02–8Dmr fm 1⅛ Ⓣ :493 1:133 1:364 1:481 3↑ⒻMbe/RnaH-G1 102 4 52¼ 64 73¼ 44 2nk Gomez G K LB120 2.50 92–04 Affluent118nk *Golden Apples*120½ Janet1181½ Waited bit,surged late 7
20Apr02–9SA fm 1¼ Ⓣ :504 1:152 1:39 2:012 4↑ⒻSntBrbrH-G2 96 5 53½ 54 63 32 22 Gomez G K LB121 *.90e 84–12 *Astra*1212 Golden Apples121no Polaire1154 Altered path 1/8 6
23Mar02–9SA fm 1⅛ Ⓣ :482 1:122 1:353 1:47 4↑ⒻSntaAnaH-G2 107 9 96 96¼ 95¼ 42 11¼ Gomez G K LB119 3.40 94–12 Golden Apples1191¼ Starine1222 *Astra*1221½ Split foes,rail rally 9
25Nov01–5Hol yl 1⅛ Ⓣ :503 1:142 1:38 1:50 +3↑ⒻMatriarc-G1 95 4 99½ 810 87¾ 54¾ 32¾ Gomez G K LB120 *2.00e 75–20 Starine1232½ Lethals Lady120nk *Golden Apples*1203 4wd into str,missed 2d 12
4Nov01–7SA fm 1⅛ Ⓣ :472 1:104 1:343 1:463 3↑ⒻLsPlmasH-G2 103 2 98¼ 913 911 64¾ 1¾ Gomez G K LB115 2.90 98–06 Golden Apples115¾ Dancingonice1131½ Janet120no Closed with a rush 9
13Oct01–8Kee gd 1⅛ Ⓣ :48 1:132 1:381 1:50 ⒻQEIICup-G1 98 5 74½ 73½ 62¼ 3½ 2nk Gomez G K L121 3.40 87–18 *Affluent*121nk *Golden Apples*1212¼ *Snow Dance*1211¼ Hop in air strt,gamely 10
18Aug01–8Dmr fm 1⅛ Ⓣ :491 1:124 1:362 1:474 ⒻDMrOaks-G1 101 5 65½ 66 66¼ 62¼ 11 Gomez G K LB121 21.00 94–10 Golden Apples1211 *Affluent*1211 ReinedeRomance121nk Swung out,rallied 8
Previously trained by David Hanley
30Jun01 Curragh (Ire) yl 1¼ Ⓣ RH 2:083 3↑ Pretty Polly Stakes-G2 32 Egan J F 119 10.00 Rebelline1192 Molomo131hd *Golden Apples*1191 12
Timeform rating: 107+ Stk 108000 *Rated in 9th,finished well w/o threatening.Toroca 5th,Dearly 12th*
7Jun01 Gowran Park (Ire) gd 1⅛ Ⓣ RH 1:582 3↑ Victor McCalmont Meml St(Lstd) 41¼ Smullen P J 119 *2.00 Dearly119no Chiming119nk Alexander Express1191 8
Timeform rating: 100 Stk 43200 *Tracked leader,led 3f out,dueled 2f out,headed 1f out,gamely*
16May01 Gowran Park (Ire) gd 1⅛ Ⓣ RH 2:064 3↑ Ormonde Maiden 18 Kinane M J 123 *1.00 Golden Apples1238 Alassio1236 *Silver Risks*1239 17
Timeform rating: 104 Maiden 10100 *Dueled,led 3f out,clear 2f out,handily*
3May01 Tipperary (Ire) hy 1⅛ Ⓣ LH 2:193 Monard Maiden 21½ O'Dwyer J M 123 25.00 *Adonesque*1231½ *Golden Apples*12330 Giocomo1282½ 16
Timeform rating: 104 Maiden 14100 *4th on rail,2nd 3f out,held by winner.Giocomo distanced.Flag strt*

Gourmet Girl
Own: Tanaka Gary A

Dk. b or b. m. 6 (Apr)
Sire: Cee's Tizzy (Relaunch) $10,000
Dam: Rhondaling*GB (Welsh Pageant*Fr)
Br: Carl Cannata & Olivia Cannata (Cal)
Tr: Perdomo A. P

Life	33	9	7	10	$1,255,373	110	D.Fst	27	8	7	9	$1,130,709	110
2001	6	3	1	0	$554,950	110	Wet(399)	3	1	0	1	$120,000	103
2000	10	0	2	5	$205,865	104	Turf(192)	3	0	0	0	$4,664	83
	0	0	0	0	$0	–	DstⓉ(323)	0	0	0	0	$0	–

5Aug01–6Dmr fst 1 1/16 :23 :461 1:10 1:413 3↑ⒻCLHrschH-G2 99 2 2½ 2½ 2½ 22½ 23 Solis A LB122 b *1.10 92–11 *TrnquilityLke*1203 GourmetGirl1222½ NnysSwep116hd Speed,vied,2nd best 4
30Jun01–8Hol fst 1⅛ :48 1:12 1:362 1:491 3↑ⒻVanityH-G1 100 2 11 12 11½ 13½ 15 Stevens G L LB119 b 3.10 86–12 Gourmet Girl1195 Lazy Slusan1221½ Setareh1141½ Bit off rail,riddn out 5
8Apr01–9OP fst 1 1/16 :23 :454 1:10 1:42 4↑ⒻAplBlsmH-G1 110 3 21 2½ 11 13½ 14½ Borel C H L113 b 10.60e 94–13 *Gourmet Girl*1134½ Lu Ravi114½ *Lazy Slusan*1163 Stalked, stayed clear 11
10Mar01–6SA fst 1⅛ :474 1:112 1:354 1:482 4↑ⒻSMrgrtaH-G1 93 5 53¼ 53 53 53½ 53¾ Gonzalez R M LB116 b 3.10e 89–11 Lazy Slusan116½ Spain122½ Critikola116nk Pulled,no late bid 7
3Mar01–8GG fst 1 :224 :46 1:102 1:353 3↑ⒻSacramntoH58k 96 5 64½ 55¼ 53 2hd 12 Gonzalez R M LB120 b 2.60 94–08 Gourmet Girl1202 Linda Love117½ *Puerto Plata*1151 Wide trip, handily 9
6Jan01–8GG yl 1 Ⓣ :252 :50 1:141 1:384 4↑Ⓕ[S]WorkCrowdH100k 76 4 21½ 21 31 45½ 57½ Gonzalez R M LB122 3.20 69–19 LazySlusan1202½ MindforGold117no ShoeCrazy1154 Prssd pace 2w, empty 6
23Dec00–8Hol fst 1 1/16 :232 :462 1:102 1:421 3↑ⒻBayakoaH-G2 104 1 41½ 3½ 1hd 2hd 2hd Espinoza V LB118 *3.30 89–19 *Feverish*119hd Gourmet Girl1181 *Lazy Slusan*117½ Rail trip,gamely 9
15Nov00–7Hol fm 1 Ⓣ :23 :462 1:094 1:34 3↑ⒻAlw 55620N$MY 83 2 56 53 52¼ 53¾ 64½ Espinoza V LB123 5.00 88–12 Coracle123½ Dyna's Club118no *Rare Charmer*1171 4wd into lane,wkened 7
28Oct00–5SA fst 1 1/16 :234 :472 1:113 1:424 3↑Ⓕ[S]CalCupMatH150k 96 1 33½ 33 31 32 35 Espinoza V LB123 *1.90 84–16 QueenieBelle118no Feverish1205 GourmtGirl1233½ Loomed 3wd,no match 5
16Sep00–9Bel fst 1 1/16 :234 :47 1:104 1:401 3↑ⒻRuffianH-G1 102 4 41 51¾ 41¾ 46 27½ Espinoza V L114 18.00 88–14 *Ribolett*1257½ GourmetGirl1141¾ *CountryHidewy*114no Game finish outside 7
12Aug00–7Dmr fst 1 1/16 :232 :47 1:11 1:42 3↑ⒻCLHrschH-G2 103 5 13 1½ 1hd 21½ 32 Delahoussaye E LB115 8.30e 91–12 *Riboletta*1251½ Bordelaise115½ Gourmet Girl1152 Inside,lost 2nd late 6
31Jly00–7Dmr fst 6½f :22 :441 1:083 1:15 3↑Ⓕ[R]FntstcGirl72k 90 4 5 510 511 410 38 Delahoussaye E LB116 3.80 90–12 Hookdonthflin1163 OlympcChrmr1225 GourmtGrl1161 Broke in air,slowly 5
30Apr00–5Hol fst 7f :214 :44 1:083 1:214 4↑Ⓕ[S]BThoughtfl150k 95 6 4 53¼ 45 34 34 Smith M E LB124 3.20 86–11 *La Feminn*1182 *Theresa's Tizzy*1202 Gourmet Girl1243 Bested rest outside 8
5Mar00–8SA sly 1⅛ :47 1:112 1:37 1:502 4↑ⒻSMrgrtaH-G1 76 3 2hd 1hd 2½ 58½ 514½ Gonzalez R M LB115 3.00 68–20 Riboletta1153 Bordelaise1144 Snowberg114½ Pulled,bid btwn,wkened 5
13Feb00–8SA wf 1 1/16 :232 :471 1:11 1:423 4↑ⒻSntMriaH-G1 101 2 31½ 42 1hd 2hd 32 Desormeaux K J LB116 7.50 88–13 Manistique125½ Snowberg1141½ GourmetGirl1162½ Bid inside,wkened late 8
22Jan00–8SA fst 7f :22 :441 1:082 1:212 4↑ⒻSntMncaH-G1 97 7 3 75 67¼ 76¼ 46 Valenzuela P A LB118 11.30 92–10 *HonestLdy*1141 KlooknQuen1162 EnjoythMomnt1183 Off rail,imp position 9
31Dec99–2SA fst 6f :22 :443 :563 1:084 3↑ⒻAlw 66950N$Y 93 1 2 51¾ 54 53½ 32¼ Valenzuela P A LB122 2.00 94–11 WoodmnsDncer122nk HerShKisss1172 GourmtGirl122½ Late foot outside 5
26Jun99–9Hol fst 1⅛ :462 1:101 1:35 1:48 3↑ⒻVanityH-G1 84 6 44 55½ 54½ 47 611¼ Delahoussaye E LB118 2.30 75–09 Manistique1224½ YoloLady1152 BellaChiarr1162½ 3wd 2nd turn,weakened 6
31May99–8Hol fst 1 1/16 :231 :454 1:093 1:404 3↑ⒻMladyBCH-G1 109 4 21 32 1hd 11½ 12 Delahoussaye E LB115 4.60 96–04 Gourmet Girl1152 Yolo Lady1151¾ VictoryStripes1174 Inside,clear,driving 5
15May99–8Hol fst 7f :222 :443 1:084 1:212 3↑Ⓕ[S]BThoughtfl100k 97 3 6 22 34½ 23½ 24 Delahoussaye E LB122 2.20 91–06 Censored1224 *Gourmet Girl*1222½ Funallover1222½ Angled in, second best 8
10Apr99–8GG wf 1 ⊗ :223 :453 1:093 1:353 3↑ⒻMissAmrcaH150k 103 2 21 2½ 2hd 13 13½ Gonzalez R M LB116 *1.20 94–15 Gourmet Girl1163½ Call Me1151½ Hot Lear116¾ Stlkd 2w, rddn out 8
7Feb99–5SA fst 1⅛ :471 1:111 1:36 1:484 ⒻLaCanada-G2 99 5 31½ 32½ 32 42¾ 35 Desormeaux K J LB117 5.70 86–11 *Manistique*1192½ MagicIAllure1192½ *GourmetGirl*117¾ Stalked pace,held 3rd 7
17Jan99–3SA fst 1 1/16 :224 :462 1:104 1:43 ⒻElEncino-G2 95 1 21½ 22½ 2½ 2hd 2hd Desormeaux K J LB117 5.40 88–13 *Manistique*119hd Gourmet Girl1175½ Magical Allure119 3 wide bid,game try 3
27Dec98–8SA fst 7f :224 :444 1:09 1:22 ⒻLaBrea-G1 97 1 4 63¼ 64 54 2½ Desormeaux K J LB117 14.50 94–06 MgiclAllure121½ GourmetGirl1171¼ TrnquilityLk1161¼ 4 wide into stretch 7
13Dec98–3Hol fst 6f :221 :45 :571 1:094 3↑ⒻOC 62k/N$Y -N 89 3 4 42 56 3½ 11 Delahoussaye E LB116 *1.50 88–16 GourmetGirl1161 DixieHoliday1173 ZendasDiablo1121¾ 5 wide into stretch 6
17May98–7Hol fst 7f :22 :441 1:082 1:204 ⒻRailbird-G2 91 5 2 31½ 31½ 23 26 Desormeaux K J LB119 b 5.90 92–08 Brulay1156 *Gourmet Girl*119no Unreal Squeal1161 Loomed 1/4, hung 6
24Apr98–6Hol fm 1 Ⓣ :244 :481 1:113 1:351 ⒻSenorita-G3 73 3 1hd 31 41½ 31½ 54½ Douglas R R LB120 4.70 82–11 DncingRhythm117¾ PhoneAlex1151 StrsProudPnny122¾ Blocked 1/4 pole 7
28Mar98–10BM fst 1 1/16 :23 :46 1:101 1:432 ⒻBMOaks-G3 91 6 21½ 21 1hd 16 112 Gonzalez R M LB115 3.10 87–24 Gourmet Girl11512 Reign On Rainier1143¼ Code Love116½ Handily 6
14Mar98–5SA fst 6½f :211 :433 1:091 1:161 Ⓕ[S]Alw 42000N$Y 84 5 7 63½ 52¾ 33 31 Douglas R R LB115 *2.60 87–09 *CherryMoon*117½ *CourtroomAntics*117½ *GourmtGirl*1152 Gaining late stretch 12
21Feb98–7SA fst 6f :211 :434 :561 1:093 Ⓕ[S]BooLaBoo109k 79 5 7 67½ 68¾ 310 38 Douglas R R LB115 4.50 84–11 MothersMeeting1172 Loveontherod1196 GourmetGirl115hd In tight early 8
31Dec97–7SA fst 7f :222 :45 1:10 1:24 Ⓕ[S]CalBrdrsCh168k 81 2 6 54½ 53½ 2½ 31½ Douglas R R LB114 5.20 82–18 *Nijinsky's Passion*1161 *Sassy*115½ Gourmet Girl1141 Got through, inside 11
29Nov97–7Hol fst 7f :214 :443 1:094 1:23 ⒻAlw 40000s 74 9 7 74¾ 32 12 11 Desormeaux K J 120 3.60 87–10 Gourmet Girl1201 *Nijinsky's Passion*1153½ Cookin Vickie1201½ Driving 12
7Nov97–1Hol fst 6½f :213 :442 1:101 1:164 ⒻMd 32000(32-28) 74 5 5 31½ 32 21 13½ Douglas R R B119 14.30 82–09 *GourmetGirl*1193½ RunawayVal1195½ MlibuMry1194 Angled out, drew clear 8

Halfbridled
Own: Wertheimer Farm LLC

Dk. b or b. f. 3 (Feb)
Sire: Unbridled (Fappiano) $200,000
Dam: Half Queen (Deputy Minister)
Br: Wertheimer & Frere (Ky)
Tr: Mandella Richard E

Life	6	4	2	0	$959,400	99	D.Fst	6	4	2	0	$959,400	99
2004	2	0	2	0	$110,000	93	Wet(421)	0	0	0	0	$0	–
2003	4	4	0	0	$849,400	99	Turf(302)	0	0	0	0	$0	–
	0	0	0	0	$0	–	DstⓉ(336)	0	0	0	0	$0	–

8Apr04–8Kee fst *7f :214 :442 1:103 1:27 ⒻBeaumont-G2 76 4 5 89¼ 87¼ 33 28¼ Solis A L123 *.40 83–09 VctoryUSA1188¼ Hlfbrdld1231½ WldwodFlwr1181¾ Drift out turn,2ndbest 8
13Mar04–8SA fst 1 1/16 :224 :462 1:104 1:424 ⒻSAOaks-G1 93 1 32½ 43½ 41¾ 22 21½ Stevens G L LB117 *.50 89–08 SilentSighs1171½ Halfbridled1171½ A.P.Adventure117½ Bit off rail,willingly 7
25Oct03–3SA fst 1 1/16 :224 :464 1:104 1:423 ⒻBCJuvFil-G1 99 14 74½ 51¾ 31 1½ 12½ Krone J A LB119 *2.30 91–07 Halfbridled1192½ *Ashado*119nk *Victory U. S. A.*1199¼ Wide trip, drew off 14
28Sep03–9SA fst 1 1/16 :24 :48 1:122 1:433 ⒻOakLeaf-G2 98 4 11½ 2½ 11 12 14½ Krone J A LB119 *.30 86–16 *Halfbridled*1194½ Tarlow119½ Hollywood Story1196½ Inside,clear,gamely 7
30Aug03–8Dmr fst 7f :224 :451 1:093 1:221 ⒻDMrDeb-G1 99 1 4 42 2hd 11½ 15 Krone J A LB116 1.60 91–13 *Hlfbridld*1165 HollywoodStory115no VictoryUSA1161½ Re-bid rail 1/4,clear 6
27Jly03–3Dmr fst 5½f :22 :451 :574 1:04 ⒻMd Sp Wt 49k 87 1 4 65 64¼ 31 14½ Krone J A B118 3.60 95–10 *Halfbridled*1184½ UppityKitty1182 HaleakalSunrise1182 4wd rally,drew off 6

High Chaparral (Ire)
Own: Tabor Michael and Magnier, Mrs. John

B. c. 4 (Mar)
Sire: Sadler's Wells (Northern Dancer)
Dam: Kasora (Darshaan*GB)
Br: S. Coughlan (Ire)
Tr: O'Brien Aidan P

Life	13	10	1	2	$5,331,231	112	D.Fst	0	0	0	0	$0	–
2003	4	3	0	1	$1,717,124	112	Wet(280)	0	0	0	0	$0	–
2002	6	5	0	1	$3,436,410	111	Turf(346)	13	10	1	2	$5,331,231	112
	0	0	0	0	$0	–	Dst(T)(398)	0	0	0	0	$0	–

25Oct03–8SA fm 1½ (T) :483 1:112 2:00 2:241 3↑ BCTurf-G1 **112** 3 52 31 32 32 1hd Kinane M J LB126 4.90 105–04 DH HighChaparral126 DH Johar126hd *Falbrv*1265½ Came out str,game btwn 9
5Oct03 Longchamp (Fr) hy *1½ (T) RH 2:321 3↑ Prix de l'Arc de Triomphe-G1 35¾ Kinane M J 131 2.60 Dalakhani123¾ *Mubtaker*1315 *High Chaparral*1311½ 13
Timeform rating: 124 Stk 1851000 *4th on rail,3rd 2f out,no chance with first two.Ange Gabriel 9th*
6Sep03 Leopardstwn (Ire) gd 1¼ (T) LH 2:031 3↑ Irish Champion Stakes-G1 1nk Kinane M J 130 4.00 High Chaparral130nk *Falbrav*130hd *Islington*1271½ 7
Timeform rating: 128 Stk 1110000 *Trckd 4th,2nd 2f out,led 1f out,drftd left,held well.Alamshar 4th*
10Aug03 Curragh (Ire) gf 1¼ (T) RH 2:044 3↑ Royal Whip Stakes-G2 1¾ Kinane M J 139 *.90 *High Chaparral*139¾ Imperial Dancer132nk In Time's Eye1322 6
Timeform rating: 128+ Stk 147000 *Tracked in 3rd,2nd 1-1/2f out,led 1f out,driving*
26Oct02–9AP yl 1½ (T) :511 1:17 2:054 2:30 3↑ BCTurf-G1 **111** 5 51½ 53½ 33 1hd 11¼ Kinane M J L121 *.90 89–09 *HighChaparrl*1211¼ WithAnticiption126¾ FlconFlight1261 Split horses turn 8
6Oct02 Longchamp (Fr) gd *1½ (T) RH 2:263 3↑ Prix de l'Arc de Triomphe-G1 31¼ Kinane M J 123 *2.20e Marienbard131¾ *Sulamani*123½ *High Chaparral*123½ 16
Timeform rating: 127 Stk 1566000 *Tracked leaders,bid 1-1/2f out,one-paced late.Islington 5th*
30Jun02 Curragh (Ire) gd 1½ (T) RH 2:321 Irish Derby-G1 13½ Kinane M J 126 *.33 High Chaparral1263½ Sholokhov1261½ Ballingarry126hd 9
Timeform rating: 127+ Stk 1280000 *Tracked in 4th,carried left 1-1/2f out,led 1f out,drew clear*
8Jun02 Epsom (GB) yl 1½ (T) RH 2:392 Epsom Derby-G1 12 Murtagh J P 126 3.50 *High Chaparral*1262 *Hawk Wing*12612 *Moon Ballad*1261 12
Timeform rating: 130 Stk 2083000 *Rated towards rear,rallied to lead over 2f out,driving.Bandari8th*
12May02 Leopardstwn (Ire) gd 1¼ (T) LH 2:032 Derrinstown Stud Derby Trial-G3 11 Heffernan J A 130 *.20 *High Chaparral*1301 In Time's Eye1231½ Ahsanabad1233 5
Timeform rating: 118 Stk 86300 *Tracked in 3rd,led over 1f out,comfortably*
14Apr02 Leopardstwn (Ire) gd 1¼ (T) LH 2:054 Ballysax Stakes (Listed) 17 Kinane M J 131 *.65 *High Chaparral*1317 Twentytwoandchange124½ Rahn1243 7
Timeform rating: 123 Stk 43900 *Rated in 5th,3rd 2f out,led over 1f out,drew clear*
27Oct01 Doncaster (GB) hy 1 (T) Str 1:451 Racing Post Trophy-G1 1¾ Darley K 126 4.50 *High Chaparral*126¾ Castle Gandolfo1265 Redback1263 6
Timeform rating: 115+ Stk 276000 *Rated in last,progress into 2nd 1-1/2f out,led late.Camp David5th*
7Oct01 Tipperary (Ire) sf 7f (T) LH 1:411 Nenagh EBF Maiden 12½ Heffernan J A 128 *.33 *High Chaparral*1282½ Querin Pier1234 Dexileos128hd 16
Timeform rating: 93 Maiden 16300 *Slowly away,soon tracking ldrs,2nd hfwy,led 150y out,going away*
30Sep01 Punchestown (Ire) gd 7½f (T) RH 1:41 EBF Maiden 2no Kinane M J 126 *.55 Hot Trotter126no *High Chaparral*1264 Bounce Back1261 18
Timeform rating: 92 Maiden 16300 *Dwelt,soon 7th,wide bid 2f out,close 2nd 1f out,just failed*

Hirapour (Ire)
Own: Eldon Farm LLC

B. g. 9 (Apr)
Sire: Kahyasi*Ire (Ile de Bourbon) $8,140
Dam: Himaya*Ire (Mouktar)
Br: His Highness the Aga Khans Studs S. C. (Ire)
Tr: Fout Paul D

Life	36	15	6	3	$581,426	–	D.Fst	0	0	0	0	$0	–
2005	4	2	1	1	$208,025	–	Wet(173*)	0	0	0	0	$0	–
2004	4	2	2	0	$199,625	–	Turf(349)	19	5	2	1	$53,109	–
	0	0	0	0	$0	–	Dst(T)(269)	0	0	0	0	$0	–

2Sep05–1Sar yl 2⅜ (T) Hurdles 4:244 4↑ NYTurfWH-G1 – 9 89¼ 85¼ 51¼ 1½ 13¾ McCarron M O L158 *1.25 – – Hirapour1583¾ Three Carat1401¾ Party Airs1421 When ready, clear 9
8Aug05–1Sar fm 2 1/16 (T) Hurdles 3:434 4↑ APSmthMm-G2 – 6 44 32 37 26 33 Miller F B Jr L158 *1.15 – – Paradise's Boss1502½ Serazzo150½ *Hirapour*1583¾ Stayed on well 8
22Apr05–9Kee fm 2½ (T) Hurdles 4:42 4↑ RylChsHd-G1 – 3 75¾ 52 53 11 11¼ McCarron M O L160 2.40 – – Hirapour1601¼ *Sur La Tete*1563½ McDynamo16215 4-5w,bobble,driving 8
2Apr05–6Cam fm 2⅜ (T) Hurdles 4:33 4↑ Crl1Crln-G3 – 1 21½ 31½ 31½ 2hd 2hd McCarron M O L158 – – – Sur La Tete154hd *Hirapour*1583¾ *Preemptive Strike*15858 Battled lane, hung 4
21Nov04–7Cam fm 2¾ (T) Hurdles 5:043 4↑ ColonlCp-G1 – 4 624 418 42 1hd 12¾ McCarron M O L156 – – – Hirapour1562¾ Preemptive Strike1565 *Sur La Tete*1569 Settled, stiff drive 7
23Oct04–5FH fm 2⅝ (T) Hurdles 5:064 4↑ BrCupStp-G1 – 2 76½ 77½ 44 21½ 21½ McCarron M O L156 – – – McDynamo1561½ *Hirapour*156½ Sur La Tete15615½ Loomed, finished well 7
16Apr04–8Kee fm 2½ (T) Hurdles 4:412 4↑ RylChsHd-G1 – 1 69 67 41¼ 2hd 11¾ Chipperfield C L148 *1.20 – – Hirapour1481¾ Preemptive Strike1507 *Dancewel*1421 Driving,clear 8
27Mar04–6Cam fm 2⅜ (T) Hurdles 4:23 4↑ Crl1Crln-G3 – 3 65 35½ 21½ 11 2¾ Chipperfield C L146 – – – PreemptiveStrike146¾ *Hirpour*1467 *AlSkywlkr*15812 Led strch, outfinished 6
1Nov03–3Pmt fm *2⅜ (T) Hurdles 3:513 4↑ (R) ChampHur-G1 – 2 34 32½ 2½ 1½ 1¾ Massey R L165 – – – Hirapour165¾ *Preemptive Strike*1535 Party Airs150nk Fully extended 9
18Oct03–8GrM gd *1¾ (T) 3:403 3↑ Alw 12500NC – 4 33 25 31½ 16 113 Boisgontier J L160 – – – *Hirapour*16013 Potro Sol1602½ La Grande Ballade1572 Handily 14
21May03 Kelso (GB) gd 2 13/16 (T) LH 5:31 4↑ Intermediate Hurdle 122 Dennis D R 159 *.25 *Hirapour*15922 *Tramantano*15630 Eyze154 3
Alw 33600 *Tracked leader,led at 7th,ridden clear*
16May03 Aintree (GB) gs 2½ (T) LH 5:03 4↑ Radio City Novices Hurdle 13½ Dennis D R 154 *.22 *Hirapour*1543½ Algarve1548 Overlord15123 6
Alw 12300 *Tracked leaders,cruised to lead 3 out,in a canter*
24Apr03 Perth (GB) gd 2 9/16 (T) RH 5:054 4↑ Conditional Jockeys Hcp Hurdle 19 Worthington W A8 152 *.57 *Hirapour*1529 Scarletti1488 Bodfari Signet13530 5
Hcp 20600 *Prompted pace,led at 5th,clear 2 out,handily*
8Apr03 Exeter (GB) gf 2⅛ (T) RH 4:012 4↑ Conditional Jockeys Hcp Hurdle 122 Worthington W A8 165 *.40 *Hirapour*16522 Western Ridge1402 Timidjar1374 6
Hcp 7900 *Led to 2nd,prompted pace,led 5th,soon clear,easily*
2Apr03 Ludlow (GB) gd 2⅝ (T) RH 5:043 4↑ Cndtnl Jckys Novice Hp Hurdle 112 W A Worthington8 158 *1.75 *Hirapour*15812 Dragut Torghoud14313 Xellance1438 11
Hcp 11700 *Behind,prgrss to lead 3 out,clear & mistake 2 out,handily*
7Mar03 Sandown Park (GB) hy 2 9/16 (T) RH 5:391 4↑ HMS Sandown Novices Hurdle 36 Dennis D R 154 5.00 Sherbet Lad1545 Briar1501 *Hirapour*1542½ 12
Alw 12400 *Tracked leaders,led 2 out,soon headed,one-paced*
23Feb03 Hereford (GB) gd 2⅜ (T) RH 5:03 4↑ Betfair.com Maiden Hurdle 25 Dennis D R 156 3.50 Home James1515 Hirapour15616 Alvino15611 14
Maiden 9300 *Tracked leader,led after 6th,soon clear,headed 2 out*
24Jan03 Doncaster (GB) gs 2 1/16 (T) LH 4:054 5↑ Cusworth Novices Hurdle 415 Dennis D R 152 6.00 *Demi Beau*1526 Mythical King1584 Valeureux1525 16
Alw 9000 *Twrds rear,prgrss over 3 out,close up 2 out,one-paced*
Previously trained by Amanda Perrett
19Oct02 Newmarket (GB) gd 2¼ (T) RH 3:511 3↑ Cesarewitch Handicap 1717 Murtagh J P 130 50.00 Miss Fara112hd Direct Bearing1173½ Dubai Seven Stars103¾ 36
Timeform rating: 93 Hcp 185000 *In touch,weakened 2f out*
6Oct02 Longchamp (Fr) gd *2½ (T) RH 4:234 4↑ Prix du Cadran-G1 159½ Eddery Pat 128 48.00 Give Notice128hd Pushkin128¾ (D) Polish Summer128¾ 16
Timeform rating: 103? Stk 195000 *Tracked in 3rd,weakened 2f out.Plcd 13th via DQ*
Placed 13th through disqualification
21Sep02 Newbury (GB) gf 1 11/16 (T) 2:471 3↑ Farewell To Graham Kendrick Autumn Cup 1123 Quinn T 140 4.50 Windermere125½ *Typhoon Tilly*108¾ Wait for the Will1241½ 11
Hcp 36400 *Chased leader, challenged from 4f out til weakened 2f out*
16Aug02 Newbury (GB) gf 1½ (T) 2:362 3↑ Stan James European Breeders Fund Classified S25 Quinn T 134 6.00 Systematic1285 Hirapour13414 In Disguise126 3
Alw 27900 *Tracked leader, led inside final 3f, headed 2f out*
20Oct01 Newmarket (GB) gs 2¼ (T) 4:001 3↑ Tote Cesarewitch H. 811¾ Eddery P 130 16.00 Distant Prospect120nk Palua1031¾ Give Notice1261¼ 31
Hcp 172000 *Midfield: rdn and outpcd over 5f out: styd on again appr fnl f: n*
21Sep01 Newbury (GB) gf 2 (T) 3:272 3↑ Dubai Duty Free Finest Surprise Handicap S. 13 Eddery P 136 3.50 Hirapour1363 Gold Standard1051½ Browning121nk 5
Hcp 15800 *Chsd ldr 2f: styd in 3rd: hdwy over 3f out: led over 2f out: drvn*
1Sep01 Chester (GB) gd 1 11/16 (T) 2:55 3↑ Bet Direct on Channel 4 Teletext Page 613 Rated S61¼ Ryan W 119 10.00 Flossy1194 Jalousie1131¼ Garden Society122hd 11
Stk 46900 *Trckd ldrs: lost pl over 6f out: rallied u.p over 3f out: kpt on*
19Jun01 Ascot (GB) gd 1½ (T) 2:302 3↑ Duke of Edinburgh Handicap 117¾ Duffield G 128 20.00 Takamaka Bay126no *Akbar*137½ Gallery God1311½ 20
Hcp 77000 *Led tl hdd and wknd over 1f out*
2Jun01 Newmarket (GB) gf 1½ (T) 2:31 3↑ Mix-it Classified S. 11½ Eddery P 133 3.30 Hirapour1331½ Carlys Quest1337 Hudood1331¾ 8
Alw 14700 *Mde all: sn clr: drvn out*
22Oct00 Naas (Ire) yl 1⅜ (T) 2:323 3↑ Coughlan E.b.f. H. 10 Smullen P J 136 b 8.00 Tarwila1241½ Golden Fact1312 Common Kris130½ 15
Hcp 16000
9Sep00 Leopardstwn (Ire) gd 1¾ (T) 2:582 3↑ E.B.F. September H. 13 Berry F M 136 16.00 Kate Emily1082 Just Wondering121½ Crystal Springs111nk 13
Hcp 44100
2Jly00 Curragh (Ire) gd 1½ (T) RH 2:363 3↑ World Sports Handicap 1027½ Smullen P J 140 12.00 *Tragic Lover*1243 Bamford Castle1361 Mudaa-Eb1362½ 15
Hcp 24200

20Jun00 Ascot (GB) gd 1½ Ⓣ RH 2:31^{3} 3↑ Duke of Edinburgh Handicap 17 28¾ Smullen P J 134 b 20.00 *Katiykha*135no Gallery God121 2½ Veridian116½ 20
Hcp 83500 *A bhd*

24May00 Leopardstwn (Ire) gd 1¾ Ⓣ RH 2:57 3↑ Saval Beg Stakes (Listed) 3 2½ Smullen P J 132 6.00 Royal Rebel136^{no} Enzeli141 2½ Hirapour132 2½ 5
Stk 28800

15Apr00 Listowel (Ire) sf 1½ Ⓣ 3:19^{4} 4↑ Dawn Pure Orange Juice S. 1¾ Smullen P J 133 5.50 Hirapour133¾ Morning Breeze128^{5} Minella Hotel125^{hd} 8
Alw 15300

26Mar00 Curragh (Ire) sf 2 Ⓣ 3:52^{1} 4↑ Kildare Race 9 Shanahan P 126 16.00 Knife Edge121^{8} Endless Magic121^{hd} His Song121^{8} 17
Alw 9900

21Aug99 Fairyhouse (Ire) gd 1⅝ Ⓣ 2:51^{3} 3↑ Ratoath Maiden S. 1 4½ Murtagh J P 128 2.00 Hirapour128 4½ *Scottish Memories*128^{12} Amocachi139 2½ 11
Maiden 6000

7Jun99 Leopardstwn (Ire) yl 1¼ Ⓣ 2:10^{2} 3↑ Wexford Maiden S. 2 2½ Murtagh J P 128 3.00 *Halcyon*128 2½ *Hirapour*128^{7} Playing Hours128 2½ 6
Maiden 7800

Islington (Ire)

Own: Executors Of The Late Lord Weinstock

B. f. 4 (Feb)
Sire: Sadler's Wells (Northern Dancer)
Dam: Hellenic (Darshaan*GB)
Br: Ballymacoll Stud Farm Ltd (Ire)
Tr: Stoute Sir Michael R

Life	15	6	0	4	$1,553,043	109	D.Fst	0	0	0	0	$0 –
2003	6	2	0	2	$955,142	109	Wet(280)	0	0	0	0	$0 –
2002	7	4	0	1	$594,316	105	Turf(346)	15	6	0	4	$1,565,260 109
	0	0	0	0	$0	–	DstⓉ(398)	0	0	0	0	$0 –

30Nov03 Tokyo (Jpn) yl *1½ Ⓣ LH 2:28^{3} 3↑ Japan Cup-G1 9 13½ Fallon K 121 18.90 Tap Dance City126^{9} That's The Plenty121¾ *Symboli Kris S*126^{hd} 18
Timeform rating: 102 Stk 4342000 *Tracked in 4th,weakened over 1f out.Denon 8th,Johar 16th*

25Oct03-6SA fm 1¼ Ⓣ :46^{3} 1:10^{2} 1:35^{1} 1:59 3↑ⒻBCF&MTrf-G1 **109** 4 5^{8} 6^{11} 6 3¼ 2^{hd} 1^{nk} Fallon K **LB**123 *2.90 98-04 Islington123^{nk} L'Ancresse118 2½ Yesterday118^{no} Pulled,bid,led,gamely 12

6Sep03 Leopardstwn (Ire) gd 1¼ Ⓣ LH 2:03^{1} 3↑ Irish Champion Stakes-G1 3^{nk} Fallon K 127 16.00 High Chaparral130^{nk} *Falbrav*130^{hd} *Islington*127 1½ 7
Timeform rating: 124+ Stk 1110000 *Rated at rear,pushed along after 4f,gaining late.Alamshar 4th*

20Aug03 York (GB) gf 1½ Ⓣ LH 2:27^{2} 3↑ ⒻYorkshire Oaks-G1 1^{1} Fallon K 130 *.70 Islington130^{1} Ocean Silk120^{3} Summitville120 1¾ 8
Timeform rating: 120 Stk 398000 *3rd on rail,led over 2f out,held well.L'Ancresse5th,CasualLook7th*

5Jly03 Sandown Park (GB) gf 1¼ Ⓣ RH 2:05^{2} 3↑ Coral Eclipse S.-G1 6^{3} Fallon K 130 4.50 Falbrav133¾ Nayef133 1¼ Kaieteur133^{no} 15
Timeform rating: 118 Stk 616500 *Mid-pack on rail,3rd 1-1/2f out,faded late.Grandera 8th*

18Jun03 Ascot (GB) gd 1¼ Ⓣ RH 2:05^{1} 4↑ Prince of Wales's Stakes-G1 3 3½ Fallon K 123 7.00 Nayef126 2½ *Rakti*126^{1} Islington123^{1} 10
Timeform rating: 118 Stk 587000 *Trckd ldrs,angld out 1f out,drftd lft,held by first two.Falbrav5t*

26Oct02-7AP yl 1¼ Ⓣ :49 1:13^{2} 1:38^{2} 2:03^{2} 3↑ⒻBCF&MTrf-G1 **105** 2 9^{11} 7 8½ 8^{4} 6^{2} 3 1¾ Fallon K 118 4.00 87-09 Starine123 1½ Banks Hill123^{nk} Islington118^{nk} Steadied repeatedly 12

6Oct02 Longchamp (Fr) gd *1½ Ⓣ RH 2:26^{3} 3↑ Prix de l'Arc de Triomphe-G1 5^{2} Fallon K 120 7.20 Marienbard131¾ *Sulamani*123½ *High Chaparral*123½ 16
Timeform rating: 123 Stk 1566000 *Rank early tracking clear leader,led ovr 2f out to 100y out,faded*

21Aug02 York (GB) gd 1½ Ⓣ LH 2:26^{3} 3↑ ⒻYorkshire Oaks-G1 1^{5} Fallon K 120 2.00 Islington120^{5} Guadalupe120^{hd} Sulk120^{hd} 11
Timeform rating: 120+ Stk 382000 *Trckd in 3rd,dueled 3-1/2f out,led 2-1/2f outdrew clear.Kazzia4th*

3Aug02 Goodwood (GB) gd 1¼ Ⓣ RH 2:04^{3} 3↑ ⒻNassau Stakes-G1 1^{4} Fallon K 118 3.30 *Islington*118^{4} Sulk118½ Quarter Moon118^{1} 10
Timeform rating: 119+ Stk 211000 *Tracked in 4th,led 2f out,soon well clear,handily.Golden Silca7th*

7Jun02 Epsom (GB) sf 1½ Ⓣ LH 2:44^{2} ⒻEnglish Oaks-G1 8 18½ Fallon K 126 3.50 Kazzia126½ Quarter Moon126^{14} Shadow Dancing126^{nk} 14
Timeform rating: 99 Stk 511000 *Tracked leaders,2nd halfway,brief bid 3f out,weakened 2f out*

14May02 York (GB) gd 1 5/16 Ⓣ LH 2:09 ⒻMusidora Stakes (1 1/4m,85y)-G3 1^{1} Fallon K 120 *.85 Islington120^{1} Spinnette120^{1} Alexander Three D120^{3} 5
Timeform rating: 112+ Stk 72400 *Tracked in 3rd,led 3f out,held well*

19Apr02 Newbury (GB) gd 1¼ Ⓣ LH 2:09^{3} ⒻSanctuary Group Maiden Stakes 1 1½ Fallon K 123 *.65 *Islington*123 1½ *Fragrant View*123¾ Mexican Hawk123 3½ 16
Timeform rating: 89+ Maiden 12000 *Tracked leaders,roused to lead 2f out,quickened clear 1f out*

6Oct01 Newmarket (GB) gd 7f Ⓣ Str 1:26^{3} ⒻOh So Sharp Stakes (Listed) 3½ Fallon K 121 5.00 Protectress121^{hd} Snowfire121½ *Islington*121 2½ 12
Timeform rating: 100+ Stk 32600 *Slowly away,rated at rear,rallied to lead briefly 2f out,gamely*

17Aug01 Newmarket (GB) gd 7f Ⓣ Str 1:28^{1} ⒻQ103 Maiden Stakes 6 5½ Fallon K 123 2.25 Bright And Clear123 2½ *Helloimustbegoing*123 1½ Cozy Maria123^{nk} 10
Timeform rating: 73 Maiden 9200 *Tracked leaders,weakened 1f out*

Johannesburg

Own: Mr Michael Tabor & Mrs John Magnier

B. c. 3 (Feb)
Sire: Hennessy (Storm Cat) $35,000
Dam: Myth (Ogygian)
Br: W. G. Lyster III & Jayeff B Stables (Ky)
Tr: O'Brien Aidan P

Life	10	7	1	0	$1,014,585	99	D.Fst	2	1	0	0	$520,000 99
2002	3	0	1	0	$11,691	95	Wet(353)	0	0	0	0	$0 –
2001	7	7	0	0	$1,002,894	99	Turf(297)	8	6	1	0	$494,585 –
	0	0	0	0	$0	–	DstⓉ(330)	0	0	0	0	$0 –

22Jun02 Ascot (GB) gf 6f Ⓣ Str 1:14^{1} 3↑ Golden Jubilee S.-G1 9^{10} Kinane M J 123 *3.00 Malhub130 1½ Danehurst127½ Three Points130 1¾ 12
Timeform rating: 90 Stk 404100 *Trckd ldrs,drifted right over 2f out,soon weakened.Continent 5th*

4May02-9CD fst 1¼ :47 1:11^{3} 1:36^{3} 2:01 KyDerby-G1 **95** 1 10 6½ 10 5¼ 9 8¼ 8^{8} 8^{13} Stevens G L **L**126 8.10 81-05 *War Emblem*126^{4} Proud Citizen126¾ Perfect Drift126 3¼ Inside trip,no rally 18

7Apr02 Curragh (Ire) yl 7f Ⓣ Str 1:31^{3} 3↑ Gladness Stakes-G3 2no Kinane M J 125 *.30 *Rebelline*136no Johannesburg125^{1} Shoal Creek133¾ 7
Timeform rating: 114 Stk 61500 *Rank early tracking in 3rd,led 1f out,headed on line*

27Oct01-8Bel fst 1 1/16 :23^{3} :46^{4} 1:11 1:42^{1} BCJuvnle-G1 **99** 3 5 1¾ 5 1¾ 5 1¼ 4^{nk} 1 1¼ Kinane M J **L**122 7.20 86-12 Johannesburg122 1¼ *Repent*122 1¼ *Siphonic*122¾ Split rivals, driving 12

4Oct01 Newmarket (GB) yl 6f Ⓣ Str 1:11^{3} Middle Park Stakes-G1 1^{3} Kinane M J 123 *.30 *Johannesburg*123^{3} Zipping123^{3} Doc Holiday123¾ 7
Timeform rating: 121+ Stk 221500 *Tracked in 4th,quickened to lead 1-1/2f out,soon clear*

26Aug01 Deauville (Fr) yl *6f Ⓣ Str 1:10^{2} Prix Morny-G1 1 1½ Kinane M J 126 *.60e *Johannesburg*126 1½ Zipping126 1½ Meshaheer126 1½ 11
Timeform rating: 120+ Stk 194900 *Tracked in 5th,rallied to lead 170y out,handily.Firebreak 4th*

12Aug01 Leopardstwn (Ire) sf 6f Ⓣ Str 1:13^{1} Phoenix Stakes-G1 1^{5} Kinane M J 126 *.40 *Johannesburg*126^{5} Miss Beabea123 1½ Agnetha123^{nk} 11
Timeform rating: 119+ Stk 255300 *Tracked in 5th,led over 1f out,quickly clear.Wiseman's Ferry 4th*

14Jly01 Curragh (Ire) yl 6f Ⓣ Str 1:16^{4} Anglesey Stakes (6f,63y)-G3 1^{4} Kinane M J 127 *.80 *Johannesburg*127^{4} Wiseman's Ferry124^{nk} High Society121^{3} 8
Timeform rating: 114+ Stk 65100 *Tracked in 3rd,angled right 1-1/2f out,led 1f out,quickly clear*

21Jun01 Ascot (GB) gd 5f Ⓣ Str 1:02 Norfolk Stakes-G3 1 1¼ Kinane M J 124 *1.35 *Johannesburg*124 1¼ Waterside124^{no} Lord Merlin124 1½ 10
Timeform rating: 100+ Stk 77900 *Slowly away,soon tracking leaders,drifted right 2f out,led 1f out*

30May01 Fairyhouse (Ire) fm 6f Ⓣ RH 1:14^{4} Ratoath EBF Maiden 1 3½ Kinane M J 128 *.30 *Johannesburg*128 3½ Minaun Heights123^{5} Leinster Mills123^{4} 8
Timeform rating: 84+ Maiden 15200 *Well placed in 4th,led 1-1/2f out,drew clear in hand*

Kalanisi (Ire)

Own: H.H. Aga Khan

Dk. b or b. h. 5 (Mar)
Sire: Doyoun*Ire (Mill Reef) $5,520
Dam: Kalamba*Ire (Green Dancer)
Br: His Highness the Aga Khan's Studs S.C. (Ire)
Tr: Stoute Sir Michael R

Life	11	6	4	1	$2,148,836	110	D.Fst	0	0	0	0	$0 –
2001	2	0	1	1	$96,568	–	Wet(275*)	0	0	0	0	$0 –
2000	6	3	3	0	$2,014,773	110	Turf(324)	11	6	4	1	$2,148,836 110
	0	0	0	0	$0	–	Dst(T)(291)	0	0	0	0	$0 –

20Jun01 Ascot (GB) gd 1¼ (T) RH 2:042 4↑ Prince of Wales's Stakes-G1 Stk 349500 2½ Fallon K 126 *2.00 Fantastic Light126½ Kalanisi126¾ Hightori126 1¼ 9
Wide in 5th,6th 2-1/2f out,bid 1-1/2f out,2nd best.Observatory4th

27May01 Curragh (Ire) yl 1⅝ (T) RH 2:132 4↑ Tattersalls Gold Cup-G1 Stk 218600 3¼ Fallon K 126 *1.75 *Fantastic Light*126nk Golden Snake1263 Kalanisi1261 6
Rated in 5th,brief bid 1-1/2f out,soon beaten.Bach 5th

4Nov00- 9CD fm 1½ (T) :5011:151 2:0332:264 3↑ BCTurf-G1 110 1 106 95¾ 74 42½ 1½ Murtagh J P 126 4.60 109 - Kalanisi126½ Quiet Resolve126no John's Call126hd Stead early,going away 13
Previously trained by Stoute Michael R

14Oct00 Newmarket (GB) yl 1¼ (T) Str 2:052 3↑ Champion Stakes-G1 Stk 580700 1½ Murtagh J 128 5.00 *Kalanisi*128½ Montjeu128 2½ Distant Music123 1½ 15
Timeform rating: 130 Mid-pack,rallied to lead 2f out,held gamely.Slickly 8th

22Aug00 York (GB) gd 1 5/16 (T) LH 2:09 3↑ Juddmonte International Stakes-G1 Stk 667600 2hd Eddery P 131 1.25 *Giant's Causeway*123hd *Kalanisi*1317 *Lear Spear*131½ 6
Timeform rating: 130 Tracked in 3rd,led 1f out,drifted left,headed near line

8Jly00 Sandown Park (GB) gd 1¼ (T) RH 2:051 3↑ Eclipse Stakes-G1 Stk 544800 2hd Eddery P 133 3.50 *Giant's Causeway*122hd Kalanisi133 2½ Shiva130 1½ 8
Timeform rating: 130 7th early,rallied,led 100y out,headed near line.FantasticLight5th

20Jun00 Ascot (GB) gd 1 (T) Str 1:393 3↑ Queen Anne Stakes-G2 Stk 182200 1½ Fallon K 128 5.50 Kalanisi128½ Dansili131no *Swallow Flight*128 3½ 11
Timeform rating: 125 Behind,angled out 2f out,led 100y out.Muhtathir6th,IndianLodge7th

15May00 Windsor (GB) gd 1 70 (T) RH 1:42 3↑ Royal Windsor Stakes (Listed) Stk 34500 2½ Fallon K 133 *2.00 *Swallow Flight*128½ *Kalanisi*133nk Showboat1284 8
Timeform rating: 117 Mid-pack,outpaced over 3f out,late rush,up for 2nd

29May99 Kempton (GB) gd 1 (T) RH 1:353 Heron Stakes (Listed) Stk 35200 1hd Mosse G 124 *1.35 Kalanisi124hd Mensa1242 Peculiarity124½ 6
Timeform rating: 112 Trckd 4th,ridden 3f out,late rush,led on line.Killer Instinct 4th

2May99 Newmarket (GB) gd 7f (T) Str 1:254 Who's 60 Tomorrow? Cndtns Stks Alw 15800 13 Fallon K 127 *1.60 *Kalanisi*1273 *Hawriyah*122 1¼ Subeen122no 4
Timeform rating: 110+ Tracked in 3rd,led over 1f out,drew clear

20Apr99 Folkestone (GB) sf 7f (T) Str 1:34 Norman Poole Meml Mdn St(Div2) Maiden 7800 18 Ffrench R 126 *.70 *Kalanisi*1268 Compensation126nk Haymaker1266 7
Timeform rating: 92+ Tracked in 3rd,led 2f out,quickly clear

Kitten's Joy

Own: Ramsey Kenneth L. and Sarah K

Ch. c. 4 (May)
Sire: El Prado*Ire (Sadler's Wells) $100,000
Dam: Kitten's First (Lear Fan)
Br: Kenneth L. Ramsey & Sarah K. Ramsey (Ky)
Tr: Romans Dale L

Life	13	9	3	0	$1,875,791	114	D.Fst	2	0	1	0	$10,550 74
2005	1	1	0	0	$169,880	105	Wet(349)	0	0	0	0	$0 –
2004	8	6	2	0	$1,625,796	114	Turf(330)	11	9	2	0	$1,865,241 114
	0	0	0	0	$0	–	Dst(T)(318)	0	0	0	0	$0 –

4Jly05-10CD fm 1 (T) :242 :482 1:1221:351 3↑ FrckrBCH-G2 105 4 44 43½ 44 21½ 11 Prado E S L124 *.60 93- 10 Kitten's Joy1241 Old Forester115½ America Alive119 1¼ Inside,hand urging 6
30Oct04- 8LS yl 1½ (T) :49 1:134 2:04 2:293 3↑ BCTurf-G1 108 4 37 32½ 32 31½ 21¾ Velazquez J R L121 *.70 121- 07 BettrTlkNow126 1¾ *KittnsJoy*1211 Powrscourt126 2¼ Inside move, 2nd best 8
2Oct04- 9Bel yl 1½ (T) :5041:171 2:0712:294 3↑ TfClscIv-G1 114 5 42½ 41¾ 21½ 1hd 12½ Velazquez J R L121 2.40 72- 22 Kitten's Joy121 2½ Magistretti126¾ Tycoon1213 Strong when set down 7
14Aug04-11AP fm 1¼ (T) :4631:11 1:3511:593 Secretar-G1 113 1 611 610 52¾ 1½ 13¼ Bailey J D L123 *.90 113 - *KittensJoy*123 3¼ GreekSun121 1¼ MoscowBallet1191 5w, vigorous hand ride 7
10Jly04- 9Cnl fm 1¼ (T) :4711:112 1:3642:011 VaDby-G3 108 2 616 413 33½ 1½ 12¾ Prado E S L117 1.70 99- 16 *Kitten'sJoy*117 2¾ *ArtieSchiller*117 4¾ *PrinceArch*119 12¾ 4wd move,drifted out 8
12Jun04- 5CD yl 1⅛ (T) :49 1:134 1:3811:503 JfrsnCup-G3 101 8 85 64 41 1hd 2hd Bailey J D L122 *.70 80- 25 PrncArch120hd *KttnsJoy*122 4¾ CoolCondctor116 1¼ 5w,bid,clear,outgamed 9
30Apr04- 9CD gd 1 1/16 (T) :243 :492 1:1311:431 AmerTurf-G3 93 4 93¾ 82¾ 42½ 1½ 12½ Bailey J D L123 *1.10 88- 11 Kitten's Joy123 2½ *Prince Arch*123½ Capo117 2¼ Bmp gate,6w,driving 9
21Feb04-11GP fm 1⅛ (T) :4941:133 1:3711:483 PalmBch-G3 91 1 43½ 43 52½ 3½ 11¾ Bailey J D L122 *.60e 92- 06 *Kitten's Joy*122 1¾ Prince Arch118nk Pa Pa Da118¾ Angled out, clear 12
1Jan04- 9Crc fm 1⅛ (T) :4711:112 1:3511:464 + TrPDerby-G3 91 9 43 64½ 41½ 1hd 14½ Bailey J D L119 3.60 95- 08 *KittensJoy*119 4½ BrodwyView112nk SoverignHonor117hd 3wd bid,drew off 11
16Nov03- 7CD yl 1 1/16 (T) :234 :49 1:1421:463 Alw 67100NC 86 8 64¼ 54½ 31½ 21½ 1hd Perret C L120 2.20 71- 26 *Kitten's Joy*120hd Bogangles120nk *Grand Heritage*1205 4-5w,stiff drive 8
9Oct03- 5Bel fm 1⅛ [T] :4821:133 1:3841:504 Md Sp Wt 46k 81 1 42 32 52¼ 2hd 14½ Bridgmohan S X L120 *2.50 76- 24 *KittensJoy*120 4½ ThPnnyDrops120no KnnlUp115 1¾ Drew away when roused 10
24Sep03- 6Bel fst 1 ⊗ :23 :472 1:1341:384 Md Sp Wt 46k 74 2 31 41¼ 2hd 11 2hd Santos J A L119 *.95 72- 25 Big Booster119hd *Kitten's Joy*119½ *Gradepoint*119 9¼ Got through on rail 9
20Aug03- 4Sar fst 5f :212 :444 :572 Md Sp Wt 45k 62 3 4 48 56¾ 68 56¼ Luzzi M J 119 16.40 96- 06 Cat Buster119 2¾ Breakaway1192 Relato Del Gato119 1¼ Inside trip, no rally 9

Kona Gold

Own: Headley, Bruce, Molasky, Irwin and Andrew, et al

B. g. 8 (Mar)
Sire: Java Gold (Key to the Mint) $7,462
Dam: Double Sunrise (Slew o' Gold)
Br: Carlos Perez (Ky)
Tr: Headley Bruce

Life	30	14	7	2	$2,293,384	123	D.Fst	29	14	6	2	$2,261,074 123
2003	4	1	0	1	$95,680	109	Wet(327)	1	0	1	0	$32,310 109
2002	3	1	0	0	$128,340	113	Turf(261)	0	0	0	0	$0 –
	0	0	0	0	$0	–	Dst(T)(314)	0	0	0	0	$0 –

26Jly03- 6Dmr fst 6f :214 :44 :5531:074 3↑ BCrsbBCH-G2 103 5 7 95¾ 75½ 56 54¾ Solis A LB119 3.50 97- 07 BeusTown119 1½ CptlnSquire117nk Bluesthstndrd1172 No late bid outside 9
29Mar03- 8SA fst 6½f :212 :44 1:0821:144 4↑ PtrGrBCH-G2 99 6 6 64½ 53¼ 32 32½ Nakatani C S LB121 *1.50 96- 10 *Bluesthestandard*1152 *JoeyFrnco*116½ KonGold121 5½ 3wd into str,missed 2d 7
26Jan03- 7SA fst 6f :212 :434 :5521:074 4↑ PlsVrdsH-G2 102 3 4 54½ 33 33 65¾ Solis A LB124 *1.40 93- 10 Avnzdo116 4½ MellowFllow117½ Disturbingthpc120nk Rail move,no late bid 6
1Jan03- 7SA fst 5½f :212 :442 :5621:023 4↑ ElCnejoH-G3 109 1 7 74½ 64¾ 41½ 1nk Solis A LB123 *1.30 99- 09 Kona Gold123nk Radiata115¾ No Armistice116hd Rail bid,up late,game 7
26Oct02- 6AP fst 6f :212 :434 :56 1:084 3↑ BCSprint-G1 106 9 7 118½ 96¼ 64 43¼ Solis A L126 7.30 99 - Orientate126½ Thunderello123½ Crafty C. T.126 2¼ Bumped break 13
6Jly02- 8Hol fst 7f :222 :444 1:0831:21 3↑ TrBndBCH-G2 96 5 3 3nk 21 33 66¾ Solis A LB126 *.80 87- 11 *Disturbingthepeace*1133 D'wildcat115 2½ Mellow Fellow120no Dueled,tired 9
2Jun02- 8Hol fst 6f :212 :433 :56 1:083 3↑ LsAnglsH-G3 113 4 4 45 32 1½ 11¼ Solis A LB125 *.80 97- 13 Kona Gold125 1¼ No Armistice116nk Komax114 3½ Rid out,in hand late 6
17Nov01- 9Lrl fst 6f :212 :441 :5621:09 3↑ DeFrncsM-G1 106 7 3 46 36½ 43 44 Solis A L125 *2.10 90- 19 DelawareTownship1253 EarlyFlyer115¾ *XtrHet*117nk 4wd trip, no response 7
27Oct01- 6Bel fst 6f :222 :443 :5611:082 3↑ BCSprint-G1 108 4 5 116¾ 137½ 86 74 Solis A L126 *3.50 92- 03 Squirtle Squirt124½ Xtra Heat121nk Caller One126nk Inside trip, no rally 14
6Oct01- 8SA fst 6f :211 :432 :5531:073 3↑ AnTtlBCH-G1 115 6 1 43½ 45 21 22½ Solis A LB127 *.60 98- 12 SweptOverboard116 2½ KonGold1273 *ILoveSilver*1161 Led past 1/8,2nd best 6
22Jly01- 8Dmr fst 6f :22 :441 :5541:081 3↑ BCrsbBCH-G2 119 4 2 25 21½ 21½ 1¾ Solis A LB126 *.90 99- 07 KonaGold126¾ CllerOne124½ SweptOverbord1155 Wore down rival,gamely 4
1Apr01- 7SA fst 6½f :211 :44 1:0821:15 4↑ PtrGrBCH-G2 112 2 2 34½ 32 2hd 1nk Solis A LB126 *.30 93- 12 *Kona Gold*126nk [DH]Hollycombe114 [DH]Explicit1164 3wd bid,gamely 4
4Mar01- 7SA fst 7f :221 :444 1:0841:211 4↑ SnCrlosH-G1 112 7 3 41¼ 31 11 12 Solis A LB125 *.30e 99- 12 *KonaGold*1252 *BldeProspector*1132 GreyMemo115hd 4wd,cut inside,cleared 7
4Nov00- 6CD fst 6f :204 :432 :5511:073 3↑ BCSprnt-G1 114 10 5 52½ 22 21½ 1½ Solis A L126 *1.70 107 - *KonaGold*126½ HonestLady123½ BetOnSunshine1262 Stalked,4w,stiff drive 14
14Oct00- 3SA fst 6f :214 :442 :56 1:08 3↑ AnTtlBCH-G2 117 2 3 22½ 2hd 11½ 13 Solis A LB124 *.30 99- 14 *Kona Gold*1243 Regal Thunder117no Elaborate116 2½ Bid betwn, led,driving 4
29Jly00- 7Dmr fst 6f :22 :443 :5631:082 3↑ BCrsbBCH-G2 118 4 2 34 21½ 1hd 1¾ Solis A LB123 *.60e 98- 10 *Kona Gold*123¾ *Love That Red*1187 *Lexicon*1171 Brushed 1/16,gamely 6
8Apr00- 3SA fst 6½f :221 :441 1:0811:143 4↑ PtrGrBCH-G2 119 2 1 22½ 21½ 12½ 14½ Solis A LB122 *.70 95- 14 *Kona Gold*122 4½ Old Topper1162 Your Halo116½ Inside bid, drew off 4
4Mar00- 4SA gd 7f :232 :462 1:10 1:22 4↑ SnCrlosH-G2 109 5 2 1hd 1hd 1hd 2no Solis A LB122 *.40e 95- 10 Son of a Pistol117no *Kona Gold*122 2½ OldTopper116no Dueled btwn,gamely 6
29Jan00- 8SA fst 6f :214 :441 :5611:082 4↑ PlsVrdsH-G2 112 2 1 31½ 22 21 12 Solis A LB121 *1.10 97- 12 Kona Gold1212 *Big Jag*1213 Freespool115¾ Stalked,bid,led,clear 5
6Nov99- 6GP fst 6f :22 :44 :5541:074 3↑ BCSprint-G1 123 2 8 64¼ 52¾ 31½ 2½ Solis A L126 7.70 102 - Artax126½ *Kona Gold*126 2¾ Big Jag126½ Bump foe,rail trip 14
17Oct99- 7SA fst 6f :214 :44 :5541:074 3↑ AnTtlBCH-G2 115 5 3 22 21½ 2hd 22 Solis A LB120 *.80 99- 11 Lexicon1162 Kona Gold1206 Regal Thunder117½ Bid rail,2nd best 8
6Mar99- 7SA fst 7f :224 :451 1:0841:21 4↑ SnCrlosH-G2 115 3 1 2½ 2½ 2hd 2½ Solis A LB120 *1.10 99- 05 *Big Jag*118½ Kona Gold120½ *Dramatic Gold*1172 Bit tight 3/16 5
30Jan99- 7SA fst 6f :212 :434 :5541:08 4↑ PlsVrdsH-G2 115 1 4 11 11 11½ 2hd Solis A LB121 *.30 100- 07 *Big Jag*116hd Kona Gold1218 Swiss Yodeler114 1½ Drifted lane,caught 5
3Jan99- 8SA fst 5½f :213 :44 :5531:013 4↑ ElConejoH107k 115 2 5 2hd 1hd 11½ 12¼ Solis A LB119 *1.00 101- 11 Kona Gold119 2¼ *Big Jag*117 4½ *Mr. Doubledown*118½ Dueled,clearly best 6
7Nov98- 6CD fst 6f :21 :441 :5611:09 3↑ BCSprnt-G1 106 8 6 73 43 22½ 32 Solis A L126 16.80 96- 03 *Reraise*1242 Grand Slam124hd *Kona Gold*1261 Close up, lacked rally 14
17Oct98- 5SA fst 6f :212 :44 :56 1:082 3↑ AnTtlBCH-G3 99 1 6 72¾ 63¼ 53 52¼ Solis A LB115 *1.30 96- 09 Gold Land117¾ A. P. Assay116¾ Swiss Yodeler114no Tight 1/2,stdied lane 8
5Sep98- 9Dmr fst 6f :22 :444 :57 1:091 3↑ OC 62k/N$Y -N 108 2 7 1hd 11 13½ 16½ Solis A LB117 *.30 93- 13 Kona Gold117 6½ Venus Genus1171 Wrekin Pilot114hd Off slow, ridden out 8
15Aug98- 8Dmr fst 6f :214 :442 :5621:083 3↑ Alw 42000N$Y 112 5 2 2½ 2hd 13 17 Solis A LB119 *.40 96- 09 *KonaGold*1197 BrassAmbssdor119½ Robynhood1196 Drew off impressively 7
26Jly98-10Dmr fst 6½f :22 :442 1:0831:144 3↑ Md Sp Wt 37k 110 4 2 31 21 13½ 115 Solis A LB122 *.80e 97- 06 *Kona Gold*12215 Comic Trick118½ Belal118 1½ In hand late 10
31May98- 1Hol fst 6½f :22 :441 1:0831:144 3↑ Md Sp Wt 37k 88 5 6 52½ 42½ 43 27 McCarron C J LB122 5.30 85- 14 *Regal Thunder*1227 *Kona Gold*122hd Skibo Castle116 1¼ Up for place 7

Left Bank

Own: Tabor Michael B

Ch. h. 5 (May)
Sire: French Deputy (Deputy Minister) $30,126
Dam: Marshesseaux (Dr. Blum)
Br: John Youngblood & Fletcher Gray (Ky)
Tr: Pletcher Todd A

Life	24	14	2	0	$1,402,806	121	D.Fst	22	14	1	0	$1,394,606	121
2002	4	3	0	0	$626,146	121	Wet(377)	2	0	1	0	$8,200	93
2001	8	4	1	0	$524,200	118	Turf(288)	0	0	0	0	$0	–
	0	0	0	0	$0	–	Dst(T)(331)	0	0	0	0	$0	–

3Aug02-9Sar	fst	1⅛	:454 1:091 1:34 1:47	3↑WhitneyH-G1	121	1	22	23	21½	12½	11¼	Velazquez J R	L118 fb	3.60	104-07	Left Bank1181¼ Street Cry123no *Lido Palace*1191½	Speed outside, driving	6
4Jly02-8Bel	fst	7f	:214 :441 1:074 1:20	3↑TomFoolH-G2	121	4	3	31½	3nk	12½	16¼	Velazquez J R	L121 fb	*1.60	103-03	*LeftBnk*1216¼ *AffirmedSuccess*1205¾ SummerNot1131¼	Vigorous hand ride	6
27May02-9Bel	fst	1	:222 :443 1:083 1:331	3↑MtropltH-G1	97	4	1hd	2hd	54	512	513	Velazquez J R	L121 fb	*2.20	90 -	Swept Overboard1174¾ Aldebaran1151½ Crafty C.T.1164¼	Vied 4 wide, tired	10
11May02-6Bel	fst	6f	:222 :45 :57 1:091	3↑BoldRlrH-G3	109	4	3	3½	1hd	1½	11	Velazquez J R	L121 fb	*.35	92-13	Left Bank1211 Silky Sweep114½ SayFloridaSandy1169	Vied 3 wide, driving	4
24Nov01-8Aqu	fst	1	:232 :453 1:092 1:331	3↑CigarMiH-G1	118	6	2hd	2hd	1½	12½	13¼	Velazquez J R	L120 fb	*2.45	101-16	*Left Bank*1203¼ Graeme Hall118hd Red Bullet1181¾	When roused, driving	9
27Oct01-6Bel	fst	6f	:222 :443 :561 1:082	3↑BCSprint-G1	112	8	10	51¼	62¼	64	52½	Velazquez J R	L126 fb	8.90	93-03	Squirtle Squirt124½ Xtra Heat121nk Caller One126nk	3 wide, good finish	14
22Sep01-10Bel	fst	7f	:223 :442 1:081 1:203	3↑Vosburgh-G1	118	6	2	21½	22½	21½	1½	Velazquez J R	L126 fb	3.75	100-11	Left Bank126½ *Squirtle Squirt*1239¾ Big E E126nk	Game outside, driving	6
1Sep01-9Sar	fst	6½f	:213 :44 1:084 1:152	3↑ForegoH-G1	106	3	7	52¾	52¾	61¼	21¼	Velazquez J R	L115 b	4.60	97-03	*Delaware Township*1161¼ *Left Bank*115¾ Alannan1172¼	Tough trip, gamely	9
13Aug01-3Sar	fst	6f	:222 :444 :562 1:082	4↑Alw 55000N$Y	114	1	4	1hd	11½	13½	17¾	Velazquez J R	L118 b	*.70	102-05	Left Bank1187¾ *Rich Reward*118½ ValiantStyle1162¾	Stumbled start, inside	5
28May01-9Bel	my	1	:221 :45 1:102 1:37	3↑MtropltH-G1	93	5	4nk	31	5¾	63¼	87¾	Velazquez J R	L115 b	10.20	74-26	Exciting Story115¾ Peeping Tom1192 Alannan1182¾	Between rivals, tired	10
14Apr01-7Kee	fst	7f	:22 :443 1:092 1:221	3↑CmwlthBC-G2	70	6	7	31	54	79	713¾	Velazquez J R	L118 b	*.90	77-13	*Alannan*1184 Valiant Halory118¾ Liberty Gold1181¼	Drft in bmp start,tire	8
11Mar01-4GP	fst	6½f	:214 :434 1:082 1:151	4↑Alw 52000N$Y	114	6	1	31½	1½	13½	17¼	Velazquez J R	L122 b	*.70	102-11	Left Bank1227¼ Salty Glance1163¾ Ice Agent116nk	Drew away, handily	6
25Nov00-8Aqu	fst	1	:23 :454 1:10 1:343	3↑CigarMiH-G1	100	7	1hd	2hd	1½	31½	56¼	Velazquez J R	L116 b	8.80	89-17	*ElCorredor*1161¾ *PeepingTom*111nk *AffirmdSuccss*1203½	Bobbled start, vied	11
25Oct00-8Aqu	fst	1⅛	:464 1:10 1:342 1:471	DiscvryH-G3	103	3	1½	11	12½	12½	12¼	Velazquez J R	L119 b	*.30	101-13	Left Bank1192¼ Perfect Cat114hd Open Sesame1154	Pace, clear, driving	4
30Sep00-3Bel	fst	1 1/16	:233 :46 1:094 1:411	3↑Alw 57000C	109	3	11	1½	12½	110	113¼	Velazquez J R	L115 b	*1.40	91-13	*LeftBnk*11513¼ AbovetheCrowd117hd PhonthKing1194	Drew away, handily	5
26Aug00-8Sar	fst	7f	:214 :441 1:092 1:222	KngsBshp-G1	91	3	3	2hd	2hd	3nk	45½	Bailey J D	L116 b	1.90	87-09	MoreThnRedy1241½ VlintHlory1143¾ Millencolin121nk	Vied outside, tired	6
5Aug00-7Sar	fst	7f	:221 :45 1:091 1:214	3↑Alw 54000N$Y	106	5	4	1hd	11	12	12¾	Sellers S J	L116 b	*1.20	96-13	Left Bank1162¾ Laredo123¾ *Ican'thearyou*1193	Pace, clear, driving	9
28Jun00-8Bel	fst	7f	:233 :462 1:10 1:222	3↑Alw 45590N3X	107	2	3	1½	1½	15½	18¾	Velazquez J R	L117 b	*.65	91-16	*Left Bank*1178¾ Muqtarib123½ Momsmercedes1193¼	Pace, rail, ridden out	4
10Jun00-1Bel	fst	7f	:212 :453 1:102 1:23	3↑Alw 45000N2X	98	1	3	2hd	1hd	12	14¼	Velazquez J R	L115 b	11.10	88-13	*Left Bank*1154¼ *Trajectory*117nk Valiant Halory1172½	Vied inside, driving	9
21Feb00-10GP	fst	6½f	:22 :45 1:093 1:161	GrtNavigtr54k	65	6	7	33	32	712	715¼	Bailey J D	115 b	2.20	82-13	UltimateWarrior1195½ BLsAppeal119no RichCelebrtion1152	3 wide, faded	7
29Jan00-8GP	fst	1 1/16	:231 :463 1:104 1:442	Alw 34000N2X	67	9	43	32	32	79½	813¼	Bailey J D	119 b	*2.20	73-14	Un Fino Vino1191 Rupert Herd1222 Valiant Style119nk	3 wide, faltered	9
8Jan00-9GP	fst	7f	:221 :451 1:102 1:233	Alw 32000N2L	87	10	2	1hd	2hd	13	12¼	Bailey J D	122 b	3.40	82-19	Left Bank1222¼ *Polish Miner*122¾ Admiral Perry1223¾	Vied, drew clear	12
12Dec99-6Aqu	fst	6f ⊡	:231 :464 :59 1:113	Md Sp Wt 41k	84	5	8	21	21	21½	12¾	•Chavez J F	120 fb	*1.20	84-19	DH*Left Bank*120 DH*Binnifactor*1202¾ Alf1202	Hit gate start, wide	8
27Nov99-4Aqu	my	6f	:223 :454 :582 1:11	Md Sp Wt 41k	71	8	3	53	54	33½	23¼	Velazquez J R	119	2.90	80-16	FrenchFable1193¼ *LeftBank*1192¾ Justifiction1194¾	Off pace, no gain lane	8

Lemon Drop Kid

Own: Vance Jeanne G

B. c. 4 (May)
Sire: Kingmambo (Mr. Prospector) $300,000
Dam: Charming Lassie (Seattle Slew)
Br: W. S. Farish & W. S. Kilroy (Ky)
Tr: Schulhofer Flint S

Life	24	10	3	3	$3,245,370	118	D.Fst	18	9	1	2	$2,366,870	117
2000	9	5	0	1	$1,673,900	118	Wet(370)	6	1	2	1	$878,500	118
1999	9	3	1	1	$1,349,400	111	Turf(326)	0	0	0	0	$0	–
	0	0	0	0	$0	–	Dst(T)(356)	0	0	0	0	$0	–

4Nov00-10CD	fst	1¼	:472 1:12 1:36 2:003	3↑BCClasic-G1	108	6	41¼	41¼	43	54	55¼	Prado E S	L126 b	6.20	102 -	*Tiznow*122nk Giant's Causeway1223¼ *Captain Steve*122hd	Empty in drive	13
14Oct00-10Bel	fst	1¼	:464 1:101 1:342 1:591	3↑JkyClbGC-G1	105	4	63¼	63¾	54½	48½	59½	Prado E S	L126 b	*.95	88-09	AlberttheGret1226 Gnder1263 VisionndVers126no	Bumped start, steadied	7
16Sep00-8Bel	fst	1⅛	:461 1:104 1:364 1:502	3↑Woodward-G1	105	5	51¾	3½	1hd	1hd	1hd	Prado E S	L126 b	*.70	79-14	Lemon Drop Kid126hd Behrens126¾ Gander1263¾	4 wide, resolutely	5
6Aug00-9Sar	gd	1⅛	:463 1:101 1:35 1:481	3↑WhitneyH-G1	118	1	51¾	52½	41	11½	12	Prado E S	L123 b	*2.05	100 -	*Lemon Drop Kid*1232 Cat Thief1174¼ Behrens1221½	4 wide move, driving	6
4Jly00-9Bel	fst	1¼	:463 1:094 1:341 1:584	3↑SuburbnH-G2	117	2	21	21	1hd	12½	12½	Prado E S	L122 b	*.80	100-13	*Lemon Drop Kid*1222½ Behrens1224¼ Lager1131	Speed outside, driving	6
11Jun00-8Bel	fst	1⅛	:47 1:114 1:371 1:494	3↑BroklynH-G2	115	4	3½	31	2hd	12½	17¼	Prado E S	L120 b	2.10	82-29	*Lemon Drop Kid*1207¼ Lager114hd *Down theAisle*112hd	Speed 3 wide, driving	7
13May00-10Pim	fst	1 3/16	:472 1:111 1:361 1:543	3↑PimSpclH-G1	112	4	61¾	62¾	52¼	4¾	32	Prado E S	L120	4.10	90-18	*GoldenMissile*1162 PlesntBreeze111no *LmonDropKid*1204	3wd trip, willingly	8
15Apr00-3Aqu	fst	1⅛	:463 1:102 1:353 1:491	4↑Alw 60000C	98	5	44	44½	21½	1½	11½	•Santos J A	L122	*.65	91-10	DHLmonDrpKd122 DHEndfthRd1131½ GldStrDpty11616¼	4 wide first turn	5
18Mar00-10GP	sly	1⅛	:474 1:12 1:373 1:513	3↑WidenerH-G3	105	3	32½	31	3½	12	12	Santos J A	L119	*.60	79-21	D*LemonDropKid*1192 BlazingSword112hd WithAnticipation1112½	Duckd in	4
Disqualified and placed 4th																		
6Nov99-10GP	fst	1¼	:453 1:094 1:341 1:592	3↑BCClasic-G1	111	11	98¼	95¾	64½	53¼	64½	Santos J A	L122	6.30	109 -	CatThief1221¼ Budroyle126hd GoldenMissile1262	Swerve in start,bumped	14
10Oct99-6Bel	sly	1¼	:462 1:101 1:352 2:012	3↑JkyClbGC-G1	103	7	54½	52½	52½	56	59¼	Santos J A	L121	5.30	78-23	River Keen1263¼ Behrens126hd Almutawakel1264¼	Inside run second turn	8
28Aug99-9Sar	fst	1¼	:481 1:122 1:364 2:02	Travers-G1	110	6	31	3½	2hd	1hd	1¾	Santos J A	L126	3.65	98-13	LemonDropKid126¾ VisionndVerse1261¾ Menif1261¾	Close 3w, hard drive	8
8Aug99-8Sar	sly	1⅛	:474 1:12 1:364 1:492	JimDandy-G2	103	5	5¾	41	42¼	22½	25¼	Santos J A	L124	3.25	84-18	EctonPrk1165¼ *LmonDropKid*1242 BdgrGold1141¾	Came wide, game finish	7
5Jun99-9Bel	fst	1½	:473 1:12 2:014 2:274	Belmont-G1	109	6	83¾	84¾	41¼	1½	1hd	Santos J A	L126	29.75	105-06	LmonDropKid126hd VisonndVrs1261½ Chrsmtc1264¾	Swung wide 1/4pl,drv	12
23May99-8Bel	my	1⅛	:451 1:09 1:344 1:474	PeterPan-G2	103	6	41½	43	42	3½	32½	Santos J A	L120	3.60	89-27	BestofLuck1131 TrsurIslnd1141½ *LmonDropKid*1202	Tight quarters stretch	9
1May99-8CD	fst	1¼	:474 1:122 1:372 2:031	KyDerby-G1	100	19	167	178¼	158¼	1510	95½	Santos J A	L126	11.60e	83-14	*Charismatic*126nk Menifee126¾ Cat Thief1261¼	No threat,8wide,drive	19
10Apr99-9Kee	fst	1⅛	:47 1:104 1:36 1:483	BlueGras-G1	97	5	62¾	62¾	52¼	63¾	55¾	Velazquez J R	L123	4.30	86-19	Menifee1231¼ Cat Thief123½ Vicar1232½	In close 7/16 pole	8
27Feb99-3GP	fst	1 1/16	:234 :474 1:121 1:443	Alw 34000N2X	98	2	32	31½	2hd	11½	13½	Velazquez J R	L119	*.80	84-14	LmonDropKid1193½ Cryptodiplomcy1194 *Alnnn*119¾	Jumped tracks 1/16 pl	6
7Nov98-4CD	fst	1 1/16	:231 :463 1:113 1:44	BCJuven-G1	86	2	89	79½	63¼	64	56½	Velazquez J R	122	3.70	84-07	Answer Lively122hd Aly's Alley122¾ Cat Thief1225½	No late bid	13
10Oct98-9Bel	sly	1 1/16	:222 :451 1:10 1:424	Champagn-G1	88	3	43½	33	43	2½	22¾	Velazquez J R	122	2.55	82-14	ThGroomIsRd1222¾ LmnDrpKd1222 WkndMny122½	Wide move, game fin	7
20Sep98-9Bel	fst	1	:24 :473 1:121 1:372	Futurity-G1	92	5	41	31	21	22	1½	Velazquez J R	122	6.40	77-26	LemonDropKid122½ YesItsTrue1229 MedivilHro1225	Speed 3w, along late	5
21Aug98-4Sar	fst	7f	:224 :46 1:102 1:23	Alw 37000N2L	68	4	2	51¾	31½	34½	313½	Santos J A	116	2.75	76-13	*Menifee*1163 Cat Thief11610½ *Lemon Drop Kid*1164½	Wide trip, lugged in	5
1Aug98-3Sar	fst	6f	:223 :461 :582 1:104	Md Sp Wt 35k	88	2	5	31	2hd	2½	1nk	Santos J A	116	*1.00	87-12	Lemon Drop Kid116nk Arrested1169 Kipling116nk	3 wide move, driving	10
12Jly98-2Bel	fst	5½f	:224 :454 :574 1:041	Md Sp Wt 35k	89	9	7	42½	3½	21	2no	Santos J A	115	3.25	94-10	Treasure Island115no *Lemon Drop Kid*1151¾ Arrested1151	Gamely,outside	9

Macho Uno

Own: Stronach Stables

Gr/ro. c. 4 (Apr)
Sire: Holy Bull (Great Above) $15,000
Dam: Primal Force (Blushing Groom*Fr)
Br: Adena Springs (Ky)
Tr: Orseno Joseph F

Life	14	6	1	3	$1,851,803	116	D.Fst	14	6	1	3	$1,851,803	116
2002	6	2	0	1	$519,600	116	Wet(423)	0	0	0	0	$0	–
2001	4	1	1	1	$563,400	110	Turf(277)	0	0	0	0	$0	–
	0	0	0	0	$0	–	Dst(T)(335)	0	0	0	0	$0	–

26Oct02-10AP	fst	1¼	:463 1:101 1:352 2:011	3↑BCClasic-G1	101	6	75¾	75	63¼	46½	510¼	Stevens G L	L126 b	19.80	87 -	Volponi1266½ *Medagliad'Oro*121nk MilwaukeeBrew1263	Angled 5 wide turn	12
29Sep02-7AP	fst	1 3/16	:472 1:114 1:353 1:55	3↑WashPkH-G2	97	2	33	32	31½	45¼	57¼	Stevens G L	L119 fb	*.70	- -	*Tenpins*116nk Generous Rosi1151¼ *Bonus Pack*1154	No response	5
3Aug02-9Sar	fst	1⅛	:454 1:091 1:34 1:47	3↑WhitneyH-G1	116	5	612	611	510	43½	42¾	Day P	L118 b	4.60	101-07	Left Bank1181¼ Street Cry123no *Lido Palace*1191½	Good finish inside	6
6Jly02-10Bel	fst	1¼	:483 1:124 1:37 2:004	3↑SuburbnH-G2	111	5	53¼	42½	31	33	31¾	Stevens G L	L119 b	*1.10	88-10	E Dubai116¾ Lido Palace1191 Macho Uno1193¾	Game finish outside	7
1Jun02-13Suf	fst	1⅛	:462 1:103 1:37 1:502	3↑MassH-G2	110	2	43½	53	51¾	41½	11¾	Stevens G L	LB117 b	2.10	91-13	Macho Uno1171¾ Evening Attire114nk Include1201¼	Altrd crs 1/8, in hand	9
23Mar02-9GP	fst	170	:23 :461 1:11 1:41	4↑Alw 46000C	111	4	64	73¾	52¾	33	1½	Douglas R R	L120 b	*.70	96-17	*Macho Uno*120½ *Hail The Chief*1204¼ Proper Man1168¾	Up final strides	8
27Oct01-10Bel	fst	1¼	:47 1:111 1:354 2:003	3↑BCClasic-G1	110	7	94¾	93¾	63¾	43	44½	Stevens G L	L122 fb	19.50	86-12	Tiznow126no *Sakhee*1261¾ Albert the Great1262¾	Even finish	13
29Sep01-11Tdn	fst	1⅛	:471 1:104 1:353 1:483	OhioDrby-G2	104	4	52¾	54½	43½	21½	3¾	Stevens G L	L119 fb	*.20	102-11	*WesternPride*119½ Woodmoon113nk MchoUno1194	Brushed,bid,outfinishd	6
3Sep01-11Pha	fst	1⅛	:483 1:123 1:371 1:493	PaDerby-G3	104	5	42½	43½	42½	3nk	11½	Stevens G L	L116 fb	*.90	90-17	Macho Uno1161½ Unbridled Elaine119½ Touch Tone1226¾	Outside, easily	6
25Jly01-8Sar	fst	7f	:222 :442 1:083 1:214	3↑Alw 47000N3X	94	1	6	32½	32½	1hd	2no	Bailey J D	L116	*.95	96-05	Wicked Will116no *Macho Uno*1162 Country Only120½	Erratic deep stretch	7
4Nov00-8CD	fst	1 1/16	:232 :464 1:111 1:42	BCJuven-G1	99	4	42	51¼	41½	21	1no	Bailey J D	L122	6.30	100 -	Macho Uno122no *Point Given*1221½ *Street Cry*122½	Shied, ducked out wire	14
9Oct00-8WO	fst	1 1/16	:242 :48 1:13 1:44	GreyBC-G1	94	2	22	22	2½	12½	17	Bailey J D	L115	*.40	87-21	*Macho Uno*1157 *Indygo Shiner*1115¼ Stage Classic1136	Much the best	4
2Sep00-9Sar	fst	7f	:223 :461 1:111 1:242	Hopeful-G1	85	7	6	71½	61¼	21½	3nk	Prado E S	122	9.10	83-14	DHYonaguska122 DHCity Zip122nk *Macho Uno*1227¼	5 wide move, gamely	11
26Jly00-6Sar	fst	5½f	:224 :462 :58 1:042	Md Sp Wt 41k	84	7	4	2½	2½	1½	12¾	Prado E S	117	*.75	95-10	MchoUno1172¾ DevilsDomin1178¼ Mercenry1174½	Wrapped up under wire	7

McDynamo

Own: Moran Michael J

B. g. 8 (Apr)
Sire: Dynaformer (Roberto) $75,000
Dam: Rondonia (Monteverdi*Ire)
Br: Richard Fox, Nathan Fox & Richard Kaster (Ky)
Tr: Hendriks Sanna N

Life	25	11	6	1	$677,994	88	D.Fst	0	0	0	0	$0 –
2005	4	0	3	1	$65,425	74	Wet(291)	0	0	0	0	$0 –
2004	2	1	0	0	$101,250	–	Turf(343)	9	2	2	0	$44,890 88
	0	0	0	0	$0	–	Dst(T)(336)	0	0	0	0	$0 –

Date/Race	Cond	Dist	Time	Race	Fig	PP	Calls	Jockey	Wt	Odds	Figs	Finishers	Comment	Fld
1Oct05-3Med	fm	2½ (T) Hurdles	4:173	4↑SMCSRG-G2	74	6	332 230 215 23 25	Massey R	L158	*1.80	- -	PreemptiveStrike1525 McDynmo158¾ ThreCrt1449¾	Rallied, second best	7
17Jly05-3Cnl	gd	2¼ (T) Hurdles	4:304	3↑FrgsnMem-G3	–	4	56½ 53½ 35 34 25¼	Massey R	L154	*.50	- -	Paradise's Boss1465¼ McDynamo1542 Understood1542½	No threat	5
14May05-6PW	fm	3 (T) Hurdles	5:472	4↑Iroquois-G1	–	1	76 57 43 2½ 22¼	Thornton C	L158	-	- -	Sur LaTete1582¼ McDynamo15811½ BowStrada158½	Bid to lane,outfinishd	8
22Apr05-9Kee	fm	2½ (T) Hurdles	4:42	4↑RylChsHd-G1	–	6	22½ 2½ 1½ 21 34¾	Thornton C	L162	*1.50	- -	Hirapour1601¼ Sur La Tete1563½ McDynamo16215	Tracked,led,weakened	8
21Nov04-7Cam	fm	2¾ (T) Hurdles	5:043	4↑ColonlCp-G1	–	7	322 316 31½ 45½ 416¾	Thornton C	L156	-	- -	Hirapour1562¾ Preemptive Strike1565 SurLaTete1569	Early run, weakened	7
23Oct04-5FH	fm	2⅝ (T) Hurdles	5:064	4↑BrCupStp-G1	–	4	32½ 33 11½ 11½ 11½	Thornton C	L156	-	- -	McDynamo1561½ Hirapour156½ Sur La Tete15615½	Prevailed, right hand	7
16Nov03-6Cam	fm	*2¾ (T) Hurdles	5:052	4↑ColonlCp-G1	–	7	57½ 53¼ 12 12 14	Thornton C	L156	-	- -	McDynamo1564 Lord Zada15615½ Pelagos1561¼	Much the best	7
18Oct03-4FH	gd	*2⅝ (T) Hurdles	5:24	4↑(R)BrCupStp-G1	–	5	22 11½ 12 14 115¼	Thornton C	L156	-	- -	McDynamo15615¼ Pelagos156½ Mulahen1569½	Easily	7
25Apr03-8Kee	fm	*2½ (T) Hurdles	4:441	4↑RylChsHd-G1	–	1	76 76 66 11½ 17½	Thornton C	L158	4.60	- -	McDynmo1587½ ShmrockIsle1585 PrisethPrinc158nk	Drew off,hand urging	8
2Nov02-3Pmt	gd	*2⅜ (T) Hurdles	3:50	4↑(R)ChampHur-G1	–	3	45½ 57 44 2½ 11½	Brown Gus	L159	-	- -	McDynamo1591½ Gallant Turk151nk Mr Perkolater147hd	Strong drive	6
19Oct02-2FH	sf	*2½ (T) Hurdles	5:103	4↑(R)Foxbrook-G2	–	3	66½ 53 12 18 119	Brown Gus	L156	-	- -	McDynamo15619 Mr Perkolater1455¾ Trebizond15325	Ridden out	9
Previously trained by Neilson Sanna 2002(as of 6/6): (27 9 6 4 0.33)														
6Jun02-9Bel	fm	2½ (T) Hurdles	4:371	4↑(R)MedowBrk-G1	–	6	27 - - - -	Thornton C	L154	3.00	- -	Sharp Face1511 Anofferucantrefuse1544 Najjm1601½	Fell over 7th	10
17May02-3Pim	fm	*2⅛ (T) Hurdles	3:413	4↑(R)JAchsnHr-G1	–	6	21½ 21½ 22½ 21½ 22	Thornton C	L154	*.90	- -	Anofferucntrefus1512 McDynmo1545¾ EthicIActions1512½	Stalked, gamely	10
2May02-10CD	yl	*2 1/16 (T) Hurdles	3:48	4↑(R)HrdScufl-G1	–	3	2hd 11½ 11½ 11½ 12¼	Thornton C	L151	5.60	- -	McDynamo1512¼ Najjm16011½ Miles Ahead148½	Bmp,5th jump,driving	8
13Apr02-4Cnl	fm	*2¼ (T) Hurdles	4:163	4↑Alw 20000N$Y	–	7	215 25 12½ 14 17	McCarron M O	L152	-	- -	McDynamo1527 Comanche Raider1564½ Safe Viewing144½	Clear, driving	7
20Oct01-1FH	fm	*2⅛ (T) Hurdles	4:031	3↑Md Sp Wt 25k	–	6	33½ 22 2½ 11½ 14¼	Thornton C	L150	-	- -	McDynamo1504¼ Storm Touch1544½ Indy Fever1503¼	Vigorous hand ride	10
Previously trained by Moran Michael J 2001(as of 9/8): (57 12 10 8 0.21)														
8Sep01-4Bel	fm	1¼ [T]	:4931:133 1:3712:01	3↑Alw 46000N2X	88	6	22½ 21½ 31 53¼ 64	Day P	L120	24.75	82- 17	Megantic1161 Tiger Trap1162 Sestino120no	Attended pace, tired	7
12Aug01-7Sar	gd	1½ [T]	:4831:134 2:0332:283	3↑Alw 46000N2X	86	5	21½ 3½ 2½ 22 42¾	Day P	L120	11.10	90- 12	ZfonicsSong120nk LodgHill1202¼ Glyndbourn120nk	With pace, stubbornly	11
3Aug01-10Cnl	fm	1¼ (T)	:4831:12 1:3642:023	3↑Alw 26000N1X	83	1	21½ 21½ 1hd 1hd 11¼	Verge M E	L119	*1.30	86- 16	McDynmo1191¼ ForstSrvc1212¾ OrBoyChmp119nk	2wd bid 3/8,duel,drvng	8
9Jly01-9Cnl	fm	1¼ (T)	:4921:141 1:3842:024	3↑Alw 31928N1X	77	8	56½ 54 3½ 11 23	Verge M E	L119	2.90	82- 15	ProspectGreen1163 McDynamo1191 ResontoSqull1241½	Wide,left lead late	10
16Jun01-1Mth	fm	1⅛ (T)	:4741:114 1:3621:481	3↑Alw 37000N1X	77	6	95¾ 97¾ 94¼ 52¼ 22	Marquez C H Jr	L118	8.50	90- 04	Alotabull1182 McDynamo1181 Don't Box Me In1181	Outside, closed well	10
12Jly00-9Bel	fm	1¼ [T]	:5031:154 1:3932:022	3↑Alw 44000N1X	74	3	1½ 1½ 2hd 44 78	Prado E S	L117	13.60	71- 21	A. P. Delta1171½ Call It Off115no Knock Again1174	Set pace, tired	8
25Jun00-5Bel	fm	1⅜ [T]	:4831:131 1:3812:151	3↑Alw 44000N1X	73	2	66 56¼ 85¾ 96¼ 97	Davis R G	L115	12.60	72- 17	Hotspur115nk Go Go Juice121no Indy Shuffle115½	Had no rally	10
3Jun00-3Pim	fm	1½ (T)	:4941:164 2:0842:332	3↑Md Sp Wt 26k	71	7	84¾ 62¾ 43½ 2½ 1no	Johnston M T	116	4.30	74- 16	McDynamo116no Safari Racer122½ Celtic Reign1224¼	Wide, driving	10
13May00-3Pim	fm	1 1/16 (T)	:231 :471 1:1141:43	3↑Md Sp Wt 26k	50	3	11141010 89½ 812 78½	Castanon J L	115 f	4.40	80- 09	Northbridge1152½ Brass Off1221¾ Bold Crossing122hd	Slow start,bore in	11

Mineshaft

Own: Farish, William S., Elkins Jr., James A. and Webber, Jr., W. Temple

Dk. b or b. c. 4 (May)
Sire: A.P. Indy (Seattle Slew) $300,000
Dam: Prospectors Delite (Mr. Prospector)
Br: W. S. Farish, James Elkins & W. T. Webber Jr. (Ky)
Tr: Howard Neil J

Life	18	10	3	1	$2,283,402	118	D.Fst	10	8	2	0	$1,856,046 117
2003	9	7	2	0	$2,209,686	118	Wet(438)	1	1	0	0	$400,000 118
2002	9	3	1	1	$73,716	104	Turf(312)	7	1	1	1	$27,356 –
	0	0	0	0	$0	–	Dst(T)(392)	0	0	0	0	$0 –

Date/Race	Cond	Dist	Time	Race	Fig	PP	Calls	Jockey	Wt	Odds	Figs	Finishers	Comment	Fld
27Sep03-10Bel	fst	1¼	:4731:11 1:3442:001	3↑JkyClbGC-G1	114	3	32 2½ 11½ 15 14¼	Albarado R J	L126	*.40	93- 09	Mineshaft1264¼ Quest1262¾ Evening Attire1266½	When asked, ridden out	5
6Sep03-9Bel	fst	1⅛	:4721:111 1:3421:461	3↑Woodward-G1	117	2	43½ 42½ 32 12½ 14¼	Albarado R J	L126	*.30	99- 13	Mineshaft1264¼ Hold That Tiger1224¾ Puzzlement12611½	3 wide move, clear	5
5Jly03-9Bel	fst	1¼	:4831:123 1:37 2:012	3↑SuburbnH-G1	115	1	21½ 2½ 1hd 1½ 12¼	Albarado R J	L121	*.75	87- 13	Mineshaft1212¼ Volponi1214 Dollar Bill1152¼	Cruised when asked	8
14Jun03-10CD	fst	1⅛	:4641:102 1:35 1:472	3↑SFosterH-G1	117	10	52½ 53½ 11½ 11 2hd	Albarado R J	L123	*.70	101- 04	Perfect Drift115hd Mineshaft1239½ Aldebaran120½	Bmp start,outgamed	10
16May03-11Pim	sly	1 3/16	:4631:11 1:3621:56	4↑PimSpclH-G1	118	3	42 42¾ 21 11½ 13¾	Albarado R J	L121	*1.30	93- 23	Mineshaft1213¾ Western Pride116hd Judge's Case1131¾	Driving	9
25Apr03-9Kee	fst	1⅛	:4741:12 1:3621:482	4↑BenAli-G3	116	1	32½ 33 2hd 12½ 19	Albarado R J	L120	*.30	98- 02	Mineshaft1209 AmericanStyle1161½ Mettron1161¾	Hand urging,much best	4
2Mar03-9FG	fst	1⅛	:4741:121 1:3621:484	4↑NwOrlnsH-G2	116	6	21½ 22½ 1hd 11½ 13½	Albarado R J	L115	5.00	100- 17	Mineshaft1153½ Olmodavor1172½ Strive1141½	Took over, driving	11
9Feb03-9FG	fst	1 1/16	:24 :474 1:1241:433	4↑WirlwayH-G3	107	7	57¼ 45½ 53½ 42½ 22¼	Albarado R J	L116	2.70	89- 20	Balto Star1182¼ Mineshaft116¾ Bonapaw1153½	Up for second	8
19Jan03-9FG	fst	1 1/16	:241 :472 1:1131:434	4↑DiplmtWayH75k	103	2	32½ 31½ 1hd 11 1no	Albarado R J	116	*1.00	91- 13	Mineshaft116no Learned1161½ Discreet Hero1131	Shook free, all out	7
20Dec02-9FG	fst	140	:232 :47 1:12 1:384	3↑OC 40k/N2X-N	104	2	22 22 11 12½ 13½	Albarado R J	119	*.90	100- 09	Mineshaft1193½ Halo's Tiger1181¾ Majestic Thief118¾	Charged gate	9
27Nov02-9CD	fst	1	:224 :454 1:1041:361	3↑Alw 41720N1X	96	5	61½ 61¾ 51¼ 21½ 11½	Albarado R J	114	*2.70	86- 19	Mineshaft1141½ Revised Note114hd RoaroftheTiger1111½	Bmp start,5w,drvg	11
Previously trained by John Gosden														
13Sep02 Doncaster (GB)	gd	1 (T) Str	1:383	CPL Industries Chllnge Trophy Alw 18600 (Timeform rating: 109)			22	Hughes R	126	*1.35		Tikkun1232 Mineshaft1262½ Funfair Wane1232	Led to 200y out,chased winner home	8
15Aug02 Salisbury (GB)	gd	1 (T) Str	1:41	3↑Sovereign Stakes (Listed) Stk 64500 (Timeform rating: 108)			61¼	Hughes R	119	*3.00		Priors Lodge126¾ Bourgainville126hd Vicious Knight126no	Trailed,progress 3f out,bid 1f out,not good enough.Lahooq 9th	9
28Jly02 Maisons-Laffitte (Fr)	gd	*1⅛ (T) RH	1:542	Prix Daphnis-G3 Stk 65200 (Timeform rating: 109)			42	Hughes R	121	14.00		Bernebeau1211½ Guys And Dolls125½ Cielago121no	Rated rear,sharp bid to duel 1f out,bumped,gamely.Plcd 3rd via DQ	9
Placed third through disqualification														
20Jun02 Ascot (GB)	gd	1 (T) Str	1:41	Britannia Handicap Hcp 82500 (Timeform rating: 100)			106	Dettori L	133	8.00		Pentecost117nk Ghannam125nk Shot to Fame128nk	Rank at rear,prgrss into 5th ovr 1f out,wknd.Bit Of Luck(126)13th	31
1Jun02 Newmarket (GB)	gd	1¼ (T) Str	2:054	Fairway Stakes (Listed) Stk 35400 (Timeform rating: 107)			42½	Robinson P	124	1.60		Bustan124no Al Moulatham1242 Fraulein122½	Tracked leader,faded final furlong	5
5May02 Newmarket (GB)	gd	1 (T) Str	1:37	Hastings Maiden Stakes Maiden 15900 (Timeform rating: 105+)			1nk	Robinson P	126	4.50		Mineshaft126nk Hero's Journey126½ Izdiham1262½	Tracked leaders,led over 1f out,held gamely	17
20Apr02 Newbury (GB)	gd	1 (T) Str	1:384	Dubai Intl Airport Mdn S(Div2) Maiden 16200 (Timeform rating: 77)			45¾	Robinson P	126	16.00		Disco Volante1213 Scent of Victory1262 Welsh Diva121¾	Slowly away,trailed,progress 3f out,never catching leaders	14

Orientate

Own: Lewis Robert B. and Beverly J

Dk. b or b. c. 4 (Mar)
Sire: Mt. Livermore (Blushing Groom*Fr) $25,000
Dam: Dream Team (Cox's Ridge)
Br: Gainesway Thoroughbreds Ltd. (Ky)
Tr: Lukas D. W

Life	19	10	3	0	$1,716,950	116	D.Fst	14	7	3	0	$1,283,410 116
2002	10	6	1	0	$1,412,970	116	Wet(371)	2	2	0	0	$357,100 109
2001	7	4	1	0	$293,700	105	Turf(267)	3	1	0	0	$76,440 102
	0	0	0	0	$0	–	Dst(T)(335)	0	0	0	0	$0 –

Date/Race	Cond	Dist	Time	Race	Fig	PP	Calls	Jockey	Wt	Odds	Figs	Finishers	Comment	Fld
26Oct02-6AP	fst	6f	:212 :434 :56 1:084	3↑BCSprint-G1	114	10	2 41½ 21 21 1½	Bailey J D	L126	*2.70	102 -	Orientate126½ Thunderello123½ Crafty C. T.1262¼	4 wide, up late	13
1Sep02-9Sar	fst	6½f	:212 :441 1:09 1:153	3↑ForegoH-G1	116	3	4 2½ 1hd 13½ 12¼	Bailey J D	L122	*1.80	97- 15	Orientate1222¼ Aldebaran1153¾ Multiple Choice1142¼	Vied, clear, driving	8
11Aug02-9Sar	fst	6f	:224 :454 :5711:093	3↑AGVndbtH-G2	112	5	2 1½ 1½ 13½ 12	Bailey J D	L121	*.45	94- 17	Orientate1212 SyFloridSndy1153 MultipleChoice112½	Set pace, ridden out	6
13Jly02-9Crc	fst	6f	:212 :441 :5641:094	3↑SmilSprntH400k	115	7	2 1hd 1hd 11½ 16	Smith M E	L119	2.10	95- 07	Orientate1196 Echo Eddie117hd Crafty C. T.1171½	Pressured, drew away	7
29Jun02-9CD	fst	6½f	:22 :442 1:0811:142	3↑AristdsH-G3	115	2	2 1½ 1½ 12½ 14½	Albarado R J	L118	1.70	99- 08	Orientate1184½ Binthebest1141 No Armistice1161	Pace,inside,driving	5
27May02-8Hol	fm	1 (T)	:233 :461 1:0921:331	3↑ShoeBCM-G1	102	3	11½ 2½ 21½ 3½ 44	Solis A	LB124	14.90	94- 09	LadiesDin1243 Redttore1241 Spinelessjellyfish124no	Re-bid btwn,lost 3rd	10
3May02-6CD	gd	5f (T)	:214 :45 :571	3↑TurfSprt-G3	92	8	4 2½ 2½ 42 93¾	Day P	L119	*2.40	89- 07	Testify119hd Texas Glitter122nk Gone Fishin1161½	Exch brushes late,tire	10
14Apr02-8Kee	sly	7f	:213 :442 1:0911:212	3↑CmwlthBC-G2	109	2	2 13 13 12 11¼	Day P	L120	2.60	97- 12	Orientate1201¼ Aldebaran1184¼ Twilight Road118½	Fast pace,hand urg	7
2Feb02-9SA	fst	1⅛	:45 1:091 1:3431:471	Strub-G2	103	10	11 11 1hd 31½ 69¾	McCarron C J	LB119	12.30	90 -	MizzenMast1214 GiantGentlemn1174½ FncyAs119nk	Inside trip,weakened	11
12Jan02-8SA	fst	1 1/16	:221 :444 1:0841:411	SnFndoBC-G2	109	10	11 2½ 2hd 2½ 21	McCarron C J	LB120	8.00	97- 13	Western Pride1221 Orientate1203 Fancy As1202	Dueled, willingly	10
26Dec01-8SA	fm	1 (T)	:233 :473 1:1141:361	SirBeufort77k	94	3	13½ 13 11 11½ 12	McCarron C J	LB122	4.60	86- 13	Orientate1222 Sigfreto1221½ Blue Steller1222	Speed,inside,gamely	10
27Oct01-10Bel	fst	1¼	:47 1:111 1:3542:003	3↑BCClasic-G1	73	1	1½ 42 1314 1321 1229¾	Day P	L122	34.25	61- 12	Tiznow126no Sakhee1261¾ Albert the Great1262¾	Dueled inside, tired	13
6Oct01-9Hoo	gd	1 1/16	:221 :46 1:1021:421	IndianaDby314k	105	11	12 11 11½ 13 13¼	Albarado R J	LB115	15.30	98- 20	Orientate1153¼ SaratogGmes121no TrionGeorgi1242¼	Speed to inside, drvg	11
25Aug01-9Sar	fst	7f	:22 :441 1:0831:214	KngsBshp-G1	65	1	8 52¼ 54½ 712 719	Guidry M	L115	9.10	77- 08	Squirtle Squirt1213¼ Illusioned1191¼ City Zip1245	In tight backstretch	8

11Aug01-8Sar fst 6f :214 :443 :5641:093 3↑ Alw 43000N1x 104 8 2 2hd 12½ 17 13¾ Bailey J D L118 *.65 96-08 Oriente118 3¾ MountIntrpid120 3½ EvningAttir116 1¼ Vied outside, driving 10
28Jly01-2Sar fst 6f :222 :452 :5711:092 3↑ Md Sp Wt 41k 103 7 1 12 12 17 16½ Bailey J D L118 *.40 97-06 *Orientate*118 6½ Cherokee Beau118hd Strandhill118 1 Set pace, ridden out 8
24Jun01-5Hol fst 7f :22 :444 1:0911:211 3↑ Md Sp Wt 42k 104 10 2 11 12 11 21 Nakatani C S LB117 3.80 92-15 *Kela*117 1 *Orientate*117 7½ High and Low Vixen117 3½ Speed,angld in,2d best 10
31Dec00-1SA fst 1 1/16 :23 :47 1:12 1:444 Md Sp Wt 48k 64 2 43½ 33½ 52¼ 43½ 47½ Espinoza V LB120 *1.10 71-21 Indy Lead120 2½ Thunder Bull120 4 Thunder Ghost120 1 Saved ground to 1/4 6
18Nov00-6Hol fst 7f :224 :462 1:1111:234 Md Sp Wt 37k 84 6 4 1hd 2hd 21½ 23 Espinoza V LB120 4.90 77-19 Millennium Wind120 3 Orientate120 2½ Decision120 8 Vied btwn,2nd best 8

Ouija Board (GB)

Own: Lord Derby

B. f. 4 (Mar)
Sire: Cape Cross*Ire (Green Desert) $34,430
Dam: Selection Board*GB (Welsh Pageant*Fr)
Br: Stanley Estate and Stud Co (GB)
Tr: Dunlop Edward A

Life	10	6	0	3	$1,713,013	108	D.Fst	0	0	0	0	$0	-
2005	2	1	0	0	$41,245	-	Wet(280*)	0	0	0	0	$0	-
2004	5	4	0	1	$1,659,958	108	Turf(267*)	10	6	0	3	$1,713,013	108
	0	0	0	0	$0	-	Dst(T)(287)	1	0	0	1	$3,728	-

24Sep05 Newmarket (GB) gd 1½(T) 2:322 3↑ (F)Princess Royal John Doyle S.-G3 12½ Dettori L 126 *1.35 Ouija Board126 2½ Briolette118 1 Asawer118no 13
Timeform rating: 114+ Stk 71100 *Midpack,progress to lead over 2-1/2f out,clear 1-1/2f out,driving*
15Jun05 York (GB) gf 1 5/16(T) LH 2:08 4↑ Prince of Wales's Stks(1 1/4m,88y)-G1 729½ Spencer J P 123 3.50 *Azamour*126 1½ Ace126 5 Elvstroem126 4 8
Stk 632000 *Trailed,wknd 3f out,not persevered with.NorseDancer6th*
30Oct04-6LS yl 1⅜(T) :5221:182 1:4212:181 3↑(F)BCF&MTrf-G1 108 5 55½ 43½ 43 2hd 11½ Fallon K L118 *.90 98-07 Ouija Board118 1½ *Film Maker*123nk Wonder Again123 2¾ Drew off late 12
3Oct04 Longchamp (Fr) gd *1½(T) RH 2:25 3↑ Prix de l'Arc de Triomphe-G1 31½ Murtagh J P 120 9.00 *Bago*123½ Cherry Mix123 1 *Ouija Board*120 2 19
Timeform rating: 124+ Stk 1986000 *Rated in 14th,lacked room 2f out,sharp late run into 3rd*
18Jly04 Curragh (Ire) gf 1½(T) RH 2:281 (F)Irish Oaks-G1 11 Fallon K 126 *.57 Ouija Board126 1 Punctilious126¾ Hazarista126 7 7
Timeform rating: 116+ Stk 498000 *Dwelt,rated in 5th,led 1-1/2f out,handily.AllTooBeautiful4th*
4Jun04 Epsom (GB) gd 1½(T) LH 2:352 (F)English Oaks-G1 17 Fallon K 126 3.50 *Ouija Board*126 7 All Too Beautiful126 3½ *Punctilious*126 1½ 7
Timeform rating: 124 Stk 644000 *Dwelt,rated in 6th,led 2f out,surged clear.Necklace4th*
2May04 Newmarket (GB) gd 1¼(T) Str 2:024 (F)Pretty Polly Stakes (Listed) 16 Fallon K 120 *2.00 *Ouija Board*120 6 Sahool120½ *Rave Reviews*120 1¼ 9
Timeform rating: 116+ Stk 53300 *Rated in 5th,led over 1f out,ridden clear*
1Nov03 Newmarket (GB) gs 1 (T) Str 1:382 (F)EBF Montrose Stakes (Listed) 34 Spencer J P 120 *2.75 Spotlight120 4 St Francis Wood121no *Ouija Board*120 1 12
Timeform rating: 91 Stk 33900 *Dwelt,soon mid-pack,2nd 1f out,lost 2nd on line*
21Oct03 Yarmouth (GB) gf 7f (T) Str 1:28 EBF Novice Stakes 14 Spencer J P 119 *1.00 Ouija Board119 4 *Rydal*124 2 Naaddey128 2 6
Timeform rating: 90+ Alw 9600 *Rated in 5th,led and drifted left over 1f out,drew clear*
3Oct03 Newmarket (GB) gf 7f (T) Str 1:253 Beech House Stud EBF Mdn Stks 31½ Ahern E 121 20.00 *Secret Charm*121nk Gravardlax126 1¼ *Ouija Board*121 1½ 23
Timeform rating: 81+ Maiden 18200 *Never far away,led over 1f out,headed 100y out*

Perfect Sting

Own: Stronach Stables

B. m. 5 (Apr)
Sire: Red Ransom (Roberto) $43,038
Dam: Valid Victress (Valid Appeal)
Br: Adena Springs (Ky)
Tr: Orseno Joseph F

Life	21	14	3	0	$2,202,042	106	D.Fst	2	1	0	0	$38,369	79
2001	2	1	0	0	$120,000	106	Wet(328)	0	0	0	0	$0	-
2000	6	5	1	0	$1,367,000	105	Turf(335)	19	13	3	0	$2,163,673	106
	0	0	0	0	$0	-	Dst(T)(331)	0	0	0	0	$0	-

9Jun01-9Bel fm 1¼ [T] :4841:132 1:3712:003 3↑ ManhttnH-G1 94 2 54½ 71¾ 73¾ 59¼ 67¼ McCarron C J L115 2.30 81-10 Forbidden Apple117¾ *King Cugat*120½ Tijiyr115 2 Bumped second turn 10
14Apr01-11Hia fm 1⅛ (T) 1:47 3↑(F)BlkHelnH-G2 106 4 410 416 313 2hd 12 Coa E M L122 *.30e 97-08 PerfectSting122 2 *ClerlyQun*111 1 SpookExprss115 9½ Edged away late, drvg 5
4Nov00-7CD fm 1⅜ (T) :4821:122 1:3622:13 3↑(F)BCF&MTrf-G1 105 8 84¼ 95¼ 52¼ 11½ 1¾ Bailey J D L123 5.00 100 - *Perfect Sting*123¾ *Tout Charmant*123¾ Catella123 1½ Drifted, steady urging 14
13Oct00-8Kee fm 1 3/16 (T) :4821:132 1:3741:543 3↑(F)Galaxy-G3 101 4 43 41¼ 21½ 21 21¼ Bailey J D L121 *.50 95-07 Tout Charmant117 1¼ *Perfect Sting*121 2½ License Fee119 4 4wide,2ndbest 7
4Sep00-10Sar fm 1⅛ (T) :4741:112 1:3421:47 3↑(F)DianaH-G2 102 6 63½ 61½ 51¾ 1hd 1¾ Bailey J D L123 *.65 94-11 Perfect Sting123¾ License Fee116½ Hello Soso113 1 Quick 3 wide move 7
15Jly00-8Bel sf 1¼ [T] :5021:143 1:39 2:051 3↑(F)NewYorkH-G2 101 2 63¼ 41½ 21½ 21½ 1hd Bailey J D L122 *1.15 65-35 *PerfectSting*122hd *SnowPolin*116 4½ PicoTeneriff115 1¼ Determined outside 8
10Jun00-5Bel gd 1 (T) :241 :48 1:1131:342 3↑(F)JsAGmBCH-G3 101 4 51¼ 52½ 61¼ 5½ 1no Bailey J D L121 *.65 86-16 *Perfect Sting*121no Ronda116 2 Snow Polina116no Resolutely outside 7
7May00-7Aqu fm 1 1/16 (T) :233 :481 1:1211:421 3↑(F)BeaugayH-G3 101 4 55 32½ 31 1hd 1½ Bailey J D L119 *1.00 98-08 *Perfect Sting*119½ License Fee114 1½ Fictitious114 3¼ 3 wide move, driving 7
6Nov99-7GP gd 1⅜ (T) :4911:14 1:3832:134 3↑(F)BCF&MTrf-G1 100 10 52¼ 53½ 52¼ 66 62½ Day P L119 4.00 84-09 Soaring Softly123¾ *Coretta*123hd Zomaradah123hd Lacked late response 14
9Oct99-8Kee yl 1⅛ (T) :4811:132 1:3821:503 (F)QEIICup-G1 103 7 63¼ 41½ 3nk 21 12 Day P L121 *1.60 76-22 PerfctSting121 2 ToutChrmnt121 2 WnnbGrnd121 2½ 7wide lane,hand urged 9
12Sep99-9Bel sf 1⅛ [T] :4731:121 1:37 1:492 (F)GrdCyBCH-G1 101 2 66 53½ 64½ 2½ 12¼ Day P L120 3.30 81-19 *Perfect Sting*120 2¼ Nordican Inch116nk Ronda121½ Came wide, clear late 12
2Aug99-8Sar fm 1 1/16 (T) :23 :461 1:0941:40 (F)LakeGrgH-G3 99 3 44 44 33½ 23 2½ Day P L122 2.95 95-04 Nani Rose122½ *Perfect Sting*122¾ Intrigued122 4 Came wide,game finish 8
4Jly99-8Mth gd 1 1/16 (T) :241 :482 1:12 1:432 (F)CaptivMiss50k 93 5 63¾ 85¼ 64½ 31 12 Day P L121 *.30 84-14 Perfect Sting121 2 Fresh Aire112no Boca Juniors116 4 Much the best 9
6Jun99-8Bel fm 1⅛ [T] :4731:111 1:35 1:464 (F)SandsPnt-G3 95 6 22½ 21½ 22½ 1hd 11½ Day P L118 2.70 94-06 *PerfectSting*118 1½ PicoTeneriff121 1¼ *Illiquidity*113½ Drew clear, ridden out 6
22May99-7Bel gd 1⅛ [T] :4911:131 1:3731:492 3↑(F)Alw 47000N3x 94 4 21½ 21½ 21½ 1hd 1hd Day P L113 *1.75 81-17 *PerfectSting*113hd Terrevign118 3 HighlndStrik118no Dug in gamely,driving 8
Previously trained by Byrne Patrick B 1999(as of 4/15): (23 4 6 2 0.17)
15Apr99-8Kee yl 1⅛ (T) :4711:123 1:3711:493 (F)Palisades111k 86 9 4¾ 31 32½ 33½ 51½ Day P L115 2.20 79-19 WildHertDncing115nk *RivierColleen*115¾ Suffrgtt115no Forced out 1st turn 9
2Apr99-8Kee fm 1 (T) :231 :47 1:1141:351 (F)Applachian111k 90 3 42½ 32 3½ 21 21 Day P L114 *.80 95-03 Tres Coronas114 1 Perfect Sting114 2½ Seducer119¾ Lacked late bid 9
7Mar99-3GP fm 1 (T) :233 :464 1:1041:341 (F)Alw 34000N2x 91 2 33½ 44 41½ 11½ 12¼ Day P L118 *.50 - - PerfectSting118 2¼ MysteryPlace118 6¼ Valarone118¾ Svd grnd, ridden out 7
29Oct98-8Kee fm 1 1/16 (T) :224 :463 1:1141:433 (F)GreenRiver71k 90 4 54¼ 43 32 1½ 13½ Day P L113 3.10 85-15 *Perfect Sting*113 3½ On a Soapbox116 1½ DanceDiane121 1 3 wide, bid, driving 9
11Oct98-8Kee fst 1 1/16 :224 :454 1:1041:421 (F)Alcibiad-G2 79 10 86¾ 711 76¾ 46 410½ Day P L118 9.30 86 - *Silverbulletdy*118 2½ ExtendedAppluse118 7 GrndDed118 1 Bid, flattened out 11
26Sep98-3TP fst 6f :221 :463 :5921:12 (F)Md Sp Wt 24k 68 7 7 84¼ 21 11 16 Day P L121 *.90 81-13 PrfctSting121 6 RockyPoint121 7 TropiclRnbow121nk Inside turn, drew off 12

Point Given

Own: The Thoroughbred Corporation

Ch. c. 3 (Mar)
Sire: Thunder Gulch (Gulch) $40,000
Dam: Turko's Turn (Turkoman)
Br: The Thoroughbred Corporation (Ky)
Tr: Baffert Bob

Life	13	9	3	0	$3,968,500	117	D.Fst	12	8	3	0	$3,518,500	117
2001	7	6	0	0	$3,350,000	117	Wet(330)	1	1	0	0	$450,000	110
2000	6	3	3	0	$618,500	101	Turf(293)	0	0	0	0	$0	-
	0	0	0	0	$0	-	Dst(T)(284)	0	0	0	0	$0	-

25Aug01-10Sar fst 1¼ :4731:111 1:3542:012 Travers-G1 117 7 31½ 3½ 2½ 1hd 13½ Stevens G L L126 br *.65 98-02 Point Given126 3½ E Dubai126 1½ *Dollar Bill*126¾ 3 wide trip, driving 9
5Aug01-11Mth fst 1⅛ :4641:111 1:3621:493 HsklInvH-G1 106 6 56¾ 55½ 31½ 31 1½ Stevens G L L124 br *.30 88-10 *PointGiven*124½ TouchTone115no BurningRom119¾ Outside,lugged in,drvg 6
9Jun01-10Bel fst 1½ :48 1:113 2:0032:262 Belmont-G1 114 9 31 1hd 12 17 112¼ Stevens G L L126 b *1.35 107-02 *Point Given*126 12¼ A P Valentine126¾ Monarchos126 1 5 wide, strong urging 9
19May01-11Pim fst 1 3/16 :4711:114 1:3621:552 Preaknes-G1 111 11 910 67½ 3nk 1½ 12¼ Stevens G L L126 b *2.30 94-11 *Point Given*126 2¼ A P Valentine126nk *Congaree*126 1½ Brk slw,5wd,lug in str 11
5May01-8CD fst 1¼ :4441:091 1:35 1:594 KyDerby-G1 99 17 76¼ 73¾ 21½ 44½ 511¼ Stevens G L L126 b *1.80 92 - Monarchos126 4¾ Invisible Ink126no Congaree126 4 Broke in bmp,flattened 17
7Apr01-5SA wf 1⅛ :4621:104 1:3521:473 SADerby-G1 110 1 21 21 11 12½ 15¼ Stevens G L LB122 b *.70 97-08 Point Given122 5¼ CraftyC.T.122 3 ILoveSilver122 2¼ Led in hand,ridden out 6
17Mar01-7SA fst 1 1/16 :223 :461 1:1021:414 SnFelipe-G2 105 8 55 54 1hd 12 12¼ Stevens G L LB122 b *.40 95-13 *PointGiven*122 2¼ ILoveSilver116 1½ JamicnRum119 7 5wd move, led, cleared 8
16Dec00-4Hol fst 1 1/16 :23 :464 1:1041:421 HolFut-G1 101 4 45 3½ 3½ 2hd 11 Stevens G L LB121 b *.30 89-15 *PointGiven*121 1 *MillnniumWind*121 7 GoldnTickt121 5 3wd,lugged in bit,best 4
4Nov00-8CD fst 1 1/16 :232 :464 1:1111:42 BCJuven-G1 99 1 106½ 127 1410 67 2no Stevens G L L122 b 8.10 100 - Macho Uno122no *Point Given*122 1½ *Street Cry*122½ 10w strtch,closed fast 14
14Oct00-9Bel fst 1 1/16 :223 :45 1:0921:412 Champagn-G1 95 2 41 1hd 3nk 2hd 21¾ Desormeaux K J L122 b 4.60 88-09 A P Valentine122 1¾ Point Given122¾ Yonaguska122 1 Vied inside, gamely 10
16Sep00-12TP fst 1 1/16 :221 :453 1:12 1:47 KyCupJuv-G3 81 7 89½ 67½ 53 13 13½ Sellers S J L114 b 3.30 68-23 Point Given114 3½ Holiday Thunder114 4 *The Goo*116½ Broke a bit in air 11
26Aug00-7Dmr fst 7f :223 :452 1:1021:232 Md Sp Wt 47k 93 1 6 4¾ 1½ 11 12 Espinoza V LB118 b *1.20 88-10 *PointGiven*118 2 HighandLowVixen118 4 Qwqeb118 8 Inside duel,clear,dvng 7
12Aug00-6Dmr fst 5½f :221 :451 :5721:04 Md Sp Wt 47k 74 9 6 109¾ 99½ 79¾ 25½ Take Y LB118 b 19.00 86-17 HighCascade118 5½ *PointGiven*118 2½ WestwrdAngel118no 4wd turn,late 2nd 11

Pompeyo (Chi)

Own: Augustin Stable

Dk. b or b. g. 7 (Sep)
Sire: Nureyev Dancer (Nureyev)
Dam: Pouliche*Chi (Domineau)
Br: Haras Santa Amelia (Chi)
Tr: Neilson Sanna

Life	33	11	6	5	$528,325	95	D.Fst	0	0	0	0	$0 –
2001	2	2	0	0	$141,525	–	Wet(320*)	2	0	1	0	$28,924 68
2000	9	5	2	2	$211,755	–	Turf(429)	20	4	3	3	$146,121 95
	0	0	0	0	$0	–	Dst(T)(480)	2	1	0	0	$5,661 –

27Apr01- 7Kee fm *2½ (T)Hurdles 4:342 4↑RylChsHd-G1 – 3 64 53½ 2½ 13½ 13 Brown Gus L158 2.90 - - Pompeyo1583 All Gong1581 Rand1581¼ 5w,drew off,steady drv 10
31Mar01- 2Cam fm *2 (T)Hurdles 4:121 4↑(R)WdwrdKrC-G3 – 6 44½ 33½ 1hd 13 16½ Brown Gus L160 - - - Pompeyo1606½ Flasher154¾ Emancipate1492¾ Handily 6
9Dec00- 1Crc fm *2¼ (T)Hurdles 4:084 4↑TrPStplH-G2 – 3 55½ 42 2hd 11 11 Brown Gus L158 *.80 - - Pompeyo1581 Clearance Code14013 War Talk142¾ Driving 6
19Nov00- 3Cam fm *2¼ (T)Hurdles 4:28 4↑Hcp 20000C – 2 34½ 31½ 21 1½ 13½ Brown Gus L158 - - - Pompeyo1583½ Allan Prell14610¾ Poor Porgy14410 Driving 7
28Oct00- 2FH fm *2½ (T)Hurdles 4:454 4↑(R)Foxbrook-G2 – 5 38½ 32 2hd 21 22¼ Brown Gus L156 - - - Yellowroad1592¼ Pompeyo1565 Flasher156no Bid, weakened 7
6Oct00- 2Cnl fm *2¼ (T)Hurdles 3:591 4↑FrgsnMHH-G2 – 7 819 513 41¾ 37 38½ Brown Gus L148 *1.50 - - Spring Salute1427¾ Al Skywalker140¾ Pompeyo1485½ Wide, flattened out 9
8Jun00- 9Bel sf 2½ (T)Hurdles 4:414 4↑(R)MedowBrk-G1 – 2 105¾1016 83¼ 42½ 32¾ Brown Gus L152 *1.90 - - Yellowrod1521 Indispensble1501¾ Pompeyo1521¾ Awkward brk, wide trip 12
18May00- 4Pim fm *2⅛ (T)Hurdles 3:522 4↑(R)JAchsnHr-G1 – 4 65 67½ 1hd 11 11¾ Brown Gus L150 *.90 - - Pompeyo1501¾ Banjo Man1483½ Shahrahere148½ Wide trip,mild drive 7
4May00-10CD gd *2 1/16 (T)Hurdles 3:451 4↑(R)HrdScufl-G1 – 7 86 74¼ 64 2hd 12¼ Brown Gus L148 8.80 - - Pompeyo1482¼ Shahrahere1481 Turkish Corner1426 5wide, driving,clear 9
15Apr00- 3Cnl yl *2¼ (T)Hurdles 4:202 4↑Md Sp Wt 14k – 5 96½ 74 33 2½ 110¾ Brown Gus L154 - - - Pompeyo15410¾ Ponsonby1549 El Campeon14917¼ Drew off 12
25Mar00- 1Aik fm *2⅛ (T)Hurdles 4:19 4↑Md Sp Wt 14k – 3 15 18 18 2hd 23½ Brown Gus L154 - - - Jack Flash1543½ Pompeyo1544 Banjo Man1553½ Bobbled, 2nd best 7
11Nov99- 8Lrl yl 1½ (T) :5211:182 2:0922:332 3↑LrlTrfCp-G3 79 6 1111116¼ 96¾ 912 911¼ Rice D S L115 27.70 54- 35 John's Call1173¼ Brightwood115nk Pay Zone115½ Rank early,lost ground 12
Previously trained by Drysdale Neil 1999(as of 5/29): (124 21 19 22 0.17)
29May99- 9CD fm 1⅜ (T) :4721:12 1:3642:14 3↑LouisvillH112k 70 6 69½ 79½ 77½ 811 718 Espinoza V L112 11.70 77- 08 Chorwon114no Buff1141¼ Keats and Yeats110½ Not a factor 8
25Apr99- 9Hol fm 1¼ (T) :4921:132 1:37 2:003 4↑Alw 65000N$MY 95 3 75½ 73¾ 64¼ 52½ 31½ Espinoza V LB114 18.90 91- 09 SpecialQuest115½ StrPerformnce1161 Pompeyo114nk Pulled early,rallied 7
11Apr99- 7SA wf 1⅛ :4631:10 1:3441:473 4↑SnBrdnoH-G2 68 1 32½ 43 44½ 410 426½ Desormeaux K J LB116 10.10 70- 14 Classic Cat1223½ Budroyale1198 Klinsman11515 Saved ground, gave way 4
15Feb99- 8SA fm 1½ (T) :50 1:144 2:0332:28 4↑SLsObspH-G2 80 6 54 53 52½ 78½ 714½ Desormeaux K J LB116 20.00 66- 21 Kessem Power115¾ Brave Act1211¾ Lazy Lode1204½ Hugged rail, no rally 7
12Dec98- 5Hol fm 1½ (T) :5011:16 2:0432:281 3↑HolTrfCp-G1 79 3 84¾ 84½ 86½ 1010 1016½ Solis A LB126 15.50 59- 20 Lazy Lode1261½ Yagli1264 Ferrari126½ 5 wide into lane 10
25Nov98- 2Hol fm 1¼ (T) :5011:16 1:4012:032 3↑OC 100k/N$Y-N 95 4 32½ 33 31½ 3nk 1hd Desormeaux K J LB116 *2.10 80- 19 Pompeyo116hd Belgravia116hd Silverani1184 Threw head start,game 5
Previously trained by J Allende
30Mar98 Club Hippico (Chi) fm *1⅜ (T) RH 2:104 Clasico Luis Cousino-G3 Stk 15500 36 Munoz L 123 2.40 Prince Albert II1234½ Tono1231½ Pompeyo123133¾ 4
16Mar98 Club Hippico (Chi) fm *1¼ (T) RH 1:59 3↑ Clasico Verano-Arturo Cousino-G2 Stk 21400 11½ Munoz L 123 - Pompeyo1231½ Sahumerio132no Jaque Mate13226¾ 4
26Feb98 Club Hippico (Chi) fm *1⅛ (T) RH 1:47 Clasico Raul Ovalle U (Listed) Stk 12500 35 Munoz L 123 3.10 Prince Albert II1233¼ Nazarita1171¾ Pompeyo1233½ 5
1Feb98 Valparaiso (Chi) fm *1½ (T) LH 2:26 Chilean Derby-G1 Stk 103900 1115¼ Munoz L 128 4.50 Sidon1284 Mash One1282 India Divina1211¼ Nazarita 5th,As de Copas 6th 16
20Dec97 Hipodromo (Chi) gd *1⅜ LH 2:19 Chilean St Leger-G1 Stk 115600 21 Munoz L 123 11.70 FontnellBorghese1171 Pompyo123nk ApoloDordo1231 Puerto Madero 4th 12
9Nov97 Club Hippico (Chi) fm *1½ (T) RH 2:241 Clasico El Ensayo-G1 Stk 120300 1½ Barrera H 123 25.30 Pmp123½ Nrt117no Rt123no Santona 8th,Mash One 9th,Prince Albert II 13t 15
28Sep97 Club Hippico (Chi) fm *1¼ (T) RH 2:01 Gr Prmio Nacional Ricardo Lyon-G1 Stk 45400 42¾ Munoz L 123 17.60 Nazarita1171½ Simona1171½ Prince Albert123no 14
15Sep97 Club Hippico (Chi) fm *1⅛ (T) RH 1:481 - Alw 7300 21¾ Munoz L 119 6.10 Riquet1191¾ Pompeyo119½ Prince Albert II128 12
3Sep97 Club Hippico (Chi) fm *1 (T) RH 1:394 Clasico Ignacio Urrutia (Lstd) Stk 11000 59¼ Vera P 123 - Henares1234 MrinoAltivo123no Victorino1233¾ Pompeyo 5th,Fierrazo 10th 12
25Aug97 Club Hippico (Chi) fm *1 (T) RH 1:36 - Alw 0 2 jockey u 123 - Prince Albert II123 Pompeyo123 2
6Aug97 Club Hippico (Chi) sf *6f (T) RH Allowance Race Alw 0 9 NO RIDER 117 - 0
19May97 Club Hippico (Chi) fm *6½f (T) RH Allowance Race Alw 0 4 NO RIDER 119 - 0
5May97 Club Hippico (Chi) fm *1 (T) 1:34 Clasico Alvaro Covarrubias-G3 Stk 13700 42¼ Vera P 123 - Cruzeiro123nk Palazzo Ducale123no Real Congress1232 6
24Apr97 Club Hippico (Chi) fm *6½f (T) - Maiden 0 1 NO RIDER 123 - Pompeyo123 0
13Apr97 Club Hippico (Chi) fm *6f (T) - Maiden 0 2 NO RIDER 123 - Pompeyo123 0

Riboletta (Brz)

Own: Jones Aaron U. and Marie D

B. m. 5 (Jul)
Sire: Roi Normand (Exclusive Native)
Dam: Joy Valley*Brz (Ghadeer*Fr)
Br: Haras Santa Ana do Rio Grande (Brz)
Tr: Inda Eduardo

Life	28	13	3	3	$1,555,103	115	D.Fst	10	6	0	1	$1,200,183 115
2000	11	7	0	2	$1,384,860	115	Wet(280*)	6	4	1	0	$216,514 100
1999	6	1	0	1	$82,226	98	Turf(336)	12	3	2	2	$138,406 98
	0	0	0	0	$0	–	Dst(T)(333)	1	0	1	0	$1,320 –

4Nov00- 3CD fst 1⅛ :4611:102 1:3441:473 3↑(F)BCDistaf-G1 93 8 54 45 52 78½ 78¾ McCarron C J L123 *.40 89 - Spain1201½ Surfside1201½ Heritage of Gold123¾ 4 wide, lacked rally 9
14Oct00- 8Bel fst 1⅛ :46 1:091 1:3311:46 3↑(F)Beldame-G1 115 1 24½ 25 22 12 12 McCarron C J L123 *.50 101- 09 Riboletta1232 BeautifulPlesure12314½ Penttonic1232¼ Not fully extended 5
16Sep00- 9Bel fst 1 1/16 :234 :47 1:1041:401 3↑(F)RuffianH-G1 115 3 2hd 1hd 1hd 15½ 17½ McCarron C J L125 *1.05 96- 14 Riboltt1257½ GourmtGirl1141¾ CountryHidwy114no When asked, ridden out 7
12Aug00- 7Dmr fst 1 1/16 :232 :47 1:11 1:42 3↑(F)CLHrschH-G2 107 6 23 2½ 2hd 11½ 11½ McCarron C J LB125 *.40 93- 12 Riboletta1251½ Bordelaise115½ Gourmet Girl1152 Bid,led,clear,driving 6
25Jun00- 6Hol fst 1⅛ :4741:113 1:3541:482 3↑(F)VanityH-G1 111 3 21 2½ 1hd 15 15½ McCarron C J LB123 *.60 87- 20 Ribolett1235½ SpekingofTime1082½ ExcellntMting120½ Bid btwn,ridden out 6
28May00- 9Hol fst 1 1/16 :23 :454 1:1021:42 3↑(F)MladyBCH-G1 110 1 2hd 1hd 11 12½ 13½ McCarron C J LB120 *1.00 90- 10 Riboltt1203½ Bordelise1171½ ExcellentMeting121no Rail,strong hand ride 6
7May00- 4Hol fst 1 1/16 :233 :464 1:1111:421 3↑(F)HawthrnH-G2 105 5 3½ 31 1½ 13 17 McCarron C J LB117 3.20 89- 15 Riboltt1177 ExcellentMting122nk SpkingofTim1118 3wd,drew clear,drvng 5
9Apr00- 8GG fm 1 (T) :24 :471 1:1031:344 3↑(F)MissAmrcaH100k 69 5 31½ 31½ 46 47 313 Alvarado F T LB118 3.40 84- 03 Penny Marie115no Dianehill11413 Riboletta1182 Stalked 3w, empty 5
5Mar00- 8SA sly 1⅛ :47 1:112 1:37 1:502 4↑(F)SMrgrtaH-G1 100 1 1hd 2hd 1½ 12½ 13 Nakatani C S LB115 5.80 83- 20 Riboletta1153 Bordelaise1144 Snowberg114½ Rail,clear,held gamely 5
13Feb00- 8SA wf 1 1/16 :232 :471 1:11 1:423 4↑(F)SntMriaH-G1 97 6 63 73¾ 62¾ 42¾ 44½ Blanc B LB114 25.40 85- 13 Manistique125½ Snowberg1141½ Gourmet Girl1162½ Angled in,no late bid 8
17Jan00- 8SA fm 1⅛ (T) :4911:123 1:3621:483 4↑(F)SnGrgnoH-G2 98 2 21 23 23 21½ 31½ Nakatani C S LB116 11.20 84- 16 Lady At Peace1151½ SpanishFern119no Riboletta1161½ Stalked rail,held 3rd 5
Previously trained by Baffert Bob 1999(as of 12/11): (692 162 118 89 0.23)
11Dec99- 8Hol fst 1 1/16 :24 :473 1:1131:43 3↑(F)BayakoaH-G2 98 5 41½ 2hd 1hd 21½ 34 Flores D R LB116 11.10 81- 15 Manistique1243 Snowberg1151 Riboletta1161½ Bid,dueled,held 3rd 7
7Nov99- 8SA fm 1⅛ (T) :48 1:123 1:3631:481 3↑(F)LsPlmasH-G2 94 3 43½ 44 21 2hd 52¾ Gomez G K LB115 12.30 85- 12 Sapphire Ring1182 Cyrillic117no CountryGarden113hd Bid btwn,outkicked 11
15Oct99- 7SA fm 1 (T) :233 :463 1:10 1:333 3↑(F)Alw 65000N$MY 91 1 74¾ 73¾ 63¾ 3nk 11 Flores D R LB116 8.20 91- 10 Riboletta1161 Lexa1163 Golden Arches117nk Split foes 1/8,cleared 8
2Sep99- 7Dmr fm 1⅜ (T) :4631:113 1:3722:144 3↑(F)CTT&TOCH76k 35 6 1hd 2hd 74¾ 814 833 Antley C W LB117 5.20 61- 07 Sterling Heights1153½ Andoya115no Celibataire1151 Dueled, gave way 8
8Aug99- 8Dmr fst 1 1/16 :231 :454 1:1021:432 3↑(F)ChlaVstH-G2 82 3 32 45½ 44½ 46 49 Flores D R LB116 7.30 78- 21 A Lady FromDixie116½ Manistique124½ YoloLady1168 Angled in, weakened 5
24Jly99- 8Dmr fm 1 1/16 (T) :233 :474 1:1111:413 3↑(F)(R)OsunitasH111k 91 3 44 45 56 44 52¾ Antley C W LB117 4.90 94- 08 Que Belle118no Bella Chiarra1161¾ Cyrillic115½ Off bit slow,mild bid 8
21Nov98 Gavea (Brz) gd *1 1/16 LH 1:591 3↑ Classico Mariano Procopio-G3 (F)Stk 24800 13½ James J 123 1.30 Riboletta1233½ Panchellita1334½ Vitalina1333½ 6
17Oct98 Ciudad Jardim (Brz) gd *1¼ (T) LH 2:041 Grande Premio Diana (Brz Oaks)-G1 (F)Stk 545001no James J 123 2.70 Riboletta123no La Rascasse12310½ Lantejola Equilia1233 12
20Sep98 Gavea (Brz) hy *1¼ (T) LH 2:103 Clsco C T & C G da Rocha Faria-G2 (F)Stk 33400 115½ James J 123 3.30 Riboletta12315½ Sweet Eternity1231¼ Andaina123½ 13
15Aug98 Gavea (Brz) sf *1 (T) LH 1:353 Clsco J A & N de Almeida Prado-G3 (F)Stk 25300 2½ James J 123 2.50 Adrienne123½ Riboletta1232¼ Imperial Lady1231¼ 11
5Jly98 Gavea (Brz) gd *7f LH 1:252 Allowance Race Alw 0 12 James J 119 1.40 Riboletta1192 Bekmesity123no Bar King1237 8
13Jun98 Gavea (Brz) gd *7f LH 1:251 Maiden Race (F)Alw 0 119¾ James J 121 1.60 Riboletta12119¾ Heaven Baby121no Argile1213 12
30May98 Gavea (Brz) sf *7½f (T) LH 1:342 Cls F Vilella de Paula Machado-G2 (F)Stk 39000 58½ James J 121 52.90 French Opera1212 Fanciulla Del West1211¾ Regua Mestra121nk 7
3May98 Gavea (Brz) fm *7f (T) LH 1:222 Clssco Henrique de Toledo Lara-G3 (F)Stk 29400 47¾ James J 121 15.90 Candy Lonly1212¾ Fanciulla Del West1213 Regua Mestra1212 6
28Mar98 Gavea (Brz) fm *6½f (T) LH 1:17 Maiden Race (F)Maiden 0 23¼ NO RIDER 121 - Candy Lonly1213¼ Riboletta12141½ Opus Quatro1235 12
7Mar98 Gavea (Brz) ft *6f LH 1:111 Cl Luiz Alves de Almeida(Lstd) (F)Stk 21800 414½ James J 117 - Fanciulla Del West12111½ Royal Jade1172¾ Imperial Lady121nk 11
20Feb98 Gavea (Brz) my *6f LH 1:132 Maiden Race Alw 0 21¾ James J 119 - Royal Jade1191¾ Riboletta119no Retta Finale11716¼ 6

Smarty Jones
Own: Someday Farm

Ch. c. 3 (Feb)
Sire: Elusive Quality (Gone West) $86,075
Dam: I'll Get Along (Smile)
Br: Someday Farm (Pa)
Tr: Servis John C

Life	9	8	1	0	$7,613,155	118	**D.Fst**	7	6	1	0	$1,128,355 118
2004	7	6	1	0	$7,563,535	118	**Wet(358)**	2	2	0	0	$6,484,800 109
2003	2	2	0	0	$49,620	105	**Turf(300)**	0	0	0	0	$0 –
	0	0	0	0	$0	–	**Dst(T)(347)**	0	0	0	0	$0 –

Date/Race	Cond	Dist	Fractions	Race	Fig	PP	St	1C	2C	Str	Fin	Jockey	Wt	Odds	Spd-Var	Top Finishers	Comment	Fld
5Jun04-11Bel	fst	1½	:483 1:113 2:002 2:272	Belmont-G1	**100**	9	31	1½	13½	11½	21	Elliott S	**L**126 f	*.35	94-10	*Birdstone*1261 Smarty Jones1268 Royal Assault1263	Vied, clear, gamely	9
15May04-12Pim	fst	1 3/16	:471 1:112 1:362 1:552	Preaknes-G1	**118**	6	21½	22½	21	15	111½	Elliott S	**L**126 f	*.70	100-13	SmrtyJons126111½ RockHrdTn1262 Eddington126hd	3-4w,angled in,driving	10
1May04-10CD	sly	1¼	:463 1:114 1:371 2:04	KyDerby-G1	**107**	13	42½	21½	2hd	1hd	12¾	Elliott S	**L**126 f	*4.10	79-21	*Smarty Jones*1262¾ Lion Heart1263¼ Imperialism1262	Stalked,bid,clear	18
10Apr04-9OP	my	1⅛	:464 1:113 1:364 1:492	ArkDerby-G2	**109**	11	2½	2½	1hd	13	11½	Elliott S	122 f	*1.00	91-17	*Smarty Jones*1221½ Borrego1181½ Pro Prado1223½	Cleared at will,drivng	11
20Mar04-10OP	fst	1 1/16	:232 :473 1:12 1:42	Rebel200k	**112**	7	21	21	2½	11	13¼	Elliott S	122 f	3.50	100-16	*Smarty Jones*1223¼ Purge1173¾ Pro Prado1173¾	Kicked strongly clear	9
28Feb04-9OP	fst	1	:224 :454 1:111 1:372	Southwest100k	**95**	6	21½	22½	2hd	12	1¾	Elliott S	122 f	*.50	97-18	*SmrtyJons*122¾ *TwoDownAtomtc*112½ ProPrd1177¼	Chased,took over,drvng	9
3Jan04-8Aqu	fst	170 ⊡	:231 :47 1:113 1:412	CountFleet81k	**97**	7	31	31	2hd	1½	15	Elliott S	116 f	*.40	91-21	*Smarty Jones*1165 Risky Trick1166 Mr. Spock116½	Stumbled start, 3 wide	7
22Nov03-9Pha	fst	7f	:214 :441 1:083 1:214	(S)PennaNurse56k	**105**	1	10	12	12½	18	115	Elliott S	117 f	*.70	98-17	*SmartyJones*11715 SaltyPunch1172¼ IsleofMirth1171½	Off slow, dominated	11
9Nov03-6Pha	fst	6f	:221 :451 :574 1:11	Md Sp Wt 23k	**84**	8	4	2hd	15	16	17¾	Elliott S	118 f	*1.10	84-22	*Smarty Jones*1187¾ *Deputy Rummy*1132¾ Speedwell Beau1186	Handy score	10

Speightstown
Own: Melnyk Eugene and Laura

Ch. h. 6 (Feb)
Sire: Gone West (Mr. Prospector) $150,000
Dam: Silken Cat (Storm Cat)
Br: Aaron U. Jones & Marie Jones (Ky)
Tr: Pletcher Todd A

Life	16	10	2	2	$1,258,256	117	**D.Fst**	13	8	1	2	$1,064,600 117
2004	6	5	0	1	$1,045,556	117	**Wet(404)**	3	2	1	0	$193,656 116
2003	2	1	1	0	$56,020	105	**Turf(331)**	0	0	0	0	$0 –
	0	0	0	0	$0	–	**Dst(T)(403)**	0	0	0	0	$0 –

Date/Race	Cond	Dist	Fractions	Race	Fig	PP	St	1C	2C	Str	Fin	Jockey	Wt	Odds	Spd-Var	Top Finishers	Comment	Fld
30Oct04-5LS	fst	6f	:211 :432 :552 1:08	3↑BCSprint-G1	**112**	2	8	41½	31	11½	11¼	Velazquez J R	**L**126	3.70	100-04	Speightstown1261¼ Kela126¾ My Cousin Matt126½	Rail trip,edged clear	13
2Oct04-8Bel	fst	6f	:223 :453 :571 1:093	3↑Vosburgh-G1	**102**	2	2	1½	2hd	2½	34½	Velazquez J R	**L**124	*.80	86-22	Pico Central1244 Voodoo124½ *Speightstown*124hd	Bobbled start, between	5
14Aug04-7Sar	fst	6f	:22 :442 :554 1:08	3↑AGVndbtH-G2	**117**	2	5	1hd	2hd	12½	11½	Velazquez J R	**L**120	*.90	102-12	Spghtstown1201½ ClockStoppr1151½ GtrsNBrs1182	Vied inside, kept busy	6
5Jun04-7Bel	fst	6f	:212 :433 :551 1:08	3↑TrNthBCH-G2	**115**	3	1	22½	1½	11½	11½	Velazquez J R	**L**119	*1.80	99-07	*Speightstown*1191½ Cat Genius1161¾ *Pohave*117nk	When roused, driving	9
1May04-5CD	gd	7f	:222 :451 1:084 1:211	4↑CDH-G2	**116**	1	3	11	11	12½	13½	Velazquez J R	**L**115	5.40	96-06	*Speightstown*1153½ McCannsMojve1172 Publiction1162	Speed,inside,clear	7
27Mar04-11GP	fst	7f	:221 :444 1:09 1:22	3↑ArtaxH100k	**106**	1	1	1hd	1hd	13½	14½	Coa E M	**L**116	*3.20	92-16	*Speightstown*1164½ *PrttyWild*111no WckyforLov1153¼	Dueled rail, drew off	9
26May03-8Bel	sly	7f ⊗	:213 :434 1:091 1:232	3↑JaipurH112k	**82**	2	1	1hd	2hd	2hd	21¼	Velazquez J R	**L**121	2.05	82-19	Grnered1161¼ *Speightstown*121½ Whitewterspritzr115no	Dueled, held place	5
9May03-8Bel	fst	7f	:221 :451 1:10 1:223	4↑Alw 56000N4X	**105**	1	1	1hd	2hd	2hd	1nk	Velazquez J R	**L**116	4.70	87-22	Speightstown116nk Volponi1224 Reason to Hail1166½	Came again gamely	6
Previously trained by England Phillip 2001(as of 8/3): (67 15 9 8 0.22)																		
3Aug01-8Sar	fst	6f	:213 :444 :572 1:11	Amstrdam-G2	**97**	5	2	1hd	1hd	2hd	21	Bailey J D	**L**118 f	5.40	88-15	City Zip1231 *Speightstown*1181 Smile My Lord1182¼	Bumped 1/4 pole	6
24Jun01-8WO	fst	7f	:22 :442 1:09 1:22	3↑Alw 67200N$Y	**99**	4	3	2hd	2hd	12½	12	Husbands P	**L**115 f	*1.25	94-10	Speightstown1152 Grand End Sweep119½ Catahoula Parish1192	Driving	7
3Jun01-6WO	my	6f	:22 :451 :571 1:094	3↑OC 62k/N2X-N	**98**	7	3	11½	12	12½	12½	Landry R C	**L**114 f	*.55	91-13	*Speightstown*1142½ Bridgeport1193¼ Jet Drive1162¼	Ridden out	7
8Apr01-6WO	fst	7f	:222 :444 1:10 1:233	Alw 52800N1X	**96**	4	2	22	2½	12½	16	Landry R C	**L**118 f	*.70	86-20	*Speightstown*1186 *Lucky Tec*1155 End Wisely118¾	Ridden out	8
18Mar01-9Aqu	fst	1	:224 :46 1:103 1:35	Gotham-G3	**54**	2	2½	4¾	87¼	717	724¾	Gryder A T	**L**116	15.10	67-12	Richly Blended1165¼ Mr. John116nk Voodoo1166¼	Speed inside, tired	8
24Feb01-9GP	fst	6f	:22 :444 :572 1:103	Alw 36000N1X	**78**	6	5	33	36	35½	35	Smith M E	122	*.70	81-13	Mr. John1202 Hana Highway1223 Speightstown122½	Lacked a rally	8
3Feb01-4GP	fst	6f	:221 :451 :573 1:10	Md Sp Wt 32k	**96**	5	3	1hd	11½	13	16¾	Smith M E	122	13.50	89-11	Speightstown1226¾ *CobraCeltic*1221 DnherSteve1221¼	Vigorous hand ride	10
Previously trained by Pletcher Todd A 2000(as of 8/26): (469 82 77 46 0.17)																		
26Aug00-3Sar	fst	6f	:22 :46 :582 1:112	Md Sp Wt 41k	**41**	5	13	41½	63	1211	1315	Bailey J D	118	*2.45	73-09	Ommadon1181½ Smart Pick1181½ Pure Prize118½	Greenly, tired	13

Squirtle Squirt
Own: Lanzman David J

Dk. b or b. c. 4 (Feb)
Sire: Marquetry (Conquistador Cielo) $7,500
Dam: Lost the Code (Lost Code)
Br: Dr. Audrey Narducci (Ky)
Tr: Frankel Robert J

Life	16	8	4	0	$1,112,220	119	**D.Fst**	15	8	3	0	$1,082,220 119
2002	2	0	1	0	$45,000	106	**Wet(340)**	1	0	1	0	$30,000 106
2001	6	3	3	0	$817,720	119	**Turf(308)**	0	0	0	0	$0 –
	0	0	0	0	$0	–	**Dst(T)(336)**	0	0	0	0	$0 –

Date/Race	Cond	Dist	Fractions	Race	Fig	PP	St	1C	2C	Str	Fin	Jockey	Wt	Odds	Spd-Var	Top Finishers	Comment	Fld
1Sep02-9Sar	fst	6½f	:212 :441 1:09 1:153	3↑ForegoH-G1	**96**	2	3	1½	2hd	23½	48¼	Chavez J F	**L**122	3.40	89-15	*Orientate*1222¼ Aldebaran1153¾ Multiple Choice1142¼	Vied inside, tired	8
27Jan02-8SA	wf	6f	:21 :431 :551 1:073	4↑PlsVrdsH-G2	**106**	3	3	2hd	2½	21½	24	Bailey J D	**LB**122	*.80	96-12	*Snow Ridge*1164 Squirtle Squirt122½ Ceeband1171	Dueled,just held 2nd	7
27Oct01-6Bel	fst	6f	:222 :443 :561 1:082	3↑BCSprint-G1	**119**	3	2	3½	31½	31	1½	Bailey J D	**L**124	9.60	96-03	Squirtle Squirt124½ Xtra Heat121nk Caller One126nk	Split rivals, driving	14
22Sep01-10Bel	fst	7f	:223 :442 1:081 1:203	3↑Vosburgh-G1	**117**	3	4	11½	12½	11½	2½	Bailey J D	**L**123	*.75	99-11	Left Bank126½ *Squirtle Squirt*1239¾ Big E E126nk	Set pace, gamely	6
25Aug01-9Sar	fst	7f	:22 :441 1:083 1:214	KngsBshp-G1	**107**	6	2	1½	11½	13½	13¼	Bailey J D	**L**121	*1.50	96-08	Squirtle Squirt1213¼ Illusioned1191¼ *City Zip*1245	Set pace, driving	8
1Jly01-10Hol	fst	7f	:213 :433 1:081 1:21	3↑TrBndBCH-G2	**111**	8	1	1hd	1½	14	2½	Pincay L Jr	**LB**114	*2.10	93-10	Ceeband110½ *Squirtle Squirt*1142½ Elaborate118½	Dueled,clear,caught	10
28May01-9Hol	fst	7f	:213 :434 1:074 1:202	LBrreraM-G3	**108**	5	3	11	1hd	1hd	2¾	Pincay L Jr	**LB**123	1.70	96-06	Early Flyer123¾ Squirtle Squirt1233½ Top Hit1184½	Fought back,gamely	7
2May01-4Hol	fst	6f	:212 :432 :552 1:083	Alw 58800NC	**103**	1	3	11	13	13	11½	Pincay L Jr	**LB**122	1.70	97-09	SquirtleSquirt1221½ *BeyondBrillint*1201½ TopHit1202½	Speed,inside,driving	4
Previously trained by Garcia Joe A Jr 2000(as of 9/24): (78 9 4 5 0.12)																		
24Sep00-10Fpx	fst	6½f	:213 :451 1:104 1:172	(R)BrrettsJuv101k	**84**	2	6	31	1½	13	16½	Black C A	**B**123	*1.20	91-15	*SquirtlSqurt*1236½ KngGorgsWy115nk ChnookCt1172	Off bit slow,rail,dvng	7
13Sep00-8Dmr	fst	7f	:22 :441 1:09 1:22	DMrFut-G2	**78**	8	2	3nk	42	55	711¼	Delahoussaye E	**B**121	7.80	84-08	*FlameThrower*119hd StreetCry1163½ *ArbinLight*1195	4wd to turn, weakened	8
23Aug00-7Dmr	fst	6½f	:214 :444 1:094 1:162	BestPal-G3	**64**	5	3	41	42½	47	413¾	Pincay L Jr	**B**121	*1.00	77-13	*FlmeThrower*1172¾ *Trilthefox*1215 LegendryWeve1176	Broke out,weakened	7
23Jly00-9Hol	fst	6f	:214 :443 :57 1:094	HolJuvCh-G3	**93**	5	1	12	12½	13	12	Pincay L Jr	**B**120	*.40	88-14	SquirtleSquirt1202 LegendryWeve1171¾ *Drumcliff*1171	Speed,clearly best	5
25Jun00-2Hol	fst	5½f	:213 :45 :572 1:04	Haggin84k	**89**	2	4	1½	12½	15	16	Pincay L Jr	**B**119	*1.30	90-16	*SquirtleSquirt*1196 PintedAvenu1161½ SlwHsMssg1161½	Inside, ridden out	6
29May00-7Hol	fst	4½f	:214 :453 :514	WProctrMem79k	**84**	2	2	31½		21	11½	Pincay L Jr	**B**119	*.80	96-13	*SquirtleSquirt*1191½ OurMagistrate1193½ Maxin119hd	3wd bid,bumpd,game	8
5May00-4Hol	fst	4½f	:22 :451 :512	Md Sp Wt 43k	**91**	2	1	11		11½	11½	Pincay L Jr	**B**118	7.80	98-10	*SquirtleSquirt*1181½ *BldwinCounty*1183½ HedWest1181	Speed,inside,driving	10
21Apr00-2SA	fst	2f	:111 :212	Md Sp Wt 47k	**–**	9	7			73	42	Pincay L Jr	**B**120	12.60	96-11	Trailthefox120no *Breoni*1201½ *Kenny Mais*120½	Drifted out bit	10

Storm Flag Flying
Own: Phipps Ogden M

Dk. b or b. f. 4 (Apr)
Sire: Storm Cat (Storm Bird) $500,000
Dam: My Flag (Easy Goer)
Br: Phipps Stable (Ky)
Tr: McGaughey III Claude R

Life	14	7	3	3	$1,951,828	103	**D.Fst**	11	5	2	3	$911,828 103
2004	8	3	2	3	$963,248	103	**Wet(426)**	3	2	1	0	$1,040,000 102
2003	2	0	1	0	$21,580	79	**Turf(354)**	0	0	0	0	$0 –
	0	0	0	0	$0	–	**Dst(T)(420)**	0	0	0	0	$0 –

Date/Race	Cond	Dist	Fractions	Race	Fig	PP	St	1C	2C	Str	Fin	Jockey	Wt	Odds	Spd-Var	Top Finishers	Comment	Fld
30Oct04-2LS	gd	1⅛	:463 1:102 1:352 1:481	3↑(F)BCDistaf-G1	**100**	7	104½	114¾	83¾	52	21¼	Bailey J D	**L**123	4.60	107-02	Ashado1191¼ StormFlgFlying123nk *StellrJyne*1191½	Svd grnd,finished well	11
9Oct04-9Bel	fst	1⅛	:482 1:124 1:364 1:493	3↑(F)Beldame-G1	**94**	5	2hd	21	2½	46½	34	Velazquez J R	**L**123	4.40	79-20	Sghtsk1232¾ SoctySlcton1201¼ StormFlgFlyng123¾	Stayed on stubbornly	5
27Aug04-9Sar	fst	1¼	:461 1:093 1:354 2:033	3↑(F)PrsnlEnH-G1	**99**	1	37½	37	31½	1hd	11¼	Velazquez J R	**L**116	2.15	89-11	Storm Flag Flying1161¼ *Azeri*122½ Nevermore1144½	3 wide move, resolute	5
1Aug04-9Sar	fst	1⅛	:473 1:104 1:35 1:474	3↑(F)GoFWandH-G1	**100**	1	31½	31	42	33½	33¾	Velazquez J R	**L**117	3.05	92-14	Azeri1201¾ *Sightseek*1222 *Storm Flag Flying*1177	Steadied rail 1st turn	5
19Jun04-9Bel	fst	1 1/16	:231 :453 1:10 1:412	3↑(F)OPhippsH-G1	**93**	4	31	3½	3½	26	23¼	Velazquez J R	**L**117	3.00	90-20	Sightsek1203¼ StormFlgFlying1176½ PssingShot1162	3 wide bid, no match	4
15May04-8Bel	fst	1	:234 :463 1:111 1:36	3↑(F)ShuveeH-G2	**103**	2	42½	31	41	31½	1½	Velazquez J R	**L**116	*1.00	81-19	StormFlgFlyng116½ PssngShot117no RorEmoton1178¼	Along late outside	6
27Mar04-8Aqu	fst	7f	:224 :461 1:10 1:223	3↑(F)DistfBCH-G2	**87**	2	3	2½	32	36½	35¾	Prado E S	**L**118	2.10	86-17	Randaroo1213½ Chirimoya1102¼ *StormFlgFlying*11811¼	Inside, no response	4
26Feb04-8GP	fst	170	:224 :462 1:114 1:423	4↑(F)OC 100k/c-N	**92**	7	31	21½	2½	11	13¾	Velazquez J R	**L**115	*.80	84-28	StormFlgFlying1153¾ RdoubldMiss1191¼ KiSkur1153¼	Drew away, driving	7
6Jun03-10Bel	fst	1	:232 :461 1:102 1:351	(F)Acorn-G1	**75**	1	4¾	72	77½	713	611	Velazquez J R	**L**121	*1.70	79-16	Bird Town121hd *Lady Tak*1211 Final Round1213¼	Between rivals, empty	7
18Apr03-8Aqu	fst	1	:231 :451 1:10 1:354	(F)Comely-G3	**79**	1	31	21½	32½	27	25½	Velazquez J R	**L**122	*.25	80-13	Cyber Secret1225½ Storm Flag Flying1223 Bonay1162¼	Chased, stayed on	5
26Oct02-4AP	gd	1⅛	:461 1:101 1:354 1:493	(F)BCJuvFil-G1	**102**	3	22	32	21	2hd	1½	Velazquez J R	**L**119	*.80	100 -	StormFlagFlying119½ Composure1199¾ *SantCtrin*1192	Headed, very game	10
5Oct02-6Bel	fst	1 1/16	:233 :472 1:121 1:441	(F)Frizette-G1	**98**	3	31	2½	2½	1½	12	Velazquez J R	**L**120	*.60	79-22	*StrmFlgFln*1202 SntCtrn12011¼ ApplbGrdns1203	When asked, shown whip	7
15Sep02-6Bel	gd	1	:222 :46 1:122 1:382	(F)Matron-G1	**94**	2	31½	32	2hd	13	112¾	Velazquez J R	**L**119	*1.40	77-22	*Storm Flag Flying*11912¾ *Wild Snitch*1191 Fircroft1195¼	Greenly, kept busy	7
18Aug02-6Sar	fst	6f	:221 :453 :58 1:11	(F)Md Sp Wt 45k	**86**	3	6	56½	42	21½	11	Velazquez J R	**L**119	3.65	87-13	*StormFlgFlyng*1191 SomthngSlvr1195 OrNncyL1194½	4 wide move, greenly	9

Surfside

Own: Overbrook Farm

B. f. 4 (Jan)
Sire: Seattle Slew (Bold Reasoning) $300,000
Dam: Flanders (Seeking the Gold)
Br: Overbrook Farm (Ky)
Tr: Lukas D. W

Life	15	8	3	2	$1,852,987	116	D.Fst	12 6 3 1	$1,468,987 116
2001	2	0	0	1	$28,000	92	Wet(392)	3 2 0 1	$384,000 94
2000	7	4	2	0	$1,147,637	116	Turf(276)	0 0 0 0	$0 -
	0	0	0	0	$0	-	Dst(T)(398)	0 0 0 0	$0 -

Date/Race	Cond	Dist	Fractions	Race	Fig	Running line	Jockey	Wt	Odds	Figs	Top finishers	Comment	Fld
18Feb01-7SA	fst	1 1/16	:224 :46 1:103 1:431	4↑(F)SntMriaH-G1	86	2 2hd 2hd 2½ 55½ 58	Day P	LB121 b	*.60	80-12	Lovellon116nk Feverish119¾ Critikola1153	Dueled, gave way	5
27Jan01-8SA	wf	7f	:213 :441 1:091 1:222	4↑(F)SntMncaH-G1	92	5 4 52½ 43 34½ 34	Day P	LB121 b	*.60	89-10	Nany's Sweep1171 Serenita1153 Surfside121½	3wd turn,held 3rd	7
24Nov00-11CD	fst	1⅛	:472 1:113 1:361 1:483	3↑ClarkH-G2	116	7 12 12½ 12 11½ 14	Day P	L113 b	1.60	93-14	Surfside1134 *Guided Tour*1141¼ Maysville Slew1131¾	Pace, 4-5 wide,driving	9
4Nov00-3CD	fst	1⅛	:461 1:102 1:344 1:473	3↑(F)BCDistaf-G1	105	6 12½ 13½ 11 2½ 21½	Day P	L120 b	10.30	96 -	Spain1201½ *Surfside*1201½ *Heritage of Gold*123¾	Drifted late, gamely	9
11Oct00-8Kee	fst	7f	:212 :432 1:081 1:204	(F)RavenRun82k	102	3 3 1hd 1½ 11 21¼	Day P	L123 b	1.70	97-08	Darling My Darling1171¼ Surfside1232 Cat Cay117¾	Dueled,inside,2ndbest	6
8Apr00-5SA	fst	1⅛	:471 1:112 1:362 1:49	SADerby-G1	95	1 11 1½ 1½ 32½ 58½	Day P	LB115 b	5.60	81-16	The Deputy1201 War Chant1202 Captain Steve1203	Inside duel,weakened	6
12Mar00-7SA	fst	1 1/16	:224 :454 1:102 1:44	(F)SAOaks-G1	95	3 2hd 1hd 2hd 11 1¾	Day P	B117	*.40	83-14	Surfside117¾ *KumariContinent*117no *ClassyCr*1171¾	Dueled,inchd away,held	5
12Feb00-6SA	my	1	:23 :464 1:112 1:37	(F)LsVrgnes-G1	94	1 2½ 11 1½ 11 1¾	Day P	LB122	*.20	86-17	*Surfside*122¾ Spain115½ Rings a Chime1167	Met bid, gamely	4
9Jan00-8SA	fst	1 1/16	:232 :47 1:111 1:432	(F)SntYsabl-G3	103	3 2hd 1hd 1½ 13 18	Day P	LB123	*.20	86-20	*Surfside*1238 Rings a Chime1152 She's Classy11812	Drew clear, handily	4
19Dec99-8Hol	fst	1 1/16	:232 :463 1:11 1:432	(F)HolStrlt-G1	100	3 1hd 2hd 1hd 13 17	Day P	LB120	*.50	83-17	*Surfside*1207 She's Classy1201 *Abby Girl*1205½	Inside, ridden out	5
6Nov99-4GP	fst	1 1/16	:223 :454 1:101 1:431	(F)BCJuvFil-G1	90	7 64 85 75¾ 55¼ 31¾	Day P	L119	2.50	89 -	Cash Run1191¾ Chilukki119½ *Surfside*119½	Wide trip, closed well	9
10Oct99-4Bel	sly	1 1/16	:231 :464 1:112 1:43	(F)Frizette-G1	94	1 11 11 2hd 2hd 1hd	Day P	L119	1.95	82-23	Surfside119hd DarlingMyDarling11910 *MrchMgic*1194¼	Came again gamely	5
3Sep99-8Sar	fst	7f	:221 :444 1:094 1:231	(F)Spinaway-G1	88	4 2 31 32½ 32 21¼	Day P	L121	*1.15	88-13	Circle of Life1211¼ *Surfside*1211¾ Miss Wineshine1213¼	3 wide, game finish	6
20Aug99-4Sar	fst	6f	:222 :461 :58 1:102	(F)Alw 42000N1x	91	2 3 1hd 1hd 1½ 11½	Day P	117	*.45	89-11	Surfside1171½ DatYouMizBlue1176¾ *MrgInte*1172	When asked, ridden out	8
4Aug99-2Sar	fst	5½f	:22 :452 :573 1:034	(F)Md Sp Wt 40k	99	1 4 11 1½ 11 14¾	Day P	117	*.95	99-11	*Surfside*1174¾ You and I Babe1171¾ Wedding Weekend1173½	Ridden out	7

Sweet Catomine

Own: Wygod Mr. and Mrs. Martin J

B. f. 3 (Feb)
Sire: Storm Cat (Storm Bird) $500,000
Dam: Sweet Life (Kris S.)
Br: Mr. & Mrs. Martin J. Wygod (Ky)
Tr: Canani Julio C

Life	7	5	1	0	$1,059,600	102	D.Fst	7 5 1 0	$1,059,600 102
2005	3	2	0	0	$259,800	96	Wet(428)	0 0 0 0	$0 -
2004	4	3	1	0	$799,800	102	Turf(381)	0 0 0 0	$0 -
	0	0	0	0	$0	-	Dst(T)(392)	0 0 0 0	$0 -

Date/Race	Cond	Dist	Fractions	Race	Fig	Running line	Jockey	Wt	Odds	Figs	Top finishers	Comment	Fld
9Apr05-6SA	fst	1⅛	:471 1:111 1:362 1:49	SADerby-G1	90	2 41½ 72½ 52¼ 52½ 55	Nakatani C S	LB117 b	*1.00	84-08	Buzzards Bay122½ General John B122no Wilko1221½	Bumped 1/2,no rally	11
13Mar05-9SA	fst	1 1/16	:232 :482 1:14 1:442	(F)SAOaks-G1	96	1 64 62½ 2hd 12½ 13	Nakatani C S	LB121 b	*.20	83-20	SweetCtomine1213 Memorette1215 ShSings1211¼	3wd bid, powered clear	7
16Jan05-3SA	fst	1 1/16	:224 :461 1:103 1:433	(F)SntYsabl-G3	88	4 41¾ 31 1½ 11 12½	Flores D R	LB124 b	*.10e	87-16	*SwtCtomin*1242½ PussyctDoll1154 OnLondonTim1158	Bid btwn,led,gamely	5
30Oct04-3LS	fst	1 1/16	:224 :462 1:103 1:413	(F)BCJuvFil-G1	102	9 75½ 74¼ 71¾ 2hd 13¾	Nakatani C S	L119 b	*2.30	94-02	*SweetCatomine*1193¾ Balletto1191¼ *RunwyModel*119¾	Blocked 5/16,checked	12
2Oct04-9SA	fst	1 1/16	:23 :464 1:111 1:424	(F)OakLeaf-G2	91	9 72¾ 66 52¼ 12½ 14	Nakatani C S	LB119 b	2.00	91-08	*SweetCatomine*1194 *SplendidBlended*1192½ Memorette1194	4wd surge,clear	9
28Aug04-8Dmr	fst	7f	:22 :442 1:102 1:24	(F)DMrDeb-G1	76	7 9 96¼ 78¼ 33 1¾	Espinoza V	LB114 b	*1.60e	82-13	*SwtCtomin*114¾ SouvnirGift1201½ HlloLucky1162½	Hopd brk,5w,nailed foe	9
31Jly04-1Dmr	fst	5½f	:221 :451 :574 1:042	(F)Md Sp Wt 50k	64	9 3 42¾ 42½ 33½ 25	Flores D R	LB118 b	5.70	88-09	She's Salty1185 *Sweet Catomine*118nk Wild Humor118½	5wd,3wd,late 2nd	9

Tempera

Own: Godolphin Racing, Inc.

Dk. b or b. f. 3 (Mar)
Sire: A.P. Indy (Seattle Slew) $300,000
Dam: Colour Chart (Mr. Prospector)
Br: Darley Stud Management, LLC. (Ky)
Tr: bin Suroor Saeed

Life	7	3	2	2	$770,240	107	D.Fst	7 3 2 2	$770,240 107
2002	2	0	2	0	$100,000	-	Wet(438)	0 0 0 0	$0 -
2001	5	3	0	2	$670,240	107	Turf(313)	0 0 0 0	$0 -
	0	0	0	0	$0	-	Dst(T)(393)	0 0 0 0	$0 -

13Apr02 Nad Al Sheba (UAE) ft *1⅛ LH 1:493 (F)UAE Oaks (Prestige) Stk 250000 — 23¼ Flores D 126 - Imperial Gesture1263¼ Tempera1266 Seba12618 — 5
Timeform rating: 106
Tracked pacesetting winner,3rd and wide 2-1/2f out,second best

14Mar02 Nad Al Sheba (UAE) ft *1 LH 1:374 (F)UAE 1000 Guineas (Prestige) Stk 250000 — 25 Dettori L 126 - Infinite Spirit1265 Tempera1261¾ E. B.'s Sweep126nk — 6
Timeform rating: 99+
Tracked leaders,brief bid 1-1/2f out,faded.Seba 4th

Date/Race	Cond	Dist	Fractions	Race	Fig	Running line	Jockey	Wt	Odds	Figs	Top finishers	Comment	Fld
27Oct01-4Bel	fst	1 1/16	:232 :464 1:104 1:412	(F)BCJuvFil-G1	107	9 41 5¾ 31 2hd 11½	Flores D R	L119	11.90	90-12	Tempera1191½ *Imperial Gesture*1193½ *Bella Bellucci*119½	5 wide trip, driving	9
26Aug01-8Dmr	fst	7f	:223 :451 1:094 1:221	(F)DMrDeb-G1	90	3 1 21 1½ 3½ 34	Flores D R	LB119	*.50	90-09	Habibti1152 Who LovesAleyna1162 *Tempera*1197½	Inside bid,btwn,wkened	5
4Aug01-7Dmr	fst	6½f	:22 :451 1:094 1:16	(F)Sorrento-G2	95	8 3 31½ 31 12½ 19	Flores D R	LB117	*.80	93-09	Tempera1179 Respectful1151 *Roaring Blaze*1173½	3wd bid,mild hand ride	8
4Jly01-1Hol	fst	5½f	:22 :45 :57 1:031	(F)Md Sp Wt 42k	92	3 2 1hd 11½ 11½ 13	Flores D R	LB118	*.60	97-11	*Tempera*1183 *Newport Beach*1185 Cat Ballado1183½	Bit off rail,riddn out	8
10Jun01-10Hol	fst	5f	:213 :443 :57	(F)Md Sp Wt 42k	67	4 9 78¼ 710 58 310	Nakatani C S	LB118	3.10	87-08	September Secret1181 Ayanna1189 *Tempera*1182½	Crowded early & 3/16	10

Tiznow

Own: Cees Stable LLC

B. c. 4 (Mar)
Sire: Cee's Tizzy (Relaunch) $10,000
Dam: Cee's Song (Seattle Song)
Br: Cecilia Straub Rubens (Cal)
Tr: Robbins Jay M

Life	15	8	4	2	$6,427,830	119	D.Fst	15 8 4 2	$6,427,830 119
2001	6	3	1	2	$2,981,880	117	Wet(396)	0 0 0 0	$0 -
2000	9	5	3	0	$3,445,950	119	Turf(239)	0 0 0 0	$0 -
	0	0	0	0	$0	-	Dst(T)(319)	0 0 0 0	$0 -

Date/Race	Cond	Dist	Fractions	Race	Fig	Running line	Jockey	Wt	Odds	Figs	Top finishers	Comment	Fld
27Oct01-10Bel	fst	1¼	:47 1:111 1:354 2:003	3↑BCClasic-G1	117	10 31½ 31½ 21 3½ 1no	McCarron C J	L126	6.90	91-12	Tiznow126no *Sakhee*1261¾ Albert the Great1262¾	Prevailed, gamely	13
7Oct01-8SA	fst	1⅛	:452 1:092 1:352 1:484	3↑GdwdBCH-G2	106	5 32½ 31½ 31 32½ 31½	McCarron C J	LB124	*1.10	89-09	Freedom Crest1161 Skimming123½ *Tiznow*1244	Bid 3wd,slow gain late	6
8Sep01-9Bel	fst	1⅛	:463 1:101 1:343 1:472	3↑Woodward-G1	110	2 2½ 2½ 2½ 3½ 31½	McCarron C J	L126	2.40	91-14	Lido Palace1261 Albert the Great126½ Tiznow1268¼	Speed inside, gamely	5
3Mar01-9SA	fst	1¼	:462 1:103 1:354 2:012	4↑SAH-G1	117	5 2½ 2hd 1hd 12½ 15	McCarron C J	LB122	*1.00	96-10	Tiznow1225 Wooden Phone1171½ Tribunal1162	Dueled, drew clear	12
3Feb01-8SA	fst	1⅛	:471 1:102 1:352 1:482	Strub-G2	105	6 31 3nk 4¾ 22½ 22	McCarron C J	LB123	*.30	91-12	Wooden Phone1172 *Tiznow*1233½ Jimmy Z117¾	Vied 3wd,4wd,2nd best	6
13Jan01-8SA	fst	1 1/16	:231 :463 1:104 1:42	SnFndoBC-G2	108	6 2½ 2hd 2½ 21 11¼	McCarron C J	LB122	*.30	94-12	Tiznow1221¼ Wlkslikeduck120¾ *WoodenPhone*1162	3wd bid,brushd,gamely	6
4Nov00-10CD	fst	1¼	:472 1:12 1:36 2:003	3↑BCClasic-G1	116	12 1hd 2hd 1hd 1hd 1nk	McCarron C J	L122	9.20	107 -	*Tiznow*122nk GiantsCusewy1223½ *CptinSteve*122hd	Duel,headed,gamely,drv	13
15Oct00-7SA	fst	1⅛	:47 1:104 1:35 1:471	3↑GdwdBCH-G2	119	7 11½ 11 1½ 1hd 1½	McCarron C J	LB116	*1.20	99-13	*Tiznow*116½ Captain Steve1171½ Euchre1154	Rated, repulsed rival	7
30Sep00-6LaD	fst	1¼	:471 1:102 1:351 1:594	SuperDby-G1	114	4 1½ 1hd 11 13 16	McCarron C J	L124	*.80	103-05	*Tiznow*1246 Commendable1241 Mass Market1249	Restrained, ridden out	6
26Aug00-8Dmr	fst	1¼	:452 1:094 1:35 2:011	3↑PacifcCl-G1	115	4 33½ 21 21½ 22½ 22	McCarron C J	LB117	4.00	93-14	Skimming1242 *Tiznow*1171¼ Ecton Park124½	Chased,bid, 2nd best	7
23Jly00-6Hol	fst	1⅛	:464 1:103 1:352 1:48	Swaps-G1	107	1 41½ 42 41 21½ 22½	Espinoza V	LB118 b	2.90	86-11	Captain Steve1202½ Tiznow1181 Spacelink1182	Pulld,trapped rail 3/8	6
1Jly00-8Hol	fst	1 1/16	:231 :46 1:101 1:421	AffirmdH-G3	103	3 42 31 3½ 2hd 1nk	Espinoza V	LB111 b	10.80	89-18	Tiznow111nk *Dixie Union*1222 Millencolin1172	Tight rail 7-1/2 & 3/8	6
31May00-4Hol	fst	1 1/16	:233 :462 1:104 1:424	3↑Md Sp Wt 52k	95	5 2½ 2hd 12 14½ 18½	Solis A	LB115 b	*1.30	86-21	*Tiznow*1158½ *ColdwterCnyon*1163½ FctulEvidenc115hd	Drew off, ridden out	9
11May00-6Hol	fst	1 1/16	:232 :47 1:12 1:431	3↑Md Sp Wt 47k	99	3 73¼ 41¼ 42 21 2nk	Solis A	LB115 b	*2.20	84-15	*SpicyStuff*115nk *Tiznow*1154 ColdwaterCanyon116½	Crowded strt,waitd 1/4	9
22Apr00-7SA	fst	6f	:212 :441 :563 1:10	Md Sp Wt 47k	82	8 5 63¾ 810 78¼ 63	Solis A	B122 b	13.80	86-13	MrWondrful1222½ *ProgrmmdAppl*122no *CocontWlly*122hd	Steadied near 3/8	10

Vindication
Own: Padua Stables

Dk. b or b. c. 2 (Jan)
Sire: Seattle Slew (Bold Reasoning) $300,000
Dam: Strawberry Reason (Strawberry Road*Aus)
Br: Payson Stud Inc. (Ky)
Tr: Baffert Bob

Life	4	4	0	0	$680,950	102	D.Fst	4	4	0	0	$680,950 102
2002	4	4	0	0	$680,950	102	Wet(381)	0	0	0	0	$0 -
2001	0	M	0	0	$0	-	Turf(301)	0	0	0	0	$0 -
	0	0	0	0	$0	-	Dst(T)(373)	0	0	0	0	$0 -

26Oct02-8AP	fst	1⅛	:46 1:094 1:354 1:493	BCJuvnle-G1	102	6 1hd 1½ 2hd 12½ 12¾	Smith M E	L122	4.10	100 -	Vindication1222¾ Kafwin1222½ HoldThtTiger1221¼	Steady urging, drifted	13
14Sep02-10TP	fst	1 1/16	:232 :471 1:13 1:463	KyCupJuv-G3	87	4 59 58 1hd 13 16	Smith M E	L116	*1.10	79- 20	*Vindication*1166 Private Gold118¾ Tito's Beau114hd	Broke in air, 5w move	8
22Aug02-2Dmr	fst	6f	:22 :451 :58 1:112	OC 80k/N1x -N	84	2 4 1hd 11 12½ 11½	Smith M E	LB121	*.10	83- 20	*Vindication*1211½ Pine for Java1185 *Jimmy O*1184	Drifted bit,ridden out	5
27Jly02-7Dmr	fst	6f	:221 :451 :5721:103	Md Sp Wt 47k	87	1 5 11 11 13 15½	Smith M E	LB120	2.30	87- 13	*Vindiction*1205½ ListenIndy120hd AplchinThunder1201	Drew clear, handily	11

War Emblem
Own: The Thoroughbred Corporation

Dk. b or b. c. 3 (Feb)
Sire: Our Emblem (Mr. Prospector) $10,000
Dam: Sweetest Lady (Lord At War*Arg)
Br: Charles Nuckols Jr. & Sons (Ky)
Tr: Baffert Bob

Life	13	7	0	0	$3,491,000	114	D.Fst	12	7	0	0	$3,491,000 114
2002	10	5	0	0	$3,455,000	114	Wet(338)	0	0	0	0	$0 -
2001	3	2	0	0	$36,000	83	Turf(320)	1	0	0	0	$0 44
	0	0	0	0	$0	-	Dst(T)(333)	0	0	0	0	$0 -

26Oct02-10AP	fst	1¼	:463 1:101 1:352 2:011	3↑BCClasic-G1	89	3 21½ 21 3½ 57½ 818¼	Espinoza V	L121	4.00	79 -	Volponi1266½ *Medaglia d'Oro*121nk Milwaukee Brew1263	Bid turn, faltered	12
25Aug02-5Dmr	fst	1¼	:452 1:094 1:352 2:012	3↑PacifcCl-G1	110	6 31½ 32 2hd 2hd 64¼	Espinoza V	LB117	*1.20	88- 13	CameHome117¾ Momentum1241½ MilwaukeeBrew124½	3wd bid,weakened	14
4Aug02-11Mth	fst	1⅛	:471 1:103 1:352 1:481	HsklInvH-G1	112	4 1½ 1½ 11½ 14½ 13½	Espinoza V	L124	*.30	99- 01	WarEmblem1243½ MagicWeisner118¾ LikeHero1173¾	Bit fractious in gate	5
8Jun02-10Bel	fst	1½	:48 1:121 2:032 2:293	Belmont-G1	82	9 41½ 2hd 52¼ 712 819½	Espinoza V	L126	*1.25	64- 12	Sarava126½ *Medaglia d'Oro*1269½ Sunday Break1261	Stumb brk,rank,tired	11
18May02-12Pim	fst	1 3/16	:46 1:103 1:361 1:561	Preaknes-G1	109	8 2hd 2hd 2hd 11½ 1¾	Espinoza V	L126	*2.80	90- 14	WrEmblem126¾ MgicWeisnr126¾ ProudCitizn1261½	Rated 3wd, stiff drive	13
4May02-9CD	fst	1¼	:47 1:113 1:363 2:01	KyDerby-G1	114	5 11½ 11½ 11½ 11½ 14	Espinoza V	L126	20.50	94- 05	*WrEmblem*1264 ProudCitizen126¾ PerfectDrift1263¼	Pace, 3w,hand urging	18
Previously trained by Springer Frank R 2002(as of 4/6): (29 8 4 3 0.28)													
6Apr02-8Spt	fst	1⅛	:481 1:13 1:373 1:494	IllDerby-G2	112	4 11½ 11½ 12½ 15 16¼	Sterling L J Jr	L114	6.30	92- 17	*War Emblem*1146¼ Repent1244½ Fonz's1176½	Ridden out	9
17Mar02-8Spt	fst	1	:233 :47 1:122 1:391	Alw 48600NC	98	1 11 11½ 11½ 13 110¾	Juarez A J Jr	L118	*.80	87- 20	*War Emblem*11810¾ *Colorful Tour*1213 Boston Common1158	Driving	6
17Feb02-9FG	fst	1 1/16	:23 :46 1:111 1:43	RisenStr-G3	85	3 31 42 41¾ 76 69¾	Theriot H J II	L117	38.80	85- 08	*Repent*1222¼ BobsImage1153 Esyfromthegitgo1222¼	Ranged up 3w, faded	9
26Jan02-9FG	fst	1	:24 :472 1:12 1:374	Lecomte100k	86	3 2hd 1½ 1½ 2½ 52¼	Theriot H J II	L117	12.40	93- 07	Esyfromthgitgo114no SkyTrrc119¾ Itsllinthchs1221¼	Faltered final 1/16th	11
23Nov01-8FG	fst	1	:231 :471 1:122 1:39	Alw 32000N1x	83	6 53¼ 3nk 11 13 14½	Theriot H J II	L119	2.00	84- 19	War Emblem1194½ No Trouble1196 Ski Hero1191	Kept to task	6
20Oct01-8AP	gd	1 (T)	:233 :474 1:123 1:393	Manila75k	44	10 21 1hd 2hd 75¾ 717½	Juarez A J Jr	116	8.00	65- 20	Rylstone1163 U S S Tinosa1201½ Jaha1164	Tired, bled	12
4Oct01-5AP	fst	1	:23 :454 1:111 1:391	Md Sp Wt 28k	69	1 1hd 11 1½ 14 11¾	Juarez A J Jr	121	16.40	78- 23	War Emblem1211¾ Castner1212 Thrym1211½	Driving	9

Xtra Heat
Own: Classic Star Stable LLC

B. m. 5 (Mar)
Sire: Dixieland Heat (Dixieland Band) $4,000
Dam: Begin (Hatchet Man)
Br: P. McLean Sr., P. McLean Jr., M. McLean, P. Feringa Jr (Ky)
Tr: Salzman J E Sr

Life	35	26	5	2	$2,389,635	120	D.Fst	32	24	4	2	$2,163,305 120
2003	2	2	0	0	$150,000	105	Wet(322)	3	2	1	0	$226,330 108
2002	11	7	2	1	$965,485	111	Turf(284)	0	0	0	0	$0 -
	0	0	0	0	$0	-	Dst(T)(343)	0	0	0	0	$0 -

22Feb03-10Lrl	sly	7f	:224 :452 1:103 1:243	3↑(F)BFrtcheH-G2	99	3 11¾	Wilson R	L125	*1.00	84- 14	Xtra Heat1251¾ *Carson Hollow*1191¼ Spelling113hd	Fog,when rdy 2w,drvng	7
18Jan03-8Lrl	fst	6f	:23 :46 :572 1:092	4↑(F)WhatASummr52k	105	4 1 11 12½ 12 12¾	Wilson R	L122	*.20	92- 26	*Xtra Heat*1222¾ Gazillion1193½ Bernie's Gold1172	Rail, mild hand ride	6
14Dec02-8Aqu	my	6f [•]	:222 :452 :571 1:10	3↑(F)GrlndORssH81k	102	2 4 1hd 2hd 22 22¼	Wilson R	L127	*.60	92- 16	DtYouMizBlue1162¼ *XtrHet*1275¾ BelleArtist1148¼	Dueled inside,no match	5
26Oct02-6AP	fst	6f	:212 :434 :56 1:084	3↑BCSprint-G1	101	6 4 31 32 53½ 65	Vega H	L123	6.40	97 -	Orientate126½ Thunderello123½ Crafty C. T.1262¼	Saved grd, tired	13
5Oct02-7Kee	fst	6f	:211 :443 :564 1:10	3↑PhoenxBC-G3	107	4 1 2hd 1hd 11½ 13	Vega H	L123	*.70	89- 20	Xtra Heat1233 Day Trader120¾ Touch Tone119hd	Dueled,4w,drvg,clear	5
7Sep02-8Del	fst	6f	:22 :453 :582 1:104	3↑(F)Endine-G3	99	1 1 1hd 1½ 13 15	Vega H	L121	*.20	89- 17	*XtraHet*1215 OutstndingInfo1181 UrbnDncer118¾	Good energy,ridden out	5
10Aug02-8Lrl	fst	7f	:221 :451 1:10 1:23	3↑(F)StrDealBCH122k	100	3 1 1½ 1½ 14 12½	Vega H	L126	*.05	92- 21	*Xtra Heat*1262½ OutstandingInfo114½ *WinterLeaf*110½	Dictated rail, handily	5
13Jly02-12Crc	fst	6f	:212 :442 :57 1:101	3↑(F)PrcsRnyH-G2	111	3 4 2hd 11½ 12 2½	Vega H	L127	*.40	92- 07	Gold Mover115½ *Xtra Heat*1277½ Fly Me Crazy112½	Off rail, outfinished	6
9Jun02-8Bel	fst	6½f	:222 :45 1:093 1:162	3↑(F)VagrncyH-G2	106	4 1 1hd 1½ 11½ 1nk	Vega H	L127	*.65	93- 17	Xtra Heat127nk *Gold Mover*1154 *Shine Again*1175½	Pace, dug in, driving	5
12May02-8Bel	gd	6f	:221 :45 :57 1:101	3↑(F)GnunRskH-G2	108	5 5 1½ 1½ 12½ 11	Vega H	L126	*.85	87- 20	*Xtra Heat*1261 Shine Again1173¾ La Galerie1141¼	Pace, clear, driving	6
23Mar02 Nad Al Sheba (UAE)	ft	*6f	Str 1:094	3↑Dubai Golden Shaheen-G1 Stk 2000000		33½	Vega H	126	-		Caller One130hd Echo Eddie1303½ *Xtra Heat*1261¾	*Quickly away, stayed on same pace from 1f out*	13
16Feb02-9Lrl	fst	7f	:224 :452 1:093 1:223	3↑(F)BFrtcheH-G2	101	2 1 11½ 11½ 14 12¾	Vega H	L128	*.70	94- 16	Xtra Heat1282¾ Prized Stamp114nk *Kimbralata*1141½	Rail, pace, driving	8
1Jan02-8Aqu	fst	6f [•]	:223 :461 :582 1:11	3↑(F)InterbrghH81k	102	2 4 12 12½ 15 15½	Vega H	L125	*.35	89- 16	*Xtra Heat*1255½ *City Fair*114nk Look of the Lynx114nk	Kept to drive	6
17Nov01-9Lrl	fst	6f	:212 :441 :562 1:09	3↑DeFrncsM-G1	106	2 2 1½ 1½ 1½ 33¾	Vega H	L117	2.70	90- 19	DelawareTownship1253 EarlyFlyer115¾ *XtraHet*117nk	Pace ins, grudgingly	7
27Oct01-6Bel	fst	6f	:222 :443 :561 1:082	3↑BCSprint-G1	118	1 1 1hd 11 11 2½	Chavez J F	L121	17.50	95- 03	Squirtle Squirt124½ Xtra Heat121nk Caller One126nk	Set pace, gamely	14
29Sep01-6Del	fst	6f	:221 :453 :573 1:101	3↑(F)SweetnSasy97k	120	1 1 1½ 13 17 111½	Wilson R	L118	*.05	92- 18	XtrHet11811½ IvysJewel1142½ SuperduperMiss1164	Quick lead,ridden out	4
8Sep01-5Del	fst	6f	:212 :44 :562 1:093	3↑(F)Endine-G3	117	5 1 1½ 11 12½ 15¼	Wilson R	L118	*.60	95- 15	*Xtra Heat*1185¼ Ivy's Jewel1182½ Big Bambu1214¾	Ridden out	5
18Aug01-9Pim	fst	6f	:23 :453 :571 1:09	3↑(F)StrDealBCH112k	113	5 3 12 12 14 16	Wilson R	L120	*.30	101- 12	*XtrHet*1206 SuperduprMiss1176¼ ShutupndDnc1172¼	Rail,pace,ridden out	5
28Jly01-8Sar	fst	7f	:212 :44 1:084 1:213	(F)Test-G1	100	5 3 1hd 1½ 2hd 23¼	Wilson R	L123	2.30	94- 06	*Victory Ride*1163¼ *Xtra Heat*1233 *Nasty Storm*120nk	Vied inside, gamely	8
4Jly01-9Bel	fst	6f	:214 :443 :56 1:081	(F)Prioress-G1	113	6 3 2hd 1hd 1hd 1nk	Wilson R	L121	*1.85	97- 09	XtrHet121nk *AbovePerfection*1166 HrmonyLodg116½	Vied outside, driving	7
3Jun01-9Pim	fst	6f	:224 :453 :573 1:10	(F)ArticCloud36k	87	1 1 1hd 12½ 16 116¼	Wilson R	L122	*.05	96- 11	*Xtra Heat*12216¼ *Musical Times*11512¼ Bewixed115	Brushed start,handily	3
9May01-8Bel	fst	7f	:223 :45 1:094 1:23	(F)NassauCo-G2	95	2 4 1½ 11 13½ 2no	Wilson R	L122	*2.00	88- 13	Cat Chat114no *Xtra Heat*1222¼ *Shooting Party*1145¼	Pace, clear, gamely	6
22Apr01-8Kee	fst	*7f	:22 :444 1:102 1:274	(F)Beaumont-G2	89	3 1 1½ 11 14 12¾	Wilson R	L120	3.20	85- 13	XtraHeat1202¾ MountainBird1163¼ *RgingFever*1233¼	2-3 path,steady drive	5
25Mar01-6Aqu	fst	7f	:224 :46 1:101 1:231	(F)Cicada-G3	90	1 2 1½ 11 13 11¾	Wilson R	L122	*.35	84- 14	*Xtra Heat*1221¾ Erin Moor1164¼ Chasm116½	Pace, clear, driving	4
17Feb01-8Aqu	fst	6f [•]	:23 :46 :582 1:114	(F)DrlyPrcius79k	84	1 4 1hd 12 14½ 11	Wilson R	L122	*.55	86- 15	*Xtra Heat*1221 Schatzeli118nk I'm a Little Busy1185¼	Pace, clear, driving	5
7Jan01-8Aqu	fst	6f [•]	:224 :46 :573 1:111	(F)Ruthless80k	89	4 1 2hd 12 15½ 1¾	Wilson R	L122	*.95	89- 13	*Xtra Heat*122¾ *Major Wager*1181 Montana Cat1183½	Held on, driving	5
29Dec00-8Lrl	fst	7f	:233 :473 1:122 1:253	(F)KattgtPrid75k	78	4 1 12 14 15½ 13¼	Johnston M T	L119	*.70	79- 18	*Xtra Heat*1193¼ *Ultravase*114½ *Strike It Up*11210¾	Rail,steady hand ride	6
3Dec00-8CT	fst	7f	:234 :473 1:131 1:263	(F)SnowWhite40k	77	6 4 2½ 11 12½ 13¾	Johnston M T	L119	*.20	91- 15	*Xtra Heat*1193¾ Carni's Luck1143¼ *Curve Ahead*1144¼	Clear,kept to task	8
4Nov00-4CD	fst	1 1/16	:23 :462 1:11 1:423	(F)BCJuvFil-G1	54	7 95¼ 85¾ 108½ 1011 1021½	Johnston M T	L119	30.10	75 -	*Caressing*119½ Platinum Tiara1191¾ She's a Devil Due1191¼	Outrun	12
15Oct00-9Bel	fst	6½f	:214 :442 1:094 1:163	(F)Astarita-G2	85	2 2 4¾ 1hd 1½ 1nk	Johnston M T	L117	7.90	89- 12	Xtra Heat117nk GoldMover120nk MajorWager1174½	Bumped start, driving	8
16Sep00-7Del	fst	6f	:213 :453 :583 1:114	(F)BlueHen75k	88	5 5 2½ 11 15 12¾	Johnston M T	L121	*1.50	84- 20	*Xtra Heat*1212¾ Outstanding Info1164¾ *Trial Fighter*1161¼	Ridden out	8
26Aug00-9Pha	fst	6f	:22 :452 :573 1:103	(F)CriticalMs42k	78	4 2 11 1½ 12½ 12	Potts C L	122	*.50	87- 13	*Xtra Heat*1222 Foxy Red1209½ Elusive Dream1121¼	Set pace in hand, drvg	6
13Aug00-8Lrl	fst	6f	:221 :461 :582 1:112	(F)LauraGal42k	76	6 3 2hd 1½ 13 1¾	Johnston M T	120	1.50	85- 18	*Xtra Heat*120¾ Scarlet Tango114¾ *Sea Dragoness*1134¼	Hit gate,3wd,driving	7
16Jly00-9Lrl	fst	5½f	:223 :452 :572 1:034	(F)Toddler41k	79	6 3 11½ 12½ 15 14¾	Johnston M T	114	16.10	95- 18	*Xtra Heat*1144¾ Zonk1132 Sea Dragoness1131¾	Pace, driving	9
30Jun00-3Lrl	fst	5f	:224 :464 :593	(F)Md 25000(25-20)	57	5 8 43 21 1½ 1nk	Wilson R	120	2.40	91- 12	*XtraHeat*120nk *FrostyRox*1206¼ TwoPinkRoses1203½	Slow start,3wd,driving	8

CHAMPIONS

APPENDICES

PAST PERFORMANCES INDEX

Explanation of Past Performances

Name of horse, Country of origin (if foreign)

Color, sex, year of birth, sire, sire's sire, dam, dam's sire

Owner, Breeder, state where bred

Speed rating and track variant

Starts, 1st, 2nd, 3rd, earnings

Secretariat

ch. c. 1970, by Bold Ruler (Nasrullah)–Somethingroyal, by Princequillo

Lifetime record: 21 16 3 1 $1,316,808

Own.– Meadow Stable
Br.– Meadow Stud Inc (Va)
Tr.– L. Laurin

Fractional times

28Oct73- 8WO	fm $1\frac{5}{8}$ Ⓣ	$:47^2$	$1{:}37^3$		$2{:}41^4$	3↑ Can Int'l-G2	12	2	$2^{1\frac{1}{2}}$	1^5	1^{12}	$1^{6\frac{1}{2}}$	Maple E	117	b	*.20	96-04	Secretariat$117^{6\frac{1}{2}}$BigSpruce$126^{1\frac{1}{2}}$GoldenDon$117^{\frac{3}{4}}$	Ridden out 12
8Oct73- 7Bel	fm $1\frac{1}{2}$ Ⓣ	$:47$	$1{:}11^3$	$2{:}00$	$2{:}24^4$	3↑ Man o' War-G1	3	1	1^3	$1^{1\frac{1}{2}}$	1^3	1^5	Turcotte R	121	b	*.50	103-01	Secretariat121^5Tentam$126^{7\frac{1}{2}}$Big Spruce$126^{\frac{1}{2}}$	Ridden out 7
29Sep73- 7Bel	sly $1\frac{1}{2}$	$:50$	$1{:}13^2$	$2{:}01^4$	$2{:}25^4$	3↑ Woodward-G1	5	2	$2^{\frac{1}{2}}$	1^{hd}	$2^{1\frac{1}{2}}$	$2^{4\frac{1}{2}}$	Turcotte R	119	b	*.30	86-15	ProveOut$126^{4\frac{1}{2}}$Secretariat119^{11}CougarII$126^{\frac{1}{2}}$	Best of rest 5
15Sep73- 7Bel	fst $1\frac{1}{8}$	$:45^3$	$1{:}09^1$	$1{:}33$	$1{:}45^2$	3↑ Marl Cup Inv'l H 250k	7	5	$5^{1\frac{1}{4}}$	$3^{\frac{1}{2}}$	1^2	$1^{3\frac{1}{2}}$	Turcotte R	124	b	*.40e	104-07	Secretariat$124^{3\frac{1}{2}}$Riva Ridge127^2Cougar II$126^{6\frac{1}{2}}$	Ridden out 7
4Aug73- 7Sar	fst $1\frac{1}{8}$	$:47^4$	$1{:}11$	$1{:}36$	$1{:}49^1$	3↑ Whitney H-G2	3	4	3^1	$2^{\frac{1}{2}}$	2^{hd}	2^1	Turcotte R	119	b	*.10	94-15	Onion119^1Secretariat$119^{\frac{1}{2}}$Rule by Reason119^2	Weakened 5
30Jun73- 8AP	fst $1\frac{1}{8}$	$:48$	$1{:}11^1$	$1{:}35$	$1{:}47$	Invitational 125k	4	1	1^3	$1^{2\frac{1}{2}}$	1^6	1^9	Turcotte R	126	b	*.05	99-17	Secretariat126^9My Gallant120^{nk}Our Native120^{17}	Easily 4
9Jun73- 8Bel	fst $1\frac{1}{2}$	$:46^1$	$1{:}09^4$	$1{:}59$	$2{:}24$	Belmont-G1	1	1	1^{hd}	1^{20}	1^{28}	1^{31}	Turcotte R	126	b	*.10	113-05	Secretariat126^{31}TwiceaPrince$126^{\frac{1}{2}}$MyGllnt126^{13}	Ridden out 5
19May73- 8Pim	fst $1\frac{3}{16}$	$:48^1$	$1{:}11^2$	$1{:}35^3$	$1{:}54^2$	Preakness-G1	3	4	$1^{\frac{1}{2}}$	$1^{2\frac{1}{2}}$	$1^{2\frac{1}{2}}$	$1^{2\frac{1}{2}}$	Turcotte R	126	b	*.30	98-13	Secretariat$126^{2\frac{1}{2}}$Sham126^8Our Native126^1	Handily 6
	Daily Racing Form time 1:53 2/5																		
5May73- 9CD	fst $1\frac{1}{4}$	$:47^2$	$1{:}11^4$	$1{:}36^1$	$1{:}59^2$	Ky Derby-G1	10	11	$6^{9\frac{1}{2}}$	$2^{\frac{1}{2}}$	$1^{\frac{1}{2}}$	$1^{2\frac{1}{2}}$	Turcotte R	126	b	*1.50e	103-10	Secretariat$126^{2\frac{1}{2}}$Sham126^8Our Native$126^{\frac{1}{2}}$	Handily 13
21Apr73- 7Aqu	fst $1\frac{1}{8}$	$:48^1$	$1{:}12^1$	$1{:}36^4$	$1{:}49^4$	Wood Memorial-G1	6	7	6^6	$5^{5\frac{1}{2}}$	$4^{5\frac{1}{2}}$	3^4	Turcotte R	126	b	*.30e	83-17	Angle Light126^{hd}Sham126^4Secretariat$126^{\frac{1}{2}}$	Wide,hung 8
7Apr73- 7Aqu	fst 1	$:23^1$	$:45^1$	$1{:}08^3$	$1{:}33^2$	Gotham-G2	3	3	1^{hd}	1^2	$1^{\frac{1}{2}}$	1^3	Turcotte R	126	b	*.10	100-08	Secretariat126^3ChampagneCharl117^{10}Flush$117^{2\frac{1}{2}}$	Ridden out 6
17Mar73- 7Aqu	sly 7f	$:22^1$	$:44^4$	$1{:}10$	$1{:}23^1$	Bay Shore-G3	4	5	5^6	5^3	1^{hd}	$1^{4\frac{1}{2}}$	Turcotte R	126	b	*.20	85-17	Secretarit$126^{4\frac{1}{2}}$ChmpgnChrl$118^{2\frac{1}{2}}$Impcunous126^{no}	Mild drive 6
18Nov72- 8GS	fst $1\frac{1}{16}$	$:24^1$	$:47^2$	$1{:}12$	$1{:}44^2$	Garden State 298k	6	6	$4^{6\frac{1}{4}}$	3^3	$1^{1\frac{1}{2}}$	$1^{3\frac{1}{2}}$	Turcotte R	122	b	*.10e	83-23	Secretariat$122^{3\frac{1}{2}}$Angle Light$122^{\frac{1}{2}}$Step Nicely$122^{\frac{3}{4}}$	Handily 6
28Oct72- 7Lrl	sly $1\frac{1}{16}$	$:22^4$	$:45^4$	$1{:}11^2$	$1{:}42^4$	Lrl Futurity 133k	5	6	5^{10}	5^3	1^5	1^8	Turcotte R	122	b	*.10e	99-14	Secretariat122^8Stop the Music122^8Angle Light122^1	Easily 6
14Oct72- 7Bel	fst 1	$:22^4$	$:45^1$	$1{:}09^4$	$1{:}35$	Champagne 146k	4	11	$9^{8\frac{1}{2}}$	$5^{3\frac{1}{2}}$	$1^{\frac{1}{2}}$	1^2	Turcotte R	122	b	*.70e	97-12	D Secretariat122^2StoptheMusic122^2StepNicly$122^{1\frac{1}{2}}$	Bore in 12
	Disqualified and placed second																		
16Sep72- 7Bel	fst $6\frac{1}{2}$f	$:22^3$	$:45^3$	$1{:}10$	$1{:}16^2$	Futurity 144k	4	5	$6^{5\frac{1}{2}}$	$5^{3\frac{1}{2}}$	1^2	$1^{1\frac{3}{4}}$	Turcotte R	122	b	*.20	98-09	Secretariat$122^{1\frac{3}{4}}$StoptheMusic122^5SwiftCourr$122^{2\frac{1}{2}}$	Handily 7
26Aug72- 7Sar	fst $6\frac{1}{2}$f	$:22^4$	$:46^3$	$1{:}09^4$	$1{:}16^1$	Hopeful 86k	8	8	$9^{6\frac{1}{2}}$	1^{hd}	1^4	1^5	Turcotte R	121	b	*.30	97-12	Secretariat121^5FlighttoGlory121^{nk}StopthMusc121^2	Handily 9
16Aug72- 7Sar	fst 6f	$:22^4$	$:46^1$		$1{:}10$	Sanford 27k	2	5	5^4	4^1	$1^{\frac{1}{2}}$	1^3	Turcotte R	121	b	1.50	96-14	Secretariat121^3Lnd'sChf121^6NorthstrDncr$121^{3\frac{1}{2}}$	Ridden out 5
31Jly72- 4Sar	fst 6f	$:23^1$	$:46^2$		$1{:}10^4$	Alw 9000	4	7	$7^{3\frac{3}{4}}$	$3^{\frac{1}{2}}$	1^{hd}	$1^{1\frac{1}{2}}$	Turcotte R	118	b	*.40	92-13	Secretariat$118^{1\frac{1}{2}}$Russ Miron118^7Joe Iz$118^{2\frac{1}{2}}$	Ridden out 7
15Jly72- 4Aqu	fst 6f	$:22^1$	$:45^2$		$1{:}10^3$	©Md Sp Wt	8	11	$6^{6\frac{1}{2}}$	4^3	$1^{\frac{1}{2}}$	1^6	Feliciano P^5	113	b	*1.30	90-14	Secretariat113^6Master Achiever$118^{\frac{3}{4}}$Be on It118^4	Handily 11
4Jly72- 2Aqu	fst $5\frac{1}{2}$f	$:22^2$	$:46^1$	$:58^4$	$1{:}05$	©Md Sp Wt	2	11	10^7	$10^{8\frac{3}{4}}$	$7^{5\frac{1}{2}}$	$4^{1\frac{1}{4}}$	Feliciano P^5	113	b	*3.10	87-11	Herbull118^{nk}Master Achiever118^1Fleet 'n Royal118^{no}	12
	Impeded,rallied																		

Odds to $1 (* indicates favorite)

Age, sex restrictions, class of race, purse

Date, race, track abbreviation, track condition, distance, surface

Post position, fractional calls with margins, finish with margins

Jockey, weight carried, equipment

First three finishers with weight carried and margins, comment line number of starters

ABBREVIATIONS FOR TYPES OF RACES

Alw 15000	Allowence race, $15,000
Alw 15000s	Starter allowance (number indicates minimum claiming price horse must have started for to be eligible)
Clm 10000	Claiming race (entered to be claimed for $10,000)
Hcp 10000s	Starter handicap race. Number indicates minimum claiming price horse must have started for to be eligible
Md Sp Wt	Maiden Special Weight race (for non-winners)
MCl 32000	Maiden Claiming race (entered to be claimed for $32,000)
Handicap 40k	Overnight handicap race (purse of $40,000)
Ky Derby-G1	Graded Stakes race, with name of race (North American races are graded in order of status,with G1 being the best)
PrincetonH 40k	Ungraded, but named Stakes race (H indicates handicap) Purse value is $40,000

SYMBOLS

[•]	=	Inner dirt track
[D]	=	Disqualified (symbol located next to odds and in company line)
[DH]	=	Dead-Heat (symbol located in company line if horses are among first three finishers)
ɩ	=	Dead-Heat (symbol used next to finish position)
3↑	=	Race for 3-year-olds and up
♦	=	Foreign race (outside of North America)
[S]	=	Race for state-breds only
[R]	=	Restricted race for horses who meet certain conditions
Ⓒ	=	restricted to colts and geldings
Ⓕ	=	Race for fillies, or fillies and mares
Ⓣ	=	Main turf course
[T]	=	Inner turf course
⊗	=	Race taken off turf
*	=	About distance
+	=	Start from turf chute
wc	=	Widener Course

FRACTIONAL TIMES

Distance	Fractional Times			
3½ f	—	1/4	3/8	*finish*
4f	—	1/4	3/8	*finish*
4½ f	—	1/4	1/2	*finish*
5 f	—	1/4	1/2	*finish*
5½ f	1/4	1/2	5/8	*finish*
6 f	1/4	1/2	5/8	*finish*
6½ f	1/4	1/2	3/4	*finish*
7 f	1/4	1/2	3/4	*finish*
7½ f	1/4	1/2	3/4	*finish*
1 mile	1/4	1/2	3/4	*finish*
1 m70 yds	1/4	1/2	3/4	*finish*
1 1/16	1/2	3/4	*mile*	*finish*
1 3/16	1/2	3/4	*mile*	*finish*
1¼	1/2	3/4	*mile*	*finish*
1⅜	1/2	3/4	*mile*	*finish*
1½	1/2	3/4	1¼	*finish*
1⅝	1/2	*mile*	1¼	*finish*
1¾	1/2	1¼	1½	*finish*
1⅞	1/2	1¼	1¾	*finish*
2 miles	1/2	1½	1¾	*finish*
2⅛	1/2	1½	1¾	*finish*

TRACK CONDITIONS

DIRT TRACKS

fst	=	**Fast**
wf	=	**Wet-Fast**
gd	=	**Good**
sly	=	**Sloppy**
my	=	**Muddy**
sl	=	**Slow**
hy	=	**Heavy**
fr	=	**Frozen**
cpy	=	**Cuppy**

TURF & STEEPLECHASE

hd	=	**Hard**
fm	=	**Firm**
gd	=	**Good**
yl	=	**Yielding**
sf	=	**Soft**
hy	=	**Heavy**

EQUIPMENT & MEDICATION

b	=	**Blinkers**
f	=	**Front bandages**
r	=	**Bar shoe**
w	=	**whip**
s	=	**spurs**
B	=	**Butazolidin**
L	=	**Lasix (furosemide)**

Track Abbreviations

ABBREV	TRACK NAME	STATE
AC	Agua Caliente	MX
Agm	Agawam	MA
Aik	Aiken	SC
Aks	Aksarben	NE
Alb	Albuquerque	NM
AP	Arlington Park	IL
Aqu	Aqueduct	NY
AtH	Atlanta Hunt	GA
Atl	Atlantic City	NJ
BB	Blue Bonnets	QU
Bel	Belmont Park	NY
Ben	Bennings	DC
BM	Bay Meadows	CA
Bmf	Bay Meadows Fair	CA
Bow	Bowie	MD
BPT	Belmont Park Terminal	NY
Bri	Brighton Beach	NY
Bue	Butte	MT
Cam	Camden	SC
Cby	Canterbury	MN
CD	Churchill Downs	KY
CDA	Coeur d'Alene	ID
Cen	Centennial	CO
CI	Coney Island	OH
Clm	Clemmons	NC
Con	Connaught Park	ON
Crc	Calder Race Course	FL
Dad	Dade Park	KY
Dal	Dallas	TX
Dar	Darby Downs	OH
Del	Delaware Park	DE
Det	Detroit	MI
Dev	Devonshire Park	ON
Dmr	Del Mar	CA
DoP	Douglas Park	KY
Dor	Dorval Park	QU
DRn	Deep Run	VA
Due	Dueling Grounds	KY
ElP	Ellis Park	KY
Emp	Empire City	NY
Esx	Essex Park	AR
EvD	Evangeline Downs	LA
Fai	Fair Hill	MD
Fax	Fairfax	VA
FE	Fort Erie	ON
FG	Fair Grounds	LA
FH	Far Hills	NJ
FL	Finger Lakes	NY
Fon	Fonner Park	NE
FP	Fairmount Park	IL
Fx	Foxfield	VA
GG	Golden Gate	CA
GP	Gulfstream Park	FL
Gra	Gravesend	NY
Grd	Greenwood	ON
GrM	Great Meadows	VA
GS	Garden State Park	NJ
Ham	Hamilton	ON
Haw	Hawthorne	IL
HdG	Havre de Grace	MD
Hel	Helena	MT
Hia	Hialeah Park	FL
Hol	Hollywood Park	CA
HP	Hazel Park	MI
Hrm	Harlem	IL
Jam	Jamaica	NY
JnD	Jefferson Downs	LA
Jua	Juarez	MX
Kee	Keeneland	KY
Key	Keystone	PA
Knw	Kenilworth	ON
LA	Los Alamitos	CA
LaD	Louisiana Downs	LA
Lag	Lagoon	UT

ABBREV	TRACK NAME	STATE
Lak	Lakeside	IN
Lat	Latonia	KY
LD	Lincoln Downs	RI
Lex	Lexington	KY
LF	Lincoln Fields	IL
Lga	Longacres	WA
Lib	Liberty Bell Park	PA
Lig	Ligonier	PA
Lrl	Laurel	MD
LS	Lone Star	TX
Lxt	Lexington	KY
Mal	Malvern	PA
MBr	Meadow Brook	NY
Med	Meadowlands	NJ
Mgo	Marengo	VA
Mid	Middleburg	VA
Mor	Morven Park	VA
MP	Morris Park	NY
Mth	Monmouth Park	NJ
Mtp	Montpelier	VA
Nar	Narragansett	RI
Nvl	Nashville	TN
Nwp	Newport	KY
Oak	Oakland	CA
Oky	Oakley	OH
OMP	Old Monmouth Park	NJ
OP	Oaklawn Park	AR
OWP	Old Washington Park	IL
Pal	Palmetto	SC
Pen	Penn National	PA
Pha	Philadelphia Park	PA
Pim	Pimlico	MD
PiR	Piping Rock	NY
Pln	Pleasanton	CA
PM	Portland Meadows	OR
Pmt	Pine Mountain	GA

ABBREV	TRACK NAME	STATE
PR	El Commandante	PR
Pro	Prospect	KY
Pur	Purchase Hunts	NY
PW	Percy Warner	TN
Ran	Randall Park	OH
RB	Red Bank	NJ
RD	River Downs	OH
Rkm	Rockingham Park	NH
SA	Santa Anita Park	CA
Sac	Sacramento	CA
SAP	Old Santa Anita Park	CA
Sar	Saratoga	NY
SH	Strawberry Hill	VA
She	Sheepshead Bay	NY
Sol	Solano	CA
SoP	Southern Pines	NC
Spt	Sportsman's Park	IL
SR	Santa Rosa	CA
StL	St. Louis	MO
Suf	Suffolk Downs	MA
Syr	Syracuse	NY
Tam	Tampa Bay Downs	FL
Tan	Tanforan	CA
Tdn	Thistledown	OH
Tij	Tijuana	MX
Tim	Timonium	MD
TP	Turfway Park	KY
TrP	Tropical Park	FL
Try	Tryon	NC
TuP	Turf Paradise	AZ
UH	United Hunts	NY
Uni	Unionville	PA
War	Warrenton	VA
Was	Washington Park	IL
Wnr	Windsor	ON
WO	Woodbine	ON

About the Authors

GLENYE CAIN has been the bloodstock correspondent for *Daily Racing Form* since May of 1999. Previously Cain was news editor and features editor of the *Thoroughbred Times*; was the editor of *Equine Athlete*; and worked for the Thoroughbred Owners and Breeders Association and National Thoroughbred Racing Association. Cain received the 1995 Story of the Year Award for *The Chronicle of the Horse* and was the 1999 winner of the Kent Hollingsworth Award for reporting excellence. Cain is the author of the 2004 title *The Home Run Horse.*

STEVEN CRIST was named CEO, editor, and publisher of *Daily Racing Form* in August 1998. Crist covered horse racing as a *New York Times* reporter and columnist from 1981 through 1990; was founding editor-in-chief of *The Racing Times* in 1991-92; served on Governor Mario Cuomo's Commission on Racing in the 21st Century from 1993 to 1995; and was a vice president of the New York Racing Association from 1995 to 1997. He is the author of three books: *Offtrack*, *The Horse Traders*, and *Betting on Myself.*

DAVID GRENING has covered Thoroughbred racing since 1991. He worked the Delaware Valley circuit for *The Trentonian* and was also the correspondent in that area for *The Blood-Horse* from 1991-94. In May 1994, he joined the *New York Post*, where he covered New York racing and the national scene for four years before joining *Daily Racing Form* as its New York correspondent in September 1998. He also worked as the New York correspondent for the *Thoroughbred Times* during his four-year tenure at the *Post*.

JOE HIRSCH, an internationally recognized racing figure for most of the last 50 years, is considered the dean of America's turf writers. *Daily Racing Form*'s longtime executive columnist, who worked for the paper from 1948 through 2003, has covered more major American races than any other journalist. Hirsch's work has been honored with virtually every major award in his profession. He is the only turf writer to win both the Eclipse Award and the Lord Derby Award from the Horse Race Writers of England. His many other accolades include The Jockey Club Medal, the Walter Haight Award, the William H. May Award from the Association of Racing Commissioners International, and an entire day in his name from the state of Kentucky. Hirsch wrote *The First Century*, a history of Thoroughbred racing from 1894-1994, and collaborated with Jim Bolus on *Kentucky Derby: The Chance of a Lifetime.*

JAY PRIVMAN has been the national correspondent for *Daily Racing Form* since October 1998. He is the lead writer on events such as the Triple Crown and Breeders' Cup. Prior to that, he was a West Coast correspondent for *The New York Times* for six years, and a staff writer with the Los Angeles *Daily News* for nine years. Privman served as the West Coast editor for *The Racing Times*, and was also a West Coast correspondent for the *Thoroughbred Times* from 1985 to 1998. Privman does extensive television work, most notably as an analyst for ESPN and ABC. Privman is a five-time winner of the Red Smith Kentucky Derby Writing Contest, and three times has received honorable mentions in the Eclipse Awards for his writing

DAVE LITFIN was a call-taker with *Daily Racing Form* from 1982 until the fall of 1984, when he joined the New York Racing Association's publicity department just as Slew o' Gold was setting out to sweep the Woodward, Marlboro Cup, and Jockey Club Gold Cup. Four years later, he left the NYRA to serve brief stints at *Racing Action* and the New York *Daily News*, but came back to the *Form* in 1990 and has been the lead New York handicapper since the spring of 1991. In addition to a twice-weekly column entitled "Handicapper's Corner," Litfin has authored two well-received handicapping books: *Dave Litfin's Expert Handicapping*, and *Real-Life Handicapping*.

JAY HOVDEY, executive columnist for *Daily Racing Form*, is a four-time Eclipse Award winner for writing whose work also has appeared in *Reader's Digest*, *The New York Times*, the *Los Angeles Times*, and such Thoroughbred-racing publications as *The Blood-Horse*, *Thoroughbred Times*, *The Racing Times*, *The Horsemen's Journal*, *Spur* magazine, *Pacemaker International*, and *Keiba Book* of Japan. He is the author of three books on horse racing, including *Whittingham: A Thoroughbred Racing Legend* and *Cigar: America's Horse*. Hovdey is a two-time winner of the David F. Woods Award for coverage of the Preakness Stakes, a two-time winner of the Joe Hirsch Award for coverage of the Breeders' Cup, winner of Canada's Sovereign Award for feature writing, and winner of the Charles Englehard Award for turf writing. In 1995 he was honored by his peers with the Walter Haight Award for career excellence in racing journalism.

PAULA WELCH was the special-projects editor for *Daily Racing Form* from 1996 to 2000. In addition to researching and collecting the data for the past performances in *Champions*, Welch also coordinated the material for the *Graded Stakes Yearbook* from 1995 through 1998. A 1992 graduate of the Racetrack Industry Program at the University of Arizona, Welch currently is the editor for *The American Racing Manual*.